INTERNATIONAL ENCYCLOPEDIA OF THE SOCIOLOGY OF EDUCATION

Resources in Education

This series of Pergamon one-volume Encyclopedias draws upon articles in the acclaimed *International Encyclopedia of Education, Second Edition*, with revisions as well as new articles. Each volume in the series is thematically organized and aims to provide complete and up-to-date coverage on its subject. These Encyclopedias will serve as an invaluable reference source for researchers, faculty members, teacher educators, government officials, educational administrators, and policymakers.

This *Encyclopedia* is intended to be a specialist collection, in considerable depth, for use as a convenient reference book and resource book for courses in the sociology of education. Because of the breadth and depth of its offerings, the volume is a suitable resource for use in many subareas within the sociology of education, for example, sociological theory, the study of the family, educational structures, and educational processes.

The sociology of education is a rapidly expanding area within sociology and in educational studies generally, and cuts across many other disciplines. Within colleges of education it is often known as the social foundations of education, or sometimes as the social context of education. In research, the sociology of education has been the arena for significant developments in theory and methods and in many instances has led the other sociological, social science, and educational fields. This *Encyclopedia* draws together many of the articles from the parent encyclopedia, and provides an opportunity for updating and filling in gaps brought about by new developments.

The primary aim of this *Encyclopedia* is to provide a state-of-the-art resource, for an international audience, of the cumulative results of research and to identify the substantive developments which will take the sociological study of education into the next century. This *Encyclopedia* presents the full range of paradigms, theoretical points of view, together with many research methodologies.

As in the *International Encyclopedia of Education, Second Edition*, the articles are research based, but will be accessible to a range of readers, including students, professors, researchers, educational practitioners, teachers, and policymakers.

Other titles in the series include:

POSTLETHWAITE (ed.)
International Encyclopedia of National Systems of Education, Second Edition

CARNOY (ed.)
International Encyclopedia of Economics of Education, Second Edition

ANDERSON (ed.)
International Encyclopedia of Teaching and Teacher Education, Second Edition

TUIJNMAN (ed.)
International Encyclopedia of Adult Education and Training, Second Edition

PLOMP & ELY (eds)
International Encyclopedia of Educational Technology, Second Edition

DE CORTE & WEINERT (eds)
International Encyclopedia of Developmental and Instructional Psychology

KEEVES (ed.)
Educational Research, Methodology, and Measurement: An International Handbook, Second Edition

INTERNATIONAL ENCYCLOPEDIA OF THE SOCIOLOGY OF EDUCATION

Edited by

LAWRENCE J. SAHA

Australian National University, Canberra, ACT, Australia

PERGAMON

UK   Elsevier Science Ltd., The Boulevard, Langford Lane,
Kidlington, Oxford OX5 1GB, UK

USA   Elsevier Science Inc., 655 Avenue of the Americas,
New York 10010, USA

JAPAN   Elsevier Science Japan, 9-15 Higashi-Azabu 1-chome,
Minato-ku, Tokyo 106, Japan

First edition 1997

Library of Congress Cataloging in Publication Data
International encyclopedia of the sociology of education /
edited by Lawrence J. Saha. —1st ed.
    p.   cm.
  ISBN 0-08-042990-4 (hc)
   1. Educational sociology—Encyclopedias. I. Saha,
Lawrence J.
LC191.I49 1997
306.43'03—DC21   97-24837

British Library Cataloguing in Publication Data
A catalogue record for this book is available from the
British Library.

ISBN 0–08–042990–4 (hard: alk. paper)

∞™   The paper used in this publication meets the minimum requirements of the
American National Standard for Information Sciences—Permanence of Paper for Printed
Library Materials, ANSI Z39.48–1984.

Printed and bound in Great Britain by BPC Wheatons Ltd., Exeter,
UK.

Contents

Contents

Contents

Contents

Contents

Contents

xiv

Preface

The purpose of this preface is to locate the sociology of education in both sociology and in education research. In the process of identifying the distinctiveness of the sociology of education, this discussion will also identify its subfields and the ways the area is structured and integrated. The preface will conclude with a brief explanation of how this *Encyclopedia* is organized with respect to the integration of the sociological of education. A specific discussion of the major theoretical themes and research agendas within the sociology of education is found in another article in this *Encyclopedia* (see *Sociology of Education: An Overview*).

1. Introduction

The sociology of education is perhaps one of the broadest fields within sociology itself. It cuts across almost all of the other sociological fields and is found represented in departments of sociology and departments of education. One reason for this wide-ranging presence is the almost universal experience of schooling today by most members of modern societies. Because of the breadth of research topics within the sociology of education, the boundaries of the field within sociology and education are difficult to determine. If the topical areas are numerous, then so too are the theoretical paradigms through which sociologists of education study and interpret the objects of their research.

One of the most uncomfortable divisions within the sociology of education has been the extent to which the field is seen as a "science," represented by the dispassionate investigation of educational phenomena, or as the policy-related and reform-oriented approach to the study of education. About three decades ago this basic division was characterized as that between the empirical and normative "modes" in the study of education.

> Empirical inquiry is dedicated to the establishment of verified knowledge, internally consistent, cogent, and adequate to its subject. In such inquiry and from such theory emerge statements of what is, what has been, what is possible, and what is likely. In contrast, normative inquiry is dedicated to the establishment of imperatives for the development of policies, programs and actions, and to the establishment of normative theory; that is, to an internally consistent and cogent body of prescription, adequate to the realization of desired goals and consistent with a valid ethic. (Hansen 1967)

This division continues to the present day. There are many within the sociology of education who see the discipline primarily as a change agent in education, either through the formulation of policy, or through the effects of research itself. In this respect, the sociology of education is seen primarily as a normative subject which is concerned with specifying what education or schools "ought" to be or do in carrying out the educative function. This point of view seems to have dominated the early development of the sociology of education, at least in the United States. Hansen (1967) comments that this approach was usually known as "educational sociology" rather than the "sociology of education."

On the other hand, there are others who view the sociology of education from a more scientific perspective, where the discipline is seen to produce scientific knowledge about the relationship between education and society, and about the causes and effects of schooling. Thus the label "sociology of education" has its roots in the sociological tradition which attempted to create a "science of society," and emulate the natural sciences.

Lest too much be put in a name, Hansen (1967) argues that the distinction is useful and can minimize confusion about the nature of the sociology of education.

> Such confusion is avoided and more critical gains promised if the term "educational sociology" is used to refer to the pursuit of a normative theory of education and to research that is primarily directed to furthering that normative theory or to direct application. "Sociology of education" would then refer to the pursuit of empirical theory and to research that is essentially directed toward furthering it. (Hansen 1967 p. 22)

For all practical purposes, the dominant label currently is the sociology of education, and that is the label used in this *Encyclopedia*.

However, the issue underlying Hansen's concern continues today in the sociology of education is the preoccupation over its normative application, even at the expense of its scientific claim. Noblit and Pink, for example, comment that "The sociology of education is a field in which the concern to improve education seems to have undercut the wider discipline moves for distinctiveness and science" (Noblit and Pink 1995 p. 3).

2. *The Origins of the Sociology of Education*

It is generally acknowledged that the sociology of education, as we know it today, began with the work of Emile Durkheim. Although Durkheim's place in sociology largely is due to his other writings, in particular *The Division of Labor in Society* (1893), *The Rules of the Sociological Method* (1895), *Suicide* (1897), and *The Elementary Forms of Religious Life* (1912), much of his lecturing and writing also focused on education, and in this context he applied a sociological perspective (see *Classical Sociological Theories of Education*). Because Durkheim was both a sociologist and a pedagogist, his approach to the study of education was eminently sociological. His work on moral education, on the sociological forces which affect educational development, and his focus on the link between education and society, have produced a body of sociological literature which is yet too little known or explored by sociologists of education. Furthermore, many of Durkheim's book reviews, correspondence, and other public exchanges touched on educational issues. In this regard, Durkheim must have been one of the first, if not the first sociologist who adopted a view on such wide-ranging issues as the education of women and sex education, even though his views are challenged today (Lehmann 1995).

As a result of Durkheim's sociological teaching and research in education, the subject of sociology was taught in the teacher-training colleges in France by the 1920s. Two of Durkheim's followers and colleagues in the production of *L'annee sociologique*, Celestin Bougle and Paul Lapie, were important contributors to this development (Filloux, 1993).

But the sociology of education was also growing in the United Kingdom and the United States. Banks (1971) records this rapid growth, and provides figures which are impressive, for example, that between 1910 and 1927 the number of universities offering courses in the sociology of education (taken broadly) was from 40 to 194, and over the 20 year period between 1916 and 1936, the number of textbooks published was 25.

By the end of this century the sociology of education has become a major subdiscipline within the sociology of education. It is one of the largest sections in many professional sociological associations, such as the American Sociological Association, The Australian Sociological Association, The British Sociological Association, and the International Sociological Association. It supports specialist journals, two of the most visible being *Sociology of Education* and *The British Journal of Sociology of Education*, and a journal of abstracts, the *Sociology of Education Abstracts*.

3. *Defining the Field*

Clearly, the sociology of education is a broad and vigorous field within sociology generally. There are few areas within sociology which, at some point or another, do not treat education as an independent or dependent variable. Regarding the former, stratification and class research, research on race and ethnicity, crime and deviance, formal organizations, and others all use education in some form as an explanatory variable. The sociology of education is also interdisciplinary. In a recent attempt to evaluate the current state of the sociology of education in the United States, Apple commented that he would "construct a picture of the sociology of education that is broad and that cuts across disciplinary boundaries—including important work in education in curriculum studies, history, gender studies, cultural studies, postcolonial studies, critical race theory, and so on" (1996 p. 125).

Socialists of education themselves focus on education both as a causal variable as well as an outcome variable. Thus, research on the way education affects other social behaviors, and the factors which determine education outcomes, that is, educational attainment, achievement, and performance, all fall within the sociology of education.

The sociologists of education also has been at the forefront of theoretical and methodological developments. Such has been the emergence of the sociology of education within sociology itself that in the United States Karabel and Halsey (1977), over 20 years ago, could observe that "over the last generation education research has come from the humblest margins of the social sciences to occupy a central position in sociology . . ." (p. 1). Karabel (1979) could later argue that the sociology of education had become "one of the most vibrant and respected areas of sociological research" because of the theoretical developments taking place within it (p. 85). In Canada, Tepperman (1979) commented that ". . . the sociology of education is important in helping to understand inequality, and in the last twenty years, the sociological study of education has become a battleground for theories about inequality" (p. v). Finally in Britain, where the sociology of education had only recently become re-established, Demain (1981) observed that "in recent years sociology of education has been transformed and the state of theoretical debate invigorated by the influx of Marxist, neo-Marxist and radical theories and concepts" (p. 1).

In spite of these optimistic assessments of the impact of the sociology of education, there is much dissatisfaction within the discipline which suggests that many theoretical and research tasks remain. Shilling (1992), in a plea for a resolution of the macro–micro gap in educational studies, has commented that "sociologists of education have still to sort out precisely how 'grand' theoretical narratives (e.g. feminism, Marxism) can or should be applied to particular pieces of micro-level research" (p. 50). He has argued that the structuration theory of Giddens, when applied to educational analyses, might offer a new direction for the sociology of education.

Yet, in spite of these criticisms, Noblit and Pink (1995) describe the sociology of education as "extremely rich, vibrant and diverse" (p. 27). Furthermore, they regard the field as "emergent rather than static and multidimensional rather than unitary" (p. 27).

These latter comments highlight difficulties in defining the field of the sociology of education. Often when sociologists turn their attention to education, either as an independent or dependent variable, they rub shoulders with researchers from other disciplines. What then, makes a sociological approach to the study of education unique and distinctive?

Like sociologists generally, a sociological approach is one which focuses on social factors rather than psychological, biological, or physical ones. Furthermore, the social factors of interest to sociologists include those which are related to social structures as well as social processes. In this respect the study of schools as social organizations and bureaucracies is a well-established field in the sociology of education which provides the framework for studies of processes which occur within the school, such as the acquisition of attitudes, values, identity, achievement, discipline, and the like. But so is the study of educational and school processes.

Sociologists and educational researchers alike recognize the importance of the family in educational processes and outcomes. Any study which neglects the importance of family or origin is likely to be seen as incomplete, or at least limited in some way. The importance of the family in early socialization, the provision of family resources, including material, social, and psychological, and the continued interest in school progress remain among the most important factors in explaining variations in school success.

Teachers and students also receive their share of attention from sociologists and educational researchers, and interests range from the study of inputs, process, and outputs of both the teaching profession and of schools.

But sociologists of education also take an interest in a more macro view of education. In this respect there have been sociological studies of educational systems, educational expansion, education in different ideological systems, and the relationship between stratification and class structures and educational systems.

Still at the macro level, sociologists have directed attention to the relationship between education and social change. This includes a wide range of topics, including social and economic development, the relationship between technology and education, and the factors related to the formation of educational policy and planning.

4. The Plan of this Encyclopedia

4.1 How to Organize a Discipline

There is hardly ever an agreement over the ways a discipline should be subdivided or organized. This is also true for the discipline of sociology, and within it, the sociology of education. Naturally the manner of organizing a discipline depends on the purpose or goal of the exercise. Thus if one wanted to organize a discipline on the basis of its theoretical paradigms, the divisions would differ from a structure based on research methodologies. The same would be true if one wanted to emphasize dominant themes or research areas.

It follows, then, that no organization of a discipline into subparts is value free or neutral, for each attempt reflects the interests and goals of the researcher or writer. This problem was recognized by Noblit and Pink (1995) when they reviewed three overviews of the sociology of education, namely Karabel and Halsey (1977), Trent et al. (1985), and Wexler (1987).

> Karabel and Halsey revealed the contradictions within the field that promoted a new sociology of education. Trent, Braddock, and Henderson's view reasserted the view of sociology as a science and projected, instead of alternative sociologies of education, an emerging unity, even as they blamed the new sociologists of education for divisiveness. Wexler's thesis, by contrast, was that this divisiveness, as central as it was to establishing the new sociology of education, contained the seeds for the destruction of the new sociology of education. (Noblit and Pink 1995 p. 25)

Each of these sets of authors organized their discussion of the discipline in a different but useful manner. The approaches were diverse enough for Noblit and Pink to make their main point, namely that all attempts to organize a discipline are a form of construction: "Considering the past is an act of cultural production, of making the present and projecting the future" (p. 8). In the end, borrowing from Wexler, Noblit and Pink organized their own edited work around the notion of "paths" or major domains, of which they identified five: the empirical–analytic path, the interpretive path, the critical path, the policy path, and the postmodern path. They regarded these paths as "heuristic" and as conceptually blurred at the boundaries, but as nonetheless pointing to a unified discipline.

4.2 Organizing the Sociology of Education

The organization of the sociology of education in this *Encyclopedia* departs from those discussed above. In order to provide maximum coverage of the discipline, the *Encyclopedia* is divided into 10 sections which seem best to describe the discipline, and at the same time represent the areas in which sociologists mainly focus their teaching and research. These areas are as follows:

Social Theories in the Sociology of Education
Sociological Fields in the Sociology of Education
Research Traditions in the Sociology of Education
The School as a Social System
The Structure of Educational Systems
School Processes
Family and Schooling
Teachers in Society
Youth in Schools
Educational Policy and Change

4.2.1 Social Theories in the Sociology of Education. The key to unlock the sociology of education is the set of theories which provide the windows through which sociologists see the educational world. These theories in one form or another permeate all attempts by sociologists to understand education, whether it be the students in the classroom, the teacher, or the parents. Instead it would be impossible to fully understand much of the writing on substantive areas within the sociology of education without some knowledge of the theoretical frameworks which sociologists adopt, or are committed to, in their research.

The two overview articles on classical sociological theories of education (Saha and Zubrzycki) and contemporary sociological theories of education (Turner and Mitchell) open the section and put other theoretical perspectives into a temporal and theoretical framework. These are followed by a series of more focused treatments of specific theoretical approaches such as hermeneutics and reproduction theory, or specialized areas within the sociology of education such as education administration (Foster) and social psychological theories of education (Bank and Biddle).

4.2.2 Sociological Fields in the Sociology of Education. The purpose of this section is to present the diversity in the sociology of education. There are many subfields which can be included under the broad umbrella of the sociology of education which, to some extent, have developed their own specialist methodologies, highly specialized research and policy agendas, and specialist personnel. In some cases journals have emerged which are largely sociological in nature but which are highly focused in subject matter.

This section starts with a general overview to the sociology of education, which is thematically organized, followed by 15 articles which provide an overview and state-of-the-art discussion of "sociologies of education."

4.2.3 Research Traditions in the Sociology of Education. Research methodologies in one respect might be said to be discipline free: they are applicable to most research problems, human or nonhuman. This can be said about research traditions in the sociology of education. For the most part those who conduct research in social aspects of education tend to use standard methodologies and conventional techniques. However, this is only a partial truth, for the study of education poses unique problems for the researcher. In the first place, the objects of research can be students, teachers, or the school or educational systems themselves. The human subjects can be of any age, sex, or socioeconomic status. Furthermore, the study of education can produce unique research problems, particularly as schools are not randomly structured or organized. Because they are organized by classes, which in turn are often selective, it is difficult to obtain truly random samples, or for that matter typical subjects, whether students, teachers, or principals. Thus, educational research is problematic from the outset.

It is because of these challenges that educational research has been the developing ground for new methodologies, both quantitative and qualitative. Attempts to account for the effects of home and background, classrooms, peers, teachers, and school climates and cultures on the social academic experiences and outcomes of students have resulted in a rich variety of approaches and methodologies. At the same time, researchers have had to struggle with the more fundamental epistemological questions of research knowledge itself.

This section provides the reader with a wide coverage of these research problems and methods within the sociology of education. The coverage of articles range from questions of research knowledge and the nature of scientific enquiry, to general trends in qualitative and quantitative methods, to specific methods such as highly quantitative education production functions to the qualitative biographical research methods. The trend articles suggest that developments to further refine our ability to conduct valid and reliable research on the sociological dimensions of educational structures and processes will continue.

4.2.4 The School as a Social System. In sociology, a social system is defined as any patterned way of doing things in society. In this respect, the articles in this section focus upon the ways that the school can be seen as a social system, and in this respect how society influences the patterned behaviors which take place within the school.

The 10 articles in this section are varied, ranging from the manner in which the state influences the patterned ways of behavior in schools to the influence of school size on what goes on in schools. In like manner, the difference between capitalist and socialist schooling relates to system differences. Even though some of the distinctions may be primarily of historical interest, over the past 70 years there have been in the world clear differences between the capitalist and socialist systems, and these differences have attracted much attention from sociologists of education. In the end, the system level of analysis focuses on those factors which explain how schools function like a social organism, that is a set of patterned behaviors which reflect how individuals within the system behave.

4.2.5 The Structure of Educational Systems. In contrast to social systems, the study of social structures focuses on the ways through which social life is bounded by the organizational patterns of a system, and how these patterns impinge on individual, group, or organizational behavior. These organizational patterns can be formal or informal, and therefore include deliberate decisions to structure a social activity in a particular way, such as a company, or informal patterns which emerge from social behavior, but which nonetheless structure social or organizational behavior, such as informal promotion criteria which affect promotions, but which are never formally approved or written down.

The study of social structures by sociologists is extensive, and this applies no less to the study of education and schooling. Educational administration, schools as bureaucracies, and many other areas of enquiry fall within this field.

In this section the 15 articles focus on various organizational patterns in educational systems and include both formal and informal patterns. The topics address both the ways students are organized in classrooms, as well as the ways in which education is organized across educational systems, and the consequences of these patterns.

4.2.6 School Processes. Much research on schools focuses on the social characteristics which students bring with them into schools, the inputs, or what they bring with them when they leave, the outputs. However, the study of school processes focuses on what is going on within the "black box" of education. It could be argued that what goes on inside schools, that is these processes, provides ". . . the arena where the structures of the educational system converge in the daily face-to-face encounters between teacher–student and student–student in the classroom, the corridors, in the courtyards and on the playing fields" (Saha 1990 p. 113). It is also the area of schooling that attracts researchers of varying theoretical and methodological approaches.

These processes affect many dimensions of the experience of the students, and this is reflected in the 19 articles which are included here. The discussion of school processes includes a wide range of topics from the hidden curriculum in schools to the ways that young people experience the danger of dropping out of school altogether.

4.2.7 Family and Schooling. The family is generally regarded as the most important factor which explains if and how young people experience school. However, even though the research on family effects is extensive, there are many aspects of family influence that are little understood. Obviously the resources available in the family, which are related to the social and occupational status of the parents, have a great influence on the ability of the family to support the child's educational opportunities. But there is much more than this. The culture of the family, or what is sometimes called the family environment, can operate independently of the status of family background. It is areas such as these that have yet to be adequately researched.

The 13 articles in this section address the many dimensions of family influence on the educational experiences of young people. These range from a general overview of the relationship between the family and schooling, the importance of the home environment, and the impact of single-parent families on children's educational experiences.

4.2.8 Teachers in Society. Sociologists and educational researchers generally have debated the relevance of teachers in the educational process. Indeed it has been sometimes suggested that teachers are a minor factor in the determination of educational outcomes. However, like all professions, teachers are an object of research in their own right, and their roles, career patterns, and school practices have been extensively researched.

The 13 articles in this section cover a range of topics relating to teachers: from teacher recruitment, teacher roles, their professional lives, and the factors which sometimes lead to their burnout from the teaching profession. Given that teachers form a major component in the educational costs to a society, and given that their input into the educational process is central to the sociological study of education, no account of sociological research in education can neglect them.

4.2.9 Youth in Schools. Sociological research on school students generally focus on them solely within an educational context. However, what is often overlooked is that students have a life outside of schools, or at least outside the classroom. In this respect the study of youth is more than the study of school students. It is the study of peer groups, and it is the study of a social category that exists independently of the school. However, the life of students outside of school has a profound relationship with what goes on within schools. The impact of the wider society and its appeal to youth, leisure activities, and contact with other youth through participation in youth subcultures all have an impact on how youth will interact with schooling.

The 11 articles in this section cover a wide range of topics which touch upon the above considerations. Furthermore, the articles follow youth after schooling and include their political and occupational careers as well.

4.2.10 Educational Policy and Change. The concluding section of the *Encyclopedia* addresses a macro perspective of the role of education generally, and schools in particular, as change agents in society. Much has been written about the contribution that education, in producing a learned and skilled population, makes to the economic development of a country. It is often argued that an educated population is more politically informed, more flexible in employment skills, and more productive in work output. Social and economic development are seen as the long-term consequences of this process. Seven articles address these issues in the first subsection.

In addition to the role of education as a change agent, the impact of technology on education (and the reverse) and on society are pressing issues in the adjustments of education to modern society. These issues are reviewed and discussed in the five articles of this subsection.

Finally, the principles of education policy and planning are as much a part of the sociology of education as are the topics of the previous nine sections of this *Encyclopedia*. The development of policy and planning are social in nature, and therefore any understanding of these processes must take into account these social factors. The four articles in this section focus on these issues in a variety of contexts.

In this respect the 16 articles in Section X provide a fitting conclusion to the *Encyclopedia*.

5. Themes and Other Topical Areas

As indicated earlier, those involved in the sociology of education and educational research would no doubt suggest other ways of organizing an encyclopedia. In particular, one might ask about the representation of particular themes which have made recent impact on our sociological thinking about education and schools, for example, race, gender, and class. In reply, it needs to be said that these are indeed well represented, but are grouped in the sections which seem most appropriate. For example, there are a dozen articles which specifically address sex/gender effects and women's issues in education, and these are found in seven of the 10 sections of the *Encyclopedia*. In like manner, race, ethnic, and social class issues are addressed in articles in at least five sections.

The same can be said for the newer perspectives (and indeed some "old" ones) in the sociology of education, such as the "new" sociology of education or the "critical" sociology of education. The reader is encouraged to search both the table of contents and the index in order to locate those topical areas of interest. In this way, not only will specific relevant articles be located, but treatments of topics within wider contexts will be available.

6. Acknowledgments

An encyclopedia of this magnitude could not have been produced without the help of many people. In the first place, I wish to express gratitude to Torsten Húsen and T. Neville Postlethwaite who not only provided valuable feedback on the proposal for this volume, but invited me several years ago to be a section editor for the sociology of education for *The International Encyclopedia of Education, Second Edition*. Participation in that very ambitious and mammoth project provided me with the opportunity to work with an international team of researchers, and to meet and become familiar with the work of other educational researchers throughout the world. It was that project which equipped me with the academic contacts and knowledge needed for the production of this volume. Second, I am also grateful to Barbara Barrett and her staff at Elsevier Science Ltd., in particular Michele Wheaton, Glenda Pringle, and Helen Collins, who worked on this project at various times. Third, I owe gratitude to John P. Keeves of Flinders University, himself a Pergamon author, who listened patiently to my ideas for this volume and gave me much valuable advice. Finally, my gratitude goes to the many authors who produced the highly specialized and excellent articles for this volume. I hope they derived as much satisfaction in their own contributions as I had in working with them, and in seeing this volume come together. To all of them, my sincere gratitude.

References

Apple M W 1996 Power, meaning and identity: critical sociology of education in the United States. *Br. J. Sociol. Educ.* 17(2): 125–44

Banks O 1971 *The Sociology of Education*, 2nd edn. Batsford, London

Demaine J 1981 *Contemporary Theories in the Sociology of Education* Macmillan, London

Filloux J-C 1993 Emile Durkheim. *Prospects: Quarterly Review of Education* XXIII (1/2): 303–20

Hansen D A 1967 The uncomfortable relation of sociology and education. In: Hansen D A, Gerstle J E (eds.) 1967 *On Education: Sociological Perspectives*. John Wiley & Sons, New York

Karabel J, Halsey A H (eds.) 1977 *Power and Ideology in Education* Oxford University Press, New York

Karabel J 1979 The sociology of education: perils and possibilities. *Am. Sociol.* 14(May): 85–91

Lehmann J M 1995 The question of caste in modern society: Durkheim's contradictory theories of race, class, and sex. *Am. Sociol. Rev.* 60(August): 566–85

Noblit G W, Pink W T 1995 Mapping the alternative paths of the sociology of education. In: Pink W T, Noblit G W (eds.) 1995 *Continuity and Contradiction: The Futures of the Sociology of Education*. Hampton Press, Cresskill, New Jersey

Saha L J 1990 Schools as youth-processing institutions. In: Saha L J, Keeves J P (eds.) 1990 *Schooling and Society in Australia: Australian Perspectives*. Australian National University Press, Sydney

Shilling C 1992 Reconceptualising structure and agency in the sociology of education: structuration theory and schooling. *Br. J. Sociol. Educ.* 13(1): 69–87

Tepperman L 1979 Editor's Introduction. In: Murphy R (ed.) 1979 *Sociological Theories of Education*. McGraw-Hill Ryerson Ltd., Toronto

Trent W, Braddock J, Henderson R 1985 Sociology of education: a focus on education as an institution. In: Gordon E (ed.) 1985 *Rev. Res. Educ.* 12: 295–335

Wexler P 1987 *Social Analysis of Education*. Routledge, New York

June 1997

LAWRENCE J. SAHA
Canberra, Australia

Social Theories in the Sociology of Education

Introduction: Theoretical Developments in the Sociology of Education

L. J. Saha

Up to three decades ago, it was said that what was then called educational sociology should not be allowed to perpetuate itself (Conant 1963, cited in Banks 1971 p. 2), that it was "ivory tower nonsense" (Hansen 1967), and that it was characterized by the "sterility of the questions that it asked" (Corwin 1965). Somewhat later, however, Karabel (1979) argued that the sociology of education had become ". . . one of the most vibrant and respected areas of sociological research," largely because of the theoretical developments taking place within it. Richardson (1986) observed that by the end of the 1970s, "the sociology of education experienced a revitalization of theory which placed the field at the forefront of sociology itself" (p. xvi). More recently, Noblit and Pink (1995) offered a view of the sociology of education "that is extremely rich, vibrant, and diverse" with "an exciting range of substantive issues for investigation, *as well as an equally exciting range of theoretical considerations* and methodological tools for undertaking these investigations . . ." (p. 27, italics mine). Clearly, the sociology of education appears destined to enter the next millennium in a healthy theoretical state.

The 14 articles in this section provide support to the view that theoretical developments in the sociology of education are "rich, vibrant, and diverse." The section is divided into two subsections, the first of which consists of three overview articles which complement the more focused articles in the second subsection.

1. Theoretical Overviews

The origins of the sociology of education go back almost to the origins of sociology itself. The overview article on *Classical Sociological Theories of Education* by Saha and Zubrzycki shows that all three of the founding fathers of sociology, Durkheim, Weber, and Marx, have had considerable influence in the origins of the sociological study of education, although it was Durkheim who held a specific interest in education. Weber and Marx were less interested than their followers in the study of education, and with them it is more a question of the application of their theory than a specific interest in education.

The legacy of the classical theorists is apparent in the second overview article by Turner and Mitchell, *Contemporary Sociological Theories of Education*, which traces the development of theoretical paradigms in the sociology of education, for example, functionalism, conflict theorizing, including the Marxian and Weberian inspired conflict theories, and finally forms of interactionist theories. The authors suggest that there may be a hiatus between theorizing in the sociology of education and actual research. The latter, because it is often problem- and reform-oriented, may use theory in a more vague and less precise manner.

A third theoretical overview of an area closely interrelated with the sociology of education is found in Bank and Biddle's article, *Social Psychological Theories in Education*. Considerable research in the sociology of education has focused on, or used, social psychological variables to explain academic and educational achievement. Examples of these variables are the aspirations and expectations of students, forms of self-image or self-confidence, and beliefs about the causes of success and failure. In particular, the Wisconsin status attainment model which has dominated quantitative research in the last two decades relied heavily on social psychological variables (see, for example, Haller 1982).

2. Theoretical Perspectives

A number of focused discussions about theoretical perspectives are found in Section Ib. In some cases these articles expand on the discussions found in one of the overview articles, for example, the articles *Administration of Education: Critical Approaches* (Foster), *Critical Theory and Education* (Lakomski), *Marxism and Educational Thought* (Burbules), *Positivism, Antipositivism, and Empiricism* (Phillips), *Reproduction Theory* (Teese), and *Resistance Theory* (Walker). On the other hand, several articles focus on theoretical approaches to education which are less commonly represented in sociological and educational analyses, and in some cases represent new theoretical developments in explanations of education, such as the articles on *Hermeneutics* (Ödman and Kerdeman), *Gender Theories in Education* (Davies), *Phenomenology and Existentialism* (Small), and *Postmodernism and Education* (Marshall and Peters). Finally. Luke, in his *Critical Discourse Analysis*, represents a theoretically-based approach (borrowing from psycholinguistics, sociolinguistics, and poststructuralism) to study written and verbal language communication, and is characterized by keywords such as *text, discourse, intertexuality, genre, subjectivity, hegemony,* and *ideology*.

The articles in this section support the observations made by writers that the sociology of education has indeed been a fertile ground for theoretical development. This does not mean, of course, that all research in the sociology of education is well grounded in theory, but rather that many of the important questions about education and schooling have received attention by theorists. There is good reason to believe that the richness and the tradition of theoretical development in the sociological study of education will continue well into the future.

References

Banks O 1971 *The Sociology of Education*, 2nd edn. Batsford, London
Corwin R G 1965 *A Sociology of Education*. Appleton-Century Crofts, New York
Haller A O 1982 Reflections on the social psychology of status attainment. In: Hauser R M, Mechanic D, Haller A O, Hauser T (eds.) 1982 *Social Structure and Behavior*, Academic Press, New York
Hansen D A 1967 The uncomfortable relation of sociology and education. In: Hansen D A, Gerstle J E (eds.) 1967 *On Education: Sociological Perspectives*. John Wiley & Sons, New York
Karabel J 1979 The sociology of education: perils and possibilities. *Am. Sociol.* 14 (May): 185–91
Noblit G W, Pink W T 1995 Mapping the alternative paths of the sociology of education. In: Pink W T, Noblit G W (eds.) 1995 *Continuity and Contradiction; The Futures of the Sociology of Education*. Hampton Press, Cresskill, New Jersey
Richardson J G 1986 Introduction. In: Richardson J G (ed.) 1986 *Handbook of Theory and Research for the Sociology of Education*. Greenwood Press, New York

(a) Theoretical Overviews

Classical Sociological Theories of Education

L. J. Saha and J. Zubrzycki

This article will focus on the sociological writings about education by the three founding fathers of sociology, Durkheim, Marx, and Weber, and will briefly discuss four other important writers, Spencer, Mannheim, Veblen, and Znaniecki. These early sociologists continue to influence contemporary thought through the main sociological theoretical traditions of functionalism, conflict theory, interpretive sociology, and critical theory.

1. Education in Social and Political Theory

From the time philosophers and social thinkers began to consider the major questions of society, education has been a part of their concern, particularly in relation to social and political matters. Often references were made to education in the broadest sense, including forms of socialization, as in Plato's *Republic*, Aristotle's *Politics*, and Adam Smith's *The Wealth of Nations*. In some cases, references to education and learning pertained to the writer's own education, as in Augustine's *Confessions* or Descartes's *Discourse*. In many instances, education was the central focus of the treatises themselves, as in Augustine's *Concerning the Teacher*, Milton's *Of Education*, Locke's *Some Thoughts Concerning Education*, Comenius's *The Great Didactic*, and Rousseau's *Emile* (see Adler and Gorman 1952). The nineteenth century produced educational writings such as Newman's *The Idea of a University*, Arnold's *Culture and Anarchy*, and Spencer's *Education: Intellectual, Moral and Physical*, while the twentieth century produced the writings of Russell, Dewey, and Whitehead.

These early classical works of social and political thought usually related the notion of education to teaching and learning, the cultivation of character (in particular the acquisition of values such as virtue and truth) and habits of the mind, and, above all, the exercise of citizenship. These concerns were both pedagogical and sociological, and in many respects the understanding of education can be traced back to these early writers.

2. Emile Durkheim and the Origins of the Sociology of Education

Modern sociology of education had its formal beginnings in the writings of Emile Durkheim, who seems to have been one of the first to have systematically examined the relationship between education and society. This is not to say that earlier social philosophers ignored the social context of education. Nothing could be further from the truth, as any history of educational thought makes patently clear. Much of this earlier concern, however, focused on the social and moral development of the child, as did Rousseau, for example. It was the sociologists, however, who began to explore the social link between education and society, particularly in terms of education's role in social integration, social cohesion, social conflict, and social inequality. Durkheim, as a teacher of teachers, was preoccupied with some of these aspects of education's link with society.

Emile Durkheim (1858–1917) was born in the Alsace-Lorraine region of France into a Jewish rabbinical family. He attended the best of the Parisian schools, leading to entry to the Ecole normale supérieure, the training ground for the French elite, and there he prepared for a teaching career and also embarked on doctoral studies. Durkheim spent a number of years teaching in French *lycées*, spent a year on scholarship in Germany, and in 1887 was appointed to the University of Bordeaux, where he taught social science and pedagogy. In 1902 he transferred to the Sorbonne, where he was appointed Professor of Pedagogy in 1906, and to the Chair of Pedagogy and Sociology in 1912. He remained there for the rest of his life.

Through his main sociological works, *The Division of Labor in Society* (1893), *The Rules of Sociological Method* (1895), *Suicide* (1897), and *The Elementary Forms of Religious Life* (1915), Durkheim not only firmly established sociology as a legitimate academic discipline, but also laid the foundation for a sociological perspective which continues to influence contemporary sociological theory and research.

Durkheim's primary sociological preoccupation was the study of social solidarity and social order. Although not sympathetic to revolutionary Marxism, Durkheim was aware of conflict and inequality in industrial society, and believed that reform was possible by means of new forms of occupational associations and social cohesion. Although Durkheim was basically

a functionalist in his analysis of major social institutions (like the division of labor and religion), his
sociology is much more complex. His functionalism
has caused him to be regarded, until recently, as a
conservative (Nisbet 1965) when in fact he held left-
wing political views and was not solely concerned with
the conservative forces in society (see, for example,
Pearce 1989, Lehmann 1995).

2.1 Durkheim, Sociological Functionalism, and Education

Put simply, functionalism is a type of social theory
which explains a social phenomenon in terms of its
contribution to the operations of a larger social phenomenon, institution, or society. A pattern of behavior
is said to be "functional" when it can be explained
in terms of its beneficial effects on the integration
or survival of the larger society; it is said to be
"dysfunctional" when it exercises negative effects
on the integration or survival of a society. Various functionalist arguments have become common in
the sociological literature, for example, in terms of
manifest and latent functions, system maintenance or
stability, and the satisfaction of basic societal needs or
prerequisites for the survival of society.

The origins of functionalism are usually traced to
the notion of society compared to a biological organism, seen as a system made up of many interdependent
parts. Some have argued that its first impetus and use
came from the early sociologists Auguste Comte and
Herbert Spencer, since they tended to take a more
holistic and biological view of society. However, the
dominance of functionalism owes much more to Emile
Durkheim (although Durkheim never used the term
"functionalism"). In his work *The Rules of Sociological Method* Durkheim commented: "When, then, the
explanation of a social phenomenon is undertaken,
we must seek separately the efficient cause which
produces it and the function it fulfils" (Durkheim
1964 p. 95).

For Durkheim, the importance of a focus on function
is that it represents a methodology for the analysis
of what he called "social facts," that is, patterns of
behavior in society which exercise external constraints
on individual behavior. The importance of a functional
approach is thus evident in his argument that "to
explain a social fact it is not enough to show the cause
on which it depends; we must also, at least in most
cases, show its function in the establishment of social
order" (p. 97).

It is important, however, to appreciate that
Durkheim was not wholly deterministic in his view
of the force of social facts. Liberty and freedom,
for Durkheim, were not inhibited by "social facts."
As he saw it, "Liberty is the daughter of authority
properly understood. For to be free is not to do
what one pleases; it is to be master of oneself, it
is to know how to act with reason and to do one's
duty" (pp. 89–90). In this context, one can understand

Durkheim's opposition to those such as the Epicu-
reans and Montaigne who saw education as pleasure.
For Durkheim, education was the mechanism through
which the child learned to exercise strong control
and restraint in order to become an "ideal adult" and
thus ensure the survival of a differentiated society. In
such a society, dominated by the ideals of moral individualism, conformity must "not amount to passive
resignation, but to enlightened allegiance" (Durkheim
1961 p. 115).

From these principles, it is clear that Durkheim's
functionalist sociology and his understanding of education in society have exercised considerable influence on much of twentieth-century educational theory
and research. The development of the functionalist
view of society in sociology, particularly through
the work of Talcott Parsons and Robert Merton,
was important for the study of how the young are
integrated into adult society. Socialization generally,
and the family and school in particular, became essential components of modern functionalist analysis
of schooling and of society. Indeed, for Durkheim,
education was the "methodical socialization" of young
members into society (Halls 1994) (see *Contemporary
Sociological Theories of Education; Socialization*).

2.2 Durkheim on Education and Society

The earliest of Durkheim's educational writings, *Education and Sociology* (1922) and *Moral Education*
(1925), were published posthumously, and for decades
were taken to represent the corpus of Durkheim's
theory of education and society. However, with the
growing awareness of his work following the publication of a series of later lectures given between 1904–05
and 1914, *The Evolution of Educational Thought:
Lectures on the Formation and Development of Secondary Education in France*, Durkheim's sociology of
education has become the focus of renewed interest.
In France, Cherkaoui (1976, 1981) has argued that a
different Durkheim is found in this volume: not one of
consensus, order, equilibrium, and functionalism, but
rather one of struggle and ideological conflict. Fenton
(1984) comments that there remains much of value to
be found in a closer analysis of Durkheim's sociology
of education.

In *Education and Sociology*, Durkheim put forward
his broadest interpretation of the link between education and society. It is an eminently functionalist interpretation. Durkheim reserved the term "education"
to mean the influence exercised by adult generations
on those not yet ready for social life, in other words,
the methodological socialization of the young. Every
society, according to Durkheim, has adapted education
to conform to its values and goals. This is why,
he argued, educational systems have displayed such
variety both across societies and in the same societies
over time. For Durkheim, it was unthinkable that
education could function differently: "Of what use is
it to imagine a kind of education that would be fatal

for the society that put it into practice?" (Durkheim 1956 p. 64).

Durkheim, then, saw education and society as inextricably linked, the former as an element in the latter's overall structure. Furthermore, Durkheim argued that the educational system contributes to the survival of society: "Education is, then, only the means by which society prepares, within the children, the essential conditions of its very existence" (p. 71). In this respect, Durkheim admired great educational thinkers such as Comenius, Rousseau and Condorcet, because they saw education as oriented to the external world, to the needs of society, and in this sense they took a utilitarian perspective. He was less impressed with Montaigne, Erasmus, and the Jesuits, because they were too humanistic, antiscience, and other-wordly in their educational goals. Thus Durkheim maintained that every society has its own "ideal of man, of what he should be, as much from the intellectual point of view as the physical and moral" (p. 70). This ideal included religious and moral priorities, national traditions, and group consciousness (or what he called a "conscience collective"). In other words, the function of education is to produce "ideal adults" for society (Fauconnet 1923).

2.3 Durkheim and Moral Education

It is precisely in this context that one can understand Durkheim's observation that all education is moral education, for the notion of morality lay at the heart of his theory of society and was "a subject to which he was completely dedicated" (Pickering 1995 p.20). Durkheim regarded morality as the set of duties and obligations which influences the behavior of individuals. Although earlier notions of morality were linked with religious beliefs, Durkheim contended that modern industrial society requires a secular morality, one resting on reason. The future of a cohesive society rests on the maintenance of a moral code of social obligations and duties which benefit the individual as well as society. "In a word," he argued in his Sorbonne lectures of 1902–03, "we must discover the rational substitutes for those religious notions that for a long time have served as the vehicle for the most essential moral ideas" (Durkheim 1961 p. 9).

For Durkheim, then, formal or systematic education lay at the center of his larger concern for the creation and maintenance of consensus and solidarity in an increasingly differentiated, specialized, and heterogeneous industrial society. Furthermore, Durkheim's personal commitment, as well as his view of academic sociology, was that it should be used to "help us determine the way in which we ought to orient our conduct" (cited in Wilson 1961 p. ix). Given his concern for the practical uses of basic research, Durkheim therefore constructed a theory of educational practice which included what he considered the three basic elements of morality: discipline, attachment to social groups, and autonomy. Durkheim believed that discipline was

essential to ensure consistency and regularity of conduct, as well as a sense of authority which would serve to evoke both the desired responses and restraints in human behavior. This moral discipline is relevant only insofar as it is oriented to a particular group or society. Thus Durkheim argued that moral behavior requires an attachment (or belonging) to a social group. Finally, Durkheim did not believe that moral behavior could be coerced or forced behavior. In other words, the individual must freely choose to behave in a manner which reflects obligation and responsibility toward society as a whole. He saw moral behavior, then, as based on the "desirability" of the object of that behavior, or what might be called "moral motivation" (Hall 1993), even though there might also be "effort, pain, and sacrifice," for ". . .a moral action which is too easy to carry out is not a moral action" (Durkheim 1995 p.29). Durkheim, even in his concern for the integration of the larger society, wished to preserve individual and self-determined behavior.

2.4 Durkheim, Conflict, and Education

In two works, *Professional Ethics and Civic Morals* (1957) and *The Evolution of Educational Thought* (1977), Durkheim dispels the notion that his sociology is purely conservative and functionalist.

In the former, Durkheim recognized the need for social change in the France of his day. As a nonrevolutionary socialist, Durkheim was concerned that the goals of the French Revolution (liberty, equality, and fraternity) had not been achieved. Durkheim observed that the economic structure of modern society was changing: "There has been talk, and not without reason, of societies becoming mainly industrial" (1957 p. 11). Furthermore, Durkheim was mistrustful of the self-interest with which individuals carried out their economic activities. He recognized the possibility of continual conflict between members of economic groups and argued that stability and order constituted a "moral task." As he wrote: "It is therefore extremely important that economic life should be regulated, should have its moral standards raised, so that the conflicts that disturb it have an end" (p. 12). For Durkheim, this moral regulation could only come about through the formation of organizational groups which would foster a moral code of behavior which would protect the rights of individuals and groups. Durkheim saw education as one of the professional activities connected with the state which required regulation. Therefore, while Durkheim saw the functional importance of education in terms of its production of the "ideal adult" and moral consensus in society, he was also aware that education was an occupation (a profession) within which self-interest and conflict were endemic, and, furthermore, that conflict between education and the state could be expected.

This Janus-faced view of education is most apparent in *The Evolution of Educational Thought*. In this important analysis Durkheim was concerned with historical struggle and ideological conflict. As with the rest of society, Durkheim believed that the struggle over educational ideas (and as he calls it here, the production of "the man of his times") has always existed, and explains the forms of education found in France in the first part of the twentieth century. For Durkheim, the history of education was in reality the history of secondary education, and this secondary education had its origins in the cathedral and cloister schools of the pre-Carolingian period. Because these schools incorporated the church's need both to perpetuate its teachings (through the training of priests) and to preach and convert, they contained both sacred and profane elements, or what Durkheim called "the germ of that great struggle" (1977 p. 26). In this sweeping sociological and historical analysis of French education, Durkheim wove a convincing argument that it was conflict, rather than consensus, out of which French secondary education originated and developed. From the beginning, even though the influence of the church prevailed, education was hierarchically structured, starting with parish schools on the bottom, equivalent to elementary schools, then the cathedral schools, and finally the elite Ecole du Palais at the top (Durkheim 1977).

Thus for Durkheim there were two main struggles in the development of French education: that between the sacred and the profane, and that between the various social groups in their access to and participation in schooling.

Ultimately, however, Durkheim never lost his conviction that a strong society required a strong educational system, and the "ideal adult" was a person who was integrated and committed to the goals of the society as a whole. Toward the end of his life Durkheim lamented the weak moral integration of French society during the First World War. The solution rested in the school, through which the moral fiber of France was to be reawakened. Thus the future French school should inculcate "respect for legitimate authority," the "joys of acting in conjunction with others" in accordance with a law common to all, and a school discipline which would appear to children as "something good and sacred." In this way, Durkheim argued, "when they are men, they will accept spontaneously and consciously that social discipline which cannot be weakened without endangering the community" (Durkheim 1977 pp. 160–61).

Durkheim's belief that the moral fabric of a society rested on its educational system is one that survives in much of modern educational thought. In spite of the instrumental (vocational) aspects of education which have dominated much debate in the 1980s and 1990s over the functions of education, the concern with moral aspects of education survive. The belief in the "ideal adult" is as prevalent in the 1990s as it was in Durkheim's day. However, what has been lost among many modern educational functionalists is the awareness that the notion of the "ideal adult" is the product of competing (and conflicting) beliefs and interests in society as a whole.

3. Karl Marx and Education as Conflict

In many respects, the Marxist view of schooling, and particularly of school processes, shares much with its functionalist counterpart. Like functionalism, Marxist and neo-Marxist theories focus primarily on structural aspects of society in order to understand what is happening within society and its institutions. Underlying the Marxist theory is the added conviction that social structure and social processes can be explained in terms of the economic base of society. Both the superstructure of society (social institutions such as political, religious and military institutions) and "forms of consciousness" (ideas and knowledge) are ultimately to be understood in terms of the dominant mode of economic production (for example, feudalism, capitalism, or communism) and the relation of individuals and groups of individuals to that mode of production.

3.1 Marx's Writings on Education

While Karl Marx (1818–83) never made any systematic reference to education as part of the capitalist class system which he saw as dominating Western industrial societies, the importance of education is nevertheless implicit in his theory. Comments about education and schooling are scattered throughout Marx's writings. For example, an examination of the volumes of the collected works of Marx and Engels reveals many substantial discussions of education and schooling (Cleverly 1985). For the most part these comments are in the context of other, more central features of his theory of society, particularly those of class struggle and alienation. Marx apparently held education in high regard. It was rather the content of education and the way its facilities were distributed and used in industrializing societies of the late nineteenth century that concerned him.

Marx's early writings about education are almost functionalist, for he regarded education as an important agent for the socialization of the young into the roles they would assume as adults. Indeed, Marx regarded the outside world as a wider classroom than the narrower classroom of the school, but he also recognized the specific functions of formal education. In 1842, writing in the *Kölnische Zeitung*, Marx commented that through education the state converts "the aims of the individual into general aims, crude instinct into moral inclination, natural independence into spiritual freedom, by the individual finding his good in the life of the whole, and the whole in the frame of mind of the individual" (Marx 1842 p. 193).

Both Marx and his colleague, Frederick Engels, advocated education for all. Even more, they regarded the general education of children to be the responsibility of the state and an essential factor for the attainment of "practical communism." However, the main concern of Marx was with the type of education working-class youth received. It was in this context that he regarded education in capitalist societies as a tool which the ruling class, the bourgeoisie, used to their advantage. According to Marx, the bourgeoisie regarded the education of the workers as a form of "indoctrination with bourgeois principles, and that . . . the bourgeois class neither has the means, nor if it had them would it use them, to offer the people a real education" (Marx 1847 p. 427).

One of Marx's main concerns was the monopoly which the ruling class had on education, and by which it created a working class which was useful for it. The ruling class, through education, became noble, wise, and articulate, while the working class was kept silent and inarticulate. Thus Marx gradually began to understand the educational system of the capitalist industrial period as a means of perpetuating the advantaged position of the ruling class and the disadvantaged position of the working class.

3.2 Marx and Contemporary Theories of Education

Marx and Engels never fully integrated their views on education into their theory of capitalism and the transition of capitalist to socialist and communist societies. Nor did they clearly develop a model of an educational system which would not act as a tool for the ruling class. This was left to later generations of Marxists and neo-Marxists, particularly in the 1960s and 1970s, when Marxist sociology was in the ascendant in the discipline. It was during this period that socialist and liberation pedagogies, as alternatives to capitalist education, were developed among Western Marxists (see, for example, Norton and Ollman 1978). Furthermore, two identifiable Marxist sociological traditions emerged, each with relevance for education: the structuralists and the voluntarists.

Structural Marxists argue that patterns of social behavior are "determined" by the structures of society, especially the economic structure. In the 1960s and early 1970s, the person most responsible for developing this view was Althusser (1972). Althusser argued that in capitalist societies most social institutions, such as religion, education, and the military, serve the interests of the state. In turn, the state is controlled by the ruling capitalist class. In a capitalist system an important component is the reproduction of labor power and the reproduction of the conditions of production, that is, the reproduction of the relations of production. Althusser's application of his perspective to schooling is particularly important in this regard.

According to Althusser, capitalist state apparatuses such as schools operate through "ideological" means rather than repressive means or force. In this respect, schools serve to maintain the status quo not by force (as might the police or the military) but through nonphysical means. Thus through the inculcation of the ruling class ideology, schools "will provide for the domination of the ruling class 'in words'" (Althusser 1972 pp. 245–46).

The significant aspect of Althusser's Marxist interpretation of the educational system is that it functions in a "deterministic" manner. Althusser argued that human behavior is determined by the structures and processes of society, and in this context he represents "scientific Marxism," which regards schools as a tool or apparatus of the ruling class through which the "means of production" and the "relations of production" are maintained. Further developments of education as an agent of social reproduction are found in the writings of Bourdieu in France and Bowles and Gintis in the United States (see *Reproduction Theory*).

An alternate "humanistic" form of neo-Marxism with respect to schools and school processes is exemplified by the ideas of Gramsci (1891–1937). Writing during Italy's Fascist period, Gramsci argued that subjective factors, such as beliefs, values, aspirations, and culture in general, could not be ignored in trying to understand capitalism and human behavior. Thus Gramsci contended that schools do not simply reflect the dominance of the ruling class (as Althusser argued), but can be instruments of general social change and, in particular, instruments for overthrowing the dominance of the capitalist system (see Entwistle 1979). In this respect, Gramsci's "voluntarist" theory is closely related to the views of the Frankfurt School of sociology, which argued that the transformation from capitalism to socialism could be accomplished through nonrevolutionary means, primarily through the development of "critical consciousness" or "awareness" which would lead to emancipation from capitalist oppression. Represented by the writings of Habermas, Marcuse, and others, the members of the Frankfurt School have tended to oppose positivism and quantitative research and endorse social criticism and social transformation. Although the writings of these latter so-called "critical theorists" do not fall into a tidy homogeneous category, they have exerted an influence on the sociological study of education, which has resulted in critiques of the process of schooling in capitalist societies (see *Critical Theory and Education*).

According to some, it would be inappropriate to assume that the influence of a Marxist framework on educational theory and practice has waned in recent years. Rikowski (1996) contends that Marxism remains influential, and he differentiates between the "old" and the "new" Marxist educational theory. The former, he argues, consists of reproduction and resistance theories, and the latter of newer approaches which focus their critiques on the marketization of education, and a "return to class" in confronting educational postmodernism. According to Rikowski, these new forms may eventually replace the "old" forms of

Marxist educational theory in the analysis of schooling in capitalist societies.

4. Max Weber and Education

Max Weber (1864–1920), a German sociologist who is often regarded as the third of the founding fathers of modern sociology, never wrote a specific treatise about education. Nevertheless, his concerns regarding the changes taking place in Germany and Europe during the nineteenth century resulted in an approach to sociological analysis which has had an important impact on contemporary sociology of education.

Weber is best known for his rejection of Marx's historical materialism, the class struggle, and the notion that working-class domination was the desired end-state of conflicts in Western society. The topics addressed by Weber in his sociological writings were wide ranging, including the increasing rationalization and bureaucratization of modern society, value freedom in the social sciences, and the subjective meaningfulness of human action. Because of the breadth of his inquiries, and the absence of a unified integrated theory of society, Weber's influence on modern sociology of education has tended to be indirect and multistranded. The three most relevant areas of impact derive from Weber's understanding of conflict in society and his multifactor interpretation of social stratification, from his concern with the subjective nature of human action, and from his concern with value freedom.

4.1 Weber, Credentialism, and Social Exclusion

Weber's rejection of Marx's economic determinism and the latter's belief in the inevitability of proletarian dominance of the class struggle in Western capitalist society led Weber to adopt a more complex three-fold conceptualization of the conflict base in society: property ownership (class), cultural position in society (status), and differences in power derived from cultural and organizational position in society (power). While Marx saw one form of conflict dominating society (class), Weber saw conflict emerging from all three dimensions. Furthermore, Weber saw social groups in a constant state of struggle to preserve their control over one or more of these dimensions and thereby "exclude" access to them by nongroup members. One way of exercising this control was through the use of knowledge credentials which certified claim or access. Thus for Weber, knowledge, and the proof of possessing that knowledge (credentials), was a major mechanism for the struggles between groups in society.

4.2 Weber and the Subjective Meaning of Human Action

One of Weber's contributions to sociology was his notion of *verstehen*, that is, the observation and theo-

retical interpretation of the subjective "states of mind" of actors (Parsons 1947). For Weber, sociology could be defined as a "science which attempts the interpretive understanding of social action in order thereby to arrive at a causal explanation of its course and effects" (Weber 1947 p. 88). Most importantly, social action, in turn, includes "all human behaviour when and in so far as the acting individual attaches a subjective meaning to it" (Weber 1947 p. 88). Although the notion of subjective meaning for Weber was not straightforward, the essential component of *verstehen*, and interpretive sociology, is that subjective meanings must be differentiated from "objectively 'correct'" meanings, or from truth in a metaphysical sense.

From this approach to the study of human behavior, a strong tradition of an interpretive sociology of education has developed since the late 1960s. The study of the meaning of the classroom experience through the eyes of teachers and students, and the implications of these meanings, stem directly from Weber's preoccupation with social action as he defined it. Teacher expectations and the process and implications of labeling have been a focal point of a sociological study of education based on a Weberian perspective. Although Weber himself never applied this perspective to schooling, it remains an important and rich tradition in the sociology of education (see *School and Classroom Dynamics; Sociology of Teaching*).

4.3 Weber and Bureaucracy

The study of schools as organizations owes much to Weber's concern with the increasing bureaucratization of modern society. This process of bureaucratization is linked to what Weber saw as changing forms of legitimate authority, namely, the traditional, the charismatic, and the rational. Whereas traditional authority is based on belief in the "sanctity" of tradition, and charismatic authority on the devotion to unique characteristics of a specific person, rational authority rests on the believed legality of rules and the rights of those in positions to issue commands.

Weber saw rational authority as emerging from a new form of organizational structure which he called "the bureaucracy." Modern bureaucracy empowers persons in legitimate positions with an authority of office. The main characteristics of bureaucracy are: (a) a division of labor which includes obligations and tasks, (b) an elaborate system of rules and regulations which governs behavior, (c) a hierarchical structure with clear lines of authority, (d) an impersonal and detached approach in dealing with others, (e) a system of record keeping, (f) an administrative staff who do not "own" the organization, and (g) a career structure within the organization (Weber 1947).

Weber's writings on types of authority and bureaucracy have become a central subdiscipline within sociology. However, this same focus has influenced much research into the organization of schools, and the roles and functions of principals and teachers, and the interactions between them. The extent to which teachers are seen as professionals in their own right or as officers of an organization has a direct link with Weber's arguments about bureaucracy. In addition, the study of mobility within the educational system is often analyzed in the context of bureaucratic career structures. Finally, the extent to which the chain of command from central educational authorities, through school principals or head teachers to classroom teachers, is "loosely" or "tightly" coupled is directly related to Weber's notion of bureaucracy (see *Loose Coupling and Educational Systems*).

4.4 Some Applications of Weberian Sociology to the Study of Schools

It has been suggested that one of the reasons why Weber has been relatively neglected by sociologists of education has been the fact that he never developed a unified theory of society. In this respect, Durkheim and Marx have been more utilized (King 1980), although it has been argued that much of what has been labeled as Marxist sociology of education is, in reality, closer to a Weberian perspective. In spite of the fact that there has been no attempt to develop a distinctive Weberian sociology of education, examples of a Weberian approach are numerous.

In the United States, Collins (1971, 1979) contended that a Weberian model of conflict, using the concepts of class, status, and power, provides a plausible explanation for the link between education and occupations. Collins demonstrated that employers use educational qualifications as indicators of characteristics which they consider most important for their jobs. Collins argued that the conflicts over education are more a manifestation of conflict between status groups and less a factor of class struggle. Thus for Collins, "the main activity of schools is to teach particular status cultures, both in and outside the classroom" (1971 p. 1010). It is the conflict between status groups which motivates group members to establish barriers against those outside the group: "the interests of the members in wealth, power, and prestige motivate them to institute strong collective controls over insiders and to seek monopolistic sanctions against outsiders" (1979 p. 135). Collins argued that it is therefore not surprising that "educational credentials are most heavily emphasized within organizations stressing normative control —that is, cultural socialization—and in the large national bureaucracies; nor is it surprising that these are stronger determinants than technological change" (1979 p. 48).

A similar observation was made by Murphy (1982) in his studies of Canadian education. Murphy supported the Weberian notion of education as a mechanism of "closure" whereby the interests of particular status groups are protected. In this respect he regarded schools as more autonomous than the Marxist theories have postulated.

In Australia, Etzioni-Halevy (1987) argued that in-equalities in Australian education are better interpreted from a Weberian rather than Marxist perspective. Using data from the Australian census, she demonstrated that status and cultural variables differentiate better between various measures of educational resources and attainments than Marxist economic variables.

Finally, an example from the United Kingdom of a Weberian influence on education is found in Archer's (1979) analysis of the expansion of the educational systems of the United Kingdom, Denmark, France, and Russia. Archer's study is based largely on a Weberian interpretation of educational change as a result of purposeful action or, in Weber's terminology, the subjective meanings of action. At the same time, while critical of the structural or determinist interpretations of education (for example, derived from Durkheimian and Marxist perspectives), Archer recognized the need to understand purposeful change within a structural context. In this respect, by emphasizing both micro and macro perspectives, she foreshadowed much of the sociological debate of the 1980s and 1990s over agency and structure as explanations of human behavior. Thus she argued that educational change in these countries profoundly affected the behaviors of individuals, but within a structural context.

5. Other Social Theories of Education: Spencer, Mannheim, Veblen, and Znaniecki

Although most contemporary sociological theories of education can be traced back to one of the three founding fathers, there were others who were in part contemporaries, and who also made contributions to the development of the sociological study of education. Four sociologists, who might be considered among the "classics," and whose work continues to influence contemporary educational theory and research, merit attention, namely Herbert Spencer, Karl Mannheim, Thorstein Veblen, and Florian Znaniecki.

5.1 Herbert Spencer: Social Darwinism and Education

Herbert Spencer (1820–1903), along with Auguste Comte, has been called one of the two great systematic sociologists of the nineteenth century (Peel 1971). In contrast to Marx, Weber, and Durkheim, Spencer was systematic in his attempt to develop a unified sociology. Spencer was a social evolutionist who believed that society was like an organism which passed through stages of development. Because of this, he argued against social or state intervention and espoused a *laissez-faire* approach to dealing with social problems. Spencer is best known for his *Principles of Sociology* which had a profound effect on social thought in the United States during the late nineteenth century, and was largely responsible for the dominance of what was known as Social Darwinism.

Spencer was also one of the few nineteenth-century sociologists who wrote specifically about education, in particular a work called *Education: Intellectual, Moral and Physical* (1861). As an evolutionist, Spencer regarded education in much the same way as he did other social institutions, that is, as a mechanism to promote the beneficial evolution of society. Thus Spencer did not believe in universal primary (or secondary) education. Nor did he believe that the state should be involved in education. Spencer championed a *laissez-faire* policy regarding all activities of the state (Peel 1971).

Spencer's treatise on education was focused on the value of different kinds of knowledge. Spencer was critical of the education in schools and universities in the United Kingdom in the nineteenth century. He believed that most education was useless in that it was oriented to "bring applause" from others rather than to have any practical value to the individual or society (Spencer 1949). Although he did not promote intervention in the development of school curricula, Spencer favored science education over other subjects, as he saw it as more beneficial for the individual and for the development of society as a whole: "the study of surrounding phenomena is immensely superior to the study of grammar and lexicons" (Spencer 1949).

Although Spencer's influence today hardly compares to that of Durkheim, Marx, or Weber, his *laissez-faire* approach to education parallels much of contemporary debate about privatization of schooling, streaming, and the importance of vocational over academic curricula.

5.2 Karl Mannheim: Education for Social Reconstruction

Karl Mannheim (1893–1947) was a German-born sociologist who spent much of his professional life in the United Kingdom. He is known for his work on ideology and irrationalism. Like Spencer before him, Mannheim also wrote a treatise on education in which many of his ideas are found (Mannheim and Stewart 1969). In this regard, Mannheim is perhaps most well-known for his work on the social context of knowledge, or what is known as the sociology of knowledge (*Ideology and Utopia* 1962). In this work he argued that education is a "living struggle, a replica, on a small scale of conflicting purposes and tendencies which rage in society at large" (p. 156). Thus for Mannheim, there are two kinds of educated persons, those who participate directly in the production of knowledge, and others who simply absorb the dominant world-view (*Weltanschauung*) of their particular social group, and act within it without question. In many ways, this approach to education was a precursor to the "new" sociology of education which emerged in the late 1960s, and within it, the sociology of the curriculum, in which definitions of legitimate school knowledge, by whom, and for whom,

became central questions (Young 1971, Saha 1978, Sharp 1980).

5.2.1 Education as a tool. Mannheim considered education to be one of the social techniques, a general category of methods for influencing human behavior so that it fits into the prevailing patterns of social intention and organization. He saw this technique of education as an instrument of social reconstruction. Mannheim was much influenced by American education, which, under the influence of John Dewey's pragmatism, placed less emphasis on the conservative social function of education and more on the part it had to play in social change. Mannheim, more than the other classical theorists, visualized education as an essential tool for the social reconstruction of mass society which he saw as composed of disconnected groups of atomized individuals with no social ties.

5.2.2 Education as process. Mannheim's formal treatise on the sociology of education, which was published posthumously from his lecture notes (Mannheim and Stewart 1969), reflects his ongoing concern with education as a broad social process, that is, the reflection of a society's social and philosophical values. He made the distinction between the "school in society" and the "school and society" in an effort to emphasize the existence of what he called the "educative society." Mannheim's primary concern with knowledge and ways of knowing meant that he directed attention not only to formal education and schooling, but also to other educative processes. Thus, being influenced by Cooley and Mead, he focused on the impact of primary groups on the educative process, and because he was also influenced by Waller (1965), he attempted an analysis of classroom interaction, all consistent with his own overarching concern with ideology and the social context of knowledge and knowledge transmission.

Although he was more of a "new generation" classical sociologist, Mannheim has indirectly exercised an impact on thinking about education by and large through his writings about ideology and knowledge, and his sociology of knowledge. Late-twentieth-century sociologists of education who take a sociology of knowledge perspective or who see the curriculum as negotiated knowledge are followers, in some degree, of the pioneering work of Mannheim in this area.

5.3 Thorstein Veblen: Education and the Leisured Classes

Thorstein Veblen (1857–1929) was a United States sociologist and economist, sometimes labeled as a technological evolutionist, who was primarily concerned with the leisured classes and the industrial classes. Veblen was particularly critical of the leisured classes which were unproductive but privileged, and the industrial classes which were productive. Because honor and prestige are related to the possession of wealth and material goods, Veblen used the phrase "conspicuous consumption" to argue that even the lowest classes consume goods in order to indicate or increase their social position in society (Veblen 1970).

Although not a specialist on education, Veblen did consider the manner in which the various classes experienced education, and he was particularly concerned with the influence of business on higher education (Veblen 1957). With respect to the latter, Veblen saw United States universities in the early twentieth century as in a process of transition, from institutions of liberal education and intellectual curiosity, to institutions which reflect the interests of business and industry.

Veblen considered education to be the site where the contradictions of the classes were resolved. In this respect, his interpretation of education foreshadowed much of neo-Marxist thinking in the 1970s and 1980s. The children of the industrial classes received an education which prepared them for their future work roles in industry, while the children of the leisured classes were educated in a way that prepared them for a lifestyle of leisure.

Veblen's impact on subsequent sociological approaches to the study of education has not been as direct as that of Durkheim, Weber, or Marx. There is no Veblen theory or perspective about education, either at the individual or societal level. Nevertheless, current neo-Marxist research mirrors much of Veblen's thought about the class structure and its relation to education. Furthermore, his writings on both school education and higher learning bear a strong resemblance to contemporary reproduction theory. Although not as influential as the three major classical sociologists in the study of education, it is nevertheless appropriate to include Veblen as an intellectual precursor of some important aspects of contemporary sociological thought about education.

5.4 Florian Znaniecki: The Role of Educating Institutions

Florian Znaniecki (1882–1958) was a philosopher turned sociologist whose career spanned two countries, his native Poland and the United States. He rose to prominence first in Poland as a philosopher through the publication of two works (*The Problem of Values in Philosophy* 1910; *Humanism and Knowledge* 1912) that foreshadowed the dual focuses of his subsequent sociological inquiries: the significance of values rather than actions for heuristic purposes, and the notion of the "humanistic coefficient" representing his conviction that any student of cultural life can only understand the data he or she observes if one takes into account the experiences of the human agent. These methodological insights served as Znaniecki's original contribution in the monumental two-volume study in empirical sociology written jointly with W I Thomas, *The Polish Peasant in Europe and America* (1927) and

in his own masterpiece published shortly after he was forced to seek refuge in the United States during the Second World War, *The Social Role of the Man of Knowledge* (Znaniecki 1965).

The latter work, and especially its chapter titled "Schools and Scholars as Bearers of Absolute Truth," together with the two-volume *Socjologia wychowania* (*Sociology of Education*) (Znaniecki 1928, 1930), published 10 years earlier, provide a comprehensive and fully integrated theory of education as a social process. Writing in the mid-1920s and restating his position in 1940, Znaniecki attempted to treat the entire sociological question of education with its methodological and educational foundations as a branch of sociology. In a manner comparable to Durkheim's work, Znaniecki traced the development of the sociological functions of the family, teacher, and school as components of the "educating institutions in society." Where he departed from Durkheim's argument was in pinpointing the modern phenomenon of the growing isolation of these institutions from the broader social context, and the resulting threat to their educational functioning. Znaniecki's analysis of contradictions in educational goals and tasks among diverse ideological and political groupings, and the impact of these contradictions on the educating institutions, is paralleled by his treatment of the process of socialization to which the "educand" is subject. The conjunction between the two sides of the problematic (or feedback) has anticipated and prepared the theoretical basis for the subsequent proliferation of studies of the mechanisms and phases of the socialization process not only in the school but through the life course of the individual.

Thus, already in the interwar period in Poland, and later at Columbia and the University of Illinois, Znaniecki was addressing problems which only later came to prominence: the links between the school and its environment; the recognition of the functioning of the family within the overall system of socialization; the recognition of the importance of the local community within the educational environment; and the role of the peer group in the process of socialization. Znaniecki's insights are not only convincing at a theoretical level, but also still amazingly apt and influential, more than half a century after their initial appearance in Poland.

6. Conclusion

The concern of sociology with aspects of education, taken broadly, is as old as sociology itself. However, in classical sociological discourse there is a degree of "tension" between pedagogy and moral education, between education as practice and education as an instrument of social cohesion and social stability. In this sense, education in much of the writings of these early sociologists includes activities of all social institutions—the family, the church, schools, and (perhaps in Marx) the state—which socialize individuals of all ages. This particular tension was resolved to some extent by Mannheim in his view of education as a technique, a tool of social reconstruction, and a tool of social engineering. In another sense, this tension also manifested itself in views of education as part of the dynamic of both social stability and social change, particularly in the writing of Durkheim.

The influence of these early writers, particularly Durkheim, Marx, and Weber, continues to exercise direct impact on current interpretations of education. To a lesser extent, and in different countries and schools of thought, Spencer, Mannheim, Veblen, and Znaniecki have also left behind intellectual legacies which can be detected in much of current sociology of education. Although none of these writers, except perhaps Durkheim, developed a coherent social theory of education, coherent theories have been developed from the corpus of their work. It is likely that the influence of the classical sociological theorists on social interpretations of education will continue.

See also: Contemporary Sociological Theories of Education; Critical Theory and Education; Marxism and Educational Thought; Reproduction Theory; Resistance Theory

References

Adler M J, Gorman W 1952 Education. In: Adler M J, Gorman W (eds.) 1952 *The Great Ideas. A Syntopicon of Great Books of the Western World.* Encyclopedia Brittanica, Chicago, Illinois

Althusser L 1972 Ideology and ideological state apparatuses. In: Cosin B R (ed.) 1972 *Education, Structure and Society.* Penguin, Harmondsworth

Archer M S 1979 *Social Origins of Educational Systems.* Sage Publications, London

Cherkaoui M 1976 Socialisation et conflict: les systemes educatifs et leur histoire selon Durkheim. *Revue Francaise de Sociologie* 17(2): 197–212

Cherkaoui M 1981 Consensus or conflict? Return to Durkheim's proteiform theory. *Theory and Society* 10(1): 127–38

Cleverly C 1985 Marx-Engels on education: Some lesser and better known writings. In: Maddock J, Hindson C (eds.) 1985 *Quality and Equality in Education.* Proc. 13th Annual Conf. Australian and New Zealand Comparative and International Education Society. Flinders University of South Australia, Bedford Park

Collins R 1971 Functional and conflict theories of educational stratification. *Am. Sociol. Rev.* 36(6): 1002–19

Collins R 1979 *The Credential Society: An Historical Sociology of Education and Stratification.* Academic Press, New York

Durkheim E 1956 (1st edn. 1922) *Education and Sociology.* Free Press, Glencoe, New York

Durkheim E 1957 *Professional Ethics and Civic Morals.* Routledge and Kegan Paul, London

Durkheim E 1961 (1st edn. 1925) *Moral Education.* Free Press, Glencoe, New York

Durkheim E 1964 (1st edn. 1895) *The Rules of Sociological Method.* Free Press, Glencoe, New York

Durkheim E 1977 (1st edn. 1938) *The Evolution of Educational Thought: Lectures on the Formation and Development of Secondary Education in France.* Routledge and Kegan Paul, London

Durkheim E 1995 The teaching of morality in primary schools. In: Pickering W S F (ed.) 1995 Durkheim and moral education for children: a recently discovered manuscript. *J. Moral Educ.* 24(1): 19–36

Entwistle H 1979 *Antonio Gramsci.* Routledge and Kegan Paul, London

Etzioni-Halevy E 1987 Inequalities in Australian education: A neo-Weberian perspective. *Australian and New Zealand Journal of Sociology* 23(2): 199–216

Fauconnet P 1923 The pedagogical work of Emile Durkheim. *Am. J. Sociol.* 28(5): 529–53

Fenton S 1984 *Durkheim and Modern Sociology.* Cambridge University Press, Cambridge

Hall R T 1993 Introduction. In: Durkheim E (ed.) 1993 *Ethics and the Sociology of Morals.* Prometheus Books, New York

Halls W D 1994 The educational legacy of Durkheim. *Oxford Rev. Educ.* 20(2): 253–57

King R 1980 Weberian perspectives and the study of education. *Br. J. Sociol. Educ.* 1(1): 7–23

Lehmann J M 1995 The question of caste in modern society: Durkheim's contradictory theories of race, class and sex. *Am. Sociol. Rev.* 60(4): 566–85

Mannheim K, Stewart W A C 1969 *An Introduction to the Sociology of Education.* Routledge and Kegan Paul, London

Marx K 1842 Leading article in no. 179 of *Kölnische Zeitung.* In: 1987 *Karl Marx Frederick Engels: Collected Works*, Vol. 1. Lawrence & Wishart, London

Marx K 1847 Wages. In: 1987 *Karl Marx Frederick Engels: Collected Works*, Vol. 6. Lawrence & Wishart, London

Murphy R 1982 Power and autonomy with sociology of educaton. *Theory and Society* 11(2): 179–203

Nisbet R A 1965 *Emile Durkheim.* Prentice-Hall, Englewood Cliffs, New Jersey

Norton T M, Ollman B (eds.) 1978 *Studies in Socialist Pedagogy.* Monthly Review Press, New York

Parsons T 1947 Footnote 2. In: Weber M (ed.) 1947

Pearce F 1989 *The Radical Durkheim.* Unwin Hyman, London

Peel J D Y 1971 *Herbert Spencer: The Evolution of a Sociologist.* Heinemann Educational, London

Rikowski G 1996 Left alone: end time for Marxist educational theory? *Br. J. Sociol. Educ.* 17(4): 415–51

Saha L J 1978 The "new" sociology of education and the study of learning environments: Prospects and problems. *Acta Sociol.* 21(1): 47–63

Sharp R 1980 *Knowledge, Ideology and the Politics of Schooling: Towards a Marxist Analysis of Education.* Routledge and Kegan Paul, London

Spencer H 1949 *Education: Intellectual, Moral and Physical.* Hurst, New York

Thomas W I, Znaniecki F 1927 *The Polish Peasant in Europe and America*, 2nd edn., 2 Vols. Alfred A Knopf, New York

Veblen T 1957 *The Higher Learning in America.* Academic Reprints, Stanford, California

Veblen T 1970 *The Theory of the Leisure Class: An Economic Study of Institutions.* Allen and Unwin, London

Waller W 1965 *The Sociology of Teaching.* Wiley, New York

Weber M 1947 *The Theory of Social and Economic Organization.* The Free Press, New York

Wilson E K 1961 Editor's introduction. In: Durkheim E (ed.) 1961 *Moral Education.* Free Press, Glencoe, New York

Young M F D 1971 An approach to the study of curricula as socially organized knowledge. In: Young M F D (ed.) 1971 *Knowledge and Control: New Directions for the Sociology of Education.* Collier-Macmillan, London

Znaniecki F 1928 1930 *Socjologia wychowania*, Vols I and II. The Ministry of Education of Poland, Warsaw

Znaniecki F 1965 *The Social Role of the Man of Knowledge.* Octagon Books, New York

Further Reading

Blackledge D, Hunt B 1985 *Sociological Interpretations of Education.* Croom Helm, London

Cladis M S 1995 Education, virtue and democracy in the work of Emile Durkheim. *J. Moral Educ.* 24(1): 37–52

De Gaudemar P, Cardi F, Plantier J (eds.) 1993 *Durkheim, Sociologue del'Education.* L'Harmattan/INRP, Paris

Filloux J-C 1993 Emile Durkheim. *Prospects: Quart. Rev. Educ.* XXIII (1/2): 303–20

Liston D P 1988 *Capitalist Schools: Explanation and Ethics in Radical Studies of Schooling.* Routledge and Kegan Paul, London

Lukes S 1975 *Emile Durkheim, His Life and Work: A Historical and Critical Study.* Penguin, Harmondsworth

Mannheim K 1940 *Man and Society in an Age of Social Reconstruction.* Routledge and Kegan Paul, London

Mannheim K 1943 *Diagnosis of Our Time.* Kegan Paul, London

Sarup M 1978 *Marxism and Education.* Routledge and Kegan Paul, London

Weber M 1958 The "rationalization" of education and training. In: Gerth H H, Mills C W (eds.) 1958 *From Max Weber: Essays in Sociology.* Oxford University Press, New York

Weber M 1968 Bureaucracy and education. In: Roth G, Wittich C (eds.) 1978 *Max Weber: Economy and Society.* University of California Press, Berkeley, California

Contemporary Sociological Theories of Education

J. H. Turner and D. E. Mitchell

The development of social theory in any particular domain of human endeavor typically reflects more general movements in sociology. This is especially true in education, where both professionals and scholars tend to see themselves as engaged in applying social analysis to a practical field of activity—using and evaluating theory rather more than creating it. As a result, there has been an ebb and flow in the prominence and popularity of various general theories as they have been pressed into service to interpret the complex and often controversial dynamics of educational institutions and practices in modern societies.

As might be expected, the popularity of particular theoretical perspectives has varied with national settings and political ideologies. Over the long term, however, a general diffusion of major theoretical alternatives has produced a robust debate about the virtues and limitations of each in accounting for the social meaning and ends of education. Virtually all major theories have been called upon to explain some aspects of educational phenomena in all countries where sociology is an established discipline.

1. General Theoretical Perspectives and the Sociology of Education

Social theories generally tend to emphasize one or more of three distinct levels of human activity. At the micro level, sociological theory tackles the problem of individual actions. Such micro theories treat societies and institutions as contexts or constraints which elicit, interpret, direct, or constrain individual actions. Attention is focused on the acquisition of social consciousness, the creation of patterns of interaction and meaning, the differentiation and taking of social roles, or the study of leadership and other mechanisms of individual influence.

At an intermediate level, sociological theories tackle the analysis of institutions and social organizations. These meso theories focus attention on social groups and structures, analyzing such phenomena as authority development and decision-making, role formation, work and play, social careers, occupational identities, or program and policy impacts. Organizational and occupational sociologists confine their attention almost entirely to this level of analysis.

At the broadest level of social behavior, sociological theories tackle questions of social order, social stratification, and the nature of interactions among social institutions. These macro theories concentrate on the foundations of social orderliness and influence and probe the relationships between social activity and the physical, historical, cultural, political, and economic forces shaping human societies.

The emphasis in the sociology of education on applied problems has tended to blunt theoretical development at the micro and meso levels. At the macro level, however, education theorists have displayed a more systematic interest in the development and elaboration of theoretical thought. Thus, the review presented here concentrates on macro social theory as it has been developed and applied to education, although micro level approaches will also be examined.

Contemporary macro social theories can be categorized into a number of broad frameworks or theoretical orientations—sometimes loosely described as competing sociological "paradigms" (Turner 1991). Four of these frames of reference dominate modern sociological theorizing about education. One is functional theory, in which the institution of education and its various organizational components are analyzed with respect to their consequences for the needs or requisites of the larger society. A second perspective is utilitarianism, in which educational systems are analyzed with respect to cost–benefit calculations and exchanges of resources among actors. Another general perspective, which often takes functional and utilitarian theory as its critical foil, is conflict theory, in which the effects of educational structures on maintaining inequality and stratification are emphasized. The final perspective is interactionism, in which face-to-face interactions of individuals in school contexts and the nature of the construction of meanings are given prominence. Within each of these four general perspectives lies a wide range of competing theories. Moreover, considerable overlap, borrowing, and diffusion occur across the borders of each overarching perspective.

2. Functional Theorizing on Education

All functional theorizing is ultimately concerned with how social structures meet the needs or requisites of a more inclusive social system (Turner and Maryanski 1979). In the context of the macro level sociology of education, this mode of theorizing analyzes the consequences of educational structures on the society as a whole. The most common type of functional analysis is a listing of the functions of education in modern societies. For example, Goslin has argued that "each of the different institutions within the society, including educational systems, have important functions in relation to the system as a whole and to its other parts" (1965 p. 1); he then proceeded to list three basic functions of education for society: the maintenance and transmission of culture (knowledge, beliefs, values, etc.); the innovation, discovery, and transmission of new knowledge; and the allocation of individuals to positions in society.

Macro functional analysis has developed substantially through efforts to analyze the problem of modernization. Analysts ask why political leaders of modernizing and developing societies institutionalize systems of mass education; their answer to this inquiry is a list of the functions of schools for these societies.

For instance, functionalists in the area of development are likely to stress that education teaches new skills, preserves intellectual systems, indoctrinates the young into a political culture, and generates as well as transmits new technologies necessary for development (Turner 1972). Somewhat more theoretically sophisticated modernization approaches have examined the evolutionary trend toward increased structural differentiation and the effects of education on such differentiation—concerns that go back to the early works on education by Spencer (1874–96) and Durkheim (1893, 1922). In these types of analyses, structural differentiation generates needs for separate structures that can facilitate the integration of individuals into the more complex system. Education evolves as a response to this broader system's need for specialized training and the credentialing of individuals who are then inserted into the economy, while simultaneously inculcating individuals into a common civic culture or societal community (Parsons 1971). Parsons (1959) was the most persistent advocate of this position, arguing that educational structures nurture the value of achievement so necessary for a market-oriented economic system, while legitimating inequalities associated with differential rewards attached to varying levels of achievement.

While the most familiar functionalist theories have treated education as a source of social integration, others have emphasized functional differentiation and the "selective functions" of the educational system. From this perspective, education is viewed as the mechanism by which various categories of people are selected for particular positions in society. For example, Turner (1971) compared the norms of the British and American educational systems in terms of "sponsored" as opposed to "contest" mobility. In contest systems, such as the United States, upward mobility is a race in which the rules are known by all, the sorting of individuals is delayed as long as possible, the hope for mobility is kept alive, and the responsibility for failure falls on the individual. In sponsored systems, new and future elites are assigned to positions by existing elites who use high prestige schools to sort the designated out early. In either case, the norms of the educational system have the function of selecting, while also mitigating the inequalities associated with differential mobility and privilege.

Still relying on macro level functionalism, some scholars have focused on the effects of specific aspects of education on society as a whole. One of the most prominent of these more focused explorations was the investigation of American universities conducted by Parsons and Platt (1973). In their analysis, the general theory of action as developed by Parsons (1949, 1952) and various colleagues (e.g., Parsons et al. 1953) was used to analyze the nature of the American university. In this kind of analysis the overall functions of the university system in America were established: universities have consequences for the "fiduciary" subsystem by virtue of their effects on the value of "cognitive rationality." Next, American higher education was seen as a "full university" composed of four differentiated units corresponding to Parsons' four functions scheme: undergraduate education, research and graduate training, professional schools, and relations with the broader society. Each of these was viewed as employing specialized media of exchange, such as influence and intelligence, to produce commitments to the value of cognitive rationality. In turn, such commitments facilitated the operation of other institutional structures: economy, polity, and law.

Macro level functional theorizing about education reached its zenith in the 1960s and early 1970s. A revival of conflict sociology in the 1960s challenged the adequacy of functional analysis which thereafter receded significantly. Though functionalists then often became the "straw men" for various conflict theories, functionalism did not so much disappear as move to the meso level of organisation analysis, becoming a dominant theoretical framework for graduate training programs and surfacing in the day-to-day "folk orientations" of those who administer school systems. That is, while theoretical discourse moved to conflict theories, actual practices within the schools themselves continued to be concerned with the "functions of" this or that structure or program. A key work facilitating this transition was Waller's (1961) largely functionalist analysis of how sociological processes shape teaching and learning in schools. Despite Durkheim's (1893) and Parson's (1949) early polemics, much functional analysis was imported and blended with its arch enemy—utilitarianism—to produce a new way for the conceptualization of how education functions for the general social body.

3. Utilitarian Theorizing on Education

As a theoretical doctrine, utilitarianism emphasizes that actors reveal clear hierarchies of value (i.e., preferences for resources or "utilities"). Actors are also rational in that they calculate the resources to be used (costs) to secure those valued resources high in their preference hierarchy. Most utilitarian theories add a "maximization of utilities" corollary, arguing that actors seek to maximize their profits in exchanges of resources with other actors. This simple set of assumptions, borrowed from the Scottish economist Adam Smith (1776) and subsequent thinkers in the eighteenth and nineteenth centuries, has been elaborated into a number of general theoretical approaches in sociology, most notably exchange theory (e.g., Emerson 1986, Cook 1986, Willer 1987) and rational choice theory (Coleman 1990, Hechter 1987). None of these theories has penetrated theorizing in the sociology of education in nearly as a comprehensive way as have various functional or conflict theories. However, the basic assumptions of utilitarianism can be found in both conceptual and policy statements as enumerated by economists and economically oriented theorists.

A prominent application of utilitarian assumptions in the field of education has been the "human capital" approach (e.g., Levin and Shank 1970, Juster 1975, Becker 1975, Schultz 1961, United States National Commission on Excellence in Education 1983, Sobel 1978). Often using analytic techniques borrowed from quantitative economics, this approach operates at both the micro and macro levels. At the micro end, individuals are conceptualized as calculating the benefits of attending school (i.e., the likelihood of obtaining higher pay and a prestige job) against the costs of school (e.g., time and lost income). Such calculations are facilitated by media-sponsored information on the income differentials between college and noncollege graduates, as well as by marketing by both colleges and trade schools. Moreover, the types of schools and majors in schools (e.g., business vs. humanities) can be explained in terms of such calculations. Thus the amount and type of "human capital" represented by educational credentials can be viewed as a resource that individuals use in their exchanges with employers who, for their part of the bargain, assume that these credentials increase the productivity of their workers. At the macro end, societies as a whole are seen as "investing" in education in order to improve the pool of human capital that can increase productivity. Thus expenditures on education, especially technical and higher educational facilities, can be considered by political leaders to be an investment that will be returned through higher productivity and economic growth.

In policy debates in the 1970s and 1980s utilitarian theory shifted from discussions of the rate of return on educational investment to analysis of individual and group decision-making behavior. Buchanan (1978) is credited by Sichel (1989) with the development of modern public choice theory. This utilitarian theory has been applied to such diverse topics as school desegregation (Rossell 1990), educational vouchers (Levin 1991), parental choice plans (Goldring 1991), and the behavior of school board members (Rada 1988) and of school administrators (Crowson 1989). Public choice theory draws attention to the logic of participation in decisions and the formation of public conceptions of efficiency and effectiveness in educational service provision. It has been extended through agency theory (Crowson and Morris 1990) to address the behavior of individuals whose utility functions depend on costs and benefits that actually accrue to others. While this approach has been applied to schooling in most developed nations only during the 1970s and 1980s, its roots can be traced in the United States to Callahan's (1962) vitriolic critique in *Education and the Cult of Efficiency*.

There have been many criticisms of utilitarian explanations of educational system performance—those in more general sociological theory (Blaug 1976,

O'Toole 1977, Hurn 1985 pp. 54–61). These criticisms question, at the micro level, the rationality of actors' calculations in the light of imperfect information and sociocultural constraints. At more macro level, they question assumptions about the payoffs of education for societal productivity and economic development. Many of those who offer these critiques propose an alternative to both functionalism and utilitarianism: conflict theory.

4. Conflict Theorizing on Education

The conflict perspective is far and away the dominant mode of theorizing about educational processes. Conflict theories are highly diverse, although they all emphasize that the dynamics of education revolve around, and are implicated in, the unequal distribution of resources in society. Conflict theories have been utilized to explore such diverse educational phenomena as local vs. state control; labor relations; class, ethnic, and racial segregation; student grouping or tracking; teacher–student conflict; and the distribution of educational attainment. It is difficult to establish clear labels for all of the conflict theories within the sociology of education, but intellectual poles can be established toward which various theories gravitate. One set of approaches, inspired by Karl Marx, has emphasized the ways in which schools reproduce class relations (Sarup 1978, Levitas 1974). Another set of theories, more indebted to Weber, stresses the effects of education on the formation of, and competition among, status groups whose boundaries are more permeable and less enduring than those attributed to Marx's conception of social classes.

4.1 Marxian-inspired Conflict Theories

Marxian theories on educational processes tend to be mediated by European adaptations of Marx, especially the works of Gramsci (1971) and Althusser (1971). In both of these scholars' works, emphasis is given to the impact of ideology and its transmission on the maintenance of capitalist class relations. For while Marx's concept of "false consciousness" anticipated some of this emphasis, his actual work on ideology— for example, *The German Ideology* (Marx and Engels 1845–46)—does not fully capture the shift to the analysis of superstructural processes.

Althusser (1971) has remained closest to Marx in emphasizing that social structure consists of an infrastructure of economic forces and relations of production linked to a superstructure consisting of a political–legal repressive apparatus and an ideological state apparatus. Ultimately the political–legal and ideological apparatuses are grounded in conditions within the material economic infrastructure, but they also operate with a certain autonomy. The ideological state apparatus influences all institutional spheres, but its power is especially evident in the schools in which children learn the "know-how," "logics," and "dispositions" appropriate to the material relations of production.

Gramsci (1971) argued in a similar vein, but his work has given much more emphasis to the autonomy of ideology and the role of intellectuals in society (Mouffe 1979). Intellectuals, Gramsci argued, elaborate the dominant culture into complex ideologies, hiding and obfuscating the connection between symbols and power. The result is that intellectuals produce knowledge, logics, and ideas that are hegemonic, subtly justifying a system of domination. This thrust on the role of intellectuals has come to be generalized to consideration of the role of teachers in the schools. Teachers have hegemony in the classroom: they impart and impose the ideas of the ruling class into the minds of children, thereby reproducing a system of domination. Since schools and ideology become the most significant repressive forces in society, it should not be surprising that many of the conflicts over the material base (both the forces and relations of production) manifest themselves in the cultural arena and in the schools.

These kinds of arguments, which can also be found in a number of other continental European interpreters of Marx, have perhaps had the greatest influence on Anglo-American scholarship, especially in the United States where the decline of the Cold War McCarthyism of the 1950s combined with civil rights politics during the 1960s to produce a burst of Marxian theorizing in the 1970s and 1980s.

As Hurn (1985) noted, there are two types of radical theories that, to some degree, take off from the positions of Althusser and Gramsci. One is the "hidden curriculum" position or, as it is sometimes called, the "correspondence" argument, in which the school produces the traits and attitudes necessary for the maintenance of the capitalist class system. The most prominent advocates of this theoretical position are Bowles and Gintis (1976) and such empirical researchers as Anyon (1980). A somewhat different, though overlapping, type of radical theory has stressed the effects of the more "explicit curriculum" in the "reproduction of a consciousness" that helps sustain or reproduce the capitalist system. The most prominent scholars who have maintained this position are Illich (1971), Apple (1979, 1982a, 1982b, 1988) and Giroux (1981). Others, such as Carnoy (1974, 1984, 1989) as well as Carnoy and Levin (1978) have taken a position between the Althusserian and Gramscian poles, though leaning toward Althusser. To provide a sense for these theoretical differences, the discussion will emphasize Bowles and Gintis's correspondence theory and Apple's more Gramscian argument, closing with a review of Carnoy's and Levin's more intermediate position.

Bowles and Gintis's conceptualization is more Althusserian in that it emphasizes the correspondence between the material relations of production in capitalist societies and the superstructural processes operating in schools. In essence, the structure of the workplace is mirrored in the classroom where there is an emphasis on obedience to rules, deference to authority, punctuality, and external evaluation (Gintis 1972). For example, the authoritarian structure corresponds to the hierarchy of corporate organizational structures and the system of grades corresponds to wage incentive systems. Such a structure penalizes students who are creative, aggressive, and independent and rewards those who obey and conform. In so doing, the school trains students from different class backgrounds to adapt to their ultimate occupational niche, thereby perpetuating the relations of production and class structure of capitalist societies.

Later empirical work by Anyon (1980, 1983) has added refinements to the kinds of arguments made by Bowles and Gintis. For example, a comparison of different types of schools serving the children of varying social classes (working class, middle class, affluent professional, and elite executive) revealed that there is a hidden agenda, revolving around curricular, pedagogical, and evaluation processes that emphasize different cognitive and behavioral skills and which, thereby, develop dispositions to act toward physical and symbolic capital, authority, and work processes in ways corresponding to their class background. This differentiation is particularly poignant in schools that track children into different academic programs (Oakes 1985).

At the more Gramscian end of the Marxist spectrum is Apple (1979, 1982a, 1982b, 1988) who has argued that there is no simple correspondence between the material infrastructure and superstructure. Rather, schools operate to produce the ideological hegemony of the dominant classes. The economy influences these ideological processes, but they reveal a certain independence; their effects on the reproduction of class relations is subtle and indirect. Moreover, schools are the major sites in which ideological conflicts are often fought. While these to some degree reflect material class interests, they often reveal a more autonomous ideological character concerning the ends and goals a society should pursue and deciding which means for realizing these goals are legitimate. Schools thus become a place where complex ideological struggles occur; and these struggles result from contradictions between the material and ideological superstructure as well as contradictions within both. Thus, the texts, curriculum, pedagogy, and other facets of the educational system work to reproduce class relations, but because of their autonomy as "cultural institutions," they become themselves arenas for conflicts emanating from complex relations between base and superstructure (McLaren 1989).

Giroux (1981, 1990a, 1990b) has added refinements to this Gramscian line of argument. The school is an oppressive system that, to a degree, corresponds to class relations, but it has a certain degree of independence. Hence it is best to examine school processes precisely, especially those in the classroom, in order to assess how they reproduce and contradict prevailing ideologies and social relations in the broader society (Giroux and McLaren 1989). One can see, Giroux argued, both contradiction and correspondence between the school, on the one side, and sociocultural arrangements in the larger society, on the other, with respect to such matters as curricula, teaching techniques, texts, and administrative philosophies and practices.

Between this attack on Bowles and Gintis's Althusserian correspondence approach and the more Gramscian autonomy of ideology and superstructure position are several mediating positions. Carnoy and Levin's writings (1978, 1985), as well as independent work by Carnoy (1984), best illustrate this moderation.

For Carnoy and Levin, conflict in schools is ultimately between the dominant and the dominated sectors of society. Much of this conflict is ideological because the dominant business class seeks to impose its values, norms, purposes, and goals on schools and to socialize the young into its ideology, thereby perpetuating the social relations of production and the class system. Schools thus operate to "colonize" students and their parents into accepting the legitimacy of the meritocracy implemented by the schools (as in the use of "objective tests," "tracking," and "grades") which reproduces the class system (Carnoy 1975). Yet the schools reflect the contradiction between capitalism and the modern democratic state which, on the one hand, uses schools to socialize children in ways reproducing relations of production and, on the other hand, must respond to protests and movements demanding greater equality in the distribution of resources. Thus, there are both "reproductive" and "democratizing" forces operating in capitalist societies (Carnoy 1989) and these can work at cross purposes with each other in the schools because dominant educational ideologies must make concessions to the demands of the dominated for greater access to those credentials and other resources provided by the schools. This is ultimately a conflict over relations of production and access to material resources, but it often occurs at an ideological level as dominant and dominated struggle over school organization, curricula, grades, tests, tracks, and other tools perpetuating the ideology of the business class (i.e., the belief in "meritocracy"). While the schools often coopt the dominated by making it seem as though greater fairness and access to resources have occurred, some real gains in equality of opportunity are recorded. As a consequence, the school structure and its culture do not completely mirror the interests of the business class but rather some negotiated compromise with various dominated populations who have mobilized to pursue their interests and who, because of the "forces of democracy," can realize at least some of those interests against those of the dominant business class. Thus the school is an arena for intense ideological conflicts over credentials, curriculum, pedagogy, and other aspects of school culture and structure; these conflicts reflect the contradictions of a democratic state apparatus that seeks to reproduce relations of production and, at the same time, to respond to the pressures of dominated subpopulations. Therefore, while much struggle is ideological, it is nonetheless connected to the material relations of production and distributions of resources.

4.2 Weberian-inspired Conflict Theories

Like all Marxist theories, those inspired by Weber's (1922) analysis of domination also address the question of how schools "reproduce" the class system and how cultural ideas or ideology are implicated in this reproduction. Yet there is a clear shift in emphasis toward concerns with competition among "status groups," or how subpopulations compete over honor, prestige, and cultural capital. For to the degree that the economic class system is reproduced by the educational system, the intervening mechanisms revolve around the formation of status groups.

Collins (1979) has developed the most explicitly Weberian conflict approach. For Collins, schools are not so much a tool or "apparatus" of the capitalist class as they are instruments for maintaining cultural differences among individuals. Status groups compete with each other for honor and prestige, and the distribution of educational credentials is one major arena in which this conflict occurs. In contrast to functional approaches, where the expansion of the school system is seen as related to societal needs, Collins has argued that the expansion of the school system, especially the higher educational system, reflects status group competition that has little to do with actual societal needs or job requirements. The educational establishment has encouraged the use of credentials as "markers" of honor and prestige; as it has been sucessful in this pursuit of its own interests, educational credentials and the cultural capital they imply have become necessary for access to jobs with higher pay and power which, in turn, further denote status group membership. As a result, the pursuit of credentials becomes more intense as people seek markers of status and access to jobs with higher paying-power; as more and more people demand and earn ever more credentials, inflation occurs, lowering the value of credentials for both status group membership and job access. Ironically, as the value of one level of credential declines (e.g., a university degree), then more credentials are sought, thereby ratcheting up the inflationary cycle and the competition for markers of cultural capital. Thus, the conflicts in schools and the demands for ever greater access to more credentials are not just a class-driven process; status group membership as defined by educational credentials is also involved and, in advanced capitalist systems, becomes a mechanism for gaining access to class positions.

Bourdieu (1984), and Bourdieu and Passeron (1977) approached this kind of argument in a somewhat different way. The dynamics of education, Bourdieu argued, must be understood in terms of more general stratifying processes in which various types of "capital"—economic (money, objects), social (positions, networks, group affiliations), cultural (skills, credentials, tastes, speech), and symbolic (legitimating codes)—are unequally distributed. Social class position is determined by the total amount as well as the configurations of these four types of capital. Moreover, divisions within classes are also reflected in the amount and configuration of capital. Hence, the dominant class is high in all forms of capital, although its three factions reveal different amounts of various types of capital; similarly, the middle class has moderate amounts of capital, with factions evidencing somewhat different levels and configurations of capital; and the same is true of the lower classes who have, on the whole, low levels of all forms of capital. For each class and faction, there is a distinct culture or "habitus" which is the largely unconscious perceptions, choices, preferences, and behaviors of members with a given level and configuration of economic, social, cultural, and symbolic capital. Children learn within the habitus, and they acquire capital from their parents and peers that they can then use to acquire academic credentials (a type of cultural capital) which, in turn, can be exchanged for other forms of capital. Thus, educational credentials become one of the key media of exchange for converting one kind of capital into another. By virtue of acquiring from parents and from class peers levels and types of economic, social, symbolic, and cultural capital, children are able to perform with varying degrees of success in schools, thereby acquiring differentially valued credentials. The credentials are then used to "purchase" other types and amounts of capital—jobs, networks, money, prestige, tastes, life-styles, speech, legitimacy, status group membership—which maintain class position. Thus, not only is class itself a composite of varying types of capital, the processes of class reproduction are subtle and indirect, operating through habitus and school structures. Upper-class children start with high levels of all forms of capital and can use these to secure prestigeful educational credentials that can sustain their class position. Lower-class children can be upwardly mobile, but their lack of economic capital (money), social capital (networks, group memberships), and most importantly, cultural capital (speech, styles, manner, knowledge, tastes, demeanor) ultimately keeps them from penetrating the dominant classes in any numbers. Middle-class children encounter similar obstacles, especially with respect to their lower levels of cultural capital. These processes operate in an educational system that, itself, is stratified and that has its own interests in producing and reproducing itself as the arbitrator of cultural capital. Because of this fact, there is a lack of tight correspondence and synchronization between relations of economic production and educational processes.

Meyer (1977) has extended this theme, arguing that education is not the passive servant of elites but, in fact, is an active agent in creating "new classes of knowledge and personnel." Moreover, as modern capitalist economies have increasingly become "knowledge economies," this power to create and certify positions that bring income, prestige, and power has grown. Indeed, educational levels become status positions, entitling individuals to certain resources and responses from others, while shaping how adult roles are played. Since educational credentials bestow membership in a status group, people in modern societies demand increasing access to the educational system. This pressure for education to provide access to elite positions cannot be fully successful because of the tendency for higher access to deflate credential values (Collins's argument) without overcoming the persistence of unequal distribution of other types of capital (Bourdieu's position). The critical conclusion from Meyer's theory, however, is that education cannot be merely a tool of elites for class reproduction; it remains institutionally too autonomous as a creator of status and too vulnerable to demand for the extension of credentials to ever more people.

In sum, then, the major difference between Marxian and Weberian conflict theories is over the degree to which school structures and processes correspond to, reflect, or reproduce relations of the means of production. For both Gramscian and Althusserian Marxists, there is a relatively tight connection between sub- and superstructure, even if this connection is mediated by somewhat autonomous cultural and ideological forces. Within the Weberian tradition, however, class itself is a multidimensional phenomenon, involving more than relations of production, with the result that schooling creates and sustains class relations (through credentialing) as much as it is controlled by class interests. While the vocabularies and thrusts of the theories vary, their concerns are the same: to document how the distribution of status and resources in the larger society are sustained and reproduced, or challenged and redistributed, as schools mediate life chances in modern, capitalist societies. So long as theorists like Meyer convincingly argue that schools themselves have the power to create new high income-prestige positions, despite mass pressures for increasing access to the system, education will continue to be seen as more than merely an "apparatus" of the state used to promote the interests of a dominant elite.

5. Interactionist Theorizing on Education

While functional and conflict theories emphasize attention to the macrolevel relationship between school and society, symbolic interaction sociologies tend toward meso and micro level analysis of individual behavior within educational settings. Interactionist theorizing has three distinct traditions, each of which makes a significant contribution to understanding contemporary work in education. One is the tradition initiated by Mead and Morris (1962) and personified in the 1990s in symbolic interactionism and role theory. Another is the line of work inspired by the late Durkheim (1912, Durkheim and Mauss 1903) which has evolved into either linguistics and structuralism or interaction ritual theory. The third has resulted from Schutz's (1932) sociological adaptation of Husserl's phenomenological project, creating modern-day phenomenology and ethnomethodology (see *Phenomenology and Existentialism*).

With the applied emphasis of most educational research, distinctions among these interactionist approaches tend to become blurred, but a conceptual emphasis on one of the three approaches is typically dominant. In general, symbolic interactionists' emphasis on self and definition of the situation is, by far, the most common conceptual imagery. The dramaturgy of Goffman that Durkheim inspired is given less emphasis than the linguistic structuralism stimulated by Durkheim via Saussure (1949). The phenomenology emphasis on categorization and knowledgeability, coupled with ethnomethodological concerns about the construction of a sense of reality, is often stressed but is frequently blended into symbolic interactionist concerns about definitions of situations. What emerges, therefore, is a somewhat eclectic mix of interactionist traditions. Moreover, these more micro approaches are often infused with concerns of functional theory (e.g., Woods 1983) and Marxist conflict theorizing (e.g., Bernstein 1977) making them even more eclectic.

5.1 Symbolic Interactionism and Role Theory

Hargreaves's early work (1967, 1975) laid out the basic tenets of interactionist role theory: the self-conception of teachers and pupils, the perceptions of relevant roles by teachers and pupils, the categorizing or stereotyping of others, the playing of roles, and the creation and maintenance of definitions of situations. All of these processes interact and intersect in complex ways, but like all interactionist theory, particular emphasis is given to self-conceptions as a mediating influence on definitions of situations, categorizations of other, and performances in roles. As teachers and pupils interact, these can be renegotiated, but given the power and authority of teachers, it is their self, definitions, stereotypes, and role performances that have a disproportionate influence on pupils.

Works by various interactionist sociologists have examined all of the forces enumerated by Hargreaves, but the most prevalent have focused on categorizations by teachers, definitions of situations, and role-playing style (e.g., Hammersley 1977, Hammersley and Turner 1984, Delamont 1976, Nash 1976, Sharp and Green

1975). There is also a large literature on pupils' self-conceptions, definitions of the classroom/school situation, and role-playing styles (e.g., Pollard 1984, Woods 1983, Furlong 1976). Of particular note is a large body of theory and research, inspired by Lemert's seminal work (1951), on the effects of labeling processes by teachers, testing systems, and school culture on students' self-conceptions and consequent role-playing and performance in schools (e.g., Rosenthal and Jacobsen 1982, Eder 1981, Rist 1977, McDermott 1977, Entwhisle and Hayduk 1981, Mercer 1992) (see *Social Psychological Theories in Educaton*).

As micro level analysis of school structures, especially classroom interactions, proliferated, some began to emphasize that macro level processes set parameters for roles, definitions of situations, and categorizations and stereotypes. For example, Archer (1984) has argued that the historical processes creating educational systems "structurally conditions" the interaction processes; and while such interactions can "structurally elaborate" macro level structural conditioning, it is still essential to visualize micro level encounters among teachers, students, and administrators as highly circumscribed by the larger system of education as it evolved as a result of political and economic forces.

5.2 Dramaturgical Interactionism

One line of analysis runs from Durkheim's interpretation of rituals and their effects on social structure to Goffman's dramaturgical perspective which, in turn, has influenced educational research and theory. This perspective has emphasized that ordered interactions or encounters among individuals are embedded in a more macro context. Analysis of these encounters has focused on the presentations of "self" and "face," the constructions of lines of conduct (Goffman 1959), the strategic nature of interaction (Goffman 1972), the importance of talk and ritual in interpersonal relations (Goffman 1972), and the framing of situations in terms of what is to be excluded and included (Goffman 1975). No single conceptualization exists of how all of these dynamics operate in school, but researchers have included a number of these processes in their analyses. For example, Woods (1983) made the connection to Durkheim explicit in adopting and then adapting to the school context Merton's (1938) famous classification of responses to cultural success goals and institutional means to reach them. Perhaps in response to criticisms that such a classification of students' responses did not capture the complexity of pupil–teacher interaction, Woods (1990) moved more explicitly into the Goffmanian tradition, invoking the concepts of encounters and strategic interactions. Yet in Woods's and other work, the full Goffmanian legacy has yet to be employed systematically to the study of the school and classroom encounters (for exceptions to this conclusion see Pollard 1985, Hatch 1987).

5.3 Interactionist Structuralism

A second Durkheimian legacy is structuralism, as this evolved through Saussure (1949), Levi-Strauss (1953), and a host of modern French thinkers (Lemert 1990). Bernstein (1977) has been perhaps the most prominent thinker in education, using quasi-structuralist ideas with a Marxian twist (another well-established French tradition, including Althusser's work and that of later Europeans). Moreover, he also added what appear to be some Goffmanian elements to his analysis, reflecting the dramaturgical lineage from Durkheim.

Bernstein's most famous idea is the distinction between "restricted" and "elaborated" linguistic codes. Restricted codes operate to leave implicit much of the meaning and context of utterances, whereas elaborated codes work to make explicit and universalistic the context, meaning, and intent of utterances. Since schools are biased toward the elaborated code, and since the use of such codes is more typical among children from the middle classes, lower-class children, who are more likely to use restricted codes, are placed at a disadvantage. Differential socialization practices—"positional" with "strong classification" versus "personal" and "weak classification"—produce these differences. Positional socialization has generated a restricted code and classification schema that partitions the world, whereas personal socialization fosters an elaborated code and weak classification system that enables relationships among elements of the world to be seen and spoken. In schools, which have moved from a mechanical basis of solidarity (common values, one class, ascribed teacher status and authority, tight external control) to a more organic basis of solidarity (plurality of values, ability groupings instead of classrooms, achieved teacher authority, and weakened external control), those who use elaborated codes, weak classification systems, and weak frames (over what is to be included and excluded from the classroom) will enjoy an advantage over those who use restricted codes, strong classification, and strong frames. Bernstein's analysis is vague, like so much structuralism, but his debts to Durkheim and, to a lesser extent, Goffman and Marxian class analysis are clear.

5.4 Interactionist Phenomenology

Alfred Schutz's (1932) reconstruction of Husserl's (1913) phenomenological project has produced a concern for the "taken-for-granted" nature of much reality and the interpersonal processes that produce and sustain people's sense of reality. At a more general theoretical level, this line of argument is found in constructionist theory (Berger and Luckman 1967), ethnomethodology (Garfinkel 1967) and its offspring, conversational analysis (e.g., Schegloff 1968), and more modern versions of phenomenology. When applied to educational processes, this more phenomenological version of interactionist theory emphasizes how knowledge, truth, ability, intelligence, and other supposedly "objective" realities are, in fact, socially constructed (Blackledge and Hunt 1985, Young 1971, Keddie 1971, Esland 1971, Mehan 1987).

As Young has emphasized, schools are structured around a biased view of knowledge: that academic, abstract knowledge is superior to commonsense or everyday knowledge (Young 1971). This view of knowledge is imposed upon students, with those able to enter the teachers' realm of abstracted knowledge being defined as bright, intelligent, and motivated. In contrast, those who remain at the everyday level are defined as less bright and less able to achieve in school. Tracking in schools on ability thus involves an implicit assumption about superior knowledge which defines and labels students, pushing them into ability tracks in terms of whether or not they can enter the realm of abstract knowledge.

Keddie (1971), for example, examined "classroom knowledge" in these terms, noting that subtle and implicit class labels put on students affect judgments about which students can and will enter the realm of academic and abstracted knowledge and which cannot. The reality of school tracking, then, is not so much based on actual abilities but on a constructed framework which differentially values and rewards certain types of knowledge, usually to the disadvantage of non-middle-class students. The seeming "rationality" of the evaluation systems in schools is nothing more than an imposition of one form of knowledgeability on students.

6. Conclusion

Sociological theorizing about education has tended to reflect the ebb and flow of broader theoretical perspectives. The application of these perspectives has generally involved the extraction of certain analytical elements and application of these elements to either macro or micro level processes in schools. Though more educational researchers have relied on functional or interaction theories in interpreting problems of practice, conflict theory has been the focus of more theoretically oriented scholars. The ascendance of conflict theory may have peaked, however. At the very least it is being supplemented in many countries by a shift from concern about class inequalities to those revolving around sex/gender and race/ethnicity (e.g., Weis 1988).

Virtually all educational sociology is only loosely theoretical. Theoretical work focuses primarily on macro processes, with little theoretical attention given to meso and micro level analyses. Most theorizing on education is highly derivative, rarely offering to general theory comprehensive analysis or new insights. The reason for this situation is that research in education is overwhelmingly applied to problems of policy and practice, frequently by the ideological questions of research sponsors or professional reformers. In such an environment, theory will be used for ad hoc policy and ideological purposes. The result will be loose, imprecise, and vague use of theory to interpret educational processes.

See also: Classical Sociological Theories of Education; Critical Discourse Analysis; Marxism and Educational Thought; Phenomenology and Existentialism; Reproduction Theory; Resistance Theory; Social Psychological Theories in Education; Sociology of Education: An Overview

References

Althusser L 1971 Ideology and ideological state apparatuses. In: Althusser L (ed.) 1971 *Lenin and Philosophy and Other Essays*. New Left Books, London
Anyon J 1980 Social class and the hidden curriculum of work. *J. Educ.* 162(1): 67–92
Anyon J 1983 *Social Class and Gender in U.S. Education.* Routledge and Kegan Paul, London
Apple M W 1979 *Ideology and Curriculum.* Routledge and Kegan Paul, Boston, Massachusetts
Apple M W 1982a *Education and Power.* Routledge and Kegan Paul, Boston, Massachusetts
Apple M W (ed.) 1982b *Cultural and Economic Reproduction in Education: Essays on Class, Ideology and the State.* Routledge and Kegan Paul, London
Apple M W 1988 *Teacher and Texts: A Political Economy of Class and Gender Relations in Education.* Routledge and Kegan Paul, London
Archer M 1984 *Social Origins of Educational Systems.* Sage, London
Becker G 1975 *Human Capital*, 2nd edn. Columbia University Press, New York
Berger P, Luckman T 1967 *The Social Construction of Reality.* Allen Lane, London
Bernstein B 1977 *Class, Codes and Control. Vol. 3: Towards a Theory of Educational Transmission*, 2nd edn. Routledge and Kegan Paul, London
Blackledge D A, Hunt B D 1985 *Sociological Interpretations of Education.* Routledge and Kegan Paul, London
Blaug M 1976 The empirical status of human capital theory: A slightly jaundiced view. *J. Econ. Lit.* 14(3): 827–55
Bourdieu P 1984 *Distinction: A Social Critique of the Judgement of Taste.* Routledge and Kegan Paul, London
Bourdieu P, Passeron J 1977 *Reproduction in Education, Society and Culture.* Sage, London
Bowles S, Gintis H 1976 *Schooling in Capitalist America: Educational Reform and the Contradictions of Economic Life.* Routledge and Kegan Paul, London
Buchanan J M 1969 *Cost and Choice: An Inquiry into Economic Theory.* University of Chicago Press, Chicago, Illinois
Callahan R E 1962 *Education and the Cult of Efficiency.* University of Chicago Press, Chicago, Illinois
Carnoy M 1974 *Education as Cultural Imperialism.* McKay, New York
Carnoy M (ed.) 1975 *Schooling in a Corporate Society:*

The Political Economy of Education in America. McKay, New York

Carnoy M 1984 Marxism and education. In: Ollman B, Vernoff E (eds.) 1984 *The Left Academy: Marxist Scholarship on American Campuses*, Vol. 2. Praeger, New York

Carnoy M 1989 Education, state, and culture in American society. In: Giroux H, McLaren P (eds.) 1989 *Critical Pedagogy. The State and Cultural Struggle.* SUNY Press, Albany, New York

Carnoy M, Levin H (eds.) 1978 *The Limits of Educational Reform.* Longman, New York

Carnoy M, Levin H (eds.) 1985 *Schooling and Work in the Democratic State.* Stanford University Press, Stanford, California

Coleman J S 1990 *Foundations of Social Theory.* Belknap, Cambridge, Massachusetts

Collins R 1979 *The Credential Society.* Academic Press, New York

Cook K S (ed.) 1986 *Social Exchange Theory.* Sage, Newbury Park, California

Crowson R L 1989 Managerial ethics in educational administration: The rational choice approach. *Urban Educ.* 23(4): 412–35

Crowson R L, Morris V C 1990 *The Superintendency and School Leadership. The National Center for School Leadership Project Report.* Office of Educational Research and Improvement, Washington, DC

Delamont S 1976 *Interaction in the Classroom.* Routledge and Kegan Paul, London

Durkheim E 1933 (1st edn. 1893) *The Division of Labor in Society.* Free Press, Glencoe, Illinois

Durkheim E 1961 (1st edn. 1922) *Moral Education.* Free Press, New York

Durkheim E 1976 (1st edn. 1912) *Elementary Forms of the Religious Life,* 2nd edn. Allen and Unwin, London

Durkheim E, Mauss M 1969 (1st edn. 1903) *Primitive Classification.* Cohen and West, London

Eder D 1981 Ability grouping as a self-fulfilling prophecy: A micro-analysis of teacher–student interaction. *Sociol. Educ.* 54(3): 151–62

Emerson R 1986 Toward a theory of value in social exchange. In: Cook K S (ed.) 1980 *Social Exchange Theory.* Sage, Beverly Hills, California

Entwhisle D, Hayduk L 1981 Academic expectations and the school attainment of young children. *Sociol. Educ.* 54(1): 34–50

Esland G 1971 Teaching and learning as the organization of knowledge. In: Young M F D (ed.) 1971 *Knowledge and Control.* Collier-Macmillan, London

Furlong V 1976 Interaction sets in the classroom. In: *Hammersley M*, Woods P (ed.) 1976 *The Process of Schooling.* Routledge and Kegan Paul, London

Garfinkel H 1967 *Studies in Ethnomethodology.* Prentice-Hall, Englewood Cliffs, New Jersey

Gintis H 1972 Toward a political economy of education. *Harv. Educ. Rev.* 42: 1–24

Giroux H A 1981 *Ideology, Culture, and the Process of Schooling.* Falmer Press, London

Giroux H A 1990a *Schooling and the Struggle for Public Life.* University of Minnesota Press, Minneapolis, Minnesota

Giroux H A 1990b *Teachers as Intellectuals: A Critical Pedagogy for Practical Learning.* Bergin and Garvey, South Hadley, Massachusetts

Giroux H A, McLaren P (eds.) 1989 *Critical Pedagogy, the State and Cultural Struggle.* SUNY Press, Albany, New York

Goffman E 1959 *The Presentation of Self in Everyday Life.* Doubleday, New York

Goffman E 1972 *Interaction Ritual.* Allen Lane, London

Goffman E 1975 *Frame Analysis.* Penguin, Harmondsworth

Goldring E B (ed.) 1991 Parental involvement and public choice in education. *Int. J. Educ. Res.* 15(3–4): 229–352

Goslin D A 1965 *The School in Contemporary Society.* Scott, Foresman, Boston, Massachusetts

Gramsci A 1971 *Selections from The Prison Notebooks of Antonio Gramsci.* Lawrence and Wishart, London

Hammersley M 1977 Teacher perspectives. *Schooling and Society (Unit 9 of E202).* Open University Press, Milton Keynes

Hammersley M, Turner G 1984 Conformist pupils. In: Hammersley M, Woods P (eds.) 1984 *Life in Schools: The Sociology of Pupil Culture.* Open University Press, Milton Keynes

Hargreaves D H 1967 *Social Relations in a Secondary School.* Routledge and Kegan Paul, London

Hargreaves D H 1975 *Interpersonal Relations and Education.* Routledge and Kegan Paul, London

Hatch J A 1987 Impression management in kindergarten classrooms. *Rev. Educ. Res.* 57: 437–66

Hechter M 1987 *Principles of Group Solidarity.* University of California Press, Berkeley, California

Hurn C J 1985 *The Limits and Possibilities of Schooling,* 2nd edn. Allyn and Bacon, Boston, Massachusetts

Husserl E 1969 (1st edn. 1913) *Ideas: General Introduction to Pure Phenomenology.* Allen and Unwin, London

Illich I 1971 *Deschooling Society.* Calder and Boyars, London

Juster T (ed.) 1975 *Education, Income and Human Behavior.* McGraw-Hill, New York

Keddie N 1971 Classroom knowledge. In: Young M F D (ed.) 1971 *Knowledge and Control: New Directions for the Sociology of Education.* Collier-Macmillan, London

Lemert C C 1990 The uses of French structuralisms in sociology. In: Ritzer G (ed.) 1990 *Frontiers of Social Theory: The New Syntheses.* Columbia University Press, New York

Lemert E 1951 *Social Pathology.* McGraw-Hill, New York

Levin H M 1991 Views on the economics of educational choice. A reply to West. *Econ. Educ. Rev.* 10 (2): 171–75

Levin M R, Shank A 1970 *Educational Investment in An Urban Society: Costs, Benefits and Public Policy.* Teachers College Press, New York

Levi-Strauss C 1953 Social structure. In: Kroeber A (ed.) 1953 *Anthropology Today.* University of Chicago Press, Chicago, Illinois

Levitas M (ed.) 1974 *Marxist Perspectives in the Sociology of Education.* Routledge and Kegan Paul, London

Marx K, Engels F, Arthur C J 1947 (1st edn. 1845–46) *The German Ideology.* Lawrence and Wishart, London

McDermott R P 1977 Social relations as context for learning. *Harv. Educ. Rev.* 47(2): 198–213

McLaren P 1989 *Life in Schools: An Introduction to Critical Pedagogy in the Foundations of Education.* Longman, New York

Mead G H, Morris C W 1962 *Mind, Self, and Society: From the Standpoint of a Social.Behaviorist.* University of Chicago Press, Chicago, Illinois

Mehan H 1987 Language and schooling. In: Spindler G,

Spindler L (eds.) 1987 *Interpretive Ethnography of Education*. Erlbaum, Hillsdale, New Jersey

Mercer J R 1992 The impact of changing paradigms of disability on mental retardation in the year 2000. In: Rowitz L (ed.) 1992 *Mental Retardation in the Year 2000*. Springer-Verlag, New York

Merton R H 1938 Social structure and anomie. *Am. Sociol. Rev.* 3(6): 672–82

Meyer J W 1977 The effects of education as an institution. *Am. J. Sociol.* 83(1): 55–77

Mouffe C (ed.) 1979 *Gramsci and Marxist Theory*. Routledge and Kegan Paul, London

Nash R 1976 *Teacher Expectations and Pupil Learning*. Routledge and Kegan Paul, London

Oakes J 1985 *Keeping Track: How Schools Structure Inequality*. Yale University Press, New Haven, Connecticut

O'Toole J 1977 *Work, Learning and the American Future*. Jossey-Bass, San Francisco

Parsons T 1949 *The Structure of Social Action*. Free Press, Glencoe, Illinois

Parsons T 1952 *The Social System*. Free Press, New York

Parsons T 1959 The school as a social system: Some of its functions in American society. *Harv. Educ. Rev.* 29(4): 297–318

Parsons T 1971 *The System of Modern Societies*. Prentice-Hall, Englewood Cliffs, New Jersey

Parsons T, Bales R F, Shils E A 1953 *Working Papers in the Theory of Action*. Free Press, Glencoe, Illinois

Parsons T, Platt G 1973 *The American University*. Harvard University Press, Cambridge, Massachusetts

Pollard A 1984 Goodies, jokers, and gangs. In: Hammersley M, Woods P (eds.) 1984 *Life in Schools: The Sociology of Pupil Cultures*. Open University Press, Milton Keynes

Pollard A 1985 *The Social World of the Primary School*. Cassell, London

Rada R D 1988 A public choice theory of school board member behavior. *Educ. Eval. Policy Anal.* 10(3): 225–36

Rist R C 1977 On understanding the process of schooling: The contributions of labelling theory. In: Karabel J, Halsey A H (eds.) 1977 *Power and Ideology in Education*. Oxford University Press, New York

Rosenthal R, Jacobsen L 1982 *Pygmalion in the Classroom*. Irvington, New York

Rossell C H 1990 The carrot or the stick for school desegregation policy? *Urban Affairs Q.* 25(3): 474–99

Sarup M 1978 *Marxism and Education*. Routledge and Kegan Paul, London

Saussure F de 1949 *Course in General Linguistics*. Payot, Paris

Schegloff E A 1968 Sequencing in conversational openings. *American Anthropologist* 70(4): 1075–95

Schultz T 1961 Investment in human capital. *Am. Econ. Rev.* 51(March): 1–17

Schutz A 1932 (republished 1967) *The Phenomenology of the Social World*. Northwestern University Press, Evanston, Illinois

Sharp R, Green A 1975 *Education and Social Control*. Routledge and Kegan Paul, London

Sichel W (ed.) 1989 *The State of Economic Science: Views of Six Nobel Laureates*. W E Upjohn Institute for Employment Research, Kalamazoo, Missouri

Smith A 1937 (1st edn. 1776) *An Inquiry into the Nature and Causes of the Wealth of Nations*. Random House, New York

Sobel I 1978 The human capital revolution in economic development: Its current history and status. *Comp. Educ. Rev.* 22(2): 278–308

Spencer H 1969 (1st edn. 1874–96) *The Principles of Sociology*. Macmillan, London

Turner J H 1972 *Patterns of Social Organization*. McGraw-Hill, New York

Turner J H 1991 *The Structure of Sociological Theory*, 5th edn. Wadsworth, Belmont, California

Turner J H, Maryanski A 1979 *Functionalism*. Benjamin-Cummings, Menlo Park, California

Turner R H 1971 Sponsored and contest mobility in the school system. In: Hopper E (ed.) 1971 *Readings in the Theory of Educational Systems*. Hutchinson, London

United States National Commission on Excellence in Education 1983 *A Nation at Risk*. United States Government Printing Office, Washington, DC

Waller W 1961 *The Sociology of Teaching*. Wiley and Sons, New York

Weber M 1968 (1st edn. 1922) *Economy and Society*. University of California, Berkeley, California

Weis L (ed.) 1988 *Class, Race and Gender in American Education*. SUNY Press, Albany, New York

Willer D 1987 *Theory and the Experimental Investigation of Social Structures*. Gordon and Breach, New York

Woods P 1983 *Sociology and the School: An Interactionist Viewpoint*. Routledge and Kegan Paul, London

Woods P 1990 *The Happiest Days? How Pupils Cope with Schools*. Falmer Press, London

Young M F D (ed.) 1971 *Knowledge and Control*. Collier-Macmillan, London

Further Reading

Apple M W (ed.) 1982 *Cultural and Economic Reproduction in Education*. Routledge and Kegan Paul, London

Becker G 1975 *Human Capital*, 2nd edn. Columbia University Press, New York

Bennett K, LeCompte M D 1990 *The Way Schools Work: A Sociological Analysis of Education*. Longman, New York

Blackledge D, Hunt B 1985 *Sociological Interpretations of Education*. Routledge, London

Carnoy M, Levin H 1985 *Schooling and Work in the Democratic State*. Stanford University Press, Stanford, California

Hurn C 1985 *The Limits and Possibilities of Schooling*, 2nd edn. Allyn and Bacon, Boston, Massachusetts

Karabel J, Halsey A H (eds.) 1977 *Power and Ideology in Education*. Oxford University Press, New York

McLaren P 1989 *Life in Schools*. Longman, New York

Social Psychological Theories in Education

B. J. Bank and B. J. Biddle

There is nothing so practical as a good theory (Lewin 1951 p. 169)

The field of social psychology concerns the ways in which individuals think about and react to social events and how those persons, in turn, affect and reconstruct events through interaction with others. Since textbooks for the field did not appear until 1908, social psychology is actually quite young. Nevertheless, during its brief history it has involved many leading scholars and generated a great deal of research in psychology, sociology, and allied disciplines. Since education is both ubiquitous and of vital importance in modern societies, a good deal of that effort has focused on education—on its students, teachers, and other actors who participate in its activities, as well as on its classrooms, schools, school systems, and other types of social events that make up the education system.

Reviewers have noted that social psychology has reflected various traditions of theory over the years. Despite common concerns, these traditions have made quite different assumptions about human nature and the causes of social events, and each has generated its own vocabularies and research histories. At least four of these traditions have made, and continue to make, significant contributions to educational thought, and most of this article concerns those four traditions. However, other traditions have also appeared within social psychology that are less relevant to education today, and it is worth mentioning two of these here.

One early theoretical tradition, psychoanalytic theory, derived originally from the contributions of Sigmund Freud. This perspective gave stress to early childhood experiences, physiological development, basic drives associated with sex and aggression, the unconscious, repression, the mechanisms of neurotic adjustment, and the use of psychotherapeutic counseling to promote adult mental health. It has had an enormous impact on Western thought generally (particularly in Europe), as well as on developmental, clinical, and counseling psychology (in the United States). It also had significant effects within social psychology in the years immediately following the Second World War—witness, for example, social psychologists' interests in the origins of Fascism and the large body of research stimulated by publication of *The Authoritarian Personality* (Adorno et al. 1950). Because of its stresses on early socialization in the family and adult therapy, however, psychoanalytic theory has not been applied often to education, and it has less apparent impact on social psychology in the late 1990s than in earlier years.

A second tradition, behaviorism and reinforcement theory, has had more influence on social psychology than the psychoanalytic approach, and in the past that influence also generated applications in education. This second tradition began among experimental psychologists who studied animal behavior, and as a result it gave stress to associations among observable stimuli and behaviors, to patterns of reinforcement, and to drive states, rewards, punishments, and the concept of satiation. Past research by behaviorists on imitation generated applications in classrooms where modeling is practiced (see Bandura 1969). As well, leading behaviorists such as Skinner (1960) became advocates for programmed instruction and computer-assisted education, and others applied reinforcement ideas to designs for remedial education and "tough love" approaches for coping with rebellious adolescents. However, behaviorists did not give much stress to the complexities of human thinking or to the idea that one might discover useful information by interviewing people about their thoughts and feelings. Moreover, effectiveness of reinforcement schedules for human behavior seems to differ sharply depending on social context, which means that what works as a "reward" or "punishment" in one setting may not have similar effects elsewhere. As a result, interest in this tradition has never been as strong among most educators as research traditions that give more attention to the ways in which people interpret the contexts in which they find themselves. The behaviorist and reinforcement tradition continues in social psychology largely in the form of research concerned with social exchange processes, but exchange theory seems to have attracted minimal attention among educational researchers.

In contrast, four other traditions of theory have appeared in social psychology that are both alive today and continue to generate important contributions to education.

1. Cognitive Social Psychology

The strong influence of Gestalt Psychology on the work of such important social psychologists as Kurt Lewin, Solomon Asch, and Fritz Heider virtually insured that social psychology would have a strong cognitive orientation. They, their students, and their students' students continued a tradition in which perception, beliefs, and mental processes were seen as largely responsible for overt behavior. So pervasive is the cognitive orientation in social psychology that some analysts have suggested that the phrase "cognitive social psychology" is redundant. All of social psychology, they suggest, is concerned with thinking, meaning, and interpretation.

Explicitly or implicitly, much of educational research is influenced by the language and concerns of cognitive social psychology. Such concepts as attitudes, values, affect, aspirations, cognitive consistency, attributions, and social cognitions quickly made their way from social psychological theories into educational research. Although they often favored laboratory experiments, some cognitive social psychologists deliberately chose educational settings as venues in which to develop and test their theories. Two important examples are studies of the impact of schooling on student attitudes and values and studies of the effects of attributions on student behaviors.

1.1 Student Attitudes and Values

An early and now-classic set of studies examining the effects of schooling on student attitudes and values was conducted by Newcomb (1943) and Newcomb et al. (1967) at Bennington College, an elite women's college in Vermont, beginning in the 1930s. The basic findings of the study have been summarized quite clearly by Ross and Nisbett (1991 pp. 35–6):

> Young women from predominantly upper middle-class families entered Bennington College between 1935 and 1939, sharing the generally conservative Republican political views and voting preferences of their parents. Within a couple of years, after having been exposed to the Bennington milieu, the students' views and preferences had shifted far to the left of those of their family members and of most other Americans of their social class . . . More than 20 years later, in the 1960 election, when John Kennedy received scant support from other well-to-do Protestant college graduates in the Northeast (30 percent is a generous estimate . . .), roughly 60 percent of the Bennington 1935–39 graduates voted for Kennedy. When asked to describe their present political views, over 60 percent said that on most issues they were "liberal" or "left of center," while only about 16 percent labeled themselves "conservatives" (the remainder described themselves as "middle of the road").

Not surprisingly, these dramatic findings stimulated a large literature, reviewed by Newcomb and Feldman (1969), concerned with the impact of college on the attitudes and values of college students. Subsequently, Pascarella and Terenzini (1991 pp. 269–334) reviewed the "torrent of additional studies of attitude and value change among college students" reported since the publication of Newcomb and Feldman's book. They conclude their review by noting that "Glaring weaknesses—conceptual and methodological—are apparent in the existing research . . . Many studies are atheoretical, apparently proceeding as much from mild curiosity as any systematic set of hypotheses based on some theory of how students learn or develop. Given their objectives, many studies are based on woefully weak research designs . . ." (Pascarella and Terenzini 1991 p. 330).

This conclusion is particularly disappointing given the longitudinal design and strong theoretical grounding of Newcomb's pioneering study. Drawing on both cognitive balance theory and the groups and reference groups traditions of social psychology (reviewed below), Newcomb was able to show that the attitude and value changes of the students he studied were due to characteristics of the social situation at Bennington, especially group cohesion, self-sufficiency, and relative isolation from the surrounding community, a dynamic, politically liberal faculty that wanted to increase social awareness and involvement among the students, and pressures to uniformity enforced by the promise of social acceptance and the threat of rejection. In cognitive balance theory, disagreeing with those one admires is uncomfortable. To rid oneself of this discomfort, attraction is likely to produce communication about disagreements which is likely, in turn, to increase agreement. Thus, Newcomb's analysis stressed the adaptive social functions of the students' political conversions: adopting liberal or radical views was a way to fulfill their desire for social approval.

It seems likely that social approval continues to be a major motive for the cognitive changes experienced by contemporary college students. Direct tests of this proposition need to be conducted, however, and there is a need for careful studies of the relationships between the situational characteristics of schools and colleges and the kinds of attitudinal and value changes that occur (or do not occur) among their students. As Pascarella and Terenzini (1991 p. 330) note, "The evidence is clear that changes occur during the college years and that the collegiate experience is responsible for at least *some* of those changes. But much remains to be done. It is now time for higher education researchers to look more closely and rigorously at the magnitudes, origins, timing, and durability of those changes."

1.2 Attributions and Student Behaviors

By the 1970s, cognitive consistency theories, including the cognitive balance theory central to Newcomb's research, tended to give way to an increasing emphasis within cognitive social psychology on attribution processes. As originally formulated, attribution theory was concerned primarily with the ways in which an individual understands the causes of another person's behaviors. The location of these causes can be internal, within the individual, or external, associated with the situation. At least within American society, the attribution process tends to be subject to systematic errors and biases, such as the fundamental attribution error in which people are prone to overlook situational causes of actions and outcomes in favor of dispositional ones.

One of the more surprising findings of attribution research is that people tend to use the same inferential strategies and are susceptible to many of the same errors and biases when they are trying to understand their own behaviors as when they are trying to understand someone else's. Further, it has been found that the kinds of attributions a person makes about his or her own behaviors can have implications for his or her subsequent behaviors. Thus, a person who attributes her success on a particular task to luck may be less likely to persist at that task than a person who attributes her success to ability. Similarly, a person who attributes his failure on a particular task to lack of effort may be more likely to persist at that task than a person who attributes his failure to the difficulty of the task. Not surprisingly, educators were quick to grasp the implications of such propositions for student learning, and a large body of research and theorizing has appeared showing how attributions by both students and their teachers can affect students' motivations and performance (Dweck and Goetz 1978, Dweck and Leggett 1988, Weiner 1974, 1986).

2. Symbolic Interactionism

Whereas cognitive social psychology stresses the ways in which individuals interpret their environments, symbolic interactionists stress the ways in which meanings are constructed in social interaction. Although individuals are deemed capable of interacting with themselves, most interaction takes place among two or more persons. Even interaction with oneself (the symbolic interactionist definition of thinking) requires language and other symbols that have been learned from and with others through processes of socialization and interaction. Thus, symbolic interactionism is both less individualistic and less psychologistic than cognitive social psychology. Not surprisingly, it has its roots in sociology, particularly in the teachings and writings of George Herbert Mead, Charles Horton Cooley, W.I. Thomas, Herbert Blumer, and Erving Goffman. Its impact on social psychological research conducted by psychologists has been limited to only a few topics, but these have included some very important topics in psychology such as self-presentation and self-concept that also have important implications for education.

2.1 Self-presentation and Self-labeling

From its inception, symbolic interactionism has stressed the importance of the self. In any given situation, selves are the most important social objects that must be defined, and these definitions will depend on the responses that actors make to themselves and to others. Thus, the self is both a social product and a social force. Individuals actively try to manipulate their self-presentations to other people in order to achieve a particular impression. Efforts at impression management will not be successful, however, unless other people in the situation are willing to support the presented self by acting toward the individual in ways that validate the impression she or he is trying to create. If other people invalidate the self-presentation of the individual, conflict may occur ("You're a liar." "No, I'm not.") or a negotiation may follow in which all parties try to arrive at enough agreement about self-definitions for the interaction to proceed.

Within symbolic interactionism, the process of childhood socialization is seen as one in which socializing agents such as parents and teachers try to assign to children self-labels that will help them succeed in life. The process can be illustrated by a set of familiar exhortations: "Don't be a crybaby." "Don't be a grouch." "Act like a lady/gentleman." "Be a good sport." Such expressions do not only describe the person at whom they are directed or tell that person how to behave, they also give (or deny) a self-label to that person. Such statements go beyond the expression of expectations for behaviors ("You should do X") such as those stressed in role theory (discussed below). Instead, the expectations are embedded in a label describing the person: "Because you are such a good student, I know you will do X."

How successful are self-labels of this sort, and how does their effectiveness compare with persuasive messages? To answer these questions, Miller et al. (1975) conducted two studies in classroom settings. The first study focused on classroom littering. One classroom was assigned to a control condition in which the investigators simply measured the percentage of litter that was deposited into the wastebasket. A second classroom was assigned to a "persuasion" condition. Over an eight-day period students in this classroom received various written and oral appeals from school personnel to keep their classroom neat and to deposit litter in the wastebasket. The third classroom was assigned to a "positive self-label" condition. Over the same eight-day period students in this classroom were told by school personnel not that they should be neat, but rather that they actually were neat. They were commended for being litter-conscious and for keeping their classroom cleaner than some others in the school.

The percentage of litter (including some deliberately created by the researchers) that was deposited into the wastebaskets was measured at the beginning and end of the eight-day period and two weeks later. During the pretest period the percentage of litter deposited in wastebaskets was equally low (less than 20 percent) in all classrooms. At the time of the immediate post-test, both the persuasion condition and the positive self-label condition showed a decrease in littering with the decrease being considerably greater in the self-label condition (80 percent of litter in wastebaskets) than in the persuasion condition (45 percent of litter in wastebaskets). Even more impressive were the results for the delayed post-test, two weeks after the littering messaged ended. At that time, students in the persuasion condition had reverted to the high levels of littering characteristic of their own pre-test period and of the control group across all three periods. In contrast, the positively labeled students continued to behave in a manner consistent with their self-label by continuing to deposit most of their litter in the wastebaskets.

In a follow up study, Miller and his co-workers showed that mathematics achievements and corresponding changes in self-esteem were similarly responsive to manipulations of self-identity labels and similarly unresponsive, in the long run, to persuasion and to influence tactics recommended by reinforcement theories (rewards, punishments). The findings of this study, like those of the littering study, show the importance of self-labeling processes. Positive behaviors were larger and more sustained when the school children attributed those behaviors to their own self-identities rather than to instructions from teachers and other school personnel.

2.2 Self-concepts and Self-esteem

Whereas the literature concerned with self-presentation and self-labeling tends to focus on the self as a social process, writings concerned with the self-concept tend to treat the self as a social product. In research, the self-concept is usually taken to be a set of descriptive statements about the self that can vary in importance, salience, and specificity. Closely related to the self-concept is self-esteem, usually defined as an evaluation of oneself generally or of particular self-concepts. In the field of education much attention has been paid to the relationship between self-esteem and academic performance. Reviews of such studies (e.g., Wylie 1979) usually report a positive, albeit moderate, correlation between self-esteem, on the one hand, and IQ scores, achievement test scores, or school marks, on the other. These correlations increase in size when measures of academic self-esteem, rather than general self-esteem, are used.

Findings such as these have been interpreted in two contradictory ways. Some educators have argued that positive self-esteem should be a major educational goal. Related to this argument is the assumption that students cannot learn if their (academic) self-esteem is too low, and raising their self-esteem will help to improve their academic performance. In sharp contrast to this position is the argument advanced by Lee (1997 pp. 142–3): "Within the educational world, I question the trend in gender-equity studies to pursue self-esteem as a 'stand-alone' educational outcome. I regard self-esteem or, as it is commonly referred to, 'self-concept' as an attitude that is developed as a byproduct of success in school, rather than a substitute for success. It could be simplistic, but I believe that when students experience solid and demonstrable success in school, their self-esteem will take care of itself." Support for Lee's argument can be found in research by Calsyn and Kenny (1977) which used a cross-lagged panel design to show that performance affected self-concept more than the other way around.

Educators with a strong commitment to the improvement of students' self-esteem are unlikely to be persuaded by Lee's argument to abandon their efforts

to make students feel better about themselves, and such educators can take some comfort in the fact that Calsyn and Kenny's evidence also indicated that the self-concept had significant effects on academic performance. The fact that this effect was weaker than the effect of academic performance on self-concept does suggest that efforts to improve self-esteem should be coupled with efforts to improve academic performance. Failure to do so could lead to a type of victim blaming in which students from disadvantaged backgrounds are said to do poorly in school because of deficient self-esteem rather than because of deficient schools.

2.3 Qualitative Research

The contributions of symbolic interactionism to educational research have been epistemological and methodological as well as theoretical and substantive. The interest of symbolic interactionists in the construction of social meaning and the ways in which people create identities for themselves and one another is consistent with the use of qualitative research methods designed to get inside the world of the research subjects and to see the world as they see it. This stress on qualitative research was particularly strong in that branch of symbolic interactionism associated with the University of Chicago during the first 60 years of the twentieth century (see Bulmer 1984).

Among the practitioners of qualitative methodology in the Chicago Sociology Department were Robert Park and Ernest Burgess who pioneered in the 1920s what later became known as "participant observation." This research method was an attempt to overcome ethnocentrism by getting to know research subjects from the inside out. The goal of research should be to penetrate beneath the conventional self-presentation of people in order to determine what they really thought and felt. Neither Park nor Burgess rejected quantitative research methods, however, and neither of them had strong qualifications as a social psychologist. Instead, it fell to Herbert Blumer to make the case for qualitative social psychology.

Blumer was a graduate student and then a member of the sociology faculty at the University of Chicago from 1927 to 1952 in which year he moved to the University of California at Berkeley where he remained until his retirement. Blumer's doctoral dissertation, called *Method in Social Psychology*, argued that social research was a process of symbolic interactionism in which researchers came to see the world through the eyes of whatever group they were studying. Because people's behaviors depend upon how they define the situation in which they find themselves, researchers should seek to understand these definitions not just to observe words and deeds. Blumer's stress on sympathetic introspection led him to advocate the use of such research techniques as life histories, autobiographies, case studies, letters, open-ended interviews, and participant observation.

According to Collier et al. (1991), Blumer's methodology can be seen as both a critique of traditional statistical and quantitative procedures and as a justification for the kinds of research developed and widely used at the University of Chicago. Blumer's opposition to quantitative procedures was based on the fact that they typically start with preconceived theories and neglect the process of interpretation. Such preconceptions bias the researcher's interpretation of events, and the meaning of the situation as seen by participants tends to be ignored. Blumer was highly critical of operational definitions because they focus on a single quantifiable characteristic and ignore the total context in which social behavior occurs. He felt that the ambiguity of concepts used by social psychologists, such as attitudes, introduced a gap between theory and research, leading to either empty theorizing or detached and frequently pointless research. To the contrary, he argued that concepts should sensitize researchers to the task of "working with and through the distinctive nature of the empirical instance, instead of casting the unique nature aside . . ." (Blumer 1954 p. 8).

The qualitative methodology advocated at the University of Chicago found its way into educational research through the work of Chicago students and those they influenced. One example is Howard Becker whose dissertation, completed at Chicago in 1951, was concerned with role and career problems of Chicago public school teachers. In addition to his well-known work on higher and professional education (Becker et al. 1961, 1968), Becker (1958) published an influential article concerned with problems of inference and proof in participant observation. The many researchers influenced by this article included Smith and Geoffrey (1968) whose now-classic study of an urban classroom became a model for qualitative research in education.

Many qualitative researchers in education are unaware of the debt they owe to the traditions of the Chicago school of symbolic interactionism. This is partly due to a tendency among qualitative researchers, especially ethnographers, to write at a descriptive level that ignores both theoretical and methodological issues. Among those qualitative researchers of education who do place their work in the theoretical frameworks (e.g. Eder et al. 1995), many ignore symbolic interactionism per se in favor of one or more of the newer theories that have branched off from symbolic interactionism since the late 1950s. These include ethnomethodology, discourse analysis, social constructionism, ethogenics, and critical social psychology (see Collier et al. 1991 pp. 281–90 for a review). Although differing in their emphases, these variants of symbolic interactionism share the assumptions that thought and communication are part of a social process, that actors give meaning to their own behaviors, that action depends on how actors define situations, and that qualitative research methods are a good way to study and to understand these processes.

3. Role Theory

The social psychological concept of role arose from the vocabulary of the theater and was first proposed for use in social analysis at the turn of the century by the German sociologist, Georg Simmel. This challenge was taken up in the 1920s and 1930s by leading scholars in several fields, notably George Herbert Mead (a social philosopher), Ralph Linton (an anthropologist), and Jacob Moreno (a psychologist). As a result of this mixed heritage, the role concept is widely used in social analysis today, but its usage is subject to some confusion and dispute.

In current writings, the "role" term is used to refer to at least three associated concepts:

(a) the "identity" that a person assumes in a given social context (i.e., whether one appears in the school as a student, a teacher, a principal, a nurse, or perhaps a janitor);

(b) "characteristic behaviors" that are exhibited by persons who share an identity term (e.g., what the typical student is observed to do);

(c) "expectations" that are held for the behaviors of those who share an identity term (e.g., what persons would prefer students to do, think they are likely to do, or perhaps what they ought to do).

Needless to say, it is awkward to expect one term (role) to encompass these three, different concepts, so from here on in this selection we shall refer to "identities" as social positions, "characteristic behaviors" as roles, and "expectations for members of social positions" as role expectations.

In addition, confusion and disputes have arisen because groups of role theorists differ somewhat in the assumptions they make about roles and associated events. The version of role theory having greatest impact on education stemmed originally from the writings of Talcott Parsons who argued that social systems and their component roles tend to persist because people conform to normative role expectations for their social positions (i.e., rules about what they "should" and "should not" do). Moreover, Parsons assumed that those involved in the system understand and can express those norms, they teach those norms to newcomers in the system, they enforce those norms through willingness to sanction others, and they largely agree on the norms they hold and express.

Subsequent events have challenged many of these assumptions. It is now known that disagreement about norms (or "role conflict") is common in many social contexts, that sanctioning behavior is quite rare in many supportive settings, and that people also form other kinds of role expectations (e.g., beliefs, preferences, values, attitudes, and the like) which can also affect conduct. Nevertheless, the general thrust of normative role theory has tended to persist among social psychologists interested in the study of formal organizations and has been applied extensively in education.

3.1 Role Expectations for Teachers

A good deal of research has appeared concerned with role expectations that are held for common social positions in education (i.e., for school superintendents, school board members, school principals, school counselors, coaches, students, and the like), but the bulk of this literature has focused on teachers (see Biddle, in press).

This effort has explored many issues. Contrasts have been unearthed among the role expectations held for teachers by various types of respondents—teachers themselves, student teachers, faculty members in colleges of education, school principals, school superintendents, members of the public, students, even pre-school children! Panel studies have explored how the role expectations of teacher trainees shift as they go through their undergraduate years and then enter the teaching profession. Other research has examined relations between teacher-held role expectations and teachers' actual roles in classrooms and schools. Contrasts have been sought among role expectations that are held for primary and secondary teachers, teacher "specialists" and other professionals in schools, and teachers who offer specific subjects. Studies have examined the impact of various types of innovative and reform programs on role expectations held for and by teachers.

Although much of this research effort has examined norms, it has also explored other forms of role expectations (e.g., "attitudes," "conceptions," "beliefs," "ideals," "perspectives," and the like). It has also generated a good deal of useful knowledge ranging from broad-scale portraits of the culture of teaching to information about why young people choose careers in education (see Brookhart and Freeman 1992, for example), the effects of teacher-education programs, how teacher thinking is related to teacher conduct, and how teachers (and others in education) are affected by current innovations in schools and turmoils over educational policy.

3.2 Role Conflicts for Educators

One of the earliest challenges to Parsonian role theory came from a massive study of role expectations conducted in an educational context (Gross et al. 1958). This work, focused on norms held for school superintendents in Massachusetts, established that these persons often were subjected to contradictory norms from others who were important in their professional lives (e.g., school board members, teachers, union representatives, etc.), that they were aware of these "role conflicts," and that when experiences of role conflict appeared they were a source of worry and a cause for low morale. Moreover, superintendents

pursued various strategies for "resolving" these role conflicts, and the investigators explored techniques for predicting their strategies for conflict resolution.

This innovative research had impact in both social and industrial psychology, and it was to be followed by hundreds of other studies in formal organizations exploring role conflicts, their effects on morale, and strategies for their resolution. Nor surprisingly, a number of these studies have focused on social positions in education, particularly teachers and school principals, and most of these latter works have also reported that many respondents have experienced role conflicts and that those conflicts were, indeed, associated with worry and low morale. In fact, it is now argued that role conflicts among teachers are a major source of teacher burnout (see, for example, Starnaman and Miller 1992).

Role conflict research has been associated strongly with formal organizations, so it is not surprising that its major applications in education have been to teachers, school principals, and other adults who work in school systems. It might also be useful to explore whether the role conflict concept generates insights if applied to standards for student behavior or achievement, or to norms for conduct in classroom interaction.

3.3 Teacher Expectations for Students

Lack of research on student role conflicts does not mean that investigators have ignored role expectations for students. On the contrary, a good deal of research has appeared concerned with teacher-held expectations for students and with the effects of those expectations on teacher conduct and student response. This latter research began with publication of a now classic work, *Pygmalion in the Classroom* (Rosenthal and Jacobson 1968) that reported an experimental study in which teachers were given falsely positive information about the prospects of a few, randomly-selected students in their classrooms, and it was found that those students thereafter displayed significant gains in achievement.

Why should this have happened? Rosenthal and Jacobson argued that the experimental treatment had caused teachers to form new expectations for students, that these new expectations had generated inadvertent differences in the ways they treated students, and that students had responded "appropriately" to the inadvertent cues teachers had given off. Or to recast the argument in role terms, teachers had been led to form role expectations—in this case, beliefs—about certain students, they had responded to those expectations by shifting the ways in which they sanctioned students (although they did not know they were doing so), and the targeted students had thereafter conformed to the new expectations that teachers were signaling through their sanctioning behaviors.

This reasoning suggested a disturbing corollary—that other teachers may also form inappropriate beliefs about students' abilities from rumors, minimal cues, or racist and ethnic stereotypes, and that these inappropriate beliefs may also generate inadvertent sanctioning that converts those beliefs into self-fulfilling prophesies. Worries about this possibility generated interest among educators, and other investigators quickly sought to replicate Rosenthal and Jacobson's study (reporting mixed results).

The major problem with this early effort was that the Rosenthal and Jacobson study design had provided no evidence to confirm details of their argument about teacher expectations and their effects, and it took studies with different research designs to examine these crucial processes. Much of the latter work was pioneered by Brophy and Good (1974) who interviewed teachers to learn about the details of their expectations for students and then observed their classroom behaviors to see how they treated those students. These studies have established that some teachers do, indeed, treat students differently in their classrooms depending on whether they think those students are "dull" or "bright," thus providing signals to those students (and others) concerning their expectations, and that those teachers who do this seem to be largely unaware of the process. However, not all teachers do this, and when those who do it are told about what they have been doing, they tend to change their behaviors.

Useful studies exploring relations between teacher-held expectations, classroom events, and student learning continued to be published in subsequent years. In some of these (e.g. Cooper and Good 1983), efforts were made to develop explanatory frameworks that combined role theory with cognitive social psychology, especially attribution theory (discussed above), and some aspects of group (e.g., classroom) structure and processes (discussed below). Although such efforts have not always been successful, interest in the effects of teacher-held expectations remains high as evidenced by continuing stress given to this issue in recent handbooks, encyclopedias, and texts concerned with teaching and teacher education.

4. Groups and Reference Groups

The effects of social groups on human thinking and action have interested social theorists throughout history, but it was not until the 1930s that Kurt Lewin, Jacob Moreno, Muzafer Sherif, and other social psychologists, began a tradition of systematic research into group processes. This research has involved at least two conceptions of social group: sets of real people who interact with each other in face-to-face settings—groups, and classes of real or fictitious persons whose presumed standards influence the individual—reference groups. Despite the fact that these conceptions are clearly distinct, theories and research concerning them have overlapped, and knowledge concerning both is generally subsumed under the rubric of "group dynamics."

Theories concerning groups and reference groups have generally stressed the high degree to which others provide a context for action, indeed provide much of the "definition of the situation" for the person. Thus, both types of groups are argued to generate beliefs, attitudes, norms, values, and other types of thought materials for the individual, to provide a social context for viewing and evaluating oneself, to create opportunities and constraints, rewards and costs, and structuring for interactions with others. For example, real groups may be structured so as to encourage leadership, followership, cooperation, competition, or outright conflict with others, whereas reference groups provide the person with normative standards for conduct as well as beliefs about behavioral possibilities and the likely outcomes of action.

Over the years this broad outline of ideas has been fleshed out with many different concepts, formal theories of group processes, and traditions of research; and a good deal of knowledge has now appeared concerning how groups and reference groups function in both laboratory and real-world settings. Not surprisingly, these traditions of effort have also been applied to education, and we turn now to examples of this application.

4.1 Leadership Theory and Classroom Research

In the late 1930s, Lewin et al. (1939) began a series of experimental studies on group leadership. This research took place during a stressful time when the Western democracies were being challenged by fascist ideologies. Thus, these studies examined the effects of "democratic," "autocratic," and *"Laissez-faire"* leadership on the behaviors of group members, and although conducted with young boys assembled for recreational purposes, their results were thought to apply widely to other "leadership" contexts.

One such context was thought to be the classroom, where teachers might also behave in a "democratic," "autocratic," or *"laissez-faire"* manner, so various investigators, such as Harold H. Anderson, James Withall, and Ned A. Flanders, shortly began to study how various teaching styles affect the conduct and learning of students in classrooms. In so doing they pioneered techniques for observing behavior in face-to-face situations (such as classrooms) and touched off a massive tradition of research that has generated literally hundreds of studies over the years reviewed by Dunkin and Biddle (1974) and Good (1996).

Early studies in this tradition tended to seek simple, noncontingent relations between variations in teacher behaviors and differences in student learning, but recent research has given greater stress to context features (e.g., subject matter, grade level, or student characteristics) that mediate the effects of teaching. Other studies have examined relations between teacher thought and teacher conduct, while recent efforts have also focused on the ways in which students mediate instructional behaviors and outcomes. This broad tradition of research continues today and has generated massive amounts of useful knowledge (see for example, Weinert and Helmke 1995).

4.2 The Sociometry of Classrooms and Schools

Shortly after escaping from Nazi germany, Moreno (1934) published a book with the provocative title, *Who Shall Survive?* This work pioneered various innovative ideas, among them the notion of sociometry—the study of group properties that are estimated by collating and juxtaposing the responses of individuals in the group. Moreover, in his book Moreno illustrated the promise of sociometry by applying it to primary-level classrooms representing different grade levels. Students in those classrooms were asked to nominate their "best friends," and Moreno then drew diagrams to show which students were linked to which others through friendship. When this was done, first-grade classrooms were found likely to have diffuse friendship structures (although some students were bound together in friendship "cliques," whereas others were "isolates"). In contrast, third- or fourth-grade classrooms tended to exhibit structures characterized by two antagonistic friendship groups—boys and girls—who liked others of their own gender but claimed few if any cross-sex friendships.

This insight and methodology touched off a host of other studies applying sociometric techniques to groups in alternative settings. Kurt Lewin and his students also began to conduct experiments demonstrating the effects of different group structures on such outcomes as group cohesiveness, information flow, morale, and productivity. By the mid-1960s Harary et al. (1965) were able to provide a mathematically-expressed theory concerning group structure and its effects, a development that touched off many studies of "networks" in various social contexts.

These contexts include schools, and interest in studying group structures particularly in elementary, middle, and junior high schools has generated a robust research tradition. Hallinan and Sorenson (1992), and others, have conducted extensive research on sociometric processes in American schools focusing on the effects of student background characteristics, such as race, gender, and age, and various school characteristics, such as ability tracking, on the formation and development of children's friendships (see Hallinan 1981, 1992, Hallinan and Sorenson 1992).

4.3 Conflict and Cooperative Learning

Meanwhile, other social psychologists have focused on the striking effects that groups may have on creating and resolving conflicts. Although these potentials had been known for some years, a striking demonstration of their potency appeared in the famous "Robbers Cave experiment" (Sherif et al. 1961), involving groups of boys in a summer camp. By manipulating the structures of their groups, the researchers were able to promote and then to resolve intense conflicts among those boys, and it was not long before other researchers began to apply similar processes in educational settings.

An early example of this work appeared in the "Jigsaw Classroom" experiment, reported by Aronson et al. (1978), in which the researchers reported reducing inter-racial tensions in classrooms through the use of cooperative learning groups. Extensive research on conflicts in classrooms has also been conducted by Johnson et al. (1986), and Slavin (1986) and Cohen (1994) have continued to explore the effects of co-operative learning groups in classrooms—contrasting such grouping structures with more traditional classrooms that stress individual effort and competition among students.

4.4 Peer Groups and Cultures in Schools

Drawing from social psychological research on both sociometric choices and intergroup conflicts, a large amount of research has appeared concerned with peer groups and peer cultures in schools. In general, peer groups are defined as two or more peers who are linked together by more than their common identity label (e.g., student, adolescent). These linkages usually include contact, interaction, and positive, sociometric choice (Who are your friends? Whom do you like?). The increasingly popular term "peer culture" consists of the descriptive and evaluative meanings that peer groups assign to behaviors and relationships, both those of their own peer group and those of "outsiders." These meanings are never static, and the interactions among peer group members consist of talk and behaviors that construct, maintain, consolidate, challenge, or change these meanings. The literature on peer cultures in schools has yielded a colorful array of identity labels. These include lads, ear'oles, jocks, sporties, burnouts, druggies, normals, freaks, politicos, rads, greasers, rah-rahs, crispies, grits, brains, trendies, grinds, hoods, populars, dweebs, workers, nerds, outcasts, musicians, preppies or preps, debaters, executioners, the power clique, and the leading crowd. This list does not exhaust all the names that appear in the existing literature nor would an exhaustive list necessarily be a useful basis on which to construct a systematic typology of peer cultures. Some of the identity labels (e.g., crispies) appear in only one study, and others take on different meanings as one moves from school to school. In addition, many of the labels reflect the national context in which the research was done.

What seems more likely to be comparable across national and school contexts is information about the origins and originators of peer cultures. Three originating methods have appeared in the relevant literature: peer choice, reputational techniques, and school-initiation. Whereas cultures based on peer choice are constructed out of the behaviors and interpretations of the peer group members themselves, cultures identified by reputational techniques are defined by outsiders. These outsiders may be other students, parents, teachers, school administrators, or researchers. A classic example of a researcher-identified peer group may be found in the study of ten American high schools by Coleman (1961). Although Coleman (1961 pp. 173–219) presents considerable information about the peer groups that are chosen by the students he studied, the primary argument of his work is that an adolescent culture is emerging in industrial societies. Adolescents are becoming increasingly peer-oriented, and they share values (e.g., prizing athletics above scholarship) that are contrary to the values of their parents and teachers.

Coleman's arguments parallel many of the arguments about the international youth culture that were advanced in the decade following the publication of his book. He also fueled the flames of an on-going debate in the research literature about parental, teacher, and peer influence. Although much of that research simply asked whether adults had more or less influence than peers on children, adolescents, and young adults, some investigators have incorporated social psychological dimensions for characterizing types of social influence into their research designs. One such dimension proposed by Biddle and Bank (Biddle et al. 1980a, 1980b, Bank et al. 1985) contrasts modeling (what peers do) and normative influence (what peers think I should do). Their research in the United States found that peers influenced adolescents' alcohol use by modeling more than by their norms, but parents influenced adolescents' alcohol use more by their norms than by their behaviors. They were able to predict this pattern of results on the basis of findings from more than 20 American studies (reviewed in Biddle et al. 1980a) that had compared either the normative standards or the behaviors of parents and peers as predictors of adolescent behaviors.

A second dimension for characterizing types of influence is the distinction between compliance and internalization (Kelman 1958). Compliance refers to the tendency to do or say what the other does or says or wants you to say or do. Compliance is a response to influence which does not include psychological changes. One complies in speech or action, but one does not agree that this compliant behavior is good or appropriate. Compliance is either automatic and thoughtless or is done for instrumental reasons. In contrast, internalization involves not only overt compliance but also psychological changes. The target of the influence attempt comes to accept the values, norms, or preferences of the influential other. As a result, the target person is likely to do what the other does or expects even when that other is absent.

In their research on alcohol use in four countries, Bank et al. (1985) found that internalization was a more common form of influence among peers than compliance. For the topic of violence, however,

Felson et al. (1994) found that the violent behaviors of the adolescent boys whom they studied were directly affected by the values (favoring aggressive responses) prevalent among students in their high schools, independent of their own values (regarding aggressive responses). They label the process of compliance in which the values of the group predict individuals' behaviors, independent of the values of those individuals, a social control process. This social control process, more than individual values, affected not only the amount of violence in which a student engaged but also the amount of other forms of delinquency (theft, vandalism, truancy, cheating). They conclude that "(d)elinquency involves public compliance and impression management, rather than private acceptance or internalization of one's schoolmates' values" (Felson et al. 1994 p. 168).

Unlike chosen peer cultures or reputational techniques for identifying peer cultures, school-initiated peer cultures are rooted in groups that are deliberately created by teachers or administrators to foster particular kinds of interpersonal relationships. Most instructional groupings in schools are not formed for these reasons. Instead they are formed to achieve academic goals, such as improved student motivation and performance. A common and controversial form of academic grouping is curricular tracking. Such tracking includes specialized programs for academic and vocational students; student placements in core subjects on the basis of ability; and elective courses for students with particular talents or interests. Although academic tracking is not designed to create peer groups, it does alter opportunities for peer interaction. Evidence for the effects of these opportunity structures has emerged from studies (e.g. Epstein 1989, Epstein and Karweit 1983, Hallinan and Sorenson 1985, Hargreaves 1967) showing that students are more likely to select friends from their own curricular track than from other tracks. These studies suggest that schools can shape peer relationships and peer cultures even when such effects are unintended.

5. Conclusion

As suggested by the famous quote from Kurt Lewin with which we began this article, good theories from social psychology are not only deemed "practical" but also have had great influence on how education is viewed and conducted in the 1990s. Since much of this thinking about education hinges upon the ways in which individuals (be they teachers, students, educational administrators, or others) interact, cope with, and affect one another within the context of classrooms and schools, social psychology will surely continue to have substantial effects in the future.

See also: Acquiring Attitudes and Values; Children and Youth at Risk; Development of Achievement Motivation; Dropouts, School Leavers, and Truancy; Gender Theories in Education; Sex Differences and School Outcomes; Social Foundations of School Choice; Social Psychological Theories of Teaching; Student Roles in Classrooms; Teachers' Expectations; Teachers' Roles; Youth and Conflict in School

References

Adorno T W, Frenkel-Brunswik E, Levinson D J, Sanford R N 1950 *The Authoritarian Personality.* Harper, New York

Aronson E, Blaney N, Stephan, C Sikes J, Snapp M 1978 *The Jigsaw Classroom.* Sage, Beverley Hills, California

Bandura A 1969 *Principles of Behavior Modification.* Holt, New York

Bank B J, Biddle B J, Anderson D S, Hauge R, Keats D M, Martin M M, Valantin S 1985 Comparative research on the social determinants of adolescent drinking. *Soc. Psychol. Q.* 48: 164–77

Becker H S 1958 Problems of inference and proof in participant observation. *Am. Sociol. Rev.* 28: 652–60

Becker H S, Geer B, Hughes E C 1968 *Making the Grade: The Academic Side of College Life.* Wiley, New York

Becker H S, Geer B, Hughes E C, Strauss A 1961 *Boys in White.* University of Chicago Press, Chicago, Illinois

Biddle B J in press Recent research on the role of the teacher. In: Biddle B J, Good T L, Goodson I J (eds.) in press *International Handbook of Teachers and Teaching.* Kluwer, Dordrecht, The Netherlands

Biddle B J, Bank B J, Marlin M M 1980a Parental and peer influence on adolescents. *Soc. Forces* 58: 1057–79

Biddle B J, Bank B J, Marlin M M 1980b Social determinants of adolescent drinking: What they think, what they do and what I think and do. *J. Stud. Alcohol* 41: 215–41

Blumer H 1954 What is wrong with social theory? *Am. Sociol. Rev.* 19: 3–10

Brookhart S M, Freeman D J 1992 Characteristics of entering teacher candidates. *Rev. Educ. Res.* 62(1): 37–60

Brophy J E, Good T L 1974 *Teacher–Student Relationships: Causes and Consequences.* Holt, New York

Bulmer M 1984 *The Chicago School of Sociology.* University of Chicago Press, Chicago, Illinois

Calsyn R J, Kenney D A 1977 Self-concept of ability and perceived evaluation of others: Cause or effect of academic achievement? *J. Educ. Psychol.* 69: 136–45

Cohen E 1994 *Designing Groupwork: Strategies for the Heterogeneous Classroom,* 2nd edn. Teachers College Press, New York

Coleman J S 1961 *The Adolescent Society: the Social Life of the Teenager and its Impact on Education.* The Free Press of Glencoe, New York

Collier G, Minton H L, Reynolds G 1991 *Currents of Thoughts in American Social Psychology.* Oxford University Press, New York

Cooper H M, Good T L 1983 *Pygmalion grows up: Studies in the Expectation Communication Process.* Longman, New York

Dunkin M J, Biddle B J 1974 *The Study of Teaching.* Holt, Rinehart and Winston, New York

Dweck C S, Goetz T E 1978 Attributions and learned helplessness. In: Harvey J H, Ickes W, Kidd R F (eds.) 1978 *New Directions in Attribution Theory,* Vol. 2. Earlbaum, Hillsdale, New Jersey

Dweck C S, Leggett E L 1988 A social-cognitive approach to motivation and personality. *Psychol. Rev.* 95: 256–73

Eder D, Evans C C, Parker S 1995 *School Talk: Gender and Adolescent Culture.* Rutgers University Press, New Brunswick, New Jersey

Epstein J L 1989 The selection of friends: Changes across the grades and in different school environments. In: Berndt T J, Ladd G W (eds.) 1989 *Peer Relationships in Child Development.* Wiley, New York

Epstein J L, Karweit N (eds.)1983 *Friends in School: Patterns of Selection and Influence in Secondary Schools.* Academic Press, New York

Felson R B, Liska A E, South S J, McNulty T L 1994 The subculture of violence and delinquency: Individual vs. school context effects. *Soc. Forces* 73: 155–73

Good T L 1996 Teaching effects and teacher evaluation. In: Sikula J, Buttery T, Guyton E (eds.) 1996 *Handbook of Research on Teacher Education,* 2nd edn. MacMillan, New York

Gross N, Mason W S, McEachern A W 1958 *Explorations in Role Analysis: Studies of the School Superintendency Role.* Wiley, New York

Hallinan M T 1981 Recent advances in sociometry. In: Asher S R, Gottman J M (eds.) 1981 *The Development of Children's Friendships.* Cambridge University Press, Cambridge

Hallinan M T 1992 Determinants of students' friendship choices. *Advances in Group Processes* 9: 163–83

Hallinan M T, Sorensen A B 1985 Ability grouping and student friendships. *Am. Educ. Res. J.* 22: 485–99

Hargreaves D H 1967 *Social Relations in a Secondary School.* Routledge and Kegan Paul, London

Harary F, Norman R Z, Cartwright D 1965 *Structural Models: An Introduction to the Theory of Directed Graphs.* Wiley, New York

Kelman H 1958 Compliance, identification, and internalization: Three processes of attitude change. *J. Conflict Resolution* 2: 51–60

Johnson D W, Johnson R T, Smith K A 1986 Academic conflict among students: Controversy and learning. In: Feldman R S (ed.) 1986 *The Social Psychology of Education: Current Research and Theory.* Cambridge University Press, Cambridge

Lee V E 1997 Gender equity and the organization of schools. In: Bank B J, Hall P M (eds.) 1977 *Gender, Equity, and Schooling: Policy and Practice.* Garland Publishing New York

Lewin K 1951 *Field Theory in Social Science.* Harper and Row, New York

Lewin K, Lippitt R, White R 1939 Patterns of aggressive behavior in experimentally created "social climates." *J. Soc. Psychol.* 10: 271–99

Miller R L, Brickman P, Bolen D 1975 Attribution vs. persuasion as a means for modifying behavior. *J. Per. Soc. Psychol.* 3: 430–41

Moreno J L 1934 *Who Shall Survive?* Nervous and Mental Disease Publication, Washington, DC

Newcomb T M 1943 *Personality and Social Change.* Dryden, New York

Newcomb T M, Feldman K A 1969 *The Impact of College on Students.* Jossey-Bass, San Francisco, California

Newcomb T M, Koenig K E, Flacks R, Warwick D P 1967 *Persistence and Change: Bennington College and its Students after Twenty-five Years.* Wiley, New York

Pascarella E T, Terenzini P T. 1991 *How College Affects*

Students: Findings and Insights from Twenty Years of Research. Jossey-Bass, San Francisco, California

Rosenthal R, Jacobson L 1968 *Pygmalion in the Classroom: Teacher Expectation and Pupils' Intellectual Development.* Holt, New York

Ross L, Nisbett R E 1991 *The Person and the Situation: Perspectives of Social Psychology.* McGraw-Hill, New York

Sherif M, Harvey O J, White B J, Hood W R, Sherif C W 1961 *Intergroup Conflict and Cooperation: The Robbers Cave Experiment.* Institute of Group Relations, Norman, Oklahoma

Skinner B F 1960 Teaching machines. In: Lumsdaine A A, Glaser R (eds.) 1960 *Teaching Machines and Programmed Learning.* National Educational Association, Washington, DC

Slavin R E 1986 Cooperative learning: engineering social psychology in the classroom. In: Feldman R S (ed.) 1986 *The Social Psychology of Education: Current Research and Theory.* Cambridge University Press, Cambridge

Smith L M, Geoffrey W 1968 *The Complexities of an Urban Classroom.* Holt, Rinehart and Winston, New York

Starnaman S M, Miller K I 1992 A test of a causal model of communication and burnout in the teaching profession. *Commun. Educ.* 41(1): 40–53

Weiner B (ed.) 1974 *Achievement Motivation and Attribution Theory.* General Learning Press, Morristown, New Jersey

Weiner B 1986 *An Attributional Theory of Motivation and Emotion.* Springer-Verlag, New York

Weinert L, Helmke A 1995 Interclassroom differences in instructional quality and interindividual differences in cognitive development. *Educ. Psychol.* 30: 15–20.2

Wylie R 1979 *The Self-Concept*, rev. edn., Vol. 2. University of Nebraska Press, Lincoln, Nebraska

(b) Theoretical Perspectives

Administration of Education: Critical Approaches

W. Foster

The contemporary history of the field of educational administration has exhibited considerable divisiveness; indeed a major debate has developed in the field internationally, regarding the appropriate theoretical constructs that should guide it and the types of research programs that should be conducted. At issue, largely, has been a debate between traditional perspectives, as these have been interpreted by theorists in educational administration, and those perspectives aligned with more critical views. This article reviews the arguments that theorists critical of the orthodox perspectives have made for the rethinking of educational administration as a field of study. It looks at various views informed by critical theory, constructivism, feminism, and poststructural ideas. Each of these is, in some way, a response to the dominant perspective in educational administration.

The dominant perspective tends to accept a neoscientific view of administration informed by a social science agenda that incorporates an empiricist, and often positivist, view of the role of science in creating knowledge for a practical field. Those critical of this perspective argue that such a view is largely pseudoscientific, that it forecloses other ways of knowing, and that it does little to further a deeper understanding of administrative practice.

1. Historical Dimensions from a Critical Perspective

According to the critics of the field, educational administration traditionally has chosen to become a science in the positivist sense: it has aspired to develop law-like generalizations which have predictive power regarding the practice of administration in schools. It was hoped that a positivist program of this kind, which was of particular significance in the 1950s and 1960s, would yield grand theories of human behavior in school settings. As far as administrative researchers were concerned the late twentieth century was a period during which a grand, unifying theory of administration was sought; one which suggested to practitioners the positive ways of administering organizations and which departed from the folklore of administrative practice that Simon (1945) so eloquently criticized. It was a period hallmarked by a search for certainty;

a period of attempting to find positivist knowledge regarding social issues. Furthermore, it was a period of enquiry into the laws that must govern human behavior, and that accepted logical positivism as the true way of knowing about human behavior.

Positivism itself, which has been long discredited even among its former supporters, suggested that "true" knowledge was only obtainable through empirical verification or through analytic logic; other forms of truth were, indeed, "non-sense," insofar as they did not correspond to either of the two criteria. Positivism asserted that the methodology of the natural sciences was appropriate for the social sciences, that the goal of social researchers was to develop law-like explanations for human behavior, and that research must be value-free and instrumentally useful (that is, research findings will lead to technical procedures for controlling social institutions) (Giddens 1978). A positivistic approach to administration therefore required its adherents to engage in systematic, empirical research, to justify conclusions about administrative behavior in terms of certain laws that applied, and to reject any valuational basis for administration. However, positivism itself, it has been observed, could not sustain the weight of its own arguments: its claims were shown to be themselves fallacious. Critics of positivism said that these claims were not susceptible to either empirical verification nor were they analytically deducible.

Yet positivism remained a potent, if declining, force in the shaping of administrative theory. The history of the field, according to critical analysts, is one of a progression from models based on Taylor's *Scientific Management* (1947) and the development of a "best" system (Tyack 1974) to models concerned with the development of a theory base which would yield scientific, predictive laws of administrative behavior in the positivist sense. Indeed, the "theory movement" of the 1950s and 1960s indicates the degree to which educational administration professors in university settings hoped to develop an all-encompassing explanation of how things worked in school settings. The search for a unifying theory of administrative behavior continues in the early 1990s, though significant challenges have appeared.

Culbertson (1988 p.24) observed:

After a century's pursuit of knowledge, scholars of educational administration still look to science, with its multifaceted and changing definitions for a legitimizing cloak, facilitator of inquiry, and a tool to be used in the *continuing* quest for knowledge about the ends, means, and settings of a very complex social process.

While the canons of science (broadly taken as a public process of providing explanations about social phenomena) may apply, they do so for the challengers to the orthodox, positivist approach in radically different ways (see *Positivism, Antipositivism, and Empiricism*).

2. Critical Reactions

Many of the theorists in educational administration who started the "theory movement" were later to signal its demise. Indeed, it was admitted that the field of educational administration was in "intellectual turmoil" (Griffiths 1979). This, in a sense, opened the door for a wider hearing of alternative perspectives on the field. These began to emerge in the late 1970s. Among the first was the Canadian researcher Greenfield who, in an address delivered in 1974, claimed that organizations were not the researchable, concrete realities that educational administration theorists assumed; rather, he asserted, they were constructions of the human imagination, and, as such, were not predictable (Greenfield 1975). Greenfield continued to pursue this line of investigation, showing that rules of administrative logic were reconstructed ones, based on agreements that were neither particularly logical nor rational: rather, they expressed the consent of the parties to such rules, and only such consent.

In Canada, such deviations from dominant thinking became acceptable, and a number of institutions there began to question the value of standard paradigms for researching the practice of school administration. A similar movement arose in Australia at about the same time.

Bates, a New Zealander who had emigrated to Australia, and had studied in England, adopted the perspective of what was then labeled the "new sociology of education," one which stressed the political and socioeconomic dimensions of schooling. Bates transported many of these ideas into the field of administration, adding his own version of the nature of education and administration in a democratic society (Bates 1983, 1984). In particular, Bates developed a series of arguments quite critical of dominant administrative theory in Australia and the United States and, through a variety of presentations (especially at the annual meetings of the American Educational Research Association) was able to attract a following of adherents to his opinions. Bates also organized a team of scholars at Deakin University in Australia who produced substantive ideas, monographs, and associated works on these concepts.

In Brazil at about the same time, Freire (1972) had begun writing on the nature of education in a class-based society. While not concentrating on administration, his writings had particular significance for both educators and administrators in all countries. Freire argued that the poor and oppressed in Third World societies were victims of a "banking" model of education in which dominant and usually socially oppressive ideas were "deposited" in the heads of the poor without a chance on their part to reflect critically about how such dominant concepts aided in keeping regimes in power and their own situation helpless. Freire, by contrast, endorsed a model of education based on the politicization of curricula and on the raising of consciousness (*conscientizaçao*) which requires that acting subjects acknowledge the conditions of their lives and reject the passive acceptance of such conditions. Freire's work received international acclaim, and has influenced substantially critical perspectives on administration (see *Conscientization and Mobilization*).

A similar movement developed in the United States. Here, functionalist sociology and an attendant positivism was far more warmly received than in Europe, and its tenets were carried over into educational administration. A critical perspective, however, has emerged as an important alternative. Foster (1986) developed a view of educational administrative reflective of the ideas of critical theorists. Shakeshaft (1987), Ortiz and Marshall (1988), and others also adopted an alternative perspective based on feminist thought. Other scholars took a critical standpoint, ranging from mild to radical critiques.

These movements demonstrate a rejection of the abstract formalism of administrative theories, a sense of crisis in both education and society, and a concern for social justice, equality, and emancipation. Critical perspectives, while they may differ in many ways, do share these as a common ground for both breaking away from the dominant regime of administrative theory and for proposing different ways of conceptualizing administration and education.

3. Foundations of Critical Approaches

For the most part, critical perspectives on educational administration have been informed by philosophy and sociology, with a special reliance on neo-Marxist social thought. Critical approaches have depended on the seminal thought of, among others, Habermas (1976, 1984) in Germany, Bourdieu and Passeron (1977) and Foucault (1980) in France, Freire (1972) in Brazil, and Giddens (1978, 1984) in the United Kingdom. MacIntyre (1984) and Fay (1987) in the United States have also had considerable impact on contemporary critical thought in educational administration.

Habermas (1976, 1984) was influential in his development of several arguments critical of modern social structures, particularly, with regard to administration, the idea that an instrumental and bureaucratic rationality has become dominant in the modern state and has contributed to the erosion of normative bonds that formerly held communities together. Bourdieu and Passeron (1977) are credited with developing the idea of "cultural capital," that is, that the cultural knowledge of dominant groups is asymmetrically distributed in a society, with the result that oppressed groups are at a disadvantage when they enter educational institutions that only value the dominant culture. Foucault (1980) has written extensively on the relationship between power, domination, and social forms. Freire (1972) has discussed the means by which social systems maintain structures of domination. Giddens (1984) has developed a theory of "structuration," which explains how social structures are created and recreated over time and space. MacIntyre (1984) and Fay (1987) are philosophers who developed different arguments critical of both modern philosophy and modern organization, and which have found their way into critical analyses of administration and administrative theory.

Both the scholars mentioned above and many others have provided the seminal work which has allowed the development of what might be labeled an "alternative paradigm" in educational administration. This paradigm is one that incorporates perspectives and ways of thinking oppositional to much of the mainstream literature in the field. This paradigm may be said to be composed of the following major areas: constructivist approaches, critical theory, feminist theory, and poststructuralism. Each of these will be addressed in turn.

3.1 Constructivist Approaches

While mainstream administrative theory draws on the resources provided by functionalist sociology, with its claims that organizations, such as schools, are real, concrete institutions whose regularities can be both investigated and predicted (Burrell and Morgan 1979), constructivist approaches assert that organizations are phenomena that are socially constructed; they exist as aspects of human will and imagination. Such organizations, and their administration, are essentially arbitrary; they follow no preordained law of organization, nor are they immune from changes wrought by human intervention. Educational organizations, then, are created by the consensual actions of organizational members; it is their acceptance of the symbology, culture, and "logic" of the organization that allows it to continue as an entity supported by the activities and consciousness of the members.

This approach to organizations draws on various sources, but largely on the symbolic interactionist approach advocated by Blumer (1969). Symbolic interactionism argues that social reality is always negotiated between actors, who draw on a repertoire of possibilities. In this sense, this approach provides a detailed critique of the standard orthodoxy in educational administration. It does so by arguing that the administrative world is not subject to the canons of positivist science, but is in fact created and recreated through the actions of agents who are historically and socially located in a particular moment of time and space. As Gronn (1986) has stated, "social reality is a 'negotiated order' in which conflicting definitions of the situation or meanings are construed and reconstrued by the actors as part of their ongoing role performances. The properties of the social world are taken to be emergent, shifting, and in flux, rather than fixed" (p. 6). Consequently, for Gronn (1983) and others in this tradition, the essence of educational administration is talk; that is, the continual negotiation of power, status, and control with others through language. By understanding what it is that administrators say, it is possible to begin to understand what it is they do.

The late T. Greenfield (1975) is recognized largely as the first and foremost proponent of a constructivist approach to educational administration. As Culbertson (1988 p. 20) said, Greenfield "fired a shot at the theory movement that was heard around the world." Greenfield's (1975) main theses were aimed at a systems model of organization and administration. He claimed that such models reified the organization and removed the concept of action from them. Organizations are not things, he maintained, but are human constructs. It is individuals who act, and through efforts of will and determination it is they, and they alone, who construct distinctions of power and status in organizations. An understanding of organizations, then, requires an understanding of how individuals construct and then interpret their worlds, and this is done, for Greenfield, much more meaningfully through a phenomenological attempt at understanding than it is through an abstract and formalistic theory.

One implication of Greenfield's work is that the preparation for, and conduct of, administration should be guided more by a knowledge of the humanities than of the methodologies of the natural sciences. A belief that social reality is a constructed reality would suggest that one understands the social histories that actors bring with them, and this can best be accomplished through the study of the arts, philosophy, history, and the law. It is these that provide one with a sense of human power and of human frailty, and it is this sense that would profit administration most.

3.2 Critical Theory

Administrative scholars influenced by critical theory have addressed the role of administration in the creation of just and equitable social orders within schools. Critical theorists have largely been influenced by the work of the German theorists associated with the Frankfurt School: in particular by the social philosopher and sociologist Jürgen Habermas (1976, 1984). Critical theorists have asserted that schools are based in social class distinctions which, through their very structure, are replicated within generations. Thus, certain schools have a tendency to replicate the underclass while others are servants to the elite, and the difference between the two is the amount of cultural and economic capital that students bring to each site, as well as the system of reproduced economies in school settings wherein the major function of schooling becomes the creation of workers eligible to join the pool of labor a society needs to sustain its economic development.

Critical theorists in administration decry this limited vision of schooling; many of them return to a Deweyan emphasis on the purpose of schools as forming a democratic populace where issues and concerns of a democratic society are reconsidered. Critical theorists, then, are particularly suspicious of arrangements of administration prevailing in the late twentieth century. They suggest that the bureaucratic apparatus of schooling is not conducive to the formation of political consciousness and that the accepted structure of administration neglects a variety of moral and ethical issues.

In particular, an approach to administration informed by critical theory would take issue with those dimensions of the orthodox approach which are positivistic in nature and which suggest that certain and true knowledge of administration can be discovered and an administrative "science" established. Critical theorists in educational administration argue that such attempts to obtain certain knowledge are not only doomed to failure, because of the lack of predictability in human affairs, but also because they divert attention away from the essentially moral basis of educational administration.

Instead, critical theorists ask administrative scholars to focus on the bureaucratization of the organization and on the instrumental rationality so prevalent therein. Critical theorists are largely concerned with the emancipation of all persons, and to this end they examine the process of bureaucracy insofar as it removes from agents the possibility of democratic will. In administration, this means the exploration of alternate ways of organizing schools, such as localizing decision-making at a level wherein all participants can have a voice.

However, one issue which tends to preclude this possibility is the development of instrumental reason. Here, a distinction is made by critical theorists, drawing upon the work of Habermas (1976), between communicative rationality and instrumental rationality. Communicative rationality has to do with the use of reason to establish bonds between people, to develop forms of interaction where they can live in respect with each other. Instrumental rationality, on the other hand, involves the use of reason to achieve objectives and goals; it is a rationality designed for a purpose. Bureaucracies tend to emphasize purposive or instrumental rationality to the detriment of communicative rationality. Procedural and technical aspects, aimed at student performance, have come to replace discursive methods aimed at establishing forms of community in

schools. Such an instrumental reason displaces those attempts by teachers and administrators to establish meaningful communities in their schools, with the result that democratic forms of governance become considered obsolete for school sites. In their place state and national rules and procedures assume dominance, with a concomitant reduction in local control. Instrumental reason, then, comes to subsume communicative action, and in so doing establishes a technocratic dominancy within school settings. To the extent that administrators accede to this, schooling becomes a mere form of meeting those objectives established by existing hierarchies, rather than a fundamental way of improving the human condition.

Thus, critical theory in administration suggests that many of the fundamental purposes of education, such as the development of citizens and the formation of political consciousness, have become subjugated to economic interests determined by a capitalistic state. Formal educational institutions, in this respect, have come to serve as training grounds for the corporate sector, and, as such, these institutions reproduce the inequalities of class, race, and gender that have come to be hallmarks of a capitalistic economy.

However, critical theorists also have an optimistic appraisal of the possibilities for change. They suggest that through the critical evaluation of educational practices, a certain consciousness about those practices can be developed, and that an administration concerned with issues of a social nature can be developed through preparation programs. A goal of critical theorists in educational administration has therefore become the development of intellectuals who, engaging in administration, can take steps appropriate to the transformation of institutions. Such administrators, in a critical theoretic perspective, can engage teachers, students, and parents in a dialogue about the nature of schooling in a class-based society and about the possibilities of achieving democratic representation in such institutions (see *Critical Theory and Education*).

3.3 Feminist Approaches

Feminist approaches draw upon the resources of feminist theory, critical theory, and various sociological and psychological perspectives in order to present a sustained and perceptive attack on the positivist and largely male-dominated issues in educational administration. Of concern here has been the neglect by establishment scholars of the different perspectives that feminism could contribute to the practice of administration. As Ortiz and Marshall (1988) put it:

> An alternative explanation for the failure to see the potential value of women's contributions to educational administration is that the chiefs want to retain the power inherent in defining what is valuable, good, and proper. *Different* values and behaviors can simply be defined as deficient, devalued, and wrong when they are displayed by people who appear to pose threats to those in control. (p. 136)

Such "different" values have largely to do with male hierarchies and the suppression of women in the profession. Initial concern tended to focus on the presence of what were labeled "old boy networks," and the inability of women to penetrate these networks in order even to secure appointment to administrative posts. More recent work, while not abandoning the importance of access to administration, has focused more on the ingrained nature of male-oriented patterns of domination within the workplace. Thus, the modern school organization rewards individualism more than community, competitiveness more than cooperation, and justice more than caring; each characteristic that is rewarded tends also to be associated more with a male worldview (see, e.g., Noddings 1984).

A feminist perspective on administration would thus present a number of fundamental challenges to the field. First, these perspectives would question the idea of administration as a "control" mechanism for maintaining the operation of schools. In place of control, such perspectives would suggest that administration should be considered a "constructing" endeavor, one that attempts to build bonds between all parties involved in the schooling effort. Further, feminist perspectives would challenge the notion of schools as agents of cultural transmission, arguing instead that the culture transmitted is one saddled with a history of masculine domination and insensitivity to the needs of other groups. Rather, these perspectives would argue, schools should become places for cultural transformation, for the raising of consciousness about issues of power and domination. Finally, and certainly without exhausting the supply of challenges, feminist perspectives might observe that the centralized, bureaucratic nature of schooling in many countries contributes to a hierarchical model of administration more appropriate to the militaristic "father" image of conquest than it is to a more urgently needed "mother" image of support and nurturance. Schools, and administration, it might be argued, should no longer be sites for training the young in the ways and means of securing world supremacy, but rather places for kindness, where the young are taught their own worth and the value of all humans. Noddings (1984), for example, has illustrated cogently the value of caring within human relationships; her work suggests that schools and their administration be sites for the development of respectful relationships between adults and children, rather than the sites for the control of others (see *Gender Theories in Education*).

3.4 Poststructuralism

Another development in educational administration is the application of poststructuralist, or postmodern, thought to the field of educational administration. Poststructuralism, as applied to administration, is critical of the traditional orthodoxies in the field and begins to question the foundational assumptions of educational administration. Poststructuralism argues against the principle of foundationalism; namely, that there are fixed, transcendent first principles upon which all other knowledge is based. In administration, for example, there has been a tendency to accept the structural features of school organization as "natural" and to then look for the underlying "laws" which hold these structures together and which allow for administrative action to be effective. Poststructuralists would argue that attempts to determine foundational laws of administrative (or other) behavior are not only misplaced but dangerous. Such attempts are dangerous because they conceal the point that such structures arise out of discursive practices (i.e., speech acts) which compete with each other for power and the right to define what is true and proper. Paternalistic discourse, for example, is an attempt to establish the man as dominant and to place the woman in a subservient relationship of power difference. Cherryholmes (1988) explored these issues when he wrote:

> Modern, analytic, and structural thought seek rationality, linearity, progress, and control by discovering, developing, and inventing metanarratives, metadiscourses, and metacritiques that define rationality, linearity, progress, and control. Postmodern, postanalytic, and poststructural thought are skeptical and incredulous about the possibility of such metanarratives. (p. 11)

Such metanarratives or metadiscourses provide the framework within which administrators, researchers, and teachers conduct their business. Certainly a dominant narrative in education and administration, and contained in the texts of the field, has been that of control. Thus, the idea of "scientific management" proved a popular one for early administrators, and continued as a major theme for later administrative practice, lurking in the shadows of such popular administrative notions as management by objectives, accountability systems, performance-based teaching and administration, and so on. Poststructuralism attempts to reveal the idea of control as an ideological front which arises from largely written discourse and which becomes used to establish, or shore up, different structures of power. Control and power become the (not entirely covert) reasons for putting into place in school systems a variety of technical accounting and behavioral systems.

Poststructuralist thought has been most prevalent in philosophy, architecture, literature, and the arts, and from these has carried over into education and educational administration. Poststructuralism attempts to debunk the dominant hierarchies of power, whether linguistic or artistic, and to suggest that it is in the continual reformation of language and power relationships that "truth" is to be found. Indeed, "truth" become a somewhat vacuous concept, one which depends more on the regnant power establishments than it does on any actual substantive connections (see *Critical Discourse Analysis; Postmodernism and Education*).

4. Implications of Critical Approaches

These critical perspectives carry a number of implications for educational administrative practice as well as for the formal preparation of educational administrators. Among these, there is first a movement from the idea of administration to the idea of leadership. Administration tends to mean the establishment of systems of control over bureaucratic institutions; leadership implies the voluntaristic achievement of mutual goals. The emphasis in critical approaches has often been on the formation of democratic communities where decision-making is achieved through participatory involvement of all members. This implies that leadership must be taken in order to facilitate the often difficult process of soliciting the involvement of all parties and in empowering in particular those traditionally disenfranchised by the system. Whereas dominant theories in educational administration have tended to emphasize the control of educational institutions, the critical perspectives have tended to suggest that it is leadership that is needed. By "leadership," such alternative perspectives do not mean the generally accepted definition of the term, that is, a position held by an administrator. Rather, the idea of leadership denotes what Burns (1979) termed "transformational leadership," namely, that which seeks to raise the consciousness of followers with the goal of achieving real and intended changes. Such leadership requires the voluntary cooperation of followers in a mission identified by both followers and leaders as one of significance; critical perspectives suggest, then, that such a mission is one intended to cause real and substantive change in the operating procedures of institutions.

There is also a movement from value-neutral beliefs in administration to value-laden beliefs. This means that the search for various laws of administrative behavior should end; there are no such laws and the search for them has become a vain quest without end. MacIntyre (1984), for example, observed that "the salient fact about those sciences is the absence of the discovery of any law-like generalization whatsoever" (p. 88). The effort to find predictable laws and generalizations has proved futile, for there are none, except perhaps for the most trivial. What is left, then, are efforts at coming to terms with the value-laden sets of beliefs that professionals in education, including administrators, bring with them to their jobs. What are the beliefs and values that are held? How do they inform the everyday practices of administrators, teachers, and students? In what way do such beliefs impact upon the course of education? These are the questions that critical perspectives would ask of administrative researchers, and then ask them to further examine the answers in terms of their contribution to the formation of democratic practices within the institution.

To continue to search for generalizable and value-free laws of administrative behavior is, in a critical framework, to search for what cannot ever be found.

To recognize that everyone has values and beliefs, and that these inform people's very being, as well as their workday performances, is to accept a perspective that alternative ways of viewing administration would consider very important. Of course, in a critical perspective, not all values are created equal; the end value of human emancipation from various forms of oppression (whether educational, cultural, ethnic, gender, or other forms) takes precedence and it becomes incumbent on preparation programs to incorporate such a value into their curriculum.

The perspectives addressed above also suggest that the field of educational administration is moving from a foundationalist perspective to a nonfoundationalist one. This means that the foundations of the field, the knowledge-base for what is understood about administration, is never firmly established but shifts as social forces and concerns shift. The field of educational administration is thus distinguished from such fields as law and medicine because there are no particularly important "first principles"; rather, there are only general guidelines regarding possibilities.

One such general guideline is that certain knowledge regarding education and administration, which could be codified in technical rules and procedures, will not be forthcoming. While a great deal can be learned about the specific, this will not result in universalizable maxims. For critical theorists, this is an acceptable state of affairs because, as developed previously, there is strong connection between knowledge and power. Coming to the realization that knowledge can never be conclusive in the field may mean that power too may never be fully conclusive. This, in turn, means that power may be able to be more widely distributed and the knowledge possessed by dominated groups become valued and valuable.

The further acceptance of critical perspectives on educational administration leads to a fourth implication. Administrators should be primarily educators, engaged in the process of consciousness-raising rather than of consciousness-control. This implies a whole new dimension to how administrative practice is conceptualized and to how the preparation of educational administrators is to be regarded. It becomes less important to develop technical expertise in the content of traditional administrative programs than to engage in processes of intellectual inquiry and critical evaluations of prevailing social practices.

5. Conclusion: Toward Postadministration?

This entry has reviewed the various concepts and traditions conveyed by the term "critical approaches" when applied to educational administration. These have included viewpoints on administration derived from constructivism, critical theory, feminism, and poststructuralism. Each has been shown to be critical of the traditional, orthodox view of administration that has been positivist in orientation, instrumental in practice, and largely dedicated to the control and maintenance of social institutions and the people in them.

What an examination of these positions critical of traditional administrative thought seems to lead to is a theory of antiadministration. If administration is to be identified with the current, orthodox definitions of it, then critical perspectives must be defined in opposition to this.

"Administration" is the establishment of order in a somewhat disorderly, but largely harmonious world. It accepts the regnant ideas and narratives as true, and these foundational assumptions are not to be examined, let alone challenged. "Administration" assumes a certain soundness to the world order; problems that are identified can be rectified through more research, or through the more efficient application of what is already known. "Administration" puts a certain faith in technical rules of procedure, assuming that human error and variance can be adjusted to the norm by the application of standard ways of operating.

"Antiadministration," as critical perspectives might have it, is at variance with the tenets of "administration." Antiadministration believes that human beings live in a world of both physical and emotional pain, that they live within and firmly subscribe to ideologies which will later be shown to have been of historical significance in maintaining regimes of inequality. Antiadministration further holds that the modern state and its administration have focused on only one dimension of human agency—people's productive power—and have created instrumental systems designed both to harness that power and suppress other dimensions of the human experience.

In "administration" and "antiadministration" a tension of opposites generated by different theoretical stances may be observed, as well as the dialectics of the positive and the negative. Each critical perspective, taken individually, contributes to this dialectic. Administration claims that it is a necessary component for establishing order in a complex world, for generating the levels of productivity that developed nations demand. The response of administration is that this world represents the zenith of instrumental rationality.

Perhaps the critical perspectives drawn from critical theory, constructivism, feminism, and poststructuralism can be combined into a coherent theory of "postadministration," one that transcends the limits of orthodox administration and those of individual critical alternatives. Postadministration would argue the need for the creation of order within community, but would also look for the contributions of all members to the formation of such a community. Postadministration would accept that humans are, in Fay's words, "not only active beings, but they are also embodied, traditional, historical, and embedded creatures" (1987 p. 9) and thus change occurs spo-

radically and with effort. Postadministration would be conscious of the patriarchical nature of modern systems and practices, and engage in a detailed critique of these. Finally, postadministration would be aware of the tendency for its pronouncements to become law, to become a metanarrative about how our institutions should be run and, while this is always a temptation, perhaps the postadministrator can recognize that their leadership is, ultimately, only an attempt to improve the human condition.

See also: Conscientization and Mobilization; Critical Theory and Education; Gender Theories in Education; Positivism, Antipositivism, and Empiricism

References

Bates R 1983 *Educational Administration and the Management of Knowledge.* Deakin University Press, Geelong

Bates R 1984 Towards a critical practice of educational administration. In: Sergiovanni T J, Corbally J E (eds.) 1984 *Leadership and Organization Culture.* University of Illinois, Urbana, Illinois

Blumer H 1969 *Symbolic Interactionism: Perspectives and Method.* Prentice-Hall, Englewood Cliffs, New Jersey

Bourdieu P, Passeron J-C 1977 *Reproduction in Education, Society, and Culture.* Sage, London

Burns J M 1979 *Leadership.* Harper and Row, New York

Burrell G, Morgan G 1979 *Sociological Paradigms and Organizational Analysis: Elements of the Sociology of Corporate Life.* Heinemann, London

Cherryholmes C H 1988 *Power and Criticism: Poststructural Investigations in Education.* Teachers College Press, New York

Culbertson J A 1988 A century's quest for a knowledge base. In: Boyan N (ed.) 1988 *Handbook of Research on Educational Administration.* Longman, New York

Fay B 1987 *Critical Social Science: Liberation and its Limits.* Polity Press, Cambridge

Foster W 1986 *Paradigms and Promises: New Approaches to Educational Administration.* Prometheus, Buffalo, New York

Foucault M 1980 *Power & Knowledge: Selected Interviews and Other Writings 1972–1977.* Harvester Press, Brighton

Freire P 1972 *Pedagogy of the Oppressed.* Sheed and Ward, London

Giddens A 1978 Introduction. In: Giddens A. (ed.) 1978 *Positivism and Sociology.* Heinemann, London

Giddens A 1984 *The Constitution of Society: Outline of the Theory of Structuration.* Polity Press, Oxford

Greenfield T B 1975 Theory about organization: A new perspective and its implications for schools. In: Hughes M (ed.) 1975 *Administering Education: International Challenge.* Athlone, London

Griffiths D E 1979 Intellectual turmoil in educational administration. *Educ. Admin. Q.* 15(3): 43–65

Gronn P 1983 Talk as the work: The accomplishment of school administration. *Adm. Sci. Q.* 28(1): 1–21

Gronn P 1986 *The Psycho-Social Dynamics of Leading and Following.* Deakin University, Geelong

Habermas J 1976 *Legitimation Crisis.* Heinemann Educational, London

49

Habermas J 1984 *The Theory of Communicative Action: Reason and the Rationalization of Society*, Vol. I. Beacon Press, Boston, Massachusetts

MacIntyre A 1984 *After Virtue: A Study in Moral Theory*, 2nd edn. University of Notre Dame Press, Notre Dame, Indiana

Noddings N 1984 *Caring: A Feminine Approach to Ethics and Moral Education*. University of California, Berkeley, California

Ortiz F I, Marshall C 1988 Women in educational administration. In: Boyan N (ed.), *Handbook of Research on Educational Administration*. Longman, New York

Shakeshaft C 1987 *Women in Educational Administration*. Sage, Beverly Hills, California

Simon H 1945 *Administrative Behavior: A Study of Decision-making Processes in Administrative Organization*. Macmillan, New York

Taylor F W 1947 *Scientific Management*. Harper, New York

Tyack D B 1974 *The One Best System: A History of American Urban Education*. Harvard University Press, Cambridge, Massachusetts

Critical Discourse Analysis

A. Luke

Critical discourse analysis is a contemporary approach to the study of language and discourses in social institutions. Drawing on poststructuralist discourse theory and critical linguistics, it focuses on how social relations, identity, knowledge, and power are constructed through written and spoken texts in communities, schools, and classrooms. This article describes the historical contexts and theoretical precedents for sociological models for the study of language, discourse, and text in education. It then outlines key terms, assumptions, and practices of critical discourse analysis. It concludes by describing unresolved issues and challenges for discourse analysis and sociology of education.

1. Language and Discourse in Contemporary Education

In a context of unprecedented educational expansion and population growth, postwar sociology of education focused urgently on issues around institutional structure, the production of skilled workers, and increased educational access and participation. By the 1960s, attempts to explain and redress educational inequality for minority and lower socioeconomic groups generated major debates in sociolinguistics and the ethnography of communication. Much of that work focused on language development and literacy acquisition as key factors in differential student achievement and the intergenerational reproduction of educational inequality. Debates over the role of social class-specific "speech codes," "linguistic deficits," the educational consequences of multilingualism, and the institutional status of nonstandard English are still not fully resolved.

Some thirty years later, educators face the challenges of "new times" (Hall 1996): new cultural practices and media texts, hybrid cultural identities, emergent social formations and institutions, and changing structures of work and economy. In postindustrial and newly industrializing nation-states, the rapidity and depth of many of these changes have drawn anew many sociologists' attention to language, texts, and discourses. There is an increasing recognition that these now form the central media of community life, education, and work.

Large-scale immigration and the emergence of multicultural, multilingual nation states have marked the postwar era. In urban and suburban areas, schools and educators are facing new student bodies and rapidly changing community demographic profiles. These conditions have called into question the relevance and efficacy of longstanding administrative, curriculum, instruction, and evaluation practices, many of which were developed in early and mid-century secular school systems designed for monocultural, homogenous nation-states. The recognition and enfranchisement of linguistic and cultural minority students has generated a host of practical issues around new dynamics of ethnic, cultural, and gender difference in communities, families, and institutional life, differential power in pedagogic relations in classrooms, and the knowledge and epistemological claims of historically disenfranchised groups over what should count as curriculum knowledge (see Apple 1996).

At the same time, the commodification of Western popular culture and the multinational globalization of economies have changed the patterns and practices of work and leisure in many communities. In an emergent "post-Fordist" economic and sociological context, new industrial conditions and information technologies have begun to alter the requisites and parameters of what might count as educationally produced skilled labor. In service, information, and media sectors of the economy, the exchange of symbols, discourses, and texts have become key modes of value and exchange. Current definitions of educationally produced skills, competences, and knowledges appear to be in transition, with the emergent requisites of new technologies and reorganized labor practices and markets making new demands on academic and vocational education. In response, research and theory in many areas of the social sciences and applied human services have shifted from a focus on traditional labor markets to an analysis of the economic and cultural consequences of new modes of information.

These conditions raise questions about the relevance and value of the structures and practices of early and mid-twentieth century schooling. These include questions about apparent disjunctions between community and school cultures; the appropriateness of curricular, instructional models for new student populations; and the practical requirements and challenges of new workplaces and civic spheres where these students live and work. However, many prevailing social and cultural theories of education and their affiliated practices are based on historical critiques of industrial-era schooling and work, and sociological analyses of the late nineteenth and early twentieth century monocultural monolingual nation-state. The move towards discourse analytic approaches to education thus begins from the assumption that many of these challenges can only be addressed by a focus on how language, discourse, and text figure in educational processes, practices, and outcomes (New London Group 1996).

2. *Poststructuralist and Postmodern Discourse Theory*

The development of the "new" sociology of education in the early 1970s was a key moment in the application of Western social philosophy and sociology to educational theory and problems. Phenomenological, symbolic interactionist, and neo-Marxian approaches to the study of identity, knowledge, and institutional change in turn led to the development and application of various interpretive methods in educational research. These include action research, literary analysis, revisionist historiography, and critical ethnography. Yet these various approaches are often conflated, erroneously, with later poststructuralist and postmodern social theory under the general category of "critical theory."

The application of French discourse theory to educational research followed from the translation and dissemination of the work of Michel Foucault and Jacques Derrida in England and America during the 1970s and 1980s. What distinguishes French and Anglo-American poststructuralist theory is a recognition of the centrality of language and discourse. According to Foucault and Derrida, language and discourse are not transparent or neutral means for describing or analyzing the social and biological world. Rather they effectively construct, regulate, and control knowledge, social relations, and institutions,

and indeed, such analytic and exegetic practices as scholarship and research. By this account, nothing is outside of or prior to its manifestation in discourse.

Foucault asks whether the natural and social worlds are indeed knowable, accessible, and analyzable without recourse to the constitutive forces of discourse. He does not limit his notion of discourse to language, but refers more generally to reiterated key words and statements that recur in local texts of all kinds. Such statements appear intertextually across texts and comprise familiar patterns of disciplinary and paradigmatic knowledge and practice. For instance, one might speak of discourses of "physics" or "politics," but also might specify more fine-grained categories of discourse, like "quantum mechanics" or "socialist politics," depending on the texts in question and the purposes of the analysis. Discourses have both disciplinary and, to use Foucault's term "disciplining" effects. They enable and delimit fields of knowledge and inquiry, and they govern what can be said, thought, and done within those fields.

Poststructuralist discourse theory examines how writing, texts, and discourses are constructive phenomena, shaping the identities and practices of human subjects. In his historical studies of asylums, governments, prisons, and schools, Foucault focused on how historical configurations of discourse constructed new kinds of human subjects. He argued that institutionalized discourses consist of categorical "grids of specification" that classify and regulate peoples' identities, bodies, domestic and civil spaces, and social practices in different relations of knowledge and power. These discourses, he goes on to argue, work in the local situations of social institutions in ways that cannot be explained by reference to any individual's or group's roles, intents, or motivations. Indeed, poststructuralist theory questions whether there are essential human subjects, individual agents, and social realities independent of their dynamic historical construction in social and cultural discourses.

By this account, social institutions such as schools and universities are comprised by and through discourses. Discourses make up a dense fabric of spoken, written, and symbolic texts of institutional bureaucracies (e.g., policies, curriculum documents, forms) and their ubiquitous face-to-face encounters (e.g., classroom interaction, informal talk). Within these institutions, human subjects are defined and constructed both in generic categories (e.g., as "children" and "teachers") and in more specialized and purposive historical categories (e.g., as "professionals," "adolescents," "linguistic deficit," "preoperational"). These discourse constructions act both as institutional "technologies of power," implemented and enforced by official authorization, and they act as "technologies of the self" (Foucault 1980), internalized means for the self-discipline of action, practice, and identity. According to Foucault, these technologies potentially have both productive and negative material, bodily

51

and spatial consequences for human subjects and communities.

While Foucault's work shifts our attention to the regulatory nature of discourses, Derrida questioned whether any cultural texts can have intrinsic authority or canonical status as accounts of "truths" about the phenomenal world. That is, Derrida's approach to philosophic and literary "deconstruction" queries whether definitive or authoritative interpretations are possible in the first place. All texts comprise a dynamic play of "*differance*" which necessarily renders them polysemous: multiple and potentially quite idiosyncratic meanings can be generated by readers in particular social contexts. Each text's distinctive features and differences thus are reconstructed and reconstituted into distinctive "readings" in "local institutional sites" (Baker and Luke 1991).

Poststructuralist work thus forms a critique of ontology and epistemology in empirical approaches to social science. It makes the case that: (a) all inquiry is by definition a form of discourse analysis; and (b) all research consists of a "reading" and "rewriting" of a series of texts from a particular historical and epistemological standpoint. In so doing, it provides a radically different perspective on students and teachers, policy and curriculum, schools and classrooms. If its premises are accepted then an appropriate focus on sociological studies would be on how the texts of schooling construct such taken for granted phenomena as individuals, skills, knowledge, and institutions. At the same time, it raises significant methodological questions about the status of data and the epistemological standpoint of the educational researcher. Given the primacy of discourse, the social facts studied by sociologists are constructed artefacts of researchers' own discourses and "naming," and any data collected in the field needs to be treated as a "readable" text, subject to interpretation.

This theoretical shift has the potential for destabilizing dominant paradigms and theories. Prevailing models of educational research and practice comprise what Lyotard (1984) has called "metanarratives": stories about human progress and scientific development that prescribe, rather than describe in any empirical sense, what will count as individual and institutional development. Consequently, the very foundational theories that have been used to study the child, education, curriculum, and instruction may be viewed as discourses, taken-for-granted "truths" that "systematically form the objects about which they speak" (Foucault 1972 p. 39). Following a postmodern radical scepticism towards "metanarratives," no disciplinary or commonsense source of "truth claims" would be exempt.

Poststructuralist theory thereby encourages a counterontological critique of those broad theories of human development, social agency, and social structure that were used in the nineteenth century to analyze and develop educational interventions. In this way, it enables a self-reflexive critique of the modernist and industrial-era administrative and curricular models mentioned at the onset of this article. At the same time, it encourages the further development of experimental, interpretive modes of inquiry to examine new educational phenomena.

The insight of philosophic poststructuralism, then, is that there are no educational truths, practices, or phenomena that can be studied outside of discourse. By such an account, educational institutions could be seen as complex sites constructed by and through discourses expressed in various texts: from policy statements and textbooks to face-to-face talk in classrooms. These texts are seen as "heteroglossic" articulations of various historical, class, and cultural interests contending for social power and capital. The question of how to collect, read, and interpret these texts and how to analyze and situate their "symbolic power" is complex. It requires the study of the diverse "linguistic markets" and "social fields" where educationally acquired competence is used (Bourdieu 1992 pp. 51–65). For while poststructuralism provides a wide-ranging epistemological critique of how discourse works, Foucault and Derrida assiduously avoided offering more than broad theoretical directions for the study of discourse in specific local institutions.

3. Educational Applications of Discourse Analysis

As noted at the onset of this article, the heralded "linguistic turn" in the social sciences had a significant impact on educational research in the postwar era. Discourse analysis describes an interdisciplinary family of methodologies and approaches to the study of language and text that draws variously upon linguistics, literary theory and cultural studies, philosophy of language, sociology, and psychology. Initially, the term was used in the 1950s to describe linguistic analysis of semantic structures above the level of the sentence. In the 1960s and 1970s, it was applied by english teachers to the systematic analyses of the error patterns of second language learners' spoken and written texts and by educational psychologists to the development of cognitive text processing models.

American and European psycholinguistics and sociolinguistics in the 1960s focused on the development of linguistic models that describe how people produce and use language. However, interactional sociolinguistics and its various subdisciplines (e.g., ethnography of communication, language planning) have tended to draw extensively from structural functionalist and symbolic interactionist sociological theory (see Williams 1992). The principal focus of discourse analysis in education in the 1970s and 1980s was on instances of face-to-face talk between, for instance, care-givers and children as key moments in language socialization, and the development of literate competence and cultural identity (see Cazden 1988). Application of ethnomethodological approaches to the study of classroom talk (see Mehan 1979) and to educational texts (see Baker and Freebody 1989) further showed how normative categories of gender, student disability, deficit, and disadvantage were constructed in the exchange structures and themes of classroom talk.

Sociolinguistic and ethnomethodological discourse analysis yielded detailed studies of language in classrooms, supplanting psychological "deficit" models with descriptions of cultural difference and the regulatory effects of schooling and classroom language. As sociological research, however, this work stops short of addressing larger questions about the unequal social production of "cultural capital," and about relationships of power among social actors and classes. In sum, this work provided a detailed description of everyday language use and textual practice but struggled to reconnect these systematically to larger ideological issues in what by the late 1980s appeared to be an increasingly conflict-ridden and heterogeneous social institution of schooling.

At the same time, Foucault's work had begun to provide a framework for describing how educational texts construct children, teachers, students, and human subjects in different relations of power and knowledge. Henriques et al. (1984) began to meld poststructuralist and neo-Marxist educational analysis to describe the hegemonic power of educational discourses in the construction of gender, cultural identity, and child development. A range of studies described the broad development and intellectual history of particular paradigms and networks of ideas as "genealogical" discourses that build institutions of "governmentality" and moral order. These included historical studies of childhood, progressive education, and mental measurement as well as contemporary studies of educational policy and curriculum fields including mathematics, physical education, language, and literacy teaching (see Ball 1990).

There is, additionally, a growing corpus of feminist and postcolonial work that, following Derrida and Foucault, attempts to write and hear historically marginalized speakers and voices. This includes significant work in educational autobiographies of women and members of indigenous, cultural, and ethnic minority groups. One of the shared tenets of poststructuralist feminist and postcolonial theory is the need to generate a public and intellectual "space" for the critique of dominant discourses and for the speaking and writing of the "unsaid," "subaltern" voices and stories that have been silenced historically. Within the fields of "critical pedagogy" and "feminist pedagogy," this work is seen to serve educative and emancipatory political projects (see Luke and Gore 1993).

The development of discourse analysis of educational texts thus mirrors some of the unresolved theoretical dilemmas in the sociology of education and in the emergence and application of cultural studies to education. While sociolinguistic work has stressed microanalyses of face-to-face language use in classrooms, textbooks, and student texts, genealogical studies of curriculum and policy have tended to provide broad interpretive analyses of the historical development of institutional and knowledge structures with less detailed textual analysis. By contrast, much feminist and postcolonial writing has focused on the production of situated accounts of experience and identity formation, marginality, and exclusion. The outstanding task for critical discourse analysis, then, is to provide detailed analysis of cultural voices and texts in local educational sites, while attempting to connect theoretically and empirically these with an understanding of power and ideology in broader social formations and configurations. In many ways, this is a restatement of an archetypal task of the sociology of education: to link specific educational processes with systemic sociological outcomes. But that task has been reframed by the challenge of poststructuralism: to theorize and describe the relationships between discourse change and social change, between the word and the material world.

4. Critical Discourse Analysis

Critical discourse analysis refers to the use of an ensemble of techniques for the study of textual practice and language use as social and cultural practices (Fairclough 1992b). It builds from three broad theoretical orientations. First, it draws from poststructuralism the view that discourse operates laterally across local institutional sites, and that texts have a constructive function in forming up and shaping human identities and actions. Second, it draws from Bourdieu's sociology the assumption that actual textual practices and interactions with texts become "embodied" forms of "cultural capital" with exchange value in particular social fields. Third, it draws from neo-Marxist cultural theory the assumption that these discourses are produced and used within political economies, and that they thus produce and articulate broader ideological interests, social formations, and movements within those fields (see Hall 1996).

The practical techniques of critical discourse analysis are derived from various disciplinary fields. Work in pragmatics, narratology, and speech act theory argues that texts are forms of social action that occur in complex social contexts. Research and theory in systemic functional linguistics (Halliday 1985) shows how linguistic forms can be systematically related to social and ideological functions. Critical discourse analysis uses analytic tools from these fields to address persistent questions about larger, systemic relations of class, gender, and culture. In educational research, this work has been turned to the examination of how knowledge and identity are constructed across a range of texts in the institutional "site" of the school.

Critical discourse analysis begins from the assumption that systematic asymmetries of power and resources between speakers and listeners, readers, and writers can be linked to their unequal access to linguistic and social resources. In this way, the presupposition of critical discourse analysis is that institutions like schools act as gatekeepers of mastery of discursive resources: the discourses, texts, genres, lexical, and grammatical structures of everyday language use. What this suggests is a reframing of questions about educational equality in terms of how systematically distorted and ideological communication may set the conditions for differential institutional access to discursive resources, the very educational competences needed for social and economic relations in information-based economies.

Discourse and language in everyday life may function ideologically. They may be used to make asymmetrical relations of power and particular textual portrayals of social and biological worlds appear given, commonsensical, and "natural." Accordingly, the task of critical discourse analysis is both deconstructive and constructive. In its deconstructive moment it aims to disrupt and render problematic the themes and power relations of everyday talk and writing. In its constructive moment, it has been applied to the development of critical literacy curriculum that aims towards an expansion of students' capacities to critique and analyze discourse and social relations, and towards a more equitable distribution of discourse resources (Fairclough 1992a).

The principal unit of analysis for critical discourse analysis is the text. Texts are taken to be social actions, meaningful and coherent instances of spoken and written language use. Yet their shape and form is not random or arbitrary. Specific text types of "genres" serve conventional social uses and functions. That is, particular kinds of texts attempt to "do things" in social institutions with predictable ideational and material effects. These include functional written texts (e.g., business letters, forms, policies, textbooks), spoken face-to-face interactions (e.g., clinical exchanges, service exchanges, classroom lessons), and multimodal visual, electronic, and gestural texts (e.g., Internet home pages). Taken as historically and culturally specific social actions, genres are dynamic and continually subject to innovation and reinvention. They remain affiliated nonetheless with particular conventionalized discourses. For example, business letters are likely to feature discourses of finance and business; tabloid news reports would be sites for discourses of romance and sexuality. As conventional forms, then, genres and subgenres thus both constrain and enable meanings and social relations between speakers and listeners, writers, and readers.

All genres can be analyzed in terms of their sequenced structures of propositions, their textual macrostructures. The structures of spoken and written narratives have identifiable segments, movements or "chunks." In the case of, for example, children's reading or science textbooks, the sequencing and montage of key actions, portrayals, and claims follows an identifiable order. The resultant text structures tend to operate as large-scale "grammars" of actions and events chained together, as expressions of a "cultural logic," and taken for granted assumptions about historical and human agency, social, and natural causality. The study of narrative structures has been used to study the representation of gender relations, cultures and cultural groups, wars, and other major historical events, and civic and political structures in textbooks (see Luke 1995).

Studies of UK, US, and Australian classrooms have focused on how classroom talk can shape and reshape what will count as knowledge, subjectivity, legitimate social relations, and textual practices. Classroom talk is a primary medium through which teachers and students construct "readings" of textbooks, in effect reshaping text structures, features, and knowledge into authoritative interpretations. The turn-taking structure of classroom lessons and other spoken texts can be analyzed for its topic and propositional macrostructure, to document patterns of who can speak, when, about what topics, and with what officially recognized authority and force. As noted, ethnomethodological studies of classroom talk detail many of the typical discourse moves and techniques with which teachers regulate classroom knowledge. Studies of gender and cultural identity document how students' resistance can reshape school knowledge and social relations (see, for example, Gutierrez et al. 1995).

Critical discourse analysis also focuses on sentence and word-level analysis, drawing analytic methods from systemic functional linguistics. Halliday (1985) argues that lexical and grammatical features of texts have identifiable functions: (a) they represent and portray the social and natural world ("field"); (b) they construct and effect social relations ("tenor"); and (c) they develop conventions as coherent, identifiable texts in particular media ("mode"). A range of other descriptions of language functions have been developed. According to Kress (1989), written and spoken texts represent particular selective views of the world or "subject positions" (i.e., field) and they set out social relations of "reading positions" (i.e., tenor). By establishing reading positions, texts can interpellate readers, situating and positioning them in identifiable relations of power and agency in relation to texts.

The study of subject positions of textbooks has focused on selective traditions of values, ideologies, "voices," and representations. In addition to describing the cultural assumptions expressed in the text macrostructure, analysis can describe particular lexical choices (e.g., "wordings," "namings") and the grammatical representation of agency and action (e.g., transitivity, mode, and modality). The use of an active or passive voice in a history textbook description of the "colonization" of the Americas, for example, may have the ideological effect of foregrounding or backgrounding Anglo/European agency. The lexical choice of "colonization" rather than "invasion," and the verbs and adjectives affiliated with indigenous people would represent a particular version of the historical event. Critical discourse analysis, thus, can document how the world is portrayed and how human, biological, and political actions are represented, sanctioned, and critiqued in the official texts of educational institutions (see for example, Muspratt et al. 1997).

At the same time, texts can be analyzed in terms of how they structure and stipulate social relations between human subjects. As noted, teachers and students in classroom talk tend to reconstruct text features and knowledge, often in resistant and idiosyncratic ways. However, educational texts hail readers, and position them in ideological relations through various lexical and grammatical devices. Texts operate pragmatically through the use of pronominalization, modal auxiliaries, and the selection of speech acts such as questions and commands, orders, and injunctions. Consider, for example, how the aforementioned history textbook might define and position the reader through the use of "We" to refer to Anglo/European settlers. Or perhaps, like many other textbooks, it directs its readers' analyses and actions with questions and imperatives (e.g., "Answer these questions after reading"). These lexical and grammatical choices build differential relations of power and agency between readers and writers, between students and textbooks.

Critical discourse analysis thus employs interdisciplinary techniques of text analysis to look at how texts construct representations of the world, social identities, and social relationships. This has already enabled the detailed study of policy texts, official curriculum documents, textbooks, teachers' guidebooks, and student writings. It has also been used to look at a range of formal and informal spoken texts, including classroom talk, administrators' public talk, staffroom talk, and parent–teacher interviews. Several studies of the social construction of school knowledge attempt to track different discourses across a range of texts within school systems (Corson 1995). In her study of social science education in Australian secondary schools, Lee (1996) examined syllabus documents, textbook forms, teacher commentaries on students and student work, classroom talk, and students' written assignments. Operating from a poststructuralist feminist perspective, she documented the construction of gender and gendered textual practices. This research design, used by many Australian and UK researchers, involves a series of text analyses that use different analytic tools, but which are nested within an overall set of social theoretic frameworks and sociological questions.

In its constructive moment, critical discourse analysis is being used as the basis for the teaching of "critical language awareness" and "critical literacy" to students in Australia and the UK (Fairclough 1992a). Critical deconstruction and social critique are key teleological principles of, respectively, poststructuralist discourse theory and Frankfurt School social analysis. The assumptions of such curricula are: (a) that students can be taught how to analyze critically the texts of the culture around them as part of literacy and social science education; and (b) that critical literacy is the "new basic" for postmodern conditions.

5. Conclusion

Discourses constitute what Wittgenstein called "forms of life," ubiquitous ways of knowing, valuing, and experiencing the world. They can be used for the assertion of power and knowledge and they can be used for purposes of resistance and critique. They are used in everyday local texts for building productive power and knowledge and for purposes of regulation and normalization, for the development of new knowledge and power relations, and for hegemony. If the poststructuralist view of primacy of discourse is accepted, then critical discourse analysis is necessary for describing and interpreting, analyzing, and critiquing social life.

Critical discourse analysis provides an interdisciplinary analytic approach and a flexible metalanguage for the sociological analysis of texts and discourses. The emergence of critical discourse analysis has at least three interrelated implications for educational studies and the sociology of education. First, it marks out a retheorization of educational practice. Educational theory and practice has relied historically on foundational metaphors of the unfolding child, the industrial machine, the individual rationalist mind, and, most recently, the digital computer. The metaphor offered by poststructuralism is that of the text as an interpretable phenomenon that is constitutive of all educational and intellectual endeavors.

Second, critical discourse analysis marks out a new set of methodological techniques and possibilities. The assumption shared by many quantitative and qualitative approaches to sociological research has been that observable realities, truths, and social facts have an essential existence prior to discourse. Critical discourse analysis begins from a recognition of language and discourse as nontransparent, opaque ways of studying and representing the world. It recasts all data and research artefacts as discourse. It raises and addresses the question of self-reflexivity by making researchers' own uses of discourse a key problematic in design and inquiry.

Third, critical discourse analysis marks out the grounds for rethinking pedagogical practices and outcomes as discourse. The assumption underlying many postwar curriculum development and instructional models is that the purpose of education is to produce behaviors, skills, and competences required for industrial-era workplaces and civic spheres. Critical discourse analysis suggests that mastery of discourse is the principle educational process and outcome, and that this mastery can be reshaped normatively to introduce teachers and students to critical analyses of text-based, postmodern cultures and economies.

This article began by describing the challenges posed by information-based multicultural economies and nation-states for the sociology of education. Critical discourse analysis provides a means for the sociology of education to examine new phenomena, including:

(a) New workplaces, communities, and civic spheres: shifting population demographics, new social geographies, multiculturalism, and new information technologies are altering social relations and how discourse is learned and used. There is a need for detailed study of new textual demands and practices in these institutions;

(b) New texts, genres, and discourses: these conditions are encouraging the articulation and comodification of new, unprecedented modes of expression. There is a need for the study and critique of hybrid written forms (e.g., newspaper formats that emulate TV "soundbites"), intercultural and "creolized" communications, new popular cultural forms of textual expression (e.g., rock videos, infomercials), electronic communications;

(c) New social identities: in these contexts, youth have access to unprecedented symbolic and material means for the construction of social values, beliefs, and identities. From the discourse analytic perspective presented here, youth identities and affiliated phenomena such as "class," "race," and "gender" cannot be viewed as having prior essential characteristics independent of their formation and representation in discourse. There is a need for study of how and to what end youth are using texts and discourses to construct and reconstruct new identities and communities.

The application of critical discourse analysis to educational research will require nothing less than the development of a new sociology of educational discourse. Critical discourse analysis enables modeling of how language, text, and discourse figure in the production and reproduction of educational outcomes. The focus of the sociology of education historically has been on the structures, processes, and consequences of educational institutions. A turn to the study of languages, discourses, and texts will be needed if indeed we are to understand how educational institutions might make a difference in postmodern economies, nation-states, and cultures.

See also: Contemporary Sociological Theories of Education; Critical Theory and Education; Hermeneutics; Marxism and Educational Thought; Postmodernism and Education; Trends in Qualitative Research Methods

References

Apple M W 1996 *Cultural Politics in Education*. Teachers College Press, New York

Baker C D, Freebody P 1989 *Children's First Schoolbooks*. Blackwell, Oxford

Baker C D, Luke A (eds.) 1991 *Towards a Critical Sociology of Reading Pedagogy*. Benjamins, Amsterdam

Ball S (ed.) 1990 *Foucault and Education*. Routledge, New York

Bourdieu P 1992 *Language and Symbolic Power*, Polity Press, Cambridge

Cazden C 1988 *Classroom Discourse*. Heineman, Portsmouth, New Jersey

Corson D (ed.) 1995 *Discourse and Power in Educational Organizations*. Hampton Press, Creskill, New Jersey

Fairclough N (ed.) 1992a *Critical Language Awareness*. Longman, London

Fairclough N 1992b *Discourse and Social Change*. Polity Press, Cambridge

Foucault M 1972 *The Archaeology of Knowledge*. Harper and Row, New York

Foucault M 1980 *Power/Knowledge*. Pantheon, New York

Gutierrez K, Larson J, Kreuter B 1995 Cultural tensions in the scripted classroom: The value of the subjugated perspective. *Urban Educ.* 29: 410–42

Hall S 1996 The meaning of New Times. In: Morley D, Chen K (eds.) 1996 *Stuart Hall: Critical Dialogues in Cultural Studies*. Routledge and Kegan Paul, London

Halliday M A K 1985 *An Introduction to Functional Grammar*. Edward Arnold, London

Henriques J, Hollway W, Urwin C, Venn C, Walkerdine V 1984 *Changing the Subject: Psychology, Social Regulation and Subjectivity*. Methuen, London

Kress G 1989 *Linguistic Processes in Sociocultural Practice*. Oxford University Press, Oxford

Lee A 1996 *Literacy, Gender and Curriculum*. Taylor & Francis, London

Luke A 1995. Text and discourse analysis in education: An introduction to critical discourse analysis. *Rev. Res. Ed.* 21: 1–48

Luke C, Gore J (eds.) 1992 *Feminism and Critical Pedagogy*. Routledge, New York

Lyotard J F 1984 *The Postmodern Condition: A Report on Knowledge*. University of Minnesota Press, Minneapolis, Minnesota

Mehan H 1979 *Learning Lessons*. Harvard University Press, Cambridge, Massachusetts

Muspratt S, Luke A, Freebody P (eds.) 1997 *Constructing Critical Literacies* Hampton Press, Creskill, New Jersey

New London Group 1996 A pedagogy of multiliteracies: Designing social futures. *Harv. Educ. Rev.* 66: 60–92

Williams G 1992 *Sociolinguistics: A Sociological Critique*. Routledge and Kegan Paul, London

Further Reading

Fairclough N 1989 *Language and Power*. Longman, London

Gee J P 1995 *Social Linguistics and Literacies*. Taylor & Francis, London

Harvey D 1989 *The Condition of Postmodernity*. Blackwell, Oxford

Lash S 1990 *Sociology of Postmodernism*. Routledge and Kegan Paul, London

Mey J L 1985 *Whose Language? A Study in Linguistic Pragmatics*. John Benjamins, Amsterdam

Poster M 1990 *The Mode of Information*. Polity Press, Cambridge

Critical Theory and Education

G. Lakomski

Among the various theories competing for acceptance, if not dominance, in the field of education, critical theory is a vigorous and ambitious contender. It is the purpose of this article to ask just how serious a contender critical theory is by examining its validity as a theory and its usefulness as an approach to educational research.

As a relative newcomer to education theory, the critical theory of society—whether in its original, or later Habermasian, form—has already marshaled significant support and won over a dedicated group of educators. Its arrival in educational research was greeted enthusiastically by writers such as Bredo and Feinberg (1982), for example, who believe that critical theory is able to transcend the distance between the dominant positivist school and its challenger, the interpretivist paradigm. Both schools of educational research have come under attack. Positivist research has been challenged both from within analytic philosophy of science and from interpretivists who criticize its reductionism, while the implicit relativism of the interpretivist approach is said to make it an unsuitable successor to positivism. Critical theory, as seen by its advocates, promises to solve the problems of both schools in a higher order synthesis which allocates the empirical–analytical and the historical–hermeneutic sciences to their own, mutually exclusive, object domains, complete with their respective methodologies.

In addition to relegating the sciences to their respective spheres of influence and thus deflating any claims for the superiority of one or the other methodology, critical theory has a distinctive political orientation. It suggests that the dominance of science and the rise of technology and bureaucracy are developmental tendencies of late capitalism which increasingly encroach on the domain of social life (Habermas 1976b). As a result of such imperialism which is accompanied by the decline and erosion of traditional institutions and legitimations, the legitimatory vacuum thus created is filled by the new belief in science (Habermas 1972c). What is obliterated in this process, according to Habermas, is the possibility of raising questions about social norms and values, and questions about "the good life" in the public domain. Where they are raised, they can only be perceived through the distorting lens of instrumental action, or the technical interest, which makes them appear solvable by the application of Weber's means–end scheme. Unmasking the illegitimate intrusion of science into the realm of social norms, Habermas believes, makes critical theory "critical" in the sense Marx understood the term, since science and technology have thus been shown to be ideological. The perspective which makes such insight possible is that of critical reflection which liberates or emancipates actors from false beliefs and subsequently leads to concrete proposals for overcoming oppression.

It is not difficult to see the attraction of critical theory for a number of educators who, critical of positivism, wary of the implicit relativism and conservatism of the interpretive school, and disenchanted with the so-called "economism" of Marxist education theory (e.g., Bowles and Gintis 1976), have been searching for a more appropriate foundation for a socially just educational theory and practice. Critical theory, consequently, has found application in, for example, curriculum theory (Apple 1982, Van Manen 1977), educational administration (Foster 1980, 1986, Bates 1983, Giroux 1983), action research (Carr and Kemmis 1986), teacher education (Baldwin 1987), educational policy analysis (Prunty 1985) and planning (Weiler 1984), educational theory (Young 1989), and adult education (Mezirow 1985). It has also been used to explain the crisis in formal schooling (Shapiro 1984). (for a more comprehensive list, see Ewert 1991).

Applying critical theory to curriculum making, Van Manen (1977 p. 209) notes that "Curriculum is approached as a nexus of behavioral modes which must be monitored, objectified, rationalized, and made accountable." Questions about the practical relevancy of, for example, teacher education programs, in Van Manen's view are then directly translatable into demands for increasing teacher competency and curriculum effectiveness.

In educational administration, writers such as Bates, Foster, and Giroux argue that the administration of schools, when carried out from within the scientific theory of administration (which they equate with positivism), merely emphasizes the technical–procedural aspects of their operations which are then taken as the only relevant and legitimate focuses of analysis. They contend that schools ought to be studied in all their interactional complexities. This is to be done by the method of "cultural analysis" with its emphasis on understanding and critical reflection. The rationale for cultural analysis is that, in Giroux's words, "the notion of culture . . . a political force . . . a powerful moment in the process of domination" (Giroux 1983 p. 31).

The advantage of critical theory as seen by those who adopt its central concepts are, as Foster (1980 p. 499) notes, that "it is possible to have a social science which is neither purely empirical nor purely interpretative," on the assumption that critical theory thus escapes the criticisms leveled at positivism and interpretivist theory respectively. The stakes, then, are high, and the goal ambitious, for if critical theory could achieve what is claimed on its behalf, and what it claims for itself, then it would indeed be an outstanding candidate for a new, comprehensive social theory in general, and for education in particular.

The version of critical theory considered here is that presented in the work of Habermas, since it is his version which provides the source material for most educators interested in critical theory, Giroux's emphasis on the older school notwithstanding. The task is then not only to examine critical theory's central claims, but also to explicate briefly what it sets itself to achieve. This is important since critical theory is presented by its advocates as both theoretically superior to positivist social and educational theory and as practically and politically more desirable. While neither claim is considered justified, the first will be examined since the validity of any theory depends on the justification not only of its claims to knowledge, but also on the grounds on which these claims are made. If these are inadequate, then any claims derived from them, be they "practical" or "political," are equally unjustified. If critical theory turns out to be incoherent, so is any educational theory which seeks to derive its justification from it.

This article examines two central doctrines of the theory: (a) the conception of interests, and (b) the notion of communicative competence which culminates in the "ideal speech situation." The first concept provides justification of the theory as knowledge, and the second is Habermas's proposed solution to the "theory–practice" problem, that is, the proposal for overcoming domination.

1. Habermasian Interests

Central to understanding Habermas's approach to social theory is what he takes to be the fundamental problem of contemporary social science, the relationship between theory and practice (Habermas

1974). He means by this that the connection between knowledge and social action has become an instrumentalist one, a relation which assumes the neutrality of science. Science is considered to be free of values and cannot, therefore, give people any guidance on how to conduct their lives. This development is the result of the victory of "scientism," or positivism, which, Habermas argues, presents itself as the only valid form of knowledge. As a consequence, it has become impossible, he suggests, to reflect critically on current forms of domination since even they appear as problems which are solvable by technical means. Habermas's aim is to restore to theory the dimension of reflection eclipsed by positivism and present a social theory which, as "ideology–critique," reunites theory with practice.

The quest for a comprehensive theory of social evolution as a theory of rationality leads Habermas to examine recent developments in the social sciences and in the analytic philosophy of science on the one hand (Habermas 1985b), and investigations in the field of philosophy of language and theoretical linguistics on the other (Habermas 1972a, Habermas 1972b, Habermas 1976a, Habermas 1979). In addition, he also re-examines the crisis potential of late capitalism (Habermas 1976b, Habermas 1976c) and the foundations of the older school of critical theory (Habermas 1982). These issues are outside the scope of this article. For present purposes, the concept of "interests" (*Interessen*) is most important since it is the cornerstone of critical theory, aiming as it does at the re-examination of the connection between knowledge and human interests in general.

Interests, Habermas contends, are not like any other contingent empirical fact about human beings; neither are they rooted in an ahistorical subjectivity. Rather, they are grounded in the fundamental human conditions of work (following Marx) and interaction. What Habermas also calls a "cognitive" interest is consequently:

> a peculiar category, which conforms as little to the distinction between empirical and transcendental or factual and symbolic determinations as to that between motivation and cognition. For knowledge is neither a mere instrument of an organism's adaptation to a changing environment nor the act of a pure rational being removed from the context of life in contemplation. (1972a p. 197)

Cognitive, or knowledge-constitutive, interests are hence ascribed a "quasi-transcendental" status, an ascription Habermas acknowledges as being problematic (1974 p. 8). Critical theory claims three such interests: the technical, the practical, and the emancipatory. These three are asserted to correspond to the three types of sciences. The natural sciences, in Habermas' view, incorporate a technical interest; the historical–hermeneutic sciences the practical interest; and the critical sciences (such as sociology and Freudian psychoanalysis) the emancipatory. The technical interest guides work, the practical guides interaction, and the emancipatory guides power. Work, or purposive–rational action, is defined as:

> either instrumental action or rational choice or their conjunction. Instrumental action is governed by technical rules based on empirical knowledge. In every case they imply conditional predictions about observable events, physical or social. These predictions can prove correct or incorrect. The conduct of rational choice is governed by strategies based on analytic knowledge. They imply deductions from preference rules (value systems) and decision procedures; these propositions are either correctly or incorrectly deduced. Purposive rational action realizes defined goals under given conditions. But while instrumental action organizes means that are appropriate or inappropriate according to criteria of an effective control of reality, strategic action depends only on the correct evaluation of possible alternative choices, which results from calculation supplemented by values and maxims. (Habermas 1972c pp. 91–92)

The second cognitive interest—the practical—enables the grasping of reality through understanding in different historical contexts (Habermas 1972a Chaps. 7, 8). It involves interaction patterns which provide a reliable foundation for communication. What Habermas terms "interaction" or "communicative action" is, like the technical interest, a distinct, nonreducible kind of action which demands specific categories of description, explanation, and understanding. It is this conception which provides the justification for the method of "cultural analysis" employed by some writers in education.

Habermas argues that just as human beings produce and reproduce themselves through work, so they shape and determine themselves through language and communication in the course of their historical development. While he emphasizes with Marx the historically determined forms of interaction, he nevertheless insists that symbolic interaction, together with cultural tradition, forms a "second synthesis" and is the "only basis on which power (*Herrschaft*) and ideology can be comprehended" (1972a p. 42). Marx is accused of not understanding the importance of communicative action since it does not play a separate role in, and is subsumed under, the concept of social labor which Habermas claims fits his own notion of instrumental action. Nevertheless, undistorted communication which, in Habermas's view, is the goal of the practical interest inherent in the hermeneutic sciences, requires the existence of social institutions which are free from domination themselves. On Habermas's own admission, these do not yet exist. By adding the model of symbolic interaction, he wishes to expand epistemologically Marx's conception of labor.

Finally, the notion of the emancipatory cognitive interest leads one to the most fundamental, yet also derivative, interest. It must be understood in the context of the German idealist tradition whose underlying theme, Habermas asserts, is that reason, once properly understood, "means the will to reason. In self-reflection, knowledge for the sake of knowledge attains congruence with the interest in autonomy and responsibility. The emancipatory cognitive interest aims at the pursuit of reflection as such" (1972a p. 314). It is this interest which provides the epistemological basis for Habermas's notion of critique which is alleged to be the function of the critical social sciences. Consequently, this interest is of equal importance for educational theory which aims to be "interested" in just this way.

2. Interests and Their Epistemological Status

Habermas's conception of interests was developed in critical response to positivism. The peculiar status of the interests resulted from his desire to avoid a naturalistic reduction of quasi-transcendental interests to empirical ones. Habermas wants to say, on the one hand, that humans have transformed nature, built social systems, and developed science in the course of their evolution, a process which is analogous to the evolution of claws and teeth in animals (1972a p. 312). On the other hand, he is not content with such naturalism and claims that these achievements of human evolution are not merely accidental or contingent but have developed the way they have because of a priori knowledge–constitutive interests. These cognitive interests are described as being of "metalogical necessity . . . that we can neither prescribe nor represent, but with which we must instead come to terms" (p. 312). They are "innate" and "have emerged in man's natural history" (p. 312) and are located in "deeply rooted (invariant?) structures of action and experience—i.e. in the constituent elements of social systems" (p. 371). From the observation that humans have in fact transformed nature, built social systems, and created science, it does not follow that they have done so because of transcendental interests. In other words, there is no equivalence between asserting that the technical, practical, and emancipatory interests have emerged in human natural history, and asserting that they are true and provide the transcendental framework for all human knowledge. How could such a transcendental framework be justified?

Two alternatives are possible. Habermas can resort to another transcendental framework or, alternatively, concede that there is a framework which exists a priori. In the case of the first alternative, Habermas argues that cognitive interests are rooted in the depth structures of the human species. This is merely another transcendental, anthropological concept which is itself in need of justification. This solution leads to an infinite regress of transcendental frameworks since one can press the point of justification with each new framework. This means that in the end, no justification is provided. If this regress is to be avoided, one would need to fall back on an a priori framework, a solution

Habermas wants to avoid. It would seem that no matter which of these two alternatives is chosen, the status of interests which are neither amenable to empirical demonstration nor to be sought in the transcendental realm (being "*quasi*-transcendental" entities) remains unclear. If the epistemological status of the interests remains in such jeopardy, the consequences for critical theory are serious, since the interests were meant to provide the foundation for the claims made on behalf of the sciences. This means that Habermas's assertion of the existence of two categorially distinct forms of knowledge and inquiry lapses for want of adequate justification.

In the light of various criticisms of the epistemological status of the interests (e.g., McCarthy 1981, Evers and Lakomski 1991, in particular Chap. 7), Habermas felt compelled to note: "My view is today that the attempt to ground critical theory by way of the *theory of knowledge*, while it did not lead astray, was indeed a round-about way" (1982 p. 233). This assessment leads him to ground his theory in the theory of language instead (Habermas 1979, 1985a).

3. Communicative Competence and the Ideal Speech Situation

The concept of communicative competence culminating in the ideal speech situation is the centerpiece of critical theory, since here the various strands of Habermas's investigations are drawn together. Parallel to Marx's critique of political economy, Habermas attempts to elucidate contemporary forms of alienation expressed in distorted communication. He wants to show that the potential for emancipation inheres in ordinary language which both presupposes and anticipates an ideal speech situation in which communication free from domination is possible. The full impact of Habermas's theory of communicative competence cannot be grasped adequately without taking recourse to its three underlying tenets which need further explication: (a) the notion of discourse and its relation to interaction, (b) the consensus theory of truth, and (c) the conception of an ideal speech situation.

Habermas argues that one can proceed from the fact that functioning language games, in which speech acts are exchanged, are based on an underlying consensus which is formed in the reciprocal recognition of at least four claims to validity. These claims comprise the "comprehensibility of an utterance, the truth of its propositional component, the correctness and appropriateness of its performatory component, and the authenticity of the speaking subject" (Habermas 1974 p. 18, 1979 Chap. 1). Habermas contends that in normal communication these claims are accepted uncritically. Only when a background consensus is challenged can all claims be questioned. Their justification is subject to "theoretical discourse" which is

an intersubjective enterprise within a community of inquirers. This concept is adapted from Habermas' interpretation of Pierce's model of empirical science (Habermas 1972a Chaps. 5, 6). Although theoretical discourse demands the "virtualization of constraints on action," it still remains implicitly presupposed in interaction because Habermas assumes that the subjects are in fact capable of justifying their beliefs discursively. Such a capability is characteristic of a functioning language game. Yet he is also aware of the fact that there is no complete symmetry of power among the partners of communication.

If one considers a consensus to be rational and discovers after further reflection and argumentation that it is not, how is one to decide what does constitute a rational consensus? Habermas claims that the only recourse one has is to discourse itself. He is aware that this answer might lead into a vicious circle and contends that not every achieved agreement is a consensus, that is, can be considered a criterion for truth. If, for example, an agreement is reached on the basis of what Habermas calls (covert or open) "strategic" action, then that consensus is a "pseudo-consensus" (Habermas 1982 p. 237). Strategic action is that which is undertaken primarily to safeguard an individual's personal success by means of conscious or unconscious deception. In the case of systematically distorted communication (i.e., unconscious deception), Habermas believes that "at least one of the participants is deceiving *himself* or *herself* regarding the fact that he or she is actually behaving strategically, while he or she has only apparently adopted an attitude orientated to reaching understanding" (p. 264). Even in this case, he contends, the actors themselves can know—even though only "vaguely and intuitively"—which of the two attitudes they were adopting. Both kinds are seen as "genuine types of interaction" and may be mixed up with each other in practice. As a result, Habermas asserts: " . . . it is often difficult for an observer to make a correct ascription" (p. 266). If one wants to reach a true (or "founded") consensus, he argues, one must admit as the only permissible compulsion the force of the argument, and consider as the only permissible motive the cooperative search for truth (1972a p. 363).

An argument, then, qualifies as rational when it is cogent and motivates one in one's search for truth. Implicit in this thesis is Habermas's belief that there must be increased freedom for discourse to reach higher levels, that truth claims and claims to correctness of problematic statements and norms must be able to be assessed discursively, and in the course of assessment, also be able to be changed or rejected. The conditions under which such freedom can be attained are, in Habermas's view, given in the "ideal speech situation" because "the design of an ideal speech situation is necessarily implied with the structure of potential speech; for every speech, even that of intentional deception, is oriented towards the idea of truth" (1972b

p. 144). The ideal speech situation is attained when the requirements of symmetrical relations are obtained which involve all speakers having equal chances of selecting and employing "speech acts" and their being able to assume interchangeable dialogue roles. Since practical discourse is generally distorted, according to Habermas, and since the ideal speech situation can only be anticipated, it is difficult to assess empirically whether or not, or to what extent, the conditions of an ideal speech situation are actually obtained. This problem, Habermas contends, cannot be solved in any a priori way. There is no single decisive criterion by which one can judge whether a consensus reached is "founded," even under ideal conditions; one can only determine in retrospect whether the conditions for an ideal speech situation are obtained. This difficulty resides in the fact that:

> the ideal speech situation is neither an empirical phenom-enon nor simply a construct, but a reciprocal supposition or imputation (*Unterstellung*) unavoidable in discourse. This supposition can, but need not be, contra-factual; but even when contra-factual it is a fiction which is operative-ly effective in communication. I would therefore prefer to speak of an anticipation of an ideal speech situation[.]. This anticipation alone is the warrant which permits us to join to an actually attained consensus the claim of a ra-tional consensus. At the same time it is a critical standard against which every actually reached consensus can be called into question and checked. (Habermas in McCarthy 1976 p. 486)

What, exactly, does this notion amount to? Stripped of its abstractions, one is left with a procedural model of negotiation which has the following characteristics in practice: (a) not everyone can participate in a given negotiation because of the existing power differential in society; (b) even when one reaches agreement practically, one is not sure whether it really is a consensus, nor does one have the means to check this (presuming that that is a worthwhile thing to do in the first place); and (c) the language one uses to reach con-sensus is itself a carrier of ideology. While Habermas emphasizes that his model is only an "anticipation" possessing the status of a "practical hypothesis" which does not refer to any historical society (Habermas 1982 pp. 261–62), one is nevertheless entitled to press the point regarding its potential for realization in the here and now. Recall that the solution to this dilemma is that one can only determine with hindsight whether or not its conditions are obtained. Recall further that these are the postulates of symmetrical relations in which all speakers have equal chances of "selecting and employing speech acts." This still does not solve the problem because one has to repeat the question of how one would ever know that these "equal chances" were obtained. Since all one has to go by are self-reports which may be consciously or unconsciously misleading, or even false, even a retrospective assessment would not avoid the skeptical regress.

Habermas calls his model a "constitutive illusion" and an "unavoidable supposition of discourse" which, however, is possibly always counterfactual. From this, McCarthy draws the conclusion that: "Nonetheless this does not itself render the ideal illegitimate, an ideal that can be more or less adequately approximated in reality, that can serve as guide for the institu-tionalization of discourse and as a critical standard against which every actually achieved consensus can be measured" (1981 p. 309).

While this is not an uncommon defence of the ideal speech situation, it is nevertheless invalid. This is so because the ideal speech situation is in principle unrealizable. It cannot be "more or less" adequate-ly approximated in reality because the condition of retrospectivity does not get Habermas out of the problem of stopping an infinite skeptical regress, as was argued above. It follows that one cannot even achieve what self-reflection and the emancipatory in-terest promised: the liberation from dogmatic attitudes which is, in any case, only the formal precondition for practical, political action in Habermas's scheme of things. For his theory to work, one must assume as already given, what, on his own account, does not yet exist but is supposed to come into existence as the result of the theory: namely, a world in which power and control are equalized. On the issue of social change then, this theory, which makes so much of its historical–materialist heritage, is silent (for further critical comment on this aspect see Evers and Lakomski 1991 Chap. 7).

4. Conclusion

It is perplexing that this model of rationality (i.e., rational persons discussing their differences in an ideal speech situation) has been hailed as at least potentially the solution to the so-called "theory/prac-tice problem" which holds that traditional (positivist) theory is incapable of informing and guiding practice. If the preceding analysis is correct, it seems that critical theory is similarly incapable of doing so. While the reasons outlined above go a considerable way toward explaining the problems of the theory of communicative competence, and hence critical theory, it finally fails because truth-as-consensus is removed from direct confrontation with the "objects of possible experience." In other words, the consensus theory of truth rules out the possibility of making true statements about empirical reality. If one cannot, in principle, know whether or not there is, as Habermas asserts, distorted communication and oppression in contemporary society, then one is left with mere speculation. However intuitively convincing this may be, speculation comes a poor second to knowledge. These fundamental problems need to be resolved if the critical theory of society is to be relevant for this world.

See also: Action Research; Administration of Education: Critical Approaches; Contemporary Sociological Theories of Education; Critical Discourse Analysis; Hermeneutics; Participatory Research; Research Paradigms in Education

References

Apple M W 1982 *Education and Power*. Routledge and Kegan Paul, London

Baldwin E E 1987 Theory vs. ideology in the practice of teacher-education. *J. Teach. Educ.* 38(1): 16–19

Bates R J 1983 *Educational Administration and the Management of Knowledge*. Deakin University Press, Geelong

Bowles S, Gintis H 1976 *Schooling in Capitalist America*. Basic Books, New York

Bredo E, Feinberg W (eds.) 1982 *Knowledge and Values in Social and Educational Research*. Temple University Press, Philadelphia, Pennsylvania

Carr W, Kemmis S 1986 *Becoming Critical: Education Knowledge and Action Research*. Falmer Press, London

Evers C W, Lakomski G 1991 *Knowing Educational Administration*. Pergamon Press, Oxford

Ewert G D 1991 Habermas and education: A comprehensive overview of the influence of Habermas in educational literature. *Rev. Educ. Res.* 61(3): 345–78

Foster W P 1980 Administration and the crisis of legitimacy: A review of Habermasian thought. *Harv. Educ. Rev.* 50(4): 496–505

Foster W P 1986 *Paradigms and Promises: New Approaches to Educational Administration*. Prometheus, Buffalo, New York

Giroux H 1983 *Critical Theory and Educational Practice*. Deakin University Press, Geelong

Habermas J 1971 *Toward a Rational Society*. Heinemann, London

Habermas J 1972a *Knowledge and Human Interests*. Heinemann, London

Habermas J 1972b Towards a theory of communicative competence. In: Dreitzel H P (ed.) 1972 *Recent Sociology, No. 2: Patterns of Communicative Behavior*. Macmillan, New York

Habermas J 1972c *Toward a Rational Society*. Heinemann, London

Habermas J 1974 *Theory and Practice*. Heinemann, London

Habermas J 1976a Systematically distorted communication. In: Connerton P (ed.) 1976 *Critical Sociology*. Penguin, Harmondsworth

Habermas J 1976b *Legitimation Crisis*. Heinemann, London

Habermas J 1976c *Zur Rekonstruktion des historischen Materialismus*, 2nd edn. Suhrkamp, Frankfurt

Habermas J 1979 *Communication and the Evolution of Society*. Beacon Press, Boston, Massachusetts

Habermas J 1982 A reply to my critics. In: Thompson J B, Held D (eds.) 1982 *Habermas: Critical Debates*. Macmillan, London

Habermas J 1985a *The Theory of Communicative Action I: Reason and the Rationalization of Society*. Beacon Press, Boston, Massachusetts

Habermas J 1985b *Zur Logik der Sozialwissenschaften*. Suhrkamp, Frankfurt

McCarthy T A 1976 A theory of communicative competence. In: Connerton P (ed.) 1976 *Critical Sociology*. Penguin, Harmondsworth

McCarthy T A 1981 *The Critical Theory of Jürgen Habermas*. MIT Press, Cambridge, Massachusetts

Mezirow J 1985 Concept and action in adult-education. *Adult Educ. Q.* 35(3): 142–51

Prunty J J 1985 Signposts for a critical educational policy analysis. *Aust J. Educ.* 29(2): 133–40

Shapiro S 1984 Crisis of legitimation: Schools, society and declining faith in education. *Interchange* 15(4): 26–39

Van Manen M 1977 Linking ways of knowing with ways of being practical. *Curric. Inq.* 6(3): 205–28

Weiler H N 1984 The political economy of education and development. *Prospects* 14(4): 467–77

Young R E 1989 *A Critical Theory of Education: Habermas and Our Children's Future*. Harvester Wheatsheaf, New York

Gender Theories in Education

B. Davies

Gender theories in education attempt to analyze how and why oppressive gender relations are formed, what part schools play in reproducing these, and why some strategies for change work in the ways that they do. Central to these analyses are liberal, radical, socialist, and poststructuralist feminist theories. These theories appeared, historically, in that order and each was formed, at least in part, in reaction to the perceived theoretical, ideological, and practical flaws in the preceding theory. Yet each theoretical position is still current in the early 1990s and exists in creative tension with each of the others. Collectively and individually these theories continue, for example, to influence the socialization of teachers, the construction of curricula, the organizational patterns of schools, and the way the sexes relate to each other at all levels of schooling. In this article, the primary emphasis is on the nature and assumptions of each gender theory with specific educational implications and examples cited in each section.

1. Feminist Theories Defined

The central feature of liberal feminism is women's assertion of their equality with men and their demand for access to those roles and positions of public life traditionally regarded as the province of men. Liberal feminism in education has been primarily a political/legislative battle against the rules of exclusion. Through such strategies, women and girls have gained access to public life, which nevertheless tends to remain male. The problem with liberal feminism, considered within other theoretical frameworks, relates to the ideological and practical dilemmas involved in learning to do "male" things in a male world while retaining one's female identity. This has led to a heightening of individual femininity along with a marking up of skills relevant to the masculine world to which access has been gained (Walkerdine 1989). In this position, it is difficult to join with other women to call in question that male world, or to celebrate or revise the form of femininity that must be accentuated to offset acquired male characteristics.

Radical feminism developed in response to this dilemma, and has involved a personal and collective struggle fueled by the alienation and marginalization that women have experienced, and continue to experience, within the public world as it is defined through the male symbolic order. In the traditions of masculinist thought the oppositional and hierarchical dualisms through which maleness and femaleness are understood tend to locate the male side of the equation in the positive pole and the female in the negative pole (Davies 1990b). Radical feminists, through the celebration of femaleness and the calling in question of maleness, have confronted and in some cases reversed the poles, at the same time leaving the oppositional meaning of maleness and femaleness intact.

Radical feminism, in particular, has made the personal and the everyday relevant within feminist thought. How each woman lives her life becomes central to the feminist debate. "The personal is political" is the slogan that best expresses this position. Socialist feminists, usually with a Marxist background, acknowledged this relevance of the personal, but brought into focus the social structures of capitalism and patriarchy. In doing so they have called in question the liberal humanist assumptions of liberal feminism and the sex/gender essentialism of the radical feminists. At the same time, their structuralist focus made patriarchy appear inevitable in both social and psychic terms, thus dampening the radical potential of feminist action.

Poststructuralist feminism shifts the ground again by calling in question the very terms "male" and "female." Change is understood as taking place at the structural level through changes in the *discursive practices* through which structures are created and maintained. Discourse is also examined in its relation to each individual psyche, revealing the ways in which gendered patterns of desire are discursively constituted (Davies 1990b). The individual's personal confrontation with the psychic implications of shifting their identity through the deconstruction of male/female dualism is regarded as fundamental. The rejection of the dichotomy male/female has also

profound linguistic and structural implications insofar as social structures are created and maintained through the discursive and textual practices which are being challenged. It is primarily, then, to the deconstuction of maleness and femaleness as a dualism that feminist poststructuralist thought is turned. This theoretical position has had much popularity throughout the 1980s and into the 1990s but is problematic in a number of ways if it presumes that it can stand alone without the other feminisms. This problem will be addressed in the conclusion of this article.

2. *Liberal Feminism*

Access, in the first place, means the right to attend an educational institution. Rules of exclusion operate through legislation, through institutional structures and practices, through funding practices, and so on. Struggles to remove rules of exclusion have taken place at every level of education. Removal of rules of exclusion has thus consumed, and continues to consume, most of the energy of those who are actively trying to bring about gender equity. Women and girls have faced a long history of resistance as they have sought, and continue to seek, entrance to the "male world." The gains have often been made on the understanding that the gender order will not change as a result of the concessions. Because the discursive practices through which the gender order, and in particular male/female dualism, is constructed and maintained remain intact, each battle for access has had to be fought afresh.

Access to primary and then secondary education made no difference to the way women were viewed when they tried to gain access to universities. When they appealed to the courts for a ruling that as people they should have access to universities, using the argument that university acts were framed in terms of "people" rather than "men," and that women were clearly included in the category "people," judges in some instances ruled that women were not included in the category "people," comparing them to children, animals, imbeciles, and even inanimate objects rather than give way to women's arguments for inclusion (Sachs and Hoff Wilson 1978).

In some places, when women finally gained access to universities, they were allowed in on condition that they did not gain degrees. When they won that battle, they found that they could have their degrees but not use them in professional practice. Liberal feminists mobilized central concepts within liberal thought, such as justice and equity, to support their arguments, but could only be heard after much struggle. Feminist poststructuralist analysis attempts to explain this inability of the male resistance to hear and act straightforwardly in response to the women's arguments. Their failure can be seen as a result of the ingrained position of male/female dualism in social structures and in language. Men's conceptions of themselves as superior to women was threatened by actions which might allow women to be constituted as the same. This threat is not necessarily experienced at a conscious or rational level, but more likely as an emotional (disguised as moral) resistance to any disruption to the status quo. As Moi (1985 p. 29) points out, those who want gender equity must both engage in reasoned debate and confront the "recalcitrant unconscious . . . liberation can no longer be seen solely as the logical consequence of a rational exposure of the false beliefs on which patriarchal rule is based."

There are several reasons, then, why access alone is insufficient to redress female oppression. First, liberal feminism relies on the dominance and centrality of rational thought in the human psyche. As poststructuralist theory makes clear, people are constituted through a number of discourses, and being a person entails more than having a "rational mind." People are also body and emotion and unconscious mind; they have histories in terms of male/female dualism; and their own "identity," something which they take to signal their essential and "natural" selves which they have a right and even a duty to express, according to liberal humanist theory.

Second, because male/female dualism is left intact, women and girls find themselves continually compromised as they attempt to find ways to make the masculine requirements of the structures in which they work compatible with the requirement of maintaining their female identities. That presentation of themselves as female/feminine comes at a high price, not just because of the inherent contradictions, but because the female is constituted as of less value than the male. Inevitably, within such a structure, the ways in which others interact with females is qualitatively different from the way they interact with males. One telling example of the patterns of belief that lead to this difference in interaction is elaborated in Adams and Walkerdine (1986). Teachers frequently assume that if boys are noncooperative or do their work badly, it is because they are "really" very bright and thus bored by the lessons. In contrast, girls behaving cooperatively and producing good work are interpreted as not "really clever," but simply trying to please the teacher.

Third, and closely related to each of the above, liberal feminism fails to challenge that which women and girls have wanted access to, therefore allowing it to remain masculinist in assumptions, structures, processes, and outcomes. When female students eventually find themselves in the same classrooms as male students, studying the same courses, they find that the theoretical frameworks for the disciplines they study, the content of the courses they study, the discursive practices through which they are taught, and ultimately the way in which they are located as gendered beings in the social world of schools and of tertiary institutions, militate against the construction of themselves as in any sense equal to male students (Baker and Davies 1989, Davies 1989). At the same time as they learn to

regard themselves as equal subjects with the male students, they learn, through the processes of schooling, that only males have access to nongendered subjectivity (Lees 1986). This insight derives from the study of the relation between subjectivity and discourse within poststructuralist theory. Linguistically, "man" is the unmarked category, just as "White" is the unmarked category in relation to "Black" (Connell 1987). In practice this means that a White man viewing himself in the mirror will probably see "a person," since his gender and color are unmarked. In contrast, a White woman will probably see herself as "a woman," since her sex is marked, while a Black woman will probably see both her gender and color. The discourses through which linguistic (and subjective) markings are created and sustained are made available to students through school text and talk. Further, women and girls learn, through the gendered discourses that take place in schools, that as female, they are sexualized beings, objects of male attention. Such a positioning powerfully counteracts the discourses to which they also have access, that they are persons capable of acting powerfully in their own right (Lees 1986).

Thus access to schooling, accompanied by the maintenance of the traditional structures and practices, while it may give girls formal equality of educational opportunity, tends to lead to their being deeply embedded in their subordinate position, since they learn more thoroughly through their education to construe the world in male terms. At the same time, however, as they learn to take up as their own their allocated female subject position, they are given the contradictory opportunity to position themselves, at least in their imagination, as agents (Davies 1990a). In a further twist, this enables them to split themselves off from their femaleness and to see the world and themselves through male eyes.

Strategies for change within liberal feminism, apart from the legal access battles noted above, have, when it comes to schooling itself, generally been based on individualistic liberal humanist modes of thought. Teachers acting within this framework have told girls that they can do as well as boys, that they can do well in mathematics, science, and technology, and when the girls have apparently failed to hear or to act upon this message, a failure of some kind is located in the individual child. She is assumed to have low self-esteem, which should be remedied, or her parents or the media or the books she is reading are giving her the "wrong thoughts," or more often, she is after all female and it is "natural" for her not to want male things. This kind of thought has been criticized by Kenway and Willis (1990). Another strategy, oriented toward individual teachers and their practices, has involved teachers learning not to discriminate against girls by, for example, ensuring that they interact with male and female students the same number of times. In all of these the interpretation of equity is understood as sameness, and in particular, the rights of girls to receive the same treatment as boys, and the capacity of girls to be the same as boys.

Another obvious solution to gender inequities, working within this framework, is the provision of individual role models or women in high status positions. The absence of women in high status positions is an observable part of the inequitable social structure, and children are highly observant of, and absorb the details of the way inequity appears, as the basis of their understanding of the way the world "really is." Clearly, part of any gender equity strategy needs women in positions of authority, but not as exceptions. Ultimately, their presence should signal that there is no structural impediment nor set of practices nor interpretive strategies which exclude them.

In terms of curriculum, one of the important changes compatible with liberal feminist thought has been the inclusion of women of note in school texts (McMurchy et al. 1983).

3. Radical Feminism

In radical feminist theory the male symbolic order, to which women gained access through liberal feminist strategies, is seen as constitutive of women's oppression and not something in which women can or should function in the ways men do. Maleness is questioned and female ways of being are extolled.

In terms of social structure, single-sex classes have been one of the most prominent elements of radical feminist strategies. Removing women and girls from an oppressive male presence and giving them the space in which they can come to value themselves in their own way, has been an ideal informing such separatist strategies. Single-sex schools, in contrast, are not necessarily seen as compatible with these ideals and may well create class divisions, such that middle-class girls can establish themselves as superior to working-class ones. Further, single-sex schools have not decreased the sexism of boys, rather the reverse.

Examples of the kinds of strategies that have been developed to allow female students to come to know themselves and to acquire knowledge outside of patriarchal knowledge systems include, in the Netherlands, Hablé's (1985) rewriting of science teaching strategies; in Germany, Haug's (1987) development of collective memory work in which groups of women reconstruct the stories through which their lives as females have been constituted; in the United States, Chicago's (1982) development of art teaching that begins with and expresses women's ways of being; and in the United Kingdom, Stanley and Wise's (1983) development of women's strategies for doing social science.

The most profound work accomplished by radical feminists is the radical revaluing of what it is that women do. This has led to a proliferation of women's studies courses, particularly at university level, in which women's knowledge and women's ways of teaching and learning and doing research have been developed and passed on to new students. Partly as a result of such strategies and the consequent elevation of feminist knowledge, and partly as a result of radical feminists working in mainstream disciplines, the traditional separation between schooling and the feminine has been eliminated. Previously devalued ways of interacting, of teaching, and of thinking have become an accepted part of school and university curricula. This in turn affects activity in the everyday world. The fact that some men and boys are now taking up traditional female activities, such as childcare, is one indicator of the success of this reordering. The outcomes of these strategies make a significant contribution to the poststructuralist project of deconstructing male/female dualism.

But liberal and radical feminisms, in some fundamental ways, leave the social structures of the gender order intact. Male and female still take their meaning in hierarchical opposition to each other. In liberal feminism maleness or male ways of being and male knowledge have unquestioned superiority and are desired and appropriated by women, while in radical feminism the opposite is maintained, in that the feminine becomes the superior way of being. Neither of these theories have the conceptual means to analyze the processes through which macro social structures such as capitalism and patriarchy create and maintain themselves. The inability of their strategies to create radical and lasting change is seen as a fundamental problem. It is to this problem that the socialist feminists were able to address themselves.

4. Socialist Feminism

The material force of capitalist structures, along with the material and psychic force of patriarchal structures, are first introduced to feminist thought through a socialist feminist analysis. Drawing on Marxist and psychoanalytic theory, the previously invisible ways in which individual consciousness and social practices are shaped by the structures in which they find themselves can be located. This set of insights has become fundamental for feminist theory and practice. The humanism fundamental to liberal and radical feminisms did not lead their proponents to call in question the way in which their beliefs and desires were constituted by the structures in which they found themselves. Although radical feminist groups had engaged in "consciousness raising," through which aspects of patriarchal language were revealed as such and rejected, and new terms and related forms of consciousness were developed, these processes were generally limited by lack of access to a theory through which they could analyze how ideologies are shaped. Consciousness raising, however, provided a basis for understanding the socialist feminist insights into the power and control that ideologies have over individuals. That control results, in no small part, from the humanist orientation of the education systems in which students learn to read their ideological positions as "their own," that is, as both arising from their "inner selves" and as signaling who they are. The embeddedness of patriarchal discourses, of capitalist discourses, and of humanist discourses in educational text and talk, and the relation of these discourses to individual subjectivity has been taken up and developed by the feminist poststructuralists.

A second central contribution of socialist feminist theory has been a recognition of the tendency of feminism to be "owned" and propagated by White middle-class women to the exclusion of other classes and cultures (Barbre et al. 1989, Cohen and Somerville 1990, Sanghatana 1989).

5. Feminist Poststructuralism

Feminist poststructuralist theory and practice in relation to schooling is relatively new. However, it has had a profound effect on feminist theorizing since it is almost impossible to talk about each of the other theoretical positions without introducing a feminist poststructuralist critique. In order to explore the material effects of social structures further, and the effects of these on the individual psyche, feminist poststructuralist writers have turned their attention to discourse and have begun the complex process of deconstructing male/female dualism. Many of the changes that have already begun to take place in the subject matter taught in schools and universities is being picked up and developed in this process. The recognition of the hegemonic disciplines as essentially masculinist constructions is being further revealed through an analysis of the narrative structures which inform the sciences, the humanities, and the arts (Martin 1991). There are concurrent changes in the disciplines, for example in history, where the traditional periodization is no longer automatically organized around male events such as war and the succession of male leaders, nor is it any longer automatically written as if these men caused history. Instead, an understanding of the constitutive force of language leads to quite different tellings in which, for example, changes in popular discourses lead to the positioning of certain individuals in positions of leadership—such people, in a sense, being spoken into existence as leaders by the prevailing discourses of the time. Such revisions lead to profound insights not only into the general absence of women in traditional histories but also into the constructed nature of the men who have not been absent.

Similarly, the idea of discourses of resistance is being developed to deal with modes of interaction that lock students into male/female dualism. The development of the discourse of sexual harassment is an example of this process. With the aid of poststructuralist analysis it is possible to see how the sexual harassment discourse worked. First, the traditional storyline of male hero/predator and attractive female/victim was called in question. A new storyline was put in its place about the rights of women to work and to study without being sexually molested and without having their sexuality made central to their identity. At the structural level, laws were changed to establish the rights of women over their own bodies, and institutions such as women's shelters were created for them to go to, thus making practically possible the refusal of molestation and physical abuse. Again, from a feminist poststructuralist perspective, it is possible to explain the partial failure of the new discourse in terms of the material force of unconscious patterns of desire, not understood at the time the new discourse was being developed.

The manner in which teaching is done is also shifting in the light of feminist poststructuralist theory, through the inevitable questioning of the authoritative voice of both male and female authors and teachers who make claims to universal truths. Students, authors, and teachers are developing skills with which to recognize the constitutive force of spoken and written text and learn strategies of resistance to being constituted in unitary and oppressive ways (Cixous 1988, Davies 1993).

6. Conclusion

Feminist discourses provide necessary counters to the hegemonic discourses that constitute oppressive structures and relations. Though they disagree with each other in some fundamental ways, they have become so interwoven in their influences on each other that they can only really be separated out for analytic purposes. In strategic terms they are each fundamental to understanding and explaining what feminist practice is about. The possibility of attempting to hold and even act in terms of contradictory theoretical positions at one and the same time is a radical position and emerges directly from the feminist poststructuralist critique of enlightenment discourse. Poststructuralist theory reveals the inevitability of contradiction, given the contradictory discourses and positionings within those discourses through which theories are continually being constituted and reconstituted.

The explanatory frameworks of the earlier feminisms must, for a number of reasons, be looked at in parallel with poststructuralist feminism. First, the task of evolving identity and discursive and social practices which go beyond male/female dualism is almost unthinkable because of the embeddedness of such dualism in people's conscious and unconscious ways of knowing themselves and the world. Until this possibility has been elaborated and explored more fully it will be neither desirable nor practicable to move solely to a set of discursive practices in which sex is not named. As long as sex is the basis of oppressive relations, that oppression must be named as such if attention is to be drawn to it in order to change it. There is a deep level of resistance to rejecting male/female dualism, both from the conservative/liberal right and, ironically and for opposite reasons, from radical feminists. For both of these groups, the naming of male/female difference is essential; for the former, as a basis for the maintenance of oppressive gender relations, and for the latter, to engage in the essential task of valuing that which is feminine. This radical feminist work is and will remain essential as long as male and female are understood as opposite, each taking its meaning in relation to the other. Deconstructing male/female dualism, if it were ever complete, could seem to negate that work, but as Kristeva (1979) points out, both are essential. The deconstructive work and the celebratory work must run parallel, "even interwoven, one with the other," if there is to be a move toward gender equity.

See also: Coeducation versus Single-sex Schooling; Critical Discourse Analysis; Critical Theory and Education; Feminist Approaches to the Curriculum; Feminist Research Methodology; Gender and Education

References

Adams C, Walkerdine V 1986 *Investigating Gender in the Primary School: Activity Based* INSET Materials for Primary Teachers. Inner London Education Authority, London

Baker C, Davies B 1989 A lesson on sex roles. *Gender and Education* 1(1): 59–76

Barbre J W et al. (eds.) 1989 *Interpreting Women's Lives. Feminist Theory and Personal Narratives.* Indiana University Press, Bloomington, Indiana

Chicago J 1982 *Through the Flower. My Struggle as a Woman Artist.* The Women's Press, Oxford

Cixous H 1988 Extreme fidelity. In: Sellers S (ed.) 1988 *Writing Differences. Reading from the Seminar of Helene Cixous.* Open University Press, Milton Keynes

Cohen P, Somerville M 1990 *Ingelba and the Five Black Matriarchs.* Allen and Unwin, Sydney

Connell R W 1987 *Gender and Power: Society, the Person and Sexual Politics.* Polity Press, Cambridge

Davies B 1989 The discursive production of the male/female dualism in school settings. *Oxford Rev. Educ.* 15(3): 229–41

Davies B 1990a Agency as a form of discursive practice. A classroom scene observed. *Br. J. Sociol. Educ.* 11(3): 341–61

Davies B 1990b The problem of desire. *Soc. Prob.* 37(4): 801–16

Davies B 1993 Beyond dualism and towards multiple subjectivities. In: Christian-Smith L (ed.) 1993 *Texts of Desire: Essays on Fiction Femininity and Schooling.* Falmer Press, Lewes

Hablé R 1985 *Female Logic.* University of Amsterdam, Amsterdam

Haug F (ed.) 1987 *Female Sexualization: A Collective Work of Memory.* Verso, London

Kenway J, Willis S 1990 *Hearts and Minds: Self-esteem and the Schooling of Girls.* Falmer Press, London

Kristeva J 1979 Le temps des femmes 33/44: Cahiers de Recherche Sciences des Textes et Documents 5: 5–19

Lees S 1986 *Losing Out: Sexuality and Adolescent Girls.* Hutchinson, London

Martin E 1991 The egg and the sperm: How science has constructed a romance based on stereotypical male–female roles. *Signs* 16(3): 485–501

McMurchy M, Oliver M, Thornley J 1983 *For Love or Money. A Pictorial History of Women and Work in Australia.* Penguin, Ringwood

Moi T 1985 *Sexual–Textual Politics: Feminist Literary Theory.* Methuen, London

Sachs A, Hoff Wilson J 1978 *Sexism and the Law: A Study of Male Beliefs and Legal Bias in Britain and the* US. Martin Robertson, Oxford

Sanghatana S S 1989 *'We Were Making History . . .' Life Stories of Women in the Telangana People's Struggle.* Kali for Women, Delhi

Stanley L, Wise S 1983 *Breaking Out: Feminist Consciousness and Feminist Research.* Routledge and Kegan Paul, London

Walkerdine V 1989 Femininity as performance. *Oxford Rev. Educ.* 15(3): 267–80

Further Reading

Davies B 1989 *Frogs and Snails and Feminist Tales. Preschool Children and Gender.* Allen and Unwin, Sydney

Tong R 1989 *Feminist Thought. A Comprehensive Introduction.* Unwin Hyman, London

Walkerdine V 1990 *Schoolgirl Fictions.* Verso, London

Weedon C 1987 *Feminist Practice and Poststructuralist Theory.* Blackwell, Oxford

Hermeneutics

P.-J. Ödman and D. Kerdeman

Until the nineteenth century, "hermeneutics" was commonly defined as "the art (or science) of interpretation (especially of the Bible)." As a consequence of contributions by Schleiermacher, Dilthey, and late existential philosophers such as Heidegger and Gadamer, the meaning of the term has changed. No longer does hermeneutics refer solely to methods of textual exegesis and interpretation. Hermeneutics also describes a philosophical position which regards understanding and interpretation as endemic to and a definitive mark of human existence and social life.

For this article hermeneutics will be defined as the

theory and practice of interpretation and understanding (German, *Verstehen*) in different kinds of human contexts (religious as well as secular, scientific, and quotidian). Several different topics fall under the rubric of this definition. Hermeneutics embraces discussions about: (a) the methodological foundation of the human sciences (German, *Geisteswissenschaften*); (b) the phenomenology of existence and existential understanding; (c) systems of interpretation, used by people to reach the meaning behind myths, symbols, and actions (Palmer 1969). To this list might be added debates concerning: (d) theories of the process of interpretation and the validity of interpretative claims; (e) empirically oriented schools of research that study people in social contexts. It should be noted, however, that many still define hermeneutics as the theory of biblical exegesis, general philological methodology, and the science of linguistic understanding (Palmer 1969).

1. Differences in Relation to Other Traditions of Thought

Hermeneutics is not the only philosophical tradition that regards understanding and interpretation as central to social life. During the twentieth century, a number of other philosophies have come to embrace this position. While they and hermeneutics share many of the same assumptions, it is helpful to sketch some of the differences that make hermeneutics unique.

1.1 Phenomenology

Like hermeneutics, phenomenology is concerned with the structure of understanding. Phenomenology, however, construes understanding primarily in terms of cognitive constructs and functions. For hermeneutics, by contrast, understanding is not only a cognitive function: it also is the ontological condition of human existence. Moreover, while hermeneutics stresses the social nature of meaning, it is not altogether clear whether meaning for phenomenology is primarily subjective or social (see *Phenomenology and Existentialism*).

1.2 Wittgenstein's Later Philosophy

Both hermeneutics and the later philosophy of Ludwig Wittgenstein (1889–1951) posit that meaning resides in the conventions and practices of ordinary social life. Meaning, in other words, is not fixed by the rules of an ideal grammar or calculus but instead is negotiated, conditioned, practical, and fluid. Wittgenstein, however, believed that there is no structure common to all "language games" which philosophical analysis could uncover and use to mediate between different life-forms. Hermeneutics, by contrast, holds that mediation between different life-forms is possible. Indeed, articulating the conditions that make mediation

or translation possible constitutes a central problem of hermeneutics. Additionally, hermeneutics looks upon language as the mode by which Being is revealed. No such concern for Being characterizes linguistic analysis.

1.3 Critical Theory

Both hermeneutics and critical theory maintain that understanding and meaning are constitutive of social life. Hermeneutics, however, holds that since one's present situation always is involved in any process of understanding, it is impossible to grasp in any final or definitive form all of the meanings embedded in a tradition. Hermeneutics thus eschews the quest to ground understanding in a theoretical framework or method and concentrates instead on interpreting cultures from within given situations and contexts. Critical theory, by contrast, regards understanding as only one interest in the constitution of culture. It aims, therefore, to situate understanding within a broader or more universal explanatory framework, the purpose of which is to make transparent the ways in which ideology informs and conditions not only understanding but all of the interests and relations that constitute social life (see *Critical Theory and Education*).

1.4 Marxism

Unlike Marxism, the underlying theory of hermeneutics is not primarily materialistic. Moreover, hermeneutics does not focus on the question of historical determinism. Rather, several branches of hermeneutics emphasize freedom in human action (see *Marxism and Educational Thought*).

1.5 Postmodern Deconstructionist Hermeneutics

According to postmodern hermeneuticists such as Jacques Derrida (1930–) (1978, 1979), meaning is understood only insofar as it is deconstructed. On this view, meaning (together with the metaphysical categories of humanism and power that meaning impies) does not consist in a revelation of Being or truth. In the end, all we have is an endless play of signifiers. Understanding, in turn, is not constituted in a circular tension between familiar and strange, past and future, that ultimately produces wider or deeper agreement. Understanding instead both denotes and is made possible by disruption and difference (*différance*). According to Paul Ricoeur (1965), the restorative and transformative dimensions of understanding are not mutually exclusive. Both trust and suspicion represent tendencies of hermeneutic activity.

2. Purpose of Hermeneutics

The purpose of hermeneutics is to increase understanding as regards other cultures, groups, individuals, conditions, and life-styles, present as well as past. The process must be mutual, implying an increase in self-understanding on the part of subject and interpreter alike. Moreover, hermeneutics aims to clarify its own working principles, to "understand understanding." This goal is realized not through the application of method but by bringing into focus the deep assumptions and meanings that inform everyday existence.

Hermeneutics can contribute much to both the practice of education and to educational research. A hermeneutically oriented educator would endeavor, for example, to interpret the meaning that educational practices and conventions hold for those who experience and participate in them. Such an educator might also try to understand various groups of pupils and their life-styles. Additionally, he or she would accentuate the significance of mutual understanding, such as that between teachers and pupils or between pupils of different backgrounds.

Insofar as research is concerned, hermeneutics can deepen the understanding of education by focusing on the meanings that underlie specific educational strategies and practices. A hermeneutic approach to inquiry would explore questions such as the following. How should certain administrative practices be understood? What are their hidden meanings? How might phenomena such as time-scheduling or the separation of learning into different subject-areas be interpreted in a broader cultural and historical context? By means of which educational and teaching strategies is cultural reproduction realized (Bourdieu and Passeron 1970)? Answers to such questions often are given as interpretations through which understanding is promoted.

3. Understanding, Preunderstanding, and Interpretation

The concept of "understanding" can only be defined with the help of analogies and synonyms. The original literal meaning of the term may have been, "to stand close to or under something," or "to place something close to or under oneself." To stand close to something breeds a sense of familiarity. One knows well that to which one is close; one is understanding it. In other words, one is seeing it. The analogy with seeing is appropriate, because it coincides with linguistic practice. In many languages, "to see" connotes "to understand." Often, in fact, the two verbs are used interchangeably.

According to hermeneutics, the idea of familiarity is essential to the interpretative process. Insofar as familiarity obtains, a person to some extent already has understood that which he or she is trying to interpret. This preliminary understanding is known in the hermeneutic tradition as "preunderstanding."

To illustrate the notion of preunderstanding, it is helpful to think about how sense is made of problematic sections in texts. When a difficult passage or word in a narrative is encountered the reader tries to see how that particular part of the text fits within the pattern of the work as whole. Now, the reader may not completely understand the whole text. Indeed, insofar as he or she finds certain passages opaque, understanding is precluded from being complete or absolutely clear. Nonetheless, on some level the reader already does understand the text, albeit in a preliminary way. For without at least a dim sense of familiarity with the work as a whole, there would be no context within which to make sense of or relate individual parts. In this respect, preunderstanding makes reflective understanding possible: it functions as a structure, a whole within the limits of which reflective understanding evolves.

If preunderstanding of an entire text makes it possible to grasp its parts, so the clearer the reader becomes with respect to its parts, and the more clearly the whole narrative will be understood. New dimensions of the text may be noticed. Thus in coming reflectively to understand the parts, the sense of the whole is revitalized.

In short, hermeneutic understanding begins with an inchoate sense of a text in its entirety. At the same time, it is only by probing and analyzing its parts that the whole of a text can be constituted. In this respect, preunderstanding and understanding mutually inform and refine each other. The dialectical relationship of preliminary and reflective understanding is known as the "hermeneutic circle." By means of the hermeneutic circle, texts are clarified or interpreted. According to contemporary hermeneutics, the circular process of preunderstanding, understanding, and interpretation describes more than a method of textual exegesis. Insofar as understanding is central to human existence, the hermeneutic circle captures how ordinary people experience and make sense of life.

4. Historical Background

The word "hermeneutics" derives from Greek antiquity. The Greek verb *hermeneuein* (to interpret) and the noun *hermeneia* (interpretation) are the sources of the modern concept. Additionally, hermeneutics is associated with Hermes, who was both the messenger of and interpreter for the Greek gods. Hermes is also associated with the discovery of language and writing, the most important tools for grasping meaning and conveying it to others (Palmer 1969).

4.1 Hermeneutics as Biblical Exegesis

Biblical exegesis has a very long tradition, dating back to the time of the Hebrew Bible. Indeed, canons for interpreting the Hebrew Bible already had been developed by the first century AD. By the Middle Ages, two main approaches to interpreting both the Hebrew and Christian Bibles had come into use. One approach endeavored to interpret the text literally, spelling out meanings that were already more or less explicit. Over time the literal approach to biblical exegesis became more directed toward reconstructing the historical meaning of biblical texts. The second approach was more concerned with symbolic content. Since the text was regarded as a message from God, it had to be interpreted allegorically. The purpose of allegorical interpretation was to reconstruct or uncover divine meanings not literally apparent.

With the Enlightenment, the scope of hermeneutics broadened. Entering the field of philological research, hermeneutics took a critical first step into the world of modern science. This move had important consequences for biblical exegesis. As an object of philological interpretation, the Bible became simply one among many objects of interpretation; classical and legal texts also were subjected to interpretative philological exegesis. In this respect, literal interpretation constituted an important bridge between interpretation as biblical exegesis and interpretation as a tool for scientific purposes.

4.2 Hermeneutics as "The Art of Understanding"

The German theologian and philosopher Friedrich Schleiermacher (1768–1834) was the first to formulate a new direction for hermeneutics. In Schleiermacher's view, understanding was not automatic: it was an achievement, a coming to grips with meaning which was opaque and problematic. Accordingly, Schleiermacher did not focus on hermeneutics as a body of practical rules: his aim, rather, was to examine the conditions that make understanding possible. How was it, Schleiermacher wondered, that understanding was accomplished? Answering this question, Schleiermacher hoped to establish hermeneutics as the discipline of understanding.

For Schleiermacher, understanding consisted of two elements, one grammatical and one psychological. The relationship between these two elements is dialectical. In grammatical interpretation, the work is interpreted in terms of its linguistic principles, while psychological interpretation aims to interpret a text with regard to the thoughts and feelings of its author. The interpreter does this by identifying with the author's life and situation.

Schleiermacher's conception of understanding was rooted in the principle of the hermeneutic circle. In grammatical interpretation, a work is regarded as a context of meaning. Within this context, specific parts are elucidated, even as the explication of parts makes the entire context intelligible. For its part, psychological interpretation is founded on intuition. In the act of divining an author's intended meaning, the interpreter grasps an inchoate sense of the whole text which he or she will subsequently refine.

4.3 Hermeneutics as the Theoretical Foundation of the Human Sciences

The German philosopher Wilhelm Dilthey (1833–1911) extended the application of hermeneutics from the interpretation of texts to the whole field of human studies. His line of thought led in ontological as well as methodological directions. Dilthey's thinking can be summarized as an enormous widening of the hermeneutic circle. His central concepts were experience (*Erlebnis*), expression (*Ausdruck*), and understanding (*Verstehen*). Experience for Dilthey had a much broader connotation than it has today: "one may call each encompassing unity of parts of life bound together through a common meaning for the course of life an 'experience'—even when the several parts are separated from each other by interrupting events" (Palmer 1969). Dilthey, in other words, held that people understand discrete life-experiences by assigning them a special place within an experiential whole. At the same time, one singular experience can change the way a person understands himself or herself and his or her life. The very experience of life, in short, is characterized by Dilthey as a continuous interaction between "wholes" and "parts."

The following example illustrates Dilthey's ideas. A teacher wishes to understand why a certain pupil is having difficulty. In order to make sense of the phenomenon, the teacher situates the problem within the context of his or her experience as an instructor. The teacher has previously seen that lack of interest on the part of parents greatly influences a child's progress in school. This understanding prompts the teacher to ask the child how he or she gets along at home; the teacher learns that relations between the child and the parents are very cold. By drawing on his or her experience to clarify the child's situation, the teacher achieves a better understanding of how to help the student. By the same token, understanding the situation of this particular student refines and enriches the teacher's entire instructional experience.

By "expression" Dilthey had in mind all the manifestations or "objectifications" of human experience, even those that are unintentional and nonverbal. Life-expressions, in other words, objectify or make concrete a person's understanding of life. Although expressions of meaning are personal, they are not created in a vacuum, Dilthey says. It is only by drawing on the common stock of meanings embedded in one's culture that an individual is able to express what experience means to him or her.

According to Dilthey, reflective understanding or "interpretation" consists in recovering the intimate connection between experience and expression. In explicating the meaning of a concrete expression, the interpreter brings to light not only the way a particular individual has understood his or her life-experience: because life-expressions are embedded in historical contexts, the interpreter illuminates a cultural milieu as well. As a consequence, an otherwise distant world comes alive in the present. The following example illustrates Dilthey's theory.

A Swedish educational historian seeks to interpret

the meaning of some financial accounts which a gymnasium student in the seventeenth century gave to his headmaster. The accounts tell how much money the student collected during one of his wanderings. (Wanderings were common during this period and formed an important source of income for Scandinavian schools.) The interpreter's first task is to clarify the expressions; that is, the meaning of the symbols used in the student's accounts. Second, an attempt should be made to detect the personal experiences that these particular accounts express. Finally, the interpreter must reconstruct the context of forgotten meanings which characterized the practice of wandering and shaped the lives of Scandinavian students during the seventeenth century. In so doing, the interpreter unites the past (the student and his historical context) with the present world of contemporary readers and their preunderstandings.

In extending the hermeneutic circle to the domain of life experience, Dilthey at once both deepened and broadened the concept of "understanding." In particular, Dilthey's vision underscored the situational nature of the interpretative precess. This insight profoundly influenced the development of existential hermeneutics in the twentieth century. No longer was understanding seen as the result of interpretation: with Dilthey, ordinary understanding was transformed into the existential ground from which reflective interpretation derives.

Dilthey hoped to demonstrate how the understanding that occurs in quotidian experience could ground a theory of human science. For Dilthey, however, the scientific study of social life posed an intractable dilemma. Ordinary understanding makes use of part–whole relations conditioned by particular historical contexts. Science, however, demands objectivity, the overcoming of situation. Can an interpretation be at once historically conditioned and also objectively valid? To avoid the threat of relativism, Dilthey felt he had to forgo the condition of historicity. In so doing, he gave up his most profound and influential insight.

5. *Hermeneutics as a Phenomenology of Existence*

With the German philosophers Martin Heidegger (1889–1976) and Hans-Georg Gadamer (1900–), the existential implications latent in Dilthey's thought became fully developed. According to Heidegger and Gadamer, understanding and interpretation denote how human beings define themselves as beings in the world. In understanding, self and world emerge together: they are fundamentally related.

Understanding is relational in another way as well. Understanding constantly refers to the future. At the same time, it is conditioned by a person's situation: it operates within a totality of already interpreted relations. This relational totality Heidegger called the "world." A teacher entering a classroom can serve as an example. The teacher's understanding of the situation is referenced toward the future: he or she anticipates, for instance, how the pupils will respond to instruction and fears that some of them may cause trouble. Understanding for the teacher also is conditioned by his or her former experience of this class, or by earlier experiences he or she had during the day. In this respect, the teacher's present understanding at once calls up the future and recalls the past.

The linguisticality of understanding is a point stressed by Gadamer (1975). According to Gadamer, language is like a storehouse of assumptions or "prejudices." In this respect, language forms a parameter or "horizon" of possible understandings. This does not mean that language confines individuals to the meanings of particular times and places. Indeed, by means of language, past and present understandings are mediated. Gadamer calls the mediation of past and present a "fusion of horizons."

For Gadamer, a "fusion of horizons" is an interpretative event which demands an attitude of openness on the part of the interpreter. This openness is similar to the kind of attitude with which a person confronts great art. In Gadamer's view, both the encounter with art and the interpretation of historical texts are marked by genuine questioning, founded on a sense of expectancy and a readiness to be changed or transformed by the meaning of a work.

An historian trying to understand a diary written by an elementary school teacher in the nineteenth century illustrates this principle. Based on the way the teacher describes himself in his diary, the historian initially concludes that the teacher was a nice man. As the historian reads further, however, she discovers that in some passages of the the diary, the teacher discusses how he used corporal punishment to discipline his students. When confronted with this information, the historian experiences a clash between her "horizon" of understanding and the world of the teacher. The historian could react by shutting off further efforts to understand. Or, she could ask herself: "How is it possible to make sense of these actions when performed by such a nice person?" In order to reduce her conflict, the historian reads books about the role of corporal punishment in earlier eras of education. Gradually, she comes to see that the teacher in the past was only doing what other teachers and school authorities of his day thought best. The historian also learns that children in the late nineteenth century were not looked upon in the same way as they are in her time. Through a series of questions, then, for which there is a real need to know answers, the historian develops new understanding. In so doing, she extends the limits of her meaning-horizon and lays the groundwork for future understanding.

According to Gadamer, every hermeneutical endeavor proceeds from a stance of openness. In this respect, the interpreter does not "take possession" of the text that he or she interprets. Rather, the interpreter must let the text reveal its world.

6. The Model of the Text

The contribution of the French philosopher Paul Ricoeur (1913–) to interpretative theory is all-encompassing. It can be described as an effort to synthesize the problems and insights of hermeneutics from Aristotle to the late twentieth century. In one of his definitions, Ricoeur calls hermeneutics "the theory of rules that governs an exegesis, that is to say, an interpretation of a particular text or collection of signs susceptible of being considered as a text" (Palmer 1969 p. 43). For Ricoeur, the literal meaning of a text or system of symbols constitutes a closed world. This view parallels that of structural analysis, which studies language as a closed system of signs. A text also represents an open system, Ricoeur explained, because it refers to a world that exists outside of itself. In this respect, texts-as-discourse are similar to oral discourse, which is characterized by nonverbal signs and cues that direct the attention of the participants to circumstances and facts beyond the immediate discourse situation (Ricoeur 1971). Unlike oral discourse, however, texts are not limited to particular contexts. This is because texts refer not to situations but to worlds.

Texts, therefore, can be regarded in two different ways. First a text can be viewed as representing a closed system of signs. From this perspective, the aim of interpretation is to clarify the meaning inherent in words. Ricoeur calls this the "archaeological" aspect of hermeneutics. Owing to the referential function of words, however, texts also can be viewed as pointing to an existential space. Thus, once the meaning of a text's words has been made evident, the interpreter can focus on the existential world to which the text points. Put differently, once the "what" of the text has been explicated, the "about what" of the text can be sought.

According to Ricoeur, the interpreter in this way moves from what the text says to what it is talking about. This movement, Ricoeur stressed, does not result in an identification with an unknown mentality through acts of empathy (as Schleiermacher thought). On the contrary, the interpreter confronts a world: the world about which the text is talking. Interpretation for Ricoeur is thus not a matter of detecting secrets behind a text. Rather, interpretation is a process of reading the references that constitute a text's existential space. This often entails confronting new perspectives on life through the lifestyles of other existential worlds. As a consequence of interpretation and understanding, something heretofore alien becomes part of the interpreter's world, and the interpreter comes to understand himself or herself in a new way. The hermeneutic circle is moving between the interpreter's way of being and the being disclosed by the text.

In Ricoeur's view, all aspects of human communication and activity, including cultural products and artifacts, are analogous to texts. Accordingly, Ricoeur conceived his interpretative schema as pertaining not only to literature but also to the human sciences.

7. Hermeneutic Social Science

Since the late 1960s philosophers and practitioners alike have joined Ricoeur and Gadamer in exploring the implications of hermeneutics for the investigation of social life. A particularly influential contribution was advanced by Taylor (1971). Taylor's conception of human inquiry is anchored by a crucial premise of existential hermeneutics: meaning is not located in the minds of individuals. Rather, meaning consists in matrices of specific intersubjective agreements and understandings which are both constitutive of and expressed in social institutions and practices. Meaning, in short, is not private or subjective in Taylor's model: it is public, relational, and contextual.

This premise, Taylor argues, implies that the logic of hermeneutic inquiry is fundamentally different from the logic of positivistic science which has dominated social research since the nineteenth century. These differences become salient when one compares how hermeneutic and positivistic social science conceive the data of inquiry, the interpretation or explanation of data, and the justification and assessment of interpretative claims.

In the positivist model, physical behavior is distinguished from values, intentions, and goals. The former is observable and "brute identifiable"; the latter are hidden within the psyche, unavailable to sight. Positivist social science, Taylor said, strives to correlate public behaviors with subjective states of mind (Taylor 1971 pp. 18–21). When a significant convergence obtains, events and phenomena are said to be explained.

Such a science is extremely limited, Taylor declares. Because the positivist model regards meaning as hidden and subjective, it vastly underestimates and often just misses the import of social events. Breakdowns in fundamental institutions and practices such as voting, negotiation, and work, for example, represent more than the "public eruption of private pathology." These breakdowns, Taylor says, signal deep crises which represent "a malady of society itself, a malaise which affects its constitutive meanings" (Taylor 1971 p. 41). Like Ricoeur, Taylor argues that changes and crises of meaning per se are not grasped through acts of empathy. Nor can they be explained by subsuming observable sequences of "brute" behavior under general laws. Insofar as the data of social science express "a certain vision of the agent and his relation to others and to society" (Taylor 1971 p. 26), such a science will be unavoidably hermeneutic, less an application of theory and law than a reading of social meaning.

According to the hermeneutic model of inquiry, the only way researchers can justify their interpretations is by pointing to other readings. Man "is a self-interpreting animal," Taylor writes. "He is necessarily so, for there is no such thing as the structure of meanings for him independent of his interpretation of them . . . already to be a living agent is to experience one's situation in terms of certain meanings" (Taylor 1971 p. 16). For Taylor, in short, the justification and acceptance of interpretative claims—no less than their formulation—cannot appeal beyond the hermeneutic circle. Failure to grasp an interpretation is not due to an insufficiency of evidence or an inability to follow the logic of an argument. Inability to see instead derives from a fundamental inadequacy of self-definition which marks out the parameters of possible understanding. It follows, Taylor concludes, that in a hermeneutical science, "a certain measure of insight is indispensable" (Taylor 1971 p. 46). Some interpretations, as a consequence, simply will be "nonarbitrable."

8. Hermeneutics and Validity

The idea that interpretations may resist arbitration is disputed by a number of hermeneuticists. Betti (1967), for example, holds that without theoretical rules of verification, interpretation becomes anarchic. Betti tries to define a method that would allow interpretations to be assessed with "relative objectivity." Since human expressions are objectifications of the human spirit, Betti reasons that it is possible for an interpreter to reconstruct the meaning an author intended. The principle of authorial intention also is propounded by Hirsch (1967). It stands in clear contradiction to the view of Ricoeur, who argues that the author's intention is of secondary interest. This is because texts, when completed, must be regarded as autonomous from their authors.

Whether or not one agrees with Hirsch and Betti, the problem with which they wrestle is crucial. As Heidegger and Gadamer have noted, interpretation is a function of situated engagement: without a context of already interpreted meanings, understanding is impossible. At the same time, emphasis on the situatedness and finitude of interpretative understanding raises the question of whether or not interpretations in principle are decidable (Connolly and Keutner 1988). Is it possible for a hermeneutic philosophy to stay within a historically conditioned circle of understanding and at the same time posit rational principles as conditions for the possible validity or truth of particular claims to understanding (Hoy 1978)? Unless such principles can be articulated, is it clear how competing or conflicting interpretations can be adjudicated, or how the specter of relativism can be avoided?

9. Criteria of Interpretation

One important response to the above questions has been put forward by Ricoeur. In an essay on the relation between explanation and understanding, Ricoeur argues that the contradiction between the natural and human sciences to a great degree is an artifact (Ricoeur 1986). Texts and other human products can be subjected to explanation in a way similar to that used by the natural sciences. In fact, understanding is impossible without explanation, and, of course, vice versa. Interpretation and understanding are thus promoted by means of logic and argumentation. Moreover, interpretation and understanding often play important roles in the introductory and final stages of scientific research.

The question regarding situatedness and rationality therefore may be wrongly put. Because of its dependence on interpretation and understanding, physical science, no less than hermeneutic philosophy, is always situated within a particular time and place. As Gadamer has stated, there is no position outside our historicity. Humans, therefore, must make themselves aware of their historical situatedness and the preunderstandings that attend this condition (Gadamer 1975). Canons of interpretation, Gadamer maintains, help to achieve this awareness. In Gadamer's view, interpretative processes employ the very rationality and reason that contributed to the birth of the natural sciences.

The main interpretative principle, of course, is that of the hermeneutic circle: the parts of a text and its whole must be checked against each other. By means of the hermeneutic circle, a text can be interpreted mainly in two ways. It can be interpreted literally; or an attempt can be made to reconstruct the world of the text. With respect to literal interpretation, the logic of sentences and actions is often rather strict. It is therefore possible to apply strict logic to check interpretations. One such logical canon holds that an interpretation of phenomena and actions cannot be accepted unless it explains all available relevant information (Trankell 1972). If some important action or meaning in the text as a whole is excluded or only vaguely taken into consideration, the interpretation must be rejected. A second canon holds that an interpretation cannot be fully accepted unless it is the only one that explains the meaning of a research object. In many cases, this second criterion is difficult to satisfy. Even in those successful situations where only one interpretation remains after scrutiny in light of other competing interpretations, there is no guarantee that the interpretation will remain the correct one.

With respect to reconstructing the world to which a text or text-analog refers, the canon of the hermeneutical circle functions as a contextual criterion. According to this principle, every single interpretation must be checked against all available relevant facts, sources, and circumstances in connection with the interpreted object. If knowledge of those facts, sources, and circumstances contradicts the interpretation, it must be rejected or modified. By creating alternative interpretations of the same phenomena, cultural products, actions, or events from the very start, the interpretative process can be systematized. Concomitant with testing his or her main interpretation, then, the interpreter also can judge the validity of alternative interpretations. He or she thereby gradually refines his or her conceptions of the interpreted object.

10. The Position of Hermeneutics

The explosion of existential hermeneutics in the twentieth century has served to challenge a number of dualisms that are deeply rooted in modern epistemology and scientific method. Distinctions between facts and values, explanation and understanding, knowledge and self-knowledge, theory and practice were once regarded as inviolable; now these basic categories are being reconceptualized (Bernstein 1978, Dallmayr and McCarthy 1977). In the process, the relationship between hermeneutics and science with respect to the definition and determination of knowledge has been undergoing change. Some, such as Taylor (1971), have held that the logics driving hermeneutics and science are separate and incompatible. Others, such as Rorty (1979) and Gadamer (1975), have held a very different view. Overturning the old positivist position regarding the universality of science, Rorty and Gadamer have maintained that all knowledge is interpretative. There thus is no essential distinction between science and hermeneutics. Still others, such as Habermas (1973) and Apel (1973), have argued for the integrity of each domain but have posited a dialectical relationship between them.

Within the world of education, hermeneutics has flourished since around 1970, particularly with respect to educational research. The rise of so-called qualitative methods has broadened not only the scope and aim of educational research: it has also prompted investigators to reexamine the principles and aims of social inquiry (see, for example, Erickson 1986 and the *International Journal of Education Research* 1991.) A surge of interest in interpretative inquiry has prompted a number of important debates with the education community. Issues that have been discussed include the nature of the relationship between interpretative inquiry and more traditionally scientific designs; standards for adjudicating competing or conflicting interpretative claims; and the continued development of interpretative methods.

See also: Critical Discourse Analysis; Phenomenology and Existentialism; Positivism, Antipositivism, and Empiricism; Research in Education: Epistemological Issues

References

Apel K-O 1973 *Transformation der Philosophie.* Suhrkamp Verlag, Frankfurt [1980 *Towards a Transformation of Philosophy.* Routledge and Kegan Paul, London]
Bernstein R J 1978 *The Restructuring of Social and Political Theory.* University of Pennsylvania Press, Philadelphia, Pennsylvania
Betti E 1967 *Allgemeine Auslegungslehre als Methodik der Geisteswissenschaften.* Mohr, Tübingen
Bourdieu P, Passeron J-C 1970 *La Reproduction: éléments pour une théorie du système d'enseignement.* Editions de Minuit, Paris
Connolly J M, Keutner T (eds.) 1988 *Hermeneutics versus Science? Three German Views.* University of Notre Dame Press, Notre Dame, Indiana
Dallmayr F R, McCarthy T A (eds.) 1977 *Understanding and Social Inquiry.* University of Notre Dame Press, Notre Dame, Indiana
Derrida J 1978 (trans. Bass A) *Writing and Difference.* University of Chicago Press, Chicago, Illinois
Derrida J 1979 (trans. Harlow B) *Spurs: Nietzsche's Styles.* University of Chicago Press, Chicago, Illinois
Erickson F 1986 Qualitative methods in research on teaching. In: Wittrock M C (ed.) 1986 *Handbook of Research on Teaching*, 3rd edn. Macmillan, New York
Gadamer H-G 1975 *Wahrheit und Methode: Grundzüge einer Philosophischen Hermeneutik*, 4th edn. Mohr, Tübingen [1993 (trans. and revised Weinsheimer J, Marshall D G) *Truth and Method*, 2nd rev. edn. Continuum Press, New York]
Habermas J 1973 *Erkenntnis und Interesse*, 6th edn. Suhrkamp Verlag, Frankfurt [1987 *Knowledge and Human Interests*, 2nd edn. Polity, Cambridge]
Hirsch E D 1967 *Validity in Intepretation.* Yale University Press, New Haven, Connecticut
Hoy D C 1978 *The Critical Circle: Literature, History, and Philosophical Hermeneutics.* University of California Press, Berkeley, California
International Journal of Educational Research 1991 15(6): (special issue)
Palmer R E 1969 *Hermeneutics: Interpretation Theory in Schleiermacher, Dilthey, Heidegger, and Gadamer.* Northwestern University Press, Evanston, Illinois
Ricoeur P 1965 *De l'interpretation: essai sur Freud.* Editions du Suil, Paris [1970 (trans. Savage D) *Freud and Philosophy: An Essay on Interpretation.* Yale University Press, New Haven, Connecticut]
Ricoeur P 1971 The model of the text: Meaningful action considered as a text. *Soc. Res.* 38 (3): 529–62
Ricoeur P 1986 Essais d'herméneutique, Vol 2: *Du texte à l'action.* Editions du Seuil, Paris
Rorty R 1979 *Philosophy and the Mirror of Nature.* Princeton University Press, Princeton, New Jersey
Taylor C 1971 Interpretation and the sciences of man. *Rev. Metaphysics* 25 (1): 3–51
Trankell A 1972 *Reliability of Evidence: Methods for Analyzing and Assessing Witness Statements.* Beckman, Stockholm

Further Reading

Bauman Z 1978 *Hermeneutics and Social Science.* Columbia University Press, New York
Bernstein R J 1988 *Beyond Objectivism and Relativism: Science, Hermeneutics, and Praxis.* University of Pennsylvania Press, Philadelphia, Pennsylvania
Bleicher J 1980 *Contemporary Hermeneutics: Hermeneutics as Method, Philosophy and Critique.* Routledge, Chapman and Hall, New York

Bruner J 1990 *Acts of Meaning.* Harvard University Press, Cambridge, Massachusetts

Bruns G L 1992 *Hermeneutics Ancient and Modern.* Yale University Press, New Haven, Connecticut

Bubner R 1981 (trans. Matthews E) *Modern German Philosophy.* Cambridge University Press, Cambridge

Caputo J D 1987 *Radical Hermeneutics: Repetition, Deconstruction, and the Hermeneutic Project.* Indiana University Press, Bloomington, Indiana

Dilthey W 1883/1922/1989 In: Makkreel R A, Rodi F (eds.) *Selected Works Volume 1 Introduction to the Human Sciences.* Princeton University Press, Princeton, New Jersey

Engdahl H et al. 1977 *Hermeneutik.* Rabén and Sjörgren, Stockholm

Ermarth M 1978 *Wilhelm Dilthey· The Critique of Historical Reason.* University of Chicago Press, Chicago, Illinois

Ermarth M 1981 The transformation of hermeneutics: Nineteenth century ancients and twentieth century moderns. *Monist* 64(2): 175–94

Føllesdall D 1979 Hermeneutics and the hypothetico-deductive method. *Dialectica* 33 (3–4): 319–36

Gadamer H-G 1977 (trans. and ed. Linge D E) *Philosophical Hermeneutics: Hans-Georg Gadamer.* University of California Press, Berkeley, California

Gadamer H-G 1981 (trans. Lawrence F G) *Reason In The Age of Science* MIT Press, Cambridge, Massachusetts

Gadamer H-G 1992 In: Misgeld D, Nicholson G (eds.) *Hans-Georg Gadamer On Education, Poetry and History: Applied Hermeneutics.* State University of New York Press, Albany, New York

Gallagher S 1992 *Hermeneutics and Education.* State University of New York Press, Albany, New York

Grondin J 1995 *Sources of Hermeneutics.* State University of New York Press, Albany, New York

Guignon C (ed.) 1993 *The Cambridge Campanion to Hedeigger.* Cambridge University Press, Cambridge

Habermas J 1981 *Theorie des Kommunikativen Handelns,* Vol. 1, *Handlungsrationalität und Gesellschaftliche Rationalisierung.* Suhrkamp Verlag, Frankfurt [1984 *The Theory of Communicative Action,* Vol 1, *Reason and the Rationalization of Society.* Beacon Press, Boston, Massachusetts]

Habermas J 1981 *Theorie des Kommunikativen Handelns,* Vol. 2, *Zur Kritik der Funktionalistischen Vernunft,* 3rd edn. Surhkamp Verlag, Frankfurt [1987 *The Theory of Communicative Action,* Vol. 2, *Lifeworld and System: A Critique of Functionalist Reason.* Beacon Press, Boston, Massachusetts]

Heidegger M 1977 *Sein und Zeit.* Klostermann, Frankfurt

Hiley D R, Bohman J F, Shusterman R (eds.) 1991 *The Interpretive Turn: Philosophy, Science, Culture.* Cornell University Press, Ithaca, New York

Meehan J (ed.) 1995 *Feminists Read Habermas.* Routledge, New York

Mueller-Vollmer K (ed.) 1985 *The Hermeneutics Reader.* Continuum, New York

Natanson M 1973 *Edmund Husserl: Philosopher of Infinite Tasks.* Northwetern University Press, Evanson, Illinois

Ödman P-J 1979 *Tolkning, Förstaåelse, Vetande: Hermeneutik i teori och praktik.* AWE/Gebers, Stockholm

Ödman P-J 1992 Interpreting the Past. *Int. J. Qualitative Stud. Educ.* 5(2): 167–84

Ormiston G, Schrift A (eds.) 1990 *The Hermeneutic Tradition: From Ast to Ricoeur.* State University of New York Press, Albany, New York

Rabinow P, Sullivan W M (eds.) 1987 *Interpretive Social Science: A Second Look.* University of California Press, Berkeley, California

Ricoeur P 1974 In: Ihde D (ed.) 1974 *The Conflict of Interpretations.* Northwestern University Press, Evanston, Illinois

Ricoeur P 1981 (trans. and ed. Thompson J) *Hermeneutics and the Human Sciences.* Cambridge University Press, Cambridge

Ricoeur P 1984–88 (trans. McLaughlin Pellauer D) *Time and Narrative,* 3 Vols. University of Chicago Press, Chicago, Illinois

Ricoeur P 1992 (trans. Blamey K) *Oneself as Another.* University of Chicago Press, Chicago, Illinois

Thompson J B 1981 *Critical Hermeneutics: A Study in the Thought of Paul Ricoeur and Jürgen Habermas.* Cambridge University Press, Cambridge

Wachterhauser B (ed.) 1986 *Hermeneutics and Modern Philosophy.* State University of New York Press, Albany, New York

Warnke G (ed.) 1987 *Gadamer: Hermeneutics, Tradition, and Reason.* Stanford University Press, Stanford, California

Marxism and Educational Thought

N. C. Burbules

In the 1990s, given the dissolution of the Soviet Union and the abandonment of communist ideology by many other countries around the world, one would have to identify the direct influence of Marxism on educational theory and practice more as an historical event than as a topic of contemporary relevance. Even where national educational systems retain a Marxist label (for example, in China or Cuba), actual practices are shaped as much by specific national, religious, and cultural influences as by Marxist doctrine. Nevertheless, concepts and modes of analysis typical of Karl Marx's thought have played a pivotal role in the critical analysis of schooling in capitalist societies, and remain influential in such critical studies even when the broader theory and politics of Marxism are not. This article focuses primarily on this line of influence.

1. Marxism and the Genesis of Critical Educational Studies

Marx himself wrote almost nothing about education; hence much of his legacy must be read from the interpretations and educational implications others have drawn from his work. Two central lines of influence can be distinguished: that within communist societies, where Marxism has constituted the official ideology of the state (and hence of schooling); and that with capitalist societies, where Marx's theory has served primarily as a lens through which institutions of schooling can be analyzed and critiqued.

Within the communist world, Marxism provided a framework for conceiving education as an instrument of revolution: the responsibility of schools was to prepare workers, to inculcate appropriate socialist attitudes, and to promote the ideology of the Party. This has been true not only in the former Soviet Union (Sulimov et al. 1984, Lenin 1920), but in China (Mao 1949), Eastern Europe, and smaller communist societies in the Third World (such as Cuba, Nicaragua, and Tanzania). Often outside of formal schooling contexts, Marxist theory and practice have also informed revolutionary activities in these countries that can be seen as "educational" in a broader sense, such as adult literacy campaigns and community development programs.

Marxism in the 1990s, however, is almost everywhere in retreat; and while elements of socialist and social democratic policy continue to have broad appeal, the specific ideology and politics of Marxism do not. Nevertheless, even in capitalist societies elements of Marx's theory have had a profound and lasting influence on the critical study of schools. Three Marxian notions have been especially influential.

1.1 Class

In Marx's theory, the basic structure of capitalist society is the division of classes, and their fundamental conflict establishes the dynamic of all social and economic life. Owners of capital require a disciplined and dependent work force; but workers, when they become aware of the exploitative character of their work situation, resist and disrupt the smooth operation of capitalist production (for example, by striking). Hence a stable capitalist system requires the reproduction of a dependable class of workers, which first entails the purely physical supply of new generations of able-bodied men and women; and second, a class that is reproduced as an appropriate work force, sufficiently skilled and compliant to continue performing its role in the industrial process (Marx 1967).

This latter sense of reproduction has been crucial in the development of critical educational studies (see *Critical Theory and Education*). Althusser (1971) argued, that the reproduction of a class of workers was the central task of schools in capitalist societies, and that this task had two components: the training of vocational skills and the development of appropriate attitudes and dispositions (the most important of which is the acceptance of one's class role as fair, or at least as unavoidable). In capitalist societies, working-class students receive an education in routine and largely manual work skills, within the context of a structure of classroom relations—relations of authority, obedience, and orderly discipline—that prepare them for their later roles as supervised workers in an industrial system. Correspondingly, students from more privileged classes receive an education that stresses independence, self-reliance, creativity, and initiative (Anyon 1980, Bourdieu and Passeron 1977, Bowles and Gintis 1976).

1.2 Ideology

A second feature of Marx's theory is the significance of ideology as a central element in the dynamics of class; ideology comprises the "ruling ideas," which are in turn the "ideas of the ruling class"; and these serve to legitimate or to obscure the real class order, so that it continues to operate relatively consensually (Marx 1974; see also Althusser 1971).

Two aspects of Marx's theory of ideology have had a direct impact on critical studies of schooling. First, at a general level, the very existence of a publicly accessible school system functions ideologically, since it maintains the form of a meritocratic route of opportunity, sustaining the hope that any student can improve his or her lot in life through ability and effort. This meritocratic hope forestalls dissatisfaction with the class system and channels resistant worker energies into seeking to obtain a "better life" for themselves or for their children through education. The obverse aspect of this meritocratic ideology is that, because school is open to nearly everyone, when working-class students do not excel in school (which is usually the case), they are more likely to see this as their own failure, and so perceive their lot in life as appropriate and deserved. When workers acquiesce to their class position, stable capitalist relations can be maintained through the appearance of consent, rather than through the overt use or threat of force; this line of analysis depends directly on the work of the Italian Marxist, Antonio Gramsci (1971).

The second, and more specific, role that the Marxian conception of ideology has played in the development of critical educational studies has been in the analysis of curriculum (Apple 1990, Young 1971). With the expansion of tracking programs in schools that sort students into different course sequences, depending ostensibly on ability but in fact reflecting a clear stratification by class (as well as by race), the teachers, modes of instruction, and curriculum content to which students are exposed differ markedly. The ideological character of this content reflects, again, the different skills, dispositions, and attitudes appropriate to working-class and privileged students' respective class destinies. Working-class students are exposed to more concrete and reified bodies of fact, upon which they are drilled and tested continuously; they are generally given much less discretion in their choices among academic options. Students from more privileged and professional classes are presented with a curriculum of much higher academic content, requiring greater cognitive skill and flexibility; they are generally granted a broader range of choices, which they are encouraged to make for themselves (Anyon 1981). A Marxian analysis notes the ideological congruence between such content and specific work roles.

1.3 The State

A third factor in Marx's theory that has influenced critical educational studies is his conception of the state in capitalist society: for Marx the state, like other "superstructural" institutions, must be analyzed not as a discrete and autonomous political sphere, but as an arena in which the classes "become aware of their different interests and fight them out" (Marx 1986). This arena is not equally hospitable to all, and by transferring class conflicts to an ostensibly "neutral" playing field (which is in fact biased to advantage the wealthy and powerful), capitalist society deflects class resentments into relatively safe and ineffectual forms of political contestation.

Marx himself had a rather instrumental view of the state, believing that it responded fairly directly to the imperatives of the economic ruling class. Neo-Marxian theorists have emphasized the "relative autonomy" of the state (Althusser 1971, Poulantzas 1978): that there are a range of meliorative interventions that the state might undertake to minimize some of the unequal consequences of capitalism, but which do not challenge the fundamental character of capitalist relations and, in the long term, actually help to support them by forestalling more threatening expressions of opposition. More recently, other neo-Marxian theorists have argued that the state has a discrete set of interests and prerogatives which it strives to maintain even in the face of pressure from economic forces (Offe 1984); and that real tensions can emerge between the state's role in maintaining the social and economic conditions of capitalist production (for example, through Keynesian interventions in the economy), and its self-interest in protecting jobs, work conditions, and bureaucratic prerogatives within the state sector itself (for example, within regulatory agencies). These tensions can produce unexpected forms of resistance within state policy to unbridled capitalist expansion per se.

Because schooling in contemporary societies is generally a publicly funded and administered institution, many neo-Marxian theorists have drawn from this general theory of the state a framework for understanding why school policies, administration, and funding have the shape that they do. These vary, as before, from the more instrumental (Miliband 1969, 1977), to the structural–functional (Althusser 1971, Bowles and Gintis 1976), to regarding the state's educational

policies as a potential terrain of active struggle and contestation among classes, in which substantial concessions might still be won (Carnoy and Levin 1985, Shapiro 1990).

2. From Class to Culture: Trends in Critical Educational Studies

Because Marx's theory of capitalism purports to be comprehensive, accounting not only for the fundamental dynamics of the political economy but for its relation to all other social, political, and cultural institutions, its perspective on revolutionary social change tends to be somewhat daunting. The transition from capitalism to a more just socialist system cannot be evolutionary, but must be sudden and complete. At the theoretical level, this totalizing perspective leads to a view of social change that rejects "reform" in favor of "revolution," scorning by implication meliorative proposals or pragmatic compromises.

For educators, the implications of this theoretical framework are especially discouraging: significant change in educational institutions must follow, and cannot cause, more fundamental social or economic change. As superstructural institutions, schools are seen as the "direct efflux" of the imperatives of work roles and relations, and of the broader demands of capitalist production and consumption. What happens in schools is either directly controlled (via the state) or indirectly shaped (via the influece of ideology) to conform to the needs of reproducing and maintaining a stable class system.

This view has not rested easily with educators who, first, do not consider themselves to be the agents of capitalism and, second, generally believe in the potential of schools to improve the lot of individual students and disadvantaged groups, and thereby to promote the justice and equality of society at large. Educators tend to be optimists and incrementalists; yet classical Marxism implies that their hopes for significant social reform through school efforts are illusory.

Accordingly, critical educational theorists have looked more and more for guidance and inspiration to the neo-Marxian theories of authors such as Gramsci and Raymond Williams (1959, 1980), who stress the importance of culture in the workings of capitalist society and who describe a much broader terrain for politics and resistance in the class struggle.

Gramsci's work (1971) has been especially influential on critical educational studies in three ways. First, where Lenin's view of communist revolution involved the leadership of a cadre or vanguard who directed political action, Gramsci stressed the role of "organic intellectuals," members of the working class who bring to their leadership an imminent relation to and understanding of the experiences and outlook of other workers. The development of such organic intellectuals, drawn from the membership of particular class, racial, or ethnic groups, is often presented as a progressive educational goal. Second, where Marxian theory traditionally emphasizes the struggle over economic stakes ("control of the means of production"), Gramsci stressed ideological struggle as well. Gramsci emphasized the capacity of capitalist societies to secure worker cooperation by apparent consent, rather than through coercion or force. By maintaining certain unquestioned popular beliefs and values through the media of public influence, privileged groups promote a hegemonic order in which there may be a degree of discussion and choice, but bounded within a circumscribed range. Such hegemony is difficult to disclose and challenge, because of the appearance (and, to some extent, reality) of public diversity and debate; also, the restrictions built into such an ideological order have to do mainly with silences and gaps, with what is not on the agenda. Radical educators have taken it as a significant educational goal to promote counterhegemonic ways of thinking. Finally, rather than conceiving of revolution as the seizure of state power, or of a sudden and complete overturning of society, Gramsci urged action across various institutions of civil society, in a perpetual "war of position" across different terrains of radical political struggle—including schools. Despite the fact that Gramsci's own educational recommendations are surprisingly conservative (Gramsci 1959, see also Entwistle 1979), for educators interested in making schools the site of political struggle Gramsci's work has provided a convincing theoretical rationale within a broader neo-Marxian framework (each of these three themes can be seen in Aronowitz and Giroux 1985).

2.1 Beyond Reproduction

Rather than focusing on the functions of schooling that perpetuate social position and legitimate this in the eyes of students, radical educational theorists have emphasized the opportunities for schools to become sites of "resistance." Because students in school situations form social groups and construct identities in contexts that stand outside the official curriculum, their class identity—especially for working-class students—is often read as a manifestation of active cultural construction and contestation, not as passively receiving the edicts of the school (Giroux 1983, Willis 1977). While these forms of resistance, such as adopting particular styles of speech or dress, or refusing certain school assignments, may not constitute any fundamental challenge to the school (and may in fact serve to reinforce the sorting functions that shape their future life options; see Walker 1985), they do have two main features that belie the simple reproduction thesis. First, they reflect a struggle for independence, self-definition, and pride that significantly complicates the basic picture of schools as reproducing and legitimating institutions: students often do not accept the labels and judgments schools place on them. Second, these resistant attitudes and

activities can, among working-class students, be seen as expressing a protoclass consciousness, one that is cognizant and critical of the injustice and false promises of capitalism, and one that produces a certain class solidarity among working-class students; this solidarity is manifested first in opposition to the teacher and school, and might later be extended against the authorities and institutions of capitalist society generally (see *Reproduction Theory; Resistance Theory*).

2.2 Beyond Class

A related theme in current educational theory is a deemphasis on class as the central explanatory category for describing and accounting for why schools teach as they do. Schools also sort students and their educational opportunities by race, ethnicity, and gender. While these interact with class characteristics in many instances, they also represent distinct forms of disadvantage that cannot be reduced entirely to the dynamics of class.

Hence, for example, young girls are frequently taught differently, taught different subjects, and advised into different career paths than are boys with similar abilities (see *Gender Theories in Education*). There is no simple way for a Marxian theory to explain this pattern, since it largely cuts across all categories of class and frequently conflicts with what a purely class-based capitalist rationale would predict: namely, that increasing the supply of qualified workers and the competition for jobs would hold salaries down. (For attempts to reconcile Marxist and feminist perspectives, see Barrett 1988 and MacKinnon 1989).

Similarly, members of certain racial or ethnic groups are frequently stereotyped in ways that prejudge (and hence help confirm) their educational destinies. Even when educators sincerely desire the advancement of members of disadvantaged groups in schools, the content and manner of teaching are so foreign to the cultural styles, concerns, and experiences of these students that it is unlikely that their effort will succeed. In fact, when school is seen as a fundamentally alien and dehumanizing experience, the very value of school success is often inverted; students from these groups who do succeed in scholastic terms often face ostracism from their own peers.

These sorts of dynamics may, as noted, partly grow out of class cultures: certainly when students from racial or ethnic minorities are also disadvantaged by low income or poverty the likelihood is increased that they will not succeed at school, or will succeed only to a degree that reaffirms their class status position and limited scope of opportunities. Nevertheless, these cultural characteristics operate differently within different realms of school experience, and constitute aspects of identity that supercede class identity per se. Moreover, for resistance theorists, these other cultural dimensions of identity and group association may yield strong sources of opposition to school-sanctioned behavior. This culturalist perspective has received increasing emphasis in postmodern studies in education, as multiple characteristics of class, race, gender, ethnicity, and sexual orientation are seen as coequal elements of an increasingly fragmented identity, in which class is given no primacy whatsoever; in this context, Marx's theory comes to be seen as largely irrelevant, or even retrograde (see *Postmodernism and Education*).

3. The Marxian Legacy in Critical Educational Studies

While many critical educational theorists have been quick to abandon the totalizing character of Marxist theory, its somewhat reductionist focus on class dynamics, and its frequently mechanistic explanation of the impact of the political economy on schools, they have often neglected to recognize the more fundamental style of analysis, argumentation, and critique that they have derived from Marx even when they apply it in other domains, such as gender.

The Marxian world view describes society in terms of a fundamental conflict among groups divided by political power, economic resources, and social status. Whether one draws these lines by class, gender, race, or ethnicity—or some complex interaction among these factors—what remains is still an image of society bifurcated between oppressors and the oppressed, and of perpetual struggle against a "ruling class" of disproportionate power and privilege.

Additionally, while the Marxian tendency to explain all other social institutions in terms of the dynamics of the political economy is surely too simple and mechanistic a model, the Marxian conception of "historical materialism" nevertheless has influenced most social theorists to see the effects of "material conditions" (the processes of production and consumption in society) as crucial to social explanation. Certainly the existence of wide disparities of economic well-being and class privilege remains a central grievance among groups seeking expanded opportunities and benefits within capitalist systems.

Finally, the Marxian conceptions of ideology and the relation of the state to the political economy, while they cannot be accounted for simply as the instruments of "ruling class interests," remain powerful explanatory concepts for understanding how capitalism persists, despite the conditions of economic crisis that cyclically arise in all advanced capitalist societies. A major question of interest is the role of ideational influences, particularly the media, and of state intervention, in facilitating and legitimating the ongoing processes of capitalist production and consumption, even within societies that are (ostensibly) democratically controlled.

Each of these elements has shaped discourse concerning schools and educational policies; and the influence of Marxian theory has raised critical questions about the shortcomings and failures of schools that even nonradical scholars have needed to acknowledge. While the collapse of communist societies all over the world has led many observers to proclaim "the death of Marxism," it is important to distinguish Marxism as a prescriptive theory of revolution and the pursuit of a communist utopia, from the elements within Marxian theory that provide a trenchant diagnosis and critique of the injustices of capitalism. From this latter perspective, Marx's work has provided a vocabulary, a set of concepts, and a mode of social analysis that have fundamentally shaped contemporary understandings of capitalist society.

In the case of critical studies of schools, this line of reasoning has challenged the traditional view of schools as well-intended if ineffective avenues of opportunity, in favor of a view of schools as institutions largely dedicated to sorting students and justifying to them the restricted opportunities that society offers. This challenge, it appears, has yet to be answered.

See also: Political Socialization and Education; Socialist and Capitalist Schooling: Comparative Perspectives; Socialist Education Systems

References

Althusser L 1971 Ideology and ideological state apparatuses. In: Althusser L (ed.) 1971 *Lenin and Philosophy, and Other Essays*. Monthly Review Press, New York

Anyon J 1980 Social class and the hidden curriculum of work. *J. Educ.* 162(1): 67–92

Anyon J 1981 Social class and school knowledge. *Curric. Inq.* 11(1): 3–42

Apple M W 1990 *Ideology and Curriculum*, 2nd edn. Routledge, New York

Aronowitz S, Giroux H 1985 *Education Under Siege: The Conservative, Liberal and Radical Debate Over Schooling*. Bergin and Garvey, South Hadley, Massachusetts

Barrett M 1988 *Women's Oppression Today: The Marxist-Feminist Encounter*, rev. edn. Verso, New York

Bourdieu P, Passeron J-C 1977 *Reproduction in Education, Society, and Culture*. Sage, Beverly Hills, California

Bowles S, Gintis H 1976 *Schooling in Capitalist America: Educational Reform and the Contradictions of Economic Life*. Basic Books, New York

Carnoy M, Levin H M 1985 *Schooling and Work in the Democratic State*. Stanford University Press, Stanford, California

Entwistle H 1979 *Antonio Gramsci: Conservative Schooling for Radical Politics*. RKP, London

Giroux H 1983 *Theory and Resistance in Education: A Pedagogy for the Opposition*. Heinemann Educational, London

Gramsci A 1959 The organization of education. In: Marks L (ed.) 1957 *The Modern Prince and Other Writings*. International Publishers, New York

Gramsci A 1971 *Selections from the Prison Notebooks*. Lawrence & Wishart, London

Lenin V I 1971 (1st edn. 1920) The tasks of the Youth Leagues. In: Fineberg J (ed.) 1971 *Selected Works*.

International Publishers, New York

MacKinnon C A 1989 *Toward a Feminist Theory of the State.* Harvard University Press, Cambridge, Massachusetts

Mao Tse-Tung 1949 On the people's democratic dictatorship. In: *Selected Works*, Vol. 5. International Publishers, New York

Marx K 1974 (1st edn. 1845–46) *The German Ideology.* International Publishers, New York

Marx K 1967 (1st edn. 1887) *Capital: A Critique of Political Economy, Vol. One: The Process of Capitalist Accumulation.* International Publishers, New York

Marx K 1986 (1st edn. 1859) Preface to A Critique of Political Economy. In: Elster J (ed.) 1986 *Karl Marx: A Reader.* Cambridge University Press, New York

Miliband R 1969 *The State in Capitalist Society.* Weidenfeld and Nicholson, London

Miliband R 1977 *Marxism and Politics.* Oxford University Press, New York

Offe C 1984 *Contradictions of the Welfare State.* MIT Press, Cambridge, Massachusetts

Poulantzas N 1978 *State, Power, Socialism.* NLB, London

Shapiro S 1990 *Between Capitalism and Democracy: Educa-*

tional Policy and the Crisis of the Welfare State. Bergin and Garvey, South Hadley, Massachusetts

Sulimov E F et al. 1984 *Teorya y praktika Kommunisti chkova vospitanya.* Visshnaya Shkola, Moscow

Walker J C 1985 Rebels with our applause? A critique of resistance theory. *J. Educ.* 167(2): 63–83

Williams R 1959 Marxism and culture. In: Williams R (ed.) 1959 *Culture and Society 1780–1950.* Chatto and Windus, London

Williams R 1980 *Problems in Materialism and Culture: Selected Essays.* Verso, London

Willis P E 1977 *Learning to Labour: How Working-Class Kids Get Working-Class Jobs.* Saxon House, Farnborough

Young M F D (ed.) 1971 *Knowledge and Control: New Directions for the Sociology of Education.* Collier-Macmillan, London

Further Reading

Marx K 1975 *On Education, Women, and Children.* McGraw-Hill, New York

Phenomenology and Existentialism

R. Small

This article provides a brief survey of the philosophical traditions of phenomenology and existentialism, and a discussion of their relevance to educational thought. Although Jean-Paul Sartre is better known to the general public, it is Martin Heidegger who figures centrally in this discussion.

1. Phenomenology

Often associated with each other, phenomenology and existentialism are nevertheless distinct tendencies. Phenomenology is a philosophical methodology, arising from the work of Edmund Husserl (1859–1938).

Franz Brentano (1838–1917) had revived the scholastic concept of "intentionality" (*esse intentionale*) as the defining feature of psychical phenomena (Brentano 1973). On this view, mental acts are always directed towards an object, though not necessarily an existing thing. In classifying representation, judgment, and feeling as differing modes of intentionality, Brentano considered he had made a genuinely scientific psychology possible for the first time.

Husserl applied Brentano's concept of intentionality to a broader philosophical program, a radical empiricism characterized by his slogan: "To the things themselves!" ("*Zu den Sachen selbst!*"). He used the term "phenomenology" for a science of ideal meanings, based on a direct intuition achieved through successive "reductions" of given experience. By setting aside (or "bracketing") the reality of the objects

of experience, the investigator could isolate mental phenomena in their purity. A further "transcendental reduction," bracketing the reality of mental acts themselves, revealed that the world and its meanings are constituted in transcendental subjectivity. Transcendental phenomenology could thus provide the basis of all other sciences, in accordance with the traditional ideal of philosophy.

In his 1911 manifesto "Philosophy as Rigorous Science" Husserl reaffirmed this systematic program, repudiating "profundity" in favor of scientific clarity, and claiming that only phenomenology could answer the challenges of relativism and naturalism (Husserl 1981). In works such as *Ideas Towards a Pure Phenomenology* (1982) and *Cartesian Meditations* (1960), as well as many unpublished writings, he continued to extend and apply his ideas. The 1935 Vienna lecture "Philosophy and the Crisis of European Humanity" announced the themes of his important final work, *The Crisis of European Sciences and Transcendental Phenomenology* (Husserl 1970). In addressing the historical situation of European culture, Husserl introduces the idea of the pre-given, taken-for-granted "life-world," within which both philosophy and science arise as human activities. The modern crisis of rationality, he argues, is due to its estrangement from this basis. The sciences have become abstract and formal sets of ideas, irrelevant to human life and its meaning. Meanwhile, philosophy is misled by "naturalistic objectivism" into assuming the status of the world, without inquiring into its origins in subjectivity. Only transcendental phenomenology, Husserl concludes, can restore philosophy, and the European culture that depends on it, to their true path (Husserl 1970).

Phenomenology has had a wide influence in philosophy and related disciplines such as psychology and sociology, due to the work of Alfred Schutz. However, the term "phenomenology" is often used loosely: Ivan Illich's claim to offer a "phenomenology of school" in his *Deschooling Society* is a case in point. Phenomenology has been used to explore educational issues by a group of American philosophers, amongst whom Maxine Greene, Leroy Troutner, and Donald Vandenberg are prominent. Here the existential version of phenomenology is a main influence. The contributions of European writers are not readily available in English, but Vandenberg (1971) provides a useful guide to their ideas.

2. Existentialism

"Existentialism" is a misleading word if it suggests either a unified school or a clearly definable set of beliefs shared by its members. Who counts as an existentialist depends on who is making up the list. Certainly it would be necessary to include literary figures, such as Dostoyevsky and Kafka, as well as philosophers; and Nietzsche is often included, if only because he cannot easily be put in any other category. Some philosophers are clearly central to the existential tradition: in the nineteenth century, Søren Kierkegaard (1813–55); and in the twentieth, Karl Jaspers (1883–1969), Martin Heidegger (1889–1976), and Jean-Paul Sartre (1905–80).

There are sharp differences between these thinkers: for instance, Kierkegaard and Jaspers were Christians, Sartre a militant atheist. In politics, Sartre was a left-wing activist, while Heidegger's tragic misjudgment in aligning himself with the Nazi regime is still a topic of heated controversy. There are common preoccupations, however. Individuality, subjectivity, and freedom are key themes in existential thought. This is why existentialists are sharply opposed to any kind of naturalism, which diminishes or eliminates the distinction between the human beings and other things.

While predecessors such as Blaise Pascal or J G Hamann can be found, the initiator of modern existentialism is Kierkegaard. His thinking can be seen as one revolt against the domination of philosophy by the systemic rationalism of Hegel. Marx rejected absolute idealism as a mystification of social life in its material reality; Kierkegaard thought it had left out the irreducible individuality of the thinking subject. The system in its totality took no account of this finite, imperfect, and temporal individual. Kierkegaard does not deny an absolute and eternal truth: on the contrary, it is precisely the tension between this truth and humans' finite being that constitutes the human predicament. He

writes: "Two ways, in general, are open for an existing individual: *Either* he can do his utmost to forget that he is an existing individual, by which he becomes a comic figure, since existence has the remarkable trait of compelling an existing individual to exist whether he wills it or not . . . *Or* he can concentrate his entire energy on the fact that he is an existing individual" (Kierkegaard 1941 p. 109). To do this is to become "subjective," choosing and committing oneself to what must remain an objective uncertainty, and so grasping truth as a passionate appropriation.

Kierkegaard's philosophical writing differs considerably from that of conventional treatises. His continual use of humor and irony, his dramatic devices and highly personal tone, are all deliberately adopted in order to create a discourse appropriate to what he wants to communicate. Existential reality, Kierkegaard states, is incommunicable (Kierkegaard 1941 p. 320). There he is referring to just one mode of communication: the direct sort appropriate to objective thinking, but not to a truth of inwardness and appropriation. For that Kierkegaard proposes instead another, *indirect* mode of communication. As he explains, "A communication in the form of a possibility compels the recipient to face the problem of existing in it" (Kierkegaard 1941 p. 320). It is up to the recipient to recognize such a communication as pointing to a possibility of his or her own existence.

The existential influence has flourished in religious thought, with the Jewish thinkers Martin Buber and Franz Rosenzweig, and the Protestant Paul Tillich. The twentieth-century philosopher who stands closest to Kierkegaard is Karl Jaspers, whose sensitive treatment of what he terms the "boundary situations" of human existence—death, suffering, struggle, and guilt—is of particular value (Jaspers 1969–71). His "elucidation" of human existence makes no attempt to eliminate ambiguity and paradox. Not surprisingly, Jaspers rejected the existential phenomenology of Heidegger as a misguided exercise. He wrote: "Heidegger's thought is presented in objective terms, as a doctrine, and as a result it commits us no more than the traditional systems. What we have, then, is a noncommittal, phenomenological knowledge, and by the same token, a learnable, usable knowledge that is a perversion of philosophy" (Jaspers and Bultmann 1958 p. 8).

3. Existential Phenomenology

The confluence of phenomenology with existentialist thought began with Martin Heidegger's *Being and Time*, first published in 1927. The stated aim of the work is to open up what Heidegger called "the question of Being" (Heidegger 1962). The "ontological difference" between Being and beings (or entities) is crucial here. Because most thinking is directed towards beings, Heidegger begins with an interpretation (or "hermeneutic") of a particular kind of Being: our own.

Heidegger calls the human mode of Being *Dasein*. The German word, usually left untranslated, means "Being-there." In the course of an analysis whose richness of detail can only be hinted at here, he elaborates this into a concept of "Being-in-the-world." People are always already in the world, not in the sense of simple location, but of living there, dwelling alongside and caring about things and other people. Heidegger's method is phenomenological; what he means by "phenomena" are not the usual objects of experience, however, but rather the hidden background which is usually overlooked, or apprehended only in exceptional moods, such as joy or anxiety. In uncovering the inconspicuous structures of everyday life, Heidegger shows how *Dasein* is absorbed into an anonymous public world. This is its "inauthentic" mode of Being, which nevertheless points out an alternative. The temporality of human existence is not that of the world of objects, the time measured by clocks; *Dasein* always runs ahead of itself into the future, and retrieves its past possibilities. Above all, its temporality differs from objective time in being finite. On the one hand, one is thrown into the world, delivered over to one's situation; on the other, one faces the indefinite yet inevitable prospect of one's death. Authenticity (*Eigentlichkeit*) means taking over one's own existence as uniquely one's own, in a resolute appropriation of past and future possibilities.

Jean-Paul Sartre's *Being and Nothingness*, first published in 1943, takes up themes from Hegel, Husserl, and Heidegger; its dominant concern is Sartre's own preoccupation with freedom and responsibility. Sartre's literary flair is seen in his vivid treatment of inauthenticity, which he renames "bad faith." In one well-known passage, he describes the cafe waiter who is a little too attentive and assiduous in performing his tasks; Sartre explain that this person is "playing at being a waiter in a café" (Sartre 1957 p. 59). After all, his being a waiter is always in question, never a settled fact. So why does he act as if it were? Social pressure may be a factor: the public needs to be reassured that the waiter is "only" a waiter. There is a deeper reason, though: the realization of one's own freedom is alarming and uncomfortable. Since one's existence precedes one's essence, one is continually creating oneself anew, with no higher authority to validate one's choices. The anguish of this freedom is just the human condition: Sartre insists that one face one's absolute responsibility without the comforts of self-deception.

The popular success of the French school of Sartre, Albert Camus, and Simone de Beauvoir, all literary figures as well as philosophers, made "existentialism" a household word in the postwar period. In a popular lecture, Sartre claimed existentialism as a form of humanism (Sartre 1948). Heidegger was provoked into repudiating both "existentialism" and "humanism" as misleading labels (Heidegger 1977). By then, his own work had taken a different turn, still pursuing

"the question of Being," but through a "destruction" of the Western tradition of thought, extending to an abandonment of terms such as "phenomenology" and even "philosophy" (in favor of "thinking"). This later work of Heidegger remains a powerful influence in the current postmodern and deconstructionist movements.

4. Problem Areas in Education

While existential phenomenology is relevant to many aspects of education, three particular areas in which it raises significant issues can be noted.

4.1 Childhood as a Mode of Existence

Where education has to do with children, it must take into account the nature of childhood. A biological model, in which learning is one aspect of growth, comes to mind readily. An alternative is to identify childhood as a social category, contrasting its forms in different societies. These still leave open the question: what *is* the child, as an individual person?

No existentialist writer has shown a greater awareness of the fragility of individual identity than Franz Kafka. His observations on education are of particular interest in identifying the family as the greatest threat to the separate identity of the child. He writes:

> The love that parents have for their children is animal, mindless, and always prone to confuse the child with their own selves. But the educator has respect for the child; and for the purposes of education that is incomparably more, even if there is no love involved. I repeat: for the purposes of education. For when I call parental love mindless and animal, that is not to denigrate it. It is as much an inscrutable mystery as the intelligent creative love of the educator. Only for the purposes of education we cannot denigrate it enough. (Kafka 1977 p. 296)

Kafka insists on respect for the child both as an individual and as a child, and sees the educator as uniquely placed to protect and enhance both aspects. Other existential writers on education have explored the character of childhood as a mode of existence, to be grasped in terms of its own possibilities (Denton 1978).

4.2 The School as a Social Institution

Education is seen as part of the everyday world. Schools are public institutions, more or less bureaucratic in character; teaching and learning are routine activities, plausibly characterized as social "roles." Existential thought is sharply critical of the "one-dimensionality" of modern societies. As happens in other professions, a teacher may be absorbed within everyday functions, often reinforced by an administrative policy which minimizes individual autonomy. Can authenticity be achieved in such a setting? It seems unlikely. Yet Kierkegaard describes the "knight of faith," an individual whose deep spirituality requires no external expression, so that to the observer he or she is indistinguishable from a conventional member of society. Introduced to this individual, Kierkegaard says, one murmurs to oneself: "Good Lord, is this the man? Is it really he? Why, he looks like a tax-collector!" (Kierkegaard 1941 p. 53). Authenticity is not something to be addressed by empirical research; it is an issue for the existing individual alone. It cannot be directly linked with particular social or political arrangements, or with one model of schooling.

4.3 Teaching and Learning as Interpersonal Relations

Whatever its setting may be, education eventually comes down to the relation between teacher and learner. Given its radically individualistic character, can existential thinking assist people in grasping the interpersonal character of education? Heidegger's analysis of "Being-with-others" is mainly concerned with its inauthentic mode. When it comes to an authentic mode of communication, for example, he suggests that reticence and even silence are preferable to "idle talk." One's aim must be to free others for their own possibilities, rather than taking them over by open or hidden domination. The problem of domination is prominent in Sartre's *Being and Nothingness* (1957), where an elaborate construction of interpersonal relations is offered—but no solution. Sartre's play *No Exit* includes a memorable line: "Hell is other people."

In place of these discouraging ideas, existential writers on education often invoke the concept of dialogue. Any suggestion of a Socratic pedagogy needs care, however. Franz Rosenzweig contrasts the thinking of past philosophy, seemingly autonomous and timeless, with a thinking which is bound to speech and to life with others in a common world. A comparison between the Gospels and the Socratic dialogues, Rosenzweig suggests, brings out the point: since Socrates already knows what is to be thought, his conversation is merely a concession to the limitations of communication: nothing actually happens in it. In contrast, genuine dialogue is open to the unforeseen: "I do not know in advance what the other person will say to me, because I do not even know what I myself am going to say. I do not even know whether I am going to say anything at all" (Glazer 1961 p. 199).

One writer who has emphasized "dialogical education" is Paulo Freire, whose *Pedagogy of the Oppressed*, mixing themes from existentialism, Marxism, and Christianity, appealed to a wide audience (Freire 1972). Criticizing "a mechanistic, static, naturalistic, spatialized view of consciousness," he appealed to the Husserlian notion of intentionality (as interpreted by Sartre) for an alternative. Freire is both eclectic and selective: yet for all his passionate attack on oppression, he is a positive thinker, treating

problems as soluble through action; so many existential themes find no place in his thinking. Just as important for him is Marx's third thesis on Feuerbach, with its warning that "the educator must himself be educated," and recommendation of a "revolutionary praxis" which transforms both the agent and the world. Freire denounces a "banking concept" of education, which treats knowledge as a ready-made product, to be transferred into the empty mind of a passive learner; he argues for a pedagogy of dialogue between equals, aiming primarily at social and political liberation.

The overlap between these ideas and existential thought can be gauged from one lecture of Heidegger in which his own pedagogy is outlined with exemplary clarity. Teaching is an offering and giving, Heidegger explains, but learning is not just a taking:

> If the student only takes over something which is offered he does not learn. He comes to learn only when he experiences what he takes as something he himself already has. True learning only occurs where the taking of what one already has is a self-giving and is experienced as such. Teaching, therefore, does not mean anything else than to let the others learn, i.e., to bring one another to learning. Learning is more difficult than teaching; for only he who can truly learn—and only as long as he can do it—can truly teach. The genuine teacher differs from the pupil only in that he can learn better and that he more genuinely wants to learn. In all teaching, the teacher learns the most. (Heidegger 1968 p. 73)

See also: Conscientization and Mobilization; Hermeneutics; Research Paradigms in Education

References

Brentano F 1973 *Psychology from an Empirical Standpoint.* Routledge and Kegan Paul, London
Denton D E (ed.) 1978 *Existentialism and Phenomenology in Education: Collected Essays.* Teachers College Press, New York
Freire P 1972 *Pedagogy of the Oppressed.* Penguin Books, Harmondsworth
Glazer N N (ed.) 1961 *Franz Rosenzweig: His Life and Thought* 2nd rev. edn. Schocken Books, New York
Heidegger M 1962 *Being and Time.* SCM Press, London
Heidegger M 1968 *What is a Thing?* Henry Regnery, Chicago, Illinois
Heidegger M 1977 (ed. Krell D F) *Basic Writings.* Harper and Row, New York
Husserl E 1960 (1st edn. 1929) *Cartesian Meditations.* Martinus Nijhoff, The Hague
Husserl E 1970 *The Crisis of European Sciences and Transcendental Phenomenology: An Introduction to Phenomenological Philosophy.* Northwestern University Press, Evanston, Illinois
Husserl E 1981 Philosophy as rigorous science. In: McCormick P, Elliston F A (eds.) 1981 *Shorter Works.* Harvester Press, Brighton
Husserl E 1982 (1st edn. 1913) *Ideas Pertaining to a Pure Phenomenology and to a Phenomenological Philosophy,* First Book. Martinus Nijhoff, The Hague

Jaspers K, Bultmann R 1958 *Myth and Christianity: An Inquiry into the Possibility of Religion without Myth.* Noonday Press, New York

Jaspers K 1969–71 *Philosophy*, 3 vols. University of Chicago Press, Chicago, Illinois

Kafka F 1977 *Letters to Friends, Family, and Editors.* Schocken Books, New York

Kierkegaard S 1941 *Concluding Unscientific Postscript.* Princeton University Press, Princeton, New Jersey

Kierkegaard S 1941 *Fear and Trembling.* Princeton University Press, Princeton, New Jersey

Sartre J-P 1948 *Existentialism and Humanism.* Methuen, London

Sartre J-P 1957 *Being and Nothingness.* Methuen, London

Vandenberg D 1971 *Being and Education: An Essay in Existential Phenomenology.* Prentice-Hall, Englewood Cliffs, New Jersey

Further Reading

Bollnow O F 1959 *Existenzphilosophie und Pädagogik: Versuch über unstetige Formen der Erziehung.* W. Kohlhammer Verlag, Stuttgart

Cooper D E 1983 *Authenticity and Learning: Nietzsche's Educational Philosophy.* Routledge and Kegan Paul, London

Greene M 1973 *Teacher as Stranger: Educational Philosophy for the Modern Age.* Wadsworth, Belmont, California

Manheimer R J 1978 *Kierkegaard as Educator.* University of California Press, Berkeley, California

Morris V C 1966 *Existentialism in Education: What it Means.* Harper and Row, New York

Murphy T F 1984 *Nietzsche as Educator.* University Press of America, Lanham, Maryland

Positivism, Antipositivism, and Empiricism

D. C. Phillips

During the closing decades of the twentieth century, members of the international educational research community have displayed a growing interest in the philosophical underpinnings of their work—especially of the methodological aspects. One line of evidence for this is readily available in the pages of the *Educational Researcher*, the "house journal" of the American Educational Research Association, where since the mid-1970s a large number of articles on philosophical and methodological matters have appeared, many written by nonphilosophers; another indication is the special issue of the *International Journal of Educational Research*, which, in 1991, was given over entirely to philosophical issues in research (Lakomski 1991). Special symposia have even been held to allow researchers to discuss these matters (see Guba 1990). Amongst the topics most frequently referred to has been the "demise of positivism" (see, for example, Phillips 1983, Miller and Fredericks 1991, Schrag 1992); in much of this literature, however, there has been confusion about the relationships between positivism, logical positivism, and empiricism, and also about how these positions relate to realism and relativism.

1. Empiricism

Empiricism is one of the two major, classic positions in epistemology—the other being rationalism, which, crudely put, holds that the main underpinning of human knowledge is the "light of reason." (Descartes is a quintessential figure in the history of rationalism; as is well-known, he searched through his ideas to find one which was clear and distinct to the light of reason, and which could not be doubted. Thus he arrived at his famous "cogito ergo sum," which became the ultimate foundation for his knowledge.) Both classic positions are complex, in the sense that within each there are many subschools of thought.

Empiricism, according to one authority, may be characterized as "Any of a variety of views to the effect that either our concepts or our knowledge are, wholly or partly, based on experience through the senses and introspection. The basing may refer to psychological origin or, more usually, philosophical justification" (Lacey 1976 p. 55).

Thus, one form of empiricism holds that human knowledge originates from sense experience; a representative figure here is the British philosopher of the seventeenth century, John Locke, who held that at birth the mind of the individual was a "tabula rasa" (blank tablet)—and that the origin of every simple idea could be traced to sense experience or to introspection (inner experience). Locke had a view that later followers came to call "mental chemistry," for he envisioned simple ideas being combined in various ways to form more and more complex ideas; but there was no idea whose genealogy could not be traced back down the descending path from complex to simple to eventual origin in sense experience. A person who had never experienced the color lilac could not have the idea of lilac (although the person might know the word "lilac" from having heard or read it).

Thus, for Locke, the sequence of knowledge-growth was as follows: a newborn baby, devoid of ideas but with a cognitive mechanism that was potentially able to manipulate and work with ideas (a crucial point), might experience coldness, loudness, redness, and roundness (from the surrounding environment, a toy hanging over the crib, and so forth), and these would give rise to the corresponding simple ideas; gradually complex ideas like "red ball" would be built up—but only if the requisite simple ideas had been formed. Introspection, or reflection, or inner experience, would similarly produce simple ideas like "pain" or "anger." As should be evident, Locke was a strong opponent of the view that there could be innate ideas.

As the quotation from Lacey indicates, however, there are other forms of empiricism. A person might be more interested in the question of justification than of origin. Consider the claim that unadulterated water, at normal pressure, boils at 100°C. A narrow Lockean might want to emphasize the fact that the concepts here—"water," "boils," "pressure," and so on—must all have had their ultimate origin in sense experience; but others (and, for that matter, a Lockean as well) might want to know what justifies or warrants this particular claim—why is pure water believed to boil at 100°C rather than at 90°C? Empiricists would want to say that this claim is justified by experience, or by the empirical evidence that is available.

At first sight, this justificatory version of empiricism has a lot going for it—for it is hard to see how any philosopher could advocate a position that did not in some way allow for the fact that knowledge of the world must be constrained in some fashion by the way the world is, or appears to be. (Even so strong a contemporary critic of simplistic empiricism as Paul Feyerabend admits that he is prepared to march in company with empiricism at least this far; see Feyerabend 1980.) In the second half of the twentieth century, however, some severe problems have come to the fore, especially as philosophers have pursued issues of justification with respect to the theoretical knowledge of the advanced sciences.

2. Challenges to Empiricism

Perhaps the most important challenge to empiricism has been the realization that the items constituting knowledge—theories, hypotheses, and so on—are always underdetermined by the evidence that is available. In other words, knowledge always goes beyond the evidence; or, to turn the point around, the evidence at hand at hand is always compatible with a variety of theories or hypotheses. So it cannot be claimed that the belief in theory T1 is justified by a particular body of empirical evidence, because theories T2, T3, and so on, are also justified or warranted by this same evidence. To take an oversimple example, one might claim to know that there is a golf ball lying on the table, and by way of justification one offers the fact that one experiences seeing the ball there. However, another person may claim that it is not a golf ball, but a hologram; and another might offer the opinion that it is one of those light plastic replicas that are sometimes used to play practical jokes on golfers. The point is, the evidence that warrants one's own claim can also be used to warrant the other people's. If new

evidence is collected, these alternative theories may be ruled out, but others might be dreamt up that are still compatible with the finite body of evidence that is available. These rival theories might be ruled out on the grounds that they are unreasonable or improbable, given the situation in which the observations are being made, but then it is evident that the knowledge that this is indeed a golf ball is based on more than the empirical evidence that is available—for some additional principle or principles have also been drawn on (in this example, concerning what is reasonable or probable under the circumstances). (For an important discussion of the limitations of the argument concerning underdetermination, see Laudan 1990.)

Another problem concerns the status of theoretical entities; such things as quarks, or subnuclear forces, are not directly observable, and to claim that they are "indirectly" observable is also to oversimplify the chains of reasoning involved. How, then, can it be claimed that knowledge of these things "originates" in experience, or is "justified" by experience? Locke's successor Hume (1711–76) raised a similar issue about knowledge of causation in nature: Causes are not actually observed at work, rather what is seen is mere "constant conjunction" (event A seems always to be followed by event B). As a consequence of all this, there is an antirealist tendency for empiricism to lead to the view that the only realities are the empirically observable phenomena, and that the entities postulated within theoretical physics are "convenient fictions." (Empiricists differ over this, and other, matters.)

A further difficulty for empiricisms of both types outlined above is the fact that observation, or the gathering of empirical evidence, is not the pristine process that is presupposed by such philosophies. The varieties of empiricism discussed above make the assumption that sense experience is unadulterated, in that it is completely uncontaminated by theory; after all, experience can hardly be the origin of knowledge, or the justificatory "court" to which one appeals when one is asked to warrant knowledge claims, if prior beliefs or theories or knowledge can be shown to have influenced it. This is precisely what has been shown (by Wittgenstein, Popper, Hanson, Kuhn, and others; see Phillips 1987 for further discussion)—observation is theory-laden, and is not theory-neutral. What is seen (or felt or heard or tasted or smelled), and how it is seen (or felt . . .), is influenced by knowledge the experiencer already possesses.

Finally, given the centrality of the notion of "experience," it has been crucial for empiricists to grapple with the issue of what is actually experienced during experience. Different answers have been forthcoming: only sense data are experienced (such things as "red patch here now," although the precise formulation is a matter of learned debate); actual objects are directly experienced; objects and the relations between them are experienced.

As a result of these and other problems (see

Morick 1980), an epistemological position known as nonfoundationalism or nonjustificationism has been developed (by Popper and others), according to which knowledge is not to be regarded as being based upon some indubitable and neutral foundation such as experience or the light of reason; rather, those theories or hypotheses that have been adequately tested are tentatively accepted as knowledge—with the caveat that no knowledge is ever absolutely established. Knowledge, in short, is inherently hypothetical (which is not to say that people do not usually have substantial reasons for believing the things that they do) (see *Research in Education: Epistemological Issues*).

3. Positivism

Positivism—itself a complex of several subpositions—is merely one form of empiricsm, despite the fact that critics of positivism in educational research tend to identify it as being coextensive with empiricism. In order words, while all forms of positivism are forms of empiricism, it is a mistake to infer back that all empiricisms are forms of positivism. As a consequence, not all problems facing positivism necessarily face other forms of empiricism.

The term "positivist" is used very loosely in the contemporary educational research literature to which reference was made at the outset: it has become a more or less generalized and vague term of abuse. A positivist is likely to be identified, inter alia, as someone who is an empiricist, a realist, a believer in the value of objectivity in research, a believer that truth is a sustainable ideal for research, an adherent of the experimental method, a supporter of quantitative/statistical methods, and a skeptic about qualitative methodologies. That such identifications are fantasies, and in some cases are directly the opposite of the true state of affairs, generally escapes notice. Certainly positivists believe a few of the things here attributed to them, but so do many others—so once again it is invalid to argue backwards and infer that anyone who holds one of these particular positions must be a positivist. Furthermore it is hard to follow the logic that leads to the conclusion that a positivist must be a lover of statistical methods and an opponent of qualitative/observational studies.

Classic positivism can be traced back to the writings of the Frenchman Comte (1798–1857), who in a multivolume work developed a position with three important prongs. First, that human knowledge has developed through three stages marked in each case by the distinctive way knowledge was established—the theological or fictitious stage, the metaphysical or abstract stage, and the scientific or positive stage (Comte 1970 p. 1). Clearly, in Comte's view, the third stage is the one which is epistemologically most adequate.

Second, that the "positive sciences" can be classified in a manner which displays their mutual dependence (and which also relates to the order in which they have been developed)—mathematics, astronomy, physics, chemistry, physiology, and social physics (sociology) (Comte 1970 pp. 46–52).

Third, that scientific knowledge "gives up the search after the origin and hidden causes of the universe and a knowledge of the final causes of phenomena" (Comte 1970 p. 2). Instead, science focuses upon observation, and what can be gleaned by reasoning about observed phenomena. (This was his "positive" method.) Here it is clear that Comte was trying—unsuccessfully—to avoid the problem of classic empiricism concerning the status of inferred theoretical entities; by eschewing the search for hidden causes in nature, he worked himself into the same corner as Locke and Hume. Comte may have allowed scientists to reason, but he did not encourage their thoughts to wander too far from the realm of the observable. (For further discussion, see Phillips 1992 Chap. 7.)

Comte's work had a marked impact on late-nineteenth- and early-twentieth-century thought about the nature of the sciences (and especially about the social sciences).

4. Logical Positivism

It is clear that Comte's ideas were strongly empiricist, and that they had an antimetaphysical thrust—as indicated by his refusal to condone the search for "hidden causes" or "final causes." These interrelated elements were taken even further by an interdisciplinary group that formed in the 1920s around Mortiz Schlick in Vienna—a group that became known as the Vienna Circle. Schlick came from physics, Carnap and Waissman from mathematics and philosophy, Neurath from sociology, Godel and Hahn from mathematics, Kraft from history, Frank from physics. Later Reichenbach, Hempel, and Ayer, among others, became associated with the group; Karl Popper was resident in Vienna then, but was a strong critic of their ideas (this is significant, for antipositivists in the educational literature sometimes include Popper among the logical positivists). The early work of Wittgenstein was a great stimulus to the group, especially his "picture theory" of language, according to which the logical structure of meaningful statements must be directly isomorphic with the elements in reality (Wittgenstein 1961).

The group flourished into the 1930s, when the rise of Hitler and the murder of Schlick by a deranged student (who was not prosecuted by the authorities) led to its disbandment; many members took refuge in the English-speaking world. Their ideas became very influential, especially in North America where they shaped the image of the nature of science for several decades: the young Skinner met logical positivism (or logical empiricism, as it was sometimes called) while a graduate student, and his behaviorism clearly bears its stamp (Skinner 1953). The physicist Bridgman also succumbed, and developed his operationism; as a result of his work, the need for researchers to clarify their concepts by means of operational definitions (i.e., by precise specification of the procedures to be used in measuring them) became an item of faith.

Like Comte before them, the logical positivists were strongly antimetaphysical; and to expunge all traces of metaphysical from science they hit upon the strategem of defining metaphysical claims as being meaningless —literally, "nonsensical." To this end they devised the well-known logical positivist verifiability criterion of meaning. This criterion started out being quite simple, but over the years it was complexified as various problems with it were recognized. Its pristine version was as follows: "A statement is held to be literally meaningful if and only if it is either analytic or empirically verifiable" (Ayer 1966 p. 9). Colloquially this can be stated even more directly: "If it can't be seen or measured, it is not meaningful to talk about." The impact of this doctrine was colorfully described by Scriven:

> The Vienna Circle or *Wiener Kreis* was a band of cutthroats that went after the fact burghers of Continental metaphysics who had become intolerably inbred and pompously verbose. The *Kris* is a Malaysian knife, and the *Wiener Kreis* employed a kind of Occam's razor called the verifiability principle. It performed a tracheotomy that made it possible for philosophy to breathe again. (Scriven 1969 p. 195)

As already mentioned, behaviorism and operationism are related forms of this "cutthroat" doctrine in educational research.

Finally, the logical positivists, and fellow travelers such as operationists, needed to give an account of what an acceptable "verification or measurement procedure" was; and although there was much debate over details, the agreed-upon theme—reminiscent of classic Lockeanism—was that verification must be via reduction to basic "sense data."

5. Difficulties of Logical Positivism and Antipositivism

It should be evident that the logical positivists faced the same kinds of problems that confronted all classic empiricists, only they faced these in particularly virulent forms. One additional issue concerns the status of the "verifiability criterion of meaning" itself, for it cannot be shown to be meaningful in the way that it prescribes itself; furthermore, the notion of meaningfulness embodied in this principle seems a truncated and unnecessarily narrow one. Clearly the chief embarrassment for the logical positivists was that their philosophy—which was devised to strengthen science, and to make scientific method more rigorous —actually threatened the existence of key elements of theoretical science. Laws of nature, for example,

cannot be verified in terms of sense experience, for such experience can show at best only that a regularity holds in specific observed cases—experience cannot show that the purported laws hold at all times and in all places (for all times and all places can never be observed). A parallel problem exists with respect to theoretical entities: the sciences have developed theories about realms that are unobservable (the realms of quarks, the conditions inside black holes, the events in the microseconds following the big bang, and so on). It is one thing to say that one does not accept some of these theories as true; but it seems shocking to say that one regards such speculation or theorizing as literally meaningless.

To overcome such problems, many logical positivists were led in antirealist directions; they argued that such theoretical entities as subatomic particles and subnuclear fundamental forces are not to be thought of as real—they have the status of "logical constructions," or "instruments" for making calculations or predictions. Thus, for many positivists, truth and reality were restricted to the domain of the phenomenal, to the realm of sense-experience. And yet the erroneous belief persists among many educational researchers that logical positivists are, quintessentially, realists who believe in "Truth." To cite one example, a well-known contributor to the *Educational Researcher* wrote (in a passage that displays several common misapprehensions): "Philosophers of the positivist school, Carl Hempel and Karl Popper particularly, have posited that propositional statements of lawful relationship are the closest approximations of Truth— whether we are talking about physical matter or human" (Stake 1978 p. 6). (For further examples drawn from the educational literature, see Phillips 1983, and Phillips 1987 Chaps. 4, 8.)

Indeed, it can be argued that many vocal antipositivists are closer than they realize to the spirit of the logical positivists (although, of course, there are significant differences as well)—what unites them is their mutual antirealism.

See also: Research in Education: Epistemological Issues; Research Methodology: Scientific Methods; Research Paradigms in Education

References

Ayer A J 1966 *Language, Truth and Logic*. Gollancz, London

Bridgman P W 1927 *The Logic of Modern Physics*. Macmillan, New York

Comte A 1970 (ed. Ferre F) *Introduction to Positive Philosophy*. Bobbs-Merrill, Indianapolis, Indiana

Feyerabend P 1969 How to be a good empiricist. In: Morick H (ed.) 1980

Guba E (ed.) 1990 *The Paradigm Dialog: Options for Inquiry in the Social Sciences*. Sage, London

Lacey A R 1976 *A Dictionary of Philosophy*. Routledge and Kegan Paul, London

Lakomski G 1991 (ed.) *Int. J. Educ. Res.* 15(6): whole issue

Laudan L 1990 Demystifying underdetermination. In: Savage C W (ed.) 1990 *Scientific Theories*, Minnesota Studies in the Philosophy of Science, XIV. University of Minnesota Press, Minneapolis, Minnesota

Miller S, Fredericks M 1991 Postpositivistic assumptions and educational research: Another view. *Educ. Researcher* 20(4): 2–8

Morick H (ed.) 1980 *Challenges to Empiricism*. Hackett, Indianapolis, Indiana

Phillips D C 1983 After the wake: Postpositivistic educational thought. *Educ. Researcher* 12(5): 4–12

Phillips D C 1987 *Philosophy, Science, and Social Inquiry*.

Pergamon Press, Oxford

Phillips D C 1992 *The Social Scientist's Bestiary*. Pergamon Press, Oxford

Schrag F 1992 In defense of positivist research paradigms. *Educ. Researcher* 21(5): 5–8

Scriven M 1969 Logical positivism and the behavioral sciences. In: Achinstein P, Barker F (eds.) 1969

Skinner B F 1953 *Science and Human Behavior*. Free Press, New York

Stake R 1978 The case study method in social inquiry. *Educ. Researcher* 7(2): 5–8

Wittgenstein L 1961 *Tractatus Logico-Philosophicus*. Routledge and Kegan Paul, London

Postmodernism and Education

J. Marshall and M. Peters

"Postmodernism" is an increasingly used term to describe certain intellectual and cultural tendencies. Its use remains somewhat controversial.

There is a tendency to regard the thought of Immanuel Kant as providing the critical reference point for postmodern perspectives, especially the critique of both narrow versions of reason (including a total identification with scientific reason) and of the autonomous and rational subject. The necessity of Kantian reason is replaced by a view of conventionality and contingency of the rules and criteria of daily speech and action. Against the universality of Kantian reason is pitted a conception of the irreducible plurality of "language games" and "forms of life." Postmodernism, in this sense, is seen to emphasize the discursive character of truth and argument, the "local" character of narrative knowledge, a heterogeneity and cultural variation against the a priori, certainty, universality, and historical invariancy characterizing foundational thought and the search for metaphysical first principles.

The postmodern critique of the rational autonomous subject is also an attack on the Kantian and Hegelian premises of universality, abstractness, autonomy, individuality, and rationality. The postmodern perspective, by contrast, emphasizes the corporeality, the finitude, and the temporality of the human subject.

In this article the ideas of three postmodernist thinkers will be introduced, and the direct implications of their works for education identified. There are also implicit implications, for they discuss knowledge and its legitimation (which is relevant for thinking about the nature of the school curriculum), and there are discussions which bring into question liberal notions of freedom through rational autonomy.

1. Defining the Postmodern

The term "postmodernism" surfaced in the 1930s and 1940s mainly in relation to the arts, including architecture and history (Rose 1991). However, to talk of modernism and postmodernism as periods or epochs implies by itself a modernist stance, namely, that it is possible to delineate the characteristics of a period and, thereby, to be beyond that period. It may be better to see postmodernism as a complex intellectual map of late-twentieth-century thought and practice rather than any clear-cut philosophic, political and/or aesthetic movement.

Is the distinction between the modern and the postmodern a polemical or a philosophical distinction? If it is the latter, and a "Kuhnian"-style paradigm shift is occurring in philosophy and social theory, then some theorists may be "left behind." The paradigm shift question has been formulated and debated by, among others, Lyotard and Habermas. Whereas Lyotard rejoices in the shift away from post-Enlightenment thought and the philosophical "certainty" of meta-narratives, Habermas wishes to preserve what was important in the Enlightenment's view of reason. Jameson begins his foreword to Lyotard (1984) by saying: "[postmodernism] involves a radical break, both with dominant culture and aesthetic, and with a rather different moment of socioeconomic organization against which its structural novelties and innovations are measured: a new social or economic moment (or even system)." Lyotard's (1984) well-known definition is that "postmodern" is an "incredulity towards meta-narratives" (a meta-narrative being a theoretical or justificatory discussion about narratives or "lower level" discourse or practices). It is this sense of the term which will be followed below (see *Research in Education: Epistemological Issues*).

2. Postmodernists

Whilst three French thinkers will be identified as representatives of postmodernism, it should not be assumed either that they are exclusively representatives of postmodernism, or that they share anything in common other than this label (which itself is a modern "object").

2.1 Lyotard and the Postmodern Condition

Lyotard's (1984) major hypothesis maintains that the status of knowledge is altered as societies enter what is known as the postindustrial age and cultures enter what is called the postmodern age. He uses the term "post modern" to describe the condition of knowledge in the most developed societies. He follows sociologists and critics who have used the term to designate the state of Western culture "following the transformations which, since the end of the nineteenth century, have altered the game rules for science, literature and the arts" (1984 p 3). Lyotard places these transformations within the context of the crisis of narratives, especially those Enlightenment meta-narratives concerning meaning and emancipation which have been used to legitimate both the rules of knowledge of the sciences and the foundations of institutions.

By "transformations," Lyotard is referring principally to the effects of the new technologies since the 1950s and their combined impact on the two functions of knowledge—research and the transmission of learning. Significantly, the leading sciences and technologies have all been based on language-related developments—theories of linguistics, cybernetics, informatics, computer languages, telematics, theories of algebra—and their miniaturization and commercialization. In this changed context the status of knowledge is permanently altered: its availability as an international commodity becomes the basis for national, commercial, and military competitive advantage and security. Knowledge has become the principal force of production, changing the composition of the workforce in developed countries. The commercialization of knowledge will further widen the gap between nation-states and the information-rich multinationals, thereby raising new legal, ethical, political, and educational problems.

2.2 The Legitimation of Knowledge

As knowledge becomes a question of government, the problem of legitimation necessarily arises: who decides what is "true" or "scientific"? The postmodernist maintains that knowledge and power are simply two sides of the same question. The problem of legitimation is highlighted with a recognition of the crises of narratives and specifically the inability of the sciences to legitimate themselves by reference to the grand narrative of philosophy. Postmodernism is characterized by an incredulity towards meta-narratives—a distrust of stories which purport to justify certain practices or institutions by grounding them upon a set of transcendental, ahistorical, or universal principles. The postmodern concept of knowledge begins with skepticism about the rules of consensus: that the truth value of a statement between the sender and addressee is acceptable if there is unanimity between rational minds. The crisis of narratives is symbolized in the postmodern dispersal of language elements. There is no universal meta-language, for there are many languages—a multiplicity of language games each with specific pragmatic valencies. Lyotard's reading of Wittgenstein emphasizes the pluralistic and incommensurable nature of language games, each with its body of rules defining its properties and uses (Lyotard 1988). There is an agonistics of language in which utterances are understood not as the transmission of information or messages, but rather as an unstable exchange between communicational adversaries. The rules do not have a bedrock justification; they are the object of a contract between players. If there are no rules, there is no game. Every utterance is a "move" in the game where to speak is to fight (in the sense of playing). Progress in knowledge is conceived of in two ways: the first is construed as a new move within the established rules; the second is construed as the invention of new rules, that is, the development of a new game.

This basic conflict model of language, then, challenges the rules of consensus—not only as it underlies the Enlightenment narrative of the hero of knowledge working towards good ethico-political ends, but also contemporary accounts of the fully transparent communicational society as advanced by Habermas, on the basis of the ideal speech community, where validity claims are said to be discursively redeemable at the level of discourse. The conflict model is ultimately used for understanding the nature of the social bond: everyone lives at the intersection of many games.

The interpretation of language games as heteronomous (untranslatable) and paralogous (undermining rules) shatters the grand legitimating meta-narrative of science as the supreme voice of reason. Science is not only incapable of legitimating other language games but is incapable of legitimating itself, and metaphysical philosophy is forced to relinquish its role as legitimizer in face of the proliferation and splintering of language games. The idea of modernity, of science as the exemplification of rationality, is revealed as just one narrative among others—the grand narrative, but one which has broken apart and splintered into many different forms.

In the postmodern age, however, decision makers still proceed on the assumption that there is commensurability and that the whole is determinable. The legitimation of knowledge and of practices is formulated in terms of performativity. Increasingly, science has fallen under the sway of another game, technology, whose goal is not truth, but optimal performance, and whose criteria are minimizing input and maximizing output, rather than truth or justice. Increasingly performativity is being applied to practices and social institutions in new forms of managerialism. Research and progress in knowledge are relegitimated in terms of the performative or efficiency criterion (Lyotard 1993).

2.3 Michel Foucault

Foucault attempts to avoid the trap of thinking in terms of epochs by viewing Enlightenment (following Kant) as an attitude. While he did not care much for the term, "modernity" for him refers to a form of "post-Enlightenment slumber" whereby Kant's notion of modernity as an attitude has been reified into a certain view of humankind—the version of human nature to be found in the social sciences—and also into a certain view of rationality (post Descartes, Rousseau, and Kant). On these issues, and in his associated treatment of governmentality, Foucault (1979b) presents a dark face of the Enlightenment and the path it has taken.

Foucault (1984) believed that by following Kant's attitude and critically interrogating the present, there is a way out. He does not accept the Enlightenment view of the improvement of human beings through the advancement of reason, for he rejects the form that reason has taken. In his first major book (1961), he launches an attack upon Western reason—and on Descartes in particular, arguing that by excluding madness in the *Meditations*, Descartes has attempted to confine reason, thereby limiting the potential of the imagination (see also Foucault 1986c), and limiting creativity and freedom.

Nevertheless, Foucault maintains that there is no universal form that reason must take. Rather, there are multiplicities of reason, and multiplicities of theories in relation to specific local issues. If there are no metanarratives, in this sense, then the role of intellectuals must be local and specific (see 1972a). Yet, Foucault believes, Kant was correct in urging that theory must be critical. Slumber was caused by a failure to continually respond to socio-historical conditions and failure to question the development of responses to human dilemmas through the critical questioning of the application of universal reason. Hence a source of his objections to Marxism and Sartre, for example.

Rather than reason unfolding, Foucault the archeologist would say (1972b), arbitrary formations of discourse—especially those which he designates as the human sciences—have frozen Kant's notion of an unfolding freedom and everyone has become embroiled in a senseless dynamic of power (modern power or bio-power) which continues to dominate and subjugate them as human beings (1979b). These arbitrary discourses are the result of the breakdown of the notion of language as representation (1970) and its dispersion and fragmentation. To be modern is to attempt to control this dispersion and fragmentation. Yet Foucault takes no general stand (1970 p. 307).

The human being, as the knowing subject and the object of knowledge of the human sciences, was, according to Foucault, permitted to emerge by the decline of the classical regime (at the end of the eighteenth century). Foucault believes that the modern individual has in part been "constructed" by techniques of examination, measurement, and categorization in disciplinary blocs by professionals in the human sciences; so individuals are normalized, that is, they become beings who lead useful, docile, and practical lives because they are politically dominated or subjugated (1979a).

Modern individuals also construct themselves through care of the self (Foucault 1980, 1986a, 1986b). The way out is to reject the "truths" of the human sciences in care of the self, thereby promoting forms of freedom different from the morally autonomous person of Kant and modern pedagogy. This is an aesthetic attitude towards personal identity. Foucault is not rejecting modernity *simpliciter*, but only those practices and discourses within the Enlightenment tradition that he calls "humanism" (as against Habermas's interpretation of a total rejection).

Foucault has been criticized for not providing norms for distinguishing between dominating and nondominating forms of power/discourse. On Foucault's grounds, it is only possible to distinguish intensity of domination and, lacking some normative stance, it is unclear when resistance is the proper ethical or political path to adopt. Furthermore, with no normative stance, it is not clear how one can engage the complex problems of modern societies. If, indeed, one can resist oppressive forms of power, this is not to give insight into the ways in which the problems and issues which resulted in such exercises of power can be resolved.

2.4 Derrida and Deconstructionism

Deconstruction begins by questioning the almost received assumption that "philosophy" is a superior kind of truth, especially in relation to literature. This claim can be traced to Plato and his attack upon poetry as a form of irrational seizure (Norris 1983 p. 1). It denies that philosophy has a privileged access to truth which literature does not, or which literature can only pervert or destroy. It is not, however, a mere traditional defense as mounted, for example, by Shelley, for these also are undermined by deconstructionism.

Hermeneutics goes beyond the foundationalism of Kantian epistemology (especially the privileged position of speaker and/or author) to claim that understanding involves an interpretation. Deconstruction claims that any system of thought is itself based upon contradictions. "Any reading" must therefore be capable of multiple and contradictory readings. Thus texts do not just say "something" but many different things, some of which may be contrary to the writer's intentions. Texts do not have meanings which can be "read off"; for the traditional relationship between text and meaning is severed, and Derrida's deconstruction shows that the text can tell a different, new story (see *Hermeneutics*).

Derrida stressed how different his position was from hermeneutics and used the term "grammatology" to capture this difference. His critical readings of texts—and of philosophy in general (1982)—were designed to bring out the underlying contradictions that undermine the apparent coherence of texts and philosophical systems. Following Nietzsche, he rejected binary logic (the principles of identity and noncontradiction) and read philosophy as a history of certain oppositions privileging one side of the binary opposition and establishing a "violent hierarchy" and "order of subordination." This hierarchy must be overturned, he felt, but not in a simple valorization of the opposing pole.

Derrida's starting points (1981a, 1981b) are basic words which have different and opposed meanings and syntactic contexts in which one of the meanings is not unequivocally eliminated. Because "the" meaning cannot be determined from the context this opens up a play of possibilities of different and contrary readings of the text. Thereby texts are deconstructed. Foucault (1983) criticized Derrida for ignoring social practices that texts employ and reflect.

Derrida, along with Foucault and Lyotard, sees the traditional metaphysic of Western philosopy as being at an end. It is not so clear that he sees philosophy per se as being ended, but he certainly concentrates on the periphery of traditional philosophy (1982), on metaphor and rhetoric, rather than the central logical and epistemological concerns within the tradition. Along with Foucault, he attacks the humanistic notion of humankind central to phenomenology, existentialism, and some versions of Marxism.

3. Educational Implications

Foucault's critique of the human sciences directs the attention toward how education shapes individual subjects, normalizing them through the exercise of power/knowledge in disciplinary blocs. There are strong implications here for issues related to gender and education. Foucault provides a sharp critique of the notion of the morally autonomous person and of the roles of educational professionals in shaping identities. He directs attention at the use of power in education, rather than taking the traditional liberal approach to notions of social control and control of knowledge through discussions of authority (Marshall 1996). He provides a basis for analyzing the relations between truth and power in educational discourse and discursive practices (see Foucault 1983).

Lyotard's critique also covers the natural sciences. His account of knowledge and its changed form of legitimation has implications for education, for it will change the ways in which learning is acquired,

stored, assessed, and classified. Learning, no longer entirely falling within the purview of the state, will be geared toward the production of knowledge to be sold. Knowledge is exteriorized with respect to the "knower," and the status of the learner and teacher is transformed into a commodity relationship of "supplier" and "consumer." Knowledge ceases to be an end in itself. On the basis of Lyotard's critiques, theorists would want to identify the main meta-narratives in education and the ways in which they have excluded local knowledge.

Derrida poses questions about the curriculum—and curriculum priorities—with his emphases on literature, rhetoric, and metaphor, rather than logic, mathematics, and the priority of the senses for knowledge and understanding.

All three writers emphasize the plurality of reason, the demise of grand totalizing theory, and the march of modern power and technocratic rationality.

An effect of the march of technocratic rationality has been a crisis of value. Conservatives have attempted to reassert traditional values in education, as elsewhere, blaming postmodernist tendencies for this crisis. Postmodernism, however, would merely assert that values cannot be legitimated by meta-narratives, not that there are no values to be held.

See also: Critical Discourse Analysis; Phenomenology and Existentialism

References

Derrida J 1981b *Dissemination*. Athlone Press, London
Derrida J 1981a (trans. Bass A) *Positions*. Chicago University Press, Chicago, Illinois
Foucault M 1961 *Folie et Deraison: l'histoire de la folie a l'age classique*. Plon, Paris
Foucault M 1970 *The Order of Things*. Tavistock Publications, London
Foucault M 1972a Intellectuals and power. In: Foucault M, Bouchard D (eds.) 1972 *Language, Counter-Memory, Practice*. Cornell University Press, Ithaca, New York
Foucault M 1972b *The Archaeology of Knowledge*. Tavistock, London
Foucault M 1979a *Discipline and Punishment: The Birth of the Prison*. Penguin Books, Harmondsworth
Foucault M 1979b On governmentality. *Ideology and Consciousness* 6: 5–26
Foucault M 1980 *The History of Sexuality*, Vol. 1. Vintage, New York
Foucault M 1983 Afterword: The subject and power. In: Dreyfus H L, Rabinow P (eds.) 1983 *Michel Foucault: Beyond Structuralism and Hermeneutics*. University of Chicago Press, Chicago, Illinois
Foucault M 1984 What is enlightenment? In: Rabinow P (ed.) 1984 *The Foucault Reader*. Pantheon, New York
Foucault M 1986a *The Use of Pleasure*. Penguin, Harmondsworth
Foucault M 1986b *The Care of the Self*. Penguin, Harmondsworth
Foucault M 1986c Introduction to Binswanger Ludwig 1986

Dream and Existence. Review of Existential Psychology and Psychiatry

Habermas J 1981 Modernity versus postmodernity. *New German Critique* 22: 3–14

Lyotard J-F 1984 *The Post Modern Condition: A Report on Knowledge.* University of Minnesota Press, Minneapolis, Minnesota

Lyotard J-F 1988 *The Differend.* Manchester University Press, Manchester

Lyotard J-F 1993 *Political Writings.* UCL Press, London

Marshall J 1996 *Michel Foucault: Personal Autonomy and Education.* Kluwer, Dordrecht

Norris C 1983 *The Deconstructive Turn: Essays in the Rhetoric of Philosophy.* Methuen, London

Rose M A 1991 *The Post Modern and the Post Industrial.* Cambridge University Press, Cambridge

Further Reading

Derrida J 1963 Cogito and the history of madness. In: Derrida J (ed.) 1978 *Writing and Difference.* University of Chicago Press, Chicago, Illinois

Derrida J 1977 *Of Grammatology.* Johns Hopkins University Press, Baltimore, Maryland

Eribon D 1991 *Michel Foucault.* Harvard University Press, Cambridge, Massachusetts

Foucault M 1971 *The Discourse on Language.* In: Foucault M (ed.) 1972b

Hoy D C (ed.) 1986 *Foucault: A Critical Reader.* Basil Blackwell, Oxford

McLaren P (ed.) 1991 Post-modernism, post-colonialism and pedagogy. *Educ. Soc.* 9(2): special issue, parts I and II

Nicholson L (ed.) 1990 *Post-Modernism/Feminism.* Routledge and Kegan Paul, London

Peters M 1966 *Poststructuralism, Politics and Education.* Bergin and Garvey, New York

Peters M (ed.) 1995 *Education and the Postmodern Condition.* Foreword by J-F Lyotard. Bergin and Garvey, New York

Peters M (ed.) 1997 *Naming the Multiple: Poststructuralism and Education.* Bergin and Garvey, New York

Peters M, Marshall J 1992 Beyond the philosophy of the subject: Liberalism, education and the critique of individualism. *Educ. Phil. Theor.* 25(1): 19–39

Reproduction Theory

R. Teese

Reproduction theory arose in the 1960s and 1970s in response to the failure of mass systems of secondary education in Europe to achieve greater social equality. Previously the failure of children from lower status backgrounds had been interpreted in terms of individual differences in intelligence, language, or motivation. Attention had been paid mainly to the presenting characteristics of children, rather than to the operation of schools as institutions. With reproduction theory, the focus shifted to the teaching relationship, the use of language, unstated expectations about learning style and achievement at home, and the influence of implicit models of "good" and "bad" pupils.

1. The Historical Context

Reproduction theory takes its name from a number of highly influential works published in the 1960s by the French sociologists, Pierre Bourdieu and Jean-Claude Passeron—in particular, *Les héritiers: les étudiants et la culture* (1964) and *La reproduction: éléments pour une théorie du système d'enseignement* (1970). Both works have been widely translated, *The Inheritors* in five languages, *Reproduction* in nine languages, including Japanese. The earlier work is perhaps the most accessible.

In *The Inheritors* the authors document the extent of social inequality in contemporary French higher education. In the early 1960s the child of an agricultural laborer in France had less than one chance in 100 of reaching university as compared to a 60 percent chance for the children of senior managers and upper professionals, such as doctors, lawyers, and architects.

With changes in economic structures and in business organization, all social groups were coming to depend increasingly on formal education to protect inherited wealth and position, to achieve status advancement, or simply to maintain basic economic security (Bourdieu *La distinction* 1979 pp. 145–88; English translation 1984 pp. 125–68).

Success at school was thus crucial for all groups, though much more likely for the upper middle classes. The question of why children from these backgrounds were more effective in using school needs to be examined.

2. Social Class and Culture

While recognizing the importance of economic factors connected with class position—income, living conditions, resources for study, time, and physical constraints—Bourdieu and Passeron argue that cultural differences are more important. In *The Inheritors* (1964) the authors identify two major ways in which educational opportunities were constrained or enhanced by cultural factors linked to social class.

Family attitudes, values, and experiences were well-documented influences on the likelihood of a child succeeding at school. In France the organization of the secondary school curriculum into a hierarchy of streams or tracks, at the apex of which stood Latin and Greek, provided a framework for families (and teachers) to interpret what was relevant and appropriate for the individual child. This framework shaped educational and occupational expectations, provided a standard for assessing achievement and potential, and acted as the basis for planning either a long-term career in education or a more or less truncated interlude before work.

While the curriculum framework of classical, modern, and practical streams was part of school as an institution, it also articulated basic differences in lifestyle. Families used this framework to interpret the signs of failure at school or to raise their expectations according to an institutional grading of possibilities. Thus the cultural model of the bright working-class boy included the choice of Latin, which signified a major and exceptional step forward for his family into learned culture. More fundamental, however, was the work of the family in inculcating different attitudes to learning and different learning styles, depending on social position. In *Reproduction* a strong emphasis is placed on these differences as laying the basis for subsequent achievement in school.

In upper middle-class families, the teaching process within the home took the form of initiating the child into a world of important distinctions (*La distinction* Chap. 3). In art, music, literature, food, in fact in all fields of cultural consumption, discernment and good taste were essential. The ability to make sound distinctions by reference to an appropriate standard—an academic authority, a recognized journal—constituted the outward mark of membership of a social group, and had to be cultivated from the beginning. Through the pedagogical work of the family, a predisposition was established in the child to pursue learning as the basis of personal distinction and to view knowledge in an academic way as the creation and celebration of distinctions. The terms "cultural ethos" and later "habitus" were used to describe this intellectual predisposition, the most important manifestation of which was the use of language.

3. Language Differences

To examine the importance of language as a source of cultural advantage, Bourdieu and his colleagues studied the teaching relationship in French higher education and in particular the efficiency of communication between teachers and students in faculties of arts. The results of this study are reported in the monograph, *Rapport pédagogique et communication* (Bourdieu et al. 1965; English translation 1993), and also extensively in *The Inheritors* (Bourdieu

and Passeron 1964) and *Reproduction* (Bourdieu and Passeron 1970).

First-year students displayed marked differences in their knowledge of scholastic vocabularies, technical terms, and most strikingly the language of their own lecturers. Learning in universities took place in a context of "linguistic miscomprehension," with many students proving unable to explain key terms and concepts employed by their teachers. The language of communication was quite inefficient. It was adapted more to emulating academic form and style than to reporting and verifying accurately student comprehension.

The code of communication was rhetorical. As such it favored young people from upper middle-class backgrounds in whom an "aristocratic" orientation to language use had been cultivated. Students from white-collar and manual working-class backgrounds displayed a different kind of approach to language—studious rather than refined, prudent rather than confident, and lacking style. In writing essays or answering examination questions, they more often aimed at a naïve exposure of their knowledge, rather than seeking personal distinction through an elegant and assertive style as displayed by upper middle-class students.

The cultivation of a particular disposition to learn is central to Bourdieu and Passeron's arguments about the origins of educational inequality. Language training is the core of the family's pedagogical work, and the type of language patterns laid down by the family determine how far away in cultural terms a child will be from school, or how close.

> Language is not simply an instrument of communication: it also provides, together with a richer or poorer vocabulary, a more or less complex system of categories, so that the capacity to decipher and manipulate complex structures, whether logical or aesthetic, depends partly on the language transmitted by the family. (Bourdieu and Passeron 1977 p. 73)

The language facility of children brought up in well-educated homes represents part of their "cultural capital." Using the term "capital" underlines the importance, not only of language as a resource capable of profitable investment, but of school as a market on the lookout for resources and driven by expectations about their quality or potential. Cultural capital includes both "linguistic capital" and other forms of knowledge built up by the family in a variety of domains and which represent so many years of investment in the child.

While documenting language differences among students who had survived the long process of selection and elimination during primary and secondary education, Bourdieu and Passeron—referring to the seminal work of the English sociolinguist, Basil Bernstein (1971)—emphasize that the early years of school are crucial.

Of all the cultural obstacles, those which arise from the language spoken at home are without doubt the most serious and the most insidious, especially during the first years of schooling, when comprehension and manipulation of words are the focus of teacher judgement. (Bourdieu 1966 pp. 329–30)

A particularly telling illustration of class differences in orientation to language use is given in *Reproduction*. Students were asked to define the word *gérophagie*. Those from lower status backgrounds were willing to admit ignorance or attempted a definition timidly and with carefully worded reservations. This behavior contrasted sharply with the approach adopted by upper-class students from Paris, who were bold and categorical, and who exploited to the full their background knowledge of Greek and Latin. Though the word did not exist, they quickly and confidently established a meaning for it.

The best results on the battery of language tests administered by Bourdieu and his team were achieved by students who studied the classical languages in secondary school. This result confirmed the basic argument put forward by the researchers on the origins of educational inequality.

Initial advantages in cultural capital and cultural ethos, both linked to social class, are rewarded by schools and are decisive at the key turning points in a child's school career, especially allocation to curriculum stream—"the disadvantage attached to social origin is primarily mediated by educational channelling and streaming" (Bourdieu and Passeron 1970 p. 106). Schools act as relays. Cultural capital is progressively translated into scholastic capital—marks, school record, qualifications, prizes—and scholastic capital controls access to the most profitable parts of the curriculum in school and the most prestigious institutions of higher education.

4. Teachers and Teaching

The translation of cultural capital into scholastic capital could not occur except through the medium of teacher judgment and the particular nature of the teaching relationship in the academic secondary school.

Again the social and institutional context needs to be taken into account to appreciate the role of teachers in the conversion of cultural capital into academic success. Secondary-school teachers in France have traditionally been drawn from an elite of highly successful pupils. They mastered a series of selective public examinations, were trained in prestigious establishments, and qualified through the *agrégation* to teach, not only in secondary schools, but in higher education as well. The *lycée* was very closely aligned to the universities and the *grandes écoles* (elite higher professional schools). It was through the teachers who taught in the *lycées*—the *agrégés*—that the intellectual and cultural expectations and demands of higher education were communicated downward to aspiring pupils.

In a highly selective system, the role of the *professeur* was to cultivate the underlying talents or "gifts" of the prized elite under his or her charge. Teaching took the form of evoking the latent powers of the pupil, drawing upon the store of interests and tastes, and literary, artistic, logical and mathematical skills already accumulated in the child through the cultural universe of his or her family. As a former successful pupil, the teacher's task was really to rediscover and to relive his or her own history by arousing and developing the talents of his or her pupils. At the upper levels of the *lycée*—especially the post-*baccalauréat* classes preparing for admission to the *grandes écoles*—the teacher's role was essentially to co-opt into the *corps professoriel* the most gifted and brilliant students. It was the responsibility of the teacher to select the best (the *élite*) and immense pride was taken in a duty which was nothing less than the celebration of humanistic culture.

This was the institutional and cultural framework which, in the 1960s, was besieged by the mounting social demand for secondary and higher education. Secondary teachers were being asked to completely transform their role from inspiring, charismatic representative of an aristocratic culture to master of rational and methodical communication, accessible to the most diverse and unprepared populations. The nearest professional equivalent to this democratic role was the primary school teacher (*instituteur*), whose social status, training, and whole outlook differed totally from those of the *professeur*.

Seen in this perspective, the more secondary teachers sought to fulfill their task, to devote themselves to their work, to invest themselves completely in its moral and spiritual significance, the more they would tend to exclude and reject students whose social background, culture, and communication skills differed from their own. Rather than implying any conspiracy on the part of teachers to defend the social order, their conservatism lay in the fullness and explicitness with which they lived their role as awakeners and illuminators of moral reason and intellectual sensibility. The freer they were to pursue this role through all the institutional and social pillars which safeguarded the operation of the *lycée*, the more selection would tend to be severe and socially biased.

It would be too much to expect secondary teachers to abandon the traditional teaching relationship on which their own success as past pupils had been built and to adopt the methodical and didactic ways of the *instituteur*. To create talent through teaching efficiency, rather than arousing and cultivating pre-existing gifts, would imply that those past pupils who had distinguished themselves—and who had often become teachers in their turn—could have been part of a more numerous crowd, but for the hazards of teaching practice. Their success would then appear to be founded on the way institutions worked, including underlying cultural biases, rather than on their innate talents.

Teachers could not adopt a fundamentally different approach to teaching without surrendering the theory that they themselves had been successful as pupils thanks to the "discovery" of their talents by their teachers. Any shift to an explicit methodology would simultaneously expose the issue of how they themselves had learnt and basically how much their success owed to their family background and social advantages, rather than to purely individual qualities and innate "gifts."

5. Academic Autonomy and Reproduction

It is against this background that Bourdieu and Passeron argue that schools reproduce social inequalities, not through deliberate manipulative practices or through overtly antidemocratic bias on the part of teachers, but rather by striving conscientiously to do what they are good at.

The search for the "gifted," conducted through the traditional teaching relationship, did not exclude the new nontraditional populations entering the secondary schools in the 1950s and 1960s primarily through formal mechanisms of ability grouping and "streaming" or "tracking." On the contrary, these selection practices were themselves based upon and simply articulated and made official the underlying relationship of cultural distance separating the *professeur* from lower middle-class and working-class pupils.

Institutional segregation through subject streams ("classical," "modern," "practical"), or relegation into separate establishments, such as vocational training schools, were important in implementing the verdict of professorial judgment. This judgment was based on the continual manifestation of cultural distance, above all in the form of pupils' language use and orientation. More fundamentally, the way in which children used language reflected a deep division in behavioral expectations. Implicitly teachers expected a display, not simply of grammatically correct speech and an impressive vocabulary, but of a personality projected through speech, where the qualities of speech established the presence of a distinctive cast of mind, the child able to externalize his or her spirit (or "potential") through the objective medium of artistically and intellectually controlled speech.

Thus, while Bourdieu and Passeron argue that "the disadvantage linked to social origin is primarily relayed by academic streaming (*orientations scolaires*)" (Bourdieu and Passeron 1970 p. 106)—and their attention to these mechanisms is often ignored by their critics—structure acquires its importance only thanks to deeper cultural advantages established through the teaching relationship itself. To the extent that teachers strive only to achieve the best in their pupils, which amounts to re-establishing the history of their own relationship to the best in culture ("aristocratic," learned, or academic culture), they will tend to reward the advantages of cultured family background and to penalize children who can acquire "culture" only through school. Teachers' commitment to discovering the best—an apparently meritocratic project —leads mainly to rediscovering the cultural best, and thus to conferring upon an aristocracy of culture the meritocratic crown of academic best.

6. Cultural Demands of Schooling

This assessment of the ways in which schools reward cultural advantages and thus play a socially conservative role was developed during the 1960s, when mass systems of secondary education in Europe had not yet been fully established. Because reproduction theory focuses on underlying processes of cultural selection, both in family background and in school, it is of great relevance in understanding the phenomena of social inequality which characterize the systems of the 1980s and 1990s when most children complete school.

Success in the academic curriculum of secondary school requires children to recognize and satisfy a range of intellectual and behavioral expectations which are foreign to the family culture and community of the majority of them. The notions of "cultural capital" and "cultural ethos" relate to these demands on how children should interpret the use of language and the functions of communication in the classroom, how they should view school work and the role of the teacher, and the place which school learning should occupy in their public and private lives.

According to the expectations of teachers, scholarship should become the objective medium through which the child establishes his or her identity and which governs the child's relationship with the world of others. Beyond the acquisition of school knowledge comes a scholarly orientation toward cultural life as a whole and the recognition of "legitimate culture"— learned culture and its extensions (such as film and photography). To enter this world of cultural distinctions, good taste, and erudition, the child has to meet demands in the classroom which are fashioned on the unstated assumption that his or her family already occupies the particular social space in which these distinctions are a way of life.

Besides the ability to manipulate language in complex ways, the "good pupil" in the course of his or her school career needs to fulfill other, more diffuse intellectual requirements—to appreciate properties of form and structure (e.g., literary form as against narrative content); to recognize the theoretical dimensions of a problem (implying distance and abstract hypothetical reasoning, the testing of assumptions, the recognition of implications, etc.); to manage symbolic and technical language (e.g., mathematical notation); to establish perspectives on a problem by supplanting personal reactions in favor of academic authorities.

These demands on intellectual behavior saturate the academic curriculum and impose other, more overt physical and mental pressures and conditions—the need to concentrate for long hours, to be well-organized, to be personally confident and secure, and to be free of excessive family stress and personal anxiety.

To be shaped as an instrument of cultural consumption, with the teacher as the master craftsman, requires the pupil to be made of the right material. Inculcating a basic disposition towards learning (a "habitus") requires the germ of this feeling to be already present.

From the perspective of the intellectual demands made upon the child in order to acquire this outlook through school, the curriculum takes on the features of an arbitrary imposition. Bourdieu and Passeron use the term "cultural arbitrary" to describe a set of expectations which the working-class child is implicitly meant to satisfy, but which are foreign to his or her way of life. Imposed on family and child, who are penalized for failure and often driven out of the system, they amount to a form of "symbolic violence" in which particular ways of seeing and communicating, in which values and associations foreign to the work of schools, are forcibly repressed through the discipline of learning.

7. Origins of Change

In describing how the traditional teaching relationship tends to lock out new populations, Bourdieu and Passeron do not imply that no change can or does occur. The process of cultural reproduction through schooling takes place in the context of major economic and social changes which throw into relief the rigidities of the education system, while at the same time they challenge and weaken established perceptions and practices.

Reproduction implies ongoing tension and adjustment, by no means smooth and functional, in which individuals and families have to develop strategies either for conserving advantages bestowed on them by past generations or for establishing interests and claims never asserted by their forebears.

The "inheritors" do not have their inheritance guaranteed by a hidden hand of social determinism. They have to work to secure their inheritance because they, too, are exposed to selection. Indeed, Bourdieu and Passeron show how strategies such as the use of private schools or enrollment in the less academically esteemed disciplines in French universities—like sociology (Bourdieu and Passeron 1970 p. 122)—are responses to failure in privileged families, where failure should not occur if a strict social determinism applied. Conversely, working-class and lower middle-class children can and do succeed, thanks to particular advantages of background or "counter handicaps."

If teachers appear locked into an inherently conservative project, based on their own success as past pupils and on their social role as repositories of the humanistic tradition, the institutional framework of mass secondary schooling has profoundly altered the context in which the project of selecting an elite can be executed. Past certainties, buttressed by overt segregation of populations in a clearly defined hierarchy of institutions, have been greatly undermined.

As the period of effective compulsory schooling has been extended upward to the end of secondary school and draws in all population groups, the pressure increases for the *professeur* to become the *instituteur*. At the same time both the social origins and personal experiences (including political and cultural life) of a once-elite professorial corps are changing. New teachers display less distance in social and cultural terms from their pupils than they themselves typically experienced toward their own teachers.

Bourdieu and Passeron argue that teaching needs to shift in a fundamental way toward a methodology in which intellectual demands and learning criteria are made explicit. Assessment practices need to reflect what is actually taught. Students need to be trained in the techniques of intellectual and scholarly work. This demand for a rational teaching methodology in which the aim is to create "talent" (rather than seeking to discover it) would seem to have found a supportive environment, if not in the actual working conditions of teachers—burdened by past structures, often poor resources, and continuing conflict over goals—at least in their own biographies and in the biographies of their parents.

8. Importance of Reproduction Theory

Reproduction theory arose as the first efforts in the postwar era to democratize secondary education were shown to be failing. Much contemporary research, including the early work of Bernstein (1971), sought to explain this by documenting cultural deficiencies in working-class children. This extremely important work was conducted, however, within a "provider perspective." It tended to take for granted the intellectual expectations which schools, as the providers of education, made on all pupils, irrespective of their backgrounds.

With the writings of Bourdieu and Passeron, a major shift occurs from the "provider perspective" to the "client perspective." From the point of view of the families and children seeking to access secondary education, the school's implicit expectations on language training in the home, on scholastic orientation, and on cultural capital amount to a "culturally arbitrary system" which inevitably disadvantages them.

In exposing the provider perspective on educational inequality as part of the process of social reproduction itself, Bourdieu and Passeron contributed to a major redirection in research away from the psychology of individual differences (where the "client" is the problem) to the sociology of knowledge (where the "provider" of education becomes central to the problem).

This change is exemplified above all in the sociology of the curriculum. Once taken for granted as an institutional given, the curriculum is now recognized as the decisive link in the construction of relationships between class and culture. How the curriculum is established and conserved as the legitimate body of school knowledge, the divergence between economic and social imperatives in the definition of school knowledge, how regimes of scholastic assessment and selection are maintained in the face of persistent social and gender inequalities in success and failure have become major avenues of investigation since the 1970s and represent the maturing of the sociology of education as an independent, scholarly discipline.

See also: Contemporary Sociological Theories of Education; Curriculum: Sociological Perspectives; Family, School, and Cultural Capital; Resistance Theory; Sociology of Education: An Overview

References

Bernstein B 1971 *Class, Codes and Control.* Routledge and Kegan Paul, London

Bourdieu P 1966 L'école conservatrice. Les inégalités devant l'école et devant la culture. *Revue française de sociologie* 7(3): 325–47 [1974 *Contemporary Research in the Sociology of Education.* Methuen, London]

Bourdieu P 1979 *La distinction: critique sociale du jugement.* Les Editions de Minuit, Paris [1984 *Distinction. A Social Critique of the Judgement of Taste.* Harvard University Press, Cambridge, Massachusetts]

Bourdieu P, Passeron J-C 1964 *Les héritiers: les étudiants et la culture.* Les Editions de minuit, Paris [1979 *The Inheritors. French Students and Their Relation to Culture.* University of Chicago Press, Chicago, Illinois]

Bourdieu P, Passeron J-C, De Saint Martin M 1965 *Rapport pédagogique et communication.* Mouton, Paris [1993 *Academic Discourse.* Polity Press, Cambridge]

Bourdieu P, Passeron J-C 1970 *La reproduction: elements pour une théorie du système d'enseignement.* Les Editions de Minuit, Paris [1977 *Reproduction in Education, Society and Culture.* Sage, London]

Further Reading

Bourdieu P 1989 *La noblesse d'E[ac]tat. Grandes Ecoles et esprit de corps.* Les Editions de Minuit, Paris

Bourdieu P, Wacquant L J D 1992 *An Invitation to Reflexive Sociology.* University of Chicago Press, Chicago, Illinois

Harker R, Maher C, Wilkes C (eds.) 1991 *An Introduction to the Work of Pierre Bourdieu: The Practice of Theory.* MacMillan, Basingstoke

Robbins D 1991 *The Work of Pierre Bourdieu: Recognizing Society.* Open University Press, Milton Keynes

Resistance Theory

M. G. McFadden and J. C. Walker

Any account of schooling outcomes has to take into consideration the dynamic relationship between students' cultural background and the society of which they are a part. Resistance theory is a valuable but limited attempt to explain the effects of schooling on individuals and society.

Three things stand out about the use of "resistance" in contemporary educational discussion. First, talk of resistance in education has become very popular. Second, there is confusion about the use of the term "resistance." There is no one consistent body of theory or research in which there is a clear understanding of what constitutes resistance. Third, therefore, given both the fashion and the confusion, the status of "resistance theory" remains problematic.

The term "resistance" and the development of resistance theory have to be understood in an historical context. Initially this comprised attempts in the sociology and political economy of education to explain the outcomes of schooling, specifically the inequality of achievement of students with different social class, race, ethnic, and gender backgrounds. What is now often referred to as "resistance theory" has in large part emerged as a reaction against an earlier view, "reproduction theory." These two views reflect distinct, albeit not entirely coherent, approaches to explaining how the members of different social groups respond to and are affected by schooling.

In general terms, reproduction theory suggests that schools contribute quite straightforwardly to the maintenance of the status quo, by reproducing the existing relationships between social groups and between their cultures. Thus, for example, schools serve to produce educational outcomes in which the children of working-class parents remain in the working class, and those of the middle class stay in the same class as their parents.

Resistance theory suggests that if such "reproduction" occurs it is not at all straightforward, and that students in fact resist the demands, pressures, and offers of schools. It is problematic whether the result of this resistance is that they escape from the social structures and cultural patterns in which they are presently located, or whether despite or even because of their resistance to school finish up in the same location. However, at least resistance theory tries to address the question of change.

In this entry, the movement from a focus on reproduction to a focus on resistance is examined, and it is argued that although resistance theory is an advance on reproduction theory, it is still an inadequate viewpoint. This is because to the extent that the theory picks out and explains actual behavior in schools, it does not tend to pick up the kind of behavior which is likely to lead to a change in the lives of individuals and in the social relationships of groups. There is a need to move beyond the limited perspectives summed up under both "reproduction" and "resistance," and to focus on individuals and groups as creative agents capable of transcending both social "structures" and cultures. In other words, a more dynamic theory of individual, social, and cultural change is needed, a theory which enables the understanding of what needs to be changed in school curriculum, pedagogy, and organization to bring about better and fairer social outcomes for students.

1. Reproduction Theory

During the 1970s, radical educational theorists drew attention to the apparent failure of liberal educational reform to bring about structural changes in society which would produce more equitable distributions of wealth and power. Marxist explanations of social and economic inequality, arguing that the school either did not or could not contribute to the elimination of inequality and injustice, became popular. Schools reflected the class structure of society, either directly in their own structures, or more subtly and indirectly through the ideologies on which they were based and which they instilled in students. Thus theories of ideology have been consistently associated with reproduction theory, as they have with resistance theory.

A major source of thinking about ideology was the work of the French Marxist philosopher Althusser (1971). Influenced by French structuralism, particularly the work of Bachelard, Althusser saw individuals as the effects of structures which were held together by ideology, which for Althusser is a set of practices embodying understandings of social relations as well as cultural symbols. In this overwhelmingly deterministic view, structure, through ideology, forms the individual. Althusser's work was influential in the sociology of education, particularly in the United Kingdom. Although it is a clear example of reproduction theory, some resistance theorists, such as Giroux (1983), have persisted with elements of the Althusserian theory of ideology (see also Giroux and McLaren 1994).

1.1 Social Reproduction

The American political economists Bowles and Gintis, in their influential book, *Schooling in Capitalist America* (1976), argued that there was a correspondence between the structure of relations in schools and the structure of relations in the capitalist economy. Hence their position came to be known as "correspondence theory." Schools, by sorting students into strata based on social class origins (even though ostensibly based on such criteria as achievement, intelligence, and other concepts of ability, which Bowles and Gintis argued acted as surrogates for social class) in fact served to reproduce the social relations of the workplace in a capitalist society.

1.2 Cultural Reproduction

French sociologists Bourdieu and Passeron, in their book, *Reproduction in Education, Society and Culture* (1977), denied that schools simply mirrored capitalist society. They saw schools as largely autonomous institutions indirectly influenced by powerful economic and political forces. Schools, they said, reproduced the *cultural* relations of society through symbolic mechanisms, for example, the uses of certain kinds of language and the legitimation of certain kinds of texts reflecting the interests, values, and tastes of the dominant social class. Through its schools, society recognized the language and cultural resources of the dominant social class, its cultural capital, and disregarded the cultural capital of those in the working class. The cultural capital which working-class students brought with them to school was seen to disadvantage them in the school situation. Under the guise of neutrality and impartiality, students were again sorted into strata along similar lines to those described above, but the determining factor this time was their cultural background. Again, this was seen to reproduce the social relations of the workplace because position in the school academic hierarchy mirrored that of the workplace.

The radical theorists of social and cultural reproduction intended their analysis as a form of critique of schooling in a capitalist society, but the deterministic accounts they produced seemed to imply that there was nothing one could do, especially within the schools themselves, to change the situation. (For concise summaries of the literature on cultural and social reproduction see Willis 1981, Hargreaves 1982, Weis 1985, Woods 1990, Marjoribanks 1991; see also *Contemporary Sociological Theories of Education; Reproduction Theory*.)

2. Resistance Theory

By the late 1970s, there was a strong reaction against ideas of smooth social and cultural reproduction through schooling. Although schools "made a difference" (Connell et al. 1982), this occurred through a process of contestation in which there was resistance to schools and teachers, their culture, and the social structures of school and society. Reproduction theory oversimplified this complex reality.

2.1 Beginnings of Resistance Theory

Influential work on the resistance of a variety of youth cultures to the dominant structures of society was carried out by the University of Birmingham Centre for Contemporary Cultural Studies (CCCS). Seminal work was Hall's and Jefferson's *Resistance Through Rituals: Youth Subcultures in Post-war Britain* (1976) which dealt with cultural resistance in general, and Willis's work on school resistance, in particular, *Learning to Labour: How Working Class Kids Get Working Class Jobs* (1977) (see also Willis 1981).

2.2 Ironic Resistance

Willis studied the cultural relations of working-class males in an inner-city English school. He argued that the students he studied, "the lads," resisted the dominant social values and meanings of society by resisting the form of education which school offered. Willis believed that the resistance of students to what it was that schools were teaching, and to the educational practices in schools, was a creative cultural response to a "teaching paradigm" whose social relations and cultural form embodied the essence of capitalist society. Ironically, the form of the teaching paradigm promised upward mobility through education, but in resisting school, the working-class boys rejected this promise, and of their own volition, cemented their existing class position. For Willis, resistance reproduced structural relations of oppression at an even deeper level than that suggested by either Bowles and Gintis or Bourdieu (Weis 1982). A major problem for resistance theorists is how resistance can avoid such reproductive outcomes, or how one gets beyond what might be called "ironic resistance."

Willis's lads constructed a "counter-culture" in opposition to the culture of schooling. This valorized manual work and manualist forms of action and despised intellectual work as "feminine." Thus, a superiority of masculine over feminine forms of knowledge relegated females to second-class others, therefore reproducing the sexism of the workplace.

Neither reproduction theory nor Willis's class resistance theory, however, attempted to explain the perpetuation of oppressive social relations other than those of social class. McRobbie (1991), researching the culture of working-class girls in an English high school, used the CCCS culturalist framework to study the reproduction of oppressive gender relations in society. She found that the girls' resistance was characterized by a rejection of the school ethos of passivity and femininity, for one of sexuality, in which popular culture, boys, and appearance became all important. Again, as in Willis's work, the resistance of the girls

was seen to be the seed for their own domestic oppression, but also as positive because it indicated an opposition to the essential evils of patriarchy.

2.3 Critical Resistance

Many substantial contributions to the debate on resistance theory have been made by Giroux, particularly, *Theory and Resistance in Education: A Pedagogy for the Opposition* (1983). He sees resistance as indicative of a basic struggle in the wider society between the dominant and exploited classes. Giroux makes use of the notion of hegemony to explain the reasons why structural disadvantage of certain groups in society is reproduced from generation to generation. Hegemony is a relation between one set of beliefs, values, and ideas—for example, that of the ruling class—and another set—for example, that of the working class—where the first actively defines and shapes the content of the latter.

For Giroux, schools are sites where the struggle between the two sets of beliefs takes place. Therefore, schools are sites for the propagation of liberal democratic ideals where education is reconstructed in terms of a political struggle for social justice and democratic citizenship and where oppressions like sexism and racism can be overcome (Giroux 1983). However, drawing on Freire's (1972) notion of a "pedagogy of the oppressed," Giroux argues that the conditions must be right to enable such progressive social change. Both believe that change is only possible at moments of critical awareness. Giroux refers to the "critical moment of critique." In such a moment, the individual or the group understands the construction of their own social positioning and recognizes their ability to change their situation through critical reflection on lived experience and related social action.

2.4 Research

Research in education in the late 1980s and into the 1990s reflects the popular use of resistance theory as an analytical tool in attempting to explain the dynamic relationship between student background, culture, society, and schooling. An example is Baron's (1989) study of street punks of the Canadian west coast. Quigley (1990) used the concept of resistance in literature to explain nonparticipation of working-class adult learners in literacy classes, while others prefer to see resistance as active behavior which crosses class boundaries (Grahame and Jardine 1990, Alpert 1991).

Tanner (1990) focused on the reported school experiences of 162 male and female high school dropouts in Edmonton, Alberta to explore attitudes to schooling, while Cordeiro (1991) focused on high-achieving at-risk Hispanic youth at two urban high schools in the United States to identify positive influences in their collective school experience. (For a comprehensive overview of ethnographic United Kingdom and Canadian studies exploring student resistance and the relationships of class, gender, and race to wider economic and social structures, see Woods 1990.)

3. Problems with Resistance Theory

Like theories of reproduction, resistance theories are open to criticism for oversimplifying the relations between schools, culture, and society. This applies both to the response to school by students from different social groups, and to the outcomes of schooling. As McFadden (1995) argues, "What resistance theory fails to capture is the variation in the responses to schooling which arise from the intersection of student and teacher perspectives, perceptions, and expectations, particularly when such intersections involve a variety of modes of masculinity, femininity, class, race, and ethnicity" (p. 297).

3.1 Problems from Research Findings

Numerous studies reported in the literature underscore this point. For example, Connell et al. (1982), investigating a cross section of schools in two Australian cities, found no standard set of expectations within social class groups as to the educational outcomes appropriate or likely for their children, nor standard beliefs as to the appropriate attitude to school. Walker's (1988) study of an inner-city Australian boys' high school, found that responses to school and postschool employment destinations varied more along complex cultural lines, where concrete youth cultures were formed on several interacting dimensions, including ethnicity, gender, and sporting and other recreational preferences. A similar finding in relation to teenage girls was made by Moran (1988). Students were not so much "resisting" schooling as working out solutions to social and personal problems encountered in their lives.

In his study of girls in an English inner-city secondary school, Meyenn (1980) found that resistance to the demands of teachers and schools was not especially class based; antischool behavior was not necessarily associated with poor academic performance; positive attitudes to pop culture were not necessarily associated with antischool behavior; and most pro- and antischool students were able successfully to negotiate school rules. Brown (1987) investigating three schools in Wales, found that the majority of working-class students neither accepted nor rejected school; they simply complied with it.

Folds (1987) shows the positive attitude to education, if not to schooling, of Pitjantjatjara (tribal Aboriginal) children in South Australia. Pro- and antischool attitudes to school were discovered among Afro-Caribbean boys in an English school (Furlong 1984). Studies of Australian girls by Samuel (1983) and of Asian and Afro-Caribbean "resisters" by Mac an Ghaill (1989) suggest that success or failure at school and attitudes to school are more products of teachers' perceptions and labeling than of any prior characteristics brought to school by the students.

Cordeiro's (1991) ethnography of high achieving Hispanic youth in two inner-city high schools in the southwestern United States found them committed to education, though not necessarily to school.

3.2 Theoretical Problems

There is considerable evidence from these and other studies that working-class students implicitly and sometimes explicitly distinguish between, on the one hand, education, and especially its credentialist, utilitarian value and, on the other, the form and content of actual pedagogy, curriculum, and organization of schooling. As Weis (1990) puts it, students engage and react to the form rather than the substance of schooling. It would be reasonable to assume that this is not confined to working-class students (Alpert 1991).

If this is so, there are serious theoretical problems surrounding the explanatory use which has been made of the term "resistance" (Hargreaves 1982). In his discussion of Willis's theory of resistance, Walker (1985, 1986) argues that the theory suffers from two major errors—dualism and essentialism. The dualism between structure and agency is a persistent theme of contemporary social theory (Giddens 1979). Given the existence of social structures which impinge on individual and group consciousness and action, how is free action possible, and especially (the problem for the radical reformer) how is action to change the structures possible? Resistance theory can only go so far with this problem: resistance to oppressive structures is all very well, but to what does it lead? Walker argues that this whole framework of analysis—the dualism of agency and structure—is mistaken, and that structures are the creations of free agents, not independently determined patterns of social space within which agents act. Agents are constantly creating—and destroying—structures.

Walker claims that Willis romanticizes working-class culture by postulating that whatever the negative and self-defeating actions of working-class people—such as "the lads"—there is at the heart of working-class culture a set of pure insights into the oppressive nature of capitalism. This cultural essence, which unconsciously penetrates the masks with which capitalist ideology blurs and hides social reality, is the hope for future change at some opportune moment. It may be that this sort of romanticism is what leads many resistance theorists to become stuck in critique and unable to suggest action for educational improvement.

4. Beyond Resistance

Students, regardless of their class, race, or gender, express a belief in the utility of education for the pursuit of their future goals. However, this belief does not necessarily coincide with acceptance of the form which schooling takes, that is, the practices of real teachers and real schools. What students are constantly rejecting, or sometimes at best, merely complying with regardless of class, gender, race, and ethnicity, is schooling which depowers them. Practices and procedures like streaming, which leads to differentiation and polarization (Woods 1990) are often followed on the basis of a teacher's perception of ability. The perception can be influenced by race, ethnicity, class, and gender, which then has an influence on the curriculum offered, the pedagogy employed, and the evaluation procedures used. For example, students placed in low ability classes tend to endure reductivist teaching characterized by "repetition of drill and practice and the accumulation of fragmented bits of information with no apparent relevance to either real world problems or the kinds of thinking tasks productive adults perform" (Wehlage et al. 1992).

4.1 Student Resistance: Interpreting the Evidence

This limits students' access to knowledge and therefore their power to determine the options in their lives. Studies by Alpert (1991) and Grahame and Jardine (1990) show students, regardless of gender, race, ethnicity, or class, reacting against what they perceive as poor teaching methods. Foley (1991) sees resistance as dependent upon the context, the subject being taught, the teacher, and their particular teaching style. The most common criticism made by students of schooling was that work was not challenging and was seen as boring.

An alternative interpretation of the empirical evidence is that students from certain kinds of backgrounds have experiences of schooling which restrict their opportunity to extend their knowledge. This occurs because of the educational practices of the school. For example, streaming on perceived ability, and the pedagogical practices of teachers, such as setting rote learning tasks for those perceived as unable to learn, affect the process of learning. Perceptions of student capabilities are made by teachers often on the basis of race, ethnicity, class, and gender, and operate to restrict opportunity to learn in the first place (McFadden 1996).

It may be that a key factor in students' response to schooling, and in determining educational outcomes, is the capacity of teachers to understand the students, their backgrounds, social and economic circumstances, needs for knowledge, and intellectual capacities, and to build on that understanding with pedagogical and curriculum practices which challenge and engage students, expand their options, and assist them to solve their problems and achieve their goals (Walker 1988). Such an approach, while not denying the existence of cultural constraints, moves beyond the negativity of a focus on resistance alone.

5. Conclusion

Within the sociology and political economy of education, resistance theory is a clear advance on its predecessor, reproduction theory, in drawing attention to the capacity of people to make choices about education and other significant options in their lives. They may choose to reject the status quo and to resist what is demanded or expected of them, and to disagree with the entire set of practices of schooling as they encounter it. Explanations as to what happens next, and why, vary and are problematic. Ironic resistance lands people right back where they were, with nothing changed. The limitation of the framework of analysis to the social theory, sociology, and political economy of education makes consideration of the next step almost impossible, because what is required is an understanding not just of how and why people resist, but how they can change both themselves and their relations with others and produce *new* social relations and cultural practices. Above all, an understanding is required of how individual and group creativity arises and how it can be used to create new structures of schooling. If so, then what is missing in the search for empowering education and just outcomes is not additional resistance and proposals as to what to do with it, but attention to the capacity to create the empowerment and desired outcomes.

See also: Sociology of Education: An Overview

References

Alpert B 1991 Students' resistance in the classroom. *Anthropol. Educ. Q.* 22(4): 350–66
Althusser L 1971 Ideology and the state. In: Althusser L 1971 *Lenin and Philosophy and Other Essays*. New Left Books, London
Baron S 1989 Resistance and its consequences: The street culture of punks. *Youth Soc.* 21(2): 207–37
Bourdieu P, Passeron J C 1977 *Reproduction in Education, Society and Culture*. Sage, London
Bowles S, Gintis H 1976 *Schooling in Capitalist America*. Routledge and Kegan Paul, London
Brown P 1987 *Schooling Ordinary Kids: Inequality Unemployment and the New Vocationalism*. Tavistock, London
Connell R, Ashenden D J, Kessler S, Dowsett G W 1982 *Making the Difference: Schools Families and Social Division*. Allen and Unwin, Sydney
Cordeiro P A 1991 An ethnography of high achieving at-risk Hispanic youths at two urban high schools: Implications for administrators. Paper presented to the annual meeting of the American Educational Research Association, Chicago, Illinois
Folds R 1987 *Whitefella School: Education and Aboriginal Resistance*. Allen and Unwin, Sydney
Foley D E 1991 Rethinking school ethnographies of colonial settings: A performance perspective of reproduction and resistance. *Comp. Educ. Rev.* 35(3): 532–51
Freire P 1972 *Pedagogy of the Oppressed*. Penguin, Harmondsworth
Furlong V J 1984 Black resistance in the liberal comprehensive. In: Delamont S (ed.) *Readings on Interaction in the Classroom*. Methuen, London
Giddens A 1979 *Central Problems in Social Theory: Action,*

Structure and Contradiction in Social Analysis. Macmillan, London

Giroux H 1983 *Theory and Resistance in Education: A Pedagogy for the Opposition.* Bergin and Harvey, South Hadley, Massachusetts

Giroux H, McLaren P (eds.) 1994 *Between Borders: Pedagogy and the Politics of Cultural Studies.* Routledge, New York

Grahame P R, Jardine D W 1990 Deviance, resistance, and play: A study in the communicative organisation of trouble in class. *Curric. Inq.* 20(3): 283–304

Hall S, Jefferson T (eds.) 1976 *Resistance Through Rituals: Youth Subcultures in Post-war Britain.* Hutchinson, London

Hargreaves A 1982 Resistance and relative autonomy theories: Problems of distortion and incoherence in recent Marxist analyses of education. *Br. J. Sociol. Educ.* 3(2): 107–26

Mac an Ghaill M 1989 Beyond the White norm: The use of qualitative methods in the study of Black youths' schooling in England. *Qualitative Stud. Educ.* 2(3): 175–89

McFadden M G 1995 Resistance to schooling and educational outcomes: Questions of structure and agency. *Br J. Soc. Educ.* 16(3): 293–308

McFadden M G 1996 'Second chance' education: Accessing opportunity or recycling disadvantage? *Int. Stud. Soc. Educ.* 6(1): 87–111

McRobbie A 1991 *Feminism and Youth Culture: From "Jackie" to "Just Seventeen."* Macmillan, Basingstoke

Marjoribanks K (ed.) 1991 *The Foundations of Students' Learning.* Pergamon Press, Oxford

Meyenn R J 1980 School girls' peer groups. In: Woods P (ed.) 1980 *Pupil Strategies: Explorations in the Sociology of the School.* Croom Helm, London

Moran P 1988 Female youth culture in an inner city school. Occasional Paper No 17. Department of Education, University of Sydney, Sydney

Quigley A 1990 Hidden logic: Reproduction and resistance in adult literacy and adult basic education. *Adult Educ. Q.* 40(2): 103–15

Samuel L 1983 The making of a school resister: A case study of Australian working class secondary schoolgirls. In: Browne R K, Foster L E 1983 *Sociology of Education*, 3rd edn. Macmillan, Melbourne

Tanner J 1990 Reluctant rebels: A case study of Edmonton high school drop-outs. *Can. Rev. Soc. Anthrop.* 27(1): 74–94

Walker J C 1985 Rebels with our applause? A critique of resistance theory in Paul Willis's ethnography of schooling. *J. Educ.* 167(2): 63–83

Walker J C 1986 Romanticising resistance, romanticising culture: Problems in Willis's theory of cultural production. *Br. J. Soc. Educ.* 7(1): 59–80

Walker J C 1988 *Louts and Legends: Male Youth Culture in an Inner City School.* Allen and Unwin, London

Wehlage G, Smith G, Lipman P 1992 Restructing urban schools: The New Futures experience. *Am. Educ. Res. J.* 29(1): 51–93

Weis L 1982 Educational outcomes and school processes: Theoretical perspectives. In: Altbach P G, Arnove R F, Kelly G P (eds.) 1982 *Comparative Education.* Macmillan, London

Weis L 1985 *Between Two Worlds: Black Students in an Urban Community College.* Routledge and Kegan Paul, Boston, Massachusetts

Weis L 1990 *Working Class Without Work: High School Students in a De-industrializing Economy.* Routledge, New York

Willis P 1977 *Learning to Labour: How Working Class Kids Get Working Class Jobs.* Saxon House, Farnborough

Willis P 1981 Cultural production is different from cultural reproduction is different from social reproduction is different from reproduction. *Interchange* 12(2–3): 48–67

Woods 1990 *The Happiest Days? How Pupils Cope With School.* Falmer Press, London

Sociological Fields in the Study of Education

Introduction: The Diversification of the Sociology of Education

L. J. Saha

The purpose of this section is to provide overviews of the many fields which have developed within the sociology of education. Questions of whether the sociology of education is itself a discipline or a field, and whether the diversity of activities within it constitute subfields is not the issue here, for these are matters of academic debate and not likely to be easily resolved.

> Academic boundaries are themselves culturally produced and are often the results of complex "policing" actions by those who have the power to enforce them and to declare what is or is not the subject of "legitimate" sociological enquiry. (Apple 1996 p. 125)

As Apple argues, the manner in which a discipline is structured into fields and subfields is a social construct. However, one of the characteristics of the postmodern era is that the boundaries of traditional disciplines have blurred so that what constitutes the sociology of education itself might be contested. "Postmodernity can be described as a time of cultural and epistemological *coupure*, a time during which cultural and epistemological borders are breaking down and disciplinary genres are becoming blurred" (McLaren 1995 p. 10).

On the other hand, sociologists and educational researchers are accustomed to identify with specific academic fields and subfields as traditionally and administrationally defined, and they look to those teachers and researchers in similar fields as their peers or reference groups, and they tend to publish in specialist journals. This occurs in spite of the fact that much interdisciplinary activity takes place in the sociology of education, and both within and between its subfields. Thus, in the sociological study of education, there are a number of subfields which have developed, and in so doing have developed their own academic communities and in some cases have their own journals, professional associations, and conferences.

1. Overview

In this section the diversity of the sociology of education is reflected in 15 articles which focus on the sociology of education and the traditional fields within its boundaries. The section begins with an overview article which presents a survey of the origins and development of the sociology of education, and some of the dominant themes within it (see Saha, *Sociology of Education: An Overview*). The overview article traces the manner in which the development of the sociology of education is also related to the emergence of theoretical and methodological traditions within it, for example, the "new" sociology of education, the status attainment tradition, and "critical" sociology of education, to name a few. Likewise, a number of themes have dominated the field in theoretical debate, for example, that between structure and agency, critical pedagogy, equality and efficiency, and the importance of gender in sociological analyses of schooling. The overview of the discipline substantiates the observation made by writers that sociology the of education has become a vibrant field within sociology, and it reflects and contributes to many of the intellectual and methodological currents which operate within sociology generally.

2. *Specific Fields Within the Sociology of Education*

The overview is followed by 14 articles which discuss in greater detail the concentration of sociological research in specialized educational areas. Willower, for example, in *Administration of Education as a Field of Study*, locates the study of educational administration in the social sciences, and identifies several major alternative perspectives which have influenced its recent development, for example, subjectivism and critical theory. The three articles on the curriculum clearly indicate the centrality of this educational field for sociological activity. Musgrave, in *Curriculum: Sociological Perspectives*, provides an overview of the sociological approaches to the study of the curriculum, which as he points out, has become more broadly defined to include not only curriculum content, but also pedagogy, organization, and forms of evaluation. This broader definition of the curriculum becomes particularly relevant in Gordon's article, *Neo-Marxist Approaches to Curriculum*, in which he elaborates on the neo-Marxist critique of the school curriculum and suggests new directions that this perspective might take in future theoretical development and research. Donn also takes a broad view of the curriculum in *Feminist Approaches to the Curriculum* and reviews the relevance of the various feminist theories for a critique of current curricular practices, and raises the question of whether there is a need for a change from "male-centeredness" toward "girl-centeredness" in curriculum change.

Several of the articles in this section do not include "sociology" in their titles, but nonetheless flag the importance of sociological approaches in the relevant theoretical and research activities within them. Thus, for example, Trow's article, *Policy Analysis*, does in fact identify sociologically relevant issues in his discussion of the factors which result in policy decisions. In similar manner, Thomas' discussion of religious education (*Religious Education*) not only documents the various forms of religious education in the world today, but also discusses many sociologically relevant variables necessary to understand the processes of religious education, such as pedagogical practices, teaching personnel, administration, and the curriculum. The same is true for Diorio's discussion of sex education in the article, *Sex Education*. Here sex education is discussed within current theories of sexuality, and their implications for programs in sex education.

The six "sociology of" articles, like Musgrave's curriculum article, reflect concentrated sociological theory and research activities in their respective topical areas. Thus, Jarvis' article, *Sociology of Adult Education*, provides an overview of the social aspects of various forms of adult education, as well as the dominant theoretical perspectives which have arisen in the adult education literature. Meek's article on the *Sociology of Higher Education* provides an important continuity between school and postschool education, and further demonstrates how well this field has developed in its own right within the sociology of education. In *Sociology of Learning in School*, Broadfoot surveys social theories of learning and reviews the sociologically relevant literature on the learning environment and shows how learning is an interpersonal activity. A sociological approach to special education addresses macro societal questions. Milofsky, in his article, *Sociology of Special Education*, argues that it derives from the contrast between a "medical model" of disability and a "social systems model." From a sociological perspective, assumed personal defects and disabilities can be seen as largely socially constructed and categorized, with important policy implications related to student learning and the organizational structure of special education.

Kirk's article, *Sociology of Physical and Health Education*, brings into the mainstream a field of study which, until recently, has not often received the sociological attention that it merits. Kirk's overview of recent developments in the field of physical education focuses upon the status of physical and health education in schools, the importance of teacher recruitment and teacher education, and curriculum policy and practice. Health education, in turn, has experienced increased attention from sociologists because of the emergence of topics such as drug education and HIV/AIDS education in school curricula.

In contrast to some of the above fields, the sociological study of teaching has had a somewhat longer and broader tradition. Spencer, in her article *Sociology of Teaching*, provides an overview of the many areas within this field, including the social characteristics of teachers, the social mobility of teachers, and aspects of teaching as a profession. What emerges from her article is the clear sociological nature of teachers' roles and activities in schools, and the ways they are affected by societal conditions and expectations for schools.

Johnson and Johnson's article on *Social Psychological Theories of Teaching* extends the strictly sociological approaches documented above by Spencer. As was made clear in Bank and Biddle's article in Section I (see *Social Psychological Theories in Education*), an approach which takes into account the interpersonal, small group, and organizational dynamics of teaching complements the more strictly sociological approaches which locate teaching in a social and structural context. In this respect, social psychological theories such as role theory, achievement motivation theory and attribution theory, among others, are important for research into, and the understanding of, the teaching process. As Johnson and Johnson point out, a social psychological approach can have relevance for the implementation of innovative changes in schools.

One of the reasons for the diversity within the sociology of education must lie in the pervasiveness of the educational experience itself. There is hardly an aspect of social life that is not affected, either positively or negatively, by education. Thus the sociology of education not only cuts across other sociological fields, such as social stratification, social class, race and ethnicity, sociology of religion, and so on, but it has also developed its own set of core activities which gives it legitimacy in its own right. The articles in this section demonstrate both the diversity of the sociology of education and also the consistency of themes and approaches which dominate the specific subfields within it.

References

Apple M W 1996 Power, meaning and identity: critical sociology of education in the United States. *Br. J. Sociol. Educ.* 17(2): 125–44

McLaren P 1995 Introduction: Postmodernism, postcolonialism and pedagogy. In: MacLaren P (ed.) 1995 *Postmodernism, Postcolonialism and Pedagogy*. James Nicholas Publishers, Albert Park, Victoria

(a) Overview

Sociology of Education: An Overview

L. J. Saha

By the late nineteenth and early twentieth centuries, the precursors of modern sociology had established the foundation for a sociological analysis of education. This was especially true of the three major founding fathers of sociology, Emile Durkheim, Karl Marx, and Max Weber.

The sociology of education, with its origins embedded in the early development of sociology, has become a major subfield in the discipline. No survey of educational research can ignore the contribution of the sociology of education, both in terms of its contribution to the sociology discipline, as well as its contribution to educational theory, research, and policy. Much of sociological theory and research takes into account the importance of education, either as cause or consequence. Education, in all of its levels and structures, is a key variable in sociological research. The study of education is as important to sociology as the sociological study of education is important for understanding education and the formulation of educational policy.

The aims of this article are: (a) to discuss the basic characteristics of a sociological perspective of education, (b) to present an overview of the sociology of education in the context of the development of the sociology discipline, (c) to point to trends in modern sociology of education, and (d) to discuss the contribution of the sociology of education to educational change, policy, and planning. Specialized articles in this *Encyclopedia* discuss in depth many other topical fields in the sociology of education.

1. The Sociological Perspective in the Study of Education

It is difficult to give a single, comprehensive definition of the sociology of education as practiced in the discipline. Marjoribanks (1985) traced the first definition of the field, called "educational sociology" at the time, to Suzallo's (1913) definition in the *Cyclopedia of Education*, which focused on methodology, that is, "one of the four special approaches utilized in that scientific study of education which founds its philosophy or inclusive theory upon detailed observation and analysis" (cited in Marjoribanks 1985 p. 4680).

Seventy-five years later an attempt to define the field emphasized its eclectic and broad scope. According to Bidwell and Friedkin (1988), the most central focus of the sociology of education is "the analysis of educational activities—their form and content, their embeddedness in broader social structures, and their outcomes for individuals and collectivities" (p. 449). From this latter perspective, the field includes the study of virtually every aspect connected with all levels of the educational structures and processes in society, and includes family background, socialization, teacher and classroom processes, educational organizations and hierarchies, and short- and long-term educational outcomes.

In this respect, Durkheim was correct when he argued that education was "an eminently social matter," and that no aspect of education can be understood without taking into account the social forces and consequences which characterize it.

1.1 Sociology of Education as the Study of Social Control

Bidwell and Friedkin (1988) contend that underlying the variety of topics and perspectives addressed by sociologists of education is the theme of social control. This theme was the dominant concern of the European sociologists of the nineteenth century. For example, Durkheim saw education primarily as a mechanism through which the "ideal adult" would be produced for society. He believed that education, as an instrument of moral integration, is the means whereby the norms and values of society are transmitted from one generation to the next.

Marx believed that education was a way of imposing a dominant ideology on members of society, particularly the working classes, so that they would accept, and not question, their position in society. Althusser (1972), a French Marxist of the late twentieth century, referred to this process as one of symbolic violence, particularly as compared to the physical and repressive violence exercised by the military and the police, for example.

Weber too, among the classical sociological thinkers, saw education largely in control terms. Thus, even though Weber focused his analysis of society on bureaucracy and rationality, for him education served as a credential whereby an appropriate way of life would be prepared for.

Much of the research in modern sociology of education continues to focus on the control aspect of education, although not necessarily in an exclusive manner. Socialization in schools, studies of the classroom, and social aspects of the curriculum are examples of areas which focus on the extent to which education serves as an integrative or control mechanism in society.

1.2 Sociology of Education as the Study of Opportunity

Views other than that of education as social control have become commonplace. A major focus of much research is the extent to which education serves as an agent of opportunity or, conversely, as an agent which reproduces the inequalities in society.

Included in this context are studies of education and various aspects of social stratification. Topics such as education and social mobility, status attainment, empowerment skills, and education and national development are examples of education seen as an agent of opportunity in society.

Insofar as sociology is the study of patterns of human relationships, particularly as they emerge from the tensions and conflicts of group life and contradictions in social structures, the sociology of education applies this perspective to the study of education.

The often heated debates about these two processes —education as opportunity and education as social reproduction—have thrust the sociology of education into the forefront of sociological enquiry generally, particularly with respect to questions of social inequality. Many writers have seen the oppositional forces in the sociology of education as a virtual battleground for theoretical development and research effort, and even for the adoption of educational policies about inequality and educational reform (Collins 1977a, 1977b, Halsey et al. 1980).

Thus, from a sociological point of view, there is little social life that is untouched by the experience of formal education. In most contemporary societies, virtually everyone has experienced at least primary and some secondary schooling. Thus education not only forms individuals, but through individuals has an impact on the very fabric of society. In like manner, the nature of education in any society is affected by the culture and structure of each society's institutions. This interactive relationship between individuals, educational institutions, and society means that education is one of the most relevant of the social institutions, and it penetrates virtually all aspects of society which are sociological (see *Classical Sociological Theories of Education*).

2. The Sociology of Education: From Margin to Mainstream

2.1 Origins

Virtually all social thinkers, since the time of Plato and Aristotle, have considered the education of the young as part of their theory of society. From a social point of view, the process of education has always been linked with other social processes, either as a source of social stability or a source of social conflict. However, given that the discipline of sociology itself did not emerge until the early nineteenth century with the writings of Auguste Comte (1798–1857), what could be called a sociology of education did not emerge until Emile Durkheim (1858–1917) began to teach, and write about, education and educational institutions to students at the Sorbonne, where he was made Professor of Pedagogy and Sociology in 1913. Durkheim quite rightly can be called the father of the sociology of education. The other major nineteenth-century sociologists, in particular Max Weber (1864–1920) and Karl Marx (1818–83), did not write directly about education, either as a process, or social institution, or formal organization. Nevertheless, all three have had considerable influence on the development of schools of thought within contemporary sociology of education. Thus functionalism, Marxist conflict theory, Weberian conflict theory, phenomenology and the sociology of knowledge, and critical theory have their origins in these early writers, and can be found in the orientations and perspectives used in contemporary educational research.

Just as the sociology of education was marginal to most of the founding fathers of sociology, so too were its origins in the discipline of sociology, as well as in educational theory and research. In its early stages, that is, from the 1920s to the 1940s, the ambivalence of educational sociology, as it was then called, was reflected in the presumption by sociologists that the study of schools and of education was of little importance and therefore of low status in the sociology discipline, and in the presumption by educators that research into education by sociologists was "ivory-tower nonsense" and had little to say about the day-to-day functioning of teaching and learning (Hansen 1967).

This was particularly true regarding the development of the sociology of education in the United States and the United Kingdom. Banks (1971) points out that between 1910 and 1926 the number of courses in United States colleges and universities increased from 40 to 194, and between 1916 and 1936, 25 textbooks were published. However, the number of courses had declined by 1940, partially because most of the teaching took place outside of departments of sociology and thus outside of the mainstream of sociology. Furthermore, the subject was often taught with emphasis on prescriptions about proper pedagogical methods, that is, in teaching teachers how and what to teach and why. Courses were therefore steeped in practical ideology, and directly counter to the scientific and positivist spirit which prevailed in United States sociology during these decades. The normative and descriptive orientation of what was then called educational sociology conflicted with the notion of value-freedom and scientific analysis which dominated the other fields of sociology.

Even the journal *Educational Sociology*, founded in 1927, reflected these two approaches, and the contrast between the orientation of its contents before and after 1963, when it came under the jurisdiction of the American Sociological Association, is obvious to even the most casual observer. Also significant is the fact that after 1963 the journal was called *Sociology of Education*, and the retiring editor confessed to being concerned about the direction the new journal might take. Of the original orientation of the journal, he observed that it was conceived "as a magazine of theory and practice which would 'bridge the gap' between sociology as a science and education as an art" (Dodson 1963 p. 407). It was feared, however, that the journal might be taken over by sociologist theoreticians who spin out theory "with no responsibility for testing it —to say nothing about the extent of its applicability" (p. 408). Furthermore, concern was expressed that the journal should report research conducted on schools and not on university captive populations. Dodson hoped that the new journal would encourage academic sociologists out of their "cloistered environs and aid them in getting their hands dirty with the 'raw meat' of education in its broader spectrum" (p. 409). Clearly at this time there was a mistrust as to what might happen to the journal if taken over by academic sociologists.

Also the field was considered to be theoretically impoverished. In 1963 James Conant, the United States educator, commented: "As to whether the present group of professors who consider themselves educational sociologists, should perpetuate themselves, I have the greatest doubts" (cited in Banks 1971 p. 2). Likewise, Corwin, in his assessment of the field, observed that "the early limitations of the sociology of education do not lie so much in the inadequacy of its conclusions as in the sterility of the questions that it asked" (Corwin 1965 p. 65).

Even in the United Kingdom, where sociological research into education played a central role in the reform of schooling through the studies of Halsey, Douglas, and others, it had little impact on the preparation of teachers or the better understanding of classroom processes (Banks 1971). Archer (1972) lamented that the sociology of education was among the "least adventurous specialisms" in sociology, and remained "tightly shackled to its subject matter, reflecting the priorities and preoccupations of educators rather than the theoretical concerns of sociologists" (p. v). Her complaint was that sociologists had been too preoccupied with analyses of "the classroom, the school and social differentials in achievement and interaction, and thus shown a complementary neglect of research about educational systems." In other words, there was no macrosociology of education. She partly remedied this criticism in her study of the origins of educational systems in the United Kingdom, Denmark, France, and Russia, in which she combined a micro

and macro approach (Archer 1979), and also in her edited volume containing analyses of the expansion of educational systems (Archer 1982).

The ambivalence about the sociology of education prevailed elsewhere in the English-speaking world. In Australia and New Zealand in 1980 it was noted that the sociology of education held a "distinctly minor place" in educational research generally (Bates 1980). Furthermore, it was argued that Australian sociologists of education were noncritical, atheoretical, and practical in their teaching and research orientations, being dominated by a "paucity of criticism" and a research orientation described as "political arithmetic" (Musgrave 1980). These views existed at a time when the sociology of education dominated the interests of Australian and New Zealand sociologists, with 25 percent giving sociology of education as one of their three main areas of interest (Saha 1990). Also, the study of education was ranked second in popularity among United Kingdom sociologists but was not mentioned among the top 10 areas of interest among United States sociologists (Simon 1969).

However, by the mid-1980s, the sociology of education was one of the most popular and productive areas within sociology. There are three dedicated journals in the English language: *Sociology of Education* (Vol. 1: 1927), the *British Journal of Sociology of Education* (Vol. 1: 1980), and *International Studies in Sociology of Education* (Vol. 1: 1991). *The Sociology of Education Abstracts* (Vol. 1: 1965) annually abstracts 600 journal articles and books, and draws upon over 370 journals from a large number of countries and in at least nine languages. The reasons for the increasing popularity, productivity, and vitality of sociology of education from the 1960s onward lay in a number of theoretical and methodological developments which, while sometimes in conflict with each other, nevertheless contributed to the increasing importance of the field and its move into the mainstream of sociology generally.

2.2 Theoretical and Methodological Developments

During the 1950s and 1960s, when most advanced societies regarded schools as strategic institutions for implementing change, the central concern for research in the sociology of education was with school reform, equality, and social mobility. The methodology and absence of theory in these early studies, which were characteristic in both the United States and the United Kingdom, were labeled "political arithmetic" (Karabel and Halsey 1977, Marjoribanks 1985). It was only after the mid-1960s and early 1970s that developments emerged which were to have a considerable effect on the rejuvenation of the sociology of education.

2.2.1 The "new" sociology of education. During the above period a new strand of the sociology of education was developing, but with a focus on micro phenomena. During this period Bernstein was conducting research on language codes and learning, and pointed to the hitherto ignored symbols and meanings in the classroom situation as a possible locus of inequality in educational processes. Bernstein's research gradually led him to focus on the ways knowledge is valued, classified, and controlled in various kinds of pedagogic processes (Bernstein 1971, 1975).

However, the actual watershed of what became known as the "new" sociology of education occurred at the 1970 British Sociological Association Conference, where the papers in the sociology of education "reflected the very interesting fact that the definition of this whole field of sociological enquiry was changing in important ways" (Brown 1973 p. 2). In the minds of some, this "new" approach, which combined other antipositivist sociological movements such as symbolic interactionism, phenomenology, ethnomethodology, Marxist sociology, and the sociology of knowledge, constituted a paradigm shift in the sociology of education comparable to a scientific revolution in the Kuhnian sense (Saha 1978). Perhaps the most important aspect of the "new" sociology of education was that it directed attention to the study, using mainly qualitative methods, of classroom interaction, classroom language, and the curriculum, the last having been a hitherto neglected field for sociological research (Young 1971). Knowledge itself became the main focus of study: how knowledge was defined, controlled, and transmitted to students.

During the 1970s and 1980s the "new" sociology of education stood in opposition to the "old" and was manifested particularly in resistance theory and social and cultural reproduction theories. Although it is clear that developments in the sociology of education have moved into other "newer" directions (Wexler 1987, Noblit and Pink 1995), the influence of the "new" sociology of education continues in much of current theoretical debate and research (see *Reproduction Theory; Resistance Theory*).

2.2.2 Education and status attainment.
A second direction in the sociology of education emerged in the United States at about the same time that the "new" sociology of education was developing in the United Kingdom: the use of causal models to investigate the multiple determinants of educational outcomes, and subsequently, the effect of educational attainments on occupational and career attainments. Although the use of highly quantifiable data and statistical techniques was not new in the sociological study of education on either side of the Atlantic, the development of status attainment models added social–psychological variables to the educational and occupational attainment process (Haller 1982). The use of causal (path) models dominated one aspect of sociology of education research from the 1970s to the early 1990s in many countries, including the United States (Sewell and Hauser 1980), the United Kingdom (Halsey et al. 1980), the Netherlands (Bakker et al. 1989), Sweden

(Tuijnman 1989), Australia (Saha 1985), and Canada (Boyd et al. 1985) (see *Aspirations and Expectations of Students; Measurement of Social Background; Social Mobility, Social Stratification, and Education; Stratification in Educational Systems*).

2.2.3 Critical theory.
A movement which emerged in the sociology of education during the late 1970s was critical theory, with a focus on the study of education as a form of oppression by dominant groups. Writers such as Freire (1985), Giroux (1992), and Apple (1982) are well-known to educationists and educational researchers. However, critical theory as a sociological theory of society is probably less known, and its implications for educational policy and planning are less apparent. Nevertheless, this theoretical development has become important and deserves attention as a useful framework for formulating and identifying educational planning objectives and strategies.

Critical theory emerged out of the Frankfurt School which was established in Frankfurt, Germany, in 1923. During the ensuing years, including a period of dispersion during the Second World War, members of the Frankfurt School, particularly Horkheimer, Adorno, Fromm, Marcuse, and Habermas, developed a range of theoretical approaches which, on the one hand, are a reaction to the scientism of positivist sociology and, on the other, are an attempt to develop a general theoretical approach which combines theory and practice (Bottomore 1984). Although the focal points and precise details of writers vary, the general perspective and its implications for education are coherent and relevant.

Critical theory is based on the assumption that the power of capitalism has come to dominate all aspects of both social life and the mechanisms of social control in society. Concepts such as "the totally administered society," "one-dimensional man," and "communicative competence" typify the portrayal of social life in modern capitalism. The purpose of critical theory is not to explain and analyze, but to help emancipate and transform society through the process of education. This process includes what is known as identity politics, or the study of the school as the site for the production of identities (Apple 1996) (see *Critical Theory and Education*).

2.2.4 Education as an institution.
An approach to the sociological study of education which focuses on cultural rules, otherwise known as institutions, has been developed by Meyer and his colleagues (Meyer et al. 1987). This approach assumes that observed patterns of activity are manifestations of the institutionalization of rules which give meaning and value to particular entities and activities. Thus even structural characteristics which constrain behavior, such as organizational structures, are seen as themselves constrained by wider institutionalized rules. Phenomena such as educational expansion (Meyer et al. 1992),

the growing power of the state (Boli 1989), or the increase of female enrollments, can be understood as manifestations of the emergence of rules according to which these phenomena occur.

Research using this perspective has focused on education and citizenship (Boli 1989), the curriculum, and the increasing participation of women (*see Institutional Approach to the Study of Education*).

By the late 1970s, as a result of these and many other developments, the sociology of education had moved into the mainstream of sociological debate generally. One writer called it "one of the most vibrant and respected areas of sociological research" (Karabel 1979 p. 85). During this period, sociologists of education focused much of their research on questions of equality of opportunity for education and career, and also on the role of education for social mobility and social reproduction (Saha 1987). These debates became so important that some writers suggested that the sociology of education had become a battleground for theories and policies about inequality and social reform (Tepperman 1979, Halsey et al. 1980). By the mid-1980s the sociology of education had become very much a mainstream area in the discipline of sociology generally.

2.3 Sociology of Education as an International Discipline

The sociology of education has changed considerably since its early development in various Western societies. Insofar as schooling has now become a universal experience, its place in social processes is crucial. The sociological study of education contributes to the location of this social institution and process in a wider societal context.

There is growing documentation about the development of the sociology of education in Western countries. Surveys of research in the sociology of education, for example, in the United States (Dreeben 1994), the former Federal Republic of Germany (Chisholm 1996), the Netherlands (Wesslingh 1996), the United Kingdom (Swift and Acland 1969) and South Africa (Muller 1996), to name a few, present a picture of a rapidly growing discipline with shifting and multiple paradigms. Likewise in France the work of Boudon (1974) most closely approximated traditional sociology of education, but it was also in France that Marxist approaches were developed.

In many other countries the sociology of education was developing at about the same time. In India, for example, the earliest identifiable studies in the sociology of education were conducted in 1953 and 1967 (Chitnis 1982). In 1974, 89 studies were identified and reviewed, but by 1980 the number had more than doubled. The themes addressed by these studies were: (a) the backgrounds, attitudes, and values of students and teachers, (b) the socializing functions of schooling, (c) the expansion and growth of education in India, (d) equality and social mobility, (e) the organization

and structure of education, and (f) the role of teachers and students (Chitnis 1982). Chitnis considered the future of the sociology of education in India to have promising potential.

The sociology of education in Spain, like many countries outside the United States and the United Kingdom, has a relatively short history. Early studies occurred in the 1960s and were typified by an emphasis on human capital theory, particularly in relation to economic development in Spain (Subirats 1990). After 1970 and the Education Act, the sociology of education began to develop more radical topics. Much influenced by French sociology, the sociology of education since the mid-1970s has been dominated by neo-Marxist interests, with research being conducted on schooling and social reproduction, into the effectiveness (or ineffectiveness) of schools, on the link between school and work, and particularly on the role of universities in social reform. Empirical research has since followed themes common to other Western countries, for example, the sexist character of education, socialization, democracy in education, and classroom interaction. As Spanish sociology entered the 1990s, Subirats (1990) argued that the two requirements for the continued relevance of Spanish sociology of education was more communication between researchers, and more dialogue between academics, educators, and politicians to discuss educational problems.

The international character and importance of the sociology of education is reflected in the strength of the field in the International Sociological Association. The Research Committee on Sociology of Education in the early 1990s was one of the largest and most active of 34 research committees. The vitality of the field is further indicated by the number of texts produced in various countries which summarize research, for example in the United States (Bennett and LeCompte 1990, Ballentine 1993), Canada (Mifflen and Mifflen 1982), France (Cherkaoui 1989), Australia (Saha and Keeves 1990, Foster and Harman 1992), and Africa (Datta 1984). An international survey of the teaching of the sociology of education found that the five most popular topics were: (a) theory in the sociology of education, (b) the school as organization and system, (c) the functions of education, (d) the social foundations of education, and (e) stratification and education (Ballentine et al. 1984). Clearly, these priorities in the field vary between countries, and they change over time as research and theoretical developments occur within particular cultural and political systems.

3. Themes and Developments in the Sociology of Education

Although the sociology of education has branched out into a number of identifiable subfields, such as the sociology of the curriculum and the sociology of teaching, there are a number of themes and developments which have dominated both theory and research across all subfields. The identification of these themes can sometimes be problematic, and authors divide the field in many ways, for example into major domains or paths, such as the empirical-analytic path, the interpretive path, and so on (Noblit and Pink 1995). In this section some of the themes, or domains, which have generated debate in the sociology of education are discussed, particularly in the context of their relevance for theoretical development and research.

3.1 Structure and Agency

For over 20 years, one of the major issues in sociology has been the dualism between macro and micro approaches to the study of human behavior. Macro approaches typically focus upon aspects of social structures as explanatory variables, and thus tend to adopt deterministic and constraining theories about human behavior, with little or no acknowledgment of individual autonomy or freedom. Typical variables for the macro-oriented sociologists are those of social class, gender, ethnicity, capitalism, and organizational hierarchies. Conversely, micro-oriented sociologists tend to focus upon individual actors, regarding them as autonomous with few or no constraints by the outside social and structural environment. Typical variables for the microsociologists are the subjective meanings of human interaction, resistance, aspects of action, and voluntaristic behavior.

Each of these approaches has been linked, in a simplistic manner, to quantitative and qualitative methodologies. Thus those who tend to take a macro approach also tend to use survey data or similar types of quantitative data. Conversely, those who take a micro-oriented approach tend to use ethnographic methods and focus on subjective interpretations or articulations of social situations. Although there have been attempts to combine macro and micro approaches, the dualism has been difficult to overcome.

In the study of education this has meant an almost irreconcilable gulf between those who have produced studies of classroom interaction, peer group interaction, and similar behaviors, and those adopting a macro-perspective, who have tended to study the statistical relationships between variables, largely measuring structural characteristics such as socioeconomic status, social class, gender, ethnicity, and the like. The impasse between the two approaches has prompted some researchers to observe that the only solution is to continue to develop both macro- and microsociology (Archer 1979).

Related to the macro/micro controversy, and perhaps an obstacle to solving it, has been the question of structure and agency. The conceptualization of these two dimensions of social action also represents a dualism in the sociological study of education. This dualism focuses on alternative explanations of social action: large-scale structural forces or individual voluntaristic forces. In other words, social action is seen as existing on two distinct levels (Shilling 1992). Examples of the former in the sociology of education are structuralist neo-Marxists, such as Althusser (1972) and Bowles and Gintis (1976), who explain social reproduction in schools in terms of the contradictions of the capitalist economic system. Regarding the agency frame of reference, those who adopt an interpretive perspective tend to see the source of action in the individual at the micro level.

Although Shilling (1992) identifies three attempts to overcome this impasse, the most successful and best-known is that put forward by Giddens in his structuration theory. According to Giddens (1984), it is necessary to distinguish between systems and structures. Most sociologists confuse the two and refer to social systems when they mean structures. Giddens contends that social structures are both a cause and an outcome of social interaction. In the production of social action, structures are reproduced. Thus the structures are the rules and resources of social action which both influence and are reproduced by action. Giddens therefore preserves both the notion of constraints on human behavior by outside forces, as well as the agency of human actors in that same behavior.

The solution of the structure/agency dualism is important for the future of the sociology of education, for otherwise there will remain the division, the compartmentalization, of studies of macro educational processes and micro-level aspects of behavior in classrooms, on playgrounds, or in families.

3.2 Critical Pedagogy and Postmodernism

It would be difficult to assume that the sociological study of education would be unaffected by the intellectual movements of the late twentieth century, such as postmodernism, deconstructionism, and critical pedagogy. These intellectual movements approach the study of education from a critical, oppositional, and sometimes neo-Marxist perspective.

Critical pedagogy, derived from the critical theory perspective, advocates that the classroom should become the arena for "intellectual resistance towards the ways in which our roles, our lives, and our subjectivities are defined and constituted" (Shapiro 1995). Ultimately, those who espouse critical pedagogy in classrooms aspire to the emergence of a truly democratic culture through a form of education which is empowering and liberating from the dominant ideology. An early application of critical theory to educational practice was described in Shor (1980), and more theoretically elaborated in Giroux (1992). Those who espouse a critical pedagogy regard educational processes as social and political, and thus any analysis of the deception inherent in capitalist schooling is inherently sociological, though far from the sociology of education that dominates the mainstream of the discipline.

Postmodernism, as a social theory and intellectual movement, differs from critical pedagogy and critical theory in that the notion of an underlying reality is denied. The notion of a postmodernist break or rupture with modernity has occurred through the penetration of the media, advertising, and television. The surface signs (language) take on a meaning of their own without an underlying meaning. It has been argued that postmodernist social theory makes the notion of intellectual resistance and liberation meaningless (Shapiro 1995) and thus devoid of educational relevance. Modernism refers to the industrial revolution, the artistic and literary movements of the twentieth century and the beliefs and values of the Enlightenment, such as the idea of progress, and belief in reason and principles such as equality, liberty and justice. In contrast, postmodernism rejects linear views of progress, relies more on a dialectical analysis of the opposing forces in society, and stresses a democratic, emancipatory and antitotalitarian theory and practice, particularly with respect to education (Sadovnik 1995).

As developing theoretical movements, it remains to be seen how critical pedagogy and postmodernism will influence the understanding of educational processes and educational policy and practice (see *Critical Discourse Analysis; Critical Theory and Education; Postmodernism and Education*).

3.3 Equality and Efficiency

In most Western societies, the concepts of equality and inequality have been central to much of the planning for and expectations from educational systems. Generally speaking, inequality is defined as a social problem, and education is usually seen as a way of resolving social inequality. Furthermore, most modern democracies espouse the principles of meritocracy for opportunity, rewards, and self-betterment. In this context, education plays a double role, for not only is it expected to provide a major mechanism for bringing about greater equality, but it also serves as a mechanism for self-betterment, and therefore for social mobility.

Clearly then, since education is linked to equality and inequality, it is essential to clarify what is meant by the term. Oxenham (1985) argues that two seemingly contradictory dimensions underlie notions of equality with respect to education. The first of these includes the notions of fairness and equity, and generally means that "random inequalities of nature" should be acknowledged and taken into account in the educative process. Thus, naturally bright children should be treated in ways which will allow that brightness to be developed to its full potential. Not to do so would be unequal and inefficient.

However, in contrast to the first is a second dimension, that education should help to rectify (mitigate) the "random inequities of nature." In other words, insofar as is possible, every person should have an equal opportunity to excel in ways that are not constrained by natural differences.

Sociological research in education has addressed the origins of inequality in education, the consequences of inequality, and policies which may make educational access and outcomes more equitable but also more efficient. Much of the research into the importance of family background and schooling in educational and occupational attainments has the question of inequality underlying it. The extent to which education either creates or reinforces inequalities means that ultimately it operates in an inequitable and possibly inefficient manner. Thus the subfields of adult education, the curriculum, learning, special education, and teaching are all concerned, in one form or another, with equality and efficiency in the educational system.

3.4 Gender and Education

The process of differentiation by sex in education occurs early in schooling and continues throughout the education process. In most countries, the attainments and achievement of males and females at different education levels, and in different subject areas, differs considerably. In a study of science achievement in nine countries (Australia, the United Kingdom, Finland, Hungary, Italy, the Netherlands, Sweden, Thailand, and the United States) between 1970 and 1984, Keeves and Kotte (1992) found that not only had the social roles of women changed in all countries (with respect to participation in the labor force and the declining fertility rate), but that the participation of women at the secondary and tertiary levels had also increased, and in some countries, female students had passed the males.

Keeves and Kotte (1992) found that in all countries boys outperformed girls in science, even when other variables were taken into account, such as home background, aptitude of student, values and motivation to do science, and attitudes toward science. The authors concluded, however, that their model left much unanswered in explaining why it is that boys do better in science than girls: "it is not firmly established exactly how the effects of being male or female operate to influence achievement outcomes in science" (p. 163).

Although it can be argued that sex differentiation has its origins in the family during infancy and childhood, the school remains a key institution which accounts for unequal educational outcomes. Connell et al. (1982) have argued that the school both constructs and reconstructs gender relations such that the subordinate status of females is continually confirmed. The fact that females are staying in school longer in many countries does not mean that gender differences are being eradicated. Questions of gender in education apply to teachers as well as students. Sex inequalities in student academic and career outcomes have often been related to the influence, subtle or otherwise, of the sex of teachers. More importantly, the sex inequalities among teachers regarding their work experience and career opportunities have become topics of importance for understanding the influence of gender in education generally (Acker 1995–96).

Continued research into the processes which maintain or break down the sexual division of labor will remain high on the agenda of sociologists of education. Furthermore, social policies to eradicate gender inequalities in education can only become effective when they are based on sound research evidence, which is scanty (see *Sex Differences and Educational Outcomes*).

3.5 Cultural Pluralism and Multicultural Education

The increasing movement of peoples across and between national boundaries continues to pose important research issues for sociologists of education. While the schooling of minority groups within countries has been a long-standing item on the sociology research agenda, particularly in countries such as the United States, the United Kingdom, Canada, and Australia, the emergence of heterogeneous populations through voluntary and nonvoluntary migration has called into question again whether education serves as an assimilationist mechanism or a protector of unique cultural systems and identities. In reality the debate over the notion of a core curriculum and a multicultural curriculum has yet to be resolved, particularly with respect to learning among members of racial and ethnic minorities (Ogbu 1992).

Considerable research has been conducted on the factors which contribute to the academic achievement of minority groups in various countries, but these studies have often assumed homogeneity within minority groups themselves, and have also assumed that members of minority groups share with the dominant group similar values regarding education and its outcomes. The cumulative research findings make it clear that this is not the case, and that for indigenous groups and other racial and ethnic minorities, "differentness" and "otherness," both between and within groups, are major factors in explaining educational processes and outcomes (Deyhle and Swisher 1997, Tate 1997). Ogbu (1992) has argued that those who advocate a strong core curriculum (as in Germany, Japan, South Korea, and Taiwan) and those who support a more pluralistic multicultural curriculum overlook the wider societal and dominant cultural impact on the learning processes of minority students.

A further dimension of plural societies is that of religion. The issues surrounding the existence of private schools, in particular issues of funding, school choice, and efficiency and effectiveness of educational systems, have highlighted the impact of dual or plural structures. Sociologists of education have directed considerable attention to the study of public and private schools and have yet to reach a consensus as to the impact of the private sector on the public sector. While it is not clear whether private schools themselves are responsible for the higher attainments of their students, it is clear that the social and cultural environments of these schools do impart cultural and social capital which may be socially advantageous (see Coleman and Hoffer 1987).

Future sociologists of education will focus more on the educational processes related to the education of refugees, the consequences of new international economic and social alliances, such as the European Community, and improved knowledge about the determinants of academic achievement across and within minority groups of all types (see *Multicultural Education; Public and Private Schools: Sociological Perspectives; Race and Ethnicity in Education*).

3.6 Dropouts and Burnouts: Alienation in Schools

School retention rates have steadily risen since the 1960s in almost all countries of the world. Nevertheless, there remains considerable concern over those students in the 1990s who do not complete secondary school. There are numerous reasons for this concern. Rumberger (1987) gives five: (a) the short-term increase in dropouts since 1968, at least in the United States, (b) the participation of minority group students with high dropout rates is increasing, (c) as academic standards rise, dropout rates will also rise, (d) the standard of educational credentials required for virtually all jobs can be expected to rise, and (e) completion rates will increasingly be used as an indicator of performance for secondary schools.

Most of the research on school dropouts has regarded the phenomenon as pathological, and as representing a loss to the individual as well as to society. Lee and Burkam (1992) group the causes of dropping out into three categories: (a) the personal and psychological characteristics of dropouts, (b) the academic and psychological behaviors of dropouts, and (c) schools as contributors to dropping out. Thus, they argue that dropouts (or "at risk" students) tend to come from low-status, minority backgrounds and from single parent or stepparent households, have high levels of alienation, have higher rates of truancy, and do not attend schools (such as Catholic schools) which have lower dropout rates (pp. 422–23).

LeCompte and Dworkin (1991) confirm these findings, but draw attention to the equivalent phenomenon among teachers, namely burnout. They argue that teachers also experience alienation and often leave the profession because of burnout. However, they also observe that many teachers who experience burnout and lose their commitment do not leave the profession, a process they call role entrapment. This phenomenon poses two problems for the quality of teaching in schools: first, new programs are difficult to implement with unenthusiastic teachers, and, second, staffing becomes a problem when teachers who should leave do not. The authors suggest that school reforms fail because of inappropriate measures of school success or failure, mismatched reforms, quick-fix reforms, or reforms which leave the alienating structure unchanged.

In short, alienation in schools, both from individual and structural causes, results in problems which are only beginning to be researched. Sociologists of education in most countries will continue to research these processes as long as there are school dropouts and burned-out teachers (see *School and Classroom Dynamics; School Dropouts; Teacher Burnout*).

3.7 Democracy and Education

Citizenship education has become a key objective among educators, politicians, and sociologists in many countries. The advent of plural societies in Europe and elsewhere and the radical critiques of education in capitalist societies have caused citizenship as an educational objective to become an issue since the 1980s. Citizenship education not only concerns the development of an appropriate curriculum, but also the democratic process of the classroom itself.

There is wide variation between countries in the extent to which political education is explicit in the curriculum, whether it is a required subject and centrally controlled (e.g., in Germany), or whether it is left up to local state or school district levels (e.g., in the United States). In many countries, political education of any kind is not a requirement for school students, in spite of the fact that as adults the students will be expected to participate actively in the political life of the country (e.g., Australia), or not to participate at all (e.g., Hong Kong). However, even in the latter two countries, the issue of the introduction of political education is controversial.

The issue of citizenship education focuses attention on noncognitive outcomes of schooling and is concerned with democratic curricula and the acquisition of empowerment skills. Although not yet studied in great depth by sociologists, this form of noncognitive outcome, sometimes considered a part of moral or values education, will be higher on the research agenda by the beginning of the twenty-first century (see *Political Socialization and Education; Student Political Activism and Student Movements*).

4. Sociology of Education and Educational Policy and Planning

Educational planning is generally understood to be the identification, development, and implementation of strategies designed to attain, efficiently and effectively, the educational needs and goals of students and society (Coombs 1970). The practice of educational planning is not a new phenomenon, and according to some, can be traced to the writings of Plato, to Renaissance scholars, and, more recently, to post-Second World War experts.

What characterizes current planning activities is that planners have tended to rely upon nonsocial assumptions in formulating their planning models. Demographic projections, workforce models, rate-of-return approaches, and school mapping all approach the task of educational planning as though the social aspects of educational behavior are irrelevant. Each of these techniques has at its base an implicit theory which assumes that the needs of society can be clearly specified and measured in economic terms, and that the social behavior of individuals in response to these needs is unproblematic. It is for this reason that Windham (1980) and Lenhardt (1985) argue that educational planning needs a social theory of society which includes both structure and process, and both macro and micro dimensions.

4.1 Sociological Theories and Educational Planning

What has sociology of education research contributed toward a better understanding of the "social" aspects of education? To begin with, research from the functionalist perspective has demonstrated that education is related to other social institutions and cannot be manipulated without affecting and being affected by them. Any attempt to change education without taking into account family structures, the economy, the labor market, and other institutions runs the risk of resistance on the part of individuals and the failure of the reform program.

Also from within this framework, it is clear that education does serve as an agent (although sometimes moderate) in the selection and allocation process of individuals into the marketplace, and that generally the more education a person acquires, the better his or her life chances. As indicated earlier, there is a large body of literature documenting the positive relationship between education and social mobility, and the role of education in the status attainment process. In spite of some reservations about this research, it is difficult to deny that education plays a major role in expanding the opportunities and choices of individuals, and research findings have been used to support programs aimed at the disadvantaged, and at expanding equality in society generally.

Research from within the conflict perspective, especially from the Marxist-oriented sociologists, has documented the bias in the educational process in favor of the already advantaged, who seem to get the better opportunities. From this research it is also apparent that education can sometimes be used by those in power to achieve goals favorable to themselves. Although some social reproduction does occur through the educational system, so does the expansion of opportunity and social mobility.

Research from the interactionist perspective has documented the importance of classroom interaction in the educational process. The expectations of teachers have been found to exert considerable influence on the attitudes and performance of students (the "self-fulfilling prophecy" effect). Furthermore, it is from this kind of research that one can understand how well-planned curriculum reforms can fail to change what goes on in the classroom. Teachers, parents, and peer groups must be included in any program designed to change educational processes within schools, and ultimately within classrooms.

4.2 The Social Process of Planning

Research from these sociological perspectives has documented that the actors in the planning process—the politicians, bureaucrats, and planners—are part of the very system they want to change. The functionalists can explain how it is that these persons act largely to preserve the status quo, even though the planning programs may appear very radical. The Marxists can explain in whose interests planning decisions are made, while the interactionists can explain at the micro level how and why the actors in the planning process come to define planning objectives in particular ways, and how competing views are "defined away."

Finally, sociological research has helped explain the importance of consultation with all interested parties in the educational planning process. Coleman (1976) has argued that the compensatory education and desegregation programs in the United States during the 1960s and early 1970s were flawed by lack of adequate information about objectives and methods. Resistance to any social reform can indicate conflicting interests which could have been avoided had adequate information been obtained beforehand. It is only by understanding these social forces that means can be taken to ensure that the objectives and strategies of educational planning are appropriately, efficiently, and effectively formulated and implemented.

5. Sociology of Education in the Twenty-first Century

The rapid development of the sociology of education during the late nineteenth century and the twentieth century has resulted in considerable accumulated knowledge about educational systems and how they work in different cultural and organizational settings. The discipline has become increasingly relevant for policy-making, as well as for theoretical development and methodological application. It is also a field of study which is increasingly comparative, as knowledge about educational systems across national and cultural boundaries adds to both the knowledge of consistencies in educational processes, and the idiosyncratic properties of education in different structural and cultural settings.

Although it would be erroneous to assume that the sociology of education will develop in all societies according to the directions indicated here, the development of the field will continue to reflect the preoccupation of countries in the performance of schools and the educational needs of society. In this respect, Durkheim was correct in arguing that education was eminently social. It will continue to be so, and will continue to attract the vigorous attention of sociologists.

See also: Curriculum: Sociological Perspectives; Educational Expansion: Sociological Perspectives; Sociology of Adult Education; Sociology of Special Education; Sociology of Teaching

References

Acker S 1996 Gender and Teachers' Work. In: Apple M W (ed.) 1996 *Review of Research in Education.* 21: 99–162. American Educational Research Association, Washington DC

Althusser L 1972 Ideology and ideological state apparatuses. In: Cosin B R (ed.) 1972 *Education, Structure and Society.* Penguin, Harmondsworth

Apple M W 1982 *Education and Power.* Routledge and Kegan Paul, Boston, Massachusetts

Apple M W 1996 Power, meaning and identity: critical sociology of education in the United States. *Br. J. Sociol. Educ.* 17(2): 125–44

Archer M S 1972 Foreword. In: Archer M S (ed.) 1972 *Students, University and Society: A Comparative Sociological Review.* Heinemann Educational Books, London

Archer M S 1979 *Social Origins of Educational Systems.* Sage, London

Archer M S 1982 Introduction: Theorizing about the expansion of educational systems. In: Archer M S (ed.) 1982 *The Sociology of Educational Expansion: Take-Off, Growth and Inflation in Educational Systems.* Sage Publications, Beverly Hills, California

Bakker B F M, Dronkers J, Meijnen G W 1989 *Educational Opportunities in the Welfare State. Longitudinal Studies in Educational and Occupational Attainment in the Netherlands.* Instituut Voor Toegepaste Sociale Wetenschappen, Nijmegen

Ballentine J H 1993 *The Sociology of Education: A Systematic Analysis,* 2nd edn. Prentice-Hall, Englewood Cliffs, New Jersey

Ballentine J, Wagenaar T, King E 1984 Teaching about the sociology of education: Cross cultural variations in content and style. Paper presented to the International Sociological Association Interim Conf. of the Research Committee on Sociology of Education, Paris

Banks O 1971 *The Sociology of Education,* 2nd edn. Batsford, London

Bates R J 1980 Problems and prospects for a sociology of New Zealand education. *The Australian and New Zealand Journal of Sociology* 16(2): 4–8

Bennett K P, LeCompte M D 1990 *How Schools Work: A Sociological Analysis of Education.* Longman, New York

Bernstein B B 1971 *Class, Codes and Control. Vol. 1: Theoretical Studies Towards a Sociology of Language.* Routledge and Kegan Paul, London

Bernstein B B 1975 *Class, Codes and Control. Vol. 3: Towards a Theory of Educational Transmissions.* Routledge and Kegan Paul, London

Bidwell C E, Friedkin N E 1988 The sociology of education. In: Smelser N J (ed.) 1988 *Handbook of Sociology,* Sage Publications, Newbury Park, California

Boli J 1989 *New Citizens for a New Society: The Institutional Origins of Mass Schooling in Sweden.* Pergamon Press, Oxford

Bottomore T 1982 *The Frankfurt School.* Tavistock, London

Boudon R 1974 *Education, Opportunity, and Social Inequality. Changing Prospects in Western Society.* John Wiley-Interscience, New York

Bowles S, Gintis H 1976 *Schooling in Capitalist America.* Routledge and Kegan Paul, London

Boyd M et al. (eds.) 1985 *Ascription and Achievement: Studies in Mobility and Status Attainment in Canada.* Carleton University Press, Ottawa

Brown R 1973 Introduction. In: Brown R (ed.) 1973 *Knowledge, Education and Cultural Change: Papers in the Sociology of Education* Tavistock, London

Cherkaoui M 1989 *Sociologie de l'éducation.* Presses Universitaires de France, Paris

Chisholm L 1996 A singular history? The development of German perspectives on the social analysis of education. *Br. J. Sociol. Educ.* 17(2): 197–211

Chitnis S 1982 Sociology of education in India: Emerging trends and needed research. In: Nayar P K B (ed.) 1982 *Sociology in India: Retrospect and Prospect.* B R Publishing, New Delhi

Coleman J S 1976 Policy decisions, social science information, and education. *Sociol. Educ.* 49(4): 304–12

Coleman J S, Hoffer T 1987 *Public and Private High Schools: The Impact of Communities.* Basic Books, New York

Collins R 1977a Functional and conflict theories of educational stratification. In: Karabel J, Halsey A H (eds.) 1977 *Power and Ideology in Education.* Oxford University Press, New York

Collins R 1977b Some comparative principles of educational stratification. *Harv. Educ. Rev.* 47(1): 1–27

Connell R W, Ashenden D J, Kessler S, Dowsett G W 1982 *Making the Difference: Schools, Families and Social Division.* Allen and Unwin, London

Coombs P H 1970 *What Is Educational Planning?* International Institute of Educational Planning, UNESCO, Paris

Corwin R G 1965 *A Sociology of Education.* Appleton-Century Crofts, New York

Datta A 1984 *Education and Society: A Sociology of African Education.* Macmillan, London

Deyhle D, Swisher K 1997 Research in American Indian and Alaska Native education: from assimilation to self-determination. In: Apple M W (ed.) 1997 *Review of Research in Education.* 22: 113–94. American Educational Research Association, Washington, DC

Dodson D W 1963 Valedictory. *J. Educ. Sociol.* 36(9): 407–9

Dreeben R 1994 The sociology of education: its development in the United States. *Res. Sociol Educ. Socialization* 10: 7–52

Foster L, Harman K 1992 *Australian Education: A Sociological Perspective,* 3rd edn. Prentice-Hall, Sydney

Freire P 1985 *The Politics of Education.* Macmillan, London

Giroux H 1992 *Border Crossings: Cultural Workers and the Politics of Education.* Routledge, New York

Haller A O 1982 Reflections on the social psychology of status attainment. In: Hauser R M, Mechanic D, Haller A O, Hauser T S (eds.) 1982 *Social Structure and Behavior.* Academic Press, New York

Halsey A H, Heath A F, Ridge J M 1980 *Origins and Destinations: Family, Class and Education and Modern Britain.* Clarendon Press, Oxford

Hansen D A 1967 The uncomfortable relation of sociology and education. In: Hansen D A, Gerstle J E (eds.) 1967 *On Education: Sociological Perspectives.* Wiley, New York

Karabel J 1979 The sociology of education: Perils and possibilities. *Am. Sociol.* 14(2): 85–91

Karabel J, Halsey A H 1977 Educational research: A review and an interpretation. In: Karabel J, Halsey A H (eds.) 1977 *Power and Ideology in Education.* Oxford University Press, New York

Keeves J P, Kotte D 1992 Disparities between the sexes in science education: 1970–1984. In: Keeves J P (ed.) 1992 *The IEA Study of Science III: Changes in Science Education and Achievement: 1970 to 1984.* Pergamon Press, Oxford

LeCompte M D, Dworkin A G 1991 *Giving Up on School: Student Dropouts and Teacher Burnouts.* Corwin Press, Newbury Park, California

Lee V E, Burkam D T 1992 Transferring high schools: An alternative to dropping out? *Am. J. Educ.* 100(4): 420–53

Lenhardt G 1985 Ideology in educational planning. In: Husen T, Postlethwaite T N (eds.) 1985 *The International Encyclopedia of Education.* Pergamon Press, Oxford

Marjoribanks K 1985 Sociology of education. In: Husén T, Postlethwaite T N (eds.) 1985 *International Encyclopedia of Education.* Pergamon Press, Oxford

Meyer J W, Boli J, Thomas G M 1987 Ontology and rationalization in the Western cultural account. In: Thomas G M, Meyer J W, Ramirez F O, Boli J (eds.) 1987 *Institutional Structure: Constituting the State, Society, and the Individual.* Sage Publications, Newbury Park, California

Meyer J W, Ramirez F O, Soysal Y N 1992 World expansion of mass education, 1870–1980. *Sociol. Educ.* 65(2): 128–49

Mifflen F J, Mifflen S C 1982 *The Sociology of Education: Canada and Beyond.* Detselig Enterprises, Calgary

Muller J 1996 Dreams of wholeness and loss: critical sociology of education in South Africa *Br. J. Sociol. Educ.* 17(2): 177–95

Musgrave P W 1980 The sociology of the Australian curriculum: A case study in the diffusion of theory. *Aust. NZ J. Sociol.* 16(2): 15–19

Noblit G W, Pink W T 1995 Mapping the alternative paths of the sociology of education. In: Pink W T, Noblit G W (eds.) 1995 *Continuity and Contradiction: The Futures of the Sociology of Education.* Hampton Press, Cresskill, New Jersey

Ogbu J U 1992 Understanding cultural diversity and learning. *Educ. Researcher* 21(8): 5–14

Oxenham J 1985 Equality, policies for educational. In: Husén T, Postlethwaite T N (eds.) 1985 *The International Encyclopedia of Education.* Pergamon Press, Oxford

Rumberger R W 1987 High school dropouts: A review of issues and evidence. *Rev. Educ. Res.* 57(2): 101–21

Sadovnik A R 1995 Postmodernism in the sociology of education: closing the rift among theory, practice and research, In: Pink W T, Noblit G W (eds.) 1995 *Continuity and Contradication: The Futures of the Sociology of Education.* Hampton Press, Cresskill, New Jersey

Saha L J 1978 The "new" sociology of education and the study of learning environments: Prospects and problems. *Acta Sociol.* 21(1): 47–63

Saha L J 1985 The legitimacy of early school leaving: Occupational orientations, vocational training plans, and educational achievement among urban Australian youth. *Sociol. Educ.* 58(4): 228–40

Saha L J 1987 Social mobility versus social reproduction: Paradigms and politics in the sociology of education. *New Educ.* 9(1, 2): 14–28

Saha L J 1990 Towards an Australian sociology of education. In: Saha L J, Keeves J P (eds.) 1990

Saha L J, Keeves J P (eds.) 1990 *Schooling and Society in Australia: Sociological Perspectives*. Australian National University Press, Sydney

Sewell W H, Hauser R M 1980 The Wisconsin longitudinal study of social and psychological factors in aspirations and achievements. In: Kerckhoff (ed.) 1980 *Research in the Sociology of Education and Socialization*, Vol. 1. JAI Press, Greenwich, Connecticut

Shapiro S 1995 The end of radical hope? Postmodernism and the challenge to critical pedagogy. In: McLaren P (ed.) 1995 *Postmodernism, Postcolonialism and Pedagogy* James Nicholas Publishers, Albert Park, Australia

Shilling C 1992 Reconceptualising structure and agency in the sociology of education: Structuration theory and schooling. *Br. J. Sociol. Educ.* 13(1): 69–87

Shor I 1987 *Critical Teaching and Everyday Life*. University of Chicago Press, Chicago, Illinois

Simon R J 1969 A Comment on sociological research and interest in Britain and the United States. *Sociol. Rev.* 17: 5–9

Subirats M 1990 Sociology of education in Spain. In: Giner S, Moreno L (eds.) 1990 *Sociology in Spain*. Consejo Superior de Investigaciones Científicas, Madrid

Suzallo H 1913 Sociology, educational. In: Moore P (ed.) 1913 *A Cyclopedia of Education*, Vol. 5. Macmillan, New York

Swift D F, Acland H 1969 The sociology of education in Britain, 1960–1968: A bibliographical review. *Social Sci. Information* 8(4): 31–64

Tate W F 1997 Critical race theory and education: history, theory, and implications. In: Apple M W (ed.) 1997 *Review of Research in Education* 22: 195–247. American Educational Research Association, Washington DC

Tepperman L 1979 Editor's introduction. In: Murphy R 1979 *Sociological Theories of Education*. McGraw-Hill Ryerson, Toronto

Tuijnman A 1989 *Recurrent Education, Earnings and Well-being*. Almqvist and Wiksell, Stockholm

Wesselingh A 1996 The Dutch sociology of education: its origins, significance and future. *Br. J. Sociol. Educ.* 17(2): 213–26

Wexler P 1987 *Social Analysis of Education*. Routledge, New York

Windham D M 1980 Micro-educational decisions as a basis for macro-educational planning. In: Weiler H N (ed.) 1980 *Educational Planning and Social Change*. International Institute for Educational Planning, UNESCO, Paris

Young M F D 1971 An approach to the study of curricula as socially organized knowledge. In: Young M F D (ed.) 1971 *Knowledge and Control: New Directions for the Sociology of Education*. Collier-Macmillan, London

(b) Specific Fields Within the Sociology of Education

Administration of Education as a Field of Study

D. J. Willower

This article deals with broad intellectual forces that have influenced educational administration as a field of study. It begins by examining the emphasis on the use of the social sciences in educational administration, which began in the mid-1950s and has continued to the present day. It then explores criticisms of that emphasis, mainly from subjectivists and critical theorists, which marked the 1970s and 1980s. Finally, it considers the scene in the 1990s. Trends are hard to pin down, but they feature a variety of specialties, theories, and methodologies, along with an enduring practical empiricism in matters of inquiry.

The major controversies have dealt with fundamental questions about scholarship in the field: what topics should it address and what methods should it employ? The issues are philosophical as well as scientific. The different positions taken in the debates have often corresponded in a general way to established perspectives in philosophy.

1. The Social Sciences

The events leading to the adoption in educational administration of the social sciences as sources of concepts, theories, and methods have been well-documented (see Campbell et al. 1987, Culbertson 1988). Several efforts were underway, especially in North America, to strengthen and professionalize educational administration as a university field of graduate preparation and of research. They were reinforced by a widespread belief that the literature of educational administration had been for too long dominated by hortatory and opinion pieces by those in leadership positions in the field. The notion that the social sciences could provide subject matter that would put graduate study in educational administration and scholarship in the field on firmer ground fitted the goal of professionalization. Furthermore, since school administrators accomplished their work through people in group, organizational, and community settings, the relevance of disciplines devoted to the study of such settings made sense.

These ideas were diffused and implemented rapidly, first in North America, then in the British Commonwealth nations, with Australia taking the lead. Organizations in which educational administration professors participated, such as the National Conference (now Council) of Professors of Educational Administration (NCPEA) and the University Council for Educational Administration (UCEA) in the United States and the Commonwealth Council for Educational Administration, were important vehicles of diffusion. For instance, NCPEA sponsored the book *Administrative Behavior in Education*, edited by Campbell and Gregg (1957), and UCEA organized the first of a continuing series of seminars for professors. On the subject of "Administrative Theory in Education," it was held in 1957 at the University of Chicago and resulted in a monograph of the same name edited by Halpin (1958). Among the social scientists who presented papers were Talcott Parsons, James D Thompson, and J W Getzels. Moreover, two new journals were established which were to become outlets for research and theory: the *Journal of Educational Administration*, established at the University of New England in Australia, and the *Educational Administration Quarterly*, sponsored by UCEA.

All this was to lead to a great deal of scholarship, much of it reviewed in the *Handbook of Research on Educational Administration* (Boyan 1988), the most comprehensive document of its kind to date. While empirical studies often used survey instruments and quantitative procedures to measure the variables under inquiry, there was a sprinkling of qualitative field studies in educational administration from the early 1950s on, and many calls for more of this kind of research (Everhart 1988).

Indeed, the notion that the period from approximately the mid-1950s to the mid-1970s, when the influence of the social sciences in educational administration was particularly strong, was single-mindedly devoted to quantitative research and social science theory, ignoring other methods, philosophical concerns, and administrative practice, is incorrect. An examination of UCEA documents on professorial and institutional activities of that time shows a great variety of projects. Much energy went into the development of realistic instructional materials, including cases and simulations, and seminars and publications were devoted to such topics as philosophy, values, and the humanities in addition to the attention given to the social sciences and the knowledge base in educational administration. Moreover, writing on social science applications commonly included discussions of relevance, an issue then as well as now.

Nor was it the case that the field was dominated by one theory. For example, various social system theories that emphasized culture, processes, and social structures were widely employed, role theory was briefly popular, exchange theory was much discussed, leadership theories from social psychology guided numerous studies, and theories oriented to political relationships guided some. In the 1970s "garbage can" and "organized anarchy" theory, the "loose coupling" concept, institutional theory, and ideas from political economy or public choice entered the literature of the field (Boyan 1982, Boyd and Crowson 1981). Despite claims to the contrary by some critics, functionalism never developed into a strand of substantive scholarship in educational administration, although theorists such as Hills (1982) argued for its value and relevance. While some research was guided by a particular theory, much of the empirical work in the field was theoretically eclectic, using whatever theory (or diverse elements of several theories) helped with the problem at hand. A good example of the latter was the "in basket" study of principals' decision-making (Hemphill et al. 1962).

In sum, social science influences in educational administration brought conceptual and methodological variety. An additional legacy was that the field became more specialized, often in line with social science interests (Willower 1988).

2. Changing Social Science

Meanwhile, the social sciences were changing. In the United States, Western Europe, and elsewhere the 1960s and 1970s were marked by political activism, especially in the universities. Antiwar, antigovernment, antibusiness, and antitechnology activists sought a wide range of social and economic reforms, including equity for underrepresented groups of all kinds.

In the social sciences, two perspectives that had been marginal fitted the tenor of the times, and both rapidly became much more popular. These perspectives, subjectivism and neo-Marxism, were quite dissimilar but shared some important antipathies. A major one was antipathy toward science, seen by the former as serving a dehumanizing objectivity and by the latter as a tool of the dominant social classes.

Subjectivism was traditionally represented in philosophy by forms of idealism and, especially in the twentieth century, by phenomenology and existentialism. While Marxism originated with a single thinker, numerous versions have evolved, ranging from orthodox dialectical materialism to critical theory to analytic Marxism. Revitalized forms of subjectivism and Marxism became increasingly influential in the social sciences and the humanities as well. For instance, both were formidable forces in sociology in the 1960s and 1970s and beyond (Alexander 1988, Smelser 1988).

3. Educational Administration and the Changing Social Sciences

Both of these perspectives eventually reached educational administration where they were presented as criticisms of its emphasis on the social sciences. Ironically, their rise in educational administration and the arguments presented on their behalf faithfully mirrored what had occurred in the social sciences.

3.1 Subjectivism

Although Hartley (1970) proposed humanistic existentialism as an appropriate philosophy for educational administration, the most vocal advocate for subjectivism has been Greenfield (e.g., 1975, 1986). Greenfield's position has been centered on his critique of science and positivism, which he appeared to equate. He argued that the field of administration is dominated by a scientistic view that excludes values, emotions, and personal travails. This state of affairs he blamed in large part on the influence of the American Herbert A Simon, because of what he regarded as that scholar's emphasis on rational decision-making and the separation of the descriptive and normative (Greenfield 1986).

Another target was most of the research in the field, especially quantitative research. Greenfield contended that such research is irrelevant to administration because it fails to deal with themes such as will, intention, and compulsion. For Greenfield (1986), research should be concerned with issues of right and wrong in administration and such topics as the language and social realities of administration and organization. It appears that the style of research he saw as appropriate for subjectivism is qualitative inasmuch as he cited studies of this kind as exemplars.

Greenfield also argued that the scientific approach to administration is limited to descriptive studies while the subject matter of the field is fundamentally normative. Greenfield has not presented a theory of valuation, but wrote approvingly of Hodgkinson's (see 1991) hierarchical conception of values, which was developed with educational administration in mind. Hodgkinson contended there are three types of values: subrational preferences, those based on rational analysis, and the highest, transrational values, which are principles that are grounded metaphysically. Such a view seems consistent with the kind of philosophical idealism that is often congenial to subjectivists.

There appears to be no line of empirical inquiry in educational administration explicitly identified with Greenfield's ideas, although field studies that plumb the pressures faced by individuals in school organizations fit the general tenor of his thought. However, the surge in field studies in educational administration (Everhart 1988, Willower 1988) stemmed from a variety of sources, many unrelated or opposed to subjectivism. For instance, the most influential ethnography concerned with educational administration is probably Wolcott's (1973) study of an elementary principal, completed before subjectivism became a factor in educational administration and written from a traditional cultural anthropology perspective. It is clear, however, that whatever the influence of Greenfield's views on research methods, it has been on the side of qualitative studies.

While Culbertson (1988 p. 3) credits Greenfield with a "searching critique of inquiry in educational administration," others have taken issue with Greenfield. Just as Greenfield's views more or less reflected subjectivist thinking in the social sciences, with applications to educational administration, the criticisms of his subjectivism mirror antisubjectivist thinking in the social sciences. Among the main criticisms are that he attacks a straw man, an outdated mechanistic, positivistic scientism that is without advocates, while he ignores the open, self-corrective processes of empirical science and those philosophies that reject positivism, but accept science; that his epistemology must end in relativism since it does not provide criteria for the assessment of ideas; that he separates values from their empirical context and is left either with a relativistic approach to values, grounded only in individual preferences, or, if he adopts Hodgkinson's system, confusion over potentially competing "principles." One of the broadest treatments of Greenfield's position is Evers and Lakomski (1991). Other sources are cited therein and in Willower (1991).

3.2 Critical Theory

This form of neo-Marxism was developed at the Institute for Social Research founded at Frankfurt am Main in 1923. Its proponents have been called the "Frankfurt School" since the 1950s. The schools' version of Marxist thought is found in the work of Max Horkheimer, Theodor Adorno, and Herbert Marcuse, among others. Jürgen Habermas is perhaps its best-known more recent figure, although his later work in some respects is atypical of the School. The major project of the Frankfurt School was the revitalization of Marxism in the light of modern technological and societal changes. Critical theorists recognized the failure of Marxian historical necessity and of the predictions Marx made that were grounded in that conception of history, and wished to develop more contemporary versions of Marxism.

More specifically, critical theorists proposed to deal with the failure of the proletariat in Western democracies to exhibit class consciousness and revolutionary fervor. They embarked on analyses of "false consciousness," which they believed was fostered by subtle societal mechanisms that permeated all aspects of life including the most basic social relationships and structures. Institutionalized in the workplace, education, mass media, entertainment, and patterns of recreation and consumption, these relationships and structures served the interests of the ruling classes at the expense of the working class and other disempowered groups. The British "new sociology of education" promulgated many of these ideas, but they did not enter educational administration in a substantive way until the 1980s. Bates (1980) and Foster (1986) were among the most notable proponents of critical theory in educational administration. They both argued that schools treated students differentially according to class and influence and that school administrators mainly represented the interests of those in power, often failing to work for equity for the disadvantaged. Critical theorists also stressed reproduction theory, which held that the schools tended to reproduce the status quo, a view shared by many non-Marxist theorists.

Some Marxists argued that reproduction theory neglected the radical ardor of the oppressed and studies appeared that documented the resistance of working-class youth to authority. One of the best known was by Willis (1977), who chronicled the predicament of some working-class boys in an English high school: their rejection of the school's values effectively cut off the main possibility of upward mobility for them.

Despite such studies, and others in the ideological style of what is often called "critical ethnography," neo-Marxists tend to be suspicious of empirical research and ordinarily depict social science as serving class interests. In this connection, favorite targets are positivism, because it ignores values, and functionalism, because it favors the status quo. Much of the literature of critical theory is in the form of social criticism, often in a polemical style. Such criticism reflects the Marxian emphasis on *praxis*. In philosophy this term means informed or thoughtful practice, but in Marxism it has additional meaning—political action on behalf of causes that fit the agenda of that point of view. Hence, political argumentation and social commentary are favored forms of scholarship.

One of the criticisms of this view is that it is harder to tell what it stands for than what it is against. Other standard criticisms are that neo-Marxism, including critical theory, is basically an ideology devoted to a political agenda rather than a theory presenting ideas to be tested in inquiry; that the assumption of a monolithic ruling class in society is incorrect in the light of the pluralistic politics and multiple interest groups of modern society; that upward mobility in democratic countries is ignored; and that nations with Marxist governments had their privileged classes along with oppressive state controls.

Specifically in regard to educational administration, critical theorists have been described as utopian, censorious, and out of touch with the realities of school life. They fail to recognize that in democratic societies, school administrators, in their official capacities, are expected to be fair in their treatment of different political views, not proponents of any one view, let alone one that has been popularly rejected in many countries because it was seen as antidemocratic and oppressive. Critical theorists have also been faulted because empirical studies have called into question the theory that schools reproduce the status quo. (More elaborate treatments of these topics can be found in Evers and Lakomski 1991 and Willower 1991; see also *Critical Theory and Education*.)

3.3 Other Influences

While subjectivism and critical theory have been the main manifestations in educational administration of the antiestablishment and antiscientific thought that became prominent in the social sciences in the 1960s and 1970s, there have been a number of other intellectual influences. They have frequently been more indirect than the two views considered, but are nonetheless forces that merit attention in their own right, and because they likely contributed to the spread of those two views.

Kuhn's (1970) work on the history of science was widely cited. Kuhn argued that his study of what he termed "paradigm shifts" in the physical sciences indicated that new theory became established as a result of its accommodation to changing intellectual and social patterns. Rather than being disproved, old theory simply tended to become dated, lacking as it did connection to contemporary styles of thinking. Kuhn was criticized for the various meanings he gave to the term "paradigm," ranging from scientific theory to worldview, and because he failed to recognize the cumulative nature of science. However, his views were used, especially by social scientists, to counter the notion of objectivity in science. Other ideas employed in opposition to scientific determinism included the physicist Werner Heisenberg's uncertainty principle and chaos theory.

Additional work, often in the humanities, influenced the social sciences in similar directions. For example, postmodernism, characterized by an antirational, antisystems focus, has been critical of science and of most forms of organization and administration. Having some philosophical ties to the thought of Friedrich Nietzsche, this type of thought is represented in the work of the French scholar Jacques Derrida (e.g. 1973), among others. Highly relativistic, postmodernism (or "poststructuralism," as it is often called, especially in reference to the work of Derrida and other French thinkers) is perhaps best known for the deconstruction of language and meaning. Popular but controversial in the humanities, especially in literary studies, this strand of thought has not yet exerted any serious influence in educational administration.

More visible in education and in educational administration than any of the other ancillary influences

have been lines of scholarship devoted to studying and improving the circumstances of certain groups. This work has been devoted mainly to gender, race, and ethnicity. One thrust has been to seek a more prominent voice for the groups in question. This type of inquiry often documents inequities suffered by the members of the groups studied, but it has also sometimes been critical of social science. Criticisms range from suggestions that social theory exhibits subtle biases, or lacunae that do not fit or work against certain categories of people, to a more extreme view that argues for different science for different groups. In educational administration, much of the literature deals with underrepresentation and equity. (There are three chapters in Boyan 1988 reviewing these matters.)

Another category of individuals who had some influence on change in the social sciences consisted of those who accepted science but rejected scientism and positivism (see Willower 1991). Their views were typically compatible with philosophical pragmatism, naturalism, descriptive phenomenology, or some forms of realism or empiricism. They commonly rejected the narrowness of positivism, especially its labeling of certain abstract ideas as meaningless and the separation of valuation and science. These scholars held a conception of science that emphasized its tentative, changing, self-critical character. Within the social sciences, they argued for openness to multiple theoretical approaches and methods; they believed that a variety of theories and methods should have the opportunity to show what they can contribute as well as be subjected to public scrutiny in scientific terms. In addition, they were often concerned with the connections of social science to everyday life and sought to enhance those connections and the relevance of social science to existing social problems.

All of these forces, as well as the prevailing *Zeitgeist*, influenced the intellectual landscape of the social sciences and eventually of educational administration. These ancillary forces provided alternative critical perspectives on rigidities in science, while the main, usually more extensive and often more polemical attacks were carried forward by subjectivists and neo-Marxists.

4. Still Changing Social Science and Educational Administration

Subjectivism and neo-Marxism have enjoyed a prominent place in the social sciences since the 1960s, but if sociology can be taken as a bellwether, they have run their course and begun to wane. Alexander (1988), for instance, argued that these lines of thought have lost their momentum and that they started to decline because of their one-sidedness. He stated that radical and one-sided theories have been giving way to a kind of theorizing that he described as synthetic rather than polemical. Furthermore, a number of writers have noted the enduring character of the commitment to a kind of practical empiricism on the part of rank-and-file social scientists. For example, Smelser (1988) observed that attacks on sociological empiricism have not been successful because most scholars, even those who are phenomenological or Marxist critics, adopt the methods of science when they conduct empirical studies.

The same tendencies can be found in educational administration. Thus, Culbertson (1988 p. 24) asserted that the field's scholars "still look to science . . . for a legitimating cloak, facilitator of inquiry and as a tool," and in his review of the organizational theory literature Griffiths (1988) came to a similar conclusion.

If educational administration continues to follow trends in the social sciences, it is quite likely that subjectivism and critical theory will decline in influence. However, there are differences between educational administration and a social science such as sociology. Educational administration has a weaker intellectual culture and a stronger attachment to practice. In the past, both of these characteristics have meant that a segment of the professoriate in educational administration has been quite detached from the kind of debates chronicled here, and has been mainly devoted to teaching about the more practical aspects of administration. Such professors often work with school personnel, most of whom, it seems reasonable to conjecture, would find many of the criticisms made by subjectivists and critical theorists arcane or objectionable.

The weak intellectual culture of the field has also meant that it has been vulnerable to trendy ideas, whether old, new, or old presented as new. There has also been a tendency to misunderstand philosophical and theoretical contexts. For instance, Greenfield at first used the term "phenomenology" in connection with his views, although they bore only the most limited relation to the philosophical phenomenology associated with the founder of that school of thought, Edmund Husserl. A more significant example is the association of positivism and functionalism, despite the fact that the latter "arose as a form of antipositivistic holism" (Martindale 1965 p. 145).

These considerations suggest that intellectual fashions in educational administration might be relatively unstable. If intellectual traditions are not deeply rooted in the field, are not always well understood, and are sometimes considered to be irrelevant or only marginal contributors to improved practice, the way seems more open to a kind of "easy-come, easy-go" situation than would be the case in the opposite circumstances.

None of this provides a compelling reason why subjectivism or critical theory would continue to remain as influences in educational administration while declining in the social sciences. If anything, in educational administration these views have seemed as indiscriminate in their criticisms as writers such as Alexander indicate they have been in sociology. At the same time, it should be kept in mind that universities are sheltered places where schools of thought sometimes continue to find expression long after they have lost favor elsewhere. Furthermore, the decline of a point of view is not the same as its total demise. It seems likely that these two perspectives will, in one form or another, be part of the intellectual scene in educational administration for some time to come, though less influential ones.

5. Emergent Trends

As the controversies that have marked the intellectual literature of educational administration since the 1950s run their course and the protagonists change, what can be expected? A very general answer is that, as in the past, theorizing and research will probably continue to follow the spirit of the times, developments and trends in the social sciences, and the special circumstances of educational administration.

5.1 Wider Influences on Educational Administration

Examples of the changing times include the ascendancy of more moderate and sometimes more conservative political perspectives and regimes, the collapse of Marxism as a contending ideology of governance, and the replacement of old ideological issues such as the antagonism between capitalism and socialism with new ones such as global ecology and the environment.

Another example is the matter of the uses of equality. As various groups and even nationalities achieve success in their struggles for recognition and power, the issues shift from the attainment of equity to the sharing of desirable futures in a more diverse world. Crucial questions are how to avoid cultural exclusivity, intolerance, and conflict, and how to promote cultural reflexivity, civility, and humane values.

Yet another example of change is found in the realm of international conflict, which since the end of the Second World War has threatened to unleash nuclear conflagration possibly through misadventure. This threat has decreased as a result of the rapprochement between the Western democracies and the former Soviet Union. However, at the same time as the threat of war between the superpowers has diminished, so the possibility of conflict between smaller states or nationality groups appears to have increased. This possibility is all the more ominous in the light of the potential for nuclear proliferation.

Speculation on how such broad changes will impact on society and its intellectual and academic pursuits is, of course, a very uncertain undertaking. However, it appears that neo-Marxist views of all kinds will become less relevant and less popular. It is possible that some of them will evolve toward a kind of social criticism that is less recognizably Marxian. Although critical theory is historically Marxist in origin and outlook, it could move in such a direction, especially in areas such as education where Marxism as a philosophical and political perspective is often not well-understood. If such an evolution were to occur, it would likely result not only in a more diffuse, less readily identifiable philosophical perspective, but in a less cohesive set of adherents. However, this is hardly an aberration since it is already the case with most "schools" of philosophy.

Other predictions are more difficult to make. It is possible that a surge toward more democratic, more pluralistic forms of governance would favor philosophies such as pragmatism with its Deweyan emphasis on democracy and community, and its view of reflection and inquiry as vehicles of societal and personal growth. Philosophies of this kind, which reject absolutes and formal systems, might also benefit from more peaceful, and tolerant times, (which are far from certain). On the other hand, various kinds of subjectivism might benefit from a continued emphasis on cultural independence and whatever enhancement of relativism that might engender.

5.2 Prospects for the Influence of Social Sciences

The decline of subjectivism and neo-Marxism has been noted above, as has the persistence of a kind of practical empiricism in the conduct of research. These trends have been discussed by scholars in sociology. While that discipline usually exerts a strong influence on educational administration, other social sciences and some of the humanities are also potential sources of influence. At the same time, subjectivism and neo-Marxism have perhaps been more central in the recent past to sociology than to other social sciences, so their decline in those domains has some significance.

According to Alexander (1988), the less polemical and more synthetic theorizing which is emerging in sociology will blend structural and cultural analysis and draw upon both micro and macro modes of discourse. He noted such directions especially in the work of revisionists within the various theoretical camps, work that he saw as a reaction to theoretical weaknesses and limitations. He gave many examples, including efforts by symbolic interactionists to emphasize linkages between actors and social systems, and the leavening of macrostructuralist theories, especially Marxian ones, with conceptions of culture.

Whatever the form of newer theories in the social sciences, it appears likely that when theory is used to guide inquiry, the practical empiricism noted earlier will continue to set the standards aimed at by most of the scholars who conduct the research. These standards are human creations that differ somewhat from one community of scholars to another. Obviously, they are likely to be more demanding when prediction can be clearly assessed and replication readily undertaken. Nevertheless, every field has standards that are used to make judgments about the plausibility and compellingness of its empirical studies. Underlying these standards are the more general norms of science which ordinarily include skeptical open-mindedness, impersonal criteria of evaluation, and the public communication of results (Zuckerman 1988).

It seems clear that scientific methods remain a critical part of the armamentarium of social scientists who do empirical studies. Attacks on science from various sources have probably heightened awareness of science as a human enterprise, with all of the limitations that implies. However, these attacks have not been very effective. Researchers commonly appeal to science to justify their work to their peers. Logical theorizing and credible empirical evidence continue to be the coin of the realm among scholars.

A reasonable conclusion for sociology in particular, and probably the social sciences in general, is that theories will be less one-sided, less polemical, and more likely to draw on rival traditions to shore up weaknesses. As in the past, a variety of theories and methods will be featured in the social sciences. Such multiplicity should ensure the flow of new ideas. Those that persist will eventually be subject to critical scrutiny, since scientific standards of public assessment will remain the principal form of intellectual accountability.

5.3 Trends in Educational Administration

In the concluding chapter of the *Handbook of Research on Educational Administration* (Willower 1988), six trends were inferred, based on the scholarship reported in this collection of major reviews. The trends were: (a) increased diversification, fragmentation, and specialization among scholars in the field; (b) more research, typically qualitative, that deals with people in real-life settings; (c) an enhanced awareness of the complexity of the subject matter of educational administration along with a variety of strategies to comprehend complexity more adequately; (d) a growing recognition of administration as a means to attain organizational and social aims; (e) more attention to values in administration; and (f) greater interest in the philosophical bases of inquiry.

If these trends and those noted earlier are taken at face value, a number of speculations can be made concerning the study of educational administration. First, it seems plausible that polemical perspectives such as neo-Marxist critical theory and versions of subjectivism such as Greenfield's will both decline and soften. More tolerant, more flexible, and more sagacious philosophies could become more prominent, from pragmatism to more sophisticated versions of subjectivism such as phenomenological analysis to versions of realism or naturalism that avoid reductionism to theories of social justice that do not carry the burdens of Marxist dogma. Whether postmodernism will win more than passing attention and the extent to which feminist thought will develop, as an independent force or within theoretical schools, are not clear. However, philosophical perspectives will probably continue to be overshadowed in educational administration by specific considerations of policy, practice, and valuation.

In line with past criticisms and trends, values

seem sure to continue to be recognized as crucial. However, relevant scholarship most likely will occur in the context of administrator decision-making and in the scanning of alternative futures rather than in terms of the abstract examination of competing value systems. Concern with values should benefit from a trend not yet mentioned, the effort to make preparation programs more realistic and more relevant. In this connection, enhanced interest in values could also spur studies of how administrators make choices from among potential courses of action, studies that could be influenced by developments in cognitive psychology, and by efforts to understand deliberation and reflective thought of the kind discussed by philosophers such as John Dewey. While much writing in educational administration has merely lamented the lack of attention to values, it seems reasonable to conjecture that future work will confront issues of values in their organizational, community, and societal contexts. Thus, the focus of work on values will be the recurring choices and quandaries of everyday administrative life and, at a broader level, the social problems of the times that impact on education and that education might help to resolve.

Debates about qualitative versus quantitative research, probably exaggerated by philosophical disputes in educational administration, seem likely to become less strident in the face of recognition of the utility of a variety of methodologies, each serving distinctive purposes and scholarly specializations. Emphasis on the improvement of methods in use, rather than on debates over the intrinsic values of particular methods, would presumably be seen as constructive by many researchers.

It is not surprising that greater attention is already being given to appropriate regimens for qualitative studies. Their popularity has created a demand for more rigorous standards of assessment, as well as for more searching analyses of their several purposes. In a time that values qualitative studies, but also features more sophisticated quantitative techniques buttressed by computer technologies, it appears probable that there will be methodological advances in both areas. Overall, trends in research should continue to reflect the emphasis on practical empiricism already discussed. However, this kind of practical empiricism will be a touchstone mainly for those engaged in inquiry. Given the relatively weak commitment to research in the field, ideological agendas could continue to be the primary concerns of some scholars.

6. Conclusion

In sum, emergent trends in educational administration as a field of study may feature less polemical, more tolerant, and more sophisticated philosophical and theoretical perspectives, greater attention to values and valuation in the context of school, community, and societal aims and decision-making, and more widespread recognition of the utility of a variety of research methods, along with efforts to enhance the scientific credibility of qualitative studies. Educational administration has had its share of intellectual conflict and confusion since the 1960s. A period of consolidation and renewal may be in the offing.

See also: Administration of Education: Critical Approaches; Contemporary Sociological Theories of Education; School and Classroom Dynamics

References

Alexander J C 1988 The new theoretical movement. In: Smelser N J (ed.) 1988 *Handbook of Sociology*. Sage, Newbury Park, California
Bates R J 1980 Educational administration, the sociology of science and the management of knowledge. *Educ. Admin. Q.* 16(2): 1–20
Boyan N J 1982 Administration of educational institutions. In: Mitzel H E (ed.) 1982 *Encyclopedia of Educational Research*. Macmillan Inc. and Free Press, New York
Boyan N J (ed.) 1988 *Handbook of Research on Educational Administration: A Project of the American Educational Research Association*. Longman, New York
Boyd W L, Crowson R L 1981 The changing conception and practice of public school administration. In: Berliner D (ed.) 1981 *Review of Research in Education*, Vol. 9. American Educational Research Association, Washington, DC
Campbell R F, Fleming T, Newell L J, Bennion J W 1987 *A History of Thought and Practice in Educational Administration*. Teachers College Press, New York
Campbell R F, Gregg R T (eds.) 1957 *Administrative Behavior in Education*. Harper and Brothers, New York
Culbertson J A 1988 A century's quest for a knowledge base. In: Boyan N J (ed.) 1988
Derrida J 1972 *La Voix et le phénomène: Introduction au problème du signe dans la phenomenologie de Husserl*, 2nd edn. Presses Universitaires de France, Paris
Everhart R B 1988 Fieldwork methodology in educational administration. In: Boyan N J (ed.) 1988
Evers C W, Lakomski G 1991 *Knowing Educational Administration: Contemporary Methodological Controversies in Educational Administration Research*. Pergamon Press, Oxford
Foster W P 1986 *Paradigms and Promises: New Approaches to Educational Administration*. Prometheus, Buffalo, New York
Greenfield T B 1975 Theory about organization: A new perspective and its implications for schools. In: Hughes M (ed.) 1975 *Administering Education: International Challenge*. Athlone, London
Greenfield T B 1986 The decline and fall of science in educational administration. *Interchange* 17(2): 57–80
Griffiths D E 1988 Administrative theory. In: Boyan N J (ed.) 1988
Halpin A W (ed.) 1958 *Administrative Theory in Education*. Macmillan, New York
Hartley H J 1970 Humanistic existentialism and the school administrator. In: Lutz F W (ed.) 1970 *Toward Improved Urban Education*. Jones, Worthington, Ohio

Hemphill J K, Griffiths D E, Frederiksen N 1962 *Administrative Performance and Personality: A Study of the Principal in a Simulated Elementary School*. Teachers College Press, New York

Hills R J 1982 Functional requirements and the theory of action. *Educ. Admin. Q.* 18(4): 36–61

Hodgkinson C 1991 *Educational Leadership: The Moral Art*. State University of New York Press, Albany, New York

Kuhn T S 1970 *The Structure of Scientific Revolutions*. University of Chicago Press, Chicago, Illinois

Martindale D 1965 Limits of and alternatives to functionalism in sociology. In: Martindale D (ed.) 1965 *Functionalism in the Social Sciences*. American Academy of Political and Social Science, Philadelphia, Pennsylvania

Smelser N J 1988 Introduction. In: Smelser N J (ed.) 1988 *Handbook of Sociology*. Sage, Newbury Park, California

Willis P E 1977 *Learning to Labour: How working-class kids get working-class jobs*. Saxon House, Farnborough

Willower D J 1988 Synthesis and projection. In: Boyan N J (ed.) 1988

Willower D J 1991 *Educational Administration: Philosophy, Praxis, Professing*. National Conference of Professors of Educational Administration, Madison, Wisconsin. Revision reissued 1994 as *Educational Administration: Inquiry, Values, Practice* (rev. ed.) Technomic, Lancaster, Pennsylvania and Basel, Switzerland

Wolcott H F 1973 *The Man in the Principal's Office: An Ethnography*. Holt, Rinehart, and Winston, New York

Zuckerman H 1988 The sociology of science. In: Smelser N J (ed.) 1988 *Handbook of Sociology*. Sage, Newbury Park, California

Further Reading

Held D 1980 *Introduction to Critical Theory: Horkheimer to Habermas*. University of California Press, Berkeley and Los Angeles, California

Willower D J 1992 Educational administration: Intellectual trends. In: Alkin M C (ed.) 1992 *Encyclopedia of Educational Research*. Macmillan Inc., New York

Curriculum: Sociological Perspectives

P. W. Musgrave

In the past the curriculum has been defined in terms of the content of what was taught in schools or other educational institutions, but increasingly there has been a realization that pedagogy, organization, and methods of evaluation also greatly affect what students learn. This has led to curriculum being defined more widely. These changing definitions have in large part influenced the focus of the research done in this field. Elements of the curriculum such as content or pedagogy have been termed variously as "open," "manifest," or "visible" or as "hidden," "latent," or "invisible" depending upon whether intention was declared or not. Furthermore, the learning intended or achieved might also be termed "academic" or "moral" depending upon whether it was thought to be cognitive or behavioral in nature.

Much of the writing done in this field, sometimes also called the sociology of school knowledge, has been conceptual rather than empirical. The aim of such work was summarized by Young (1971) as the relating of the principles of selection and organization that underlie curricula to their institutional and interactional setting in schools and classrooms and to the wider social structure. Prior to that date important work was done on the sociology of the curriculum, but since then there has been a greater emphasis and more work of a conceptual nature has been undertaken. There have been three main influences: the renewal of interest in the phenomenological tradition; the birth of what came to be called reproduction theory; and, in its various strands, the growth of the application of Marxist theory to education.

1. Work up to 1970

From the start of the twentieth century, historians have worked on the curriculum and their writing has increasingly been informed by sociological concepts (Musgrave 1988a). However, from the 1920s the main focus of sociologists of education has become the inequality of educational opportunities seen in terms of political arithmetic, underpinned by an implicit organicist theory. It was this theory that informed early sociological thinking on the curriculum.

1.1 The Organicist Tradition

The earliest, and still an outstanding, exemplar of this tradition, is Durkheim's (1977) book taken from a series of lectures he gave in 1902 on the development of secondary education in France from the time of the early Church to the nineteenth century. He relates education and the secondary curriculum to the changing social structure of France, and especially to the functions of the Church throughout this period.

In the United Kingdom, work in this mode, then the conventional theoretical one, was done at the London Institute of Education after 1950. This resulted in the books by Banks on the changing prestige and content of English secondary education from 1900 to 1950, by Cotgrove on the equivocal place of British professional and technical curricula in this period, and by Musgrave on the importance of a general curriculum in easing economic change in Britain and Germany since 1860 (Banks 1974). Much of this work can also be seen in terms of the sociology of knowledge. Karl

Mannheim, to whom that theoretical tradition owes so much, was at the London Institute of Education from 1940 to 1947, though his published work from that period does not emphasize the curriculum or, particularly, the way in which it might change in response to different forms of social structure. This approach would nevertheless be generated from a Mannheimian view of the sociology of knowledge (see *Classical Sociological Theories of Education*.

1.2 The Sociology of Knowledge

The Mannheimian approach encouraged the position that such systems of knowledge as academic subjects, vital in determining much curricular content, depended upon the social structure, thereby implying a relativistic view of knowledge. However, in this view, natural science was always privileged as a special case, seen as more nearly absolute. This position was challenged by Kuhn (1961), whose work on the history of physics led him to reconceptualize how academic subjects should be viewed. These were now seen to be governed by a framework of what was called "the normal science," comprising their paradigms—the askable questions, methods of research, and accepted past findings. Around these paradigms grew social systems of powerful figures—professors, examiners, and readers for publishers—who decided what was acceptable knowledge and who should be licensed bearers or transmitters of any normal science. The concept of paradigms was applied, often rather loosely, to disciplines other than the natural sciences and even to the moral dimensions, where "dangerous knowledge" was sanctioned by agents of respectability.

Work in this tradition was continued in three main directions. First, the way in which academic subjects, particularly in the forms of school knowledge, have developed has been investigated. Cooper (1985) has shown how powerful groups within emerging or developing subjects negotiate from positions based on resources to define or redefine what is for the time being the paradigm that governs relevant texts and examinations. Second, Musgrave (1988b) has indicated the important role secondary examination boards play as a battlefield where struggles are fought between the ever-changing coalitions of the interests involved. Third, Gilbert (1984) has shown how deeply the ideology that broadly justifies a society's structure can influence school textbooks; his research on English secondary social science texts reveals that, though those writing and sponsoring the texts aimed to teach students to be socially critical, the epistemological underpinnings of the books were fundamentally conservative. From the mid-1980s to the mid-1990s, some emphasis has been given to work on textbooks by sociologists, and Stray (1994) has begun the conceptualization of this area by formulating a historical sociology of the textbook.

1.3 The Phenomenological Tradition

The range of the sociology of knowledge was widened in the 1960s by the increasing popularity of the sociological phenomenology of Schutz, and more particularly by the publication of Berger and Luckmann's *The Social Construction of Reality* (1967), subtitled "A Treatise in the Sociology of Knowledge." This book extended the concerns of this branch of sociology to, as its dust cover put it, "everything that passes for knowledge in society" and because of its emphasis upon the social construction of knowledge forced those considering curricular content both to take a more relativistic stance and to look more closely at the way meanings were constructed at the interpersonal level, especially in classrooms.

This new strand in the sociology of the curriculum was strongly represented in Young's (1971) important and influential collection by theoretical references in his own paper and in that by Esland. In addition, Keddie's reported empirical work showed how teachers' perceptions of pupils' ability, closely linked to interpretations of their behavior in terms of social class, determined what was taught and learnt. Much research, ethnomethodological in nature, has fed into this strand; though focused on classroom interaction, it has had relevance for work on the curriculum.

Initially those following this tradition saw implications for radical reconstruction of knowledge and the curriculum, a message clearly expressed by Young (1971) himself. These hopes were soon disappointed, largely owing to weaknesses within the phenomenological approach itself. The emphasis was put so much on interpersonal interaction that both the power that could be brought to bear from outside on these small-scale situations and the historical legacies in meanings were forgotten, so that radical curricular policies failed. Those with power could defeat such change and most teachers were governed by the cultural influences of their upbringing to reject radical curricular change.

2. Reproduction Theories

In the 1960s work on educational inequality, formerly carried out in the political arithmetic tradition, was reconceptualized in terms of how the selection of cultural meanings, known as "the curriculum," were passed on or reproduced in different strata, especially social classes. Two workers, both tending to write in theoretical terms—Bernstein in Britain and Bourdieu in France—have been influential in the development of this approach to the curriculum (see *Reproduction Theory*).

2.1 Bernstein

In a now classic paper in Young (1971), Bernstein used the concept of "code" to analyze the ways in which curricula were built and knowledge was transmitted in various educational systems. He posited a "collection code" which is based on a bundle of strongly separated specialist subjects and an "integrated code" in which the boundaries between subjects are weak. In Durkheimian fashion, the type of code used is much influenced by the social structure, more particularly by the degree of the division of labor, contemporary changes in which Bernstein thought were moving curricula from the typical academic secondary school collection code to more integrated offerings.

These ideas have proved very fertile in that they have inspired theoretical writings in the field and some empirical work has resulted. Despite this harvest some criticism has followed. At the empirical level, King (1976) has thrown doubt on the existence of the two curriculum codes in the English educational system. At a methodological level, Bernstein's use of historical data in his paper (1971) on curricular codes can be faulted, in that he seems to quote only favorable data and then use it without systematizing the features of the various societies cited. Furthermore, here at least he tends mistakenly to see the middle and working classes as homogeneous entities. In addition, the predictive power of his theories has been low. He suggests that integrated codes will raise the potential for support for conservative regimes; yet the French and German radical generations of the late 1960s came from schools marked by strongly integrated curricula. On the other hand, Bernstein suggested that integrated codes will increase the likelihood of social criticism, but the more integrated curricula of the United States have not led to a strong radical tradition.

2.2 Bourdieu

In 1970 Bourdieu and Passeron published *Reproduction in Education, Society and Culture* in France. Their work began to be available in English when two papers by Bourdieu appeared in Young (1971). The book was published in English in 1976. It is largely conceptual in content, but does contain some simple supporting statistical data. Bourdieu's position is that schools take "pedagogical action" which ensures by "symbolic violence" the imposition of the "cultural arbitrary" of the dominant groups. The outcome of this process depends on the "habitus" of the clients, by which Bourdieu means the more or less permanent dispositions that generate a unified structure of practices. Habitus varies by social class. In most educational systems the middle class, but not the working class, find the school oriented to its habitus. Thus in school work the middle class succeed, whilst the working class fail, and this result is seen as a reality because of the immense legitimacy of the school. In it cultural differences come to be defined as cultural deprivations.

Work on school textbooks is relevant to reproduction theories. One study is that by Balibar (1974) which shows how the language used in a scene from George Sand's novel, *The Devil's Pool* (1846), was edited to meet the habitus of the working class in a

text for French elementary schools, but retained its bourgeois, humanist overtones in the version used in the *Lycées*. In a British study of secondary social science texts used between the 1900s and the 1960s, Ahier (1988) demonstrated how much more complex theoretically was the reproduction process than that assumed by a thesis often advanced that ruralism in British schools has lowered industrial efficiency.

Bourdieu's work, like Bernstein's, has produced a rich harvest of theoretical writing, but problems have soon become apparent. Social classes again are seen as homogeneous, human agency is underplayed, and the potentially powerful concept of "habitus" is not clarified. Above all, Bourdieu's theory assumes a black box within which reproduction occurs, and one is never told how the process occurs. Furthermore, despite the apparent stress on social class, other groups in conflict are ignored. Power struggles in schools, in the wider educational field, or even outside it, about curriculum, pedagogy, or assessment are ignored. It is in such contradictions and struggles that curricular change is born and Bourdieu says nothing of this.

3. Theories Influenced by Marxism

3.1 Early Work

Despite the centrality of social class to work in the sociology of education, only since the late 1960s have various Marxist theories had much influence. In 1961 Williams published *The Long Revolution*, in which he traced the coming to the United Kingdom of the revolution of mass literacy. The curriculum was a major focus in his cultural approach. He saw its content to be determined by a series of negotiations between three groups, each holding different values: the industrial trainers, the old humanists, and the public educators. More recent work has added a fourth group—the state bureaucrats. This categorization has increasingly been used in analyses of curricular decision making.

Work of a more structural nature in this tradition has been influenced by the French Marxist, Althusser, who, writing mainly in the 1960s, saw education as one part of the ideological social formation with "relative autonomy" from other formations and with the economy only exercising full power "in the last resort." The search for an exact meaning for these terms has produced much work. The first major work in this tradition was by Bowles and Gintis (1976). Their thesis, supported by a massive analysis of secondary material, was that schools played a crucial part in preparing labor for the stratified capitalist workforce, thereby perpetuating inequality rather than providing opportunity. They posited a correspondence principle between the structural relations of education and those of production. This work, initially influential, was soon criticized on various grounds, but particularly because it was marked by the weakness of any correspondence theory, statistical or qualitative; the direction of causality and processes involved are not specified. In addition, some of the evidence was poor. This was especially so in the case of historical data concerning whether literacy preceded industralization, which the authors disbelieved though it was empirically supported in some cases (see *Neo-Marxist Approaches to Curriculum*).

3.2 Apple and his Followers

Marxist theorizing about the curriculum in the United States has been much influenced by the work of Apple. His first major work, *Ideology and Curriculum* (1979), was a conceptual analysis of the way in which the power of the dominant class worked, consciously and unconsciously, to preserve their hegemony in such a way that, for example, conflict theories were omitted from syllabuses in the natural and social sciences in the United States schools. Apple's work, influential throughout the English-speaking world, came to give more weight to the power of students themselves to resist teachers, creating their own meanings at school. More recently, Apple (1986) has examined textbooks, educational publishing, and the way in which the curriculum development movement, particularly its key product —the kit—have constrained teachers' professional freedom in the classroom. Apple's writings highlight the complexity of the process of reproduction, but he has not backed his research by much empirical work, though he has used his experiences in radical reform as data.

Apple's colleagues and students have, nevertheless, produced a body of research in the field. Apple and Weiss (1983) contains some of this research. Papers included cover the omission of labor history from secondary social science texts (Anyon), the mode of portrayal of the American Revolution in children's fiction (Taxel), the gendered education of clerical workers (Valli), and the influence of color as cultural reproduction (Weiss).

Resistance has become an important concept for these writers, but the concept itself is undertheorized. Giroux (1983) has indicated the problems implicit in what has come to be called "resistance theory." The conditions that do or do not breed resistance are not specified; more particularly (though Apple and his followers are exceptions here), gender, race, or ethnicity are rarely introduced into analyses; the focus is put upon overt rebelliousness, whereas all teachers know the power of dumb insolence; and, lastly, no explanation is ever given of how most school rebels become compliant citizens (see *Resistance Theory*).

3.3 Other Relevant Work

An important concept has emerged from a large-scale series of Australian ethnographic studies in state and private schools (Connell et al. 1982), as a result of which the authors recommended a curriculum that is "organic" to the social class learning from it. The idea raises problems for the specification of any core curriculum for all schools; in some societies this is a commonly advocated policy among right-wing decision makers, marking a move away from the popular policy of school-based curricula. Such organic curricula for the working class are often seen as being aimed to teach students to be socially critical. This raises the whole question of whether the state is willing to subsidize the possibility of its own demise through the teaching of radical curricula in its schools, which are seen by the dominant classes as agents of their hegemony since their offspring usually succeed in what Connell et al. (1982) see as the competitive academic curriculum.

In this respect, the normal position has been described by Anyon's (1980) work in the United States. Her ethnographic studies of five elementary schools showed how teachers unconsciously met the needs of their students differently in their curricula according to the social class nature of the school's catchment area: rote-type learning in the working-class area, a "bureaucratic" emphasis for the middle class, and a more creative and independent style for the professional classes.

Another form of Marxist conceptualization is the development of a critical theory of curriculum. This strand of work is based in the Frankfurt School, and especially on the thinking of Habermas, who has given prominence to analyzing the ideologies of those who construct knowledge. Critical theorists aim to uncover the ideologies at work in education, especially in such neutral areas as the natural sciences. Furthermore, they are constantly on the watch for the influence of their own ideologies on their work. A relevant study would be that by Karier (1972) on the hegemonic functions of psychological testing in capitalist states. Also relevant, though socialist rather than Marxist in tenor, is Whitty's (1985) series of studies on those English public examinations based on school-based assessment of their own syllabuses. His original hypothesis was that teachers using this mode were seen as left-wing and those in power worked against them as purveyors of dangerous knowledge. He found rather that a number of very different forces were at work, including legacies of the past, administrative difficulties, cost, and even a lack of skill among the teachers concerned.

4. Directions

Under contemporary political conditions, education in most societies is under such constraints that great economy is needed. Expenditure in this field must be directed toward the development of curricular materials that are seen as relevant for perpetuating the hegemony or toward research to aid this process, for example, assessment of learning core curricula. Despite this constraint, however, present interests and strengths hint at the possibility of work along three dimensions:

(a) The mass of conceptual work done during the 1970s and 1980s in all the strands of which weaknesses are apparent, needs grounding in empirical studies. These can be either qualitative or quantitative in nature. Despite the growing popularity of the former, there is still room for such statistical work as that undertaken by Lynch (1989) on the hidden curriculum in Irish secondary schools. In this she showed how the hidden curriculum is not "a unitary, undifferentiated entity" (p. 4), but is variously experienced by students and also how, despite "the universalistic character of knowledge selection, organisation and evaluation" (p. 32) teachers and administrators practice a "particularism of knowledge distribution and consumption" (p. 32). Such research obviously adds to the complexity, but also to the applicability, of the key concept of hidden curriculum.

(b) Educational administration is an obvious focus when conservative forces are trying to recapture ground perceived as lost to various brands of progressive, for example, to those advocating school-based curricula. The administration of curricular change could become an important focus, particularly through the application of sociological theory to problems of management of school knowledge. This is particularly so at a time when the greater use of computers in the classroom must influence curricular content (Luke 1996).

(c) Discourse analysis, often structuralist in nature, has become a more common technique in sociology. Relevant work has been reported above (e.g., that of Taxel on children's fiction), but Wexler (1987), who has worked with Apple, sees the semiotic emphasis as a crucial basis for a new sociology of the curriculum. He defines "the student a subject, making and being made, within the history of discourse and production" (p. 101). Certainly this is a comparatively cheap research technique and, in view of the popularity of structuralist criticism in language studies, this would seem a highly probable direction for development.

See also: Critical Discourse Analysis; Feminist Approaches to the Curriculum; Hidden Curriculum; Social, Cultural, and Economic Factors Affecting Curriculum; Socialization; Sociology of Education: An Overview

References

Ahier J 1988 *Industry, Children and the Nation.* Falmer Press, Lewes

Anyon J 1980 Social class and the hidden curriculum of work. *J. Educ.* 162(1): 67–92

Apple M W 1979 *Ideology and Curriculum.* Routledge and Kegan Paul, London

Apple M W 1986 *Teachers and Texts.* Routledge and Kegan Paul, London

Apple M W, Weiss L (eds.) 1983 *Ideology and Practice in Schooling.* Temple University Press, Philadelphia, Pennsylvania

Balibar R, Meslin G, Tset G 1974 *Les Francais Fictifs.* Hachette, Paris

Banks O 1974 The "new" sociology of education. *Forum* 17(1): 4–7

Berger P, Luckmann T 1967 *The Social Construction of Reality.* Penguin, Harmondsworth

Bernstein B 1971 On the classification and framing of educational knowledge. In: Young M F D (ed.) 1971

Bourdieu P, Passeron J C 1977 *Reproduction in Education, Society and Culture.* Sage, London

Bowles S, Gintis H 1976 *Schooling in Capitalist America.* Routledge and Kegan Paul, London

Connell R W, Ashenden D J, Kessler S, Dowsett G W 1982 *Making the Difference.* Allen and Unwin, Sydney

Cooper B 1985 *Renegotiating Secondary School Mathematics.* Falmer Press, Lewes

Durkheim E 1977 *The Evolution of Educational Thought.* Routledge and Kegan Paul, London

Gilbert R 1984 *The Impotent Image.* Falmer Press, Lewes

Giroux H 1983 Theories of reproduction and resistance in the new sociology of education: a critical analysis. *Harv. Educ. Rev.* 53(3): 257–93

Karier C 1972 Testing for order and control in the corporate liberal state. *Educ. Theory* 22(2): 154–80

King R 1976 Bernstein's sociology of the school—some propositions tested. *Br. J. Sociol.* 27(4): 430–43

Kuhn T S 1961 *The Structure of Scientific Revolutions.* University of Chicago Press, Chicago, Illinois

Luke C 1996 Ekstasis & cyberia. *Discourse* 17(2): 187–208

Lynch K 1989 *The Hidden Curriculum.* Falmer Press, Lewes

Musgrave P W 1988a Curriculum history: Past, present and future. *History of Educ. Rev.* 17(2): 1–14

Musgrave P W 1988b *Whose Knowledge?* Falmer Press, Lewes

Stray C 1994 Paradigms regained: towards a historical sociology of the textbook. *J. Curric. Stud.* 26(1): 1–29

Wexler P 1987 *Social Analysis of Education.* Routledge and Kegan Paul, London

Whitty G 1985 *Sociology and School Knowledge.* Methuen, London

Williams R 1961 *The Long Revolution.* Chatto and Windus, London

Young M F D (ed.) 1971 *Knowledge and Control.* Collier Macmillan, London

Feminist Approaches to the Curriculum

G. Donn

Curriculum development has become an essential concern for feminists who wish to see changes in the apparently unequal assessment of achievement of males and females. This article examines various feminist approaches to the curriculum before looking at equal opportunity curriculum policymaking.

1. The Curriculum

There are many definitions of what a curriculum actually is. These examine and analyze curriculum (a) as a document describing content, aims, and learning situations, involving the learner, society, and organized subject matter; (b) as a system, dealing with the context of human actions and decisions; (c) as a set of related statements giving meaning to a school's program of learning by pointing up the relationships between its elements and by directing its development, its use, and its evaluation; (d) as a set of norms and rules which provides a rationale for reasoning about decisions and learning; (e) as norms and rules of interaction to be shared by everyone involved in the learning process; (f) as a systematic link between curriculum and instruction; and (g) as a device which has to explain the relevance of content in connection with methods of learning.

These definitions result in a number of basic questions: What educational purpose should the school seek to attain? How can learning experiences be selected which are likely to be useful in attaining these objectives? How can learning experiences be organized for effective instruction? How can the effectiveness of learning experiences be evaluated?

These definitions and this set of questions can be situated within the framework of "curriculum content." This has been defined as the first of two major curriculum issues. The second fundamental issue concerns "curriculum control." It is argued that these issues result in different approaches to curriculum policy and educational change. This entry recognizes that the gender-related concerns may be coalesced around both of these analytical concepts. The first concept lends itself to an egalitarian-oriented, liberal feminist analysis of the role and place of gender and the curriculum; the second to more radical, socialist, and Marxist analyses of gender and the curriculum (see *Curriculum: Sociological Perspectives; Neo-Marxist Approaches to Curriculum*).

2. Feminist Approaches

2.1 Liberal Feminist Approach

The egalitarian and liberal feminist approach stresses equal opportunities for all children, pupil competencies, and school objectives. Its focus is on learning objectives, changes in pupil behavior, standards, measurement, and competencies; it develops concepts intended to enhance the success and achievement of various groups, particularly women, through the curriculum. It does not address the issue, delineated later in this entry by socialist feminists, of the inherent male bias of the curriculum; neither does it address the issue of changing structures which maintain inequalities. Instead, it aims to aid greater access to, and achievement through, these structures.

The egalitarian, liberal feminist position has developed out of the philosophy of liberalism which, with the rise of *laissez-faire* capitalism in the nineteenth century, argues that merit, not birth, should be the basis for social advancement and achievement. The role of education, and the curriculum in particular, has been seen as crucial to an egalitarian society.

Much research has been conducted through this perspective, detailing how gender becomes a defining factor in educational "success" or "failure." Writers have examined the density and implications of sex-role steretypes and gendered socialization (Stanworth 1983, Weiner and Arnot 1987, Walkerdine 1989). More recently research has examined gender portrayal in school books, in language, and in subject choice, in an attempt to indicate the ways in which girls are "disadvantaged" through the curriculum. The absence of images of women and female exemplification is found to correlate highly with those subject areas which girls find most alienating, and this in turn contributes to the sense of difficulty which girls express in learning certain subjects (Kelly 1987). Girls follow a curriculum which tends to exclude mathematics, physical science, and trade-related subjects. A British study has shown that when girls undertook O-level physics and chemistry, they obtained a higher proportion of A-grade passes than boys. However, girls acting on the image, if not the content of these subjects, tend to follow courses which are considered more "feminine," such as home economics, arts, and business studies. Their occupational and educational horizons are limited but remain "appropriate" to their occupational roles in the family and the labor market.

Further, in a study of eight major textbooks used in the Australian history curriculum, males were depicted as the active agents, seen as making and shaping history. The content of syllabuses from the 1940s to the 1970s were seen to show the public world of men, in politics, culture, diplomacy, and the economy.

Gendered subject choice has been studied particularly in the fields of mathematics and science. Data on Scottish pupils noted relatively small differences in the take-up of science subjects at 10 and 11 years of age, but increasing differentiation was apparent in secondary school. Data on England and Wales by the Assessment and Performance Unit (Schofield 1989) shows differential attainment in physics, but not in biology and chemistry, developing between boys and girls, between the ages of 13 and 15.

Kelly (1987), writing on the Girls into Science and Technology (GIST) project, describes the interventionist strategies—including school visits by women scientists, girl-friendly materials introduced into the written curriculum, teachers' workshops and career information—employed by eight coeducational English comprehensives designed to encourage more girls to continue with the physical sciences and technical craft subjects when these became optional at school. Positive results from the project were that there was less endorsement of sex stereotyping; there was a more favorable attitude to science by all pupils; and for girls taking particular subject choices there was less stereotyping than previously. The greatest disappointment of the project was the limited change in teachers' classroom practice, in spite of the project team's close involvement with teachers in workshops, observation, and the design of interventions. In her conclusion, Kelly offers a range of specific strategies for changing the masculinity of science: a male–female balance both in those studying and teaching science; different packaging and presentation of science, so that boys' orientations to life are no longer taken as the norm; and behavioral reconstruction of science so that it is no longer perceived as a male preserve.

However, research in England (Riddell 1992) has shown that subject choice itself owes more to teacher appraisal of pupil's potentials and pupils' own horizons of expectations, than to formalized curriculum structures. She notes the role of sex and achievement as the basis of selection for option choice, despite the rhetoric of free choice. Boys, whatever their level of achievement, were encouraged to choose subjects in relation to the area of work they aspired to, and they had clearer ideas of what they wanted to do. Girls tended to be much more vague, or else suggested sex-stereotyped jobs such as hairdressing. She noted little or no attempt being made to encourage them to think of alternatives.

In addition to gender portrayal in school books, language, and subject choice, timetabling has been identified as an important influence on gender inequality and curriculum choice. Research in Scotland has identified structuring of the upper secondary schools' timetables so that arts and science specializations were mutually exclusive, as were the traditional "boys" and "girls" subjects. This study also drew attention to beliefs held by pupils, parents, teachers, and headteachers about "appropriate" subjects for boys and girls.

These concerns also apply to girls in the Indian subcontinent where the dearth of female role models in

books, and in society at large, constrains girls' school-based achievement. Studies are now emerging which address the issue of equality of opportunity through educational provision but recognize the limitations in a society where so many sociocultural factors conspire to minimize girls' interest and involvement in education (Brock and Cammish 1991). It has been suggested that in India, the distant location of the school, care of siblings by sisters, and the male gender of most teachers have the effect of producing a cultural bias in favor of male attendance at, and success within, school. These social factors in addition to the underrepresentation of girls in textbook pictures, mean that girls have little with which to identify if they do manage to attend school. Brock and Cammish (1991) note that in wealthier families, female school attendance is seen as an advantage towards a "good marriage"; such concerns do not apply to poorer families in India. The cost of educating a girl which is met by the first family gives benefit to her family-by-marriage. This ensures that there is little, if any, familial pressure for a gender-relevant curriculum.

2.2 Radical Feminist Approach

Critics of the liberal feminist position point to an absence in analysis of existing structural inequalities. A radical feminist perspective focuses on *control* of the curriculum, recognizes that sex-stereotypes are themselves cultural constructs in need of analytical study, and supports a curriculum based on theoretically justified antisexist concepts.

By focusing on control over the curriculum, antisexist perspectives locate questions about the purpose of schooling and curricular decisions within a sociopolitical framework of competing educational and economic interests. Further, developing out of this perspective are two feminist positions derived from a Marxist account of reproduction—the radical feminist and the socialist feminist. Both address, in different ways, the question of how to justify, develop, and locate an antisexist curriculum in schools. Feminist writers (Kelly 1987) argue that classical Marxist reproduction theory, while analyzing class inequality, fails to address the issue of gender inequality in capitalism and the subsequent and inherent crisis of legitimation.

Both radical and socialist feminist writers address these issues, and in so doing direct attention to the hidden curriculum. The "hidden curriculum," whereby implicit and covert facets of socialization are reproduced through control of the curriculum, is central to this perspective. Unequal distribution of power between men and women in schools is one aspect of the hidden curriculum. It confirms "common sense knowledge" which legitimizes the oppression of women. For radical feminists, analysis of the hidden curriculum enables discussion of the role the curriculum plays in maintaining and enhancing a patriarchal ideology and patriarchal social structures (see *Hidden Curriculum*).

Radical feminists argue against the central role that Marxists allocate to the capitalist mode of production. Instead, they locate patriarchy as the root of women's oppression. They see patriarchy as socially constructed and seek to analyze schooling and curriculum in this context (Acker 1989). This position is developed from the interactionist and phenomenological perspectives on education which examine how pupil identities become formed through classroom interaction, and how the rhetoric of cultural deprivation has been replaced by the discourse of cultural relativism. The curriculum is examined as a means whereby knowledge and skills representing dominant cultural values are transmitted. Spender (1983) argues that men have been ascribed "prestigious" qualities such as reason, objectivity, leadership, independence, and authority, while women have been allocated "stigmatized" qualities such as emotion, irrationality, passivity, and dependence (Spender 1983 p. 42). In this way, differential behavioral expectations of males and females are underpinned by official ideology regarding appropriate gendered behavior. Further, these behaviors are made appropriate through a gendered curriculum of logical, rational, technicological and numerate subjects being counterposed with more literate, sensitive, and insightful subjects (Barrett 1987).

Spender (1983) states that the entire curriculum consists of masculine knowledge; it is men who have decreed what is known. This, she argues, puts men in the privileged position of continuing to create the knowledge of society, of continuing to appropriate "superiority" for themselves, to perpetuate patriarchy and to reinforce oppression. In support of this position, Stanworth (1983) notes that out of the enormous range of ideas, values, and knowledge available in any culture, only a fraction is selected as suitable for transmission in schools. She draws attention especially to Bourdieu and Passeron (1977) who have attempted to show that the intellectual styles espoused by schools, and the forms of expression which are valued and rewarded, correspond more closely to dominant groups' experiences of the world than to the experiences of other groups.

Radical feminist writers stress the importance of curriculum innovations which delineate mechanisms of current patriarchal control and focus on "female subjects" and concerns, be they female history, the "androcentricity" of male-dominated academic disciplines, the experience of "femininity" in the classroom under a system of patriarchy, or the role of the school in the reproduction of patriarchy. Radical feminist researchers attempt to derive a school curriculum which is less concerned with traditional epistemologies and patriarchal research methods and more with feminist approaches to generating theory, notably through personal reflection and consciousness-raising.

Current concern is with the role of the curriculum in reproducing suitably qualified and satisfactory numbers of female labor for production in advanced capitalist markets (Hartmann 1981). However, this position is criticized as not addressing the issue of how gender divisions in labor actually originated.

2.3 Socialist Feminist Approach

The radical feminist position is, in part, criticized by socialist feminists whose task is to understand femininity and masculinity as constructs of capitalism and hence describe and explain the complex interrelationships between capitalism and patriarchy (Barrett 1987). Education policies are seen as the response of the state to deal with complex and contradictory problems of fiscal management and political legitimation (Habermas 1976). The relationship between the historical and contemporary nature of state ideology and the provision of women's education is analyzed, particularly between female education and the "dual" location of women in the family and the waged labor process. It has been suggested that this socialist feminist paradigm contains within it theories of social reproduction and theories of cultural reproduction.

It is debateable whether reproduction theory allows for discussions about gender, but it does move the discourse on feminist approaches to the curriculum from psychological and phenomenological concerns about patriarchy to more structurally located frameworks. However, that structuralism has itself been criticized as being overdeterministic in its examination of schooling in capitalist society. The transmission of ideologies, and the ideology of the woman's role is embedded, not only in state educational policy, but also in frameworks and practices, with teachers performing as agents of the state.

When this analysis is related to gender issues, it is suggested that the culture of the school helps to develop concepts of masculinity and femininity. The roles allocated to female children in the classroom may have a huge impact on general self-perception. This can affect material aspects of perception, such as subject choice and career paths (Riddell 1992).

Tomlinson (1987) suggests, in the case of children with special educational needs, that it is possible through the lens of critical theory to locate curricular practice as cultural practice. Concepts such as domination, emancipation, alienation, and repression can be studied along with an analysis of the curriculum (Giroux 1983).

3. Curriculum Policy-making and Equal Opportunities

It is suggested that it is not sufficient to hold out a curriculum derived from a commitment to compensatory education as the means of engendering equal opportunities. There are many other sites of gender discrimination. In the home and at work, gender inequality has also been found to replicate that found in schooling and in the curriculum (Acker 1989).

Legislation has been introduced in many countries in an attempt to reduce—if not abolish—the social bases of gender inequality. In the United Kingdom, since the introduction of the Equal Pay Act in 1970, the establishment of an Equal Opportunities Commission, and the 1975 Sex Discrimination Act, no school may offer any subject to one sex only. Boys and girls are meant to be able to share a common curriculum. The Education Reform Act 1988 in the United Kingdom, which introduced a national curriculum, is seen by some as an example of this determination. By others it is seen as further evidence of an absence of concern for gender issues and inequality in the curriculum.

British National Curriculum legislation ensured that all children from the age of 11 or 12 followed certain core and foundation subjects. In England and Wales the 1988 legislation established a national curriculum of three core subjects (mathematics, english, and science) and six foundation subjects (history, geography, technology, music, art, and physical education). For each subject, programs of study have been developed which reflect either academic subject boundaries, as with mathematics, or broad areas and frameworks, as with technology. Anxiety has been expressed about the privileged status that this type of curriculum might bestow on traditionally masculine areas such as science.

Others are critical of the British government's dismissal of gender as a serious concern in the construction of the curriculum: traditional assumptions and discriminatory practices "happily co-exist" (Arnot 1989). The possibility has been raised of the curriculum reverting to an old-style option-choice system, particularly in the light of a 1988 amendment allowing pupils to take science for 10 percent rather than 20 percent of the timetable. However, there has been some attempt to address the issue of gender in curriculum subjects as the Department of Education and Science (DES) proposals make clear.

Further, attention is drawn to the ideological climate pre-1988 where moral education, preparation for parenthood, and an adult role in family life were all on the curriculum agenda. These subjects were most notable in the development of the TVEI curriculum, introduced in 1982, through the Manpower Service Commission. They indicated the government's commitment to prepare children not only for their later economic role, but also for differential gender roles in adulthood. The notion of the family portrayed in the moral education curriculum is patriarchal, of unequal gender relations, with the male working outside and the female working inside the home.

In Scotland, where there has been a parallel development with the introduction of curriculum guidelines for 5–14-year olds, there has been less public debate on the impact of recent legislation on gender issues. Indeed, in the education policy community, comprising the Scottish Consultative Committee on the Curriculum, a General Teaching Council, and the Scottish Office Education Department, there are few, if any, women members or representatives, and even less discussion about gender issues (Brown and Riddell 1992). Concern has been expressed about the absence of women on various task groups on the curriculum (Barton and Weiner 1990). Women who are successful in educational and political careers tend to come from supportive middle- and upper-middle class backgrounds and from professional occupations.

In South Africa little has been done to correct gender bias and to eliminate gender discrimination in the South African system (Jansen 1990). Although the current transformation of education offers opportunities to tackle gender discrimination, it is suggested that state intervention is unlikely. More probable is the drive for an emancipatory curriculum from local women's organizations.

In New Zealand, in contrast to the United Kingdom, Australia, and many other countries, there has been a centrally determined curriculum for schools, with a core curriculum for secondary schools. However, during the 1980s concern developed about the nature and efficacy of the curriculum, resulting in documents for a new national curriculum. In a 1991 discussion document, gender was mentioned, along with race and ethnicity, as something to be "recognized, respected, and responded to." However, many New Zealand writers have suggested that the importance of a focus on the curriculum is to ensure a complementarity between schooling and the changing economy (Codd 1991, Lauder et al. 1988) rather than to address an alleged inherent male bias in the current curriculum. Research indicates, however, that girls' aspirations are changing (Burnhill and McPherson 1984) and that their performance in traditional male subjects is improving.

4. Conclusion

Is there a need for major curriculum change away from male-centeredness toward girl-centered education (Whyte et al. 1992)? In arguing for single-sex schools, advocates noted that while the early champions of mixed-sex education recognized that both sexes would bring different sets of social experiences to the classroom, hoping that this would be beneficial, they did not consider the possibility that one sex (male) would derive much greater benefit from this situation.

The assumption is now questioned that there are social advantages in mixed-sex schools by asking "social advantages for whom?" The possibilities of a wider curriculum in mixed-sex schools is also questioned (Shaw 1985). Shaw notes that school inspectors in the United Kingdom (HMIs) reported that girls were less likely to choose a science subject if they attended a mixed school than they would if they attended a single-sex girls' school, even though in a mixed school they are more likely to be offered science. The HMI report went on to show that the popularity of an arts subject was markedly greater in mixed-sex schools. This is particularly important in the light of evidence that the child who takes science subjects has a greater chance of remaining longer at school than the child who takes arts subjects (Shaw 1985).

Further, interaction in the classroom has been studied to examine whether teachers do, indeed, spend greater amounts of time with, and addressing boys. In an experiment, teachers made a deliberate attempt to give girls more attention. The taped results disclose that, on average, teachers interacted with the girls 38 percent of the time, the maximum time devoted to girls being 42 percent. During the experiment, despite the fact that the boys were still getting a substantially greater amount of the teachers' time, the teacher and male pupils all felt that the girls had been unfairly favored.

In Australia, girl-friendly schooling has focused on language and classroom dynamics, and campaigns to promote nontraditional careers, in an attempt to address issues of equality of opportunity through the curriculum (Yates 1992). Reports had shown how girls did not receive an equal share of educational resources: less money was spent on them; they had access to less space and equipment; they were debarred from certain studies, and marginalized in classroom activity by forms of language of teachers, use of space, types of encouragement and disencouragement, and conversational politics (Stanworth 1983).

In response to this situation a number of writers support a "feminist curriculum" (Spender 1981). It is suggested that such a curriculum would be explicitly political; it would involve a major critique of existing educational institutions, and be concerned not merely with equal access to education but with offering a different experience of education. In this way, traditional subjects have been reconstructed offering feminist insight into both content and activity. Yates (1992) illustrates this approach by noting the project in Victoria, Australia, which reconstructed the history of Australian squatters by giving attention to the experience of women in colonial life. The project included games and physical activities in an attempt to work out how a culturally, geographically, and historically specific concept like squatters could have any meaning for migrant adolescent schoolgirls. It may be that the most creative and girl-friendly curricula can be developed outside formal educational arenas. In the United States, women's groups, although having access to only limited resources, have introduced into the girl-centered curriculum issues such as domestic violence, authoritarianism in the family, abortion, motherhood as an ideology, and unequal pay. It is suggested that to the extent that these issues gain prominence, so will there be greater understanding of sexual oppression and female subordination in society with increasing pressure on the state to respond to the needs of women for a transformed society. Whether such pressure will produce a girl-friendly school curriculum is precisely the issue debated by the three feminist perspectives discussed above.

See also: Coeducation versus Single-sex Schooling; Gender Theories in Education; Sex Equity: Assumptions and Strategies

References

Acker S 1989 Women and teaching: A semi-detached sociology of a semi-profession. In: Walker S, Barton L (eds.) 1989

Acker S (ed.) 1989 *Teachers, Gender and Careers.* Falmer Press, Lewes

Arnot 1989 A cloud over coeducation: An analysis of the forms of transmission of class and gender relations. In: Walker S, Barton L (eds.) 1989

Barton L, Weiner R 1990 Social justice and the national curriculum. *Research Papers in Education* 5(3): 203–07

Barrett M 1987 Gender and class: Marxist feminist perspectives on education. In: Arnot M, Weiner G (eds.) 1987 *Gender and the Politics of Schooling.* Open University Press, Milton Keynes

Bourdieu P, Passeron J-C 1977 *Reproduction in Education and Culture.* Sage, London

Brock C, Cammish N K 1991 *Factors Affecting Female Participation in Education in Six Developing Countries.* Overseas Development Administration, London

Brown S, Riddell S (eds.) 1992 *Gender, Race and Class in Schools.* SCRE, Edinburgh

Burnhill P, McPherson A 1984 Careers and gender: The expectations of able Scottish school leavers in 1971 and 1981. In: Acker S, Piper D W (eds.) 1984 *Is Higher Education Fair to Women?* Society for Research in Higher Education, London

Codd J 1991 Curriculum reform in New Zealand. *J. Curric. St.* 23(2): 177–80

Giroux H 1983 *Critical Theory and Educational Practice.* Deakin University Press, Geelong

Habermas J 1976 *Legitimation Crisis.* Heinemann, London

Hartmann H 1981 The unhappy marriage of Marxism and feminism. In: Sargent L (ed.) 1981 *Women and Revolution.* Pluto, London

Jansen J (ed.) 1990 *Knowledge and Power in South Africa: A critical Perspective Across the Disciplines.* Skotaville Press, Johannesburg

Kelly A 1987 The construction of masculine science. In: Arnot M, Weiner G (eds.) 1987 *Gender and the Politics of Schooling.* Open University Press, Milton Keynes

Lauder H, Middleton S, Boston J, Wylie I 1988 The third wave: A critique of the New Zealand Treasury's Report on Education. *NZ J. Educ. Stud.* 23: 15–33

Riddell S 1992 *Gender and the Politics of the Curriculum.* Routledge and Kegan Paul, London

Shaw J 1985 Politics of single sex schools. In: Deem R (ed.) 1985 *Coeducation Reconsidered.* Open University Press, Milton Keynes

Spender D (ed.) 1981 *Men's Studies Modified: The Impact of Feminism on Academic Disciplines.* Pergamon Press, Oxford

Spender D 1983 *Invisible Women: The Schooling Scandal.* Writers and Readers Publishing Cooperative, London

Stanworth M 1983 *Gender and Schooling.* Open University Press, Milton Keynes

Tomlinson S 1987 Why Johnny can't read: Critical theory

and special education. *Eur. J. Spec. Needs Educ.* 3 (1): 45–98

Walkerdine V 1989 *Counting Girls Out.* Virago, London

Weiner G, Arnot M (eds.) 1987 *Gender under Scrutiny: New Inquiries in Education.* Open University Press, Milton Keynes

Whyte J, Deem R, Kant L, Cruikshank M (eds.) 1985 *Girl-friendly Schooling.* Methuen, London

Yates L 1992 The theory and practice of counter-sexist education in schools. *Discourse* 3(2): 33–44

Further Reading

Apple M 1979 *Cultural and Economic Reproduction in Education.* Routledge and Kegan Paul, London

Apple M 1986 *Ideology and Curriculum.* Routledge and Kegan Paul, London

Byrne E 1987 Gender in education: Educational policy in Australia and Europe (1975–1985). *Comp. Educ.* 23 (1): 11–22

Elliot J, Powell C 1987 Young women and science: Do we need more science? In: Kelly A (ed.) 1987 *The Missing Half: Girls and Science Education.* Manchester University Press, Manchester

Hills C 1989 The Senga syndrome: Reflections on 21 years in education. In: Patterson F, Fewell J (eds.) 1989 *Girls in their Prime—Scottish Education Visited.* Scottish Academic Press, Edinburgh

Schofield B (ed.) 1989 *Science at Age 13.* HMSO, London

Spender D, Sarah E (eds.) 1988 *Learning to Lose: Sexism and Education.* Womens Press, London

Walker S, Barton L (eds.) 1989 *Gender, Class and Education.* Falmer Press, Lewes

Neo-Marxist Approaches to Curriculum

D. Gordon

The neo-Marxist approach to education is concerned first and foremost with education's contribution to the reproduction of the means and the relations of production in society (particularly capitalist society). In other words neo-Marxists are concerned with the process of reproduction of class structure. They are also interested in the possibilities of contesting this reproductive process, and thus in education's potential for radical political change. The neo-Marxists' concerns have led them to stress the prime importance of skills taught, knowledge and ideologies transmitted, and also of the centrality of the reproduction of consciousness in the general reproduction process. Inevitably this has led them to investigate the school's overt and hidden curricula, and in general to stress the significance of curriculum as a mechanism for reproduction.

1. Reconceptualism and the "New" Sociology

The first-generation neo-Marxist group flourished in the mid-1970s and was in fact a part and, to an extent, an extension of the reconceptualist approach to curriculum in the United States (Giroux et al. 1981), and the "new" sociology of education in Great Britain. It is the group's relationship to the latter which best demonstrates the contribution and limitations of their particular neo-Marxist theory to curriculum research, and to educational thought in general.

The new sociology of education (Young 1971) arose as a reaction to the dominant paradigm in sociology of education in the late 1960s, that is, the functionalist, educational input–output approach. The "new" sociologists of education rejected functionalism and

charged sociologists with having ignored the process of schooling itself, and in particular condemned their ignoring what goes on in classrooms. A central aspect of classroom life is the way knowledge is transmitted, and thus the "new" sociologists developed a sociology of education which was largely a sociology of curriculum, using ideas from the sociology of knowledge. They tended to eschew a grand theory and a macrolevel of analysis. The reproduction theorists' contribution was to fill this gap by linking the sociology of curriculum to macrosocietal processes, within the framework of Marxism, that is, one of the major grand themes in the sociological tradition. This paradigm rapidly became perhaps the most influential and flourishing paradigm of the 1970s in educational sociology and in curriculum studies.

2. The Reproduction Theory

The classic statement of the neo-Marxist position vis-à-vis school and curriculum is Althusser's *Ideology and Ideological State Apparatuses* (1971). Althusser distinguishes between (a) repressive state apparatuses (police, military, etc.) which ensure the political conditions of the reproduction of relations of production primarily through the use of force, and (b) ideological state apparatuses (church, mass media, family, schools, etc.) which work more covertly through ideology, or as Bourdieu has put it—through symbolic violence (Bordieu and Passeron 1977). Of these, the most important for Althusser is the school:

> One ideological State apparatus certainly has the dominant role, although hardly anyone lends an ear to its music: it is

so silent! This is the school. It takes children from every class at infant-school age, and then for years, the years in which the child is most "vulnerable"... it drums into them, whether it uses new or old methods, a certain amount of "know-how" wrapped in the ruling ideology (French, arithmetic, natural history ...)... or simply the ruling ideology in its pure state (ethics, civic instruction ...)... Each mass [of children] ejected en route is practically provided with the ideology which suits the role it has to fulfill in class society...[It] is by [this] apprenticeship that the relations of production in a capitalist social formation, i.e., the relations of exploited to exploiter are largely reproduced. The mechanisms which produce this vital result ... are ... concealed by a universally reigning ideology of the school ... which represents the school as a neutral environment purged of ideology. (Althusser 1971 pp. 155–56)

This quote encapsulates three of the central ideas characteristic of the writings of a first generation of neo-Marxist thinkers concerned with curriculum, who became known as reproduction theorists. These ideas are outlined below.

2.1 Knowledge as a Form of Capital

Knowledge is viewed as part of what has been called cultural capital (Bourdieu and Passeron 1977). Thus the knowledge (procedural and substantive) that a person "owns," like all capital, determines, at least in part, their position within the class structure. One of the mechanisms whereby societies reproduce the class structure is through control of access to cultural capital. That is, children of different social classes are given access to different forms of knowledge, the status of the various sorts of knowledge reflecting the social status of those who "own" them. This is accomplished in at least three ways:

(a) *Different curricula.* Children from different social backgrounds who attend different sorts of schools (e.g., vocational vs. academic high schools) will study different subjects.

(b) *Middle-class subject bias.* The content of high-status subjects, studied in school by all students, will be easier for middle-class students to master because they have already acquired at home a familiarity with the language of school and the content of the high-status subject (Bourdieu and Passeron 1977, Bernstein 1977). This is not to say that the contents of one school subject is intrinsically superior to another but that the kinds of knowledge with which the working-class students would be more likely to be familiar are not included in the common curriculum. Thus Vulliamy (1976) has argued, for example, that school music generally means "serious," that is, classical music in the western tradition, and that a "culture clash" exists between school music and working-class pupils' nonclassical musical interests outside school.

(c) *Middle-class language.* The presentation of information in school is often couched in a language and/or style with which middle-class students are more familiar (Bourdieu and Passeron 1977, Bernstein 1977). Again, what is being claimed is that this language and/or style is not intrinsically superior to that of the working class, but rather acts to maintain class structure.

2.2 The Ideological Nature of the School Curriculum

The ostensibly ideologically neutral content of the school curriculum is, in fact, highly ideological in nature and reflects the need to reproduce class structure. Take, for example, natural science. The study of physics, chemistry, and biology would appear as far from being ideological in content as one could imagine. Yet Apple (1979) has argued that science is taught in such a way as to play down the role of scientific revolutions in research. This results in a general deemphasis of revolution, encourages political acquiescence, and thus helps maintain the status quo.

2.3 The Hidden Curriculum

The hidden curriculum, consisting of unacknowledged but highly consistent messages transmitted to the students (Bloom 1972, Gordon 1982), is assumed to be the most powerful and effective means available in schools to help reproduce class structure. These unacknowledged messages derive both from implicit aspects of the manifest curriculum and also from structural properties of the school. The latter, and in particular the hierarchical structure of social relations in the school, have been seen as exhibiting a correspondence with the hierarchical division of labour [this is known as the correspondence principle analysed by the Marxist economists Bowles and Gintis (1976)].

The interests of the reproduction theorists in the "hidden curriculum" follows from their interest in the theory of "working class false consciousness," a theory developed by Lukács (Lukács 1968). The notion that schools silently and covertly transmit concealed but powerful messages to the students also links closely with the concept of class hegemony developed by the Italian Marxist Gramsci (Gramsci 1971). Hegemony, which refers to "the successful attempt of a dominant class to utilize its control over the resources of state and civil society ... to establish its view of the world as all-inclusive and universal" (Giroux 1981b p. 23) in fact became a central concept of neo-Marxist educational thought.

3. Criticisms of Reproduction Theory

Naturally the reproduction approach came in for a considerable amount of criticism from thinkers who rejected the entire Marxist framework. However, by the late 1970s the reproduction approach was also being criticized by neo-Marxists and even by some of the original reproduction theorists themselves (e.g., Apple

1982). These criticisms centered particularly on the assertion that in arguing that the reproduction process in general, and in schools especially, is so powerful that it seems to be an almost inevitable and inescapable result of the way societies and schools work, Althusser and his fellow reproduction theorists seemed to be adopting a deterministic stance to societal processes. Thinkers like Anyon (1981), Apple (1982), and Giroux (1981a) saw this stance as overly pessimistic, and as denying the possibilities of political and social change. These criticisms of the second generation group of neo-Marxist educators led them to an interest in the phenomenon of resistance.

4. Resistance Theory

The trigger for the work around resistance theory was Paul Willis' (1977) classic study *Learning to Labour: How Working Class Kids Get Working Class Jobs.* This is an ethnographic study of a group of working-class teenagers both in school and, after they leave school, in the work place. This group—known as "the lads"—simply wrought havoc in their school. Willis shows that their behavior stemmed in fact from a sophisticated awareness of the hegemonic function of the school, and in particular of its hidden curriculum. Their rebellion derived from their refusal to "buy" the school's ideology and is, for Willis, a form of political resistance. Ironically however, this resistance was self-defeating. The "lads" ended up with an official education of so low a standard that it led them inevitably to getting menial, low-status jobs when they left school. Thus their sort of resistance in fact helps perpetuate the existing class structure.

Willis' study has invited the resistance theorists to set themselves the following tasks:

(a) To identify and document (mainly through ethnographic studies) examples of student resistance to schooling and to the hidden curriculum in particular.

(b) To differentiate between self-defeating and productive examples of resistance (i.e., resistance which can lead to political change).

(c) to suggest ways of mobilizing the resistance phenomenon for political change.

5. Recent Trends

Resistance theory gave the neo-Marxist approach to curriculum a new direction, and in the late 1970s and early 1980s this was once again probably the dominant school of thought in curriculum studies. However, it is an approach that has had to try to counter some telling criticisms. Hargreaves (1982) has published a

powerful attack on resistance theorists. In his view, their assumptions and activist political stance has led them to the absurd position of reading "resistance" into every conceivable sign of disaffection, boredom, or passivity on the part of pupils in school. Thus, in his opinion, their empirical work is loose and methodologically weak.

From the vantage point of the late 1980s, resistance theory, and, in fact, neo-Marxist approaches to curriculum in general, seem to be at the crossroads. It may be that their paradigm has exhausted the interesting questions it is capable of asking and answering. On the other hand, there have been attempts to link the approach to modern work in discourse analysis and to the work of Foucault (Whitty 1985). These may once again encourage a further development of the neo-Marxist paradigm in curricular work.

See also: Classical Sociological Theories of Education; Contemporary Sociological Theories of Education; Hidden Curriculum; Marxism and Educational Thought; Reproduction Theory; Resistance Theory

References

Althusser L 1971 Ideology and ideological state apparatuses: Notes towards an investigation. In: Althusser L (ed.) 1971 *Lenin and Philosophy and Other Essays.* New Left Books, New York
Anyon J 1981 Elementary schooling and distinctions of social class. *Interchange* 12(2/3): 118–32
Apple M W 1979 *Ideology and Curriculum.* Routledge and Kegan Paul, London
Apple M W 1982 *Education and Power.* Routledge and Kegan Paul, London
Bernstein B 1977 *Class Codes and Control* Vol 3. *Towards a Theory of Educational Transmissions.* Routledge and Kegan Paul, London
Bloom B S 1972 Innocence in education. *Sch. Rev.* 80(3): 333–52
Bourdieu P, Passeron J C 1977 *Reproduction in Education and Society.* Sage, London
Bowles S, Gintis H 1976 *Schooling in Capitalist America: Educational Reform and the Contradictions of Economic Life.* Basic Books, New York
Giroux H A 1981a Hegemony, resistance and the paradox of educational reform. *Interchange* 12(2/3): 3–26
Giroux H A 1981b *Ideology, Culture and the Process of Schooling.* Temple University Press, Philadelphia, Pennsylvania
Giroux H A, Penna A N, Pinar W F (eds.) 1981 *Curriculum and Instruction: Alternatives in Education.* McCutchan, Berkeley, California
Gordon D 1982 The concept of the hidden curriculum *J. Phil. Educ.* 16(2): 187–98
Gramsci A 1971 *Selections from the Prison Notebooks.* International Publishers, New York
Hargreaves A 1982 Resistance and relative autonomy theories: Problems of distortion and incoherence in recent Marxist analyses of education. *Br. J. Sociol. Educ.* 3(2): 107–26
Lukács G 1968 *History and Class Consciousness: Studies in Marxist Dialectics* MIT Press, Cambridge, Massachusetts

Vulliamy G 1976 What counts as school music? In: Whitty G, Young M F D (eds.) 1976 *Explorations in the Politics of School Knowledge.* Nafferton Books, Nafferton

Whitty G 1985 *Sociology and School Knowledge: Curriculum Theory, Research and Politics.* Methuen, London

Willis P E 1977 *Learning to Labour: How Working Class Kids Get Working Class Jobs.* Saxon House, Farnborough

Young M F D (ed.) 1971 *Knowledge and Control: New Directions for the Sociology of Education.* Collier-Macmillan, London

Policy Analysis

M. Trow

Husén (1984) has argued that the relation of research to policy is far more complex, far more indirect than it formerly appeared. Drawing on the informed writings of Weiss (1979) and Kogan et al. (1980) among others, and from rich experience, he dismisses as irrelevant, at least to the field of education, two classical models of the application of research to policy that Weiss lists among seven different models or concepts of research utilization: the "linear" model, which leads neatly from basic knowledge to applied research to development to application, and the "problem-solving" model, in which research is done to fill in certain bodies of knowledge needed to make a decision among policy alternatives. These are dismissed on the grounds that they simply do not even roughly describe what happens in the real world. The remaining models are merged into two. One is an "enlightenment" or "percolation" model, in which research somehow (and just how is of greatest interest) influences policy indirectly, by entering into the consciousness of the actors and shaping the terms of their discussion about policy alternatives. The second, the "political model," refers to the intentional use of research by political decision-makers to strengthen an argument, to justify positions already taken, or to avoid making or having to make unpopular decisions by burying the controversial problem in research.

Of these two models, the first or "percolation" model is the more interesting, since it is the way through which research actually has an influence on policy, rather than merely being used to justify or avoid making decisions. Moreover, the percolation model and its mechanisms and processes are so subtle that they challenge study and reflection.

1. Researchers and Policy Analysts

The decade between the mid-1970s and mid-1980s saw in the United States, and to some extent elsewhere, the emergence of a profession, that of the policy analyst, whose training, habits of mind, and conditions of work were expressly designed to narrow the gap between the researcher and the policymaker and to bring systematic knowledge to bear more directly, more quickly, and more relevantly on the issues of public policy. This entry attempts to compare and contrast the researcher and the policy analyst to see how this breed of staff analyst/researcher, inside as well as outside government, may affect the ways in which research comes to bear on policy. The comparison is not intended to be invidious, that is, there is no implication that the invention of policy analysis has in any way solved the problems of the relation of research to policy that Husén, Weiss, and others have identified. But it may be of interest to see how this emerging profession affects that process, and how it generates new problems—intellectual, political, and moral—as it solves some of the old.

Policy analysis developed as a formal discipline in the mid-1970s through the coming together of a number of strands of work and thought in the social sciences. These included operations research developed during the Second World War on a strongly mathematical basis for improving the efficiency of military operations—the deployment of submarines, bombing raids, and convoy management. Added to this were new forms of microeconomics developed in the 1950s and 1960s; the long-standing tradition of work in public administration; the newer and increasingly strong strain of behaviorism in the political sciences; organizational theory; certain lines of applied sociology and social psychology; and the emerging interest in the role of law in public policy. Graduate schools of public policy were established in a number of leading American universities around 1970. Some leading universities now have genuine graduate schools of public policy; there are literally hundreds of others which offer programs which include some measure of policy analysis in their schools of management, public administration, or business administration. To the mix of social science and law, some schools have added scientists, engineers, and others interested in public policy problems. These graduate schools for the most part offer a two-year postgraduate professional degree, ordinarily the Master of Public Policy. Their graduates go directly into public service at national, state, or local levels, or get jobs in think-tanks or private agencies concerned with public issues—for example, organizations concerned with the preservation of the environment, with education, overseas trade, and so forth. These latter "private" organizations, however, are directly involved for the most part in public policy —indeed, much of what they do is to try to influence public policy, so the conditions of work for public policy analysts in them resemble those of analysts who enter governmental service itself.

There are several aspects of the training of policy analysts that need to be emphasized. As must already be clear, the training of the policy analyst is intensely interdisciplinary. This is required first because of the diverse nature of its intellectual antecedents; the field itself reflects the coming together of diverse currents in what Lasswell (Lerner and Lasswell 1951) called the "policy sciences." But more important, the training has to be interdisciplinary because that is the way the problems present themselves to decision makers. Real decisions, as we all know, do not respect the boundaries of the academic disciplines: they always have political, economic, and organizational components; they may well also have legal, educational, biological, or other technical implications as well.

Perhaps the most important distinguishing characteristic of policy analysts as contrasted with academic research social scientists is that they are trained, indeed required, to see and to formulate problems from the perspectives not of the academic disciplines, but of the decision makers. In their work, they accept the constraints and values of decision makers—the political pressures on them, the political feasibility of a proposal, its financial costs, the legal context within which it will operate, the difficulties of implementing it, of shaping organizations, and of recruiting, training, and motivating people to work in the service of its purposes. They are, if effectively trained, sensitive to the costs and benefits of programs, to the trade-offs in any decision, and to the alternative advantages of government and the market in achieving social purposes. In a word, they try to see problems from the perspective of the decision maker, but with a set of intellectual, analytical, and research tools that the politician or senior civil servant may not possess. They are, and are trained to be, the researchers in government at the elbow of the decision makers, or if not in government, then serving the "government in opposition" or some think-tank or interest group which hopes to staff the next administration or agency on the next swing of the political pendulum. Of course, not all policy analysts are "researchers," as the university conceives of research. But what they do, bringing ideas and information to bear on social "problems" in a search for "solutions," is the kind of "research" that has the most direct influence on public policy.

By contrast, the faculty members of schools of public policy are not, for the most part, like the students that they train: the former are almost without exception academics with PhDs, trained in and drawn from the social science disciplines, specialists originally who have a particular interest in public policy, and who do research on policy issues, but not on the whole like the research that their students will be doing in their

government or quasi-government jobs. The faculty members of these schools are for the most part what Wilson (1981 p. 36) has called "policy intellectuals," while their students are policy analysts—the staff people and bureaucrats serving their policy-oriented clients in and out of governments. The relationship of the policy intellectual in the university to the policy analyst in government bears on the issue of "knowledge creep" and "research percolation" that Husén and Weiss speak of, and to which this entry will return.

Let us look at some of the characteristics of "researchers" as Husén describes them, and at some of the "disjunctions" between research and policy that the nature of the researcher in the university gives rise to. The field of policy analysis and the new profession of policy analyst were, one might say, invented precisely to meet the need of policymakers for analysis and research carried out within the same constraints that the policymaker experiences. Policy analysis thus aims to narrow those "disjunctions" between research and policy of which Husén speaks. He describes three conditions under which researchers work that are different for policy analysts:

(a) Researchers are usually performing their tasks at . . . universities . . . . They tend to conduct their research according to the paradigms to which they have become socialized by their graduate studies. Their achievements are subjected to peer reviews which they regard as more important than assessments made by the customers in a public agency. (Husén 1984 p. 10)

Analysts, by contrast, work for the most part in government or in shadow governmental agencies, or in large private business organizations. The paradigms of research that they acquire in graduate school emphasize the importance of serving the client, of defining or clarifying the nature of the problem, or identifying the policy options available, of evaluating those alternatives in terms of their cost, probable effectiveness, political feasibility, ease of implementation, and the like—the same criteria which the decision maker would use in planning and choosing a course of action. The analyst is trained then to make recommendations among the action alternatives that have been identified, supporting the recommendations made with appropriate arguments and evidence.

Much, perhaps most, of what such analysts do is not published, is not reviewed by peers, and will almost certainly appear, if at all, in greatly modified form, either anonymously or under someone else's name. The analyst's reputation will be made *not* in an academic setting, but in his or her agency, and more importantly among the small but active community of analysts in government agencies, on legislative staffs, in think-tanks, and special interest organizations who know of the analyst's work and its quality. Incidentally, it is in that arena of discussion and assessment—the analyst's analog to the scholar's "invisible college"— that we need to look for the mechanisms of information

139

"drift" and "creep," and for the processes of percolation through which research and evidence come to influence policy.

> (b) Researchers operate at a high level of training and specialization, which means that they tend to isolate a "slice" of a problem area that can be more readily handled than more complicated global problems. (Husén 1984 p. 10)

By contrast, analysts are trained to be as interdisciplinary as possible, to follow the requirements of a problem in their choice of ideas, theories, and research methods, rather than to allow the theories and methods of their discipline select and shape their problems. This is not wholly successful, in part because their teachers in these schools are not themselves equally familiar with the variety of research methods and perspectives across disciplinary lines, and because their students, the fledgling analysts, inevitably come to be more familiar and comfortable with some kinds of analysis rather than others. Nevertheless the requirement that they see problems as the policymakers would were they analysts, requires analysts to transcend the constraints of a single discipline and to tackle problems as wholes rather than by "slices."

> (c) Researchers are much less constrained than policy makers in terms of what problems they can tackle, what kind of critical language they can employ and how much time they have . . . at their disposal to complete a study. (Husén 1984 p. 10)

Analysts, by contrast, ordinarily are assigned their studies, or do them within circumscribed policy areas. That does not wholly preclude their exercise of discretion; and indeed, they may exercise very important amounts of initiative in how they formulate their problems, and in the range of responses to the problems they consider (Meltsner 1976 pp. 81–114). From the researcher's perspective, the captive analyst is merely "a hired gun" doing what he or she is told by political or bureaucratic superiors. But from the perspective of the analyst, discretion, even within the constraints of a given policy problem or area, may be very considerable. How to control air pollution in a given area, for example, allows a variety of regulatory solutions, from setting standards for allowable emissions for different kinds of plants and industries to setting charges on pollutants requiring polluters to pay for each unit of pollutant emitted. The issues are political, technical, economic, legal, and normative—and they are not always decided a priori by political or administrative decision-makers.

It is true that analysts are ordinarily held to a closer time frame than are academic researchers; it is not unusual for students to become accustomed to doing analyses of various policy problems, drawing upon the best available data, research, and advice, within 48 or 72 hours, exercises designed to prepare them for the fierce time pressures of legislative hearings or the negotiations that accompany the writing and revision of legislation. Other exercises allow them a week, and a major piece of research equivalent to a master's essay will take up to six months. Time constraints on the job also vary; analysts become skillful in knowing who has been working on a given problem area, and where published or unpublished research or data on the issue can be found. For the analyst, knowledgeable people are a central research resource, and the telephone is part of the student's equipment alongside computers and the library.

But as they develop the skill of rapidly bringing ideas to bear on data, and data on ideas, analysts become heavily dependent upon existing statistics and on research done by others. They are often skillful, and even bold, in drawing analogies between findings in different areas of social life, allowing them thus to use the findings of research in one area for informing decisions in another. These analysts cannot often meet the scholar's standards of depth and thoroughness in their research—for example, in the review of the research literature, or in the critical evaluation of the findings of relevant research. Yet working under time and other pressures in the political milieu, the analysts know that the alternative to what they are doing is not a major university-based research project, but more commonly the impressions, anecdotes, and general wisdom of a staff conference. Their own reports, which include discussions of alternative lines of action based on data regarding their comparative costs and benefits, must, they believe, be better than an unsystematic discussion among friends and advisers.

Policy analysts in government as we have described them have some of the characteristics of researchers, but are more narrowly constrained by their bureaucratic roles. They also have some of the characteristics of Kogan's middle-men, professionals who serve a liaison function (Kogan et al. 1980 pp. 36–38), though they are more active and ready to take research initiatives than the term "middle-man" implies. But they also are not infrequently the decision-makers themselves.

2. Example from the Field of Education

One almost always talks about research *influencing* decision makers—and if the researcher is a university social scientist then the decision maker is almost certainly someone a distance away with his or her own concerns, political commitments, interests, and prejudices. But the policy analyst has the advantage of acting within the bureaucracy to make or directly affect a myriad of administrative decisions that rarely get into the newspapers, are not debated by politicians or on floors of legislatures, but nevertheless have very large consequences.

One illustration comes from the University of California, half of whose budget—the half which pays the operating costs of the University, faculty salaries, and the like—comes from the state of California. The preparation of the University's budget and its incorporation into the governor's budget is a complicated procedure. Very substantial parts of the University's budget are governed by formulas, relating, for example, support levels to enrollment levels, that have been negotiated over the years between the budget analysts in the central administration of the University and their counterparts in the State Department of Finance. These formulas, essentially bureaucratic treaties, are mutual understandings which give the university a greater degree of fiscal security and predictability than one would ever guess from reading the newspapers, which almost never report these matters, but only the visible debates in the legislature and speeches by the governor.

The formulas, of course, do not cover all contingencies, especially in an institution as fluid and diverse as the University of California with so many different sources of energy and initiative creating new programs, facilities, and claims on public funds all the time. Claims for resources, old and new, are argued out or negotiated annually between the University analysts and the State Department of Finance analysts; they speak each other's language, and often have been trained in the same graduate schools and departments, not infrequently in Berkeley's School of Public Policy. In these negotiations, "good arguments" by the University are rewarded; that is, requests for additional support funds that are supported by a good bureaucratic argument are often accepted, and new activities are built into the governor's budget. The arguments made for these programs are the arguments of analysts, often based on analogies with existing state-funded activities, and backed by data showing the actual nature of the activity and its costs. For example, the University wants the state to revise the formula allocating funds for the replacement of scientific equipment used in teaching; it wants more generous provision for teaching assistants; it wants the state to assume the costs of certain athletic facilities; it wants the state to support remedial courses for underprepared students; and so on. In support of these claims the University analysts do research on the actual useful life of laboratory instruments in different scientific departments and on how that record compares with the life of instruments in other universities and in commercial labs; it studies the use and distribution of teaching assistants in the University and how their work contributes to the instructional program; it studies who uses the athletic facilities and for what purposes; and so on. These are not matters of high principle; there exists a broad area of value consensus between the negotiators, but the quality of the research backing those claims is crucial to whether they are accepted, and indeed whether they ought to be accepted. The sums of money that are allocated in these ways are in the aggregate very large. There are many areas of public life in which civil servants exercise wide discretion in decision-making,

though they are often wise enough to deny that they are in fact making policy or decisions, but merely "implementing" them. Nevertheless, when we reflect on the influence of research on policy, we should not neglect the realm of bureaucratic and technocratic decision-making in the public sector where researcher and decision maker come together in the person of the policy analyst. University-based researchers need to be reminded that not all research has to percolate down through a complex network of relationships to enter another complex process of "decision accretion"; some research has access to decision-makers quickly and directly, and is done for and by them.

The newly emergent field of policy analysis seems to be thriving in the United States, at least in a modest way, even in the face of budget cuts and hiring freezes in the federal and in many state and local governments. Policy analysts are in demand whether public expenditures are rising or falling; the problems posed to government by budgetary constraints are even more severe than those posed by expansion and the proliferation of public programs and services. And with all the cuts, most governments are not reducing the absolute level of public expenditures on social services, but merely reducing their rates of growth. In any event, public life is becoming increasingly more complex and there is no shortage of work for policy analysts.

3. Four Problems Facing the Policy Analyst

It should not be thought that the emergence of policy analysis, and of the infrastructure of graduate schools, journals, professional associations and meetings which give it definition and self-consciousness, solve all the problems of the relation of research to policy. For if policy analysts solve some of those problems, they also create new ones. This section outlines four such problems in the realm of policy analysis as currently practiced, though this does not imply that there are only four. These are all problems which in significant ways affect the quality of the analyst's work and his or her influence on policy and decision-making.

First, and this is a problem that the analyst shares with academic research in education, policy analysis makes relatively little use of ethnographic research methods, the method of direct observation of customary behavior and informal conversation. One consequence of this is that the policy analyst is a captive of existing and usually official statistics; where those statistics are wrong or misleading or inadequate, the analyst's work is flawed, misleading, and inadequate also. By contrast, university researchers are more likely to question the quality of research data, though it is likely that they rarely question the quality of official statistics.

Second, the outcome of public policy analysis, its reports and recommendations, is affected not only by

141

the analyst's own preferences and biases and those of the client, but also by how the analyst bounds the problem, the phenomena and variables that will be taken into account. These boundaries are sharply constrained by the analyst's position within the bureaucratic work setting, more so than for the university-based researcher.

Third, for every policy analyst outside the university there is tension between the needs and requirements of the client, on one hand, and their own professional commitments to intellectual honesty, to the searching out of negative evidence, and to their freedom to speak and publish what is known or has been learnt, on the other. Bureaucratic research settings put severe strains on those scholarly and professional values. Indeed, the moral issue of how policy analysts deal with dual loyalty to their professional identity as analysts and to their political masters and clients is at the heart of policy analysis and not, as moral issues often are, at the margins.

Finally, there is the relation between policy analysts and policy intellectuals which bears on the nature of communication and persuasion in the political arena, and more broadly on the processes of "decision accretion" through enlightenment and the percolation of research findings, ideas, and assumptions in the decision-making process.

4. Policy Intellectuals and Policy Analysts

In his paper identifying several models of connections between research and policy, Husén (1984) is drawn to the enlightenment or "percolation" model. He quotes Weiss to describe research as permeating the policy making process, entering the policy arena not through specific findings or recommendations, but by its "generalizations and orientations percolating through informed publics in coming to shape the way in which people think about social issues" (Weiss 1979).

There is, I think, broad agreement that much of the impact of research on policy (I would not say all) occurs in this subtle, difficult-to-measure way. But is this not at variance with the image of the policy analyst directly at the policy maker's elbow, preparing papers and reports at his or her request, speaking to issues and problems that the policy-maker will be facing even if not yet recognizing their character or the available options? This image of the policy analyst is in fact compatible with the metaphor of the "percolation" of research, and of the notion of research entering into the general debate and discussion about an issue going on among interested publics, an ongoing debate that crystallizes into policy at a moment when a political actor chooses to place it on the agenda for action and not merely discussion. The analyst in government cannot often do basic research or long-range studies; he or she is to a large extent a consumer and adapter of research, part of the attentive audience for research, and among the most active participants in the critical discussion about the issue and the literature that grows up around it. In the United States, analysts who are educated at schools of public policy are especially trained to take part in that discussion because their teachers and their teachers' peers in other policy schools and professional and academic departments do the research and comment on the research of others in such journals as *The Public Interest, Policy Analysts, Public Choice, Policy Studies Journal*, and *The Journal of Policy Analysis and Management*, among others. These university-based writers and researchers, some of whom teach in the schools of public policy, are what Wilson calls "policy intellectuals." And his view of their influence on policy is not far from that of Weiss and Husén's notion of the percolation model. Reviewing the role of policy intellectuals over the past decade, Wilson observes that

> If the influence of intellectuals was not to be found in the details of policy, it was nonetheless real, albeit indirect. Intellectuals provided the conceptual language, the ruling paradigms, the empirical examples . . . that became the accepted assumptions for those in charge of making policy. Intellectuals framed, and to a large degree conducted, the debates about whether this language and these paradigms were correct. The most influential intellectuals were those who managed to link a concept or a theory to the practical needs and ideological dispositions of political activists and governmental officials. (Wilson 1981 p. 36).

Wilson goes further than most of us in downplaying the role of research per se as against the power of the arguments of skillful intellectuals.

> At any given moment in history, an influential idea—and thus an influential intellectual—is one that provides a persuasive simplification of some policy question that is consistent with a particular mix of core values then held by the political elite . . . Clarifying and making persuasive those ideas is largely a matter of argument and the careful use of analogies; rarely . . . does this process involve matters of proof and evidence of the sort that is, in their scholarly, as opposed to their public lives, supposed to be the particular skill and obligation of the intellectual in the university. (Wilson 1981 p. 36)

The role of the policy intellectual in policy debates, independent of his or her research, is of great importance and deserves to be studied more closely. The influence of such informed discussion and argument will, I think, vary in different policy fields. But of special interest is the combined effect of policy intellectuals based in the universities and the policy analysts whom they have trained, or who were trained to read them, to understand them, and to use their arguments in the preparation of their reports for decision makers in government. These staff papers, reports, and memoranda give the policy intellectuals' ideas and work access, in ways that the intellectuals themselves do not always have, to the committee rooms and governmental conversations where decisions are made.

5. *Policy Analysts versus Interest Groups*

The structure of government in the United States, both in Washington and in the state capitols, is changing, becoming even more open and responsive than it has been to vocal, well-organized special interest groups, less and less managed by traditional elites. In the field of education, states Murphy,

> State policy systems, no longer the captive of state educa-tion establishments, are now far more accessible to interest groups and open to public view. The adoption of a large number of policy reforms reflects a new responsiveness on the part of state government to these groups.
>
> Within government, the most important change is the heavy involvement of legislators and governors in educa-tional matters. Spurred on by worries about money, school quality, and social issues (e.g., integration), general state government has used its new staff and expertise to chal-lenge education professionals and to remove education from its privileged perch "above politics."
>
> There's a different cast of participants outside gov-ernment as well . . . Some of the new lobbies promote equality, representing such interests as urban areas, the poor, blacks, Hispanics, the disadvantaged, the handi-capped, girls. Reform of state school finance laws has been promoted for the past decade by a network of schol-ars, foundation executives, lawyers, government officials, community organizers, and citizen groups. Other groups work for efficiency and effectiveness, lobbying for com-prehensive planning, improved budgeting, accountability laws, standards for graduation, competency tests for stu-dents and teachers. More recently, some of these groups have been promoting tax limitation measures and controls on expenditures. Still other lobbies promote "the public interest." (Murphy 1981 p. 128)

All this energy and activity (in part a consequence of mass higher education) generates an extraordinary level of noise, demands, charges and counter-charges, court actions, and so forth. Pressures of every kind are felt by legislators, elected officials, and their staffs. Policy analysts inside government provide some counterweight, some degree of stability, pre-dictability, and rationality through their professional patterns of response to these pressures and demands. This is not to say that the political activists and their pressure groups are not often successful. But how a government agency responds to organized politi-cal pressure may well be shaped by the anonymous analysts in the executive and legislative staffs and agencies. And it is through them that a large or at least a different, set of ideas comes into play in these discussions, and these ideas at their best are less narrow and parochial, more likely to be illuminated by historical and comparative perspectives and by the ongoing discussion that policy intellectuals carry on among themselves in the professional journals.

The structure of politics, the character of the policy areas in which discussions and debate about policies are carried on, are quite different in, for example, Sweden than they are in the United States. Careful studies of actual policy formulation and implementa-tion in specific areas must illuminate the patterns of "social interaction" that more often than not are the major determinants of outcomes in the policy arena. In these increasingly complex networks of social interaction, the relations between policy analysts in government and policy intellectuals in the university are of large and growing importance in the United States, with close analogues in Sweden and other western societies.

6. *Conclusion: Research and the Rhetoric of Politics*

It is natural that members of the research community are concerned that the research they do provides true and illuminating accounts of the institutions and processes that they study. Some researchers are also interested in whether research has any influence on the shaping of policy and the making of decisions, and if it does, how it enters the decision process and affects the outcomes of those decisions.

But it may be useful, and not wholly subversive of the research itself, to reflect that policy research has value independent of its truth or quality or its influence on policy. That is because social research is one of the ways in which political discussions are carried on in democratic societies, a way that is supportive of liberal democratic politics. Political argument is increasingly conducted in the language of research and analysis; concepts like "cost–benefit" and "trade-off" have found their way into the daily language of politicians and bureaucrats. Moreover, social research and democratic politics have some close affinities. For one thing, like democratic politics, social research is a process not of assertion or demonstration, but of persuasion. Moreover, it is a form of persuasion that appeals to reason and evidence rather than to supernatural authority, or tradition, or the charisma of an individual, or the authority of a legal order. The appeal to research findings is very far from the coercive domination of others by force or threat, and equally far from political manipulations which depend on the exploitation of a differential of knowledge and awareness between manipulator and the manipulated. The appeal to "research findings" is the appeal to the authority of reason, to a rationality that connects means and ends in ways that are consistent with strongly held social values. Max Weber has said that the contribution of sociology to politics is not to affirm ultimate ends, but to help clarify, if possible to "make transparent," the connections between means and ends so that choices can be made in greater awareness of the consistency of the means chosen with the ends intended. Insofar as social science attempts to do that, it becomes part of the persuasive mechanism of politics, rooting politics, at least in part, in persuasion based on an appeal to reason and knowledge. It need not weaken professional concern for the quality and truth of research to suggest that social research makes its largest contribution to liberal society not through its findings, but by its steady affirmation of the relevance of reason and knowledge to the politics of democracy.

See also: Educational Research and Policy-making; Policy-oriented Research

References

Husén T 1984 Issues and their background. In: Husén T, Kogan M (eds.) 1984 *Educational Research and Policy: How do They Relate?* Pergamon Press, Oxford
Kogan M, Korman N, Henkel M 1980 *Government's Commissioning of Research: A Case Study*. Department of Government, Brunel University, Uxbridge
Lerner D, Lasswell H (eds.) 1951 *The Policy Sciences*. Stanford University Press, Stanford, California
Meltsner A J 1976 *Policy Analysts in the Bureaucracy*. University of California Press, Berkeley, California
Murphy J T 1981 The paradox of state government reform. *Public Interest* 64: 124–39
Weiss C H 1979 The many meanings of research utilization. *Publ. Admin. Review* 39: 426–31
Wilson J Q 1981 Policy intellectuals and 'public policy'. *Public Interest* 64: 31–46

Further Reading

Kallen D B P et al. (eds.) 1983 *Social Science Research and Public Policy Making: A Reappraisal*. NFER–Nelson, Windsor

Religious Education

R. M. Thomas

Because there exists no universal agreement about the meaning of either religion or education, there is likewise no agreement about what constitutes the field of religious education. Therefore, at the outset of this review of religious education studies, it is useful to identify which meanings will be assigned to these two terms.

Writers who conceptualize religion in a broadly inclusive way define it variously as "the collective expression of human values," as "the zealous and devout pursuit of an objective," or as "a system of values or preferences—an inferential value system." Such definitions are so broad that they encompass not only the belief systems of Christianity, Islam, and Hinduism but also those of communism, democracy, logical positivism, and even anarchism.

Other writers place far greater limitations on the term "religion," proposing that a conceptual scheme qualifying as religion must be an integrated system of specified components, including the nature of a supreme being or of gods (theology), the origin and condition of the universe (cosmology), rules governing human relations (ethics, morals), the proper behavior of people toward superhuman powers (rites, rituals, worship), the nature of knowledge and its proper sources (epistemology), and the goal of life (teleology). Under this second sort of definition, Christianity, Islam, and Hinduism are religions but communism, democracy, logical positivism, and anarchism are not.

The second of these conceptions of religion seems to be the one intended by most people who write or speak about religious education, so it is the one adopted here for identifying matters that rightly belong in the field of religious education.

Just as religion has been defined in various ways by different writers, so has education. In its broadest sense, education can be equated with learning. Learning can be defined as "changes in mental process and overt behavior as a result of experience." However, for the purposes of the following review, education is defined in a narrower sense to mean "the activity carried on by a society's institutions of systematic, planned instruction." Such a definition eliminates from consideration kinds of learning informally acquired during people's daily social interaction, as through their conversations in the family or through models of behavior offered by their companions. It eliminates as well learning acquired through the incidental use of libraries, bookshops, newspapers, and recreational radio and television.

When the foregoing preferred definitions are combined, they identify the realm of religious education as being that of "systematic, planned instruction in beliefs about the nature of the cosmos and of a supreme power, about rites and worship, about personal moral values and the ethics of human relations, and about the meaning and goal of life."

It is well at the beginning also to recognize a distinction between religious instruction and instruction about religions, since both of these types can be classified under the rubric "religious education." The term "religious instruction" traditionally has meant teaching the doctrine of a given religion with the intention of convincing the learners that this religion is the true one, and its tenets and practices are to be honored as the correct ones. Such religious instruction, aimed at converting learners both intellectually and emotionally to a set of convictions, continues to be by far the dominant form of religious education in all parts of the world. In contrast, instruction about religions is a relatively recent development, with the teacher describing various religions rather than seeking to convert learners to a particular faith. Studies bearing on both of these varieties of religious education are included in the following pages.

The review of studies is organized around seven aspects of religious education. Each aspect is described and trends in its development are traced. The seven are: (a) forms of religious education; (b) aims or objectives; (c) instructional methods and media; (d) educational personnel; (e) administration and finance; (f) evaluating religious education; and (g) effects of social change. The review of these seven is prefaced by a brief overview of the estimated number of followers of the major religions of the world. The article closes with an estimate of the state of recent research on religious education.

1. Major Religions and Their Followers

The magnitude of the educational task faced by the world's religions is suggested by the numbers of followers of the major faiths. By the mid-1990s, in an estimated total world population of 5,800 million, the following quantities of adherents were reported for the principal religions (with the percentages of the world population represented by each religion indicated in parentheses). Christianity had 1,955 million (33.7 percent), Islam 1,114 million (19.2 percent), no-religion and atheism 1,073 (18.5 percent), Hinduism 795 million (13.7 percent), Buddhism 331 million (5.7 percent), Chinese folk religions 226 million (3.9 percent), new religions 122 million (2.1 percent), ethnic religions (tribal and shamanist faiths) 116 million (2 percent), Judaism 12 million (0.2 percent), and other religions 58 million (1 percent) (Edwards 1996, p. 298). Compared to estimates in 1900, Christianity's percentage of the world population by the mid-1990s had diminished only slightly (34.4 to 33.7), while the percentages of Moslems, Hindus, and new religions had grown slightly. The greatest increase of any category over the 95-year period was in people professing either no religion or else atheism (from 0.2 to 18.5). Chinese folk religions had dropped dramatically (23.5 to 3.9). Buddhism had decreased by 1.6 percent and Judaism by 0.6 percent. While these figures illustrate gross trends in religious affiliation, they fail to make clear the changes that have occurred within a given religion. Christianity, in particular, has experienced a marked shift in the proportion of adherents from one denomination to another. For example, Barrett (1982) reported that in 1900 two-thirds of all Christians lived in Europe and Russia, but he estimated that by the early twenty-first century three-fifths of them will live in Africa, Asia, and Latin America. Furthermore, the traditional Reformation denominations (Lutherans, Presbyterians, and the like) no longer have the majority of followers, but are outdistanced by evangelical groups.

The continuing strength of religions and the changes in the percentages of adherents in different groups are partially the result of differing degrees of success of religious education. The marked growth in nonreligious people is likewise a result of educational efforts that discredit religion. Often these efforts are sponsored by such political movements as communism.

2. Forms of Religious Education

The term "forms" refers to the various combinations of time and location used for providing religious instruction. The following overview proceeds from forms that involve the largest amounts of time to those that involve the least, a range extending from full-time boarding schools to only occasional religious study. The limited research about the relationship between the amount of time spent on instruction and the thoroughness of religious learning supports the commonsense notion that the more time spent in religious study, the greater the religious knowledge acquired and the deeper the religious conviction (Hartman 1979, Himmelfarb 1977). Consequently, the forms described early in this overview can be expected to lead to greater achievement of the religious goals than is attained by the ones described later.

2.1 Full-time Boarding Schools

The institutions that provide the greatest amount of time for religious instruction are schools in which students live full-time, following a curriculum that is entirely or dominantly religious. In such settings, students' class time and out-of-class study hours not only focus on religious issues, but mealtimes and leisure hours are often imbued with religious teachings and rituals as well.

Full-time boarding schools trace their beginnings back to ancient days. In modern times most residential schools of this type are found in Asia and Africa, attended almost exclusively by boys and young men. While such institutions also exist in Europe and in the Americas—principally at the college or seminary level—they are far fewer in number and more often include secular subjects in the curriculum (mathematics, social science, science) than do the traditional Asian and African varieties.

In Islamic regions the residential schools are much alike, focusing chiefly on the Koran and other Islamic scriptures and on the Arabic language, even though the schools are known by different titles in different regions—*madrasah* in Arabic countries, *khalwa* in the Sudan, *pesantren* in Indonesia, and *pondok* in Malaysia. In Hindu India, where the schools center on the study of the Vedas and other Hindu writings and often on techniques of meditation, they are known as *ashrams*. In Buddhist Thailand they are *wat* schools.

In terms of worldwide trends, full-time religious schools have been diminishing both in number and in the proportion of their religious subject matter in comparison to secular subjects. In developing nations, this decrease in religious schools apparently has been caused chiefly by the developing societies' "modernization programs," with modernization meaning the adoption of the socioeconomic values and technology of industrialized Western nations. Graduates of a traditional religious curriculum find themselves poorly equipped for the job requirements of the newly evolving vocational world, so that learning to be a "good person" in a religious sense no longer suffices for succeeding socially and economically in a society stressing new values.

2.2 Full-time Day Schools

Next to boarding schools, the intensity of religious education is greatest in full-time day schools that concentrate exclusively on religious studies. They are much like the religious boarding schools in curricula and organization. Often the two types are identical, with the same school enrolling both resident students and ones who live at home and attend classes only during the day.

More numerous than day schools that teach only religious subjects are those whose curriculum includes a combination of religious and secular studies. An example of this type is the Islamic *madrasah* in Indonesia, the nation with the largest Moslem population in the world at over 175 million. The Indonesian version of the *madrasah* was inaugurated in the second decade of the twentieth century by Islamic reformers to make religious education more relevant to the requirements of modern secular life, yet retain the essential elements of traditional Moslem schooling. Over the years the quantity of secular studies in *madrasahs* has gradually increased. By the 1990s, at least 70 percent of class time in the nation's 35,000 *madrasahs* was devoted to secular studies (Indonesian language, mathematics, science, social studies, local language or English, the arts) and the remaining 30 percent to Moslem topics (the Koran, the Hadith or sayings of the Prophet Muhammad, principles of Islamic faith, Islamic law, Arabic language, and others).

The fact that a day school includes both secular and religious studies fails to reveal the amount of religious education students receive, since the amount of time dedicated to religious subjects varies so greatly from one school to another. In fact, the practice of combining religious and secular subjects in most school systems consists of dedicating only one class hour a day or only one or two hours a week to religious topics, with the rest of the school hours focusing entirely on secular studies. In school systems that enroll pupils from various religious sects, religious studies are often provided through a released-time arrangement, with pupils released an hour or so a week from their secular studies to follow instruction offered by a religious teacher of their own persuasion. Such teachers are often priests, pastors, or knowledgeable laypersons. Under these arrangements, religious education is systematic but in a relatively small amount (Carper and Hunt 1984).

2.3 Supplementary Day Schools

In many parts of the world, pupils not only attend a secular school, but also daily attend one that concentrates on religious studies. Such a pattern of paralleling secular schooling with religious education appears to have evolved in two principal ways in different societies.

In one case a dominant, traditional religious school system has been largely displaced by a secular public system. The displacement has occurred either because parents have come to judge religious education as inadequate preparation for youths to progress in a modernizing socioeconomic system or because the government requires that all children follow a curriculum that includes an array of secular subjects not taught in the traditional religious schools. Under such conditions, the displaced religious school assumes a supplementary education role, offering its daily lessons during hours before or after the secular school sessions. One example of this pattern is provided by the *faifeau* (pastor) or catechist schools in the Samoan Islands of the South Central Pacific. These schools were introduced in the mid-nineteenth century by Christian missionaries, who established the institutions in villages throughout the islands to give instruction in religious topics and in reading the Bible in the Samoan language. Eventually such secular topics as geography, history, and arithmetic were added to the curriculum. *Faifeau* schools served as the chief educational institutions in the islands until far into the twentieth century. However, they have been largely replaced by secular public schools, particularly in American Samoa. *Faifeau* schools, as a way of adjusting to changing times, are conducted for only an hour or two in the early morning or evening and/or when pupils are on vacation from secular schools. In Malaysia a similar pattern of development has occurred, with pupils attending in parallel both a secular school and a traditional Islamic *pondok*.

The second type of parallel school has developed, not from religious schools gradually being displaced by secular education, but rather from parents' desire to have their children obtain systematic religious education in addition to the secular instruction received in a public school system. An example is the Jewish supplementary school in the United States, a common type of religious education in the nation which by 1990 contained the world's largest Jewish population at 7 million. The typical supplementary school meets in the late afternoon twice during the week, such as on Tuesday and Thursday for an hour or two, and on Sunday for perhaps three hours. At the elementary level the subjects of study are Jewish history and culture, the biblical Old Testament, and Hebrew language. At the secondary level such subjects as Jewish law, ethics, and comparative religion are frequently added.

2.4 Occasional Classes

Much religious education, particularly since the spread of secular schooling, has been only an occasional event, such as a child's attending Sunday school or an adult's attending a church, mosque, temple, or synagogue for an hour or so once a week. People may engage in religious study at home by means of radio or television broadcasts, self-instructional lessons distributed by a religious organization, or a small group of adherents meeting to analyze holy scripture.

3. Aims and Objectives of Religious Education

The goals of religious education can be viewed from a variety of perspectives, three of which are: (a) the overt versus the implied; (b) indoctrination versus comparison; and (c) the cognitive versus the affective.

3.1 Overt versus Implied Objectives

The objectives of religious education may either be stated directly or only be implied by the methods of instruction and the observed outcomes of religious training programs. Typical openly stated objectives are illustrated by the following examples drawn from official descriptions of religious groups' educational goals or from proposals by scholars in the field.

An example from Islam is a statement endorsed by 313 Moslem scholars attending the First World Conference on Moslem Education held at Mecca in 1977:

Education should aim at the balanced growth of the total personality of Man through the training of Man's spirit, intellect, the rational self, feelings, and bodily senses. Education should therefore cater for the growth of man in all its aspects: spiritual, intellectual, imaginative, physical, scientific, linguistic, both individual and collectively and motivate all these aspects towards goodness and the attainment of perfection. The ultimate aim of Muslim education lies in the realization of complete submission to Allah on the level of the individual, the community, and humanity at large. (Husain and Ashraf 1979 p. 44)

A widely adopted Christian statement of goals derives from a National Council of Churches of Christ (USA) study paper:

The objective of Christian education is to help persons to be aware of God's self-disclosure and seeking love in Jesus Christ, and to respond in faith and love—to the end that they may know who they are and what their human situation means, grow as sons of God rooted in the Christian community, live in the Spirit of God in every relationship, fulfill their common discipleship in the world, and abide in the Christian hope. (Cully 1963)

As a more detailed proposal, Miller (1977 pp. 54–58) has suggested five goals as appropriate for Christian education. First is the objective of developing an attitude of respect and concern for others: "If we are persuaded to love God and to love others as ourselves, we are dealing with an attitude toward the whole of life." Second is creating amicable relationships, "the I-thou relationship." Third is learning religious content, in the sense of education as an intellectual discipline—"to develop beliefs that are consistent with our view of the world as derived from all sources, especially science." Fourth is establishing personal morality by recognizing religion's "supreme importance for the meaning of living." Fifth is developing social ethics so that the individual is not just personally "good" but also works for the common welfare—"civil rights, racial harmony, open housing, or the liberation of oppressed groups."

In contrast to overt objectives are those that can only be inferred as being pursued, for they are not openly described. The inference is drawn from the nature of the methods and materials used, or from the beliefs and behaviors the learners eventually exhibit. There are at least three reasons why goals may be left unstated.

First, the program planners may believe that their objectives are self-explanatory, that is, so obvious to anyone that they need not be explained. For example, religious educators may feel it unnecessary to state that the aim of studying the Torah for Jews, the Koran for Moslems, the Vedas for Hindus, or the Bible for Christians is to understand God's will and thereby know how to attain a desired life after death.

A second reason is that religious educators may not recognize that certain unintended outcomes result from the methods and materials they are using. In this case, the goals are being attained unintentionally or out of ignorance. For instance, Adamu (1973 p. 54) quotes Alhaji Aminu Kano as criticizing the Koranic schools of Northern Nigeria for having a curriculum:

"arbitrary in form, bookish in style, and hopeless for promoting social ideals and usefulness. It has done nothing but make the work in the school lifeless and killing." The Koranic schools, he points out, have utterly failed to appeal to the child, "but succeeded in promoting drudgery, loading the child's mind with fantastic facts which she or he never understands." Consequently, the child becomes mentally disabled, and the products of such schools are a mass of static adolescents "who make a static society."

In leveling these charges at the religious schools, Aminu did not propose that the teachers were intentionally producing dolts and laggards, but rather that they were unwittingly achieving such undesirable ends.

The present-day Koran teacher, beside being a most disqualified teacher or educator, appears to be a menace to the children's world and in the educational field; for not only is he hopelessly ignorant of modern conceptions, but is not ready to accept them. (Aminu in Adamu 1973 p. 55)

It should be noted, however, that not all unintended outcomes are negative ones. For example, the Buddhist *wat* schools of Thailand serve as a vehicle of upward social mobility for boys of lower-class families, an outcome not advertised as a purpose of the schools but one which, nevertheless, most parents likely recognize when they enroll their sons.

A third reason certain objectives may be left unstated is that the religious educators or their sponsors are intentionally exploiting their followers. That is, the leaders promote their own welfare rather than that of the learners, a condition that the leaders do not wish their followers to discover. Such educators have been accused of intentionally teaching in ways that cause learners to: (a) be afraid to inquire into controversial theological and social issues, (b) feel guilty about ever doubting the leaders' word, (c) obey the leaders without question, (d) accept a subservient or degrading role in life as being the learners' just due, (e) hate people of other sects or ethnic groups, and (f) sacrifice one's own needs and desires in order to enhance the leaders' wealth, comfort, and power. The traditional Hindu caste system has been used by critics as an illustration of this phenomenon. Critics have claimed that the system was created in ancient times by the conquering Aryans who devised the caste features of Hinduism as a way of ensuring their own superior power and welfare in relation to the peoples they sought to dominate. Much of traditional Hindu education for the upper castes has consisted of students' mastering the rules and rituals that define the rights and responsibilities for each caste as described in such writings as the *Laws of Manu (Manu Smriti)* (Bühler 1886) and the *Rules of Vedic Domestic Ceremonies (Grihya-Sutras)* (Oldenberg 1886). Although the caste system—and particularly its relegating certain groups to untouchable status—has been repudiated in modern times by the Indian government, the system and its educational components live on.

Charges of fostering similar unstated exploitative aims have been directed at other religious groups as well. Some of the most caustic charges have been issued by followers of such social commentators as Karl Marx who have viewed religion as "the opiate of the masses."

While it is possible that the originators of a particular sect—like the originators of certain socioeconomic and political systems—may consciously devise methods that foster their own welfare at the expense of their followers, people who subsequently perpetuate the religion's educational techniques may not be moved by such a motive, at least not consciously. They may simply propagate the faith and its methodology because they accept the particular religious tradition as the true way. In that case, such educators qualify for inclusion in the second category described above, that of religious instructors who unwittingly further unstated ends.

Accusations about exploitative unstated goals—or what has sometimes been called a hidden curriculum—have been important in religious education for several reasons. First, they have stimulated reforms in objectives and in instructional methods within those religions at which the accusations have been directed. (Illustrative reforms are described below under Sect. 4.) Second, criticism has motivated religious educators who believe such accusations are undeserved to develop more convincing rationales and explanations of their work. Third, the accusations have sufficiently alienated some followers from a particular religion that they have either rejected organized religion entirely or else have adopted markedly different religious education practices. One different practice is that of replacing the goal of religious indoctrination with one of comparing religions so that each learner can achieve a "free, enlightened choice of faith," as explained in Sect. 3.2.

3.2 Indoctrination versus Comparison

The dominant, almost exclusive purposes of religious education programs have been: (a) to convince learners that a particular religion is the one true faith and (b) to school the learners in the doctrine and practices of that faith. In short, the goal of such programs is evangelism or indoctrination. However, a growing number of programs have been designed to teach students about various religions and even about such nonreligious philosophical positions as humanism, which stresses a commitment to human values without necessitating belief in a god, in religious ritual, or in a life hereafter. The goal of this second variety—the comparative religion approach—is to help students "find a faith to live by." They are to find this faith not as a result of indoctrination in a single religion but by their own enlightened choice, which "can only be made when the pupils have studied with some seriousness the nature of religious and nonreligious systems of belief and the grounds which men of goodwill and sincerity on both sides find convincing" (Holm 1975).

The aim of such religious study, which is both nondenominational and comparative, is illustrated in the syllabus ratified by the Swedish parliament in 1969 to guide the religious instruction required at all levels of Sweden's comprehensive school system. Under this reformation of religious education:

> Instruction shall be broadminded and objective in a way that factual knowledge concerning different religious beliefs and philosophies is presented without seeking to exert pressure on the students to embrace one particular ethic. This instruction should be carried out in such a way that the students understand the seriousness and importance of the questions with which they are dealing. It should enhance their personal development and help bring about an understanding of the value of a personal ethic. The students should also gain understanding and respect for different points of view in questions of ethics and religion. (Fägerlind 1974 p. 38)

The comparative religion approach is rarely the type

conducted within an established sect or denomination, such as in a Sunday school or in a church-sponsored day school. Nearly all church-sponsored schools limit teaching to their own doctrine or else they compare other belief systems unfavorably to their own. In contrast, comparative religion programs are most often found in secular schools—public or private—of nations like the United Kingdom, Australia, Germany, and Sweden that: (a) require religious education in all schools, and (b) have varied religious and nonreligious groups represented in the society, with enough adherents in the major groups to threaten political disorder if a single religion's doctrine were imposed on students in the schools.

3.3 Cognitive versus Affective Objectives

The term "cognitive" refers here to intellectual comprehension, to those parts of religious education that can be communicated to someone else in words, committed to memory for later recall, analyzed, and used for guidance in making decisions in life. Students are most frequently expected to achieve cognitive objectives by memorizing holy scripture and answers to common doctrinal questions (catechisms) and by hearing an expert apply religious doctrine to life situations. Some programs, particularly at the more advanced levels, move beyond the passive–receptive mode of cognitive learning to the more active–productive intellectual activities of debating, analyzing, and synthesizing religious issues.

In contrast to the cognitive aspect, the affective is the emotional component of religious education, the array of feelings that cannot be conveyed adequately in words, like the sensation referred to in a Christian hymn as "the peace that passeth understanding." Such affect includes mysticism, in the sense of realities beyond perception and intellectual comprehension, realities that are directly accessible through intuition, inspiration, or meditation.

While for purposes of analysis, the cognitive and affective have been contrasted, religious education programs generally attempt to achieve both types of goals. As Brink (1977 p. 409) has suggested, "Religion does not and should not aim at intellectual conversion. Religion should strive for total conversion, that is, one which involves feeling, willing, and acting as well as thinking."

Different religious education programs consist of different proportions of cognitive and affective goals, just as different religious sects may place more emphasis on one type of goal than another. For example, within the typical Unitarian and Christian Science versions of Christianity there has been a greater emphasis on intellectual comprehension and cognitive analysis than was found in the Catholic Church's ritual of the past which was conducted in Latin for non-Latin-speaking congregations who were expected to gain more affectively—or spiritually—than cognitively as a result of their religious experience. In a similar

fashion, affective outcomes, as contrasted to cognitive ones, have been particularly important components of the Sufism movement in Islam, the Yoga version of Hinduism, and the Zen variety of Buddhism. The instructional methods in programs emphasizing affective objectives typically depend less on intellectual analysis and more on the generation of altered states of consciousness (meditation), on visual and tactile symbols (a cross, a star, a crescent moon, a statue, beads), and on the repetition of prayers, chants, and mantras (sacred verbal formulas).

Often a religious body emphasizes cognitive goals in one portion of the church program and affective goals in another. For example, Christian churches frequently provide Bible-study classes whose chief purpose is to teach the history and tenets of the religion, while separate prayer meetings or revival sessions are conducted to further the sect's emotional or spiritual outcomes.

4. Instructional Methods and Media

The predominant—and often exclusive—methods of instruction are those of having students: (a) memorize passages of the holy scriptures, (b) participate in rituals, and (c) read or listen to sermons or interpretations of what the scriptures mean and how they can be applied to one's life. The interpretations are usually presented by someone in a position of authority—a priest, minister, teacher, or religious scholar. At the more advanced stages of study, students may engage in discussions or debates in which they actively analyze theological and ethical issues, supporting their opinions with quotations from the scriptures.

While such traditional instructional methods continue throughout the world to be by far the most popular teaching techniques, their dominance has been challenged by a variety of different instructional methods. The new techniques are chiefly adaptations of innovative methodology developed in secular schools and founded on recent advances in educational psychology and instructional technology. As a consequence, increasing numbers of programs, particularly in Western nations, have focused their curricula on children's interests (student-centered approaches) or on problems in society (social-issue approaches) rather than on direct study of the holy scriptures. Religious educators' interest in thus replacing or supplementing traditional teaching methods has been motivated by their dissatisfaction with what they judge are serious shortcomings of conventional methodology.

One of the most common topics of pedagogical debate has been that of the effectiveness of rote memorization. In virtually every religious tradition, memorizing passages of scripture or catechisms and being able to repeat them word-for-word has been considered a keystone of religious instruction. In typical Moslem schools, children spend years memorizing the entire Koran and chanting it in a prescribed manner. Pride in the ability to perform this act continues to be so great that in such a country as Malaysia, where Islam is the official state religion, an annual nationally televised contest is conducted to determine which youths intone passages of scripture most eloquently.

Supporters of rote-memorization methodology contend that a student's committing scriptures to memory not only makes them constantly available as guides to living but that the demanding feat of memorization itself builds character. Advocates of such mastery also often hold that the literal repetition of holy words itself conveys mystical values that extend beyond the analytical meaning of the passages themselves.

> Every Muslim agrees that the Quran itself as the word of God is untranslatable, not only in the ordinary sense in which all great literary works are untranslatable, but because its meaning cannot be divorced from its rhythms and the incomparable harmony which its sounds create. (Husain and Ashraf 1979 p. 116)

However, critics have charged that too often students memorize phrases whose meaning they do not truly comprehend—they simply parrot the words—so the material fails to furnish the guidance and consolation needed in their daily lives. Schmitt (1982 pp. 94–95), commenting on German parents' opinions of the mandated religious education classes they had attended in secondary school, reports that "adults often express dissatisfaction and unpleasant memories. They recall that much memorizing of biblical texts and hymns was required, absolute but hardly practicable moral principles were laid down, and uncritical acceptance of church teachings demanded."

Linked to the issue of rote memorization is the claim that religious education is too often seen by the learners as irrelevant to their interests and needs. Youths frequently consider religious instruction old fashioned, perhaps pertinent in the past but inappropriate to the present as they experience it. This problem has become particularly acute with the spread of advanced technology that finds secular subjects taking precedence over religious studies in preparing youths for the goals they hope to achieve.

Furthermore, traditional methods of instruction—reading and memorizing scripture, listening to sermons, performing rituals—often seem less appealing than newer instructional approaches found in secular education, such as simulation games, sociodrama, motion pictures, television, and discussions focusing on problems important to modern youth. Not only has the cognitive significance of conventional methodology been cast in doubt, but traditional ways of achieving the desired affective or mystical outcomes of religious experience have also been questioned (Sarno 1987).

Stimulated by such criticisms, religious educators have sought new methods and media to replace or, more often, to supplement traditional approaches, new methods that better ensure that (a) learners truly understand the meaning of scriptures and not merely memorize the words, (b) the methods and materials capture the learners' interest in competition with other attractions in their environment, (c) the learners know how to apply religious teachings in their daily lives, and (d) religious education reaches as large an audience as possible. The following samples of six types of innovative practice illustrate the range of methods with which religious educators have experimented.

4.1 Participatory Sermons and Study Groups

Stokes (1977) has described a variety of innovations in certain American Protestant churches in the 1970s intended to elicit more active learning than likely occurs when a congregation listens passively to a sermon. One approach has been the participatory sermon during which the members of the audience respond to questions posed by the minister during the sermon. The response may take the form of a minister–congregation dialogue during the sermon or may follow the sermon as an open discussion, debate, or panel discussion. In some cases the discussion takes place in small groups later in the week.

4.2 Student-centered Projects

One trend, particularly in Western societies, has been that of identifying interests of young people at different age levels, then designing religious study projects directed at those interests. An example of such student-centered instruction is a Swedish program which began with an investigation of the personal concerns of pupils aged 10 to 12 years, an investigation that involved pupils completing unfinished stories about children in pictured conflict situations. The survey showed that two of the primary concerns of pupils were about loneliness and about the effects of violence, suffering, and war. The results of the survey were then used to formulate themes for religious education projects enabling instructors to identify passages of the Bible that bore on these concerns and to devise discussions that engaged children in identifying ways the themes and Bible passages could influence their lives. In effect, the starting point for specifying topics to study was not the Bible or adult interests, but rather was a series of children's interest, in matters of life and death, responsibility and guilt, suffering and compassion, fear and security, loneliness and fellowship (Fägerlind 1974).

4.3 Social-action Programs

The 1960s witnessed marked social unrest in many nations, an unrest reflected in religious education programs often turning from Bible study to social action. The action took the form of political demonstrations and direct social service intended to redress the neglect or oppression being suffered by minorities, or to correct conditions detrimental to the general quality of life in the community.

According to a survey of North American Protestant churches (Stokes 1977), the social involvement of the 1960s changed in the 1970s to include greater attention to Bible study and serious theological thinking, so that the version of the 1970s deserved the label "action/reflection" model. In keeping with this conception of religious education, a film produced by the United Presbyterian Church suggested four models of adult learning that might be combined: (a) the conventional Bible class in church, but taught in newer ways (cognitive learning); (b) helping others, as in giving service in a teenage crisis center (personal–social skill training); (c) small, intimate discussion group (affective learning), and (d) participation in issue oriented movements, such as gaining equal rights for women or for minority groups (action/involvement learning).

4.4 Dramatics

The use of drama in religious education is nothing new, for drama and pageantry have long been used to portray religious events. The present-day term for string-operated puppets—"marionettes"—derives from the description of the supporting characters (little Marys) in medieval Christian plays which featured the Virgin Mary. However, the variety of ways dramatics contribute to religious instruction today is far greater than in the past.

Formal dramas in which actors memorize speeches created by a playwright continue to be popular. Puppetry also continues in use. However, in their modern form, dramatics are not confined to stage productions but can be audio recorded on tape to simulate radio drama or video recorded through a television camera to form a motion picture. Or, as another approach, members of a study group may read aloud segments of a play, then use the segments as the subject of a discussion of theological or moral issues.

Less traditional forms of drama, requiring greater ingenuity on the part of the actors, are creative dramatics, role playing, sociodrama, and psychodrama. In each of these, the actors spontaneously devise their own speeches and actions in response to the behavior of the others in the play. Such dramatic forms can reflect daily life and thereby furnish the actors' practice in ways of responding to real-life decision-making demands. Creative dramatics is a general term identifying modes of spontaneously developing characters and their actions. Typically the characters are told whom they represent and the conflict situation in which they find themselves. Then they are to interact with each other as they imagine such characters would in real life. Role playing, as a form of creative dramatics, emphasizes the kind of person a character is and the way that person would feel and behave under various conditions. Sociodrama lays stress on the social interaction of characters, and psychodrama emphasizes the internal struggles that operate within an individual's personality (Fogle 1989, Glavich 1989). In some Christian denominations, educational activities have included dance and movement, features that have traditionally played a prominent role in many ethnic religions (Jones 1988).

4.5 Multimedia Approaches

A significant feature of many religious education programs has been the introduction of a broad variety of communication media found in modernized secular education and in public information and entertainment fields. These media have included such stimuluses for discussion sessions as filmed interviews with famous personalities or with people who have had striking religious experiences, posters illustrating personal and social issues, photographs of people in problem situations, "you-are-there" radio broadcasts of Biblical occasions, comic-book versions of religious history, picture Bibles for children, and filmstrips of places and events associated with a religion. Increasing numbers of motion pictures have been produced by religious organizations, and regular entertainment films have been used in movie forums as subjects of analysis to determine to what degree the films reflect values advocated in religious education. To aid European educators in conducting such forums, the Dutch-based Interfilm organization furnishes information about available films and ways they can serve in religious instruction.

4.6 Radio and Television

Since the early 1970s an unprecedented increase in the use of radio and television for religious education has been witnessed on an international scale. While in many nations occasional religious programs appeared on radio and television in the past, it was not until the latter 1970s that evangelical religious programs achieved the prominence they currently display. By the beginning of the 1980s in the United States there were more than 300 radio stations dedicating their entire time to religious material, and hundreds of commercial stations sold portions of their broadcast time to religious groups.

More dramatic than radio has been the growth of television broadcasting. By 1981 in the United States there were 36 television stations maintaining full-time religious schedules, with some stations operating 24 hours a day. Hundreds of additional commercial-television stations sold their entire Sunday morning and much of their late evening time to religious groups. As a consequence, evangelical programs now reach into millions of homes on a regular basis. While most broadcasts have originated in the United States, their influence has not been confined to that nation. One religious leader's radio and television programs have been broadcast on 650 stations in 18 countries and translated into seven languages (Hadden and Swann 1981).

As a result of these developments, religious education—particularly of an evangelical variety—reaches a larger audience than ever before, is available to listeners in their homes, and is produced in a format that matches the technical and dramatic quality of modern-day commercial television.

5. *Educational Personnel*

Religious education instructors throughout the world are more diverse in their qualifications than are instructors teaching secular subjects. Teachers of religion range in background from those with advanced university degrees in theology and in teaching methodology to others who have had no teacher training and who hold only a slight knowledge of religion. There appear to be several reasons for such diversity.

First, religious instruction is carried on in more varied ways than is secular schooling. As noted earlier, religious education assumes many forms—full-time study in school, part-time study in school, once a week in a church or mosque, in casual study sessions of a small group, during an informal visit to a neighbor's home, and others. The skills a person needs to offer religious instruction in one of these settings can differ markedly from those needed in another.

Second, governments usually maintain more official control over secular than over religious instruction. Part of the reason for this is that freedom of religious belief is a far more common political policy than freedom of secular education. Whereas governments commonly regulate what is taught in schools and stipulate who is qualified to teach (especially in state-supported or public schools), they are far less likely to set regulations about who is qualified to offer religious instruction, particularly in countries with sects that might pose a political threat if their independence was hampered. Thus, even in as formal a setting as the school, marked diversity exists in the kinds of people offering religious instruction. For example, in the Netherlands, laypersons teach in the Sunday school, regular classroom teachers provide religious instruction in primary schools, and clergymen or theologically trained laymen teach religion in secondary schools. Furthermore, in Moslem regions there is a long tradition of permitting anyone who has attended a Koran school to set up such an instructional center of his own without his having any formal teacher training. Governments seeking to change such a tradition could expect stiff resistance from the Islamic community. In short, few if any nations that endorse the practice of religion will prevent anyone from organizing at least informal religious instruction sessions.

Third, there is greater consensus about what should constitute teacher education for giving instruction in secular subjects than for teaching religion. In other words, educators agree more on the content and skills needed for teaching such subjects as geography, physics, or music than for teaching religious doctrine. Hence, it has been easier to specify qualifications that should be met by instructors for secular subjects than

those to be met by religious educators.

For the future, it seems likely that the issue of what preparation is needed by religious education personnel will continue to be debated. However, because of widespread governmental policies of religious freedom and the lack of agreement about the skills and knowledge needed for offering religious instruction, it seems unlikely that the present diversity in qualifications for teaching religion will diminish.

6. *Administration and Finance*

A wide variety of systems for administering religious education operate throughout the world. In some cases a large international network of churches of a particular denomination, such as those within Catholicism, is administered through a hierarchy of authorities that provide goals, curriculum materials, teacher training, supervisory personnel, interchurch conferences, newsletters, evaluation procedures, and financial aid to the religious education programs within the network. In other cases a national or regional body performs these services. In still other instances, individual churches independently devise their own religious instruction, drawing upon whatever materials and methodologies they choose from those available in the general field of religious education.

Organizational trends have moved in two opposite directions. On the one hand, formerly independent groups have linked together to produce larger, overarching administrative units. This has been the ecumenical movement in which different denominations have sought to emphasize their likenesses rather than differences and to cooperate in such activities as the production of syllabuses and the conduct of interfaith religious education conferences. At the same time, segments of existing large administrative units have broken away from the parent body, or have at least loosened their administrative ties, to gain more autonomy. This kind of splitting off from an established structure, which over the centuries has produced a multitude of subsects and denominations, has been particularly evident in developing nations; that is, in formerly colonized regions which, after the Second World War, gained political independence. During colonial times in these countries, Christian missionaries had conducted much of the available religious and secular schooling, with the administration of both churches and schools controlled by the sponsoring denominations in Europe or North America. Since the early 1950s, however, as part of the general movement of colonized peoples toward political independence, an increasing number of church groups within formerly colonized countries have chosen to become self-sufficient in church administration. Nevertheless, while assuming more administrative control, such groups still usually maintain at least a liaison relationship with their original church abroad, availing themselves of both funds and religious education practices from Europe and the Americas.

An administrative issue of continuing importance throughout the world has been the relationship between church and state. Some nations have a state religion (either official or unofficial), with the authority to oversee religious education vested in a central ministry or department of education or subsumed under the authority of a minister of general education. The governments in such countries frequently mandate the teaching of religion as a regular subject of instruction in all schools, public and private. Such is the practice in Finland, Norway, France, Germany, the Netherlands, Italy, Spain, much of Latin America, Thailand, Indonesia, countries of the Middle East, and others. Although religious instruction is officially required in these nations, provision is often made—as in the United Kingdom, Finland, Germany, and Italy—for children to be exempt from the requirement if their parents are either nonbelievers or if an instructor is not available for the faith to which the parents subscribe. New Zealand is one of the countries that follow a released-time policy by which pupils are released from their secular studies each week for sessions of religious instruction offered by someone of their faith.

In some countries, religious instruction policy is not uniform throughout the nation but varies from one region to another. In Canada religious instruction in the schools has been obligatory in three provinces, permitted in three others, not permitted in two, and offered as an elective course in the remaining two. In Scotland the responsibility for implementing religious instructional policy rests with local authorities.

In still other nations, religious instruction—in the form of espousing a particular faith—is prohibited in the schools. Such is the case in the United States and in countries ruled by single-party Marxist governments, such as the People's Republic of China, the Democratic People's Republic of Korea, and others.

Financing religious education has always depended heavily on private sources, chiefly on contributions that followers of a religion voluntarily make to the church and on fees parents pay to support their children's studies. However, public funding is also often involved, with the role of government in financing religious education varying greatly from one nation to another. In the Netherlands, both secular state schools and ones operated by religious groups (confessional schools) are completely underwritten by the government. In Indonesia, the Ministry of Religion fully finances Islamic *madrasahs* in certain sections of the country, while the Ministry of Education subsidizes Christian schools that meet government standards. In the United States, schools below the university level that are sponsored by religious bodies receive no government funds, although they enjoy tax-free status by virtue of their religious nature.

It seems apparent that the financial viability of religious education programs is significantly influenced by the funding policies of the governments under which they operate. The chance that religious education will thrive appears greater in nations that contribute public funds toward its support.

7. Evaluating Religious Education

Many kinds of data and methods of data collection have been used for evaluating the success of religious education. Some assessments are in simple quantitative terms. One crude measure of success is the total number of professed followers of a religion. A second is the number of converts or new church members enrolled during a particular period of time. A third is the number of people enrolled in religious education programs. However, because such figures, even when accurately reported, tell nothing of the quality of religious education, other sorts of assessment have been used to appraise qualitative aspects.

Perhaps the most obvious approach to judging quality has been that of assessing an individual's religious training by how well his or her behavior matches the model of a true adherent of the faith. In the case of a traditional Hindu man, this means observing him to learn how well he follows his caste's rules pertaining to occupation, social intermingling, marriage, food taboos, and prayers and rituals for various occasions. In the case of a Moslem man, it means observing how well he fulfills the five pillars of faith (declaring that there is no God but Allah and that Muhammad is his messenger, praying five times daily, giving alms to the poor, fasting during the prescribed lunar month each year, and making a pilgrimage to the holy city of Mecca at some time during his life). In addition, the proper Moslem abides by a variety of other expectations, such as attending services in the mosque at midday on Friday and abstaining from drinking alcoholic beverages.

Assessing the adequacy of religious education by observing individuals' behavior has typically been an informal mode of evaluation, popular since the earliest days of religions. However, more formal evaluations have also been performed, as in the Catholic practice of believers confessing to a priest the ways in which they have fallen short of the goals of their religion. Another formal mode of long standing is the oral examination in which a religious teacher questions the learner over doctrine and church history. In more recent times, such examinations have been in written form, permitting the simultaneous testing of a group of learners by a single instructor.

Finally, built-in assessment is provided by all instructional methods that require an active response on the part of learners. Observing the learners' performance during group discussion, role playing, social-action projects, picture or story interpretation, and creative-writing assignments informs the instructor of how well the students have mastered the knowledge and skills being taught.

8. Effects of Social Change

Religion as an institution is essentially conservative, expected to hold steadfast in the face of assaults by alternative philosophies and by social change. A chief strength of religious doctrine is its representation as eternal truth which people can always count on in times of personal and public distress. However, social conditions often change in ways that cause followers to dispute the validity of their religion's tenets and practices. When the pressure of such distrust becomes sufficiently strong, leaders of the faith may propose innovations intended to accommodate the criticism of the discontented. The innovations are then incorporated into the group's religious education programs (Abu-Rabi 1989, Farley and Wheeler 1991). The following are instances of this phenomenon in the realms of curriculum content, teaching personnel, and terminology.

8.1 Curriculum Content

In selecting topics to be studied in religious education programs, authorities have been confronted with a pair of opposing demands: to add more secular subject matter that keeps up with changing times while still maintaining the strong doctrinal components that have distinguished their particular religious faith over the centuries. An example from Great Britain illustrates the introduction of new topics, while one from Germany demonstrates the effort of religious leaders to resist the diminution of traditional religious content.

In 1992 the head of the Roman Catholic Church in Great Britain, Cardinal Basil Hume, urged participants at a Catholic education conference to include the topics of sexuality and AIDS (acquired immune deficiency syndrome) in religious education classes so that pupils might achieve a moral awareness extending beyond the physiological knowledge taught in science classes.

With the unification of Germany in 1990, schools in the eastern sector that had followed state atheism for 40 years were now obliged to reintroduce religion as a regular part of the curriculum. Under the German constitution that was already operating in the western sector, students were to be taught "in accordance with the tenets of the religious communities," which in most western schools meant Catholic and Protestant instruction. Four new federal states in the east adopted this pattern, but the state of Brandenburg intended to integrate religion into a new life-orientation and ethics course that was being introduced in 44 schools on a trial basis. Church leaders objected to the Brandenburg plan on the grounds that religion was in danger of receiving short shrift in a course that focused also on such topics as unemployment, tolerance for minorities, ethics, and sexuality.

8.2 Teaching Personnel

The question of what kinds of people are qualified to offer religious instruction has become a source of controversy in a variety of Christian and Jewish denominations. The debate has been waged chiefly over the issue of who should be permitted to hold such authoritative instructional positions as those of ordained minister, priest, or rabbi.

Conflict over the ordination of women became particularly volatile in the 1970s, with the controversy extending into the 1990s, resulting in a growing number of denominations yielding to the demand of women for equal rights to leadership positions (Ashe 1991, Fischer 1988, Tamez 1989).

More recently the question of ordination has extended to the matter of homosexuals. In 1991, Conservative Jews in New York City were confronted with the most divisive issue they had faced since agreeing in the early 1980s to ordain women as rabbis. Their 1991 debate focused on the case of a lesbian rabbi seeking to be assigned to a synagogue that counted a large proportion of homosexuals in the congregation. In pursuing the issue, the authorities were faced with two problems: (a) admitting homosexuality as an acceptable sexual orientation (although condemned in biblical text) and (b) appointing a homosexual rabbi as a suitable spiritual guide for Jews.

In Eastern Europe after communist regimes were replaced in the 1990s by governments that encouraged religious freedom, the matter of staffing religious education programs with suitable teachers became an immediate problem. For example, in Germany church authorities charged that teachers trained under the former atheistic regime of East Germany were unqualified to teach religion in the nation's schools.

8.3 Terminology

Examples from the *Oxford Dictionary of New Words* (Tulloch 1991) illustrate neologisms that enter the religious educator's lexicon because of changing times. The term "televangelist" was created to designate anyone who uses television as the medium for propagating a particular religious persuasion. The word "womanspirit" was coined to identify the spiritual sensibilities and teachings shaped by feminists' rejection of the traditional male religious imagery and authority that has dominated most religions. The phrase "vision quest" was borrowed from American Indian lore to indicate an individual's use of meditation, and perhaps such austerities as fasting and the denial of pleasure, as a means of searching for one's inner self or personal calling in order to reach a higher level of maturity.

9. *Religious-education Research*

Studies of religious education have been of many varieties. A large number qualify as think pieces, philosophical proposals or analyses based on authors' casual observations, personal experiences, or logical reasoning. Often the authors' purpose is to convince readers to adopt a viewpoint they espouse. Wyckoff offered three reasons why Germany may well be the leader in this type of study.

> First, the size and cohesiveness of the corps of professional teachers makes feasible production of books and journals of high scholarly quality. Second, the theologians and educators who train the teachers in theological faculties and in the faculties of graduate educational institutes constitute a large coterie of scholar-teacher-writers. Third, there is in each German state a highly trained supervisory group of scholar-administrator-writers. The result is a volume and quality of writing on religious education that exceeds that of any other country in the world. (Wyckoff 1979 p. 101)

In a variety of nations, historical research is also common, with authors attempting to explain the evolution of such institutions as the Sunday school, the Salvation Army, and catechetical instruction. Other studies are descriptions of educational practice, often based on data gathered by means of a survey of a variety of programs. Surveys are also conducted of people's attitudes on religious issues.

Another type of investigation utilizes content analysis, a process consisting of a researcher examining published materials to discover how much their content fits selected analytical categories. For example, history and science textbooks may be analyzed to determine whether the way they picture the creation of the world fits the view given in holy scripture. Or motion pictures may be inspected to determine if moral values they reflect are in keeping with values advocated in religious doctrine. A further kind of study seeks to show ways learners have changed as a result of religious instruction, with comparisons sometimes made of the effects of instruction at different age levels.

The question of how many studies have been carried out across the world in recent years cannot be answered, because research has been conducted in so many different places and issued in such diverse forms. There appears to be no agency dedicated to the task of cataloguing the myriad studies. However, a growing number of lists of research have been published so that some information is available about types and numbers of investigations for limited sections of the world (Hull 1984, Lynn and Moberg 1989, Peatling 1984). A volume edited by Strommen (1971) reviewed studies readily available in Western published sources prior to the 1970s. In 1979 Peatling (1979) updated Strommen's work by listing 134 empirical investigations on religious and moral education topics reported in European, North American, and Australian sources over the period 1968–79.

Beginning in 1978, the journal *Religious Education* issued brief yearly reviews of empirical research but discontinued the practice in 1984.

Periodically *Religious Education* has also published abstracts of doctoral studies reported in *Dissertation Abstracts International*. However, because *Dissertation Abstracts* draws chiefly on work done in North American universities, its coverage of studies in religious education is quite limited. The author of this entry's observations of universities in Asia suggest that most research on educational matters in many countries is carried out in the form of masters degrees or doctoral theses which never enter lists of research and therefore have little chance of coming to the attention of either the regional or worldwide academic community.

While the cataloguing of research continues to be incomplete, those listings that have been compiled provide some limited notion of trends in methodology, at least in Western nations. For example, Peatling (1979) concluded from his review of empirical investigations that objective assessments, rather than only subjective appraisals, are being increasingly used in religious education research, which is a development he commended. Furthermore, researchers have utilized a broad variety of tests and rating devices, many of which are in sufficiently standard use in psychology and education that they provide the basis for reliable comparisons across different studies. However, Peatling also noted two methodological shortcomings. One was a paucity of studies that provide pretesting followed by a carefully designed educational intervention or treatment which, in turn, is followed by posttesting to determine the effect of the intervention. The other was a shortage of:

> creative methods peculiarly suited to exploratory research. . . . If this indicates any feeling that the important questions have been explored, then a lot more realism and some serious thinking is an urgent necessity. Large samples, rigorous designs, and sophisticated analyses all build upon careful exploratory research: the two have a true symbiotic relationship. (Peatling 1979 pp. 425–26)

Peatling (1984 p.114) also noted that (a) a substantial amount of research pertinent to religious education is found in journals of such cognate fields as psychology, sociology, anthropology, and general education; and that (b) the field of religious education "is most often a consumer of research done by others and is not too often a stimulator or supporter of its own research."

Webster (1984) identified four major focuses of research in religious education: child development, religious experience, moral growth and faith development, and curricula. His review of studies up to the mid-1980s led him to conclude that much improvement is needed in the field.

> Research in religious education has generally been sporadic, haphazard, and unsystematic. It tends to be highly

derivative and much of it is poor in quality. There is very little of any significance which is empirically sound, which employs large stratified samples and a rigorous research design, which uses sophisticated analyses or objective assessment procedures. Since the mid-1970s the picture has begun to improve slowly, though there remain many one-off studies which suffer from serious conceptual inadequacies and which fail to control important variables. . . . Despite does ignore significant areas. One of the most important of these concerns is the sense of mystery or awe at the heart of religious education, though there are foundations for its investigation in the available research. (Webster 1984 pp. 293, 295)

What appear to be needed in the future are more investigations of religious education issues, wider application of modern research techniques, and better methods for providing access to studies from around the world. Advances in data-storage and retrieval techniques by electronic computers linked into a network of the world's libraries promise greater availability of studies on religious education in the years ahead.

See also: Public and Private Schools: Sociological Perspectives

References

Abu-Rabi I M 1989 Modern trends in Islamic education. *Relig. Educ.* 84(2): 168–200

Adamu H A 1973 *The North and Nigerian Unity*. Daily Times, Lagos

Ashe K 1991 The feminist revolution and religious education. *Relig. Educ.* 86(1): 99–105

Barrett D B (ed.) 1982 *World Christian Encyclopedia: A Comparative Study of Churches and Religions in the Modern World, AD 1900–2000*. Oxford University Press, London

Brink T L 1977 A pscyhotherapeutic model for religious education. *Relig. Educ.* 72(4): 409–13

Bühler G 1886 The laws of Manu: Manu Smriti. Vol. 25 of Müller F M (ed.) 1886 *The Sacred Books of the East*. Clarendon Press, Oxford

Carper J C, Hunt T C (eds.) 1984 *Religious Schooling in America*. Religious Education Press, Birmingham, Alabama

Cully K B (ed.) 1963 *The Westminster Dictionary of Christian Education*. Westminster Press, Philadelphia, Pennsylvania

Edwards G M (ed.) 1996 *Encyclopedia Britannica Book of the Year*. Encyclopaedia Britannica, Chicago, Illinois

Fägerlind I 1974 Research on religious education in the Swedish school system. *Character Potential* 7(1): 38–47

Farley E, Wheeler B G (eds.) 1991 *Shifting Boundaries: Contextual Approaches to the Structure of Theological Education*. Westminster/John Knox Press, Louisville, Kentucky

Fischer K 1988 *Women at the Well: Feminist Perspectives on Spiritual Direction*. Paulist Press, New York

Fogle J S 1989 *Teaching the Bible with Puppets*. Twenty-Third Publications, Mystic, Connecticut

Glavich M K 1989 *Gospel Plays for Students: Thirty-Six Scripts for Education and Worship*. Twenty-Third Publications, Mystic, Connecticut

Hadden J K, Swann C E 1981 *Prime Time Preachers: The Rising Powers of Televangelism*. Addison-Wesley, Reading, Massachusetts

Hartman E E 1979 A follow-up study of graduates of selected Hebrew elementary educational institutions. *Relig. Educ.* 74(4): 416

Himmelfarb H S 1977 The non-linear impact of schooling: Comparing different types and amounts of Jewish education. *Sociol. Educ.* 50(2): 114–32

Holm J L 1975 *Teaching Religion in the School: A Practical Approach*. Oxford University Press, London

Hull J 1984 *Studies in Religion and Education*. Falmer, London

Husain S S, Ashraf S A 1979 *Crisis in Muslim Education*. King Abdulaziz University, Jidda

Jones M 1988 *God's People on the Move: A Manual for Leading Congregations in Dance and Movement*. Christian Dance Fellowship of Australia, Broadway, New South Wales

Lynn M L, Moberg D O (eds.) 1989 *Research in the Social Scientific Study of Religion*, Vol. 1. JAI Press, Greenwich, Connecticut

Miller R C 1977 Theology and the future of religious education. *Relig. Educ.* 72(1): 46–60

Oldenberg H 1886 The Grihya-Sûtras: Rules of vedic domestic ceremonies. Vols. 29–30 of Müller F M (ed.) 1886 *The Sacred Books of the East*. Clarendon Press, Oxford

Peatling J H 1979 Annual review of research: Religious education, 1979. *Relig. Educ.* 74(4): 422–41

Peatling J H 1984 Research in religious education. In: Taylor M J (ed.) 1984 *Changing Patterns of Religious Education*. Abingdon, Nashville, Tennessee

Sarno R A 1987 *Using Media in Religious Education*. Religious Education Press, Birmingham, Alabama

Schmitt G 1982 Teaching religion in German secondary schools. *Relig. Educ.* 77(1): 88–100

Stokes K E 1977 Protestantism. *Relig. Educ.* 72(2): 121–32

Strommen M P (ed.) 1971 *Research on Religious Development: A Comprehensive Handbook*. Hawthorn, New York

Tamez E (ed.) 1989 *Through Her Eyes: Women's Theology from Latin America*. Orbis, New York

Tulloch S 1991 *Oxford Dictionary of New Words*. Oxford University Press, Oxford

Webster D 1984 Research in RE. In: Sutcliffe J M (ed.) 1991 *A Dictionary of Religious Education*. SCM Press, Philadelphia, Pennsylvania

Wyckoff D C 1979 German religious education: An analysis. *Relig. Educ.* 74: 100–05

Further Reading

AAAS 1988 *Religion and Education*. American Association of Arts and Sciences, Cambridge, Massachusetts

Cully I V, Cully K B (eds.) 1990 *Harper's Encyclopedia of Religious Education*. Harper and Row, San Francisco, California

Gates, B (ed.) 1996 *Freedom and Authority in Religions and Religious Education*. Cassell, London

Roeder P M, Richter I, Fussel H P (eds.) 1995 *Pluralism and Education: Current World Trends in Policy, Law,* and Administration. Max Planck Institute for Human Development and Education, Berlin

Spiecker B, Straughan R (eds.) 1991 *Freedom and Indoctrination in Education: International Perspectives*. Cassell, London

Tulasciewicz W, To C-Y (eds.) 1993 *World Religions and Educational Practice*. Cassell, London

Wyckoff D C, Brown J (eds.) 1995 *Religious Education, 1960–1993: An Annotated Bibliography*. Greenwood, Westport, Connecticut

Sex Education

J. A. Diorio

Arguments about sex education commonly ignore feminist writing about sexuality. This article challenges prevailing biological assumptions about the nature of sexuality and its role in society, and questions the functions and objectives of sex education. This entry discusses the significance of feminist theories of sexuality to sex education.

1. The Sex Education Controversy

Sex education is controversial in many societies, though it is opposed only by minorities (Meredith 1989 p. 2, Kenny and Orr 1984 p. 492, Fantini 1983 pp. 1–2). Some parents fear that sex education will instill improper attitudes in children and will promote precocious or promiscuous sexual activity (Reppucci and Herman 1991 p. 130). Proponents of sex education argue that this fear should not block young people from obtaining the information which they need to avoid unwanted pregnancies and sexually transmitted diseases (STDs) (Herz et al. 1986 p. 202, Brooks-Gunn and Furstenberg 1989 p. 255).

This controversy is part of a broader dispute over the permissiveness of the so-called "sexual revolution" (Weeks 1985 pp. 17–21). From the mid-1950s to the mid-1970s opposition to contraception, abortion, divorce, extramarital sex, and homosexuality decreased (Weeks 1985 p. 19). Sex was more widely accepted as a positive aspect of life, and was freed increasingly from reproductive contexts and restrictive traditional attitudes (Katchadourian 1985 pp. 429–46, Weeks 1981 pp. 249–72). Many sex educators adopted more liberal attitudes (Obstfeld and Meyers 1984 p. 69), and strove to teach young people to understand their "emerging" sexuality as natural and positive (Silverstein and Buck 1986 p. 979). Liberal educators tended to acknowledge the sexual activity of young people, even if they did not always approve of it. They aimed to provide information about sexuality and contraception, rather than to curtail adolescent sexual activity (Strouse and Fabes 1985 p. 251).

Much of the debate in the early 1990s involves "progressive" and "traditional" approaches to sex education. Progressivists argue that sex education should eliminate needless ignorance and repression, and promote sexual confidence and responsibility among young people (Meredith 1989 p. 16). Many progressivist sex educators employ the notion of "sexuality comfort," which they want parents and teachers to embody and adolescents to acquire. Sexuality comfort involves "joyfully" affirming sexuality, and expressing it in a tolerant and sharing manner (Fetter 1987 p. 6). Traditionalists, on the other hand, believe that sex education ought to be delayed, and rather act as a "deterrent."

2. Essentialism versus Constructionism

It has been claimed that there has been a "paradigm shift" from traditional to progressive approaches to sex education over the past few decades (Scales 1986 pp. 265–74). Whatever the other differences between them, however, both approaches see sexuality as a natural drive. The controversy between these approaches does not reflect a more fundamental shift in the understanding of sexuality which has arisen during the 1970s and 1980s. This shift arose from growing skepticism toward positivist–empiricist conceptions of knowledge (Gergen 1985 p. 266, Tiefer 1987 p. 71). These conceptions saw knowledge as the accurate mental mirroring of the external world, and assumed that seemingly correct ideas in the mind must reflect real phenomena in the world. Ideas, including those about sexuality, thus easily became reified as reality. Our thoughts about sex were believed to correspond to, and even to be caused by, natural sexual features and forces in our bodies. This understanding of sex, commonly called "essentialism," views sex as a universal, biological reality which shapes personal as well as social life. Essentialism predominates among both traditional and progressive theorists of sexuality and sex education.

Challenges to positivist–empiricist conceptions of

knowledge have supported a "social constructionist" understanding of sexuality which is fundamentally different from essentialism. Constructionists claim that sexual ideas and behaviors are not generated naturally within bodies, but are produced by variable social and cultural forces (e.g., Diorio 1985 p. 245). One of the most influential progenitors of the constructionist approach is Michel Foucault (e.g., 1980 pp. 103, 105), who denies that sexuality is a forceful natural phenomenon which requires restraint by social institutions. Rather, sexuality is *made* by social institutions and practices.

Foucault attacks the common claim that we are witnessing a sexual revolution which has accepted natural sexual urges as positive, and freed them for more open expression. The idea of a sexual revolution, he argues, requires a sex drive inherent in human nature. The existence and social repression of this drive are not objective facts about the world, but socially produced beliefs. Society has not suppressed real sex, but produced suppressed sex. Interests, drives, and behaviors have to be generated within bodies and defined as sexual by social forces before they can be *felt* as sexual. Society makes us feel sex, and it also makes us feel that our sex is suppressed.

Since there is no natural sexuality for society to repress, there cannot be a revolution to free natural sexuality from social repression. The belief that we are in the midst of such a revolution does not reflect reality. It is a socially generated idea which, once held collectively, induces people to feel and act in ways compatible with itself. People mistakenly perceive the world to provide positive evidence of the social repression of natural sexuality and of a revolt against this repression, regardless of whether they support the revolution (Foucault 1980 pp. 17–49).

Sexuality is of major interest to feminist theorists, and constructionism has attracted overwhelming support among them. Feminism is not a monolithic movement, however, and not all feminist considerations of sexuality are constructionist, nor do all constructionist feminists apply this theory to sexuality in the same way. Nonetheless, a substantial feminist–constructionist literature about sexuality was published during the 1970s and 1980s, which has problematized the nature of sexuality in ways which are potentially important for sex educators. "Sexuality today," one author has noted, " . . . has become a moral and political battlefield" (Weeks 1985 p. 4).

Sex, though contested, has also become a major feature of how individuals understand themselves. Despite this, and despite the significance of constructionist arguments to our conception of sexuality, many writers about sexuality show little awareness of constructionism. Sex educators in particular, while self-consciously aware of working in a highly controversial field, have paid little attention to the essentialist–constructionist debate over sexuality or to feminist contributions to it.

3. Feminism and Sexuality

Feminist writers generally agree that sexuality is implicated in patriarchy's oppression of women, which it cloaks with mystifying beliefs about natural male–female differences (e.g. Hanmer 1990 p. 444, Martin 1982 p. 3). "Sexuality," MacKinnon (1989 p. ix) claims, is "central to women's status," and she links the constructionist theory of sex with the feminist theory of patriarchy as follows:

the molding, direction, and expression of sexuality organizes society into two sexes . . . This division underlies the totality of social relations. Sexuality is the social process through which social relations of gender are created . . . creating the social beings we know as women and men . . . A theory of sexuality becomes feminist methodologically . . . to the extent it treats sexuality as a social construct of male power: defined by men, forced on women, and constitutive of the meaning of gender. (MacKinnon 1989 pp. 3, 128)

The oppressiveness of sexuality is opaque, because most people have been socialized to think of sex primarily as a domain of pleasure. Feminist theorists have noted the tension between the socially constructed expectation that sex is pleasure, and the experience of many women that sex is a vehicle for their subordination. Many feminists argue that since patriarchy is a male-dominated social system, its construction of sexuality—and especially of women's sexuality—necessarily serves "to complement and service the dominant ideology of masculinity and men's sexual pleasure" (Holland et al. 1990 p. 129).

According to this feminist view, sexuality is constructed in patriarchy by male-dominated forces and practices which define women as sources of men's enjoyment. Being a source of male sexual enjoyment is what makes a person a woman, and women are *made*, not born. Without sexuality, there would be no subordinate women. The reproduction of patriarchy requires the ongoing construction of women as the sexual objects of men, and of sexuality as the enjoyment of women by men. Women and sexuality are defined in terms of each other. As the primary arena in which women are constituted *as* women, sexuality is central to their oppression. Sexuality and women are produced in general through the collective exercise of socially institutionalized male power. The practice of sex in particular relationships also involves the exercise of this same power by individual men over specific women. Women are thus oppressed both generally by the institution of sexuality, and individually when they function sexually *as* women within specific personal relationships. Women in patriarchy are unable to define the nature of sexuality, or to control what goes on within sexual relations (Holland et al. 1990 p. 130).

While feminist analyses of sexuality insist on the centrality of power within this domain, very little sex education literature discusses the power relations between males and females. The essentialist orientation of most sex educators deflects their attention away from the role of power in sexuality. For feminists, this failure to consider power helps to explain the lack of success obtained by sex education programs which aim to lower adolescent pregnancy and STD rates by providing information about contraception and safe sex (Meredith 1989 pp. 2–3, Herz et al. 1986 pp. 202–203, Strouse and Fabes 1985 p. 242). According to feminist–constructionist analyses, essentialist sex education programs cannot change adolescent sexual behavior because they are based on misunderstandings of where these behaviors originate and how their popularity is maintained. Simply providing information about the deleterious effects of socially designated sexual activities will not enable young people to behave differently, because these young people have been socialized to see and to feel these same activities as inevitable expressions of their own supposedly basic sexual nature. It is especially unrealistic to expect girls to change their sexual behaviors on the basis of such information. The male-based social pressures under which girls live induce them to interact sexually with boys, while withholding from them the ability— and even the idea—of taking control of these interactions (Holland et al. 1990 pp. 129–32).

4. Heterosexism and Women's Oppression

From a feminist point of view, patriarchy leads people to believe that they are naturally sexual, and that sex is naturally heterosexual. Heterosexuality defines women as different from and subordinate to men, and draws them into seemingly necessary sexual and social relationships with men. Heterosexuality is thus seen as a cornerstone of patriarchy. Many feminists argue that people are not born into, but acquire, heterosexuality. Heterosexuality constructs women into sexual gratifiers at the disposal of men. By masking the subordination of women behind sexual pleasure, heterosexuality serves as "the strongest arm and most powerful manifestation of patriarchy; and therefore one of its most important objects is the oppression of women" (Overall 1990 p. 8).

Heterosexuality makes sex sexist. It makes the difference of women from men appear to be the cause, rather than the effect, of women's sexual subordination (MacKinnon 1989 pp. 218–19). Anything which reinforces the belief that sexuality is naturally heterosexist supports patriarchy's exercise of concealed power over women. In feminist eyes, this is what sex education does. By seeking to lower adolescent pregnancy rates, sex educators concentrate on heterosexual copulation as the most natural and inevitable form of sex. This encourages students to see male–female genital copulation as an essential source of sexual gratification and personal sexual identity. Educating women into heterosexuality "colonizes"

them with male-defined ideas and behaviors, and constructs them into willing participants in their own oppression (Hartsock 1990 pp. 160–64).

The feminist understanding of heterosexuality as a constructed institutionalization of patriarchal power rejects the progressive essentialist view of sex as a socially repressed but inherently liberating force. Rather than sex being repressed by society, women are seen by feminists as oppressed *by* and *within* socially constructed sexuality. Attempting to free contemporary forms of sexuality from social restraint, and seeking to help people feel "sexually comfortable" with these forms through sex education, simply reifies their apparent naturalness and contributes to the oppression of women.

The following comment, from a widely used textbook on sexuality, illustrates the division between progressive essentialist and feminist understandings of women's sexuality:

> The major changes of the sexual revolution have primarily influenced women . . . The behavior of men has not changed that much, and what has changed has been in large part in reactions to alterations in female sexuality. Women are now sexually more candid, interested, tolerant, active, and fulfilled than probably at any earlier period of the nation's history. (Katchadourian 1985 p. 437)

For progressive essentialists, the apparent increase in sexual willingness and activity by women is a stride forward in freeing sexuality from social repression. For feminists, however, this passage documents the growing power of patriarchy to construct women as the sexual servants of men. It would not surprise feminists if the sexual activities of men have not changed. Patriarchy has not retreated in the face of feminist challenges in their view, but has maintained its heterosexist power, while working to induct women into more active participation in the very sexuality which defines and enforces their subordination. This difference is epitomized in conflicting evaluations of the impact of contraception on women's sexuality. For progressive essentialists, contraception frees women to participate actively in sexuality without fear of unwanted pregnancies. For many feminists, contraception has placed women *more* at the sexual disposal of men by eliminating one of their grounds for refusing male sexual advances.

5. Sex Education, Subjectivity, and Power

For feminists, sex educators must encourage a critical perspective toward sexuality on the part of young people. They must alert students to the socially contingent foundations of contemporary sexual practices and attitudes, and they must seek to transform social and sexual relationships by empowering young women within them (Holland et al. 1990 p. 141). From the feminist point of view, therefore, sex educators should explain the reality of contemporary sexuality, and challenge the qualities of heterosexist institutions, attitudes, and relationships that oppress women (Klein 1992).

Feminist writers have produced at least two different approaches to achieving these objectives. The first condemns patriarchy for denying women a sexuality of their own, and seeks to use sex education for the construction and expression by young women of self-generated sexual desires and behaviors. This approach accepts the existence of women's potential sexuality apart from the influence of patriarchy, and implies that there is something about sexuality which stands outside social construction. The second approach rejects the possibility of a socially independent women's sexuality, because it sees the very idea of sexuality as produced totally by patriarchy. Within patriarchy, sexuality and heterosexism are identical. This is true even for homosexuals, since homosexuality depends on the prior, heterosexist division of the population into two falsely natural genders. Without heterosexism, homosexuals could not know which kinds of people with whom to interact sexually, or even what kinds of activities to recognize as sexual. Since the possibility of sexuality of any kind requires heterosexist understandings of human nature and behavior, and since heterosexism *is* the oppression of women, any form of sexuality inescapably would subordinate women.

These two approaches support quite different programs for sex education. The first uses sex education for developing the sexual subjectivity of young women. It accepts that sexuality in the early 1990s is oppressive of women, but it finds room within a broader—and seemingly natural—"space" of sex for nonoppressive desires and pleasures. It aims to lead young women to enjoy these pleasures, by helping them to generate new desires and to validate and voice inchoate ones which can be felt only in vague and unarticulated ways. Existing sex education programs are acknowledged to promote oppressive heterosexism. Since heterosexism does not exhaust the potential of sexuality, however, there can be feminist sex education programs which subvert heterosexism and initiate pleasurable, nonoppressive sexuality for girls (Lenskyj 1990 pp. 222–23).

The second approach, since it denies that there is any natural "space" for sexuality apart from that filled by the social constructions of heterosexism, must also deny the possibility of sex-positive, counteroppressive sex education which could encourage sexual pleasures in any way. The only way sex education could contribute to the liberation of women would be for it to expose the inescapable oppressiveness of sexuality, and to work for its elimination. Eliminating sexuality does not necessarily entail eliminating reproductive behavior. Reproduction, for many feminist writers, is linked only contingently with the constructions of sexuality. Sexuality could be destroyed, but

reproductive activity could continue without being thought of as "sexual," or serving as the keystone in the gendered structuring of social relationships.

These two feminist approaches to sexuality and sex education parallel differing reactions to Foucault's analysis of power. Foucault claims that our current understanding of the nature of power is derived from revolutionary movements against the monarchs of the *ancien régime* in Europe. This has led us to understand power as something held by persons in dominant positions in a social order, and exercised over those who are subordinate. He argues that we must conceive of power differently. Far from being the exclusive possession of dominant individuals or groups, power is everywhere: it is exercised in every human relationship and conversation. Rather than its exercise being primarily negative and repressive, it constructs us into what we are (Foucault 1980 p. 136). It is the medium in and through which our lives and our thoughts are shaped.

Foucault's conception of power is problematic for feminism. If the ultimate agenda of feminism is rebellion against the dominance of men over women, Foucault undermines this agenda by refusing to locate power exclusively in the hands of any one group (Hartsock, 1990 p. 169). If men do not really hold power over women, then women cannot sensibly seek liberation from men. Foucault's attack on the idea of a sexual revolution is the result of applying his analysis of power to sexuality. Foucault argues that sexuality is not naturally opposed to social power, such that any expression of sexuality subverts that power.

Sexuality is produced by power, and the more people talk about and engage in it the more they construct it. Speaking about and performing sex are not revolutionary acts which subvert the power of dominant groups, for such acts themselves are exercises of omnipresent, diffuse power (Singer 1989 pp. 141–43). "We must not think," Foucault (1980 p. 157) writes, "that by saying yes to sex, one says no to power . . ." Rather than setting sexuality and politics against each other, Foucault merges them, blurring the parallel distinctions between the individual and society, and between subversion and repression (Martin 1982 p. 6).

In order to subvert political power, sexuality would have to stand at least partially outside the domain constructed *by* power. Only then could sexuality— and especially women's sexuality—be juxtaposed to power, and its expression provide a natural leverage point from which to subvert dominant, male-defined sexual institutions and practices. The basic question for feminism, then, from the point of view both of the analysis of patriarchal power and of the definition of sex education, is whether there is any real sexuality or sexual potential present in women apart from that which has been socially produced.

A major theme in feminist writing is that patriarchy constructs women as "objects" in a world that is defined by and centered upon men. Patriarchy thereby silences women's subjectivity, which is their ability to define and speak for themselves, and to express the world as it is to them. Subsequently, feminist theorists have criticized the disciplines of learning for serving as the voice of men in their confrontations with the world, and for pushing women to the sidelines in human attempts to know the world. Patriarchy constructs knowledge in terms of the interests and attitudes of men, making women into things known rather than active knowers: objects, rather than subjects of knowledge. When male-centered knowledge is transmitted through school curricula, schooling—including male-defined sex education—participates in this de-subjectifying of women.

Foucault's analysis of power may be complicitous in this denial of women's subjectivity. For him, subjectivity only exists if it is constructed through the operation of power. There can be no silenced subjectivity apart from the actual subjectivity which is produced by power, just as there can be no socially independent sexuality which is suppressed by social power. But some feminist analyses assume that there is real female subjectivity apart from, and silenced by, the constructions of power. Denying that such subjectivity exists, it is charged, is just another exercise of power by patriarchy's dominant group—an exercise which Foucault himself leads, while cleverly covering his own tracks with the denial that power really is exercised by any dominant group. Hartsock (1990) puts the point as a question:

> Why is it that just at the moment when so many of us who have been silenced begin to demand the right to name ourselves, to act as subjects rather than objects of history, that just then the concept of subjecthood becomes problematic? (pp. 163–64)

If women are to be subjectified, however, thereby dislocating men from the center of knowledge and speech, what is it that is to take up this new subjectivity, and where is it now (Hanmer 1990 p. 445)? If there is nothing within the subject apart from what has been placed there by power, then power can never be said to have suppressed or silenced the subject. If sexuality is *completely* constructed by power, then there can be no female sexuality outside of this construction which power denies or represses. Similarly, independent female sexuality could never be *voiced* in opposition to power or in an attempt to subvert patriarchy.

Feminist theorists who believe in an independent female subjectivity distance themselves from Foucault, and limit the extent to which constructionism can account for sexuality. These theorists accept the possibility of liberationist sex education programs which can develop and express female sexuality, thereby subverting the dominant, patriarchal construction of sex. They share with progressive essentialist educators a belief that sex and power *are* antagonistic.

Theoretical support for this approach is provided by Hélène Cixous, who argues that women should "write"

their bodies: putting into words the sexuality which has been denied them by the male-authored speech and knowledge about sex which pervades our culture. Cixous does not discuss sex education, but in her view this male knowledge must be what fills the textbooks and discussions of contemporary sex educators. Women must break out of this discourse: "If woman has always functioned "within" the discourse of man . . . it is time for her to dislocate this "within," to explode it, turn it around, and seize it; to . . . invent for herself a language to get inside of" (Cixous 1981 pp. 256–57; see also Singer 1989).

In the view of these writers, existing sex education programs have silenced female desire by teaching knowledge about sexuality that is based solely on male perspectives. These programs construct girls to see themselves as recipients of male desires and attentions, rather than as generators of their own self-conceived sexual desires. Seen in this way, feminist sex education must provide girls with opportunities to develop and voice their own "discourse of desire," and to build their own sense of sexual agency (Fine 1988 pp. 29–44). The mounting of this discourse will de-center men from the middle of the sexual universe, and provide for the construction of a new sexuality based on women's experience and desires. It will promote a sexual revolution against the imposed, male-defined model of sex through which women are silenced and under which they suffer.

But *from where*, Foucaultians will ask, is this discourse to be voiced, and *who* is to speak it? Promoting female sexual subjectivity through sex-positive feminist sex education requires a female subjectivity which exists unvoiced but is not produced. But subjectivity for Foucault cannot come from nowhere. It must be produced by power, and once it has been produced it necessarily must be caught up in the nexus of power relations which produces and maintains it (Foucault 1980 p. 100, Singer 1989 p. 141, Horowitz 1987 pp. 63–64, Hartsock 1990 p. 170). Subjectivity cannot be found outside of power, and any subjective voicing of sexual desire cannot be juxtaposed against power. There are simply different power relations producing different subjectivities and generating different sexual desires and voices. For Foucaultians, advocates of subversive female sexuality have reverted to thinking of power in terms of the *ancien régime*, just like progressive essentialist sex educators and advocates of the sexual revolution. But Foucault is not a revolutionary or a liberationist (McWhorter 1989 p. 613).

6. Conclusion

Traditionalist and progressivist approaches to sex education share a belief in the biological essentialness of human sexuality, while disagreeing over how expressions of this sexuality should be viewed. Both traditional and progressive essentialists disagree with social constructionists over the foundations of sexuality, and most feminist writers about sex adopt a constructionist approach. In criticizing the patriarchal construction of sexuality as part of the oppression of women, however, some feminists seek grounds for developing female sexual subjectivity, and in doing so are led to seemingly essentialist commitments regarding the potential sexuality of women. These feminists share with progressivists a belief in the liberating potential of sexuality, and in the positive role of sex education within a modified sexual revolution. Other feminists, however, reject real female sexuality, and see the only subversive role of feminist sex education in exposing all forms of sexuality as artificial vehicles of patriarchy.

Whether sex-positive feminist sex education has any role in the political agenda of feminism is therefore disputed by feminist writers. This debate will continue, as feminist theorists grapple with the concepts of sexuality, society, power, and personal subjectivity, and with the relationships among them. Constructionist and feminist arguments in this debate are central to sex education theory and research, however, and they deserve more serious consideration by others working in the sex education field than they have as yet received.

See also: Gender Theories in Education

References

Brooks-Gunn J, Furstenberg F F Jr. 1989 Adolescent sexual behavior. *Am. Psychol.* 44(2): 249–57

Cixous H 1981 The laugh of the Medusa. In: Marks E, de Courtivron I (eds.) 1981 *New French Feminisms*. Harvester Press, Brighton

Diorio J A 1985 Contraception, copulation domination, and the theoretical barrenness of sex education literature. *Educ. Theory* 35(3): 239–54

Fantini M D 1983 Sex education: Alternative modes of delivery. *J. Res. Dev. Educ.* 16(2): 1–7

Fetter M P 1987 Reaching a level of sexual comfort. *Health Education* 18(1): 6–8

Fine M 1988 Sexuality, schooling, and adolescent females: The missing discourse of desire. *Harv. Educ. Rev.* 58(1): 29–53

Foucault M 1980 *The History of Sexuality*, Vol. 1. Vintage Books, New York

Gergen K J 1985 The social constructionist movement in modern psychology. *Am. Psychol.* 40(3): 266–75

Hanmer J 1990 Men, power, and the exploitation of women. *Women's Studies Int. Forum* 13(5): 443–56

Hartsock N 1990 Foucault on power: A theory for women? In: Nicholson L J (ed.) 1990 *Feminism/Postmodernism*. Routledge, New York

Herz E J, Reis J S, Barbera-Stein L 1986 Family life education for young teens: An assessment of three interventions. *Health Educ. Q.* 13(3): 201–21

Holland J, Ramazanoglu C, Scott S 1990 Managing risk and experiencing danger: Tensions between government AIDS education policy and young women's sexuality. *Gender and Education* 2(2): 125–46

Horowitz G 1987 The Foucaultian impasse: No sex, no self, no revolution. *Political Theory* 15(1): 61–80

Katchadourian H A 1985 *Fundamentals of Human Sexuality*, 4th edn. Holt, Rinehart and Winston, New York

Kenny A M, Orr M T 1984 Sex education: An overview of current programs, policies and research. *Phi Del. Kap.* 67(7): 491–96

Klein S S (ed.) 1992 *Sex Equity and Sexuality in Education*. State University of New York Press, Albany, New York

Lenskyj H 1990 Beyond plumbing and prevention: Feminist approaches to sex education. *Gender and Education* 2(2): 217–30

MacKinnon C A 1989 *Toward a Feminist Theory of the State*. Harvard University Press, Cambridge, Massachusetts

McWhorter L 1989 Culture or nature? The function of the term 'body' in the work of Michel Foucault. *J. Phil.* 86(11): 608–14

Martin B 1982 Feminism, criticism, and Foucault. *New German Critique* 27: 3–30

Meredith P 1989 *Sex Education: Political Issues in Britain and Europe*. Routledge and Kegan Paul, London

Obstfeld L S, Meyers A V 1984 Adolescent sex education: A preventive mental health measure. *J. School Health* 54(2): 68–70

Overall C 1990 Heterosexuality and feminist theory. *Can. J. Phil.* 20(1): 1–18

Reppucci N D, Herman J 1991 Sexuality education and child sexual abuse prevention programs in the schools. In: Grant G (ed.) 1991 *Rev. Res. Educ. 17*. American Educational Research Association, Washington, DC

Scales P 1986 The changing context of sexuality education: Paradigms and challenges for alternative futures. *Fam. Relat.* 35(2): 265–74

Silverstein C D, Buck G M 1986 Parental preferences regarding sex education topics for sixth graders. *Adolescence* 21: 971–80

Singer J 1989 True confessions: Cixous and Foucault on sexuality and power. In: Allen J, Young I M (eds.) 1989 *The Thinking Muse*. Indiana University Press, Bloomington, Indiana

Strouse J, Fabes R A 1985 Formal versus informal sources of sex education: Competing forces in the sexual socialization of adolescents. *Adolescence* 20: 251–63

Tiefer L 1987 Social constructionism and the study of human sexuality. In: Shaver P, Hendrick C (eds.) 1987 *Sex and Gender*. Sage, Newbury Park, California

Weeks J 1981 *Sex, Politics and Society: The Regulation of Sexuality since 1800*. Longman, London

Weeks J 1985 *Sexuality and Its Discontents: Meanings, Myths and Modern Sexualities*. Routledge and Kegan Paul, London

Social Psychological Theories of Teaching

D. W. Johnson and R. T. Johnson

Education is fundamentally an interpersonal process involving teachers and students, aimed at transmitting knowledge, skills, and culture from one generation to the next. Thus social psychology (the study of interpersonal, small-group, and organizational dynamics) is perhaps the most relevant social science for educators. The social nature of education is the first issue described in this article. The application of social psychological knowledge to educational practice is then discussed. The theories and research findings included in this article were chosen on the basis of their relevance to educational practice.

1. The Social Nature of Education

A defining characteristic of the human species is the transference of knowledge and tradition from one generation to the next. The process of transferring accumulated knowledge, skills, and cultures across generations is fundamentally a social process, requiring communication and interaction among people who exchange ideas, skills, attitudes, and feelings. Schools have been developed and have evolved to enhance and systematize this transfer. The transfer is conducted not by computers, teaching machines, textbooks, laboratory equipment, and videotapes; rather it is the direct result of interaction between human beings—between teachers and students, and students themselves. Teachers in the middle grades, for example, typically engage in about 200 interpersonal interchanges per hour (Jackson 1968). How much students learn and how successful teachers are depends on the nature and the quality of these classroom interactions.

2. Educational Social Organizations and Role Theory

The transfer of culture from one generation to the next is organized within schools. Schools are social organizations—a planned set of interpersonal relationships structured to achieve certain goals. The better teachers understand how the school works as a social organization, the more effectively they can teach. All social organizations are based on cooperation among members to achieve goals, maintain effective working relationships, and adapt to change. The success of the school depends on cooperative relationships among its members. Relationships are structured through the assignment of roles and the establishment of norms.

The school, like all social organizations, contains a variety of positions, such as teacher, student, and administrator. For each position there is a "role"—a set of prescribed behaviors that anyone who occupies that position should perform. The roles define how adults, children, and adolescents are to relate to one another in repeated and reliable ways so that the school's goals are achieved. The roles are interdependent and complementary. Roles contain both obligations, which individuals in complementary roles expect from a person, and rights, which individuals in complementary roles will do for a person. A teacher, for example, is obligated to structure instructional situations so that students learn; students in turn have the right to expect the teacher to do so.

People in certain roles are expected to behave in certain ways, both by themselves and by those in other roles. When a person holds positions in two different groups that make contradictory demands, there is "interrole conflict." If a student, for example, is in a science class that requires a major report to be written tonight and is also on the football team and is expected to go to rest for tomorrow's game, then there is a conflict between the roles of student and football player. "Intrarole conflict" occurs when other roles hold incompatible expectations of a particular role. If the history teacher, for example, expects students to complete three hours of homework tonight and the science teacher expects the same students to complete a major report, then students have a role conflict.

"Norms" define general expectations for everyone in the school. "No running in the halls" is an example of a school norm. Norms make explicit what behavior is appropriate or inappropriate within the school, and they have a specific "ought" or "must" quality. Roles and norms influence educators' actions so that a coordinated division of labor results within schools.

Because schools are organizations, all the social psychological knowledge contained within the fields of organizational psychology and group dynamics is relevant to educational practice. The continual effectiveness of schools, furthermore, depends on their ability to change and develop over time. Social psychologists have applied organizational development and change theory to schools (Miles 1964). Based on the research, schools are being encouraged to change to team-based cooperative organizational structures (Johnson and Johnson 1994).

Organizational and role theories help educators understand a wide variety of dynamics within schools. By redesigning roles the effectiveness of schools may be increased. By identifying and reducing role conflicts the productivity of individual members may be increased. Teachers, for example, may coordinate when tests are given and reports are due so that students are not faced with competing assignments on any one night. By changing individuals' roles their perspectives, attitudes, and behavior can change. When students are given the responsibility of teaching other students, for example, their attitudes toward homework may change.

3. Interpersonal Expectations and Performance

Closely related to role theory is expectancy theory. Students have a tendency to live up (or down) to teacher expectations. Expectancy theory predicts that what teachers and classmates expect from students tends to influence how much students actually learn (Rosenthal and Jacobson 1968). A number of studies have confirmed this prediction. In addition, there is evidence that people will believe and do what prestigeful others suggest. In order to maximize achievement, both the teacher and classmates should expect students to achieve realistic but challenging learning goals.

4. Social Interdependence Theory

Perhaps the most influential social psychological theory for educational practice is social interdependence theory. For each lesson, teachers must decide whether to structure the learning goals cooperatively, competitively, or individualistically. The first experimental studies on social interdependence were conducted in the 1890s in England, Germany, and the United States. The basic theory, based on Kurt Lewin's (1935) field theory, was formulated by Morton Deutsch (1949). Social interdependence exists when each individual's outcomes are affected by the actions of others. Within any social situation, individuals may join together to achieve mutual goals, compete to see who is best, or act independently on their own.

There are two types of social interdependence: cooperative and competitive. The absence of social interdependence results in individualistic efforts. Cooperation exists when one perceives that one is linked with others in a way so that one cannot succeed unless others succeed (and vice versa), and/or one's work benefits others and others' work benefits one. Competition exists when one perceives that one cannot succeed unless others fail (and vice versa) and/or one's work decreases others' chances for success and others' work decreases one's chances for success. Individualistic efforts exist when one perceives that one's success is unrelated to the success or failure of others.

Over 550 experimental and 100 correlational studies have been conducted on this theory (Johnson and Johnson 1989). These studies demonstrate that working cooperatively, compared with competitive and individualistic efforts, will result in higher student achievement, more positive relationships among students (including between White and minority students, and nonhandicapped and handicapped students), and greater psychological adjustment, social competencies, and self-esteem. Cooperative learning has such consistent, powerful, and numerous effects on educational outcomes that it should probably be used the majority of the school day. A number of social psychologists have worked with schools in implementing cooperative learning within the classroom and cooperative teaching teams within the school (see Johnson et al. 1993). Teachers at all grade levels need to be trained in how to structure lessons cooperatively.

5. Distributive Justice

Closely related to social interdependence theory are theories of distributive justice (Deutsch 1985). Distributive justice deals with how benefits such as grades are granted to group or organizational members. The equity (or merit or competitive) view is that a person's rewards should be in proportion to his or her contributions to the group's effort. The equality (or cooperative) view is that all group members should benefit equally. The need view is that group members should be rewarded in proportion to their need. Whether teachers utilize an equity, equality, or need system, students have to perceive the system as "just." When rewards are distributed unjustly, the group may be characterized by low morale, high conflict, and low productivity. The evidence indicates that before a task is performed the equity reward system is perceived to be fairest, while after a task is performed the equality system is perceived to be most just. Before starting a project, members of a learning group may wish to be ranked from best to worst and given grades accordingly. After the project is completed, students will wish to have all members receive the same grade, believing that the diverse contributions cannot be "justly" ranked from most to least valuable. With increased experience, students tend to achieve higher under the equality system. When a groupmate suffers a life crisis (such as parents getting a divorce), furthermore, students usually wish to have the teacher take "need" into consideration. In terms of giving grades to students and rewarding educators, an equality system or some combination of the three would probably be most effective.

6. Conflict Theory

For instructional effectiveness and classroom order, teachers both create intellectual conflict to improve instruction and teach students how to negotiate and mediate in order to reduce discipline problems and improve the quality of life within schools. Controversy exists when one person's ideas, information, conclusions, theories, or opinions are incompatible with those of another, and the two seek to reach an agreement. When academic controversies are structured in the classroom, students are required to conduct research and prepare a position; rehearse orally the relevant information; advocate a position; teach their knowledge to peers; analyze, critically evaluate, and rebut information; reason both deductively and inductively; and synthesize and integrate information into factual and judgmental conclusions with which all sides can agree (Johnson and Johnson 1989). Controversy theory is based on developmental theories of Piaget (1950), Berlyne (1965), Hunt (1964), and others, who posit that cognitive and social development as well as learning depend on creating cognitive disequilibrium, conceptual conflict, cognitive uncertainty, and epistemic curiosity. Controversy (compared with individualistic and competitive learning, debate, and concurrence-seeking) creates higher achievement, problem-solving, critical thinking, creativity, motivation to learn, and task involvement. Instead of suppressing intellectual conflict among students by lecturing, competition, and individualistic work, according to this theory teachers should structure and encourage it to promote learning.

There are times when the wants and goals of students conflict and procedures for negotiating integrative agreements are needed (Johnson and Johnson 1995). Social psychology has provided a long history of theorizing and research on negotiating integrative agreements (Deutsch 1973). The traditional family, neighborhood, and community procedures for teaching children how to manage conflicts have broken down. Students come to school with diverse ideas about how conflicts should be managed. Teachers need to teach all students to use the same set of procedures and skills in negotiating wise resolutions to their conflicts. Such training programs consist of two steps: (a) teaching all students a negotiation procedure, and (b) involving students in a peer mediation program where they help their classmates negotiate wise agreements to their conflicts (Johnson and Johnson 1995). Students need to be taught to state what they want and how they feel, provide the reasons underlying their wants, accurately take their opponent's perspective, propose at least three options for an agreement, and reach a mutually satisfying agreement. Teaching students how to resolve their conflicts constructively reduces discipline problems and empowers students to regulate their own behavior rather than rely on adult authorities to do so.

7. Achievement Motivation Theory

The instructional methods teachers use affect how motivated students are to achieve. Motivation to achieve is the degree to which individuals commit effort to achieve goals they perceive as meaningful and worthwhile. While humans may be born with a motivation to increase their competencies, how meaningful goals appear to be and how much effort individuals decide to exert are basically determined by internalized past relationships, present relationships, or current interaction patterns within the learning situation (Johnson and Johnson 1989). The two most important theories of achievement motivation were formulated by Atkinson and Feather (1965) and David McClelland (1965). Atkinson states that achievement motivation is a balance between the tendency to achieve success and the tendency to avoid failure. The tendency to achieve success is assumed to be a function of the general motive to achieve success, the subjective probability of success, and the incentive to succeed. McClelland has demonstrated that, with training, the achievement motivation of adults can be increased. Together, their work provides a basis for educators to ensure that students develop a high level of achievement motivation.

One application of achievement motivation to education is Richard DeCharms' (1976) work with personal causation. Students can see their behavior as originating in themselves (they are an origin) or as being the result of external pressure (they are a pawn). Students treated as origins tend to like school tasks, work hard at them, and be more involved in them than are students treated as pawns. Students, furthermore, want to be the origin of their behavior and constantly struggle against the constraint of external causes. The more students believe they are studying because they freely choose to do so, operate under their own control, and are personally committed to learn, the greater their task motivation (see *Development of Achievement Motivation*).

8. Attribution Theory

Causal attributions answer "why" questions, such as "Why did I fail this exam?" "Why" questions are asked more frequently after negative, unexpected, or atypical outcomes. The reasons to which students attribute their failures influence how hard they work on subsequent tasks. Attribution theory is concerned with people's explanations of the causes of (a) their own and other's behavior and (b) events (Graham 1991, Heider 1958). Growing out of the social psychological theories on social perception, attribution theory focuses on whether people attribute the causes of behavior to the situation or the individual, ways in which responsibility for success or failure is determined, and how attributional decisions affect subsequent behavior. Causes can be dispositional (within people) or situational (within environment). Students can claim their success is due to their ability or the amount of effort they exerted (dispositional causes) or because the task was easy or they were lucky (situational causes). In most cases, students should be trained to attribute their success to themselves and their failures to situational causes.

Generally, there are three dispositional causal dimensions: locus, stability, and controllability (Weiner

1986). The locus dimension defines the location of a cause as internal or external to the individual. The stability dimension designates causes as constant or varying over time. The controllability dimension refers to whether a cause is subject to one's own volitional influence. Ability is an internal, stable, and uncontrollable cause. Effort is internal, unstable, and controllable.

Teachers should ensure that students think through why they succeeded or failed, while guiding them toward the conclusion that their failure is caused by a lack of effort or using the wrong strategy. What emotions teachers express toward students seems to affect the attributions students make about the causes of their success or failure. Teacher sympathy for failure tends to be interpreted as indicating low ability, while teacher anger towards failure seems to be interpreted as indicating low effort.

9. Self-esteem Theory

Students who are confused as to who they are or who lack confidence in themselves hesitate to attempt difficult and challenging learning tasks. Teachers make their jobs easier in many ways by helping students gain a clear and positive sense of identity and self-esteem. Every student needs to acquire a positive self-identity, a sense of self that remains the same over time no matter what else has changed in one's life and environment (Erikson 1968). A person is not born with a sense of self. It is during the first two or three years that a kind of crude self-awareness develops, such as being able to make distinctions between what is part of his or her body and what is part of something else. It takes many years of maturation before full adult self-awareness comes into being. As people develop self-awareness, they formulate a self-conception and develop processes through which they derive conclusions about their self-worth. Self-esteem and self-identity develop primarily from relationships with other people, including working with others to achieve challenging goals; being known, liked, and respected by others; and knowing others well enough to identify similarities and differences. The more teachers involve students in joint projects that allow personal and supportive relationships to develop, the more positive will be students' self-identity and self-esteem.

Self-esteem may also be approached from a social-learning perspective that emphasizes students' perceived competence and self-efficacy, which influence students' choices of tasks, willingness to invest effort in task accomplishment, and persistence in the face of subsequent failure (Bandura 1986). Perceived competence is heavily influenced by initial encounters with novel tasks or new subjects. Individuals who experience initial success or failure in some new undertaking tend to infer that they possess relatively high or low aptitude/competence in that area. Once formed, these beliefs in one's competence are resistant to change. The implication for teaching is that at the beginning of each new class, students should be given success experiences in ways that lead them to believe they have an aptitude for the subject area.

10. School Culture

There is considerable evidence that the work environment can affect the meaning of work to the worker. Schools are no exception. The way the school is managed and the policies it espouses tend to affect staff and student motivation. Within each school a culture has to be built based on shared perceptions of (a) desired goals worth striving to achieve and (b) how these goals may be attained. Differences in school culture help explain why some schools are better than others. School culture comprises four interdependent dimensions (Maehr and Braskamp 1986): (a) goal structures (for both students and staff, cooperative efforts are more productive than are competitive or individualistic efforts), (b) roles and power relationships (students and staff should see themselves as autonomous and self-reliant individuals who are the "origin" of their efforts to achieve, rather than as passive pawns who are controlled), (c) evaluation and feedback systems (internal, student-centered evaluation creates greater task orientation and intrinsic motivation to achieve than does external, teacher-dominated evaluation), and (d) symbols of identity and purpose (effective schools stand for something—goals, values, and expectations for student behavior are expressed through slogans, posters, songs, and role models). A clear and strong school culture is especially important when students are culturally diverse.

11. Social Psychology of Education

Almost all social psychological knowledge could contribute to educational practice. In order to help teachers, social psychologists have (a) specifically operationalized social psychological knowledge into teaching and managing practices and (b) implemented organizational change procedures to ensure innovations are adopted by schools.

Education takes place through interpersonal interactions structured through roles and norms to achieve the school's goals. Understanding the nature of social organizations and role theory helps teachers clarify the rights and obligations of themselves and their students. The expectations teachers hold for students not only help define their role but also influence how much students learn. The school by its very organizational nature is a cooperative enterprise, but within any lesson teachers may structure students' learning goals cooperatively, competitively, or individualistically. Related to social interdependence theory are theories of distributive justice that help teachers give rewards in ways that are perceived to be "just," and conflict theory which has relevance for improving instruction (especially higher level reasoning) and decreasing discipline problems within the school. Social psychology has developed several theories of achievement motivation that influence how curriculum is designed and how teaching is conducted. Like all organizations, schools develop cultures around the goals they consider worth achieving and how the goals are to be attained.

Social psychology has much to offer teachers. Both preservice and inservice teacher education should emphasize social psychological knowledge. Social scientists interested in education should both advance social psychological theories through systematic research programs and operationalize their findings into more effective teaching procedures. Each of the theories discussed requires considerably more research to maximize its value to teachers. Key studies are especially needed on the ways a cooperative structure provides the context in which the impact of the other theories is maximized. The major problems facing education, furthermore, are inherently social psychological and provide a fertile field for new social psychological research. Ensuring that diversity among students results in mutual understanding, respect, creativity, and sophistication is an inherently social psychological problem. Reducing destructive antisocial behaviors such as drug abuse, suicide, criminality, sexual promiscuity, and so forth requires the application of social psychological knowledge. Motivating at-risk students, lowering dropout rates, and ensuring that women and minorities become interested in mathematics and science require social psychological interventions. Both in its basic nature and in its need to solve major problems, education relies heavily on social psychological knowledge.

See also: Social Psychological Theories in Education

References

Atkinson J, Feather N (eds.) 1966 *A Theory of Achievement Motivation.* Wiley, New York

Bandura A 1986 *Social Foundations of Thought and Action.* Prentice-Hall, Englewood Cliffs, New Jersey

Berlyne D 1965 Curiosity and education. In: Krumboltz J (ed.) 1965 *Learning and the Educational Process.* Rand-McNally, Chicago, Illinois

DeCharms R 1976 *Enhancing Motivation.* Irvington, New York

Deutsch M 1949 A theory of cooperation and competition. *Human Relations* 2(2): 129–52

Deutsch M 1973 *The Resolution of Conflict.* Yale University Press, New Haven, Connecticut

Deutsch M 1985 *Distributive Justice.* Yale University Press, New Haven, Connecticut

Erikson E 1968 *Identity: Youth and Crisis.* Norton, New York

Graham S 1991 A review of attribution theory in achievement contexts. *Educ. Psychol. Rev.* 3(1): 5–39

Heider F 1958 *The Psychology of Interpersonal Relations.* Wiley, New York

Hunt J 1964 Introduction: Revisiting Montessori. In: Montessori M (ed.) 1964 *The Montessori Method.* Schocken Books, New York

Jackson P W 1968 *Life in Classrooms.* Holt, Rinehart and Winston, New York

Johnson D W, Johnson R 1989 *Cooperation and Competition: Theory and Research.* Interaction Book Company, Edina, Minnesota

Johnson D W, Johnson R 1994 *Leading the Cooperative School,* 2nd edn. Interaction Book Company, Edina, Minnesota

Johnson D W, Johnson R 1995 *Teaching Students to be Peacemakers,* 3rd edn. Interaction Book Company, Edina, Minnesota

Johnson D W, Johnson R, Holubec E 1995 *Circles of Learning.* Interaction Book Company, Edina, Minnesota

Lewin K 1935 *A Dynamic Theory of Personality.* McGraw-Hill, New York

Maehr M, Braskamp L 1986 *The Motivation Factor: A Theory of Personal Investment.* Lexington Press, Lexington, Massachusetts

McClelland D 1965 Toward a Theory of Motive Acquisition. *Am. Psychol.* 20(5): 321–33

Miles M 1964 *Innovation in Education.* Teachers College Press, New York

Piaget J 1950 *The Psychology of Intelligence.* Harcourt, New York

Rosenthal R, Jacobson L 1968 *Pygmalion in the Classroom.* Holt, Rinehart, and Winston, New York

Weiner B 1986 *An Attributional Theory of Motivation and Emotion.* Springer-Verlag, New York

Further Reading

Bar-Tal D, Saxe L (eds.) 1978 *Social Psychology of Education.* Hemisphere, Washington, DC

Feldman R 1986 *The Social Psychology of Education.* Cambridge University Press, Cambridge, Massachusetts

Johnson D W 1970 *The Social Psychology of Education.* Holt, Rinehart and Winston, New York

Sociology of Adult Education

P. Jarvis

While the sociology of school education is a well-developed study, sociological studies of adult education are much more infrequent. This entry seeks to demonstrate the complexities of the concept of adult education and, thereafter, to examine ways by which it might be analyzed and in the process will refer to some well-known works in studies of children's education.

There are many ways in which adult education differs from school education, but perhaps the most obvious sociological difference is that whereas school education occurs almost entirely in that sector of society called "education," this is not the case for adult education: adults are educated in college, in their work, in their leisure, at home, in and by a variety of different organizations, and so on. Educators of children are schoolteachers, but educators of adults might be adult educators, university teachers, human resource developers, vocational educators, trainers, or even political activists seeking to educate the general public about specific political concerns. Hence, it may be seen that there are many fields of practice in which the teaching and learning process occurs among adults, but many of them are not within the education sector of society.

Adult education is operationally defined here as the institutionalized processes of teaching and learning that exist for those individuals who are regarded as adults, irrespective of the sector of society in which it occurs. Such a broad and imprecise definition suggests that the boundaries of the concept are blurred, which reflects the social reality. Indeed, as societies have become more complex through the growth in technological knowledge, the division of labor, and the subsequent creation of pluralism, so the education of adults has expanded to perform educative functions in each of the different social institutions.

Following Coombs and Ahmed (1974) (see also LaBelle 1982), the education of adults may be broadly divided into three categories: (a) formal, where the education occurs in educational institutions, for example, schools, vocational schools, colleges, and universities; (b) nonformal, where the education takes place outside of such organizations, for example, in the community, or popular education; and (c) informal, where the education occurs through personal interaction or participation. While this distinction does not adequately categorize adult education, it does provide a framework for the first three sections of the following discussion, although it is recognized that some forms may be located in more than one division, for example, adult basic education, or study circles. In Sect. 4 the emergence of distance education is taken as an example of a form of education for adults which reflects late modernity. In Sect. 5 some of the dominant theoretical areas of study that have been addressed by adult education scholars will be discussed, and in the final section the professionalization of adult education will be examined.

1. Formal Adult Education

Formal education for adults is conducted within an organizational context, with there being a variety of providers. Obviously the state is a major provider of formal adult education, which may be either vocational or nonvocational, but there are others, such as employers, professional organizations, trades unions, private and voluntary educational agencies, and voluntary agencies such as the churches. By definition, educational providers organize and run educational programs for adults, although they do not necessarily have to be the funding agency—often the providers act as agents of the state, although others are independent, financially and otherwise.

While it is possible to find similarities between the sociological analyses of formal adult education and school education, it would be simplistic to suggest that the two were the same, as the following example demonstrates. Governments with right-wing political ideologies have influenced the curriculum of schools so that they include a greater emphasis on science and technology, but this change in curriculum has not had a great effect upon the structures of schooling. However, in some instances the implementation of the same policies in the education of adults has resulted in continuing professional education and liberal adult education being almost totally separated from each other and regarded as different forms of education, with the former being treated as important and centrally funded, while the latter is regarded as a leisure-time pursuit to be followed at the learners' own expense in their own free time. Such a division is rather artificial: all forms of education can assist learners to develop self-confidence which may have effects on both work and leisure, and some people may learn a subject, such as a foreign language, as a leisure-time pursuit, but then use it in the course of employment. However, the fact that this separation has occurred illustrates that formal education funded by the state, whether it be for children or adults, is controlled and functions to produce the outcomes desired by government. Such conclusions allow for Marxist analyses of adult education, of which there have been a limited number (e.g., Youngman 1986).

It could be argued that all technological societies need a highly skilled and knowledgeable work force and that one of the functions of formal adult education is to produce this. By contrast, it would be possible to argue, following Althusser (1971), that the elite ruling capitalist class controls the apparatus of state and that it uses the formal education of adults to ensure that there is a highly skilled work force that will perpetuate the capitalist system. Hence the emphasis on vocational education to this end, rather than the liberal adult education which might produce articulate adults who might question the whole system.

All organizations operate systems of control, so that the education provided by the churches, and some other similar organizations, is designed either to initiate or socialize the participants into the culture and beliefs of the organization, or else to prepare the workers in the organization to be more efficient in what they do. This form of education is thus an agency of cultural, or subcultural, hegemony in the sense Gramsci used the concept, since it does not involve physical coercion (Entwistle 1979 p. 12). This interpretation is applicable to a great deal of adult educational activity. Consequently, it can be argued that formal education for adults serves as a mechanism of cultural reproduction (Bourdieu and Passeron 1977), whether it occurs at the level of the state or the organization.

In the United Kingdom there are only a few voluntary organizations, such as the Workers' Educational Association and the Women's Institute, which seek to offer education for personal and social development, much of which is a leisure-time pursuit, and it is significant that the right-wing government of the 1980s restricted the funding of both liberal adult education and the Workers' Educational Association, and their future was immediately placed in jeopardy.

Personal and social development is also the theme of much adult education for women (Thompson 1983) and ethnic minorities (Cassara 1990). In these instances, adult education can be viewed as an instrument of empowerment, providing a sense of identity and purpose for those who are underprivileged and oppressed.

Some forms of education may, therefore, be viewed as dysfunctional, and in these instances those who exercise power seek to control or to curtail these activities. It may thus be concluded that the formal education of adults is recognized by those who exercise power as a potentially significant political phenomenon, which is precisely the argument put forward by Freire (1972), who claimed that education could be both oppressive and liberating. There are two distinct sociological paradigms, the functionalist and the conflict, which have been used by scholars analyzing formal adult education, and when contrasted in this way it is easy to place value judgments upon it, from whatever ideological persuasion it is analyzed.

One of the common criticisms of functionalism is that it implies an unchanging society, whereas conflict is trying to generate change. However, it is also possible to argue that, although there is a tendency to inertia in bureaucratic organizations, including the state, one of the aims of the formal education of adults is to produce change and through the implementation of the government policy of supporting vocational education, this is being achieved. Adult educators, who tend to adopt a more individualistic and psychological approach to education, often claim that education produces change agents, but clearly the education of adults is being used by government as an agent of social change (moreover in accord with its own ideological predispositions) rather than individual change. There are similar examples, such as the use of formal adult education to acculturate immigrants to their new country, for example, in the United States, where Carlson (1987) called it "Americanization education" (see also Thomas 1991). Therefore, the education of adults in its formal sense is often an instrument in governmental policy. Griffin (1987) has provided the most complete analysis of adult education and social policy.

Since formal adult education is organizational it is hardly surprising that a great number of studies have been conducted about enrollment and participation. Many of these have tended to adopt a psychological approach because this has been the dominant perspective in United States adult education. Even so, there has been a general acceptance that adult education tends to be a middle-class pursuit, since it is middle-class people who have sufficient cultural capital to benefit from it (Bourdieu 1973). Courtney (1992), however, began to analyze participation in sociological terms and noted that some of the functions of participation included social mobility and the reinforcement of the cultural values acquired during the mobility process. In Sweden, in a continuation of the Malmö longitudinal study which was commenced in 1938, Tuijnman (1989) has shown that male attendance at adult education classes throughout the life span influences career prospects, job satisfaction, well-being, and, indirectly, earnings.

A great deal of the formal education of adults which has been discussed in this section may also be categorized as "education from above" (Jarvis 1985a); the same could not be claimed for the nonformal education of adults, which is much more a form of "education of equals."

2. Nonformal Education of Adults

Nonformal education for adults occurs outside of the formal educational institution and may be discovered in a variety of different forms, such as adult literacy, study circles, personal development training, health education, community development, and even social action campaigns. They are not all regarded as educational, but all have an educative function which may be intended or unintended. Many of these activities are fully institutionalized, even to the extent of there being departments and units of government for nonformal education in some countries, and in most societies in the world adult literacy is at least partially government funded. Nonformal education, therefore, is a recognized type of education occurring outside of the formal structures of the educational system. It need not take place in a classroom or even in a building, and it often involves a teacher and a small group of students.

Each of these types of nonformal education for adults is different and has varying social functions, some of which are discussed here. While the individual benefits of literacy may be self-evident, the social functions are less obvious. Its social significance, for instance, is acknowledged by the term "functional literacy," which tends to mean that individuals should acquire the necessary literacy skills to play their part in society, including its occupational and economic life. At this level, literacy programs can help individuals play a full part in society, but such programs serve other functions, for example, the modern state is bureaucratic and its language is writing, so it is important for the smooth operations of the state that its citizens can read and write. Indeed, illiterate citizens cannot read instructions, census returns, or even their tax returns, so that surveillance cannot be effective nor can these matters be recorded or controlled easily. Thus literacy education has a number of less frequently acknowledged functions. Perhaps the term "computer literacy" indicates how the concept is relative and changing as society becomes increasingly technological. This is more fully discussed by Levine (1986).

In certain democracies in the world, the state also provides financial support for nonformal liberal adult education in the form of study circles. The support of the state for such activities demonstrates something of the democratic nature of society, although the control of the funding indicates that there are limits placed on the democratic process. Where the support is enshrined within a legal framework, as it is for the study circles in Scandinavia, then liberal adult education may serve a democratic political function in society.

Nonformal adult education also occurs through the educative function of certain movements and pressure groups. The fact that these groups, however radical, see themselves as having an educative function indicates that they have not moved to a revolutionary position—for education is a prerevolutionary activity and, in this sense, while appearing to be radical, it acts as a focus for discontent and dissatisfaction within society. Hence the twofold nature of this educative exercise: (a) to focus and manage discontent, and (b) to perform a democratic function of educating people to be more active in changing their society. Many of these movements and groups are discussed in the adult education literature under the rubric of radical adult education (Lovett 1988). Occasionally, however, there is the recognition that community education must spill over into social, even revolutionary, action (Freire 1972). There are many similar nonformal radical adult education groups performing the same functions and having aims in society, however, working primarily and peacefully for community development. These are generally classified as forms of community education (see Fletcher and Thompson 1980).

Additionally, nonformal education has been institutionalized in some professions through the use of trained mentors or teacher–practitioners whose work function is to train new recruits to occupations and professions in the workplace. In these instances, skilled practitioners receive some training in teaching techniques so that they can mentor new recruits. Naturally, this serves to ensure that practical knowledge and skills are transmitted to new recruits, but it also has a socializing function—new recruits are socialized into the current practices of the workplace without disrupting the work situation and so cultural reproduction is facilitated.

3. Informal Education

Some scholars might question the extent to which informal education is actually education, since it is individualistic, noninstitutionalized, and experiential. In this sense they seek to distinguish clearly between education and learning in a way that some adult education literature fails to do. However, there are institutionalized processes of teaching and learning that are more informal. For instance, there have been a number of studies of learning in the workplace (Marsick 1987), where the institutionalized supervisory role is educative.

The growth of the affective adult education movement, often regarding itself as experiential education and going under a number of names from encounter groups to human potential development, is certainly one major development in informal education, although it might also legitimately be categorized as nonformal education. This movement combines both educational and therapeutic functions of group dynamics. One of its major exponents has been Rogers (1983), and this movement has provided therapy, a sense of belonging, and even a sense of religious purpose to its participants. In this context, it is a form of sedative, and yet it also helps prevent the growth of alienation, which is a feature of contemporary society.

LaBelle (1982 p. 162) actually suggests that peer group participation and daily experience provide informal education situations. Certainly they provide the basis of informal learning, but the extent to which this is education is debatable. Certainly it is sometimes claimed that the mass media provide another form of ideological control and so there have been a number of papers advocating that critical reflection is an important part of the learning process (Jarvis 1985b, Brookfield 1987).

However, this does also indicate that as society has become more individuated there has been a corresponding emphasis upon individual and experiential learning. Indeed, there have been sociological studies of adult learning (Jarvis 1987) in which it has been recognized that learning is itself a social phenomenon. One of the major influences underlying this approach is the work of Mead (Strauss 1964). However, one other factor which has played a significant part in this emphasis on learning has been the work on reflection by Freire (1972) and Habermas (1972), among others. Habermas, for instance, was instrumental in Mezirow's (1981) discussion of levels of reflective learning. This approach to adult learning has become central to much discussion and thinking about adult learning, and it also mirrors Giddens's (1979) emphasis on reflexivity as a crucial element in understanding human action in contemporary society. While some adult educators tend to relate their thinking about reflective learning and individual criticality to critical theory, it would be true to claim that there have been very few studies of adult education from this perspective, the exceptions being Collins (1991) and Hart (1992) (see *Conscientization and Mobilization*).

4. Distance Education: An Educational Structure for Late Modernity

Distance education has its beginnings at the end of the nineteenth century but it was in the mid twentieth century that this approach to education really developed. Although distance education has been utilized in school education, its expansion has taken place in the field of adult education. It may be regarded as a production of industrial capitalism. Peters (1988) has argued for many years that distance education is rationalistic, entrepreneurial, and involves the division of labor and the technological production and transmission of teaching materials. This argument can be extended to demonstrate that the teaching materials are now an educational commodity and sold in a marketplace which is becoming increasingly international. Since the law of the market is operating, there is a danger that the weak will suffer—hence the possibility exists that a new form of cultural imperialism could reassert itself.

However, it is not only the production of teaching materials and the market-place that is significant about the distance-teaching universities for adults: they manifest the structural symbols of modernity. Giddens (1990) has suggested that late modernity is characterized by three elements: the separation of time and space; the development of disembedding mechanisms; and the reflexive appropriation of knowledge. It is suggested here that distance education epitomizes all three of these symbols: there is space–time distancing in teaching and learning, a disembedded structure, and reflective learning.

5. Dominant Theoretical Perspectives

Having analyzed four specific forms of adult education, this section is designed to examine from a sociological perspective some of the major adult educational theories that have arisen in literature, such as andragogy, self-directed learning, empowerment, and liberation.

Theoretical perspectives on adult education were emerging in the earlier part of the twentieth century —the first doctorate in the study of adult education being given by the University of London in the early 1920s on a topic, "Adult Education and Spiritual Values," which reflects many of its origins. However, it was not until graduate programs were commenced in the United States that theoretical perspectives really developed and since this was at Teachers College, University of Columbia, it is hardly surprising that Dewey's influence can be detected. The dominant theories of the later part of the century have also been influenced by the culture of the time when they emerged—the 1960s— which embraced the values of humanism, individualism, and self-achievement.

Two American scholars, Cyril Houle and Malcolm Knowles, have been the key figures in this development. Houle (1961) wrote a small book which stimulated a great deal of research on self-directed learning. Malcolm Knowles, a doctoral student of Houle, introduced the concept of andragogy to United States adult education in a number of books and articles. In a sense, self-directed learning reflects the American culture of individualism and self-achievement, so that research in this area has become central to much United States thinking. Knowles learned the term "andragogy" from a Yugoslav adult educator, as andragogy has been prominent there for many years. Unfortunately Knowles did not use the term in the same way as the Yugoslavian adult educators, but it is the United States version which has become well-known in the English-speaking world. Knowles (1970, 1980) originally postulated four assumptions about andragogy: (a) adult learners are self-directed, (b) they have experience which is a reservoir for future learning, (c) they are ready to learn, and (d) they will learn more readily the things relevant to their lives. Immediately it may be seen that Knowles was reflecting some of the same aspects of the 1960s United States culture as Houle, but he also emphasized the humanistic element. There is a sense in which the term "andragogy" itself was as important as its content. United States adult education was growing in the 1960s, many new university departments were being established, and adult education needed an identity which made it distinct from school education; the term "andragogy" provided it. Andragogy, as a concept, emerged when the time was ripe for it, and while Knowles has changed and developed his ideas and heavily criticized the concept itself (Jarvis 1984), andragogy provided adult education with an identity, and its content reflected the culture of the time during the growth period of adult education in the United States.

Radical adult educators, working with the underprivileged and with oppressed groups, have adopted the dominant theme of empowerment to describe a great deal of their work. Clearly, adult education does act to change people, helping them to see themselves as more significant in society.

6. Professionalization of Adult Education

There have been attempts by the Commission of Professors of Adult Education in the United States to professionalize adult education, but such a move is fraught with difficulties because of the nature of the occupation. Unlike more traditional occupations, adult education has neither a single structure nor a controlling body. As was pointed out at the beginning of this entry, adult education occurs in many different sectors of society, each sector being able to control its own educators. Hence, nursing education, for instance, can recruit, train, and license its own educators without reference to any other branch of adult education. Indeed, in the higher status professions the educators are much more likely to identify with their profession than they are with a lower status occupation like adult education. Thus the education of adults might be conceptualized as a functional occupation or profession which will not professionalize along any of the paths that students of the professions have, at various times, suggested (e.g., Wilensky 1964). Different sectors may professionalize within their own profession, but this will not directly affect any other branch of adult education.

7. Conclusion

As the population ages, so adult education assumes new forms, but performs similar functions with different age groups. For instance, as people leave their work on retirement and enter what will be for many a prolonged period of leisure, many employers are introducing preretirement education to prepare their workers for the future. Indeed, educational gerontology is a rapidly developing field of adult education, with its own journals and research interests, as it is performing a leisure-time function for the elderly (see, e.g., Glendenning and Percy 1990).

Even at its peak, however, adult education was undergoing change, from adult education to continuing education and lifelong education. But now, and very significantly, the term "education" is being replaced by "learning" and so lifelong education becomes lifelong learning, and the providers of learning materials are certainly no longer, if they have ever been, educational institutions. New learning materials are market commodities to be purchased by anyone in their lifetime.

It may be seen, therefore, that the forms and structures of adult education are related to the structures and the levels of development of the societies in which they occur. This is leading to the development of comparative studies in the education of adults (see Lichtner 1989). At the same time, the functions that it performs are similar throughout but, naturally, there is a greater concentration upon leisure-time pursuits among the elderly, compared with those who are still in employment.

See also: Adult Education for Development; Education and Development; Sociology of Education: An Overview

References

Althusser L 1971 (trans. Brewster B) *Lenin and Philosophy and Other Essays*. New Left Books, London
Bourdieu P 1973 Cultural reproduction and social reproduction. In: Brown R (ed.) 1973 *Knowledge, Education, and Cultural Change*. Tavistock, London
Bourdieu P, Passeron J-C 1977 (trans. Nice R) *Reproduction in Education, Society and Culture*. Sage Publications, London
Brookfield S D 1987 *Developing Critical Thinkers*. Jossey-Bass, San Francisco, California
Carlson R A 1987 *The Americanization Syndrome: A Quest for Conformity*, rev. edn. Croom Helm, London
Cassara B (ed.) 1990 *Adult Education in a Multicultural Society*. Routledge, London
Collins M 1991 *Adult Education as Vocation*. Routledge and Kegan Paul, London
Coombs P H, Ahmed M 1974 *Attacking Rural Poverty: How Non-Formal Education Can Help*. Johns Hopkins University Press, Baltimore, Maryland
Courtney S 1992 *Why Adults Learn: Towards a Theory of Participation in Adult Education*. Routledge and Kegan Paul, London
Entwistle H 1979 *Antonio Gramsci: Conservative Schooling for Radical Politics*. Routledge and Kegan Paul, London
Fletcher C, Thompson N (eds.) 1980 *Issues in Community Education*. Falmer Press, Lewes
Freire P 1972 (trans. Ramos B) *Pedagogy of the Oppressed*. Penguin, Harmondsworth
Giddens A 1979 *Central Problems in Social Theory: Action, Structure and Contradiction in Social Analysis*. Macmillan, London
Giddens A (1990) *The Consequences of Modernity*. Polity Press, Cambridge
Glendenning F, Percy K (eds.) 1990 *Ageing, Education and Society*. Association for Educational Gerontology, University of Keele, Keele
Griffin C 1987 *Adult Education as Social Policy*. Croom Helm, London
Habermas J 1972 (trans. Shapiro J J) *Knowledge and Human Interests*. Heinemann Educational, London
Hart M U 1992 *Working and Educating for Life*. Routledge and Kegan Paul, London
Houle C O 1961 *The Inquiring Mind*. University of Wisconsin Press, Madison, Wisconsin

Jarvis P 1984 Andragogy—a sign of the times. *Stud. Educ. Adults* 16: 32–38

Jarvis P 1985a *The Sociology of Adult and Continuing Education*. Croom Helm, London

Jarvis P 1985b Thinking critically in an information society: A sociological analysis. *Lifelong Learn.: An Omnibus of Practice and Res.* 8(6): 11–14

Jarvis P 1987 *Adult Learning in the Social Context*. Croom Helm, London

Knowles M S 1970 *The Modern Practice of Adult Education: Andragogy versus Pedagogy*. Association Press, Chicago, Illinois

Knowles M S 1980 *The Modern Practice of Adult Education: From Pedagogy to Andragogy*, rev. edn. Follett, Chicago, Illinois

LaBelle T J 1982 Formal, non-formal and informal education: A holistic perspective on lifelong learning. *Int. Rev. Educ.* 28(2): 159–75

Levine K 1986 *The Social Context of Literacy*. Routledge and Kegan Paul, London

Lichtner M (ed.) 1989 *Comparative Research in Adult Education*. Centro Europeo dell'Educazione, Frascati

Lovett T (ed.) 1988 *Radical Approaches to Adult Education: A Reader*. Routledge and Kegan Paul, London

Marsick V J (ed.) 1987 *Learning in the Workplace*. Croom Helm, London

Mezirow J A 1981 Critical Theory of Adult Learning and Education. *Adult Educ.* 32(1): 3–24

Peters O 1988 Distance teaching and industrial production: A comparative interpretation in outline. In Sewart D, Keegan D, Holmberg B (eds.) *Distance Education: International Perspectives*, 2nd edn. Routledge and Kegan Paul, London

Rogers C 1983 *Freedom to Learn for the 80's*. Merrill, Columbus, Ohio

Strauss A (ed.) 1964 *George Herbert Mead on Social Psychology*. University of Chicago Press, Chicago, Illinois

Thomas A M 1991 *Beyond Education: A New Perspective on Society's Management of Learning*. Jossey-Bass, San Francisco, California

Thompson J L 1983 *Learning Liberation: Women's Response to Men's Education*. Croom Helm, London

Tuijnman A 1989 *Recurrent Education, Earnings and Well-being*. Almqvist and Wiksell International, Stockholm

Wilensky H A L 1964 The professionalization of everyone? *Am. J. Sociol.* 70: 137–58

Youngman F 1986 *Adult Education and Socialist Pedagogy*. Croom Helm, London

Sociology of Higher Education

V. L. Meek

Throughout history, civilizations have developed various forms of advanced training for their ruling, priestly, military and bureaucratic elites, "but only in medieval Europe did an institution recognisable as a university arise: a school of higher learning combining teaching and scholarship and characterised by its corporate autonomy and academic freedom" (Perkin 1991 p. 169). The durability of the university as a social institution is often remarked upon. Some seventy ancient universities "are still in the same locations with some of the same buildings, with professors and students doing much the same things, and with governance carried on in much the same ways" (Kerr 1982 p. 152).

The Western university inherited what appears to be a remarkably stable institutional form, along with a propensity to transgress national and cultural boundaries. In the thirteenth century, scholars from the most distant parts of Europe migrated to the main centers of higher learning at Paris, Bologna, and Salerno. Later, universities themselves migrated to every corner of the globe.

In a sense, the university is a "schizophrenic" organization. While it has preserved many of its basic characteristics, the university has also proved to be quite innovative and adaptive, incorporating entirely new bodies of knowledge as well as flourishing in cultural milieux quite different from that of its medieval European home. According to Perkin (1991 p. 170), the adaptation of the university can be told in five historical stages:

1. The rise of the cosmopolitan European university and its role in the destruction of the medieval world order at the Reformation (twelfth century—1530s)
2. The 'nationalisation' of the university by the emerging nation states of the Religious Wars, and its decline during the eighteenth-century Enlightenment (1530s–1789)
3. The revival of the university after the French Revolution and its belated but increasing role in Industrial Society (1789–1939)
4. The migration of the university to the non-European world and its adaptation to the needs of developing societies and the anticolonial reaction (1938–1960s)
5. The transition from elite to mass higher education and the role of the university and its offshoots in post-industrial society (1945–1990s).

The sociology of higher education can be applied to each of Perkins historical stages, but this article is concerned primarily with post-Second World War developments and particularly with the transition from elite to mass higher education and the role of the university in postindustrial society. The reason for this choice is that with the close of the twentieth century, higher education institutions the world over are under intense pressure to radically transform their role in society. This pressure is the result of financial stringency, increased demand, effective articulation between higher and other education sectors, labor market priorities, aging populations, changes in the structure of the "welfare state" and reform of the public sector, and the interests of minority groups. Increasing participation (both numerically and in terms of the variety of different client groups) and the transformation of higher education from elite to mass systems inevitably leads to much larger community involvement and makes higher education more of a political issue. Financial pressures, and the wish of governments to get more value per dollar, appear to be driving higher education systems to change, as does the wish for higher education to be more closely tied to national economies, both in terms of meeting national labor market needs and through research discovering new products and resources. As what Daniel Bell (1973) terms "knowledge workers" replace factory workers in the production of wealth, both government and industry interest in higher education increases enormously. Paradoxically, however, knowledge as the primary form of wealth production may pose the ultimate threat to the survival of the Western university in postindustrial society—a topic explored in more detail in the conclusion.

Before continuing, a few words need to be said about definitions. First, it should be noted that the term higher education is used quite differently in different countries. In some places it refers to all forms of post compulsory education and is used interchangeably with the term tertiary education, while in other countries higher education means university education. Second, it should also be recognized that the organization of higher education differs widely between societies and over time within societies. There are, for example, formally unified systems recently created in Australia and the UK where all higher education institutions are called universities, well-entrenched formal binary divisions between university and nonuniversity institutions in Canada, The Netherlands, and Germany, highly centralized systems in France, and the USA with its great variety of institutional types. A third and related point is that the mere reference to a system of higher education in the absence of a specific national context can be misleading. Too often, description of events in higher education assumes implicitly the existence of some sort of universal system of higher education that has no substance in reality. Nonetheless, higher education has always had an international flavor, and there appears to be a remarkable degree to which diverse and often divergent national systems of higher education are experiencing common problems and dilemmas.

Thus, finally, for the purpose of analysis it will be assumed that higher education constitutes a specific field of social activity with its own particular norms, values, patterns of interaction, culture, and authority structures. According to DiMaggio and Powell (1983 p. 148), an organizational field consists of "those organizations that, in the aggregate, constitute a recognized area of institutional life: key suppliers, resource and product consumers, regulatory agencies, and other organizations that produce similar services or products." Or, as Dahrendorf (in Clark 1983 p. 2) puts it: "certain areas of human activity have evolved their own action patterns; the world of science, or of painting. There is, in other words, such a thing as sectoral hegemony."

If the aim of this article was comparative empirical research, then a more rigorous definition of higher education would be necessary, along with a clear specification of the level of aggregation that would be the subject of observation. The discussion here, however, will be more generic, using "higher education" as an ombudsman term for all education that is "postschool," although the underlying concept is university education unless otherwise specified. Nonetheless, the following caveat offered by Neave (1996 p. 26) is kept well in mind:

> One of the most ticklish problems that face the analyst of higher education is the dynamic of systems—how they move from one state to another and indeed, in which direction they are moving. The situation is vaguely reminiscent of the episode in *Alice's Adventures in Wonderland* when Alice meets up with the Cheshire cat. The Cat, like education itself, is a singular creature. From afar, its profile looks pretty solid. The nearer the analytic 'Alices' come to the university Cat, the less solid it seems so that, in the end, at the level of the individual establishment, often all we have is a grin at best or a *rictus sardonicus* at worst.

1. What is the Sociology of Higher Education

While the study of most if not all of the main issues of concern to sociology in general—social structure and social reproduction, status, power, gender, race, resource distribution, class, etc.—are applicable to higher education in the specific, "a specific sociology of higher education hardly exists" (Wolthuis 1992 p. 1858). This does not mean, however, that higher education lacks sufficient substance to warrant the development of a disciplinary subfield interested in it, if not a separate discipline altogether. Quite the contrary. Higher education is so intricate, diverse and complex that no one discipline, much less a disciplinary subfield, has sufficient intellectual resources to understand and analyze all aspects of it. Moreover, what intellectual tools that are brought to bear depend on what aspect of higher education the researcher is interested in. For example, there is a vast psychological literature directed at an understanding of student learning and knowledge aquisition (Ramsden 1988, Entwhistle 1987, Marton et al. 1984, 1993, Dunkin and Barnes 1986), as there is an economic literature devoted to higher education financial and funding issues (Williams et al. 1974, Williams 1990, Psacharopoulos and Woodhall 1985, Woodhall 1989), a management literature directed at higher education administration and organization (Cohen and March 1974, Riley and Baldridge 1977, Salancik and Pfeffer 1974, Moodie and Eustace 1974), a political science literature that examines higher education policy development and implementation (Lane and Fredriksson 1981, Premfors 1981, Cerych 1984), a historical literature that traces the evolution of higher education as a social institution (Geiger 1986, 1993, Rudis 1984, Rothblatt 1968), a philosophical literature that attempts to define the "essence" of the university (Newman 1976, Jaspers 1959, Niblett 1974, Brubacher 1978), and so on. Higher education even features in literary studies, with authors such as Barth (1982), Bradbury (1975) and Lodge (1988), to name but a few, featuring higher education in their novels. The four-volume *Encyclopedia of Higher Education* (Clark and Neave 1992) is clear testament to the vast array of disciplinary interests in higher education.

The sociology of higher education necessitates an eclectic approach and, of coarse, sociology itself is far from possessing a single unifying paradigm: it bring several different and sometimes contradictory theoretical frames of reference to bear on the study of any social phenomenon. One way of presenting the sociology of higher education would be to concentrate solely on the historical foundations to current theoretical approaches and debates. But this has been accomplished quite adequately elsewhere at both the micro (Lewis 1977, Hammack and Heyns 1992) and macro (Wolthuis 1992) levels. Some mention, of course, of the underlying theoretical arguments and traditions pertinent to the study of higher education is necessary, and will be presented briefly below. This is followed by a more detailed sketch of the broad social trends in higher education since the Second World War, particularly its transportation to developing countries, the later internationalization of higher education, and the changing relationship between higher education and government/society at the close of the twentieth century. The article concludes with a few observations about the future of higher education in postindustrial society.

2. Theoretical Approaches and Traditions

As already stressed, there are numerous sociologists and sociologies of higher education. For example, a number of sociologists have been interested in the socio-political characteristics of the academic profession (Altbach 1996, Neave 1983, Halsey and Trow 1971, Halsey 1992, Metzger 1977, Riesman et al. 1970), while others have been more concerned with the cultural characteristics of disciplines (Becher 1989, Blau 1973). Particularly in the USA there is a long tradition of research on the cultural impact of colleges and universities on students (Pace and Stern 1958,

Pace 1987, Kuh 1990, Tierney 1990), and over a number of years the work of Astin (1993) has profiled the characteristics of entering students. The prominent North American sociologist Talcot Parsons was particularly interested in the university as a source of cultural cohesion within society and as a transmitter of cultural values (Parsons and Platt 1973). The French sociologist Bourdieu (1988) has also been interested in the culture of the academy, but not in terms of social unification but as a source of social stratification and potential hostility as individuals and groups in vying for power draw upon different social capital resources according to their location in the higher education field.

Two areas very closely related to the sociology of higher education are the sociology of science and the sociology of education in general. In that the sociology of science is concerned with the organization and structure of knowledge and research, the academy has to be a focus of study since in most countries the bulk of all scientific research takes place in universities and related institutions. Clark (1983, 1996) goes so far as to maintain that the control, production, and proliferation of knowledge define the higher education enterprise.

2.1 Participation and Intersector Relationship

Although higher education has a sector hegemony, it nonetheless influences and is influenced by other education sectors. In fact, in some countries, higher education has been strongly criticized for having undue influence on the school sector. In the United States where it is fairly easy to gain access to some form of higher education, "the relatively open HE systems . . . appear to exert comparatively little pressure on the organization of schools" (Mortimore 1992 p. 1016). In other countries, universities' strict control over the public examination system and entry standards has resulted in senior secondary schools preparing students almost solely for university entrance. This situation did not present a problem when only a small social elite reached the last years of secondary schooling and an even smaller proportion of the age cohort went on to higher education. But now in nearly every OECD country, universal participation in secondary education has been achieved. In some places, this has resulted in a tension in secondary schools between preparing students for higher education and preparing them for the world of work and citizenship. In turn, this tension may dissipate as countries go from mass to universal participation in higher education.

The "massification" of higher education is more about finance, governance, regulation, student recruitment and the curriculum, academic standards, control, and accountability of higher education than about participation rates per se. But suffice it to say here that the phenomenon is generally conceptualized in terms of the proportion of the relevant age cohort in higher education institutions: below 15 percent is considered to typify "elite" higher education, between 15 and 35 percent "mass" systems and over 35 percent "universal" access (Trow 1974).

Probably the United States is the only OECD country that has yet approached anything like universal participation in higher education. In the United States it is interesting to note that over 90 percent of higher education institutions permit matriculation without a high school certificate (Hammack and Heyns 1992 p. 1876). Also within the United States system, many of the tensions and questions regarding selective participation have been pushed up to the postgraduate level.

But little can be said with any reliability about participation in higher education and the benefits attached to it, or about other elements in the higher education–school relationship in the absence of a detailed country-specific analysis. Again in the United States, for example, it is often not clear whether participation rates refer to all forms of higher education, including the thousands of community colleges which have no entry requirements, or only to universities. Because of the advanced nature of the schooling system, in some European countries the first degree at university is considered to be equivalent to a masters, which is not the case in Anglo-Saxon systems. A few gross generalizations are possible, such as it remains true that the more education an individual receives the higher the life-long earnings, though the salary gap between the educated and the noneducated has narrowed substantially since the 1960s (Murphy and Welch 1989). Hammack and Heyns (1992 p. 1876) note that:

> While evidence of the positive contribution of education to occupational advancement and income is available, the reasons for that contribution are not fully clear. On the one hand, the theory of human capital (Becker 1964) links increases in the educational attainment of workers with rising levels of economic productivity in the society at large. On the other hand, much research undertaken in the 1970s and 1980s questions the degree to which these two are correlated and, furthermore, questions whether expansion in education beyond basic literacy and numeracy is associated with economic growth. (Berg 1971, Blaug 1976, Collins 1971, Dore 1976, Fagerlind and Saha 1989, Squires 1977)

Moreover, "access to higher education has grown and has become more equal, yet the relative amount of social mobility and the patterning of economic inequality remains largely unchanged" (Hammach and Heyns 1992 p. 1880). There have been some significant movements in aspects of participation. Male domination of the student body, for example, has given way to a situation where now in most OECD countries females constitute 50 percent or more of the higher education students. But the "social class milieu in which an individual is reared [continues to impose nearly everywhere] major constraints upon educational aspirations and achievements" (Hayden and Carpenter 1993 p. 506). As important and interesting as these generalizations are, it would be dangerous indeed to attempt to explain them out of context.

2.2 Theoretical Foundations

Though sociological interest in higher education is wide and varied, the number of theoretical underpinnings are more restricted. The theoretical foundations of the sociological study of higher education, as with most other areas, can be traced back to the classical writings of Weber, Durkheim, and Marx. Weber was one of the first sociologists to analyze higher education as a social institution (Shils 1974). Weber's writings on higher education were somewhat fragmented and covered such diverse topics as university autonomy, academic freedom, and the professionalization of science, and he "argued for the cultural, civilising effect of higher education, as against obedience to the state" (Wolthuis 1992 p. 1859). As with his other sociological works, Weber was consistently interested in relating developments in higher education to large-scale social movements within and between nations. Weber was particularly concerned with how the structure of higher education and the values and beliefs of its members were being transformed by the entrenchment of industrial capitalism and the bureaucratic state (Meek 1990 p. 192).

Durkheim too was interested in the cultural role of higher education in the broader society, and maintained that the function of higher education "is to prepare for moral life" and the establishment of moral solidarity within society (Walthus 1992 p. 1859). Much of the sociology of higher education relies on Durkheim and his analysis of the importance of division of labor in the creation of modern industrial society and the grand sociological theory of structural-functionalism which Durkheim helped father (Meek et al. 1996).

In contrast to the "moral order" of pre-industrial society based on religion, the solidarity of modern society is based, according to Durkheim, on a division of labour that creates solidarity within groups and mutual dependencies between groups despite inequalities. As society becomes more differentiated according to expanding numbers of occupational groups, the solidarity of the whole is maintained as these groups become increasingly dependent upon one another for goods and services. Durkheim, like Comte before him and many other sociologists after him, explains the "organic solidarity" of society by analogy to the human body: the component parts of society like the organs of the body function to ensure the continued existence of the whole (Giddens 1989 pp. 691–96).

As stated above, many social theories of education either implicitly or explicitly draw heavily on Durkheim. Clark (1996 p. 422), for example, maintains that it is the very division of labor in higher education based on professional knowledge and professional expertise that provides higher education institutions with their essential social characteristics:

"Disciplinary fragmentation is arguably *the* source of ever-growing system complexity, a source more powerful in its effects than the expanded inputs of students and the more varied outputs to the labor force . . . ." "A national system of higher education is also a set of disciplines and professions" (Clark 1983 p. 29), but each isolated from the others, and with their own particular set of norms, values, and culture. As Clark (1983 pp. 14–15) states: "the harsh fact is that those who handle the materials of microbiology and those who deal in medieval history do not need one another to get on with the work, either in teaching or research or service." Pressures and conflicts produced by increasing professionalism and specialization in higher education have been met with increasing differentiation, not unification. "In separating tasks, specialisation pulls apart groups that otherwise may have to fight it out . . ."; for example, "biochemists and chemists do not have to fight over turf within a chemistry department if biochemists can develop their specialty to the point of a separate department" (Clark 1983 p. 219).

At the other end of the spectrum from Durkheim is classical Marxist theory which regards all forms of education as an instrument of the capitalist ruling class used for maintaining domination and ownership of the means of production. Neo-Marxists, such as Althusser (1971), Bowles and Gintis (1976), and Poulantzas (1973), have been concerned with the ideological and socialization functions of education. Education as an instrument of a capitalist state socializes members of society into accepting the attitudes and values of class relationships and the inequalities they create (see *Education and the State*). From a Marxist perspective, university education is directed more at instilling the attitudes and values necessary to maintain a hierarchical class structure than imparting specialist skills. With respect to knowledge, Marxist theory regards science also as an instrument of the bourgeoisie for the purpose of domination (Aronowitz 1989).

One seeming paradox of the Marxist perspective is that the vast majority of Marxist critics of the university and society are employed by public supported higher education institutions. Moreover, while much of the practice of modern higher education, including that of science, may be influenced by the capitalist mode of production, this article assumes that higher education has an existence independent of the productive relations (see *Classical Sociological Theories of Education*).

2.3 Towards a Theoretical Frame of Reference

Can the eclectic nature of the sociology of higher education be unified through theory and can such disparate theories as Marxism and structural-functionalism be brought together? If by theory it is meant one grand, universal, overarching, and unifying paradigm, then the answer is no. Nonetheless, no observation is entirely independent of theory despite the fact that most studies of higher education appear to be atheoretical (Huisman 1995).

The great task for the sociology of higher education as for sociology in general is to understand simultaneously "voluntarism" and "determinism," social action (i.e., the creative, autonomous, and purposeful behavior of the individual) and the structure of the social context in which action occurs. One approach to this task is to view action and structure as a duality. Structure is both the medium and product (outcome) of social interaction:

> [Structures] are the medium, because structures provide the rules and resources individuals must draw on to interact meaningfully. They are its outcome, because rules and resources exist only through being applied and acknowledged in interaction—they have no reality independent of the social practices they constitute . . . (Riley 1983 p. 415)

Every national system of higher education is dependent on the society that sponsors it, but also contributes significantly to society in terms of knowledge, trained personnel, advice, and ideas for new products and industrial processes. Higher education is influenced by societal values and norms and by the various demands placed on it by both the broader social and political structure. But higher education is also a source of innovation and change within society. One important source of innovation and change is linked to higher education's international dimension. Knowledge and new ideas generally are not constrained by national boundaries. Academic disciplines are organized internationally as well as nationally, and trained professionals often move easily from one country to another. To a large extent, the international community benefits from significant research discoveries, whether they be in medicine or laser physics.

According to Wolthuis (1992 p. 1865), "higher education has become more stratified and vocationalized. Just like other types of schooling, it has become integrated into the wage-labor system and has lost its place as an exclusive, cultural community, marginal to society." Although it appears that higher education is increasingly interdependent on other parts of society, this does not necessarily mean that higher education is (or is becoming) a subsystem of the sociopolitical superstructure, dependent entirely on the state for its norms and authority. The construct that higher education is no more than a subsystem of the state may have validity in some cases but, "it has no logical inevitability and it preempts the issue of how far higher education institutions are licensed to be free to set their own norms, or even to be in conflict or tension with the society that sponsors them to be its antibodies" (Kogan 1984 p. 67).

Explanations with respect to the ability of higher education institutions to exercise initiative in the context of system-wide authority structures have often been organized on a continuum. At one end of the continuum is the "bottom-up" type of system where government policy follows rather than leads a change process initiated at the departmental, faculty, or institutional level; at the other end of the continuum is the "top-down" type of system where institutions merely respond to government-inspired policy initiatives which are enforced by the power of the state. "Bottom-up" systems are characterized by high institutional autonomy, and control mechanisms that rest more on a competitive market than on state legislative authority; "top-down" systems are characterized by the opposite (Clark 1983). Such a conceptualization of change, however, has limited explanatory value for it ignores the duality of structure (Meek 1991). The location of a national system of higher education on the continuum may assist in the identification of the relative power of individuals and groups, but this explains little of the dynamics of change and social interaction.

In a "top-down," centrally funded, national system of higher education, government is a highly significant actor. But no government has absolute power over higher education, or at least, it cannot exercise it absolutely. Governments are themselves part of the higher education system, and their policies are either constrained or furthered by the norms, values, and interests of other parties within the system. The degree and extent of change in a complex system, such as higher education, is dependent upon the intersection of interests, strategic behavior, norms and values, and ideologies of all concerned. The question is not solely one of government intervention (effective or otherwise), but one of how and why conditions prevail to the extent that systems do engage in extensive and far-reaching change. It is the dynamics and complexities of the interrelationship between higher education policy and the structure of higher education systems which should be at issue. The extent of change (or, for that matter, nonchange) is the resultant of the interactions between various groups located within the higher education system, whose actions and interests (including ideological ones) are constrained or furthered by the structure of the academic system and their specific location in it. Bourdieu (1988 pp. xvi–xvii) makes a related point when he states that "it is not, as is usually thought, political stances which determine people's stances on things academic, but their positions in the academic field which inform the stances that they adopt on political issues in general as well as on academic problems."

There are various ways in which higher education can be typified structurally, but the work of Becher and Kogan (1980) and Clark (1983) seems particularly relevant here because of the way in which they merge micro- and macrosociological aspects. For the purpose of analysis, the structure of higher education can be disaggregated into three levels: what Becher and Kogan (1980) call the basic unit, the institutional level and the central authority level; or what Clark (1983) terms as the understructure (basic academic or disciplinary units); the middle or enterprise structure (individual organizations in their entirety); and the superstructure (the vast array of government and other system regulatory mechanisms that relate organizations to one another).

From the perspective outlined above, the structure itself is viewed as a source of change (cf. Bourdieu 1988, Giddens 1977). Structure influences action, and where individuals are placed in the higher education field (understructure, middle structure, and superstructure) largely determines (though does not necessarily predetermine) their interests and the power which they may exercise to protect those interests. The exercise of power and the pursuit of interests by individuals and groups may in turn change the structural requisites. In considering the following outline of current trends and issues in the sociology of higher education, this theoretical frame of reference should be kept in mind. The pressures and dilemmas faced by higher education institutions and systems arise from a structure where interaction between individuals and groups intersect at many different levels, both internal and external to the institutions themselves.

3. Trends and Issues in Higher Education

An outline of basic trends and issues in higher education is necessarily arbitrary and selective. The following choice of topics is restricted by space and by a desire to present what appear to be major, world-wide trends and movements. The discussion will first address how higher education has and continues to transgress national boundaries through (a) its transportation to former colonial dependencies, and (b) later movements to internationalize higher education. The discussion then shifts to what appear to be major policy issues involved in the relationship between higher education and government/society.

3.1 Transgression of National Boundaries

3.1.1 The transportation of higher education to developing countries. The role of higher education in so-called developing countries has attracted considerable sociological interest. Prior to the Second World War, the establishment of higher education in the colonial dependencies was patchy, and for the most part the role of higher education was confined to the training of a small indigenous elite to assist with the administration of the colony. Moreover, universities initially established in colonial dependencies were cultural outposts under the direct control of governing bodies residing in the mother country. After the Second World War and with the push for independence by colonial dependencies, the establishment of universities in less developed countries gained momentum. During this period the trend shifted towards creating higher education institutions that were either fully autonomous institutions from the beginning, or were initially attached to an indigenous university.

The role of higher education in the immediate postcolonial era attracted both praise and harsh criticism. The proponents and critics fell into two broad and opposing theoretical camps: the "diffusionist" or "development" theorists and the "dependency" theorists. The former school of thought maintains that the university as a Western cultural institution which permeated societies lacking in Western traditions of higher education during the nineteenth and twentieth centuries is a primary force for modernization and development. The argument basically is that because the university is a Western institution—an institution supposedly having ideas and values of "universal reference"—it will bring about "modern" attitudes and habits in the indigenous population fortunate enough to participate. Once begun, modernization is a continuous process leading to successive stages of development, paralleling those that occurred in the industrialized West.

Clearly, higher education has helped transform traditional societies through, for example, providing the high-level manpower necessary for many of these societies to achieve nationhood. But in some cases the introduction of higher education has helped to create inequitable social structures that tended to mirror those of the metropolis. Van den Berghe (1973), for example, has argued that the lack of adaptability of the Oxbridge model to Nigerian society was accompanied by a considerable adaptation of the country to the kind of elitist social system that the transfer of the British model of higher education helped create. But the more fundamental criticism of modernization theory is that it is based on a Western ethnocentric assumption of a universal response to similar organizational forms which trivializes and obscures the difference in meaning which people from different cultures may attach to similar structures and forms of social organization (Meek 1982).

Advocates of dependency theory, on the other hand, question whether higher education is a mechanism for nation building and modernization. Dependency theorists regard higher education as a means for controlling knowledge and maintaining Third World countries in a state of neocolonial subjugation to the metropolis. Mazrui (1975), for example, has argued that the African university is basically a multinational corporation that serves interests other than indigenous ones. Higher education in developing countries fosters dependency through, for example, reliance on expatriate academic staff, use of the metropolitan language for publication and instruction, and reliance on a core of knowledge that is largely not produced locally.

Dependency theory also assumes universal responses to similar organizational form despite the culture and form of social organization of specific places. Both dependency and modernization theory adopt a linear view of history, assuming that the intro-duction of Western higher education either sponsors successive stages of development or ever-deepening circles of dependency. Although the debate between the two schools of thought has not been resolved, the focus has shifted somewhat. No longer are the main protagonists former colonial powers and their dependencies, but aid donating nations and international bodies, such as the World Bank.

The structure of aid to higher education in developing countries has changed dramatically over the last four decades, although many of the problems inherent in the donor–recipient relationship linger. But expansion and diversity, as with many other facets of higher education, have directly intervened in the aid relationship. Initially, most of the universities created in sub-Saharan Africa, Asia, and the Pacific were more or less a direct transfer of the models familiar to the former colonial powers. But during the postindependence period, there was a proliferation of donors, which in turn, sponsored institutional experimentation and innovation: land grant universities, open universities, liberal arts colleges, technical universities, etc. (Eisemon and Kourouma 1991).

Foreign aid has allowed the dramatic expansion of higher education in developing countries. But there are cases where aid has benefited the donors more than the recipients, and expansion has threatened the quality of higher education. Eisemon and Kourouma (1991 p. 3) observe that:

> In the 1980s, developing countries began reaping the consequencies . . . of the investments which governments and foreign donors made in expanding infrastructures for higher education. The negative consequences are now receiving much attention from the donor community: uncontrolled growth of expenditures for higher education (Salmi 1991), poor quality of instruction (Commbe 1990, Eisemon 1991) and declining levels of research activity and production of postgraduates in applied scientific fields. (Eisemon and Davis 1991)

Studies indicate that investment in higher education in developing countries has been ineffective, largely due to poor planning at both the systems and institutional levels (Rondinelli et al. 1990). It appears that higher education absorbs a disproportionate amount of the resources going to all forms of education, while being the least productive of the different education sectors (Psacharopoulos and Woodhall 1985, World Bank 1988). Other studies claim that higher education curriculum is often irrelevant to local needs, producing graduates unsuited to the demands of the labor market and with little prospect of finding suitable employment (Sanyal 1991 pp. 147–68). Many economists themselves have abandoned the "True Believer" status of the human capital theorists of the 1950s and 1960s who assumed a direct relationship between educational investment and economic productivity (see Blaug 1987). It is now recognized that the relationship between investment in higher education and economic productivity is far more complicated and complex than once thought. Some have argued that "there is evidence, deriving from the effect of schooling on earnings and productivity, that in many countries the average dollar invested in primary education returns twice as much as the one invested in higher education" (Psacharopoulos et al. 1986 p. 1). Others such as Klees (1991) and Blaug (1987) dispute this conclusion. Many studies maintain that education subsidies benefit the rich more than the poor: "public subsidies for higher education in developing countries have the perverse effect of transferring income from poor taxpayers to rich families, whose children benefit from subsidised education" (Psacharopoulos and Woodhall (1985 p. 141). Others disagree with such findings both on technical grounds (Bowman et al. 1984, Blaug 1983) and through appeal to the argument that it is the wealthy who pay the highest taxes. About the only thing that can be said with any certainty is that everywhere there has been a dramatic rise in student participation coupled with a fall in public expenditure per student unit.

Since the 1950s higher education systems have expanded and worldwide enrolments have increased dramatically. In the history of the universities, the greatest expansion of higher education has occurred since the Second World War. According to Ramirez and Riddle (1991 p. 91), "out of 1,854 universities founded between 1200 and 1985, 1,101 (59 percent) were established between 1950 and 1985." They also note that many of these universities were established in the less developed countries either at the time of independence or shortly thereafter. The older universities have also doubled and tripled in size and nearly everywhere an increasing proportion of the relevant age group is participating in higher education. But public expenditure has not kept pace with growth in enrollments. According to Salmi (1991), "the majority of universities in developing countries are confronted today with a difficult situation of uncontrolled growth of enrollments and expenditures against a background of diminishing financial resources. During the 1980s, student numbers continued to rise rapidly whereas real expenditures followed a downward trend . . ."

In addition to placing intense pressure on infrastructure and facilities, rising enrollments, paradoxically, have done little to assist equity of participation in higher education, while they appear to exacerbate other problems, such as internal institutional efficiency. While publicly funded higher education is financed by the entire population, in many developing countries the sons and daughters of the high and middle-income urban-based professional families are the primary beneficiaries of higher education. In the Congo, for example, "30% of the budget is allocated to 2% of the student population; in Rwanda, 15% of the budget goes to 0.2% of the student population; in Burkina Faso, the figures are 28% and 1.2%, respectively" (Salmi 1991 p. 5). Another paradox with respect to equity is that scholarships provided to students in less developed countries by aid donors for overseas study often widen the gap between the rich and the poor. Often it is the children of the more well-to-do who are more likely to complete secondary school and are thus able to compete for scholarships (Luteru 1991 p. 88).

The problems facing higher education institutions and systems in developing countries are indeed acute. But, as will be discussed, they are not categorically different from those confronting OECD nations.

3.1.2 Internationalization. The transportation of higher education during both the colonial and neo-colonial periods was by definition an international phenomenon, and became a structural component of international relations during the Cold War era as East and West vied for influence amongst the developing nations. Now, the internationalization of higher education is being driven as much by economic factors and the creation of a world market as by particular national political and military priorities.

Higher education institutions have always encouraged international cooperation and the free flow of ideas and professional personnel between countries. They have appreciated that science and scholarship do not recognize national boundaries and that progress in research will be facilitated by effective international sharing of ideas and discoveries.

The need to promote such cooperation is even greater in the 1990s than in the past. National economies generally are becoming increasingly interdependent, while each year new technological advances in communication and transport mean that nations generally are in closer contact with one another. Added to this is the realization that many areas of scientific, technological, and medical research are becoming increasingly expensive, and that facilitating mobility of professional personnel is, on balance, likely to advantage rather than disadvantage most countries economically.

Curiosity still motivates a large number of students to seek study abroad, but in the later half of the twentieth century, international higher education endeavors have increasingly become tied to the development of global markets and worldwide economic restructuring. The internationalization of higher education seems to be growing and, as the production of wealth increasingly becomes based on knowledge rather than mechanization, it can be expected that the exploitation of international "knowledge markets" will assume greater importance. For example, the recruitment of fee paying overseas students has become a multibillion dollar business for such countries as Australia, Canada, Great Britain, and the United States. However, the flow of overseas students is mainly in one direction: of the over one million overseas students studying in OECD countries, about 80% are nationals from developing countries.

So far, international activities in higher education have mainly been between nations rather than involving supranational structures. International agencies such as the World Bank and UNESCO attempt to influence higher education provision on a global scale. In Western Europe, the internationalization of higher education has been legally constituted amongst EC (European Community) member states through such programs as ERASMUS (Action Program of the European Community for the Mobility of University Students). While the vast majority of higher education students and staff are nationals, higher education provision appears to be increasingly transcending nation-state boundaries.

Governments, particularly those in OECD countries, have financed in one form or another various higher education cooperative efforts. Many governments expend a proportion of their international aid in the form of overseas fellowships and scholarships (by so doing, of course, they recoup some of the international aid via overseas student financial expenditure at the host institutions). Many cultural treaties between nations contain explicit provision for exchange of higher education staff and students, and several government ministries of education have created formal programs to further the international activities of their respective higher education systems.

However, governments are supporting international cooperative schemes not merely for the cultural and academic enhancement of students and staff who participate in them. Governments are becoming increasingly concerned that they occupy for economic and political purposes an advantageous position in the international knowledge-market. Higher education cooperation is taking place in a changing economic market environment, and markets are based on principles of competition. As Wagner and Schnitzer (1991 p. 276) note, the "keywords are *competition* and *development* with economics assuming pride-of-place alongside cultural and social values in the internationalization of higher education."

Competition amongst nations for the control and productive utilization of knowledge is increasing. Moreover, the power to shape and influence the direction of internationalization and cooperation in higher education clearly rests with the larger and more powerful institutions and systems of the advanced countries. These countries do not present a united front; they compete amongst themselves for foreign students, control of knowledge, and influence in the international higher education arena. What they do have in common, however, is an emphasis on market relations and a related set of attitudes and values that seem to be influencing higher education policy everywhere.

3.2 Government–Higher Education Relationships

3.2.1 Policy trends and debates. According to Teichler (1992 pp. 39–40), planning and policy in higher education at the system level in most countries since the Second World War has been driven by three interrelated phenomena:

(a) the quantative expansion of the higher education system;

(b) the increased belief in the need and the potential of macrosocietal planning and steering of the higher education systems;

(c) concerns about teaching and learning in higher education and reform efforts in curricula, teaching, and learning.

During the 1950s and early 1960s, the higher education policymakers were preoccupied with questions of expansion and the means of expansion of higher education. From the late 1960s to the mid-1970s, attention shifted to "a search for a modern structure of the higher education system" in a climate of student criticism of prevailing teaching, research, and decision-making patterns. From the mid-1970s to the mid-1980s, there was a "shift from optimism or euphoria regarding the needs and virtues of educational expansion toward pessimism and renewed scepticism and a collapse of faith in societal planning, both in terms of understanding sufficiently the complexity of higher education and its environment and of carrying through plans of reshaping higher education" (Teichler 1992 p. 43).

During the later half of the 1980s, there was a marked diversification in the higher education policies between countries, and though there was no single topic dominating the higher education agenda, several issues did have particular prominence in a number of countries. These issues included an emphasis on the need for quality improvement; increased support for diversity in higher education; increasing attention to more efficient management of higher education institutions; growth in the use of performance indicators to measure quality and efficiency in the allocation of resources; greater interest in the utility of higher education to the private sector; and the internationalization of higher education. The demise of the influence of buffer bodies such as the University Grants Committee in Britain, and the Commonwealth Tertiary Commission in Australia, also characterized this period and raised concern from within the academic community in particular about the autonomy of higher education institutions.

The early 1990s as a fourth phase in higher education planning and policy development is characterized by: reductions in public expenditure; increased emphasis on efficiency of resource utilization and management; and a strengthening of the policy and planning role of individual institutions (Teichler 1992). Higher education institutions must now, as Kogan (1992) observes, justify their existence more in economic rather than in social terms.

Similarly, Berdahl (1991 p. 50) observes that in Western Europe, current government intervention in higher education reflects economic needs rather than the social demands of the previous decades. According to Berdahl "three concerns drove this intervention; a shift from policies determined primarily by social demand to policies that are expenditure driven; strong pressures for greater efficiency in internal management; and the rise of what Neave has coined the 'evaluative state.'"

The continuing pressures for rapid expansion in student enrollments and for higher education institutions to serve a greater range of functions increase the need for higher education systems to improve their capacity for effective planning and for efficient management of resources, both financial and human. But system level planning in higher education has proved to be a difficult endeavor. As a result, there is now far less enthusiasm for centralized, large scale, long-term planning efforts than there was in the 1960s. Moreover, concern with higher education reform has become a part of a broader government agenda of microeconomic reform of the public sector and, similarly, the changes proposed are framed in the language of "efficiency" and "productivity." This is reflected in many OECD and developing countries alike in a shift from what has been termed state control to state supervision models of higher education steering.

3.2.2 State control and supervision models of higher education.
Higher education institutions have never been left entirely to their own devices with respect to their core activities of teaching, research, and community service. One of the major policy challenges for governments in managing their higher education systems has been how best to obtain the appropriate balance between the needs of centralized funding, planning, coordination, and accountability on the one hand, and the need for institutional autonomy and appropriate discretion in goal setting and management on the other.

Since the 1970s, two broad policy strategies are evident in relation to higher education. The first can be characterized as strong government planning and control through the application of "stringent regulations" and tightened budget allocations. The second policy strategy can be seen more as a "stepping back" by governments from detailed centralized control through encouraging higher education institutions to be more autonomous, self-regulating, and market oriented in their operations—albeit within an overall framework of government priorities (Kogan 1988, Kells 1989, Neave 1987, van Vught 1989, Jappinen 1989). The claimed advantage of this second, self-regulation strategy is that institutions are able to:

> obtain an autonomy relative to central government, but at the same time be forced to go into the market in which they must seek sponsorship. They have the freedom to compete for funds. This enlargement of institutional autonomy is assumed to result in a better adjustment to changing societal conditions but at the same time, governments still have to protect the interests of the 'consumers' (i.e. students) and formulate the 'overall targets' of the higher education system. (Askling 1989 p. 293)

Self-regulatory higher education systems are also considered to be more innovative than those subject to detailed centralized control (van Vught 1989, Cerych and Sabatier 1986).

3.2.3 Collegial vs. corporate management models.
Coupled with a shift at the national system level from state control to state supervisory models of higher education has been the strengthening of corporate management models at the institutional level. The two phenomena are directly interrelated. Under the state supervisory model, a large degree of responsibility and authority is transferred to institutional management, which is expected to provide strong and decisive leadership. But in higher education institutions, traditional academic norms and values concerning control over working conditions are not easily modified (Meek and Wood 1997).

There is one school of thought that considers management principles as universal: good management practice can be transferred from organization to organization despite the line of business of a particular organization. Coupled with this is the belief that large organizations require corporate style management, strong leadership, and clear lines of authority. According to Scott (1993 p. 47), "the 'collegial' university governed by the academic guild assisted by low-profile administrators has been succeeded by the 'managerial' university dominated by an increasingly expert cadre of senior managers" which, according to him, is caused in particular by the size of the present day institutions. "Universities must be managed as businesses not because they are businesses but because they are on a corporate scale" (Scott 1993). A contrary argument points to the unique features of higher education institutions as making a corporate style of management not only difficult but inadvisable. Indeed, there are numerous assertions that since the ultimate goal of higher education institutions is the creation, preservation, and transmission of knowledge, they cannot be managed like private corporations. According to this view higher education governance rests ultimately on collegial concensus rather than on executive priority. Academics rather than "managers" know best how to run the university and must be given the freedom and autonomy to pursue knowledge wherever it may lead them.

The collegial model of academic governance probably has always been a well-perpetuated myth. Nonetheless, higher education institutions do have their own particular norms and values that must be taken into account in devising effective management structures and practices. As with society in general, academic norms and values often are more potent in their violation than in their day-to-day conformation. Moreover, much of the general literature on management of change argues for a degree of congruence between policy goals and the values of those who are to implement them (Cerych and Sabatier 1986, Hage and Aiken 1970, Levine 1980, Rogers 1983).

Trow (1994) distinguishes between two distinct approaches to managerialism in higher education: "hard" and "soft" management. According to Trow (p. 11): ". . . the "soft" managerialists still see higher education as an autonomous activity, governed by its own norms and traditions, with a more effective and rationalised management still serving functions defined by the academic community itself." But it appears that it is the "hard" concept of managerialism that has won the day and has the most powerful voice. The hard managerialists:

> are resolved to reshape and redirect the activities of [the academic] community through funding formulas and other mechanisms of accountability imposed from outside the academic community, management mechanisms created and largely shaped for application to large commercial enterprises. Business models are central to the hard conception of managerialism; when applied to higher education, as the current government does, the commitment is to transform universities into organisations similar enough to ordinary commercial firms so that they can be assessed and managed in roughly similar ways. (Trow 1994 p. 12)

The new managerialist approach to higher education inevitably creates tensions between administrators and academics. But what needs to be recognized is that the push towards corporate styles of management is not idiosyncratic to particular countries, nor can it be divorced from broader socioeconomic forces that are reshaping higher education globally. Miller (1992 p. 21), for example, sees similarities in management structures in Australia and the United Kingdom: "there are elements which would seem to relate to deep structures of economy, polity and language which affect both countries." These in turn extend across institutions of many nations because of similar external influences that are worldwide:

> underlying the particular dynamics of management of a higher education institution, lie not only the characteristics of the culture of the nation state and region in which it is located, but a much broader set of external movements which in its cultural aspect are becoming increasingly similar so that the language of management is familiar to academics across continents and is regarded by many with similar suspicion. (Miller 1992 p. 21)

Both the corporate management push within higher education institutions and the deregulation of state control at systems level are driven by a more or less universal trend towards privatization and market relations in higher education.

3.2.4 Privatization and market relations. One of the central themes in the sociology of higher education at the close of the twentieth century is the assumption that higher education is made more effective and cost-efficient in an environment of deregulated state control and enhanced institutional entrepreneurship where market relations, consumer control, user-pays, and institutional competitiveness help further innovation, quality, and relevance.

"Privatization" (taken here to mean the growth of "privateness" within public higher education) and market-like relations have arisen on the higher education agenda of many countries, whether primarily public or with dual public–private sectors. Also, shifts in public–private relationships have changed in many spheres, not only within higher education. With respect to higher education, as Levy (1991 p. 7) notes, "privateness is . . . seen as providing more incentives for efficiencies for actors from students to administrators. Supporters of privatization find vindication in the trends of the last fifteen years or so. In the [most developed countries], this marks a striking reversal of the decreasing privateness of postwar decades. Thus, the public universities of Europe have come to look much more favorably on private finance to augment resources, offset lost government funds, and provide energising competition."

Privatization is being embraced as an ideology in its own right and as a reaction to what is perceived as "public failure." Behind many of the changes in the relationship between governments and higher educational institutions is the philosophy of "economic rationalism;" this reflects a belief that market forces, rather than state intervention, will make institutions more cost-effective and better managed, as well as making higher education systems more fluid and responsive to client needs and demands. Market competition "is posed as the solution to good government, the condition for a healthy economy, and the chance for a better education" (Perkins 1987 p. 1).

Private investment in higher education and market competition are not confined to OECD nations. Many of the former Eastern Block countries and some nations still controlled by a communist party, such as Vietnam, are also encouraging the privatization of their higher education systems (see Sloper and Can 1995), as are many developing nations (Neave and van Vught 1994). As growth in participation and thus cost of higher education continue to rise, governments will pressure higher education institutions to find more of their costs from users, particularly students, and from selling their services, such as research products, to industry. But there is some question of whether the market will achieve for higher education all that is expected of it. The way in which market relations are being employed in higher education appears somewhat contradictory in a number of respects. First, there is no such thing as a pure market in higher education anywhere. All governments intervene in higher education, and it is more a question of the degree of intervention than one of intervention versus nonintervention. Also, deregulation of higher education has been accompanied by increased emphasis on accountability and quality control. Too much emphasis on accountability and quality can undermine the objectives of market competition and introduce centralized control in a different guise (Neave 1996). Second, one of the purposes of deregulation of higher education in many countries has been the bolstering of private investment in higher education. Several countries have been successful in getting private money to help offset the decline in government support of higher education. But this has not necessarily improved or even maintained teaching quality. A study of private investment in higher education in France, Germany, The Netherlands, Sweden, Britain, the United States, and Japan demonstrates that the bulk of private money is consumed by research and services, with little private investment going towards teaching. The authors of the report conclude that: "the teaching function will bear the full burden of future reductions in public higher education funding, as it has already done in the recent past. Combined with the trend to increased participation this will lead to catastrophic effects in the foreseeable future: institutions will no longer be able to provide adequate education to students as available funds, under changed circumstances, will become absolutely insufficient to provide the necessary [teaching] infrastructure ..." (Goedegebuure et al. 1994). While there has recently been substantial increase in private investment in higher education, its effect on teaching quality is largely unknown. Third, market competition can result in one of two types of institutional behavior: each university attempting to better the other by attempting to seize the same market, or diversification of function in order to avoid direct competition. There is some evidence to suggest that market competition may have the unintended consequence of sponsoring sterile institutional imitation and conformity rather than innovativeness (Meek et al. 1996). Finally, the challenge for universities is how to maintain an appropriate balance between free and open scholarly inquiry in teaching and research and the more immediate demands and priorities that can be imposed by the private sector. It has been argued that academic autonomy is related to the multiplicity of funding sources. But what appears to be at issue is not the multiplicity of funding sources per se, but the structures of control embedded in particular types of funding mechanisms. In this sense, market forces may be more of a threat to academic freedom than government policy ever was (Slaughter 1990, Wood 1992).

4. Conclusion

The massive and unprecedented expansion of higher education during the second half of the twentieth century is being fueled by global economic restructuring and the advent of postindustrial or "knowledge society." In the knowledge society, knowledge supersedes agriculture and manufacturing as the main means for wealth production, and knowledge replaces energy from coal, oil, nuclear power, etc. as the primary resource of society (Bell 1973, Scott 1997). It is not that agriculture and manufacturing disappear, but rather that technology has made both agriculture and manufacturing so efficient that they demand the attention of only a minority of the workforce (Perkin 1991).

Obviously, higher education organizations, particularly universities as cutting edge research institutions, have a key role to play in the knowledge society. "In the course of the present century," as Scott (1997 p.6) explains, the university:

> has become the main (even the monopoly producer) and reproducer, of human and cultural capital. Older routes to acquiring higher-level skills ... have fallen into disuse. Similarly, older forms of socialisation into élite social roles ... have also been abandoned. Anyone who aspires to be an 'expert' or join an élite now has to be a university graduate. Moreover the university has established itself as the leading scientific institution of our age. Its dominance is both organisational and epistemological. It employs more scientists than any other institution ... And its cognitive values and social practices ... have been widely accepted as the conditions for world-class research.

But the university may not be able to maintain its monopoly as knowledge producer as postindustrial society continues to develop. Mass participation in higher education has already challenged many of the traditional academic values of the university and questioned the legitimacy in the traditional intellectual structures. Nybom (1996 p. 3) goes so far as to maintain that "the loss of legitimacy in the traditional university, has to do with the fact that this institution in its basic, historical structure, is a sub-optimal system." But, even more importantly, as the knowledge society continues to develop, market relations based on knowledge production increasingly permeate all aspects and institutions of society, and the university is faced with a growing number of competitors in both research and training. What is at question is the continuing importance and centrality of the university as knowledge is increasingly brought within market and political exchanges (Scott 1997).

> It is not just that universities are having to adapt, willingly or unwillingly, to a market environment, by competing for students or research funds or adopting more business-like forms of operation. It is that they have been absorbed into, been taken over by, market relations. But in the process, those market relations have been profoundly changed. Higher education has taken over the market, just as much as the other way round. (Scott 1997 p. 14)

But, as Scott indicates, the interesting sociological question is whether higher education institutions, universities in particular, will continue to be recognized as such as postindustrial society moves into the twenty-first century.

See also: Authority and Power in Educational Organizations; Benefits of Education; Education and the State; Educational Expansion: Sociological Perspectives; Institutional Approach to the Study of Education

References

Altbach P G (ed.) 1996 *The International Academic Profession: Portraits From Fourteen Countries.* Carnegie Foundation for the Advancement of Teaching, Princeton, New Jersey

Althusser L 1971 Ideology and ideological state apparatuses. In: Althusser L 1971 *Lenin and Philosophy and Other Essays.* New Left Books, London

Aronowitz S 1989 *Science as Power.* Macmillan, London

Askling B 1989 Structural uniformity and functional diversification. *Higher Educ. Q.* 43(4): 289–305

Austin A W 1993 What matters in college. *Lib. Educ.* 79(4): 4–15

Barth J 1982 *Sabbatical.* Penguin, Harmondsworth

Becher T 1989 *Academic Tribes and Territories.* Open University Press, Milton Keynes

Becher T, Kogan M 1980 *Process and Structure in Higher Education.* Heineman, London

Bell D 1973 *The Coming of Post-Industrial Society.* Basic Books, New York

Berdahl R 1991 Higher education and government relations in Western Europe. *Educ. Rec.* 72(4): 50–54

Blau P M 1973 *The Organisation of Academic Work.* Wiley, New York

Blaug M 1983 A methodological appraisal of radical economics. In: Coats A (ed.) 1983 *Methodological Controversies in Economics.* JAI Press, Greenwich, Connecticut

Blaug M 1987 *The Economics of Education and the Education of an Economist.* New York University Press, New York

Bourdieu P 1988 *Homo Academicus.* Polity Press, Cambridge

Bowles S, Gintis H 1976 *Schooling in Capitalist America: Educational Reform and the Contradictions of Economic Life.* Basic Books, New York

Bowman M, Millet B, Schiefelbein E 1984 *The Political Economy of Higher Education Studies in Chile, France and Malaysia.* World Bank, Washington, DC

Bradbury M 1975 *The History Man.* Arena, Arrow Books, London

Brubacher J S 1978 *On the Philosophy of Higher Education.* Jossey-Bass, San Francisco

Cerych L 1984 The policy perspective. In: Clark B R (ed.) 1984 *Perspectives on Higher Education.* University of California Press, Berkeley, California

Cerych L, Sabatier P 1986 *Great Expectations and Mixed Performance.* European Institute of Education and Social Policy, Trentham Books, Stoke-on-Trent

Clark B R 1983 *The Higher Education System.* University of California Press, Berkeley, California

Clark B R 1996 Substantive growth and innovative organization: new categories for higher education reseach. *High. Educ.* 23: 417–30

Clark B R, Neave G (eds.) 1992 *The Encyclopedia of Higher Education.* Pergamon Press, Oxford

Cohen M, March J 1974 *Leadership and Ambiguity: The American College President.* McGraw-Hill, New York

DiMaggio P J, Powell W W 1983 The iron cage revisited: institutional isomorphism amd collective rationality in organizational fields. *Am. Sociol. Rev.* 48: 147–60

Dunkin M J, Barnes J 1986 Research on teaching in higher education. In: Wittrock M C (ed.) 1986 *Handbook of Research on Teaching,* 2nd edn. Macmillan, New York

Eisemon T O, Kourouma M 1991 Foreign assistance for university development in Sub-Saharan Africa and Asia. Paper for the World Bank Senior Policy Seminar on Improvement and Innovation of Higher Education in Developing Countries, 30 June–4 July, Kuala Lumpur

Entwhistle N J 1987 A model of the teaching–learning process. In: Richardson J T E, Eysnek M W, Warren Piper D (eds.) 1987 *Student Learning: Research into Education and Cognitive Psychology.* Open University Press, Milton Keynes

Geiger R L 1986 *To Advance Knowledge: The Growth of American Research Universities, 1900–1940.* Oxford University Press, New York

Geiger R L 1993 *Research and Relevant Knowledge: American Research Universities Since World War II.* Oxford University Press, New York

Giddens A 1977 *Central Problems in Social Theory: Action Structure and Contradiction in Social Analysis.* Macmillan, London

Giddens A 1989 *Sociology.* Polity Press, Oxford

Goedegebuure L, Kaiser F, van Vught F 1994 Disaster warning. *Times Higher Education Supplement,* 7 October, 1–3

Hage J, Aitken M 1970 *Social Change in Complex Organizations.* Random House, New York

Halsey A H 1992 *Decline of Donnish Dominion. The British Academic Profession in the Twentieth Century.* Clarendon Press, Oxford

Halsey A H, Trow M 1971 *The British Academics.* Faber and Faber, London

Hammack F M, Heyns B 1992 Microsociology. In: Clark B R, Neave G (eds.) 1992, Vol. III

Hayden M, Carpenter P 1993 The attainment of higher education in Australian society. In: Najman J M, Western J S (eds.) 1993 *A Sociology of Australian Society,* 2nd edn. Macmillan, Melbourne

Huisman J 1995 *Differentiation, Diversity and Dependency in Higher Education.* Lemma, Utrecht

Jappinen A 1989 University and government in Finland: complementary roles. *High. Educ. Mang.* 1(3): 333–36

Jaspers K 1959 *The Idea of the University.* Peter Owen, London

Kells H R 1989 University self-regulation in Europe. *Eur. J. Educ.* 24(3): 299–309

Kerr C 1982 *The Uses of the University.* Harvard University Press, Cambridge, Massachusetts

Klees S J 1991 The economics of education: is that all there is? *Comp. Educ. Rev.* 33(4)

Kogan M 1984 The political view. In: Clark B R (ed.) 1984 *Perspectives on Higher Education.* University of California Press, Berkeley, California

Kogan M 1988 Government and management of higher education: an introductory review. *Int. J. Inst. Mang. Higher Educ.* 12(1): 5–15

Kogan M 1992 New trends in higher education in research in Europe and their relationship to key issues in European higher education and higher education policy. In: Frackmann E, Maassen P (eds.) 1992 *Towards Excellence in European Higher Education in the Nineties.* Lemma, Utrecht

Kuh G D 1990 Assessing student culture. In: Tierney W G (ed.) 1990 *Assessing Academic Climates and Cultures, New Directions for Institutional Research.* Jossey-Bass, San Francisco, California

Lane J-E, Fredriksson B 1981 *Higher Education and Public Administration.* Almqvist and Wiksell, Stockholm

Levine A 1980 *Why Innovation Fails, The Institutionalization and Termination of Innovation in Higher Education.* State University of New York, Albany, New York

Levy D C 1991 Problems of privatization. Paper prepared for the World Bank Senior Policy Seminar on Improvement and Innovation of Higher Education in Developing Countries, 30 June–4 July, Kuala Lumpur

Lewis L S 1977 Sociology of higher education. In: Knowles A S (ed.) 1977 *The International Encyclopedia of Higher Education*, Vol III. Jossey-Bass, San Francisco, California

Lodge D 1988 *Nice Work.* Penguin, Harmondsworth

Luteru P H 1991 The impact of foreign aid on Pacific mores, ideas and traditions. In: Jones D R, Meek V L, Weeks J (eds.) 1991 *Explorations in Higher Education: A South Pacific Critique.* University of Melbourne, Parkville

Martin F, Dall'Alba G, Beaty E 1993 Conceptions of learning. *Int. J. Educ. Res.* 19: 277–300

Martin F, Houndsell D, Entwhistle N (eds.) 1984 *The Experience of Learning.* Scottish Academic Press, Edinburgh

Mazrui A 1975 The African university as a multinational corporation: problems of penetration and dependency. *Harv. Educ. Rev.* 45(2): 191–210

Meek V L 1982 *The University of Papua New Guinea: A case Study in the Sociology of Higher Education.* University of Queensland Press, St. Lucia

Meek V L 1990 Differentiation in higher education. In: Saha L J, Keeves J P (eds.) 1990 *Schooling and Society in Australia: Sociological Perspectives.* Pergamon, Sydney

Meek V L 1991 The transformation of Australian higher education from binary to unitary system. *High. Educ.* 21: 461–94

Meek V L, Goedegebuure L, Kivinen O, Rinne R 1996 Conclusion. In: Meek V L, Goedegebuure L, Kivinen O, Rinne R (eds.) 1996 *The Mockers and Mocked: Comparative Perspectives on Diversity, Differentiation and Convergence in Higher Education.* Pergamon, Oxford

Meek V L, Wood F Q 1997 *Higher Education Governance and Management: An Australian Study.* AGPS, Canberra

Metzger W P 1977 *Reader on the Sociology of the Academic Profession.* Arno Press, New York

Miller H 1992 The state of the academic profession: an Australian–United Kingdom comparison. *Aust. Univ. Rev.* 35(2): 21–25

Moodie G, Eustace R 1974 *Power and Authority in British Universities.* Allen and Unwin, London

Mortimore P 1992 Schools and higher education. In: Clark B R, Neave G (eds.) 1992, Vol III

Murphy K, Welch F 1989 Wage premiums for college graduates: Recent growth and possible explanations. *Educ. Researcher* 18(4): 17–26

Neave G 1983 The changing face of the academic profession in Western Europe. *Eur. J. Educ.* 18(3): 217–27

Neave G 1987 Editorial. *Eur. J. Educ.* 22(2):121–22

Neave G 1996 Homogenization, integration and convergence: the cheshire cats of higher education analysis. In: Meek V L, Goedegebuure L, Kivinen O, Rinne R (eds.) 1996

Neave G, van Vught F (eds.) 1994 *Government and Higher Education Relationships Across Three Continents: The Winds of Change.* Pergamon, Oxford

Newman J H 1976 (1st edn. 1873) *The Idea of a University.* Oxford University Press, Oxford

Niblett W R 1974 *Universities Between Two Worlds.* University of London Press, London

Nybom T 1976 The future relations between research and higher education. Paper presented to the 13th General Conference of IMHE Member Institutions Setting New Priorities for Higher Education Management, 2–4 September, Paris

Pace C R 1987 *CSEQ: Test Manual and Norms: College Student Experiences Questionnaire.* Centre for the Study of Evaluation, Graduate School of Education, University of California, Los Angeles, California

Pace C R, Stern G G 1958 An approach to the measurement of psychological characteristics of college environments. *J. Educ. Psych.* 49: 269–77

Parsons T, Platt G M 1973 *The American University.* Harvard University Press, Cambridge, Massachusetts

Perkin H 1991 History of universities. In: Altbach P G (ed.) 1991 *International Higher Education, An Encyclopedia.* Garland, New York

Perkins J A 1987 Privatization. *Newsletter.* International Council for Educational Development, p. 1

Poulantzas N A 1973 *Political Power and Social Classes.* New Left Books, London

Premfors R 1981 National policy styles and higher education in France, Sweden and the United Kingdom. *Eur. J. Educ.* 16(2): 253–62

Psacharopoulos G, Tan Jee-Peng, Jimenez E 1986 *Financing Education in Developing Countries.* World Bank, Washington, DC

Psacharopoulos G, Woodhall M 1985 *Education for Development: An Analysis of Investment Choices.* Oxford University Press, New York

Ramirez F O, Riddle P 1991 The expansion of higher education. In: Altbach P G (ed.) 1991 *International Higher Education, An Encyclopedia.* Garland, New York

Ramsden P (ed.) 1988 *Improving Learning: New Perspectives.* Kogan Page, London

Reisman D, Gusfield J, Gamson Z 1970 *Academic Values and Mass Education.* McGraw-Hill, New York

Riley G, Baldridge J 1977 *Governing Academic Organizations.* McCutchan, Berkeley, California

Riley P 1983 A structurationist account of political culture. *Adm. Sci. Q.* 28: 414–37

Rogers E M 1982 *Diffusion of Innovations.* The Free Press. New York

Rondinelli D A, Middleton J, Verspoor A M 1990 *Planning Education Reforms in Developing Countries.* Duke University Press, Durham, North Carolina

Rothblatt S 1968 *The Revolution of the Dons: Cambridge and Society in Victorian England.* Faber and Faber, London

Rudis W 1984 *The Universities of Europe 1100–1914.* Associated University Press, London

Salancik S, Pfeffer J 1974 The bases and use of power in organizational decision making: the case of a university. *Adm. Sci. Q.* 19: 453–73

Salmi J 1991 *Perspectives on the Financing of Higher Education.* Education and Employment Division, Population and Human Resources Department, World Bank, Washington, DC

Sanyal B C 1991 Higher education and the labor market. In: Altbach P G (ed.) 1991 *International Higher Education, An Encyclopedia.* Garland, New York

Scott P 1993 Respondent. *The Transition from Elite to Mass Higher Education.* Occasional Paper Series, DEET Higher Division, AGPS, Canberra

Scott P 1997 The changing role of the university in the

production of new knowledge. *Tertiary Educ. Mang.* 3(1): 5–14

Shils E (ed. and trans.) 1974 *Max Weber on Universities.* University of Chicago Press, Chicago, Illinois

Slaughter S 1990 *The Higher Learning and High Technology.* State University of New York Press, New York

Sloper D, Can Le Thac 1995 *Higher Education in Vietnam: Change and Response.* St. Martin's Press, New York

Teichler U 1992 Research on higher education in Europe: some aspects of recent developments. In: Frackmann E, Maassen P (eds.) 1992 *Towards Excellence in European Higher Education in the Nineties.* Lemma, Utrecht

Tierney W G (ed.) 1990 *Assessing Academic Climates and Cultures, New Directions for Institutional Research.* Jossey-Bass, San Francisco, California

Trow M 1974 Problems in the transition from elite to mass higher education. *Policies for Higher Education.* OECD, Paris

Trow M 1994 Managerialism and the academic profession: the case of England. *Higher Educ. Policy* 7(2): 11–18

van der Berghe P 1973 *Power and Privelege at an African University.* Schenkman, Cambridge, Massachusetts

van Vught F 1989 Government strategies in practice. In: van

Vught F (ed.) 1989 *Government Strategies and Innovation in Higher Education.* Jessica Kingsley, London

Wagner A, Schnitzer K 1991 Programmes and policies for foreign students and study abroad: the search for effective approaches in a new global setting. *High. Educ.* 21(3): 275–88

Williams B 1990 The crucial question of how we should run our universities. *Australian* 20 July, 14

Williams G, Blackstone T, Metcalf D 1974 *The Academic Labour Market: Economic and Social Aspects of a Profession.* Elsevier Scientific Publishing Company, Amsterdam

Wolthuis J 1992 Macrosociology. In: Clark B R, Neave G (eds.) 1992 *The Encyclopedia of Higher Education,* Vol. III. Pergamon Press, Oxford

Wood F Q 1992 The commercialisation of university research in Australia: issues and problems. *Comp. Educ.* 28(3): 293–313

Woodhall M (ed.) 1989 *Financial Support for Students: Grants, Loans or Graduate Tax?* Kogan Page, London

World Bank 1988 *Education in Sub-Saharan Africa: Policies for Adjustment, Revitalization and Expansion.* World Bank, Washington, DC

Sociology of Learning in School

P. Broadfoot

Most learning is a social activity in which parents, friends, and teachers provide the encouragement and the framework within which learning can take place. This article explores the social influences which affect learning both within the classroom and outside it.

1. The Nature of Learning

All societies, if they are to endure, must make provision for children to be taught the knowledge, skills, and values which they will need to become competent, adult members of that society. In most traditional societies it seems to have been accepted that the vital tasks of language acquisition, of the development of appropriate modes of behavior, of the learning of necessary skills, and of gaining knowledge and understanding about the world could safely be achieved informally through the child's participation in the daily life of the society. This process of informal learning that sociologists term "socialization" (see *Socialization*) is frequently complemented, however, by more explicit provision for formal instruction or practical training. The nature of such provision has traditionally varied enormously, including, for example, the formal religious schools run by holy men in temples and monasteries which have been a feature of most of the world's major religions, the explicitly vocational training associated with apprenticeships and

the attachment of an individual to a particular "master," and those periods of specific training organized by individual tribes as a precursor to initiation into adulthood.

Despite their enormous diversity, however, such traditional forms of educational provision appear to have one feature in common—an acceptance of the process of learning as essentially unproblematic. It is only with the advent of formal educational provision on a mass scale, which is associated with the process of industrialization, that questions have arisen concerning how the necessary learning may most effectively and efficiently be provided.

1.1 Early Studies of Learning Potential

Interest in systematic inquiry into the delivery of education increased dramatically at the end of the nineteenth century and was associated with the very evident differences between individuals in their learning achievement. Such differences were for a long time linked to the search for a physiological explanation of mental capacity. This in turn gave rise to the field of psychometrics and the search for ways of measuring intellectual ability and performance.

When toward the middle of the twentieth century sociologists also began to turn their attention to the empirical study of education the very significant relationship between home background and educational achievement, which studies such as those of Floud et al. (1956), Douglas (1964), and Coleman et al. (1966) were able to document, made it impossible to view differences in student learning outcomes purely as a function of innate intellectual capacity. There followed a protracted debate between leading scholars as to the proportion of intellectual capacity which was genetically determined in the form of an inherited characteristic like eye or hair color and was thus immutable and the degree to which such capacity is a reflection of the environment—especially the social context—to which the individual is exposed which helps or hinders the development of the intellect (see Husén 1975).

1.2 Social Class and Educational Achievement

The ramifications of the nature–nurture debate have been considerable. The evidence provided by a series of major sociological studies of education since the 1950s associated with, for example, Bernstein, Goldthorpe, and Halsey in the United Kingdom; Bourdieu and Establet in France; Jencks and Bowles and Gintis in the United States; and Connell in Australia has pointed to a powerful relationship between social class and educational achievement. It is clear from the mass of evidence that has been generated that "ability to learn," while being to some extent influenced by heredity, is strongly affected by circumstantial factors rooted in the cultural experiences to which an individual is subject. In addition to social class, it is now recognized that these circumstantial factors include ethnicity and gender which also exercise a strong influence on educational achievement.

1.3 Interactionist Perspectives

The early studies of social inequality in education were largely concerned to demonstrate the existence of a correlation between home background and educational outcomes. It was not until the 1970s that attempts to document how the correlation was actually produced achieved prominence in the rapid growth of interest in interactionist perspectives and associated microsociological studies of the details of educational processes. Although a number of theoretical traditions had long been established under the general umbrella of interactionist perspectives such as symbolic interaction, phenomenology, and ethnomethodology, in the 1970s these perspectives began to be used as the foundation for what could now properly be called a sociology of learning.

Detailed interactionist studies of learning as an interpersonal activity have revealed some of the dynamic factors that affect learning as realized in interaction. Such studies build on quantitative evidence concerning patterns of differential student learning outcomes—according to social groups based on class, race, gender, or geographic location as well as by institution—and seek to explain these in terms of the processes which lie behind such outcomes. By so doing they link the traditional interest of psychologists

in individual perspectives and ability and in teaching and learning strategies with the important sociological perspective that a student's ability to respond to a given stimulus or situation is significantly affected by a variety of social factors. These factors include the more or less permanent influence of home background, race, and gender as well as the more ephemeral impact of the classroom, the quality of teaching, and peer group relations.

1.4 Social Theories of Learning

Haste (1987) provides a model of learning which relates these various influences. She identifies three domains of influence—the "intra-individual," the "interpersonal," and the "sociohistorical." The first of these concerns the way in which the individual assimilates experiences and constructs understanding; the second is the domain of social interaction in which meanings are negotiated and through which cultural norms and social conventions are learned; the third concerns the wider sociohistorical context in which learning takes place, its origins, and the circumstances of the learner. This is dealt with later in this article.

1.4.1 The intra-individual. One important contribution to the understanding of learning as a social process comes from the work of Vygotsky. Vygotsky emphasizes the central role of language in mediating the culture in which an individual lives by enabling them to make sense of their surroundings by the attribution of concepts and ideas drawn from that culture. Language is thus the mechanism individuals use to make sense of their world and to inform action. There is now a very considerable body of research that explores the relationship between language and the process of learning (see for example, Barnes 1976, Cazdan 1988, Wells 1987).

Vygotsky introduced the concept of the Zone of Proximal Development (ZPD), which distinguishes between the learning which would have taken place given no outside help and the potential development associated with learning under adult guidance or with the support of more capable peers. As Tharp and Gallimore (1988) suggest, social interaction is a crucial part of this process since a deliberate intervention by a teacher or other adult can assist the learners by providing a scaffold for the learners to build across their ZPD.

Vygotsky's emphasis on the interrelatedness of thought, language, and culture as part of a perspective in which social interaction is seen as the central foundation for learning links to the second element in the model—the interpersonal.

1.4.2 The interpersonal. The emphasis on learning as grounded in the assumption that people need to "make sense" of a given situation so that, through the attribution of meaning, they can incorporate new knowledge into their existing understanding has much in common with the symbolic interactionist perspective which the American social psychologist George Herbert Mead originally popularized in the 1930s. Both this approach and that of Vygotsky stress the crucial role of the individual's own perception of any particular situation and the actions that follow from their perception of the meaning of it. Mead argues that people act together on the basis of meanings which have been generated by their experiences in interaction. These meanings become socially patterned and are sustained through cultures. The same process also produces a perception of oneself—a sense of personal identity which not only influences the way people interact with others, but also, crucially, influences their view of themselves as learners.

This emphasis on the relationship between the social context and student learning is in stark contrast to the concept of learning as a function of innate ability or what Bonniol (1991) refers to as "the old demon of innate IQ." It stresses the dynamic possibilities of any learning situation and thus the need to maximize those social factors which will produce a successful learning environment.

2. The Learning Environment

Most learning is likely to take place in one of three main areas of social life: the home, the school or workplace, or during leisure activities. In relation to each of these settings a number of key concepts may be distinguished which help to explain the nature and significance of the interaction that takes place. Within the fundamental distinction between structure and action, between external reality and the response which is the individual's interpretation of that reality, which characterizes all sociological analysis, influences on learning may be structured in terms of two main groups —the characteristics of the teaching provided and the factors that influence students' response.

2.1 Effective Teaching

A great deal of research has been devoted to identifying the qualities of effective teaching and teachers (Kyriacou 1986). Although significant communalities can be identified in this respect across many different countries (Fraser 1986), variations in the age of the learners and the educational setting, and cultural differences mean that there can be no one recipe for success in this respect. Knowledge of the matter to be taught and being well-organized are two of the variables which consistently appear. Beyond this, however, the emphasis is very much on interactional variables—being able to communicate effectively, being fair, treating learners with respect, having a sense of humor, being approachable. All these commonly identified factors reinforce once again the social nature of the teaching–learning process. In particular

they emphasize that the teacher is of major importance in the quality of the opportunity to learn that is provided.

This accords with the social constructivist theory of learning outlined above, which suggests that the teacher needs to provide the means necessary for the learner to traverse the ZPD as effectively as possible by providing instruction and guidance that matches the individual learner's needs in terms of their existing understanding and skill. Teachers must also provide a social setting in which individuals have the confidence to engage in problem-solving activity and to ask the teacher questions, and are motivated to persevere in the face of difficulty.

2.2 The Impact of Evaluation

Evaluation skills are clearly crucial in all these respects. The research of Bennett et al. (1984) in primary schools emphasizes the importance of feedback that highlights what a learner can do to correct unsatisfactory results—a skill that many teachers in conventional classrooms find difficult because of the large numbers of students involved, their lack of knowledge of formative assessment techniques, and the objective constraints of expectations, time, and resources to which they are subject. It is perhaps for these reasons that Tharp and Gallimore find the kind of carefully targeted assistance that learners need to make effective progress is much more common in the one-to-one setting of the parent–child relationship in the home than in the average classroom where there is "too little time for interaction, conversation and joint activity among teacher and children" (1988 p. 80).

A detailed survey of research concerning the impact of evaluation on student learning which was undertaken by Crooks (1988) reinforces the importance of evaluative strategies, suggesting that feedback in the form of global grades or simply confirming correct answers has little effect on subsequent performance. In place of the vague, implicit, and incomplete criteria that teachers frequently use or an emphasis on neatness, conduct, or encouragement which diverts vital intellectual feedback, learners need clear and explicit performance criteria which detail what they are expected to do.

Crooks also highlights the importance of the role played by evaluation and feedback in promoting learning through the affective domain. Self-esteem has long been recognized by psychologists as a major influence on motivation and thus on learning, since students with high self-esteem are likely to try harder and persist longer in the face of difficulties. Of central interest to sociologists is the fact that a major determinant of self-esteem is feedback from significant others. Teachers' evaluations are crucial in this respect, particularly in the early years of schooling when learners are developing their self-image of themselves and of their identity as typically successful or unsuccessful learners.

2.3 Coping Strategies

The kind of one-to-one interactive situation between teacher and taught that often characterizes parent–child or master craftsman and apprentice learning situations makes it relatively easy both to "scaffold" the individual's intellectual progress and to provide the necessary affective conditions which will reinforce the learner's confidence and motivation. In the kind of classroom situation that characterizes most formal educational provision, however, a teacher typically has to deal with a large number of students simultaneously. In this situation a teacher's first priority is to control the class, to impose his or her definition of the situation so that the conditions can be created for some common learning activity to take place. Typically too, the teacher will be obliged to implement external directives concerning what is to be taught and often school-based, or external, policies as to how it should be taught. Limited in time for one-to-one interaction, in resources, and often in the necessary skills needed to diagnose the learning needs of individual students, teachers typically resort to a range of coping strategies which allow them to reconcile the conflicting demands that this kind of formal learning situation inevitably places upon them. Such coping strategies may involve ignoring nondisruptive lapses in discipline, initiating unequal amounts of interaction between more and less demanding pupils, and allowing a whole range of activities to take place which have as their primary function keeping the students occupied and quiet rather than the extension of their learning. Furthermore, given the interactional constraints of the typical classroom situation most teachers feel obliged to pitch their instruction at what they perceive to be the average level; alternatively they may categorize the students into groups according to perceived ability and provide them with differentiated learning tasks. Teachers are often aware of the disadvantages of all these strategies in terms of both students' intellectual progress and their self-concept but feel obliged to adopt these and many other similar compromises between the ideal and the practical if they are to cope with the range of expectations to which they are subject.

2.4 Stereotype Formation

A great deal of the impact of teachers on student learning is not deliberate or overt. Much is embedded in the quality of the routine interaction of the classroom and, in particular, in the process of categorization and, ultimately, stereotyping of individual students. Symbolic interactionist theory emphasizes the need for actors to be able to predict the likely outcome of any given action they may take in order that the desired goal of the action may be achieved. The necessary ability to make such predictions depends on a process of categorization of situations and of individuals according to a range of culturally determined criteria. How a teacher

responds to a particular student is thus likely to depend on his or her expectations for that student built upon a range of background information, personal characteristics, and previous evaluations. Teachers' attitudes to and expectations of individual students will be expressed in their varying interactions with students so that individuals and the other members of a particular class quickly come to learn what the teacher thinks of them. Research has shown, for example, that teachers give different feedback to those for whom they have high or low aspirations.

How any one student reacts to this information is certainly influenced by a host of factors including the individual's existing self-image, aspirations, and attitude both to the particular teacher and to learning in general. To the extent that the student accepts a teacher's identification of them as "able," "dull," or "disruptive" and acts accordingly, the initial label will be reinforced and have a compounding effect on all subsequent interactions between that teacher and student. Typically, as a result of both written and verbal reports, impressions will be passed on from teacher to teacher so that the initial stereotype becomes progressively reinforced. It may also be further reinforced by the organizational arrangements of the school in which tracking or streaming provide a structural basis for the grouping together of students who are perceived to have similar learning characteristics. Having been publicly categorized in this way, not only will it be increasingly hard for students to resist accepting and acting upon the imputation of a particular identity, but this identity will tend to be related to preexisting stereotypes of student "types." Teacher actions based on such typification may well ignore important individual characteristics of the learner.

3. Social Differences and Learning

The above schematic account of the process of stereotype formation through interaction tends to imply that students start from an equal baseline, whereas it is now well-known from a wide variety of sociological research studies that this is not so. Structurally determined inequalities of race, class, and gender allow teachers to begin to categorize students almost as soon as they meet them and long before they can make any formal assessment of their intellectual performance. Classroom-based research has found that learners receive different types of feedback according to gender and ethnic group. For example, teachers typically give different kinds of feedback to boys and girls, allowing boys to explain their failure in terms of lack of effort whereas girls are led to attribute their failure to lack of ability. This latter tends to lead to an unwillingness to persist on the part of the learner, which has been termed "learned helplessness" (see *Sex Differences and School Outcomes*). A range of other studies have identified an independent effect of stereotyping operating against working-class children.

To suggest that the process of interaction between student and teacher exerts an independent effect on any individual student's capacity to learn is not to deny the very real differences in ability to profit from schooling and other forms of education and training with which students have been equipped by their previous experience. A substantial body of sociological research has shown that in many ways teachers are justified in expecting the middle-class child to be more "able" since the entire ethos of the school, having its origins in the dominant culture, tends to reflect that culture in its values, its curriculum, its pedagogy, and its language. It is rather to argue that existing social inequalities are compounded by the differential expectations teachers have of their students. Research into the effects of both the independent and the combined effects of race and gender demonstrate the same tendency for inequalities which exist in the wider society to be reproduced in the process of schooling, not least through the powerful influence of teacher expectation as this influences classroom interaction.

3.1 Cultural Differences in Teacher Expectations

While teacher expectations undoubtedly operate as a powerful influence in all learning situations, there are important cultural differences which inform the nature of those expectations and hence their impact. In Japan, for example, where it has been the tradition in society as a whole to emphasize communality rather than individuality, both teachers and students are more likely to regard differences in educational achievement as a result of relative effort rather than of differences in initial ability and home background. The effect of this appears to be that teachers are able to sustain high expectations of a much greater number of students than in those countries where class and ethnic differential patterns of achievement are more in evidence (White 1987). It is perhaps for this reason that more Japanese students reach the higher levels of the education system than in many other industrialized countries.

Important differences in this respect can also be demonstrated even in near-neighbor countries like the United Kingdom and France. The strong belief in equality of opportunity and national homogeneity that has traditionally informed French education leads to considerably more uniform expectations of students than in the United Kingdom, where a deep-rooted philosophy of responding to the needs of individual learners has at times led to a lowering of teacher expectations and thus of student achievement (Broadfoot et al 1993).

3.2 Cultural Differences in Learning Style

Cultural differences are also an important factor in the creation of successful learning environments. A number of studies have shown that different emphases in child-rearing patterns in terms of, for example, the value placed on students being articulate, or persevering, or docile will influence the kind of learning environment that best suits an individual learner. Comparing the learning behavior of United States and Japanese children, for example, Hess and Azuma (1991) were able to show marked differences, with United States children requiring significantly more regular positive reinforcement in terms of perceived success than their Japanese counterparts who had been socialized to value commitment to the task more than achieving a successful outcome.

Cultural differences such as these may well be intranational as well as international, that is, the product of ethnic or social class differences in cultural style within one country. If this is so, the effect is likely to be far more significant because it leads to the relative disadvantage of particular students who are faced with both uncongenial teaching strategies and the compounding effect of this expressed in negative teacher expectations as discussed above. Cultural differences also find expression in values as well as preferred modes of behavior. Extensive research by Raven in England, Scotland, and Ireland underlines the key role played by values in the motivation of students, leading him to argue that as part of the important task of "scaffolding" individual learning through the ZPD, teachers need to recognize that learners will function most effectively when they themselves value the goals they are striving to achieve (Raven 1991).

3.3 Sources of Cultural Differences

In place of the psychologists' emphasis on individual ability or personality characteristics as the major determinant of learning outcomes, sociological analyses of learning thus take student and teacher perspectives and their often differing attributions of meaning to a given social situation as the starting point for explaining differences in students' problem-solving behavior and hence, learning outcomes. The patterning of such interaction is on the basis of previous social experience. For teachers, the most significant elements in this respect are likely to be their own cultural background including their own experience as a student, their professional training, and their contact with dominant professional and institutional ideologies (Broadfoot et al. 1993). For students, their attribution of meaning within social settings, their values, and their preferred modes of behavior are initially, as has been seen, likely to be strongly influenced by ascriptive criteria of gender, race, and socioeconomic background. These variables are likely to influence the "scripts" chosen by individual learners as they come to a definition of their social identity. Classroom studies have shown how students' common cultural understandings, values, and aspirations lead them to adopt a particular "script"—norms of behavior which make the students identifiable as a group in terms of their actions. The relationship between structure and action which is embodied in the concept of "script," highlights the interrelationship of social class, race, and gender in the formation of individual social identities. More generally socio-cultural research has gained prominence in recent years in highlighting the importance of culture as a mediating process in educational transmissions (Wertsch 1985, Lave 1988).

3.4 Student Subcultures

Sociologists use the term "subculture" to refer to groups which form on the basis of shared values and modes of social behavior. Although it is clear from the above that many subcultural groups found in schools and colleges are rooted in social experiences outside formal educational settings as a result of common ascribed characteristics such as race or gender or in shared cultural backgrounds, many subcultures are also formed in response to experiences within the process of education itself. The student who is constantly in receipt of negative evaluations either in response to behavior or lack of achievement is likely to try to protect his or her self-esteem by devaluing the goals of the institution and substituting an alternative set of values in which he or she can experience success. Such strategies are likely to be enhanced by the extent to which individuals can group together with other similarly disaffected students, producing the all-too-familiar reality of groups of recalcitrant students typically found in bottom streams. Earlier studies of how the structural organization of the school—notably the impact of streaming—influenced the creation of such subcultural identities have now been complemented by more interactionist accounts which document the creation of more or less enduring subcultures on the basis of the values students bring with them from the outside world. Particularly important in this respect is the influence of elements of youth subculture as this is represented in modes of dress, music, language, and leisure pursuits.

4. Conclusion

Sociological research concerning learning takes as its starting point the idea that learning is an interpersonal activity. The successful promotion of learning thus requires the teacher to be sensitive both to the intellectual needs of the learner and to the role played by the student's own self-image.

Research in the sociology of learning highlights the considerable range of social factors within the classroom, the school, the home, and the peer group which affect the process of learning. It provides insights into the organizational imperatives which determine many of the characteristic features of classroom interaction and thus of the extreme difficulties teachers face in seeking to respond appropriately within such learning contexts to students' individual and social differences. It leads to the conclusion that there is often a deep incompatibility between current forms of formal educational provision and the learning needs of students. The effect of this is that many students turn away from formal education without fulfilling their potential as learners.

See also: Classical Sociological Theories of Education; Contemporary Sociological Theories of Education; Social Mobility, Social Stratification, and Education; Social Psychological Theories in Education; Socialization; Stratification in Educational Systems; Youth Cultures and Subcultures

References

Barnes D 1976 *From Communication to Curriculum*. Penguin Education, Harmondsworth

Bennett N, Desforges C, Cockburn A, Wilkinson B 1984 *The Quality of Pupil Learning Experiences*. Lawrence Erlbaum Associates, London

Bonniol J J 1991 The mechanism regulating the learning process of pupils. In: Weston P (ed.) 1991 *Assessment of Pupil Achievement, Motivation and School Success*. Council of Europe/Swets and Zeitlinger, Amsterdam

Broadfoot P, Gilly M, Osburn M, Brucher A 1993 *Perceptions of Teaching: Primary School Teachers in England and France*. Cassell, London

Cazden C 1988 *Classroom Discourse: The Language of Teaching and Learning*: Heinemann, Portsmouth, New Hampshire

Coleman J S et al. 1966 *Equality of Educational Opportunity*. US Government Printing Office, Washington, DC

Crooks T J 1988 The impact of classroom evaluation practices on students. *Rev. Educ. Res.* 58(4): 438–81

Douglas J W B 1964 *The Home and the School. A Study of Ability and Attainment in the Primary School*. MacGibbon and Kee, London

Floud J, Halsey A H, Martin F M 1956 *Social Class and Educational Opportunity*. Heinemann, London

Fraser B J 1986 *Classroom Environment*. Croom Helm, Sydney

Haste H 1987 Growing into rules. In: Bruner J, Haste H 1987 *Making Sense: The Child's Construction of the World*. Methuen, London

Hess R D, Azuma H 1991 Cultural support for schooling: Contrasts between Japan and the United States. *Educ. Researcher* 20(9): 2–9

Husén T 1975 *Social Influences on Educational Attainment*. Organisation for Economic Co-operation and Development, Paris

Kyriacou C 1986 *Effective Teaching in Schools*. Blackwell, Oxford

Lave J 1988 *Cognition in Practice: Mind Mathmetics and Culture in Everyday Life*. Cambridge University Press, Cambridge

Raven J 1991 *The Tragic Illusion: Educational Testing*. Trillium Press, New York

Tharp R, Gallimore R 1988 *Rousing Minds to Life: Teaching, Learning and Schooling in a Social Context*. Cambridge University Press, Cambridge

Wells C G 1987 *The Meaning Makers: Children Learning Language and Using Language to Learn*. Hodder and Stoughton

Wertsch J V 1985 *Vygotsky and the Social Formation*

of Mind. MA Thesis, Harvard University, Cambridge, Massachusetts

White M 1987 *The Japanese Educational Challenge. A Commitment to Children*. The Free Press, New York

Further Reading

Bernstein B 1961 Social class and linguistic development: A theory of social learning. In: Halsey A H, Floud J, Anderson C A (eds.) 1961 *Education, Economy and Society*. The Free Press, New York

Bernstein B 1996 *Pedagogy, Symbolic Control and Identity*. Taylor and Francis, London

Bourdieu P 1964 *Les herétiers: Les étudiants et la culture*. Editions de Minuit, Paris

Coleman J S 1961 *The Adolescent Society*. The Free Press, Glencoe

Goldthorpe J H 1980 *Social Mobility and Class Structure in Modern Britain*. Clarendon Press, Oxford

Osborn M, Broadfoot P M 1992 A lesson in progress? Primary classrooms observed in England and France. *Oxford Rev. Educ*. 18(1): 3–15

Sociology of Physical and Health Education

D. Kirk

1. Introduction: Definitions and Clarifications

The widely reported marginality of physical education and health education to the educational purposes of schools present some initial difficulties in identifying the work sociologists are currently undertaking in these areas of the curriculum. Part of the difficulty lies in their problematic status as school subjects. For instance, it is not uncommon in system and school policies and programs to see the terms "physical education" and "sport" used interchangeably. While physical educationists generally insist that these terms refer to quite separate sets of practices, in the daily activities of schools such distinctions may not be so sharply evident, further reinforcing a blurring of concepts. The problems besetting health education are rather different, but no less troublesome. While physical education at least, in most government schools systems in Western nations, enjoys the status of a distinct category of curriculum activity, health education is often incorporated into school practices as a cross-curricular theme.

A further difficulty in identifying the work of sociologists in these curriculum areas is that sociological concepts and research strategies are frequently used by researchers who neither identify themselves as sociologists nor do they publish the results of their investigations in recognizably sociological journals, preferring to locate their work instead within the more generic categories of curriculum, instructional, or educational research. Moreover, it is increasingly the case that researchers utilize traditionally sociological and anthropological research methods in hybrid forms, such as the "condensed case study" that involves short field visits to observe and interview participants in preference to prolonged immersion in a site, or utilize multimethod research designs that involve various combinations of surveys, case studies, structured, semistructured, or ethnographic interviews, field notes and respondent diaries, and historical with contemporary data sources.

In physical education where sociology has only relatively recently begun to challenge educational psychology as the dominant source of theoretical frameworks among North American researchers, it is not uncommon to find sociological methods used in studies framed by psychological theories and concepts. Evans (1986) has noted that social phenomenology has formed the dominant paradigm in the sociology of physical education in the last decade, in which actors' attempts to negotiate and make meaning through interactions with others in everyday situations are highlighted. Sparkes's (1992) more recent edited collection signaled the emergence of critical and feminist paradigms in sociological research.

It is the case that the marginal educational status of physical education is due to its grounding in practical physical activity and the often unspoken assumption among researchers that this area of education is of little sociological importance. The same troubles have bedeviled the sociological study of sport, a field of research that now seems to be overcoming this earlier neglect. At the same time, and ironically, there are few scholars in the sociology of sport field who have considered school physical education or school sport worthy of their attention. It is easy to see in this neglect or oversight the insidious workings of Cartesian dualism. However, as some of the emerging sociological research in physical education reveals, the dominant practices of teachers of physical education suggest that they too see little educational or any other relevance for their subject.

Health education has been handicapped by the tendency of curriculum developers to treat this field as a cross-curricular theme that should be integrated into other, better established curriculum activities such as physical education. In addition, school health education has been overshadowed by developments in the field of health promotion. Within this paradigm dominated by epidemiological methods, involving correlational studies with large population samples, schools tend to be conceptualized as one site among many others in which health promotion activities might take place. The concept of the health promoting school, which is currently prominent among Australian health promoters, quite appropriately views the complete school environment, including canteens or tuck shops, classroom conditions, school ethos, physical education, and so on, as vital to the success of efforts to facilitate school pupils leading healthy lifestyles. However, while advocacy for the implementation of this concept is strong, there is little sociological research that focuses on health education in schools, which some writers in this field argue is not quite the same thing as health promotion. The relative paucity of health education in school curricula may be both cause and effect of the neglect in this area.

Curriculum development in these fields in Australia has, on the one hand, raised the profile of health education, and on the other, located health education and physical education in the same key learning area of the "national curriculum," under the title Health and Physical Education. In England and Wales, in contrast, health education has become a cross-curricular activity. However, this conjoining of fields of study in contemporary curriculum development in Australia re-affirms a traditional relationship between these fields. In both Australia and Britain, physical training and school medical inspection were closely associated in educational policy between 1909 and the 1930s, with physical training in Britain under the direct control of school medical services. More recently, physical educators have embraced a form of their subject in Australia, Britain, and North America that has been health based and has taken as its central goal the improvement of children's health through exercise.

These problems contributing to the location and identification of sociological research in physical education and health education are not insurmountable, however, and in physical education particularly there is an emerging body of sociological knowledge within some clearly discernible strands of programmatic research. At the same time, these problems do help to explain, at least in part, why sociological research in these fields of education is relatively recent.

2. Physical Education

Since the late 1960s, there has been an emerging and diverse literature in the sociology of physical education. An excellent overview of this early research is provided by Evans and Davies (1986). The focus in this article is on the accelerating production of research-based material since the early 1980s in those areas of the sociology of physical education that have attracted the interests of a critical mass of researchers. These key areas are teaching and teacher education, the construction of gender, and curriculum policy and practice. In the space available for this article, it has only been possible to cite some of the key studies in each of these areas, and I make no claims to an exhaustive overview of the literature. There are three categories of publication cited here. Priority and greatest attention has been given to publications that are data-based and report findings of original sociological research. A second category is the review paper, and where these are available they have been cited to direct the readers' attention to syntheses of bodies of data-based reports. A third category is the conceptual paper, that is concerned with the analysis of concepts and ideas, and a smaller number of these have been cited.

2.1 Teaching and Teacher Education

The study of teachers and teaching makes up a substantial category of research activity in the sociology of physical education. This interest in teachers is not surprising given that many researchers began their careers as teachers of physical education, and as teacher educators as well as researchers, many have ready access to student teachers. Within this literature, socialization into teaching has been a central organizing concept in research programs. It has also been influential in steering researchers towards a more recent interest in teachers' lives and careers and, more recently still, researchers have turned their attention to teachers' work and to their interpretations of the forces that operate on their day to day practices.

A substantial literature also exists that comprises the results of systematic observations of teacher behavior and teacher thinking. This research is not included here since it is almost entirely informed by psychological theories and untilizes psychometric instrumentation or similar techniques for data collection. The sociological research conducted to date on teaching, particularly in relation to teachers' work, is outlined below.

The cyclical process of recruitment of physical education teachers, their acquisition of the knowledges, values, and practices of the profession during preservice teacher education courses, their induction into the workplace, and their subsequent career paths have been subject to much critical scrutiny by sociologists who have conceptualized this process as one of the socialization into physical education teaching. In two important collections of research studies edited by Templin and Schempp (1989) and Stroot (1993), socialization is considered to be a dialectical process involving the dynamic interplay between self-identity and collective practices of physical educators that results in the production of professional identities. Research into each of these key stages of the socialization process have been overviewed by the authors contributing to the Stroot (1993) collection, and some of the key findings summarized.

2.1.1 Recruitment into teaching. At the recruitment stage, the early work of Lawson (1983) and Dewar and Lawson (1984) reported that the subjective warrant for entering a career in physical education teaching included the prospects of continuing association with sport and physical activity at which prospective student teachers has already excelled, opportunities to work with people and offer a service to the community, and the promise of good working conditions. More recent research reported by Hutchinson (1993) suggests that these and other orientations formed before entry to the field are likely to persist throughout and beyond a teacher education course. In a critical analysis of the recruitment phase, Dewar (1989) argued that a prospective recruit's experience of school physical education has a significant influence on the early formation of beliefs about the work of teachers of physical education.

2.1.2 Teacher education. Professional preparation has been recognized as an agent of socialization into teaching (Graber 1989), and Templin and Schempp (1989) report that as a consequence considerable attention has been directed to the structure of preservice teacher education courses (e.g., Fernandez-Balboa 1997, Kirk et al. 1997, Evans 1995). However, Doolittle et al. (1993), in their consideration of the effects of teacher education programs on altering the entry beliefs of student teachers, suggest that preservice courses typically have a low impact on these beliefs. This claim is supported by Rovegno (1992, 1993) who has shown that preservice teacher education can with some difficulty assist student teachers to overcome cultural templates and adopt a socially critical perspective in teaching physical education. Doolittle and Schwager (1989) and Tinning et al. (1996) have made tentative claims that inservice teacher education can make a positive contribution to ongoing professional development.

2.1.3 Entry into the workforce. Stroot et al. (1993) provide an overview of the research on the induction of beginning physical education teachers into the workforce and note that young teachers experience reality shock, role conflict, isolation, and a washout effect during the first year of teaching. Macdonald (Macdonald 1995, Macdonald et al. 1994, Hutchins and Macdonald 1993) has extended this research by reporting on factors contributing to a high attrition rate among beginning teachers of physical education, including a trend towards proletarianization in the context of the rise to prominence of other vocational applications of the field of human movement studies such as exercise management and prescription.

2.1.4 Teacher's work, lives, and careers. An emerging program of research has begun to attend increasingly to teachers' work, building on Lawson's (1989) framework for understanding workplace conditions (Stroot and Lawson 1993). Additional research, pioneered by Sparkes and his colleagues (Sparkes et al. 1993, Squires and Sparkes 1996), has used a life history approach to understanding teachers' lives and careers, and has produced explanations of teachers' motivations for and interests in remaining in or leaving teaching. Supplemented by interview and survey-based research (e.g., Evans and Williams 1989, Macdonald 1993), these studies suggest that gender and social class play a key role in the formation of teacher professional identity and teachers' abilities to access opportunities that enhance promotion prospects. Ennis and her colleagues (Ennis and Chen 1993, Ennis 1992) have developed a research program centered on the investigation of teacher value orientations for teaching physical education and the effects of value orientations on teaching practices and program development. They have also noted the influence of experience on value orientations of teachers. Rovengno's (Rovegno and Bandauer 1997) two-year participant observer study with a collaborating school teacher in which researcher and teacher together developed and taught a critical approach to child-designed games in an elementary school signals a new participatory form of sociological research on teaching. Rovegno's program might be viewed as a development of Tinning's work with action research in teacher professional development (Tinning 1987, Tinning et al. 1996).

2.2 The Social Construction of Gender

As a professional body of physical educators began to emerge in the first half of the twentieth century, they were strictly segregated in their training according to the sex of the individual (Kirk 1992). Due to this single-sex training, gendered forms of physical education have vied with each other for a dominant place in school programs. In the last 30 years, a form of physical education sponsored principally by male physical educators with competitive team games at its core has come to dominate school programs in Australia, Britain, and parts of North America. Fletcher's historical sociology of the female tradition in English physical education has shown that progressive desegregation of courses from the mid-1960s has resulted in the marginalization of a distinctly feminine version of the subject, best exemplified by activities such as modern educational dance and educational gymnastics (Fletcher 1984). In this context, a significant research program has developed around the topic of the social construction of gender in and through physical education, focusing particularly on girls' and women's experiences of physical education and physical education teacher education.

Griffin utilized ethnographic methods in a study of gender in coeducational middle school physical education (Griffin 1984, Griffin 1985). She noted that patterns of interaction between students and subsequent opportunities to learn were heavily influenced by the sex of the students. While she noted considerable variation in participation styles within the sexes, much of the boys' conduct was characterized by overtly physical and aggressive forms of behavior and public clowning, while girls' behavior was characterized by cooperation and verbal communication. She noted that girls were regularly hassled by boys to give up equipment or for taking an activity seriously, and that boys often delimited the range of their own potential learning experiences by ridiculing as "sissy" or for "wimps" some forms of physical activity. As a result of these studies, Griffin (1989) argued that gender is a key socializing agent in physical education and a major mediating factor in student learning.

Scraton's study of gender and girls' physical education, completed as a Ph.D. in 1988 and published in book form in 1992 (Scraton 1992), sought to locate girls' experiences of physical activity in schools within a broad framework of women's oppression within a patriarchal society. She also intended to contribute to feminist theory at a time when there was little serious attention being paid to "the physical" by feminist scholars. Scraton showed how images of femininity and gender-appropriate behavior were constructed and legitimated through girls' experiences of physical education. Methodologically, Scraton attempted to examine together both the structures of power and ideological positions represented within them and their instantiation within school practices. Her research had political purposes, and sought to outline possibilities in and through physical education for the emancipation of women (Scraton and Flintoff 1992).

Given the long history of sex segregation in physical education teacher education, studies by Flintoff (1993) and Dewar (1990) have been particularly important. Both studies, again utilizing ethnographic methods, examined the social construction of gender and the reproduction of gender inequalities at a time when physical education teacher education institutions have been required through legislation to move towards desegregated, coeducational arrangements both in Europe and North America. In both studies, the researchers found that women were forced to negotiate forms of gender and sexual identity that were regarded as appropriate to the dominant masculinist ethos of the institutions. In Dewar's study, for example, women negotiated identities within the physical education teacher education peer group that could be grouped around a "prissy," ultrafeminine identity, a "jock" identity that involved some women displaying strongly masculine behaviors, and a "dyke" identity of lesbian students. Flintoff's and Dewar's studies have important implications for school physical education and suggest that physical education teacher education faces serious future challenges in addressing issues of the social construction of gender.

Wright's study of teacher talk and its contribution to the construction of gendered subjectivity in physical education is one of the few sociological studies of physical education to employ the analytical tools of social semiotics utilizing audio and video recordings of lessons in addition to standard ethnographic methods (Wright 1993, Wright and King 1991). Her findings supported those of Griffin and Scraton to the extent that girls were represented through teacher talk as being in deficit of qualities the teachers valued, such as skillfulness, perseverance and application, and toughness. The language teachers used to communicate with students revealed deeply entrenched expectations of appropriate gendered behavior of girls and boys, lending support to Martinek's (1981) earlier research on the Pygmalion effect. Wright's research, informed by a feminist poststructuralist methodology that attempts to contain researcher biography and political purposes, temporal and structural moments, and discursive and reflexive consciousness within the frame of analysis (Wright 1997), demonstrates the increasing sophistication of sociological research in physical education.

Feminist studies on girls' and on the construction of femininity remain the predominant form of research on gender within the sociology of physical education literature. While boys have been included in some studies of gender, such as Griffin's, their participation in physical education has tended not to be conceptualized as a means of the social construction of masculinity. An emerging line of research has now begun to examine boys' experiences of physical education and sport (Fitzclarence 1995, Kirk and Wright 1995, Connell 1989, Walker 1988) and outdoor adventure activities (Humberstone 1990) in the making of masculinities. However, this research has yet to match the volume of studies on masculinity and sport (cf. Messner and Sabo 1990).

2.3 Curriculum Policy and Practice

A third substantial program of research in the sociology of physical education has been concerned with curriculum policy and practice. These two points of focus have sometimes been treated as distinct topics of study. However, Evans et al. (1996) have proposed that they form a continuum of activities in which policy is made in a range of sites, including the offices of specialized curriculum developers and policymakers, and also in school and classroom practice. Much of the research in this strand has tended to focus on specific contemporary curriculum developments and their impact on school practices, and this has led some researchers to examine explicitly the processes of change in physical education, both within specific sites such as schools, and across sites and systems. In this section, we overview studies of contemporary curriculum policy and practice before examining the specific issue of the processes of innovation and change. The section concludes with a brief summary of a relatively neglected dimension in the continuum of curriculum research, which is student perspectives on and participation in physical education.

2.3.1 Contemporary practices. The combined results of research studies of contemporary practice since the mid-1980s demonstrate accelerating curriculum development in physical education as a result, in some cases, of shifts in social values and in others, of system wide changes to education in a number of countries. A feature of much of this research has been attempts by sociologists to locate and understand the particular forms of physical education instantiated in curriculum documents and in school policies and practices within broader social or system wide forces.

The emergence of health-based forms of physical education have been a widely investigated development in the first category. Studies by Colquhoun (1990), Tinning and Kirk (1991), Devis and Piero (1992), and Kimiecik and Lawson (1996) have utilized data from surveys, document analysis, and teacher and student interviews to locate these developments within a new health consciousness among the middle classes of many Western countries. These studies report that a typical outcome of health-based developments has been a narrowing of program goals and content to focus almost exclusively on improving the physical fitness of children through exercise while ignoring or reducing the importance of other potential educational outcomes for physical education.

A second and more recent development of major significance in this former category has been sport education. The series of interventive studies by Alexander and his colleagues in Western Australia has involved national and international collaboration with researchers in New Zealand and the USA. Alexander et al. (1996) have reported that this form of physical education which models competitive sport competitions, including the allocation of roles such as player, coach, administrator, and reporter, and competitions between teams and leagues played within seasons, can produce wide-ranging changes to school practices, such as improved student participation and learning and new forms of teaching.

Physical educators' attempts to respond to system wide changes in education have been widely researched by sociologists. Fitzclarence and Tinning (1990) found considerable resistance from teachers to the development of a new form of physical education in conjunction with the Victorian Certificate of Education for Years 11 and 12 students. They suggested that the former High School Certificate version of physical education was based on a hegemonic form of the competitive academic curriculum in which high status, scientific and propositional knowledge is valued, which worked against the successful implementation of the new curriculum. Macdonald and Brooker (1997a, 1997b) studied the trailing of a new Senior School Syllabus in Physical Education in Queensland and concluded that a strength of the Syllabus, based on Arnold's model of learning in, through, and about physical activity, was its integration of "theory" and "practice" and its challenge to the mind/body dualism

that often characterizes thinking about curriculum in physical education. However, they warn that the syllabus's strong academic foundations and intensive assessment procedures, factors frequently seen as the panacea for the subject in terms of its status and credibility, bring their own problems with respect to students' access and outcomes. Questions of how schools select and assess subject matter in ways which are equitable for students of, for example, different sexes, abilities, socio-cultural backgrounds, and body shapes remained unresolved as the development project entered the pilot phase.

An Australian study that ran parallel to the implementation of the Health and Physical Education Statement and Profile through teacher professional development in Queensland and Victoria reported that the success of a teacher-inquiry approach was uneven across schools and highly vulnerable to the levels of support made available to teachers within schools, particularly support from colleagues and administrators. This project also reported that the conceptualization of the curriculum as a series of key learning areas rather than as subjects had significant consequences for the implementation process. In particular, researchers reported that teacher professional identities were threatened, knowledge boundaries and responsibilities were ambiguous and a source of conflict, and new forms of teacher collaboration were required to overcome these problems (Macdonald and Kirk 1996, Macdonald and Glover 1997).

Evans and his colleagues have focused much of their research since the late 1980s on the effects of the Educational Reform Act (ERA) of 1988 in England and Wales on the provision of physical education and sport in schools and on the implementation of a National Curriculum for Physical Education. This research program has produced an analysis of the ideological forces shaping the government's positioning of physical education within the school curriculum which has tended towards a conservative, traditional orientation celebrating masculine values and competitive sport (Evans 1990). It has also produced a thorough examination of the interdependent roles of government agencies, local education authorities, and schools in constructing a delimited range of forms physical education might take, restricted predominantly to performance in sport and games. Evans et al. (1996), and Penney and Evans (1995, 1996) argue that as a result of the interactions between these three levels of policy creation and implementation, serious inequities remain in terms of children's access to a broad and balanced experience of physical education that the ERA was intended to assure.

2.3.2 Innovation and change. In this context of accelerating developments in physical education due to societal and education system changes, some researchers have focused on the change process itself, the ways in which change is managed by teachers, and some of the broader forces that create changes in curriculum policy and practice. Given the considerable number of potential vantage points from which the change process might be viewed, researchers have employed a range of approaches to understanding change, including studies of the micropolitics of change within schools, the nature of change processes within systems of education, and the processes of change across time.

Studies by Bell (1986) Kirk (1988), and Sparkes (1990) used ethnographic research methods to investigate the micropolitics of innovation within school physical education departments and reported on teachers' attempts to manage change. Bell reported that in the schools he studied, the prescriptions of some advocates for rational change were irrelevant and that teachers reacted to new situations and circumstances in an ad hoc fashion. Investigating change processes initiated by teachers, both Kirk and Sparkes demonstrated the complex micropolitics of teachers' participation within a professional context structured by costs and rewards. In both studies, teachers constructed a formal doctrine or used strategic rhetoric to represent their innovative work to others that did not match their practices, signaling that change was in some ways superficial. All three studies revealed that change at local levels is a complex process and that the possibilities of bringing about what Sparkes (1990) described as deep change is extremely difficult, since this required a fundamental shift in teachers' values.

Further layers of complexity are added when the impact on schools of system-wide change is considered. In this context, researchers such as Williams (1985), Evans (1990), and Kirk (1990) have utilized the work of sociologists of education such as William Reid and Basil Bernstein in order to theorize the interdependent relationships between sites in education systems. Each of these studies has demonstrated tensions between the ideological and bureaucratic structuring of teachers' actions on the one hand, and the significant transformation of innovative ideas by teachers on the other. Research into teachers' lives and careers discussed in Section 2.1.4 adds further layers of complexity to the change process.

Utilizing a combination of historical materials and sociological concepts, a final set of studies has focused on the change process in physical education over longer cycles of time than the studies previously mentioned. Hargreaves (1986), drawing on a post-Marxist framework, argued that physical education and sport in schools has been a key site for the production of unequal relations of class, race and sex, and that it remains instrumental in reproducing power and culture through practices of schooling bodies. More recently, Kirk (1992, 1994) and Wright (1996) have used historical materials to understand change processes over time that have resulted in various forms of crisis in contemporary physical education discourse.

2.3.3 Student perspectives and participation. The study of students has appeared somewhat erratically in the sociology of physical education literature, perhaps due to the dual effects of the dominance of disciplines such as psychology in the measurement of student behavior and to the overwhelming interest of sociologists in other topics such as teachers, gender, and curriculum. Sociologists have conducted two forms of research that has included students, studies of participation, and studies of attitudes and identity. In the case of the latter focus, much of this research is dispersed throughout the research literature and linked to other topics such as gender (Kirk and Tinning 1994), drop-out from sport (Robertson 1988), and student alienation (Carlson 1995).

The majority of research on students has involved surveys of participation. Research using surveys usually require students to self-report their participation levels and various likes and dislikes in relation to school physical education and sport. This form of research tends to conceptualize participation and attitudes as indicators of the effects of physical education programs. Surveys by Clough and Trail (1993) and the Australian Sports Commission (1991) are good examples of this genre of research. Participation results from individual studies are by themselves difficult to interpret. One of the few significant patterns to emerge from these studies is that levels of participation begin to taper significantly along with positive attitudes towards physical education with the onset of adolescence, a process that disproportionately involves girls. Another finding that emerges regularly from such surveys is that young people in the main have positive attitudes towards participation in physical activity but are often discouraged by overcompetitive attitudes among peers, teachers, and other adults.

3. Health Education

Approaches to health education through physical education have been a feature of new programs in schools during the 1980s, and research on this topic has been reviewed earlier in the article. There exists a burgeoning literature on the sociology of health, though almost none of that material addresses issues of health education. There is also a growing literature on health education and allied topics such as drug education, AIDS education, and so on, but only a fraction of this research could be characterized as sociological. In some cases, such as the study by Poltnikoff et al. (1996), questionnaire data is used to supplement exercise, dietary, and other data. Much of this literature consists of reports of large-scale epidemiological studies of variables affecting health. For the reasons outlined in the introduction to this article, the meagre output of sociological research in health education cannot match the relatively extensive body of knowledge that has been produced by researchers in physical education. It is difficult to imagine conducting extensive curriculum policy and practice research on a curriculum topic that, until recently, rarely existed as a distinct school subject. Since there have been few cases of health education as a subject in school curricula, it is not surprising to find that there have been few health education teachers designated as such, and virtually no specialist teacher education programs.

Colquhoun (1995) outlines one of the few programs of sociological research in health education that is currently underway in Australia. The collection of evaluation reports of the Health in Primary Schools Project edited by Went (1991) contains some studies that clearly utilized sociological concepts and research methods, while the series of case studies in drug education by Garbutcheon-Singh (1989) are mostly interview and observation based. Lawson's research program in the United States (Lawson 1992, 1994) draws extensively on sociological concepts within a community action framework.

The fact that this situation has begun to change suggests that there may well be an upsurge in interest in sociological research in health education during the next decade. In the Australian states of Victoria and Queensland, where Health Education is offered as a senior school subject that counts towards university entrance, sociological research is already in progress in masters and doctoral research programs. In New South Wales, where a key learning area (KLA) approach was adopted earlier than other Australian states, an interview-based study using focus groups investigated the integration of formerly separate subject areas through the Personal Development, Health and Physical Education KLA (Williams et al. 1994). If health education gains greater prominence in the school curriculum through either means, it seems likely that there will be an increase in research in this area.

4. Conclusion

A critical mass of sociological research in physical education has developed in relation to teaching and teacher education, the social construction of gender and curriculum policy and practice. Other noteworthy research activities can also be found in the research literature, such as research on youth culture and physical education, and the relationship between school and junior community based sport participation. However, systematic research programs conducted by a critical mass of scholars have yet to emerge in this area. The establishment of journals such as *Sport, Education and Society* and *Pedagogy in Practice* have provided new outlets for sociological research in physical education, while established journals such as *The Journal of Teaching in Physical Education* are now publishing more sociological material. These developments augur well for a field of research in the sociology of education that is fast growing to maturity. As this article

suggests, sociological research in health education is still in its infancy, though new possibilities appear to be emerging with curriculum developments in school systems. It remains to be seen whether the outlets for publication of research in this field will become available.

See also: Sociology of Teaching; Teacher Recruitment and Induction; Teaching, Social Status

References

Alexander K, Taggart A, Thorpe S 1996 A spring in their steps? Possibilities for professional renewal through sport education in Australian schools. *Sport, Educ. and Society* 1(1): 23–46
Australian Sports Commission 1991 *Sport for Young Australians.* Australian Sports Commission, Canberra, Australia
Bell L 1986 Managing to survive in secondary school physical education. In: Evans J (ed.) 1986
Carlson T B 1995 We hate gym: Student alienation from physical education. *J. Teach. Phys. Educ.* 14: 467–77
Clough J, Trail R 1993 A mapping of participation rates in junior sport. *The ACHPER Nat. J.* 40(2): 4–7
Colquhoun D 1990 Images of healthism in health-based physical education. In: Kirk D, Tinning R (eds.) 1990 *Physical Education. Curriculum and Culture* Falmer, Lewes
Colquhoun D 1995 Post positivist research in health education. In: Jensen B B (ed.) *Research in Environmental and Health Education.* The Royal Danish School of Educational Studies, Copenhagen
Connell R W 1989 Cool guys, swots and wimps: the interplay of masculinity and education. *Oxford Rev. Educ.* 15(3): 291–303
Devis J, Piero C 1992 Exercise and health in a Spanish PE curriculum. In: Williams T, Almond L, Sparkes A (eds.) 1992 *Sport and Physical Activity* Spon, London
Dewar A 1989 Recruitment in physical education teaching: Toward a critical approach. In: Templin T J and Schempp P G (eds.) 1989 *Socialization into Physical Education Indianapolis*: Benchmark, Indianapolis, Indiana
Dewar A 1990 Oppression and privilege in physical education: Struggles in the negotiation of gender in a university program. In: Kirk D, Tinning R (eds.) 1990 *Physical Education, Curriculum and Culture.* Falmer, Lewes
Dewar A, Lawson H A 1984 The subjective warrant and recruitment into physical education. *Quest* 36: 15–25
Doolittle S A, Dodds P, Placek J H 1993 Persistence of beliefs about teaching during formal training of preservice teachers. *J. Teach. Phys. Educ.* 12(4): 355–64
Doolittle S, Schwager S 1989 Socialization and inservice education. In: Templin T J, Schempp P G (eds.) 1989
Ennis C D 1992 The influence of value orientations in curriculum decision making. *Quest* 44: 317–29
Ennis C D, Chen A 1993 Domain specifications and content representativeness of the revised Values Orientation Inventory. *Res. Q. Exercise and Sport* 64: 436–46
Evans J 1986 (ed.) *Physical Education, Sport and Schooling: Studies in the Sociology of Physical Education.* Falmer, Lewes
Evans J 1990 Defining the subject; The rise and rise of the New PE. *Br. J. Sociol. Educ.* 11(2): 155–69

Evans J 1995 Reconstructing teacher education *Eur. Phys. Educ. Rev.* 1(2): 111–21

Evans J, Davies B 1986 Sociology, schooling and physical education. In: Evans J (ed.) 1986

Evans J, Penney D, Davies B 1996 Back to the future? Education policy and PE. In: Armstrong N (ed.) 1996 *New Directions in Physical Education: Change and Innovation*. Cassell, London

Evans J, Penney D, Bryant A, Hennick M 1996 All things bright and beautiful? PE in primary schools post the 1988 ERA. *Educ. Rev.* 48(1): 29–40

Evans J, Williams T 1989 Moving up and getting out: The classed and gendered career opportunities of physical education. In: Templin T J, Schempp P G (eds.) 1989

Fernandez-Balboa J-M 1997 Knowledge base for physical education teacher education: A proposal for a new era. *Quest* 49(2): 161–81

Fletcher S 1984 *Women First: The Female Tradition in English Physical Education, 1880–1980* Althone, London

Flintoff A 1993 Gender, physical education and initial teacher education. In: Evans J (ed.) 1993 *Equality, Education and Physical Education*. Falmer, London

Fitzclarence L 1995 Education's shadow? Towards an understanding of violence in schools. *Aust. J. Educ.* 39(1): 22–40

Fitzclarence L, Tinning R 1990 Challenging hegemonic physical education: Contextualising physical education as an examinable subject. In: Kirk D, Tinning R (eds.) 1990 *Physical Education, Curriculum and Culture*. Falmer, Lewes

Garbutcheon-Singh L 1989 *Case Studies in Drug Education* (6 Volumes). Deakin Institute for Studies in Education, Geelong, Australia

Graber K C 1989 Teaching tomorrow's teachers: Professional preparation as an agent of socialization. In: Templin T J, Schempp P G (eds.) 1989 *Socialization into Physical Education*, Benchmark, Indianapolis, Indiana

Griffin P 1984 Girls' participation patterns in a middle school team sports unit *J. Teach. Phys. Educ.* 4(1): 30–8

Griffin P 1985 Boys' participation styles in a middle school team sports unit. *J. Teach. Phys. Educ.* 4(2): 100–10

Griffin P 1989 Gender as a socializing agent in physical education. In: Templin T J, Schempp P G (eds.) 1989

Hargreaves J 1986 *Sport, Power and Culture*. Polity Press, Cambridge

Humberstone B 1990 Warriors or wimps? Creating alternative forms of PE. In: Messner M, Sabo D (eds.) 1990

Hutchins C, Macdonald D 1993 Beginning physical education teachers and early career decision-making. *Phys. Educ. Rev*, 16(2): 151–60

Hutchinson G E 1992 Prospective teachers' perspectives on teaching physical education: An interview study on the recruitment phase of teacher socialization. *J. Teach. Phys. Educ.* 12(4): 244–54

Kimiecik J, Lawson H A 1996 Toward new approaches for exercise behavior change and health promotion. *Quest* 48(1): 102–25

Kirk D 1988 Ideology and school-centred innovation: A case study and a critique. *J. Curric. St.* 20(5): 449–64

Kirk D 1990 School knowledge and the curriculum package-as-text. *J. Curric. St.* 22(5): 409–25

Kirk D 1992 *Defining Physical Education: The Social Construction of a School Subject in Postwar Britain*. Falmer, London

Kirk D 1994 Making the Present Strange': Sources of the current crisis in physical education. *Discourse: The Aust. J. Educ. Studies* 15(1): 46–63

Kirk D, Macdonald D, Tinning R 1997 The social construction of pedagogic discourse in physical education teacher education in Australia. *Curric. J.* 8(2): 269–96

Kirk D, Tinning R 1994 Embodied self-identity, healthy lifestyles and school physical education. *Sociol. Health and Illness: J. Med. Sociol.* 16(5): 600–25

Kirk D, Wright J 1995 The social construction of bodies: Implications for the health and physical education curriculum. *Unicorn* 21(4): 63–73

Lawson H A 1983 Toward a model of teacher socialization in physical education: The subjective warrant, recruitment and teacher education. *J. Teach. Phys. Educ.* 2(3): 3–16

Lawson H A 1989 From rookie to veteran: Workplace conditions in physical education and induction into the profession. In: Templin T J, Schempp P G (eds.) 1989

Lawson H A 1992 Toward a socioecological conception of health. *Quest* 44: 105–21

Lawson H A 1994 Toward healthy learners, schools and communities. *J. Teach. Educ.* 45: 62–70

Macdonald D 1993 Knowledge, gender and power in physical education teacher education. *Aust. J. Educ.* 37(3): 259–78

Macdonald D 1995 The role of proletarianization in physical education teacher attrition. *Res. Q. Exercise Sport* 66(2): 129–41

Macdonald D, Brooker R 1997a Moving beyond the crisis in secondary physical education: An Australian initiative. *J Teach. Phys. Educ.* 16(2): 155–75

Macdonald D, Brooker R 1997b Accountability issues in a performance-based subject: a case study of senior physical education. *Stud. Educ. Eval.* 23(1): 83–102

Macdonald D, Glover S 1997 Subject matter boundaries and curriculum change in the Health and Physical Education key learning area. *Curric. Perspectives.* 17(1): 23–30

Macdonald D, Kirk D 1996 Mapping current practice against the Curriculum Profile in the Health and Physical Education key learning area. *ACHPER Healthy Lifestyles J.* 43(3): 8–11

Macdonald D, Hutchins C, Madden J 1994 To leave or not to leave: Health and physical education teachers' career choices. *ACHPER Healthy Lifestyles J.* 41(3): 19–22

Martinek T 1981 Pygmalion in the gym: a model for the communication of teacher expectations in physical education. *Res. Q. Exercise Sport* 52: 58–67

Messner M, Sabo D 1990 (eds.) *Sport, Men and the Gender Order*. Human Kinetics, Champaign, Illinois

Penney D, Evans J 1995 The National Curriculum for Physical Education: Entitlement for all? *Br. J. Phys. Educ.* 26(4): 6–13

Penney D, Evans J 1996 When breadth and balance means balancing the books: Curriculum planning in schools post-ERA. In: Pole C, Chawla R (eds.) 1996 *Educational Change in the 1990s: Perspectives on Secondary Schooling*. Falmer, London

Poltnikoff R, Williams P, Higginbotham N 1996 An evaluation of the Kurri Kurri public schools healthy heartbeat project. *ACHPER Healthy Lifestyles J.* 43(2): 21–5

Robertson I 1988 *The Sports Drop-Out: A Time for Change?* Australian Sports Commission, Belconnen

Rovegno I 1992 Learning a new curricular approach: Mechanisms of knowledge acquisition in preservice teachers. *Teaching and Teacher Educ.* 8: 253–64

Rovegno I 1993 Content knowledge acquisition during undergraduate teacher education: Overcoming cultural templates and learning through practice. *Am. Educ. Res. J.* 30: 611–42

Rovegno I, Bandauer D 1997 Psychological dispositions that facilitated and sustained the development of knowledge of a constructivist approach to physical education. *J. Teach. Phys. Educ.* 16: 136–54

Scraton S 1992 *Shaping Up to Womanhood: Gender and Girls' Physical Education*. Open University Press, Milton Keynes

Scraton S, Flintoff A 1992 Feminist research and physical education. In: Sparkes A C (ed.) 1992

Sparkes A C 1990 *Curriculum Change and Physical Education: Towards a Micropolitical Understanding*. Deakin University Press, Geelong

Sparkes A C 1992 (ed.) *Research in Physical Education and Sport: Exploring Alternative Visions*. Falmer, London

Sparkes A C, Templin T J, Schempp P G 1993 Exploring dimensions of marginality: Reflecting on the life histories of physical education teachers. *J. Teach. Phys. Educ.* 12(4) 368–98

Squires S L, Sparkes A C 1996 Circles of silence: Sexual identity in physical education and sport. *Sport, Education and Society* 1(1): 77–102

Stroot S A 1993 (ed.) *Socialization Into Physical Education*, Special Issue. *J. Teach. Phys. Educ.* 12(4)

Stroot S A, Faucette N, Schwager S 1993 In the beginning: The induction of physical educators. *J. Teach. Phys. Educ.* 12(4): 375–85

Stroot S A, Lawson H A 1993 Footprints and signposts: Perspectives on socialization research. *J. Teach. Phys. Educ.* 12(4): 437–46

Templin T J, Schempp P G 1989 (eds.) *Socialization into Physical Education*. Benchmark, Indianapolis, Indiana

Tinning R 1987 Beyond the development of a utilitarian teaching perspective: An Australian case study of action research in teacher preparation. In: Barrette G, Fiengold R, Rees R, Pieron M (eds.) 1987 *Myths, Models and Methods in Sport Pedagogy*. Human Kinetics, Champaign, Illinois

Tinning R, Kirk D 1991 *Daily Physical Education: Collected Papers on Health Based Physical Education in Australia*. Deakin University Press, Geelong

Tinning R, Macdonald D, Boustead J, Tregenza K 1996 Action research and the professional development of teachers in the health and physical education field. *J. Educ. Action Res.* 4(2): 391–406

Walker J C 1988 *Louts and Legends*. Allen & Unwin, Sydney

Went S 1991 *A Health Start: Holistic Approaches to Health Promotion In School Communities*. Monash University, Melbourne

Williams P, Williams M, Guray C, Bertram A, Brenton R, McCormack A 1994 Perceived barriers to implementing a new integrated curriculum. *Curric. Perspectives* 14(1): 17–24

Williams A E 1985 Understanding constraints on innovation in physical education. *J. Curric. St.* 17(4): 407–13

Wright J 1993 Regulation and resistance: The physical education lesson as speech genre. *Social Semiotics* 3: 23–56

Wright J 1996 Mapping the discourse of physical education: Articulating a female tradition. *J. Curric. St.* 28(3): 331–52

Wright J 1997 A feminist poststructuralist methodology for the study of gender construction in physical education: description of a study. *J. Teach. Phys. Educ.* 15(1): 1–24

Wright J, King R C 1991 'I say what I mean', said Alice: An analysis of gendered discourse in physical education. *J. Teach. Phys. Educ.* 10: 210–25

Sociology of Special Education

C. Milofsky

The sociology of special education derives from a contrast between the "medical model" of disability and the social system model. Special education refers to school programs that serve children with physical, cognitive, or emotional disabilities through classes that are separate from those of the regular or mainstream school. Most special education programs are legitimated by the belief that the students suffer personal defects of some kind, whether they be neural lesions associated with learning disabilities or mental retardation, emotional pathologies, or physiological deficits that limit students' abilities to profit from the mainstream school environment.

Sociologists argue that these hypothesized personal defects in students are socially constructed. Research has focused on three ways in which social systems have promoted the creation of special student categories and programs: (a) class, cultural, or political conflicts in society that identify some students as threatening to the school order; (b) social problems that are "medicalized" to hide people's reluctance or inability to address social aspects of those problems; and (c) organizational dynamics from which there emerges a need to control certain students so that they do not disrupt or undermine the regular school program.

1. Special Education and the Broader Society

Since the turn of the twentieth century when Binet invented his individual intelligence scale to identify retarded children in the public schools of Paris (Sarason 1976, Sarason and Doris 1979), special education has had a significance that has transcended the difficulties of teaching children with cognitive disabilities. Explanations of why children fail in school, and why poor school performance tends to be concentrated in the lower socioeconomic classes and in certain ethnic minorities, have directly affected immigration and economic policies throughout the industrialized world.

Arguments that cognitive disabilities have a physiological basis and/or genetic causes were instrumental in the passage of immigration restrictions in the United States during the 1920s (Kamin 1974), and in developing policies of eugenic sterilization. Disbelief in physiological theories led some countries to undertake radical work-training policies for the retarded with surprising results. Labor shortages in postwar Europe led some countries to train retardates for factory work, allowing them to live independent lives in the long term. When Israel inherited a large population of war ophans, believed to be retarded because of deprivation and emotional shock, it developed programs based on the assumption of physiological normality that led to the rehabilitation of some who, in retrospect, were seriously disabled (Feuerstein et al. 1986).

In the wake of the United States civil rights movement, arguments about the heritability of intelligence began anew when some scholars argued that Afro-American children cannot learn as well as Whites because they have inherited mild mental retardation. In contrast, critics argued that intelligence tests are culturally biased. Categorization of minority children as mentally retarded became politically difficult in many United States school districts. A number of states passed laws that imposed administrative controls on the classification process and mandated that children "threatened" with placement in special education classes should be afforded due process.

From this perspective, special education is viewed as a variety of institutional racism. It is a way of controlling or oppressing children from ethnic minorities by placing them in stigmatizing classes with less rigorous curricula and a type of teaching that provides little chance for children to improve their educational fortunes. The notion that special education classes were a dumping ground for undesirable children provided an easy explanation for why, during the 1950s in the United States, so many classes for the mildly retarded contained mostly minority children.

When civil rights attacks were launched, a parallel movement began to expand special education classes to serve severely disabled children and those who were learning disabled. Despite growing restrictions on classes for the mentally retarded, special education generally continued to grow exponentially in many industrialized nations. The students were drawn increasingly from the middle classes and within a decade a dramatically different population was being served as special education became integrated by race and class.

On the surface, this shift undercut the argument that special education programs were serving social control functions in the schools. However, critical theorists (Barton 1986, Carrier 1986, Tomlinson 1982) argue differently. The civil rights conception of social control is a narrow one that focuses only at the level of particular schools. A broader perspective asks how elite classes use schools to control the poor and to reproduce the class structure from generation to generation, and how special education contributes to this societal control.

Critical theorists argue that over time, schools have become increasingly important as instruments of societal social control. Public school systems have become increasingly comprehensive and less disposed to exclude children for low academic achievement. As children are included in schools for more years of their lives, it becomes more difficult for educators to make sharp distinctions among them based on ability.

In this culture of inclusiveness, explanations of failure that focus on the incapacity of individuals become increasingly important as justifications for making educational distinctions. Physiological explanations are a useful expedient to make sense of why low-income children continue to fail in school despite compensatory eduction efforts. This is why the concept of learning disabilities has become so popular despite the lack of solid evidence that these cognitive deficits exist, or that schools can effectively address them in teaching programs (Coles 1987).

In an age when schools are supposed to make equal opportunity available to everyone, learning disabilities provide an explanation for why some children simply cannot profit from school programs. Thus, in the view of critical theory, special education programs represent a form of cultural control. This view explains why there is a loose relationship between the various concepts of educational handicap and what actually happens in school programs.

2. Labeling and the Medical Model

Closely parallel to the critical theory view is the application of labeling theory to special education. Mercer (1973) argued that most of the children labeled mentally retarded by public schools were what she called "situationally retarded." That is, they were retarded in the schools and nowhere else. She also claimed that what made them retarded in schools is that they were identified as retarded. This may or may not have much to do with actual behavior, performance, or cognitive ability. There is an organizational logic in schools that makes special education programs useful, and that leads some students to be pulled out of regular programs and put in special classes. The children selected for special classes are not necessarily (or not usually) the ones that a dispassionate screening program would select (McIntyre 1969).

Mercer's complaint is essentially that of the critical theorists. In her view, mental retardation worked primarily to limit the educational opportunity of Afro-American and Mexican-American students in the California school districts she studied. Intelligence tests and the very concept of mental retardation as applied in schools were culturally biased. Retardation is universally and spontaneously identified in human communities, but, she argued, diagnosis must include carefully collected data on a subject's social interaction performance in diverse institutional and community contexts.

This is almost never the case in schools (Milofsky 1986), and so children placed in special education classes represent students who are situationally retarded. They are classified retarded in schools, but they generally are socially normal elsewhere. There is reason to believe that special education students do not represent the most educationally disadvantaged children in their schools, nor the ones who are most clearly cognitively handicapped, nor the students most likely to benefit from intensive, specialized instruction.

There is a capricious or arbitrary nature to the selection process, hence the image of "labeling." Children are labeled like packages for the post office, in that an identifying mark is pasted on the outside of the package, but it has nothing to do with the contents. Unfortunately, being labeled can have long-term, devastating consequences for those affected. This is partly because labels persist as institutional records long after individuals have left programs.

More importantly, people who are labeled as retarded or learning disabled are treated as intellectually compromised people and respond in kind. A disability that might begin as a narrow and specific problem— or that may not exist at all when this interaction sequence or "career" (Goffman 1961) begins—becomes generalized into a role that shapes a child's whole identity. These are the processes of societal reaction and secondary deviation. To observers of school failure, it is the process by which stupidity is socially created (McIntyre 1969).

Mercer recognized that the concept "mental retardation" was itself a cause of difficulty because it was (and continues to be) treated as a physiological attribute of affected children—not unlike a broken leg or color blindness—that is thought to exist in an objectively measurable way. Intelligence quotient test scores are the strongest predictor of which children, among those referred for psychological evaluation and possible special education placement, will actually end up in special classes. The social context of a child's life, and the institutional dynamics that led up to referral, have little meaningful role in identifying the educationally handicapped or, generally, in shaping the management of their cases (Milofsky 1986).

Mercer saw that cognitive disability was treated as a medical problem in the narrowest sense. In the medical model, illness and disability are defined as a disruption to the biological system caused by disease, injuries or lesions, or insufficient development. Disability is contained in the body; it exists objectively in itself and it causes the problems for which someone has sought treatment and therapy. Coles (1987) argues that learning disability theorists continue to follow the medical model, ignoring the complex ways that social contexts and transactional processes shape students' lives in schools and the way that certain children are singled out as problems.

The medical model has long been rejected by social scientists. At a minimum, according to Wright (1960), it is necessary to distinguish between *disabilities* (specific physiological or psychological dysfunctions) and *handicaps* (the expression of a disability in a social role). A specific disability can have widely different social expressions, depending on the barriers to social independence an individual confronts, the social supports available to a person, and an individual's psychological coping resources.

A sensitivity to the social context was central in early writings about learning disabilities. Rather than seeing learning disabilities as severe limitations in cognitive functioning, they were understood to be a product of the restricted teaching environments that prevail in schools as well as of problems "in" children. Classrooms impose a host of specific cognitive demands on children, most of which are irrelevant to learning tasks; for example, receiving instructions aurally, transferring written instructions from vertical to horizontal surfaces, and learning to read and decode texts at 6 years old. Intellectually capable children may fail at these specific tasks, and this incapacity can trigger a sequence of failure experiences that gradually create secondary deviation—school failure or the perception of stupidity. By paying attention to the specifics of a child's cognitive mismatch with the school environment, it might then be possible to change the instructional environment so that a child's idiosyncratic cognitive style does not conflict with the institutional rigidities of the school and set off a career of secondary deviation and failure.

This is a "transactional" way to frame learning disabilities (Sarason and Doris 1979). As the medical model has dominated research on what learning disabilities are and how they may be remediated, however, the sociologically sensitive insights of this approach have mostly been lost. When theory and treatment of educational handicaps eschews careful transactional analysis, then special education ceases to address the ways that idiosyncratic learning styles are given expression in school roles of failure.

3. Organizational Control

This omission is devastating if the goal is pragmatically to address student learning problems. The behavior that is observed when any limitation of function occurs is the expression of that disability in a social role or handicap. The disability itself is generally invisible, and if it is not somehow made socially significant it is deemed unimportant. To ignore how a child's failure career evolved creates a devastating gap between theory and educational processes. The effects critical theorists complained about—special education being used to control and oppress low-income children and students from racial minorities—flows from this disconnection. There is a body of arcane theory that justifies the field, but that theory does not shape actual instruction. What goes on in special education classrooms, therefore, is often not very different from what goes on in mainstream classrooms.

The organizational structure of special education also contributes to the "nonspecialness" of special education. A cohesive body of research from the United States (Milofsky 1986), the United Kingdom (Barton 1986, Tomlinson 1982), Canada (Caspo 1984), and Australia (Fulcher 1989) argues that special education is primarily an instrument for social control in schools, and that this accounts for the gap between the manifest purposes of these programs and what they actually do. That is, special education programs exist primarily to help bring orderliness to mainstream or regular school programs. They do this by helping to remove troublesome students from regular classes and also by giving administrative support to teachers in the mainstream.

To call special education social control may sound accusatory to some. As with labeling, however, which in the end turned out to be intrinsic to the original conception of learning disability, the social control framework is a way of focusing on the interactional and strategic context in which special education programs function in schools. It will be shown that the mandate for social control also creates deep ethical and political dilemmas for special education. Recognizing the inherent organizational complexities of special education thus helps in understanding the macrosocial problems these programs raise for educational policy.

The social control perspective rests on several core organizational understandings—or assumptions—about how schools work.

First, the central task of public schooling is to educate "normal" children. "Normal" is a problematic term because integral to sensitivity to learning disability concepts is an awareness of the enormous variability in personal styles, problems, and interests that children bring to classrooms. These diverse styles can in many ways conflict with the operating regime of the schools, spawning failure careers. The main business of schools, however, is to teach children using a model that assumes little variation in the "raw material" (children) and an instructional regime that, controlling for age, varies little from classroom to classroom and school to school. (That is why it is possible to talk easily about a "school system" characteristic of each nation.)

Second, regular classroom teaching is an art, rather than a technology. This is to say that the logic of instruction mandates that teachers have a measure of autonomy in their work, however bureaucratic and controlling their school system supervisors might seek to be.

Third, more important than the personal variations in students, teachers need autonomy because regular classroom teaching requires that instructors forge a group consensus about work in their classrooms. Teachers must become authoritative leaders. Successful instruction depends on the organizational efficiencies that follow when the class accepts the pattern and legitimacy of a teacher's work routines.

To survive, teachers have to establish routines and avoid having individual confrontations with students or group conflicts that make the teacher seem other than an expert adviser to children about how they might best further their own educational programs. Authoritative leadership is an exercise in trust that is fragile, and perhaps not easily achieved in many contemporary public schools.

Fourth, because authority is fragile and also because classroom discipline has become accepted by teachers and supervisors alike as the legitimate measure of effectiveness, disruptiveness is often profoundly threatening to teachers. Much administrative problem solving in schools is directed at identifying sources of disruption, assigning blame (between teachers, principals, families, and student groups), and finding ways to resolve persistent or escalating disruptions.

Fifth, classroom disruption in this way can become a collective distrubance in the informal social fabric of a school. Disruptions have a contagious quality that make them dangerous, both in the sense that schools become physically threatening places, and in the sense that the task goals of schools become difficult to achieve.

Disruptions may involve students who act up and challenge teacher authority. Disruptions may also be quiet, involving students who do not learn well and whose needs are not addressed because teachers conclude they will require more time than they have to give. Thus, to some teachers the passivity associated with mild mental retardation can be as disruptive, in the sense of making a teacher feel inadequate and out of control, as direct confrontation from other students.

Ethnic difference can also make a teacher feel inadequate and out of control. Meanwhile, children who feel attacked for their ethnicity may band together in their rejection of schooling. This may become an active program of resistance in schools or a collective rejection of schooling by children from a specific ethnic community.

Sixth, in this context special education programs have to be understood as marginal school programs (Milofsky 1986). This is not to say that they are unimportant or invalid. Rather, they exist on the periphery of the institution, where regular school programs are the core of the institution. This means that for most people, in and out of schools, regular programs have higher priority than special programs.

Despite the various ways that special programs can proclaim their own autonomy, their own access to resources, and their right and obligation to define their own distinctive goals, the structure of special education programs is contingent on the way regular school programs work. In some contexts, enlightened people run the regular program. They understand and respect the needs and goals of the special program and create an organizational environment in which diagnoses and special teaching can proceed as envisioned in the idealistic world of academic research, curricular planning, and policy analysis that has created the legal, administrative, and intellectual superstructure of the field (Fulcher 1989, Weatherley and Lipsky 1992).

More commonly, the content of local special education programs is the product of ongoing, historically shaped negotiations between special and regular program staff at the local level. In some school systems these negotiations happen because a single administrative unit runs both programs. In this sort of arrangement regular educators tend to have more power in the system because they have larger numbers, larger budgets, and more ways to influence the broader political system. The public understands services the regular school program provides, and when there is debate about educational reform it almost always focuses on the success or failure of the regular program. Special education is ignored in these general debates, unless there is a focus on the seemingly unnecessary expenses involved in supporting special education.

Even where special and regular programs are administratively separate, special programs are dependent because the regular program controls the supply of students. Very few special education programs for the mildly handicapped select their students through independent screening programs. Students are generally recruited via a referral process that begins with recommendations from the regular classroom teacher, which are validated by the principal. Students are then passed on to a diagnostic team composed of specialists.

Having to rely on regular program staff for the raw material of special education programs means that special educators must confront and deal with regular educators' ways of defining specialness. Most regular classroom teachers and many school-level administrators (as well as higher-level administrators) have a primitive understanding of the concepts and criteria underlying learning disabilities and other cognitive handicaps. The children referred for special education screening tend to be either those who have severe problems or those whom regular teachers find troublesome and whose problems they think can be blamed on cognitive disabilities.

Referrals by regular teachers are problematic. It is reasonable to think that most of these instructors want to do the right thing for children and, by virtue of having worked with hundreds of children, that many have a finely honed sensitivity to differences in cognitive styles among their students. Most teachers also have an elaborate range of strategies to use on students who do not learn in conventional ways. They are not foolish or casual about how they assess children and many of the students referred for special education are identified by astute teachers.

At the same time, classroom disruption, conflict among school staff, and political chaos at the school system level—resulting in budget shortfalls, staff transfers, arbitrary policies, and the like—are commonplace in public schools in all countries. As conflicts and feelings of insecurity escalate, teachers and principals (and children) look for ways to defend themselves. Special education programs often represent unclaimed resources that regular staff think ought to be used to help make things better in the regular program. Special education staff in schools (teachers and school psychologists primarily) often are willing to help out. Oddly, the professional self-interest of special education staff is often served by their subversion of their own programs.

The transactional character of learning disabilities is one of the main reasons that special educators conspire to undermine the specialness of their own programs. There may be a specific cognitive disability that sets off a chain of events causing a child to assume the role of failure, but if learning disabilities are partly caused by the rigidities of organizational structure, then a sensible special educator is also a social psychologist for the schools. Special educators cannot just treat the child in isolation; they must also deal with the school context from which that child's failure emerged.

This requires that special educators immerse themselves in school politics and build alliances with educators. This is a matter of self-defense—trying to control the original selection of children for special education. It also is an exercise in primary prevention —treating learning problems in classrooms before they become crystallized as careers of failure. Often special educators' involvement includes working with teachers and administrators to address and resolve the complex interactive problems that cause children to be scapegoated by teachers as they justify their own failures.

From a transactional standpoint the only sensible way to do special education is to engage in this sort of aggressive bridge-building to the regular school staff. Definitions of failure are inextricably tied to issues of social control in classrooms and to the dynamic balance of control and autonomy in regular school administrations.

Unfortunately, the cultural politics of school funding does not allow for the allocation of money to pay for freelance specialist consultants or pressure valve programs in schools, which is what the best special education really is. Special education programs are legitimated by the cultural notion that some people are more intelligent than others for genetic and physiological reasons. Society's collective guilt that children from low-income and ethnic minority families do not succeed in schools is assuaged somewhat by these biological explanations. Society is willing to support special programs for these children, as well as for the physically disabled, and at the same time gains some leverage in justifying a high correlation between social class and school outcomes from these programs. The truly handicapped are skimmed out of the school program, it is argued, so that the people left behind have a level playing field. Achievement and failure then can be appropriately rewarded.

Cultural politics are central to the definition of special education because they provide the political legitimacy necessary for a stable funding and program base. Once a policy sponsoring special education exists, a program has to be created, children must be selected, theory must be generated, and workers must be trained. Understandably, there is a gap and some tension between special education as imagined and justified in the political system, and the sort of special education that makes sense in practice. Lip service must be paid to the political justifications for these programs.

There is a deep ethical problem embedded in special education, however. Although it may be acknowledged that transactionally oriented special educators provide a valuable service in schools and can be important protectors of children, it is also believed that for children to be helped they must be labeled. The legal and administrative meaning of those labels are rooted in the medical model and almost inevitably they distort the real character of students' school problems. Furthermore, to be effective, special educators often must be duplicitous in building their alliances with regular educators and intervening to shape the outcomes of particular cases. By its nature, special education is ethically compromised.

See also: Contemporary Sociological Theories of Education; Social Psychological Theories in Education

References

Barton L 1986 The politics of special educational needs. *Disability, Handicap and Society* 1(3): 273–90

Carrier J G 1986 *Learning Disability: Social Class and the Construction of Inequality in American Education.* Greenwood Press, New York

Caspo M 1984, Segregation, integration and beyond: A sociological perspective of special education. *British Columbia J. Spec. Educ.* 8(3): 211–29

Coles G S 1987 *The Learning Mystique. A Critical Look at Learning Disabilities.* Fawcett Columbine, New York

Feuerstein et al. 1986 Learning potential assessment. *Special Services in the Schools* 2(2–3): 85–106

Fulcher G 1989 *Disabling Policies? A Comparative Approach to Education Policy and Disability.* Falmer Press, London

Goffman E 1961 The moral career of a mental patient. In: Goffman E 1961 *Asylums.* Anchor, Garden City, New York

Kamin L 1974 *The Science and Politics of IQ.* Lawrence Erlbaum Associates, Potomac, Maryland

McIntyre D 1969 Two schools, one psychologist. In: Kaplan F, Sarason S B (eds.) 1969 *The Psycho-Educational Clinic,* Community Mental Health Monograph Series, Vol. 4. Massachusetts Department of Mental Health, Boston, Massachusetts

Mercer J 1973 *Labeling the Mentally Retarded.* University of California Press, Berkeley, California

Milofsky C 1986 Special education and social control. In: Richardson J G (ed.) 1986 *Handbook of Theory and Research for the Sociology of Education.* Greenwood Press, Westport, Connecticut

Sarason S B 1976 The unfortunate fate of Alfred Binet and school psychology. *Teach. Coll. Rec.* 77(4): 579–92

Sarason S B, Doris J 1979 *Educational Handicap, Public Policy, and Social History: A Broadened Perspective on Mental Retardation.* Free Press, New York

Tomlinson S 1982 *A Sociology of Special Education.* Routledge and Kegan Paul, London

Weatherley R, Lipsky M 1992 Street-level bureaucrats and institutional innovation: Implementing special-education reform. In: Hehir T, Latus T (eds.) 1992 *Special Education at the Century's End. Evolution of Theory and Practice Since 1970.* Harvard Educational Review, Reprint Series 23, Cambridge, Massachusetts

Wright B 1960 *Physical Disability—A Psychological Approach.* Harper and Row, New York

Sociology of Teaching

D. A. Spencer

The sociology of teaching and the role of teachers in society comprises one area of interest to sociologists of education. This area includes the examination of teachers' work in sociohistorical contexts, the description of teachers' social characteristics, and the process of socialization in teaching.

1. The Role of Teachers in Society: Sociological Perspectives

Three major theoretical perspectives have dominated sociology as analytic frameworks for understanding social structure and process: structural-functionalism, conflict theory, and interpretive theories. These theories point to the central role of teachers and educational institutions, whether in the transmission of cultural knowledge, values, and beliefs, in the reproduction of economic structures and stratification of the work force, or in the socialization process. A brief overview of their assumptions is presented as a backdrop to understanding sociologists' views on the role of education and teachers in society (see *Teachers' Roles*).

Structural-functionalism, a macro-sociological or large-scale approach, looks at societies and the interrelationship of their structures or institutions (such as education) and the functions they serve in preserving the status quo or well-being of a society. Societies are seen as systems of functionally interrelated and interdependent parts, held together and stabilized through adherence to basic values.

Emile Durkheim first wrote about education as the institution through which values are transmitted and internalized by societal members, and, in this sense, is moral in nature and intent. Moral education is thought to be the task of teachers, so their commitment to the mainstream values and beliefs of a society is crucial. Durkheim found teachers' roles quite powerful because, subject to little external supervision, they ensure cultural transmission of values from generation to generation. Thus they are instrumental in preserving the ongoing social order. While the functionalist perspective has been criticized for its conservative or even static view of society, sociologists continue to use its terminology in examining the functions of schooling in society, and teachers' roles in the transmission of ideas, values, and beliefs to students.

Conflict theorists, including Marxist and neo-Marxists, have found structural functionalism inadequate in explaining the dynamic nature of societies. Instead, they view society as a system characterized by social inequality, which generates social conflict and results in social change. The source of inequality in a society is determined by its economic organization and the unequal distribution of property or resources. Schools are seen as a crucial link between the economy and individuals' economic opportunities within the existing class structure. Furthermore, schools serve to reinforce inequality because they are controlled by powerful elites whose interests are served and whose children benefit most.

From this perspective, the work of Bowles and Gintis (1976) has been particularly influential in demonstrating how the rise of capitalism paralleled the growth of public education in the United States. They assert that schools served the capitalist class by supplying them with a ready, willing, and able supply of workers through the transmission of values which encouraged such traits as obedience to authority, punctuality, and responsibility for work. They believe a myth was (and is) created which leads the public to believe that equal educational opportunity is available to people of all social classes but that, in reality, schools reward students differentially according to their social class origins. This reproduces the social division of labor in society.

Teachers are instrumental in this reproduction process, and to the extent that they base judgments of students on their social class, they perpetuate inequality. Good examples of this process in schools in the United States are found in the work of Anyon (1980) and Page (1987), who look at teachers' judgments of students based on how students have been tracked in schools by their social class. The work of Metz (1990) examines the ways teachers' own social class origins affect their perceptions and treatment of students in the United States, as does that of Connell et al. (1982) among Australian teachers. Apple has written on the proletarianization of teaching as an occupation, and on teachers' roles within the social class structure (1985).

Interpretive theories, microlevel in analysis, are based on the meanings or interpretations of social situations that people construct through their interactions with others. Individuals coordinate their actions with others through shared symbol systems, the most important of which is language. Interpretive sociologists, and particularly symbolic interactionists, are interested in the development of the self-concept, the socialization process, and the ability of individuals to take the role of others in planning their own actions. Application of these theories in the sociology of education has relied on qualitative research methods to gain an understanding of day-to-day school life from the perspective of those who are a part of school organizations.

United Kingdom sociologists of education, particularly, have made significant contributions to an understanding of teacher–pupil relationships and classroom interaction patterns from an interactionist perspective (see Stubbs and Delamont 1976). A focus on teachers is found in Woods (1983), who examined the ideological basis of different teacher subcultures depending on their position within the school system. An example of the reciprocal effects of teachers' and students' behaviors on the others' actions and perceptions is found in Spencer's (1981) study of students' use of impression management in elementary school classrooms.

1.1 Characteristics of Teaching in Sociohistorical Context

Dramatic changes in social, cultural, and material patterns in the late nineteenth century and the early twentieth century provided the context in which to understand growth and changes in education systems and their effects on the professionalization of teaching. Along with rapid increases in industrialization, there were periods of significant population growth and demographic shifts from rural to urban settings. Taken together, these political, economic, and demographic transformations created changes in the labor force, which directly affected the social organization of educational systems and schools.

Throughout this period, teaching was regarded as temporary work for basically untrained people. In the United States, schools and teachers moved to where the children were located, or taught several sessions in one location. On a yearly basis, they taught only a few months (Parelius and Parelius 1987, Warren 1989). In a history of education in the United Kingdom, Musgrave (1968) has described teachers through the turn of the nineteenth century as similar to those of the United States. They basically were untrained or "sweated labour." Teachers in rural areas tended to have the lowest levels of training, while teachers in urban areas had the highest.

The adoption of compulsory school attendance policies and the growth of mass public education created a critical shortage of trained teachers and a need for more efficient mechanisms for training teachers and measuring their effectiveness in standardized ways. The development of normal schools as teacher-training institutions has served in most countries in the world to fulfill this need for a certified labor force in schools (Herbst 1989). Despite the expansion of teacher training, however, shortages of qualified teachers continued to be a serious problem. In the United States this problem was exacerbated by the shift to local control by school districts which often fell short of funds. To deal with the problem these districts looked for less expensive teachers. Male teachers began leaving schools in large numbers as the broader job market opened up, and, because most job markets were closed to women, they were hired as teachers and worked for lower wages. By the first decades of the twentieth century, teaching was seen as a revolving-door career (Rury 1989). For men who stayed in teaching, most went on to administrative positions, and turnover rates for women teachers were extremely high because of sanctions against their being married and teaching. The feminization of teaching did not occur because school districts hired only women because they were cheaper, nor because women willingly accepted low wages. Instead, "cash poor," largely rural school districts hired women because they were an available labor source, and women accepted low wages because their options in the work force were seriously limited (Warren 1985, Strober and Lanford 1986).

The feminization of teaching is a phenomenon found in all countries. Clifford (1989) found that in France between 1900 and 1936 the proportion of male teachers in elementary schools decreased from one-half to one-third, and in Germany in 1900, 85 percent of teachers were male, with significant decreases shown during the same time period. By the turn of the nineteenth century in the United States, three-fourths of all teachers were women, and by 1920, they comprised 86 percent of all teachers. From data collected around the 1930s, out of 26 nations, 41.5 percent of teachers were male. At the secondary level, however, there were higher proportions of men worldwide (71.8 percent), except for the United States and Ireland where men represented less than half of secondary-school teachers. Since that time, however, in the United States secondary teachers have become increasingly male.

Around the time of the Second World War, both because males were in short supply, and later because of the postwar baby boom's creation of rapid growth in school enrollment, teacher shortages became particularly acute. To meet these demands, sanctions against women teachers marrying were eliminated, although women continued to leave teaching to have children. High teacher turnover rates were reflected in Musgrave's (1968) description of United Kingdom teachers in the early 1960s; 19,000 teachers per year came into schools, but 18,000 left.

Although schools in all countries have depended on women as their labor pool, women teachers have been strikingly absent from the history of teaching until work in the 1980s and 1990s by feminist scholars. Historical overviews are provided by Hoffman (1981), Kaufman (1984), and Althenbaugh (1992), who examine women's personal accounts of their teaching in the United States at the turn of the century, whereas Spencer (1986) looks at accounts of contemporary women teachers. Also, a collection edited by Prentice and Theobald (1991) on women teachers in the United Kingdom, Australia, Canada, and the United States, as well as DeLyon and Migniudo's (1989) and Acker's (1989) volumes on United Kingdom teachers, add to a much more complex view of women teachers' roles in the history of schooling.

1.2 Social Characteristics of Teachers

Among the ways that sociologists have described teachers and assessed their homogeneity and heterogeneity is by their social characteristics. Overall, the teaching force comprises a significant proportion of the labor force throughout the world. A report on teachers in OECD (Organisation for Economic Co-operation and Development) countries shows that despite alarmist views the size of the teaching force has not declined over recent years (OECD 1990). Instead, a significant drop in birthrates in all countries, except Australia and Sweden, has created a shrinking student population rather than a shrinking teaching force.

As was seen in Sect. 1.1, the most distinctive social characteristic of schoolteachers is that they have been predominantly female since the early stages of industrialization. The picture in the early 1990s, however, shows considerable diversity between countries and within countries at different levels of the education system (OECD 1990). Women are predominant at preprimary and primary or elementary levels, while secondary levels show a more mixed picture. With some exceptions, women make up less than half of secondary teachers in most countries.

The most striking gender difference is found in the significant underrepresentation of women in administrative positions. This is true for all OECD countries, and in some countries, such as Canada, Australia, and the Netherlands, there has even been a reduction of women in leadership positions. In Australia, for example, between 1971 and 1983 in Victoria, the number of female secondary heads was reduced by half (Burke 1989, cited in OECD 1990). The fact that men manage most schools means they also typically earn significantly higher salaries than women teachers. Thus the gender gap creates and perpetuates a parallel wage gap within teaching.

Another social characteristic of teachers is their age. Historically, during periods of teacher shortages and low levels of teacher training, teachers entered teaching at 15 or 16 years of age. As requirements for training increased, the age of entrance to teaching also increased. Rury (1989) points out that the influence of changing roles for women in this century is reflected in a bimodal age distribution of teachers. This is created by entrance into teaching at a young age, and re-entry after marriage and raising children.

The report of teachers of OECD countries concludes that aging as a factor affecting the teaching force may be exaggerated (OECD 1990). For example, in the United States the median age of teachers was the same in 1961 as in 1986: 41 years. Rather than aging, teachers are now at a historical norm. In general, to say teachers are an "aging" population reflects shifts in credentialing requirements rather than the lack of new entrants in the profession. The report acknowledges that although the long-term effects of an aging teaching population can result in such problems as teacher shortages and more teachers at higher salary levels, there is no evidence to support the notion that younger teachers are better than older teachers. In fact, the opposite would seem to be the case because older teachers are also more experienced.

1.3 Social Mobility of Teachers

An important indicator of a person's position in the social structure is his or her occupation. For many sociologists, occupational mobility is considered the most important measure of social mobility. However, social mobility, or the movement from one position to another in a social system, is too complex a factor on which to base international comparisons of teachers. Such comparisons are particularly difficult, given the vast differences in economic systems and their effects on the classification and characteristics of social classes within countries.

In the United States, there has been a shift in teachers' social class background since the turn of the nineteenth century from farm and blue-collar backgrounds to middle- and upper-middle-class backgrounds. Havighurst and Levine (1979) found that by 1939 teachers were mostly from the lower middle class, and in the decades after that time, teachers came increasingly from more heterogeneous backgrounds. By 1986 teachers' fathers' occupations were as follows: farmers, 13.1 percent; unskilled workers, 8.7 percent; skilled or semiskilled workers, 29.9 percent; clerical or sales workers, 5.0 percent; managerial or self-employed, 21.5 percent; professional or semi-professionals, 21.9 percent (NEA 1987). As teachers' backgrounds have become more similar to those of their parents, the extent to which they show intergenerational mobility, has reduced.

A study of Polish teachers showed their level of satisfaction with teaching and pay was correlated to their qualifications, to the location of their job, and to their social class background—primarily farming or manual work (Górowska-Fells 1991). The explanation for greater dissatisfaction among teachers from higher social class backgrounds is that they see the discrepancy between their current position and that of their families. Dissatisfaction among teachers with blue-collar backgrounds may be due to discrepancies between their positions within the country's intelligentsia and their low pay when compared to other white-collar workers, between their salary and the many duties they must perform, and between their low salaries and the high prestige level afforded teachers in Polish society.

The occupational prestige (that is, societal judgments or social approval accorded to an occupation) of teachers has been low. For example, the findings of a rating system of occupational prestige developed in the United States in 1947 by the National Opinion Research Center (NORC) show that since that time teachers have ranked below professions such as medicine and law and above other public service semiprofessions. In Poland, where social prestige is solely dependent on one's occupation, teachers, with other professions requiring high levels of education, have ranked high on surveys of occupational prestige (Górowska-Fells 1991).

A factor in ranking occupational prestige is teachers' salaries, which are used as indicators of the value a society places on teachers' work. International comparisons of teachers' salaries are extremely difficult given differences in currencies, as well as geographical location and types of school within countries (rural to urban, public and private schools), responsibilities in and out of the classroom, length of working day, years of teaching experience, and level of teacher qualifications. However, in the European Community several organizations have compared teachers' salaries both within and between countries. Peck (1992) has summarized their findings and found that teachers' pay in the mid- to late-1980s was less than industrial workers in Italy (58 percent of industrial workers' pay), Austria (66 percent), England and Wales (75 percent), and Norway (95 percent). The best teachers' pay was found in Switzerland (128 to 312 percent of industrial workers' pay), the Netherlands, West Germany, and Denmark. Comparisons between countries showed the highest paid teachers were in Luxembourg, West Germany, and Denmark, and the lowest paid in Scotland, Belgium, France, and Italy. These data assume teachers are a homogeneous group, but gender differences in pay are found across all OECD countries; teachers' salaries have been high for women compared to other women workers, but low for men (OECD 1990).

Salmon (1987) has concluded that in the United States, not only are teachers' salaries lower than other professions, but during the 10-year period between 1976–77 and 1986–87, teachers lost gains in salary in relation to inflation rates. Anthony (1987) takes this pattern a step further and found that, not only are teachers' salaries less then other professions which require a four-year college education, but teachers are also no better off than people in occupations that do not require a college degree. Lawton (1987) estimates it would require a 25 percent increase in pay to place teachers at international norms for the position of teachers in the overall occupational structure.

Despite teachers' low pay in the United States, in a study conducted by the International Consortium for Cross-cultural Research in Education of nearly 4,000 teachers in the United States, the United Kingdom, West Germany, Japan, Singapore, and Poland, the least frustration with working conditions was reported among teachers in the United States (Wiśniewski 1991). In fact, 40 percent of teachers in the United States reported high levels of satisfaction with their work, while only about 20 percent of teachers in Singapore and the United Kingdom, 14 percent of those in West Germany and Poland, and 9 percent of those in Japan reported high levels of satisfaction. At the same time West German teachers reported the most satisfaction with their pay (50 percent), while only one-third of the teachers in Singapore, 30 percent of those in the United States, 7 percent of those in the United Kingdom, and 2 percent in Japan and Poland reported satisfaction.

In the United States about one-half of all teachers have second jobs. This varies by gender, with 72 percent of the males having second jobs, and 33 percent of the females. Peck (1992) reports that Greek teachers, among the lowest paid in Europe, also frequently hold second jobs. The effect of teachers taking second jobs which are not necessarily commensurate with their education is that it diminishes the status of teachers in the eyes of the public (Anthony 1987).

In summary, teachers have suffered from low pay and low prestige in most societies throughout the history of teaching (Herbst 1989). As the overall level of education of societies increases, and teachers come from higher social classes, both their intergenerational and intragenerational mobility becomes more limited. Within teaching, social mobility continues to be mostly horizontal, particularly for women, just as Becker (1952) described it in the 1950s (see *Teaching, Social Status*).

2. Teaching as a Profession

Whether or not an occupation is considered a profession has been measured by different, yet arbitrary, sets of standards. Sociologists characterize a profession as having a specialized body of knowledge based on systematic theories and transmitted through a formalized educational process, a clearly defined code of ethics which serves as a basis for monitoring by others in the profession, an orientation to serving the public, authority over clients, and autonomy and control over the work environment.

Through the 1970s, sociologists of education examined teaching from this definition and deemed it short of fulfilling these characteristics (Etzioni 1969, Lortie 1975). Some, but not all, of the characteristics of a profession are found; teaching has no specialized body of knowledge, teachers have less training

than the traditional professions, and they work in isolated environments with little autonomy over working conditions. These problems, as well as teachers' presumed lack of commitment to their work and unstructured work patterns, were attributed to the fact that most teachers are women. Therefore, teaching was labeled a "semiprofession" and grouped with other female-dominated occupations, including nursing and social work.

It has been suggested that attempts to evaluate whether teaching is a profession are of use only to sociologists for the sake of comparisons with other work, but are of "limited practical value" (OECD 1990, Griffin 1992). Among the suggestions for reexamination of professionalism among teachers are that the concept should not be used as a dichotomous categorization, but instead should describe points along a continuum or that the term "open professionalism" be used to indicated blurred distinctions in categorization (OECD 1990). It has also been suggested that because commitment to teaching has been assessed through the use of arbitrary standards, it does not reflect the balance of women's commitments to their families and to their work (Grant 1989, Spencer 1986). Rather than lack of commitment to their work, women show nontraditional career patterns. And last, there is a need for the reconceptualization of teachers' careers, which typically do not follow a linear path and should be considered in relation to changing labor markets for women. Teachers' careers are in a state of constant change as teachers adapt to new situations and organizational contexts (Goodson and Walker 1991). Careers, then, should be regarded as "a series of experiences in coming to terms with situations and making choices subject to constraints" (Acker 1989 p. 9).

2.1 Teacher Recruitment

The single most powerful recruiter of teachers is the schools themselves. People who have had positive experiences in school can prolong that experience by becoming teachers. Their many years of observation of teachers serves as a basis for their career decision and a model for their own behavior in the classroom.

In view of teachers' low salaries in most countries it is not surprising that they are attracted to teaching for its intrinsic rewards. In the United States teachers' altruism is seen as one of the most common reasons given for entering teaching in annual surveys administered to teachers in the latter half of the twentieth century (Lortie 1975). The results of the 1987 poll reflect this continuity in attractors to teaching: a desire to work with young people (65.6 percent), belief in the value of education in society (37.2 percent), and interest in a particular subject (37.1 percent) (NEA 1987).

While interpersonal and service themes have been prevalent over time, other factors which have influenced recruitment to teaching have been crosscut by gender issues. The restriction of occupational choices for women in the work force has served as an attractor to teaching, as well as the flexibility of work schedule which women find more compatible with family life (see *Teacher Recruitment and Induction*).

2.2 Teacher Training and Socialization

Teacher socialization, or the process through which teachers learn and internalize accepted patterns of behavior in schools, has remained remarkably similar across time, beginning with Waller's (1984) seminal work, first published in 1932, through Lortie's (1975) highly influential work, to studies by Spencer (1986) and Johnson (1990). Griffin (1992) divides this process into three stages: the prospective teacher stage, the new teacher stage, and the experienced teacher stage.

The prospective teacher stage includes teacher education, plus what Lortie calls the period of "mini-apprenticeship" and others call practicum or student teaching experience. An examination of the social characteristics of teacher education students shows that teachers are much more highly educated than in the past. However, standardized test scores among students in the United States show they do much less well when compared to others who earn college degrees. Parelius and Parelius (1987) report that teachers have always scored poorly on standardized tests of academic ability and achievement. They claim that standards for becoming a teacher have never been high as a result of historical periods when demand for teachers was high and schools of education lowered standards to meet the demand. Standards were also lowered during periods when students have been attracted to other fields. Kerr (1983) explains that the talent pool for teaching has diminished, or a "brain drain" has occurred. This has created dual problems in which those with the best teaching credentials do not enter teaching at all, and of those who are hired, the best teachers leave because of the loss in teacher salary buying power and changes in job opportunities for women. In response to these criticisms of teacher education students, it should be borne in mind that about 11 percent of them are drawn from the highest quintile of the Scholastic Aptitude Test (SAT), which is a much higher proportion than one would expect for an occupation which is characterized by low pay and low status (Schlechty and Vance 1983).

Sykes (1983) characterizes this stage of teacher socialization by its "ease of entry" into teaching through minimal expenditures of time, money, and effort, and goes on to say that, "In fact, the current limitations of teacher education represent a nicely calibrated adaptation to the economic status of teachers. As constituted, teacher education continues to be a recruitment incentive by virtue of its very *lack* of rigor" (p. 581).

An ongoing debate across countries focuses on whether more emphasis should be placed on the extension of teacher training in subject matter or on pedagogical methods (OECD 1990). There are marked differences between countries in terms of the quality and relevance of teacher education courses, as well as the length of teacher training. Countries which have extended the length of teacher preparation are the Republic of Ireland, France, Austria, Finland, Switzerland, and Portugal. Counter to the trend in the United States to require secondary-level teachers to complete more rigorous training in their subject area, in the Netherlands there has been a reduction of training in an academic area from six to four years and more emphasis on teaching practice.

The final phase of the prospective teacher stage is student teaching or practicum, which serves as a transitional phase of anticipatory socialization which aids adaptation to the first teaching experience (Hoy 1968). Mickelson (1990) cites a study at the University of Victoria, British Columbia, Canada, in which 86 percent of education students placed much higher value on their practicum than on their university course work.

The new teacher stage includes the first year of teaching. This stage has been described as a survival stage in which teachers resort to trial-and-error methods for solving classroom problems. Their problems are exacerbated by the lack of collegial support networks for new teachers in schools and the inhibitions teachers have of asking other teachers for help. It is at this stage that teachers are socialized into the school culture and to the norms and expectations for their behaviors.

The experienced teacher stage is an ongoing phase of socialization. As their experience increases, teachers learn strategies for coping and learn to live with the isolated structure of classrooms within schools. Their attitudes toward their work, students, and work environment are shaped through experience as well as through interactions with other teachers. Comments of other teachers in informal settings, such as teachers' workrooms and lounges, are particularly powerful forums for the transmission of expectations for students and for the school as a workplace.

3. Conclusion

Teaching as an occupation and the social characteristics of teachers have been and will continue to be affected by social conditions and societal expectations for schools and for teachers' roles. Sociologists of education will chart those changes as they pay increasing attention to micro-level analyses which focus on the perspectives of teachers about their work.

See also: Contemporary Sociological Theories of Education; Political Sociology of Teachers' Work; Professional Socialization of Teachers; Teachers' Work and Political Action; Women and the Professionalization of Teaching

References

Acker S (ed.) 1989 *Teachers, Gender and Careers*. Falmer Press, London
Altenbaugh R J (ed.) 1992 *The Teacher's Voice*. Falmer Press, London
Anthony P 1987 Teachers in the economic system. In:

Alexander K, Monk D (eds.) 1987 *Attracting and Compensating America's Teachers*. Ballinger, Cambridge, Massachusetts

Anyon J 1980 Social class and the hidden curriculum of work. *J. Educ.* 162(1): 67–92

Apple M W 1985 Teaching and "women's work": A comparative historical and ideological analysis. *Teach. Coll. Rec.* 86(3): 455–73

Becker H S 1952 The career of the Chicago public school teachers. *Am. J. Sociol.* 57: 470–77

Bowles S, Gintis H 1976 *Schooling in Capitalist America*. Basic Books, New York

Burke G 1989 Teachers in Australia: Teacher supply and teacher quality: Social and economic aspects. OECD Working Document, Paris

Clifford G J 1989 Man/woman/teacher: Gender, family and career in American educational history. In: Warren D (ed.) 1989

Connell R W, Ashenden D J, Kessler S, Dowsett G W 1982 *Making the Difference: Schools, Families and Social Division*. George Allen and Unwin, Sydney

DeLyon H, Migniudo F W (eds.) 1989 *Women Teachers: Issues and Experiences*. Open University Press, Milton Keynes

Etzioni A (ed.) 1969 *The Semi-Professions and Their Organization: Teachers, Nurses, Social Workers*. The Free Press, New York

Goodson I F, Walker R 1991 *Biography, Identity and Schooling: Episodes in Educational Research*. Falmer Press, London

Górowska-Fells M 1991 The financial position of the Polish teachers in the mid nineteen-eighties. Zeszyt 49, University of Warsaw, Warsaw

Grant R 1989 Women teachers' career pathways: Towards an alternative model of "career." In: Acker S (ed.) 1989

Griffin G 1992 Teacher education. In: Alkin M (ed.) 1992 *Encyclopedia of Educational Research*, 6th edn. Macmillan, New York

Havighurst R J, Levine D U 1979 *Society and Education*, 5th edn. Allyn and Bacon, Boston, Massachusetts

Herbst J 1989 *And Sadly Teach: Teacher Education and Professionalization in American Culture*. University of Wisconsin Press, Madison, Wisconsin

Hoffman N (ed.) 1981 *Woman's "True" Profession: Voices from the History of Teaching*. The Feminist Press, Old Westbury, New York

Hoy W K 1968 The influence of experience on the beginning teacher. *Sch. Rev.* 76(3): 312–23

Johnson S M 1990 *Teachers at Work: Achieving Excellence in Our Schools*. Basic Books, New York

Kaufman P W 1984 *Women Teachers on the Frontier*. Yale University Press, New Haven, Connecticut

Kerr D 1983 Teaching competence and teacher education in the United States. In: Shulman L S, Sykes G (eds.) 1983 *Handbook of Teaching and Policy*. Longman, New York

Lawton S 1987 Teachers' salaries: An international perspective. In: Alexander K, Monk D (eds.) 1987 *Attracting and Compensating America's Teachers*. Ballinger, Cambridge, Massachusetts

Lortie D C 1975 *Schoolteacher: A Sociological Study*. University of Chicago Press, Chicago, Illinois

Metz M 1990 How social class differences shape teachers' work. In: McLaughlin M W, Talbert J E, Bascia N (eds.) 1990 *The Contexts of Teaching in Secondary Schools: Teachers' Realities*. Teachers College Press, New York

Mickelson N I 1990 The role of the practicum in the preparation of teachers. In: Orteza y, Miranda E, Magsino R F (eds.) 1990 *Teaching, Schools, and Society*. Falmer Press, London

Musgrave P W 1968 *Society and Education in England Since 1800*. Methuen, London

NEA (National Education Association) 1987 *Status of the American Public School Teacher, 1985–86*. NEA, Westhaven, Connecticut

OECD 1990 *The Teacher Today: Tasks, Conditions, Policies*. Organisation for Economic Co-operation and Development, Paris

Page R 1987 Teachers' perceptions of students: A link between classrooms, school cultures, and the social order. *Anthropol. Educ. Q.* 18(2): 77–99

Parelius R J, Parelius A P 1987 *The Sociology of Education*. Prentice-Hall, Englewood Cliffs, New Jersey

Peck B T 1992 Perspectives on teachers' pay. *Phi Del. Kap.* 73(9): 734–35

Prentice A, Theobald M R (eds.) 1991 *Women Who Taught: Perspectives on the History of Women and Teaching*. University of Toronto Press, Toronto

Rury J L 1989 Who became teachers? The social characteristics of teachers in American history. In: Warren D (ed.) 1989

Salmon R G 1987 Teacher salaries: Progress over the decade. In: Alexander K, Monk D (eds.) 1987

Schlechty P C, Vance V S 1983 Recruitment, selection, and retention: The shape of the teaching force. *Elem. Sch. J.* 83(4): 469–87

Spencer D A 1981 Looking behind the teacher's back. *Elem. Sch. J.* 81(5): 281–89

Spencer D A 1986 *Contemporary Women Teachers: Balancing Work and Home*. Longman, New York

Strober M H, Lanford A G 1986 The feminization of public school teaching: Cross-sectional analysis 1850–1880. *Signs* 11(2): 212–35

Stubbs M, Delamont D (eds.) 1976 *Explorations in Classroom Observation*. Wiley, London

Sykes G 1983 Caring about teachers. Response to Donna Kerr. *Teach. Coll. Rec.* 84(3): 579–92

Waller W 1984 What teaching does to teachers: Determinants of the occupational type. In: Hargreaves A, Woods P (eds.) 1984 *Classrooms and Staffrooms: The Sociology of Teachers and Teaching*. Open University Press, Milton Keynes

Warren D 1985 Learning from experience: History and teacher education. *Educ. Researcher* 14(10): 5–12

Warren D (ed.) 1989 *American Teachers: Histories of a Profession at Work*. Macmillan, New York

Wiśniewski W 1991 Job satisfaction of secondary school teachers in six countries: the USA, England, West Germany, Japan, Singapore, and Poland. Zeszyt 49, University of Warsaw, Warsaw

Woods P 1983 *Sociology and the School: An Interactionist Viewpoint*. Routledge and Kegan Paul, London

Further Reading

Dreeben R 1970 *The Nature of Teaching*. Scott Foresman, Glenview, Illinois

Popkewitz T S 1991 *A Political Sociology of Educational Reform: Power/Knowledge in Teaching, Teacher Education and Research*. Teachers College Press, New York

Research Traditions in the Sociology of Education

Introduction: Methodological Developments in the Sociology of Education

L. J. Saha

The sociology of education has been a research-oriented field within sociology generally. Furthermore, the nature of the research tasks, particularly the challenge of studying the diverse structures and processes of education, with varying levels of selectivity, both between and within institutions and classrooms, has contributed to the field becoming a leader in the development of research methodology, both qualitative and quantitative. Furthermore, emerging insights into the complex processes of the educational experience, and the rapid development of computer technology, has opened doors to newer approaches of data gathering and analyses probably without parallel in the social sciences.

1. Issues and Trends in Research Methods

This section consists of two subsections with a total of 17 articles. In Section IIIa the focus on the seven articles is on issues and trends in research methodology. The issues are primarily those which concern the underlying assumptions of empirical research in education, starting with Walker and Evers' article on the epistemological and paradigmatic issues underlying educational research (*Research in Education: Epistemological Issues*). Kaplan provides a different kind of enquiry in his discussion of the scientific underpinnings of educational research (*Research in Education: Scientific Methods*). Husén, on the other hand, provides an overview of the two main paradigms in education research, one modeled on natural science (*Erklären*) and the second on humanistic and interpretive approaches (*Verstehen*). In his article, *Research Paradigms in Education*, Husén argues for the compatibility and unity of the two paradigms. Acker provides an overview of feminist critiques of research methodology in *Feminist Critiques of Educational Practices and Research*, and calls into question some of the assumptions underlying much of educational research. Finally, Keeves and Saha, in *Measurement of Social Background*, raise a number of issues related to the measurement of social background, one of the basic variables used in educational research.

These articles serve as a reminder that research practices should be reviewed constantly, and that the validity and reliability of educational research, whether qualitative or quantitative, cannot be maintained and improved without an open mindedness to the weaknesses which come about by the assumptions that we make.

The impressive gains in sociological research methodology are apparent in the two trend articles which review developments in qualitative and quantitative methods. An issue which surfaces in the reading of these two articles concerns the so-called divide which exists between the two approaches. Husén, in *Research Paradigms in Education*, adheres to the distinction between *Verstehen* and *Erklären*, or between explanation and understanding (Húsen 1988). LeCompte, in her article *Trends in Qualitative Research Methods*, suggests a struggle between the two research paradigms, while Keeves in his *Trends in Quantitative Research Methods* argues on behalf of a continuum rather than a divide, for complementarity rather than conflict (see Keeves 1988), since the distinction between categorical, categorized, and continuous appears to be breaking down with the emergence of new techniques of measurement and analysis. Apart from this issue, the two articles provide complementary sweeping overviews of the developments in the two research paradigms.

2. Research Traditions

The 10 articles in Section IIIb provide more detailed discussions of individual research traditions, which for the most part, complement the two trend articles. These contributions include both qualitative and quantitative research approaches, but are not intended to represent accounts of all possible research methodologies available to educational researchers. An excellent source for a comprehensive account of these methodologies can be found in Keeves' *Educational Research, Methodology, and Measurement: An International Handbook, Second Edition*, 1997.

Two of these methods, Kemmis' *Action Research* and Hall's *Participatory Research*, represent attempts to break down the distance between researchers and practitioners and to combine theory and practice. Both methods are forms of *collaborative research* in which the traditional research "subjects" participate in the research which will lead to the improvement of educational practices, including a heightened consciousness about, and understanding of, the practices being researched.

In *Biographical Research Methods*, Denzin includes a family of methods which use, in one form or another, life documents or histories, including oral history, which provide the data for the study of a person. In *Content and Text Analysis*, on the other hand, Anderson also uses documents to systematically study forms of human communication, whether written or oral. The techniques are wide ranging and include both qualitative and quantitative approaches.

To the extent that feminism has rejected the positivism of traditional science, the article by Haig, *Feminist Research Methodology*, might be seen as more qualitative than quantitative, and certainly postpositivist. In this respect, the discussion shows how feminism, by adapting existing research methods to advance research on women, creates a new kind of research methodology.

Quantitative research approaches are represented by four articles, three of which represent applications of input–output, cost-benefit approaches, namely Tachibanaki's *Education, Occupation, and Earnings*, Hanushek's *Education Production Functions*, and Willms and Raudenbush's *Effective Schools Research: Methodological Issues*. The methods and related issues discussed in these articles represent the backbone of much of quantitative educational research, particularly with respect to studies of educational and occupational attainment, social mobility, school effectiveness and efficiency, the impact of teacher quality, and so on. A fourth article by Suarez, *Needs Assessment*, describes techniques for the identification and collection of social needs data specifically oriented to policy or planning-oriented research.

The final article in this section, Nisbet's *Policy-oriented Research*, relates research and policy and makes the distinction between pure or fundamental research and policyoriented research. The focal point of Nisbet's article is that research which is intended to guide policy decisions must be planned and designed in consultation with the policymakers themselves, or at least with the knowledge of how the results are to be used. Naturally, this raises questions about the use of research, and the manner in which anticipated use may compromise the research itself. In this respect, the issues which emerge relate, to some extent, to the articles in the first part of this section.

References

Husén T 1988 Research paradigms in education. *Interchange* 19(1): 2–13
Keeves J P 1988 The unity of educational research. *Interchange* 19(1): 14–30
Keeves J P (ed.) 1997 *Educational Research, Methodology, and Measurement: An International Handbook*, 2nd edn. Pergamon, Oxford

(a) Issues and Trends in Research Methods

Feminist Critiques of Educational Practices and Research

S. Acker

This article reviews feminist criticism of the practice of education and of the typical conceptual and methodological approaches in educational research. Feminism addresses the question of women's subordination to men. Proposed explanations of this differ, the main ones being traditional and attitudinal barriers to equality, the tendency of capitalism to exploit other social divisions, and men's entrenched patriarchal privileges.

1. Critiques of Educational Practice

1.1 Liberal Feminist Critiques

Liberal feminism argues for the removal of barriers embodied in laws, government policies, tradition and religion and fostered through socialization stereotyping and sex discrimination. Equal access to educational institutions is a particular concern, especially in the Third World, where female participation is often dramatically below that of males and prospects are becoming bleaker as poverty increases. The educational policies of many governments have been criticized for downplaying gender or being poorly matched to the needs and wants of women (see Jayaweera 1987). Women teachers' and academics' career opportunities are also a liberal feminist topic.

1.2 Socialist Feminist Critiques

Socialist feminists (in capitalist states) argue that together with other social institutions, the school perpetuates ("reproduces") sexual divisions and associated inequalities across the generations. Some researchers have called attention to the complex ways in which gender and social class interact and structure school life, influencing values, timetabling, grouping, teacher deployment, curriculum and examinations. A few studies look at adolescent girls' "resistance" to the dominant ideologies.

1.3 Radical Feminist Critiques

Radical feminists argue that the curriculum at all levels of education is the embodiment of male knowledge, the experiences and participation of women having been excluded or disparaged (Spender 1982). The Women's Studies movement is a response to such analysis, seeking to build an alternative woman-centred curriculum and pedagogy. Another concern is the sexual politics of everyday life in educational institutions. Teachers are said to give boys more attention than girls and to tailor activities to boys' interests. Recent British radical feminist writing has pointed to the presence of sexual harassment in schools, sometimes combined with racial harassment or homophobia.

1.4 Current Developments

Current feminist thought, influenced by poststructuralism and postmodernism and the critiques of racial or ethnic minority women, has moved away from typologies such as liberal, socialist, and radical feminism. All-embracing theories are less often seen as convincing claims to truth. Debate rages over how to understand the concept of "woman" as it is recognized that women possess multiple subjectivities based on race, class, age, sexual orientation, religion, and so forth. Educational practices, by extension, do not simply apply to homogeneous groups of "girls" and "boys" (Davies 1989). Classrooms and schools are now often seen as sites where knowledge and power are constructed and reconstructed, and traditional and alternative discourses are in competition (Weiler 1988). The possibility of a feminist pedagogy, especially at postsecondary level, has also received considerable attention (Luke and Gore 1992).

2. Critiques of Educational Research: The Research Process

Feminist critiques specifically of educational research procedures are relatively uncommon. This section deals with the criticisms of the various stages of research, from identifying a problem to writing up a report.

2.1 The Research Problem

"Problems" may be derived from previous research, applications of theory to a particular setting, or be based on personal experience. If most researchers are men, and if they draw upon their own experiences and upon bodies of literature and theory also constructed by men, it follows that other perspectives may be excluded (Smith 1987). For example, for years British sociology of education relied on a series of studies of adolescent boys, conducted by male researchers, to provide knowledge of pupil subcultures. Studies which focused on the consequences of the supposed low commitment of women teachers for the occupation's claims to professionalization provide another example. Only recently have perspectives changed, and the problems teaching presents for women been examined. In the process concepts such as "career" and "commitment" have had to be rethought. Feminist perspectives provide a range of "new" research problems as well as the impetus to rethink old ones.

2.2 Concepts

The definition of a research problem involves identifying key concepts to guide the research. In the example above, "commitment" and "career" for teachers have frequently been defined in ways that are at odds with women's lives and experiences. Ignoring such differential experiences is what Eichler (1987) calls "gender insensitivity."

"Sex differences" is a concept in educational research often criticized by feminists (Hare-Mustin and Marecek 1990). Reporting of sex differences in abilities or examination results often implies that girls and boys form discrete groups. Average scores on tests are reported disregarding the spread. Even if the boys do "better" (on average) than girls on, say, a test of spatial ability, some girls will have higher scores than some boys. Thinking of differences as sex-linked (biological) tends to minimize the heavy cultural input that shapes notions of appropriate "masculine" and "feminine" behavior and temperament. There is evidence that some teachers believe that political neutrality requires them to eschew tampering with "natural" sex differences, for example in students' subject preferences.

2.3 Research Design

Basically a research design consists of answers to a series of questions, such as: Will the study be theoretical or empirical? Will it rely on data available in libraries or collections, community action, surveys? How and from whom will data be collected? What instruments will be used? How will the analysis proceed? Eichler (1987) shows how frequently sexist approaches – gender overgeneralization or overspecificity, gender insensitivity, double standards—are built into research designs.

Two points for particular mention are sampling and method. Feminist work shows how incomplete much sampling has been. Women have in many instances been left out of research when their answers did not fit existing theory. Classic examples here are

research on achievement motivation and moral development. Another example concerns the measurement of socioeconomic status. Women do not always work continuously and their occupations cluster in narrow bands; thus, conventional measurements of occupational status may not suit them. Educational studies have therefore tended to use father's occupation exclusively as an indicator of a child's social class background, or have only studied the social mobility of men. A review of educational articles in British journals from 1960 to 1989 (Acker 1994) produced examples of sampling excluding women. Of 143 articles using empirical data, 58 percent were mixed male and female, 37 percent male only and 5 percent female only (the latter mostly surveys of mothers about their children).

Method refers to the use of particular techniques. In empirical research this is basically some form of observing behavior, asking questions, or looking at documents. Feminist discussions of method often compare quantitative and qualitative approaches, often suggesting that the latter is a more suitable feminist choice because of its sensitivity to context and greater likelihood of allowing the interpretations of participants to emerge. However, others argue that there is nothing inappropriate about using any technique if the purpose is a feminist one. What emerges in such discussions is the need to remodel the relationships of researcher and researched.

2.4 Interpretation and Report

Research reporting of both quantitative and qualitative data relies to a large extent on the interpretation of its originator. Researchers impose all kinds of categories, codes, and themes in order to derive an account which is comprehensible by others. This is a small selection of what might be reported. A feminist perspective (or simply a gender-sensitive one) can totally alter an interpretation. For example, studies of classrooms before the mid-1970s depict boys as victims of a stifling feminine atmosphere and report teacher preferences for girls, but later studies reach the opposite conclusions. Is this a historical change, an artifact of methods used, or due to an altered researcher consciousness?

3. Critiques of Educational Research: Underlying Issues

There are several additional problems which cut across all stages in the research process: language, purposes and politics, and the social conditions research production.

3.1 Language

A familiar criticism of social science (and others) research focuses on language, especially the use of "he" for both he and she and the generic use of "man." These uses were at one time near-universal but are much less often encountered in the late 1990s. The main argument for nonsexist language is that language structures realize moreover, that those reading the word "man" often cannot be sure whether generic man or biological man is intended.

3.2 Purposes and Politics of Research

According to Harding (1987), both methodological and epistemological issues must be tackled. Methodological questions ask how research should proceed; epistemological questions consider who can know, what can be known and by what criteria we evaluate knowledge. Harding argues that the essential features of feminist research are that it: (a) derives its research problems from women's perspectives and experiences, (b) allows the researcher to enter into the same "plane" as the subjects, and (c) is for women, aiming to give answers to questions asked by women.

For Stanley (1984), the researcher's own experience of oppression as a woman is the necessary starting point—and thus in her opinion men cannot do feminist research, although Harding (1987) disagrees on this point. The women's movement slogan, "the personal is political," is relevant to Stanley's version of feminist research. Various writers elaborate on Harding's second point, rejecting the model where the researcher stays aloof from the "subjects," suggesting instead that self-disclosure and reciprocity should be a part of the research relationship (Lather 1991). Lather tackles the third point too, arguing that research must be directed towards political ends, explicitly critiquing the status quo. For Lather, research must serve the emancipatory purpose of empowering others, not just contributing to the career advancement of researchers.

3.3 Social Relations of Research Production

Who does the judging of standards? Who are the gate-keepers? (Smith 1987). The social conditions under which research is produced and its results conveyed must be considered. Although there are now a number of feminist journals, including *Gender and Education*, many feminist books on education and examples of feminist research in mainstream education journals, there are still forces working against this type of work. First, research funding is limited and governments and funding bodies decide what kind of work is to be encouraged and rewarded. In some countries, political considerations limit freedom of expression. Second, editors and reviewers work within their disciplinary cultures and not all fields have been friendly to feminism. Third, women academics are in a minority in universities. With cutbacks and economic retrenchment in many countries, full-time, tenured academic numbers have declined or stayed stable, while contractually limited appointments, with tenuous job security, have increased. Hierarchical university organization places power in the hands of small numbers of highly placed professors and managers. Typically, women are better represented at the lower than higher levels, and they have not held many of the powerful positions. Feminist research may not be well-regarded in a male-dominated structure and academics may avoid doing work that is seen to carry a price in career terms.

Conclusion

Feminist scholarship has extended and redefined issues for educational practice and research. Reasons for resistance to feminist perspectives might be sought in the practices of higher education which give form and direction to educational research.

See also: Feminist Approaches to the Curriculum; Gender Theories in Education

References

Acker S 1994 *General Education: Sociological Reflections on Women, Teaching and Feminism.* Open University Press, Milton Keynes

Davies B 1989 *Frogs and Snails and Feminist Tales.* Allen and Unwin, Sydney

Eichler M 1987 *Nonsexist Research Methods: A Practical Guide.* Allen and Unwin, Boston, Massachusetts

Harding S 1987 Is there a feminist method? In: Harding S (ed.) 1987 *Feminism and Methodology.* Open University Press, Milton Keynes

Hare-Mustin R, Marecek J 1990 *Making a Difference: Psychology and the Construction of Gender.* Yale University Press, New Haven, Connecticut

Jayaweera S (ed.) 1987 *Int. Rev. Educ.* 33(4): Special issue devoted to women and education

Lather P 1991 *Getting Smart: Feminist Research and Pedagogy Within the Postmodern* Routledge, New York

Luke C and Gore J (eds.) 1992 *Feminisms and Critical Pedagogy.* Routledge, New York

Smith D E 1987 *The Everyday World as Problematic: A Feminist Sociology* Northeastern University Press, Boston, Massachusetts

Spender D 1982 *Invisible Women: The Schooling Scandal.* Writers and Readers, London

Weiler K 1988 *Women Teaching for Change.* Bergin and Garvey, South Hadley, Massachusetts

Further Reading

Blair M, Holland J (with Sheldon S.) (eds.) 1995 *Identity and Diversity: Gender and the Experience of Education.* Multilingual Matters, Clevedon, Ohio

hooks b 1988 *Talking Back: Thinking Feminist, Thinking Black.* Between the Lines, Toronto

Marshall C (ed.) 1997 *Critical Policy Analysis: Dismantling the Master's House,* Vols. 1 and 2. Falmer, London

Sadker M, Sadker D 1994 *Failing at Fairness: How Our Schools Cheat Girls.* Touchstone, New York

Stone L (ed.) 1994 *The Education Feminism Reader.* Routledge, New York

Weiner G 1994 *Feminisms in Education.* Open University Press, Milton Keynes

Wrigley J (ed.) 1992 *Education and Gender Inequality.* Falmer, London

Measurement of Social Background

J. P. Keeves and L. J. Saha

Since the early 1930s it has been increasingly recognized that in most countries differences in social background are strongly related to educational outcomes. In recognition of this relationship many countries have introduced compensatory programs to assist with the provision of educational services to those who are seen to be socially and economically disadvantaged. Underlying these developments has been the work undertaken primarily in the area of sociology concerned with the study of social stratification and social mobility and the measurement of social status. This article is concerned with the measurement of social background and social status, and the problems encountered in the development of consistent and valid measurement.

1. Measurement Issues

Meaningful measurement requires that the properties being measured have a sound conceptual basis within an established theory, and that the operational definitions linking the theory and the scaling techniques employed yield both valid and reliable measures. However, social stratification and social mobility are fields in which there is considerable controversy. Haug (1977) has pointed out that there are at least two types of characteristics which are used to cluster persons into strata or groups that are hierarchically ordered. First, there are biologically based characteristics such as age, sex, race, and ethnic origin. Second, there are acquired characteristics such as power, wealth, and social prestige. Societies differ in the emphasis given to particular characteristics, both biological and acquired, in the process of stratification within them. Even within a given society the emphasis on these characteristics changes over time. Consequently, there is little consensus regarding which characteristics should form the basis of a general theory of social stratification. Nevertheless, the theories of Marx, that class categories are derived from the relation of a group to the means of production and thus are based on differences between ownership of property and the provision of labor, have greatly influenced thinking in this area. Another prominent view advanced by Weber is that position in society is built around the three concepts of status, power, and class, with status being related to prestige ascribed by the community, power being associated with a political context, and class having an economic basis. These three dimensions of status, power, and class are conceptually interrelated and might be expected to be highly correlated with one another. As a consequence they have provided the

main foundation on which the measurement of social stratification has proceeded, particularly in industrial societies.

Two broad approaches have been employed in the investigation and measurement of social background and social status. Warner et al. (1949) have identified these two approaches, distinguishing between the approach in which an assessment is made of social standing by the observed and evaluated participation of an individual in the social system of a community, and the approach in which indexes of the status level of the individual in the community are developed using information obtained directly from the individual by either objective or subjective responses.

As a result, in undertaking the task of measuring social status it is necessary not only to consider the theoretical basis of the concepts to be employed but also how information related to an individual with respect to those concepts might be obtained. The most commonly used single indicator of a person's relative standing with respect to the concepts of status, power, and class is that of occupational status. Thus information on the social standing of an occupation can be obtained either by the use of the subjective perceptions of members of the community, or by the use of concomitant objective characteristics of the occupation associated with the level of skill required, the level of education necessary to engage in the occupation, and the income received from regular employment in the occupation. These three characteristics are interrelated insofar as economic return is determined, in part, by both level of skill and level of education, and together they form a basis for objective measurement.

2. Measurement of Occupational Status

In general, the starting point for the measurement of occupational status involves the setting up of a classification of the full range of occupations which exist in a society. Since such a large number of classified occupations exist, it is necessary to group them into categories. Once occupational categories have been formed they must be assigned to a rank order. The simplest grouping in industrialized societies is into two categories: white-collar workers and blue-collar workers. This reflects the wearing of blue denim clothing by workers in many countries especially the United States. White-collar occupations typically require a high proportion of the work to be carried out within an office. Blue-collar occupations involve a high proportion of the work being undertaken out of doors or away from an office desk. In most societies white-collar occupations are perceived to require a higher level of education and skill. In the main, they are more highly rewarded and are thus accorded higher status than blue-collar occupations. A more extensive categorization, again based essentially on levels of education, skill, and income, involves six categories of occupation: professional, managerial, clerical, skilled, semiskilled, and unskilled. The first three named are white-collar occupations; the last three are blue-collar occupations.

Broom et al. (1977) have identified five main approaches which have been involved in the measurement of occupations beyond the simple categorizations referred to above. First, it is possible to develop a more extensive set of occupational categories based on level of education, skill, and income and to assign integer scores to the hierarchically ordered occupational categories (Jones 1971). A second approach has been to derive socioeconomic scores for each occupation by combining average years of education and average income associated with each occupation, customarily with equal weight (e.g.: for Canada, Blishen [1958]; for New Zealand, Elley and Irving [1972]; and for the United States, Nam and Powers [1968]). A third strategy has been to carry out an auxiliary study of occupational prestige, and, using regression analysis, to estimate the weights for such characteristics as years of education and income in order to predict the prestige score for major occupations. Scores for those occupations not estimated directly may be obtained by interpolation (Duncan 1961, Pineo and Porter 1967). A fourth approach is to make direct estimates of social standing or prestige using information obtained from a single study which provides data for all occupations, or to use previous rating studies to provide some of the necessary data (Siegel 1971). A fifth procedure that has been employed is to compute scores for occupational categories from the analysis of measures obtained on several separate characteristics (e.g., level of education, income, level of occupational skill) using the interrelations between the measures to generate the scores. The statistical techniques of principal components analysis, factor analysis, and canonical analysis have been employed to this end (Keeves 1972).

In the remainder of Sect. 2 the procedures which have been employed in selected countries are described briefly.

2.1 Australia

The starting point of the work of Broom et al. (1965) was the classified list of occupations which had been developed for use in the national census. As a first step, Broom and colleagues grouped the 342 occupational titles into 100 clusters on the basis of interrelations between occupations, and then into 16 broad categories using as the main criterion that each group should contain jobs involving the same level of skill or skill type. These 16 categories were ordered to form a prestige scale broadly in agreement with the findings of an earlier study into occupational prestige by Congalton (1963) that had produced an occupational prestige scale. Subsequently, Broom et al. (1977) extended this work using the third strategy described above, namely that of fitting an equation to prestige scores for measures of age, sex, birthplace, schooling and qualifications, housing and vehicle ownership, and interpolating for a wider set of occupations.

2.2 The United Kingdom

The first attempt in the United Kingdom to form an occupational classification was carried out for the census in 1911 when five occupational categories were defined. This classification was revised in 1971 to six classes which were: I—professional; II—intermediate occupations; III N—skilled occupations (nonmanual); III M—skilled occupations (manual); IV—partly skilled occupations; V—unskilled occupations. In addition, a stratification measure was developed by Hall and Caradog Jones (1950) based on community perceptions of occupational prestige. Initially, this scale was constructed for 30 occupational categories, and was later extended to include approximately 650 occupations (Oppenheim 1966). Subsequently, Goldthorpe and Hope (1974) grouped all the occupations in the United Kingdom census classification into 125 categories which were as homogeneous as possible with respect to both intrinsic and extrinsic rewards. They then selected a representative sample of occupational titles from each category, and in a single study obtained rankings of the prestige of each of the occupational groups. From these rankings a single scale was formed, but no attempt was made to group the final 124 categories into a smaller number of classes or strata.

2.3 The United States

In the United States, the major system of classifying occupations developed by the Bureau of Census was used as the basis for setting up measures of stratification. Edwards (1938) developed the first scale. Using education and income as criteria, he grouped together all occupations into 10 hierarchically ordered classes. Such a scale, employing income in the formation of socioeconomic groups, has become known as a scale of "socioeconomic status" (SES). This term is now widely used even where the measures employed do not strictly involve income. For the 1971 United States Census a 12-category scale was developed from Edwards's scale, but whether it retains the socioeconomic groupings of the earlier scale is open to question.

Perhaps the most frequently used measure of social stratification in the United States is the Duncan Socio-Economic Index (SEI) (Duncan 1961), which is based on occupational prestige as evaluated by public opinion, using the third strategy outlined above. However, the estimated prestige scores showed many shortcomings and Siegel (1971) sought to obtain a more secure empirical basis for the prestige ratings from a public opinion survey for as many of the major census occupations as possible.

In addition to these two measures, Miller (1991) presents four other scales for use in the United States: (a) Nam—Powers Socioeconomic Status Scores, (b) Hollingshead's Two-Factor Index of Social Position, (c) the Revised Occupational Rating Scale from Warner Meeker, and Eell's Index of Status Characteristics, and (d) Edwards's Social—Economic Group of Occupations.

2.4 Canada

The construction of measures of stratification in Canada has followed closely the work carried out in the United States. Blishen (1958) initially developed an occupational scale by combining the mean standard scores for both education and income for members of occupational groups using Canadian census classifications and data from a national census. Blishen (1967) then followed the procedures used by Duncan (1961) to obtain regression weights for education and income measures in the prediction of prestige scores. The weights obtained by Blishen for education exceeded those for income, where Duncan had obtained approximately equal weights. Furthermore, Pineo and Porter (1967) sought to obtain information on occupational prestige through a national survey. Subsequently, Pineo, Porter, and McRoberts developed an occupational classification of 16 categories for the Canadian Mobility Study, that was condensed by McRoberts (1985) into 10 categories for the examination of mobility and attainment.

3. The Standard International Occupational Prestige Scale

Husén (1967) used an occupational scale developed at the University of Chicago with considerable success in the First Mathematics Study for the International Association for the Evaluation of Educational Achievement in 1964. One problem with this scale was that it did not allow for the societal and cultural differences between countries. Subsequently, Treiman (1977) sought to combine the many diverse scales of prestige employed in different countries into a single scheme that could be used in cross-cultural research and other comparative studies. Treiman obtained information from prestige studies in 55 countries and recoded the occupational titles according to the appropriate categories employed in the International Standard Classification of Occupations (ISCO) published by the International Labor Office in 1969. After conversion to a common standard metric, the scores obtained from the 55 countries for each occupational group were averaged across countries to obtain the international scale. Treiman claimed that the concurrent validity

of the scale was high because the average coefficient obtained by correlating each country's occupational scale scores with those for the international scale with that country removed was 0.89. In addition, with the exclusion of a few developing countries and some socialist countries, the correlations between scales were unrelated to level of industrialization as measured by gross national product. In common with most of the scales in current use there are short-comings in the scales with respect to the positions of farm and rural workers. Thus, for a country with a high percentage of the workforce engaged in primary industry, it must be anticipated that some problems will be encountered.

4. The Occupational Power Scales

Erickson et al. (1979) have proposed an occupational scale that has been presented in detail by Goldthorpe (1980) which was developed as a class schema for the study of occupational mobility. In this scale, Classes I and II represent what has become known as the "Service Class." The Service Class comprises those with expertise who exercise power on behalf of corporate bodies, together with independent professionals and self-employed business people. Class I is the higher level and Class II the lower level of the service class. Class III comprises routine, non-manual employees associated with the service class, who do not exercise authority, or if they do, the authority is exercised within a limited field. Class IV comprises persons in self-employment with Class IVa consisting of those self-employed persons who have employees working for them; Class IVb consists of those self-employed persons who are engaged in rural occupations. Class V consists of lower level technicians and foremen, while Class VI comprises skilled manual workers. Class VII consists of some skilled and unskilled manual workers while Class VIIa comprises those not in agriculture, and Class VIIb those employed in agriculture. This class scale is now being used in cross-national studies of occupational mobility, but has not been used widely in educational research. The occupational class categorization proposed by Goldthorpe (1980) has a very different meaning from the scales that use concepts of SES, prestige, and skill level of occupation. Consequently, this scale has some advantages in causal modeling where other measures of economic circumstances are also included.

5. Some Special Problems for Educational Research

There are many issues of both a methodological and substantive nature associated with the use of social background data in educational research. Although such information has been found to have considerable explanatory power, problems have been encountered that limit the usefulness of such measures.

5.1 Confidentiality of Information

During the 1970s and the 1980s there was growing awareness of the confidential nature of much of the data that were collected in large-scale surveys. The ease with which data could be stored and subsequently accessed through computerized data banks has led to widespread protest with respect to the confidentiality of personal information. In many countries research workers have had experience of data files being destroyed or mutilated. Information regarding occupation, years of education, and level of income are collected in national censuses where there is a public guarantee of confidentiality. However, in educational surveys teacher unions and parent organizations sometimes refuse permission for such data to be collected from students with respect to their parents on the grounds of invasion of privacy. Little damage is done in cases where the parent of an isolated student prevents this information being supplied in response to questionnaire items in a survey. Where the data are withheld for individual schools or groups of schools, the validity of the data that are collected is quickly cast into doubt. In some countries, for example, Japan, it is no longer possible to collect information on parental occupation from students in large-scale surveys.

5.2 Response Error in Student Reports

It has been accepted generally that most students by the age of 10 years are able to provide information on father's occupation, that some students are unable to report accurately on father's and mother's education, and that few students can provide accurate data on level of father's or mother's income. As a consequence, information on level of income is rarely sought directly from students. However, in order to obtain accurate information on parental occupation and education, students are commonly requested to check their responses with their parents on the night prior to responding to a questionnaire. This procedure is not only a courtesy to parents, informing them that such data are being sought and seeking authorization for participation in the survey, but it also helps to ensure that the data collected are accurate.

Considerable work has been carried out to study response error in student reports of parental socioeconomic characteristics (see, for example, Coleman et al. 1966, Jencks et al. 1972). Subsequently, Mason et al. (1976) developed a conceptual and analytic model and examined measurement error for White and Black students at different grade levels in the United States. For only one group, namely 12th grade White students, were the measurement errors shown to be random. It is clear that substantial bias commonly exists in such data. Nevertheless, data on socioeconomic characteristics have been found to have considerable explanatory power.

5.3 Occupational Status Scales for Women

An increasing proportion of the workforce in most countries is made up of women, and increasing proportions of women are now engaged in occupations that were formerly the preserve of males. However, the occupational scales that have been constructed in most countries, including the Treiman scale, were developed with data from samples of adult males. These scales are not necessarily appropriate for female occupations. First, there are substantial proportions of women in many countries who are not in the labor force. These women are commonly engaged in home duties, and the reasons for their nonparticipation in the labor force differ across countries. In some countries it is only the unskilled who are not able to obtain employment. In other countries substantial numbers of the better educated women do not need to seek employment to augment the family income. Secondly, in spite of gains in female labor force participation, and educational preparation, substantial differences persist in most countries in the average earnings of men and women in the same occupational group. It is evident that women are still not ascribed the same status as men in a particular occupation. Nevertheless, valuable information is available for both prediction and explanation of student achievement in data collected from students on the occupation and level of education of their mothers as well as their fathers.

The Nam–Powers Socioeconomic Status Scores provides combined scales for men and women in the United States, in contrast to the other major scales used in that country, which provide scores for men only (Miller 1991 p. 329).

5.4 Single-parent Families

In the late twentieth century there has been a marked increase in many countries in the incidence of divorce and the establishment of single-parent families. While this has the effect of lowering family income, its effects on intellectual development and educational achievement are more complex. In part, this is a consequence of the fact that in some countries one-parent families occur more frequently among lower socioeconomic groups, and are confounded with racial differences in countries such as the United States. Research does not show unequivocally that living in a single-parent home results in lower educational achievement (Scott-Jones 1984) (see *Children of Single-parent Families*).

5.5 Occupational Status and Race

In many countries there has been a marked change during recent decades in the racial and ethnic composition of the labor force as a result of cross-national migration. This has also resulted in certain occupations being taken by persons from particular ethnic groups, who for a variety of reasons are assigned a lower status. As a consequence, the occupational status scales that were constructed using data from a more homogeneous population within a particular country are no longer as meaningful as they were formerly. Furthermore, in the examination of the effects of race or ethnic composition on educational outcomes it would seem necessary to control for occupational status to obtain meaningful relationships. However, such statistical control may not be fully appropriate if occupational status in the land of adoption were rather lower than it would have been in the land of origin for particular racial and ethnic groups.

5.6 Robust Measures of Occupational Status

Much effort went into developing refined measures of occupational status during the decades from 1960 to 1990. However, in studies where information with respect to the occupation of their parents is obtained from students at levels of schooling below the age of noncompulsory attendance, it is found that a simple 4-category classification: (a) professional and managerial, (b) clerical, (c) skilled blue-collar, and (d) semiskilled and unskilled worker, to which rank scaled scores of 4, 3, 2, and 1, respectively are assigned, yields just as strong relationships with educational outcomes as do more refined occupational status scales. The reason for these apparently anomalous results would appear to lie in the greater robustness of the classificatory scheme and a reduction in errors of misclassification. Generally, with a simple four-category scale, missing data and nonresponse are best assigned to the scale value, 1 or 0, as determined by criterion scaling (Keeves 1992).

5.7 Sensitive Measures of Occupational Status

A 4-category scale is, however, of little value at levels beyond the age of compulsory schooling, because of the lack of discrimination of such a scale for father's occupation, mother's occupation, and expected occupation data. The Treiman international scale provides greater discrimination at the upper-secondary-school level which yields stronger relationships with other measures (Keeves 1992).

5.8 Differences in Relationships between Occupational Status and Achievement Outcomes in Developed and Developing Countries

The Six Subject Study conducted by the International Association for the Evaluation of Educational Achievement (IEA) in 1970–71 showed that the relationship between occupational status measures and achievement outcomes was generally greater in the more industrialized countries than in the less industrialized and developing countries (Walker 1976). Several reasons can be advanced which help to account for this difference. First, there is a lack of variance in the outcome measure in the developing countries, arising from the greater difficulty level and lower

discriminating power of the tests used. Second, there is a lack of variance in the occupational status measures in the developing countries, arising from high proportions in the low-status categories and low proportions in the high-status categories. Third, there are effects of selection bias in the developing countries, with less able students from low-status homes either dropping out from school or being required to repeat grades. Fourth, there is the possibility that the occupational classification and the occupational status measure employed are conceptually inappropriate in the developing countries. Heyneman and Loxley (1983) have considered the confounding effects of selection bias and contend that this is not a plausible explanation. However, the other possible grounds for a reduced relationship remain.

5.9 Changes in the Magnitude of Relations between Measures of Social Background and Achievement Outcomes over Time

Keeves and Saha (1992) examined the magnitudes of the relationships between science achievement and measures of social background between 1970 and 1984. Data for large random samples from 10 countries were available for both occasions on a range of measures, which included father's occupation, father's education, mother's education, books in the home, use of dictionary in the home, and family size. While the measures on both occasions were similar, they were not in many cases identical. Marginally stronger relationships were recorded for 1984 than for 1970. It would appear possible that this is evidence that the effects of home background on educational achievement increased over this period of 14 years. Such a change would be consistent with the development of a more meritocratic society where education was becoming more important for the attainment of high social status. While the explanation of this stronger relationship recorded might lie in improved measurement and the use of slightly more meaningful questions, or in more variance in the outcome measure, the possibility of greater inequalities over time in the societies being studied cannot be gainsaid.

However, Peterson (1982) contends that a marked drop in such relationships occurred in the United States in the late 1970s. Since most of the decline reported took place during a brief five-year period from 1973 to 1978, some doubt must exist regarding the quality of the samples used.

6. The Cultural Level of the Home

Floud (1961) has pointed out that the French have a phrase, *la famille éducogéne*, to describe families who provide an educative environment that reinforces the intellectual pressures exerted by the school. It is widely recognized that the educative climate of the home influences the intellectual development of the child not only during the years of schooling, but more particularly during the early years of childhood (Bloom 1964). Subsequently, Bloom (1976) argued that family background may be considered to involve three components, which are: (a) a cultural component such as the number of books in the home, visits to the theatre or museum, use of a public library; (b) a social component which comprises the parents' educational and occupational status; and (c) an economic component which refers to the family income and possessions.

In the IEA Six Subject Study in 1970–71, recognition of the cultural as well as the social component led to the development of an index of social background, which was based upon six measures: father's occupation, father's education, mother's education, use of the dictionary, number of books in the home, and family size. These six variables were weighted by criterion-scaling procedures using achievement on tests of science, reading, and word knowledge as criteria to form a composite measure assessing the sociocultural level of the home (Comber and Keeves 1973). Keeves (1972) had previously employed a similar index using five measures: family size, father's occupation, father's education, mother's occupation before marriage, and religious affiliation, combining the variables by principal components analysis. The incorporation of a scaled measure of religious affiliation led to the acceptance that the index developed involved a cultural rather than an economic emphasis. Likewise, the inclusion of mother's occupation before marriage was seen to be associated with the competence of the mother rather than being related to the contribution that she made to the total family income.

7. Educational Resources of the Home

Difficulties associated with measuring socioeconomic status, and general acceptance of the importance of the cultural level of the home, led the IEA Reading Literacy Study in 1991 to employ a variable concerned with reading resources of the home. The measures employed in the construction of this variable were: (a) number of books at home, (b) use of test language at home, and (c) home possessions (Postlethwaite and Ross 1992).

8. Conclusion

It should be noted that indexes of occupational status and socioeconomic status correlate positively and significantly with the educational outcomes of both achievement and attainment in cases where the school population has not been truncated by the removal of less able students. Even where the school population has been reduced or censored in this way these indexes are, in the main, positively related to educational outcomes. Research since the 1980s shows a clear tendency for indexes of sociocultural level to be more strongly related to educational outcomes than are indexes of occupational and socioeconomic status, and thus they have greater explanatory power. The evidence available strongly supports the contention that it is not the occupational status of the home per se that influences educational outcomes but rather the related sociocultural level of the home with its emphasis on reading and the use of language.

See also: Family, School, and Social Capital; Social Mobility, Social Stratification, and Education; Stratification in Educational Systems

References

Blishen B R 1958 The construction and use of an occupational scale. *Can. J. Econ. Polit. Sci.* 24: 519–31
Blishen B R 1967 A socioeconomic index for occupations in Canada. *Can. Rev. Soc. Anthropol.* 4: 41–53
Bloom B S 1964 *Stability and Change in Human Characteristics.* Wiley, New York
Bloom B S 1976 *Human Characteristics and School Learning.* McGraw-Hill, New York
Broom L, Jones F L, Zubrzycki J 1965 An occupational classification of the Australian workforce. *Aust. N. Z. J. Sociol.* 1 (supplement)
Broom L, Duncan-Jones P, Jones F L, McDonnell P 1977 *Investigating Social Mobility.* Australian National University Press, Canberra
Coleman J S et al. 1966 *Equality of Educational Opportunity*, 2 vols. US Government Printing Office, Washington, DC
Comber L C, Keeves J P 1973 *Science Education in Nineteen Countries: An Empirical Study.* Wiley, New York
Congalton A A 1963 *Occupational Status in Australia.* School of Sociology, University of New South Wales, Kensington
Duncan O D 1961 A socioeconomic index for all occupations. In: Reiss A J (ed.) 1961 *Occupations and Social Status.* Free Press, New York
Edwards A 1938 *A Social-Economic Grouping of the Gainful Workers of the United States, Gainful Workers of 1930 in Social-Economic Groups, by Color, Nativity, Age, and Sex, and by Industry, with Comparative Statistics for 1920 and 1910.* GPO, Washington, DC
Elley W B, Irving J C 1972 A socioeconomic index for New Zealand based on levels of education and income from the 1966 Census. *N.Z. J. Educ. Stud.* 7: 153–67
Erikson R, Goldthorpe J H, Portecarero 1979 Intergenerational class mobility in three Western European societies: England, France and Sweden. *Br. J. Sociol.* 30(4): 415–41
Floud J 1961 Social class factors in educational achievement. In: Halsey A H (ed.) 1961 *Ability and Educational Opportunity.* OECD, Paris
Goldthorpe J H 1980 *Social Mobility and Class Structure in Modern Britain.* Clarendon Press, Oxford
Goldthorpe J H, Hope K 1974 *The Social Grading of Occupations: A New Approach and Scale.* Clarendon Press, Oxford

Hall J, Caradog Jones D 1950 Social grading of occupations. *Br. J. Sociol.* 1: 31–55

Haug M R 1977 Measurement in social stratification. *Ann. Rev. Sociol.* 3: 51–78

Heyneman S P, Loxley W A 1983 The effects of primary school quality on academic achievement across twenty-nine high- and low-income countries. *Am. J. Sociol.* 88(6): 1162–94

Husén T (ed.) 1967 *International Study of Achievement in Mathematics: A Comparison of Twelve Countries.* Almqvist and Wiksell, Stockholm

Jencks C S et al. 1972 *Inequality: A reassessment of the effect of family and schooling in America.* Basic Books, New York

Jones F L 1971 Occupational achievement in Australia and the United States: A comparative path analysis. *Am. J. Sociol.* 77: 527–39

Keeves J P 1972 *Educational Environment and Student Achievement.* Almqvist and Wiksell, Stockholm

Keeves J P (ed.) 1992 *The IEA Study of Science III. Changes in Science Education and Achievement. 1970–1984.* Pergamon, Oxford

Keeves J P, Saha L J 1992 Home background factors and educational outcomes. In: Keeves J P (ed.) 1992

Mason W M et al. 1976 Models of response error in student reports of parental socioeconomic characteristics. In: Sewell W M, Hauser R M, Featherman D L (eds.) 1976 *Schooling and Achievement in American Society.* Academic Press, New York

McRoberts H A 1985 Mobility and attainment in Canada: The effects of origin. In: Boyd M et al. 1985 *Ascription and Achievement.* Carleton University Press, Ottawa

Miller D C 1991 *Handbook of Research Design and Social Measurement*, 5th edn. Sage, Newbury Park, California

Nam C B, Powers M G 1968 Changes in relative status of workers in the United States, 1950–60. *Social Forces* 47: 158–70

Oppenheim A N 1966 *Questionnaire Design and Attitude Measurement.* Heinemann, London

Peterson P E 1982 Effect of credentials, connections, and competence on income. In: Kruskal W H (ed.) 1982 *The Social Sciences: Their Nature and Uses.* University of Chicago Press, Chicago, Illinois

Pineo P, Porter J 1967 Occupational prestige in Canada. *Canadian Rev. Sociol. Anthropol.* 4: 24–40

Postlethwaite T N, Ross K N 1992 *Effective Schools in Reading: Implications for Educational Planners.* IEA, Hamburg

Scott-Jones D 1984 Family influences on cognitive development and school achievement. *Rev. Res. Educ.* II: 259–304

Siegel P M 1971 Prestige in the American occupational structure. PhD thesis, University of Chicago

Treiman D J 1977 *Occupational Prestige in Comparative Perspective.* Academic Press, New York

Walker D A 1976 *The IEA Six Subject Survey: An Empirical Study of Education in Twenty-One Countries.* Almqvist and Wiksell, Stockholm

Warner W L, Meeker M, Eells K 1949 *Social Class in America: A Manual of Procedure for the Measurement of Social Status.* Science Research Associates, Chicago, Illinois

Research in Education: Epistemological Issues

J. C. Walker and C. W. Evers

Epistemology is the study of the nature, scope, and applicability of knowledge. Educational research, in being concerned with the conduct of educational inquiry and the development and evaluation of its methods and findings, embodies a commitment to epistemological assumptions—at least it does if its findings are expected to command attention, serve as a sound basis for action, or constitute legitimate knowledge claims. These matters are the subject of epistemological theories which deal more systematically with such general corresponding issues as justification, truth, and the accessibility of reality in the search for knowledge.

In educational research, obviously, there are different methods of inquiry, ranging from controlled laboratory experiments through participant observation to action research, from historical studies to logical analysis. These have been organized in different research traditions, such as "quantitative" and "qualitative," or associated with different theoretical positions, such as behaviorism and critical theory. In practice, the categories of method, tradition, and theoretical position cut across each other to some extent.

The major epistemological question here is whether these distinctions are associated with different ways of knowing or forms of knowledge, which partition educational research so that research traditions, for example, turn out to be radically distinct epistemologically, each having its own theories and rules of justification, meaning, and truth. If so, the next question is whether findings produced by the different traditions can be rationally integrated, rendered coherent, or even compared. For this to be possible, for traditions to be commensurable, there will have to be some shared concepts and standards of justification, meaning, and truth: some epistemological touchstone. If, however, the traditions are so fundamentally disparate that any choice between them in educational research is arbitrary or the result of nonrational commitment— an act of faith—there is no touchstone. The research traditions are incommensurable.

There has long been controversy over these issues,

in educational research and the social sciences generally, as advocates of research traditions variously described as "scientific," "humanistic," "quantitative," "qualitative," "positivist," and "interpretative" have tried to sort out the respective epistemological merits of these approaches and the methodological, practical, and even political relations between them.

There are three major views available, which have emerged in educational research in more or less the following historical order. First, it can be asserted that there are epistemologically different paradigms, which are incommensurable in that neither educational research nor any other form of inquiry can provide a rational method for judging between them. Moreover, they are mutually incompatible, competitive ways of researching the same territory. This may be called the "oppositional diversity thesis." Second, it could be decided that there are epistemologically distinct paradigms, but that though incommensurable they are complementary, not competitive: equally appropriate ways of approaching different, overlapping, or perhaps even the same research problems. This may be called the "complementary diversity thesis." The first and second views agree that there is a fundamental epistemological diversity in educational research. The third alternative, the unity thesis, denies this. It disagrees with the view that different research methods can be grouped under incommensurable paradigms, and asserts that the very idea of such paradigms is mistaken, even incoherent. It claims there is touchstone for judging the respective merits of different research traditions and bringing them into a productive relationship with one another. It asserts a fundamental epistemological unity of educational research, derived from the practical problems addressed.

This article argues for the unity thesis. After a discussion of the term "paradigm," and of the oppositional and complementary diversity theses, it is shown that the theory that there are research paradigms—call it the "P-theory"—is largely responsible for both forms of diversity thesis. Some reasons are offered for believing that P-theory is incoherent, and it is argued that a coherentist epistemology sustains the thesis of the epistemological unity of educational research. A feature of this epistemology is its account of touchstone in educational research.

1. Epistemology and Paradigms

Numerous educational researchers have been drawn to the view that research traditions are best regarded as different paradigms. Indeed, as Shulman (1986 p. 3) observes, in writing about the different research programs of communities of scholars engaged in the study of teaching, "the term most frequently employed to describe such research communities, and the conceptions of problem and method they share is *paradigm.*"

As the quantitative/qualitative debate shows, many writers in education distinguish two fundamental

paradigms of research: the "scientific" which is often erroneously identified with positivism, and the "interpretative" or "humanistic." Husén associates the distinction with divergent forms of explanation and understanding:

> The twentieth century has seen the conflict between two main paradigms employed in researching educational problems. The one is modeled on the natural sciences with an emphasis on empirical quantifiable observations which lend themselves to analyses by means of mathematical tools. The task of research is to establish causal relationships, to explain (*Erklären*). The other paradigm is derived from the humanities with an emphasis on holistic and qualitative information and to interpretive approaches (*Verstehen*). (1988 p. 17)

In offering a broader, three-way taxonomy of research to account for diversity in inquiry, Popkewitz (1984 p. 35) says: "the concept of paradigm provides a way to consider this divergence in vision, custom and tradition. It enables us to consider science as having different sets of assumptions, commitments, procedures and theories of social affairs." He assumes that "in educational sciences, three paradigms have emerged to give definition and structure to the practice of research." After the fashion of "critical theory" (Habermas 1972), he identifies the paradigms as "empirical-analytic" (roughly equivalent to quantitative science), "symbolic" (qualitative and interpretative or hermeneutical inquiry), and "critical" (where political criteria relating to human betterment are applied in research).

Noting the influence of positivism on the formation of research traditions and the paradigms debate, Lincoln and Guba (1984 p. 15) mention another common three-way distinction, which they apply to "paradigm eras," "periods in which certain sets of basic beliefs have guided inquiry in quite different ways," rather than directly to paradigms as such. They identify these paradigm eras as "prepositivist," "positivist," and "postpositivist." Now the term "positivist" also has a history of varied usage (Phillips 1983) but, because of the practice common among educational researchers of defining their perspectives in relation to one or more of the varieties of positivism, it is important to note some of the issues involved in the transition to postpositivism.

In philosophy of science, views of the nature of science commonly described as positivist have characterized science as value-free, basing its theories and findings on logically simple and epistemically secure observation reports, and using empirical concepts themselves deriving directly from observation (Hooker 1975). Positivism in this sense, as a form of empiricism, involves a foundational epistemology. Knowledge claims are justified when they are shown to be based on secure foundations, which for positivist empiricism are the sense data acquired through empirical observation. Some positivists—the logical positivists—maintained that only the sentences of science thus conceived, and the "conceptual truths" of logic and mathematics, were objectively meaningful, and that therefore here were to be drawn the limits of genuine knowledge, not simply scientific knowledge. Thus delimited, the domain of knowledge excluded morals, politics, and indeed any field where value judgments were made, which would include much educational research. The movement to postpositivist philosophy of science has occurred because of the undermining of all such doctrines (House 1991).

This use of "positivist" needs to be clearly distinguished from use of the term to describe any view that science (and perhaps conceptual truths of logic and mathematics) is the only way to knowledge, and that the task of philosophy—which is not sharply distinguished from but continuous with empirical science—is to find general principles common to all sciences and even to extend the use of such principles to the regulation of human conduct and the organization of society. The move to a postpositivist (in the first sense) philosophy of science is quite compatible with such a view of the nature of science and its role in human affairs.

Unfortunately, this distinction is not always clearly observed in epistemological discussions of educational research. It is one thing to say, with Lincoln and Guba (1984), that since it has been recognized that science is more complex than building on theory-free and value-free observations, qualitative inquiry may be recognized as a legitimate approach; that the latest paradigm era sanctions more than one paradigm. It is another thing to identify science with positivism (in the first sense) and on the basis of this identification to attack all views suggesting an epistemological continuity between the natural and the social sciences including educational research. Ironically, many writers, while they claim to reject positivism (in both senses), retain a positivist (in the first sense) view of natural science (e.g., Habermas 1972). In this entry "positivist" is used in the first sense, to refer to positivistic empiricism, including logical positivism.

In summary, the move from a positivist to a postpositivist philosophy of science has been paralleled by a move from a view of educational research dominated by the quantitative tradition to a more pluralistic view. The advent of the postpositivist era has been characterized by an acceptance of epistemological diversity which, however, insofar as it is formulated in terms of P-theory, leaves educational research epistemologically divided. The question, then, if there are such divisions as have been noted, is whether the diversity must be oppositional, or can it be harmonious?

2. The Oppositional Diversity Thesis

Quantitative researchers have often seen qualitative research as lacking in objectivity, rigor, and scientific controls (Kerlinger 1973 p. 401). Lacking the resources of quantification, qualitative research cannot produce the requisite generalizations to build up a set of laws of human behavior, nor can it apply adequate tests for validity and reliability. Moreover, the positivist fact/value distinction is often employed to discredit the claims of qualitative inquiry to produce knowledge, since knowledge is value-free whereas qualitative research is irreducibly value-laden and subjective. In short, qualitative research falls short of the high standards of objectivity and the tight criteria for truth of the quantitative, or "scientific," paradigm. Given the prestige of science, and a positivist view of science, it is easy to see why quantitative researchers have sometimes even seen qualitative research as opposed to sound scientific method.

In reply, many qualitative researchers, invoking the explanation/understanding distinction, claim that the genuinely and distinctively human dimension of education cannot be captured by statistical generalizations and causal laws. Knowledge of human affairs is irreducibly subjective. It must grasp the meanings of actions, the uniqueness of events, and the individuality of persons. From this perspective, it is easy to see the quantitative tradition as an intrusive, even alien and antihuman, approach to the study of education. "Science" may be appropriate to the study of nature, but it distorts the study of human affairs. It is easy to see why, given a perceived *de facto* domination of educational research by the quantitative tradition, qualitative researchers have sometimes seen it in oppositional, even antagonistic, terms.

Thus the debate over whether so-called quantitative research methodology is in conflict with qualitative research methodology does not revolve simply around the use of numbers, of mathematical and statistical procedures. Rather, it concerns the relation of quantification to more basic questions about objectivity, validity, reliability, and criteria for truth. For example, according to Smith and Heshusius (1986 p. 9), who have reasserted the oppositional diversity thesis against the increasing popularity of the other two: "For quantitative inquiry, a logic of justification that is epistemologically foundational leads to the position that certain sets of techniques are epistemologically privileged in that their correct application is necessary to achieve validity or to discover how things really are out there." They also state: "From the perspective of qualitative inquiry, this line of reasoning is unacceptable. The assumptions or logic of justification in this case are not foundationalist and, by extension, do not allow that certain sets of procedures are epistemologically privileged." There are two key epistemological distinctions here. First, "logic of justification" (grounds for making claims) is distinguished from research procedures (techniques used to gather, analyze, and interpret data). Second, foundational epistemologies, which provide a logic or justification basing knowledge claims on supposedly secure or certain foundations (such as empirical observations), are distinguished from nonfoundational epistemologies whose logic of justification involves no foundations. Later in this entry the assumption that quantitative inquiry must be foundationalist is queried.

The key epistemological dilemma posed by Smith and Heshusius is that for the quantitative researcher there exists a mind-independent reality "out there" that is to some extent knowable. Disciplined observation of it provides epistemic foundations. Qualitative researchers, they assert, are committed to denying this. By following certain practices of inquiry that enjoy a cluster of related theoretical advantages—the advantages of internal and external validity, reliability, and objectivity—the quantitative researcher increases the likelihood of discovering something important about that reality. Its properties and the causal structures governing the orderly behavior of its interrelated parts constitute typical goals of quantitative inquiry. What makes these goals possible, and indeed holds together the theoretical features of such inquiry, is a belief that people can know when a correspondence obtains between the sentences of a theory and the world "out there." It is this correspondence that makes knowledge claims true.

It is precisely this belief that is most often questioned by qualitative researchers. Reality, or at least social reality, they frequently maintain, is something constructed with the mind as a product of theorizing. Theorizing shapes reality, rather than the other way around. There is simply no mind-independent or theory-independent reality to match up with or correspond to sentences, to serve as a check on their acceptability. Under this assumption, the theoretical apparatus employed to characterize epistemically virtuous inquiry will apparently have little use for familiar quantitative notions. Instead, distinctly alternative networks of theoretical requirements for qualitative research will need to be devised, tied to procedures for getting at subjective, or intersubjective, symbols, meanings, and understandings.

Critical theorists go one step further in this philosophical opposition to the "intrusion" of the quantitative tradition into the search for knowledge of the "genuinely human." In addition to being unable to capture the necessary relation between the human mind and social reality, critical theorists maintain that the quantitative (or empirical-analytic) tradition cannot capture the essential role of values in that kind of knowledge needed to improve the human condition. Thus Bates (1980) argues that epistemically adequate educational research must be research that makes for "human betterment." The "praxis" tradition in epistemology, well-exemplified in the theoretical writings of Freire (1972), and more particularly in the action research tradition (Carr and Kemmis 1983), provides a rich theoretical context for elaborating further nonquantitative criteria to replace quantitative notions of validity, reliability, and objectivity. In contrast to the usual lines drawn in the quantitative/qualitative debate, the elimination of social injustice, for example, is not merely a matter of constructing alternative realities, or alternative theories. Nor is validity simply a matter of establishing a correspondence between theory and the world, when the goal is social improvement. Rather, what counts as valid inquiry, as epistemically progressive, is limited to what the surrounding epistemology counts as promoting human well-being.

3. The Complementary Diversity Thesis

Within the epistemologically softer climate of the postpositivist era, many educational researchers believe that the various research traditions, even if incommensurable, are equally legitimate and in no necessary conflict. The "scientific" and "humanistic" approaches, "are not exclusive, but complementary to each other" (Husén 1988 p. 20). Indeed Shulman (1986 p. 4) goes so far as to suggest that "the danger for any field of social science or educational research lies in its potential corruption . . . by a single paradigmatic view." Against what they have regarded as the unwarranted "positivist," quantitative domination of educational research, proponents of the qualitative/interpretative paradigm have succeeded in convincing a number of scholars whose work has been within the quantitative tradition (e.g., Campbell and Overman 1988, Cronbach 1975) that the qualitative approach has its own merits.

Some writers have suggested that complementarity must be recognized in view of various distinct desiderata in educational research, not all of which can be met by any one single paradigm. For example, there are pressing educational and social problems requiring policy and practical responses. The information necessary for policy formulation might not be available for controlled laboratory experiments of limited generalizability (or external validity), but might be provided by "quasi-experiments" (Cook and Campbell 1979) or qualitative research. Moreover, given the rate of social change, or the constant interactive effects of educational treatments and student aptitudes, generalizations yielded by a quantitative approach might become rapidly out of date. The project of developing a stable set of scientific educational laws may not be viable (Cronbach 1975).

For other writers espousing complementary diversity, the multifactorial complexity of educational problems supports epistemological pluralism. Keeves acknowledges that some approaches are more holistic, embracing greater complexity than others:

> The techniques employed in educational research must be capable of examining many variables at the same time, but not necessarily through the use of complex statistical procedures . . . although these have their place. Anthropologists have evolved procedures for analyzing and presenting information from a situation which involves many factors that are very different from those

used by psychologists, and different again from those that might be employed by economists and sociologists. (1986 p. 390)

Nevertheless, according to Campbell and Overman (1988), P-theoretical differences are still unavoidable because there remains a need for the kind of research produced by the tools of descriptive science and formal logic, which cannot embrace the value judgments characteristic of much nonquantitative educational inquiry. For other writers, fundamental epistemological differences between explanation and interpretation, of course, remain.

In educational research acceptance of the epistemological integrity of a nonquantitative paradigm has largely been the result of efforts by qualitative researchers to spell out alternative networks of theoretical requirements for qualitative research. These have tended to run parallel to elements in the received epistemological scheme of quantitative research (validity, reliability, etc.). One influential example, elaborated by Lincoln and Guba (1984), employs the notions of credibility, applicability (or transferability), consistency, and neutrality, as analogies respectively for internal validity, external validity, reliability, and objectivity.

The point here, however, is not so much that there is some loose analogical connection between corresponding terms in these sets. Rather, despite détente, the point to note is the persisting apparent epistemological distinctiveness of these theoretically interanimated clusters and their respective embeddings in different epistemologies. Some complementary diversity theorists might think that they can have fundamental epistemological diversity without subscribing to something as strong as the P-theory and its incommensurability doctrine. Here, perhaps, epistemological diversity is being confused with methodological diversity, a diversity of techniques of inquiry. Of course the latter is possible but, in the opinion of the authors, is best underwritten by a "touchstone" account of epistemic justification, not several incommensurable epistemologies. Such an account does not have to be fixed and absolute; it can change. The point is that at any given time it embraces those epistemological commitments that are shared by researchers. This is the unity thesis. If complementary diversity theorists wish to eschew such epistemological touchstone, then they remain committed to P-theory.

It should be noted that many advocates of equal rights for qualitative research have wished to play down the epistemological differences (Lincoln and Guba 1984, Miles and Huberman 1984). It may be that exponents of the complementary diversity thesis who persist with the term "paradigm" do not embrace P-theory's doctrine of incommensurability, although this is rarely made explicit. If they disavow incommensurability, their position would seem to collapse into the unity thesis, with revisionary consequences for the

way they draw the distinctions between paradigms. These may be more drastic than at first appears. In the case of the explanation/understanding distinction, for instance, Keeves (1988), in arguing for complementarity, has adopted Giddens's (1984) reworking of this distinction. Not all complementarists have recognized the seriousness of the problem, however. As Smith and Heshusius (1986 p. 7) put it, there has been a tendency to "de-epistemologize" the debate or even ignore paradigmatic differences. Given that paradigms exist, Smith and Heshusius may well be right—but do paradigms exist?

4. Criticisms of the Paradigms Theory

It is apparent that there is some confusion over both the term "paradigm" and the problem of unambiguously identifying paradigms of educational research. Some of the confusion comes from the ambiguity of the term "paradigm" itself. On the one hand, as Husén (1988 p. 17) points out, there would be wide agreement that the most influential use of "paradigm" stems from the work of Kuhn (1970). However, Masterman (1970) identified some 21 different uses of the term in Kuhn's book; Kuhn subsequently published revisions, some substantial, to his original theory (e.g., Kuhn 1974); and finally, not all methodologists embrace Kuhn's ideas uncritically.

Kuhn has also put the principal argument for regarding paradigms as incommensurable, as incapable of being compared or measured against some touchstone standard:

> In learning a paradigm the scientist acquires theory, methods, and standards together, usually in an inextricable mixture. Therefore when paradigms change, there are usually significant shifts in the criteria determining the legitimacy both of problems and of proposed solutions.
>
> That observation . . . provides our first explicit indication of why the choice between competing paradigms regularly raises questions that cannot be resolved by the criteria of normal science . . . will inevitably talk through each other when debating the relative merits of their respective paradigms. In the partially circular arguments that regularly result, each paradigm will be shown to satisfy more or less the criteria that it dictates for itself and to fall short of a few of those dictated by its opponent. (1970 pp. 109–10)

The key claim being made here is that paradigms include both substantive theories and the standards and criteria for evaluating those theories, or paradigm-specific epistemologies. As such, it is also claimed, there is no priviledged epistemic vantage point from which different paradigms can be assessed; there are only the rival epistemic standards built into each paradigm.

Kuhn's early comments on the task of adjudicating the merits of competing paradigms are instructive: "the proponents of competing paradigms practise their trade in different worlds" (Kuhn 1970 p. 150); "the transfer of allegiance from paradigm to paradigm is a conversion experience that cannot be forced" (Kuhn 1970 p. 151); such a transition occurs relatively suddenly, like a gestalt switch "just because it is a transition between incommensurables" (Kuhn 1970 p. 150).

Moreover, the belief that some research traditions are incommensurable can be made to look initially plausible by noting the kind of tradition-specific vocabularies that are used to characterize matters epistemological. As has been seen, methodological reflection on quantitative research commonly trades in such terminology as "scientific," "positivist," "foundational," "correspondence-truth," "objective," "realist," "validity," "reliability," "reductionist," and "empiricist." The qualitative network of such terms includes "nonpositivist," "antifoundational," "interpretation," "understanding," "subjective," "idealist," "relativist," and "antireductionist." The fact that key terms of epistemic conduct in one cluster are formed by negating terms in the other cluster readily suggests no common basis for the conduct and assessment of inquiry, and hence the incommensurability of these traditions.

Clearly, for a defense of the epistemological unity of educational research, the most important obstacle is this P-theoretical analysis of research traditions. So the first point to make in a defense of the unity thesis is that in philosophy, and philosophy of science in particular, P-theory is widely regarded as false. In a major review of the literature following a 1969 symposium on the structure of scientific theories, Suppe (1977 p. 647) remarks: "Since the symposium Kuhn's views have undergone a sharply declining influence on contemporary work in philosophy of science." He goes on to claim that contemporary work in philosophy of science, that is, postpositivist philosophy in science, "increasingly subscribes to the position that it is a central aim of science to come to know how the world *really is*" (Suppe 1977 p. 649). In social and educational research, however, especially among qualitative researchers and critical theorists, antirealist belief in paradigms remains strong. In the authors' opinion, the apparent ubiquity of "paradigms" in educational research occurs because the epistemological assumptions of the P-theory itself, or its P-epistemology, are largely responsible for structuring differences among research traditions into putative paradigms.

Of course epistemologists in general agree that inquiry structures knowledge of the objects of inquiry; this is part of what is involved in maintaining that all experience is theory-laden. Contrary to Smith and Heshusius (1986), it is not a feature peculiar to qualitative inquiry. The interesting question is whether there is any reason to believe that different research traditions partition into paradigms the way P-theory requires. However, it is rarely noted that whether it is even appropriate to give reasons, to marshal evidence, to analyze research practices and inquiry contexts in

order to justify such a belief, will depend on whether P-theory is, by its own lights, a paradigm (or part of a paradigm), or not. If it is, then the relevant standards of reasoning, evidence, and analysis will be peculiar to P-theory (or its encompassing paradigm) and so will have rational epistemic purchase on none but the already committed. To the unbeliever, P-theory would literally have nothing to say for itself. For one to believe that educational research comes in paradigms would require an act of faith: to come to believe it after believing the contrary would require a conversion experience.

There are interesting problems with this view. For example, what happens if one is converted to it? Does one then say that it is true that educational research divides into paradigms? Unfortunately the term "true" is P-theoretical and so one needs to determine first whether, for example, the sentences of P-theory correspond to a world of real educational researchers really engaged in incommensurable research practices. If so, then P-theory is not after all a paradigm distinct from those that employ correspondence-truth. If not, then there is a genuine equivocation over the term "true" which will permit the following claims to be made without contradiction: (a) it is correspondence-true that the different research traditions are not epistemologically distinct; and (b) it is P-true that the different research traditions are epistemologically distinct.

In conceding the equal legitimacy of incommensurable rivals (whether oppositional or complementary), however, particularly a correspondence-truth rival, the P-theorist seems to be surrendering the capacity to say anything about actual educational research practices and the historical and theoretical context of current research traditions. Worse still, in eschewing any schema for determining the ontological commitments of P-theory, there seems to be no way of knowing what the P-theorist is talking about. As such, P-theory hardly provides a challenge to a realist view of the unity of educational research.

To avoid the dilemma that threatens when P-theory becomes self-referential, several options are available. Two are considered here. First, a less parsimonious attitude to rival epistemologies can be adopted by maintaining that correspondence-true theories, which caused all the trouble, are false, wrong, or, as hard-hitting relativists are fond of saying, inadequate. Indeed, getting rid of correspondence-truth may be a condition for meaningful P-theoretical claims about theorists' living in different worlds; after all, talk of a real world tends to make other worlds pale into nonexistence. A second, opposite, strategy is to say that P-theory is not a distinct paradigm at all, but rather a set of carefully argued, evidentially supported, correspondence-true claims about the existence of paradigmatic divisions among the major research traditions. It is instructive to note that some methodologists run both these strategies simultaneously (e.g.,

Lincoln and Guba 1984, Eisner 1979). (For damaging criticism of Eisner's running the two strategies together, see Phillips 1983.)

Arguments for the first option are by now familiar enough. Correspondence-truth is assumed to be located in a network of terms usually associated with the quantitative research tradition. Valid and reliable knowledge about the world is said to be that which is, in some way, derivable from some epistemically secure (or even certain) foundation; in positivistic empiricism usually observations or first person sensory reports. Objectivity consists in intersubjectively agreed matchings between statements and experience. And, of course, these objectively known statements are correspondence-true just in case the required matching occurs (although often the only reality admitted was sense data).

There are many objections to foundational empiricist epistemologies (e.g., Hesse 1974, Churchland 1979), but a version of the earlier argument from self-reference will suffice to illustrate the problems. Although this is not widely recognized in positivistic empiricism, epistemology is a task that requires (as Kant saw) a theory of the powers of the mind. What one can know will depend, to some extent, on what sort of creature one is and, in particular, on what sort of perceptual and cognitive capacities one has. A theory of the mind, however, is something one has to get to know. In the case of empiricist foundationalism, it is necessary to know that one's own sensory experiences will provide one with epistemically secure foundations. Unfortunately for the foundationalist, the theory of mind required to underwrite this claim is not itself an item of sensory experience, nor an observation report. This means that knowledge of how the class of epistemically privileged items is known is not itself epistemically privileged. Indeed, the sophisticated neurophysiological models of brain functioning now typical of accounts of perception and cognition are quite ill-suited to serving the regress pattern of foundational justification. For they so far outrun the purported resources of any proposed foundation that the whole point of foundational justification here collapses. More generally, knowledge of perceptual powers, or possible foundations, like knowledge of everything, is theory-laden. The result is that there is no epistemically privileged, theory-free, way of viewing the world. There is thus no reality that can be seen independent of competing theoretical perspectives. This applies as much to the empirical sciences (and the quantitative tradition in educational research) as to other areas (see Walker and Evers 1982, Walker and Evers 1986).

From the fact that all experience is theory-laden, however, that what one believes exists depends on what theory one adopts, it does not follow that all theories are evidentially equivalent, or equally reasonable. There is more to evidence than observation, or as Churchland (1985 p. 35) argues: "observational

excellence or 'empirical adequacy' is only one epistemic virtue among others of equal or comparable importance." The point is that some theories organize their interpretations of experience better than others. A humdrum example employing subjectivist scruples on evidence will illustrate this point. A theory which says that I can leave what I interpret to be my office by walking through what I interpret to be the wall will cohere less well with my interpreted desire to leave my office than a theory which counsels departure via what I take to be the door. It is all interpretative, of course, but some organized sets of interpretations, or theories, are better than others. The theory that enables a person to experience the desired success of departing the perceived enclosure of an office enjoys certain epistemic advantages over one that does not. With all experience interpreted, though, the correct conclusion to draw is not that there is no adequate objective standard of reality, but that objectivity involves more than empirical adequacy. Theoretically motivated success in getting in and out of rooms is about as basic as objectivity ever gets. There are superempirical, theoretical tests which can be couched in a "coherence epistemology." One advocate of coherence epistemology, the postpositivist philosopher Quine, sums up this standard of reality.

> Having noted that man has no evidence for the existence of bodies beyond the fact that their assumption helps him organize experience, we should have done well, instead of disclaiming evidence for the existence of bodies, to conclude: such, then, at bottom, is what evidence is both for ordinary bodies and molecules. (Quine 1960a p. 251)

Quine's point here foreshadows a significant epistemological consequence of this attack on foundationalism. According to Quine, and many coherence theorists, we need to distinguish sharply between the theory of evidence and the theory of truth (Quine 1960a, Quine 1960b, Quine 1969, Quine 1974, Williams 1980). Theory of evidence is concerned with the global excellence of theory, and involves both empirical adequacy, inasmuch as this can be achieved and the superempirical virtues of simplicity, consistency, comprehensiveness, fecundity, familiarity or principle, and explanatory power. Once the best theory according to these coherence criteria has been established, it is the resulting theory itself that is used to state what exists and how the theory's sentences match up with that posited reality. What corresponds to true sentences is therefore something that is determined after the theory of evidence has done its work. It is not something that figures a priori, or in some privileged foundational way in the determination of the best theory.

The evidence suggests that P-theory critiques of foundationalism draw too radical a conclusion. In terms of the quantitative/qualitative debate, for example, the coherence epistemology sanctioned by the most powerful criticisms of empiricist foundationalism cuts across this familiar methodological (putatively paradigmatic) bifurcation. In acknowledging the theory-ladenness of all experience it is nonpositivist and nonfoundational. It agrees that people's window on the world is mind-dependent and subject to the interpretations of theorists. On the other hand, it can be realist, scientific, objective, reductionist, and embrace correspondence-truth. This possibility raises serious doubts about P-theorists' claims concerning the diversity of educational research, whether oppositional or complementary.

A more systematic objection to P-theory can be raised, however, by examining the epistemological warrant for incommensurability. The belief that research methodologies comprising incommensurable networks of theoretical terms are epistemically autonomous is sustained in large measure by a particular theory of meaning, notably that terms gain what meaning they possess in virtue of their role in some network or conceptual scheme. Where conceptual schemes or theories are said to be systematically different, no basis exists for matching the terms of one theory with those of another. So expressions such as "validity" or "truth," which appear as orthographically equivalent across different schemes, are really equivocal, with systematic differences emerging as differences in conceptual role.

Both Kuhn and Feyerabend maintain versions of the conceptual role theory of meaning. The trouble, however, is that they maintain implausibly strong versions of it, for if meaning is determined entirely by conceptual role then incommensurable theories become unlearnable. This all turns on the modest empirical fact that as finite learners people need some point of entry into an elaborate systematically interconnected vocabulary like a theory. In order to learn some small part of the theory, say a handful of expressions, however, P-epistemology requires mastery of the whole theory in order to appreciate the conceptual role played by these expressions. It is at this point that the theory of meaning begins to outrun its own epistemological resources: it posits learned antecedents of learning that cannot themselves be learned. The parts cannot be understood without mastery of the whole, and resources are lacking to master the whole without first scaling the parts. An implicit feature of the epistemology driving P-theory's account of meaning as conceptual role is thus an implausibly strong theory of the powers of the mind. (A P-theoretical attack on correspondence-truth appears to depend on a correspondence-true theory of mind.)

Once again P-theory may be observed getting into difficulty over self-reference. In this case an epistemology should come out knowable on its own account of knowledge. The chief advantage of arguments from self-reference is that they focus directly on the superempirical virtues or weaknesses of a theory.

Inasmuch as one is impressed by such theoretical shortcomings as inconsistency, lack of explanatory power in relation to rivals, use of ad hoc hypotheses, and so on, one is allowing these criteria to function as touchstone in the evaluation of epistemologies and research methodologies. Of course one can ignore these vices in theory-construction: they are not extratheoretical privileged foundations by which all theorizing can be assessed. Methodologists in the main research traditions, however, who expect their inquiries to command attention, serve as a sound basis for action, or constitute a particular or definite set of knowledge claims, have been unwilling to play fast and loose with such virtues as consistency (usually on the formal ground that a contradiction will sanction any conclusion whatever) or simplicity and comprehensiveness (on the ground that ad hoc or arbitrary addition of hypotheses can be used to explain anything whatsoever, and hence nothing at all). Indeed a theory cannot be empirically significant unless it is consistent. With P-theory's theory of meaning exhibiting the superempirical weakness of lack of explanatory power in relation to what it sets itself to explain, and with that weakness being traceable to a theory of mind, it should be observed that whether epistemologies or methodologies are incommensurable turns on such things as empirical theories of mind or brain functioning, or theories of learning and cognition. Epistemology itself is therefore continuous with, and relies upon, empirical science. In Quine's words (1969), epistemology is "naturalized." One consequence is that interpretative theorists, for example, must rely partly on the "scientific" paradigm in order to show the incommensurability of their own paradigm with the "scientific."

5. The Unity Thesis

Although the paradigms perspective is seriously flawed, some account of the kind of unity educational research actually enjoys still needs to be given. In arguing against P-theory, coherence epistemology has already been considered. To conclude this discussion a brief outline will be given of a particular version of coherentism, or epistemological holism, which has achieved considerable prominence in postpositivist philosophy (Quine 1974), has been applied to educational philosophy (Walker and Evers 1982), and systematically to educational administration (Evers and Lakomski 1990) and research methodology (Lakomski 1991).

A more positive epistemological agenda for educational research can be provided by responding to the second strategy a P-theorist can adopt in defending diversity. This strategy involved denying P-theory was a distinct paradigm, conceding correspondence-truth, but arguing that fundamental epistemological diversity still occurred in educational research. In replying to this claim it can be noted that the strategy will need to employ superempirical epistemic virtues to be persuasive. To be effective against a wide range of theoretical perspectives these virtues (consistency, simplicity, fecundity, etc.) will need to be recognized as such by rival epistemologies and hence function as touchstone. As a result the P-theorist's strategy is already compromised. To complete the job, however, a coherence epistemology is needed that yields a touchstone-coherent account of itself and its own epistemic virtues, that is unproblematically self-referential in scope, and that can account for the touchstone-recognized successes of alternative epistemologies and their research extensions.

In the view of the authors, the epistemology that best accounts for knowledge, its growth, and evaluation is a form of holistic scientific naturalism (in Quine's "epistemology naturalized" sense of "naturalism")—a theory that makes ready use of the best or most coherent theories of perception and cognition. According to this view, people are acquiring their theory of the world from infancy onward. Indeed, as Quine (1960b) has shown, theory precedes all learning and hence commences with the innate complement of dispositions to respond selectively to the environment. What one can know is dependent on the kind of creature one is and, as human beings, everyone is one kind of creature. Everyone shares genetically derived, though culturally expressed, refined and modified touchstone standards and procedures. Added to these is further culturally produced touchstone that people acquire as social beings sharing material problems in concrete social contexts. Knowledge is made up of theories, whose existence is to be explained causally, as problem-solving devices. There are numerous philosophical accounts (e.g., Laudan 1977) of how theories can be analyzed as problem-solving devices. In the case of epistemological theories, the problems arise from theoretical practice, including empirical (e.g., educational) research. Clearly, there are certain issues concerning whether a theory is addressing the right problems, and a theory is needed of how to distinguish between real problems and pseudoproblems, and between better and worse formulations of problems. Here the epistemology would lean on a theory of evidence and experiment, on the pragmatic relations between "theory" and "practice" (Walker 1985a).

One real problem, shared by all educational researchers, is how best to conduct inquiry into human learning itself. Without this problem there could be no debate about whether educational research is epistemologically diverse. For there to be an issue at all presupposes at least some sharing of language, including general epistemological terminology such as "truth," "meaning," "adequacy," "interpretation," "paradigm," and so on.

Competition remains, of course, but competition between theories, including theories of educational research methodology, not paradigms. Competition arises because, in addition to touchstone, there are unshared (which is not to say incommensurable) concepts, hypotheses, and rules of method. Indeed, this is part and parcel of being able to distinguish one theory from another in a competitive situation. There can be genuine competition between theories, however, only when they have an issue over which to compete, some shared problem(s). Theory A is in competition with theory B when one or more of its sentences is contrary to sentences in theory B. For this situation to obtain, theories A and B must be attempts at solving at least one common problem. To identify a shared problem involves some conceptual common ground and, if only implicitly at first, some shared method; the concepts have to be deployed. Thus one begins to discover and negotiate touchstone theory which, unlike the privileged epistemic units of foundational epistemologies, is merely the shifting historically explicable amount of theory that is shared by rival theories and theorists. Beginning with identification of common problems, one can proceed to identify further touchstone and elaborate the touchstone frameworks within which theories compete.

Having identified common ground between theories, their differences are next rigorously set out and tested against that touchstone by empirical research and theoretical analysis, seeking to identify the strengths and weaknesses of each, and reach a decision on the theory which is strongest under present circumstances (Walker 1985b), taking into account past achievements and likely future problems (Churchland 1979).

Other features of this epistemology include its capacity to survive its own test of self-reference (Quine 1969), its unified account of validity and reliability (Evers 1991), its denial that all science consists of sets of laws, and of any fundamental epistemological distinction between explanation and understanding (Walker 1985c) or between fact and value judgments (Evers and Lakomski 1990).

Finally, although in this entry it has been maintained that such a coherentist naturalistic epistemology is a sound way of underwriting the epistemological unity of educational research, achieved through touchstone analysis, it should be stressed that it is as much a competing theory as any other, and subject to theory testing (Walker 1985a). Granted that it shares touchstone with other epistemologies, arguments can of course be mounted against it; to engage in such arguments, however, all participations would be implicitly conceding the epistemological unity of research.

See also: Critical Theory and Education; Positivism, Antipositivism, and Empiricism; Research Methodology: Scientific Methods; Research Paradigms in Education

References

Bates R J 1980 New developments in the new sociology of education. *Br. J. Sociol. Educ.* 1(1): 67–79
Campbell D T, Overman S E 1988 *Methodology and Epistemology for Social Science: Selected Papers.* Chicago University Press, Chicago, Illinois

Carr W, Kemmis S 1983 *Becoming Critical. Knowing Through Action Research*. Deakin University Press, Geelong

Churchland P M 1979 *Scientific Realism and the Plasticity of Mind*. Cambridge University Press, Cambridge

Churchland P M 1985 The ontological status of observables. In: Churchland P M, Hooker C A (eds.) 1985 *Images of Science: Essays on Realism and Empiricism*. University of Chicago Press, Chicago, Illinois

Cook T H, Campbell D T 1979 *Quasi-Experimentation. Design and Analysis Issues for Field Settings*. Rand McNally, Chicago, Illinois

Cronbach L J 1975 Beyond the two disciplines of scientific psychology. *Am. Psychol.* 30(2): 116–27

Eisner E 1979 *The Educational Imagination*. Macmillan, New York

Evers C W 1991 Towards a coherentist theory of validity. *Int. J. Educ. Res.* 15(6): 521–35

Evers C W, Lakomski G 1990 *Knowing Educational Administration*. Pergamon Press, Oxford

Freire P 1972 *Cultural Action for Freedom*. Penguin, Harmondsworth

Giddens A 1984 *The Constitution of Society: Outline of the Theory of Structuration*. Polity Press, Cambridge

Habermas J 1972 (trans. Shapiro J) *Knowledge and Human Interests*. Heinemann, London

Hesse M 1974 *The Structure of Scientific Inference*. Macmillan, London

Hooker C A 1975 Philosophy and meta-philosophy of science. Empiricism, Popperianism and realism. *Synthèse* 32: 177–231

House E R 1991 Realism in research. *Educ. Researcher* 20(6): 2–9

Husén T 1988 Research paradigms in education. In: Keeves J P (ed.) 1988 *Educational Research, Methodology, and Measurement: An International Handbook*. Pergamon Press, Oxford

Keeves J P 1986 Theory, politics and experiment in educational research methodology. A response. *Int. Rev. Educ.* 32(4): 388–92

Keeves J P 1988 Social theory and educational research. In: Keeves J P (ed.) 1988 *Educational Research, Methodology, and Measurement: An International Handbook*. Pergamon Press, Oxford

Kerlinger F N 1973 *Foundations of Behavioral Research. Educational and Psychological Inquiry*, 2nd edn. Holt, Rinehart and Winston, New York

Kuhn T S 1970 *The Structure of Scientific Revolutions*, 2nd edn. University of Chicago Press, Chicago, Illinois

Kuhn T S 1974 Second thoughts about paradigms. In: Suppe F (ed.) 1977

Lakomski G (ed.) 1991 Beyond paradigms: Coherentism and holism in educational research. *Int. J. Educ. Res.* 15(6): 449–97

Laudan L 1977 *Progress and its Problems. Towards a Theory of Scientific Growth*. Routledge and Kegan Paul, London

Lincoln Y S, Guba E G 1984 *Naturalistic Inquiry*. Sage, Beverly Hills, California

Masterman M 1970 The nature of a paradigm. In: Lakatos I, Musgrave A (eds.) 1970 *Criticism and the Growth of Knowledge*. Cambridge University Press, London

Miles M, Huberman M 1984 Drawing valid meaning from qualitative data. Towards a shared craft. *Educ. Researcher* 13(5): 20–30

Phillips D C 1983 After the wake: Postpositivistic educational thought: The social functions of the intellectual. *Educ. Researcher* 12(5): 4–12

Popkewitz T 1984 *Paradigm and Ideology in Educational Research*. Falmer Press, London

Quine W V 1960a Posits and reality. In: Uyeda S (ed.) 1960 *Bases of Contemporary Philosophy*, Vol. 5. Waseda University Press, Tokyo.

Quine W V 1960b *Word and Object*. MIT Press, Cambridge, Massachusetts

Quine W V 1969 Epistemology naturalized. In: Quine W V 1969 *Ontological Relativity and Other Essays*. Columbia University Press, New York

Quine W V 1974 The nature of natural knowledge. In: Guttenplan S (ed.) 1975 *Mind and Language*. Clarendon Press, Oxford

Shulman L 1986 Paradigms and research programs in the study of teaching. A contemporary perspective. In: Wittrock M C (ed.) 1986 *Handbook of Research on Teaching*, 3rd edn. Macmillan, New York

Smith J K, Heshusius L 1986 Closing down the conversation. The end of the qualitative/quantitative debate among educational inquirers. *Educ. Researcher* 15(1): 4–12

Suppe F (ed.) 1977 *The Structure of Scientific Theories*, 2nd edn. University of Illinois Press, Chicago, Illinois

Walker J C 1985a The philosopher's touchstone. Towards pragmatic unity in educational studies. *J. Philos. Educ.* 19(2): 181–98

Walker J C 1985b Philosophy and the study of education. A critique of the commonsense consensus. *Aust. J. Educ.* 29(2): 101–14

Walker J C 1985c Materialist pragmatism and sociology of education. *Br. J. Sociol. Educ.* 6(1): 55–74

Walker J C, Evers C W 1982 Epistemology and justifying the curriculum of educational studies. *Br. J. Educ. Stud.* 30(2): 213–29

Walker J C, Evers C W 1986 Theory, politics, and experiment in educational research methodology. *Int. Rev. Educ.* 32(4): 373–87

Williams M 1980 Coherence justification and truth. *Rev. Metaphys.* 34(2): 243–72

Further Reading

Chalmers A 1990 *Science and its Fabrication*. Open University Press, Buckingham

Keeves J P (ed.) 1988 *Educational Research, Methodology, and Measurement: An International Handbook*. Pergamon Press, Oxford

Miller S I, Fredericks M 1991 Postpositivistic assumptions and educational research: Another view. *Educ. Researcher* 20(4): 2–8

Phillips D C 1987 *Philosophy, Science and Social Inquiry*. Pergamon Press, Oxford

Salomon G 1991 Transcending the qualitative-quantitative debate: The analytic and systemic approaches to educational research. *Educ. Researcher* 20(6): 10–18

Research Methodology: Scientific Methods

A. Kaplan

Methodology as a discipline lies between two poles. On the one hand is technics, the study of specific techniques of research—interpreting a Rorschach protocol, conducting a public opinion survey, or calculating a correlation coefficient. On the other hand is philosophy of science, the logical analysis of concepts presupposed in the scientific enterprise as a whole—evidence, objectivity, truth, or inductive inference. Technics has an immediate practical bearing, but only on the use of specific techniques. Philosophy of science, though quite general in application, has only remote and indirect practical bearings. Though philosophy is much exercised about the problem of induction, for instance, behavioral scientists would be quite content to arrive at conclusions acceptable with the same confidence as the proposition that the sun will rise tomorrow.

Methodology is a generalization of technics and a concretization of philosophy. It deals with the resources and limitations of general research methods—such as observation, experiment, measurement, and model building—with reference to concrete contexts of inquiry. No sharp lines divide methodology from technics or from philosophy; particular discussions are likely to involve elements of all three.

The behavioral sciences' concern with methodology has lessened: more and more the researchers do their work rather than working on how they should do it. There has been a corresponding lessening of belief in the myth of methodology, the notion that if only the student of human behavior could find "the right way" to go about research, the findings would be undeniably "scientific."

Anxious defensiveness heightened vulnerability to the pressure of scientific fashions. Scientism is an exaggerated regard for techniques which have succeeded elsewhere, in contrast to the scientific temper, which is open to whatever techniques hold promise for the particular inquiry at hand. Computers, mathematical models, and brass instruments are not limited to one subject matter or another; neither is their use necessary for scientific respectability.

Methodology does not dictate that the soft sciences be hardened or abandoned. Neither does methodology exclude human behavior from scientific treatment. The task is to do as well as is made possible by the nature of the problem and the given state of knowledge and technology.

Fashions in science are not intrinsically objectionable, any more than fashions in dress, nor are they intrinsically praiseworthy. What is fashionable is only one particular way of doing things; that it is in the mode neither guarantees nor precludes effectiveness.

Cognitive style is a characteristic way of attaining knowledge; it varies with persons, periods, cultures, schools of thought, and entire disciplines. Many different styles are identifiable in the scientific enterprise; at different times and places some styles are more fashionable than others. Successful scientists include analysts and synthesizers; experimenters and theoreticians; model builders and data collectors; technicians and interpreters. Problems are often formulated to suit a style imposed either by fashion or by personal predilection, and are investigated in predetermined ways. Scientism in the behavioral sciences is marked by the drunkard's search—the drunkard hunts for the dropped house key, not at the door, but under the corner streetlamp, "because it's lighter there." Widespread throughout the sciences is the law of the instrument: give a small child a hammer and it turns out that everything the child sees needs pounding. It is not unreasonable to do what is possible with given instruments; what is unreasonable is to view them as infallible and all-powerful.

1. Scientific Terms

Closely associated with the myth of methodology is the semantic myth—that all would be well in the behavioral sciences if only their terms were defined with clarity and precision. The myth does not make clear precisely how this is to be done. Scientists agree that scientific terms must bear some relation to observations. There is no consensus on exactly what relation, nor even on whether a useful scientific purpose would be served by a general formulation of a criterion of cognitive meaning. In particular cases the issue is not whether a term has meaning but just what its meaning might be.

For some decades the behavioral sciences were dominated by operationism, which held that terms have meaning only if definite operations can be performed to decide whether the terms apply in any given case, and that the meaning of the terms is determined by these operations. "Intelligence" is what is measured by an intelligence test; "public opinion" is what is disclosed in a survey. Which details are essential to the operation called for and which are irrelevant presupposes some notion of what concept the operations are meant to delimit. The same presupposition underlies attempts to improve tests and measures. A more serious objection is that the validation of scientific findings relies heavily on the circumstances that widely different measuring operations yield substantially the same results. It is hard to avoid the conclusion that they are measuring the same magnitude. Most operations relate terms to observations only by way of other terms; once "symbolic operations" are countenanced, the semantic problems which operationism was meant to solve are reinstated.

Ambiguities abound in the behavioral sciences. The behavioral scientist is involved with the subject matter in distinctive ways, justifiably so. The involvement makes for widespread normative ambiguity, the same term being used both normatively and descriptively—"abnormal" behavior, for example, may be pathological or merely deviant. Also wide spread is functional ambiguity, the same term having both a descriptive sense and an explanatory sense—the Freudian "unconscious" may be topographical or dynamic. Ambiguity is a species of openness of meaning, perhaps the most objectionable. Vagueness is another species. All terms are more or less vague, allowing for borderline cases to which it is uncertain whether the term applies—not because what is known about the case is insufficient, but because the meaning of the term is not sufficiently determinate. All terms have some degree of internal vagueness, uncertainties of application, not at the borderline but squarely within the designation; some instances are better specimens of what the term designates than others (closer to the "ideal type"), and how good a specimen is meant is not wholly determinate. Most terms have also a systemic vagueness: meanings come not singly but in more or less orderly battalions, and the term itself does not identify in what system of meanings (notably, a theory) it is to be interpreted. Significant terms are also likely to exhibit dynamic openness, changing their meanings as contexts of application multiply and knowledge grows.

As dangerous as openness is the premature closure of meanings. The progressive improvement of meanings—the semantic approximation—is interwoven with the growth of knowledge—the epistemic approximation. The advance of science does not consist only of arriving at more warranted judgments but also of arriving at more appropriate concepts. The interdependence of the two constitutes the paradox of conceptualization: formulating sound theories depends on having suitable concepts, but suitable concepts are not to be had without sound theoretical understanding. The circle is not vicious; it is broken by successive approximations, now semantic and now epistemic.

Meanings are made more determinate by a process of specification of meaning. This is sometimes loosely called "definition"; in a strict sense definition is only one way of specifying meanings—providing a combination of terms, whose meaning is presumed to be already known, which in that combination have a meaning equivalent to that of the given term. Definitions are useful for formal disciplines, like mathematics; for empirical disciplines, their usefulness varies inversely with the importance of the term.

In simple cases, meanings can be specified by ostension: making what is meant available to direct experience. Empiricism regards ostensions as the fundamental anchorage for theoretical abstractions. Meanings in the behavioral sciences are often specified by description of the thing meant, especially when this is included in or is close to everyday experience. Most scientific terms have a meaning specified by indication: a set of indices, concrete or abstract, often the outcomes of specified tests and measures, which constitute, not *the* meaning of the term, but some of the conditions which provide ground for applying the term. Each index carries its own weight; each case exhibits a profile, whose weight is not necessarily the sum of the weights of the constituent indices. As contexts of application change as well as what knowledge is available, so do the indications and their weight, and thereby also the meaning specified. Premature closure of meaning by definition is likely to provide false precision, groundless or unusable.

Which type of specification is appropriate depends on the scientific purposes the term is meant to serve. Observables, terms denoting what can be experienced more or less directly, invite ostension. Indirect observables lend themselves to description of what would be observed if our senses or other circumstances were different from what they are: in the behavioral sciences such terms are sometimes known as "intervening variables." Constructs have meanings built up from structures of other terms, and so are subject to definition. Theoretical terms have a core of systemic meaning which can be specified only by an open and ever-changing set of indications. Many terms have sufficient functional ambiguity to exhibit characteristics of several or all of these types of terms; they call for various types of specification of meaning.

2. *Classes*

Empirical terms determine classes; because of openness of meaning these classes are only approximations to well-defined sets in the sense of mathematical logic, where everything in the universe of discourse definitely belongs to or is excluded from the class. The approximation to a set can be made closer (the term made more precise) by restricting its meaning to what is specifiable by easily observable and measurable indices. The danger is that such classes are only artificial, delimiting a domain which contributes to science little more than knowledge of the characteristics by which it is delimited. Natural classes correspond to an articulation of the subject matter which figures in theories, laws, or at least in empirical generalizations inviting and guiding further research. Artificial and natural classes lie at two poles of a continuum. A classification closer to being artificial is a descriptive taxonomy; one closer to being natural is an explanatory typology. Growth of concepts as science progresses is a movement from taxonomies to typologies—

Linnaeus to Darwin, Mendeleef to the modern periodic table, humors to Freudian characterology.

3. Propositions

Knowledge of a subject matter is implicit in how it is conceptualized; knowledge is explicit in propositions. Propositions perform a number of different functions in science.

First are identifications, specifying the field with which a given discipline deals, and identifying the unit elements of the field. In the behavioral sciences "idiographic" disciplines have been distinguished from "nomothetic," the former dealing with individuals, the latter with general relationships among individuals (history and sociology, for instance, or clinical and dynamic psychology). Both equally involve generalizations, because both demand identifications—the same "state" with a new government, or different personalities of the same "person": sameness and difference can be specified only by way of generalizations. Which units are to be selected is the locus problem; political science, for instance, can be pursued as the study of governments, of power, or of political behavior. What is to be the starting point of any given inquiry cannot be prejudged by other disciplines, certainly not by methodology. It is determinable only in the course of the inquiry itself—the principle of the autonomy of the conceptual base.

Other propositions serve as presuppositions of a given inquiry—what is taken for granted about the conceptual and empirical framework of the inquiry. Nothing is intrinsically indubitable but in each context there is always something undoubted. Assumptions are not taken for granted but are taken as starting points of the inquiry or as special conditions in the problem being dealt with. Assumptions are often known to be false, but are made nevertheless because of their heuristic usefulness. Hypotheses are the propositions being investigated.

4. Generalizations

Conclusions of an inquiry, if they are to be applicable to more than the particular context of the inquiry, are stated as generalizations. According to the logical reconstruction prevailing in philosophy of science for some decades (but recently coming under increasing criticism), generalizations have the form: "For all x, if x has the property f, then it has the property g." The content of the generalization can be specified only in terms of its place in a more comprehensive system of propositions.

A simple generalization moves from a set of propositions about a number of individual cases to all cases of that class. An extensional generalization moves from a narrower class to a broader one. Both these types are likely to be only descriptive. An intermediate generalization moves from propositions affirming relations of either of the preceding types to one affirming a relation of both relata to some intermediate term. It begins to be explanatory, invoking the intermediate term to account for the linkage recorded in its premises. A theoretical generalization is fully explanatory, putting the original relata and their intermediates into a meaningful structure. The conclusion of a successful inquiry may produce any of these types of generalization, not only the last.

All empirical findings, whether appearing as premises or as conclusions, are provisional, subject to rejection in the light of later findings. Philosophy of science divides propositions into a priori and a posteriori; for methodology it is more useful to replace the dichotomy by degrees of priority, the weight of evidence required before a finding is likely to be rejected. In increasing order of priority are conjectures, hypotheses, and scientific laws. A law strongly supported by theory as well as by the empirical evidence may have a very high degree of priority, often marked by calling the law a principle. In a logical reconstruction of the discipline in which it appears it may be incorporated in definitions, and so become a priori in the strict sense.

5. Observations and Data

Unless a proposition is a definition or a logical consequence of definition, it must be validated by reference, sooner or later, to observations. Reports of observation—data—must themselves be validated; what was reported might not in fact have been observed. A magician's performance can never be explained from a description of the effect, for the effect is an illusion; a correct description would not call for an explanation.

Errors of observation are virtually inevitable, especially in observations of human behavior; in the fashionable idiom, there is noise in every channel through which nature tells us something. In some contexts, observation can be insulated, to a degree, from error—it might be made, for instance, through a one-way mirror, so that data would not be contaminated by the intrusiveness of the observer. Error can sometimes be cancelled—reports from a large number of observers are likely to cancel out personal bias or idiosyncracy. In special cases error can be discounted: its magnitude, or at least its direction, can be taken into account in drawing conclusions from the data—memories are likely to be distorted in predictable ways.

There is a mistaken notion that the validity of data would be guaranteed if interpretations were scrupulously excluded from reports of what is actually seen. This mistake has been called "the dogma of immaculate perception." Observation is inseparable from a grasp of meanings; interpretation is intrinsic to perception, not an afterthought. It has been well said that there is more to observation than meets the eye.

Two levels of interpretation can be discriminated (in the abstract) in behavioral science. First is the interpretation of bodily movements as the performance of certain acts—the grasp of an act meaning. Raised hands may be interpreted as voting behavior rather than as involuntary muscular contractions (such contractions may be act meanings for a physiologist). A second level of interpretation sees observed acts in the light of some theory of their causes or functions—the grasp of an action meaning. Dress and hairstyle may be seen as adolescent rebelliousness.

Both levels of interpretation are hypothetical in the literal sense—they rest on hypotheses as to what is going on. Such hypotheses in turn rest on previous observations. This is the paradox of data: hypotheses are necessary to arrive at meaningful data, but valid hypotheses can be arrived at only on the basis of the data. As with the paradox of conceptualization, the circle is broken by successive approximation.

Because observation is interwoven with interpretation, what is observed depends on the concepts and theories through which the world is being seen. Whatever does not fit into the interpretive frame remains unseen—invisible data, like pre-Freudian male hysteria and infantile sexuality. The data may be noted but be dismissed as meaningless—cryptic data, like dreams and slips of the tongue. Observation also depends on what instruments of observation are available. Techniques like mazes, projective tests, and opinion surveys have had enormous impact on behavioral science research.

6. Experiments

Creating circumstances especially conducive to observation is an experiment. Not all experiments are probative, meant to establish a given hypothesis or to select between alternative hypotheses (crucial experiment). Some may be methodological, like pilot studies or the secondary experiments performed to determine factors restricting the interpretation of the primary experiment. Heuristic experiments may be fact finding or exploratory. Other experiments are illustrative, used for pedagogy or to generate ideas, a common function of simulations.

The significance of experiments sometimes appears only long after they were performed. Experiments have meaning only in a conceptual frame. Scientific advance may provide a new frame in which the old experiment has a new and more important meaning. The secondary analysis of an experiment already performed may be more valuable than a new experiment.

Experiments in the behavioral sciences have often been criticized on the basis of an unfounded distinction between the laboratory and "life." There are important differences between the laboratory and other life situations—for instance, significant differences in scale.

Only moderate stresses are produced—subjects may be given, say, only a small amount of money with which to play an experimental game, whose outcome may therefore have only questionable bearings on decisions about marriage, surgery, or war. Secondary experiments may be useful to assess the effect of the differences in scale. All observations, whether in the laboratory or not, are of particular circumstances; applying the findings to other circumstances always needs validation.

Not all experiments are manipulative; in some, the manipulation is only of verbal stimuli—administering a questionnaire can be regarded as an experiment. Events especially conducive to observation even though they were not brought about for that purpose are sometimes called nature's experiments—disaster situations or identical twins separated at birth. The relocation of workers or refugees, school bussing, and changes in the penal code are instances of social experiments. Experimentation and field work shade off into one another.

7. Measurement

The more exact the observations, the greater their possible usefulness (possible, but not necessary). Widespread is a mystique of quality—the notion that quantitative description is inappropriate to the study of human behavior. True, quantitative description "leaves something out"—precision demands a sharp focus. But what *is* being described is more fully described by a quantitative description. Income leaves out of account many important components of a standard of living, but a quantitative description says more about income than "high" or "low."

There is a complementary mystique of quantity—the notion that nothing is known till it has been weighed and measured. Precision may be greater than is usable in the context or even be altogether irrelevant. Because quantitative data are more easily processed, they may be taken more seriously than the actually more important imponderables. The precision may be spurious, accurate in itself but combined with impressionistic data. Fashion in the behavioral sciences may invite the use of quantitative idioms even if no measurements are available to determine the implied quantities.

Measurement is the mapping of numbers to a set of elements in such a way that certain operations on the numbers yield results which consistently correspond to certain relations among the elements. The conditions specifying the mapping define a scale; applications of the scale produce measures which correspond to magnitudes. Just what logical operations on the numbers can be performed to yield empirical correspondence depends on the scale.

Numbers may be used only as names—a nominal scale—in which case nothing can be inferred about the elements save that they are the same or different if their names are such. The numbers may be used so as to take into account relations of greater and less—an ordinal scale—allowing the corresponding elements to be put into a definite order. An interval scale defines a relation of greater and less among differences in the order. Operations may be defined allowing measures to be combined arithmetically, by which magnitudes can be compared quantitatively—a ratio or additive scale. Scales can be freely constructed, but there is no freedom to choose what they logically entail. Equally restrictive are the empirical constraints imposed by the operations coordinating measures and magnitudes.

One measuring operation or instrument is more sensitive than another if it can deal with smaller differences in the magnitudes. One is more reliable than another if repetitions of the measures it yields are closer to one another. Accuracy combines both sensitivity and reliability. An accurate measure is without significance if it does not allow for any inferences about the magnitudes save that they result from just such and such operations. The usefulness of the measure for other inferences, especially those presupposed or hypothesized in the given inquiry, is its validity.

8. Statistics and Probability

No measures are wholly accurate. Observations are multiple, both because data are manifold and because findings, to be scientific, must be capable of replication by other observers. Inevitably, not all the findings are exactly alike. Inferences drawn from any measure are correspondingly inconclusive. Statistics are the set of mathematical techniques developed to cope with these difficulties.

A problematic situation is one inviting inquiry. The situation itself does not predetermine how the problem is to be formulated; the investigator must formulate it. A problem well-formulated is half solved; badly formulated, it may be quite insoluble. The indeterminacy of a situation, from the point of view of statistics, is its uncertainty. When a specific problem has been formulated, the situation is transformed to one of risk. A card game involves risk; playing with strangers, uncertainty. Moving from uncertainty to risk is the structuring problem; it may be more important than computing and coping with risk once that has been defined. How to compute risk is the subject matter of the theory of probability; how to cope with it, the theory of games, and more generally, decision theory.

The calculation of probabilities rests on three different foundations; alternatively, three different conceptions or probability may be invoked. Mathematical probability is expressed as the ratio of "favorable" cases (those being calculated) to the total number of (equally likely) cases. Statistical probability is the (long-run) frequency of favorable cases in the sequence of observations. Personal probability is an expression of judgments of likelihood (or degree of confidence) made in accord with certain rules to guarantee consistency. For different problems different approaches are appropriate. Mendelian genetics or the study of kinship systems makes use of mathematical probability. Studies of traffic accidents or suicides call for statistical probabilities. Prediction of the outcome of a particular war or labor dispute is a matter of personal probability.

Statistics begin where assignment of probabilities leaves off. A multiplicity of data are given. The first task is that of statistical description: how to reduce the multiplicity to a managable unity with minimal distortion. This is usually done by giving some measure of the central tendency of the data, and specifying in one way or another the dispersion of the data around that central measure (like the mean and the standard deviation). Inferences drawn from the data are statable as statistical hypotheses, whose weight is estimated from the relation between the data and the population about which inferences are being made (sampling theory). Depending on the nature of the sample and of its dispersion, statistical tests assign a measure of the likelihood of the hypothesis in question. Explanatory statistics address themselves to the use of statistical descriptions and hypotheses in formulating explanations (for instance, by way of correlations).

9. Theories and Models

Once a problematic situation has been structured and the data measured and counted, a set of hypotheses may be formulated as possible solutions to the problem. Generalized, the hypotheses are said to constitute a theory. Alternatively, it is possible to begin with a set of hypotheses formulated in the abstract, then interpret them as applying to one or another problematic situation. Such a set is called a model.

Often the result of structuring the problematic situation is called a model. Structure is the essential feature of a model. In an interpretation of the model, a correspondence is specified between the elements of the model and those of some situation, and between certain relations holding within each set of elements, so that when two elements of the model are in a certain relation the corresponding elements stand in the corresponding relation, and vice versa. A set of elements related in certain ways is a system; a structure is what is shared by corresponding systems (or it may be identified with the set of all possible systems corresponding to a given one and thus to each other).

A model can be a physical system (like an airplane model in a wind tunnel), in which case it is an analog. An analog computer is a device which allows such systems to be easily constructed—systems consisting, for instance, of electrical networks with certain voltages, resistances, and current flow. Operations on the analog which preserve its structure show what would happen in any other system having the same structure. If the model is a system of symbols it may be called a map. Behavioral science models are maps of human systems.

When the correspondences are only suggested rather than being explicitly defined, the symbolic system is an extended metaphor; intermediate between a metaphor and a model is an analogy, in which correspondences are explicit but inexact. All three have roles in the actual conduct of inquiry; the view that only models have a place in science makes both terms honorific.

In another honorific usage "model" is a synonym for "theory" or even " hypothesis." The term is useful only when the symbolic system it refers to is significant as a structure—a system which allows for exact deductions and explicit correspondences. The value of a model lies in part in its abstractness, so that it can be given many interpretations, which thereby reveal unexpected similarities. The value lies also in the deductive fertility of the model, so that unexpected consequences can be predicted and then tested by observation and experiment. Here digital computers have already shown themselves to be important, and promise to become invaluable.

Two dangers in the use of models are to be noted. One is map reading, attaching significance to features of the model which do not belong to its structure but only to the particular symbolization of the structure (countries are not colored like their maps; psychoanalytic models do not describe hydrodynamic processes of a psychic fluid: "psychic energy" is not equal to mc^2).

The other danger is, not that something is read into the map which does not belong to the structure, but that something is omitted from the map which does. This error is called oversimplification. All models simplify, or they would not have the abstractness which makes them models. The model is oversimplified when it is not known by how much nor even in what direction to correct the outcomes of the model so that they apply to the situation modeled. In an economic model, ignoring differences in the worth of money to the rich and to the poor is likely to be an oversimplification; ignoring what exactly the money is spent on may not be.

Theories need not be models; they may present a significant content even though lacking an exactly specified structure—as was done by the theory of evolution, the germ theory of disease, and the psychoanalytic theory of the neuroses. A theory is a concatenation of hypotheses so bound up with one another that the proof or disproof of any of them affects that of all the others. The terms in which the hypotheses are couched are likely to have systemic meaning, specifiable only by reference to the entire theory. Knowledge may grow by extension—applying a theory to wider domains. It may also grow by intension—deepening the theory, specifying more exactly details previously only sketched in or even glossed over.

Theory is not usefully counterposed to practice; if it is sound, a theory is of practice, though the theoretical problems may be so simplified that the theory provides only an approximate solution to the problems of practice, and then only under certain conditions. A theory, it has been said, is a policy, not a creed. It does not purport to provide a picture of the world but only a map. It guides decisions on how best to deal with the world, including decisions on how to continue fruitful inquiry. It raises as many questions as it answers; the answers themselves are proposed directives for action rather than assertions for belief.

10. Explanation, Interpretation, and Validation

Validation of a theory is a matter, first, of coherence with knowledge already established. A new theory may raise difficulties of its own, but it must at least do justice to the facts the older theory accounted for. Validation means, second, a certain correspondence with the world as revealed in the continually growing body of data—it must successfully map its domain. Validation, finally, lies in the continued usefulness of the theory in practice, especially in the conduct of further inquiry.

A valid theory provides an explanation of the data, not merely a shorthand description of them. The latter, even if comprehensive, is only an empirical generalization; a theory gives grounds for expecting the generalization to be indefinitely extendable to data of the same kind. A dynamic tendency is quite different from a statistical trend. The theory may allow the prediction of data not yet observed, though it may be valid without successful prediction if this is precluded by the intervention of factors outside the theory, or by cumulation of the inexactness to be found in all theories when applied to empirical findings. Conversely, an empirical generalization may suggest successful predictions even though it is unable to say why the predictions should succeed.

Deductive explanation deduces predictions from the premises postulated by the theory (together with the initial conditions of the particular situation). This type of explanation is characteristic of models. Pattern explanation makes the data intelligible by fitting them into a meaningful whole (predictions might then be made of what would fit the gaps). This is characteristic of disciplines concerned with action meanings.

Behavioral interpretation is grasping such meanings, as distinguished from model interpretation, which is setting up correspondences that give content to an abstract structure. In behavioral interpretation actions are understood as purposive, goal directed. Goals need not be conscious, deliberate, intentional—in short, motivational; they may be purely functional, as are the telic mechanisms of cybernetic systems. Interpretation in the behavioral sciences often suffers from mistaking functions for motives, then introducing abstract agents to have the putative motives—neuroses are said to defend themselves, ruling classes to perpetuate a social order, economies to seek to expand.

All explanations, at best, leave something to be desired. They are partial, dealing with only a limited class of situations. They are conditional, depending on special circumstances in those situations. They are approximate—no explanation is wholly precise. They are indeterminate, having only a statistical validity—there are always apparent exceptions. They are inconclusive, never validated beyond any possibility of replacement or correction. They are intermediate, pointing always to something which needs to be explained in turn. They are limited, serving in each instance only some of the purposes for which explanations might be sought—a psychologist's explanation of a death (as, say, a suicide) is very different from a pathologist's explanation (as, say, a poisoning). Both explanations may be equally valid. All this openness of theory corresponds in the epistemic approximation to the openness of meaning in the semantic approximation.

11. Values and Bias

Inquiry itself is purposive behavior and so is subject to behavioral interpretation. The interpretation consists in part in specifying the values implicated in specific processes of conceptualization, observation, measurement, and theory construction. That values play a part in these processes does not in itself make the outcomes of these processes pejoratively subjective, nor otherwise invalidate them. A value which interferes with inquiry is a bias. Not all values are biases; on the contrary, inquiry is impossible without values.

A distinction between facts and values remains; the distinction is functional and contextual, not intrinsic to any given content. Descriptions may be used normatively. They are also shaped by norms which guide not only what is worth describing but also what form the description should take—for instance, the degree of precision which is worthwhile, the size of sample which is worth taking, the confidence level to be demanded, and the like. Values play a part not only in choosing problems but also in choosing patterns of inquiry into them. The behavioral sciences have rightly become concerned with the ethics of the profession, as bearing, for instance, on experimentation with human beings.

A myth of neutralism supposes that scientific status requires rigorous exclusion of values from the scientific enterprise. Even if this exclusion were desirable (a value!), it is impossible. The exclusion of bias, on the other hand, *is* an operative ideal. Bias is only hidden by the pretense of neutrality; it is effectively minimized only by making values explicit and subjecting them in turn to careful inquiry.

The danger that values become biases is especially great when values enter into the assessment of the results of inquiry as distinct from what is being inquired into and how. A truth may be unpleasant, even downright objectionable, yet remain true for all that. Science must be granted autonomy from the dictates of political, religious, and other extra scientific institutions. The content of the pursuit of truth is accountable to nothing and no one not a part of that pursuit.

All inquiries are carried out in specific contexts. Validation of the results of any particular inquiry by reference to the outcomes of other inquiries is important. How important varies with the distance between their respective subject matters, concepts, data, and other components of the process of inquiry. The behavioral sciences have become increasingly willing to affirm their autonomy with respect to the physical and biological sciences. Science suffers not only from the attempts of church, state, and society to control its findings but also from the repressiveness of the scientific establishment itself. In the end, each scientist must walk alone, not in defiance but with the independence demanded by intellectual integrity. That is what it means to have a scientific temper of mind.

See also: Hermeneutics; Positivism, Antipositivism, and Empiricism; Research Paradigms in Education

Bibliography

Bailey K D 1978 *Methods of Social Research*. Free Press, New York

Black J A, Champion D J 1976 *Methods and Issues in Social Research*. Wiley, New York

Braithwaite R B 1953 *Scientific Explanation: A Study of the Function of Theory Probability and Law in Science*. Cambridge University Press, Cambridge

Campbell N R 1928 *Measurement and Calculation*. Longman, New York

Durkheim E 1950 *The Rules of Sociological Method*, 8th edn. Free Press, New York

Ellingstad V S, Heimstra N W 1974 *Methods in the Study of Human Behavior*. Brooks Cole, Monterey, California

Gellner E 1973 *Cause and Meaning in the Social Sciences*. Routledge and Kegan Paul, London

Hanson N R 1972 *Observation and Explanation: A Guide to Philosophy of Science*. Harper and Row, New York

Hempel C G 1965 *Aspects of Scientific Explanation, and Other Essays in the Philosophy of Science*. Free Press, New York

Kaplan A 1964 *The Conduct of Inquiry: Methodology for Behavioral Science*. Chandler, New York

Kuhn T S 1970 *The Structure of Scientific Revolutions*. University of Chicago Press, Chicago, Illinois

Lachenmeyer C W 1973 *Essence of Social Research: A Copernican Revolution*. Free Press, New York

Myrdal G 1969 *Objectivity in Social Research*. Pantheon, Westminster, Maryland

Nachmias D, Nachmias C 1976 *Research Methods in the Social Sciences*. St. Martin's Press, New York

Nagel E 1961 *The Structure of Science: Problems in the*

Logic of Scientific Explanation. Harcourt Brace, and World, New York

Neale J M, Liebert R M 1973 *Science and Behavior: An Introduction to Methods of Research*. Prentice-Hall, Englewood Cliffs, New Jersey

Popper K R 1959 *The Logic of Scientific Discovery*. Basic Books, New York

Popper K R, Eccles J C 1983 *The Self and its Brain*. Rout-

ledge and Kegan Paul, London

Quyine W V, Ullian J S 1978 *The Web of Belief*, 2nd edn. Random House, New York

Runkel P J, McGrath J E 1972 *Research on Human Behavior: A Systematic Guide to Method*. Holt, Rinehart and Winston, New York

Weber M 1949 *Methodology in the Social Sciences*. Free Press, New York

Research Paradigms in Education

T. Husén

Thomas Kuhn, himself a historian of science, contributed to a fruitful development in the philosophy of science with his book *The Structure of Scientific Revolutions* published in 1962. It mapped out how established thinking, research strategies, and methods in a scientific field, in Kuhn's terminology "normal science," were established. It brought into focus two streams of thinking about what could be regarded as "scientific," the Aristotelian tradition with its teleological approach and the Galilean with its causal and mechanistic approach. It introduced the concept of "paradigm" into the philosophical debate.

"Paradigm" derives from the Greek verb for "exhibiting side by side." In lexica it is given with the translations "example" or "table of declensions and conjugations." Although Kuhn himself used paradigm rather ambiguously, the concept has turned out to be useful in inspiring critical thinking about "normal science" and the way shifts in basic scientific thinking occur. A paradigm determines the criteria according to which one selects and defines problems for inquiry and how one approaches them theoretically and methodologically. Young scientists tend to be socialized into the precepts of the prevailing paradigm which to them constitutes "normal science." In that respect a paradigm could be regarded as a cultural artifact, reflecting the dominant notions about scientific behavior in a particular scientific community, be it national or international, and at a particular point in time. Paradigms determine scientific approaches and procedures which stand out as exemplary to the new generation of scientists—as long as they do not oppose them.

A "revolution" in the world of scientific paradigms occurs when one or several researchers at a given time encounter anomalies, for instance, make observations, which in a striking way do not fit the prevailing paradigm. Such anomalies can give rise to a crisis after which the universe under study is perceived in an entirely new light. Previous theories and facts become subject to thorough rethinking and re-evaluation.

In well-defined disciplines which have developed over centuries, such as the natural sciences, it is relatively easy to point out dramatic changes in paradigms, such as in astronomy from Ptolemy through Copernicus to Galileo or in physics from Aristotle via Galileo and Newton to Einstein. When the social sciences emerged in the nineteenth century, people like Comte tended to regard the natural sciences as scientific models, but without awareness that the social scientist is part of a process of social self-understanding. Educational research faces a particular problem, since education, as William James pointed out, is not a well-defined, unitary discipline but a practical art. Research into educational problems is conducted by scholars with many disciplinary affiliations. Most of them have a background in psychology or other behavioral sciences, but quite a few of them have a humanistic background in philosophy and history. Thus there cannot be any prevailing paradigm or "normal science" in the very multifaceted field of educational research. However, when empirical research conducted by behavioral scientists, particularly in the Anglo-Saxon countries, in the 1960s and early 1970s began to be accused of dominating research with a positivist quantitatively oriented paradigm that prevented other paradigms of a humanistic or dialectical nature being employed, the accusations were directed at those with a behavioral science background.

1. The Two Classical Paradigms

The twentieth century has seen the conflict between two main paradigms employed in researching educational problems. The one is modeled on the natural sciences with an emphasis on empirical quantifiable observations which lend themselves to analyses by means of mathematical tools. The task of research is to establish causal relationships, to explain (*Erklären*). The other paradigm is derived from the humanities with an emphasis on holistic and qualitative information and interpretive approaches (*Verstehen*).

Briefly, the two paradigms in educational research developed historically as follows. By the mid-nineteenth century, when Auguste Comte (1798–1857) developed positivism in sociology and John Stuart Mill (1806–1873) empiricism in psychology, there was a major breakthrough in the natural sciences at the universities with the development of a particular logic and methodology of experiments and hypothesis testing. They therefore came to serve as models and their prevailing paradigm was taken over by social scientists, particularly in the Anglo-Saxon countries (see, e.g., Pearson 1892). However, on the European Continent there was another tradition from German idealism and Hegelianism. The "Galilean," mechanistic conception became the dominant one, particularly with mathematical physics as the methodological ideal. Positivism was characterized by methodological monism. Philosophers at the University of Vienna (such as Neurath), referred to as the "Vienna Circle," developed what is called "neopositivism" or "logical empiricism." Around 1950 they founded a series of publications devoted to the study of what they called "unified science." Positivism saw the main task for the social sciences as being the making of causal explanations and the prediction of future behavior on the basis of the study of present behavior. Neopositivism emanated from the stong influence of analytical philosophy.

There are at least three strands for the other main paradigm in educational research. The Continental idealism of the early nineteenth century has been mentioned. Around the turn of the century it had a dominant influence at German universities with philosophers, such as Wilhelm Dilthey (1833–1911), who in the 1890s published a classical treatise in which he made the distinction between *Verstehen* and *Erklären*. He maintained that the humanities had their own logic of research and pointed out that the difference between natural sciences and humanities was that the former tried to explain, whereas the latter tried to understand. He also maintained that there were two kinds of psychology, the one which by means of experimental methods attempted to generalize and predict, and the one that tried to understand the unique individual in his or her entire, concrete setting. Other philosophers with similar conceptions were Heinrich Rickert and Wilhelm Windelband. A counterpart in France was Henri Bergson (1859–1941) who maintained that the intellect was unable to grasp the living reality which could only be approached by means of intuition. In Sweden, John Landquist advanced an epistemology of humanities.

A second strand was represented by the phenomenological philosophy developed by Edmund Husserl (1859–1938) in Germany. It emphasized the importance of taking a widened perspective and of trying to "get to the roots" of human activity. The phenomenological, and later the hermeneutic, approach is holistic: it tries by means of empathy (*Einfühlung*) to understand the motives behind human reactions. By widening the perspective and trying to understand human beings as individuals in their entirety and in their proper context it also tries to avoid the fragmentation caused by the positivistic and experimental approach that takes out a small slice which it subjects to closer scrutiny.

The third strand in the humanistic paradigm consists of the critical philosophy, not least the one of the Frankfurt school (Adorno, Horckheimer, and Habermas) which developed with a certain amount of neo-Marxism. Marx himself would probably have felt rather ambivalent in an encounter between the two main scientific philosophies. On the one hand, he felt attracted to positivism. On the other hand, Marx belonged to the German philosophical tradition and the neo-Marxists have not had great difficulties in accepting hermeneutics and merging it with a dialectical approach.

The paradigm determines how a problem is formulated and methodologically tackled. According to the traditional positivist conception, problems that relate, for example, to classroom behavior should be investigated primarily in terms of the individual actor, either the pupils, who might be neurotic, or the teacher, who might be ill-prepared for his or her job. The other conception is to formulate the problem in terms of the larger setting, that of the school, or rather that of the society at large. Furthermore, one does not in the first place, by means of such mechanisms as testing, observation, and the like, try to find out why the pupil or the teacher deviates from the "normal." Rather an attempt is made to study the particular individual as a goal-directed human being with particular and unique motives.

The belief that science, particularly social science, would "save us" was expressed as late as in the 1940s by George Lundberg (1947), a sociologist who represented a consistent positivist approach. In the long run, the study of human beings would map out the social reality and provide a knowledge base for vastly improved methods of dealing with human beings, be they pupils in the classroom or workers in the factory. A similar hope still guided the establishment of research and development centers with massive resources at some North American universities in the 1960s. What experience and enlightened empathy could tell was somehow regarded as inferior to the knowledge provided by systematic observations and measurements.

2. A Historical Note

In his *Talks to Teachers on Psychology*, given in the 1890s, James (1899 p. 9) pointed out: "To know psychology . . . is absolutely no guarantee that we shall be good teachers." An additional ability is required, something that he calls the "happy tact and ingenuity," the "ingenuity in meeting and pursuing the pupil, the tact for the concrete situation." He mentions the demands of making systematic observations that some "enthusiasts for child study" have burdened the teachers with, including "compiling statistics and computing the percent." In order to avoid such endeavors resulting in trivialities they must be related to the "anecdotes and observations" which acquaint the teachers more intimately with the students.

What James refers to is something that in the terminology of the late twentieth century would be seen as a conflict between two main research paradigms. By the end of the nineteenth century, the scientific paradigm emerged that has since then been the prevailing one, at least in the Anglo-Saxon world. It was part of a larger movement toward "scientific management" in industry.

The new scientific approach emerging at the end of the nineteenth century was spelled out by the leading educational psychologist, Edward Lee Thorndike of Columbia University, in the preface to his seminal book *Educational Psychology* in 1903. He set out to apply "the methods of exact science" to educational problems, reject "speculative opinions," and emphasize "accurate quantitative treatment" of information collected (Clifford 1984). He acknowledged the influence on his thinking of people who have advocated the quantitative and experimental approach, like James McKeen Cattell and R S Woodworth in the United States and Francis Galton and Karl Pearson in England. In a brief concluding chapter he dealt with the problem of education as a science and presented the main characteristics of what he regarded as scientific in education:

> It is the vice or the misfortune of thinkers about education to have chosen the methods of philosophy or of popular thought instead of those of science . . . The chief duty of serious students of the theory of education today is to form the habit of inductive study and learn the logic of statistics. (Thorndike 1903 p. 164)

Part of the new scientific paradigm was to make a clear-cut distinction between the descriptive and the normative. Research conducted according to "logic of science" was supposed to be neutral with regard to values and policy-making.

The prevailing paradigm in North America spelled out by Thorndike was further developed by John Franklin Bobbitt, professor at the University of Chicago, who in 1912 advanced the notion that schools could be operated according to the methods of "scientific management" which had been developed in industry by Frederick Taylor. Bobbitt also played an important role in attempts to determine empirically the content of curriculum by analyzing what people needed as holders of occupations and as citizens in order to arrive at a common denominator of skills and specific pieces of knowledge with which the school had to equip them.

With an eye on the natural sciences, social science has for more than a century made the claim to be an "objective" and "explaining" science. It purported to be able to make a clear-cut distinction between aims and means of achieving these aims. It maintained that in handling social realities it was able to do it without any moral commitments. Its representatives claim like in the natural sciences to reside outside the system they observe. Such a claim has been brought into question. Gunnar Myrdal (1969) did so in a book (first published in Swedish in the 1930s) on science and politics in economics. He showed that the social researcher could not be free from his or her own values and political convictions, but could arrive at more valid conclusions and gain in credibility by making his or her value premises explicit and by making clear what those biases were in describing reality. Thereby the researcher can also give the "consumers" of his or her research an instrument for correction.

Social research, not least that in education, consists of data collection and reflection about societal problems, with their dilemmas and paradoxes, tensions, and so on, as well as alternatives for political action which offer themselves. Not even in the ideal case can a consensus be expected around theoretical paradigms as separated from practical problems. Social science researchers are part of the social process which they set out to investigate. They share social and political values of the surrounding society. In a way, they participate in the process of social self-understanding. This means that there is no such thing as a "social technology" in the same sense as a technology based on natural science. This does not imply, however, that educational research endeavors are of very limited value or entirely futile. The "aloofness" of the researchers in terms of dependence on interest groups and politics with shared social values is a relative matter. The task of the academic of "seeking the truth" can become institutionalized. This is what happens when fundamental, discipline-oriented research is established in institutions where the researchers can pursue their tasks of critical review without jeopardizing their positions.

There were those who, in contrast to William James, thought that it would be possible to make education a science. One of them was Charles H Judd (a student of Wundt), who in *Introduction to the Scientific Study of Education* in 1918, tried to explain how research was related to teacher training and educational practice. In 1909 the Department of Education at the University of Chicago had abandoned course requirements for prospective teachers in the history of education and psychology. These courses had been replaced by one course called "Introduction to Education" and one in "Methods of Teaching." Thereby the teacher candidates could be introduced to the school problems in "a more direct, concrete way." Each chapter in Judd's book presents practical school problems and gives sources of information for the solution of these problems. Much of this information is very incomplete, but as a whole Judd thinks that it is justified to speak about a "science of education." To use the term "science" he thinks would be justified, even when the information available is very scanty, "for the essence of science is its methods of investigation, not its ability to lay down a body of final rules of action" (Judd 1918 p. 299).

A research paradigm similar to the one advanced by Galton, Pearson, and Thorndike developed in Germany and France under the influence of experimental psychology. Ernst Meumann, a student of Wilhelm Wundt and a leading experimental psychologist, published at the beginning of the twentieth century his monumental three-volume work *Vorlesungen zur Einführung in die experimentelle Pädagogik* (1911) (*Introduction to Experimental Pedagogy*). He meant by "experimental education" largely the application of the systematic, empirical, and statistical methods to educational data. Alfred Binet in France had a similar influence in both child study and intelligence testing.

3. The Two Main Paradigms and Their Compatibility

One can distinguish between two main paradigms in educational research planning and with different epistemological basis (Adams 1988). On the one hand, there is the functional–structural, objective–rational, goal-directed, manipulative, hierarchical, and technocratic approach. On the other hand, there is the interpretivist, humanistic, consensual, subjective, and collegial one.

The first approach is derived from classical positivism. The second one, which in recent years has gained momentum, is partly derived from the critical theory of the Frankfurt school, particularly from Habermas's theory of communicative action. The first approach is "linear" and consists of a straightforward rational action toward preconceived problems. The second approach leaves room for reinterpretation and reshaping of the problem during the process of dialogue prior to action and even during action.

Phillips (1983) has contributed to a valuable conceptual clarification of "positivism." He distinguishes between four varieties of it: (a) the classical Comtean positivism with its belief that the scientific method established in the natural sciences can be applied in the study of human behavior and human affairs in general; (b) logical positivism embodied by the Vienna Circle which had a strong impact among psychologists and sociologists in the middle of the twentieth century with its quest for verification and operational definitions; (c) behaviorism of the Watsonian or Skinnerian type; and (d) positivism as a general label for empiricism, which covers a broad spectrum of epistemological positions.

Phillips (1983) argues that some of the many ardent critics of allegedly positivist researchers are them-

selves "more positivistic than they recognize," some of them by using an instrumentalistic criterion of truth. They tend to make the mistake of "identifying positivism with particular research methods," such as experimental design or statistical analysis methods. Thus, there is basically not such an unbridgeable gap between the two paradigms as is often purported by representatives of the respective camps.

Keeves (1988) argues that the various research paradigms employed in education, the empirical–positivist, the hermeneutic or phenomenological, and the ethnographic–anthropological are complementary to each other. He talks about the "unity of educational research," makes a distinction between paradigms and approaches, and contends that there is, in the final analysis, only one paradigm but many approaches. The teaching–learning process can be observed and/or video-recorded. The observations can be quantified and the data analyzed by means of advanced statistical methods. Content can be studied in the light of national traditions and the philosophy underlying curriculum constructions. Both the teaching–learning process and its outcomes can be studied in a comparative, cross-national perspective.

Depending upon the *objective* of a particular research project, emphasis is laid more on the one or on the other paradigm. One could quote the following as an example of how quantitative and qualitative paradigms are complementary to each other. It is not possible to arrive at any valid information about a school or national system concerning the level of competence achieved in, for instance, science by visiting a number of classrooms and thereby trying to collect impressions. Even a highly experienced science teacher is not able to gain information that would allow accurate inferences about the quality of outcomes of science teaching in the entire system of education. Sample surveys like the ones conducted by the IEA (International Association for the Evaluation of Education Achievement) would be necessary instruments. But such surveys are too superficial when it comes to accounting for factors behind the differences between school systems. Here qualitative information of different kinds is required.

But the choice or "mix" of paradigm is also determined by what *kind of knowledge* one is searching for. The ultimate purpose of any knowledge arrived at in educational research is to provide a basis for action, be it policy action or methods of teaching in the classroom. The former type of knowledge must by definition be of a more general nature and apply to a lot of local and individual situations, such as reforming the structure of the system or the relationship between home background and school attainments. But the classroom teacher deals with a unique child in a unique teaching–learning situation and is not very much helped by relying on generalized knowledge.

Policymakers, planners, and administrators want generalizations and rules which apply to a wide variety of institutions with children of rather diverse backgrounds. The policymaker and planner is more interested in the collectivity than in the individual child. They operate from the perspective of the whole system. Educational research has made significant contributions to reforms of entire national systems of education. Sweden and Germany are cases in point.

Classroom practicioners are not very much helped by generalizations which apply "on the whole" or "by and large" because they are concerned with the timely, the particular child here and now. Research on the teaching–learning process can at best give them a perspective on the particular teaching–learning situation with which they are faced. The pedagogical steps taken have to be guided by the qualitative information that Eisner (1982) refers to as "connoisseurship" which is a body of experiences and critical analysis which may well also be guided by research insights.

4. The Need for Pluralism in Approaches

In the late 1960s and early 1970s critical, dialectical, hermeneutical, and neo-Marxian paradigms were advanced as alternatives or even replacements for the prevailing neopositivist paradigm of quantification, hypothesis testing, and generalizations. The latter had dominated the scene of social science research in the Anglo-Saxon countries for many decades and had taken the lead at many Continental universities as well. The new approaches were espoused by many from these universities to the extent that a group of younger researchers in education even prepared an international handbook of educational research that deliberately challenged the prevailing Anglo-Saxon research paradigms. The behavioral sciences have equipped educational researchers with an arsenal of research tools, such as observational methods and tests, which help them to systematize observations which would otherwise not have been considered in the more holistic and intuitive attempts to make, for instance, informal observations or to conduct personal interviews.

Those who turn to social science research in order to find out about the "best" pedagogy or the most "efficient" methods of teaching are in a way victims of the traditional science which claimed to be able to arrive at generalizations applicable in practically every context. But, not least through critical philosophy, researchers have become increasingly aware that education does not take place in a social vacuum. Educational researchers have also begun to realize that educational practices are not independent of the cultural and social context in which they operate. Nor are they neutral to educational policies. Therefore, dogmatic evangelism for particular philosophies and ideologies espoused as "scientific" and not accessible to criticism is detrimental to the spirit of inquiry. The two main paradigms are not exclusive, but complementary to each other.

See also: Educational Research and Policymaking; Hermeneutics; Policy-oriented Research; Positivism, Antipositivism, and Empiricism

References

Adams D 1988 Extending the educational planning discussion: Conceptual and paradigmatic explorations. *Comp. Educ. Rev.* 32: 400–15
Clifford G J 1984 *The Sane Positivist: A Biography of Edward L Thorndike.* Wesleyan University Press, Middletown, Connecticut
Eisner E 1982 *Cognition and Curriculum: A Basis for Deciding What to Teach.* Longman, London
James W 1899 *Talks to Teachers on Psychology: And to Students on Some of the Life's Ideals.* Longmans Green, London
Judd C H 1918 *Introduction to the Scientific Study of Education.* Ginn, Boston, Massachusetts
Keeves J P 1988 The unity of educational research. *Interchange* 19(1): 14–30
Kuhn T S 1962 *The Structure of Scientific Revolutions.* University of Chicago Press, Chicago, Illinois
Lundberg G 1947 *Can Science Save Us?* Longmans Green, London
Meumann E 1911 *Vorlesungen zur Einführung in die experimentelle Pädagogik und ihre psychologischen Grundlagen.* Engelmann, Leipzig
Myrdal G 1969 *Objectivity in Social Research.* Pantheon, New York
Pearson K 1892 *The Grammar of Science.* Adam and Charles Black, London
Phillips D C 1983 After the wake: Postpositivistic educational thought. *Educ. Res.* 12(5): 4–14, 23–24
Thorndike E L 1903 *Educational Psychology.* Scientific Press, New York

Further Reading

Cronbach L J 1975 Beyond the two disciplines of scientific psychology. *Am. Psychol.* (30): 116–27
Eisner E (ed.) 1985a *The Educational Imagination.* Macmillan, New York
Eisner E (ed.) 1985b Learning and teaching the ways of knowing. In: National Society for the Study of Education 1985 *Eighty-fourth Yearbook.* Chicago University Press, Chicago, Illinois
Fritzell C 1981 *Teaching Science and Ideology: A Critical Inquiry into the Sociology of Pedagogy.* Gleerup, Lund
Fromm E (ed.) 1965 *Socialist Humanism: An International Symposium.* Doubleday, Garden City, New York
Gage N L 1989 The paradigm wars and their aftermath: A "historical" sketch of research on teaching since 1989. *Educ. Res.* 18(7): 4–10
Galtung J 1977 *Essays in Methodology, Vol. 1: Methodology and Ideology.* Ejlers, Copenhagen
Guba E 1978 *Toward A Methodology of Naturalistic Inquiry in Educational Evaluation.* University of California, Center for Study in Evaluation, Los Angeles, California
Habermas J 1972 *Knowledge and Human Interests.* Heinemann, London

Heidegger M 1962 *Being and Time*. Harper, New York

Home K R 1988 Against the quantitative–qualitative incompatability thesis or dogmas die hard. *Educ. Res.* 17(8): 10–16

Husén T 1979 General theories in education: A twenty-five year perspective. *Int. Rev. Educ.* 25: 325–45

Husén T 1988 Research paradigms in education. *Interchange* 19(1): 2–13

Husén T 1989 Educational research at the crossroads? An exercise in self-criticism. *Prospects* 19(3): 351–60

Jaeger R M 1988 *Complementary Methods of Research in Education*. American Educational Research Association (AERA), Washington, DC

Landquist J 1920 *Människokunskap*. Bonniers, Stockholm

Lindholm S 1981 *Paradigms, Science and Reality: On Dialectics, Hermeneutics and Positivism in the Social Sciences*. Department of Education, Stockholm University, Stockholm

Landsheere G de 1986 *La recherche en education dans le monde*. Presse Universitaire de France, Paris

Palmer R E 1969 *Hermeneutics: Interpretation Theory in Schleiermacher, Dilthey, Heidegger, and Gadamer*. Northwestern University Press, Evanston, Illinois

Phillips D C 1992 *The Social Scientist's Bestiary*. Pergamon Press, Oxford

Rapoport A 1950 *Science and the Goals of Man: A Study in Semantic Orientation*. Harper, New York

Rizo F M 1991 The controversy about quantification in social research: An extension of Gage's "historical sketch." *Educ. Res.* 20: 9–12

Shulman L S 1986 Those who understand knowledge growth in teaching. *Educ. Res.* 15(2): 4–14

Smith J K, Heshusius L 1986 Closing down the conversation: The end of the quantitative–qualitative debate among educational inquirers. *Educ. Res.* 15(1): 4–12

Soltis J F 1984 On the nature of educational research. *Educ. Res.* 13(10): 5–10

Tuthill D, Ashton P 1983 Improving educational research through the development of educational paradigms. *Educ. Res.* 12(10): 6–14

Wright G H von 1971 *Explanation and Understanding*. Routledge and Kegan Paul, London

Trends in Qualitative Research Methods

M. D. LeCompte

There is a long, if often ignored qualitative tradition in the sociology of education. Philosophers and social theorists such as Durkheim, Weber, and Dewey provided a rationale for examining the relationship between the internal workings and external objectives of school systems and the structure and destiny of society at large, as well as the impact of schooling on individuals. In turn, this work legitimated the empirical study of school and educational processes. Sociological field methods developed in community studies and by the interactionists of the Chicago School and the University of Iowa undergirded qualitative studies of schools as components of community systems (Hollingshead 1947, Lynd and Lynd 1929, Vidich and Bensman 1958, Warner et al. 1963, Warner and Lunt 1941, Wylie 1974) and as systems in their own right (Gordon 1957, Waller 1932). These works were traditional functionalist studies, using participant observation and survey research as well as document, demographic, and sociometric analysis to examine schools as one of the many interdependent social institutions constituting a community

The symbolic interactionist tradition of the Chicago School provided a conceptual and theoretical framework for exploring the internal dynamics of educational systems; it examined relationships between the mind and society, or how the social "got into the mind" of the individual (following G.H. Mead); for exploring how individuals create social roles and identities, and for identifying patterns of meaning and interaction. In their examination of microlevel relationships within and among social groups, the symbolic interactionists created models for contemporary field research in schools. The "second" Chicago School also provided models for studies of schooling, teachers, and students informed by interactive and interpretive frameworks and utilizing the participative methods characteristic of the symbolic interactionist approach (Becker 1953, Becker et al. 1961, Becker et al. 1968, Lortie 1969, 1975, Jackson 1968, Cicourel and Kitsuse 1963). Postmodern perspectives in the late 1980s and 1990s narrowed the focus of research to the level of individuals. In works often termed "interpretive" biographies (Denzin 1989) or narratives (Manning and Cullum-Swan 1994, Richardson 1991 1994) sociologists have concentrated, much as oral historians and anthropologists do, on the experiences of single individuals, told more or less in their own words.

It is perhaps unfortunate that mid-century enthusiasm for large-scale, positivistic, and quantitative studies of education eclipsed the qualitative tradition in sociology until the 1990s. With a few notable exceptions, sociologists from the United States have, in fact, abdicated the arena of qualitative studies in education to educators, anthropologists, psychologists, and evaluation researchers. In this article, an attempt is made to reclaim that tradition, showing, to the extent possible, how some sociologists have continued to use qualitative methods and summarizing how some new directions in qualitative research have affected work in the sociology of education. In so doing, many important qualitative works done by nonsociologists have been omitted, and other important works, or influences from, sociologists may have been overlooked. But this article is intended only as an overview. Important work in cultural studies and the semiotic tr dition (see, for example, Apple 1995, Roman 1996) has been omitted because it is less based on observations of human behavior although it has influenced profoundly how scholars view the schools and their impact.

This article is organized into four parts. First is a definition of what qualitative research is and for what it is best suited. Too often, qualitative research has been stigmatized as "soft" research, reserved for studies less rigorous than, or done only preparatory to, a quantitative or experimental study. In the 1990s, however, the defensive posture into which qualitative researchers had been forced is obsolete, and the value of such approaches to knowing now is properly defined in terms of questions they are intended to address, rather than as matters of, research competence and credibility.

Second, more traditional qualitative studies of education in sociology are discussed. A description is included about how they evolved from their inception in the 1920s and 1930s. Their emergence is traced as new research questions were asked by new faces in the academy. The theoretical evolution from functionalism and conflict theory to interpretivism is discussed. In this section, the argument is advanced that most current changes in qualitative research are epistemologically, rather than methodologically, inspired and that what is new under the sun in sociological studies comes from changes in how the known and knowable are construed, rather than from how we collect information on what is known, once the known is defined.

Third, a shift from interpretivism to critical theory and postmodernist approaches is discussed, with concomitant changes how terms used to interpret research findings are chosen and privileged. Often phrased in terms of the question, "Whose story is being told?" this change altered both how reality is construed and how researchers relate to their informants. It also opened the door to new directions in the interpretation and presentation of research data. Finally, some of these experimental modes of data presentation are discussed.

1. A Definition of Qualitative Research

Qualitative research can be executed in many ways. It can be implemented as a project in its own right. Commonly, it is used as a way to provide context for an otherwise quantitative or experimental study (see Eder and Parker 1987; Eder and Kinney 1995), or as the preliminary fieldwork necessary to identify the parameters of a population or the constructs and questions which will ultimately frame a quantitative study or be used to construct a survey.

However it is used, qualitative research generally is construed to be a loosely defined set of approaches to inquiry, all relying on the elicitation of verbal, visual, tactile, auditory, and gustatory data. These data are presented in descriptive narratives such as field notes, recordings, or other transcriptions from audio and video tapes, other written records including surveys and questionnaires, and photographs and films. Artifacts, consisting of products people use or make, and records of what they do, say, produce, or write also constitute qualitative data (LeCompte and Preissle 1993, LeCompte and Preissle 1994). In fact, qualitative researchers have been described as "omnivores" (Spindler and Spindler 1992), capable of devouring and putting to use virtually anything that could remotely be described as data.

The term qualitative research is an umbrella term for a group of specific designs, including case studies, field studies, community studies, life histories, document analyses, ethnographies, clinical studies, and some kinds of content analyses and surveys. Such designs are distinguished by factors such as the size of the population, the boundedness of the research site, and the degree to which research problems and categories of meaning are defined by the study participants rather than the investigator. They also require an interpretive or semiotic mode of interpretation. Qualitative research can be eclectic (Wilson 1977) in its use of methods (as are case studies, field studies, and ethographies) or based on one method alone, such as in-depth interviews (clinical case studies, biography, oral history, life history), or analysis of texts, diaries, journals. Qualitative data can be found in studies which range from surveys and ethnographies to "stories" and narratives; it includes virtually anything that is not test scores or other nominal, or easily quantified categorical data.

Qualitative data is collected primarily to address the following general questions: "What kinds of things can be found here in this setting?" "What kinds of events are happening here in this setting?" "What are people doing, thinking, and believing in this setting?" These questions can be asked about anything: ordinary occurrences, extraordinary events, or circumstances that simply puzzle the investigator.

Data collection methods notwithstanding, there are three principal characteristics determining whether or not research is defined as qualitative. First, such research is based on and grounded in descriptions of the qualities of things garnered through direct or indirect observation (Sherman and Webb 1988). That is, it is concerned with the characteristics and meanings people ascribe to things and events in their world and to how they experience them.

The second characteristic involves attention paid to the immediacy of unfolding events in the natural or unmanipulated flow of human activity. As a rule, qualitative researchers do not manipulate subjects to create the effects they wish to observe. The third characteristic is that the researchers themselves serve as the key instrument, or data collection device, the principal filter through which all information is sifted, abstracted, and subsequently defined as relevant to the question at hand. Even if the data collection tools seem at first to record information unedited—as might appear to be so in films and audio- or videotape recording—the researcher still aims the camera or positions microphones to privilege some perspectives or vantage points to the disadvantage of others. Even when surveys used by researchers have been pretested, piloted, and administered by well-trained field assistants whose activities are impeccably uniform, technical rigor alone cannot compensate for questions which are vague or lack construct validity because the researcher did not construct them with knowledge of the community whose members were being queried. Furthermore, even when the researcher is trying to account for or record all influences on a particular scene, some are hidden inevitably from view or otherwise inaccessible to the researcher.

All of these issues subject qualitative researchers to charges that they are only observing what they want to see, that they are biased in their perceptions, and that their perceptions or observations are incomplete. Inability to collect all information about a given scene and consequent charges of bias have been treated in two ways: first, as a problem of technical rigor, and second, as an inevitable Heisenbergian consequence of the uncertainty principle, wherein access to some kinds of knowledge precludes access to other kinds of knowledge. Of course, critical and postmodern perspectives posit that all knowledge, regardless of discipline or how it is collected, is partial, that all data are filtered through researcher biases, and that no technique for data collection is infallibly accurate.

The first strategy for eliminating bias follows positivistic or postpositivistic canons regarding reliability, validity, and procedural correctness. This strategy was more common throughout the 1970s and 1980s, when qualitative research was only beginning to find a foothold in educational research. Those who practiced it often found themselves on the defensive, held accountable to canons more properly used to assess the quality of quantitative or experimental research (see, for example, Campbell and Stanley 1971, Cook and Campbell 1979). Qualitative researchers often tried to demonstrate the rigor of their qualitative methods by describing them in great detail, recognizing that the intuitive character of much qualitative data and its analysis often seemed careless to researchers more accustomed to working with easily measured factoids and data bits.

The second strategy began to gain ascendancy in the 1980s, with the appearance of a series of articles which contested the appropriateness of positivistic standards

for research which was not, after all, trying to answer the same questions about education which interested experimental and quantitative researchers (LeCompte and Goetz 1982, Lincoln and Guba 1984, Lather 1988, Eisenhart and Howe 1992). Instead, qualitative researchers advocated the use of self-reflective strategies more congenial to postmodern and critical perspectives, including attempts to achieve disciplined subjectivity, interrogating and making transparent or explicit the biases and standpoints of researchers, and decentering the interpretations of researchers by incorporating into the analysis perspectives of multiple informants from the field. Qualitative researchers currently celebrate the difference between their approaches and more quantitative or experimental ones, and often reject as outmoded what they believe to be inappropriate canons of positivism. Total rejection of canons for rigor may be inappropriate, however (e.g., LeCompte and Goetz 1981). Although the specifics of the positivist canon often cannot be applied to much qualitative research, its general plea for well-conceptualized and executed research whose methods and constructs are intelligible to others and whose conclusions can be subject to scrutiny by peers (Shulman 1988) still is relevant.

1.1 The Emergence of Pedagogical Materials in Qualitative Methods

Until the mid-1980s, the methodological treatises available to teach neophyte researchers how to study students, teachers, schools, and schooling processes came from sociology. Notwithstanding, academic departments of sociology were not particularly interested in qualitative studies of schooling. Schools of education carried out the greatest number of studies of educational processes, but they were dominated by psychologists who did few qualitative, and even fewer sociologically informed studies. Anthropologists, who had really pioneered "fieldwork," still argued that people learned how to do field work by doing it; competence was acquired by osmosis, or by watching others "do ethnography." Ruth Benedict, for example, described how her "methods" classes really consisted of learning the functionalist frameworks with which she would be expected to classify data once she had collected it; these frameworks were supposed to alert her as to what was important to note in the field, and to guide what subsequently she would collect for data. Her mentors and other early anthropologists sent students into the field with best wishes, standardized notebooks, and fileboxes in which to keep data neatly organized, but with no prior training as to what they should write in the notebooks or organize in the boxes (Mead 1959).

In 1976 this author organized probably the first "field methods" course in a school of education. The field, or qualitative, methods course was a major innovation, but there were literally no pedagogical materials in education to use for the students. Instead, field methods materials from sociology were adapted. Materials were borrowed from everywhere, from the Royal Anthropological Institute of Great Britain and Ireland's *Notes and Queries on Anthropology*, to works on how to construct surveys (Goode and Hatt 1952, Babbie 1973), to treatises on the ethics of field work (Glazer 1972; Rynkiewich and Spradley 1976), to ways systematically to carry out fieldwork (Filstead 1979, Bogdan and Taylor 1975, Lofland 1971, McCall and Simmons 1969, Schatzman and Strauss 1973). Students used these disparate materials to inform qualitative evaluations and studies of everything from cultural mismatches between schools and students; school failures and dropouts; teacher professionalization; innovative curricula and instruction; educational policy and school reform; and classroom processes. In addition, for those students interested in studies of communities, organizations, or social groups, the interpretive traditions of the Chicago School were made to appear sufficiently rigorous and systematic to satisfy experimental researchers (see LeCompte and Goetz 1982). The latter was aided by publication of the renowned *"Spindler series"* of monographs in education, ethnographic studies of schooling processes published by Holt, Rinehart, and Winston, edited by anthropologists George and Louise Spindler, and carried out primarily by anthropologists and sociolinguists. Books in this series continued the community studies tradition once most common in urban and rural sociology.

The materials used in this course still were rooted in positivistic tenets governing the implementation of survey research and observational protocols; they emphasized "objectivity," operationalization, and measurability of variables, and the canons of reliability. Perhaps this was fortuitous, because they used canons and terms familiar to the educational psychologists who dominated the school and made more acceptable the use of field methods, which otherwise were derogated as "journalistic" efforts lacking control groups.

These teaching experiences are described because the course in sociological field methods was one of the first which focused specifically on educational issues and certainly one of the first in an American school of education. At that time, the field of sociology in the United States was sufficiently hostile to qualitative research that publication in sociology journals was difficult and legitimacy was a dicey proposition.

It is not, of course, that qualitative studies of education did not exist in the USA; after 1968, quite a few observational studies of innovative curricula, classroom processes, at-risk students, and teacher professionalization as well as a plethora of qualitative or "ethnographic" evaluation studies were carried out in education. It is just that they were not done by sociologists nor, for the most part, were they informed by sociological concepts. In fact, qualitative research in education drew its most powerful conceptual frames from ecological and clinical psychology, curriculum theory, sociolinguistics and anthropology, not from the more interpretive or phenomenological and critical perspectives now coming to dominate sociological research on educational issues. In fact, anthropologists and evaluators assumed the vanguard of development of qualitative methods for the study of education. This article now discusses the work of anthropologists, and then the influence of evaluation researchers.

1.2 Influences from Anthropology

In the late 1970s, those researchers, from whatever discipline, who were interested in qualitative research in education began to find a more congenial home in the Council on Anthropology and Education (CAE) of the American Anthropological Association. Many people who joined the CAE were not anthropologists or even sociologists; they included psychologists, educational administrators, and persons from the health, physical education, and nursing fields, bilingual and muticultural educators, curriculum theorists, and evaluators. This diversity came to characterize the world of qualitative research in education.

The CAE's newsletter, which later evolved into the *Anthropology and Education Quarterly*, regularly featured a column called *Singara*, which published syllabi and reading lists from teachers of qualitative methods in education. *Singara* established an interchange among methods teachers and was instrumental in creating a body of pedagogical knowledge about field research training; the *Quarterly* itself became one of the earliest, and at that time, the only publication devoted entirely to qualitative studies in education.

1.3 Influences from Evaluation Research

Evaluation research had a profound impact on the degree to which qualitative methods achieved legitimacy in education, and on its increasing popularity as a research strategy. In the late 1960s, as part of the "War on Poverty," the United States government funded a wide variety of compensatory education programs. Program developers were , in turn, required to evaluate their programs for effectiveness as a condition of funding. In bidding for these research/evaluation monies, Robert Stake and other educational researchers soon found that the experimental designs they used in evaluation research projects did not answer the questions that educators asked about process and why programs did or did not work. Stake is an educational psychologist and experimental researcher; it was the publication of his article on a "breakthrough" design he called "case study" research (Stake 1978) in the *Educational Researcher* that really helped qualitative research take hold in schools of education. *Educational Researcher* is the monthly journal of the American Educational Research Association and reaches some 10,000 educators.

A less widely read, but no less prestigious educational journal, the *Review of Educational Research*, had published an article on "ethnographic" methods the year before (Wilson 1977), and shortly thereafter, the mainstream of educational research began to hold seminars and workshops on "case study" research and "ethnographic evaluation," strategies which still relied on the same sociological methods books which this author had used in 1976. Simultaneously, "ethnographic" evaluation—by which was meant evaluation which used participant and nonparticipant observation and surveys grounded in field data—had become mandated for virtually all federally funded educational programs. As a consequence, quite a few traditionally experimental and quantitative researchers had to learn about naturalistic inquiry and participant observation; their students and research teams likewise had to be trained in the new approaches. Because they came from a wide range of disciplines, their studies were informed by concepts and constructs from their own disciplines, not sociology; they only borrowed the methods from sociology. Nonetheless, their studies legitimated the use of qualitative methods and led to a demand for journals which would publish the articles and papers they generated.

1.4 The Creation of Pedagogical Materials

A measure of the success of the qualitative revolution has been the number of methods textbooks informed by anthropological and sociological fieldwork traditions published since the 1980s. Dobbert (1982), Patton (1980, 1990), Goetz and Le Compte (1984), Bogdan and Biklen (1986, 1992), Fetterman (1984), Fetterman and Pitman (1986), Lincoln and Guba (1985), Merriam (1988), Sherman and Webb (1988), Miles and Huberman (1984, 1994), Le Compte et al. (1992), Glesne and Peshkin (1992), and LeCompte and Preissle (1993). These are only the earliest and are most clearly written by social scientists. They have been accompanied by the very successful and voluminous Sage Publications series of small volumes on qualitative methods, each of which addresses a single aspect, method, or issue of qualitative research.

2. Early Traditions in Qualitative Research

Research traditions can be influenced to change in many ways, and change in such traditions has been the hallmark of the late 1980s and 1990s. One influence is, of course, the introduction of new ways of thinking. Thus, comments above should not be construed as an obituary for qualitative sociological research in education. The qualitative tradition did continue in England and in Australia (see Hargreaves and Woods 1984, Sikes et al. 1985, McRobbie 1978, Willis 1977, Keddie 1971, Fuller 1980, Lacey 1970, 1977, Furlong 1985, Woods 1984 1992), often informed by more theoretical work from Europe (e.g., Bourdieu 1977, 1990, Foucault 1972, 1980, Derrida 1976) and, by

the work of Third World scholars from a critical and postmodern tradition of cultural studies (e.g., Trinh 1989, Mohanty 1988, Said 1978, 1994, Spivak 1988).

It was not, however, until the publication of Michael Apple's (1978) *Harvard Educational Review* article, "The New Sociology of Education: Analyzing Cultural and Economic Reproduction," that an alternative to existing frameworks became clear. Apple's article introduced North American researchers in education to the symbolic interactionist studies done by sociologists in England (see Woods review article, 1992), and to the work of Continental cultural theorists such as Boudon (1974) and Bourdieu (Bourdieu and Passeron 1977, Bourdieu 1973). These two influenced the emphasis of qualitative studies toward sociological concepts of class and power, made explicit the impact of social stratification of language, knowledge, and behavior, and began a move from studies of systems to small groups and individuals. It took, however, 15 more years of struggle by qualitative researchers for such studies to become the norm in educational research and to become reasonably accepted in United States' sociology.

These differences in research traditions derive, at least in part, from differences in cultural and political contexts. The United States, whose cultural ideology characterizes it as an egalitarian melting pot with few divisive class distinctions (see Persell 1978) despite its long history of both racial and ethnic diversity and tension, has tended to foster much research on race relations and little, until the 1990s, seriously addressing the impact of social class and its determinants in the political economy. By contrast, researchers from England and Europe, and their counterparts in the Anglophone world, have spent less energy examining issues of race and ethnicity and more on class and cultural differences. The United States, whose scientific enterprises tend to be informed by a belief in the efficacy of technical solutions to all human problems, pioneered in computer technology and emphasized large-scale, quantitative studies and speed in solving problems. By contrast, European and British researchers focused on less technocentric studies informed more by theory than by the speed with which data could be crunched. These cultural differences in ideology not only led to different research traditions, but to differences in the way in which reality was conceptualized and knowledge apprehended. It took, however, the introduction of feminist, postmodern, and Third World theorists to really change the epistemological underpinnings of qualitative research in education.

2.1 New Faces in the Academy

The arrival in the United States of the "New Sociology of Education" (Apple 1978) with its emphasis on the social construction of meaning and its focus on class, race, and gender inequities in England and Australia coincided with considerable social class and racial unrest in the United States. The "new sociology" challenged traditional theoretical frameworks which legitimized the status quo ante. It also inspired researchers from ranks hitherto absent from the Academy: nonmainstream researchers—women, homosexuals, persons from the lower socioeconomic strata, and people of color—who found that much research on human problems did not provide results congruent with their own experience. They contested research which concluded that public schools created equality of educational opportunity and contributed to democracy and social mobility when all around them, they saw evidence to the contrary. They had friends who did not make it into the Academy. If they did gain entry, they were denied scholarships and mentorship and often discouraged from continuing their studies, if not outright barred from educational opportunity by racist policies. Because these newcomers held standpoints (Hartsock 1983, Smith 1974, 1987) which differed from those held by previous investigators, they introduced new ways of thinking about and looking at the world.

The newcomers focused on increasingly apparent economic racial, linguistic, and gender inequities present in American society, as well as issues such as workplace conditions for teachers (Ginsburg 1988, Connell 1985), the increasing numbers of school dropouts (Weis 1990, Fine 1991), the absence of females and minorities in academic and professional career tracks in school (Oakes 1985), and the high rates of school failure among ethnic and linguistic minority students (Delgado-Gaitan 1990). They also explored the social construction of identity: identities of failure and success, of gender, of ethnicity, differential professional status, and of social class (Eckerd 1988, Gibson 1988, Herr 1991, Holland and Eisenhart 1990, Fine and Zane 1989, Macleod 1987, Willis 1977). In so doing, they brought feminist and Third World perspectives to bear on topics formerly viewed only through more traditional lenses. They also narrowed the focus of research in education from systems and their functions to the experiences of individual participants in those systems, expressed as authentically as possible in their own words.

In contrast to the interests of the newcomers was the "old guard." The Academy had been dominated by white, male, middle-to-upper class, and European-American scholars, and it was governed by norms and expectations which typified such individuals. Since scientists typically only raise those questions of interest to or congruent with the experience of other scientists currently in their profession, they tended to legitimate results or interpretations of data which coincided with their own lives and the experiences and biases of existing researchers. Thus, research which questioned benevolent assumptions about the egalitarian nature and democratizing purposes of schooling in the United States was considered erroneous in the 1960s and 1970s, and only came to be questioned when the complexion and composition of the professorate

itself began to be transformed.

This set the stage for academic conflict between the old and new guard, even in departments of sociology and anthropology and in schools of education, which had led the way in diversifying their professorate. The conflict was expressed in bitter battles over the supremacy of paradigms and control of "rigor" and academic standards by intellectual elites. Battles for control of the research question and assessment of research quality often were disguised as arguments over preserving standards of quality, alluded to earlier in comments about the defensive posture qualitative researchers assumed in the pre-1980s. In such discussions, the term "quality" often served as a synonym for work legitimated by and most often carried out by white male members of the academic elite. Later, academic battles were redefined as questions about who has the right to speak for others, for science and for the oppressed. The term "voice" became a synonym for power and legitimacy; having one's voice "silenced," whether by researchers or by society, meant one was powerless and that one's work, one's perspective, and even one's right to professional recognition was denied. Remedy was found in studies which elicit that voice, presented in stories and narratives about personal experience and lives. These works still are controversial, and still are denied legitimacy in some circles as mere "story-telling."

2.2 New Questions for the Academy

This article has given indications that changing social, economic, and cultural conditions can create new problems to be investigated. In the case of education, increasing awareness of the relationship between education and social inequity led to a study of that relationship; a further development was the failure of traditionally positivistic and quantitative studies to answer questions of interest to researchers. In the 1960s and 1970s, the relationship between ability, educational attainment, and occupational status (e.g., Blau and Duncan 1967, Bowles and Gintis 1976, Coleman 1966, Jencks 1972, Carnoy 1972), and in particular, the explanation of such relationships in terms of meritocratic hypotheses (Young 1958) of ability was tested quantitatively (e.g., Blau and Duncan 1967, Sewell et al. 1969) in the United States and in political arithmetical studies (Karabel and Halsey 1978) in the United Kingdom. The latter examined the representation of individuals from across the social class spectrum in occupations ranging from the most to the least prestigious. Quantitative data showing over-representation of persons of color and from the lower classes in lower educational tracks and correspondingly low occupational niches contradicted the meritocratic hypothesis.

The existence of inequities in what had been believed to be a "fair game" puzzled educators, policymakers, and researchers alike. Teasing out the causes was important, because unless educators and social scientists accepted hypotheses positing the genetic inferiority of individuals or groups whose members ended up systematically at the bottom of the heap, this meant that demonstrated merit alone was insufficient for meritorious members of poor and minority groups to achieve their educational and occupational potentials.

The quantitative studies of meritocracy raised questions that could not be answered using quantitative methods. Schools were defined as "black boxes" whose inner workings defied exploration via then conventional means. While clearly they had a differential impact on attitudes and achievement that was confounded by race, class, gender, ethnicity, and other ascriptive characteristics, discovering how that impact was effected was impossible without more in-depth and observational research strategies. This led to a quest for ways to enter the black box by using more observational, interpretive, or phenomenological, that is, qualitative strategies for collecting and interpreting data, though the new strategies did not in any way supplant quantitative analyses of the same ideas.

The qualitative revolution in education certainly changed how research was done in schools, and it changed greatly the kinds of questions which could be asked, and reasonably answered, by researchers. However, the methods used themselves have changed very little since the advent of the field or "ethnographic" study. Qualitative methods include surveys, questionnaires, participant and nonparticipant observation, formal and informal interviews, document analysis, sociometric analysis, mapping, photo and video documentary, sociometric analysis, and collection of artifacts. While there have been substantial advances in the sophistication of technical tools used to collect these data, and in the speed and ease by which data can be analyzed, the basic bag of tricks of the qualitative researcher has not been transformed.

In fact, it can be argued that the least changed of all aspects of qualitative research in education has been the methods themselves. "Old" or traditional methods continue to be used appropriately and to be informed fruitfully by conceptual frameworks used decades ago, at the same time that legitimacy has been accorded to newer forms of research.

2.3 Some "Old-style" Qualitative Research Which Provided a Vanguard for the New

Some outliers in the general predominance of quantitative studies in education were sociologists who focused on the biases in and social class stratification of both the hidden and the overt curriculum. Anyon's content analysis of textbooks, and her later observational study of how instruction and management systems in public schools varied according to the social class background of the students taught, were landmarks in beginning to understand and how schools worked to perpetuate privilege (1980, 1983). Similarly, Oakes' (1985) Page's (1987), and Powell et al.'s, (1985) studies of tracking and how it affects aspi-

rations and achievement of low-income and minority students showed how formal educational structures reinforced the existing socioeconomic structure of society, just as Clark's early study (1960) of the "cooling out" function of counseling tended to dampen the aspirations of college students, rather than help them to achieve mobility. Works by Weis and Apple and edited volumes by them (e.g., Apple and Weis 1983) also focused on the impact of gender, class, and ethnic stratification on curriculum.

Other outliers were groups of sociologists and anthropologists who did qualitative studies of the impact of desegregation efforts on attitudes and patterns of interaction among white and black students (Metz 1978, Grant 1989, Schofield 1982); on school politics and reform (Brouillette 1996, Hess 1991, LeCompte and McLaughlin 1994, McQuillan 1997, Muncey and McQuillan 1996, McNeil 1988, Sarason 1971, Rogers 1968); on the inner workings of small and rural schools; on classroom processes (LeCompte 1978, 1981, Borman 1982, Bossert 1979); school-to-work transitions (Borman 1991, Weis 1990); teacher socialization (Lacey 1977, Ginsburg and LeCompte 1988, Ginsburg 1988, Newman 1980); and peer group influences in middle and high schools (Eder 1985, Eder and Parker, 1987. Eder and Evans 1993, Eder and Kinney 1995, Cusick 1973, Stinchcombe 1964, Adler et al. 1992, Adler and Adler 1991).

While the methods themselves have changed little from those used in the studies listed above, what has changed is the questions researchers are called upon to answer. In addition, the levels of analytic units which researchers use have changed from a focus on systems to a focus on individuals, and researchers have changed perspectives on how they participate in the collection of data, their stance toward research subjects/participants, the place and privilege of researcher conceptual frameworks, and the epistemological perspectives taken during the work itself. These, more than issues of method, have led to a transformation of qualitative research. The article will now discuss the conceptual and epistemological factors which led to this transformation.

3. From Functionalism and Positivism to Critical Theory and Postmodernism

Since the 1960s, social science research has undergone a shift from functionalism to conflict theory, from conflict theory to interpretivism, and from there to critical theory and poststructuralism. It has also shifted from positivistic to more phenomenological and constructed perspectives on how to apprehend social reality. These shifts have been reflected in moves in conceptual focus from structure to agency, and from objective detachment to passionate involvement and self-reflection on the part of researchers. It also relocated the origins of conceptual frameworks from exclusive reliance on researcher definitions to subject meanings, and from the latter to ones whose interpretive frames are either established collaboratively between researchers and subjects or simply told in the terms of the subjects alone.

In research informed by functional or conflict paradigms, interpretive frameworks derive from the disciplinary frameworks of the researchers. Individual behavior and belief are conceived of as determined by system norms and expectations. Individuals play little role in enacting their own destiny; to understand individuals one must understand how the systems in which they participate operate. The focus of research is on ways to describe system processes and components so as to understand the behavior of individuals. The functionalist and conflict perspectives are shaped by naturalism, or a belief that human phenomena in their natural contexts can be studied in the same objective manner as can physical phenomena. Such a formulation leads researchers to be unaware of their own implicit frameworks; hence, functionalists, for example, could believe that their systems metaphors were not, in fact, social constructions hegemonically applied, but were simply a dispassionate portrayal of "the way things were." Thus construed, researchers could develop concepts and constructs "objectively," searching for them in the human universe by using the same controlled observation and experimentation they used to unlock the secrets of the physical universe. Construed this way, research becomes "top down;" that is, even when data are approached inductively, the frameworks informing the investigation are imposed by the researcher.

"Top down" research in education facilitated the continued hegemony of positivism and its privileging of patriarchal, Eurocentric ways of knowing (Keller 1983, Keller and Grontkowski 1983). This was especially true in the United States, where researchers contended with an educational establishment primarily interested in psychological testing and in the quantitative measurement of educational effects. However, as indicated earlier, positivistic and quantitative approaches encountered two obstacles. One was methodological; test scores and categorical data simply could not answer questions about processes, and examination of processes was the only way to answer questions about what was occurring in schools and classrooms to create the effects that researchers had observed.

The second was conceptual: social scientists found they could not treat human beings as if they were rocks and plants. Since the behavior of human beings was considerably more complex than the behavior of rocks and most plants, it had to be reconceptualized to include the inner lives and feelings that human beings create and participate in. Accessing these inner lives and feelings required an altogether different stance on the part of researchers. It was not possible for human scientists to achieve the stringent "objectivity"

and detachment apparently mandated for the "hard" sciences. Regardless of how difficult it might be to access inner lives and feelings, these still were the genesis of the very behavior and belief of interest to investigators. It became clear that mere observation of phenomena was insufficient to elicit all the determinants of human behavior. It was totally inadequate for explorations of how people define and socially construct their identities and the worlds in which they live. Rather, following Simmel, Dilthey, Weber, and others, researchers found that they needed to develop *verstehen*, or intersubjective understanding, in order to fully apprehend, or step into, the inner lives and minds of the subjects under investigation.

3.1 Searching for New Theoretical Frameworks

A solution was found in alternative theoretical frames. Since the 1980s, researchers have sought out critical theory, phenomenology, and symbolic interactionism as counters to the overly deterministic approaches of functionalism and conflict theory. This shift has permitted researchers to broaden their perspectives on schools and learning and to ask a much wider range of questions. Changing the frames has had some methodological implications, for the shift from macro- to microprocesses and from examination of larger structures to a focus on small groups and individuals has meant an emphasis on nuances of language, belief, and behavior, and a shift away from simple descriptions of behavior. While the methods still involve participant and nonparticipant observation, interviews and interview surrogates such as surveys, journals, and diaries, they often are put to new uses and employ much more intensive forms of observation, including in-depth interviewing and videotaping. Their implementation in much more intimate settings and relationships also has altered the roles which researchers play vis-à-vis their informants or subjects and altered locus of meanings and definitions by which they have framed their investigations.

3.2 Emergence of "Interpretive" Perspectives

Just as Stake's (1978) article on case study research altered research traditions from sole reliance on quantitative and experimental designs to acceptance of qualitative research, Frederick Erickson's (1986) article, "Qualitative Methods in Research on Teaching" in the *Third Handbook on Research in Teaching* shifted the focus of qualitative research in education from a positivistic attempt to justify rigor to an interpretive attempt to elicit meaning and achieve understanding. Erickson's article used the term interpretive almost synonymously for work seen as qualitative, phenomenological, emic, interactionist, or constructivist, depending on the discipline.

Erickson argued that instead of first developing a deductive framework and imposing it on what they observed, researchers should try to hold their own conceptual frameworks in abeyance, at least for the duration of initial fieldwork. In this way, they could "let the field talk back" to them, gaining an understanding of how research subjects structured, defined and talked about their worlds and what rules they used to guide their behavior. Researchers needed to do more than simply think they understood what subjects were about; they also had to intersubjectively understand, which meant checking with the people under study to make sure that the researchers' notions of what they had found made sense to, and were defined the same way as, those of the subjects themselves. Only then could a study be said to have internal validity (see LeCompte and Goetz 1982), and only then could the researcher step back out of the subject's world and begin to create interpretations based on etic, or externally created, sets of concepts or definitions.

Erickson's article introduced many researchers in education to the concept and importance of *verstehen*. Jacob's (1987) article, "Qualitative Research Traditions" in the *American Educational Research Journal*, widened the discussion, as did the rejoinder a year later by Atkinson et al. (1988), English sociologists who argued that Jacob, a cognitive anthropologist, had omitted both the qualitative traditions in sociology and concurrent influences of *verstehen* led, in turn, to divergence in the epistemological frameworks of qualitative researchers in education. *Verstehen*, or intersubjective understanding, became the fulcrum around which revolved varying approaches to qualitative research, ranging from post-positivistic adherence to objectivity to interpretive and phenomenological privileging of meanings and definitions held by the persons being studied.

3.3 Verstehen and the Problem of Meaning and Interpretation

For some researchers, *verstehen* is a means to an end. That is, one needs to "get into the heads" of subjects in order to learn why they do what they do, but once researchers have figured out the correlates of the "natives'" behavior, they "back out" of the subject mind and reformulate that they have learned in terms of categories and frameworks deriving from their disciplinary training. Such a position is postpositivistic. Researchers retain their commitment to objectivity, but they suspend it temporarily in the interest of better understanding of the topic or people under investigation. This school of thought privileges researcher concepts, such that researchers might explain subjects' behavior to the outside world in terms of concepts which, in fact, might not make sense to the subjects. For example, Rogers's description (1968) of the New York City School District as a "pathological bureaucracy" might seem accurate to outsiders who read Rogers's account of the district's checkered history of desegregation efforts, but it probably not only did not make sense to many bureaucrats in the institution, but may have been offensive to them as well. Similarly,

Weis's (1990) working-class male students who were "without work" or its prospect found it difficult to envision a world in which the highly paid blue-collar employment they expected was nonexistent.

Other researchers attempt to provide a synthesis (Lincoln and Guba 1985) of perspectives or at least to present conflicting perspectives, including that of the researchers themselves. For still other researchers, *verstehen* is a way to focus on the "immediate and local meanings of actions, as defined from the actors' point of view, using them as a basic criterion for validity" (Erickson 1986 p. 119). Such a perspective places the subject's perspectives within one of a number of "nested" interpretive contexts (Lubeck 1988), presenting the perspective of the subjects first, in their own terms, and then gradually embedding that perspective in the context of larger and more structural and historical interpretations.

In her study of preschool programs, Lubeck contrasts the authoritarian structure of a program for African-American children with another serving middle-class white children. The latter was more child-centered and allowed considerably greater movement, freedom, and exploration for children. The African-American teachers had rejected this model, even though they were supposed to be using it. Lubeck initially proclaimed that the African-American teachers were "bad teachers." Later, she explained what she had observed in the terms of the African-American teachers themselves, who argued that their teaching was designed to help the children survive in what the teachers felt was an oppressive, racist, and often dangerous adult world. They believed the children had to learn "proper" and compliant behavior which would not offend white people, even though this approach contradicted white middle-class norms about child rearing and programs based on them. Lubeck described her embedded contexts in terms of a progression from researcher determined meanings to meanings that were interpretively negotiated and constructed, to a critical interpretation which located the day care centers within historical patterns of asymmetry and racial discrimination in United States' society.

One might also describe Lubeck's "nested contexts" in terms of the emic "experience near" and etic "experience distant" perspectives of Geertz (1983), in which the experience distance perspectives include both the pejorative initial reaction of Lubeck to the teaching strategies of the African-American teachers and her subsequent critical locating of that same behavior in its proper historical and social context. Notwithstanding their attention to subject meanings, and even their altered interpretations in light of those meanings, both Lubeck and Geertz retain control over the story; in their work, the perspectives, interpretive frameworks, and concepts of the researcher remain the structuring ones and the researchers have the "last word."

In an attempt to move beyond functional and interpretive perspectives, researchers have turned to work informed by phenomenologists, symbolic interactionists, and postmodernists. In general, these approaches hold that knowledge of the world can only be accessed through human experience and understood through the mediating influence of the human mind. Thus the researcher is a translator, or hermeneut, eliciting meanings from people in one cultural setting and then rendering them comprehensible to people in another and different cultural setting. This is, in fact, what ethnomethodologists such as Garfinkle (1967) do as they seek out the semiconscious and even unconscious rules which create the patterns for, and permit prediction of, human behavior (Jacob 1987). The symbolic interactionists, especially those whose work is influenced by neo-Marxism and critical theory, have been particularly helpful in understanding educational processes, insofar as they locate their work less inside the head and more in structural frameworks of class, power, and other asymmetries.

The move away from positivism initiated an appreciation for such local definitions of the situation. Reality began to be viewed not as fixed, but as relational, something that is person specific and socially constructed. Representing reality then became more than an epistemological problem; it also was an existential one: Whose reality is to be represented and by whom? If reality is seen as personally constructed and located in the combined experiences of many people, then truth resides in full presentation of their reality, or multiple realities, voices, or stories, including that of the researcher. This requires the researcher to make explicit his or her own interpretive frames and to be clear where the latter differ from explanations and interpretations offered by the people under study.

Critical theorists and postmodernists argue against the time-honored practice of "writing the author out" of the story, either by having the text written in the third person, as if it wrote itself, or in the first person, as if the subject were the author of the study, rather than the "absent" researcher (Clifford and Marcus 1986, Marcus and Fischer (1986). For many such works, the emic perspective prevails in these works as long as the rules and behaviors under study are described in terms that make sense to the actors studied, but an etic perspective takes over as the researcher translates this sense into terms comprehensible to larger audiences. Unfortunately, writing conventions often obscure just who is talking for whom and under what conditions.

Many critical, feminist, and postmodern researchers believe that the relationship between researchers and those they study is inherently asymmetrical. They argue that the predominance of power is held by researchers, even in those rare cases when researchers "study up," or investigate people whose status and power are greater than their own. This is because researchers always have the last word: they are the ones who write the report or tell the story. Postmodernists advocate recognition of and confrontation with the fact of this power asymmetry, suggesting that researchers work collaboratively with those they study to make sure that the story they tell is one of which the investigatees approve, or at least understand, even if they disagree with its conclusions. Some researchers even suggest that no-one has the right to speak for someone else, especially if the "other" being spoken for is from an oppressed or marginalized group. To that end, researchers struggle for a way to foreground the story told by the informant, while still presenting it in the context of valid social science theory, and where it seems important, locating what researchers observe and what informants say within social and historical relationships of power.

More and more often, critical and postmodern researchers privilege the perspective of subjects, rather than that of the researcher, and collaborate with subjects on the construction of portrayals of themselves and their worlds. None of these portrayals expresses the whole story, or the whole truth, but it is hoped that a combined telling of the groups' stories can more closely approximate reality (Marcus and Fischer 1986).

Much serious work in this vein has been done by sociologists and anthropologists whose work is informed by critical theory or "critical ethnography" (Anderson 1989, Quantz 1992). These studies emphasize the study of subordinate groups, identifying the conditions and social forces which create inequities among individual groups; in particular, race, class, professional status, age, gender, and sexual orientation. They describe also how the individual subjects respond to and construct their own identity and lives in the context of those forces. This work goes beyond social critique, and, informed considerably by the work of feminist researchers, melds social activism, interpretive epistemology, and research methods characteristically used by symbolic interactionists. Among the many examples are Foster's studies of African-American teachers (1993, 1994); Granfield's (1991), and Fine and Weis's studies of dropouts, at-risk youth, and white working class adults (Fine 1991, Kelly and Nihlen 1982, Weis and Fine 1993, Weis 1990, Fine and Zane 1989); studies of persons with HIV/AIDS (Lather 1996, Tierney 1994); examinations of American-Indian students in prebaccalaureate programs and colleges (Deyhle 1986, 1991, 1992, Tierney 1993); gay and lesbian students (O'Conor 1993–1994, Friend 1993); untenured university faculty (Gumport 1993), working class female teachers (Kelly and Nihlen 1982), female punks (Roman 1993), and the disconnect between schooling and the training of rock-n-roll musicians (Holloway 1996).

Such an appreciation for the diversity of human values and norms could lead to relativism, a position that human behavior ought to be judged morally, ethically, and esthetically within the framework of the culture or context that produced it (Rorty 1985).

It can also lead to poor research. Privileging subject meanings rather than researcher meanings often has led novice qualitative researchers to assume that all they need to do is to present results exclusively from the perspective of the "other," that is, the subject or group under study. The problem remains that it is difficult to do this and still be viewed as science. Much qualitative research remains "top down;" the story told may seem to be recounted by the "natives," but the interpretive constructs and definitions that frame the account are those of the investigator, imposed upon the narrative. The consequence has been a great deal of handwringing by researchers who lament the fact that they cannot avoid speaking for the "other" and feel guilty doing so, even as they write (see Geertz 1989–1990, for a discussion of these issues). Some such researchers deliberately leave data under- and unanalyzed to give the appearance that the informant really is telling the story, and that the researcher had no role in eliciting or shaping it. This is done by researchers who are reluctant to impose external frameworks on the definitions and constructions of the people they are studying, to categorize them through lenses not developed indigenously, or to judge them by an external set of standards. The result is often mere story telling.

3.4 "Story" Research

In both sociology and education, some researchers have become preoccupied by the life experiences of single individuals, whether they be practicing or neophyte teachers, students, or members of oppressed groups. In education, such research is informed by constructivism. Constructivism is a philosophical perspective which holds that because humans are thinkers who know things, any actions they undertake are shaped by this knowing (Magoon 1977). Constructivism is important for discussion of sociological qualitative research, because it uses the language of the "social construction" of knowledge and "situated cognition," without much reference to the social or to the situation in which cognition is embedded. It also borrows ideas from critical sociology, though without the structural underpinnings of that discipline.

Constructivists in education are primarily trained in psychology. To them, the "social" aspects of social construction are limited to immediate, dyadic, or small group contexts; the "situation" in which cognition is located is not embedded in more social or historical structures. For this reason, their work is somewhat unsatisfactory to sociologists because it lacks a social structural referent to which all sociological work at least implicitly refers, and it does not situate conditions of teaching and learning within contexts beyond specific and limited contemporary moments in classrooms. Nonetheless, constructivism has also provided experimental works and ways of portrayal and presentation of data which inform research more clearly sociological in nature.

The task of the constructivist researcher is to find out what people know, and then to use that information to understand their behavior. Further, constructivists assume that if what people know can be changed, then their behavior will change accordingly. They try to get teachers to reflect on and then to describe what they are doing, and then to identify the knowledge base upon which their actions are predicated. This, in turn, forms the basis for trying to alter the knowledge base of teachers in ways more conducive to innovative teaching. Often using discourse or sociolinguistic analysis, "story" research or narrative inquiry in education (Clandinin and Connelly 1994, Connelly and Clandinin 1990) focuses on teacher practice, teacher change, research on teaching and learning in maths, science, reading, and writing, and on oppressed participants in educational systems.

Notwithstanding its lack of a historical or structural perspective, some researchers have melded constructivism with parts of the critical tradition, such that they argue that teachers have been silenced or disempowered in their jobs. They believe that the act of participating in research on their own practice can help them to become more efficacious (see Gitlin and Smyth 1989, Gitlin et al. 1992). Elsewhere, there is criticism of this kind of "feel good" approach to social mobilization (LeCompte and DeMarrais 1992), especially when it is relegated to schools and classrooms. Notwithstanding, "story" research or "story-telling" does shift the level of analysis from systems to individuals. It privileges the meanings of the story-teller, even without situating them within external referents, and it has been the catalyst for much collaborative work between academic researchers and practitioners and persons in the community. To these ends, it informs the practice of sociologists, discussed below.

3.5 Biography and Narrative Inquiry

In his book on "interpretive biography," Denzin (1989) argues for the reclaiming of sociology's long history of biographical method. Beginning with Dilthey's interest in biography (1900/1976), Denzin suggests that works which should be of interest to sociologists include "studied use and collection of life documents" (1989 p. 7), which include autobiographies, diaries, letters, obituaries, life histories and stories, personal experience stories, oral histories, and personal histories. Citing Mills (1959), he notes that applying the sociological imagination to the intersections of history and biography within a given society permits the sociologist to locate fully and understand the individual within their contexts. Denzin suggests that the Chicago School researchers made considerable use of biography; in his own recent writings (1989, 1994), he argues not for a method of *doing* biography, but for an analytic strategy aimed at understanding how to analyze life data and then write it up in ways that take advantage of literary conventions while recognizing the degree to which they impose constraints upon the use of literature as social science/sociology.

In another vein, Richardson (1990) argues for the use of narrative by sociologists, based on her assertion that it is the single most pervasive way that humans organize their experience. "Narrative," she says, "is everywhere" (1990 p. 117). Citing Polkinghorne (1988), she suggests that it is the primary way through which humans organize their experience, link events, and constitute meaning. She suggests that the narrative mode is contextually embedded and looks for particular connections between events; the connection itself constitutes the meaning. She distinguishes narrative from logico-empirical codes that dominate scientific writing and aim at universal truths. Richardson's argument, then, differs little from the constructivists in its privileging of local meanings, its focus on "experience-near," and its apparent aversion to imposed frameworks. She also argues, as do critical ethnographers and constructivists, that the act of creating and presenting the "collective story," or the story of people who are silenced or marginalized, can be transformative, in that it offers "new narratives. . .[as] the patterns for new lives" (1990 p. 129).

Richardson states that children learn to tell stories at a very early age, and that from the time they begin doing so, their stories can and should become a major focus for sociological researchers seeking to understand human behavior and belief. Such research, as is the case with constructivists, uses conventional analytic methods common to discourse or text analysis and sociolinguistics, or the theme-and-domain analyses of cultural anthropologists such as Spradley (1979).

Her argument comes close to suggesting that narrative itself is genetically programmed in the human species. An alternative view is that any "good" narrative is structured by tacit cultural understandings and judged by canons derived from Western traditions of temporality and causality. Richardson herself discusses the components of narrative in these terms, suggesting that narratives are "time made human," and that narrative functions to mark off the lives of individuals as unique from all other individuals in a collective. Narratives also, according to Richardson, have plots, characters, dialogue, complicating actions, and settings. They have as well an order or sequence which is causally and temporally determined (Richardson 1990). Thus, stories go forward and they carry their characters and plots forward with them.

This emphasis on time, individualism, progress, and on the importance of plot, sequence, and characters is characteristic of a particular kind of cultural thinking, one that constitutes a tacit or implicit framework informing story or narrative research. Rather than having no framework at all, rather than simply being the conduit through which the voice of the informant flows, these researchers are instead steeped in a grand historical narrative, a metaphor which has governed life and thought in the Western world since the En-

lightenment. Life, in the grand narrative tradition, has beginnings, endings, and a trajectory between the two; it makes progress. So does the history of humankind. Thus, the work of story or narrative researchers is no less informed by implicit or tacit frameworks than that of the unaware functionalists referred to earlier.

As long as researchers do their work with persons who are also steeped in the grand narrative tradition, few problems arise; most people schooled in Western academic traditions are so steeped. They learn what a story is or should be by fourth grade, and if they forget, they are forcefully reminded by every elementary school teacher who ever reshaped a child's inchoate tellings in accordance with conventional norms about how a story should be structured (Heath 1996a). Researchers seek to find stories with the same form as their own or those they have been taught, and when they do not find such stories intact, they keep talking to informants until they have enough data to reformulate the material into a "real" story (see Mishler 1986) with a beginning, end, trajectory, plot, and characters. Only then can they begin to analyze or "make sense" of it.

Such reformulating, however, really differs little from the act of imposing researcher categories on informant data which so discomfits many postmodernists. The task of making sense becomes increasingly problematic and difficult as the kinds of people with whom researchers work become more and more out of the mainstream and more and more unlike them. They now encounter people who do not tell stories or frame what they say as narratives. Angrosino's mentally handicapped, low-income informant, Vonnie Lee, left the researcher

> stumped . . . I could form no clear sense of who or what Vonnie Lee Hargrett thought he was . . . Vonnie Lee worked in an anecdotal style of narrative . . . he would . . . relate an encapsulated anecdote that was meant to represent his life as a "real little kid'. Then we would go on and say, 'So then I got a little older. Yeah. Here's what it was.' And he would launch into another encapsulated story . . . almost devoid of characters . . . and of plot, even of the most attenuated type. (1994 p. 17)

Similarly, Heath's (1996b) teenage informants in afterschool arts organizations refused to "tell stories"

> Their discourse is thematically organized . . . the familiar narrative strands of time and sequencing . . . are replaced by segments interlinked by theme, like stanzas of poetry. The poetics of their talk, instead of being an esoteric object within a snippet chosen by examiner for analysis, remains constant, moving back and forth across chunks that carry within them particular strands of content that provide chaining of these segments . . . predictabilities of narratives give way to parallels. (p. 12)

Both Heath and Angrosino link these communicative styles to the lived experiences of their informants; they talked as they lived.

Heath argues that they really live in a fragmented postmodern world, lacking canons or logic, even a future. They could not describe their world in ways that were not congruent with the way they lived it. Thus, by refusing to "tell stories," they resisted all attempts by a researcher to impose another order upon their lives. This resistance creates a dilemma for researchers: either they must reframe the talk of their informants into a narrative, or they must create a different genre for presenting it. However different genres often are not recognized as science.

4. Alternative Forms of Presentation

Having just suggested that alternative or experimental genres often are not thought of as science, this article now discusses ways in which some social scientists are struggling with the dilemma posed above. From most to least "scientific," there are "messy texts" (Marcus 1994), narratives of the self, fictional representations, poetic representations, mixed genres (Richardson 1994), and ethnographic drama (McCall and Becker 1990, Richardson 1994). Proponents of these genres justify them in terms of the social science imperative to present, as clearly and directly as possible, the lived experience of the informants as they understand it. As I have indicated, many contemporary informants do not experience life in ways conducive to clear presentation following conventions of sociological writing. Further, postmodern ethics forbid treating such lives as social scientists once did: as discordant, deviant, superstition-ridden, or irrational. Given the complexity and often intractability of postmodern life, these research practitioners argue that only by moving beyond conventional text-based presentations can justice be done to their life stories.

4.1 "Messy" Texts and Mixed Genres

"Messy texts" have three characteristics. First, they mix the global and local levels of analysis, since they address the problem of how difficult it is to give a simple account of daily life when the global is interpenetrated by the local and vice versa in postmodern life. Second, messy texts present a partial kind of holism; they give a "sense of the whole without evoking the totality" to which research often alludes. Finally, they are incomplete, open-ended, unwilling to tell the end of a story, or draw it to a close (Marcus 1994 p. 567). Messy texts are created in an attempt to address some of the postmodern dilemmas of inconstancy, change, and partiality described earlier in this article. When they go beyond the presentation of a work in text form only, they often result in what Richardson (1994) calls "mixed genres."

Mixed genres are works that freely intermingle literary, artistic, and scientific genres. They might include poetry, ethnographic account, fieldnotes, and fiction, or they could mix cartoons, photographs, essays, and

annotated transcripts into what otherwise is a field study report (1994).

Regardless of whether texts are messy or mixed, their aim is to represent more clearly the lived experience of informants, on the one hand, and to communicate to and across varied audiences, on the other. Thus, these forms of experimental genres try for intelligibility more than merely for an academic constituency.

4.2 Narratives of Self

Many sociologists and anthropologists have been accused of giving up on writing about the "other" by writing, instead, about themselves (Geertz 1989–1990). These writings take the form of "highly personalized, revealing texts in which the author tells stories about his or her own lived experience" (Richardson 1994), often as they lived it in the research site. The anthropological literature is replete with such self-reflective works; other disciplines are also now capitalizing on the "tales from the field" genre. These often are useful for neophyte researchers; they also help, if read in conjunction with an author's less self-oriented field studies, to elucidate interpretations which the author might have made.

4.3 Fiction

Ever since the fictitious Carlos Castaneda published his accounts of learning to be a shaman in the *Tales of Power* series, researchers have argued whether a story which was fictitious as to person and perhaps place, but accurate as to practices and beliefs, was legitimate social science. Some social science writing does read like good fiction; there are, in fact, conventions in ethnographic writing that argue for the telling of a "good story." Further, much ethnographic writing does, in fact, contain elements of fiction, if only insofar as characters in the story are disguised to protect their identity. Under some conditions, fictionalized accounts may be the only way in which an author can tell a tale.

4.4 Poetry

Richardson (1994) argues that presenting interviews in poetic form often preserves the feel of the informant's speech as well as its "punch;" quoting Frost, she notes that "a poem is the shortest emotional distance between" the reader and the speaker. She also suggests that poems are a concentrated method of evocative communication; they can communicate more in their brevity than any long dreary monograph.

4.5 Drama and Performance

Similarly, when the material to be presented is emotionally laden, intractable, or multileveled, drama may be the most effective way to recapture the experience. Becker (McCall and Becker 1990, Paget 1994) and others have experimented with acting out or performing material on certain kinds of events or issues which their qualitative research has unearthed, arguing against "the odd way in which in sociology we have privileged the written text as though the written text is the only model for how we can communicate our understanding of the life world." (Paget 1994 p. 137). Like Marcus and Richardson and others, they suggest that the conventions of sociological writing are so tightly controlled that they obscure the relationship which writers have to their work; yet unlike Marcus and Richardson, who still utilize text-based genres, however messy or mixed they might be, they reject text altogether, except insofar as it serves as a script to be acted out.

4.6 Going Beyond Text

Even farther from text is presentation which goes straight to the visual. While a written plan of action still might guide what is to be presented, the use of films, CD-ROM, videotape, and even paintings and sculpture have been suggested as alternatives for presentation of sociological field work. In general, these materials are presented at conferences, rather than referenced in texts, and are, therefore, fugitive materials. They move the visual from its use as a means to create description in order to create a product, to its use as an end or a product, such as a film, painting, website, or video, in itself. A case might be made for including Internet technology in this category, though not eletronic journals; while these are an alternative distribution mode, they are, in fact, not different forms of representation. Presentation in hypertext like websites on the Internet, however, constitutes both alternative forms of presentation and distribution.

4.7 Problems with Alternative Modes of Presentation

Some obvious limitations appear in the use of such modes of presentation and representation. Such works are less accessible by conventional means. Most cannot be confined within the covers of a book or journal, and thus are less available through conventional channels of distribution. This means that they are less subject to canonical evaluation. Critics also contend that while such formats certainly are evocative and thought-provoking, they are not scientific. Their supporters, however, might argue that breaking both the strictures of conventional textual presentations and the power of the canon is exactly the point. More problematic, however, is the issue of analysis and interpretation. In conventional text presentations, and even in messy texts and mixed genres, poems, songs, visuals, and other materials are presented in support of a point which is made clear by the researcher. Analytic and interpretive strategies are made more or less transparent to the reader and rendered for critique as to their credibility, authenticity, representativeness, validity, and care in exercise of the craft. Thus, scientists can use artistic works of others whom they are studying, but they have to say what use is being made of them or place them in some sort of meaningful context. Such is not the case when the product being evaluated is the artistic work of the scientist himself or herself, which then raises the question of the purpose of the work itself. Whether a work is science or art, or instead, is some sort of alternative or mixed genre, may be beside the point; more important may be to find appropriate venues for a wide variety of presentations on similar subjects but intended for different audiences. Such a strategy might, indeed, help the social sciences preach less to the choir and more to communities who might make wider use of their insights.

See also: Biographical Research Methods; Critical Discourse Analysis; Feminist Research Methodology; Participatory Research; Research Paradigms in Education; Trends in Quantitative Research Methods

References

Adler P A, Adler P 1991 *Blackboards and Backboards: College Athletes and Role Engulfment.* Columbian University Press, New York

Adler P A, Kless S J, Adler P 1992 Socialization to gender roles: popularity among elementary school boys and girls. *Sociol. Educ.* 65: 169–87

Anderson G L 1989 Critical ethnography in education: its origins, current status and new directions. *Rev. Educ. Res.* 59(3): 249–70

Angrosino M V 1994 On the bus with Vonnie Lee. *J. Contemp. Ethnography* 23(1): 14–29

Anyon J 1980 Social class and the hidden curriculum of work. *J. Educ.* 162: 62–92

Anyon J 1983 Workers, labor and economic history, and textbook content. In: Apple M W, Weis L (eds.) 1983

Apple M W 1978 The new sociology of education: Analyzing cultural and economic reproduction. *Harv. Educ. Rev.* 48: 495–503

Apple M W, Weis L (eds.) 1983 *Ideology and Practice in Schooling.* Temple University Press, Philadelphia, Pennsylvania

Atkinson P, Delamont S, Hammerley M 1988 Qualitative research traditions: A British response to Jacob. *Rev. Educ. Res.* 58: 231–50

Babbie E R *Survey Research Methods.* Wadsworth, Belmont, California

Becker H S 1953 The teacher in the authority system of the public school. *J. Educ. Sociol.* 27: 128–41

Becker H S, Geer B, Hughes E C 1968 *Making the Grade: The Academic Side of College Life.* Wiley, New York

Becker H S, Geer B, Hughes E C, Strauss A L 1961 *Boys in White: Student Culture in Medical School.* University of Chicago Press, Chicago, Illinois

Blau P, Duncan O D 1967 *The American Occupational Structure.* Wiley, New York

Bogden R C, Biklen S K 1986 *Qualitative Research for Education: An Introduction to Theory and Methods.* Allyn and Bacon, Boston, Massachusetts

Bogdan R C, Biklen S K 1992 *Qualitative Research for Education: An Introduction to Theory and Methods,* 2nd edn. Allyn and Bacon, Boston, Massachusetts

Bogdan R C, Taylor S J 1975 *Introduction to Qualitative Research Methods: A Phenomenological Approach to the Social Science*. Wiley, New York

Borman K M (ed.) 1982 *The Social Life of Children in a Changing Society*. Erlbaum, Hillsdale, New Jersey

Borman K M 1991 *The First Real Job: A Study of Young Workers*. State University of New York Press, Albany, New York

Bossert S T 1979 *Tasks and Social Relationships in Classrooms: A Study of Instructional Organization and its Consequences*. Cambridge University Press, Cambridge

Boudon R 1974 *Education, Opportunity, and Social Inequality: Changing Prospects in Western Society*. Wiley, New York

Bourdieu P 1973 Cultural reproduction and social reproduction. In: Brown R (ed.) *Knowledge, Education and Cultural Change*. Tavistock, London

Bourdieu P 1990 *The Logic of Practice*. Stanford University Press, Stanford, California

Bourdieu P, Passeron J-C 1977 *Reproduction in Education, Society and Culture* (trans. R. Nice). Sage, London

Bowles S, Gintis H 1976 *Schooling in Capitalist America: Educational Reform and the Contradictions of Economic Life*. Basic Books, New York

Brouillette L 1996 *A Geology of School Reform*. State University of New York Press, Albany, New York

Campbell D T, Stanley J C 1963 Experimental and Quasi-experimental Designs for Research on Teaching. In: Gage N L (ed.) 1963 *The Handbook of Research on Teaching*. Rand McNally, Chicago, Illinois

Carnoy M 1972 *Education as Cultural Imperialism*. McKay, New York

Cicourel A V, Kitsuse J I 1963 *The Educational Decisionmakers*. Bobbs-Merrill, Indianapolis, Indiana

Clark B R 1960 The cooling out function in higher education. *Am. J. Sociol.* 15: 569–76

Cook R D, Campbell D T 1979 *Quasi-Experimentation: Design and Analysis Issues for Field Settings*. Rand McNally, Chicago, Illinois

Connell R W 1985 *Teachers Work*. Allen and Unwin, Winchester, Massachusetts

Connelly F M, Clandinin D J 1990 Stories of experience and narrative inquiry. *Educ. Researcher* 19(5): 2–14

Clandinin D J, Connelly F M 1944 Personal experience methods. In: Lincoln Y, Denzin N K (eds.) 1994 *The Handbook of Qualitative Research*. Sage, Thousand Oaks, California

Clifford J, Marcus G E 1986 *Writing Culture: The Poetics and Politics of Ethnography*. University of California Press, Berkeley, California

Coleman J S 1966 *Equality of Educational Opportunity*. US Government Printing Office, Washington DC

Cusick P A 1973 *Inside High School: The Student's World*. Holt, Rinehart, and Winston, New York

Delgado-Gaitan C 1990 *Literacy for Empowerment*. Falmer Press, Bristol, Pennsylvania

Denzin N K 1989 *Interpretive Biography*. Sage, Newbury Park, California

Denzin N K 1994 The art and politics of interpretation. In: Lincoln Y, Denzin N K (eds.) 1994 *The Handbook of Qualitative Research*. Sage, Thousand Oaks, California

Derrida J 1976 On Grammatology (Spivak GC, trans.). Johns Hopkins University Press, Baltimore, Maryland

Deyle D M 1986 Break dancing and breaking out: Anglos, Utes and Navajos in a border reservation school. *Anthropol. Educ. Q.* 17: 111–27

Deyhle D M 1992 Constructing failure and maintaining culture identity: Navajo and Ute school leavers. *J. Am. Indian Educ.* January 24–47

Dilthey WL 1900/1976 *Selected Writings*. Cambridge University Press, Cambridge

Dobbert M L 1982 *Ethnographic Research: Theory and Application for Modern Schools and Societies*. Praeger, New York

Eckerd P 1988 *Jocks and Burnouts: Social Categories and Identity in the High School*. Teachers College Press, New York

Eder D 1985 The cycle of popularity: Interpersonal relations among adolescents. *Sociol. Educ.* 58: 154–65

Eder D, Evans D 1993 No exit: Processes of social isolation in the middle school. *J. Contemp. Ethnography* 22(2) 139–71

Eder D, Kinney D A 1995 The effect of middle school extracurricular activities on adolescents' popularity and peer status. *Youth Soc.* 26(3): 298–325

Eder D, Parker S 1987 The cultural production and reproduction of gender: The effect of extracurricular activities on peer group culture. *Sociol. Educ.* 60: 200–13

Eisenhart M A, Howe K R 1992 Validity in educational research. In: LeCompte M D, Millroy W L, Preissle J (eds.) 1992 *The Handbook of Qualitative Research in Education*. Academic Press, San Diego, California

Erickson F 1986 Qualitative methods in research on teaching. In: Wittrock M C (ed.) 1986 *The Handbook of Research in Teaching*, 3rd edn. MacMillan, New York

Fetterman D M (ed.) 1984 *Qualitative Approaches to Evaluation in Education: The Silent Revolution*. Praeger, New York

Fetterman D M, Pitman M A (eds.) 1986 *Educational Evaluation: Ethnography in Theory Practice and Politics*. Sage, Newbury Park, California

Filstead W J 1979 Qualitative methods: A needed perspective in evaluation research. In: Cook T C, Reichardt C S (eds.) 1979 *Qualitative and Quantitative Methods in Evaluation Research*. Sage, Beverly Hills, California

Fine M 1991 *Framing Dropouts: Notes on the Politics of an Urban High School*. State University of New York Press, Albany, New York

Fine M, Zane N 1989 Being wrapped too tight: Why low-income women drop out of high school. In: Weis L, Farrar E, Petrie H (eds.) 1989 *Dropouts From School: Issues, Dilemmas, and Solutions*. State University of New York Press, Albany, New York

Foster M 1933 Resisting racism: Personal testimonies of African-American teachers. In: Weis L, Fine M (eds.) 1993 *Beyond Silenced Voices: Class, Race and Gender in United States Schools*. State University of New York Press, Albany, New York

Foster M 1994 The power to know one thing is never the power to know all things: Methodological notes on two studies of Black American teachers. In: Gitlin A (ed.) 1994 *Power and Method*. Routledge, New York

Foucault M 1972 *The Archeology of Knowledge and the Discourse on Language*. Pantheon, New York

Foucault M 1980 Power/Knowledge. In: Gordon D (ed.) 1980 *Power/Knowledge: Selected Interviews and other Writings*. Pantheon, New York

Friend R A 1933 Choices, not closets: Heterosexism and homophobia in schools. In: Weis L, Fine M (eds.) 1993

Fuller M 1980 Black girls in a London comprehensive.

In: James A, Jeffcoate R (eds.) 1980 *The School in Multicultural Society*. Harper and Row, London

Furlong V 1976 Interaction sets in the classroom: Towards a study of pupil knowledge. In: Stubbs M, Delamont S (eds.) 1976 *Explorations in Classroom Observations*. Wiley, London

Garfinkle H 1967 *Studies in Ethnomethodology*. Prentice-Hall, Englewood Cliffs, New Jersey

Geertz C 1983 *Local Knowledge*. Basic Books, New York

Geertz C 1989–1990 *Works and Lives: The Anthropologist as Author*. Stanford University Press, Stanford, California

Gibson M A 1988 *Accommodation Without Assimilation: Sikh Immigrants in an American High School*. Cornell University Press, Ithaca, New York

Ginsburg M B 1988 *Contradictions in Teacher Education and Society*. Falmer, New York

Ginsberg M B, LeCompte M D 1987 How students learn to become teachers: An exploration of alternative responses to a teacher training program. In: Noblit G W, Pink W T (eds.) 1987 *Schooling in Social Context: Qualitative Studies*. Ablex, Norwood, New Jersey

Gitlin A, Bringhurst K, Burns M, Cooley V, Myers B, Prise K, Russell R, Tiess P 1992 *Teachers' Voices for School Change*. Teachers College Press, New York

Gitlin A, Smyth J 1989 *Teacher Evaluation: Schooling and Everyday Life*. Bergin and Garvey, Westport, Connecticut

Glesne C, Peshkin A 1992 *Becoming Qualitative Researchers*. Longman, White Plains, New Jersey

Glazer N 1972 *The Research Adventure*. Random House, New York

Goetz J P, LeCompte M D 1984 *Ethnography and Qualitative Design and Educational Research*. Academic Press, New York

Goode W J, Hatt P K 1952 *Methods in Social Research*. McGraw-Hill, New York

Gordon C W 1957 *The Social System of the High School*. Free Press, Glencoe, Illinois

Granfield R 1991 Making it by faking it: Working-class students in an elite academic environment. *J. Contemp. Ethnography* 20(3): 331–52

Grant G 1989 *The World We Created at Hamilton High*. Harvard University Press, Cambridge, Massachusetts

Gumpost P 1993 Fired faculty: Reflections on marginality and academic identity. In: McLaughlin D, Tierney W (eds.) 1993 *Naming Silenced Lives*. Routledge, New York

Hargreaves A, Woods P 1984 *Classrooms and Staffrooms*. Open University Press, Milton Keynes

Hartsock N C M 1983 The feminist standpoint: Developing the ground for a specifically feminist historical materialism. In: Harding S, Hintikka M (eds.) 1983 *Discovering Reality: Feminist Perspectives on Epistemology, Metaphysics, Methodology and Philosophy of Science*. Reidel, Boston, Massachusetts

Heath S B 1996 Postmodern narrative and its consequences in knowledge transition. Lecture 1, University of Colorado, Boulder, Colorado, September 11

Heath S B 1996 The ideology of narrative and youth. Lecture 2, University of Colorado, Boulder, Colorado, September 30

Herr K 1991 Portrait of a teenage mother. In: Donmoyer R, Kos R (eds.) 1991 *Students At-Risk: Portraits and Policies*. State University of New York Press, Albany, New York

Hess G A 1991 *School Reform Chicago Style*. Corwin Press, Newbury Park, California

Holland D, Eisenhart M 1990 *Educated in Romance* University of Chicago Press, Chicago, Illinois

Hollingshead A B 1947 *Elmtown's Youth*. Wiley, New York

Holloway D L 1996 Constructing identity and community through rock-n-roll: The influence of popular culture and the politics of schools. Paper presented at the annual meeting of the American Educational Studies Association, Montreal, Quebec, Canada, November 8

Jackson P W 1968 *Life in Classrooms*. Holt, Rinehart, and Winston, New York

Jacob E 1987 Qualitative research traditions. *Rev. Educ. Res.* 57: 1–51

Jencks C 1972 *Inequality: A Reassessment of the Effect of Family and Schooling in America*. Basic Books, New York

Karabel J, Halsey A H 1978 *Power and Ideology in Education*. Oxford University Press, New York

Keddie N 1971 Classroom knowledge. In: Young M F D (ed.) 1971 *Knowledge and Control: New Directions for the Sociology of Education*. Collier Macmillan, London

Keller E 1983 Gender and science. In: Harding S, Hintikka M (eds.) 1983 *Discovering Reality: Feminist Perspectives on Epistemology, Metaphysics, Methodology and Philosophy of Science*. Reidel, Boston, Massachusetts

Keller E, Grontkowski C R 1983 The mind's eye. In: Harding S, Hintikka M (eds.) 1983 *Discovering Reality: Feminist Perspectives on Epistemology, Metaphysics, Methodology and Philosophy of Science*. Reidel, Boston, Massachusetts

Kelly G, Nihlen A S 1982 Schooling and the reproduction of patriary: Unequal workloads, unequal rewards. In: Apple M W (ed.) 1982 *Cultural and Economic Reproduction in Education*. Routledge and Kegan Paul, London

Lacey C 1970 *Hightown Grammar: The School as a Social System*. Manchester University Press, Manchester

Lacey C 1977 *The Socialization of Teachers*. Methuen, London

Lather P 1986 Research as praxis. *Harv. Educ. Rev.* 56: 257–77

Lather P 1996 Troubling clarity: The politics of accessible language. *Harv. Educ. Rev.* 66(3): 525–45

LeCompte M D 1978 Learning to work: The hidden curriculum of the classroom. *Anthropol. Educ. Q.* 9(1): 23–37

LeCompte M D 1981 The civilizing of children: How young children learn to become students. *The Journal of Thought* 15(3): 105–27

LeCompte M D, DeMarrais K B 1992 The disempowering of empowerment: Out of the revolution and into the classroom. *Educ. Foundations* 6(3): 5–33

LeCompte M D, Goetz J P 1982 Problems of reliability and validity in ethnographic research. *Rev. Educ. Res.* 52: 31–60

LeCompte M D, McLaughlin D 1994 Witchcraft and blessings, science and rationality: Discourses of power and science in collaborative work with Navajo schools. In: Gitlin A (ed.) 1994 *Power and Method: Political Activism and Educational Research*. Routledge, New York

LeCompte M D, Millroy W, Preissle J 1992 *The Handbook of Qualitative Research in Education*. Academic Press, Orlando, Florida

LeCompte M D, Preissle J 1993 *Ethnography and Qualitative Design in Educational Research*, 2nd edn. Academic Press, San Diego, California

LeCompte M D, Preissle J 1994 Qualitative research: What it is, what it isn't, and how it's done. In: Thompson B (ed.) 1994 *Advances in Social Science Research,* Vol. 3. JAI Press, New York

Lincoln Y, Guba E 1985 *Naturalistic Inquiry.* Sage, Beverly Hills, California

Lofland J 1971 *Analyzing Social Settings: A Guide to Qualitative Observation and Analysis,* 2nd edn. Wadsworth, Belmont, California

Lortie D 1969 The partial professionalization of elementary teaching. In: Etzioni A (ed.) 1969 *The Semi-Professions and Their Organization.* Free Press, New York

Lortie D 1975 *Schoolteacher.* University of Chicago Press, Chicago, Illinois

Lubeck S 1988 Nested contexts. In: Weis L (ed.) 1988 *Class, Race and Gender in American Education.* State University of New York Press, Albany, New York

Lynd R S, Lynd H M 1929 *Middletown: A Study in Contemporary American Culture.* Harcourt Brace, New York

MacLeod J 1987 *Ain't no Makin' It.* Westview Press, Boulder, Colorado

Magoon G E 1977 Contructivist approaches in educational research. *Rev. Educ. Res.* 47: 651–93

Manning P K, Cullum-Swan B 1994 Narrative, content and semiotic analysis. In: Lincoln Y, Denzin N (eds.) 1994 *The Handbook of Qualitative Research.* Sage, Thousand Oaks, California

Marcus G E 1994 What comes (just) after "post"? The case of ethnography. In: Lincoln Y, Denzin N K (eds.) 1994 *The Handbook of Qualitative Research.* Sage Publications, Thousand Oaks, California

Marcus G E, Fischer M M J 1986 *Anthropology as Cultural Critique: An Experimental Moment in the Human Sciences.* University of Chicago Press, Chicago, Illinois

McCall M, Becker H S 1990 Performance science. *Social Problems* 32: 117–32

McCall G J, Simmons J L (eds.) 1969 *Issues in Participant Observation: A Text and Reader.* Addison-Wesley, Reading, Massachusetts

McNeil L 1988 *Contradictions of Control: School Structure and School Knowledge.* Routledge, New York

McQuillan P 1997 *Educational Opportunity in an Urban American High School: A Cultural Analysis.* State University of New York Press, Albany, New York

McRobbie A 1978 working class girls and the culture of feminity. In: Women's Studies Group, Center for Contemporary Cultural Studies (ed.) 1978 *Women Take Issue: Aspects of Women's Subordination.* Hutchinson, London

Mead M 1959 *An Anthropologist at Work: The Writings of Ruth Benedict.* Houghton Mifflin, Boston, Massachusetts

Merriam S B 1988 *Case Study Research in Education: A Quantitative Approach.* Jossey-Bass, San Francisco, California

Metz M H 1978 *Classrooms and Corridors: The Crisis of Authority in Desegregated Secondary Schools.* University of California Press. Berkely, California

Miles M B, Huberman A M 1984 *Qualitative Data Analysis: A Sourcebook of New Methods.* Sage, Beverly Hills, California

Miles M B, Huberman A M 1994 *Qualitative Data Analysis: A Sourcebook of New Methods.* Sage, Beverly Hills, California

Mills C W 1959 *The Sociological Imagination.* Oxford University Press, New York

Mishler E G 1986 *Research Interviewing: Context and Narrative.* Harvard University Press, Cambridge, Massachusetts

Mohanty C 1988 Under Western eyes: Feminist scholarship and colonial discourses. *Feminist Rev.* 30: 60–88

Muncey D E, McQuillan P 1996 *Reform and Resistance in Schools and Classrooms: An Ethnographic View.* Yale University Press, New Haven, Connecticut

Newman K K 1980 Stages in an unstaged occupation. *Educ. Leadership* 37: 514–16

Oakes J 1985 *Keeping Track: How Schools Structure Inequality.* Yale University Press, New Haven, Connecticut

O'Conor A 1993–1994. Who gets called queer in school? Lesbian, gay and bisexual teenagers, homophobia and high school. *The High School J.* 77(2): 7–13

Page R 1987 Lower-track classes at a college preparatory high school: A caricature of education encounters. In: Spindler G, Splinder L (eds.) *Interpretive Ethnography of Education at Home and Abroad.* Lawrence Erlbaum, Hillsdale, New Jersey

Paget M A 1994 Performing the text. *J. Contemp. Ethnography* 19(1): 136–55

Patton M Q 1980 *Qualitative Evaluation Methods.* Sage, Newbury Park, California

Patton M Q 1990 *Qualitative Evaluation and Research Methods,* 2nd edn. Sage, Newbury Park, California

Persell C 1977 *Education and Inequality: The Roots and Results of Stratification.* Free Press, New York

Polkinghorne D E 1988 *Narrative Knowing and the Human Sciences.* State University of New York Press, Albany

Powell A G, Farrar E, Cohen D K 1985 *The Shopping Mall High School.* Houghton Mifflin, Boston, Massachusetts

Quantz R A 1992 On critical ethnography (with some postmodern considerations. In: LeCompte M D, Millroy W L, Preissle J (eds.) 1992 *The Handbook of Qualitative Research In Education.* Academic Press, San Diego, California

Richardson L 1991 Narrative and sociology. *J. Contemp. Ethnography* 19(1): 116–36

Richardson L 1994 Writing: A method of inquiry. In: Lincoln Y, Denzin N K (eds.) 1994 *The Handbook of Qualitative Research.* Sage, Thousand Oaks, California

Rogers D 1968 *110 Livingston Street: Politics and Bureacracy in the New York City School System.* Random House, New York

Roman L G 1993 Double exposure; The politics of feminist materialist ethnography. *Educ. Theory* 43(3): 278–309

Roman L G 1996 Spectacle in the dark: Youth as transgression, display and repression. *Educ. Theory* Winter: 1–23

Rorty R 1985 Solidarity or objectivity? In: Rajchman J, West C (eds.) 1985 *Post-Analytic Philosophy.* Columbian University Press, New York

Rynkiewich M A, Spradley J P (eds.)1976 *Ethics and Anthropology: Dilemmas In Fieldwork.* Wiley, New York

Said E W 1978 *Orientalism.* Pantheon, New York

Said E W 1994 *Culture and Imperialism.* Alfred Knopf, New York

Sarason S 1971 *The Culture of the School and the Problem of Change.* Allyn and Bacon, Boston, Massachusetts

Shatzman L, Strauss A L 1973 *Field Research: Strategies for a Natural Sociology.* Prentice-Hall, Englewood Cliffs, New Jersey

Schofield J 1982 *Black and White in School.* Praeger, New York

Sewell W H, Haller A O, Portes A 1969 The educational and early occupational attainment process. *Am. Sociol. Rev.* 34: 82–92

Sherman R R, Webb R B 1988 *Qualitative Research in Education: Focus and Methods*. Falmer, New York

Shulman L 1988 Disciplines of Inquiry. In: Jaeger R M (ed.) 1988 *Complementary Methods for Research in Education*. American Educational Research Association, Washington, DC

Sikes P, Measor L, Woods P 1985 *Teacher Careers: Crises and Continuities*. Falmer Press, London

Smith D E 1974 Women's perspective as a radical critique of sociology. *Sociological Inquiry*, 4: 1–13

Smith D E 1987 *The Everyday World as Problematic*. Northeastern University Press, Boston, Massachusetts

Spindler G D, Spindler L 1992 Cultural process and ethnography: An anthropological perspective. In: LeCompte M D, Millroy W L, Preissle J (eds.) 1992 *The Handbook of Qualitative Research in Education*. Academic Press, San diego, California

Spivak G C 1988 Subaltern studies: Deconstructing historiography. In: Spivak G C (ed.) 1988 *In Other Worlds*. Routledge, London

Spradley J P 1979 *The Ethnographic Interview*. Holt, Rinehart and Winston, New York

Stake R E 1978 The case study method in social inquiry. *Educ. Researcher* 7: 5–8

Stinchcombe A L 1964 *Rebellion in a High School*. Quadrangle Books, Chicago, Illinois

Tierney W G 1993 The college experience of Native Americans: A critical analysis. In: Weis L, Fine M (eds.) 1993

Tierney W G 1994 On method and hope. In: Gitlin A (ed.) 1994 *Power and Method*. Routledge, New York

Trinh M T T 1989 *Woman, Native, Other: Writing Postcoloniality and Feminism*. Indiana University Press, Bloomington, Indiana

Vidich A J, Bensman J 1958 *Small Town in Mass Society: Class, Power and Religion in a Rural Community*. Princeton University Press, Princeton, New Jersey

Waller W 1932 *The Sociology of Teaching*. Wiley, New York

Warner L, Lunt P S 1941 *The Social Life of a Modern Community*. Yale University Press, New Haven, Connecticut

Warner L, Low J O, Lunt P S, Strole L 1963 *Yankee City*. Yale University Press, New Haven, Connecticut

Weis L 1990 *Working Class Without Work: High School Students in a De-industrializing Economy*. Routledge, New York

Weis L, Fine M (eds.) 1993 *Beyond Silenced Voices: Class, Race, and Gender in United States Schools*. State University of New York Press, Albany, New York

Weis L, Farrar E, Petrie H (eds.) 1989 *Dropouts from School: Issues, Dilemmas and Solutions*. State University of New York Press, Albany, New York

Willis P E 1977 *Learning to Labour: How Working Class Kids Get Working Class Jobs*. Saxon House, Farnborough

Wilson S 1977 The use of ethnographic techniques in educational research. *Rev. Educ. Res.* 47: 245–65

Woods P 1992 Symbolic interactionism: Theory and method. In: LeCompte M D, Millroy W L, Preissle J (eds.) 1992 *The Handbook of Qualitative Research in Education*. Academic Press, San Diego, California

Wylie L 1974 *Village in the Vaucluse*. Harvard University Press, Cambridge, Massachusetts

Young M F D 1958 *The Rise of the Meritocracy*. Thames and Hudson, London

Trends in Quantitative Research Methods

J. P. Keeves

Sociology is the study of societies, social groups, and human social life. It seeks to provide understanding and explanation of the behavior of humans as social beings. Its scope is wide and is complicated by the fact that it is also involved with phenomena at the level of individuals. The sociology of education, as a consequence, is concerned with stability and change in the characteristics of both individuals and groups, insofar as they are influenced by educative processes. This dual nature of the sociology of education and its consideration of multilevel phenomena that involve both individuals and groups, as well as intraindividual and intragroup stability and change, has not in the past been widely appreciated or openly acknowledged. This has been a direct consequence of the lack of effective methods and procedures for the investigation of problems and the analysis of related data of a multilevel nature. However, over the past decade, from the mid-1980s to the mid-1990s, marked advances have occurred primarily in the field of education to resolve the issues and difficulties that arise in the investigation of multilevel phenomena. This entry examines these developments and argues that they have the potential to transform the sociology of education.

Major advances have taken place in quantitative research methods since electronic computing devices were made available for research purposes in universities and research institutes in the early 1960s. Today, in the late 1990s, powerful computers are now so readily accessible on the office desk or at home, which have the capacity to store large amounts of data, and to carry out complex statistical analyses very rapidly, that the limitations to the conduct of research lie in the effective use of computers, rather than in an inability to investigate complex problem situations. The use of computers involves not only the analysis of data, but also the collection of data both efficiently and accurately through the use of data-recording procedures that check the accuracy of the information as it is recorded, as well as the storage of the data. In addition, many problem situations can be investigated by simulation studies or by the examination of census files, without the collection of new data, simply because computers are now available to perform very rapidly the tasks involved. Unfortunately, however, the ubiquity of computers and the complex skills required to be mastered for their effective use has led to a polarization of the approaches employed in the conduct of research in the sociology of education, in particular, into quantitative and qualitative methods. It is necessary from the outset in this article to challenge this artificial and spurious dichotomy.

1. Removing the Quantitative and Qualitative Divide

In a discussion of the bifurcation of research methods into the quantitative and the qualitative, four aspects of the issue need to be addressed. First, there is the question of the difference between quantities and qualities. Second, there are the distinctions between data that are categorical, categorized, and continuous. Third, there are the little considered questions that relate to the analysis of categorical or qualitative data. Fourth, there are considerations concerned with the role of measurement in research.

1.1 Quantities and Qualities

It is frequently claimed that there are two different modes of inquiry in the behavioral and social sciences which lead to the quantitative and qualitative approaches to research. However, this simple dichotomy involves a serious failure to understand the nature of both quantities and qualities. Kaplan (1997) argues that it is necessary to emphasize that measurement is not an end in itself, it merely performs an instrumental function in inquiry. He also argues that there is a danger of assuming that measures have an inherent value, without regard for the nature of the object being measured, and the intrusion of the observer into the measurement process. Furthermore, there is a tendency to disregard how the number assigned in measurement should be used in analysis. The treatment of measurement as if it had intrinsic scientific value is referred to by Kaplan (1964) as the "mystique of quantity." There is, however, a more pervasive "mystique of quality," which considers that any attempt that is made to measure in educational research is a gross distortion or obfuscation of both objects and events. Those who adhere to this perspective regard qualitative methods as the only meaningful way to investigate an educational problem.

If these two views are considered as alternatives or even as opposites that are complementary, then a serious misunderstanding of the nature of both quantities and qualities has occurred. Kaplan (1964, p. 207) has clarified the point at issue in the following terms:

Quantities are *of* qualities, and a measured quality *has* just the magnitude expressed in its measure.

Every measurement demands some degree of abstraction. The assigning of a number to an observable characteristic or relationship requires the refinement of that characteristic or relation before measurements can be made. This is not an assumption of measurement, it is a *requirement* that the characteristic or relation should be accurately specified and should be unidimensional before measurement is attempted.

1.2 Categorical, Categorized, and Continuous Data

When the characteristics of individuals and groups are examined, prior to the making of observations and the collecting of data, it is necessary to consider the nature of each particular characteristic and the observations that can be made. For some characteristics of an individual, such as the sex of an individual, there are two distinct categories occurring in nature, and the data must be considered to be categorical. However, if observations are to be made and data are to be collected on the influence of educational attainment, or the number of years of education completed, the underlying characteristic involves a continuous variable, but the data are for convenience categorized in terms of years of education completed. Alternatively, if observations are to be made on a student's age, then the data collected involve a continuous measure that can be expressed readily in terms of years and months or possibly further refined to days. These distinctions between categorical, categorized, and continuous data are of considerable importance at the stage of data analysis. Moreover, the analytical procedures to be used influence the manner in which data are collected and as a consequence the way in which the research study is conducted and the methods of investigation employed.

Continuous or quasicontinuous data can be analyzed by many statistical procedures that are readily available for use on a computer. When choosing the analytical procedures to be employed, it is also necessary to consider whether collectively they are distributed with multivariate normality. Most computer packages provide information on the normality of the distribution of single variates or observed variables. However, only PRELIS2 (Jöreskog and Sörbom 1993) currently provides tests for the multivariate normality of a variance–covariance matrix. The normality of a distribution of an observed variable influences the analysis of data in two ways. First, significance tests require that the observed variables are normally distributed, and in more complex analyses that the residuals are normally distributed. Second, maximum likelihood analytical procedures assume the normality of the distribution of the variates employed as well as multivariate normality, except for exogenous variables which may be dichotomous or polychotomous under certain conditions.

Where observations have been categorized from an underlying normal distribution, the variance and covariance or correlation terms employed in analysis can be corrected for the categorization involved through the use of the PRELIS2 computer program, and the analysis proceeds with an assumption of underlying normality. Nevertheless, it should be noted that least-squares statistical procedures would appear to be robust when categorized variables are assumed to have a continuous mode, and when such variables diverge from normality, except in circumstances where the divergence is extreme with outlying observations. With increasingly complex analytical procedures being made available, it is becoming necessary to examine both the observations and the underlying variables under investigation for normality and for outlying values that might have to be given special consideration in analysis, for example, with robust regression procedures (Huynh Huynh 1997).

It is indeed fortunate that many human characteristics result from the operation of a large number of subordinate factors which give rise to an underlying normal distribution of the characteristic in the population. Likewise, when the characteristics of individuals are aggregated to form the characteristic of a group, then the aggregation and averaging of observations to the group level generally yields a measure that has an underlying normal distribution. While some analytical procedures have to be used with great care if the assumptions of normality and of an underlying interval scale are violated, the problems encountered are being overcome through new approaches to measurement and to the analysis of categorical data. It is here that important developments have occurred in Europe that have not received widespread recognition in North America.

1.3 New Methods for the Examination of Categorical Data

In Continental Europe it is widely accepted that much data which are obtained in sociological investigations are categorical in nature, and as a consequence analytical procedures have been developed for the examination of categorical data as distinct from categorized or continuous data. Where in the analysis of data associated with a continuous variable, the variance is partitioned into components to be analyzed systematically, the newly developed statistical procedures seek to analyze and partition the chi-square statistic or preferably the likelihood-ratio statistic into its components. This has led to the development of a family of procedures for statistical analysis that include: (a) CHAID (Kass 1980, Magidson 1989) which involves a sample splitting technique: (b) log-linear modeling (Kennedy and Hak Ping Tam 1997) which involves the hierarchical analysis of contingency table data; (c) configural frequency analysis (Kristof

1997, von Eye 1990, Krauth 1993) which is a procedure for the identification of types and antitypes in the analysis of cross-classifications; and (d) correspondence analysis (Everitt and Dunn 1991, Henry 1997) which employs a procedure for the extraction of principal components from a body of categorical data. There are further analytical procedures for analyzing the hierarchical structure of categorical data which have also been developed in Europe: (a) Galois lattices (Ander et al. 1997) which use a graphical method for representing hierarchical structures; and (b) partial order scalogram analysis (Shye 1997) which is a procedure for analyzing order relations among nonmetric data.

These procedures when added to the battery of analytical techniques that have been used traditionally in sociology of: (a) sociometric methods (Saha 1997); (b) social network analysis (Klovdahl 1997); and (c) mobility tables (Erikson 1997) for the analysis of categorical data, provide a valuable battery of techniques to examine bodies of data that were formerly not analyzed in a rigorous way because appropriate methods of analysis were not readily available. These computer programs are gradually being incorporated into statistical packages such as SPSS (Norusis 1996).

2. Advances in Measurement

Greater attention is now being paid in the field of the sociology of education to the use of new approaches to measurement, so that more efficient and more powerful procedures for the statistical analysis of data can be employed. Studies in the sociology of education have been severely restricted by the inability to measure important predictor and criterion variables with sufficient consistency, other than performance on multiple choice achievement tests, and thus to achieve strong levels of prediction and explanation. However, advances have been made, through the use of item response theory (Stocking 1997) and, in particular, the Rasch model (Allerup 1997, Andrich 1997, Masters 1997), in order to obtain measures on an interval scale from ratings, attitude scales, and checklists. These developments are largely unknown outside the field of achievement testing in which they are now being used in institutions where there are groups of research workers with expertise in educational and psychological measurement. In arguing a case for improved measurement in the field of the sociology of education, several issues must be addressed, namely: (a) the advantage of using measurement, (b) single or multiple measurements, (c) bandwidth and fidelity, (d) precision in measurement, and (e) Rasch scaling.

2.1 The Advantage of Using Measures

The great advantage of using numbers to specify the degree or extent of a characteristic or relationship is that mathematics has provided the rules and procedures for working with numbers and matrices in order to examine relationships. In addition, statistics has provided the rules and procedures for examining the probabilities with which results might be observed and the levels of magnitude and importance of such results. These mathematical and statistical procedures are necessary, not only because the interrelations between variables in educational research are complex, but also because measurements made in educational research often involve considerable error and require large samples of observations or persons for a hypothesized relationship to be detected. The rules and procedures provided by mathematics and statistics permit both the hypothesizing of relationships between measured variables and the subsequent examination of these hypothesized relationships, together with the estimation of the magnitude of the effects.

2.2 Single or Multiple Measurements

A general distinction must be drawn between measurements that are made through a single observation or judgment and measurements that are made by combining in an appropriate way multiple observations or judgments. Errors in measurement arise from three distinct sources: (a) variability in the making of the observation or judgment by the observer, (b) variability in the making of the observation or judgment due to the instrument being employed, and (c) variability in the characteristic being measured. Errors arising from the third source demand the making of multiple measurements by the sampling of behaviors or observable phenomena associated with the characteristic or relationship under survey. It is, however, not uncommon to make multiple measurements in order to estimate and allow for observer errors and instrumental errors. Such procedures necessarily lead to the combination of multiple measurements in an appropriate way.

Consequently, reliance on a single observation or judgment is relatively rare in measurement in both research and practice, and the use of multiple observations or judgments is widespread. Substantial problems arise because the multiple measurements must be combined. Cronbach (1960), using an analogy with recording of music, draws attention to the distinction made between *bandwidth* and *fidelity*. Thus, in measurement with multiple observations or judgments, it is necessary that the range of measurements recorded is sufficiently wide to provide a meaningful indicator of the variability in the characteristic or relationship under investigation. The range of measurements is associated with the bandwidth of the recording. However, it is also necessary with multiple measurements to ensure that the range of measurements obtained is sufficiently narrow to provide a high degree of fidelity. Only thus is it possible to ensure that the measurements are unidimensional and that it is meaningful to combine them. This balance between bandwidth and fidelity becomes increasingly important as advances

occur in educational research where multiple measurements are made.

2.3 Bandwidth and Fidelity

The terms bandwidth and fidelity have some overlap in meaning with the more technical terms of validity and reliability, but they are not synonymous with these more familiar terms. Moreover, they are increasingly being used in situations where validity and reliability do not suffice, since they are more directly related to the combining of observations and judgments in the making of measurements.

Fidelity demands that not only should a characteristic or relationship be accurately defined, but that the measurements should satisfy the requirement of *unidimensionality*. The development of procedures for confirmatory factor analysis (Spearritt 1997) provides a useful test of unidimensionality that is based on the variability existing in the sample employed. Bejar (1983 p. 31) has, however, drawn attention to the fact that unidimensionality as tested under these conditions does not imply that only a single characteristic is involved in responding or that a single process operates. If several characteristics or processes were to operate in unison, then unidimensionality would also hold. However, if the characteristics or processes did not operate together then it would not be meaningful to assign numbers to any combination of the measurements obtained, unless another operation such as that of prediction were to provide the rule for combination. If a set of measurements lacked this necessary fidelity, and if several identifiable dimensions were involved, then each dimension would need to be considered separately and a profile of measures recorded.

The idea of *bandwidth* is employed to ensure that there is a sufficient range of manifestations of the characteristic being measured for meaningful representation of that characteristic. If variability exists in the characteristic, a range of instances is required to represent adequately that characteristic. Consequently, under some circumstances, observations and judgments can be said to supply redundant information and serve no useful purpose and must be rejected. Observations and judgments can also supply information that can be shown not to relate to the specified characteristic and they must also be rejected. Thus, decisions need to be made prior to the undertaking of measurement on the bandwidth of acceptable observations and judgments when variability exists in the characteristic being measured.

The power of measurement is that once a characteristic or relationship has been specified in detail and in a meaningful way with sufficient bandwidth and fidelity, then the quantities that are obtained as measures of two objects or events can be compared. Where measurement is made through a single observation or judgment, the issues of bandwidth and fidelity do not apply. Consequently, there is a heavy burden placed on the single measure.

Similar issues must be considered when multiple measurements are made because of random variability due to the observer, or because of the random variability that arises from the instrument employed. Thus, most measurements involve error. However, the word *error* implies not a mistake, but like the "knights errant" of old, a wandering about a central position. Where random error is associated with measurement, then statistical procedures can be employed which, according to established conventions, enable the precision of the measurement to be established. It is, however, the issues of bandwidth and fidelity that must be tackled in the improvement of measurement in sociological and educational research.

2.4 Precision

In educational and sociological research it is common to make measurements in the form of graded responses or ratings. It is also common in the use of rating scales to assign numbers to response categories that imply equal spacing, and to assume that the error involved in rating is the same across response categories. It is also generally assumed that greater precision is obtained through the use of a greater number of response categories that have each been carefully specified. In more advanced treatments of measurement in education (Andrich 1995a, 1995b), it is argued that categories do not have equal spacing, that errors in choice of response categories cannot be ignored, and that the response categories employed are meaningful and have been carefully specified. In general, the larger the number of response categories the more precise the measurement. However, there is commonly a limit to the number of response categories that can be employed effectively in measurement by the observers making the measurement or by respondents to a rating scale.

2.5 Conjoint Measurement

One of the major problems in measurement in education and in the social and behavioral sciences is that there is an interaction between the person being measured and the instrument involved in measurement at the time measurements are made. As a consequence the measure obtained is not independent of the measuring instrument employed. An important development has occurred since 1960 in the treatment of this problem. This uncertainty or confounding that arises between the person and the instrument is to some degree removed by the procedures of conjoint measurement proposed by Ferguson (see Lawley 1943) and developed by Rasch (1960). In conjoint measurement it is always the performance of a person relative to a particular task that is being considered in terms of probabilities. Thus a person's performance level is set at the same level as the difficulty of a task if that person has a specified probability, commonly 50 percent, of responding correctly to the task.

Furthermore, clear benefits would be gained in measurement if the persons measured by an instrument and the tasks included in that instrument were located on a common scale. In this way performance with respect to particular tasks could be measured. Specific levels or standards of performance on a scale of this type could also be stated and shown in terms of either the characteristics of the tasks, or the characteristics of the persons, or alternatively by a defined level on the scale. The logistic transformation of the response odds enables the task and person parameters and their estimated values to be placed on a conjoint measurements scale. Conditional probabilities are then used to separate the person parameters from the task calibration, and the task parameters from the estimation of the person parameters. The requirement for this estimation procedure to provide meaningful results would be that both the tasks and the persons must fit a unidimensional model and behave in a consistent way across different samples.

It should be noted that the Rasch scale is not only an interval scale, but also has its own natural metric, with the scale unit referred to as a logit. All that is required is that a fixed point should be specified in order to determine the location of the scale. In addition, the errors involved in the estimation of both the task difficulty parameters and the person performance parameters are obtained for each individual task and person, rather than for the instrument as a whole, provided conditions of independence of observation of tasks and persons are maintained. This scaling procedure eliminates the dependence of the task parameters on the sample of persons used in calibration, and the dependence of the person parameters on the sample of tasks used. Under these circumstances, the scale so formed has some properties of an absolute scale, but fails to have an absolute zero, being an interval, but not a ratio scale. Such a scale has substantial advantages in educational and sociological measurement, with the only requirement that the tasks and the persons used in the calibration of the scale must satisfy the condition of unidimensionality.

2.6 The Advantages of Rasch Measurement

Some of the immediately obvious advantages of this important development which involves the Rasch scaling of observations and judgments can be listed. First, different instruments measuring the same underlying dimension can be readily equated through common tasks or common persons. Second, bias associated with specific tasks can be readily identified. Thirdly, persons with inconsistent behavior can also be easily identified, since a particular person might be expected to respond correctly to those tasks whose difficulty levels are below that person's level of performance and to respond incorrectly to those tasks at a higher level of performance.

Furthermore, these scaling procedures can be employed for the rating of a set of tasks where there is: (a) a dichotomous rating of "can perform the task" or "cannot perform the task" (using the simple Rasch model) (Allerup 1997); (b) a polychotomous rating associated with frequency of performance or degree of success in performance, without necessarily equal spacing on the scale between response categories (using the rating scale model) (Andrich 1997); (c) a polychotomous rating scheme with different numbers of ratings for different tasks (using the partial credit model) Masters 1997); (d) discontinuities in levels of performance (using the saltus model) (Wilson 1997); (e) differences between different raters or judges (using the facet model) (Linacre 1997); and (f) in situations where more than one dimension is involved (using a multidimensional model) (Swaminathan 1997). The necessary requirement is that the tasks which are employed to form a particular scale must satisfy tests of unidimensionality. Under certain circumstances it may be necessary to eliminate some persons and tasks in the calibration of a scale. However, it is also possible to estimate the level of performance of persons who perform correctly all tasks, or alternatively none of the tasks, or omit specific tasks.

It should also be noted that these procedures can be applied to the scaling of attitudes and values as well as to ratings of performance, or views towards a specific object and the climate of an institution, provided that the components forming the scale satisfy the conditions for unidimensionality. The benefits of the use of these scaling procedures are those of measurement on an interval scale, and a generality of measurement that extends beyond the particular tasks considered and the particular sample of persons under investigation. Nevertheless, it is generally necessary to have at least 10 tasks in order to specify the dimensionals of a particular scale, and approximately 50 times as many persons responding as the number of response categories employed.

The strengths of the Rasch model lie in the simplicity of the algebra involved as well as in the extension of the model to cover a range of situations. No longer is unidimensionality a restriction, provided a limited number of dimensions has been hypothesized, and the items and persons are constrained to these dimensions (Swaminathan 1997). There is no place for noise or for items and persons that do not conform to the dimensions specified in a model. If the necessary requirements of the model are satisfied, the benefits are substantial and involve the shift from deterministic approaches to measurement in education to the use of probabilistic and stochastic models in order to advance the accuracy of measurement. There remain some limitations associated with a ceiling or floor for a particular instrument when respondents answer correctly all items or no items respectively. However, the ceilings or floors are false insofar as the use of further items that conform to the unidimensional scale involved would permit the accurate estimation of

performance. Thus unlike classical test theory, where the test or instrument is the scale, in Rasch scaling the scale is independent of the items in the test and the sample employed in calibration.

It must be recognized that problems are encountered if a latent trait under consideration does not remain invariant over the population being investigated. However, the capability exists to develop a scale that has the property of invariance, as well as to construct multidimensional scales. Insufficient work has been carried out in the field of the sociology of education into the use of such scales to determine the limitations imposed on the research questions that can be meaningfully investigated. In addition, further research is required into the robustness of scales measuring sociological characteristics and behavior in contrast to tightly defined cognitive abilities and educational achievement, as well as the validity of the results obtained under different circumstances. Nevertheless, the potential exists for research in this area, because computer programs for the necessary analyses are now readily available. Particular benefits are likely to arise from the repeated measurement of performance over time with scales that make allowance for the learning that might occur. From such measurements made over more than two occasions, stability and change in human characteristics can be more effectively investigated.

3. Developments in Methods of Research using Measures and Categorical Data

In this section consideration is given to developments in those methods of inquiry employed in the sociology of education that involve the collection of both measures and categorical data.

3.1 Survey Research Methods

Survey research seeks, in the main, to provide a description of the properties and relationships that are characteristic of the situation under survey. However, most problem situations of interest in the area of the sociology of education involve many variables, which operate at more than one level. Consequently, there is limited interest in univariate statistics and the simple bivariate relationships which are obtained for descriptive purposes. There is growing interest in prediction and the use of statistical control in a situation that is multivariate in nature, as well as the teasing out of a causally based explanation of the forces operating. While it may be argued that prediction implicitly involves an acknowledgment of causal relationships, the trend during recent decades has been towards the formulation of a model of the hypothesized relationships between the factors that are considered to be operating, and the testing of that model and alternative models, as well as the estimation of the parameters of the model that best fits the data obtained from the real world (Lietz and Keeves 1997, Rosier 1997).

The strength of a well-planned and well-conducted survey arises from the use of a probability sample which is drawn from a well-defined target population to which generalization is sought. Only through the use of a probability sample and a high response rate to the survey in excess of 80 percent of the designed sample is it possible both to claim representativeness as well as to estimate accurately the magnitude of the errors involved in sampling and in measurement. It should be noted that the magnitude of the error which is estimated does not, in general, depend upon the proportion of the target population that is sampled, but on the effective size of the sample. The effective size commonly differs markedly from the actual size of the sample, assessed in terms of individuals, because of the cluster nature of the samples used in studies in the sociology of education in which groups are employed as the primary sampling unit and individuals are sampled at a second level from within groups. Failure to consider the design effects of cluster samples leads to a very high proportion of sociological and educational studies currently reporting errors and applying tests of statistical significance that are clearly wrong. Standard computer packages and widely used statistical texts do not consider these issues, but the *WesVar PC* (Brick et al. 1996) computer program has been made available that permits sampling errors to be accurately estimated.

Major problems arise in survey research where the target population employed suffers from the effects of selection, or where the response rate falls below a widely recognized response level of 80 percent. In such situations the extent of bias is likely to be substantial and difficult if not impossible to estimate. Some of the effects of bias can be partly removed by statistical control in analysis, if appropriate control variables are employed. Nevertheless, a high response rate is important if the findings of a survey are to have meaning and generality.

3.2 Longitudinal Research Methods

Studies in the sociology of education are frequently concerned with stability and change in human characteristics or in the characteristics and relationships operating between individuals within groups, as well as between groups. As a consequence investigations are increasingly being conducted over time with measurements made at several points in time. In the past, relatively few investigations into problem situations in the area of the sociology of education have used longitudinal designs, in part, because of the difficulties encountered in maintaining contact over time with the individuals selected in the samples. Furthermore, there has been an inability to analyze effectively data which are essentially multilevel in nature, with levels operating within individuals, between individuals, and between groups. However, the development

of procedures for multilevel analysis resolves some of these problems, provided that measurements are made at more than two time points. Moreover, the developments that have occurred in the field of logistic regression, permit the consideration of data at two time points only, provided the criterion variable is dichotomous in nature (Bryk et al. 1996).

There are three major systems of influence that affect stability and change in human development and learning. These influences have their origins in (a) biological factors, (b) environmental factors, and (c) planned learning experiences or interventions. However, these three different sets of influences interact with each other in significant ways. Moreover, while it is possible to undertake intervention studies that have an experimental design, the interactions with biological and environmental factors are highly complex and tend to prevent the undertaking of long term experimental or intervention studies, even if they were both ethically and financially feasible (see Keeves 1997).

Time is the key variable in longitudinal research and it is employed in such studies in two different ways. First, time is a characteristic of the subject, when chronological age is employed as a basis for the selection of an individual or an age group for study, or when the members of an age cohort are studied at successive times during their lives. However, the major problem with this use of time is that it cannot be manipulated and individuals cannot be randomly assigned to different time periods. Consequently, it is not possible to control for environmental effects by randomization. Nevertheless, the use of time in this way has the advantage that causal relationships demand that earlier events influence later events and it is possible to control statistically for hypothesized causal effects. Secondly, time can be employed as a design characteristic in a learning study. Not only does time operate as an arrow in a learning study, but time can also be used as an alterable variable, whose effects on learning can be analyzed. Furthermore, time used in this way is not only a continuous variable, but equal intervals of time are readily determined and a zero point for measurement purposes can be readily identified.

Longitudinal research studies are increasingly being used in educational and sociological research, which are conducted over longer time periods with more observation points, because of the ease with which data can be stored on a computer. Furthermore, the availability of computer programs for the analysis of complex causal models, permits sets of hypothesized relationships to be tested and the magnitude of effects to be estimated after the application of statistical controls, as well as allowance being made for differences in levels of operation.

3.3 Experimental and Intervention Research Methods

Experimental and intervention methods are highly

regarded in research studies in the sociology of education because of the strength of the causal inferences that can be drawn from such studies if they have been carefully designed. Important studies to use this design have been: (a) the Ypsilanti Perry Pre-School Project with a long-term follow up, conducted by the High Scope Educational Research Foundation and reported by Weikart and his colleagues (Weikart 1984) to evaluate Head Start Programs in the United States, and the Sustaining Effects Study concerned with the evaluation of Title I Programs for the educationally disadvantaged in the United States (Carter 1984). There are five important characteristics of an experimental and intervention study.

First, in order to generalize the findings of a study to a larger population the subjects chosen for experimentation must be selected at random from the target population. Second, the subjects chosen must be assigned randomly to the groups formed for study in the experiment. Third, the intervention or treatment must be administered to one group, selected at random (the treatment group) and withheld from the other group (the control group). Fourth, the treatment must be administered with consistency and rigor throughout the period of experimentation, and the dangers of corruption of the treatment condition avoided. Finally, the effects of the treatment must be measured with a high degree of validity and reliability to form the dependent variable in the analysis of the data. The determination of the treatment conditions and the choice of a meaningful and valid criterion variable must be governed by a well-developed theory, since the administration of the treatment must be carefully designed, and the outcome must be measured accurately, if a strong effect is to be observed. In the design of the study, consideration must be given to the size of the treatment and control groups and the manner in which the treatment is administered to groups of students for effects of sufficient magnitude to have practical significance as well as statistical significance. Once the size of the change in the criterion variable, which would be considered to be of practical significance has been estimated, power calculations should be employed to determine the size of the treatment and control groups, with consideration also given to the design effect of the subgroups within which the treatment and control conditions are administered.

Tightly controlled experimental studies are difficult to conduct successfully in the sociology of education, and it is commonly necessary to modify or relax some of the conditions necessary for an optimal design. Under these circumstances the experimental study is described as an intervention study or a quasi-experimental study. An intervention study is generally considered to be one in which measurements are made on the criterion variable at several time points, with the treatment being maintained over time. A quasi-experimental study is one in which fully random allocation of individuals to treatment and control groups is not undertaken, and the experiment is administered with naturally occurring groups which are randomly assigned to treatment and control conditions.

Consequently, in quasi-experimental and intervention studies, the effects of the many unknown factors that could give rise to spurious results are not fully controlled by randomization, and statistical control must be exercised. There are two general approaches to statistical control. First, in covariance adjustment a covariate that is related to the criterion measure is identified, and the effects of prior performance assessed on the covariate measure are removed by regression from the criterion variable, before the effects of the treatment condition are examined. However, it is possible that performance associated with the covariate might influence the administration of the treatment. The second approach to statistical control involves regression analysis in which the criterion is regressed on both the covariate and on the treatment and control conditions, which permits the effects of prior performance to be removed from the estimation of the treatment effects (see Lawson 1997).

3.4 Evaluation Research Methods

In recent decades, evaluation research has been developed as a significant and separate field of research activity. It is not uncommon for an evaluation study to have a clearly identifiable quantitative component, although it is not essential that an evaluation study should be quantitative in nature. Furthermore, it might be contended that evaluation studies do not necessarily contain an investigatory or research component. However, since many evaluation studies are set in a theoretical context, and seek answers to questions that are of theoretical significance, it is clear that those studies which do, must be regarded as research. The findings of such studies should not only be examined to provide evidence for decision-making and the passing of evaluative judgments, but they should also provide evidence and findings that assist in the making of generalizations and further the understanding of educative processes (see Smith 1997).

There are other methods of investigation and research, such as the case study method, action research, historical research, and policy research that could well incorporate the use of quantitative data into their research design. However, these methods of inquiry do not commonly do so, and they would generally be considered to be associated with qualitative studies. The dichotomy between a quantitative and a qualitative approach is difficult to maintain in practice. Consequently, it is necessary to emphasize that in the investigation of a particular problem situation the methods of investigation employed are not limited to a quantitative or qualitative approach, or by any one of the research methods considered above. The most appropriate methods of inquiry should be identified in order to provide answers to the research questions, and persons selected to conduct a study with a particular orientation should have the necessary skills and experience to maintain high standards of research and effective analysis of the data collected. The strength of the findings of research are assessed in terms of: (a) coherence with what is known; (b) simplicity, in which the results are not submerged in a congerie of detail; (c) generality, insofar as the results apply more broadly than the situation in which the study was conducted; and (d) fruitfulness, insofar as the research findings give rise to other ideas and relationships that warrant further investigation.

4. New Techniques for Analyzing Models of Processes and Structure

The data collected in quantitative studies in the sociology of education have commonly been sought with a substantial number of key hypotheses being advanced to direct the investigation. Because the problem situation involves many criteria as well as many predictors, and because it commonly involves effects that operate at more than one level, the key hypotheses must be combined together in a model that permits not only the testing of each hypothesis separately, but also the testing of the hypotheses collectively. The essential feature of such a model that combines together many hypotheses is the causal structure which is built into the model to provide a coherent explanation in terms of acknowledged theory. Since the late 1960s and early 1970s procedures have been developed in the fields of sociology and education respectively to test models of increasing complexity as well as the estimation of the parameters of such models and the examination of these estimates for practical and statistical significance.

4.1 Mediating, Moderating, and Reciprocal Effects

In the construction of a causal model, there are three different ways in which variables U, V, and W can interact. These three modes of interaction are shown in Fig. 1. Figure 1(a) presents a mediating effect in which variable U acts directly on the criterion variable W, but also operates indirectly through variable V to influence the criterion variable W. The indirect effect of variable U through variable V is referred to as a *mediating effect*. In Fig. 1(b) variables U and V not only influence the criterion variable W directly, but they have a joint effect in which variable U is moderated by variable V to influence variable W. The *moderating effect* is carried in analysis by the product of U and V and this is shown in Fig. 1(b) by the new variable formed (as shown by broken lines) from the product of U and V, variable I. In order to estimate the moderating effect correctly, variables U and V must be centered but need not be standardized prior to forming the product. When the regression of W on U, V, and I is undertaken the unstandardized or metric solution to the regression analysis should be reported even though variables U and V might or might not have been standardized (Aiken and West 1991). In Fig 1(c) a *reciprocal effect* is shown in which both variables V and W are influenced by variable U. In addition, variable V influences variable W and variable W exerts a reciprocal effect back on variable V. The model shown in Fig. 1(c) is underidentified with more parameters to be estimated than there are data available for estimation. Problems of model identification must be resolved before estimation of the parameters of the model can be undertaken by indirect regression analysis or two-stage least square analysis (Sellin and Keeves 1997).

4.2 The Production of Latent Variables

In the construction of a causal model, there are commonly several indicator or manifest variates that must be combined together to produce a latent variable in order to simplify the model and to avoid problems of multicollinearity in the testing of the model. The indicator or manifest variates may involve variables that can be measured directly and that can be used

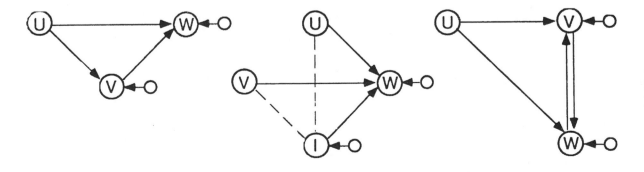

Figure 1
Three modes of interaction between three variables. (a) A mediating effect, (b) a moderating effect, (c) a reciprocal effect.

as indicators of a construct or latent variable, which cannot be directly measured. The production of the latent variable can be carried out in three ways, which are illustrated in Fig. 2.

In Fig. 2(a) there is a single manifest variate (shown as a square or rectangle) which is employed to produce a latent variable χ (shown as a circle). This is referred to as the *unitary mode* with the loading of χ on U given by 1.0. In Fig. 2(b) the three manifest variates U, V, and W combine together to form the latent variable χ in a manner referred to as the *formative mode*. The weights for combining U, V and W to form χ are obtained by regressing χ on U, V, and W. The three manifest variates act as alternatives in the formation of χ. Fig. 2(c) shows a third way in which a latent variable can be produced from manifest variates. In this mode the three manifest variates, U, V, and W reflect the latent variable χ in what is referred to as the *reflective mode*. In this case the effects of the observed variates are additive and the loadings are estimated by regressing the variates U, V, and W on χ. It should be noted that a latent variable generally has greater validity than the observed variates taken separately, and the validity of the latent variable can be estimated in the analysis.

There are several recently developed procedures available for causal modeling in the sociology of education with latent variables and two general strategies of analysis have been advanced.

4.3 Partial Least-squares Path Analysis

The first strategy involves a least squares regression based approach in which the process employed is based on the maximization of explained variance in the outcome measures. This is achieved by the formation of latent variables using either a factor analytic method for the reflective mode or by using the latent variables to carry regression relationships through from the observed variates to the latent variable for the formative mode, and on to explain the variance of the outcomes. In addition, a path analytic or regression approach is also employed between the latent variables to estimate

the magnitude of the relationships involved (Wold 1982). Two computer programs, LVPLS (Löhmuller 1983) and PLSPATH (Sellin 1990), have been prepared in Germany for this strategy of analysis, which is highly flexible, but less rigorous than the alternative strategy (see Sellin and Keeves 1997).

4.4 Linear Structural Relations Analysis

The second approach involves the detailed specification of a structural equation model and the use of maximum likelihood procedures of analysis to estimate the parameters of the model and to examine whether the model provides a high degree of fit to the observed data (Jöreskog and Sörbom 1993). This approach is conceptually more rigorous insofar as a well-specified model of the processes involved is required before any examination of the model is undertaken. Since the procedure and the statistical tests applied are very sensitive to sample size, the data collection must be carefully planned with the model of analysis in mind and with a sample of approximately 400 students for optimal results. The computer programs available at the time of writing are LISREL 8 (Jöreskog and Sörbom 1993), AMOS (Arbuckle 1995), and EQS (Bentler 1985). These programs are increasingly making the analysis of data readily managed and user-friendly. Nevertheless, while this approach to the analysis of data is complex, it does provide a rigorous alternative to an experimental study in those situations, which pervade research in education and sociology, where an experimental study cannot be undertaken (see Tuijnman and Keeves 1997).

4.5 Multilevel Analysis Procedures

The procedures of analysis, discussed above, do not take into account the multilevel nature of most data sets that are analyzed in research in the sociology of education. As a consequence, both the significance tests employed and the estimates of effect are erroneous and frequently seriously wrong. Several

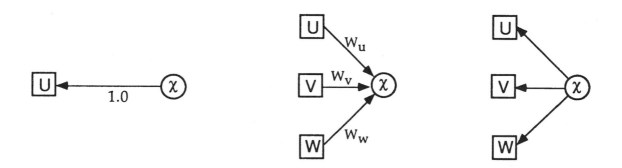

Figure 2
The production of latent variables from manifest variates. (a) The unitary mode, (b) the formative mode, (c) the reflective mode

procedures that have been developed for multilevel analysis, HLM (Raudenbush and Bryk 1986) MLn (Goldstein 1987) and VARCL (Aikin and Longford 1986) provide a major advance for educational research with two modes of analysis.

The first mode in which multilevel analysis programs can be employed is in the separation of effects that operate at the student, classroom or teacher, and school levels. Experience with HLM2L and HLM3L (Bryk et al. 1996) has shown that the models being tested must be well specified in order to tease out effects at these three levels of analysis. With well specified models it is possible to examine the effects of student, classroom or teacher, and school factors on student performance. It is important to note that there must be sufficient parameter variance at each level for the effective estimation of effects. Generally, there is sufficient variance at the student level for sound analyses. However, at the level of classroom or teacher within school there may well be inadequate variance to make analysis at this level worthwhile. Likewise, at the school level where the schools are very similar to each other and there is little variance between them, the analyses carried out may be unrewarding. In part, these conditions are dependent on the number of cases at each level. Thus, if there are only two classrooms within each school, or only two students in a classroom, the data for those classrooms or those students cannot be effectively analyzed. Nevertheless, the computer program HLM3L, which has the capability for the analysis of data at three levels, provides an analytic procedure that has not previously been available to estimate accurately the effects of the conditions of instruction at the classroom and school levels. The examination of these effects in a sound way has previously been denied to research workers.

The second mode in which multilevel analysis programs can be employed is in the investigation of student learning. Studies of student learning in schools that have relied on gain scores between two occasions have commonly given rise to data of insufficient reliability for the analysis of absolute gain, although the analysis of relative gain has generally been profitable. Willett (1997) has argued that the difficulties encountered in studies which have employed gain scores in the detection of classroom, teacher, and school effects, arise from an inability to estimate the reliability of the gain score and from its probably low value. This implies that a substantial proportion of the variance of the gain score is error variance, which cannot be allowed for in analysis.

Bryk and Raudenbush (1987) have shown that if measures of student learning have been made on three or more occasions, it is possible to estimate the slopes of the regression lines across occasions and to analyse the effects of factors that are considered to influence student learning, and thus to influence the within student slopes and intercepts. The analysis of data using HLM3L (Bryk et al. 1996) can be extended to a third level, namely the between classroom level, and hierarchically above the between and within student levels, in order to examine the effects of teachers and classrooms on student learning. Moreover, it is not the absolute level of performance of a classroom group that is of importance in education, because this inevitably depends on the quality of the students taken into a classroom, particularly their ability and aptitude. It is rather what the teacher and the classroom conditions do to promote student learning between occasions that is of consequence. Such effects can now be investigated, and the data analyzed in a sound way, that is capable of detecting and estimating effects that are hypothesized to operate.

A further development of considerable interest in the multilevel analysis of data is the extension of the LISREL program to test multilevel models, by partitioning the variance into appropriate levels and analyzing the data at the two levels simultaneously. The computer program STREAMS achieves this by analyzing the data partitioned into two levels for analysis as if it were comparing two data sets at a single level (Gustafsson and Stahl 1996). However, this procedure does not permit the estimation of cross level effects that influence the slopes of the regression lines at the lower or student level, and merely examines factors that influence the intercepts at the macro level. Nevertheless, this approach provides an important advance in the rigorous analysis of causal models with latent variables in a way that takes into consideration the multilevel structure of the data.

5. Advances in the Development of Theory on the Sociology of Education

While marked advances have been achieved in the methods available for research in the field of sociology of education, investigations that employ quantitative approaches are likely to be productive only if based on sound theoretical foundations.

During the 50-year period from the end of the Second World War to the late 1990s, there has been a marked development in theoretical perspectives in the field of education, and in the sociology of education, in particular. As a consequence, it is increasingly important to consider both theoretical perspectives as well as the findings of previous research when designing a new study. The aim of research in the sociology of education is not only to influence policy and practice, but also to contribute to a cumulative body of knowledge. The field of educational sociology is now very extensive, and this volume provides an introduction to the many theoretical perspectives and frameworks that are available for working over. The aim of rigorous quantitative research is the examination and estimation of models and hypotheses derived from theory against data from the real world in order to consolidate and extend theoretical knowledge.

See also: Education Production Functions; Effective Schools Research: Methodological Issues; Research Methodology: Scientific Methods; Research Paradigms in Education; Trends in Qualitative Research Methods

References

Aiken L H, West S G 1991 *Multiple Regression. Testing and Interpreting Interactions.* Sage, Newbury Park, California

Aitken M A, Longford N 1986 Statistical modelling issues in school effectiveness studies. *J. Roy. Stat. Soc.* Series A 149(1): 1–43

Allerup P 1997 Rasch measurement theory. In: Keeves J P (ed.) 1997 *Educational Research, Methodology, and Measurement: An International Handbook,* 2nd edn. Elsevier, Oxford

Ander C, Joó A, Mérö L 1997 Galois lattices. In: Keeves J P (ed.) 1997 *Educational Research, Methodology, and Measurement: An International Handbook*, 2nd edn. Elsevier, Oxford

Andrich D 1995a Models for measurement, precision and the non-dichotomization of graded responses. *Psychometrika* 60: 7–26

Andrich D 1995b Further remarks on the non-dichotomization of graded responses. *Psychometrika* 60: 36–46

Andrich D 1997 Rating scale analysis. In: Keeves J P (ed.) 1997 *Educational Research, Methodology, and Measurement: An International Handbook*, 2nd edn. Elsevier, Oxford

Arbuckle J L 1995 *Amos User's Guide.* Small Waters Corporation, Chicago, Illinois

Bejar I I 1983 *Achievement Testing: Recent Advances.* Sage, Beverly Hills, California and London

Bentler P M 1985 *Theory and Implementation of EQS: A Structural Equation Program.* BMDPS Statistical Software, Los Angeles, California

Brick J M, Broene P James P, Severynse J 1996 *A User's Guide to WesVar PC.* Westat, Rockville, Massachusetts

Bryk A S, Raudenbush S W 1987 Applications of hierarchical linear models to assessing change. *Psych. Bull.* 101(1): 147–58

Bryk A S, Raudenbush S W, Congdon R 1996 *HLM. Hierarchical Linear Modeling with the HLM/2L and HML/3L Programs.* Scientific Software International, Chicago, Illinois

Carter L F 1984 The sustaining effects study of compensatory and elementary education. *Educ. Res.* 13(7): 4–13

Cronbach L J 1960 *Essentials of Psychological Testing.* Harper and Row, New York

Erikson R 1997 Mobility tables. In: Keeves J P (ed.) 1997 *Educational Research Methodology, and Measurement: An International Handbook*, 2nd edn. Elsevier, Oxford

Everitt B S, Dunn G 1992 *Applied Multivariate Data Analysis.* Edward Arnold, London

Goldstein H 1987 *Multilevel Models in Educational and Social Research.* Oxford University Press, Oxford

Gustafsson J E, Stahl P A 1996 STREAMS. University of Gotenborg, Molndal, Sweden

Henry G 1997 Correspondence analyses of qualitative data. In: Keeves J P (ed.) 1997 *Educational Research, Methodology, and Measurement: An International Handbook*,

2nd edn. Elsevier, Oxford.

Huynh Huynh 1997 Robust statistical procedures. In: Keeves J P (ed.) 1997 *Educational Research, Methodology, and Measurement: An International Handbook*, 2nd edn. Elsevier, Oxford

Jöreskog K G, Sörbom D 1993 *LISREL8 and PRELIS2, for DOS, DOS EXTENDER and WINDOWS.* Scientific Software International, Chicago, Illinois

Kaplan A 1964 *The Conduct of Inquiry.* Chandler, San Francisco

Kaplan A 1997 Educational research: Scientific methods. In: Keeves J P (ed.) 1997 *Educational Research, Methodology, and Measurement: An International Handbook*, 2nd edn. Elsevier, Oxford

Kass G 1980 An exploratory technique for investigating large quantities of categorical data. *Appl. Stat.* 9: 119–27

Keeves J P 1997 Longitudinal research methods. In: Keeves J P (ed.) 1997 *Educational Research, Methodology, and Measurement: An International Handbook*, 2nd edn. Elsevier, Oxford

Kennedy J J, Hak Ping Tam 1997 Log-linear models. In: Keeves J P (ed.) 1997 *Educational Research, Methodology, and Measurement: An International Handbook*, 2nd edn. Elsevier, Oxford.

Klovdahl A 1997 Social network analyses. In: Keeves J P (ed.) 1997 *Educational Research, Methodology, and Measurement: An International Handbook*, 2nd edn. Elsevier, Oxford.

Krauth J 1993 *Einführing in die Kongifurations—frequenz analyse (KFA).* Beltz, München

Kristof W 1997 Configural frequency analysis of categorical data. In: Keeves J P (ed.) 1997 *Educational Research, Methodology, and Measurement: An International Handbook*, 2nd edn. Elsevier Oxford.

Lawley D N 1943 On problems connected with item selection and test construction. *Proc. Roy. Soc. Educ.* 61: 273–87

Lawson M J 1997 Experimental studies. In: Keeves J P (ed.) 1997 *Educational Research, Methodology, and Measurement: An International Handbook*, 2nd edn. Elsevier, Oxford

Lietz P, Keeves J P 1997 Cross-sectional research methods. In: Keeves J P (ed.) 1997 *Educational Research, Methodology, and Measurement: An International Handbook*, 2nd edn. Elsevier, Oxford

Linacre M J 1997 Judgments, measurement of. In: Keeves J P (ed.) 1997 *Educational Research, Methodology, and Measurement: An International Handbook*, 2nd edn. Elsevier, Oxford

Löhmuller J B 1983 *LVPLS Program Manual Version 1.6.* Zentralarchiv Universtät Köln, Köln

Magidson J 1989 *Statistical Package in Social Science.* /PC +CHAID. SPSS, Chicago, Illinois

Masters G N 1997 Partial credit model. In: Keeves J P (ed.) 1997 *Educational Research, Methodology, and Measurement: An International Handbook*, 2nd edn. Elsevier, Oxford

Norusis M J 1996 *SPSS Base System. User's Guide* SPSS, Chicago, Illinois

Rasch G 1960 *Probabilistic Models for Some Intelligence and Attainment Tests.* (reprinted 1980). University of Chicago Press, Chicago, Illinois

Raudenbush S W, Bryk A S 1986 A hierarchical model for studying school effects. *Sociol. Educ.* 59(1): 1–17

Rosier M J 1997 Survey research methods. In: Keeves J P (ed.) 1997 *Educational Research, Methodology, and*

Measurement: An International Handbook, 2nd edn. Elsevier, Oxford

Saha L J 1997 Sociometric methods. In: Keeves J P (ed.) 1997 *Educational Research, Methodology, and Measurement: An International Handbook*, 2nd edn. Elsevier, Oxford

Sellin N 1990 *PLSPATH Version 3.01 Program Manual*, University of Hamburg, Hamburg

Sellin N, Keeves J P 1997 Path analysis with lateral variables. In: Keeves J P (ed.) 1997 *Educational Research, Methodology, and Measurement: An International Handbook*, 2nd edn. Elsevier, Oxford

Shye S 1997 Partial order scalogram analyses of non-metric data. In: Keeves J P (ed.) 1997 *Educational Research, Methodology, and Measurement: An International Handbook*, 2nd edn. Elsevier, Oxford

Smith N L 1997 Evaluation models and approaches. In: Keeves J P (ed.) 1997 *Educational Research, Methodology, and Measurement: An International Handbook*, 2nd edn. Elsevier, Oxford

Spearritt D 1997 Factor Analysis. In: Keeves J P (ed.) 1997 *Educational Research, Methodology, and Measurement: An International Handbook*, 2nd edn. Elsevier, Oxford

Stocking M L 1997 Item response theory. In: Keeves J P (ed.) 1997 *Educational Research, Methodology, and Measurement: An International Handbook*, 2nd edn. Elsevier, Oxford

Swaminathan H 1997 Latent trait measurement models. In: Keeves J P (ed.) 1997 *Educational Research, Methodology, and Measurement: An International Handbook*, 2nd edn. Elsevier, Oxford

Tuijnman A, Keeves J P 1997 Path analysis and linear structural relations analysis. In: Keeves J P (ed.) 1997 *Educational Research, Methodology, and Measurement: An International Handbook*, 2nd edn. Elsevier, Oxford

von Eye A 1990 *Introduction to Configural Frequency Analysis*. Cambridge University Press, Cambridge

Weikart D P (ed.) 1984 *Changed Lives: The Effects of the Perry Preschool Program on Youths through Age Nineteen*. High Scope Press, Ypsitanti, Michigan

Willett J B 1997 Change, measurement of. In: Keeves J P (ed.) 1997 *Educational Research, Methodology, and Measurement: An International Handbook*, 2nd edn. Elsevier, Oxford

Wilson M 1997 Developmental levels, measurement of. In: Keeves J P (ed.) 1997 *Educational Research, Methodology, and Measurement: An International Handbook*, 2nd edn. Elsevier, Oxford

Wold H 1982 Soft modelling: The basic design and some extensions. In: Jöreskog K G, Wold H (eds.) 1982 *Systems under Indirect Observation. Part II*. North-Holland Press, Amsterdam

(b) Research Traditions

Action Research

S. Kemmis

The lively debates about educational research methodology in the 1970s and 1980s raised fundamental questions about the connections between educational theory and educational practice, between the conduct of research and the improvement of educational practice, and between researchers and teachers and learners. Around the world, a number of theorists of educational research have fostered the development of action research as an approach that provides ways of making these connections. Action research aims to help practitioners investigate the connections between their own theories of education and their own day-to-day educational practices; it aims to integrate the research act into the educational setting so that research can play a direct and immediate role in the improvement of practice; and it aims to overcome the distance between researchers and practitioners by assisting practitioners to become researchers.

This article outlines a view of action research as a form of participatory and collaborative research aimed at improving educational understandings, practices, and settings, and at involving those affected in the research process. It describes a variety of international perspectives on educational action research, linking it to participatory action research for community development and ideas about critical social and educational science. Some of the contemporary contests about how action research is to be understood are described in terms of a debate between two main schools of thought about action research, one (more collaborative) based on the idea of a critical educational science and the other (more individualistic) based on ideas about practical reasoning and "the reflective practitioner."

1. Definition of Action Research

Kemmis and McTaggart (1988) defined action research as a form of collective self-reflective enquiry undertaken by participants in social situations in order to improve the productivity, rationality, and justice of their own social or educational practices, as well as their understanding of these practices and the situations in which the practices are carried out. Groups of participants can be teachers, students, principals, parents and other community members—any group with a shared concern. Kemmis and McTaggart stress that action research is collaborative, though it is important to realize that the action research of a group depends upon individual members critically examining their own actions. In education, action research has been employed in school-based curriculum development, professional development, school improvement programs, and systems planning and policy development (e.g., in relation to policy about classroom rules, school policies about noncompetitive assessment, regional project team policies about their consultancy roles, and state policies about the conduct of school improvement programs).

Based on the work of Kurt Lewin, frequently described as "the father of action research," Kemmis and McTaggart (1988) presented an introductory sketch of the process of action research, outlining a spiral of cycles of reconnaissance, planning action, enacting and observing the planned action, reflecting on the implementation of the plan in the light of evidence collected during implementation, then replanning (developing a changed or modified action plan), taking further action and making further observations, reflecting on the evidence from this new cycle, and so on. These steps are (of course) far too mechanical and procedural to be more than a starting point: they are best thought of as tips for beginners.

Kemmis and McTaggart also set out some possible questions to be asked by intending action researchers as they plan and conduct their enquiries, linking each stage of the process (reconnaissance, planning, enacting and observing, reflecting) to three interdependent domains of social and educational life: (a) language and discourse; (b) activities and practices; and (c) social relationships and forms of organization. The first of each of these pairs of terms relates to events and states of affairs in the lifeworld of a setting; the second to its more formal, institutional, systemic aspects (on the distinction and relationships between lifeworld and system, see Habermas 1984, 1987). To address the complexity of the relationships within and between these pairs of terms requires reflective and critical judgment—a kind of judgment incompatible with a mechanical view of the action research process.

In action research, teachers (and others) are encouraged to treat their own educational ideas and theories, their own work practices, and their own work settings, as objects for analysis and critique. On the basis of careful reflection, it is argued, teachers may uncover theoretical ideas or assumptions that turn out to be unjustified and liable to lead them astray in their teaching (e.g., if they hold too rigid assumptions about the nature of students' innate abilities). Similarly, concerning their practices, teachers may find ways in which practices shaped by habit or tradition have become irrelevant or useless (e.g., finding that practices of classroom discipline, formerly seen as appropriate, may now be unacceptable or even counterproductive). Similarly, concerning the educational settings in which they practice, teachers may discover how the structure of the settings may place obstacles in the way of attaining educational goals (e.g., that the physical structure of the conventional classroom may hinder mixed ability grouping or the use of new technologies, or the management structure of a school may mitigate against new forms of curriculum organization).

The activities in this spiral of cycles aim at the improvement of practices, understandings, and situations, and at the involvement of as many as possible of those intimately affected by the action in all phases of the research process. Especially when they collaborate with other teachers in action research focused on their ideas, practices, and settings, teachers regularly find new ways of thinking, practicing, and structuring educational settings that will allow them to overcome obstacles and difficulties. In this way, action research contributes directly to the improvement of practice.

The involvement of teachers and others in the action research process—in data-gathering, analysis, and critique—creates an immediate sense of responsibility for the improvement of practice. Participation in action research is thus a form of professional development, linking the improvement of practitioners with the improvement of practices. It enhances the professional role of the teacher, even where beginning teacher–researchers are assisted by outside consultants or facilitators.

Many of the improvements that have flowed from teacher action research, in Australia and elsewhere, have escaped notice in the conventional educational research literature. Teachers have not generally been comfortable in contributing to educational research journals, nor are they frequent readers of such journals. Nevertheless, there is a growing body of action research work authored by teachers. It remains fugitive largely because its justification is the improvement of practitioners' own practices, and writing for others is seen as secondary to this purpose. Moreover, the action research "movement" has contributed to a subtle change in the educational research literature; as a consequence there are many more references to the research work and research problems of teachers in the "official" research literature, and there is a growing number of citations of work on the theory and practice of educational action research. A number of the

journals of learned societies for educational research in Australia, Spain, the United Kingdom, and the United States of America, for example, have become more "teacher friendly," making particular efforts to carry reports of teachers' action research projects. Moreover, some specialist action research journals have sprung up (e.g., *Educational Action Research*), and some more conventional research journals have offered special issues on action research (e.g., the *Peabody Journal of Education*, which offered two special issues on action research in 1989). Nowadays, educational researchers outside schools also seem less likely to regard the teacher as "other" or "object" in their reporting of educational research, and are more likely to regard teachers as readers of and contributors to the improvement of education through research. This may be only a subtle effect, but it is an important one in the realignment of the relationship between educational research and educational practice.

2. Key Points about Action Research

Kemmis and McTaggart (1988) outlined a number of key features of action research:

(a) Action research is an approach to improving education by changing it and learning from the consequences of changes.

(b) Action research develops through a self-reflective spiral of cycles of planning, acting (implementing plans), observing (systematically), reflecting, and then replanning, further implementation, observing, and reflecting. It is a systematic learning process in which people act deliberately, though remaining open to surprises and responsive to opportunities.

(c) Action research is participatory: it is research through which people work toward the improvement of their own practices.

(d) Action research is collaborative: it involves those responsible for action in improving it, widening the collaborating group from those most directly involved to as many as possible of those affected by the practices concerned. It establishes self-critical communities of people participating and collaborating in all phases of the research process.

(e) Action research involves people in theorizing about their practices—being inquisitive about circumstances, action, and consequences, and coming to understand the relationships between circumstance, action and consequence in their work and lives.

(f) Action research requires that people put their practices, ideas, and assumptions about institutions to the test by finding out whether there is compelling evidence that could convince them that their previous practices, ideas, and assumptions were false or incoherent (or both).

(g) Action research is open-minded about what counts as evidence (or data), but it always involves keeping records, and collecting and analyzing evidence about the contexts, commitments, conduct and consequences of the actions and interactions being investigated. It involves keeping a personal journal recording progress in, and reflections about, two parallel sets of learnings: learnings about the practices being studied, and learnings about the process of studying them (the action research process itself).

(h) Action research allows participants to build records of their improvements: (a) records of changes in activities and practices; (b) records of changes in the language and discourse in which practices are described, explained, and justified; (c) records of changes in the social relationships and forms of organization which characterize and constrain practices; and (d) records of change and development in the action research process itself. It thus allows participants to provide reasoned justifications of their educational work because it allows them to show how evidence and reflection have provided a basis for a developed, tested, and critically examined rationale for what is being done.

(i) Action research starts small. It normally begins with small changes which even a single person can try, and works toward more extensive changes; with small cycles of planning, acting, observing, and reflecting which can help to define issues, ideas, and assumptions more clearly so that those involved can define more powerful questions for themselves as their work progresses; and it begins with small groups of collaborators at the beginning, but widens the community of participating action researchers so that it gradually includes more and more of those involved in and affected by the practices in question.

(j) Action research involves people in making critical analyses of the situations (classrooms, schools, systems) in which they work—situations that are structured socially, historically, and institutionally. Critical analyses aim to recover how a situation has been socially and historically constructed, as a source of insight into ways in which people might be able to reconstruct it.

(k) Action research is a political process, because it involves making changes in the actions and interactions that constitute and structure social life (social practices); such changes typically have effects on the expectations and interests of others beyond the immediate participants in these actions and interactions.

3. International Perspectives on Action Research

One view of educational action research is associated with the work of a group at Deakin University in Australia. The views of this group derive from the ideas of social psychologist Lewin (1946), the thinking of Stenhouse and his colleagues at the University of East Anglia in the United Kingdom (e.g., Stenhouse 1975, Elliott 1978), and the ideas of the Frankfurt School in critical social science (see Carr and Kemmis 1986). This view of action research emphasizes the importance of collaboration, believing that some action research work of the past has been rather too individualistic, too little aware of the social construction of social reality, and too poorly attuned to the social processes and politics of change. It also understands action research to be a cultural process, in similar terms to Freire's (1970) notion of "cultural action for freedom." On this view, action researchers are understood as groups of people who participate systematically and deliberately in the processes of contestation and institutionalization which are always at work in social and educational life, aiming to help in the improvement of social or educational life by the reflective and self-reflective ways they participate in it.

This Australian view of action research is far from being the only extant view of action research, however. There are many other groups around the world with different views about the development of the theory and practice of action research; indeed, it has become something of a worldwide movement.

A great deal of action research work goes on in the United Kingdom, for example—much of it inspired by Stenhouse's (1975) notion of the teacher as researcher. The Ford Teaching Project of Elliott and Adelman (1973) broke new ground in action research in education in the 1970s, and their work has spawned a great diversity of action research work in schools and colleges around the United Kingdom—some of which can be accessed through publications and conferences of the Classroom Action Research Network based initially at the Cambridge Institute of Education and now at the University of East Anglia. British action research work ranges from the enquiries of individual teachers into their own practice to shared work by groups of teachers (e.g., Hustler et al. 1986, McKernan 1991); from work focused on the analysis of contradictions in practitioners' own theories and practices (Whitehead 1989) to work more critically relating these to wider social, cultural, and political trends (Elliott 1991); and from work informed by practical and interpretative views of social science and its possibilities for professional development (Nixon 1981) to work more closely allied with reflexive sociology and critical theory (Winter 1987, 1989). Despite Stenhouse's

(1975) disquiet about "movements" and the possibility of a curriculum development movement based on the notion of teachers as researchers, there can be no doubt that there is an action research movement in the United Kingdom, nor can there be any doubt that it has provided an important source of professional inspiration for teachers and school administrators throughout the country.

There has also been a resurgence of interest in action research in the United States and Canada. Early United States views of action research in education were inspired by the work of Corey (1949); later it was influenced by Schwab's (1969) ideas about practical reasoning, by Schön's (1983) ideas about "the reflective practitioner," by concerns to recognize and develop teachers' craft knowledge, by the desire of university educational researchers to employ field methods that engage teachers in research for their own professional development (Oja and Smulyan 1989), and by teacher educators committed to exploring action research in pre-service and in-service teacher education (Zeichner and Liston 1987). In general, educational action research in the United States has been less responsive to the arguments of critical social and educational theory, but the themes of critical theory have been taken up by a number of American advocates of action research (Noffke and Brennan 1988, Noffke 1991). In addition to this critical work in education, there is a strong tradition of critical action research for community development in the United States, exemplified by the work of Horton, Gavena, and their colleagues at the Highlander Center in Tennessee (Gaventa 1991, Horton and Freire 1990).

In Canada, one strong current of educational action research is based in the phenomenological tradition (Van Manen 1990), and there is also a strong movement in participatory action research in adult education and community development which shares the critical communitarian commitment of the participatory action research of Gaventa in the United States and of Freire and others in Central and South America (see *Participatory Research*).

By the beginning of the 1990s there were many European advocates of educational action research, for example in Germany (Klafki 1988a, 1988b, Finger 1988), Austria (Altrichter and Posch 1990), and Asturias, Spain (Rozada et al. 1989, Cascante 1991). Some of these theorists have been influenced by the ideas of Habermas (1972, 1974) about "sciences of social action" (now known as critical social science), though others have clearly been influenced by the British action research movement, and others by phenomenological approaches.

In Central and South America there has been a tradition of participatory action research work which has been strongly influenced by Freirean ideas, in Mexico, Colombia, Venezuala, Nicaragua, Brazil, and elsewhere. The social and political commitments of the participatory action research movement in

these countries (see Fals Borda 1990, Fals Borda and Rahman 1991, Serra 1988) have extended from community development to popular education and action research in education. The extent to which the forms and content of these community development efforts through action research are realizable in the reconstruction of institutionalized schooling in the developed industrial nations of the West is, of course, a matter for continuing exploration, but the communitarian ethic they embody provides a powerful model of ordinary people reconstructing the circumstances of their own lives.

The Central and South American tradition of participatory action research in community development has spread, through the work of Freire, to other parts of the world; for example, to Africa, India, Nepal, the Philippines, Sri Lanka, and Thailand. There is now a substantial tradition of action research in community development in India (Tandon 1988, Handay and Tandon 1988), and in Southeast Asia (e.g., in Singapore, Malaysia, and Thailand). Some of this work is associated with nongovernment organizations, while other work is associated with official educational projects. In the Southeast Asian context, for example, there has been an exploration of action research for community development through adult education and the Freireian participatory action research movement, on the one hand, and a somewhat separate development of action research in institutional contexts of school improvement and evaluation on the other (a good example of the latter being a project in the initial and postinitial education of nurses; see Chuaprapaisilp 1989). The latter trend seems more closely aligned with the kinds of interests in the educational profession that inspired the British action research movement in its early days.

As this brief review suggests, there is a wide diversity of motivations, forms, and contents of action research around the world. It would be mistaken, therefore, to regard educational action research as expressing a single school of thought or as embodying a coherent and unified point of view on social or educational research.

4. Contest over the Term "Action Research"

Like any significant theoretical term, the idea of "action research" is contested. Its meaning and significance cannot be fixed by any one person or group. It is the subject of continuing argument and debate within and outside the relevant traditions and professions.

There is an internal debate between two main contemporary "schools" of action research internationally, one adopting a critical social science view of action research, while the other draws more on the Schwabian tradition of practical reasoning and, more recently, on Schön's (1983) notion of "the reflective practitioner." The debate between these two schools of thought may have reached the point where they now relate to one another as "external" critics of each other's positions, rather than as "internal" critics who share broad agreements about the nature and conduct of action research, though they also keep these agreements under critical review. When there is uncertainty about whether participants in the field share a common system of beliefs, values, and commitments, it is uncertain whether they are members of and participants in a single tradition. As disagreements about fundamental issues in a field accumulate, it is pushed toward a division into two or more new and opposed traditions. Perhaps it is already true that debates previously regarded as "internal" debates within the field of action research—clarifying and continuously revitalizing a more or less coherent tradition—are now "external" debates between advocates of opposed traditions.

Since the early 1980s, the critical social science view of action research has been subjected to sharp criticism (e.g., Gibson 1985, Elliott 1991). This reaction was partly caused, no doubt, by the drawing of distinctions between "technical," "practical," and "emancipatory" (or critical) action research (Carr and Kemmis 1986), and the insistence of advocates of "emancipatory" view that action research undertaken primarily by individual teacher–researchers was less significant than action research undertaken by collaborating groups in "self-critical communities." Reaction was further fanned by advocacies (like those of McTaggart and Garbutcheon-Singh 1988, Kemmis and Di Chiro 1989) of connections between action research groups and the critical efforts of activists in broader social movements. While at first such advocacies were treated as "utopian" and "idealistic," and as attempting to "capture" action research to a particular view of critical educational science and a particular understanding of the relationship between theory and practice (see, e.g., Gibson 1985, Lewis 1987), they have since been regarded by some as "dangerous" (Elliott 1991). Arguably, some of these criticisms are based on a misunderstanding of critical social science and the possibility of a critical educational science.

A key element of the difference between the two main contemporary schools in educational action research lies in how the aspirations of action research are to be interpreted: whether (on the one hand) they are to be interpreted as a means of improving professional practice primarily at the local, classroom level, within the capacities of individuals and the constraints of educational institutions and organizations, or (on the other) whether they are to be interpreted as an approach to changing education and schooling in a broader sense. Like other choices of principle, this is a choice between different views of human nature and different views of the good for humankind. Like other such debates, it will be resolved not by argument alone, but by the judgment of history.

5. Shortcomings of Some Contemporary Advocacies for Action Research

The critical social science view of action research emphasizes the connections between particular elements of action research in theory and practice, not the separations between them, regarding these elements as dialectically related, not as dichotomies. In particular, the critical view has sought to emphasize the connections between:

(a) the individual and the social (the social construction of social realities and practices) in the practice of action research and in the practice of education (see, e.g., Kemmis and McTaggart 1988);

(b) the cognitive (practitioners' ideas) and the theoretical (formal discourses, whether employed by researchers or by others involved in education; see, e.g., Kemmis 1990);

(c) theory and method in action research practice (the role of action research as a systematic social practice that provides a way of formulating and attacking educational research problems in an educational and social context; see, e.g., McTaggart and Garbutcheon-Singh 1988).

When these terms are regarded as dichotomies, not as dialectically related, advocates and practitioners of action research may be led into fallacies of dualistic, black and white reasoning. Some of these fallacies arise when advocates and practitioners of action research believe, or appear to believe:

(a) that action research can involve the work of individuals without being, simultaneously, intrinsically social (rooted in the fundamental connections between individuals embodied in and shaped by the social media of language, work, and power, though social practices of communication, production, and organization);

(b) that action research can deal with practitioners' ideas without simultaneously recognizing that these ideas are theoretical (or at least pretheoretical or prototheoretical), in the sense that they draw on public discourses which give meaning and significance to their work as educators or as researchers;

(c) that action research is a relatively "neutral" research technology which can be separated from particular intellectual traditions, involving particular notions and theories about society, education, and social and educational change (especially participatory views about social practices, education, democracy, and change).

When views of action research become structured

by dichotomized thinking about these relationships, their advocates may fall into the trap of focusing too much on the individual action researcher and her or his development (e.g., as an individual professional) without also taking a critical view of the social context in which the individual works. They may focus too much on individuals' ideas and thinking without giving sufficient critical attention to the ordinary language and formal discourses that give form and content to individual thinking. Moreover, they may focus too much on action research as a method or procedure without giving critical attention to the social framework in which the procedure operates, and to the way the procedures of action research actively connect with and coordinate processes of change in history which is to say, politically. Some contemporary action research literature seems to have fallen into these traps.

6. Conclusion

Understanding of action research has been, and will continue to be, reconstructed anew for changing times and circumstances. The idea of action research may be no more perfectible than the idea of the perfectibility of humankind, but over 50 years it has offered and demonstrated possibilities for linking social research and social action, and it has made worthwhile contributions to the improvement of education, science, and society. As Sanford (1970) argued, action research is a social practice that still contains possibilities that may prove useful in addressing the social, cultural, and educational problems of contemporary times.

The notion of action research is just that: it is a notion, not a thing. As a notion, it does no more than give form to a particular kind of democratic aspiration to engage in changing the world as well as interpreting it. It offers an embryonic, local form of connecting research with social, educational, and political action in complex practical circumstances. In this, it is similar to the aspiration sloganized by the environmental movement in the words "think globally, act locally," and, as such, it may be a social form that can help educators address the contradictions, constraints, and limitations of their theories and practices, of their words and our world.

See also: Participatory Research; Research in Education: Epistemological Issues; Research Methodology: Scientific Methods; Research Paradigms in Education

References

Altrichter H, Posch P 1990 *Lehrer Erforschen Ihren Unterricht. Eine Einführung in die Methoden der Aktionforschung.* Klinkhardt, Bad Heilbrunn
Carr W, Kemmis S 1986 *Becoming Critical: Education, Knowledge and Action Research.* Falmer, London
Cascante Fernandez C 1991 Los ámbitos de la práctica educativa: Una experiencia de investigación en la acción. *Revista Interuniversitaria de Formación del Profesorado* 10: 265–74
Chuaprapaisilp A 1989 Critical reflection in clinical experience: Action research in nurse education (Doctoral dissertation, University of New South Wales)
Corey S 1949 Action research, fundamental research and educational practices. *Teach. Coll. Rec.* 50: 509–14
Elliott J 1978 What is action-research in schools? *J. Curric. St.* 10(4): 355–57
Elliott J 1991 *Action Research for Educational Change.* Open University Press, Milton Keynes
Elliott J, Adelman C 1973 Reflecting where the action is: The design of the Ford Teaching Project. *Educ. Teach.* 92: 8–20
Fals Borda O 1990 Social movements and political power: Evolution in Latin America. *Int. Sociol.* 5(2): 115–28
Fals Borda O, Rahman M A 1991 *Action and Knowledge: Breaking the Monopoly with Participatory Action-Research.* Apex, New York
Finger M 1988 Heinz Moser's concept of action research. In Kemmis S, McTaggart R (eds.) 1988
Freire P 1970 *Cultural Action for Freedom.* Center for the Study of Change, Cambridge, Massachusetts
Gaventa J 1991 Toward a knowledge democracy: Viewpoints on participatory research in North America. In: Fals Borda O, Rahman M A (eds.) 1991
Gibson R 1985 Critical times for action research. *Camb. J. Educ.* 15(1): 59–64
Habermas J 1972 *Knowledge and Human Interests.* Heinemann, London
Habermas J 1974 *Theory and Practice.* Heinemann, London
Habermas J 1984 *The Theory of Communicative Action. Vol.1: Reason and the Rationalization of Society.* Beacon, Boston, Massachusetts
Habermas J 1987 *The Theory of Communicative Action. Vol.2: Lifeworld and System: A Critique of Functionalist Reason.* Beacon, Boston, Massachusetts
Handay G, Tandon R 1988 *Revolution through Reform with People's Wisdom.* (videotape) Society for Participatory Research in Asia, Khanpur, New Delhi
Horton M, Freire P 1990 *We Make the Road by Walking: Conversations on Education and Social Change.* Temple University Press, Philadelphia, Pennsylvania
Hustler D, Cassidy A, Cuff E (eds.) 1986 *Action Research in Classrooms and Schools.* Allen and Unwin, London
Kemmis S 1990 Some Ambiguities of Stenhouse's Notion of "the Teacher as Researcher": Towards a New Resolution. 1989 Lawrence Stenhouse Memorial Lecture to the British Educational Research Association, School of Education, University of East Anglia, Norwich
Kemmis S, Di Chiro G 1989 Emerging and evolving issues of action research praxis: An Australian perspective. *Peabody J. Educ.* 64 (3): 101–30
Kemmis S, McTaggart R (eds.) 1988 *The Action Research Reader,* 3rd edn. Deakin University Press, Geelong
Klafki W 1988a Decentralised curriculum development in the form of action research. In: Kemmis S, McTaggart R (eds.)
Klafki W 1988b Pedagogy: Theory of a practice. In: Kemmis S, McTaggart R (eds.) 1988
Lewin K 1946 Action research and minority problems. *J. Soc. Issues* 2(4): 34–46
Lewis I 1987 Encouraging reflective teacher research: A review article. *Br. J. Sociol. Educ.* 8(1): 95–105
McKernan J 1991 *Curriculum Action Research: A Handbook*

of Methods and Resources for the Reflective Practitioner. Kogan Page, London

McTaggart R, Garbutcheon-Singh M 1988 A fourth generation of action research: Notes on the Deakin seminar. In: Kemmis S, McTaggart R (eds.) 1988

Nixon J (ed.) 1981 *A Teachers' Guide to Action Research*. Grant McIntyre, London

Noffke S E 1991 Hearing the teacher's voice: Now what? *Curriculum Perspectives*

Noffke S E, Brennan M 1988 Action research and reflective student teaching at U W -Madison: Issues and examples. Paper presented at the Annual Meeting of the Association of Teacher Educators, San Diego, California

Oja S N, Smulyan L 1989 *Collaborative Action Research: A Developmental Approach*. Falmer, London

Rozada Martínez J, Cascante Fernández C, Arrieta Gallastegui J 1989 *Desarrollo Curricular y Formación del Profesorado*. Cyan Gestión Editorial, Gijón

Sanford N 1970 Whatever happened to action research? *J. Soc. Issues* 26(4): 3–23

Schön D A 1983 *The Reflective Practitioner: How Professionals Think in Action*. Temple Smith, London

Schwab J J 1969 The practical: A language for curriculum. *Sch. Rev.* 78: 1–24

Serra L 1988 Participatory research and popular education. Paper presented to the North American Adult Education Association Research Conference, University of Calgary

Stenhouse L A 1975 *An Introduction to Curriculum Research and Development*. Heinemann, London

Tandon R 1988 Social transformation and participatory research. *Convergence* 21(2,3): 5–18

Van Manen M 1990 *Researching Lived Experience: Human Science for an Action-Sensitive Pedagogy*. State University of New York Press, Albany, New York

Whitehead J 1989 Creating a living educational theory from questions of the kind, "How do I improve my practice?" *Camb. J. Educ.* 19(1): 41–52

Winter R 1987 *Action-Research and the Nature of Social Inquiry*. Gower, Aldershot

Winter R 1989 *Learning from Experience: Principles and Practice in Action-Research*. Falmer, London

Zeichner K, Liston D P 1987 Teaching student teachers to reflect. *Harv. Educ. Rev.* 57(1): 23–48

Biographical Research Methods

N. K. Denzin

The biographical method which is considered in this article is defined as the studied use and collection of life documents, or documents of life that describe turning-point moments in individuals' lives. These documents include autobiographies, biographies, diaries, letters, obituaries, life histories, life stories, personal experience stories, oral histories, and personal histories. The subject matter of the biographical method is the life experiences of a person, and biographical methods provide the very foundations for the study of educative processes. When written in the first person it is called "autobiography," life story, or life history. When written by another person it is called a "biography." An "auto-ethnography" is a partial first-person text, based on the cultural study of the person's own group. There are many biographical methods, or many ways of writing about a life. Each form presents different textual problems and leaves the reader with different messages and understandings. A life or a biography is only ever given in the words that are written about it.

1. Historical Development

The biographical, life history, case study, case history, or ethnographic method has been a part of sociology's history since the 1920s and 1930s when University of Chicago sociologists, under the influence of Robert E Park and others, were trained in the qualitative, interpretative, interactionist approach to human group life.

Sociologists in succeeding generations turned away from the method. They gave their attention to problems of measurement, validity, reliability, responses to attitude questionnaires, survey methodologies, laboratory experiments, theory development, and conceptual indicators. Many researchers combined these interests and problems with the use of the life history, biographical method. The result often produced a trivialization, and distortion of the original intents of the method.

In the 1980s and 1990s, sociologists and scholars in other disciplines have evidenced a renewed interest in the biographical method, coupled with a resurgence of interest in interpretative approaches to the study of culture, biography, and human group life. In 1978 a "Biography and Society Group" formed within the International Sociological Association (ISA) and met in Uppsala, Sweden. In 1986 that Group became a research committee within the ISA (see *Current Sociology* 1995). The journal *Oral History*, of the Oral History Society, also regularly publishes life history, biographical materials. Within sociology and anthropology, *Qualitative Sociology*, *Qualitative Inquiry*, The *Journal of Contemporary Ethnography*, *Dialectical Anthropology*, and *Current Anthropology* frequently publish biographically related articles, as does *Signs*. The autobiography has become a topic of renewed interest in literary criticism. Feminists and postcolonial theory (Trinh 1989, 1991) have led the way in this discussion (Personal Narratives Group

1989). Moreover, a number of sociological monographs using the method have appeared. In short, the method has returned to the human disciplines.

Central to the biographical–interpretative view has been the argument that societies, cultures, and the expressions of human experience can be read as social texts; that is, as structures of representation that require symbolic statement. These texts, whether oral or written, have taken on a problematic status in the interpretative project. Questions concerning how texts are authored, read, and interpreted have emerged. How authors, lives, societies, and cultures get inside interpretative texts are now hotly debated topics.

In 1959 Mills in *The Sociological Imagination* argued that the sociological imagination "enables us to grasp history and biography and the relations between the two within society." He then suggested that "No social study that does not come back to the problems of biography, of history and of their intersections within a society has completed its intellectual journey" (Mills 1959).

A basic question drives the interpretive project in the human disciplines: how do men and women live and give meaning to their lives, and capture these meanings in written, narrative, and oral forms? As Karl Marx observed, men and women "make their own history, but not . . . under conditions they have chosen for themselves; rather on terms immediately existing, given and handed down to them." How are these lives, their histories and their meanings to be studied? Who are these people who make their own history? What does history mean to them? How do sociologists, anthropologists, historians, and literary critics read, write, and make sense of these lives?

2. The Subject and the Biographical Method

From its birth, modern, qualitative, interpretive sociology, which links with Max Weber's mediations on *verstehen* (understanding) and method, has been haunted by a "metaphysics of presence" which asserts that real, concrete subjects live lives with meaning and these meanings have a concrete presence in the lives of these people. This belief in a real subject, who is present in the world, has led sociologists to continue to search for a method that would allow them to uncover how these subjects give subjective meaning to their life experiences. This method would rely upon the subjective, verbal, and written expressions of meaning given by the individuals being studied; these expressions being windows into the inner life of the person. Since Wilhelm Dilthey (1833–1911) this search has led to a perennial focus in the human sciences on the autobiographical approach and its interpretative biographical variants, including hermeneutics (see *Hermeneutics*).

Jacques Derrida has contributed to the understanding that there is no clear window into the inner life of a person, for any window is always filtered through the glaze of language, signs, and the process of signification. Moreover, language, in both its written and spoken forms, is always inherently unstable, in flux, and made up of the traces of other signs and symbolic statements. Hence there can never be a clear, unambiguous statement of anything, including an intention or a meaning. The researcher's task is to reconcile this concern with the metaphysics of presence, and its representations, with a commitment to the position that interpretative sociologists and anthropologists study real people who have real lived experiences in the social world.

3. A Clarification of Terms

A family of terms combine to shape the biographical method. The terms are: method, life, self, experience, epiphany, case, autobiography, ethnography, autoethnography, biography, ethnography, story, discourse, narrative, narrator, fiction, history, personal history, oral history, case history, case study, writing presence, difference, life history, life story, self-story, and personal experience story. Table 1 summarizes these concepts and terms which have historically defined the biographical method.

The above terms require discussion. The word "method" will be understood to refer to a way of knowing about the world. A way of knowing may proceed from subjective or objective grounds. Subjective knowing involves drawing on personal experience, or the personal experiences of others, in an effort to form an understanding and interpretation of a particular phenomenon. Objective knowing assumes that an individual can stand outside an experience and understand it, independent of the persons experiencing the phenomenon in question. Intersubjective knowing rests on shared experiences and the knowledge gained from having participated in a common experience with another person. The biographical method rests on subjective and intersubjectively gained knowledge and understandings of the life experiences of individuals, including a person's own life. Such understandings rest on an interpretative process that leads a person to enter into the emotional life of another. "Interpretation"—the act of interpreting and making sense out of something—creates the conditions for "understanding," which involves being able to grasp the meanings of an interpreted experience for another individual. Understanding is an intersubjective, emotional process. Its goal is to build shareable understandings of the life experiences of another. This is also called creating verisimilitudes or "truth-like" intersubjectively shareable emotional feelings and cognitive understandings.

3.1 Lifes, Persons, Selves, Experiences

All biographical studies presume a life that has been lived, or a life that can be studied, constructed, reconstructed, and written about. In the present context a "life" refers to two phenomena: (a) lived experiences, or conscious existence, and person (a self-conscious being, as well as a named, cultural object); (b) cultural creation. The consciousness of the person is simultaneously directed to "an inner world of thought and experience and to an outer world of events and experience." These two worlds, the inner and the outer, are termed the "phenomenological stream of

Table 1
Terms/forms and varieties of the biographical method[a]

Term/method	Key features	Forms/variations
1 Method	A way of knowing	Subjective/objective
2 Life	Period of existence; lived experiences	Partial/complete/edited/public/private
3 Self	Ideas, images, and thoughts of self	Self-stories, autobiographies
4 Experience	Confronting and passing through events	Problematic, routine, ritual
5 Epiphany	Moment of revelation in a life	Major, minor, relived, illuminative
6 Autobiography	Personal history of one's life	Complete, edited, topical
7 Ethnography	Written account of a culture, or group	Realist, interpretative, descriptive
8 Autoethnography	Account of one's life as an ethnographer	Complete, edited, partial
9 Biography	History of a life	Autobiography
10 Story	A fiction, narrative	First, third person
11 Fiction	An account, something made up, fashioned	Story (life, self)
12 History	Account of how something happened	Personal, oral, case
13 Discourse	Telling a story, talk about a text	First, third person
14 Narrator	Teller of a story	First, third person
15 Narrative	A story, having a plot and existence separate from life of teller	Fiction, epic, science, folklore, myth
16 Writing	Inscribing, creating a written text	Logocentric, deconstructive
17 *Différance*	Every word carries traces of another word	Writing, speech
18 Personal history	Reconstruction of life based on interviews and conversations	Life history, life story
20 Oral history	Personal recollections of events, their causes, and effects	Work, ethnic, religious personal, musical, etc.
21 Case history	History of an event or social process, not of a person	Single, multiple, medical, legal
22 Life history	Account of a life based on interviews and conversations	Personal, edited, topical, complete
23 Life story	A person's story of his or her life, or a part thereof	Edited, complete, topical, fictional
24 Self-story [mystory]	Story of self in relation to an event	Personal experience, fictional, true
25 Personal experience story	Stories about personal experience	Single, multiple episode, private or communal folklore
26 Case study	Analysis and record of single case	Single, multiple

a Adapted from Denzin (1989)

consciousness" and the "interactional stream of experience." The phenomenological stream describes the person caught up in thoughts and the flow of inner experience. The outer, interactional stream locates the person in the world of others. These two streams are opposite sides of the same process, or chiasma, for there can be no firm dividing line between inner and outer experience. The biographical method recognizes this facticity about human existence, for its hallmark is the joining and recording of these two structures of experience in a personal document.

"Epiphanies" are interactional moments and experiences that leave marks on people's lives. In them personal character is manifested. They are often moments of crisis. They alter the fundamental meaning structures in a person's life. Their effects may be positive or negative. They are like the historian Victor Turner's "liminal phase of experience." In the liminal, or threshold moment of experience, the person is in a "non-man's-land betwixt and between . . . the past and the . . . future." These are existential acts. Some are ritualized, as in status passages; others are even routinized, as when a person daily batters and beats his or her spouse. Still others are totally emergent and unstructured, and the person enters them with few—if any—prior understandings of what is going to happen. The meanings of these experiences are always given retrospectively, as they are relived and re-experienced in the stories persons tell about what has happened to them.

There are four forms of the epiphany: (a) the major event which touches every fabric of a person's life; (b) the cumulative or representative event which signifies eruptions or reactions to experiences that have been going on for a long period of time; (c) the minor epiphany which symbolically represents a major, problematic moment in a relationship, or a person's life; and (d) those episodes whose meanings are given in the reliving of the experience. These are called, respectively, the "major epiphany," the "cumulative epiphany," the "illuminative or minor epiphany," and the "relived epiphany."

A "case," as indicated in Table 1, describes an instance of a phenomenon. A case may be even a process or a person. Often a case overlaps with a person; for example, the number of AIDS cases in a local community. "History" is an account of an event and involves determining how a particular event, process, or set of experiences occurred. A "case history" refers to the history of an event or a process; for example, the history of AIDS as an epidemic in the United States. A "case study" is the analysis of a single case, or of multiple instances of the same process, as it is embodied in the life experiences of a community, a group, or a person.

An "autobiography," as noted earlier, is a first-person account (which actually takes the third-person form) of a set of life experiences. A "biography" is an account of a life, written by a third party.

The poet John Dryden (1631–1700) defined the word biography in 1683 as "the history of particular men's lives." A biographer, then, is a historian of selves and lives. Autobiographies and biographies are structured by a set of literary, sociological, and interpretative conventions. They are formalized expressions of experience. An "autoethnography" is an ethnographic statement which writes the ethnographer into the text in an autobiographical manner. This is an important variant in the traditional ethnographic account, which positions the writer as an objective outsider in the texts that are written about the culture, group, or person in question. A fully grounded biographical study would be autoethnographic, and contain elements of the writer's own biography and personal history. Such an autoethnography would be descriptive and interpretative (Ellis 1995, 1996).

Several critical points concerning the autobiographical and biographical method may be drawn from these extended excerpts. Autobiographies and biographies are conventionalized, narrative expressions of life experiences. These conventions, which structure how lives are told and written about, involve the following problematic presuppositions, and assumptions that are taken for granted: (a) the existence of others; (b) the influence and importance of gender and class; (c) family beginnings; (d) starting points; (e) known, and knowing authors and observers; (f) objective life markers; (g) real persons with real lives; (h) turning point experiences, and (i) truthful statements distinguished from fictions.

These conventions serve to define the biographical method as a distinct approach to the study of human experience. They are the methods by which the "real" appearances of "real" people are created. They are Western literary conventions and have been present since the invention of the biographical form. Some are more central than others, although they all appear to be universal, while they change and take different form, depending on the writer, the place of writing, and the historical moment. They shape how lives are told. In so doing they create the subject matter of the biographical approach. They were each present in the biographical and autobiographical excerpts just presented. Each is treated in turn below.

Ethnographies, biographies, and autobiographies rest on "stories" which are fictional, narrative accounts of how something happened. Stories are fictions. A "fiction" is something made, or fashioned, out of real and imagined events. History, in this sense, is fiction. A story has a beginning, a middle, and an end. Stories take the form of texts. They can be transcribed, written down, and studied. They are "narratives" with a plot and a story line that exists independently of the life of the storyteller, or "narrator." Every narrative contains a reason, or set of justifications for its telling. Narrators report stories as narratives. A story is told in and through "discourse," or talk, just as there can be discourse about the text of a story. A text can be part of a larger body of discourse

A "life history" or "personal history" is a written account of a person's life based on spoken conversations and interviews. In its expanded form the life history may pertain to the collective life of a group, organization, or community. An "oral history" focuses chiefly on events, processes, causes, and effects, rather than on individuals whose recollections furnish oral history with its raw data. Since oral histories are typically obtained through spoken conversations and interviews, they often furnish the materials for life histories, and case histories. Oral histories should not be confused, however, with personal histories, for the latter attempt to reconstruct lives based on interviews and conversations. Life histories and personal histories may be topical, focusing on only one portion of a life, or complete, attempting to tell the full details of a life as it is recollected.

"Life stories" examine a life, or a segment of a life, as reported by the individual in question. A life story is a person's story of his or her life, or of what he or she thinks is a significant part of that life. It is therefore a personal narrative, a story of personal experience. A life story may be written or published as an autobiography. Its narrative, story-telling form gives it the flavor of fiction, or of fictional accounts of what happened in a person's life.

The life story turns the subject into an author; an author, or authoress being one who brings a story into existence. The subject-as-author is given an authority over the life that is written about. After all it is their life. This means the author has an authority in the text that is given by the very conventions that structure the writing or telling of the story in the first place. But where in the text of the story is the author? Clearly he or she is everywhere and nowhere. For an author is always present in personal name, and signified in the words that he or she uses. But the author is not in those words; they are only signs of the author, the self, and the life in question. They are inscriptions on and of the self or life that is being told about. The author is in the text only through the words and the conventions he or she uses. The languages of biography structure how biographies are written. There is no fixed, ever-present author.

"Self-stories" are told by a person in the context of a specific set of experiences. A self-story positions the self of the teller centrally in the narrative that is given. It is literally a story of and about the self in relation to an experience. The self-story is made up as it is told. It does not exist as a story independent of its telling; although after it has been told, it can take on the status of a story that can be retold. Its narrative form typically follows the linear format; that is, beginning, middle, end. These tellings build on the assumption that each person is a storyteller of self-experiences. These oral histories of self are often mandated by social groups. When a self-story joins with an author's account of

popular culture and scholarly discourse on the individual's life experiences it becomes a "mystory"; that is, my story about how my life has been represented by others. ("Mystory" is Gregory Ulmer's term.)

"Personal experience narratives" are stories people tell about their personal experience. They often draw upon the public, oral story-telling tradition of a group. These stories are based on personal experience. They have the narrative structure of a story (i.e., a beginning, middle, and end). They describe a set of events that exist independently of the telling. The experiences that are described draw their meaning from the common understandings that exist in a group, although they do express the "private" folklore, or meanings of the teller. When told, they create an emotional bond between listener and teller. They express a part of the "inner life" of the storyteller.

Personal experience narratives differ from self-stories in several ways. These narratives do not necessarily position the self of the teller in the center of the story, as self-stories do. Their focus is on shareable experience. Personal experience narratives are more likely to be based on anecdotal, everyday, commonplace experiences, while self-stories involve pivotal, often critical life experiences. Self-stories need not be coherent, linear accounts. They need not be entertaining, or recreate cherished values and memories of a group, while personal experience narratives do. Self-stories are often mandated by a group; personal experience narratives are not. Self-stories are often told to groups, while personal experience narratives may only be told to another individual. These two biographical forms are alike, however, in that they both rest on personal experiences.

4. Representing Lives

Lives and their experiences are represented in stories. They are like pictures that have been painted over, and when paint is scraped off an old picture something new becomes visible. What is new is what was previously covered up. A life and the stories about it have the qualities of pentimento: something painted out of a picture which later becomes visible again. Something new is always coming into sight, displacing what was previously certain and seen. There is no truth in the painting of a life, only multiple images and traces of what has been, what could have been, and what now is.

These stories move outward from the selves of the person and inward to the groups that give them meaning and structure. Persons are arbitrators of their own presence in the world, and they should have the last word on this problem. Texts must always return to and reflect the words that persons speak as they attempt to give meaning and shape to the lives they lead. The materials of the biographical method resolve, in the final analysis, into the stories that persons tell one another.

These stories are learned and told in cultural groups. The stories that members of groups pass on to one another are reflective of understandings and practices that are at work in the larger system of cultural understandings that are acted upon by group members. These understandings contain conceptions of persons, lives, meaningful and subjective experience, and notions of how persons and their experiences are to be represented. There are only stories to be told, and listened to. These stories resolve the dilemmas surrounding the metaphysics of presence that haunts the individual as he or she attempts to give shape to this thing called a life and a biography. A person becomes the stories he or she tells. The elusive nature of these stories calls the person back to the understanding that this business of a life story is just that, a story that can never be completed.

Stories then, like the lives they relate, are always open ended, inconclusive, and ambiguous, subject to multiple interpretations. Some are big, others are little. Some take on heroic, folktale proportions in the cultural lives of groups members; others are tragic; and all too few are comic. Some break fast and run to rapid conclusions. Most slowly unwind and twist back on themselves as persons seek to find meaning for themselves in the experiences they call their own. Some are told for the person by others who are called experts, be these journalists, or professional biographers. Some the person keeps to herself or himself and tells to no one else. Many individuals are at a loss as to what story to tell, feeling that they have nothing worthwhile to talk about. Within this group there are persons who have no voice, and no one to whom to tell their story.

This means that biographical work must always be interventionist, seeking to give voice to those who may otherwise not be allowed to tell their story, or who are denied a voice to speak. This is what *écriture feminine* attempts; a radical form of feminist writing which "transgresses structures of . . . domination—a kind of writing which reproduces the struggle for voice of those on the wrong side of the power relationship." This stance disrupts the classic oedipal logic of the life-history method which situates subjectivity and self-development in the patriarchal system of marriage, kinship, and sexuality (Clough 1994). This logic underwrites the scientist, positivistic use of life histories, and supports institutionalized sociological discourse on human subjects as individuals who can tell true stories about their lives. *Écriture feminine*, and certain versions of the "queer theory" (Clough 1994) moving from a deconstructive stance, make no attempt at the production of biographical narratives which fill out the sociologist's version of what a life and its stories should look like. It accepts sociology as fictive writing, and biographical work as the search for partial, not full identities.

Students of the method must begin to assemble a body of work that is grounded in the workings of these various cultural groups. This is the challenge and the promise of this project. In order to speak to the Fourth Epoch, so called by Mills as the "postmodern period," it is necessary to begin to listen to the workings of these groups that make up our time. It is necessary also to learn how to connect biographies and lived experiences, the epiphanies of lives, to the groups and social relationships that surround and shape persons.

5. *Personal Writing*

As we write about our lives, we bring the world of others into our texts. We create differences, oppositions, and presences which allow us to maintain the illusion that we have captured the "real" experiences of "real" people. In fact, we create the persons we write about, just as they create themselves when they engage in story-telling practices. As students of the biographical method we must become more sensitive to the writing strategies we use when we attempt to accomplish these ends. And, as readers, we can only have trust, or mistrust in the writers that we read, for there is no way to stuff a real-live person between the two covers of a text.

Biographical studies should attempt to articulate how each subject deals with the problems of coherence, illusion, consubstantiality, presence, deep, inner selves, others, gender, class, starting and ending points, epiphanies, fictions, truths, and final causes. These recurring, obdurate, culturally constructed dimensions of Western lives provide framing devices for the stories that are told about the lives that we study. They are, however, no more than artifices; contrivances that writers and tellers are differentially skilled at using. As writers we must not be trapped into thinking that they are any more than cultural practice.

As we learn to do this we must remember that our primary obligation is always to the people we study, not to our project, or to a larger discipline. The lives and stories that we hear and study are given to us under a promise. That promise being that we protect those who have shared with us. In return, this sharing will allow us to write life documents that speak to the human dignity, the suffering, the hopes, the dreams, the lives gained and the lives lost by the people we study. These documents will become testimonies to the ability of the human being to endure, to prevail, and to triumph over the structural forces that threaten, at any moment, to annihilate all of us. If we foster the illusion that we understand when we do not, or that we have found meaningful, coherent lives where none exist, then we engage in a cultural practice that is just as repressive as the most repressive of political regimes.

See also: Hermeneutics; Postmodernism and Education; Trends in Qualitative Research Methods

References

Clough P T 1994 *Feminist Thought: Desire, Power and Academic Discourse.* Blackwell, Cambridge, Massachusetts

Current Sociology 1995 Special Issue Biographical Research 43: (2/3) Autumn/Winter. Simeoni D, Doana M (eds.)

Ellis C 1995 *Final Negotiations.* Temple University Press, Philadelphia, Pennsylvania

Ellis C 1996 Evocative Authoethnography: Writing Emotionally About Our Lives. In: Lincoln Y S, Tierney W (eds.), *Representation and the Text: Reframing the Narrative Voice.* SUNY Press, Albany, New York

Mills C W 1959 *The Sociological Imagination.* Oxford University Press, New York

Personal Narratives Group 1989 *Interpreting Women's Lives: Feminist Theory and Personal Narratives.* Indiana University Press, Bloomington, Indiana

Trinh T. Minh-ha 1989 *Woman, Native, Other: Writing Postcoloniality and Feminism.* Indiana University Press, Bloomington, New York

Trinh T. Minh-ha 1991 *When the Moon Waxes Red: Representation. Gender and Cultural Politics.* Routledge, New York

Further Reading

Denzin N K 1987 *Interpretive Biography.* Sage, Newbury Park, California

Denzin N K 1989 *The Research Act: A Theoretical Introduction to Sociological Methods*, 3rd edn. Prentice-Hall, Englewood Cliffs, New Jersey

Denzin N K 1989 *Interpretive Interactionism.* Sage, Newbury Park, California

Denzin N K 1997 Interpretive ethnography. *Ethnographic Practices for the 21st Century.* Sage, Thousand Oaks, California

Feagin J R, Orum A M, Sjoberg G (eds.) 1991 *A Case for the Case Study.* University of North Carolina Press, Chapel Hill, North Carolina

Journal of Applied Behavioral Science 1989 vol. 25 (4) (issue devoted to Autobiography, Social Research, and the Organizational Context)

Reinharz S, Davidson L 1992 *Feminist Methods in Social Research.* Oxford University Press, New York

Roman L G 1992 The political significance of other ways of narrating ethnography: A feminist materialist approach. In: LeCompte M D, Millroy W L, Preissle J (eds.) 1992 *Handbook of Qualitative Research in Education.* Academic Press, San Diego

Smith L M 1994 Biographical methods. In: Denzin N K, Lincoln Y S (eds.) 1994 *Handbook of Qualitative Research.* Sage, Newbury Park, California

Content and Text Analysis

J. Anderson

Content analysis, sometimes referred to as document analysis, includes the methods and techniques researchers use to examine, analyze, and make inferences about human communications. Typically, communications consist of printed or written text but may also comprise photographs, cartoons, illustrations, broadcasts, and verbal interactions. Text analysis, by contrast, has a narrower focus and is restricted to analysis of text features, and usually as these relate to comprehensibility or writing style. The widespread use of computers has seen a resurgence of research studies using methods of content and text analysis.

The techniques of content and text analysis are used by researchers across a range of disciplines: anthropology, psychology, sociology, psychiatry, history, literature, political science, education, linguistics, artificial intelligence. This entry adopts an educational, psycholinguistic perspective and, although there is often overlap, content and text analysis are discussed separately. The focus in this article is on written communication, on purposes and techniques commonly employed by educational researchers, and on methodological issues.

1. Definitions of Content Analysis

Berelson's chapter in *Handbook of Social Psychology* Vol. 1 (1952) is still regarded as a basic reference for content analysis. (This chapter is a condensed version of Berelson's book *Content Analysis in Communication Research* published two years previously and republished in 1971). Here Berelson defines content analysis as a "a research technique for the objective, systematic, and quantitative description of the manifest content of communication" (p. 489). In a further major review of content analysis in the second edition of *The Handbook of Social Psychology*, Holsti (1968) adopts essentially the same definition.

A slightly different interpretation was made by Osgood who defined content analysis as "a procedure whereby one makes inferences about sources and receivers from evidence in the messages they exchange" (Osgood 1959 p. 35).This changed emphasis was taken up by Weber who defined content analysis as "a research methodology that utilizes a set of procedures to make valid inferences from text" (Weber 1985 p. 9). Weber continues: "These inferences are about the sender(s) of message, the message itself, or the audience of the message."

In successive editions of *Foundations of Behavioral Research*, Kerlinger adopts this wider view of content analysis as going beyond description to making inferences about variables. Thus, content analysis is defined by Kerlinger (1986 p. 477) as "a method of studying and analyzing communications in a systematic, objective, and quantitative manner to measure variables." While many earlier studies using content analysis focused on descriptions of various communications—for instance,analyzing the content of newspapers,radio and television programs, studies of propaganda, public opinion, bias and prejudice, and studies of literary style, reading difficulty, and error analysis—for Kerlinger, content analysis is also a method of observation and measurement. "Instead of observing people's behavior directly, or asking them to respond to scales, or interviewing them, the investigator takes the communications that people have produced and asks questions of the communications" (p. 477).

2. A Framework for Studies of Content Analysis

A model widely applied to biological,psychological, social, and other systems was that proposed by Shannon and Weaver (1949). Developed to deal with signal transmission, this model incorporates a source, transmitter, channel of communication, noise, receiver, and destination. The model has been adapted to language communication (Anderson 1976), as shown in Fig.1, and provides a framework for studies of content analysis, both in its narrower and wider connotations.

Not only does the language communication model in Fig.1 provide a useful framework for reviewing the field of content analysis, it can also serve as a fruitful source for generating hypotheses. First, studies that focus primarily on the source system typically deal with the psychological states, motivations, or characteristics of encoders and the effects of these upon messages produced. Many of these studies fall into the category of "language style." Second, studies focusing mainly on the receiver system and which investigate attitudes, values, motives, and other psychological characteristics of decoders in relation to messages

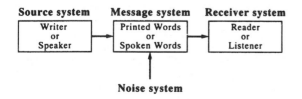

Source system   **Message system**   **Receiver system**

Writer or Speaker → Printed Words or Spoken Words → Reader or Listener

Noise system

Figure 1
A model for the correspondence of source, message, noise, and receiver systems

received, come into the realm of "audience analysis." Third, other studies where the primary focus is on the message itself or on noise and the effect of distortion in the message upon receivers belong to the field of content analysis in its narrower sense. Insofar as these three categories of studies involve the message system however, they are all embraced by content analysis in its wider connotation as a method of observation and measurement.

Typical of numerous studies in the first category noted, where the focus of attention is on the message in order to make inferences about encoders of messages, is that of Mahl (1959) who examined the speech of psychotherapy patients in order to assess their anxiety. Exemplifying the second category, where the focus of attention is again on the message but this time to make inferences about decoders, is a study of supporters' and critics' reactions to a television news program aimed at high school students (Wulfemeyer and Mueller 1991). Focusing more directly on the message itself is Anderson and Yip's (1987) study which examined the content of two editions of an Australian reading scheme to see what changes took place in the presentation of sex roles over a decade and a half when the roles of women in western societies changed quite markedly. The numerous investigations into methodological questions relating to "cloze procedure" (a measure of reading comprehension discussed below where subjects attempt to replace deleted parts of text), such as the effect on comprehension of frequency of deletions, type of deletions, and scoring procedures, are illustrative of studies into noise or message distortion.

3. Purposes and Techniques of Content Analysis

The research investigations cited demonstrate the wide range of uses of content analysis. Content analyzed by researchers covers the gamut of human communication: letters, stories, poetry, essays, diaries, obituaries, minutes, biographies, newspapers, radio, television, conversations, cartoons, drawing, photographs, film. As others have remarked, communication content is the what in the classic description of communication: who says what to whom, how, and with what effect. The widespread use of computers, together with the increasing ease of inputting text via scanners and text recognition software, are multiplying the number of studies utilizing text analysis.

Although there are several ways to do content analysis, there are, nevertheless, recognized procedures that do not differ markedly from many other procedures in educational research. These procedures are illustrated by reference to specific studies. First and foremost is the need to identify the corpus or universe to be studied. In the investigation cited of sex roles in young children's books (Anderson and Yip 1987), the corpus of reading content for analysis comprised the first nine books from the *Young Australia Language Scheme* (first published in 1966) and the first nine basic readers from *Young Australia Readers* (published in 1980). These 18 books constituted the content for analysis.

The second essential step is to define the categories into which the universe is to be partitioned. According to Kerlinger (1986), this is the most important part of content analysis because it reflects the purposes of the research and the theory underlying it. Categories must be objectively defined and mutually exclusive. Further, if comparisons are to be made with other studies, generally agreed upon or standard categories need to be adopted. Considerations like these led Stone and co-workers to develop *The General Inquirer*, a computerized approach to content analysis (Stone et al. 1966). The bases of this approach are specially developed dictionaries which allow computer tagging of words of text entered into the computer program. The tagged words then serve as indicators of, for example, need-achievement, or discipline, or for whatever the dictionary has been designed.

After defining categories, the next step is to determine units for analysis. In the preceding example, the computer tags words indicating need-achievement. Other units may be themes (often phrases or even sentences), characters, items, or space-and-time measures (like the number of pages in a book or the length of a discussion in minutes). Anderson and Yip (1987) adopted as one form of category the total number of characters (human, animal, fantasy figure, inanimate object) presented in the text and/or accompanying illustrations. Characters were counted for each story in each of the readers, noting the gender of all characters. Where the gender of characters was ambiguous, it was recorded as "other." As another form of category, all activities of male and female characters were categorized under a number of themes established in another study: themes like leadership, triumphing over foe or adversity, rescuing, exploring, showing bravery, showing fear, and so on. The units of analysis determine the level of measurement in statistical analyses.

The techniques of content analysis such as defining categories and determining units for analysis prove useful, too, in a number of investigations where the focus is not primarily on analyzing content. One example is in coding open-ended questionnaire responses. In an evaluation of curriculum materials, for example, rather than ask teachers to tick or otherwise indicate their views by choosing from a series of predetermined responses or multiple-choice questions, Anderson (1981) preferred to ask users to write down their views. The copious detail provided a rich data source, but to capture the depth of detail and allow responses to be analyzed by computer, some data reduction was necessary. Users' comments to individual questionnaire items became the universe. Each universe was examined and a set of categories or a coding scheme developed, as illustrated below in a request for suggestions to produce further language materials.

Code

10–19	Produce materials other than those already available
11	Special materials for "enquiry–approach" projects
12	Materials for infants/younger children
13	Accompanying comprehension exercises or workbooks
14	More evaluation materials
15	Extending the scheme to accommodate advanced students
16	Review workbooks
17	Very basic materials for non-English-speaking children
18	Miscellaneous exercises (e.g., music with sentence drills)

Further codes were for suggestions to expand existing materials (20–29), for suggestions about general presentation (30–39), and for missing data where the question was not answered (99).

Following a decision about units of analysis, a further step is to determine which units may be reliably quantified. In early studies of readability, for instance, researchers looked for factors thought to contribute to reading difficulty, such as sentence complexity, vocabulary load, interest level, and so on. Reliably quantifying the different factors often resulted in a much reduced list. Questions of reliability inevitably raise questions of validity since some argue that there is little use in achieving high reliability if what is left to be measured has little utility or content validity.

Quantification may take the form of a simple "frequency count," as in counting the number of male and female characters per story. Ranking texts in terms of perceived reading difficulty is "ordinal measurement." Space measures like inches of newspaper type, or time measures such as minutes of teacher talk, are "interval measurement."

4. Text Analysis and Comprehensibility

Teachers and librarians have an obvious interest in content analysis since best results in learning are usually achieved by judicious matching of student with appropriate learning materials. This interest has long been manifest, particularly in analyses of characteristics of text as these relate to "comprehensibility." One characteristic of appropriate learning materials in this context is text reading difficulty or "readability." This entry focuses on this aspect, though the interest level of reading materials and students' motivation clearly impact on comprehensibility.

The readability movement was born in the 1920s with the publication of Thorndike's epic work on word frequency, *A Teacher Wordbook of 10,000 Words*. Shortly after this book was published, the first formula for ranking books in relative order of difficulty appeared, a formula based on Thorndike's word list. Since then many readability formulas have been developed for estimating the reading difficulty of texts in English, Japanese, Spanish, French, and other languages. The method used to construct a readability formula essentially comprises four steps, the first two of which are similar to the procedures of content analysis described above. The first is to search for factors thought to contribute to reading difficulty like, for instance, use of affixes, sentence complexity, or unfamiliar vocabulary. This step is what content analysts term "defining the categories." The second step is to determine which of these factors or categories can be reliably quantified. The third, and possibly the most difficult step, is to establish a criterion or exterior measure of reading difficulty against which the quantified factors may be validated. The final step is to incorporate into a regression equation those quantified factors which predict the criterion best. The regression equation becomes the readability formula. Two readability formulas described in Klare (1975) are those by Flesch and Spache:

$$\text{Reading Ease} = 206.835 - 0.846wl \qquad \text{[Flesch]}$$
$$- 1.015sl$$

$$\text{Grade Level} = 0.141 X_1 + 0.086 X_2 + 0.839 \quad \text{[Spache]}$$

where wl, sl, X_1, and X_2 are all text factors (different measures of word difficulty and sentence complexity). The widely used Fry readability graph (see Klare 1975) is also a regression equation in graphical form.

The use of computers has had a marked effect on readability measurement, as on measurement generally. Thus, while word length in Flesch's formula (developed in 1948) involved a count of syllables which is relatively easy for human analysts, more recent formulas compute word length by counting characters. Such character counts would rarely have been conceived when analyses were done manually since they were too time-consuming and unreliable.

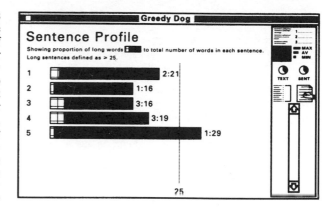

Figure 3
Sentence profile for Aesop's *The Greedy Dog*

For computers though, character counts are quicker and certainly more accurate than counting syllables.

A research instrument developed at Flinders University for use on microcomputers to analyze text features (Anderson 1992) displays the following text counts when the Text Count icon (the one selected in Fig. 2) is clicked.

Similarly, clicking on the Sentence Profile icon (seen in Fig. 3) displays a sentence profile for a given text.

The same text analysis tool computes an estimate of text reading difficulty, base on the "Rix" index, a measure that traces its origins to an index termed "Lix" which was developed in Sweden by Björnsson (1968). Clicking on the Text Difficulty icon (see Fig. 4) displays information about text difficulty.

Further options compute the reading difficulty of individual sentences and list the number of different words in a text (ordered alphabetically, by frequency, or by word length).

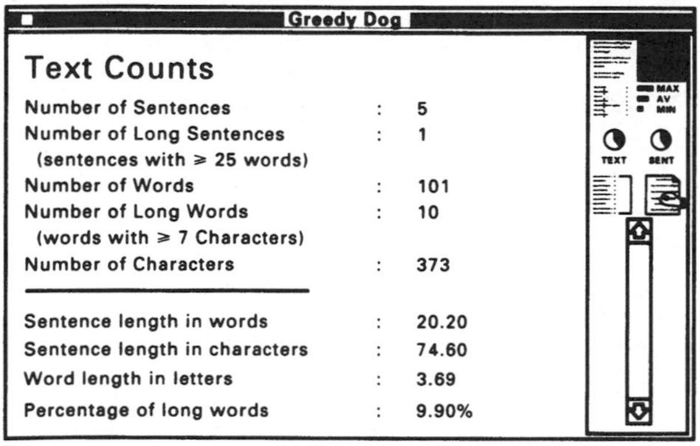

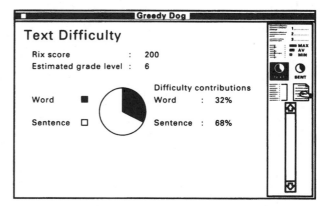

Figure 2
Text counts in Aesop's *The Greedy Dog*

Figure 4
Text difficulty for Aesop's *The Greedy Dog*

5. Cloze Procedure and Cohesion

Readability measurement as a form of text analysis has obvious advantages and equally obvious short-comings. Among the advantages are that it is objective and, with computers, quick and easy to apply. Indices such as Flesch, Lix, or Rix provide estimates of readability, that is, predictions of the ease or difficulty that readers are likely to experience in comprehending texts. Herein, however, lies the inherent weakness of such measures because no account is taken of the reader, at least in any direct way.

5.1 Cloze Procedure

Cloze procedure was developed to overcome this precise problem and to involve readers directly. It is basically a straightforward technique, consisting of a set of rules for constructing cloze tests over samples of written (or spoken) materials, administering these tests to subjects and scoring them, and determining from the cloze scores the degree of comprehension of the written (or spoken materials). To construct a cloze test, the words of a passage are systematically deleted in some mechanical way, for example, every seventh word, and replaced by blanks, usually of a standard length (though this condition is not a necessary one). The task for subjects is then to replace the missing words, and their scores, that is, the number of words correctly replaced, is an index of the comprehension of the passage. Thus the technique measures two aspects: the readability or reading difficulty of text and subjects' comprehension of text.

There are many reviews of cloze procedure since it is now included in the repertoire of techniques employed by classroom teachers, as well as being a useful measure in language research. The application of cloze procedure in foreign language testing, and especially with English learned as a foreign language in Southeast Asia as well as with Malay and Mandarin Chinese, is comprehensively reviewed in Anderson (1976).

5.2 Cohesion

"Cohesion" is yet another aspect of text which is receiving increased attention from educational researchers. Cohesion is based on the linguistic concept of cohesive ties, the mechanisms in text that make a text a text, thus differentiating connected discourse from a set of unrelated sentences. The most complete linguistic description of cohesive ties in English is to be found in Halliday and Hasan (1976). Researchers at The Open University in the United Kingdom, in a large-scale longitudinal study and in a series of fine-grained analyses, have tested the educational and psychological validity of cohesion by demonstrating that students' perception of cohesive ties in text is related to other measures of linguistic and verbal ability (see especially Chapman 1983). The *Australian Journal of Reading* (1983) devoted a special issue to the topic of cohesion and the reading teacher.

6. Content and Text Analysis: Retrospect and Prospect

Content and text analysis deal with essential forms of human interaction, the messages that the human species has developed for communication. As Holsti (1969 p. 1) remarked:

> It therefore follows that the study of the processes and products of communication is basic to the student of history, behavior, thought, art, and institutions. Often the only surviving artifacts that may be used to study human activity are to be found in documents.

Yet, as Berelson (1952 p. 518) even earlier remarked: "Content analysis, as a method, has no magical qualities." The methods of the content or text analyst are open to the same strictures faced by all educational researchers: the need to select the universe of materials for analysis carefully if unwarranted generalizations are not to be made, to select categories that are meaningful, and to pay heed to questions of reliability and validity.

The computer, as a research tool, has had an enormous impact on content and text analysis and this impact is likely to increase even further. Not only does the computer facilitate all statistical analyses, it is a tool that is ideally suited for making routine counts of whatever categories researchers adopt, provided these can be fully defined and therefore quantified. The bottleneck that used to exist when entering text into computers is fast losing force as an obstacle, as scanners linked to computers become more widespread. Improvements in software are making text recognition more rapid and efficient, across a range of languages and alphabets. When voice recognition becomes a reality, the amount of human communication content available for ready analysis will increase even more dramatically.

See also: Trends in Quantitative Research Methods

References

Anderson J 1976 *Psycholinguistic Experiments in Foreign Language Testing*. University of Queensland Press, St Lucia

Anderson J 1981 *A National Survey of User Opinion of Commonwealth-produced Curriculum Materials for Teaching English as a Second Language*. Flinders University, Adelaide

Anderson J 1992 *MacTexan a Tool to Analyze Texts*. Flinders University, Adelaide

Anderson J, Yip L 1987 Are sex roles represented fairly in children's books? A content analysis of old and new readers. *Unicorn* 13(3): 155–61

Australian Journal of Reading 1983 Vol. 6, No. (issue devoted to Cohesion and the Reading Teacher)

Berelson B 1952 Content analysis. In: Lindzey G (ed.) 1952

Handbook of Social Psychology. Vol. 1; Theory and Method. Addison-Wesley, Reading, Massachusetts

Björnsson C H 1968 *Läsbarhet.* Bokförlaget Liber, Stockholm

Chapman L J 1983 *Reading Development and Cohesion.* Heinemann, London

Halliday M A K, Hasan R 1976 *Cohesion in English.* Longman, London

Holsti O R 1968 Content analysis. In: Lindzey G, Aronson E (eds.) 1968 *The Handbook of Social Psychology. Vol. 2: Research Methods*, 2nd edn. Addison-Wesley, Reading, Massachusetts

Holsti O R 1969 *Content Analysis for the Social Sciences and Humanities.* Addison-Wesley, Reading, Massachusetts

Kerlinger F R 1986 *Foundations of Behavioral Research*, 3rd edn. Holt, Rinehart, and Winston, New York

Klare G R 1975 Assessing readability. *Read. Res. Q.* 10(1): 62–102

Mahl G F 1959 Exploring emotional states by content analysis. In: Pool I D S (ed.) 1959 *Trends in Content Analysis.* University of Illinois Press, Urbana, Illinois

Osgood C E 1959 The representational model and relevant research methods. In: Pool I D S (ed.) 1959 *Trends in Content Analysis.* University of Illinois Press, Urbana, Illinois

Shannon C E, Weaver W 1949 *The Mathematical Theory of Communication.* University of Illinois Press, Urbana, Illinois

Stone P J, Dunphy D C, Smith M S, Ogilvie D M 1966 *The General Inquirer: A Computer Approach to Content Analysis.* MIT Press, Cambridge, Massachusetts

Weber R P 1985 *Basic Content Analysis.* Sage, Beverly Hills, California

Wulfemeyer K T, Mueller B 1991 Television commercials in the classroom: A content analysis of Channel One ads. *Commun. Journalism Educ. Today* 24(4): 10–13

Education, Occupation, and Earnings

T. Tachibanaki

Education, occupation, and earnings are interrelated. Most analyses of these phenomena, however, have focused on either the relationships between education and earnings or that between education and occupation. The relationship between occupation and earnings has also been studied. There are several explanations for why these relationships have been studied separately. One important explanation is that the relationship between education and occupation has been researched mainly by sociologists, whereas the relationship between education and earnings has been researched largely by economists.

1. Factors Affecting the Determination of Earnings

The effect of education on the determination of wages and earnings has been analyzed by employing the concept of human capital. The concept emphasizes the importance of not only formal education but also job training. A basic premise behind the concept is that higher levels of educational attainment increase individuals' productivity and, consequently, their earnings capacity. Since formal education and job training are costly, it is impossible to invest in human capital endlessly. Many studies have been devoted to examining the effect of education on earnings within the framework of human capital theory.

The relationship between occupation and earnings has been analyzed extensively in many countries. It may be described as "pay difference by occupation" or "pay structure by occupation." It is important to stress that occupation is the variable that has received the most attention in studies investigating earnings differ-

ence. Researchers were interested in studying whether there were earnings differences between occupations by estimating the magnitudes of such differences, if any. They usually suggested social and economic reasons to explain occupational earnings differentials.

It is possible to conclude that difference of earnings by occupation can be observed in all societies in all periods of history. In modern times pattern of pay difference by occupation is common to many countries, particularly capitalist countries, suggesting that occupations which pay higher wages and those which pay lower wages do not differ significantly from country to country. For example, white–collar workers receive higher wages than manual workers in nearly all countries. This situation is found even when a wider range of occupations is considered. What kind of justifications can be offered to explain earnings difference by occupation?

Brown (1977) provides a useful survey of the causes for pay difference by occupation. The starting point for explaining pay difference by occupation can be found in the usual functions of supply and demand, consisting of both wage rates and the number of jobs available for any occupation. Economics asserts that the intersection of the supply and demand curves determines the equilibrium wage and the number of jobs for each occupation. When adjustments of both supply and demand for all occupations are made smoothly, nearly all occupations produce equilibrium wage rates. In some occupations, however, the effects of supply and demand are often limited for various reasons. This limitation is responsible for pay differences between occupations. Several institutional and economic factors can be suggested that prevent free and perfect adjustments of supply and demand.

(a) Perfect monopoly in supply: the number of people available for a particular occupation is perfectly controlled by a group of people who engage in the same occupation. In other words, there is an entry barrier to working in a particular occupation to protect the benefits of workers already engaged in it. This is a variation of the guild system developed in medieval Europe. It continues to be commonly observed.

(b) License: a public authority grants special privileges to a particular occupation such that only people who have received licenses or other types of certification can engage in the occupation. Examples include medical doctors and airline pilots.

(c) Compensating wage differentials: some types of occupations involve dangerous tasks, require special physical abilities, or are located in unfavorable environments. It is expected that higher wages are paid in these occupations to compensate for unfavorable or excessively demanding working conditions. This concept is called "equalizing" or "compensating" wage differentials. The idea goes back to Adam Smith's *The Wealth of Nations* (published in 1776). The concept can be analyzed by supply–demand relations. It suggests that jobs or occupations that offer favorable working conditions attract many workers at lower wages than average wages, while jobs or occupations that offer unfavorable working conditions must pay premiums (i.e., higher wages) to compensate for such undesirable working conditions in order to attract workers. Examples of the working conditions concerned are: unsocial working hours, high risk levels, high skill levels, locations of factories and offices, and unemployment risk. This kind of theory can be explained by the demand–supply relationship between a firm and a worker who has certain preferences, and the number of firms and of workers. A simple economic equation can describe theoretically this idea of compensatory wage differentials, as Rosen (1986) has elegantly shown. The results of empirical observations are, however, considerably mixed, with only some supporting the theory.

(d) Risk: this refers to the personal traits of individuals that affect their choice of occupation. Individuals' attitudes toward risk have been included in studies by several economists, such as Friedman and Kuznets (1954) and Weiss (1972). Friedman, for example, suggested that skewness in earnings distribution arises from the fact that while most persons are risk averse, some persons are risk lovers. By employing Von Neumann and Morgenstern's notion of expected utility maximization, he was able to show that risk lovers choose an occupation in which there is a small chance of success at a higher income, while risk-averse people choose an occupation in which there is a large chance of receiving a lower income. Consequently, the degree of risk determines an individual's occupation, and thus produces the observed difference in earnings.

The effects of compensatory wage differentials caused by various occupations and the risk element are somewhat conflicting because the latter is a rationale for wage differentials, while the former is a rationale for equalizing wages by occupations. The actual earnings differentials by occupation may be a hybrid of the two. Discovering which of the two is dominant may be an interesting area for further empirical research.

(e) Imperfect or asymmetrical information: individuals in the labor market do not have perfect access to all available information. When they seek jobs they often lack sufficient information on both wage levels and the number of jobs available. Such imperfect information creates a distortion and causes pay difference by occupation.

(f) Formal education and training costs: several occupations require higher formal education or more training to obtain them and to perform the tasks involved successfully. Formal education and training incur cost; thus a proportion of workers cannot afford the education and training when they have to bear the cost. In such cases the situation may be observed where one group of people can engage in higher wage occupations because they were able to pay the cost, while another group of people is obliged to engage in lower wage occupations because they are unable to bear the cost.

(g) Ability: some jobs or occupations require special talent or ability, such as artistic activities and professional sport. Work in these fields cannot be gained through education and training alone. In other words, innate ability is essential. It is quite natural that extra money is paid to talented people in such fields because the supply is very limited.

(h) Regional immobility: even if information is perfect, there are significant transaction costs for both employers and employees, which restrict the movement of workers and/or offices or factories. This influences the determination of wages and produces pay differences: two identical people engaged in the same occupations but who live in different locations may receive different wages.

Other reasons may be advanced to explain pay differences by occupation. Among these is the "occupation matching" theory. This is influenced by the notion of "job matching," which emerged as an alternative explanation for several labor market phenomena explained by human capital theory. The job matching model arose from dissatisfaction with human capital theory in explaining the wage–tenure profiles and turnover–tenure relations. Human capital theory predicts the positive growth of wage by length of job tenure, but job matching theory proposes that this positive rate appears because only those workers who are well-matched to their jobs stay in their jobs. If workers who changed jobs because of mismatching were included, the positive wage growth would not appear. The occupation matching model is an extension of the job matching model. Therefore, it is likely that it can deny the human capital interpretation of the effect of education and job tenure on earnings, or it can give an alternative understanding of education in relation to earnings which has not been disclosed by the human capital model. Since these issues have not yet been exhaustively analyzed in the literature, fuller analyses and examinations of the relationship between the occupation matching model and earnings are tasks for the future (but see the pioneering work by Miller 1984).

2. Education and Occupation

The effect of education on determining a person's occupation can be analyzed from various perspectives. One approach is to examine the relationship between educational attainment and jobs obtained (or simply occupation). A second approach is to investigate the relationship between education and earnings without necessarily referring to occupation. The second approach was applied frequently when the concept of human capital was used to investigate the economics of education. Using this approach, the internal rates of returns to various education levels were estimated. It should be emphasized, however, that the first approach actually examined the effect of education on earnings because average earnings of each occupation are used to represent occupations quantitatively. In other words, jobs (or occupations) are ranked by their average earnings. Consequently, both the first and second approaches in fact applied the same approach, namely that of focusing on the relationship between education and earnings.

Apart from the relationship between education and earnings, it is important to explain the effect of "credentialism" and the "screening hypothesis" when the relationships between education, occupation, and earnings are investigated. They are particularly important for understanding the effect of education on the determination of occupation.

The screening hypothesis is sometimes referred to as "educational signaling," a concept proposed by Arrow (1973) and Spence (1973). It argues that education serves as an informational device for distinguishing between talented and untalented people. It does not indicate any direct effect of education on a person's skill. A person who has a higher educational attainment is judged to be an able person because he or she can purchase the educational signal on more favorable terms, whereas a less able person cannot. Credentialism is a more direct form of educational signaling, which guarantees certain benefits for a person who had a higher education or who graduated from a particular school or university. Some of the implications of these signaling and credential effects were described above in the discussion of the relationship between occupation and earnings. It should be remembered that education or education in a particular school is used as a prerequisite for certain occupations or for obtaining a higher status since it conveys a signal to employers of the job applicant's capability.

The relationship between the signaling hypothesis and occupation can be understood easily by considering occupations such as flying and law. There are often particular schools that produce pilots and lawyers. In Japan, pilots attend an airline pilots' school; in almost every country, lawyers must attend law school or university faculties. Those universities or schools select entrants (i.e., students) by means of tough physical and/or intellectual examinations. Students who are admitted and graduate from these schools convey, through their credentials, the information that they will conduct their professional lives successfully. Of course, several further examinations have to be passed even after eligibility to become a pilot or lawyer has been secured. The great majority pass such entry examinations after they graduate from these schools. Thus, the examinations are only formal matters. Graduation (i.e., education) is more important. The education of medical doctors also proceeds along similar lines.

It should be emphasized, however, that the meaning of educational screening, signaling, and credentialing is much more general than is suggested by the discussion in the previous paragraph. They signify a device for identifying more or less able persons. Three comments can be offered about the implications of the signaling aspect of education, following the arguments of Rosen (1987).

First, although the human capital interpretation of education and the signaling (or screening) interpretation of education are proposed on different theoretical grounds, they have very similar implications for the rational choice of schooling. In particular, empirical studies of income and schooling cannot distinguish between the human capital interpretation of education and the signaling interpretation of education. In other words, it is nearly impossible to identify which interpretation is more appropriate to explain empirical evidence of the relationship between education and earnings. This is due partly to the fact that a person's productivity or earnings capacity cannot be observed in the production process. Thus it is impossible to test directly the effect of education (i.e., schooling) on earnings capacity, as the theory of human capital proposes. Therefore, Rosen (1987) understands that schooling has little social value when it serves as a signal and much social value when it produces real human capital. Second, schooling contributes only a very marginal part of earnings differentials. Other important variables, such as ability, job tenure, and family background, contribute significantly to the variance of earnings. The limited explanatory power of schooling in the determination of earnings obscures the value of education as a signal. Third, if people are identified and classified properly by using schooling and education as a signaling device, it may be socially productive because such sortings of people are likely to allocate both talented and untalented people to the most relevant places in the market.

As was noted previously, the relationships between education, occupation, and earnings have traditionally been examined separately. When the comprehensive relationship between these variables is investigated by applying econometric techniques to individual survey data, a recursive-type simultaneous equation system is used. Typical examples of the endogenous variables are education, occupation, and earnings. The theory behind this system implies that education determines occupational attainment and occupation then determines earnings. If these observations together with other information on various exogenous variables are available, the ordinary least squares method or the two-stage least squares method can be applied, depending upon the correlation among the error terms. Representative examples are shown by Griliches and Mason (1972) for the United States, by Tachibanaki (1980) for France, by Hubler (1984) for Germany, and by Tachibanaki (1988) for Japan. Before discussing these issues, several observations should be made about this econometric approach.

First, many sociological studies strongly suggest that sociological background (such as father's or mother's educational attainment and occupational level and family income) are important determinants of an individual's educational level. Thus it is customary to consider social background variables prior to the determination of educational attainment (see Duncan et al. 1968).

Second, occupational level is a difficult variable for quantification. Several United States studies use the sociologist Duncan's socioeconomic index, which gives a weighted average of income and corresponding educational attainment for occupations in order to quantify occupations. Griliches (1976) posed a serious question concerning the introduction of occupation, claiming that it correlates with dependent variables, such as earnings or education. Thus, he urged ignoring occupation, if occupational attainment were quantified like Duncan's socioeconomic index. This elimination causes an omitted-variable problem. Thus it would be preferable not to ignore occupation

in a recursive type simultaneous equation system. A variable such as "prestige," which was used by Tachibanaki (1980, 1988), may be an alternative idea to quantify occupation. Needless to say, prestige is measured independently of education and/or income.

Third, when an estimate is made of the earning function which enters as part of a recursive simultaneous equation system, the ability (innate ability) of an individual cannot be ignored because it affects not only earnings but also occupation and other variables which may raise earnings capacity. This subject has received considerable attention, discussed in the following way.

Ignoring other variables, a simple earnings function can be written:

$$Y = \alpha + \beta S + \gamma A + u \qquad (1)$$

where Y is income, S is education and A is a measure of ability. When we ignore ability, we obtain a biased estimator of β as follows:

$$Eb_{YS} = \beta + \gamma b_{AS} = \beta + \gamma \ \text{cov}(AS)/\text{var}A, \qquad (2)$$

where the return to education is estimated with a bias. Thus, it is necessary to include A when ability has an independent positive effect on earnings, and the relationship between the excluded ability and included schooling variable is positive. However, Griliches (1977) proposed that the "ability bias" caused by the excluded ability was minor. Therefore, it is not so serious even if ability is excluded. Moreover, serious problems remain for the ability variable even if it is included. First, even if a popular variable such as IQ is included, there is a question about whether this indicates a proper measure of ability. A professional baseball player has a particular ability rather than IQ. Therefore the ability variable should be fairly multi dimensional. Second, even if we assume that IQ is a relevant measure, it includes considerable measurement errors. In other words, errors-in-variables may be more serious than the previous left-out-problem bias. "Ability" is a difficult subject and needs to be investigated seriously.

3. Conclusion

Although the above problems cannot be ignored, empirical estimates of earnings functions together with other variables which are included in recursive type simultaneous equation models suggest the following conclusions. First, the social background variable is a very important factor and affects a student's success. Second, education determines the level of occupational attainment fairly directly. In other words, the higher the educational attainment, the higher the occupational attainment. Third, both educational attainment and occupational achievement contribute to providing people with higher earnings. Fourth, many exogenous variables must be included to obtain a better estimate of earnings function, in addition to social background, education, and occupation. They include age, tenure, family status, region, religion, and working hours. Fifth, the recursive model is fairly successful in explaining the relationship between education, occupation, and earnings in Japan and European nations such as France and Germany judging from the estimated R^2 of earnings functions. However, the result for the United States is less impressive because the estimated R^2 of earnings functions are not so high but fairly low (0.1–0.3). In other words, there are "unexplained factors" or large residuals in the estimation of earnings functions in the United States (see, for example, Taubman 1975). Jencks (1972) once attributed this residual to "luck." The determination of which variables are left out in explaining earnings differentials in the United States requires investigation, even though more empirical studies have been made in the United States than in other countries.

Three important variables which need more attention in research are hierarchy (or position) in a firm, the size of firm, and industry. The first variable is strictly related to the relationship between supervisory job and incentive. The second is related to the ability of firms to pay higher wages, and the third is related to efficiency wage hypothesis. Representative works dealing with these variables include Lazear and Rosen (1981), Rosen (1982), Brown and Medoff (1989), Akerlof (1982), and Katz (1986).

See also: Benefits of Education; Social Mobility, Social Stratification, and Education; Sociology of Education: An Overview

References

Akerlof G A 1982 Labor contracts as partial gift exchange. *Q. J. Econ.* 97(4): 543–69
Arrow K J 1973 Higher education as a filter. *J. Publ. Econ.* 2(3): 193–216
Brown C, Medoff J 1989 The employer size-wage effect. *J. Pol. Econ.* 97(5): 1027–59
Brown H P 1977 *The Inequality of Pay.* Oxford University Press, Oxford
Duncan O D, Featherman D L, Duncan B 1968 *Socio-economic Background and Occupational Achievement: Extensions of a Basic Model.* US Department of Health, Education and Welfare, Washington, DC
Friedman M, Kuznets S 1954 *Income from Independent Professional Practice.* National Bureau of Economic Research, New York
Griliches Z 1976 Wages and earnings of very young men. *J. Pol. Econ.* 84 (4 pt.2): 569–86
Griliches Z 1977 Estimating the returns to schooling: Some econometric problems. *Econometrica* 45: 1–22
Griliches Z, Mason W 1972 Education, income and ability. *J. Pol. Econ.* 80 (3 pt.2): S74–103
Hubler O 1984 Zur empirischen Uberüfung alternativer Theorien der Verteilung von Arbeitseinkommen. In: Bellman L, Gerlack K, Hubler O (eds.) 1984 *Lohnstruktur in der Bundesrepublik Deutschland.* Campus Verlag, Frankfurt
Jencks C 1972 *Inequality: A Reassessment of the Effect of Family and Schooling in Practice.* Basic Books, New York
Katz L 1986 Efficiency wage theories: A partial evaluation. In: Fischer S (ed.) 1986 NBER Macroeconomics Annual. MIT Press, Cambridge, Massachusetts
Lazear E P, Rosen S 1981 Rank–order tournaments as optimum labor contracts. *J. Pol. Econ.* 89(5): 841–64
Miller R A 1984 Job matching and occupational choice. *J. Pol. Econ.* 92(6): 1086–1120
Rosen S 1982 Authority, control and the distribution of earnings. *Bell J. Econ. Manag. Sci.* 13: 311–23
Rosen S 1986 The theory of equalizing differences. In: Ashenfelter O, Layard R (eds.) 1986 *Handbook of Labor Economics* Vol. 1. North-Holland, Amsterdam
Rosen S 1987 Human capital. In: Eatwell J, Milgate M, Newman P (eds.) 1987 *The New Palgrave: A Dictionary of Economics*, Vol. 2, Macmillan, London
Spence M 1973 Job market signalling. *Q. J. Econ.* 87(3): 355–74
Tachibanaki T 1980 Education, occupation and earnings: A recursive approach for France. *Euro. Econ. Rev.* 13: 103–27
Tachibanaki T 1988 Education, occupation, hierarchy and earnings. *Econ. Educ. Rev.* 7: 221–29
Taubman P 1975 *Sources of Inequality in earnings.* North-Holland, Amsterdam
Weiss Y 1972 The risk element in occupational and educational choice. *J. Pol. Econ.* 80(6): 1203–13

Education Production Functions

E. A. Hanushek

Although research into the determinants of students' achievement takes various approaches, one of the most appealing and useful is what economists call the "production function" approach. (In other disciplines it is known as the input–output or cost–quality approach.) In this, attention is focused primarily on the relationship between school outcomes and measurable inputs into the educational process. The method of providing instruction—that is, the educational process—is presumed to adjust to use available resources in the best way possible. If the production function for schools were known, it would then be possible to predict what would happen if resources were added or subtracted, and to analyze what actions should be taken if the prices of various inputs were to change. The problem is that the production function for education is unknown and must be inferred from data on students and their schools.

1. The Coleman Report and its Influence

The origin of estimating input–output relations in schools is usually traced to the monumental United States study *Equality of Educational Opportunity* (commonly known as the Coleman Report—Coleman et al. 1966). Designed explicitly to study equity, this report was the United States Office of Education's response to a requirement of the Civil Rights Act of 1964, namely to investigate the extent of inequality (by race, religion, or national origin) in the nation's schools. The study's fundamental contribution was to direct attention to the distribution of student performance—the outputs under consideration in this entry. Instead of addressing questions of inequality simply by producing an inventory of differences among schools and teachers by race and region of the country, the Coleman Report sought to explain those differences; it delved into the relationship between inputs and outputs of schools.

The Coleman Report was widely interpreted as finding that schools have little importance in determining student achievement. Families and, to a lesser extent, peers were seen to be the primary determinants of variations in performance. The findings were clearly controversial (see critiques by Bowles and Levin 1968 and Hanushek and Kain 1972) and immediately led to an extensive research effort to compile additional evidence about the relationship between school resources and school performance. As described below, the common interpretation of the Coleman Report in fact results from a misinterpretation of the statistical findings.

The underlying model guiding the Coleman Report and most subsequent studies is straightforward. It postulates that the output of the educational process —that is, the achievement of individual students— is directly related to a series of inputs. Policymakers directly control some of these inputs; for instance, the characteristics of schools, teachers, and curricula. Other inputs—those of families and friends plus the innate endowments or learning capacities of the students—generally cannot be affected by public policy. Further, although achievement is usually measured at discrete points in time, the educational process is cumulative; past inputs affect students' current levels of achievement.

Starting with this model, statistical techniques, typically some form of regression analysis, are employed to identify the specific determinants of achievement and to make inferences about the relative importance of the various inputs into student performance. The accuracy of the analysis and the confidence the answers warrant depend crucially on a variety of issues regarding measurement and technical estimation. This summary sets aside these issues (see Hanushek 1979, 1981, 1986). Instead it highlights the overall findings and the major unanswered questions from this research.

Most studies of educational production relationships measure output by students' scores on standardized achievement tests, although significant numbers have used other quantitative measures, such as student attitudes, school attendance rates, and college continuation or dropout rates. The general interpretation is that they are all plausible indicators of future success in the labor market.

The reason for concentrating on achievement for students in school is straightforward. The policy question centers on how different teachers and school resources affect student performance. It would be generally impractical to have to wait a decade or two after observing educational inputs to measure any subsequent outcomes that will be related to those inputs. Data and analytical necessities dictate concentration on immediate measures of student performance such as test scores. Other research, however, indicates that these in-school measures are related to subsequent performance in the labor market and that they are thus reasonable proxies of economically pertinent skills.

Test measures have been included in standard models that explain earnings differences in the population. Studies of adult earnings in developed countries typically show significant direct effects of achievement. These come, however, in statistical models that also include years of schooling, and test achievement is an important determinant of continuation in schooling, implying an important additional indirect effect. The evidence on returns to different measured skills has tended to be stronger in developing countries (see review in Harbison and Hanushek 1992). Second, studies have found direct links with productivity, particularly in agriculture (Welch 1970, Jamison and Lau 1982). In short, there is reasonably broad support for the notion that school quality as measured during schooling is directly related to productivity and earnings when students enter the labor force. Thus, although most attention is focused on the ability of schools to raise students' academic performance, there is reason to interpret this in the broader context of increasing economic performance of the students and of the overall economies.

Empirical specifications of production functions have varied widely in details, but they have also had much in common. Family inputs tend to be measured by sociodemographic characteristics of families, such as parental education, income, and family size. Peer inputs, when included, are typically aggregate summaries of the sociodemographic characteristics of other students in the school. School inputs include measures of the teachers' characteristics (education level, experience, sex, race, and so forth), of the schools' organization (class sizes, facilities, administrative expenditures, and so forth), and of district or community factors (e.g., average expenditure levels). Except for the original Coleman Report, most empirical work related to developed countries has relied on data, such as the normal administrative records of schools, that were constructed for other purposes. In developing countries, special analytical surveys have been more common, but other constraints have tended to limit data quality.

2. Schools, Expenditures, and Achievement in the United States

The production function approach has been employed broadly to investigate the effect on school performance of the core factors that determine expenditure on education. Instructional expenditures make up about two-thirds of total school expenditures in the United States. Instructional expenditures are, in turn, determined mostly by teacher salaries and class sizes. Finally, in most United States school districts, teacher salaries are directly related to the years of teaching experience and the educational level of the teacher. Thus, the basic determinants of instructional expenditures in a district are teacher experience, teacher education, and class size. Most studies, regardless of what other school characteristics might be included, analyze the effect of these factors on outcomes. (These are also the factors most likely to be found in any given data set, especially if the data come from standard administrative records.)

Because the analyses have such common specifications, the effects of the expenditure parameters can easily be tabulated. An exhaustive search of publications through 1994 uncovered 37 separate qualified studies found in 90 separate published articles or books. (Qualified studies satisfy certain minimal quality standards—being published in a book or journal, providing direct information about the effects of school resources on student performance, and providing information about the statistical significance of any findings.) These studies, while restricted to public schools, cover all regions of the United States, different grade levels, different measures of performance, and different analytical and statistical approaches. About one-third draw their data from a single school district, while the remaining two-thirds compare school performance across multiple districts. About half of the studies (182) use individual students as the unit of analysis; the remainder rely upon aggregate school, district, or state level data. The studies are split about evenly between primary schooling (Grades 1–6) and secondary schooling (Grades 7–12). Three-quarters of the studies measure school performance by some kind of standardized test. However, those that use nontest measures (such as dropout rates, college continuation, attitudes, or performance after school) are for obvious reasons concentrated in studies of secondary schooling. There is no indication that differences in sample and study design lead to differences in conclusions.

Table 1 summarizes the expenditure components of the 377 studies (Hanushek 1997). Since not all studies include each of the expenditure parameters, the first column in the table presents the total number of studies for which an input can be tabulated. For example, 277 studies provide information about the relationship between the teacher–pupil ratio and student performance. The available studies all provide regression estimates of the partial effect of given inputs, holding

Table 1
Percentage distribution of estimated resource parameter coefficients from 377 studies of educational production functions: United States

| Resources | Number of estimates | Statistically significant | | Statistically insignificant | | |
		Positive	Negative	Positive	Negative	Unknown sign
Real classroom resources						
Teacher–pupil ratio	277	15%	13%	27%	25%	20%
Teacher education	171	9	5	33	27	26
Teacher experience	207	29	5	30	24	12
Financial aggregates						
Teacher salary	119	20%	7%	25%	20%	28%
Expenditure per pupil	163	27	7	34	19	13
Other resources						
Administrative inputs	75	12	5	23	28	32
Facilities	91	9	5	23	19	44

Source: Hanushek (1989)

constant family background and other inputs. These estimated coefficients have been tabulated according to two pieces of information: the sign and the statistical significance (5 percent level) of the estimated relationship. Statistical significance is included to indicate confidence that any estimated relationship is real and not just an artifact of the sample of data employed.

According to both conventional wisdom and generally observed school policies, each tabulated factor should have a positive effect on student achievement. More education and more experience on the part of the teacher cost more and are presumed to improve individual student learning; smaller classes (more teachers per student) are also expected to be beneficial. More spending in general, higher teacher salaries, better facilities and better administration should also lead to better student performance. The quantitative magnitudes of estimated relationships are ignored here; only the direction of any effect is analyzed.

Of the 277 estimates of the effects of class size, only 28 percent are statistically significant. Of these, only 15 percent show a statistically significant positive relationship, whereas 13 percent display a negative relationship. An additional 72 percent of the estimates show that class size is not significant at the 5 percent level. Nor does ignoring statistical significance help to confirm the benefits of small classes. The insignificant coefficients are almost evenly split between positive and negative effects (if the sign was reported).

The entries for teacher education tell a similar story. The statistically significant results are split between positive and negative relationships, and in a vast majority of cases (147 out of 171) the estimated coefficients are statistically insignificant. Forgetting about statistical significance and looking just at estimated signs again does not make a case for the importance of added schooling for teachers.

Teacher experience is possibly different. A clear majority of estimated coefficients point in the expected direction, and 29 percent of the estimated coefficients are both statistically significant and of the conventionally expected sign. These results, however, are hardly overwhelming; they only appear strong relative to the other school inputs. Moreover, they are subject to interpretative questions. Specifically, these positive correlations may result from senior teachers having the ability to locate themselves in schools and classrooms with good students. In other words, causation may run from achievement to experience and not the other way around.

Overall, the results are startlingly consistent. No compelling evidence emerges that teacher–pupil ratios, teacher education, or teacher experience have the expected positive effects on student achievement. It cannot be stated with confidence that hiring teachers with more education or having smaller classes will improve student performance. Teacher experience appears only marginally stronger in its relationship.

The remaining rows of Table 1 summarize information on other expenditure components, including administration, facilities, teacher salaries, and total expenditure per student. The quality of administration is measured in a wide variety of ways, ranging from characteristics of the principal to expenditure per pupil on noninstructional items. Similarly, the quality of facilities is identified through both spending and many specific physical characteristics. The absence of a strong relationship between these two components and performance may result in part from variations in how these factors are measured. If only because of the preponderance of positive signs among the significant coefficients, administration appears marginally stronger in its relationship than facilities. Nevertheless, the available evidence on both again fails to support convincingly the conventional wisdom.

Finally, explicit measures of teacher salaries and expenditure per student are tabulated. These measures are less frequently available and are more difficult to interpret because they are included along with their underlying determinants. Nevertheless, it is not surprising that they do not suggest that they have a potentially important role in determining achievement. After all, the underlying components of this expenditure were themselves unrelated to achievement.

The research reveals no strong or systematic relationship between school expenditures and student performance. This is the case both when expenditure is decomposed into underlying determinants and when it is considered in the aggregate. Some controversies have surrounded this analysis (see Hanushek 1997). Nonetheless, they do not affect the policy conclusion that some pure policies are unlikely to be effective.

3. Other Inputs into Education—United States Studies

Since the publication of the Coleman Report, intense debate has surrounded the fundamental question of whether schools and teachers are important to the educational performance of students. That report has been commonly interpreted as finding that variations in school resources explain only a negligible portion of the variation in students' achievement.

A number of studies provide direct analyses of this overall question of differential effectiveness of teachers and schools (Hanushek 1971, 1992; Murnane 1975; Armor et al. 1976; Murnane and Phillips 1981). They do this by estimating differences in the average performance of each teacher's (or school's) students after allowing for differences in family backgrounds and initial achievement scores. The findings are unequivocal: teachers and schools differ dramatically in their effectiveness. The formal statistical tests employed in these studies confirm that there are striking differences in average gain in student achievement across teachers. The faulty impressions left by the Coleman Report and by a number of subsequent studies about the importance of teachers have resulted primarily from a confusion between the measures of effectiveness and true effectiveness itself.

These production function analyses have also investigated a wide variety of other school and nonschool factors. Although it is difficult to be specific in any summary of other factors because the specifications are quite idiosyncratic, three generalizations are possible. First, family background is clearly very important in explaining differences in achievement. Second, while considerable attention has been given to the characteristics of peers or other students within schools, the findings are ambiguous. Finally, studies have examined many additional measures of the effects of schools; teachers, curricula, and, especially, instructional methods on achievement, but few consistent results have emerged.

4. Schooling in Developing Countries

Research on school achievement in developing countries is less extensive, less rigorous, and more difficult to interpret than that for the United States. Nevertheless, some conclusions can be drawn from school operations in developing countries from such research.

Dissimilar findings about the determinants of school performance in developing countries, as contrasted with developed countries, might be expected. The dramatic differences in the level of educational support provided by families and schools imply that the educational production process could be very different in developed and developing countries. In particular, while the effect of marginal resources on achievement may be hard to discern when average school expenditure in the United States is US$7,000 per year per pupil, they might be much larger and more noticeable when expenditure is one tenth or one hundredth that level.

At the same time, the standards of data collection and analysis are so variable that the results from this work tend to be uncertain. Much of the analysis of input–output relationships for developing countries is not published in standard academic journals, and thus it does not have that basic level of quality control. Even more important, the data for many of these studies do not come from regular collection schemes, are difficult to check for quality, and miss key elements of the educational process.

Different researchers have attempted to summarize key aspects of these studies, frequently providing qualitative discussions of the analyses, their results, and their interpretation. Here, however, an overall quantitative summary of the available analyses will be presented, which parallels that for the United States studies. The starting point is the comprehensive review of studies by Fuller (1985). This is supplemented by additional studies that have appeared since that review or were omitted from it. There are limitations, however. Because this discussion and analysis relies chiefly on secondary materials, the reporting of results has to be accepted. Consequently, the results cannot be presented in the same depth as those for the United States. Additionally, there is virtually no control over the selection of papers (i.e., according to explicit minimal quality standards) or over the interpretation of the statistical results.

A total of 96 underlying studies form the basis for the analysis (about half the number utilized in the United States analysis). Table 2 divides the available studies into statistically significant (by sign) and statistically insignificant. (The insignificant findings, unfortunately, cannot be divided by direction of effect.) The table is laid out similarly to that for the United States studies. It begins with the characteristics directly related to instructional expenditure per student and then treats other attributes of schools.

Table 2

Percentage distribution of estimated resource parameter coefficients from 96 studies of educational production functions: developing countries

Resources	Number of estimates	Statistically significant		Statistically insignificant
		Positive	Negative	
Real classroom resources				
Teacher–pupil ratio	30	27%	27%	46%
Teacher education	63	56	3	41
Teacher experience	46	35	4	61
Financial aggregates				
Teacher salary	13	31	15	54
Expenditures per pupil	12	50	0	50
Other resources				
Facilities	34	65	9	26

Source: Harbison and Hanushek (1992)

The studies differ from the United States studies in terms of the overall significance of the estimated school effects. Simply put, compared with the results presented in Table 1, a higher proportion of the tabulated coefficients for the 96 studies in developing countries is statistically significant. (It must be emphasized, however, that the proportion of results that are "correct"—statistically significant by conventional standards and in the right direction—never reaches two-thirds; moreover, the general conclusion of no strong evidence of a systematic relationship between these factors and performance will not change.) The relative robustness in statistical findings could reflect analysis of settings where there is either greater variation in the tabulated educational inputs or greater sensitivity to these inputs by students. Alternatively, the differences could reflect attributes and, specifically, biases of the analyses themselves.

The evidence in Table 2 from developing countries provides no support for policies of reducing class sizes. Of the 30 studies investigating teacher–pupil ratios, only eight find statistically significant results supporting smaller classes; an equal number are significant but have the opposite sign; and almost half are statistically insignificant. These findings are particularly interesting because class sizes in the studies of developing countries are considerably more varied than those in the United States studies and thus pertain to a wider set of environments.

The analysis of the effect of teacher experience yields results that are roughly similar to those in the United States studies. Although 35 percent of the studies display significant positive benefits from more teaching experience (the analogous figure for United States studies is 29 percent), the majority of the estimated coefficients still are statistically insignificant. The primary difference between the two sets of tabulations arises from the relative support implied for the different school inputs. The United States studies are the most supportive of the conventional wisdom regarding the effects of teacher experience on performance. Similar support compared to other factors is not found in developing country studies.

The results for teacher education, on the other hand, diverge in relative terms from those seen for the United States. A majority of the studies (35 out of 63) support the conventional notion that providing more education for teachers is valuable. In the United States studies, teacher education provided the least support of all the inputs for the conventional wisdom. Although still surrounded by considerable uncertainty (since 26 estimates are insignificant and 2 display significantly negative effects), these noticeably stronger results in developing countries clearly suggest a possible differentiation by stage of development and general level of resources available.

The teacher salary findings in developing countries contain no compelling support for the notion that better teachers are systematically paid more. Since the studies aggregate findings across very different countries, school organizations, and labor markets, however, it is difficult to take these results too far. For policy purposes, it would be desirable to seek information on what happens if the entire salary schedule is altered (as opposed to simply moving along a given schedule denominated, say, in experience, education, or other attributes of teachers). It is impossible to distinguish, however, between studies reflecting differences in schedules and those reflecting movements along a schedule.

Data for total expenditure per pupil are rarely available in analyses of education in developing countries. The 12 studies in which estimates can be found are evenly split between statistically significant and statistically insignificant. Given questions about the quality of the underlying data, not too much should be inferred from the findings for direct expenditure measures.

One of the clearest divergences between the two sets of findings is for facilities, again suggesting that differences in school environments are of some importance. The measures of facilities in developing countries (which incorporate a wide range of actual variables in specific studies) indicate more likely effects on student performance than found in United States studies. Some 22 of the 34 investigations demonstrate support for the provision of quality buildings and libraries.

In summary, the results of studies in developing countries do not make a compelling case for specific input policies. They do, however, indicate that direct school resources might be important in developing countries. Nevertheless, as in the United States research, the estimated models of educational performance undoubtedly fail to capture many of the truly important inputs to the educational process.

5. Other Factors—Developing Countries

As with the United States studies, a variety of other factors has been investigated in the course of the analyses of developing countries, including an assortment of curriculum issues, instructional methods, and teacher training programs. Many of these are difficult to assess (at least in a quantitative, comparative way) given the evidence from many countries and the probable importance of local institutions.

One intervention that has widespread endorsement, although as much for conceptual reasons as for solid empirical ones, is the provision of textbooks. The relationship of textbooks and writing materials to student performance is found with reasonable consistency to be important in developing countries, but there are relatively few studies of this (see Lockheed and Hanushek 1988, Lockheed and Verspoor 1989).

Investigations of technological or organizational differences have led to mixed results. Because of scattered settlement in many rural areas, several approaches to "distance education" have been invest-igated. In three extensive investigations (Nicaragua, Kenya, and Thailand), the use of interactive radio has proved effective (Lockheed and Hanushek 1988). However, this conclusion should not be generalized to all possible uses of new technology. In particular, there is little evidence at this time that the widespread introduction of computers is sensible (Lockheed and Verspoor 1989).

6. Conclusion—Implications for Policy

Somewhat surprisingly, perhaps, the available re-search from both developed and developing countries leads to many of the same conclusions. Two potential policy conclusions spring immediately from the over-all results. First, since within the current institutional structure expenditures are not systematically related to performance, policies should not be dictated simply on the basis of expenditure. Second, since common surrogates for teacher and school quality—class size, teachers' education, and teachers' experience being among the most important—are not systematically related to performance, policies should not be dictated simply on the basis of such surrogates.

Moreover, these results strongly suggest that poli-cies based solely on inputs—such as general reduc-tions in class size or uniform increases in spending—are unlikely to be successful. This underscores the importance of moving toward policies based on performance; that is, output-based policies. Such poli-cies would emphasize the importance of performance incentives (see Hanushek et al. 1994).

See also: Effective Schools Research: Methodological Is-sues; Needs Assessment; Policy-oriented Research; Re-source Allocation in Schools and School Systems; School Size and Small Schools; Trends in Quantitative Research Methods

References

Armor D et al. 1976 *Analysis of the School Preferred Reading Program in Selected Los Angeles Minor-ity Schools.* R-2007-LAUSD, Rand Corporation, Santa Monica, California

Bowles S, Levin H M 1968 The determinants of scholastic achievement: An appraisal of some recent evidence. *J. Hum. Resources* 3(1): 3–24

Chubb J E, Hanushek E A 1990 Reforming educational reform. In: Aaron H J (ed.) 1990 *Setting National Pri-orities: Policy for the Nineties.* Brookings Institution, Washington, DC

Coleman J S et al. 1966 *Equality of Educational Opportunity.* US Government Printing Office, Washington, DC

Fuller B 1985 *Raising School Quality in Developing Coun-tries: What Investments Boost Learning?* Report No. EDT7, Education and Training Series, World Bank, Washington, DC

Hanushek E A 1971 Teacher characteristics and gains in student achievement: Estimation using micro-data. *Am. Econ. Rev.* 61(2): 280–88

Hanushek E A 1979 Conceptual and empirical issues in the estimation of educational production functions. *J. Hum. Resources* 14(3): 351–88

Hanushek E A 1981 Throwing money at schools. *J. Policy Analysis and Management* 1(1): 19–41

Hanushek E A 1986 The economics of schooling: Produc-tion and efficiency in public schools. *J. Econ. Lit.* 24: 1141–77

Hanushek E A 1989 The impact of differential expenditures on school performance. *Educ. Res.* 18(4): 45–51

Hanushek E A 1992 The trade-off between child quantity and quality. *J. Pol. Econ.* 100(1): 84–117

Hanushek E A et al. 1994 *Making Schools Work: Im-proving Performance and Controlling Costs.* Brookings, Washington, DC

Hanushek E A 1997 Assessing the effects of resources on student performance: An update. *Educ. Eval. Policy Anal.* 19(2)

Hanushek E A, Kain J F 1972 On the value of "equality of educational opportunity" as a guide to public policy. In: Mosteller F, Moynihan D P (eds.) 1972 *On Equality of Educational Opportunity.* Random House, New York

Harbison R W, Hanushek E A 1992 *Educational Perfor-mance of the Poor: Lessons from Rural Northeast Brazil.* Oxford University Press, New York

Jamison D, Lau L 1982 *Farmer Education and Farm Efficiency.* Johns Hopkins University Press, Baltimore, Maryland

Lockheed M E, Verspoor A 1989 *Improving Primary Edu-cation in Developing Countries: A Review of Policy Options.* World Bank, Washington, DC

Lockheed M E, Hanushek E A 1988 Improving Educational efficiency in developing countries: What do we know? *Compare* 18(1): 21–38

Murnane R J 1975 *Impact of School Resources on the Learning of Inner City Children.* Ballinger, Cambridge, Massachusetts

Murnane R J, Philips B 1981 What do effective teachers of inner-city children have in common? *Soc. Sci. Res.* 10(1): 83–100

Welch F 1970 Education in production. *J. Pol. Econ.* 78(1): 35–59

Effective Schools Research: Methodological Issues

J. D. Willms and S. W. Raudenbush

Since the 1960s researchers have been trying to identify the policies and practices that contribute to successful school performance. Research in several countries has shown that schools differ in their outcomes, even after taking account of the characteristics of pupils attending them (Gray 1989, Raudenbush and Willms 1991). But efforts to determine why schools differ have been less successful. Some of the early studies in this area suggested that the effects of school resources and organizational factors were weak, and a number of studies produced inconsistent or inconclusive findings (Bridge et al. 1979). Research in this domain entails several complex methodological issues, which probably contributed to the failure to identify the attributes of effective schools. This entry discusses developments in educational measurement, research design, and statistical techniques which have enabled researchers to address these issues.

Research on effective schools has been based on a theory that presumes schooling outcomes are affected by pupils' ability, their family background, and their experiences at school. The goal of the research has been to determine whether schools vary in their outcomes after taking account of ability and background and, if so, whether particular school policies and practices account for these differences. The research has been criticized as being atheoretical because it failed to specify the links between particular school policies and classroom instruction (Barr and Dreeben 1983). Also, the research treated many complex schooling processes as unidimensional concepts, and examined only their direct effects on outcomes. Factors such as "principal leadership" or "teacher morale" are multifaceted and are difficult to define and measure (Anderson 1982, Boyd 1983). Some factors have relatively weak direct effects on schooling outcomes, but are important in that they create a school atmosphere conducive to learning (Rosenholtz 1989). The study of schooling processes requires a multilevel formulation because factors at different levels of the schooling system can affect outcomes, and their effects can interact across levels (Meyer 1980). The identification of schooling outcomes is also problematic. Some educators contend that the emphasis on academic achievement has deterred educators from critically examining the goals of schooling, and how they might best accomplish these goals. Thus, the extent to which research in this domain is productive depends first on the adequacy of theories about how schools work. Valid measurement, strong designs, and powerful statistical techniques require a solid theoretical foundation.

Nearly all studies of school effects have been, in essence, quasi-experiments with pupils receiving different "treatments" in their respective schools. Some of the designs are nested, with sets of schools each applying a certain treatment (e.g., different approaches to school organization, public or private schools). The researcher observes pupil outcomes after treatment, and asks whether differences in outcomes are related to differences in treatment. Such designs are quasi-experimental because pupils are not randomly assigned to schools. Cook and Campbell (1979) described a number of threats to the validity of this and other types of quasi-experiments. The most important threats to the validity of studies of school effectiveness concern the definition and measurement of schooling constructs, the differential selection of pupils into different types of schools, and the nested structure of the schooling system. During the 1980s researchers developed promising techniques for ameliorating these threats. These techniques are discussed below.

1. Definition and Measurement of Schooling Constructs

Many studies of school effectiveness have been based on data collected by school districts or government bodies as part of their general monitoring systems. These data are often derived from multipurpose surveys designed to serve a number of constituents. Usually these surveys emphasize contextual and setting variables such as school size, pupil–teacher ratio, racial balance, and levels of education of the staff. Generally the information pertaining to school processes has been too "thin" to be useful for explaining why some schools perform better than others. Researchers have recognized the need to collect detailed information on the climate or culture of a school. Recent work has attempted to describe the inner workings of school life: how pupils are organized for instruction, the relationship between curriculum and instructional activities, the formal and informal rules influencing behavior, the interactions between pupils and staff, and the values, expectations, and attitudes they hold. Rather than collecting thin data for a large sample of schools and pupils, some researchers have attempted to obtain detailed information on one or two school processes for a small number of pupils and schools.

Plewis's (1991) study of curriculum coverage in 42 English primary classrooms serves as an example. Results from some national studies had suggested that the match between the intended and enacted curriculum was one of the most important school processes (Lee and Bryk 1989, McKnight et al. 1987). Plewis and his colleagues asked teachers to identify which curricular items in written language and mathematics had been covered by each of the sixth-year (P6) pupils during the year. Plewis's analysis of the pre- and post-test scores in mathematics showed that pupils made more progress when information on their initial achievement was used to group children for instruction, and when the curriculum was closely matched to initial levels of achievement. Because the researchers had collected detailed information on this process, they were able to show that gains in achievement were not simply a function of how much of the curriculum had been covered.

A number of studies have shown the need to control also for the social composition of schools (see Willms 1986 for a review). The aggregate characteristics of a school, such as the average socioeconomic status (SES) of its pupils, have an effect on pupils' outcomes over and above pupils' individual characteristics. This effect, referred to as a "contextual effect," is not fully understood. Researchers are attempting to discern whether there is some critical proportion of high-ability or high-SES pupils necessary for a positive contextual effect, whether the effect is the same for different types of pupils, and whether the effect is confounded by other school factors such as disciplinary climate or teachers' expectations.

Work is also underway to improve the measurement of schooling outcomes. Most previous studies limited their outcome measures to achievement tests of basic skills, often to tests of reading and arithmetic. Few studies employed measures pertaining to the social, personal, and vocational goals of schooling. Many educators have argued that the multiple-choice tests that are commonly used in school effectiveness studies emphasize lower order skills that are isolated from a wider context. These critics have called for more "authentic" forms of assessment based on longer term accomplishments (Wolf et al. 1991). These include, for example, in-depth projects, journals, portfolios, recitals, debates, and oral presentations. The challenge for researchers is to collect data that are more directly related to what is taught and learned in school. These data will inevitably be more expensive to collect, and therefore researchers require designs that are powerful even with small samples of pupils and schools.

2. Promising Approaches to Design

Another major threat to the validity of studies of school effectiveness is selection bias. Selection bias occurs when schools differ in their intakes, such that estimates of the effects of attendance at particular schools are biased by differences in the background and aptitude of the pupils entering the schools. Also,

estimates of the effects of particular policies or practices are affected by differences among schools in their intakes (Raudenbush and Willms 1995).

2.1 True Experiments

The best method of controlling for differences among groups is to randomly assign pupils to schools, and schools to treatment conditions. However, "true" experiments of the effects of educational policies and practices are the exception, not the norm. Often political considerations override the desire for valid and reliable assessment. In some settings, though, researchers have been able to conduct true experiments. A notable example in the United States is the Tennessee study of the effects of class size on primary school pupils' achievement, self-concept, and academic motivation (Finn and Achilles 1990). The researchers randomly assigned pupils to one of three types of classes: small (13–17 pupils), regular (22–25 pupils), and regular with a teacher aide. Teachers were also assigned randomly to three class types. Their design ensured that teacher and school effects were not confounded with the effects of class size. Test results at the end of the first grade indicated large and statistically significant effects of class size on achievement. Moreover, the design was powerful enough to detect differences in the class size effect for minority and White pupils.

2.2 Longitudinal Designs with Repeated Measures on Pupils

Without random assignment, researchers can address the problem of selection bias by collecting data on pupils' ability and family background, and making a statistical adjustment for schooling intake. There are several adjustment techniques (Anderson et al. 1980); regression techniques, particularly analysis of covariance, are most common. Researchers have shown that measures of family socioeconomic status (e.g., prestige of parents' occupation, levels of parental education, family income) are by themselves insufficient; measures of pupils' academic achievement or general ability upon entry to school are also necessary. Cross-sectional data tend to yield biased estimates of the effects of schools (Willms 1992). The necessity for longitudinal data that include a premeasure of ability or achievement suggests that most of the earlier studies of school effectiveness produced biased findings. It also implies that many of the comparisons made among schools, districts, or states using cross-sectional data on school performance are misleading and invalid.

In making a statistical adjustment for prior achievement or ability, researchers are attempting to ask whether schools differ in the rate at which pupils acquire knowledge and skills, and whether differences among schools are attributable to policy and practice. A more direct way of examining learning rates is to collect data on the same set of pupils on at least three occasions (Bryk and Raudenbush 1987, Willett 1988). With this design, pupils are tested with the same test, or with a parallel form of the test, on each occasion. Alternatively, the researcher can use a set of vertically equated tests which map scores onto a long continuous scale covering several years of schooling.

Designs that provide estimates of individual growth rates have several advantages over cross-sectional or two-time point designs. For example, Bryk and Raudenbush (1988) examined the rate of pupil growth in reading and mathematics from grades one to three for a sample of over 600 pupils in the Sustaining Effects Study. Their research showed that the variation among schools in their pupils' growth rates was considerably larger than in pupils' status at a particular grade level. With a similar design, Willms and Jacobsen (1990) examined pupils' growth in three separate domains of mathematics skills between grades four and seven. The work showed that males and females varied in their patterns of growth in each domain, even though average differences between the sexes were small. Variation in growth rates was related to pupils' age at entry to primary school, their cognitive ability, and the school they attended. Both studies suggested that researchers' attempts to uncover the effects of school policies and practices are more likely to meet with success if they have longitudinal data covering three or four years.

2.3 Longitudinal Designs with Repeated Measures on Schools

Another way of strengthening the quasi-experimental design is to use data describing schooling inputs, processes, and outcomes for successive cohorts of pupils attending the same set of schools. The aim of the design is to determine whether changes in school performance are associated with changes in school policy and practice. The longitudinal design is stronger because each school essentially serves as its own control.

Schools vary in their performance from year to year for a number of reasons. Some of the variation is due to changes in school organization, and to changes in the involvement and effort of school staff. But some of the variation is due to changes in the social and economic conditions of the wider community, or due to measurement error or random fluctuations associated with the interests and abilities of particular cohorts of pupils. In earlier work, the authors set out a design for separating variation due to policy and practice from other sources of variation (Willms and Raudenbush 1989). The design provided estimates of each school's effect on each occasion, and its long-term average effect. It also provided estimates of the effects of policies and practices on changes in school performance. This design was applied to data describing pupils' attainment in one Scottish education authority's secondary schools. The results suggested that the authority's effort to reduce

differences among schools in their mean SES resulted in smaller variation among schools in their performance.

3. Multilevel Analysis

The policies and practices that affect schooling outcomes are implemented in organizational settings (e.g., classrooms and schools) which are nested within a hierarchical structure (e.g., school districts or educational authorities). Moreover, the actions of educators and policymakers at one level of the system affect processes at other levels. Researchers have long debated whether the pupil, classroom, or school was the correct unit of analysis for assessing school effects. Most analyses ignored the hierarchical structure of educational data. However, advances in statistics and computing have provided appropriate multilevel statistical methods for analyzing hierarchical data (Aitkin and Longford 1986, Goldstein 1995, Raudenbush and Bryk 1986).

The new statistical and methodological techniques have generated another wave of school effectiveness studies (Raudenbush and Willms 1991). The work has been directed at answering four principal questions, set out by Willms (1992 p. 178): (a) To what extent do schools vary in their outcomes? (b) To what extent do outcomes vary for pupils of differing status? (c) What school policies and practices improve levels of schooling outcomes? (d) What school policies and practices reduce inequalities in outcomes between high- and low-status groups?

The same set of questions can be asked of other organizational units, such as the school district or classroom. The first two questions concern quality and equity. They require only descriptive techniques; however, they are often extended to ask how much schools vary after adjusting for pupils' family background. The last two questions concern the *causes* of quality and equity.

The underlying logic of multilevel models is that data at one level (e.g., pupils) are fit to a regression model within each of a number of second-level units (e.g., schools). Parameter estimates for the first-level regressions then become dependent variables in second-level regressions fit to data describing the second-level units. The estimation technique combines the regression models for both levels into a single multilevel model, and estimates the parameters simultaneously.

Lockheed and Longford's (1991) study of primary school effectiveness in Thailand provides an example of the basic two-level model. They employed data from the International Association for the Evaluation of Educational Achievement's Second International Math Study, which covered over 4,000 pupils. At the first level they regressed pupils' mathematics scores on a number of pupil-level background variables (mathematics pretest, age, sex, father's occupation, mother's education, and a number of attitudinal variables). The pretest was the most important control variable. Before entering any school-level variables, they addressed the first two questions above. The multilevel model provided estimates of the extent to which background-adjusted school means vary across schools, and the extent to which outcome/pretest regression slopes vary across schools. The background-adjusted means are an indicator of quality: they are the expected score for pupils with average initial achievement and average background. The slopes are an indicator of equity: they show whether schools exaggerate or reduce initial differences in achievement. Lockheed and Longford (1991) found that the schools varied significantly in their background-adjusted means: the highest background-adjusted means were about eight points higher than the lowest adjusted means (standard deviation=2.224) for a test that had a pupil-level standard deviation of about nine points. However, the researchers did not find significant differences among schools in their outcome/pretest slopes.

Variables describing a number of school-level characteristics were then added to the model in an attempt to explain the significant variation among background-adjusted school means. These included a number of variables describing the school setting (e.g., school size, student–teacher ratio, staff qualifications), and process variables describing school organization (e.g., whether the school practiced ability grouping, the time teachers spent on administration) and teacher practices (e.g., time spent on maintaining order, time on seatwork, use of materials). Their model accounted for nearly all of the among-school variation. The most important explanatory variables were the proportion of teachers who were qualified to teach mathematics, whether teachers used an enriched curriculum, and the frequent use of textbooks as opposed to workbooks.

Three-level models can also be constructed to describe effects at three levels, such as pupil-, classroom-, and school-level effects. Moreover, multilevel models can be used to depict pupils' rates of growth, or changes in school performance over time. The combination of longitudinal designs with multilevel techniques could provide a powerful means of overcoming some of the methodological problems associated with the study of schooling.

4. Interpretation

Many of the studies of school effectiveness have found statistically significant effects of certain school factors, but they have not specified the magnitude of the effects. To facilitate interpretation, it is useful to report results both as standardized "effect sizes" (Hedges and Olkin 1985), and in unadjusted units of the outcome variable. The same applies to estimates of the differences among schools or school districts in their outcomes.

5. Conclusions

Most of the research on school effectiveness has been based on quasi-experimental or correlational designs. Therefore, the validity of causal statements about relationships between schooling processes and outcomes has been easily challenged—usually there are a number of rival hypotheses. Measurement problems and selection bias have been endemic. However, the new approaches to examining questions about school effectiveness provide a stronger basis for making causal inferences.

Progress in this area will come first through the development of stronger theories about how processes at each level of the system affect processes and outcomes at other levels. The testing of these theories will require thicker data than have been typically available in large national studies. Recent studies describing school culture and climate have already contributed to our understanding of what constitutes an effective school.

Researchers now have available some powerful methods for the analysis of educational data. These methods enable researchers to study the rate at which pupils acquire skills and knowledge, and to determine the extent to which changes in school performance are related to changes in school policies and practices. The techniques also provide a systematic way to test whether schools differ in their performance, and whether they have differential effects for pupils with differing status.

See also: Education Production Functions; Needs Assessment; Trends in Quantitative Research Methods

References

Aitkin M, Longford N 1986 Statistical modelling issues in school effectiveness studies. *J. Royal Stat. Soc. A* 149(1): 1–26

Anderson C S 1982 The search for school climate: A review of the research. *Rev. Educ. Res.* 52(3): 368–420

Anderson et al. 1980 *Statistical Methods for Comparative Studies: Techniques for Bias Reduction* Wiley, New York

Barr R, Dreeben R 1983 *How Schools Work.* University of Chicago Press, Chicago, Illinois

Boyd W L 1983 What school administrators do and don't do: Implications for effective schools. *The Canadian Administrator* 22(6): 1–4

Bridge R G, Judd C M, Moock P R 1979 *The Determinants of Educational Outcomes: The Impacts of Families, Peers, Teachers, and Schools.* Ballinger, Cambridge, Massachusetts

Bryk A S, Raudenbush S W 1987 Application of hierarchical linear models to assessing change. *Psych. Bull.* 101(1): 147–58

Bryk A S, Raudenbush S W 1988 Toward a more appropriate conceptualization of research on school effects: A three-level linear model. *Am. J. Educ.* 97(1): 65–108

Cook T D, Campbell D T 1979 *Quasi-experimentation: Design and Analysis issues for Field Settings.* Rand McNally, Chicago, Illinois

Finn J D, Achilles C M 1990 Answers and questions about class size: A statewide experiment. *Am. Educ. Res. J.* 27(3): 557–77

Goldstein H 1995 *Multilevel Statistical Models*, 2nd edn. Arnold, London

Gray J 1989 Multilevel models: Issues and problems emerging from their recent application in British studies of school effectiveness. In: Bock D R (ed.) 1989 *Multilevel Analyses of Educational Data*. Academic Press, San Diego, California

Hedges L V, Olkin I 1985 *Statistical Methods for Meta-analysis*. Academic Press, San Diego, California

Lee V E, Bryk A S 1989. A multilevel model of the social distribution of high school achievement. *Sociol. Educ.* 62(3): 172–92

Lockheed M E, Longford N T 1991 School effects on mathematics achievement gain in Thailand. In: Raudenbush S W, Willms J D (eds.) 1991 *Schools, Classrooms, and Pupils: International Studies of Schooling from a Multilevel Perspective*. Academic Press, San Diego, California

McKnight C C et al. 1987 *The Underachieving Curriculum: Assessing U.S. School Mathematics from an International Perspective*. Stipes, Champaign, Illinois

Meyer J W 1980 Levels of the educational system and schooling effects. In: Bidwell C, Windham D (eds.) 1980 *The Analysis of Educational Productivity*, Vol. 2. Ballinger, Cambridge, Massachusetts

Plewis I 1991 Using multilevel models to link educational progress with curriculum coverage. In: Raudenbush S W, Willms J D (eds.) 1991 *Schools, Classrooms, and Pupils: International Studies of Schooling from a Multilevel Perspective*. Academic Press, San Diego, California

Raudenbush S W, Bryk A S 1986 A hierarchical model for studying school effects. *Sociol. Educ.* 59(1): 1–17

Raudenbush S W, Willms J D 1991 The organization of schooling and its methodological implications. In: Raudenbush S W, Willms J D (eds.) 1991 *Schools, Classrooms, and Pupils: International Studies of Schooling from a Multilevel Perspective*. Academic Press, San Diego, California

Raudenbush S W, Willms J D 1995 The estimation of school effects. *J. Educ. Behav. Stat.* 20(4): 307–35

Rosenholtz S J 1989 Workplace conditions that affect teacher quality and commitment: Implications for teacher induction programs. *Elem. Sch. J.* 89(4): 421–39

Willett J B 1988 Questions and answers in the measurement of change. In: Rothkopf E Z (ed.) 1988 *Review of Research in Education*, Vol. 15. American Educational Research Association, Washington, DC

Willms J D 1986 Social class segregation and its relationship to pupils' examination results in Scotland. *Am. Sociol. Rev.* 51(2): 224–41

Willms J D 1992 *Monitoring School Performance: A Guide for Educators*. Falmer Press, Lewes

Willms J D, Jacobsen S 1990 Growth in mathematics skills during the intermediate years: Sex differences and school effects. *Int. J. Educ. Res.* 14(2): 157–74

Willms J D, Raudenbush S W 1989 A longitudinal hierarchical linear model for estimating school effects and their stability. *J. Educ. Meas.* 26(3): 209–32

Wolf D, Bixby J, Glenn J III, Gardner H 1991 To use their minds well: Investigating new forms of student assessment. In: Grant G (ed.) 1991 *Review of Research in Education*, Vol. 17. American Educational Research Association, Washington, DC

Feminist Research Methodology

B. D. Haig

Since the 1960s, feminist scholars have made significant contributions to educational and social science research methodology. These contributions are varied in nature and wide-ranging in scope. This article describes and evaluates some of the central developments in feminist methodology that are relevant to educational research. These include: (a) the feminist critique of standard empiricist research; (b) a consideration of methods used by feminist researchers; (c) the three major feminist epistemologies and their methodological implications; and (d) the relevance of pragmatist thought for the further development of feminist methodology.

1. Is There a Distinctive Feminist Methodology?

A number of feminist researchers have debated the issue of whether there is a distinctive feminist methodology. Interestingly, few feminists have claimed that there is, or could be, though Reinharz (1983) has developed a communal approach to research called "experiential analysis," contending that it is distinctively feminist in character. However, most feminists appear to accept the view that it is a mistake to portray feminist methodology as distinctive. Clegg (1985) contends that there is no unified feminist methodology and that attempts to suggest otherwise run the risk of missing the real value of feminist contributions. Peplau and Conrad (1989) evaluate a number of proposals for distinctively feminist methods and conclude that any method can be misused in sexist ways. Similarly, Harding (1989) argues that attempts to identify a distinctively feminist method are misguided. She contends that feminist researchers use a variety of existing research methods, adapted to their own purposes, and that the arguments against a specifically feminist methodology are largely beside the point.

2. Common Features of Feminist Methodology

Although feminist methodology comprises a diversity of offerings, a number of common themes have been identified in presentations of feminist methodology (e.g., Cook and Fonow 1986, Mies 1983). The following features are often included in these presentations:

2.1 The Rejection of Positivism

Despite their many disagreements, feminist methodologists appear united in their opposition to the many positivist strands of orthodox educational and social science research.

This opposition ranges from efforts to improve on standard empiricism's positivist image by the development of a feminist empiricism, through the endorsement of extant postempiricist methodologies such as the "new" social psychology of Harré and Secord (Wilkinson 1986), to the extreme postpositivism of skeptical postmodernism (Rosenau 1992). The common features of feminist methodology mentioned immediately below are a part of its postpositivist commitments.

2.2 The Pervasive Influence of Gender Relations

Probably the most central feature of feminist methodology is its ubiquitous concern with gender. It is because of differences in the social position and power of women and men that gender relations are held to pervade social life. For this reason feminist researchers are committed to describing, explaining, and otherwise interpreting the female world. From these considerations feminist methodology has urged researchers to acknowledge and portray women's experiences, to identify the patriarchal bias of orthodox research and, relatedly, to assess the ways in which gender relations impact on the conduct of research (Cook and Fonow 1986).

2.3 The Value-ladenness of Science

The persistent positivist myth that science is value-free has never been true to science and has been repeatedly challenged by feminist scholars. From their belief that science is a human social endeavor, feminists maintain that such inquiry takes on the values of the people who do the research as well as the values of the institutions that sustain it. Positivist empiricist research has been undertaken to produce secure factual knowledge bereft of explanatory power, which has served to maintain the status quo in respect of women's oppression. In stressing the value-ladenness of research, feminist methodologists have also been concerned to articulate a feminist ethic (Cook and Fonow 1986) that is concerned with the way gender-biased language subordinates women, the fairness of practices which prevent the publication of feminist research and stifle career opportunities, and problems of researcher intervention into participatory research relationships.

2.4 The Adoption of Liberatory Methodology

The feminist movement characterizes itself as being primarily concerned with the emancipation of women from oppression. In consequence, it is often claimed that research-based knowledge should be employed to help liberate women from their oppression. Mies (1983) forcefully expresses this view by claiming that, in order to change the status quo, feminists must integrate their research with an active participation in the struggle against women's oppression. Consistent with this, Mies claims further that the worth of a theory is to be judged, not through the application of methodological principles, but on its ability to assist the emancipatory process.

Liberatory methodologists are often critical of the use of attitude surveys in gathering knowledge about women on the grounds that they tell us little about women's true consciousness. In formulating a liberatory methodology, feminists have sometimes insisted that the research process must become a process of "conscientization" in Freire's (1972) sense (Mies 1983, Lather 1988). This process involves "learning to perceive social, political, and economic contradictions, and to take action against the oppressive elements of reality" (Freire 1972 p. 15). As a problem-solving methodology, conscientization involves the study of oppressive reality by the subjects of oppression, where the social science researchers give their research resources to the oppressed so that they can formulate and come to understand their own problems. In these ways feminist liberatory methodology is seen to issue in action research.

2.5 The Pursuit of Nonhierarchical Research Relationships

A fifth common feature of feminist methodology is its strong endorsement of a nonhierarchical relationship between the researcher and the researched. This contrasts with positivist empiricism's penchant for assigning the researcher a position of epistemic privilege. In particular, feminist methodology seeks to replace the epistemic privilege of the professional researcher by democratic participatory inquiry where the researcher and researched enter into a social relationship of reciprocity in which there is a complementary recognition of their equal agency. The establishment of a relationship of nonhierarchy also requires the replacement of a spectator view of knowledge with "conscious partiality" (Mies 1983) which the researcher achieves by partially identifying with the researched. Because the identification is not complete, the mutual correction of distortions remains possible.

3. Research Methods

The conclusion that there are no distinctively feminist research methods is borne out by the widespread use of a variety of existing research methods by feminist researchers. However, feminist researchers tend to view these methods critically and deploy them in the light of their particular value commitments.

3.1 Experimentation

Feminists have criticized the use of experimental methods in the social sciences, both for assigning power and privilege to experimenters in their relationships with subjects, and for the artificiality of the laboratory experiment with its simplification of context (e.g., Parlee 1979). For these reasons, feminist methodologists have tended to favor nonexperimental methods in natural settings. However, it should be noted that a plausible case has been advanced by Greenwood (1989) for the constructive use of role-playing experiments in social psychological contexts in a way that can avoid the artificiality of altered social relations in laboratory experiments.

3.2 Meta-analysis

The extended history of research on gender differences has entered its latest phase with the adoption of meta-analytic procedures to summarize the disparate findings of numerous empirical studies in this controversial area. Meta-analysis is a recently developed approach to research integration that involves the statistical analysis of the results of data analyses from many individual studies in a given domain in order to synthesize those findings. Some (e.g., Hyde 1990) see meta-analysis making a significant contribution to feminist research by providing strong quantitative conclusions about the extent and magnitude of gender differences. However, the empiricist basis of its most popular form should temper the widespread view that meta-analysis is a powerful method of research synthesis.

3.3 Ethnography

With the tendency of feminist methodologists to recommend qualitative methods over quantitative alternatives, ethnographic methods have frequently been used by feminist researchers. Such methods are attractive because they acknowledge the importance of the research context, focus on the experiential reports of women, and seek collaborative relationships between the researcher and researched. Glaser and Strauss's grounded theory perspective on ethnography (e.g., Strauss 1987) has been used by a number of feminist social science researchers. Their approach to qualitative research breaks from the prevalent hypothetico-deductive practice of testing existing theories and encourages researchers to generate their own theories inductively to explain patterns in systematically obtained data. However, while acknowledging the methodological advantages that accrue to such ethnographic perspectives on the research process, some feminists worry about the possibilities of serious exploitation, betrayal, and abandonment of the re-search subject by the researcher in their collaborative relationship (e.g., Stacey 1988).

4. Methodology and Epistemology

In the early 1980s, feminism seemed more willing to spell out its methodology than develop its theory of knowledge. However, since then developments in feminist methodology have proceeded more slowly than advances in feminist epistemology. Indeed, much of the content in feminist methodological writings has come to focus on general epistemological issues implicated in the feminist critiques of positivist research and the proposed alternatives. A consideration of feminist methodology, therefore, requires one to attend to the relevant epistemological literature. Harding (1986) has distinguished three major alternative feminist epistemologies: feminist empiricism, feminist standpoint epistemology, and feminist postmodernism. A good deal of debate in feminist methodology in the early 1990s involves the ongoing elaboration and evaluation of these positions.

4.1 Feminist Empiricism

Although some feminist scholars have criticized the positivist features of traditional science and sought to replace postpositivist science with a feminist successor, others have looked to reshape traditional science in the belief that it can serve feminist ends. "Feminist empiricism," as the modified account has been called, contends that the sexism and androcentrism evident in much research are social biases that result from doing bad science, but that they can be overcome, or minimized, by following the methodological norms of good orthodox science.

The attainment of these norms has been sought by the construction of guidelines for the conduct of gender-fair research (e.g., Eichler 1988), and by efforts to identify and guard against gender differences in the sex composition of research participants as well as assessment of treatment conditions for gender neutrality.

Feminist research has sanctioned the continued use of many standard experimental, quasiexperimental, and observational methods, as well as a variety of qualitative methods, but with a heightened appreciation of the importance of bias in the deployment of these methods. New methods have also been enthusiastically accepted as improvements on the acknowledged limitations of older methods. For example, meta-analytic review procedures have been employed as a more effective gauge of gender differences than traditional tests of statistical significance (Hyde 1990).

Although research from a feminist empiricist perspective helps to include women in science and can contribute to the improvement of conventional science, it has been criticized for improving the "masculinist conception of objectivity" (Heckman

1990 p. 129) and for ignoring the important connection between science and politics.

4.2 Feminist Standpoint Epistemology

Feminist standpoint epistemologies are seen by their adherents to undergird a successor science that overcomes the inadequacies of both traditional empiricist science and its feminist improvement. In contrast to feminist empiricism, feminist standpoint theorists contend that the characteristics of researchers are crucial determinants of their understanding of reality. Drawing from Marxist, and/or psychoanalytic theorizing about gender, feminist standpoint epistemologies regard the subjugated social position of women as a privileged vantage point from which to view social reality. One explanation for women's epistemic privilege draws from object relations theory within psychoanalysis and claims that the formation of a distinctively female identity in infancy leads to a distinctive and superior form of knowing than that of men. However, the idea that women have a superior ability to reflect on and comprehend reality has been criticized by feminists and nonfeminists alike. For example, object relations theory has been judged to have weak evidential support, while the general claim of women as better knowers has been criticized as an untenable endorsement of cognitive privilege (Chandler 1990).

4.3 Feminist Postmodernism

Feminist postmodernism rejects the epistemological assumptions of modernist, Enlightenment thought. Thus, it stands opposed to the foundationalist grounding of knowledge, the universalizing claims for the scope of knowledge, and the employment of dualistic categories of thought. By contrast, postmodern feminism is an epistemology that is non-foundationalist, contextualist, and nondualist, or multiplist, in its commitments.

Feminist postmodernists sometimes maintain that language cannot really be used to refer, predicate, identify, and individuate an extralinguistic reality. This view of language underwrites an approach to discourse analysis research which substitutes the study of texts for the broader study of social reality.

Critics of postmodern feminism (e.g., Hawkesworth 1989) argue that this flight to the text is inconsistent with its radical political aspirations. To shift the focus from the study of oppression suffered by women to the interpretation of texts is to abandon the real world for a relativist world of ideas. It is maintained that such a retreat can only serve to reinforce the status quo.

5. A Pragmatist Turn

Harding (1986) believes that because of the unstable nature of the categories they use, feminists should accommodate the tensions between these alternative epistemologies for now. However, Nelson (1990) has combined important insights from Quine's influential philosophy of science with feminist criticisms of science, to formulate an enriched feminist empiricism that she believes has the ability to resolve the differences among these epistemologies. With Quine, Nelson rejects foundationalist thinking and maintains that science should justify its claims in accordance with a coherence theory of evidence. While foundationalism maintains that theories are justified by being appropriately related to some privileged source, such as observation statements, coherentism maintains that knowledge claims are justified in virtue of their coherence with other accepted beliefs.

Relatedly, Nelson's neo-Quinean perspective regards knowledge as a seamless web with no boundaries between science, metaphysics, methodology, and epistemology. Thus, philosophy does not lie outside science, but is instead contained in, and is interdependent with, other parts of science. From this perspective it can be appreciated that epistemologies and methodologies do not function in isolation, but actually make metaphysical commitments. Traditional empiricist methodology, for example, regards the knower as an abstract and autonomous individual. However, Nelson breaks with Quine at this point and, by joining science and politics, she insists that it is communities rather than individuals who know; that it is the standards of a community that determines what counts as evidence for a knowledge claim.

Feminist scholars have been criticized for seeking distinctively feminist conceptions of science. Lakomski (1989), for example, has criticized Harding for pursuing such a project and suggests that progress in feminist theorizing will come from a consideration of mainstream epistemology and philosophy of science. Indeed, Nelson's radical feminist empiricism may be viewed in part as an advancement of the feminist understanding of science by exploiting Quinean epistemology.

6. Pragmatist Realist Methodology

Seigfried (1991) has lamented the fact that United States feminists have not appropriated their own country's philosophy of pragmatism, a philosophy that has resources suitable for the development of feminist theory. Of importance, however, is the fact that a number of writers in a pragmatist realist tradition have made significant contributions to methodology that are suitable for appropriation by feminist and other postpositivist researchers. This section of the article outlines some of these developments and briefly links them to feminist concerns about methodology.

6.1 Research Problems

In her forceful plea for overcoming the uncritical employment of method, Daly (1973) suggests that the common practice of having the research problem determined by the method should be reversed so that the method is chosen to fit the problem. However, this reasonable suggestion fails to depict research adequately as a problem-solving enterprise.

Nickles (1981) has developed a constraint inclusion theory of problems which assigns to scientific problems a positive methodological role. On this account a problem is taken to comprise all the constraints on the solution (plus the demand that the solution be found). With this theory the constraints do not lie outside the problem, but are constitutive of the problem itself; they actually serve to characterize the problem and give it structure. This constraint inclusion account of problems stresses the fact that, in good scientific research, problems typically evolve from an ill-structured state and eventually attain a degree of well-formedness, such that their solution becomes possible. Incorporating such an account of problems into research method itself allows the problem to guide inquiry and explain how it is possible.

6.2 Generative Methodology

Most traditional philosophies of science have insisted on drawing a strong distinction between the context of discovery and the context of justification. The context of discovery is concerned with the origin of scientific hypotheses and is thought to be a psychological, but not a methodological, affair. The context of justification is concerned with the validation of hypotheses and is the domain to which methodology properly belongs. Some feminist methodologists such as Harding (1989), for example, have argued that understanding the origin of scientific hypotheses requires one to admit that methodology can rightly operate in the context of discovery. Other advocates of discovery have argued for the same conclusion. This traditional methodological distinction, combined with the dominance of the hypothetico-deductive method, has resulted in a half methodology whereby researchers evaluate knowledge claims solely in terms of their consequences.

However, a methodology adequate to the full range of scientific reasoning must supplement consequentialism with a conception of methodology that is also generative in nature. In contrast to consequentialist thinking, generative methodologies reason to, and accept, the knowledge claims in question from warranted premises (Nickles 1987). The widely used procedure of exploratory factor analysis serves as an example of a method that facilitates generative reasoning by helping to reason forward from correlational data to the plausible factorial theories that they occasion. The endorsement of generative methodologies will be an essential part of feminist methodologists' resolve to acknowledge and scrutinize the entire research process.

6.3 Heuristics

Feminists frequently have criticized positivist empiricism for its rather idealized portrayal of the researcher as a computationally adept being whose behavior is strongly guided by rules. However, this unrealistic picture has been rejected by pragmatist methodologists in favor of a more modest conception of themselves as knowers. A view of the researcher as a "satisficer" has been influential in this regard. The rational behavior of the satisficer is bounded by temporal, computational, and memorial constraints and, as a result, involves the frequent use of heuristic procedures. Heuristic procedures are "rules of thumb" which have the following characteristics (Wimsatt 1981): (a) the correct use of heuristics does not guarantee a correct solution, nor even that a solution will be found; (b) heuristics are cost-effective procedures, making considerably fewer demands on time, effort, and computation than equivalent algorithmic procedures; (c) errors made in using heuristic procedures are systematically biased. Glaser and Strauss's grounded theory perspective on ethnographic methodology, which has been endorsed and used by a number of feminist methodologists, makes considerable use of heuristic procedures.

6.4 Coherence Justification

Feminist scholars have frequently attacked positivist empiricism for justifying its knowledge claims by appealing to a privileged base of observational data. However, foundationalist theories of justification have been widely rejected in contemporary philosophy, and coherentist approaches to justification are being presented as an attractive option. As noted above, Nelson's (1990) neo-Quinean framework for feminist science explicitly adopts a coherence perspective on justification. Also, coherence justification has begun to receive consideration within educational research methodology (Lakomski 1991). And in an important contribution to scientific methodology, Thagard (1989) has developed a new theory of explanatory coherence that is capable of evaluating competing hypotheses in science as well as in everyday affairs. Based on principles that establish the local coherence between a hypothesis and other propositions, Thagard's approach is able to integrate considerations of explanatory breadth, simplicity, and analogy into an overall gauge of explanatory coherence. Thagard's view of theory appraisal as explanatory coherence is a significant postpositivist contribution to a neglected aspect of research methodology that can be implemented widely in areas of research that boast competing explanatory theories.

These are just some of the features of a contemporary pragmatic realist methodology. A comprehensive formulation of such a methodology has been outlined by Nickles (1987) and is exemplified in Wimsatt's (1981) study of reductionism in biology. With its rejection of the methodologies of positivist empiricism, naive realism, and strong versions of social constructivism, pragmatic realism recommends itself as an attractive option. The feminist research enterprise stands to strengthen its hand by taking the pragmatic realist turn in methodology. For its part, pragmatic realism would be enriched by assimilating the gains made by feminist methodology since the late 1970s.

7. Conclusion

Feminist social science research in the 1970s operated largely from the confines of positivist empiricist methodology, but since that time virtually all developments in feminist methodology have been critical of positivism. Feminist methodology in the early 1990s is postpositivist in a number of ways. Although some feminists have sought to develop a distinctively feminist approach to methodology, most have adapted existing research methods to their own purposes. Feminist methodology has broadened to include discussion of the three epistemologies of feminist empiricism, feminist standpoint epistemology, and feminist postmodernism. In the light of criticisms of these theories of knowledge, a pragmatic realist perspective on science recommends itself with a methodology that is appropriate for advancing feminist inquiry and social science research generally.

See also: Feminist Critiques of Educational Practices and Research; Positivism, Antipositivism, and Empiricism; Postmodernism and Education; Research in Education: Epistemological Issues

References

Chandler J 1990 Feminism and epistemology. *Metaphilosophy* 21(4): 367–81
Clegg S 1985 Feminist methodology: Fact or fiction? *Quality and Quantity* 19(1): 83–97
Cook J, Fonow M 1986 Knowledge and women's interests: Issues of epistemology and methodology in feminist sociological research. *Sociol. Inq.* 56(1): 2–29
Daly M 1973 *Beyond God the Father: Toward a Philosophy of Women's Liberation.* Beacon Press, Boston, Massachusetts
Eichler M 1988 *Nonsexist Research Methods.* Allen and Unwin, Boston, Massachusetts
Freire P 1972 *Pedagogy of the Oppressed.* Penguin, Harmondsworth
Greenwood J 1989 *Explanation and Experiment in Social Psychological Science.* Springer-Verlag, New York
Harding S 1986 *The Science Question in Feminism.* Cornell University Press, Ithaca, New York
Harding S 1989 Is there a feminist method? In: Tuana N (ed.) 1989 *Feminism and Science.* Indiana University Press, Bloomington, Indiana
Hawkesworth M 1989 Knowers, knowing, known: Feminist theory and claims of truth. *Signs* 14(3): 533–57
Heckman S 1990 *Gender and Knowledge: Elements of a Postmodern Feminism.* Polity Press, Cambridge
Hyde J E 1990 Meta-analysis and the psychology of gender differences. *Signs* 16(1): 55–73
Lakomski G 1989 Against feminist science: Harding and the science question in feminism. *Educ. Phil. Theor.* 21(2): 1–11

Lakomski G (ed.) 1991 Beyond paradigms: Coherentism and holism in educational research. *Int. J. Educ. Res.* 15(6): 499–597
Lather P 1988 Feminist perspectives on empowering research methodologies. *Womens' Studies International Forum* 11(6): 569–81
Mies M 1983 Towards a methodology for feminist research. In: Bowles G, Klein R D (eds.) 1983 *Theories of Womens' Studies.* Routledge and Kegan Paul, London
Nelson L 1990 *Who Knows: From Quine to a Feminist Empiricism.* Temple University Press, Philadelphia, Pennsylvania
Nickles T 1981 What is a problem that we might solve it? *Synthese* 47(1): 85–118
Nickles T 1987 Methodology, heuristics and rationality. In: Pitt J, Pera M (eds.) 1987 *Rational Changes in Science.* Reidel, Dordrecht
Parlee M 1979 Psychology and women. *Signs* 5(1): 121–33
Peplau L, Conrad E 1989 Beyond nonsexist research: The perils of feminist methods in psychology. *Psychol. Women Q.* 13(4): 379–400
Reinharz S 1983 Experiential analysis: A contribution to feminist research. In: Bowles G, Klein R D (eds.) 1983 *Theories of Womens Studies.* Routledge and Kegan Paul, London
Rosenau P 1992 *Postmodernism and the Social Sciences.* Princeton University Press, Princeton, New Jersey
Seigfried C 1991 Where are all the pragmatist feminists? *Hypatia* 6(2): 1–20
Stacey J 1988 Can there be a feminist ethnography? *Womens' Studies International Forum* 11(2): 21–27
Strauss A 1987 *Qualitative Analysis for Social Scientists.* Cambridge University Press, Cambridge
Thagard P 1989 Explanatory coherence. *Behav. Brain Sci.* 12(3): 435–67
Wilkinson S 1986 Sighting possibilities: Diversity and commonality in feminist research. In: Wilkinson S (ed.) 1986 *Feminist Social Psychology.* Open University Press, Milton Keynes
Wimsatt W 1981 Robustness, reliability, and overdetermination. In: Brewer M, Collins B (eds.) 1981 *Scientific Inquiry and the Social Sciences.* Jossey-Bass, San Francisco, California

Further Reading

Fonow M, Cook J (eds.) 1991 *Beyond Methodology.* Indiana University Press, Bloomington, Indiana
Jayaratne T E 1983 The value of quantitative methodology for feminist research. In: Bowles G, Duelli Kline R (eds.) 1983 *Theories of Women's Studies.* Routledge and Kegan Paul, London
Lather P 1991 *Getting Smart: Feminist Research and Pedagogy within the Postmodern.* Routledge, New York
Reinharz S 1992 *Feminist Methods in Social Research.* Oxford University Press, New York
Stanley L, Wise S 1983 *Breaking Out: Feminist Consciousness and Feminist Research.* Routledge and Kegan Paul, London
Tomm W (ed.) 1989 *The Effects of Feminist Approaches on Research Methodologies.* Wilfrid Laurier University Press, Waterloo

Needs Assessment

T. M. Suarez

Needs assessment is an information-gathering and analysis process which results in the identification of the needs of individuals, groups, institutions, communities, or societies. In education, the process of needs assessment has been used, for example, to identify the needs of students for instruction in a given subject area; to determine weaknesses in students' overall academic achievement; to determine the needs of teachers for additional training; and to determine the future needs of local, regional, and national educational systems. It is the intent of needs assessments to identify areas in which deficits exist, desired performance has not been attained, or problems may be expected in the future. The results of needs assessments are then used for further action such as planning or remediation to improve the situation.

Educational needs have been assessed and analyzed for centuries. However, formalized assessments of educational needs were not conducted on a widespread basis until the middle of the twentieth century (Suarez 1981). At that time, public and professional demands for more systematic and accountable processes of providing education led to the emergence of information-based models for educational planning and evaluation. This was particularly true in the United States where widespread federal aid to education with accompanying accountability requirements was instituted in the mid-1960s. Among the information-based processes which emerged during that time was the systematic determination of needs as a basis for program planning and development. This process was called "needs assessment."

The determination of needs is such a broad concept, applicable in so many situations, that a common conceptual model and set of needs assessment procedures have not emerged. Instead, the literature describes a number of conceptual and procedural approaches. Some are drawn from definitional and philosophic differences while others seem based on the task at hand. Major variations in needs assessments appear in: (a) the definition used for the term "need," (b) the purposes for which needs assessments are conducted, (c) the standards by which needs are identified, and (d) the strategies and procedures used in the process.

1. The Concept of Need

A variety of concepts of the term "need" are used in both the discussions and practice of needs assessment. Controversy regarding the definition of "need" for needs assessments, together with a proliferation of studies using different definitions, has limited the development of universally accepted conceptual or theoretical models of the process. The majority of needs assessment studies, however, has been based on a variation of one of three definitions of the term "need."

The most widely used definition of "need" for needs assessments is that of a discrepancy. This definition, introduced by Kaufman (1972), suggests that needs are areas in which actual status is less than targeted status. Targeted status has come to encompass ideals, norms, preferences, expectations, and perceptions of what ought to be. Needs assessments based on this definition require procedures for selecting or determining targeted status, gathering information to determine current status relative to the target status, and comparing the two to discover discrepancies and identify needs.

Another commonly used definition of "need" is that of a want or preference. Stufflebeam et al. (1985) refer to this definition as the "democratic view" of needs (i.e., a need is a change desired by a majority of some reference group). Identification of needs using this definition does not require the determination of a discrepancy. Instead, it requires determination of the perceptions of needs of selected individuals or groups. Although there are writers who oppose the use of this definition, many needs assessments are based on this definition, particularly in those situations where public and professional opinion regarding needs are used as a basis for establishing educational goals or policy.

A more stringent and less used concept of need for needs assessment studies is that of a deficit. A need is said to exist if the absence or a deficiency in the area of interest is harmful. Scriven and Roth (1978) have expanded this definition to describe a need as a state in which a minimum satisfactory level has not been reached or cannot be maintained. Few needs assessment studies have been conducted using this definition due to the difficulty in determining the point at which a deficit or minimum satisfactory level can be said to exist.

Stufflebeam et al. (1985) argue for a broader concept of need using the standard dictionary definition of a need as something that is necessary or useful for a defensible purpose. They do not see needs as objective, scientific truths but as the outcomes of human judgments, values, and interactions within a given context. Mattimore-Knudson (1983) debates the use of the term "need" altogether because of its multiple and ambiguous meanings, calling instead for a "situation assessment, identification, and analysis."

Surprisingly, the debate over the definition of

"need" does not seem to have interfered with the use of the needs assessment process. Some, such as Kaufman (1987), have built procedures around a particular definition of the term. Most, however, use a variety of procedures to help identify, assess, and analyze a current situation in order to provide direction for the future.

Original discussions of needs and the needs assessment process were based on a rational planning model which was perceived as being contaminated if personal views and values were dominant. Later writers (e.g., Witkin 1984, Guba and Lincoln 1982, and Stufflebeam et al. 1985) suggest that needs are relative to points in time, reference groups, and context, and thus cannot be described without consideration of the views, preferences, and values of the individuals whose needs are of concern, the staff of programs designed to meet needs, and the decision and policymakers who provide direction to programs and systems of services designed to address needs.

2. The Purposes of Needs Assessments

Providing information for planning is the most common reason given for conducting needs assessments. Needs assessments for planning may result in the identification of goals, the determination of the extent to which desired goals are being achieved, or the specification of areas in which efforts and resources should be placed. Such assessments may be used to develop plans for immediate action or to develop long-range plans for the future.

The diagnosis or identification of problems or weaknesses is another common purpose of needs assessments. Needs assessments for this purpose focus on identifying the areas in which the educational process or system is ineffective so that remedial actions may be taken.

Needs assessments are components of several evaluation models. These assessments are part of the evaluation process and may have as their purpose determining areas of weakness prior to the implementation of a given form of instruction or treatment, determining gaps in implementation, or determining the status of performance at intervals during the development or implementation of a treatment. The results of these assessments become part of the evaluation findings or, in the case of needs assessments prior to treatment, the basis upon which the evaluation criteria for judging the effectiveness of treatments are determined.

Needs assessments are also conducted to hold educational institutions accountable for their efforts. The most common forms of these types of needs assessments are mandated large-scale assessments of student educational outcomes. Results of these assessments are used to determine if the educational efforts of schools or school systems are effective and to iden-tify subject areas or locations in which educational achievements are less than desired.

3. Common Standards by which Educational Needs are Identified

When planning is the purpose of a needs assessment, educational goals are often the standards against which status is compared to determine needs. A common practice for these types of needs assessments is the determination of goals prior to the assessment of needs. When goals have been determined, the needs assessment is then conducted to determine if there are discrepancies between identified goals and current status. The process of goal determination involves identifying the individuals and/or groups who should participate in the determination of goals and involving them in the process. Two major procedures for goal determination are usually used: (a) generating the set of goals, and (b) selecting goals from present lists of goal statements. When goals already exist in the area of interest, this step is omitted and current status is compared to the existing goals.

Norms are another standard often used in the determination of educational needs. The norms most often used are those associated with standardized tests. Needs are determined by comparing performance on the tests with existing norms, that is, the performance of the population upon which the test was standardized. Other norms used for needs assessments are previous behaviors of similar groups, for example, number of graduates entering college in previous years.

Minimum satisfactory level is another standard used for needs assessments. Determining minimum satisfactory levels of performance requires determining the level of performance at which goals cannot be met or harm due to educational deficits will be the result. These types of standards are most often applied in biological and medical situations and are based on research evidence or experience. There is little research evidence regarding the minimum level of education that is needed to predict future achievement with certainty. Most minimum educational levels are therefore determined on the basis of experience as represented by public and professional opinion.

Other standards used to determine needs are desires or wants, perceptions of what should be the status of performance, and requirements. The first two are determined by public or professional opinion. Requirements are found in existing laws, policies, and regulating procedures.

4. Needs Assessment Strategies and Procedures

Because needs assessments are conducted for a variety of reasons in many different settings and to identify many types of needs, the strategies and procedures used to conduct such assessments also vary a great deal. There are, however, several procedures or stages which are common to many needs assessment studies.

4.1 Preparing to Conduct a Needs Assessment

Like other forms of inquiry, preparing to conduct a needs assessment requires decisions to conduct such a study, determining the purposes the assessment is to serve, and delimiting the areas in which the study is to concentrate. In addition, because educational needs are based to a large extent on the values of the institution or society in which they are to be determined, procedures must be incorporated into the process to ensure that these values are represented. This is most often accomplished by involving a variety of interested or involved individuals or groups in the process. A preparation activity for these assessments is the identification of those who will be involved in or affected by the study and the procurement of their commitment to participate.

4.2 Designing the Needs Assessment

Good designs for needs assessments begin with a clear specification of the focus of the study. This includes a delineation of the specific purposes of the study, the areas in which needs are to be assessed, and the type of needs to be identified.

A clear focus for the assessment will dictate most of the data collection, analyses, and reporting procedures. Needs assessments designed to gather community opinions of educational needs, for example, might suggest the methods of opinion-survey research, the use of public hearings or forums, or the use of focus groups. Data collection procedures might include the administration of surveys, conducting interviews, or the use of ranking procedures such as card sorts or budget allocation simulations. To conduct assessments designed to determine student performance needs, one might administer tests, analyze school work, survey teachers, or examine existing records. Other assessments might require using educational indicators such as drop-out rates, post-graduation placements, and other demographic and statistical data. Those using forecasting and future methods might choose scenarios or Delphi techniques. Needs assessments designed to determine the cause of needs might use strategies such as fault tree analyses.

Complete designs would include procedures for analyzing data and reporting results. For many needs assessments, it is necessary to conduct discrepancy analyses to identify needs. These may be conducted by determining differences among two sets of data, combining analyses of several sets and types of data, and developing criticality indices or functions (Witkin 1984).

4.3 Assigning Priorities to Needs

Needs assessment studies may result in the identification of many needs. To be of maximum use, identified needs should be placed in order from most to least crucial. Quantitative procedures for setting priorities include ordering needs by the strength of their ratings of importance, by the extent of the discrepancy between targeted and actual status, and by the importance ratings and extent of discrepancy (Witkin 1984).

Others see the process of setting priorities as a complex analytical process. Lund and McGechan (1981), for example, suggest specific criteria for analyzing needs that include: (a) How many people are affected? (b) What would be the consequences if the needs were not met? (c) Is this a need that can be met by an educational activity? (d) Is this a critical need that should be met before other educational needs are addressed? (e) Will resources (funds, staff) be adequate to meet those needs?

4.4 Reporting and Using the Results

A particular characteristic of needs assessment studies is the intended utility of the results. Whether for planning, problem-solving, setting criteria for evaluation results, or praising or censuring education efforts, the final stage in the process is intended to be one of active use of the findings.

Witkin (1984) suggests enhancing the use of needs assessment findings by communicating information about the study during all of its phases, from planning to use. Most writers encourage the use of effective communication strategies—that is, identifying the audiences for the information, tailoring the information to the audience and the media being used, and attending to the timing of the release of information relative to audience needs.

5. Trends and Issues

Changes in funding mechanisms, the worldwide recession, and emphases on testing and other forms of pupil assessment have reduced the emphasis on the development and use of needs assessments in education. Methodological development in this area was arrested just as philosophical debates regarding approaches used in behavioral science emerged. Much work remains to be done in developing models and procedures of determining needs in context, of incorporating values which often conflict into the process, and of establishing ways of determining the priority of multiple needs, many of which interact with one another.

See also: Education Production Functions; Effective Schools Research: Methodological Issues; Resource Allocation in Schools and School Systems

References

Guba E G, Lincoln Y S 1982 The place of values in needs assessment. *Educ. Eval. Policy Anal.* 4(3): 311–20

Kaufman R A 1972 *Educational System Planning*. Prentice-Hall, Englewood Cliffs, New Jersey

Kaufman R A 1987 Needs assessment primer. *Train. Dev. J.* 41(10): 78–83

Lund B, McGechan S 1981 CE Programmer's Manual. Continuing Education Division, Ministry of Education, Victoria

Mattimore-Knudson R 1983 The concept of need: Its hedonistic and logical nature. *Adult Educ. Forum* 33(2): 117–24

Scriven M, Roth J 1978 Needs: Concept and practice. *Ex-ploring Purposes and Dimensions: New Directions for Program Evaluation* 1:1–11

Stufflebeam D L, McCormick C H, Brinkerhoff R O, Nelson C O 1985 *Conducting Educational Needs Assessment*. Kluwer Nijhoff, Boston, Massachusetts

Suarez T M 1981 Needs assessment. In: Lewy A, Nevo D (eds.) 1981 *Evaluation Roles in Education*. Gordon and Breach, London

Witkin B R 1984 *Assessing Needs in Educational and Social Programs*. Jossey-Bass, San Francisco, California

Participatory Research

B. L. Hall

Participatory research has been described most generally as a process that combines three activities: research, education, and action (Hall 1981). Participatory research is a social action process that is biased in favor of dominated, exploited, poor, or otherwise left-out people. It sees no contradiction between goals of collective empowerment and the deepening of social knowledge. The concern with power and democracy and their interactions are central to participatory research. Attention to gender, race, ethnicity, sexual orientation, physical and mental abilities, and other social factors are critical.

With the early support of the International Council for Adult Education, which initiated a global network in participatory research in 1977, and widespread interest over the years, the concept has been elaborated and developed much further. Fals Borda initially referred to a similar process in which he and his colleagues were engaged in Colombia and elsewhere in Latin America in the mid-1970s as "action research" (Fals Borda and Rahman 1991). When Vio Grossi, now of Chile but earlier working in Venezuela, organized a vigorous and dynamic Latin American network under the label "participatory research," Fals Borda joined forces and modified his label to "participatory action research." Both the "participatory action research" of Fals Borda and "participatory research" refer to the same general process. Fals Borda, Rahman of Bangladesh, and scores of other colleagues have been and continue to be central figures in the international participatory research community.

Authors have characterized the nature of participatory research in the following terms.

> Participatory research attempts to present people as researchers themselves in pursuit of answers to the questions of their daily struggle and survival. (Tandon 1988 p. 7)

> Participatory Research is a way for researchers and oppressed people to join in solidarity to take collective action, both short and long term, for radical social change.

Locally determined and controlled action is a planned consequence of inquiry. (Maguire 1987 p. 29)

> The final aims of this combination of liberating knowledge and political power within a continuous process of life and work are: (1) to enable the oppressed groups and classes to acquire sufficient creative and transforming leverage as expressed in specific projects, acts and struggles; and (2) to produce and develop socio-political thought processes with which popular bases can identify. (Fals Borda and Rahman 1991 p. 4)

> Participatory research attempts to break down the distinction between the researchers and the researched, the subjects and objects of knowledge production by the participation of the people-for-themselves in the process of gaining and creating knowledge. In the process, research is seen not only as a process of creating knowledge, but simultaneously, as education and development of consciousness, and of mobilization for action. (Gaventa 1988 p. 19)

> Participatory research is collaborative, endogenous, heuristic and experiential. Transculturally, this implies an ability to accept the idea of native science and a sensitivity to the process-oriented, communally-based indigenous methodology. Through joint research projects between equal partners, participatory research can act as a flow-through mechanism for scientific findings from both worlds. (Colorado 1988 p. 63)

> An immediate objective . . . is to return to the people the legitimacy of the knowledge they are capable of producing through their own verification systems, as fully scientific, and the right to use this knowledge, but not be dictated by it—as a guide in their own action. (Fals Borda and Rahman 1991 p. 15).

1. Origins of Participatory Research

It is important to recognize that, while the term "participatory research" may be new, the concerns being expressed have a history and continuity in social science (see Hall 1992). Many of the ideas that are finding new opportunities for expression can be traced as far back as the early fieldwork of Frederick Engels, who investigated conditions in the early factories of Manchester in the United Kingdom in the mid-nineteenth century. Marx's use of the structured interview—*L'Enquête ouvrière*—with French factory workers is another sometimes forgotten antecedent. In later times aspects of the work of John Dewey, George Herbert Mead, and the Tavistock Institute in London have outlined methods of social investigation that are based on other than a positivistic epistemology.

By the late 1950s and early 1960s, the dominant international research paradigm was a version of the North American and European model based on empiricism and positivism and characterized by an attention to instrument construction and rigor defined by statistical precision and replicability. Through the elaborate mechanisms of colonial and postcolonial relations, international scholarships, cultural exchanges, and training of researchers in Europe and North America, this dominant paradigm was extended to the dependent and poorer nations. Research methods, through an illusion of objectivity and scientific credibility, became one more manifestation of cultural dependency.

The reaction of the Third World—beginning in Latin America—has taken many forms. Dependency theorists, such as Dos Santos, Frank, Amin, and Leys outlined some of the mechanisms of economic and cultural dependency. Hence, in the field of research methods, Third World perspectives have grown in part out of a reaction to approaches developed in North America and Europe; approaches that have not only been created in different cultural settings but which contribute to already existing class distinctions. The Third World's contribution to social science research methods represents an attempt to find ways of uncovering knowledge that can be applied in societies where interpretation of reality must take second place to the changing of that reality.

Practical experience in what was becoming known as participatory research occurred in the work of the Tanzanian Bureau of Research Allocation and Land Use Planning. Here, Marja-Liisa Swantz and teams of students and village workers were involved in the questions of youth and employment in the coast region and later in studies of socioeconomic causes of malnutrition in Central Kilimanjaro. A visit by Paulo Freire to Tanzania in 1971 was a stimulus to many social scientists who might not otherwise have been as impressed by the existing experience of many adult educators or community development workers.

What happened in Tanzania in a small way had already begun in Latin America in the early 1960s. Stimulated in part by the success of the Cuban revolution, Latin American social scientists began exploring more committed forms of research. One of the most

useful roles of Paulo Freire has been to bring some of the current ideas of Latin American social scientists to the attention of persons in other parts of the world. His work on thematic investigation, first in Brazil and later in Chile, was an expression of this search. Others, such as Beltran and Gerace Larufa, have explored alternatives through concepts of horizontal communication (Beltran 1976, Gerace Larufa 1973). Fals Borda (1980) and others in Colombia have been engaged in *investigación y acción*, while the D'arcy de Oliveiras have made people aware of the value of militant observation (D'Arcy de Oliveira and D'arcy de Oliveira 1975).

2. Not the Third World Alone

While the specific term "participatory research" developed in the South, consciousness was growing in Europe and North America (see Hall 1992). Critiques of positivistic research paradigms began to surface in the 1970s. The Frankfurt School was rediscovered through the work of Jürgen Habermas and Theodor Adorno. The International Sociological Association, with encouragement from Peter Park of the United States and Ulf Himmelstrand of Sweden, began to place action-oriented sociology on the agenda of many academic meetings. In Switzerland, researchers in curriculum development adapted methodologies from political research to their needs. In Canada, Stinson developed methods of evaluation along action research lines for community development (Stinson 1979). In the Netherlands, de Vries explored research alternatives as an adult educator. Brown, of the United States, brought participatory research to the world of organizational development (Brown and Kaplan 1981). The National Institute for Adult Education in the United Kingdom pioneered participatory research through its evaluation of the United Kingdom adult literacy campaign (Holmes 1976). In Italy, Paulo Orefice and colleagues at the University of Naples applied the methodology in the context of growing political decentralization (Orefice 1981). In the United States, the Highlander Center in Tennessee has used participatory research for many years to deal with issues of land ownership and use (Horton 1981) and environmental deterioration. In Canada, the Toronto-based Participatory Research Group worked with a wide variety of groups, including First Nations peoples (Jackson 1980, Jackson et al. 1982), adult educators (Cassara 1985), immigrant women (Barndt 1981), and health workers (Hall 1981). The 1991 bibliography on participatory research by the Center for Community Education and Action provides the best perspective on the use and geographic spread of the approach (Center for Community Education and Action 1991). One of the newest books on participatory research reviews the North American experiences during the 1980s (Park et al. 1993).

3. Question of Methods

The literature on participatory research has always been vague on the question of methods. This is so because for participatory research, the most important factors are the origins of the issues, the roles those concerned with the issues play in the process, the emersion of the process in the context of the moment, the potential for mobilizing and for collective learning, the links to action, the understanding of how power relationships work, and the potential for communications with others experiencing similar discrimination, oppression, or violence. In addition, participatory research is based on the epistemological assumption that knowledge is constructed socially and therefore that approaches that allow for social, group, or collective analysis of life experiences of power and knowledge are most appropriate.

This means that for participatory research there are no methodological orthodoxies, no cookbook approaches to follow. The principle is that both issues and ways of working should flow from those involved and their context. In practice a creative and very wide variety of approaches have been used. All approaches have been selected because of their potential for drawing out knowledge and analysis in a social or collective way (Participatory Research Network 1982). They include: community meetings, video documentaries, community drama, camps for the landless in India, use of drawings and murals, photonovels, sharing of oral histories, community surveys, story-telling, shared testimonies, and many more. Even questionnaires have been used at times as a first step in a group-controlled process of reflection. Barndt and the Jesuit Centre for Faith and Social Justice in Canada have developed an approach to social movement research called "Naming the Moment" which offers a method for determining the political space available to them for action (Barndt 1989). Participatory Research in Asia (PRIA) reviewed the methods and results used by 10 different grassroots groups in India (PRIA 1985). The Society for the Promotion of Education and Research (SPEAR) of Belize, Central America, produced a participatory research training guide (SPEAR 1990). Fals Borda discussed many methodological issues on a videotape produced by the University of Calgary in 1990.

4. Issues and Debates

4.1 The Feminist Advance

Feminist critiques of research have contributed to the understanding and practice of participatory research. Both feminist approaches and participatory research are concerned with knowledge creation in ways that empower those engaged rather than maintaining the status quo. Both feminist research and participatory research seek to shift the center from which knowledge is

generated (Joyappa and Martin 1997). Spender (1978 pp. 1–2) has described the field of women's studies as follows:

> Its multi-disciplinary nature challenges the arrangements of knowledge into academic disciplines; its methodology breaks down many of the traditional distinctions between theoretical and empirical and between objective and subjective. It is in the process of redefining knowledge, knowledge gathering and making . . .

In addition, Callaway has demonstrated that women have been largely excluded from producing the dominant forms of knowledge and that the social sciences have been not only a science of male society but also a male science of society (Callaway 1981). Spender urged women "to learn to create our own knowledge." It is crucially important, she states:

> that women begin to create our own means of producing and validating knowledge which is consistent with our own personal experience. We need to formulate our own yardsticks, for we are doomed to deviancy if we persist in measuring ourselves against the male standard. This is our area of learning, with learning used in a widely encompassing, highly charged, political and revolutionary sense. (Spender 1978 pp. 1–2)

Maguire has bridged feminist research approaches and participatory research in her 1987 book which points out what she has called the "Androcentric filter" in participatory research writing (Maguire 1987). Maguire has pointed out the distinct silence around gender and women in the participatory research discourse. She noted that women's ways of seeing were not mentioned until 1981 and that in the general discourse women have been excluded.

Maguire put forward a number of specific guidelines for feminist participatory research:

> (1) the critique is both of positivist and androcentric research paradigms;
> (2) gender needs to be a central piece of the issues agenda;
> (3) integrative feminism which recognizes diversity should be central to theoretical discussions on participatory research;
> (4) the role of gender needs to be taken into account in all phases of participatory research;
> (5) feminist participatory research would give explicit attention to how women and men as groups benefit from a project;
> (6) attention to gender language use is critical;
> (7) gender, culture, race and class all figure in questions about the research team;
> (8) gender should be a factor in considering evaluation;
> (9) patriarchy is a system to be dismantled along with other systems of domination and oppression. (Maguire 1987 pp. 105–08)

Smith has suggested that feminist sociology, like participatory research, must "begin where we are" with real, concrete people with actual lives if it is to do more than reproduce patriarchal patterns of relations

(Smith 1979). Oral history as a particular approach to feminist research has been used in participatory research as well (Anderson et al. 1990).

4.2 *Question of Voice*

Participatory research fundamentally is about who has the right to speak, to analyze, and to act. It is about rural Black women in southern cooperatives in the United States speaking for themselves in obtaining loans for planting. It is about shantytown mothers in Bombay speaking for themselves. It is about citizens of Turkish descent in Germany looking at and articulating their own needs in the face of neo-Nazi revival. It is about women in Thailand's hill country protecting forests. It is about indigenous people of the First Nations of North America researching land rights. It is about people who do not read and write taking control of literacy programs. It is a process that supports the voices from the margins in speaking, analyzing, building alliances, and taking action. As Lourde's (1984) poem "Litany for Survival" says:

and when we speak we are afraid
our words will not be heard
nor welcomed
but when we are silent
We are still afraid

So it is better to speak
remembering
we were never meant to survive

According to hooks, critical theorist and Afro-American woman, "It is our responsibility collectively and individually to distinguish between mere speaking that is about self-aggrandizement, exploitation of the exotic "other", and that coming to voice which is a gesture of resistance, an affirmation of struggle" (hooks 1988).

Participatory research argues for the articulation of points of view by the dominated or subordinated, whether from gender, race, ethnicity, or other structures of subordination. Participatory research posits that an individual's position in structures of subordination shapes the ability to see the whole. hooks reflected thus on growing up Black in the United States:

Living as we did—on the edge—we developed a particular way of seeing reality. We looked both from the outside in and from the inside out. We focused our attention on the center as well as on the margin. We understood both. This mode of seeing reminded us of the existence of a whole universe, a main body made up of both margin and center. Our survival depended on an ongoing private acknowledgment that we were a necessary, vital part of that whole.

This sense of wholeness, impressed upon our consciousness by the structure of our daily lives, provided us an oppositional world view—a mode of seeing unknown to most of our oppressors, that sustained us, sided us in our struggle to transcend poverty and despair, strengthened our sense of self and our solidarity. (hooks 1984 p. 9)

5. *Participatory Research as Counterhegemonic Practice*

Disturbed by the fact that dissatisfaction of the working class in Italy produced fascism instead of a socialist transformation as happened in the Soviet Union in 1917, Antonio Gramsci undertook a lengthy study, though this was partly brought about by his imprisonment. The translation of his work into English in the early 1970s allowed greater access to his complex and fascinating ideas (Hoare and Nowell-Smith 1971). Hegemony is one of the major concepts that helps individuals to understand participatory research. According to Gramsci, humans are controlled by both coercion and consent. Laws exist that limit actions that can be taken in redressing structural imbalances, but in fact demand most often "consent" to structures of domination or hegemony. Dominated classes, genders, races, sexual orientations, or different-ability groups internalize the views of what is "acceptable" resistance, "realistic" strategy, their own fault or the natural order of things and thereby participate in the maintenance of hegemony.

But unlike orthodox Marxism, Gramsci saw a more dialectical relationship between consciousness and reality. While not accepting the idealist position that consciousness determines reality, Gramsci allowed that human agency does have a role and that the construction of counterhegemonic patterns was what was needed. In the construction of counterhegemonic ideas there is a role for intellectuals, but new kinds of intellectuals, what he called "organic intellectuals," who are deeply rooted to and part of the class- or other dominated structures from which they come. The knowledge produced in participatory research processes can be seen as part of the counterhegemonic process.

6. *Restoration of Ancient Knowledge*

The growing awareness globally about environmental and ecological deterioration has reinforced many of the claims and aspirations for participatory research. Shiva of India, for example, has noted that the scientific revolution of Isaac Newton and Francis Bacon was a male, Eurocentric, white science that by its invention immediately created nonscience or ignorance among people or in places that did not share in this particular way of knowing. Western science rendered invisible ancient, feminine, proearth ways of knowing (Shiva 1989).

There is widespread interest in the recovery of ancient ways of knowing that seem more fully integrated into the world and nature as opposed to those ways that view nature as separate and needing to be conquered for human beings to prosper. There is a role for participatory research with people and by people who still have links to ancient knowledge. In this case can participatory research be part of such a recovery or restoration process (Colorado 1988)?

7. Co-optation and the Role of the University

What is the role of the academy in participatory research? What has the academy done with participatory research? What is the status of the knowledge generated in a participatory research process? Participatory research originated as a challenge to positivist research paradigms as carried out largely by university-based researchers. The position has been that the center of knowledge generation needed to be in what dominant society described as the margins: in communities, with women, with people of color, and so forth. Experience has shown that it is very difficult to achieve this kind of process from a university base; hence the need for alternative structures such as community-based networks or centers. But how can this be reconciled with the fact that so many of those who publish are university based?

If the research process is genuinely and organically situated in a community, workplace, or group that is experiencing domination, there is no need to be afraid that the knowledge being generated will be used for purposes that the community or group does not need or wish for. The difficulty arises because there are different uses of knowledge in the academy from those in community or workplace situations. According to the discourse of participatory research, knowledge generated, whether of localized application or larger theoretical value, is linked in some ways with shifts of power or structural changes. But intentions do not always produce desired results, and those who have been working along these lines for a number of years share these assumptions. It is necessary to hope for a fuller understanding of the context and conditions of both work and life.

Knowledge within the academy serves a variety of purposes. It is a commodity by which academics do far more than exchange ideas; it is the very means of exchange for the academic political economy. Tenure, promotion, peer recognition, research grants, and countless smaller codes of privilege are accorded through the adding up of articles, books, papers in "refereed" journals and conferences. Academics in the marketplace of knowledge know that they must identify or become identified with streams of ideas that offer the possibility of publishing and dialogue within appropriate and recognized settings. Collaborative research or at least collaborative publishing is informally discouraged because of the difficulty in attributing authorship. Collaborative research with persons who are not academics by the standards of the academy is uncommon. While academics in fact gain financially through accumulated publications of appropriate knowledge, community collaborators seldom benefit from such collaboration in financial terms. As can be seen, academics are under economic, job survival, or advancement pressures to produce in appropriate ways. It is this structural pressure that plays havoc with academic engagement in the participatory research process. Is it not possible that in spite of personal history, ideological commitment, and deep personal links with social movements or transformative processes that the structural location of the academy as the preferred location for the organizing of knowledge will distort a participatory research process?

Does this mean that there is no role for university-based people to be engaged in participatory research processes? Arguments exist on both sides of this question. Universities or similarly accredited researchers are clearly not required to animate a participatory research process. Participatory research is a tool which social movements, activists, trade unionists, women on welfare, the homeless, or any similar groups use as part of a variety of strategies and methods for the conduct of their work. If they wish to invite a university-based group to become involved they need to set up the conditions at the start and maintain control of the process if they wish to benefit as much as possible. Countless groups make use of processes that resemble participatory research without naming it or certainly without asking for outside validation of the knowledge produced.

Participatory research deserves to be taught in universities, and is increasingly being taught. The academic community deserves to discuss and challenge and be challenged by these and other ideas which raise questions of the role of knowledge and power. Adult educators, community workers, social workers, primary healthcare personnel, solidarity cooperators, cooperative movement workers, multicultural workers, teachers, and countless others who begin working after a university education deserve to study, read, and experience the ideas that make up participatory research.

Academics also do not cease to be members of the community by going to work in a university. There are countless community issues, whether related to toxic dumping, homelessness, high drop-out levels in local schools, or unfair taxation policies, that engage us all as citizens. Academics have some skills that can contribute to community action along with the skills of others in the community.

The concern with co-optation is not limited to the academy, but runs through the professional circles of those involved in international development. Rahnema, a former senior Iranian official turned advisor on nongovernmental activities for the United Nations Development Program (UNDP) and visiting university professor, has criticized participatory action research as "The Last Temptation of Saint

Development" (Rahnema 1990). He says that in its most generalized form, the call for participation is naı[um]ve and by now accepted by all international agencies. He suggests that participatory research can at best only change external factors affecting people's lives and not touch the deeper conditioning that causes people to do what they do; "It serves no one to make a new fetish out of participation, only because nonparticipatory development has failed in every way" (Rahnema 1990).

8. Historical Materialism, Critical Theory, and Other Philosophical Support

Vio Grossi wrote in 1981 that:

> some . . . understood that participatory research was implicitly rejecting . . . historical materialism. We were accused of integration and reformism. Participatory research is not, and has never intended to be, a new ideological and scientific holistic system, an alternative to historical materialism. On the contrary, it attempts to start the research from the concrete and specific reality, incorporating the people's viewpoints, in order to contribute to a type of social transformation that eliminates poverty, dependence and exploitation. This assertion requires a further analysis of its components. Historical materialism has been stated as a method for investigating reality with the intent of revealing the main tendencies of changes in order to orient action. (Vio Grossi 1981)

As Gramsci has said:

> The starting-point of critical elaboration is the consciousness of what one really is, and in "knowing thyself" as a product of the historical process to date which has deposited in you an infinity of traces, without leaving an inventory. (Hoare and Nowell-Smith 1971 p. 326)

Early efforts to place the evolving practice of participatory research within appropriate or supportive theoretical frameworks focused on debates between pragmatic or historical materialist epistemological frameworks (Kassam and Mustapha 1982). The majority of participatory research writers found themselves agreeing that class, power, ideology, and other social structural elements were critical to understanding change and hence drew upon historical materialist sources. In the mid-1980s, and particularly in North America, contributions linked participatory research to the critical theory streams of Horkheimer, Adorno, and Habermas (Comstock and Fox 1993, Park 1993). Additional linkages were made between the concepts of "critical pedagogy," particularly as both Giroux of the United States and Simon of Canada began to move the focus of their work beyond schooling and into cultural politics and the notions of "border" pedagogies.

It is necessary to stress that the basis for a critical pedagogy cannot be developed merely around the inclusion of particular forms of knowledge that have been suppressed or ignored by the dominant culture, nor can it only center on providing students with more empowering interpretations of the social and material world. Such a pedagogy must be attentive to ways in which students make both affective and semantic investments as part of their attempts to regulate and give meaning to their lives (Giroux and Simon 1992).

9. Local Autonomy and Broader Struggles

Additional debates exist in the field. For example, there is tension between the requirement of local autonomy for a given participatory process and the demand for coordinated social action at the national or regional levels. A national action must be more than an aggregate of local experiences. At certain critical moments, will a local-level participatory research process hinder the progress of broader social movements by overemphasizing the localized nature of the problem? There is a need to understand the relationships of different kinds of knowledge and information generating from different levels and aspects of society.

10. Question of Power

Emerging from the discussions, debates, and activities of participatory research is the central question of power. Participatory research is intended to contribute to processes of shifting power or democratizing a variety of contexts. Power can be expressed in several ways: A exercises power over B when A affects B in a manner contrary to B's interests; in other words A gets B to do what he or she does not want to do. But A also exercises power by influencing, shaping, or determining B's very wants, by controlling the agenda through a complex interplay of social control (Gaventa 1979).

How, then, can participatory research be useful in shifting power? Practitioners have suggested at least three possibilities.

10.1 Unmasking the Myths

Vio Grossi (1981) has written of participatory research as initiating a process of disindoctrination that allows people to detach themselves from the myths imposed on them by the power structure and which have prevented them from seeing their own oppression or from seeing possibilities for breaking free. Transformative action can be seen as the strategic goal to be reached in the medium or long term. A participatory research process carried out in conjunction with popular groups (and under their control) is designed to facilitate the analysis of stages toward that goal.

10.2 Creation of Popular Knowledge

Fals Borda has contributed to the discussion of popular

knowledge in his paper on "Science and the Common People" (Fals Borda 1980). He says the creation of knowledge that comes from the people contributes to the realization of a people's science which serves and is understood by the people, and no longer perpetuates the status quo. The process of this new paradigm involves: (a) returning information to the people in the language and cultural form in which it originated; (b) establishing control of the work by the popular and base movements; (c) popularizing research techniques; (d) integrating the information as the base of the organic intellectual; (e) maintaining a conscious effort in the action/reflection rhythm of work; (f) recognizing science as part of the everyday lives of all people; and (g) learning to listen.

In Gaventa's terms popular knowledge can be seen as a contribution toward limiting the ability of those in power to determine the wants of others, thus in effect transferring power to those groups engaged in the production of popular knowledge (Gaventa 1979).

10.3 Contributing to Organizing

Participatory research is conceived to be an integral process of investigation, education, and action. When the question of power is addressed, it is clearer than ever that the first two aspects are empty without the third. But action must be explained still further. From several years of sharing information and results it has become clear that the most common action and the critical necessity is that of organizing, in its various phases. It has meant building alliances and strengthening links within various progressive sectors.

It would be an error to assume that naïve or uncontrolled use of participatory research results in strengthening the power of the powerless at the base of society. Where control over the participatory research process is missing, experience has shown that power can easily accrue to those already in control. There has been ambiguity in some earlier writings on participatory research which has resulted in misunderstanding and manipulation.

See also: Feminist Research Methodology; Trends in Qualitative Research Methods

References

Anderson K, Armitage S, Jack D, Wittner J 1990 Beginning where we are: Feminist methodology in oral history. In: Nielson J M (ed.) 1990 *Feminist Research Methods.* Westview, Boulder, Colorado

Barndt D 1981 *Just Getting There: Creating Visual Tools for Collective Analysis in Freirean Education Programmes for Migrant Women in Canada.* Par Res Group, Toronto

Barndt D 1989 *Naming the Moment: Political Analysis for Action—A Manual for Community Groups.* Moment Project, Toronto

Beltran L R 1976 Alien premises: Objects and methods in Latin American communication research. *Commun. Res.* 3(2): 107–34

Brown L D, Kaplan R E 1981 Participatory research in a factory. In: Reason P, Rowan J (eds.) 1981 *Human Inquiry: A Sourcebook of New Paradigm Research.* Wiley, London

Callaway H 1981 Women's perspectives: Research as revision. In: Reason P, Rowan J (eds.) 1981 *Human Inquiry: A Sourcebook of New Paradigm Research.* Wiley, London

Cassara B 1985 *Participatory Research: Group Self-directed Learning for Social Transformation.* Adult Education, University of Georgia, Athens, Georgia

Center for Community Education and Action 1991 *Participatory Research: An Annotated Bibliography.* CCEA and Center for International Education, Amherst, Massachusetts

Colorado P 1988 Bridging native and western science. *Convergence* 21(3/4)

Comstock D, Fox R 1993 Citizen's action at North Bonneville Dam. In: Park P, Brydon-Miller M, Hall B, Jackson T (eds.) 1993

D'arcy de Oliveira R, D'arcy de Oliveira M 1975 *The Militant Observer: A Sociological Alternative.* Institut d'Action Culturelle, Geneva

Fals Borda O 1980 *Science and the Common People.* International Forum on Participatory Research

Fals Borda O, Rahman M A 1991 *Action and Knowledge: Breaking the Monopoly with Participatory Action-Research.* Apex, New York

Gaventa J 1979 *Power and Powerlessness: Quiescence and Rebellion in an Appalachian Valley.* University of Illinois Press, Urbana, Illinois

Gaventa J 1988 Participatory research in North America. *Convergence* 21(2/3): 19–48

Gerace Larufa F 1973 *Comunicación Horizontal.* Librería Studium, Lima

Giroux H, Simon R 1992 Popular culture as a pedagogy of pleasure and meaning: Decolonizing the body. In: Giroux H (ed.) 1992 *Border Crossings: Cultural Workers and the Politics of Education.* Routledge, New York

Hall B 1981 Participatory research, popular knowledge and power. *Convergence* 14(3)

Hall B 1992 The development and purpose of participatory research *Am. Sociol.* 23(4): 15–28

Hoare Q, Nowell-Smith G (eds. and trans.) 1971 *Selections from the Prison Notebooks of Antonio Gramsci.* Lawrence and Wishart, London

Holmes J 1976 Thoughts on research methodology. *Stud. Adult Educ.* 8(2): 149–63

hooks b 1984 *Feminist Theory: From Margin to Center.* South End, Boston, Massachusetts

hooks b 1988 *Talking Back: Thinking Feminist Thinking Black.* South End, Boston, Massachusetts

Horton B D 1981 On the potential of participatory research: An evaluation of a regional experiment. Paper prepared for annual meeting of the Society for Study of Social Problems, Toronto, Canada

Jackson T 1980 Environmental assessment in big trout lake, Canada. Paper for International Forum on participatory research

Jackson T, McCaskill D, Hall B 1982 Learning for self-determination: Community-based options for native training and research. *Can. J. Native Studies* 2(1) (special issue)

Joyappa V, Martin D 1997 Exploring alternative research epistemologies for adult education: participatory research, feminist research and feminist participatory research. *Adult Educ. Q.* 47(1): 1–14

Kassam Y, Mustapha K 1982 *Participatory Research: An Emerging Alternative Methodology in Social Science Research.* ICAE, Toronto

Lourde A 1984 *Sister Outsider: Essays and Speeches.* Crossing Press, Trumansburg, New York

Maguire P 1987 *Doing Participatory Research: A Feminist Approach.* Center for International Education, University of Massachusetts, Amherst, Massachusetts

Orefice P 1981 Cultural self-awareness of local community: An experience in the south of Italy. *Convergence* 14: 56–64

Park P 1993 What is participatory research? In: Park P, Brydon-Miller M, Hall B, Jackson T (eds.) 1993

Park P, Brydon-Miller M, Hall B, Jackson T (eds.) 1993 *Voices of Change: Participatory Research in the United States and Canada* Greenwood, Westport, Connecticut

Participatory Research Network 1982 *An Introduction to Participatory Research.* ICAE, New Delhi

PRIA 1985 *Knowledge and Social Change: An Inquiry into Participatory Research in India.* PRIA, New Delhi

Rahnema M 1990 Participatory action research: The "last temptation" of saint development. *Alternatives* 15: 199–226

Shiva V 1989 *Staying Alive: Women, Ecology and Development.* Zed Books, London

Smith D 1979 A sociology for women. In: Sherman J, Bock E (eds.) 1979 *The Prism of Sex: Essays in the Sociology of Knowledge.* University of Wisconsin Press, Madison, Wisconsin

SPEAR 1990 *You Better Belize It! A Participatory Research Training Guide on a Training Workshop in Belize.* SPEAR and PRG, Toronto

Spender D 1978 Editorial. *Womens' Studies International Q.* 1: 1–2

Stinson A (ed.) 1979 *Canadians Participate: Annotated Bibliography of Case Studies.* Centre for Social Welfare Studies, Ottawa

Tandon R 1988 Social transformation and participatory research. *Convergence* 21(2/3): 5–18

Vio Grossi F 1981 The socio-political implications of participatory research. Yugoslavia. *Convergence* 14(3): 34–51

Policy-oriented Research

J. Nisbet

Policy-oriented research is best defined in terms of its instrumental function rather than by its topics of study. When research in education is designed, managed, and reported with the specific purpose of informing a policy decision, or assisting or monitoring its implementation, or evaluating its effects, the term "policy-oriented" is used to distinguish this approach from "fundamental" research which is designed primarily to extend the frontiers of knowledge. This definition of policy-oriented research may be extended to include research which is closely tied to educational practice as well as policy.

The implicit model is that the function of research is to provide an information base for decision-making, to establish the "facts"; administrators, politicians, or teachers then add the necessary value judgments, supposedly so that policy and practice are firmly based on empirical evidence from experiment and survey. Thus "good" research provides answers to "relevant" problems. In this approach, educational issues which are of current concern are accepted as priority topics for research. This instrumental view of the function of research, however, makes naive and simplistic assumptions about how policy and practice are determined (see *Educational Research and Policy-making*). If adopted uncritically, the emphasis on relevance constrains inquiry within the limits of existing policy and risks a trivialization of research and centralization

of control over the choice of topics for inquiry. But with a clearer understanding of the relation of research and policy and with enlightened administration of research funding, the trend toward policy-oriented research could enable research to make a more effective contribution to educational practice.

1. Definitions

The definition of policy-oriented research is usually expressed by contrasting it with fundamental research, on the analogy of pure and applied science. A variety of terms can be used to express the contrast: applied versus basic research, policy-oriented versus curiosity-oriented studies, instrumental versus enlightenment functions, work directed toward decision or action versus work directed toward knowledge or theory. Less charitably, "relevant" research may be contrasted with "academic" research. Cronbach and Suppes (1969) criticized these "popular labels," arguing instead for a distinction in terms of the audience to whom the research is directed. Their concepts of "decision-oriented" and "conclusion-oriented" research have been widely adopted. Decision-oriented research is designed to provide information wanted by a decision-maker; the findings of conclusion-oriented research are of interest primarily to the research community. "The distinction between decision-oriented and conclusion-oriented research lies in the origination of the inquiry and the constraints imposed by its institutional setting, not in topic or technique" (p. 23). Thus, Cooley and Bickel (1985) define decision-oriented research as "a form of educational research that is designed to be directly relevant to the current information requirements of those who are shaping educational policy or managing educational systems" (p. xi).

Whichever terms are used, they carry value judgments which can be misleading if they are not made explicit. The distinction between pure and applied research in education is itself misleading, in that theoretical studies provide concepts for the analysis of problems and may even help to identify and define problems. It may be argued that educational research must be set in the context of an educational system: if it is general, it may be better described as psychological or sociological or management research. "From one point of view, *all* educational research is applied research, designed to bring about changes in the way education is carried on, rather than simply to add to our existing stock of knowledge" (Taylor 1973 p. 207). Defined narrowly, policy-oriented research is research which has direct application to current issues in educational policy or practice. A wider definition (and, to anticipate the argument of this analysis, a better one) is that policy-oriented research consists of careful, systematic attempts to understand the educational process and, through understanding, to improve its efficiency.

Listing the procedures involved is one way of defining. Policy-oriented research includes surveys or any comparable data-gathering which enables policy-makers or practitioners to base their decisions on evidence rather than on prejudice or guesswork. This includes the search for solutions to pressing educational or social problems, identifying and resolving the problems involved in implementing policy decisions, pilot studies to test new initiatives, monitoring and evaluating initiatives in educational practice, and experimental studies to compare alternative educational methods. It also includes policy studies and retrospective analyses of past policy where the purpose is to help make better policy decisions in the future.

Thus the essential distinction between policy-oriented and other forms of educational research is in terms of purpose, rather than in choice of subject or method. Since the perception of educational issues as being of current concern is subject to volatile popular fashion, an aspect of learning may be regarded as a theoretical issue this year but a topic of policy-oriented research next year. The end products of policy-oriented research are recommendations for decision or action. The products of fundamental research are contributions to knowledge, understanding, or theory. Since decisions and action necessarily imply the adoption of some theory or interpretation, and theory likewise has long-term implications for action, the distinction between the two categories is not as sharp

as is sometimes assumed. However, policy-oriented research usually operates within the context of accepted theory: it does not aim to modify theory, though it may do so incidentally. Similarly, fundamental research does not aim to affect practice, but it may do so indirectly. Policy-oriented research is responsive, whereas fundamental research is autonomous.

Autonomous educational research, which does not have to be accountable in the sense of producing useful or usable findings, runs the risk of producing results which are of interest only to other researchers. In its extreme, it is concerned with attacking other people's theories, irrespective of whether the points at issue are of any importance outside the research sphere. Responsive research, designed as a response to a practical need, is no less likely to raise and illuminate fundamental issues, and there is the added bonus that it can be useful at the same time. However, it runs the risk of being left behind by the rapid course of events, since by the time results are available the problem which they were designed to answer is liable to have changed or to be no longer seen as important. The resolution of this dilemma may lie in the concept of "strategic research" (Bondi 1983): "that grey zone of researches that . . . are not immediately of use to the customer, but lay the foundations for being able to answer questions that may be put in the future" (p. 3). Unfortunately, however, the precise nature of strategic research remains uncertain.

Since responsive research operates within the context of existing policy or practice, it is limited in its generalizability, but it is more likely to have an impact on the specific policy or practice for which it is designed. The impact of this kind of research, however, is incremental rather than radical. Policy-oriented research modifies (and hopefully improves) the existing situation, protecting it from running into trouble by identifying or anticipating problems. It may challenge established policy by demonstrating its impracticability, or may develop or explore alternative policies. But it is essentially concerned with movement from a present situation, and therefore it obliges researchers to relate their work to "reality," usually in the form of empirical studies or fieldwork.

2. Trends

Although pressure toward policy-oriented research has increased since the early 1970s, many of the early educational research studies had a strong practical orientation. Binet's work, for example, which laid the foundations of psychometry, began with the problem of early identification of slow-learning children. The work of Thorndike and others in the 1920s on the psychology of the elementary school curriculum aimed to influence educational policy and classroom practice. The "scientific movement" in the 1930s envisaged the creation of a science of education based on experimentation, which would be used to improve decision-making at all levels, from day-to-day classroom practice to long-term educational planning. National studies in the 1930s, such as the Eight-year Study to test the feasibility of school accreditation and the international program of research on examinations, were directed to produce practical recommendations for improvement of the system. The distinction between practical and theoretical research was not stressed at this time. The two kinds of research were seen as complementary; and since there was practically no public funding of research, the choice of topic was left to academic researchers in universities and colleges.

The situation changed dramatically in the years after 1950, first with the growth of publicly financed research (1955–65) and a massive expansion of funding in 1965–70, and subsequently with the demand for accountability and a trend toward central control of research. Initially (and relatively slowly) there was acceptance that educational research could make a significant contribution to policy and practice. The social sciences had come of age and their potential value was recognized. (Perhaps it was merely that administrators found themselves at a disadvantage in controversies if they could not produce empirical evidence to support their decisions.) In Sweden, the linking of research to policy began in the 1940s. In the 1960s, in the United States and the United Kingdom (and subsequently in many other countries), formal institutional structures were created for channeling public funds into educational research and development, particularly for curriculum development and intervention programs. As a result, between 1964 and 1969, expenditure on research in education in the United Kingdom multiplied tenfold; and in the United States, expenditure doubled each year from 1964 through 1967. Almost all this funding was for policy-oriented research.

The increase in funding soon led to a demand for accountability, and for a greater say in how the funds were to be spent. Since public funding was for policy-oriented research, policymakers began to demand the right to decide which policy aspects should be researched, and also how the research should be oriented. In 1970 in the United Kingdom, for example, the Secretary of State for Education and Science demanded that research policy in education "had to move from a basis of patronage—the rather passive support of ideas which were essentially other people's, related to problems which were often of other people's choosing—to a basis of commission . . . the active initiation by the Department on problems of its own choosing, within a procedure and timetable which were relevant to its needs" (DES 1970). This was followed in 1971 by the crude customer–contractor formula of the Rothschild Report (1971): "The customer says what he wants; the contractor (the researcher) does it if he can; and the customer pays" (p. 3). This method of deciding how research should be funded was widely challenged at the time. But the

protests could not survive the energy crisis of 1973 and the economic constraints of the years which followed. The need to cut back expenditure made decisions on priorities inevitable, and increasingly these decisions were made by central government. Perhaps too much had been expected, or promised, and disillusionment was allied with suspicion of "academic drift," in which preoccupation with theory was given priority over pressing practical issues. In the early 1990s, research which is not linked to policy is at risk of being seen as a dispensable luxury, and major policy issues are seen as the only topics worth studying.

Thus, to quote from a review of developments in eight countries (Nisbet 1981a), "Across the world, educational research is now an integral part of modern administrative procedure. Increased investment in research has led to . . . a concern that the conduct, organisation and funding of research should be directed towards maximising its effect on policy and practice. The major questions to which answers are still sought are, What forms of research should have priority? and, Who is to decide?" (p. 104).

Since then, decisions increasingly have been made centrally by those who control public funds, not only on what should be researched but also on the method and scale (everything short of the results expected), and often with restrictions on the right to publish without official approval. Central decision-making on research priorities runs the risk of restricting the scope of inquiry. The Organisation for Economic Co-operation and Development in a report (OECD 1988 p. 23) expressed its concern at the trend toward a "practical, short-term and commercial orientation" in the national research programs of its member states. However, as Cuban (1992) noted, "the frameworks which educational researchers use . . . often overlook unwittingly the enduring tension-ridden dilemmas that practitioners and policymakers must manage in their organizations" (p. 7). Restrictions on dissemination, though increasingly common in research contracts, run counter to the basic principle of "critical debate," defined in a policy statement of the British Educational Research Association (Bassey 1992) as "opening one's work to the scrutiny of others in order first to search for errors and fallacies, and secondly to seek creative insights into its future development" (p. 8).

If policy-oriented research is to be effective, it needs cooperation between policymakers and researchers; but it also requires a degree of independence. A warning of the danger inherent in central control was given in the United Kingdom in 1982, when a second Rothschild Report (1982) was published, on the work of the government-sponsored Social Science Research Council: "The need for independence from government departments is particularly important because so much social science is the stuff of political debate . . . It would be too much to expect Ministers to show enthusiasm for research designed to show that their policies were misconceived. But it seems obvious that in many cases the public interest will be served by such research being undertaken" (p. 12). This raises the issue of how research can best be used in the framing and monitoring of policy.

3. Utilization

How can research best contribute to policy and practice in education? This question is the central theme of the 1985 *World Yearbook of Education* (Nisbet et al. 1985), which reviews contrasting perspectives in 14 countries. People have different expectations of research, and these are often unrealistic. Policymakers and teachers tend to look to research to provide answers to their problems; but research can perform this function only when there is consensus on values, within the framework of accepted policy or in the context of established practice. Researchers are more likely to see the role of research as identifying new problems, or new perspectives on problems—problem-setting rather than problem-solving (Rein and Schon 1977). But implementation will happen only when the findings are seen as relevant to the issues which concern those with the responsibility of action. If it is not to be just an esoteric activity, research in education must have a context. But whose context is it to be?

If research is undertaken in the context of those who are expected to make use of the findings, the likelihood of implementation is much greater. The Australian *Karmel Report* (Karmel 1973) summarized the requirements for impact: "The effectiveness of innovation . . . is dependent on the extent to which the people concerned perceive a problem . . ., are knowledgeable about a range of alternative solutions, and feel themselves to be in a congenial climate" (p. 126). How people perceive a problem is itself influenced by research publications. Thus research shapes people's perceptions, and provides them with concepts to use in thinking about the work they do. In this way, research creates an agenda of concern.

Weiss (1979), reviewing the contribution of social research to public policy, identified seven models of research utilization:

(a) the linear model, which assumes that basic research leads into applied research, followed by development and implementation;

(b) the problem-solving model, in which research identifies the missing knowledge to guide action;

(c) the interactive model, involving researchers and policymakers in constructive cooperative dialogue;

(d) the political model, where research is used to provide justification for an already favored policy;

(e) the tactical model, in which the need for research is used as an excuse to delay decision or action;

(f) the enlightenment model, envisaging research

ideas filtering through and shaping how people think;

(g) the intellectual model, by which the activity of research widens horizons and raises the quality of public debate.

The first two models are naive; the third and seventh overhopeful; the fourth and fifth cynical. In an earlier work, Weiss (1977) argued for the sixth of these models—the enlightenment model—seeing the most important effect of research as indirect and long-term, through "a gradual accumulation of research results" (p. 16), shaping the context within which policy decisions are made. Husén and Kogan (1984) in *Educational Research and Policy: How Do They Relate?*, the most comprehensive review of the issue in the 1980s, accept this "percolation" model, but ask how the percolation of ideas can be engineered. Research can clarify issues, raise awareness, and create space for testing policies before they are put into action; but there is a lack of institutional structures for independent research to have impact on the formulation of policy.

The problem-solving model is implicit in one of the most widely read educational publications of the 1980s, *What Works: Research about Teaching and Learning* (US Department of Education 1986). This 65-page booklet listed 41 research findings about how best to teach and improve learning. Each finding was stated, briefly elaborated, and supported by five references to research literature. In the Preface, the President of the United States commended it as providing practical knowledge based on "some of the best available research for use by the American public." Published in January 1986, 300,000 copies were in circulation within 6 months. Glass (1987) criticized this selection of "useful findings" as "an expression of conservative philosophy" (p. 6), arguing that its popular appeal was due to the possibility of applying the findings within the existing framework of educational assumptions.

Husén and Kogan (1984) identify a major dilemma in the different worlds of policy and research. The two worlds have different and conflicting values, different reference groups and reward systems, and even different languages. Policy decision-making must be firm and authoritative, whereas research is essentially questioning and uncertain.

> A political decision will lead to closure on an issue. Research findings add to, rather than reduce, uncertainty for decision-makers. The interplay between decision-making which must be authoritative and firm and the questioning and uncertainty implicit in the research is an important phenomenon. It leads to a central policy question: can national authorities sponsor the generation of uncertainty? . . . Policy-makers may foreclose on issues too quickly: social science can keep open the space between the dissemination of ideas which might lead to policy changes and their enforcement. (p. 52)

327

Bell and Raffe (1991) offer a resolution of this dilemma by distinguishing a changing balance between research and policy in three phases of the policy cycle:

(a) recognition of a problem and shaping a policy;

(b) implementing a policy;

(c) evaluating the outcomes and reshaping the policy.

In the first phase, before outlines of a new policy have emerged, "wide-ranging critical research is welcomed, because it will help to win support for change." In the second phase, the government needs to build support for its chosen policy: "research which calls into question the wisdom of the policy or the assumptions on which it is based is not welcome." Here, the policy world is most restrictive and control tightest. In the third phase, "there is a degree of relaxation: the policy is no longer so politically sensitive (it is now the flavour of last month) . . . and critical research findings are less potentially damaging" (p. 141). Bell and Raffe ask why so little policy-related research is commissioned in the first phase of the policy cycle.

The answer lies in who is seen as holding power. The policymakers seek to establish a policy which is acceptable to those with power to influence its implementation. Their concern is not so much a matter of being "right" (for there are different "right" solutions, depending on one's values), but rather of reconciling divergent views in a solution which is seen as "fair" by a maximum number of those affected by it. In this, the aims and values of those with access to power must carry greatest weight.

In the amorphous process of policy-making, there are several functions which research can perform. First, insofar as information conveys power, research strengthens the hand of any group which can produce research findings to support its preferred viewpoint. (Even to describe assertions as "research" strengthens their impact.) Coleman (1984) noted that this strategy "is most often used by those without direct control over policy, who challenge the policies of those in positions of authority" (p. 132); and this may be one reason for policymakers' hostility to research. Administrators commission policy-oriented research to strengthen their hand against the many pressure groups in the policy-making arena. In the view of the administrators, pressure groups are those who seek to further their own policies, whereas administrators see themselves as neutral to the policy they implement. Information thus weakens the power of those who play on ignorance or twist facts to suit their private ends. This, however, assumes that research is value-free, or at least that research makes explicit the values on which it is based.

A second function for research is to ensure that action will achieve what is intended in a policy. For this purpose, research is used to work out the details of how to implement decisions, by identifying obstacles, including the opinions and attitudes of those who might oppose the policy, and by testing out solutions to overcome these obstacles in trials with pilot groups. Using Bell and Raffe's three phases of the policy cycle: in phase 1, surveys gather relevant "facts" as a database for decision; in phase 2, pilot studies establish feasibility and identify likely obstacles; and in phase 3, evaluation provides monitoring and guidance for future decision or modification.

In all three phases, the most valuable research design is one which focuses on analysis of problems, rather than simply seeking to supply answers to questions. There are of course some who still hold the unrealistic expectation that research should provide ready-made incontrovertible solutions. The Secretary of State of the Department of Education and Science for England and Wales, for example, once complained: "It is exceptional to find a piece of research that really hits the nail on the head and tells you pretty clearly what is wrong or what should be done" (Pile 1976 p. 3). Weiss (1977) describes this as the "linear model" of research utilization and criticizes its "instrumental naivety." The sequence implied is: "A problem exists; information or understanding is lacking; research provides the missing knowledge; a solution is reached" (pp. 11–12). There are relatively few situations in which this model is applicable. Halsey's (1972) interpretation is nearer the truth: "Action research is unlikely ever to yield neat and definitive prescriptions from field-tested plans. What it offers is an aid to intelligent decision-making, not a substitute for it. Research brings relevant information rather than uniquely exclusive conditions" (p. 179).

However, the claim that the prime use of research lies in the analysis of problems may be seen only as an academic abdication of responsibility, and may encourage the suspicion that the only ones who derive benefit from investment in research are the researchers themselves. Being isolated from the practical realities of the "real world," as it is termed, they divert public money to academic interests of their own instead of to the problems which require solutions. The solution adopted has been to take the decisions on research priorities out of the hands of the researchers and put them in the hands of the administrators. If research cannot give direction to policy, then the influence should be reserved and policymakers should be given control of research, allowing policy priorities to determine the choice and design of research. If those who are in contact with the "real world" take over the management of research, so the assumption goes, impact will be improved, relevance will be greater, and the risk of wasted money will be avoided.

Consequently, decisions on research priorities are often made by those who are not themselves directly involved in research. This mode of working is familiar to the economist, the engineer, and the agricultural specialist; it is not accepted generally in legal and medical matters. The administrator who controls research funds now expects to be involved in the initial decisions on the topic of inquiry, the design, the time scale, the personnel required, and of course the cost. When a project is funded, there will be continuing interest (or interference, as it may seem to the researcher) in monitoring what is being done through an advisory committee (often designated as a steering committee) and regular reporting on progress. Tighter control may be imposed by "stepped funding," in which funds for each stage are conditional on approval of a report on the previous one. Arrangements for publishing and discussing the findings will be specified in the contract, which may require surrender of copyright and "moral rights" to the sponsor and acceptance of their right of veto should they find the results not to their liking.

It is difficult to stand against these pressures. Not only can sponsors withhold funds: even access to schools is usually made conditional on approval of the research project as a whole and of the research instruments in detail. Thus policy-oriented research can become wholly directed and censored by people who are not themselves researchers and who have a vested interest in the outcomes. Clearly, the dangers here are that criticism of a policy is not likely to be encouraged and that important issues are organized out of debate. Fortunately, many of those responsible for the funding of research are aware of these dangers. In some countries at least, the relationship between researchers and the providers of funds is quite close, both sides understanding the requirements and constraints of the other.

4. Conclusion

Two functions of research in education can be distinguished: one long-term, creating the theoretical context in which day-to-day issues are perceived, writing an agenda of concern; the other more immediate, working out routine problems within the context of the current educational provision and prevailing views. These are the basic and policy-oriented modes of research, but the distinction between them is not as sharp as might appear. The applied sciences have often resulted in significant contributions to theory, and theoretical studies may have profound impact on perceptions of practical needs.

Academic status tends to be accorded to those who make contributions to theory. In the social sciences, their ideas and new concepts are gradually absorbed into popular thought and discussion until they become a new climate of opinion, variously described as a "prevailing view" (Cronbach and Suppes), "a cumulative altering of conceptions of human behavior" (Getzels), "sensitizing" (Taylor), or "ideas in good currency" (Schon). Administrators and politicians respond to the "resonance" of research findings, often to a filtered, out-of-date perception. In the early 1990s, however, research funding is available almost exclusively for policy-oriented studies. Research of this kind can be a powerful instrument of reform, testing out new ideas, modifying them or rejecting them if they are at fault, and if the evidence shows them to be feasible, establishing their credibility all the more widely and quickly. The results are more likely to have impact and thus create in the long term a favorable climate of opinion as to the value of educational research. In a time of financial constraint and accountability, it is difficult to justify the expenditure of public funds on any other kind of research in education.

The danger, however, is that if research is too closely tied to existing educational provision and practice, where the concept of "relevance" implies implementation without radical change, the effects may be only marginal and may even be an obstacle to reform. The restrictions increasingly imposed on researchers in policy-oriented funding are seen by many as running counter to the basic requirement of open, critical study. There is also a danger of accepting a purely technocratic role for research, creating an elite group of researchers in alliance with bureaucrats to manage the system. Though at first sight this may seem an attractive role for the researcher, it is potentially divisive, since it divides the researcher and his or her powerful partner from the teaching profession and the public. An alternative style of research is the "teachers as researchers" movement or "action research" (see *Action Research*). In this school-based research, teachers are encouraged to apply the techniques of research to their own work: they define the problems to be researched and they investigate and reflect on their own practice. This style of research also has its risks, of restricting research within the limits of inflexible classroom traditions and narrow professional perspectives. But it could also "be the most fertile soil for educational research to grow in . . . If it can be developed so as to provide teachers (and administrators and parents and all those concerned with education) with the means of improving their own understanding, then its effect will be to put educational studies into a questioning framework" (Broadfoot and Nisbet 1981 p. 121).

An interactionist model of this kind for educational research applies also to the relation of research to policy. The association of policy, administration, and research could be developed in such a way that each illuminates the others. Cronbach et al. (1980) argue for an intermediate structure between research and application to promote this interaction, some institutional means of arguing about the policy relevance of ambiguous results in a "context of accommodation" rather than a "context of command" (pp. 83–84). If policy-oriented studies can be developed in this enlightened way, educational research stands to gain from its closer association with both policy and practice. "Two worlds of educational research may be distinguished, the practical and the theoretical, pure and applied; but we are more likely to have a balanced attitude if we have a foot in both worlds" (Nisbet 1981b p. 175). The contributions of research to policy, to practice, and to theory are not easily reconciled; but the research enterprise would suffer if any one of these three is regarded as of lesser importance.

See also: Educational Research and Policymaking; Policy Analysis; Politics of Educational Planning

References

Bassey M 1992 Educational research and politics: A viewpoint. *Research Intelligence* 43: 8–9

Bell C, Raffe D 1991 Working together: Research, policy and practice. In: Walford G (ed.) 1991 *Doing Educational Research*. Routledge and Kegan Paul, London.

Bondi H 1983 Research funding scrutinized. THES August 19: 3

Broadfoot P M, Nisbet J 1981 The impact of research on educational studies. *Br. J. Educ. Stud.* 29(2): 115–22

Coleman J S 1984 Issues in the institutionalisation of social policy. In: Husén T H, Kogan M (eds.) 1984

Cooley W, Bickel W 1985 *Decision-oriented Educational Research*. Kluwer-Nijhoff, Boston, Massachusetts

Cronbach L J, Suppes P (eds.) 1969 *Research for Tomorrow's Schools: Disciplined Inquiry for Education*. Macmillan, New York

Cronbach L J et al. 1980 *Toward Reform of Program Evaluation*. Jossey-Bass, San Francisco, California

Cuban L 1992 Managing dilemmas while building professional communities. *Educ. Researcher* 21(1): 4–11

Department of Education and Science (DES) 1970 Press release December 1, 1970, for speech to National Foundation for Educational Research. In: Taylor W (ed.) 1973 *Research Perspectives in Education*. Routledge and Kegan Paul, London

Glass G V 1987 What works: Politics and research. *Educ. Researcher* 16(3): 5–10

Halsey A H 1972 *Educational Priority*, Vol. 1. HMSO, London

Husén T H, Kogan M (eds.) 1984 *Educational Research and Policy: How Do They Relate?* Pergamon Press, Oxford

Karmel P H (Chair) 1973 *Schools in Australia*. Australian Government Printing Service, Canberra

Nisbet J 1981a The impact of research on policy and practice in education. *Int. Rev. Educ.* 27(2): 101–04

Nisbet J 1981b Educational research and educational practice. In: Simon B, Taylor W (eds.) 1981 *Education in the Eighties: The Central Issues*. Batsford, London

Nisbet J, Megarry J, Nisbet S (eds.) 1985 *World Yearbook of Education 1985: Research, Policy and Practice*. Kogan Page, London

OECD 1988 *Science and Technology Policy Outlook*. OECD, Paris.

Pile W 1976 Some research called "rubbish." THES January 23: 3

Rein M, Schon D A 1977 Problem setting in policy research. In: Weiss C (ed.) 1977

Rothschild Report 1971 *A Framework for Government Research and Development*. HMSO (Cmnd 4814), London

Rothschild Report 1982 *An Enquiry into the Social Science Research Council*. HMSO (Cmnd 8554), London

Taylor W (ed.) 1973 *Research Perspectives in Education*. Routledge and Kegan Paul, London

US Department of Education 1986 *What Works: Research about Teaching and Learning*. Washington, DC

Weiss C (ed.) 1977 *Using Social Research in Public Policy Making*. Heath, Lexington, Massachusetts

Weiss C 1979 The many meanings of research utilization. *Public Administration Review* (Sept/Oct): 426–31

SECTION IV

The School as a Social System

Introduction: The Systemic Approach to the Study of Education

L. J. Saha

It is common to talk about differences in educational systems. Often we do this in a comparative context, but by doing so we are acknowledging that there are macro level characteristics which allow us to describe differences between education in different social, structural, and cultural contexts. These contexts may be countries, political boundaries such as states or provinces, or local education authorities in Britain and local school districts in the United States.

In sociology, the term "social system" refers to any patterning of social relations across temporal or spatial boundaries. In this context a social system can refer to a social group, social organization such as a company or firm, a political entity such as state or country, or a larger global entity, such as the British Commonwealth. Often the notion of social system is equated with functionalism which postulates that society is like a system which is composed of integrated parts which function together to form a well-integrated whole. However, that is not the understanding of social system which is found in much of educational research.

The 10 articles in the section focus upon aspects of education as a social system, and therefore in one way or another focus upon patterned ways of ordering education systems and the implications for students, teachers, and administrators within them.

The two most obvious places to begin such an analysis is with cultural systems and the state. With respect to the first, Erickson defines a sociocultural system as ". . . one in which interactions within and across system boundaries are social and cultural, rather than physical or chemical" (*Schools as Sociocultural Systems*). Obviously one type of boundary is the political, and in particular the kind of social system which is brought about by the link between education and the state, which Meek discusses in his article *Education and the State*. Meek observes that the relations between education and the modern state are "infinitely complex and continually changing."

Another way of analyzing educational systems is discussed by Benavot in *Institutional Approach to the Study of Education*. This relatively new perspective focuses upon the ways in which nation-states empower schools to classify young people in different ways, such as classrooms, grade levels, education credentials, and curricular tracks, and how these institutionalized systems of meaning exercise an impact on other aspects of society, such as definitions of the self, relations within families, and the rights of different groups within society.

Clearly, state policies affect aspects of educational and school systems, such as race and ethnic differences in schools, and educational programs to encourage multiculturalism in heterogeneous societies are a reflection of such policies, as Ekstrand discusses in *Multicultural Education*. Likewise, Bray addresses issues related to school size in *School Size and Small Schools*, and Hallinan focuses on the social context of school choice in *Social Foundations of School Choice*, both of which are important dimensions in current debates about ways that school systems should be organized. Additional system-level characteristics of education concern the issues relating to the link between education and occupations, discussed by Peschar in *Stratification in Educational Systems*. These links affect the patterns of social mobility within a society, that is, the extent to which the society is "open" or "closed." Dronkers summarizes the ways in which societies differ in the relationship between education and social mobility in *Social Mobility, Social Stratification, and Education*.

Political ideologies often bring about considerable variation in educational systems. For 70 years one could argue that there were two major educational systems which dominated the developed world, namely that based on Marxist–Leninist ideology and that based on Western capitalism. The former, often known as the socialist educational model, and the latter, known as the capitalist model, are described by Lofstedt and Zhao in *Socialist and Capitalist Schooling: Comparative Perspectives*. Their article contrasts the two systems in terms of ideological origins and the ways that these ideologies are reflected in the structures and practices within the school systems themselves. Their prototype of the socialist model is largely derived from China. Kuebart, on the other hand, in *Socialist Education Systems*, focuses on the Eastern European socialist educational systems before 1989 and 1990. He describes the socialist educational system in terms of general structure, curriculum, administration, and the status of teachers, and identifies ways in which aspects of the socialist system still remain after the reforms of these educational systems in postsocialist Eastern Europe.

The sociological study of education and of schools from a system perspective does not yet exist as a coherent body of knowledge, although the recognition of education and schools as systems does receive attention in specialized research and policy areas. The articles in this section, when seen as a totality, make a contribution towards generating a more integrated system-level approach to the study of schooling.

Education and the State

V. L. Meek

The relationship between education and the state is infinitely complex and continually changing, and generalizations are difficult to make. Analysis is complicated by the fact that there is no agreement on what actually constitutes the state or on how it operates. The substance of the relationship varies greatly according to theoretical perspective. It is also necessary to distinguish between public perceptions on how the state operates and theoretical views. Nevertheless, the consequences of different theoretical views of the state can be identified and broad trends in the relationship between education and the state can be discerned.

This article first examines the concept of the state and the various and sometimes contradictory theories which attempt to explain how it operates. The way in which theory and perception of the function and structure of education interact are highlighted. Then the discussion turns to trends in the relationship between education and the state, such as moves toward marketplace discipline, deregulation, national curriculum, key competencies, managerialism, and centralization/decentralization. Higher education, particularly university education, is treated as a special case. In conclusion, future directions are examined. The discussion here is mainly concerned with Western state systems and public sector education. Mass public education, with its roots in the nineteenth and early part of the twentieth centuries, is a product of the modern state. However, it should be noted that the distinction between public and private sector education is largely artificial; the state impinges on private sector education in a number of ways—through regulation, accreditation, finance, and subsidies.

1. Conceptual and Theoretical Issues

There is no one accepted definition of the state or agreement on how it operates, but it is possible to discern the parameters within which much of the debate occurs. Before turning to an outline of the main theoretical traditions that have been applied to an understanding of the relationship between education and the state, the concept itself requires examination.

State theorists usually draw a distinction between the state as such and state organizations. Typical state organizations are: the elected representatives meeting in congress, parliament, cabinet, or some such forum; the departments of state, such as treasury, foreign affairs, health, housing, and education; the judiciary and courts; the military and police; state or provincial governments/parliaments in federated systems; state owned companies, such as airlines; and regulatory bodies and statutory authorities, such as the BBC in the United Kingdom and the ABC in Australia. The state, as an analytical concept, is not synonymous with state instrumentalities, government, or the public sector although, in everyday language, the terms are often used interchangeably. Moreover, the state cannot be thought of as all that is not private. The interrelationship between private interests—particularly private property interests—and the state is a focal point for analysis. Students of public policy draw a clear line between government instrumentalities and civil society, whereas state theorists make a much less fine distinction. As a concept, the state transcends the notion of particular nation-states. In fact, since the 1950s, much of the structure and curriculum content of education, particularly in developing countries, have been shaped by international organizations, such as The World Bank and UNESCO. Of course, the political agenda of these agencies and of the United Nations itself is greatly influenced by the interests of particular nation-states, such as the United States.

Thus, "in analytical terms the state is an agency of control, social order and cohesion, legitimacy, socialisation and economic intervention" (Davis et al. 1988 p.16). The state is best understood "as the sphere of direct enforceable social relationships . . . which underlie markets and also provide the basis for the construction of the state organizations such as courts, parliaments and government departments" (Connell 1977 p.6). Whose interest state-enforced social relationships serve is the subject of much debate. Although an oversimplification, the debate can be divided between those who see the state as serving the interests of the entire body-politic of society, and those who regard the state as oriented to the interests of the ruling class in a structure of capitalist social and economic relations. More will be said about this in a later section but first the issue of the power of the state needs to be addressed.

1.1 State Power

Given the above definition, the question arises as to how the state enforces a set of social relationships. The power of government both rests on and is constrained by the legislative and legal fabric of society, but, on a more analytical plane, the state can be viewed as having access to the three primary instruments of power: condign power (physical), compensatory power (economic), and conditioned power (belief) (Galbraith 1983).

Condign power, the legitimate use of physical coercion and violence, belongs to the state, and usually is exercised by the military, police, and judiciary. But the state may also sanction (or deny) the use of coercion by other public or private instrumentalities, such as education. In most industrialized countries, for example, attendance at school until a citizen reaches a set age is legally enforceable. Some states may sanction the use of corporal punishment within schools, while others deny its use, but legitimate violence plays a minor role in the maintenance of social order in modern society. As Bismarck is reputed to have once said: you can do several things with bayonets, except sit upon them.

Compensatory power, the power to allocate resources (property, capital, money), is a fundamental role of the state. The state is both an economic force in its own right and intervenes in private business and markets in a number of ways. As will be discussed further below, the wealth of the state is used to support particular economic relations within society. Neo-Marxists maintain that capitalist economic principles shape all other institutions in society, including the state. Nevertheless, mass public education is, by definition, only possible through the economic wealth of the state, whether capitalist or socialist. A nation's commitment to education is often measured in terms of the percentage of GDP it allocates to this activity. More important than money are the basic principles underlying its allocation and society's belief in their inherent worth.

Conditioned power is the most important form of power in modern industrial society, and the state is the locus of conditioned power. It is through "persuasion, education, or the social commitment to what seems natural, proper or right" that the corporation, educational institution, church, and the state "cause the individual to submit to the will of another or of others." Conditioned power is central "to the functioning of the modern economy and polity, and in capitalist and socialist countries alike" (Galbraith 1983 p. 23).

No individual or group in modern industrial society can sustain power over a long period of time solely on the basis of the threat of physical violence or the promise of economic reward. If power is to be sustained over time then at least a proportion of the population must believe in the social order that results in the subordination of some groups to the will and interest of others. People are never completely conditioned to unquestioningly accept the beliefs and values of others, and groups may be in conflict because they hold competing beliefs and values. People nonetheless submit, probably to a greater extent than they know or are willing to admit, to the authority and interests of others because they believe it is the right thing to do.

The ubiquity of conditioned power means that it is difficult to analyze. One way to approach the problem is to look behind generally accepted ideas and beliefs to see what power relations they support and whose interests they serve. Take, for example, the general social support which early industrial capitalism received despite the striking inequalities that it produced. As industrial capitalism developed so did certain ideas

about the nature of humankind that tended to support the power of the capitalist. From religion, ideas were introduced that said God rewarded the righteous on this earth and that the righteous had a God-given right to rule (see Weber *The Protestant Ethic and the Spirit of Capitalism*). The social scientists and economists introduced similar ideas and gave them a pseudoscientific legitimacy. The ultimate case for industrial capitalism was made by the social Darwinist, Herbert Spencer: "[capitalism] was the manifestation of Darwin in the social order; its governing principle was the survival of the fittest. The great industrial capitalists . . . were great because they were biologically superior; the poor were poor because they were inferior" (Galbraith 1983 p. 117).

It was classical economics, and its architect Adam Smith, that provided an enduring set of ideas that has supported capitalism throughout its development from industrial to corporate capitalism. From classical economics comes the idea of the inherent good of a free market, and that it is the "invisible hand of the marketplace" that adjusts all social relations for the greatest social good. With the development of classical economic theory:

> went the continuing celebration of the market. Not only did its uninhibited operation accord the greatest good to the greatest number, but it was also an effective solvent— and concealment—of the power of industrial capitalism. Prices were set by the market. Wages were set by the market. So were the prices of all the other requisites to the market. On none of these matters did the industrialist have power; hence there could be no legitimate concern as to its exercise. . . . Here was the supreme conditioning achievement of what has come to be called classical economics. It guided the power of the industrialist, however, against his intention, to good social ends; it also denied the existence of such power. And it taught this to all who sought to understand the workings of the system. . . . This instruction, needless to say, still persists. Nothing is so important in the defense of the modern corporation as the argument that its power does not exist—that all power is surrendered to the impersonal play of the market, all decision is in response to the instruction of the market. And nothing is more serviceable than the resulting conditioning of the young to that belief. (Galbraith 1983 pp. 119–20)

The two basic concepts used by state theorists to examine conditioned power are ideology and hegemony. Ideology is defined by the *Shorter Oxford Dictionary* as "a system of ideas concerning phenomena, esp. those of social life; the manner of thinking characteristic of a class or an individual." While different writers use the word in various ways, underlying most sociological use of the word is the notion that ideology somehow masks or hides the real nature of social relations. Marx, for example, maintained that in every historical period the ruling ideas were the ideas of the ruling class. As noted above, under capitalism a set of ideas which legitimates the exploitation of the laboring class and the protection of private property is promoted as the right and natural way of viewing the world. Its acceptance and the way in which it masks the true nature of the social relations of material production is termed as false ideology or false consciousness. From this point of view, one of the primary functions of a state-sponsored system of mass education is to socialize one generation of children after another into accepting as natural the ideology of the ruling class, thus reproducing the exploitive social relations over time.

The concept of hegemony, as developed by the Italian dissident Antonio Gramsci, goes beyond that of ideology in that it attempts to explain how the ruling class attempts to incorporate the interests of potentially divergent groups within its own ranks, establishing "*their* view of the world as universal, thus imposing their own conception of reality on all subordinate classes" (Porter 1991 p. 15). According to Whitson (1991 p. 79):

> the concept of hegemony would be superfluous if it meant nothing more than domination through the combined effects of diverse ideological and coercive factors. The essential and unique contribution of "hegemony" is its revelation of how the program of dominant groups is advanced, not simply by excluding oppositional programs, but by locating the opposition within the total ideological and sociopolitical structure in places where the opposition may be harmless or even supporting to the structure's viability.

Bourgeois values and norms dominate not through the coercive arm of the state, but through its educative purpose. According to Gramsci (quoted in Torres 1985 p. 4793) "rule by intellectual and moral hegemony is the form of power which gives stability and . . . wide-ranging consent and acquiescence; every relationship of hegemony is necessarily a pedagogical relationship."

1.2 Theories of the State

There are several theories of the state: Marxist, neo-Marxist, corporatism, elitist, liberal democratic, organizational, bureaucratic, and so on (Jessop 1990). The theoretical complexity in understanding the state/education relationship can be grasped by placing theory on a continuum, with radical left interpretations at one end and conservative new right theory at the other.

Classical Marxist theory views the state—the superstructure—basically as an instrument of the capitalist ruling class, but even if the state does ultimately serve the interests of the ruling class, it must appear to do otherwise. Here, ideology and the socialization function of education are central factors. Althusser (1971), for example, maintains that the socioeconomic relations of capitalism are produced and reproduced through what he terms the "ideological state apparatus." The state, particularly through the instrument of education, socializes society into accepting the attitudes and values of class relationships and the inequalities they create. Schools not only produce the skills necessary for an industrialized labor force, but are agents of domination, repression, and exploitation through socializing the working class into accepting their role within a hierarchical class structure. Poulantzas (1973) also regards education as a repressive instrument of the superstructure, forcing students into accepting both the skills and attitudes and values necessary for maintaining the social relations of material production. Bowles and Gintis (1976), in their historical study of education in the United States, attempt to demonstrate how schooling at different points in time supports the social relations of production. There are many other writers who have argued that the family and schools socialize the young into accepting the "culture" of their class position.

Connell (1977 p. 187), in his examination of education in Australia, criticizes an instrumentalist and overly deterministic approach to schooling adopted by some writers, maintaining that it is not so much that schools socialize the young into accepting their class position but: "what seems more important is the learning of social practices, such as a specific style of work, and a prudential respecting of (rather than an attitude of respect for) authority and private property." In other words, class relations are based on first-hand knowledge of the material world, with both members of the working class and the bourgeoisie holding the same attitudes toward class and the benefits or otherwise of particular class membership. Connell's questioning of the degree to which the "norms of compliance are thoroughly internalized" opens up the possibility of contradiction and conflict within the superstructure.

The liberal democratic or liberal pluralist theories of the state can be placed somewhere in the middle of the theoretical continuum. The liberal pluralist tradition views the state more or less as a neutral instrument for mediating and adjudicating between the competing demands of various interest groups within society. The state does not favor one group or coalition over another, but allows and protects the expression of interests of various groups through the democratic process. Power within society is fairly evenly distributed and does not coalesce around class interests. The state exists to protect the rights of all citizens. According to liberal pluralists, education serves three primary functions: cognitive development and skills formation, training for citizenship and participation in the democratic process, and rewarding the meritorious. According to the principle of meritocracy, education does not serve the interest of any one group or class, but allows every citizen to achieve according to his or her innate ability. The role of the state is to ensure equity in educational provision, though not necessarily in outcome.

On the other end of the theoretical continuum from the Marxists is the new right or conservative interpretation of the state. Not unlike Marxists, the conservative position regards economic relations as the dominant force shaping society and the state as interventionist, protecting and promoting particular interests and values. The conservatives rapidly depart company from the Marxists in their emphasis on the inherent good of the private market. For conservatives, the state is a necessary "evil," but its sphere of influence should be kept to a minimum in order to allow social relations to be adjusted through market competition. For conservatives, the private market, not the state, should be the final arbitrator of social relations. The state should not have a central planning function, it should only ensure that the rules of market competition are fair. Market competition promotes both cost efficiency and individual freedom. Education is not so much a public good to be subsidized by the state, as it is a consumable item to be paid for by the individual. Thus, individuals should be allowed to pay for the best education that they can afford. Under market rules, equity of educational provision is not an issue.

The above theoretical approaches to the state are, of necessity, oversimplifications. What each tends to ignore is, on the one hand, the degree to which the state has autonomy from the means of production, and, on the other, the state and state organizations as sites for contests and conflicts over values and norms. In most Western countries, the state does much more than merely serve the interests of private capital. As well as being a site for power struggles between different class interests, the state promotes reforms and the protection of general human rights. The state is contradictory in that it is simultaneously a repressive agent of the bourgeoisie and an autonomous and progressive promoter of reform:

> Thus contradictions are inherent in the action of educational systems and policy can be, at one and the same time, progressive and reproductive. In this formulation the state is given both reflectivity *and* autonomy from the economic base. Furthermore, it is credited with some real progressive impact via its liberal democratic discourse of natural rights. Given that education is a key arm of the state, this conception allows us to explain how educational authorities can be both progressive and conservative with regard to class and gender divisions. It also illuminates the way the state is both a site of social struggle *and* the prize itself. (Porter 1991 p. 17)

To conclude the theoretical discussion, it should be noted that, since the 1970s what has been termed as postmodernism or poststructuralism has attempted to usher in a new set of understandings of the relationship between education and the state. Neither postmodernism nor poststructuralism constitutes a coherent set of theoretical assumptions, and, while some writers use the two words interchangeably, others draw a firm distinction between postmodern and poststructural theories (Whitson 1991 p. 73). Basically, the postmodern movement is a reaction against modernism, against overly deterministic grand theory of either the right or left persuasion, against

the assumption of the ubiquitous nature of Western humanism and scientific rationalism and against equating change with progress and modernization. For postmodern theorists, there are no universals:

> postmodernism presents itself as a critique of all forms of representation and meaning that claim transcendental and transhistorical status. It rejects universal reason as a foundation for human affairs, and poses as alternative forms of knowing that are partial, historical, and social in nature. . . . postmodernism points to a world in which the production of meaning has become as important as the production of labor in shaping the boundaries of human existence . . .
>
> Postmodernism not only views the subject as contradictory and multi-layered, it rejects the notion that individual consciousness and reason are the most important determinants in shaping human history. It posits instead a faith in forms of social transformation that understand the historical, structural, and ideological limits that shape the possibility for self-reflection, agency and action. (Giroux 1991 p. 24)

Thus, the postmodern education agenda looks not to universal structural relationships between education and the state, but toward empowering the individual with the means of deconstructing a world that is entirely of a social nature: "there is no single, predetermined relationship between a cultural code and the subject position that a student occupies. One's class, racial, gender, or ethnic position may influence but does not irrevocably predetermine how one takes up a particular ideology, reads a particular text, or responds to particular forms of oppression" (Giroux 1991 p. 29).

2. Trends

Throughout the 1980s and into the 1990s, new right ideology, supported by monetarist economic philosophy and strategies, has been the dominant influence on the relationship between education and the state. The new right ideology, with its emphasis on the marketplace and privatization, has helped restructure the state/education relationship in many countries. This movement has been popularly characterized as Thatcherism in the United Kingdom and Reaganomics in the United States. However, the influence of new right ideology neither began with Margaret Thatcher or Ronald Reagan, nor has it ceased with their departure from the world political stage. Elements of this ideology—particularly its emphasis on the market as the most efficient mechanism for coordinating the affairs of society—can be traced back to Adam Smith, and are found in such diverse political systems as Australia, Canada, New Zealand, Sweden, and the United States (Lawton S 1992).

The new right has gained prominence, on the one hand, as a response to economic downturn and rising trade deficits and, on the other, as a reaction against the perceived failure of centralized planning and the excesses of the welfare state. Also, the collapse of communism in Eastern Europe and the former USSR has left the impression in the West that the free market is the only enduring mechanism for organizing socioeconomic relations. The celebration of the marketplace vis-à-vis central planning is typified in the following quotation from Sir Keith Joseph, one-time Minister of Education and Science in the Thatcher government:

> The blind, unplanned, uncoordinated wisdom of the market . . . is overwhelmingly superior to the well-researched, rational, systematic, well-meaning, cooperative, science-based, forward-looking, statistically respectable plans of government. . . . The market system is the greatest generator of national wealth known to mankind: coordinating and fulfilling the diverse needs of countless individuals in a way which no human mind or minds could ever comprehend, without coercion, without direction, without bureaucratic interference. (Lawton D 1992 p. 6)

In many countries, the reassertion of traditional conservative values stands in opposition to those of the "permissive society" of the 1960s and early 1970s. Progressive education and child-centered learning are being replaced by an emphasis on standards, discipline, and consumer choice. Self-reliance and the pursuit of personal gain within a free market context, rather than state welfare and centralized planning, are being regarded as the best approach to social ills and inequalities.

New right ideology and its emphasis on marketplace discipline have had several consequences for the state/education relationship. In many countries, the emphasis has shifted from centralized control to consumerism and devolution of authority within the context of a deregulated educational environment. Whereas it was once believed that quality and equity in educational provision could only be achieved through centralized state authority, in countries like Australia and New Zealand, much of the responsibility for these matters has been placed on local communities. Educational reforms in New Zealand are premised on the belief that "by gaining more control over the education system, parents would be able to ensure their children would get a good education. In this approach, control by the central state was seen as a barrier to equality" (Gordon 1992 p. 191). The 1988 Education Reform Act in the United Kingdom not only gave schools the option of being released from their Local Education Authorities (LEAs) and creating stronger, parent-dominated councils, but also gave parents the choice as to which school they would send their children (Walford 1992). What is at issue is not choice, as such, but the assumption that the marketplace "is a more efficient method of matching the needs and desires of investors (or consumers) with the products and services that are available" (S Lawton 1992 p. 143). Writing on the school choice movement in the United States, Cookson (1992 p. 303) maintains that: "If we are able to select our schools the way we select our laundry detergents, then state regulation must be minimal, unobtrusive and probably insignificant. . . . by their very nature free-market school-choice plans are designed to limit the power of the state in determining where students will attend school."

Devolution of authority and control to the schools themselves and the introduction of school-based management have been accompanied by what has been termed the managerial revolution. For the sake of enhancing efficiency and effectiveness, politicians are turning away from the advice of professional educators toward the managerial norms and values of private enterprise. In the Australian state of Victoria, for example, the title of Director-General of Education has been changed to General Manager of Schools. Some writers view the managerial movement in education as a way for politicians to wrest control from professional educators. Others, such as S Lawton (1992), regard it more in terms of a general dissatisfaction with centralized bureaucratic planning. Aucoin and Bakvis state that:

> Almost everywhere, from Ottawa to Moscow and Washington to Paris, highly regulated and centralized structures and processes of public administration have been subject to plans or proposals to deregulate management and to decentralize administrative systems. At the heart of this global concern is the capacity of the modern state, as a complex organization, to respond effectively to turbulent environments on the one hand and to overcome as much as possible the rigidities and pathologies of bureaucratic structures on the other. (Lawton S 1992 p. 146)

No state, however, has or intends to entirely relinquish control over mass public education. Market-driven education policy is full of contradictions. It is appropriate to look at the special case of higher education, for it throws the tensions between education and the state into sharp relief.

2.1 Higher Education and the State

The relationship between higher education, university education in particular, and the state is a special case in that higher education is presumed to be a forum for an autonomous critique of society. Writers such as Kogan have argued against the idea that higher education is a subsystem of the sociopolitical superstructure, dependent entirely on the state for its norms and authority. While such a construct may have validity in some cases, "it has no logical inevitability and it preempts the issue of how far higher education institutions are licensed to be free to set their own norms, or even to be in conflict or tension with the society that sponsors them to be its antibodies" (Kogan 1984 p. 67).

Public higher education institutions receive their charter from the state and, thus, the state is the ultimate authority. Even in countries like the United States with a large private higher education sector, most institutions are nonprofit and are regulated and accredited by the state in various ways. Nevertheless, higher education has developed a tradition of academic autonomy and self-governance that has been respected by most governments in Western countries. Despite higher education's autonomy, governments in several countries are bending their higher education systems in a similar direction: toward marketplace discipline, enhanced efficiency and effectiveness through stronger management, greater competition between institutions, accountability, and tying the goals of higher education more closely to those of industry and private enterprise. Higher education has not escaped many of the state reforms applied to the schools sector.

Several countries have experienced a radical restructuring of their higher education systems, and what is interesting is the high degree of similarity in the reforms across different countries (Meek and Goedegebuure 1991). Both Australia and the United Kingdom, for example, have abolished their binary systems of higher education, called for stronger institutional management based on private enterprise principles (including staff appraisal), introduced user-pays mechanisms (student loans in the United Kingdom and a form of graduate tax in Australia), and set in place policies that enhance institutional competition within a competitive market environment. A comparative study of higher education in eleven countries—Australia, USA (California), Denmark, France, Germany, Japan, the Netherlands, Canada (Ontario), Sweden, Switzerland, and the United Kingdom— concluded that:

> behind many of the changes in the relationships between governments and higher educational institutions is the philosophy of "economic rationalism"; a belief that market forces, rather than state intervention, will make institutions more cost-effective and better managed, as well as making higher education systems more fluid and responsive to client needs and demands. (Goedegebuure et al. 1993 p. 323)

With respect to state/education relationships, two lessons emerge from the higher education experience. First, it highlights the reversal in direction in the relationship between education and the state. Trow (1984 p. 143) maintains that during the 1950s, 1960s, and 1970s most Western governments were not willing to trust to the private sector the achievement of basic social goals: "governments since World War II have intervened directly in higher education systems to democratize access and governance, to increase the relevance of studies for the economy and careers, and, perhaps above all, to increase their own influence over the size, shape, costs, and future direction of the higher education system." And Trow goes on to claim that "states on the whole do not like the market principle: its results are unpredictable; it gives power to institutions and their members, or to students and their parents, rather than to society and state officials" (1984 p. 143). It appears that there has been a remarkable change in attitude by many states toward the market principle.

Second, the higher education experience demonstrates the importance of conditioned power in the state–education relationship. Higher education institutions, universities in particular, are in a much stronger position than schools to resist reform and government intervention if they so wish. However, in most of the countries mentioned above, while there has been criticism of government policy, there has been no concerted and systematic campaign for the wholesale rejection of the reform packages. Higher education institutions have not merely bowed to the power of the state; significant actors within the higher education systems have actively supported the reforms and accepted many of the premises upon which they are based (Meek 1991). Ideological acceptance, more than the coercive legislative power of the state, is reshaping higher education in many countries.

2.2 Contradictions in the New Right Ideology

The trends in the state–education relationship identified above are neither totally one-directional nor unambiguous. The new right discourse on the role of the state in public education is full of contradiction. For every step toward deregulation and reliance on marketplace discipline to govern educational provision and outcome, there is one in the opposite direction of increased centralized state control. At best, it is a regulated deregulation. For example, the move toward school-based management in several countries, such as Australia, the United Kingdom, and New Zealand, has been accompanied by a counter move toward the introduction of a national curriculum and centralized testing. While the 1988 Reform Act in the United Kingdom released schools from the LEAs and increased parental control, it also encouraged schools to apply for central government funding. In many countries, competitive market competition among higher education institutions has been accompanied by the introduction of centralized quality control mechanisms. The deregulation of higher education in Australia and the United Kingdom was accompanied by the abolition of buffer-type coordinating authorities —the Commonwealth Tertiary Education Commission and the University Grants Commission respectively— placing higher education much more under the direct authority of the relevant government departments and ministries. In Australia, a new bureaucracy has been established in the form of the Australian National Training Authority, headed by an industrialist, to oversee the funding and coordination of technical and further education (TAFE), and, toward the end of 1992, the Mayer Committee (1992) recommended the introduction of a national set of employment-related key competencies into the curriculum of the schools and vocational training sectors. The apparent contradiction in many governments' educational policy is fuelled, in part, by the desire to relegate educational efficiency and effectiveness, and as much of the cost as possible, to the marketplace, while simultaneously firmly tying the goals of education at all levels to economic growth and prosperity. Education as investment in human capital has lost none of its appeal.

3. The Future

New right ideology calls for a minimalist state, deregulation, reduced state intervention, and, most importantly, reduced public spending, particularly in the area of social welfare. It is an expression of basic bourgeois social values and transcends governments of particular political persuasion. Elements of the ideology guide education policy in countries under Labour controlled governments, such as in Australia, and under Conservative governments, such as in the United Kingdom. Governments nearly everywhere have had to cope with rising costs in the areas of health, education, and welfare, while simultaneously being placed under intense political pressure to reduce taxes. Governments have found new right beliefs appealing both for ideological and pragmatic reasons. Governments are elected by the bourgeois middle class, not by what Galbraith (1992) terms the disenfranchised underclass, and politicians are likely to appeal to the values and wishes of the bourgeoisie.

The state as "the sphere of direct enforceable social relationships" does not create ideology however. Ideology arises from the total structure of social relations within society, including the relations of material production. The argument here is that while many contradictions exist, the relationship between education and the state, as Western countries head toward the twenty-first century, is being shaped primarily by a resurgence of new right ideology, with its emphasis on individualism and the inherent good of the private market. The ideals of collective socialism are on the wane, both in the West and in the former communist countries of Eastern Europe, as is the notion that the state can effectively intervene in socioeconomic relations for the good of society as a whole. It must be recognized, however, that new right ideology benefits those who already enjoy an advantageous position in society. It is, as Galbraith maintains, based on *The Culture of Contentment*:

individuals and communities that are favoured in their economic, social and political condition attribute social virtue and political durability to that which they themselves enjoy. That attribution, in turn, is made to apply even in the face of commanding evidence to the contrary. The beliefs of the fortunate are brought to serve the cause of continuing contentment, and the economic and political ideas of the time are similarly accommodated. There is an eager political market for that which pleases and reassures. Those who would serve this market and reap the resulting reward in money and applause are reliably available. (Galbraith 1992 p. 2)

The ultimate contradiction of new right ideology is

that it may contain the seeds of its own destruction. At critical times in the past, such as during the Great Depression, had the state not intervened in the areas of welfare, unemployment, prices, and other forms of market relations, it is doubtful that capitalism could have survived. Such intervention was resisted at the time, as it is in the 1990s. At present, states are shifting more and more toward serving the interests of the already advantaged, who are the majority in most Western societies (although some groups are much more advantaged than others). However, substantial minorities remain in severe poverty, the inner cities of many American metropolises resemble more a battleground than a liberal democratic state, and fascism is on the rise in Western Europe. If the fate of the disadvantaged and disenfranchised underclass is left solely to the private market, it is likely that many nations will need to use substantial coercive force in the form of the police and military to maintain social order and the position of the advantaged. History has demonstrated that few if any states can survive for long where condign power dominates.

See also: Administration of Education as a Field of Study; Critical Theory and Education; Institutional Approach to the Study of Education

References

Althusser L 1971 Ideology and ideological state apparatuses. In: Althusser L 1971 *Lenin and Philosophy and Other Essays*. New Left Books, London

Bowles S, Gintis H 1976 *Schooling in Capitalist America: Educational Reform and the Contradictions of Economic Life*. Basic Books, New York

Connell R W 1977 *Ruling Class Ruling Culture*. Cambridge University Press, Cambridge

Cookson P W 1992 The ideology of consumership and the coming deregulation of the public school system. *J. Educ. Policy* 7(3): 301–11

Davis G, Wanna J, Warhurst J, Weller P 1988 *Public Policy in Australia*. Allen and Unwin, Sydney

Galbraith J K 1983 *The Anatomy of Power*. Houghton Mifflin, Boston, Massachusetts

Galbraith J K 1992 *The Culture of Contentment*. Houghton Mifflin, Boston, Massachusetts

Giroux H A 1991 Border pedagogy and the politics of postmodernism. *Educ. Soc.* 9(1): 23–37

Goedegebuure L, Kaiser F, Maassen P, Meek L, van Vught F, de Weert E 1993 International perspectives on trends and issues in higher education policy. In: Goedegebuure L, Kaiser F, Maassen P, Meek L, van Vught F, de Weert E (eds.) 1993 *Higher Education Policy: An International Comparative Perspective*. Pergamon Press, Oxford

Gordon L 1992 The state, devolution and educational reform in New Zealand. *J. Educ. Policy* 7(2): 187–203

Jessop B 1990 *State Theory*. Polity Press, Cambridge

Kogan M 1984 The political view. In: Clark B R (ed.) 1984 *Perspectives on Higher Education*. University of California Press, Berkeley, California

Lawton D 1992 *Education and Politics for the 1990s: Conflict or Consensus?* Falmer Press, London

Lawton S 1992 Why restructure? An international survey of the roots of reform. *J. Educ. Policy* 7(2): 139–154

Mayer E (chair) 1992 *Putting General Education to Work.* The Australian Education Council/Ministers for Vocational Education, Employment and Training, Canberra

Meek V L 1991 The transformation of Australian higher education: From binary to unitary system. *High. Educ.* 21(4): 11–43

Meek V L, Goedegebuure L (eds.) 1991 Policy change in higher education: Intended and unintended outcomes *High. Educ.* 21(4): 451–59

Porter P 1991 The state–family–workplace intersection: Hegemony, contradiction and counter-hegemony in education. In: Dawkins D (ed.) 1991 *Power and Politics in Education.* Falmer Press, London

Poulantzas N A 1973 *Political Power and Social Classes.* New Left Books, London

Torres C A 1985 State and education: Marxist theories In: Husén T, Postlethwaite T N (eds.) 1985 *The International Encyclopedia of Education*, 1st edn. Pergamon Press, Oxford

Trow M 1984 The analysis of status. In: Clark B R (ed.) 1984 *Perspectives on Higher Education.* University of California Press, Berkeley, California

Walford G 1992 Educational choice and equity in Great Britain. *Educ. Policy* 6(2): 123–38

Whitson J A 1991 Post-structuralist pedagogy as counter-hegemonic praxis (can we find the baby in the bathwater). *Educ. Soc.* 9(1): 73–85

Further Reading

Carnoy M 1984 *The State and Political Theory.* Princeton University Press, Princeton, New Jersey

Chubb J E, Moe T M 1990 *Politics, Markets and America's Schools.* The Brookings Institution, Washington, DC

Dale R 1989 *The State and Educational Policy.* Open University Press, Milton Keynes

Dunleavy P, O'Leary B 1987 *Theories of the State.* Macmillan, Basingstoke

King R 1986 *The State in Modern Society.* Chatham House Publishers, Chatham, New Jersey

Shapiro S 1991 The end of radical hope? Postmodernism and the challenge to critical pedagogy. *Educ. Soc.* 9(2): 112–34

Institutional Approach to the Study of Education

A. Benavot

1. Introduction

Educating young people according to deliberate pedagogical principles, whether in one-room schoolhouses or elaborate campuses, has become a standardized, taken-for-granted activity in the modern world. Facilitated by powerful ideological notions that education makes a difference in the lives of individuals and in the direction of national development and increasingly viewed as a basic human right by international organizations, formal schooling has become an ubiquitous feature of twentieth century social life. These features underscore the nature of schooling as an institution: "a socially embedded idea defined by well-known structures and shaping the consciousness of the community that holds and supports it" (Reid 1992 p. 12) or as "standardized activity sequences that have taken-for-granted rationales, that is, some kind of common social 'account' of their existence and purpose" (Jepperson 1991 p. 145).

The institutional approach to the study of education, a relatively recent addition to this field, highlights three interrelated themes concerning education and schooling in the contemporary period (see Meyer 1977, 1980, Meyer and Rowan 1983, Ramirez and Boli 1987, Boli and Ramirez 1988, Boli 1989). First, it focuses on the origins and expansion of modern, secular mass systems of schooling in Europe and North America and their worldwide institutionalization during the course of the twentieth century. Second, it analyzes the institutional underpinnings of education in society: for example, why schools are empowered to sort and classify young people in socially meaningful ways; why education has become a powerful and legitimate social force in the allocation of status in society; and how the components of schooling (e.g., classrooms, grades, curricular tracks, school subjects, transcripts, credentials, etc.) are deeply embedded in standardized and institutionalized systems of meaning. Third, this approach examines the ways in which mass and elite education alter important social constructions and institutional arrangements in society (e.g., definitions of the modern self, the broadening roles of women in society, the changing economic value of work and nonwork activities, the character of the modern nation-state, global models of progress and development). In short, the institutional approach to education focuses on the institutionalization of schooling in the modern world and the institutional-level effects of education on society, both at the national and global levels.

2. The Rise and Institutionalization of Mass Schooling

The institutional approach emphasizes the transnational and ideological character of universal mass education, whose origins are closely linked to the propping up of the nation-state model, the celebration of the sovereign individual, and the extension of citizenship rules (see Ramirez and Meyer 1980, Ramirez and Boli 1987, Boli 1989, Meyer et al. 1997). This account of the rise of mass education is contrasted with functional theories, on the one hand, which emphasizes the spread of education to meet the growing demand for highly skilled labor in urban, industrializing societies (see Clark 1962) and conflict theories, on the other, which stress the importance of schools as a means of reproducing hierarchical class divisions in capitalist societies and minimizing inherent conflicts and struggles generated by the spread of capitalism (Bowles and Gintis 1976, Carnoy 1975).

Empirical studies lending qualified support to the institutional approach have focused on the European origins and worldwide institutionalization of compulsory school rules (Soysal and Strang 1989; Ramirez and Ventresca 1992), the global expansion of primary education (Meyer et al. 1977, Benavot and Riddle 1988, Meyer, Ramirez and Soysal 1992), the standardization of national educational purposes (Fiala and Gordon-Lansford 1987, McNeely 1995), the transformation of vocational educational education (Benavot 1983) and the expansion of universities (Riddle 1992).

The institutional character of the school curriculum has also been the focus of considerable analysis and empirical research (Benavot et al. 1991, Meyer, Kamens and Benavot 1992, Kamens et al. 1996, Reid 1990, Reid 1992, Frank et al. 1994). The official contours of primary and upper secondary school curricula have been compared across national space and found to be surprisingly standardized. Apart from some interesting variants, curricular categories at the primary level and curricular programs/tracks at the secondary levels have become increasingly similar over the course of the twentieth century. The fact that the curricular outlines of mass education are closely linked to educational ideologies institutionalized at the world level provides additional evidence of the growing isomorphism of national education systems.

3. The Institutional and Organizational Nature of Schools

While other approaches view education as a process of socialization (the transmission of a particular cultural heritage from one generation to the next), training (the inculcation of general cognitive capacities and specific skills in young people), allocation (the rational assigning of individuals to work positions in labor market), or reproduction (an inequitable process of matching talents and work positions resulting in an unequal class structure dominated by economic or cultural elites), the institutional approach emphasizes other dynamic features of schooling. A central

assumption of the approach is that education shapes society by classifying young people into socially meaningful, and institutionally embedded, categories with distinct social status. In other words, educational levels (primary, secondary, tertiary), school grades (1st, 3rd, 9th, etc.), curricular tracks (e.g., academic, vocational, comprehensive), and academic disciplines (history, geography, physics, etc.) are types of institutional categories, which, in and of themselves, denote differential social status. Of the various statuses individuals attain in the course of their productive lives, they acquire considerable social status based on the variety of institutionalized educational categories they pass through.

Most institutional categories are commonplace and confer minimal social status; others, however, denote statuses judged to carry significant positive or negative social value: a "college graduate," a "high school dropout," a "gifted seventh grader," a "special education pupil," and for a select few, a "doctor of philosophy." While all schools confer commonplace statuses, some schools acquire the right to confer "special" statuses on their students—a "certified public accountant," a "clinical psychologist," or a "master of business administration"—each of which is codified in the formal educational credentials or diplomas they receive upon graduation. Special statuses, often due to the substantial market value they possess, mark those individuals who have acquired expertise in a field and who expect to be distinguished from others who have not attained similar credentials and who therefore cannot make such claims of expertise.

Where do schools receive the authority to confer social status on their pupils and graduates? According to the institutional approach, schools receive a charter (or socially defined mission) from a legitimate political authority in society—frequently a central or federal state but sometimes a colonial administration or religious organization—to define and classify individuals in special ways (Meyer 1970). These charters specify, in effect, the labels (social statuses) that each educational institution can confer on those who pass through its classrooms. School charters have also been found to influence the ways in which parents manage their children's school careers (Oswald et al. 1988). Schools belong to a select group of institutions empowered and chartered by society to grant social status to individuals. This relatively exclusive societal mandate reflects the conviction that education is an efficient and legitimate way to allocate status in the modern world. Thus, an important effect of education lies in the power it holds to certify and sanction differences between groups, positions, statuses, and individuals based on their educational achievements and attainments, on the one hand, and the authority to create new positions and categories of status on the other.

Moreover, the categories that schools apply as well as the labels they confer are deeply embedded in wider institutional environments. Local schools are local in name only: they are tightly connected to rationally organized, national, and international systems of education. Thus, for example, if a child completes third grade, and moves to another jurisdiction, the school authorities are expected to recognize the child's "third gradeness." Universities and colleges are expected to recognize the "high school graduateness" of students who have completed academic programs varying significantly in breadth and depth. Employers are expected to recognize as nominally equivalent the educational credentials of candidates, be they local, national, or foreign, who have completed university programs with widely varying degrees of rigor. In this sense, major educational categories such as classroom, grade, curricular track, ability group, school subject, curricular timetable, transcript, and credential carry broad symbolic meanings due to their strong institutional moorings. They are public in character, guided by notions of rationality and purposive action and modeled on nationally, as well as internationally, recognized entities, rather than local or particularistic ones.

An interesting implication of the institutional approach is that curricular classifications created by schools can have powerful socializing effects on pupils, based on the institutional status of the school and curricula, effects which frequently transcend the actual experiences of pupils in the classrooms. For example, ability groups in the elementary grades (see Gamoran 1986, Pallas et al. 1994), high-school curricular tracks and college-level academic programs (see Kamens 1977) carry differential symbolic meanings which can independently affect pupil achievements either through anticipatory socialization or due to the fact that those enrolled in high-status curricular programs believe, act, and are treated by others as if the socially constructed differences produced by the schools and colleges are real. Thus, pupils' educational careers are subject to significant institutional effects.

As previously noted, select educational categories such as the high school diploma or college degree come to be associated with special entitlements (e.g., prestigious jobs in the labor market) and privileges (income, job security, etc.). The rationale for bestowing such rights and privileges on a certain category is often driven home to student and public alike during official school rituals or rites of passage such as the graduation ceremony. These formal rituals give special recognition to the successful pupils who have persevered. Speeches by school officials stress the excellence of the graduates, the honorable quality of their motivations, as well as their noteworthy achievements and accomplishments.

Subsequent to the conferral of new statuses by educational institutions—statuses which can rarely be rescinded—graduates are empowered to make certain claims of expertise and authority over specialized bodies of social knowledge. For example, holders of a social work degree can begin recommending specific welfare policies; psychologists, who have been authorized to make inventories of the human personality, can label some people mentally deranged and others in perfect health; sociologists can make authoritative statements about the social ills of society; economists about the interests, motivations, and behavior of workers and consumers, and so on. In short, the acquisition of educational qualifications enables newly constituted "experts," "specialists," or "professionals" to make authoritative statements in their area of expertise and to advance new knowledge claims.

Another important implication of the institutional approach concerns the ripple effects of the conferral of status on some (the graduates) and not others. While credentialled individuals acquire the power and authority to make certain claims on society, noncredentialled persons learn that they cannot make such claims. Thus, one of the critical impacts of schooling, one overlooked in other theoretical approaches, is to delegitimate and deflate the natural, common sense knowledge of the "uneducated" or nongraduates at the same time that it legitimates and inflates the "supposed" knowledge of the graduates.

Ironically, the institutional embeddedness of schools in a rational system of classification and legitimation suggests that attention to the key purposes of schooling—teaching skills and imparting knowledge—is reduced in order to safeguard the continued viability of the institution. To be sure, educational officials and political leaders insist that the inculcation of values, skills, and knowledge is vital, while educational reformers bemoan the deficiencies of the schools and promulgate new initiatives to tinker with the educational system. In the end, however, surprisingly little actually changes in schools and classrooms. Most educational reforms, while symbolically important, have a certain cosmetic quality: rarely do they alter the day-to-day rhythms of school life.

Why? According to the institutional approach, schools are a type of loosely-coupled organization in which the core activity, classroom instruction, is removed from tighter forms of supervision, coordination, and control usually found in bureaucratic organizations or large corporations (Meyer and Rowan 1983). While classroom activities are relatively secluded, that is, "buffered," from public view, institutional classifications are recorded in great detail. School principals, district officials, and government administrators spend considerable time and energy preparing large quantities of aggregate statistical data on the constituent elements of schooling, for example, the number of students processed, the number of full- or part-time teachers and their qualifications, instructional time spent on various curricular subjects, the number of books in the school library, the number of programs for the disadvantaged or the gifted. Rarely, however, do these officials know what actually goes on behind the closed doors of the classrooms.

Rational depictions of the educational enterprise, as reflected in the "hard data" accounts of educational officials, helps to reassure the public and stabilize the allocation of school monies and outside funding, while, at the same time, buffering classroom activities from outside interference and protecting the weak professionalism of teachers from unwarranted criticism. But conforming to ritual classifications and institutional rules exacts a price: often it means that the skills and knowledge base of the graduates are shallow and superficial, a state of affairs increasingly criticized by the public. Broad movements to bolster accountability, that is, tighter coupling, can be viewed in this light, though rarely do schools "fail" due to incompetence. The high survival rate of poor schools reflects the valuable resources gained by schools that conform to the official guidelines of their institutional environment and buffer their classroom activities from outside inspection.

4. The Macrosocietal Effects of Education

Proponents of the institutional perspective maintain that the expansion of formal schooling directly alters important social understandings and institutional arrangements in society (see Meyer 1977, Boli, et al. 1985, Thomas et al. 1987). Educational expansion, for example, constructs a more standardized life course while creating new and more expanded definitions of the individual and the self (Meyer 1986); it creates new positions in the labor market and intensifies the use of education-related rules for the allocation of jobs and promotions; it also enlarges the social arenas over which state bureaucracies direct their administrative attention (Meyer 1992).

For developing nations in the Third world, the advent and expansion of compulsory primary education is particularly crucial in this regard. Mass education extends citizenship rights and duties to traditionally marginal segments of society (e.g., women, minorities, and the nonpropertied classes), thereby increasing their integration into the economy and polity (Ramirez and Rubinson 1979, Ramirez and Weiss 1979). It also restructures the corporate identity and authority relations in the family since the cost of raising children increases, children's potential for work (both inside and outside the home) is reduced, and children come to be seen by adults as future rather than present producers (Caldwell 1982). These institutional changes, it is argued, have an impact on the nonschooled as well as the schooled, on the parental generation as well as the school-age generation, and on the status of social classes who are not directly exposed to schooling as well as the status of those who are.

In economic terms, the institutional perspective focuses on the macroeconomic effects of education, without belaboring the obvious relationship between years of schooling completed by individuals and their entrance into high-status or high-wage jobs. First, while educational expansion creates skills and enhances productivity, these effects are neither uniform nor consistent, but are conditioned by the institutional context in which schools produce future workers (Rubinson and Fuller 1992). Second, educational expansion contributes, both directly and indirectly, to the social construction of the national economy (Benavot 1989, 1992). Universities certify experts who legitimate new occupational niches by creating new categories of economic value, delegitimate "traditional" economic pursuits usually isolated from the wage economy and redefine formerly private or communal pursuits as deserving renumeration. In this way, education contributes directly to economic growth, independent of individual-level effects, by altering the economic value attached to a wide range of economic and social activities that, ultimately, become incorporated in aggregate measures of national wealth such as the gross national product (GNP).

These arguments have important implications for the changing status of women in developing economies. The provision of mass education for girls, and the ideology undergirding its expansion with an emphasis on citizenship, individualism, and national progress, erodes the role of women in the traditional family economy and constructs new rights and duties for women as potentially productive wage earners in the national economy (Benavot 1989, Ramirez and Cha 1990). On a global level, there are signs that the "invisible" work traditionally done by women becomes incorporated into national and international accounts of economic value (see Joekes 1987). Thus, expanding school places for girls, even in extremely patriarchal societies, comes to be seen as rational because school-age girls are viewed as potentially valuable assets of the nation-state in its pursuit of social progress. Although gender inequalities and inequities in education and wages persist, the primary education of girls and young women clearly has important institutional effects in Third World nations.

Institutional theories of education and development also discuss the political consequences of educational expansion (Meyer 1977, Kamens 1988). Here too, institutionalists view national educational systems not only in terms of their socialization and allocation effects on society, but as part of a broader process of the political construction of society, in which highly institutionalized social roles and categories are created and legitimated. For example, Meyer and Rubinson (1975) argue that the political impact of education is not just the aggregation of political-related changes at the individual level (e.g., an increased sense of political efficacy, the strengthening of democratic attitudes, values and behaviors), but also the direct effects of education on the overall expansion of political authority in society, on the range and depth of state jurisdiction over civil society, and on the overall distribution of political power between elites and the masses.

Though their participation in the mass educational system, which is compelled in over 85 percent of all countries, young people become "modern citizens," a socially constructed identity linking them to the increasingly powerful and authoritative nation-state. Thus, education becomes a mechanism for the construction of loyal and efficacious citizens who are endowed with legitimated capacities to participate in the social and political life of the nation, a deeply institutionalized principle of democratic regimes (see Ramirez and Rubinson 1979).

Other significant political effects result from the expansion of higher education. Universities and colleges increase levels of activity among students regarding a wide array of political issues and concerns, reflecting their anticipation of future elite status. Since their studies often involve explicit comparisons between existing political systems, including democratic ones, students become more knowledgeable of and concerned with their own political rights and civil liberties. University faculties generate new political discourses in which political structures are evaluated in a more critical light. Political elites legitimated by university institutions are more directly involved in the creation and running of existing political institutions and in guaranteeing basic political liberties and civil rights. In short, higher education, by changing the character of political culture and debate among elites, plays a crucial role in the emergence of democratic regimes and their consolidation (see Benavot 1996).

5. Conclusion

Overall, institutionalists view education as contributing to the construction of new categories of social value and to the redistribution of political and economic power in national societies. Educational institutions provide convincing rationales for community and social action and, in doing so, they contribute to the expansion of social arenas in which political authority can be employed. Institutions of mass and elite education certify which members of society can legitimately use their authority and power in these new spheres of action. The political effects of education, though deserving greater research attention, represent an important future focus of the institutional approach to the study of education.

See also: Educational Expansion: Sociological Perspectives; Sociology of Education: An Overview

References

Benavot A 1983 The rise and decline of vocational education. *Sociol. Educ.* 56: 63–76

Benavot A 1989 Education, gender, and economic development: A cross-national study. *Sociol. Educ.* 62: 14–32

Benavot A 1992 Educational expansion and economic growth in modern world. 1913–1985. In: Fuller B, Rubinson R (eds.) 1992 *The Political Construction of Education.* Praeger, New York

Benavot A 1996 Education and political democratization: A cross-national and longitudinal study. *Comp. Educ. Rev.* 40: 377–403

Benavot A, Riddle P 1988 The expansion of primary education 1870–1940: Trends and issues. *Sociol. Educ.* 61: 190–210

Benavot A, Cha Y, Kamens D, Meyer J W, Wong S 1991 Knowledge for the masses: World models and national curricula 1920–1986. *Am. Sociol. Rev.* 56: 83–100

Boli J 1989 *New Citizens for a New Society: The Institutional Origins of Mass Schooling in Sweden.* Pergamon, Oxford

Boli J, Ramirez F 1988 World culture and the institutional development of mass education. In: Richardson J (ed.) 1988 *Handbook of Theory and Research for the Sociology of Education.* Greenwood Press, New York

Boli J, Ramirez F, Meyer J W 1985 Explaining the origins and expansion of mass education. *Comp. Educ. Rev.* 29: 145–70

Bowles S, Gintis H 1976 *Schooling in Capitalist America.* Basic Books, New York

Caldwell J 1982 *Theory of Fertility Decline.* Academic Press, London

Carnoy M 1975 *Schooling in a Corporate Society.* McKay, New York

Clark B 1962 *Educating the Expert Society.* Chandler, San Francisco, California

Fiala R, Gordon-Lansford A 1987 Educational ideology and the world educational revolution 1950–70. *Comp. Educ. Rev.* 31: 315–32

Frank D J, Schofer E, Torres J C 1994 Rethinking history: Change in the university curriculum 1910–90. *Sociol. Educ.* 67(4): 231–42

Gamoran 1986 Instructional and institutional effects of ability grouping. *Sociol. Educ.* 59: 185–98

Jepperson 1991 Institutions, institutional effects and institutionalism. In: Powell W, DiMaggio P (eds) 1991 *The New Institutionalism in Organizational Analysis.* University of Chicago Press, Chicago, Illinois

Joekes S 1987 *Women in the World Economy*: An INSTRAW Study. Oxford University Press, New York

Kamens D 1977 Legitimating myths and educational organization. *Am. Sociol. Rev.* 42: 208–19

Kamens D 1988 Education and democracy: A comparative institutional analysis. *Sociol. Educ.* 61: 114–27

Kamens D, Meyer J W, Benavot A 1996 Worldwide patterns in academic secondary education curricula. *Comp. Educ. Rev.* 40: 116–38

McNeely C 1995 Prescribing national education policies: The role of international organizations. *Comp. Educ. Rev.* 39(4): 483–507

Meyer J W 1970 The charter: Conditions of diffuse socialization in schools. In: Scott W (ed.) 1970 *Social Processes and Social Structures.* Holt, Rinehart & Winston, New York

Meyer J W 1977 The effects of education as an institution. *Am. J. Sociol.* 83: 55–77

Meyer J W 1980 Levels of the education system and schooling effects. In: Bidwell C, Windham D (eds.) 1980 *The*

Analysis of Educational Productivity, Vol. 2. Ballinger, Cambridge

Meyer J W 1980 Institutional control over education: Origins and effects. In: Blalock H (ed.) 1980 *Sociological Theory and Research*. Free Press, New York

Meyer J W 1986 The self and the life course: Institutionalization and its effects. In: Sorensen A, Weinert F, Sherrod L (eds.) 1986 *Human Development and the Life Course*. Erlbaum, Hillsdale, New Jersey

Meyer J W 1992 The social construction of motives for educational expansion. In: Fuller B, Rubinson R (eds.) 1992 *The Political Construction of Education*. Praeger New York

Meyer J, Boli J, Thomas G, Ramirez F 1997 World society and the nation-state. *Am. J. Sociol.* 103: 144–81

Meyer J, Kamens D, Benavot A 1992 *School Knowledge for the Masses*. Falmer Press, Washington, DC

Meyer J, Ramirez F, Boli J 1977 The world educational revolution 1950–75. *Sociol. Educ.* 50: 242–58

Meyer J, Ramirez F, Soysal Y 1992 World expansion of mass education 1870–1980. *Sociol. Educ.* 65: 128–49

Meyer J, Rowan B 1983 The structure of educational organizations. In: Meyer J, Scott W R (eds.) 1983 *Organizational Environments*. Sage, Beverly Hills, California

Meyer J, Rubinson R 1975 Education and political development. *Rev. Res. Educ.* 3: 134–62

Oswald H, Baker D, Stevenson D 1988 School charter and parental management in West Germany. *Sociol. Educ.* 61(4): 255–65

Pallas A, Entwisle D, Alexander K, Stlucka M F 1994 Ability-group effects: Instructional, social or institutional. *Sociol. Educ.* 67(1): 27–46

Ramirez F, Boli J 1987 The political construction of mass schooling: European origins and worldwide institutionalization. *Sociol. Educ.* 60: 2–17

Ramirez F, Cha Y H 1990 Citizenship and gender: Western educational development in comparative perspective. *Res. Sociol. Educ. Socialization* 9: 153–74

Ramirez F, Meyer J W 1980 Comparative education: The social construction of the modern world system. *Annu. Rev. Sociol.* 6: 369–99

Ramirez F, Rubinson R 1979 Creating members: The political incorporation and expansion of public education. In: Meyer J W, Hannan M (eds.) 1979 *National Development and the World System*. University of Chicago Press, Chicago, Illinois

Ramirez R, Ventresca M 1992 Building the institution of mass schooling: Isomorphism in the modern world. In: Fuller B, Rubinson R (eds.) 1992 *The Political Construction of Education*. Praeger, New York

Ramirez F, Weiss J 1979 The political incorporation of women. In: Meyer J W, Hannan M (eds.) 1979 *National Development and the World System*. University of Chicago Press, Chicago, Illinois

Reid W 1990 Strange curricula: Origins and development of institutional categories of schooling. *Curric. St.* 22: 203–16

Reid W 1992 *The Pursuit of the Curriculum: Schooling and the Public Interest*. Ablex Publishing Corporation Norwood, New Jersey

Rubinson R, Fuller B 1992 Specifying the effects of education on national economic growth. In: Fuller B, Rubinson R (eds.) 1992 *The Political Construction of Education*. Praeger, New York

Soysal Y, Strang D 1989 Construction of the first mass education systems in 19th century Europe. *Sociol. Educ.* 62: 277–88

Thomas G, Meyer J W, Boli J, Ramirez F 1987 *Institutional Structure: Constituting the State, Society and the Individual*. Sage, Beverley Hills, California

Multicultural Education

L. H. Ekstrand

This article will describe and discuss aspects of education in racially and ethnically pluralistic societies. It will examine the ideologies, practices, and consequences of educating young people from heterogeneous cultural backgrounds. The issue of preserving national unity and promoting cultural diversity through education will be discussed, and various curriculum practices in some well-known multicultural societies will be examined.

1. Definitions and Delineations

1.1 Introduction

Initially, multicultural education will be defined as "education, usually formal, in which two or more cultures are involved," and specifications will be given during the discussion. Because there exists no universally accepted definition of multicultural education, it is defined here in a broad sense to include a variety of programs for immigrants, minorities, refugees, and majority members. It is important to note that because of increasing international contacts, even monocultural and monolingual countries experience a need for some kind of multicultural education. Multicultural education is neither a well-delineated, nor a conceptually clear area. Both as a direction in education movements and as a scientific discipline, multicultural education consists of a number of areas and specialties. It may not be possible, nor desirable, to make it a homogeneous, practical, or scientific concept or area.

1.2 Terminology

The terminology is not uniform. In addition to "multicultural education," the terms "intercultural education," "interethnic education," "transcultural education," "multiethnic education," and "cross-cultural education" may be found in the literature. These terms are taken here to have largely the same meaning, although not all authors agree (Velasquez and Ingle 1982, Banks 1985). The first two terms, multicultural education and intercultural education, are much more common than the others.

There are also a number of related or subordinate terms referring to types of education that may be included in the concept of multicultural education. One collection of such terms includes immigrant education, bilingual education, community education, migrant education, and minority education. All these terms refer to the education of immigrants, although minority education also may refer to the education of indigenous minorities.

Another list of terms includes immersion education (a type of bilingual education for indigenous ethnic groups), monolingual or mother tongue classes (classes for immigrant children in one language, either in the host language or the mother tongue), composite or compound classes (consisting of native and immigrant children mixed in bilingual education classes), mother tongue education (referring normally to the teaching of indigenous children, but also immigrant children), and minority schools.

1.3 The Link between Multicultural Education and Society

There is a link between multicultural education and the social and cultural concept in any particular society, with the specific goals of that society. For instance, the United States, Canada, and Australia were multicultural societies from their political beginnings, with native minority populations and one or two majority populations. They welcomed immigrants and refugees, so that a number of immigrant (minority) populations emerged. In contrast many small nations, such as the Scandinavian countries, are basically monocultural countries, possibly with small enclaves of indigenous populations (such as the Lapps in Scandinavian countries). Many countries have comparatively recently opened up to immigrants and refugees.

The United Kingdom is a country with a history of recent colonialism, as are Germany and France. Israel is a country which includes Jews from industrialized countries in the West, as well as immigrants from agrarian countries in the East, and also Arabs. In reality, very few countries in the world, if any, are completely monocultural. Well-known examples of "supermultilingualism" are China and India. These are also examples of the Third World situation which is fairly complex. India, for instance, has 179 distinct languages (the numbers vary depending on the source), out of which 15 are official languages. English is the common language in practice, although it is not an official language.

Because of the link between multicultural education and society, many of the terms and concepts listed above are culture-bound. Bilingual education as a label for immigrant education is predominantly used in the United States, whereas it has broader connotations in other countries. Community languages, as a term for immigrant languages, is mostly used in Australia, whereas other expressions are used elsewhere. Bilingualism in the former Soviet Union was used for the "Russification" of incorporated areas, and hence it was very unpopular in republics such as the Baltic states. Transcultural education is a term used in the Netherlands. Multicultural education in the United States is used to refer to general multicultural competency, but it is also a broad term which includes the education of any minority, including social class or sex minorities. Multicultural education in the United Kingdom is very much concerned with racial and ethnic issues.

The existing terms have arisen from practical situations and needs, such as the experience of immigration, or the occurrence of indigenous minorities. This has resulted in a traditional understanding of multicultural education, as reflected in the definitions cited below.

Within multicultural education, new specialties are developing, in addition to traditional areas such as immigrant/minority educational research and programs. One prominent area is intercultural communication, in part applied teaching, in part a research discipline, with a North American emphasis. This discipline still lacks a scientific tradition in other parts of the world, except in some European countries.

1.4 Some Existing Definitions

The concept of multicultural education is relatively new, although the phenomenon as such is not. The *Dictionary of Education* (Good 1959) does not list it, nor does the *Encyclopedia of Education* (Deighton 1971) (although the latter has both "Immigrants—" and "Migrants—Education of"). Neither the German *Lexikon der Pädagogik* (1971) nor the Danish *Pedagogisk Oppslagsbok* (Ness 1974) includes the term. The words appear in the *Encyclopedia of Educational Research* (Mitzel 1982) and in *The International Encyclopedia of Education* (Husén and Postlethwaite 1985). *A Critical Dictionary of Educational Concepts* (Barrow and Milburn 1986) has an entry entitled "Multiculturalism," but the discussion is predominantly concerned with multicultural education.

Some of the several definitions of multicultural education will be cited and briefly commented on here to establish what they include and do not include. None of the definitions is completely satisfactory, however, and the question is whether it is possible to formulate a precise definition for such a complex field. The entry by Banks (1985) in the *International Encyclopedia of Education* under the entry for "Multicultural States Education": "Programs and practices designed to help improve the academic achievement of ethnic and immigrant populations and/or teach majority group students about the cultures and experiences of the minority groups within their nations are referred to as multicultural education" (p. 3440). This definition limits the concept of multicultural education to the majority/minority situation within a country, but leaves out the relation to cultures outside the country. In a multicultural world the aspect of education for increasing official, commercial, cultural, and individual interdependence must be taken into consideration.

The second definition of multicultural education in that Encyclopedia is given under the entry "Immigrant Children, Policies for Educating" (Ekstrand 1985): "Multicultural education involves both majority and minority children. Majority children are expected to learn at least one foreign language, and to become acquainted with one or more foreign cultures. Preferably, majority and minority children should be integrated within the school system" (p. 2401). This definition is broader than the first, but is still incomplete.

The *Encyclopedia of Educational Research* (Mitzel 5th edn., 1982) discusses multicultural education from the American perspective under the entry "Multicultural and Minority Education." Although criticizing other definitions, the entry avoids giving a clear definition. It states:

> Multicultural education is a broader term than "multiethnic" or "bilingual" education. In the United States "culture" has been used to include "ethnic heritage", "linguistic background", employment status (as in blue-collar culture), sex, age, race, and condition of handicap, as well as collective experience, such as "drug culture". Clearly the majority of studies that focused on multicultural phenomena are related to ethnic and linguistic cultures. (p. 1267)

This description leaves unclear what multicultural education in the United States is. Should subcultures such as "youth culture" or "gay culture" be included in the definition or not?

The *International Dictionary of Education* (Page and Thomas 1977), under the entry "Multiethnic education," refers the reader to "Crosscultural education/training," defined as "involving a mix of cultures as when a student brought up in one culture receives education at an institution which has the values of another culture" (p. 92). This definition is clearly not adequate for the multicultural education concept.

The difficulties in defining multicultural education are vividly illustrated by the Swedish Committee on Linguistic and Cultural Heritage (*Språkoch Kulturarvsutredningen* 1983) which in its report states that "the term 'Intercultural Education' is specified and described, when necessary, in different contexts" (p. 158). The Committee does, however, say that multicultural education is knowledge and consciousness of one's own, and different, cultures and values. However it also defines multicultural education in terms of goals, such as solving conflicts and improving relations between minority and majority groups.

Pusch (1979) provides a different type of definition. Not only does she stress knowledge and awareness of different cultures, but she also includes the practical experience of cultural differences as part of multicultural education.

These definitions are typical of what may be called "direct multicultural education" (see below), but they do not cover the teaching of subject matter, for example physics, to minority students, although this too must be considered an important part of multicultural education.

Finally, multicultural education can also be seen as a strategy, policy, or a set of organizational measures and applied teaching activities.

1.5 Delineations

A first delineation is to observe that multicultural education predominantly refers to cultures defined by national, linguistic, ethnic, or racial criteria. Social class, sex, and dialectal or geographical regions are seen as normal subcultural variations, the education of which does not belong to multicultural education. Regions within a nation are regarded as normal variations, and are not usually included in definitions of multicultural education. Nor does the education of minorities other than those defined by nation, language, ethnicity, or race, such as the handicapped or sexual minorities, belong to multicultural education.

Certain other delineations might be useful. Firstly, it is possible to differentiate between formal, informal, and nonformal multicultural education. Formal multicultural education occurs within the formal educational system, within special multicultural education programs such as bilingual education, or for example through arranged study tours. Nonformal multicultural education occurs via the mass media, or as private study or tourist travels, private reading, private radio listening and television watching. Informal education occurs via informal contacts with ethnic groups.

A further differentiation may be made between direct and indirect multicultural education. Direct multicultural education would be action taken directly to influence intercultural attitudes and competency, such as simulation and role-playing games, or comparative culture studies. Much of the literature deals with this type of instruction. Indirect multicultural education would include all the cultural information conveyed through the teaching of foreign (second) languages, and in the teaching of subject matters. Much of the direct multicultural education is closely linked to programs and training activities for intercultural communicative competency, a rapidly developing area with a growing literature.

A distinction can also be made between a general and a specific type of multicultural education. Some direct multicultural education aims at a general, nonspecific cultural awareness, typically through simulation games, films, and cultural assimilators, not related to any culture in particular. Specific multicultural education is directed to a specific culture or to a specific need.

1.6 A Comprehensive Definition

Drawing on the observations above, a new and comprehensive definition is proposed here. Multicultural education is an educational process or a strategy involving more than one culture, as defined by national, linguistic, ethnic, or racial criteria. Multicultural education may take place within formal or informal education settings, directly or indirectly. Multicultural education is supposed to create awareness, tolerance, understanding, and knowledge regarding different cultures as well as the differences and similarities between cultures and their related world views, concepts, values, beliefs, and attitudes. It is intended to provide cognitive, verbal, and nonverbal skills in coping with different cultures or cultural groups, and skills in communicating with members of these groups. It is also intended to promote academic and social achievement in intercultural settings. The ultimate goal of multicultural education is to accomplish increased communication and understanding between cultures, nations, groups, and individuals.

2. Categories, Goals, and Methods of Multicultural Education

2.1 Categories

The type of multicultural education should be distinguished from its goals, contents, methods, and special school types. At least the following types of basic multicultural education situations can be discerned: (a) education of or about indigenous linguistic and/or ethnic minorities; (b) education of or about immigrated national, linguistic, or ethnic groups, including refugees and other temporary residents; (c) the teaching of foreign languages (for the majority as well as the minorities); (d) the teaching of second languages; (e) domestic and/or foreign culture knowledge, theory, and analysis where two or more cultures are involved; (f) programs designed for multicultural awareness and skills training; (g) education of students abroad; (h) teaching with a second or foreign language as the medium of instruction; (i) Third World knowledge, included in school curricula as well as in the training of development workers and volunteers; (j) the teaching of subject matter with international or cross-cultural components; (k) multicultural education-related areas such as cross-cultural counseling and psychology, especially in the schools; (l) specific multicultural education training of professionals such as teachers, counselors, and psychologists; (m) education and training of administrators, workers, and others into established or developing international systems; (n) peace and conflict education; (o) desegrega-

tion programs; (p) a host of other education and training needs and activities that can be summarized as "internationalization"; and (q) concern with human, ecological, environmental, or biological questions about the world, that can be summarized as "globalization."

Listing these educational contexts presents a paradox: some programs for the education of immigrants or indigenous minorities clearly aim at maintaining the mother tongue and culture of origin, and hence are made as monocultural as possible. However, their inclusion in multicultural education is justified, as these programs are carried out in another culture, and the students cannot avoid interacting with the majority culture outside the protected or sheltered programs.

Indigenous minorities may be of ancient origin, for example the aboriginals of Australia, the indigenous people of North America, the Lapps of Scandinavia, or of more recent origin, the Blacks in the United States. It is difficult to say when an immigrated group passes from immigrant status to an indigenous ethnic minority status. Opinions varying from several years to several generations are found in the literature (Vecoli 1972, Ekstrand 1978).

Foreign language teaching usually means the teaching of a language not spoken in the country. Second language teaching may include several varieties. It may mean the teaching of a second language in a bilingual country, such as French/Flemish in Belgium, English/French in Canada, or Finnish/Swedish in Finland. Which language is regarded as the second is relative to the mother tongue of each group. In many Third World countries, English or French is used as a second language, and as a medium of instruction in the schools. Normally, second language teaching also means teaching with the language as the medium of instruction, for example, English in India.

Education in domestic or foreign cultures aims at a practical working knowledge of one or more cultures, whereas culture knowledge and analysis aims at finding specific or universal principles. The two areas often overlap. The education of students abroad, which may often be mother tongue education of children of families (temporarily) living abroad, is organized by many countries. There are American, British, French, German, and other minority schools in many countries. Such schools also attract students from other nationalities too small to form a school, or from the majority population because the parents want to give their children foreign language proficiency and, in fact, a good multicultural education. Student-exchange programs like ERASMUS or COMMETT should be included in this category. Many school subjects naturally contain multicultural components. Examples are geography, religion, history, or economics. One example of problems of training for new systems is the difference in standards and rules between EU and non-EU countries. Internationalization activities can be anything from conferences to intercultural song and dance programs, twin school programs, student group study tours, and pen friends.

The multicultural education training of professionals usually occurs as short-term courses. In the case of teacher training, full programs may occur. Some countries insist on the teacher trainees coming from the actual target cultures, whereas others prefer members of their own culture. Some countries have special programs for multicultural education teacher training while others integrate this training in regular programs, or do not give any training.

Multicultural education can be implemented at the preschool, primary, secondary, and tertiary education levels.

2.2 Goals, Content, Methods, and School Types

The goals of multicultural education are manifold and sometimes overlapping. They include:

(a) attitudinal goals: cultural awareness and sensitivity, cultural tolerance, respect for cultural identity, culture-responsive attitude, skill in conflict avoidance and conflict resolution;

(b) cognitive goals: academic achievement, second and foreign language learning, knowledge of specific cultures, competency to analyze and interpret cultural behavior, awareness of one's own cultural perspective;

(c) instructional goals: correcting distortions, stereotypes, omissions, and misinformation about ethnic groups in text books and teaching media; providing strategies for dealing with differences among people, providing the conceptual tools for intercultural communication, developing interpersonal skills, providing evaluative techniques, helping with values clarification, explaining cultural dynamics.

The content of courses or programs will relate to the type and goal of multicultural education as described above. It is not possible to go into a more detailed discussion of content in this context.

The methods display a large diversification. Methods for direct, specific multicultural education are case studies, immersion in a particular culture (e.g., school practice abroad and study tours), and problem-solving. One type of method deserves particular mention: the comparative approach, where at least two cultures are compared, described, and analyzed in some respect by the students, through reading, interviews, questionnaires, or visits. Examples from classes on comparative analysis are "Christmas in Arab and Western Countries," and "The Death Concept in Holland and Sweden." Other methods, also used for the direct, nonspecific multicultural education, are simulations (of cultural groups, or culture-conflict situations), films, other audiovisual presentations, seminars (oc-

casional or series), lectures, games, critical incidents, and role playing.

Some specific school types designed for multicultural education are international schools, minority schools, and language schools. International schools are (a) national international schools, as found in Switzerland and elsewhere; (b) privately owned, parent-owned, or foreign-government-owned schools in another nation, such as the French, German, or English schools in many countries, the Anglo-American schools in the Indian subcontinent, the French *lycées* of Africa, and a host of mother tongue minority schools, all of them primarily intended for the children of abroad-based personnel; (c) schools founded by two or more governments or national groupings in cooperation; (d) schools belonging to the International Schools Association (ISA), aiming at educating young people to be at home in the world everywhere (Leach 1969). Minority schools are intended for permanently settled, indigenous, or immigrated minorities. Language schools of many kinds exist, for example the Berlitz schools, constituting a type of international language school.

3. What is "Culture" and "Multiculturalism?"

3.1 Defining Culture

Many authors define culture as the sum of behaviors and artifacts among a group of people. Often, definitions contain references to the values, rules, perceptions, and symbols that members of a group have in common. Other researchers advocate structural definitions, such as culture consisting of "isolates, sets, and patterns," patterns meaning rules (Hall 1959) or "elements, structures, patterns, and rules" (Ekstrand and Ekstrand 1986). Culture is shaped by, and in itself creates, behavior, thoughts, and feelings, in constant interaction. Thus, culture is constantly changing. What seems to be most important in a culture is (a) what unites members of the group; and (b) what distinguishes them from other groups. What is typical for a culture is not necessarily what is frequent; something very infrequent can be typical if it is not found in any other culture.

3.2 Multiculturalism

Smolicz (1981) distinguishes between three main types of "multiculturalism." First, "transitional multiculturalism" is a temporary support where children can keep up their academic skills while learning the majority language. The French-Canadians were the first to regard this as a danger and as an effective and painless way to achieve Anglo-uniformity. The traditional United States policy has been transition rather than maintenance; where maintenance occurs, it is the result of local or state initiatives. Second, "residual multiculturalism" is the kind that takes into account all kinds of subcultural groups: for example, gay culture, pop culture, and shift workers' culture. Ethnic cultures are then added to the list. The result is that all these groups will be part of the majority way of life, which is regarded by some as a camouflaged assimilation strategy. The logical fallacy is that any ethnic group includes most of these subcultural divisions. Third, "internal multiculturalism" recognizes that culture includes structural as well as institutional aspects. Hence national cultures cannot remain intact in a plural society. Some institutional and cultural facets have to be shared by each ethnic group.

The retention and development of ethnic cultures is compatible with the evolution and acceptance of shared values for the whole society. It must be remembered that the original culture of the home country will also change, as migrants returning after a long time will discover, often painfully, as the ideal image no longer matches reality. The modification of national cultures in another country is not equivalent with their reduction into residues. Learning the majority language and fitting into a matrix of shared values need not endanger the core values of the cultures concerned. The core values themselves provide the boundary line between the cultural accommodation that must take place to make different groups fit into the shared value matrix, and the cultural retention necessary to maintain cultural pluralism. This kind of multiculturalism is applicable both to groups and individuals.

A somewhat different categorization of multiculturalism is found in Robinson (1981). First, "assimilation and bilingual education" refers to transition models marked by assimilation, defined as "the process of social and psychological adherence to a 'core society'." Second, "cultural pluralism and bilingual education" argues the right for different cultures to maintain their cultural identity. Distinct cultures remain and coexist. Third, "multicultural synthesis" means a combination and modification of the assimilationist position and the pluralist position. It describes a "melting pot" type of society, but differs from the assimilationist position in that there is no "dominant mold" or "core" society to which other cultures are attracted. This position strives for cultural eclecticism and synthesis within the individual as well as for the society *in toto*, and promotes continuous change in the various cultures. The clientele is both majority and minority members.

4. Multicultural Adaptation

4.1 Systems Level: Integration Processes

The intercultural adaptation process is central to the concept of multiculturalism and hence to multicultural education. Multicultural education is a consequence of interethnic and international interaction, but is also instrumental in promoting it. Broadly, two types of multicultural adjustment can be discerned, namely, of individuals and groups, and of systems and nations. Individuals and groups are involved in interaction processes of a cognitive and psychosocial nature, whereas systems, namely nations, associations of nations, and multinational organizations, are involved in organizational and diplomatic interaction. The individual may have to learn languages and acquire cultural competency, and systems have to be developed and harmonized, such as in the cases of the EU, or the integration of the East European states into the rest of Europe. There is an interplay between the individual and systems levels: to develop and understand systems, individuals have to learn, formally or informally, and systems development reflects, and is dependent on attitudes.

Two opposite processes took place in the early 1990s on the international stage at the systems level, namely, integration and disintegration. Parallel with the integration of different states, other nations or associations of nations were falling apart because of internal diversity in ethnicity, culture, and/or language.

The systems level of the integration/disintegration paradox consists of many components. Integration components are, first, increasingly improved means of communication, through travel, television, radio, mobile or otherwise improved telephones, and what is known as electronic mail, such as fax, telex, and computer networks. Second, there is the everincreasing network of commercial exchange. Third, national jurisdictions and barriers are being superseded by international organizations, such as the United Nations with its specialized agencies (UNESCO, WHO, and the World Bank), the OECD (Organisation for Economic Co-operation and Development), the EU (European Union), OPEC (Organization of Petroleum Exporting Countries), GATT (General Agreements on Tariffs and Trade), the humanitarian organizations such as the Red Cross and Amnesty International, all the national development organizations such as the Canadian International Development Agency (CIDA), the Swedish International Development Authority (SIDA), USAID, and all the private organizations, such as the Ford Foundation, the Lutheran World Service, and CARE.

In most nations, interethnic and/or religious conflicts create problems. In India, there are ethnic controversies, as well as the communal conflicts between Hindus and Muslims. Iraq, Iran, and Turkey have problems, most prominently in the strained relations with the Kurds, but also among themselves. Myanmar, Indonesia, Cyprus, Sri Lanka, and Lebanon are examples of other Asian or Middle-Eastern nations with ethnic problems. The whole continent of Africa is a stage of interethnic, tribal, racial, and political conflicts within virtually every state.

The situation in Europe in the early 1990s was a particularly positive example of integration, both regarding the far-reaching harmonization of rules, laws, and administration within the EU, and the democratization of the East European states, in spite of the many problems involved. The latter was preceded, however, by a disintegration process, namely the dissolution of the Warsaw Pact in the summer of 1991.

4.2 Systems Level: Disintegration Processes. Ethnicity or Ethnocentrism?

The disintegration process of the Communist systems has passed into national disintegration processes. Ethnic, religious, and cultural diversity are at the core of the disintegration processes. The increasing ethnic consciousness has led to demands for increased autonomy. The beginning of the 1990s witnessed the disintegration of the Soviet Union and Yugoslavia, due to ethnic differences. In the former Soviet Union, all the republics declared autonomy, and announced elections. These republics deleted the term "socialist" from their names, as did indeed the whole former Soviet Union, before its dissolution on December 25, 1991. However, some of these republics agreed to form a new Slavic Commonwealth. The three Baltic republics, formerly autonomous states, declared themselves, and were recognized by most countries, as autonomous countries, not wanting to be members of the new Commonwealth. In Yugoslavia, countries such as Slovenia and Croatia declared themselves independent, and were also recognized by many countries, and expressed their wish to develop relations with the rest of Europe and to gain membership of the EU. In the cases of both Russia and Yugoslavia, a combination of ethnicity and economy explains the disintegration. In former Yugoslavia, the strivings for autonomy tragically led to the war between Serbs, Croats and Bosnian Muslims.

Apparently stable countries such as France, the United Kingdom, and the United States were also shaken by the force of the new ethnicity. In the United States, to the old diversification of American Indians, Blacks, and European immigrant groups, two new groups were added, by the influx of Hispanics from Mexico, Cuba, Puerto Rico, and elsewhere in the Caribbean, and the reception of a large number of refugees from all over the world (Gray 1991, Schlesinger 1991). By 1991 Hispanics formed 9 percent of the United States population, and in the same year, students from 123 countries were being educated in Dade County in Florida.

Radical multiculturalism seems to have upset old values, that so far had been the cement of the nation, that is the principles of freedom to create a new personal identity and the chance to become part of a nation of people who are doing the same (Gray 1991). Whereas a certain degree of multiethnic awareness is healthy and contributes to pluralism, when pressed too far, it creates disintegrative problems (Schlesinger 1991). Historians such as Schlesinger are, however, optimistic. The historic forces driving toward "one people" remain powerful, and most United States-born

ethnic group members see themselves as Americans. Similar principles probably apply to many of the other nations in crisis. It would seem that a truly multicultural education of a pluralistic nature would help the situation. Demands for separate schools for ethnic groups is a type of multicultural education that strives for monoculturalism rather than pluralism, and does not seem to be able to improve the situation.

4.3 Individual and Group Level

On the individual and group level, the basic problem and subject of debate concerns the choice between integration or segregation of the minority vis-à-vis the majority. This adaptation process is of a psychosocial, interpersonal, or intergroup nature. The process is assumed to have far-reaching consequences for the mental health of minority members (see Ekstrand 1978, for a research review and references). Multicultural education is supposed to help in this process, but there is a controversy as to how to proceed. This controversy is discussed in some detail by Ekstrand (1978, 1983, 1986, 1989), and will be sketched here only briefly.

In this context, a number of concepts are used, such as integration, assimilation, adaptation, absorption, discrimination, segregation, separation, and identity. Early social scientists, such as Eisenstadt (1955), viewed assimilation as desirable, and differentiated between cultural and social assimilation. "Cultural assimilation" means the internalization by the minority members of the norms and behavior patterns of the majority. "Social assimilation" is the absorption of the minority members into the primary groups of the majority, that is, they can vote, they can become politicians or officials, and they are accepted in all social contexts. The opposite to this state of affairs is segregation, a common event long before it was scientifically studied. Some authors have differentiated between assimilation and integration, indicating that the former term means giving up ethnic identity, whereas the latter term means social assimilation but with ethnic identity retained. In 1937, Stonequist introduced the concept of marginality. Perhaps groups such as the Gypsies and Jews are the best examples of marginality because they have managed to preserve their culture and keep to themselves in spite of living in other societies.

Since the 1970s increasing ethnic awareness has produced advocates who resent assimilation on the grounds that it means totally giving up ethnic identity. This position is more political than scientific, as the advocates do not leave the decision to the individuals concerned. In any event, ethnic identity is difficult to remove. An alternative that has been advocated is "ethnic autonomy." Sweden and the province of Bavaria in Germany were first to experience the effects of a policy of ethnic autonomy on multicultural education. The Bavarian multicultural education system has been heavily criticized and subsequently modified (Rist 1978).

In Scandinavia, as discussed in Ekstrand (1983), certain Finnish sociologists, educators, and linguists argued that immigrant children should be brought up in a segregated environment (also called positive segregation). This segregation policy manifested itself as monolingual or mother tongue classes in schools. The task of these classes was as much to protect the students from the alleged harmful influence of exposure to a second language as to promote the mother tongue. As shown in much research (see Ekstrand 1983), this type of education proved disastrous to the students. Their mother tongue declined and the host language did not develop properly, hence the children's school achievements suffered. However, students who followed mainstream education, with mother tongue tuition, did about as well as indigenous students.

In Canada, some researchers have argued that mother tongue education is superior, and that less training in the second language will improve the latter's proficiency through assumed mother tongue improvement (Cummins and Swain 1986). However, research has indicated otherwise. Some interesting research evidence suggests what will happen in the future with students from segregated ethnic school models. Nelleman (1981) interviewed about 800 Polish immigrants who came to Denmark at the beginning of the twentieth century. About 1,250 of their adult children also answered a questionnaire. They had followed Polish or Danish education. Those who had followed Polish education had preserved the Polish language and culture to a higher degree, but had also suffered more discrimination. Many were critical of their parents' choice of schooling. Their command of the Danish language had not developed satisfactorily, and they felt they had been hampered in their social careers, with difficulties in getting jobs and positions.

In Fig. 1, the interdependence of the majority's and the ethnic group's attitudes toward maintenance is summarized, and some of the terms used in the debate are defined. The ethnic group may be positive or negative toward society and toward cultural maintenance. This gives three meaningful combinations, as the fourth, being negative to both, will be rare. The mainstream society can accept or reject the ethnic group(s).

Regarding multicultural education and strategies for multicultural adaptation, long-term, specific formal or informal exposure to more than one language or culture seems to have greater impact than various direct, nonspecific approaches. This is natural, as the latter by necessity will be of a limited and mostly short-lasting nature. Several experiments (reviewed in Ekstrand 1978) indicate that sensitivity, attitudes, and cognitive development prosper from bilingualism. However, in several ambitious desegregated classroom experiments in Israel (Dar and Resh 1986, Rich et al. 1986), results so far have been poorer than expected, mainly because ethnicity is associated with socioeconomic status, IQ, and schooling, which seem to be more powerful factors.

5. Multiculturalism, Multicultural Education, and Testing

The first cross-cultural study with tests was probably the one conducted in 1899 on the Torres Straits islands off northern Australia (Biesheuvel 1972). In the United States, cross-cultural tests were used as early as 1910 (Anastasi 1968). These tests were developed for the large waves of immigrants, mostly for placement purposes, and particularly for military needs. The best-known test was the Army Alpha, which was found too verbal, hence too biased for non-English speaking groups; thus the subsequent nonverbal Army Beta was developed. Later, Cattell (1971) developed the Culture Fair Intelligence Test, with nonverbal characteristics.

Multicultural Education		
Ethnic group's attitude to majority society	Majority society's attitude toward ethnic group	
	Accepts	Rejects
Positive to majority society/Positive to maintenance	Integration	Segregation
Positive to majority society/Negative to maintenance	Assimilation	Separation
Negative to majority society/Positive to maintenance	Self-separation	Marginalization

Figure 1
The interdependence of interethnic relations and attitudes toward ethnic maintenance

Eventually testing became widely accepted in the United States, for employment and for school purposes. Immigrant children were often placed in special classes because of low scores on IQ tests. Yet the use of testing in the schools has been controversial, because tests have been accused of being biased. However, it is not so much the tests per se that should be criticized, but rather the poor practices in using the tests. Malpractices in test application have been strongly attacked by many authors, such as Samuda (1975) and Samuda and Kong (1986).

6. Some Case Studies

6.1 Germany

The case of Germany may be discussed from four different aspects: the education of immigrants; education in the European context, which mostly concerns higher education; schools abroad; and the reunion between the former East and West Germany. In 1992 Germany had a population of some 77 million, 61 from the former West Germany and 16 from the former East Germany. In the then West Germany, the school system was unprepared for the wave of some 4.5 million foreign immigrants and their families, starting in the late 1960s. The authorities did not recognize the permanency of this *de facto* immigration, but labeled the migrants as "guest workers" (Rist 1978).

The German states have individual educational policies and systems. Most of the states of the federation limited the number of immigrants they would receive, but this limit was frequently changed according to economic fluctuations. Now and then, groups of "guest workers" were sent away, and hence acted as regulators of the economy. Immigrants from Turkey, Greece, and Yugoslavia by 1990 constituted 12 percent of the total workforce. In cities such as Berlin and Frankfurt, the proportion of permanent foreign citizens was close to 25 percent. Since the beginning of the 1980s, virtually no labor immigration has been allowed; only immigration for family reunion or refugee reasons occurs. In 1991, 200,000 asylum applications came to the Ministry of the Interior, while another 900,000 were being processed.

Educational practices have changed substantially over the years. From models of separate education, especially found in Bavaria, there has been a tendency toward integrated models. In Nordrhein-Westfalen, the most populous state, 65 percent of all foreign children were taught in ordinary schools in 1980 compared to 95 percent in 1986. During the same period the failure rate declined from 60 percent to 30 percent. The proportion of foreign students in the high schools has doubled, hence 3 percent of the students at the most selective *Gymnasiums* are of foreign origin. Bavaria still continued to follow the separatist education policy, providing schools with the mother tongue as the predominant medium of instruction, but it has been substantially modified since the early 1970s, so that much more instruction in and with the German language is given from the very start, and German dominates by Grade 9.

Germany has shifted largely from a separatist to a transitional system of immigrant education. There is a clear goal of some cultural maintenance, but progress is slow. Mother tongue education is mostly given after school hours, only in the major immigrant languages, and to a small proportion of students. Mother tongue or home language teachers are recruited among Germans, rather than from the ethnic groups themselves, meaning that they do not have full command of the ethnic language or culture. In the informal sector, German attitudes are fairly ethnocentric. Virtually all foreign movies are dubbed into German. Germany tries to create German words for new phenomena, rather than borrow the foreign terms. As reported in the press in the early 1990s, attitudes toward immigrants are often suspicious, and interaction occurs rarely. Hence, in Berlin and other major cities ghettos have developed, with unrest and social disturbances.

With the new European integration, certain changes are perceptible. There is, on principle, free exchange of labor within the European Union, so that workers from, for example, the United Kingdom can go to Germany as guest workers. The most prominent change is the exchange program at the higher education level, namely ERASMUS, COMMETT, and the language study program LINGUA. ERASMUS (European Community Action Scheme for the Mobility of University Students) is a system for the EU to exchange students for studies, but not research. The studies at a foreign university are fully accepted for national examinations, the program is open for all faculties and subjects, it is permanent, and the goal is that at least 10 percent of European students shall conduct part of their studies in another country. COMMETT (Community Action Program for Education and Training for Technology) is a program for work experience in companies, and to transmit knowledge between companies and universities.

Germany has an old tradition of establishing schools abroad, in very different countries such as Chile, Finland, Spain, and Sweden. Although most of the teaching is done in German, native language development never becomes fully natural, but a high degree of advanced bilingualism is achieved.

In the united Germany of the early 1990s, two different school systems are being integrated, and in the former East Germany, new values and perspectives are being taught. Teachers are to undergo a complete transformation and teach new contents and values. The integration is supposed to take from five to ten years. The West German school system is the norm for the new Germany.

6.2 Canada

Canada has 12 educational systems. The country has an indigenous native population, and two major ethnic groups, the Anglophone and the Francophone Canadians. In addition, there have been for many generations a number of immigrant groups, mainly from Europe, but in smaller numbers from almost all over the world. Immigration is still encouraged, in particular from Southeast Asia. However, bilingual education programs for immigrants are not numerous. It seems that most immigrant children are placed in ordinary English- or French-medium classes. In several metropolitan Toronto schools less than 50 percent of the students have English as their first language. In Vancouver this figure is around 40 percent. The proportion seems to be increasing, and is no longer restricted to urban areas. During the 1980s, there were transitional programs for Italian children in Toronto, Ukrainian and German programs in the west, and ethnically oriented schools for many different groups in several cities. The Heritage Language Program in Ontario involved the teaching of community languages during or after regular school for up to 2.5 hours per week. A program in Quebec taught Italian, Greek, Portuguese, and Spanish to immigrant children for about 30 min a day. It is not known how large a proportion of all immigrant children receive some kind of bilingual education.

Adam-Moodley (1986) argues that the discussions about pluralism in Canada are merely rhetoric. Multicultural education is seen as superimposed upon a mainstream Anglo-Saxon curriculum. High-level social and political positions are closed to ethnic minorities, especially the visible minorities.

The best-known multicultural programs are the immersion programs. These consist mainly of teaching English-speaking children in French, but there are a few programs where English immersion classes are available to French-speaking children, and also a few trilingual programs in English-French-Hebrew. In the mid-1980s, more than 75,000 students were assumed to have been exposed to immersion programs (Samuda and Kong 1986). The mother tongue of these students does not suffer, and their academic achievement and cognitive development are in fact very good (Lambert et al. 1973). Total immersion seems to be better than partial immersion.

6.3 The United States

The United States has a native minority population, that is various tribes of American Indians; a large English-speaking White minority; a Black population originating from the African slaves; a large number of immigrants from all over the world; and a number of refugees. In 1968 the Bilingual Education Act was passed, giving the right to bilingual education to minority students. After the Lau versus Nichols case

in the Supreme Court in 1974, bilingual programs expanded over the entire country, for immigrant as well as for indigenous minority students. In this court case, a Chinese family claimed that its child was denied equal educational opportunity because he was not sufficiently proficient in English. This claim was upheld in the Supreme Court. Statistics and projections estimate that the number of persons of non-English language background was 28 million in 1976 (13 percent), 30 million in 1980 (14 percent), 35 million in 1990 (16 percent), and will be 40 million by 2000 (18 percent). The projected number of children aged 5–14 of limited English proficiency was 2.5 million in 1976, 2.4 million in 1980, 2.8 million in 1990, and will be 3.4 million in 2000. These figures may be too low because of a heavy influx of refugees. There was also a large number of "undocumented aliens," mostly Spanish speaking.

The expansion of bilingual programs, especially the more maintenance-directed ones, has slowed down, owing to a number of experiences and evaluations. More maintenance does not seem to contribute to academic or linguistic achievement. Students are more affected by the social, physical, and cultural environment which will support that particular language. A bilingual educational model with an emphasis on the actual language, but with continued support in the original language, seems to be optimal (Anderson and Boyer 1978, Linde 1986, Linde and Löfgren 1988, review in Ekstrand 1983). Only very few researchers in Canada and Finland argue that more mother tongue education will give better proficiency in a second language. Results of the Finnish and Canadian studies seem to point the other way.

More and more direct multicultural education programs, aiming at intercultural sensitization, competency, and communication, have appeared in the United States. It is difficult to estimate their extent, but this movement is clearly expanding, and spreading to other countries. Finally, a strong demand for ethnic, segregated schools for Blacks and Hispanics has emerged in contrast to pressures during the 1950s to the 1980s for desegregated schools.

See also: Race and Ethnicity in Education; Students in Classrooms, Gender and Racial Differences Among; Education of Indigenous Peoples

References

Adam-Moodley K 1986 The politics of education in three multicultural societies: Germany, South Africa and Canada. In: Samuda R J, Kong S L (eds.) 1986
Anastasi A 1968 *Psychological Testing*, 3rd edn. Macmillan, London
Anderson T, Boyer M 1978 *Bilingual Schooling in the United States*, 2nd edn. National Educational Laboratory Publishers, Austin, Texas
Banks J A 1985 Multicultural education. In: Husén T,

Postlethwaite T N (eds.) 1985 *The International Encyclopedia of Education*. Pergamon Press, Oxford

Barrow R, Milburn G (eds.) 1986 *A Critical Dictionary of Educational Concepts*. Wheatsheaf, Brighton

Biesheuvel S 1972 Adaptability: Its measurement and determinants. In: Cronbach L J, Drenth P J D (eds.) 1972 *Mental Tests and Cultural Adaptation*. Mouton, The Hague

Cattell R B 1971 *Abilities: Their Structure, Growth and Action*. Houghton Mifflin, Boston, Massachusetts

Cummins J, Swain M 1986 *Bilingualism in Education*. Longman, London

Dar Y, Resh N 1986 Dimensions of student-body composition and academic achievement: An Israeli experience. In: Ekstrand L H (ed.) 1986

Deighton L C (ed.) 1971 *Encyclopedia of Education*. Free Press, New York

Eisenstadt S N 1955 *The Absorption of Immigrants*. The Free Press, Glencoe, Illinois

Ekstrand L H 1978 Migrant adaptation: A cross-cultural problem. In: Freudenstein R (ed.) 1978 *Teaching the Children of Immigrants*. Didier, Brussels

Ekstrand L H 1983 Maintenance or transition—or both? In: Husén T, Opper S (eds.) 1983 *Multicultural and Multilingual Education in Immigrant Countries*. Pergamon Press, Oxford

Ekstrand L H 1985 Immigrant children, policies for education. In: Husén T, Postlethwaite T N (eds.) 1985 *The International Encyclopedia of Education*. Pergamon Press, Oxford

Ekstrand L H (ed.) 1986 *Ethnic Minorities and Immigrants in a Cross-Cultural Perspective*. Swets and Zeitlinger, Lisse

Ekstrand L H 1989 Bilingualism in education—A book review. *J. Language Social Psychol.* 8(2): 131–36

Ekstrand L H, Ekstrand G 1986 Developing the emic and etic concepts for cross-cultural comparisons. *Educational and Psychological Interactions* 86. Malmö School of Education, Malmö

Good C V (ed.) 1959 *Dictionary of Education*, 2nd edn. McGraw-Hill, New York

Gray P 1991 Whose America? *Time International* 138(27): 20–25

Hall E T 1959 *The Silent Language*. Doubleday, New York

Lambert W E, Tucker G R, D'Anglejan A 1973 Cognitive and attitudinal consequences of bilingual schooling. *J. Educ. Psychol.* 65: 141–59

Leach R J 1969 *International Schools and Their Role in the Field of International Education*. Pergamon Press, Oxford

Lexikon der Pädagogik 1971 Herder, Freiburg

Linde S G 1986 The relationship between different forms of bilingual education and achievement among Finnish minority sixth-grade students in Sweden. In: Ekstrand L H (ed.) 1986

Linde S, Löfgren H 1988 The relationship between medium of instruction and school achievement for Finnish-speaking students in Sweden. *Language, Culture and Curriculum* 1(2): 131–45

Nelleman G 1981 *Polske Landarbeidere i Danmark og Deres Efterkommere*. Nationalmuseet, Copenhagen

Ness E (ed.) 1974 *Pedagogisk Oppslagsbok*. Gyldendal, Oslo

Page G T, Thomas J B 1977 *International Dictionary of Education*. Kogan Page, London

Pusch M D (ed.) 1979 *Multicultural Education. A Cross-cultural Training Approach*. Intercultural Press, Chicago, Illinois

Rich Y, Amir Y, Ben-Ari R, Mevarech Z 1986 Cooperation strategies for mixed-ethnic groups in the Israeli desegregated classroom. In: Ekstrand L H (ed.) 1986

Rist R C 1978 *Guestworkers in Germany: The Prospect for Pluralism*. Praeger, New York

Robinson G L N 1981 Bilingual education in Australia and the United States. In: Garner M (ed.) 1981 *Community Languages*. River Seine Publications, Melbourne

Samuda R J 1975 *Psychological Testing of American Minorities: Issues and Consequences*. Harper and Row, New York

Samuda R J, Kong S L (eds.) 1986 *Multicultural Education: Programs and Methods*. Intercultural Social Sciences Publications, Toronto

Schlesinger A 1991 The cult of ethnicity, good and bad. *Time International* 138(27): 26

Smolicz J J 1981 The three types of multiculturalism. In: Garner M (ed.) 1981 *Community Languages*. River Seine Publications, Melbourne

Språkoch Kulturarvsutredningen 1983 Ministry of Education, Stockholm

Stonequist E V 1937 *The Marginal Man*. Scribner's, New York

Vecoli R J 1972 European Americans: From immigrants to ethnics. *International Migration Review* 6: 403–34

Velasquez A G, Ingle H T 1982 Multicultural and minority education. In: Mitzel H E (ed.) 1982 *Encyclopedia of Educational Research*, 5th edn. Free Press, New York

Further Reading

Ekstrand L H 1990 Children in India and Sweden. *Reprints and Miniprints* 708. Malmö School of Education, Malmö

Ekstrand L H, Foster S, Olkiewicz E, Stankovski M 1981 Interculture: some concepts for describing the situation of immigrants. *J. Multilingual Multicultural Dev.* 2(4): 269–95

Husén T, Opper S (eds.) 1983 *Multicultural and Multilingual Education in Immigrant Countries*. Pergamon Press, Oxford

Löfgren, H (ed.) 1995 *Peace Education and Human Development*. Malmö School of Education, Malmö

Schools as Sociocultural Systems

F. Erickson

Schools both create sociocultural order and respond to the ordering of their environments within society. Culture, shared within local human groups, can be seen as the sedimentation of the collective learning that occurs within the group's historical experience. It arises through the recursive, situated practice of persons in everyday life. That practice is constrained by the contingencies of processes in society at large. This article focuses upon the nature of culture and of cultural practice in schools and upon the school's relations with its environments. After discussing the basic concepts of sociocultural systems as they pertain to schools, the article gives an illustrative overview of international research bearing on the topic. This overview highlights issues of equity and of class and cultural conflict connected to schools.

1. Basic Conceptions

The notion of "system" is that of a set of entities linked by interactions within boundaries that keep the system distinct from and connected with its external surround. A "sociocultural system" is one in which interactions within and across system boundaries are social and cultural rather than physical or chemical. Such interactions take place through modalities of resources (e.g., legitimacy and taste, power, knowledge, technique) whose values are defined and encoded semiotically, that is, in symbol systems. Schools are institutions in which meanings and semiotic capacities are transmitted and created; hence the workings of schools partake of the same modalities and resources whose distribution and exchange constitute the workings of the wider social system of which the school is a part.

A fundamental shift in emphasis has been taking place in the social and behavioral sciences and in organization theory which is changing conceptions of sociocultural systems. Formerly, in the organization theory derived from structural or functionalist social theory, it was presumed that social processes were inherently homeostatic. There is now an alternative to the image of an organization maintaining an internal steady state in the midst of transactions with an external environment. This is the image of an organization as a set of relations among conflicting subsystems (see Morgan 1986). Diverse interests and situated perspectives can run along lines of official and unofficial social networks within and across subsystem units such as departments.

Clear organizational goals and coherent internal arrangments in the pursuit of them also seem less characteristic of organizations than they did previously.

Since the work of J G March and Simon and their followers (e.g., March and Olsen 1976) organizations and their operations are seen as inherently limited in their means–ends rationality. The same is true for notions of individual cognition, for contemporary cognitive psychology emphasizes the boundedness of attention and memory.

Ways of thinking about the distribution of culture and language in society are also changing. Rather than being seen as a unitary, internally consistent system of symbols or values that is shared uniformly among members of a social group and is reproduced intact across generations, culture, language, and other semiotic systems are coming to be seen as inherently diverse and partial. Subcultures and stylistic dialects are seen as interpenetrating; overlapping not only within the social group or network but within the individual person. These cultural subsystems are conceived of as being held in tension within the individual as well as within the group, diverse registers being organized as repertoires of performance variation to which the person or group has access. Sets of cultural knowledge are acquired successively across the life cycle. One learns a cultural and linguistic register within the nuclear family of origin, another upon entering school, others among networks of peers, and still others among colleagues at work. From this point of view everyone is multicultural.

Culture refers to customary ways of making sense—that is, lines of interpretation—which are learned rather than innate. Goodenough (1981) has defined culture as sets of learned and shared standards for perceiving, believing, acting, and evaluating the actions of others. Through cultural learning humans develop a taken-for-granted ontology. This influences interpretations of what is, what ought to be, what is likely to happen, and why it will happen.

One way to think of culture is by analogy to information bits in a computer's memory or to genetic information as distributed within a breeding population. From this perspective culture consists of many small items of knowledge that are stored as a large pool of information within a bounded social group. Although the bearers of cultural knowledge are individuals, no single member of the group has learned all of the knowledge that is possessed within the group as a whole.

Another perspective sees culture as consisting of large chunks of knowledge—conceptual structures. These are core symbols that constitute what is taken as "reality" and "purpose" by members of a group. Within the group routine ways of acting and making sense repeat the major framing patterns again and again, just as within a musical composition many variations can be written on a few underlying thematic elements (for elaboration, see Geertz 1983). In the former conception of culture as information bits, the amounts and kinds of information known by individuals are seen as varying widely across persons and subgroups within a given population. In the latter conception (the more classically held view among anthropologists and sociologists) systemic coherence is emphasized, with an assumption of closely shared understanding of core symbols among the individuals that make up the bounded social group.

In a third view cultural sharing and nonsharing across individuals are seen as strongly patterned along lines of power and rank relationships and across institutional boundaries within a social group. In societies structured by inequality, not all cultural variants are equally valued. Prestige accrues to some sets of knowledge and taste, and stigma to others. What is valued by the general society serves particular subgroups and individuals as "cultural capital" (see Bourdieu and Passeron 1977). From this point of view cultural diversity within a society is seen as an exact reproduction of the distribution of power within the society.

Each of the three previous views emphasizes the intergenerational transmission of culture, de-emphasizes human agency, and leaves little analytic room for the possibility of cultural change within and across generations. From these perspectives, an individual's ways of acting and making sense are overdetermined by socialization, as if the individual social actor were an automaton.

A fourth view takes more account of human agency than do any of the previous three. Rather than viewing culture as epiphenomenal of pre-existing power relationships in society (i.e., as "superstructure" in traditional Marxist terms) this perspective considers culture, social structure, and human agency as mutually constitutive. The individual constructs culture in immediate experience through the recursive enactment of practices; that is, sets of actions strategically intended toward the accomplishment of desired ends or projects. The practices are situated; that is, they take place within the contingencies of immediate circumstances. Recalling Marx's dictum that persons make history in circumstances not of their own choosing, one must note that the conditions of immediate experience in a cultural learning environment are not created *ex nihilo* by the individual learner. Rather, in the production of culture within practice the individual makes use of pre-existing production resources, among them the knowledge and meaning perspectives that result from deliberate and nondeliberate socialization by elders and by peers. The individual also "makes sense," that is, creates new production resources (unique knowledge and meaning perspectives) by learning the consequences of his or her own efforts through trial and error.

Since the situation of practice itself is partly determined by past history, the cultural knowledge the individual is able to construct through practice is influenced by general social structure. This takes place in at least two ways. First, by influencing the constitution of the kinds of activities that occur recursively in a cultural learning environment (hence influencing the consequences of the learner's actions in practices), the general social structure profoundly influences the learner's opportunity to learn within processes of inventing new culture. Second, by influencing the message contents and forms that will be used by socializing agents in the learning environment, the general social structure influences the learner's opportunity to learn within processes of acquiring old culture. Thus cultural production can be seen as a mediating activity within which, as Giddens (1984 p. 25) put it, "social structures are both constituted by human agency, and yet at the same time are the very medium of this constitution."

It should be emphasized that in cultural production not all the intentions nor all the knowledges acquired are deliberate. Some of the limits on awareness come from processes elucidated by clinical psychology; for example, denial and projection. In addition, anthropologists identify as implicit culture the results of teaching and learning that take place outside conscious awareness for reasons other than clinical ones (e.g., the sense of how long after the beginning of a stated meeting time it is not inappropriate to be late, or the presupposition of lateness itself as a phenomenon). Implicit culture, whether it is the result of invention or of socialization, is learned and taught outside conscious awareness. Moreover, there are unintended consequences of practices that may be overlooked by the culture learner and there are consequences of practices that may only be apparent at later points in time, far beyond the understanding of the learner who is immersed in the conduct of situated cultural practice.

Thus the notions of intention, project, socialization, and trial and error learning in the above discussion should not be construed as implying that conscious reflection is involved. Indeed, from this perspective what is "natural" about cultural learning and practice is not that it is rational but that it is, in formal terms, irrational. The practicing subject takes an inherently situated (i.e., nonobjective) stance when engaged in everyday life. That insight has been apparent since Plato invoked the metaphor of the cave. Modern philosophy and social scientific work goes much further, however, by suggesting that the situated condition of the perceiving subject is fundamentally irremediable, or at least is incapable of remedy by a retreat to the objectivist stance of disembodied and disinterested observation and reflection.

The same insight applies to current perspectives on organizational functioning. In an earlier era, the emphasis in organization theory was on organizational rationality. Now it is on what may appear, at first glance, as organizational irrationality. Increasing attention is being paid to discrepancies between an organization's stated aims and unstated aspects of its actual functioning, between organization charts and the organization's informal underlife, between putative inputs and putative outputs. It is precisely because the individuals within organizations are using situated fuzzy logics of practical sense-making and decision-making (some of which become recursively shared and sedimented in interacting groups and networks) that organizations develop a sociocultural life of their own in their transactions with the wider social and cultural systems of their environment. In addressing this local complexity, contemporary organizational research attempts to treat the formal organization as something other than a black box.

In sum, a modern emphasis in social and cultural theory, cognitive theory, and organization theory is on the bounded, the tacit and situationally embedded, the reflexive, and the conflictual. Culture is seen as being acquired within and across generations both by transmission (and acquiescence) and by invention (and resistance). Diversity of voices and interests is seen as inherent within human societies, within the formal organization, and within the person. Direct observation is seen as necessary—of organizations and their environments, of specific situations of interaction within the organization, and of persons in those situations. Hence, it should come as no surprise to find that, upon taking a firsthand look in schools, diversity of socially organized voice and interest becomes apparent and indeed appears ubiquitous in the cultural practices that arise and endure there.

One of the concomitants of local practice by teachers and students appears to be the development of mutual cynicism in attribution of motive and ability. With increasing school experience many teachers become less and less optimistic in their views of the intentions and capacities of their students. Students reciprocate this. Especially among those students who become disaffiliated in their early school years, distrust and dislike of teachers and of school become increasingly openly felt and expressed. The same pattern is seen in relations between administrators and teachers and between school staff and parents—mutual distrust often increases across time. It appears that the practices of school life are often alienating. People at school tend to adopt coping strategies that include hiding one's true thoughts, feelings, and actions as well as acting in ways that are visibly hostile. Yet, in some schools, mutual trust and respect appear to flourish, which shows that nonalienating school experience is possible. Such schools appear to be the exception rather than the rule (Sarason 1971).

In the educational literature there are various explanations for the alienated experience of participants out of which school cultures form as complex webs of trust and mistrust. Some of these explanations are considered in the section below.

2. Focal Issues and Topics of Research

Because of space limitations, this review of empirical research will focus on qualitative studies. (The reader is referred to more extensive reviews of qualitative research by Jacob 1987, Atkinson et al. 1988, and Mehan 1992.)

If the school is a sociocultural system, what are its boundaries? This has been a crucial question for research. Does the school simply repeat and reproduce the sociocultural order of the wider society or is the school to some extent socioculturally distinct from it? The view that increased education leads directly to individual and social betterment has come to be seen as naively optimistic. The contrary view, that increased schooling produces greater inequality and alienation in society, has some empirical warrant but may be overly cynical. On these issues the results of research are mixed. One way to survey the literature is to consider what various streams of inquiry have to say about the boundaries of schools as sociocultural systems.

2.1 Community—School Focus

Community studies were especially characteristic in the United States immediately after the Second World War, and that work has continued. Some community studies focused on the local school have emphasized continuity between national culture, local community culture, and school culture. Among these are studies of American communities (e.g., Hollingshead 1975, Varenne 1977) and studies of villages in various nations, for example, France (Wylie 1964), Germany (Spindler and Spindler 1987), and China (Chance 1984). This stream of work suggests that local schools, especially when staffed by local residents, differ little from local community cultural perspectives and values.

2.2 Class and Culture Conflict

Another way in which the boundaries of schools can be seen as highly permeable is for research to portray conflicts that occur in the wider society as being played out face-to-face inside schools, especially in relations between teachers and students. Since the 1960s there have been numerous studies of sociocultural discontinuity and conflict in schools. As Atkinson et al. (1988) have noted, school studies outside the United States, notably in the United Kingdom, have tended to emphasize conflict that runs along class lines, while studies in the United States have emphasized conflict between the minority ethnic culture of students and the school culture. The notion is that conflict and inequality between various interest groups within the larger society becomes focused and repeated inside the school.

Case studies of class conflict in British schools include Lacey (1970) and Ball (1981; see also the collection by Hammersley and Woods 1984). This stream of work tends toward accounts that suggest that the reproduction of existing inequalities happens almost automatically in schools. A study by Willis (1977) took a slightly different tack. He interviewed and observed working-class "lads" in a technical high school. His study shows that by refusing to affiliate with the middle-class ethos of the school, "the lads" engaged in self-defeating resistance that constructed a working-class future. Their school failure was not automatic; it could be seen as being achieved (see also McDermott and Gospodinoff 1979 for an American argument along similar lines). Yet Willis's account is still heavily determinist. The "lads" are portrayed as having no option but to collude in their own educational demise. A more nuanced position is taken in Connell et al.'s study (1982) of social reproduction in a variety of elite and nonelite Australian schools. That study shows variation in school affiliation within as well as between classes. Connell attributes this to two factors; what he calls the distinctive "projects" toward education held by particular families for their children and, especially for working-class students, the positive influence of some unusually empathic teachers. Such teachers were encountered randomly, however, within the school careers of the students, suggesting that school organizations were by no means systematically organized to foster educational improvement among working-class students.

There have also been school studies of class reproduction and resistance in the United States. Often the school conflict is shown to combine class, race, ethnicity, and gender, taking a more complex and less determinist view of the relations between class and school achievement that is akin to that of Connell et al. In linked papers, Ogbu (1993) and Erickson (1993) discussed a racially based culture of school resistance by African-Americans that is analogous to the class-based culture of resistance identified by Willis. Foley's (1990) school community study in a South Texas town showed how issues of Mexican-American and Anglo ethnic identity combined in complex ways with issues of social class. In a discussion of these studies, Mehan (1992) also reported his own research on the institutionalized judgment processes by which students who do not "fit," for a variety of reasons (including cultural ones), were streamed into a remedial track. These studies in the United States showed how active sense-making in specific situations of practice is entailed in the reproduction of inequality in schools.

A number of United States studies have focused on ethnic and racial culture clash between schools and their local communities. Much of this work has been sociolinguistic in orientation, identifying cultural patterns of communication style that become grounds for conflict in the classroom. (Many of the studies are reviewed in Cazden 1988.) Culturally responsive pedagogy appears to be one way to reduce such classroom conflict, especially in elementary schools.

Considerable work on classroom discourse has also been done in the United Kingdom, emphasizing class differences more than ethnic differences. Theoretical and empirical work is reviewed in Stubbs (1983) and Atkinson et al. (1988). Some studies of classroom interaction have emphasized national culture differences in conceptions of children's abilities and assumptions about appropriate pedagogy; for example Anderson-Levitt (1987) on French classrooms, Spindler and Spindler (1987) on German and United States classrooms, and Tobin et al. (1989) on Japanese, Chinese, and United States classrooms.

2.3 Focus on School Roles

Various American studies have considered the distinctive professional culture of teachers, beginning with the classic essay by Waller (1932; see also Sikes et al. 1985, a collection of British studies). Wolcott (1984) focused an entire ethnography on the work life of a school principal (see also Gronn 1983). Lareau (1989) compared working-class and middle-class families as they interacted with teachers and principals at school. It is perhaps in this line of work, together with classroom research, that the boundaries of schools and local school communities as systems can be most clearly identified. As a distinctive local school microculture develops within a given building in networks of teachers interacting with building administrators, as it develops at the classroom level, and as families develop distinct microcultures that include particular educational projects (in Connell's sense), there is an opportunity to see not only the determining influences of large-scale social forces—the weight of history on actual lives—but the emergence of counterdetermining, and counterhegemonic practices at the local level where actual persons can be seen to be making history.

3. Conclusion

Schools as sociocultural systems appear to be loosely organized (Bidwell 1965, Weick 1976) (see *Loose Coupling and Educational Systems*). Mass schooling is a recent occurrence in human history and so the contradiction and incoherence of school practice is not entirely surprising. Schools can be seen as sites where diversity of societal interests and cultural perspectives is both collected from the environmental surround and invented in the situated practices of the various participants within the organization. The question of whether schools can play a progressive role in social change is as yet unanswered.

Future empirical work might well focus on multiple conflicting interests as they are engaged within the school. Past work has emphasized differences between teachers and students, and to some extent between administrators and teachers. Yet schools contain additional aspects of diversity of interest and practice within their walls; for example, faculty politics that run along lines of pedagogical philosophy and political belief, and the influences and interests of custodians, classroom aides, and lunchroom and playground aides in relations with the professional staff of the school. Gender, race, ethnicity, and class are entailed in the organization of these relatively unstudied phenomena, just as they are in the everyday conduct of curriculum and instruction.

Transactions between the school and its external environment have also been understudied from a sociocultural point of view. Relations with parents are the most immediate of these transactions. In the United States relations with local taxpayers are especially crucial and relations with the local business community have become increasingly important. Moreover, there are local and national conflicts over curricular content; for example, in the United States conflicts over sex education, creationism in teaching biology, and the "Euro-American canon" in teaching literature and history. Other arenas in which competing interests in society become focused on education and schooling are regional and national political processes by which educational policy is determined, and state and market influences bearing on the publishing of educational materials. At this level of social organization education becomes articulated with the political economy and with deeply held ontological assumptions concerning human nature, conduct, and purposes.

Yet there is evidence that these articulations are not determined in simple, linear ways. Schools, considered as sociocultural systems, appear to be producing, as well as reproducing, the culture and society in which they exist. The ways in which persons make history within sociocultural systems are various on a worldwide range. Moreover, alienation from learning and teaching, while prevalent within schools, is not universal. Thus the diversity of ways in which school morale is organized socially and culturally remains to be understood more fully.

See also: Administration of Education: Critical Approaches; Reproduction Theory; Sociology of Education: An Overview

References

Anderson-Levitt K 1987 Cultural knowledge for teaching first grade: An example from France. In: Spindler G, Spindler L (eds.) 1987 *Interpretive Ethnography of Education: At Home and Abroad.* Erlbaum, Hillsdale, New Jersey

Atkinson P, Delamont S, Hammersley M 1988 Qualitative research traditions: A British response to Jacob. *Rev. Educ. Res.* 58(2): 231–50

Ball S 1981 *Beachside Comprehensive.* Cambridge University Press, Cambridge

Bidwell C E 1965 The school as a formal organization. In: March J G (ed.) 1965 *Handbook of Organizations.* Rand-McNally, Chicago, Illinois

Bourdieu P, Passeron J C 1977 *Reproduction in Education, Society, and Culture.* Sage, London

Cazden C B 1988 *Classroom Discourse.* Heinemann, New York

Chance N 1984 *China's Urban Villagers: Life in a Beijing Commune.* Holt, Rinehart, and Winston, New York

Connell R W, Ashenden D J, Kessler S, Dowsett G W 1982 *Making the Difference: Schools, Families and Social Division.* Allen and Unwin, Sydney

Erickson F 1993 In: Jacob E, Jordan C (eds.) 1993 *Minority Education: Anthropological Perspectives.* Ablex, Norwood, New Jersey

Foley D E 1990 *Learning Capitalistic Culture: Deep in the Heart of Texas.* University of Pennsylvania Press, Philadelphia, Pennsylvania

Geertz C 1983 From the native point of view: On the nature of anthropological understanding. In: Geertz C 1983 *Local Knowledge.* Basic Books, New York

Giddens A 1984 *The Constitution of Society.* University of California Press, Berkeley, California

Goodenough W 1981 *Culture, Language and Society.* Benjamin-Cummings, Menlo Park, California

Gronn P C 1983 Talk as the work: The accomplishment of school administration. *Admin. Sci. Q.* 28: 1–21

Hammersley M, Woods P (eds.) 1984 *Life in Schools.* Open University Press, Milton Keynes

Hollingshead A 1975 *Elmtown's Youth and Elmtown Revisited.* Wiley, New York

Jacob E 1987 Qualitative research traditions: A review. *Rev. Educ. Res.* 57(1): 1–50

Lacey C 1970 *Hightown Grammar.* Manchester University Press, Manchester

Lareau A 1989 *Home Advantage: Social Class and Parental Intervention in Elementary Education.* Falmer Press, Philadelphia, Pennsylvania

March J G, Olsen J P 1976 *Ambiguity and Choice in Organizations.* Universitetsforlaget, Bergen

McDermott R P, Gospodinoff K 1979 Social contexts for ethnic borders and school failure. In: Trueba H, Guthrie G, Au K H (eds.) 1981 *Culture and the Bilingual Classroom.* Newbury House, Rowley, Massachusetts

Mehan H 1992 Understanding inequality in schools: The contribution of interpretive studies. *Soc. Educ.* 65(1): 1–20

Morgan G 1986 *Images of Organization.* Sage, Newbury Park, California

Ogbu 1993 In: Jacob E, Jordan C 1993 *Minority Education: Anthropological Perspectives.* Ablex, Norwood, New Jersey

Sarason S 1971 *The Culture of the School and the Problem of Change.* Allyn and Bacon, Boston, Massachusetts

Sikes P, Measor L, Woods P 1985 *Teacher Careers: Crises and Continuities.* Falmer Press, London

Spindler G, Spindler L 1987 Schonhausen revisited and the rediscovery of culture. In: Spindler G, Spindler L (eds.) 1987 *Interpretive Ethnography of Education: At Home and Abroad.* Erlbaum, Hillsdale, New Jersey

Stubbs M 1983 *Language, Schools and Classrooms.* Methuen, London

Tobin J, Wu D, Davidson D 1989 *Preschool in Three*

Cultures: Japan, China, and the United States. Yale University Press, New Haven, Connecticut

Varenne H 1977 *Americans Together: Structured Diversity in a Midwestern Town*. Teachers College Press, New York

Waller W 1932 *The Sociology of Teaching*. Wiley, New York

Weick K E 1976 Educational organizations as loosely coupled systems. *Adm. Sci. Q.* 21: 1–19

Willis P 1977 *Learning to Labour*. Saxon House, Farnborough

Wolcott H 1984 *The Man in the Principal's Office: An Ethnography*. Waveland, Prospect Heights, Illinois

Wylie L 1964 *Village in the Vaucluse*. Harvard University Press, Cambridge, Massachusetts

School Size and Small Schools

M. Bray

Determining the optimum size of schools is an important but complex task. Policies have to take account of economic, educational, and social factors. This article discusses these three groups of factors.

1. The Economics of School Size

Reliable research evidence on the economics of school size is rather scarce. Partly because of the way in which government budgets are constructed, identifying all costs of specific institutions is frequently a complex matter. Researchers also encounter problems of institutional comparability, for it is often difficult to isolate variations in costs that are solely attributable to school size. However, some important studies are worth highlighting.

One of the best was conducted by the Commission for Local Authority Accounts in Scotland (see Bell and Sigsworth 1987), and has some general implications. The Commission examined 85 schools with enrollments ranging from 8 to 457. The research showed sharply escalating unit costs when enrollments fell below 25, but also showed wide variation. Some institutions with 20 pupils, for example, had double the unit costs of other institutions with 20 pupils. Wide variation also existed among larger schools, and ones with more than 200 pupils found their costs varying by up to 65 percent. Because of these variations, unit costs in some small schools were substantially lower than in many larger institutions.

Three principal factors accounted for this situation. First, because education is relatively labor-intensive, teachers' salaries commonly absorbed over 60 percent of annual recurrent expenditure. Scottish salary scales allowed significant differences in teacher costs, with a teacher at the top of the scale earning nearly 3,000 more than a newly appointed colleague. A two-teacher school with a recently appointed head and a young assistant could have a salary bill 5,500 less than a similar school with experienced staff.

Second, variation was caused by the system of cut-off points beyond which schools qualified for extra staff. Whereas a two-teacher school with just under 50 pupils would have a pupil–teacher ratio close to the average, a slightly larger school would be entitled to three teachers and a much lower ratio. Confirming this feature in another part of the United Kingdom, a survey in Norfolk (reported in Bell and Sigsworth 1987) indicated substantially lower average unit costs in schools with 40 to 50 pupils than in either smaller two-teacher schools or three-teacher schools with up to 60 pupils.

Third, unit costs vary because of factors specific to each institution and community. Transportation costs may vary widely according to population density and other geographic features, and many schools inherit high costs from the existence of large playing fields, the nature of their buildings, and so on. Features of this sort are common to school systems throughout the world.

Further light has been shed on unit costs by studies in the United States. One of the first was by Riew (1966). He began by trying to control for school quality because, in the absence of such control, variations in costs might merely reflect variations in quality. Although some aspects of Riew's research method remain questionable (see Fox 1981, Bray 1988), the attempt to control for quality makes this study particularly important.

Riew found that expenditures per pupil declined fairly steadily from US$531 to US$374 as enrollment rose from below 200 to 701–900. They then rose to US$433 in the next size-category, 901–1,100. However, this rise in expenditure was accompanied by a rise in the proportion of teachers with masters' degrees, and by a considerable broadening of the school curriculum. Because of these accompanying factors, Riew pointed out, it was arguable that large schools were still providing value for money.

Further research was conducted by Osburn (1970) in Missouri. Although he showed significant cost savings, they were much lower than those indicated by Riew. He found that schools with 500 pupils had unit costs US$12.74 less than schools with 200. Corresponding reductions were US$16.74 in schools with 1,000 pupils, US$11.14 in schools with 1,500 pupils, US$5.53 in schools with 2,000 pupils, and US $0.66 in schools with 2,244 pupils. Although this suggested ongoing economies of scale, the majority of savings had been achieved when student numbers reached 1,500. Osburn suggested that one factor explaining the difference between his figures and Riew's might have been the omission of transportation costs from Riew's analysis.

Dawson and Dancey's (1974) Canadian work also provided useful evidence, and also attempted to control for school quality. The researchers concluded that among secondary schools economies of scale existed up to an enrollment of 4,000. After that point, calculations based on some assumptions about quality indicated diseconomies of scale, though this was not consistent in all schools. At the elementary level, the researchers found little evidence of economies of scale at any point in the system.

Space limitations do not permit more detailed review of these and other studies. Readers are therefore referred to the literature reviews by Fox (1981), Bell and Sigsworth (1987), and Bray (1988). The research may be summarized as follows:

(a) Studies are inconsistent in their findings. Some find evidence of economies of scale, while others do not. Some find evidence of *dis*economies of scale beyond a certain point, while others do not. In general, however, very small schools (e.g., with an enrollment below 50) do have higher costs than larger institutions.

(b) The detailed picture from the Scottish research helps explain why aggregated figures often present a confusing picture. The structure of salary scales and cut-off points beyond which schools qualify for extra staff lead to wide variations among institutions. Individual small schools *may* have unit costs considerably lower than those of individual large schools.

(c) The Scottish research also highlighted the impact of the specific features of individual schools. These features include large sports fields and aging buildings requiring expensive maintenance.

(d) Researchers have also pointed out that it is essential for cost estimates to control for variations in quality. This, however, is easier said than done. It is difficult both to measure qualitative differences and to assign monetary values to the inputs creating these differences. Failure to control for quality in a convincing way casts doubt on the validity of many research studies.

(e) Some school consolidation programs (e.g., in Europe and North America) have undoubtedly reduced unit costs. However, this does not necessarily mean that consolidation will always reduce costs. In some cases, consolidation *increases* costs because pupils have to travel longer distances each day between home and school. Some studies of unit costs have presented a misleading picture by failing to take transportation into account.

Overall, the research indicates that relationships are rarely straightforward. General rules of thumb are unreliable, and in most cases administrators have to consider the individual circumstances of specific institutions.

2. The Educational Implications of School Size

The educational implications of school size are also more complex than they appear at first sight. Large schools are widely considered qualitatively superior because they can have broader curricula and because they can give their teachers more support. This view has some validity, but should be treated with caution.

2.1 Curriculum

Small schools are often able to offer only a limited range of subjects. This may be especially serious at the secondary level. The range is limited by the facts that:

(a) Small schools have few teachers, and thus small pools of talent. The smallest schools have only one teacher. They can only offer what that teacher can teach.

(b) Even when teachers do have specialist skills, the number of interested pupils may be too small. For example, a small secondary school may have staff who can teach both French and Russian, but may have too few pupils to justify organizing classes in both subjects.

(c) Small schools find it hard to justify costly investment in libraries, computers, science equipment, and so on.

(d) Very small schools may not even have enough children to form a pair of football teams. Thus, small schools may be handicapped in sporting activities.

However, these problems can often be reduced, and sometimes avoided altogether. Many governments supplement teachers' skills with radio and television broadcasts, and they encourage schools to join school clusters to share staff and equipment.

2.2 The Internal Environment

Small schools are also accused of having a restricted internal social environment. It is claimed that pupils lack competition, interact with relatively few peers, and may get stuck with the same teacher for an entire school career. The latter feature may be particularly unfortunate if the pupils and teacher suffer personality clashes. In a large school both pupils and teachers get a partial new start every academic year when the pupils move up one grade, but in a small school this is less likely to happen.

The picture has another side, however. Large schools are often impersonal, and may suffer from discipline problems. In contrast, teachers in small schools can get to know their pupils more easily. Small schools also usually have a much more cooperative environment. This may be particularly important for children who lack self-confidence, and can help both academic and extracurricular activities. Children can learn from their peers how to do arithmetic or recite poetry, for example, and they have better chances of being included in the school basketball team and the school play.

2.3 Teachers and Teaching

Since the quality of education chiefly depends on the quality of formal teaching, it must be asked whether small schools can be expected to provide better or worse teaching than large ones. Although the answer, of course, depends on individual contexts, several factors are common. First, in many countries, teachers in rural areas (where small schools predominate) have fewer formal qualifications. This is because: (a) ambitious and well-qualified staff are able to arrange postings in desirable environments, which usually means suburban or urban ones; (b) because suburban and urban communities often have more political power, administrators find themselves under strong pressure to post the good teachers to those areas; (c) remote areas are sometimes used as dumping grounds for teachers who are incompetent or rebellious.

Second, teachers in small rural schools are professionally more isolated than staff in larger institutions. They have fewer colleagues with whom to exchange ideas, and it is harder for the central administration to give them professional support.

A third factor is that small schools cannot stream pupils according to ability. Indeed, teachers may be faced by multigrade classes and wide age ranges. This makes teaching more challenging, yet it is uncommon for training colleges to give much attention to these matters.

However, small schools do not always suffer. When administrators ensure that good teachers are posted to small schools, and when the teachers are well-supported, the quality of staff and their work can be at least as high as in large schools. Indeed, many teachers feel that their efforts are noticed more readily in

small schools. In the more personal atmosphere, they become more committed to their work.

2.4 Educational Achievement

It is clear from this discussion that large schools usually have resource advantages that help improve the breadth of the curriculum. However, many analysts feel that this should not be given too much weight. Research suggests that small schools can still provide good (or even better) quality education, with a depth that can more than compensate for lack of breadth.

One study in the United States, for example, found that students from large schools were exposed to a larger number of school activities, and the best of them achieved standards that were unequaled by students in small schools. However, pupils in small schools participated in more activities, both academic and extracurricular. The versatility and performance of pupils in small schools were consistently higher. The pupils reported more satisfaction and displayed more motivation in all areas of schools activity (see Barker and Gump 1964, Campbell 1980).

This finding matches similar ones from the United Kingdom. For example, after investigating small schools in Cambridgeshire, Howells (1982 p. 8) concluded that "there is no evidence to support the view that small schools are any less educationally viable than large schools." Moreover, a research team at the University of Aston, Birmingham, recorded that it:

> had received several well-founded reports that secondary schools have found [pupils from small rural schools] not only as well prepared academically as pupils from other schools, but that they generally had a better attitude to work. Having been accustomed to working much of the time on their own, they could be given more responsibility for the organisation of their work. (quoted in Howells 1982 p. 4)

Strong support for small schools was also given by a careful and substantial project coordinated by the University of Leicester (Galton and Patrick 1990).

It appears, therefore, that small schools may suffer some educational limitations, particularly at the secondary level. However, they also have strong advantages, and supportive education authorities can help the schools to overcome their problems. By themselves, arguments about the quality of education are rarely strong enough to justify either refusal to open or decisions to close small schools.

3. Social Considerations in Policymaking

Since the 1980s, decision-makers have tended to give more weight to social factors in policy formation. Social factors usually favor small schools more than large ones. Schools are always major centers for social development. It is usually desirable to have as many centers as possible, and they are especially necessary in rural areas which lack alternative focuses for community attention. Thus, if the choice is between: (a) several small schools, which allow each village to have one; or (b) a large school in one village but no schools in the others, the social arguments will almost always favor the former.

Of course, it cannot be said that several small schools are always preferable to a single large one. For example, if a village has two schools, it may suffer from social division and would be more united if there were only one. Also, large schools sometimes widen pupils' and parents' horizons, helping them to meet people outside their immediate neighborhood.

However, the generalization that it is important for every community to have its own school still holds. Recent recognition of this fact has led to significant policy swings in such countries as Australia, Finland, Norway, and the United Kingdom (see Bell and Sigsworth 1987).

4. Conclusion

A universal optimum school size that is applicable to all countries or even to all regions within a single country cannot be determined. Different governments must have different policies reflecting their specific circumstances and individual preferences. This entry has suggested that policies should take separate account of economic, educational, and social factors.

At first sight both economic and educational factors would seem to favor medium-sized and large schools, while social factors would seem to favor small schools. However, in practice matters are not so simple. Small schools may have unit costs just as low as large schools; and decision-making on quality depends very much on personal interpretations of the meaning of quality. Social arguments are more likely to support small than large institutions, but even this cannot be taken as a universal generalization.

One possible conclusion is that the advantages of medium-sized or large schools are stronger at the secondary than at the primary level. First, it is at the secondary stage that pupils begin to specialize, and it is easier to offer a wide range of options when a school is fairly large. Second, because the libraries, laboratories, and workshops required for specialization are expensive, it is important for them to be fully utilized.

Yet even this conclusion would to a large extent depend on personal judgment about the weight of specific factors. Moreover, it may not be easy to create medium-sized or large institutions. In areas with reasonably high population densities and good road networks, pupils can be transported by special school buses; but in other areas it might be necessary to introduce boarding, which would have its own social and financial implications. To reiterate, therefore, it is impossible to derive universally applicable rules of thumb. What may be appropriate in one locality may be less appropriate in another.

See also: Effective Secondary Schools; Resource Allocation in Schools and School Systems

References

Barker R G, Gump P V (eds.) 1964 *Big School, Small School: High School Size and Student Behavior.* Stanford University Press, Stanford, California
Bell A, Sigsworth A 1987 *The Small Rural Primary School: A Matter of Quality.* Falmer Press, London
Bray M 1988 Small size and unit costs. International evidence and its usefulness. *Res. Rural Educ.* 5(1): 7–11
Campbell W J 1980 School size: Its influence on pupils. In: Fitch A, Scrimshaw P (eds.) 1980 *Standards, Schooling and Education.* Hodder and Stoughton, London
Dawson D A, Dancey K J 1974 Economies of scale in the Ontario public school sector. *Alberta J. of Educ. Res.* 20(2): 186–97
Fox W F 1981 Reviewing economies of size in education. *J. Educ. Finance* 6(3): 273–96
Galton M, Patrick H (eds.) 1990 *Curriculum Provision in the Small Primary School.* Routledge, London
Howells R A 1982 *Curriculum Provision in the Small Primary School.* Institute of Education, University of Cambridge, Cambridge
Osburn D D 1970 Economies of size associated with public high schools. *Rev. Econ. Stat.* 11(1): 113–15
Riew J 1966 Economies of scale in high school operation. *Rev. Econ. Stat.* 48(3): 280–87

Further Reading

Bray M 1987 *Are Small Schools the Answer? Cost-effective Strategies for Rural School Provision.* Commonwealth Secretariat, London
ERIC Clearinghouse on Educational Management 1982 *School Size: A Reassessment of the Small School.* Research Action Brief No. 21, Eugene, Oregon
Forsythe D (ed.) 1983 *The Rural Community and the Small School.* Aberdeen University Press, Aberdeen
Gregory T B, Smith G K 1987 *High Schools as Communities: The Small School Reconsidered.* Phi Kappa Delta Educational Foundation, Bloomington, Indiana
Harrison D A 1995 Small schools, big ideas: primary education in rural areas. *Br. J. Educ. Stud.* 43(4): 384–97
Lewis J R 1989 *The Village School.* Hale, London
Marshall D G 1985 Closing small schools, or when is small too small? *Education in Canada* 25(3): 10–16
Meier D W 1996 The big benefits of smallness. *Educ. Leadership* 54(1): 12–15
Monk D H 1990 Educational costs and small rural schools. *J. Educ. Finance* 16(2): 213–25
Vulliamy G, Webb R 1995 The implementation of the national curriculum in small primary schools. *Educ. Rev.* 47(1): 25–41

Social Foundations of School Choice

M. T. Hallinan

One of the most controversial policy issues in contemporary education is that of school choice, that is, the right of parents or guardians to select their child's school. The expressed aim of school choice is to improve student learning and academic achievement by improving the quality of education provided by schools. The mechanism of school improvement is competition—schools must compete for students to obtain government funding to operate.

1. School Choice Plans

School choice plans have been proposed or implemented in several countries. In the United Kingdom a free-market policy has governed school selection since the Education Reform Act of 1988 (Walford 1992). Here, less than 10 percent of schools are private (elite, independent, nonreligious schools) and these are not supported by the government. The majority of schools are state or religiously affiliated schools. The national government provides 80 percent of the cost of these schools, funneling most of the funds through local educational authorities (LEAS). The LEAS, which provide the remaining 20 percent of school costs, must distribute 85 percent of the national funds to schools on the basis of enrollment. Schools also have the option of choosing total autonomy from the local authorities and receiving all their support directly from the national government. A somewhat similar situation exists in Canada where the government supports the large Catholic school system as well as the public schools, but does not fund other private or religious schools (Lawton 1992).

With most of the schools in the United Kingdom and Canada supported by the government, the school choice issue is not related to public/private school questions. Rather, debate about school choice centers on the effectiveness of the competition among schools created by the policy of government funding of private education. Early impressions are that the new school choice plan in the United Kingdom is popular, but its success in improving poor schools has not yet been demonstrated. While parents enjoy their ability to select among schools, and while individual schools enjoy their greater autonomy, not enough good schools are available. Competition among schools for students seems to reduce bureaucratic inefficiency at the district level but many question whether educational quality has been affected.

In Australia, both public and private schools are supported primarily by the state, but private schools have less accountability. This raises questions about freedom of choice, evaluation standards, school quality, and the impact of a dual school system on society. The argument in favor of continuing the dual system is primarily to maintain school choice. Anderson (1990) summarizes three major arguments against the public/private division: existing research shows little difference in the achievement of students in public and private schools; private schools have the potential to discriminate against certain sectors of society; and a dual school system where private schools disproportionately enroll higher-achieving students makes it more difficult for the public schools to provide quality education for all students.

In the United States, in response to *A Nation at Risk* (1983), a report critical of United States education, President Bush proposed school choice as one of the ways to improve the quality of education. In 1993 students had to attend their neighborhood public school, which is fully supported by the government, or pay tuition to attend a private (religious or nondenominational) school. Four basic school choice plans have been proposed, varying in degree of departure from the present educational structure. These are magnet schools, open enrollment, tuition tax credits, and voucher plans.

Magnet schools are alternative schools that offer specialized curricula. Parents can choose between their local public school and a magnet school within their district. While popular, magnet schools have a limited number of openings which makes this choice available to only a small proportion of families. Open enrollment plans are either district-wide, allowing parents to choose any public school within their residential area, or interdistrict, permitting the selection of any public school within the state. While magnet schools and open enrollment plans increase parental power over school selection, both plans lack market principles. Schools are not rewarded or penalized for performance, and consequently, are not really in competition with one another.

Tuition tax credit is a plan that gives parents credit against federal or state taxes for some portion of the tuition they pay for private schools. Voucher plans provide subsidies for all students, which may be applied to public or private school tuition. Both of these plans make private schools more affordable, thus increasing their competitiveness with public schools. Neither plan, however, insures access to private schools for all families. Private schools may require a higher tuition fee than the amount of the voucher, which would restrict the freedom of choice of low-income families. They also could have exclusionary admission criteria, unless government regulations mandated otherwise.

Reactions to school choice proposals and experiments have been mixed. Advocates of school choice claim that choice encourages parental involvement, promotes diversity, improves the curriculum, and expands educational opportunities for underprivileged children (Armor 1989). Opponents of choice argue that it violates civil liberties and democratic principles through the support of religiously affiliated schools, and fails to increase the educational opportunities of the poor who are constrained by lack of information about the schools, by transportation difficulties, and by a family structure that makes the neighborhood school more convenient and practical (Honig 1990). School personnel generally oppose school choice because they believe it weakens their control over their schools and threatens their job security.

Given the far-reaching consequences of school choice policies for restructuring schools and their potential impact on educational quality, a comprehensive examination of the social principles underlying school choice is imperative. Only a reasoned analysis of the school choice issue will raise the debate above the level of biases, fears, and political persuasions. This should lead to informed judgments and decisions about school choice plans that improve the quality of education for all students.

2. School Choice and Conflicting Societal Values

One reason the school choice debate has been so intense is that the issue is related to values strongly endorsed by various members of society. One of these values is that of equality. Most people believe, in principle, that all students should have equal access to schooling, regardless of their social origins. Another deepseated value is that of meritocracy. It is widely held that ability and achievement, rather than background, should determine a person's position in society. Belief in both of these principles makes the issue of school choice complex.

While commitment both to equality of educational opportunity and to upward mobility based on ability and achievement are valued, these two principles can conflict because they rest on diverse assumptions about what is best for society. A commitment to equality is built on the assumption that equal opportunity for all citizens is in the best interests of society as a whole, and possibly, in the long run, of each member of society. Thus it is just to ask members of society to set aside self-interest for the sake of the common good. The idea of a meritocracy is built on the assumption that individuals are entitled to use their resources to maximize their opportunities in society. Personal entitlement is just because it is believed to serve best the common good in the long run.

Disagreement over school choice arises when the common good is seen to conflict with personal entitlement. Since both values are viewed as good, the issue becomes one of priorities. Those who attach higher priority to equal opportunity for the sake of the common good judge that unequal access to schooling is unjust. Those who see a greater good in insuring a meritocratic society find nothing inherently unjust in an individual's using rightfully acquired resources to obtain an educational advantage. The two viewpoints reflect a philosophical difference, resting on one's concept of justice.

3. Theoretical Perspectives on Justice and School Choice

Two treatises on justice by the moral philosophers Rawls and Nozick are useful in explicating the justice issues surrounding the school choice debate. In Rawls' *Theory of Justice* (1972) and Nozick's *Anarchy, State and Utopia* (1974), the authors analyze the concept of justice and reach fundamentally different conclusions. Applied to the school choice debate, their works have very different policy implications.

In *A Theory of Justice*, Rawls (1972) is concerned with what, if any, inequalities are justified in society; that is, what is a just distribution of resources. He concludes that only those inequalities are justified that benefit the least advantaged. This conclusion is based on two principles: first, "each person is to have an equal right to the most extensive basic liberty compatible with a similar liberty for others" (p. 60), and second, that "social and economic inequalities are to be arranged so that they are both (a) reasonably expected to be to everyone's advantage, and (b) attached to positions and offices open to all" (p. 60). He gives priority to the first principle, claiming that liberty can be restricted only for the sake of greater liberty, not for the sake of increased social gains. In short, Rawls argues that inequalities are "just" only if they improve everyone's well-being, particularly that of the disadvantaged. Thus, if an unequal distribution of resources, for example of educational opportunities, leads to greater productivity than an equal distribution of resources, it is fair and just. Rawls' prescription for a just society assumes that resources are a public good and should, under certain circumstances, be redistributed.

In contrast to Rawls' position, Nozick, in *Anarchy, State, and Utopia* (1974), argues that inequalities stem from individual differences in abilities, skills, and other resources. These capabilities can be inherited or acquired. Control over these resources belongs totally to each individual, rather than to the collectivity. Nozick concludes that justice permits each person to have full entitlement to what he or she justly has attained.

These two theories of justice have direct implications for education. Carried to its extreme, Rawls's argument implies that children should be removed from their families at birth, in order to eliminate differences in family background which provide one child with more opportunities than another. All children should become wards of the state and attend schools which are total institutions, such as boarding schools. At the other extreme, Nozick's arguments suggest that there be no system of public education, because public schools aim to be redistributive. Since children are entitled to the full benefits of their families' resources, education should be private, with each family paying for the school of its choice in accordance with its resources.

Several examples of the conflict between these two theories of justice, or more specifically between the parental right to entitlement and the common good, can be cited. A striking example was played out with school desegregation in the United States. In this case, the exercise of the parental right of school selection through residential mobility resulted in White flight. As a result, busing plans were enforced which limited parents' rights to select their children's school through residential choice.

Another example is found in the way many countries finance public education. In this section, public school refers to a government-financed school, the usage given the term in the United States and Australia. In the United Kingdom, the referent would be a state or religiously affiliated school, while a private school would be one not supported by the government, regardless of religious affiliation. Most people would agree that parents or guardians should have the right to send their children to private schools. This is an inherent right, in Nozick's sense. At the same time, few would question the right of the government to tax citizens to provide a free public school system for all children. This practice is consistent with Rawls' conceptualization of justice because it benefits the collectivity. The conflict arises when families who would prefer private schools cannot choose them because of the double financial burden of taxes and private school tuition. In this case, tax policies restrict parental rights in favor of the common good.

Countless other examples of the tension between individual rights and the collectivity could be mentioned. These include conflicts over sex education in the schools, dress codes, curriculum content, and corporal punishment. The policy decisions that emerge from these debates can be located on a continuum on which Rawls's concept of justice is at one end and Nozick's on the other. Some policies stress individual rights more than the common good, while others accommodate the common good or the disadvantaged while restricting individual rights. Whether an individual is satisfied with the way any one of these issues is resolved depends basically on that person's philosophical position on the definition of justice and its implications for educational opportunity.

The tension between Rawls's and Nozick's concepts of justice is dramatically evident in the school choice debate. Rawls would claim that parental choice plans are just only if they promote the common good. Nozick would argue that choice plans are just only if parents have the right to secure for their children the best possible education that their means permit, arguing that in the long run, this benefits the collectivity. School choice plans can be evaluated from each of these perspectives.

Ideally, school choice would insure better education for all students by forcing schools to improve through the mechanism of competition. Allowing parents unrestricted choice of public or private schools would represent the greatest equality of educational opportunity, and thus benefit the collectivity. If all schools improved as a result, families should no longer feel the need to provide family resources to insure a quality education. This would be considered a just outcome from both Rawls's and Nozick's perspective.

In practice, however, no school choice plan would satisfy perfectly those who endorse either Rawls's or Nozick's concept of justice. Working out a school choice plan requires taking into account the interests of individuals who attach different priorities to personal entitlement and the collective good. Consequently, one group is likely to find a particular plan more attractive than another, depending on the individuals' concept of justice.

School choice plans that extend to private as well as public schools are viewed as the most radical and, not surprisingly, are the most controversial. Generally, these plans provide financing for families to choose private or public schools. Removing finances as a barrier to school choice provides the greatest equality of access to schools. This should also maximize competition among schools, which should be in the best interest of the collectivity. Unrestricted access to schools nonetheless limits personal entitlement by denying parents the opportunity to use their personal resources to provide an educational advantage for their children. Thus, while benefiting the common good, the plans place limitations on the educational opportunities associated with personal entitlement.

Moreover, most school choice plans that extend to private schools generally provide only limited financial support for private schooling. While these plans increase educational opportunity for some families, they have little effect on families who cannot afford any private school tuition. These plans may be attractive to those concerned about the common good because they do increase educational opportunity beyond a common school model. However, they may be opposed by those who attach higher priority to personal entitlement, because they decrease the economic advantages held by higher income families.

More conservative school choice plans that limit choice to public schools are less controversial, although they deviate more from Rawls's and Nozick's concepts of justice. Removing geographic boundaries to school selection gives parents access to the best public schools available, subject only to governmental regulations governing school composition. While this represents an improvement over the neighborhood school concept, it still fails to insure equality of educational opportunity for all students. Most dramatically, it does not provide access to private schools.

Even aside from their failure to make private schools more accessible, public school choice plans leave room for inequities within the public school sector. Families have differential access to information about the quality of schools, vary in their ability to evaluate school programs, have family situations that are better served if a child attends a school in a particular geographical area, and have different transportation requirements. Family circumstances such as these can lead to a family's choosing a lower quality school. Over time, inferior schools may deteriorate further, as more advantaged students transfer to better schools. Thus, even choice plans that exclude private schools permit personal entitlement to operate.

The regulations placed on access to schools by the government or school authorities also affect the extent to which a school choice plan approximates a full entitlement model or a common good model. Regulations that limit free choice govern most existing or proposed school choice plans. For example, regulations may determine a school's admissions criteria, establish quotas to insure racial and ethnic balance in the schools, require alternate employment plans for teachers who lose their jobs due to school closings, and require that certain characteristics of students be related to the amount of a tuition voucher. These restrictions aim to insure the equitable distribution of students across schools.

Regulations are imposed on school selection for the sake of insuring the common good and protecting the rights of all students. The more restrictions that are placed on a school choice plan, the closer the plan will approximate to Rawls's common good model. Plans with fewer restrictions will be better expressions of Nozick's entitlement model. Regulations are a primary mechanism through which school choice plans are tailored to reflect prevailing beliefs about justice and equality. They often represent an effort to insure that a school choice plan is acceptable to the interests of both those who ascribe to Rawls's theory of justice and those who favor Nozick's.

No school plan reflects perfectly either Rawls's or Nozick's definition of justice. An individual's willingness to accept a particular school choice plan depends on the extent to which a school choice plan is consistent with that person's concept of justice. Making explicit the assumptions about justice underlying various school choice plans lends clarity to the debate about school choice and helps contain the fears and biases that have characterized much of the rhetoric surrounding the topic of school choice. Compromises that accommodate the philosophical beliefs of persons committed to a common good model and those

wedded to an entitlement model are possible if the extent to which a particular school choice plan reflects either of these two positions on justice is clearly understood.

4. Conclusion

The fundamental issue underlying the school choice debate is that of justice. The philosophical treatises of Rawls and Nozick permit a conceptualization of school choice issues in terms of the concept of justice. Rawls's focus on the common good directs attention to the extent to which a school choice plan provides for the collectivity and accommodates the disadvantaged. Nozick's emphasis on personal entitlement points to the role of choice plans in a meritocratic society. An exposition of these philosophical positions permits an evaluation of school choice plans in terms of what is fair and just for all interested parties.

In principle, many persons who agree with Nozick's definition of justice are likely to support unrestricted school choice because it provides greater freedom for parents to use societal institutions to maximize the personal benefits of their own resources. Others of the same philosophical persuasion but with the economic resources to select desirable private schools for their children may be indifferent to school choice, since it should not affect their school selection. In practice, however, particular school choice plans may restrict parents' rights and limit their economic advantage through the regulations they impose on school selection. When this occurs, parents who would be expected to support school choice in theory may oppose it in practice.

Similarly, individuals who agree with Rawls' concept of justice might be expected to support school choice because it redistributes access to schooling in a more equitable manner. This aims to benefit all students while markedly increasing the educational opportunities of the disadvantaged. Again, however, in practice the plans may deviate from this ideal. The pervasiveness of poverty and other societal pathologies seriously constrain equal access to education. Family background remains a major influence on opportunity, despite structural chances to promote equality. Regulations governing school choice attempt to take these initial inequities into account, but it is impossible to eradicate their influence. Consequently, school choice plans tend to be criticized by some who espouse the common good model because they do not provide greater equality, despite provisions designed to attain that end.

In general, persons of either philosophical persuasion can find fault with any school choice plan because it deviates from the ideal. The challenge is to find an acceptable compromise that represents an improvement over the status quo. If school choice is to be attempted as a large-scale social experiment, it must balance regulation and freedom, without seriously violating the citizenry's concept of justice.

In general, individuals are willing to support the common good, but unwilling to compromise their own advantages to do so. For this reason, they oppose school choice, believing that the assumption is faulty that competition will improve all schools. They fear that permitting school choice will ultimately make all schools mediocre. Carefully designed longitudinal studies of the effects of school choice plans on student opportunity and achievement in a large number of school districts, states, and countries will support or alleviate this fear.

The conceptualization of justice outlined here is intended to inform and elucidate the highly charged debate on school choice. Making explicit one's understanding of justice and its implications for equality of educational opportunity should help reduce the confusion and empty rhetoric that has characterized many of the arguments to date. While it may seem bold to stress rationality in the discussion of an issue that has such far-reaching personal consequences for all interested parties, the importance of the issue and its potential impact on the welfare of children demand that it receive careful analysis.

See also: Equality, Policies for Education

References

Anderson D S 1990 The public/private division in Australian schooling: Social and educational effects. In: Saha L J, Keeves J P (eds.) 1990 *Schooling and Society in Australia: Sociological Perspectives*. Australian National University Press, Sydney

Armor D J 1989 After busing: Education and choice. *Public Interest*. 95: 24–37

Honig B 1990 School vouchers: Dangerous claptrap. *NY Times*, June 29, p. 25

Lawton S 1992. Issues of choice: Canadian and American perspectives. In: Cookson P (ed.) 1992 *The Choice Controversy*. Corwin Press, Newbury, California

Nozick R 1974 *Anarchy, State, and Utopia*. Basic Books, New York

Rawls J 1972 *A Theory of Justice*. Clasendon Press, Oxford

National Commission on Excellence in Education 1983 *A Nation at Risk*. National Commission on Excellence in Education, Washington, DC

Walford G 1992. Educational choice and equity in Great Britain. In: Sadovnik A, Sewel S (eds.) 1992 *International Handbook of Educational Reform*. Greenwood Press, Westport, Connecticut

Further Reading

Boyd W L, Kerchner C T (eds.) 1987 *The Politics of Excellence and Choice in Education*. Falmer Press, Lewes

Boyd W L, Walberg H J (eds.) 1990 *Choice in Education: Potential and Problems*. McCutchan, Berkeley, California

Chubb J E, Moe T M 1990 *Politics, Markets and America's Schools*. Brooking Institution, Washington, DC

Clune W H, Witte J F (eds.) 1990 *Choice and Control in American Education*, Vols. 1, 2. Falmer Press, London

Coleman J 1990 *Equality and Achievement in Education*. Westview Press, Boulder, Colorado

Everhart R B (ed.) 1982 *The Public School Monopoly*. Ballinger, Cambridge, Massachusetts

Gardner W D 1990 *The Trouble in Canada: A Citizen Speaks Out*. Stoddard, Toronto

Glass G V, Mathews D A 1991 Are data enough? Review of "Politics, markets and America's schools." *Educ. Res.* 20(3): 24–27

Illich I 1983 *Deschooling Society*. Harper & Row, New York

Tyack D B 1974 *The One Best System: A History of American Urban Education*. Harvard University Press, Cambridge, Massachusetts

Social Mobility, Social Stratification, and Education

J. Dronkers

All human societies known so far are divided into different ranks corresponding to the social positions occupied by their individual members. Directly or indirectly, these ranks have derived from the division of labor in the respective societies, at the same time being influenced by their historical circumstances. Sociologists call this vertical social ranking "the social stratification of a society." Education is, in many cases, one of the building blocks for social stratification because the amount of knowledge, skills, and attitudes acquired in school are considered important for the survival and growth of a society; this importance is reflected, in part, in the relative honorific standings of occupations.

In their life course, individuals can move up and down this social stratification system as a consequence of either forced or free changes in their social position. This movement within an individual's life course is called intragenerational vertical mobility, and it is different from intergenerational vertical mobility. The latter represents the difference between the position of parents and that of their children in a social stratification system. The first question to be asked concerns the role played by education in promoting or obstructing the degree of vertical mobility of individuals. The second question concerns whether the influence of education upon the degree of vertical mobility has increased as a consequence of the evolution toward a society in which knowledge, skills, and attitudes acquired in school have become more important for the survival and growth of the respective society.

The opportunities of individuals for using education as an avenue for their own vertical mobility or for that of their children cannot be seen as separate from the unequal distribution of commodities (for example, income, housing, cultural heritage, or the quality of teaching in schools) among individuals, or from the unequal distribution of individual characteristics (for example, intelligence, motivation, or health). Therefore, it is important to unravel the contribution offered by these commodities and characteristics, on the one hand, and the contribution of education, on the other, to the degree of vertical mobility experienced by individuals and society. Because of the interrelationships between education and these commodities and characteristics, it is easy to make wrong estimations regarding the importance of education. A major part of the study of education and social mobility is devoted to unraveling the effects of commodities, characteristics, and education upon the opportunities of individuals for intragenerational or intergenerational mobility in societies with different sociopolitical regimes and educational systems. Another part of this type of study is directed toward the changes occurring in these effects as a result of the development from ascription to achievement as a base for the selection and allocation of individuals in relation to increasing educational participation.

1. Social Stratification

1.1 Definition

Social stratification is the hierarchical ranking of people within a society along one or more dimensions of inequality, based on a certain combination of real and perceived income, wealth, power, social standing, age, and ethnicity, as well as other social (and sometimes physical) characteristics. Because, directly or indirectly, these inequalities have derived from the division of labor, and also because occupations have become the most distinguishing characteristic of modern societies, in most cases occupations are used as the basis for social stratification scales. This means that most social stratification scales are hierarchical rankings of occupations along one or more dimensions of inequality based on a certain combination of real and perceived characteristics (see above) of all the individuals within that occupation.

The importance of such rankings is that occupations differ systematically in point of resources (for example, income, wealth, or power), which partly explains, apart from other factors (intelligence, for instance), the resulting differences in people's life chances (such as health) and those of their offspring (such as children's educational attainment). The study of the relations between different occupational resources (as measured by social stratification) and different life chances of people and of their offspring is one of the major research topics in sociology and also a topic which has made a most important contribution to understanding educational structures and processes.

1.2 Different Scales of Social Stratification

The measurement of the hierarchical ranking of occupations along one or more of these dimensions of inequality has resulted in a large number of various scales of social stratification. The most widely used scales can be grouped into two families: prestige scales and socioeconomic scales (Grusky and Van Rompaey 1992).

Prestige scales are the oldest type of social stratification scale and, perhaps, the best known. Prestige scales refer to the symbolic domain of stratification. The purpose of these scales is to represent "collective perceptions and beliefs" about the ranking of occupational hierarchies (Hope 1982 p. 1012). The usual way to measure these perceptions and beliefs is to ask individuals or judges to rank a number of well-known occupations according to their honorific standing in society. These individual rankings are then combined into one type of scale: the occupational prestige scale. This type of scale has been developed in various societies since 1950; in the United States, East and West Europe, and in Asia (see Treiman 1977 for a review). Despite the large differences between these societies, the similarities between these nationally based prestige scales are striking and important. Treiman (1977) used these highly correlated prestige scales to produce one international prestige scale, which suggests that the honorific standing of occupations was more or less the same in societies at the time, even though there were large differences in stage of socioeconomic development, political–economic systems, and historical backgrounds. Changes occurring over time in the relative scaling of occupations are smaller than expected if one compares various scales which were constructed in the same society in different decades (Sixma and Ultee 1984).

The main problem with these prestige scales is the disagreement regarding the underlying causes of occupational ranking. One argument is that judgments about social standing are sensitive to honorific considerations which cannot be equated with socioeconomic factors like income and education (Hope 1982); an alternative argument suggests that socioeconomic factors play such a dominant role in ranking occupational perceptions (Hauser and Featherman 1977, Goldthorpe and Hope 1974), that the prestige scales measure more or less the generalized desirability of occupations.

Socioeconomic stratification scales try to capture the cultural and economic resources connected with occupations. In their simplest but still effective form they are constructed by the averaging of the mean income and educational level of all individuals within an occupation, and then these averages of occupations are projected into one socioeconomic scale. One of the best-known examples of this kind of socioeconomic scale is the prestige-based socioeconomic scale of Duncan (1961). Given the average income and educational level of all individuals within a limited number of well-known occupations (derived from census data), and the score of the same occupations on the prestige scale, Duncan estimated the effects of average income and educational level on occupational prestige. From these effects it was then possible to estimate the prestige of all occupations which were not included in the occupational prestige scale, given the average income and educational level of all individuals within those occupations.

There have been updates and transformations of these prestige-based socioeconomic scales (often known as an SEI or Social–Economic Index). Comparable socioeconomic scales have been developed in other societies. The main problem in these societies is the somewhat ad hoc and arbitrary nature of the SEI. Why only use average income or educational level as indicators? A larger number of indicators which measure resources of occupations might produce another one-dimensional scale or a two-dimensional scale. What is/are the common factor(s) underlying these indicators, such as prestige scores or social and economic life chances, which people experience in their occupations?

2. Vertical Mobility

The two types of vertical mobility within social stratification systems (intragenerational and intergenerational) must be distinguised from other forms of mobility, for instance, geographical mobility (a change in the residence of an individual). Furthermore, not every change of occupation results in an upward or downward movement. It can happen that a change of occupation constitutes a sideways shift, and does not result in a change of rank in the social stratification system.

2.1 Intergenerational Mobility and Education

From the very beginning, mobility studies have regarded education as one of the most important mechanisms (apart from the inheritance of money and commodities, or marriage) for transmitting parental social stratification positions to their children in those societies not based upon hereditary occupations, as was the case with most agrarian and feudal societies. Among the first to empirically analyze the assumed importance of this transmitting function of education were Blau and Duncan (1967). They used path analysis to estimate the effects of father's occupation on son's education and on son's occupation in the United States. These effects could be disaggregated into indirect effects (from father's occupation via son's education to son's occupation), and a direct effect (from father's occupation to son's occupation, controlling for indirect effects). The major component of the total effects of father's occupation on son's occupation (the sum of direct and indirect effects) was indirect. That means that the largest part of the overall relationship between the occupations of fathers and sons in the United States is transmitted by the educational level of the sons, which is influenced by the occupational level of the fathers also influencing the occupational level of the sons.

Blau and Duncan interpreted their findings as a consequence of the rising meritocracy in society: the idea that in modern, industrialized societies the selection for higher ranked occupations is increasingly shaped by achievement standards (expressed in educational attainment) and less directly by family background. They found some evidence, for the United States, that such a change towards a smaller direct effect of father's occupation on son's occupation actually existed. However, the importance of the indirect effect of father's occupation via son's education on son's occupation underlines the point already made by Young (1958), namely, that a more meritocratic society does not mean a classless society nor a society with equal opportunities for all.

This original study of Blau and Duncan's was only the starting point for a wave of studies in many societies which elaborated on the importance of education in transmitting the rank in social stratification systems from one generation to the next. Four elaborations based upon the basic model of Blau and Duncan can be identified: (a) the refinement in measuring parental resources; (b) the addition of intelligence or scholastic ability to the other variables in the model; (c) the addition of social-psychological factors; and (d) the distinction between between-family variance and within-family variance.

Because parents have slightly different resources than that measured by social stratification (due to the within-occupation variance), one of the first additions to the Blau and Duncan model were other parental resources such as father's and mother's education, financial income, occupation of the mother, residence, and so on. The addition of these individual resources increased the explanatory power of the model because these factors, especially parental education, financial income, and the occupation of the mother, could partly explain the educational level of the offspring which could not be explained by father's occupation. However, the addition of these individual resources did not nullify the importance of father's occupation for the educational attainment of his children, although this importance decreased with the addition of these other individual resources. This means that education transmits the father's occupational ranking to the occupational ranking of his offspring, but that this transmission is also partly explained by other individual resources. The addition of mother's occupation showed that the ranking of her occupation in the stratification system had independent effects on the educational level of her offspring (and thus on intergenerational mobility), comparable to that of her partner, although these effects tended to be smaller. (Married women tend to take part-time jobs more often and treat their jobs as less important than their partner's.) This underlines the importance of taking into account the occupations of all relevant adults when analyzing the vertical mobility of their children.

The importance of parental financial resources for intergenerational mobility is not as great as is often assumed if one takes into consideration the effects of other parental resources, although this finding differs somewhat between societies. In other words, compared to other resources, such as parental education and occupation, financial resources are less important for the educational attainment of the children, and, given the educational level of the children, parental income does not, directly, add much to the occupational level of the children. However, there are indications that in nations that have more financial thresholds or fewer personal grants in their educational systems, the effects of parental financial resources are somewhat greater than in nations where there are fewer financial thresholds or a higher level of personal grant. These differences between modern societies are not so large as to allow parental income to become the most important factor in explaining the chances for intergenerational mobility in any modern society. A good example of this type of study is that of Halsey et al. (1980) which was carried out in England and Wales.

The effects of parental occupation and other resources on the educational level of the children can be explained by the intelligence or scholastic ability of the children, which in turn is dependent on parental resources and intelligence. The relationship between son's education and occupation can also be partly explained by intelligence or scholastic ability, which can lead to an overestimation of the importance of education for occupational attainment and, thus, for intergenerational mobility. These considerations lead to the addition of intelligence or scholastic ability to the intergenerational mobility model. The best-known example of models which include intelligence or scholastic ability is that developed by Jencks et al. (1972, 1979) for men in the United States. This model has been replicated for different societies and has provided results which, in part, deviate from those of the United States model.

The scholastic ability of children depends, in most studies, on parental resources, and it mediates a major part of the relationship between these parental resources and the educational attainment of their children. The direct effects of scholastic ability on occupational standing or income are not very large, with controls for educational attainment, although these effects are mostly significant. This means that either educational attainment is a good indicator of ability, or that, given a certain educational level, scholastic ability does not really increase one's opportunities for a better job or larger income, due to the strong allocation function of schooling in most societies. This model, incorporating scholastic ability, has influenced a large number of other studies.

The addition of social-psychological factors, apart from scholastic ability and other parental resources, to the basic model of Blau and Duncan, has been achieved in the so-called Wisconsin model. Sewell and Hauser (1975) included neighborhood and school contexts, educational aspirations, the influences of "significant others," and scholastic ability to the basic model. They used longitudinal data of 1957 male and female high-school seniors in Wisconsin, who were followed up during their educational and occupational careers in 1964, 1975, and 1992. This Wisconsin model provided a more complete and powerful explanation of these careers than less elaborate models, but did not alter the interpretations of intergenerational mobility significantly. The model stimulated very different research activities, mostly directed to unraveling the different contributions of parental resources and children's abilities to the educational and occupational attainment of different groups. Others have used the Wisconsin model for different samples of United States, Canadian, Latin American, European, Asian, and Middle East populations. Although there have been interesting differences with regard to the obtained results, one is more impressed by their similarity given that the same or similar variables and measurement models are used across societies. (For a review of these studies, see Sewell and Hauser 1980.)

These data and models also promoted the study of the influence of family structure on intergenerational mobility. The main question concerned the importance of a "family bias," as occurs when measuring sibling resemblance in terms of ability, educational attainment, occupational status, and earnings, compared to the ability, educational attainment, occupational status, and earnings of each individual sibling. The models used in these studies are complex and the results are not yet final (Hauser and Wong 1989). However, it is clear that parental resources affect, by way of a common family background, the educational and occupational attainment of all their children. This common family background of siblings (irrespective of their gender) is only partly determined by parental occupational and educational status, while individual siblings (again, irrespective of their gender) vary in their educational and occupational attainment, despite their common family background. A conclusion from these studies is that the family structure adds to the inequality in intergenerational mobility opportunities just like the occupational status of the parents, but that there is still considerable room for differences in intergenerational mobility between siblings despite the common family and parental resources. A few European studies on siblings (De Graaf and Huinink 1992) found comparable outcomes, which were somewhat different for different generations.

2.2 Intragenerational Mobility and Education

The study of intragenerational mobility (vertical mobility within one generation) is less developed than the study of intergenerational mobility (vertical mobility between two generations), although the models of Jencks and the Wisconsin study do separate the first occupation after leaving school from the actual occupation at the time of the study. Generally, one finds large effects of the status of the first job on that of the actual job, even after controlling for the effects of educational attainment and scholastic ability, indicating the strong channeling influence of education and that of the first job on the labor market. The direct effects of educational attainment and scholastic ability on actual occupation are relatively small, after controling for first occupation. This indicates that intragenerational mobility is less important than intergenerational mobility and that educational attainment affects the intragenerational mobility opportunities mostly indirectly. An important study of the effect of education on intragenerational mobility was conducted by Tuijnman (1989). Tuijnman tried to establish the effect of adult or recurrent education on the occupational attainment, earnings, and well-being of Swedish men. He found increasing positive effects of adult education on occupation but not on earnings, after controling for youth education, first occupation, scholastic ability, and parental resources. (For comparable results in the Netherlands, see van Leeuwen and Dronkers 1992). An implication of this research is that adult education might promote intragenerational mobility, although the positive effect of youth education (and thus indirectly of parental resources) on adult education is strong and thus decreases intergenerational mobility.

2.3 Structural and Circulation Mobility

One important question in mobility research is whether mobility differs between societies or between generations. This question is closely related to theories about the relationship between the degree of industrialization of a society and the degree of vertical mobility (Erikson and Goldthorpe 1992). Liberals see a positive relationship between industrialization and mobility and a resulting increase in equality of opportunity. Marxists often argue that there was no relationship at all, or, if any, a negative one, between industrialization and mobility in capitalist societies, but a positive relation existed in socialist societies. Others have claimed a different degree of mobility for a particular society, related to its history or institutions (e.g., the United States as a society with a high level of mobility, and the United Kingdom as one with a low level). The first

empirical comparative studies of cross-national variation in mobility ended in the conclusion of Lipset and Zetterberg (1959) that the overall pattern of mobility is "much the same" in Western societies.

These first empirical studies did not distinguish between two possible causes of cross-national variation in vertical mobility. The first cause for a change in intergenerational mobility in a society is the difference between the available positions for older generations and those for the succeeding generations. If, in a society, there are more high-ranking positions available for the younger generation compared to the older generation (due perhaps to changes in the socioeconomic development of that society), there is more upward intergenerational mobility, which is "forced" or structural, because it originates from a change in the structure of occupations. The opposite is true if there are fewer high-ranking positions available for the younger generation compared to the older generation in a society. In that case, there is more downward intergenerational mobility which is also "forced" or structural because it also originates from a change in the structure of occupations. The second cause of variation in intergenerational mobility is a change in the boundaries between certain positions in the social stratification system between two generations, namely circulation or exchange mobility. This change can be stimulated by educational reforms, which open certain avenues to higher positions, or by closing the access to higher positions by introducing extra thresholds, for instance, selective schooling. Both causes for changes in intergenerational mobility can be relevant at the same time and, in studying mobility, one must try to disentangle these two causes. This distinction is also relevant for educational reforms because they mostly attempt to promote circulation mobility by increasing educational opportunities for children from lower-ranking positions. Featherman et al. (1975) argue, on the basis of this distinction between structural and circulation mobility, that the latter is basically the same in all industrial societies with a market economy and a nuclear family system (both capitalist and socialist). Erikson and Goldthorpe (1992) find basically the same circulation mobility pattern (or trendless variations) for Western and Eastern Europe, North America, Australia, and Japan, and reject both liberal and Marxist theories about the relationship between industrialization and mobility. They also conclude that arguments for culturally caused differentiations in mobility are overstated, although to dismiss cultural influences on mobility entirely would be to go too far. (For instance, they found some long-term effects of the German apprentice system.) They admit that political intervention (income policy and/or educational reforms) may be a source of cross-national differences in mobility, but reject the assumption that this variation must necessarily be systematically related to regimes or governments of various types. The relevance of this conclusion for education is that claims regarding the effectiveness of an educational system in promoting or obstructing more equal educational opportunities are not justified.

3. The Declining Effects of Parental Status

Despite this negative conclusion from cross-national studies of mobility, researchers often find changes in the effects of parental occupational status on the educational attainment of their children. Although the trend is not always very clear, these effects seem to decrease over time (Blau and Duncan 1967, Featherman and Hauser 1978, Vrooman and Dronkers 1986). Mare (1981) argues that this decrease of parental effect could be explained by the higher educational participation of younger generations. The longer a generation participates in education, the more hurdles it will overcome. In particular, overcoming hurdles (e.g., completing primary school; leaving junior high school with qualifications) in the early school career depends more on parental resources than overcoming hurdles in the late school career (going to college or university; graduating from college or university). If more children from a younger generation can overcome these hurdles in their early school career, the effect of parental resources will decrease. This decrease does not occur because overcoming hurdles has become less dependent on parental resources, but because more children manage to overcome these hurdles. Mare (1981) derives this idea from the distinction between structural and circulation mobility.

Comparative research on education and intergenerational mobility of different generations in different societies in Europe, the United States, and Asia (Shavit and Blossfeld 1993) shows that, in most cases, the decline in the effect of parental occupational status on the educational attainment of children can be explained fully by educational upgrading, which raises increasingly large proportions of generations to a level of schooling where the effects of parental resources are comparatively modest. A decrease in the importance of parental resources for overcoming hurdles in the educational career was found only in two societies, Sweden and the Netherlands, countries with different educational systems. In other societies the importance of parental resources had not changed between generations. This means that an increase in educational participation would be a good means to promote equal educational opportunities in a society.

See also: Aspirations and Expectations of Students; Family and School Environmental Measures; Family Status and Economic Status; Measurement of Social Background; Stratification in Educational Systems

References

Blau P M 1967 *The American Occupational Structure*. Wiley, New York

De Graaf P M, Huinink J J 1992 Trends in measured and unmeasured effects of family background on educational attainment and occupational status in the Federal Republic of Germany. *Soc. Sci. Res.* 21(1): 84–112

Duncan O D 1962 A socioeconomic scale for all occupations. In: Reiss A J (ed.) 1962 *Occupations and Social Status*. Free Press of Glencoe, New York

Erikson R, Goldthorpe J H 1992 *The Constant Flux. A Study of Class Mobility in Industrial Societies*. Clarendon Press, Oxford

Featherman D L, Jones F L, Hauser R M 1975 Assumptions of social mobility research in the US: The case of occupational status. *Soc. Sci. Res.* 4(4): 329–60

Featherman D L, Hauser R M 1978 *Opportunity and Change*. Academic Press, New York

Goldthorpe J H, Hope K 1974 *The Social Grading of Occupations. A New Approach and Scale*. Clarendon Press, Oxford

Grusky D B, Van Rompaey S E 1992 The vertical scaling of occupations: Some cautionary comments and reflections. *Am. J. Sociol.* 97(6): 1712–28

Halsey A H, Heath A F, Ridge J M 1980 *Origins and Destinations: Family, Class, and Education in Modern Britain*. Clarendon Press, Oxford

Hauser R M, Featherman D L 1977 *The Process of Stratification*. Academic Press, New York

Hauser R M, Wong R S-K 1989 Sibling resemblance and intersibling effects in educational attainment. *Sociol. Educ.* 62(3): 149–71

Hope K 1982 A liberal theory of prestige. *Am. J. Sociol.* 87: 1011–31

Jencks C et al. 1972 *Inequality. A Reassessment of the Effect of Family and Schooling in America*. Basic Books, New York

Jencks C et al. 1979 *Who Gets Ahead? The Determinants of Economic Success in America*. Basic Books, New York

Lipset S M, Zetterberg H L 1959 Social mobility in industrial societies. In: Lipset S M, Bendix R (eds.) 1959 *Social Mobility in Industrial Society*. University of California Press, Berkeley, California

Mare R D 1981 Change and stability in educational stratification. *Am. Sociol. Rev.* 46(1): 72–87

Sewell W H, Hauser R M 1975 *Education, Occupation, and Earnings: Achievement in the Early Career*. Academic Press, New York

Sewell W H, Hauser R M 1980 The Wisconsin longitudinal study of social and psychological factors in aspirations and achievements. In: Kerckhoff A C (ed.) 1980 *Research in Sociology of Education and Socialisation*. JAI Press, Greenwich, Connecticut

Shavit Y, Blossfeld H-P 1993 *Persistent Inequality: Changing Educational Stratification in Thirteen Countries*. Westview Press, Boulder, Colorado

Sixma H, Ultee W C 1984 An occupational prestige scale for the Netherlands in the eighties. In: Bakker B F M, Dronkers J, Ganzeboom H B G (eds.) 1984 *Social Stratification and Mobility in the Netherlands*. SISWO, Amsterdam

Treiman D 1977 *Occupational Prestige in Comparative Perspective*. Academic Press, New York

Tuijnman A 1989 *Recurrent Education, Earnings, and Wellbeing. A Fifty-Year Longitudinal Study of a Cohort of Swedish Men*. Almqvist and Wiksell International, Stockholm

van Leeuwen S, Dronkers J 1992 Effects of continuing

education: A study on adult education, social inequality, and labor market position. *Int. J. Educ. Res.* 17: 609–24.
Vrooman J C, Dronkers J 1986 Changing educational attainment processes: Some evidence from the Netherlands.

Sociol. Educ. 59(2): 69–78
Young M 1958 *The Rise of the Meritocracy, 1870–2033; An Essay on Education and Equality.* Penguin, Harmondsworth

Socialist and Capitalist Schooling: Comparative Perspectives

J.-I. Löfstedt and S. Zhao

Since the coming of age of the first socialist state—the USSR in the 1930s—and, especially after the Cold War period, the polarized antagonistic relationship between socialism and capitalism has changed radically, and the two competing systems have undergone considerable transformation in many respects. Rather than transition from capitalism to socialism, the reverse now seems to be on the agenda. More brutal characteristics of capitalism, such as extreme exploitation, child labor, and conquering wars have been modified significantly and limited, and socialist/communist calls for violent class struggle and the elimination of the world capitalist system by force are no longer widely heard.

In spite of the changed—and still changing—global scenario, and at a time when socialism and capitalism as competing development models may be of more historical than current interest, the time is perhaps ripe for an attempt at a brief analytical assessment and comparison of the two systems in terms of some of their basic ideological assumptions regarding politics, economy, and education.

This article tries first to outline a definitional framework of two different paradigms and then to place schooling in its socioeconomic and ideological context in the respective systems of ideas and practice. Needless to say, most of the concepts discussed here are heavily loaded with political bias and have over time been used in a variety of rhetorical contexts where definitions have depended on the ideological affiliation of the writer. This certainly makes a neutral, exact, and "objective" treatment of the subject most difficult.

For the discussion of socialist/communist thinking, this article has drawn mainly on the writings of Marx, Engels, Lenin, and Mao Zedong and most examples of socialist schooling have been taken from the USSR, China, and Korea. The general frame of reference for capitalist thinking has been provided by writers (both advocates and critics) such as Adam Smith, John Locke, George Reisman, Ayn Rand, Milton Friedman, John Dewey, Burrhus Skinner, Samuel Bowles and Herbert Gintis, Martin Carnoy, and John Chubb and Terry Moe, and most examples of capitalist schooling have been taken from the United States and the United Kingdom.

1. The Socialist/Communist Paradigm

In the historic development of socioeconomic systems,

socialism is in Marxist theory seen as a chronological, transitory stage between (a) a capitalist system of private ownership and a competitive market economy with minimum state interference and (b) a communist system without class conflict, with people's collective ownership of the means of production, and with distribution of welfare according to the needs of the individuals. In the socialist stage, the state apparatus and the communist party are supposed to represent the interests of the broad masses and thus claim control over the main social and economic activities in society. Solidarity and loyalty are expected from the citizens in the socialist society, whereas the capitalist system puts more stress on individual rights and freedoms—and even self-interest—than on common interests. In contrast to the Marxist definition, socialism, according to Ayn Rand from the opposite camp,

> is the doctrine that man has no right to exist for his own sake, that his life and work do not belong to him, but belong to society, that the only justification of his existence is his service to society, and that society may dispose of him in any way it pleases for the sake of whatever it deems to be its own tribal, collective good.

Unlike capitalism, socialism/communism is antireligious and atheistic. This has implications for curricula, syllabi, and instruction in socialist schools, which teach historical materialism refuting all kinds of religious thinking and transcendental or supernatural ideas. According to Marxism, the history of mankind can never be influenced by gods or any other supernatural forces. Whether Man is in full control of his destiny is, however, controversial and has constantly been discussed by Marxist theoreticians who sometimes lean towards determinism and sometimes towards voluntarism: Man has a free will, and can act accordingly, but is also formed by social circumstances and through social interaction (including education).

1.1 Socialist Education

Classical Marxist writers (such as Marx, Engels, Lenin, and Mao Zedong) have usually dealt with educational issues within a parameter which can perhaps best be described as a system of views and concepts of Man, Knowledge, Society, Dialectics (i.e., the lawlike emanation of synthesis from contradictions), and Ideology. Mao Zedong believed in the given class nature of human beings but also emphasized malleability and the importance of upbringing and education as the fostering of the good Man in preparation for Communist Society.

Marx and Engels saw education (in capitalist society) as an ideological instrument of the state apparatus and ruling class with the function of ideological control and reproduction of class society (where one class can oppress and exploit others). The role of the education system was thus to reproduce socioeconomic class differences through selection according to background ("cultural capital" in Bourdieu's words) and to recreate the different competencies, qualifications, and attitudes needed in a stratified society. Also Lenin regarded education as "political" in the sense that it serves the interests of the ruling class—be it the capitalist class in capitalist society, or the proletariat in socialist society.

1.1.1 Concerning theory and practice. For the young socialist system in the USSR, Lenin, in his time, advocated "polytechnic" education by which he meant that vocational elements should be integrated into basic or elementary education and that students should acquaint themselves with all the main branches of production (1969 p. 9). The teaching method of the Labor School in the USSR was once described by Lunacharsky, Chairman of the People's Commissariat of Education, in the following words:

> The labor character of the school consists in the fact that labor pedagogical as well as productive labor, will be made the basis for teaching. In the primary school it will be mostly work within the walls of the school: in the kitchen, in the garden, in special workshops, etc. The labor must be of a productive character—in this way, in particular, that the children serve the needs of the community so far as their strength will permit them . . .

The Labor School system was discontinued, however, and labor was abolished as an independent subject in Soviet primary and secondary schools already in the 1930s but, some decades later, the Chinese further developed the ideas of combining theory with practice and education with production in the teaching–learning process. Translated into educational policy, this meant that

> in order to strengthen labor education and the development of laboring or vocational skills, starting Grade 3 of primary school, pupils should be taught some relevant basic labor knowledge and techniques; and develop a labor viewpoint as well as good working habits and love for the working people. (Renmin Jiaoyu 12/1986 p. 17).

The combination of theory and practice, the integration of labor in education, and the relationship between education and production have been frequent—but often controversial—themes in socialist education theory. Exactly how should theoretical and practical elements be integrated in the teaching learning process in a feasible way? How should productive labor be included in the timetable of the school without taking too much time away from the core theoretical subjects? How should a sound balance between general and vocational streams in education be maintained in order to best meet the needs for high-level and middle-level manpower, and how should the school and the world of work cooperate and coordinate their activities?

China provides a good illustration of the development and implementation of important pedagogical principles regarding theory-and-practice and education-with-production within a socialist framework. A variety of educational models were tested during different periods: schools would run their own workshops, factories operated schools, and schools and factories linked up in education-cum-production units. The underlying principles did, however, have several different, and sometimes even conflicting, applications and were extended to different relationships and dimensions in education and production. At least four different relationships were of special importance, viz. between: (a) theory and practice in the teaching–learning process; (b) education (as a didactic activity) and production (as a producing activity); (c) general education and vocational training; and between (d) the world of education and the world of work.

The theory–practice axis was of a pedagogical, and even epistemological, nature and related to the integration of theoretical and practical elements in class, such as, for instance, the illustration of mathematical laws and concepts through measurement exercises inside or outside the school. This principle was based on the assumption that learning is a dialectical process of reinforcement of theoretical knowledge through practical application and testing. In the implementation of the education–production principle, productive labor was part of the school timetable for economic and political (ideological) reasons. The school would earn income; students would be socialized into workers and possible future conflicts between workers and intellectuals could be avoided. The third principle related to the balance between general and vocational streams or tracks in education and had bearings on the division of labor in society and on manpower needs. The education–work dimension, finally, had to do with a number of aspects, such as job assignments for school leavers and the use of workers and technicians for the work places as teachers in schools.

It should perhaps be noted that different rationales would be offered for the different arrangements discussed above: the political and ideological advantage was supposed to be that the sociocultural barriers between workers and intellectuals would be eliminated and socialist consciousness be promoted; the expected pedagogical benefit was that the learning process would be cognitively more effective, resulting in better performance; the human development argument was that the arrangement would promote all-round harmonious development of mental, physical, emotional, and moral qualities in students; and, finally, the manpower needs rationale was that workers and staff would be better prepared for a variety of different tasks and flexible deployment or rotation in their work places.

Mao Zedong often dealt with the topics of intellectual and manual work and the sociopolitical relationship between intellectuals and workers. He pointed to processes of teaching and learning not only in schools but in society at large and often emphasized the need for intellectuals, including teachers, to teach and learn in a constantly ongoing process. As early as in 1937 Mao said, on the question of the intellectuals:

Unless they rid themselves of what is unsound, intellectuals cannot shoulder the task of educating others. Naturally we have to learn while teaching and be pupils while serving as teachers. To be a good teacher, one must first be a good pupil. There are many things which cannot be learnt from books alone; one must learn from those engaged in production, from the workers, from the peasants, and, in schools, from the students, from those one teaches. (Selected Works V 1957 pp. 425–26)

1.1.2 The individual and the collective. The relationship between the individual and the collective has been another important theme in socialist educational theory. The basic assumption is that the collective and the public take precedence over the individuals. In the words of Kim Ilsung (1977):

In socialist society, where the means of production are owned by the state and society and educational institutions are directed by the state, educational work can be successful only when the state guarantees it responsibly.

The collective is the main frame factor also at the classroom level. Makarenko was an early exponent in the USSR of the view that collective discipline should be used as a pedagogical method. The ideas he developed in the 1930s do, of course, bear the marks of war communism, and his emphasis on the subordination of the individual to the collective and on in-group solidarity mirrored a system of industrialization, centralized leadership, and needs for individual sacrifices for economic construction and national defence.

The formative element of Marxism stresses, as noted above, the need to foster physically, mentally, and morally all-round and fully developed human beings. Education should impart a proletarian ideology and political awareness as well as knowledge. Political awareness here implies sense of duty and commitment to collective interests in addition to knowledge of Marxist theory. In Mao's China, the slogan was to be "Red and Expert" that is, both politically conscious and professionally competent.

1.2 Comtemporary Socialist Education

Even in the late 1990s, the normative and ideologically formative elements of education are underlined in China, where the basic aim of education is to train students to become citizens with high ideals and good moral standards, well educated and disciplined, with love for their socialist motherland and the cause of socialism, who devote themselves to attaining prosperity for the country and the people, and who pursue new knowledge and cultivate the spirit of seeking truth from facts. Schools in China are not only expected to develop cognitive competencies but also to foster good socialist attitudes and form good behaviors in a collectivist spirit in students. The main themes in moral education in China are; love for the motherland, for the people, for work, for science, and for socialism. As stated in Zhou et al. (1990):

The cultivation of talents in ideals, morality, culture and discipline, as well as the cultivation of successors to the proletarian revolutionary cause, would not be possible if moral education became lax. Therefore, it is indispensable to place moral education before everything else in persisting in the political direction of socialist education.

A striking feature in socialist higher education has been the priority given to the sciences as opposed to the humanities and the social sciences. High-level manpower trained in natural science and technology were needed in the industrialization effort, and social sciences like sociology and psychology were condemned outright as totally contaminated with bourgeois ideology. In the case of China, the social sciences were revived slowly only in the late 1970s. Likewise, typical of the socialist model, was the extreme specialization in natural science. In the case of China, which had inherited the Soviet system, in the broad field of mechanical engineering, to take one example, engineers were trained in separate streams for manufacturing and fabrication and for design and/or research and development. Many specialists were also organized along product or process lines (e.g., internal combustion engines, steam turbines, cranes, and other machines). Specialities concerned with, for instance, internal combustion engines, were then further subdivided into automobile, agricultural machine-building, aviation, and ship-building industries (Löfstedt 1990 p. 68, Price 1987, Hayhoe and Bastid 1987).

Few Marxist writers on education have dealt with classroom didactics and teaching methods (besides what has been said above about the combination of theory and practice). Kim Ilsung, however, did outline general didactic guidelines, which he termed "heuristic" (1977 pp. 26–29). Mao Zedong has also referred in passing to the "enlightenment method." Heuristic instruction, according to Kim, should "give an illuminating explanation through talks and conversations." Discussions and debates should be held in the form of questions and answers. Teaching should make use of visual aids and demonstration plays. But at the same time, "ideological education of students should be given through explanation and persuasion."

The idea of strict guidance of the pupils combined with hierarchical and paternalistic traditions have tended to produce a pedagogical practice in socialist societies characterized by teacher-centered and somewhat spoon-feeding methods. Classroom or school democracy allowing for pupil or student influence on school management has rarely been seen in socialist countries, and the well-known criticism–self-criticism meetings frequently held have in most cases been forum for the promotion of good moral standards rather than examples of school democracy.

2. The Capitalist Paradigm

Capitalism, as ideology and a cluster of politico-economic subsystems, is linked closely with industrialization which was basically a transition from a subsistence economy to a money-market economy based on private ownership, commerce, and factory production. Its pattern and structure have varied in different national contexts. In the Anglo-Saxon countries, capitalism was generally driven by individual profit maximization, whereas in Germanic and Francophone Europe, industrialization was state-sponsored and served national, economic, and military objectives.

In a capitalist system, private individuals and companies own the means of production, organize and execute production with the help of employees, and carry on the exchange of goods and services through market mechanisms for profit maximization. Nonsocialist/communist systems commonly describe themselves as free enterprise and market systems. A combination of self-interest, private property, and competition is expected to lead to the well-being of society.

> Capitalism asserts that the ownership of property in private hands, exchanged in the market place in accordance with the mechanism of prices, leads to a state of affairs in which most people's 'welfare' is vastly improved. (Kelley 1992)

The role of the state and the public sector in capitalist systems is often unclear and controversial and, as indicated above, varies from country to country. Mixed economies usually allow a considerable amount of state intervention in the "free" market and see the state as the guarantor for minimum equity and social justice and as a mediator between conflicting interests.

Its more radical advocates believe that (*laissez-faire*) capitalism can make social harmony possible through the pursuit of self-interest. From the tenet of individual rights and freedoms follows that natural resources and basic means of production should be privately owned and that the national economy should be uncontrolled and unregulated. According to this somewhat fundamentalistic stand, the only purpose of government is to protect citizens from violence and fraud. The concept of the welfare state is rejected by the *laissez-faire* capitalist on the grounds that it requires the unjustified appropriation of income through taxation for redistribution to others, which

is an infringement on the rights and freedoms of the individual. The basic function of the capitalist in his capacity as businessman is to

> . . . raise the productivity, and thus the real wages, of manual labor by means of creating, coordinating, and improving the efficiency of the division of labour. (Reisman 1996 pp. 17–18)

2.1 Capitalist Education

The early capitalist View of Man, also reflected frequently in school curricula, may be illustrated by the following propositions:

> 1. Labour is unreliable, lazy and will only work when tightly controlled and closely supervised. 2. The main controllable business cost is labour; therefore the key to increased profits is to make labour cheaper, and/or increase its productivity, by getting employees to work harder, or for longer hours, for the same, or less money. (Burns 1996 p. 7)

Another version of the capitalist View of Man is that people are economic beings:

> They are solely motivated by money. This instrumental orientation means that they will try to achieve the maximum reward for the minimum work, and will use whatever bargaining power their skills or knowledge allow to this end. (Burns 1996 p. 27)

2.1.1 Education and the class structure. Educational thinking in capitalist societies usually has its main roots in two basically opposite traditions corresponding to the division of society in "upper" and "lower" classes, or owners of capital and means of production, on the one hand, and workers and employees, on the other. Intermingled with these two traditions has been a sometimes strong religious, mainly Christian, force which has exerted considerable influence on education, and at certain historical stages the Church has been the institution mainly responsible for the education of the poor (children should be taught to respect God, the King, and the Nation).

As long as political power was entirely in the hands of the upper classes, two parallel educational streams existed in society, one for the poor and one for the wealthy. A good example of this policy in the context of the United Kingdom is provided by Robert Low who said:

> The lower classes ought to be educated to discharge the duties cast upon them. They should also be educated that they may appreciate and defer to a higher cultivation when they meet it, and the higher classes ought to be educated that they may exhibit to the lower classes that higher cultivation to which, if it were shown to them, they would bow down and defer.

The main purpose of general basic education was thus to keep the poor in their place. For the industrialists (capitalists) of England, education for the lower classes beyond the elementary stage was a luxury that could not be afforded. Such schooling would mean that needed labor would be absorbed in schools and that workers may be encouraged to get ideas above their station. In the eyes of the conservatives, education for the masses would threaten culture and the established order. It also followed from this that there should be a minimum of mixing of working class and middle class children in schools.

Whereas the conservatives saw the ideology of egalitarianism as the main threat to educational quality, educational thinking with roots in the working class and trade union movements, however, have emphasized aspects such as free and public education for all, equality of opportunity, multiculturalism, fair provision of educational opportunities, egalitarianism in all respects, and so on. Concern with the working class tradition in education has for instance, been expressed by the National Education Association in the United States which believes that

> . . . the influence of the labor movement and unionism on the growth of the United States should be an integral part of the curriculum in our schools. (NEA Resolutions)

Capitalist schooling has thus developed in many directions depending on a variety of historical, national, social, and cultural factors and traditions. Most of its pedagogical systems have been founded in behavioristic, interactionistic, or cognitivistic psychological paradigms or Views of Man. Important branches on this "tree of pedagogy" have been "child-centered" pedagogy, "progressive" teaching, "progressivism" or "Plowdenism," "learner-centered teacher education," and "discovery learning" (Dewey 1916/1963, Freedman 1993, Bruner 1966). Other branches on the tree have been "mastery learning" and "personalized system of instruction," and "programmed instruction" (Kulik et al. 1990, Bloom 1976, Skinner 1958). Capitalist pedagogy has seen a variety of different didactic approaches ranging from teacher-centered to subject and learner-centered modes.

Although oriented in several different directions, what unifies the above pedagogical systems is that their point of departure is a psychological definition of the learner, the child, based on a conception of how human beings function. There are other capitalist thinkers who are more concerned with a normative or programmatic visionary perspective. In Rand's words:

> The only purpose of education is to teach a student how to live his life, by developing his mind and equipping him to deal with reality. The training he needs is theoretical, i.e., conceptual. He has to be taught to think, to understand, to integrate, to prove. He has to be taught the essentials of the knowledge discovered in the past—and he has to be equipped to acquire further knowledge by his own effort. Rand (1967)

2.1.2 Education, individual choice, and the market. The strong belief in personal freedom and the objection to government interventions in the capitalist paradigm also entail rejection of compulsory tax-financed education and insistence on parents' free choice of schools for their children. Even when education is wholly or partly publicly financed, the general idea, as expounded in the "public choice theory," is that

through rational decision-making by parents combined with decentralization, school autonomy, and antibureaucratization, and perhaps a form of a voucher program, the best possible education will be provided. According to many capitalist educators and writers in the school choice movement (e.g., Chubb and Moe 1990), private schools offer greater teacher and administrator autonomy and this has a positive influence on student achievement in contrast to the bureaucracy of public schools which stifles autonomy and thus has a negative effect on student performance. The important factors in improving the schools are total autonomy of teachers and principals and freedom from bureaucratic government regulations, and even from school boards. One problem area referred to by Chubb and Moe is the difficulty for others than those directly involved in the teaching–learning process to measure the results of education. Public education entailing top-down hierarchical management is counterproductive to good education because of the measurement problem:

> Effective bureaucracy is commonly built around rules that specify appropriate behavior, rewards, and sanctions that encourage such behavior, and monitoring to ascertain whether goals are being met, whether rules are being followed, and whether the rules and incentive system need to be adjusted. All are rendered highly problematic in education, because good education and the behaviors conducive to it are inherently difficult to measure in an objective, quantifiable, formal manner. The measurement problem makes it difficult or impossible for education administrators to know what they are doing—and their controls, as a result, threaten to be ill-suited to the ends they want to achieve. (1990 p. 36)

The educational policy of the World Bank may be seen as a typical expression of the capitalist paradigm in education. The Bank, which has adopted some of its main (economistic) assumptions from the Human Capital Theory of the 1960s and 1970s, "finances education because it is sound economic investment with high returns . . ." and invests in education because it raises per capita GNP (Choksi 1995).

The firm belief in competitive markets in the capitalist paradigm also applies to education, and the Reagan and Thatcher eras have displayed many illustrative examples of measures aimed at promoting market-driven education (primarily at secondary and tertiary levels). Even Herbert Gintis, who in the 1970s criticized capitalist education from the left and claimed that education prepared individuals for social relations of dominance and subordination in the economic sphere and made the majority of them accept the degree of powerlessness that they would face as adults (1976 p. 265), in the 1990s, expressed his faith in the role of free market competition as the solution to educational problems (see, for instance, the Internet discussion on http://olam.ed.asu.edu/epaa/v2n6.htm).

The "Charter School" in the United States is a typical example of the belief in competition in education. These schools have been created on the assumption that students would benefit from increased competition in the educational arena because poor quality schools would not be able to survive in a competitive market where the superior schools would attract more students and thus take over. With more school choices available, charter schools would have to offer superior curricula and focus on student performance in order to meet parental demands.

Another trend indicative of the individualistic trait in capitalist education is the homeschooling movement in the US. This is in an area where strong religious influence is still felt in education after the Church had been more or less ousted from the public educational system. Homeschooling is based on the assumption that individual parents are better equipped to take care of the education of their children than the public sector. Homeschooling is legal in all states in the United States and it is estimated that around half a million (1 percent of the school-aged children) in the country are taught outside of formal schools (Lines 1991).

3. Summary and Conclusions

A truly systematic comparison of socialist and capitalist systems is extremely difficult since they are conditioned by so many different historical, cultural, ethnic, and other factors. A tentative comparison of some of their respective educational features will, however, be attempted here.

This brief overview shows that socialist schooling has been based on values of collectivism (including subordination to the common good), solidarity, and atheism as well as the combination of theory and practice, and has been state and/or party controlled. Capitalist schooling, in contrast, is founded in self-interest, individualism, competition, and free choice, and is to varying degrees market driven, but also allows considerable religious influence. Socialist education basically is part of a monolithic political system with top-down planning and administration, whereas capitalist schooling reflects a bipolar, and also pluralistic, system with different, often competing, socioeconomically determined traditions.

In terms of educational performance, the two systems have weak as well as strong points. Socialist societies, on the whole, have performed better in the promotion of literacy. Especially the USSR, China, and Cuba are examples of countries which implemented well-organized and effective nationwide literacy campaigns.

Basically, both systems have failed to equitable distribution of educational provisions. Considerable disparities are found in both socialist and capitalist societies in terms of the provision of education along gender, ethnic, regional, and socioeconomic dimensions.

The launching of the *sputnik* in the USSR in the late 1950s made it clear to the world that the socialist educational system could produce impressive medium- and high-level manpower competence. Capitalist societies have likewise scaled high peaks in knowledge- and competence-driven areas. In the USSR, the high priority given to natural science and technology in combination with the extremely narrow specialization in technical fields were important factors explaining the *sputnik* success, but overspecialization also raised barriers and created communication obstacles between different disciplines which sometimes in the end resulted in coordination and management problems in the execution of large research and development projects.

Pedagogy and didactics in capitalist societies tend to be more pluralistic, dynamic, and experimental, whereas teaching in socialist societies, with some exceptions, have been more geared to discipline, rules, and regulations, and rote learning. Socialist teaching has on the whole been distinctly teacher-centered, whereas capitalist schools have allowed more room for learner-centered approaches.

Somewhat ironically, both socialism and capitalism have common, although conflicting, roots in the same early stages of industrial capitalism. The relationship between the two systems may sometimes be understood as that of thesis–antithesis. Antithesis in one system has become thesis in the other in the way that Marx for instance, was antithesis in the capitalist system but became thesis in the socialist system, and Rand was antithesis in relation to the socialist system but became thesis in the capitalist system. However, after more than a hundred years of hostility between the two systems, perhaps the time now is appropriate for a dispassionate evaluation and appreciation of the strong points of both.

See also: Marxism and Educational Thought; Socialist Education Systems

References

Bloom B S 1976 *Human Characteristics and School Learning.* McGraw-Hill, New York
Bruner J S 1966 *Toward a Theory of Instruction.* Norton, New York
Burns B 1996 *Managing Change—A Strategic Approach to Oreganisational Dynamics.* Pitman, London
Choksi A M 1995 The World Bank and Education. Speech published on the Internet: http://www.worldbank.org/html/hcovp/speeches/choksp.htm
Chubb J, Moe T 1990 *Politics, Markets and America's Schools.* The Brookings Institution, Washington, DC
Dewey J 1916/1963 *Democracy and Education.* Macmillan, New York
Freedman J 1993 Failing grades, *Canadian Schooling in a Global Economy.* Red Deer, Alberta
Hayhoe R, Bastid M (eds.) 1987 *China's Education and the Industrialized World.* Sharpe, Armong, New york
Kelley M W 1992 Capitalist morality & the politics of socialism. *Contra Mundum* 4 (http://www.wavefront.com-contra_m/cm/features/cm04_capitalist.html)

Kim Ilsung 1977 *Theses on Socialist Education*. Foreign Languages Publishing House, Pyongyang

Kulik C L, Kulik J A, Bangert-Drowns R L 1990 Effectiveness of mastery learning programs: A meta-analysis. *Rev. Educ. Res.* 60(2): 303–7

Lenin 1969 *On Youth*. Novostni Press Agency Publishing House, Moscow

Lines P 1991 *Estimating the Home Schooled Population*. Working Paper. US Department of Education, Washington, DC

Löfstedt J-I 1990 *Human Resources in Chinese Development: Needs and Supply of Competencies*. IIEP Research Report No. 89, Paris

Mao Zedong 1965 The Debate on the Co-Operative Transformation of Agriculture and the Current Class Struggle. In: *Selected Works*. Foreign Languages Press, Peking

Price R F 1979 *Marx and Education in Russia and China*. Routledge and Kegan Paul, London

Rand A 1967 *Capitalism: The Unknown Ideal*. Penguin, London

Reisman, G 1979 *The Government Against the Economy*. Caroline House, Ottawa, Illinois

Reisman G 1996 *Capitalism: A Treatise in Economics*. Jameson, Ottawa, Illinois

Renmin Jiaoyu (People's Education) 1986 12: 17

Skinner B F 1958 Teaching machines. *Science* 128: 967–77

Zhou Y et al. (eds.) 1990 *Education in Contemporary China*. Hunan Education Publishing House, Changsha

Further Reading

Bowen J 1962 *Soviet Education: Anton Makarenko and the Years of Experiment*. University of Wisconsin Press, Madison, Wisconsin

Bowles S, Gintis H 1976 *Schooling in Capitalist America: Educational Reform and the Contradictions of Economic Life*. Basic Books, New York

Capitalism: Frequently Asked Questions—Theory 1997 http://www.ocf.berkeley.edu/~shadab/capit-2.htm

Deineko M 1956 *Public Education in the USSR. Facts and Figures*. Progress, Moscow

Goncharov N K 1967 Theory of education: Lenin and pedagogy. *Sovietskaia Pedagogika* 11

Hawkins J N 1974 *Mao Tse-Tung and Education*. Shoe String Press, Hamden, Connecticut

Liston D P 1990 *Capitalist Schools: Explanations and Ethics in Radical Studies of Schooling*. Routledge, New York

Lu Tingyi 1964 *Education Must Be Combined with Productive Labour*. Foreign Languages Press, Peking

Löfstedt J-I 1977 *Röd och Expert (Red and Expert)*. Wahlström and Widstrand, Stockholm

Löfstedt J-I 1980 *Chinese Educational Policy: Changes and Contradictions 1949–79*. Almqvist and Wiksell, Stockholm, New Jersey

Mao Zedong 1957 On the Correct Handling of Contradictions Among the People. In: *Selected Readings From the Works of Mao Tse-Tung*. Foreign Languages Press, Peking

Miron G (ed.) 1993 *Towards Free Choice and Market Oriented Schools—Problems and Promises*. Institute of International Education, Stockholm University

Reisman G 1984 Classical economics versus the exploitation theory. In: Leube K, Zlabinger A (eds.) 1984 *The Political Economy of Freedom: Essays in Honor of F.A. Hayek*. Philosophia Verlag, Munich

Shore M 1947 *Soviet Education*. Philosophical Library, New York

Skinner B F 1968 *The Technology of Teaching*. Appleton Century Crofts, New York

Skinner B F 1978 *Reflections on Behaviorism and Society*. Prentice-Hall, Englewood Cliffs, New Jersey

Socialist Education Systems

F. Kuebart

The revolutionary changes that shook Central and Eastern Europe in 1989 and 1990 and reverberated throughout the Asian continent marked the end of socialism as a socioeconomic and political world system. The collapse of multinational states such as the Soviet Union and Yugoslavia changed the political map with new independent states emerging in their wake while the GDR ceased to exist altogether as a consequence of German reunification. In these parts of the world socialism as the ideological basis determining the social and political order of the various states has become a historical phenomenon, as has East–West rivalry which also shaped education, its goals, organization, contents; and outcomes.

The countries that labeled themselves "socialist" never constituted a united or homogeneous block from a political economic, or cultural point of view, although they converged in a number of basic tenets incorporating Marxism–Leninism as the official ideology, state ownership of the means of production and the concentration of power in the hands of a Communist party. In the socialist transformation of society—as an interim stage on the way to Communism—the education system was allotted a crucial role: the creation of a "new person" who would combine broad knowledge with ideological conviction and political loyalty and who would be prepared actively to serve the interests of society.

Some countries such as the People's Republic of China or Yugoslavia which had originally been under the influence of the Soviet model of development, later built their own, specific types of socialism.

Others, especially in the Third World, though emulating Soviet socialist experience and practice in many fields, including education, had not developed beyond the status of a "socialist orientation." In this article, the notion of socialist education systems is mainly confined to education in those European socialist countries which belonged to the international organizations dominated by the Soviet Union, e.g., the Warsaw Pact and the Council for Mutual Economic Assistance (CMEA; "Comecon"), and which claimed to represent "real" (or "mature") socialism as opposed to other strands of socialist ideology and practice. It, therefore, focuses on the now historic experiences of these countries rather than dealing with problems of those socialist education systems that continue to exist, as in China or in Cuba and Vietnam as former non-European members of the CMEA.

1. Historical Background and Common Principle

After a period of "revolutionary transformation" in the 1920s, an education system was established in the Soviet Union during the 1930s conforming to the socialist demand for a unified school structure, and with the overriding aim of producing the specialist "cadres" required by the rapidly developing economy. Curricula and organization of instruction were reminiscent of the traditional bourgeois academic school while the formalized and ritualized inculcation of the doctrine of Marxism–Leninism was arrived at producing loyalty towards the political regime. By the end of the 1930s the compulsory primary school had been established nearly everywhere and illiteracy almost vanished.

When the East European countries and the then Soviet zone of occupation in Germany embarked on the transformation of their education after 1945, they first aimed at "democratizing" the education systems by opening them up for all social classes and by giving special priority to the underprivileged. The next stage of development was reached in the late 1940s and early 1950s when increasing Soviet influence made itself felt on the education systems of the new "people's democracies," particularly with respect to pedagogical theory, curricula and textbooks, the linking of the education system to economic planning and administrative forms and styles. A certain degree of unification was thus achieved, although organizational structures remained relatively unaffected in each country. Since the end of the 1950s, cultural, educational, and national traditions regained influence and specific national requirements received more attention in educational strategies. The reform processes set in motion in the late 1970s and early 1980s by the pressures of technological and economic modernization once more moved all the East European education systems with their common ideological basis in the same direction, but specific national arrangements varied in detail.

In the 1980s, however, which began with the crisis of the political system in Poland, decisions on educational policy tended to be come more exclusively geared to the conditions and interests of the national education systems and their specific political and economic ramifications, even if in political rhetoric the Soviet Union continued to be regarded as the model to be followed. This common denominator was further eroded with the advent of *perestroika* in the Soviet Union which heralded system changes regarded as potentially threatening by some of the CMEA member states, especially the GDR. "Unity in diversity" became the slogan aimed at bridging the widening gaps created by centrifugal dynamics before they resulted in the final breakdown of the system.

The fundamental principles governing the structures and contents of the education systems in the socialist states were derived from the Marxist–Leninist program of transforming society, as formulated in the Soviet Union during the Stalin era and later applied to all states of the Soviet block. However, patterns of interpretation have differed, producing sometimes contradictory results. The program was advertised in the socialist countries as being straightforward, logical, internally consistent, and pointing to a clearly linear and progressive path of educational and social development. In practice, however, it proved to be not without some grave internal contradictions, that had a number of unexpected and ambiguous consequences. For example, one of the most important principles was the uniformity of the education system both with regard to structures and content which produced constant tension with the need to foster and to differentiate talent. The egalitarian principle of open access to education was limited by the selective nature of higher and some aspects of secondary education. The principle of the unity of teaching and upbringing supported the inculcation of a closed system of political and moral values often at variance with real life experience of young people, while the principle of linking school with life which entered the curriculum in the shape of polytechnical instruction and labor training, frequently resulted in students being used as cheap labor needed to remedy the deficiences of state planning mechanisms.

2. General Structures of Educational Systems

In the socialist states, the educational system was planned as a uniform system integrating every stage of education from the preschool to tertiary level and opening up educational channels for all age-groups. To improve educational opportunity, evening and correspondence courses were assigned an important role and rapid economic change has brought a new emphasis on lifelong education, personnel development, and retraining efforts.

As the earliest level of the national systems of

education, preschool education served both social and educational goals. Crèches accommodated children below the age of three and nursery schools took children between the ages of three to six or seven the age of transfer to school. The degree of priority allotted to expansion of preschool provision varied from country to country, but growth was more or less steady from the 1960s on. At least three goals were pursued: the early moral and political socialization of children to complement upbringing in the family; provision of compensatory conditions for learning and development prior to starting school; and a better utilization of female labor. In the 1980s the German Democratic Republic (GDR) provided nursery school places for about 90 percent of all infants and in Bulgaria, Czechoslovakia and Hungary too the existing demand was largely to have been met. In the Soviet Union this was only the case in some of the large cities. As in Poland, efforts were concentrated on providing special preparation for children starting school.

The school system in the socialist countries was basically divided into a common unified elementary school comprising the primary and the lower secondary stages, and an upper secondary stage, consisting of various parallel general and vocational schools. This structural principle applied to the systems in all the European CMEA countries, including Yugoslavia, though there were differences in detail, particularly at the upper secondary level.

The educational reforms of the 1980s retained the unified "elementary school" as the cornerstone of the educational system. Over a period of generally eight years (10 in the GDR) it provided a common general education for nearly all pupils. The three to four year primary stage differed from the subsequent lower secondary level by employing the class teacher principle and by its curricular organization. In most countries, compulsory schooling was formally extended to 10 years so that pupils as a rule continued their education at one of the schools of the upper secondary level. Only the Soviet Union set about introducing 11 years compulsory schooling (nine plus two years) as a goal for the 1984 reform, but as early as 1988, return to a 10-year course of general secondary education and a reduction of compulsory schooling was advocated by influential planners. In Poland, the reform which aimed to introduce 10 years of compulsory schooling was abandoned in the early 1980s, but at least 90 percent of all young people continued their education beyond the 8-year elementary school.

The structure of the upper secondary stage showed considerable variations among individual countries with regard to the different types of school, their goals, and length of courses. Basically there were three parallel educational pathways: (a) a general education school, the name of which in some countries ("gymnasium" in Czechoslovakia and Hungary, "lyceum" in Poland and Romania) pointed to its academic tradition; (b) a secondary specialized school providing training for technicians and subacademic staff in the social sphere along with a certificate of secondary education (in the GDR it offered courses only at postsecondary level, and in the USSR at both levels); (c) the vocational schools which provided training for skilled workers, which could, in most countries, also be combined with a certificate of secondary education.

The proportions of the age-group enrolled in these schools varied considerably from one country to another, as did their scope and procedures of selection. In the GDR, for instance, access to the extended secondary schools was based on rigid planning and selection, while in other countries there is broader opportunity for individual choice in accordance with pupils' interests and career aspirations. The so-called special schools were a type of general secondary school aimed explicitly at catering for gifted children. With admission on a selective basis, they offered intensive and more advanced teaching in certain subjects (foreign languages, mathematics and natural sciences, sports, art, or music). Their social importance by far exceeded their numbers and though their elitism was at variance with the egalitarian nature of the common school principle and therefore sometimes attracted criticism on social grounds, they politically legitimized as a means of fostering talent indispensible for economic advancement. In some countries integrating all the schools at the upper secondary level to form a single overarching structure was expected to provide an improved capacity for directing pupils, particularly towards blue-collar jobs. However, both in Bulgaria and Yugoslavia the lessons learned from implementing the reforms soon led to their modification and in the Soviet Union the idea of an integrated general and vocational secondary school projected as a reform goal in 1984 was silently dropped.

At the tertiary level the task of higher education was to train a "socialist intelligentsia," the specialists and leaders required in every sector of society. Higher education was thus regarded as the uppermost level of vocational training. Structurally the higher education sector characterized by the parallel existence of universities, some with century-old traditions, and a large number of specialized higher education institutions. Amongst these latter are colleges of technology, agriculture, economics, medicine, education, some of them rather narrowly geared to the needs of individual branches of industry.

The quantitative development of higher education was strictly subject to government educational planning. Priority was given to the labor requirements of the economy, rather than to individual educational aspirations. Planning to meet the demands of the employment system showed limited success, however, and by no means all graduates from higher education were able to find a job in line with their specialisms and qualifications. In some countries (e.g., Hungary, Poland, Czechoslovakia) the social and cultural functions of higher education were stressed more explicitly alongside the goals of employment policies. After a long period of expansion, the 1980s saw a contraction, or at least stagnation, of student numbers due to changing economic conditions and the fact that saturation point had been reached or even passed in the demand for graduates, most particularly for engineers. Issues of the quality and effectiveness of training increasingly supplanted concern for producing sheer numbers of graduates and efforts to adjust the availability of courses to changes in the demand for qualifications were stepped up, especially in the field of technology.

Planning student numbers according to demand affected selection procedures for entry to higher education. Except in the GDR where selection took place in the schools of the upper secondary level, admission to higher education was regulated by a competitive examination system based mainly on performance criteria. The weight given to social criteria varied from country to country in the course of time and the political involvement of applicants also allotted a varying degree of significance. The encouragement of certain social groups—workers and peasants—as for example, reflected in special privileges in the admission procedure. To compensate for academic performance deficits among applicants from groups with work experience some countries (Czechoslovakia, Hungary, USSR to some extent the GDR, too) introduced preparation departments or courses at higher education institutions. These policies undoubtedly contributed to improving social mobility. However, due to pressure for higher education to improve the quality of its output, certain countries later turned to performance-based admission criteria at the expense of egalitarian considerations. Increasingly, technological and economic change also required modernizing of course contents and organization. Particular attention was paid to the new technologies, as was the case in the reform of courses for engineers and economists launched in 1983 in the GDR or in the more comprehensive higher education reforms started in the USSR in 1986.

3. Curriculum

Curriculum and teaching in the socialist education systems were influenced strongly by the overall government control of education and the uniform character of schooling. Mandatory curricula for the individual types of schools were laid down by the central education authorities, prescribing the range of subjects and number of lessons to be allocated to them per year and allowing only for minor variations in the case of multinational societies such as the USSR or Czechoslovakia. Subject syllabi were developed by central institutions and required the approval of the state authorities, as did textbooks. The curricula which encompassed a wide range of subjects, followed a broadly similar pattern in most socialist countries. Their structure and contents were based on the concept of "socialist general education," which aim at imparting "scientific" knowledge derived from academic disciplines along with the inculcation of Marxist–Leninist doctrine and a "scientific world outlook." Overt political socialization was embedded in ideological "key subjects" such as civics (social studies) or history. The organization of school life, where the official youth organizations played a significant role, was likewise meant to produce the convictions and attitudes of a "socialist personality." In some countries (e.g., Bulgaria, GDR, USSR) basic military training also formed part of the school curriculum. As an exception for a socialist state, "religious studies" were introduced in the late 1980s as a compulsory subject in Polish upper secondary schools.

Another distinctive feature of socialist general education based on Marxist–Leninist principles was polytechnical instruction, the theoretical foundations of which were, however, subject to varying interpretations and for the practical realization of which there were no generally accepted solutions. Thus, educational reforms were repeatedly attempted to find new specific forms of "combining school and productive labor." Owing to the expansion of general schooling and the growing number of young people wishing to enter higher education, in the late 1970s a number of countries returned to the policy of strengthening the polytechnical element in the general education schools and reinforcing vocational preparation, in order to direct career aspirations back to blue-collar jobs. An extreme solution was adopted in the Soviet school reform of 1984 by expecting schools to provide vocational skills alongside a general education certificate, but this proved unworkable and was abandoned in 1988.

In the 1980s, the rapidly growing computer literacy gap in the socialist countries compared to the West could no longer be ignored. With the realization that microtechnology and computer science had become the centerpiece for the "scientific–technological revolution" and were key factors for economic modernization and progress, governments undertook great efforts to harness schools to the new task of teaching computer science. Approaches to meeting this challenge varied. In some countries computer science was introduced as a separate subject (USSR, Czechoslovakia, Bulgaria), in others it was only offered as an optional course or on an experimental basis, whilst in the GDR it was integrated into polytechnical instruction. However, in addition to a lack of qualified teachers, instruction everywhere suffered from shortages of both hard- and software which tended to focus teaching on theoretical knowledge rather than usage skills.

Although the ideologically based principle of a common general education for all pupils was constant by uphold, it was gradually modified by the introduction of various forms of differentiation from the 1960s on. Following the Soviet Union's example of optional courses in the lower and upper secondary schools, most countries introduced these in various forms alongside the compulsory core, Hungary having been one of the trail-blazers. The aim was to allow for some choice within an otherwise strictly prescribed curriculum in order to promote pupils' special interests and to foster talent, as was done in the above-mentioned special schools. Teaching methods were still characterized by teacher-centered instruction and systematic learning of subject matter as presented by teacher and textbook. Theoretical discussion of problem solving and other active methods. It was not until Soviet *perestroika* in the late 1980s that discussion on education reforms was able to publicly advocate the liberation of teachers from methodological control and demand new and open approaches to pupil–teacher interaction ("pedagogy of cooperation") as opposed to a tightly supervised teaching and learning process.

4. Administration and Supervisory Structures

In the socialist countries, educational institutions were almost exclusively in the hands of the state with the exception of a few church schools and preschool institutions in Hungary, Poland, and the GDR. Fundamental decisions on educational policies were taken by the central leadership bodies of the ruling Communist or workers' parties, while administration is the job of the government authorities responsible for education. In most of the socialist states the educational administration was organized on a strictly centralized basis. In the multinational, theoretically federal Soviet Union the general directive functions were in the hands of central Union bodies, whilst the republics were merely responsible for executing Union policies in most educational matters. However, in federal Czechoslovakia with its two republics (Czech SSR and Slovak SSR) there was no central body for educational administration at a national level.

After the educational administration had been integrated in one top-level department in both Poland (1987) and the Soviet Union (1988), the entire educational system in socialist countries was the responsibility of one single agency, with the exception of the GDR which retained three parallel agencies (in charge of schools, vocational training, and higher education). In some sectors, such as vocational training and higher education, the economic branch ministries also had considerable powers concerning planning, finance, and personnel resulting in a complex power structure in the field of educational decision making. However, by the end of the 1980s, the hierarchical, top-down character of educational governance was on the wane. In order to encourage more flexibility in administering the educational system and to improve the quality and efficiency of its work, most of the states were moving towards decentralization and a devolution of power at various levels of the administration. This went hand-in-hand with the idea of supporting power-sharing and self-government on local and institutional levels. In particular, grassroots initiatives and innovations were to be given greater scope for development and to introduce a dynamic element into rigid bureaucratic structures. In the wake of *perestroika*, there was a clear trend in the Soviet Union, especially towards providing legal and institutional guarantees for the "democratization" of educational administration by mobilizing the involvement of societal forces vis-à-vis state bureaucracy.

5. Education and Status of Teachers

There used to be two distinct sectors of teacher training in socialist countries. Future primary school teachers generally took a 3- to 4-year course at a teacher training college (normal school) below the level of higher education, as did teachers of technical subjects, art, and music for secondary schools. The majority of teachers for the secondary schools took 4- to 5-year courses at institutions of higher education, such as colleges of education or universities. Despite considerable efforts to expand teacher training, very few countries (GDR, Czechoslovakia) had enough teachers to meet their requirements. The degree of teacher shortage depended on factors such as demographic developments, the additional requirements of educational reforms, and the effects of wage policies. Increasingly, mobility of teaching staff exacerbated the situation when the teaching profession became less and less attractive.

While official proclamations stressed the high social esteem with which teachers were regarded, teachers' salaries were allowed to drop well behind the general level of incomes, particularly when compared to those of manual workers. Poor pay and too heavy a work load—frequently encompassing nonteaching duties—contributed to the drop in social prestige and teachers' dissatisfaction with their work. Strict bureaucratic control with its effect on stifling creativity did little to enhance motivation. Rather than representing the interests of the teaching profession vis-à-vis the state administration, teachers' unions were mainly concerned with providing service-related benefits to teachers.

6. Educational Cooperation Among Socialist States

When the ideological and political foundations of the "socialist world system" were built in the postwar decades under the hegemonial influence of the Soviet Union, cooperation took place on a largely bilateral basis, coordinated by the party machineries of the ruling Communist parties. The long-term program of "socialist economic integration" within the CMEA, launched in the 1970s, provided encouragement for an increase in multilateral cooperation among the member states in the field of education. It was expected that parallel processes of political, social, and cultural development based on a common ideology would result in a *rapprochement* of the CMEA countries. On a theoretical level it was claimed that within the "Socialist Community of Nations" educational development would necessarily follow general "laws" and some experts even envisaged an ideal type of a socialist education system which would emerge as a result of the processes of socialist internationalization.

However, the organizational structure of the CMEA in reality only offered a very limited institutional framework for devising common educational strategies or program and allowed mainly for mutual information and consultation. This was the main agenda of regular conferences of the ministers responsible for the various sectors of education. As these conferences had no powers of decision-making binding on participating member countries, they were largely confined to declarations of principles or political intentions. Multilaterial cooperation took place on a more practical level and resulted, for example, in the mutual recognition among socialist countries of the certificates, diplomas, and academic degrees gained in one of the member states. The most intensive domain of cooperation was in educational research coordinated by "council of experts" and carried out by the leading research institutions of member countries. There was also an increasing number of contacts among representatives of educational administration, including direct links between similar institutions, particularly in higher education, and an extensive exchange of students and postgraduates. But in spite of the emergence of closely knit networks of those engaged in similar areas of administration and research, educational planning and decision-making remained a national prerogative, the more so, as willingness among member states to agree to any serious approaches to supranational coordination of policies remained distinctly low.

7. Socialist Legacy and Postsocialist Transformation

After the collapse of the state socialist regimes, the course was set for the transition to a market economy and a democratic political order. In education the first steps into an inevitably long-term transformation process consisted of legislation to support sweeping reforms generally aimed at getting rid of some of the most salient features of the former system. Thus, reforms were directed at the de-ideologization of the system by the elimination of the teaching of Marxism–Leninism from the curricula of schools and universities, the decentralization of decision-making and the removal of bureaucratic control by granting educational institutions a wide scope of autonomy,

the demise of the unitary character of the school system following the emergence of a variety of new, often academically and socially selective educational institutions including the mushrooming of private educational provision, the humanization of education by encouraging "bottom-up" innovations and a child-centered, individualized approach to teaching and communication at schools.

The directions of change point to some of the major deficiencies of education under "real socialism" which had led to an obvious crisis during the 1980s and encouraged the search for fundamental alternatives among liberal-minded educationists and researchers. The political struggles surrounding the new liberal paradigm for educational transformation along with the factual continuity of an institutional framework and established educational practice deeply rooted in the socialist past have not been conducive to a differentiated evaluation of the legacy of the socialist education systems. A critical assessment would have to take into account the complex historical circumstances of their development and cannot be reduced to a simple debit and credit balance sheet. All the same, a tentative appraisal of general achievements would point to the eradication of illiteracy in the Soviet Union and some East European countries, the expansion of schooling, the extension of educational opportunity promoting upward social mobility for young people from social groups hitherto largely excluded from more than a basic education, a generally high level of formal educational attainment, and the promotion of academic excellence in mathematics and the sciences. This was in many ways counterbalanced by a rigid subordination of educational provision and aspirations of the individual to the interests of the state and the requirements of the planned economy. Through a weighty input of overt ideological education along with collectivist and authoritarian methods of socialization that were able to produce a conformist type of personality, education could for a long time, be seen to contribute to regime stabilization. On the other hand, this type of socialization with its underlying value system was not only unable to immunize youth against external, Western ideas, it was also at the roots of the disaffection and alienation from the system that became widespread in the 1980s and that advanced the collapse of socialism.

Educational reforms introduced since the demise of socialism, widespread experimentation, and innovations at the grass-roots level have profoundly changed the face of the former socialist education systems, providing a great variety of national approaches and solutions, some them borrowed from Western models. All the same, in a time of flux the features of the past are still easily recognizable and coexist, often uneasily, with new developments with regard to organizational and institutional structures as well as to habits and practices. There has been a tendency to fill the vacuum left by the removal of socialist ideology with national or nationalistic doctrines in order to enlist the support of education in creating new state ideologies. A tendency to differentiate educational provision on a basis of academic performance reflects the growing social differentiation of societies; however, in most postsocialist states the extensive reduction of funds devoted to education in the wake of the economic transition crisis poses the most severe problems for the development of the education systems.

See also: Marxism and Educational Thought; Socialist and Capitalist Schooling: Comparative Perspectives

Further Reading

Anweiler O (ed.) 1986 *Staatliche Steuerung und Eigendynamik im Bildungs- und Erziehungswesen osteuropäischer Staaten und der DDR.* Berlin Verlag Arno Spitz, Berlin

Anweiler O, Kuebart F (eds.) 1984 *Bildungssysteme in Osteuropa. Reform oder Krise?* Berlin Verlag Arno Spitz, Berlin

Birzea C 1994 *Educational Policies of the Countries in Transition.* Council of Europe Press, Strasbourg

Dunstan J (ed.) 1992 *Soviet Education under Perestroika.* Routledge, London and New York.

Filippov F R, Mitev P E (eds.) 1984 *Molodzeh i vysshee abrazovanie v sotsialisticheskikh stranakh* [Youth and higher education in socialist countries]. Nauka, Moscow

Grant N 1969 *Society, Schools, and Progress in Eastern Europe.* Pergamon, Oxford

Hegedüs L, von Kopp B, Schmidt G 1982 *Hochschulstudium und Berufseingliederung in Sozialistischen Staaten.* Böhlau, Cologne and Vienna

Hofman H G, Malkova, Z 1990 The socialist countries. In: Halls W D (ed.) 1990 *Comparative Education Contemporary Issues and Trends.* Jessica Kingsley, London and UNESCO, Paris

Karsten S, Majoor D (eds.) 1994 *Education in East Central Europe, Educational Changes after the Fall of Communism.* Waxmann Münster, and New York

Klarkina T F (ed.) 1982 *Vospitatel'naia rabota v shkolach stran sotsializma* [Upbringing in the schools of socialist countries]. Pedagogika, Moscow

Kienitz K 1984 Fortschritte des Bildungswesens in der Etappe des entwickelten Sozialismus: Ein Überblick über internationale Tendenzen. *Vergl. Pädag.* 20(2): 140–63; 20(3): 263–79

Kluczynski J 1985 Research on higher education in European socialist countries. In: Altbach P G, Kelly D H (eds.) 1985 *Higher Education in International Perspective.* Mansell, London.

Mal'kova Z A 1983 *Shkola i pedagogika za rubezhom* [School and education in foreign countries]. Pedagogika, Moscow

Matthews M 1982 *Education in the Soviet Union: Policies and Institutions Since Stalin.* George Allen and Unwin, London

Mitter W 1976 *Secondary School Graduation: University Entrance Qualification in Socialist Countries.* Pergamon, New York

Mitter W 1983 Schulreform in Osteuropa. In: Lenzen D (ed.) 1983 *Enzyklopädie Erziehungswissenschaft*, Vol. 8. Klett, Stuttgart

Phillips D, Kaser M (eds.) 1992 *Education and Economic Change in Eastern Europe and the Former Soviet Union.* Triangle Books, Wallingford, Oxfordshire. Oxford Studies in Comparative Education, Vol. 2(1)

Pivovarov V M (ed.) 1989 *Problemy obshchego obrazovaniia v stranakh sotsializma* [Problems of general education in the socialist countries], Pedagogika, Moscow

Vladislavlev P A 1989 *Sistema obrazovaniia v evropeiskikh stranakh SEV. Ekonomicheskie i sotsialnye problemy* [The system of Education in the European Comecon countries. Economic and social problems]. Nauka, Moscow

Waterkamp D 1987 *Handbuch zum Bildungswesen der DDR.* Berlin Verlag Arno Spitz, Berlin

Stratification in Educational Systems

J. L. Peschar

This article will first address the issue of what is meant by stratification. Conceptual issues and corresponding empirical indicators at the individual level are introduced. This is followed by a discussion of the relationship between an individuals' position in the stratification and the educational system. Different connotations of "education" are distinguished. The third section considers whether these relationships are stable or differ between schools. On a more general level the structures of educational systems are also relevant. Do systems induce stratified patterns and lead to specific strategies of social groups, and are these changed after reforms in educational systems?

There has been much empirical progress in this area which merits that some attention be given to methodological issues.

1. Stratification

In discussions about stratification, five issues arise. First, there is the question of whether social privileges are connected to certain discrete social classes which can be clearly distinguished, or whether social privileges are linked with a dimension of status which ranks individuals in a more or less continuous way.

The former view is associated with the classical theory of Karl Marx and mostly applied to preindustrial societies with clear-cut social dividing lines. The latter view is based on the work of Max Weber, who introduced the concept of life-styles to indicate class and status.

After agreement is reached on the meaning of class and status, the second issue is the question of how many classes must be distinguished, or whether more or less homogeneous strata of persons with similar life-styles can be identified. Do persons belonging to these classes share (or lack) the same privileges? Or can individuals be ordered in a hierarchical way, where people at the top enjoy more privileges? Usually social position is defined in terms of the occupation held, even though this implies that information is available on the active employed population of men and women between 20 and 65 years of age.

The third issue is descriptive: how many persons belong to which category and what are the correlates of this class or status position with respect to other socially scarce goods, such as education, income, wealth, or consumption? Here, there are many studies which document social distributions, ranging from the classical Yankee City and Middletown studies to the contemporary social indicator reports of many countries.

A fourth issue is the degree of stability of the above-described patterns. Due to changing social conditions and economic growth, the distributions of privileged positions and occupations are changing, which creates opportunities for individuals to move upward or downward in social hierarchies. These mobility patterns may be observed during an individual's life course (intragenerational), but also between the generations of parents and children (intergenerational). The degree to which mobility within and between generations is realized is often considered an indicator for the openness or rigidity of a society. The more mobility, the less an individual is determined by his or her origins. It will be clear that much openness does not challenge the legitimacy of the social hierarchy or class system; it only means that many persons travel across socially defined borderlines.

The fifth issue is therefore whether these borderlines, the classifications or dimensions of class or status themselves, are subject to change over time. In the development of industrial societies the division of labor has led to an increased specialization and differentiation of work. Especially in the twentieth century, many occupations have disappeared due to the mechanization and automation of work. Also, new occupations have been created that did not formerly exist. This has resulted in a complete rearranging of the social hierarchies and thus of the paths according to which social mobility could develop. One of the difficult tasks in sociology is to set apart the various components of mobility: absolute versus relative rates of mobility; changes resulting from different classifications versus "real" changing patterns of mobility.

These issues are not limited to theoretical importance. Empirical research in this area is determined by the distinction between classes, status, prestige, and socioeconomic position. Socioeconomic position (and also social standing) is frequently indicated by some kind of composite measure that includes the weighted sums of occupational prestige, educational level and income. It will be clear that these kinds of indicators are unsuitable for studies of stratification in education because these variables are interrelated.

In the 1990s principally two different instruments are accepted as a standard in international and comparative research. For national research local versions of socioeconomic position are available. The *Standard International Occupational Prestige Scale* was developed by Treiman (1977) to normalize the many national status scales into one that could be used in comparative research. The scale is based on the aggregated national prestige scales that were available and in use in the 1950s and 1960s.

A further observation about status and prestige scales is that persons with the same prestige score hold a wide variety of jobs and vice versa. Thus a prestige score does not refer to a social group with more or less cohesion. Erikson and Goldthorpe (1992) therefore developed a ten-category (EGP) class scheme on the basis of four different job attributes: sector, employment status, skill level, and supervisor status (see Table 1).

Similarly Ganzeboom et al. (1989) applied a compressed version of this scheme to 149 mobility tables from 35 countries to discover a modest general trend toward societal openness since the Second World War. For both the Treiman and EGP scales, detailed recoding schemes are easily available from knowledge about levels of occupations (see Sect. 5).

Some authors consider gender and race as special dimensions for social stratification. These can also be considered as specifications of a general pattern of stratification. The criteria discussed, however, refer to

Table 1
The Erikson–Goldthorpe–Portocarero Class Scheme (EGP)

I	Large proprietors; higher professionals and managers
II	Lower professionals and managers
III	Routine nonmanual workers
IVa	Small proprietors with employees
IVb	Small proprietors without employees
IVc	Self-employed farmers
V	Lower grade technicians and manual supervisors
VI	Skilled manual workers
VIIa	Unskilled and semiskilled manual workers
VIIb	(Unskilled) agricultural workers

Source: Erikson and Goldthorpe (1992)

the occupational domain and it has been argued that other criteria might be equally relevant as indicators to distinguish stratified societies. Marriage patterns (homogamy and heterogamy) have been suggested and applied, as well as educational criteria (educational mobility).

2. *Stratification and Educational Outcomes*

An important question is whether persons with higher educational performance or achievements have better mobility chances? To answer this, it is first necessary to elaborate on the meaning of "education." For the individual, the notion of educational competencies is the most relevant concept. While several distinctions regarding education can be made (cognitive, technical instrumental, noncognitive, social normative, cross-curricular), stratification studies by and large concentrate on the cognitive outcomes of education (achievement, performance). As this information is not always available, educational certification (diploma), or simply the time spent in school (number of years), are chosen as proxies. These proxies, however, are not always comparable, as they reflect local or national characteristics, and are not stable over time. In cross-national research it is very difficult to use educational criteria and indicators which are equivalent enough to allow reliable comparisons. The practice of using number of years of education as an indicator has been frequently discussed and rejected (see Allmendinger 1989).

When educational certification is chosen, other problems arise: the cross-national comparison of diplomas includes both an individual component (performance) and system characteristics. Müller et al. (1995) developed a special version for their study of class (EGP) and education in nine industrial nations (see Table 2). From this scheme it is clear that the ranking of diplomas of different school types can only partially be achieved in educational systems where both a general and a vocational track exist. In addition, a separate translation table must be constructed to match national certificates to the scheme. This can be done only by experts (see Müller et al. 1995).

Table 2
Educational scheme according to Müller et al. 1995

1a	Inadequately completed general elementary education
1b	General elementary education
1c	General elementary education and basic vocational qualification
2a	Intermediate vocational qualification
2b	Intermediate general qualification
3a	Higher education—maturity level
3b	Higher education—lower-level tertiary certificate
3c	Higher education—upper-level tertiary certificate

What is the relation between stratification and educational outcomes? Blau and Duncan (1967) developed a model of status attainment, where educational attainment is determined by social background (occupation and education of the father), but in turn the achieved job and income of a person is determined by the level of education attained. There have been numerous replications and extensions of this basic model (for a discussion, see Treiman and Ganzeboom 1990 or Breiger 1991). This causal model approach has led to many new questions which need to be addressed. The relationship between education and mobility has been clarified, but studies on the effects of the composition of the paternal family, siblings, and peer group or educational attainment have also been carried out. In later research, studies included the role of school factors (such as organization, teachers, management style, curriculum) in the attainment process, which has led into what is known as research into effective schools.

Though considered a very productive approach, the main criticism of this research has been that progress, especially in methodology (see Sect. 5), has been at the expense of theory and explanatory power. The reason why and through which mechanisms the position of parents in a social hierarchy can affect a student's performance and achievement has thus not been solved: the research has documented mainly the degree to which this pattern exists. Various theoretical approaches have attempted to open this black box and have more or less been subject to empirical research. The influence of parents' attitudes, aspirations, and expectations was initially seen as the main determinant of educational success. Later, theories on conformity values, language codes, cultural reproduction, social capital, and networks were proposed. The limitation of space restricts the elaboration of these explanations of differential educational success. It must be noted, however, that empirical support for these explanations is not always impressive. Little research has been done to test the combined effects of different or alternative explanations.

A main characteristic of these attainment studies in stages of the life-cycle is the application of models using individual longitudinal data. One of the objections to Jencks's famous *Inequality* study (Jencks et al. 1972) was to the lack of such data. A replication of this study revealed that the influence of family and schooling on earnings becomes much stronger over time, when based on longitudinal data (Jencks and Bartlett 1979).

The above approach to the study of stratification and education is typically an individualized one. The personal characteristics of the family and the student are assumed to determine to what extent he or she may be successful in school and career. Contextual information is introduced into the models at the level of interaction with peers or teachers, but a job will only be attained in competition with others, and an employer will only pay the wage that is reasonable in certain labor markets. Thus the strength of these models, that is, the rigorous testing of hypotheses by conducting appropriate analyses, is at the same time its weakness: structural and institutional effects are left out.

Others have emphasized precisely these institutional aspects. Boudon (1974) developed a dynamic model of educational and social opportunity that accounts for the increase of numbers of students with higher educational credentials. He demonstrated that an increase in educational opportunities is not necessarily matched with an increase in occupational opportunities, because at the structural level only a fixed number of vacancies (opportunities) are available. A similar point was made by Thurow (1975), who argued that employers do not select according to the absolute educational level attained, but on the relative position of an individual within a queue of applicants. Although these views have been challenged, they do direct attention to the possible importance of the institutional aspects of stratification.

3. Schools and Stratification

Schools may contribute to different educational outcomes in various ways. A stronger selection of students according to previous performance at entrance to schools (input) will raise the level of educational outcomes. As this level of performance is highly correlated with social backgrounds, the selective schools will become less heterogeneous. Within these schools, therefore, the effect of social background on educational outcomes will decrease, if not disappear. Thus the reduction of social variation within schools can be seen as a result of restricted admission, which might explain the absence of strong correlations between social background and performance at the highest educational levels (restriction of range).

However, this raises the question of whether the school is a neutral institution that only transmits inequality from the parents' generation to that of the child. Does the school act independently to weaken or reinforce the effects of stratification? Do educational outcomes still vary, having controlled for the social composition of the student body? The influence of school factors, such as organization, curriculum, or general well-being has been the focus of much school effectiveness research. In general these factors contribute up to 10 to 15 percent of the variance in addition to that already accounted for by other influences.

Research has shown that sometimes interesting contextual effects show up after controlling for student body composition. For example, Coleman and Hoffer (1987) confirmed earlier studies which focused on the higher relative performance of students in Catholic schools in the United States. Similar results were reported in Scotland by McPherson and Willms (1986),

and again the question arises as to how these findings can be explained. Coleman and Hoffer (1987) have argued that stronger Catholic social capital and networks explain the difference; the Scottish authors suggest that the minority status of Catholics may be the cause. Other research, however, has resulted in inconsistent contextual effects of school, religious background, or neighborhood.

Multilevel techniques that separate the effects of individual and school variation are becoming the appropriate tools to study the issue of whether schools reinforce or weaken the ties between stratification and education. It is still too early to determine whether school effects are substantive, and to what extent they relate to properties of the school (tracking, denominational, selectivity) or of the school system (comprehensiveness).

4. Educational Systems and Stratification

Educational systems throughout the world show a large variety of structures. Systems vary with regard to the length of compulsory schooling, but also on the age that different curriculum tracks have to be chosen by the student. Some systems are decentralized, while others are highly centralized; some have little or no selection for entry, while others are very selective at early ages. It might well be that for any given society the variation in system characteristics coincides with the strength of stratification effects on education. Such inference, however, cannot be found by simply studying the blueprints of educational structures in detail, as has often been done in the past. Whether the correlation between social background and educational achievement or performance varies between educational systems can only be established by empirical research. This, however, assumes the availability of large-scale cross-national data sets with equivalent measures and samples. Unfortunately these types of data are rare and very expensive to collect.

The various IEA (International Association for the Evaluation of Educational Achievement) studies, some in more than 40 countries, are one exception, but little attention has been given to the stratification issue. The study of Passow and et al. (1976) attempted to establish the relationship between average academic performance and educational system characteristics using country as the unit of analysis. They found no clear relationships, possibly because the variation between countries is much smaller than that within countries. Keeves et al. (1991) conducted a study on individual student IEA data for the 10 countries which participated in the two science studies in 1970–71 and 1983–84. They reported that educational expansion has resulted in a general increase of educational opportunity, particularly in Sweden with a marked equality policy.

An alternative approach is the application of large-scale national surveys that contain data on the social background and education of respondents and their parents. These data usually are collected from individuals between 15 and 65 years old, so one can compare the relationship between social background and education for persons born in the same year in several countries. Though the number of variables in past surveys of this kind is restricted (and usually only contains achievement and no measures of performance), this cohort approach leads to interesting findings over a long time-span. In standardized analyses the change in educational opportunity seems to be comparable and constant over time for many Western countries. Exceptions to this rule are Sweden and the Netherlands where opportunities seem to have increased (Shavit and Blossfeld 1993).

Such studies on the level of educational opportunity over time become more interesting when used to evaluate the effects of specific educational transformations. Sato (1991) studied the educational system in Japan, which was transformed after 1945 from a highly selective system to a nonselective secondary school system. She concluded that while social selection in secondary education had diminished, it returned again at the university level. In this respect the system preserved its social selection mechanism, only at a later age.

In Eastern and Central Europe, great social changes took place after the Second World War. The transformation to state socialist societies with much emphasis on equal opportunity implied that the old educational systems had to be abolished and replaced by systems where selection on social grounds would not occur. Education was seen as the engine of social change and greater social justice. Unfortunately no evaluations are available on the effectiveness of these massive educational reforms. When comparing the educational achievement of generations from before and after the great transformations, the average absolute educational level has increased for every younger generation. The transformation itself provided an expansion of opportunity, but the anticipated relative improvement for lower-class children has not been observed at all. Patterns of inequality proved to be the same and almost constant over time in Hungary, Czechoslovakia, and Poland, but also in the Netherlands, where no educational change was introduced during the period under study (Peschar 1991). In fact the old patterns of school choice and achievement hardly changed, in spite of explicit policies (e.g., quota systems) to promote better individual chances for children from working-class families. New studies are underway to evaluate the effects of the 1990 breakdown of the communist regimes in Central Europe.

A few studies have focused on cross-national differences in the qualification structure of countries and the consequences of these structures for educational careers. Müller et al. (1989) concluded in their nine-country study that nations which have a relatively low degree of credentialism (as in the United Kingdom or Poland) show a low degree of class inequality and educational opportunity. In other nations (as Germany, France, or Hungary) the association between qualification and class position seemed to be stronger. This suggests that there are structural and institutional effects present. Also Allmendinger (1989) shows that the effects of educational attainment on occupational rewards are clearly dependent on characteristics of the educational system. For example, the relation is stronger in more stratified educational systems.

These latter studies underline the relevance of context and social structure when comparing educational systems and their outcomes. Studies on many countries from a macro perspective, with aggregated data, are unlikely to find much variation between systems. In addition to the ecological fallacy, one should be careful not to generalize from cross-national comparisons from one point in time, to developments over time in a comparative perspective. The best strategy would seem to be one which is restricted to an intensive study of a few countries over a longer period of time (Blom 1995).

5. Methodological Issues

The area of stratification and education is a crossroad between subject matter and methodology and statistics. Path analysis and structural equation modeling were applied first in the study of this research problem (Blau and Duncan 1967, Featherman and Hauser 1978). These developments resulted in numerous studies on the effects of social background on education, which later served as bases for large-scale evaluation programs in compensatory education.

The analysis of mobility tables, or more generally panel data, was taken up again in the beginning of the 1980s when log-linear modeling was developed (Hagenaars 1990). This procedure has led to particular progress in the area of comparative studies. To study, for instance, the effects of educational reform on social equality one needs data on educational attainment and social background for different birth cohorts. When comparing before- and after-reform cohorts, the effects of the reform can be tested rigorously with log-linear analysis, and the absolute and relative educational improvement can be identified and measured (for an application on Eastern Europe see Peschar 1991).

By 1990 more attention was being devoted to the analysis of complete life histories over time. Event history analysis has proven to be a powerful tool to investigate the role of education in career attainments for different generations (Blossfeld and Rowler 1995) (see *Biographical Research Methods*).

The development of multilevel models has been referred to previously. It may be expected that the further advancement of these models will make possible the separation of effects on the individual by factors at different contextual levels more precise (Bryk and Raudenbush 1992).

The growth of knowledge about stratification and education has been facilitated by the development of information technology. Apart from newly designed statistical techniques, the manipulation and processing of large data sets with numerous variables from one or more countries is now possible. This is most important as research in this area heavily depends on the (re-)analysis of existing (census) data. In addition, large (inter)national surveys about the labor market can now be made accessible for this type of research problem.

Finally, new standards and coding systems for occupations and key attainments in educational careers have been developed. Occupations can now be coded using the *International Standard Classification of Occupations* (ISCO) of the International Labour Organisation, and coding is being implemented by most national central bureaus of statistics. Sophisticated systems allow the transformation of the ISCO code into most other major coding systems, such as Treimans' international prestige scale or the EGP (Popping 1991). It is only a matter of time before the same will hold for information from the *International Standard Classification of Education* (ISCED).

See also: Family and School Environmental Measures; Family and Schooling; Effective Schools Research: Methodological Issues; Measurement of Social Background; Social Mobility, Social Stratification, and Education; Trends in Qualitative Research Methods; Trends in Quantitative Research Methods

References

Allmendinger J 1989 Educational systems and labor market outcomes. *Eur. Sociol. Rev.* 5: 231–50

Blau P, Duncan O D 1967 *The American Occupational Structure*. Wiley, New York

Blom S V 1995 *Intellectuele vorming in Nederland en Frankrijk (Intellectual Development in the Netherlands and France)*. Wolters-Noordhoff, Groningen

Blossfeld H-P, Rowler G 1995 *Techniques of Event History Modelling: New Approaches to Causal Analysis*. Erlbaum, Mahwah, New Jersey

Boudon R 1974 *Education, Opportunity, and Social Inequality*. Wiley, New York

Breiger R L (ed.) 1991 *Social Mobility and Social Structure*. Cambridge University Press, Cambridge, Massachusetts

Bryk A S, Raudenbush S W 1992 *Hierarchical Linear Models: Applications and Data Analysis Methods*. Sage, Newbury Park, California

Coleman J S, Hoffer T 1987 *Public and Private High Schools. The Impact of Communities*. Basic Books, New York

Erikson R, Goldthorpe J H 1992 *The Constant Flux: A Study of Class Mobility*. Clarendon Press, Oxford

Featherman D L, Hauser R M 1978 *Opportunity and Change*. Academic Press, New York

Ganzeboom H B G, Luijkx R, Treiman D J 1989 Intergenerational class mobility in comparative perspective. *Research in Social Stratification and Mobility* 9: 3–85

Goldstein H 1987 *Multilevel Models in Educational and Social Research*. Oxford University Press, New York

Hagenaars J A 1990 *Categorial Longitudinal Data: Loglinear Panel, Trend and Cohort Analysis*. Sage, Newbury Park, California

Jencks C S, Bartlett S 1979 *Who Gets Ahead? The Determinants of Economic Success in America*. Basic Books, New York

Jencks C S et al. 1972 *Inequality: A Reassessment of the Effect of Family and Schooling In America*. Basic Books, New York

Keeves J P, Morgenstern C, Saha L J 1991 Educational expansion and equality of opportunity: Evidence from studies conducted by IEA in ten countries in 1970–71 and 1983–84. *Int. J. Educ. Res.* 15(1): 61–80

McPherson A, Willms J D 1986 Certification, class conflict, religion, and community: A socio-historical explanation of the effectiveness of contemporary schools. *Research in Sociology of Education and Socialisation* 6: 227–302

Müller W, Lüttinger P, Koenig W, Karle W 1989 Class and education in industrial nations. *Int. J. Sociol.* 19: 3–39

Müller W, Ishida H, Ridge J 1995 Class Origin, Class Destination and Education *Am. J. Sociol.* 101: 145–93

Passow A H, Noah H J, Eckstein M A, Mallea J R 1976 *The National Case Study: An Empirical Comparative Study of Twenty-One Educational Systems*. Almqvist and Wiksell, Stockholm

Peschar J L 1991 Educational opportunities in East–West perspective: A comparative analysis of the Netherlands, Hungary, Poland and Czechoslovakia. *Int. J. Educ. Res.* 15(1): 107–121

Popping R 1991 *A Knowledge-Based System for Occupational Classifications*. iecProGAMMA, Groningen

Sato J 1991 Family background and school continuation decisions in Japan *Int. J. Educ. Res.* 15: 81–105

Shavit Y, Blossfeld H-P 1993 *Persistent Inequality. Changing Educational Attainment in Thirteen Countries*. Westview Press, Boulder, Colorado

Thurow L 1975 *Generating Inequality. Mechanisms of Distribution in the US Economy*. Basic Books, New York

Treiman D J (ed.) 1977 *Occupational Prestige in Comparative Perspective*. Academic Press, New York

Treiman D J Ganzeboom H B G 1990 Cross-national comparative status attainment research. *Research in Social Stratification and Mobility*. 9: 105–27

Further Reading

Erikson R, Jonsson, J O (eds.) 1996 *Can Education be Equalized? The Swedish Case in Comparative Perspective*. Westerview Press, Boulder, Colorado

Müller D K, Ringer F, Simon B (eds.) 1987 *The Rise of the Modern Educational System: Structural Change and Social Reproduction 1870–1921*. Cambridge University Press, Cambridge

The Structure of Educational Systems

Introduction: The Organizational Structure of Educational Systems

L. J. Saha

By organizational structure, social scientists refer to stable and enduring features of a social system. Although there is a wide range of understandings as to what is meant by organizational structure, it is here taken in a strict sense to refer to the more or less deliberate arrangements according to which activities are ordered. In this context one can include bureaucracies of all types, companies, firms, and the like. Thus the relations of authority, communication, and career patterns are all examples of the ways behavior is structured in organizations. Sociologists of education continue to be influenced by the ideas of Weber (1946) in their understanding of educational organizational structures, and in particular the notion of bureaucratic or rational structures upon which to plan efficient and effective decision-making and career processes in schools.

Educational systems are structured activities, and schools are types of formal organizations with both formal and informal structures. Sociologists of education have directed considerable attention to the ways that educational systems and schools are organized. The study of educational administration is one of the more dominant fields in which the organizational structures are the focal point of teaching and research.

The organization of education systems and schools affects both students, teachers, administrators, and education systems. The 15 articles in this section are divided into two groups: those relating to the ways that students are organized in the process of schooling and those relating to the structure of schooling itself.

1. The Organization of Students

One of the characteristics of Western schooling is the way that students are grouped according to age and, sometimes, according to ability. As noted by Oakes and Heckman (*Age Grouping of Students*), the practice of age grouping emerged in Europe and the United States in the seventeenth and eighteenth centuries and was based on the notion that it was beneficial for the learning process and made the task of teachers easier. On the other hand, Oakes notes that the practice of ability grouping is of more recent origin and is based on the assumption that students with different capacities to learn require separate treatments in terms of curriculum and teaching methods (*Ability Grouping and Tracking in Schools*). Both of these organizational practices have been the subject of much research and debate, both on ideological and pedagogical grounds.

Similar observations might be made about the incorporation of discipline in school practices. As Lewis points out in *Discipline in Schools*, there have been at least three models or approaches to the problem of discipline: influence, management, and control. Each reflects an approach to structuring the experience of students in schools, and each has been the subject of ideological and pedagogical debate.

Finally, the important area of equality between the sexes depends on the structuring of the experience of males and females in schools. As Sadker and Sadker point out (*Sex Equity: Assumptions and Strategies*), the choice of textbooks, the structuring of teacher–student interaction, and the academic reward system are three strategic focal points where the equality of experience between males and females can be built into the organizational structure of schools.

2. The Organization of Schooling

The general organization of schooling is addressed by 11 articles which can be loosely grouped into three: the formal organizational structure of schools, the organization of access into schools, and the organization of educational provision.

The first is represented by four articles, Mitchell and Treiman's *Authority and Power in Educational Organizations*, Wong's *Bureaucracy and School Effectiveness*, Lee's *Effective Secondary Schools*, and Sturman's *Loose Coupling and Educational Systems*. In each of these, attention is directed to the manner in which the decision-making processes in schools are structured, and these include questions of hierarchical versus shared decision-making structures within schools, and centralized versus decentralized structures between the school and community. Sturman's discussion of loose coupling in the organizational structure of schools is particularly relevant, since the concept helps understand what is sometimes called "slippage" in the structure, that is, the extent to which the forces of autonomy and independence work against tight administrative control. These aspects of school organization have clear relevance for the experience of administrators, teachers, and students, who interact within and between schools, and also the interaction between schools and their communities.

The structuring of school access is addressed by Lockheed and Lee's discussion of sex segregation in schooling (*Coeducation versus Single-sex Schooling*), Anderson's discussion of public and private schools (*Public and Private Schools: Sociological Perspectives*), and Oxenham's and Farrells's focus upon policies which concern equal access to schools (*Equality, Policies for Educational; Social Equality and Educational Planning in Developing Nations*).

The organization of educational provision is not unrelated to access, but focuses more specifically on the availability of schooling, the resourcing of schooling, and the flexibilities for students to change options once they have embarked upon their educational careers. In this context, Dronkers and van der Ploeg document the rapid expansion of schooling in a global context (*Educational Expansion: Sociological Perspectives*), while Monk addresses the equitable resourcing of schools once they are established (*Resource Allocation in Schools and School Systems*). Finally, Yogev addresses an issue often neglected in the study of educational organizational structures, and this relates to the "openness" of the structure to allow students a range of options after they have begun their educational careers. In *Second Chance Education and Alternative Routes*, Yogev documents some international differences in the permeability of educational structures and relates this aspect of educational organizations to school dropouts and other forms of inefficiencies to individuals and societies.

The study of educational organizations from a sociological perspective is an important and rich source of data for understanding the performance of educational systems for societies as a whole. As reflected in the articles in this section, within the sociology of education there is a wide range of important organizational questions which structure the educational experience of administrators, teachers, and students. Because organizational structures are changeable through policy decisions, many school reform programs are addressed to this level in an attempt to direct the performance of educational structures to achieve desired goals and objectives.

References

Weber M 1946 *From Max Weber: Essays in Sociology*. Oxford University Press, New York

(a) The Organization of Students

Ability Grouping and Tracking in Schools

J. Oakes

Since the early part of the twentieth century, schools in the United States and most other developed nations have separated students into groups, classrooms, programs of study, or schools according to indicators of their intellectual ability or promise. This widespread practice has seemed logical because it responds to a century-old conviction that students' capacities differ sufficiently to require distinct curricula and separate instruction. In developed, industrialized nations this educational differentiation also has conformed to societal expectations that schools will prepare students for a differentiated economy that requires workers with diverse knowledge and skills. By and large, educators and publics have generally viewed ability-related grouping practices as both democratic and functional. This article reviews the state of knowledge about these practices within comprehensive schools, including their academic and social consequences (for a more comprehensive review, see Oakes et al. 1992a).

1. What is Ability Grouping and Tracking?

In the United States (in contrast to countries such as Japan), ability grouping begins very early. A number of school systems administer "readiness" tests to determine which 5-year olds should be placed in academically focused kindergartens and which should be placed in less demanding classes. Many systems use such tests (often in combination with teacher recommendations) to guide first grade placements. Elementary schools in the United States exhibit a wide range of ability-related grouping practices, including grouping within classes or regrouping among classes (sometimes across grade levels) for selected subjects (such as reading and mathematics) and assigning students to self-contained ability-homogeneous classrooms for the whole day (Slavin 1987). The virtual absence of grouping by ability within or among classrooms in Japanese elementary and junior high schools differs conspicuously from practices in the United States and many European countries (Cummings 1980, Rohlen 1983).

Many comprehensive secondary schools assign students to each class separately, using measures of their ability in each subject; others enroll students in blocks of classes relying on general ability measures. By age 14, most students are members of curriculum "tracks" that are comprised of sequences of courses intended to prepare them for different postsecondary destinations; simultaneously, students enroll in different "levels" of those academic subjects taken by all students (Oakes 1985). Offering different tracks within comprehensive high schools is the most common practice in the United States, while most other nations, including Japan and West Germany, typically sort students into different schools (e.g., public, academically-oriented high schools; public vocational schools; private academic high schools) (Rohlen 1983, Kariya and Rosenbaum 1987). A few nations, including the United Kingdom and Israel, provide both comprehensive and specialized schools.

2. Effects on Academic and Social Outcomes

Since the 1930s, researchers have amassed numerous studies on ability grouping and tracking. While much of this work investigates whether these methods enhance achievement, a significant and growing number of studies investigate their social implications. These latter studies consider how ability grouping and tracking affect students' attitudes, peer associations, and educational and occupational careers.

2.1 Impact on Achievement

Conventional wisdom holds that brighter students race ahead when they are taught separately, and that students with lesser abilities profit from being insulated in classes where teachers target instruction to their deficiencies. However, the bulk of evidence contradicts both assumptions. In most instances, ability grouping and tracking fails to boost learning outcomes. Whole-class grouping of elementary students provides no measurable achievement benefits for any group —high-, average-, or low-achieving—over ability-heterogeneous classes. Some limited and flexible regrouping schemes yield positive effects on average achievement in the elementary grades (particularly plans that promote student mobility between "levels" with a multigrade structure): however they also create achievement inequalities. Children in high groups benefit most, and those in low groups least. Over time, the gap between them widens (Barr and Dreeben 1983, Gamoran 1986, Slavin 1987).

Similarly, research comparing grouped and ungrouped secondary programs fails to demonstrate the efficacy of ability-groups or tracking. A meta-analysis by Kulik and Kulik (1982) indicates a small positive effect on average achievement. However, most reviews of controlled studies that compare grouped and ungrouped settings do not find this trend (Slavin 1990). For example, Slavin (1990) concludes that no group of secondary students benefits academically from being in ability grouped or tracked classes.

At the same time, studies employing large-scale survey data to compare the outcomes of high- and low-track students within tracked secondary schools (employing controls for student background and prior achievement) find increasing disparities between high- and low-track students as time goes by (see, e.g., US studies by Hotchkiss and Dorsten 1987, Vanfossen et al. 1987, Lee and Bryk 1988, and Gamoran and Mare 1989; UK analyses by Kerckhoff 1986; and Israeli research by Shavit and Featherman 1988, and Yoger 1981).

The seeming contradiction between these two types of studies can be better understood in view of the fact that tracked schools both separate students, and, as will be described below, provide considerable advantages to the top groups. Moreover, in tracked schools, high-track students' within-class advantages are augmented by their completion of more academic courses (Lee and Bryk 1988).

2.2 Effects on Students' Associations and Attitudes

Grouping and tracking create social as well as academic divisions among students. Hallinan and Sorensen (1985) found, for example, that elementary students were more likely to choose "best friends" from their classroom ability groups, and that the overlap between group membership and friendship networks increased over time. Secondary students' friendship networks also tend to coincide with their ability group levels (Hargreaves 1967, Lacey 1970, Rosenbaum 1976).

Researchers in the United Kingdom report that secondary students exhibit "polarized" attitudes, with high-stream students more pro-school and those in the low stream more resistant. Most studies in the United States agree that high-track students show greater enthusiasm for school than their low-track peers (Rosenbaum 1976). Whether grouping actually causes these attitude differences remains uncertain, since Waitrowski et al.'s (1982) longitudinal analyses found no such track-related effects.

2.3 Implications for Educational Careers and Attainment

Track membership has a long-lasting influence on educational attainment and, indirectly, on life chances. In this regard, grouping practices in the United States are probably less restrictive than those in countries such as Japan and Germany where the type of high school one attends virtually determines the postsecondary experience one can expect.

Nevertheless, research supports the claim that, even in comprehensive schools, ability-related placements influence students' future educational opportunities and life chances, independent of subsequent achievement. Mobility between ability levels at both the elementary and secondary levels is limited, suggesting that early grouping largely determines succeeding placements. College-track membership increases students' likelihood of high school graduation (Waitrowski et al. 1982, Hotchkiss and Dorsten 1987, Vanfossen et al. 1987). Gamoran and Mare (1989) show that, other things being equal, college-track students are about 10 percent more likely to graduate.

Research also casts doubt on claims that vocational tracks enhance students' educational attainment or subsequent opportunities. Shavit and Williams (1985) found that, except for very low-achieving students, vocational education in Israel failed to keep students in school longer than their counterparts in academic programs. Most studies in the United States find that vocational course completion falls short of helping students secure training-related employment, avoid unemployment, or command higher wages than other high school graduates.

Finally, academic-track students more often aspire to and actually enroll in college than otherwise similar high school students. Further, track effects persist through college: academic-track graduates complete college at higher rates than nonacademic-track peers with comparable college-going plans, pre-college test scores, and early college grades (Velez 1985).

3. Ability Grouping and Tracking as Opportunity Structures

In addition to examining grouping effects on student outcomes, research has also investigated how ability grouping and tracking function as "opportunity structures" within schools that enhance or limit students' access to knowledge, teachers, and classroom learning opportunities. In the United States, researchers have been particularly interested in whether these practices create schooling inequalities that mirror, and perhaps perpetuate, social and economic inequalities related to race and class.

3.1 Access to Curriculum

Ability grouping propels elementary school children through the curriculum at different speeds—even though slower groups typically claim the rather illogical goal of helping students "catch up." Differences in pace through a sequenced curriculum (particularly in mathematics and reading) lead to differences in coverage. In reading, for example, low groups spend relatively more time on decoding activities, whereas high groups move on to consider the meanings of stories (Hiebert 1983). The high-group advantage accumulates as the years pass, and students with a history of membership in high-ability groups are more likely to have covered considerably more material by the end of elementary school.

In this way, elementary school ability grouping influences much of what students experience later. Pace and coverage differences result in low-group students falling further and further behind, and, receiving increasingly different curricula (Barr and Dreeben 1983, Gamoran 1986). Before long, students in slower groups lack the prerequisite curricular experiences needed to qualify for or to succeed in faster or higher groups. Moreover, they are likely to have internalized the judgement that they are less able and less likely to succeed, and, as a consequence, are no longer eager to put forth the hard work it might take to do well in a higher ability class.

Early in secondary school, there begins an intentional shift away from the goal of propelling children through the same curriculum at different speeds. Instead, schools change their "curricular intentions" for students. Now, not only is the speed different, but so is the substance. Courses with different names—sometimes prefixed with "basic," "regular," "pre-," "honors," or "gifted"—are clearly different in both content and rigor. Lower-track classes maintain no pretense of preparing students to move into higher tracks.

Lower track secondary courses consistently offer less demanding topics and skills, while high-track courses typically include more complex material (Hargreaves 1967, Keddie 1971, Burgess 1983, Oakes 1985). In a large-scale national study, Oakes (1990) also found that teachers of low-track mathematics and science place less importance than teachers of higher level classes on students' learning science concepts, developing interest in mathematics and science, gaining inquiry and problem-solving skills, and being prepared for further study in these subjects. Remarkably, such goals need not depend on students' prior knowledge or skills. On the contrary, these goals are increasingly considered essential for all. These findings complement earlier work documenting that high-track teachers in most subjects more often stress competent and autonomous thinking, while low-track teachers tend to place greater emphasis on rule-following (Oakes 1985). Such studies describe clear national patterns. At the same time, however, interpretive research provides considerable insight into local variations (Page and Valli 1990, Page 1991).

3.2 Teachers and Teaching

Ability groups and tracks exhibit differences in teaching consistent with documented curricular differences. Typically, teachers allocate less time to instruction

(compared to routines, discipline, and socializing) in low tracks, and learning activities more often consist of drill and practice emphasizing trivial bits of information, seatwork, and worksheets (Oakes 1985). Technology in low tracks is most often used in conjunction with low-level tasks, such as computation. Computer activities, for example, often mimic texts and worksheets (Oakes 1990).

The allocation of teaching assignments most often results in low-track students having less exposure than their high-track peers to well-qualified teachers. For example, Oakes (1990) found teachers of secondary low-ability science and mathematics classes to be less experienced, and less likely to be certified or hold degrees in mathematics or science, have less training in the use of computers, and less often report themselves to be "master teachers" than their colleagues in upper track classes. These patterns frequently result from a jockeying among teachers for high-track assignments, or from principals' use of class assignments as rewards and sanctions (Hargreaves 1967, McPartland and Crain 1987). In both the United States and the United Kingdom, teachers tend to prefer high-ability classes because students are more amenable to academic demands (Hargreaves 1967, Lacey 1970, Ball 1981).

3.3 Classroom Social Relationships

Researchers also find track-related differences in the relationships and general climates of classrooms. Vanfossen et al. (1987) note that college-track students are more likely than others to describe their teachers as patient, respectful, and enjoying their work. Consistently, Oakes (1985) documents a greater emphasis on discipline and control in lower track compared with upper track classes. Related differences included greater student disruption, hostility, and alienation in low-track classes. Here, too, however, qualitative studies supplement these general patterns from survey research by describing situations under which lower track classes have emphasized caring over conflict, and learning over control (Page and Valli 1990).

4. Connections Between Group Placement, Race, and Social Class

Assignment of elementary students to groups and classes follows from formal assessments (usually tests) of students' aptitudes, readiness, and past achievement, and from informal observations of students' classroom performance and behaviors. Formally at least, grouping in high schools permits a high degree of choice. However, researchers question the extent to which students actually chose their tracks, even when they report having done so. In England, for example, Ball (1981) describes practices in which students' choices almost always followed the school staff's recommendations, and educators in the United States consistently report that other criteria accompany and often pre-empt students' preferences: standardized test scores, teacher and counselor recommendations, prior placements, and grades.

In the United States, the students' assignments link to race, ethnicity, and social class, although the links are not sufficiently understood. Early in the twentieth century, low-level academic and vocational training were thought to be more appropriate for immigrant, low-income, and minority youth, while rigorous academic preparation was seen as better meeting the needs of more affluent Whites (Oakes 1985). Few questioned this pattern, just as few questioned the many other social and economic barriers faced by African-American and Latino minorities before the 1960s. In the early 1990s, however, educators and policymakers in the United States express concern about the likely role of ability grouping and tracking in constraining the educational and occupational futures of low-income, African-American, and Latino students, and, in racially mixed schools, perpetuating stereotypes of minority students as less intelligent than Whites.

This concern has been triggered by consistent findings that, from their earliest school years, African-American and Latino students are overrepresented in low-ability groups, remedial classes, and special education programs. Some qualitative studies suggest that elementary teachers are biased against poor children when they assign students to within-class ability groups (Rist 1970). However, quantitative studies fail to support this claim. For example, Sorensen and Hallinan (1984) uncovered no direct effects of race or social class on assignment to ability groups at the elementary level. It appears that schools rely heavily on test results to form and legitimate judgements about elementary students' intellectual capacities, and African-American and Latino students typically perform less well on these measures.

However, test scores may not be as color-blind as they appear. Because children's prior opportunities have considerable influence on test scores, it is not surprising that young children with academically rich preschool and school-like home environments do better on tests and are more likely to be judged as developmentally "ready" for "regular" kindergartens and suited for high-ability first grade classrooms. Thus, tests place low-income and most minority children at a clear disadvantage, since fewer of them have advantaged preschool opportunities. It is therefore no surprise that disproportionate numbers of young minority children are placed in low-ability primary classrooms. Such practices begin a pattern that persists throughout elementary schools.

As students proceed through secondary schools, increasingly disproportionate percentages of African-Americans and Latinos enroll in low-ability tracks (Braddock 1989, Oakes 1990). For example, Oakes (1990) found that in the United States, all-minority secondary schools enroll far greater percentages of students in low-track classes compared to all-White schools. Moreover, racial separation by track within mixed-raced schools across the nation is striking. For example, two-thirds of science and mathematics classes with disproportionately large minority enrollments (compared to the minority representation in the student body as a whole) were low-track classes, compared with only 5 percent of the disproportionately White classes. In contrast, only 9 percent of the disproportionately minority classes were high track, compared to 57 percent of the disproportionately White classes. Results consistent with these findings were observed in a study of middle-school tracking in urban districts, wherein minority students were three times as likely as White students to be enrolled in low-track mathematics classes and Whites were more than one-and-one-half times as likely to be enrolled in high-track classes (Villegas and Watts 1991).

Students' prior achievement most strongly predicts their secondary school track placement—a factor not unrelated to their prior group placements and the opportunities provided therein. In part, then, minority students' disproportionate secondary school placements stem from their diminished opportunities and achievements in low-ability groups and classes in elementary school. Disproportionate placements are exacerbated by schools' reliance on standardized tests in assessing students' achievements and potential. Even though such tests likely underestimate minority students' capabilities, they may carry more weight than information about students' past classroom performance or teachers' recommendations, particularly when students move into new schools where counselors may have little or no contact with students' former teachers (Oakes et al. 1992b, Villegas and Watts 1991).

Most studies also find that race and social class exert a direct, if considerably smaller, effect on track placement. For example, data from the Second International Mathematics Study show that the assignment of United States students with comparable past achievement among four types of eighth grade mathematics courses (algebra, pre-algebra, general, and remedial) varied with students' social background. Girls, Whites, and students whose fathers held high- rather than low-level occupations were more likely to be placed in algebra than were other students (McKnight et al. 1987). In contrast, other researchers have found positive effects of being Black on high school track enrollment, net of social class background and prior achievement (Gamoran and Mare 1989).

Two additional and related factors play a role in creating a racially skewed pattern of placements in the United States. One is the pervasive stereotypical expectations that society and schools hold for students of different social class and racial groups. For example, some research suggests that race and class are linked to track placement because students from different backgrounds receive different information, advice, and attention from guidance counselors. Cicourel and

Kitsuse (1984) observed that, even though counselors consistently assigned low-income students with low grades and test scores to low-ability classes, students exhibiting similar performance, but who were from middle- or high-income families were sometimes placed in higher groups. Oakes et al. (1992b) found school counselors and teachers respond to comparable achievement scores of Asian and Hispanic students quite differently, with Asians far more likely to be placed in advanced classes than Hispanics. In addition, low-track, minority students most often report that others make coursetaking decisions for them (Villegas and Watts 1991).

A second factor likely to skew track placements is the frequent "politicking" by knowledgeable parents who want their children placed in the top classes. Although such parents are not exclusively White, in most schools White parents, especially middle-class White parents, better understand the inequalities in the school structure and feel more confident that the school will respond positively to their pressure (Cicourel and Kitsuse 1984, Oakes et al. 1992b).

Until the late 1980s, most studies have found either no significant relationship between gender and track-placement or that boys had a slight advantage in securing high-track placements (e.g., Alexander et al. 1978). Gamoran and Mare (1989), however, suggest a small but significant advantage for girls. Further, an ethnographic account (Page and Valli 1990) notes that some teachers permit girls who do not make trouble to stay in regular classes, but shift more difficult, equally able girls to a lower track.

Not all researchers agree that students' placements are strongly directed by potentially biased practices, however. For example, Davis and Haller (1981) found that ninth-grade students chose their track levels based on their aspirations and that aspirations were closely linked to ability. The result was a strong association between track level and student ability and a much weaker link between social class and assignment.

In a different vein, other studies emphasize how characteristics of school contexts diminish the influence of individual characteristics—ability, social class, gender, or race—on students' group or track assignments. For example, DeLany (1986) found that the placement of students of different backgrounds in mathematics and science courses at different track levels differed considerably at four high schools as a consequence of schools' tracking policies and the composition of their student bodies. Similarly, Oakes (1990) and Oakes et al. (1992b) found that while schools serving very different populations all tend to offer a full range of tracks, schools with large minority populations typically have larger proportions of low-track academic classes. Even so, because students at these schools typically have lower average test scores, competition for positions in high-track classes is less formidable. (This may partially explain Gamoran and Mare's (1989) finding, noted above,

that Black students in the High School and Beyond sample had a 10% greater chance of being placed in college tracks than White students with comparable prior achievement and social backgrounds.) Garet and DeLany (1988) also found the logistics of creating a master schedule and the limitations of the teaching staff impose constraints on schools' efforts to offer well-developed, separate tracks and on their ability to match students with courses across subject fields. As a consequence, they suggest that placements may be more accurately described as a result of constraints and organizational choices than as a consequence of predetermined placement criteria or individual choices.

5. Ability Grouping and Tracking as a Target of School Reform

Partly because of the disappointing outcomes described above, many policymakers, national opinion leaders, and educators in the United States are adding tracking to the list of school practices that need to be "restructured." Clearly, tracking has not solved the problem of workforce preparation, evidenced by employers' increasing disenchantment with students' knowledge, skills, and attitudes. Rapidly changing work technologies and out-of-date equipment limit middle and high schools' capacities to prepare students with specific occupational skills. And, as more jobs require greater sophistication in literacy, numeracy, and problem-solving, schools are under fire for failing to provide entry-level workers with the academic and thinking competencies that many jobs require. Confidence that a tracked high school curriculum will ready noncollege bound students for work has been shaken. At the same time, sequences of special classes designed to prepare students for college have also come under scrutiny as the nation becomes increasingly concerned that even its "best" students may not be academically competitive with their peers in other countries.

Pressure to eliminate tracking in the United States, however, is not based solely on disillusion with its effectiveness with regard to achievement. Increasingly, policymakers and educators are questioning the fairness of the uneven opportunity structure tracking creates, particularly since many of the most obvious inequalities cannot be justified as educationally appropriate adaptations to variation in students' learning aptitude, speed, or style. Yet, it is not surprising that, when students are separated and provided with different knowledge and learning conditions, students in the top groups experience greater learning gains than the others; lower track students get less and learn less. Most salient in the United States is that this distribution places the burden of such schooling inequalities most heavily on immigrant, low-income, and minority children.

Despite growing dissatisfaction with existing, widespread grouping methods, little research provides specific evidence about the nature of effective and fair approaches for organizing and teaching diverse groups of students in heterogeneous settings, particularly approaches that include a more even distribution of knowledge, resources, and learning opportunities. Neither are there systematic studies of the technically demanding and politically sensitive processes that schools might use to create and implement such alternatives effectively. These are promising avenues for future research.

See also: School and Classroom Dynamics; Stratification in Educational Systems

References

Alexander K L, Cook M A, McDill E L 1978 Curriculum tracking and educational stratification. *Am. Sociol. Rev.* 43: 47–66

Ball S J 1981 *Beachside Comprehensive: A Case-study of Secondary Schooling.* Cambridge University Press, Cambridge

Barr R, Dreeben R 1983 *How Schools Work.* University of Chicago Press, Chicago, Illinois

Braddock J H 1989 *Tracking of Black, Hispanic, Asian, Native American and White Students: National Patterns and Trends.* Johns Hopkins University, Center for Research on Effective Schooling for Disadvantaged Students, Baltimore, Maryland

Burgess R G 1983 *Experiencing Comprehensive Education: A Study of Bishop McGregor School.* Methuen, London

Cicourel A V, Kitsuse J I 1963 *The Educational Decision-Makers.* Bobbs Merrill, Indianapolis, Indiana

Cummings W 1980 *Education and Equality in Japan.* Princeton University Press, Princeton, New Jersey

Davis S A, Haller E J 1981. Tracking ability and SES: Further evidence on the "revisionist–meritocratic debate." *Am. J. Educ.* 89(3): 283–304

DeLany B 1986 Choices and chances: The matching of students and courses in high school. Doctoral dissertation, Stanford University, Stanford, California

Gamoran A 1986 Instructional and institutional effects of ability grouping. *Sociol. Educ.* 59(4): 185–98

Gamoran A, Mare R D 1989 Secondary school tracking and educational inequality: Compensation, reinforcement, or neutrality? *Am. J. Sociol.* 94(5): 1146–83

Garet M, DeLany B 1988 Students, courses, and stratification. *Sociol. Educ.* 61(2): 61–77

Hallinan M T, Sorensen A B 1985 Ability grouping and student friendships. *Am. Educ. Res. J.* 22(4): 485–99

Hargreaves D H 1967 *Social Relations in a Secondary School.* Routledge and Kegan Paul, London

Hiebert E H 1983 An examination of ability grouping for reading instruction. *Read. Res. Q.* 18(2): 231–55

Hotchkiss L, Dorsten L 1987 Curriculum effects on early post high school outcomes. In: Corwin R G (ed.) 1987 *Sociology of Education and Socialization.* JAI Press, Greenwich, Connecticut

Kariya T, Rosenbaum J E 1987 Self-selection in Japanese junior high schools. *Sociol. Educ.* 60: 168–80

Keddie N 1971 Classroom knowledge. In: Young M F D (ed.) 1971 *Knowledge and Control.* Collier–Macmillan, London

Kerckhoff A C 1986 Effects of ability grouping in British secondary schools. *Am. Sociol. Rev.* 51(6): 842–58

Kulik C L, Kulik J 1982 Effects of ability grouping on secondary school students: A meta-analysis of evaluation findings. *Am. Educ. Res. J.* 19(3): 415–28

Lacey C 1970 *Hightown Grammar: The School as a Social System.* Manchester University Press, Manchester

Lee V E, Bryk A S 1988 Curriculum tracking as mediating the social distribution of high school achievement. *Sociol. Educ.* 61(2): 78–94

McKnight C C et al. 1987 *The Underachieving Curriculum: Assessing US School Mathematics from an International Perspective.* Stipes Publishing Co., Champaign, Illinois

McPartlan J M, Crain R L 1987 Evaluating the trade-offs in student outcomes from alternative school organization policies. In: Hallinan M T (ed.) 1987 *The Social Organization of Schools: New Conceptualizations of the Learning Process.* Plenum, New York

Oakes J 1985 *Keeping Track: How Schools Structure Inequality.* Yale University Press, New Haven, Connecticut

Oakes J 1990 *Multiplying Inequalities: The Effects of Race, Social Class, and Tracking on Opportunities to Learn Math and Science.* The RAND Corporation, Santa Monica, California

Oakes J, Gamoran A, Page R N 1992a Curriculum differentiation: Opportunities, outcomes, and meanings. In: Jackson P (ed.) 1992 *Handbook of Research on Curriculum.* Macmillan, New York

Oakes J, Selvin M, Karoly L, Guiton G 1992b *Educational Matchmaking: Academic and Vocational Tracking in Comprehensive High Schools* The RAND Corporation, Santa Monica, California

Page R 1991 *Low-track Classes.* Teachers College Press, New York

Page R, Valli L 1990 (eds.) *Curriculum Differentiation: Interpretive Studies in US Secondary Schools.* State University of New York Press, Albany, New York

Rist R 1970 Student social class and teacher expectations: The self-fulfilling prophecy in ghetto education. *Harv. Educ. Rev.* 40 (3): 411–51

Rohlen T P 1983 *Japan's High Schools.* University of California Press, Berkeley, California

Rosenbaum J E 1976 *Making Inequality: The Hidden Curriculum of High School Tracking.* Wiley, New York

Shavit Y, Featherman D L 1988 Schooling, tracking, and teenage intelligence. *Sociol. Educ.* 61: 42–51

Shavit Y, Williams R 1985 Ability grouping and contextual determinants of educational expectations in Israel. *Am. Sociol. Rev.* 50 (1): 62–73

Slavin R E 1987 Ability grouping and student achievement in elementary schools: A best-evidence synthesis. *Rev. Educ. Res.* 57 (3): 293–336

Slavin R E 1990 *Achievement Effects of Ability Grouping in Secondary Schools: A Best-Evidence Synthesis.* Wisconsin Center for Education Research, Madison, Wisconsin

Sorensen A B, Hallinan M T 1984 Race effects on the assignment to ability groups. In: Peterson P L, Wilkerson L C, Hallinan M T (eds.) 1984 *The Social Context of Instruction.* Academic Press, San Diego, California

Vanfossen B E, Jones J D, Spade J Z 1987 Curriculum tracking and status maintenance. *Sociol. Educ.* 60 (2): 104–22

Velez W 1985 Finishing college: The effects of college type. *Sociol. Educ.* 58 (3): 191–200

Villegas A M, Watts S M 1991 Life in the classroom: The influence of class placement and student race/ethnicity. Paper presented at the annual meeting of the American Educational Research Association, Chicago, Illinois, April

Wiatrowski M D, Hansell S, Massey C R, Wilson D L 1982 Curriculum tracking and delinquency. *Am. Sociol. Rev.* 47: 151–60

Yogev A 1981 Determinants of early educational career in Israel: Further evidence for the sponsorship thesis. *Sociol. Educ.* 54: 181–95

Further Reading

Metz M H 1978 *Classrooms and Corridors: The Crisis of*

Authority in Desegregated Secondary Schools. University of California Press, Berkeley, California

Gamoran A, Berends M 1987 The effects of stratification in secondary schools: Synthesis of survey and ethnographic research. *Rev. Educ. Res.* 57 (4): 415–35

Husén T 1974 *Talent, Equality and Meritocracy.* Nijhoff, The Hague

Powell A, Farrar E, Cohen D K 1986 *The Shopping Mall High School: Winners and Losers in the Educational Marketplace.* Houghton-Mifflin, Boston, Massachusetts

Rosenbaum J E 1980 Social implications of educational grouping. In: Berliner D C (ed.) 1980 *Rev. Res. Educ.* 8: 361–401

Svensson N E 1962 *Ability Grouping and Scholastic Achievement.* Almqvist and Wiksell, Stockholm

Age Grouping of Students

J. Oakes and P. E. Heckman

Since the mid-nineteenth century, most schools have placed students into groups with the objective of reducing student variability, thereby easing the teaching task. While most choose to place children of the same age together into grades, multigraded and nongraded school structures are alternatives that yield at least comparable achievement outcomes and nearly always enhance social growth. Many of these alternative ways of grouping students attempt to pursue simultaneously the goals of reduced variability and of increased individualization. New knowledge about learning, however, combined with the increased diversity of school populations, has prompted educators to reconsider these goals as well as the practices they have spawned.

1. The Age-graded School

Age-graded schooling practices first emerged in Europe and the United States during the late seventeenth and early eighteenth centuries, replacing a less formalized arrangement whereby children and young adults learned together with a single schoolmaster over several years (Aries 1962). Over time, the practice of separating students into age-specific classrooms, each with its prescribed and standardized curriculum, brought a specialized and hierarchical structure into schools. Each grade level's work was a building block necessary to construct an educated adult. By the late nineteenth century, age-graded schools mimicked practices in newly bureaucratized factories, where manufacturing was being made more "scientific" and efficient by being broken down into discrete steps to ensure the uniform production of parts that could be

assembled into a whole product (Pratt 1983).

Educators hoped that age-specific groups would decrease the variability of both students and the curriculum and provide a better match between the two. Curriculum guides suggested topics, knowledge and skills, and activities appropriate for each grade, which, in turn, generated textbooks, workbooks, and supplemental materials with grade level designations. Standardized achievement test scores were transformed into grade equivalency scores, so that any child's performance can be interpreted in light of the graded school structure.

Some children of the same age still inevitably learned more quickly than others. In order to reduce this inefficient variability, educators have commonly employed a tracking strategy. Children of the same age and grade are assigned to homogeneous subgroups based on ability, achievement, and/or interest. Children who failed to keep pace with even the slowest groups typically are not promoted to the next grade. The next year, these retained children repeat the curriculum with younger children. Sometimes slower children repeat several grades. Educators have supported these practices in the belief that each curricular building block must be mastered before a new layer of learning can be added; these practices continue to dominate schools.

2. Alternatives to Age Grouping

Goodlad and Anderson (1959) note that educators have questioned these grouping practices and have sought alternatives to the graded school structure since shortly after its formation. The alternatives have included multigrade classrooms, cross-grade regrouping, individualized instruction, and nongraded schools. Like traditional graded structures, these alternatives seek to cope with the variability in achievement, ability, motivation, and interest among learners. Early experimenters—including John Dewey in the United States, Peter Petersen in Germany, Maria Montessori in Switzerland, and the founders of the British infant and primary schools—sought alternatives that mitigate the problems associated with variability by promoting students' social, personal, and cognitive development.

2.1 Multigrade/Combination Classes

In many nations, schools place children from two or three grade levels together in "combination" classes, most often to keep classes at roughly the same size. Similarly, small schools with few students at each grade level combine classes, especially in sparsely populated rural areas of the United States, Canada, and many developing nations. Most multigrade classes depart only slightly from traditional age-grading, since teachers usually teach students as distinct subgroups and work with them on "grade-level" material.

2.2 Nongraded Schooling

With the publication of *The Nongraded Elementary School* in 1959, Goodlad and Anderson created a comprehensive model for elementary education in the United States that drew upon prior American and European attempts to overcome problems in the graded school design. Essentially, Goodlad and Anderson sought a school structure that would "implement a theory of continuous pupil progress: since the differences among children are great and since these differences cannot be substantially modified, school structure must facilitate the continuous educational progress of each pupil. Some pupils, therefore, will require a longer period of time than others for achieving certain learnings and attaining certain developmental levels" (p. 52). These ideas spawned an elementary school structure with fewer major divisions—for example, primary, intermediate, and upper elementary—with classes in each division comprised of students spanning a three- to four-year age range. Here, children of different ages would progress continuously as individuals through a curriculum unbound by grade-level distinctions. Initially, teachers were assigned one class of multiage students and stayed with them for three or more years; later, team teaching enhanced the model. Concurrent with this activity in the United States, similar conceptions of continuous progress and individual development advocated by Peter Petersen and the German Progressive School movement formed the basis of the Dutch *Jenaplan* nongraded schools, of which there were more than 200 by 1990 (Anderson 1992).

Not suprisingly, given the preoccupation with student variability as an instructional obstacle, most nongraded schools attempted to "reduce the range of abilities with which the teacher must cope" (Goodlad and Anderson 1959 p. 65). For example, many educators assumed that language arts and mathematics were sequential and skill-based subjects that demanded homogeneous groups of learners, even in nongraded settings. Others, however, disagreed with any form of homogeneous grouping and advocated the random assignment of children to multiage groups. Still others considered personality, interests, and other factors in making assignments.

2.3 Cross-grade Regrouping

One nongraded variant was to regroup students across grade levels for instruction in reading and language arts. Many traditional schools adopted plans (usually referred to as "Joplin plans," owing to their origin in Joplin, Missouri) wherein students who spent most of their day in single-grade classrooms were regrouped by reading skills into multigrade groups. Thereby, schools reduced the variability in students' reading skills and provided students with more direct instruction than was permitted by traditional within-class reading groups. In nongraded schools, Joplin plans eased the logistical difficulties of moving away from graded materials and practices in reading and language arts, and called attention to students' abilities and rates of learning, rather than age or grade (Floyd 1954). Subsequently, educators approached mathematics and other curriculum areas by delineating skills, allowing for various rates of learning, and then grouping according to the skills and the rate of learning without regard to age (Provus 1960).

2.4 Mixed-age Groupings

Katz et al. (1990) distinguish between nongrading and mixed-age grouping: "The former is primarily intended to homogenize groups for instruction by ability or developmental level rather than by age; the latter is intended to optimize what can be learned when children of different—as well as the same—ages and abilities have opportunity to interact" (p. 1). Thus, mixed-age grouping challenges nongrading's focus on continuous progress and sequential, predetermined curricula.

Katz et al. also advocate promoting rather than narrowing differences among individuals in a group because children's construction of knowledge is enhanced as they interact and share meanings through talk and activity. Mixed-age grouping permits children to draw on a wide range of expertise from peers and adults.

2.5 Individualized Instruction

Given the emphasis on individual learners (rather than on the group as a whole) in nongraded schools, it is not surprising that individualized instruction gained popularity during the early years of nongrading. Individually Guided Education (IGE) is perhaps the most highly technological attempt to provide individualized instruction in nongraded school structures (Klausmeier et al. 1977). One of many individualized programs that required students to use self-paced materials, study guides, and pre- and posttests (Bangert et al. 1983), IGE specified that nongraded units of 100 students work with a team of four teachers, a unit leader, teaching aides and clerks, and appropriate curriculum materials. Its proponents considered the nongraded structure well-matched to a complex technology for identifying objectives, estimating how many objectives students could attain, and diagnosing students' levels of achievement relative to these objectives, their motivation, and learning styles.

2.6 Open Schools

Far less technological than individualized instruction plans, open schools also sought to accommodate variation among children's learning rates and styles, the curriculum, and individual goals (Pavan 1973). Teachers in open-space schools " . . . work with individuals or small groups, allow more peer interaction, have less need to direct pupil behavior, use more supplementary materials, and respond to individuals more frequently" (Pavan 1973 p. 340).

3. Effects of Alternatives to Age Grouping

In spite of the limited implementation of alternatives to age-grouping, research permits some conclusions about their effects. Effects on both achievement and noncognitive outcomes have been studied.

3.1 Effects on Achievement

Researchers draw conflicting conclusions about the effects of alternatives to age-grouping on student achievement. For example, Pavan's (1977) review of studies comparing traditional and multigrade structures concludes, "There is definitive research evidence to confirm the theories underlying nongradedness" (p. 340). In contrast, after reviewing the research on multiage grouping before 1981 (including those studies examined by Pavan), Pratt (1983) reported that multiage grouping showed no consistent relationship with academic achievement.

Gutierrez and Slavin (1992) have completed a "best evidence" review. Sorting nongraded plans into different types, they report positive effects for nongraded, one-subject programs (i.e., Joplin plans) and for more comprehensive nongraded plans that are regrouped by skill levels. In contrast, nongraded schemes incorporating individualized instruction, including IGE, yielded no achievement advantages over age-grading. Gutierrez and Slavin conclude that nongrading enhances achievement because it allows teachers to reduce the number of within-class groups in reading and mathematics, thereby increasing the amount of direct instruction students receive. Other research suggests that mixed-age grouping may enhance learning because such settings increase the variability of knowledge and skills on which members of the group can draw (Rogoff and Lave 1984).

3.2 Noncognitive Outcomes

Research on social and emotional effects shows clearer patterns of benefits for nongraded settings. For example, Pavan (1973) reviewed 16 studies that included measures of noncognitive outcomes and reported that only three studies favored traditional settings. More recently, Katz et al. (1989) concluded from their review of 17 studies that mixed-age group interactions promote helping, sharing, and taking turns; they provide older children with important leadership opportunities and younger children with more complex play opportunities than they experience in age-homogeneous settings. Other studies reveal that, outside of school, many societies—including the United States (Barker and Wright 1955), the United Kingdom (Sluckin 1981), and other non-Western cultures (Whiting and Whiting 1975)—socialize children and encourage them to develop friendships in age groups wider than traditional age-graded schools permit.

4. Issues for Theory, Research, and Practice

New scholarship about how children learn, the impact of increased student diversity in contemporary schools, and demands on schools to prepare students for a postindustrial world all call into question schools' efforts to create groupings that reduce learner variability and support standardized, sequential curricula. For example, developments in cognitive science suggest the importance of social interaction between experts and novices as a way of acquiring knowledge (Katz et al. 1990, Rogoff and Lave 1984, Newman et al. 1989). Hence, interactions among individuals with a range of experience and expertise allow greater opportunities to acquire important elements of the culture. This work suggests that the goal of limiting variability is not only illusive, but unproductive.

In most highly industrialized Western countries, for example, poverty has increased dramatically, and immigrants have infused once homogeneous societies with new languages and cultures. Whether this increased variability among students promotes or interferes with learning seems to depend upon the characteristics of the schools that children attend. School practices grounded in new conceptions of learning may prove more powerful in educating diverse school populations. For example, Rosenholtz and Simpson (1984) distinguish between unidimensional and multidimensional classrooms, providing evidence that the latter more effectively accommodated variability among learners. Yet, both traditional age-graded and many nongraded schools tend toward the unidimensional—narrow definitions of academic ability, hierarchical arrangement of the curriculum, and homogeneous ability or achievement groups that result in the tacit or overt stratification of students into high and low status groups.

In contrast, Katz et al.'s mixed-age grouping model more closely approximates multidimensionality with its promotion of a broad conception of ability, achievement, and intelligence; multiple performance criteria and diverse methods for achievement, and a high degree of student autonomy and peer interaction resulting in less pressure to perform (Rosenholtz and Simpson 1984).

Finally, school structures that attempt to reduce variability among individuals and standardize learning run counter to the demands of a postindustrial age. For example, cooperation and group problem-finding and problem-solving in nonroutine circumstances with people of diverse backgrounds and abilities are essential skills if organizations are to flourish in turbulent economic, political, and social systems. Taken together, these trends suggest that school structures that mimic or attempt to improve upon assembly-line models of production require further scrutiny by educators and researchers.

See also: Ability Grouping and Tracking in Schools

References

Anderson R H 1992 The nongraded elementary school: Lessons from history. Paper presented at the Annual Meeting of the American Educational Research Association, San Francisco, California

Aries P 1962 *Centuries of Childhood*. Vintage, New York

Bangert-Drowns R L, Kulik J, Kulik C C 1983 Individualized systems of instruction in secondary schools. *Rev. Educ. Res.* 53: 143–58

Barker R G, Wright H F 1955 *Midwest and its Children: The Psychological Ecology of an American Town*. Row, Peterson, Evanston, Illinois

Floyd C 1954 Meeting children's reading needs in the middle grades. A preliminary report. *Elem. Sch. J.* 55: 99–103

Goodlad J I, Anderson R H 1959 *The Nongraded Elementary School*. Teachers College Press, New York

Gutierrez R, Slavin R E 1992 Achievement effects of the nongraded elementary school: A retrospective and prospective review. *Rev. Educ. Res.*

Katz L G, Evangelou D, Hartman, J A 1990 *The Case for Mixed-Age Grouping in Early Childhood Education Programs*. ERIC Clearinghouse on Elementary and Early Childhood Education, Urbana-Champaign, Illinois

Katz L G, Evangelou D, Hartman, J A 1990 *The Case for Mixed-Age Grouping in Early Childhood Education*. National Association for the Education of Young Children, Washington, DC.

Klausmeier H J, Rossmiller R A, Saily M (eds.) 1977 *Individually Guided Education*. Academic Press, New York

Newman D, Griffin P, Cole M 1989 *The Construction Zone Working for Cognitive Change in School*. Cambridge University Press, New York

Pavan B N 1973 Good news: Research on the nongraded elementary school. *Elem. Sch. J.* 73: 333–42

Pavan B N 1977 The nongraded elementary school: Research on academic and mental health. *Texas Tech. J. Educ.* 4: 91–107.

Pratt D 1983 Age segregation in the schools. Paper presented at the Annual Meeting of the American Educational Research Association, Montreal, Canada

Provus M M 1960 Ability grouping in arithmetic. *Elem. Sch. J.* 60: 391–98

Rogoff B, Lave J (eds.) 1984 *Everyday Cognition: Its Development in Social Context*. Harvard University Press, Cambridge, Massachusetts

Rosenholtz S, Simpson C 1984 Classroom organization and student stratification. *Elem. Sch. J.* 85: 21–37.

Sluckin A 1981 *Growing up in the Playground: The Social Development of Children*. Routledge and Kegan Paul, London

Whiting B B, Whiting J W M 1975 *Children of Six Cultures: A Psycho-Cultural Analysis*. Harvard University Press, Cambridge, Massachusetts

Discipline in Schools

R. Lewis

Discipline is a major component of a school's activity, and is critical in establishing an environment which facilitates students' academic achievement as well as their socialization. It is an important factor in parents' evaluation of schooling and in the quality of students' and teachers' lives, consuming a substantial proportion of teachers' and administrators' time and energy. Discipline can be distinguished from the broader area of classroom management in that the latter emphasizes the provision of quality instruction as a means of minimizing disruption in classrooms, whereas discipline is generally represented as what teachers do in response to students' misbehavior. There are, however, some who argue that it can be a means of imposing on students an institutional culture, regardless of its relevance or appropriateness. In exercising discipline in schools, teachers select from a range of models and techniques. Some of the factors influencing their choice are associated with the assumptions underlying competing models, the impact of models on students' attitudes, behavior, and achievement, and the relative extent to which the aim of the disciplinary interaction is to establish order or to teach values. Each of these issues is explored below.

1. Functions of Discipline

As early as 1914, Bagley identified a number of functions of discipline when he examined the then, current educational scene. He described the functions of discipline as, first "The creation and preservation of the conditions that are essential to the orderly progress of the work for which the school exists" (p. 10). Bagley viewed a second function of discipline as "The preparation of the pupils for effective participation in an organized adult society which while granting many liberties balances each one with a corresponding responsibility" (p. 10).

Currently, a view that appears to be consistent with Bagley's definition which promotes discipline as a collection of techniques and strategies employed by teachers to facilitate order in the classroom is termed a managerial orientation (Lewis 1997). Such order is necessary so that an environment is developed which maximizes the learning of school subjects.

In contrast, an educational orientation (Lewis 1997), corresponding to Bagley's second definition, emphasizes the impact of disciplinary interactions on students, and views discipline as a learning experience via which students learn about human values.

Since the 1960s there have been varying levels of tension between the two, at times opposing orientations described above with by far the greater emphasis being devoted to the managerial orientation. Even though both aim to minimize student misbehavior, the sort of discipline which might most efficiently establish order in the classroom may not be best suited to the development of self-discipline and a sense of responsibility in students.

2. Student Misbehavior in Schools

Student misbehavior takes many forms, some of which are believed to have increased over time due to a range of factors. It is a source of concern for the community and a source of stress for teachers. Views about why students misbehave vary. Factors identified relate to students, teachers, schools, and the broader society.

2.1 Development in Theorists' Beliefs About the Causes of Misbehavior at School Since the Second World War

From the 1950s to the 1970s, the misbehavior of any children who did not "fit the system" was seen as

wilful behavior which needed to be controlled. From the 1970s to the 1980s a new set of assumptions was added. It suggested that children who were unable to adjust to the demands of a school had a deficit of some kind (for example, a poor home life), and needed support, understanding, and remediation. They had to rethink their positions within the group, and to decide to conform to the behavior standards required to ensure acceptance by the school community. Since the 1980s a third set of assumptions has been added to the preceding two sets, namely that children who were misbehaving were doing so because they had not been engaged by the school curriculum, and were therefore reacting to an institution which was not providing for their legitimate learning needs.

As indicated above, the development of theorizing about discipline has been one where a new set of assumptions about causes of misbehavior has been added to the existing set; until in the 1990s the three sets of assumptions outlined above are competing for the attention of those reflecting on the reasons for unacceptable behavior in schools. This analysis does not argue that each of these assumptions has not had some currency at all times, but simply reflects the change in emphasis accorded different understandings.

2.2 Reasons for Alleged Increases in Levels of Student Misbehavior

Although it is commonly believed that the incidence of misbehavior in schools is on the increase, there is little research evidence reported to support the claim. Nevertheless, a range of reasons has been proposed to account for the hypothetical increase. These include:

(a) High mobility of students contributing to disruption in school programs and dislocation of school communities.

(b) Increasing breakdown of the nuclear family and community norms, undermining community support for the work of schools.

(c) A shift from a framework of social justice to one of economic rationalism leading to a decrease in resources for schools.

(d) Young people's access to technology-assisted learning and entertainment opportunities rendering classroom learning mundane by comparison.

(e) Greater heterogeneity of students in classrooms attributed to factors such as increased student mobility and retention, resulting in more ethnic tensions between students.

(f) Fewer job opportunities for students who are very unhappy at school which causes them to remain at school despite their dissatisfaction with it.

In summarizing the research about causes of misbehavior, it can be argued that student misbehavior is partly a function of student characteristics (for example, attitudes to school, career aspirations, and academic performance), partly related to classroom factors (for example, physical setting, clarity of instruction, levels of accountability, and complexity of task) and partly related to features of the school (for example, extent of clarity of expectations for student behavior and of discipline policy, teachers' attitudes, and resources).

One particularly contentious reason for misbehavior that has gained prominence in the last decade is attention deficit disorder (ADD or ADHD). Although the prevalence of this disorder appears to have grown exponentially, the extent of its occurrence varies from study to study. The proportion of children so identified nationally has varied from less than 0.1 percent to over 30 percent of the sample examined, depending on which country is the site of the investigation. The proportion of children in the US reported as suffering from a chronic short attention span is approximately 4 percent. Despite the advantages of an ADD diagnosis, which includes the removal of responsibility for inappropriate behavior from the student, parent, and teacher alike, some researchers strongly argue that care needs to be exercised in prescribing drugs (such as Ritalin) too readily. A discussion of relevant literature comprises almost half of a recent issue of *Phi Delta Kappan* (77(6), 1996).

2.3 How Students Misbehave

Despite a tendency for the media to sensationalize students' misbehavior in schools, and an increasing concern by school communities about violence in schools, teachers generally continue to cite as their main cause of concern minor student misconduct such as repetitive talking, moving, and noise-making. These misbehaviors are more likely to be displayed by male students who take up most of teachers' disciplinary time in the classroom. Since the 1970s however, a number of more serious types of misconduct have gained prominence in the literature. Among these are issues such as drugs-related behavior, the possession of guns and knives at school, the intrusion into schools of nonstudent gangs, and bullying. Of these, the last is most commonly reported. Bullying, which is defined in the literature as the unjustified, cruel, and repeated physical or psychological oppression of the powerless by the powerful, was highlighted in the 1970s in Scandinavia and in the 1980s in the US, Britain, Canada, Holland, Italy, Spain, Japan, and Australia. It appears to have been tolerated in schools until the 1970s. The level of bullying affects many children although there are national differences, with Australia recording highest levels. In Australia for example, about one child in five reports that there are weekly incidents of harassment, although the amount of bullying of girls is slightly less than that of boys. The nature of bullying varies, with boys more likely to experience physical or verbal assault and girls more

likely to experience systematic exclusion. Its extent and nature is also age related, peaking in the age range 10–14 years and moving from physical and verbal abuse to systematic exclusion with increasing age (Rigby 1997).

2.4 Student Misbehavior and Teacher Stress

Student misbehavior is cited as one of the main concerns of teachers as well as being reported as one of the primary reasons for teacher burnout and resignation from the profession. For example, in an investigation in Israel, the strongest predictor of teacher burnout was student disrespect. The specific behavior characterizing disrespect included talking out of turn, chatting, shouting, violence to other students, impudence, and tardiness. It is of interest to note that in this study, student disrespect was a greater source of stress for women teachers than for men. It was also more stressful for beginning teachers than for experienced ones (Friedman 1995). Nevertheless, despite general support in the literature for the belief that student misbehavior is an inevitable source of teacher stress, there is one major contrary piece of research. Hart et al. (1995), report a study in which over 4,000 Australian teachers in 32 primary and 52 secondary schools were involved in discussions leading to the development and adoption of a schoolwide discipline approach. They report that even though the teachers in their sample report, on average, as much student misbehavior as ever, as a result of feeling supported by their peers, "student misbehavior is not overtly stressful for most teachers" (p. 44). Consequently, it can be argued that even when student misbehavior disrupts teachers' attempts to instruct students, the teachers' levels of stress are reduced when they feel part of a community which is responding systematically to such behavior.

2.5 Community Concern about Student Misbehavior

As usual, according to the *Phi Delta Kappan* poll (Langdon 1996), "Both teachers and the public agree that student discipline is one of the biggest problems schools face" (p. 244). Inspection of the data presented indicates that lack of discipline is rated as the major problem identified by 20 percent of teachers and 15 percent of the public. Although it is not the main problem cited by either group, a complicating factor is the additional 7 and 14 percent of teachers and the public, respectively, who highlight the issue of fighting/violence/gangs as their major concern. Even without the inclusion of this latter category, lack of discipline rates higher for teachers in 1996 than it did in 1984 or 1989.

There would appear to be good reason for general concern about the quality of school discipline as it is not only significantly associated with school learning but there is also evidence that students who misbehave while at school have greater likelihood of dropping out, substance abuse, and engaging in crime in later life (Gottfredson et al. 1993).

2.6 Avoiding Classroom Misbehavior by Students

In order to minimize student misbehavior in classrooms, much research emphasizes not only the corrective aspects of classroom discipline but also a preventative component. For example, in a review of research on classroom management, emphasis is given to the importance of integrating good instructional techniques with good discipline (Evertson and Harris 1992). A further contribution is made by research which documents the preferences of students for alternative disciplinary techniques and their affective reaction to those they view as unjust or hostile (Lewis and Lovegrove 1987). Such research indicates that techniques such as displays of anger, lack of adequate recognition for good behavior, the use of sarcasm and even the use of group punishments may be effective in the provision of order in the classroom but do not promote an effective learning environment.

3. Discipline

Despite teachers' best attempts at averting misbehavior, it appears that there will always be some students who are difficult to manage. Consequently, it is not surprising that teachers in a number of different countries report that classroom management skills are of major importance, and many teachers are interested in further development in this area (Merrett and Wheldall 1993).

3.1 Discipline Models

The range of strategies available to respond to misbehavior vary widely, but basically comprise five categories of responses which reflect increasing levels of teacher intervention. The least interventional category consists of techniques such as the teacher verbally cueing students, or pausing, or looking at students who misbehave. The next contains nondirectional descriptions of unacceptable behavior such as "someone is speaking." The third category includes questions directed at the misbehaving students, asking what they are doing, and what they should be doing. The next contains assertive demands, and the last is comprised of logical consequences, arbitrary punishments, and rewards. These techniques give rise to three theoretical approaches to discipline, each of which is based on one of the set of assumptions about why students misbehave, outlined in Sect. 2.1.

The approaches can be distinguished by reference to the answer to two questions. First, who should be responsible for deciding on what constitutes acceptable behavior in the classroom and second, who should be considered responsible for seeing that students act appropriately? Such an analysis yields three dominant models of discipline, namely that the responsibility for both sets of decisions resides solely with the teacher, the teacher together with the class, or the individual students together with the teacher. These approaches to discipline, traditionally referred to as interventionist, interactionist, and noninterventionist, have been identified as models of control, management, and influence (Lewis 1997).

3.2 Comparing Discipline Models

A useful way to compare the three approaches is to line them up along an imaginary continuum with the model of influence at one end, the model of management in the middle, and the model of control at the other end.

Teacher influence, which is based on the earlier articulated assumption that misbehavior is due to a lack of fulfilment of students' legitimate needs, consists of the use of techniques such as telling students the impact of their misbehavior on others, listening to and clarifying the student's perspective, and negotiating a solution to the problem that satisfies the needs of both teacher and student.

The second approach, the model of management, is based on the assumption mentioned earlier that students are primarily motivated by a desire to be accepted or recognized by the group. The techniques relevant to this model, which takes up the center of the continuum are: the use of questions such as "What are you doing?" and other forms of reality tests; the application of logical consequences rather than arbitrary punishments; the use of a nonpunitive space where children can go to plan for a better future; and finally, class meetings at which students and the teacher will debate and determine classroom discipline policy.

At the end of the continuum opposite the model of influence is the model of control. This approach is predicated on the assumption described earlier that misbehavior is wilful. A model of control consists of the application of clear rules, a range of both individual and class recognitions and rewards for good behavior, and a hierarchy of rewards and increasingly severe punishments.

Only since the 1960s have models of discipline based on these three approaches been designed as "packages" to be marketed. In accord with the changing views about the causes of a lack of discipline, the packages have varied. The earliest were developed as alternatives to the prevailing culture of control through punishments and they took two forms. The first provided ways of establishing order by the exercise of influence and negotiation, and the second stressed the use of group decision-making and group processes in general. One of the most popular recent packages, however, returns to the model of control. Each of these competing alternatives is alive and well in the 1990s.

3.3 Evaluation of the Competing Models of Discipline

Very few studies have systematically evaluated the effectiveness of alternative styles of discipline. Probably one of the best evaluations has been contributed by Emmer and Aussiker (1989) who conducted a meta-analysis of reported evaluations of the effects of four types of discipline packages on students' school-related attitudes and behavior. The styles considered included a model of influence, a model of group management, and a model of control. In the words of Emmer and Aussiker,

> Considered as a whole, the research on the four models provides some evidence for positive effects on various *teacher* attitudes, beliefs and perceptions . . . when the outcome measures were teacher *behaviors*, results were mixed, although TET studies, particularly—and to a lesser degree Assertive discipline—did find at least short term changes. . . . Studies of effects on *students* produced variable results across the models. (pp. 118–19)

The inability of discipline packages to bring about a change in student behavior is also noted by Hart et al. (1995), who evaluated the impact of a one and a quarter million dollar staff development program in Australia, called the Whole School Program–Discipline. Their evaluation involved the collection of longitudinal data from over 4,000 teachers in 86 schools. Hart et al. conclude that

> . . . although it is generally believed that schools' discipline policies and procedures will influence student misbehavior . . . a series of structural equation models based on large samples of teachers failed to support this view. (p. 44)

To further substantiate this contention, they also report that over the 12 month period that schools were involved in the intervention there was significant improvement in their discipline policies but no corresponding change in the mean level of student on-task behavior. This finding is partly contradicted, however, by those of Veenman and Raemaekers (1995) who report that five years after an intervention designed to influence the way teachers deal with classroom disturbances, they continue to discipline students in a way which differs from the ways practised by teachers who were in the control group. Similarly, a positive example of an evaluation of a discipline package is provided by Freiberg et al. (1995) who report the effect of the "Consistency Management Program" in an inner-city elementary school. They report a significant change in teachers' behavior, students' perceptions of classroom climate, and students' motivation and achievement one year after the program was implemented.

One of the possible shortcomings of such analyses, however, is that the amount of order in the classroom, the students' attitude to their learning environment, the classroom climate, the amount of lesson content covered, or even the students' achievement may not be the only and perhaps not even the most significant criterion for the evaluation of various forms of classroom discipline. Even though it is acknowledged that schools are primarily agents designed to promote cog-

nitive growth in students, when it comes to evaluating the appropriateness of an approach to discipline, what may need to be assessed is the political and other values that children learn as a result of being exposed to discipline models of different sorts.

3.4 Changes in the Use of Alternative Models of Discipline Since the Second World War

Despite the developments in theorizing about the reasons for student misbehavior and classroom discipline, and despite a relatively small number of schools in the US, England, Canada, Australia, etc., where teachers have tried to act in accord with the shifting assumptions about the causes of student inattention and disruption outlined in Sect. 2.1, there is little reported research evidence of change in the dominant approach to discipline used in schools. In general, schools have sought, and continue to seek, to control students. There has, however, been substantial modification of the types of rewards and punishments used. First, the use of rewards for appropriate behavior has generally increased since the 1950s. Second, in light of an increasing awareness of human rights in general, and the children's rights in particular, the use of punishment aimed at physical and/or emotional hurt has been progressively reduced, and in some countries eliminated, and the use of temporary isolation within school and suspension from school has increased. It is important to note that most current models of control do not support the use of corporal punishment even though it is still legal in most countries, including almost half the states of America.

Since the 1970s there would appear to be an increasing discrepancy between teachers' professed orientation for models of management and their practice, which emphasizes models of control. This is not surprising given that the results of research into the effect of staff development in this area indicate that although it is relatively easy to influence teachers' attitudes, it is difficult to bring about systematic change in their classroom behavior (Joyce and Showers 1988).

Current debate about classroom discipline packages arises primarily as a result of the widespread adoption of models of control. Most of those supporting models of control argue from the perspective that they are efficient in establishing order in the classroom and consequently facilitate school learning. The critics fall into two main camps. The least successful criticisms of the model of control focus on its emphasis on extrinsic motivators and its consequent undermining of the development of students' intrinsic motivation (see for example, the *Review of Educational Research*, 1996, 66(1)).

A more damaging criticism centers on the educational value of such models in terms of the values they transmit regarding who is responsible for whom in the classroom. Such critics argue that models of control at best make students obedient, at worst make them resistant, but never make them responsible. Such a view appears not only to be promoted by teachers within countries such as the USA, Britain, and Australia but also Japan (Lewis 1995).

4. Initiatives Aimed at Increasing the Level of Student Responsibility in Schools

A number of innovations in schools appear to be aimed at increasing students' sense of responsibility by making them responsible for much of the decision-making that accompanies day-to-day schooling. One current, systematic attempt is called educational responsibility (Schneider 1996). It is an approach to classroom management which is designed to strengthen student empowerment and responsibility and reduce the emphasis on obedience and coercion. It focuses on both classroom instruction and classroom discipline. In both arenas the recommended procedures reflect the interactional perspective and rely on participative decision-making. Consequently, when it comes to misbehavior, educational responsibility highlights the use of I-messages, negotiated, win–win solutions, the identification of alternative, acceptable ways of expressing negative feeling, and class meetings at which norms are established, past performances evaluated, and plans for a better future designed. Time is spent on attempting to develop students' moral thinking by having them discuss the impact of one's behavior on others. The process relies heavily on the assumption outlined in Sect. 2.1, that misbehavior is closely related to low self-concept and unfulfilled need. A second example of an empowering orientation is provided by Glasser (1990). Until 1987, Glasser promoted a limited version of empowerment which saw classroom meetings responsible for reflection and policy formation on issues related to social problems, instruction and curriculum, and any other matters of intellectual interest. Since then he has substantially expanded his vision to promote control theory and quality schools as a way in which students' legitimate needs can be met in the classroom, thereby alleviating classroom disruption.

Another initiative which also calls for more student participation does so by identifying discipline as part of students' political education. It dismisses all three models of discipline identified in Sect. 3.1 as models of control, arguing that they are all used for "generating compliance for organizational harmony" (Slee 1995 p. 91) and are too frequently implemented to "make up for what is essentially ineffective schooling" (p. 91). Proponents of democratic classrooms highlight not only student participation in decision-making but also democratically defined rights and responsibilities, inclusiveness, and equal encouragement, a problem-solving curriculum, and an intellectual appreciation of the importance of democracy (Pearl and Knight in press).

Another very popular response to some kinds of misbehavior, which aims at maximizing students' responsibility, is one which removes the teacher from the picture completely. Peer mediation is a process which has students facilitating negotiated solutions to disputes which involve other students. There are two main approaches to peer mediation. One involves preparing as mediators only a small proportion of the students in a school. The other approach involves training all the students in the process of negotiated solutions. The sort of conflicts which can be managed by peer mediation are those which occur between students. Typically these take the form of physical or verbal harassment or disputes over access to, or possession of, resources.

An evaluation of peer mediation in an inner urban elementary school notes that the types of between-students conflicts reported in a nine-month period fell mainly into two categories (Johnson et al. 1996). The first was physical aggression and the second insults and put downs. There were no significant differences between male–male and female–female disputes, and those involving a member of both sexes. The conflicts were successfully mediated by trained peer mediators in 98 percent of cases. In general, the solutions were structural, involving a semipermanent separation of the antagonists. Therefore, rather than reaching a solution to the problem and restoring a quality relationship between students, most students opted for a palliative solution and adaption to an unfortunate situation.

5. School Discipline Policies

Generally, within the field of education, there is a move to decentralized decision-making and flatter decision-making structures. In the US there are now New American schools and American Charter schools (David 1996). In Britain one finds British grant-maintained schools. In Victoria, Australia, there are "Schools of the Future," which are required to develop charters which address all aspects of a school's functioning and include aims, processes, and procedures. Disciplinary policy is but one component. In developing these policies, school staff ensure a consistency across classrooms by adopting a schoolwide approach. A school's code of conduct for students provides a general framework within which teachers may be expected to develop their own specific procedures.

An analysis of approximately 300 Victorian primary and secondary schools' codes highlights a number of components, and the extent to which primary and secondary schools include each component (Lewis in press). In analyzing codes of conduct attention was focused on eight areas. These were:

(a) The aim or rationale of the code of behavior

(b) The rights (students', parents', or teachers') which formed a basis for the code

409

(c) The responsibility of students, teachers, and parents under the code

(d) The rules

(e) Elements of student participation in the definition of the rights, rules and processes to be implemented

(f) Preemptive strategies aimed at minimizing the likelihood of inappropriate student behavior

(g) The consequences to be applied to appropriate and inappropriate student behavior

(h) The models of discipline implicitly or explicitly being defined within the code.

The results of these analyses resulted in the following recommendations. First, although nearly all schools based their codes on the rights of students, over a third made no reference to students' associated responsibilities. Second, most school communities were excluding students from the decision-making process which surrounds the implementation of school discipline and those which did involve students restricted their involvement to rule definition. Third, despite the fact that approximately two-thirds of codes mentioned reinforcement of appropriate student behavior, there was little reference to specific rewards and recognitions. Consequently, the results are interpreted as indicating that there is greater opportunity for schools to emphasize the use of rewards in schools.

Another finding of the study is that schools highlight student self-discipline as a desired outcome of their codes of behavior, yet nearly all codes are characterized by a model of control consisting primarily of a hierarchy of increasingly severe punishments. The implicit assumption appears to be that students who are coerced into appropriate behavior patterns will internalize the values underlying such behavior. That is, although it is the teacher who is initially responsible for the behavior of students, ultimately the students will become responsible for their own behavior. Two components of the codes analyzed which were reported as facilitating such a transfer of responsibility from teacher to student were the emphasis on discussion and explanation, and an expectation that students apologize for their misbehavior. It is argued that these reasons are important because they may help promote the development of guilt and shame in students, two ingredients essential to the internalization of external strictures.

In reporting this analysis, a stereotypical distinction is noted between primary and secondary schools. The former are reported as focusing more on involving, supporting, and educating the whole child, while the latter emphasize more surveillance and punishments to secure the establishment of the order necessary to facilitate the learning of school subjects. This tendency for teachers to recommend less participation by older children in school-based decision making is noted as not surprising, given the results of related research which report similar findings. For example, it has already been noted that in the US not only do students have less opportunity to legislate for their behavior in schools as they grow older, but this occurs despite an increase in their say over the curriculum content and process (McCaslin and Good 1992). Given the role that schools play in preparing students to take their position in society, it may be useful for school communities to reconsider the extent of students' involvement in decision-making.

6. Summary

Discipline in schools is a major concern of teachers, students, and the community at large. Despite an increasing interest in violence in schools, most discipline is aimed at minor but repetitive types of misbehavior, like students talking out of turn or arguing with teachers. Disciplinary techniques range from low intervention strategies such as negotiating win–win solutions with students, through moderately interventional strategies like questions to miscreants and descriptions of unacceptable behavior, to high interventional strategies, for example, rewards and punishments. Combinations of these strategies produce three styles of discipline called models of influence, group management, and control, each of which is based on different assumptions about what causes student misbehavior and how students best learn. There are two main criteria for model selection, first, the efficiency with which each model will promote order in the classroom, and second, the values students will learn from respective models. The results of evaluating the impact of different discipline models on teachers' and students' attitudes and behavior is mixed, with little evidence that models influence levels of student misbehavior. Debate on the relative merit of models of discipline, and a number of initiatives aimed at involving students in decision-making about their behavior in schools, have arisen primarily as a reaction to the popularity of models of control, and a concern about how successful these models can be in developing students' self-discipline and a sense of responsibility.

See also: Adolescence; Aggression, Development and Socialization; Children and Youth at Risk; Dropouts, School Leavers, and Truancy; Socialization; Youth Cultures and Subcultures; Youth Friendships and Conflict in Schools

References

Bagley W C 1914 *School Discipline*. Macmillan, New York
David L 1996 The who, what, and why of site based management. *Educ. Leadership* 53(4): 4–9
Emmer E, Aussiker A 1989 School and classroom discipline programs how well do they work? In Moles O C (ed.) 1989 *Strategies to Reduce Student Misbehavior* US Department of Education, Washington, DC

Evertson C M, Harris A H 1992 Synthesis of research: What we know about managing classrooms. *Educ. Leadership* 49:(April) 74–78

Friedman I A 1995 Student behavior patterns contributing to teacher burnout. *J. Educ. Res.* 88(5): 281–89

Freiberg H J, Stein T A, Huang S 1995 Effects of a classroom management intervention on student achievement in inner-city elementary schools. *Educ. Res. Evaluation* 1(1): 36–66

Glasser W 1990 *The Quality School: Managing Students Without Coercion*. Thomas Nelson, Melbourne

Gottfredson D, Gottfredson G D, Hybl L G 1993 Managing adolescent behavior: A multi-year, multischool study. *Am. Educ. Res. J.* 30(1): 179–215

Hart P M, Wearing A J, Conn M 1995 Conventional wisdom is a poor predictor of the relationship between discipline policy, student misbehavior and teacher stress. *Br. J. Educ. Psychol.* 65(1): 27–48

Johnson D W, Johnson R, Mitchell J, Cotter B, Harris D, Louison S 1996 Effectiveness of conflict managers in an inner suburban elementary school. *J. Educ. Res.* 89(5): 280–85

Joyce B R, Showers B 1988 *Student Achievement Through Staff Development*. Longman, New York

Langdon C A 1996 The third Phi Delta Kappann poll of teachers' attitudes towards the public schools. *Phi Delta Kappan* 78(3): 244–50

Lewis C C 1995 The roots of Japanese educational achievement: Helping children develop bonds to school. *Educ. Policy* 9(2): 129–51

Lewis R 1997 *The Discipline Dilemma*, 2nd edn. The Australian Council for Educational Research, Melbourne

Lewis R (in press) Preparing students for democratic citizenship: Codes of conduct in Victoria's schools of the future. *Educ. Res. Evaluation*

Lewis R, Lovegrove M N 1987 The teacher as disciplinarian: How do students feel? *Aust. J. Educ.* 31(2): 173–86

McCaslin M, Good T L 1992 Compliant cognition: The misalliance of management and instructional goals in current school reform. *Educ. Res.* 21(3): 4–6

Merrett F, Wheldall K 1993 How do teachers learn to manage classroom behavior? A study of teachers' opinions about their initial training with special reference to classroom behavior management. *Educ. Stud.* 19(1): 91–105

Pearl A, Knight A (in press) *Democratic Schooling: Theory to Guide Educational Practice*. Hampton Press, New Jersey

Rigby K 1997 *Bullying in Schools and What to Do About It*. The Australian Council for Educational Research, Melbourne

Schneider E 1996 Giving students a voice in the classroom. *Educ. Leadership* 54(1): 22–26

Slee R 1995 *Changing Theories and Practices of Discipline*. Falmer Press, London

Veenman S, Raemaekers J 1995 Long-term effects of a staff development program on effective instruction and classroom management for teachers in multigrade classes. *Educ. Stud.* 21(2): 167–85

Further Reading

Braithwaite J 1989 *Crime, Shame and Reintegration*. Cambridge University Press, Cambridge

Curwin R L, Mendler A N 1989 Packaged discipline programs: Let the buyer beware *Educ. Leadership* 46: 68–71

Johnson B, Whitington V, Oswold M 1994 Teachers' views on school discipline: A theoretical framework. *Camb. J. Educ.* 94(2): 261–76

Kelman H C, Hamilton V L 1989 *Crimes of Obedience: Toward a Social Psychology of Authority and Responsibility*. Yale University Press, New Haven, Connecticut

Knight T 1988 Student discipline as a curriculum concern. In: Slee R (ed.) 1988 *Discipline and Schools: A Curriculum Perspective*. Macmillan, Melbourne, Australia

Kohn A 1993 *Punished by Rewards: The Trouble with Gold Stars, Incentive Plans, A's, Praise and Other Bribes*. Houghton Miffin, Boston, Massachusetts

Lovegrove M N, Lewis R (eds.) 1991 *Classroom Discipline*. Longman, Cheshire, Melbourne

McLaughlin J 1994 From negation to negotiation: moving away from the management metaphor. *Action in Teacher Educ.* 16(1): 75–84

Sex Equity: Assumptions and Strategies

D. Sadker and M. Sadker

The 1960s through the 1980s witnessed unparalleled progress in knowledge concerning the educational barriers confronting girls and women. This article will review four areas of gender research in school: curriculum, teacher–student interaction, educational outcomes, and strategies to achieve gender equity in education. Because of space limitations, only salient studies and findings will be discussed, but suggestions for further reading and related references are provided.

1. Curriculum

Classroom teaching revolves primarily around instructional materials such as commercially produced textbooks. The importance and accessibility of textbooks have made them a prime area for analysis. The curriculum was the first educational area to undergo significant investigation concerning sexism.

Beginning in the early 1970s, textbooks were the focus of several content analysis studies. These studies indicated that females were generally under-represented in elementary basal readers (See Women on Words and Images 1972, Weitzman and Rizzo 1974). An early and influential study of 134 basal readers from 16 different publishers indicated that for every five stories focusing on male characters, there were only two stories with a female-centered theme. Moreover, there were three times more adult male main characters than female, six times more male biographies, four times more male folk or fantasy stories, and twice as many male animal stories. Other studies of elementary textbooks in social studies, mathematics, and spelling found that women represented only 31 percent of the illustrations in these books. Studies conducted at the secondary level reflected similar inequities, with fewer females being included and the experiences and contributions of women given little attention or space.

When girls and women were included in textbooks, their presentation was often stereotypic. One investigation revealed that elementary textbooks portrayed men in 150 roles, while women were depicted only as homemakers. Secondary textbook studies revealed similar findings. As a result of the underrepresentation and stereotypic presentation reported, publishers issued guidelines which offered authors and illustrators strategies to increase the numbers of female characters while decreasing their stereotypic portrayal (Sadker and Sadker 1980). The impact of these guidelines was mixed. Elementary reading, science and mathematics texts published during the 1980s were more equitable in numbers of females and were also less sex-role stereotyped. However, females were still portrayed less frequently in scientific careers and presented as generally more passive than men. In history textbooks, progress has been particularly slow, and the contributions of women continue to be omitted or minimized.

In addition to textbooks, a number of studies have examined children's literature, books that are presently used to expand and enrich the school curriculum. Results indicated gender bias through omission and stereotyping. Caldecott Award winners selected by the American Library Association as the best picture books published between 1953 and 1971 were analyzed. The ratio of male to female characters in illustrations was 11 to 1; when female and male animal characters were included, the male to female ratio grew to an astounding 95 to 1. Most common roles for females were those of fairy godmother and mermaid. Content analyses of Newbery Medal winners and honor books awarded by the American Library Association for the best book for older readers published each year also revealed sex-role stereotyping. However, studies conducted during the 1980s have found a significant shift towards more equal representation of females in award-winning children's literature.

It is not surprising that award-winning children's books, usually selected by a committee of professionals, would reflect sensitivity to issues of sexism and racism. But in most children's books, other than the few selected to win distinguished prizes, progress has been more difficult. Best-selling fiction marketed for adolescent girls depicts female characters with little interest in careers and motivated mainly by the desire to fall in love. Moreover, a study of 254 elementary teachers indicated that when choosing books to read aloud to their classes, most chose traditional books with males as main characters and females in minor roles. Negative portrayals of girls and women affect the attitudes and aspirations of students (Scott 1986). A summary of the research on gender in instructional materials indicates:

(a) Textbooks and other children's literature published before the 1980s and still widely used in schools today reflect a world populated mostly by males, with females relegated to minor, stereotypic roles.

(b) The creation of nonsexist guidelines and a more heightened awareness to bias has led to more representation and less stereotyping of females in both textbooks and award-winning children's literature. However, sex bias still persists in some subject areas (e.g., history texts and science texts), in best-selling adolescent books that do not win awards, and in the books most commonly read aloud to children.

(c) In the 1980s fewer researchers have analyzed textbooks and children's literature. It is important that new content analysis research be conducted to ensure the fairness of instructional materials during the 1990s.

2. Teacher–Student Interaction

Before 1970 the small number of gender studies focused on the penalties suffered by males in what was characterized as a feminine school environment. The 1970s marked a profound change in the amount and nature of research on gender in classroom interaction. Early concern about discipline problems involving male students was extended to awareness of the quieter, more passive behaviors of girls.

Studies focusing on the frequency and nature of classroom interaction at the preschool, elementary, secondary and college levels indicate that teachers interact more with male students than female students. Across subject areas including mathematics, science, language arts, social studies, and others, this pattern of disproportionately greater attention to males persists.

The importance of active and direct teacher attention has been well documented. Direct, precise and frequent teacher attention is positively associated with student achievement. If boys receive more active teacher attention, they are more likely to excel academically. Cross-cultural studies of achievement test scores indicate that as male students progress through school, they outperform girls on many academic measures. Attention to male students provides one explanation for this gender performance gap.

Some educators explain that the more frequent teacher attention given to boys is a result of their more aggressive classroom behavior. Male students are more likely to call out answers and comments than females, and they are more likely to create discipline problems. Other educators suggest that teachers unknowingly display a subtle cultural bias in favor of males.

There are also gender differences in the precision of teacher comments. Teachers are more likely to praise, criticize, and correct the answers offered by male students, and give them more specific and useful evaluation. Males receive more quantity and quality of the teacher's active verbal attention (Sadker and Sadker 1986). Some studies suggest that males may also receive more of the teacher's nonverbal attention, that is, a longer wait-time to answer questions. Other studies, however, find no difference in the length of time teachers wait for female and male students to respond.

The concepts of learned helplessness and attribution theory have been applied to classroom interaction. Females have been reported as approaching learning situations with less self-confidence and lower expectation of success. Boys are more likely to attribute success to ability, whereas girls are more likely to attribute success to luck. On the other hand, females are more likely to attribute failure to lack of ability, while males attribute failure more often to lack of effort. In short, males view tasks with a sense of mastery and confidence and demonstrate greater persistence in academic efforts. Some researchers believe that the more central and active role boys play in classroom interaction serves to strengthen their confidence and their sense of academic mastery. The more specific teacher evaluation given to males (e.g., praise, criticism, and remediation) may provide them with a clearer view of the quality of their performance and therefore greater opportunity to improve that performance. In contrast, the more diffuse acceptance reactions given to girls (e.g., "OK" or nonverbal acknowledgment) do not provide information on how to modify behavior and improve performance (Sadker and Sadker 1995).

In summary, classroom interaction studies indicate that:

(a) From preschool through college, male students receive more teacher interactions. One reason for this inequitable distribution of attention is that boys are more assertive in calling out answers, questions, and comments. However, when girls call out, teachers are likely to remind them of appropriate classroom behavior.

(b) Teachers not only interact more frequently with male students, but they also give them more precise and helpful evaluation of their performance through praise, criticism, and remediation.

(c) Studies on teacher effectiveness and student achievement indicate that the frequency and precision of teacher interactions with students is related to academic success. Since male students receive more frequent and precise teacher comments, this inequitable teaching behavior may contribute to higher male performance on standardized tests.

3. Educational Outcomes

Until about the late 1960s, educators often assumed that gender differences in academic performance, personality traits, and career paths were primarily biologically determined. Maccoby and Jacklin's *The Psychology of Sex Differences* (1974) provided a comprehensive literature review which challenged traditional assumptions about female and male behavior.

The nature–nurture controversy continues to this day with gender differences in intellectual and psychological areas ascribed to hormonal or brain differences by some researchers, while others seek explanations in socialization and education. Recent meta-analyses indicate that intellectual gender differences are limited to four areas and that these differences have declined dramatically during the 1970s and 1980s. These four areas include mathematics, science, spatial visualization, and verbal skills. This section will not explore the embryonic and controversial biological explanations but will focus on the educational and sociological causes, more appropriate to the concerns and responsibilities of educators.

In the early grades girls are equal to boys in quantitative skills. However, by the time they reach secondary school, boys are outperforming girls on standardized mathematics tests. Some studies indicate that higher levels of male enrollment in advanced mathematics courses explain these outcome differences; others suggest that girls have less interest in mathematics and do not perceive its usefulness. Finally, some educators have attempted to tie poorer female mathematics performance to difficulties in spatial visualization. Studies conducted in several different countries indicate that the gender gap in mathematics has been closing at a relatively rapid rate, underscoring the importance of environmental influence. If biological factors were more significant, such a rapid performance change would be far less likely (Friedman 1989).

Male–female differences in science performance are explained by factors similar to those potentially causing mathematics differences. Males are more likely to enroll in advanced science courses; they report enjoying science more; curricular materials frequently show a male orientation; boys are more active class participants; and some researchers believe a link exists between spatial visualization and science.

Spatial ability refers to a wide range of skills from mentally rotating objects to reasoning about spatially presented information. Females lag behind males in mentally rotating and visualizing objects in space; however, their performance is similar to males in spatial reasoning problems. A debate continues as to the relationship between spatial visualization skills and mathematics and science performance. Several researchers claim that biological factors influence spatial ability, but studies indicate that direct training in this area can lead to improved performance by both female and male students. Few schools, however, include training for spatial ability in the curriculum.

Females have traditionally outperformed males on tests of verbal skills. However, as males progress through school, they close this gap. Some researchers attribute this to the large number of remedial reading courses and a general mobilization of school resources to improve verbal performance. Since boys exhibit weaker ability in reading and language skills in the earlier grades, they are more likely to benefit from these resources. By high school graduation, males are generally equal to females in verbal skills. On some measures they are ahead. These academic differences may in part contribute to self-esteem differences, differences which indicate that as females progress through school, their self image declines (Greenberg-Lake Analysis Group 1990, Peterson et al. 1991). As one might expect, researchers have pointed to a number of nonacademic areas of gender difference, including moral reasoning (Brown and Gilligan 1992). The discussion in this review, however, has been limited to academic differences. To summarize:

(a)   Traditional gender differences in academic achievement have existed in four areas: mathematics, science, spatial visualization, and verbal skills. Females score behind males in all areas but verbal abilities.

(b)   In the mid-1990s, meta-analyses indicate that the gender differences in academic performance have been declining. Other studies suggest that these differences do not occur in all cultures. Both of these findings underscore the importance of environment, socialization, and education as key factors contributing to the gender gap in academic performance.

4. Strategies to Achieve Gender Equity in Education

A number of strategies have been explored to achieve gender equity in schools. These approaches include:

(a)   *Reforming teacher education*—Some pre- and inservice teacher preparation programs now incorporate efforts to create more equitable teacher–student interaction. For example, the Principal Effectiveness Pupil Achievement (PEPA) program at the School of Education, American University, Washington DC is a skills-oriented program that has achieved statistically significant results for attaining gender equity in teacher performance. Teachers are taught strategies to involve male and female students equally in classroom discussion, to increase their wait-time and to offer more thoughtful and precise evaluation of student responses. They are also taught a classroom observation system which objectively tracks the frequency, precision, and equity of teacher reactions.

(b)   *Curricular guidelines*—Commercial publishers and school administrations have adopted nonsexist guidelines to improve the quality and equality of instructional materials. Such guidelines strive to eliminate sexist language, increase coverage of the barriers confronting women and the contributions women have made to each field of study, and insure that illustrations and other text features provide equitable coverage to males and females. Such guidelines have resulted in textbooks less likely to omit girls and women or promote stereotypic portrayals.

(c)   *Instructional and legal equity efforts*—School districts have instituted affirmative strategies to promote equity. Special science and mathematics courses and activities designed to recruit and retain females have been initiated. Other schools have attempted to increase the number of female administrators. Still others sponsor special activities, such as women's history week or nontraditional career counseling, to promote equity goals. The effectiveness of these activities has varied. Also, several governments have passed legislation designed to prohibit discrimination based on gender, including sexual harassment (Stein 1993). While useful, the effectiveness of these laws is often determined by the strength or absence of enforcement and penalty provisions.

(d)   *Single-sex schools versus coeducation*—In the 1990s almost all nations have adopted coeducation as the model for fair and equal education. In the United States the number of single-sex schools declined sharply during the 1960s and 1970s. In the United Kingdom, where middle- and upper-class families had traditionally sent their children to single-sex schools, educators consciously adopted the United States model of coeducation; as a result the number of single-sex schools dropped. However, even as coeducation has become the model of schooling around the globe, those concerned about gender equity have begun to re-examine its effectiveness for girls and women. During the 1970s and 1980s, research revealed the academic and psychological benefits of single-sex schools, especially for girls. In the First International Science Study, Comber and Keeves (1973) found that in the majority of countries studied, girls from single-sex schools had higher science achievement than those in mixed schools. In a more recent and carefully controlled study Lee and Bryk (1986) compared single-sex and coeducational Catholic schools in the United States. They found that girls in single-sex schools had higher achievement and saw themselves in less sex-stereotyped roles (see also Hollinger 1993, Riordan 1990). Feminists in the United Kingdom and other countries have expressed concern about single-sex schools as a vanishing educational option. The controversy over single-sex versus coeducation will continue and perhaps intensify during the 1990s and beyond.

See also: Coeducation versus Single-sex Schooling; Gender and New Technology; Sex Differences and School Outcomes; Students in Classrooms, Gender and Racial Differences Among

References

Brown L M, Gilligan C 1992 *Meeting at the Crossroads: Women's Psychology and Girls' Development.* Harvard University Press, Cambridge, Massachusetts

Comber L C, Keeves J P 1973 *Science Education in Nineteen Countries.* International Studies in Evaluation 1. Wiley, New York

Friedman L 1989 Mathematics and the gender gap: A meta-analysis of recent studies on sex differences in mathematical tasks. *Rev. Educ. Res.* 59(2): 185–213

Greenberg-Lake Analysis Group 1990 *Shortchanging Girls, Shortchanging America.* American Association of University Women, Washington, DC

Hollinger D (ed.) 1993 *Single-Sex Schooling: Perspectives from Practice and Research.* OERI Department of Education, Washington, DC

Lee V E, Bryk A S 1986 Effects of single-sex secondary schools on student achievement and attitudes. *J. Educ. Psychol.* 78(5): 381–95

Maccoby E E, Jacklin C N 1974 *The Psychology of Sex Differences.* Stanford University Press, Stanford, California

Petersen A, Sarigiani P and Kennedy R 1991 Adolescent Depression: Why More Girls? *J. Youth Adoles.* 20(2): 247–71

Riordan C 1990 *Girls and Boys in School: Together or Separate.* Columbia University, New York

Sadker M, Sadker D 1980 Sexism in teacher education texts. *Harv. Educ. Rev.* 50(1): 36–46

Sadker M, Sadker D 1986 Sexism in the classroom: From grade school to graduate school. *Phi Del. Kap.* 67(7): 512–15

Sadker M, Sadker D 1995 *Failing at Fairness: How Our Schools Cheat Girls.* Touchstone Press, New York

Scott K P 1986 Effects of sex-fair reading materials on pupils' attitudes, comprehension, and interests. *Am. Educ. Res. J.* 23(1): 105–16

Stein N 1993 Sexual harassment in schools. *The School Administrator* (January) 14–21

Weitzman L, Rizzo D 1974 *Biased Textbooks: Images of Males and Females in Elementary School Textbooks.* National Foundation for the Improvement of Education, Washington, DC

Women on Words and Images 1972 *Dick and Jane as Victims: Sex Stereotyping in Children's Readers.* Carolingian Press, Princeton, New Jersey

Further Reading

Dale R R 1974 *Mixed or Single-Sex School? Vol. III: Attainment, Attitudes, and Overview.* Routledge and Kegan Paul, London

Klein S (ed.) 1985 *Handbook for Achieving Sex Equity through Education.* Johns Hopkins University Press, Baltimore, Maryland

Lee L 1987 The scarecrows that frighten women: The myths in science. *R. Quebecoise Psychol.* 8(3): 154–64

Linn M C, Hyde J S 1989 Gender, mathematics and science. *Educ. Researcher* 18(8): 17–19, 22–27

Mann J 1994 *The Difference: Growing Up Female in America.* Warner Books, New York

Sadker M, Sadker D, Klein S 1991 The issue of gender in elementary and secondary education. In Grant G (ed.) 1991 *The Review of Research in Education*, 17. American Educational Research Association, Washington, DC

Stage C 1988 Gender differences in test results. *Scand. J. Educ. Res.* 32(3): 101–11

Tavris, C 1992 *The Mismeasure of Women.* Simon and Schuster, New York

Tyack D, Hansot E 1990 *Learning Together: A History of Coeducation in American Schools.* The Russell Sage Foundation, New York

Whyte J, Deem R 1985 *Girl Friendly Schooling.* Methuen, London

(b) The Organization of Schooling

Authority and Power in Educational Organizations

D. E. Mitchell and J. E. Treiman

The structuring and restructuring of educational authority and power arrangements is a major theme in school administration and policy analysis. As basic mechanisms for establishing social order and control, authority and power are universal concepts in the lexicons of both practical politics and theoretical analysis. Differences in how these terms are conceptualized, defined, and acted upon dramatically affect both the nature and the outcomes of social and political conflicts over school organization and operations. This article explores these issues and illustrates their practical significance for teacher professionalism and empowerment, transformational leadership, and gender differences in school leadership.

1. The Nature of Power and Authority

How power and authority are used to create social control systems that structure role relationships and influence school performance is at the heart of many school reform issues worldwide, such as school-based management, teacher empowerment and professionalism, effective organizational leadership, and equal opportunity for various ethnic, language, race, and gender groups. The bedrock problem is how to create a system of social order and control that not only respects individual rights and liberties but also supports and sustains effective teaching and learning without generating personal alienation or organizational rigidity and inefficiency.

To understand these issues, it is necessary to clarify some basic confusions and contradictions that surround discussions of power and authority. Although all analysts agree that authority is a mechanism for encouraging subordinates to behave in accordance with the wishes of social and organizational leaders, there is sharp disagreement regarding how this mechanism is to be distinguished from power, persuasion, and exchange, the other basic mechanisms of social influence and control (Mitchell and Spady 1983). After reviewing the conceptual complexity of the issue, one popular textbook concluded that the relationship between authority and power is "subtle" and "murky" (Sergiovanni et al. 1992 p. 232). Clarification of this relationship is an important prerequisite to the development of meaningful theories of school organization and policy.

1.1 Two Theories of Authority

Two incompatible conceptions of the relationship between power and authority are found in organizational theory. The dominant theory conceptualizes authority as the social legitimation of power-based influence—influence garnered through "control over and effective use of certain resources" (Kimbrough and Nunnery 1988 p. 423). This view was developed at length by Friedrich (1958) and skillfully applied to educational organizations by Dornbusch and Scott (1975). Theorists in this camp assert that all social influence is grounded in the manipulation of power resources. They define authority by reference to the social circumstances under which power-based influence is exercised. Hoy and Miskel (1986 p. 109) adopted this theory and summarized it to mean that "authority is a legitimate kind of power. . . . Authority exists when a common set of beliefs (norms) in a school legitimizes the use of power as 'right and proper'."

A competing and incompatible theory holds that authority is fundamentally different from social power. Theorists holding this second view often trace the concept historically (Arendt 1968, Nisbet 1975). They noted, for example, that the English word for authority is derived from Latin (*auctor*) rather than earlier Hebrew or Greek roots that guide modern thought about power (Arendt 1968, Mitchell and Spady 1983).

This second concept of authority asserts that it is a uniquely human form of social influence. Authoritative influence arises when one individual provides certain core social experiences—security, intimacy, self-worth, and personal potency—that attract and engage others. As Mitchell and Spady (1983 p. 12) put it: "Individuals move toward social relationships that promise to provide these experiences and come to accept as legitimate the right of anyone who can create such experiences to guide and direct their behavior." These authors further argued that power is actually derived from authority through the psychological process of displacement from the authority experiences themselves to objective and manipulable symbols that come to represent them. Power resources consist of manipulable symbols whose potency to influence behavior rests on their capacity to make subordinates feel that their security, personal capacities, self-worth, or opportunities for intimacy are subject to control by the power-wielder.

The differences between the two competing theories of authority are of crucial significance to the development of administrative control systems. If the first theory is right, administrative control is derived through acquisition and judicious use of critical power resources. Authority-based control, achieved by generating popular support for the exercise of power, is important only as a means of stabilizing influence and reducing the costs of maintaining organizational control. Sergiovanni et al. (1992 p. 232) put this point succinctly by asserting that: "The advantage of using authority, rather than power, is that it costs little or nothing."

If the second theory is right, however, administrators who focus their attention on gaining influence through the acquisition and use of power resources are likely to miss entirely the importance of being able to generate for their subordinates the types of personal experience that encourage enthusiastic support for organizational goals and voluntary compliance with the wishes of administrative leaders. At its core, this second conception of authority insists that legitimate social influence arises from personal substance and character, and from the willingness and capacity of leaders to develop relationships that create meaning for their subordinates—not from the accumulation of symbolic or material resources or the development of a capacity for reward and punishment.

1.2 Four Modes of Authority

Whether they embrace the direct experience or the social-approval conceptions of authority, virtually all theorists agree that there are multiple types or modes of authority, and that the nature of the influence exercised by persons occupying superordinate roles depends on the particular mode of authority being used. Early in the twentieth century Weber explored this issue in depth, distinguishing three modes of authority: traditional, charismatic, and rational–legal (Weber 1946). He argued that modern social organizations (the bureaucratic forms common to modern social institutions, governments, armies, and private corporations) were organized on the basis of rational–legal authority systems. The traditional authority systems of feudal society and the important, but unstable, influence of charismatic individual leaders were, he argued, systematically replaced in the systems of modernity, based on division of labor, formal rules, and meritocratic status.

Later work demonstrated that Weber's conception of authority is flawed in two important respects. First, his "rational–legal" mode of authority failed to distinguish two quite different meanings of the term "rational." In what is probably the most common usage of the term, a rational action is one that relies on expert knowledge to link the means and ends of action. A second common meaning of the word "rational" refers to the imposition of a conventional or deliberate order on a situation that is otherwise unorganized. Executive or democratic decision-making, rather than expert knowledge, is used to provide the content and rationale for this type of order. In this use, "rational" means measured, routine, or standardized action, conventional order created through consensus or convenience. From this perspective, the twin elements of Weber's term are pulled apart. Authority utilizing the first notion of rationality is "expert" authority, whereas "legal" authority springs from reliance on social relationships to develop acceptable guidelines for action. In sum then, there are four, not three, basic modes of authority: traditional, charismatic, legal, and expert. The American sociologist Parsons (1937, 1947) was the first to recognize the importance of this problem in Weber's thinking. He pointed out that Weber's conception of bureaucracy assumed that the greatest expertise in an organization would always be found in the highest levels of formal (legal) authority, making management of professionalized expert workers by general-purpose managers hard to conceive.

The second problem with Weber's discussion of authority modes is his tendency to view charisma, and to a lesser extent tradition, as awesome and extraordinary, arising only rarely in human experience. Actually, these modes of authority influence behavior in a wide variety of ordinary everyday social settings. All human groups develop traditions soon after they are formed. The "old hands" interpret these traditional norms to newcomers, and their authority is confirmed through acceptance of their right to do so. Charisma is also an everyday experience. Personal charm, friendship, camaraderie, entertainment, and spontaneous leadership all depend on the easy availability of a certain amount of charismatic authority. Anyone who, by force of personality, engages the spirit or shapes the behavior of others relies on charismatic authority or its power derivative, psychological domination.

1.3 Persuasion and Exchange

It is important to recognize that the mechanisms of persuasion and exchange in social influence emerge from the fact the multiple modalities of authority (and power) are most effective in influencing particular domains of human behavior. (For a more detailed discussion of this issue, see Mitchell and Spady 1983, or Spady and Mitchell 1979). Legal authority, for example, serves to create behavioral rules and establish conventional order, but traditional authority is more effective at creating cultural values and norms or moralizing social responsibilities. Legal authority and its derivative power mode, official coercion, can be used to establish organizational routines, but they have little effect on the development of self-worth and identity. Reliance on traditional authority conveys to subordinates a sense of group identity, but it can get in the way of a rational attack on operational problems and opportunities for change. Expert authority generates control when leaders and followers are both concerned with effective action, but charismatic authority establishes influence where intimacy and warmth of social relationships are necessary prerequisites to the achievement of specific outcomes. Expert authority and its derivative power mode, technical control, guide behavior when subordinates sense they have an intellectual problem or need help in overcoming technical obstacles. However, charismatic authority and its the power-based derivative, psychological domination, are more effective when social isolation, alienation, or disengagement are the principal impediments to cooperation.

Persuasion is a mechanism of social influence that relies on using one mode of authority to guide behavior ordinarily shaped by another. Thus, for example, teachers whose subject-matter expertise is recognized can often persuade students to follow classroom rules on the ground that it will lead to effective learning, even if they cannot provide the students with the sense of order and personal security that lead to direct support for rule-making legal authority. Similarly, teachers who are experienced as charismatic personal mentors may be able to establish preliminary control over classroom participation by persuading students to study hard, even if they do not initially provide them with the experiences of personal potency that come from insightful sharing of subject-matter expertise.

As distinct from persuasion, which relies on authority trade-offs, exchange is mechanism of influence that relies on the ability to trade power resources. Though some power relationships are characterized by the complete capitulation of subordinates, most involve trade-offs. One person or group with technical superiority may confront another with stronger public moral acceptance, or one with the power of law may oppose another with the psychological advantage of a dominant personality. The result is usually an accommodating exchange of power rather than a simple contest of strength. Except where power resources are overwhelming, exchanges of psychological, moralistic, legal, or technical power resources are the norm in power-based situations concerning social influence.

2. Modern Issues

Different patterns or styles of social influence are developed through reliance on various combinations of authority, power, persuasion, and exchange. While the variety of influence mechanisms and modalities produces a complex and often subtle system of influence in all social institutions, the most painful and intractable control problems facing modern leaders and policymakers are those generated by disagreement over whether authority or power is the more

basic influence mechanism. Those who view authority as socially approved power will misunderstand the underlying frame of reference and the specific ideas and concerns involved in educational reform put forth by anyone who sees social authority grounded in leader character and direct social experience. Although many important topics have been covered in the 1980s and 1990s in discussions of how power and authority relationships could be restructured in education, three specific issues are particularly useful in illustrating the source and importance of this misunderstanding: (a) teacher professionalism and empowerment; (b) organizational culture and administrative leadership; and (c) the impact of gender on organizational goal-setting and management. (While the specifics of other equity issues—such as race, ethnicity, language minorities, and handicapping conditions—differ from that of gender, they all involve continued confusion of authority and power-based social control.)

2.1 Teacher Professionalism and Empowerment

During the first half of the twentieth century, professionalism for teachers was thought to depend on extended training and educator control over school organizations. Since many teachers had no advanced training for their work and school organizations were under lay political control, this view led to rapidly expanding teacher preparation and training requirements, and to the creation of tenure laws protecting their control over classroom activities. Though the conception was dramatically challenged by militant teacher unionism during the 1960s and 1970s, mid-century professionalism for teachers meant separating schools from community control and family involvement while concentrating on individual job performance and occupational career opportunities. Teaching career structures remained rather flat, however, encouraging teachers to leave the classroom in order to gain in social status. Principals and higher-level administrators tended to gain professional status while classroom teachers remained functionaries or, at best, "semi-professionals" (Etzioni 1969). There was reasonably widespread confidence that the professionalized administrators faithfully represented teacher needs and interests to governing bodies and to the public.

This early definition of professionalism was dismantled by teachers who turned to industrial unionism to cope with problems of alienation, frustration, and persistent low status in the workplace (Kerchner and Mitchell 1988). From the traditional perspective, the newly militant teachers were decidedly antiprofessional. They sought to use organizational power to improve their working conditions rather than to gain legitimacy for their social status. They adopted the organizing tactics and contractual stance of industrial laborers (which are quite different from those used by craft and artist unions), and also used traditional blue-collar unionist political tactics—intense public organization and overt support for favored political parties and candidates.

Curiously, while the new labor union strategies were successful in enhancing teacher political power, they produced little sense of professional authority or personal empowerment for rank-and-file teachers. Measured objectively, organized teacher power rose dramatically. In the United States, for example, teaching became one of the most thoroughly unionized occupations in either the public or private sector. Building on earlier tenure laws, labor contracts increased job protection and gave teacher organizations effective access to a wide range of decisions about school policy and practice. As business and political leaders pressured for improved school performance during the 1980s, however, policies aimed at teacher competence and accountability gained more support than those advocating higher authority and status. Indeed, the earlier emphasis on professionalism as skilled performance of complex tasks was revitalized to rationalize teacher testing and training reforms. Additionally, performance-based certification standards were proposed along with a number of attempts to create multistage career "ladders" for classroom teachers.

From the teachers' perspective, most of the 1980s reforms carried an emphasis on political and workplace accountability rather than professionalism (Shedd and Bacharach 1991). Reforms seemed to emphasize monitoring and validation of teacher capacity and willingness to produce results, not an expansion of their autonomy and control. Frequently defended as necessary for the development of the public confidence and occupational prestige that would assure professional empowerment, these policies have often been perceived by teachers and the public alike as having the opposite effect. Apparently, professional status cannot be produced using power-based accountability mechanisms: it must be granted to an occupational group as a precondition for the development of the personal and organizational empowerment features associated with authoritative professional work roles.

Observers who hold the view that authority is legitimated power have expected teacher empowerment to emerge from broadened social support for their expanded control over work roles and working conditions. For those who see authority as springing from character and manifested in direct experience, however, the evolution of the unionism–professionalism issue demonstrates that social approval for power-based social control cannot define or create authentic professionalism and, therefore, cannot lead to the expanded influence and social control suggested by the concept of teacher empowerment. From the power perspective, control comes first and its social acceptance produces authoritative empowerment. From the direct social experience perspective, authoritative teacher–student–family relationships come first and empowerment arises from the increased capacity of these relationships to provide security, self-worth, competency, and intimacy experiences in the schools (see *Teachers' Work and Political Action*).

2.2 Transformational Leadership and Organizational Culture

Leadership research provides a second issue illustrating the importance of resolving the contradictions between the conceptions of authority as direct experience or legitimated power. Leadership studies have focused attention on how principals and other school administrators set about establishing robust school cultures capable of confirming social values and guiding the beliefs as well as the behavior of school staff, students, families and interested citizens. Grounded in the work of Burns (1979), discussions of the problem have become dominated by a concern with "transformational" rather than merely "transactional" relationships between leaders and their followers—see the special issue of *Educational Leadership* devoted to this topic (Brandt 1992).

Transformational leadership involves eliciting new beliefs and commitments from followers rather than merely controlling their behavior. In institutions such as schools, where the very reason for their establishment involves changing the thinking and feeling of its members, transformational leadership is increasingly seen as a fundamental requirement. Scholarly interest in transformational leadership has emphasized analysis of qualitative relationships and interpretation of organizational cultures. As Mitchell (1990 p. 244) put it: "genuine educational leaders are bound up in the realm of existence of the educational constituency through the voluntary commitment of heart and soul."

This new leadership framework has encouraged decentralization of power-based control resources—reduction of behavior regulation and hierarchical status systems associated with formal organization. The most prevalent form of this emphasis is associated with the development of school-based management, with its attendant emphasis on separating local decision-making from external regulations and remote superordinates.

The competing theories of authority provide entirely different explanations for the leadership reform problem and lead to very different approaches to its future development. For those who hold a view of authority as socially legitimated power, the purpose of reform is to move power from places where it is not legitimately held into the hands of those now disenfranchised. From the direct experience view, however, the goal is to bring power resources into line with experienced authority. The former want to shift power resources, the latter to encourage development of authority-generating experiences.

2.3 Gender Differences in Educational Leadership

Gender differences in administrative orientation and behavior provide a third perspective on the complex problem of administrative power and authority.

Research on school principals has documented substantial and persistent differences in the working approaches of men and women (Kanthak 1991). Women give closer attention to instructional matters and to the direct supervision of teachers and other staff members. Men, by contrast, give greater attention to the environmental and political dimensions of the work. Additionally, women administrators see the building of a community to be at the core of their work responsibilities, where men tend to rely more on independent action and group regulation. Shakeshaft (1987) argued that administrative theory and training are flawed because they ignore the experiences of women. She urged a rewriting of the literature and a restructuring of training experiences for administrators.

Differences in male and female approaches to school administration and policy do not, of course, automatically lead to success or failure for either gender group. The differences, however, do tend to change the overall character of educational programs and school operations. While women continue to be substantially underrepresented in positions of educational leadership, the balance of public and professional support has shifted dramatically toward the women's perspective. This shift is linked to a broad-based social reconsideration of the appropriate bases of legitimate social influence and control.

For several hundred years—roughly from the emergence of feudalism until the French and American revolutions—Western societies were organized through reliance on clan loyalties and cultic belief systems. This form of social organization, which Weber called *Gemeinschaft* or community-based organization, gave way at the dawn of the modern period to the creation of formalized, power-based social organizations dominated by hierarchical control systems. Western societies rebelled against the betrayal of authority in the hands of kings and church leaders and created a new form of social order, which Weber labeled *Gesellschaft* organization, characterized by a belief in the division of labor, democratic allocation of power resources, and substitution of rationalism and legalism for communal and emotional bases of decision-making.

In effect, Western societies ceased to trust in relationships and began instead to put faith in structural arrangements and material resources to guide social action. Conflict and competition for resources were legitimated and incorporated into the new bourgeois entrepreneurial economy. Males were socialized to operate within the *Gesellschaft* social order—reducing their attention to, and dependence upon, direct experience while emphasizing accumulation of power resources. Women were largely kept from this new socialization process. They were expected to retain the social-experience-based approach to influence and control of the *Gemeinschaft* social order. The result has been sharp divergence in male and female

approaches to social organization. Males generally have a harder time recognizing the importance of experienced relationships and attribute their influence to resource management rather than character. These characteristics, most useful when formal organizational development is the dominant problem, create blind spots when productivity and performance are impeded more by alienation and disengagement than by weak structures. By attending more to direct experience, women more often than men approach organizational development through close management of relationships. They are less comfortable with resource-based power relationships, but more effective in creating the direct experiences from which interpersonal authority is born.

3. Conclusion

Sharply divergent interpretations of school organizations and operations result from the two competing conceptions of social power and authority. Theorists and education professionals who rely on the conception of authority as socially legitimated power neglect the important personal character and equate leadership with socialization and resource management. Those who see authority as a uniquely human form of social control, rooted in the essentially social character of security, self-worth, competency, and intimacy, emphasize the importance of personal character and interpersonal experience in creating and sustaining social authority systems.

The contrast between these two views is not just a matter of theoretical complexity. Issues of teacher empowerment, organizational leadership and social equity are radically recast by the choice of one theory (or its associated strategies) over the other.

In the first view, empowerment is the result of resource control, leadership a matter of getting social support for organizational structures and regulations, equity a matter of balanced access to resources and opportunities.

In the second view, teacher empowerment begins in self-regulation, personal character, and skill and is institutionalized through structures that support their development and enactment. Empowering organizations embrace and nurture these characteristics rather than simply imposing and regulating them. Individual differences are not seen simply as sources of inequity or as problems to be resolved, but are valued as essential aspects of the character of the desired social order. From this perspective, leadership is manifested in the quality of human experience generated within an organization.

See also: Acquisition of Empowerment Skills; Administration of Education: Critical Approaches; Contemporary Sociological Theories of Education; Political Sociology of Teachers' Work

References

Arendt H 1968 *Between Past and Future: Eight Exercises in Political Thought.* Viking, New York

Brandt R S (ed.) 1992 Transformational Leadership. *Educ. Leadership* 49(5): (whole issue)

Burns J M 1979 *Leadership.* Harper and Row, New York

Dornbusch S, Scott W R 1975 *Evaluation and the Exercise of Authority.* Jossey-Bass, San Francisco, California

Etzioni A (ed.) 1969 *The Semi-professions and their Organizations: Teachers, Nurses, Social Workers.* Free Press, New York

Friedrich C J (ed.) 1958 *Authority.* Harvard University Press, Cambridge, Massachusetts

Hoy W K, Miskel C G 1986 *Educational Administration Theory, Research and Practice,* 3rd edn. Random House, New York

Kanthak L M 1991 The effects of gender on work orientation and the impact on principal selection. Doctoral dissertation, University of California, Riverside, California

Kerchner C T, Mitchell D E 1988 *The Changing Idea of a Teachers' Union.* Falmer, London

Kimbrough R B, Nunnery M Y 1988 *Educational Administration: An Introduction,* 3rd edn. Macmillan, Inc., New York

Mitchell D E, Spady W G 1983 Authority, power and the legitimation of social control. *Educ. Admin. Q.* 19

(1): 5–33

Mitchell J G 1990 *Re-visioning Educational Leadership: A Phenomenological Approach.* Garland, New York

Nisbet R A 1975 Authority. In: Monahan W G (ed.) 1975 *Theoretical Dimension of Educational Administration.* Macmillan Inc., New York

Parsons T 1937 *The Structure of Social Action.* Free Press, New York

Parsons T 1947 Introduction. (trans. and ed. Henderson A M, Parsons T) In: Weber M 1947 *The Theory of Social and Economic Organizations.* Macmillan, New York

Sergiovanni T J, Burlingame M, Coombs F S, Thurston P W 1992 *Educational Governance and Administration,* 3rd edn. Allyn and Bacon, Boston, Massachusetts

Shakeshaft C 1987 *Women in Educational Administration.* Sage, Beverly Hills, California

Shedd J B, Bacharach S B 1991 *Tangled Hierarchies: Teachers as Professionals and the Management of Schools.* Jossey-Bass, San Francisco, California

Spady W, Mitchell D 1979 Authority and the management of classroom activities. In: Duke D (ed.) 1979 *Classroom Management.* Seventy-Eighth Yearbook of the National Society for the Study of Education, Part II. University of Chicago Press, Chicago, Illinois.

Weber M 1946 *From Max Weber: Essays in Sociology.* Oxford University Press, New York

Bureaucracy and School Effectiveness

K. K. Wong

Bureaucracy has long been the predominant mode of public school organization in virtually every country. To provide daily services to hundreds of thousands of children, the school system tends to follow a bureaucratic structure—centralization of decision-making, routinization of task performance, and standardization of resource generation and allocation (Weber 1964, Bidwell 1965). Bureaucratic power has served important institutional functions in the public school system: it manages competing interests, routinizes service delivery, distributes comparable resources to schools, enforces national and state or provincial mandates on basic academic standards and equity issues, and, above all, provides organizational stability to a complex operation that serves a diverse clientele (Boyd 1983, Wong 1992b). Despite its many accomplishments, the central bureaucracy is increasingly viewed as excessive in interfering with instructional and curricular activities at the school and classroom levels—the task of producing learners.

The public's growing distrust of school bureaucracy is embedded in the broader climate of rapid political and economic changes that swept both the East and the West in the 1980s and 1990s. The repeated electoral endorsement of Thatcherism in the United Kingdom,

the practice of Reaganomics in the United States, and the rise in popular support for conservative coalitions in other industrialized countries during the 1980s called into question the tradition of the "social welfare state" and its ever-expanding administrative agencies. The disintegration of the former Soviet Union, the introduction of market economies in formerly Soviet-dominated Eastern Europe, and the extensive deregulation in Latin American countries have raised new hopes that market-oriented initiatives can be effective in solving social and economic problems. Within this political context, the public school system becomes a target of the antibureaucratic sentiments. Increasingly, policymakers, business leaders, and parents blame central bureaucracy for the decline in student performance. At the same time, demographic trends and economic restructuring also heighten public concerns about the future performance of public schools. Will high school graduates acquire adequate skills to compete with their peers in other countries in the global economy? Does the projected labor force shortage mean that employers have to hire the less skilled in the future? Can the new work force perform well in a technologically complex world? The public seems uncertain that bureaucratized school organizations are effective in meeting these challenges.

This article reviews the literature on the relationship between bureaucratic organization and school effectiveness. There are, to be sure, different perspectives on this complex, and often controversial, issue. For analytical purposes, two contrasting approaches are examined: the "exit" or school choice argument and the "voice" or school-site empowerment perspective (Hirschman 1970). The choice argument looks for market solutions that enable parents and students a choice of both public and private schools; the voice perspective supports a shared authority system within the public sector that empowers parents and the professional staff at the school level.

1. The School Choice Perspective

Although private schools are available in most countries, the public or state school system usually is the key provider of educational services. There is, of course, substantial cross-national variation in school enrollment in the private sector. According to a UNESCO survey originally undertaken in 1988 (UNESCO 1991), countries with a significant private education sector (as measured by percentage of primary student enrollment in private schools) included Ireland (100 percent), Zimbabwe (87 percent), the Netherlands (69 percent), Belgium (56 percent), Chile (37 percent), Spain (34 percent), Australia (25 percent), and Singapore (24 percent). In contrast, the private sector is modest in Japan (1 percent), Turkey (1 percent), Sweden (1 percent), Norway (1 percent), Switzerland (2 percent), Luxembourg (1 percent), Austria (4 percent), Canada (4 percent), the United Kingdom (5 percent), Greece (6 percent), Mexico (6 percent), and Portugal (7 percent). The survey did not differentiate between types of schools (e.g., Catholic or independent) within the private sector. At the time of the survey, socialist countries were dominated by the state educational sector. Following the disintegration of the Communist bloc, religious institutions have played an active role in organizing schools in Eastern Europe.

In the United States, private schools account for slightly over 10 percent of the total school enrollment. Although the public sector continues to dominate educational services, a growing number of empirical studies in the United States have identified bureaucratic power and its regulatory functions at all levels of the school policy organization as key barriers to improving student performance. (For earlier theoretical works, see Friedman 1962, Coons and Sugarman 1978.) Beginning in 1980, the National Center for Education Statistics of the United States Department of Education surveyed a national sample of high school sophomores and seniors in both the public and nonpublic sectors. With the availability of the High School and Beyond (HSB) surveys, researchers are able to compare student performance between the public and the nonpublic sectors. These studies engage in a more systematic search for organizational variables that are likely to contribute to better outcomes, thus taking an important step beyond the earlier input–output studies that found limited school effects on student achievements at the school level (Coleman et al. 1966, Hanushek 1986).

The first such large-scale, cross-sector comparison was conducted by a research team led by sociologist James Coleman at the University of Chicago in the United States. In analyzing the first set of HSB survey data (collected in 1980), Coleman et al. (1982) found that students in Catholic and independent private schools outperformed students with similar socioeconomic backgrounds in public schools by one grade level on standardized tests in basic skills. These differential outcomes, according to the study, are less linked to income segregation, because only a very small number of private schools retains a predominantly upper-middle class clientele. Instead, different modes of organization between public and nonpublic schools are said to be pivotal. While the public schools are predominantly based in geographical attendance areas, and are governed by exceedingly cumbersome mandates, parochial schools are organized around religious identity and are relatively free from external regulatory constraints. Parochial schools can more freely enforce student discipline standards and impose greater academic demands. Parents who select parochial schools are expected to reinforce the educational goals of the chosen school. In contrast, public schools operate in a bureaucratic system and lack the authority to make academic and disciplinary demands on their clients.

Coleman's study generated a great deal of controversy. Aside from student self-selection in nonpublic schools and other issues related to sample characteristics, skeptics pointed out the need to compare students who begin with similar levels of achievements and the importance of considering outcomes other than the standardized test scores. With the 1982 HSB survey, the Coleman team was able to examine students' academic growth in public, private, and Catholic sectors. The second Coleman study (1987) found virtually no difference in student outcomes between public and independent private schools. Catholic high schools, however, continued to show the highest rates in students' academic progress in verbal and mathematical skills, although student outcomes in science knowledge and civics were comparable to those in the public sector. Students with disadvantaged backgrounds were found to have made substantial progress in Catholic schools. Catholic schools also maintained the lowest dropout rates and their students were more likely to attend four-year colleges. In explaining these successes among students in Catholic schools, Coleman and Hoffer suggested the benefits of social integration of both adults and children that is based on religious identity. They argued that the close social relations among youth, parents, and teachers in parochial schools are likely to generate "social capital," an informal system of value transmission and social support that is largely lacking in public and independent private schools. By frequently spending time in a variety of activities that facilitate the child's intellectual development, parents, grandparents, and other adults in the broader social (religious) community provide collective support for educational purposes. In contrast, public schools are based largely in rules and mandates and generally lack the social and normative basis for frequent interaction among youth, families, and teachers.

In an attempt to link politics and bureaucracy explicitly to school effectiveness, two United States political scientists, Chubb and Moe (1990), examined the relationship between school autonomy (as opposed to direct electoral and bureaucratic control) and student performance. They saw public schools as far too responsive to external political demands. This resulted because "public schools are governed by institutions of direct democratic control" (p. 67). These institutions are "inherently destructive of school autonomy, and inherently conducive to bureaucracy" (p. 47). In their view, educational governance is an open system where political interests have successfully expanded the bureaucracy and proliferated programmatic rules to protect their gains.

Using the HSB surveys for 1982 and 1984 and the Administrator and Teacher Survey data for 1984, Chubb and Moe found that politics and bureaucracy in public schools do not contribute to the desirable forms of school organization associated with higher academic performance. Instead, the more market-oriented nonpublic schools were far more likely to produce what they call effective organizations. These high-performance schools, mostly nonpublic, can be distinguished from low-performance schools (mostly urban public): "Their goals are clearer and more academically ambitious, their principals are stronger educational leaders, their teachers are more professional and harmonious, their course work is more academically rigorous, and their classrooms are more orderly and less bureaucratic" (p. 99). Consequently, Chubb and Moe suggested parental choice in education as a way of eliminating the adverse effects of democratic politics and bureaucracy.

The Chubb and Moe perspective, like the Coleman studies, has generated a great deal of controversy. Skeptics pointed to their argument's heavy reliance on the 116 items on 5 sets of tests that took 63 minutes to complete (Kirst 1990). In fact, their analysis focused on interschool variation on gains over a total of 23 items between the sophomore and the senior years. Further, school organization—a constructed index in the Chubb and Moe analysis—explains a very small portion of the variation in student achievement gains between the sophomore and senior year. As Glass and Matthews (1991 p. 26) pointed out, "A school that

moves from the 5th percentile to the 95th percentile on autonomous organization would be expected . . . to climb only a month or so in grade equivalent units on a standardized achievement test." Above all, their argument solely relies on school-level characteristics and ignores the enormous variation among tracks and classes within a school. In fact, the within-school organization can be seen as the critical link to the task of producing learners. According to Barr and Dreeben (1983), school-level properties create only the conditions for, but do not directly produce, student learning. Enjoying autonomy from bureaucratic interference is one thing; how teachers use their discretion in applying instructional strategies—grouping, tracking, curricular coverage, allocating teaching time, and employing other instructional technologies—to their students is a completely different set of issues. Clearly, the internal organization of production both within a school and within a classroom holds the key to school effectiveness.

The Chubb and Moe recommendation on transforming public education into a market place is even more controversial. Opposition to choice has been based on concerns over equal educational opportunities and the perpetuation of elitism. Choice programs tend to "cream off" better students and take other resources out of neighborhood schools. Local residents may perceive that the conversion of their neighborhood school to a choice program deprives them of direct access to their community-based service institution. Questions have been raised about the implementation of a system-wide choice plan, with regard to distribution of school information to all parents, transportation costs, and compliance with civil rights provisions. In short, choice programs may come into conflict with other restructuring efforts in public schools and may destabilize school governance.

At the same time, the case for school choice seems to be supported partially by studies on the relatively small number of "magnet schools" in the United States —public schools with specialty academic programs that admit students (often selectively) from throughout the system. It should be noted that the early "voucher" experiment in Alum Rock (California) produced no discernible difference in students' academic outcomes between choice and nonchoice programs (Capell and Doscher 1981). Evaluation of later small-scale magnet school programs, however, offers some evidence that connects choice to educational improvement. Better student performance is said to be linked to greater school autonomy, better curricular planning, greater parental involvement, higher level of racial integration, and more effective instructional practices. (For a review of the literature, see Raywid 1985, Wong 1992a). However, evaluation of the small-scale choice experiment in Milwaukee after its first year has yielded mixed results for the program participants (Witte 1991).

The real challenge is whether student gains can be sustained when small-scale choice programs become system-wide (or national) policy. In this regard, lessons from the European experience in educational pluralism have been inconclusive. The extensive school choice practices in the Dutch system, for example, have enhanced school accountability at the expense of social integration (Glenn 1989). In Scotland, six years after the implementation of the 1981 Education Act that granted parents school choice, nine out of 10 students remained in their neighborhood schools. Parents with high educational backgrounds and high socioeconomic status were more likely to move their children out of the designated school. Indeed, choice has led to enrollment increase in some of the older formerly selective schools. Moreover, "while the 1981 Act has led to the integration of some pupils from areas of multiple deprivation into schools with adjacent catchment areas, it has probably increased the segregation of those who remained at the district school" (Adler et al. 1989 p. 215).

However, in assessing the first three years of implementation of the 1988 Education Reform Act (ERA) that affected 33,000 British public schools, Chubb and Moe (1992) claimed that school autonomy is producing positive results. Although ERA standardizes student assessment and the national curriculum for all "state maintained" schools, the 1988 reform allowed parents and governing boards of individual schools the choice to "opt out" of the existing bureaucratic system, "taking students, money, and all relevant decision-making power with them" (Chubb and Moe 1992 p. 28). During the first three years of the reform, about 100 schools opted out and another 140 were in the process of becoming "grant-maintained" schools. Schools that chose to sever ties with the bureaucratic system were twice as likely to be found in districts that were dominated by the Conservative Party than by the Labour Party. Although "opted-out" schools represent a tiny fraction of the 33,000 schools in the country, Chubb and Moe (1992) believed that "if enough schools were to follow this path, the existing system would collapse and a very new and different one would take its place—a system whose hallmark is . . . school autonomy" (p. 28). Their interviews with several school heads suggested that opted-out schools, given strong leadership, were likely to facilitate a working relationship with the local community, recruit better teachers, respond to their particular needs (e.g., roof repair), attract a student-applicant pool that exceeds the number of classroom seats, and gain control over student disciplinary problems. Perhaps their most important conclusion was that choice did not discriminate against pupils with disadvantaged backgrounds. Instead, the opted-out schools were drawing students from "all ability levels," and were catering to the educational interest of their clients, who were seen as "ordinary people by class-based standards" (Chubb and Moe 1992 p. 40).

2. The School-site Empowerment Perspective

In contrast to school choice, giving more powers to parents and the professionals in school operation represents a different approach in containing bureaucratic influence. Instead of seeking to dismantle the public–private boundary, many school reformers support the notion of power reallocation within the public sector.

Shared decision-making in school policy has different roots and has taken different forms in various countries. In Norway, teacher organizations and other "corporate groups" across a wide political spectrum have pushed for decentralization in educational policy for decades. Decentralization in school appropriations, curriculum, and student assessment has been fully implemented since the 1980s. Since 1986 the national government has lumped its educational subsidies with grants for other social programs into a general block grant, where allocative priorities are determined by the local governments. In amending the 1974 Model Plan for the primary schools, reforms in 1985 and 1987 granted teachers greater authority over curricular design, instructional practices, and assessment standards. Consequently, Norwegian teachers have substantial influence over school life, promoting "different and more personalized teaching styles and unique learning approaches" (Rust and Blakemore 1990 p. 512).

In Spain, the new constitution in 1978 laid the groundwork for the restructuring of public education in the post-Franco regime. The previously centralized system was replaced by 17 autonomous regions, within which regional and local authorities exercise substantial control over educational matters. Since 1985 each school has been governed by a local school council. One-third of its members are elected parents, another third is the teaching staff, and the rest consists of administrators and politicians (Hanson 1990). The council enjoys extensive power, including budgetary allocation and hiring and firing the school director. Based on interviews with members of the councils, Hanson concluded that teachers have gained control over the council, thereby politicizing the decision-making process—"Friendship groups, power blocks, and coalitions often dominate the voting, and elections have less to do with education than alliances" (Hanson 1990 p. 535).

The political culture of democratic participation in Sweden has facilitated the practice of "democratic discourse" in the public schools (Ball 1988). Citizenship education is seen as a major function of the public schools. To achieve this goal, pupils participate in "decision-making and the negotiation of the curriculum. Subjects and subject departments are reduced in importance and the need for teachers and pupils to act in working-groups is emphasized" (Ball 1988 p. 80). For example, the 1980 national curricular guidelines (LGR 80) required equal attendance by pupil and teacher representatives in educational planning meetings that are organized by the school headmaster. Thus, the notion in school-level management in Sweden seems to be consistent with the notion of political equality in a social democracy.

In the United States, in the aftermath of the Brown decision in 1954 (eliminating racial segregation in schools) and during the Civil Rights movement of the 1960s, reformers began to focus on bureaucratic responsiveness to minorities. From the 1960s onward, interest in site-level decision-making has grown because principals and teachers are seen as possessing the knowledge and the technology to improve student performance. Similarly, from the 1960s on, the federal government required citizen advisory bodies at the program sites in compensatory education and special education. In the 1980s, parental involvement at the school sites gained widespread support from reform interest groups, businesses, and elected officials. Community involvement was further facilitated by state mandates on performance reporting on a school-by-school basis. By the 1990s virtually all major urban districts had some form of shared governance in which parents and community representatives participate in decision-making structures at the school sites. Examples of these governance arrangements include community control in New York City; site-based management in Dade County (Florida), Rochester (New York), and Salt Lake City (Utah), and the Chicago experiment in establishing a locally elected parent council in each school.

Research on the politics of decentralization in the United States has examined two key issues: (a) whether parents have substantive power in making major decisions at the school site; and (b) the effects, if any, of school-site governance on educational improvement. So far, there is more evidence about the first issue than the second.

School professionals almost always become the key decision-makers in decentralized governance. The process of decentralization does not necessarily lead to parent empowerment. Participation rates for parents in school affairs and school elections are usually low, and particularly so for parents from low-income, minority groups. School elections in the 31 decentralized districts in New York have usually attracted very low turnouts. Even when the community and parents are included in school governance, their authority in personnel issues is seriously challenged by the teachers' union. This was most evident in the intense conflict between the union and the community governing board in the Ocean Hill–Brownsville experimental district in New York City during the late 1960s. When the locally elected board fired 10 teachers, the union responded with what came to be the first of a series of major strikes. After several strikes and numerous incidents that escalated racial conflict in the community, a state supervisory board was created to protect teachers' union rights from any community board decisions.

Personnel matters that were related to collective bargaining were placed outside of the local governing body under a revised notion of community governance in New York.

Union rights and electoral barrier notwithstanding, parental participation can be further constrained by institutional arrangements. One of the best recent examples on parents' limited influence in school site decisions is provided by Malen and Ogawa (1988). Based on an in-depth analysis of eight schools in Salt Lake City in the United States, the two researchers concluded that decentralized governance did not "substantially alter the relative power" relationship between the school principal and the parents. Their study suggested several constraints on parental power. First, the site-level partnership consisted of two structures: one for the principal and staff, the other for both professionals and parents. Naturally, the professionals dominated decision-making because they controlled the agenda, maintained privileged access to information on school operation, and possessed expert knowledge. Second, parents were not given the discretionary power over the bulk of the school expenditures. They were not involved in the hiring (and firing) of the principal, and only occasionally were they asked to evaluate the performance of the school staff. Third, parents were not elected, but received "invitations" from the principal to participate. Consequently, parent-members shared similar values with the principal and acted primarily as supporters of "system maintenance."

The best recent effort to make sure that parents are indeed the key decision-makers is found in the local school councils in the Chicago Public Schools. Following a long legislative process, the 1988 Chicago School Reform Act mandates comprehensive reforms that restructure governance in all 530 public schools in Chicago. This reform represents an opportunity for parents, school staff, and community groups to work together on educational improvement. It is designed to restore public confidence by granting parents substantial "ownership" over schools. To enhance accountally, ability, the central office has decentralized policy-making to locally elected parent councils and the principal at each school site. The 11-member councils consist of six parents (i.e., the majority), two community representatives, two teachers, and the principal. There is also one student member at the high school level. Members of the local council are given substantial authority—they can hire and fire the principal, allocate school funds, and develop school improvement plans. With training and support from business and public interest groups, local councils have written their bylaws (i.e., rules), approved school budgets, and successfully reviewed and ratified the principal's contract.

Turning to the issue of school effectiveness, there are few empirical studies on the connection between democratic governance and urban school improvement, particularly when parents do gain substantive power. Research in the United States offers a good example. Those who studied community control generally painted an unfavorable picture—patronage, low voter turnout, mixed staff morale, and politicized leadership. In strong disagreement with most of the observations on the Ocean Hill–Brownsville community control experiment, Fantini et al. (1970) saw positive results. They found that the district was able to fill leadership positions with minorities, to develop a reform climate of community input to schools, and to implement innovative programs that were designed to improve educational performance. Furthermore, in a longitudinal study of the decentralization experience in New York City, Rogers and Chung (1983) concluded that locally elected boards (those that were reflective of racial and ethnic composition of the communities) were more effective in managing ethnic succession in schools because these boards were more politically stable and enjoyed greater legitimacy. Their eight case studies also suggested that, in the long run, decentralized boards were able to tackle education programming and staff development (including raising staff morale).

It is too soon to know whether Chicago's experiment in parental empowerment will lead to better student performance. Schools are only in their early years of reform and are still in the process of incorporating new mechanisms of governance. Preliminary observations suggest that principals, parents, teachers, and other key actors are learning more about the new organizational life, and are seeking ways to work with one another. This process of institution-building takes time and is likely to be uneven—constrained by neighborhood differences in socioeconomic resources, the availability of competent and dedicated principals, the commitment of parents, and the supply of minority teachers. In the long run, new governing practices may substantially shape organizational life within schools, for example, faculty–parent–community collaboration in curricular planning. Parent participation on locally elected councils may even stimulate positive feelings toward school life, which should lead to better attendance rates and higher student and teacher morale. If successful, Chicago reform may revive public education in inner-city neighborhoods and may offer a viable alternative to choice in improving school effectiveness at the national level.

3. Conclusion

There are two major strategies to reduce centralized power in public education—school choice and mechanisms for voice or shared decision-making at the school-site level. The literature suggests that the specifics and the scope of these reform strategies tend to vary from country to country, and, within the United States, from district to district. Since the early 1980s, public schools have gradually moved away from strong bureaucratic control. Increasingly, school systems have adopted a variety of power-sharing strategies—the Swedish model of democratic education, teacher control in Norway, Spain, and several big-city districts in the United States, and parent empowerment in Chicago. In contrast, parental choice of private schools has yet to be widely adopted as a real alternative to the public sector. Nonetheless, the current debate in the United States and the reform in the United Kingdom clearly suggest that choice is likely to become increasingly prominent as the political support for the "social welfare state" declines. In sum, diversity in governing structures—not only between public and private schools but also within the public sector—will remain for some time and will continue to shape our understanding of school organization and its effectiveness.

See also: Authority and Power in Educational Organizations; Effective Schools Research: Methodological Issues; Effective Secondary Schools; Social Foundations of School Choice

References

Adler M, Petch A, Tweedie J 1989 *Parental Choice and Educational Policy*. Edinburgh University Press, Edinburgh
Ball S J 1988 Costing democracy: Schooling, equality and democracy in Sweden. In: Lauder H, Brown P (eds.) 1988 *Education in Search of A Future*. Falmer Press, London
Barr B, Dreeben R 1983 *How Schools Work*. University of Chicago Press, Chicago, Illinois
Bidwell C 1965 The school as a formal organization. In: March J G (ed.) 1965 *The Handbook of Organizations*. Rand McNally, Chicago, Illinois
Boyd W L 1983 Rethinking educational policy and management: Political science and educational administration in the 1980s. *Am. J. Educ.* 92(1): 1–29
Capell F, Doscher L 1981 *A Study of Alternative in American Education. Vol. 6: Student Outcomes At Alum Rock 1974–1976*. Rand Corporation, Santa Monica, California
Chubb J, Moe T 1990 *Politics, Markets, and America's Schools*. Brookings Institution, Washington, DC
Chubb J, Moe T 1992 *A Lesson in School Reform from Great Britain*. Brookings Institution, Washington, DC
Coleman J S et al. 1966 *Equality of Educational Opportunity*. United States Department of Health, Education and Welfare, Washington, DC
Coleman J S, Hoffer T 1987 *Public and Private High Schools: The Impact of Communities*. Basic Books, New York
Coleman J S, Hoffer T, Kilgore S 1982 *High School Achievement: Public, Catholic, and Private Schools Compared*. Basic Books, New York
Coons J, Sugarman S 1978 *Education By Choice: The Case for Family Choice*. University of California Press, Berkeley, California
Fantini M, Gittell M, Magat R 1970 *Community Control and the Urban School*. Praeger, New York
Friedman M 1962 *Capitalism and Freedom*. University of Chicago Press, Chicago, Illinois

Glass G V, Matthews D A 1991 Are data enough? *Educ. Researcher* 20(3): 24–27

Glenn C L 1989 *Choice of Schools in Six Countries: France, Netherlands, Belgium, Britain, Canada, and West Germany*. United States Department of Education, Washington, DC

Hanson E M 1990 School-based management and educational reform in the United States and Spain. *Comp. Educ. Rev.* 34(4): 523–37

Hanushek E 1986 The economics of schooling: Production and efficiency in the public schools. *J. Econ. Lit.* 24(3): 1141–77

Hirschman A 1970 *Exit, Voice, and Loyalty: Responses to Decline in firms, Organization, and States*. Harvard University Press, Cambridge, Massachusetts

Kirst M 1990 Review of "Politics, markets, and America's schools." *Politics of Education Bulletin* (Fall issue)

Malen B, Ogawa R 1988 Professional-patron influence on site-based governance councils: A confounding case study. *Educ. Eval. Policy Anal.* 10(4): 251–70

Raywid M A 1985 Family choice arrangements in public schools: A review of literature. *Rev. Educ. Res.* 55(4): 435–67

Rogers D, Chung N 1983 *110 Livingston Street Revisited: Decentralization in Action*. New York University Press, New York

Rust V D, Blakemore K 1990 Educational reform in Norway and in England and Wales: A corporatist interpretation, *Comp. Educ. Rev.* 34(4): 500–22

UNESCO 1991 *World Education Report 1991*. UNESCO, Paris

Weber M 1964 *The Theory of Social and Economic Organization* (trans. Parsons T, Henderson A M). Free Press, Glencoe

Witte J 1991 *First Year Report: Milwaukee Parental Choice Program*. La Follette Institute of Public Affairs, University of Wisconsin–Madison, Madison, Wisconsin

Wong K 1992a Choice in public schools: Their institutional functions and distributive consequences. In: Wong K (ed.) 1992 *Politics of Policy Innovation in Chicago*. JAI Press, Greenwich, Connecticut

Wong K 1992b The politics of urban education as a field of study: An interpretive analysis. In: Cibulka J, Reed R, Wong K (eds.) 1992 *The Politics of Urban Education in the United States*. Falmer Press, London

Coeducation versus Single-sex Schooling

M. E. Lockheed and V. E. Lee

Single-sex education refers to three types of schooling, classified according to the gender composition of the school, classroom, and teaching staff. The purest type of single-sex education is where the entire student body of the school and the teachers are the same sex. Examples are Roman Catholic convent education for girls, or traditional, elite boarding schools for boys. The next type of single-sex configuration includes a mixed-sex teaching staff. Most single-sex schools are of this type. A third type of single-sex education occurs when school buildings are coeducational, but all instruction occurs in gender segregated classes. This form of instruction is common in many coeducational schools in the Third World, particularly in Asia.

1. Historical Trends with Respect to Single-sex Education

In the United States; a movement away from single-sex education at both the secondary and postsecondary levels was experienced in the 1960s and 1970s. These developments were motivated by both social and economic considerations. Single-sex education was viewed as a barrier to successful adolescent cross-sex socialization, and the declining demand for single-sex education led to institutions either closing or converting to coeducation in order to stabilize enrollments (Astin 1977). This trend occurred at precisely the time that research on American postsecondary institutions was beginning to document positive effects—especially for young women—for single-sex education on students' academic and occupational achievement pattern, self-image, and career choice (Astin 1977, Furniss and Graham 1974, Oates and Williamson 1978, Tidball and Kistiakowsky 1976). In countries where education systems are still expanding, as in many developing countries, coeducation is also advocated for economic reasons. The cost of providing parallel single-sex education is seen to outweigh possible benefits, except in countries such as Saudi Arabia, where coeducation is culturally unacceptable.

2. Effects of Single-sex Education

Provision of single-sex education is of interest for two reasons, both related to the education of women. First, where female participation; in schooling is low, as in much of the Third World, single-sex education enhances the probability of female school participation. Second, where female school performance is depressed in comparison with male performance, single-sex schools boost female achievement and enhance female academic attitudes and self-esteem.

Most research on single-sex education has examined its effects on student attitudes and achievement only, and has not addressed its effects on increasing participation. With the exception of a few studies, research on single-sex education is limited to: (a) studies at the tertiary level in the United States, and (b) studies at the secondary level in the United States and other developed Western countries. Only very few studies have examined single-sex education in developing countries.

2.1 Tertiary Education in Developed Countries

Summarizing the results of a large longitudinal study of more than 200,000 students in over 300 colleges, Astin concluded that, "Single-sex colleges show a pattern of effects that is almost universally positive" with respect to a large array of academic and pre-professional outcomes (Astin 1977 p. 41): the effects of single-sex schooling were generally stronger for women than men. Astin speculated that such effects were probably due to the more circumscribed heterosexual activity and to a greater sense of identification and communal feeling when both students and faculty are predominantly of the same sex. Other studies have found that undergraduate education in a women's college, particularly highly selective private sector schools, is a major explanatory factor for women's career achievement patterns (Graham 1970, Oates and Williamson 1978, Tidball 1980, Tidball and Kistiakowsky 1976).

2.2 Secondary Education in Developed Countries

Most research comparing single-sex with coeducational schooling has been conducted in secondary schools in developed Western countries. The focus has been more on students' attitudes about the social and psychological environments of their schools than on academic attitudes and behaviors, and most studies have not measured achievement differences between students attending the two school types.

Whereas single-sex schools, especially those for girls, were considered to emphasize control and discipline to a greater extent, coeducational schools were found to have a more relaxed and friendlier atmosphere. However, there is some disagreement about actual academic emphasis between the two school types, with some researchers finding girls' schools to evidence a more academic orientation, and other studies finding no positive relationship between single-sex status and academic orientation. Finn (1980) reported on a cross-national study, using 1970 data from the International Association for the Evaluation of Educational Achievement (IEA) of attitudes and achievement in science and reading among 14-year olds in both single-sex and coeducational schools in the United States and the United Kingdom. While no differences were found between coeducational and a small sample of single-sex schools in the United States ($n=8$), noticeable effects appeared in the British sample, which included 47 single-sex schools. Girls in coeducational schools in the United Kingdom showed a decline in science and vocabulary relative to male peers, while girls in single-sex schools excelled in reading and science.

Two studies in the 1980s have focused on large,

randomly selected, samples of United States Roman Catholic secondary schools. Lee and Bryk (1986) examined 75 Roman Catholic schools from the High School and Beyond study, which included longitudinal information on student background, attitudes, behaviors, and achievement. Whether concerning academic achievement, achievement gains, educational aspirations, locus of control, sex-role stereotyping, or attitudes and behaviors related to academic study, results indicated that single-sex schools delivered specific advantages, especially to their female students. All analyses included considerable adjustment for student background and contextual differences between schools. Riordan (1985) compared White students in public schools with Roman Catholic single-sex and coeducational school students, using 1972 National Longitudinal Study data, and controlling for students' social class and census region. Positive effects were found for achievement in single-sex schools, particularly for girls.

The relation between sex-stereotyped attitudes and behaviors and United States sex-segregated education has received some research attention. Girls in girls' schools were found to have less stereotypic views of women's role than their coeducational counterparts, and showed a decrease in sex-role stereotyping over the last two years of high school (Lee and Bryk 1986). Girls in single-sex Roman Catholic high schools in suburban Chicago held less stereotypic views of scientific professions than did a comparable group of public school girls. High school girls in single-sex schools had a significantly higher interest level in the feminist movement than their coeducational female counterparts. Fear of success was greater among girls in a coeducational than all-girls New York Jewish high school, with fear of success even less for girls who had also attended a single-sex elementary school. Adolescent female participation rates and leadership behavior in a laboratory game-playing situation increased when preceded by game experience in a single-sex condition. Positive effects of single-sex grouping in both the cognitive and affective domains have also been found for girls in the first grade. No significant single-sex effects for boys were reported in any of these studies.

2.3 Developing Countries

Research on the comparative effects of sex-segregated and coeducational schooling in developing countries is scarce, although single-sex education is somewhat more common in those countries than in developed countries. One study compares the relative advantages of the two types of school grouping on male and female eighth-graders in Thailand, using longitudinal data on mathematics achievement before and after eighth-grade (Jimenez and Lockheed 1989). These researchers found that single-sex schools were more effective for female students, whereas coeducational schools were more effective for male students. The longtitudinal nature of the data and the econometric two-stage modeling of choice into school and effects of school on achievement make these findings particularly strong.

A second study from a developing country analyzes the effectiveness of single-sex and coeducational schools with respect to student mathematics achievement and gender-stereotypic attitudes toward mathematics, for secondary students in government-owned schools in Nigeria (Lee and Lockheed 1990). After controlling for student background, student attitudes, and teacher characteristics and practices, single-sex schools were found to have a positive effect for female students, but a negative effect for male students, with an effect size of approximately one tenth of a standard deviation in both cases.

3. Utility of Single-sex Education for Girls in Developing Countries

Women's education in developing countries is of interest to policymakers because of its important contribution to national economic development directly through increased productivity and indirectly through lowered fertility, increased child health and nutrition, and increased child school participation. In most developing countries, however, female participation in education lags well behind male participation, with fewer females than males entering, remaining in, or completing every level of schooling. The situation is most acute in the nonindustrialized countries of East Africa, South Asia, and Southern Europe. Moreover, female participation rates in the lowest income countries decline precipitously between primary and secondary educational levels. Explanations for this decline emphasize the role that female maturation, marriage, and anticipated marriage plays in family decisions to remove girls from (largely coeducational) schooling. Single-sex secondary education, therefore, could not only facilitate female achievement, but could also promote greater female participation in schooling where the physical safety of adolescents is an issue.

4. Schooling Factors Affecting Participation

Previous policy research on female participation has touched on single-sex education only lightly. Instead, studies seeking to understand differences in male and female school participation rates have concentrated on household economic decision-making and the opportunity costs of child schooling, particularly in rural farm households. This research has emphasized: (a) the role that the demand for female child labor plays in determining school participation, and (b) the absence of anticipated returns to the family for investment in female education. Policy efforts to increase female school participation in developing countries have

therefore sought to lower the direct and indirect costs to families. Projects have subsidized families' out-of-pocket expenses for such things as schools fees, uniforms, textbooks, and other materials, and have tried to reduce the opportunity costs incurred by loss of child labor by such strategies as changing the school calendar to coincide with agricultural schedules, modifying the designs of primary schools to include preschools where students' childcare responsibilities could be met, and building more schools—particularly girls' schools—located in closer proximity to children's homes.

Of these approaches, school availability has been most studied for impact. Policy interventions have not been designed to increase the particular within school factors which might be differentially more facilitating for girls, nor has school effects research in developing countries consciously searched for such factors. Instead, school effects research has focused on inputs having uniform effects on achievement of both girls and boys, and the issue of differentiating effects has been limited to identifying factors that increase female participation in school: the presence of a (female) school, distance to school, and school safety.

4.1 Presence of a School

The actual presence or availability of schools is, of course, a major determinant of whether or not a child attends school. For example, the presence of primary schools has been found to increase the probability of children's school attendance and to increase the number of years of attained schooling in Indonesia and Brazil. However, village-level school availability was found to have no effect on primary school participation in Nepal. In many developing countries, schooling is available for the overwhelming majority of primary school-age children, including girls. On the other hand, in 1983 there were still at least 30 countries in which fewer than 80 percent of the primary school-age population had access to primary school places, and over 35 countries for which this was the case for girls. At the secondary level, access is restricted for both girls and boys, with only 31 percent of children aged 12 to 17 enrolled in the lowest income countries.

4.2 Distance to School

The distance between the child's home and the nearest appropriate school is also an important factor for participation, and distance to school has been found to be negatively associated with female school enrollment in Egypt, Philippines, Nepal, and Thailand. In all cases, children residing further from school were less likely to enroll in school than children living closer to school. Once enrolled, children living further from school were more likely to drop out than children living closer. Finally, children living further from school completed fewer years of schooling than children living closer to school; this was found in studies in Egypt, Philippines, and Thailand, but not in Nepal, principally because distances were, on average, quite short.

4.3 Safety within Schools

While school availability is certainly important for participation, the safety of students—particularly girls —within schools is emerging as a determinant of participation. There is little empirical evidence regarding unsafe schools, but anecdotal evidence abounds. For example, Deble (1980 p. 89) notes that "many people still hesitate to trust the school where girls are concerned." Lycette (1986) cites a survey of rural households in India that found about one-fifth of girls were withdrawn from school at the onset of puberty, often because parents felt it was dangerous for an unmarried girl to appear in public. The danger is, not surprisingly, sexual in nature. For example, a study of factors affecting repetition and dropout in Papua New Guinea identified "rape and coercion" as a major fear of parents about sending daughters to school. Furthermore, "about 75 percent of parents interviewed indicated a preference for sending their daughters to a mission school," since "mission schools generally provided closer supervision of both pupils and teachers, and more stringent punishment for misdemeanors —lessening the likelihood of sexual involvement" (Yeoman 1985 p. 24).

See also: Gender and Education; Sex Differences and School Outcomes; Students in Classrooms, Gender and Racial Differences Among

References

Astin A W 1977 *Four Critical Years: Effects of College on Beliefs, Attitudes, and Knowledge*. Jossey-Bass, San Francisco, California

Deble I 1980 *The School Education of Girls*. UNESCO, Paris

Finn J D 1980 Sex differences in educational outcomes: A cross-national study. *Sex Roles* 6(1): 9–26

Furniss W T, Graham P A (eds.) 1974 *Women in Higher Education*. American Council on Education, Washington, DC

Graham P A 1970 Women in academe. *Science* 169(3952): 1284–90

Jimenez E, Lockheed M E 1989 Enhancing girls' learning through single-sex education: Evidence and a policy conundrum. *Educ Eval. Policy Anal.* 11(2): 117–42

Lee V E, Bryk A S 1986 Effects of single-sex secondary schools on student achievement and attitudes. *J. Educ. Psychol.* 78(5): 381–95

Lee V E, Lockheed M E 1990 The effects of single-sex schooling on student achievement and attitudes in Nigeria. *Comp. Educ. Rev.* 34(2): 209–31

Lycette M A 1986 *Improving Basic Educational Opportunities for Women in Developing Countries*. International Center for Research on Women, Washington, DC

Oates M J, Williamson S 1978 Women's colleges and women achievers. *Signs: J. Women Culture Soc.* 3(4): 795–806

Riordan C 1985 Public and Catholic schooling: The effects of gender context policy. *Am. J. Educ.* 93(4): 518–40

Tidball M E 1980 Women's colleges and women achievers revisited. *Signs: J. Women Culture Soc.* 5(3): 504–17

Tidball M E, Kistiakowsky V 1976 Baccalaureate origins of American scientists and scholars. *Science* 193(4254): 646–52

Yeoman L 1985 Universal primary education: Factors affecting enrolment and retention of girls in Papau New Guinea community schools. Paper presented at the UNESCO Regional Review Meeting, Bangkok

Further Reading

Carpenter P, Hayden M 1987 Girls' academic achievements: Single-sex versus coeducational schools in Australia. *Sociol. Educ.* 60(3): 156–67

Dale R R 1974 *Mixed or Single-sex School? Vol. III: Attainment, Attitudes and Overview*. Routledge and Kegan Paul, London

Educational Expansion: Sociological Perspectives

J. Dronkers and S. W. van der Ploeg

In nearly every society growing numbers of pupils take part in education, stay longer in school, and reach higher levels of education. This process is referred to as educational expansion. This article sets out to describe the process of educational expansion in various societies, and give an overview of its causes and main consequences.

1. Educational Expansion in Figures

Although educational expansion nowadays is present in nearly every society, societies differ in terms of the time when educational expansion began to occur, at what speed this expansion has taken place, and at what stage is the expansion process at in the late 1990s. In general, educational expansion starts to occur at the primary level (preprimary and primary school), followed by expansion at the secondary level (secondary education, and junior and senior vocational education), and subsequently at the tertiary level (university and vocational colleges). The figures for this expansion before 1980 are given by Craig (1981), although the international comparability of these older figures is always disputable. The most reliable figures for educational expansion during the 1980s and the

1990s in different countries have been gathered by the OECD (1996 p. 113). The figures in Table 1 give the degree of participation of the relevant age group in upper secondary education and in tertiary education. Although these figures may be influenced by rapid changes in the size of the relevant age group due to demographic developments (for instance the post-1945 baby boom, both in the USA and in some parts of Europe), they give a clear picture of educational expansion during this period.

Table 1 shows clearly that between 1975 and 1994 tertiary education expanded in nearly all countries, even if the expansion at the upper secondary educational level lagged behind. But Table 1 also clearly reveals that the expansion of education does not occur at the same rate in all countries, even if countries are quite close to each other, both culturally and economically. Nor can one say that the most advanced countries have the highest level of educational participation at the upper secondary or tertiary levels (compare Germany, Japan, or United States with France, Italy, or Spain). Both this general trend of an increased educational participation in nearly all countries, and the diversity between countries, make the causes of educational expansion difficult to identify.

2. Causes of Educational Expansion

The causes of educational expansion have been the subject of scientific research over the last few decades. In general, the available research approaches can be divided into two categories: the first category emphasizing economic factors and the second emphasizing cultural and institutional factors.

Table 1
Number of full-time students enrolled in public and private upper secondary and tertiary education per 100 persons in the population aged 5 to 29 in 1975 and 1994 for different countries

	Upper secondary education		Tertiary education	
	1975	1994	1975	1994
Australia	6.9	6.5	4.5	6.2
Canada	12.5	11.9	6.7	10.8
France	8.7	12.4	4.9	10.3
Germany	11.0	11.4	4.4	8.2
Italy	10.0	15.5	4.6	9.3
Japan	9.7	12.2	4.3	8.5
Netherlands	5.1	12.3	4.9	7.5
Spain	9.0	18.2	3.7	10.1
Sweden	7.4	12.0	5.6	5.7
Turkey	3.3	6.0	1.5	3.7
United Kingdom	11.2	12.9	2.5	5.3
United States	7.3	10.7	6.6	8.8

Source: OECD 1996 p. 113

2.1 Economic Factors of Educational Expansion

The technical functional approach views education expanding in response to the increasing demand for more highly skilled labor. Two processes are responsible for this growth. First, a shift in the occupational structure towards white collar employment requires a larger proportion of better skilled, and therefore more highly educated, workers. Second, technological innovations and increasing complexity of production processes cause an upgrading of skill requirements within jobs. Trow (1961), for example, argues that the growth in American secondary schooling is largely caused by "the pull of the economy for a mass of white collar employees with more than elementary school education" (p. 145). Furthermore, he states that the rapid increase in the number of professional technical, and kindred workers, occupations that call for at least a partial college education, caused a demand for more highly trained and educated people (p. 154).

This explanation heavily emphasizes the qualification function of education. It is assumed that instrumental knowledge and skills, necessary for the performance of work, have risen and since those are taught in school the demand for education has increased. Also Clark (1962) links educational expansion to the emergence of the expert society:

> ... the educational threshold of employment has been increasingly raised since the advent of the Industrial Revolution and especially in the last half-century. Labor on the family farm did not demand literacy, but skilled jobs and clerical work in the factory required literacy and more. Now in a society where automation is taking over the tasks of routine labor, a larger proportion of jobs increasingly falls into the upper ranges of skill and expertise, in the range from profession to technician. Large scale enterprises—big business, big government, big labor, big education—demands managers, professionals and technicians, and these posts demand training beyond high school for the most part. (p. 48)

Human capital theory adds to this approach with the argument that through education, future laborers acquire knowledge and skills that have economic value. An increase in human capital leads to higher marginal productivity (Schultz 1961). Pupils invest in their own human capital by attaining higher levels of education because of its future returns, for higher marginal productivity will be rewarded by higher income. So, an increasing demand for more highly skilled workers in this view will lead to higher wages for this group, which is an incentive for youngsters to continue schooling. If the costs of education (e.g., tuition fees and foregone earnings) fall behind expected returns, young people will decide to invest in additional schooling. Again in this view education is clearly approached from its function of qualification.

Although this technical–functional approach has

met with much criticism, various findings from empirical research have shown that this explanation proves to be true for different societies and different time periods. A Dutch study has shown that the shift in the composition of the labor force towards service-oriented occupations has positively influenced growth in enrollments after 1945 (Dronkers and Van der Stelt 1986). Thus the expansion of the service and government sector is, among other processes, responsible for the expansion of secondary and tertiary education. A study of France, covering the period 1881–1970, also points out that socio-economic variables indicating shifts in the occupational structure are important in explaining educational expansion (Garnier et al. 1989). Also the effects of technological progress on educational expansion have been proven. Rubinson and Ralph (1984) found, for the United States, a positive influence of technological change on enrollments in primary education from 1890 until 1922, and on enrollments in secondary education from 1922 until 1977. The authors conclude that the impact of technological progress manifests itself only when education turns into a mass institution.

Another approach emphasizing the relation of educational expansion with economic changes stresses the controlling aspects of the expansion. In this view the rise of formal education is related to the needs of industrializing societies. Education legitimizes the existing balance of power within society and the adjustment of persons to distinct social positions. An industrial economy uses the educational system to socialize young people in order to integrate them in a hierarchical and rational economic system. The structure of the social relationships in school teaches the pupil discipline, attitudes, types of behavior, presentation, and class consciousness that are essential for the workforce. The correspondence between the relationships in the educational system and the production system creates a socialization of people into an industrious working class. So here school expansion is directly related to industrialization.

This approach is criticized by several authors, since empirical research has shown that in several cases the growing participation in education has preceded industrialization (Meyer et al. 1979, Craig 1981). So although a better educated labor force might have positively influenced industrialization, it is highly questionable whether education expanded as the result of the need for a docile working class.

An alternative theory for the explanation of educational expansion, opposing the technical–functional explanation and the human capital approach, was formulated by Collins (1971, 1979). He criticizes the assumption that skill requirements have been constantly rising over time and states that "education is often irrelevant to on-the-job productivity and is sometimes counter-productive" (1971 p. 1007). What can be observed is a rise in credential requirements over time for the same jobs and a proliferation of the

need of educational qualifications for employment. From this observation, Collins formulates his status competition model. According to his theory, education is commonly perceived as a means for upward social mobility:

> It is . . . a political process: the expansion of schools has been due to pressures from the population to expand opportunities to acquire status . . . Competition between different religious sects, ethnic groups and local governments has resulted in educational expansion; the combination of a decentralized democracy and a market for status credentials has made education into a kind of business, selling opportunities for educational degrees. While the possession of education was once confined to relatively upper-status groups (clergy and some of the leisured gentry), the creation of this competitive market made the whole system dynamic. As the older credentials became more widespread, they no longer carried the same connotation of elite status. Job requirements began to shift, requiring higher credentials since more educated people were available for jobs. (1988, p. 178)

Once this process has started, it keeps itself in motion. Credentials lose their value in terms of probabilities of obtaining higher status positions since more people become available for the same jobs. This inflation of credentials in turn causes more people to attain higher levels of education, and so on.

Thurow's labor market theory (1975) explains why employers tend to shift towards higher educational requirements if the supply of more highly educated people available for jobs rises. Collins pays no heed to this point. Thurow argues that for all vacant jobs, persons compete for the first position in the "labor queue." Those responsible for selection rank applicants in order of preference. The most preferable are generally not the ones asking for the lowest wages—since this has become invariable due to legislation and collective labor treaties—but the ones that will reduce training costs once they are employed. Consequently, wage competition is substituted by job competition. One of the major indicators for low training costs is the educational level of candidates. Those who are more highly educated tend to have good relative positions in labor queues. Candidates are aware of the value of education and credentials in this respect, so they search for additional education to beat their competitors. Thurow even speaks of education as a defensive necessity "to protect one's market share" (p. 97). Again at the aggregate level this process will lead to credential inflation, forcing new entrants to the labor market to complete even higher educational levels and thus keeping this process in motion.

Collins has founded his own theory empirically (1979) and others have interpreted their results as confirming his approach. In a contribution analyzing the American educational system from 1890 to 1970, the effect of immigrant groups on participation in schooling was examined (Ralph and Rubinson 1980). From 1890 to 1924, enrollment in private education rose as the result of the immigration of Eastern, Central, and Southern Europeans. Established groups were closing public education for these new citizens so the latter were forced into private schools. From 1924 until 1970, this negative effect of immigration on public educational expansion turned into a positive one which, according to the authors, was the result of the changing characteristic of immigration. From then on, Western European immigrants in particular were added to the American population, who were not considered a threat like the earlier immigrants. Ralph and Rubinson interpret these findings as a confirmation of the status competition approach. Privileged groups are trying to keep ahead of less privileged groups who are trying to come up.

Baker, et al. (1985), who studied the effects of immigrant workers on educational stratification in Germany, also provide arguments for effects from status competition. Investigating the period from 1960 until 1982 at the national, federal, and community level, they found that immigrant children were mainly incorporated at the bottom of the German educational system. The inflow of immigrants at the lowest levels of the system pushed German children up to higher levels of education, who were trying to keep distance in order to maintain their status. Also Van der Ploeg (1994) found competition effects at the tertiary level after 1945 until 1980 in the Netherlands.

Herweijer and Blank (1986), who examined the effect of unemployment on educational expansion using Dutch data on flows in secondary education between 1967 and 1984, also found effects from credential inflation. They argue, however, that this trend component in their analysis is limited by the existence of a "natural" level of flow to higher levels of education. According to the authors this limit had been reached at the end of the 1970s. The subsequent expansion in the 1980s therefore must be attributed to the increase in unemployment. When employment is restored, the flow rate to higher levels will return to the natural level (p. 85). Furthermore, the effect of unemployment on flow rates to higher levels appears to be positive. On the one hand, there are growing numbers of young people who seek better qualifications through education to maximize their chances of finding employment. On the other hand, schools provide a warehouse function in times of unemployment. In this latter view the educational system absorbs persons who otherwise would have entered the labor market, but who are discouraged by the relatively low chances of finding employment. A tight labor market pulls pupils out of school to fill vacant occupational positions, and pushes them back or prevents them from leaving the educational system when jobs are more difficult to obtain.

The concept of the warehouse function of education has been used earlier by Walters (1984). She only found an effect from unemployment on secondary enrollments rates before 1950 for the United States.

After 1950 this effect disappeared. Her explanation for this finding is that secondary education had become nearly universal by about 1950. When education has not already become universal for an age group, participation is discretionary. That is, the choice between pursuing an education and finding a job is real, so unemployment can have positive effects on enrollments. If a particular educational level is opened up to a large segment of the population, however, unemployment loses this impact because entering the labor market is not seen as a serious alternative.

2.2 Cultural and Institutional Factors

Garnier et al. (1989) conclude from their analysis of French educational expansion that social economic variables indicating shifts in job opportunities are only important in explaining elite expansion, not mass expansion. They attribute the expansion of mass schooling instead to state policy and the spread of the middle class standards as the relevant ones for success in education, and the attachment of educational success to occupational placement (which they label as the "myth of education"). Hage and Garnier (1990) replicated this study on French educational expansion for Great Britain and found only modest confirmation for the earlier results. They attribute this to the more hesitant government in Britain.

Ramirez and Rubinson (1979) argue that education is seen and used by political elites to generate an integration in national political cultures. States use education to construct a direct and equal political relationship with all citizens. In this way education contributes to the formation of a national identity. Often education is the single aspect of citizenship which is made compulsory, as opposed to, for example, the right to vote or the right of assembly. Therefore it plays a central role in the formation of citizenship and thus national identity. In this view the integrative function of education plays a central role. Schooling provides the development of common values and norms that ensure societal balance.

A view emphasizing cultural forces behind expansion is elaborated by Ramirez and Boli (1987) who try to explain why mass education was sponsored by states in nearly every modern Western European society at the end of the nineteenth century. They argue that as the result of three related transformations in European culture, the Reformation, and Contra Reformation, the construction of nation states and the rise of capitalistic exchange economy, five myths emerged as part of the model of Western European national societies: the myth of the individual, the myth of the nation as the aggregate of all individuals, the myth of progress, the myth of socialization, and the myth of the state as protector of the nation. These elements led to the origin of state educational systems. The progress of a nation in this view is the progress of all individuals by socializing them, with the state having primary responsibility for this socialization as protector of the nation.

This European model of national societies has been accepted worldwide: all societies incorporated into the World System organized their nations according to this model.

Why this model is accepted so widely is explained by the World System view on educational expansion which had already been developed somewhat earlier. In an attempt to explain the "world educational revolution" between 1959 and 1970 it appeared that cross-national variation in political, social, and economic characteristics hardly explained any differences in the rise of educational participation between societies (Meyer, Ramirez et al. 1979). Meyer and his colleagues view educational expansion primarily as the result of population and organization characteristics of the educational system itself. The cross-national similarity is caused by the incorporation of all states into the World System. In this system a highly educated population legitimizes established governments since there is a broad convergence in beliefs and values attached to progress. Progress is directly connected to success in economic competition, and elites who do not strive for economic and political development run the risk of losing power.

Meyer, Tyack et al. (1979) also stress cultural forces behind school expansion, but do not agree that the central government plays a key role. They conclude from their analysis of the founding of the public mass educational system in the United States in the nineteenth century that neither industrialization nor urbanization were prerequisites for this development. In fact, the less industrialized and rural North and West showed higher enrollments than towns and cities. According to these authors the early expansion in the rural areas was the result of a commonly held ideology regarding nation building: small entrepreneurs who combined evangelical Protestantism with an individual conception of polity were the basis for nation building. So it was not a political elite or powerful state that erected schools but rather hundreds of small groups trying to organize local communities.

Craig and Spear (1982) developed a hypothesis from a modernization perspective. The determinants of educational expansion must be sought in the transition from traditional to modern societies. Modernization is a kind of compounded concept referring to various more or less simultaneously occurring processes: development of nation states, industrialization, large-scale labor division, growing interdependence between different social institutions, expanding communication and transport networks, disappearance of specific regional cultures, and so on. Along with the rise of modern economic, political, and social structures, people, on the one hand, are forced to accommodate to specialized and complex assertions of a changing society, and on the other, must attain general skills necessary for communication over differentiated social and physical boundaries. In the nineteenth century schools provided for this demand. Children

were taught to handle uncertainty, autonomy, and new information. Education also played a central role in the provision of integrative aspects, for example, a common language. Garnier et al. (1989) and Hage and Garnier (1990) relate this modernization to the proliferation of the "myth of education," or the increasing valuation of education by the rising educational level of parents.

3. The Consequences of Educational Expansion

Empirical research into the consequences of educational expansion is rather scarce. Hardly any scientific attempts have been made to measure the effects of an increasingly better educated population on various societal developments. This is surprising since education draws a large part of the population from other social activities, and expenditures on education consume a great part of the national income. One would anticipate a great deal of attention being paid to the societal returns from educational expansion, because of the large investments in time and money.

There are a large number of potential effects from a rising educational level of the population. Craig (1981) and Haveman and Wolfe (1984) offer lists of possibilities. Education might, for example, result in higher earnings, greater national integration, economic growth, greater life expectancy, a more efficient working and marriage market, a reduction of fertility rates, and so forth. In the rest of this section two possible effects are discussed that are relatively well studied: the economic effects of educational expansion and the effects on credential inflation.

3.1 Economic Effects

It is commonly believed that educational expansion is a prerequisite for economic development. This belief can be traced back to the technical functional approach of educational expansion discussed in the previous section which states that the growing complexity of work demands a more highly skilled labor force, and thus a more highly skilled labor force generates economic development. Empirical research into the relationship between educational expansion and the economic behavior of societies, however, is not unequivocal. Positive effects of educational expansion are found, but in many cases they appear to be absent (Denison 1967, Lundgreen 1976, Walters and Rubinson 1983, Fuller et al. 1986, Dronkers 1988, Hage et al. 1988, Garnier and Hage 1990, Liu and Armer 1992). Furthermore, variations in periods and societies do not seem to provide possible explanations. The effects of educational expansion have been investigated in various countries (France, Germany, Mexico, The Netherlands, Taiwan, United States) and at various time points (from the nineteenth century until the late 1990s) without any clear conclusions.

One of the major obstacles for the analysis of the economic effects of educational expansion is the right level of investigation. The assumed effects of educational expansion are formulated at societal level, which leads to the calculation of a Cobb–Douglas function at a macrolevel:

$$\text{Production} = \text{Capital}^{\beta_1} * \text{Labor}^{\beta_2}$$

In this equation production is indicated by gross national product, capital by capital stock, and labor by the labor volume at different educational levels, as can be found in national statistics. Time series analysis is often used to estimate the parameters of this equation, using gross national product, capital stock, and the educational levels of the working population. Although this Cobb–Douglas function is a correct reformulation of the belief that educational expansion is a perquisite for economic development, its application is surrounded by problems, which can make the results invalid. One needs a substantial number of years with available data on gross national product, capital stock and the educational levels of the working population to make a stable and reliable estimation of the parameters. However, the more years one can use in the time analyses, the greater is the possibility that the social and economic conditions have changed dramatically (for instance a world war or the oil crises of the 1970s) which can destroy the assumptions of this Cobb–Douglas function. Another problem is that this equation is very simple and thus begs for more independent variables. However, more variables in the equation would also require more years of data. The same holds for the statistically more sophisticated models of the macrorelations between production and the educational level of the working population.

Another means of estimating the economic effects of educational expansion is a comparison between countries of their educational productivity and their educational expansion. This approach has even more limitations than the time series analysis, given the fact that the number of countries with reliable and comparable data on gross national product, capital stock, and educational levels of their working population is limited, while the number of explanations of between-country variance of gross national product is larger than simply the capital stock and the educational level of their working populations.

Given all of these problems in measuring the economic effects of educational expansion at the macrolevel, one often must resort to measurement of the long-term relation between individual educational attainment and individual income. In this case one assumes that this well-established relationship is not only true at the microlevel but also at the macrolevel. However, this assumption avoids the crucial question of whether one is allowed, in this type of case, to aggregate a relationship from a microlevel to another level, the macrolevel. Even sociologists who advocate an individual rational choice approach in the social and economic sciences (Coleman 1990) would not accept such an assumption without further empirical proof.

In conclusion, the empirical evidence for the positive economic effects of educational expansion is scarce, despite the strong belief, in policy circles around the world, of its existence.

3.2 Institutional Effects

One of the most interesting effects of educational expansion is the returns on educational credentials. Collins (1971) has argued that returns on credentials decrease as education expands. This decrease is caused by the growing supply of higher skilled workers where the demand for these skills grows at a slower rate. The subsequent substitution of lower skilled workers with higher skilled workers is described by Thurow (1975). Empirical evidence for this process is given by Van der Ploeg (1994). He shows that additional credentials always pay off in terms of attained occupational level. Furthermore, the additional returns of diplomas appear to depend on the level of proliferation of these credentials. As the proliferation rate grows, returns first grow as well until an inflation point is reached after which continuing proliferation brings about decreasing returns. The initial growth of returns when proliferation is relatively low is caused by a process described by Seidman (1984). He argued that when educational attainment at a particular educational level is small, the returns of the particular credentials would be small as well because they are not used as a prerequisite for job entry or promotion. However, returns increase as the attainment at a particular level grows, because credentials will be required more frequently for job entry, job security, and promotion. There is a point, however, at which the supply of attainers will outstrip the demand, resulting in lower returns on credentials. Here the inflation of credentials brings about a situation in which everyone has attained a particular level and consequently its additional benefit has become zero.

This process of credential inflation clearly shows how educational expansion can perpetuate itself. People tend to strive for high educational levels, for these pay off most. To achieve these high levels of education one cannot avoid first attaining the lower hurdles. The enormous spread of diplomas from these lower levels of education results in a rapid inflation of their usefulness in the labor market. In the end they may be useful only as entrance tickets to higher levels of education. Because the inflation of credentials continues, people have to attain even higher levels of education in order to gain the best relative position in the educational credential distribution

4. Conclusion

Educational expansion is not a self-evident process, neither in its causes nor its effects. This suggests a need for a critical approach to educational expansion, both for the well-being of the individuals as well as for the functioning of societies. There are clear indications in the literature that a large part of educational expansion is the result of unintended processes and consequences. This can make the positive societal effects of unconditional educational expansion, at its best, dubious and at its worst, counterproductive. But the empirical evidence for these causes and effects is still fraught with serious methodological problems (data, levels of analyses). This makes it difficult to make policy recommendations about the best approach to educational expansion. It is clearly too hazardous to restrain educational expansion with arguments about its dubious or counterproductive effects. But it is also too hazardous to promote educational expansion unconditionally with economic, social, or cultural arguments.

See also: Basic Education: Comparative and International Studies; Benefits of Education; Education and Development; Institutional Approach to the Study of Education

References

Baker D P, Esmer Y, Lenhart G, Meyer J W 1985 Effects of immigrant workers on educational stratification in Germany. *Sociol. Educ.* 58: 213–27

Clark B R 1962 *Educating the Expert Society.* Chandler, San Francisco

Collins R 1971 Functional and conflict theories of educational stratification. *Am. Sociol. Rev.* 36: 1002–19

Collins R 1979 *The Credential Society. An Historical Sociology of Education and Stratification* Academic Press, New York

Collins R 1988 *Theoretical Sociology* Harcourt Brace Jovanovich, San Diego

Coleman J 1990 *Foundations of Social Theory.* Harvard University Press, Cambridge, Massachusetts

Craig J E 1981 The expansion of education. *Rev. Res. Educ.* 9: 151–13

Craig J E, Spear N 1982 Explaining educational expansion: An agenda for historical and comparative research. In: Archer M S (ed.) 1982 *The Sociology of Educational Expansion; Take-off, Growth and Inflation in Educational Systems.* Sage, Beverly Hills, California

Denison E 1967 *Why Growth Rates Differ: Postwar Experiences in Nine Western Countries.* Brookings Institute, Washington, DC

Dronkers J, Van der Stelt H G 1986 Economische groei en onderwijsdeelname: een empirisch macro-sociologische analyse van de groei van het Nederlandse secundaire en tertiaire onderwijs sinds 1945 [Economic growth and educational enrollments: an empirical macro sociological analysis of Dutch secondary and tertiary educational expansion] In: van Wieringen A M L (ed.) 1986 *Innovatie van onderwijs en arbeid,* Swets en Zeitlinger, Lisse

Dronkers J 1993 Educational expansion and economic output in a European industrial nation during 1960–1980: the Netherlands. In: Yogev A, Dronkers J (eds.) 1993 *International Perspectives on Education and Society. Education and Social Change.* JAI Press, Greenwich, Connecticut

Fuller B, Gorman K, Edwards J 1986 The Influence of school investment quality on economic growth: An historical look at Mexico, 1880–1945. In: Heyneman S, White D (eds.) 1986 *School Quality in Developing Countries.* World Bank, Washington, DC

Garnier M A, Hage J, Fuller B 1989 The strong state, social class, and controlled school expansion in France, 1881–1975. *Am. J. Sociol.* 95: 279–306

Garnier A M, Hage J 1990 Education and economic growth in Germany. In: Corwin R G (ed.) 1990 *Research in Sociology of Education and Socialisation.* JAI Press, Greenwich, Connecticut

Hage J, Garnier M A 1990 Social class, the hesitant state, and the expansion of secondary schools in Britain, 1870–1975. In: Corwin R C (ed.) 1990 *Research in Sociology of Education and Socialization. Historical Approaches.* JAI Press, Greenwich, Connecticut

Hage J, Garnier M A, Fuller B 1988 The active state, investment in human capital and economic growth. *Am. Sociol. Rev.* 53(6): 824–37

Haveman R H, Wolfe B L 1984 Education, productivity and well-being. On defining and measuring the economic characteristics of schooling. In: Dean E (ed.) 1984 *Education and Economic Productivity.* Ballinger, Cambridge

Herweijer L J, Blank J L T 1986 De groei van het mbo: de invloed van werkgelegenheid op onderwijsdeelneming [The growth of senior vocational education: the effects of employment on educational participation] In: Wieringen A M L van (ed.) 1986 *Innovatie van onderwijs en arbeid.* Swets and Zeitlinger, Lisse

Lui C, Armer J M 1992 *Educational effects and non-effects on economic growth in Taiwan, 1953–1985.* Paper presented at the Annual Congress of the American Sociological Association

Lundgreen P 1976 Educational expansion and economic growth in nineteenth century Germany: a quantitative study. In: Stone L (ed.) 1976 *Schooling and Society.* Johns Hopkins University Press, Baltimore, Maryland

Meyer J W, Ramirez F O, Rubinson R, Boli-Bennett J 1979 The world educational revolution, 1950–1970. In: Meyer J W, Hannan M T (eds.) 1979

Meyer J W, Tyack D, Nagel T, Gordon A 1979 Public education as nation-building in America: Enrollments and bureaucratization in the American States, 1870–1930. *Am. J. Sociol.* 85: 591–613

OECD 1996 *Education at a Glance.* OECD Indicators. OECD, Paris

Ramirez F O, Boli J 1987 The political construction of mass schooling: European origins and worldwide institutionalization. *Sociol. Educ.* 60: 2–17

Ramirez F O, Rubinson R 1979 Creating members: The political incorporation and expansion of public education. In: Meyer J W, Hannan M T (eds.) 1979

Ralph J, Rubinson R 1980 Immigration and the expansion of schooling in the United States, 1890–1970. *Am. Sociol. Rev.* 45: 943–54

Rubinson R, Ralph J 1984 Technical change and the expansion of school in the United States, 1890–1969. *Sociol. Educ.* 57: 134–52

Schultz T W 1961 Investment in human capital. *Am. Econ. Rev.* 51: 1–17

Seidman R H 1984 The logic and behavioral principles of educational systems: social independence or dependence. In: Archer M S (ed.) 1984 *The Sociology of Educational Expansion.* Sage, Beverly Hills, California

Thurow L C 1975 *Generating Inequality; Mechanisms of Distribution in the US Economy*. Basic Books, New York

Trow M 1961 The second transformation of American secondary education. *Int. J. Comp. Sociol.* 2: 144–66

Van der Ploeg S W 1994 Educational expansion and returns on credentials. *Eur. Sociol. Rev.* 10(1): 63–78

Walters P B, Rubinson R 1983 Educational expansion and economic output in the United States, 1890–1969: a production function analysis. *Am. Sociol. Rev.* 48: 480–93

Walters P B 1984 Occupational and labour market effects on secondary and postsecondary educational expansion in the United States: 1922 to 1979. *Am. Sociol. Rev.* 49: 659–71

Further Reading

Grossman M 1975 The correlation between health and schooling. In: Terleckyi N E (ed.) 1975 *Household Production and Consumption*. National Bureau of Educational Research, New York

Meyer J W, Hannan M T (eds.) 1979 *National Development and the World System: Educational, Economic and Political Change 1950–1970*. University of Chicago Press, Chicago, Illinois

Rubinson R 1986 Class formation, politics and institutions: Schooling in the United States. *Am. J. Sociol.* 92: 519–48.

Effective Secondary Schools

V. E. Lee

Although the definition of school effectiveness has changed over time, attention to student outcomes—especially achievement—is constant. After defining "effectiveness," this article explores both the external and internal factors that influence a school's organizational effectiveness, for both the students who attend and the teachers who work there. This summary is based on a broad review of school organizational effects in the United States by Lee et al. (1993).

1. Background of Research on Effective Secondary Schools

The conceptual framework for this entry sees schools as influenced by both external and internal forces. While schools are shaped by external factors, their organizations also mediate the influence of those factors on the experiences of school members: teachers and students. The primary focus is on the internal organization of secondary schools, and how these factors influence the work of teachers and students. After defining "effectiveness," two distinct streams of research related to school organization are identified: (a) the rational–bureaucratic; (b) the communitarian. Using the contrasting views, external and internal features of school organization are related to effectiveness.

The history of school effects studies is a short one. Early studies, which followed from the publication of Coleman et al.'s (1966) seminal work *Equality of Educational Opportunity*, were framed as input–output studies. Such studies were disappointing, in that they were unable to show that inputs (primarily such resources as library books or per-pupil expenditure) were nearly as influential on student outcomes as family background. The next wave of studies focused on social stratification (by race and class) in educational attainment, mostly measured by years of education. Neither type of study attempted to explore the internal organization of schools. More promising was the wave of "effective schools" research in the late 1970s and early 1980s, which began to look inside schools for explanations of differences in student performance, especially for disadvantaged students. These studies, which focused primarily on elementary schools, are summarized in two strong reviews (Rosenholtz 1985, Purkey and Smith 1983).

Unfortunately, past studies on school effects "have collected and analyzed data in ways that conceal more than they reveal. The established methods have generated false conclusions in many studies" (Cronbach 1976 p.1). As Bidwell and Kasarda (1980) noted, most studies of school effects failed to make the crucial distinction between the school as an organization and the instructional process of schools. Fortunately, statistical advances, combined with a sociological perspective, have facilitated a more productive approach to school effects research. The difficulties of past efforts, and the formulation of the new studies, are summarized by Lee et al. (1993). The present entry is selective in the research reviewed, in that studies displaying the methodological weaknesses described are afforded less credence than those using newer approaches. In short, valid research on school effects must allow: (a) the appropriate statistical estimation of organizational effects; and (b) examination of distributional effects within schools. Past research, most of which focused on means differences between schools, has systematically either underestimated or ignored these important issues.

2. Contrasting Sociological Views of Schools

2.1 Formal Organizations versus Small Societies

Schools as organizations may be conceptualized through two contrasting lenses (Bidwell 1965). From a rational–bureaucratic perspective, schools are "formal" organizations, with authority defined by roles rather than persons, labor divided into specialized tasks, teachers seen as subject-matter specialists, and rules defining behavior with little personal discretion. The comprehensive public high school, first described by Conant (1959) and very common in contemporary society (Powell 1986) epitomizes the rational–bureaucratic view of schooling. In sharp contrast is the communal perspective, where schools are seen as "small societies." Under this conception, informal social relationships are emphasized, with schools operating under unique sets of values (instead of rules) which all members support. Adult roles are diffuse rather than specialized, with a minimal division of labor. Contemporary Catholic high schools (Bryk et al. 1993) are representative of the "small society" view of schools.

Schools seen as "good" or "effective" under the two definitions evidence very different characteristics. Where efficiency is paramount in the first view, strong social ties characterize the second. Until the late 1980s, both school organization itself and research on school effectiveness have been dominated by the bureaucratic view. However, some writings on schools have begun to question the very aims of schooling, the societal values that undergird these aims, and the meaning of the work of adults and students in schools. Such questioning lends support to the alternative view.

2.2 Definition of an "Effective Secondary School"

In attempting to take the "small society" view seriously, this entry defines "effectiveness" rather broadly. While not ignoring students as the primary clients of schools, adults who work there (mainly teachers) are also seen as important members of school organizations for whom the school and its work must have meaning. Although academic achievement is acknowledged as the primary component of "effectiveness," the definition is expanded to include students' engagement in the schooling enterprise. Moreover, the operant definition also includes a focus on the internal distribution of these outcomes inside each school. Who achieves? Who is engaged? In other words, besides high average levels of achievement and engagement, the effective secondary school should include an equitable distribution of these outcomes among students of different social and intellectual backgrounds. Such a definition presupposes that, in general, schools should not be serving entirely homogeneous clienteles —racially, socially, or intellectually.

3. External Influences on Organizational Effectiveness

3.1 School Size

How the size of a school influences its effectiveness depends on one's perspective. Much research on school size favors the bureaucratic view, presuming that larger schools are more efficient. Historically, economy of scale has provided the major argument for school and district consolidation (Conant 1959, Guthrie 1979). It is also clear that increased size leads to program specialization and differentiation (Lee and Bryk 1989). Large schools are characterized by social stratification in both learning opportunities and academic outcomes, with the potential that both students and teachers become alienated from the school and its aims. While it is certainly the case that a broader set of offerings is more likely in larger schools, it is unclear that a broader curriculum necessarily benefits students (Powell 1986). At least in comparison to the trend toward larger schools in urban settings, it would appear that smaller schools are preferable. This is consistent with Goodlad's (1984) suggestion that the ideal high school size is 500 to 600 students, considerably smaller than today's comprehensive high schools.

3.2 Diversity of Attendance

A basic organizational challenge is how schools should respond to the diversity of students who attend them. The limited research on student body composition focuses on three distinct features: race/ethnicity, social class, and student ability. The most useful focus is on students as a resource for learning. A school's population shapes the curriculum and the policies that map students to that curriculum. It is clear that schools respond differently to students with similar entry characteristics. The academic structure of a school and its underlying belief system about who can learn what shape students' academic experiences, their engagement with learning, and their subsequent achievement.

Research conducted in the United States on racial composition is primarily focused on the effects of school desegregation. Reviews by Mahard and Crain (1983) and Schofield and Sagar (1983) examined effects of desegregation on, respectively, achievement and human relations. In short, while minority students are somewhat advantaged academically by attending mostly white schools, social relations are isolating for minority students. More important, desegregating schools usually does not result in multiracial learning experiences, since students are almost always grouped by ability for instruction, usually resulting in racially separate learning experiences (Eyler et al. 1983).

High concentrations of disadvantaged students affect the maintenance of social order, often fomenting a peer culture actively opposed to learning. Social class composition is most often seen as a proxy for fiscal and human resources, seldom examined independently from race and ethnicity. Lee and Bryk (1989) found that while average school social class is positively related to higher achievement, it also increases the relationship between student social class and achievement.

School social class plays a much stronger role in public than Catholic schools, with affluent public schools being strongly socially differentiating environments.

The most important compositional research focuses on ability. Rutter et al. (1979) found that an "academic balance in intakes to the schools" was crucial in developing a positive ethos in secondary schools with high proportions of disadvantaged students (p.178). This view is expanded conceptually in "vacancy theory" (Sorensen 1987). Resources within schools (teachers, materials, time) are distributed through ability groups. As the number of places in each instructional group is also limited, the structure of ability groups is not necessarily matched to the distribution of student ability in each school.

3.3 Governance Structure

Research comparing public and private schools is subject to criticism on grounds of selectivity bias, no matter how many controls are introduced to adjust statistically for intake differences. Nevertheless, a large body of research comparing Catholic and public schools suggests that the considerable organizational differences between schools in the two sectors are responsible for favorable student and teacher outcomes in Catholic schools (summarized in Bryk et al. 1993, Lee et al. 1993). Control over entry and exit (i.e., the ability to select and remove students and teachers) is seen as an inherent advantage of private schools, although only one study (Bryk and Driscoll 1988) has examined this question empirically, finding that selectivity did exercise considerable organizational advantage. It is clear that the overly legalistic response of public high schools in the 1970s to disruptive student behavior, and their inability to remove the most troublesome, acted as a major obstacle to their smooth operation (Grant 1988).

3.4 Parents and the Community

While it is impossible to ignore the larger societal context within which schools operate, limited space in this entry constrains thorough treatment of the subject. Parental involvement operates in three contexts: (a) through parental support of the school and its aims; (b) through family lifestyles, which offer support for education; and (c) more specifically through parents' direct efforts to help their children with their academic work. All are important, though less likely to occur in schools enrolling large numbers of disadvantaged students. If poor children are to have access to the opportunities of mainstream life in the United States, then socialization toward that end must occur both in school and at home.

It is common, particularly under the bureaucratic view, to see home environment as a potential problem that may be "solved" through parent education. In this view, control of education remains with professionals, and possible disjunction of home and school

values is not addressed directly. This view has been challenged, increasingly manifested through efforts toward community control of schools in poor communities. Another option, the functional community (Coleman and Hoffer 1987), combines the bureaucratic and communitarian perspectives. While productive social relations between families and schools are stressed, the school is seen as a limited community focused on educational aims. The professional expertise of school staff retains a special role which is respected by families.

4. Internal Influences on Organizational Effectiveness

The external influences on schools affect teacher and student outcomes indirectly, mostly through their effects on the school's internal organization. Four broad considerations guide the discussion here of internal organization. The most important of these centers on a school's formal organization (see Sect. 4.3): how are schools organized as workplaces for teachers and students?

4.1 School Culture

What are the belief systems in schools, the goals that schools set for themselves, and how are these cultural beliefs and goals distributed among staff and students? Most of this work centers on "school climate"— teacher commitment, peer norms, academic emphasis and expectations, and goal consistency. Two types of research are typical: (a) empirically based but theoretically weak studies; and (b) more recent ethnographic and anthropological work. Rather than implying any particular configuration of beliefs, research on school cultures tends to emphasize the unique aspects of each school. Research on this topic from a bureaucratic view has focused on organizational goals, and effective schools research has used a goal model perspective (e.g., Hoy and Ferguson 1985). However, this research focus is more appropriate for elementary than secondary schools, which often have concurrent but conflicting goals.

The presence of shared values among a school's staff has received attention, including norms for instruction and civility (Bird and Little 1986). Good examples of this type of work include ethnographic accounts of schools, such as those by Grant (1988) and Lightfoot (1983). In general, consistent academic and social norms favor the communal over the bureaucratic perspective. The commonality of these goals is characterized by a routine expression of feelings about the welfare of others.

4.2 Administration

While the research base on secondary school administration is vast, very few studies are empirically based or published in scholarly journals. The research may be categorized in terms of roles:

(a) management role (allocating resources, developing and enforcing rules, and supervising staff development and evaluation);

(b) mediation role (facilitating communication between the school and its external constituencies, buffering the technical core of instruction, communicating policy decisions and problems); and

(c) leadership role (shaping and defining the operant and official goals, providing guidance and supervision of instruction).

Most of this research has a definite bureaucratic inclination. In general, schools organized communally tend to have a thinner administrative structure. In highly bureaucratized schools, such attitudes as "Just tell me what you want me to do" are not uncommon. Such risk-averse behaviors are not productive to advancing quality teaching and good schooling. The inherent ambiguity and uncertainty in teaching induce dependence on students' efforts for teachers to feel successful, a situation fostered by strong social supports from colleagues and parents. The communitarian perspective here offers a strong contrast to the more common bureaucratic approach.

Issues of leadership in secondary schools are complicated by the size and diversity of academic purpose often operant in a single school. Most research on leadership in effective schools centers on elementary schools. The bureaucratic and communitarian views stand in sharp contrast here. Bureaucratic notions of school leadership are expressed primarily through the formulation of clear educational goals. From the communitarian perspective, the cultural rather than the managerial dimensions of leadership are paramount. One view concentrates on rules, policies, and procedures; the other on situations, personalities, and a developed set of norms and understandings. While the research base linking characteristics of leadership directly to teacher and student outcomes is weak, the importance of leadership in any school's organization is undisputed.

4.3 Formal Organization of Work

An important aspect of secondary compared with elementary schools is the organization of instruction through the subunits of departments. Departments play an important role in teachers' lives, forming the locus of their primary social and professional ties. Case studies suggest that important decisions about what courses are offered, and about who will teach and who will take which courses, occur within departments. Under bureaucratic theory, departmentalization is a deliberate organizational device to enhance academic learning, although little is known about the social consequences that may accrue. It seems reasonable that some differentiation in goal consensus, program coherence, and social structures within a high school may occur as a result of strong departmentalization. This is important if it detracts from teachers' loyalty to the school community, since teachers in communally organized schools are more satisfied with their work and experience a higher sense of staff morale (Bryk and Driscoll 1988, Lee et al. 1991) (see *Teachers' Work and Political Action*).

Work specialization in secondary schools is a central aspect of their organization as bureaucracies. The contemporary comprehensive high school has a highly differentiated staff catering to students' specialized needs (Powell et al. 1985). Under bureaucratic theory, staff specialization allows a school to deliver its services in an efficient manner. Another perspective is offered by Newmann (1981), however, who describes the considerable alienation that may result in an organization fostering transient interactions between teachers and students rather than more affiliative adult–student relationships. An alternative role for teachers gives them broad responsibilities extending beyond classroom duties and subject specialties. A more extended or diffuse teacher role recognizes the responsibility of schools to influence students' social and personal development, as well as their academic prowess. Developing warm personal relationships outside of class catalyzes students' engagement in class. Such personal relationships also benefit teachers, providing a source of the intrinsic rewards so important to them (Lortie 1975). A diffuse teacher role characterizes Catholic high schools (Bryk et al. 1993).

A critical feature differentiating effective from ineffective schools is how schools organize academic work for their students. A large body of research in the 1980s described the general atmosphere of secondary schools: students as passive recipients of teaching that is often characterized as routinized and deadening (Goodlad 1984, Grant 1988, Powell et al. 1986). These accounts also describe instruction as highly stratified, with top-track students much more likely to be found in small classes characterized by stimulating teaching and engaged students. Exceptions to this general pattern have been reported, however (Lightfoot 1983), especially in field accounts of Catholic high schools (Bryk et al. 1993).

This research builds on a well-established base of work on a particular organizational feature of high schools, tracking, and how schools control students' opportunities to learn through this mechanism. Traditional tracking structures, where courses are organized into a small and well-defined number of specific curricular programs and students mapped to courses through the curricular programs, changed during the 1970s and 1980s. With a virtual explosion of the high school curriculum, students had to confront many more options in selecting their courses of study, with enormous diversity in student programs even within the same high school. As a result, research has begun to focus on actual course enrollments rather than tracking. A research focus on either course taking or tracking shares a similar concern, however: the differential exposure to academic subject matter and the consequences deriving from this exposure.

Conclusions from this research, most of which has employed the large longitudinal database on 1980s American high schools and their students called "High School and Beyond" are similar. Quite simply, student course-taking and tracking are the most powerful predictors of academic achievement, surpassing the effects of personal background and a wide array of personal attitudes and behaviors (Gamoran 1987, Lee and Bryk 1988 are examples of this work). The policy implications of this research are clear: any effort to affect academic achievement must target policies and practices that determine students' exposure to subject matter.

The "student side" of the specialization of labor discussed earlier for teachers focuses on the role of school organization in creating differentiating learning opportunities. Three studies are particularly prominent in this area. Garet and Delaney (1988), who showed that there were substantial school-by-school differences in the probability of equivalent students taking advanced courses, concluded that stratification in students' opportunities to learn resulted, in part, from school decisions about courses and offerings. In parallel analyses for students in Catholic and public high schools, Lee and Bryk (1988) examined how student background and ability mapped onto academic experiences, and how those experiences, in turn, influenced achievement. Holding student background constant, they found that a much larger proportion of Catholic high school students were placed in the academic curriculum track, and that background was less strongly related to track placement in Catholic high schools. In fact, the largest Catholic–public differences in academic course enrollments were in the nonacademic tracks. In other words, much less internal differentiation in course-taking (and subsequent achievement) was found in Catholic high schools because of their proactive policy of encouraging an academic curriculum for all students.

Direct empirical evidence about the role of curriculum organization in effecting an equitable distribution of achievement was presented by Lee and Bryk (1989). The constrained academic structure in Catholic high schools acts to minimize the normal differentiating effects that accompany wide latitude in course choices. The smaller size of these schools helps play a role in this, since it is easier to create a more internally differentiated academic structure in a larger school. Moreover, other aspects of the normative environment of schools were important. For example, achievement (especially for minorities) was higher in schools with orderly and safe environments. Achievement was also positively affected by schools with lower teacher absenteeism and higher teacher commitment. It is important to note that this research takes a new methodological approach, where the effects of schools on students are estimated with statistical methods that take this hierarchical structure into account.

4.4 Social Relations

A focus on social relations, influenced strongly by the work of Waller (1932) and Dewey (1966), is an important topic in research on secondary schools. Faculty collegiality, from a bureaucratic view, is a vehicle for promoting horizontal communication within the organization, aiming to bring collective technical expertise to bear on specific school problems. However, collegiality has both formal and informal dimensions, the informal social networks providing professional and personal support to teachers who otherwise suffer from severe isolation in their jobs. Cooperative relations among faculty are seen as critical to accomplishing the academic work of the school.

From the student perspective, peer influence may operate either to promote or to inhibit positive educational outcomes (Epstein 1983). The social structure of student interactions may operate either in opposition to, or in sychronization with the orientation of the school, which is related strongly to such organizational features as ability grouping and tracking, the cultural environment, and students' interactions with teachers. Schools can also quite consciously promote common activities and rituals which foster positive adult–student relations. Moreover, student participation in a common curriculum, where students have little choice (and which changes little over time), constitutes a ritual in itself, as students interact with one another and with past members as a part of the school's tradition.

The alienating quality of high schools has received some attention (Grant 1988, Newmann 1981), particularly in the context of problems in urban schools. While teachers and students are mutually dependent, the excessively bureaucratic role of teachers as subject specialists does not foster the important relationships needed for both groups to thrive. Several factors may break the common cycle of alienation: students perceiving what they learn as relevant to their lives; mutual respect between teachers and students; high expectations for student success; and faculty influence over decisions important in their professional lives.

5. Conclusion

The two perspectives introduced in this entry provide different orientations toward schools. Within the bureaucratic perspective, internal organizational factors are seen as instrumental, with efficiently organized and formally defined activities aimed at the academic ends of schools. Social relations are organizational features to be managed, rather than ends in themselves, which is how they would be viewed from a communitarian perspective.

It should be clear that the preference of this review is, generally, toward the communitarian view fostering more effective secondary schools. This orientation is primarily directed toward altering the historical development toward comprehensive high schools. Larger school size, greater curriculum complexity, and a dense external policy network seem to have resulted in organizational environments characterized by distrust, social conflict, and a lack of meaningful human relations. This trend has been most marked in urban public school districts, where demands are typically greater and resources to address them more constrained.

Contrasted with this trend is a view of schooling that emphasizes community–cooperative work, effective communication, and shared goals. While this perspective seems possibly reflective of an idealized past, and contains a danger of particularization (closeness within implying closure to the outside), the modern Catholic high school in the United States seems to have achieved many of the positive aspects of effective schools described here without closure. Field research on these schools describes them as having strong institutional norms linked to basic religious beliefs about the dignity of each person and a shared responsibility for advancing a just, caring society. While it is obviously easier to espouse these ideals from a religious base, it is also clear that such norms are entirely in line with basic democratic ideals.

In short, the effective secondary school should be relatively small, with a constrained academic program followed by all students regardless of their family background, their academic preparation, or their future aspirations. Teachers in such schools should see themselves as developers of character rather than simply as subject specialists. The communitarian critique of contemporary schooling is most important in drawing attention to individual commitment, and how such commitment is grounded in particular beliefs, values, and understandings. Current reform movements toward such issues as "school choice," "school-site autonomy," and "community control" will fail in their efforts to achieve important change in schools until these more fundamental issues are addressed.

See also: Bureaucracy and School Effectiveness; Effective Schools Research: Methodological Issues

References

Bidwell C E 1965 The school as a formal organization. In: March J G (ed.) 1965 *Handbook of Organizations*. Rand-McNally, Chicago, Illinois

Bidwell C E, Kasarda J D 1980 Conceptualizing and measuring the effects of schools and schooling. *Am. J. Educ.* 88(4): 401–30

Bird T, Little J W 1986 How schools organize the teaching occupation. *Elem. Sch. J.* 86(4): 493–511

Bryk A S, Driscoll M E 1988 *The High School as Community: Contextual Influences, and Consequences for Students and Teachers*. National Center on Effective Secondary Schools, University of Wisconsin–Madison, Madison, Wisconsin

Bryk A S, Lee V E, Holland P B 1993 *Catholic Schools and the Common Good*. Harvard University Press, Cambridge, Massachusetts

Coleman J S et al. 1966 *Equality of Educational Opportunity*. National Center for Educational Statistics/US Government Printing Office, Washington, DC

Coleman J S, Hoffer T 1987 *Public and Private High Schools: The Impact of Communities*. Basic Books, New York

Conant J B 1959 *The American High School Today: A First Report to Interested Citizens*. McGraw-Hill, New York

Cronbach L J 1976 *Research on Classrooms and Schools: Formulations of Questions, Design, and Analysis*. Stanford Evaluation Consortium, School of Education, Stanford University, Stanford, California

Dewey J 1966 *Democracy and Education: An Introduction to the Philosophy of Education*. Free Press, New York

Epstein J L 1983 The influence of friends on achievement and affective outcomes. In: Epstein J L, Karweit N (eds.) 1983 *Friends in School: Patterns of Selection and Influence in Secondary Schools*. Academic Press, New York

Eyler J, Cook V J, Ward L E 1983 Resegregation: Segregation within desegregated schools. In: Rossell C H, Hawley W D (eds.) 1983 *The Consequences of School Desegregation*. Temple University Press, Philadelphia, Pennsylvania

Gamoran A 1987 The stratification of high school learning opportunities. *Sociol. Educ.* 60(3): 135–55

Garet M S, Delaney B 1988 Student courses and stratification. *Sociol. Educ.* 61(2): 61–77

Goodlad J I 1984 *A Place Called School: Prospects for the Future*. McGraw-Hill, New York

Grant G 1988 *The World We Created at Hamilton High*. Harvard University Press, Cambridge, Massachusetts

Guthrie J 1979 Organizational scale and school success. *Educ. Eval. Policy Anal.* 1(1): 17–27

Hoy W K, Ferguson J 1985 A theoretical framework and exploration of organizational effectiveness of schools. *Educ. Admin. Q.* 21(2): 117–34

Lee V E, Bryk A S 1988 Curriculum tracking as mediating the social distribution of high school achievement. *Sociol. Educ.* 61(2): 78–94

Lee V E, Bryk A S 1989 A multilevel model of the social distribution of high school achievement. *Sociol. Educ.* 62(3): 172–92

Lee V E, Dedrick R F, Smith J B 1991 The effect of the social organization of schools on teachers' efficacy and satisfaction. *Sociol. Educ.* 64(3): 190–208

Lee V E, Bryk A S, Smith J B 1993 The organization of effective high schools. *Rev. Res. Educ.* 19:171–267

Lightfoot S L 1983 *The Good High School: Portraits of Character and Culture*. Basic Books, New York

Lortie D C 1975 *Schoolteacher*. University of Chicago Press, Chicago, Illinois

Mahard R E, Crain R L 1983 Research on minority achievement in desegregated schools. In: Rossell C H, Hawley W D (eds.) 1983 *The Consequences of School Desegregation*. Temple University Press, Philadelphia, Pennsylvania

Newmann F M 1981 Reducing student alienation in high schools: Implications of theory. *Harv. Educ. Rev.* 51(4): 546–64

Powell A G, Farrar E, Cohen D V 1985 *The Shopping Mall High School: Winners and Losers in the Educational Marketplace.* Houghton Mifflin, Boston, Massachusetts

Purkey S C, Smith M S 1983 Effective schools: A review. *Elem. Sch. J.* 83(4): 427–52

Rosenholtz S J 1985 Effective schools: Interpreting the evidence. *Am. J. Educ.* 93(3): 352–88

Rutter M, Maughan B, Mortimore P, Ouston J 1979 *Fifteen-Thousand Hours: Secondary Schools and Their Effects on Children.* Harvard University Press, Cambridge, Massachusetts

Schofield J W, Sagar H A 1983 Desegregation, school practices, and student race relations. In: Rossell C H, Hawley W D (eds.) 1983 *The Consequences of School Desegregation.* Temple University Press, Philadelphia, Pennsylvania

Sorensen A B 1987 The organizational differentiation of students in schools as an opportunity structure. In: Hallinan M T (ed.) 1987 *The Social Organization of Schools.* Plenum, New York

Waller W 1932 *The Sociology of Teaching.* Russell & Russell, New York

Equality, Policies for Educational

J. Oxenham

. . .empirical data show that all Western industrial societies have been characterized since the end of World War II both by a steady decrease in Inequalities of Educational Opportunity and by an almost complete stability of Inequalities in Social Opportunity. . . Indeed, the educational growth witnessed in all Western industrial societies since 1945 has been accompanied by an increase rather than a decrease in economic inequality, even though the educational system has become more equalitarian in the meanwhile. (Boudon 1973 pp. xii–xiii)

The subject of this article is policies for educational equality. Yet the quotation above illustrates that educational equality is generally not viewed as an end in itself. Rather, it is treated as one means of reducing economic and social inequality. Accordingly, some perspective on its place among other means and ends and among factors which promote or militate against them is a desirable preliminary.

1. Origins

What educational equality might mean in practice will be examined a little further on. At this point, the origins of concern with it need to be recalled. The concept has risen to sustained prominence only since the nineteenth century, policies to realize it have become general only in the twentieth century, and research and publication on the topic have risen to a flood only in the second half of the twentieth century. Its elaboration has coincided with or followed the increasing industrialization and bureaucratization of societies and rise of various forms of elected representative government.

Six factors seem to explain it. The first is the perception that certain forms and degrees of inequality constitute a social problem. Inequality exists and persists in the distribution of wealth, incomes, social status, occupational status, and political power in all known major societies. Although the range of inequality in any aspect varies from society to society, no

state has yet been able to abolish inequality. That states or societies might want to abolish it, or at least reduce it, implies the second factor, namely the idea and powerful appeal of egalitarianism. Expressions of it can be found in capitalistic polities, like that of the United States, in so-called social democratic welfare states like that of Sweden, and in socialistic ones like that of the Soviet Union.

Concomitant but not wholly consistent with the second is the third factor, the twin notions of meritocracy and social mobility: those who deserve to should be able to gain promotion through the various strata of a society to whatever position they desire. Merit is to be measured by impartial, objective criteria. Meritocracy concords with equality insofar as it supposes equal treatment for equally deserving. It diverges from equality insofar as it implies the probability of unequal merit and, thus, unequal promotion.

Fourth are the associated notions that education improves the quality of a person, that an educated person is more productive economically and socially than one who is uneducated—and that a more educated person is more productive than a less educated person; and hence that an educated nation is likely to be a more productive and generally better nation. Education then is in both the public and the private interest. Fifth is the apparently consequent direct link created between education, on the one hand, and merit and eligibility for socioeconomic promotion, on the other. Education has been made a prime public and objective criterion for qualifying (and disqualifying) people for particular ranges of occupations and incomes. The means is a schedule of correspondence between scholastic attainment and eligibility for specific jobs or training for such jobs and their associated salaries, careers, and connections.

This link between education, employment, and incomes is clearly a phenomenon of a particular organization of employment and a particular organization of education—which is the sixth factor. It does not appear where independent household, individual, or even small enterprise employment are the only forms of livelihood. It presupposes instead relatively large-scale, bureaucratized employers selecting from among numerous would-be employees, and therefore actively attempting to distinguish inequalities of eligibility. The employers offer jobs on certain conditions, a major one of which is an educational qualification—particularly for young entrants to the employment market. Those who seek the jobs must of necessity satisfy the conditions. As societies have industrialized, so large-scale employers have increased and independent employment declined and wage-salary employment spread. An important consequence has been that educational qualifications have become more and more necessary to more and more people.

Correspondingly, the organization of education has shifted from being a concern solely of the family or household and perhaps of religious bodies to being a matter of the state. Education has become increasingly, almost exclusively, identified with a set of institutions called schools, universities, and the like. Most of them are now provided by the state from public funds, although in many countries significant private sectors flourish. They have enabled the establishment and elaboration of objective educational standards, credentials, and qualifications by which employers can distinguish between and select from numbers of applicants for employment. Further since occupational status heavily influences social status as well, the credentials are doubly important. Hence access to qualifications has become an important political issue, for which policies need to be devised.

It will have been noted that education has been ranked only fourth and fifth among six factors. Even then, a sixth has followed, which again appears to explain, rather than be explained by, education. The inference is plainly that the concern for educational equality is a dependent phenomenon, deriving its importance less from educational, and more from economic and social considerations. A further inference may be that the educational system is itself subordinate to other forces in society and is less able to influence them than they it. Consequently, policies for educational equality may succeed in reducing educational inequality without—as the introductory quotation suggests—having the slightest effect on other inequalities.

That said, two points remain crucial. Both apply to all societies, which have moved away from inheritance as the major overt determinant of occupational and social status. The first is that, however unequal the society in economic or social terms, social mobility is considerable. Substantial proportions of people can move up the occupational, income, and social scales and similarly substantial proportions can move down. The observation may be truer of the currently industrializing countries than it is of the industrialized. The second point is that educational attainment is as yet the most important determinant of mobility. With-

out a good education, a person of low social status will find promoting himself (or particularly herself) extremely difficult. A person of higher social status correspondingly will have difficulty maintaining his or her position and will probably need to be protected by his or her family and peers. These difficulties will be more or less severe, according to the degree of meritocracy and bureaucratization in a society. In all cases, however, access to and the utilization of education remain issues of high concern for individuals intent on improving, or at least retaining, their status and that of their children. The aggregation of that intent creates the social demand for education, which in turn makes demands on social resources and so creates the need for policies. Policies in their turn are better oriented by clear values, concepts, and goals.

2. Educational Equality—Definitions

The values behind the idea of educational equality are clear enough. One the one hand, there are general notions of fairness and equity. On the other there is the view that human rationality should as far as possible rectify the random inequities of nature and social history. As education can make such large differences in life chances and as it can be provided rationally, fairness seems to demand that (randomly) bright children born into (randomly) unfavoring environments should have the education to enable them to equal equally bright children born into favoring circumstances. Even more does fairness seem to require that such children should not be constrained by their unfavoring environment to do worse than less bright children born into favoring environments. This view is well-encapsulated in Section 26 of the United Nations Declaration of Human Rights which claims access to education for children irrespective of the social class, economic conditions and place of residence of their parents.

Fairness does not of course stop with the bright children. The less bright children also are the products of random distributions of genes and environments. For them, the sense of fairness demands that they should have such education as will enable them at least to maintain at a constant level their deficits vis-à-vis the brighter. Education should at least not widen the gaps between the bright and the less bright. At best, it might even enable some narrowing of the gap (Rawls 1971).

This illustration of values now highlights a cardinal and double difficulty with the concept of educational equality itself. If it is true that there are inequalities of "brightness"—the vague word is used deliberately—what can educational equality mean? For inequalities of brightness can be associated with inequalities of learning ability, talent, interest, motivation, energy, diligence, or manual dexterity. Should, indeed could, educational equality require the equalization of all these aspects?

At this point—and before proceeding to the second part of the difficulty—a debate needs to be noted. The preceding paragraph implies an assumption that at least part of brightness and other abilities is inborn or due to genetic inheritance. One school of thought would argue that, whatever the inheritance, its effects are negligible in relation to those of the environment. Social class, economic conditions, the education of parents, place of residence, the preferred peer group are all likely to provide the overwhelming influences on the development of brightness. A second school of thought, on the other hand, would point to the disparities of brightness not only within families, as between siblings born of the same parents, but even between identical or monozygotic twins, and even more between fraternal or dyzygotic twins. Here, environments are held virtually constant, yet considerable inequalities appear not only in educational attainments, but also in later occupations and incomes. On balance, ascribing only a residual importance to genetic inheritance seems implausible. Hence, the question remains of the possible role of education in compensating for genetic inequality (Husén 1974).

The second component of the double difficulty is that inequality is compounded by difference. Children observably vary in their personalities, temperaments, abilities, and interests. A plausible inference might be that a single form of education for all children would be excessively procrustean. Therefore, educational provision should be as varied as the pupils taking it. The drawback here is that the elements of educational diversity tend to become ordered or ranked in association with particular bands of occupation, income, and social status. The lower the latter, the more likely the former to be reserved for the less bright. Diversity is confused with inequality. That is, the inequalities of the larger society intrude upon and dominate educational choice and practice. All the same, the question remains whether educational equality might be feasibly delineated in terms of similar education for similar people, and different education for different people.

Only a little less difficult than the genetic question is the major component of environment, namely the social class of the family. Evidence from the industrialized countries and those with well-defined and established hierarchies suggests strongly that the higher the social class of a family, the more education it is likely to secure for its children and, conversely, the lower the social class, the less the education secured. In all classes, the actual amount of education taken by a particular child varies with its ability and scholastic performance—again at least partially reflecting the influence of the larger economy. However, there are significant differences. An upper-class child of only mediocre ability and performance is nevertheless likely to receive much more than average education. In contrast, children of lower classes often need to attain exceptionally high performance, before they go beyond even an average education. On the face of it, the phenomenon offends the value of fairness. That conclusion, however, assumes that the lower-class children of high ability are indeed interested in social and economic mobility, wish to achieve it through the normal avenue of educational credentials and would indeed take more education, if only they were not unfairly handicapped in some way. If this assumption is correct, what might be the handicaps?

There is certainly evidence from both industrialized and industrializing countries that biases within educational institutions do undermine the progress of children from less privileged social classes and rural areas. Educational personnel, their language, procedures, and norms may be strange and intimidating. It seems also to be the case that the milieu of the schools, largely reflecting that of the more privileged classes, is often uncongenial. Reciprocally, many teachers try to avoid and to escape from teaching in schools with large majorities of lower-class children. The consequence can be that such schools have staff, who are unwilling, unstable, and possibly below average in professional competence. Taken together, these factors would certainly constitute an unwarranted handicap on less privileged children who aimed at upward mobility.

There is, however, also evidence that the social milieu of the children in question has apart in shaping their horizons and aspirations. They may not wish to achieve mobility at all, or at least not on the usual terms. They may judge they can make their way by other means and be able to point to successful models in their parents or older siblings. They may be unwilling to risk alienation from their families and peers. Or they may set their ambitions at a level modestly above their present status but below their full potential. Their families—and they themselves—may prefer that they earn money earlier, rather than spend more time on education for possibly only slightly better paid employment and prospects. To the extent that these suggestions are accurate, the notions of handicap and unfairness are weakened. The issue is then whether such judgments are valid on their own terms, or the result of "false consciousness," misguided and damaging to their makers, or possibly defensive rationales against risking failure in attempts at social promotion.

Whichever explanation is the more applicable in a particular society at a particular time—and both are likely to be valid to some extent—the unequal use of education by people who are apparently equal in educational terms but unequal in social class has its sources not in schooling as such, but in the wider society. The variegation of values, cultures, stratifications, prejudices, and conflicts generates drives and inhibitions which affect education. If educational equality is viewed partly as a matter of equal use of educational resources by people who are equal in some appropriate standard, irrespective of social class and social ambition, then clearly educational policy will be insufficient on its own. However, it is possible that deliberately mixing social and ethnic groups in schools, in proportions approaching those in which they are found in a defined geographical area, may simultaneously promote social equality as well as equality in educational demand and use. If this were accepted, educational policy would certainly have a role in arranging for the mixing. Forms of community, neighborhood, and comprehensive schools and arrangements to transport children of one socioeconomic area to schools in another ("busing") are attempts to do precisely that.

Connected with social class, and also with economic and political power, is another phenomenon. It can be observed in both industrialized and industrializing or developing countries, but is much more marked in the latter. Some schools, used in the main by the more affluent, better educated, and politically more influential groups, tend to attract higher levels of resources in terms of texts, equipment, other teaching resources and quality and experience of teachers. The contrast extends to urban vis-à-vis rural schools, but remains even within the urban group. Indeed, the less favoured urban schools—whether they be the inner-city schools of the industrialized countries or the city-fringe slum schools of the developing countries—can be at a disadvantage even against rural schools. The inequalities of resources tend to be paralleled both with inequalities of internal efficiency—differences in the rates of attendance, repetition, desertion, graduation—and also with inequalities of attainment: the poorer schools do worse at standard tests and selection examinations.

There is, however, debate on the extent to which the correspondence reflects causal relationships between resources, processes, and outcomes. Some research in both industrialized and developing countries suggests that material resources such as money, buildings, laboratories, and books have little effect on internal efficiency or attainment, and neither do the formal qualifications and training of teachers. Inequalities in these aspects apparently do not necessarily give rise to inequalities in others. On the other hand, other research, again in both industrialized and developing countries, suggests that the commitment, quality, and leadership of teaching staff and availability of at least basic, good quality texts do influence efficiency and attainment. Where the balance of probability might plausibly lie in this apparent conflict of evidence cannot be pursued here. Nevertheless, estimates of it should clearly be elements of policy (Rutter et al. 1979).

The two preceding paragraphs have introduced four further factors of educational inequality and have also shifted the focus from individual learners and social groups to inequalities between schools, or more generally between educational institutions. The first is the extension of the will for education to the willingness to use political power to secure good education for oneself or more commonly for one's protégés and allies. Again, this is a factor extrinsic to education itself. The second is inequalities in the distribution of resources between educational institutions. An additional dimension here is inequalities between different levels of educational institution, for example, between primary and secondary schools or between polytechnics and universities. In some countries, one secondary school place may absorb resources equivalent to two primary-school places. Elsewhere, the ratio may be as high as 1:15. Disparities in ratios of the cost of university to the cost of primary-school places can range from 1:10 to 1:200. As the bulk of recurrent costs is absorbed by the salaries of personnel, the disparities are again largely due to economic inequality within a society but they reflect on the scale and quality of educational provision.

The third factor is inequalities in the effectiveness of teachers. In part, these may arise from genetic variation among the teachers, in part from inequalities in the teachers' own education, in part from inequalities in the effectiveness of teacher trainers, and in part from inequalities of morale and commitment possibly induced by inequalities of resources, other forms of professional support and encouragement, and cooperation from the parents of students. The fourth factor is in part a product of the third and is the inequalities between schools or various indices of efficiency and effectiveness.

The discussion so far seems to have assumed implicitly that simple access to education is assured everywhere. The provision of sufficient primary schools and competent teachers to afford every child a place and adequate pedagogical attention and support has been taken for granted, as have enough secondary school and tertiary education places for those who want them. Implicit also has been the assumption that there are no barriers to access, either direct or indirect, and that the choice whether or not to take education is umcomplicated and free. Such is by no means universally the case, as even a glance at the UNESCO *Statistical Yearbooks* will show. To be sure, there are many countries, particularly but not exclusively among the industrialized, where such postulates would be safe. But there are also many countries, where the primary schools cannot cope with all the eligible children, where many children live too far from schools to be able to attend, and where what schools there are, are overcrowded, grossly underequipped, and unevenly distributed. In the very simplest sense of the term, access to education in the form of schooling is not equal.

Access is often made unequal also by both the direct and opportunity costs of schooling. Some governments feel constrained to charge fees even for primary education, so that, no matter how low the fees are, some households feel unable to afford them. Others are able to provide free tuition, but call upon the families to pay for textbooks, and writing materials—modest costs, indeed, but enough to exclude a proportion of households from participation. Some schools find it necessary to insist on uniform, sports charges, maintenance contributions, and the like which also exclude the very poor families.

The opportunity costs include forgoing the assistance of children in the maintenance and livelihood of the family. Household, agricultural, pastoral, artisan, and industrial tasks within the family, as well as forms of casual, more or less permanent, wage labor can constitute indispensable contributions to family welfare and so reduce the opportunities (and increase the inequalities) for access to education for considerable proportions of children.

Much of the deficiency and maldistribution of educational provision, as well as much of the need for and inegalitarian impact of fees and charges, can be ascribed to the relative poverty of the societies concerned. A number of governments simply cannot afford to pay for a full system of education or to meet full costs of what provision is afforded. (Here of course is inequality on the international plane.) Additionally, there are historical and political contributions to the explanation. Possession by a colonial power and penetration by Christian missionaries had a large role in introducing scholastic education, in determining its patchy distribution, and in restricting and slowing its dissemination and universalization in most countries of Africa and Asia. For colonial governments, after all, equality could scarcely be a consideration, let alone a priority. Elsewhere, where colonial subjugation was either not experienced or terminated well before the twentieth century, other causes must be sought. Feudal or agrarian societies, for example, might have no interest in education, and their regimes might fear its spread. Examples could also be given for modernizing governments which, openly or surreptitiously, neglect or even discriminate against particular groups and areas, and favor others at the expense of the former. For equality or reduced inequality is not yet an objective common to all governments and societies, nor equally assiduously pursued by all who profess it. Educational inequality due solely to history or poverty is susceptible to mitigation by a steady application of policy and resources. when rooted in political and social values and interests, it is amenable only to political and social change, reformist or revolutionary. This observation again echoes the dependence of education upon the workings of the larger society.

An important aspect of provision is the ratio between different levels of education. Most developing countries provide many more primary school places than secondary; all countries provide many more secondary places than tertiary. By that fact alone, of course, inequality is built into education, whatever the political philosophy of a society or its government. In poorer countries, that inequality may be exacerbated by the sacrifice of universal primary education to ensure some provision of the secondary and tertiary stages. However defended as necessary and temporary, such inequality cannot help but reinforce and prolong the other inequalities between those social groups who can use all the educational layers and those who cannot use even the first.

The fact of diminishing layers also requires selection between candidates. By definition, selection implies and requires inequality, whatever the criterion applied. There is in effect unequal provision, because there is an apparently inescapable and apparently universal belief in unequal abilities, expressed through unequal scholastic attainment. The discussion is thus taken back to its starting point about one of the major sources of educational inequality.

However, a partially countervailing belief has been emerging into higher prominence. It rejects the permanent validity of measurements of ability taken at particular moments early in life. Stated more positively, it is a belief in the "late developer," the person whose intellectual, cultural, or occupational interests are stimulated to grow at an age later than the conventional span of schooling. The social background and educational experience of a person may have stunted her or his capacities, while later social or occupational experiences may have brought them into play and demonstrated a need for guided development. This belief has been increasingly reinforced by the rates of technological and social changes since the late nineteenth century. Educational provision for adults at all stages of their lives and for all changes and adaptations in their livelihoods is a rising demand. It goes beyond the earlier provisions of adult education for occupational improvement or a vocational interest. Indeed, it asserts itself as an element indispensable to the ability of a society to generate wider and greater well-being for its members and to keep abreast of advances in well-being elsewhere. Since adult education almost everywhere secures only very small proportions of the resources allocated to education, the "late developer" or "recurrent education" is in effect posing an issue of equality between generations: should there be more equality in provisions for children, adolescents, and young adults, on the one hand, and older adults on the other?

As a dozen or so aspects of educational inequality have been touched so far, a paragraph of review may be helpful, before proceeding to consider policy. The sources of inequality have been suggested to be:

(a) The genetic inheritance of individuals in terms of the variety of constellations of abilities, which are differently valued by societies and inequalities in specific abilities important for scholastic education.

(b) The social class of individuals in terms of perceptions of the values of education for life goals, actively securing education and assuring its quality, discouraging others from education, utilizing what education is made available, and succeeding in education.

(c) The political power of governments, social classes, and individuals in both providing and securing education.

(d) State and private resources for the provision of education.

(e) The allocation of resources between levels of education.

(f) Differences in the provision of educational institutions across geographical areas and social groups.

(g) Differences in the resources, efficiency, and attainments between educational institutions and groups of them.

(h) Differences between teachers in effectiveness.

(i) Direct and indirect costs to households in utilizing education.

(j) Selection for different levels of education.

(k) The allocation of resources between generations

3. Equality of Opportunity

This array of inequalities is perplexing for any educational policy maker to confront. Certainly some of them seem within the practical grasp of governments truly intent on reducing whatever inequalities give rise to inequities. Others, however, arguably more important, seem to be such as no government or society can prevent. Indeed, a pessimist might argue that the inequalities which are manipulable are unlikely to be as important as those which are not. Not surprisingly, recourse has been had to the concept of "equality of educational opportunity." In brief, the suggestion is that a society's duty is merely to ensure that, as far as can be managed, educational facilities of equal quality should be equally available to every member of the eligible group. Thereafter, what use is made of educational opportunity is entirely up to the individual with the explicit or implicit concession that the utilization of opportunity will necessarily be unequal, because of differences of efficiency. As a first move towards educational equality, such a view is reasonable.

However, it is widely regarded as inherently flawed because it assumes implicitly that all eligible individuals are equally free and capable of being efficient in using or declining opportunity. If that were indeed the case, no objection could be advanced. Yet the summary list above suggests that most individuals are not wholly free and independent agents, equally capable of appraising and utilizing opportunities. On the contrary, most are heavily dependent on the resources of their households and wider social groups for information, orientation, guidance, and support—and households are widely unequal in all these matters. Equal opportunity offered in circumstances of inequalities of endowment and environment will perpetuate existing patterns not only of inequality, but of inequity as well, for equals on a given set of criteria will be able to respond unequally to opportunity because of inequalities in environment. In parallel, the more powerful groups will be able to protect their less able members at the expense of the more able members of the less powerful groups. This school of thought would argue that, in order to respond equitably in educational terms to inequalities in people and their environments, a state should provide unequal educational opportunities: those at a disadvantage through genetic endowment, environment, or other accident should be offered and enabled to use greater educational opportunities than those who are more privileged.

A separate point of objection is the meaning of equal opportunity in a situation of diversity in constellations of ability. On the one hand, a uniform education is bound to favor those whose constellations it fits closely and to discriminate in varying degrees against the rest. On the other, given an unequal society, where diversity of occupation overlaps to a large degree with inequality of status and income, diversity of education will come inescapably to correspond with social inequality. Indeed, by degrees it will grow to help predetermine eventual status. In doing so, it would come to offend against the value or principle of mobility. It would in effect overdetermine a child's future, before its range of potential could be fully assessed. Further the very inequalities of society would constrain the better informed and more determined social groups to ensure that their offspring, whatever their abilities, avoid those programs which seem oriented to what they would regard as lower-status futures.

A dilemma is presented which is insoluble, once again, because a subordinate institution cannot easily operate on principles contradictory to those of the organisms on which it depends and for which it prepares its charges.

4. Issues of Policy

In moving to a discussion of policy for educational equality, an assumption has to be made about a society and its government. In part, it is that there is sufficient consensus in the society about the need for at least greater—if not absolute—equality to achieve greater equity among its members. In part, it is that there is sufficient agreement that education should be used as an instrument for equality and equity. The third part is that the government and its agents have the intent, sincerity, power, and capacity to implement whatever policies seem necessary, both in education and more widely, for greater equality and equity. If the assumption is invalid, the discussion is of course vain. At the same time, "sufficient consensus" does not require total consensus or the absence of all resistance from groups with interests vested in various forms of inequality and even of inequity. Indeed, part of policy will need to include measures to mitigate, buy off, circumvent, neutralize, or even crush such resistance.

Granted that assumption, a government has four major areas to consider: provision, access, utilization, and outcomes. Each of course has to be weighed against the resources available—material in terms of finance and equipment, human for the administrative and professional aspects. The availability of the resources themselves is of course a function of the trade-off between the various goals and priorities a government has. Although education is everywhere a major element of public expenditure, it has to compete against the claims of law and order, defense, economic development, and so on. Within education itself, however, the likely ordering of priority for resources coincides with the order of the list of areas above. For that is both a sequence of time and a ranking of importance. It is also a ranking of difficulty. The physical provision of educational personnel and facilities, for instance, is a prior and an easier matter than assuring that the outcomes of tuition and learning across schools or polytechnics are sufficiently equal.

4.1 Provision

The earlier discussion pointed out the need for a balance between two conventional requirements of provision. The first is the amount and quality of education which needs to be provided for every member of the society. The second is the pattern and volume of provision for successive stages of education to ensure that enough skills are formed to generate and sustain socioeconomic development. The poorer the society, the more acute will be this choice, for its consequences for social and economic inequality will be great. In an extreme case, the question could be at what sacrifice of quantity and quality should education for the many today be restricted to secure the education of the "necessary" few, in order to build a better future for the many of a succeeding generation? The wealthier the society, the less will choices of this nature need to be made.

The secondary choice follows, determining the phasing and speed of provision, so that all sections of the eligible population are eventually equally provided for. In the transition, however, inequality is necessarily involved. For allocating provision is in effect allocating privilege, however temporarily, and offering a form of "head start." The choice then is whether a fresh privilege should reinforce other privileges or be used to compensate for other disadvantages. In most countries, for instance, the already wealthier urban areas—and wealthier suburbs within—or already privileged locations of accessible settlement have benefited first and most from educational provision. There are few instances where education has been used to pioneer the reduction of disadvantage.

After the physical provision follows the question of equality in quality. Where trained teachers are in short supply and very mobile, and where educational provision is being expanded rapidly, equalizing quality will be impossible and variation will be wide. At the same time, experience in the industrialized countries so far suggests that, although some reductions in inequalities of quality are feasible, some degree of variation will persist.

4.2 Access

Granted the educational personnel and facilities, do the eligible members of the society have sufficiently equal access to them? As with provision, this is a question of more acute importance to the developing countries, as the wealthier states can pay for measures to ensure virtually equal access. Are schools, for example, sited so that all their prospective pupils find it relatively equally feasible to enrol in and attend them? Or do inordinate distances, rivers, or mountains preclude some? Barriers to access are not restricted to geography. As already remarked, fees and charges of various kinds, even nominal payments for learning materials can debar many children even from primary education—as has been demonstrated by increases in primary-school enrolments, as soon as enrolment fees were abolished, in a number of countries. The need to pay for lodging and board can exclude a number of the officially eligible from secondary school.

Dependent on quantitative provision is the decision whether access to successive stages of education is to be determined by formal criteria of selection or can be left open for all comers. Linked with the provision of quality is the question whether such criteria should apply equally to all aspirants, or whether compensatory adjustments should be introduced to allow for variations in educational quality, which affect educational attainment. For instance, it is well-known in many countries that children from rural and poorer suburban schools do markedly worse on examination for selection from primary to secondary schools. The reasons are thought to be a combination of social background and the quality of teaching, with the latter playing a very important part. Some governments judge that nothing can be done about the matter, except gradually to improve the quality of the less successful schools. Others, on the contrary, judge that the bias needs to be countered and operate systems to do so. Students from designated schools or districts can then be selected for secondary schools with lower attainments on the selection exams than students from better equipped districts. A natural consequence is that an apparent inequity is created: some students who are more qualified for secondary education have to give way to others less qualified than themselves. Governments have to choose which evil is the lesser. Similar provisions have been made in some countries to protect the access of particularly underprivileged social and ethnic groups. In at least one case, long-term political considerations entered to discriminate against students of privileged social backgrounds. In all such instances, as might be expected, there is public controversy, sometimed violent.

4.3 Utilization

Provision and access may be thought of as the "supply side" of education. The "demand side" is expressed in utilization: what use do people make of the education provided? As remarked earlier, utilization tends to be very unequal across social groups, within social groups, and also within households. Further, girls tend to utilize—or be allowed to utilize—education less than boys and the order of birth of a child also appears to influence what use she or he will make of education.

The reasons may be, as suggested, economic in three different senses. The direct and indirect or opportunity costs may be beyond a household's capacity to afford. Part of irregular attendance and premature leaving can be ascribed here. There may also be an assessment that the economic returns to education will be no greater than those offered by other ways of applying effort and time. There may be in addition more particular judgments that particular children are or are not capable of taking sufficient advantage from particular stages of education. More generally, among the lower-status groups, there may be overestimates of the magnitude of ability required for further education.

Other reasons may have cultural elements. In some societies or among some social groups, there may be a rejection of the school as an alien institution, which propagates values incompatible with those of the host society. At least part of the lagging participation of girls in a number of countries is explained by this. So too, is part of the failure for school enrolments to grow, even among boys and even where schools and teachers are provided.

A contributory, perhaps underestimated, cause is simply the deficient dissemination of information on which appraisals of the benefits of education can be founded. More potent, and more intractable, particularly in strongly stratified societies, might be social prejudice. The more strongly the different strata stress their differences, and the more strongly particular levels of education are associated with particular social strata, the more reluctant or diffident will other strata be to utilize those levels and the more will the user strata discourage or repel the others.

What a given government does in any of these circumstances clearly will depend on its view of the importance of the particular program of education in question. If the government is anxious that more general advantage should be taken of a particular provision, it can apply either coercion or inducements to increase participation. A span of education might be declared compulsory and laws and resources applied to ensure that all those eligible do use it. Alternatively, participants in education may have not only their tuition fees paid, but receive in addition subsistence, lodging, and book and other allowances to relieve their households of at least the direct costs. Social differences in outlook and achievement may be evened out by special arrangements for socially mixed schools. Evidently, the degree and distribution of such support and inducement will be a function of the resources a government feels able to appropriate for such purposes at the expense of others. Evidently too, wealthier societies will be able to afford more positive support than less wealthy—although, to be sure, the wealth of a society is no sure guide to its policies on support for compensatory or positively discriminatory educational measures.

4.4 Outcomes

So far as is known, no society intends that its educational system should produce wholly homogenous graduates, even though some societies permit no pluralism in education, while others permit much. Indeed, the very fact that every society has differentiated branches and successive layers of education, each later stage accessible to fewer people, implies the acceptance of differentiation and inequality in abilities, knowledge, and skills, That said, it remains possible to interpret equality in terms of minimums or floors of competence: each graduate of a particular program of education should have attained a defined minimum of skills and perhaps knowledge. For example, every young person who completes the 6-, 9-, or 12-year course of basic education available to all, might be expected to have developed at least self-sustaining skills and interest in reading, writing, and whatever numeracy is deemed essential not to be at a disadvantage in day-to-day commerce. Those who, for whatever reason, have difficulty in mastering even the minimum, could be accorded whatever pedagogical resources they need to bring themselves to the common level.

If equality is regarded as a floor, how might policy deal with the notion of excellence? More concretely how might it allocate resources between assuring the floor and promoting excellence? By definition, excellence connotes inequality. Indeed, it could be said to praise inequality and urge it to even greater lengths. On the other hand, it has been argued that excellence is not, in practical terms, incompatible with equality because those who do not excel—by definition a majority—benefit from the excellence of the few. By raising the ceiling, so to speak, the excellent also raise the floor by pressing forward the boundaries of the possible. That is, the private inequality of individual achievement can be offset by greater wellbeing in the public domain. The task of policy then would be to multiply and diversify opportunities for excellence, while simultaneously safeguarding the minimums for all.

However persuasive the argument, the need for the safeguard requires emphasis. For the tendency in most societies has been to provide generously for excellence and much less adequately for the other tail of the distribution. (Ensuring that inequality on one dimension does not generate undue inequalities in other spheres may also be a matter for policy, but is wider than the remit of education.)

Equality of educational outcomes between individuals may be neither feasible nor even desirable. However, equality of outcomes between similar educational institutions is both. Absolute equality may be beyond human grasp, given the variations in the effectiveness of teachers, professors, and educational administrators such as principals. However, reducing inequalities, on whatever the dimensions measured, would appear a reasonable objective. A sharper conflict between equality and excellence can occur here. A number of experiments with "centers of excellence" have been attempted. They may indeed be pathfinders and provide stimulus for less excellent institutions. On the other hand, they also, perhaps necessarily, tend to deprive the less excellent of the wherewithal to develop excellence. For they attract not only disproportionate material resources, but also the more effective teachers and more able students.

4.5 Measures and Monitoring

A final comment is called for on an aspect common to all four areas of concern just discussed. Experience so far suggests that equality, or significant reductions in inequality, is not an easy objective to achieve. Nor, once achieved, is it easy to sustain. The social—some might claim, natural—forces remain powerful enough to reassert themselves, at any relaxing in efforts for equality. Accordingly, policies for educational equality generally provide for mechanisms and measures to monitor the progress, stagnation, or regression of equalization in each of the areas of provision, access, utilization, and outcomes.

References

Husén T 1974 *Talent, Equality and Meritocracy: Availability and Utilization of Talent*. Martinus Nijhoff, The Hague
Rawls J 1971 *A Theory of Justice*. Harvard University Press, Cambridge, Massachusetts
Rutter M, Maughan B, Mortimore P, Ouston J, Smith A 1979 *Fifteen Thousand Hours: Secondary Schools and Their Effects on Children*. Open Books, London

Further Reading

Avalos B, Haddad W 1979 *A Review of Teacher Effectiveness Research in Africa, India, Latin America, Middle East, Malaysia, Philippines and Synthesis of Results*. International Development Research Center, Ottawa, Ontario, ERIC Document No. ED 190 551
Bardouille R 1982 The mobility patterns of the University of Zambia graduates: The case of the 1976 cohort of graduates. Mimeograph. University of Zambia Institute for African Studies, Lusaka
Boudon R 1973 *Education, Opportunity and Social Inequality: Changing Prospects in Western Society*. Wiley, New York
Bourdieu P, Passeron J-C 1977 *Reproduction in Education, Society and Culture*, Sage, London
Bourdieu P, Passeron J-C 1979 *The Inheritors: French Students and Their Relation to Culture*. University of Chicage Press, Chicago, Illinois
Blau P M, Duncan O D 1967 *The American Occupational Structure*. Wiley, New York
Carron G, Ta Ngoc Châu (eds.) 1980a *Regional Disparities in Educational Development*, Vol 1: *A Controversial Issue*. International Institute for Educational Planning, Paris
Carron G, Ta Ngoc Châu (eds.) 1980b *Regional Disparities in Educational Development*. Vol. 2: *Diagnosis and Policies for Reduction*. International Institute for Educational Planning, Paris
Carron G, Ta Ngoc Châu (eds.) 1981 *Reduction of Regional Disparities: The Role of Educational Planning*. International Institute for Educational Planning. Paris
Cooksey B 1981 Social class and academic performance: A Cameroon case study. *Comp. Educ. Rev.* 25: 403–18
Dandekar V M 1955 *Report of Investigation into Wastage and Stagnation in Primary Education in Satara District*. Publication No. 32. Gokhale Institute of Politics and Economics, Poona
Dyer H S 1969 School factors and equal educational opportunity. In: Harvard Educational Review 1969 *Equal Educational Opportunity*. Harvard University Press, Cambridge, Massachusetts
Eckland B K 1967 Genetics and sociology: A reconsideration. *Am. Sociol. Rev.* 32: 173–94
Frankel C 1973 The new egalitarianism and the old. *Commentary* 56
Fry G W 1980 Education and success: A case study of the Thai public service. *Comp. Educ. Rev.* 24: 21–34
Fuller W P, Chantavanish A 1977 *A Study of Primary Schooling in Thailand: Factors Affecting Scholastic Achievement of Primary School Pupils*. Office of the National Education Commission, Bangkok
Halsey A H (ed.) 1961 *Ability and Educational Opportunity*. OECD, Paris
Halsey A H, Floud I, Anderson C A (eds.) 1961 *Education, Economy and Society: A Reader in the Sociology of Education*. Macmillan, London
Halsey A H, Heath A F, Ridge J M 1980 *Origins and Destinations: Family Class and Education in Modern Britain*. Oxford University Press, London
Heyneman S P 1979 Why impoverished children do well in Ugandan schools. *Comp. Educ.* 15: 175–76
Heyneman S P 1982 Resource availability, equality and educational opportunity among nations. In: Anderson L, Windham D W (eds.) 1982 *Education and Development: Issues in the analysis and Planning of Post-colonial Societies*. Heath, Lexington, Massachusetts
Heyneman S P, Currie J K 1979 *Schooling, Academic Performance and Occupational Attainment in a Non-industrialized Society*. University Press of America, Washington, DC
Heyneman S P, Jamison D T 1980 Student learning in Uganda: Text-book availability and other factors. *Comp.*

Educ. Rev. 24: 206–20

Heyneman S P, Loxley W 1981 The effects of primary school quality on academic achievement across 29 high and low income countries. Paper presented to the Annual Meeting of the American Sociological Association, Toronto

Howard University Institute for the Study of Educational Policy 1978 *Equal Educational Opportunity: More Promise than Progress.* Howard University Press, Washington, DC

Husén T 1972 *Social Background and Educational Career: Research Perspectives on Equality of Educational Opportunity.* Centre for Educational Research and Innovation, OECD, Paris

Husén T, Saha L J, Noonan R 1978 *Teacher Training and Student Achievement in Less Developed Countries.* Staff Working Paper No. 310. World Bank, Washington, DC

Jencks C 1979 *Who Gets Ahead? The Determinants of Economic Success in America.* Basic Books, New York

Jensen A R 1972 *Genetics and Education.* Methuen, London

Kyn O 1978 Education, sex and income inequality in Soviet type socialism. In: Griliches Z, Krelle W, Krupp H-J, Kyn O (eds.) 1978 *Income Distribution and Economic Inequality.* Wiley, New York

Lipset S M, Bendix R 1959 *Social Mobility in Industrial Society.* University of California Press, Berkeley, California

Lodge P, Blackstone T 1982 *Educational Policy and Educational Equality.* Robertson, Oxford

Mosteller R, Moynihan D P (eds.) 1972 *On Equality of Educational Opportunity.* Random House, New York

Nantiyal K C, Sharma Y D 1979 *Equalisation of Educational Opportunities for Scheduled Castes and Scheduled Tribes.* National Council for Educational Research and Training, New Delhi

Neave G R 1976 *Patterns of Equality: The Influence of New Structures in European Higher Education upon Equality of Educational Opportunity.* National Foundation for Educational Research, Slough

Schiefelbein E, Farrell J P 1980 Education and occupational attainment in Chile: the effects of educational quality, attainment and achievement. Unpublished manuscript. World Bank Education Department, Washington, DC

Somerset H C A 1982 Examinations reform: The Kenyan experience. Mimeograph. Report prepared for the World Bank and Institute for Development Studies, Brighton

Taubman P 1976 The determinants of earnings: Genetics, family and other environments: A study of white male twins. *Am. Econ. Rev.* 66: 858–70

Taubman P, Behrman J, Wales T 1978 The role of genetics and environment in the distribution of earnings. In: Griliches Z, Krelle W, Krupp H-J, Kyn O (eds.) 1978 *Income Distribution and Economic Inequality.* Wiley, New York

Thurow L C 1975 *Generating Inequality.* Basic Books, New York

Tyler W 1977 *The Sociology of Educational Inequality.* Methuen, London

Unger J 1980 Severing the links between education and careers: The sobering experience of China's urban schools 1968–76. *IDS Bulletin* 11: 49–54

Wilson B R (ed.) 1975 *Education, Equality and Society.* Allen and Unwin, London

Yanowitch M, Fisher W 1973 *Social Stratification and Mobility in the USSR.* International Arts and Sciences Press, White Plains, New York

Loose Coupling and Educational Systems

A. Sturman

The concept of educational organizations as loosely coupled systems is in contrast to classical theories of organization which assume clear-cut goals, well-coordinated activities and tight lines of control. The distinguishing feature of systems that are loosely coupled is that the elements within them are responsive, that is, although they retain some separate identity, they are also attached, even though the attachment may be weak, infrequent, or unimportant. This view of organizations has been heralded as providing important understandings of educational settings, but it has also been criticized as remaining within a functionalist paradigm that focuses on organizations as rational and stable creations.

1. Models of Educational Organization

Corwin (1974) described two sets of primary models, as well as additional derivative models, which have been applied to educational organizations. The first set was the open versus closed model, and the second the rational versus natural systems model.

The open and closed models of organization are based upon different assumptions about the extent to which organizations can be autonomous from their environments, and how important these environments are for understanding the internal processes of the organizations. Closed models assume that organizations act independently from their environments, while open models assume that organizations are more influenced by those environments.

The rational and natural systems models are based upon different assumptions about the manner in which organizations conduct their business. The rational model assumes that organizations have clear-cut goals, planned and closely coordinated activities, and tight control by officials. The best example is bureaucracy as an ideal type. Writers in the 1960s applied this model to educational organizations, and they continue to do so.

The natural systems model emerged in recognition of the fact that educational organizations do not always conform to the assumptions that underpin the rational model. Rather, members in different parts of an organization often place the interest of their unit above others, official goals may become distorted and neglected, decisions may be the outcomes of bargaining and compromise, and coordination among components of the organization may be weak.

Corwin contended that most organizations range between these polar types and therefore it is possible to identify derivative models, one of which—the conflict model—assumes that patterns of tensions and autonomy in organizations are best analyzed in terms of conflict between persons or groups in different parts of the system.

Although Corwin was writing before the concept of loose coupling emerged in the literature, he clearly saw this concept as one derivative of the natural systems model. He referred to research into patterns of autonomy in schools (Katz 1964), structural looseness (Bidwell 1965), and zones of autonomy (Lortie 1969). Similarly, Weick (1976), who is credited with introducing the concept of loose coupling to the study of education, noted that it had already appeared in the literature (Glassman 1973, March and Olsen 1976).

While loose coupling is best viewed, then, as an extension of existing ideas, rather than a completely new concept, it is clear that it can be used to examine both the primary organizational models described by Corwin and derivative models.

2. Loosely Coupled Systems: The Concept Elaborated

Weick (1976 p. 3) referred to loose coupling in the following way:

> By loose coupling, the author intends to convey the image that coupled events are responsive, but that each event also preserves its own identity and some evidence of its physical or logical separateness. Thus, in the case of an educational organization, it may be the case that the counselor's office is loosely coupled to the principal's office. The image is that the principal and the counselor are somehow attached, but that each retains some identity and separateness and that their attachment may be circumscribed, infrequent, weak in its mutual affects, unimportant, and/or slow to respond. Each of these connotations would be conveyed if the qualifier loosely were attached to the word coupled. Loose coupling also carries connotations of impermanence, dissolvability, and tacitness all of which are potentially crucial properties of the "glue" that holds organizations together.

Weick commented that researchers can study "loose coupling" in educational organizations or "loosely coupled systems": the shorter phrase, "loose coupling" connotes anything that may be tied together weakly, infrequently, slowly, or with minimal interdependence.

Weick stressed that loose coupling need not be used normatively. He listed both its advantages and potential liabilities. He further argued that the overall pattern in a school is more important than the tightness of specific couplings: tight coupling between all parts of a system or the use of all forms of coupling are not necessary.

3. Applying the Concept to Educational Systems

Weick argued that the most commonly discussed coupling mechanisms in schools are the technical core of the organization and the authority of office. He suggested, however, that neither of these mechanisms is prominent in educational organizations, and a list of potential coupling elements might include intentions and action (March and Olsen 1976), the past and present (what happened yesterday may be loosely coupled with what happens tomorrow), means and ends, hierarchical positions, teachers and the materials they use, teachers and students, teachers and other teachers, and parents and teachers.

A number of studies have applied the concept of loose coupling to the study of education. For example, Firestone and Herriott (1981) in the United States and Ainley (1984) in Australia both examined the coupling mechanisms in elementary and high schools, in particular the relationship between the administration and the technical operations of the school. Firestone and Herriott conclude that, in terms of goal consensus and centralization of influence on decisions, high schools display more of the characteristics of loosely coupled systems while elementary schools more closely resemble bureaucratic organizations. Ainley's conclusions were similar, and, in interpreting these results, he draws attention to the importance of subunits, such as faculties, within high schools compared with elementary schools. Ainley also suggests that the different training backgrounds of elementary and high-school teachers may contribute to the coupling patterns that emerge: high-school principals generally have expertise in one subject area and may consider that they lack the expertise to become involved in the activities of other faculties.

What these findings suggest is that the way high schools are organized, with a primary dependence on the structure of the different disciplines, leads not only to the creation of subunits which affects the coupling structures in schools, but also to differences between teachers in their views of the disciplines and their interrelationships, which in turn affects the cohesion and unity of organizations. Sturman (1989) found that teachers from different discipline areas also held quite different epistemologies and these epistemologies could be more important in determining the curriculum that emerged in schools than organizational structures as such.

Also working in the United States, Ouchi (1977, 1979) examined control mechanisms in different

453

types of organization and applied his findings to the concept of loose coupling. He argued that in bureaucratic organizations the form of commitment to the organization is compliance; staff behavior and output are closely monitored. The informational requirement necessary to operate a bureaucracy is a set of rules. Ouchi distinguished bureaucracies from clans, the latter being a more appropriate term, he argued, for describing schools. Staff are committed to their clan because they identify with its ethos or guiding principles. Emphasis is placed on skill and value training rather than a close monitoring of behavior and output. The informational requirements necessary to operate a clan are simply the traditions which convey the values and beliefs of the organization.

Ouchi suggested that where loose coupling exists, reliable and precise measurement is not possible and control mechanisms based on such measurement are likely to reward a narrow range of behavior and lead ultimately to organizational decline. The clan system of control, he argued, is preferable.

Similarly, Meyer and Rowan (1977) argued that educational organizations in the United States lack coordination in the content and methodology of instruction. They contended that outputs of instructional tasks are seldom used to evaluate the performance of teachers or institutions and that there is a lack of consensus about what should entail an instructional program. They concluded that, although administrators have responsibility to plan and coordinate the content and methods of instruction, in practice they lack the authority to conduct these tasks.

Whereas Ouchi envisaged that organizations such as schools can be bound together through adherence to the values and beliefs of the organization, Meyer and Rowan suggested that the "myth of professionalism" provides the confidence that the system operates effectively: teachers are appropriately credentialled and subjects have a legitimacy through their origins in accredited institutions.

While these studies have focused on differences between what Corwin referred to as "natural systems" and "rational models of organization," Sturman (1989) investigated both these differences and the differences between open and closed models in a study into the effects on curriculum provision of the decentralization of curriculum decision-making in Australia. Sturman examined the type of coupling that exists between schools and state administrations, between teachers and the school administration, and between teachers and parents and the community. The study concluded that differences in the type of coupling that was evident had distinct effects on curriculum provision.

4. A Critique of the Concept

In an investigation of Weick's contribution to educational administration, Foster (1983) divides his critique into two parts: a "soft" and "radical" critique. The soft critique focuses on technical issues in relation to research into loose coupling, in particular operationalizing the concept. The radical critique, on the other hand, is concerned with epistemological assumptions that are considered to underpin the development of the concept and its application to research in education.

4.1 Technical Issues

Firestone (1985) argued that although the idea of loose coupling has raised important issues, there are difficulties in using the concept to resolve them. He noted that a major difficulty is creating a definition of looseness that facilitates research activities, and he commented on the lack of agreement among those who write about the concept.

Weick himself quotes Glassman, who defined loose coupling in the following way:

> The degree of coupling, or interaction, between two systems depends on the activity of the variables which they share. To the extent that two systems either have few variables in common or if the common variables are weak compared to other variables which influence the system, they are independent of each other. It is convenient to speak of such a situation as loose coupling. (Glassman 1973 p. 84)

As Firestone stated, such a definition is exceedingly general, and, while Weick has attempted to clarify these definitional issues by providing 15 diverse examples of situations where loose coupling exists in schools, Firestone pointed out that it is difficult to imagine a single measure of loose coupling that can cover this range of meanings.

In a later paper, Weick (1982) defined tight coupling as a situation in which there are rules on which there is consensus and which has a system of inspection combined with feedback to improve compliance to rules. Firestone acknowledged that such a definition can be operationalized, but will only cover predictable, recurring events.

While these criticisms are valid, they are not insurmountable. Firestone commented that there have been efforts to overcome conceptual ambiguities in order to operationalize coupling mechanisms and explore their causes and consequences. As one example, in his own research, Firestone and his colleagues engaged in instrument development to operationalize loose coupling in schools. The methodological properties of the scales that they developed to measure different types of linkages were described by Wilson et al. (1983).

4.2 Epistemological Assumptions

Burrell and Morgan (1979) described how the general sociological debate concerning assumptions about the nature of social science and society led to the emer-

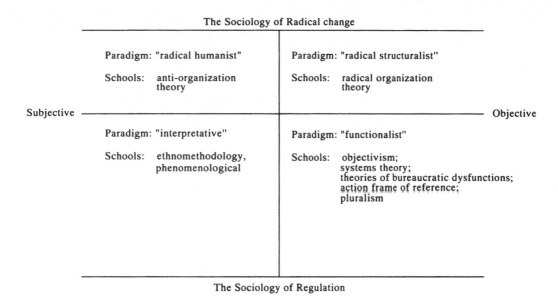

Figure 1
Paradigms for the analysis of social theory and the relationship to the main schools of organizational analysis
Source: Burrell and Morgan 1979 pp. 22, 30

gence of different sociological paradigms, which have been applied to organizational theory. Dichotomies concerning order and conflict, stability and change, and subjectivity and objectivity are found in the four sociological paradigms that Burrell and Morgan distinguished: the functionalist paradigm; the interpretative paradigm; the radical humanist paradigm; and the radical structuralist paradigm. The relationship between these paradigms and schools of organizational analysis are shown in Fig 1.

The radical critique of loose coupling (Foster 1983, Tyler 1987) argues that loose coupling sits within the functionalist paradigm and, as a result, is a limited interpretation of organizational behavior. Specifically, Foster contended that loose coupling is mainly systems theory with a new vocabulary and suffers the weaknesses of the functionalist paradigm, that loose coupling is a distorted view of organized activity, and that "it presents an ideology of conservative alienation" (p. 20). Foster maintained that an examination of education in terms of loose coupling ignores the internal effects of schooling in relation to social structures, and the relationship of the school hierarchy to the environment is seen largely in terms of efforts to maintain the stability and legitimacy of the institution in light of changing conditions. According to Foster, the place of political movements and social conflict is removed from the functionalist or systems view and individuals are not seen as active creators of their worlds but as "sense makers in a world given to them" (p. 28).

As a result of these criticisms, Foster suggested alternative approaches to the study of organizations, which relate to the other paradigms outlined in Fig 1. In particular he suggested a dialectical approach, ethnomethodology, a cultural approach, and a critical approach.

Much of the debate on organizational models and their application to education is weak because it attempts to seek one model which can describe all schools. Similarly, much of the debate on theoretical paradigms that has been a part of sociology for several decades has sought to replace one paradigm with another. What is required is acknowledgment that many models and many paradigms can assist in understanding schools.

5. Future Directions

A continuing priority for research into loose coupling is the development of appropriate conceptual tools and methodology. This was acknowledged by Weick, who also saw as important the explication of the elements available for coupling, promotion of descriptions of coupling patterns, and investigation of the manner in which people operate in loosely coupled systems.

Much of the research that has used the concept of loose coupling has been concerned with the relationship between the administration and technical core of the school. More work is needed on the coupling mechanism between teachers and students and the effects of different patterns of coupling.

See also: Authority and Power in Educational Organizations; Effective Secondary Schools

References

Ainley J 1984 Policy formulation and coordination in Australian schools. *Unicorn* 10(1): 16–28

Bidwell C E 1965 The school as a formal organisation. In: March J G (ed.) 1965 *Handbook of Organizations*. Rand McNally, Chicago, Illinois

Burrell G, Morgan G 1979 *Sociological Paradigms and Organisational Analysis: Elements of the Sociology of Corporate Life*. Heinemann Educational, London

Corwin R G 1974 Models of educational organizations. *Rev. Res. Educ.* 2: 247–95

Firestone W A 1985 The study of loose coupling: Problems, progress, and prospects. In: Kerckhoff A C (ed.) 1985 *Research in Sociology of Education and Socialization*, Vol. 5. JAI Press, Greenwich, Connecticut

Firestone W A, Herriott R E 1981 *The Bureaucratic Elementary School: Comparing Two Images of Elementary, Junior High and High Schools*. Research for Better Schools, Inc., Philadelphia, Pennsylvania (ERIC Doc. No. ED 203 532)

Foster W 1983 *Loose Coupling Revisited: A Critical View of Weick's Contribution to Educational Administration*. Deakin University Press, Geelong, Victoria

Glassman R B 1973 Persistence and loose coupling in living systems. *Behav. Sci.* 18: 83–98

Katz F E 1964 The school as a complex organization. *Harv. Educ. Rev.* 34: 428–55

Lortie D C 1969 The balance of control and autonomy in elementary school teaching. In: Etzioni A (ed.) 1969 *The Semi-Professionals and Their Organizations: Teachers, Nurses, Social Workers*. The Free Press, New York

March J G, Olsen J P 1976 *Ambiguity and Choice in Organizations*. Universitetsforlaget, Bergen

Meyer J W, Rowan B 1977 Institutional organizations: Formal structure as myth and ceremony. *Am. J. Sociol.* 83(2): 340–63

Ouchi W G 1977 The relationship between organizational structure and organizational control. *Adm. Sci. Q.* 22(1): 95–113

Ouchi W G 1979 A conceptual framework for the design of organizational control mechanisms. *Man. Sci.* 25(9): 833–48

Sturman A 1989 *Decentralisation and the Curriculum: Effects of the Devolution of Curriculum Decision Making in Australia* (ACER Research Monograph No. 35). ACER, Hawthorn

Tyler W 1987 "Loosely coupled" schools: A structuralist critique. *Br. J. Sociol. Educ.* 8(3): 313–26

Weick K 1976 Educational organizations as loosely coupled systems. *Adm. Sci. Q.* 21(1): 1–19

Weick K E 1982 Administering education in loosely coupled schools. *Phi Del. Kap.* 63(10): 673–76

Wilson B L, Firestone W A, Herriot R E 1983 *School Assessment Survey: An Introductory Guide*. Research for Better Schools, Philadelphia, Pennsylvania

Further Reading

Bates R 1982 *Towards a Critical Practice of Educational Administration*. Paper presented at the Annual Meeting of the American Educational Research Association, New York

Benson J K 1977 Organizations: A dialectical view. *Adm. Sci. Q.* 22(1): 1–21

Bittner E 1974 The concept of organization. In: Turner R (ed.) 1974 *Ethnomethodology: Selected Readings*. Penguin, Harmondsworth

Bolman L G, Deal T E 1984 *Modern Approaches to Understanding and Managing Organizations*. Jossey-Bass, San Francisco, California

Gamoran A, Dreeben, R 1986 Coupling and control in educational organizations. *Adm. Sci. Q.* 31(4): 612–32

Greenfield T B 1980 Theory about organization: A new perspective and its implications for schools. In: Bush T, Glatter R, Goodey J, Riches C (eds.) 1980 *Approaches to School Management*. Harper & Row, London

Horne S 1992 Organisation and change within educational systems: Some implications of a loose-coupling model. *Educ. Man. Adm.* 20(2): 88–98

Logan C S, Ellett C D, Licata J W 1993 Structural coupling, robustness and effectiveness of schools. *J. Educ. Adm.* 31(4): 19–32

Orton J D, Weick K E 1990 Loosely coupled systems: A reconceptualization. *Acad. Man. Rev.* 15(2): 203–23

Sturman A 1986 The application of organizational models to the study of schools. *J. Educ. Adm.* 24(2): 187–212

Public and Private Schools: Sociological Perspectives

D. S. Anderson

According to a UNESCO (1989) survey, some 50 million of the 350 million children living in countries where private education has been permitted were in private schools. At the primary level just under 12 percent in both developing and developed countries were in the private sector, but at secondary level there was a large difference with 28 percent of children in developing countries in private compared with 14 percent in developed countries. During the 1980s there were increases in the private share of enrollments in Africa, Europe, and Oceania, and a decline in Asia.

The public–private division in school systems is of interest to sociologists for two reasons. First is the question of the impact of schooling on society—in the present case the extent to which the public or private school sectors facilitate social mobility, or parallel class or subcultural divisions in the larger society, and help to reproduce them. Second, there is a question of interest to educational sociologists—the effect that class or other segregation of students into different types of school has on pupils' learning, in particular their scholastic attainment. Answers to the latter question require an understanding of the interactions between public and private systems. As will be seen, for reasons not necessarily associated with pedagogy, the average scholastic performance of socially elite private schools may be ahead of that of public schools, but if the balance of enrollments shifts to private schools the loss of a critical core of able students from public schools may contribute to an average decline in performance of the remainder, and in the system overall.

A brief review of the reasons for the growth in the size of the private sector in a number of countries will be provided and the various types of school within the public and private sectors will be examined.

1. Pressures to Privatize Schools

Economic and social pressures have caused governments to become interested in forms of privatization of schooling, in some cases leading to changes in what has been a fairly stable balance between the public and private sectors. Tight budgetary constraints are one factor. In some countries a strong private sector is a response to excess demand as governments are unable or unwilling to find the resources to build the additional schools that are needed and to staff them with trained teachers.

Pressures from minorities are a second reason for renewed interest in private schools, as organized religious and ethnic subcultures come to regard public education as an ineffective means of transmitting group identity to the rising generation.

Ideological preferences are a third reason for encouragement of the private sector. Following the global economic downturn starting in the mid-1970s belief in the efficacy of market forces as superior to regulation and planning led a number of countries to consider privatizing public institutions, including education.

Private schools may also be regarded as "lighthouse" institutions increasing the diversity of a country's stock of schools, and as a safety valve, releasing the pressure from those who may be disaffected with their government schools.

During the 1980s the terms "vouchers," "choice," and "devolution" became popular in the vocabularies of school reformers, especially in Anglo-American countries, and were deemed to represent desirable organizational arrangements, more likely to be associated with private than public schools. In the United Kingdom the government of Margaret Thatcher initiated an Assisted Places Scheme of financial assistance to help intelligent but poor students meet the costs of attending private schools (Edwards et al. 1991).

Another policy in the United Kingdom allowed state schools to opt out of the publicly managed system, becoming in effect unregulated and self-managing schools but with their resources still being supplied by government (Walford 1990). Following the election of John Major's government, the move is accelerating; however, in 1997 with the election of Tony Blair, the scheme is to be abolished.

Following what was seen to be an intractable record of poor scholastic attainment by children in the United States, in 1991 President George Bush devoted a major policy speech solely to education. He stressed that parents should be free to choose the sort of schooling they wanted for their children; and that public schools should be freed from excessive bureaucratic control. The strategy draws on market theory and an influential set of ideas to be found in a book by Chubb and Moe (1990) for reforming public schools which would extend to them the autonomy and organizational effectiveness attributed to private schools.

Some European countries are devolving authority from central government to regions and to individual schools in a way which may blur the public–private boundary. In Sweden, for example, following disenchantment with social democratic reforms, the role of central management is being diminished and, in education, management of schooling has been transferred from central government to municipalities with few restrictions being placed on the sorts of school that will qualify for funding. The small number of private schools in Sweden will gain support. Fewer than one percent of all children were in private schools in 1993 but, under the new dispensation, many more are likely to be established, for example Waldorf (Rudolph Steiner) and Christian community schools.

In the sense that privatization means rolling back the power of the state these changes imply that the management of schooling is being privatized. Privatization is a multi-faceted idea and includes the use of vouchers whereby approved consumers are given government-funded entitlements to purchase specified goods or services from a private market (Gormley 1991). In education, proposals for privatization envision a market of schools in which clients would choose and pay with a voucher for the educational service they wanted. The concept of vouchers has been discussed a great deal since it was first suggested by Milton Friedman (1962), but there are not many places where it has been tried in practice.

One variation of the voucher idea would allow schools to charge tuition fees in addition to the state-funded voucher entitlements. Fee-charging private schools which also receive per capita government subsidies represent this form of voucher funding, each additional child entitling the school to a grant. In Australia, where "freedom to choose" receives strong bipartisan political support, almost 30 percent of all children are in schools (the majority of them Catholic) which are outside the state-managed systems. These schools receive substantial government subsidies, the amount varying according to the school's resources. James (1991 p. 79) refers to this as "a policy of limited privatization with redistributive subsidies . . . like a voucher system." In countries with no direct government subsidies for private schools, the private sector is much smaller—for example, in both the United States and the United Kingdom the private sector educates approximately 10 percent of all children. The World Bank has encouraged the idea of fee-charging private schools as an alternative to government schools in some Third World countries where it is desired to extend participation in secondary education (Jones 1992).

In former Eastern Bloc countries in the early 1990s, interest in private education is growing as a reaction against state-directed schools. Impetus is added to the move as churches try to recover former school properties, ethnic groups aspire to retain their traditions among the young, elite groups move to establish their family advantage in the social order, and impoverished governments seek alternative sources of funding.

Apart from shifting the costs from the public purse to the user, the benefits which supporters of privatization claim will follow include greater effectiveness, greater efficiency, and enhancement of parents' freedom to choose. Reform programs vary in the emphases which are placed on each these objectives. Whereas effectiveness and efficiency are capable of being evaluated empirically, freedom to choose is ultimately a matter of value preference—nevertheless it is regarded as of central importance, particularly in countries where there is a pluralism of religious and ethnic communities. Advocates of a market solution to replace managed school systems view freedom of choice not so much as an end in itself, but as a mechanism for causing schools to become more efficient and effective.

2. Types of Public and Private Schools

The most common definition of a private school is one that is not managed by a state or public authority. The distinction is used by UNESCO and OECD in their statistical surveys of education: private schools are those not managed by or within the government sector; government-aided schools are classified with the private sector if they are privately managed. This definition side-steps a number of questions that are of interest to policymakers and to students of privatization: whether, for example, funding is from public or private sources, whether individual schools or subsets of schools within the public sector are exempted from directives applying to most schools, and whether the school is owned by public or private interests. The following three examples illustrate how the public–private boundary may blur depending on one's perspective.

First, in a few countries like Denmark and Australia subsidies covering most of their running costs are granted to religious and other schools that are outside the publicly managed sector. In the Netherlands the constitution guarantees citizens the right of access for their children to a "private" school of their faith, all costs being met by the government. Second, certain schools that are sponsored by subcultures, for instance Catholic and some ethnic schools in New Zealand and "direct grant" religious schools in the United Kingdom, are fully funded from the public purse but are permitted to retain their special character and to recruit children of their own faith. Third, the arrangements permitting schools in England to leave their Local Education Authorities and become self-managing means that they have the autonomy of private independent schools except that they are owned and subsidized by government.

Whether they are distinguished according to management, source of income, autonomy, or ownership, it is misleading to talk of the public and private sectors as if each is comprised of a homogeneous set of schools—in many respects there is as much variation within the sectors as there is between them. For the purposes of sociological analysis it is helpful to view schools according to their social function. The following set represent "pure types": very few schools would correspond exactly to a type, but in most cases one or at most two of the characteristics predominates. Generally a particular type is found mainly in either the conventional public or the private but there is usually some overlap:

(a) academically selective schools for pupils of above average intellectual attainment;

(b) socially selective or elite schools which, because of their location, their high fees or their selection practices, recruit children from families of greater than average social status;

(c) schools of commitment which cater for the children of particular religious or ethnic subsectors of a society;

(d) community schools which are open to all children in a particular neighborhood;

(e) "free" or alternative schools which espouse some particular educational or social philosophy;

(f) market schools run by their owners as a business enterprise; and

(g) charity or special schools sponsored by philanthropic organizations, or the state, for children who are handicapped—physically, socially, or intellectually.

Academically selective schools are to be found at secondary level in many countries, often in both the public and the privately managed sectors. In public school systems there is sometimes contention over whether all schools should be comprehensive with the full spectrum of abilities represented; whether the system should be specialized, for example into academic, general, and technical schools; or whether there should be a few "elite" schools for pupils of outstanding ability. The latter facilitate the upward social mobility of intelligent children of lower social origins.

Sometimes "technical" or "general" are used as euphemisms for schools or streams intended for children of lesser ability. It is argued, for example by James (1988), that the absence of academically selective schools in the public sector of a country is a condition favoring the development of private schools.

Socially selective schools are usually found in the private sector, high fees or covert discrimination in admissions practices helping to deter enrollment by the children of poorer families. The sociological term "elite" can be applied to this type because it functions to reproduce a sector of society with access to power and privilege (see Cookson and Persell 1985, Graetz 1988, Persell and Cookson 1990, Reid et al. 1991). Some public schools acquire an elite character due to their location in more salubrious residential areas or because of academic selection. Since many socially selective private schools also aim to prepare their pupils for university entrance there tends to be an overlap between social elite and academic elite. Of some educational significance is the power which some elite sectors are able to exert over national or state curriculum, generally pressing for academic subjects rather than those designed for the full range of interests and students.

Even though they comprise only a small fraction of the private sector it is the socially elite schools that have attracted most interest from sociologists. The impact on society of elite schools used to be particularly marked in England where "what school did you go to?" was as common as "what do you do?" as a question for getting a lead about an acquaintance's position in the social order (see Sampson 1962, Walford 1990). As will be seen later it is also the elite categories of schools which can cause difficulties for educational planning in the public sector.

Schools of commitment function to nurture and reproduce a particular religious or other subculture within the wider society, socializing the children according to the values and beliefs of the sponsoring community. Religious schools are the most common but, with the growth of ethnic minorities in many countries, there is renewed interest in using schooling as a means of promoting ethnic identity. Public schools are not necessarily precluded from teaching religion or the traditions of subcultures, but they find it difficult to devise an acceptable curriculum when their children represent diverse backgrounds. For this reason and because of the insistence of religious or ethnic leaders, most schooling of commitment is now to be found in the privately managed sector. The need to charge tuition fees means that the clientele tend to be in above-average positions on the socioeconomic scale, but not to the extent of socially elite schools. Of all types of private school, schools of commitment argue most strenuously for government subsidies as a matter of equity.

Community schools are open to all the children in a neighborhood. They are held to represent values such as equality, tolerance, and understanding of others. According to Shils (1982 p. 59) the community school may also be viewed as an instrument of social cohesion, contributing to shared values and to "the formation, diffusion, and the maintenance of the common culture." Nearly all community schools are in the public sector. In the United States the community or common school was seen and promoted, notably by Horace Mann, as an agent of social reform and a necessary component for creating a common identity among children of culturally diverse backgrounds. In more homogeneous societies such as Sweden, the public school (attended by 99 percent of all children) has been seen as an expression of common citizenship. Naturally the social mix of community schools reflects that of the local neighborhood except where there are policies designed to diversify intakes, for example, bussing in the United States, or where there are private schools recruiting children from upper status families. The claims for the common school in America has been criticized as myth by Glenn (1988) who argues that reaction against "group solidarity" has energized the creation of alternative and sectarian schools in the private sector.

Free or alternative schools espouse a particular educational philosophy, frequently one that is child centered; unlike schools of commitment the parents do not have in common membership of coherent subcultures. These schools are more likely to be in the private sector, but some have become established in public sectors where central control and zoning have been relaxed.

Market or free enterprise schools run by their owners for a profit (as well as to provide an educational service) are not found as frequently in the 1990s in economically developed countries as they were in the nineteenth and early twentieth centuries. Now the most common examples tend to be specialist or vocational schools, for example teaching computing or accountancy. Some cater for pupils who have been unable to gain entry to academic programs of regular schools or have been unsuccessful in gaining university entrance.

Charity schools are also less frequently found in developed countries, but they were once common, offering education to children who were poor or otherwise handicapped. In many countries the service once provided by charity schools has been taken over by free public schools, and by special schools for the handicapped which are most frequently found in the public sector.

In analyzing the role of schools it is useful to have in mind these various social functions (as distinct from their stated purposes) served by schools and the educational or social objectives that are at issue.

3. Effectiveness

It is rarely easy to determine how well the objectives of a school or set of schools are attained because purposes vary a great deal, and because precise statements of objectives tend to be elusive. In the argument over the relative merits of public and private schools researchers have focused their analyses mainly on scholastic attainment. For example Coleman et al. (1982) in the United States, Williams and Carpenter (1990) in Australia, and van Laarhoven et al. (1986) in the Netherlands all find that the private sector has a small but significant edge over the public.

The research findings are still being contested in the scholarly literature (see Alexander 1987, Graetz 1990, Willms 1987) but, for policy purposes, the position is pretty clear: there is no sufficiently reliable evidence which justifies the conclusion that either public or private management consistently leads to more effective pedagogy. Despite the slight statistical margin in favor of private management, critics point out that it is not justified to attribute this to superior teaching because all other things are not equal, there almost always being critical differences in the family backgrounds and abilities of pupils recruited to public and private schools. An example often cited is the freedom that private schools generally have to maximize their outcomes by selecting those pupils who are most likely to succeed and by discarding pupils whose performance or behavior is not up to scratch. These practices are more likely to be found among elite private schools. There can never be certainty that all such biasing variables have been identified and controlled for in the statistical equations.

Not only are the average statistical differences that have been reported between sectors too small to provide any practical basis for planners to favor one sector over the other, but the variation of scholastic attainment between the public and private sectors is usually considerably less than the variation within them. It follows from this that parents seeking a school which will maximize their children's scholastic chances should be advised to forget about whether a school is public or private and evaluate those schools that are available on their merits.

A clue to a social cause of good scholastic attainment may be found in a reanalysis by Murnane (1986) of the data used by Coleman and his colleagues (Coleman et al. 1982). When account is taken of the social mix of each school the difference in favor of private disappears. It appears that children of relatively poor scholastic promise are liable to have their performance lifted when they are in a class which has a critical core of able and well-motivated students. If this core is lost, for example, because of attraction to an elite school, the performance of the remaining children is likely to decline.

To the extent that this is a general phenomenon, there is a policy dilemma, because at this point individual interests and collective interests diverge. Parents who take their children from the community school and put them in an elite school could be acting rationally if their aim is to gain a competitive edge in the race for university entry. However, the aggregation of a large number of such decisions impoverishes public schools and may lead to a point where many of them lose a critical mass of able and well-motivated students with a consequent decline in average scholastic performance. The dilemma for policymakers becomes acute when private schools seek public subsidies but insist on retaining freedom about which students they may recruit and which they may expel.

Scholastic attainment is by no means the only objective of schools or of parents. Character development, religious commitment, and adherence to the sponsoring subculture are important objectives of particular types of private school. Given the importance that is attached to these aspects in schools' official statements it is surprising how little they have been evaluated. Schools of commitment place a high value on religious or cultural outcomes. The small amount of research on the effectiveness of such schools suggests that, once allowance has been made for influences from children's homes, there is very little that can be attributed to the school (Greeley and Rossi 1966). In other words schools of commitment are likely to confirm value positions but unlikely to change them.

Studies in Australia (Anderson 1986), England (Lambert and Millham 1968), and the United States (Persell and Cookson 1990) suggest that socially elite schools do impart to their pupils values and preferences of the culture from which they are drawn. These tend to include conservative political beliefs.

4. Efficiency

Efficiency means doing more with less. An efficient school or system is one which achieves its objectives with fewer dollars per pupil than another school or system, due allowance having been made for differences in intakes and composition.

Many investigations of efficiency take school organization or size as their independent variables. Although there is considerable variation, the smallest schools in urban areas tend to be in the private sector, public school authorities being inclined to amalgamate or close schools when enrollments decline below a critical point. The general conclusion with regard to size is that there is a wide range within which there are no discernible economies associated with scale. Very small schools are inclined to cost more because of fixed overheads; very large schools may also have higher unit costs because of the increasing complexities of administration.

In the Netherlands, where government policy has been very liberal with regard to funding religious and cultural groups wishing to have their own schools, there are as a consequence many small schools, especially in the nonpublic sector. James (1986) estimates that this liberal policy costs around 15 percent more than a conventionally funded system.

At a system level the coexistence of an unplanned but subsidized private sector and a planned public sector can lead to inefficiencies with respect to public outlays. Private schools are free to set up wherever they wish and are unrestricted in where they recruit their pupils. As a consequence there may be inefficient duplication, although the Netherlands experience suggests that this may not be excessively costly. There are situations where elite private schools, competing for top pupils, can acquire better pupils from a neighboring public one. Because public authorities usually have an obligation to make schooling available to all comers, the expense of maintaining a residual public school may lead to greater costs overall than where there is no competition.

In areas of demographic decline the inefficiencies associated with a dual system are liable to be exacerbated. For example, as a matter of rational planning, public authorities may decide to close or consolidate their schools. Even rumors of closure are often enough to upset parents and, if there is a private option in the neighborhood, there may be a flow of students from the public school to the private one.

It is difficult to find satisfactory empirical investigations of the effect of school organization on pupils' scholastic performance. Chubb and Moe (1990) reanalyze a national longitudinal data set and claim that the results confirm their contention that schools which are free of local democratic control and bureaucratic management also have a better record of scholastic achievement. Unfortunately their method of analysis has been shown to be flawed (Lemann 1991) and it is not possible to place any reliance on the results.

5. Value Dilemmas

Most countries are culturally pluralistic societies with a diversity of religions, ethnic affiliations, and social distinctions. The term "pluralism" sometimes refers to a descriptive account of the array of the beliefs, values, and practices associated with diverse subcultures. It can also serve in a normative sense, expressing a commitment to the preservation of these diverse attitudes and cultural practices. Either interpretation can give rise to concerns about the role of schooling in socializing the youthful members of particular subcultures. Leaders of the important subcultures, and some of the parents, want school to supplement the socializing role of family, church, and ethnic organizations. Furthermore it is widely preferred, if not demanded, by the leaders of these subcultures, that there should be separate schools for the purpose.

It is a mark of a tolerant society that pluralism is respected and that nothing is done that might undermine legitimate subcultures. To hold that pluralism is a good thing is to have a commitment to allowing diverse value positions to play themselves out in the social and political workings of society. Schools of commitment represent a tolerance for and valuing of social pluralism. A society which supports its Islamic or Catholic schools, or those of any other belief group, is respecting the right of parents to school their children according to their consciences, and of the group to transmit its culture to succeeding generations.

Pluralism in schooling has been equated with freedom of choice and is valued to the extent that in some countries the state meets all or most of the costs of private schools. Furthermore private schools outside the managed system are exempted from normal efficiency planning so that, as discussed above, small public schools may be closed to achieve economies of scale, while even smaller private schools are permitted to retain their subsidies.

Private schooling still poses dilemmas for the tolerant citizen and the tolerant state. One of these is the question of public funding. While there is almost universal support for the right of parents to school their children outside the planned sector, there is not agreement over whether that right should be subsidized. This issue is liable to become highly divisive in times of budgetary restraint.

A second dilemma arises because the exercise of rights by those choosing to opt out of public schooling may unwittingly diminish the rights of those who remain. The loss of community representativeness can threaten the core of public schooling, in the extreme case changing its function from a community to a charity service. Supporters of public schooling point out that many parents choose public schools for their children because of the above values. Students from families of diverse beliefs and social origins constitute an important part of the school experience. A central value is the learning of tolerance which is part of the curriculum in a school with a diverse mix of pupils. Thus, the exercise of tolerance by providing for choice of schools may reduce the opportunity for the children in a pluralistic society to learn that tolerance.

In similar fashion, academically selective or elite schools pose a dilemma for public planners. As has been seen, the right of parents to choose an elite school may conflict with the rights of public school parents who expect their children to be educated among an effective intellectual mix of students.

Creaming off is not limited to students. A private sector is liable to draw off the more influential and articulate parents who, if they remained, would, as stake-holders, be liable to be agents for reform. When a public–private balance sheet is drawn, the implications for public schooling due to the "exit" of able students and politically sophisticated parents should be set against the "lighthouse" and "safety valve" role attributed to the private sector.

A fourth dilemma concerns the tolerance that should be extended to groups whose values threaten those of the dominant society. An extreme example follows: presumably a private school run by a group of political dissidents with lessons on how to booby-trap cars would be refused a license. However, to take a nonfictitious example, what of a sect which, believing that girls have inferior intellects to boys, denies them an academic curriculum; or a religious group which practices physical punishment of children as an expression of its theological beliefs? The human rights issues posed by such examples are becoming more frequent in multicultural countries.

Finally there is a dilemma for governments with a commitment to both public and private education of how to present policies for assisting the private sector without appearing to diminish the value of the public. Substantial subsidies for private schools extend choice by making it easier for parents to use private schools, but there may also be an implicit message that private is better. This seems to be happening with the assisted places scheme intended to help intelligent but poor children attend private schools in England and Wales.

6. Equality versus Freedom to Choose versus Efficiency

The United Nations Declaration of Human Rights is frequently cited in defense of private schools. It asserts that parents have a prior right to choose the sort of education they wish for their children. Critics point out that this right needs to be qualified by the recognition that children also have rights and that, in extreme cases, the latter may have to take precedence; furthermore, that the freedom to choose is also limited to the extent that its exercise should not detract from the rights of others.

As the examples given above illustrate, the making of public education policy in a pluralist society is a balancing act between individual freedom and collective interest. In education, and in other areas where the state pays for a community service, the aggregation of a host of decisions made by individuals, each pursuing his or her own interests, does not necessarily result in the greatest good for the greatest number.

A private health service, or a private courier service, can cream off the lucrative end of the market, adding to the costs of a public health or postal enterprise which is obliged to service all areas. Similarly in schooling, a private sector, particularly if it is subsidized, can grow in influence and size to the point where it can have a negative impact on public schools irrespective of their efficiency or effectiveness.

See also: Effective Secondary Schools; Resource Allocations in Schools and School Systems; Religious Education; Social Foundations of School Choice

References

Alexander K L 1987 Cross-sectional comparisons of public and private school effectiveness: A review of evidence and issues. In: Haertel E D, James T, Levin H M (eds.) 1987 *Comparing Public & Private Schools. Volume 2: School Achievement.* Falmer Press, New York

Anderson D S 1986 Values, religion, social class and choice of private school in Australia. *Int. J. Educ. Res.* 12(4): 351–73

Chubb J E, Moe T M 1990 *Politics, Markets, and America's Schools.* Brookings Institution, Washington, DC

Coleman J S, Hoffer T, Kilgore S 1982 *High School Achievement: Public, Catholic, and Private Schools Compared.* Basic Books, New York

Cookson P W Jr, Persell C H 1985 *Preparing for Power: America's Elite Boarding Schools.* Basic Books, New York

Edwards T, Gewirtz S, Whitty G 1991 From assisted places to city technology colleges. In: Walford G (ed.) 1991 *Private Schooling: Tradition, Change and Diversity.* Paul Chapman Publishing, London.

Friedman M 1962 *Capitalism and Freedom.* University of Chicago Press, Chicago, Illinois

Glenn C L Jr 1988 *The Myth of the Common School.* The University of Massachusetts Press, Amherst, Massachusetts

Gormley W T Jr 1991 The privatization controversy. In: Gormley W T Jr (ed.) 1991 *Privatization and Its Alternatives.* The University of Wisconsin Press, Madison, Wisconsin

Graetz B 1988 The reproduction of privilege in Australian education. *Br. J. Sociol.* 39: 358–76

Graetz B 1990 Private schools and educational attainment: Cohort and generational Effects. *Australian Journal of Education* 34(2): 174–91

Greeley A M, Rossi P H 1966 *The Education of Catholic Americans.* Aldine Press, Chicago, Illinois

James E 1986 Public subsidies for private and public education: The Duth case. In: Levy D C (ed.) 1986 *Private Education: Studies in Choice and Public Policy.* Oxford University Press, New York

James E 1988 The public/private division of responsibility for education: An international comparison. In: James T, Levin H M (eds.) 1988 *Comparing Public and Private Schools. Vol. 1: Institutions and Organizations.* Falmer Press, New York

James E 1991 Private education and redistributive subsidies in Australia. In: Gormley W T Jr (ed.) 1991 *Privatization and Its Alternatives.* University of Wisconsin Press, Madison, Wisconsin

Jones P W 1992 *World Bank Financing of Education: Lending, Learning and Development.* Routledge, New York

Lambert R, Millham S 1968 *The Hothouse Society: An Exploration of Boarding-School Life Through the Boys' and Girls' Own Writings.* Weidenfeld and Nicolson, London

Lemann N 1991 A false panacea. *The New Yorker*, January. pp.101–05

Murnane R J 1986 Comparisons of private and public schools: What can we learn? In: Levy D C (ed.) 1986 *Private Education: Studies in Choice and Public Policy.* Oxford University Press, New York

Persell C H, Cookson P W Jr 1990 Chartering and bartering: Elite education and social reproduction. In: Kingston P W, Lewis L S (eds.) 1990 *The High-Status Track: Studies of Elite Schools and Stratification.* State University of New York Press, Albany, New York

Reid I, Williams R, Rayner M 1991 The education of the elite. In: Walford G (ed.) 1991 *Private Schooling: Tradition, Change and Diversity.* Paul Chapman Publishing, London

Sampson A 1962 *Anatomy of Britain.* Hodder and Stoughton, London

Shils E 1982 *The Constitution of Society.* University of Chicago Press, Chicago, Illinois

UNESCO 1989 *Development of Private Enrolment First and Second Level Education, 1975–1985.* UNESCO, Paris

van Laarhoven P, Bakker B, Dronkers J, Schijf H 1986 Some aspects of school careers in public and non-public primary schools. *Tijdschrift voor Onderwijsresearch* 11(2): 83–6

Walford G 1990 *Privatization and Privilege in Education.* Routledge, London

Williams T, Carpenter P G 1990 Private schooling and public achievement. *Australian Journal of Education* 34(1): 3–24

Willms J D 1987 Patterns of academic achievement in public and private schools: Implications for public policy and future research. In: Haertel E D, James T, Levin H M (eds.) 1987 *Comparing Public and Private Schools. Volume 2: School Achievement.* Falmer Press, New York

Further Reading

Boyd W L 1987 Balancing public and private schools: The Australian experience and American implications. *Educ. Eval. Policy Anal.* 9(3): 183–98

Cooper B S 1987 The uncertain future of national education policy: Private schools and the federal role. In: Boyd W L, Kerchner C T (eds.) 1987 *The Politics of Excellence and Choice in Education. 1987 Yearbook of the Politics of Education Association.* Falmer Press, Philadelphia, Pennsylvania

Glenn C L 1989 *Choice of Schools in Six Nations.* US Department of Education, Washington, DC

Halsey A H, Heath A F, Ridge J M 1980 *Origins and Destinations.* Clarendon Press, Oxford

Hansen J V 1971 *Nor Free Nor Secular.* Oxford University Press, Melbourne

Murnane R J 1986 Comparisons of private and public schools: The critical role of regulations. In: Levy D C (ed.) 1986 *Private Education: Studies in Choice and Public Policy.* Oxford University Press, New York

Sherington G, Petersen R C, Brice I 1987 *Learning to Lead: A History of Girls' and Boys' Corporate Secondary Schools in Australia.* Allen and Unwin, Sydney

Walford G (ed.) 1989 *Private Schools in Ten Countries: Policy and Practice.* Routledge, London

Whitty G 1989 The New Right and the National Curriculum: State control or market forces? *Journal of Education Policy* 4(4): 329–41

Resource Allocation in Schools and School Systems

D. H. Monk

Interest in the study of how resources are allocated at a variety of levels within school systems grew rapidly during the 1970s and 1980s. Much of this interest stemmed from concerns over equity in the distribution of fiscal resources for educational purposes. The desire to learn more about the internal allocation of resources for education has not been limited to decentralized schooling systems such as those found in the United States and Canada. Even in highly centralized school governance systems, considerable variation exists at local levels in how educational resources are ultimately utilized. Studies have begun to examine these internal distribution practices in a wide variety of nations from around the world. The results of these and a variety of American studies will be considered in this article.

In the United States, the early work on education resource allocation, dating from the early twentieth century, focused on the apportionment of state resources among constituent local education agencies or authorities (LEAs), most typically school districts. Among the products of this work are the numerous state aid distribution formulas that govern the distribution of state aid for education in the United States.

While challenges to the distribution of resources among LEAs continues (witness the flurry of constitutional challenges in the United States, considered in Benson 1991), there is interest in what happens to these resources after they reach LEAs. In other words, there is interest in how LEAs apportion state-supplied resources among constituent schools, programs, types of students, and so forth. Moreover, there is interest in what these creatures of local government do with whatever fiscal resources they raise locally.

The desire to learn more about these internal resource allocation practices has prompted two lines of research. First, there has been a focus on equity issues. This work has dealt with what fairness requires in the distribution of schooling resources. Second, efficiency concerns are prompted by the question: how can LEAs allocate their resources so that the production of a given level of desired education (and perhaps labor market) outcomes requires fewer resources?

The primary focus in this article will be on equity

issues and the associated policy implications, although some attention will be paid to the research on efficiency.

The article is organized by topic. Particular types of inequalities will be examined and the relevant research will be discussed. This is a relatively new area of research, and given the emphasis on resource allocation it is not surprising to observe that much of the research is motivated by economic models. However, as resource allocation issues reach ever closer to the actual instruction that takes place within schools and classrooms, the need for a more multidisciplinary approach is becoming more apparent. In particular, it is important for economists, political scientists, educational psychologists, and those with expert knowledge about educational organizations to work collaboratively if this work is to realize its full potential. In this light, the interest of political scientists in the micropolitics of education is heartening (see, e.g., Ball 1987, Blase 1988, 1991a, 1991b, Hoyle 1986). The few examples of joint work among political scientists and economists are very encouraging (see, e.g., Boyd and Hartman 1988).

1. Origins of Interest in the Internal Allocation of Resources

As was indicated, the conventional study of equity in the distribution of educational resources in the United States focuses on the distribution of state resources among constituent LEAs. A large literature has grown up around this topic, and significant methodological advances have been made (Barro 1989, Berne and Stiefel 1984).

Interest in what happens to resources after they reach school districts derives from several sources. First, it can be viewed as a byproduct of singling out special needs populations within schools. For example, in the United States from the 1960s a variety of student subpopulations have been singled out for special treatment. These groups include disadvantaged, handicapped, bilingual, and gifted students. Once a group is identified, questions logically follow about how that group fares compared with others in the distribution of resources. Answers to these questions require analysts to trace resource flows to their intended beneficiaries deep within regions, schools, and perhaps even classrooms.

Second, perceptions that an educational system is failing or is performing less well than was previously the case can give rise to interest in what is actually happening to resources. Again, an example can be found in the United States where there has been widespread criticism of public schools. The United States schools have been criticized for rapidly rising real expenditures per pupil coupled with declining—or at best—stable measures of educational achievement (Hanushek 1989). In partial response to this criticism, the United States federal government established a research center focused on educational finance and productivity. The research agenda followed by this center places a heavy emphasis on micro-level equity as well as efficiency issues.

The former United States Secretary of Education also criticized the schools for spending resources on the wrong inputs. In particular, he emphasized what he called the "administrative blob," a term that suggested his displeasure with how much was being spent on administration by United States schools (Kirst 1988). Allegations such as these have prompted researchers to conduct longitudinal studies of how dollars are distributed across budget categories such as central administration. Sherman (1985), for example, has found that between 1960 and 1980 the percentage spent by United States K-12 (i.e., kindergarten through secondary) school systems on administration changed from 4.1 to 4.9. A later study indicated that the percentage was slightly over 5 percent (Sherman and Suitor 1991). Fox (1987) found that local administration (the salaries of school-level administrators) plus district and state administration amounted to 6.9 percent of the total costs of operating a typical United States classroom in 1984–85. One of the frustrations associated with this type of research is related to inconsistencies across jurisdictions in what is included under broad headings such as "administrative support."

Third, schools constitute promising sites for testing emerging theories of organizational behavior, productivity, and individual as well as group behavior. Data describing school practices tend to be extensive, especially in industrialized nations, and many of these data are part of the public record. This availability of detailed information about schooling practices contrasts sharply with the inaccessibility of information about organizations operating within the private sector of many economies.

There has been an interesting byproduct of this interest in tracing resource flows to micro-levels within educational systems. Consider the United States federal government's program for disadvantaged students, which over the years has required LEAs to demonstrate that these federal dollars flowed to the intended beneficiaries. The government's demand has been cited as one of the reasons for the widespread use of "pull-out" compensatory education programs for the disadvantaged. When eligible students are "pulled out" from the regular program and sent for fixed periods of time to a special program, it becomes relatively easy to satisfy auditors that the federal dollars have not in fact been diverted to ineligible students. The irony here is that "pull-out" programs have been closely questioned and criticized in recent years on pedagogical grounds (Smith 1986).

2. Inequalities among Schools within Common Organizational Structures

Ginsburg et al. (1981) conducted one of the early

studies of how funding inequalities among schools compare with funding inequalities across the larger organizational units in which schools are located. They were particularly concerned with inequalities among individual schools located within common school districts, and they focused their analysis on data drawn from New York State. Their analyses revealed substantial variability in the decomposition of variance, depending on the attribute being considered. For example, when they examined salary attributes of teachers, they found that most of the variation existed across school districts rather than across schools within school districts. More specifically, upward of 80 percent of the total variation in teacher salaries in New York State existed at the school district level. This result is not surprising, given the widespread use of district-wide salary schedules in New York. In contrast, more within-district variation was found for staff inputs such as the supply of teacher aides, where only 31 percent of the variance existed across rather than within school districts.

Their analysis also considered correlates of the revealed variation. District-level inequalities were straightforward in the sense that, despite the infusion of state aid for education paid in inverse proportion to district wealth, the wealthier districts spent at higher levels and paid higher teacher salaries. The within-district analysis revealed a more complex distribution, where schools with a high incidence of special needs populations received substantially more professionals, but also where the professionals received were less educated and less experienced. Needy schools within districts also received larger supplies of paraprofessional support. Ginsburg and his colleagues concluded that from a resource perspective the greater quantity of teachers and teacher aides offset the lower levels of experience and training. Thus, they reached the overall conclusion that, in contrast to the interdistrict distribution, the distribution of resources within New York State school districts favored special needs populations.

Research dealing with school-level inequalities in funding has also been conducted outside the United States. Tibi (1988) reported on a comparative analysis of micro-level resource allocation that was conducted under the auspices of the International Institute for Educational Planning (IIEP), a division of UNESCO. According to Tibi, the research carried out by the Institute has demonstrated disparities in resource levels among schools within nations, as well as in the internal utilization of these resources. The results support the general thesis that even in nations with what appear at first glance to be highly centralized educational governance structures, considerable variation can exist at the local level in the distribution and utilization of financial resources.

Tibi goes on to note that ministries of education typically retain direct control over physical resources such as equipment, furniture, and textbooks. Staff deployment, in contrast, is influenced in many countries by preferences of teachers for cities, and is sometimes limited by regulations preventing redeployment when civil servants object. These factors can have a significant impact on the distribution of staff between institutions (Tibi 1988 p. 83).

He also noted that at micro-levels, the availability of physical resources as well as human resources may be quite sensitive to abrupt and hard-to-anticipate changes in demand. Perhaps the best example is an occasion where an unexpected change takes place in the number of students enrolled. Where more students than expected arrive, resources will be stretched thinly, since it will be difficult for the central authority to respond quickly. Students will face crowding, large classes, insufficient numbers of textbooks, etc. Where enrollments fall short of projections, the opposite result will obtain.

The net result, from a national perspective, is variation in the supply of resources at any given time, despite the use of perhaps quite rigid and centralized rules governing the deployment of resources. The central authority may impose a policy of one teacher per X number of students only to find substantial variation among individual schools (and within individual schools) at any one time.

Interest in school-level equity issues at the school level is growing, particularly in the United States. The United States federal government funded a five-year Research Center for the Study of Educational Finance and Productivity based at the University of Wisconsin in Madison. An important part of the center's research agenda involves tracing resource flows to micro-levels within educational systems. A substantial part of this effort will involve looking at distributions across schools within school districts.

3. Understanding the Micro Implications of Grants-in-aid

In decentralized systems of educational governance and finance, where revenues enter at different levels of government, it is important for policymakers at more centralized levels to understand decision-making processes at less centralized levels. If, for example, the central government wishes to stimulate spending on education, a program of aid can be designed. But it is not a simple matter of assuming that the new funds will be added to existing allocations since the decision-makers at more local levels may choose to withdraw locally raised revenues that were previously allocated to education.

A variety of types of grants-in-aid have been devised so that options exist regarding the manner in which a given level of resources might be made available to constituent units. Aid, for example, might be offered on a matching basis for certain special purposes. Important policy questions arise about whether this is more or less effective at stimulating spending than if the same amount of aid were offered on an entitlement basis. Two micro-level resource-allocation phenomena are at issue: (a) the stimulating effects of the outside resources on the willingness of localities to contribute their own resources; and (b) the leakage of earmarked dollars from the external source into unintended uses. Tsang and Levin (1983), in their review of the effects of alternative grant designs, demonstrated the stimulative effects of matching and other categorical forms of aid. Their analysis made it clear that decisions taken at centralized levels regarding the distribution of aid can have substantial effects on decisions that localities make about how to spend funds for educational purposes.

4. Interactions with the Private Sector

The privatization of public education has important micro-level resource-allocation implications. In the United States privatization takes several forms, which have in common the goal of more directly involving parents, students, and others (e.g., the local business community) in the operation of individual schools. These efforts include the establishment of school-level councils with some degree of autonomy (e.g., Moore 1990), enhanced opportunities for choice in the selection of schools and school districts (Clune and Witte 1990), and proposals for greater reliance on user fees as a means of financing schools (Monk 1990, Odden 1990). A related feature of privatization is more extensive involvement of the business community in school operations (McLaughlin 1988).

From a resource allocation perspective, privatization is of interest because it involves the infusion of resources under new terms and often from new sources. The school-by-school character of the privatization movement dictates a micro-level resource approach to questions about both the nature of the changes in the restrictions that arise and their consequences.

These reform efforts only began in the United States in the 1980s. Only a few micro-level resource analyses have yet been made. There is more experience with the mixing of public and private sources of revenue outside the United States. Tibi's (1988) survey of 14 countries included two countries with one or more private networks that receive partial public funding (Indonesia and Kenya). This survey also provided insight into the widespread reliance on school fees paid by parents. Tibi noted that even within a highly centralized and restricting system, such as that found in the Congo, parents make a limited direct contribution to the operation of their children's schools.

Tibi's research revealed an interesting practice regarding the collection of fees for secondary schools in Indonesia. The usual practice is to conceive of fees as what parents offer in exchange for services provided by the school. It might be a straightforward service such as the provision (or purchase) of a school uniform or a textbook, or it might be a more general activity fee where the connection to a specific service is less clear. One common characteristic of these fees is that they stay at the local level and finance services produced at that level. It is a fee-for-service notion. In Indonesia, fees are collected but only a portion of the fee, 85 percent according to Tibi's estimates, is retained by the school. The balance is collected by the central agency and is used to help finance the overall costs of the system. Tibi also found that the percentage of fees a given school surrenders to the central agency varies depending on the characteristics of the school. Tibi pointed out that this percentage variation has implications for how much inequality there is across schools within the Indonesian system.

Tibi also reported empirical evidence showing that the infusion of private resources into education is associated with larger disparities across schools in the provision of educational services. In particular, he showed that the explanatory power of size as a predictor of total expenditures is weakest in countries with significant private fund involvement. He found similar results in his analyses of unit expenditures. He contrasted Morocco, where unit expenditures varied minimally, with Indonesia, where the variation in unit expenditures was quite high. According to Tibi, the reliance on user fees contributes to the variability in spending levels per pupil in Indonesia.

5. Inequalities within Schools

Research examining inequalities within schools is hardly new. Analysts for years have been concerned with phenomena such as the tracking of students by academic specialization or the grouping of students for instructional purposes. There have been studies of high-school tracking, where findings suggest that students assigned to the nonacademic track are seriously discriminated against (see, e.g., Oakes 1985). And there have been studies of instructional grouping where the findings reveal substantial inequalities in the amount and character of the instructional resources that are supplied (for an example, see Dreeben and Barr 1988).

Less common are studies of within-school inequalities that have an explicit focus on resource allocation issues, complete with economic rationales for the observed resource allocation practices. Such a line of research has emerged. It is rooted in the economist's notion of scale economies, and is focused on inequalities in the supply of learning opportunities across discrete areas of the secondary school curriculum.

The long-standing presumption among policymakers has been that school size is strongly and uniformly related positively to the breadth and depth of curricular offerings, so that larger schools are unambiguously able to offer superior educational opportunities to their students. However, an important distinction can be drawn between the availability of scale economies and the actual willingness or ability of school officials to realize them, if and when a school's size increases (Monk 1987). Research conducted during the late 1980s and early 1990s has looked explicitly at the degree to which larger school size translates into enhanced curricular offerings (Barker 1985, Haller et al. 1990, McKenzie 1989, Monk 1987, Monk and Haller 1993). The major research findings are the following.

First, the effects of school size on curricular offerings vary depending on the subject area of the curriculum. For example, school size has much less impact on course offerings in social studies and science than it has in foreign languages and the performing and visual arts.

Second, the strength of the relationship between school size and curricular offerings diminishes as schools become larger. Increases in the size of very small schools are associated with greater curricular gains than increases in the size of larger schools.

Third, school size is related to the types of courses that are added within subject areas. In particular, school size is positively related to the share of the academic curriculum devoted to advanced and remedial courses. In most subjects, advanced courses grow more rapidly with school size than do remedial courses (Monk et al. 1996).

Fourth, substantial variation in curricular offerings among high schools remains after the effects of school size are removed. There are small schools with rich curricular offerings just as there are large schools with modest offerings. School size alone explains roughly half of the variation in course offerings among high schools. Research is also showing that curricular offerings are sensitive to measures of social class (Monk and Haller 1993, Oakes 1990).

Fifth, the mere presence of a course in a curriculum is no guarantee of widespread student participation. Remarkably small percentages of students within a school take advantage of those courses found only within large school curricula.

Collectively, these findings have important implications for the organizational structuring of secondary schools. They point out that the conventional reorganization solution is likely to pay off unevenly for different types of students. They make it clear that once schools reach relatively modest sizes, by historical standards, the case for reorganization on curricular improvement grounds becomes weak. They also underline the importance of more deeply seated phenomena such as the student demand for particular courses. Important questions can be asked and need to be answered about why so few students take advantage of the courses found only in the curricula of larger high schools.

McKenzie's (1989) Australian study extended the earlier studies in several interesting directions. In particular, he succeeded at distinguishing among grade levels in his analysis of the effects of school size on curricular offerings. He found important differences suggesting that curricular offerings at the upper end of the secondary program (for years 11 and 12 in the Australian system) were more sensitive to enrollment size than the program at the lower end of the system (years 7–10 in the Australian system). Subsequent analyses using United States data have also demonstrated the importance of grade configuration within a high school on course offerings (Monk and Haller 1993).

McKenzie's study included analyses of relationships between school size and selected aspects of teacher decision making. In so doing he was able to replicate some earlier findings from the United States suggesting that there are upper limits on the degree to which secondary school teachers specialize in the teaching of particular subjects (Monk 1987). Regardless of how large a high school becomes, it appears that there are limits on the degree to which teachers specialize in the teaching of a particular course or subject.

McKenzie (1989) also examined relationships between the size of a school and the percentage of teacher time devoted to class teaching. He reported small positive relationships in this regard, suggesting that in larger schools a slightly larger percentage of a teacher's time is assigned to class teaching duties. He explained these positive relationships as byproducts of scale economies in the provision of administrative and classroom support services (see also Monk et al. 1996).

6. Conclusion

This entry has provided an overview of developments in a relatively new area of educational research. Analysts and policymakers are realizing that it is no longer sufficient to assume that internal resource allocation practices are either unimportant or innocuous with respect to the equity targets that have been set. In addition, there are a host of productivity issues that have been touched on only briefly here.

While the research has begun and has contributed important insights, there are two major obstacles that need to be overcome. First, there is a paucity of theory to guide analysts. Much of the existing empirical analysis is primarily descriptive. This work is important, but more needs to be done than simply document the extent to which inequalities exist at various levels within educational systems. At minimum, distinctions need to be drawn between inequalities that are acceptable and those that violate fundamental notions of equity. Theoretical work is also needed to shed light on why the observed inequalities develop.

Second, there are immense data collection and availability problems. Many of the industrialized nations are making some progress toward collecting resource allocation data at school and subschool levels, but progress is slow and costly. Data availability problems in developing countries are chronic and become even more serious as analysts reach more micro-levels.

In light of these problems, it is heartening to observe that lines of research into micro-level resource allocation issues have been established and are being pursued. The potential for fruitful collaborative work among economists, political scientists, organizational theorists, and those with expert knowledge about educational systems is large. It will be an important area of research to monitor during the 1990s and beyond.

See also: Effective Secondary Schools; Public and Private Schools: Sociological Perspectives; School Size and Small Schools

References

Ball S J 1987 *The Micro-Politics of the School*. Methuen, London

Barker B 1985 A study reporting secondary course offerings in small and large high schools. Paper presented to the Rhode Island Department of Education Conference, Providence, Rhode Island (ERIC Document Reproduction Service No. ED 256 547)

Barro S M 1989 Fund distribution issues in school finance: Priorities for the next round of research. *Educ. Eval. Policy Anal.* 11(1): 17–30

Benson C S 1991 Definitions of equity in school finance in Texas, New Jersey, and Kentucky. *Harvard J. Legislation* 28(2): 401–21

Berne R, Stiefel L 1984 *The Measurement of Equity in School Finance: Conceptual, Methodological and Empirical Dimensions*. Johns Hopkins University Press, Baltimore, Maryland

Blase J 1988 The teachers' political orientation vis-à-vis the principal: The micropolitics of the school. In: Hannaway J, Crowson R (eds.) 1988 *The Politics of Reforming School Administration: The 1988 Yearbook of the Politics of Education Association*. Falmer, New York

Blase J 1991a The micropolitical perspective: A brief overview. *Politics of Education Bulletin* 17(3)

Blase J (ed.) 1991b *The Politics of Life in Schools: Power, Conflict, and Cooperation*. Corwin Press, Newbury Park, California

Boyd W L, Hartman W T 1988 The politics of educational productivity. In: Monk D H, Underwood J (eds.) 1988 *Microlevel School Finance: Issues and Implications for Policy*. Ballinger, Cambridge, Massachusetts

Clune W H, Witte J F (eds.) 1990 *Choice and Control in American Education*, Vols. 1 and 2. Falmer, London

Dreeben R, Barr R 1988 The formation and instruction of ability groups. *Am. J. Educ.* 97(1): 34–64

Fox J N 1987 An analysis of classroom spending: Or where do all the dollars go? *Planning and Changing* 18(3): 154–62

Ginsburg A, Moskowitz J H, Rosenthal A S 1981 A school based analysis of inter- and intradistrict resource allocation. *J. Educ. Finance* 6(4): 440–55

Haller E J, Monk D H, Spotted-Bear A, Griffith J, Moss P 1990 School size and program comprehensiveness: Evidence from high school and beyond. *Educ. Eval. Policy Anal.* 12(2): 109–20

Hanushek E A 1989 The impact of differential expenditures on school performance. *Educ. Res.* 18(4): 45–62

Hoyle E 1986 *The Politics of School Management*. Hodder and Stoughton, London

Kirst M W 1988 The internal allocation of resources within US school districts: Implications for policymakers and practitioners. In: Monk D H, Underwood J (eds.) 1988 *Microlevel School Finance: Issues and Implications for Policy*. Ballinger, Cambridge, Massachusetts

McKenzie P A 1989 Secondary school size, curriculum structure, and resource use: A study in the economics of education. (Doctoral dissertation, Monash University)

McLaughlin M W 1988 Business and the public schools: New patterns of support. In: Monk D H, Underwood J (eds.) 1988 *Microlevel School Finance: Issues and Implications for Policy*. Ballinger, Cambridge, Massachusetts

Monk D H 1987 Secondary school size and curricular comprehensiveness. *Econ. Educ. Rev.* 6(2): 137–50

Monk D H 1990 *Educational Finance: An Economic Approach*. McGraw-Hill, New York

Monk D H, Haller E J 1993 Predictors of high school academic course offerings: The role of school size. *Am. Educ. Res. J.* 30(1): 3–21

Monk D H, Roellke C E, Brent B O 1996 *What Education Dollars Buy: An Examination of Resource Allocation Patterns in New York State Public School Systems*. Cornell University, Ithaca, New York

Moore D R 1990 Voice and choice in Chicago. In: Clune W H, Witte J F (eds.) 1990 *Choice and Control in American Education, Vol. 2: The Practice of Choice, Decentralization and School Restructuring*. Falmer, London

Oakes J 1985 *Keeping Track: How Schools Structure Inequality*. Yale University Press, New Haven, Connecticut

Oakes J 1990 *Multiplying Inequalities: The Effects of Race, Social Class, and Tracking on Opportunities to Learn Mathematics and Science*. NSF-R-3928. Rand Corporation, Santa Monica, California

Odden A 1990 A new school finance for public school choice. Paper presented at the Annual Meeting of the American Educational Research Association, School of Education, University of Southern California, Los Angeles, California

Sherman J 1985 Resource allocation and staffing patterns in the public schools: 1959–60 to 1983–84. Paper presented at the annual meeting of the American Educational Research Association, Chicago, Illinois

Sherman J, Suitor J H 1991 Where does the money go? An analysis of state expenditures for elementary and secondary schools. Paper presented at the annual meeting of the American Education Finance Association, Williamsburg, Virginia

Smith M S 1986 *Selecting Students and Services for Chapter 1*. Stanford University School of Education, Stanford, California

Tibi C 1988 The internal allocation of resources for education: An international perspective. In: Monk D H, Underwood J (eds.) 1988 *Microlevel School Finance: Issues and Implications for Policy*. Ballinger, Cambridge, Massachusetts

Tsang M, Levin H M 1983 The impact of intergovernmental grants on educational expenditure. *Rev. Educ. Res.* 53(3): 329–67

Second Chance Education and Alternative Routes

A. Yogev

The notion of second chance education is related to the worldwide expansion of secondary and tertiary systems of education since the 1950s. This expansion, coupled with the growing demand for educational credentials in the labor market, have turned the secondary and higher institutions of education in many countries into the major selection mechanism of the labor force. The emphasis of these institutions on academic ability in the selection and promotion processes of students has left many adolescents outside the main academic track due to low ability or lack of academic motivation. These adolescents drop out of school or legitimately leave the educational system at a relatively early stage of their educational career, and are unable to pursue occupational careers requiring educational credentials. The colinearity of academic achievement and social origin means that many of these adolescents belong to lower social classes or to ethnic minorities.

Ideas and frameworks of second chance education, which have evolved in various countries since the late 1950s, are therefore closely related to the ideology of equal opportunity in education. They are based on the belief that errors made by the selection mechanisms of the educational system or by individuals who terminated their own educational career could be corrected at a later stage by the provision of second chance educational frameworks.

Since this belief denotes some sort of openness of the education system, such frameworks are more typical in some countries than others. Some of these frameworks are organized and supervised by the state, while others are left to community-level initiatives. Second chance frameworks also differ by level and scope, ranging from popular literacy campaigns to established programs in secondary schools and in institutions of tertiary education. Despite the considerable number of sociological and educational studies on individual frameworks of second chance education in various countries, there is no agreement among researchers on the exact types of programs and frameworks which constitute second chance systems. Even the term "second chance education" itself is used only in some countries (e.g., Germany, Israel, and the United States), while the term "further education" is used in the United Kingdom, and in Latin America such programs tend to fall under the heading of nonformal or popular education.

It seems reasonable, however, to divide the discussion of second chance frameworks into three categories: programs conducted on the secondary education level, those on the tertiary level, and programs of nonformal education. While the third category entirely relates to programs alongside the main education system, second chance education on the secondary level, and to some extent also on the tertiary, may be further divided into programs within the regular education system and special frameworks existing outside this system.

1. Second Chance Within and Outside the Regular Education System

There is an ongoing debate among policymakers, practitioners, and researchers, as to whether second chance programs should be administered within the regular education system. As noted by Inbar (1990), this debate represents two different approaches to second chance, mainly regarding secondary education. Advocates of the within-school programs adhere to the preventive approach to second chance. According to this approach, the provision of second chance programs within the first chance system may prevent the failure of students and their dropping out of the system. In contrast, advocates of alternative frameworks of second chance education adhere to the rehabilitation approach. From this viewpoint, students who have already failed in the regular education system or who have voluntarily dropped out of school require special treatment in order to rehabilitate their self-esteem and motivation for further education.

Arguments for and against each type of the second chance frameworks stem from the ideological differences embedded in the two approaches. Supporters of second chance opportunities within the regular education system argue that only the first chance system can provide real opportunities for second chance students, since its credentials are accepted by the labor market. The provision of such opportunities does not only prevent the potential dropout of weak students, but also enhances their self-esteem and motivation, since they are considered part of the regular education system. In addition, it is argued that second chance programs handled by regular schools are less costly and more efficient than special frameworks outside these schools.

In contrast, supporters of the alternative programs alongside the regular system claim that the regular system is based on the tracking and stratification of students by ability, and is therefore incapable of handling the particular problems of second chance students. Only outside programs, specifically aimed at these students and staffed by trained practitioners, can rehabilitate the educational careers of such students. Though such programs may be expensive, especially since they may require more years of education than in the regular system, their effectiveness in the long run may rebalance their cost.

The importance of the ongoing debate between the two approaches notwithstanding, it should be noted that most countries adhering to the second chance notion have developed both types of programs, within the regular education system and alongside it. This development is based on the belief that the two types of programs may serve different sorts of clientele. Also, developments of some frameworks of second chance education, as shown later, bring them closer to the main system, and thus turn the boundaries between the two types of second chance education into more permeable ones. As emphasized below the emerging tendency of researchers to replace the ideology of second chance education altogether with notions of alternative education routes, may turn the distinction between the two types of second chance program into a somewhat outdated notion.

2. Second Chance Frameworks at the Secondary Education Level

At the secondary school level, second chance programs may be defined as those alongside the regular academic high school track, either within or outside the regular schools.

2.1 Within-school Programs

By far the most important second chance programs within the regular high school system are the vocational ones. Students of low academic ability are frequently tracked into vocational studies in order to prevent their dropout and to enable them to obtain a high-school matriculation diploma. The notion of vocational tracking within regular high schools has occurred particularly in European and Middle-Eastern countries since the mid-1970s, partly replacing older apprenticeship programs of vocational secondary education outside the regular high school system. The decline of the latter programs during the 1970s (Benavot 1983), and the rise during the 1980s of within-school vocational programs leading toward high school matriculation diplomas, are clearly related to the ideology of equal opportunity in education.

Though this ideology is shared by many countries, the structuring of vocational education within regular high schools differs by country, and variations in this respect exist even within countries. In some countries, like the United Kingdom and Israel, distinct vocational tracks exist within comprehensive or separate high schools, and provide a full-scale study program parallel to that of the academic track. In other countries, like Germany, a work-study program is typical of the vocational high schools. An innovative modular program, which allows students to combine several modules of vocational courses in different schools and during a

prolonged period of time, has been introduced in Scotland (Raffe 1988). Yet in some other countries, like the United States, vocational tracking in high school is less distinctive altogether. Vocational courses are offered alongside the academic ones, and students not included in a college-preparatory program usually enroll in more vocational courses.

Despite the clear advantages of within-school vocational programs in providing second chance education that leads toward a matriculation diploma, they have been criticized by various researchers from the viewpoint of equal opportunity in education. These criticisms mainly relate to two issues. First, the high school matriculation diplomas obtained by graduates of the vocational tracks are not necessarily equivalent to those provided in the academic track, and are recognized less readily by institutions of higher education. Therefore, vocational tracking enhances social reproduction by channeling students of lower social strata, ethnic minorities, and girls, into terminal education routes. These social reproductive tendencies have been demonstrated not only with respect to vocational versus academic tracking, but also in relation to specific curricular stratification within the vocational track, in countries where vocational high school tracking is either distinctive (Yogev and Ayalon 1991) or less distinctive (Oakes 1985). Second, the curriculum of vocational tracks has been depicted, mainly by French and British researchers (see Dickinson and Erben 1982), as pursuing "the pedagogy of technicization," aimed at separating the students from elite knowledge and producing an obedient middle class of workers.

2.2 Programs Outside the Regular School System

Among the second chance programs outside the regular high school system, only a minority are aimed at preparing the students for a matriculation diploma. An example is the "external high schools" in Israel. These are private schools that prepare dropouts of the regular system for the matriculation examinations. It has been shown that these schools tend to attract dropouts of higher social strata and of the ethnic majority, and only a small percentage of their students are successful in obtaining the matriculation diploma (Ayalon 1990).

The majority of programs constitute endless variations of dropout recovery efforts, providing basic skills and vocational training to out-of-school youth, either employed or unemployed. As such, they are mainly targeted at disadvantaged populations. These programs may be organized by the state, by local authorities, by voluntary organizations or, less frequently, by the private sector. Rumberger (1990) reports that thousands of such programs exist in the United States alone. Surveying a variety of these programs he contends that, despite their cost, they carry long-range benefits not only in terms of employment and income, but also by reducing the social costs associated with crime rates, drug abuse, and poor health.

Since programs outside the regular school system

mainly provide terminal education to disadvantaged populations, they were traditionally considered to constitute the core of the second chance ideology. However, more recent research regards them as legitimate alternative routes to education. Saha (1985), for example, has studied the tendencies of urban high school leavers in Australia to pursue their education in vocational training programs. Finding that these tendencies are determined by specific occupational aspirations rather than by social origin, he contends that such programs may be considered by youngsters as legitimate alternatives to high school education, enabling them to pursue their future occupational plans.

3. Second Chance Frameworks at the Tertiary Education Level

At this level of the education system one may differentiate between second chance programs preparing for entrance to higher education and programs at the tertiary level itself. Preparatory programs are aimed at providing a second chance for enrollment in higher education to high school graduates whose past academic achievements do not meet the entrance criteria of these institutions. Such programs may be provided by private schools, such as the *Yobiko* schools in Japan, or by the universities themselves. In the case of the *Yobiko* schools it has been shown that, despite the high aspirations of all their students, it is mainly those of higher social strata who succeed in entering prestigious universities upon graduation from the preparatory school (Tsukada 1992). In contrast, students in the one-year academic preparatory programs offered by the Israeli universities, including students from disadvantaged social origins, tend to mingle successfully with the regular university students after completing their preparatory studies (Ayalon et al. 1992).

Institutions of higher education are beyond the scope of this entry, but it is worth mentioning briefly some trends in second chance orientations at this level because of their resemblance to equivalent trends at the secondary level of education. Of particular relevance are the gradual replacement of the second chance ideology with an alternative route orientation, and the deterioration of boundaries between programs within and outside the regular system.

The vocationalization of the United States community colleges since the 1960s, and the expansion of technical colleges since the mid-1970s in Western Europe, especially in the United Kingdom, France, and Germany, have created a basic change in attitudes toward second chance in adult education. The common idea that two-year colleges are aimed at providing a nontargeted educational enrichment to younger and older adults of low academic ability, thus serving as a second chance mechanism "cooling out" their aspirations, was replaced with the notion of targeted alternative routes to higher education (Brint and Karabel 1989). The establishment of such colleges as preparatory frameworks for mid-level managerial and technical vocations has further made them an integral part of the tertiary education system. This process has been intensified by the growing worldwide recognition of open universities, originally based on a second chance orientation, as full-scale institutions of higher education (Sewart et al. 1983).

4. Nonformal Education and Second Chance

Alongside the formal education system, nonformal education programs are also frequently considered to provide second chance education to both youth and adults. Nonformal programs are usually organized by the state, particularly in Third World countries, or by voluntary organizations, and they usually provide selected types of learning, such as basic skills and some vocational training, to specific subgroups of the population.

The main reason underlying the assumption that nonformal programs provide second chance education is their clientele. Such programs are usually aimed at disadvantaged populations, usually adolescents and adults who left school at an early stage. The particular popularity of nonformal education programs in Third World countries has strengthened their public image as second chance frameworks. This image has further expanded with the more recent emphasis of various Latin American countries on programs of popular education. These programs, initiated during the 1980s by revolutionary regimes and then spreading to other Latin American countries, are particularly aimed at marginal populations, such as subordinate ethnic minorities and women in rural areas (Fink and Arnove 1991).

However, the actual provision of second chances in education by nonformal programs may be only marginal. Such programs do not necessarily provide any certificates of graduation to their participants, and even when they do, such certificates do not usually qualify their holders to enroll in formal education programs, nor are they readily recognized by potential employers as educational credentials. Subsequently, nonformal programs tend to raise the educational and occupational aspirations of disadvantaged adolescents and adults, but do not enable them to realize their expectations (La Belle 1986, Yogev and Shapira 1990).

Moreover, nonformal education has been extensively used for manipulative purposes by political elites of Third World countries, who have sought to improve their public image and to extend their public support by launching nonformal education projects. This aspect of nonformal education has been emphasized by Yogev and Shapira (1990) in relation to national youth programs in several African and Central American countries, and by Torres (1990) regarding the nonformal education of adults in Latin America. Taking this clear political function into consideration, it is possible to conceive of nonformal education as an exemplary case of "ritualistic second-chance systems," characterized by a gap between their announced goals and actual outputs (Inbar and Sever 1986).

5. Conclusion

Despite the growing number of sociological studies on particular programs or specific aspects of second chance education, in the early 1990s there is still no systematic research on the universal scope of second chance education considering the entire range of such programs and frameworks. The typology of second chance programs, suggested by this entry, into secondary and tertiary level programs of the formal education system and nonformal education frameworks, demonstrates the complexity of existing second chance programs, and hints at trends related to conceptualizations and ideologies of second chance education.

There is, first, a clear trend toward greater permeability of traditional boundaries between second chance programs within and outside the regular education system. This trend has been especially notable on the tertiary education level, where institutions traditionally recognized as providers of second chance education are now fully or partly integrated with the regular system of higher education. This trend infiltrates the secondary education level, where high school vocational tracks take over the second chance function traditionally fulfilled by vocational programs outside the regular school system.

An even more significant trend, which deserves the special attention of researchers, is the growing recognition of second chance systems as alternative education routes by their participants and by the general public. This new orientation toward second chance education is spreading not only with respect to formal programs on the secondary and tertiary levels of formal education, but also in relation to nonformal education. The replacement of nonformal education by the popular education concept in Third World countries, though not necessarily increasing actual second chances in education, indicates an ideological shift toward programs providing alternative education to marginal groups rejected by the selective, "nonpopular," formal system. Considering the communality of this new orientation in all three types or levels of second chance systems, it is possible that in the near future the concept of second chance education, symbolizing recovery or correction of errors made within the first chance system, will be replaced altogether by the concept of alternative education routes.

See also: Aspirations and Expectations of Students; Children and Youth at Risk; Dropouts, School Leavers, and Truancy; School Dropouts; Sociology of Adult Education

References

Ayalon H 1990 The social impact of nonregular education in Israel. *Comp. Educ. Rev.* 34(3): 302–13

Ayalon H, Shapira R, Shavit R 1992 A second chance for higher education: Academic preparatory programs in Israel. *Res. Higher Educ.* 33(4): 497–510

Benavot A 1983 The rise and decline of vocational education. *Soc. Educ.* 56(2): 63–76

Brint S, Karabel J 1989 *The Diverted Dream: Community Colleges and the Promise of Educational Opportunity in America 1900–1985.* Oxford University Press, New York

Dickinson H, Erben M 1982 Technical culture and technical education in France: A consideration of the work of Claude Grignon and its relevance to British further education curricula. *Br. J. Sociol. Educ.* 3(2): 145–59

Fink M, Arnove R F 1991 Issues and tensions in popular education in Latin America. *Int. J. Educ. Dev.* 11(3): 221–30

Inbar D E 1990 The legitimation of a second chance. In: Inbar D E (ed.) 1990 *Second Chance in Education.* Falmer Press, London

Inbar D E, Sever R 1986 Second chance: Some theoretical and empirical remarks. *Issues in Education* 4(2): 121–35

La Belle T 1986 *Nonformal Education in Latin America and the Caribbean. Stability, Reform or Revolution?* Praeger, New York

Oakes J 1985 *Keeping Track: How Schools Structure Inequality.* Yale University Press, New Haven, Connecticut

Raffe D 1988 Modules and the strategy of institutional versatility: The first two years of the 16-plus action plan in Scotland. In: Raffe D (ed.) 1988 *Education and the Youth Labor Market.* Falmer Press, London

Rumberger R W 1990 Second chance for high school dropouts: The costs and benefits of dropout recovery programs in the United States. In: Inbar D E (ed.) 1990 *Second Chance in Education.* Falmer Press, London

Saha L J 1985 The legitimacy of early school leaving: Occupational orientations, vocational training plans, and educational attainment among urban Australian youth. *Soc. Educ.* 58(4): 228–40

Sewart D, Keegan D, Holmberg B (eds.) 1983 *Distance Education: International Perspectives.* Croom Helm, London

Torres C A 1990 *The Politics of Nonformal Education in Latin America.* Praeger, New York

Tsukada M 1992 Social origin, tracking, and aspirations of *Yobiko* students: A case study of supplementary education in Japan. In: Yogev A (ed.) 1992 *International Perspectives on Education and Society*, Vol. 2. JAI Press, Greenwich, Connecticut

Yogev A, Shapira R 1990 Citizenship socialization in national voluntary youth organizations. In: Ichilov O (ed.) 1990 *Political Socialization, Citizenship Education, and Democracy.* Teachers College Press, New York

Yogev A, Ayalon H 1991 Learning to labor or laboring to learn: Curricular stratification in Israeli vocational high schools. *Int. J. Educ. Dev.* 11(3): 209–19

Further Reading

Inbar D E (ed.) 1990 *Second Chance in Education.* Falmer Press, London

Social Equality and Educational Planning in Developing Nations

J. P. Farrell

This article reviews changing conceptions of how, and to what degree, provision of formal schooling contributes to greater social equality; presents a simple model for sorting out the confusing array of data regarding that question which has been generated since the Second World War; and then uses that model to identify the principle conclusions that can be drawn from that data. The aim is to provide a broad framework within which debates regarding educational policy provision designed to promote social equality can be understood. Although some reference is made to rich nations, the focus is upon poor and middle-income nations.

1. Changing Understandings of Educational Expansion and Social Equality

It was after the Second World War, and particularly during the great epoch of formal decolonization, from the mid-1950s to the early 1960s, that much of the rich industrialized world "discovered" the fact that a large portion of the world's population lived in abject poverty. A combination of moral sensibility and Cold War imperative led many to define this new discovery as a problem, to which they should and could devote attention. Although there were fierce scholarly debates during this epoch regarding the precise nature of national "development," eventually a fairly general consensus was that it entailed not only the generation of more wealth within a nation (economic development) but the more equitable distribution of such wealth (social development). This entry focuses upon social development as one of the engines which has driven the massive expansion of educational facilities during the epoch since the Second World War.

The general understanding during the 1950s and much of the 1960s was that formal education was a major producer of upward social and economic mobility among the poor, and consequently that expansion of access to such education would naturally, and rather automatically, produce greater social and economic equality in poor societies. The application of this view was at least partly responsible for massive enrolment increases. Between 1960 and 1975 the number of children in school in developing countries increased by 122 percent; the proportion of age-eligible children in primary schooling increased from 57 to 75 percent during the same 15-year period, with corresponding increases at the secondary level (14% to 26%) and postsecondary level (1.5% to 4.4%). However, because population was also growing rapidly, relative to the rate of expansion of school provision, the absolute number of primary-age children out of

school in developing nations increased in the same period from 109.2 million to 120.5 million (World Bank 1980).

Moreover, substantial inequalities in the distribution of schooling within most developing societies appeared to be persisting, and in some cases increasing. In many societies urban children appeared to benefit more from the increased school provision than rural children. In others particular ethnic or tribal groups benefited more than others. Boys frequently received more of the newly available schooling than did girls. In many societies newly opened school places, particularly at the relatively expensive secondary and university levels, were occupied predominantly, or almost exclusively, by children of the already well-to-do. The data was not especially systematic, coming primarily from unconnected case studies of different countries at different points in time, and was often interpreted differently by different scholars. Nonetheless, the newly available evidence led to a significant modification—for many observers a complete rejection—of that earlier optimistic view which had guided the actions not only of Western policymakers and advisers, but of influential individuals in the Third World, who were themselves predominantly the product of Western education, either in their own countries or in the universities of Europe and North America.

Claims about the power of formal schooling to equalize the life chances of children who are born into very different social and economic circumstances became much more cautious. Indeed, it became increasingly popular to argue that education can have no significant equalizing or mobility-generating effect in a society which is characterized generally by a high degree of structured social inequality. It was claimed that even if the children of the poor achieve a relatively high level of education, which is itself unlikely, this will not ordinarily produce in the labor market, or in their adult lives generally, the same benefits as those received by the children of the rich because: (a) the labor market (and perhaps more importantly the sociopolitical system) can be manipulated by the well-to-do to maintain their advantages for their offspring; and/or (b) as educational systems have expanded more rapidly than the modern sectors of the economy, there is increasing "educated unemployment" which has more effect upon the children of the poor than the rich, and/or (c) as the educational system expands rapidly, the educational currency becomes devalued, so the child of the poor parent is forever pursuing a receding target.

Many scholars, arguing from a Marxist, neo-Marxist, or dependency theory stance, claimed that

473

formal education could *necessarily* do little more than reproduce structural inequalities in the existing social system; that this was its basic sociopolitical and economic function; and that this was inevitably part of the normal development of capitalist nations and of developing countries linked to such nations through dependent economic, political, and social connections (see Carnoy 1974, Bowles and Gintis 1976). This view gained considerable popularity among some sectors of the scholarly community and among some policymakers in developing nations and international aid agencies. However, it never became the predominant view. By the mid-1980s some of the academic proponents of this view began significantly to modify their earlier position, arguing that formal schooling could function both to reproduce existing structural inequalities and to produce structural change (Carnoy and Levin 1985, Liston 1988).

Developing nations continued to invest major portions of their resources in educational expansion, and international donor agencies typically increased their investments in education, assuming (at least in many cases) that there would be over the long term an improvement in social equality as a result. The major effect of the revisionist argument of the 1970s was to modify the naive optimism of the previous decade and to reduce the level of expectation regarding the equalizing effect of increases in educational provision.

It also became clear that some of the basic theoretical constructs which were used to attempt to understand social equality within the experience of the industrialized nations of the West are not automatically applicable to the diverse and changing cultures and societies of the developing world. Particularly important is what is meant by the "social and economic circumstances" which children bring with them to the school.

All extant societies have some form of internal social differentiation, with some members being valued or rewarded more than others. However, the degree of such differentiation and its significance for the way individuals lead their lives varies dramatically across societies. Moreover, there are many different bases or criteria for such differentiation. Among the most common are occupation, race, ethnicity, regional origin, lineage, sex, income, political power, and religion. Both across and within societies there is considerable variation in which one of these, or which set of them, is most powerful as a determinant of how different people live their lives. Those who are creatures of the historical experience and intellectual traditions of the industrial nations of the West, whether they embrace some form of structural–functional or Marxist social theory, tend to collapse a common set of these—particularly occupation, income, and political power—into the notion of social class or social status. It is not at all clear that these theoretical constructs are generally applicable to all, or even most, less developed societies, either as accurate descriptors or

as meaningful categories of social thought and behavior among individuals in those societies. In many such societies the occupation or income of a child's parent may be much less salient as a constraint upon life chances than the parents' ethnic or tribal group, or their lineage, or the geographical region of origin.

Finally, it has become clear that the concept of equality of education is much more complex and multifaceted than had been assumed. The notion of educational equality which grew with the development of systems of tax-supported public schooling in rich nations focused on opportunity. The general assumption was that the job of the state was to ensure that all children had access to schools which were free of direct cost, with generally similar facilities and curricula, at least through the age of compulsory attendance. It was assumed that it was the responsibility of the child to use the opportunity thus provided. If children did not do well in school the responsibility was their's or their family's, not the state's. As it became increasingly apparent that large numbers of children were unable effectively to use the educational opportunity provided because of their social origins, the concept of educational equality has been gradually extended to include some notion of equal educational *results*, with the task of public policy being extended to include ensuring that all children, whatever their social origins, have an equal ability to benefit from the educational experience provided, in terms of what they learn and how they use their learning in later life, particularly in the labor market (Coleman 1968).

It has been found to be useful to make a distinction between *equality* and *equity*. As Bronfenbrenner has suggested, equity refers to social justice or fairness. It involves a subjective ethical or moral judgment. Equality deals with the actual patterns in which something, say income or education, is distributed among members of a particular group (Bronfenbrenner 1973). One can statistically assess the equality of an income distribution by measuring deviations from some hypothetically completely equal situation. But individual judgments regarding the equity or fairness of any given observed degree of inequality can and do differ; equity involves value judgments. Since societies differ in their reigning value systems a given degree of observed educational inequality may be regarded as quite fair, or equitable, in one society and very inequitable in another.

The years since the early 1960s then, have been characterized by increasing conceptual confusion. This conceptual confusion has been to a considerable degree the result of the circulation of a bewildering quantity of comparative information regarding the utilization of education by, and the effect of education upon the destinies of, different social groups in widely differing societies, especially developing nations. Untangling some of that data, and deriving meaning from it, with respect to *equality* as a rationale for educational expansion, is the task of this article.

2. A "Model" of Educational Inequality

When considering problems of educational inequality it has become increasingly common to view schooling as a long-term process in which children may be sorted at many different points and in several different ways. Recognizing that schooling operates as a selective social screening mechanism, enhancing the status of some and ratifying the status of others, raises this question: At what points in the process, to what degree, and how are children of which social groups screened out or kept in? From this point of view, several facets of equality can be usefully distinguished.

(a) *Equality of access*: the probabilities of children from different social groupings getting into the school system;

(b) *Equality of survival*: the probabilities of children from various social groupings staying in the school system to some defined level, usually the end of a complete cycle (primary, secondary, higher);

(c) *Equality of output*: the probabilities that children from various social groupings will learn the same things to the same level at a defined point in the school system;

(d) *Equality of outcome*: the probabilities that children from various social groupings will live relatively similar lives subsequent to and as a result of schooling (have equal incomes, have jobs of roughly the same status, have equal access to the sites of political power, etc.).

The first three of these types of equality refer to the workings of the school system itself. Equality of outcome refers to the junction between the school system and adult life, especially the labor market. With reference to the first three, each represents a mechanism by which children are sorted and screened by the school, and all three occur at each level or cycle of the system (i.e., a child may or may not enter primary schooling, may or may not survive to the end of the primary cycle, may or may not learn as much as other students do by the end of primary; having completed primary, a child may or may not enter secondary schooling, may or may not survive to the end of secondary, and so on). It should be noted also that in systems which have different types of schools at the same level the access question is not simply whether a student enters the cycle, but the type of institution to which the student is given access.

3. What Do the Data Say?

The task here is to try to make some sense of the welter of comparative data regarding educational equality which has been developed primarily since the early 1960s. With respect to some aspects of the model just presented, the evidence is sufficient to permit a coherent summary; with respect to other aspects the evidence is very spotty and inconsistent.

3.1 Equality of Access

For the vast majority of children in developing nations equality of access is a problem at the primary level. A major objective of educational policy at the start of the 1960s was to provide school places sufficient to permit every child to have access to at least a few years of primary schooling. By the mid-1980s considerable progress had been made. Between 1960 and 1975 the proportion of 6- to 11-year old children in developing nations who spent at least a few years in primary school rose from 57 percent to 75 percent, and by 1985 the primary enrollment ratio had reached 90 percent for middle-income nations and 76 percent among even the 40 poorest nations of the world (Farrell 1989). However, in many nations, particularly many of the largest and poorest nations, total population was growing even faster than the rate of educational expansion (which indeed decreased generally starting in the late 1970s, owing to a world-wide economic crisis). Even the most optimistic available enrollment forecasts in the early 1990s suggested that by the turn of the century no developing region as a whole would have attained universal primary schooling, although some individual countries, particularly in Latin America, may have come close to providing at least a few years of primary schooling for all of their children. Even optimistic forecasts indicate that by the year 2000 there will still be over 100 million children in the developing world with no exposure at all to formal schooling (Coombs 1985).

In those many societies which are not now able, and are unlikely for many years to be able, to provide school places for all potential entrants the salient equality question is whether the probability of entering school for any given child is independent of his or her social or economic circumstances. For such societies, wherein education is necessarily a "scarce good" which not all can acquire, the equality model becomes one of random access, with the paradigm case being a fair lottery. Even in rich societies, of course, this is the model which obtains at some point beyond the limit of compulsory schooling. Not even the wealthiest nations have yet contemplated seriously the universal provision of postsecondary formal education.

The available comparative data indicate clearly that the ideal random access situation is rarely even approximated in developing nations, although the bases for discrimination vary from society to society. In many societies rural children are much less likely to enter school than children of the towns and cities. Even in the cities poor children are less likely than well-to-do children to enter school. In a number of societies girls are much less likely than boys to enter school. Frequently, certain tribal, religious, or ethnic groups are either consciously excluded from school, or simply ignored.

A common assumption is that the problem of equality of access to primary schooling is almost entirely a question of inadequate supply of schools; that an effective demand for formal schooling exists almost everywhere, and that if the resources and political will can be found to provide an adequate number of primary schools all children will attend. The obstacles on the supply side are indeed formidable. If one were to meet the often-cited goal of universal access to basic education resources would have to be found, from shrinking national and international agency budgets, to create almost as many school places as were created in the 20 years between 1965 and 1985 (Lockheed and Verspoor 1990).

However, there are obstacles on the demand side as well. In most middle-income nations, and in some favored regions of low-income nations, there are more than enough school places, in the appropriate locations, for all age-eligible children. In such circumstances, when children do not attend school, and they often do not, it is because their parents will not send them. Parents may regard the education provided there as inappropriate (e.g., on religious or cultural grounds), or of little use, or not worth the opportunity cost of the child's labor (Bowman 1988). This is a particularly serious obstacle to the enrollment of girls in many nations.

3.2 Equality of Survival

Among middle-income developing nations, between 20 and 30 percent of an entering first grade cohort will not complete the primary cycle. In low-income nations, the completion proportions are even lower —just over 50 percent—and were actually declining during the 1980s. In some very poor nations, the primary completion ratios are far below 50 percent. These high rates of nonsurvival are a result of the combined effect of high repetition rates, and high proportions of children dropping out of school, frequently after having repeated an early grade one or more times (Schiefelbein 1975, Lockheed and Verspoor 1990). In most developing nations the survival rates at the secondary or postsecondary levels, for the very small proportions of the population who reach those levels, are also very low.

It is generally true that in any given level of the educational system poor children are less likely to survive educationally than are well-to-do children; that children born in rural areas are less likely to survive educationally than urban children; that repetition and dropout rates are higher among girls than boys. However, the evidence regarding the relationship between

any particular aspect of a child's personal or family circumstances and the probability of achieving a given level of education is so scanty and contradictory that general conclusions cannot be easily drawn. The patterns vary dramatically from country to country, in ways which are not easily accounted for. The variations in the influence of gender on survival potential are particularly striking. For example, female enrollment ratios (compared with those among males) for the postprimary age group (12 to 17) vary from lows of 1.7 percent (vs. 14.9% males) in the Yemen Arab Republic and 5.8 percent (vs. 22.3% males) in Chad to highs of 79.3 percent (vs. 91.0% males) in Bahrain and 82.9 percent (vs. 83.1% males) in Chile (World Bank 1980). Schiefelbein and Farrell have suggested that the best explanation of the Chilean pattern may lie in historical factors which are unique to that society (Schiefelbein and Farrell 1980). An explanation for the unusually high female enrollment in a society such as Bahrain is not available.

It is important to bear in mind that survival rates, for entire populations or for subgroups thereof, can only be understood correctly with respect to educational policy by also referring to access figures. For example, in both Tunisia and Tanzania, approximately 77 percent of children entering the first grade will reach the end of primary schooling. However, in Tunisia almost all eligible children enter the first grade, while in Tanzania just over half do so. In contrast, Senegal has about the same first grade access rate as does Tanzania, but 86 percent of its entrants complete primary schooling (Lockheed and Verspoor 1990). In spite of their similarity on either equality of access or equality of survival, the interaction between the two types of inequality produce three very different educational situations by the end of primary schooling.

3.3 Equality of Output

A system's output is whatever the system produces directly; in the case of an educational system, learning. Children with the same number of years of schooling (thus with equal access and equal survival) may have learned quite different things, or the same subjects to quite different levels. There is a great deal of cross-national evidence which indicates that differences in levels of achievement are systematically associated with differing social origins of children in a particular society. Generally, among those who have reached a given level of a nation's school system, children who are poor, or rural, or female, learn less. However, here too the differences among developing nations in the effect of these social characteristics on learning are impressive. The available evidence clearly indicates that the influence of gender on learning levels varies substantially across cultures. In some nations, boys outperform girls on achievement tests in almost all subject areas (Finn et al. 1979). On the other hand, a detailed 8-year longitudinal study in Chile could detect no significant sex-linked differences in achievement scores associated with the schooling process (Schiefelbein and Farrell 1980).

Since the early 1970s there have been a large number of "educational production function" studies carried out in developing nations which permit one to examine the effect of social origin, relative to other variables, on school achievement. A very systematic pattern has emerged: the less developed a society, the less the effect of social status on learning and the greater the effect of school-related variables (Heyneman and Loxley 1983). Different explanations for this pattern, one of the most systematic relationships ever discovered in the comparative study of education, have been advanced. Foster (1977) has suggested the following:

> In broadest terms, as less developed nations "modernize" the pattern of "objective" differentiation of populations becomes more complex with the growth of a monetized economy and a greater division of labour. Not only this, possession of a "modern type" occupation becomes an increasingly important factor in determining the generalized social status of an individual. In other words social strata defined in *objective* terms of occupations and income begin to emerge. Initially, however, this pattern of objective differentiation may not be accompanied by an equivalent degree of cultural differentiation as represented by increasing divergence of values, attitudes and lifestyles among various subgroups. In time, however, this may occur and we move, in effect, toward a pattern of stratification that more closely resembles that obtaining in developed societies.

What one may be observing, then, is the educational effect of the process of "class formation" (in the Western sense) as poor societies become more like Western societies. Of course it is also the case that in societies in which standard Western indexes of social status are not, or not yet, relevant to a child's education destiny, other traditional stratification patterns (e.g., tribe, caste, lineage) may be very important.

A different, but related, explanation is that there is much greater variation in the availability of school resources in developing nations than in developed nations. For example, in rich nations almost all students have complete sets of textbooks, and the differences in the formal educational levels of teachers are relatively small, while there are great variations on such indicators within developing nations. In a poor nation, even modest increments in either can thus have a major effect upon student learning, while in rich nations, increases in learning would require difficult and costly improvements in the quality of the books or the performance of teachers. From the above, Farrell has suggested that while in rich nations, which are close to the limits of perfectibility of the technology of schooling, "even modest additional gains in achievement require very difficult and costly educational effort"; in developing nations, " . . . even the very modest improvements in school quality which a poor

nation can realistically contemplate have the potential for providing important increases in student learning," particularly among the poorest students (Farrell 1989).

The possibility of improving equality of output in developing nations within the very modest resources available to them is particularly important because the evidence indicates that levels of learning among students in developing nations are systematically lower than among students in rich nations. The cross-national comparisons of student achievement levels which have been carried out, principally under the auspices of the International Association for the Evaluation of Educational Achievement (IEA), have consistently demonstrated that the achievement test scores of children from low- and middle-income nations are lower than those of children of comparable age or grade level in industrialized nations (Farrell and Heyneman 1989).

There is also evidence that the fiscal crisis in most developing nations in the 1980s, combined with expanding enrollments, dramatically decreased the instructional resources available per student, which in turn increased the "learning gap" between students in rich and poor nations (Farrell and Heyneman 1989). This has led many observers to conclude that in many poor regions, such as Africa, further progress in improving equality of access and survival may have to be sacrificed in order to restore at least minimal levels of learning output from the educational system (Symposium 1989). In sum, the argument is that neither individuals nor the society benefit from increasingly equal access to and survival through a schooling system in which students learn less and less as total available resources decrease.

3.4 Equality of Outcome

Relatively equal distributions of access to, survival through, or learning within the formal schooling system is considered socially beneficial by many only if it "pays off" for the recipients in relatively equal access to life chances (particularly jobs) as adults. To what extent does education have an intervening effect on intergenerational status transmission? To what extent and under what conditions can it produce upward social mobility rather than simply ratify or reproduce existing patterns of structural inequality? A great deal of comparative data and interpretations of theory have been produced with reference to this issue, and the results are empirically systematic but theoretically confusing. In 1975 Lin and Yauger reported data from Haiti, from Costa Rican communities at three levels of development, from the United Kingdom, and from the United States, and concluded that "the direct influence of educational attainment on occupational status is curvilinearly (concave) related to degree of industrialization" (Lin and Yauger 1975). Schiefelbein and Farrell noted that data from Uganda at three points in time and from four Brazilian communities fitted the same pattern (Schiefelbein and Farrell 1978).

More recent results from Chile reinforce the general conclusions (Farrell and Schiefelbein 1985).

In the very poorest societies, where almost everyone is engaged in subsistence agriculture, except for a few occupants of newly created civil service posts and some commercial entrepreneurs, education can have very little effect on occupational mobility because there are very few occupational destinations available into which one could be mobile (which partially explains the lack of effective demand for education among such populations, as noted above). As the local economy grows and becomes more differentiated, creating a variety of new job openings, and in the absence of a traditional dominant class which can exploit all of the new opportunities, formal education becomes a predominant influence on the level of job acquired, and significant numbers of even very poor children use education to obtain access to positions in the "modern" economy. (In many developing societies the growth of the educational system has surpassed the growth of the economy, producing a problem of "educated unemployment." Even in such societies children often continue in school as long as possible because the potential pay-off is high if, or when, they can obtain any job at all.) As societies become very developed their economies are so complex and rapidly changing, and the possible avenues to economic success are so varied, that the independent effect of formal education begins to diminish (Jencks 1973).

Evidence from advanced socialist societies suggests that there, too, this general pattern is evident (Zajda 1980). Some economists have argued that in very advanced postindustrial economies the phenomenon of the "declining middle," the elimination of well-paying industrial jobs in favor of lower paying service sector jobs, is reducing even further the mobility-generating effect of formal schooling (Kuttner 1984). Pushing this argument a step further, Farrell and Schiefelbein have claimed that all of the major studies which have provided data regarding the effect of education on intergenerational status transmission, and which form the empirical foundation for the theoretical arguments on this question, may be flawed and uninterpretable because of a failure to take into account long-term structural changes in the economy (Farrell and Schiefelbein 1985). Beyond this, a new generation of "naturalistic" studies of the ways in which youth from structurally disadvantaged backgrounds react to and use formal schooling is further confounding understanding, from all traditional theoretical frames, of the ways in which young people are affected by and use schooling to ratify or improve their inherited life chances (see Willis 1977, Bullivant 1987, Walker 1988). However, in spite of this growing empirical and theoretical confusion it is still clear that even in those societies where education has the weakest effect on intergenerational status transmission there is still some relationship; nowhere does the provision of formal education have no mobility-generating consequences.

4. Conclusion

While the available data indicate that the highly optimistic view prevalent in the early 1960s that almost any type of increased investment in education would automatically reduce social inequality does not hold, those same data also do not support the more extreme position from the "cynical 1970s," that increased provision of schooling will either have no effect upon, or actually aggravate, existing social inequalities. At the end of the 1970s, Snodgrass argued for a "guardedly optimistic view . . . As GNP per head and mean years of schooling rise, there is a broad tendency for all forms of inequality to decrease . . . there is a long term trend toward more equal distribution of schooling and probably also of earnings" (Snodgrass 1980).

By the early 1990s the most appropriate stance might have been called "guardedly pessimistic." In a sense, one could say that since 1950 educators and policymakers have learned how to use increased investments in education to improve, at least to a degree, equality on all four of the dimensions discussed above, if the available resources are used wisely by national authorities and international agencies. But the poorest nations of the world have been particularly hard hit by the world-wide financial and debt crisis of the 1980s and 1990s. As a result, educational expenditures, which were already very low in such nations, have actually been decreasing, in both total and per capita terms, rather than increasing. Among the 39 nations classified in the early 1990s by the World Bank as low income, which have approximately 60 percent of the primary school-age children in the world, public recurrent expenditures per primary student declined by 11.8 percent between 1975 and 1985, and dropped from 11.0 to 8.1 percent of GNP per capita (Lockheed and Verspoor 1990, Tables 1 and 20). As a consequence, for almost two-thirds of the world's children, educational access equality is stagnating, and survival and output equality are deteriorating. At the same time, rich and middle-income nations, where just over one-third of the world's children live, continue to increase their educational expenditures and generally to improve educational equality within their own borders. On a world basis the principal problem is how to at least maintain the gains achieved since the early 1960s.

It may be appropriate nonetheless to close this entry on a "guardedly optimistic" note. Some kinds of problems are preferable to others. As a consequence of the massive increases in educational provision, there has been a change in the critical locus of the inequality problem within many school systems. At the initial stages of development of an educational system the critical "sorting point" is entrance to primary education. As increasingly large proportions of children are able to enter primary schooling, the critical problem becomes survival: who completes and who drops out. As one approaches effective universal primary education—most children enter and most complete—

attention shifts to equality of output at the end of primary schooling and equality of access to secondary, and so on. "Earlier stage" problems are not necessarily completely eliminated, but the most critical screening point for most children moves upward through the system.

From this point of view one may see investments in educational expansion, where they can occur, not in the expectation that the educational equality problem will disappear but in the hope that it will take on a more socially tolerable form and locus.

See also: Education and Development; Educational Expansion: Sociological Perspectives; Equality, Policies for Educational; Reproduction Theory; Social Mobility, Social Stratification, and Education

References

Bowles S, Gintis H 1976 *Schooling in Capitalist America*; *Educational Reform and the Contradictions of Economic Life*. Routledge and Kegan Paul, London

Bowman M J 1988 An integrated framework for analysis of the spread of schooling in less developed countries. *Comp. Educ. Rev.* 28(4): 563–84

Bronfenbrenner M 1973 Equality and equity. *The Annals* 409: 482–95

Bullivant B M 1987 *The Ethnic Encounter in the Secondary School: Ethnocultural Reproduction and Resistance*. Falmer Press, London

Carnoy M 1974 *Education as Cultural Imperialism*. McKay, New York

Carnoy M, Levin H M 1985 *Schooling and Work in the Democratic State*. Stanford University Press, Stanford, California

Coleman J 1968 The concept of equality of educational opportunity. *Harv. Educ. Rev.* 38(1): 7–22

Coombs P H 1985 *The World Crisis in Education: The View From the Eighties*. Oxford University Press, New York

Farrell J P 1989 International lessons for school effectiveness: The view from the developing world. In Holmes M, Leithwood K A, Musella O F (eds.) 1989 *Educational Policy for Effective Schools*. Ontario Institute for Studies in Education, Ontario

Farrell J P, Heyneman S P 1989 *Textbooks in the Developing World: Economic and Educational Choices*. World Bank, Washington, DC

Farrell J P, Schiefelbein E 1985 Education and status attainment in Chile: A comparative challenge to the Wisconsin model of status attainment. *Comp. Educ. Rev.* 29(4): 490–506

Finn J O, Dulberg L, Reis J 1979 Sex differences in educational attainment: A cross-national perspective. *Harv. Educ. Rev.* 49(4): 477–503

Foster P J 1977 Education and social differentiation in less developed countries. *Comp. Educ. Rev.* 21(2–3): 211–29

Heyneman S P, Loxley W 1983 The effects of primary school quality on academic achievement across twenty-nine high income and low-income countries. *Am. J. Sociol.* 88(6): 1162–94

Jencks C 1973 *Inequality: A Reassessment of the Effect of Family and Schooling in America*. Allen Lane, London

Kuttner B 1984 *The Economic Illusion: False Choices between Prosperity and Social Justice*. Houghton-Mifflin, Boston, Massachusetts

Lin N, Yauger D 1975 The process of occupational status achievement. A preliminary cross-national comparison. *Am. J. Sociol.* 81(6): 543–62

Liston D P 1988 *Capitalist Schools: Explanation and Ethics in Radical Studies of Schooling*. Routledge, London

Lockheed M E, Verspoor A M 1990 *Improving Primary Education in Developing Nations: A Review of Policy Options*. World Bank, Washington, DC

Schiefelbein E 1975 Repeating: An overlooked problem of Latin American education. *Comp. Educ. Rev.* 19(3): 468–87

Schiefelbein S, Farrell J P 1978 Selectivity and survival in the schools of Chile. *Comp. Educ. Rev.* 22(2): 326–41

Schiefelbein S, Farrell J P 1980 Women, schooling and work in Chile: Evidence from a longitudinal study. *Comp. Educ. Rev.* 24(2, Part 2): 160–79

Snodgrass D R 1980 The distribution of schooling and the distribution of income. In: Davis R (ed.) 1980 *Planning Education for Development*, Vol 1. Harvard University Center for Studies in Education and Development, Cambridge, Massachusetts

Symposium 1989 World Bank report on education in Sub-Saharan Africa *Comp. Educ. Rev.* 33(1): 93–104

Walker J C 1988 *Louts and Legends: Male Youth Culture in an Inner-City School*. Allen and Unwin, Sydney

Willis P 1977 *Learning to Labour: How Working Class Kids Get Working Class Jobs*. Saxon House, Farnborough

World Bank 1980 *Education: Sector Policy Paper*, 3rd. edn. World Bank, Washington, DC

Zajda J 1980 Education and social stratification in the Soviet Union. *Comp. Educ. Rev.* 16(1): 3–11

Further Reading

Farrell J P 1992 Conceptualizing education and the drive for social equality. In: Arnove R, Altbach P G, Kelley G P (eds.) 1992 *Emergent Issues in Education: Comparative Perspectives*. SUNY Press, Albany, New York

School Processes

Introduction: Sociological Processes Within Schools

L. J. Saha

The articles in this section focus on what goes on within the "black box" of schooling. The organizational structures of schools, whether formal or informal, nevertheless impinge on the day-to-day experiences of school principals, teachers, and students and exercise a profound effect on the educational outcomes of students, the careers of teachers, and from a postmodernist perspective, on the conceptualizing of "groups," whether by race, class, or gender (Ladwig 1995).

Among the several processes which take place in the school on a daily basis is also that of the transmission of knowledge and of the cultural and normative heritage of society, more commonly known as socialization. It is through this process that the attitudes, values, and beliefs which are part of a cultural legacy are developed and formed in students. Finally, because the processes within schools are not determinate but dynamic, the manner in which students react to teachers and to other students can result in compliance or resistance (Saha 1990). In this respect, school truancy and school dropouts are part of the output of school processes.

The 19 articles in this section are divided in four subsections, each dealing with a dimension of the many processes which take place on a daily basis in schools: (a) Knowledge and the Curriculum; (b) Acquiring Attitudes, Values, and Skills, (c) Race, Ethnicity, and Gender, and (d) Students at Risk.

1. Knowledge and the Curriculum

The first subsection consists of four articles which focus on school knowledge and the curriculum, and the classroom context within which the instructional process occurs. The two articles which discuss the formal curriculum, Skilbeck's *Social, Cultural, and Economic Factors Affecting Curriculum*, and Lamm's *Knowledge: Conceptions of and Impact on Education*, clearly emphasize the problematic nature of school knowledge, and indeed that what counts as school knowledge is the result of a sociological process, involving forces both external and internal to the school. The processes which partly describe how the social constructions occur are described by Gordon in *Hidden Curriculum* and Hallinan in *School and Classroom Dynamics*. The factors identified by Gordon and Hallinan make clear that the processes within schooling affect not only the knowledge acquired by students, but the entirety of school life, both intellectual and social.

2. Acquiring Attitudes, Values, and Skills

The second subsection directs attention to processes of attitude, value, and belief formation within schools and consists of six articles, all involving in one form or another the process of socialization (see Sturman, *Socialization* and Braungart and Braungart, *Political*

Socialization and Education). As discussed by Oser (*Acquiring Attitudes and Values*) and Heyman and Dweck (*Development of Achievement Motivation*), the acquisition of achievement motivation attitudes and values are social psychological in nature and problematic because of the contradictory processes that occur in schools. The same can be said for the acquisition of aspirations and expectations (Saha, *Aspirations and Expectations of Students*) and empowerment skills (Land and Gilbert, *Acquisition of Empowerment Skills*). The problematic nature of the formation of attitudes, values, and beliefs includes the variations in their acquisition, and why some students acquire them differently. The question is important because of the sociological implications of these processes not only in terms of school outcomes, but also because of their impact on later career and occupational attainments.

3. Race, Ethnicity, and Gender

The third subsection consists of six articles which address race, ethnicity, and gender issues, which, as Ladwig (1995) notes, are a part of school processes, to a greater or lesser extent. Obviously, a preoccupation with these major social and educational "divides" concerns the provision and access of educational facilities, and the articles by Juan (*Education of Indigenous Peoples*), Stromquist (*Gender and Education*), and Clifton (*Race and Ethnicity in Education*) provide overviews of these issues on an international and cross-cultural level. At the same time, they touch upon the important problem of definitions, and implicitly raise questions about the "conceptualization" of these groups in the school process. Weiner (*Students in Classrooms, Gender and Racial Differences Among*) provides an overview of the dimensions of school processes which contribute to the "politics of difference" which occurs in schools. The unequal power relations which permeate language use in the classroom, the formation of self-concept, teachers' perceptions of students, the different curricula, and other similar dimensions, contribute to differing experiences of the school process by racial, ethnic, and gender groups. Finally, Keeves and Kotte (*Sex Differences and School Outcomes*) and Strober (*Gender and Occupational Segregation*) touch upon the consequences of school processes for later life attainments, and in so doing provide evidence for a continuity of processes from within schools to postschool outcomes.

4. Students at Risk

The final subsection consists of three articles which focus on two types of outcomes from school processes, namely truancy and school dropouts. Davis and McCaul (*Children and Youth at Risk*) provide an overview of social factors such as poverty, race, or ethnicity, parental background, and language proficiency, which place students "at risk." The authors use the term "at risk" broadly to include stress, maladjustment, truancy, and finally dropping from school altogether. Natriello (*Dropouts, School Leavers, and Truancy*) and Kelly (*School Dropouts*) both address the end states of being an "at risk" student. Natriello includes truancy and "early leaving" in his discussion and focuses on antecedents and consequences. Kelly, on the other hand, prefers to conceptualize the process as one of "disengagement," "pushout," and the result of a long-term interactive process in her discussion. While the end product may be the same, the two articles provide a valuable complement to each other in perspective.

Given the range of issues related to school processes, the "black-box" of schooling, it is easy to understand the centrality of this area for the sociology of education. The multiplicity of theoretical and methodological approaches in the study of school processes has made this area a rich and important source of knowledge about schooling, and has contributed substantially to attempts to devise plans and policies related to school reform and school improvement programs.

References

Ladwig J G 1995 The genesis of groups in the sociology of school knowledge. In: Pink W T, Noblit G W (eds.) 1995 *Continuity and Contradiction: The Futures of the Sociology of Education*. Hampton Press, Cresskill, New Jersey

Saha L J 1990 Schools as youth-processing institutions. In: Saha L J, Keeves J P (eds.) 1990 *Schooling and Society in Australia: Australian Perspectives*. Australian National University Press, Sydney

(a) Knowledge and the Curriculum

Hidden Curriculum

D. Gordon

The "hidden curriculum" refers to learning outcomes that are either unintended by the teacher (or the school in general) or are intended, but not openly acknowledged to the learners (Martin 1976). As can be seen readily from this definition, the hidden curriculum seems to encompass many different aspects of school life and yet is difficult to distinguish from other related concepts. This imprecision is well illustrated by the various alternative terms that have been used, such as "unwritten," "implicit," "unstudied," "covert," and "latent" curricula. The lack of precision of the concept raises a question that forms the focus of much of the writing on the hidden curriculum: why has so vague a term achieved such universal currency? Bloom suggested the following answer: "the (hidden) curriculum is in many respects likely to be more effective than the manifest curriculum. The lessons it teaches are long remembered because it is so pervasive and consistent over the many years in which our students attend school. Its lessons are experienced daily and learned firmly" (1972 p. 343).

In other words, the popularity of the hidden curriculum seems to follow from the intuitive feeling of many researchers that the term relates to the important and influential aspects of school life. Thus it cannot be ignored, despite its lack of precision, particularly as so often the hidden curriculum is illustrated by examples of its negative, pernicious effects. A great deal of the work on the hidden curriculum, specifically that which appeared in the 1980s, relates to this imputed effectiveness or power of the hidden curriculum.

1. The First Generation of Research on the Hidden Curriculum

The term "hidden curriculum" was first used by Jackson (1968) in his book *Life in Classrooms*. In the first decade of research on the hidden curriculum (as well as in the few cases before 1968 where similar notions were discussed using different terminologies), most researchers were concerned with illustrating its different aspects. One can distinguish three strands in this work: the hidden curriculum conceived as outcome, as setting, and as process.

1.1 Hidden Curriculum as Outcome

Much of the writing on the hidden curriculum is concerned with the values, dispositions, norms, attitudes, and skills students learn independently of cognitive subject matter. Jackson, for example, sees the hidden curriculum as made up of learning how to live in an environment of crowds, praise, and power. Dreeben (1968) writes about the teaching of the norms of independence, achievement, universalism, and specificity, norms necessary for efficient integration into modern industrial society. Snyder (1971) argues that successful university students are those that pick up the cues in the hidden curriculum concerning what is really required of them, rather than the official requirements of the system. The common assumption of the writers who share this view of the hidden curriculum, is that its outcomes are nonacademic learnings.

1.2 Hidden Curriculum as Setting

School learning in general can be conceived as learning which usually takes place in a particular intellectual context (the classroom), embedded within a particular physical and social setting (the school), with defined structural properties. The hidden curriculum is often viewed as learning that this setting inadvertently teaches, independently of explicit classroom learning. Dreeben (1968) suggests that the four abovementioned norms taught in the hidden curriculum result from the nature of the school as an impersonal institution, as embodied in its structural properties and institutional arrangements. For example, the norm of universalism (i.e., the treatment of individuals in terms of their membership of categories) is taught in schools by providing experiences of systematic establishment and demarcation of membership categories: students belong to a class, and as such are presented with similar sets of demands; the adults belong to a particular category (teachers) and students learn that this requires both students and teachers to behave in certain role-defined ways. A similar notion is developed by Bowles and Gintis (1976) in their discussion of the correspondence principle, the correspondence between the social relationships which govern personal interaction in the workplace and the social relationships in the school. Getzels (1974) describes the physical structure of classrooms in different types of schools, and argues that each structure presents the students with a different image of the ideal learner. The "rectangular" classroom, for example, with "the pupils' chairs . . . firmly bolted to the floor in straight rows, and the teacher's desk . . . front and center" (p. 527) presents the learner as an empty organism under the control of the teacher, who is the only source of learning experience.

The problem with both the outcome and setting approaches is that they do not encompass a particular type of cognitive learning that seems to be part of the hidden curriculum. For example, Apple (1971) argues that science textbooks underplay the role of revolution in scientific development, and thus teach that revolutions are not important. In his view, this encourages political quiescence and conservatism. Illich (1971) conceives of the hidden curriculum as teaching that "all economically valuable knowledge is the result of professional teaching and . . . (thus) transforms the explicit curriculum into a commodity" (p. 3). Another example is the sexist, stereotypic learning of masculine and feminine roles embedded in many textbooks and readers (Frazier and Sadker 1975). These are all examples of classroom-derived learning and can also be viewed as academic learnings. In order to deal with such examples, this entry now examines the third approach to the hidden curriculum.

1.3 Hidden Curriculum as Process

According to the view of hidden curriculum as process, the hidden curriculum is distinguished from the manifest curriculum by the way its teachings are transmitted. The mode of transmission is implicit or unconscious. Messages are often nonverbal, and if verbal, are embedded in the "deep structure" of discourse.

Schwab (1962), for example, writes of "meta-lessons" of science teaching, and argues that the way science is usually taught through a "rhetoric of conclusions" presents an image of science in which "the current and temporary constructions of scientific knowledge are conveyed as empirical, literal, and irrevocable truths" (p. 24). Gordon (1981) stresses the pragmatic nature of teacher-initiated classroom discourse. He argues that beyond the content of this discourse, its form militates against the school's ability to develop students' aesthetic attitudes, as the aesthetic attitude is nonpragmatic by its very nature.

The third approach to the hidden curriculum seems capable of explaining most examples of hidden curricular teaching and learning that have been given by different researchers. However, it is an approach that invites much methodological and conceptual criticism of the notion of a hidden curriculum. These and other criticisms are discussed below.

2. The Second Generation of Research on the Hidden Curiculum—Criticisms of the Concept

Lakomski (1988) criticizes most research on the hid-den curriculum for not being research in the accepted sense. There is no evidence that the learnings imputed to the hidden curriculum were actually learned through its mechanisms or, in fact, were learned in school at all. She also points out that most writing on the hidden curriculum is based on qualitative observations in classrooms and schools. This, as Vallance (1980) has argued, is as it should be, as the hidden curriculum and qualitative research are both "attuned to the subtle qualities of schooling" (p.138). However, the qualitative nature of these observations underlines their interpretive character. Lakomski argues that for most interpretations of hidden curricular learning, one can suggest an infinite number of alternative interpretations. In her view, there is no rational way of adjudicating between them, and this leads her to the conclusion that "the hidden curriculum" is a meaningless term.

Less extreme criticisms do not dismiss the term entirely, but rather question Bloom's claim that the hidden curriculum is all-pervasive and powerful. Neo-Marxist, radical, and critical pedagogical theory, for example, after first using the notion of a hidden curriculum to illustrate the powerful, pernicious hidden messages and class reproductive effects of schooling in capitalist society, went on to argue that students often resist the hidden curriculum's messages. These so-called "resistance theorists" claimed that students are far more aware of the school's hidden messages than previously suspected, and often consciously oppose them. The classic text in this regard is Willis' (1977) *Learning to Labour: How Working Class Kids Get Working Class Jobs*. This is an ethnographic study of a group of working-class teenagers both in school and, after they leave school, in the workplace. This group wreaked havoc in their school. Willis shows that their behavior stemmed from a sophisticated awareness of the hegemonic function of the school, and in particular of its hidden curriculum (see *Resistance Theory*).

Much of the writing by critical theorists after 1977 has been devoted to documenting cases where students have read the hidden curriculum and resisted it, differentiating between students who do and do not resist the hidden curriculum, and assessing the effectiveness of student resistance as a means of inducing social and political change.

A completely different tack in questioning Bloom's pervasiveness thesis has been taken by Assor and Gordon (1987). They point out that Bloom's thesis is based on an implicit learning theory which stresses the redundancy of the messages of the hidden curriculum and assumes that this redundancy is the reason for its efficiency. They argue that this learning theory is inadequate, because it ignores the reward value of learned material. Some items in the hidden curriculum have high hedonic relevance for pupils (the "hot" hidden curriculum) and others low hedonic relevance (the "cold" hidden curriculum). The former are learned through different mechanisms from the latter, which relies entirely on mechanisms related to redundancy. The learning efficiency of the hot curriculum will be high or low depending on compatibility with influences external to the school, whereas the learning efficiency of the cold curriculum will tend to be moderate.

Despite their differences, all these criticisms have in common their acceptance of the idea that the hidden curriculum, if it exists, is a social "text." In order to be of meaning, this text must be read and interpreted by the students. In contrast to Bloom, who assumed that the text's redundancy ensured that the students would decipher and naively accept the text's objective hidden meaning, Lakomski raises doubts about whether there is such an objective meaning; the critical theorists question whether the students' readings are as naive and uncritical as Bloom thought; and Assor and Gordon question the effectiveness of redundancy as a communication characteristic or mechanism.

Perhaps the most important contribution of the concept of a hidden curriculum resides in its invitation to researchers to look at education, teaching, and schooling in this hermeneutic fashion (i.e., as a text to be interpreted or have its hidden meanings disclosed). Such a perspective accords well with the increased emphasis on meaning in social action since the early 1970s (see *Hermeneutics*).

3. New Possibilities and Trends

Conceiving hidden curricula as hermeneutic in nature helps explain a curious historical fact, an explanation that also suggests a possible new line of research on the hidden curriculum. Although the term "hidden curriculum" was first introduced by Jackson (1968), the idea of such a dimension in teaching can be traced back at least as far as Kilpatrick (1925, p. 102), who introduced the distinctions among primary, associate, and concomitant learnings. The primary learnings related to an activity are those connected directly to the activity. The associate learnings are all the items learned that are related indirectly to the activity. The concomitant learnings are the general attitudes and values that people learn and adopt. There is a gap of over 40 years between Kilpatrick's work and Jackson's introduction of the term "hidden curriculum." A few writers during this period did seem to be suggesting similar ideas. However, Jackson's work can be viewed as seminal, and as a revival of a way of looking at schools that had lain dormant since Kilpatrick's time. This gap can best be explained as a case of the above-mentioned general paradigm change in the social sciences, from the positivistic concern for correlations between phenomena to the emphasis on hermeneutic meaning. Research on the hidden curriculum could only flourish in the latter kind of intellectual milieu.

Of course, the "move toward meaning" has not

signalled a total paradigm change in education. The positivistic strand is still a dominant emphasis in educational research, particularly in work on school improvement and school effectiveness (Rutter et al. 1979). There is a great difference between Kilpatrick and modern commentators. Kilpatrick, Dewey, and the other progressive educators did not distinguish sharply between concern for meaning on the one hand, and school improvement and effectiveness on the other. In the 1990s, however, there is a sharp divide between researchers concerned with the hidden curriculum, qualitative evaluation, and critical pedagogy, and those concerned with school change. The concepts used and the literatures cited are entirely different. In particular, the hidden curriculum is a term unlikely to be used by those involved in school improvement projects and interventions. They are more concerned with clearly measurable school effects and lists of easily measurable school factors that influence school improvement. However, even if Bloom is only partially correct in attributing such power to the hidden curriculum, the term still points to an aspect of schooling of crucial interest to those concerned with improving schools. There is a striking lack of research on the hidden curriculum as an obstacle to school change. Research is also needed on the mechanisms of change of the hidden curriculum itself, and how to use them to help make schools better institutions, with more positive hidden curricula than those that have been identified.

The hermeneutic perspective also suggests a second line of research and analysis. If education is a text, then the question arises: who is the audience? It has been assumed that the students are the readers of the hidden curricular text, but there are other possibilities. Perhaps the text is being written not so much for the students, but rather for society at large, or for the text's authors—the teachers themselves. These are possibilities which invite further exploration.

Finally, a relatively new notion developed by Eisner (1979), the null curriculum, seems to offer potential for further analysis. The null curriculum is that which school does not teach. The gaps are not something neutral, but have important effects on the students—they limit the alternatives and perspectives of which they are aware. Gaps can refer both to the kind of intellectual processes that students do not experience (nonverbal processes, for example, are less likely to be used in school) and to content they are not exposed to (entire disciplines, topics within disciplines, or particular bits of information). As these gaps are normally not openly acknowledged to the learners, the null curriculum can be regarded as part of the hidden curriculum, although Eisner distinguishes between the null curriculum and what he calls the implicit curriculum. The null curriculum seems a particularly important concept considering that the process of building personal, cultural, and social identity is to a large extent a process by which human beings eliminate certain options, or have them eliminated for them. Thus, pointing out those significant options that schools deliberately or inadvertently eliminate is an important research and critical task.

Here, then, is another illustration of why the hidden curriculum and its family concepts are so attractive—imprecise, difficult to measure, but important because they hint at the most profound and influential functions that education can fulfill.

See also: Critical Theory and Education; Curriculum: Sociological Perspectives; Feminist Approaches to the Curriculum; Neo-Marxist Approaches to Curriculum

References

Apple M W 1971 The hidden curriculum and the nature of conflict. *Interchange* 2(4): 27–40
Assor A, Gordon D 1987 The implicit learning theory of hidden-curriculum research. *J. Curric. St.* 19(4): 329–39
Bloom B S 1972 Innocence in education. *Sch. Rev.* 80: 333–52
Bowles S, Gintis H 1976 *Schooling in Capitalist America.* Basic Books, New York
Dreeben R 1968 *On What is Learned in School.* Addison-Wesley, Reading, Massachusetts
Eisner E W 1979 *The Educational Imagination.* MacMillan, New York
Frazier N, Sadker M 1975 *Sexism in School and Society.* Harper and Row, New York
Getzels J W 1974 Images of the classroom and visions of the learner. *Sch. Rev.* 82: 527–40
Gordon D 1981 The aesthetic attitude and the hidden curriculum. *J. Aesthetic Educ.* 15(2): 51–63
Illich I 1971 The breakdown of schools: A problem or a symptom? *Interchange* 2(4): 1–10
Jackson P W 1968 *Life in Classrooms.* Holt, Rinehart and Winston, New York
Kilpatrick W H 1925 *Foundations of Method*: *Informal Talks on Teaching.* MacMillan, New York
Lakomski G 1988 Witches, weather gods, and phlogiston: The demise of the hidden curriculum. *Curric. Inq.* 18(4): 451–64
Martin J R 1976 What should we do with a hidden curriculum when we find one? *Curric. Inq.* 6(2): 135–52
Rutter M, Maughan B, Mortimer P, Ouston J 1979 *Fifteen Thousand Hours. Secondary Schools and Their Effects on Children.* Open Books, London
Schwab J J 1962 The teaching of science as enquiry. In: Schwab J J, Brandwein P (eds.) 1962 *The Teaching of Science.* Harvard University Press, Cambridge, Massachusetts
Snyder B R 1971 *The Hidden Curriculum.* Knopf, New York
Vallance E 1980 The hidden curriculum and qualitative inquiry as states of mind. *J. Educ.* 162(1): 139–51
Willis P 1977 *Learning to Labour: How Working Class Kids Get Working Class Jobs.* Saxon House, Farnborough

Further Reading

Giroux H, Purpel D (eds.) 1983 *The Hidden Curriculum and Moral Education*: *Deception or Discovery.* McCutchan, Berkeley, California
Overly N V (ed.) 1970 *The Unstudied Curriculum. Its Impact on Children.* Association for Supervision and Curriculum Development, Washington, DC

Knowledge: Conceptions of and Impact on Education

Z. Lamm

Questions about the nature of knowledge, its validity, scope, sources, and degree of influence on the lives of people have given rise to a number of areas of research. Epistemology is a philosophical discipline which attempts to supply answers to questions concerning the nature of human knowledge and its validity; the sociology of knowledge probes the links between the social lives of people and their opinions; the psychology of learning investigates how people acquire knowledge; and the history of ideas, science, and philosophy traces the development of human knowledge. The impact of these areas of research on what is taught in schools, and on the methods used, is limited to the extent that they become part of the accepted ideologies of people.

1. Conception of Knowledge in Education

The prevailing ideologies at various times and in various societies determine the status of knowledge in education. The importance of knowledge among the other possible outcomes of education (such as character formation, inculcation of behavior patterns and good citizenship, or imparting religious beliefs) has changed numerous times in the course of history. However, even in periods and societies where knowledge was assigned a high rung on the ladder of educational objectives, this was not always a result of the same factors. During long periods of many societies' history, knowledge had a prominent place in the hierarchy of educational goals because it served as a symbol of the class to which educated persons belonged. Members of this class were differentiated from those of other, inferior classes by, among other things, the fact that they attended school and therefore were considered to have acquired knowledge. Throughout history there have been persons attracted to knowledge by their innate curiosity and their lively intellect—traits not necessarily connected to their class membership—but they did not determine the status of knowledge in society and in education. It is only in modern society that a basic change in the status of knowledge has taken place. In modern society scholastic studies were for the first time openly linked with the struggle for existence. It was no longer a symbolic connection but a concrete one. As a result, scholastic studies (namely, knowledge) were recognized as having general importance.

Most people who live in modern societies are aware of the role knowledge plays in their lives, and they seek to acquire it for themselves and their children, no longer only as a symbol of class status but as a real weapon in the battle for existence. Prior to the emergence of modern societies, the transfer of instruments in the battle for survival from one generation to the next did not require the assistance of the school. The young generation learned the methods for survival directly from the practitioners, without the mediation of the schools. The status of knowledge in the schools changed in accordance with changes in the relevant ideologies. When these ideologies changed, so did the curricula and the methods of instruction. The inclusion of the sciences in the curriculum and elimination of subjects that had been studied for many generations, as well as the gradual introduction of methods of instruction designed to foster thinking and intellectual initiative while phasing out rote learning, are manifestations of what happened in the schools when feudal ideologies gave way to those of the modern age.

2. Paradigms of the Status of Knowledge in Education

If a classification and analysis is undertaken of the various approaches to knowledge which prevailed in the schools in the past, and which prevail in the 1990s, they can be seen to rest on a small number of paradigms. These paradigms stem from the roles people assign to knowledge. The basic roles giving rise to the paradigms are social instrumentalism, ritualism, and developmental instrumentalism.

2.1 Social Instrumentalism

According to the ideology of social instrumentalism, the status of knowledge in teaching is determined by the view that the value of knowledge is in its utility. The most valuable knowledge, according to this ideology, is that which serves humanity in its struggle for survival in the widest sense. This approach is strengthened by the arguments used by utilitarian philosophy. In its application to education and curriculum, utilitarianism bases the choice of curriculum and teaching methods on the principle that the schools should teach only, or primarily, that which can be of use to people in their daily lives. A distinct proponent of this approach in modern educational thought was Spencer. In the second half of the nineteenth century Spencer posed

the question: "What knowledge is of most worth?" The answer he gave was as follows:

> The uniform reply is—Science. This is the verdict on all the counts. For direct self-preservation, or the maintenance of life and health, the all-important knowledge is—Science. For that indirect self-preservation which we call gaining a livelihood, the knowledge of greatest value is—Science. For that interpretation of national life, past and present, without which the citizen cannot rightly regulate his conduct, the indispensable key is—Science. Alike for the most perfect production and highest enjoyment of art in all its forms, the needful preparation is still—Science. (Spencer 1911 pp. 42–43)

Spencer lists the areas of knowledge which are in his view the only ones worthy of study in the schools. These are maintenance of life and health, acquiring an occupation to earn a livelihood, the rudiments of good citizenship, and the ability to enjoy art in all its forms. The last area is related to the ability to utilize leisure time. Ignorance in any of these realms would undoubtedly, in Spencer's view, adversely affect a person's life, and they should all, therefore, be included in school curricula. The extreme adherents of this view hold that these areas are the only ones that should be included in curricula studied by all pupils. The approach here is that knowledge is an instrument and should be treated as such. The relationship of persons to instruments is rational; they utilize them and learn to utilize them to the extent that they need them. The instrumentalism underlying this approach applies clearly to knowledge whose use has social value in a broad sense, primarily the struggle for survival of societies by means of people's labors to supply their needs and defend themselves. Teaching methods are an outgrowth of this approach. If knowledge is an instrument, the main purpose of acquiring it is to learn how to use it. Teaching along these lines is thus similar to what teachers do when they impart skills—they teach ways of utilization. Knowledge that does not lend itself to utilization has merely an ornamental value, and has no place in education that is controlled by this conception. The uses of various areas of knowledge that are dictated by life in society determine what knowledge is, what parts of it should be taught, and how.

2.2 Ritualism

A different conception of knowledge in education is the one determined by the ritualistic approach. According to this concept, there are categories of knowledge that possess intrinsic value and it is imperative to teach them. It is necessary to teach knowledge of this kind, not because it is of obvious utility or practical value, but because a person who does not have this knowledge is lacking in the basic essence of a human being. Acquisition of this knowledge makes a person different; it is required in order for the individual to rise to the level of human being that he or she should attain. The ritualistic approach to knowledge characterizes two conceptions which continue to be dominant in certain systems in the 1990s. These are religious and humanistic education. The educational systems of most religions are based on the teachings of their holy books. Knowledge of these holy writings is necessary, according to the educational views of the believers, in order for the individual to attain full human stature as the religion would like. One does not study the writings for any practical reason, but to make one better, in line with the ideals of the particular religion.

Humanism was originally a revolt against the limitations of knowledge imposed by religion during the period prior to the Renaissance. Humanism called for freedom to conduct research, and freedom to teach the findings of that research. Humanism was also a revolt against the limitations on humans' right to derive as much pleasure as possible from life. These limitations were imposed over the course of many centuries by religions in which God rather than humans stood at the center of the world.

Humanism introduced the study of humans (*Humana studia*), which edged out religious studies (*Divina studia*) in the universities. From the universities the study of humans rapidly spread to the secondary schools and then later to the elementary schools. Similar to religions, humanism has writings that occupy a special place, and that are taught in the educational institutions under its influence. For a long time these were the classic works of Greek and Roman literature. The adherents of this approach in the 1990s added to the list the great books in philosophy and science, literature, and history, and the outstanding works in religious thought. All of these, in accordance with this view of knowledge, should be taught for their own sake. Whitehead expressed it as follows: "The really profound changes in human life all have their ultimate origin in knowledge pursued for its own sake" (1948 p. 19). The importance of this kind of education is the transfer of knowledge from one generation to the next. It is justified by the claim that in the course of history the wise and talented people understood gradually, and to a limited extent, what life is all about and the roles and obligations of human beings in this world. What they found became the inherited body of the culture of humankind, which made possible human survival and imbued it with moral significance. The handing down of this heritage from generation to generation is the primary task of education. The cultural heritage is transmitted by study, and these studies mold the character of the members of the younger generation. If not for the transmission of knowledge by means of teaching and learning, the human race would have to begin its history from the start in each generation. Education is knowledge that liberates the human creature from its original nature and confers upon it a new, cultured nature. This role of education through knowledge is alluded to in the term "liberal education." In the schools, teachers are engaged in additional activities aside from teaching the cultural heritage of humankind. They devote time to physical education and recreation, vocational training, and political indoctrination. All these, however, according to this view, are merely secondary tasks of education. Schools exist first and foremost for the purpose of imparting knowledge.

However, not all youngsters are equally capable of acquiring knowledge. This approach to education is in essence aristocratic. One of its exponents explains it as follows:

> a liberal education aims to develop the powers of understanding and judgment. It is impossible that too many people can be educated in this sense, because there cannot be too many people with understanding and judgment. We hear a great deal today about the dangers that will come upon us through the frustration of educated people who have got educated in the expectation that education will get them a better job, and who fail to get it. But surely this depends on the representations that are made to the young about what education is. If we allow them to believe that education will get them better jobs and encourage them to get educated with that end in view, they are entitled to a sense of frustration if, when they have got the education, they do not get the jobs. But, if we say that they should be educated in order to be men, and that everybody, whether he is a ditch-digger or a bank president, should have this education because he is a man, then the ditch-digger may still feel frustrated, but not because of his education. (Hutchins 1953 pp. 73–74)

2.3 Developmental Instrumentalism

The third approach to knowledge, which has only begun to penetrate schools in the late twentieth century, is also instrumental, but in a different way. Knowledge, according to this approach, is an instrument that can help the person develop intellectual faculties. Here knowledge is not assigned any intrinsic value, as in the previous approach, nor is any ritualistic signficance attributed to it. Neither does this approach adopt a utilitarian view of knowledge which would make it serve the future social roles of the pupil. Instead, it is regarded as an instrument, not for the adjustment of the individual to life in society, but which fosters the development of the learner's mental abilities. In this approach the acquisition of knowledge is not tantamount to education, as the ritualistic approach contends. This approach holds that people are born human and education has no role to play in determining a person's essentially human nature. The task of education is to bring the person's human potential to realization. By means of knowledge a person activates and sharpens innate intellectual faculties. Knowledge is thus an instrument to realize the potential in the individual. The developmental instrumentalist concept places the pupil's needs at the center of the curricula. The desire to know is an inborn need; the expression of this need is curiosity. Learning out of curiosity is the way to acquire knowledge that fosters the learner's development. There are other modes of learning: learning out of a feeling of obligation, to win prizes, to avoid punishment, or to compete with others. However, according to proponents of this approach all these other modes, although they may have at times led people to become experts in certain areas of knowledge, do not contribute to the healthy, free development of the personality. Pupils should study what interests them and what they want to know. In this approach the pupil's motivation is considered to play a central role in learning, because satisfying the immediate intellectual needs of the learner is here considered necessary for sound development. In this view, the intellectual abilities of the students develop and grow strong as a result of learning things which they want to know. The proponents of the child-centered approach in contemporary education expressed this view in their writings. The following is an illustration:

> . . . You end up with a 'student-centered curriculum' not because it is good for 'motivation' but because you don't, in fact, have any other choice. There is no such a thing as 'subject matter' in the abstract. "Subject matter" exists in the minds of perceivers. And what each one thinks it is, it is. We have been acting in schools as if knowledge lies outside the learner, which is why we have the kind of curricula, syllabi, and text we have. But knowledge . . . is what we know *after* we have learned. It is an outcome of perception and is as unique and subjective as any other perception. Thus if you assume you are confronted by a "meaning maker" rather than by an "empty bucket" you would quite logically stop the practice of preparing and using syllabi and texts which state exactly what knowledge is to be learned. (Postman and Weingarther 1969 pp. 92–93)

3. The Eclectic Models of Knowledge in Education

The approaches to knowledge outlined above determined in the past, and continue to determine in the 1990s, the curricula and teaching methods used in schools. Only rarely, however, are curricula and teaching methods found that follow only one of the foregoing approaches. As a rule the curriculum is influenced by more than one approach, and examples exist of every possible permutation and combination. Sometimes, one subject is handled according to the ritualistic approach, while another, in the same school, is based on one of the instrumentalist approaches. Even within the same subject, some chapters are taught according to one approach while others are taught on the basis of a different one. These variations reflect the

ideological conceptions of the decision-makers in the educational system.

4. The Link Between Approaches to Knowledge and Overall Conceptions of Education

The various approaches to knowledge do not inform educational philosophy without regard to other aspects of education. Each of these approaches is anchored in an overall conception of education. The differences between the overall conceptions, which are educational ideologies, refer not only to the status of knowledge, but also to such issues as the proper place of the pupil and the teacher in the educational process, the kind of motivation desirable, or the type of leadership recommended. The social instrumentalist approach to the status of knowledge in education is typical of the conceptions of education as socialization. Ritualism as the definition of the status of knowledge characterizes conceptions of education that see the primary goal as transmitting culture. The approach of developmental instrumentalism is associated with child-centered conceptions of education (Lamm 1976).

See also: Curriculum: Sociological Perspectives; Research in Education: Epistemological Issues

References

Hutchins R 1953 *The Conflict in Education in a Democratic Society.* Harper and Row, New York
Lamm Z 1976 *Conflicting Theories of Instruction: Conceptual Dimensions.* McCutchan, Berkeley, California
Postman N, Weingartner C 1969 *Teaching as a Subversive Activity.* Delacorte, New York
Spencer H 1911 *Essays on Education.* J M Dent, London
Whitehead A N 1948 *An Introduction to Mathematics.* Oxford University Press, London

Further Reading

Dearden R F et al. (eds.) 1972 *Education and the Development of Reason.* Routledge and Kegan Paul, London
Ford G W, Pugno L 1964 *The Structure of Knowledge and the Curriculum.* Rand McNally, Chicago, Illinois
Hutchins R 1968 *The Learning Society.* Praeger, New York
Phenix P H 1964 *Realms of Meaning: A Philosophy of the Curriculum for General Education.* McGraw-Hill, New York
Scheffler I 1965 *Conditions of Knowledge: Introduction to Epistemology and Education.* University of Chicago, Chicago, Illinois
Young M F D (ed.) 1972 *Knowledge and Control.* Collier-Macmillan, London

School and Classroom Dynamics

M. T. Hallinan

Several dynamic processes occur within the school and classroom. These processes fall into two categories: cognitive and interactive. Cognitive processes involve the many dimensions of thinking and are the foundation of learning. Two developments in learning theory have increased the attention of educators to cognitive processes. First, researchers and educators are learning how to identify students' different learning styles, including auditory and visual learning, as well as use of a combination of sensory inputs. Second, researchers are broadening the concept of intelligence to include several different types. These new developments augment the large extant body of literature on learning theory.

Interactive processes in the school and classroom include instructional interactions and noninstructional or social interactions. They occur between teacher and students, and between and among students. These interactions affect a student's learning, attitudes, self-esteem, and motivation and lead to the formation of friendships and social networks.

The interactive processes that occur in the school and classroom are the subject of this article. Interactional processes are identifiable and manipulable, and can be evaluated in terms of student achievement and social development.

1. Instructional Processes

1.1 Organization of Instruction

The organization of students for instruction is a major structural determinant of interactional opportunities for teachers and students. The size and composition of the student population influence the organizational differentiation of students for instruction. Generally, the larger the school, the more likely students are to be assigned to smaller groups for instruction. Typically this takes the form of age grading. In contrast to the late nineteenth century, in the early 1990s few schools in any country group students for instruction heterogeneously with respect to age. The age distribution of the student body determines the age range of the students assigned to a particular class.

The gender, racial, and ethnic composition of a school also affects the composition of the students assigned to a particular class. In some schools, students are segregated by gender, although mixed gender classes are far more common. Generally, race or ethnicity does not act as a basis for instructional group assignment, although a correlation between race and achievement in the United States makes it appear otherwise. In some cases, students are assigned to instructional groups in such a way as to insure desegregated classes. Socioeconomic status (SES), by itself, is seldom used as a basis for instructional grouping although, like race, its correlation with achievement may affect the distribution of SES across classes.

The most common basis for assigning students to instructional groups in schools is student ability. Ability groups restrict the ability range of the students in the group in order to facilitate teacher instruction and better meet the learning needs of the students. The achievement distribution of the student population determines the number, size, and ability range of the groups that are created. The majority of schools in many countries, including the United Kingdom, the United States, Japan, and Australia, group students by ability for instruction, at least in language and mathematics. Ability grouping is known as "streaming" in the United Kingdom and as "tracking" at the high school level in the United States and elsewhere.

Ability grouping affects student learning in several ways. In general, students in high ability groups receive a greater quantity and quality of instruction than those in lower groups. High ability students spend more time on task than lower ability pupils, are interrupted less frequently for administrative or disciplinary reasons, are encouraged and rewarded more often, and participate in discussions more frequently than pupils in lower ability groups (see, e.g., Nystrand and Gamoran 1991, Oakes 1985, Barr and Dreeben 1983).

The superiority of the instruction received by students in high ability groups, and the positive social psychological dynamics that increase motivation, effort, and self-esteem, explain the greater growth in achievement of students in high ability groups and the slower growth in achievement of students in the lower ability groups. Several studies show that, controlling for ability, students assigned to high ability English and mathematics groups learn more than those in lower tracks (see Slavin 1990 for a review of these studies of grouping effects in United Kingdom and United States schools). Ability grouping generally shows no direct effect of streaming or tracking on achievement (Slavin 1987). The explanation generally given for this result is that the gains of the high ability students offset the losses of the low ability students, as supported by Kerckhoff's 1986 study of streamed and unstreamed schools in Britain.

1.2 Teacher-led Instruction

Most instruction in the classroom takes place in teacher-led groups. Teacher-led instruction occurs when the teacher is the center of communication. The teacher provides information, directs discussion, and monitors student input and behavior. The primary modes of communication are lectures, question and answer sessions, recitations, and discussion. Ordinarily, students all work on the same task. They are expected to attend to the interactions between the teacher and other pupils and to respond when it is their turn. Teacher-led instruction can take place with the class as a whole or in small groups within the class. Students can be assigned to a teacher-led instructional group on any basis, though typically homogeneous groups are formed within the classroom.

Advocates of teacher-led instruction argue that this pedagogical method insures that students are exposed to the curriculum in an orderly fashion, that they receive correct information, that their mistakes are rectified immediately, and that expectations for performance are clear and uniform. Critics of teacher-led instruction argue that the more students participate directly in the learning experience, the more interested they will be in the curriculum, the more time they will spend on-task, and the more they will learn.

One important dimension of teacher-led instruction in the classroom involves the effects of student characteristics on patterns of communication. A primary focus has been differential communication patterns between teachers and students by student gender. These patterns have been associated with differences between boys and girls in attitudes toward school, academic achievement, self-esteem, and educational aspirations.

The question of differential treatment of male and female students by teachers has long been a subject of concern and debate. As early as 1909, Ayres charged that teachers discriminated against boys in the assignment of grades in all subjects. Other early critics claimed that the learning needs of boys could not be met adequately because teachers were predominantly female. More recently, researchers and educators have attributed, at least in part, the superior mathematics test scores of boys and their more frequent election of mathematics courses to sex differences in teacher interactions and expectation (Becker 1981).

Empirical research provides evidence of differences in teacher interactions with male and female students at the elementary school level (see Brophy 1985). Teachers are found to call on boys more frequently than girls, to initiate both work-related and personal contacts more frequently with boys than with girls and to correct and discipline boys more frequently than girls. Whether these differences represent teachers' responses to student behavior or student gender is not clear. Other studies show that even when boys and girls, receive a similar amount of praise and criticism, boys receive significantly more praise for the intellectual quality of their work while girls receive more praise for its nonintellectual aspects, such as appearance, organization, and presentation.

Similar findings are reported in studies of gender-related differences in teacher interactions with adolescent students. In several studies of mathematics classes, teachers were observed to spend more time with the boys, to initiate more contacts, and to correct, praise, encourage, socialize, and joke with boys more frequently than with girls. Becker (1981) summarized these results by describing the learning environment for boys in mathematics classes as being supportive, both academically and emotionally, while the environment for girls is one of benign neglect. Classrooms vary, of course, in the extent to which gender differences are observed in teacher–student interactions. Attention given to the lower test scores and participation of females in mathematics and science is leading to a greater awareness of gender bias in instruction and to greater efforts to eliminate discrimination against students on the basis of gender.

While a large body of literature exists on gender differences in teacher–student interaction patterns, there is less research examining variance in teacher–student interaction patterns by student race or ethnicity. A few studies show that White students receive more praise for academic performance while Black students receive more directives regarding behavior. When gender–race combinations are examined, there is some evidence that White girls have the warmest, most positive contacts with teachers while Black boys receive most negative feedback about behavior. Due to the dominance of female teachers in United States schools, where most of the empirical research on teacher–student interactions have been conducted, few studies comparing teacher–student communication by gender of teacher are available. Those that do exist show no major differences in gender-related interactions with students by male and female teachers.

In general, the literature shows that female and male students, as well as students who differ in other ascribed characteristics, experience different interaction patterns with teachers. While overt teacher discrimination against students by gender is not found, subtle differences in interactions with male and female students do occur. These differences can serve to advantage students with one set of characteristics over those with another. In some cases, teachers initiate different interaction patterns with boys and girls. In other cases, teachers respond to different behaviors by boys and girls. Here teachers may reinforce already existing gender differences in behavior. These differential interaction patterns tend to create inequities in the opportunities for students to learn. They may also have a negative influence on students' attitudes toward school and their peers. Consequently, efforts need to be directed to eliminate gender and race/ethnic differences in teacher–student interaction patterns.

1.3 Peer Instructional Groups

While teacher-led instructional groups remain the most popular method of instruction in schools in nearly all countries, a growing number of teachers are also using peer instructional groups for at least part of their instructional time. In peer instructional groups, the students are seen as the primary resources for learning and student communication and exchange are the basic mode of instruction. Peer instructional groups may be homogeneous or heterogeneous with respect to student ability.

Stodolsky (1984) distinguishes five types of peer instructional groups: completely cooperative, cooperative, helping obligatory, helping permitted, and peer tutoring. In a completely cooperative group, the students have common goals and activities, are expected to work together, and produce a common product which is evaluated as a group effort. A cooperative group is similar except that it contains some division of labor among the students. In the remaining three types of group, students have individual goals, and are evaluated individually. In helping obligatory groups, peers are expected to help peers with their assignments. In helping permitted groups, students may assist peers but are not required to do so. Finally, in peer tutoring, one student is designated as the instructor who assists another student to complete assigned tasks.

Considerable research has examined the effects of peer instructional groups, especially cooperative groups, on student learning. (For a review of these studies, see Slavin 1987.) The results show that the type of peer group affects the types of interaction patterns that emerge. Asymmetric communications are more common in helping groups and peer tutoring, while symmetric interactions occur more often in cooperative groups. Student ascribed and achieved characteristics are less salient in interactions in cooperative groups than in helping groups. In terms of learning outcomes, students who work in cooperative groups are found to master higher developmental skills than those working alone, likely as a result of the discussion, argumentation, and multiple perspectives that characterize these groups.

Cooperative instructional groups also have been utilized to improve social relations among students, particularly among those with different backgrounds or social characteristics. The rationale for this approach is found in social psychological theories of contact and expectation states. Contact theory (Allport 1954) predicts that race relations will improve if members of different racial groups have the opportunity to interact with each other in situations where they are status equals. Cooperative learning groups satisfy these conditions of contact theory. Most empirical studies show that cooperative groups do promote better attitudes among students of different racial or ethnic backgrounds. Moreover, cross-race friendships are more likely to form among students in cooperative groups than in competitive groups.

Expectation states theory (Berger et al. 1972) claims that status characteristics lead to generalized expectations about individuals' behavior. The status derived from diffuse characteristics, such as race and gender, and specific characteristics, such as mathematical ability, is generalized to new situations where the characteristics are unrelated to the task at hand. As a result, higher status persons are expected to have more competence in performing the new task than lower status persons. A large body of empirical research, mostly experimental studies, supports expectation states theory.

Applied to classroom interaction, expectation states theory predicts that the higher a student's diffuse or specific status characteristic, the greater will be that student's participation and influence in performing a group task. Gender, race, ethnicity, physical attractiveness, and academic ability are believed to act as status characteristics in a classroom setting. In particular, males and Whites typically have higher rates of participation and exert greater influence in problem solving groups than females and non-Whites. Interventions that increase the skills or resources of lower status group members in performing a group task have successfully reduced the effects of diffuse status characteristics on student performance. To produce equal-status interactions, however, it appears necessary not only to equalize student competence, but also to insure that the lower status students have greater skills and resources to perform the assigned task than higher status peers.

One contribution of the research on status effects on student interactions in the classroom is that it suggests ways to alter the effects of ascribed characteristics on student behavior. While ascribed characteristics are immutable, status is manipulable. Interventions that alter the status hierarchy of a classroom have been shown to have a direct, powerful effect on changing interaction patterns and on distributing participation and influence more equally across all students.

2. Social Processes

In conjunction with the instructionally based interactions that occur in school, teachers and students engage in social interactions that play a major role in student socialization and maturation. Social interactions influence a student's self-esteem, attitudes, values, aspirations, and academic achievement. Students' social interactions are inextricably tied to the instructional processes that occur in school. The content of many interactions are curriculum related, and peer interactions affect a student's attitude toward school and learning. Student interactions are governed by social psychological factors that determine their nature, duration, and consequences. Here, attention will focus on two types of student interactions, those that result in peer influence and those that affect student friendship.

2.1 Peer Influence Processes

The influence of peers on students' attitudes and behaviors has been a topic of extensive research. Interest in peer effects is based on the belief that peers act as a significant socializing agent for students. Peers have the potential to be valuable educational resources that encourage student achievement. They also may act as obstacles to achievement that weaken a school's efforts to instruct. Much of the research on peer effects focuses on the effects of context, such as the normative climate of the school, on student achievement, aspirations, and attainment. Other studies analyze the proximate influences of peers on a student's social behavior.

The racial, ethnic, and socioeconomic composition of a school are the context variables analyzed most frequently in peer effects studies. The research generally reports context effects of small magnitude (see Spady 1973 for a review). In United States schools, higher socioeconomic composition and a higher percentage of Whites are associated with higher mean academic achievement. Educational aspirations increase for Black students in all-Black schools. For White students in desegregated schools, mean educational aspirations increase as the percentage of Blacks in a school increases. While these results appear fairly robust, a number of the studies have been criticized on methodological grounds (e.g., Hauser 1970, Campbell 1983).

The theoretical framework generally relied on to explain contextual effects is that of reference group processes. Spady (1973) argues that reference groups can operate in three ways. The first way is through normative group influences, where students respond to the norms, values, and standards that describe their environment. The second is through role modeling, where peers illustrate the behavior that is defined as acceptable to the group. The third way is through comparative group influences, whereby students compare their attitudes and behaviors to those of their peers and adjust their own to be consistent with their peers. Most, though not all, of these influences are transmitted through interpersonal interactions. The effects of the normative context of the school appear to be strongest when the norms and values are transmitted by a student's friends.

While reference group processes provide reasonable post hoc explanations of contextual effects, the theories have little predictive power. They fail to address central issues such as why students vary in their susceptibility to contextual influences. The theories lack specificity and ignore the effects of student and situational characteristics or the effects of context on student outcomes. Consequently, no major breakthrough has occurred in understanding this aspect of peer influences.

Research on proximate peer influences compares the attitudes and behaviors of students with those of their peers and explains similarities in terms of peer effects. Early proximate peer effects studies are found in status attainment research (see Sewell et al. 1970, Campbell 1983). Here, the focus is on the effects of a significant other, generally a friend, on a student's attitudes and behavior. The studies show that friends' educational aspirations and attainment have a positive effect on a student's university plans and educational attainment, regardless of the student's socioeconomic status. Moreover, significant other influences increase over time.

A number of studies, mostly observations, analyze proximate peer influences on noncognitive outcomes (e.g., Hollingshead 1949, Coleman 1961, Cusick 1973). Students form social groupings or cliques on the basis of similar characteristics, such as SES or athletic ability. These groups, once formed, tend to exert considerable power over their members' behavior. The subcultures that emerge in these groups may promote antiacademic norms.

A major weakness of most of the studies of proximate peer influence is that they fail to separate selection and influence factors. Much of the research attributes similarities among peers to peer influence. This ignores the likelihood that peers select each other because of existing similarities. As a result, observed peer effects in many studies may be inflated. Another shortcoming of this research is that it rests on the untested assumption that the same processes govern the influence by friends and nonfriends, and academic and nonacademic outcomes. Further theoretical work is needed to specify more accurately the mechanisms that govern student influence.

A heuristically richer theoretical foundation for the study of peer influences can be found in a treatise by Parsons (1963). While this work has received some attention by social psychologists, it has not been applied systematically to the study of peer influences and has not generated empirical studies. Attention to this work might enrich the study of peer influences. Parsons assumes that influence occurs in the following situation. An individual is in need of knowledge in order to adapt to and interact with the environment. The individual chooses to or needs to rely on others for the requisite information. Influence occurs when the individual accepts information from another. The necessary condition for influence, therefore, is the willingness of the individual to accept information from another.

Willingness to accept information is determined by the amount of trust the person places in the source of the information, whether that be a person or a normative system. The degree of trust depends on the amount of knowledge the individual has of the informant or of the normative system. The greater the trust, the greater the influence.

The advantage of this theoretical approach to the study of peer influences is that it specifies the conditions under which influence will occur (Hallinan

1992). Determinants of the need for information can be hypothesized, such as the newness of a situation, the need for action or decision, the visibility of the action, and its relevance to others. Determinants of the need to rely on others also can be predicted, including the availability of the information from elsewhere, the need for immediate action that precludes finding the information oneself, and the belief that the information one obtained from another would be more accurate than that obtained oneself. The extent to which these conditions for influence are present in a particular school setting can be analyzed easily to predict the likelihood of peer influence.

Empirical research on peer effects has stagnated since the early 1980s. Future insights into the peer influence process requires continued theoretical development in this area. Empirical research studies should then be derived from these new theoretical formations, rather than replicating existing designs and offering only post hoc explanations of results. The importance of peer influences to the learning process underscores the importance of these efforts.

2.2 Friendship Processes

A student's friends are likely to exert a major influence on the student's attitudes and behaviors. Consequently, identifying the determinants of friendship formation in a school setting assumes considerable importance. Characteristics of a student's environment, including school size and composition, the organizational differentiation of students for instruction, the availability of extracurricular activities, and the student status system affect whom a student chooses as a friend as well as the duration and consequences of the friendship. Individual characteristics of students, of course, are the primary determinants of friendship choice, but these characteristics may interact with school variables to influence students' social relationships (Hallinan and Williams 1990).

A necessary, but not sufficient condition, for friendship choice is proximity. Students will interact only if they have the opportunity to do so. The composition of the student body defines the ascribed and achieved characteristics of the pool of peers with whom a student can become friends. Schools and classes are typically age graded, making friendship with same-age peers more likely. The racial or ethnic composition of a school affects the probability of interracial friendships, while the SES of the students determines the social class boundaries of friendships. The ability distribution of the student population affects the likelihood of a student forming a friendship with a peer with similar ability.

The main way that schools affect the proximity of students is through the assignment of students to groups for instruction. Grouping students by ability, or by any other salient characteristic, increases opportunities for students to interact with peers who are assigned to the same group and therefore possess similar characteristics. Grouping decreases opportunities for students to interact with peers in a different group. Since proximity permits interaction which typically leads to positive sentiment (Homans 1974), more friendships are expected to develop among students in the same group than among those in different groups. Hallinan and Sorensen (1985) report empirical evidence of this grouping effect on student friendships. The availability of cocurricular and extracurricular activities in a school also affects student proximity, providing opportunities for students to interact with peers participating in the same activity.

Since proximity is only a necessary condition for friendship, other factors also affect friendship formation. Social psychological theories of interpersonal attraction point to similarity and status as major determinants of friendship. Individuals tend to choose as friends those who are similar to themselves in ascribed and achieved characteristics. Hence, one observes a preponderance of friendships in which students are the same gender, race or ethnicity, SES, and ability level.

Schools can influence what characteristics students determine are relevant bases of friendship. For example, if cross-race or cross-ethnic sociability is encouraged in a school, the salience of racial or ethnic similarity as a basis of attraction may diminish. If school authorities use gender as a basis for assigning students to instructional groups or noncurricular activities, then the importance of gender in students' social relations may increase. A number of empirical studies show that the opportunity to interact increases the likelihood of interracial friendships.

School practices can also lead to the formation of new similarities among students. When students are assigned to the same ability group, they are exposed to the same curriculum, perform the same assignments, and share ideas with group members. These shared experiences likely lead to new similarities among students assigned to the same group. The students are apt to develop similar attitudes and norms about school and to become more similar in behavior. These new similarities can stabilize and intensify existing friendships and lead to the formation of new friendships.

Schools play a major role in the formation of a status hierarchy among students. Both the normative climate of a school and its reward structure and disciplinary code identify those students that school authorities define as deserving respect or esteem. If the normative climate of a school supports academic achievement, then students who are successful academically are likely to have higher status than those who are less successful. Assigning students to instructional groups based on ability plays an important role in emphasizing academic achievement as a basis for status. Students assigned to the high ability groups usually command more respect from students and faculty than those in lower ability groups. The emphasis given to athletics, the fine arts, and other curricular and noncurricular accomplishments will affect students' status among their peers.

Since status is a basis for interpersonal attraction, students who rank higher in a status hierarchy are likely to be more popular than those with lower status. Popular friends are likely to exert a stronger influence on a student than less popular ones. If popular students endorse a school's academic goals, they are likely to have a positive influence on their friends' academic achievement. However, most schools have a subset of students who reject the dominant value climate of the school, particularly if it is based on academic achievement. Students who are part of an antiacademic subculture tend to choose friends who have a negative influence on their attitudes toward learning and academic achievement.

Of particular interest in the study of school and classroom processes that affect student friendships is school effects on interracial friendships in desegregated schools. While individual characteristics of students are the primary determinant of cross-race friendships, organizational characteristics of schools and classrooms also play an important role. Specifically, the school and classroom racial composition affects the likelihood of cross-race interactions while the organization of curricular and noncurricular activities influences how similarity and status affect interracial attraction. Several empirical studies show that the larger the Black population in a desegregated school, the more likely Whites are to choose a Black friend, although there is some evidence that this relationship does not hold for Black students. Other studies report that students assigned to small, instructional groups that are heterogeneous with respect to race and ability are more likely to make cross-race friendships than students not assigned to groups. Racial cleavage has been found to increase in schools that group students by ability for instruction. (For a review of these studies, see Hallinan 1992.)

2.3 Social Networks

The theoretical and empirical interest in social networks that emerged in the 1970s and 1980s appears in school research as well as elsewhere. Network analysts examine how the structure of the ties that link members of a group affects the likelihood that a group member will make a particular social connection. In terms of friendships in school, the question is how characteristics of a student's social network relate to that student's friendship choices. For example, how will the popularity of a student's friends affect the number of friendship choices that student gives and receives?

One of the social psychological processes that appears to govern the effects of network structure on friendship choice is a norm of reciprocity (Gouldner 1960). A person is more likely to choose another as a friend if that person chooses the individual as a friend. Thus, students are more likely to establish friendships with classmates who they perceive as liking them. Similarly, popular students are more likely to make friendship choices than unpopular ones. Hallinan (1992) finds a strong reciprocity effect in several data sets on school children's friendships.

A second theoretical base for network effects is that of dissonance theory. Certain formulations of dissonance theory claim that positive sentiment tends to be transitive: that is, if A likes B and B likes C, then A will experience psychological discomfort unless A also likes C. A tendency toward transitivity implies that the friendship choices of a student's friend affects the student's friendship choices. Moreover, students involved in intransitive triadic relationships are likely to change their friendship choices in such a way as to restore transitivity or balance. It has been also shown that the expansion of a social network requires members to be involved in intransitive relationships, at least temporarily, but that the tendency toward transitivity eventually results in a stable, cohesive social network (Sorensen and Hallinan 1984).

The structure of larger networks also affects friendship choice. Hallinan and McFarland (1975) show that, under certain assumptions, the structure of a tetrad may be such that a tetrad member cannot resolve an intransitive triadic relationship in the tetrad without inducing another intransitive relationship in the tetrad. While the effects of configurations larger than a tetrad have not been examined, due to the cumbersomeness of the data, the network approach outlined here can be extended to networks of any size. Ultimately, this approach should yield a better understanding of why certain patterns, such as cohesive groups or cliques, typically evolve in students' social networks.

These network studies are of considerable importance in terms of understanding school and classroom processes. Network studies demonstrate that the interactive processes that occur in school are determined not only by individual characteristics of students and organizational characteristics of schools, but also by structural characteristics of students' social relationships. Organizational features of schools and classrooms, such as racial composition and grouping practices, create opportunities for and constraints on students' social interactions. These interactions, in turn, generate social psychological conditions that affect friendship choice. Thus, interventions designed to alter and improve students' social relations must take into account the effect of the intervention on individual, situational, and structural determinants of friendship.

3. Conclusion

Learning occurs through both instructional and social processes. These two sets of processes occur when teachers and students interact with each other.

A dynamic, reciprocal relationship exists between interaction and learning. Consequently, a better understanding of how students learn can be obtained through an analysis of the effects of school practices on student interaction.

Organizational characteristics of a school and classroom affect the nature, content, and duration of instruction. Primary among these organizational factors is the assignment of students to groups for learning. The effects of grouping practices on student learning is transmitted through the kinds of student interactions that occur in instructional groups. Students' social interactions are determined by the pool of available peers, by opportunities and constraints on peer interactions, and by the climate and culture of the school. Organizational and social psychological theories that focus on the dynamics of student interactions explain how school and classroom processes promote student learning.

See also: Ability Grouping and Tracking in Schools; Students in Classrooms, Gender and Racial Differences Among; Youth Cultures and Subcultures; Youth Friendships and Conflict in Schools

References

Allport G W 1954 *The Nature of Prejudice*. Addison-Wesley, Cambridge, Massachusetts
Ayres L 1909 *Laggards in Our Schools: A Study of Retardation and Elimination in City School Systems*. Russell Sage Foundation, New York
Barr R, Dreeben R 1983 *How Schools Work*. University of Chicago Press, Chicago, Illinois
Becker J 1981 Differential teacher treatment of males and females in mathematics classes. *J. Res. Math. Educ.* 12(1): 40–53
Berger J, Cohen B, Zelditch M Jr 1972 Status characteristics and social interaction. *Am. Sociol. Rev.* 37(3): 241–55
Brophy J 1985 Interactions of male and female students with male and female teachers. In: Wilkinson L C, Marrett C B (eds.) 1985 *Gender Influences in Classroom Interaction*. Academic Press, Orlando, Florida
Campbell R 1983 Status attainment research: End of the beginning or beginning of the end? *Sociol. Educ.* 56(1): 47–62
Coleman J S 1961 *The Adolescent Society: The Social Life of the Teenager and its Impact on Education*. Free Press, New York
Cusick P 1973 *Inside High School: The Students' World*. Holt, Rinehart, and Winston, New York
Gouldner A W 1960 The norm of reciprocity: a preliminary statement. *Am. Sociol. Rev.* 25(2): 161–78
Hallinan M T 1992 Determinants of students' friendship choices. In: Lawler E (ed.) 1992 *Advances in Group Processes*, Vol. 9. JAI Press, Greenwich, Connecticut
Hallinan M T, McFarland D 1975 Higher order stability conditions in mathematical models of sociometric or cognitive structure. *J. Math. Sociol.* 41(7): 131–48
Hallinan M T, Sorensen A B 1985 Ability grouping and student friendships. *Am. Educ. Res. J.* 22(4): 485–99
Hallinan M T, Williams R 1990 Student characteristics and the peer influence process: A nationwide study. *Sociol. Educ.* 63(2): 122–32
Hauser R M 1970 Context and consex: A cautionary tale. *Am. J. Sociol.* 75(4): 645–64
Hollingshead A 1949 *Elmtown's Youth: The Impact of Social Classes on Adolescents*. Wiley, New York
Homans G C 1974 *Social Behavior: Its Elementary Forms*. Harcourt Brace Jovanovich, New York
Kerckhoff A C 1986 Effects of achievement grouping in British secondary schools. *Am. Sociol. Rev.* 51(6): 842–58
Nystrand M, Gamoran A 1991 Instructional discourse, student engagement and literature achievement. *Res. Teach. Engl.* 25: 261–90
Oakes J 1985 *Keeping Track: How Schools Structure Inequality*. Yale University Press, New Haven, Connecticut
Parsons T 1963 On the concept of influence. *Pub. Opin. Q.* 27: 37–62
Sewell W, Haller O, Ohlenforf G 1970 The educational and early occupational attainment process: Replication and revision. *Am. Sociol. Rev.* 35: 1014–27
Slavin R E 1987 Ability grouping and student achievement in elementary schools: A best-evidence synthesis. *Rev. Educ. Res.* 57(3): 293–336
Slavin R E 1990 Achievement effects of ability grouping in secondary schools. A best-evidence synthesis. *Rev. Educ. Res.* 60(3): 471–99
Sorensen A B, Hallinan M T 1984 Effects of race on assignment to ability groups. In: Peterson P, Wilkinson L C, Hallinan M T (eds.) 1984 *The Social Context of Instruction: Group Processes*. Academic Press, San Diego, California
Spady W G 1973 The impact of school resources on students. *Rev. Res. Educ.* 1: 135–77
Stodolsky S 1984 Frameworks for studying instructional processes in peer work-groups. In: Peterson P L, Wilkinson L C, Hallinan M (eds.) 1984 *The Social Context of Instruction*. Academic Press, Orlando, Florida

Further Reading

Barr R, Dreeben R 1983 *How Schools Work*. University of Chicago Press, Chicago, Illinois
Peterson P L, Wilkinson L C, Hallinan M (eds.) 1984 *The Social Context of Instruction*. Academic Press, Orlando, Florida
Wilkinson L C, Marrett C B (eds.) 1985 *Gender Influences in Classroom Interaction*. Academic Press, Orlando, Florida

Social, Cultural, and Economic Factors Affecting Curriculum

M. Skilbeck

In a very general sense, the school curriculum may be thought of as a map or chart of organized knowledge and experience, through whose systematic study the student is expected to learn efficiently and to apply that learning in life situations. From a social standpoint, this map or chart of experiences serves as an orderly introduction to the culture, a means whereby the student is drawn into major forms and modes of thought and experience and learns to use them—in however limited a fashion—creatively and practically as well as cognitively. These are, of course, idealized notions since, in practice, the curriculum is subject to pressures and forces which both produce imbalances and sharpen up or place in focus particular themes, issues, or aspects of contemporary life. The breadth, balance, and cohesion of the curriculum, which are commonly set as educational ideals and goals, may thereby be impaired.

How sociocultural pressures and forces affect the curriculum has been the subject of intensive investigation in many countries. Insight has been gained into the manner in which the curriculum changes in its social context, and how in practice the curriculum facilitates or inhibits the achievement of such social values as equality and mobility. Experience has been gained in ways of organizing large-scale curriculum change aimed at keeping it topical and relevant, yet there are still large gaps in understanding, and little agreement over certain key issues.

Educational theorists are divided on the question of whether the school curriculum is or can be other than a social artifact, a rather flat image, or a reflection of prevailing social values, serving dominant interest groups (reproductive), or whether, as some radical commentators assert, it is capable of sponsoring and fostering significant social and cultural change (reconstructive). There is little disagreement, however, over the extent and complexity of sociocultural factors that need to be taken into account in explaining how the curriculum relates to the sociocultural context and defining ways to change its direction and its effect on learning.

In all countries, social expectations of schooling, of further and higher education, and hence of the curriculum, are high and generally rising. Students are expected to acquire the foundations of general knowledge and ways of applying that knowledge. The curriculum is also expected to be responsive to the changing needs of the economy, especially the labor market; to equip students with transferable competences; to prepare them to meet an uncertain future; to impart civic knowledge and values; and to enable students to respond positively to trends in contemporary society as diverse as consumerism, environmentalism, and technological evolution. It is no longer possible to treat the curriculum of any educational institution as if it exists in isolation from a wider community or separate from the society from which it draws its students, teachers, and the resources needed to sustain it. What the curriculum thereby gains in relevance from such linkages, however, it is in danger of losing in form and depth. Responsiveness to an ever wider range of social factors has meant overcrowding and superficiality with consequent efforts to define the curriculum in terms of essential core learnings. While retaining openness and flexibility in the face of social and economic demand, educators must ensure that the broader claims of human personality, knowledge, and understanding are met.

1. Curriculum Exposed to Economic Forces

A common assumption among several schools of social theorists, ranging from Marxists and neo-Marxists to advocates of a market approach, is that the school curriculum either is, or can be made to be, directly responsive to forces and trends in the economy. Sometimes this point is generalized from the economy to a wider set of features of social structure, notably the interests of particular social classes or occupational groups, or specific value sets such as those associated with religious beliefs. In all such cases, the curriculum is viewed instrumentally, as a means to some ends that may or may not coincide with the developmental needs and interests of the learner (see *Neo-Marxist Approaches to Curriculum*).

From an analytic standpoint, the workings of the economy have come into greater prominence in curriculum planning and design since the early 1960s than at any previous time in history. This is true of both the developed Western economies and the developing world, where the uses of education for economic advancement have for long been actively explored by national governments and aid and development agencies as well as by educational interest groups.

The key to explaining curriculum trends, for all of these schools of thought, is to be found in the dynamics of the economy in interaction with traditional beliefs, prevailing values, and customary practices in educational institutions. These dynamics and interactions profoundly influence what institutions teach and what they give priority to, who attends them, for how long, and with what measure of success: curriculum equates with economic substructure by responding to its demands. This form of economic determinism minimizes or tends to discount the significance either of pedagogically inspired reform or of broadly based national policies which attempt to determine the curriculum according to the needs and interests of a wide array of social groups. It is most evident in specialized training programs closely tied to labor market needs, but has a growing importance through efforts to vocationalize schooling to the extent of building a dimension of preparation for working life into the curriculum of general education.

While many economists criticize the traditionalism and inflexibility they find in schooling, they see the curriculum, nevertheless, as a potentially important instrument for achieving economic ends. The human capital theorists of the late 1950s and 1960s envisaged investment in education as a factor in economic development; sociologists, at the same time, sought to redress major social inequalities through curriculum and other school structures and processes designed to improve participation levels and success rates of students who would otherwise be likely to drop out of school. Labor market economists and vocational educators have sought to raise the status and improve the quality of both general and vocationally geared education through curricular reforms, linking education and working life. Most recently, economists subscribing to "new growth" theories have returned to the argument that a concentration of reform effort and resources on schooling will pay substantial dividends in further economic growth.

In all of these movements, either implicit or explicit criticisms are made of school curricula on the grounds that their distinctive features and relationships to changing socioeconomic needs show a remarkable stability and resistance to fundamental change. In the secondary school, for example, neither new subject matter nor orientations such as environmental and health education, new information technology, work experience, nor new pedagogies based on self-managed learning, project methods, and the breakdown of the age-based class group have been successful in dislodging the traditional subjects or academic disciplines, their associated instructional methods, and the ways they are examined. In higher and further education, a similar stability is to be observed although new subject matter and new kinds of vocationally oriented institutions have emerged in response to labor market needs. Such institutions are a demonstration of the tendency of students to abandon forms of education that do not suit them or to follow options which seem most useful to them.

Economic pressure on the curriculum at all levels has grown markedly in countries experiencing faltering growth or decline. It is most visible in the demand for curricula that better equip students for the labor market, a paradox in face of the disappearing youth labor market especially in the industrialized countries. More thoughtful commentators are assessing the need for a renewed emphasis on general education throughout the years of compulsory schooling and into further and higher education, but with close attention in curriculum planning to such strategic issues as longer term trends in adult employment, education for leisure, for diverse adult roles, for citizenship, and for the increasing globalization of national life. Above all, the argument is for curriculum that fosters interest in and capacity for sustained learning and the application of knowledge, in changing work environments. From this, it is argued by some economists that people acquire an enhanced capacity to choose and select from the many options available in social and economic life.

Whether the position of economic commentators is deterministic in the sense that the curriculum is treated as a function of underlying economic values and trends, or voluntaristic, in the sense that educationalists are being urged to restructure the curriculum to address changing economic values and conditions, it is still economic processes that are operative. The curriculum is, accordingly, perceived instrumentally rather than in terms that suggest either intrinsic educational or broadly cultural considerations. The inadequacy of this view is its inattention to the diversity of sociocultural forces and their interactions, the reluctance to consider philosophical and cultural analyses which treat education and the curriculum as themselves actually or potentially being key factors in the society, and the scant attention given to the developmental needs and interests of the student as individual and future citizen. The economic approaches risk being reductionist in their treatment of culture and curriculum.

Given the scale and historically upward trend of public investment in education, and the force of the "education as investment" argument, it is to be expected that an economic critique of the curriculum would give rise to political concern followed by action. There is evidence of this in many parts of the world. In developing countries, belief in the economic as well as the wider social returns of educational investment has remained strong, if not uniformly so. In industrialized societies, the function of schooling as an agency of social and labor market placement has been questioned by empirical investigators, and more recently, through the impact of growing unemployment among youth who have completed several years of secondary schooling. The political response has been to call for accountability measures to encourage a more utilitarian approach to the curriculum, to reduce the rate of increase of educational expenditure, and to give support to those educational innovations which appear to point the way towards enhanced practical skills at the expense of a more broadly based general education. These responses are not always well focused or sufficiently strategic, given the difficulty of matching educational policy (long-term) to the shorter term fluctuations of the business cycle and labor markets. However, they do reflect community concerns, a growing public skepticism about the quality of education including those innovations in curriculum that have called into question many traditional practices. A further consequence for the curriculum has been a strengthening, in several countries, of public examinations and formal assessment procedures, a call for improved standards and their incorporation in straightforward credentials.

2. Responses to Population Shifts

The effect of demographic movements combines with economic trends and economically inspired critiques in several different ways. Where rates of population increase are declining or stable, governments experiencing economic difficulties are inclined to reduce the flow of resources into education, thus disregarding teacher union pressure for improved staffing ratios and better facilities. Major imbalances and uncertainties for the curriculum can result: declining enrollments in secondary schools, accompanied by cuts in staffing, make the delivery of certain kinds of curricula impossible. Reductions in funds for materials and texts prevent schools from updating their learning resources. Where population continues to increase in developing countries, governments struggle, as they have done for decades, to provide a basic minimum curriculum for those in schools, and are unable to prevent overall increases in the number of illiterates even where they effect percentage improvements. The problems for developing countries have been intensified by oil price increases, heavy loan debts, and recession in major Western markets. Another demographic consideration, in developed and developing countries alike, is that improvements in health care, nutrition, housing and working conditions, combined with birth rate trends, are resulting in massive increases in numbers of older people: the need for curricula for lifelong education is not a distant dream but a rapidly emerging reality.

A factor in population movements which is having a profound influence on the curriculum in many countries is the movement of ethnic and cultural groups across national boundaries. Immigrant workers in Europe and the Americas, sponsored immigration in Australia and Israel, refugees in Southeast Asia and in Central and Southern Europe, migration flows around the Mediterranean, and cultural regrouping in Africa are examples of a massive worldwide change in the ethnic and cultural components of the populations of nation states. They give rise to new pressures for and ways of teaching mother tongue and national languages and multicultural themes across the curriculum. Inequalities imposed by dominant group influence in the curriculum, and sheer pressure of space and resources are among the problems to be addressed.

3. Traditional Education and Changing Sociocultural Values

The most powerful of all curriculum traditions is the persistence of textbook-structured learning in support of separate subjects, a procedure attractive to parents and teachers, if not always to pupils. Mastery of the text is the single most important goal in education practice. This tradition derives from ancient religious practices and values in both Eastern and Western societies: all the major world religions lay emphasis on the mystical significance of sacred texts and on the need for detailed knowledge of them.

Strengthened by the impact of professionalization in society and the consequent interest of the commercial and manufacturing bourgeoisie in formal schooling, and by its attractiveness as a low-cost tool for effective mass learning, the subject text has gained the assent of all occupational groups and social classes. The text symbolizes a received and bookish character in learning and even where the curriculum has been castigated for its irrelevance, exclusiveness, and neglect of the practical and the everyday, that character has persisted. In the minds of many, the text is the curriculum.

In the 1990s, two sociocultural factors offer an increasing challenge to the book domination of learning and, more generally, to the dominance of the academic curriculum: electronic media and the drive towards vocational, trade, and practical skills training. The challenge is directed toward the assumptions that sharply differentiated subject matter—derived from a small set of cognitive subjects such as language, mathematics, history, and science, and from their codification within texts of received knowledge—is the principal base and means of learning. The social changes underlying the challenge include the widespread displacement of labor and structural unemployment, technological evolution, the growth of leisure industries, and the emergence of mass society on a world scale.

There is growing dissatisfaction with the performance and potential of the academic curriculum as a means for mass education. Television, where it is well-established, offers a challenge to the classroom as a focus of attention and a source of information; family and peer group experiences are more basic sources of social and moral values than the school. Work and life experience can provide the raw material for education and training. Increasingly, it is suggested that formal schooling is less the means of upward social mobility in the mass than in the elite society and for the older age group. Work experience, travel, television, and leisure pursuits vie with formal education as a means of learning through experience.

These challenges to, and dissatisfaction with, educational institutions notwithstanding, it is still to them that the public turn for solutions to the "values crisis."

That crisis is seldom articulated into a cogent and coherent strategy and direction of curriculum reform. Is education a preparation for life as it is, or as it might be? Whose values should permeate the curriculum and how are values best taught? There are contradictions and underlying tensions within the concept of curriculum "relevance" that create great problems for educators. On the one hand, relevance equates with curriculum that meets the economic goals and needs of society. On the other, the consequences of economic growth, such as consumerism, urbanism, and the environmental effects of the exploitation of resources, are regarded as subject matter for a kind of moral remediation by schools. Into this confused and contradictory territory, different groups have moved. Some advocate dogmatic, anti-intellectual and authoritarian value systems which challenge many of the presuppositions and procedures of social democracy; others, of a progressive tendency, are searching for a new social ethic which fosters creative ways of addressing major social issues.

4. A Sociocultural Critique of Curriculum

What is needed, if curricula are not to be weighted down by unmanageable bodies of subject matter and to become the prey of pressure groups and lobbies, is a reappraisal of the social purposes and functions of education in an era of universal schooling which extends through the years of childhood and adolescence and, increasingly, into early adulthood. First there must be a critique and, second, the setting of new directions.

Essentially, the social critique of school curricula takes the form that education in schools and colleges is, in aggregate, a high-cost activity and a heavy charge on public funds. To be justified, this cost must lead to substantial returns, including the preparation of all students for active social life, a high level of public satisfaction with the results of schooling, and a visible responsiveness of curricula to changes in the wider sociocultural environment. Yet the education system in practice seems to give high status to certain kinds of academic knowledge and ways of learning and to confer relative advantage on the minority who perform well in this curriculum. Thus it reinforces the social and economic advantage enjoyed by the more prosperous and socially powerful sections of the population and at the same time, does too little in response to the needs of all students, and the requirements of the economy and society in a state of flux. Access to knowledge via the academic curriculum is not in practice equally available to all, nor is that knowledge, as structured into separate disciplines, sufficient as a preparation for effective social participation. At the same time, this emphasis and status, by spreading into the curriculum of all students, creates a mismatch

between social, economic, and cultural need, personal development, and learning tasks.

The school curriculum, furthermore, is overloaded with information and dominated by mental processes which correspond poorly with the large social and cultural transformations that the world is undergoing. In order to train groups of specialists to operate the modern economy and provide citizens with the rudiments of general social education and personal life skills, an elaborate and expensive system has to be maintained. Yet such indicators as illiteracy rates and levels of practical social efficiency suggest that schooling is making little progress relative to factors such as population growth, structural changes in the economy, information technology, and the growth of communications media and leisure opportunities. It is social change itself that has rendered invalid the structuring of knowledge and experience through the academic curriculum and its delivery via the formal agency of schooling.

The critique draws attention to other social issues and trends to which the curriculum of educational institutions is felt to be insufficiently responsive. Discrimination against particular races and against economically less favored sectors of the population was one of the bases for the equality of opportunity movement; sex bias has been argued as a reason for changing the approach taken in teaching certain subjects, especially mathematics and the sciences, in schools, and for introducing new feminist courses and programs in higher and further education. While such curricula have gained ground, they have by no means displaced confidence in the conventional curriculum, as modified through updating of content and adjustments within the component subjects. The impact of the critique, and of the sociocultural factors in which it is grounded, is to be observed in research studies, in developments in curriculum theory, and in such practical changes as—in the developed countries—the upsurge of instrumentalist, practical, and skills-based courses and—in the developing world—the growth of administrative and political interest in recurrent or lifelong education, adult learning by informal means, and mass applications of communications technology.

5. Curriculum for Development: Human, Social, and Economic

Policies for curriculum reform and development projects have been set in motion to assist schools in their adaptation to social and economic change and in response to specific weaknesses or problems in society. These policies and projects are as much social and political as pedagogical in their intent. From the perspective of most developing countries, where exceptional population pressures combine with poverty to make even universal primary schooling an unattainable goal, the issue is the relationship of curriculum to declared targets of nation building. Inheritance of curriculum assumptions from colonial powers has been a major influence even where new national goals and development targets call into question the continuing relevance of the inheritance. "Curriculum for development" has been the theme of major regional programs of educational cooperation, for example, UNESCO'S Asian Program of Educational Innovation for Development. One of the outcomes of this program is regional collaboration in curriculum review and the quest for curricula that are more obviously relevant to contemporary life than are those inherited from the past. Development is seen as dynamic and open-ended, and new curricula for development are needed to replace those which derive from another kind of past. Another kind of regional program is the Pacific Circle Consortium of the Organisation for Economic Co-operation and Development (OECD), a group of institutions and government bodies which cooperate in curricular development aimed at strengthening Pacific regional knowledge and a sense of community.

From the perspective of developed countries, the impact of social, economic, and technological change upon the curriculum has meant that there have been many attempts to transform content in existing subject areas (the curriculum project movement centering on the United States and the United Kingdom in the 1960s, and spreading to many countries in the 1970s), and more radical schemes for rebuilding the whole curriculum in order to respond to the kinds of criticism already noted. Despite the criticism and research evidence (sometimes contradictory) on the perceived value and performance of school curricula, the changes in most of these countries have been slow and evolutionary, rather than dramatic.

The curriculum of the school has a remarkable resistance to those social and cultural factors which seem to call for or imply substantial institutional adjustments, and a receptivity toward those factors which seem to reinforce existing values and practices. It is for this reason that many who accept that the school curriculum is a significant determinant of learning and of life chances are doubtful about the reconstructionist argument that the curriculum itself should be a major force for social and cultural change. Despite this skepticism, and the intellectual popularity of neo-Marxist claims that the essential social function of the school curriculum is to reproduce the cultural order of the dominant classes in society and to ensure mass acquiescence in this state of affairs, the reconstructionist position has not been abandoned. It first gained prominence in the early twentieth-century writings of Dewey (e.g., Dewey 1916) and among his United States followers, notably Counts (1932), in the depression of the 1930s, and was also an early dimension of communist educational theory

in the Soviet Union in the 1920s. Reconstructionism has re-emerged in the context of postcolonial nation building; it is also linked with the new growth theories in economics and in face of the challenges of extended universal education is likely, once again, to become a major force in curriculum theory and in policy analysis.

Reversing the usual sociological interpretation of the curriculum as the mediator and transmitter of existing culture, the reconstructionist claim is that a radically transformed curriculum may be a major means of renewing that culture both by encouraging in students a critique of it and providing them with intellectual and practical resources for shaping the future. Such an approach would acknowledge the need for improved and more equal opportunities for personal development and incorporate the highest ideals and standards of life, as they have evolved in the experiences of different societies worldwide.

In practice, for reasons given above, the curriculum seldom lives up to the reconstructionist expectations. There are some changes, however. The continuing impact on the curriculum of technological change, of shifts of populations across national boundaries and hence the multiculturalism of schooling, and other social and cultural factors, are seen by some as evidence of the adaptability of schooling and the capacity of educators to adjust. An example of such adaptability is the "Europeanization" movement among member countries of the European Community, whereby a European as distinct from the traditional nationalist bias is being incorporated into school curriculum. Another is the effort being made in many previously decentralized education systems to introduce national core curricula and standards of attainment as targets for all schools.

The success or otherwise of such attempts will provide evidence on whether schooling is able to continue to be socially responsive through curriculum evolution. Responsiveness is not the same as mechanical adaptation or subservience. Educators must continue to find ways of maintaining the openness and flexibility of curricula, and their receptivity to changing needs in the economy and society, while at the same time satisfying the broader claims of human development, requirements for the growth of knowledge, and the fostering of understanding in all of the main fields of human endeavor.

See also: Curriculum: Sociological Perspectives; Feminist Approaches to the Curriculum

References

Counts G S 1932 *Dare the School Build a New Social Order?* John Day, New York
Dewey J 1916 *Democracy and Education: An Introduction to the Philosophy of Education.* Free Press, New York

Further Reading

Apple M W (ed.) 1982 *Cultural and Economic Production in Education: Essays on Class, Ideology and the State.* Routledge and Kegan Paul, London

Australia Ministry for Employment, Education and Training 1988 *Strengthening Australia's Schools.* Australian Government Publishing Service, Canberra

Bernstein B 1990 *The Structuring of Pedagogic Discourse: Class, Codes and Control*, Vol. 4. Routledge, Chapman and Hall, New York

Bowles S, Gintis H 1977 *Schooling in Capitalist America: Educational Reform and the Contradictions of Economic Life.* Basic Books, New York

Callahan R 1962 *Education and the Cult of Efficiency.* University of Chicago Press, Chicago, Illinois

Dewey J 1957 *Reconstruction in Philosophy.* Beacon Press, New York

Habermas J 1971 *Knowledge and Human Interests.* Beacon Press, Boston, Massachusetts

Lawton D 1980 *The Politics of the School Curriculum.* Routledge and Kegan Paul, London

MacPherson C B 1964 *The Political Theory of Possessive Individualism: Hobbes to Locke.* Clarendon Press, Oxford

Organisation for Economic Co-operation and Development 1988 *Structural Adjustment and Economic Performance.* OECD, Paris

Organisation for Economic Co-operation and Development 1989 *Education and the Economy in a Changing Society.* OECD, Paris

Rawls J 1971 *A Theory of Justice.* Harvard University Press, Cambridge, Massachusetts

Ravitch D 1977 *The Revisionists Revised: A Critique of the Radical Attack on the Schools.* Ventura Hall, Stanford, California

Schulz T W 1981 *Investing in People. The Economics of Population Quality.* University of California Press, Berkeley, California

UNESCO 1991 *World Education Report.* UNESCO, Paris

Wexler P 1987 *Social Analysis of Education.* Routledge, New York

Worth A G 1983 *Productive Work in Industry and Schools: Becoming Persons Again.* University Press of America, Lanham, Maryland

(b) Acquiring Attitudes, Values, and Skills

Acquiring Attitudes and Values

F. K. Oser

In her book *A Philosophy of Morals*, Heller (1990) included a chapter on how to live an honest life. She adopted the distinction (and then criticized its limits) between the moralist and the moral philosopher, the former analyzing a given moral situation or language, the latter describing, in a teleological sense, how morality should be achieved. She then outlined the "decent person," who needs both value description and normativity in the field of values. The decent person expresses values by facing moral dilemmas, even against their own will, by living a norm-oriented life, and by realizing an existential decision to strive for the good. Decent people set their value standards, express values in their social interactions, and sense a kind of necessity in conforming to values.

Heller's distinction resembles the situation in value education. Whereas sociologists have theories about the origins of general changes in value orientations (including generational effects; e.g., Inglehart 1977), educational psychologists discuss in which directions change should go and what conditions are required for the transformation of an individual value structure. Whereas in many sociological studies, including poll-type and secondary statistical inquiries, values are defined by a more or less determined approval of some action, person, object, norm, rule, or system, and these analyses can reveal to what degree certain values, including moral values, are shared by a society or on some subcultural level, educational psychology is more interested in inner mechanisms of acquisition and change.

1. Two Psychological Approaches to Value Acquisition

The issue of value acquisition and change has been addressed by two major theoretical approaches: social learning theory and cognitive developmentalism. In social learning theory, the focus is on learning: external influences lead to reactions of a cognitive, emotional, and behavioral nature, which in turn contribute to a person's total repertoire of capacities and the willingness to perform value-based actions in the social, moral, or aesthetic domain (e.g., Mischel and Mischel

1976). The structuralist tradition of cognitive–developmental psychology emphasizes not learning but construction. It is suggested that the understanding of values and the significance given to them are strongly dependent on active processes of construction and reconstruction of normative features of reality, which in turn always start from given levels of social understanding and sociomoral reasoning competence. According to this line of thought, understanding is not a matter of transmission of factual knowledge but a product of active reflection of experience in the interpersonal sphere. If values are to become properly integrated within a person, he or she needs experiences in solving value conflicts, in participating in a value-oriented (particularly moral) discourse, and involvement in deliberate attempts at establishing normative rule systems on an interpersonal or group level (e.g., Kohlberg 1985).

Various structural theories have attempted to describe and explain developmental change in different domains of cognitive understanding and reasoning that all have some value dimension. Against the background of Piaget's and Baldwin's theories, stage schemes have been suggested by Kohlberg for the development of moral judgment competence, by Selman, Damon, Turiel, Youniss, and others for the domain of social understanding (including, e.g., the understanding of friendship), by Loevinger, Kegan, Noam, and others for the domain of self-development, and by Oser and Fowler for the domain of religious judgment and faith. This has led to a distinction between different types of values. Philosophers and lay people distinguish between moral and nonmoral (e.g., aesthetic) values, the latter being characterized by the fact that subscribing to one or other value is of only personal rather than social or societal relevance. One major feature of moral values is their universal existence and justifiability. This marks a crucial difference from many other types of values, such as aesthetic, political, work-oriented, cultural, or religious values, which are all to a much higher degree multifaceted and context-related. Children as young as 3 or 4 years of age can distinguish between social–conventional and moral values, the first being arbitrary and a matter of social agreement, the second being perceived as unimpeachable in their validity (Turiel 1983).

2. The Interplay of Factors

While the two streams of thought mentioned so far used to be treated as opposites, it can be argued that their propositions must not be considered controversial (Gibbs and Schnell 1985). Social learning theory and research programs informed by this line of thought (e.g., most social psychological studies of prosocial behavior) start with overt behavioral stimuli and observe overt reactions; the focus of description is on interindividual differences under specific contextual conditions. Cognitive developmentalism, with its focus on structure, starts with the individual and with the person's internal modes of meaning-making and motivation; the focus is on covert competences of information processing ("the reason behind the reason given") and on interindividual similarities at universal developmental levels. In theory and research, and especially in terms of pedagogical implications, an interplay of both approaches with their ability to explain different aspects of the processes of values learning and change could be fruitful. One empirical example may illustrate this interplay and the processes that are in need of further clarification.

In an intervention study, Oser and Schlaefli (1985) attempted to influence the personal value hierarchies of apprentices. As means of intervention they designed a course involving the clarification of values and highlighting their significance (all this in accordance to social learning theory). They also sought to bring out moral dilemmas and conflicts between values in role-play situations and discussions. Results showed a general change in value hierarchies from a more hedonistic or materialist orientation (characterized by concern for salary and pleasure in sports and leisure time) to concern for more fundamental, interpersonal, or idealistic values such as health, family, self-confidence, and freedom. These changes remained relatively stable in follow-up testing after six months. The six most highly ranked values (in order of decreasing significance: love, friendship, health, tolerance, success in the profession, family) remained the same; yet interestingly, the following two values (freedom and self-confidence) were replaced by values of a more materialistic nature: money and travel.

Referring back to the two major theoretical approaches outlined above, it can be assumed that both environmental factors and processes of active reconstruction of values and their meaning play a role in this ordering and reordering of personal value hierarchies.

Cherishing a value and being ready to express it publicly thus presupposes an experiential awareness of its significance—something that can certainly be supported and encouraged by social models, by the experience that the value is ascribed high significance in a reference group, and by vivid forms of instruction. On the other hand, a full understanding of certain values, particularly immaterial values, and the ability to check their respective importance in cases of value conflicts require cognitive capacities that cannot simply be taught but, rather, must be constructed in a stepwise sequence. The meaning of the notion "freedom," for example, undergoes dramatic changes when the sociomoral perspective becomes broader (and begins to include a conception of the interdependency of human beings in groups and society), when moral thought adopts logical and social reciprocity as a leading principle in the solution of moral conflict, when the understanding of psychological processes allows the individual to understand that vulnerability exists not only on a physical level, and when experience has made clear that freedom is a highly complex political category interpreted in different ways by different people.

3. Attitudes versus Values

What about attitudes? An attitude, it has been proposed (e.g., by McGuire), is a response locating an object of thought along some dimension of judgment. Unlike the first attitude concepts (e.g., those of Allport 1935), attitudes are now usually thought of as: (a) systems with structures, including relationships within one attitude between several objects, relationships between several attitudes with regard to the same object; and (b) belief systems, that is, those involving relationships between several attitudes without necessarily referring to one single object. These systems, in turn, are in specific relationships to other personal subsytems, including affect and behavior. The inclusion of the latter makes up what is usually referred to as the "tripartite definition" of attitude: cognitive, affective, and conative.

This systems or structural approach has some resemblance to the approach used to analyze value systems, which also deal with evaluative or value judgments. The concepts of attitude and value are highly interconnected (see Tesser and Shaffer 1990 p. 488); because the concept of value is broader than the concept of attitude, values have sometimes been seen as "causing" attitudes (Rokeach 1968). For instance, everyday problems typically involve coping with dilemmas, that is, situations characterized by the presence of opposing values (Billing et al. 1988), which leads to more complex attitude or belief systems (Tetlock 1986).

Comparing the tripartite conception of attitudes to what has been said above about value systems, it turns out that attitude systems and value systems have the same structure and must be measured in similar ways. If people are said to have particular values and particular attitudes, then it is probably accepted that both are similar and have been similarly influenced. Applying the principles presented above means, then, that to change a moral attitude one can change a set of moral values, which can be done through desequilibration of people's value structure, by evaluative judgments, by "consider the opposite" techniques, or by participation and role-taking exercises (see Klauer 1991).

Knowledge transformation is only a necessary, not a sufficient condition, for attitude and value change.

4. Central Issues in Value and Attitude Education

When focusing the issue of values and attitudes acquisition on the question of how they are acquired, particular conditions of moral learning have to be addressed. Five topics seem to be of crucial importance.

First is the issue of indoctrination versus value relativism. Indoctrinative approaches hold that strong normative standpoints have to be considered necessary for societal stability and are transmitted by means of example, persuasion, or authority. Relativistic approaches reject the possibility of justifying universal criteria and emphasize the contextuality of values.

The second issue is the autonomy of persons with respect to moral norms. This refers, in philosophical terms, to the issue of freedom and determination; in psychological terms, the discussion refers to the question of whether the growing person is a passive recipient of influences or plays an active, (re)constructive role in development.

Third is the issue of defining the goals of moral education. Reflection of concrete values and value priorities, attitudes, and attitude priorities, and the demands of living up to personal, (sub)cultural, and societal standards are only formally consensual dimensions of various programs in value and moral education. The understanding of goals—as well as of appropriate educational means—differs heavily from one approach to the other (see Hersh et al. 1980).

The fourth issue is the inner mechanisms of moral learning. These have to be distinguished from the learning of attitudes that are much more open to change.

Finally, there is the issue of content and specificity of concrete values emphasized by the subject, given a specific age, context, and particular situational and cultural conditions. There are two positions concerning contextuality: (a) one in which knowledge handling as such is, in terms of orientations manifested in actions, rather irrelevant, as has been shown in many studies since the classical investigation of Hartshorne and May (1928); (b) one in which real-life moral decision-making is believed to be always embedded in a specific reality which creates sex differences with respect of the content (not the stages) and the orientation (justice vs. care) of a moral decision. New research shows also that cultural differences are larger than psychologists in general assume.

Much more research still needs to be done. It is not known how knowledge handling and structural competence are related, nor how experienced events lead to different value conceptions. Also unknown are the absolute conditions for optimal age-related development to a cognitive and performative structural level.

From a structural point of view there is no single value that can be induced by education; it always transmits a balance of contradictory values. Therefore the sociological approach in which a subject is asked about one value at a time is unhelpful for educational matters. Anyone can express a view about a value in general, but then act against the view in a conflict situation. We may all oppose stealing, but how would we react when confronted by the situation where a man has to steal to save his wife's life (Kohlberg 1984)? Thus, reconciling different theories must in future deal with many more different sources of our subjective value judgment.

A holistic approach of acquiring values and attitudes that comprehends both mentioned theoretical methods is the so-called Just Community approach. Students and teachers learn to decide on school matters in a democratic procedure which enables them to build up a highly shared value system (see Power et al. 1989). This value system is more stable than any other form of value reflection, value clarification, or value arousal. The problem with such a holistic concept is how to measure success. In the future, educational researchers must give more attention to Heller's "decent person" and to what she calls the "moralist position."

See also: Aspirations and Expectations of Students; Development of Achievement Motivation; Social Psychological Theories in Education

References

Allport G W 1935 Attitudes. In: Murchison C (ed.) 1935 *A Handbook of Social Psychology.* Clark University Press, Worcester, Massachusetts

Billing M et al. (eds.) 1988 *Ideological Dilemmas: A Social Psychology of Everyday Thinking,* 2nd edn. Sage, London

Gibbs J, Schnell S V 1985 Moral development "versus" socialization: A critique. *Am. Psychol.* 40(10): 1071–80

Hartshorne H, May M A 1928 *Studies in Deceit. Studies in the Nature of Character,* Vol. 1 Macmillan, New York

Heller A 1990 *A Philosophy of Morals.* Blackwell, Oxford

Hersh R H, Miller J P, Fielding G D 1980 *Models of Moral Education: An Appraisal.* Longman, New York

Inglehart R 1977 *The Silent Revolution: Changing Values and Political Styles among Western Publics.* Princeton University Press, Princeton, New Jersey

Klauer K C 1991 *Einstellungen: Der Einfluß der affektiven Komponente auf das kognitive Urteil.* Hogrefe, Göttingen

Kohlberg L 1984 *Essays on Moral Development. Vol. 2: The Psychology of Moral Development, The Nature and Validity of Moral Stages.* Harper and Row, San Francisco, California

Kohlberg L 1985 The just community approach to moral education in theory and practice. In: Berkowitz M W, Oser F K (eds.) 1985 *Moral Education: Theory and Application.* Erlbaum, Hillsdale, New Jersey

Mischel W, Mischel H N 1976 A cognitive social-learning approach to morality and self-regulation. In: Lickona T (ed.) 1976 *Moral Development and Behavior: Theory, Research, and Social Issues.* Holt, Rinehart and Winston, New York

Oser F K, Schlaefli A 1985 But it does move: The difficulty

of gradual change in moral development. In: Berkowitz M W, Oser F K (eds.) 1985 *Moral Education: Theory and Application.* Erlbaum, Hillsdale, New Jersey

Power F C, Higgins A, Kohlberg L 1989 *Lawrence Kohlberg's Approach to Moral Education.* Columbia University Press, New York

Rokeach M 1968 *Beliefs, Attitudes, and Values: A Theory of Organizational Change.* Jossey-Bass, San Francisco, California

Tesser A, Shaffer D R 1990 Attitudes and attitude change. *Annu. Rev. Psychol.* 41: 479–523

Tetlock P E 1986 A value pluralism model of ideological reasoning. *J. Pers. Soc. Psychol.* 50(4): 819–27

Turiel E 1983 *The Development of Social Knowledge: Morality and Convention.* Cambridge University Press, Cambridge

Further Reading

Feather N T 1975 *Values in Education and Society.* Free Press, New York

Gergen K J 1982 *Toward Transformation in Social Knowledge.* Springer-Verlag, New York

Kohlberg L 1981 *Essays on Moral Development. Vol. 1: The Philosophy of Moral Development—Moral Stages and the Idea of Justice.* Harper and Row, San Francisco, California

Modgil S, Modgil C (eds.) 1986 *Lawrence Kohlberg: Consensus and Controversy.* Falmer Press, Philadelphia, Pennsylvania

Oser F, Althof W 1992 *Moralische Selbstbestimmung: Modelle der Entwicklung und Erziehung im Wertebereich. Ein Lehrbuch.* Klett-Cotta, Stuttgart

Acquisition of Empowerment Skills

R. Land and R. Gilbert

Education for empowerment has entered the lexicon of mainstream education through a confluence of several, often conflicting, uses in research and practice. Most commonly, education for empowerment aims to provide young people with the understanding, abilities, and commitments with which they can identify and act upon their interests. When this aim is applied to education for all, and hence to some notion of universal empowerment, it becomes the base for an emancipatory approach to education for justice, equality, and human rights. Empowerment has achieved paradigmatic status in curricular discussion, figuring in debates in gender, health, literacy, adult, special, political, community, and vocational education.

This popularity derives from renewed interest in the role of power as a key element of the social dynamic. As a result, the particular form of education recommended as empowering depends largely on the associated analysis of power. Four major variants are evident in the literature on empowerment through: (a) individual competence; (b) active citizenship; (c) critical consciousness; and (d) empowering difference.

This article considers each variant in turn. The first view focuses on enhanced individual behavior through increased control. The second locates such empowered behavior within social groups and institutions through the concept of active citizenship. The third locates empowerment at the interface between ideology and individual experience, as integral to the reconstruction and transformation of both subjectivity and social structures. Finally, an emphasis on the diversity of human experience and interest in particular contexts recommends a view which is always worked out anew as people form alliances and take action in real situations.

1. Empowerment Through Individual Competence

This variant of empowerment is based on what Burbules (1986 p. 96) calls the traditional theory of power, defined as "a property of *individual* persons, wielded *instrumentally* as a means to particular *intended* outcomes." At its simplest it is synonymous with ability or capacity, and can be found in the writings of Dewey and in the popular adage that "knowledge is power." From this viewpoint, usually bolstered by psychosocial and phenomenological theories, empowerment is used as an explanatory concept to describe a set of behaviors which can be observed or reported upon for individuals undergoing a planned training experience or change process. Typically, children, young people, and others, described as previously suffering from various forms of disengagement from "the system," are said to be "empowered" through such learning experiences.

In such contexts, an empowered person was held to be "someone who believed in his or her ability/capability to act, and this belief would be accompanied by able/capable action" (Ashcroft 1987 p. 143). A sense of efficacy was said to derive from a combination of increased confidence and competence, greater self-direction, and acceptance of responsibility for self through active engagement in tasks of meaning and relevance to the individual. People who were empowered to act in and on their social circumstances were usually contrasted with others, who were variously said to feel powerless, alienated, or dependent. Each of these contrasting constructs has a rich but contested literature of its own.

The construct which attempts to combine these ideas is the psychosocial construct "locus of control"

—that is, the individual's perceived sense of power in directing the course of her or his life. This construct has been particularly influential in the field of political socialization where it has been contrasted with "need theories" as an explanatory mechanism for various levels of observed political behavior among adolescents and young adults (Carmines 1980, Sigel and Hoskin 1981, Merelman and King 1986).

One major educational implication of such ideas is the concentration on individual change through training programs which focus on possible links between attitudes and behavior through the acquisition of skills. Burbules (1986) criticizes this approach to power for its neglect of the reciprocity of power relations (famously illustrated in Hegel's master–slave example) and of the institutionalization of power relations in social systems, a form which cannot be reduced to the idea of individuals having power over others. Since historically reproduced institutionalized power relations are not explicable as matters of conscious individual choice, changing individuals' beliefs about their personal capacities is unlikely to be sufficient to change power relations. It has been argued that such change requires participation in the formal democratic political process. This raises the second form in which empowerment has been addressed in education—the idea of citizenship.

2. Empowerment Through Active Citizenship

This view of empowerment derives from innovative but diverse approaches to mainstream social education/studies/sciences in several countries. Its rationale derives from liberal democratic theory and its educational heritage (especially from Dewey 1929), with its emphasis on informed and active citizens as the cornerstone of civilized life in democratic society.

In the United States the "new social studies" movement, drawing on the work of the influential Harvard educator, Bruner (1962), moved away from dependence on exposition and memorization to the hypothetical study of problems—past and present, both within the social science disciplines and within the society at large—as providing a more appropriate and relevant way to prepare citizens in a democracy who, by definition, are expected to be active citizens. This focus on active problem-solving related to public issues (Oliver and Shaver 1966, Oliver and Newmann 1967) has been revived as a "curriculum for democratic citizenship" (Engle and Ochoa 1986), with the following broad principles:

(a) It should confront students with important questions and problems for which answers are not readily available and without pressure for closure.

(b) Topics chosen should have the greatest potential for encouraging and supporting thinking and even controversy about an important social problem.

(c) Independent depth studies organized around important social questions, problems, and topics should be the dominant feature of curriculum organization.

(d) Such studies should use varied data drawn from history, a range of social sciences, literature and journalism—and, importantly, from student firsthand experience.

(e) The school should mirror such a democratic formal curriculum by offering a good example of respect for democracy, both in its governance through the involvement of students and in reasoned, intellectual honesty as integral to scholarship and teacher–student relationships.

In the United Kingdom the approach to empowerment education advocated by the Program for Political Education (Porter 1984) was that of "political literacy." It endorsed the following principles:

(a) Political literacy is a compound of knowledge, skills, and attitudes, to be developed together, with each influencing and affecting the other. Knowledge without appropriate opportunities for action is insufficient and often disabling. Unreflective or uninformed participation is often neither constructive, nor conducive to change, nor mindful of consequences.

(b) Alternative information, opinions, attitudes, and actions concerning political issues form the basis of this approach to political education. Pluralism of perspective is a feature of contemporary life in a democracy, and the political literacy approach advocates a positive, explicit, and inclusive incorporation of alternative views.

(c) Students come to classrooms with much political information, diverse attitudes and beliefs, and variable experience of the political in life. The particular role of the school is to help students handle this information in a critical way, to form and develop their own viewpoints, to appreciate those of others, and to provide some of the motivation, means, and experiences which allow them to participate effectively and responsibly.

(d) Political literacy in schools is not synonymous with studies of politics, government, or civics, although it should closely and directly affect these. It is also a more general framework which informs and is intended to help reform some of the content and methodology of the various human and social science subjects.

(e) The approach attempts to provide an integrated framework within which significant sociopolitical issues can be selected for detailed learning (Crick and Porter 1978).

In Australia, the Senate Standing Committee on Education, Employment and Training (1989, 1991) conducted a major public inquiry into Education for Active Citizenship defined in the following way:

> To be a citizen is to participate in the public practices which sustain, and to a large extent define, a community. These practices are integral to, yet discernible within, the complex of activities and values which constitute the culture of a community, and they relate to aspects of social organisation, legal, economic and other power relationships and the distribution of goods and services within that community. For the Committee, active citizenship implies a serious, reflective engagement with such community-defining public practices. (Senate Steering Committee 1991 p. 6)

This approach through active citizenship has two major elements. Like the first variant discussed above, active citizenship emphasizes individual belief and engagement as the means of empowerment, but goes beyond this to focus on the formal channels through which action can be achieved, and on the skills and understandings required to use them. The second element is the belief in the formal legal and political processes of democratic government as the framework within which empowerment operates. This latter emphasis has the benefit of being demonstrably applicable in the dominant formal institutions of power in the mass twentieth-century democracies. However, it often excludes a critique of these institutions themselves, and has been accused of legitimizing, rationalizing, and apologizing for them (Tapper and Salter 1978, Gilbert 1984). Given the criticisms of mass democracies as "elective autocracies" (Lucas 1976) dominated by the state, and "corporatist alliances among powerful interests" (Wolfe 1977), education for empowerment may be severely restricted if it uncritically accepts as its base individual access to existing legal and political channels.

If dominant forms of democratic governance are not unambiguously acting in the interests of all, and if their organizational structures restrict access and prevent people from pursuing legitimate interests, then education for empowerment requires an orientation which not only prepares young people to participate in present institutional processes, but also provides them with the critical insights and abilities to evaluate and, where desirable, to work to change them. Power then lies not only in using existing channels, but in taking control of one's circumstances to pursue legitimate interests. A third variant of education for empowerment addresses this issue.

3. Empowerment Through Critical Consciousness

This view of empowerment owes much to the work of the Brazilian community educator, Paulo Freire (1972, 1985). He focuses on empowerment through conscientization—critical reflection on the circumstances of lived experiences together with action. For Freire and Shor (1987), the purpose of education should be human liberation so that learners can be both subjects and actors in their own lives and as members of society. Freire advocates a three-step methodology for any educational program fostering empowerment:

(a) This requires active listening to clarify and understand the felt issues or major themes of community life.

(b) It involves participatory dialogue about the investigated issues where all members are equal colearners and where critical problem-solving allows participants to uncover root causes of their place in society—the socioeconomic, political, cultural, and historical context of their everyday lives.

(c) It also demands action by both community and individuals, directed towards positive changes envisaged during the dialogue which move participants beyond powerlessness to gain greater control over the course of their lives.

Freire's ideas and methodologies have been used in diverse fields, ranging across school language education (Hasan and Martin 1988), community health education (Wallerstein and Bernstein 1989), and tertiary women's studies (Middleton 1987). Giroux and others have sought to clarify the implications of Freire's work for education for empowerment, defined as "the process whereby students acquire the means to critically appropriate knowledge existing outside of their immediate experience in order to broaden their understanding of themselves, the world, and the possibilities for transforming the taken-for-granted assumptions about the way we live" (Giroux and McLaren 1986 p. 229). Not only does this approach recommend a critical analysis of present arrangements, its critique goes beyond the more conspicuous institutional sites of power in the political and legal systems. It involves a cultural politics including the critical study of power, language, mass and popular cultures, and history.

Vital to transformation and change is the role of critical consciousness, which "lays bare the historically and socially sedimented values at work in the construction of knowledge, social relations and material practices" (Giroux 1984 p. 323). Middleton (1987) documents the use of life-history analysis as a technique in a women's studies course to help empower students to learn to link biography, history, and social structure, to "use and interpret their own experiences in a manner which reveals how the latter have been shaped and influenced by the dominant culture" (Giroux 1981 p. 124). This critical approach must be combined with a positive program, symbolized in the idea of a pedagogy of possibility. Giroux and McLaren (1986) and Simon (1987) emphasize the need to develop a vision whereby the possibility for transformation can be identified, and to provide students with the chance to engage in dialogue where their own voices can be heard and their own identities interrogated and affirmed.

The use of Freire's work has been widespread and diverse. An emphasis on conscientization can lead to the individualism of the first variant of empowerment. The focus on participation and dialogue could be read in terms of conventional democratic channels, as in the second variant. The focus on a comprehensive critique of the participant's social circumstances, and the creation of transformative possibilities through dialogue is more faithful to Freire's scheme. Again, however, aspects of this approach have been criticized. In her challenge to the radical pedagogy of empowerment and possibility, Ellsworth (1989) claims that its arguments are abstract and decontextualized, that the reliance on public dialogue in educational institutions ignores the realities of unequal power which excludes some from the debate, and that the commitment to reason implies a set of universal ideals which in the past have not prevented oppression. In circumstances where the definition of what is rational and universal has been in the hands of powerful groups, the interests of marginalized groups have not been adequately acknowledged. Ellsworth's critique illustrates a trend in the analysis of power and consequent concepts of education for empowerment based on diverse sectional rather than universal interests, and on the multiple articulations of overlapping group interests rather than an idea of consensus or holistic transformation.

4. Empowering Difference

Ellsworth (1989) argues that the partial narratives of students cannot be made whole through dialogue supervised by the ideal rational person in the form of teacher, for all narratives are partial, and all teachers are implicated in the power structures which produce the marginalization of less powerful voices. Nor can the experience of student voice be authentically expressed in the unequal relationship of student to teacher, with its tenuously abstract connection with other contexts. Until educators address these issues in their own lives and work situations, education for empowerment will not succeed. In addition, this view emphasizes that empowerment in action cannot be an individual enterprise, but neither can it be based on an abstract consensus. It requires a personal relationship of trust and an identity built up in the experience of action itself, based on shared commitments but also on the recognition that people will always have "different stakes in, experiences of, and perspectives on" issues (Ellsworth 1989, p. 318). These differences are a caution against universal solutions, but are also a resource

to enrich the search for possibilities and strategies for change.

The emphasis on empowerment through the shared experience of political action on common interests is an important feature of contemporary analyses of power. Concepts of "life" or "identity" politics (Giddens 1991, Brunt 1989) endorse one aspect of this, where the personal becomes political in ways not previously possible in the judicial–administrative idea of institutional politics. Bonding people by their lived experience of injustice in diverse spheres, rather than by commitment to an abstract ideal, identity politics has proved particularly effective in the development of social movements in which people of similar cultural orientations and experiences form alliances to contest the management of the social organization of their lives (Touraine 1988).

The critique of universalism and reason and the emphasis on partial narratives and difference are features of poststructuralist and feminist concepts of power and responses to it. Foucault's open-textured concept of localized power relations supports the comprehensive view of the critical approach to empowerment, but calls into question any notion of universal ideals (Cousins and Hussain 1984). The feminist critique of rationality as masculinist argues against reason as the only criterion for understanding (Gunew 1990). The implications of such arguments for education for empowerment are difficult to identify for a number of reasons. They are new and yet to develop a record of practice; the poststructuralist strategy avoids explicitly recommending general solutions to decontextualized problems; and the literature is clearer about its guiding principles for practice rather than practices themselves. As a result they must be regarded as relatively untested.

However, notions of critical pragmatism (Cherryholmes 1988), feminist pedagogy (Maher 1987), or pedagogy of the unknowable (Ellsworth 1989) are useful guides to empowering difference. This fourth variant is an important reminder that empowerment cannot be developed in the abstract discourses and hierarchical relations of much contemporary schooling; that the concept of human interest must be identified in context rather than in universal ideals; and that the project of empowerment will never be complete, given the myriad and contradictory ways in which power relations are articulated with each other.

5. Conclusion

The role of education for empowerment is therefore critical, as it can provide (after Nyberg 1981 and Taylor 1989):

(a) knowledge about power and how it operates;

(b) access to relevant sources of information;

(c) processes of inference based on such information but directed to long-term goals;

(d) skills of controlling and using information to achieve the possible in current circumstances.

As Hicks points out, positive freedom is a necessary outcome of empowerment education: "we cannot claim that a particular kind of schooling is empowering just because it relieves certain forms of dependency and harm, without also asking how what is taught enables students to take their place as independent individuals within our society, capable of critically interpreting the relations of power in which they live" (Hicks 1990 pp. 40–41).

See also: Conscientization and Mobilization; Critical Theory and Education; Political Socialization and Education; Socialization

References

Ashcroft L 1987 Defusing "empowering": The what and the why. *Lang. Arts.* 64(2): 142–56

Bruner J 1962 *The Process of Education*. Harvard University Press, Cambridge, Massachusetts

Brunt R 1989 The politics of identity. In: Hall S, Jacques M (eds.) 1989 *New Times: Changing Face of Politics in the 1990s*. Lawrence and Wishart, New York

Burbules N 1986 A theory of power in education. *Educ. Theory* 36(2):95–114

Carmines E 1980 A competency theory versus need theory of political involvement. In: Kourvetaris G, Dobratz B (eds.) 1980 *Political Sociology: Reading in Research and Theory*. Transaction Books, New Brunswick, New Jersey

Cherryholmes C 1988 *Power and Criticism: Poststructural Investigations in Education*. Teachers College Press, New York

Cousins M, Hussain A 1984 *Michel Foucault*. Macmillan, London

Crick B, Porter A (eds.) 1978 *Political Education and Political Literacy*. Longman, London

Dewey J 1929 *Democracy and Education*. Macmillan, New York

Ellsworth E 1989 Why doesn't this feel empowering? Working through the repressive myths of critical pedagogy. *Harv. Educ. Rev.* 59(3): 297–324

Engle S, Ochoa A 1986 A curriculum for democratic citizenship. *Soc. Educ.* 50(7): 514–25

Freire P 1972 *Pedagogy of the Oppressed*. Penguin, Ringwood

Freire P 1985 *The Politics of Education*. Macmillan, London

Freire P, Shor I 1987 *A Pedagogy for Liberation*. Macmillan, London

Giddens A 1991 *Modernity and Self-Identity: Self and Society in the Late Modern Age*. Polity, Oxford

Gilbert R 1984 *The Impotent Image: Reflections of Ideology in the Secondary School Curriculum*. Falmer Press, London

Giroux H 1981 *Ideology, Culture and the Process of Schooling*. Falmer Press, London

Giroux H 1984 Ideology, agency and the process of schooling. In: Barton L, Walkers S (eds.) 1984 *Social Crisis and Educational Research*. Croom Helm, London

Giroux H, McLaren P 1986 Teacher education and the politics of engagement: The case for democratic schooling. *Harv. Educ. Rev.* 56(3): 213–38

Gunew S 1990 Feminist knowledge: Critique and construct. In: Gunew S (ed.) 1990 *Feminist Knowledge: Critique and Construct*. Routledge, London

Hasan R, Martin J (eds.) 1988 *Learning Language: Learning Culture*. Ablex Publishing Corporation, Norwood, New Jersey

Hicks L 1990 A feminist analysis of empowerment and community in art education. *Stud. Art Educ.* 32(1): 36–46

Lucas J 1976 *Democracy and Participation*. Penguin, Harmondsworth

Maher F 1987 Inquiry teaching and feminist pedagogy. *Soc. Educ.* 51(3): 186–92

Merelman R, King G 1986 The development of political activities: Toward a model of early learning. *Soc. Sci. Q.* 67(3): 473–90

Middelton S 1987 Feminist educators in a university setting: A case study in the politics of "educational" knowledge. *Discourse* 8(1): 25–47

Nyberg D 1981 *Power Over Power*. Cornell University Press, Ithaca, New York

Oliver D, Shaver J 1966 *Teaching Public Issues in the High School*. Houghton Mifflin, Boston, Massachusetts

Oliver D, Newmann F 1967 *The Public Issues Series/Harvard Social Studies Project*. American Education Publications, Middleton, Connecticut

Porter A (ed.) 1984 *Principles of Political Literacy*. University of London Institute of Education, London

Senate Standing Committee on Employment, Education and Training 1989 *Active Citizenship*. Parliament of the Commonwealth of Australia, Canberra

Senate Standing Committee on Employment, Education and Training 1991 *Active Citizenship Revisited*. Parliament of the Commonwealth of Australia, Canberra

Sigel R, Hoskin M 1981 *The Political Involvement of Adolescents*. Rutgers University Press, New Brunswick, New Jersey

Simon R 1987 Empowerment as a pedagogy of possibility. *Lang. Arts* 64(4): 370–82

Tapper T, Salter B 1978 *Education and the Political Order: Changing Patterns of Class Control*. Macmillan, London

Taylor S 1989 Empowering girls and young women: The challenge of the gender-inclusive curriculum. *J. Curric. St.* 21(5): 441–56

Touraine A 1988 *Return of the Actor: Social Theory in Postindustrial Society*. University of Minnesota Press, Minneapolis, Minnesota

Wallerstein N, Bernstein E 1989 Empowerment education: Friere's ideas adapted to health education. *Health Educ. Q.* 15(4): 379–94

Wolfe A 1977 *The Limits of Legitimacy: Political Contradictions of Contemporary Capitalism*. The Free Press, New York

Aspirations and Expectations of Students

L. J. Saha

The importance of social-psychological predispositions for behavior is widely recognized in the disciplines of psychology and sociology. These predispositions are generally treated under conceptual labels such as attitudes, values, or beliefs, and have been linked with a wide range of behaviors, such as child rearing, voting, and aspects of interpersonal behavior. One area which has been extensively studied is career ambitions and attainment.

Much research has been conducted on the educational and occupational ambitions of young people, and their influence on subsequent attainments. This body of research has included both the determinants and the consequences of ambitions. The relationship between these career predispositions and attainments has become an important part of the study of school-to-work transitions, and in sociology, studies of education and occupational status attainment and the determinants of social mobility.

This article focuses on a specific aspect of attitudes and behaviors, namely the career aspirations and expectations of secondary school students. The notion of career is taken to include both educational and occupational attainments. Since aspirations and expectations are related to attitudes, the entry first discusses attitudes, and the relationship between attitudes and behavior. The following sections then review the main issues and findings regarding the career aspirations and expectations of students, subsequent career attainments, and finally the policy implications arising from this research.

1. Attitudes and Behavior

1.1 Components of Attitudes

A major issue regarding attitudes is the extent to which they are related to subsequent behavior. In other words, is what people say they will do related to what they do? The empirical usefulness of the attitude construct and the measurement of attitudes is directly linked with their relationship to actual behavior. This is because attitudes are thought to consist of three components: the cognitive, the affective, and the conative. The cognitive component consists of the knowledge about the object of the attitude, or the properties attributed to the object. In addition to knowledge, attitudes also incorporate an affective component, that is, the extent to which the person likes or dislikes the object of the attitude. Finally, attitudes have a conative component which relates to intended behavior regarding an object.

1.2 Correspondence Between Attitudes and Behavior

There is no evidence to suggest that there should be a perfect correspondence between attitudes and behavior. The social-psychological literature documents correlations of between 0.30 and 0.60 for a wide range of attitudes and behaviors, with suggestions that in some circumstances the attitude–behavior link could be much lower. In fact, McGuire (1985) argues that rarely do attitudes account for more than 10 percent of variation in behavior.

There are a number of reasons why attitudes may not correlate highly with behavior. The first is what writers call pseudoinconsistency, or the possibility that statements of intention and actual behavior have different situational thresholds. A second difficulty in evaluating the relationship between attitudes and behavior is the setting of what should be considered a high correlation between the two. In other words, according to what criteria does one determine whether a correlation of 0.30 is high or low, or that 10 percent of variance explained is an indication of the power of attitudes to explain actual behavior?

There are other explanations for inconsistencies between behavioral intentions and actual behavior. Fishbein and Ajzen (1975) list the following: (a) the instability of intentions over time, (b) other competing intentions, (c) the absence of ability or skills, (d) the unavailability of alternate behaviors, (e) perceptions of what is proper behavior, (f) expected consequences of behavior, (g) unexpected events which prevent one from carrying out the behavior, and (h) the lack of control over the behavior in question.

Thus there are many reasons why the correlation between behavioral intentions and actual behavior is not perfect. Conversely, there is considerable evidence for intention–behavior similarity. This means that any intervention in changing attitudes will have some impact on actual behavior, or at least on the energy and effort expended in attempting to attain the object of the intentions.

2. Aspirations and Expectations as Attitudes

2.1 Aspirations and Expectations as Affective and Conative Components of Attitudes

Aspirations and expectations, as measured and analyzed in the social-psychological literature, are forms of attitude. This is especially the case with respect to educational and occupational aspirations and expectations. An educational or occupational aspiration or expectation designates a readiness to act toward the educational and occupational goals. However, aspiration can be defined as a reflection of what is thought to be socially desirable, while an expectation reflects what the person perceives as reasonable or likely as a goal, given the person's social position and understanding of the way that society operates.

2.2 Attitudes and Motivation

Thus there are a number of similar concepts which are often related to attitudes. Ambition and motivation are two such concepts. Research on educational performance and attainments has often identified ambition and motivation as general social-psychological dimensions which explain a significant portion of the variation in educational behavior. Although ambition and motivation tend to be general concepts, they are usually operationalized in terms of some future objective or objectives which are seen as desirable by students. Most often these general notions specifically focus on educational and occupational goals which the students, at least at the time, claim to strive toward. Turner (1964) argued that the concept of ambition is related to the achievement motive, and defined it as "a desire to abandon one social position and attain another." He did not relate ambition or motivation to attitudes.

Most research into ambition and motivation variables has tended to use single indicators such as plans, aspirations, goals, expectations, and so on. Less attention has been directed toward the possibility of multiple dimensions of ambition or motivation which not only measure the desirability of objectives, but also include an assessment of the likelihood that those objectives might be achieved.

These dispositions have been seen as operative, though with continual readjustment and compromise, throughout one's social life. They are also particularly relevant for understanding the school and postschool behavior of young people. Research has shown that at relatively early ages children begin to form attitudes and values toward a wide range of objects, including the government, political parties, jobs, and sex roles. Indeed, it has been suggested that children already begin to construct ideas about their future occupations, and that these can be seen as the beginnings of occupational identities (Hutchings 1996). Although the knowledge upon which these constructions are based may be naïve, immature, and unstable, they nevertheless form the basis upon which future dispositional development takes place.

The difficulty with most research on these predispositions is the failure accurately to conceptualize and operationalize the concepts in question. Thus ambition, motives, aspirations, and expectations are used, sometimes interchangeably, in research into student predispositions to future actions and attainments. This has been the case with research into career aspirations and expectations among school students.

3. Aspirations and Expectations

3.1 Distinction Between Aspirations and Expectations

The distinction between aspirations and expectations does clarify the notion of career plans or ambitions. It has been argued that the class structure, in conjunction with race, ethnicity, and gender, and reinforced by a school system which inculcates values and imparts knowledge to the advantage of the dominant class, "socializes" youth in such a way that educational and occupational choices coincide with a person's location in the class structure. What is less certain, however, is the mechanism whereby school students recognize, or have imposed on them, the structural limits to their career ambitions.

Han (1969) contended that career expectations are strongly affected by perceptions of restricted opportunity and that the difference between career wishes and career expectations reflects the "acceptance of the societal emphasis upon success and achievement," simultaneously with a recognition of the "class differential acceptance of these values" (p.681). Clearly, the distinction between aspirations and expectations is foreshadowed here.

Empirical support for the distinction between aspirations and expectations has been found in Canada, where Desoran (1977–78) concluded that occupational expectations were more strongly related to students' home background than aspirations, and that occupational aspirations tended to be higher in status than expectations. In Australia, research has found that children are socialized early both in the home and the school into recognizing the limits to their career aspirations, and the criteria which justify those limits —for example, innate intelligence, school success, and continued participation in the school system (Connell 1977, Russell and Smith 1979).

Saha (1982) based his analysis of aspirations and expectations on two questions: "If you had a completely free choice, what occupation would you choose?" and "Describe fully the occupation you expect to have during most of your working life." He found that male students had higher status occupational aspirations and expectations than females, and that the gap between aspirations and expectations is smaller for males. Furthermore, he found that occupational expectations were more predictable than occupational aspirations, which suggests that young people, in spite of having very high aspirations, do recognize the limits to what they can hope to achieve in their careers as adults. He concluded that "realistic" expectations were more closely related to social characteristics such as socioeconomic status, sex, ethnicity, and type of school attended than were occupational aspirations.

A related phenomenon was found in a study of career plans and expectations of final-year university students. Blau and Ferber (1991) analyzed the earnings expectations of male and female students and found that while both expected similar starting earnings, the males expected higher career earnings than the females. This difference remained even when the expected number of work years were controlled. In other words, the female students seemed to recognize limitations on their careers, or put differently, "they anticipate that they will do less well in terms of promotions" (p. 599). Furthermore, the authors show that expected lower earnings are not a factor which explains shorter expected careers.

Motivated by a concern for "lost talent," Hanson (1994) found in her analysis of the High School and Beyond data that 16% of US students had educational expectations lower than their aspirations, and that between late high school and early post high school, 27% of the students had lowered their educational expectations. Hansen argued that, for able students, talent is lost to society when (a) expectations fall short of aspirations; (b) expectations drop over time; and (c) students are not able to realize their earlier expectations.

Because of the distinction between aspirations and expectations, it is possible to understand further the conative dimension of attitudes, and the importance of social and structural variables on both attitudes and the attitude–behavior relationship. These external constraints on attitudes and behavior have been the center of continuing controversy, particularly since Fishbein and Ajzen (1975) suggested that the intention to perform an action is the best predictor of that action, and that social and structural constraints, such as gender and social background, act directly on the formation of attitudes because of the impact of social norms.

Liska (1984) has disagreed with Fishbein and Ajzen, and has argued that the impact of background variables such as socioeconomic position and gender actually influence the resources available for realizing behavioral intentions, not the nature of the intentions themselves. This and other criticisms of the Fishbein/Ajzen model have led Liska and others to argue that the attitude–behavior model is more complex than the two authors contend, and must include the possibility of nonrecursive effects, such as behavior effects on attitudes. The findings of Carpenter and Fleishman (1987) in their study of secondary students' college plans and eventual college attendance supported Liska's argument: college attendance was affected by attitudes toward college, academic achievement, and parental encouragement, while the intentions were in turn affected by academic achievement, perceived academic ability, and perceived social norms.

3.2 Aspirations, Expectations, and Attainments

Like attitudes, the theoretical and empirical value of aspirations and expectations depends on the extent to which they are related to attainments.

Studies of either aspirations or expectations relating to educational or occupational attainment report correlations of a similar magnitude. There has been

research on the effect of aspirations and expectations on educational and occupational attainment in Australia. In a small follow-up study of student educational and occupational aspirations, Poole (1982) found that 36 percent of those interviewed held the jobs they expected to have when they were 14 years old. Furthermore, Carpenter et al. (1980) found that the effect of Year 12 educational aspirations on eventual university enrollment was 0.48 for males and 0.42 for females. Their findings were consistent with the findings of comparable United States and Swedish studies and showed that "aspirations not only affect attainments but also act as key mediating variables in transmitting anterior factors into subsequent behaviours" (Carpenter et al. 1981). In a study of urban Australian youth from all capital cities, Saha (1985) found that students' occupational aspirations (preferred occupations) exercised important independent effects (net of socioeconomic background and type of school attended) on both expected educational and occupational attainments. Carpenter and Fleishman (1987) found in an analysis of data from Queensland that the correlation between intentions and behavior was 0.62 for males and 0.50 for females.

In the case of aspirations and expectations, it is easier to make statements about what one aspires to, or expects, than it is to actually behave in such a way as to attain the objectives of those statements.

4. What Do Students Signify by their Aspirations and Expectations?

There is a wide range of interpretations about the meaning of student articulations of educational and occupational goals. Some argue that aspirations and expectations represent realistic assessments by young people as to what objectives are desirable and possible in society. In other words, these articulations reflect both the internalization of societal values, and the recognition of the processes (both in terms of advantages and obstacles) involved in realizing those goals.

Other researchers contend that aspirations and/or expectations reflect the values imbued by parents and can be interpreted as a form of family encouragement. Thus, apart from the realistic assessment of aspirations and expectations with respect to the "real world," one could regard them as surrogates for parental encouragement and a part of the "culture capital" passed on to young people in realizing eventual educational and occupational attainments.

Finally, there are those who reject the validity and reliability of aspirations and expectations and argue that they represent mere "flights of fancy." While it may be true that specific levels of education or specific occupations may be unrealistic, it remains true that the relationship between these "achievement motivations" and eventual attainments is too significant to be ignored in the study of educational performance and attainment, and of eventual career attainments.

5. Theoretical Perspectives Concerning Career Orientations

The subject of educational and occupational plans, either as aspirations, expectations, or both, has been studied extensively. The general concern of much of this research is the extent to which career orientations are linked with both educational and occupational attainments, and, given this link, the factors which determine these orientations. Research in industrial societies has shown that a variety of factors contribute to career orientations, the most important of which are the socioeconomic status background of the student, the peer group, and the school itself (Sewell and Hauser 1975, Kerckhoff 1976). However, other factors such as family context (Marjoribanks 1997) and learning ability (Rojewski 1996) have also been found to be important.

While social-psychological variables such as aspirations and expectations have been found to exert considerable influence on future occupational attainment (Otto and Haller 1979), there is less agreement about the origins and meanings of these variables, or the manner by which they influence attainment. Alexander and Cook (1979), for example, contend that career plans are, at most, a "rough sketch of some course of action." Nevertheless they also find that students who firmed up their career plans early in life had higher levels of educational and occupational achievement, which suggests that such plans are not necessarily unrealistic or fantasy based. Thus, they argue that career plans are not to be regarded solely as educational outcomes—that is, as consequences of educational experience and performance—but rather as intervening variables (along with school experience) between background factors and career attainment. This has been the conventional location of expressions of career plans in the Wisconsin status-attainment model of Sewell and Hauser (1980).

There have been many theories about the formation of aspirations and expectations. It has been suggested that they represent the influence of family, peer group, and school socialization on the formation of occupational "role maps" (Musgrave 1967, Ford and Box 1967) or on the assessment of personal abilities (Blau et al. 1956, Portes et al. 1978). Others have contended that career plans are spontaneous and nonrational and the result of chance events (Jencks et al. 1972) or that they represent subjective constructs and the early stages of occupational identities (Hutchings 1996). Finally, some have suggested that they are the result of a rational matching of personality characteristics with educational and occupational demands (Holland

1973). However, no approach has been able to explain fully how young people may have a thorough knowledge of, and share, society's values about occupational status, and yet expect to attain only those occupations which are consistent with their background and gender.

6. Causal Variations in the Aspirations and Expectations of School Students

Educational performance and attainments are both the object and cause of aspirations, expectations, and later attainments. With regard to the first, the motivation with which young people approach study and other tasks related to schooling is clearly related to their school performance (grades) and eventual attainment.

Specific aspirations and expectations relate to educational objectives alone, while others relate to educational objectives only in an instrumental sense, that is, as a stepping-stone to other, more long-term objectives. Thus educational aspirations and expectations may have meaning only in terms of career aspirations and expectations, such as for an occupation, wealth, or a particular lifestyle.

The ordering of aspirations and expectations with respect to educational and occupational attainments is important for research. In a causal model, the decision regarding the relative placing of these important variables can make a considerable difference both in analysis and in findings. Although it is quite likely that the actual relationship between variables is more complex than that which a linear causal model can analyze, decisions must be made about the ordering of these relationships. The ordering of the variables relates to the underlying theory which guides the research.

7. Future Directions for the Study of Aspirations and Expectations

In the end, the attitude–behavior controversy and the subsequent development of the model seem to support the distinction between aspirations and expectations. Thus, much of the inconsistency in findings might be due to a confusion, in conceptualization as well as in measurement, between aspirations, which refer to the valued norms of educational and occupational attainment, and expectations, which refer to the recognition (perceived or factual) of the social constraints which impede the attainment of aspirations. It is because of this difference that aspirations are generally higher than expectations, and why the gap between aspirations and expectations is greater for female students than male students, and possibly for other social groups as well.

It also explains why studies of aspirations, crudely defined and measured, often produce results which suggest that secondary and tertiary student aspirations far outstrip the capacity of countries to absorb them. This is especially the case in less developed countries where the gap between aspirations and prospective attainments appears the greatest (Saha 1992). Apart from the possible consequences of unfulfilled aspirations (Burris 1983, Post 1990), the problem is also due to poor measurement. Expectations more closely approximate a country's power to absorb students in those occupations which they expect to attain, rather than their aspirations, which are less constrained and more related to social and cultural desirability.

Researchers interested in the educational and occupational ambitions and life plans of students should give careful attention to the dimensions which they wish to measure. Inadvertent confusion of aspirations and expectations may result in inconsistencies which may appear to render the study of career behavioral intentions of little use in understanding career attitudes and behaviors, or in policy programs ranging from counseling to career planning. Clarification of career behavioral intentions such as aspirations or expectations, and the measurement of these accordingly, provide an additional direction for the development of models of attitude formation and behavioral attainments in educational and occupational careers.

See also: Acquiring Attitudes and Values; Development of Achievement Motivation; Family, School, and Social Capital; Social Mobility, Social Stratification, and Education; Social Psychological Theories in Education; Socialization

References

Alexander K L, Cook M A 1979 The motivational relevance of educational plans: Questioning the conventional wisdom. *Soc. Psychol. Q.* 42(3): 202–13

Blau D M, Gustad J W, Jessor R, Parnes H S, Wilcox R C 1956 Occupational choice: A conceptual framework. *Ind. Lbr. Relat. Rev.* 9: 531–43

Blau F D, Ferber M A 1991 Career plans and expectations of young women and men: The earnings gap and labor force participation. *J. Hum. Resources* 26(4): 581–607

Burris V 1983 The social and political consequences of overeducation. *Am. Sociol. Rev.* 48(4): 454–66

Carpenter P G, Fleishman J A 1987 Linking intentions and behavior: Australian students' college plans and college attendance. *Am. Educ. Res. J.* 24(1): 79–105

Carpenter P G, Western J S, Foster W G 1980 Social background, aspirations and educational achievement among Queensland youth. In: Smith I D (ed.) 1980 *Youth, Schooling and Employment.* Australian Association for Research in Education, Melbourne

Carpenter P G, Western J S, Foster W G 1981 Origins, aspirations and attainments. In: Lawson M J, Linke R (eds.) 1981 *Inquiry and Action in Education.* Australian Association for Research in Education, Melbourne

Connell R W 1977 *Ruling Class, Ruling Culture.* Cambridge University Press, Cambridge

Desoran R A 1977/1978 Educational aspirations: Individual freedom or social justice? *Interchange* 8(3): 72–87

Fishbein M, Ajzen I 1975 *Belief, Attitude, Intention and Behavior: An Introduction to Theory and Research.* Addison-Wesley, Reading, Massachusetts

Ford J, Box S 1967 Sociological theory and occupational choice. *Sociol. Rev.* 15: 287–99

Han W S 1969 Two conflicting themes: Common values versus class differential values. *Am. Sociol. Rev.* 34(5): 679–90

Hanson S L 1994 Lost talent: unrealized educational aspirations and expectations among US youth. *Sociol. Educ.* 63(3): 159–83

Holland J L 1973 *Making Vocational Choices: A Theory of Careers.* Prentice Hall, Englewood Cliffs, New Jersey

Hutchings M 1996 What will you do when you grow up? The social construction of children's occupational preferences. *Children's Social Econ. Educ.* 1(1): 15–30

Jencks C et al. 1972 *Inequality: A Reassessment of the Effect of Family and Schooling in America.* Basic Books, New York

Kerckhoff A C 1976 The status attainment process: Socialization or allocation? *Soc. Forces* 55(2): 368–81

Liska A E 1984 A critical examination of the causal structure of the Fishbein/Ajzen attitude–behavior model. *Soc. Psychol. Q.* 47(1): 61–74

Marjoribanks K 1997 Family contexts, immediate family settings and adolescent aspirations. *J. Appl. Dev. Psychol.* 18(1): 119–32

McGuire W J 1985 Attitudes and attitude change. In: Lindsey G, Aronson E (eds.) 1985 *Handbook of Social Psychology: Vol. 2 Special Fields and Applications*, 3rd edn. Random House, New York

Musgrave P W 1967 Towards a sociological theory of occupational choice. *Sociol. Rev.* 15: 33–46

Otto L B, Haller A O 1979 Evidence for a social psychological view of the status attainment process: Four studies compared. *Soc. Forces* 57(3): 887–914

Poole M E 1982 *Youth: Expectations and Transitions.* Routledge and Kegan Paul, Melbourne

Portes A, McLeod S A, Parker R N 1978 Immigrant aspirations. *Sociol. Educ.* 51(4): 241–60

Post D 1990 The social demand for education in Peru: Students' choices and state autonomy. *Sociol. Educ.* 63 (4): 258–71

Rojewski J W 1996 Occupational aspirations and early career-choice patterns of adolescents with and without learning disabilities. *Learning Disability Q.* 19(2): 99–116

Russell G, Smith J 1979 Girls can be doctors—can't they? Sex differences in career aspirations. *Austr. J. Social Issues* 14(2): 91–102

Saha L J 1982 Gender, school attainment and occupational plans: Determinants of aspirations and expectations among Australian urban school leavers. *Austr. J. Educ.* 26(3): 247–65

Saha L J 1985 The legitimacy of early school leaving: Occupational orientations, vocational training plans, and educational attainment among urban Australian youth. *Sociol. Educ.* 58(4): 228–40

Saha L J 1992 The effects of socio-economic development on student academic performance and life plans: A cross national analysis. *Int. J. Educ. Dev.* 12(3): 191–204

Sewell W H, Hauser R M 1975 *Education, Occupation and Earnings: Achievement in the Early Career*. Academic Press, New York

Sewell W H, Hauser R M 1980 The Wisconsin longitudinal study of social and psychological factors in aspirations and achievements. In: Kerckhoff A C (ed.) 1980 *Research in Sociology of Education and Socialization: A Research Annual*, Vol. 1. JAI Press, Greenwich, Connecticut

Turner R H 1964 *The Social Context of Ambition*. Chandler, San Francisco, California

Further Reading

Ajzen I, Fishbein M 1980 *Understanding Attitudes and Predicting Social Behavior*. Prentice-Hall, Englewood Cliffs, New Jersey

Carpenter P G, Western J S 1989 *Starting a Career: The Early Attainments of Young People*. Australian Council for Educational Research, Hawthorn

Howell F M, Frese W 1982 *Making Life Plans: Race, Gender and Career Decisions*. University Press of America, Washington, DC

Development of Achievement Motivation

G. D. Heyman and C. S. Dweck

Motivation drives and directs behavior; achievement motivation governs behavior relevant to achievement and learning. An understanding of achievement motivation has implications for many aspects of human life, including how individuals develop new skills, and how or whether they make use of existing skills. Consequently, issues concerning the nature and development of achievement motivation take on great theoretical and practical significance.

Many approaches have been taken to explain achievement motivational processes. Some approaches have included the examination of global achievement "motives" or broad self-concepts such as self-esteem. However, researchers have become aware of the need to examine specific concepts that illuminate motivational processes. One such approach, the "goals" approach, has begun to provide answers to the basic questions in the field.

In this article, the goals approach to achievement motivation will be described. Next, motivation will be discussed from a developmental perspective. Finally, ways to develop adaptive achievement motivation will be examined.

1. The Goals Approach

The goals approach grew out of research on adaptive and maladaptive motivation (see, e.g., Ames 1984, Diener and Dweck 1978). Findings from this research indicate that children of comparable ability often respond very differently when they encounter academic obstacles. Some children (including many with high levels of ability) interpret their difficulties to mean that they have low ability. They seem to lose hope that their efforts will lead them to success, and their performance tends to deteriorate. This constellation of responses, sometimes referred to as a "helpless" pattern, is considered maladaptive because it prevents individuals from reaching potentially attainable, valued goals. In contrast, other children respond to obstacles as challenges to be mastered. These children do not appear to be upset by their difficulties, and sometimes report feeling excited by the challenge. They typically focus their attention on modifying their effort and strategy, and they maintain or improve their level of problem-solving. These reactions, which frequently are called "mastery-oriented" responses, are considered to be adaptive because they allow individuals the time that is often necessary to overcome difficulties and to progress toward valued goals.

Converging research results suggest that these adaptive and maladaptive motivational responses can result from different goals (see Table 1); that is, from the different aims children pursue in achievement situations. Achievement motivation researchers have examined two classes of achievement goals (see, e.g., Ames 1984, Dweck and Leggett 1988, Nicholls 1984). One class of goals, sometimes referred to as "performance goals," centers on issues of performance and adequacy. When individuals hold performance goals they are concerned with documenting their competence, and they tend to view achievement situations as tests of their competence. Another set of goals, termed "learning goals," revolves around learning and task mastery. When individuals hold learning goals they strive to master new tasks and develop competencies.

Justifiably, children tend to be concerned with both learning and appearing competent. Which of these goals predominates, however, has important motivational consequences. When the focus is on performance goals, task performance is readily seen as measuring ability level. Poor performance is viewed in terms of low ability (particularly when individuals have low confidence about their abilities) and motivational helplessness may result. In contrast, when learning goals are emphasized, difficulties do not provide information about competency; rather, they guide task mastery and learning and indicate the points at which greater effort or new strategies are required. In

Table 1
Relation between beliefs about intelligence, goals, and response to obstacles in achievement situations

Theory of intelligence	Goal orientation	Response to obstacles
Entity (intelligence is fixed)	Performance (goal is to demonstrate competence)	Vulnerability to helpless pattern (low persistence; performance deterioration)
Incremental (intelligence is malleable)	Learning (goal is to increase competence)	Mastery-oriented pattern (high persistence; performance maintenance or improvement)

this way, learning goals facilitate a mastery-oriented motivational stance in the face of difficulty.

These findings concerning achievement goals are consonant with other research in the field, including the work of Kuhl (1983). This research shows that individuals who focus more on such factors as outcomes (state orientation) show greater motivational vulnerability when encountering difficulties than those who concentrate on such factors as learning processes (action orientation).

In summary, results of a great deal of research on achievement goals suggest that when individuals place an emphasis on measuring or proving their ability, they tend to show motivational vulnerability in the face of difficulties. Conversely, when individuals focus their attention on thinking about ways to learn or develop skills, they are more resilient.

Why might different individuals pursue different goals even in identical situations? One reason for this seems to be that they hold different theories of intelligence (see Dweck and Leggett 1988, Faria and Fontaine 1989, Stevenson et al. 1990). Some children tend to view intelligence as a relatively fixed and measurable quality ("entity theory"); other children believe that intelligence is a malleable quality that can be increased through effort ("incremental theory"). Findings from research on these theories suggest that when individuals view their intelligence as a fixed capacity, they are more likely to enter achievement situations pursuing performance goals, looking for ways to demonstrate that this capacity is adequate. In contrast, when individuals believe that their intelligence is malleable they are more likely to pursue learning goals, seeking ways to develop their intelligence.

In short, the entity view of intelligence and performance goals are associated with vulnerability to helplessness. Conversely, the incremental view of intelligence and learning goals are associated with the maintenance of adaptive motivational patterns in the face of difficulty.

2. Motivation and Development

There is growing recognition that motivational pro-

cesses are dynamic systems that have the potential to change over the course of development. Systematic research has been undertaken in order to understand the nature of the development of achievement motivation.

Several researchers have examined the impact of obstacles on the motivation of children in first grade and younger. In some of this work, young children, after facing obstacles, reported substantial optimism about their chances for future success and displayed motivational resilience. They did not exhibit responses characteristic of the helpless pattern.

Consistent with this notion of children's motivational resilience, some researchers have found developmental differences in the way children reason about effort and ability in relation to achievement outcomes (Nicholls 1984). This work indicates that young children do not understand or measure ability in the same manner as older children, and that young children are more likely to expect effort to lead to desired outcomes. This emphasis on effort rather than ability is characteristic of the mastery-oriented motivational response. These results suggest that young children are less likely to view effort as having negative implications for their abilities and are less apt to question the usefulness of effort. Thus, this developmental research on children's responses to obstacles and on their motivationally relevant thinking supports the idea that children start off with relative motivational resilience and become less adaptively motivated as they grow older.

2.1 Developmental Issues: A New Look

Although previous research has painted a picture of young children as a motivationally homogeneous group who think and respond like mastery-oriented older children, research in the early 1990s suggests a rather different picture. This work demonstrates that when tasks are meaningful and failures are salient, some young children, like their older counterparts, respond to difficulties with negative emotional reactions (Stipek et al. 1992) and also display the thoughts and behaviors characteristic of the helpless pattern (Dweck 1991).

How can findings of children's motivational

vulnerabilities be reconciled with findings that children lack concern with or understanding of ability? One possibility is that children think about their performance not in terms of how it reflects on their ability, but on other important aspects of themselves. If failure in achievement situations does have implications for aspects of the self early in life, it would most likely hold meaning in terms of concepts that are familiar to young children. One set of such concepts relates to goodness and badness. Since teaching children what is right and wrong is a major goal of socialization, children are likely to receive numerous messages regarding these issues. Thus, young children may develop ideas about goodness or badness that they can apply to a variety of situations, including achievement contexts (Dweck 1991).

There is some evidence to suggest that children just starting school may indeed think about what achievement outcomes mean about their goodness and badness. Heyman et al. (1992) found that kindergarten children who exhibited responses characteristic of the helpless pattern were more likely to report feeling "bad" after they made mistakes.

Just as young children are not completely protected from motivational difficulties, they are not necessarily doomed to greater risk as they age. As indicated above, children's thinking about achievement situations often becomes increasingly conductive to the helpless pattern as they get older (Nicholls 1984). However, cross-cultural research suggests that such trends in motivationally relevant thinking are not inevitable. For example, Salili et al. (1976) found that Iranian children emphasize effort more as they get older, and Hau and Salili (1990) found that emphasis on learning goals increases with age among Chinese students in Hong Kong.

In summary, research has suggested that there may be meaningful differences in the ways in which younger and older children process ability information and respond to some achievement situations. However, findings indicate that in the context of salient failure, some young children tend to show motivational responses that are very similar to those of older children. Research also suggests that for young children, differences in motivational patterns may be more closely related to conceptions of goodness and badness than to specific conceptions of intellectual competence.

2.2 The Intrinsic Motivation Approach: Parallel Findings

The intrinsic motivation approach to achievement motivation also focuses on the ways in which individuals perceive achievement situations. This approach is primarily concerned with task interest and enjoyment.

As in the goals framework, in the intrinsic motivation framework children often appear less adaptively motivated across development. In other words, children seem to find schoolwork to be less enjoyable as they progress through school. However, to describe young children as full of intrinsic motivation which slowly dissipates is to give an incomplete picture. Lepper et al. (1973) found that even preschoolers lose interest in activities for which their participation has been externally rewarded. In addition, Harter (1986) demonstrated that some children maintain the same level—or even show increases—in intrinsic motivation upon entering junior high school, when most students show the greatest decline.

3. Promoting Adaptive Achievement Motivation

How can the development of adaptive achievement motivation be encouraged? Several approaches that focus on changing achievement contexts and individuals' perceptions of these contexts have met with a good deal of success.

One general approach has focused on changing the explanations children make when they fail. As described earlier, an important aspect of the helpless motivational pattern is that it involves explaining difficulties in terms of personal deficiencies. In contrast, individuals exhibiting mastery-oriented motivation do not explain their difficulties in this way. When they do give such explanations they tend to remain focused on effort and strategy (Diener and Dweck 1978). Researchers have found that when children are taught to provide explanations in terms of factors over which they have control, adaptive motivational consequences are likely to result. Specifically, these positive effects have been demonstrated in situations in which children are taught to focus attention on their effort or strategy, rather than their ability, when they are having difficulties (Dweck 1975, Andrews and Debus 1978).

Another general approach to enhancing achievement motivation has involved a focus on goals. Researchers consistently have demonstrated that a variety of factors that emphasize performance goals often tend to be associated with negative motivational consequences, and that factors that elicit learning goals are associated with adaptive motivation. For example, Butler (1987) found that children who received information about their performance or ability level through normative grades or praise (performance goal manipulation) on a divergent thinking task showed less intrinsic motivation than children who received feedback of task-relevant comments or no feedback. In another goal manipulation, Ames (1984) gave children problems to solve in a competitive context that emphasized performance relative to a peer, as compared to an individualistic structure in which self-improvement was emphasized. She found that children who worked in the individualistic (learning goal) context were less likely to attribute failure to ability and more apt to engage in self-instruction than were children working in the competitive (performance goal) context.

More comprehensive programs are being implemented that utilize research from both the goals and intrinsic motivation frameworks. One such program emphasizes learning goals through enhancing children's interest in learning and providing them with skills to meet learning goals (Ames 1990). Students with motivational difficulties who were involved in this program showed motivational benefits in comparison to a control group of children with motivational difficulties. These benefits included higher levels of intrinsic motivation and higher perceived ability.

Adaptive motivation may also be promoted by influencing motivationally relevant theories about intelligence. Indeed, Stevenson et al. (1990) argued that the Japanese and Chinese cultural beliefs that people are very malleable help to account for the high levels of academic success achieved by many children in these countries. Preliminary research suggests that one can influence children's goal choices by influencing their beliefs about intelligence (see Dweck and Leggett 1988). Specifically, when incremental (malleable) beliefs about intelligence were emphasized, as opposed to entity (fixed) beliefs, children were more likely to endorse learning goals. Although further research is needed, it seems likely that more adaptive motivation will result if individuals can be taught to think about their abilities as malleable.

In summary, adaptive motivation can be promoted at multiple levels, incorporating individuals' explanations of their difficulties, the goals they hold for achievement situations, their beliefs about intelligence, and their intrinsic interest in achievement situations.

See also: Acquiring Attitudes and Values; Aspirations and Expectations of Students; Family, School, and Social Capital; Social Psychological Theories in Education; Socialization

References

Ames C 1984 Achievement attribution and self-instructions under competitive and individualistic goal structures. *J. Educ. Psychol.* 76(3): 478–87
Ames C 1990 Achievement goals and classroom structure: Developing a learning orientation. Paper presented at the annual meeting of the American Educational Research Association, Boston, Massachusetts
Andrews G R, Debus R 1978 Persistence and causal perceptions of failure: Modifying cognitive attributions. *J. Educ. Psychol.* 70(2): 154–66
Butler R 1987 Task-involving and ego involving properties of evaluative situations: Effects of different feedback conditions on motivational perceptions, interest, and performance. *J. Educ. Psychol.* 79(4): 474–82
Diener C, Dweck C S 1978 An analysis of learned helplessness: Continuous changes in performance, strategy, and achievement cognitions following failure. *J. Pers. Soc. Psychol.* 36: 451–61
Dweck C S 1975 The role of expectations and attributions in the alleviation of learned helplessness. *J. Pers. Soc. Psychol.* 31(4): 674–85
Dweck C S 1991 Self-theories and goals: Their role in motivation, personality and development. In: Dienstbier R (ed.) 1991 *Nebraska Symposium on Motivation: Perspectives on Motivation*, Vol. 38. University of Nebraska Press, Lincoln, Nebraska
Dweck C S, Leggett E 1988 A social-cognitive approach to motivation and personality. *Psychol. Rev.* 95(2): 256–73
Faria L, Fontaine A M 1989 Conceptions personelles d'intelligence: Elaboration d'une echelle et études exploratoires. *Cadernos de Consulta Psicologica* 5: 19–30
Harter S 1986 The relationship between perceived competence, affect, and motivational orientation within the classroom: Process and patterns of change. In: Boggiano A K, Pitman T (eds.) 1986 *Achievement and Motivation: A Social-Developmental Perspective.* Cambridge University Press, Cambridge
Hau K, Salili F 1990 Examination result attribution, expectancy and achievement goals among Chinese students in Hong Kong. *Educ. Stud.* 16(1): 17–31
Heyman G D, Dweck C S, Cain K M 1992 Young children's vulnerability to self-blame and helplessness: Relationship to beliefs about goodness. *Child Dev.* 63(2): 401–15
Kuhl J 1983 *Motivation, Konflikt und Handlungskontrolle.* Springer-Verlag, Berlin
Lepper M R, Greene D, Nisbett R E 1973 Undermining children's intrinsic interest with extrinsic rewards: A test of the "overjustification" hypothesis. *J. Pers. Soc. Psychol.* 28(1): 129–37
Nicholls J G 1984 Achievement motivation: Conceptions of ability, subjective experience, task choice, and performance. *Psychol. Rev.* 91(3): 328–46
Salili F, Maehr M L, Gilmore G 1976 Achievement and morality: A cross-cultural analysis of causal attribution and evaluation. *J. Pers. Soc. Psychol.* 33(3): 327–37
Stevenson H W et al. 1990 Contexts of achievement: A study of American, Chinese and Japanese children. *Monogr. Soc. Res. Child Dev.* 55(1–2) (221): 123
Stipek D, Recchia S, McClintic S 1992 Self-evaluation in young children. *Monogr. Soc. Res. Child Dev.* 57(1) (226): 100

Further Reading

Covington M V, Beery R G 1976 *Self-worth and School Learfrning.* Holt, Rinehart, and Winston, New York
Stipek D, MacIver D 1989 Developmental change in children's assessment of intellectual competence. *Child Dev.* 60(3): 521–38
Weiner B 1985 An attributional theory of achievement motivation and emotion. *Psychol. Rev.* 92(4): 548–73

Political Socialization and Education

R. G. Braungart and M. M. Braungart

Political socialization is the process of learning political attitudes and behavior through social interaction. Although a number of agents influence political socialization—family, education, media, peers, and groups and organizations—education is the principal institution in society formally charged with teaching the younger generation about political society and citizenship. This article explores the role of education in the political socialization process.

Because childhood and adolescence are the formative stages for developing social and political orientations, most of the focus is on political socialization in the primary and secondary school system. Reflecting empirical research as well as discussions in education, information is presented about the historical foundations of education's role in political socialization, the functions of education in contemporary society, mechanisms of political socialization, practices and trends in education, examples of political socialization in four nations, and the effectiveness of education in the political socialization process. Brief mention is made of political socialization in other educational settings, such as in higher education, national service, and adult education.

Fraught with controversy and debate, especially in democratic societies, educating young people and adults for politics and citizenship is no clear-cut matter. Contrasting perspectives are evident in political socialization theory and research as well as in educational programs designed to teach students about society and politics. For example, some researchers and educators view the relationship between political socialization and education from structural-functional and behaviorist perspectives, largely concerned with training students to fit into the political system and display conventional citizenship behavior. Input–output models of political learning reflect this perspective, with political socialization considered an important source of societal and political stability. However, cognitive and developmental theories in psychology, along with conflict theories in sociology, view the individual as actor in his or her socialization process and emphasize the struggle over political power among competing groups in society. Thus, although adults attempt to inculcate political values and norms, young people perceive, interpret, and respond in their own ways, with generational and group conflict a significant source of political change. The debate over political socialization as a force for stability or for change permeates many of the controversies in education.

1. Historical Foundations

The role of education in the political socialization process is rooted in Western thought and the evolution of democracy and citizenship. Reacting against autocratic rule in the fifth century BC, the Greek historian Herodotus defined democracy as "the rule of the many" in a society where there is "equality before the law" and where the political officeholder is "answerable for what he does" (Pennock 1979 p. 3). Plato and his pupil Aristotle stressed rational participation in the democratic process, which they noted depended on an educated citizenry—education was denied in ancient Greece to women, slaves, youth, and foreigners (Tarrant 1989).

Another milestone in the development of democracy and citizenship occurred during the Enlightenment, as philosophers in Western Europe redefined the arrangement between the individual and the state. Their discussions and debates about the social contract, liberty, equality, freedom, and the supremacy of the people's will over state authority provided the inspiration for the American Revolutionary War, the French *Declaration of the Rights of Man*, and the French Revolution. Democracy and citizenship had moved from the ideal to the real world, and from the late eighteenth century onward, the historical thrust has been the drive for nationalism and the extension of democracy and citizenship from elites to non-elites, from adults to youth, and from Europe and North America to the rest of the world. As nationhood, citizenship, and democracy evolved, so has education's role in producing the informed citizenry necessary to carry out democratic goals.

However, despite the emotional appeal of democracy and the recognized need to cultivate an educated citizenry, tension, debate, and outright conflict have ensued over the functions, goals, and practices of education in socializing individuals to politics. Much of the controversy in education reflects the inherent contradictions in democracy itself—freedom versus equality, societal order versus personal liberty, and majority rule versus minority rights. Moreover, as the twentieth century comes to an end, every type of political regime claims to be teaching democratic values and behavior through its educational system. In practice, governments are more or less democratic, with their policies and procedures measured against the democratic ideal. As Tarrant (1989) observed, there is little that is democratic in either so-called "peoples' democracies" or in laissez-faire capitalist societies. One indicator of a nation's level of democratic achievement is the functions of education and the methods employed to socialize youngsters to politics in the schools.

2. Functions of Education

A principal function of education in most societies is to legitimize and maintain the political system, although the way this function is carried out varies widely from one society to the next. In totalitarian societies, education goes beyond the system-maintenance function to indoctrinate the younger generation into the "correct" political thinking and to induce conformity to the authoritarian regime. Much of the emphasis is on rote memorization, with the educational system acting as a significant mechanism of social and political control. In societies undergoing transformations, new-nation status, or political upheavals (e.g., Eastern Europe, Africa, and the Middle East), education may be directed toward system-creation (Farah and Kuroda 1987, Heater and Gillespie 1981), rather than serving the function of system-maintenance.

Although in most democratic societies one of the foremost tasks of schools is to produce informed, critical, competent, and active citizens, there is much debate over the implementation of these goals. For example, while some educators support Thomas Jefferson's contention that education should teach individuals to be critical so they can be the guardians of their own liberty against autocratic rule, scholars such as Janowitz (1983) argue that a critical emphasis in education produces self-centered, negative, and cynical students who can agree to no position other than their own. In addition, whereas some educators define competent citizens as those who do not violate human rights, and argue that education should be directed toward world peace and improving individuals' life chances, others claim education's political socialization function should be limited to enhancing political literacy and an understanding of the role of citizen. Finally, while to many educators "active" citizenship means conventional behaviors such as letter-writing and voting, others advocate that young people should be taught the skills of grass-roots mobilization (Eveslage 1993, Remy 1980). Controversy is fundamental to democracies, and members of the adult generation no doubt will continue to haggle over the meaning, interpretation, and methodology of developing "good" citizens in schools.

3. Mechanisms of Political Socialization

In order to understand how students are socialized to politics in the educational system, some of the principal mechanisms of learning and socialization are reviewed. First, political socialization is partially a function of the young person's developmental level. Based largely on Piagetian conceptions of cognitive development, research indicates that although children may form attachments to political symbols, because of the abstract nature of politics, elementary school children have only a rudimentary grasp of political concepts. However, with the development of abstract thinking during adolescence and youth, awareness and understanding of political concepts and symbols increase. Often considered to be the "crucial stage" for the formation of political values and norms, experiences and behavior learned during adolescence and youth are especially significant and may last a lifetime (Adelson 1986, Braungart and Braungart 1986). Not surprisingly, adolescence is the time when youngsters in many countries take their civics courses and become acquainted with their rights and duties as citizens.

A second mechanism of socialization involves the various models of learning that explain the acquisition of political knowledge, attitudes, and behavior. Conditioning the learner through positive and negative associations or reinforcement is one of the simplest types of learning. Thinking is not required; rather, the individual learns by responding to stimuli in his or her environment. Prejudice, political orientations, and deliberate as well as inadvertent political learning often can be explained by this kind of respondent or operant conditioning. Social learning is one of the most powerful models. As individuals observe the conduct of others and its consequences, they are likely to imitate attractive role models and behavior perceived to be rewarded. This is why the mass media, textbooks, and the attitudes and actions of authority figures become important considerations in evaluating political socialization in the schools. Cognitive, humanistic, and psychoanalytic models posit that learning is more than responding to and copying what is observed by the individual in the social environment. Learning is a private matter, strongly influenced by personal needs, thought processes, perceptions, interpretations, and emotional conflicts. Here the focus shifts away from agents of political socialization to the learner.

Third, political socialization in the educational setting occurs in formal, rational, and direct ways as well as in informal, irrational, and indirect ways. For example, a school system may have a mandated political curriculum with clearly defined goals, objectives, content, and activities for each grade level. Yet children and adolescents acquire knowledge about politics at school not only through formal classroom training but through informal experiences and indirect kinds of learning, such as class elections, extracurricular activities, and group interactions. In addition, while adults may present material designed to socialize the younger generation to the political system, some of the pupils' political learning may be unintended, such as reacting against rather than supporting the political regime, misinterpreting or misunderstanding important concepts, and deciding that politics and government are irrelevant or uninteresting.

Another mechanism affecting the political socialization process is the larger historical and social context in which teaching and learning occur. Various levels of influence need to be considered: (a) the social background of the student (family, socioeconomic, ethnic-religious, lifestyle, peer groups, or other significant reference groups and social categories); (b) the community and school environment (local economy, culture, social structure, sources of conflict, and pressure groups and organizations); (c) regional, state, and national politics, trends, and events; and (d) global structure, changes, and influences. Each of these forces may have a direct or indirect bearing on educational policies, the process of political socialization, and the outcomes of political learning. These levels of influence also provide important sources of cross-pressure that may mitigate the political socialization efforts of the schools. In order to gain a clearer picture of how political socialization is conducted in education, some of the current practices and trends are discussed briefly.

4. Practices and Trends

As Patrick (1977) noted, the educational components of political socialization tend to be similar from one society to the next and include political knowledge, values, attitudes, and participation skills. However, the relative weight given to each of these components differs widely among and within nations, as does the degree to which the curriculum is developed at the national level, the local school level, or by the individual teacher. Moreover, nations vary in the percentage of young people enrolled in the educational system, which, in turn, determines the extent to which members of the younger generation are exposed to formal political socialization.

New educational trends are shifting the emphasis given to each of the components of political socialization in the schools. Until recently, teaching students about society, politics, and citizenship was considered a relatively simple matter, often relegated to a few courses such as history, social studies, and civics; primarily directed toward the political knowledge component and system-maintenance function; and involving traditional teaching styles and classroom activities. The focus was on what to think, not how to think. These, of course, may still be the educational orientations in many countries and localities.

In response to changing global and societal conditions as well as advances in psychology and education, innovative approaches have been introduced to enhance the political socialization function of the schools. First, an increasing number of disciplines are involved in a student's formal political course work —especially the social sciences, but also law, public affairs, and international relations. Second, a host of new topics is being incorporated into the political curriculum, such as social and environmental problems, multiculturalism, ethnicity, gender studies, and global citizenship. Third, the goals of political socialization

in educational systems are moving beyond the political knowledge component to include critical thinking, problem solving, decision-making, and citizen participation skills. Fourth, teaching students to use the scientific method to investigate political questions, issues, and problems is being encouraged. And fifth, moral education and ethics are being included to cultivate students' understanding of themselves and the handling of social and political issues (Eveslage 1993, Remy 1980).

A more proactive view of student learning is being advocated, which has implications for teaching practices. As well as routine textbook reading, teacher lecturing, and graded pupil activities, greater student involvement may be encouraged by role playing, simulation exercises, debates, and direct personal experiences. Research in a number of countries indicates that students' political knowledge and support for democratic values are greater in classrooms that encourage free discussion and participation than in traditional classrooms that emphasize rote memorization. Moreover, if the goal of political socialization is ultimately to promote democracy and competent citizenship, then the structure of the educational system, the staffing of the school, and the underlying assumptions of the curriculum, tasks, and evaluation process need to reflect the spirit of democracy. Educational practices such as relegating students to vocational or academic programs in the schools, tracking them into advanced and disadvantaged competency groups, and emphasizing competition and winning rather than cooperation and individual worth run counter to democratic principles. In addition, careful evaluation needs to be made of the messages sent to students in textbooks, classroom instructional materials, and teacher attitudes, especially those communications (overt or hidden, verbal or nonverbal) that reinforce stereotypes, discrimination, or destructive practices (Ichilov 1990, Tarrant 1989). Beyond this general discussion, examples are provided of some of the various ways that the democracies of the United States, the United Kingdom, Germany, and Japan handle political socialization in their schools.

5. Political Socialization in Four Nations

5.1 The United States

The United States has a decentralized education system, with political socialization goals and activities largely left to the determination of the 50 states and the more than 15,500 school districts. By law, almost all states require citizenship education, some states further mandate citizenship participation activities for students, and a few states have a system of compulsory testing in the area of civics. The heterogeneous composition of American society, the sharp ideological divisions, and disagreements over the meaning of citizenship and democracy complicate teaching American youth about citizen rights and duties. The function of political socialization in the education process is hotly debated at the local level, with some Americans demanding that schools teach children to be patriotic and fit into the capitalist system, whereas others want schools to teach children to be aware of social problems and critical of society and politics in order to forge a better nation and world. Historical subject matter comprises much of the information in citizenship and civics courses, and despite some innovative programs, the approach to political socialization in American education has been fragmented. National as well as international competency tests have indicated that American youth do not perform well in history, geography, or civics tests (Reische 1987). Increasing youth violence and worry about the declining moral, physical, and emotional well-being of many young people in the United States have led some schools to include programs in health care, personal awareness, and conflict resolution skills as part of citizenship education (Braungart and Braungart 1995, Carnegie Council 1995, National Research Council 1993).

5.2 The United Kingdom

Strong tradition and the social class structure have created somewhat different goals and political curricula in the bifurcated English educational system. Non-state (private) schools, largely for elites, tend to educate students for academic placement, character development, and leadership roles. State schools for the masses of students take the "informed-citizenship approach," teaching young people about local and national government, community services, and social problems. Civics education courses are usually required in middle school, but thereafter students may attend different types of secondary schools, and courses about politics and society may be optional. Waves of immigrants from the West Indies and elsewhere prompted demands to include multiculturalism in education, and there has been a movement to educate students for world peace. Innovations in the formal political socialization curriculum have been proposed—such as moral development, environment, decision-making, and interpersonal skills—but their implementation tends to occur in relative isolation, partly because teachers are not well prepared to handle such new ideas (Derricott 1979, Heater 1990). Academics and practitioners in the United Kingdom are proposing a more holistic and developmental approach to improving the transition from dependent youth status to independent adulthood. The route to responsible citizenship, according to Jones and Wallace (1992), is coterminous with meeting the educational needs, work and employment opportunities, and economic security of every young person, irrespective of class, gender, and location.

5.3 Germany

Regional and local traditions, party politics, and a differentiated educational system that tracks youngsters into higher education or into a variety of vocational and career schools result in diverse political socialization experiences for German youth. The comparatively few students preparing for a university education have the most intensive education in politics and citizenship, whereas secondary school students preparing for job training spend more effort on their "subjects" than on politics. Teachers often shy away from dealing with Germany's past, especially the Nazi era, and political topics tend to be handled in a neutral manner, emphasizing knowledge of the political system and political participation. Educational debates frequently divide into those who stress authority, order, law, and discipline and those who want German youth educated to be critical and to recognize social conflict as a legitimate source of political change (Kuhn 1979). What often results is a compromise, with students characterized by Davey (1987) as "sifting and weighing various pieces of information that they pick up in school—each of them making somewhat different sense of it all, according to his or her particular circumstances" (pp. 5–6). German reunification presented challenges to integrate and socialize East German youth into Western-style capitalism and democracy. The growing European Community prompted some German states to require students to study more geography and develop better technical skills for participation in the economically interdependent new Europe (Meyenberg 1993).

5.4 Japan

During the allied occupation of postwar Japan, efforts were made to rid education of supernationalism and militarism and to facilitate democratization by adopting an American-style educational system. The Japanese Ministry of Education prescribes the basic curricula in elementary and secondary schools, subject to the approval of the local school boards. Each school, in turn, organizes an appropriate program of study that meets government regulations and local conditions. Moral education is considered important, especially in the elementary grades, and social studies courses are required at all grade levels. Civics education is compulsory in the ninth grade, and the 90 percent of students who continue to high school must take courses in ethics, sociology, politics, and economics along with history and geography. The Ministry of Education's stated political socialization goals for students include intentions to "develop those qualities which are essential for building a democratic and peaceful society," and "strive to contribute toward world peace and the general welfare of humankind from a global perspective" (Nagai 1979 pp. 50–53). While Japanese students are noted for being well disciplined and hard-working, education is criticized for being too competitive, for reinforcing rigid conformity to the group, and for pervasive bullying and the use of severe physical and psychological punishment. Reformers demand that Japanese schools encourage greater freedom, individuality, tolerance, and creativity (Horio 1988, Schoolland 1990).

6. *Effectiveness of Political Socialization in Education*

Given the schools' mandate to prepare the next generation of youth to be knowledgeable about politics and become competent citizens, a central question is how effective education is in the political socialization process. The research results are mixed. One set of studies indicates that in the adult population, increased levels of education are associated with greater political knowledge, support for democratic values, feelings of political efficacy, and political participation. In general, level of education is associated with greater political sophistication as adolescents advance in school. However, school factors such as the civics curriculum and teacher qualifications have been reported to have little or moderate effects on students' political knowledge, values, and skills. Research findings from a number of countries caution that civics courses have a stronger impact on some groups of youngsters than on others, depending on factors such as social class, ethnicity, and gender (Adelson 1986, Heater and Gillespie 1981). There are a number of explanations why educating students about political culture and citizenship has been less than successful.

Part of the problem may lie in the way formal political socialization is conducted in the schools. As Turner (1981) noted, "most citizenship education . . . can be characterized as traditional, rooted in the values of the past, and supported by methodologies that are comfortable and easy for already overburdened teachers to implement" (p. 58). Much of the course content is weighted toward government, history, and geography, all of which may be quite remote to an adolescent. Teacher-centered lessons are the norm, and teachers often avoid issues and questions that might be controversial or open to interpretation. Moreover, teachers may not be prepared adequately for their political socialization function, and they are likely to view politics and citizenship from the perspective of their particular educational experiences, generational values, and political orientations. The developmental abilities of children, adolescents, and adults also need to be considered in sequencing course content and in selecting activities appropriate for each learner's abilities (Heater and Gillespie 1981). As Entwistle (1981) cautioned, an estimated 60 percent of the adult population in the United States "cannot read well enough, or think abstractly enough, to understand drivers' manuals, income tax forms, and many other obligations of modern citizenship" (p. 251). How then can students be expected to perform well if the adult population is lagging?

Another key factor that may lessen the impact of schools on political socialization is that family political socialization precedes and may well override the effects of education. Researchers consistently report children's early awareness of their parents' political views and a correspondence in parents' and offspring's politics. It is likely that subsequent school experiences are selectively filtered to conform to the young person's existing political beliefs. Teachers and political experiences that confirm the student's political orientations are internalized whereas those that run contrary to the student's political orientations are likely dismissed (Coles 1986, Renshon 1977).

The effectiveness of political socialization in education is also influenced by generational factors and the sociohistorical context. Each age group or cohort comes of age and develops its social and political orientations under specific conditions. When society changes rapidly, the social and political attitudes of the various age cohorts may differ, creating generational misunderstanding and miscommunication. Thus, the educational goals and political activities developed by adults on the basis of their collective experiences may not be well-received by the younger generation, which has both the youthful desire to make its own way in the world and a different set of societal growing-up experiences (Braungart and Braungart 1986). In addition, political regimes perceived as lacking in legitimacy and effectiveness are not likely to be successful in their political socialization efforts in the schools.

7. *Political Socialization in Other Educational Settings*

While primary and secondary schools are the major source of formal political learning, political socialization occurs in educational settings beyond the high school level, such as higher education, national service, and adult education. With regard to higher education, research indicates that students may change their political views during the course of higher education, especially when the college or university is viewed as a significant reference group. College major may be associated with political liberalism or conservatism, and students may shift their political values to correspond more closely to the values of professionals working in the student's chosen occupation. Time-series investigations report that college students' social and political views differ from one era to the next, often reflecting trends and changes in the larger national electorate (Braungart and Braungart 1988).

Political socialization in colleges and universities is, nonetheless, difficult to ascertain. In keeping with the spirit of academic freedom, many colleges and universities do not have a coordinated educational program directed toward political knowledge, attitudes, values, and skills, although some colleges may have more rigorous course requirements than others in history, philosophy, and the social sciences. It may be that higher education has a greater informal than formal impact on political socialization through student participation in extracurricular activities, where young people can develop and try out their skills at decision making, community volunteer work, and political activism.

When compared to higher education, more direct forms of political socialization are undertaken in a national service program than on a college campus. Viewed as an obligation of citizenship, national service is a period of active duty given by the individual to his or her country. Often stimulated by youth unemployment, lack of schooling, the demands of nation building, and meeting community needs, the majority of the 195 nations of the world have some type of national service which is either voluntary or required. Four categories of youth service have been identified: (a) military or civilian training and employment; (b) study-services (often in remote areas of a country); (c) foreign volunteer service; and (d) social and technical development. Such programs not only foster work and citizen skills, but may be designed to break down cultural and ethnic group conflicts and generate a feeling of contribution and involvement in one's country. Germany, for example, has an extensive mandatory national service, where the young person's obligation can be met by either military or civilian programs (Sherraden and Eberly 1982). Janowitz (1983) has argued that national service programs are one of the best sources of political socialization for balancing citizens' rights and responsibilities.

A further source of political socialization is through adult education, which is usually intended to be either compensatory or remedial. A variety of groups and organizations may offer formal courses or workshops to enhance adults' political knowledge, attitudes, values, and skills. The most frequent avenues for formal adult political socialization occur through: (a) government sponsorship (especially to combat adult illiteracy, integrate immigrant populations, and engender system-creation); (b) higher education, including evening classes, continuing education, and elder-study programs; (c) voluntary associations, such as political parties, labor unions, public interest groups, professional organizations, and advocacy organizations; (d) philanthropic foundations; and (e) religious organizations. Educators involved with the political socialization of adults caution that adults generally eschew political theory and teacher-centered lessons. Since politics is a more proximal concern for adults than for children and adolescents, adults respond favorably to pragmatic courses and workshops where they can enter into an exchange relationship with the instructor, integrate what they learn with their life experiences, and exercise political skills (Advisory Council for Adult and Continuing Education 1983, Entwistle 1981).

8. Implications

Several implications may be drawn from the above. First, understanding the role of education in political socialization requires an examination of the various assumptions held by educators, politicians, administrators, and parents, who determine how the younger generation will be taught politics and citizenship in the schools. Repeated controversies arise over the inherent contradictions in democracy and citizenship, whether political socialization is based on training or education, the role of the learner in the political socialization process, and the extent to which students should be directed toward political conformity or change. As an illustration, one may consider three contrasting assumptions about social and political change: the elitist view that change comes from above; the pluralist view that change emerges from a plethora of volunteer and interest groups; and the social movement view that political reform emanates from the grass roots. Which of these positions school systems and educators favor colors the goals, information, and activities used to teach students how to accomplish political change as citizens.

Second, advances in political socialization theory and research can result in meaningful educational applications. What was once considered a simple, often ineffective transmission of political information from adults to young people is increasingly appreciated for its complexity. Though progress has been made, much of the theory and research in political socialization and education continue to be based on simplified models. New directions in theory building and research include focusing on how theories and variables combine, incorporating both macro and micro approaches in a single design, and examining not only aggregate patterns but individual diversity in studies of political socialization and education. Findings based on quantitative and qualitative designs can be translated into sophisticated educational practices, such as tailoring political socialization efforts in the schools to the individual learner, which ultimately may have greater long-term positive consequences for society and for the individual.

A third implication concerns the dynamic nature of the relationship between political socialization and education. Shifting community, national, and global trends foster changes in democracy and citizenship, and, in turn, the way political socialization is implemented in the educational setting. Since the start of the nineteenth century, nationalism has been the driving force in the world order and more recently in the educational system, with political socialization in the schools largely directed toward teaching students about their country and fitting into the domestic order. Increasingly, however, new sets of economic, social, and political problems cross national boundaries. These include multinational corporate expansion; worker mobility; the global dissemination of technology, information, and culture; and a widening array of concerns, such as multiculturalism, environmental destruction, human health and cruelty, nuclear threat, political refugees, and terrorism. In direct response to these and other problems, new forms of citizenship are in the making, particularly as they relate to human and biological rights as well as citizen responsibility and government accountability. These global trends and transformations will affect educational debates and political socialization in the schools for decades to come.

See also: Acquisition of Empowerment Skills; Adolescence; Conscientization and Mobilization; Socialization

References

Adelson J 1986 *Inventing Adolescence: The Political Psychology of Everyday Schooling.* Transaction Books, New Brunswick, New Jersey

Advisory Council for Adult and Continuing Education 1983 *Political Education for Adults.* Advisory Council for Adult and Continuing Education, Leicester

Braungart R G, Braungart M M 1986 Life-course and generational politics. *Ann. Rev. Sociol.* 12: 205–31

Braungart R G, Braungart M M 1988 From yippies to yuppies: Twenty years of freshmen attitudes. *Public Opinion* 11: 53–56

Braungart R G, Braungart M M 1995 Today's youth, tomorrow's citizens. *The Public Perspective* 6: 4–7, 57

Carnegie Council on Adolescent Development 1995 *Great Transitions: Preparing for a New Century.* Carnegie Corporation of New York, New York

Coles R 1986 *The Political Life of Children.* Atlantic Monthly Press, Boston, Massachusetts

Davey T 1987 *A Generation Divided: German Children and the Berlin Wall.* Duke University Press, Durham, North Carolina

Derricott R 1979 Social studies in England. In: Mehlinger H D, Tucker J L (eds.) 1979 *Teaching Social Studies in Other Nations.* National Council for the Social Studies, Washington, DC

Entwistle H 1981 The political education of adults. In: Heater D, Gillespie J A (eds.) 1981 *Political Education in Flux.* Sage, London

Eveslage T E 1993 The social studies and scholastic journalism: partners in citizenship education. *Soc. Stud. Educ.* 57: 82–86

Farah T E, Kuroda Y (eds.) 1987 *Political Socialization in the Arab States.* Lynne Rienner Publishers, Boulder, Colorado

Heater D 1990 A state of confusion: Factors in the history of English political education. In: Claussen B, Mueller H (eds.) 1990 *International Studies in Political Socialization and Political Education,* Vol. 5. Peter Lang, Frankfurt

Heater D, Gillespie J A (eds.) 1981 *Political Education in Flux.* Sage, London

Horio T 1988 *Educational Thought and Ideology in Modern Japan.* University of Tokyo Press, Tokyo

Ichilov O (ed.) 1990 *Political Socialization, Citizenship Education, and Democracy.* Teachers College Press, Columbia University, New York

Janowitz M 1983 *The Reconstruction of Patriotism: Education for Civic Consciousness.* University of Chicago Press, Chicago, Illinois

Jones G, Wallace C 1992 *Youth, Family and Citizenship.* Open University Press, Buckingham

Kuhn A 1979 Social studies in the Federal Republic of Germany. In: Mehlinger H D, Tucker J L (eds.) 1979 *Teaching Social Studies in Other Nations.* National Council for the Social Studies, Washington, DC

Meyenberg R 1993 Political education, Germany, and Europe. In Farnen, R F (ed.) 1993 *Reconceptualizing Politics, Socialization, and Education.* Bibliotheks und Informationssystem der Universität Oldenburg

Nagai J 1979 Social studies in Japan. In: Mehlinger H D, Tucker J L (eds.) 1979 *Teaching Social Studies in Other Nations.* National Council for the Social Studies, Washington, DC

National Research Council 1993 *Losing Generations: Adolescents in High-risk Settings.* American Psychological Association, Washington, DC

Patrick J J 1977 Political socialization and political education in schools. In: Renshon S A (ed.) 1977 *Handbook of Political Socialization.* Free Press, New York

Pennock J R 1979 *Democratic Political Theory.* Princeton University Press, Princeton, New Jersey

Reische D L 1987 *Citizenship: Goal of Education.* American Association of School Administrators, Arlington, Virginia

Remy R C 1980 *Handbook of Basic Citizenship Competencies.* Association for Supervision and Curriculum Development, Alexandria, Virginia

Renshon S A (ed.) 1977 *Handbook of Political Socialization: Theory and Research.* Free Press, New York

Schoolland K 1990 *Shogun's Ghost: The Dark Side of Japanese Education.* Bergin and Garvey, New York

Sherraden M W, Eberly D J (eds.) 1982 *National Service: Social, Economic and Military Impacts.* Pergamon Press, New York

Tarrant J M 1989 *Democracy and Education.* Avebury, Aldershot

Turner M J 1981 Civic education in the United States. In: Heater D, Gillespie J A (eds.) 1981 *Political Education in Flux.* Sage, London

Further Reading

Angel W D (ed.) 1995 *The International Law of Youth Rights.* Martinus Nijhoff Publishers, Dordrecht, The Netherlands

Dawson R E, Prewitt K, Dawson K S 1977 *Political Socialization: An Analytical Study,* 2nd edn. Little, Brown, Boston, Massachusetts

Farnen R F 1990 *Integrating Political Science, Education and Public Policy.* Peter Lang, Frankfurt am Main

Handel G 1990 Revising socialization theory. *American Sociological Review* 55(3): 463–66

Percheron A (ed.) 1987 Special Issue on Political Socialization. *Int. Political Sci. Rev.* 8: entire issue

Sigel R S (ed.) 1989 *Political Learning in Adulthood: A Sourcebook of Theory and Research.* University of Chicago Press, Chicago, Illinois

Socialization

A. Sturman

Socialization, in its broadest sense, is the process whereby individuals become members of society or members of sectors of society. It is concerned with how individuals adopt, or do not adopt, the values, customs, and perspectives of the surrounding culture or subcultures.

The interactive nature of socialization, that is, the interaction of values, customs, and perspectives on individuals as well as the adaptation of those values, customs, and perspectives as a result of negotiation among members of groups, has made it fertile ground for the social sciences, but especially for psychologists and sociologists either working alone or in combination as social psychologists. Each discipline, however, has tended to approach the subject from a different angle. Psychologists have focused on how individuals learn and, in particular, on stages of development, whereas sociologists have focused on the relationships into which individuals move.

The first section in this article elaborates on the brief definition of socialization provided in this introduction. This is followed by a review of the antecedents to current theories of socialization and how they relate to more general sociological theory, a review of current theory and research on socialization, and an overview of the issues raised by research into the different contexts in which socialization takes place. Section 5 is an examination of the application to the field of education of studies into socialization, both in the sense of schooling as a socializing context and as regards the effects on schooling of other contexts such as the family.

While the discussion of the antecedents to current theory embraces psychological, anthropological, and sociological theory, most of the discussion of current theory and its application to education draws upon the sociological tradition.

1. An Elaboration of the Concept of Socialization

Bush and Simmons (1981) comment that distinctions between the concepts of maturation, development, and socialization are stressed in sociological work on socialization. Research into maturation processes and developmental stages has, however, contributed to research and theory on socialization.

Bush and Simmons also comment that maturation is depicted as entailing a more or less automatic unfolding of biological potential in a predictable sequence, while development is viewed as a set of sequential changes from simple to more complex structures within the boundaries set by both biological and social

structures. Both the concepts of development and socialization stress an interaction between individual behavior and the environment, but socialization does not necessarily entail sequential change from simple to complex structures.

Wentworth (1980 p. 83) has defined socialization as: "the activity that confronts and lends structure to the entry of nonmembers into an already existing world or a sector of that world."

As described by Musgrave (1987), embodied in this definition of the concept of socialization are the implications that it is a crucial link between the existing culture of a group and its members, that it can refer to processes at many levels, and that there is no assumption that the norms learned are believed or must be obeyed, that is, the norms are not necessarily internalized and change is therefore possible. This final implication allows for resistance to socializing forces, acknowledges that individuals may construct their own norms and, consequently, makes central to the study of socialization the issue of deviance, that is, behavior which does not meet existing norms.

Socialization is therefore interactive: the values, customs, and perspectives of cultures and subcultures influence how individuals behave but do not necessarily determine that behavior. Cultural influences and individual patterns of development both require consideration.

Related to this, Gecas (1981) notes that the concept of socialization has two fairly distinct meanings in sociology, both of which are valid and necessary for an adequate conceptualization. One stresses the individual's adaptation and conformity to societal requirements, and the other emphasizes the individual's development into a self-assertive, distinct human being. Gecas comments that the changes that individuals undergo become sociologically relevant in the context of organized social relationships and, in this sense, there is a "membership" component to socialization:

This component of socialization is most evident in the concept of identification, one of the key processes in socialization. Two aspects of socialization are relevant here: identification *of* and identification *with* . . . Identification *of* deals with the establishment of identities, that is, the determination of who one is and who the others are in the situation. Identification *with* refers to the emotional and psychological attachment that one has with some person or group. (Gecas 1981 p. 166)

Musgrave (1987 p. 3) has also referred to socialization as forward looking and to the effects of prior socializing experiences:

The outcomes are important to those involved, both to

those responsible for the continuity of groups, that is those with some power, and to those being socialised, whether unconsciously or because they hope to become members of some group. Sociologists often speak of anticipatory socialisation to highlight this forward-looking aspect. What has, however, to be noted is that prior socialisation may prepare potential members of groups well or less well for further experiences.

Individuals, during the course of their lives, do not experience one process of socialization but are subjected to many. Agents of socialization include wider cultural influences, families, and the formal organizations in which individuals work or learn (schools, military academies, prisons, public service bureaucracies, and the like). Sieber and Gordon (1981) categorize these socializing organizations into "total institutions," such as prisons, military academies, and boarding schools, and organizations that are less total in their regimes such as schools, summer camps, and the like. Goffman (1961) discusses the pervasive socializing influences of institutions with long duration and high intensity compared with other less pervasive or intensive institutions, of which schools are one example. Focusing on the contexts in which socialization takes place requires that special attention be given to the social structural features of these situations, such as patterns of interaction, group composition, and other group features like size and boundary permeability (see Gecas 1981).

Gecas comments that contexts of socialization vary in scope and duration. After Wheeler (1966), a distinction can be made between "developmental socialization systems" whose purpose is the training, education, or further socialization of individuals, and "re-socialization systems" whose purpose is to correct some deficiency in earlier socialization. A distinction has also been made (see Brim and Wheeler 1966) between "primary" and "secondary" socialization: the former refers to roles learned earlier in life and the latter to those that occur later. While the temporal distinction has some usefulness, Musgrave (1987) warns against the belief that primary socialization is necessarily more permanent than secondary and has warned that these distinctions can lead to a deterministic view, in that actors are seen to be socialized and cannot create patterns of behavior to meet needs.

2. Antecedents to Current Theories of Socialization

Bush and Simmons (1981) have traced the historical antecedents to current theory on socialization and have referred to the classical works of Freud, Piaget, Cooley, George Herbert Mead, Margaret Mead, Benedict, Erikson, and Mannheim.

Freud's (1961, originally published in 1930) psychosexual stage theory, and in particular his theory of the three inborn structures of the mind or personality (the id, the ego, and the superego), provided one of the most influential interpretations of the socialization process. The development of the ego and the superego are seen as the basic tasks of socialization and identification, that is, the act of becoming like something or someone is the key process. Each psychosexual stage identified by Freud is defined by where and upon whom an individual's libidinal energy is cathected at a given time.

Piaget's (1970) theory of development, which is concerned with the progressive construction and reconstruction of cognitive structures as the child develops, has also been influential in the field of socialization. According to Piaget, the child actively assimilates and organizes new information according to existing cognitive structures, and this produces the cognitive reorganization that constitutes the various stages of development outlined in his theory.

The work of Cooley (1964) and Mead (1934) on the emergence of the self through social interaction, and in particular their distinction of the "I" and "me," is also central to socialization, as is the work of Mead (1928) and Benedict (1938) on the ways in which the culture of a society can affect the character and outcomes of life transitions.

Erikson (1950), who conceived of eight ages of man, with each stage having its specific development task that must be accomplished for individuals to progress to the next stage, provides one of the most influential frameworks to deal specifically with the issue of socialization over the whole life span. Mannheim (1952) focuses on the effects of generations as a source of social change and as a potential influence on the socialization process.

Bush and Simmons (1981) argue that these very diverse classical theories have shaped the themes or raised points of contention that continue to pervade the study of socialization. In particular, they refer to the issues of continuity or discontinuity of processes of socialization and the universality of socialization processes over time and space.

Musgrave (1987), from a sociological perspective, has also reviewed past theories of socialization. He has argued that sociological theory, as applied to socialization, has followed two main paths. The first is the "organic" approach, which sees society as a network of interrelated positions filled by individuals who are in agreement about how they should interact. The key concept in this approach is structure, which is analyzed in terms of roles and statuses within institutions. The second is the "conflict" approach, which analyzes society in terms of groups whose interests conflict. The key concepts are logically conflict and interests, but power is also important. Both of these approaches have been used to analyze social behavior and, in particular, socialization at the societal and interpersonal levels.

Musgrave comments that until the 1960s the major tradition in considering socialization was the organic approach at the societal level. Sociologists examined how individuals became social beings by learning the different roles attached to positions they were expected to move through. As examples of this approach, Musgrave refers to the classical work of Margaret Mead, Durkheim, and Parsons. As Musgrave has reported, this approach has been criticized on the grounds that the logic tends to be teleological (a particular effect implies a particular cause), there is scant attention paid to issues of conflict and change, and, mainly because of this, the approach, knowingly or not, supports a conservative ideology.

Musgrave notes that since the 1960s some sociologists have worked at the societal level but from a conflict approach. The main emphasis of these writers has been on the way social groups with different interests come into conflict and on the results of that conflict. Musgrave refers to the work of sociologists both within the Marxist tradition and outside that tradition. Musgrave comments that there have been difficulties with both arms of this approach. He notes the internecine squabbles of the Marxist sociologists about what is true doctrine and the fact that Marxist predictions have not come to pass, and he notes theoretical and methodological problems with the approach of the non-Marxist sociologists.

Musgrave argues that it was also in the 1960s that greater emphasis was placed on interpersonal interaction, and he refers to the pioneering works of Goffman, Weber, Husserl, Schutz, and Berger and Luckman. Like societal theories, the interpersonal approach developed in both the organic and conflict traditions. Musgrave notes in fact that the work on symbolic interactionism, which focuses on the ways actors construct meanings in interaction, work usually associated with George Herbert Mead, has been applied to both organic and conflict theories

Examples of work in the organic tradition alone include the culture and personality theorists such as Margaret Mead, whose work examined the links between societal structure and personality, and the ethnomethodologists such as Garfinkel, who studied the ways in which people come to perceive and produce everyday interaction (see, e.g., Garfinkel 1967). Examples of work at the interpersonal level described by Musgrave and conducted within the conflict tradition include the work of Blau (1964) and Homans (1961) on exchange theory. In the view of these theorists, society is a network of transactions or exchanges carried out by explicit or implicit bargaining.

Musgrave comments that work at the interpersonal level has also been subjected to criticism at the theoretical and methodological level.

Musgrave concludes that each of the four approaches has helped the gradual clarification of ideas about social interaction but each has theoretical weaknesses. He argues therefore that there is a need for a unifying approach:

> In it emphasis is put upon the actor as a potentially creative subject who, depending upon how power is structured within his career, constructs rather than reconstructs

sometimes cognitive, but particularly moral knowledge, as this is communicated to him both through language and other cues. (Musgrave 1987 p. 23)

3. Current Theory and Research into Socialization

Bush and Simmons (1981) have reviewed current theory and research into socialization and have argued that underlying virtually all of the contemporary sociological views is the assumption that socialization is a continuing, lifelong process, although some writers would argue that change over time is anomalous, while others see it as a logical extension of values, norms, and the like that are formed in childhood and adolescence.

Bush and Simmons refer to the contemporary work that has revolved around the processes of role acquisition, role conflict, and role transitions, including role loss. Among the issues that have been addressed in this research have been an investigation of the stressful effects of role discontinuity, the effects on stress reduction of anticipatory socialization, the effects of the nature of role changes (do role changes that involve gains have the same effects as those involving losses?), the effects on role transition of rites of passage and being "off-time," the effects of lack of clarity on role consensus, and the effects on individuals of role conflict.

Bush and Simmons also refer to three general perspectives to socialization throughout the lifetime that have emerged: life-stage theories, lifespan developmental psychology, and life-course orientation.

4. Contexts of Socialization

Gecas (1981), while acknowledging that the number of contexts of socialization in a complex society is almost limitless, examines in some detail five contexts: the family, school, peer group, occupational setting, and radical resocialization settings. Zimmer and Witnov (1985) referred to a number of agents of socialization: culture, nations, family, formal organization, technology (television and computers), literature, and leaders. They examined in some detail three of these agents: culture, the family, and formal organization.

In Sect. 4 below a brief reference is made to the major themes that are present in theory and research with respect to three of these contexts: the family, peer groups, and occupational organizations. Section 5 deals separately with issues concerned with education and socialization.

4.1 The Family Context

Both Gecas and Zimmer and Witnov comment that the family is the context most closely associated with the topic of socialization because as an institution its major function is the socialization and care of children, both for membership of the family group and membership of the larger society. They argue that, because relationships within a family are usually intimate, intensive, and relatively enduring, socialization which takes place there is usually the most pervasive and consequential.

The issues raised in research and theory concerning socialization in the family have referred both to relationships within families and to the place of the family in society. Among the issues raised in the former are: the effects of the social organization of the family and in particular of the distribution of power within it; the processes of socialization, such as modeling, role-playing, and reinforcement, and the outcomes of these processes; the development in children of sex role identity, aggression, morality, and achievement; and the effects on socialization of different parental styles, family size and configuration, and single-parent families. With regard to the place of the family in the larger system of social institutions, one of the most common issues addressed in research and theory is the location of the family in the social class system.

4.2 The Childhood Peer Group Context

Gecas (1981) notes that the most important feature of the peer group is that it is a voluntary association, which means that boundaries of such groups are fluid. The peer group is also relatively independent of parental control, and consequently can be the context for the development of deviant or delinquent behavior. Gecas notes that association in peer groups is between status equals, and interaction is therefore more likely to be based on egalitarian norms, although informal status hierarchies, typically based on achievement in activities valued by the group, do develop. A third feature of such groups, noted by Gecas, is that they are typically segregated by sex.

Gecas argues that socialization in peer groups is characterized by its effect on three broad areas of the child's development: the development and validation of the self, the development of competence through role taking, and the acquisition of knowledge not gained in the family. The key to the importance of the peer group in these areas lies in the friendship bonds that are formed.

4.3 The Occupational Context

While the primary role of occupational organizations is not socialization, the structure of occupational settings can affect individual attitudes and values. Moreover, most large organizations have processes of induction and orientation which are designed to socialize new recruits into that organization.

Robbins et al. (1986) have described the process of occupational socialization as one of adaptation which takes place when an individual passes from outside the organization to the role of an inside member. Organizational socialization attempts to adapt the new employee to the organization's culture by conveying how things are done. From the perspective of the organization, acceptance by the employee of the organization's pivotal standards is imperative for individual performance and organizational stability. Nevertheless individuals vary in the degree to which they conform totally to the traditions and customs of the organization.

Gecas (1981) notes that occupational settings vary considerably with regard to a wide range of features such as power and authority relationships, worker participation, bureaucratization, and work complexity. One important distinction which tends to emerge in large organizations is between labor and management: workers in management are more likely to identify with the organization and nonmanagerial workers are more likely to identify with each other and may come into conflict with those in management.

It has been suggested that the conditions experienced in work can affect attitudes and values of workers. Kohn and co-workers argue that certain structural features of work, such as the amount of autonomy or complexity, can give rise to values of autonomy or conformity (see, for example, Kohn and Schooler 1978). Kanter (1977) argues that the adaptation of individuals to their work situation and their degree of commitment to work is a function of their location on three structural dimensions: the opportunity structure, the power structure, and the social composition of peer clusters.

As Gecas (1981) comments, work settings, like other socialization contexts, are affected by the larger society within which they exist. He notes that much of the sociological literature has dealt with the alienating effects of capitalism and he draws attention to the pioneering work of Marx and the research of Bowles and Gintis (1976).

5. Socialization and the School Context

The school, like the family, has an explicit socialization function. The extent of this function in the context of schooling is, however, more controversial and touches on the very nature of schooling. While it is accepted that schools have responsibilities in the affective domain as well as the academic domain, the extent of the former responsibilities are unclear and in constant flux. These responsibilities are not only controversial in the sense that they overlap with the responsibilities of the other agencies, particularly the family, but it is often argued that society loads schools with a range of responsibilities that go well beyond their academic mandate and ultimately detract from that mandate. The delicacy of these issues is not new. For example, the place of religious education in schools proved one of the most controversial issues in the development of schooling in many countries, and in the late twentieth century the teaching of sex education in schools has evoked mixed responses. There are parents who hold that this is an area of responsibility for the family, not the school.

5.1 Schooling and Other Socialization Contexts

While schooling is viewed as the major educational context for children, a great deal of education takes place outside school, and in particular in the family. In fact, the publication of the Coleman Report in the United States (Coleman et al. 1966) and subsequent confirmatory reports or reviews (see Averch et al. 1972, Jencks et al. 1972) led to the belief that schools make little difference in educational achievement, and it is the social status of the students' families that account for most of the difference in achievement levels. Subsequently, these findings have been challenged both on methodological and theoretical grounds and it is generally accepted that schooling has a greater effect on student achievement than was originally acknowledged. Research into the characteristics of effective schools has been one of the growth areas of educational research in the late 1980s and the 1990s.

Nonetheless, by the time children go to school they will have learned a great deal that will affect their schooling experience. Kerckhoff (1986) notes, for example, that families contribute greatly to the motivational and cognitive skill levels exhibited by their children, and they continue to influence those qualities throughout schooling. Important aspects of the family that contribute to these influences include parental expectations, cultural differences, social status differences, and parent–child interactions.

The cultural differences are evident both from within-nation studies and cross-nation studies. For example, research in Australia (see Sturman 1986) has consistently shown the higher educational aspirations of students whose backgrounds are from non-English-speaking countries. Similarly, Fuller et al. (1986) have argued that some of the differences between educational achievement levels in Japan and the United States can be attributed to the fact that elements of socialization in the Japanese family are more deeply agreed upon, less variable across parents, and more tightly coupled with the educational system.

Kerckhoff also draws attention to the important influence of peer groups on schooling, in particular because the organization of schooling ensures that students spend a great deal of time with their peers. He notes that friendship relations in school can affect educational aspirations and other aspects of the schooling process (see *Youth Friendships and Conflict in School*).

5.2 The Socializing Processes of Schooling

The socializing processes of schools can be overt or hidden. For example, teachers, because they tend to come from a similar social background, may unknowingly pass on to students certain attitudes and values. Other aspects of schooling may be more open.

Gecas (1981) argues that the most conspicuous socialization process in the classroom is social reinforcement such as praise, blame, privileges, and particularly the allocation of grades. From a review of the research, Gecas suggests that teachers reward students who conform to the social order of the school with higher grades. Thus, personality characteristics such as drive to achieve, citizenship, dependability, perseverance, and punctuality may be rewarded more highly than actual achievement. Gecas also refers to the research which suggests that teacher expectations of students can become important predictors of student achievement.

Gecas commented that students are, however, not necessarily passive recipients of the pressures they experience. They may engage in activities that alter these experiences to make them more favorable to their interests, such as the avoidance of failure by nonparticipation in certain activities, or participating but using the minimum of effort.

5.3 Schooling and the Larger Social Setting

One of the more influential theories that has been applied to education and which touches on the socialization effects of schooling is the idea that the educational system reproduces a system of knowledge based on the class relations which exist outside schools (Bourdieu and Passeron 1977). However, as Musgrave (1987) reports, critics argue that the theory does not explain how the process occurs at the interpersonal level and that, in fact, reproduction does not always take place. Musgrave comments that one way of conceptualizing this failure has been to examine resistance in education: both teachers and students can become alienated from a system where they are asked to do what they may not wish to do and the result of the alienation can be resistance.

Analysis of the links between education and the economy has tended to argue a structural correspondence, that is, that the educational system perpetuates the economic order (see Bowles and Gintis 1976). However, Musgrave (1987) notes that the critics of the correspondence theory point, to the difficulty in establishing the direction of causation and hence to the failure of the theory to address the mechanism of influence.

6. Conclusion

Research and theory on socialization covers a very wide area, ranging from micro studies of interpersonal relationships to macro studies of societal structures and cultural influences. The contexts of socialization range from the wider culture to the family, peer group, and occupational settings. This entry has attempted to map the area and draw attention to the complexity of the subject matter.

See also: Acquiring Attitudes and Values; Aggression, Development and Socialization; Political Socialization and Education; Professional Socialization of Teachers

References

Averch H S, Carroll J, Donaldson T S, Kiesling H J, Pincus J 1972 *How Effective is Schooling?* Rand Corporation, Santa Monica, California

Benedict R 1938 Continuities and discontinuities in cultural conditioning. *Psychiatry* 1: 161–67

Blau P 1964 *Exchange and Power in Social Life.* Wiley, New York

Bourdieu P, Passeron J C 1977 *Reproduction in Education, Society and Culture.* Sage, London

Bowles S, Gintis H 1976 *Schooling in Capitalist America.* Routledge and Kegan Paul, London

Brim O G, Wheeler S (eds.) 1966 *Socialization After Childhood: Two Essays.* Wiley, New York

Bush D M, Simmons R G 1981 Socialization processes over the life course. In: Rosenberg M, Turner R H (eds.) 1981 *Social Psychology: Sociological Perspectives.* Basic Books, New York

Coleman J S et al. 1966 *Equality of Educational Opportunity.* US Government Printing Office, Washington, DC

Cooley C H 1964 [1902] *Human Nature and the Social Order.* Scribner's, New York

Erikson E H 1950 *Childhood and Society.* Norton, New York

Freud S 1961 [1930] *Civilization and Its Discontents.* Dorsey, New York

Fuller B, Holloway S D, Azuma H, Hess R D, Kashiwagi K 1986 Contrasting achievement rules: Socialization of Japanese children at home and in school. In: Kerckhoff A C (ed.) 1986 *Research in Sociology of Education and Socialization: A Research Annual,* Vol. 6. JAI Press, Greenwich, Connecticut

Garfinkel H 1967 *Studies in Ethnomethodology.* Prentice-Hall, Englewood Cliffs, New Jersey

Gecas V 1981 Contexts of socialization. In: Rosenberg M, Turner R H (eds.) 1981 *Social Psychology: Sociological Perspectives.* Basic Books, New York

Goffman E 1961 *Asylums: Essays on the Social Situation of Mental Patients and Other Inmates.* Doubleday/Anchor, New York

Homans G C 1961 *Social Behavior: Its Elementary Forms.* Harcourt, Brace and World, New York

Jencks C et al. 1972 *Inequality: A Reassessment of the Effect of Family and Schooling in America.* Basic Books, New York

Kanter R M 1977 *Men and Women of the Corporation.* Basic Books, New York

Kerckhoff A C 1986 Family position, peer influences, and schooling. In: Richardson J G (ed.) 1986 *Handbook of Theory and Research for the Sociology of Education.* Greenwood Press, New York

Kohn M L, Schooler C 1978 The reciprocal effects of the substantive complexity of work and intellectual flexibility: A longitudinal assessment. *Am. J. Sociol.* 84: 24–52

Mannheim K 1952 The problem of generations. In: Mannheim K (ed.) 1952 *Essays in the Sociology of Knowledge.* Routledge and Kegan Paul, London

Mead G H 1934 *Mind, Self, and Society,* University of Chicago Press, Chicago, Illinois

Mead M 1928 *Coming of Age in Samoa.* Morrow, New York

Musgrave P W 1987 *Socialising Contexts: The Subject in Society.* Allen and Unwin, Sydney

Piaget J 1970 *Structuralism.* Basic Books, New York

Robbins S P, Low P S, Mourell M P 1986 *Managing Human Resources.* Prentice-Hall, Sydney

Sieber R T, Gordon A J (eds.) 1981 *Children and Their Organizations: Investigations in American Culture.* Hall, Boston, Massachusetts

Sturman A 1986 *Immigrant Australians and Education,* Australian Education Review No. 22. ACER, Hawthorn

Wentworth W M 1980 *Context and Understanding: An Inquiry into Socialization Theory.* Elsevier, New York

Wheeler S 1966 The structure of formally organized socialization settings. In: Brim O G, Wheeler S (eds.) 1966

Zimmer J M, Witnov S J 1985 Socialization. In: Husén T, Postlethwaite T N (eds.) 1985 *The International Encyclopedia of Education,* 1st edn. Pergamon Press, Oxford

Further Reading

Goslin D A (ed.) 1973 *Handbook of Socialization Theory and Research.* Rand McNally, Chicago, Illinois

Kerckhoff A C (ed.) 1983 *Research in Sociology of Education and Socialization: A Research Annual,* Vol. 4. JAI Press, Greenwich, Connecticut

(c) Race, Ethnicity, and Gender

Education of Indigenous Peoples

S. Juan

Education is the all-important process by which culture is learned by humans. As humans are the learners, culture is the curriculum. The study of education among indigenous peoples provides important insights which compliment those insights derived from studying education in our own society, in either historical or contemporary times. Thus, through studying the education of indigenous peoples, a broad perspective on the nature of humans and education is gained—perhaps the broadest.

1. Indigenous People, Culture, and Education

Indigenous peoples are those individuals living in societies relatively uninfluenced by modernization, urbanization, or industrialization. As such, indigenous peoples stand in sharp contrast to ourselves. Unlike our own, indigenous societies are generally small in population, isolated, non- or semiliterate, homogeneous, highly integrated, consensual, exhibit a simple division of labor, and enjoy strong group solidarity.

Each indigenous society possesses a distinct culture. "Culture," which is classically defined by Tylor (1871), is " . . . that complex whole which includes knowledge, belief, art, law, morals, custom, and any other capabilities and habits acquired by man as a member of society" (p.1). In Tylor's terms, education is the process by which culture is acquired.

More specifically, sociologists and anthropologists study the education of indigenous people in order to understand such things as how culture is learned and taught; how wisdom, skills, and technical information are passed on from individual to individual; how culture is transmitted from one generation to the next; how an individual is socialized or enculturated into roles as a fully participating member of the adult society; how the process of cultural transmission is related to the societal needs for biological and social reproduction; and how the cultural transmission process can assist or retard social change.

2. Cultural Transmission and Biological and Social Reproduction

All human societies face the imperatives of both biological and social reproduction in order to sustain themselves through time. Thus, each society must possess a system of cultural rules, values, norms, and sanctions regulating sexual behavior, family life, child rearing, and education. As part of the larger cultural system, the structure of the education system differs from society to society, and is shaped by such factors as the parameters set by the society's immediate physical environment, type of economy, history, religious tradition, social organization, and so on. Nevertheless, however a particular society fashions its education system, it represents one model of how humans have attempted to successfully adapt and survive. Thus, every indigenous system of education that anthropologists study is both unique and profound.

3. How Culture is Learned and Taught

Human learning involves cognitively assimilating the sensory data derived from watching, listening, and doing. Societies vary as to the emphasis placed upon each of these. In general, indigenous people are highly pragmatic in their approach to education. They practice the Deweyian notion of "learning by doing" and make little distinction between theory and practice. For example, rather than learn information from a textbook as people in developed countries might do, a child in an indigenous society would watch a skilled person perform some task and then attempt to perform it themselves.

Education is both "formal" and "informal" in character. "Formal" education occurs within specific social institutions designed for the training of skills, development of technical competencies, and amassing of knowledge necessary for adequate social functioning as an adult. Our schools would be a primary example. "Informal" education occurs outside such specific institutions and concerns, for example, the understanding of cultural symbols, values, norms, and patterns of behavior acceptable in that society. During the process of education, an individual in an indigenous society spends relatively little of their lifetime in formal educational settings, and far more in informal settings.

In all societies, rewards and punishments are employed to encourage learning and correct error. All societies encourage the learning of appropriate knowledge. In indigenous societies, the individual exists as a member of society and, by conforming to the ways of the society, both the society and the individual within it survive and prosper. As in developed societies, the fact that one has attained a level of knowledge is recognized and an appropriate higher status is gained for this accomplishment. Thus, the individual is motivated to learn.

In an indigenous society, being smaller in population, homogeneous, and often with less specialized knowledge, the culture to be learned is more specific. The majority of its members share similar knowledge and interests and are familiar with the thoughts, attitudes, and activities of the entire community. Therefore, education tends to be more straightforward, with little variation from individual to individual. In developed societies, individuals often learn from specialist teachers employed to perform this duty. In indigenous societies, there are rarely specialist teachers whose exclusive role is to teach. Instead, children learn from parents, elders, and peers. In such societies, a teacher is also a hunter, farmer, preparer of meals, and so on. Teaching, learning, and daily life are more closely connected since the object of instruction (e.g., repairing a fishing net) is usually immediate.

Nevertheless, no one is capable of learning all aspects of the culture of the society in which they live. Even the most technologically simple society may be highly complex in nontechnological domains of culture (e.g., kinship, religion, rituals, etc.). Therefore, although cultural knowledge is distributed through education, it may often be unevenly so. From the standpoint of the individual, culture must be continually learned. Education becomes a continuing process throughout life and may be viewed as the program that is part of a person's normal maturational and social development. Moreover, in general, the greater the knowledge and the more complicated the skills required in order to become a fully functioning member of society, the longer education takes.

Furthermore, all societies withhold certain crucial knowledge from some of its members, at least during certain periods of their lives. For example, knowledge of sex may be withheld from children, knowledge of folk medicine may be withheld from nonshamans and healers, knowledge of religious rituals of a male priestly class may be withheld from all females or from males of other classes, knowledge of childbirth may be withheld from males, and so on. The transmission of culture is invariably organized and controlled by social groups in society based upon the promotion and sustaining of their interests.

4. Education and Social Change

The process of cultural transmission can either help or hinder social change. Although education functions toward cultural continuity, it can also be a vehicle for cultural transformation. In general, efforts to stimulate social change through education are more likely to succeed when they are sensitive to the cultural factors existing in the indigenous society.

5. Studies in Six Major Geographical Regions of the World

Anthropologists, in particular, are interested in all aspects of the education of indigenous people and have studied them extensively in six major geographical regions of the world. The geographical region with the largest number of studies is sub-Saharan Africa, while the region with the least studies is the Mediterranean rim. Information on the education of indigenous peoples is often contained in ethnographies not specifically designed to focus upon the cultural transmission process in that society.

5.1 Sub-Saharan Africa

Perhaps the oldest study of the education of indigenous people is Kidd's (1906) classic description of education among the Kafir of South Africa. In Kafir society, education lasts from childhood to adulthood. The Kafir child learns through members of the family, peers, and other adults all the important cultural information. The rules of kinship and social organization are particularly significant as they determine all forms of social relations. Interestingly, Kidd offers suggestions as to how Kafir education could be improved in order to better prepare children to cope with problems faced as adults.

The account by Fortes (1938) of the Tallensi of Northern Ghana provides a prime example of the symbiotic relationship between education and other aspects of culture. Among the Tallensi, neither the educational system nor the complicated system of kinship and social organization would persist over time without the other. Fortes details fascinating aspects of Tallensi society showing how social and psychological factors, values, cosmological beliefs, laws, the sanctions that uphold them, household and family life, and technical abilities interact in a coherent pattern with, and are dependent upon, the educational system and social organization system that together maintain cultural continuity. In this small-scale farming society, education follows the principles of kinship and social organization inherent in the Tallensi structure of patrilineal clans and lineages.

Raum's (1940) invaluable account of indigenous education among the Chagga traces the intimate relationship between a tribal education and the culture of which it is part. The role played by children's peer groups in the process of education is highlighted. A child is taught by parents and by other children, rather than by specialists who separate out a formal program of training from their everyday life. Raum's data also illustrate how groups in a society will withhold certain information from children in order to serve their interests. In this case, male superiority is maintained by the mythical notion passed on to girls that males do not defecate.

In Nadel's (1942) classic study of the neo-feudal Nupe of central Nigeria, a formal education system exists to transmit certain aspects of culture, while an informal education system transmits other aspects. Among the Nupe, formal education is conducted by specialist teachers who instruct in the Koran, while representing both secular and spiritual authority. Informal education is carried out by age associations which are responsible for the practical education and training needed for daily life in Nupe society, and which also emphasize the acquisition of moral and social values.

The account by Herskovits (1943) of education among the Dahomeans of West Africa underscores the point that education can be used as a tool for cultural continuity as well as for cultural change. Furthermore, the process of cultural transmission can occur over long geographical distances (i.e., from Dahomey in West Africa to the New World). In the Dahomean case, as a result of slavery, there was an interruption of the traditional West African education system which was widespread and successfully functioning throughout the old kingdom. During their transportation and after their arrival in the New World, slaves and ex-slaves became responsible for holding the important elements of Dahomean culture intact and passing them on to the next generation. This exceedingly difficult task was accomplished despite the physical displacement from the homeland and the horrific oppression of slavery. Nevertheless, over time, some traditional cultural elements survived intact, others disappeared, and others were modified to suit the changing environmental and social conditions. Indeed, the elements that survived did so because they served to give the displaced Dahomeans a sense of identity and also made it easier for them to survive under the conditions of their new, unchosen, and hostile environment.

The account by Little (1967) of the "bush school" conducted by the "secret societies" of the Mende of Sierra Leone details the real role of these schools. By secluding children and instructing them in the important knowledge, values, and rituals of Mende society, Mende culture is transmitted to the next generation and preserved through time. Such instruction is the major means of preparing both male and female Mende children for adulthood. Intriguingly, Little observes that, although Mende children enjoy considerable parental affection, a child's social significance is very small. Should an infant die, there is no formal or ritual mourning process. In fact, the corpse is merely wrapped up in leaves and buried under a banana tree or in some other place where it is customary to deposit rubbish. At the end of education into adulthood within the bush (*poro*) school, initiation occurs. Mende belief holds that the young initiate is "swallowed" by the *poro* spirit and

"reborn" as an adult fully capable of self-discipline, working cooperatively with others, and taking orders.

Read's (1959) study of the Ngoni of Zambia also illustrates how education prepares the individual for the adjustment to adult life while also functioning toward the continuity of societal values. Among the Ngoni, the goal of educating the young may be summarized in one word, "respect" (*ulemu*) for the traditional values of their society. The concept of *ulemu* includes the acknowledgment that a particular person or office is entitled to honor, that all behavior to that person must express respect, and that by showing respect in language, posture, and action a child or adult shares in the honor attributed to the person. Thus, the Ngoni place great emphasis upon the rules of etiquette and decorum. Failure to show proper *ulemu* would result in loss of one's honor, and is virtually unthinkable in Ngoni society.

In another significant study, Gay and Cole (1967) report on the education of the Kpelle of Liberia. They demonstrate the effects of traditional learning upon cognition, and highlight the conflicts between indigenous and modern educational aims and methods. Mathematical knowledge among the Kpelle serves the immediate cultural needs existing in Kpelle society. By comparison, the learning of mathematics in Western education is abstract and theoretical. Thus, Kpelle children often do poorly in Western-oriented tests of mathematical skill. However, Kpelle mathematical skills are different rather than nonexistent. For example, rice is an important Kpelle foodstuff. Being able to accurately estimate the amount of rice that one is selling or purchasing in the marketplace is an important skill for the Kpelle to master. Kpelle children typically have the ability to merely look at a pile of rice and tell precisely how many cups it would fill. This would be daunting to most Western children.

Grindal's (1972) study of the Sisala of northern Ghana illustrates both the constructive and destructive consequences of the interaction between traditional and modern educational processes. The study highlights how introduced cultural change must be sensitive to the existing culture in order to avoid social disharmony and personal alienation.

Leis (1972) discusses socialization and enculturation in a small village of the Ijaw in Nigeria. There is an analysis of both the formal and informal educational processes as potential agents for social change and its acceptance.

Hollos and Leis (1989) continued this work by comparing another village with the one Leis originally studied. They point out that Western-style schooling is now commonplace and that many changes have occurred as a result. For example, girls traditionally married soon after menarche, while boys married later after acquiring the physical maturity to practice occupations and to earn money. Now, the years of 14–25 are a recognized transition period between adulthood and childhood such that a new, "invented," stage in the

Ijo life cycle has been created—adolescence.

However, the study by Ottenberg (1989) of the Afikpo of east central Nigeria illustrates that "bush schools," although perhaps similar in function, need not employ similar methods in all the societies in which they are found. In the Afikpo "bush school," boys are secluded during various periods, but they are not directly "instructed" as such.

5.2 Mediterranean Rim

Among the few studies related to this region is Ammar's (1954) account of formal and informal aspects of *fellahin* (peasant) education in a Muslim village in the Aswan province of Egypt. Indigenous styles of teaching and learning hold important implications for educational endeavors within a population of low literacy level.

The most important principle underlying education in this society is to instill an attitude of obedience and respect to all ordered authority (i.e., one's parents, elders, culture, and God).

In their study of the Moroccan town of Zawiya, Davis and Davis (1989) argue that schooling has played a major role in creating a series of new expectations among Moroccan youth. Furthermore, they point out that schooling serves to prolong the stage of adolescence in a manner previously unknown in that society. The school has also become a venue for the testing of the traditional societal norms, especially with respect to sexual behavior and gender roles.

5.3 East Eurasia

Nash's (1961) study of a northern Burmese village shows the ineffectiveness of social change introduced through government schools when changes have not taken place at the village level. This study illustrates the importance of taking into account indigenous cultural norms which may be contradictory to proposed changes. In the Burmese case, schools actually function as a conservative agent since the roles of teacher and pupil have not been distinguished from traditional social values and culture. Teachers take on traditional roles and do not understand the part they are supposed to play in the modernization desired by the government.

Freed and Freed (1981) describe the transition from traditional to school learning in a village in central India. Villagers of Shanti Nagar learn both how to learn and how to go to school. After first appearing completely alien, cooperating in the schooling process has, over several generations, become part of normal village life. Interestingly, the authors point out that a villager's relative degree of exposure to urban life and caste status are the two most important factors determining both school and life success.

5.4 Insular Pacific

Mead's (1954) famous study of Samoa emphasizes the stages of life through which Samoans pass and what is expected of them at each. Influential on all subsequent studies of education and culture, Mead shows how these expectations are acquired and fulfilled by means of interactions with peer groups, older relatives, and missionaries. Many difficulties faced by adolescents in Western society are not faced by those in Samoa. Mead's work establishes that childhood is culturally defined.

Equally famous are Mead's (1931, 1956) Manus studies showing the enculturation process at work, the relationship between traditional education and the modernization process, and how a society adapts to rapid cultural change resulting in a new way of life.

Firth's (1936) important account of the remote population of the Polynesian island of Tikopia clearly shows how education is inextricably a part of everyday family and social life. Formal education does not exist in this small society of only 1,200 individuals and education is by no means the province of the specialist educator. Nevertheless, education is vital to Tikopian child development. Becoming a Tikopian family member and adult is possible only by being fully socialized in Tikopian culture through the informal system of education. That system follows the principles of Tikopian social organization.

Whiting's (1941) monumental study of the Kwoma of the Sepik River highlands of Papua New Guinea both describes the culture of the Kwoma and presents a theory of the process of socialization based upon psychoanalytic and learning theory. The author writes that Kwoma teachers have a practical knowledge of the way in which people learn and then use certain techniques which are adapted, on the one hand, to the principles of learning and, on the other hand, to the culture and the necessity of transmitting it. Some of the techniques of teaching which the Kwoma employ stress motivation, others stress guidance, and still others reward. But all of them are in some way adjusted to the fact that learning only takes place when an individual is motivated by a drive to make a response in the presence of cues, and gains a reward for doing so. Furthermore, punishing, scolding, threatening, warning, and inciting are used by Kwoma teachers to motivate their pupils. Leading, instructing, and demonstrating are used to guide them; giving, helping, and praising are used to reward them.

Hogbin (1946) describes the pattern of informal education among the Wogeo of northern Papua New Guinea. The entire process of education is integrated into the general development of the individual child. The aims and sanctions behind education are identical to those that assist physical maturation, culminating in the Wogeo adult who is competent to marry and take on social responsibilities. The child's moral and technical education are but two aspects of the single process.

Howard's (1970) study depicts the transmission of Polynesian culture among the islanders of Rotuma. As a lifelong process, education involves family, peer groups, school, and community. The shifting of educational emphasis toward formal schooling and away from informal education is seen as a direct result of ever-increasing contact with the West.

Borofsky's (1987) account of education among the Polynesians of the island of Pukapuka illustrates how formal schooling is influenced by the intense status-rivalry which dominates that society. Pukapukan teaching and learning is based upon continuous questioning, ridicule, challenge, absence of praise, competition, defense of one's status, and the necessity to always appear knowledgeable.

5.5 North America

Eggan's (1956) study of the Hopi of the southwestern United States shows clearly the important part played by education in maintaining a strong sense of cultural identification against what is perceived by the Hopi as the encroaching outside world.

Williams (1958) presents a fascinating portrait of education and childhood among the Papago of the southwestern United States. The Papago follow six principles of education:

(a) There are few specific, overt techniques of punishment as a motivation for the child to learn appropriate social behavior.

(b) The individual is expected to show deference to all seniors in age regardless of sex, social ranking, or degree of relationship.

(c) Child rearing, including education, is shared by all members of the family.

(d) Supernatural sanctions exist to control social behavior that may disrupt the system of closely interdependent group life.

(e) Children are not to be held responsible for their social behavior until they have learned to become adults through the informal education process.

(f) The child is to be treated as a distinct person much as an adult is treated: for example, a child is consulted as to its wishes on matters which adults usually decide on.

Wolcott's (1967) study of education and village life among the Kwakiutl examines the dual system of the traditional/informal education and the formal education of the local school provided by the Canadian Indian Agency. The study highlights the relationship between parents and teachers, pupil attitudes and behavior in the classroom, and other issues which affect both the child, the villager, and the educator.

5.6 South and Central America

Redfield's (1943) major study of education and culture in the midwestern highlands of Guatemala underscores the point that education must be regarded as part of a total social process and is not merely confined to the school system. Redfield reports that in rural Guatemala, Indians and Ladinos (i.e., Spanish-speaking people of mixed ancestry) live side by side. The culture of the Indian majority is transmitted through traditional informal means. For example, moral values are learned through myths, folktales, and other nonpedagogical means. However, the culture of the Ladino minority, while lacking the same traditional informal means, is transmitted through other informal and nonpedagogical means. The schools set up by the government are seen as entirely external to the cultural transmission process of either culture. Schools are viewed as providing only purely technical training and, as such, are regarded as having little to do with growing up.

Modiano's (1973) study of education in the Chiapas highlands of Mexico examines how schooling is being introduced as a vehicle of social change. Frequently, modern educational methods are simply inapplicable to the real-life situations of the indigenous peoples, and conflicts between traditional and modern educational goals are numerous. Modiano writes that children are given more freedom than adults to satisfy their curiosity about the world. Their play is largely unsupervised and not seriously curtailed until the eve of adolescence. This allows them ample opportunity to explore their environment and come to terms with the adult world through imitative play. Almost no attempts are made to stifle their curiosity. It is the children rather than the adults who can observe strangers and strange phenomena freely and ask myriad questions. Childhood is truly an age of exploration. Modiano continues that two factors stand out in the indigenous style of education: (a) with sufficient practice at tasks that are an intrinsic part of the family's activities, the child is expected to become accustomed to work; and (b) both male and female children are given considerable leeway, even encouragement, to explore the world around them.

6. Conclusion

Sociologists and anthropologists continue to study the education of indigenous people. The more there is study of varied and different education systems, the more likely it is that elements common to all education systems will be discovered. When people understand all elements and how they interrelate in education systems, they will be better able to construct and modify those of their own.

See also: Social Change and Education

References

Ammar H 1954 *Growing Up in an Egyptian Village: Silwa Province of Aswan.* Routledge and Kegan Paul, London
Borofsky R 1987 *Making History: Pukapukan and*

Anthropological Constructions of Knowledge. Cambridge University Press, Cambridge

Davis S S, Davis D A 1989 *Adolescence in a Moroccan Town: Making Social Sense*. Rutgers University Press, New Brunswick, New Jersey

Eggan D 1956 Instruction and affect in Hopi cultural continuity. *Southwestern Journal of Anthropology* 12(4): 347–70

Firth R 1936 *We, the Tikopia: A Sociological Study of Kinship in Primitive Polynesia*. Allen and Unwin, London

Fortes M 1938 Social and psychological aspects of education in Taleland. *Africa* 1(4 Suppl.): 1–64

Freed R, Freed S 1981 *Enculturation and Education in Shanti Nagar*. American Museum of Natural History, New York

Gay J, Cole M 1967 *The New Mathematics and an Old Culture: The Study of Learning Among the Kpelle of Liberia*. Holt, Rinehart and Winston, New York

Grindal B 1972 *Growing up in Two Worlds: Education and Transition among the Sisala of Northern Ghana*. Holt, Rinehart and Winston, New York

Herskovits M 1943 Education and cultural dynamics: Dahomey and the New World. *Am. J. Sociol.* 48: 737–49

Hogbin I 1946 A New Guinea infancy: From weaning till the eighth year in Wogeo. *Oceania* 16: 275–96

Hollos M, Leis P 1989 *Becoming Nigerian in Ijo Society*. Rutgers University Press, New Brunswick, New Jersey

Howard A 1970 *Learning to be Rotuman: Enculturation in the South Pacific*. Teacher's College Press, New York

Kidd D 1906 *Savage Childhood: A Study of Kafir Children*. A and C Black, London

Leis P 1972 *Enculturation and Socialization in an Ijaw Village*. Holt, Rinehart and Winston, New York

Little K 1967 *The Mende of Sierre Leone*, rev. edn. Routledge and Kegan Paul, London

Mead M 1931 *Growing Up in New Guinea: A Comparative Study of Primitive Education*. William Morrow, New York

Mead M 1954 *Coming of Age in Samoa: A Psychological Study of Primitive Youth for Western Civilisation*. New American Library, New York

Mead M 1956 *New Lives for Old: A Cultural Transformation —Manus*. Gollancz, London

Modiano N 1973 *Indian Education in the Chiapas Highlands*. Holt, Rinehart and Winston, New York

Nadel S F 1942 *A Black Byzantium: The Kingdom of Nape in Nigeria*. Oxford University Press, London

Nash M 1961 Education in a new nation. The village school in upper Burma. *Int. J. Comp. Sociol.* 2(3): 135–43

Ottenberg S 1989 *Boyhood Rituals in an African Society: An Interpretation*. University of Washington Press, Seattle, Washington

Raum O 1940 *Chagga Childhood: A Description of Indigenous Education in an East African Tribe*. Oxford University Press, London

Read M 1959 *Children of Their Fathers: Growing up Among the Ngoni of Nyasaland*. Methuen, London

Redfield R 1943 Culture and education in the midwestern highlands of Guatemala. *Am. J. Sociol.* 48: 640–48

Tylor E 1871 *Primitive Culture: Researches into the Development of Mythology, Philosophy, Religion, Art and Custom*. J Murray, London

Whiting J 1941 *Becoming a Kwoma: Teaching and Learning in a New Guinea Tribe*. Yale University Press, New Haven, Connecticut

Williams T 1958 The structure of the socialization process in Papago Indian society. *Social Forces* 36(3): 251–56

Wolcott H 1967 *A Kwakiutl Village and School*. Holt, Rinehart and Winston, New York

Gender and Education

N. P. Stromquist

The way men and women are socialized throughout the world into gender roles, and the implications of this socialization process for educational participation, learning, social identification, and life outcomes are subjects with profound consequences for individuals and society.

1. Roles or Gender Ideology?

One definition of socialization is a "complex set of processes, covert and explicit, that train individuals to take their place as responsible members of society" (Lipman-Blumen 1984 p. 66). Socialization assumes inculcation of norms and values by agents such as family, school, and media. In this process, roles are the means by which individuals fit into the various areas of social life. Gender roles, specifically, are the behaviors and expectations based on social attributions of gender; these attributions involve a multiplicity of rules that range from what is "proper" to what is

"taboo" for men and women. Some feminist analyses would prefer the concept "patriarchal ideology" to emphasize that the values and norms inculcated through the gender socialization process are arbitrary (i.e., have no intrinsic truth) and depend on the will and power of the dominant group—men. Even though patriarchal ideology assumes various forms from society to society, its fundamental commonalities include the value placed on motherhood and domesticity, and the strong dichotomy between feminity and masculinity.

This entry is organized around six major areas at the intersection of ideology, education, and gender. They are access to schooling, attainment, the school experience, career choices, adult education, and benefits from schooling and education.

2. Access to Schooling

Most of the discussion about the unequal educational development between the sexes, especially in developing countries, has focused on access of girls to schooling (usually based on gross enrollment rates). Over time, girls have achieved parity in enrollment in primary and secondary education in most industrially advanced countries and in some parts of Latin America and East Asia. In many African, Middle Eastern, and South Asian countries, however, girls' primary and secondary school enrollment lags substantially behind that of boys. Women's participation in higher education tends to be lower than that of men in most countries.

Access to schooling is affected by cultural beliefs, the economic conditions of the family and the nation, and the educational supply. A host of factors outside the school system have been identified as affecting the enrollment and participation of girls in education, such as lack of time due to domestic work (cooking, obtaining water and wood, caring for minor siblings, etc.), child labor, early marriage, low aspirations, distance to schools, and lack of female teachers. While the entire list of factors is quite extensive (see Anderson 1988, Stromquist 1989), these "determinants" are merely manifestations of more fundamental causes and can be traced to two major enactments of patriarchal ideology: the practice of a strong sexual division of labor that circumscribes women to maternal and domestic roles, and the existence of sexuality norms that create physical and psychological boundaries for women.

2.1 Access in Developing Countries

The domestic division of labor affects the participation of girls in education in both rural and urban areas. Its effects are compounded dramatically by membership in a low social class. In countries where rural subsistence demands labor-intensive work, girls and women carry out a substantial amount of domestic and agricultural activities. Female labor makes women less available for schooling and, when they are available, they are left with reduced energy for learning. As a result, in many Middle Eastern, African, and South Asian countries both low rates of female access and high rates of female attrition in rural areas are in evidence. Urbanization favors school enrollment, and has a greater effect on the enrollment of women than of men. The available evidence, however, indicates that while urban life reduces the amount of domestic work, girls still work considerably more hours than boys.

2.2 Access in Developed Countries

In advanced industrialized countries there is gender parity in primary and secondary education, and substantial participation of women in higher education. For example, in the United States women outnumber men in enrollment in BA and MA programs; they are fewer than men at PhD level but their numbers are increasing. The main problem in industrially advanced countries is not access to higher education but the continuing segregation of women in a few fields. Throughout the world university programs in mathematics, engineering, and physical and biological sciences have an overrepresentation of men, and humanities and social sciences have a predominance of women.

In China, a socially, if not industrially, advanced country, more than 2.7 million children did not attend school in 1987, 83 percent of those being girls. Each year China produces an additional 2 million new illiterates, 80 percent of which are female. In 1988, Chinese women represented 41 percent of the total enrollment in secondary school and 33 percent of the enrollment in institutions of higher education.

Despite its high level of industrialization, Japan is a country with serious gender disparities at the tertiary level. Strong gender ideologies lead parents to believe that daughters do not need professional careers. Women represent only 35 percent of university enrollment; in contrast, they account for 80 percent of enrollment in junior colleges, which train students in many lower level, including home-oriented, occupations. A similar pattern operates in South Korea.

3. Attainment

Access to schooling is only part of the quest for equal education. Staying in school is no less important. Women undergo fewer years of education than men, a pattern observable in all developing regions. In only 3 out of 24 African countries (Botswana, Lesotho, and Swaziland) do women stay in schools longer than men (Hyde 1989). All three are states where demand for male labor in the mines of South Africa creates households headed by females, thus weakening patriarchal ideology about women's homebound roles.

The fewer years of education attained by women in Africa and other developing regions reflect the increasing demands that domestic work places on girls as they become older, and their internalization of domestic values. It is also clear that women's participation in education (both in terms of enrollment and time spent in education) is determined by the economic situation of the family to a greater extent than is that of men. A cumulative result of this fact is that among those enrolled in higher education, more women than men have parents who are highly educated or are in high income professions.

The control of women's sexuality affects women's education through parental emphasis on early marriage and their requirement that schools be close to home. In some Arab countries "girls are socialized into accepting the predominant sex-role stereotypes, with marriage and raising a family the ultimate goals. Schools continue to reinforce this differential socialization of gender divisions" (El-Sanabary 1989 p. 27). The value placed upon the honor (virginity) and safety of girls and women within Islamic and Hindu traditions limits their education; there is resistance from parents to sending girls to school away from home and a desire to marry them at an early age. Parents also fear that the assertiveness and belief in gender equality that women may develop through education will threaten their acceptance of men's superiority. This type of parental reaction has been observed in Bangladesh, India, and Nepal. Interpretations of Islamic precepts constrain the education of women by identifying the roles of mother and wife as being the most important for women. On the other hand, there is evidence that the level of economic development of a country and the distribution of income have a much stronger impact on women's education than religion (see Hyde 1989, O'Shaughnessy 1978; and for a contrary view, see Robertson 1985).

Distance from school acts as a considerable obstacle for girls whose parents feel that strict supervision of their daughters' behavior is needed. Long walking distances present an obstacle in several African countries, where there is a serious lack of primary schools in rural areas. Distance is also problem for African girls at the high school level, as most of these schools are located in urban areas, deeming it necessary for girls to live away from home in rented rooms. In other countries, a distance involving more than half-an-hour's walk may be considered too far for girls. Distance from school, however, is only one restriction against sending girls to school. In India, closeness to school is no longer an issue since 90 percent of children have access to a primary school or to a primary section in a secondary school within one kilometer of their home; however, other social forces prevent girls' access to education.

Even in more industrially advanced countries, parents are ambivalent about the education of their children. A study of parents in the United Kingdom produced the following results: they wanted their children, whichever sex, to study the same subjects at school; they wanted to have equal pay as men and women and to have equal access to occupations; but they believed that men and women had different roles in the family, with children being the main responsibility of women (Kelly 1982).

4. The School Experience

The processes by which schools transmit gender messages, and the dynamics by which students accept or modify these messages have in a few cases, been studied, and most of the research pertains to developed countries.

4.1 School Textbooks

The analysis of sexual bias in textbooks (through mechanisms such as stereotyping, rendering women invisible, and distorting reality) reveals remarkably similar findings across regions and cultural backgrounds. Sexual bias in textbooks has been found in countries as diverse as Colombia, India, and Zambia.

Since the mid-1970s textbooks have undergone changes in their sexual bias in the United States and in several other industrialized countries. Except for the careful revisions in Mexico and Sri Lanka, textbooks remain essentially unmodified in developing countries. In developed countries changes in textbooks have been generated by direct demand: progressive parents have reviewed textbooks and placed pressure on publishers to remove sexual bias; textbook changes have not been a product of legislation. In developing countries, textbooks are usually centrally produced and thus buffered from parental pressure. In addition, the economic situation in many developing countries is not conducive to actions that are perceived as relatively unimportant by those in government. In developing countries, textbooks transmit heavily stereotyped images of men and women, with women adopting low profiles and having traits of passivity, dependence on men, low intelligence, and lacking in leadership.

While textbooks have been revised at primary and secondary levels in developed countries, college textbooks are still heavily biased. United States studies of sociology textbooks (Ferree and Hall 1990) and economics textbooks (Feiner and Roberts 1990) revealed a gross underrepresentation of women. An examination of the table of contents and index of 34 textbooks of sociology of education in the United States, the United Kingdom, Australia, and Canada showed very limited references to sex differences, feminism, and sexism (Delamont 1989) although coverage improved slightly after 1975.

Textbooks shape attitudes through the continuous and authoritative representation of people and events. There is evidence, however, that it is possible to modify attitudes through relatively short-term intervention. Scott (1986) reports successful attitudinal change efforts involving students; Bonder (1991) conducted a similar successful experiment aimed at teachers.

4.2 Teachers' Attitudes

Teachers, as products of their society, often endorse patriarchal ideologies. Teachers who uphold dominant beliefs about men's superiority or women's maternal ambitions or domestic responsibilities are seldom conscious of their attitudes and practices. Various observational studies conducted in the United States have shown that teachers pay more attention to boys than girls in primary schools, and that they actively support boys when they do well. Qualitative investigations, using in-depth interviews and comparing interview data with classroom interaction, have established that teachers tend to enforce sharp feminine–masculine distinctions between students, attach greater importance to the cognitive development of boys than girls, and that female teachers hold ambivalent opinions about their own responsibilities as teachers and mothers. The fact that these findings have been obtained in Canada, the United Kingdom, Sweden, and Australia —countries substantially exposed to the women's movement—suggests that teachers' attitudes and practices may be even more biased in developing countries.

Questioning the premise that students accept all gender messages conveyed to them, a number of studies have explored the notion of resistance. The large body of data showing that girls endorse patriarchal definitions of feminity and masculinity indicates that resistance is a rare phenomenon.

4.3 Curriculum

In most countries there is a national curriculum, which implies that boys and girls are exposed to the same subjects. While this is true, schools in many countries continue to offer sex-differentiated courses, particularly with regard to practical activities. Girls continue to be placed in home economics courses and boys in mechanical and retail courses in many African and Middle Eastern countries. In Middle Eastern and North African countries, girls have little access to technical and vocational education (El-Sanabary 1989).

Schools also reinforce gender ideology by failing to offer courses for boys and girls that address sexuality in its social context. An increasing number of countries are offering sex education and population courses that deal with the need to be aware of demographic changes and the challenges they pose to a country's economic and social position. Yet these courses seem to concentrate on the anatomical and physiological features of sex, rather than on the social dynamics of sexuality and how these dynamics tend to affect women negatively.

Evidence about the role of a thorough sex education suggests that it can be quite effective in modifying preconceptions of feminity and masculinity, and that efforts to change attitudinal and behavioral approaches to sexuality are best introduced in early childhood —at five years of age, for instance, as happens in Sweden. Sex education in what was the Soviet Union occurs when children are between the ages of 15 and 17. The course advocates a moral approach to sex and the defense of the family, by stressing the maternal and domestic roles of women over their professional activities. It also calls for an expanded family, as a "one-child family is not really a collective" (Attwood 1987 p.128).

A positive development in tertiary education in the United States, the United Kingdom, Canada, a few Asian countries (particularly the Philippines), and Latin American countries (notably Brazil, Colombia, and Argentina) has been the emergence of women's studies programs that bring feminist theories and perspectives into the curriculum and thus challenge traditional gender notions. The United States is estimated to run 621 women's studies programs (1991) and to offer approximately 30,000 gender courses per year.

4.4 The School Environment

Research on the overall school environment is perhaps least often conducted. Longitudinal data from a United States survey—"The High School and Beyond"

(Maple and Stage 1991)—revealed that among Black and White male groups the school environment influenced student participation in an academic program of study but that it did not influence Black and White female groups. Interesting glimpses about the educational experience of girls and boys in the former Soviet Union is offered in a study by Attwood (1987). Her account indicates the existence of a strong school objective to shape definite "masculine" and "feminine" personalities, which translates into "placing boys in all the leading school and Komsomol posts" since some Soviet educators believed that girls should "in no event . . . become accustomed to the role of commander over boys" (Attwood 1987 p.115).

Data from both the United States and Chile suggest that schools do little to modify or challenge educational aspirations of girls and boys. Longitudinal data from Chile revealed that length of schooling tended to explain 21 percent of the variance in educational aspirations among boys, but only 1 percent of the variance among girls (Schiefelbein and Farrell 1980). It also showed that university aspirations between the eighth grade and the last year of high school decreased among girls but increased among boys. Studies in Africa have discovered that occupational aspirations among girls are consistently lower than among boys, even in the case of female students in elite schools. A study in the United States revealed that the influence of high school staff upon college plans negatively predicted science major choice for women but not for men (Gruca et al. 1988).

One issue in the debate about the experience of men and women in schools concerns the comparative merits of single-sex versus coeducational schools. Research focusing on cognitive development (particularly in relation to mathematics) indicates that single-sex schools promote greater learning among girls than coeducational schools (on the basis of evidence from Thailand, Nigeria, and Kenya). But it is not clear whether or not single-sex schools are better in other ways. Boys' schools have been found to prepare students for independence and power while girls' schools emphasize obedience rather than authority. In countries where there are strong norms about feminity and masculinity, coeducation can help to demystify the relationship between sexes and create a strong basis for companionship between them. Single-sex schools for girls, on the contrary, may restrict professional possibilities for women and, if expanded, could result in the additional cost of building schools for both men and women that eventually would generate separate, but unequal, education (van Bemmelen and van Vliet 1985).

5. Career Choices

Women often either select, or are led into, fields that emphasize care, that are socially defined as "proper" for women, and are compatible with the routine and close proximity demanded by family life. The clustering of women within a few fields commonly identified as "feminine fields" is a phenomenon evident throughout the world. While the occupations targeted as "feminine" are not always the same—for example, medicine in the former Soviet Union, and architecture, pharmacy, and psychology in some Latin American countries—the link between the presence of women in a field and the social devaluation of that field is a constant. A phenomenon reported in the United States is that while women are increasing their representation in previously male-dominated fields (e.g., medicine), they occupy the most devalued specializations within those fields. Even when women select nonconventional careers, a prime preoccupation is how their professional lives will fit with their family lives, a concern that male students report to a lesser degree (Stromquist 1991).

Academic choices are shaped by many factors, including adolescent concern with popularity and social acceptance. Ethington and Wolfle (1988) assert that occupational expectations linked to sex roles are the reason behind women's lack of enrollment in advanced mathematics and science courses, and that part of this decision is the perception of mathematics as a male domain. Women, then, may typically be selecting particular fields because of realistic expectations about the negative consequences of selecting deviant ones.

6. Adult Education

Literary skills among poor adult women are a critical area of educational concern. Except for Africa, where four out of five women over 25 years of age have never had any schooling, a major factor in the high rate of illiteracy among women is the limited participation (i.e., four or fewer years of schooling) of girls in primary school. One of the reasons for this is that illiterate parents see little value in the education of children, and of girls in particular. Rendering women literate could help break down this barrier.

Some ministries of education offer financial support for nonformal education (which includes adult literacy programs) but assistance is generally minimal (Stromquist 1997). Except for Indonesia, programs focusing on women are run only in countries where strictly defined gender roles exist (e.g., in Nepal, Bangladesh, and India). Further reducing the incentive of government and funding agencies to embark on literacy programs is the limited success of these programs, often with completion rates of less than 50 percent of those enrolled. To make matters worse, adult literacy programs aimed at women tend to emphasize traditional maternal and domestic roles.

In many developing countries, women in rural areas are not given adequate training in agricultural and other income-producing activities. Agricultural extension courses, when offered to women, concentrate on topics such as cooking, childcare, sewing, health and nutrition, home management, and vegetable gardening. In fact, home economics continues to be the basic nonformal education course offered to African women.

7. Benefits from Education

Cross-national comparisons (Benavot 1989) indicate that the expansion of female primary education, after controlling for women's fertility and women's participation in the labor force, has positive and stronger benefits than that of male primary education. The effect of the expansion of female secondary education is weak and insignificant, and this has been attributed to high schools being more elitist and selective than primary schools.

In numerous countries education has a direct influence on birth control together with a decrease in infant and child mortality. Educating women reduces the birthrate three times more effectively than educating men (Cochrane 1983). Educated women have been found to marry at a later age, and to provide their children with better childcare and much more verbal and physical stimulation than women with little or no education. Various studies have found greater benefits associated with the education of mothers than of fathers in relation to issues such as improved child nutrition. This is explained by the higher priority women tend to place on using their income to improve the family diet. Given existing family arrangements in which women have substantial childraising responsibilities, educated mothers have a greater influence on the cognitive development of their children. A study comparing maternal influences in both Japan and the United States found that the education of mothers positively affected the development of literacy, numeracy, and even intelligence in their children (Holloway et al. 1990). These findings support results documented in Le Vine (1982).

8. Conclusion

Despite women's increased access to schooling and extended years in education, the knowledge and skills they acquire in school tend to reproduce, rather than to alter, gender ideologies. In developing countries important school mechanisms such as textbooks, teachers' attitudes and behavior, curricula, and the general school environment continue to transmit gender messages, yet have not been the objects of large-scale interventions to try to modify them.

The sexual division of labor and the control of women's sexuality operating in any given society are reflected in parental decisions affecting their daughters' education. These parental decisions are rarely questioned by the schools, either because the schools are unable to overcome parental resistance or because the schools—as social products themselves—are in agreement with parental and community values and norms.

Even though society, the family, and children benefit greatly from the education of women, these "benefits" accrue only indirectly to women themselves. The liberatory type of knowledge women need is seldom given by the formal educational system. The unintended and undocumented consequences of education are the increased ability to reflect, and that having reflected on inequalities, eventually, leads to challenge them. It is here where the promise of education lies.

See also: Education and Development; Feminist Approaches to the Curriculum; Gender and New Technology; Gender Theories in Education; Sex Differences and School Outcomes; Students in Classrooms, Gender and Racial Differences Among

References

Anderson M 1988 *Improving Access to Schooling in the Third World: An Overview.* Bridges Research Report No. 1. Harvard University Press, Cambridge, Massachusetts

Attwood L 1987 Gender and Soviet pedagogy. In: Avis G (ed.) 1987 *The Making of the Soviet Citizen: Character Formation and Civic Training in Soviet Education.* Croom Helm, Beckenham

Benavot A 1989 Education, gender, and economic development: A cross-national study. *Sociol. Educ.* 62: 14–32

Bonder G 1991. Sexism in school practices: Designing and evaluating an experiment in attitudinal change among primary school teachers. In: Stromquist N (ed.) 1991 *Women and Education in Latin America: Knowledge, Power, and Change.* Lynne and Rienner Publishers, Boulder, Colorado

Cochrane S 1983 Effects of education and urbanization on fertility. In: Bulatao R, Lee R (eds.) 1983 *Determinants of Fertility in Developing Countries*, Vol. 2. Academic Press, New York

Delamont S 1989 *Knowledgeable Women: Structuralism and the Reproduction of Elites.* Routledge, London

El-Sanabary N 1989 *Determinants of Women's Education in the Middle East and North Africa: Illustrations from Seven Countries.* Document No. PHREE/89/14. The World Bank, Washington, DC

Ethington C, Wolfle L 1988 Women's selection of quantitative undergraduate fields of study. *Am. Educ. Res. J.* 25(2): 157–75

Feiner S, Roberts B 1990 Hidden by the invisible hand: Neoclassical economic theory and the textbook treatment of race and gender. *Gender and Society* 4(2): 159–81

Ferree M, Hall E 1990 Visual images of American society: Gender and race in introductory sociology textbooks. *Gender and Society* 4(4): 500–23

Gruca J, Ethington C, Pascarella E 1988 Intergenerational

effects of college graduates on career sex atypicality in women. *Res. Higher Educ.* 29(2): 99–124

Holloway S D, Fuller B, Hess R, Azuma H, Kashiwagi K, Gorman K 1990 The family's influence on achievement in Japan and the United States. *Comp. Educ. Rev.* 34(2): 196–208.

Hyde K 1989 *Improving Women's Education in Sub-Saharan Africa: A Review of the Literature.* World Bank, Washington, DC

Kelly. A 1982 Gender roles at home and school. *Br. J. Sociol. Educ.* 3(3): 281–95

Le Vine R 1982 Influences of women's schooling on maternal behavior in the Third World. In: Kelly G, Elliot C (eds.) 1982 *Women's Education in the Third World: Comparative Perspectives.* State University of New York Press, Albany, New York

Lipman-Blumen J 1984 *Gender Roles and Power.* Prentice-Hall, Englewood Cliffs, New Jersey

Maple S, Stage F 1991 Influences on the choice of math/science major by gender and ethnicity. *Am. Educ. Res. J.* 28(1): 37–60

O'Shaughnessy T 1978 Growth in educational opportunity for Muslim women, 1950 to 1975. *Anthropos* 73(5–6): 887–901

Robertson C 1985 A growing dilemma: Women and change in African primary education, 1950–1980. *J. Eastern African Res. Dev.* 15: 17–35

Schiefelbein E, Farrell J 1980 Women, schooling, and work in Chile: Evidence from a longitudinal study. *Comp. Educ. Rev.* 24 (2 pt 2): 5160–79

Scott K 1986 Effects of sex-fair reading materials on pupils' attitudes, comprehension, and interest. *Am. Educ. Res. J.* 23(1): 105–16

Stromquist N 1989 Determinants of educational participation and achievement of women in the Third World: A review of the evidence and a theoretical critique. *Rev. Educ. Res.* 59(2): 143–83

Stromquist N 1991 *Daring To Be Different: The Choice of Nonconventional Fields of Study by International Women Students.* Institute of International Education, New York

Stromquist N 1997 *Literacy for Citizenship: Gender and Grassroots Dynamics in Brazil.* State University of New York Press, Albany, New York

van Bemmelen S, van Vliet M 1985 *Coeducation versus Single-Sex Schooling: A Comparison Between Western and Third World Perspectives.* Center for the Study of Education in Developing Countries, The Hague

Further Reading

Kelly G, Elliott C (eds.) 1982 *Women's Education in the Third World: Comparative Perspectives.* State University of New York Press, Albany, New York

Kelly G, Slaughter S (eds.) 1991 *Women's Higher Education in Comparative Perspective.* Kluwer Academic Publishers, Dordrecht

Klein S (ed.) 1991 *Sex Equity and Sexuality in Education.* State University of New York Press, Albany, New York

Stromquist N (ed.) 1992 *Women and Education in Latin America: Knowledge, Power, and Change.* Lynne Rienner Press, Boulder, Colorado

Gender and Occupational Segregation

M. H. Strober

Men and women in the labor force are not distributed equally across occupations. This inequality in distribution is termed occupational segregation: the labor market segregates women disproportionately into certain occupations, men into others. In general, the occupations that are disproportionately female tend to have lower earnings and lower rates of return on education, less security of employment and fewer opportunities for promotion than do the occupations that are disproportionately male. As a result, occupational segregation by gender is a major contributor to the female–male earnings differential. Occupational segregation also inhibits men and women from choosing occupations in accordance with their talents and tastes and may thereby decrease the overall efficiency and productivity of the economy and the well-being of those whose aspirations are restricted.

1. Explanations

Theories that explain how occupational segregation develops and persists are divergent. And few theories have examined when and why segregation changes. For a review of theories see Reskin (1984) and Reskin and Hartmann (1986).

Most explanations of occupational segregation are supply-side; that is, they point to women themselves as the cause of occupational segregation. Sociological and psychological theories suggest that women's own values, aspirations, attitudes, expectations and behaviors are the cause of occupational segregation. Similarly, human capital theory in economics views women's own choices about their educational attainment and work experience as responsible for their occupations and earnings.

Other sociological theories, as well as economic theories of discrimination, locate the cause of segregation with the employer, sometimes aided by customers or other employees or unions. Although dual-labor market theories place much less emphasis on individual choice and the operation of labor markets than does neoclassical economic theory, these theories, too, locate the cause of occupational segregation with the employer.

Theories put forth by Hartmann (1976) and Strober (Strober 1984, Strober and Arnold 1987) stress that both supply and demand factors are responsible for occupational segregation. In a context of society-wide gender power relationships, employers, male employees, and female employees all play a role in initiating and maintaining occupational segregation.

Based on her studies of elementary school teaching and banktelling, Strober (Strober 1984, Strober and Arnold 1987) has put forth the relative attractiveness theory of occupational segregation to explain how and why occupations change their gender designation. In brief, the argument is as follows. The factors that affect demand and supply in the labor market are embedded in societal power relations that include male dominance. Because of these power relationships, women and men have unequal access to occupations. In particular, unequal power relations in the society at large are reflected in the labor market by employers' preference for White male workers in "relatively attractive" occupations (to be defined below). This is not to say that any White man can find employment in any occupation he fancies; job offers depend not only on race and gender, but also on having the requisite skill to perform the job (or at least the requisite educational credential to be trained to perform the job) and may also depend upon age and other factors such as social class.

Given employer preferences, White men choose to inhabit those occupations that are most attractive to them, leaving the occupations that they find less attractive available for the other race–gender groups. Minorities and White women, like White men, attempt to maximize their "utility," but their occupational choices are constrained by employers' preferences for White men in the most attractive occupations.

The relative attractiveness of an occupation depends on four occupational attributes: (a) the monetary return on workers' investments in their education and labor market experience; (b) the working conditions of the occupation; (c) the degree of power, prestige, and status the occupation holds in the society at large; and (d) the potential for future rewards in the occupation.

When White men find an occupation becoming relatively less attractive as compared to other occupations requiring similar education and training, they begin to leave, or reduce their rate of entry. Women then begin to enter the occupation, thereby increasing their representation in it. Such an occupation may eventually become resegregated as a female occupation.

2. Measurement of Occupational Segregation

The most common measure of occupational segregation is the Index of Segregation, also called the Index of Dissimilarity, and the Duncan Index (Duncan and Duncan 1955), defined as:

$$\text{Index of Segregation} = 1/2 \sum_{i=1}^{n} |x_i - y_i|$$

where x = the percentage of women in the ith category of a particular occupation and y = the percentage of men in that same occupational category. The index ranges from 0, indicating complete integration, to 100, indicating complete segregation. The value of the index may be interpreted as the percentage of women (or men) that would have to be redistributed among occupations in order for there to be complete equality of the occupational distribution by gender.

The magnitude of the index is affected by the level of aggregation of the occupations. The greater the degree of disaggregation, the higher the index is likely to be; aggregation of occupations into fewer categories tends to mask segregation. For example, although the occupational category "professional, technical, and related workers" was approximately gender neutral in the United States in 1990 (women accounted for 45 percent of the work force and 51 percent of professional, technical, and related workers, see International Labour Organisation 1991), women and men were not distributed equally across the various professional and technical occupations aggregated to form this broad category. For example, in 1989, women accounted for 97.8 percent of prekindergarten and kindergarten teachers, and 94.2 percent of registered nurses, but only 7.6 percent of engineers and only 7.8 percent of clergy (United States Department of Labor 1990).

For 1981 in the United States, Jacobs (1989) reported the segregation index by gender at 40.0 when calculated across 10 major categories, 62.7 across 426 categories, and 69.6 across more than 10,000 categories. Bielby and Baron (1984), in their study of approximately 400 establishments in California, found that in more than 50 percent of the establishments, occupations were completely segregated by gender and that only 20 percent of the establishments had segregation indexes lower than 90.

Because the index is sensitive to the degree of aggregation of occupations, and because the number of occupations often increases as an economy grows, analyzing changes in the degree of occupational segregation over time is complex. For instance, in the United States, the 1940 Census used 226 occupational categories while the 1980 Census used 503 (King 1992). Indexes based on the total number of categories used for each year will understate the degree of segregation in the earlier year and therefore understate the decrease in segregation over time.

One way to deal with this problem is to aggregate jobs into broad categories and compare changes in these broad categories over time (Albelda 1986). But, as already noted, calculating the index based on broad categories of occupations masks segregation in component occupations. A second method of dealing with the problem is to include in the indexes only those occupations that are common to each year being studied (Blau and Hendricks 1979). However, to the extent that integration is higher (or lower) in

new occupations than in existing occupations, indices calculated in this way will overstate (or understate) the degree of segregation in the later years and thus understate (or overstate) the reduction in segregation over time.

An additional measurement problem arises in making longitudinal comparisons of gender segregation broken down by race. Occupational categories in which women predominate are generally more aggregated than occupational categories in which men predominate. Men's occupations in the crafts are, for example, particularly disaggregated. As a result, segregation indexes show less racial segregation among women's occupations than among men's. To the extent that over time women's occupations become more finely defined, while men's occupations remain the same with respect to detailed definition, longitudinal comparisons of the segregation index may understate the decline in racial segregation among women relative to that among men (King 1992).

Comparing segregation across economies also presents difficulties. The only data that can be compared across countries are collected by the International Labour Organisation (ILO) for only the seven broadest categories of occupations: professional, technical and related workers; administrative and managerial workers; clerical and related workers; sales workers; service workers; workers in agriculture, forestry and fishing; and production and related workers, transport equipment operators and laborers. The measures of segregation for each country are therefore lower than those obtained from calculations with more refined data.

In countries where both women and men are heavily involved in agriculture, the index of segregation is likely to be low, even if, in fact, there is a great deal of gender segregation within agricultural employment. It is misleading to compare indexes for these countries with those for countries having a much smaller proportion of the labor force in agriculture. Moreover, when women do a great deal of agricultural work but are not included in the labor force, as is sometimes the case in the early stages of economic development, when the labor force participation rate of women may actually fall (Boserup 1974), indexes of occupational segregation, which are calculated on labor force data only, are not comparable across countries. A final component contributing to lack of comparability is that the work performed in occupations with a particular title (secretary, farmer, transport worker) varies greatly by level of economic development (Blau and Ferber 1992).

The index of segregation is calculated across occupational categories and hence provides a measure of horizontal gender or race–gender segregation. But occupations are also segregated vertically: women's representation in occupations is negatively related to occupational level, that is, women's representation is higher in the lower levels of an occupation than at the middle or upper levels. Vertical segregation is generally measured by comparing the percentages of women and men at various levels for particular occupations. However, there are no systematic data collected by occupational levels that permit the calculation of a single measure of vertical segregation for a country as a whole.

3. The Extent of Occupational Segregation by Gender and Changes Over Time

For the United States in 1988, using the most detailed occupational categories available in the Current Population Survey (CPS), King (1992) calculated that the index of segregation by gender was 56.7. Interestingly, the index was virtually the same for Black women and men (56.8) as for White women and men (56.7). When the index was calculated using only those 159 occupations that were found in the occupational coding system of the censuses for 1940 through 1980 as well as in the 1988 CPS, it was slightly higher: 60.9 for Black women and men and 60.4 for White women and men.

Comparable indexes of segregation by race are much lower (about 30 percentage points lower) than those for gender. Using the most detailed occupational categories, in 1988, among women, comparing Blacks and Whites, the index was 29.2. That is, 29.2 percent of Black women or White women would have had to change their occupation in order for Black and White women to be distributed equally across occupations. Among men, the comparable index was 31.8 (King 1992).

Over time, the index of segregation by gender has declined in the United States, but there is some disagreement about the pattern of the decline. In general there is agreement that between 1900 and 1960, the index was high—between 66 and 68—and relatively stable (Gross 1968). Between 1960 and 1970, the index fell about 3 percentage points (Blau and Hendricks 1979). In the next decade, 1970–80, the decline accelerated and the index fell about 8.5 percentage points (Beller 1984, Bianchi and Rytina 1986). In the 1980s, the decline continued, but at a slower pace than during the 1970s. Comparing the index computed on CPS data for 1983 with that computed on CPS data for 1987, the index fell about 2.4 percentage points (Blau 1989). (See King 1992 for a slightly different set of numbers.) A breakdown of the index change into two effects —changes in gender composition within occupations and changes in the occupational mix of the economy —showed that between 1970 and 1980 about three-fourths of the decline in the index was due to integration within occupations (particularly in professional and managerial occupations). Between 1983 and 1987, however, slightly less than two-thirds of the change was due to integration within occupations. Part

of the reason for the slowdown in the decline of the index in the 1980s was that several occupations that had become more integrated in the earlier period began, in the 1980s, to be resegregated as women's occupations, creating a "drag" on occupational integration (Blau 1989).

In Italy the index of segregation has also declined over time. In 1901, it was 78.0. It declined slightly, to 74.0, by 1936. But the major decline (18.5 percentage points, to 56.0) came between 1936 and 1971. Between 1971 and 1981, the index declined slightly, 4 percentage points, to 52.0. A breakdown of the change in the index into two effects, changes in gender composition within occupations and changes in the occupational mix of the economy, showed that between 1936 and 1971, the two effects were about equal. However, between 1971 and 1981, almost two-thirds of the decline in segregation within occupations was offset by the increased share of total employment of occupations in which women were preponderant: teachers, clerical employees, and shop assistants (Bettio 1988).

Using the ILO data for various years during the 1980s, over the seven broad occupational categories, the index of segregation for the United States was 36.6. The index ranged from a low of 9.7 in China and 9.9 in Thailand to a high of 62.3 in Qatar and 60.2 in the United Arab Emirates (Blau and Ferber 1992). For all advanced industrialized countries, the segregation index was 39.5; its range was wide, from the low and mid-20s for Greece, Japan, and Portugal to the high 40s for Denmark, Ireland, and Luxembourg.

Moreover, the underlying patterns of segregation varied widely across countries. Some examples of this are as follows: women were a high of 64 percent of all professional and technical workers in the Philippines, but a low of 15.2 percent of workers in this category in Pakistan; women were a high of 39.2 percent of managers and administrators in the US Virgin Islands, but had no representation in this occupation in Comoros; women were a high of 84.5 percent of clerical workers in Bulgaria and a low of 3.1 percent in Pakistan; and, finally, were a high of 89.7 percent of sales workers in Haiti and a low of 1.1 percent in Qatar (Blau and Ferber 1992).

In Anker and Hein's (1986) study of ILO data, they found that in developing countries women's share of professional occupations is relatively high, and unlike in industrialized countries is often greater than their share of clerical employment. This is partly because in developing countries teaching and nursing, highly feminized occupations, represent a higher percentage of all employment in professional occupations. At the same time, women are underrepresented in developing countries in administrative/managerial occupations and in production occupations.

In a more detailed breakdown of occupations for Peru, Cyprus, Ghana, India, and Mauritius, Anker and Hein (1986) found a large number of occupations that were almost exclusively male. This was true not only for countries where women constitute a small proportion of the nonagricultural labor force, but also where their share was relatively high.

In a case study of an urban labor market in Lima, Peru, Scott (1986) found a high degree of occupational segregation: out of 107 occupations, 44 were exclusively male, while only 13 were female-dominated.

A study of occupational segregation over time in Puerto Rico found that between 1950 and 1980, the segregation index fell considerably. For a set of detailed occupations present in all census years from 1950–80, the segregation index fell 23 percentage points over the period, from 80.06 in 1950 to 57.28 in 1980; for all detailed occupational categories for each census year, the index fell 19 percentage points, to 60.12 in 1980 (Presser and Kishor 1991).

3.1 Changes in the Gender Designation of Occupations

Elementary school teaching (Tyack and Strober 1981), and banktelling (Strober and Arnold 1987) in the United States and secretarial work in the United States (Davies 1984) and the United Kingdom (Cohn 1985) are examples of formerly male occupations that have been resegregated as women's occupations with concomitant losses in relative earnings and opportunities for upward mobility.

Reskin and Roos (1990) provide detailed case studies of 11 occupations in which women greatly increased their representation in the United States during the 1970s. Whether these occupations will resegregate as women's occupations remains to be seen.

In Ciudad Juarez, Mexico, when the first *maquiladoras* (foreign-owned border factories) opened in the late 1960s, the vast majority of factory operatives were women. Even in 1980–82, men held only 20 percent of such jobs. But, by 1986–87, after a downturn in the Mexican economy, employment provided by the *maquiladoras* became attractive to men and their percentage increased markedly. Estimates of the percentage of male production workers in the Ciudad Juarez *maquiladoras* in 1986–87 vary between 34 and 42 percent (Catanzarite and Strober 1993).

The phenomenon of gender resegregation in particular professions should also be studied at the disaggregate level in order to develop a better understanding of its effects. For example, in the United States, women have greatly increased their representation in the occupation of physician, from 7.5 percent in 1970 to 16.4 percent in 1989. But medicine provides a good example of the need to look at segregation at a detailed occupational level: women are not increasing their representation evenly across medical specialties, and the most lucrative specialties remain closed to women (Strober 1992).

Women are more concentrated than are men in the seven largest medical specialties. Of the 36 medical and surgical specialties listed by the American Medical Association, the top 7 account for 63 percent of male physicians, but 75 percent of women physicians. Moreover, women are particularly highly concentrated in two low-paid specialties: pediatrics and child psychiatry. At the other end of the spectrum, with the exception of obstetrics/gynecology, women are virtually absent from the highly paid surgical specialties (Strober 1992).

3.2 Vertical Segregation

Case studies of manufacturing plants in developing countries reveal the extent to which women workers are concentrated, not only into specific occupations, but also into particular sections and tasks within the hierarchically organized workplace. Horton and Lee (1988) examined the employment situation of women workers in Asian subsidiaries of the United States owned sector of the semiconductor industry. They found that women workers were at the lowest job levels. Similarly, Humphrey's (1985) study of blue-collar workers in manufacturing plants in Brazil showed that men and women were rarely found in the same department with the same job titles; women were excluded from almost all skilled occupations and even within semiskilled and unskilled occupations, women were concentrated on the lowest rungs of the occupational hierarchy.

In the United States, academia provides one example of vertical segregation. In 1989–90, women accounted for 27.4 percent of all faculty. However, they were concentrated in the lowest levels: 56.5 percent of instructors, 52.4 percent of lecturers, 39.5 percent of assistant professors, 26.4 percent of associate professors, and only 12.8 percent of professors were women (*Academe* 1990, as cited in Blau and Ferber 1992).

Another United States example concerns management. In 1990, although women accounted for 40.1 percent of all managers and administrators (ILO 1991), only half of one percent of the highest paid officers and directors in the 799 public companies on *Fortune* magazine's list of the 1,000 largest industrial and service companies were women. Out of 4,012 such people, only 19 were women (Fierman 1990). There is said to be a "glass ceiling" for women in management in the United States. Women are in jobs where they can "see" top management positions (that is, they are qualified to move into them and can picture themselves doing such jobs), but when they attempt to move into top management, they are prevented from doing so by strong structural forces and gender prejudices.

4. Conclusion

Several countries have made the elimination of occupational gender segregation a priority for public policy and have successfully used affirmative action policies to reduce such segregation. However, segregation is a dynamic process and occupations can resegregate. It is likely that in the near term, occupational segregation in the workplace will continue to mirror the gender power relationships in the society as a whole and that permanent reduction in occupational segregation will move hand in hand with fundamental shifts in societal power relationships between women and men.

See also: Benefits of Education; Education, Occupation, and Earnings

References

Albelda R P 1986 Occupational segregation by race and gender 1958–81. *Ind. Lbr. Relat. Rev.* 39(3): 404–11

Anker R, Hein C 1986 Sex inequalities in Third World employment: Statistical evidence. In: Anker R, Hein C (eds.) 1986 *Sex Inequalities in Urban Employment in the Third World.* Macmillan, New York

Beller 1984 Trends in occupational segregation by sex and race, 1960–81. In: Reskin B F (ed.) 1984

Bettio F 1988 *The Sexual Division of Labor: The Italian Case.* Oxford University Press, New York

Bianchi S M, Rytina N 1986 The decline in occupational segregation during the 1970s: Census and CPS comparisons. *Demography* 23(1): 79–86

Bielby W T, Barron J N 1984 A woman's place is with other women: Sex segregation in organizations. In: Reskin B F (ed.) 1984

Blau F D 1989 Occupational segregation by gender: A look at the 1980s. Unpublished paper.

Blau F D, Ferber M A 1992 *The Economics of Women, Men and Work.* Prentice-Hall, Englewood Cliffs, New Jersey

Blau F D, Hendricks W E 1979 Occupational segregation by sex: Trends and prospects. *J. Hum. Resources* 14(2): 197–210

Boserup E 1974 *Women's Role in Economic Development.* St. Martin's Press, New York

Catanzarite L, Strober M 1993 Gender recomposition of the maquiladora workforce in Ciudad Juarez. *Ind. Relat.* 32(1): 133–47

Cohn S 1985 *The Process of Occupational Sex-Typing: The Feminization of Clerical Labor in Great Britain.* Temple University Press, Philadelphia, Pennsylvania

Davies M W 1984 *Woman's Place is at the Typewriter: Office Work and Office Workers, 1870–1930.* Temple University Press, Philadelphia, Pennsylvania

Duncan O D, Duncan B 1955 A methodological analysis of segregation indexes. *Am. Sociol. Rev.* 20(2): 210–17

Fierman J 1990 Why women still don't hit the top. *Fortune* July 30: 40–64

Gross E 1968 Plus ça change . . .? The sexual structure of occupations over time. *Soc. Problems* 16(2): 198–208

Hartmann H I 1976 Historical roots of occupational segregation: Capitalism, patriarchy and job segregation by sex. *Signs: J. Women in Culture and Society* 1(3 Pt. II): 137–69

Horton J, Lee Eun-Jin 1988 Degraded work and devaluated labor: The proletarianization of women in the semiconductor industry. In: Smith J, Collins J, Hopkins T K, Muhammad A (eds.) 1988 *Racism, Sexism, and the World System.* Greenwood Press, New York

Humphrey J 1985 Gender, pay and skill: Manual workers in Brazilian industry. In: Ashfar H (ed.) 1985 *Women, Work and Ideology in the Third World.* Tavistock Publications, London

International Labour Organisation (ILO) 1991 *Yearbook of Labour Statistics.* ILO, Geneva

Jacobs J A 1989 *Revolving Doors. Sex Segregation and Women's Careers.* Stanford University Press, Stanford, California

King M C 1992 Occupational segregation by race and sex, 1940–88. *Mon. Lab. Rev.* 115(4): 30–36

Presser H B, Kishor S 1991 Economic development and occupational sex segregation in Puerto Rico: 1950–80. *Pop. Dev. Rev.* 17(1): 53–85

Reskin B F (ed.) 1984 *Sex Segregation in the Workplace: Trends, Explanations and Remedies.* National Academy Press, Washington, DC

Reskin B F, Hartmann H I (eds.) 1986 *Women's Work, Men's Work: Sex Segregation on the Job.* National Academy Press, Washington, DC

Reskin B F, Roos P A 1990 *Job Queues, Gender Queues: Explaining Women's Inroads into Male Occupations.* Temple University Press, Philadelphia, Pennsylvania

Scott A M 1986 Economic development and urban women's work: The case of Lima, Peru. In: Anker R, Hein C (eds.) 1986

Strober M H 1984 Toward a theory of occupational segregation. In: Reskin B F (ed.) 1984

Strober M H 1992 The relative attractiveness theory of gender segregation: The case of physicians. *Proceedings of the Annual Meetings of the Industrial and Labor Relations Research Association,* pp. 42–50

Strober M H, Arnold C 1987 The dynamics of occupational segregation among banktellers. In: Brown C, Pechman J A (eds.) 1987 *Gender in the Workplace.* The Brookings Institution, Washington, DC

Tyack D, Strober M H 1981 Jobs and gender: A history of the structuring of educational employment by sex. In: Schmuck P, Charters W W (eds.) 1981 *Educational Policy and Management: Sex Differentials.* Academic Press, New York

United States Department of Labor 1990 *Employment and Earnings,* Vol. 37. Washington, DC

Further Reading

Walby S 1986 *Patriarchy at Work: Patriarchal and Capitalist Relations in Employment.* Polity Press, Cambridge

Race and Ethnicity in Education

R. A. Clifton

This article describes the relationship between race and ethnicity as independent variables, and educational achievement and attainment as dependent variables. The major question is: do differences in race and ethnicity account for differences in the educational achievement and attainment of students? The main focus of this research has been on achievement in standardized examinations, average grades in elementary and secondary schools, and completing a full secondary education program.

In this research literature the concept of "race" refers to genetic differences between groups of people, and the concept of "ethnicity" refers to cultural differences. In other words, race generally refers to both genotypical and phenotypical differences while ethnicity refers to phenotypical differences (See and Wilson 1988). In the 1980s and 1990s, however, ethnicity is commonly used to refer to genotypical and/or phenotypical differences. In this article, ethnicity is used to refer to either one or both of these types of differences between groups of people (see and Wilson 1988, Yinger 1985).

1. Difficulties in Summarizing the Research on Ethnic Differences in Education

There are three difficulties with attempting to summarize the literature on the effects of ethnicity on educational achievement and attainment. First, there is difficulty in identifying people as belonging to specific ethnic groups. Ethnic differences are not as clearly defined as gender or age differences. There are three types of questions that researchers use to measure ethnicity: (a) the natal approach attempts to identify people by asking about their place of birth and/or the places of birth of their parents and grandparents; (b) the behavioral approach attempts to identify people by asking about some practices they have retained, such as languages spoken or religious membership; and (c) the subjective approach attempts to identify people by asking them to indicate the ethnic group or groups to which they belong (Smith 1980).

Generally, people are defined as belonging to ethnic groups if they say, in any one of the three ways, that they belong to specific groups. The problem with this operational definition is that people may have a number of reasons for not identifying themselves as being members of specific ethnic groups (e.g., discrimination) or they may have a number of reasons for identifying with specific ethnic groups (e.g., affirmative action programs).

This is particularly a problem for people with mixed ethnic ancestries. The significance of this problem is indicated by estimates of the mixed ancestries in the United States where Yinger (1985) suggests that 80 percent of Blacks have European ancestors, 50 percent of Mexican-Americans have European ancestors, and 20 percent of "White" Americans have Black ancestors. Moreover, Hirschman and Falcon (1985) report that in the 1980 United States census, 30 percent of the population reported having multiple ancestry. Researchers are thus not always sure that the ethnic variable has been adequately operationalized in their research.

Second, it is often assumed that ethnic groups differ in cultures and that these cultures, in interaction with the cultures of other ethnic groups, and within specific countries, affect the educational achievement and attainment of students (Clifton 1981, 1982). In other words, different ethnic groups may have similar educational achievement and attainment in one country and different achievement and attainment in another country. Such differences may result from, among an array of other things, the size, composition, and power of the various ethnic groups in the different countries.

Because ethnic groups often differ on variables such as socioeconomic status and family composition, it is important to control for these variables in order to determine whether the observed differences result from ethnicity alone and not from other variables. Thus, one cannot easily discuss ethnic effects in general without ensuring that the relevant variables which covary with ethnicity have been adequately controlled.

Finally, because the methodological procedures used in controlling for variables which covary with ethnicity are often very technical, the results of this research are often difficult for nonspecialists to understand (Pettigrew 1985). Moreover, in many countries the discussion of ethnic differences in education is controversial. Researchers may be reluctant to discuss differences between ethnic groups in educational achievement and attainment because they may be labeled as racist by people who do not understand the research methodology or by people who have certain ideological dispositions (Hurn 1978). As a result, people often disagree on both the facts and the social policies they think should be implemented to improve the education of certain ethnic groups.

2. Ethnicity and Equality of Educational Opportunity

In virtually all countries throughout history, most parents and other adults have attempted to provide what they considered to be optimal conditions for the growth and development of children. Since the mid-twentieth century, the concern for the welfare of children has often been expressed through concern for the education of children. This is especially true in countries which have highly differentiated labor forces and which also have an ideology of equality of educational opportunity (Bidwell 1989, Clifton 1981, 1982; Coleman 1990; Hallinan 1988). Concern for the education of children is especially evident in countries where education can make a difference because there are numerous occupations toward which young people can legitimately strive. In these countries, it is a short step from being concerned with the welfare of children to being concerned with the education of children.

There is a strong empirical relationship between the amount of education that individuals have and their ultimate social standing in countries which have both a highly differentiated labor force and an ideology of equality of educational opportunity. In fact, in these countries, educational attainment is one of the most powerful predictors of occupational prestige and income. In Australia, Poland, Germany, and the United States, for example, the correlations between peoples' education and their occupational status range between 0.5 and 0.6, and the correlations between education and income range between 0.3 and 0.4 (see Blau and Duncan 1967, Broom et al. 1980, Jencks et al. 1972, Krymkowski 1991).

Equally, it is not surprising that in many countries social reformers have also been concerned about the education of children, particularly children from ethnic minorities. The most notable symbol of the concern for the education of children from ethnic minorities has been the landmark court case *Brown* v. *Topeka Board of Education*, which was adjudicated by the United States Supreme Court in 1954. As a result of this case, the Supreme Court ordered that public schools in the United States must be desegregated. Another notable symbol of the concern for the education of children from ethnic minorities was the *Equality of Educational Opportunity* study conducted in the United States by James S Coleman and his colleagues (Coleman et al. 1966).

Following these two landmark events, many social reformers throughout the world have noted that some children are disadvantaged because of their ethnic backgrounds. They have also noted that the structure and funtioning of the regular educational system often does not seem to help these children (Bidwell 1989, Hallinan 1988). People from many political ideologies have noted that children from ethnic minorities can often improve their life through an integrated educational system that functions on the basis of equality of educational opportunity. This argument has been the basis for a variety of compensatory education programs, such as Head Start and ESL (English as a Second Language) programs in Australia, Canada, New Zealand, the United Kingdom, and the United States.

Because in many countries education is an important way of achieving economic success and because legislation has emphasized equality of educational opportunity, it has become important for sociologists to examine the ways in which the educational system may discriminate either against or in favor of children belonging to various ethnic groups. This research, however, is often restricted to Western pluralistic countries, which share a common emphasis on formal education, similar types of schools with similar programs, and an ideology of equality of educational opportunity. Even in these countries, though, the research has generally focused only on certain ethnic groups.

3. Ethnicity and Educational Achievement and Attainment

In this section, the relationships between ethnicity and educational achievement and attainment are discussed with regard to three countries: the United States, Australia, and Israel. Only a few of the ethnic groups which have been the focus of research are examined, but an attempt is made to focus on the major issue in each country. Nevertheless, readers must be careful in generalizing from these Western pluralistic countries to other countries, and from the specific ethnic groups which are discussed to other ethnic groups even within these countries.

3.1 United States

The major concern in the United States has been differences between Black and White students in educational achievement and attainment. Since the 1950s the patterns have changed substantially (Pettigrew 1985), but research indicates that there are still gross differences. White students generally have higher educational achievement and attainment than Black students (see, for example, Hirschman and Falcon 1985, Portes and Wilson 1976).

Specifically, the research suggests that Blacks have slightly lower socioeconomic status and scholastic ability, slightly more favorable influence from significant others, and slightly higher social psychological support for education than White students. However, when these relevant variables are included as independent and intervening variables, Black students generally have slightly higher achievement and attainment than White students with similar backgrounds.

More important, the research carried out in the 1980s and 1990s suggests that for both Black and White students (as well as for Asian and Hispanic students), education is the most important determinant of occupation and income attainment (Hirschman and Falcon 1985). In subtle ways, however, the process through which individuals attain positions within the stratification system varies by ethnicity. Through individual self-reliance and ambition, Blacks are able to succeed in the educational system to a slightly higher degree than Whites, but Whites have the substantial advantage of entering the educational system with higher socioeconomic status and higher scholastic resources. In essence, within strata of both socioeconomic status and scholastic ability, Black students have somewhat higher educational achievement and attainment than White students.

3.2 Australia

In Australia the major concern has been on the success of non-English speaking immigrants in the educational system. In two interrelated studies, Clifton et al. (1987, 1991) focused on examining the educational achievement and attainment of four ethnic groups: Australians, British, Greeks, and Italians. Australians were those born in Australia, whose mothers and fathers were born in Australia, and whose mothers and fathers spoke only English. British, Greek, and Italian subjects were identified as those with both parents born respectively in the United Kingdom, Greece, and Italy, and whose parents spoke English, Greek, and Italian. The British, Greeks, and Italians are the three largest immigrant ethnic groups in the population.

In this research, three educational achievement variables—word knowledge, literacy, and numeracy—were used as intervening variables between ethnicity (and eleven other independent variables), and completion of the secondary education program, the dependent variable. Not surprisingly, Italian and Greek students generally had slightly lower scores on all three achievement variables than Australian and British students. Compared with Australian students, Greek students had averages which were 6 percent lower on word knowledge, 3 percent lower on literacy, and 1 percent lower on numeracy; Italian students had averages which were 8 percent lower on word knowledge, 7 percent lower on literacy, and 10 percent lower on numeracy.

Nevertheless, when other things are equal, Greek students, and to a lesser degree Italian students, are more likely to complete a secondary education program than Australian students. Approximately 39 percent more Greek students and 20 percent more Italian students, as compared with their Australian peers, complete secondary school. British students have a 5 percent disadvantage in comparison with Australian students.

Academically successful students are more likely to complete secondary school than unsuccessful students. In fact, the educational achievement variables have the most powerful effects on the completion of secondary school, which is consistent with the research in other countries (Clifton 1981, Jencks et al. 1972). It is noteworthy that the achievement variables suppress the relationship between ethnicity and completion of secondary education. In other words, when word knowledge, literacy, and numeracy are added to the model, the positive effects of being Greek or Italian are substantially increased.

When ethnicity alone is used in the equations, the amount of variance explained is between 2.6 and 3.6 percent for the three educational achievement variables, and 0.7 percent for completion of the secondary education program. Moreover, when the other independent variables are added to the equations, the explained variance is substantially increased. These results are similar to the results of comparable research in other Western pluralistic countries. In essence, this line of research suggests that ethnic effects in education are small relative to other individual and social variables and that some minority ethnic groups have been able to use their cultural resources to obtain educational credentials. These results suggest that the Greek and Italian students are successful in school because of their cultural backgrounds and the social psychological support they receive from their peers, parents, and teachers.

3.3 Israel

In Israel the major concern has been with the relative success of Arabs, Oriental Jews (immigrants from North Africa and the Middle East), and Ashkenazi Jews (of European and American ancestry) in the educational system (Shavit 1984, 1990; Shavit and Kraus 1990; Shavit and Pierce 1991; Smooha and Kraus 1985). In the mid-1980s, approximately 17 percent of Israelis were Arabs, 46 percent were Orientals, and 37 percent were Ashkenazim (Smooha and Kraus 1985). Jewish immigrants from North Africa and the Middle East arrived in Israel in the early 1950s, and were met by a veteran Ashkenazi group (Shavit 1990) and a relatively large group of Arabs.

During the 1950s and 1960s, a large percentage of the Oriental students were dropping out of school before they completed their secondary education. As a result, the Israeli government established a program of integrated education for the Oriental and Ashkenazi students; they also established language programs for the Oriental students and implemented lower standards for them, in comparison with the Ashkenazi students, to pass the National Seker Examinations at the completion of elementary school (Shavit 1990). The Israeli government did not provide similar programs for Arab students. In fact, Arab students attend a segregated educational system (Shavit 1990).

In terms of educational achievement and attainment, however, Arab students outperform Oriental students, and Ashkenazi students outperform both Arabs and Orientals. Of the students who entered secondary school approximately 73 percent of the Ashkenazi students, 65 percent of the Arab students, and 44 percent of the Oriental students complete secondary school. Of the students who completed secondary school approximately 56 percent of the Ashkenazi students, 51 percent of the Arab students, and 43 percent of the Oriental students enroll in institutions of postsecondary education (Shavit and Pierce 1991).

Some of the advantage for the Arab students, in comparison with the Oriental students, has been attributed to the differences between the Arab and Hebrew educational systems. The Hebrew system involves tracking based on scholastic ability which, to a great degree, channels the Oriental students out of the matriculation stream. In the Arab system there is little tracking. As a result, over 80 percent of Arab secondary school students are in the academic track and over 50 percent take the matriculation examinations. By contrast, in the Hebrew system only 25 percent of the Oriental secondary school students are in the academic track and less than 20 percent take the matriculation examinations (Shavit 1990).

Another important difference between the Arab and Jewish students is in their family resources and the effects that these resources have on educational achievement and attainment. Specifically, Ashkenazi students have greater socioeconomic status and scholastic ability than the Oriental students, who in turn have greater status and ability than the Arab students. There is an important difference between these three groups in family size, however, which is a significant aspect of socioeconomic status. The Arabs and the Orientals have, on average, larger families than the Ashkenazim. The effect of family size is negative for the Jewish students, a finding which is consistent with previous research in other Western countries, while the effect of family size is either neutral or provides a slight advantage for the Arab students, a finding which is inconsistent with previous research (Shavit and Pierce 1991).

As in the United States and Australia, the research in Israel illustrates that education is the most important determinant of the status attainment of all three ethnic groups. This generalization, however, must be qualified, because the status attainment of Arabs is almost entirely within a segregated sector of the economy (Shavit 1990). Nevertheless, the fact that education is strongly related to status attainment in both the Arab and Jewish sectors suggests that inequality is a function of initial inequality in socioeconomic status and differential cultural values (Smooha and Kraus 1985).

4. Theoretical Perspectives

In all three of the countries that have been used to illustrate the effect of ethnicity on educational achievement and attainment, two main theoretical perspectives underlie both the research and the debate which seek to explain the differential access of ethnic groups to social and economic status positions. These two themes have been identified as the meritocratic model and the revisionist model (Hurn 1978, Rehberg and Rosenthal 1978).

The two perspectives are distinguished by their divergent positions on the nature of status attainment and the sources of ethnic group solidarity. Underlying the meritocratic model is the assumption that success in both the educational and occupational systems results, to a great degree, from competition. In other words, within countries that are pluralistic and have highly differentiated labor forces, ethnic groups interact and compete for positions within a market economy. An important factor within such a market economy is the use of universal criteria, in both the educational and occupational systems, which cut across more traditional ascribed statuses. If ethnic group solidarity emerges within this context, it is because members of different ethnic groups compete for the same educational and occupational rewards, and they realize that by working together they can increase their probability of success (Olzak 1983).

The revisionist model is based on the assumption that ethnic solidarity is a reaction of ethnic minorities to exploitation by the majority, that is, ethnic solidarity is a reaction to a division of labor, in education as well as in other institutions, that results from patterns of institutional discrimination. Specifically, individuals are assigned to classrooms, schools, and occupations on the basis of observable ethnic traits, such as accents, color, dress, and religion. Ethnic solidarity is increased as ethnic boundaries and lines of structural differentiation coincide (Olzak 1983). The greater the congruence between these two factors, as well as the relative disadvantage of the minority ethnic groups, the greater the likelihood of solidarity.

From these two basic theoretical perspectives there are three ways in which opportunities for ethnic minorities are expected to be restricted. First, it is argued that the channels for upward mobility have been blocked, that is, certain ethnic minorities have not been able to move up within the social structure because established groups have discriminated against them. Within this perspective it has been argued that schools are one of the most significant discriminatory institutions within society (see Bowles and Gintis 1976, Giroux 1981).

Second, it has been argued that the criteria used in assessing students are based on fluency in the national language (Mehan 1984, Olzak 1983), and students who do not speak the national language interact with students, teachers, and employers who evaluate them on their competency in the language (Clifton 1981, 1982; Clifton et al. 1986). Discrimination, therefore, results from the lack of proficiency in the national language rather than from factors such as accent, color, dress, or religion.

Third, it has been argued that certain ethnic groups shape the development of abilities and aspirations of youth, in order to preserve their cultures (see Clifton 1981, 1982, Mehen 1984). Specifically, students who have been socialized within the cultures of certain ethnic groups often differ on a number of important factors, such as interaction with significant others, motivation, and self-concept of ability, which together affect the possibilities of completing secondary school. Thus, it is important for this research literature to distinguish between fluency in the national language and ethnic prejudice as distinct impediments to educational attainment and occupational success.

The evidence from all three countries does not offer unequivocal support for any of these three arguments, though it seems to be more consistent with the meritocratic model. Thus, it seems that certain ethnic differences in the status attainment process in the United States, Australia, and Israel are a function of competition within educational systems which are essentially meritocratic. In other words, by the time students are in secondary school, the most important variables which mediate between their ethnicity and their educational attainment are academic ability, academic achievement, occupational goals, and the support they receive from significant others, their families, peers, and teachers (Bidwell 1989, Coleman 1990, Hallinan 1988).

Although the attainment of socioeconomic status is not a simple product of education, completion of secondary school is the single most important predictor of income and occupational status. Even if certain minority ethnic groups encounter discrimination, they do seem to understand the economic values associated with completing secondary education. In this respect, the sacrifices that parents from certain ethnic groups are willing to endure in order to support the education of their children is a persistent folk image in many pluralistic countries. Considerable research in sociology and education supports the folk image that cultural values are the primary reason why some ethnic groups have been successful in both the educational system and the socioeconomic system.

In this respect, the school is an organization which provides no more than opportunities to learn. Thus, there is *de facto* institutional discrimination, but it seems to be inadvertently directed at students who are disadvantaged or advantaged by their culture and their proficiency in the national language. Teachers do not force students to learn; the most that teachers can do is provide the opportunities for students to learn. The motivation, self-concept, and support from significant others that is necessary for students to capitalize on the opportunities provided by the school are derived from the individual student, his or her past successes and failures, particularly within school, and his or her cultural background, particularly within families and peers.

5. Conclusion

Researchers know very little about many ethnic groups in a great number of countries. To some degree, this accounts for the fact that, in the research literature on race and ethnicity in education, there are many more descriptive studies than studies which address theoretical issues (See and Wilson, 1988). In this review, research has been selected which addresses some of the significant theoretical issues in the relationships between ethnicity and educational achievement and attainment. Nevertheless, readers cannot generalize from these three countries to other countries, and they cannot generalize from these ethnic groups to other ethnic groups even within these countries.

See also: Education of Indigenous Peoples; Students in Classrooms, Gender and Racial Differences Among

References

Bidwell C E 1989 The meaning of educational attainment. *Research in the Sociology of Education and Socialization* 8: 117–38
Blau P M, Duncan O D 1967 *The American Occupational Structure*. John Wiley, New York
Bowles S, Gintis H 1976 *Schooling in Capitalist America*. Basic Books, New York
Broom L, Jones F L, McDonnell P, Williams T 1980 *The Inheritance of Inequality*. Routledge and Kegan Paul, London
Clifton R A 1981 Ethnicity, teachers' expectations, and the academic achievement process in Canada. *Sociol. Educ.* 54: 291–301
Clifton R A 1982 Ethnic differences in the academic achievement process in Canada. *Soc. Sci. Res.* 11: 67–87
Clifton R A, Perry R P, Parsonson K, Hryniuk S 1986 Effects of ethnicity and sex on teachers' expectations of junior high school students. *Sociol. Educ.* 59: 58–67
Clifton R A, Williams T, Clancy J 1987 Ethnic differences in the academic attainment process in Australia. *Ethnic and Racial Studies* 10: 224–44
Clifton R A, Williams T, Clancy J 1991 The academic attainment of ethnic groups in Australia: A social psychological model. *Sociol. Educ.* 64: 111–26
Coleman J S 1990 *Equality and Achievement in Education*. Westview, Boulder, Colorado
Coleman J S et al. 1966 *Equality of Educational Opportunity*. Government Printing Office, Washington, DC
Giroux H A 1981 *Ideology, Culture and the Process of Schooling*. Falmer Press, London
Hallinan M T 1988 Equality of educational opportunity. *Annu. Rev. Sociol.* 14: 249–68
Hirschman C, Falcon L M 1985 The educational attainment of religio-ethnic groups in the United States. *Res. Sociol. Educ. Socialization* 5: 83–120
Hurn C J 1978 *The limits and possibilities of schooling: An introduction to the sociology of education*. Allyn and Bacon, Boston, Massachusetts
Jencks C et al. 1972 *Inequality: A Reassessment of the Effect of Family and Schooling in America*. Basic Books, New York
Krymkowski D H 1991 The process of status attainment among men in Poland, the US, and West Germany. *Am. Sociol. Rev.* 56: 46–59
Mehan H 1984 Language and schooling. *Sociol. Educ.* 57: 174–83
Olzak S 1983 Contemporary ethnic mobilization. *Annu. Rev. Sociol.* 9: 355–74

Pettigrew T F 1985 New Black-White patterns: How best to conceptualize them? *Annu. Rev. Sociol.* 11: 329–46

Portes A, Wilson K L 1976 Black-White differences in educational attainment. *Am. Sociol. Rev.* 41: 414–31

Rehberg R A, Rosenthal E 1978 *Class and Merit in American High School: An Assessment of Revisionist and Meritocratic Arguments.* Longmans, New York

See K O, Wilson W J 1988 Race and ethnicity. In: Smelser N J (ed.) 1988 *Handbook of Sociology.* Sage, Beverly Hills, California

Shavit Y 1984 Tracking and ethnicity in Israeli secondary education. *Am. Sociol. Rev.* 49(2): 210–20

Shavit Y 1990 Segregation, tracking, and the educational attainment of minorities: Arabs and Oriental Jews in Israel. *Am. Sociol. Rev.* 55: 115–26

Shavit Y, Kraus V 1990 Educational transitions in Israel: A test of the industrialization and credentialism hypotheses. *Sociol. Educ.* 63(2): 133–41

Shavit Y, Pierce J L 1991 Sibship size and educational attainment in nuclear and extended families: Arabs and Jews in Israel. *Am. Sociol. Rev.* 56: 321–30

Smith T W 1980 Ethnic measurement and identification. *Ethnicity* 7: 78–95

Smooha S, Kraus V 1985 Ethnicity as a factor in status attainment in Israel. *Research in Social Stratification and Mobility* 4: 151–75

Yinger J M 1985 Ethnicity. *Annu. Rev. Sociol.* 11: 151–80

Sex Differences and School Outcomes

J. P. Keeves and D. Kotte

This article is concerned with differences between the sexes in educational outcomes. It traces changing views of such differences over time. In particular, it considers the changes in sex differences in educational outcomes that have occurred as a consequence of societal reforms.

1. Societal Changes

Keeves and Kotte (1992) have reported that, between 1970 and 1984, the evidence available indicated significant changes for the 10 countries under survey in: (a) an increase in the proportion of women in the labor force; (b) a marked decline in the total fertility rate; (c) a corresponding decline in family size; and (d) an increase in the age of women at first marriage. These changes were observed across a wide range of countries, and these changing circumstances have enabled women to continue for longer periods in employment and to return to work earlier after childbearing. The increased labor force participation among females has led both girls and women to undertake more education and more extensive occupational training than previously. As a consequence of these changes in the roles of women in society it might be argued that there should be significant changes in sex differences in observed educational outcomes over the corresponding period. The two decades from 1970 to 1990 were significant ones for change in the roles of women in society. These reforms built upon the growing body of evidence from psychological and educational research that the cognitive differences between women and men were not only smaller than had been formerly believed, but did not seem to be primarily dependent on biological differences between the sexes, and appeared to have a substantial environmental, cultural, and social component.

One important change that has occurred in this field during these two decades has been the growing preference of many authors and research workers to refer to "gender" rather than "sex" differences. Megarry (1984) argues for the use of "gender" to denote "the set of meanings, expectations and roles that a particular society ascribes to sex." Thus, gender is seen to be a social construct, while sex refers to the biological category to which a person belongs. In this article, interest is primarily in recorded differences in educational outcomes between males and females, the distinction being based on observable biological differences. The outcomes considered are those of ability, achievement, attitude, and participation. The similarities and differences in these outcomes between males and females are seen to be a consequence of an interaction between the biological differences and the effects of gender-related differences in environmental, cultural, and societal forces. However, the actual origins of the observed outcomes for males and females are not prejudged, except to the extent that males and females are biologically and recognizably different.

2. Previous Reviews of Research

Published research in the field of sex differences in educational outcomes has been dominated for much of the twentieth century by work done in the United States. Major reviews have, as a consequence, considered mainly research undertaken in North America (Petersen et al. 1982, Linn and Hyde 1989, Sadker et al. 1991, Humrich 1992). If the gender effects that these writers report are societally and culturally based, then to restrict consideration to one particular society or culture is to fail to test whether observable differences in outcomes occur across societies and cultures as might well be hypothesized. Not only have the reported generalizations been submitted to limited examination, but certain rather important environmentally based similarities and differences have not been taken into account. Furthermore, many reviews have failed, with Linn and Hyde (1989) and Feingold (1992) as notable exceptions, to examine changes in outcomes over time in a systematic way. This results not only in a failure to test whether effects are biologically (which might be expected to be stable over time) or environmentally (which might be expected to change over time) based, but also in a failure to observe the emergence of significant new problems. These problems involve the increased dominance of the classroom teaching profession in certain countries by women. In addition, there is a growing preponderance of girls in classrooms and schools at the postcompulsory level in most highly developed countries, as well as a cooling out in some countries of lower performing male youth from educational opportunities.

Since the last decades of the nineteenth century there has been discussion of the nature and origins of sex differences in ability and achievement. Moreover, during this period the orientation of the research has changed direction several times in response to changing societal views and concerns. Perhaps more studies into sex differences have been carried out and reported in the fields of psychology and sociology than on any other topic. As a consequence it is not possible to review all the studies that have examined and reported on sex differences and similarities. Unfortunately many such studies, while providing results of some interest, have suffered from the effects of selection and sampling bias. This has led to both inconsistent and anomalous findings. Nevertheless, the sheer volume of work has produced relatively consistent results. The research undertaken in the United States was successively reviewed by Tyler (1956), Anastasi (1958), Maccoby (1966), and Maccoby and Jacklin (1974). In addition, Tyler (1969) has emphasized that, at least for the United States, the differences between the sexes in the areas of verbal, numerical, and spatial abilities are, in general, not large when compared to differences within each sex group. In spite of this finding, substantial differences in participation and attitude occur. These may have their origins in long-term societal expectations. It is thus necessary to review briefly the field from a historical perspective.

3. Historical Overview

In 1873, Herbert Spencer, in an article "Psychology of the Sexes," argued in terms of the theories of Charles Darwin that the intellectual attributes of women developed differently in the course of evolution. Women were thus considered deficient in the powers of abstract reasoning and in the most abstract of the emotions, the sentiment of justice. The prevalent views in Germany were even less favorable to women,

who were considered to have developed differently in the course of evolution. Women were thus considered deficient in the powers essential for the survival of the race (Sherman 1978). In 1906, E L Thorndike rejected the view that the differences between the sexes which he had observed could be inherent, since such differences were too small to be of real significance. Hollingworth, a student and colleague of Thorndike's at Teachers College, Columbia University, contended that the small differences observed were due to social influences and not to biological causes, and that the true intellectual potential of women would only be revealed when women received a similar education and had the right to choose equivalent careers. Such views supported the claims of the feminist movement in the first two decades of the twentieth century, and generated interest in research that sought evidence for the equality of the sexes. Nevertheless, the question of why there were apparently so few women of genius and more male mental defectives, as had been pointed out by Havelock Ellis in his book *Men and Women* in 1894, remained. Ellis argued that there was social significance in the hypothesis of greater male variability for the development of civilization. However, Karl Pearson, in 1897, challenged Ellis on both empirical and conceptual grounds, and concluded that the male variability hypothesis remained unproven.

During the 1920s and 1930s, techniques for the measurement of aspects of personality were developed, and research into sex differences was concerned primarily with the study of differences in attitudes and emotional needs. This included the use of scales of masculinity and femininity in attempts to differentiate more accurately the characteristics of persons within the same sex group. Many of the studies undertaken were related to psychoanalytic theories which hypothesized that emotional differences arose from biological rather than sociological sources. However, during the 1950s the emphasis in research shifted once again to the study of sex roles in order to account for differences in personality development.

The comprehensive review by Maccoby (1966) proved to be a further turning point in the study of sex differences. This review was concerned primarily with the study of differences rather than similarities insofar as it focused on sex differences as an identifiable field of psychological and sociological inquiry. The subsequent emergence of the women's liberation movement led to new strands of research which sought to understand the implications of measured sex differences for female psychology and development. Research has sought to examine issues without using the male group as the reference group for the study of both differences and similarities. New approaches include the investigation of the processes operating within sex groups that are associated with biological, psychological, social, and cognitive development (Petersen et al. 1982).

4. Sex Differences in Participation

Over the period from 1970 to 1984, marked changes, as mentioned above, occurred in the relative participation of girls in academic schooling at the terminal secondary-school stage. This important finding has emerged from the two studies of science education conducted by the International Association for the Evaluation of Educational Achievement (IEA) (Keeves and Kotte 1992). For the 10 countries examined, by 1984, there were in all cases a higher proportion of the female age group retained at school to the terminal stage than of the male age group, although in the United Kingdom and Sweden the sex ratio (male/female) was only slightly below 1.0. In Finland and Hungary, however, in academic schooling there were for every 10 girls only 6 and 5 boys, respectively. Likewise, in these countries for every 10 female secondary-school teachers there were only 6 male teachers. Table 1 shows the changes that took place over the 14-year period. It is clear that a marked trend has occurred across the world at a time of expansion and redevelopment of secondary schooling, for girls to participate to a much greater extent in education than formerly. A degree of imbalance has clearly arisen in certain countries in the opportunities provided through education of an academic or general nature for boys. Such education generally leads to the better rewarded and higher status professional occupations. Boys would appear to be increasingly at a disadvantage in comparison with girls in both Finland and Hungary, and to a significant and growing extent in some other countries.

Change in participation in particular subject areas over time does not show a similar general pattern, being influenced not only by changes in school retention, but also by subject requirements for entry to higher education. However, in all countries, higher proportions of boys take the subject of physics, compared with the proportions of boys who take chemistry, and with those who take biology, indicating stronger female preferences to avoid the study of the physical sciences (Keeves 1992). A similar result is true for mathematics. Failure to study the physical

sciences and mathematics at school commonly precludes further study in particular courses that lead to highly rewarding occupations, and girls are thereby disadvantaged.

It has been such patterns of subject participation that have led to vigorous programs to increase the involvement of girls in the study of mathematics and the physical sciences in certain countries, such as: Australia (Commonwealth Schools Commission 1975, 1987); the United Kingdom (Kelly 1987, Whyte 1986); and Sweden (Israelsson 1991, Riis 1991). However, for the United States, Sadker et al. (1991) comment in the following terms:

> ... A significant body of research on gender equity in education has been mounted over the past two decades; although much of this research has generated interest from the press and lay public, its influence on teacher preparation and education reform remains marginal. ...
>
> Content analysis of influential reports on education reform issued during the 1980s show continued invisibility of gender equity as an issue of educational concern. (Sadker et al. 1991 p. 314)

Thus, in spite of the strength of research in the United States in the field of sex or gender differences in educational outcomes, it would not appear to have led to major change in educational policy or practice (see *Sex Equity: Assumptions and Strategies*).

5. Sex Differences in Achievement

5.1 Evidence from the United States

Tyler (1956), in a review of research in the United States, reported that in all studies girls achieved consistently higher school grades than did boys, were less frequently failed, and were more frequently accelerated through the years of schooling than boys. When batteries of achievement tests were used to assess achievement rather than using school grades for this purpose, girls continued to exceed boys in performance in language studies, and boys tended to perform better in mathematics and science. However,

Table 1
Indices of change in educational participation: 1950–1984

Sex ratio recorded: male–female	Australia	United Kingdom	Finland	Hungary	Italy	Japan	The Netherlands	Sweden	Thailand	United States
Terminal secondary school										
1970	1.4	1.4	0.8	0.8	1.3	1.1	1.8	1.1	1.1	1.1
1984	0.9	1.0	0.6	0.5	0.9	1.0	nd	1.0	0.8	0.9
Secondary-school teachers										
1970	0.8	1.3	1.9	1.3	1.3	3.3	2.3	1.3	1.0	1.1
1984	1.1	1.0	0.6	0.6	0.7	2.6	2.4	1.1	0.8	1.0

Source: Keeves and Kotte 1992

the differences between the sexes were small and frequently inconsistent within the same subject area; for example, boys performed better on problem-solving in mathematics, while girls frequently performed better on computation. Tyler contended that the magnitude of the sex differences reported afforded no justification for the setting up of different schools to provide different teaching for boys and girls.

The National Assessment of Educational Progress (NAEP) has traced the trends of differences in performance in science between boys and girls at ages 9, 13, and 17 years across the period of time from 1970 to 1986, with measurements made on five occasions. At all three age levels, and particularly at age 17, the performance of girls was below that of boys. However, over time the performance gap at age 9 years between males and females increased; at age 13 years it would appear to have more than doubled, and at age 17 years the disparity may have narrowed slightly (Mullis and Jenkins 1988 pp. 30–31). However, Linn and Hyde (1989) contend from their meta-analytic reviews that the gender gap in science achievement is decreasing. Since the NAEP results have been obtained with large, high-quality samples, the findings of this ongoing program must be accepted as valid (Stern 1987).

The NAEP testing program over four administrations from 1971 to 1984 found that girls performed consistently better on reading tests than did boys at all three age levels. Moreover, the evidence indicated that with general but slight gains in performance over time, the boys were at all three age levels reducing the gap. In the writing performance testing program in 1984 the girls outperformed the boys at all three grade levels (Grades 4, 8, and 11) (Stern 1987).

5.2 Evidence from Cross-national Studies

Keeves (1973) reported from the International Association for the Evaluation of Educational Achievement (IEA) studies of mathematics and science that, while the general pattern of results was one of superior performance by male students in both these subjects, there was considerable variation between countries in the extent to which boys exceeded girls in performance. Furthermore, the differences between the sexes in achievement in science increased markedly from primary to secondary schooling and to the terminal years of schooling (Comber and Keeves 1973). A similar relationship was observed in mathematics from the lower-secondary to the upper-secondary-school levels. However, the relationships were confounded by sex differences, both in participation rates in a particular subject and in retention rates in education among different countries. Consequently, it is important when reporting sex differences in achievement to do so for an age level where attendance at school and the study of the subject under review are compulsory, in order to ensure that the findings are not confounded by selection bias, differences in retentivity, or the effects of subject choice.

Where such differences in selection and retentivity occur, some adjustment must be made before effective comparisons can be carried out. Nevertheless, it is evident from the data recorded that the differences across countries are too great for simple explanations, for example, in terms of sampling variations, to be advanced as to why such sex differences should have been observed. The differences recorded could well be related, in part, to differences in the time given to the study of the subjects of mathematics and science, and thus to differences in opportunity to learn. Alternatively the observed differences could be ascribed to differences between countries in the patterns of provision in single-sex and coeducational schools, which would appear to reflect different expectations for the roles of men and women in society. An index of enrollment at single-sex and coeducational schools has, for example, been found to correlate (0.70) with differences between the sexes in achievement in mathematics at the lower-secondary-school level across 12 countries. It was found that the greater the ratio of single-sex to coeducational schools for a country, the greater the difference between the sexes in mathematics achievement, with boys outperforming girls at the 13-year old level.

Whatever the origins of these sex differences in achievement, it is clear that, primarily as a consequence of effects operating during the years of secondary schooling, girls are less well-prepared to enter occupations and careers that require a prior knowledge of mathematics and science.

Similar results are recorded in the studies conducted by the International Assessment of Educational Progress (Lapointe et al. 1989). In mathematics in the 1988 study at the 13-year old level, only in Korea and Spain were significant differences reported, with boys achieving at a higher level than girls. For the remaining 10 systems, in half the cases the girls performed marginally better than the boys on the mathematics tests. However, in science in the 1988 study at the 13-year old level, in all 12 systems the boys outperformed the girls. Only in two countries, the United Kingdom and the United States, were the differences not statistically significant, since with relatively small samples the standard errors were comparatively large.

Walker (1976) has reported from the IEA Six Subject Study on sex differences in other subject areas. On reading comprehension tests, boys showed lower performance than girls in a majority of countries, but the differences between the sexes were, in general, slight. On the literature tests, at both the 14-year old and the preuniversity levels and in all countries the boys did less well, and they also showed less interest in literature. Again, in the study of the teaching of English as a foreign language, the boys scored below the girls on both the reading and listening tests, but the differences were small. In the study of the teaching of French as a foreign language, it should be noted that fewer boys had chosen to study French, and showed inferior achievement in some countries. In the main, the statistically significant differences between the sexes in the learning of French were recorded in the English-speaking countries. When other factors were taken into consideration, it was only for the preuniversity students in the English-speaking countries that the sex of the student was important, with girls performing better than boys.

In the civic education achievement tests, the boys generally recorded higher scores than the girls at the 14-year old age level, and in all countries taking part in the study the boys showed higher levels of performance than girls at the preuniversity level.

5.3 Changes over Time in Cross-national Studies

Keeves and Kotte (1992) have examined the changes between 1970 and 1984 in the magnitudes of the differences in achievement between the sexes at the three age levels, 10-year old, 14-year old, and terminal secondary-school levels on the biology, chemistry and earth science, and physics subtests. On both occasions the effect sizes for difference between the sexes increase with age and are larger in physics than in chemistry or biology. Thus the size of the effect is influenced by time in schooling and the content of the field of science studied, with boys always outperforming girls.

Furthermore, at the 10-year old level there was little change in the size of the sex effect for science total score between occasions. At the 14-year old level there was a significant reduction in the effect size for science in five countries and on average across all countries, with one exception, namely the United Kingdom. The countries showing a decline were Australia, Finland, Hungary, Japan, and Sweden. At the terminal secondary-school level there was a significant reduction in the effect size in four countries, namely, Australia, the United Kingdom, Finland, and Sweden, with three of these countries being common at the 14-year old and terminal secondary-school levels. The average difference across all countries, at both the 14-year old level and terminal secondary-school levels, was associated with a reduction that was of borderline statistical significance. In general, the reductions recorded were associated with a drop in effect size for the physical sciences, more particularly in physics.

Causal relationships between the changes in societal conditions and a reduction in sex differences in science achievement cannot be proved. However, there would appear to have been a climate established since the late 1960s and early 1970s, as a result of programs for greater gender equity developed in some countries, that could well have given rise to the improved performance of girls relative to boys in the physical sciences, and as a consequence in a total science score. The finding of such changes over time in sex differences in science achievement would seem to indicate that these differences between the sexes arise, at least in part, from societal and cultural, rather than biological, factors.

6. Sex Differences in Abilities

It is of course possible that some of the sex differences recorded above have their origins not in societal and cultural factors but in differences in abilities between the sexes.

6.1 General Intelligence

Many research workers have from time to time reported differences between the sexes in performance on general intelligence tests. However, some tests have given boys a slight advantage and other tests would appear to have favored girls. Where such results have shown a consistent result favoring one sex rather than the other, the tests have sometimes been revised to remove what is considered to be a sex bias, by the deletion of items from a test that shows substantial sex differences. Tyler (1959) has noted that in an extensive and well-executed study carried out by the Scottish Council for Research in Education in 1932, using the Stanford-Binet intelligence test with children aged approximately 11 years, there was a difference in IQ in favor of boys of less than 1 point. However, when the study was repeated in 1947 using the Terman-Merrill revision of the Stanford-Binet, with a large, carefully drawn, and equivalent sample, a difference of 4 points of IQ in favor of girls was recorded. This difference, while of statistical significance, does not appear to be of marked practical significance. Nevertheless, the problem remains as to whether the differences recorded between the two occasions were a consequence of differences in the sampling and the execution of the two studies, changes in the characteristics of male and female student populations, or differences resulting from the revision of the test that was employed.

6.2 Verbal, Quantitative, and Spatial Abilities

In the context of the achievement differences discussed above it is more relevant to consider whether the sexes differ with respect to specific abilities rather than whether they differ in general intelligence. Female students would appear to perform better on tests of verbal ability than do male students (Anastasi 1958, Maccoby and Jacklin 1974, Tyler 1956). There is consistency in the results for all areas of verbal functioning, but generally the differences are relatively small. Maccoby and Jacklin (1974) describe the female advantage in the verbal areas as about 0.25 of a student standard deviation. Moreover, Maccoby and Jacklin give little credence to the long-held view that girls gain the advantage in verbal skills during the early years, before the age of 3 years. They suggest that, if girls have an early advantage, boys catch up by about age 3, and both sexes perform similarly until about

10 or 11 years of age, when female verbal superiority increases. However, Hyde and Linn (1988) concluded from a meta-analysis comparing more recent studies in the United States with the Maccoby and Jacklin (1974) studies that the sex difference in verbal ability at the high-school level was significantly smaller in the more recent studies and had become of little theoretical or practical significance.

Maccoby and Jacklin (1974) also found that males generally scored higher than females on tests of quantitative ability, when this was assessed in terms of quantitative reasoning or problem solving rather than in terms of computational skills. There were inconsistencies in the results obtained up to the age of about 12 or 13 years, when the quantitative ability of boys appeared to develop at a faster rate. More recent meta-analyses by Hyde (1981) also found such sex differences in quantitative abilities, but these differences were not large. Subsequently, Linn and Hyde (1989) and Friedman (1989) have concluded from meta-analytic work in the United States that the magnitudes of sex differences in quantitative abilities have declined over the period from when Maccoby and Jacklin (1974) reviewed the existing work.

Consideration of performance on quantitative scholastic aptitude tests, both in Australia (Adams 1984) and the United States (Friedman 1989) generally shows that male performance is superior to that of females. Adams (1984), however, showed that such differences were largely a consequence of selection bias resulting from differences in retention rates, while studies in the United States have shown that the effects were associated with differential course taking in mathematics (Sadker et al. 1991). Moreover, Friedman (1989) has reported that in the United States the sex differences in quantitative aptitude scores are decreasing over time.

In general, there are significant sex differences in spatial abilities, with boys performing better (Petersen et al. 1982). Sherman (1978), nevertheless, emphasized that the size of the differences reported was generally small, certainly much smaller than had been suggested in some of the writing on the subject. Moreover, the age at which differentiation between the sexes became clear was, as Maccoby and Jacklin (1974) had suggested, during the years of early adolescence. However, spatial ability tests generally involve a variety of more specific skills, and Linn and Petersen (1985) concluded from meta-analytic studies in the United States of spatial visualization ability that sex differences in this area have been declining to the extent that they no longer can be said to exist.

6.3 Sex Differences in Variability

Feingold (1992) has re-examined the controversy of sex differences in variability in intellectual abilities, and has found that males were consistently more variable than females in quantitative reasoning, spatial visualization, and mechanical reasoning. There

was similarity in variances for males and females on tests of verbal ability, short-term memory, abstract reasoning, and perceptual speed. However, most of the cross-generational comparisons of sex differences in variability for the batteries of tests examined showed stability in the magnitude of the difference over time.

Feingold (1992) also demonstrated that sex differences in variability and sex differences in central tendency are coupled and have to be considered together before sound conclusions can be drawn about the magnitudes of such differences. Moreover, Feingold argues that there is no reason to assume that reported sex differences in variability should be assumed to be innate. Such differences, like those associated with measures of central tendency, may be attributable to cultural factors.

7. Research into the Origins of Sex Differences in Abilities

It was formerly contended that the apparent superiority of females in verbal ability tests and of males in spatial and quantitative ability tests could account for the sex differences reported above with respect to achievement test performance. However, it was not possible to conclude from this that the observed differences in ability were the causes of the corresponding achievement differences recorded, although the results obtained were consistent with this hypothesis. As a consequence, efforts were made to investigate the origins of the sex differences in abilities, and why these differences did not become evident until adolescence. It was assumed that identifiable factors could conjointly influence both abilities and achievement, or that such factors could have effects on abilities that would become mediator variables influencing achievement. The reported decline in the magnitudes of sex differences in verbal, quantitative, and spatial abilities would appear to make redundant much of the research that has been undertaken in this field. The main areas that have been investigated in the quest for the origins of sex differences in abilities are: (a) biological factors including genetic, maturational, hormonal, and brain lateralization influences; (b) socialization factors including effects which are transmitted by parents, teachers, or the peer group and which are related to sex roles in society, as well as gender-role ideology; and (c) affective factors including expectancy of success, attitudes, career expectations, and values.

7.1 Biological Differences

For detailed discussions of the results obtained from research carried out in a range of disciplines and of the many theoretical and methodological issues associated with research into the biological basis of sex-related differences in cognitive performance, both Sherman

(1978) and Wittig and Petersen (1979) should be consulted.

(a) *Genetic differences.* Perhaps the most basic difference between the sexes is the chromosomal difference, and the evidence of a relationship between parent–child scores on spatial ability tests has led to the suggestion of a possible sex-linked genetic factor. However, the hypothesis that spatial visualization ability is sex limited has not been supported by later findings.

(b) *Maturational differences.* It has been suggested that the observed accelerated female physical development is paralleled mentally. Ljung (1965), using group data, has shown that there was general agreement between the physical growth pattern and the mental growth pattern at adolescence, and that the mental growth of girls occurred sooner than that of boys. However, psychologists have not been successful in linking maturation to cognitive ability, although this possibility cannot be overlooked.

(c) *Hormonal differences.* Since differences in abilities begin to emerge at adolescence, when hormonal differences between the sexes are increased, the possibility of a relationship between hormones and the development of cognitive abilities cannot be ignored. However, very few effects have been demonstrated, although some relations have been shown between androgen levels and cognitive performance.

(d) *Brain lateralization differences.* Studies of sex differences in brain organization have been carried out. It is generally accepted that the two hemispheres of the brain are organized more asymmetrically for speech and spatial functions in men than in women. However, the most striking sex difference in brain organization may not be related to asymmetry. The evidence suggests that men's and women's brains may be organized along very different lines from very early in life. Increased knowledge of such issues is likely to come from new ways of imaging the brain of living humans (Kimura 1992).

7.2 Socialization Differences

There is a growing body of evidence to support the theory that gender-role socialization both directly and indirectly influences sex-related cognitive differences. Moreover, gender-role socialization differences start to emerge during primary schooling and continue throughout the years of adolescence at the time when sex differences in achievement would also appear to develop. Wittig and Petersen (1979) have reviewed the effects of sex role as a mediator of intellectual functioning, as well as the relationships between sex role and cognitive functioning. It is evident that the differences in the patterns of socialization of male and female students, both across countries and across time, as well as between students within a particular country at a particular time, are likely to be the most influential factors which engender the development of the sex differences in abilities and achievement recorded above.

Meece et al. (1982) have argued with respect to the development of sex differences in achievement in mathematics that socialization agents are likely to contribute in three important ways: (a) male and female agents create differences through their power as role models; (b) agents convey through a variety of direct and indirect means different expectations and goals for boys and girls; and (c) socialization agents promote the development of different activities for male and female children and adolescents. The studies reviewed by Meece et al. (1982), particularly the studies by Parsons et al. (1982a, 1982b), strongly endorse the hypothesis that socialization agents treat girls and boys differently in a variety of ways that would seem to be related to course selection. Some of the studies reviewed assessed directly the causal relationships between these socialization experiences and both achievement and academic choices. Factors such as parental encouragement, perceptions, and expectations were related to plans to continue to take mathematics courses. However, the direction of causality has been difficult to determine (see *Socialization*).

Duncan (1989) has reviewed research into gender-role ideology and argues that the study of science and a subsequent career in science and technology is incongruent with adolescent girls' gender-role perceptions. It is contended that gender-role ideology leads to the gender typing of school subjects and thus to the recorded differences in performance between the sexes in particular subject areas. Gender-role ideology is also considered to lead to the gender typing of occupations, and to the participation by both boys and girls in particular courses at the levels of schooling where the study of specific subjects ceases to be mandatory. Moreover, gender-role ideology and the gender typing of school subjects and particular occupations are believed to influence both attitudes toward schooling and specific subjects as well as performance.

Duncan (1989) developed and tested a causal model for the study of performance in science using the general model of achievement behavior advanced by Eccles (1983, 1984). This model included constructs involving socialization context, gender-role ideology, gender typing of school science, and the gender typing of occupations. This model was tested in the situation of a rapidly developing country, Botswana, where science and technology have important roles in industrial growth. The causal relationships between these constructs were shown to differ for boys and girls in ways that were consistent with theory. While the effects observed were not strong, this work represented a significant advance in explaining how socialization differences between the sexes influenced the observed sex differences in educational outcomes.

561

8. Sex Differences in Attitudes and Their Effects

Attitudes have a dual function in the investigation of sex differences in the outcomes of education. Not only are attitudes important outcomes in their own right, but they are also involved in the mediation of the effects of instruction and socializing agencies on the outcomes of achievement and participation. Thus, where there are environmental and socialization effects which act differently with respect to male and female students to influence achievement outcomes, it is hypothesized that such effects are mediated, in part, through attitudes and values. Many attitudes and values have been investigated in relation to the learning of mathematics and science. For example, girls have been found to be more likely to be less confident about their ability to solve mathematical problems, and less likely to believe that mathematics would be personally useful to them. Such differences in attitude are hypothesized to account for achievement differences.

8.1 Sex Differences in Attitudes Toward Mathematics

Fennema and Sherman (1977) employed eight attitude scales in a study of sex differences in attitudes toward mathematics. These eight scales were: Confidence in Learning Mathematics, Effectance Motivation, Mathematics as a Male Domain, Attitudes toward Success in Mathematics, Usefulness of Mathematics, and Mother's, Father's, and Teacher's Perceived Attitude toward the Individual as a Learner of Mathematics. They found few sex-related differences in mathematics achievement but many sex-related attitudinal differences associated with these eight attitude scales. Other studies (Aiken 1985) have established that attitudes toward mathematics contribute significantly toward achievement in mathematics.

8.2 Sex Differences in Attitudes toward Science

Keeves and Kotte (1992) in the analysis of data from the Second IEA Science Study employed five attitude scales in the investigation of sex differences in attitudes toward science. These five scales were: Interest in Science, Ease of Learning Science, Career Interest in Science, Beneficial Aspects of Science, and Nonharmful Aspects of Science. In general, at all three age levels under survey, the 10-year-old level, 14-year-old level, and terminal secondary-school level, boys held more favorable attitudes to science than did girls. Moreover, the magnitudes of the sex difference in attitude increased with age. The main exceptions were in Finland and Hungary, where at the 14-year-old level girls held more favorable attitudes toward the Beneficial Aspects of Science. In addition, girls held more favorable attitudes with respect to the Nonharmful Aspects of Science in several countries at the 14-year-old level.

The causal analyses carried out and reported by Keeves and Kotte (1992) showed that sex of student acting through attitudes and values had only weak indirect effects on science achievement. Thus, the mediating effect of such attitudes and values on science achievement were of little consequence when compared with the more substantial direct effect of sex of student. Furthermore, in the limited causal analyses undertaken to test these relationships, it was shown that similar regression surfaces could be fitted to the data to account for the effects of attitudes and values on science achievement for male and female students. Consequently, there was no clear evidence to indicate that the five attitudes and values listed above operated differently for boys and girls to influence science achievement. Moreover, while these attitudes helped to account for the establishment of sex differences in achievement, they did not provide a strong explanation of the emergence of greater differences between the sexes in achievement with age. Nevertheless, through multilevel analysis Kotte (1992) has subsequently shown for two countries, Australia and the United Kingdom, where there were sufficient data for effective analyses, that science attitudes and values operated differently in single-sex boys' schools than in either single-sex girls' schools or coeducational schools to influence science achievement outcomes. Furthermore, Young (1994), using the same Australian data and multilevel analysis procedures, has examined the effects of school type and the sex composition of the school on achievement in physics. She has shown that when the socio-educational level of the school is taken into account, neither school type nor sex composition (single sex or coeducational) has an influence on achievement in physics.

8.3 Expectancy of Success

It is often hypothesized as a partial explanation of the apparently poorer achievement of girls in mathematics and science that the motive to avoid success is stronger in girls than in boys. There is a growing body of evidence that girls are higher on measures of fear of success than boys and that this attitude acts more strongly toward quantitative school subjects, which are perceived to be a male preserve, than toward verbal and language subjects. If this were a significant factor influencing performance on both quantitative ability and achievement tests, there would be some hope that gains could be effected in the performance of girls through programs to change attitudes. A study which examined the factors to which girls attributed their ability or inability to learn mathematics and their persistence or lack of persistence in the study of mathematics has been reported by Wolleat et al. (1980). A related intervention study involving change of attitudes to increase participation by both male and female students in the learning of mathematics has been reported by Fennema et al. (1981).

Adams (1984) adapted four of the Fennema–Sherman attitude scales, Confidence in Learning Mathematics, Mathematics as a Male Domain, Attitude toward Success in Mathematics, and Effectance

Motivation, in a study of factors contributing to differences between male and female students in performance on a quantitative scholastic aptitude test. It was shown that there were significant differences in Confidence in Success between males and females, and that Confidence in Success and Hours Spent in the Study of Mathematics, but not Sex of Student, contributed directly to accounting for the observed sex difference in quantitative scholastic aptitude. The effects of Sex of Student operated largely through the attitude Confidence in Success.

9. Problems in Sex Difference Research

In concluding this entry on sex differences in educational outcomes, it is necessary to draw attention to some of the problems of research that have no doubt led to the confounding of relationships and the contamination of results. First, the warning advanced by Feingold (1992) must be noted. Sex differences vary in magnitude with level of performance. As a consequence, differences in mean values must be considered along with differences in variability to arrive at sound conclusions about the size of such differences. Second, the complexities of sex identification when anomalous chromosomal arrangements occur cannot be ignored, particularly when dealing with subgroups such as the retarded. Third, the development of tests of intelligence and achievement in such a way as to eliminate items with apparent sex bias poses problems for establishing what the tests measure. Likewise there is a tendency in research into general and specific abilities to label a particular test in terms of a specific ability. However, such tests may have markedly different item types and properties when compared with other tests purporting to measure the same ability. Fourth, it is not possible to conduct an experimental study involving sex characteristics, because subjects cannot be randomly allocated to a sex group; from birth, subjects have been treated in ways considered appropriate to their sex. Fifth, many studies involving a large number of cases have reported differences which are statistically significant as a consequence of the large sample sizes, but which are associated with effects of such a magnitude as to be of little practical significance. Finally, many studies, while investigating large numbers of male and female students, involve samples that are contaminated by selection bias, such as occurs at age and grade levels beyond the completion of compulsory schooling. Unfortunately, there is no completely satisfactory way to allow for the effects of selection bias on the groups of male and female students under investigation. These are some of the concerns associated with research in this area. For further discussion of these issues the reader should consult Fairweather (1976) and Sherman (1978) (see also *Coeducation versus Single-sex Schooling*).

10. Conclusion

While biological differences between the sexes are too obvious to be ignored, there seems to be little evidence to suggest that, on their own, they are the causes of the manifold differences between the sexes in educational outcomes that are observed in all societies. Moreover, there are clear differences between cultural and societal groups in the magnitudes of the sex differences in achievement, ability, attitude, and participation rates. Furthermore, for some of these outcomes, recognizable changes have been recorded over relatively short periods of time of one or two decades. These findings would seem to support the conclusion that such sex differences in the outcomes of education are societally or environmentally and not biologically based. Nevertheless, some interaction between biological and social or environmental factors cannot be gainsaid.

From the findings presented above, it seems likely that sex differences in educational outcomes are largely culturally and societally based, and that programs of reform can have and are having recognizable effects. Decisions to sponsor change and reform to engender greater equity between men and women are basically societal decisions, and it would seem desirable that educational reform should follow social reform. One area where marked educational reform has taken place between 1970 and 1984 is in the provision of schooling in single-sex or coeducational institutions. Of the countries for which information on change over the 14-year period is available, there has been a marked reduction in the number of single-sex schools in Australia, the United Kingdom, Italy, the Netherlands, and Thailand. In the other countries studied, namely, Finland, Hungary, Sweden, and the United States, few, if any, single-sex schools existed in 1970. Only in Australia, the United Kingdom, and Japan, and in Japan only at the upper-secondary-school level, do single-sex schools continue to operate to an extent that parents and students are left with some choice.

In Finland and Hungary a situation has been reached where boys would appear to be denied opportunities to undertake schooling in academic programs that are likely to lead to higher status and better rewarded occupations based on higher or university education. While choice remains for boys in these two countries, societal pressures appear such that many boys do not avail themselves of the opportunities available and seek short-term gains rather than long-term rewards. In the 10 countries for which data were examined for 1984, girls now form the majority in secondary-school classrooms during the final year of schooling. This suggests that some boys in comparison with girls may, in the long term, be seriously disadvantaged as a result of missed opportunities, which result from failing to complete their secondary education.

See also: Gender and Education; Gender and Occupational Segregation; Students in Classrooms, Gender and Racial Differences Among

References

Adams R J 1984 *Sex Bias in ASAT?* ACER, Hawthorn

Aiken L R 1985 Mathematics: Attitude towards. In: Husén T, Postlethwaite T N (eds.) 1985 *The International Encyclopedia of Education*, 1st edn. Pergamon Press, Oxford

Anastasi A 1958 *Differential Psychology: Individual and Group Differences in Behavior*, 3rd edn. Macmillan, New York

Comber L C, Keeves J P 1973 *Science Education in Nineteen Countries: An Empirical Study*. Wiley, New York

Commonwealth Schools Commission 1975 *Girls, Schools and Society*. Commonwealth Schools Commission, Canberra

Commonwealth Schools Commission 1987 *The National Policy for the Education of Girls in Australia*. Commonwealth Schools Commission, Canberra

Duncan W A 1989 *Engendering School Learning*. Institute of International Education, Stockholm

Eccles J 1983 Expectations, values and academic behaviors. In: Spence J T (ed.) 1983 *Achievement and Achievement Motives, Psychological and Sociological Approaches*. Freeman, San Francisco, California

Eccles J 1984 Sex differences and mathematics participation. In: Steinkamp M, Maehr M L (eds.) 1984 *Women in Science*. JAI Press, Greenwich, Connecticut

Fairweather H 1976 Sex differences in cognition. *Cog.* 4(3): 231–80

Feingold A 1992 Sex differences in variability in intellectual abilities: A new look at an old controversy. *Rev. Educ. Res.* 62(1): 61–84

Fennema E, Sherman J A 1977 Sex-related differences in mathematics achievement, spatial visualization and affective factors. *Am. Educ. Res. J.* 14(1): 51–71

Fennema E et al. 1981 Increasing women's participation in mathematics: an intervention study. *J. Res. Math. Educ.* 12(1): 3–14

Friedman L 1989 Mathematics and the gender gap: A meta-analysis of recent studies on sex differences in mathematical tasks. *Rev. Educ. Res.* 59(2): 185–213

Humrich E 1992 *Sex Differences in Science Attitude and Achievement*. Teachers College, Columbia University, New York

Hyde J C 1981 How large are cognitive gender differences? A meta-analysis using ω^2 and α. *Am. Psychol.* 36(18): 892–901

Hyde J S, Linn M C 1988 Gender differences in verbal ability: A meta-analysis. *Psych. Bull.* 104(1): 139–55

Israelsson A M 1991 Comments on "Girls in science and technology." In: Husén T, Keeves J P (eds.) 1991 *Issues in Science Education*. Pergamon, Oxford

Keeves J P 1973 Differences between the sexes in mathematics and science courses. *Int. Rev. Educ.* 19: 47–63

Keeves J P 1992 *Learning Science in a Changing World*. IEA, The Hague

Keeves J P, Kotte D 1992 Disparities between the sexes in science education: 1970–1984. In: Keeves J P (ed.) 1992 *The IEA Study of Science III. Changes in Science Education and Achievement: 1970 to 1984*. Pergamon Press, Oxford

Kelly A (ed.) 1987 *Science for Girls?* Open University Press, Milton Keynes

Kimura D 1992 Sex differences in the brain. *Sci. Am.* 267(3): 81–7

Kotte D 1992 *Gender Differences in Science Achievement in 10 Countries—1970/71 to 1983/84*. Lang, Frankfurt

Lapointe A E, Mead N A, Phillips G W 1989 *A World of Differences*. ETS, Princeton, New Jersey

Linn M C, Petersen A C 1985 Emergence and characterization of sex differences in spatial ability: A meta-analysis. *Child Dev.* 56(6): 1479–1498

Linn M C, Hyde J S 1989 Gender, mathematics, and science. *Educ. Res.* 18(8): 17–19, 22–27

Ljung B O 1965 *The Adolescent Spurt in Mental Growth*. Almqvist and Wiksell, Stockholm

Maccoby E E (ed.) 1966 *The Development of Sex Differences*. Stanford University Press, Stanford, California

Maccoby E E, Jacklin C N 1974 *The Psychology of Sex Differences*. Stanford University Press, Stanford, California

Meece J L, Parsons J E, Kaczala C M 1982 Sex differences in math achievement: Toward a model of academic choice. *Psych. Bull.* 91(2): 324–48

Megarry J 1984 Sex, gender and education. In: Acker S (ed.) 1984 *Women and Education, World Yearbook of Education 1984*. Kogan Page, London

Mullis I V S, Jenkins L B 1988 *The Science Report Card*. ETS, Princeton, New Jersey

Parsons J E, Alder T F, Kaczala C M 1982a Socialization of achievement attitudes and beliefs: Classroom influences. *Child Dev.* 53(2): 310–21

Parsons J E, Kaczala C M, Meece J L 1982b Socialization of achievement attitudes and beliefs: Parental influences. *Child Dev.* 53(2): 322–39

Petersen A C et al. 1982 Sex differences. In: Mitzel H E (ed.) 1982 *Encyclopedia of Educational Research*, 5th edn. Free Press, New York

Riis V 1991 Girls in science and technology. In: Husén T, Keeves J P (eds.) 1991 *Issues in Science Education*. Pergamon Press, Oxford

Sadker M, Sadker D, Klein S 1991 The issue of gender in elementary and secondary education. In: Grant G (ed.) 1991 *Review of Research in Education*. 17. AERA, Washington, DC

Sherman J A 1978 *Sex-Related Cognitive Differences: An Essay on Theory and Evidence*. Thomas, Springfield, Illinois

Stern J D, Chandler M O (eds.) 1987 *The Condition of Education*. US Government Printing Office, Washington, DC

Tyler L E 1956 *The Psychology of Human Differences*, 3rd edn. Appleton-Century-Crofts, New York

Tyler L E 1969 Sex differences. In: Ebel R L (ed.) 1969 *Encyclopedia of Educational Research*, 4th edn. Collier-Macmillan, London

Walker D A 1976 *The IEA Six Subject Survey: An Empirical Study of Education in Twenty-One Countries*. Almqvist and Wiksell, Stockholm

Whyte J 1986 *Girls into Science and Technology*. Routledge and Kegan Paul, London

Wittig M A, Petersen A C(eds.) 1979 *Sex-Related Differences in Cognitive Functioning: Development Issues*. Academic Press, New York

Wolleat P E et al. 1980 Sex differences in high school students' causal attributions of performance in mathematics. *J. Res. Math. Educ.* 11(5): 365–66

Young D 1994 Single-sex schools and physics achievement: Are girls really disadvantaged? *Int. J. Sci. Educ.* 16(3): 315–325

Students in Classrooms, Gender and Racial Differences Among

G. Weiner

The concept of "differences" in education is problematic. The term can be used, among other things, to celebrate diversity, to denote injustice, or to ascribe inferiority and powerlessness. It is also a concept used more by educational psychologists than sociologists or teachers. The latter two groups are more likely to conceptualize the problem of educational difference in terms of how educational inequality within the school is related to how unequal power relations are manifested in schools and society generally. Studies have been infused with an understanding of how a social order maintains dominance or how school relations perpetuate existing unequal social relations. In contrast, psychologists have tended to focus on gender and race at psychological and interpersonal levels. Moreover, exploration of educational differences has a higher profile in studies of gender compared with those of race, possibly because racial differences are far more complex than the relatively clear male/female dualism.

1. Historical Perspective

It is important to see theories of difference as they have emerged historically. Biological attributions of gender and racial inferiority held in the nineteenth and early twentieth centuries have lost ground in the second half of the twentieth century as societal and educational factors emerged as more important, reliable, and acceptable. There has also been some debate about the nature and extent of gender and racial differences. For example, in their still important extensive survey of sex differences, Maccoby and Jacklin (1974) found relatively little overall difference between the performance of females and males. The emphasis on whether girls or boys are more disadvantaged by schooling has shifted over the years. Most recently, considerable media attention has been devoted in the UK to boys' underachievement, particularly in languages and the humanities (Weiner et al. 1997). Further, the educational effects of sociological factors such as low income and the relative heterogeneity of different cultural groups have rendered the identification of racial differences problematic.

Moreover, the possibility that identifying difference will lead to an increase in educational equality within a fundamentally unequal society has been challenged. Sarup (1986) poses the following question: "If society is differentiated on the basis of power, wealth, and education, how can children coming into the educational system from various parts of that differentiated society ever, as it were, line up equally?" (p. 3).

Nevertheless, researchers have explored and identified patterns of educational inequality, mostly focusing on gender but with some consideration of race. These are now provided in some detail.

2. Language

Language has been identified as one means by which male, White dominance of power relationships is sustained and recreated. Spender (1980) criticized the ways in which language, both in the classroom and more generally, is used both to subordinate girls and women and to define them sexually. The dominant male experience is both reflected and constructed through language so that women are defined principally in sexual or domestic servicing roles.

Language has also proved problematic for Black and ethnic minority students. For example, the dialects used by Black American and British African-Caribbean students were originally thought of as simply mispronounced and poorly spoken Standard English: hence, the emergence of linguistic deficit hypotheses which accord little respect to dialects. However, in the 1960s, this position was reconsidered by social scientists who began to see Black English as a valid dialect of Standard English. However, problems arising from linguistic differences still continue, as emphasis on Standard English is increasingly being promoted, for example, in the British National Curriculum. A strategy to overcome these differences suggested by Cooper and Stewart (1987), is to point out differences without critizing student speech, thus highlighting linguistic difference rather than linguistic deficit.

Further, gender differences in writing style and reading choice are also evident. Female students are likely to read more widely and gain greater enjoyment from reading fiction than their male counterparts who tend to focus their reading on informational, nonfictional texts (Gorman et al. 1988). It is argued that these reading patterns have an effect on writing styles, resulting in female students' preference for essay-type narratives in contrast to male students' preference for factual, briefer forms of communication (Stobart et al. 1992).

3. Student Self-concept

How students feel about themselves has been perceived as crucial to their school performance: thus, studies of differences in student self-concept have been of much interest. However, research evidence is inconclusive: findings range from little evidence of difference in self-perception between male and female students (Chapman and Boersma 1983) to males having far higher self-images (Connell et al. 1975).

The similar claim that Black children come to see themselves as failures and are nonachievers because of their negative self-concept and low esteem has also been challenged. Milner (1983), for example, suggests that Black people who are ashamed of their color feel this way because White society has forced them to accept its own appraisal of them. In contrast, Stone (1981) found the British research on Black self-concept and self-esteem to be inconclusive and contradictory. In her view, there is no basis for the belief that Black children have poor self-esteem and negative self-concept; rather the negative self-concept hypothesis serves to obscure the real issues which are of power, class, and racial oppression.

4. Socialization

Socialization into masculinity and femininity, and/or being Black or White, it is argued, begins within the family from the moment a child is born. Milner (1983) maintains that the socialization process is the most important determinant of prejudice. Similarly, Nash (1979) argues that children learn to apply stereotypes, whether in relation to gender or to racial differences before they start school. Cultural factors such as language, literature, and art also contribute to stereotypical and prejudicial thinking by conventionally using whiteness as a metaphor for all things good and pure, and blackness to denote badness and evil. Schools condone rather than challenge these stereotypes. Thus, just as parents give more attention to their sons and are more likely to reprimand them, the same patterns of differential treatment of the sexes is apparent at school (see *Socialization*).

5. Teachers' Perceptions of Students

Teachers are more likely to chastise male students and pay them more attention, while at the same timecreating greater dependency in their treatment of female students (Fagot 1977). Hence, both male and female teachers encourage in their female students stereotyped traits of obedience and passivity yet prefer their male students to adopt the more male-identified characteristics of aggression and independence (Etaugh and Hughes 1975).

Research has also shown that teachers have lower expectations of female students (as do parents and students themselves), are more intellectually encour-

aging and demanding of male students, and are more likely to reward female students for good behavior and tidy presentation. Teachers also direct male and female students into conventional subjects and careers and believe female careers to be less important than male ones (Arnot and Weiner 1987). Further, they are likely to be sexist in their allocation of tasks within school; for example, at elementary level, choosing girls to help keep the classroom clean and tidy and the often physically smaller boys to move furniture or equipment (Clift 1978).

Similarly, Black and ethnic minority children are perceived as problems rather than potentially enriching to school life. Teachers also have lower expectations of these children's abilities and potential achievements. For example, Proctor (1984) found that low expectations of students are associated with minority group membership, nonconforming personality, and nonstandard speech. There is a tendency to encourage Black students' sporting and musical abilities to the detriment of their academic studies. Further, teachers are apparently more severe in disciplining Black students, blaming "bad" behavior on what teachers see as the inadequacies of Black family life (Brah and Minhas 1985; Phoenix 1987).

Whether teachers are male or female has been found to be important in terms of their interactions with students in the classroom. In a study of 6th and 11th grade classes, Griffin (1972) found that male teachers were generally more direct and authoritarian, and female teachers warmer and less direct. However, there is little evidence to indicate that male and female teachers differ in their generally traditional and stereotypical treatment of male and female students.

6. Curriculum

Attention has focused on both the formal and hidden (implicit) school curriculum. In terms of the formal curriculum, syllabuses and content tend to exclude the experiences of girls and women whether Black or White; textbooks and reading schemes generally portray a traditional view of middle-class family life (Deliyanni-Kouimtzi 1992). Where choice is available, female students opt for the humanities, languages, and social sciences while male students select mathematical, scientific, and technological subjects despite various initiatives to counter this trend (Elkjaer 1992). Furthermore, the hidden curriculum exerts enormous pressure on students (and teachers) to conform in sex-specific ways.

At the institutional level there are gender-specific regulations on clothing (especially in the United Kingdom with its increasing adoption of school uniform) and discipline. Similarly, sexual harassment and verbal abuse have been found to be common features of school life (Lees 1987).

Black and ethnic minority experience is also

underrepresented in the content of school syllabuses and texts; racist institutional practices inhibit the progress of Black students in climbing the educational ladder. For example, there is evidence to show that irrespective of their actual ability, Black students are assigned to lower ability groups than their White counterparts. These students are consequently restricted in the level of school qualifications open to them (Wright 1987), and future channels into higher education, and the labor market (Brennan and McGeevor 1990) (see *Hidden Curriculum*).

7. Student Performance and Achievement

Attempts to establish differences in intelligence between various social groups have proved less than successful. In fact, Pidgeon (quoted in Goldstein 1987) argues that any differences emerging from tests are manufactured rather than "natural." Similarly, contemporary cultural assumptions and expectations influence test construction resulting in relatively poor performances from lower status groups (Gould 1981). According to Pidgeon, differences, say, between male and female students' test performances are likely to be due to differences in the balance of items favoring one sex or the other. Thus, it is possible for "fair" tests to be constructed where appropriate selection of items will yield tests without gender or cultural bias.

It has also been found that forms of testing are likely to affect the relative performance of male and female students, with male students achieving better on multiple choice examinations and female students on essay-type questions (Stobart et al. 1992). There is little research on the different test responses of different ethnic groups. Ethical decisions now confront test constructors as to whether it is legitimate, as is currently the case, to formulate a theoretical description of achievement which is sexually and culturally biased (Goldstein 1987), or should test constructors be working toward a more gender and culturally fair mode of assessment, as Stobart et al. (1992) suggest?

The appearance of differences between social groups in subject areas has been less controversial. Female students tend to perform better in reading, spelling, and verbal skills while male students, in the later school years, tend to excel in mathematics and problem solving (Maccoby and Jacklin 1974). Further, girls tend to be academically ahead in the elementary school phase. One perceived reason for this is that the elementary atmosphere is more "feminine" and thus more comfortable for girls. Another is that girls are relatively more mature than boys, though the concept of maturity in relation to academic achievement has been heavily critized by Goldstein (1987).

As female students progress through the school, however, their achievement levels slip, particularly in mathematics and science (Becker 1981). A variety of reasons have been given for this finding. For example, female students favor serialistic learning (proceeding from certainty to certainty, learning, remembering, recapitulating), whereas male students are likely to take a holistic approach (more exploratory, working towards an explanatory framework). Scott-Hodgetts (1986) suggests that male students are likely to be more successful learners, say in mathematics, because they are more versatile and capable of switching learning strategies where necessary.

Other studies have found that female students are more likely than their male counterparts to display "learned helplessness" (Licht and Dweck 1983). Whereas male students are more likely to attribute success to their ability and failure to a lack of effort, female students tend to relate success to effort and failure to lack of ability. Female students show a stronger tendency to view their successes as due to factors such as "luck," which implies some uncertainty about their ability to succeed in the future (Nicholls 1979). Where choice is reduced, for instance, with the introduction of the National Curriculum in Britain, girls' and boys' examination performance tends to equalize across subjects (Arnot et al. 1996).

8. Classroom Context

Mixed-classroom studies have repeatedly found that male students receive more teacher attention than do female students (e.g. Galton et al. 1980). Teachers tend to place more importance on male learning and give male students more teacher time. Yet, it is often male students themselves who demand attention by asking questions or by making heavier demands on the teacher in other ways. Teacher attention need not necessarily be thought of as positive. In her ethnographic study of a comprehensive school in Birmingham, England, Wright (1987) found that African-Caribbean students, both male and female, received more attention than their White counterparts, but that this attention was demoralizing and prejudicial in achievement terms.

A study by Sikes (1971) of seventh and eighth grade classrooms found that the many more contacts that male students had with teachers related not only to misbehavior (negative attention) but to academic contexts, both teacher and student initiated (positive attention). This study also found that male students were asked a higher percentage of abstract (rather than factual) questions and showed a greater willingness to guess when unsure of the answer. Female students had a higher percentage of positive contacts with their teachers, but they were more likely to remain silent in classroom discussion. While these patterns of classroom interaction have been found at all levels of education, there are some specific age-related factors.

567

8.1 Elementary or Primary Classrooms

A review of British primary schools by Brophy and Good (1974) found that, although boys are criticized more often than girls, they are praised as often and sometimes more often. Teachers not only check on boys' work more but also tend to question them more during the lesson. Further, boys are more likely to call out answers and thus, proactively, make greater demands on the teacher. A study by French and French (1984) similarly revealed that boys are far more able to make their comments heard and to be addressed by the teacher. In addition, certain boys in the class develop strategies which increase their chances of being asked a question by their teachers and which ensure, during the lesson, that they become the focus of attention for the whole class.

On average, elementary boys appear to misbehave much more often and more intensively than girls, thus eliciting more frequent criticism and punishment for misbehavior. However, this praise and criticism is not distributed equally among all boys in the classroom. Brophy and Good (1974) found that a large proportion, sometimes even the majority of the criticism, may be directed to a small group of boys who are perceived as likely to misbehave and who are often low achievers. In Britain, this group typically includes an overrepresentation of Black and ethnic minority students. Meanwhile, a high proportion of praise (for academic accomplishment) goes to another small group of generally White boys who are high achievers.

Overall, then, the data suggest that differences between elementary boys and girls in patterns of interactions with their teachers are as likely to be due to differences in the behavior of the students themselves as due to the tendency of teachers to treat the two sexes differently.

8.2 High-school or Secondary Classrooms

As has been discussed, the advantage in achievement held by girls at the elementary school level tends to level out in secondary school. Moreover, it is claimed that this leveling out is due to the prevention of older, female students from achieving their academic potential because of inappropriate teacher expectations and other aspects of institutionalized sexism in the school system (Becker 1981).

Significantly, early high school studies found striking differences in the teachers' treatment of males and females, invariably favoring the male students. Jones (1971), for example, found that all kinds of interactions favored male students. Particularly significant were the number of direct questions, open questions, student-initiated contacts, teacher-initiated work contacts, and positive teacher–student contacts. In addition, male students received more behavioral warnings and criticisms than did their female counterparts.

As male students get older and move toward college and university, the conflict that once seemed to have existed between the student role and the male sex role disappears. The converse happens to female students as their perceived future domestic role as wife and mother affects their career aspirations. Since achievement in school is perceived as a stepping stone toward later performance as either the family "breadwinner" or the family "carer" occupation becomes a basic part of student expectations. At the same time, familiar patterns of interaction between teachers and students continue. Stanworth (1983) found that British female secondary students found it more difficult to engage successfully in conversation with the teachers and that they were more "invisible." Hence, many of the teachers in Stanworth's study found difficulty in recalling girls' names and admitted to the fact that they could not, in some cases, distinguish one female student from another.

9. Social Relationships within the School

Many student experiences in the school context are shaped by the way they are perceived by their peer group. Evidence is now emerging that students are profoundly affected by these experiences. Two British studies illustrate this concern; the first regarding the subjective world of adolescent girls (Lees 1987), and the second the impact of racism on children's lives (Troyna and Hatcher 1992).

Lees' study aimed to explore the system of social relations in the school, Specifically how boys treat girls and how girls respond in the classroom. What emerged was that, regardless of social class or ethnic group, adolescent girls are concerned and anxious about their sexual reputation; that is, whether they are "slags" (girls who sleep around) or "drags" ("nice" girls who do not and who are considered by boys as marriageable rather than "easy lays"). Lees commented on the sheer volume of denigratory terms for women and the tight control exercised over female students' autonomy with the intent of protecting their sexual reputations.

Offensive labeling also plays a part in Black children's lives. In their study of predominantly White primary schools, Troyna and Hatcher (1992) found, first, that race and racism are significant features of school life, and that racist name-calling is by far the most common expression of racism.

> There is a wide variation in black children's experiences of racist name-calling. For some it may almost be an everyday happening. For others it is less frequent, with occurences remembered as significant events whose reoccurrence remains a possibility in every new social situation. For all, it is in general the most hurtful form of verbal aggression from other children. (p. 195)

Significantly, differences between the experiences of children in different schools were accounted for in terms of the effectiveness of the stance of staff and particularly the head (principal) in dealing with racist incidents. Again, as in the Lees (1987) study, verbal harassment was found to induce fear and construct systems of control over Black students.

10. Conclusion

Males and females, and students of different races, experience schooling quite differently. They are perceived and treated differently by their teachers and their classmates (particulary those of the opposite sex or from different races). They are assigned or select different curriculums. They achieve at different levels, partly because of the type and form of tests administered. They develop different subject interests and preferences, and they may come to perceive themselves and their abilities quite differently.

The importance of research on gender and racial differences is that findings derived from such research can raise consciousness about current inequalities in the schooling system and thus enable changes to be made. At the same time, however, raising consciousness does not guarantee that the necessary improvements will be made. Substantial improvement will probably require fundamental changes in the economic and social structures within which schools currently operate.

See also: Gender and Education; Sex Differences and School Outcomes

References

Arnot M, David M, Weiner G 1996 *Educational Reforms and Gender Equality in Schools.* Equal Opportunities Commission, Manchester
Arnot M, Weiner G (eds.) 1987 *Gender and the Politics of Schooling.* Hutchinson, London
Becker J 1981 Differential teacher treatment of males and females in mathematics classes. *J. Res. Math. Educ.* 12(1): 40–53
Brah A, Minhas R 1985 Structural racism or cultural difference. In: Weiner G (ed.) 1985 *Just a Bunch of Girls.* Open University Press, Milton Keynes
Brennan J, McGeevor P 1990 *Ethnic Minority and the Graduate Labour Market,* Commission for Racial Equality, London
Brophy J, Good T 1974 *Teacher–Student Relationships: Causes and Consequences.* Holt, Rinehart and Winston, New York
Chapman J W, Boersma F J 1983 A cross-national study of academic self-concept using the Student's Perception of Ability Scale. *N. Z. J. Educ. Stud.* 18(1): 69–75
Clift P 1978 And all things nice. . . . Unpublished paper, Open University Press, Milton Keynes
Connell W F, Stroobant R E, Sinclair K E, Connell R W, Rogers K W 1975 *Twenty to Twenty.* Hicks Smith, Sydney
Cooper P, Stewart L 1987 *Language Skills in the Classroom:*

What Research Say to the Teacher National Educational Association, Washington, DC
Deliyanni-Kouimtzi K 1992 "Father is out shopping because mother is at work": Greek primary school reading texts as an example of educational policy for gender equality. *Gender Educ.* 4(1–2): 67–79
Elkjaer B 1992 Girls and information technology in Denmark —An account of a socially constructed problem. *Gender Educ.* 4(1–2): 25–40
Etaugh C, Hughes V 1975 Teachers' evaluations of sex-typed behavior in children: The role of teacher sex and school setting. *Dev. Psychol.* 11: 394–95
Fagot B I 1977 Consequences of moderate cross-gender behavior in pre-school children. *Child Dev.* 48(3): 902–07
French J, French P 1984 Sociolinguists and gender divisions: In: Acker S (ed.) 1984 *World Yearbook of Education 1983–84: Women and Education.* Kogan Page, London
Galton M, Simon B, Croll P J 1980 *Inside the Primary Classroom.* Routledge and Kegan Paul, London
Goldstein H 1987 Gender bias and test norms in educational selection. In: Arnot M, Weiner G (eds.) 1987
Gorman T, White J, Brooks G, Maclure M, Kispala A 1988 *Language Performance in Schools.* Review of APU Language Monitoring 1979–83 HMSO, London
Gould S J 1981 *The Mismeasure of Man.* W W Norton, New York
Griffin J 1972 Influence strategies: Theory and research a study of teacher behavior. Doctoral dissertation, University of Missouri, Columbia, Missouri
Jones V 1971 The Influence of teacher–student introversion, achievement and similarity on teacher–student dyadic classroom interactions. Doctoral dissertation University of Texas, Austin, Texas
Lees S 1987 The structure of sexual relations in school. In: Arnot M, Weiner G (eds.) 1987
Licht B G, Dweck C S 1983 Sex differences in achievement orientations: Consequences for academic clones and attainments. In: Marland M (ed.) 1983 *Sex Differentiation and Schooling.* Heinemann, London
Maccoby E M, Jacklin C N 1975 *The Psychology of Sex Differences.* Oxford University Press, London
Milner D 1983 *Children and Race: Ten Years On.* Ward Lock Educational, London
Nash S C 1979 Sex role as mediator of intellectual functioning. In: Wittig M A, Petersen A C (eds.) 1979 *Sex Related Differences in Cognitive Functioning: Developmental Issues.* Academic Press, Orlando, Florida
Nicholls J 1979 Development of perception of any attainment and causal attributions for success and failure in reading. *J. Educ. Psychol.* 71(1): 94–99
Phoenix A 1987 Theories of gender and black families. In: Weiner G, Arnot M (eds.) 1987 *Gender Under Scrutiny.* Hutchinson, London
Proctor C P 1984 Teacher expectations: A model for school improvement. *Elem. Sch. J.* 84(4): 469–81
Sarup M 1986 *The Politics of Multiracial Education.* Routledge, London
Scott-Hodgetts R 1986 Girls and mathematics: The negative implications of success. In: Burton L (ed.) 1986 *Girls into Maths Can Go.* Holt, Rinehart and Winston, London
Sikes J 1971 Differential behavior of male and female teachers with male and female students. Doctoral dissertation, University of Texas, Austin, Texas

Spender D 1980 *Man Made Language*. Routledge and Kegan Paul, London

Stanworth M 1983 *Gender and Schooling: A Study of Sexual Divisions in the Classroom*. Unwin and Hyman, London.

Stobart G, Elwood J, Quinlan M 1992 Gender bias in examinations: How equal are the opportunities. *Br. J. Educ. Res.* 18(3): 261–76

Stone M 1981 *The Education the of Black Child in Britain: The Myth of Multiracial Education*. Fontana, London

Troyna B, Hatcher R 1992 *Racism in Children's Lives: A Study of Mainly-White Primary Schools*. Routledge and Kegan Paul, London

Weiner G, Arnot M, David M 1997 Is the future female? Female success, male disadvantage and changing patterns in educaton. In: Halsey A H, Brown P, Lander H (eds.) 1997 *Education, Economy, Culture and Society*. Oxford University Press, Oxford

Wright C 1987 The relations between teachers and Afro-Caribbean pupils: Observing multicultural classrooms. In: Weiner G, Arnot M (eds.) 1987 *Gender Under Scrutiny*. Hutchinson, London

(d) Students at Risk

Children and Youth at Risk

W. E. Davis and E. J. McCaul

Throughout history, children have endured countless hardships. They have been exposed to cruel mistreatment, excessive and brutal varieties of work, as well as physical and emotional abuse. In fact, until relatively modern times, children were considered chattel and treated as such (Hart 1991). Although the twentieth century has experienced marked changes in attitudes toward children, even in 1990 a quarter of a million children died every week from preventable illnesses and malnutrition. A UNICEF report, entitled *The State of the World's Children 1990*, indicated that "in many countries, poverty, child malnutrition and ill health are advancing again after decades of steady retreat" (committee 1990 p. 128). According to the report, every new day witnesses 6,000 children dying of pneumonia, 7,000 children dying of diarrhoeal dehydration, and 8,000 children dying of measles, whooping cough, or tetanus (p. 130). These facts have led to considerable concern over the status of the world's children, and in 1989 the United Nations held a Convention on the Rights of the Child. The articles developed at the convention outlined basic, fundamental rights for the world's children and provided a focal point for international child advocacy. While the United States was not one of the initial 54 countries to sign the articles, United States educators have become increasingly concerned over at-risk children and are engaging in considerable discussion of the many relevant issues involving this population. This article summarizes the discourse regarding children and youth in at-risk circumstances.

1. Background

Since 1980, shifting political, social, and economic forces have dramatically changed conditions for the world's children. A war in the Middle East, the fall of the Soviet Union, an end to statutory apartheid in South Africa, and other events have reshaped the global educational landscape and left children and youth in a variety of at-risk situations (Glenn 1992, Murphy 1992, New 1992, Rust 1992). Educational systems must respond to these changing circumstances if they are to address the unique, individual needs of these children.

The 1980s were a period of social change and educational upheaval in the United States. Public schools reverberated from the aftershocks created by the publication of *A Nation At Risk* (National Commission on Excellence in Education 1983). Soon after the publication of this report, school reform packages were introduced in many states. These packages included raising academic standards, increasing graduation requirements, and evaluating schools through statewide assessment. The expressed intent of the reform efforts was to produce students with the skills and knowledge that would allow them to be competitive with their counterparts from countries such as Germany and Japan in the modern, technological, and global workplace.

At some point during this decade of school reform, another movement gradually gathered momentum. At first only a few educators expressed concern over the possible negative consequences of reform efforts for some children. Soon, however, hardly a day passed without a headline proclaiming that not only schools, but children and youth in the United States were at risk —from increasing levels of poverty, homelessness, substance abuse, or youth violence. International comparisons began to include not only achievement test scores, but also such factors as infant mortality rates, maternal health indicators, and incidences of teenage pregnancy.

In spite of this sudden proliferation of information about at-risk children, many United States educators of the 1990s are seeking guidance in developing effective policies and implementing successful programs. Besides, the relevant issues encompass ethical, cultural, and political dimensions; many United States educators feel overwhelmed, paralyzed into inaction, and are asking the question: "What do we mean by a child being 'at risk'?"

2. Definitions of "At Risk"

Definitions of "at risk" must take into account the social, economic, and cultural environment of the particular child. The term "at risk" may refer to the stress experienced by a Turkish immigrant child in a Scandinavian country (Glenn 1992); it may refer to the adjustments demanded of a South African child in a postapartheid society (Murphy 1992); or it may refer to the low self-esteem and cultural devaluation experienced by an Alaskan Eskimo child (New 1992). The term "at risk" is necessarily culture bound, and in the broader sense, may refer to any child or youth whose own beliefs, values, or cultural norms conflict with the dominant culture's social and educational environment (Davis and McCaul 1990).

Not surprisingly then, most definitions of "at risk" in the literature tend to be broad and inclusive. For example, Catterall and Cota-Robles (1988) described three common conceptions of at risk: (a) children from poor families; (b) children with different cultural backgrounds or minorities; and (c) children from limited English-speaking families. Levin (cited in NSBA Monograph 1989) defined at-risk students as "those who lack the home and community resources to benefit from traditional schooling practices. Because of poverty, cultural obstacles, or linguistic differences, these children tend to have low academic achievement and high dropout rates. Such students are heavily concentrated among minority groups, immigrants, non-English speaking families, and economically disadvantaged populations" (p. 6).

Natriello et al. (1990) delineated four perspectives that underlie most common definitions of at risk: (a) culturally deprived/socially disadvantaged; (b) educationally deprived; (c) at risk according to indicators or predictors of educational difficulty; and (d) at risk as the general population of children and youth. The first perspective has its roots in the reform movements of the mid-1960s and emphasizes the relative disadvantage with which some students begin their public school experience. The disadvantage may entail some family "shortcomings" such as low socioeconomic status or lack of a stimulating environment. Proponents of this view stressed early childhood intervention in order to compensate for experiential deficits of early childhood. In addition, the funding for federal programs aimed at remedial education in the United States public schools, such as the federal Chapter 1 and Migrant Education programs, are based on this perspective. Chapter 1 funds are allocated to economically disadvantaged schools but, at the school level, any child with the potential to benefit from remedial instruction may be served by the program and receive individualized or small group instruction aimed at raising his or her educational attainment. The Migrant Education Program also provides small group or individualized instruction for the children of migrant agricultural workers.

The second perspective, that of the disadvantaged as "educationally deprived," focuses upon the school program and the social, cultural, or political factors contributing to educational deprivation. Proponents of this perspective argue that the cultural differences should not be viewed as cultural deficiencies and that proponents of the culturally deprived/socially

disadvantaged perspective have thus inadvertently promoted prejudicial treatment of minority groups such as African-Americans. Further, the cultural difference/deprivation perspective tends to "blame the victim" instead of focusing upon school reform and restructuring.

The third perspective utilizes the term "at risk" to refer to children who have certain characteristics which point to possible educational problems in the future. Hence, the presence of certain individual and/or environmental characteristics place a child at risk and may serve as a predictor of later educational outcomes such as low educational achievement, dropout behavior, or social problems in the school environment. Interventions are then tailored toward identified students. This approach resembles the special education process of identifying students and then providing them with specially designed instruction. Nevertheless, from this perspective, many students other than those with disabilities are now considered as at risk. For example, it is well-established that characteristics such as being male, being a member of an ethnic minority group, or being from a family of low socioeconomic status are correlated with higher rates of dropping out of school. While the future-orientation of this perspective allows for intervention strategies, labeling a student as at risk may lead to problems of stigmatizing students or creating lowered teacher expectations, particularly for children from minority groups.

The final perspective, that of youth in general being at risk, is the broadest and most encompassing. "This perspective essentially defines the entire population or at least the entire youth population as potentially disadvantaged. By not identifying any one segment of the population as being disadvantaged, this conceptualization of at risk places the whole burden of addressing the problems of disadvantaged youth on an examination of the institutions that are intended to support and develop young people" (Natriello et al. 1990 p. 11). This perspective also emphasizes the impact on the youth of the United States of social and demographic changes such as the rise in single-parent families, youth criminal activity, alcohol and drug use, sexually transmitted disease, and the increasing number of children living in poverty. It is a perspective that focuses upon the need for broad, national attitudinal and political changes as a precursor to addressing the problem of youth at risk.

Each of the perspectives outlined above has potential strengths and weaknesses in terms of its implied intervention strategies. The culturally deprived perspective, for example, suggests active early intervention to remediate experiential deficits. Clearly, many early intervention efforts with students determined to be at risk of educational failure—for example, the Headstart Program—have enjoyed considerable success. As noted by proponents of the educational deprivation perspective, however, there is an inherent danger in cultural deprivation approaches of assuming that culturally different is culturally deficient. Similarly, each perspective has an implicit intervention strategy with its accompanying strengths and weaknesses.

3. Circumstances of At-risk Students

As with definitions of at risk, a variety of theories and perspectives exist regarding the circumstances of children at risk. Further, the circumstances of at-risk children vary widely from culture to culture. Circumstances may vary from the stress experienced by a South American youth adjusting to Swedish society (Ehn 1990) to the abject poverty and starvation facing some children in South Africa (Murphy 1992). In the United States, considerable concern has arisen over the increasing number of children experiencing problems such as substance abuse, teenage pregnancy, alcohol or drug effects as babies, and youth violence. Nevertheless, five key indicators are commonly associated with educationally at-risk children: (a) living in an economically poor household; (b) having minority/racial group identity; (c) living in a single-parent family; (d) having a poorly educated mother; and (e) having a non-English-language background. All of these indicators are correlated with poor performance in school, although not always for commonly understood or agreed upon reasons. Moreover, the indicators are not independent, and children with several indicators are at the greatest risk of educational failure. In discussing these indicators, there is a clear danger of stereotyping and stigmatizing specific groups of children. Not all poor children, for example, are educationally disadvantaged, and neither are all minority children, nor all children living in single-parent households. Many students are survivors and manifest remarkable resilience. Further, the individual circumstances of children need to be taken into account—students may be at risk because their value systems may be in conflict with the established norm for the school or community. Their diversity from the norm may not be valued, respected, or tolerated; therefore, they too are at a high risk for poor overall adjustment to school. Nevertheless, each of the five key indicators cited above clearly is associated with low levels of educational achievement. These are discussed below.

3.1 Poverty

Children represent the largest and fastest growing group of the poor in the United States. It is estimated that there are more than 12.6 million poor children living in that country—nearly 20 percent of all children under the age of 18 (Children's Defense Fund 1990, Reed and Sautter 1990). More United States citizens are poor in the 1990s than before the War on Poverty was initiated in 1964, despite the fact that the official United States' poverty rate for all citizens

in 1989 edged slightly downward to 13.1 percent. Nearly 40 million people of all ages live in families that fall below the official poverty line (US$7,704 for a family of two; US$9,435 for a family of three; and US$12,092 for a family of four). Again, 40 percent of this population are children (Hodgkinson 1991, Reed and Sautter 1990).

Further, in the United States of the 1990s, the younger a child is the greater are his or her chances of being poor. Of all children age 3 and under, over four million children, 23 percent are poor; nearly 22 percent of 3 to 5-year olds are poor; and more than 20 percent (over 4 million) of 6 to 11-year old children are poor. Very young children who live in poor households are especially vulnerable and face threats to their health, safety, and psychological development that can have long-term effects on their chances of becoming healthy, productive adults. In fact, poverty increases the risk of infant mortality. As Zill and Rogers (1988) pointed out, "when the U.S. infant mortality rate is compared with that of other industrialized countries, the United States ranks only seventeenth, behind countries like Japan, the Scandinavian countries, France, Australia, and Britain" (pp. 55–56).

3.2 Race/Ethnicity

Of all of the factors associated with educational disadvantage, racial/ethnic minority status probably is the most commonly cited. In particular, African-American and Hispanic children and youth have traditionally performed less well than White children on various standardized academic achievement tests. For example, in the National Assessment of Educational Progress (NAEP), the reading, writing, and mathematics skills of African-American and Hispanic children are substantially below those of White children at ages 9, 13, and 17 (Davis and McCaul 1991). Although some data exist which suggest that this academic performance gap between ethnic/racial minority youth and White youth may be narrowing, there continues to be a significant discrepancy between the groups. Further, because African-American and Hispanic children are far more likely to drop out of school than are White children in the United States, the educational achievement gap between the two groups may be underestimated. Data from the October 1986 Current Population Survey indicated that 17.3 percent of African-American respondents and 38.2 percent of Hispanic respondents aged 22 to 24 were neither enrolled in school nor high-school graduates, as compared with only 13.9 percent of White respondents within the same age group. In some inner cities the dropout rate for African-American and Hispanic youth exceeds 60 percent (Natriello et al. 1990 p. 18).

3.3 Living in Single-parent Homes

Family structure in the 1990s United States is vastly different from what it was in the 1950s and 1960s.

Hodgkinson (1991) reported that over one-third of all marriages performed in 1988 were second marriages for at least one partner. Divorce is more common than it was. Hodgkinson also estimated that over one-half of all new marriages in the 1990s will end in divorce and that 23 percent of all children born in this period will be born outside of marriage. Children living in single-parent households, estimated to be one in four children, are far more likely to be impoverished than children living in two-parent households. Among children who grew up in the 1970s, nearly three-quarters of those who spent at least some time in a single-parent family lived in poverty at least part of the time. More than one-third (37.8 percent) of these children spent at least 4 years of their first decade in poverty, and one in five (21.8 percent) lived in poverty for 7 or more of their first 10 years. Conversely, children living continuously in a two-parent, male-headed family have but a 20 percent chance of living in poverty for at least 1 year in their first 10, and only a 2 percent chance of being poor continuously from birth to age 10 (Natriello et al. 1990).

3.4 Educational Level of Mother

Children of poorly educated mothers (a) perform worse academically and (b) leave school earlier than children of better educated mothers. According to 1986 NAEP test results, children of poorly educated mothers scored lower than children of better educated mothers in both reading and mathematics at every age level measured, with the most pronounced difference occurring in mathematics. For example, of the third-grade children participating in the 1986 NAEP, only 46 percent of those whose mothers had not completed high school scored above the level of beginning skills and understanding on the mathematics proficiency test, while 73 percent of those children whose mothers were at least high-school graduates attained that level of mastery (Natriello et al. 1990). Maternal education is also related to the likelihood of dropping out of school. Barro and Kolstad's 1987 study found that children in families where the mother has not completed high school are two to three times more likely to drop out of high school themselves than are children in families where the mother has obtained more schooling (Barro and Kolstad 1987).

The educational level of the mother is especially important because it is the mother who usually is the primary caretaker in single-parent households. Many of these mothers either do not work or hold low-paying jobs. Clearly, children living in single-parent households are much more likely to be poor than children who live in two-parent families.

3.5 Limited English Proficiency

Students whose primary language is other than English (PLOTE) or who have limited English proficiency (LEP) are generally at a distinct disadvantage in United States public schools. These students not only often encounter academic barriers, but many are forced to deal with emotional and social obstacles too. For example, LEP children are also more likely to drop out of school than are children from homes in which English is spoken exclusively. In a study reported in 1987, those students from homes where only a non-English language was spoken were more than twice as likely to drop out of high school as students from homes where English was the sole or primary language (Salganik and Celebuski 1987).

Further, ethnic and cultural customs of these students are often not understood by their peers and teachers. For example, children from some cultures tend to be more passive in group settings. Thus, a child's "lack of verbal responsiveness" could be misinterpreted by teachers as lack of interest or motivation. Likewise, children from other cultural backgrounds may manifest behaviors in the classroom or in the community which are perceived as being verbally or physically aggressive. In reality, these verbalizations and physical behaviors may not represent overt acts of defiance or disrespect but rather they may more accurately be reflective of cultural or subcultural norms.

4. Estimated Size of the Population

Despite the broad and imprecise nature of the available indicators of the educationally disadvantaged population, it is clear that substantial numbers and troubling proportions of United States' children may be classified as educationally at risk. A conservative estimate is that at least 40 percent of these children are at risk of failure in school on the basis of at least one of the five factors cited above. Other estimates indicate large percentages of United States children are at risk. A national study using a large, representative sample of youth indicated that 22 percent of eighth graders had one "risk factor" and 20 percent had two or more (Hafner et al. 1990). Another estimate indicated that approximately 33 percent of young children in the United States could be considered at risk before they even began formal schooling (Hodgkinson 1991). Demographic projections suggest that the birth rate is highest for populations that have traditionally suffered from poverty and low educational levels, thus suggesting that a greater percentage of students will be at risk in the near future.

5. Programming for Children in At-risk Circumstances

Traditionally, many children considered to be at risk of educational failure received services through the federal special and compensatory education programs. However, research on effective practices with many of these children at risk suggests that traditional approaches have not worked successfully. Neither retaining lower achieving students nor separating students for pull-out programs (the traditional approach employed in compensatory and special education programs) has demonstrated effectiveness. Moreover, pull-out programs have been criticized as stigmatizing (Lipsky and Gartner 1989, Slavin and Madden 1989, Stainback and Stainback 1985, Wang et al. 1988). A final criticism of pull-out programs is that the eligibility requirements for compensatory and special education have led to many at-risk students "falling through the cracks" of the two systems and thereby failing to receive needed services.

In determining what is effective programming with at-risk students, Slavin and Madden (1989) identified three broad categories for intervention: (a) prevention; (b) classroom change; and (c) remediation. With regard to the latter two categories, several attributes have been identified as characteristics of effective programs for at-risk students: comprehensiveness, intensity, flexibility, accessibility, and adaptability to specific student needs (Schorr 1989, Slavin and Madden 1989).

One of the more recent and promising reform approaches for at-risk students is that of accelerated schools. Proponents of accelerated schools argue that compensatory and remedial programs "institutionalize" students at risk as slow learners, thus reducing teacher expectations. They slow down the pace of instruction so that students at risk fall farther and farther behind. Teachers may fail to motivate students at risk, may not close the achievement gap between at-risk and mainstream students, and may not help students at risk to develop effective learning strategies. Four premises underlie these accelerated education projects: (a) high expectations and high status for the participants; (b) a specific deadline for closing the achievement gap of at-risk children; (c) a fast-paced curriculum that includes concepts, analysis, problem-solving, and interesting applications; and (d) the involvement of parents, the use of community resources, and the extensive use of parents and volunteers (Levin 1988).

At the secondary level, several authors (Hahn et al. 1987, Hamilton 1986) have suggested that schools need to individualize their instruction and curriculum for those students who are at risk of academic failure and who suffer from low self-esteem. Schools should, therefore, consider providing students with flexible options for completing their education. Some students, for example, may need a program of less concentration but a longer duration—a 5 or 6-year program with work-study options. Indeed, Hamilton (1986) argued that many at-risk students would benefit from more out-of-school experiences and more intensive work-related training. Community-based learning, he suggested, leads to enhanced positive attitudes as well as increased achievement for at-risk students.

In a related vein, Wehlage and Rutter (1986) offered three suggestions for schools interested in providing positive educational experiences for at-risk youth: (a) a sense of responsibility on the part of teachers and administrators toward the education of at-risk youth; (b) an effort to establish fair and respected discipline practices; and (c) a reconceptualization of schoolwork which allows at-risk students to achieve satisfaction and continue their schooling. Other research supports the notion that school climate and organization can substantially affect student engagement with schooling. Therefore, a school's atmosphere must emphasize positive teacher–student contact and support. Schools with considerable social disorganization, characterized by high truancy rates and substantial discipline problems, can work to change the school atmosphere by improving staff–administrator relationships and by instituting fair and consistent discipline policies. Establishing a positive ethos in which faculty and students share a sense of mission lessens student alienation as evidenced by absenteeism and dropout behavior. Further, schools that experience lower dropout rates are those in which face-to-face contact between students is the rule rather than the exception, in which there is an emphasis on academic pursuits, and in which the environment is safe and orderly. Teachers in these effective programs tend to see themselves as having a counseling role with students and encourage students toward trust relationships and social bonding with adults. Also there is some evidence that community support and involvement are key factors in establishing a positive school climate for at-risk youth. In addition, it was found that teacher commitment was a necessary ingredient for the effective education of at-risk youth (Bryk and Thum 1989).

6. Conclusion

The importance of establishing a positive school climate, characterized by teachers' active involvement and nurturing support of students, permeates the literature on children in at-risk circumstances. The same spirit infused the 1989 United Nations Convention at which the rights of the world's children were delineated. These included rights commonly afforded adults—freedom of movement, association, and belief —in addition to rights to nurturance, protection, and care (Hart 1991).

Clearly, these rights transcend the boundaries of individual classrooms and extend to the family, community, and society at large. Nevertheless, educators are in a unique position to recognize children's problems, advocate for solutions, and facilitate the provision of necessary services using resources from the school, family, and community. Further, research has indicated the value of formal education in enhancing the human capital of a nation (Husén and Tuijnman 1991). With the advent of a global economy and international interdependence, lifelong education becomes a primary consideration and educating children in at-risk circumstances has become not a luxury, but a necessity.

See also: Children of Single-parent Families; Dropouts, School Leavers, and Truancy; Race and Ethnicity in Education; School Dropouts

References

Barro S, Kolstad A 1987 *Who Drops Out of High School? Findings from High School and Beyond.* National Center for Education Statistics, US Department of Education, Washington, DC

Bryk A, Thum Y M 1989 The effects of high school organization on dropping out: An exploratory investigation. *Am. Educ. Res. J.* 26(3): 353–83

Catterall J, Cota-Robles E 1988 The educationally at-risk: What the numbers mean. In: Conference on Accelerating the Education of At-risk Students 1988 *Accelerating the Education of At-risk Students.* Center for Educational Research at Stanford University, Stanford, California

Children's Defense Fund Staff 1990 *Children 1990: A Report Card, Briefing Book, and Action Primer.* Children's Defense Fund, Washington, DC

Committee on Foreign Relations, United States Senate 1990 *State of the World's Children.* US Government Printing Office, Washington, DC

Davis W E, McCaul E J 1990 *At-risk Children and Youth: A Crisis in Our Schools and Society.* College of Education, University of Maine, Orono, Maine

Davis W E, McCaul E J 1991 *The Emerging Crisis: Current and Projected Status of Children in the United States.* Institute for the Study of At-risk Students, Orono, Maine

Ehn B 1990 The rhetoric of individualism and collectivism. In: Swedish Immigration Institute (ed.) 1990 *The Organization of Diversity in Sweden.* Invandraminnesarkivet, Helsingborg

Glenn C L 1992 Educating the children of immigrants. *Phi Del. Kap.* 73(5): 404–08

Hafner A, Ingels S, Schneider B, Stevenson D, Owings J A 1990 *National Educational Longitudinal Study of 1988: A Profile of the American Eighth Grader* National Center for Education Statistics, Washington, DC

Hahn A, Danzberger J, Lefkowitz B 1987 *Dropouts in America: Enough is Known for Action.* Institute for Educational Leadership, Washington, DC

Hamilton S F 1986 Raising standards and reducing dropout rates. In: Natriello G (ed.) 1986 *School Dropouts: Patterns and Policies.* Teachers College Press, New York

Hart S N 1991 From property to person status: Historical perspective on children's rights. *Am. Psychol.* 46(1): 53–9

Hodgkinson H L 1991 Reform versus reality. *Phi Del. Kap.* 73(1): 9–16

Husén T, Tuijnman A 1991 The contribution of formal schooling to the increase in intellectual capital. *Educ. Researcher* 20(7): 17–25

Levin H M 1988 *Accelerated Schools for At-risk Students.* Center for Policy Research Education, New Brunswick, New Jersey

Lipsky D K, Gartner A (eds.) 1989 *Beyond Separate Education: Quality Education for All.* Paul H Brookes, Baltimore, Maryland

Murphy J T 1992 Apartheid's legacy to Black children. *Phi Del. Kap.* 73(5): 367–74

National Commission on Excellence in Education 1983 *A Nation At Risk: The Imperative for Educational Reform.* US Department of Education, Washington, DC

National School Boards Association (NSBA) 1989 *An Equal Chance: Educating At-risk Children to Succeed.* NSBA, Alexandria, Virginia

Natriello G, McDill E L, Pallas A M 1990 *Schooling Disadvantaged Children: Racing Against Catastrophe.* Teachers College Press, New York

New D A 1992 Teaching in the Fourth World. *Phi Del. Kap.* 73(5): 396–98

Reed S, Sautter R C 1990 Children of poverty: The status of 12 million young Americans. *Phi Del. Kap.* 71(10): K1–K12

Rust V D 1992 Educational responses to reforms in East Germany, Czechoslovakia, and Poland. *Phi Del. Kap.* 73(5): 386–89

Salganik L, Celebuski C 1987 *Educational Attainment Study: Preliminary Tables.* Pelavin Associates, Washington, DC

Schorr L B 1989 *Within Our Reach: Breaking the Cycle of Disadvantage.* Doubleday, New York

Slavin R E, Madden N A 1989 What works for students at risk: A research synthesis. *Educ. Leadership* 46(5): 4–13

Stainback W, Stainback S 1984 A rationale for the merger of special and regular education. *Excep. Child.* 51(2): 102–11

Wang M C, Reynolds M C, Walberg H J 1988 Integrating the children of the second system. *Phi Del. Kap.* 70(3): 248–51

Wehlage G, Rutter R 1986 Dropping out: How much do schools contribute to the problem? In: Natriello G (ed.) 1986 *School Dropouts: Patterns and Policies.* Teachers College Press, New York

Zill N, Rogers C C 1988 Recent trends in the well-being of children in the United States and their implications for public policy. In: Cherlin A J (ed.) 1988 *The Changing American Family and Public Policy.* University Press of America, Washington, DC

Further Reading

Kozol J 1991 *Savage Inequities: Children in America's Schools.* Crown Publishing, New York

Dropouts, School Leavers, and Truancy

G. Natriello

Students who fail to attend school to the point of completion as defined by local norms are commonly identified as "dropouts" or "early school leavers." Those who absent themselves from school without good reason while still enrolled are termed "truants." This article discusses these phenomena as aspects of the single process of disengaging from school and considers the definitions of the process, its antecedents and consequences, and programmatic responses to the dropout problem.

1. Defining Dropouts, School Leavers, and Truants

The issues of truancy and dropping out or early school leaving are ones that become more salient as nations establish formal educational systems and develop requirements for school attendance. Only when regular attendance to a certain level in the educational system becomes the norm or the legal requirement does the failure of individuals to comply become defined as problematic. Before this point the phenomenon of children out of school is viewed as a more routine feature of the still developing educational system. Thus as formal educational systems develop and nations adopt goals and standards for universal primary education, or universal secondary education, the interests of society in truants and dropouts changes.

1.1 Definitions

There are no universally agreed upon definitions of truancy and dropping out. Although truancy is generally understood to mean absence from school without an acceptable reason, such as illness (Berg et al. 1988), the criteria used for determining what is an acceptable reason and who decides what is an acceptable reason are not always clear. Parents and students vary widely in their views on attendance and reasons for being absent. School personnel also differ in their attitudes toward attendance and absenteeism, particularly as one moves from school to school and system to system.

The definition of dropping out is even more complicated than the definition of truancy, as suggested by this definition proposed by Morrow:

> A dropout is any student, previously enrolled in a school, who is no longer actively enrolled as indicated by fifteen days of consecutive unexcused absence, who has not satisfied local standards for graduation, and for whom no formal request has been received signifying enrollment in another state-licensed educational institution. A student death is not tallied as a dropout. The designation of dropout can be removed by proof of enrollment in a state-licensed educational institution or by presentation of an approved high school graduation certificate. (Morrow 1987 p. 49)

Local standards for designating dropouts may differ in terms of the period of absence required before classifying a student as a dropout, the standards for school completion, the nature of other educational institutions deemed as acceptable for continuing one's education, and the procedures by which the institution the student leaves may be informed about subsequent enrollment in another acceptable institution. Thus, the seemingly clear-cut notion of a dropout is anything but clear and consistent in practice.

1.2 Calculating Dropout Rates

The calculations that produce dropout rates can be even more varied than the definitions of a dropout. Morrow (1987 p. 43) noted that three factors influence the mathematical computation of a dropout rate: (a) the time frame during which the number of students who drop out is counted; (b) the range of grade levels selected to represent a pool of possible dropouts; (c) the method of student accounting used—average daily attendance or average daily membership. Extending the time frame, limiting the range of grade levels representing the pool of possible dropouts to the levels where most dropping out is likely to occur (e.g., Grades 7–12 in the United States), and calculating the pool of students served by the school using average daily attendance will all increase the dropout rate.

There are at least three distinctly different types of dropout rates reported in the literature (National Education Goals Panel 1991 p. 219). The first, the event rate, provides a measure of the proportion of students who drop out in a single year without completing a certain level of schooling (e.g., typically secondary schools in developed countries). The second, the status rate, provides a measure of the proportion of pupils of the entire population of a given age who have not completed a certain level of schooling and currently are not enrolled. Because the status rate will include all those who have dropped out at any time, this rate is much higher than the event dropout rate for any one year. Finally, the cohort rate provides a measure of dropping out among a single group or cohort of students over a given period of time.

1.3 The Incidence of Truancy and Dropping Out

The reported rates of truancy and dropping out vary widely—as do the methods used to develop such rates. Because of the latter it is difficult to compare rates from different systems between and within nations.

Moreover, school attendance records may be inflated both because teachers and students tend to protect students from the negative consequences of being absent and because school attendance may be exaggerated systematically to protect the school's resources when such resources are based on measures of average daily attendance (Meyer et al. 1971).

Attendance rates often are used as an indication of truancy even though much absence from school is justifiable on grounds of illness. For example, Birman and Natriello (1978) indicated substantial absenteeism in urban schools in the United States, with 22 percent of all high school students in San Francisco in the 1970s having accumulated 10 or more unexcused absences in a single year, and close to half of the high schools in New York during that same decade reporting average daily attendance between 50 percent and 70 percent. Wehlage et al. (1989) reported that one in five students in Boston middle schools in the 1980s was absent more than 15 percent of the school year, and that 5 percent of the students were absent more than half of the time. Presenting data for the United Kingdom, Berg et al. (1988) noted that 2 percent of all 13- to 15-year olds in Leeds were absent over half of the time in 1982–83. These same authors reported on data collected as part of the National Child Development Study and the Cambridge Survey in Delinquent Development. In the former, truancy among primary school children was estimated by teachers as involving 1 percent of the student population, and among 14- to 16-year olds truancy was estimated to involve about 10 percent of the student population. The latter study revealed that about 5 percent of students at 8, 10, and 12 years of age and about 10 percent of those at 14 years of age were involved with truancy. Roberts (1984) reported that in London comprehensives on a typical school day 25 percent of fifth-year pupils are absent. In a study of at-risk youth in an alternative school program in the United States, Kronick and Hargis (1990) found that absenteeism among students averaged 1.15 days a week.

Dropout rates are subject to even more problems than truancy rates. Those interested in comparing dropout rates from two or more jurisdictions must be aware of differences in the definitions of a dropout, differences in the time periods during the school year when dropout data are collected, differences in the method of data collection, differences in procedures for tracking youths no longer in school to determine if they complete their education elsewhere, and differences in the methods used to calculate the dropout rate (United States General Accounting Office 1987).

With these problems in mind, the rates considered here are best treated as illustrative. For the United States, the 1990 event dropout rate was 4 percent, the 1990 status dropout rate was 12 percent, and the most recent national cohort dropout rate for 1980 sophomores who dropped out by the end of 12th grade was 17 percent (National Education Goals Panel 1991). Of course, there is considerable variation, with rates in urban areas in the United States being substantially higher. Rumberger (1987) noted that dropout rates for the 63 high schools in Chicago in the mid-1980s ranged from 10 percent to 62 percent.

A study of high schools in Ontario, Canada (Lawton 1989), reported that the annual dropout rates in seven schools had increased from an average of 10.6 percent in 1983–84 to 15.3 percent in 1986–87. In jurisdictions in which secondary education is not nearly universal the dropout phenomenon is of concern at even lower levels of schooling. A study of dropouts from junior high schools in the Guangzhou City districts in China during the 1984–85 academic year reported a dropout rate of 4.17 percent of the total student body (Joint Investigation Team 1988). In the Karnataka State in India, where compulsory primary education was introduced in 1961, figures from the 1980s revealed that about 35 percent of the students dropped out in the first two years of school, and that the dropout rates at the end of four years exceeded 70 percent (Seetharamu and Ushadevi 1985).

2. Antecedents of Truancy and Dropping Out of School

The apparent causes of truancy and dropping out are many. At least three different classes of causes or antecedents have been cited: the characteristics of individual students, of their schools, and of the wider environments in which both the students and the schools exist.

2.1 Individual Student and Family Characteristics

Research on truancy and dropping out has often focused on the characteristics of individual students that can be linked to nonattendance at school. Among those identified for United States students have been racial and ethnic minority status, low socioeconomic status, poor school performance, low self-esteem, lack of positive relationships with peers and adults in schools, delinquency, a history of substance abuse, pregnancy, non English-speaking families, single-parent families, and families that were less involved in the educational process (Ekstrom et al. 1986, Rumberger 1983, 1987; Rumberger et al. 1990).

A study of dropouts in Ontario schools found that high-school dropouts were more likely to come from families in which the parents were divorced, had lower household incomes, and had fathers working in lower level occupations (Sullivan 1988). An analysis of schooling patterns in Indonesia found that students from families with lower incomes, with parents who had lower levels of educational attainment, and in which the fathers had lower level occupations were more likely to leave school. In addition, girls were more likely than boys to leave school early, and this was particularly true for students whose parents had lower incomes and little or no schooling themselves (Chernichovsky and Meesook 1985).

Several theories have been offered to explain the relationships between student characteristics and truancy and dropping out. Some investigators have argued that accelerated role transitions or the earlier than normal assumption of new adult roles such as worker or parent, lead to increased likelihood of dropping out (Pallas 1986). Such new roles are seen as conflicting with the individual's ability to fulfill the responsibilities associated with the role of students. Other investigators have suggested that the articulation between participation and performance in school and student futures is an important determinant of school continuation. When students perceive that their participation and performance in school are connected to adult futures that they value, then they are more likely to continue in school (Stinchcombe 1964, Natriello and Dornbusch 1984). There are two crucial aspects to such explanations. First, successful school performance must be viewed as necessary for access to certain positions in adult life. Second, these adult positions must be viewed as valuable. It is this second aspect that Chernichovsky and Meesook (1985) used to explain differences by student gender in dropout patterns in Indonesia. They suggested that the lower hourly earnings of females in Indonesian society may be responsible for the higher dropout rates among females, as parents conclude that the education of female children has a relatively low rate of return.

2.2 School Characteristics

Researchers are increasingly interested in the characteristics of schools and school programs that lead students to drop out. Some analysts have argued that the relationships have been overemphasized between individual characteristics and dropping out which, in effect, places blame for early school leaving on students who may be victims of educational systems that do not meet their needs (Wehlage et al. 1989).

The most basic school characteristic that affects school persistence is the availability of a school. Chernichovsky and Meesook (1985) found that in Indonesia the availability of a school in a village had a significant positive effect on the years of schooling completed. The issue of school availability that is so clear in developing countries takes a more subtle form in developed nations such as the United States, where some have observed personnel in crowded urban schools pushing students out (Fine 1991).

Beyond school availability, dropping out has been linked to features of school organization and student experience within schools. Such features may be considered along two dimensions. First, it has been observed that schools often present students with limited opportunities for academic success. Indeed, one of the strongest correlates of dropping out found in studies of students is the lack of academic success in school. Students who more often get low grades, fail subjects, and are retained in grade have a much greater chance of leaving school prior to high-school completion. Students who have difficulty meeting the academic demands of the school tend to leave, rather than continue in the face of the frustration they often experience in trying to obtain good grades.

Student academic difficulties with school can derive from three sources: different aspects of the academic criteria set by the school, the student's own innate abilities in each subject area, and the student's willingness to direct efforts toward learning and performance on academic tasks. Moreover, studies of the sequence of events that often create a student dropout indicate that the mismatch between school demands and student behaviors can grow over time; thus opportunities for success become more remote and motivation to remain in school becomes weaker (Ekstrom et al. 1986, Natriello et al. 1990).

A second dimension of school organization and student experience in school that is associated with dropping out is the limited availability of positive social relationships and the lack of a climate of caring and support. Positive supportive relationships between teachers and students and among students, and a climate of shared purpose and concern have been identified as key elements of efforts to hold students in schools. As Legters et al. (1992) have pointed out, organizational features conducive to these positive relations such as small school size, a limited number of contacts between different teachers and students, and teachers who have been trained to focus on the needs of students are found more often in elementary schools than in middle and high schools. The latter are often characterized by larger size, departmentalized structures which expose students to different teachers for each subject, teaching roles defined in terms of subject matter expertise as opposed to interest in students, low levels of involvement with students' families and community, and tracking of students on the basis of academic preparation. All of these are features that present barriers to the establishment and maintenance of positive social relationships and a climate of shared purpose and concern.

2.3 Environmental Aspects

In addition to the characteristics of students and the conditions they encounter in school organizations, truancy and dropping out are affected by the larger environment in which students and schools are embedded. Such environmental aspects may be considered from two perspectives: (a) the degree to which schooling is perceived as relevant to students' current and future lives outside of school; and (b) the degree to which external conditions are supportive of students' continued participation in school.

The relevance of schooling to the current and future lives of students is the product of both the content of schooling and the nature of students' lives outside of school. Schooling may be perceived as less relevant when students see no connection between the curriculum of the school and the culture of their families and neighborhoods, when the values presented and demanded by the school are at variance with those of their peer groups, and when they see no connection between their academic work in schools and their future economic prospects (Legters et al. 1992).

Conditions outside of schools may fail to provide support for students to attend regularly and continue in school. Conditions that contribute to truancy and early school leaving include a variety of personal, familial, and community problems such as teenage pregnancy, alcohol and drug abuse, delinquent gang membership, family violence and child abuse, family social and financial needs requiring students to be at home or to work, and socially disorganized communities with high rates of crime (Natriello et al. 1990).

3. Consequences of Dropping Out of School

The consequences of dropping out of school vary depending on a number of factors, including the nature of the activities students engage in after leaving school and the nature of the social and economic environment of the nation state. In some societies dropping out does not automatically foreclose the possibility of continuing one's education at a later date; in others such opportunities are more limited. In addition, in some economies there are numerous opportunities for those who have not completed formal basic schooling; in others those opportunities are more restricted. There is, however, a growing perception that early school leavers will increasingly be at a disadvantage in the job market as economies develop (National Academy of Sciences 1984).

3.1 Cognitive Consequences

Although studies of the impact of dropping out on cognitive growth with appropriate controls are rare, there is some evidence that leaving school early has a negative impact. A United States study that tested students in the sophomore year of high school before they dropped out, and then followed and tested both those who remained in school and those who left before graduation, found, controlling for prior achievement differences, that the cognitive skills of youngsters who stayed in school improved more than those of dropouts. Moreover, the advantage for those who stayed was found across a rather broad range of skill areas (Alexander et al. 1985).

3.2 Economic and Social Consequences

The lower levels of cognitive growth experienced by dropouts result in less success in the job market. Not only are early school leavers more likely to be unemployed than those who complete their schooling, they are also likely to earn less when they are

employed. This pattern of relatively less success in the job market results in reductions in personal income as well as reductions in national income and government revenues. Moreover, individuals who leave school early are more likely to engage in criminal activity, have poorer health and lower rates of political participation, and simultaneously require more government services such as welfare and healthcare assistance (Rumberger 1987).

4. Programmatic Remedies to Prevent Dropping Out

The recognition of the human and economic costs of early school leaving have led to the development of a range of efforts designed to prevent students from dropping out before school completion. These efforts typically address the multiple causes of dropping out associated with schools, and with the larger environments in which schools and students function.

4.1 School-based Remedies

School-based remedies have included both programs and practices designed to enhance the prospects for student academic success, and ones designed to strengthen the positive social relationships and climate of support and concern students find in school. Examples of the former have included: improved diagnosis of student skills and abilities and tailoring of instruction to the needs of individual students, altering evaluation processes to recognize student effort, restructuring school tasks to draw on a wider range of human abilities, enhanced remediation programs making use of more time for instruction during the school year and during the summer, and increased use of tutoring and technology to deliver instruction to students whose needs are not met by regular classroom instruction. Examples of efforts to improve the prospects for positive social relationships and a shared climate of concern for students have included mentoring programs linking individual teachers and students, house plans in large schools to create smaller environments in which a limited number of students and teachers work on the entire academic program, and the use of older students as peer mentors for younger students (Natriello et al. 1990).

4.2 Environmental Remedies

Programs have also been developed to ameliorate some of the negative environmental factors affecting persistence in school. Attempts to reduce the problem of the lack of relevance of school to the current and future lives of students have included updated vocational education programs which integrate academic and vocational skills and have clear links to the world of work, multicultural curricula that include materials and role models from students' own ethnic or cultural backgrounds, and incentive programs which promise employment or support for further education to students who devote effort to school work. Strategies designed to address the unsupportive outside conditions have involved the development of new relationships between families and school and the integration of educational and human services to address the social and economic problems that impede progress through school (Legters et al. 1992).

See also: Children and Youth at Risk; School Dropouts

References

Alexander K, Natriello G, Pallas A 1985 For whom the school bell tolls: The impact of dropping out on cognitive performance. *Am. Sociol. Rev.* 50(3): 409–20

Berg I, Brown I, Hullin R 1988 *Off School, In Court: An Experimental and Psychiatric Investigation of Severe School Attendance Problems.* Springer-Verlag, New York

Birman B, Natriello G 1978 Perspectives on absenteeism in high schools. *J. Res. Dev. Educ.* 11(4): 29–38

Chernichovsky D, Meesook O A 1985 *School Enrollment in Indonesia.* World Bank, Washington, DC

Ekstrom R B, Goertz M E, Pollack J M, Rock D A 1986 Who drops out of high school and why? Findings from a national study. *Teach. Coll. Rec.* 87(3): 356–73

Fine M 1991 *Framing Dropouts: Notes on the Politics of an Urban High School.* State University of New York Press, Albany, New York

Kronick R F, Hargis C H 1990 *Dropouts: Who Drops Out and Why—And the Recommended Action.* Thomas, Springfield, Illinois

Joint Investigation Team 1988 Importance of updating educational thinking as seen from the problem of junior high school dropouts in Guangzhou City districts. *Chinese Educ. Soc. Bull.* 21(3): 80–7

Lawton S B 1989 *Student Retention and Transition in Ontario High Schools: Policies, Practices and Prospects.* Ontario Department of Education, Toronto

Legters N, McDill E, McPartland J 1992 *Responses to the Challenge of Educating At-risk Youth.* Center for Research on Effective Schooling for Disadvantaged Students, Johns Hopkins University, Baltimore, Maryland

Meyer J, Chase-Dunn C, Inverarity J 1971 *The Expansion of the Autonomy of Youth: Responses of the Secondary School to the Problems of Order in the 1960s.* Laboratory for Social Research, Stanford University, Stanford, California

Morrow G 1987 Standardizing practice in the analysis of school dropouts. In: Natriello G (ed.) 1987

National Academy of Sciences 1984 *High Schools and the Changing Workplace: The Employers' View.* Report of the Panel on Secondary School Education for the Changing Workplace, National Academy Press, Washington, DC

National Education Goals Panel 1991 *The National Education Goals Report: Building a Nation of Learners.* US Government Printing Office, Washington, DC

Natriello G, Dornbusch S M 1984 *Teacher Evaluation Standards and Student Effort.* Longman, New York

Natriello G, McDill E, Pallas A 1990 *Schooling Disadvantaged Children: Racing Against Catastrophe.* Teachers College Press, New York

Pallas A 1986 *The Determinants of High School Dropout.* Center for the Social Organization of Schools, Report No. 364. Johns Hopkins University, Baltimore, Maryland

Roberts K 1984 *School-leavers and Their Prospects: Youth in the Labour Market in the 1980s.* Open University Press, Milton Keynes

Rumberger R 1983 Dropping out of high school: The influence of race, sex, and family background. *Am. Educ. Res. J.* 20(2): 199–220

Rumberger R 1987 High school dropouts: A review of issues and evidence. *Rev. Educ. Res.* 57(2): 101–22

Rumberger R, Ghatak R, Poulos G, Ritter P, Dornbusch S 1990 Family influences on dropout behavior in one California high school. *Sociol. Educ.* 63(4): 283–99

Seetharamu A S, Ushadevi M S 1985 *Education for Rural Areas: Constraints and Prospects.* South Asia Books, Columbia, Missouri

Stinchcombe A 1979 *Rebellion in a High School*, 2nd edn. Quadrangle Books, Chicago, Illinois

Sullivan M 1988 *A Comparative Analysis of Drop-outs and Non Drop-outs in Ontario Secondary Schools.* Ontario Department of Education, Toronto

US General Accounting Office 1987 *School Dropouts: Survey of Local Programs.* US Government Printing Office, Washington, DC

Wehlage G, Rutter R, Smith G A, Lesko N, Fernandez R R 1989. *Reducing the Risk: Schools as Communities of Support.* Falmer Press, London

Further Reading

Bryk A, Thum Y 1989 The effects of high school organization on dropping out: An exploratory investigation. *Am. Educ. Res. J.* 26(3): 353–83

LeCompte M, Dworkin A 1991 *Giving Up on School: Student Dropouts and Teacher Burnouts.* Corwin Press, Newbury Park, California

Natriello G (ed.) 1987 *School Dropouts: Patterns and Policies.* Teachers College Press, New York

Pallas A 1989 Conceptual and measurement issues in the study of school dropouts. In: Corwin R, Namboodiri K (eds.) 1989 *Research in the Sociology of Education and Socialization*, Vol. 8. JAI Press, Greenwich, Connecticut

Wagenaar T 1987 What do we know about dropping out of high school? In: Corwin R (ed.) 1987 *Research in the Sociology of Education and Socialization*, Vol. 7. JAI Press, Greenwich, Connecticut

Weis L, Farrar E, Petrie H (eds.) 1989 *Dropouts from School: Issues, Dilemmas, and Solutions.* State University of New York Press, Albany, New York

School Dropouts

D. M. Kelly

Economists have traditionally viewed school dropout and grade repetition as measures of inefficiency or wastage. Other analysts are more interested in which groups suffer the most as a result of inefficient schooling systems, and their work focuses on how schooling often operates to the greater disadvantage of groups on the margins of power in society. Before taking up this theme, this article will discuss whether students drop out or get pushed out, how to measure school disengagement, the incidence of the problem, and some key variables that explain it.

1. Dropouts, Pushouts, and the Concept of Disengagement

Much of the research on students who fail to complete school can be divided into two imperfect schools of thought. The dominant school—which fits within the traditions of neoclassical economics, status attainment, and social psychology—conceives of early school leaving as dropping out. Researchers who use this framework favor correlation models in which students' behavior, performance in school, psychological states, and family background are independent variables (e.g., Ekstrom et al. 1986). This approach generally casts dropping out as an individual act, signifying individual, or perhaps family or cultural, failure.

The other school of thought conceives of noncompleters as pushouts. Such researchers see the variables emphasized by the status-attainment school as symptoms, not causes. They focus on unequal economic, political, and social structures and certain schooling practices like tracking and expulsion that serve to stigmatize, discourage, and exclude children. Researchers using this model have tended to document the inequities in the economic and political system and then postulate that pushouts are functional to the reproduction of the capitalist order (e.g., Bowles and Gintis 1976; for a review of Brazilian writers in this tradition, see Vershine and Pita de Melo 1988). Viewed through this lens, the way in which the schooling system achieves this and why the pushouts comply is relatively straightforward.

Both frameworks recognize that a certain failure rate is built into most schooling systems and that schools sort children hierarchically, but there is disagreement over the basis. The dropout school believes that, ideally, the sorting of students is based on merit. The curriculum basically works the same way for everyone and provides a fair means of selection into different areas of the workforce. In contrast, the pushout school argues that schools exclude students on the basis of class, race, ethnicity, and other markers of power and status, and that they rationalize this as being done on the basis of ability. So-called merit-based standards, set by the most powerful in society, serve mainly to perpetuate inequality. Wealthy children, for example, often attend high-quality schools, and their parents can afford to provide outside help and tutoring.

The term "dropout" puts inordinate blame on the individual; the term "pushout" puts inordinate blame on the institution. Dropout implies that the student makes an independent, final decision, while pushout implies that the institution acts inexorably to purge unwilling victims. Some work on early school leaving has emphasized that it is a mutual process of rejection (e.g., Fine 1990), or what can be called "disengagement." The metaphor underlying engagement is that of two toothed wheels of a gear, student and school, meshed together so that the motion in one is passed on to the other.

The concept of disengagement connotes a long-running, interactive process which may be reversible. It therefore encourages researchers to connect events in students' lives over time and look for cumulative effects. It also acknowledges the spectrum of ways in which students are engaged: one who recognizes the need for a diploma can be very different from one who likes school. The terms dropout and pushout retain some usefulness in characterizing an exit from school—often the final outcome—as more student- or school-initiated. For others—and in North America and elsewhere this is a significant group—the decisive moment of dropout or pushout never occurs; these students attend infrequently, leaving and returning several times, and thus may be more aptly described as fade-outs (Kelly and Gaskell 1996).

2. Measuring School Disengagement

Disengagement can be difficult to document because it occurs over time and may not always be observable (e.g., passive resistance to learning) or may be open to different interpretations. The literature on dropouts and pushouts suggests signs and styles of disengagement primarily displayed within school settings. These indicators of disengagement can be grouped under four major domains: academics (including teacher–student relations), peer relations, extracurricular activities, and the schooling credential itself (e.g., certificate, diploma).

Indicators of disengagement from academics include: poor academic progress, classroom withdrawal (e.g., few instructional interactions), participation in nonacademic or remedial classes and programs, grade repetition, and suspension and expulsion.

Ethnographic research has shown that peer cultures mediate student outcomes like dropout and pushout. These outcomes are not simply a function of within-school factors, as economic models often imply. Indicators of disengagement related to peers include: fighting, inability to make friends, alienation from and opposition to peer groups accorded status by the school, and bonding with peers marginalized by institutional practices.

Indicators of disengagement from extracurricular activities include lack of participation in and dislike of school-sponsored clubs, teams, and events. An example of disengagement from the credential is the belief that a diploma is either not necessary to realize future plans or will not bring promised rewards.

While school administrators keep records of some of these indicators, only recently have researchers and educators begun to think of systematically linking patterns of disengagement to individual students in an effort to identify and re-engage those "at risk" of dropping out or being pushed out. Instead, most attempts to define and measure disengagement have focused on the final outcome of the process, with one exception: grade repetition.

Dropout statistics vary widely, depending in part on the definition of dropout, the source of the data, and the method of calculating the rate (Rumberger 1987). Students who transfer to another school, who obtain an alternative certificate of achievement, or who stop attending but eventually return to school, are sometimes counted as dropouts. On the other hand, students who leave school at a young age, who leave to get married or join the military, or who pass the legal compulsory school attendance age are sometimes not counted as dropouts or pushouts. Nor are students who attend regularly but do not learn to read and write.

True dropout rates are difficult to obtain because few countries collect data on who actually drops out and who gets promoted (UNESCO 1984). Two common, but crude, proxies derive from attrition and census data. Typically, attrition rates are constructed for a class cohort out of enrollment and graduation numbers. One of the difficulties of the approach lies in determining membership in the cohort. Transfers and repeaters may get counted twice, overstating the number of students initially enrolled. Thus, attrition rates tend to overestimate the true dropout rate. One can use census data to calculate what percentage of a given age cohort has not completed, say, primary or secondary school and is not enrolled in school. But because census data are usually self-reported or second-hand and undercount marginalized groups like low-income and ethnic minorities, this approach can underestimate the true dropout rate.

3. Worldwide Patterns of Dropout/Pushout and Repetition

In general, primary school dropout rates are low in countries with a high gross national product per capita. These countries, primarily the industrialized countries of Europe, North America, Japan, Australia, and New Zealand, have also achieved universal primary school enrollment. Table 1 shows that 40 percent of students who enrolled in primary school in low-income countries such as Haiti and Mali dropped out or were pushed out before the terminal year of that cycle. Moreover, primary school completion rates declined over the 1980s in the poorest countries (Lockheed and Verspoor 1990).

Repetition rates show a similar pattern: they are highest in the poorest countries. Yet these aggregate data mask differences among countries due to educational structure and promotion practices. For example, low-income countries like Sudan and middle-income countries like the Republic of Korea, Zimbabwe, and Malaysia now practice automatic promotion. Although most industrialized countries follow automatic promotion either by law or in practice (UNESCO Office of Statistics 1984), many states in the United States have ended social promotion in response to concern over standards, making the country's annual repetition rate comparable to such low-income countries as Kenya (Shepard and Smith 1989 pp. 7–9).

Table 1
Median primary school dropout and repetition rates 1985

Countries by GNP per capita	Dropout rates (in %)		Repetition rates (in %)		
	Total	No. countries	Total	Female	No. countries
Low	40.8	13	16.3	16.5	23
Lower middle	19.5	11	10.6	8.7	20
Upper middle	14.1	7	7.5	5.5	14
High (oil exporters)			5.7	5.2	3
High (market economies)			1.5	1.1	10

Source: UNESCO database 1989, cited in Lockheed and Verspoor (1990 pp. 205–16)

In many countries of Africa and Asia, except the poorest, girls' repetition rates are lower than those of boys (UNESCO 1984). However, girls tend to drop out at higher rates and earlier, regardless of their repetition rate. Further, in many countries with limited access to primary school, girls are enrolled at lower rates, so dropout and repetition rates alone tend to understate gender inequities (Deble 1980 pp. 47–50). Several studies have shown that girls (or their parents) are more easily discouraged by repetition. In countries where access to further schooling is limited, parents more often encourage boys to repeat a grade in the hope that they will obtain better entrance exam scores (UNESCO 1979, Lewis et al. 1990, Anderson 1988).

4. Repetition: A Pushout Factor or Indicator of Academic Failure?

Many studies show that repetition and dropout/pushout are correlated. The relationship of repeating a grade to final disengagement is complex and shaped by the context of particular schooling systems and countries. Researchers, particularly those using a dropout framework, have commonly assumed that repetition and dropout were both largely attributable to academic failure. In contrast, those using a pushout framework have argued that being retained a grade sends an institutional message of rejection that contributes directly to students' disengagement from school, above and beyond their actual ability or achievement level (Fine 1991). In one of the few studies to examine the causal relationship between repetition and dropout, Grissom and Shepard (1989) found that repetition increased the probability of eventually dropping out of school—across three city school districts in the United States—by 20 to 30 percent, after achievement, socioeconomic status, and gender were controlled.

Repetition may also contribute to dropping out when it results in students being overage for their grade. As they approach the age of adulthood, which varies by culture, some students, especially girls and low-income youths, face increased domestic and work responsibilities and the prospects of early marriage and pregnancy that may pull them out of school. In some Third World countries, students may be overage for their grade due not to repetition but to late enrollment. For example, a study of 37 schools in Argentina found that eventual dropouts enrolled in school late and had irregular attendance compared with primary school completers, but they were not more likely to have repeated (Patty and Tobin 1973).

5. Key Variables Explaining Disengagement

Before discussing some key variables that help to explain disengagement, a few preliminary observations are in order. First, most school dropout research has been descriptive, either based on correlation models or surveys of dropouts and educators. The former cannot show that the factors associated with early school leaving actually cause the phenomenon. Survey data must also be interpreted with caution. Dropouts and pushouts, influenced by norms regarding socially acceptable behavior, may answer vaguely or lie. The responses of teachers and administrators also tend to reflect self-interest. As Davico (1990) found in her study of eight Brazilian schools, teachers identified the low socioeconomic conditions of students and families—seen to limit students' ability to learn—as the primary reason for dropout. This deflected attention from their own behavior and other in-school factors.

A second caveat has to do with differences among regions and countries. Much of the Third World data focuses more broadly on access and participation issues and thus has examined such factors as the number of, and distance to, schools (Stromquist 1989), whereas in highly industrialized countries like the United States, researchers have placed more emphasis on student behavior and achievement in relation to disengagement (Rumberger 1987). Nevertheless, a number of the factors that determine initial access to schooling also affect survival once enrolled, and these factors have been shown to interact with each other in roughly similar ways across countries.

Among these factors are markers of power and status such as social class, ethnicity and race, gender, and community type (urban or rural). Usually these have been treated as demographic variables, but with demands for democratization increasing, recent research has included more systematic analysis of how various disadvantaged groups have fared through the schooling system as well as in the labor and marriage markets. These outcomes have been seen to shape perceptions of the worth of further schooling.

5.1 Socioeconomic Status

Children living in poverty are less likely to complete school (for reviews, see Anderson 1988, Lockheed and Verspoor 1990, Rumberger 1987). Socioeconomic status, correlated with dropout/pushout, is often measured by parental education, father's occupation, family income, and household items available. Rumberger (1983), in a United States study, found that differences in dropout rates among ethnic groups could be explained mostly by differences in family background. The most uniform predictor among the various ethnic/gender groups was the presence in the home of reading materials.

Surveys of early school leavers underscore the importance of socioeconomic reasons (e.g., Vershine and Pita de Melo 1988). Some families cannot afford to pay for school fees, books and supplies, transportation, and uniforms. Others cannot afford the opportunity costs, that is, the earned income and domestic labor that parents forego when their children are enrolled in school. Still other children report shame at their relative poverty, reflected in their clothes or lack of lunch. In Brazil, where the dropout rate exceeds 80 percent at the primary level, low-income families make up the majority in the public school system. Davico (1990) identified a number of school-related factors that seemed to influence the disengagement process, including inadequately prepared teachers and low expectations for student success.

5.2 Race and Ethnicity

Race and ethnicity also influence who persists in school. Research has shown that groups that have been disadvantaged historically tend to leave school early. In a qualitative study in Canada, most First Nations (aboriginal) people who left school without graduating said racism, including discriminatory practices and attitudes on the part of teachers and peers, had affected their decision to leave (Canada 1990 p. 11). Ethnic and other minority groups may be faced with curricular content that does not reflect their living conditions or presents as truth a certain history and a set of personal experiences that for them is alien. Teaching in a language other than that used by students outside of school may contribute to their disengagement, although this is complicated by socioeconomic status and other factors. For example, Morocco introduces French, a nonindigenous language, in third grade, and a Ministry of Education study there found that knowledge of French was the single largest determinant of success at the end of primary school (Lockheed and Verspoor 1990 p. 106).

Discrimination in the job market and ethnic quotas in educational selection can promote disengagement. In Malaysia, the Malays saw university attendance and better job prospects as more possible and thus continued their schooling. In contrast, the Chinese, who came from higher socioeconomic backgrounds and had better examination scores, tended to discontinue their schooling more often because they perceived fewer payoffs (Wang 1982).

5.3 Gender

The sex-role division of labor within the family and society influences the persistence in school by gender. In some regions boys drop out more often and earlier to herd grazing animals and do other tasks (Stromquist 1989 p. 150). But more often, girls—particularly those in low-income and rural families—seem to be needed at home to care for younger siblings and do housework and agricultural tasks (Anderson 1988, Stromquist 1989, Lewis et al. 1990).

Recognizing that parents in Bangladesh have greater elasticity of demand for girls' schooling, a pilot project offered low-income girls scholarships to encourage them to remain in school. In the project area, the secondary school dropout rate for girls dropped from 15 percent before the program started to 3.5 percent in 1987. Interviews with parents of children both in and out of school confirmed that lack of financial resources was the single most important reason that girls do not attend secondary school (Thein et al. 1990).

Research in the United States and elsewhere has clearly demonstrated the link between early marriage and childbearing and dropping out, the magnitude of which is much stronger for low socioeconomic status youths (Rumberger 1983, Anderson 1988 p. 11). Surveys in developing countries reveal that a number of reasons for girls leaving school are related to the onset of puberty. Girls and parents cite sexual attention from, or involvement with, boys and male teachers, concerns about girls' safety due to distance from school, as well as cultural and religious values concerning early marriage and pregnancy (for a review, see Stromquist 1989 pp. 153–58). It is common for schools around the world to exclude girls who become pregnant or get married. In Malawi, for example, institutional policy and practice support the permanent expulsion of pregnant and married girls from formal schooling (Lewis et al. 1990 p. 13).

Do girls leave school due to early pregnancy and marriage, or do these options emerge as a means of escape from an institution—the school—that has failed to offer them a sense of purpose and competence? Scholars and policymakers have often assumed that the school has little influence on girls taking on adult roles early. Yet research indicates that pregnancy and marriage may be partly symptoms of, and attempts to deal with, disaffection with school. In the United States a substantial minority of female dropouts or pushouts become pregnant after they leave school. Likewise, several studies done in developing countries have challenged the widely held view that the main reason females drop out of school is due to pregnancy; this may only be the proximate cause or a post hoc explanation (Anderson 1988 p. 11, Lewis et al. 1990 p. 19).

5.4 Community Type

Rural residents, especially in developing countries and particularly in Latin America, drop out at higher rates than their urban counterparts (Anderson 1988, Stromquist 1989, Lockheed and Verspoor 1990). Lack of schools and a complement of grades, large distances between school and home, lack of flexible scheduling of classes and the school year to meet the local (typically agrarian) population's needs are some of the reasons cited by rural residents who have disengaged. Even in industrialized countries like Canada and Australia, rural dropouts say transportation difficulties and a lack of options within school contributed to their disengagement (Canada 1990). In the United States, and presumably other highly industrialized countries, dropouts and pushouts more often live in urban areas (Ekstrom et al. 1986), where schools are typically overcrowded, underfunded, and bureaucratically run. For example, Fine (1990) undertook an ethnographic study of a public high school in New York where over two-thirds of the student body dropped out or were pushed out.

6. Conclusion

Resources are limited, and demands for equality of access to schools and treatment are high. Given restricted numbers of places at higher levels of schooling, informal and formal practices have emerged as a means of rationing access and survival. These practices can convey messages of rejection to students, who, in turn, may decide to resist or leave an institution that does not engage them. Among the most easily discouraged are disproportionate numbers of those with limited access to power and resources in the wider society.

See also: Aspirations and Expectations of Students; Children and Youth at Risk; Dropouts, School Leavers, and Truancy; Race and Ethnicity in Education; Sociology of Learning in School; Sociology of Special Education

References

Anderson M B 1988 *Improving Access to Schooling in the Third World: An Overview*. Project BRIDGES Research Report No. 1. Harvard University, Cambridge, Massachusetts

Bowles S, Gintis H 1976 *Schooling in Capitalist America: Educational Reform and the Contradictions of Economic Life*. Basic Books, New York

Canada 1990 *Qualitative Research on School Leavers*. Employment and Immigration Canada and Statistics Canada, Queen's Printer, Ottawa

Davico M I 1990 The repeat and drop-out problem: A study in Brazil on the role of the teacher. *Prospects* 20(1): 107–13

Deble I 1980 *The School Education of Girls: An International Comparative Study on School Wastage Among Girls and Boys at the First and Second Levels of Education*. UNESCO, Paris

Ekstrom R B, Goertz M E, Pollack J M, Rock D A 1986 Who drops out of high school and why? Findings from a national study. *Teach. Coll. Rec.* 87(3): 356–73

Fine M 1990 *Framing Dropouts: Notes on the Politics of an Urban High School*. State University of New York Press, Albany, New York

Grissom J B, Shepard L A 1989 Repeating and dropping out of school. In: Shepard L A, Smith M L (eds.) 1989 *Flunking Grades: Research and Policies on Retention*. Falmer Press, Lewes

Kelly D M 1993 *Last Chance High: How Girls and Boys Drop In and Out of Alternative Schools*. Yale University Press, New Haven, Connecticut

Kelly D, Gaskell J (eds.) 1996 *Debating Dropouts: Critical Policy and Research Perspectives on School Leaving*. Teachers College Press, New York

Lewis S G, Horn R, Kainja C, Nyirenda S, Spratt J 1990 *Constraints to Girls' Persistence in Primary School and Women's Employment Opportunities in the Education Service*. Report No. PN-ABH-289. United States Agency for International Development, Washington, DC

Lockheed M E, Verspoor A M 1990 *Improving Primary Education in Developing Countries: A Review of Policy Options*. World Bank, Washington, DC

Patty M, Tobin A 1973 *La Desercion Escolar en la Primeria de Rio Negro, Argentina*. Centro de Investigaciones Educativas, Buenos Aires

Rumberger R W 1983 Dropping out of high school: The influence of race, sex, and family background. *Am. Educ. Res. J.* 20(2): 199–220

Rumberger R W 1987 High school dropouts: A review of issues and evidence. *Rev. Educ. Res.* 57(2): 101–22

Shepard L A, Smith M L 1989 Introduction and overview. In: Shepard L A, Smith M L (eds.) 1989 *Flunking Grades: Research and Policies on Retention*. Falmer Press, Lewes

Stromquist N P 1989 Determinants of educational participation and achievement of women in the Third World: A review of the evidence and a theoretical critique. *Rev. Educ. Res.* 59(2): 143–83

Thein T M, Kabir M, Islam M 1990 *Evaluation of the Female Education Scholarship Program*. Report No. PD-ABB-512. United States Agency for International Development, Washington, DC

UNESCO 1979 *Etude du problème de déperdition d'effectifs scolaires parmi les jeunes syriens et syriennes inscrit dans les cycles de l'enseignement préuniversitaire*. UNESCO, Paris

UNESCO Office of Statistics 1984 Wastage in Primary Education from 1970 to 1980. *Prospects* 14(3): 347–68

Vershine R E, Pita de Melo A M 1988 Causes of school failure: The case of the State of Bahia in Brazil. *Prospects* 18(4): 557–68

Wang B L C 1982 Sex and ethnic differences in educational investment in Malaysia: The effects of reward structures. In: Kelly G P, Elliott C M (eds.) 1982 *Women's Education in the Third World: Comparative Perspectives*. State University of New York Press, Albany, New York

Family and Schooling

Introduction: The Centrality of the Family in Educational Processes

L. J. Saha

The family influences education attainments in so many complex ways that researchers continue to refine concepts and measures to account for its dominance in studies of school inputs, processes, and outputs. Whether studied in terms of the socioeconomic status of home background, of parental values and home culture, of the relationship between family and school, or of the community and social networks enjoyed by the family, the pervasiveness of the family into the school, either positive or negative, has proven difficult to fully appreciate.

In a meta-analysis of almost 200 studies which examined the relationship between family socioeconomic status and school achievement, White (1982) found that the correlations between the two ranged between 0.10 and 0.80, figures which suggest a considerable range in family effects. One dimension not captured in family status studies has been that of the family process, in particular the nature of family interaction, and also the links between family the family and the wider community. Subsequent research has advanced the understanding of these complex family effects, and concepts such as family social capital (Coleman 1987) and cultural capital (Bourdieu 1986) have become commonplace in family-education studies. Comparative studies between countries and studies of high achieving minority groups have also targeted the family as a major explanatory variable (Caplan et al. 1992). In addition, while many studies have investigated family impacts on schooling using quantitative approaches with an emphasis on more refined measurement instruments of family environment, qualitative studies of family impacts have also been carried out.

The 13 articles in this section traverse the range of areas of interest to sociologists of education. The article by Kellaghan (*Family and Schooling*) provides an overview of family studies and in so doing, also locates the family in a changing social context, a factor which adds further complexity to the understanding of family effects on schooling.

Two articles focus on the complexity of family socioeconomic status and add further emphasis to the importance of this dimension. Behrman and †Taubman (*Family Status and Economic Status*) review the literature on the complex relationships between family, schooling, and occupational and economic status, while Strober (*Economics of Child Care*) examines social and economic consequences of childcare and the working mother, a growing characteristic of modern families.

The home environment, other than the economic, is represented by five articles. Behrman and †Taubman (*Kinship Studies*) provide an overview which addresses the nature-nurture question and the findings from kinship and twin studies. Twin studies have long been regarded as the keys to unlock the disaggregation of the multiple determinants, including the genetic, of school and occupational success. Schneewind (*Family Influences on Human Development*) also includes the genetic component, as well as socioeconomic and relational factors, in his review of the literature on individual human development within the family. Marjoribanks (*Family and School Environmental Measures*) discusses strategies to measure family and school social envronments, and reports findings from both quantitative and qualitative procedures. Fuligni and Stevenson's article, *Home Environment and School Learning*, focuses on the *processes* of the home environment and includes both the objective or material aspects, as well as the subjective and psychological. They conclude that our understanding of these processes remain "fragmentary and incomplete." Finally, Marjoribanks examines an aspect of the family environment which is receiving increased attention in his article *Children of Single-parent Families*.

From a different theoretical and conceptual framework, the two articles on social and cultural capital approach the sociological study of the impact of the family on schooling which has received considerable recent attention. Collins and Thompson (*Family, School, and Cultural Capital*) trace the notion of cultural capital from the French tradition and the theoretical and empirical writings of Bourdieu. They demonstrate the usefulness of the cultural perspective in the contemporary research which has incorporated it, both theoretically and empirically, in research on family impacts on schooling. †Coleman's article, *Family, School, and Social Capital*, while more theoretical, points to the importance of family social contacts and networks in the explanation of family effects on schooling.

Finally, this section includes three articles which direct attention to characteristics of parents themselves. Shimoni (*Parent Education*) addresses an issue related to the enrichment of the family environment, while Powell (*Parent Involvement in Preschool Programs*) and Payne (*School–Parent Relationships*) describe the importance of parent–school contacts for improvement of the academic motivation and achievement of students. In all three articles the implicit assumption is that the more education of parents about schooling, and more participation by parents in schooling, the more enriched will be the home environment. However, these articles also make clear the complexity of parental involvement, both from a policy as well as a social perspective. In some cases, parents may interfere with what the school hopes to achieve. Sociologists of education have tended to assume the positive nature of these aspects of family environment, but to date little direct research seems to have been carried out to confirm the assumptions.

References

Bourdieu P 1986 The forms of capital. In: Richardson J G (ed.) 1986 *Handbook of Theory and Research for the Sociology of Education*. Greenwood Press, New York

Caplan N, Choy M H, Whitmore J K 1992 Indochinese refugee families and academic achievement. *Sci. Am.* (February): 18–24

Coleman J S 1987 Families and schools. *Educ. Researcher* 16 (August–September): 32–8

White K R 1982 The relation between socioeconomic status and academic achievement. *Psych. Bull.* 91(3): 461–81

Children of Single-parent Families

K. Marjoribanks

In the United States it is predicted that with increases in divorce and nonmarital childbearing, at least 50 percent of recently born children will spend part of their childhood living with a single parent (Webster et al. 1995). Projections in Great Britain suggest that by the year 2000, one in six of all families will be headed by single mothers, whereas the proportion of two-parent families will fall to less than three in four (Harrop and Plewis 1995). Similarly, Dronkers (1994) indicated that the number of single-parent families in European countries is increasing rapidly with the most significant change being the growth in single-parent families headed by mothers. Research that has examined relationships between changing family structures and children's outcomes has shown "that students who live in one-parent households are disadvantaged on many counts. However, there is not much agreement as to why they are" (Mulkey et al. 1992 p. 48).

1. Theoretical Perspectives

Studies have indicated, for example, that in relation to two-parent families, children living in single-parent families: have higher dropout rates from high school; are more susceptible to pressure from their friends to engage in deviant behavior; have lower academic achievement; are more delinquent, especially in father-absent families; and have greater social and psychological problems. Also, the benefits of having two parents in the home have been shown to be greater for elementary school students than for high school students, while young adults from single-parent families have been shown to be more likely to enter low social-status occupations. The following theoretical perspectives have been proposed to explain such relationships.

1.1 The No-impact Hypothesis

This perspective proposes that the absence of one parent has no direct impact on children's outcomes. Instead, it is claimed that the association between changing family structures and outcomes can be attributed to a combination of other social factors such as parents' education, occupations, and incomes, and the ethnicity/race of the family. It is argued that statistical relationships between family structure and children's outcomes do not, without further exploration, necessarily support the proposition that living in a single-parent family is educationally or emotionally unfavorable for children. Dronkers (1994) observed,

for example, that mothers of single-parent families tend to have lower average educational levels than do mothers in two-parent families. If the educational attainment of children from single-parent families is lower than that of children from two-parent families, then "this difference might only be caused by the difference in the mothers' educational levels and not by the intrinsically less favorable conditions of lone parent families" (Dronkers 1994 p. 172).

The no-impact perspective also claims that much family structure research is inconclusive as it has not differentiated among various types of single-parent families such as whether they result from marital disruption (divorce or separation), parental death, or out-of-wedlock births. Also, it is suggested that the inconsistent findings from many studies relate to a failure to take into account the timing in a child's life of any family disruption; the duration of the effects of that disruption; and whether the lone parent is the father or mother. McLanahan (1985) proposed that one of the significant questions in family structure research continues to be whether differences in children's outcomes in single-parent families are due to the absence of a parent or to other social background factors that are correlated with both family structure and the outcome measures.

1.2 Economic Deprivation Hypothesis

In an analysis of income inequality in the United States, Nielsen and Alderson (1997 p. 19) indicated that "insofar as female-headed families have lower-than-average incomes, this trend inflated the proportion of poor families ... controlling for other factors, the presence of families headed by a single female is positively associated with income inequality." It is often proposed that such economic hardship, which is associated with female-headed single-parent families, is the significant factor that accounts for any unfavorable children's school outcomes. Specifically, it is suggested that economic hardship in single-parent families is likely to require adolescents to work long hours and to take greater responsibility for any younger brothers and sisters, and that such time-consuming activities are associated with early dropout from school.

In refining the economic deprivation perspective, Wu (1996) proposed that by concentrating on income levels the perspective has neglected the dynamic characteristics of income. He claimed that the association between changes in family structure and children's outcomes might be an artifact of varying economic circumstances, such as instability and downward shifts in family income, that may accompany changing family structures. Wu's research which investigated relationships between family structure and risks of premarital birth, proposed that the following hypotheses needed to be examined:

(a) *a low-income hypothesis*—that the risk of premarital birth is higher for women from disadvantaged economic backgrounds because they possess fewer or less attractive economic opportunities.

(b) *income and transitory income hypothesis*—that uncertainties generated by unexpected fluctuations in family income increase the risk of a premarital birth net of absolute income levels.

(c) *level and income change hypothesis*—that downward trends in family income reflect worsening socioeconomic opportunities that increase the risk of a premarital birth net of absolute income levels. (Wu 1996 p. 389)

Milne et al. (1986) suggested that introducing income into studies as a social-background factor may not adequately take into account the impact of economic circumstances on children's outcomes. Instead, it is argued that the effect on outcomes of living in one-parent families may operate mainly through the poorer economic conditions of those families, that is, income should be considered as a mediating variable between family structure and outcomes. Also, analyses of the economic deprivation hypothesis need to differentiate among the various forms of single-parent family. Biblarz and Raftery (1993) proposed that the impact of family disruption resulting from separation or divorce on children's outcomes may be stronger than the effects of family disruption resulting from the death of a parent. They suggested, for example, that widows might receive more financial and noneconomic assistance from friends and relatives than do divorcees. The economic deprivation hypothesis directs particular attention to the question whether changing family structure is "a 'cause' of poverty or a consequence of the deteriorating circumstances of individuals and families?" (Eggebeen and Lichter 1991 p. 802).

1.3 Family Socialization Orientation

It is generally accepted that the quality of parent–child interactions during childhood and adolescence have important associations with school-related outcomes and with the eventual social-status attainment of young adults. Kellaghan et al. concluded:

> The home environment is a most powerful factor in determining the school learning of students—their level of school achievement, their interest in school learning, and the number of years of schooling they will receive. Thus, parents and the home environment hold a major key to the learning of children.(Kellaghan et al. 1993 p. 145)

For single-parent families it is claimed that the absence of a parent results in a decrease in parental involvement which is associated with poorer learning outcomes. Biblarz and Raftery (1993) indicated, for example, that children in single-parent families were less likely than those in two-parent families to report that a parent was the most influential person in their lives. Furthermore, it is generally proposed that the absence of fathers has particular socialization influences, in that such absence decreases children's motivation for achievement and interferes with normal psychosexual development which results in poorer academic performance and earlier dropout from school. The father-absence perspective argues that the absence of a male role model is more detrimental for boys. As a result, it is hypothesized that there are gender differences in children's responses to the socialization in single-mother families with boys showing more negative effects than girls. Wu (1996) proposed that the socialization perspective indicates that women who grow up in a mother-only family during childhood and adolescence are at a greater risk of a premarital birth because they experience different interactions in their families than women raised in two-parent families.

Blau (1990) suggested that membership of social categories, such as family type, is a major factor in determining individuals' opportunity structures. Indeed, Blau (1990 p. 150) proposed that the central subject matter of sociology "is the study of these structural constraints limiting the opportunities of realizing choices for many while expanding them for some." The socialization orientation suggests that while parent–child interactions are related to children's learning outcomes, the nature of those relationships is influenced greatly by the opportunity structures created by living in differing family types. Investigations have emphasized the need to examine children's perceptions of those opportunity structures and socialization practices. Grolnick and Slowiaczek (1994 p. 248) observed, for example, that in family research, phenomenological experiences need to be stressed "as the child must experience the resources for them to have their influence. Such a viewpoint represents the child as an active processor of information rather than a passive recipient of inputs." Similarly, Wentzel (1994 p. 264) concluded that young people's school outcomes "may be more highly related to their own perceptions of parenting than to what parents think that they are doing in the home." McClelland also stated

> Socialization processes can orient individuals toward particular goals and, via the transmission of cultural capital, provide the means necessary to achieve them; however, through the calculus of the probable, such influences are constantly mediated by structural constraints in the form of perceptions of the opportunity structure. (McClelland 1990 p. 103)

1.4 Social Control Hypothesis

It is often argued that, in relation to single-parent families, two-parent families have greater resources available to them which allows more supervision and social control over their children. As a result of such social control, it is proposed that children from two-parent families have, for example, lower rates of delinquency, fewer premarital births, and lower levels of behavioral and emotional problems. The social control hypothesis considers adolescence as a particularly troublesome period of growing up. It is presumed that adolescents are likely to participate in what are considered to be inappropriate activities unless they are constrained by adults. Therefore, the number of parents becomes an important predictor of the amount and nature of control and supervision that occurs in families. The social control perspective is reflected in Jenkins' statement

> because single mothers are likely to be employed fulltime outside the home and must carry the weight of financial, psychological, and physical responsibilities that are normally shouldered by two parents, they may not have much time to deal with daily school issues, especially if they also lack financial and psychological support. (Jenkins 1995 p. 223)

An important distinction between the socialization and social control perspectives is noted by Wu and Martinson (1993). They indicated that the "socialization hypothesis stresses the effect of *prior* experience on current behavior while the social control hypothesis stresses the effect of *current* family situation on current behavior" (p. 212).

1.5 Instability, Change, and Stress Perspective

In the United States it is estimated that about 60 percent of first marriages in the 1980s and 1990s will end in divorce. Although 80 percent of those who divorce subsequently remarry, most children of divorced families spend over five years living in single-parent families headed by mothers (Biblarz and Raftery 1993). Harrop and Plewis (1995) have predicted that 40 percent of all marriages in the United Kingdom end in divorce. They also indicated that divorce rates underestimate the extent of marital breakdown as many marriages end in permanent separation.

The instability and change perspective relates to how children and adolescents cope with the stress that may accompany major family disruption such as divorce or separation. McLanahan (1985) proposed that marital disruption causes multiple role and status changes for children that often result in feelings of anger and loss. She suggested that these feelings are likely to be more intense at the time of disruption and may be associated with antisocial behavior, a loss of confidence, and a lowering of self-esteem. Similarly, Wu and Martinson (1993 p. 212) stated that "the disequilibrium following a disruption causes some adolescents to disengage from the parental household, for example, by spending less time in the home or by engaging in impulsive, rebellious, or aggressive actions."

Furthermore, Webster et al. (1995) proposed that if divorce or parental separation is preceded by interpersonal conflict then children's psychological adjustment might be influenced by that conflict. They claimed that children may react to such hostility with negative emotions or be drawn into the conflict and that they may blame themselves for the parental disruption. Mulkey et al. (1992) observed, however, that relationships among conflict, parental separation, and children's subsequent behavior may not differ greatly from the relations between parental conflict in many two-parent households and children's responses to that conflict.

Whereas the social control hypothesis emphasizes the effect of the current family situation on current behavior, the instability, change, and stress perspective emphasizes the impact of particular family events on behavior. While this article has examined parental divorce, other significant events that are likely to have short- and long-term influences on children's behavior are the death of a parent and the marriage of the single parent.

2. Research Investigations

Although the theoretical perspectives in Sect. 1 were presented as alternatives, analyses of the relationships between family structure and children's outcomes are likely to adopt combinations of those frameworks. In this section, a number of studies are presented that have tested various forms of those frameworks.

2.1 Family Structure and Academic Achievement

Using the sophomore cohort of the High School and Beyond Study, Mulkey et al. (1992) constructed a conceptual model that examined relationships among early family background (social status, ethnicity/race, suburban/urban, family size); family structure; parental involvement, students' school and after-school behavior, family economic condition; and students' academic performance. They investigated the following questions:

> (a) Are children from mother-absent versus father-absent households educationally disadvantaged, net of those ethnic, SES, and community-context variables that are not caused by family structure?
> (b) Can any educational disadvantage of children in a mother-absent versus a father-absent household be attributed to the children's maladaptive behavioral patterns?
> (c) Can the educational disadvantages to children in mother-absent versus father-absent households be attributed to the families' lower income resulting from marital dissolution? (Mulkey et al. 1992 p. 51)

The findings indicated that the associations between living in different family structures and scores on standardized tests and grades were small. Further analyses revealed that the effects of living with one parent on students' academic performance could be attributed almost entirely to the students' early family background. Once social background characteristics were taken into account, the residual effect of father or mother absence on students' grades was explained more by the students' misbehavior than by the economic circumstances of their families. Mulkey et al. concluded:

> In the absence of a mother or father in the household, economic status plays less of a role in educational performance than does a students' misbehavior [such as, school lateness, absences, not doing homework]. In fact, the loss of income because of the father's absence has virtually no effect on a students' grades or test scores. (Mulkey et al. 1992 p. 62)

It is suggested, however, that the research provides few indications as to why children of father- or mother-absent families behave in the manner that they do. The investigators speculated that the students' misbehavior may be related to frustration or to the need to express rebellious behavior because of their desire for interpersonal contact in their families. Also, they proposed that children from single-parent families might be less likely to connect with school because they may have "fewer familial controls or lack of supervision . . . or to the demands that the single-parent family structure places on the child to take an active adultlike socioemotional role at home" (Mulkey et al. 1992 p. 63). The study identified family social background and student behavior as the major factors accounting for relationships between family structure and students' academic performance, while suggesting that further investigations might profitably examine the social control and the instability and change theoretical perspectives.

Importantly, Mulkey et al. (1992 p. 61) concluded that "Consistent with previous studies, this analysis shows that the effect of single-parent upbringing on the evaluation of students in school—whether by standardized tests or grades—is small." Indeed, part of the title of their study is "explanations of a small effect." Similarly, using a sample drawn from all students in the first year of Dutch secondary schools, Dronkers (1994) indicated that "Children from natural parents families have more school success than children from lone father families, but it is not a very important difference" (p. 184), and "living in a lone [parent] or natural parents family is not a very important factor in educational success" (p. 181). The Dutch investigation revealed that parents' educational level was a more powerful predictor of children's school outcomes. Dronkers concluded, "This importance of parental education, also in a lone parent family, underlines the necessity of a sufficient control for parental characteristics" (p. 189).

2.2 Family Structure and School Graduation

In an analysis of the effect of family structure on whether 17 year olds graduated from high school,

McLanahan (1985) examined four theoretical orientations. These were (a) the no-impact hypothesis which proposed that living in a single-parent family has no direct influence on students' graduation; (b) an economic deprivation perspective which stated that current family income has an independent effect on students' graduation, which is separate from economic factors that are related to the formation of female-headed families; (c) a father-absence hypothesis derived from socialization theory which proposed that fathers are important role models and influence significantly the cognitive and emotional development of their children; and (d) a family stress orientation which stated that parents' marital disruption is related to children's stress which influences their likelihood of graduating, but that the more distant the disruption the less harmful is its eventual impact.

The findings revealed that 17 year olds who were living with single mothers were less likely to be in high school than adolescents living with both parents. McLanahan concluded:

> These findings are not an artifact of place of residence, parents' education, or race and they argue against the notion that family effects observed in past research are due entirely to the failure to control for background factors associated with the formation or presence of single-parent families. (McLanahan 1985 p. 897)

The results indicated that current family economic circumstances were an important factor in accounting for the negative relation between family structure and the graduation of students from white families. Such economic conditions were less significant in accounting for the negative consequences in African-American families. When the father-absence and family-stress hypotheses were investigated, the study revealed that the relationship between parent absence and student graduation depended on the type of single-parent family and to a lesser extent on the duration of parent absence. It is claimed that:

> These findings lend support to the family-stress hypothesis insofar as they show that parent absence does not necessarily have negative consequences and that offspring from recently disrupted households are least likely to be in school. On the other hand, the persistence of negative effects for five years and longer among some groups suggests that something other than the event of marital disruption triggers early departures from school. (McLanahan 1985 p. 897)

In a further analysis of the relationship between family structure and students' disengagement from school, Astone and McLanahan (1991) examined whether such relationships could be attributed to variations in parents' aspirations and parenting styles. The study indicated that children from single-parent families reported lower parental expectations, less monitoring of schoolwork by their mothers or fathers, and less overall supervision of social activities than children in two-parent families. It was found that these family structure differences in children's perceptions of their family environments accounted for little of the family structure differences in measures of school disengagement. Astone and McLanahan indicated, however, that their measures of parenting practices were restricted to one-item indicators and that many dimensions of parent–child interaction were not assessed. The study concluded, as do many family structure investigations, that there is a need to collect much more detailed and sensitive data on parent–child interactions in single- and two-parent families.

2.3 Family Structure, School Commitment, and School Delinquency

In an investigation involving seventh- and eighth-grade American students, Jenkins (1995) examined relationships between single-parent families and children's commitment to school and delinquent behavior. A number of theoretical perspectives were combined to form the conceptual framework for the study. It was proposed that because single mothers lack economic and psychological support, they are likely to have more negative contacts with their children and have less time to monitor and discipline them, to supervise their social activities, and to be involved in their homework.

Jenkins indicated, however, that the relationship between family structure and school delinquency might be mediated by intervening processes, that is, single mothers might develop alternative means of economic and social support, and they may have relatives or friends who have significant socialization influences on their children. The study hypothesized that, in relation to children living with both parents, children from single-parent families have a weaker commitment to school and are more involved in school delinquency.

The findings revealed that low levels of school commitment were associated strongly with increased rates of three types of school delinquency: crime, misconduct, and nonattendance. Typically, relationships between family structure and school delinquency were mediated by parental involvement, the ability group of the child, and the child's commitment to school. Jenkins (1995) concluded that "Since more and more families are experiencing family disruption, schools may also seek more effective means of identifying and counseling youngsters whose family circumstances put them at risk" (p. 236). It was noted, however, that the study was limited by the use of cross-sectional correlational data and that longitudinal analyses were required for a more plausible understanding of the relationships among family structure, mediating measures, and children's outcomes such as school commitment and delinquency.

2.4 Family Structure and Marital Quality

Webster at al. (1995) examined to what extent family structure is related to children's subsequent marital instability. They investigated two theoretical orientations: a socialization perspective and an interparental conflict framework. From the socialization perspective it was hypothesized that young adults who spend the least time with two parents when they are children express greater marital unhappiness and more marital instability. The interparental conflict model suggested that if divorce is more often related to problematic family relationships than other single-parent family types, then "we would predict greater interpersonal (marital) difficulties among children of divorce than among those from other types of single-parent families (or intact homes)" (Webster et al. 1995 p. 406).

The findings showed no substantial differences in the overall marital happiness of young adults who grew up in varying family structures. In contrast, there were significant associations between family structure and marital stability, "with children of divorce and those who never lived with their father most often expressing doubts about the stability of their marriage" (p. 246). While the results indicated that those children who never lived with their father resembled closely children of divorce, they also revealed that children who lost a parent to death did not differ from those children from intact families. Because the results suggested important differences among those children who spent time in different types of single-parent families, the study concluded that the socialization perspective received little support.

The study did, however, support the hypothesis that observing a poor parental marriage or interparental conflict is related to children's eventual marital success. Children of divorce, more than those from any other single-parent family type, expressed the most doubts about their marriage stability. It appeared that having lost a parent to death or never living with one's father were not associated with the same long-term effects. The investigators speculated that children in single-parent families, that result from divorce, might have an underlying insecurity or fear of repeating the experience of their parents which makes it difficult for them to commit fully to marriage. Again, as in many family structure investigations, the authors indicated that their study was limited by the use of cross-sectional data, when they were trying to understand a process that occurs over time.

2.5 Family Structure and Premarital Birth

In an examination of the association between growing up in a nonintact family and the likelihood of having a child before marriage, Wu and Martinson (1993) constructed a family structure measure that traced a respondent's parental history between birth and late adolescence. The findings indicated that changes in family structure had large effects on the risk of premarital births for white and Hispanic women, and smaller effects for African-American women. Also, the effects were particularly persistent, even at long durations after a change in family structure.

The results provided little support for a socialization perspective as "Contrary to expectations, the effects on the risk of a premarital birth of being born into a mother-only family were small, not significant, and often in the opposite direction expected for women in all three racial and ethnic groups" (p. 228). Also, a social control hypothesis was not supported as the effects of the current family situation on the risk of premarital births were not significant. Instead, the results indicated that frequent changes in the numbers and types of parental figures a young woman has lived with, had strong associations with the risk of the young woman bearing her first child out of wedlock, that is, the findings were consistent with an instability and change theoretical perspective.

In a subsequent investigation, Wu (1996) indicated that a limitation of the previous analysis was the failure to control for income. As a result, Wu posed the question, is the relationship between family instability and premarital births an artifact of low, unstable, or declining income in a women's family or origin? The study showed that the relationship between changes in family structure and premarital birth risks were relatively unaffected when the differing income measures were controlled, that is, family instability and income appeared to have independent associations with the risk of premarital births. Wu (1996) concluded, however, that the effects of unmeasured factors in a woman's family environment that might be associated with family instability and family income could alter the outcomes of such family structure research.

3. Future Research Directions

Increasingly, studies that examine relationships between family structure and children's outcomes are investigating differing theoretical orientations and addressing the limitations of earlier research. Investigations, for example, are beginning to: (a) discriminate among different types of single-parent families such as divorced, separated, widowed, or never married; (b) include various measures of family social status as background characteristics; (c) control for the possible effects of income as a background and mediating variable; (d) separate the social status and race/ethnicity of families; and (e) differentiate between the effects on outcomes of single-parent families that are headed by fathers or mothers. Family structure research, however, has tended not to examine adequately adult–child interactions in families, nor measure the cumulative effects of changes in family structure on children's outcomes.

The complexity of children's family environments was examined by Coleman (1990, 1993) when he developed the concept of social capital. He suggested that family background is analytically separable into components such as human, social, and economic capital. Human capital provides the potential for a supportive learning environment in the home and is measured approximately by parents' educational attainment. In contrast, family social capital is related to the strength of relationships between adults in the family and children. Coleman (1988 p. 110) claimed that "if the human capital possessed by parents is not complemented by social capital embodied in family relations, it is irrelevant to the child's educational growth that the parent has a great deal, or small amount, of human capital."

The analysis of family social capital, in the context of human and economic capital, suggests a sensitive approach to an examination of how families with differing structures create learning contexts for children. Coleman (1990) claimed that when both parents are present in a family, there are stronger parent–child relationships and thus greater social capital, than when only one parent is present. In particular, he stated:

> social capital derives from the existence of closure of a social network involving a child and two (or more) adults. Closure is present only when there is a relation between adults who themselves have a relation to the child. The adults are able to observe the child's actions in different circumstances, talk to each other about the child, compare notes, and establish norms. The closure of the network can provide the child with support and rewards from additional adults that reinforce those received from the first and can bring about norms and sanctions that could not be instituted by a single adult alone. (Coleman 1990 p. 593)

In an analysis of the effects of family migration on children, Hagan et al. (1996) proposed a theoretical framework that incorporated analyses of family social capital and life-course perspectives. Such a theoretical framework could be adopted for investigations of the relationships between changing family structures and children's outcomes. In future research, interconnections between changing family structures and variations in the economic, human, and social capital of families might be explored using a life-course perspective. As part of survival and recovery from change and instability, family members adopt varying coping strategies that differ across time and place (Elder 1974, 1994). The variable nature of social and economic capital in single-parent families might be considered, for example, as a form of family adaptation that can mediate or strengthen the effects of external stressors on the lives of parents and children.

Our understanding of the relationships between family structure and children's outcomes is likely to be enhanced if future research adopts life-span orientations that examine how parents and children cope and adapt to their changing family situations. Such longitudinal investigations need to examine how the social, economic, and human capital in various family structures relate to the outcomes of children from differing social status and ethnic/racial groups. Unless such research is undertaken, then social policies related to single-parent families are likely to be restricted in their effectiveness.

See also: Children and Youth at Risk; Family and Schooling; Family Influence on Human Development; Family, School, and Cultural Capital; Family, School, and Social Capital

References

Astone N M, McLanahan S S 1991 Family structure, parental practices and high school completion. *Am. Sociol. Rev.* 56(3): 309–20

Biblarz T J, Raftery A E 1993 The effects of family disruption on social mobility. *Am. Sociol. Rev.* 58(1): 97–109

Blau P M 1990 Structural constraints and opportunities: Merton's contribution to general theory. In: Clark J, Modgil C, Modgil S (eds.) 1990 *Robert K Merton, Consensus and Controversy*. Falmer Press, London

Coleman J S 1988 Social capital and the creation of human capital. *Am. J. Sociol.* 94: S95–S120

Coleman J S 1990 *Foundations of Social Theory*. Harvard University Press, Cambridge, Massachusetts

Coleman, J S 1993 The rational reconstruction of society. *Am. Sociol. Rev.* 58(1): 1–15

Dronkers J 1994 The changing effects of lone parent families on the educational attainment of their children in a European welfare state. *Sociology* 28(1): 171–91

Eggebeen D J, Lichter D T 1991 Race, family structure, and changing poverty among American children. *Am. Sociol. Rev.* 56(6): 801–17

Elder G 1974 *Children of the Great Depression: Social Change in Life Experience*. University of Chicago Press, Chicago, Illinois

Elder G 1994 Time, human agency, and social change: Perspectives on the life course. *Soc. Psychol. Q.* 57(1): 4–15

Grolnick W S, Slowiaczek M L 1994 Parents' involvement in children's learning: A multidimensional conceptualization and motivational model. *Child Dev.* 65: 237–52

Hagan J, MacMillan R, Wheaton B 1996 New kid in town: Social capital and life course effects of family migration on children. *Am. Sociol. Rev.* 61(3): 368–85

Harrop A, Plewis I 1995 Two decades of family change: Secondary analysis of continuous government surveys. *J. R. Statist. Soc. Series A* 158(1): 91–106

Jenkins P H 1995 School delinquency and school commitment. *Sociol. Educ.* 68(3): 221–39

Kellaghan T, Sloane K, Alvarez B, Bloom B S 1993 *The Home Environment and School Learning: Promoting Parental Involvement in the Education of Children*. Jossey-Bass, San Francisco, California

McClelland K 1990 Cumulative disadvantage among the highly ambitious. *Sociol. Educ.* 63(1): 102–21

McLanahan S 1985 Family structure and the reproduction of poverty. *Am. J. Sociol.* 90(4): 873–901

Milne A, Myers D E, Rosenthal A S, Ginsburg A 1986 Single parents, working mothers, and the educational achievement of school children. *Sociol. Educ.* 59(3): 125–39

Mulkey L M, Crain R L, Harrington A J C 1992 One-parent households and achievement: Economic and behavioral explanations of a small effect. *Sociol. Educ.* 65(1): 48–65

Nielsen F, Alderson A S 1997 The Kuznets curve and the great U-turn: Income inequality in U.S. counties, 1970 to 1990. *Am. Sociol. Rev.* 62(2): 404–32

Webster P S, Orbuch T L, House J S 1995 Effects of childhood family background on adult marital quality and perceived stability. *Am. J. Sociol.* 101(2): 404–32

Wentzel K R 1994 Family functioning and academic achievement in middle school: A socio-emotional perspective. *J. Early Adol.* 14(3): 268–91

Wu L L 1996 Effects of family instability, income and income stability on the risk of premarital birth. *Am. Sociol. Rev.* 61(3): 386–406

Wu L L, Martinson B C 1993 Family structure and the risk of a premarital birth. *Am. Sociol. Rev.* 58(2): 210–32

Further Reading

Fejgin N 1995 Factors contributing to the academic excellence of American Jewish and Asian students. *Sociol Educ.* 68(1): 18–30

Furstenberg F F, Cherlin A J 1991 *Divided Families*. Harvard University Press, Cambridge, Massachusetts

Jencks C 1992 *Rethinking Social Policy: Race, Poverty, and the Underclass*. Harvard University Press, Cambridge, Massachusetts

Marjoribanks K 1994 Family, schools and children's learning: A study of children's learning environments. *Int. J. Educ. Res.* 21(5): 439–555

Marjoribanks K 1996 Ethnicity, proximal family environment, and young adolescents' cognitive performance. *J. Early Adol.* 16(3): 340–59

Marjoribanks K 1997 Family contexts, immediate family settings and adolescents' aspirations. *J. Appl. Dev. Psychol.* 18(1): 119–32

McKenry P C, Fine M A 1993 Parenting following divorce: A comparison of black and white single mothers. *J. Comp. Fam. Stud.* 24(1): 100–11

Thompson M S, Entwisle D R, Alexander K L, Sundius M J 1992 The influence of family composition on children's conformity to the student role. *Am. Educ. Res. J.* 29(2): 405–24

Economics of Child Care

M. H. Strober

As a result of the remarkable increase in women's labor force participation and women's participation in education and training in all Western industrialized countries, mothers no longer routinely care for their young children on a full-time basis. Arrangements for the care of infants and young children during the working or school hours of their parent(s) have now become matters of public policy. Economic issues include the supply and demand for childcare; its cost, quality, and external benefits;

and alternative systems of finance, governance, and regulation.

Except for the United States, industrialized countries have developed extensive policies for dealing with the care of young children, including paid periods of maternal and parental leave (Kahn and Kamerman 1987). Bergman (1993) provided a full discussion of the French system. Kamerman (1991) provided a summary of policies and programs in an international context. The United States situation is of particular policy interest because numerous decisions have been debated at the national, state, and local levels.

1. Overview of the United States Childcare Market

The diversity of care options for preschool children is extraordinary. Children whose parent(s) are in school or in the labor force can be cared for informally or formally. Within the formal sector there is great variation in the auspices and ownership of care options. Moreover, within any given week, many parents often use combinations of types of care.

Informal care includes both paid and unpaid care: the child can accompany one or both parents to school or work; the parents can split their work and school time so that one of them is always available to care for the child in the child's own home (often referred to as "splitting shifts"); a relative (including an older sibling) can care for the child in the child's home or in the relative's home, either paid or unpaid; and a nonrelative (housekeeper, nanny, or au pair) can care for the child for pay in the child's own home, and either live in that home or not. Children also sometimes care for themselves; these are the so-called "latch-key children."

Formal care always involves payment and includes care in a family daycare home or in a childcare center. Family daycare services are offered in the home of the child care-provider; in general 2 to 12 children of mixed ages are cared for in such homes (Hayes et al. 1990). According to the 1990 National Child Care Survey (National Association for the Education of Young Children (NAEYC 1991) there are an average of six children in regulated family day homes, and an average of three in nonregulated homes. Often, the provider cares for her or his own child as well as for other children.

A childcare center generally cares for a substantial number of children, who are grouped by age or developmental stage. The average number of children cared for ranges from 50 in Head Start programs to 91 in for-profit chains (NAEYC 1991). Centers may be public, private nonprofit, or private for-profit. Some centers are operated by employers, primarily for the children of their employees, and some are operated by school districts.

In the United States in 1988, almost two-thirds of children under the age of five whose mothers worked full-time were cared for in group care; about one-third (32.6 percent) in childcare centers, nursery schools, kindergartens, extended daycare or day camp;

and about one-third (31.2 percent) in family daycare homes (Blau and Ferber 1992). The percentage of care provided by these two types of institutions increased greatly after the Second World War. For example, in 1958 less than 20 percent of children under five with full-time employed mothers were cared for in these two types of institutions (Hayes et al. 1990). The NAEYC (1991) study estimated that at the beginning of 1990 there were about 80,000 childcare centers serving about 4 million children, and about 118,000 regulated family daycare homes serving about 700,000 children. Estimates of unregulated family daycare homes ranged widely from 550,000 to 1.1 million (Hayes et al. 1990). The number of children served by unregulated family daycare homes was estimated to be about 5 million (Kahn and Kamerman 1987).

2. The Market for Formal Care

2.1 Supply

It is difficult to obtain precise estimates of the supply of childcare workers in the United States. Because many childcare workers, especially those who provide unregulated services in their own homes, do not report employment and income, it is likely that the Current Population Surveys underestimate the number of childcare workers (Blau 1992). The National Child Care Staffing Study, (Whitebrook et al. 1989) found that 97 percent of teachers and assistant teachers were female.

Relative to the female labor force as a whole, childcare workers are well-educated (NAEYC 1985). In the civilian labor force as a whole, less than half of all women have attended college, but Whitebrook et al. (1989) found that in their sample of childcare centers, more than half of assistant teachers and almost three-fourths of teachers had some college education. The NAEYC (1991) study found that among teachers in centers almost half (47 percent) had a four-year college degree, about 13 percent had a two-year college degree, about 12 percent had a Child Development Associate credential, and 15 percent had some college experience (NAEYC 1991).

Family daycare providers were found to be less well-educated than childcare center teachers and assistant teachers. Among United States parents who used family daycare facilities, less than half of those responding to a survey reported that their provider had childcare training (the survey had an 88 percent response rate). When providers were asked about their own training, only about two-thirds of regulated providers and one-third of unregulated providers said they had any training in child care (NAEYC 1991).

Relative to their education level, childcare workers were found to be poorly paid. The average hourly wage of teachers in childcare centers in the United States in 1990 was US$7.49; for providers in regulated family daycare homes, US$4.04; and for providers in unregulated homes, US$1.25 (NAEYC 1991). Moreover, the earnings structure was exceedingly flat: there was little wage variation by job level or by education. For example, the National Childcare Staffing study found that among those with some college education, aides were paid on average US$4.45 per hour, while teacher/directors were paid only about one dollar more (US$5.66) per hour. Among teachers, those with 12 years of schooling or less were paid US$4.74 per hour while those with a postcollege degree were paid only about three dollars per hour more (US$7.49) (Whitebrook et al. 1989).

A study of the determinants of earnings for childcare workers, using data from the Current Population Survey, found the surprising result that geographic location, race, and age were unrelated to earnings (Blau 1992). The result for geographic location was unexpected given the variation in fees by geographic area. The relationship between earnings and race needs further investigation.

The childcare market appears to be highly segregated by race. For example, the National Day Care Home Study found that 80 percent of children in family daycare centers were of the same race and ethnicity as their caregiver (Fosburg 1981). Given this segregation, it may be that there is an absence of the usual wage discrimination faced by minority workers, since, with all other factors held constant, female Black providers who cared for Black children appeared to be paid the same as female White providers who cared for White children.

Reasoning from a human capital framework, the absence of a significant relationship between earnings and age suggests that there may be little on-the-job learning in childcare. Alternatively, it may be that in the case of childcare workers, age is not a good proxy for experience: older workers in the field may not be any more experienced than younger workers.

The absence of a strong relationship between education and earnings for childcare workers was even more surprising. Among private household workers (including both nannies and family daycare providers) and among those who defined themselves as teachers (including teachers in childcare centers, nursery school teachers and kindergarten teachers), there was no significant relationship between education and earnings; however, for staff members in childcare centers who did not designate themselves as teachers (assistant teachers, aides, etc.) the wage rate was significantly related to education. Blau (1992) suggested that while teachers used their higher education to enter the more highly paid sector of the childcare market, once they did so their wage rate was not related to their education level.

Not only have wages been low among childcare workers, but benefits have also been minimal. In the National Childcare Staffing sample, even among full-time staff, only about 40 percent had employment-related health insurance and only about 20 percent had retirement benefits. Moreover, those earning the lowest wages had the poorest benefits packages (Whitebrook et al. 1989).

Partly as a consequence of low wages and poor benefits, turnover among childcare workers has been very high, a worrisome finding since continuity of care is an important element of childcare quality and children's well-being (Hayes et al. 1990). Moreover, high turnover increases the level of stress in the work environment and negatively affects the job performance and quality of care provided by remaining staff (Whitebrook et al. 1989, Strober et al. 1989). While the average turnover rate for all occupations is about 20 percent (Hayes et al. 1990), the estimates of turnover rates for childcare workers in centers ranged between 25 percent (NAEYC 1991) and 41 percent (Whitebrook et al. 1989).

The elasticity of the supply of childcare workers has been estimated by looking at the pattern of real earnings over time. Blau (1992) concluded that because real earnings remained constant over the period 1976–86, despite increases in government subsidies and regulation, the supply of childcare workers has been relatively elastic. Walker (1992), looking specifically at the elasticity of supply of family daycare providers, found that unlicensed providers had less attachment to the labor market than their licensed counterparts; they had less training, less experience, cared for fewer children per establishment, and were less involved in marketing their services.

The matter of supply elasticity deserves further research. If the elasticity of supply is indeed high, government attempts to improve quality of services by mandating higher educational requirements and requiring licensure could result in fewer childcare slots, and especially family daycare slots, as providers respond to these regulations and requirements by leaving the field altogether. The absence of a payoff to education among childcare workers also suggests that increased educational requirements may drive providers out of the market.

2.2 Demand for Childcare

Two key issues on the demand side of the market are the responsiveness of parental demand to changes in price and the effect of the availability and price of childcare on mothers' decisions to seek employment.

The price elasticity of the demand for childcare and the effect of price of childcare on mothers' employment decisions vary with the age of the child, in part because childcare costs are higher for younger children (Leibowitz et al. 1992), and with the marital status of the mother—single mothers are more responsive to changes in price than are married mothers (Michalopoulos et al. 1992).

Price has an important (negative) effect on parents' choice of type of care (Hofferth and Wissoker 1992). It also has a large and significant negative effect on mothers' labor supply, although researchers disagree on its size (Ribar 1992, Connelly 1991, Michalopoulos et al. 1992).

About a quarter of mothers aged 21–29 who were not in the United States labor force in 1988 cited childcare problems as the major reason for their non-participation. Among poor women, the percentage was about one-third (Cattan 1991). Connelly's estimates suggest that universal no-cost childcare in the United States would cause an increase of about 10 percentage points in women's labor force participation (Connelly 1991 p. 110).

In Sweden, research on the price elasticity of demand for childcare suggests that if the price of care were to fall (as a result of an increased subsidy), the effect on labor force participation would be small. Most of the effect would consist of mothers moving from private to public care (Gustafsson and Stafford 1992).

The income elasticity of demand for childcare is complex. An increase in family income that comes from wife's own earnings has a positive effect on labor force participation, but does not significantly increase childcare expenditures. On the other hand, increases in family income derived from husband's earnings or nonwage sources decreases wives' labor force participation but increases expenditures on center care (but not on care by a nanny or relatives) (Hofferth and Wissoker 1992).

2.3 Cost of Childcare

Childcare is labor-intensive, with personnel costs accounting for 50–80 percent of childcare centers' budgets (Willer 1987). Kagan and Glennon (1982) found that nonprofit centers spent about 73 percent of their budgets on wages, while profit centers spent about 63 percent. Since young children require a great deal of individual attention, especially if they are in childcare all day, quality care requires relatively low child–staff ratios. As a result, even though childcare providers receive low pay, childcare is expensive.

The cost of care ranges widely, by region of a country, age of child, and auspices of ownership. In 1990, average center fees in the United States ranged from US\$1.29 per hour in the South to US\$2.18 per hour in the Northeast. Average fees for regulated family daycare ranged from US\$1.32 per hour in the South to US\$2.02 per hour in the Northeast. Average fees in unregulated family daycare homes ranged from US\$0.89 per hour in the South to US\$1.83 per hour in the Midwest and Northeast (NAEYC 1991).

Among employed mothers with a child under 5, childcare costs represent about 10 percent of family income, about what the average family allocates to food expenditures (Hayes et al. 1990). For lower-income families, the fraction is even higher: in 1990, for those in families with an income less than US\$15,000 per year, childcare costs were almost one-fourth (23 percent) of income. For those in families with income between US\$15,000 and US\$25,000, childcare costs were 12 percent of family income (NAEYC 1991).

Infant care is even more expensive: The National Childcare Staffing Study in the United States found that in 1988 in 227 centers in the five metropolitan areas surveyed, full-time infant care fees ranged from US\$62.00 to US\$150 per week (Whitebrook et al. 1989).

2.4 Quality of Care

Child development experts agree that the primary ingredients of quality care are caregivers who interact with children frequently and responsively (Hayes et al. 1990). Certain structural arrangements promote such interactions: small group size, low child–adult ratios, child-related training for the caregiver, caregiver stability and continuity, hygienic physical care and food preparation, safe and attractive physical space, and a program that promotes children's emotional, social, and cognitive growth (Hayes et al. 1990). The effects on quality of parental involvement, caregiver autonomy, overall size of the facility, and multicultural curricula are still being studied (Hayes et al. 1990).

Many children in United States family daycare homes and childcare centers do not receive quality care because they are in programs that have high child–adult ratios and/or caregivers without training in group care of children. Although almost all states regulate child–staff ratios in centers, the stringency of their requirements varies greatly, from 6:1 for 3-year olds to 25:1 for 5-year olds. For children cared for in centers, the child–staff ratio for those under one year old is on average about 4:1; for those aged one to three, about 6–8:1; and for those aged three to five, about 10:1. For children up to 5 years old cared for in family daycare homes (both regulated and unregulated), the child–staff ratio is about 4:1 (NAEYC 1991).

Only 14 states in the United States require that family daycare providers have training in group care of children. Only 28 states specify educational requirements for teachers in centers, and only eight states have such requirements for teacher assistants (aides) (Hayes et al. 1990). Even where states have stringent requirements, because the turnover rate among childcare workers has been so high, and because centers have had difficulty finding adequately educated workers, teachers and teacher aides who do not have requisite training have often been hired on an "emergency" basis (Strober et al. 1989).

The evidence on the relationship between the cost of care and its quality is mixed (Hayes et al. 1990, Hofferth and Wissoker 1992, Kisker and Maynard 1991). In some instances, high-quality care is relatively low cost; low-paid teachers in effect subsidize the high-quality care. However, over time, these teachers tend to leave, contributing to discontinuity of teacher–child relationships.

Price appears to have a stronger effect on parental choice than does quality. However, Hofferth and Wissoker (1992) found that, given price, parents were more likely to choose a higher-quality center (as measured by child–staff ratio). Others found that parents trade off quality attributes from a child-development point of view for attributes such as convenience of location or hours of operation (Blau 1991).

Some argue that parents are often poorly informed about what constitutes good quality care from a child-development point of view (Blau 1991) and cannot (or do not) seek information about quality (Hayes et al. 1990). Others (Hofferth and Wissoker 1992) have suggested that even when parents choose family daycare, they may be better informed about quality than researchers think.

3. Policy Issues

The major policy issue in childcare concerns government intervention: should governments intervene in childcare markets, and if so, how?

In 1988 in the United States about $16 billion were spent on childcare by parents, other private sources, and government. The federal government spent about US$7 billion, slightly more than half of that through the dependent care tax credit. The states spent approximately US$500 million (Hayes et al. 1990). For purposes of comparison, it is useful to note that if all children under six years old were in full-time paid care, all children 6–14 years old were in paid care during non school hours, and all care measured up to quality standards that promoted emotional, social, and cognitive development (likely to cost about US$4,000 per year per preschooler and US$2000 per year per school-age child) the total cost of care would be US$126 billion (Hayes et al. 1990).

There are two economic justifications for increased government subsidization of childcare: increased efficiency and increased equity. The increased efficiency argument is that there is currently underinvestment in childcare, that parents spend too little on quality childcare, and that the negative effects of this underinvestment accrue not only to children and parents but also to society as a whole. This argument suggests that childcare has external benefits and that the populace as a whole has an interest (or should have an interest) in ensuring that young children whose parent(s) work receive high-quality childcare (Strober 1975).

External benefits of childcare include: enhanced social, emotional, and cognitive learning for young children which would reduce public social and educational expenditures for remediation later in childhood and in adulthood; improved ability for women to plan their education and employment with the expectation that market work can realistically be a permanent feature of their adult lives, even if they choose to have children; and increased productivity for employers as they experience decreases in employee turnover and absenteeism (Strober 1975).

With respect to equity, since children who come from families where there is economic and psychological stress are more often enrolled in low-quality childcare than are other children (Hayes et al. 1990),

subsidy of childcare for these children has been seen as righting an existing inequality.

Because childcare produces private as well as social benefits, an economic case can be made for cost sharing between the private and public sectors. Moreover, since employers are one of the beneficiaries of a high-quality, reliable childcare system, it is sensible to require that they pay part of the costs, either through the provision of direct services or through taxation.

Government subsidization of childcare may take one of four forms: subsidies to parents for childcare; subsidies to parents for parental leave to care for their own children; subsidies to providers, including tuition benefits for their own training and assistance with liability insurance; and subsidies for the infrastructure of the childcare system, including the improvement of provider training facilities and information networks for parents and providers.

The costs and benefits of each of these alternatives need to be studied. Each will have different effects on quality of care and different external benefits. For example, existing evidence does not suggest that subsidization of childcare on the demand side would lead parents to purchase higher-quality care. In addition, each alternative needs to be considered in conjunction with possible more stringent state regulation of staff–child ratios, group and facility size, and caregiver training. Decisions also need to be made about the levels of government that should collect taxes and provide subsidies (Yeager and Strober 1992).

Questions concerning organization and productivity of resources also need attention. For example, care in Swedish childcare centers was found to be twice the cost of such care in the other Nordic countries, in part because Swedish centers operated for longer hours, even though few children attended during early morning and evening hours (Jansson and Strömquist 1988). The Swedish authors questioned the productivity implications of these organizational arrangements.

There are other important questions. Could costs be reduced without compromising quality if childcare centers were combined with family daycare homes in integrated systems (Strober 1975)? Should states and localities be encouraged to place childcare systems under the aegis of existing school boards? What should be the role of employer-sponsored care in the larger childcare system? How can sick children best be cared for? Finally, what should be the role of parents in the governance of childcare systems?

See also: Family and Schooling; Home Environment and School Learning; Parent Involvement in Preschool Programs

References

Bergmann B B 1993 The French welfare system: An excellent system we could adapt and afford. In: Wilson W J (ed.) 1993 *Sociology and the Public Agenda*. Sage, Los Angeles, California

Blau D M 1991 Introduction. In: Blau D M (ed.) 1991 *The Economics of Child Care*. Russell Sage Foundation, New York

Blau D M 1992 The child care labor market. *J. Hum. Resources* 27(1): 9–39

Blau F D, Ferber M A 1992 *The Economics of Women, Men and Work*. Prentice-Hall, Englewood Cliffs, New Jersey

Cattan P 1991 Child care problems: An obstacle to work. *Month. Lab. Rev.* 114(10): 3–9

Connelly R 1991 The importance of child care costs to women's decisionmaking. In: Blau D M (ed.) 1991 *The Economics of Child Care*. Russell Sage Foundation, New York

Fosburg S 1981 *Family Day Care in the United States: Summary of Findings*. DHHS Pub. No. 80–30382. US Department of Health and Human Services, Washington, DC

Gustafsson S, Stafford F 1992 Child care subsidies and labor supply in Sweden. *J. Hum. Resources* 27(1): 204–30

Hayes C D, Palmer J L, Zaslow M J (eds.) 1990 *Who Cares for America's Children?: Child Care Policy for the 1990s*. National Academy Press, Washington, DC

Hofferth S L, Wissoker D A 1992 Price, quality and income in child care choice. *J. Hum. Resources* 27(1): 70–112

Jansson T, Strömquist S 1988 *Child Care in the Nordic Countries: Costs, Quality, Management*. The Swedish Agency for Administrative Development, Stockholm

Kagan S, Glennon T 1982 Considering proprietary child care. In: Zigler E, Gordon E (eds.) 1982 *Day Care: Scientific and Social Policy Issues*. Auburn House, Boston, Massachusetts

Kahn A J, Kamerman S B 1987 *Child Care: Facing the Hard Choices*. Greenwood Press, New Haven, Connecticut

Kamerman S B 1991 Child care policies and programs: An international overview. *J. Soc. Issues* 47(2): 179–96

Kisker E, Maynard R 1991 Quality, cost, and parental cost of child care. In: Blau D M (ed.) 1991 *The Economics of Child Care*. Russell Sage Foundation, New York

Leibowitz A, Klerman J A, Waite L J 1992 Employment of new mothers and child care choice: Differences by children's age. *J. Hum. Resources* 27(1): 112–33

Michalopoulos C, Robins P K, Garfinkel I 1992 A structural model of labor supply and child care demand. *J. Hum. Resources* 27(1): 166–203

National Association for the Education of Young Children (NAEYC) 1985 *In Whose Hands?: A Demographic Fact Sheet on Child Care Providers*. National Association for the Education of Young Children, Washington, DC

National Association for the Education of Young Children (NAEYC); Administration on Children, Youth and Families of the US Department of Health and Human Services; Office of Policy Planning of the US Department of Education 1991 *The Demand and Supply of Child Care in 1990: Joint Findings from The National Child Care Survey, 1990 and A Profile of Child Care Settings*. National Association for the Education of Young Children, Washington, DC

Ribar D C 1992 Child care and the labor supply of married women: Reduced form evidence. *J. Hum. Resources* 27(1): 134–65

Strober M H 1975 Formal extrafamily child care: Some economic observations. In: Lloyd C B (ed.) 1975 *Sex, Discrimination, and the Division of Labor*. Columbia University Press, New York

Strober M H, Gerlach-Downie S, Yeager K E 1989 Child care centers as workplaces. Paper presented to Annual Meeting of the American Educational Research Association, Boston, Massachusetts

Walker J R 1992 New evidence on the supply of child care: A statistical portrait of family providers and an analysis of their fees. *J. Hum. Resources* 27(1) 40–69

Whitebrook M, Howes C, Phillips D 1989 *Who Cares?: Child Care Teachers and the Quality of Care in America*. Child Care Employee Project, Oakland, California

Willer B 1987 *The Growing Crisis in Child Care: Quality, Compensation and Affordability in Early Childhood Programs*. National Association for the Education of Young Children, Washington, DC

Yeager K E, Strober M H 1992 Financing child care through local taxes: One city's bold attempt. *J. Family Issues*

Further Reading

Hartmann H, Pearce D 1989 *High Skill and Low Pay: The Economics of Child Care Work*. Institute for Women's Policy Research, Washington, DC

Spalter-Roth R, Hartmann H 1988 *Unnecessary Losses: Costs to Americans of the Lack of Family and Medical Leave: Executive Summary*. Institute for Women's Policy Research, Washington, DC

Family and School Environmental Measures

K. Marjoribanks

Families and schools are two of the most significant learning environments that influence students' school-related outcomes. In this article, methods which have been used in educational research to measure these two environments are examined. For the analysis, the methods have been classified as involving either an environmental press approach or an interpretative mode of investigation. Some theoretical orientations for future research involving environmental measures are also presented.

1. Environmental Press Approach

In the development of a theory of personality, Murray (1938 p. 16) suggested that if the behavior of individuals is to be understood then it is necessary to devise a method of analysis which "will lead to satisfactory dynamical formulations of external environments." He proposed that an environment should be defined by the kinds of benefits or harms that it provides. The directional tendency implied in Murray's framework is designated as the press of the environment. He distinguished between the *alpha* press "which is the press that actually exists, as far as scientific discovery can determine it," and an environment's *beta* press "which is the subject's own interpretation of the phenomena that is perceived" (Murray 1938 p. 122). Studies that have used measures to assess the press of family and school learning environments are considered in the following section.

1.1 The Press of Family Environments

It was not until Bloom (1964) and a number of his doctoral students examined the environmental correlates of children's affective and cognitive characteristics, that a "school" of research emerged to assess the alpha press of family environments. Bloom defined the environment as the conditions, forces, and external stimuli that impinge on individuals. As he suggests, "such a view of the environment reduces it for analytical purposes to those aspects of the environment which are related to a particular characteristic or set of characteristics" (Bloom 1964 p. 187). In other words, the total context surrounding an individual may be defined as being composed of a number of subenvironments. If the development of a particular characteristic is to be understood, then Bloom's approach indicates that it is necessary to identify that subenvironment of press variables which potentially is associated with the characteristic.

In the initial subenvironment investigations, Dave (1964) and Wolf (1964) examined relations between family environments and measures of academic achievement and intelligence respectively. Dave defined the family environment by six press variables which were labeled as achievement press, language models, academic guidance, activeness of the family, intellectuality in the home, and work habits in the family. A semistructured home interview schedule was designed to assess the variables, and scores on the total environment measure were related to approximately 50 percent of the variance in the arithmetic problem-solving, reading, and word knowledge performance of 11-year olds. Wolf defined the intellectual environment of the home by three press variables that were labeled as press for achievement motivation, language development, and provisions for general learning. When combined into a predictor set, the measures were associated with nearly 49 percent of the variation in intelligence test scores.

In a penetrating study of family alpha environments, Keeves (1972) collected data on Australian children when they were in the final year of elementary school and in their first year of secondary school. Family contexts were assessed by three dimensions that were categorized as structural, attitudinal, and process. The three dimensions had moderate to strong associations with mathematics and science achievement and low to modest concurrent validities with the children's attitudes to mathematics and science.

In a further example of the environmental press approach, Marjoribanks (1992) investigated relationships between the alpha and beta press of family environments and the aspirations of adolescents from different Australian ethnic groups. Environment data were collected initially from the parents of 11-year old children from Anglo–Australian, English, Greek, and Southern Italian families. The alpha press of family environments was defined by parents' aspirations for their children and parents' socialization. A schedule, in the form of a semistructured parent–interview inventory, was constructed to measure these dimensions of family learning contexts. Parents' aspirations were assessed by questions such as "How much education would you like your child to receive if at all possible?" and "What kind of job would you really like your child to have?" Parents' socialization was measured by an interrelated set of components that were defined as parents' press for independence, individualism–collectivism, English, and reading. Parents' press for independence was assessed using items that asked parents to indicate the age at which they would allow their children to undertake certain activities. In the press for individualism scale, parents were asked to react to statements such as "Even when children get married their main loyalty still belongs to their family," and "When the time comes for children to take jobs they should try and stay near their parents, even if it means giving up good opportunities." Press for English was assessed by items of the form "How often do you speak English in the home?" and "How particular are you about the way your child speaks English (e.g., good vocabulary, correct grammar)?" In the press for reading scale there were questions such as "When your child was small how often did you read to her/him?" and "How often would you help your child now with reading?" High parent socialization scores indicated that parents encouraged independence, were individualistic in their achievement orientations, and exhibited strong press for English and reading. Low socialization scores indicated that parents encouraged dependence, were collectivistic, and expressed lower press for English and reading.

In a follow-up study undertaken 5 years later, a structured questionnaire consisting of 5-point items was used to assess the 16-year olds' perceptions of their family learning environments. The schedule assessed three components of the beta press of families which were designated as adolescents' perceptions of their parents' aspirations for them, the encouragement they had received from their parents in relation to schooling, and their parents' general interest in their education. From the responses a family environment scale was formed which was defined as adolescents' perceptions of family opportunity structures.

As part of the analysis, relationships among the measures were investigated by plotting surfaces that were generated from hierarchical regression models. In the regression equations, product terms were included to test for possible interaction effects among the alpha and beta press measures, while squared terms were added to examine possible curvilinear relationships. Only one set of surfaces is presented here (see Fig. 1) and they show the relationships among parents' aspirations, adolescents' perceptions of family opportunity structures, and adolescents' realistic occupational aspirations.

The shape of the surface for Greek adolescents reflected results which indicated that initial relations between parents' and adolescents' aspirations were mediated by the association between adolescents' perceptions of family contexts and their aspirations. In contrast, parents' aspirations continued to have modest significant linear associations with realistic occupational aspirations in the Anglo–Australian group. For these latter adolescents, the shape of the surface reveals that at each value of parents' aspirations, the beta press measure had a curvilinear association with the aspiration scores. It appears that adolescents' perceptions of family opportunity structures acted as a threshold variable in the Anglo–Australian group. That is, at low beta press levels, adolescents' perceptions had little association with occupational

aspirations. After a mean level of perception scores was attained, however, adolescents' perceptions of family opportunity structures had strong associations with their occupational aspirations.

The possible complexity of relationships between family press variables and students' aspirations is shown in the regression surface for English adolescents. Parents' aspirations acted as a threshold variable, such that until a mean value of parents' aspirations was attained there were positive relations between the parental scores and adolescents' occupational aspirations. After that threshold level, however, further increments in parents' aspirations were not related to changes in realistic occupational aspirations. The surface also shows that at each level of parents' aspirations, adolescents' perceptions of family opportunity structures had a U-shaped association with their occupational aspirations.

These illustrative studies indicate that by defining family environments by press measures it is possible to enrich our understanding of differences in students' school-related outcomes. In future environmental press research, however, it will be important to address the concerns of Plomin, who has noted that:

> The importance of nonshared environmental factors suggests the need for a reconceptualization of environmental factors that focuses on experiential differences between children in the same family. That is, many environmental factors differ across families; these include socioeconomic status, parental education, and child-rearing practices. However, to the extent that these environmental factors do not differ between children growing up in the same family, they do not influence behavioral development. The critical question becomes, why are children in the same family so different from one another? The key to unlock this riddle is to study more than one child per family. This permits the study of experiential differences within a family and their associations with differences in outcome. (Plomin 1989 p. 109)

1.2 The Press of School Environments

In a review of studies that have investigated students' perceptions of school learning environments, Fraser (1986 p. 72) concludes that the research "provides consistent support for the predictive validity of student perceptions in accounting for appreciable amounts of variance in learning outcomes, often beyond that attributable to student characteristics such as pretest performance, general ability or both."

In contrast to methods that rely on observers, the perceptual approach defines classroom environments by the shared perceptions of students and sometimes by teachers' perceptions. The schedules are often referred to as high-inference measures, rather than low-inference techniques which assess specific explicit phenomena such as the number of questions asked by students in a certain section of a lesson. The strengths of the perceptual approach for assessing classroom and school environments are listed by Fraser as follows:

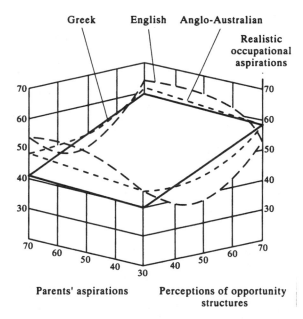

Figure 1
Fitted-realistic occupational aspiration scores in relation to parents' aspirations and adolescents' perceptions of family opportunity structures

First, paper-and-pencil perceptual measures are more economical than classroom observation techniques which involve the expense of trained outside observers. Second, perceptual measures are based on students' experiences over many lessons, while observational data usually are restricted to a very small number of lessons. Third, perceptual measures involve the pooled judgments of all students in a class, whereas observation techniques typically involve only a single observer. Fourth, students' perceptions, because they are the determinants of student behavior more so than the real situation, can be more important than observed behaviors. Fifth, perceptual measures of classroom environment typically have been found to account for considerably more variance in student learning outcomes than have directly observed variables. (Fraser 1991 p. 4)

Four of the most commonly used perceptual measures of classrooms are the Learning Environment Inventory (LEI) (Walberg 1991), the My Class Inventory (MCI) (Fraser 1991), the Classroom Environment Scale (CES) (Moos 1991), and the Individualized Classroom Environment Questionnaire (ICEQ) (Fraser and Tobin 1991).

The Learning Environment Scale, for example, consists of 15 scales that are labeled as cohesiveness, diversity, formality, speed, material environment, friction, goal direction, favoritism, difficulty, apathy, democracy, cliquishness, satisfaction, disorganization, and competitiveness. Each scale is assessed by seven Likert-type items of the form "All students know each other very well" (cohesiveness), "Certain students in this class are responsible for petty quarrels" (friction), "Students do not have to hurry to finish their work" (speed), and "The class is well organized and efficient" (disorganization). The MCI is a simplification of the LEI, designed for children between 8 and 12 years of age. It differs, however, from the LEI in a number of ways. First, to minimize fatigue among younger children it contains only five of the original LEI scales (cohesiveness, friction, satisfaction, difficulty, and competitiveness). Item wording has also been simplified and the LEI's 4-point response format has been reduced to a Yes/No answer choice.

The Class Environment Scale assesses three general categories that are designated as the relationship, personal growth, and system maintenance dimensions. In the schedule there are 9 scales, each with 10 items using True/False responses. It has been designed to measure the actual (or real) classroom environment and the preferred (or ideal) environment. Fraser (1991 p. 8) indicates that the "ICEQ differs from other classroom environment scales in that it assesses those dimensions which distinguish individualized classrooms from conventional ones." In the ICEQ there are 50 items which are assessed by 5-point scales. It has four separate forms which measure students' and teachers' perceptions of actual and preferred environments.

From an analysis of studies that have used such perceptual measures, Fraser (1991 p. 13) concludes that "Numerous research programs have shown that student perceptions account for appreciable amounts of variance in learning outcomes, often beyond that attributable to background characteristics. The practical implication from this research is that student outcomes might be improved by creating classroom environments found empirically to be conducive to learning."

Many educators will argue that learning environments need to be examined with a greater sensitivity than can be generated from perception schedules. Researchers using such perceptual scales generally suggest, however, that the measures provide a portrayal of environments that may be enhanced by adopting other measurement methods. In the following section of the analysis, interpretative models of investigating learning environments are examined.

2. Interpretative Analyses

Increasingly, in research related to analyses of family and school learning environments, concepts and methodologies are being adopted from a number of theoretical orientations such as social phenomenology, cognitive sociology, ethnomethodology, symbolic interactionism, dramaturgical sociology, and ethogenic theories of human behavior. Although there are significant conceptual differences in the orientations, Bernstein (1977) suggests that, in general, they share common features such as an opposition to structural functionalism, a view of individuals as creators of meanings, a focus on the assumptions underlying social order (together with the treatment of social categories as being problematic), a distrust of quantification and the use of objective categories, and a focus on the transmission and acquisition of interpretative procedures.

In learning environment research these interpretative perspectives have emphasized the need to examine the processes by which members of families and schools define and manage their everyday lives. Investigations typically use variations of ethnographic methods to obtain accounts of why parents, teachers, and students perform certain acts and what social meanings they give to the actions of themselves and others. For example, in a study of inequalities in educational opportunity, Connell et al. (1982 p. 17) "talked at length with a hundred 14- and 15-year olds, their parents, their school principals, and many of their teachers. Half of those hundred students were the sons and daughters of tradesmen, factory workers, truck drivers, shop workers; the other half were the children of managers, owners of businesses, lawyers, doctors. We wanted to find out why the relationship between home and school worked so much better for one group than for the other." They conclude that:

The evidence from our study is perfectly clear: families are very powerful institutions, and their influence over

603

their young members registers in every part of their lives, including schooling ... That doesn't, however, commit us to a deficit theory. One very obvious argument against it is that the same family can produce quite different educational careers for different children. (Connell et al. 1982 p. 186)

In an investigation using participant observation of first-grade classrooms, Lareau (1987) examined family–school relationships and inequalities in educational opportunities for working-class and middle-class families and concluded:

Although the educational values of the two groups of parents did not differ, the ways in which they promoted educational success did. In the working-class community, parents turned over the responsibility for education to the teacher. Just as they depended on doctors to heal their children, they depended on teachers to educate them. In the middle-class community, however, parents saw education as a shared enterprise and scrutinized, monitored, and supplemented the school experience of their children. (Lareau 1987 p. 81)

Such interpretative investigations have provided fresh and valuable insights into the relationships between family and school learning environments and students' school-related outcomes. Howe and Eisenhart (1990 p. 2) indicate, however, that "we worry that in their eagerness to embrace qualitative methods, many educational researchers do not provide adequate and clear justifications for their methods, findings, or conclusions." Chilcott also warns that ethnographic educational research must consider the often unasked and unanswered questions, such as whether or not education is addressing the goals of society. He suggests that "without such attention to such an orientation, school ethnography will remain a mere research strategy to be employed on occasion to provide description, rather than an approach to explain educational practice from a theoretical foundation" (Chilcott 1987 p. 212).

As interpretative analyses of families and schools examine how students, parents, and teachers define and manage their everyday lives, there is a need to complement the research by investigations of the social constraints that surround individuals' learning environments. That is, if the understanding of the complexity of relationships between families, schools, and students' outcomes is to be enhanced, then investigations must use more elegant theoretical frameworks and adopt more appropriate combinations of approaches to the measurement of students' learning contexts.

3. Some Directions for Research

It is suggested by Oswald et al. that:

The pivotal relationship between families and schools has generally been examined from two theoretical perspec-

tives: allocation theory and socialization theory. Allocation theory stresses the differentiation of students within formal schooling (ability grouping and track placement) and characterizes the school as active and passive. Socialization theory stresses how families provide children with characteristics (linguistic traits and cognitive development) that enhance the children's performance in school. Socialization theory characterizes the family as active and the school as passive. (Oswald et al. 1988 p. 255)

They observe, however, that the two approaches often fail to examine the characteristics of schooling which may influence the actions of families with regard to their children's education. If the measurement of learning environments is to become more sensitive, then it is important to develop a theoretical orientation in which families and schools are examined, not only as places where culture and ideology are imposed upon students, but also as sites where they are produced. Such a conceptual orientation could be constructed from Max Weber's investigation of status-group competition (see Gerth and Mills 1970). In his analysis of the structure of social groups, Weber proposed that the ideal of the cultivated person accepted in a given society is the outcome of the power of the dominant social group to universalize its particular cultural ideal. A neo-Weberian perspective suggests that if certain members of social groups have the power to determine what is valued in educational systems, then it is not surprising to find that members of subordinated social groups are disadvantaged in relation to the criteria set by the dominant group. That is, environmental measures might be constructed to assess to what extent families and schools may be viewed as teaching particular status cultures. As Aronowitz and Giroux (1988) suggest:

White middle-class linguistic forms, modes of style, and values represent honored forms of cultural capital that are accorded a greater exchange rate in the circuits of power that define and legitimate the meaning of success in public schools. Students who represent cultural forms that rely on restricted linguistic codes, working-class or oppositional modes of dress ... who downplay the ethos of individualism ... who espouse a form of solidarity ... find themselves at a decided academic, social, and ideological disadvantage in most schools. (Aronowitz and Giroux 1988 p. 192)

This analysis of environmental measures suggests the general proposition that, if families from certain social groups have the power to decide what is "valued" in schools and society, then those favored groups have greater means of passing on to their children cultural and social capital associated with the valued goals of schooling. If such a proposition is to be examined adequately, then there is a need to bring together the theoretical orientations and measurement methods of environmental press research and interpretative models of analysis within, say, a neo-Weberian conceptual framework. Unless learning environment research becomes more sophisticated and elegant in its conceptual and measurement orientations, it is unlikely that there will be a significant advance in our understanding of the complexity of family–school environment relationships. The need to enrich that understanding is summed up by Midwinter's (1975) warning that "No matter how much you do *inside* the school, you can make virtually no impact at all without the informed support of the home" (p. 61).

See also: Family and Schooling; Family Influence on Human Development; Family, School, and Cultural Capital; Family, School, and Social Capital; Home Environment and School Learning

References

Aronowitz S, Giroux H A 1988 Schooling culture and literacy in the age of broken dreams: A review of Bloom and Hirsch. *Harv. Educ. Rev.* 58(2): 172–94

Bernstein B B 1977 *Class, Codes and Control. Vol. 3: Towards a Theory of Educational Transmissions*, 2nd edn. Routledge and Kegan Paul, London

Bloom B S 1964 *Stability and Change in Human Characteristics*. Wiley, New York

Chilcott J H 1987 Where are you coming from and where are you going?: The reporting of ethnographic research. *Am. Educ. Res. J.* 24(2): 199–218

Connell R W, Ashenden D J, Kessler S, Dowsett G W 1982 *Making the Difference: Schools, Families and Social Division*. Allen and Unwin, Sydney

Dave R 1964 The identification and measurement of environmental process variables that are related to educational achievement. Unpublished doctoral dissertation, University of Chicago

Fraser B 1986 *Classroom Environment*. Croom Helm, London

Fraser B J 1991 Two decades of classroom environment research. In Fraser B J, Walberg H J (eds.) 1991

Fraser B J, Tobin K 1991 Combining qualitative and quantitative methods in classroom environment research. In: Fraser B J, Walberg H J (eds.) 1991

Gerth H H, Mills C W (eds.) 1970 *From Max Weber: Essays in Sociology*. Routledge and Kegan Paul, London

Howe K, Eisenhart M 1990 Standards for qualitative (and quantitative) research: A prolegomenon. *Educ. Researcher* 19(4): 2–9

Keeves J P 1972 *Educational Environment and Student Achievement*. Almqvist and Wiskell, Stockholm

Lareau A 1987 Social class differences in family–school relationships: The importance of cultural capital. *Sociol. Educ.* 60(2): 73–85

Marjoribanks K 1992 Ethnicity, families as opportunity structures, and adolescents' aspirations. *Ethnic and Racial Studies* 15(3): 381–94

Midwinter E 1975 Towards a solution of the EPA problem: The community school. In: Rushton J, Turner J D (eds.) 1975 *Education and Deprivation*. Manchester University Press, Manchester

Moos R H 1991 Connections between school, work, and family settings. In: Fraser B J, Walberg H J (eds.) 1991

Murray H A 1938 *Explorations in Personality: A Clinical and Experimental Study of Fifty Men of College Age*. Oxford University Press, New York

Oswald H, Baker D P, Stevenson D L 1988 School charter and parental management in West Germany. *Sociol. Educ.* 61(4): 255–65

Plomin R 1989 Environment and genes: Determinants of behavior. *Am. Psychol.* 44(2): 105–11

Walberg H J 1991 Educational productivity and talent development. In: Fraser B J, Walberg H J (eds.) 1991

Wolf R M 1964 The identification and measurement of environmental process variables related to intelligence. Unpublished doctoral dissertation, University of Chicago

Further Reading

Coleman J S 1990 *Foundations of Social Theory*. Harvard University Press, Cambridge, Massachusetts

Davies S 1995 Reproduction and resistance in Canadian high schools: An empirical analysis of the Willis thesis. *Br. J. Sociol.* 46(4): 662–87

Entwisle D R, Alexander K L, Olson L S 1994 The gender gap in math: Its possible origins in neighborhood effects. *Am. Sociol. Rev.* 59(6): 822–38

Fraser B J, Walberg H J (eds.) 1991 *Educational Environments*. Pergamon Press, Oxford

Kalmijn M, Kraaykamp G 1996 Race, cultural capital and schooling: An analysis of trends in the United States. *Sociol. Educ.* 69(1): 22–34

Kellaghan T, Sloane K, Alvarez B, Bloom B S 1993 *Home Environments and School Learning*. Jossey-Bass, San Fransisco, California

Marjoribanks K 1979 *Families and their Learning Environments: An Empirical Analysis*. Routledge and Kegan Paul, London

Marjoribanks K 1994 Families, schools and children's learning: A study of children's learning environments. *Int. J. Educ. Res.* 21(5): 439–555

Marjoribanks K 1996 Ethnicity, proximal family environment, and young adolescents' cognitive performance *J. Early Adolesc.* 16(3): 340–59

Portes A, MacLeod D 1996 Educational progress of children of immigrants: The roles of class, ethnicity, and school context. *Sociol. Educ.* 69(4): 255–75

Rumberger R W 1995 Dropping out of school: A multilevel analysis of students and schools *Am. Educ. Res. J.* 32(3): 583–625

Saha L J, Keeves J P (eds) 1991 *Schooling and Society in Australia: Sociological Perspectives*. Australian National University Press, Canberra

Family and Schooling

T. Kellaghan

Although the nature and quality of a child's educational experience and development are influenced by factors as diverse as government policy and neighborhood values, it is clear that the two institutions that impinge most directly on the child are its family and its school. Many of the wider influences of society are mediated through the opportunities and experiences provided in these institutions. Given the prominence of the family in the lives of most children, and the significance of scholastic performance for future life chances, it is not surprising that a vast amount of research now exists on the relationships between family background and school learning; nor is it surprising that the findings of that research indicate that the influence of the family on children's scholastic development is considerable. In this article, following some preliminary considerations, research findings on the nature and extent of relationships between children's scholastic development and various aspects of their family environments are described.

1. Complementary Roles of Family and School

Family and school differ from each other in their priorities, in the demands and expectations that they try to meet, in their organization of space and time, in their distinctive ways of relating to children, in their formality, and, in some cases, in their culture and language. Further, families differ from each other on a variety of characteristics. Some of the variation is related to their location (rural or urban), their socioeconomic status, and their ethnic and cultural group membership. However, within any of these categories, one is likely to find considerable variation.

The significance of variation in environments lies in the fact that the particular environmental circumstances that a child is exposed to will affect the knowledge and skills it develops. Because of differences between family environments and schools, all children will experience some discontinuity between home and school and some may have problems in adapting to the school situation. The problems are likely to be greater and more persistent when there is little overlap between the knowledge, skills, attitudes, and values fostered by family and school.

Although differences exist between family and school, they share a common concern: to ensure the optimal development of children. To achieve this objective, parents normally accept as basic obligations that they provide for children's physical needs relating to food, clothing, nutrition, and health; that they teach basic social skills; and that they lay the foundations

for, and support, children's school learning. Schools, for their part, accept the obligation of providing an adequate environment and staff and a curriculum that corresponds to the needs, interests, learning styles, and problems of participants.

Not all schools and not all families, for a variety of reasons, meet their basic obligations. Some schools may do little to promote parental involvement or to adapt their approaches to the characteristics of children who come to them from a variety of backgrounds. The concern of this article, however, is families rather than schools, though this should not be taken to imply that adaptation in schools may not be necessary to meet the needs of children, especially ones from families in which competencies, attitudes, and values are very different from those fostered in schools. Further, it should be acknowledged that families may often be unable to adapt to the educational needs of children without the assistance of other agencies, including the school. Some families have difficulty in meeting basic (e.g., nutritional) needs of children while, on a wider scale, there is extensive evidence to suggest that the effectiveness of many homes in providing conditions conducive to the educational development of children is impaired by a variety of changes that are taking place in society and in family structure and function.

2. Societal and Family Changes

Among the societal changes that affect family structure and relationships are urbanization, migration, changes in the labor force (including an increase in the number of women who work), and growth in technology (especially television). Family changes include a reduction in size, fewer households with more than two generations, an increase in single-parent families, and an increase in the number of mothers who work outside the home (Coleman 1987, Kellaghan et al. 1993).

As families have changed, social support networks in urban and suburban communities have also weakened. This is reflected in the isolation of mothers, who are often very young and may receive little or no support from the child's father or from other family members or friends. It is also reflected in a reduction in the support that was provided in the past by a variety of organizations and informal networks, including churches, youth organizations, and neighbors (Coleman 1987).

Changing family conditions are not confined to households in poor economic circumstances. In the more affluent homes of many industrialized countries, more and more children are living with only one parent (usually the mother) while the proportion of families in which both husband and wife are working has gone up sharply. Children from such homes, of course, are not necessarily at a disadvantage at school. Adequate arrangements may be made to deal with the problems of working or lone parents. However, such family conditions are often associated with other factors which tend to be unsupportive of children's formal education. For example, children being raised by single mothers in the United States have about one-third as much to spend on their needs as children in two-parent families. Further, the mothers are likely to have been poorly educated, a factor associated with children's poor achievement and early dropout. It has been estimated that at least one-third of preschool children in the United States are at risk of school failure even before they enter kindergarten because of a variety of family circumstances, including poverty, neglect, sickness, and lack of adult protection and nurturance (Hodgkinson 1991). That proportion is likely to increase in the coming decades.

While research has been carried out on the relationships between cognitive development and scholastic performance and the societal and familial changes outlined above, as well as on the effects of being reared in grossly deprived circumstances, such research is beyond the scope of this entry. However, it should be noted that the cognitive and scholastic deficits associated with gross deprivation are much greater than any that are found as a result of the normal variation in family conditions in the general population which will be considered in this entry.

3. Characteristics of Research

A very large number of studies of the effects of normal variation in family conditions on children's cognitive development and school performance have been carried out since the beginning of the twentieth century. Some were small-scale; others involved very large numbers, in some cases nationally representative samples. The vast majority of the studies were carried out in developed countries, though some data are also available from the developing world.

Studies have been carried out at all levels of the educational system from preschool through higher education—some extended their data collection to the postschool careers of individuals. Data from longitudinal as well as cross-sectional studies have been analyzed. However, several studies were limited by the fact that they employed secondary analyses of data that had been collected for other purposes. In such situations, information of interest may not be available. For example, to obtain a comprehensive picture of the effects of family size on scholastic development, it would be necessary to know not just the size of family at the time a study was carried out but also to have

information on timing of births and on when children left the household (Heer 1985).

Many studies were carried out in a purely research context. Several, however, addressed policy issues. Of particular interest in the policy context has been the effort to use the findings of studies of the relationships between home characteristics and school performance to expose injustices and to test the effectiveness of reform programs (Halsey et al. 1980). A major objective of these studies, sometimes referred to as "political arithmetic," has been to estimate the extent to which ascriptive factors (e.g., social class, race, gender) rather than individual effort and choice contribute to success in school and in later life. Such studies fall within the general ambit of studies of equality of educational opportunity. Other studies of equality of opportunity have adopted a somewhat different procedure and have examined the relative contributions of home and school factors to educational achievement (e.g., Coleman et al. 1966).

The vast majority of studies of family and schooling have used an empirical quantitative methodology, assigning numerical values to data collected about family characteristics and students' achievements. The preferred methods of analysis used correlational data and include regression analysis, canonical analysis, and path analysis. The results of a meta-analysis are also available (White 1982). Analyses have been based on different levels of aggregation of data (student, school, district). The more inclusive the aggregation, the higher the value of correlation that would be expected. In this entry, only data for student-level analyses are considered.

A number of investigators have proposed the use of ethnographic methodologies as an alternative to traditional empirical approaches in the investigation of family–school relationships. In these studies, the principal area of interest has been the social meanings that "actors" (students, teachers, parents) attach to their own goals, intentions, and actions and to the goals, intentions, and actions of others with whom they interact. Topics that have been examined using an interpretative model of analysis include teachers' knowledge of the lives of their pupils and the acceptance of responsibility by parents for school-related educational activities (Marjoribanks 1991).

In the more traditional studies, a variety of indexes of students' school performance has been used; the indexes include measures of achievement (e.g., in language, mathematics, science), of ability (e.g., general ability, verbal ability, spatial ability), of school attainment (the highest level in the educational system reached by a student), and of occupational attainment. The measures of achievement and ability most frequently used were standardized norm-referenced tests, though some studies used grade-point averages, teacher ratings, or other nonstandardized measures of school achievement.

Studies have also made use of a variety of measures

of the home or family environment. Much of the rest of this entry is organized in terms of the way in which the family environment has been measured. This is done not out of methodological interest, but for two other reasons. First, progress from the use of status measures of the home to ones that describe processes in the home has increased considerably the explanatory value of family measures in accounting for scholastic achievement. Second, analysis of family processes provides greater insights into the factors in the home that impact on school achievement. Such insights not only lead to greater understanding of family–school relationships but also provide a basis for programs that seek to assist parents in preparing their children for school.

4. Studies of Socioeconomic Variables

Among the early gross measures used to describe homes were such factors as parental occupation, level of parental education, parental income, and the prestige of a breadwinner's occupation, which were then categorized into levels of "social class" or socioeconomic status (SES). Four conclusions can be drawn from a review of studies which used such measures.

First, level of social class or SES is positively but not very strongly related to a variety of measures of scholastic ability and achievement. Children who come from homes of high SES (e.g., ones in which parents have been educated to a high level) perform better on such measures than children who come from homes of low SES. Variation in home background has been found to account for an average of under 10 percent of variance in a variety of measures of school performance in studies that used income as the index of family circumstances and an average of about 4 percent in studies that used occupation as the family index (White 1982).

Second, the effects of home differences are already in evidence when children start school and are reflected in children's preparedness to benefit from schooling. Relationships between family variables and scholastic performance tend to be higher at the elementary school level than at secondary school; to some extent this may be due to a reduction in variance in measures of home environments and scholastic performance as low-achieving students from low SES homes drop out of school. There is evidence, though it is not entirely consistent, that as children progress through school, the achievement gap between those from low and those from high SES homes tends to widen (Coleman et al. 1966, Fogelman and Goldstein 1976). While children's knowledge and skills on commencing school no doubt contribute substantially to this situation, one would expect the continuing support or lack of it that children receive during the school years to contribute as well.

Third, the level of social class or SES of a child's family is related to the child's level of school attainment (i.e. the highest level the child reaches in the educational system). In a variety of countries in Europe and in North America, it has been found that children from a high socioeconomic background are more likely than children from a low socioeconomic background to remain at school through the secondary cycle and into higher education This is true even when children's level of general scholastic ability is controlled (e.g., Adamski 1982, Greaney and Kellaghan 1984, Halsey et al. 1980, Sewell and Hauser 1976). For example, Sewell and Hauser found that socioeconomic variables accounted for 15 percent of variance in educational attainment.

Fourth, in countries that operate different types of secondary school, major selection in terms of socioeconomic background has been found to operate at the point of transfer from primary to secondary school. There is a marked tendency for children from higher socioeconomic backgrounds to transfer to an academic type of secondary school which will lead to third-level education, while children from low socioeconomic backgrounds tend to go to technical, vocational, "short-cycle," or general educational establishments (Floud and Halsey 1961, Girard 1961, Greaney and Kellaghan 1984).

Efforts to explain differences in school achievement and attainment in terms of social class or SES per se have attempted to identify characteristics on which social classes can be distinguished. Thus, it has been suggested that the values of members of lower social class groups, which tend to emphasize conformity to external prescriptions rather than self-direction, are likely to affect children's approaches to school learning (Kohn 1963). Differences in belief systems about how the world operates, which often serve to justify values and norms, may have a similar effect (McGillicuddy-DeLisi 1982). So too might the differential use by class groups of sociolinguistic codes. Such use, it has been claimed, delineates the distribution of knowledge by providing access for members of higher status groups to the "universalistic" meaning systems used in schools, while limiting lower status groups to "particularistic" meaning systems (Bernstein 1971). However, the studies of Labov (1977) have been used to challenge this position. Labov found that Black children in the United States used a form of language that differed from more standard forms; however, he also found that the Black childrens' language possessed a coherent inner logic and complex structure and permitted the expression of complicated and abstract ideas.

5. Studies of Family Configuration

Studies of family configuration examine the relationships between structural aspects of families (family size, sibling sex and spacing, and ordinal birth position) and scholastic ability, achievement, and attainment. The interaction between these family variables can be quite complex so that the influence of any one of them (e.g., birth position) may be modified by the configuration of other characteristics (e.g., sex of child or spacing between siblings). However, a number of general conclusions can be drawn from research in this area.

First, many studies report a negative correlation between family size and educational abilities, achievements, and attainment. The amount of variance accounted for by family size in these studies ranged between 4 and 10 percent. Second, increased spacing between children reduces the normal decrement in scholastic performance associated with increase in family size. Third, studies of the relationship between a child's ordinal position in the family and scholastic performance yield different conclusions when the number of siblings is held constant. Finally, the effects of family configuration variables are more marked in homes in which the father has a low occupational level than in ones in which the fathers' occupational level is high (Heer 1985, Kellaghan et al. 1993).

The mechanism through which family size might affect educational outcomes is not clearly understood. Anastasi (1956) suggested that parents have fewer resources (material and psychological) to expend on each individual child in large families than in small families. Thus, for example, children in smaller families should have more opportunities for verbal interaction with parents and there may also be emotional benefits. While findings on spacing between children support this interpretation, empirical data regarding the amount of resources that are invested in children at each point during childhood would be needed to test the validity of Anastasi's position (Heer 1985). Further, the interpretation does not take account of resources that may be available to children from other caretakers (including siblings and grandparents).

Anastasi's reasoning about the effects of family size might be extended to a consideration of the effects of a child's ordinal position in the family (Kellaghan and Macnamara 1972). If it is true that the availability of resources for individual children decreases with increased family size, and that this in turn impacts on children's scholastic performance, then one would expect a lower level of scholastic performance from later-born children than from earlier-born ones. Data that would support this view (a negative correlation between ordinal position and a measure of scholastic performance), however, are found in only some studies.

An alternative attempt to explain differences in intellectual development associated with family size and birth order was proposed by Zajonc and co-workers (e.g., Zajonc and Bargh 1980). According to their "confluence model," an explanation of the effects of family size and birth order on children's intellectual development is to be found in the "intellectual level" of the home during the course of the child's development. If the family's intellectual level is defined as the average of the current intellectual ability of all family members (including parents and children) at any given time, then the birth of an additional child will result in a drop in the average intellectual level of the family (since the newborn child's intellectual level is very low) and in a diminution of the general educational environment of the family. It is suggested that this will have negative consequences for the intellectual development of children. The model, like Anastasi's, is consistent with findings regarding the beneficial effects of spacing. While there are some research data (particularly aggregated data from large groups) that support the confluence model, there are also research data that do not. In particular, the failure to find consistent relationships between ordinal family position and educational performance raises problems for the model.

The conclusions outlined above relating to family size and educational performance are based on studies that were carried out in developed countries. One might expect the form of the functional relationships between scholastic ability and family size to vary with socioeconomic status, time, and culture. Some data from developing countries may be taken as supporting this view. Thus, studies carried out in East Africa reveal a positive rather than a negative relationship between family size and educational achievement (measured by standardized tests of ability and external achievement examinations at primary and secondary levels; e.g., Drenth et al. 1983). It is far from clear what cultural factors might help account for this finding. While it has been suggested that preference for a large family or religious beliefs that exclude family limitation might mitigate the effects of family size on educational performance, evidence from a study carried out in a European country does not support this interpretation (Kellaghan and Macnamara 1972). In the case of the African findings, it may be that extended families provide opportunities for interpersonal relationships that are not available in nuclear families.

6. Other Family Characteristics

A number of investigators have gone beyond the use of social class or socioeconomic variables and family structure and have included in their studies measures of other aspects of home environments. In an early study of the educational progress of Scottish secondary school students, Fraser (1959) employed measures of cultural background (e.g., the educational level of parents, reading habits of parents), material and economic background (e.g., family income, number of rooms), motivational background (e.g., parental encouragement in school work), and emotional background (e.g., degree of harmony in the home, interest taken by parents in the child's general welfare). The amount of variance in school progress accounted for by these home environment measures was 56 percent, which is much higher than the amount accounted for by measures of socioeconomic status or of family structure.

In a large-scale study carried out for the "Plowden Report" in England (Peaker 1967), home environmental factors were contrasted with primary school factors in predicting children's performance on standardized tests of reading and mathematics. Two aspects of the home environment were assessed: parental attitudes (e.g., hopeful and encouraging interest on the part of parents) and the material circumstances of the home (e.g., parental income, physical amenities). Parental attitudes were found to account for more of the variation in children's school achievement (28%) than either the variation in home circumstances (20%) or the variation in schools (17%). Further, parental attitudes were largely independent of home circumstances, though they were conditioned by them to some extent.

The findings of this study led to a concern with the importance of parental attitudes in education. Indeed, the Plowden Report speculated on the possibility of changing such attitudes and on the presumed effect that would have on children's achievement. However, the term "attitude" seems to have been used in a very loose sense and what precisely was measured is very difficult to say. On the basis of the instruments used, it would appear that a variety of social–psychological characteristics of the home was included.

The importance of social–psychological characteristics has been documented in other countries. In the United States, studies based on the status attainment model, elaborated as in the Wisconsin model (e.g., Sewell and Hauser 1976), examined ways in which socioeconomic background effects are mediated through social–psychological factors. The findings of numerous studies and replications carried out in the 1970s and early 1980s indicate that the effects of SES on educational attainment are mediated through parental and peer influences and students' educational and occupational aspirations. When measures of these variables were combined with SES, they accounted for more than half the variance in post-high-school attainment (compared with the 15% that was accounted for by SES alone; Sewell and Hauser 1976). Studies in the former Soviet Union, in which parental encouragement, in addition to socioeconomic status and parents' educational level, was found to affect students' educational attainment level, indicate that the educational attainment process in that country was very similar to that observed in western countries (Dobson 1977).

The relationships between family circumstances and children's scholastic performance that have been found in developed countries may not, however, obtain in all cultural contexts. The findings of some studies of students' achievements, some of which used data collected in studies of the International Association for the Evaluation of Educational Achievement (IEA), which were carried out in Africa, Asia, Latin America, and the Middle East, have been interpreted as indicating that the influence of the home, as measured by socioeconomic background, on scholastic achievement may not be as great in developing countries, particularly low-income ones, as it is in industrialized countries. For example, in a study of achievement in science in India, 27 percent of variance was attributable to variation in school factors, while only 3 percent was attributable to variation in background characteristics (Heyneman and Loxley 1983). Studies in Africa also failed to find the kind of relationship found in industrialized countries between scholastic performance and indexes of family background that included measures of material facilities and of parents' support and interest in school work (Drenth et al. 1983). There are also examples from developing countries in which the relationships between family variables and scholastic performance are similar to those found in developed countries (see Sect. 7).

7. Family Process Variables

The findings of the research considered so far point to the complexity of the interactions between individuals (parents and children) as well as to other factors in families, such as the knowledge and value systems that pervade them, that might affect the development in the child of a range of cognitive, attitudinal, and emotional characteristics relevant to scholastic performance. Such considerations have inspired a number of investigators to explore further the "curriculum" or "teaching style" of families which might account for differences in children's preparation for and guidance through the learning tasks of the school. The aim of these investigators was to identify dynamic ongoing processes within the larger network of family interactions in place of static indexes of SES as a means of improving understanding of the role of the family in the cognitive and educational development of children (Bloom 1981, Marjoribanks 1979).

The findings of many individual studies which focused on the role of particular process variables point to the importance of a range of factors embracing expectations, aspirations, reinforcement, and structure in the home. Six process variables were identified by Davé (1963) as providing a comprehensive picture of educationally relevant variables in the family which are associated with high student achievement:

(a) achievement press (e.g., high parental expectations and aspirations);

(b) language (e.g., opportunities for language development and the use of complex levels and varied styles of language);

(c) academic guidance (e.g., availability and quality of help provided by the family on matters relating to school work);

(d) activeness (e.g., parents are involved with children in a variety of activities, apart from ones with direct scholastic implications);

(e) intellectuality (e.g., children are provided with opportunities for thinking and imagination in daily activities);

(f) work habits (e.g., degree of routine and structure in home management and the emphasis on regularity in the use of time and space).

In studies that used such family characteristics and which were included in White's (1982) meta-analysis, family background factors accounted for, on average, 53 percent of variance in students' academic achievements.

Research evidence points to a number of more specific conclusions regarding relationships between family process variables and children's ability and achievement. First, family process variables are more closely related to measures of verbal ability than to measures of nonverbal ability (e.g., spatial ability). Second, they are more closely related to measures of scholastic achievement, particularly in the basic school subjects of reading and mathematics, than to measures of general scholastic ability or of verbal ability. Third, within the area of scholastic achievement, family process variables are more closely related to general areas of achievement, such as reading, than to more specialized (and presumably more school-based) areas, such as science. Fourth, relationships between family process variables and scholastic ability and achievement have been found in several countries, among different socioeconomic and ethnic groupings, and in rural as well as in urban areas. Thus, it can be concluded that there are differences in family environments within socioeconomic and ethnic groups and that what is important for children's development is not so much what parents are (e.g., in terms of SES), as what they do (Kellaghan et al. 1993).

In the above section, it was noted that some studies in developing countries failed to confirm the relationships between family variables and school performance that have been found in industrialized countries. However, there are other studies from developing countries that do tend to mirror the findings from industrialized countries on the importance of the home (Johnstone 1983, Lockheed et al. 1989, Smith and Cheung 1986). Sufficient research has not been carried out to permit identification of the factors that might account for the divergent findings from developing countries. Those factors would be expected to include characteristics of the culture in which a study was carried out, in particular the nature of families and the role of formal education. The precise family variables that have been represented in studies may also be important. As in industrialized societies, studies in developing countries that used measures that take into account family processes would seem to be more

likely than studies that use status measures to provide evidence of association between variance in family background and variance in scholastic performance.

8. Improving Home–School Relationships

Many efforts, supported by parents, teachers, school officials, and educators, have been made to strengthen home–school relationships (Epstein 1987). While it is clear that family and school have separate and distinctive roles in the education of children, much thinking about education in the late twentieth century has pointed to a need for greater collaboration between the two if the enterprise is to be successful. Most teachers foster this collaboration by sending information to students' homes about such matters as school schedules, rules, and goals, or to report on students' achievements. Teachers also may meet with parents, either individually or in groups, to discuss special events or students' progress. However, such communication, important though it is, may not always be adequate. In particular, it may not be enough to help those parents most in need of support and involvement. To provide stronger home–school links, a variety of other structures and procedures have been established in school systems throughout the world. Thus, parents may be involved in school management and decision-making or their help may be enlisted in supporting the school by participating in extra-curricular activities or fund-raising.

A more radical approach to parental involvement involves procedures that assign a "teaching" role to parents. This approach exhibits a variety of procedures to strengthen the family role and responsibility and to improve the understanding, care, and education of children. The teaching role of the parent may be exercised in the school or at home. In the school, it may involve workshops, discussion groups, and training sessions for parents, or the parents may assist teachers and students with lessons in the classroom. An example of how a parent may help in the classroom is when a parent works with individual children or a small group of children to reinforce skills already taught by the teacher while the teacher teaches another group. Such activity not only helps the teacher, it also provides parents with the opportunity of learning about the activities of the classroom which they can then reinforce with their own children at home or communicate to other parents.

Direct efforts have also been made to involve parents in learning activities with their children in their own homes. These efforts usually focus on children considered to be "at risk" and may be supported by workshops with parents or by visits to homes by teachers or other facilitators. Typically, parents are taught techniques that develop their tutoring skills, stimulate learning, involve reading and books, or encourage conversation and discussion between themselves and children. A contract may be signed by teacher and parents that specifies a particular role for the parent in connection with children's school lessons or activities.

In considering the role of improved home–school links in improving children's school learning, sight should not be lost of the fact that family and school are social units which are embedded in other formal and nonformal social units and networks. A focus on the family should not lead to a neglect of the roles that other institutions and people in the community can play in fostering children's educational development. This point was emphasized in the *Framework for Action to Meet Basic Learning Needs* (1990), adopted at the World Conference on Education for All in Jomtien, Thailand, which acknowledged the important role that community associations, cooperatives, religious bodies, and other nongovernmental organizations can play in providing and supporting basic education.

Parental programs, especially when integrated into a network of community support, have been found to have significant and positive effects on children's verbal ability, language, school-related knowledge and skills, and achievement in school subjects. They have also been found to alter parents' attitudes, self-concepts, and behavior, and to affect other members of the family and ultimately the community in which the family lives (Kellaghan et al. 1993).

9. Conclusion

Research on the relationships between the scholastic performance of children and their family environments has progressed from the use of status indexes to categorize families to an identification of family processes (i.e., interactions between parents and their children) that are associated with children's scholastic development. Descriptions of families in terms of processes account for considerably more variance in a variety of measures of scholastic performance than do socioeconomic status or family configuration variables. However, since the basis of findings is correlational, causal relationships cannot necessarily be inferred from the observed associations.

Indeed, when due consideration is given to the complexity of interactions in the home, something to which inadequate attention has been given in research to date, it is clear that research is still some way from providing a satisfactory understanding of how conditions experienced in the home affect children's development. For example, little is known about how particular aspects of the family environment affect particular aspects of cognitive or scholastic development. Similarly, little is known about how individual children react to and manipulate the behavioral elements of the family environment though differences in children's reactions presumably could have quite different consequences for development. A child's gender might be important in this; so too might its age, since children's capabilities, needs, and behavior change as they develop.

Methods other than large-scale surveys and secondary analyses of data will be required to throw more light on these issues.

Even the present state of knowledge regarding family–school relationships, however, has important policy and practical implications. The role of family factors in scholastic development has been firmly established and programs based on analyses of the factors in the family environment that are related to school progress have had some success in improving children's school performance. Apart from the important practical implications of this work, success in the alteration of family environments that is accompanied by improved scholastic performance provides stronger support than is available from correlational studies for a causal connection between the family variables that are manipulated and the scholastic performance of children.

Success in devising programs that improve children's school performance will depend on more than a greater understanding of the home processes that affect school performance. It has to be recognized that such programs operate in a political context that involves not only families but also teachers and schools and the network of other social institutions that impinge on the lives of families. It is for this reason that a strand of studies, separate from ones that examine family–school relationships, is investigating the conditions under which parents, teachers, and representatives of other community agencies can work together, often permeating long-established institutional and role boundaries, to facilitate the school performance of children.

See also: Family Influence on Human Development; Family, School, and Cultural Capital; Family, School, and Social Capital; Home Environment and School Learning

References

Adamski W W 1982 Social structure versus educational policy: Polish and European perspectives. In: Archer M S (ed.) 1982 *The Sociology of Educational Expansion: Take-off, Growth and Inflation in Educational Systems.* Sage, London

Anastasi A 1956 Intelligence and family size. *Psych. Bull.* 53: 187–209

Bernstein B 1971 *Class, Codes and Control. Vol. 1: Theoretical Studies Towards a Sociology of Language.* Routledge and Kegan Paul, London

Bloom B S 1981 *All Our Children Learning.* McGraw-Hill, New York

Coleman J S 1987 Families and schools. *Educ. Res.* 16(6): 32–8

Coleman J S et al. 1966 *Equality of Educational Opportunity.* Office of Education, US Department of Health, Education, and Welfare, Washington, DC

Davé R H 1963 The identification and measurement of environmental process variables related to educational achievement (Doctoral dissertation, University of Chicago)

Dobson R B 1977 Social status and inequality of access to higher education in the USSR. In: Karabel J, Halsey A H (eds.) 1977 *Power and Ideology in Education*. Oxford University Press, New York

Drenth P J D, van der Flier H, Omari I M 1983 Educational selection in Tanzania. *Eval. Educ.* 7(2): 95–209

Epstein J L 1987 Parent involvement: What research says to administrators. *Educ. Urb. Soc.* 19(2): 119–36

Floud J, Halsey A H 1961 Social class, intelligence tests, and selection for secondary schools. In: Halsey A H, Floud J, Anderson C A (eds.) 1961 *Education, Economy, and Society*. Free Press, New York

Fogelman K R, Goldstein H 1976 Social factors associated with changes in educational attainment between 7 and 11 years of age. *Educ. Stud.* 2(2): 95–109

Inter-Agency Commission for the World Conference on Education for All 1990 *Framework for Action to Meet Basic Learning Needs*. UNESCO House, New York

Fraser E 1959 *Home Environment and the School*. University of London Press, London

Girard A 1961 Selection for secondary education in France. In: Halsey A H, Floud J, Anderson C A (eds.) 1961 *Education, Economy and Society*. Collier-Macmillan, London

Greaney V, Kellaghan T 1984 *Equality of Opportunity in Irish Schools*. Educational Company, Dublin

Halsey A H, Heath A F, Ridge J M 1980 *Origins and Destinations: Family, Class, and Education in Modern Britain*. Clarendon Press, Oxford

Heer D M 1985 Effects of sibling number on child outcome. *Annu. Rev. Sociol.* 11: 27–47

Heyneman S P, Loxley W A 1983 The effect of primary-school quality on academic achievement across twenty-nine high- and low-income countries. *Am. J. Sociol.* 88(6): 1162–94

Hodgkinson H 1991 Reform versus reality. *Phi Del. Kap.* 73(1): 8–16

Johnstone J N 1983 Out-of-school factors and educational achievements in Indonesia. *Comp. Educ. Rev.* 27(2): 278–95

Kellaghan T, Macnamara J 1972 Family correlates of verbal reasoning ability. *Dev. Psychol.* 7(1): 49–53

Kellaghan T, Sloan K, Alvarez B, Bloom B S 1993 *The Home Environment and School Learning*. Jossey-Bass, San Francisco, California

Kohn M L 1963 Social class and parent–child relationships: An interpretation. *Am. J. Sociol.* 68: 471–80

Labov W 1977 *Language in the Inner City*. Blackwell, Oxford

Lockheed M E, Fuller B, Nyirongo R 1989 Family effects on students' achievement in Thailand and Malawi. *Sociol. Educ.* 62(4): 239–56

Marjoribanks K 1979 *Families and Their Learning Environments: An Empirical Analysis*. Routledge and Kegan Paul, London

Marjoribanks K 1991 Families, schools, and students' educational outcomes. In: Fraser B J, Walberg H J (eds.) 1991 *Educational Environments: Evaluation, Antecedents and Consequences*. Pergamon Press, Oxford

McGillicuddy-DeLisi A V 1982 The relationship between parents' beliefs about development and family constellation, socioeconomic status, and parents' teaching strategies. In: Laosa L M, Sigel I E (eds.) 1982 *Families as Learning Environments for Children*. Plenum, New York

Peaker G F 1967 The regression analyses of the national survey. In: United Kingdom, Department of Education and Science 1967 *Children and their Primary Schools: A Report of the Central Advisory Council for Education (England). Vol. 2: Research and Surveys*. HMSO, London

Sewell W H, Hauser R M 1976 Causes and consequences of higher education: Models of the status attainment process. In: Sewell W H, Hauser R M, Featherman D L (eds.) 1976 *Schooling and Achievement in American Society*. Academic Press, New York

Smith H, Cheung P 1986 Trends in the effects of family background on educational attainment in the Philippines. *Am. J. Sociol* 91(6): 1387–408

White K R 1982 The relationship between socioeconomic status and academic achievement. *Psych. Bull.* 91(3): 461–81

Zajonc R B, Bargh J 1980 The confluence model: Parameter and estimation for six divergent data sets on family factors and intelligence. *Intelligence* 4(4): 349–62

Further Reading

Alvarez B, Iriarte N 1991 *Familia y Aprendizaje. Lecciones de la Investigacion Reciente*. International Development Research Centre, Ottawa

Bronfenbrenner U 1986 Ecology of the family as a context for human development: Research perspectives. *Dev. Psychol.* 22(6): 723–42

Henderson A T Berla N (eds.) 1994 *The Family is Critical to Student Achievement. A New Generation of Evidence*. National Committee for Citizens in Education, Columbus, Maryland

Husén T et al. 1992 *Schooling in Modern European Society*. Pergamon Press, Oxford

Iverson B K, Walberg H J 1982 Home environment and school learning: A quantitative synthesis. *J. Exp. Educ.* 50(3): 144–51

Kalinowski A, Sloane K 1981 The home environment and school achievement. *Stud. Educ. Eval.* 7: 85–95

Laosa L M, Sigel I E (eds.) 1982 *Families as Learning Environments for Children*. Plenum Press, New York

Marjoribanks K (ed.) 1974 *Environments for Learning*. NFER Publishing Co., Windsor

Scott-Jones D 1984 Family influences on cognitive development and school achievement. *Rev. Res. Educ.* 11: 259–304

Swap S M 1993 *Developing Home–School Partnerships. From Concepts to Practice*. Teachers College Press, Columbia University, New York

Walberg H J, Marjoribanks K 1976 Family environment and cognitive development: Twelve analytic models. *Rev. Educ. Res.* 46(4): 527–51

Family Influence on Human Development

K. A. Schneewind

From a systems-oriented perspective, individual development within the family is conceived as a coevolutionary process. Although the family as a special group of persons and the individual family member each have their own developmental paths both mutually influence each other. Based on a rather broad psychological definition of the family, some selected topics and research findings including behavior genetics, health, relationships on different system levels, and family intervention will be presented.

1. Defining the Family

In a time when sociologists—at least in the Western world—contend that disintegration and deinstitutionalization of the family has led to a growing pluralization of family forms, defining the family is not an easy task. Many solutions have been proposed to solve this definitional dilemma. They range from conceiving of the family as a legalized two-generational unit of coresiding persons related by blood and/or adoption, to viewing it as a widely unspecified constellation of persons who of their own volition call themselves a family. For the purposes of this entry, families are defined as special variants of intimate relationship systems for which the maintenance of boundaries, privacy, closeness, and permanence are crucial, albeit empirically more or less variable, defining elements. This definition not only includes nontraditional family forms found in modern society but also focuses on a genuine psychological perspective; that is, how and to what extent people influence each other and are influenced by the relationship context in which they are living. In addition, it takes into account the dynamic nature of the codeveloping individual–family unit by explicitly considering the possibility that a person might be part of a series of quite different intimate relationship systems across his or her life course.

2. Heredity and Health in Family Life

2.1 Behavior Genetics

The fact that, unlike adopted children, consanguineous children are genetically related to their parents and siblings is of fundamental importance for the explanation of individual differences and commonalities within the family context. Quantitative behavior genetics, including developmental behavior genetics, have made great progress since the early 1980s. Based

on large data sets mainly from Anglo-American and Scandinavian countries, the following general conclusions can be drawn (Plomin and Rende 1991): (a) the variation of cognitive and socioemotional personality variables has a substantial genetic component; (b) in a developmental perspective genetic influences become increasingly more important as individual differences are determined by an active genotype–environment covariation; (c) family-related experiences such as perceived parental warmth can partially be attributed to genetic influences; (d) nonshared environmental influences (e.g., specific treatment of a child by parents or siblings) contribute to individual differences to a larger extent than family variables that are common to all offspring (e.g., socioeconomic status, generalized parenting style). The latter finding partially explains why siblings raised in the same family are so different from one another, although the siblings' specific genetic endowment may also contribute to phenotypic differences. The importance of nonshared environments has led—ironically within a behavior genetic research program—to a more detailed exploration of specific environmental influences inside and outside the family that are linked to the development of individual differences.

2.2 The Family and Health

There is ample evidence that people living in a long-term (usually marital) relationship are, on average, physically and psychologically healthier than single, divorced, or widowed persons. For instance, the data suggest that in the United States the death rates of unmarried people are up to 50 percent (females) or even 250 percent (males) higher than for married people. Causes of death with a strong behavioral component (e.g., lung cancer, suicide, accidents) have a particularly high incidence rate for unmarried people. Moreover, clinically diagnosed personality dysfunctions (e.g., anxiety, depression) are also more likely to be found among this group. Attempts to explain these differences range from mate selection (i.e., healthy people are more likely to find a partner) to the special social and emotional support provided in long-term intimate relationships (e.g., less risky life-styles, more preventive and health-enhancing activities as practiced especially by women). It should be stressed, however, that these findings are based on sample means and thus do not account for differential effects. There are some indications, for example, that the beneficial effects of living in a marriage can only be found in rewarding and nondistressed relationships.

Although living in a long-term relationship tends to be a protective factor for a person's well-being this is not the case for parenthood. On average, parents do not fare better than childless people and can even be expected to encounter somewhat higher health risks. However, differential influences must again be taken into account. Among these are the following factors: sufficient financial resources of the family, available childcare services, support from spouse or kin in sharing childcare and household chores (Ross et al. 1990).

2.3 Family Violence

In some cases the family itself may become a health risk. In Western societies this is especially true for children and women, increasingly also for older family members, whose personal integrity can be violated by physical maltreatment and sexual abuse. The expression and definition of domestic violence is different from country to country; the same holds true for corresponding laws, criminal statistics, and estimated numbers of unknown cases. Despite these differences, there is consistent evidence that domestic violence is rapidly increasing in the Western industrialized nations, quite apart from the growing neglect of children in economically deprived Third World countries. The causes and consequences of family violence and neglect are in general well-researched, suggesting a multidimensional pattern of causes among which variables like economic hardship, social and personal stress, low self-esteem, unrealistic expectations of child-rearing, and a history of experience of violence in one's own family of origin are especially salient. Several reviews concerning the consequences of child maltreatment lead to similar conclusions; that is, maltreated children tend to be more aggressive, show more internalizing and externalizing behavior problems, are less empathetic, have more troubled peer relationships, and perform lower on cognitive tasks. Preventive action seems to be imperative in view of these findings, although so far the results of corresponding programs have yielded mixed results (Gelles and Conte 1990).

3. Family Relations

The number of possible relationships within a family increases exponentially with the number of individual family members. In a four-person family, for example, there are 11 groupings of family members (i.e., six dyads, four triads, and one tetrad). In addition, relations among relationships (e.g., between the couple and the parent–child system) must be taken into account, not to mention the relationships connecting the family and its subsystems with other social units (e.g., extended family, peers). These complex patterns of relationships should be kept in mind as some of the major types of relationships within the family are briefly reviewed.

3.1 Couple Relations

Because couples are the architects of the family system, the quality of their relationship greatly influences their personal well-being, couple satisfaction, and the way they handle their children—and vice versa. One way to gain a better understanding of the concomitants, of the spouses' relationship quality is to analyze the communication experiences and corresponding behavior of distressed and nondistressed couples. Research clearly indicates that distressed couples can be characterized by a number of negative relationship skills (e.g., lack of active listening and self-disclosure, escalating conflict behavior, maintenance of irrational beliefs). Strained couple relationships and interparental conflict also seem to have a negative impact on childrens' personality development, especially for boys, although more prospective longitudinal studies are needed to disentangle causes and effects.

It should also be mentioned that the quality of couple relationships varies depending on the meaning that the spouses attach to their relationship. Fitzpatrick (1988), for instance, has found three marital types (i.e., traditionals, independents, and separates) that differ according to their preferred connectedness and autonomy, which in turn differentially influences their sense of marital satisfaction. More research is needed to determine the long-term developmental outcome of couple types both on the spouse and on the parent–child level.

3.2 Parent–Child Relations

The care and socialization of children are among the most important societal tasks that, to a great extent, are entrusted to the family. Theoretical models to explore the determinants, concomitants, and consequences of parenthood have increasingly become more complex by addressing not only specific parent–child interactions per se, but also by looking at contextual and systemic influences such as heredity, child temperament, the parents' personality and relationship history, couple relationship, workplace, social support, and economic resources. In addition, theoretical advances, especially using attachment and social-learning approaches, have shown some convergence concerning the development of competent behavior in children and adolescents. In summary, parents raising their children in a climate of affection and responsiveness, using clear and explicable rules, providing developmentally enhancing and autonomy-granting environments, are more likely to have children with a positive self-concept who are emotionally stable, socially competent, well-accepted by their peers, academically successful, and intrinsically self-responsible (Belsky 1990).

However, this general developmental pattern needs to be qualified in view of the aforementioned moderating influences, thus giving each individual

615

developmental path its very special and unique gestalt. In addition, it should be realized that these conclusions are only valid for a pattern of societal and personal values that is typical for the Western world. It has been argued that, in contrast to the West, the value system of the Eastern world is quite different, centering more on sociability, calmness, and passive contemplation. Accordingly, parental socialization practices have been shown to differ markedly from Western standards to ensure an appropriate transmission of these values.

3.3 Sibling Relations

Despite declining birthrates in industrialized countries, the sibling relationship still contributes substantially to the process of individual and family development. Beside the more structural properties of sibling constellations (i.e., spacing, distribution of sexes) and their impact on intra- and extrafamilial relationships, more fine-grained behavioral analyses have shown that differential parental treatment is strongly related to the quality of sibling relationships. Siblings who are treated differently by their parents tend to develop poorer and more conflictual relationships among themselves and also show more adaptational problems as adolescents (Dunn and Stocker 1989). This might impede the fulfillment of developmental tasks across the sibling lifecycle (e.g., caring for elderly parents, mutual support with health and financial problems). Although siblings tend to develop a closer and less competitive relationship in later life, much more knowledge is required about differential developmental paths of siblingship in a lifespan perspective.

3.4 Intergenerational Relations

With increasing life expectancies, it is becoming more probable that three or even four generations coexist. Relationships between grandparents or great-grandparents and their grandchildren or great-grandchildren are usually perceived as being rather positive by both sides. Again, differential effects seem to moderate these relationships suggesting specific systemic influences. Thus, it has been shown that, on average, grandchildren report a close relationship with their grandparents only if they also feel that the relationship between their parents and grandparents is emotionally satisfying.

However, intergenerational relations can also be less rewarding and even harmful. The experience of family violence and divorce, for example, seems to have a strong component that is transmitted from generation to generation. The work by Elder et al. (1984) is especially revealing as to the mechanisms of this intergenerational transmission process. By linking the life courses of four generations, these authors were able to demonstrate that insensitive, controlling, and hostile parenting behavior has a detrimental impact on the personality and marital relations of the off-spring, which in turn leads to inadequate parenting on their part when they have children of their own. In the same vein, Rutter's (1988) work comparing the parenting behavior of home-reared and institution-reared mothers, showed that mothers who, as children, had to be placed into an institution because of their parents' severe marital discord displayed much poorer parenting, especially if the placement happened before their fourth birthday. These results accord well with increasing research evidence stemming from an attachment theoretical approach. Nevertheless, it should be noted that there are also internal and external resources (e.g., strong personal interests, support from relatives, friends, or spouses) that serve as protective factors in coping with adverse life conditions.

4. Family Intervention

Whereas the research on family–individual codevelopment reviewed so far was noninterventive in nature, there are strong pleas for more intervention-oriented approaches for studying the individual within the family. Since the advent of family therapy as a special systemic treatment method, many hopes have been placed in this approach. Although family therapy has become a more salient example of therapeutic intervention, it needs to be complemented by other nontherapeutic, albeit interventive approaches, especially family counseling, family prevention, and family policy. All four of these approaches will be commented on briefly in the following paragraphs.

4.1 Family Therapy

Family therapy is not a monolithic treatment approach. Rather there are many different models and schools expanding almost all theoretical approaches that have been used in individual therapy by adding a systemic or relationship component to the core belief system. For family therapy in its narrower sense, it is indispensable to use sound diagnostic assessment of clinically relevant individual and/or familial dysfunctions on which family treatment can be based. Depending on the preferred theoretical orientation, research evidence on effective treatment outcomes is still scarce, although in some comparative studies it was shown that family therapy was equal or even superior to other (usually individual-oriented) treatment approaches. However, more specific research on the indication, treatment process, and outcome are clearly needed to determine their long-term impact on individual and family relations (Piercy and Sprenkle 1990).

4.2 Family Counseling

Whereas family therapy is basically aimed at therapeutic change, family counseling usually does not imply the treatment of more or less severe individual or familial dysfunctions. Instead, family counseling is a method of helping people by providing relevant information, encouraging them to clarify possible courses of action and assisting them in solving problems by themselves. Thus, family counseling is not confined only to psychosocial problems, but also extends to contexts that connect families with the outer world (e.g., school, workplace, neighborhood, and community). Although the ingredients of the counseling process such as strengthening personal and family resources or enhancing self-exploration have been shown to be beneficial for further individual and family development, more and better research on evaluation in counseling is called for.

4.3 Preventive Family Intervention

Family prevention refers to the optimization of developmental processes in nonclinical families (primary prevention) and to the prophylactic support or aftercare of high-risk families (secondary and tertiary prevention). These approaches are mainly based on providing information and imparting social skills to enhance communication and problem-solving capabilities. Research on family enrichment, divorce counseling, or families with a schizophrenic member attest to the importance and effectiveness of preventive measures for the benefit of the individual and the family alike.

4.4 Family Policy

Although at a different level, family policy is another interventive approach to helping families better cope with their lives. The quality and diversity of governmental measures taken to ensure family well-being vary greatly from country to country. Governmental intervention concerning issues such as financial transfers, support of extrafamilial child care services, parental leave, legislation on divorce, or child custody exemplifies how important family policy measures are in structuring the family's life course. It is here that the knowledge base of family psychology has much to contribute to the initiation and evaluation of programs aimed at strengthening family resources and self-regulation.

5. Conclusion

From a systemic and contextualistic point of view, it has been argued here that individual development within the family is a coevolutionary process. Elsewhere an integrative family systems model has been proposed (Schneewind 1992) that takes into account developmental stressors and resources on both a vertical axis (comprising biographically accumulated experiences) and a horizontal axis (referring to momentary and future life events). Moreover, the model relates these stressors and resources to different interconnected systems (i.e., person, couple/family, multigenerational, and extrafamilial systems). It is hoped that a conceptional framework such as this will help to instigate more interventive and noninterventive research with special emphasis on differential paths of individual development within the context of intimate relationship systems.

See also: Family and Schooling; Family, School, and Cultural Capital; Family, School, and Social Capital; Home Environment and School Learning

References

Belsky J 1990 Parental and nonparental child care and children's socioemotional development: A decade in review. *J. Marriage Fam.* 52(4): 885–903

Dunn J, Stocker C 1989 The significance of differences in siblings' experiences within the family. In: Kreppner K, Lerner R M (eds.) 1989

Elder G H, Liker J D, Cross C 1984 Parent–child behavior in the great depression: Life course and intergenerational influences. In: Baltes P B, Brim O G (eds.) 1984 *Lifespan Development and Behavior*, Vol. 6. Academic Press, New York

Fitzpatrick M A 1988 *Between Husbands and Wives: Communication in Marriage*. Sage, Newbury Park, California

Gelles R J, Conte J R 1990 Domestic violence and sexual abuse of children: A review of research in the eighties. *J. Marriage Fam.* 52(4): 1045–58

Piercy F P, Sprenkle D H 1990 Marriage and family therapy: A decade in review. *J. Marriage Fam.* 52(4): 1116–26

Plomin R, Rende R 1991 Human behavioral genetics. *Annu. Rev. Psychol.* 42: 161–90

Ross C E, Mirowsky J, Goldsteen K 1990 The impact of the family on health: The decade in review. *J. Marriage Fam.* 52(4): 1059–78

Rutter M 1988 Functions and consequences of relationships: Some psychopathological considerations. In: Hinde R A, Stevenson-Hinde J (eds.) 1988

Schneewind K A 1992 Familien zwischen Rhetorik und Realität: Eine familienpsychologische Perspektive. In: Schneewind K A, von Rosenstiel L (eds.) 1992 *Wandel der Familie*. Hogrefe, Göttingen

Further Reading

Booth A (ed.) 1991 *Contemporary Families: Looking Forward, Looking Back*. National Council on Family Relations, Minneapolis, Minnesota

Cowan P A, Hetherington M (eds.) 1991 *Family Transitions*. Erlbaum, Hillsdale, New Jersey

Hinde R A, Stevenson-Hinde J (eds.) 1988 *Relationships within Families: Mutual Influences*. Clarendon Press, Oxford

Kreppner K, Lerner R M (eds.) 1989 *Family Systems and Life-span Development*. Erlbaum, Hillsdale, New Jersey

Family, School, and Cultural Capital

J. Collins and F. Thompson

It is a common and plausible assumption that families prepare and reinforce the symbolic attributes required by schooling, and that schooling builds upon and elaborates the symbolic resources derived from family membership. Cultural capital provides a way of thinking about that process of preparation, reinforcement, development, and elaboration. It alerts analysts to the historical and contemporary dynamics of the accumulation of symbolic as well as economic resources and to the role of economic and political as well as educational institutions in creating fields of social value.

1. Cultural Capital

The concept of cultural capital originates and has been most developed in the work of Bourdieu (Bourdieu 1979, Bourdieu and Passeron 1970). Much of Bourdieu's work concerns the reproduction of social relations and institutions. Existing distributions of economic, cultural, and social resources tend to be reproduced through specific mechanisms of transmission. Educational systems provide sites for the accumulation and legitimation of cultural resources, and as the economic resources invested in education have increased throughout the twentieth century, so education had tended increasingly to mediate access to social resources. For example, where a wealthy family in the nineteenth century would transmit wealth and property directly to its offspring, an analogously situated family in the twentieth century will invest in elite education, with its children reaching the upper tiers of the corporate hierarchy via routes such as, in the United States, the Harvard Business School. Similarly, where a working-class family of the nineteenth century might hope to guarantee the father's trade for the son, perhaps through some guild structure, an analogous family in the twentieth century will find the route to industrial or service employment through the vocational school or training plan.

1.1 Forms of Capital and Fields of Value

Capital, in its broadest sense, is an attempt to capture the past in the present: "The social world is accumulated history, and if it is [to be understood] . . . one must reintroduce into it the notion of capital and with it, accumulation and all its effects" (Bourdieu 1983 [1986] p.241). Bourdieu defines capital as those resources whose distribution defines the social structure, and whose deployment figures centrally in the reproduction of that structure. Such resources are not just economic, but also social and cultural, and there are, accordingly, three basic forms of capital.

Economic capital consists of all income, and may be institutionalized in forms of inheritance. Social capital consists of influence, "networks," and "connections," and may be institutionalized in systems of noble title (1983 [1986]). Cultural capital consists of symbolic wherewithal (knowledge and possessions): it may be objectified in goods (books, artwork, high-tech playthings), institutionalized in the form of credentials and degrees, or embodied as dispositions and aptitudes (e.g., a sense of familiarity and ease with school-based schedules, forms of language, and classroom routines). The school is a primary site for institutionalizing cultural capital via degrees, and objectified and nonobjectified cultural capital are treated more fully below. The embodiment of cultural capital has been discussed by Bourdieu and others as *habitus*, basic mind and body dispositions derived from past experience, especially familial experience, and actively organizing future experience.

Given forms of capital attain their value in given markets or fields. Influential involvement, that is social capital, is not the same, for example, in academia, business, or the art world. Cultural capital similarly depends on markets or fields within which it is valued and within which it may be used advantageously. These social arenas may vary in their scope and degree of centralization. Assuming a hierarchical and highly unified schooling system, then speaking a "standard" form of the national language, having various sorts of school-relevant prior knowledge, or having attended a highly ranked school can all be seen as forms of cultural capital most valued in the national educational "market" (Collins 1989, DiMaggio 1982, Calhoun 1993). Such language, knowledge, and credentials are convertible into additional educational opportunities and into occupations.

1.2 Dominant Capital and Struggles over Value

Different social groups may have symbolic attributes and resources distinct from the dominant forms of cultural capital, and these other capitals may be valued in some social domains but not in dominant institutional arenas like public education (Hall 1992). Nonelite forms of language, knowledge, and social experience —say a working-class vernacular, knowledge of an industry or craft, and experience of wage employment —may serve youth very poorly in school, but very well in nonacademic employment situations such as getting a job on an assembly line, at a warehouse, or on a maintenance staff (MacLeod 1987, Willis 1977). Similarly, command of Black English, knowledge of African-American religious and esthetic traditions, and experience in intense verbal-interactive performance may be stigmatized or ignored in standard school curriculum, yet be valued and serve as strategic resources for competition in such fields of African–American endeavor and achievement as religion, politics, or art.

The valuing of particular symbolic attributes as cultural capital thus historically varies, depending upon the state of relations between key institutions and the state of struggles between social groups. In general, the school tends to be a conservative institution, valuing the language, cultural propensities, and social experience of dominant groups as standards, and devaluing those of dominated groups. The effectiveness of this including/excluding act depends on the relation of the school to the rest of society, and that relation is often contested (Collins 1993). The debates in the United States and United Kingdom about multiculturalism in the school curriculum are about whose history and social experience is to be included and whose excluded from school knowledge; and the controversies over bilingual education in Canada and the United States are about whose language will count in the pedagogical acts of teaching and learning.

As the concept of cultural capital points to the role of family-based symbolic accumulation in mediating the school–society relation, it raises additional questions: (a) how has the school come to define what counts as cultural capital?; and (b) when is capital activated, that is, when are resources deployed? Addressing the first requires examining the role of the state in structuring school as well as the periodic education crises that make manifest one result of that structuring: the otherwise hidden relation between cultural resources and academic achievement. Addressing the second requires examining historical and ethnographic work on families and schools. This work suggests some of the complexities underlying the use of cultural capital, and it reveals a renewal of interest in the family.

2. Schooling

2.1 The Role of the State

Public education in capitalist democracies must reconcile a fundamental contradiction between class inequality and the promise of democracy. The histories of schooling in such nation-states as France, the United Kingdom, and the United States can be read as successive efforts to control and resolve this contradiction. Shortly after major social upheavals in each country, governing bodies, working in concert with elite reformers, legislated and implemented what would count as knowledge (curriculum), how it would be known (examinations), and what populations would be affected (attendance), by right or compulsion. Since the mid-nineteenth century, the schooling systems in these countries have expanded, differentiating both school knowledge and the populations affected.

2.2 Schools and Crisis

There have been periodic crises as new populations encountered new levels of schooling. Thus in France, compulsory public education was established early in the nineteenth century with the explicit aim of inculcating a national culture and language. In this legislated order of knowledge and population, working class was subordinate to bourgeois, rural to urban, and female to male (Reed-Danahay and Anderson-Levitt 1991). Each expansion of the system to new populations, for example, the extension of higher education to working-class, rural, and female students, brought about a pedagogical crisis of curriculum and standards (Bourdieu and Passeron 1970, Bourdieu 1979). In the United States, elite coalitions argued for compulsory public schooling on the grounds that it would promote Americanism and good work habits among a restive and heterogeneous farming, artisanal and factory working class of native and immigrant origins (Nasaw 1979). Subsequent expansions and extensions of that schooling system, from compulsory primary to compulsory secondary schooling, from elite to mass postsecondary education, have been accompanied by debates over curriculum and perceived crises of standards (Nasaw 1979, Rose 1989).

2.3 Crisis and Cultural Advantage

These recurring "crises of standards" may be understood as encounters between state-established, class-, race-, and gender-selective schooling systems and new populations of students. They pose in sharp relief the question "Whose culture has more capital?," that is, whose symbolic resources are given pride of place in curriculum, testing, and classroom practice? The broad answer is "Those of the dominant groups, for a given historical period." More precise answers point to specific social categories and specific forms. Class bias in French schooling has been argued for form of language (standard/patois), experience with traditional humanist culture, and general recognition of high-culture forms such as museum art and classical music (Bourdieu and Passeron 1970, Bourdieu 1979). Class bias is amply evident in United Kingdom and Australian schooling, not just in parental knowledge of the school system and its differentiations, or children's prior experience of school-valued activities (kinds of reading and writing, attendance at museums, national and foreign travel), or the legendary differences of class and accent, but also in the pervasive, higher status, and better funded system of private schooling (Connell et al. 1982, Jackson and Marsden 1962, Willis 1977, Lamb 1990). There is also racial-ethnic bias. Indeed, much of the discussion of race relations and curriculum reform occurring in the United Kingdom since the 1970s has been concerned with what languages and national social traditions will be part of school subjects and national examinations. In the United States, class and race bias has been argued for the social knowledge presumed in standardized tests, whether at the turn of the twentieth century or the 1960s (Rose 1989); for the language of schooling more generally (Collins 1989); and for classroom-valued expressive etiquette (Heath 1983, Macleod 1987). It has been shown that knowledge of high cultural forms (e.g., the fine arts) correlates with class position and educational–occupational attainment (DiMaggio 1982) and that professional–managerial families mobilize goods, status and social connections, and sophisticated scheduling capacities, in order to advance their children's education (Lareau 1989).

The value of the concept of cultural capital is that it points not just to social-background difference in school, but to institutionally valued and devalued difference. (Does a family watch soap operas or National Geographic nature series on television, attend football matches or art galleries?) As research on the credentialing of society suggests, school-valued patterns of consumption and knowledge influence both scholastic and occupational attainment. If the presence or absence of dominant cultural capital is one significant resource in the struggle to maintain or transform social position, the question remains of when and how capital is used, and here research on the family provides special insight.

3. Families

Nearly all families care about their children's school success, but their knowledge of the system and their ability to work it to the advantage of their children varies, generally by social class but also within classes. Families can be seen to have two fronts when interacting with schools, with two overlapping but distinct amounts and types of cultural capital: (a) adults draw directly on their own resources in their dealings with the school and in their efforts to influence the education of their children, and (b) children draw on those resources that have been transmitted to them by others in the family as well as other resources they have accumulated from their experiences outside the family.

To provide their children with the maximum bases for accumulating more cultural capital in school, families need to use the capital they have at both these levels. For instance, adults with knowledge of how schools work are typically disposed to argue with school staff about the placement of their child, whereas those lacking knowledge may be inclined to accept teachers' decisions (Lareau 1989); children from families where readings are critiqued are able to use such skills in school, whereas those from families where readings are strictly literal will be at a disadvantage in many classrooms (Heath 1983). The actions and dispositions of both adults and children affect the ways teachers and other school staff make decisions which affect the education of that family's child.

3.1 Social Class Differences in Family Cultural Capital

In introducing the concept of cultural capital, Bourdieu has contributed to the theory of social reproduction; though not focused on home–school interactions, his work points to the importance of class cultures in mediating negotiations in the schooling process. As he has argued (Bourdieu 1979), selection of rising or declining fields of study (e.g. computer science versus classical languages) is typically tied to family social position. Similarly, the ability of middle and upper class families to use economic advantage and knowledge of the public system (e.g., in being able to choose the best of affluent suburban school systems, leaving the troubled urban systems to the less fortunate) means that their educational effort has more "payoff" in recognized scholastic achievement.

In a study comparing White upper-middle class and working class families in the United States (Lareau 1989), families in the upper-middle class school used a variety of resources to promote their children's educational achievement. These resources included: spending time in their child's classroom and talking to teachers; spending money on tutors in problem subjects; using their status and their education to argue with and to influence teachers to change their child's reading or mathematics group or some other aspect of the classroom program, or to argue with the principal to request specific teachers or programs; and working with their children on both school and school-like tasks at home. Not only did these families have the time, money, education, and status that helped them get what they wanted from the system, but they had even more essential resources that are so basic that they are not generally recognized as resources: the experience and the confidence to expect to get what they wanted. This model of interaction is characterized as "interconnectedness," in which "Parents' actions influenced their children's schooling and children's school experiences influenced family life" (Lareau 1989 p. 81).

By contrast, families of children in the working-class school were characterized as lacking not only in the resources of time, money, education, and status, but also in those of experience and confidence in the education field. These parents were generally intimidated by an educational system, and felt neither competent to criticize the school nor capable of helping their children with homework or other school-like tasks. This relationship between home and school is characterized as one of "separation" (Lareau 1989 p. 8).

Working class and lower-middle class families tend to be less informed as to standards of achievement than are upper-middle class families who can look to their own experience and that of their social peers (Jackson and Marsden 1962, Connell et al. 1982). Working class families tend to blame themselves or their children for school problems and to find the school difficult to challenge, whereas upper-middle class families are more apt to blame the school, to challenge the school, and to buy the services of outside experts if necessary (Lareau 1989).

In most schools, teachers and family members interact very little, regardless of class background; however, this does not preclude strong opinions from being formed. School staff seem to generalize from the characteristics of parents' achievements to a set of expectations for the children, according to social class. Lower-middle/working class parents are often considered by teachers to be lacking in parenting skills and interest, paralleling parents' actual lower level of pressure on school due to more limited resources of both families and neighborhood; in contrast, teachers are impressed by the involvement of upper-middle class families in their children's schooling: their support, suggestions, and even their criticisms are taken seriously (Reed-Danahay and Anderson-Levitt 1991, Connell et al. 1982, Lareau 1989). In addition, elite families in the United States are more aware of and responsive to the changing expectations of schools for parental participation (Lareau 1989).

3.2 Intragroup Differences in Cultural Capital

Many researchers have found the concept of cultural capital useful in trying to understand differences in home–school relationships within social classes and groups and even within families. Regardless of the level and type of interaction of parents and schools, a crucial aspect of family cultural capital is durable, embodied dispositions and aptitudes (habitus). For instance, this dimension of cultural capital has profound influences on young people's aspirations (MacLeod 1987). Of the working class families with early access to grammar-school education in the United Kingdom, those who possessed one or more of the following kinds of capital were more likely to succeed in school and afterwards: middle class grandparents; parental leadership in churches, unions, or political organizations; and parental self-education. Students from these families were more likely to develop the discipline and the assertiveness to increase the capital they had (Jackson and Marsden 1962).

> Although Bourdieu sometimes gives the impression of a homogeneity of habitus within the boundaries of social class, I understand habitus to be constituted at the level of family and thus can include, as constitutive of the habitus, factors such as ethnicity, educational histories, peer associations, and demographic characteristics (e.g., geographical mobility, duration of tenancy in public housing, sibling order, and family size) as these shape individual action. (MacLeod 1987 p. 138)

Some families provide their children with dispositions which prevent them from accumulating school-based cultural capital but which are valuable in other fields. In a study of "how working class kids get working class jobs" (Willis 1977), some working class boys' resistance in school to the ideology of individual competition was found to be based on family adherence to traditional working class cultural norms valuing manual work and group loyalty; this same habitus was the basis for acceptance when they followed their fathers into factory jobs. (This study also found that other boys from similar backgrounds were able to comply with the school's demands sufficiently to provide themselves access to office jobs.)

Until recently, minority racial and ethnic groups have tended to be treated as sharing similar levels and types of resources and dispositions. However, studies of non-White families have revealed important variations in their approach to schooling. In the United States, up-and-coming Mexicano students in the South West learn from their families to watch and imitate the behaviors of solidly middle class White students (Foley 1990). Successful low-income African-American students learn optimism, discipline, and self-esteem from their families which allows them to see themselves as able to cope with life's present exigencies and to take advantage of opportunities others might not even notice; in addition these children benefit from families who are able to be knowledgeably involved in their schooling (Clark 1983).

3.3 Use Of Cultural Capital

Though earlier studies focused on the possession of cultural capital, researchers have begun to recognize that capital must be used in order to accrue profits; this shift in perspective has necessitated an acknowledgement of the importance of social context and historical development in studies of the relationships between families, students, and schools (Connell et al. 1982, MacLeod 1987, Lareau 1989). For instance, elite fathers become more involved in the education of their independent school children as they move up the grades, whereas working class families tend to lose contact as their ability to help with homework diminishes (Connell et al. 1982); in large part, it is structural differences between schools which lead to working class parents being "frozen out" (Connell et al. 1982, Lareau 1989).

Despite limited family–school interactions, students themselves interact with schools daily. Students' interactions with their teachers are not always in line with the habitus their families have provided; for instance, some students may successfully negotiate their way through subject choices their parents cannot help with (Jackson and Marsden 1962); or others may resist classroom discipline despite the best efforts of elite parents (Lareau 1989).

4. Conclusion

As with any development in social theory, cultural capital must be explored both theoretically and through practical research. The concept helps analyze not only how privilege works through schooling but also how its workings are not so tightly determined that movement is impossible. Research has begun to uncover, for example, what kind of cultural capital is available to successful though under privileged students, and how they use what cultural capital they have to become successful despite the structured inequality of school systems (Mehan et al. 1996). If used in isolation from the larger analytic frameworks of which it is a part, the cultural capital concept can be read merely as an argument about cultural advantage and disadvantage, and as such it is susceptible to the usual criticisms about the ahistoricism and static determinism of cultural reproduction analyses (Hall 1992). Bourdieu's conceptual and empirical work suggest more historical and dynamic conceptions, however, as does much of the work in the United States, Australia, and other national contexts.

A historical perspective reveals that school knowledge is "culturally arbitrary," an imposition of specific frameworks of symbolic value onto social difference, so that the cultural correlates of class or ethnic–racial background are transformed into scholastic aptitude and ineptitude. Much of the research on family–school relationships has focused on how the conflict between the dominant-class culture of the schools and the attitudes and expectations (habitus) of nonelite students and their families work together to maintain a system in which the vast majority of these students have little opportunity to succeed. However, the concept of cultural capital lets researchers move beyond these reproduction generalizations to examine exactly what kinds of capital work in schooling, what is transmitted to students by families which helps the students do well, as well as what it is that families themselves do in their interactions with schools to the same ends. In other words, viewing home–school interactions as activations of cultural capital allows the focus of research to shift away from explaining why low-income students fail in general, and toward an explanation of how students and their families manage their school successes. The theory of cultural capital as it relates to home–school relations continues to be explored; among other researchers in the 1990s, Lareau and both authors of this entry are studying the activation of cultural capital and its historical and cumulative aspects.

See also: Family and Schooling; Family Influence on Human Development; Family, School, and Social Capital; Reproduction Theory; Resistance Theory

References

Bourdieu P 1979 *La Distinction: Critique sociale du jugement*. Les Editions de Minuit, Paris [1984 *Distinction: A Social Critique of the Judgement of Taste*. Harvard University Press, Cambridge, Massachusetts]
Bourdieu P 1983 Okonomisches Kapital, kulturelles Kapital, soziales Kapital. *Soziale Welt* 2: 183–98 [1986 The forms of capital. In: Richardson J G (ed.) 1986 *Handbook of Theory and Research for the Sociology of Education*. Greenwood Press, New York]
Bourdieu P, Passeron J-C 1970 *La Reproduction: Elements pour une theorie du systeme d'enseignement*. Les Editions de Minuit, Paris [1977 *Reproduction in Education, Society and Culture*. Sage, London]
Calhoun C 1993 Habitus, field and capital: The question of historical specificity. In: Calhoun C, Lipuma E, Postone M (eds.) 1993 *Bourdieu: Critical Perspectives*. Polity Press, New York
Clark R M 1983 *Family Life and School Achievement: Why Poor Black Children Succeed or Fail*. University of Chicago Press, Chicago, Illinois
Collins J 1989 Hegemonic practice: Literacy and standard language in public education. *J. Educ.* 172(2): 9–36
Collins J 1993 Determination and contradiction: An appreciation and critique of the work of Pierre Bourdieu on language and education. In: Calhoun C, Lipuma E, Postone M (eds.) 1993 *Bourdieu: Critical Perspectives*. Polity Press, New York
Connell R W, Ashenden D J, Kessler S, Dowsett G W 1982 *Making the Difference: Schools, Families, and Social Division*. Allen and Unwin, Sydney
DiMaggio P 1982 Cultural capital and school success: The impact of status culture participation on the grades of US high school students. *Am. Sociol. Rev.* 47: 189–201
Foley D 1990 *Learning Capitalist Culture: Deep in the Heart of Tejas*. University of Pennsylvania Press, Philadelphia, Pennsylvania
Hall J 1992 The capital(s) of culture: A nonholistic approach to status situations. In: Lamont M, Fournier M (eds.) 1992 *Cultivating Differences: Symbolic Boundaries and the Making of Inequality*. University of Chicago Press, Chicago, Illinois
Heath S B 1983 *Ways With Words: Language, Life, and Work in Communities and Classrooms*. Cambridge University Press, New York
Jackson B, Marsden D 1962 *Education and the Working Class*. Routledge and Kegan Paul, London
Lamb S 1990 Cultural selection in Australian secondary schools. *Res. Educ.* 43: 1–14
Lareau A 1989 *Home Advantage: Social Class and Parental Intervention in Elementary Education*. Falmer Press, London
MacLeod J 1987 *Ain't No Making It: Leveled Aspirations in a Low-Income Neighborhood*. Westview Press, Boulder, Colorado
Mehan H, Villeneuva I, Lintz A, Hubbard L 1996 *Constructing School Success: the Consequences of Untracking Low Achieving Students*. Cambridge University Press, New York
Nasaw D 1979 *Schooled to Order: A Social History of Public Schooling in the United States*. Oxford University Press, New York
Reed-Danahay D, Anderson-Levitt K M 1991 Backward countryside, troubled city: French teachers' images of rural and working-class families. *American Ethnologist* 18(3): 546–64
Rose M 1989 *Lives on the Boundary: The Struggles and Achievements of America's Underprepared*. Free Press, New York
Willis P 1977 *Learning to Labor: How Working Class Kids Get Working Class Jobs*. Saxon House, Farnborough

Further Reading

Bernstein B 1975 *Class, Codes, and Control*. Routledge and Kegan Paul, London

Bourdieu P 1991 *Language and Symbolic Power*. Harvard University Press, Cambridge, Massachusetts

Calhoun C, Lipuma E, Postone M (eds.) 1993 *Bourdieu: Critical Perspectives*. Polity Press, New York

Harker R K 1984 On reproduction, habitus and education. *Br. J. Social Educ.* 5(2): 117–27

Kontopoulos K 1993 *The Logics of Structure*. Cambridge University Press, New York

Lamont M, Lareau A 1988 Cultural capital: Allusions, gaps, and glissandos in recent theoretical developments. *Sociological Theory* 6: 153–68

Lamont M, Fournier M (eds.) 1992 *Cultivating Differences: Symbolic Boundaries and the Making of Inequality*. University of Chicago Press, Chicago, Illinois

Musgrave P W 1988 *Socialising Contexts: The Subject in Society*. Allen and Unwin, Sydney

Family, School, and Social Capital

† **J. S. Coleman**

The term "social capital" has been used in the study of education to refer to the social resources that children and youth have available to them outside schools in their family or community. These resources, like other forms of capital, can be productive in aiding educational growth. The term refers to a variety of different social resources, each of which may be of value for education. Forms of social capital include interests of parents in their children's development, norms held and enforced by parents or by the adult community that shape and control children's activities, relationships to adults other than the child's own parents, and the trustworthiness of those who make up the child's social environment. Social capital thus consists primarily of relationships of various categories of adults to the child and to one another.

Social capital available to the child stands in contrast to the human capital, financial capital, or physical capital of the child's parents or others in the child's environment, for it is complementary to these resources. The effective availability of these resources to the child depends on the strength of the relations of the child to those holding these resources. For example, the education of a parent (or more generally, the parents' human capital) becomes available to the child only if the relationship of the child to the parent is sufficiently strong that the human capital is transmitted.

1. Types of Social Capital

Social capital that is important for child rearing is present in three aspects of social structure. One is the intensity of relations of adults to the child, the second is the relation between two adults who have relations of some intensity with the child, and the third is continuity of structure over time. In Fig. 1, (a) illustrates the first aspect, (b), (c), (d), and (e) represent the second aspect, realized in four different ways, and (f) represents the third.

1.1 Adult–Child Relationships

In Fig. 1, (a) may represent the relation between a parent and child. The relation between John Stuart Mill and his father James Mill was one of sufficient intensity that James Mill's learning was transmitted to his son. The relation between Bertrand Russell and his grandmother who raised him (and to whose philosophical probing he attributed his own intellectual development) constituted this form of social capital. If James Mill had been doing his writing in an office rather than at home, his attention and time would not have focused so intensively on his son. The son would not have been commenting on his father's and Jeremy Bentham's manuscripts at the age of 12. If Bertrand Russell's grandmother had not engaged him in philosophical debates, his intellectual skills would not have been sharpened.

The social capital in such cases lies, in terms of the diagram, in the capability of the relation between the two nodes, adult and child, to transmit from one to the other. The adult hobbyist who transmits excitement about his or her hobby, the swimming coach or violin teacher who transmits intensity of commitment to a goal, the parent who helps a teenager over one or another obstacle, or who has carried out sufficiently strong socialization that a child has internalized the parent's goals: all of these adults illustrate the way in which social capital of the form exemplified by Fig. 1(a) can be important in a child's development.

Social capital also lies in the capability of the relation between the two nodes to transmit a different range of content. Some relations can transmit emotional content, intimate sharing of feelings which can be important for social-psychological reasons. Such relations act as protection against social isolation, a protection identified by Durkheim (1951), in his extraordinary *Suicide*, first published in 1897.

This form of social capital can have a variety of effects on children and youth, some of which would not by any criterion be characterized as beneficial to

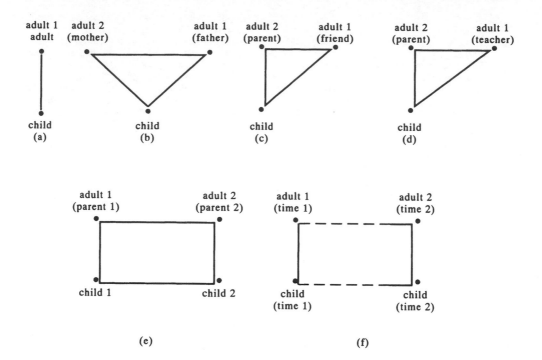

Figure 1
Social-structural forms through which social capital for childrearing is generated

the child. Sometimes a close relation between adult and child, unconstrained by incest taboos or other normative constraints on the adults, can lead to sexual exploitation of the child. Sometimes an emotional bond between child and parent can be so great that the parent has undue power over the child. Yet even with the potential for such perverse effects, the existence of a strong relation between adult and child must be regarded, on the whole, as social capital beneficial for the development of the child.

1.2 Adult–Adult–Child Relationships

Social capital of a second type is exemplified by Fig. 1(b), (c), (d), and (e). Here, the social capital resides in the existence of closure of a social network involving a child and two or more adults. It is present only when there is a relationship between two or more adults who themselves have a relationship to the child. The two adults are able to observe the child's actions in different circumstances, talk to each other about the child, compare notes, and establish norms. The closure of the relationship can both provide support and rewards for the child from additional adults that reinforce the rewards received from the first, and can bring about norms and sanctions that could not be instituted by the single adult alone.

In Fig. 1(b), the closure depends on the strength of relation between the two parents. If that relation is strong, the parents can act as a unit and consistently

toward the child. If it is weak, as in some families, or absent (as in the case of some divorced parents), the child confronts an environment with inconsistencies and conflicting signals. Nor are the parents able to reinforce each other in disciplining the child. In the extreme, the child plays off one parent against the other.

In Fig. 1(c), the closure is between a parent and another adult. The relation between the two can provide reinforcement for the parent in disciplining the child, if the other adult agrees, or a restraining influence if the other adult's experience is different. It can transmit from the parent to the other adult information about actions that the parent approves or disapproves of, and can thus strengthen the approval or disapproval the child receives; and it can transmit similar information from the other adult back to the parent.

In Fig. 1(d), the closure is between parent and teacher, a special case of the closure between the parent and another adult. This special case is of importance because in modern society school constitutes a large portion of a child's life and constitutes the major form of role differentiation that characterizes modern childhood. The teacher sees and knows the child in one context, in the role of student and of classmate to others of the same age. This is a quite different role from that observed by the parent. Thus the two have very different information about the child. The sharing of this information between them can lead them to take more mutually consistent actions toward the child, can strengthen their respective actions where their observations lead to a common conclusion, and again can lead to the creation of a norm enforced by both.

Figure 1(e) is another special case of closure, but one that is especially frequent: the closure occurs through a friend of the child, the friend's parent, and hence to the child's parent. In this case, the parents have similar tasks and similar goals in the development of their children. Without a relation to one another, these common interests—some in support of their children's activities, and some in support of one another in opposing their children's activities—have no way of mutual reinforcement. Their children have relations, develop joint strategies, and support one another in their actions. When their interests or values or tastes are opposed to those of their parents, they have the natural advantage of this mutual reinforcement if there is no comparable relationship among their parents. When their common interests demand protection from other actors (such as the school), the absence of a relationship among their parents makes each parent ineffective in opposing the school on the child's behalf.

The forms of closure shown in Fig. 1(b), (c), (d), and (e) are all forms that exist in a community in which neighbors know each other, children go to the same school, and teachers are part of the community. Such forms arise in a social structure that has the family as its basic building block.

1.3 Time-closure

The final case in Fig. 1, (f), represents social-structural closure of a different kind: time-closure. Time-closure of the relation between an adult and a child means that the adult in a particular type of relation with a child at one time is the same adult that was in this relation with this child at an earlier time. To some degree, all the relations in the figure imply continuity over time, or time-closure, in order that the relationship becomes established. However, time-closure is of importance in itself, apart from the intensity of relation it helps establish. Prospectively, it encourages investments in the other that will pay off only after some time. Also prospectively, it encourages trustworthiness, on the part of both the adult and the child, because each will have to confront the other in the future. Retrospectively, it gives the relationship a memory, which can provide the basis for placing trust, a potent form of social capital.

2. Conclusion

A number of authors have used the concept of social capital in various ways. These include Flap and De Graaf (1986), Loury (1981), Bourdieu (1980), and Coleman (1988, 1990 Chap. 12). With the decline in strength of family and community, the social capital held by a child and available for its development has become problematic, even when the other forms of capital—human, financial, and physical—have become more abundant in the child's environment.

See also: Family and School Environmental Measures; Family and Schooling; Family Influence on Human Development; Family, School, and Cultural Capital

References

Bourdieu P 1980 Le capital social. Notes provisaires. *Actes Recherche Sci. Soc.* 3: 2–3
Coleman J S 1988 Social capital in the creation of human capital. *Am. J. Sociol.* 94: S95–S120
Coleman J S 1990 *Foundations of Social Theory.* Harvard University Press, Cambridge, Massachusetts
Durkheim E 1951 (1st edn. 1897) *Suicide.* Free Press, New York
Flap H D, De Graaf N D 1986 Social capital and attained occupational status. *Netherlands J. Sociol.* 22: 145–61
Loury G 1981 Intergenerational transfers and the distribution of earnings. *Econometrica* 49: 843–67

Family Status and Economic Status

J. R. Behrman and † P. Taubman

The process by which people attain high economic status in modern industrial or postindustrial societies is a complex one. In preindustrial societies, inheritance or ascription of occupations and status were the norm. Capitalism and industrialism required a more effective utilization of talent. Ideally, jobs are to be allocated according to the match between competence and tasks. Formal education is the key instrument of such matching. However, apparently family status is an important predictor of economic status, even in industrial societies that define themselves as capitalist and meritocratic. What goes on in families and the relationship of families to the labor market seem to translate into more schooling and greater success in the labor market even when schooling is accounted for.

This article reviews the literature on the relationships between the family, education, and economic status. It focuses on developed countries, but much of the conceptual and empirical work also applies to developing countries. Although economic status can be defined either in terms of a person's income, earnings, wealth, or the quality or ranking of his or her occupation, the emphasis here is on family status, education, and occupational status. Comparisons of results are made using other concepts of status, such as earnings.

1. Occupational Status and Economic Status

1.1 Defining Occupational Status

Occupational status has been defined in a variety of ways. Duncan (1961) created an index from prestige rankings for 45 occupational titles. Using regression analysis, he related these rankings to census measures of both the percentage of male workers in each occupation who were at least high school graduates and the percentage in each occupation with a certain minimum level of income. The regression results were then used to assign status values to nearly 500 occupations. This index is stable across time and in other countries. For the 40–50 year old age group, the correlation of the index with the natural logarithm of current earnings is about 0.25 to 0.34 (Behrman et al. 1980 p.144). However, this observed correlation with earnings is lower than it might actually be. The scale of occupational status is forced into a range of 0–100 while earnings will often vary from hundreds of dollars to hundreds of thousands of dollars. Annual earnings also often have a great deal more statistical noise in them arising from the business cycle and bad or good luck in a particular year.

Occupational scales have also been created using measures of earnings and other criteria from census data in a selected year. Chamberlain and Griliches (1975), for example, used average earnings in the three-digit occupation "desired at age 30" for young men in the United States National Longitudinal Survey (NLS). (A three-digit code can specify a person's occupation and industrial sector, as well as their status as a "skilled" worker.) Alternatively, dummy (dichotomous) variables have been used, with the dummy set equal to 1 if the occupation meets a certain definition, namely "skilled" or falling between occupational code numbers N to (N + X). For example, Polachek (1981) explained women's selection into mutually exclusive occupations defined on the basis of wage level and attrition in wages when women are out of the labor force (for criticism of the Polachek model, see England 1982).

1.2 Adjusting Earnings for Occupational Characteristics

Attempts have also been made to "correct" earnings differences by adjusting them for occupational characteristics that reflect particularly dangerous or undesirable work, which therefore requires higher compensation. The theoretical basis for this "compensating differential" approach is presented in Thaler and Rosen (1975). They examine a labor market in which some jobs have a greater probability of resulting in an early death because of on-the-job accidents, murder, or ingestion of harmful substances (e.g., alcohol, asbestos, or coal dust).

They show that utility-maximizing individuals and profit-maximizing firms will adjust wages paid (to equally skilled workers) and expenditures on safety, health, and so on, until the supply and demand for each job are equalized. In this adjustment process riskier jobs pay a wage premium. The premium paid to induce the last needed worker—the worker who makes supply equal demand in any particular occupation and firm—to bear the extra risk can be estimated by comparing the wage rates of two persons alike in all other respects. However, if tastes differ, the least risk-averse individuals will be found in the most risky occupations and their premium will not be useful in determining how much more an average person would have to be paid to switch from the less to the more risky occupation under study.

The compensating variable scheme has been applied to characteristics other than likelihood of death. Examples include fluctuations in the wage or profit stream (see Taubman 1975, Weiss 1972, Hause 1974, Garen 1988); job injuries (Viscusi 1978), job turnover (Topel 1984), and disamenities (Lucas 1977). Often, controlling for these compensation variations substantially changes the estimate of the extra earnings associated with schooling.

1.3 Occupational Status during the Life Cycle

Both earnings and occupational status vary greatly during the life cycle. Mincer (1974) provided a thorough analysis for earnings changes over lifetime. Occupational status also changes over the life cycle. For example, Behrman et al. (1980 p.146) indicated that in a sample of White male twins born between 1917 and 1927, their initial full-time civilian job status index (on a scale from 0 to 100) averaged about 35, whereas in the 1960s the index averaged about 50. This difference is statistically significant. Olneck (1977), in a sample of men aged 35 – 59 years who attended school in Kalamazoo, Michigan, reported initial occupation scores of 40 and current occupational status (at age 46) of 50. He also reported results from a national representative sample—"Occupational Change in a Generation II"—for the same age range of 34 and 44. The initial status occupation measured 34 and the later status 43.

2. Explaining Occupational Success

Studies have been undertaken to "explain" both the level of occupational success and occupational success within family achievement. The analysis generally uses educational attainment, family socioeconomic status, and ability as key variables. In the within-family studies only variables that differ by individuals can be examined. Yet it is possible to adjust individual data for differences from the mean for the within variable, and then study the effects of common variables for individuals. Some of these studies estimate reduced form and/or structural equations using ordinary least squares (OLS) or some simultaneous equations method while others use path analysis (see Duncan 1966, Jencks et al. 1972). In some instances all these methods yield the same coefficients. In other cases, when the model is not statistically "just identified," the numerical estimates differ.

The studies generally focus on men. Women's occupational status and earnings are much more difficult to explain. A few studies have examined the determinants of female earnings, but the problem is complicated by the (changing) tendency of married women to drop out of the labor force. As Gronau (1974) and Heckman (1974) have shown, it is necessary to adjust for selectivity in estimating such earnings equations for women because those that stay in the labor force are a special group. Most studies of women have concentrated on earnings or wage rates and hours worked. Only a few have examined occupational status.

2.1 Occupational Success and Education

Education has been shown by many studies to exert a strong influence on the occupational attainment process. In a meritocratic society, education was assumed to be the dominant factor in social mobility. However, in the early 1960s the validity of this assumption was challenged by Anderson (1961), who argued that only a small part of a person's prospects of mobility can be explained by education. Boudon (1974) argued that a highly meritocratic society does not necessarily give those who have reached a high level of education more chance of promotion than those whose level is lower. Jencks et al. (1972) used a modification of the Duncan (1966) model to show that education is not as strong a factor in promoting social mobility as has been traditionally assumed. Using a similar model on Swedish (Malmö) longitudinal data, Fägerlind (1975) showed that the explanatory power of education and other variables of education and other variables varied according to the stage of the career being considered. Tuijnman (1989) took the same Malmö data and verified this finding, but also showed that youth education has a consistent and powerful effect on both occupational status and earnings throughout the life cycle.

2.2 Correcting for Other Variables

The relationship between occupational status and education may arise because of the underlying relationship of other variables. A major issue, therefore, in estimating the effects of education on occupational success is the bias arising from the omission of necessary controls from the equation. Controls can be either variables such as parental education or measures of family background as represented by family means or within sibling or twin pair representations. The findings in developed countries suggest that controlling for measured family background has little effect but controlling for measured ability or for genotype has a much greater effect on this relationship.

The usual measures of family background include parents' education, occupation, religion, the gender of the head of the family when the child was 14, birth order, number of siblings (which may be an endogenous variable), and residential location. When measures of the subject's own intelligence are included, most studies show that the coefficient on education decreases; yet overall, these controls generally do not have a large impact on the estimated effect of education on occupational status. However, occupational status is in part scored on the basis of average education, which may both bias the estimate of educational effects and minimize the intervening effect of other variables. Moreover, when earnings are the dependent variable, these controls reduce the effect of education by 10 percent to 25 percent, depending on what is measured and the stage of the life cycle when earnings are measured (Taubman 1989).

Several studies have tried to explain empirically occupational success using education and family background—broadly and narrowly defined—as controls. This section will consider the estimated relationships and any trends over the life cycle and time, and over generations. Many of the results are drawn from nonrandom samples, although results shown for occupational status and other dependent variables appear to be similar to those based on random samples.

The empirical results surveyed cover a wide span of years. For the United States the effect of education on occupational status is relatively time- and cohort-invariant, though there is a small negative association with age in a cohort. The major exception to this is the Chamberlain and Griliches (1975) study.

Research on occupational success was initiated in the 1960s with a study in the United States by Duncan (1961), and continued with Duncan et al. (1972). These studies mostly used the "Occupational Change in a Generation" (OCG) data, which was based on the March 1962 Current Population Survey. This was supplemented with some additional data. They obtained correlations from non-Black males in 10-year age cohorts beginning at age 25 and ending with age 64. The simple correlations between education and occupational status ranged from 0.56 to 0.65 and decreased slightly with age. The coefficient of education was about $0.5 - 0.6$ when controlling for the number of siblings, father's education, and father's occupation. This coefficient decreased with age. The same sample was analyzed by Bowles and Nelson (1974). Duncan et al. also replicated their findings in other samples, such as the Detroit Area Study of 1966 (Duncan et al. 1972).

More sophisticated results using samples with more interesting data began in the 1970s. Jencks et al. (1972) provided an excellent summary of then extant work on inequality in education, occupation, and income. They also extended much of the previous research and assembled results from previous studies using path analysis. They found that the correlation between father's and son's occupational status does not exceed 0.5. There was nearly as much status differential between fathers and sons or brothers as between randomly selected men. However, they also found that differences in education (not related to cognitive development) explained about 30 of the 60-point difference between the top and bottom fifth in occupational status. Each year of schooling added about six points to a status measure that had a standard deviation of 25 points. Jencks et al. (1972) also argued that some of the occupational success occurred because education is a credential rather than an enhancer of cognitive and other skills. They also presented some estimates of the impact of school quality on occupational quality. The best high school education could lead on to one more year of schooling and five points more in occupational status than the worst education.

Both earnings and occupational status have been correlated across the generations. Jencks et al. (1972) reported a correlation for status of about 0.5. Behrman and Taubman (1990), Solon (1992) and Zimmerman (1992) reported that annual earnings correlations are about half those for longer-run earnings.

Although estimates for parent–child correlation have focused on education, such estimates also exist for economic status. Most calculations for income or earnings are summarized in Behrman et al. (1980), Taubman (1989), or in Behrman et al. (1995). Using a year's measure of earnings taken from any point in which both generations were reporting, the correlation tended to be no higher than 0.25. However, if average earnings were used or if (in one sample) the earnings in both generations were taken from about age 40, the correlation coefficient (r) increased to more than 0.5.

Olneck (1977) presented results for both the Occupational Change in a Generation II (OCG-II), a United States random sample, and the Kalamazoo sample—data he collected. He showed that for the OCG-II sample of men aged 35 to 59, both initial occupation and current occupation displayed a positive simple correlation with test score (Kalamazoo only), father's education, and own education, whereas there were negative correlations with age and number of siblings. Moreover, the sibling correlation for initial occupation was about the same—near 0.4—for brothers born three or fewer years apart and more than three years apart. The simple sibling correlation for current occupational status was smaller for those born more than three years apart, but he did not control for the effect of age or experience in these calculations. Using number of siblings and father's education and occupation as independent variables, he found (in the Kalamazoo sample) a predicted

sibling correlation for occupational status of 0.2 for initial occupation and 0.09 for current occupational status (with no control for age or experience). He also found sibling correlation for current and initial occupation of 0.4 and 0.3. This suggested that there were important sources of sibling occupational similarity not captured by his measured variables.

The coefficients of years of schooling in initial and current occupation (in Kalamazoo) were about 0.5 when no other variables were controlled for. The coefficient was essentially unchanged when the above measures of family background were included. When regressions were estimated for pairs of siblings, the size of the impact of education on current occupation was reduced from 4.2 to 3.5, when no controls were included.

The Wisconsin Longitudinal Study (WLS), initially consisting of Wisconsin high school seniors who were administered the Hemon-Nelson intelligence test in the late 1950s, has been another important source of data in such studies (see Hauser and Mossel 1985). In the WLS, parental income was taken from the 1957 to 1960 Wisconsin tax returns and earnings were obtained from social security files (with an adjustment for the date at which the Old Age and Survivor's Disability Insurance (OASDI) tax reached its ceiling).

The results using the WLS showed—in the mid-1960s —substantial earnings returns to education. Hauser and Mossel (1985) reported that completed education (as reported by the respondent in 1975) had a correlation with 1970 and 1975 occupation of 0.6 and 0.6. They found slightly lower correlations with parent education (as reported by the parent). The slope coefficient for education was in the 0.6 and 0.7 range and was about the same when the respondents were treated as individuals or when within-sibling pair data were used.

Tuijnman's work on the Swedish data (1989), following on from Fägerlind's earlier study (1975), showed that occupational status at various ages was related significantly to adult ability, youth education, home background (family status), and adult education. Youth education continued to be highly significant even when these other variables were accounted for. This was also the case for earnings, except that neither adult or early ability (test score) were significant explainers and that family background was only significant in the prime of working life (age 35–43).

2.3 Controlling for Family Environment and Genetic Endowments

The WLS data have also been used to estimate the earnings–education relationship within and between families. In the sample of about 500 pairs, they found no significant differences in these estimates.

It is possible to use data on relatives to control for family environment and genetic endowments. Within-pair differences of identical twins control for genetic endowments and common environment. If the unmeasured specific endowment is uncorrelated with schooling, and if schooling is measured without error, the schooling coefficient estimate is unbiased. Taubman (1975) introduced the use of identical (MZ) and fraternal (DZ) twin data to economics. The difference between DZ twins and siblings is that the former are born much closer in time. For both groups, within-pair differences eliminate common environment and about half of the genetic endowment differences. In principle, the estimated coefficients need not be less biased than those based on individuals. The necessary conditions for a reduction in the bias are spelled out in Griliches (1979).

It is also possible to use other kin groups to construct controls for family environment and/or genetic endowments. For example, Scarr and Weinberg (1977) used data on adopted children. They showed that standard measures of family background have much smaller effects on children's occupational status than in data sets based on children living with their biological parents. Behrman and Taubman (1989) also showed how data on many different kin groups, including siblings and cousins, can be used to control for genotypic differences. However, they only applied their model to years of schooling.

Chamberlain and Griliches (1975) constructed a model using data for brothers, collected in 1927. They found that schooling had a coefficient of about 0.1 both in equations for individuals and in within-sibling pairs.

Behrman et al. (1980) used a large sample of White male twins (all veterans) born between 1921 and 1927 to formulate a latent variable decomposition model. The dependent variables were schooling, initial occupation, occupation in 1967, and the natural logarithm of earnings in 1973. When the twins were treated as individuals, the coefficient on schooling was 0.4 for initial occupation and 0.35 for 1967 occupation. When a long list of family background measures was included, the two coefficients fell to 0.37 and 0.33 (with the latter including the indirect effects from initial occupation).

The within-pair results were calculated separately for identical (MZ) and fraternal (DZ) twins. The effects of educational differences for initial occupation were 0.3 and 0.2 for DZ and MZ pairs respectively. For 1967 occupation, the total effect was 0.3 and 0.3 respectively. The system estimates were similar to those of the MZ within equation. Ashenfelter and Krueger (1994), using twins data collected at a twins convention and sib reports of schooling to control for measurement error, reported that measurement error accounted for the reduction in within-pair schooling effects and that there was no evidence of family endowment effects. But Behrman et al. (1994, 1996) and Miller et al. (1995) find that important family endowment effects remain even with control for measurement error in three twins sample (one birth-certificate-based, one census-based, and the one with White male veterans described above).

2.4 Conclusion

The statistical analyses indicate that education is strongly related to occupational status and earnings especially for men. However, much though not all of the relationship is attributable to the more educated differing in important characteristics from the less educated. Various techniques have been used to control for these characteristics including measures of intelligence, parental education, and studying outcomes within family groupings such as twins or brothers. Intergenerational correlations for education and economic status are positive and relatively large.

See also: Benefits of Education; Education, Occupation, and Earnings; Family and Schooling; Family, School, and Cultural Capital; Family, School, and Social Capital; Social Mobility, Social Stratification, and Education

References

Anderson C A 1961 A skeptical note on education and mobility. In: Halsey A H, Floud J, Anderson C A (eds.) 1961 *Education, Economy, and Society: A Reader in the Sociology of Education*. Free Press, New York

Ashenfelter O, Krueger A 1994 Estimates of the economic return to schooling from a new sample of twins. *Am. Econ. Rev.* 84(5): 1157–74

Behrman J R, Hrubec Z, Taubman P, Wales T J 1980 *Socioeconomics Success: A Study of the Effects of Genetic Endowments, Family Environment, and Schooling*. North-Holland, Amsterdam

Behrman J R, Pollak R A, Taubman P 1995 *From Parent to Child: Intrahousehold Allocations and Intergenerational Relations in the United States*. University of Chicago Press, Illinois

Behrman J R, Rosenzweig M R, Taubman P 1994 Endowments and the allocation of schooling in the family and in the marriage market: The twins experiment. *J. Pol. Econ.* 102(6): 1131–74

Behrman J R, Rosenzweig M R, Taubman P 1996 College choice and wages: Estimates using data on female twins. *Rev. Econ. Stat.* 73(4): 672–85

Behrman J R, Taubman P 1989 Is schooling mostly in the genes? Nature–nurture decomposition using data on relatives. *J. Pol. Econ.* 97(6): 1425–46

Behrman J R, Taubman P 1990 The intergenerational correlation between children's adult earnings and their parent's income: Results from the Michigan Panel Survey of Income Dynamics. *Rev. Inc. Wealth* 36(2): 115–27

Boudon R 1974 *Education, Opportunity, and Social Inequality: Changing Prospects in Western Society*. Wiley, New York

Bowles S, Nelson V 1974 The inheritance of IQ and the intergenerational reproduction of economic inequality. *Rev. Econ. Stat.* 56: 39–51

Chamberlain G, Griliches Z 1975 Unobservables with a variance components structure: Ability, schooling and the economic success of brothers. *Int. Econ. Rev.* 16(2): 422–29

Duncan O D 1961 A socioeconomic index for all occupations. In: Reiss A J (ed.) 1961 *Occupations and Social Status*. Free Press, New York

Duncan O D 1966 Path analysis: Sociological examples. *Am. J. Sociol.* 72(1): 1–16

Duncan O, Featherman D, Duncan B 1972 *Socioeconomic Background and Achievement.* Seminar Press, New York

England P 1982 The failure of human capital theory to explain occupational sex segregation. *J. Hum. Resources* 17(3): 358–70

Fägerlind I 1975 *Formal Education and Adult Earnings: A Longitudinal Study on the Economic Benefits of Education.* Almqvist and Wiksell, Stockholm

Garen J 1988 Compensating wage differentials and the endogeneity of job riskiness. *Rev. Econ. Stat.* 70(1): 9–16

Griliches Z 1979 Sibling models and data in economics: Beginnings of a survey. *J. Pol. Econ.* 87(5 pt.2): 537–64

Gronau R 1974 Wage comparison—A selectivity bias. *J. Pol. Econ.* 82(6): 1119–43

Hause J 1974 The risk element in occupation and educational choices: Comment. *J. Pol. Econ.* 82(4): 803–7

Hauser R, Mossel P 1985 Fraternal resemblance in educational attainment and occupational status. *Am. J. Sociol.* 91(3): 650–73

Heckman J 1974 Shadow prices, market wages, and labor supply. *Econometrica* 42(4): 679–94

Jencks C S et al 1972 *Inequality: A Reassessment of the Effect of Family and Schooling in America.* Basic Books, New York

Lucas R E B 1977 Hedonic wage equations and psychic wages in the returns of schooling. *Am. Econ. Rev.* 67(4): 549–58

Miller P, Mulvey C, Martin N 1995 What do twins studies tell us about the economic returns to education? A comparison of US and Australian findings. *Am. Econ. Rev.* 85(3): 586–99

Mincer J 1974 *Schooling Experience and Earnings.* National Bureau of Economic Research, New York

Olneck M 1977 On the use of sibling data to estimate the effects of family background, cognitive skills, and schooling: Research from the Kalamazoo brothers study. In: Taubman P (ed.) 1977 *Kinometrics: Determinants of Socioeconomic Success Within and Between Families.*

North-Holland, Amsterdam

Polachek S 1981 Occupational self-selection: A human capital approach to sex differences in occupational structure. *Rev. Econ. Stat.* 58(1): 60–69

Scarr S, Weinberg R 1977 The influence of "family background" on intellectual attainment: The unique contribution of adoptive studies to estimating environmental effects. Yale University, New Haven, Connecticut, Minnesota (mimeo)

Solon G R 1992 Intergenerational income mobility in the United States. *Am. Econ. Rev.* 82(3): 393–408

Taubman P 1975 *Sources of Inequality in Earnings: Personal Skills, Random Events, Preferences towards Risk, and other Occupational Characteristics.* North-Holland, Amsterdam

Taubman P 1989 Role of parental income in educational attainment. *Am. Econ. Rev.* 79(2): 57–61

Thaler R, Rosen S 1975 The value of saving a life: Evidence from the labor market. In: Terleckyj N (ed.) 1975 *Household Production and Consumption.* National Bureau of Economic Research, Cambridge, Massachusetts

Topel R 1984 Equilibrium earnings, turnover and unemployment: New evidence. *J. Labor. Econ.* 2(4): 500–22

Tuijnman A 1989 *Recurrent Education, Earnings, and Well-being: A Fifty-Year Longitudinal Study of a Cohort of Swedish Men.* Almqvist and Wiksell, Stockholm

Viscusi W 1978 Wealth effects and earnings premiums for job hazards. *Rev. Econ. Stat.* 60(4): 408–16

Weiss Y 1972 The risk element in occupational and educational choices. *J. Pol. Econ.* 80(6): 1203–13

Zimmerman D J 1992 Regression toward mediocrity in economic stature. *Am. Econ. Rev.* 82(3): 409–29

Further Reading

Orazen P, Matilla J 1986 Occupational entry and uncertainty: Males leaving high school. *Rev. Econ. Stat.* 68(2): 265–73

Home Environment and School Learning

A. J. Fuligni and H. W. Stevenson

Among the most important influences on children's academic achievement is their home environment. Until the 1970s, interest centered on determining the relation between school learning and demographic factors, such as gender, socioeconomic status (SES), family size, and birth order. Although demographic factors have remained of interest, the major concern is no longer the description of correlates of school learning but the analysis of the *processes* whereby demographic and other variables exert their effects. When demographic factors are studied, they are likely to be those that are relevant to contemporary families, such as mothers' working status, fathers' presence in the home, and the time spent in different types of parent–child interaction. These changes in interest

have led to research that encompasses a broader range of variables than was the case in the past.

1. Perspectives

The study of the effects of home environment on school learning, once almost the exclusive province of sociologists, has captured the attention of increasing numbers of developmental psychologists (see the review by Hess and Holloway 1984). By training and tradition, sociologists are interested in sociostructural variables. Psychologists are more likely to be interested in fine-grained analyses of behavior within the home environment. Both approaches are obviously important, and their combination is leading to a more detailed picture of the rich variety of ways in which the home environment can influence children's performance at school.

Contemporary sociologists such as Marjoribanks (1979) and Alexander and Entwisle (1988) have sought to bridge the gap between sociological and psychological approaches. Supplementing their work are analyses by psychologists of how environmental factors influence psychological processes, such as children's motivation, personality characteristics, attitudes, and beliefs, and how these in turn influence learning. The comprehensive nature of this research is illustrated in the collection of studies edited by Parke (1984).

The field has also benefited from the work of developmental psychologists who have highlighted the importance of the developmental status of the child. The home environment influences learning differentially according to the child's age. Variables affecting a 6- or 7-year old's learning do not necessarily operate in the same manner after the student has been in school for several more years. Moreover, the home environment may change markedly over this period. For example, parent–child interaction declines as children grow older. Parents may spend less than half the time in caretaking and interacting with children during the middle years of childhood than they did during the preschool years (Maccoby 1984). The meaning of other variables, such as paternal absence or parental level of education, may also differ according to the age of the child. By studying academic progress in conjunction with the rest of children's development, studies have yielded a better portrayal of the complex ways in which children may benefit or are impeded in their school learning by different types of home environments.

There has also been a growing interest in examining how home environments influence school learning in different cultures. This interest has its basis in both practical and theoretical concerns. The dramatic differences in academic achievement often found among children in different cultural groups has compelled researchers to look more closely at the environments in which these children live. Of more general theoretical concern is the interest in questions of whether the findings can be generalized across and within different cultural groups. The questions are of the following types: Does the amount of time spent assisting children at home with their schoolwork have an equally positive effect in cultures that place great value on education and in those where formal education is considered to be less important? Are variables that account for differences in achievement across cultures equally effective in explaining differences in achievement within cultures?

2. Changes in the Home Environment

The last half of the twentieth century has witnessed profound changes in family life throughout the world. Transitions from agrarian to industrialized economies, rapid advances in technology and automation, and breakdowns in traditional family structures have had ineradicable effects on the home life of families in both developing and industrialized societies. Stable, hierarchical organizations of family life have in many cultures given way to radical changes in the roles of parents and children. Traditional two-parent families have been replaced by single-parent households. Even in two-parent families, many mothers work full time and are unavailable during the day. The greater independence and at times estrangement of children from their parents is heightened in many societies by the high percentage of children who work in part-time jobs while attending school. As a consequence, factors outside the home come to play more important roles in children's lives. Peers often replace parents as the primary source of values and goals, and children's learning may depend more on their own social world than on what occurs at home.

These dramatic changes have required a new conceptualization of the home environment. Rather than considering the family as a firm structure in which roles are clearly defined and the direction of influence is predominantly from parents to children, the family is viewed as a dynamic system in which there is the potential for mutual influence among all participants. This view has added vitality to research on home influences, but there is only a vague understanding of how the complex interactions among family members influence the processes and outcomes of school learning.

3. Processes of Transmission

The influence of the home environment is transmitted to children in many different ways. These range from the effects of the objective, physical environment in which the child lives to the subjective, psychological environment created by parents through their child-rearing practices. Each of these will be explored in the following sections.

3.1 The Physical Environment

Little attention has been paid to the physical environment of the home as a contributor to school progress. Homes in industrialized countries are typically equipped with reasonable amounts of space, electricity, and other modern amenities. In contrast, homes in many developing countries lack even the most fundamental necessities, including adequate food and fresh water. It is hard to imagine how children living in these unhealthy environments can learn effectively at school. In many developing countries, the dramatic differences between the home environments of rural people, who lack nearly all modern conveniences, and those in the cities are accompanied by striking differences in what children are able to accomplish in school.

Even when economic conditions are not so dire, many parents in developing countries spend significant portions of their limited resources on tuition, books, and school uniforms. Their willingness to do this offers a much stronger indication to children of how their parents value education than is the case in more affluent societies where these expenditures place few limitations on other aspects of family life. Providing space for study imposes little sacrifice on families in industrialized societies, but places severe restrictions on the activities of other family members when the whole family must live in one or two rooms.

Children in economically sound families that do not allocate a quiet place in the home for studying or that fail to provide their children with desks or workbooks demonstrate their family's lack of support for education. Such conditions are less likely to occur in societies where strong emphasis is placed on education than in those where education is given a less central role in children's lives (Stevenson and Lee 1990).

3.2 The Child-rearing Climate

Explorations of the relation between the psychological climate within the family and children's development have a long tradition in research about children. One popular view is that of Baumrind (1973), who describes two important dimensions of family climates: (a) the degree of parental guidance and control; (b) the amount of emotional support and encouragement parents give to their children. A series of studies revealed small but consistent effects of child-rearing practices on children's academic performance during high school (Dornbusch et al. 1987, Steinberg et al. 1991). Students from "authoritative" households (those high in support and control) tended to have the highest grade-point averages. Their performance was better than that of students in either "authoritarian" households (those low in support and high in control) or in "permissive" households (those low in both support and control).

The relation between child-rearing and school performance is assumed to be mediated partly by the effects of child-rearing on other variables. For example, authoritative parenting is predictive of adolescents' self-reliance and feelings of autonomy. Thus, moderate amounts of parental control along with positive emotional support help to produce a sense of competence and confidence in children. These characteristics, in turn, are ones considered to be important for success in school.

Efforts have been made to ascertain whether the effects of authoritative parenting transcend cultural groups. Results from the Dornbusch et al. (1987) study of United States students suggest that the benefits are greatest for children from White households. Authoritative parenting was only slightly predictive of aca-

demic success among Hispanic-American adolescents, and not at all predictive among Asian- and African-American adolescents. Hess and Azuma (1991 p. 4) make a distinction between two modes of cultural transmission that influence the family climate: osmosis, where "nurturance, interdependence, and close physical proximity provide exposure to adult values and instill a readiness on the part of the child to imitate, accept, and internalize such values," and teaching, where "direct instruction, injunctions, frequent dialogue, and explanations are used." Japanese parents were much less willing than United States parents to assume the role of teacher. They tended to rely more strongly on modeling as the means of socialization, while parents in the United States depended upon a reward-based training strategy.

Children's success in school may depend, in part, on the extent to which mother–child interaction fits the cultural model and thereby matches the style of instruction in school. Hess and Azuma found, for example, that persistence in children, a highly admired trait among the Japanese, was significantly related to later academic achievement for Japanese children but not for children in the United States. In contrast, early independence, which is fostered in American culture, was a significant predictor for American, but not for Japanese children.

3.3 Parental Involvement

As children with increasingly diverse family backgrounds have begun to attend school, discord between the values and goals espoused by parents and by the schools has increased. For example, parents in many indigenous cultural groups appear to believe that a quiet child is preferable to a talkative one and may rely more closely on modeling and other nonverbal forms of instruction in teaching their children. Teachers at school, on the other hand, expect children to be able to express themselves verbally, and their teaching style relies heavily on verbal instruction. In attempting to reduce this discord between styles of teaching, efforts have been made to involve parents more closely in the activities of the school.

The degree of parental involvement varies widely. In some cases, teachers simply want to inform parents about their educational procedures and practices. In other cases, increased parental involvement means that parents are urged to become familiar with their children's daily assignments and progress. This may consist of attending parent–teacher meetings or of communicating daily with the teacher through the notebooks children carry back and forth between home and school. In still other cases, parents are expected to assume direct responsibility for establishing educational policies.

While the benefits of parental involvement in their children's education seem obvious, there has been little research to document the utility of the various forms this can take. Typical of the research that has been reported is the study of Stevenson and Baker (1987), who found that the extent to which parents were involved in school activities, such as parent–teacher organizations and parent–teacher conferences, was positively related to children's school performance. Involvement was greater among parents of younger children and among more highly educated mothers.

3.4 Cognitive Stimulation and Academic Assistance

More direct ways in which the home environment can influence school learning are through cognitive stimulation and assistance with schoolwork. Although in many societies these responsibilities lie with the mother, this is not always the case. In three-generation homes these tasks often become the province of grandparents; in other societies all members of the family, including siblings and other relatives, share these duties.

Despite the potential for cognitive stimulation that exists in all homes, some families do not provide their children with experiences that help assure their success in school. Efforts have been made to remedy these deficiencies by instructing parents about ways in which they can help their children, by talking with them, reading stories, providing toys, and playing games. In some programs, mothers also participate in groups that involve instruction and mutual support. Many of these home-based intervention programs have been found to improve children's later performance in school and, at times, to enhance their cognitive functioning (McCartney and Howley 1992). For example, simply having children read to their parents improves children's reading skills beyond what is achieved through ordinary instruction at school.

Parents' provision of out-of-home experiences, including taking children shopping, visiting zoos, museums, and libraries can also stimulate cognitive development. These opportunities for informal learning about the everyday world increase the fund of general information available to the child—a factor that has frequently been found to be predictive of skill in such subjects as reading and language arts.

The influence of direct assistance by parents on children's schoolwork is little understood. It is generally agreed that parental involvement and interest are necessary ingredients for academic success, but the form they take varies widely. Most parents in industrialized societies are capable of offering direct help to their children during the early years of elementary school, but fewer are able to do this when their children are in the later grades. Because of this, the primary way in which this interest is expressed is through the supervision of homework and the creation of an environment conducive to study. The "education moms" in many societies are distinguished not by direct forms of teaching but by the intense interest in education they convey to their children and the support they give to their children's efforts to achieve.

The value of practicing what has been learned in school by doing homework is regarded differently in different cultural groups. This was one of the most extreme differences found by Stevenson et al. (1990) in their comparisons of White, Black, and Hispanic parents. When asked about the value of increasing the amount of homework for improving elementary schoolchildren's performance, 88 percent of Black mothers, 74 percent of Hispanic mothers, but only 46 percent of White mothers answered affirmatively. This occurred despite the fact that, according to estimates made by the children's teachers, homework assignments given the previous week to children enrolled in minority schools required twice as much time to complete as the assignments given to children enrolled in all-White schools.

3.5 Beliefs and Attitudes

More subtle in their influence are the beliefs and attitudes parents hold about ways in which the home environment can influence school learning. Several reviews (Goodnow and Collins 1990, Miller 1988) have documented how beliefs held by family members affect children's development and how these, in turn, are related to their success in school.

One focus has been on parental expectations and their satisfaction with their children's academic progress. In a study of Chinese and American children and their parents, Chen and Uttal (1988) sought to discover sources of Chinese children's high achievement. Mothers were asked what score they would expect their children to obtain on a test with a maximum score of 100 and an average score of 70. Chinese and American mothers were equally positive in their expectations, but when they were asked about the score with which they would be satisfied, American mothers reported a score lower than the expected score and Chinese mothers reported a score higher than the expected score. High standards are critical in establishing high levels of motivation for achievement; children cease to be motivated to work harder when they believe they are already meeting the standards set by their parents and teachers.

Parents also hold strong beliefs about the relative contribution of innate ability and effort to children's achievement. The importance of effort is acknowledged by parents in all cultures. What differs is the degree to which parents in different cultures believe innate abilities limit what children are capable of accomplishing. As part of their cross-cultural studies of students' achievement, Stevenson and Lee (1990) examined mothers' beliefs about the roles of ability and effort in Japan, Taiwan, and the United States. Japanese and Chinese mothers gave greater emphasis to effort than did American mothers. Conversely, American mothers placed greater emphasis on the importance of innate abilities than the Japanese and Chinese mothers. A strong belief in innate ability undermines children's motivation to study hard. Parents, teachers, and children themselves believe that highly able children do not need to study hard to perform well and that intensive study is not especially productive for children with low levels of ability.

Beliefs and attitudes about ability and effort are also related to gender differences in academic achievement, especially in mathematics. Eccles (1983) is among those who have suggested that the gap in mathematics achievement between boys and girls in high school is due primarily to beliefs about their abilities and to the types of activities and classes in which they participate. Many parents believe that boys have innately superior abilities in mathematics. They believe that boys require less effort to do well in mathematics than do girls and they hold higher expectations for boys' performance. This is true even during the elementary school years, a period when boys and girls generally perform equally well. These beliefs about gender differences in mathematics ability exist in different cultures, even in such achievement-oriented countries as Japan and Taiwan (Lummis and Stevenson 1990).

4. Conclusion

The understanding of the relation of home environments to school learning is fragmentary and incomplete, despite its great practical importance to policymakers. Moreover, what is known comes primarily from studies undertaken in the West, which are often of little value to policymakers in other societies. There is great need for further expansion of research. Refinements in the meaning of categorical variables such as socioeconomic class have occurred. However, the means by which the economic and social status of families influence school learning is far from clear. The conceptualization of the home environment has expanded to include important factors such as belief systems and parent involvement, but research dealing with such topics needs to become more systematic and coherent.

Disentangling the direct and indirect ways in which factors within the home environment influence children's learning in school will be a slow process. Nevertheless, the increase in the number of cross-cultural and longitudinal studies, the greater interest in the interplay between children's developmental status and the characteristics of the home, and the trend toward studying variables that mediate between the home environment and school learning should gradually permit more comprehensive statements about this important topic.

See also: Family and School Environmental Measures; Family and Schooling; Family Influence on Human Development; Parent Involvement in Preschool Programs; Socialization

References

Alexander K L, Entwisle D R 1988 Achievement in the first two years of school: Patterns and processes. *Monogr. Soc. Res. Child Dev.* 53(2): 1–157

Baumrind D 1973 The development of instrumental competence through socialization. In: Pick A D (ed.) 1973 *Minnesota Symposium on Child Psychology*, Vol. 7. University of Minnesota Press, Minneapolis, Minnesota

Chen C, Uttal D 1988 Cultural values, parents' beliefs, and children's achievement in the United States and China. *Hum. Dev.* 31(6): 351–58

Dornbusch S, Ritter P, Leiderman P, Roberts D, Fraleigh M 1987 The relation of parenting style to adolescent school performance. *Child Dev.* 58(5): 1244–57

Eccles J 1983 Expectancies, values, and academic behaviors. In: Spence J T (ed.) 1983 *Achievement and Achievement Motivation*. Freeman, San Francisco, California

Goodnow J, Collins W A (eds.) 1990 *Development According to Parents: The Nature, Sources, and Consequences of Parents' Ideas*. Erlbaum, Hove

Hess R D, Azuma H 1991 Cultural support for schooling: Contrasts between Japan and the United States. *Educ. Researcher* 20(9): 2–8

Hess R D, Holloway S D 1984 Family and school as educational institutions. In: Parke R D (ed.) 1984

Lummis M, Stevenson H 1990 Gender differences in beliefs and achievement: A cross-cultural study. *Dev. Psychol.* 26(2): 254–63

Maccoby E 1984 Middle childhood in the context of the family In: Collins W A (ed.) 1984 *Development During Middle Childhood: The Years from 6 to 12*. National Academy Press, Washington, DC

Marjoribanks K 1979 *Families and Their Learning Environments: An Empirical Analysis*. Routledge and Kegan Paul, London

McCartney K, Howley E 1992 Parents as instruments of intervention in home-based preschool programs. In: Okagaki L, Steinberg R J (eds.) 1992 *Directors of Development: Influences on the Development of Children's Thinking*. Erlbaum, Hillsdale, New Jersey

Miller S 1988 Parents' beliefs about their children's cognitive development. *Child Dev.* 59(2): 259–85

Parke R D (ed.) 1984 *Review of Child Development Research. Vol. 7: The Family*. University of Chicago Press, Chicago, Illinois

Steinberg L, Mounts N, Lamborn S, Dornbusch S 1991 Authoritative parenting and adolescent adjustment across varied ecological niches. *J. Res. Adol.* 1(1): 19–36

Stevenson D, Baker D 1987 The family–school relation and the child's school performance. *Child Dev.* 58(5): 1348–57

Stevenson H W, Chen C, Uttal D 1990 Beliefs and achievement: A study of Black, White, and Hispanic children. *Child Dev.* 61(2): 508–23

Stevenson H W, Lee S Y 1990 Contexts of achievement: A study of American, Chinese, and Japanese children. *Monogr. Soc. Res. Child Dev.* 55(1,2): 1–116

Further Reading

McAdoo H P, McAdoo J L (eds.) 1985 *Black Children: Social, Educational, and Parental Environments*. Sage, Beverly Hills, California

Mussen P H, Flavell J, Markman E (eds.) 1983 *Handbook of Child Psychology. Vol. 4: Socialization, Personality, and Social Development.* Wiley, New York

Rooparnine J L, Carter D B 1992 *Parent–Child Socialization*

in Diverse Cultures. Ablex, Norwood, New Jersey

Stevenson H W, Stigler J W 1992 *The Learning Gap: Why our Schools are Failing and What We Can Learn from Japanese and Chinese Education.* Summit, New York

Kinship Studies

J. R. Behrman and †P. Taubman

Analysis of kin data provides valuable insights into four questions about education: (a) To what extent is there intergenerational mobility in schooling? (b) What role does family background, and in particular genetic endowments and family-determined environment, play in determining educational attainment? (c) What determines the family's expenditures on each child? (d) How are estimates of education's impact on socioeconomic outcomes biased by not controlling for factors such as ability and motivation?

While several kin data sets permit exploration of the first question, few adult sibling data sets permit full investigation of the last three questions. Most analysis has been on samples that are not representative. In most studies education is represented by grades of schooling. Some potentially important statistical issues affect the estimates based on kin samples.

Intergenerational variability is less for schooling than for other observed measures of welfare, such as socioeconomic status (SES) and may be a brake on socioeconomic mobility. Sibling studies suggest that, for the United States, the variance in family background accounts for about three-quarters of schooling's intragenerational variance for White males born in the early twentieth century. Twin data indicate this family background contribution can be decomposed into genetic and family-determined environmental factors of about equal impact. Sibling studies indicate that the pattern of intrafamily expenditures on children's education reflects a mixture of expected returns and inequality aversion. Intrafamilial allocations are not consistent with pure investment models of education. Analyses of sibling data suggest that standard estimates of increased earnings due to education may be overstated—perhaps by a factor of two to three—because there was no controlling for partially unobserved abilities and motivations.

Kin data generally imply considerably less optimism than standard analyses about the extent to which education affects socioeconomic outcomes and leads to greater equality of opportunity.

1. Siblings, Twins, and Other Kin Data for Studies of Education

Education is the process through which individuals learn about their environment, how it functions, and how it can be altered. On-the-job training, reading, exposure to media of communication, verbal interchange, and many other experiences may make important contributions to education. Different individuals have different learning aptitudes because of differing genetic and nonschooling endowments. Individuals with identical grades of schooling may have highly varying education. Nevertheless, most studies define education in terms of grades of formal schooling completed.

Schooling is a better representation of education the more it is associated with the capacity for learning from other experiences. Schooling is of particular interest because it is amenable to policy.

In many surveys, respondents provide information on their parents' and their own schooling that can be used to study intergenerational mobility. Although some data sets are for special populations, others are representative of large populations and have sufficient observations to permit statistical testing of hypotheses. Contemporaneously collected (as opposed to recalled) data on more than two generations are relatively rare.

Many data sets do not have sufficient information to examine many dimensions of the last three questions in the introductory paragraph of this entry, which require information on adult socioeconomic outcomes. Brief descriptions of most of the major relevant data sets are given below (more details concerning the first five items and item (k) are in Taubman 1977, and details on items (b), (d), and (h)–(j) are in Jencks and Bartlett 1979).

(a) 156 pairs of brothers from Indianapolis with income measured in 1927 (Gorseline data, Chamberlain and Griliches 1975).

(b) 2,478 pairs of White male twins (about half identical) born in the United States in 1917–27, both veterans; health and some socioeconomic data from military records and repeated surveys from 1967 onwards (National Academy of Science–National Research Council , Twin Registry (Behrman et al. 1977, 1980). Offspring data are available so it is possible to obtain correlations for other kin groups such as first cousins (Behrman and Taubman 1989).

(c) 292 pairs of brothers from the United States surveyed in 1966–71 and biannually (National Longitudinal Survey of Young Men, Chamberlain and Griliches 1975).

(d) 346 pairs of brothers in sixth grade between 1928 and 1950 in Kalamazoo, Michigan with socioeconomic data collected in 1973–74 (Olneck 1977).

(e) 2,000 brothers and sisters, one member a senior in secondary school in Wisconsin, United States, in 1957, with socioeconomic data from school records, parental income tax data, and surveys over the next two decades (Wisconsin Data, Sewell and Hauser 1977).

(f) About 500 pairs of sisters from Nicaragua in 1977–78 with socioeconomic data (Behrman and Wolfe 1984, 1989).

(g) About 80,000 people in some 270 "families" one member of which was institutionalized in 1900–18 because of mental retardation. A family contains all the descendants and spouses of each set of grandparents over the period 1800 to 1960. The data includes education, occupation, and IQ scores. (Reed and Reed 1965).

(h) 150 pairs of brothers in the United States age 35–64 in 1973 (National Opinion Research Center, Eagersfield 1979).

(i) 50 pairs of brothers in grades 11 and 12 in 1960 in the United States interviewed in 1971–72 (Jencks and Brown 1977).

(j) 151 individuals from 66 families in which one of the parents died in Cleveland, United States, in 1964–65 (Lindert 1977, Brittain 1976).

(k) 312 New Jersey 55–61-year old male employees of a utility company who gave information on their siblings' age, sex, education, and most recent occupation (Lindert 1977).

(l) About 5,000 siblings in the National Longitudinal survey of young men and women studied from the late 1960s through the early 1980s (Neumark 1988, Altonji and Dunn 1990).

(m) About 4,000 siblings, brothers and sisters, in the Panel Study of Income Dynamics (PSID) studied from 1968 through 1987 (Solon et al. 1987, Behrman and Taubman 1990).

(n) About 8,400 male and female twin pairs born in Minnesota between 1936 and 1955 with some 1,200 male pairs born between 1971 and 1981 (Lykken et al. 1990).

Thus, sibling data sets with information on adult outcomes are few in number, come largely from the United States, and are often small and based on sample designs that may not be representative of larger populations. The sibling samples cannot be completely random since they do not include representatives of single-child households. Most of the relevant studies address the question of representativeness by comparing sample characteristics or regression coefficients with those from random samples. Such comparisons indicate that most of these data sets have more general validity. Within-sibling estimates control for selectivity based on unobserved family characteristics.

2. Kin Data and Intergenerational Schooling Mobility

Intergeneration mobility refers to the relative position of a family in one generation versus their children's relative position. If the absolute value of the correlation between generations is close to one, there is almost no intergenerational mobility. If it is close to zero, there is considerable intergenerational mobility. Social mobility is usually regarded as a desirable characteristic.

Intergenerational correlations for schooling from a number of quite different samples—including (b), (d), (f), (h), (l), (m), and (n) in Sect. 1 and several others in Jencks and Bartlett 1979—are in the 0.3–0.5 range. The intergenerational correlations for SES are never larger, and are in the 0.2–0.4 range. Thus there is considerable intergenerational mobility for schooling. Fewer samples are available to make comparisons for income or earnings measured at the same point in the life cycle. Dwyer and Phelan (1976) estimate the intergenerational earnings correlation in sample (e) at about 0.33. Behrman and Taubman (1985) estimate this correlation R as no more than 0.2 using sample (b) augmented with children's data. However, these estimates are based on a single year's earning measure that can be atypical of a person's average income because of life cycle and business cycle factors. Adjusting for these in the PSID leads to an R of up to about 0.7 (Behrman and Taubman 1990).

3. Investment Model of Education and Role of Family

The economic analysis of education often focuses on its investment dimension (but see Sect. 7). There is an expected return to education, which depends on motivations and abilities that vary with genetic endowments and nonfamily environment. The downward sloping curve (DD) in Fig. 1 gives an individual's locus of such returns.

An individual with greater capabilities has a curve above the indicated one. The horizontal curve (SS) in Fig. 1 gives the marginal cost of investment in education. The maximizing investment is E_0, where the expected marginal return is equal to the marginal

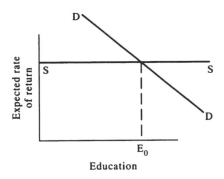

Figure 1
Determinants of education within investment model with horizontal marginal costs

cost. This framework has been refined to explore more complex issues (Becker 1967, Rosen 1976), but Fig. 1 captures its essence.

Across families there may be differences in capabilities that imply systematic differences in average family marginal return curves and (given capital market imperfections) in marginal costs of educational investments.

Siblings may have different expected returns because of different capabilities or because of imperfections in labor markets (discrimination against women implies that a girl's expected returns may be less than those for her equally capable brother).

4. Variance Decomposition Estimates

The simplest form of variance decomposition analysis assumes that the optimal schooling (S) for a given individual reflects his or her genetic endowments (G), family-determined environment (N), and other random environmental determinants (U) in an additive relation:

$$S = G + N + U \qquad (1)$$

Taubman (1981) argues that variation in N may be an important component of inequality of opportunity, the elimination of which improves economic efficiency. Generally, it is not possible to determine how important each of the right-side components are in determining schooling, because these variables are unobserved.

Data on twins make possible one somewhat controversial approach to at least a partial decomposition of the variance of each of the right-side variables. First rewrite equation (1) with the environmental variables combined into one (N + U = V):

$$S = G + V \qquad (2)$$

Schooling is an observed phenotype that equals the sum of G and N, which are assumed to be uncorrelated. The total phenotypic variance is:

$$\sigma_S^2 = \sigma_G^2 + \sigma_V^2 \qquad (3)$$

The alphabetical order of first names can be used to designate twin 1 and twin 2. By arranging all twin 1's by family number and doing the same for all twin 2's, the cross-twin covariance can be calculated by treating schooling for twin 1 and twin 2 as two separate variables. Then, by calculating the covariance separately for monozygotic (identical) and dizygotic (fraternal) twins, each of the two twin covariances can be expressed in terms of σ_G^2 and σ_V^2 and other unknown parameters. In the most general form, there are seven unknown parameters. The observed variance and covariances can be used to estimate no more than three unknowns; therefore a much simpler model must be employed (or more outcomes observed; see Sect. 5).

Heritability is defined as the proportion of the observed variance that comes from genotypic variation:

$$h^2 = \frac{\sigma_G^2}{\sigma_S^2} \qquad (4)$$

The calculation and interpretation of heritability estimates has generated considerable controversy (Goldberger 1977, 1979, Taubman 1978, 1981). In the simplest model, h^2 is estimated as twice the difference in the two twin correlations.

The assumption that the expected covariance in environments does not vary between types of twins is critical. There is some direct evidence that monozygotic twins are more alike in some respects than are dizygotic twins (for example, clothing). However, environmental differences may be in response to genetic differences and not just a desire to treat identical twins more alike. Scarr-Salapatck (1965) has examined cases in which parents have been mistaken regarding their twins' zygosity and has concluded that the parental choices are responsive to genetic factors whether or not parents correctly know the twin type.

While some researchers have been comfortable with this assumption, others have been extremely critical and have argued that heritability is overestimated since more similar environments for monozygotic twins are wrongly attributed as genetic effects. However, Taubman (1981) and Behrman et al. (1980) argue that it is legitimate to count that part of the environment that is a response to genetic differences as due to genetic differences.

Some researchers have interpreted high heritability estimates to mean that the phenotypic outcome could not be changed by variations in the environment. Such an inference is clearly wrong. Figure 2 provides an illustrative example.

The horizontal axis measures the environment (V), the vertical axis a phenotypic outcome such as schooling, and the curves A and B give the reaction of schooling to different environments for the only two

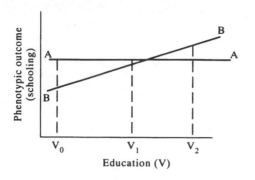

Figure 2
Reaction functions for genetic groups A and B with environment to determine schooling

genetic groups in the relevant population. Assuming that environment is identical for everyone, say at V_0, in this case a calculation of heritability indicates that all of the variance in schooling is due to genetic differences between group A and group B. However, that does not imply that environmental changes are ineffective, since these are measured by the slope of the curves A and B. Schooling inequality could almost be eliminated, for example, by changing everyone's environment to V_1, or the inequality could be reversed by changing only group B's environment to V_2. Heritability refers to a given distribution of other factors. It describes a particular situation, but does not indicate what phenotypic changes would occur if there were environmental changes.

5. Extended Latent Variable—Variance Decomposition Models

Heritability studies have been extended to a multi-equation context that allows better control for, and estimation of, the effects of unobserved or "latent" variables, such as family background, genetic endowments, and environment (Behrman et al. 1980, Chamberlain and Griliches 1975). This extension provides better estimates both of the determinants of schooling and of possible biases in the estimation of the impact of schooling.

If a latent variable is associated with enough observed variables, its variance may be estimated. For example, in Eqn. (3) above there are two unobserved variances that cannot be estimated since the only observable datum is the variance of schooling. But suppose that in addition to Eqn. (2) there were a series of other outcomes (Y_i) that depend on the same genetic endowments (G), schooling (s) and independently distributed environmental factors (V_i) in an additive manner:

$$Y_i = a_i s + b_i G + V_i \qquad (5)$$

For each additional relation three unknowns are added (i.e., a_i, b_i, and σ_v^2) However, observable data also increase; there are variances of the new variables, and their covariances with all other observed variables. With enough relations there are enough data points to estimate all of the unknown parameters. For example, with Eqn. (2) and 4 additional observed indicators determined as in Eqn. (5), there are 15 observed variances or covariances and 15 unobserved variances to be estimated (i.e., 4 a_i's, 4 b_i's, and 5 σ_v^2, σ_{SG}, and σ_G^2).

The latent variable methodology requires a relatively large number of observed variables to identify a fairly simple model (for example, genetic and environmental factors are uncorrelated, and environmental factors are independent across relations). However, sibling data increase substantially the observed covariances for a given number of Y_i because of the additional covariances among siblings. Related models have been developed by Chamberlain and Griliches (1975) for siblings and by Behrman et al. (1977) for twins. In the sibling models the researchers identify the latent variables as family factors (common to all siblings) and individual factors. In the twin models the researchers identify them as genetic endowments and family environmental factors.

The latent variable twins model is a more satisfactory framework for obtaining heritability estimates than the procedures reviewed in this section because it requires weaker assumptions. However, the controversial assumption regarding equal expected environmental correlations for the two types of twins still cannot be tested.

Behrman and Taubman (1989) adopt a model proposed by Fisher (1918) and use a larger group of kin groups to obtain heritability estimates. Fisher develops a three-parameter model of genotypic correlation of various kin groups under the assumption that (except for assortative mating) there is no correlation in the environments of kin. Behrman and Taubman partial out the effects of measured "environmental" variables such as father's occupation using a regression and then apply Fisher's method. They exploit the fact that first cousins whose fathers are identical twins are, from a genetic viewpoint, half sibs. They use both generations in the NAS–NRC sample to estimate an h^2 for years of schooling of about 0.8.

6. The Family Role in the Intragenerational Variance of Schooling

While there are a large number of estimates of heritability of IQ based on the model in Sect. 4 (Jencks et al. 1972), estimates for schooling are much less common. The correlations for schooling for monozygotic and dizygotic twins are 0.78 and 0.53 in the NAS–NRC sample used by Behrman et al. (1980). About half of the intragenerational variance in schooling for white males is accounted for by variance in the genetic components (h^2 about 0.5).

With the latent variable extended-twin model (Sect. 5) and a distinction in the schooling relation between family-determined environment and other environment as in Eqn. (1), Behrman et al. (1980) decompose this same schooling variance into 32 percent from genetic variance, 45 percent from family-determined environmental variance, and 23 percent from other environmental variance.

7. Pure Investment versus Inequality Aversion

The investment model of education in Sect. 3 assumes pure maximization of expected returns from education without any consideration of allocation within the family.

Behrman et al. (1982) develop a model that permits the testing of whether a family's allocation of schooling among children reflects pure maximization of expected returns, pure inequality aversion, or some combination. The model posits that the distribution of schooling among children in a family is the outcome of the maximization of parental utility that depends upon each child's earnings capacity. The utility function is maximized subject to both a budget constraint and the earnings production function that depends on schooling, other parental investments, and genetic endowments. Figure 3 illustrates this model.

The axes refer to expected earnings of the ith and j^{th} children in a family. The curve UU is a parental indifference curve based on the distribution of expected returns between these children. The case drawn reflects a balance between pure investment and pure inequality aversion concerns. If the parents were concerned only with the child with the lowest expected earnings, this curve would be square-cornered along the 45 degree line from the origin. If the parents were indifferent about the distribution of expected earnings, this curve would be a straight line from a given ex-

pected earnings level for one child to an identical level for the other.

The curve EE is the expected earnings frontier between these two children, given the budget- and earnings-capacity production-function constraints and the relative genetic endowments of the two children. This curve is drawn to reflect the relatively better genetic endowment of the ith child. Curve E'E' is for a different family in which the genetic endowment of the jth child is relatively better. The variance in such relative genetic endowments across families enables one to trace the curvature of the parental indifference curve, and to estimate the parental weight on inequality aversion versus pure investment maximization in their allocation of schooling among their children.

The extent of parental inequality aversion can be estimated with data on siblings' education and their expected earnings. Behrman et al. (1982) estimate this model using adult earnings as a proxy for expected earnings for the adult male United States dizygotic twins in item (b) in Sect. 1. The estimates are substantially and significantly different from the extremes of complete inequality aversion (Rawls 1971) and of pure returns maximization. Such estimates imply that parental allocation of resources to their children's schooling mitigates substantially the intrafamilial inequality of genetic endowments as compared with the pure investment model outcome.

Becker and Tomes (1976) have proposed a similar model in which parents' utility derived from each child depends on the sum of that child's expected earnings and returns from financial bequests. Since it is assumed that there are no diminishing returns to financial investments but diminishing returns to schooling investments, parents who plan to leave bequests should only spend for schooling on each child to a point where its return equals the return earned on financial investments. Parents should invest efficiently in each child's education and then compensate the less able with larger financial bequests.

Behrman et al. (1991) show that the Becker–Tomes conclusion only holds if parents have enough wealth to equalize children's income. Since they find that average annual absolute differences in siblings' earnings are in the US $6,000–$10,000 ranges, very large wealth differentials would be needed to generate offsetting annual returns from capital. They evaluate the available empirical evidence regarding patterns of bequest differentials, earnings differentials, and transfer differentials to discriminate between these models. They conclude that the evidence is less consistent with the Becker and Tomes (1976) model than with the Behrman et al. (1982) model.

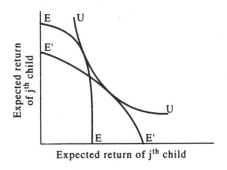

Figure 3
Parental preferences (UU) and two alternative expected returns frontiers (EE, E'E') reflecting differential relative genetic endowments

8. Biases in Standard Estimates of the Impact of Schooling

There are many estimates of the impact of schooling on earnings, and other factors. However, such estimates may be biased because of the failure to control for unobserved variables (e.g., ability and motivation). Consider estimation of Eqn. 5. With ordinary estimation techniques, estimates of the schooling coefficient are biased upward if significant genetic and environmental variables, which are positively correlated with schooling, are omitted. In multivariate estimates of the impact of schooling, an attempt has been made to include available measures of ability and of family background. Generally, the inclusion of these variables has resulted in lower estimates of the effects of schooling. These findings suggest that there are important variables that are positively correlated with schooling (Jencks and Bartlett 1979).

Sibling data permit controlling for certain dimensions of family background that are usually unobserved and that may cause biases. For the special case of monozygotic twins, Eqn. (6) controls for genetic background and common environment (where ΔU_i is assumed to be noncommon environment):

$$\Delta Y_i = a_i \Delta S + \Delta U_i \qquad (6)$$

For fraternal twins and other siblings, the differenced version controls for common environment, but not for differences in genetic background:

$$\Delta Y_i = a_i \Delta S + b_i \Delta G + \Delta U_i \qquad (7)$$

The latent variable models of Sect. 5 provide a somewhat more satisfactory control for unobserved variables (they permit combining monozygotic twins with other siblings in the same estimate).

Measurement error also leads to biased estimates. Such "noise" in independent variables tends to bias their estimated coefficients toward zero (Griliches 1979). When sibling differences are the unit of observation, measurement error may be more prominent, and biases from this source may be increased. However, measurement error does not seem to account for most of the difference between the differenced siblings estimates and the nondifferenced estimates (Behrman et al. 1980, Jencks and Bartlett 1979). Moreover, if measurement error is correlated between the siblings (due to schooling quality, for example), the bias is much smaller and may be in the other direction (Behrman 1984)

The estimated results from sibling data do not suggest large omitted variable bias if applied to samples (a) and (c) in Sect. 1 (Chamberlain and Griliches 1975). However, it is not possible to generalize from the samples since the former is regionally localized with overrepresentation of occupations in which nonpecuniary returns are relatively important (e.g., teaching), and the latter is of men at very early stages of their life cycle with expected, not actual, occupations used in the analysis.

Other sibling studies suggest that standard methods overestimate considerably the impact of education on later socioeconomic outcomes (Olneck 1977,

Behrman et al. 1977, 1980, Behrman and Wolfe 1984, 1989, Wolfe and Behrman 1986, 1987). For sample (d), controlling for common background of brothers reduces the estimated schooling impact on early occupational status by 11 percent, on mature occupational status by 20 percent, and on earnings by 33 percent. For sample (b), controlling for common environment and common genetics reduces the estimated schooling impact on early occupation status by about 33 percent and on earnings by about 25 percent. In the same sample controlling for all genetic endowments and common environment reduces the estimated schooling effect on early occupational status by 50 percent, on mature occupational status by 12 percent, and on earnings by 70 percent. For sample (f), controlling for common genetics and common environment reduces the estimated schooling effect on income by about 40 percent and on fertility and child health by 100 percent.

Such evidence is not conclusive because of the special nature of existing sibling samples and possible measurement bias and contradictory results. However, it does suggest the possibility that standard estimates substantially overestimate the impact of education on important socioeconomic outcomes.

9. Conclusion

Samples of twins, siblings, and other kin have been used to study issues related to the determinants of schooling and subsequent socioeconomic outcomes. There is considerable but incomplete intergenerational schooling mobility. The family plays a major role in determining intragenerational inequality in schooling and in earnings. There is some evidence, not accepted by all researchers, that much of this inequality is attributable to differences in genetic endowments. Evidence also exists that parents care about inequality of earnings capacity among their offspring, and provide more schooling to the less able than would be the case if they were only concerned about the total earnings of their offspring.

Finally, these kin-related samples have been used to eliminate or reduce the bias in estimates of the impact of schooling. While the evidence is mixed, these studies suggest the possibility that studies of the schooling effects based on individuals may be strongly biased upward.

See also: Family Status and Economic Status

References

Altonji J, Dunn T 1990 Relationships among the family incomes and labor market outcomes of relatives. Northwestern University, Evanston, Illinois (mimeo)

Becker G S 1967 *Human Capital and the Personal Distribution of Income: An Analytical Approach* (Woytinski Lecture). Institute of Public Administration, Ann Arbor, Michigan

Becker G S, Tomes N 1976 Child endowments and the quantity and quality of children. *J. Pol. Econ.* 84(4 Pt.2): S143–62

Behrman J R 1984 Sibling deviation estimates, measurement error and biases in estimated returns to schooling. University of Pennsylvania, Philadelphia, Pennsylvania (mimeo)

Behrman J R, Hrubec Z, Taubman P, Wales T J 1980 *Socioeconomic Success: A Study of the Effects of Genetic Endowments, Family Environment, and Schooling.* North-Holland, Amsterdam

Behrman J R, Pollak R A, Taubman P 1982 Parental preferences and provision for progeny. *J. Pol. Econ.* 90 (1): 52–73

Behrman J R, Pollak R A, Taubman P 1991 Some causes and consequences of death. University of Pennsylvania, Philadelphia, Pennsylvania (mimeo)

Behrman J R, Taubman P 1985 Intergenerational earnings mobility in the US: Some estimates and a test of Becker's intergenerational endowments model. *Rev. Econ. Stat.* 67: 144–51

Behrman J R, Taubman P 1989 Is schooling "mostly in the genes"? Nature nurture decomposition using data on relatives. *J. Pol. Econ.* 97(6): 1425–46

Behrman J R, Taubman P 1990 The intergenerational correlation between children's adult earnings and their parents income: Results from the Michigan panel survey of income dynamics. *Rev. Income and Wealth* 36(2): 115–27

Behrman J R, Taubman P, Wales T J 1977 Controlling for and measuring the effects of genetics and family environment in equations for schooling and labor market success. In: Taubman P (ed.) 1977

Behrman J R, Wolfe B L 1984 The socioeconomic impact of schooling in a developing country. *Rev. Econ. Stat.* 66(2): 296–303

Behrman J R, Wolfe B L 1989 Does more schooling make women better nourished and healthier? Adult sibling random and fixed effects estimates for Nicaragua. *J. Hum. Resources* 24(4): 644–63

Brittain J 1976 *The Inheritance of Economic Status.* Brookings Institution, Washington, DC

Chamberlain G, Griliches Z 1975 Unobservables with a variance-component structure: Ability, schooling and the economic success of brothers. *Int. Econ. Rev.* 16(2): 422–49

Dwyer J, Phelan T 1976 Education in America and the reproduction of social inequality: A method divergent model of indicator error. State University of New York, Stony Brook, New York (mimeo)

Eagersfield D 1979 The NORC brothers sample. In: Jencks C S, Bartlett S (eds.) 1979

Fisher R A 1918 The correlation between relatives on the supposition of Mendelian inheritance. *Transactions of the Royal Society Edinburgh* 52(2): 399–433

Goldberger A 1977 Twin methods: A skeptical view. In: Taubman P (ed.) 1977

Goldberger A 1979 Heritability. *Economica* 46(184): 327–47

Griliches Z 1979 Sibling models and data in economics: Beginnings of a survey. *J. Pol. Econ.* 87(5 Pt. 2): S37–64

Jencks C S, Bartlett S 1979 *Who Gets Ahead? The Determinants of Economic Success in America.* Basic Books, New York

Jencks C S, Brown M 1977 Genes and social stratification: A methodological exploration with illustrative data. In: Taubman P (ed.) 1977

Jencks C S et al. 1972 *Inequality: A Reassessment of the Effect of Family and Schooling in America.* Basic Books, New York

Lindert P 1977 Sibling position and achievement. *J. Hum Resources* 12(2): 198–219

Lykken D T, Bouchard T J Jr, McGue M, Tellegen A 1990 The Minnesota twin family registry: Some initial findings. *Acta Geneticae Medicae et Gemellologiae* 39(1): 35–70

Neumark D 1988 Employer's discriminatory behavior and the estimation of wage discrimination. *J. Hum. Resources* 23(2): 279–95

Olneck M 1977 On the use of sibling data to estimate the effects of family background, cognitive skills and schooling: Results from the Kalamazoo study. In: Taubman P (ed.) 1977

Rawls J 1971 *A Theory of Justice.* Belknap Press, Cambridge, Massachusetts

Reed E, Reed S 1965 *Mental Retardation: A Family Study.* Saunders, Philadelphia, Pennsylvania

Rosen S 1976 A theory of life earnings. *J. Pol. Econ.* 84(4 Pt. 2): 545–67

Scarr-Salapatck S 1965 Twin method: Defense of a critical assumption. University of Minnesota, Minneapolis, Minnesota (mimeo)

Sewell W, Hauser R 1977 On the effects of families and family structure on achievement. In: Taubman P (ed.) 1977

Solon G et al. 1987 The effect of family background on economic success: A longitudinal analysis of sibling correlations. NBER Working paper 2282, Cambridge, Massachusetts (mimeo)

Taubman P (ed.) 1977 *Kinometrics: Determinants of Socioeconomic Success Within and Between Families.* North-Holland, Amsterdam

Taubman P 1978 What we learn from estimating the genetic contribution to inequality in earnings: Reply. *Am. Econ. Rev.* 68(5): 970–76

Taubman P 1981 On heritability. *Economica* 48(192): 417–20

Wolfe B L, Behrman J R 1986 Child quantity and quality in a developing country: The importance of family background endogenous tastes and biological supply factors. *Econ. Dev. Cultural Change* 34: 703–20

Wolfe B L, Behrman J R 1987 Women's schooling and children's health: Are the effects robust with adult sibling control for the women's childhood backgrounds? *J. Health Econ.* 6(3): 239–54

Further Reading

Husén T 1974 *Talent, Equality and Meritocracy.* Nijhoff, The Hague

Parent Involvement in Preschool Programs

D. R. Powell

The idea that programs for young children should work closely with parents has been an integral part of early childhood education since the field's inception. Many diverse and pioneering strategies have been employed to involve parents in different kinds of early childhood programs. Some research on the effectiveness of various parent involvement practices has also been conducted, although the theoretical grounds are significantly stronger than the research base of rationales for establishing and maintaining cooperative relations between families and early childhood programs (Powell 1989). Research evidence points to a range of parent behaviors and attitudes that contribute to positive developmental outcomes in young children.

1. Rationales for Parent Involvement

The case for parent involvement in preschool programs reflects three basic premises: (a) parental rights doctrines which place responsibility for determining the child's best interest first and foremost with parents; (b) the assumption that families exert a significant influence on a child's development, and therefore the effects of preschool experiences are strengthened when they are extended and reinforced in the home; and (c) the principle of citizen participation in community institutions.

Rationales for close relations between parents and preschool programs typically expect improved outcomes in child functioning because important adults in a child's life are consistent in the way they deal with the child. Parents' feelings of competence and self-worth are also to be enhanced through participation in programs that foster partnerships between parents and program staff. In addition, it is anticipated that preschool programs will be more responsive and resourceful due to parent contributions to decisions about program practices and participation in roles that provide additional resources such as classroom assistance.

2. Approaches to Working with Parents

Three types of strategies for facilitating close ties between home and preschool have been pursued: (a) parent–teacher communication, (b) parent education, and (c) parents serving as program participants. The prevalence or use of these strategies tends to vary according to the type of early childhood program. Parent involvement in program positions is greater typically in parent cooperative preschools such as playcenters in New Zealand and the United Kingdom (Smith 1980), and in some early intervention programs such as Head Start in the United States, than in full-day childcare centers, which generally enroll children of parents who work full-time.

2.1 Parent–Teacher Communication

Frequent communication between parent and teacher has been viewed as an essential method for fostering supportive linkages between home and school. Standards of professional practice developed by the National Association for the Education of Young Children in the United States indicate that in high-quality early childhood programs: (a) information about program philosophy and operating procedures should be given to new and prospective families; (b) children and parents should be oriented to the center through pre-enrollment visits, parent meetings, or similar means; (c) staff and parents should communicate regarding home and center child-rearing practices; (d) parents should be welcome as visitors in the center at all times; and (e) a communication system should be established to share day-to-day exchanges between parents and staff (National Academy of Early Childhood Programs 1984).

For example, at the community-based childcare programs in Reggio Emilia, Italy, teachers secure from parents information about each child's daily routines and sleeping and eating preferences, and if possible, encourage parents to stay in the classroom for the first few weeks of school, until the child is comfortable with the new setting. There are also opportunities for parents to develop supportive relationships with other parents. The home–school relationships have the flavor of a traditional Italian extended family (New 1988, 1990).

Theoretical support for practice guidelines regarding parent–teacher communication is found in Bronfenbrenner's (1979) argument that the potential for settings to enhance child development is strongest when there are supportive linkages between the various settings in which the child is a participant. These supportive linkages include open two-way communication, and a personal mode of information exchange (face-to-face vs. printed announcement). Research testing these propositions is virtually nonexistent.

The highest frequency of parent–teacher communication has been found to occur when parents leave and retrieve their child at the early childhood program. One study of full-day childcare programs in the United States indicates that child-related topics were discussed with greater frequency than parent- or family-related topics, and increases in parent–staff interaction were related to increases in the diversity or range of topics discussed (Powell 1978b). Parent–teacher conferences and staff visits to the child's home appear to be infrequent types of exchanges. A study of parental presence at a university-based childcare center committed to parent involvement found that parents spent an average of 7.4 minutes a day at the center, including time spent dropping off and picking up their child, conferences with center staff, observation of children, and participation in group meetings. During the 70 consecutive days observed for this study, there were three parent–teacher conferences lasting no more than ten minutes each (Zigler and Turner 1982).

Questions need to be asked about the quality of parent–teacher exchanges that occur during the child drop-off and pick-up times. This is a time when adults may be preoccupied with other matters and, for late afternoon or evening retrievals in full-day programs, the childcare staff on duty may not have been with the child all day and therefore may have limited information on the child's day. Not surprisingly, one study found a high level of parent and teacher dissatisfaction with discussion of activities at full-day childcare centers (Powell 1978a).

Relations between parents and childcare providers may be stronger in family daycare than in center-based arrangements. A Canadian study found parents using family daycare to report closer personal relationships with providers than parents using childcare centers (Pence and Goelman 1987). A United States study found that family daycare providers spent on average about 54 minutes per week talking with each parent while center providers reported talking with each parent about 13 minutes per week (Hughes 1985).

Another set of recommended parent involvement practices is for parents to help ease their child's entry into an early childhood program. Child and parent are encouraged to visit a preschool classroom prior to the start of classes, and parents are encouraged to remain in the classroom for a period of time (e.g., 20 minutes) during the child's first session. A study of these two practices with middle-class mothers of four-year olds enrolled in a half-day nursery school found no effects on children's adaptation to the preschool (Schwarz and Wynn 1971). However, toddlers have been found to show more distress behaviors during the parents' departures than infants and preschool-age children (Field et al. 1984), and parents' provision of information to two-year old children about an impending transition to a new setting has been found to be associated with reduced distress during the separation (Weinraub and Lewis 1977).

Many early childhood educators find relations with parents to be one of the most difficult aspects of work with young children (Almy 1982). A professional ethics survey of *Young Children* readers found relationships with parents to be the greatest area of ethical concern among teachers at all job categories (Feeney and Sysko 1986), and studies suggest early childhood teachers generally hold negative judgments regarding the parenting abilities of parents using a center (Kontos and Wells 1986). These findings are consistent with sociologist Willard Waller's early observation in 1932 that parents and teachers are "natural enemies" due to the qualitatively distinct relationship each maintains with the same child. Also, efforts to increase the professional status of early childhood teachers may hinder parent involvement in early childhood programs if there is adherence to traditional conceptions of professionalism such as freedom from client control (Shimoni 1991).

2.2 Parent Education

Providing parents with expert knowledge about child growth and development has long been the goal of most early childhood programs. One of the original purposes of the nursery school was to serve as a forum for educating parents about the nature and nurture of young children. In the United States, the nursery school was used as a laboratory to train parents in child development and appropriate child-rearing practices. The parent education activities of a typical nursery school in the 1920s, for instance, included conferences with teachers, home visits, parent group meetings focused on child-rearing topics, and a consultation service for parents to explore child-rearing problems and concerns on an individual basis with a professional. Observation of children in the nursery school was also encouraged (Committee on Preschool and Parental Education 1929). Parent educators would meet weekly with parents to discuss family issues, help parents identify and use community resources, and provide support for their self-development and learning (Almy 1989).

Parent cooperative preschools offer a major opportunity for parents to learn about child development by assuming responsibility for and participating in a preschool classroom. Historically, cooperative preschool programs enabled parents to engage in "practice teaching for parenthood" by working alongside an experienced early childhood educator. Programs also provided frequent lecture and discussion sessions on child development topics, guided observation and study of children's behavior, and experience in planning program activities for young children (Whiteside-Taylor 1968).

Parent education was a major component of early intervention programs established in the 1960s and 1970s to support children who were disabled or living in high-risk conditions such as poverty. Nearly all of the major intervention program models include parent education. For example, the well-known Perry Preschool program in the United States supplemented the preschool classroom with a weekly home visit in which teachers worked with child and parent for one and a half hours (Schweinhart and Weikart

1983). An international survey in the mid-1980s of 14 home-based preschool programs in 6 countries revealed a variety of program objectives, target populations, methods of operation, and staffing patterns (Lombard 1988).

Today some early childhood programs are focused primarily on the parent's role as a teacher of the young child. In the state of Minnesota in the United States, for example, nearly every community has an Early Childhood and Family Education program that provides parent group discussions, home visits, child development classes, and other approaches to educating and supporting parents (Cooke 1992).

It appears that parents of children enrolled in part- or full-time early childhood programs view parent education activities as less important than other program components. A recent New Zealand study of parents associated with kindergarten, childcare, and playcenter programs found that the provision of parent education was among the least important goals of an early childhood program. Research in the United States suggests parent education components of half-day nursery schools (Joffe 1977) and full-day childcare centers (Coelen et al. 1984) were offered and used on a limited basis.

Early childhood programs may support parents in their child-rearing roles through informal helping relationships among parents and between parents and staff. Both center-based and family daycare providers have been found to assume an active helping role in responding to parents' questions and concerns regarding a range of child-related topics. Staff responses include asking questions, offering sympathy, presenting alternatives, and just listening (Hughes 1985, Joffe 1977).

In spite of the long history of providing parent education in the early childhood field, there is a limited amount of research evidence on the effectiveness of parent education activities that are part of a preschool program. Most of the studies do not directly assess the relative impact of a parent education component in a program that includes direct work with both the child and parents. Available studies focus primarily on low-income populations involved in early intervention programs. An early review of this research literature in the United States concluded that the involvement of the child's family as an active program participant is critical to the success of early intervention initiatives (Bronfenbrenner 1974). Evaluations of early childhood programs focused primarily on parents have found positive short-term effects on child competence and maternal behaviors (e.g., Slaughter 1983), and long-term effects on such family characteristics as mothers pursuing higher levels of formal education (Seitz et al. 1985).

2.3 Parents as Program Participants

Parents have served as program participants by functioning as classroom aides, and by participating in committees and councils charged with making decisions about program policies and practices. These parent involvement practices are an integral part of parent cooperative preschool programs, and are common characteristics of early childhood programs targeted at disabled children and children from low-income families. In full-day childcare programs, parents generally do not participate as regular classroom aides, due to work commitments.

Much of the interest in parents as program participants stems from a desire to establish substantive continuity between home and preschool for the child. The responsiveness of early childhood programs to child and family characteristics is a particularly critical issue for programs serving low-income and ethnic minority populations whose cultural values may not be represented in the program. Discontinuity between home and school has been proposed as a major cause of poor academic achievement among low-income and some ethnic minority populations (Laosa 1982). With regard to programs for children with disabilities, United States laws call for parents to assume decision-making roles about child testing and placement in special education programs, and the right to initiate due process hearings.

In the United States, the federal program "Head Start" has served as a field-based laboratory for experimenting with parents in program participant roles. Programs are required to involve parents in decisions about program operations by constituting a policy council comprising at least 50 percent parents of Head Start children enrolled in the program. Programs are also mandated to involve parents in classrooms as paid employees, volunteers, or observers. Similarly, all states in the Federal Republic of Germany provide for parent participation in the form of elected boards of parents who advise on organizational and pedagogical matters as well as on personnel hiring decisions (Tietze et al. 1989).

Research on low-income populations in the United States suggests that higher levels of parent involvement in early childhood programs are related to positive aspects of parent functioning. Active parent involvement in Head Start has been found to be positively associated with parents' psychological well-being, including greater feelings of mastery and life satisfaction (Parker et al. 1987), and reduced levels of anxiety and depression (McKey et al. 1985). It appears that sizable proportions of parents participate in various paid and volunteer activities in Head Start, but a core of parents is involved in a disproportionate share of the time (McKey et al. 1985). Available research is limited in determining whether the program is a causal factor in these relationships between program participation and individual functioning.

One of the expected outcomes of placing parents in program roles is that parents would strengthen their skills in dealing with other institutions such as schools. Anecdotal reports indicate that parent cooperative preschools have produced "mother graduates" who readily assumed positions of leadership as parent–teacher association officers and volunteers in public schools, for instance (Whiteside-Taylor 1953).

3. Parent Contributions to Young Children's School Experiences

There is compelling research evidence from the United States to indicate that parents' child-rearing practices and beliefs in the early years of a child's life are related to the child's subsequent performance in school. Maternal behaviors and attitudes when children are four years of age have been found to be related to school readiness when children are 5 and 6 years of age, and to school achievement when children are 12 years of age (Hess et al. 1984). Also, the quality of the home environment when children are 12 and 24 months of age has been linked to children's first-grade performance in reading, language, and mathematics.

Positive child outcomes have been associated with a parental view of human development as a complex process involving the child as an active contributor to development (Johnson and Martin 1983, McGillicuddy-DeLisi 1985), and with parent teaching strategies that stimulate children's thinking and promote verbal problem-solving (Sigel 1982). Also, parents' accurate judgments about their child's intellectual abilities (Hunt and Paraskevopoulos 1980) have been associated with children's cognitive skills.

Parents contribute directly and indirectly to children's literacy skills. Indirect contributions include providing children with access to reading and writing materials such as picture dictionaries and alphabet books (Hess et al. 1982), parents' own reading habits (Clark 1976), and enforcement of television viewing rules (Morrow 1983). Parents' direct contributions to children's literacy focus on reading to their young child. Parent–child interaction during storybook reading involves such parental behaviors as variety in voice, asking the child to identify objects in storybook pictures, describing storybook pictures, pausing for a child to respond, and involving the child in holding and managing the book (Ninio and Bruner 1978). Parents' contributions to children's early literacy experiences are embedded within the routine social interactions of a family (e.g., shopping, planning a wedding, etc.), and seldom occur as isolated literacy events (Teale 1986).

Parenting style also contributes to children's school experiences. Attentive, warm, and nonrestrictive maternal behaviors have been found to foster the intellectual development of young children (Belsky 1981) and to relate to school readiness at age 5 and 6 years and with school achievement at age 12 years (Estrada et al. 1987). Mothers' use of direct control tactics in teaching and disciplinary situations with 4-year old children has been found to be negatively related to children's school-related abilities at ages 4, 5, and 12 years (Hess and McDevitt 1984).

One parent factor cannot be identified as more important than others in influencing young children's school performance (Hess et al. 1984). Parent behaviors and attitudes that contribute to young children's school experiences are inextricably interwoven in daily exchanges between parent and child.

4. Conclusion

The philosophical and theoretical arguments for parent involvement in preschool programs are considerably stronger than the available research base. A limited amount of research has been conducted on this topic, and existing studies offer equivocal support for many recommended practices in the field of early childhood education.

It is difficult to generalize about the state of parent involvement in preschool programs because there is considerable variation within and across programs regarding patterns of parent participation. Within the same program, there can be a high level of involvement among one set of parents and low involvement among another set of parents. Further, different kinds of preschool programs employ various approaches to parent involvement. Parent education is a significant component of early childhood programs targeted primarily at parents as teachers but this forms a minor or absent part of many half-day and full-day programs. Similarly, parent participation in program roles such as classroom aide is integral to parent cooperative preschools and many early intervention programs, but generally is not a characteristic of full-day childcare centers.

In general, it appears that communication between parents and early childhood program staff falls short of professional recommendations regarding content and frequency. It also seems the parent–teacher relationship is problematic for many early childhood educators. Dramatic changes in the structure, functions, and lifestyles of families throughout the world require a rethinking of parent involvement practices that stem from increasingly outdated images of families. At the same time, compelling research evidence points to the significant influence of families on young children's short- and long-term school outcomes.

See also: Family and Schooling; Family Influence on Human Development; Family, School, and Cultural Capital; Parent Education

References

Almy M 1982 Day care and early childhood education. In: Zigler E F, Gordon E W (eds.) 1982 *Day Care: Scientific and Social Policy Issues*. Auburn House, Boston, Massachusetts

Almy M 1989 Foreword. In: Powell D R (ed.) 1989 *Families and Early Childhood Programs*. National Association for the Education of Young Children, Washington, DC

Belsky J 1981 Early human experience: A family perspective. *Dev. Psychol.* 17(1): 3–23

Bronfenbrenner U 1974 *Is Early Intervention Effective? A Report on Longitudinal Evaluations of Preschool Programs*, Vol. 2. Department of Health, Education and Welfare, Office of Child Development, Washington, DC

Bronfenbrenner U 1979 *The Ecology of Human Development: Experiments by Nature and Design.* Harvard University Press, Cambridge, Massachusetts

Clark M M 1976 *Young Fluent Readers: What Can They Teach Us?* Heinemann Educational Books, London

Coelen C, Glantz F, Calore D 1984 *Day Care Centers in the US: A National Profile.* University Press of America, Lanham, Maryland

Committee on Preschool and Parental Education 1929 Training for the field of parental education. In: Whipple G M (ed.) 1929 *Preschool and Parental Education.* Twenty-eighth yearbook of the National Society for the Study of Education, Part I. Public School Publishing Co., Bloomington, Indiana

Cooke B 1992 *Changing Times, Changing Families: Minnesota Early Childhood Family Education Parent Outcome Interview Study.* Minnesota Department of Education, St. Paul, Minnesota

Estrada P, Arsenio W F, Hess R D, Holloway S D 1987 Affective quality of the mother–child relationship: Longitudinal consequences for children's school-relevant cognitive functioning. *Dev. Psychol.* 23(2): 210–15

Feeney S, Sysko L 1986 Professional ethics in early childhood education: Survey results. *Young Children* 42(1): 15–22

Field T, et al. 1984 Leave-takings and reunions of infants, toddlers, preschoolers, and their parents. *Child Dev.* 55(2): 628–35

Hess R D, Holloway S D, Dickson W P, Price G G 1984 Maternal variables as predictors of children's school readiness and later achievement in vocabulary and mathematics in sixth grade. *Child Dev.* 55(5): 1902–12

Hess R D, Holloway S D, Price G G, Dickson W P 1982 Family environments and the acquisition of reading skills: Toward a more precise analysis. In: Laosa L M, Sigel I E (eds.) 1982 *Families as Learning Environments for Children.* Plenum, New York

Hess R D, McDevitt T M 1984 Some cognitive consequences of maternal intervention techniques: A longitudinal study. *Child Dev.* 55(6): 2017–30

Hughes R 1985 The informal help-giving of home and center childcare providers. *Family Relat.* 34: 359–66

Hunt J M, Paraskevopoulos J 1980 Children's psychological development as a function of the inaccuracy of their mothers' knowledge of their abilities. *J. Genet. Psychol.* 136(2): 285–98

Joffe C E 1977 *Friendly Intruders: Childcare Professionals and Family Life.* University of California Press, Berkeley, California

Johnson J E, Martin C 1983 Family environments and kindergarten children's academic knowledge. Paper presented at the meeting of the Northeastern Educational Research Association, Ellenville, New York

Kontos S, Wells W 1986 Attitudes of caregivers and the day care experiences of families. *Early Childhood Research Quarterly* 1(1): 47–67

Laosa L 1982 School, occupation, culture, and family: The impact of parental schooling on the parent–child relationship. *J. Educ. Psychol.* 74(6): 791–827

Lombard A D 1988 Home-based early childhood education

programs. *Int. J. Early Child.* 20(2): 23–35

McGillicuddy-DeLisi A V 1985 The relationship between parental beliefs and children's cognitive level. In: Sigel I E (ed.) 1985 *Parental Belief Systems.* Erlbaum, Hillsdale, New Jersey

McKey R H et al. 1985 *The Impact of Head Start on Children, Families and Communities* (DHHS Publication No. 85-31193), CSR Inc./Administration for Children, Youth, and Families, Washington, DC

Morrow L 1983 Home and school correlates of early interest in literature. *J. Educ. Res.* 76(4): 221–30

National Academy of Early Childhood Programs 1984 *Accreditation Criteria and Procedures of the National Academy of Early Childhood Programs.* National Association for the Education of Young Children, Washington, DC

New R 1988 Parental goals and Italian infant care. In: Levine R A, Miller P, West M (eds.) 1988 *New Directions for Child Development*, No. 40. Jossey-Bass, San Francisco, California

New R 1990 Excellent early education: A city in Italy has it. *Young Children* 45(6): 4–10

Ninio A, Bruner J 1978 The achievement and antecedents of labeling. *J. Child Lang.* 5(1): 1–15

Parker F L, Piotrkowski C S, Peay L 1987 Head Start as a social support for mothers: The psychological benefits of involvement. *Am. J. Orthopsychiatry* 57(2): 220–33

Pence A R, Goelman H 1987 Silent partners: Parents of children in three types of day care. *Early Childhood Res. Q.* 2(2): 103–18

Powell D R 1978a The interpersonal relationship between parents and caregivers in day care settings. *Am. J. Orthopsychiatry* 48(4) 680–89

Powell D R 1978b Correlates of parent–teacher communication frequency and diversity. *J. Educ. Res.* 71(6): 333–41

Powell D R 1989 *Families and Early Childhood Programs.* National Association for the Education of Young Children, Washington, DC

Schwarz J C, Wynn R 1971 The effects of mothers' presence and previsits on children's emotional reaction to starting nursery school. *Child Dev.* 42: 871–81

Schweinhart L J, Weikart D P 1983 Effects of the Perry Preschool programs on youths through age 15. In: Consortium for Longitudinal Studies (ed.) 1983 *As the Twig is Bent: Lasting Effects of Preschool Programs.* Erlbaum, Hillsdale, New Jersey

Seitz V, Rosenbaum L K, Apfel N 1985 Effects of family support intervention: A ten-year follow-up. *Child Dev.* 56(2): 376–91

Shimoni R 1991 Professionalization and parent involvement in early childhood education: Complementary or conflicting strategies? *Int. J. Early Child.* 23(2): 11–26

Sigel I E 1982 The relationship between parental distancing strategies and the child's cognitive behavior. In: Laosa L M, Sigel I E (eds.) 1982 *Families as Learning Environments for Children.* Plenum, New York

Slaughter D T 1983 Early intervention and its effects on maternal and child development. *Monogr. Soc. Res. Child Dev.* 48(4): Serial No. 202

Smith T 1980 *Parents and preschool.* Vol 6 of Oxford Preschool Research Project. Grant McIntyre, London

Teale W H 1986 Home background and young children's literacy development. In: Teale W H, Sulzby E (eds.) 1986 *Emergent Literacy: Writing and Reading.* Ablex, Norwood, New Jersey

Tietze W, Rossbach H-G, Ufermann K 1989 Child care and early education in the Federal Republic of Germany. In: Olmsted P P, Weikart D P (eds.) 1989 *How Nations Serve Young Children: Profiles of Child Care and Education in 14 Countries*. High/Scope Press, Ypsilanti, Michigan

Weinraub M, Lewis M 1977 The determinants of children's responses to separation. *Monogr. Soc. Res. Child Dev.* 42(4): Serial No. 172

Whiteside-Taylor K 1953 Cooperative nursery schools educate families. *Teachers College Record* 54(6): 332–39

Whiteside-Taylor K 1968 *Parents and Children Learn Together*. Teachers College Press, New York

Zigler E F, Turner P 1982 Parents and day care workers: A failed partnership? In: Zigler E F, Gordon E W (eds.) 1982 *Day Care. Scientific and Social Policy Issues*. Auburn House, Boston, Massachusetts

Further Reading

Berger E H 1987 *Parents as Partners in Education: The School and Home Working Together*. Merrill, Columbus, Ohio

Joffe C E 1977 *Friendly Intruders: Childcare Professionals and Family Life*. University of California Press, Berkeley, California

Powell D R 1989 *Families and Early Childhood Programs*. National Association for the Education of Young Children, Washington, DC

Powell D R 1991 Parents and programs: Early childhood as a pioneer in parent involvement and support. In: Kagan S L (ed.) 1991 *The Care and Education of America's Young Children: Obstacles and Opportunities*. Ninetieth yearbook of the Society for the Study of Education. National Society for the Study of Education, Chicago, Illinois

Parent Education

R. Shimoni

Parent education has a long history. Historically, expectations of parent education have ranged from the elimination of poverty (Clarke-Stewart 1988) and the reduction of social ills to more modest expectations such as helping families provide an environment adequate for the task of child rearing (Fein 1980).

1. Background

North American parent education programs have tended to fall into two main categories. One was entirely voluntary, developed by the middle class for the middle class. The other was for the lower class, developed by the middle class or by professionals. These differences, evident mainly in the recruitment procedure and in the content of the education programs, have persisted throughout the twentieth century (Schlossman 1976). While the middle-class mothers "discussed," the poor were "instructed" in the "do's and don'ts" of child rearing and home management. Attendance at the middle-class parent education meetings was voluntary, while receiving home instruction was often imposed on the poor as a condition for the receipt of welfare benefits.

For much of past and present middle-class parent education, the role of experts has been to provide an inspirational, advisory role, providing scientific (research-based) information about child development, and interpretations regarding child-rearing implications. The role of experts conducting parent education of the disadvantaged has been that of both conceptualizers and implementers. The "experts" identify the issues, and design, implement, and evaluate parent education programs.

The rationale for contemporary compensatory parent education is that the experiences of children in their early years are crucial to subsequent physical, emotional–social, and cognitive development, and that the parents are the most significant influence on the child during those formative years. Second, due to the isolation of modern families, and the difficulty in understanding and interpreting psychological literature, many parents require help. Finally, the underlying assumption is that certain kinds of parental behavior (particularly concerning styles of verbal interaction and provision of stimulation) result in better school achievement in later years. Parents lacking these skills can, it is presumed, acquire them through parent education.

2. Methods of Parent Education

Middle-class parent education since the 1960s has been largely psychotherapeutic in nature, focusing on communication and behavior management in children. Followers of psychologists such as Dreikurs and Soltz (1964) and Ginott (1965) hold group sessions for parents in a variety of settings, such as schools, churches, and community centers. In these parent education sessions, group leaders facilitate parents learning from each other while also providing them with information about child development and management. While there is no overt class orientation to this kind of parent education, and in fact some authors adhere to its cross-class suitability, most of the evaluative or descriptive studies indicate that the participants were largely middle class (Dembo et al. 1985).

A variety of compensatory parent education programs for the disadvantaged were initiated in the United States during the Head Start era, as one of the major strategies in the Johnson administration's war on poverty. Some were extremely comprehensive, combining health, social, and educational services, while others were much more concise in conception, implementation, and duration. However, the prime objective of most programs was the same: to teach parents a repertoire of behaviors that would primarily foster their children's cognitive development, and to promote the kind of attitudes in parents that would be likely to help them help their children. This generally included an understanding of the importance of their own role as the primary educators of their children, and the acquisition of the self-confidence needed to carry out that role. The format and methods of parent education varied, and included parent participation in preschool settings, home visiting programs, and group meetings.

Examples of parent education programs can be seen around the globe. Lombard (1988) has described 14 programs in 6 countries (France, the United Kingdom, Israel, Poland, Spain, and the United States), which, although varying in scope, method of implementation and evaluation, staffing, and target population, are generally based on the assumption that either improving the well-being and "general functioning of the parent will improve the child's potential for healthy normal growth . . ." (or) that by "improving the parent's role as educator . . . will improve the child's chances for success in school" (Lombard 1988 p. 28). Programs with a similar focus are also being implemented in Third World countries, such as in the Sudan (Grotberg et al. 1987).

An example of a parent education program used in several countries (United States, the Netherlands, Germany, Mexico, South Africa, New Zealand, Chile, and Turkey) is the Home Instruction Program for Preschool Youngsters (HIPPY). It is a home-based program aimed at providing "educational enrichment of disadvantaged preschool children and for the promotion of increased awareness by their mothers of their own strengths and potential as home educators." It also utilizes paraprofessionals who provide weekly instruction to mothers, based on prepared material. These meetings are augmented by biweekly group meetings. The design, coordination, and supervision of the program is university-based, while funding and administrative infrastructure are provided at the government and community level (Lombard 1981).

Since the late 1980s a number of programs for parents of young children have been developed which embody the ideology of empowerment. These programs address a shift in the balance of power between parents and staff in early intervention programs toward collaborative, co-equal relations (Powell 1989). The term "empowerment" is frequently used when staff serve as facilitators of goals and activities which are determined jointly by parents and staff (Powell 1989), rather than having the goals and activities for parents determined by "experts."

Cochran (1988) describes an early childhood model program based on the concept of parental empowerment in which the families' strengths and differences (including historical, cultural, and social traditions) are respected, and the parent is viewed as one who knows more about the child than anyone outside the family. This program includes home visits, designed to give recognition to the parenting role, to reinforce and enrich parent–child activities already being carried out, and to share information about community services. Another aspect of the program is the establishment of "cluster building neighborhoods," aimed at reducing feelings of isolation, at sharing information and pooling resources, and at providing a forum for parents to express the need for changes in the neighborhood.

The notion of empowering parents—more often mothers, who are described as "very deprived and powerless members of society" (Canning 1989)—through techniques of popular education underlies a parent education project being carried out in the Dominican Republic (Canning 1989). This approach is aimed at raising the mothers' level of consciousness, and facilitating their own and their children's development through a flexible approach that adapts to changing local conditions and needs, and shows promise in that setting.

3. Evaluation of Parent Education

Very few reliable evaluative studies have been conducted about "middle-class" parent education programs. However, it seems that families with very specific child-rearing problems or who are not middle class tend to drop out (Anchor and Thomason 1977). Although there are reports of positive effects on the attitudes of parents, there is no indication of the effect of these changed attitudes on the family dynamics, or more specifically on the children. There are also no salient data which point to varying degrees of effectiveness of the different psychological approaches behind the various parent education groups (Dembo et al. 1985).

Sorting out the fairly extensive evaluative literature on compensatory parent education is exceedingly difficult. Several studies have demonstrated short-term positive effects of parent education on children's IQ. These gains, however, are generally not sustained beyond one year. Longer term positive outcomes relating to a decrease in the likelihood of being involved in special education classes (Jester and Guinagh 1983) and reduced rates of juvenile delinquency (Lally et al. 1988) have been reported. However, one very thorough evaluative study carried out in Bermuda (Scarr and McCartney 1988) failed to reveal any positive effects on the children. Perhaps more heartening is the reporting of positive effects of parent education programs on parents, such as an increased sense of competence, and improvement in economic and life circumstances (Powell 1989).

Evidence about the effectiveness of parent education is small in comparison to the abundance of programs that have been in operation over the years (Stevens 1978). However, it is important to identify the characteristics of programs that have proven to be effective as a guard against "zeal in setting unrealistic expectations" onto a variety of parent programs (Stevens 1978).

First, according to Stevens (1978), most of the programs shown to be effective were substantially funded, and conceptualized and implemented under the direction of leaders in the field of early childhood development. Second, the programs were fairly intensive and extensive. Successful home visiting programs, for example, comprised weekly visits for a period of 18 months to 2 years. Objectives of the programs were clearly specified, and activities were carefully derived, pilot tested, and modified. Systematic supervision of those instructing the parents, a continuous monitoring of project activities, and a careful documentation of what happens in the educational program are common characteristics of effective parent education programs (Stevens 1978).

There are virtually no longitudinal studies pertaining to the shorter term, less intensive parent educational projects. In spite of claims of success of shorter projects, it would not seem reasonable to expect long-term effects. The manner in which parents relate to their children is complex and unlikely to be affected by a few parent education sessions.

Several authors have cautioned against overenthusiasm regarding parent education (Clarke-Stewart 1988, Brim 1965, Schlossman 1976). One major concern is that it may undermine parents' confidence (Clarke-Stewart 1988). The most serious criticism of parent education relates to the concern that enthusiasm regarding its potential to reduce educational disadvantages may disregard other necessary social reforms.

One major issue to be addressed is when to begin parent education. Although a convincing argument has been set forth that parent education should begin in the schools, as a central component of high school curricula, there seems to be little advancement in that area (O'Connor 1990).

Although it may be argued that the empirical foundation for justifying the continued investment in parent education is somewhat shaky, there are strong recommendations not to give up on parent education programs (Scarr and McCartney 1988). Powell (1989)

suggests that the term parent support may be replacing "parent education." This shift in terminology reflects a growing awareness that dissemination of information to parents is less likely on its own to influence positively parent functioning than is the provision of social support.

The challenge of the 1990s could perhaps be to redefine realistic goals of parent education, to continue to strive to develop programs that are more sensitive to the needs, life-styles, and culture of parents. The aim should be the continued research and development of a variety of programs with a view to achieving a balance between cost effectiveness, participant satisfaction, and benefits to the children.

See also: Family and Schooling; Parent Involvement in Preschool Programs

References

Anchor K N, Thomason T C 1977 A comparison of two parent training models with educated parents. *J. Community Psychol.* 5(2): 134–41

Brim O G 1965 *Education for Child. Rearing.* Free Press, New York

Canning P M 1989 Helping mothers in the Dominican Republic to become facilitators of their own preschoolers' development. *Early Child Devel. Care* 50: 159–66

Clarke-Stewart K A 1988 Evolving issues in early childhood education: A personal perspective. *Early Childhood Res. Q.* 3(2): 139–49

Cochran M 1988 Parental empowerment in family matters: Lessons learned from a research program. In: Powell D R (ed.) 1988 *Parent Education as Early Childhood Intervention.* Ablex, Norwood, New Jersey

Dembo M H, Sweitzer M, Lauritzen P 1985 An evaluation of group parent education: Behavioral, PET 7 and Adlerian Programs. *Rev. Educ. Res.* 55(2): 155–200

Dreikurs R, Soltz V 1964 *Children, The Challenge.* Hawthorn, New York

Fein G 1980 The informed parent. In: Killmer S (ed.) 1980 *Adv. Early Education Day Care*, Vol. 1. JAI Press, Greenwich, Connecticut

Ginott H G 1965 *Between Parent and Child: New Solutions to Old Problems.* Macmillan, New York

Grotberg E H, Badri G, King A D 1987 Changing childrearing practices in Sudan. *Child. Today* 16(1): 26–9

Jester R E, Guinagh B J 1983 The Gordon parent education infant and toddler program. In: The Consortium for Longitudinal Studies 1983 *As the Twig is Bent: Lasting Effects of Preschool Programs.* Erlbaum, Hillsdale, New Jersey

Lally J R, Mangione P L, Honig A S 1988 The Syracuse University family development research program: Long-range impact of an early intervention with low-income children and their families. In: Powell D R (ed.) 1988 *Parent Education as Early Childhood Intervention.* Ablex, Norwood, New Jersey

Lombard A D 1981 *Success Begins at Home.* Lexington Books, Lexington, Massachusetts

Lombard A D 1988 Home-based early childhood education programs. *Int. J. Early Child.* 20(2): 23–35

O'Connor L 1990 Education for parenthood and the National Curriculum: Progression or regression? *Early Child. Devel. Care* 57: 85–8

Powell D R 1989 *Families and Early Childhood Programs.* National Association for the Education of Young Children, Washington, DC

Scarr S, McCartney K 1988 Far from home: An experimental evaluation of the mother child home program in Bermuda. *Child Dev.* 59(3): 531–43

Schlossman S L 1976 Before Home Start: Notes toward a history of parent education in America, 1897–1929. *Harv. Educ. Rev.* 46(3): 436–67

Stevens J H 1978 Parent education programs: What determines effectiveness? *Young Children* 33(4): 59–65

School–Parent Relationships

M. A. Payne

It is widely agreed that good relationships between schools and their students' parents are desirable and important, for a variety of reasons. Research from many parts of the world repeatedly suggests that parents are more willing to play an active part in their children's education than many professional educators believe. However, few countries have clearly established policies and procedures for improving home–school collaboration, at either national or regional levels. As a result, the nature and scope of such collaboration tends to vary widely between and within school districts, depending on the types of initiative taken by local educational personnel and/or research groups. However, even within individual schools, relationships are typically much stronger with some parents than with others. For this and other reasons the potential negative as well as positive outcomes of schemes to enhance parental involvement must be recognized.

1. Nature and Scope of Relationships with Parents

Positive relations with parents serve many purposes. The nature of these relationships can vary widely. There are, however, some general trends in the types of relationships that are established.

1.1 Objectives

The primary objective of establishing and maintaining good relationships with parents is to promote the motivation and academic achievement of children in school. However, other important goals may be identified, such as providing support for parents, putting parents in touch with other community resources, bringing together parents whose children have similar special educational needs, and providing incentives for parents to upgrade their own academic skills or take other action to improve their quality of life (Brantlinger 1991, San Diego County Office of Education 1986). In communities in which existing curriculum materials are very limited, students and their families may be recruited to play a critical role in the development of resource materials for schools (Schiefelbein 1991).

1.2 Types of Relationships

Home–school interaction takes several forms to meet these various objectives. Some characteristically involve much higher levels of consultation with parents than others (Davies et al. 1992, Ramsay et al. 1990).

Schools may provide assistance to families in relation to their basic responsibilities for children's health, safety, supervision, discipline, and guidance. Schools may also inform parents about services available in the wider community. Parents may be regularly informed about school programs and events, and about their child's progress, via memos, telephone calls, newsletters, report cards, and special meetings. They may also be encouraged to provide or request specific information. Modern telecommunications technology can greatly enhance this aspect of home–school relations in terms of quantity of information exchanged and proportion of parents reached. An example is the Trans-Parent School model developed in Tennessee, in the United States, which uses computer-based automated telephone dialing systems and answering machines to handle daily teacher–parent messages (Bauch 1990). Discussion of children's needs and progress may also be conducted via established schemes of school conferences, home visiting, and Parent Teacher Associations.

Parents sometimes participate in activities to assist teachers, administrators, and children in classrooms and other areas of the school. They also help organize and attend student performances and school events. At home, parents monitor or assist their children in learning activities that can be coordinated with school-based instruction, and ensure that suitable conditions are provided for homework. Activities may be relatively informal, such as reading to children or visiting places of local interest. Some projects involve parents more formally, such as the Paired Reading technique in which parents act as tutors following clearly specified procedures (Topping 1986) or the "Portage" model now used in over 30 countries worldwide, which involves parents of special needs children in a systematic process of assessment and teaching (Hornby 1995).

Parents' views are invited when decisions affecting their children are made. They help decide the content and emphasis of school programs. At the highest level of consultation they can be involved in both planning and evaluation of curricula and other aspects of school policy.

1.3 General Trends

Economic conditions, together with prevailing political and educational ideologies, determine general views regarding the desirability and feasibility of various types of home–school relationships. In most Western societies, relationships traditionally were limited to the one-way transfer of information and advice from teachers to parents. Extensive contact between schools and parents typically occurred only when problems arose regarding a child's school attendance, behavior, or performance. During the 1970s and 1980s, however, schools began to encourage parents to come beyond the school gate on a more regular basis. At first, visits were typically limited to formal discussions of children's progress or fairly unskilled supervisory assistance to teachers. Parents were then offered opportunities to play more constructive and responsible roles in classroom learning activities and to consult with their children's teachers on a more informal and friendly basis.

In the 1990s legislative changes in several countries increased parents' rights to be involved in educational decision-making—there were calls for parental "empowerment" at all levels of home–school relationships. The calls were based on the assumption that parents as well as teachers have strengths, are able to assess their own needs, and will make responsible choices when given the opportunity (Cochran and Dean 1991). Moreover, there was growing recognition of the influence of all family members, not just parents, on children's progress in school. For all these reasons many contemporary writers have preferred the term "school and family partnerships" to those of "parent involvement" or "home–school relationships" (Epstein 1992).

2. Factors Influencing the Quality of Relationships with Parents

Even when prevailing ideologies support and promote parental involvement, relationships between schools and a large proportion of their students' parents are often minimal. A general trend for parent involvement to decline dramatically after the early elementary grades has also been reported.

2.1 Common Barriers

Several barriers to good school and home partnerships have been identified. These barriers lie in the areas of communication, culture, and personal feelings.

Communication difficulties result from the scheduling of school meetings and events at times when many parents cannot attend; from unreliable or unsatisfactory communication routes between school and home; and from teachers' lack of communication skills. This last problem is particularly acute when teachers work with low-income families or parents whose home language is different from that of the school.

Recalling their own unhappy or unsuccessful school experiences, many parents often feel intimidated by school buildings, organizational structures, and personnel. They may doubt their ability to influence either their child's educational progress (especially at high school level), or school policy more generally to any significant extent.

Insensitivity to traditional customs, or to cultural differences in multicultural societies, may cause many parents to be unwilling or unable to interact with school personnel or participate in school-based activities.

Many teachers still doubt the wisdom of involving parents in certain partnership roles, fearing they may teach things incorrectly, put students under undue pressure at home, or impose undesirable or unworkable policies on schools. They may feel that their school's policy for increased interaction with parents puts unwarranted and stressful demands on their time.

2.2 Strategies for Improvement

None of the above barriers is insurmountable. Case studies of individual schools, reports of research projects, and papers delivered at national and regional conferences have identified a wide variety of developmental and remedial strategies. The following issues seem to be particularly critical.

Schools benefit from conducting periodic systematic assessment of the type, level, quantity, and quality of their home–school relations, in order to pinpoint gaps and weaknesses. The "Home–School Relations Planner" (San Diego County Office of Education 1986) is an example of an instrument devised for this purpose.

Strategies for making parents feel more welcome in schools are often needed. Examples of such strategies include the provision of attractive and friendly settings for meetings and consultations, introducing opportunities for unscheduled discussions with staff, training in interpersonal skills for receptionists, telephonists, and secretaries, and using teachers or others as interpreters and translators. In multicultural contexts it also requires a willingness to accept the validity of diverse traditions and to experiment with culturally appropriate procedures (e.g., Tripcony 1994).

Once in school parents must feel able to contribute freely to discussions and have confidence that their contributions will be valued. At the beginning of an ambitious project in New Zealand to increase parental participation in curriculum decision-making, Ramsay et al. (1990) observed that most attempts by schools to disseminate information or promote debate of important issues involved large parent–teacher meetings at which parents were either afraid, or given little opportunity, to speak. Alternative strategies, involving use of smaller groups, location of meetings on alternative sites in the community, and opportunities for parents to practice their contributions to collaborative decision-making in nonthreatening environments (often in the absence of teachers) met with considerable success in terms of increased parental confidence and increased staff willingness to listen.

Additional priorities arise when the objectives include parent tutoring or teaching responsibilities. Schools need to identify systematic and detailed procedures to ensure that parents understand the relevance of what they are asked to do, are properly trained to perform tasks confidently, and obtain sufficient ongoing support.

Research clearly suggests that pre- and inservice training programs must pay much more attention to equipping teachers and administrators with both the knowledge of how good relationships with parents can enhance school effectiveness and the interpersonal skills to work with families. Teachers need more knowledge of family dynamics and the organization of schools and communities. They need to learn how to empathize with parents and recognize their strengths, make the most of parent–teacher conferences, and find creative ways to involve parents in school activities (Cochran and Dean 1991). If working with parents of children with special needs, they must also be more knowledgeable about legal issues, the nature of handicapping conditions, and services provided by agencies other than schools (Brantlinger 1991).

To promote parental involvement in school decision-making, administrators and teachers need skills to chair meetings, encourage dialogue, and relieve tensions. Since this level of collaboration requires a reworking of the delicate boundary that exists between professional prerogative and parental right, care will be needed to ensure that both parents and teachers feel "empowered" rather than "deskilled." Research suggests that a systematic process emphasizing interpersonal communication and policy-shaping skills for administrators, teachers, and parents helps each group to recognize the benefits of shared decision-making and provides an orderly mechanism for transferring tightly held power among groups (Cochran and Dean 1991, Ramsay et al. 1990). Additionally, carefully constructed inservice courses are needed which provide opportunities for analyzing successes and failures (Ramsay et al. 1990).

Schools that have low rates of parental involvement may find it difficult to initiate change by themselves. Opportunities should therefore be created for the staff of schools to meet, brainstorm, and share tested ideas. Alternatively, some projects have introduced outside personnel into schools over a more extended period to act as facilitators. In their New Zealand project, for example, Ramsay et al. (1990) imported experienced senior teachers into schools as "developers." In some cases developers merely legitimated what some teachers were already doing and empowered them to spread their practices more widely; in other cases they had the more substantial task of constructively challenging the existing school order.

2.3 Negative Outcomes

Despite widespread advocacy of the benefits of greater interaction between schools and families, possibilities for negative outcomes do exist. First, research clearly shows that almost all initiatives to date have been instigated by educators, with parental participation, at least at the initial stages, being very much on the teachers' terms. Expansion of programs in anything other than the spirit of genuine partnership therefore runs the risk of sustaining a "patronizing image of the professional expert benevolently guiding the ignorant parent" (Brantlinger 1991 p.257).

Second, there are potential dangers in expanding family support networks and using parents as teachers. An unintended consequence of increasing teachers' spheres of influence within the family can be the "deskilling" of parents by making too many suggestions as to how they might behave differently toward their children and reducing their input into decision-making regarding their child's education. Alternatively, parents who are encouraged to take on more formal responsibilities for their children's learning may end up feeling less, rather than more, competent. In the special needs situation in particular there is also the danger that overemphasis on the educative role of parents can interfere with nurturing or enjoying playful activities together (Brantlinger 1991).

Third, expansion of opportunities for home–school relationships, in the absence of sufficient effort to ensure participation of all parents, may serve to disadvantage further already disadvantaged families and groups. If the parents involved in the school process are not representative, then it may be likely that the knowledge and opinions valued by the dominant elite persist. Schools that on the surface appear to be happy, pleasant places with considerably enhanced learning may be such places because they conform to collaborative goals set by the power groups of the community (Ramsay et al. 1990).

3. Conclusion

Researchers and policymakers continue to struggle to identify key strategies for enhancing school effectiveness. The rapidly growing literature on relationships with parents attests to the critical contribution this factor is now thought to play in determining student achievement and attitudes to school. The 1990s have seen a marked upsurge of policymaker interest in this area (Palanki et al. 1992).

Nevertheless, establishment of successful programs of family–school collaboration remains to a great extent a function of the vision and dynamism of individual school principals and the willingness of teachers to accept additional responsibilities. However personally rewarding and mutually beneficial such efforts may be, greater coordination of policy and practice at local, regional, state, and national levels is essential to ensure, among other things:

(a) the provision of appropriate systematic and comprehensive pre- and inservice training programs for teachers and administrators;

(b) the establishment of guidelines for appointment of school staff to positions of responsibility for home–school liaison, the provision of additional staff to allow release of teachers for out-of-class consultation and support activities, and/or the employment of ancillary staff with particular skills (e.g., translators, community elders/mediators); and

(c) the establishment of guidelines for provision of physical resources such as convenient and comfortable rooms in schools for parents attending meetings, and hospitality centers to facilitate parent–teacher consultations.

Issues of funding are, of course, critical. Discussing the situation in the United States, Palanki et al. (1992) noted that the potential for federal and state initiatives to be sustained and make a difference was endangered by changes in economic conditions and the inability of political leadership to agree about how to pay the bill to meet the needs that are increasingly being recognized.

For all these reasons, the need for further research is crucial. Innovative projects need to be carefully designed, implemented, and monitored, and existing practices carefully evaluated. Evaluation may be essentially objective, relating to specific outcome criteria such as levels of student absenteeism, student achievement, parental attendance at school meetings and events, or more subjective, including assessments of the views and opinions of the major participants.

In working with special needs children, for example, some professionals have estimated that parents need more services than parents themselves believe they require, and these professionals tend to assume that all forms of family outreach and intervention will prove worthwhile (Brantlinger 1991). Davies et al. (1992) noted on visits to schools that principals and staff generally assumed their outreach activities to be beneficial, but only rarely had them carefully documented and evaluated. Davies et al. also pointed to a lack of clarity and agreement about key definitions and concepts: words such as parent, family, involvement, community, collaboration, partnership, home visitors, family support, restructuring are used with very different meanings at the school level, as well as among researchers and policymakers.

Schools lack the time to pursue all possible strategies, and funding agencies do not have the money to finance them. Hence, it is critical that research informs policymakers and practitioners as to which strategies are most likely to yield the most positive outcomes, within the short and long term, within particular communities, and with particular partnership objectives in mind. Studies are beginning to suggest, for example, that many parents have neither the time nor inclination to respond positively to current initiatives to involve them more widely in matters of school governance (Skau 1996), and that more theoretical analysis of the deeper organizational issues implicated in collaborative ventures is crucial if projects are to avoid pitfalls deriving from institutional territoriality and the operation of "turf-maintaining incentives" (Crowson and Boyd 1993)

See also: Family and Schooling; Family, School, and Social Capital

References

Bauch J P 1990 The TransParent school: A partnership for parent involvement. *Educational Horizons* 68: 187–89

Brantlinger E 1991 Home–school partnerships that benefit children with special needs. *Elem. Sch. J.* 91(3): 249–59

Cochran M, Dean C 1991 Home–school relations and the empowerment process. *Elem. Sch. J.* 91(3): 261–69

Crowson R L, Boyd W L 1993 Coordinated services for children: Designing arks for storms and seas unknown. *Am. J. Educ.* 101(2): 140–79

Davies D, Burch P, Johnson V R 1992 *A Portrait of Schools Reaching Out: Report of a Survey of Practices and Policies of Family-Community-School Collaboration.* Report No. 1, Center on Families, Communities, Schools and Children's Learning, Johns Hopkins University, Baltimore, Maryland

Epstein J L 1992 *School and Family Partnerships.* Report No. 6, Center on Families, Communities, Schools and Children's Learning, Johns Hopkins University, Baltimore, Maryland

Hornby G 1996 *Working with Parents of Children with Special Needs.* Cassell, London

Palanki A, Burch P, Davies D 1992 *Mapping the Policy Landscape: What Federal and State Governments are Doing to Promote Family–School–Community Partnerships.* Center on Families, Communities, Schools and Children's Learning, Johns Hopkins University, Baltimore, Maryland

Ramsay P et al. 1990 *"There's no going back": Collaborative decision-making in education.* Education Department, University of Waikato, Hamilton

San Diego County Office of Education 1986 *Strategies for Enhancing School Effectivenes: Focus on Home–School Relations.* San Diego County Office of Education, San Diego, California

Schiefelbein L 1991 *In Search of the School of the XXI Century: Is the Columbian Escuela Nueva the Right Pathfinder?* UNESCO/UNICEF, Santiago, Chile

Skau K G 1996 Parental involvement: Issues and concerns. *Alberta J. Educ.* 42(1): 34–48

Topping K 1986 *Parents as Educators*. Croom Helm, London

Tripcony P 1994 Completing the circle: Towards valued Aboriginal and Torres Strait Islander participation in schooling. In: Limerick B, Nielsen H (eds.) 1994 *School and Cummunity Relations: Participation, Policy and Practice*. Harcourt Brace, Sydney

Further Reading

Azmitia M et al. 1994 *Links between Home and School among Low-income Mexican-American and European-American Families*. National Center for Research on Cultural Diversity and Second Language Learning, Santa Cruz, California

David M E 1993 *Parents, Gender and Education Reform*. Polity Press, London

Evans I M, Cicchelli T, Cohen M, Shapiro N P (eds.) 1995 *Staying in School: Partnerships for Educational Change*. Brookes, Baltimore

Kellaghan T, Sloan K, Alvarez B, Bloom B S 1993 *Home Environments and School Learning*. Jossey-Bass, San Francisco, California

McLeod F (ed.) 1989 *Parents and Schools: The Contemporary Challenge*. Falmer Press, Lewes

Montandon C 1991 *L'Ecole dans la vie des familles*. Report No. 32, Service de la Recherche Sociologique, Geneva

Munn P (eds.) *Parents and Schools: Customers, Managers or Partners?* Routledge and Kegan Paul, London

Payne M A, Hinds J O 1986 Parent–teacher relationships: Perspectives from a developing country. *Educ. Res.* 28(2): 117–25

Phi Delta Kappan 1991 72(5) (issue on parental involvement in schools)

Richardson B 1989 *Negotiating Your Child's Experience in the Public Schools: A Handbook for Black Parents*. The National Black Child Development Institute Inc., Washington, DC

Teachers in Society

Introduction: The Changing Social Role of the Teacher

L. J. Saha

The teacher occupies a central position in the classroom and in the school. The study of teaching and teachers, both as a profession and as a career, and also as co-facilitators in the educative process, has been of central interest to sociologists of education (see in Section II, *Sociology of Teaching*). In this respect, the sociological study of teachers has been theoretically grounded and approached using both qualitative and quantitative research methods.

There are 13 articles in this section which can be grouped into three general sociological dimensions with respect to teachers: (a) the profession and careers of teachers, (b) teachers in the classroom, and (c) political aspects of teachers work.

Studies of the profession and careers of teachers in effect examine the life-cycle of teachers. There are five articles in this section which address issues related to this aspect of teachers. Bolam, in *Teacher Recruitment and Induction*, relates the question of teacher recruitment to that of the quality of schooling. He also notes, however, that the extent to which the profession can attract high-quality teachers depends on a number of external factors, such as the status and economic rewards which it attracts. In this respect Hoyle's article on the social status of teachers (*Teaching, Social Status*) concludes that teachers demand relatively high social status in most societies, but is low when compared to the other professions.

Lacey's article on the *Professional Socialization of Teachers*, and Weiler's *Women and the Professionalization of Teaching* represent somewhat opposite perspectives on the professionalization of teachers. Whereas Lacey describes the process of professionalization in a sociological context and applies it to teachers, Weiler presents feminist critiques of the professionalization of teachers, which regards moves in this direction as attempts to impose an essentially male-dominated model on the teaching profession. Feminists, in turn, advocate a "feminist professionalism" which would incorporate familial and child-caring responsibilities into the structure of the workplace.

At the end of the life-cycle of teachers lies the exit from the profession. One form of social–psychological exit is discussed by Dworkin who focuses attention on teacher burnout (*Teacher Burnout*). According to Dworkin, teachers who experience excessive job stress and the lack of support from school administrators develop a sense of alienation and loss of enthusiasm for teaching. Burnout is particularly important as teachers who experience it are often "entrapped" in the job and cannot leave.

A second group of six articles focus on sociological aspects of the practice of teaching. Biddle (*Teachers' Roles*) describes the social roles of teachers in terms of their expectations and duties and locates areas of role strain. Hargreaves (*Teaching, Realities of*) points out that the rhetoric of teaching is not often matched by reality, even though Grossman (*Teachers' Knowledge*) examines the complexity of this knowledge and its implications for the increasing professionalization of teachers. Good (*Teachers' Expectations*) examines the manner in which teachers' expectations of students influence their interaction and judgement of them, while Marx and Collopy (*Student Influences on Teaching*) examine how students can change the teaching practice of teachers. Finally, Watson and Hatton (*Teacher Placement and School Staffing*) review the literature related to the manner in which teachers are allocated to schools, and show the implications the mechanisms of placement have for school quality.

The final group of two articles addresses the work of teachers and locates it within a political context. Both Ginsberg and Kamat (*Political Sociology of Teachers' Work*) and Seddon (*Teachers' Work and Political Action*) adopt a critical perspective in their analyses of the day-to-day activities of teachers, not as professionals but as workers. Whereas Ginsberg and Kamat examine the political nature of what teachers do and do not do in the classroom, Seddon relates teachers' work to the industrial arena and discusses how teachers, like students, resort to resistance and other means to blunt control over their work by administrators.

The articles in this section provide a summary of how sociologists of education approach the study of teachers and the teaching profession. Theoretical perspectives range from role theory to critical theory, and the reviews of the literature give evidence of cumulative research findings on significant aspects of teaching.

Political Sociology of Teachers' Work

M. B. Ginsburg and S. G. Kamat

Teachers work and live within unequal relations of power. Capitalism, patriarchy, racial, or ethnic group stratification; authoritarian, religious, or secular states, and/or imperialism, are embedded not only in local, national, and global communities but also in teachers' immediate work sites (classrooms and campuses) as well as in the educational system more generally. What teachers do in and outside their workplaces is dialectically related to the distribution of both: (a) the material and symbolic resources; and (b) the structural and ideological power used to control the means of producing, reproducing, consuming, and accumulating material and symbolic resources (Ginsburg 1995, Ginsburg and Lindsay 1995).

In these terms teachers can and should be considered as political actors (Carlson 1987). At its core politics consists of power relations. Politics "concerns the procedures by which scarce resources are allocated and distributed . . . [and the struggles] between groups who uphold and those who challenge the status quo" (Dove 1986 p. 30). Teachers are engaged in political action in their pedagogical, curricular, and evaluative work with students in classrooms and corridors; in their interaction with parents, colleagues, and administrators in educational institutions; in their occupational group dealings with education system authorities and state elites; and in their role as citizens in local, national, and global communities.

It is sometimes believed that teachers can and should be "apolitical" (see Zeigler 1967). Such a belief rests partly on a distinction between professional or technical activity and political action. A related foundation for this belief is the contrast between personal and political matters or between activity in the public versus the private sphere (Weiler 1987). Teachers' work is thus characterized as professional or technical, involving personal relationships among individuals in the private sphere of the classroom or school. From this perspective, it is atypical or undesirable for "professional" teachers to venture into the public sphere, either in the educational system as members of organizations or in the community as members of political parties or social movements.

The alternate perspective on which this article is based views teachers as political actors regardless of whether they are active or passive; autonomous or heteronomous vis-à-vis other political forces/groups; conservative or oriented toward change; seeking individual, occupational group, or larger collectivities' goals; and/or serving dominant or subordinate group interests. The literature reviewed in this article sheds light on the various ways in which teachers can be understood as political actors in different historical periods in various societies. The discussion is organized around the following loci of action: classrooms, educational institutions, teacher organizations, and communities.

1. Political Work in the Classroom

Giroux (1988 p. 126) states: "Rather than being objective institutions removed from the dynamics of politics and power, schools actually are contested spheres that embody and express a struggle over what forms of authority, types of knowledge, forms of moral regulation and versions of the past and future should be legitimated and transmitted to students." Thus, teachers' curricular, pedagogical, and evaluation activities are viewed as forms of political action, in that they have consequences for power relations and the distribution of material and symbolic resources. Due to the constraints of space, the focus of this review is on curriculum choices, although similar issues could be developed in relation to pedagogy (e.g., Connell 1985, Lawn and Grace 1987) as well as evaluation activity (e.g., Dove 1986, Jansen 1990, Weiler 1988).

Curriculum content represents a selection of topics and a selection of ways of viewing these topics. Power relations are embedded in curriculum both in terms of who makes the decisions and whose interests are served by the topics and perspectives included or excluded. The content of the curriculum is emphasized here, but it should be remembered that the process of constructing the curriculum is a power struggle in which teachers play a more or less active role. While teachers generally do not have full autonomy to determine officially the curriculum, they do choose to accommodate themselves to, resist, or create alternatives to the curriculum determined by others (Apple 1988, Ozga 1988, Ginsburg 1988).

The knowledge included in or excluded from the curriculum may legitimate or challenge existing relations of power; curriculum is not neutral. A variety of studies in North America have shown how capitalist relations are preserved by promoting its "positive" features, ignoring or rationalizing as individuals' failings its "negative" features, or limiting what is known about groups who have struggled to create a more just and humane economic arrangement (see Zeigler 1967). In contrast, Sultana (1991) reports how some teachers in New Zealand, who were active in social movements, developed their curriculum in order to stress the "exploitation" of workers and indigenous groups under capitalism and the role of trades union activity and class and ethnic struggle in seeking to change or transform the system.

Studies in a range of societies have documented how unequal gender relations have been legitimated through the knowledge that teachers include in or exclude from the curriculum, portraying in an unproblematic manner males' paid labor and dominance in the economy and government and females' unpaid labor with respect to family care and house maintenance. Other teachers have been concerned to stress the problematic nature of gender relations, and have developed or used antisexist curricular materials, focused attention on how patriarchal relations limit females' (and males') lives, and encouraged students to consider alternatives to stereotyped gender roles in schools and society (Lawn and Grace 1987, Weiler 1988).

Teachers have developed or transmitted curricular knowledge that has either supported or undermined unequal racial or ethnic group relations. For example, in South Africa some teachers have promoted racist stereotypes and ideologies in their classrooms, while others have sought to "redefine curriculum content from its racist, sexist, and classist bias to the empancipatory goal of social relevance, political liberation, and social equality" (Jansen 1990 p. 67). Jarausch (1990) reports similar efforts by different groups of teachers in Nazi Germany to legitimate or criticize racial stereotypes and ideologies.

The knowledge and perspectives that teachers communicate to students may encourage support or critique of the governing elites and their actions. During the First World War, teachers who were affiliated to the revolutionary syndicalist movement in France challenged the authorities and sought to replace positive and romantic images of war with a view of it as barbaric, destructive, and futile for resolving disputes (Feeley 1989). There is also evidence that during the Second World War teachers waged "spiritual warfare for the fatherland" in Germany (Jarausch 1990 p. 29), carried out "ultranationalist indoctrination" for the military regime in Japan (Blum 1969), and in the United Kingdom, implemented curricular changes which were dictated by central government and were needed to support the war effort both materially and ideologically (Lawn and Grace 1987).

The concept of "cultural imperialism" seems useful in describing teachers' roles in legitimating colonial and neocolonial rule through their curriculum choices. Such political activity by teachers has occurred both before and after Independence in African countries (Bagunywa 1975). Moreover, many teachers in the Philippines, who were tightly controlled through training, curriculum guides, and inspection, acted as conduits of the technical and cultural knowledge and skills required by the colonial administration of the United States (Caniesco-Doronila 1987). There is also contrasting evidence of teachers' curricular work challenging imperialism. For example, rural teachers in Vietnam, despite efforts by French colonial authorities to impose a curriculum that met the needs of the colonizing power and denigrated Vietnamese culture, resisted and developed a curriculum which criticized French colonialism, celebrated Vietnamese culture, and stressed the capacity for self-rule (Kelly 1982) (see *Education and Development*).

2. Institutional Politics: The Politics of the Workplace

It is generally agreed that teachers are workers and educational institutions are workplaces (Connell 1985, Ozga 1988). Like those employed in other organizations, teachers, administrators, and others who work in schools are enmeshed in interpersonal or micropolitics, involving the tactical use of power to seek and maintain control of material and symbolic resources (Blase 1991). At the same time, because education and educational workers are part of a broader set of social relations, life in schools constitutes and is constituted by power relations on a micro as well as on a macro level.

In the United Kingdom different groups of teachers —namely, those whose careers are tied to academic subjects, as opposed to those identified with pastoral care or counseling responsibilities—have competed for material resources (salary levels and program funds), symbolic resources (status and recognition), and the power to shape the direction of their schools (Ozga 1988). Collegial relations among teachers in the United States are seen to involve strategies to acquire or protect symbolic resources, such as status and psychic rewards that come from feelings of success in working with students. Diplomatic friendliness, avoiding controversy and conflict, and mutual recognition of the sanctity of individual teachers' classrooms enable teachers to survive and obtain some level of satisfaction and control by retreating from the larger institutional setting that might otherwise be overtly fraught with struggles over material and symbolic resources (Blase 1991). However, although teachers' retreat into the security of the classroom is a creative strategy, it is one that likely allows miseducative and inequality-reinforcing aspects of the system to go unchallenged (Lawn and Grace 1987).

Research in Australia, the United Kingdom, and the United States has illuminated how administrative power over teachers has been constructed, accommodated, and resisted. Focusing on the context of Latin America, Oliveros (1975 p. 231) makes clear that these power struggles have implications for material resources, including employment, salary, and promotions, in that teachers "depend on the goodwill of their supervisors . . . to remain in the profession that goodwill in turn is paid for in loyalty and by 'not creating problems.' "

Power relations between teachers and administrators partially reflect the struggle over the educational labor process. Several studies in Canada, the United Kingdom, and the United States have focused on the sometimes contested developments through which many teachers have become "proletarianized" (i.e., their work has been deskilled and divested of power) and also on how some teachers have become "professionalized" (i.e., their work has been reskilled and they have been empowered again) (Ozga 1988, Ginsburg 1988). Seen from such a perspective, it becomes apparent that administrator–teacher relations reflect and have implications for class relations. Given the gender regime of schools where men often manage women, administrator–teacher relations also constitute a terrain on which patriarchy is reproduced and struggled over (see Apple 1988, Connell 1985).

3. Teacher Organizations and Political Work

Teachers all over the world have formed associations and unions, at least in part as a collective response to their shared experiences as employees involved in the politics of educational workplaces. In a variety of European, North American, and Third World societies teachers comprise the most highly organized category of workers (Dove 1986).

Teacher organizational activity is political in the sense that it involves relations with national and local states to shape the distribution of material resources (to teachers as opposed to other groups). Teachers have worked through their organizations to demand and/or obtain higher salaries, pensions, or other material benefits (Blum 1969, Feeley 1989, Lawn and Grace 1987, Oliveros 1975, Ozga 1988, Warren 1989). However, teacher organizations have sometimes accepted passively or even legitimated the decisions of state elites (Ginsburg 1991, Rosenthal 1969).

Part of the collective political activity of teachers has been concerned with winning the right to organize and engage in negotiations with the state, collective bargaining, strike, and other forms of "militant" action (Feeley 1989, Kelly 1982). At various times in many societies it has been illegal for teachers to withhold their labor. Historically, in Japan teacher unionism was repressed by the government before the Second World War, encouraged by the United States and allied occupying forces and the Japanese Socialist government from 1945–48, and then undermined when the Conservative Party assumed power in 1948 (Blum 1969).

Teacher organizations have also struggled with local and national state elites, educational administrators, parents, and other citizens as well as other teacher organizations over issues of power, control, and autonomy. Such struggles have concerned the capacity to determine working conditions, teachers' responsibilities, and management practices; pedagogy and curriculum, and examination systems; teacher appraisal systems; educational policy and salary determination mechanisms; and level of funding for education in general (Blum 1969, Ginsburg 1991,

Lawn and Grace 1987, Oliveros 1975, Ozga 1988, Rosenthal 1969, Warren 1989).

Organized teachers have also engaged in political action in relation to the state to obtain symbolic resources, such as professional status associated with university-based preparation. Such status symbols have been seen to be valuable assets in teachers' (and other educated workers') professionalization projects, in which increased power or autonomy and remuneration are also sought. While state action has sometimes functioned to reinforce teacher professionalization, teachers have also been the targets of deprofessionalizing or proletarianizing efforts by the state (Dove 1986, Ginsburg 1991, Jarausch 1990, Lawn and Grace 1987, Nwagwu 1977).

A major ideological weapon used both by teachers and by the state in such struggles, at least in the United Kingdom and former British colonies, is "professionalism." While there are multiple and contradictory meanings of the term "professionalism," both in social scientific literature and in everyday discourse, the notion of a hierarchical division of labor, legitimated by a meritocratic conception of educational attainment, is often a central element. In drawing on and reproducing this ideology, teachers help to legitimate a division of labor required by at least capitalist relations of production (Ginsburg 1988). This tendency is strengthened by the fact that some conceptions of professionalism distinguish professionals' organizational efforts from the "unionism" of members of the working class (Ozga 1988). This is part of the reason why in some societies the issue of teachers being affiliated to the broader labor movement stimulates such controversy, even though organized teachers have played a major leadership role in the labor movement in certain societies (Blum 1969, Feeley 1989, Ginsburg 1991).

Race relations have also affected and been shaped by the discourse and action of organized teachers. For instance, De Lyon and Migniuolo (1989) conclude that the interests of Black teachers in England and Wales were less well served by the various teacher unions and associations during the 1970s and 1980s, although the National Union of Teachers developed materials to be used by teachers in the classrooms to encourage multiculturalism and combat racism. Similarly, throughout the 1940s in the United States teachers' organizations were racially segregated, and many organized White teachers did not play a supportive role in Black teachers' organizations' struggles for equal pay (Warren 1989). The struggle by organized teachers in New York City in 1968 against Black community efforts to control their schools locally also indicates that teachers' desire for professional autonomy is related to the distribution of power among racial groups.

Teacher organizations' activity is also political as regards the perpetuation and challenging of gender relations. In Germany, the predominantly male secondary teacher organization sought to achieve and maintain professional status for their members by excluding and distancing themselves from corps of predominantly female primary teachers (Jarausch 1990). In the United Kingdom teacher organizations have tended to reflect male approaches to dealing with issues accorded more importance by male than female teachers, while ignoring concerns, such as childcare and domestic responsibilities, that affect women more than men (De Lyon and Migniuolo 1989). Historically in the United Kingdom, France, and the United States some teacher organizations have fought for equal pay for male and female teachers, while others have worked against it (Feeley 1989, De Lyon and Migniuolo 1989, Warren 1989). More-over, while women have served in leadership roles in teacher organizations in some societies, females are often underrepresented in high positions in teacher organizations in even the same countries (De Lyon and Migniuolo 1989, Warren 1989, Weiler 1987, Zeigler 1967). This point, however, must be qualified insofar as male and female teachers may play different, yet active and essential, roles in organizing collective action such as strikes (Lawn and Grace 1987, Weiler 1987).

4. Political Work in the Community

Both individually and through their associations and unions, and due to either the dictates of political and economic elites or their own values and convictions, teachers have come to play an active political role in the community. It should be borne in mind that nonparticipation may also constitute a political act—a point well illustrated by the fact that governments have occasionally sought to restrict certain types of teachers' community-based political action (Blum 1969, Dove 1986, Jarausch 1990, Zeigler 1967).

In Africa, Asia, Europe, and Latin America teachers have played leading or active participatory roles in nationalist and independence movements, and in anticolonial or anti-imperial struggles (Blum 1969, Dove 1986, Kelly 1982, Lauglo 1982). Teachers have also been prominent actors in revolutions, such as in China (White 1981), France (Feeley 1989), Mexico (Blum 1969), and Russia (Seregny 1989) during the early decades of the twentieth century, as well as in recent years in Cote d'Ivoire and Hungary (Ginsburg 1991). As Jansen (1990 p. 63) reports about his own and his colleagues' experiences in the revolutionary context of South Africa, at "moments of student–teacher–police confrontation [we] made the transition from the technocratic teacher to political activist and, on occasion, to comrade in armed struggle."

More generally, teachers have served as community leaders, *animateurs*, and agents of social change (Dove 1986, Lauglo 1982). Sometimes they have challenged the political and cultural hegemony of dominant groups and at other times they have operated as agents of state and economic elites. Similarly, teachers have functioned as mediators between national state elites and the local citizenry, while trying to find room for autonomous action in the middle of a conflict between a secular state and the Church (Blum 1969, Meyers 1976). Dove (1986) concludes that teachers more often served in community leadership roles during the pre- and immediately post-Independence periods in "developing" countries than is the case in latter years, and Lauglo (1982) reports that, historically, European and North American rural teachers have varied widely in the extent to which they performed such roles. In both cases the relative level of education of teachers compared to community members is seen as the key variable, with teachers being more active when they are more educated than community members.

In a variety of contexts heads of state, legislators, and other government officials have worked as teachers at one point of their lives (Berube 1988, Dove 1986, Jarausch 1990, Lawn and Grace 1987, Nwagwu 1977). Teachers have also been leaders of political parties as well as being overrepresented, compared to other occupational groups, as active party members (Ginsburg 1991). To varying degrees individual and organized teachers devote time to lobbying and candidate electoral work (Blum 1969, Warren 1989, Zeigler 1967).

Teachers' community-based political work has focused on a variety of issues. Teachers in the United States and the United Kingdom have been active members in the feminist and civil rights movements fighting for universal suffrage, emancipation, racial desegregation, and tax reform (Lawn and Grace 1987, Warren 1989). In contrast to these more progressive actions, those secondary school teachers who had not been purged from their organization endorsed the Nazi regime in Germany in 1933. Jarausch (1990) also indicates that some teachers took a public stand against the Nazis' fascist and racist project, while others rationalized their duty to make at least minimal concessions to Hitler's demands.

During this same period teachers in Germany and the United Kingdom contributed time and energy to community-based work to support their respective nations in the war effort (Jarausch 1990, Ozga 1988). Teachers have also become involved in antimilitarist peace movements, as in the case of Japanese teachers after the Second World War (Blum 1969) and French primary school teachers at the time of the First World War (Feeley 1989).

5. Conclusion

The actions that teachers engage in, or refrain from, in classrooms, educational institutions, teachers' organizations, and communities can be viewed as political. Although each has been discussed separately, these arenas in which teachers engage in political action should not be treated as discrete or unrelated. For example, teachers' involvement in community-based social movements may be reinforced or contradicted by how they select and organize curriculum knowledge. Their activity or inactivity in the community may be related to focusing students' attention on or ignoring inequalities, exploitation and oppression, and the role subordinate groups play in challenging such relations of power (Blum 1969, Connell 1985, Kelly 1982, Sultana 1991, Zeigler 1967).

In discussing the political work of teachers this entry has acknowledged that teachers are not a homogeneous group, and thus has endeavored to identify multiple means and ends of teachers' political work. Although some patterns and similarities obtain across a range of countries, over time, and among different groups of teachers in the same location and time period, there are also important differences internationally, historically, and intra-occupationally (Ginsburg 1995).

This entry has emphasized international comparisons, but historical comparisons are also instructive. For example, it has been noted that the relations between organized teachers and the state have varied according to historical period in the United Kingdom, Cote d'Ivoire, Germany, Hungary, Japan, Mexico, and the United States (see Berube 1988, Blum 1969, Ginsburg 1991, Jarausch 1990, Lawn and Grace 1987).

Divisions among teachers and their organizations also make general statements about their political work problematic. In a range of societies there are examples of teacher organizations fractionated by gender, race/ethnicity, social class-related differences in the level of the educational system in which their members work or were educated, subject matter taught, regional location, religious identification, political ideology or party affiliation, militancy and orientation to alliances with other groups of organized labor (Blum 1969, Feeley 1989, Ginsburg 1991, Lawn and Grace 1987, Jarausch 1990, De Lyon and Migniuolo 1989, Nwagwu 1977, Ozga 1988, Warren 1989, Zeigler 1967).

Thus, different groups of teachers at different times and places have engaged and continue to engage in a wide range of active and inactive forms of political work (Ginsburg and Lindsay 1995). The variation among teachers also means that the consequences of political work by different groups of teachers may sometimes reinforce and at other times challenge the existing distribution of material resources, symbolic resources, and power among various groups from the local to the global level. Moreover, because of the contradictions in power relations that are constitutive of and constituted by teachers' individual and collective action, it is often the case that a given teacher in a given time and place operates in a manner, for example, that partially serves the interests of both dominant and subordinate groups. The issue to be addressed, therefore, is not whether teachers should be political actors, but to what ends, by what means, and in whose interests teachers should engage in political activity.

See also: Authority and Power in Educational Organizations; Teachers' Work and Political Action

References

Apple M W 1988 *Teachers and Texts: A Political Economy of Class and Gender Relations in Education.* Routledge and Kegan Paul, New York

Bagunywa A 1975 The changing role of the teacher in African educational renewal. *Prospects* 5(2): 220–26

Berube M 1988 *Teacher Politics: The Influence of Unions* Greenwood Press, New York

Blase J (ed.) 1991 *The Politics of Life in Schools: Power Conflict and Cooperation.* Sage, Newbury Park, California

Blum A (ed.) 1969 *Teacher Unions and Associations: A Comparative Study.* University of Illinois Press, Urbana, Illinois

Canieso-Doronila M L 1987 Teachers and national identify formation: A case study from the Philippines. *J. Educ. Equity and Leadership* 7(4): 278–300

Carlson D 1987 Teachers as political actors: From reproductive theory to the crisis of schooling. *Harv. Educ. Rev.* 57(3): 283–307

Connell R 1985 *Teachers' Work.* Allen and Unwin, Sydney

De Lyon H, Migniuolo F W (eds.) 1989 *Women Teachers: Issues and Experiences.* Open University Press, Milton Keynes

Dove L 1986 *Teachers and Teacher Education in Developing Countries.* Croom Helm, London

Feeley F M 1989 *Rebels With Causes: A Study Of Revolutionary Syndicalist Culture Among The French Primary School Teachers Between 1880 and 1919.* Peter Lang, New York

Ginsburg M 1988 *Contradictions In Teacher Education and Society: A Critical Analysis.* Falmer Press, New York

Ginsburg M (ed.) 1991 *Understanding Educational Reform In Global Context: Economy Ideology and the State.* Garland, New York

Ginsburg M (ed.) 1995 *The Politics of Educators' Work and Lives.* Garland Publishing, New York

Ginsburg M, Lindsay B. (eds.) 1995 *The Political Dimension in Teacher Education: Comparative Perspectives in Policy Formation, Socialization and Society.* Falmer Press, New York

Giroux H 1988 *Teachers as Intellectuals: Toward a Critical Pedagogy of Learning.* Bergin and Garvey, Granby, Massachusetts

Jansen J 1990 In search of liberation pedagogy in South Africa. *J. Educ.* 172(2): 62–71

Jarausch K 1990 *The Unfree Professions: German Lawyers, Teachers and Engineers 1900–1950.* Oxford University Press, New York

Kelly G 1982 Teachers and the transmission of state knowledge: A case study of colonial Vietnam. In: Altbach P, Arnove R, Kelly G (eds.) 1982 *Comparative Education.* Macmillan, New York

Lauglo J 1982 Rural primary teachers as potential community leaders? Contrasting historical cases in Western countries. *Comp. Educ.* 18(3): 233–55

Lawn M, Grace G (eds.) 1987 *Teachers: The Culture and Politics Of Work.* Falmer Press, Lewes

Meyers P 1976 Professionalization and societal change: Rural teachers in nineteenth century France. *J. Soc. Hist.* 9(4): 542–58

Nwagwu N 1977 Problems of professional identity among African school teachers. *J. Educ. Admin. Hist.* 9(2): 49–54

Oliveros A 1975 Change and the Latin American teacher: Potentialities and limitations. *Prospects* 5(2): 230–38

Ozga J (ed.) 1988 *Schoolwork: Approaches To The Labour Process Of Teaching.* Open University Press, Milton Keynes

Rosenthal A 1969 *Pedagogues and Power: Teacher Groups in School Politics.* Syracuse University Press, Syracuse, New York

Seregny S 1989 *Russian Teachers and The Peasant Revolution: The Politics Of Education In 1905.* Indiana University Press, Bloomington, Indiana

Sultana R 1991 Social movements and the transformation of teachers' work: Case studies from New Zealand. *Research Papers in Education* 6(2): 133–52

Warren D (ed.) 1989 *American Teachers: History of a Profession at Work.* Macmillan, New York

Weiler K 1988 *Women Teaching For Change: Gender Class and Power.* Bergin and Garvey, South Hadley, Massachusetts

White G 1981 *Party and Professionals: The Political Role of Teachers in Contemporary China.* M E Sharpe, New York

Zeigler H 1967 *The Political Life Of American Teachers.* Prentice-Hall, Englewood Cliffs, New Jersey

Professional Socialization of Teachers

C. Lacey

The term "professional socialization of teachers" refers to the process of change by which individuals become members of the teaching profession and then take on progressively more mature roles, usually of higher status, within the profession. It is clear from this description that the particular characteristics of this process depend on the nature and structure of the teaching profession. Hence, the radical changes that affected the education systems of many countries in the 1980s will be seen to have had a clear effect on the professional socialization of teachers.

The term does not refer to a single period of transformation from student to teacher. Rather, it is a progressive, continuous process with options and choices and sometimes with recognizably different career channels. Nevertheless, there are important similarities in this process which make the study of professional socialization of teachers a rewarding field for researchers. Furthermore, the field is also of great interest to an audience of administrators and teachers whose consciousness of international issues and comparisons is constantly on the increase.

This article is organized into four major sections: definition, descriptions of research models, research findings, and recent educational changes and international comparisons. The account is enriched by weaving in a number of the themes which illustrate conflicts of ideology and purpose. These themes permeate the subject matter of each section, and relate to contemporary social issues and likely future crises. For example, the question arises as to whether teachers should be more like functionaries of the state, namely bureaucrats who merely carry out the designs and purposes of those who control the state, or whether, as

professionals, they should be predominantly educators and visionaries in their own right, whose common purpose is guided and modified by their personal philosophy and individual appraisal of the priorities of education for an increasingly uncertain future. This dilemma underlies many of the contemporary conflicts and disputes within education. The different directions in which this contest is moving has produced contrasting outcomes in many countries, both developed and developing.

1. The Definition of Professional Socialization

In an early classical study of medical students, Merton et al. (1957) produced an important definition of socialization: "The process by which people selectively acquire the values and attitudes, the interests, skills and knowledge—in short the culture—current in groups to which they are, or seek to become a member" (p. 287). The process of professional socialization into teaching therefore amounts to far more than just learning to teach. By including values, attitudes, and interests, Merton indicates that becoming a teacher involves more than the simple acquisition of academic knowledge and the skills necessary to conduct lessons.

Despite the undoubted strength and usefulness of Merton's definition, it falls short of modern practice in a number of respects. There is a strong suggestion in the definition that teaching is a single culture, an agreement about the basic values and practices within the profession; in technical terms, a "central value system." Researchers who have adhered to this view have usually also adopted a "functionalist" model of society and their research can often be described as central tendency analysis.

The major weakness of this viewpoint is that it glosses over the variations and disagreements that almost inevitably arise in any profession, but are particularly marked in teaching. Merton's definition refers to selective acquisition of values, but does not give the process much emphasis. Nor does the definition give prominence to the interactive, conflictual, and situational elements in this process of acquisition and practice. All of these elements have been stressed in later studies of the professional socialization of teachers and therefore need to be examined carefully. In fact, substantial and fundamental conflicts do exist; individuals are active in choosing and selecting from this variety of values and practices; and these individuals are often careful about to whom and in what situation they reveal their views and practices.

2. Early Research Models in the Study of Professional Socialization

As mentioned above, early studies of professional socialization were almost entirely based on functionalist models of society and used relatively crude central tendency methods of analysis. The basic assumptions underlying functionalist views of society are best expressed in the analogy of society as an organism. Parts of society are seen as functioning parts of the whole, carrying out essential tasks in harmony with the main purpose of society. In practical terms, adherence to this model implies that experienced and responsible members of society or members of the profession can recognize "good practice" or "good teachers." This assumption of a widely held and recognizable consensus lay at the root of a research tradition established in the 1950s and 1960s which "arose from a practical interest in finding better methods for selecting persons who would make 'good' teachers and in improving the training and assessment of students and practitioners" (Morrison and McIntyre 1969 p. 13).

This research tradition failed because of its theoretical and methodological weakness. It embodied a philosophy of education and a view of professional socialization that was subjected to increasing critical scrutiny in the 1970s. In addition, it failed in a practical sense to predict the best new teachers and improve the quality of training (Morrison and McIntyre 1969).

Nevertheless, this research tradition is always capable of resuscitation and rebirth. Since the 1980s governments have shown a growing tendency to intervene in reshaping education systems. They have also funded and shaped research into education to supply answers to their major concerns, which may be categorized broadly as making teachers more "efficient" and education more relevant to the needs of industry and production. These pressures have had the effect of regenerating functionalist approaches to research.

The transition from student to professional person has often been characterized as dramatic and abrupt. In Western societies the obvious change in dress from casual or eccentric student styles to the neat relatively formal dress required in schools is easily recognized and often regarded as signifying a more profound transformation of the person to accepting more socially conservative values and practices. Early studies of teacher socialization stressed the relative lack of power of initiates to the profession and gave prominence to the differences between the idealistic and radical opinions of students and the realistic and practical orientations they developed as they became teachers. Teaching appeared to produce an even more dramatic transformation than most professions because the conservative influence of senior colleagues was coupled with the chastening experience of unruly classes for those who failed to adopt authoritarian classroom discipline. Functionalist theories coupled with predominantly central tendency questionnaire designs conspired to legitimate and substantiate these findings.

3. Developments in Adult Socialization

Two publications in the early 1960s paved the way for substantial advances in the study of adult socialization. Becker et al. (1961) undertook a detailed participant observation study of medical students. Earlier socialization research had usually been based on questionnaire studies, designed to allow comparisons to be made over time or with some expected outcome. Becker et al. were more concerned with detailed observation of social processes and identifying a set of concepts that accurately portrayed their understanding of a complex process. They established a tradition of research within the study of professional socialization and a set of usefully applied concepts (e.g., culture, latent culture, perspective, and commitment) that could be used in the study of the professional socialization of teachers.

Wrong's (1961) contribution was very different. His seminal essay points to the oversocialized conceptualization of "man" (sic). He portrayed culture as a violation of human nature and as a consequence described socialization as an imperfect or partial process in which essential elements of individuals can, through choice, stay outside. His conceptualization represents an important modification of early functional theories of socialization in which individuals are assumed to conform or fail because of inability or deviance.

These two contributions represented an important stimulus to later research and although Becker et al. still emphasized the power of the socializing institution (through the concept of situational adjustment, in which individuals transform themselves "into the kind of person the situation demands"), the basis for a deeper, more complex understanding of professional socialization had been established.

4. Modern Research Tradition and its Findings

The modern research tradition in professional socialization can be characterized as bringing together a wider range of research methodologies and a richer framework of concepts and theory, including less determinant notions of culture. It has also broadened the scope of relevant factors to be included in major studies. Earlier studies focused on:

(a) the quality of the training or learning experience;

(b) the stresses experienced in the classroom as students or young teachers struggle with the problems of classroom control, pupil learning difficulties, and a heavy workload;

(c) the influence of important "others" (e.g., tutors, fellow students or teachers, head teachers).

The modern tradition has included these factors, often obtaining deeper insights into these processes and their significance through the use of participant observation as well as questionnaire and interview techniques. This tradition has also given greater emphasis to other factors that have enabled new theoretical insights and concepts to be developed. For example:

(a) the process of selection by which students choose training courses or schools in which to start their careers;

(b) the importance of personal agendas, relating to individuals' purposes in teaching, their ideas about career and their values as well as the contribution that individuals make to building institutions and cultures;

(c) the external influences of government or markets that shape the institutions in which teachers teach, and enlarge or constrict their choices in the various areas of teaching.

4.1 Modification of Early Models of Professional Socialization of Teachers

As noted above, the functionalist social theory and questionnaire methodologies established a picture of teacher socialization as a reversion to the conservative practices of the classroom that new teachers experienced as pupils and that they reexperienced as relatively powerless neophyte teachers. This analysis depended on seeing teaching as a relatively monolithic culture heavily constrained by agreements on what constituted "good practice" and classroom situations that were able to deliver substantial punishment to new

teachers who failed to conform: the "reality shock."

During the 1960s and 1970s changes took place within education that made these assumptions less valid. Educational provision expanded in almost all industrial and developing countries. Large numbers of pupils experienced levels of education unknown to their parents' generation. Educators searched for new pedagogies and new subject matter to cater to the new cohorts of pupils, and education entered a phase of flux and experimentation.

Some studies failed to take serious account of these changes. Shipman (1967) felt able to explain student "progressivism" as "impressional management" that withered away as soon as the college situation no longer existed and the reality of the staffroom and classroom became relevant. Similarly, Hanson and Herrington (1976) summarized their conclusions from their study of probationary teachers as follows: " . . . the only way apparently open to the probationers was to conform to the conventional wisdom and recipe knowledge of those around them, and this was largely an accumulation of the indigenous traditions and folkways of (the) staffroom" (p. 61).

The modern tradition has not totally negated these findings nor shown that they do not exist. Rather, it has demonstrated their partial nature and their exclusion of many competing processes. The modern picture of professional socialization emerges from the literature as being closer to a struggle in which individuals confront institutions and make their purposes felt. While this struggle often occurs on an individual basis, it can also arise from group action. The results of these studies reveal the complexity of the interactive process in which individuals may change while at the same time maintaining some stable and unchanging element in their practice and purpose. The studies also demonstrate a link between adult socialization and social change through microchanges produced within institutions.

4.2 Process of Selection and Anticipatory Socialization

Professions are frequently differentiated on the basis of status. Prestigious training institutions are able to attract high-flying individuals from social elites who will go on to obtain prominent positions within their professions and therefore ensure the reputation and high standing of the training institution with the next generation of aspirants. Where competition for entry is fierce this hierarchy of institutions, usually backed by real advantages in career and income, can have a marked socializing effect. It is necessary for individuals to prepare themselves quite carefully to become the kind of person that the professional norms demand. This process of preparation, often termed "anticipatory socialization," is most marked in the older, better paid professions. It is less marked in teaching and it is important to understand the reasons for this.

In all modern societies teaching is a large, relatively open profession. It is difficult for it to become or remain socially exclusive. Most children obtain detailed insights into teaching by attending school. It is therefore the obvious profession for aspiring working class or low caste children to enter. Thus, teaching acts as a channel for social mobility in many societies. It is also a profession with a "caring" as well as a "technical" role. Teaching has traditionally attracted a high proportion of women. While it is possible to demonstrate that in most countries women are discriminated against in terms of promotion and senior posts, it is often the case that teaching represents a relatively good career for women. The reverse is the case for men, where the availability of careers in the older, usually more lucrative, professions of medicine, law, and engineering means that teaching represents only one among many alternative careers. While this pattern is changing slowly, particularly in the rich industrialized countries, it remains a general phenomenon.

Teaching is a divided profession in other respects. It is differentiated according to subject discipline, the qualifications and training that the professionals bring to the classroom, the status of the schools in which they teach, the professional associations and unions that represent the profession, and disagreements over the aims, purposes, and philosophy of education. Some of these divisions are particularly important for the process of professional socialization.

Disputes over the aims and purposes of education have always existed. Education prepares young people for entry into society. As differences of opinion have emerged about the nature of society, so their effect has been felt in education and the training of teachers. One recurring dispute concerns a difference of opinion about the very nature of knowledge. Is knowledge easily defined within subject boundaries, authoratively laid down within the curriculum, and properly passed on as a series of skills and facts? Or is knowledge less easily defined, subject to individual interpretation, and best "discovered" by the learner who is assisted by the teacher? In the United Kingdom in the 1960s and 1970s, these and other similar questions gave rise to recognizably different approaches to the training of teachers. Some university courses became recognizably innovative; others remained relatively traditional. In turn these differences were registered by students, who were able to choose a course that suited their philosophy.

In a study of five university departments of education in the United Kingdom, Lacey et al. (1973) were able to demonstrate this process at work. The five courses in the study had been selected along a traditional–innovatory course dimension derived from course descriptions. The reasons for students choosing their courses were examined and coded according to whether they took the educational content or organization of the courses into account.

The results suggested that students clearly used their knowledge of the way in which the courses were taught to obtain the kind of socializing experience they desired. As a consequence, they influenced the student membership in each course and hence attended a course in the company of students who were more like themselves than would have been the case on other courses. This aspect of student choice is often neglected in studies of socialization.

4.3 Social Strategies

The use of participant observation and intensive interviewing within studies of professionalization gave rise to a wealth of data, much of which could not be explained by existing theories or described using existing concepts. In particular, the complex behavior of individuals observed in seminars or classrooms often could not be reconciled with the descriptive statistics derived from questionnaires. In addition, case studies of individuals showed that action in one situation apparently contradicted action in another. It was not until the individual's purpose in and definition of the situation were taken into account that the actions were capable of interpretation.

The concept of social strategy, developed by Blumer (1969) within interactionist theory, was adopted by a large number of researchers (Lacey 1977, Woods 1977, Hargreaves 1977, 1980). This concept suggests that individuals are purposeful beings, choosing between different courses of action which offer (apparent) solutions to the problems they face. Lacey (1977) developed the concept of situational adjustment into three broad strategies that incorporate the innovatory aspect of human action as well as the conforming aspects stressed by functionalists. They are: (a) internalized adjustment, (b) strategic compliance, and (c) strategic redefinition.

In the internalized adjustment strategy, the individual complies with the constraints and believes that the constraints of the situation are for the best.

Strategic compliance is the strategy where the individual complies with the authority figure's definition of the situation and the constraints on his or her action but retains private reservations about them. This latter strategy is exemplified by the student teacher who, in a written response, explained,

> Although I disagreed with my teacher-tutor, the only way to cope was to concur with her when she was present i.e., discipline of children, approach to timetable, artwork, and importance of art and the story in the curriculum. (Lacey 1977 p. 93)

Strategic redefinition is a strategy in which the individual engages in innovating within situations and, in some measure, actually changes the situation. Strategic redefinition strategies were pursued by individuals who did not possess the formal power to change situations but who nevertheless did succeed in changing them. They achieved this in most cases by causing or enabling those with formal power (tutors or head teachers) to change their interpretation of what was appropriate in any given situation.

Cooper (1990) and Zeichner and Tabachnick (1985) explored the strategies employed by student teachers and new teachers in pursuit of innovatory teaching techniques during practice teaching and early employment. Detailed case studies of a small number of teachers were made. The results suggested that individuals were able to pursue innovatory teaching methods despite substantial difficulty in doing so. Cooper found that when trying to implement investigations within mathematics teaching the main problem was the student teachers' own inexperience with a new and complex methodology. Zeichner and Tabachnick found that, within the closed system of the classroom, teachers had substantial freedoms and were able to maintain subsystems that conflicted with the expectations of the main school.

5. Educational Change and International Comparisons

Since the mid-1970s the economic expansion that followed the Second World War has been interrupted by a series of recessions. The optimistic support of educational expansion, accompanied by measures designed to produce greater equality of opportunity, has given way to criticism. Education has sometimes been made the scapegoat for economic failure. Throughout the world, education has been put under pressure to serve the economic needs of society rather than the educational needs of children. While such pressure has been similar in both rich and poor countries, the outcomes have been surprisingly different.

The education systems of the poor, predominantly agricultural countries, have been characterized by very few resources, including a lack of adequately trained teachers who are restricted to didactic, recitative methods of teaching. Teachers' freedom is often strictly circumscribed by bureaucracy, with little autonomy accorded them in shaping the curriculum. Teachers are usually at the bottom of a formidable hierarchy of political and administrative control and have little choice where and whom they teach. This system has been shown to alienate both teachers and pupils and is largely held responsible for the low levels of literacy and educational achievement in many poor countries.

After the World Conference on Education for All was held in Jomtien, Thailand in 1990, a new consensus emerged. The emphasis was now placed heavily on primary education and a drive for literacy and basic numeracy in poor rural and urban areas was instigated. Changes in educational policy, supported by donor organizations, have produced changes in teacher training and professional socialization. In India and Indonesia, for example, large-scale state-wide projects have been set up to provide inservice training for teachers. This training introduces child-centered techniques, group work, discussion, working with materials, and similar activities. The professional socialization of teachers has moved toward the model of teaching developed in the Western industrialized countries in the 1960s and 1970s and could represent a radical change if it proves to be successful.

In contrast, the critique of education in industrialized countries has occasionally centered on the very teaching methods being adopted in these new projects. The United Kingdom government has been most radical in this respect and has attempted to introduce market mechanisms as a source of competition and control. Schools are expected to publish examination results (including results of new tests introduced by the government), the curriculum has been centralized, and the proportion of the nation's resources allocated to schools reduced. The effects on the professional socialization of teachers will be most marked as teachers and schools compete in a market for pupils and resources. The change from a bureaucratic–professional milieu in which educational and social issues were highlighted to a market–competitive milieu in which a premium is placed on examination results and pupil numbers represents one of the most radical experiments ever undertaken in education. It will have important, and as yet unknown, effects on the patterns of teacher socialization. Now that the mechanisms and processes of adult socialization are better understood, much material for discussion and dispute is set to emerge from this field of study in the 1990s.

See also: Socialization; Women and the Professionalization of Teaching

References

Becker H S, Geer B, Hughes E 1961 *Boys in White: Student Culture in Medical School.* University of Chicago Press, Chicago, Illinois

Blumer H 1969 *Symbolic Interactionism: Perspective and Method.* Prentice-Hall, Englewood Cliffs, New Jersey

Cooper B 1990 PGCE students and investigational approaches in secondary maths. *Research Papers Educ.* 5(2): 127–51

Hanson D, Herrington M 1976 *From College to Classroom: The Probationary Year.* Routledge and Kegan Paul, London

Hargreaves A 1977 Progressivism and pupil autonomy. *Sociol. Rev.* 25(3): 585–621

Hargreaves A 1980 Synthesis and the study of strategies: A project for the sociological imagination. In: Woods P (ed.) *Pupil Strategies.* Croom Helm, London

Lacey C 1977 *The Socialization of Teachers.* Methuen, London

Lacey C, Horton M, Hoad P 1973 *Tutorial Schools Research Project: Teacher Socialization, the Post Grad Training Year.* Social Science Research Council, London

Merton R K, Reader G G, Kendall P L (eds.) 1957 *The Student Physician: Introductory Studies in the Sociology of Medical Education.* Harvard University Press, Cambridge, Massachusetts

Morrison A, McIntyre D 1969 *Teachers and Teaching.* Penguin, Harmondsworth.

Shipman M D 1967 Theory and practice in the education of teachers. *Educ. Res.* 9(3): 208–12

Woods P E 1977 Teaching for survival. In: Woods P E,

Hammersley M (eds.) 1977 *School Experience*. Croom Helm, London

Wrong D H 1961 The oversocialized conception of man in modern sociology. *Am. Sociol. Rev.* 26(2): 183–93

Zeichner K M, Tabachnick B R 1985 The development of teacher perspectives: Social strategies and institutional control in the socialization of beginning teachers. *J. Educ. Teaching* 11(1): 1–25

Student Influences on Teaching

R. W. Marx and R. M. B. Collopy

Teaching and learning in classrooms are complex, multiply determined phenomena. It is generally assumed that teachers, through their teaching, influence the learning of students. It is equally true, however, that students influence the ways in which they are taught. When in their classrooms, teachers may act or react on the basis of means–ends reasoning or "bounded rationality." That is, teachers adapt their methods of teaching (the means) to achieve certain goals (the ends) to differences among students. Similarly, teachers may teach students according to the expectations they have of them (see *Teachers' Expectations*).

The ways in which students influence teachers have been studied by many researchers using a variety of research methodologies. The results of these studies are presented and examined in this article in terms of two guiding questions. First, what characteristics and behaviors of students influence teachers' classroom behavior and instructional practices? Second, what theoretical mechanisms account for teachers' differential behavior and practices?

1. Assumptions

There are two basic assumptions that guide this review. First, much of teaching is assumed to be a mindful enterprise. That is, teachers modify their actions toward different students based on some sort of means–ends reasoning. Second, teachers are assumed to be subject to influences other than those that are rational. Much theoretical and empirical work has examined the expectations of teachers, the ways in which these expectations are communicated to students, and the ways in which these expectations, once communicated, influence students. While the second assumption has been discussed widely (e.g., Rosenthal and Jacobson 1968), the first needs some elaboration.

Schools are institutions with particular social purposes (e.g., developing basic literacy and numeracy skills, cultivation of mind, socialization to cultural norms and practices, preparation for participation in the local and national economy). As the primary agents of this institution, teachers act in ways that are consistent with the attainment of some or all of these goals. This is not to say that all interactions between teachers and students are influenced by such a "bounded-rationality" conception, nor that such interactions actually optimize outcomes. Rather, it means that many of the interactions are influenced by such a conception.

Several instructional theories have been developed to examine how a bounded rationality of teaching might work in classrooms. One of the more elegant has been developed since the late 1960s by Snow (1988). The elegance in Snow's work lies in both its psychological sophistication and in its explicit reliance on how instruction can be adapted to individual differences in learners. Snow refers to these individual differences as "aptitudes," which are characteristics of the learner prior to instruction that influence the extent to which the instruction will be effective. Individual differences in characteristics such as sex, ethnicity, and prior achievement can serve as devices that teachers use to connect goals with instruction, learning, and, assessment.

2. Research on Students' Influence on Teaching

Studies of students' effects on teachers tend to focus on three characteristics of students: their sex, ethnicity, and prior level of educational achievement. Some studies have examined two, or in a small number of cases, all three of these characteristics. In a few studies, researchers have investigated interactions among these characteristics of students and the same characteristics of teachers (e.g., how the sex or ethnicity of the teacher interacts with sex or ethnicity of the students). Two lines of inquiry have been used in these studies: process–product and teacher expectancies. Much of the process–product research on classroom teaching has been based on a behavioral conception of classroom interaction. The goal of this research tradition is to identify those teacher behaviors and their antecedents that are associated with higher levels of student attainment. The research methodology is quantitative, relying on correlational and descriptive studies as well as subsequent field-based experiments to demonstrate the impact of particular teacher behaviors or clusters of behaviors on student learning. The second line of inquiry directly relevant to the ways in which students affect teaching is the research on teacher expectancies. Work along this line addresses more global or inferential dimensions of classroom action and relies on qualitative research methods such as ethnographies, case studies, and teacher narratives.

2.1 Process–Product Studies

An example of a process–product study based on a behavioral approach to studying students and teachers is that conducted by Nafpaktitis et al. (1985). These researchers were interested in teacher approval and disapproval of student behavior as a function of the students' on-task and off-task behavior. Their research methods included an interval time sampling observation procedure whereby 84 intermediate school teachers (Grades 6–9) and their students were observed for two or three 30-minute periods. Teacher approval and disapproval rates were calculated and correlated with rates of student off-task and on-task behavior. Nafpaktitis et al. found that teachers who tended to approve of off-task student behavior more often also had lower rates of on-task behavior. Similarly, teachers who tended to disapprove of off-task behavior had higher rates of student on-task behavior. Working in a similar tradition, Simpson and Erickson (1983) found that White teachers in the United States directed more verbal praise, nonverbal praises and verbal criticism toward first-grade males than toward first-grade females. However, they directed more nonverbal criticism to Black males than to any other sex–race grouping.

One of the problems with work in the genre of the Nafpaktitis et al. and the Simpson and Erickson studies is that the potential role of subject matter in conditioning the types of interactions between teachers and students and among students is ignored (Stodolsky 1988). Weber and Shake (1988), for example, examined teacher rejoinders (i.e., teachers' responses to students' answers) in the comprehension phase of reading instruction in second-grade classrooms. In the overwhelming majority of these rejoinders, teachers accepted students' answers as correct. Only about 6 percent of the rejoinders indicated that the students' answers were incorrect.

By and large, the finding that teachers tend to accept or approve of students' response has been replicated over a large number of studies, at least in United States classrooms. However, because students' understanding of these teacher responses interacts in many different ways with personal (e.g., beliefs about self as learner or what one considers valuable or worthwhile), social (e.g., norms for peer support), and situational (e.g., goal structures associated with grading practices) factors, it is difficult to make generalizable, theoretically robust predictions about student behavior based on such findings.

In a study of 36 fourth-grade mathematics classes in the United States, Fennema and Peterson (1986) found very complex interactions involving teachers' differential behavior toward boys and girls. The teachers' differential behavior also interacted with achievement differently for boys and girls, depending on whether the achievement was assessed by tasks that required higher or lower level thinking. As an example of the complexity of these findings, Fennema and Peterson stated that for lower level tasks, teachers' praise for girls' correct responses was positively related to test scores on these tasks. For boys, on the other hand, teacher praise following a correct answer to higher level tasks was associated with higher scores on high-level test items. This finding was one of several dozen complex interactions.

Undaunted by this complexity, Fennema and Peterson made a number of specific recommendations for specific teacher reaction to student responses depending on whether the goal is to increase higher or lower level achievement and if the student is a boy or a girl and if the task is higher or lower level. Over a dozen specific teacher responses were suggested.

2.2 Expectation Studies

Purely behavioral accounts of student and teacher interaction beg the question of the mechanisms that might mediate the effects of student characteristics and behaviors on the way teachers respond to students. Teaching decisions are not always based on rational decisions. They may stem from inappropriate or extraneous information such as stereotypical expectations for student behavior and performance. Such expectations may, in turn, lead to expectancy effects or self-fulfilling prophecies; that is, unwarranted differential treatment of students that reinforces or alters student outcomes. Since Rosenthal and Jacobson's (1968) study, a plethora of studies have examined the determinants and outcomes of teachers' differential expectations of students.

Studies indicate that teacher expectancies for student performance can be affected by a range of student characteristics including students' race, attractiveness, socioeconomic status, classroom conduct, and previous academic record (Dusek and Joseph 1983). Equivocal evidence has been found for expectancy effects based on several categories of student characteristics such as student gender, name stereotypes, and siblings' previous performance.

Differences in results may be attributed to several causes. First, teacher characteristics such as race and gender may influence expectancy effects (Irvine 1985). Teachers also differ on the importance they place on various student characteristics. In a study of 21 first-grade teachers, for example, Fedoruk and Norman (1991) found wide variance in the rankings teachers gave to 86 student descriptors as contributors to student success or failure. Furthermore, some teachers may be more susceptible to biasing information and expectancy effects than others (Babad and Inabr 1982). In addition, most studies of teacher expectancies have been experimental, not naturalistic. Because experimental studies neglect contextual elements, their validity has been questioned. They usually use nonteachers as participants, are not conducted with intact classrooms, and do not consider multiple, interactive determinants of teacher expectancies.

Students' behavior or performance may confirm teachers' original expectations because of expectancy effects, perceptual biases on the part of teachers, or because teachers tend to predict achievement accurately without influencing it (Jussim 1989). Some researchers have argued that teachers tend to be accurate predictors of student achievement and that differential treatment may reflect appropriate responses to needs of individual students. It may also reflect students' frequency of participation and quality of contributions to classroom discourse (e.g., it is more difficult to call on students who do not raise their hand). Research in Canada by Clifton and Bulcock (1987) has shown that expectations of students held by ninth-grade teachers are based more on judgments of intellectual ability and prior performance than ethnicity (in this case, Yiddish- and French-speaking adolescents). In addition, there is evidence that teachers tend to modify their expectations as their experience with individual students increases (Brophy 1983, Raudenbush 1984).

2.3 Qualitative Studies

Since the early 1980s, research on teachers and classrooms has expanded to include more detailed, qualitative studies, usually with smaller sample sizes than those used in process–product or expectation studies. These studies provide a rich understanding of teachers' beliefs and conceptions and how they influence the ways in which teachers modify their teaching in reaction to students. These studies also provide information about how social, institutional, and personal contexts influence the work of teachers.

In a simulation study of expert, novice, and postulant (subject matter experts who wish to teach, but who have not yet been prepared formally) teachers, Carter et al. (1987) have shown that the expert teachers differ with respect to their understanding of students and classrooms. They further explicate the role that this understanding plays in classroom decisions and subsequent classroom interaction. For example, while all three groups use categories to describe students (e.g., discipline problems), expert teachers have a far richer understanding of the meaning that these categories have for their actions in the classroom. It is this more detailed understanding of teacher's beliefs, conceptions, and understandings that qualitative research methods uncover.

One of the findings from process–product and expectation studies is that teachers' judgments about students and their expectations for future performance are as likely to be based on realistic information from prior performance and classroom participation as they are to be based on bias and unfounded stereotype. This finding is supported by Barakett (1986) in her ethnography of English-speaking elementary school teachers in an inner-city school in Montreal, Canada. Barakett found that teachers' theories of students and instruction are to a large part based on teachers' experiences with students in their classrooms with respect to the type of activities and tasks that the teachers develop and use with these students. For example, the teachers in this school grouped children for learning using what, on the surface, might seem like conventional criteria (e.g., ability, motivation, family background). However, closer analysis suggested that classroom performance plays an even more powerful role than these conventional labels.

In a very different context, Abagi and Cleghorn (1990) found that rural and urban teachers in Kenya interpret and implement government policy about language of instruction in ways that are heavily influenced by their students' classroom performance. The policy for urban areas required that English be used as the language of instruction. The urban school teachers conformed to this policy. One of the rural schools in this study was situated geographically in the urban language policy jurisdiction. However, the students in this school largely spoke Kikuyu, not English, and the primary-grade teachers in this school used Kikuyu as the language of instruction, in violation of official policy. Clearly, in this as in many other instances in the literature, teachers modify their practices in conformance with their understanding of the students with whom they work more so than in reaction to official policy.

3. Conclusion

Early research on student effects on teaching and teachers was predicated on the search for behavioral regularities, that is, replicable statistical relationships between student and teacher behaviors. Since the early 1980s, researchers and theorists have recognized that an understanding of teachers and teaching requires an understanding of the minds of teachers and students. It is the beliefs, theories, and understandings of teachers that underlie whatever predictability that will be found between student and teacher behavior. Teachers' perceptions of students are filtered through their belief systems and mediate their behavior. Teachers continually change their teaching practice in response to students' needs and in reaction to the development of their own professional knowledge and expertise (Richardson 1991).

See also: Student Roles in Classrooms; Teachers' Expectations

References

Abagi J O, Cleghorn A 1990 Teacher attitudes towards the use of English, Kiswahili, and mother tongue in Kenyan primary classrooms. *Can. Int. Educ.* 19(1): 61–71

Babad E Y, Inabr J 1982 Pygmalion, Galatea, and the Golem: Investigations of biased and unbiased teachers. *J. Educ. Psychol.* 74(4): 459–74

Barakett J M 1986 Teachers' theories and methods in structuring routine activities in an inner city school. *Can. J. Educ.* 11(2): 91–108

Brophy J E 1983 Research on the self-fulfilling prophesy and teacher expectations. *J. Educ. Psychol.* 75(5): 631–61

Carter K, Sabers D, Cushing K, Pinnegar S, Berliner D C 1987 Processing and using information about students: A study of expert, novice, and postulant teachers. *Teach. Teach. Educ.* 3(2): 147–57

Clifton R A, Bulcock J W 1987 Ethnicity, teachers' expectations, and student performances in Ontario schools. *Can. J. Educ.* 12(2): 294–315

Dusek J B, Joseph G 1983 The bases of teacher expectancies: A meta-analysis. *J. Educ. Psychol.* 75(3): 327–46

Fedoruk G M, Norman C A 1991 Kindergarten screening predictive inaccuracy: First-grade teacher variability *Excep. Child.* 57(3): 258–63

Fennema E, Peterson P L 1986 Teacher–student interactions and sex-related differences in learning mathematics. *Teaching and Teacher Educ.* 2(1): 19–42

Irvine J J 1985 Teacher communication patterns as related to the race and sex of the student. *J. Educ. Res.* 78(6): 338–45

Jussim L 1989 Teacher expectations: Self-fulfilling prophecies, perceptual biases, and accuracy. *J. Pers. Soc. Psychol.* 57(3): 469–80

Nafpaktitis M, Mayer G R, Butterworth T 1985 Natural rates of teacher approval and disapproval and their relation to student behavior in intermediate school classrooms. *J. Educ. Psychol.* 77(3): 362–67

Raudenbush S W 1984 Magnitude of teacher expectancy effects on pupil IQ as a function of the credibility of expectancy induction: A synthesis of findings from eighteen experiments. *J. Educ. Psychol.* 76(1): 85–97

Richardson V 1991 Significant and worthwhile change in teaching practice. *Educ. Researcher* 19(7): 10–18

Rosenthal R, Jacobson L 1968 *Pygmalion in the Classroom: Teacher Expectation and Pupils' Intellectual Development.* Holt, Rinehart, and Winston, New York

Simpson A W, Erickson M T 1983 Teachers' verbal and nonverbal communication patterns as a function of teacher race, student gender, and student race. *Am. Educ. Res. J.* 20(2): 183–98

Snow R E 1988 Aptitude-treatment intervention as a framework for research on individual differences in learning. In: Ackerman P L, Sterberg R J, Glaser R (eds.) 1989 *Learning and Individual Differences.* Freeman, New York

Stodolsky S 1988 *The Subject Matters: Classroom Activity in Math and Social Studies.* University of Chicago Press, Chicago, Illinois

Weber R, Shake M C 1988 Teachers' rejoiners to students' responses in reading lessons. *J. Read. Behav.* 20(4): 285–99

Teacher Burnout

A. G. Dworkin

A sense of alienation and loss of enthusiasm about teaching characterize a significantly large number of teachers in urban schools in many developed nations. Excessive job stress and the absence of support by school administrators lead many teachers to feel exhausted, unproductive, and prone to denigrate their students. Organizational and individual factors determine which teachers are most likely to burn out. Burnout has been implicated in teacher absenteeism, entrapment, and the desire to quit teaching; it also makes difficult any school district's efforts to implement new programs to raise student achievement.

1. Two Perspectives on Burnout

Both psychologists and sociologists hypothesize that excessive stress associated with the teaching role precipitates burnout. However, the psychological view sees burnout as a clinical problem with the proactive development of coping skills as the suggested treatment. The sociological view emphasizes the nature of organizational and social support mechanisms which affect burnout and proposes organizational, rather than individual, solutions to the problem of burnout.

1.1 Psychological View of Burnout

The concept of burnout was first coined by Freudenberger (1974), who described it as a condition in which human service professionals wear out. Maslach and Jackson (1981) developed the most widely used scale for assessing burnout, the Maslach Burnout Inventory (MBI), an instrument that taps three central psychological dimensions of the construct: exhaustion, the loss of a sense of personal achievement, and depersonalization. The first reflects Freudenberger's view that burnout represents a sense of wearing out. Individuals report being too tired and too drained to maintain enthusiasm for their work. Maslach and Jackson's second dimension of burnout is expressed as a sense that one is not achieving one's goals; that one's work efforts produce no satisfying results; in essence, that one sees one's work as meaningless. Finally, burnout involves an emotional separation of the worker (in this case the teacher) from the client (or student). The student is viewed as an object to be processed and a nuisance, rather than as a person of worth. Further, a blaming mechanism evolves in which burned-out teachers fault their students for the teachers' own sense of failure. Thus, students are also seen as enemies who deflect one from achieving desired ends. Research by Friesen et al. (1988), using a sample of teachers from Australia and Canada, suggests that the dimensions of burnout assessed by the MBI may not function in unison, nor may they be caused by the same factors. Their study reveals that job-related stress is more associated with exhaustion than with either depersonalization or the lack of personal accomplishment.

Investigators have identified five progressive stages in burnout: physical, intellectual, social, psycho-emotional, and spiritual (Cedoline 1982 pp. 23–37). Numerous symptoms characterize each of the stages, with fatigue and exhaustion being most common in the first stage; impaired decision making and obsessive thoughts about work during the second stage; social withdrawal, cynicism, irritability, and rudeness at the third stage; denial, blame, anger, and depression in the fourth stage; and poor work quality, absenteeism, the desire to escape, and the tendency to see the needs of students as a threat during the last stage.

Central to many of the views of burnout is the role of stress (or distress) as noted by Cedoline (1982), or strain as portrayed by Cherniss (1980). While some level of stress characterizes most human endeavors, excessive stress that is perceived by the individual as threatening and dysfunctional (hence, distress) is likely to tax the individual's coping capacity. The linkage between stress and burnout has led some investigators to use the terms interchangeably (see, e.g., the work on stress burnout by Riggar 1985, or the work of Kyriacou and Sutcliffe 1978). Farber (1984) and Pines and Aronson (1988) note, however, that stress per se does not produce burnout. Individuals can thrive and achieve substantially in stress-laden environments, provided that they have a sense of doing meaningful work. However, Pines and Aronson (1988) point out that when the activities appear to be devoid of meaning, they become tedious. Most recently, Pines (1993) has proposed that job burnout creates existential crises for employees. Because many professionals come to define themselves in terms of their work, a loss of meaningfulness of work leads to a loss of meaningfulness of self-identity.

The psychological view is generally clinical in nature and offers clinical solutions to problems of burnout. With burnout often seen as the end-product of distress, stress-reduction strategies are offered to individuals to mitigate such strains and reduce burnout (see, e.g., Maslach 1976, Spaniol and Caputo 1979, Cherniss 1980, and Cedoline 1982).

While still offering clinical solutions to burnout, several researchers have viewed burnout as the product of elevated stress caused by the conjoined effects of work overload, role conflict, and role ambiguity. Kahn et al. (1964), Schwab and Iwanicki (1982), and Haney and Long (1989) view excessive work demands, demands that are mutually exclusive and/or contradictory, and demands in instances where resources are lacking or where one is not given the necessary authority to secure the cooperation of others, as causes of distress, which then results in burnout. By focusing upon roles and organizational variables, these investigators provide the beginnings of a sociological perspective on burnout.

1.2 Sociological View of Burnout

The sociological view does not deny the significant role of stress or distress in the creation of burnout. However, its emphasis is upon societal and demographic factors, and elements in the school setting and the nature of the training of teachers which heighten the likelihood of burnout. The importance of feelings of meaninglessness and powerlessness, which are found in some psychological views of burnout, is even more salient to sociologists. Burnout is thought of as a form of role-specific alienation, generally driven by stressors, which themselves have origins in the social structure of the society and the organizational structure of the school. As such, sociologists look to structural and organization changes as mechanisms which can reduce burnout.

As a form of alienation, teacher burnout is the product of a perceived gap between expectations, often developed during the preservice training of teachers, and the teacher's experiences in the classroom (Dworkin 1985, 1987; LeCompte and Dworkin 1991). Many enter teaching because of a desire to make a significant difference in the lives of children. Preservice teachers often expect that they will be able to educate and influence children, plan and develop new curricula, evaluate student learning, manage classrooms, maintain discipline, and perhaps, serve as role models and surrogate parents for children. Most important is the assumption that teachers are granted professional status and autonomy. Cherniss et al. (1976) and Sarason (1977) see colleges of education as failing to prepare teachers for educational bureaucracies in which autonomy is severely restricted. Teachers are also unprepared for an environment in which there is an excess of paperwork, where the children, their parents, other teachers, and administrators appear to be unconcerned about learning, where there are significant class and cultural differences between the teachers and their students, and where the larger community does not respect teachers. Hence, teacher burnout is often greatest in large, urban school districts, and especially among inexperienced teachers (Cedoline 1982, Russell et al. 1987, Dworkin 1987).

Agreements across the psychological and sociological paradigms support a view of burnout as composed of each of Seeman's (1975) dimensions of alienation: meaninglessness, powerlessness, isolation, normlessness, and estrangement. However, on the basis of a large sample of urban teachers, Dworkin (1987) concluded that feelings of meaninglessness and powerlessness were central to the responses of burned-out urban teachers. Dworkin defined teacher burnout as " . . . an extreme form of role-specific alienation characterized by a sense that one's work is meaningless and that one is powerless to effect changes which could make the work more meaningful" (1987 p. 28). Dworkin and Townsend (1991) utilized both the MBI and Dworkin's own scale, finding that the exhaustion and depersonalization components of psychological burnout diminish as the meaninglessness and powerlessness components of sociological burnout increase among experienced teachers. The result is that burnout, as alienation, can insulate teachers from the psychological element of exhaustion, and thus can be a coping mechanism for more experienced teachers.

2. Magnitude of the Burnout Problem

It is difficult to arrive at an accurate figure to assess the burnout rate among public school teachers, although most researchers agree that the rates are high. Furthermore, much of the research estimates stress rather than burnout levels. Litt and Turk (1985) report that 79 percent of public school teachers feel that their job is a major source of stress in their lives, compared with 38 percent for other college-educated workers. There is some variation in stress levels across school districts and societies (Menlo and Poppleton 1990). In the Consortium for Cross-cultural Research in Education's five-nation study of job attitudes, conducted between 1986 and 1988, only 10 or 11 percent of the teachers in England, the United States, Japan, and Singapore reported low levels or no stress, while 21 percent of the West German teachers reported the relative absence of stress (Poppleton 1990). Furthermore, one-third or less of the teachers (and only 15% in England) reported that staff morale in their schools was generally good (Poppleton 1990). The five-nation survey did not address burnout per se.

Many burnout studies are based upon small ethnographic and case studies, thereby mitigating generalizability. Cedoline (1982) estimated that the burnout rate among teachers in the United States is somewhere between 10 percent and 80 percent, a range too great to be of value. Dworkin (1987) and LeCompte and Dworkin (1991) rely upon data on urban and suburban teachers to arrive at a burnout rate of 37.3 percent prior to the implementation of educational reforms, which mandated more accountability of teachers, and 64.1 percent after the reforms. Rates for urban teachers were slightly higher than for suburban teachers. Kalekin-Fishman's (1986) study of metropolitan secondary school teachers suggests that burnout is widespread in Israel; however, percentages are not available.

Some researchers have compared the components of the MBI across several nations, not so much to ascertain burnout rates, as to determine differences among the components of burnout. Sarros and Sarros (1990) found that Australian teachers experienced less of the emotional exhaustion aspect of burnout than teachers in the United States, but more emotional exhaustion than Canadian teachers. In contrast, the depersonalization form of burnout was highest in some samples of teachers in the United States, and lower both among Australian and Canadian teachers. Finally, Australian teachers suffered the highest levels of diminished personal accomplishment, followed by the Canadian teachers, and finally teachers in the United States.

3. Teachers Most Likely to Burn Out

While burnout is a widespread phenomenon in urban schools in many societies, not all groups of teachers are equally susceptible to burning out. Psychologists have isolated personality and individualistic factors associated with the likelihood of burnout, while sociologists have concentrated on group, organizational, and social structural factors. Both psychologists and sociologists agree that these factors, either directly serve as, or heighten the impact of, job-related stressors.

3.1 Individualistic Factors

Many psychologists have looked for personality types who are more likely to burn out because they cannot cope as easily with stress as other individuals. Kahn et al. (1964) suggested that neurotics and introverts experience more stress in teaching, and may be more likely to experience the loss of job idealism. They also held that flexible and democratic thinkers (who often cannot say "no" to excessive organizational demands and who have difficulty working under rigid and autocratic administrators) tend to experience increased stress and a heightened chance of burnout when they are assigned to teach in rigid school systems. Finally, Mazur and Lynch (1989) noted that Type A personalities (individuals who have trouble relaxing), as well as individuals with an external locus of control (who believe that their life chances are controlled by fate or by powerful others) are more likely to burn out than are individuals with Type B personalities and individuals with an internal locus of control. Kyriacou's (1980) teachers in the United Kingdom and Dworkin's (1987) teachers in the United States were more likely to burn out if they had an external locus of control.

3.2 Demographic and Organizational Factors

Demographic factors refer to membership categories to which groups of teachers belong that affect their social status in the larger society, or in the work setting (school) to which they are assigned. Included among such demographic factors are age and teaching experience, race, ethnicity, social class, and gender.

Among the organizational factors are school size (as well as the extent of bureaucratization of the school), grade level taught, and the management style of the campus administrator.

Generally, burnout is more a malady of inexperienced teachers than of those with five or more years in the classroom (Cedoline 1982, Dworkin 1987, Mazur and Lynch 1989). Cherniss et al. (1976) reported that the absence of adequate preservice training, a problem of many new teachers, increased the chance of burnout. Russell et al. (1987) found that the number of reported stressors (sources of burnout) diminished with age and experience.

Schwab (1994) identified a range of student attitudes and behaviors that exacerbated teacher burnout. These included negative student attitudes about school and school work, lack of student motivation to learn, misbehavior, and lack of attentiveness. Unmotivated students reinforce for teachers the perception that their work as educators is meaningless. When attempts to increase student motivation fail, teachers come to recognize that they are powerless to effect changes in school that will increase the meaningfulness of their work.

Racial isolation contributes to teacher burnout (Dworkin 1987). In urban schools in the United States, White movement to the suburbs and/or to private schools has resulted in urban districts in which most students are members of racial and ethnic minorities. Many White teachers find themselves racially isolated from their students and even feel threatened by them. Likewise, minority teachers in suburban school districts, where the majority of the students are White, report feelings of racial isolation. Frequently, parents voice preferences that their children be taught by teachers of their own race, with the result that racially isolated teachers feel intimidated, unwanted, and alienated. However, minority teachers are less likely to experience burnout than are majority teachers; this is due, in part, to the greater degree of racial isolation of White teachers in the inner city than of minority teachers in the suburbs (Dworkin 1987).

Social class differences between teachers and students often observed in American urban schools contribute to a sense of culture shock for teachers, regardless of their race (LeCompte 1985). While most public school teachers come from middle-class backgrounds (Dworkin 1980), the majority of students in urban schools are from working-class or lower-class families. These differences reflect distinctive lifestyles, expectations, aspirations, values, and even communication patterns (see LeCompte and Dworkin 1991). Many parents feel that the teachers are inaccessible and unresponsive (Richardson-Koehler 1989). Ogbu (1974) noted that when middle-class teachers made extra efforts to help low income, minority children, they were shown no appreciation. In fact, the parents, with incomes substantially lower than that of the teachers, felt that the teachers were sufficiently well-paid and needed no additional thanks. Kyriacou (1980) and Kyriacou and Sutcliffe (1978) found similar frustrations among teachers in inner-city schools in the United Kingdom.

There is mixed evidence regarding the relationship between burnout and gender. Male teachers in Canada (Burke and Greenglass 1989) and the United States (Russell et al. 1987) report more stress associated with the teaching role and were more likely to experience the depersonalization form of burnout than were female teachers. Women in the study reported experiencing greater amounts of social support than did men, and this support reduced the risk of burnout. By contrast, gender differences evaporated in a multivariate model (Dworkin 1987).

The size of a school affects its likely level of bureaucracy. In turn, bureaucratization increases the sense of isolation of teachers; it also increases the likelihood of role conflicts, role ambiguities, and ultimately burnout, as teachers are forced to comply with mandates from many organizational layers. Jackson (1968) and Maslach and Pines (1979) find lower stress levels and less burnout in small schools, while Russell et al. (1987) find that larger class sizes contribute to burnout.

If burnout is associated with class and organizational size, then it might be expected that burnout levels should be highest in secondary schools, which are generally large, and lowest in elementary schools, which are generally small. However, the data are not conclusive, suggesting that the relationship between grade level and burnout is complex. Some investigators noted that male secondary school teachers reported greater levels of depersonalization burnout than did elementary school teachers (Russell et al. 1987). In contrast, Anderson and Iwanicki (1984) noted a curvilinear relationship between grade level and burnout, with early secondary (middle or junior high) school teachers displaying more burnout than did elementary and secondary school teachers. Other investigations found that, while middle school is characterized by high levels of job stress, burnout levels are highest in elementary schools (Dworkin 1987). This is because elementary school teaching tends to be quite intense, with the children placing greater interpersonal demands upon the teacher. In the absence of departmentalization, teachers have day-long contact (without even a free period) with the same students. Such prolonged interactions are stressful (Jackson 1968).

Some researchers have noted that the management style of the principal significantly affects teachers morale and burnout levels in schools (Kyriacou 1980, Murphy and Paddock 1986, Dworkin 1987, Firestone and Rosenblum 1988, Dworkin et al. 1990). Authoritarian principals and those whose styles are too *laissez-faire* are associated with higher levels of burnout among their teachers than are those whose styles are more democratic (Murphy and Paddock 1986). In addition, any substantial discrepancy between the administrative style of the principal as desired by the teachers and the actual style of that principal contributes to teacher burnout (Dworkin 1987). Further, management styles that are perceived by teachers to be unsupportive and that treat teachers as dispensable and diminish the teacher's role in campus decision-making contribute to burnout.

4. Social Support and Burnout

Much of the medical sociology literature on stress has suggested that an effective buffer against stressful events is a network of social support (see Kaplan 1983 for a survey of this research). Investigators have also spoken of the significant role of social support in mitigating burnout (see, e.g., Maslach 1976, Freudenberger 1974, Cherniss 1980, and Cedoline 1982). However, there is a disagreement about the persons who can be most supportive. The above-mentioned investigators have argued that co-worker support provides an effective buffer for teachers. By contrast, Russell et al. (1987), Dworkin (1987), and Dworkin et al. (1990) found that supportive principals, who offered positive feedback to teachers and treated them as valued colleagues, involving them in campus decision-making, retarded burnout. Supportive co-workers, however, did not reduce burnout. In fact, in the absence of principal support, co-worker support can elevate stress and burnout among younger teachers (Dworkin et al. 1990). This is due to the tendency for co-workers to feed on one another's stress and anxiety, creating rumors and emotional contagion. In a survey of burnout in 21 Dutch companies (rather than schools), Marcelissen et al. (1988) reported that strain tends to heighten negative interactions and burnout among co-workers, rather than co-worker interactions reducing strain and burnout.

In one study of principal support (Dworkin 1987), teachers who were assigned to a school where the principal was seen as supportive experienced lower levels of burnout than teachers who were assigned to schools where the principal was seen as unsupportive. When burnout did occur among teachers with supportive principals, individual teacher characteristics, rather than job stress, were implicated in the burnout; however, burnout among teachers assigned to unsupportive principals was driven by job stress. It is important to note that the reported job stress levels were statistically equal in schools with supportive and unsupportive principals. It appears that a supportive principal, who treats teachers as valued colleagues, informs them that their work is meaningful, thereby breaking the functional connection between stress and burnout. Support by co-workers alone did not affect the relationship between stress and burnout. In light of the role of principal support in mitigating burnout, it seems reasonable to rethink the clinical strategy to reducing burnout levels among teachers. The clinical solutions involve the teaching of coping skills

(Maslach 1976, Cherniss 1980), the use of holistic health practices (Tubesing and Tubesing 1982), and relaxation and self-suggestion therapy (Swick and Hanley 1983). However, if the improvement of managerial skills among principals can retard burnout, then in large school districts with thousands of teachers and hundreds of principals, it is more cost-efficient to change the management styles of the principals than to provide therapy for the multitude of teachers. Changed administrator behaviors will also reduce the need to offer additional classes in coping skills for each new cohort of teachers.

Collegial support varies somewhat across the five-nation survey (Poppleton 1990). While over 80 percent of the teachers reported their colleagues to be supportive at least some of the time, only in England and the United States did more than half of the teachers report that their colleagues were supportive most of the time. By contrast, only in England were immediate superiors seen as helpful most of the time by at least half of the sample of teachers. In West Germany, a mere 17 percent of the teachers felt that their immediate superiors were helpful most of the time (Poppleton 1990).

5. Teacher Burnout, Turnover, and Entrapment

Public school teachers tend to have an above-average job turnover rate, but one that is similar to that in other female-dominated semi-professions (Price 1977). In the United States, the turnover rate grew during the 1980s as a result of educational reform efforts that demanded greater teacher accountability and paperwork (LeCompte and Dworkin 1991), and the expansion of job opportunities in other, better-paying, fields (Mark and Anderson 1985). However, one-third of all teachers who quit eventually return to the classroom, with many recycling back and forth throughout their careers (Heyns 1990).

Burnout is strongly implicated in the desire to quit a job (Calamidas 1979, Cherniss 1980, Cedoline 1982, Dworkin 1987). It is also linked to high rates of absenteeism (Calamidas 1979). However, actual turnover does not seem to be caused by burnout (Cherniss 1980, Jackson et al. 1986, Dworkin 1987). In fact, the most burned-out teachers are quite unlikely to quit (Jackson et al. 1986). Job turnover appears to depend upon the availability of other job opportunities outside of teaching. With the exception of teachers whose specialties can translate into valued skills in the corporate sector (e.g., mathematics, science, industrial arts, business, etc.), most teachers must either retrain or accept lower-status, poorer-paying employment if they leave the field of education (Dworkin 1987, LeCompte and Dworkin 1991).

The five-nation study by the Consortium for Cross-cultural Research in Education found that slightly less than half of the teachers from West Germany and the

United States, around one-fifth of the teachers from England, and fewer than one-fifth of the teachers from Japan and Singapore would, if given the chance, again choose to become teachers (Poppleton 1990). Nevertheless, Poppleton (1990) reports that two-thirds of the teachers from the United States and three-fourths of the teachers from Japan and Singapore expect still to be teaching five years from when they were surveyed (the results for England and West Germany were not reported).

Burned out, wanting to quit, but unable to find work elsewhere, many teachers remain in disliked jobs much of their working lives. In fact, in a five-year follow-up study of urban public school teachers, Dworkin (1987) found that nearly three-fourths of the burned-out teachers who wanted to quit had not left teaching. In another study, 37 percent of the burnouts attempted to leave but could not find satisfactory work (LeCompte and Dworkin 1991). They were clearly entrapped.

Teacher entrapment represents a problem for both teachers and school districts. It is a human problem for the teacher, as there are many personal, emotional, and psychophysical costs associated with the continuation of a career that is disliked or even hated. It is an organizational problem for schools. Teacher entrapment exacerbates staffing problems. School districts, which depend upon turnover to balance budgets through the replacement of higher-paid teachers with lower-paid new teachers, discover that some of the teachers they might like to see quit do not. Furthermore, it becomes all the more difficult for school systems to introduce new programs aimed at raising student achievement when, to implement the programs, districts must rely upon unenthusiastic burned-out teachers who depersonalize their students.

One anomaly in the studies of teacher burnout is that, while stress is directly implicated in burnout and strongly associated with intentions to quit and actual quitting behavior, the association between burnout and actual quitting is generally not statistically significant. While it is reasonable to assume that actual quitting will occur only when there are career alternatives, there may be another social psychological factor involved. Dworkin suspected that the relationship between stress and burnout might become nonlinear over time, and as such, may ultimately insulate individuals from further job stress. In a recent analysis, Dworkin (1996) examined the relationships among job stress, emotional exhaustion (a psychological indicator of burnout), and sociological burnout. The study compared the relationships among the variables for four cohorts of teachers (those with 0–5, 6–10, 11–15, and 16 or more years of experience) over three waves of data collected between 1977 and 1991. While the relationship between stress and exhaustion remained stable across cohorts and across time, the relationship between sociological burnout and stress and between sociological burnout and exhaustion generally diminished among more experienced cohorts. For teachers with more than five years experience in two of the waves and teachers with more that 15 years experience in a wave during which time major school reforms were occurring, the relationships among sociological burnout and job stress and sociological burnout and exhaustion became statistically nonsignificant. Further work is needed to determine whether the linkage between burnout and stress will ultimately change directions. In such instances, the relationship would change from "the greater the stress the greater the burnout" to "the greater the burnout the less the stress." However , the notion that increased burnout insulates individuals from additional job stress and emotional exhaustion helps to clarify the finding of Cherniss (1992) that the long-term consequences of burnout did not include a heightened tendency toward quitting.

See also: Sociology of Teaching; Teachers' Work and Political Action; Teaching, Realities of

References

Anderson M B, Iwanicki E F 1984 Teacher motivation and its relationship to burnout. *Educ. Admin. Q.* 20(2): 109–32

Burke R J, Greenglass E 1989 The client's role in psychological burnout in teachers and administrators. *Psychol. Rep.* 64(3): 1299–1306

Calamidas A 1979 Distress and burnout will kill productivity. In: Cedoline A J (ed.) 1982

Cedoline A J (ed.) 1982 *Job Burnout in Public Education: Symptoms, Causes, and Survival Skills.* Teachers College Press, Columbia University, New York

Cherniss C 1980 *Professional Burnout in Human Service Organizations.* Praeger, New York

Cherniss C 1992 Long-term consequences of burnout: An exploratory study. *J. Org. Behav.* (13): 1–11

Cherniss C, Egnatios E S, Wacker S 1976 Job stress and career development in new public professionals. *Prof. Psychol.* 7(4): 428–36

Dworkin A G 1980 The changing demography of public school teachers: Some implications for faculty turnover in urban areas. *Sociol. Educ.* 53: 65–73

Dworkin A G 1985 *When Teachers Give Up: Teacher Burnout, Teacher Turnover, and Their Impact on Children.* Hogg Foundation for Mental Health, Austin, Texas

Dworkin A G 1987 *Teacher Burnout in the Public Schools: Structural Causes and Consequences for Children.* State University of New York Press, Albany, New York

Dworkin A G 1996 Coping with reform: The intermix of teacher morale, teacher burnout, and teacher accountability. In: Biddle B J, Good T L, Goodson I F (eds.) 1996 *The International Handbook of Teachers and Teaching.* Kluwer, The Hague

Dworkin A G, Haney C A, Dworkin R J, Telschow R L 1990 Stress and illness behavior among urban public school teachers. *Educ. Admin. Q.* 26(1): 60–72

Dworkin A G, Townsend M L 1991 Burnout as a coping mechanism: Or how to survive in an urban public school. Paper presented at the Southwestern Sociological Association meetings, San Antonio, Texas

Farber B A 1984 Teacher burnout: Assumptions, myths, and issues. *Teachers College Record* 86(2): 321–38

Firestone W A, Rosenblum S 1988 Building commitment in urban high schools. *Educ. Eval. Policy Anal.* 10(4): 285–99

Freudenberger H J 1974 Staff burn-out. *J. Soc. Issues* 30(1): 159–65

Friesen D, Prokop C M, Sarros J C 1988 Why teachers burn out. *Educ. Res. Q.* 12(3): 9–19

Haney C J, Long B C 1989 Role stress, coping effectiveness, and health concerns of physical education teachers. *Educ. Res. Q.* 13(4): 34–42

Heyns B 1990 The changing contours of the teaching profession. In: Hallinan M T, Klein D M, Glass J (eds.) 1990 *Change in Societal Institutions*. Plenum, New York

Jackson P 1968 *Life in Classrooms*. Holt, Rinehart, Winston, New York

Jackson S E, Schwab R L, Schuler R S 1986 Toward an understanding of the burnout phenomenon. *J. Appl. Psychol.* 71(4): 630–40

Kahn R L, Wolfe D M, Quinn R P, Snoek J D, Rosenthal R A 1964 *Organizational Stress: Studies in Role Conflict and Ambiguity*. Wiley, New York

Kalekin-Fishman D 1986 Burnout or alienation? A context specific study of occupational fatigue among secondary school teachers. *J. Res. Dev. Educ.* 19(3): 24–34

Kaplan H B 1983 Psychological distress in sociological context: Toward a general theory of psychosocial distress. In: Kaplan H B (ed.) 1983 *Psychosocial Stress: Trends in Theory and Research*. Academic Press, New York

Kyriacou C 1980 Sources of stress among British teachers: The contribution of job factors and personality factors. In: Cooper C L, Marshall J (eds.) 1980 *White Collar and Professional Stress*. John Wiley, New York

Kyriacou C, Sutcliffe J 1978 Teacher stress: Prevalence, sources, and symptoms *Br. J. Educ. Psychol.* 48(2): 159–67

LeCompte M D 1985 Defining the differences: Cultural subgroups within the educational mainstream. *The Urban Rev.* 17(2): 111–28

LeCompte M D, Dworkin A G 1991 *Giving Up On School: Student Dropouts and Teacher Burnouts*. Corwin Press, Newbury Park, California

Litt M D, Turk D C 1985 Sources of stress and dissatisfaction in experienced high school teachers. *J. Educ. Res.* 78(3): 178–85

Marcelissen F H G, Winnubst J A M, Buunk B B, de Wolfe C J 1988 Social support and occupational stress. *Soc. Sci. Med.* 26(3): 365–73

Mark J H, Anderson B D 1985 Teacher survival rates in St. Louis, 1969–1982. *Am. Educ. Res. J.* 22(3): 413–21

Maslach C 1976 Burned-out. *Hum. Behav.* 5(9): 16–22

Maslach C 1978 Job burnout: How people cope. *Public Welfare* 36(4): 56–58

Maslach C, Jackson S 1981 The measurement of experienced burnout. *J. Occ. Behav.* 2: 99–113

Maslach C, Pines A 1979 Burnout: The loss of human caring. In: Pines A, Maslach C (eds.) 1979 *Experiencing Social Psychology*. Knopf, New York

Mazur P J, Lynch M D 1989 Differential impact of administrative, organizational, and personality factors on teacher burnout. *Teaching Teacher Ed.* 5(4): 337–53

Menlo A, Poppleton P 1990 A five-country study of the work perceptions of secondary school teachers in England, the United States, Japan, Singapore, and West Germany (1986–88). *Comp. Educ.* 26(2–3): 173–82

Murphy J W, Paddock J T 1986 The "burnout syndrome" and management style. *The Clinical Supervisor* 4(4): 35–44

Ogbu J U 1974 *The Next Generation*. Academic Press, New York

Pines A M 1993 Burnout: Existential perspectives. In: Schaufeli W B, Maslach C, Marek T (eds.) 1993 *Professional Burnout: Recent Developments in Theory and Research*. Taylor and Francis Washington, DC

Pines A, Aronson E 1988 *Career Burnout: Causes and Cures*. The Free Press, New York

Poppleton P 1990 The survey data. *Comp. Educ.* 26(2–3): 183–210

Price J L 1977 *The Study of Turnover*. Iowa State University Press, Ames, Iowa

Richardson-Koehler V (ed.) 1989 *School Children At-Risk*. Taylor and Francis, Philadelphia, Pennsylvania

Riggar T F 1985 *Stress Burnout*. Southern Illinois University Press, Carbondale, Illinois

Russell D W, Altmaier E, Van Velzen D 1987 Job-related stress, social support, and burnout among classroom teachers. *J. Appl. Psychol.* 72(2): 269–74

Sarason S B 1977 *Work, Aging, and Social Change*. The Free Press, New York

Sarros A M, Sarros J C 1990 How burned out are our teachers? A cross-cultural study. *Aust. J. Ed.* 34(2): 145–52

Schwab R L 1994 Teacher stress and burnout. In: Husen T, Postlethwaite T N (eds.) 1994 *The International Encyclopedia of Education*, 2nd edn. Pergamon, Oxford

Schwab R L, Iwanicki E F 1982 Received role conflict, role ambiguity, and teacher burnout. *Ed. Admin. Q.* 18(1): 60–74

Seeman M 1975 Alienation studies. *Ann. Rev. Sociol.* 1: 91–123

Spaniol L, Caputo J 1979 *Professional Burn-out: A Personal Survival Kit*. Human Services Associates, Lexington, Massachusetts

Swick K J, Hanley P E 1983 *Teacher Renewal: Revitalization of Classroom Teachers*. National Education Association, Washington, DC

Tubesing N L, Tubesing D A 1982 The treatment of choice: Selecting stress skills to suit the individual and the situation. In: Paine W S (ed.) 1982 *Job Stress and Burnout: Research, Theory, and Intervention Perspectives*. Sage, Beverly Hills, California

Further Reading

Maslach C 1982 Understanding burnout: Definitional issues in analyzing a complex phenomenon. In: Paine W S (ed.) 1982 *Job Stress and Burnout: Research, Theory, and Intervention Perspectives*. Sage, Beverly Hills, California

Poppleton P (Issue ed.) 1990 Work perceptions of secondary teachers: International comparisons. *Comp. Educ.* 26(2–3)

Teacher Placement and School Staffing

A. J. Watson and N. G. Hatton

Teacher placement refers to the activity of locating a teacher in a particular school within an educational system. School staffing refers to broader issues involved in managing teacher placement. Staffing must not only enable teachers to go where they are needed, but must also provide the conditions and support necessary to keep them there long enough to be effective. Thus, while placement focuses on the individual teacher, staffing focuses on the administrative policies and practices of a school or a system.

Both placement and staffing have a bearing on the quality and equality of educational provision. While the issues related to placement and staffing are complex, demanding, and problematic in all countries, research in the area is seriously lacking. As a consequence, this article relies primarily on general descriptions of current practices and alternatives. It is divided into three major sections: (a) methods of teacher placement in schools; (b) problems of staffing related to those methods; and (c) concerns with staffing for effective teaching.

1. Methods of Placement

Two staffing questions preliminary to the actual placement of teachers must be answered. First, how many teachers should be allocated to a particular school? Second, what kinds of teachers should they be?

1.1 Number and Kinds of Teachers for a School

The determination of the number of teachers for a school (the teacher–pupil ratio) is inevitably a decision of the funding body for the school. This statement holds true even in highly decentralized systems such as that of Switzerland where the cantons (under which local boards of education operate with a high level of independence) set a formula for funding based on the number of pupils and the kind of school. In systems with locally managed schools (e.g., "grant maintained" schools in the United Kingdom or, "schools of the future" in Victoria, Australia), the school council has scope to determine staff numbers, but in practice is limited by the funding formula.

With regard to the kinds of teachers employed (e.g., specialist staff), systems generally allow some local initiative within the limits of the staffing formula. In a centralized system such as that of Germany, while specialists may be allocated locally, there are also some central initiatives for which schools receive additional staff. One recent example in Brandenburg has been the central funding of support teachers to assist the integration of children with disabilities into the mainstream of education. While systems may vary in determining the *number* of teachers for a school and the *kinds* of teachers they will be, much greater differences between systems arise when the question is asked, which teacher should be employed in a particular school?

1.2 Teacher Placement

The methods adopted in different countries for the placement of teachers are as varied as the history, cultural attitudes, and political policies which guide their formulation. At some risk of oversimplification, they may be represented along a continuum from central to local control, although comparison of the extent of central or local authority must be qualified, *inter alia*, by the size of the system. To give some sense of how systems differ, approaches to teacher placement in five countries will be described: Germany, Canada, Switzerland, United Kingdom, and Australia.

The German education system, in which the state employs teachers and appoints them through the regional administration and district school inspectors, is centralized and hierarchical in nature. The local school or community has no authority in the placement of teachers. A similar pattern seems to operate across all German states, including the five in the former German Democratic Republic which have adopted the West German system since reunification (see Lehmann 1994). In Bavaria, for example, new graduates apply to the state, are ranked (with equal weight being given to academic marks and practicum results), and subsequently allocated to schools that need teachers.

In Canada, both central and local influences operate. Staffing is a responsibility of the district boards which have a range of from 2 to approximately 40 schools in their care. School principals notify the district office of their specific staffing needs and new teachers apply for a job to the district office. In most districts, the principal is included in the interviewing committee and is very influential in determining who is placed at his or her school.

In Switzerland, where local autonomy has deep historical and cultural roots and is very jealously guarded, there is no federal system of education. Rather, there are 26 cantonal systems, some of which serve a very small population; Uri, for example, has 35,000 inhabitants and about 7,000 children in schools (see Organisation for Economic Co-operation and Development 1991). For staffing and other educational management decisions most cantons delegate authority to elected community educational boards on which teachers have

677

a consultative voice. Each board may have many schools under its care. A vacancy is advertised in the cantonal gazette and new teachers apply to the board, which appoints a subcommittee to select candidates on the basis of their academic and practicum reports, their performance in demonstration lessons, and their responses in an interview. Although there are likely to be teacher representatives on the subcommittee, they are usually not from the school with the vacancy. School staffing in Switzerland, while determined in the local community, is not as devolved as it has become in the United Kingdom.

In England and Wales (and in Scotland by 1997, as a result of the 1988 Education Reform Act), the school's governing body (which includes parents and teachers) has responsibility for all staffing. In practice the governors delegate the task of interviewing and choosing to a subcommittee which usually includes the principal.

In Australia, where education is a state responsibility, all administrative decisions including staffing were highly centralized until around 1990. Since then, however, as part of an attempt to improve the quality of schooling, a major devolution has taken place in most states. Different states now approach teacher placement in different ways, representing the entire range from central to local control. Queensland, for example, with some 550,000 children enrolled in primary and secondary schools, retains a highly centralized approach whereby all staff appointments are made by the Department of Education to which new teachers must apply for work. In contrast, New South Wales, with just over 1 million children, has devolved authority for the choice of the principal and senior staff to the local school council. However, a government suggestion that other staff be chosen locally met with stiff opposition from the teachers' union and parent groups.

2. Problems in School Staffing

Staffing problems related to three issues will be discussed in this section. They are: difficult-to-staff locations; fluctuations in teacher supply and demand; and staff turnover.

2.1 Difficult-to-staff Locations

Strong teacher preference to work in some geographical areas but not others creates locations that are difficult to staff. Such areas are likely to be found where there are distinct subpopulations, such as recent immigrants, indigenous people, the poor, or isolated rural dwellers. While it is likely that most countries with such groups of people have difficult-to-staff locations, little research has been conducted to identify and study their educational experiences. Nevertheless, some evidence for their existence does exist. In the United Kingdom, for instance, many overseas teachers have been recruited in recent years

by private agencies for inner-London schools to teach immigrant and poor sectors of the population, because insufficient English graduates have been prepared to teach there. The difficult-to-staff places in the United States have been identified as central districts of big cities (Darling-Hammond 1990), while in Canada most occur in remote, rural locations (Canadian Education Association 1992). In Australia, such locations have been identified on the growing fringes of large urban populations and in distant rural areas (Hatton et al. 1991).

At a time when there is no teacher shortage, this phenomenon may not be noticed. However, the study of longitudinal teacher movements and of teacher locational preferences for short- and long-term appointments is likely to reveal a strong persistent movement away from schools in less favored areas to those in more favored ones (Hatton et al. 1991).

As a consequence, children in less favored areas are taught by the least experienced teachers who stay for the minimum time. Thus, systems with central staffing methods which grant priority of location to those with the longest service could seriously disadvantage children in difficult-to-staff locations unless there are compensatory provisions to overcome this staffing pattern.

The problems of difficult-to-staff locations, however, become most acute when there is a teacher shortage and excessive teacher turnover. These issues will be considered in the next two sections.

2.2 Fluctuations in Teacher Supply and Demand

Sudden shifts between shortage and surplus have become a characteristic of the teacher labor market in much of the developed world. Economic upturn, bringing with it attractive opportunities for work in other industries, a rise in teacher resignations, and a surge in the school population can turn today's surplus quickly into tomorrow's shortage. The fluctuations of teacher supply and demand are a good test of staffing policy. A policy which works well during surplus may be quite inadequate when the cycle turns.

2.2.1 Teacher surplus. When there is a surplus of teachers a critical task for staffing policy is to enable schools to get the best teachers. The question is: does the policy allow selection of those teachers who are the strongest in terms of each particular school's needs? Local matching is desirable because teacher roles are increasingly complex and specific to a school and its existing staff, especially in countries with diverse populations. If the demands of the job are to be met, specialization and team work are called for. For this reason, a local selection process that includes input from existing staff and community members, as operates in "grant maintained" schools of the United Kingdom or in the "locally governed" schools of New Zealand, would be more likely to make a suitable match.

Whether selection is central or local, however, it is possible to use merit as its basis and so select the best in general terms. Some centralized staffing systems, such as Germany's, use academic work and practice teaching to select staff on merit. However, a staffing policy does not always allow this to happen. In New South Wales, until the 1990s, all new teachers were employed in the chronological order in which they applied for a job without any reference to quality. When it was recognized that private schools were engaging the best and most creative teachers, the employing authority began to interview final-year students and the best were given priority for appointment as "targeted graduates." Likewise, in British Columbia, Canada, which had a surplus of teachers in the mid-1990s, new graduates, even the best, were not given any priority but had to form a queue behind those teachers returning from leaves of absence and those who had acted as substitutes.

During a surplus of teachers, unless a mechanism is found to employ the most promising new graduates, the system will suffer an adverse long-term cohort effect of this loss of teaching talent as they find employment elsewhere. A time of surplus is an opportunity to strengthen the quality of the teaching service. The issue is whether the staffing method grants enough freedom to achieve this purpose.

2.2.2 Teacher shortage. A staffing policy receives its most critical test when facing a shortage. In this regard, two questions can be raised. Can schools be staffed without compromising professional standards? Can they be staffed without major disadvantage to schools in difficult-to-staff locations?

With respect to the compromise of standards, a widespread teacher shortage has the capacity to undermine the quality of education in several ways. Systems or schools, glad to hire any teachers, are not as discriminating about the quality of staff they engage. Class sizes may be increased, classes in some subjects may be cancelled, and teachers may be required to teach outside their area of competence. The effect that has greatest relevance to staffing policy is that unqualified or ill-qualified teachers may be hired. For example, Ingersoll (1995) and Ingersoll and Gruber (1996) suggest that equality of educational provision has been compromised and a teacher shortage masked by the extent of out-of-field teaching in US secondary schools.

A general shortage requires central system-wide measures. A local staffing method is clearly unable to take effective action. Furthermore, systems with centralized staffing are likely to be more quickly sensitive to the problem and better able to provide a coordinated response. The range of strategies used to boost teacher supply include attracting more students into teacher education courses by scholarships (which, however, may take too long), salary increases, recruitment from other states or systems, and enticing those who have left teaching for a time to return (e.g., mothers). None

of these need imply a compromise of professional standards.

On the other hand, the lowering of entry requirements by providing short course certification or on-the-job training is very likely to compromise standards. As an example of an emergency entry response to teacher shortage in the United States, Darling-Hammond (1989) reported that 46 states offered "emergency teaching certificates" and 23 had created alternative modes of preparation which enable a recruit to begin teaching after a course of four to six weeks. If there is a knowledge base for teaching and a range of pedagogical skills that teachers should possess, such emergency certification cannot but lower professional standards. Darling-Hammond, with biting irony, comments (1989 p. 3): "If one disallows any criterion of quality, qualified teachers are not difficult to find." This seems more likely to occur when local staffing is coupled with the absence of a strong centralized professional or union body to resist central government inclinations to implement solutions to urgent staffing problems at the cost of professional standards.

Shortage affects different systems in different ways. In systems where staffing decisions were devolved to the school's governing body, as in the United Kingdom, New Zealand, and Victoria, Australia, there is little scope for effective local action to address shortage without additional budget allowance or the acceptance of emergency certification. The problem is made worse if the school happens to be in an area difficult to staff. Devolution in these three countries happened to be introduced at a time of teacher surplus. There is some reason to fear that policy changes in the United Kingdom have mostly consolidated inequalities of educational opportunity (Halpin and Troyna 1994). A shortage of teachers will provide the acid test of devolved staffing methods.

In Switzerland, where teacher salaries are amongst the highest in the world and teaching conditions are very favorable (there are 17–25 students in a primary school class), teacher shortage does not provide a major problem. However, a report on Swiss education (Organisation for Economic Co-operation and Development 1991) points to staffing difficulties in some cantons resulting from obstacles to teacher mobility such as the lack of recognition of qualifications across cantons. In this example, a country faces difficulty in providing equal educational opportunity for all its citizens because it has no national policy of education (Gretler 1994).

With respect to the effect of shortage on difficult-to-staff schools, it is clear that shortage does not make its impact across a system in a random way. When there are fewer teachers than there are jobs, teacher preference for some locations above others means that the difficult-to-staff places are more likely to miss out. Indeed, it is a common phenomenon that even when there is an overall surplus of teachers in a system there can be a shortage of teachers for some locations or subject disciplines. Furthermore, simply preparing more teachers may not solve the problem. They may not be inclined to go to the places where they are most needed.

To remedy a selective shortage, it is first necessary to discover the basis of teacher preference for some locations and refusal of others and to devise strategies guided by that knowledge. The difficulty of getting new teachers to accept rural appointments in New South Wales led to a study which illustrates the issues involved (Watson et al. 1987). Final semester students who were surveyed indicated that the most important reasons for refusal to accept a rural appointment were fear of the unknown and isolation from family and friends. Another highly significant reason was an expectation that the climate and setting would be harsh and unfavorable. Measures proposed to address the problems included provision of more effective information about rural teaching, opportunity for more students to do their teacher education in a rural university or to do a rural practicum, and a range of incentives. It was concluded that financial incentives, though necessary for some locations, would neither address the principal cause of the reluctance to go, namely, fear of the unknown, nor help teachers with a city background prepare to be effective rural teachers.

2.2.3 Staff turnover. While a moderate level of staff turnover is desirable in a school to allow the introduction of new ideas and to permit unsuitable staff to move on, a high rate of staff turnover is quite harmful. The stagnation which may result from too little turnover is a common problem in times of teacher surplus, while the instability stemming from excessive turnover is most likely in times of shortage. A staffing system is put to a good test by its capacity to manage turnover.

With respect to maintaining a moderate level of turnover, many systems, even when staff are inefficient or unsuitable, have little scope to require a formal staff review and find it nearly impossible to terminate employment. For example, in Germany, where staff are civil servants (*Beamte*) with secure tenure and status controlled by federal law, and in Switzerland (Zürich), where they are elected by vote of the local community every six years and very rarely disapproved, it is virtually impossible to remove or move a teacher. The use of renewable contracts for senior leadership positions in New South Wales and for principals in British Columbia makes it easier to remove or replace staff, but employing all teachers on contract is difficult to implement, meeting with understandable opposition from teachers who see security of tenure as a compensation for salaries lower than those of their peers with the same length of training in other occupations. Limiting the period for which a teacher is allowed to stay in one school, say to 7 or 10 years, has proved difficult to implement. For example, it was tried in South Australia but discontinued. Requiring a 7- (or 10- year) appraisal and review before teachers can continue at a school may prove more workable.

Sustained high staff turnover has adverse effects upon schooling at several levels. It results in excessive transfer costs to the system, longer settling-in time for the school, greater difficulty maintaining staff cohesion, and weaker ties with the community. These factors are likely to have a harmful impact on student learning. Evidence suggests that there is a negative relationship of teacher turnover to pupil achievement (Walberg 1974).

These adverse effects are heightened by related factors. Most schools with high turnover are difficult to staff and the least experienced teachers, lowest in the staffing pecking order, are the most likely to be sent there, as experienced teachers transfer to more congenial schools. Furthermore, children in such places are more likely to be from disadvantaged backgrounds, requiring the most expert teaching. The result is a disproportionate number of beginning teachers being asked to teach some of the most demanding students but with few experienced teachers to advise them. While the greater stability induced by teacher surplus may ameliorate this problem, it can be very harmful during a shortage.

3. Staffing for Good Teaching

There are two basic approaches to solving problems of staffing. One is the "deficit model," the other, the "challenge model" (Ankhara-Dove 1982). Each operates from a different set of assumptions and proposes a different set of practical recommendations. The deficit model assumes that teachers are reluctant to go to areas perceived to be difficult and uses compulsory minimum terms of appointment and incentives of various kinds to compensate for the deficits of the posting. In contrast, the challenge approach assumes teachers can gain intrinsic motivation from working in difficult locations if they adjust well, find the job satisfying, and can make career progress in that place. Although in practice a system is likely to use aspects of both models, the deficit approach is usually a response to some urgent need and often implies short-term expediency, while the challenge approach requires longer-term planning and emphasis upon qualitative implications of staffing decisions, not just the quantitative concern to fill all vacancies.

3.1 The Deficit Approach

The strengths and limitations of staffing incentives need to be understood. Higher salaries can increase the number of applicants seeking to enter teaching and the length of time teachers will stay in the profession (Murnane 1994). Incentives will also increase teacher willingness to accept and remain in difficult appointments; for example, priority of transfer for next appointment, lump sum on completion of term (Hatton et al. 1991). However, incentives are not very effective for improving the quality of teaching. Though the numbers of students interested in enrolling in teacher education have increased when there are teacher salary increases, the quality of applicants is likely to be unchanged (Murnane 1994). Furthermore, competitive aspects of incentives, which pit individual against individual, or, to a lesser extent, individual against a fixed standard, undermine commitment to the job. This, together with related evidence, led Firestone and Pennell (1993) to conclude that measures other than incentives be used to foster good teaching.

3.2 The Challenge Approach

While compulsory postings and incentives may in some measure be necessary for the difficult-to-staff locations, the need for them can be reduced by establishing programs specifically designed to prepare teachers for such places. The programs will be more effective if students enrolled in them can be recruited from among the subpopulation groups situated in areas which are hard to staff (Darling-Hammond 1990). If the teacher education of these recruits can take the form of a university off-campus extension program, such as occurs in British Columbia, Canada, or an on-campus special focus program, as occurs in New South Wales, they are more likely to teach voluntarily where they are most needed and to be well-informed and soundly equipped for that location. Furthermore, such teachers are likely to stay longer, further their careers there, and, as a consequence, help to overcome problems associated with high turnover.

Good teaching requires persistence in such unglamorous and routine tasks as lesson planning and preparation, careful marking, and detailed record keeping. A deep sense of work satisfaction and a strong commitment are needed to nourish the will to sustain the long-term effort needed.

A strong body of evidence suggests that the central source of satisfaction for teachers is the relationships associated with the job—with fellow staff, with students, and perhaps with parents and the community (Chapman et al. 1993, Firestone and Pennell 1993, Watson et al. 1991). An impersonal central staffing process is less likely to provide a suitable match with staff and community than a process that includes local staff and community representatives. Satisfaction, however, is subtle, rather subjective, and may not be readily amenable to efforts aimed at its improvement. Adjustment, though related to it, is more objective and may be a more productive focus for efforts to raise satisfaction. Once staff have been selected and placed, the adequacy of the induction (see *Teacher Recruitment and Induction*), the usability of resources, the quality and availability of inservice education, and the support of fellow staff, are all important for good adjustment and satisfaction (Watson et al. 1991).

However, increased career satisfaction may not in itself lead to improved teaching. It may produce complacency when there is a need to improve instructional

practices (Chapman et al. 1993). Commitment and the stimulus to improve are also required. Commitment, which is voluntary attachment to a purpose or person that produces effort beyond the call of duty, seems to be a deeper and more abiding source of motivation than satisfaction, though nourished by it. Firestone and Pennell (1993) present evidence that commitment in teaching is best nurtured by increasing teacher participation in decision-making (at school and district levels), encouraging collaboration between staff (e.g., scheduling time for work-group meetings and planning), and increasing feedback on teaching from mentors and senior staff. It is this last source in particular that provides the stimulus for improvement.

4. Conclusion

Many systems have devolved staff decision-making to a local body, in the plausible belief that better teacher fit will help promote satisfaction and commitment and so lead to better teaching. Teacher placement should also be concerned to provide equality of opportunity in difficult-to-staff locations. The critical test is whether the staffing system can allow local participation and at the same time provide high-quality education for all students, not just those in schools attractive to teachers.

See also: Teacher Recruitment and Induction

References

Ankhara-Dove L A 1982 The development and training of teachers for remote rural schools in less developed countries. *Int. Rev. Educ.* 28: 3–27

Canadian Education Association 1992 *Teacher Recruitment and Retention: How Canadian School Boards Attract Teachers: A Report.* Canadian Education Association, Toronto

Chapman D W, Snyder C W, Burchfield S A 1993 Teacher incentives in the third world. *Teaching and Teacher Education* 9: 301–16

Darling-Hammond L 1989 Teacher supply, demand, and standards. *Educ. Policy* 3(1): 1–17

Darling-Hammond L 1990 Teachers and teaching: Signs of a changing profession. In: Houston W R (ed.) 1990 *Handbook of Research on Teacher Education.* Macmillan, New York

Firestone W A, Pennell J R 1993 Teacher commitment, working conditions and differential incentive policies. *Rev. Educ. Res.* 63: 489-526

Gretler A 1994 Switzerland: System of education. In: Husén T, Postlethwaite T N (eds.) 1994 *The International Encyclopedia of Education,* 2nd edn. Pergamon, Oxford

Halpin D, Troyna B 1994 Lessons in school reform from Great Britain? The politics of education policy borrowing. Paper prepared for the symposium "Lessons in school reform from Great Britain?: The politics of educational policy appropriation and transfer." Annual meeting of the American Education Research Association, New Orleans, Louisiana, 6 April 1994

Hatton N G, Watson A J, Squires D S, Soliman I K 1991

School staffing and the quality of education: Teacher stability and mobility. *Teaching and Teacher Education* 7: 279–93

Ingersoll R 1995 Teacher supply and demand in the US In: *Proceedings of the American Statistical Association 1995.* American Statistical Association, Alexandria, Virginia

Ingersoll R, Gruber K 1996 *Out-of-Field Teaching and Educational Equality.* US Department of Education, National Center for Educational Statistics, Washington, DC

Lehmann R H 1994 Germany: System of education. In: Husén T, Postlethwaite T N (eds.) 1994 *The International Encyclopedia of Education*, 2nd edn. Pergamon, Oxford

Murnane R J 1994 Supply of teachers. In: Husén T,

Postlethwaite T N (eds.) 1994 *The International Encyclopedia of Education*, 2nd edn. Pergamon, Oxford

Organisation for Economic Co-operation and Development 1991 *Reviews of National Policies for Education: Switzerland.* OECD, Paris

Walberg H 1974 *Evaluating Educational Performance.* McCutchan, Berkeley, California

Watson A J, Hatton N G, Squires D S, Grundy S 1987 Graduating teachers and their attitudes towards rural appointments. *South Pac. J. Teach. Educ.* 15: 1–17

Watson A J, Hatton N G, Squires D S, Soliman I K 1991 School staffing and the quality of education: Teacher adjustment and satisfaction. *Teaching and Teacher Education* 7: 63–77

Teacher Recruitment and Induction

R. Bolam

There is widespread agreement that the achievement of successful schooling is crucially dependent on the quality of the teaching force. This quality, in turn, is significantly influenced by the effectiveness of the processes of recruiting and inducting beginning teachers. This article focuses on these two processes, outlining the factors that affect their formulation, implementation, and effectiveness, including those in the broader policy context. It does not deal directly with such related matters as the supply and demand for teachers, teacher accreditation, the characteristics of beginning teachers, or the induction of experienced teachers who have changed schools.

1. Recruitment

Teacher recruitment policies of all governments are affected by basic factors such as their economic policies (specifically, the amount of money they allocate to education), increases or decreases in birthrates, and teacher supply and demand. These policies are also influenced by country-specific factors. Normally, for example, strategic decisions about the numbers to be recruited into initial teacher education and the qualifications needed to be a teacher are made nationally within the context of each government's policy for teacher supply. Thus, teachers are usually required to be college graduates, but this is not always true in developing countries. In Pakistan, for instance, only 9 percent of primary school teachers held a bachelor's degree in 1989. Similarly, although the majority of teachers are usually female, especially in the primary school sector, in Islamic countries qualifications are not the essential ingredient since a common aim is to recruit more women to teach girls. In some African

countries, recruitment and selection decisions may be influenced by tribal allegiances, in India, caste is important; and in several countries, political and union affiliations may be considered.

The status of teachers in the eyes of society at large and, more concretely, their salaries and career prospects, must also be taken into account. Teachers are often civil servants with severely restricted "professional" autonomy. Indeed, the very concept of the "professional," about which so much is written in English-speaking countries, has no apparent equivalent in many other languages. Hence, teaching is much more likely to be regarded as just another occupation in non-English-speaking countries.

The nature of the career structure also varies a great deal among countries. In the United Kingdom the head teacher of a school may earn over four times the salary of a beginning teacher and the intervening career ladder offers substantial salary incentives at each stage. In Spain, by contrast, headteachers are elected by their colleagues, receive only a nominal salary increase, and there are no salary incentives, nor any significant career ladder, for teachers. Women have relatively poor career prospects in teaching and are significantly underrepresented in senior positions. Nevertheless, they continue to constitute the majority of teachers in most countries.

In those countries such as Germany, Ireland, Belgium, and Japan, where there was an overall surplus of teachers in the 1980s and 1990s, teacher unemployment, linked to a highly competitive entry process, has been the main issue in recruitment policy. In other countries there has been an overall shortage. However, the notion of a shortage is problematic. A shortage may occur for demographic or economic reasons, because of inaccurate forecasting and planning, or because of related policy decisions. The indisputable shortage that exists in developing countries is due quite simply to the fact that there is an insufficient number of qualified people.

In countries such as the United Kingdom, the numbers entering teacher training are strictly controlled on the basis of national demographic projections. In others, such as Italy, effectively no initial training for secondary teachers existed until relatively recently. In some countries, such as Greece, there is a pool of unemployed, qualified teachers. However, this is not true in those countries, particularly in the Third World, in which a teaching qualification is sought primarily as a means to a better paid job in industry or commerce. Virtually all countries have shortages in highly marketable subjects such as science, mathematics, and computing, but even here there are exceptions. Again in Greece, there has been an oversupply of physics teachers in the late 1980s and early 1990s. Shortages in particular student age-ranges or geographic regions are also common, but the reasons are often country-specific. The nature and scope of these shortages are partly contingent on related policy decisions; for example, those on teacher–student ratios and class size, which affect the number of teachers to be recruited.

1.1 Teacher Recruitment and Teaching Quality

Most governments aim to improve the quality of their teaching force via teacher recruitment. Once again, their approaches vary. For instance, in most European countries candidates for higher education and teacher training must pass a rigorous academic examination at age 18 and, as a result, the national debate about quality is focused on subject knowledge and teaching skills rather than on basic academic competence. By contrast, many states and some school districts in the United States have introduced their own entry testing procedures to try to ensure that prospective teachers have a satisfactory level of competence in basic literacy and numeracy skills. In Europe, each member state of the European Community is now able to recruit teachers from the other states, thanks to mutual recognition of national teacher training qualifications. This in itself is a powerful new factor in promoting teacher recruitment and teaching quality throughout Europe.

1.2 Approaches to Teacher Recruitment

In centralized systems of education, including those in developing countries, teachers are usually recruited by a national unit within the framework of a national plan and then deployed by national, state, or regional administrators. The individual teacher and school have little say in the decision. Thus, new teachers are recruited to the total teaching force and may then be allocated to a school in a remote part of the country. Redeployment and promotion decisions are frequently taken in the same manner.

In systems that are relatively decentralized, such as those of the United States and the United Kingdom, on the other hand, such decisions are taken at the local or school level. Specific vacancies are advertised locally or nationally and the successful candidates are appointed after passing through a selection process conducted by the local education authority or by the governing body of the individual school. Hence, both new and experienced teachers have optimum choice over where they can apply to teach, while schools and local authorities can decide whom to select.

In general, several recruitment methods are being tried out by national and local authorities. They include the following. First, flexible entry routes and preparatory access courses are used to help candidates who are underqualified on normal criteria. Second, new forms of initial training and teacher licensing are being introduced. Third, courses for qualified candidates from other fields, for teachers wishing to switch subjects or types of school, and for married women "returners" are being converted and updated. Fourth, qualified teachers from other countries are being recruited. Fifth, specific incentives such as higher salaries, job sharing, creche facilities, and inexpensive housing are being offered to increase recruitment in shortage areas. The relative effectiveness of these various methods is unclear and, in any case, most of the available research is highly context-bound.

2. Induction

The term "induction" refers to the process of support and training that is increasingly being seen as necessary for a successful first year of teaching. Policymakers tend to be more interested in induction when there are recruitment problems, regarding it as a means of improving retention rates by encouraging a greater proportion of beginning teachers to stay on beyond the first year. Professionals tend to be interested in it as a bridging period between initial and inservice training and, hence, as the foundation of continuing professional development.

The first year of teaching has been the focus of considerable research and development since the 1960s, although principally in only a few countries (e.g., the United Kingdom, the United States, Australia, New Zealand, Canada, and Hong Kong). In other developed countries, interest in induction into teaching varies. In Germany, for example, the final two years of initial training have for many years incorporated what is, in effect, an induction period. Similarly, in the Netherlands, induction has been the subject of much research. In developing countries, induction is far less important than the improvement of initial teacher training.

The first year of teaching has several strands to it. The term "beginning teacher" is commonly used in North America, and to a lesser extent elsewhere, to refer to teachers who have completed their initial training, have received some form of professional accreditation, are employed by a school district, and are in their first year of service, with a more or less normal teaching work load. The first year is often coterminous with a period of probation during which the provisional licensure acquired by the teacher during or at the end of initial training is subject to ratification.

2.1 Principal Components of Induction Programs

By the end of the 1970s informed professional opinion and published research in the United States, United Kingdom, and Australia were, broadly speaking, in agreement regarding the principal components of a successful induction program. They are as follows: (a) additional release time, that is, time away from teaching for the beginning teacher; (b) school-based support from a colleague acting as a mentor or professional tutor, who also receives some additional release time plus training; (c) planned and systematic school-based activities, including discussion groups, classroom observation and support; (d) planned and systematic externally based activities organized by the local education authority (LEA) and university staff; and (e) the explicit and active support of school principals and other administrators. During the 1980s induction increasingly came to be considered within the broader context of staff development; since schools only recruit beginning teachers periodically, staff development is the most cost-effective way of managing the organization and staffing of the school's induction scheme.

There was, and probably still is, less operational agreement about the fundamental aims of induction. Where it is coterminous with probation, the two tend, in practice, to become conflated and confused. This situation is related to a more basic dilemma, namely, should the aim be to induct new teachers into the knowledge, skills, and values promoted by the national system, the employing LEA, the particular school, or the wider profession? The understandable response from program organizers is that a balance must be struck between all four. However, in practice, they are usually influenced by the program's funding body (i.e., the Government, the LEA, or the school) and consequently it is the fourth aim which tends to be underplayed or even omitted. Thus, few induction programs follow the approach adopted by many initial training institutions in aiming to equip new teachers to make informed, independent, professional judgments about a range of curricular and pedagogical issues or about the worthwhileness of the current policies and practices of their national or local system or school.

This "fact of life" is hardly surprising, not only from the perspective of *realpolitik*, but also because the evidence is clear that new teachers are overwhelmingly concerned with the practical problems with which they have to deal in their classrooms, departments, and schools. This concern of new teachers can be attributed largely to the "reality shock" they encounter when they move from their relatively sheltered position in initial training to a situation where they are accountable for all aspects of their professional work. Specifically they are responsible for the learning of groups of students who are frequently uncooperative or even actively hostile, while simultaneously undergoing what may be radical change in their personal lives. Small wonder that the first year of teaching is often experienced and portrayed as traumatic. Unlike most other beginning professionals, teachers work in relative isolation, behind the classroom door.

2.2 Induction Programs, Relevance, and Mentoring

Beginning teachers judge the effectiveness of induction programs primarily in terms of their practical relevance to their own current problems. They tend to be skeptical about external courses which emphasize administrative and legal information or are overly theoretical. They do value the opportunity to meet with other new teachers in "neutral" settings, such as a university, where they may be relieved to discover that their problems are not peculiar to them, and where they are able to discuss them with sympathetic peers and supportive, more experienced group leaders. Above all, they value time to plan, to mark students' work, and to think. Thus, a reduced teaching load coupled with the provision of practical help given by colleagues whom they respect and who have the skills and time to help them, are needed.

It is partly for this reason that there has been much greater emphasis since the early 1980s on mentoring. The importance of support teachers was evident much earlier, for example in the British professional tutor role. During the 1980s, however, the mentor concept was developed, partly in the light of industrial models, in relation to initial training and principal training as well as induction. While definitions vary, mentors are experienced school colleagues who are responsible for helping beginning teachers. This help may be given directly or indirectly. Mentors may provide information, conduct orientations, observe classrooms and give feedback on what they saw and heard, engage in discussion groups, provide liaison with other staff, the LEA, and the university, and, sometimes, perform assessments and evaluations. Although this list would probably attract general agreement, there are many program-specific approaches to mentoring. They include, for example, the degree of emphasis on subject knowledge (and, hence, on whether or not the mentor should have expertise in the same subject or age-range specialism as the inductee) and pedagogical expertise. Many of the skills needed by mentors (for instance, those associated with classroom observation, clinical supervision, reflective practice, and coaching) are familiar in other contexts but they do require careful adaptation to mentoring.

3. Emerging Trends, Issues, and Research

Many trends are, of necessity, specific to particular countries. In England and Wales, for example, the abolition of the probationary year, the introduction of a national teacher appraisal scheme, the introduction of school-controlled and school-based initial training, and the possible introduction of a General Teaching Council, all have significant implications for both recruitment and induction. More generally, several countries are introducing forms of restructuring that will have direct consequences for recruitment and induction, again as illustrated by experience in England and Wales. Under the system of school-based management that is now well-established there, school governors, advised by parent and community representatives, are responsible for staff appointments and for both the overall school and staff-training budgets.

The risk of a parochial and inward-looking recruitment policy being adopted in this situation is evident. Moreover, given the limited budgets available, there are strong pressures for governors to appoint less costly beginning teachers, often on short-term contracts, in preference to experienced but more expensive teachers. Governors are also likely to be reluctant to spend money from the training budget on induction training and support unless it is earmarked for that purpose within the funding formula. The logical next step in this system of school self-management, especially since it is associated with the promotion of competition between schools within a regulated market approach, is the introduction of site-level pay bargaining together with performance-related pay linked to appraisal. The implications of such developments for recruitment and induction will be considerable.

While these policy-related issues will require careful monitoring, there are several technical matters that also should be studied. Recruitment and retention are underresearched topics, partly because they are so context-bound within particular national systems. Nevertheless, it would be instructive to see which selection methods, including the interview, were effective and under what circumstances; to do the same for innovative recruitment strategies, such as the articled and licensed teacher schemes in the United Kingdom; and to study the implications of these methods and strategies for other national systems.

Several theoretical perspectives can be used profitably to study induction, including those arising from work on teacher socialization, adult learning, teacher cognition, teacher effectiveness, and teacher biographies. There is a need for further research on the roles and training needs of mentors; the role of competence-based methods in induction; the implications of the distinctive features of curriculum subjects for induction; and the relationship of induction to staff development and human resource development.

However, the most fundamental research priority arises from an issue of policy. Although the research evidence is sometimes less than robust and must always be interpreted in relation to the national context within which it was produced, the messages about the value of induction, the main components of an effective induction scheme, and, to a lesser extent, the impact of induction on retention rates, are consistently positive. It comes as some surprise, then, that so few induction programs have become established. In the United States, for example, Conant's (1963) report advocated systematic induction and six years later the National Association of Secondary School Principals (Hunt 1969) produced a set of practical guidelines which were, in their essentials, indistinguishable from those still being advocated in the early 1990s. Similarly, in England and Wales, following the recommendations of the influential James Report on the need for systematic induction (United Kingdom, Department of Education and Science 1972), a series of government-funded research and development activities resulted, by 1978, in national agreement on the nature, scope, and practical details of successful teacher induction. At the same time, however, several subsequent studies by the national inspectorate reported that induction support is patchy and sometimes nonexistent.

In both countries, induction has moved up and down the policy agenda since the 1960s, apparently depending on the perceived scale and political significance of the teacher recruitment and retention problem. A major task for policy researchers, therefore, should be to study two issues. First, how can better use be made of existing technical knowledge about the design and implementation of effective induction schemes? Second, what kind of policy and structural changes are needed for such schemes to become firmly institutionalized in a national inservice teacher education system? Only when these issues are resolved will educators be in a position to establish whether or not induction can make a consistent and positive impact on teacher recruitment and retention.

See also: Teacher Placement and School Staffing

References

Conant J B 1963 *The Education of American Teachers.* McGraw-Hill, New York
Hunt D W 1969 *Project on the Induction of Beginning Teachers*, Booklets 1–3. National Association of Secondary School Principals, Reston, Virginia
United Kingdom, Department of Education and Science 1972 *Teacher Education and Training* (James Report). HMSO, London

Further Reading

Ashton P T (ed.) 1992 Editorial—Special issue: Induction and mentoring. *J. Teach. Educ.* 43(3): 162

Bolam R 1987 Induction of beginning teachers. In: Dunkin M J (ed.) 1987 *International Encyclopedia of Teaching and Teacher Education*. Pergamon Press, Oxford

Cooke B L, Pang K C 1987 Experiences and needs of trained and untrained beginning teachers in Hong Kong: A pilot study. *Educ. Res. J.* 2: 18–27

Earley P 1992 *Beyond Initial Teacher Training: Induction and the Role of the LEA*. National Foundation for Educational Research (NFER), Slough

Education, Science and Arts Committee 1990 *Second Report: The Supply of Teachers for the 1990s*, Vol. 1. HMSO, London

Huling-Austin L, Odell S J, Ishler M, Kay R S, Edelfelt R A 1989 *Assisting the Beginning Teacher*. Association of Teacher Educators, Reston, Virginia

Instance D 1990 *The Teacher Today: Tasks, Conditions, Policies*. Organisation for Economic Co-operation and Development, Paris

Le Métais J 1990 *The Impact on the Education Service of Teacher Mobility*. National Foundation for Educational Research, Slough

Little J W, Nelson L (eds.) *Mentor Teacher: A Leader's Guide to Mentor Training*. Far West Laboratory for Educational Research and Development, San Francisco, California

Maclean R 1992 *Teachers' Careers and Promotional Patterns: A Sociological Analysis*. Falmer, London

Oldroyd D, Hall V 1991 *Managing Staff Development: A Handbook for Secondary Schools*. Chapman, London

United Kingdom Department of Education and Science 1988 *The New Teacher in School*. HMSO, London

Veenman S 1984 Perceived problems of beginning teachers. *Rev. Educ. Res.* 54(2): 143–78

Wise A E, Darling-Hammond L, Berry B 1987 *Effective Teacher Selection: From Recruitment to Retention*. Rand Corporation, Santa Monica, California

Zeichner K, Gore T 1990 Teacher socialization. In: Houston W R, Howsam R, Sikula J (eds.), 1990 *Handbook of Research on Teacher Education*. Macmillan, New York

Teachers' Expectations

T. L. Good

In the 1960s, an experiment conducted in the United States by Rosenthal and Jacobson (1968) resulted in one of the most exciting and controversial reports in the history of educational research. These investigators presented data suggesting that teachers' experimentally induced expectations for student performance were associated with student performance. That is, students whom teachers expected to achieve at higher levels did in fact achieve at higher levels, even though there was no real basis for these expectations. The study was criticized on several methodological grounds. For example, no observations were conducted in the teachers' classrooms, so there was no basis on which to determine whether teachers interacted differently with the students based on their expectations.

This article focuses on research on teachers' expectations that has been conducted since the publication of the Rosenthal and Jacobson study. It begins with a definition of teachers' expectations, discusses the major types of research on those expectations and the conceptual frameworks underlying this research, and examines ways in which different expectations are communicated to students, and the perceptions students have of these different teacher behaviors. The entry concludes with a discussion of possible directions for research on teachers' expectations.

1. Defining Teachers' Expectations

Teachers' expectations are inferences that teachers make about the future behavior or academic achievement of their students, based on what they currently know about these students. Teachers' expectations affect student outcomes because of actions that teachers take in response to their expectations. Expectations are an inescapable and important part of daily life (Jussim 1990a), influencing many social issues. Research on expectancies has examined such topics as gender role socialization, affirmative action, political person perception, and equality of educational opportunity. (For discussions of research on the role of expectancies in diverse social areas see Jussim 1990a, 1990b, Oyserman and Markus 1990.)

Cooper and Good (1983) noted that researchers have examined two types of teacher expectation effects. The first is the self-fulfilling prophecy effect, in which an originally erroneous expectation leads to behavior that causes the expectation to become true. The Rosenthal and Jacobson (1968) study deals with this type of expectation effect. In contrast, the sustaining expectation effect occurs when teachers expect students to sustain previously developed behavior patterns to the point that teachers take these patterns for granted and fail to see and capitalize on changes in student potential. Self-fulfilling prophecy effects are more powerful than sustaining expectation effects because they introduce significant change in student behavior (and thinking) instead of merely sustaining established patterns. Self-fulfilling effects can be powerful when they occur, but the more subtle sustaining expectation effects occur more often.

2. Two Types of Research on Teachers' Expectations

To understand the research on teacher expectation effects, two types of studies must be distinguished. The first involves experimental attempts to induce teacher expectations by providing teachers with fictitious information about students. The second type of study uses the expectations that teachers form naturally on the basis of whatever information they have available (e.g., test scores).

Numerous studies have induced expectations in teachers and have explored the consequent effects on student learning (Good and Brophy 1990). Some studies did not produce changes in student outcomes, apparently because the teachers did not acquire the expectations the experimenters were trying to induce. Induced-expectation experiments have produced clear-cut positive results often enough, however, to demonstrate that teacher expectations can have self-fulfilling prophecy effects on student achievement. Such demonstrations are important, because studies of teachers' naturally formed expectations cannot establish cause-and-effect relationships. These experimental studies in classrooms have been enriched by laboratory research in social psychology that has focused on the formation, communication, and interpretation of expectancies (see Jones 1990, Jussim 1990b for reviews).

However, studies linking teachers' naturally formed expectations to their classroom interactions with students are also needed, because they provide information about how teachers' expectations can become self-fulfilling. As Good and Brophy (1990) noted, most studies of teachers' naturally formed expectations have related such expectations to teacher–student interaction rather than to student outcomes. These studies typically demonstrate that many teachers interact differently with students for whom they hold high expectations than they do with students for whom they hold low expectations. They also suggest the mechanisms that mediate sustaining expectation effects.

3. The Brophy–Good Model

In their early research on teacher expectation effects on individual students, Brophy and Good (1970) suggested the following model of the process by which teachers' expectations become self-fulfilling prophecies.

(a) Early in the year, the teacher forms differential expectations for student behavior and achievement.

(b) Consistent with these differential expectations, the teacher behaves differently toward various students.

(c) This treatment tells students how they are expected to behave in the classroom and to perform on academic tasks.

(d) If the teacher's treatment is consistent over time, and if students do not actively resist or change it, it will likely affect their self-concepts, achievement motivation, levels of aspiration, classroom conduct, and interactions with the teacher.

(e) These effects generally will compliment and reinforce the teacher's expectations, so that students will conform to these expectations more than they might otherwise have done.

(f) Ultimately this reciprocal process will affect student achievement and other outcomes. High-expectation students will achieve at or near their potential, but low-expectation students will not gain as much as they could have if taught differently.

The model begins with the assumption that teachers form differential achievement expectations for various students at the beginning of the school year. Teachers use many cues for forming expectations, including track or group placement, classroom conduct, physical appearance, race, socioeconomic status, ethnicity, gender, speech characteristics, and various diagnostic labels (e.g., see Baron et al. 1985, Jussim 1989).

Self-fulfilling prophecy effects of teacher expectations can occur only when all elements in the model are present (Good and Brophy 1990). Often, however, one or more elements is missing. The teacher may not have clear-cut expectations about every student, or those expectations may change continually. Even when expectations are consistent, the teacher may not necessarily communicate them through consistent behavior. Finally, students might prevent expectations from becoming self-fulfilling by counteracting their effects or resisting them.

4. Communicating Differential Expectations

Given that teachers form differential expectations, how do they express those expectations to students in ways that might influence students' behavior? On the basis of several literature reviews, Good and Brophy (1990) suggested that the following behaviors sometimes indicate differential teacher treatment of high and low achievers: (a) waiting less time for "lows" to answer questions before giving the answer or calling on someone else; (b) giving lows answers or calling on someone else rather than trying to improve their responses by giving clues or repeating or rephrasing questions; (c) providing inappropriate reinforcement (e.g., rewarding inappropriate behavior or incorrect answers by lows); (d) criticizing lows more often for failure; (e) praising lows less often for success; (e) failing to give feedback to the public responses of lows; (f) paying less attention to lows or interacting with them less frequently; (g) calling on lows less often to respond to questions, or asking them only easier, nonanalytical questions; (h) seating lows further from the teacher; (i) demanding less from lows (e.g., teaching them less content; accepting lower quality or even incorrect responses from lows; providing excessive sympathy or unneeded help); (j) interacting with lows more privately than publicly, and monitoring and structuring their activities more closely; (k) grading tests or assignments differently (e.g., highs but not lows are given the benefit of the doubt in borderline cases), (l) engaging in less friendly interaction with lows, including less smiling and fewer other nonverbal indicators of support; (m) providing briefer and less informative feedback to questions of lows; (n) using less eye contact and other nonverbal communication of attention and responsiveness (forward lean, positive head nodding) in interactions with lows; (o) using less effective and time-consuming instructional methods with lows when time is limited; (p) accepting and using lows' ideas less often; and (q) exposing lows to an impoverished curriculum (e.g. limited and repetitive information, emphasis on factual recitation).

Three points should be noted when considering these forms of differential treatment. First, these teacher behaviors do not occur in all classrooms. Some teachers do not communicate low expectations; some provide appropriate expectations for all or most students. Second, some of the differences are due to students rather than to the teacher. For example, if lows volunteer less often, it is difficult for teachers to be sure that lows get as many response opportunities as highs. Third, some forms of differential treatment are necessary at times and may even represent appropriate individualizing of instruction rather than inappropriate projection of negative expectations. Low-achieving students in elementary schools appear to require more private structuring of their activities and closer monitoring of their work than do their peers.

When several of these differential communication patterns are observed in a classroom, however, and if the differentiation is significant, the teacher may be communicating inappropriately low expectations to some students. This is especially the case if the differential treatment directly affects students' opportunity to learn. For example, if lows receive less new information and feedback about their performance, they are almost certain to make less progress than highs, regardless of whether lows are aware of such differential treatment.

While research has focused on inappropriately low expectations, teachers can hold too high or too "narrow" expectations so that some students are pushed to do more but not allowed to take time to understand or enjoy academic work. The key is to challenge and guide students in appropriate ways to do more than they are at that time able to achieve (Vygotsky 1978).

5. The Importance of Teachers' Expectations

The effects of teachers' expectations on student learning have often been exaggerated. Indeed, in the popular press the effects have sometimes been touted as almost magical. For example, Good and Brophy (1977) lampooned an advertisement that appeared in *Reader's Digest*: "Just make a wish. Read about how it can come True." Although there is no clear way to predict with certainty the effects of teachers' expectancies on student learning, there is growing consensus among experts that expectancy effects are usually modest (e.g., Jussim 1990b estimates an average effect size of 0.2 to 0.3 standard deviations), but important (Brophy 1983). Even an effect size of 0.2 suggests that 10 percent of students who receive high expectations will show notable improvement, and that 10 percent of students exposed to low expectations will exhibit a significant decline in performance (Jussim 1990b).

There is no doubt that expectancies are common. Rosenthal and Rubin (1978) reported that some type of teacher expectancy effect occurred in about two-thirds of the 345 studies they reviewed. Although the potential importance of expectancies is shown by such reviews (and expectancy effects may compound over time), most students do not receive "average effects"; students are likely to be in classrooms where effects are very high, moderate, or nonexistent.

6. Students' Perceptions of Teachers' Differential Behavior

Unfortunately, many studies that have assessed the effects of teacher expectancies on student performance have not included process or interview data to determine students' perceptions of differential teacher behavior. In addition to expectation effects that occur directly through differences in exposure to content, indirect effects may occur as a result of teacher behavior that affects students' self-concepts, performance expectations, or motivation. Although numerous studies have examined students' achievement motivation and aspirations in classrooms, little of this research has studied these affective variables in relation to teacher behavior. Thus, little is known about how students interpret teacher behaviors and how those behaviors influence students' motivation and effort.

Studies that have been conducted suggest that students are aware of differences in teachers' patterns of interaction with students. Interview and questionnaire data indicate that elementary students see their teachers as projecting higher achievement expectations and offering increased opportunity and choice to high achievers, while structuring the activities of low achievers more closely and providing them with additional help and with more negative feedback about their academic work and classroom conduct (Cooper and Good 1983).

Furthermore, students are more aware of such differentiation in classes in which it occurs frequently (Weinstein et al. 1987). Brattesani et al. (1984) compared classrooms where the students described the teachers as differentiating considerably in their treatment of high and low achievers with classrooms in which students reported little such differentiation. They found that including teacher-expectation measures added from 9 to 18 percent to the variance in year-end achievement beyond what could have been predicted from prior achievement in the high-differentiation classes, but added only 1–5 percent in the low-differentiation classes.

7. Good's Passivity Model

Some students receive low expectations so consistently that they appear to internalize these expectations. Studies of expectations have increasingly emphasized how students internalize teachers' expectations, and models have been developed for exploring mediation effects (e.g., Cooper 1985). Good's (1981) passivity model suggested that certain forms of teacher treatment induce passivity in low-achieving students. Over time, differences in the ways teachers treat low achievers (e.g., in the third grade a student is praised or finds teacher acceptance for virtually any verbalization, but in the fourth grade the same student is seldom praised and is criticized frequently) may reduce the efforts of lows and contribute to a passive learning style. Other teacher behaviors may compound this problem. Low-achieving students who are called on frequently one year but infrequently the following year may find it confusing to adjust to different role definitions. Ironically, those students who have the least capacity to adapt may be asked to make the most adjustments as they move from classroom to classroom.

Greater variation among teachers in their interaction with low achievers may occur because teachers agree less about how to respond to students who do not learn readily. Teachers may treat lows inconsistently over the course of the school year as they try one approach after another in an attempt to find something that works.

When teachers provide fewer chances for lower achievers to participate in public discussion, wait less time for them to respond when they are called on (even though these students may need more time to think and form an answer), or criticize lows more per incorrect answer and praise them less per correct answer, the implications are similar. It seems that a good strategy for students who face such conditions would be not to volunteer or not to respond when called on. Students are discouraged from taking risks under such an instructional system (Good 1981). To the extent that students are motivated to reduce risk and ambiguity—and many argue that students are strongly motivated to do so (Doyle 1983)—students would likely become more passive in order to reduce the risk of critical teacher feedback.

Good et al. (1987) found that low achievers were just as likely to ask questions as other students in kindergarten classes, but that lows asked significantly fewer questions than their classmates in upper-elementary and secondary classes. Similarly, in a study involving grades two, four, and six, Newman and Goldin (1990) found that among sixth-graders, the lowest achievers had both the greatest perceived need for help and the greatest resistance to asking for help. Students' ambivalence about asking questions or getting help from teachers becomes especially acute during adolescence, when they are both more concerned about how they are perceived by peers and more sensitive to the costs as well as the benefits of seeking help.

8. Variation in Teachers' Expectations Over Time

Relatively little research has focused on students' classroom experiences over consecutive years, and no study examined students' reactions to differential teacher expectations over consecutive years prior to the work of Midgley et al. (1989). Midgley et al. conducted a longitudinal study in the United States of 1,329 elementary and junior high students, examining their self- and task-related beliefs in mathematics as a function of teachers' efficacy beliefs. They found that students who moved from high- to low-efficacy mathematics teachers during the transition from elementary to junior high school ended the junior high year with the lowest expectancies in perceived performance (even lower than students who had low-efficacy teachers both years) and the highest perceptions of task difficulty. Furthermore, the differences in pre- and posttransitional teachers' views of their efficacy had more of an effect on low-achieving than on high-achieving students' beliefs about mathematics.

9. Increasing Expectations

There is growing evidence that when (a) low achievers are allowed to enroll in more challenging courses or (b) course content is altered to include more challenging material that is traditionally not available to low-performing students, student performance improves. The decision to allow students to engage in more challenging academic work (e.g., move to a higher reading group) is potentially a powerful strategy for increasing teacher and student performance expectations.

Mason et al. (1992) described a study in which 34 average-achieving eighth-grade mathematics students in an urban junior high were assigned to prealgebra classes rather than placed in traditional general mathematics classes. Results showed that students placed in prealgebra classes benefited from advanced placement in comparison to average-achieving eighth-graders

689

from the previous year who took general mathematics (the cohort comparison group). Specifically, prealgebra students outperformed the comparison cohort group on a concepts subtest while maintaining equivalent performance on the problem-solving and computation subtests of the Comprehensive Assessment Program Achievement Series Test. Particularly important was that prealgebra students, in comparison with the cohort of general mathematics students, subsequently enrolled in more advanced mathematics classes during high school and obtained higher grades in these classes. Moreover, the presence of average achievers in prealgebra classes did not lower the performance of higher-achieving students in these classes.

Mason et al. qualified their findings. For example, the school in which the study took place was implementing a comprehensive school-improvement plan (higher expectations, active mathematics teaching). Hence, it was impossible to determine what instructional, curriculum, or peer effects were most influential in improving student performance. Further, the authors were aware of potential selection and history effects that can occur in a cross-sectional cohort design. Other investigators, however, have obtained similar results. Peterson (1989) found that remedial students who were placed in a prealgebra program for accelerated students achieved significantly higher results on all three mathematics subtests of the California Test of Basic Skills than did comparable students who were assigned to remedial and general mathematics classes. Such results strongly argue the need for educators to assess carefully the standards they use for assigning students to courses, since current standards may limit unnecessarily many students' access to mathematical knowledge, and potentially their access to future careers and advanced study.

Efforts to change low expectations for student performance can go beyond altering the practices of one teacher or a few teachers to include an entire school. For example, Weinstein et al. (1991) reported positive findings from a comprehensive intervention program designed to raise expectations for student achievement. This quasi-experimental field study involved collaboration between university researchers and teachers and administrators at an urban high school. The cooperating teachers attended university classes that focused on ways in which teachers can inadvertently maintain low expectations, and on the special motivational problems of low-achieving students. Teachers and researchers collaborated to develop a program for preventing and remediating low expectations.

The eight areas of the intervention program are: (a) task and curriculum (minimize tasks that heighten ability comparisons, give low achievers frequent opportunities to work on higher-order thinking and application of knowledge); (b) grouping (minimize ability grouping, make use of heterogeneous grouping and cooperative learning activities); (c) evaluation (emphasize qualitative evaluation, provide private feedback that stresses continuous progress achieved through a combination of ability and effort); (d) motivational climate (minimize competition, stress intrinsic rewards in addition to extrinsic rewards); (e) student role in learning (provide opportunities for students to make choices and to assume increasing responsibility for managing their own learning); (f) class relationships (develop a sense of community among the students that includes valuing diversity); (g) parent–teacher communication (emphasize students' positive attributes and progress rather than their deficiencies or problems); and (h) school-level supports (with cooperation from school administrators, establish increased and varied opportunities for low achievers to participate in school activities and get recognition for their achievements in and out of the classroom). The research procedures and organizational issues associated with this complex and innovative intervention cannot be presented here. However, both a rich description of the project (Weinstein et al. 1991) and an extensive analysis of the program (Weinstein 1991) are available.

The program has had some notable positive effects. For example, teachers were able to implement procedures designed to increase communication of positive expectations to low achievers. Project teachers' expectations for students, as well as their attitudes toward their colleagues, became more positive. Project teachers also expanded their roles and worked to change school tracking practices. Positive changes were also evident for the 158 project students. In contrast to 154 comparison students, project students had improved grades, fewer disciplinary referrals, and increased retention in school one year later. Weinstein et al. (1991) noted, however, that progress was not uniform. Students' absences rose and their improved academic performance was not maintained over the 9-month period of the study. According to the researchers, the limited length and breadth of the intervention and evaluation (students' performance was evaluated only in English and history), although sufficient to retain students, may have been insufficient to affect students' attendance and performance. Moreover, some teachers left the project because of excessive time requirements and lack of administrative support.

10. Directions for Research

Expectations research can be expanded in many ways to enhance understanding of classroom teaching and learning. Two of the most promising research areas are teachers' decisions about content assignments and teachers' knowledge of subject matter.

10.1 Selection of Curriculum Content

Many educators have contended that textbooks define the curriculum, although some research challenges this simplistic view and suggests that teachers act as decision-makers, modifying the curriculum in relation to factors such as teachers' beliefs about students' aptitude, their instructional intentions, and their subject-matter knowledge. If teachers influence the curriculum, then their decisions about curriculum partially determine performance expectations for students, just as teacher behaviors and activity structures do. Subsequent research could profitably attempt to integrate teachers' decisions about how much and what type of content to present with teachers' expectations for students (e.g., how students are likely to learn).

10.2 Teachers' Subject-matter Knowledge

Teachers' subject-matter knowledge is likely an important factor affecting the performance expectations they communicate to students. Because some teachers know more about some subjects or concepts than others, teachers' beliefs about subject matter and how to present it to students would probably affect whether or not they set appropriate performance expectations for students. Carlsen (1991) documented the effects of four novice biology teachers' subject-matter knowledge on discourse in their classrooms as they taught eight science lessons. The findings imply that choice of instructional activity affects students' participation in classroom discussion. Teachers used lectures and laboratory activities, which are characterized by high rates of student questioning, with topics about which they were knowledgeable. They tended to use classroom activities that involved few student questions when they were unfamiliar with the subject matter.

Carlsen's results are especially intriguing in that they illustrate that, because all teachers, and especially novice teachers, have inadequate knowledge in some areas, teachers must develop strategies for teaching content that they are still learning themselves. These strategies might include using sources additional to the textbook, bringing in guest teachers who are more knowledgeable, telling students that this is an area about which they are still learning, and presenting to students the questions that the teachers are using to structure the unit (and their own learning).

Research that examines teachers' performance expectations for individual students along with teachers' subject-matter knowledge would be profitable. When teachers instruct students in topics about which teachers have little knowledge, they may exaggerate differential treatment (i.e., avoid unpredictable questions by low achievers; overly depend on students believed to be more capable). Furthermore, the accountability systems and task structures that teachers select may be a function of their subject-matter knowledge.

10.3 Societal Expectations and Co-regulation

Historically, the research focus on teacher expectations has primarily explored how teachers communicate low expectations to students. Recent theory has argued that teachers and students reciprocally create expectations through a process of co-regulation (McCaslin 1996). McCaslin and Good (1996) note that under certain conditions teachers can help students to develop positive and realistic performance expectations and strategies for acomplishing those goals.

However, societies (especially parents and the media) construct images of what students are like—their competence and their motivation—and communicate these expectations to students. Indeed, beliefs about students (e.g., their academic performance in comparison to students in other cultures) are linked to beliefs about the economy and even national security. There is fairly consistent evidence that the popular culture does not seem to trust students to do what is "best" for the culture (McCaslin and Good 1996). More research is needed to explore how teachers can help students to integrate societal, school, and personal expectations in realistic and positive ways.

For a comprehensive summary of other emerging directions in teacher expectation effects, see Good and Thompson (in press).

11. Conclusion

Research on teacher expectancies in the classroom was a rich and exciting area in the 1970s and 1980s and many useful constructs have been derived from this work. Although the importance of teacher expectation effects have sometimes been overstated, it is clear that they are important, especially when considered with other teaching abilities and other general variables (e.g., home–school correspondence). In the 1980s there has been growing interest in the active role that students play in interpreting, internalizing, or rejecting expectations that are conveyed through teacher behavior or classroom structures. In the 1990s and beyond researchers need to study teacher expectancies and student mediation simultaneously. Such work will be enriched if researchers are also willing to explore how curriculum content and teachers' and students' knowledge of content mediate both the communication and interpretation of performance expectations.

See also: Social Psychological Theories in Education; Social Psychological Theories of Teaching

References

Baron R, Tom D, Cooper H 1985 Social class, race and teacher expectations. In: Dusek J (ed.) 1985 *Teacher Expectancies*. Erlbaum, Hillsdale, New Jersey

Brattesani K, Weinstein R, Marshall H 1984 Student perceptions of differential teacher treatment as moderators of teacher expectation effects. *J. Educ. Psychol.* 76(2): 236–47

Brophy J 1983 Research on the self-fulfilling prophecy and teacher expectations. *J. Educ. Psychol.* 75: 631–61

Brophy J, Good T 1970 The Brophy–Good System (dyadic teacher–child interaction). In: Simon A, Boyer E (eds.) 1970 *Mirrors for Behavior: An Anthology of Observation*

Instruments Continued, 1970 Supplement, Vols. A and B. Research for Better Schools, Inc., Philadelphia, Pennsylvania

Carlsen W 1991 Subject-matter knowledge and science teaching: A pragmatic perspective. In: Brophy J (ed.) 1991 *Advances in Research on Teaching*, Vol. 2. JAI Press, Greenwich, Connecticut

Cooper H 1985 Models of teacher expectation communication. In: Dusek J (ed.) 1985 *Teacher Expectancies*. Erlbaum, Hillsdale, New Jersey

Cooper H, Good T 1983 *Pygmalion Grows Up: Studies in the Expectation Communication Process*. Longman, New York

Doyle W 1983 Academic work. *Rev. Educ. Res.* 53(2): 159–200

Good T 1981 Teacher expectations and student perceptions: A decade of research. *Educ. Leadership* 38(5): 415–23

Good T, Brophy J 1977 *Educational Psychology: A Realistic Approach*. Holt, New York

Good T, Brophy J 1990 *Looking in Classrooms*, 5th edn. Harper and Collins, New York

Good T, Slavings R, Harel K, Emerson H 1987 Student passivity: A study of student question-asking in K-12 classrooms. *Sociol. Educ.* 60(4): 181–99

Good T, Thompson E (in press). New directions in classroom expectation studies. In: Brophy J (ed.) (in press), *Teacher Expectations in the Classroom. Advances in Teaching* Vol. 6. JAI Press, Greenwich, Connecticut

Jones E 1990 *Interpersonal Perception*. Freeman, New York

Jussim L 1989 Teacher expectations: Self-fulfilling prophecies, perceptual biases, and accuracy. *J. Pers. Soc. Psychol.* 57(3): 469–80

Jussim L 1990a Expectancies and social issues: Introduction. *J. Soc. Issues* 46(2): 1–8

Jussim L 1990b Social reality and social problems: The role of expectancies. *J. Soc. Issues* 46(2): 9–34

Mason D, Schroeter D, Combs R, Washington K 1992 Assigning average-achieving eighth graders to advance mathematics classes in an urban junior high. *Elem. Sch. J.* 92(5): 587–99

McCaslin M 1996 The problem of problem representation: The Summit's conception of student. *Educ. Res.* 25(8), 13–15

McCaslin M, Good T 1996 *Listening in Classrooms*. Longman, Whiteplains, New York

Midgley C, Feldlaufer H, Eccles J 1989 Change in teacher efficacy and students' self- and task-related beliefs in mathematics during the transition to junior high school. *J. Educ. Psychol.* 81(2): 247–58

Newman R, Goldin L 1990 Children's reluctance to seek help with school work. *J. Educ. Psychol.* 82: 92–100

Oyserman D, Markus H 1990 Possible selves in balance: Implications for delinquency. *J. Soc. Issues* 46(2) 141–58

Peterson J 1989 Remediation is no remedy. *Educ. Leadership* 46(6): 24–25

Rosenthal R, Jacobson L 1968 *Pygmalion in the Classroom: Teacher Expectation and Pupil's Intellectual Development*. Holt, Rinehart, and Winston, New York

Rosenthal R, Rubin D 1978 Interpersonal expectancy effects: The first 345 studies. *The Behavioral and Brain Sciences* 1(3): 377–86

Vygotsky L 1978 *Mind in Society: The Development of Higher Psychological Processes*. Harvard University Press, Cambridge, Massachusetts

Weinstein R 1991 Caught between paradigms: Obstacle or opportunity—a comment on the commentaries. *American J. Community Psychol.* 19(3): 395–404

Weinstein R, Marshall H, Sharp L, Botkin M 1987 Pygmalion and the student: Age and classroom differences in children's awareness of teacher expectations. *Child Dev.* 58(4): 1079–93

Weinstein R et al. 1991 Expectations and high school change: Teacher–researcher collaboration to prevent school failure. *Am. J. Community Psychol.* 19(3): 333–64

Teachers' Knowledge

P. L. Grossman

While researchers have long been interested in issues related to teachers' knowledge, research in this area proliferated in the decade from 1983 through 1992. As research on teaching moved from investigations of teacher behavior to considerations of the thinking and decision-making that accompany action, questions concerning the knowledge and beliefs that inform teachers' decision-making quickly arose. Issues related to what teachers know, how they acquire and store that knowledge, and how knowledge informs classroom practice are central to the work of all concerned with the initial preparation and continuing professional development of teachers.

The renewed interest in teachers' knowledge also parallels the movement within several countries to transform teaching into a recognized profession. Evidence of a specialized knowledge base necessary for the work of professionals is one hallmark of a profession. The interest in teacher knowledge since the early 1980s is motivated by practical, political, and academic concerns. Teachers' knowledge has been examined in terms of its domains, its forms or structures, and its relation to classroom practice. This article will address these areas separately, although many of the issues are interrelated.

1. Domains of Teacher Knowledge

A number of researchers have proposed frameworks for domains of teacher knowledge (Carter 1990, Leinhardt and Smith 1985, Wilson et al. 1987). Although represented as discrete domains in these frameworks, the knowledge domains are usually regarded as interwoven in practice. One possible typology of teacher knowledge includes six domains: (a) knowledge of content, (b) knowledge of learners and learning, (c) knowledge of general pedagogy, (d) knowledge of curriculum, (e) knowledge of context, and (f) knowledge of self.

Content knowledge includes both subject matter knowledge and more explicitly pedagogical knowledge of the subject matter, termed "pedagogical content knowledge." Knowledge of learners and learning includes knowledge of learning theories; the physical, social, psychological, and cognitive development of students; motivational theory and practice; and ethnic, socioeconomic, and gender diversity among students. Knowledge of general pedagogy includes knowledge of classroom organization and management, and general methods of teaching. Curricular knowledge includes knowledge both of the processes of curriculum development and of the school curriculum within and across grade levels.

Knowledge of context includes knowledge of the multiple and embedded situations and settings within which teachers work, including the school, district, or area, and state or region. Knowledge of context also includes teachers' knowledge of their students and their families, as well as the local community. It can also include knowledge of the historical, philosophical, and cultural foundations of education within a particular country. Finally, knowledge of self includes teachers' knowledge of their personal values, dispositions, strengths, and weaknesses, and their educational philosophy, goals for students, and purposes for teaching.

While all of these domains are important to the work of teachers, research has concentrated on content knowledge, general pedagogical knowledge, and knowledge of self. For example, while much research within educational psychology has focused on topics related to learners and learning, relatively few studies have looked directly at what teachers know or believe in this area. For this reason, this article will include discussions of the three domains in which the most research exists.

1.1 Knowledge of Content

While subject matter knowledge seems intuitively important for good teaching, early correlational research did not find a relationship between teachers' knowledge and student achievement. Later researchers critiqued the lack of conceptual frameworks to guide this early work and turned their attention to the relationships between teachers' subject matter knowledge and the processes of planning and instruction (Leinhardt and Smith 1985, Shulman 1987). This line of predominantly qualitative research suggests that teachers' knowledge of the content they teach affects both what teachers teach and how they teach it.

In developing curriculum for students, teachers are likely to emphasize those areas in which they are more

knowledgeable and to avoid or de-emphasize the areas in which they have relatively less content knowledge (Carlsen 1991, Smith and Neale 1991). Teachers' content knowledge may also influence how they exploit the curriculum potential of a subject (Ben-Peretz 1975, Gudmundsdottir 1990, Wilson and Wineburg 1988). For example, studies of secondary-school social studies teachers have demonstrated how teachers' own disciplinary backgrounds affect how they adapt a given curriculum to match their own disciplinary knowledge (Wilson and Wineburg 1988).

Teachers' content knowledge also influences their interactive teaching. Teachers' knowledge of subject matter affects how they represent the nature of knowing within a content area to their students. Ball (1991), for example, demonstrated that teachers with relatively weak conceptual understanding of mathematics are likely to represent the nature of mathematical knowing as arbitrary and rule bound. Teachers' content knowledge also influences their ability to construct new explanations or activities for students (Leinhardt and Smith 1985, Smith and Neale 1991), as well as the kinds of questions they ask students (Carlsen 1991, Hashweh 1987). For example, in a study of beginning science teachers, Carlsen (1991) found that teachers were more likely to ask cognitively lower level questions in areas in which they were less knowledgeable and higher level questions in those areas where they felt themselves to be knowledgeable.

Studies of teachers' subject matter knowledge also revealed that teachers possess pedagogical knowledge of the content they teach, termed "pedagogical content knowledge" (Shulman 1987). Research on pedagogical content knowledge has examined teachers' beliefs and conceptions regarding purposes for teaching subject matter, their knowledge of students' understandings and misunderstandings of particular topics within a subject matter, and their curricular and instructional knowledge related to specific content. Research in this area suggests that teachers' pedagogical content knowledge is related to teachers' planning and to classroom instruction. Most researchers found a great deal of congruence between teachers' own conceptions of the purposes for teaching a subject and their instructional practice, especially in the case of experienced teachers. Work in mathematics also suggests a tentative link between teachers' pedagogical content knowledge and student learning (Peterson et al. 1991).

1.2 Knowledge of General Pedagogy

Knowledge of general pedagogy includes knowledge about classroom organization and management, general knowledge of lesson structure, and general methods of teaching. Researchers in the area of classroom knowledge have focused on teachers' efforts to establish and maintain order in the classroom during the process of instruction. Successful classroom managers are teachers who are more attuned to student signals and conscious of the overall flow and purpose of classroom activity (Carter 1990). In addition, effective teachers swiftly establish routines for classroom activities at the beginning of the school year (Leinhardt et al. 1987).

Related to work on teachers' routines is teachers' general knowledge of lesson structure, which includes the knowledge necessary to plan and teach lessons, to make smooth transitions between different components of a lesson, and to present clear explanations of content (Leinhardt and Smith 1985). While this kind of knowledge has been designated as general, it is possible that knowledge of lesson structure is implicitly tied to the content to be taught.

Finally, work on expertise in teaching suggests that experienced teachers process information about classrooms differently than do novices (Berliner 1986). For example, when shown slides of classroom activities, the experienced teachers were more likely to identify patterns and to make inferences about the activities they observed than were novices, who provided more literal and superficial descriptions of the activities.

Much of this work has focused more on what teachers do in classrooms and how they process information than what they know explicitly or implicitly about classroom organization and management. Some researchers have explored the relationship between classroom management and teachers' implicit metaphors regarding the role of the teacher. These researchers argue that changes in teachers' classroom management must begin with reconsiderations of these underlying metaphors.

Relatively little work has investigated teachers' knowledge of various instructional strategies or methods of teaching. One line of correlational research on teaching has attempted to isolate general teaching strategies used by effective teachers (Brophy and Good 1986). While this research has produced a set of generalizations about the correlations between particular teaching behaviors and student achievement, it did not investigate what teachers knew or believed that led them to adopt such strategies. Studies of teacher planning suggest that teachers organize their planning around the development of classroom activities (Clark and Peterson 1986), but little research has investigated how teachers think specifically about issues of method in teaching.

Some researchers have argued that teachers' knowledge of teaching methods is organized into curriculum scripts for particular topics (Putnam 1987); both the content and method of teaching are included in these scripts. The European tradition of *Didaktik* also emphasizes the integration of curriculum and method in teacher thinking (Hopmann 1992). Knowledge of teaching method may be filtered through teachers' understanding of the particular content to be taught and their own goals for teaching that content, suggesting an overlap between pedagogical content knowledge and this aspect of general pedagogical knowledge.

1.3 Knowledge of Self

In an early study of teacher knowledge, Elbaz (1983) identified knowledge of self as an important facet of teachers' practical knowledge. This knowledge of self includes teachers' awareness of their own values, goals, philosophies, styles, personal characteristics, strengths, and weaknesses as they relate to teaching. Some researchers have described how teachers draw upon and use this personal knowledge to negotiate classroom dilemmas and to reflect upon their practice (Lampert 1985). Others have documented how issues of self and identity are implicated in the process of learning to teach (Britzman 1986) and how teachers' personal values underlie other forms of knowledge such as pedagogical content knowledge (Gudmundsdottir 1990). Work on teachers' metaphors also stresses the importance of teachers' implicit beliefs in understanding how teachers view their own practice (Munby 1986).

Knowledge of self differs in important ways from the knowledge domains discussed above as it represents neither theoretical nor abstract knowledge, but a more personal and inevitably idiosyncratic domain. Work on many domains of teacher knowledge suggests that abstract or theoretical knowledge about teaching is filtered through teachers' own values, goals, and personal philosophies, leading some researchers to argue that all aspects of teacher knowledge are grounded in personal perspectives and experience (Clandinin and Connelly 1987). This line of research suggests the importance of individual biography in the process of teaching and learning to teach.

1.4 Integration of Knowledge Domains and the Creation of New Knowledge

While each knowledge domain has been addressed separately for analytic purposes, in actual use by teachers, these domains are not as clearly distinguishable. For example, lesson structure knowledge, categorized under general pedagogical knowledge, intersects with pedagogical content knowledge in determining particular content to be taught. Curricular knowledge, pedagogical content knowledge, and general pedagogical knowledge all play a role in creating curriculum scripts for particular topics. The need for teachers to draw from and integrate a number of knowledge domains under conditions of uncertainty has important implications for teacher learning. Teaching these knowledge domains in isolation from one another may misrepresent the interconnected quality of knowledge use, posing difficulties for teachers who must integrate these various domains in practice.

Work on teacher knowledge also reveals its dynamic nature. Teachers' knowledge is not static. In the process of teaching and reflecting upon teaching, teachers develop new understandings of the content, of learners, and of themselves. While teachers can acquire knowledge from a wide variety of sources, they also create new knowledge within the crucible of the classroom. Because teaching has lacked a method for capturing and recording such knowledge, both researchers and practitioners have turned their attention to documenting the wisdom of practice of experienced teachers.

2. Forms of Teacher Knowledge and Relation to Classroom Practice

Researchers have argued about the various forms of teachers' knowledge; some researchers argue for the need for generalizable knowledge of principles of teaching and learning, while others contend that teachers' knowledge is inherently situational and personal, stored in the tacit forms of metaphors or images or the more explicit forms of stories or cases. In describing different potential forms for teachers' knowledge, this section uses Bruner's (1986) distinction between paradigmatic and narrative ways of knowing to describe at least two general forms of teacher knowledge.

Paradigmatic ways of knowing emphasize generalizable laws and principles applicable across a wide variety of contexts. Knowledge within the natural sciences has been described as paradigmatic knowledge. In contrast, narrative ways of knowing are more contextualized and situation-specific. Research on teaching has experienced a shift from the search for paradigmatic knowledge to an interest in narrative knowledge, a shift that has affected research on teacher knowledge.

2.1 Paradigmatic Forms of Knowledge

Some researchers on teaching have argued that teachers need to possess scientific principles regarding teaching, knowledge that has proved to be applicable across different contexts and settings (Gage 1978). These researchers stress the power of propositional knowledge about teaching and learning. Such principles might consist of propositions regarding the importance of "wait-time" for encouraging higher-order thinking, for example. These principles could be derived from large-scale research programs on effective teaching (e.g., Brophy and Good 1986) and taught directly to teachers.

Some researchers in this area have argued that research knowledge can directly affect practice by providing teachers with new principles or rules of practice to use in their own teaching. A number of experimental studies have attempted to teach experienced teachers such generalizable principles derived from correlational classroom research. While many of the studies were successful in the short run, there is little evidence that teachers continued to implement these principles of teaching over time.

Alternative ways in which paradigmatic knowledge can inform practice have also been suggested. Some researchers have argued that results of research on teaching can inform teachers' reasoning about classroom actions rather than dictate teachers' instructional practice (Fenstermacher 1986). Knowledge gained from research can influence classroom practice by influencing teachers' beliefs or by introducing new knowledge and beliefs into teachers' reasoning. Theoretical knowledge thus becomes one, but not the sole, source of knowledge that can guide teachers' curricular and instructional decision-making. A number of studies of knowledge use suggest that teachers sift generalizable principles through the filter of their own perspectives and situations; thus, this approach to using research knowledge may show promise for understanding the relationship between propositional knowledge and classroom practice.

2.2 Narrative Forms of Knowledge

Another line of work rejects the idea of generalizable knowledge and argues that teachers' knowledge is inherently personal and organized in terms of stories or narratives (Clandinin and Connelly 1987, Elbaz 1991). These researchers believe that teachers' knowledge can be best understood through their own stories of teaching, which preserve both the teachers' voice and perspective. Researchers in the area of personal practical knowledge argue that much of teachers' knowledge is inherently tacit, contained within the rituals, routines, and cycles that comprise teachers' work, and embedded within particular local contexts.

From this perspective, knowledge is embodied within classroom practice; distinctions between knowledge and classroom practice are not clear-cut. Others acknowledge a distinction between knowledge and practice, but argue that practice informs knowledge as much as knowledge influences practice. Studies of personal practical knowledge are not intended to inform as much as to illuminate classroom practice from teachers' perspectives. While narratives of personal practical knowledge offer a way of making sense of individual teachers' practice, readers can learn from these narratives through reflecting upon similar issues that arise in their own practice.

Another form of narrative knowledge might take the form of case knowledge, knowledge composed of experiences with a number of cases of particular pedagogical situations (Shulman 1991). Like personal practical knowledge, case knowledge is inherently situational and contextual. Researchers who study knowledge acquisition in ill-structured domains such as medicine or teaching believe that knowledge in these areas is organized into networks of concepts and cases. More general concepts are embedded within specific instances from actual practice. Practitioners within these ill-structured domains must integrate multiple knowledge domains in constantly shifting circumstances. From their experiences in classrooms, teachers construct a contextual understanding of classroom situations that allows them to recognize familiar features of new situations. The process of reasoning from case knowledge, then, is likely to be analogical.

Like personal practical knowledge, case knowledge has usually been represented in narrative form. However, most of these case narratives have explicitly pedagogical purposes. Advocates of case-based methods in teacher education stress the usefulness of cases in learning to teach. Cases can inform practice by offering precedents for handling particular pedagogical situations. The use of case methods can also develop pedagogical ways of reasoning, according to advocates. Most researchers in this area stress the importance of using multiple cases of a similar phenomenon to illustrate more accurately the complexity of practice.

3. The Future of Research on Teacher Knowledge

Research on teacher knowledge has clear implications for teacher education and continuing professional development. What teachers need to know and how they can best construct this knowledge are central questions facing policymakers and teacher educators alike. Considerations of the content, form, and sources of teacher knowledge are likely to become increasingly important as efforts to reform teacher education and to create a teaching profession gain momentum.

Future research will need to investigate further all of the domains of teacher knowledge, including the areas of curricular knowledge, knowledge of learners and learning, and knowledge of educational contexts. While work has been done in each of these areas, questions regarding issues such as what teachers know about motivating students, for example, remain unanswered. Documenting teachers' existing knowledge in all of the domains is essential, as teachers' prior knowledge and belief are likely to influence their future acquisition of knowledge.

Future research will also need to study the connections among teacher knowledge, school context, and student learning. Much of the research on teachers' subject matter knowledge, for example, has investigated the relationship between teachers' knowledge of the content and the processes of planning and instruction, but, with a few exceptions, has stopped short of looking for connections to student learning. As research provides increasingly sophisticated approaches to the assessment of student learning, the connection between teachers' and students' understandings may be studied more effectively.

Finally, research on teacher knowledge must continue to be informed by ongoing explorations into the nature of knowledge and cognition. Work in cognitive psychology and anthropology has demonstrated the contextual nature of cognition, a finding that has direct implications for investigations of teacher knowledge.

Work on knowledge acquisition in ill-structured domains also holds implications for research on teacher knowledge. Theorists from both critical and feminist theory pose epistemological issues with which future research must grapple. Finally, work on the narrative aspects of cognition is likely to continue to inform research on teacher knowledge.

See also: Student Influences on Teaching; Teachers' Roles; Teaching, Social Status; Technology and the Classroom Teacher

References

Ball D L 1991 Research on teaching mathematics: Making subject matter knowledge part of the equation. In: Brophy J. (ed.) 1991
Ben-Peretz M 1975 The concept of curriculum potential. *Curric. Theo.* 5: 151–59
Berliner D C 1986 In pursuit of the expert pedagogue. *Educ. Researcher* 15(7): 5–13
Britzman D P 1986 Cultural myths in the making of a teacher: Biography and social structure in teacher education. *Harv. Educ. Rev.* 56(4): 442–56
Brophy J E, Good T L 1986 Teacher behavior and student achievement. In: Wittrock M (ed.) 1986 *Handbook of Research on Teaching*, 3rd edn. Macmillan, New York
Bruner J 1986 *Actual Minds, Possible Worlds.* Harvard University Press, Cambridge, Massachusetts
Carlsen W S 1991 Subject matter knowledge and science teaching: A pragmatic perspective. In: Brophy J (ed.) 1991
Carter K 1990 Teachers' knowledge and learning to teach. In: Houston W R (ed.) 1990 *Handbook of Research on Teacher Education.* Macmillan, New York
Clandinin D J, Connelly M F 1987 Teachers' personal knowledge: What counts as personal in studies of the personal. *J. Curric. St.* 19(6): 487–500
Clark C M, Peterson P L 1986 Teachers' thought processes. In: Wittrock M (ed.) 1986 *Handbook of Research on Teaching*, 3rd edn. Macmillan, New York
Elbaz F 1983 *Teacher Thinking: A Study of Practical Knowledge.* Croom Helm, London
Elbaz F 1991 Research on teachers' knowledge: The evolution of a discourse. *J. Curric. St.* 23(1): 1–19
Fenstermacher G D 1986 Philosophy of research on teaching: Three aspects. In: Wittrock M (ed.) 1986 *Handbook of Research on Teaching,* 3rd edn. Macmillan, New York
Gage N L 1978 *The Scientific Basis of the Art of Teaching.* Teachers College Press, New York
Gudmundsdottir S 1990 Values in pedagogical content knowledge. *J. Teach. Educ.* 41(3): 44–52
Hashweh M Z 1987 Effects of subject matter knowledge in the teaching of biology and physics. *Teach. Teach. Educ.* 3(2): 109–20
Hopmann S 1992 Starting a dialogue: Roots and issues of the beginning conversation between European didaktik and the American curriculum tradition. Paper presented at the annual meeting of the American Educational Research Association, San Francisco, California
Lampert M 1985 How do teachers manage to teach? Perspectives on problems in practice. *Harv. Educ. Rev.* 55(2): 178–94

Leinhardt G, Smith D A 1985 Expertise in mathematics instruction: Subject matter knowledge. *J. Educ. Psychol.* 77(3): 247–71

Leinhardt G, Weidman C, Hammond K M 1987 Introduction and integration of classroom routines by expert teachers. *Curric. Inq.* 17(2): 135–76

Munby H 1986 Metaphor in the thinking of teachers: An exploratory study. *J. Curric. St.* 18(2): 197–209

Peterson P L, Fennema E, Carpenter T P 1991 Teachers' knowledge of students' mathematics problem-solving knowledge. In: Brophy J (ed.) 1991

Putnam R T 1987 Structuring and adjusting content for students: A study of live and simulated tutoring of addition. *Am. Educ. Res. J.* 24(1): 13–48

Shulman L S 1987 Knowledge and teaching: Foundations of the new reform. *Harv. Educ. Rev.* 57(1): 1–22

Shulman L S 1991 Toward a pedagogy of cases. In: Shulman J (ed.) 1991 *Case Methods in Teacher Education*. Teachers College Press, New York

Smith D C, Neale D C 1991 The construction of subject-matter knowledge in primary science teaching. In: Brophy J. (ed.) 1991

Wilson S M, Shulman L S, Richert A E 1987 150 differ-ent ways of knowing: Representations of knowledge in teaching. In: Calderhead J (ed.) 1987 *Exploring Teachers' Thinking*. Cassell Education, London

Wilson S M, Wineburg S S 1988 Peering at history through different lenses: The role of disciplinary perspectives in teaching history. *Teach. Coll. Rec.* 89(4): 525–39

Further Reading

Britzman D P 1991 *Practice Makes Practice: A Critical Study of Learning to Teach*. SUNY Press, Albany, New York

Brophy J (ed.) 1991 *Advances in Research on Teaching, Volume 2: Teachers' Knowledge of Subject Matter as it Relates to their Teaching Practice*. JAI Press, Greenwich, Connecticut

Calderhead J (ed.) 1991 *Teachers' Professional Learning*. Falmer Press, London

Grossman P L 1990 *The Making of a Teacher: Teacher Knowledge and Teacher Education*. Teachers College Press, New York

Shulman J (ed.) 1991 *Case Methods in Teacher Education*. Teachers College Press, New York

Teachers' Roles

B. J. Biddle

The phrase "teacher role" appears in hundreds of studies. In addition, chapters on teacher role may be found in both theoretical and hortative works concerned with teaching, its contexts, and its effects. Unfortunately, use of this phrase is also vague, and several different concepts have been intended by authors who have written about teacher roles. Many who have used this phrase have seemed unaware that it has other uses than the one they intended; thus, the first task facing those reading about it is to distinguish among the major concepts to which the phrase has been applied. Three such concepts are distinguished in this article. In addition, the use of the phrase "teacher role" declined during the 1980s, and alternative vocabularies have since been employed for teacher-role issues. As a consequence, this review stresses broad concerns rather than specific literature from the 1980s and 1990s that might also be interpreted as concerned with the roles of teachers.

1. Concepts of Teacher Role

Technical use of the social role concept appeared in the 1920s and reflected the influence of at least three seminal contributors: Ralph Linton, Jacob Moreno, and George Herbert Mead. These three men represented different disciplines in the social sciences and used the role concept somewhat differently. For simplicity, three separate concepts are distinguished here that may be designated by the phrase "teacher role" (see Biddle 1979).

1.1 Role as Behavior

Some authors use "teacher role" to refer to behaviors that are characteristic of teachers. Most who use "role" in this sense focus their interests on teacher behaviors in the work context (i.e., in the school or classroom). Nevertheless, teachers may also be found in nonwork contexts, and a few authors have discussed the role behaviors of teachers in their homes, the marketplace, or the political arena. Authors using "role" in this first sense presume that teacher behaviors are existential events that can be observed directly. Moreover, teacher roles may also be observed by other actors, hence are assumed to have the potential for affecting, and being affected by, the behaviors of pupils and other persons who interact with teachers.

1.2 Role as Social Position

Other authors use the phrase "teacher role" to refer to the identity or social position that is shared by teachers. In this usage the word "role" refers to the designating term ("teacher") and the set of persons who are designated by that occupational title. This second usage focuses on static characteristics of teachers —on the recognition of teachers as a separate social position, the composition of the teacher population, the status of the teaching profession, or conditions for entry into or departure from the field. Authors who intend this second meaning often speak of teachers as "occupying" their roles.

1.3 Role as Expectation

A third group of authors use the phrase "teacher role" to refer to expectations that are held for teachers. Some of these expectations are held by teachers themselves, whereas others are held by parents, school administrators, pupils, politicians, and members of the public. Some expectations are normative in mode, but others may represent beliefs, preferences, or other modes of thought. Some may be widely shared, while others may reflect divergent opinions and generate role conflicts for the teacher. Authors who follow this third usage tend to view teachers (and those with whom they interact) as persons capable of rational, reflective thought. Expectations are thought to be learned through experience and, once they are formed, will affect the behaviors of those who hold them in predictable ways.

None of these three concepts for teacher role precludes the others. Each represents a facet of the complexities that embed the teacher, and each is capable of generating information for educators and other social scientists. Each has also generated research literature. Nevertheless, the fact that such different concepts have all been designated by the same phrase poses problems for investigators and consumers alike. One must read each source carefully to establish the concept a given author intended by the phrase "teacher role," and one must be prepared to discount confusion that has been generated because some authors forgot their conceptual definition or misunderstood those of others.

2. The Behavioral Role of the Teacher

The behavioral role of the teacher may be defined as those behaviors that are characteristically performed by teachers. Like persons in other occupations and professions, teachers respond in characteristic ways. Most are regularly found in classrooms during the working day, and most spend much of that day supervising the instruction of pupils. When not in classrooms, teachers are likely to be found in the hallways or offices of the school building, or in the lunchroom or teachers' lounge. During the evening, teachers are likely to be grading papers, preparing lessons, or attending school-related functions. This does not mean that all teachers behave identically, but to learn that a person teaches for a living means that he or she is more likely to do certain things and less likely to do others, and it is the former that constitute the teacher's behavioral role.

Teachers characteristically do a great many things, so studies of the role of the teacher are normally limited in some fashion. Sometimes that limitation is contextual. For example, an investigator may examine the teacher's role in the classroom, the school, or in some other context in which membership of the teacher's social position is recognized and relevant. Sometimes, also, a sectoral limitation may be placed on the definition, in which case the investigator examines that portion of the teacher's role directed toward members of another social position, such as pupils. (Other sectors of the role are directed toward the school's principal, other teachers, or members of the public.) In contrast, if authors choose to discuss the teacher's role in noneducational contexts, usually that discussion focuses on behaviors that are presumed to be unique to teachers, that is, are not exhibited by other comparable actors.

Sometimes, also, functional limitations may be placed on the definition of the teacher's behavioral role. Like other professionals, teachers may accomplish a variety of things, and authors may single out one or more of those things for discussion. For example, many teachers are called upon to disseminate information to pupils, to serve as pupil counselors, and to grade pupils' performances on a regular basis. Each of these tasks requires somewhat different activities on the part of teachers, and simultaneous performance of these different activity sets may be difficult for the teacher to manage. The difficulty with functional analysis of the teacher's role is that no definitive set of functions is prescribed for most teachers, and behaviors characteristic of teachers may contribute to more than one identifiable function. As a result, many different lists of functions have been suggested for the teacher's role, and behavioral evidence concerning these functional distinctions is hard to find.

The issue of evidence raises another question concerning the behavioral role of the teacher. What is the best way to study such roles? Since behaviors are observable events, then surely the best way of studying them is to observe them directly. Until about 1960, it was difficult to find studies of behavioral roles that were based on observation, but this has since changed (see Dunkin and Biddle 1974 and many subsequent reviews). Literally thousands of studies have appeared in which the classroom behaviors of teachers and pupils were observed, and these provide a wealth of data concerning the role of participants in that context.

It is more difficult to observe teacher behaviors elsewhere in the school, however, and more difficult still to study teacher activities in nonschool contexts. As a result, studies still appear in which the teacher's behavioral role is examined by asking teachers or others to discuss those activities in interviews and questionnaire responses. Technically, the latter forms of data are measures of what respondents think about the teacher's role and are more validly interpreted as measures of their expectations for teachers. To interpret them as measures of teacher role behavior assumes a simple relationship between role expectations and role behaviors, an assumption that is questioned below. Nevertheless, indirect evidence is better than no evidence, and much of what researchers presume to know about the teacher's behavioral role in the 1990s is based on it.

3. The Social Position of the Teacher

A social position relates to a set of persons who share some characteristic and who are given a recognized label within the society. Teachers are those persons who regularly instruct pupils, thus the social position of the teacher may be defined as membership of the set of persons who regularly instruct pupils and are given such designations as "teacher," "instructor," "master," and the like. Occasionally the concept of teacher is also extended to include persons who teach students in postsecondary education. However, the teaching of adults involves activities quite different from those involved in the teaching of nonadult pupils, and those who teach adults are normally recruited and trained for their occupations in quite different ways than are teachers. Consequently, most persons who write about the social position of the teacher confine their attention to those who teach at the primary and secondary levels.

Several confusions surround the social position concept. As mentioned, some authors use the term "role" to refer to social position, so one may find articles in which "teacher role" is used to designate those who teach rather than the activities of teaching or expectations for the latter. Other authors use the term "status" to refer to social position, which is also confusing because the word "status" has another meaning concerned with the ranking of social positions vis-à-vis one another. (The status-ranking of teachers is discussed below.) Finally, some authors define the social position concept as a "location" or "niche" in a division of labor. Such definitions are confusing because they presume that all social positions are occupations. Whereas "teacher" is a recognized occupation in industrialized societies, teachers are not always paid for their services elsewhere but may still be recognized, even honored, for their activities.

3.1 The Status of Teachers

A number of characteristics of social positions have been studied over the years. One of these is status, which concerns the ranking of social positions in terms of characteristics deemed desirable. As a rule, three criteria for status ranking have dominated the literature: prestige, wealth, and authority. Members of social positions have prestige when they are able to attract deferential behavior from others who are not members of their social position. They have wealth when they are given or are allowed to control commodities. They have authority when they can get others to follow their dictates.

It is widely assumed that prestige, wealth, and authority go together and that social positions which have one of these qualities in abundance will also have the others. Although this is true on average, there are some social positions that are high on one or two of these criteria but not the others (e.g., church dignitaries, Mafiosi). Studies of the status of social positions may either focus on status as a presumed unitary concept or may involve separate investigations of prestige, wealth, and authority.

3.2 The Prestige of Teachers

Relatively few studies of the prestige of teachers have yet appeared, but these tend to place teachers toward the lower end of middle-class occupations and at the bottom of those occupations deemed to be professions. Moreover, this status ranking tends to hold throughout industrialized countries. A number of reasons have been suggested for the relatively low prestige of teachers: prevalence of women in the teaching profession, lack of specificity in the role expected of teachers, the fact that teachers work primarily with the young, devaluation of the knowledge deemed necessary to teach well, the large numbers of persons employed or available for employment as teachers, and so forth.

Lortie (1975) views teachers as having a "special but shadowed" prestige position. On the one hand, teachers' work is seen as having the aura of a "special mission," but on the other, teachers have largely lost whatever autonomy they once had to manage pedagogical theory and their classrooms because they have become functionaries in hierarchical organizations. Whatever may be the reason, teachers clearly do not attract as much deference as do the other, more secure professions: medicine, the law, the ministry. At the same time, however, teachers receive more deference than do most blue-collar occupations.

3.3 The Wealth of Teachers

Like all occupations, teachers are paid for their services. Most teachers in the West are the employees of organizations that receive public funds, so their salaries are a matter of public record. Not surprisingly then, many studies of the wealth of teachers have appeared and continue to appear on a regular basis. These studies suggest that teachers tend to be paid at about the scale appropriate to their prestige position—above the scale paid to blue-collar workers but below the scale paid to most professionnals. In fact, the wages paid to many teachers are probably sufficient to support a single person but insufficient to support a family. Since many married women do not work, this fact presumably explains why many male teachers find it necessary to work at a second job to supplement their teaching incomes.

The economic systems of most Western countries are capitalistic, and the relative wages paid to teachers tend to rise during periods of teacher shortage. Thus, probably the major reason why teachers are not paid better wages is that they have never formed cartels to prevent entry of "unqualified" persons into the profession—as is done widely in medicine. Teachers have begun to unionize, however, and teacher wages have sometimes been improved through collective bargaining and industrial action.

3.4 The Authority of Teachers

Studies of the authority of teachers are quite rare, but as a rule that authority is confined to pupils, the school, and curricular matters. Like the hospital, prison, or university, the school is a people-processing organization, and most school systems feature a bureaucratic hierarchy in which the teachers are the "workers." Given this lowly authority-position, teachers must take orders from most of the rest of the personnel: department heads, subject specialists, principals and their assistants, superintendents, and school board members. Teachers have traditionally been assigned considerable power in the classroom, but this has recently been eroded through laws that constrain teacher conduct, administrative control over the curriculum, and pupil violence.

Despite these erosions, the teacher retains an authority in the classroom that is generated through custom, law, the teacher's expert knowledge, and the teacher's control over grades and promotions for pupils. Teachers also have some authority over parental conduct in matters relating to education, although teacher/parent relationships vary considerably among countries. (Within some countries, such as the United Kingdom, parents are often discouraged from "interfering" with the school, whereas in others, such as the United States, they are usually urged to involve themselves in the education of their children.)

4. The Expected Role of the Teacher

The expected role of the teacher may be defined as the set of expectations that are held for teacher behaviors by both teachers and other persons. Like persons in other social positions, teachers are subjected to a number of expectations for their conduct that reflect law, custom, habit, desires, and theories concerning their activities. These expectations form a context in which teacher conduct is interpreted, and role expectations for the teacher are presumably a major motivator for teacher conduct. On the one hand, those who hold expectations for teacher behavior are presumed likely to pressure teachers to conform to those expectations; on the other, teachers presumably want to follow their own expectations.

The concept of expected role is deceptively simple and hides several issues that should be exposed. First, expectations may be expressed in several different forms. Some expectations are expressed verbally, some are written down in news accounts or codes of conduct, and some are presumably held as covert thoughts by participants. Most authors who write

about expectations for the teacher have the last form in mind, but covert expectations cannot be perceived directly. One learns about them by listening to respondents talk about teacher conduct or by asking questions about the topic. Consequently, studies of the expected role of the teacher are normally conducted by means of interviews or standardized questionnaires.

Second, at least three different modes of expectation appear in the literature on teacher role. Some investigators study norms for teacher conduct—statements that express what teachers ought to do. Others study preferences, that is, likes and dislikes, for teacher conduct. Still others study beliefs—statements that express subjective probability for the appearance of teacher behavior. Many investigators confuse these three modes or assume that they are interchangeable, but an expression of what teachers ought to do may not be what is preferred or what is thought likely, and evidence has appeared indicating that these three modes of expectation are not interchangeable (Bank et al. 1977).

Third, expectations for teachers may either be held by persons themselves or may be attributed by those persons to other actors. To illustrate, teachers normally hold expectations for their own conduct and attribute expectations for it to the principal of their school. The principal also holds expectations, of course, and usually he or she also attributes expectations to the teachers. These four different types of expectations are sometimes confused by researchers, or researchers may assume that by measuring one of them a good estimate is also obtained of another. Such assumptions are questionable.

Fourth and last, some authors assume that expectations for teachers are largely shared within the school or society, and teachers or other actors in the school may make similar assumptions. Such assumptions are unwise. Whereas some expectations are surely shared for teacher conduct, others are not. Moreover, teachers may be made quite uncomfortable when they are faced with contradictory expectations that are held by two or more persons who have authority over them. Such situations produce what is termed "role conflict" and have been widely studied for teachers and other employees of organizations.

4.1 Shared Expectations for Teachers

Teachers are employed to instruct pupils because of shared values concerning the importance of education and beliefs concerning the efficacy of schools for fulfilling those valued outcomes. Not surprisingly then, various authors have presumed that agreement also appears on functions or tasks that teachers are expected to perform. Several lists of such functions have been proposed, many of them drawn from the insights of Waller (1932) and Parsons (1959). An example of such a list appeared in Kelsall and Kelsall (1969) who argued that teachers are (consensually) expected to emancipate pupils from their home environments, encourage achievement among pupils, sort out and socialize "winners" and "losers" in the achievement game, inculcate societal norms in pupils, teach technical skills, instill interpersonal sensitivity and discipline, and aid pupils in making decisions and training for occupations.

The Kelsalls' list focused on tasks associated with pupils. Other authors have stressed functions generated by structural properties of the school as an organization or values in the wider society. Thus, it is presumed that teachers are also expected to maintain order in their classrooms, accept and promote a common curriculum, follow the orders of supervisors, maintain effective communication with parents, and exhibit "loyalty" for their schools.

Research has also appeared concerning shared expectations for the teacher. Some of this research concerned beliefs or stereotypes about classroom conduct. To illustrate, Mackie (1972) reported that Canadians believe teachers are sympathetic and supportive of pupils, but are also inclined to dominate the classroom. American studies summarized by Biddle (1969) found that teachers were presumed to be nonaggressive, acquiescent, and to sin largely by omission rather than by commission. Other United States studies uncovered shared preferences for fairness in grading, neatness, and willingness to help pupils (Wright and Alley 1977) and shared norms that teachers should not discriminate among pupils, should be thoughtful and friendly, and should maintain order and discipline in the classroom (Biddle et al. 1961). Such expectations may be fairly universal among Western countries, but the evidence so far available is insufficient to test this proposition. Unfortunately, most of these studies were conducted in the 1960s and 1970s, and research on role expectations for teachers seems to have declined since then.

4.2 Role Conflict, Strain, and Resolution

Not all expectations for teachers are shared, of course, and studies have also reported nonconsensual expectations for teachers. Most of these studies also appeared in the 1960s and 1970s, most focused on norms, and most authors interpreted their findings as indications of role conflict. Several forms of role conflict were suggested in this literature.

A common form of finding concerned evidence that persons in various social positions hold differing norms for teacher conduct. Such disparities were reported in both the United Kingdom and the United States among such social positions as teachers, school principals, parents, pupils, teacher trainees, teacher trainers, persons from differing social classes, and persons from rural and urban communities (see Kelsall and Kelsall 1969, Biddle 1979). Most of this research argued that these disparities pose problems for teachers because those who hold differing norms will presumably bring conflicting pressures to bear on teachers for conformity. However, it was not clear

from most of these studies that others would actually produce such pressures, that teachers were aware of these disparate norms, or that teachers were actually made uncomfortable by their appearance.

Some teachers know when others hold disparate norms for their conduct, of course, and this awareness was also interpreted by other authors as role conflict. Studies reporting such awareness have appeared in various countries, and a major investigation appeared reporting equivalent findings from Australia, New Zealand, and the United Kingdom, and the United States that were obtained from national samples of teachers (Adams 1970). This investigation found normative disparities in all four countries. Some findings were common in the countries studied; in particular, teachers everywhere were likely to view teachers as being at odds with principals and other school officials over such issues as willing acceptance of nonprofessional duties, and with parents over curricular matters. Other findings were unique to specific countries. Presumed conflict between teachers and school officials was greatest in Australia, while conflicts involving parents were strongest in the United Kingdom.

The fact that teachers perceive normative disparities among differing groups of persons does not mean that these perceptions are accurate . Biddle et al. (1966) provided data indicating that teachers distort the actual views of principals, parents, and other actors concerned with schools in systematic ways. On the other hand, perceived normative disparities have been found associated with indicators of strain among both teachers and members of other occupations (see Biddle 1979).

Other expectational disparities are generated when a teacher also holds membership in alternative social positions whose tasks are at odds with those of teaching. Studies have appeared reporting role conflict between norms associated with teaching and coaching, teaching and counseling, and teaching and administrative responsibilities, but most of the research has concentrated on the conflicting demands of teaching and home making. Most studies of this latter topic have appeared in the United States, where the bulk of teachers are women, and interest in role conflicts involving women has blossomed. Such conflicts have also been found to be associated with strain.

What does the teacher do when confronted by situations of role conflict? When serious and persisting, such experiences may interfere with the teacher's performance or may cause the teacher to leave the profession. However, many teachers manage to resolve role conflicts in one way or another, by choosing to conform to one of the disparate norms in their behavior, or by compromising among the alternatives advocated.

A general theory of role conflict resolution was originally proposed by Gross et al. (1958) and has since been tested in many contexts. Dunkin (1972) examined reported role conflict resolution among Australian teachers and found that he could predict resolution strategies from personality characteristics. "Self-oriented" teachers appeared to be more likely to resolve conflicts in terms of their own needs whereas "other-oriented" teachers apparently paid more attention to the needs and authority of other persons to whom norms were attributed.

4.3 Role Expectations and Behaviors

Role expectations may be studied for themselves, as a major indicator of the subjective culture of persons who are members of social positions. However, most people who study role expectations do so because they presume that expectations predict behavior. Teachers are presumed to conform (or at least to "want" to conform) to expectations for their social position. Furthermore, others who hold expectations for teachers are thought to exert pressures on teachers for compliance.

The interesting thing about these "reasonable" propositions is that so little evidence is available to support them. Although many studies have been reported on both teacher role expectations and teacher role behavior, little of a systematic nature is known about relationships between these two realms of investigation.

A fundamental attraction of role theory for educators is that it presumes that persons are capable of thinking rationally about their own and others' conduct and that those rational thoughts will affect their behaviors in predictable ways. Unless there is a willingness to conduct more research on the relationships between role expectations and role behaviors, that attraction will remain based merely on speculation.

See also: Social Psychological Theories in Education; Social Psychological Theories of Teaching; Sociology of Teaching; Student Influences on Teaching; Teachers' Work and Political Action; Teaching, Realities of; Technology and the Classroom Teacher

References

Adams R S (ed.) 1970 Symposium on teacher role in four English-speaking countries: Introduction. *Comp. Educ. Rev.* 14(1): 5–64

Bank B J, Biddle B J, Keats D M, Keats J A 1977 Normative, preferential, and belief modes in adolescent prejudice. *Sociol. Q.* 18: 574–88

Biddle B J 1969 Teacher roles In: Ebel R L (ed.) 1969 AERA *Encyclopedia of Educational Research*, 4th edn. Macmillan Inc., New York

Biddle B J 1979 *Role Theory: Expectations, Identities, and Behaviors*. Academic Press, New York

Biddle B J, Rosencranz H A, Rankin E F Jr. 1961 *Studies in the Role of the Public School Teacher*. University of Missouri Press, Columbia, Missouri

Biddle B J, Rosencranz H A, Tomich E, Twyman J P 1966 Shared inaccuracies in the role of the teacher. In: Biddle B J, Thomas E J (eds.) 1966 *Role Theory: Concepts and Research*. Wiley, New York

Dunkin M J 1972 The nature and resolution of role conflicts among male primary school teachers. *Sociol. Educ.* 45(2): 167–85

Dunkin M J, Biddle B J 1974 *The Study of Teaching*. Holt, Rinehalt and Winston, New York

Gross N, Mason W S, McEachern A W 1958 *Explorations in Role Analysis: Studies of the School Superintendency Role*. Wiley, New York

Kelsall R K, Kelsall H M 1969 *The School Teacher in England and the United States: The findings of Empirical Research*. Pergamon Press, Oxford

Lortie D C 1975 *Schoolteacher: A Sociological Study*. University of Chicago Press, Chicago, Illinois

Mackie M 1972 School teachers: The popular image. *Alberta J. Educ. Res.* 18(4): 267–76

Parsons T 1959 The school class as a social system: Some of its functions in American society. *Harv. Educ. Rev.* 29(4): 297–318

Waller W 1932 *Sociology of Teaching*. Wiley, New York

Wright R, Alley R 1977 A profile of the ideal teacher. *Natl. Assoc. Sec. Sch. Princ. Bull.* 61(406): 60–64

Teachers' Work and Political Action

T. Seddon

Most research on teachers has focused on the teacher–student relationship or student teachers in training, and has explored teaching techniques and their presumed sources in personality or training. It has addressed ways of improving teachers' responses, usually through better supervision and the reform of technique or changes in teacher education. In this area of research, the industrial and political dimension of teaching has been curiously lacking.

A new perspective on teachers has been emerging from several disparate research traditions: the sociology of the school as an institution, studies of teachers as a social and economic group, and the history of teaching. This new approach has taken research a great deal further and recognizes that teachers are workers engaged in a labor process in classrooms, schools, and school systems—their workplaces. Their work involves them, either consciously or unconsciously, in social and political projects which have effects within and well beyond the walls of the classroom and the lives of each individual.

1. Converging Research Traditions

The classic study of teachers by Waller (1961) offered a sociology of teaching concerned with the impact of teaching on teachers as people. Waller pointed to some distinctive features of teaching as an occupation: its low remuneration and social standing, and the way in which relationships with students press those entering teaching to show reserve, dignity, and an acceptance of routine.

Organizational research on schools, which in the past has tended to be teacher-blind, has led to a concern with schools as workplaces (Dreeben 1973). Similarly, interactionist sociology of the school, which has focused on interactions between teachers and pupils, has turned attention to interactions among teachers. Both approaches address the constraints on teaching, and on teachers' decision-making and coping strategies. This research has highlighted the work context of teaching (Denscombe 1980).

Research concerned with improving schools has taken the view that teachers are constrained by their work contexts. The school effectiveness movement has sought to enhance schools through a top-down reorganization of the conditions of teachers' work. In contrast, the school improvement movement has taken a more bottom-up approach and has emphasized teachers' experience in their efforts to change education. This concern with teachers' experience has fed back into research that uses life-cycle and biographical approaches to explore teachers' careers and the construction of their identities (Goodson and Ball 1985).

Both organizational research and movements seeking to improve schools reflect a view of schools as institutions that must be managed. Critics of this hierarchical view have also become concerned with teachers' work. Drawing on studies of the labor process (e.g., Braverman 1974), they have presented the impact of top-down reforms as "deskilling," an example of the economy-wide dynamic by which paid work is subdivided, information and control are concentrated among managers, and most employees are redirected to the mechanical execution of "detail-work." With such a degradation of teaching, the teachers' craft has been replaced by a battery of technical procedures. Work is intensified as the number of tasks increases and teachers' control of task and time declines. Some critics have described this process as "proletarianization," suggesting that teachers have become more like industrial workers than middle-class professionals; more technicians than technologists (Apple and Teitlebaum 1986).

Research on teachers as a social group, and on the labor markets governing their employment, have also constributed to the picture. Statistical research has highlighted the social composition of the teaching work force. The higher percentage of women, for example, has been described as the "feminization" of teaching, a concept, however, that has been subject to criticism (Danylewycz and Prentice 1986).

The most elaborate picture of teachers' work is found in social and labor histories of teaching (e.g., Grace 1978, Lawn and Ozga 1981, Theobald and Selleck 1990). This approach has highlighted the fact that most teachers are now employees of the state, and has explored their changing work conditions. Union histories have shown struggles around teachers' work as employers and employees have sought to define and redefine their interrelationship (Lawn 1985). Taking a long historical view has shown gradual changes in teachers' work and has revealed the double-edged character of changes in teachers' work organization in the late twentieth century. Such ambiguities have encouraged questions about complacent assumptions of teacher "professionalism" and the alarmist cries of teacher "proletarianization."

On the whole, the insights gained from these different research traditions have been isolated from each other. Some attempts at synthesis (e.g., Connell 1985, Apple 1986, Acker and David 1994, and the social and labor histories mentioned above) indicate that a more powerful social analysis of teaching is possible. It can be built upon methodological and theoretical developments in educational inquiry, discussed below.

2. Trends in Educational Inquiry

Waller's (1961) study of teaching in 1932 provided a rich description of the world of schools, written from the viewpoint of teachers and based on anthropological techniques, realist fiction, diaries, and life histories. Waller, however, viewed statistics with distrust, noting: "possibly the understanding of human life will be as much advanced by the direct study of social phenomena as by the study of numerical symbols abstracted from those phenomena" (Waller 1961 pp.v–vi). Research after the Second World War favored abstract "scientific" political arithmetic studies. Variables such as social class, achievement, and criteria of professionalism were bracketed from their social context and assessed in a way that left the interaction and processes of schooling as an unstudied "black box" between input and output. Then, from the late 1960s onward, qualitative and ethnographic approaches again prevailed.

Since the 1960s school and classroom ethnographies have revealed the complex relationships and interaction between teachers and students, as well as teachers' part in the active construction of institutional and social life in schools. These observations have been informed by an interactionist perspective, which emphasizes the following points: (a) the meaning things

703

have for people is central to human action; (b) the attribution of meaning is a continuous process of understanding and acting, not a one-off consequence of individual psychology or social structure; and (c) this process is social and localized, being based in specific contexts of interaction. It makes the study of teachers and the teachers' viewpoint important (Woods 1979).

Ethnographies have also revealed teachers' involvement in conflicting realms of interaction and the way in which their strategies and accommodations have obstructed equality of opportunity—the core principle in liberal views of education. Such insights have challenged postwar functionalist notions of education as a means of socialization in a consensual society and the views of teachers as functionaries playing coherent teacher roles. Rather than being institutions offering universal benefit, schools have been seen to favor some over others in an unequal society. The state has not neutrally arbitrated in pluralist politics, but it has systematically favored ruling interests. Instead of assuming that educational development shows a gradualist, evolutionary progress toward enlightenment and teacher professionalism, the process of educational change has seemed contradictory and crisis-ridden. Questions of social justice have become central.

Structuralist research has examined the way conflict and distortion have been systematically patterned and given order by underlying relationships, organizations, and cultural and linguistic codes that are not immediately evident in experience. Marxist structuralism, for example, has analyzed how schools and teachers have contributed to the maintenance and reproduction of unequal class societies that are governed by the pursuit of profit, cyclical crises, and constant problems of control. These characteristics have put contradictory demands on schools which must be resolved within economic (e.g., fiscal) limits. Their resolution has created patterns and trends in social life such as unequal education for different social groups and the proletarianization of teachers. These resolutions are always imperfect, however. Participants have developed class consciousness as they have seen through the ideology of liberal education. They have come to understand that class society is systematically unequal and exploitative, and that political action is the way to change it. However, the structures of class power in the wider society overwhelm the microdynamics of school life. It has been argued that schooling is an arm of the state that serves ruling class interests, and that teachers are its agents. Class struggle is the assumed premise of this perspective and its explanation of change. This view marginalizes teachers as significant political actors, both individually and as an occupational group, but sees them as contradictory class actors whose politics are a consequence of their location within the class structure (Harris 1982).

Liberal, Marxist, and structuralist views of school-

ing have been challenged by feminist research. Woman's oppression within patriarchal society has meant that she knows herself in two ways: experientially and through dominant social science, which has been developed by men and has established male experience as a universal norm. Mainstream social science is sometimes termed "malestream," to highlight its roots in male experience and the way it has defined women and their experience as deviant, marginal, or simply absent. Consciously recognizing themselves as women, rather than people, has allowed women to recognize their subordination within gender relations. The personal is political because womens' lived experience provides a standpoint, distinct from mens' experience, from which traditional (i.e., patriarchal) understandings of the world can be challenged. Feminists have criticized the separation of the public and private realms of social life because it falsely divorces and privileges employment over family and authority over care. Women's apparent absence from history is shown to be a consequence not of their incapacity to act but of their political subordination (Weiler 1988).

Feminist research methodologies have made women's experience visible (de Lyon and Widdowson 1988). Life histories and personal narratives have allowed teachers to tell of their lived experience in opposition to dominant social science. It is consciously partial, stressing not the study *of* teachers, the majority of whom are women, but research *for* the subordinated (women, people of color, the old and young) which gives them a voice in cultural politics.

New research on teachers' work has drawn on, and moved on from, these methodological and theoretical trends to develop a perspective on teachers' work that attends explicit to the sexual and social division of labor. The integration of statistical, demographic, ethnographic, and life-history data has been guided by theoretical insights arising from the contradictions of interactionism and structuralism, Marxism and feminism, micro and macro sociology, teacher and researcher perspectives. It has placed teachers at the center of research and it has valued their lived experience as a corrective to researchers' outsider assumptions. It has taken work as a useful lens which focuses teachers' active making of schooling as an economy integrated in the sexual and social division of labor and as a realm of cultural products. The perspective on teachers' work has stressed that these productions, which include students, are made within relations of power, and it has presented teachers and their work in a complex and contradictory field of social forces. Whereas much research has emphasized teachers as individuals, the more integrated teachers' work perspective has stressed the way by which teachers and teaching are shaped by social relationships.

The individualist framework has attempted to classify work and people in more or less static (essential) categories. Teaching is characterized as "professional" or "unprofessional," teachers' work as "proletarianized," the teacher labor market as "feminized." These descriptive categories are easy to apply both in research and in polemic debates, but they are often vague, lacking rigorous definition and clear limits. Above all, the sorting into categories makes the things sorted appear obvious and simple. They are taken as the starting point of analysis rather than as things to be questioned and researched. The category "teacher" is a good example. People are categorized as teachers, something so simple it is easy to take for granted. Teacher behavior or attitudes then become the point from which research commences, neglecting the fact that teachers are not born teachers, but become teachers through social processes which exist because of the broader patterns of social relationships existing in a social order.

A focus on these relationships is characteristic of the new, more relational, approach. It has sought to develop an integrated understanding by examining the pattern of social relationships and processes that constitute, shape, and constrain teachers' work. This means that while simple categories are identified (representing particular arrangements, practices, ideologies, occupations, or individuals), they cannot be taken for granted in an ahistorical way. Instead, descriptive categories are seen as more or less transient social phenomena which appear in lived experience because of the way antagonisms, tensions, and contradictions in a given pattern of social relationships have been accommodated at a particular point in history. This becomes clear in the debate over the meaning of "professionalism" for teachers. The notion of professionalism is not fixed. It has changed historically and has been used to different effect by both teachers and the state (Lawn 1996). Teachers have used professionalism as an ideology to enhance and defend their workplace autonomy. Holders of state power have sometimes encouraged teacher professionalism, and the devolution of power over curriculum, as a solution to their own dilemmas. In other circumstances there has been a sharp reaction, with moves to reimpose central control of teachers and their work. Attempts to force "creationism" into science and to define a national curriculum indicate shifting control of content. New patterns of control can also be effected through changing forms of schooling; for example, in pressure for curriculum packages, competency-based approaches, and accountability.

Three further aspects of the relational framework are significant. First, teachers' work is determined by intersecting social relations of, at least, class, gender, race, and age. However, this is not a strong determination which mechanistically stamps individuals and institutions with an enduring imprint of gender or class. It is, rather, a softer process by which individuals and institutions are positioned in historically specific ways within lived and large-scale social relations and structures. These relations and structures cut across one another, creating distinctive and changing constellations of social forces which constitute, shape, and constrain individuals and institutions. This positioning and patterning sets limits and possibilities for action which, again, changes over time.

Secondly, the intersection of these social structures and relationships creates a relatively autonomous space within which teachers can negotiate constraints and develop strategies within personal life and within institutional and broader social settings. The concepts of "constraint" and "strategy" are crucial, but their conceptualization is ambiguous (Scarth 1987). Individualists stress individuals' intentional action in pursuit of their interests and commitments. The relational framework sees individuals as constructions, formed within relations of power. Interests and commitments are also constructions produced within the relatively autonomous space between limits and possibilities. Constraints and strategies may therefore be consciously recognized or go unrecognized by the individual actor.

Finally, teachers' work, which involves conscious and unconscious processes and effects, is both shaped within, and in turn shapes, relations of power. Teachers' practice in economic and cultural production creates asymmetries in individuals' and groups' capacities to define and realize their needs. Teachers' work is therefore also political action because, consciously or unconsciously, it serves to confirm or contest the prevailing social order.

The relational teachers' work perspective has opened up the study of teachers and their work. Four major dimensions of research are emerging: (a) teachers as workers and teaching as an occupation; (b) the teaching labor process; (c) the industrial dynamics of schooling; and (d) the culture and politics of teachers' work.

3. Teachers and their Work

3.1 Teachers as Workers: Teaching as an Occupation

Seeing the teacher as a worker immediately raises questions about the teacher as an employee and about relations with other groups of workers, employers, and the state. Teachers are workers with distinctive attitudes to students, to teaching, and to education. The relational perspective sees teacher ideologies arising from relationships that make up the life of a group, rather than being individual attitudes and opinions. These ideologies are not only the emanation of groups of teachers, however. Teacher ideologies are also shaped by social relationships in the broader society (Connell 1985).

Labor market research and historical studies of teaching as an occupation have revealed the social structuring of teachers' work. Teachers' work is patterned by salary scales, avenues for promotion, and status hierarchies. These shape a division of labor within teaching. Teacher supply and demand are further organized by the external labor market, governed by a general availability of jobs and opportunities for transferring between occupations (Warren 1989).

The labor market for teachers (both inside education and beyond) is different for men and women. Wider employment opportunities for men have contributed to the overrepresentation of women in teaching. This has been termed "feminization" but the picture is not straightforward because the concentration of women is not uniform. Historically there have been different regional gender patterns. In nineteenth-century Canada and the United States, for example, urban school systems favoured men, whereas rural schools showed larger numbers of women. These patterns arose partly because in a frontier context men could find alternative work, but also because of expectations about womens' work and existing traditions of domestic tuition in which women worked as teachers. Men and women are usually also distributed differently in the internal labour market: infant schools are strongly feminized, but secondary science departments and school management are masculinized. There are many women teachers, but they are most commonly guided, directed, and controlled by men (Danylewycz and Prentice 1986).

This view of teachers as workers reveals that a teacher's career is not just a matter of choices that shape the course of the individual's life. It is the consequence, at an individual level, of labor market dynamics, patterns of incentives (salary structure and promotion), institutional orthodoxies, organizational structures, and alternative employment opportunities. Men and women make career choices, but they are made within socially defined limits and opportunities. Widely held assumptions about womens' capacities, their domestic and family responsibilities, and interpretations of their different ways of working mean that women and men teachers experience quite different "careers."

3.2 The Labor Process of Teaching

The core of teachers' daily work is a practice so familiar it is easily taken for granted. There are more or less standard techniques for classroom control, for expounding what is to be learned, and for testing. The conventional ways of looking at teachers' methods have emphasized individual variations in these techniques; that is, personal "teaching styles." Classroom observation and teachers' accounts have shown considerable variation in the encouragement of student initiative versus class drill, or formal knowledge versus practical application. The relational approach to teachers' work has argued that these variations in the labor process are not idiosyncratic but are systematically produced by the social relationships surrounding the classroom. They arise in the history of interaction of a school's staff with its particular clientele, such as the emphasis on "drill" in teaching working-class

students, in the classroom strategies characteristic of science teachers, or in broad divisions within the curriculum, for example in the teaching of "academic" as compared with "practical" subjects.

Around the business of face-to-face instruction is a battery of other tasks necessary to keep schools running, from playground "police" duty to book-keeping and inservice training. A good deal of this school work is done with other teachers, a fact that counterbalances the much-discussed "isolation" of classroom work.

The core of the teaching enterprise—getting pupils to learn—is a highly complicated process, involving emotional relationships, intellectual interaction, group dynamics, and the exercise of practical judgement in a constantly changing context. It is also difficult to pin down as "work." This is partly because it is a labor process without a clearly defined object (in the sense of the physical product produced in factory work). The teacher's skill often appears as pure intuition, although this appearance underestimates the sophistication with which the skill may be developed (Connell 1985).

For these reasons, teachers' work, in comparison with jobs that have simpler technical parameters (e.g., manufacturing ballistic missiles), is vulnerable both to limitless expansion or intensification. Because the nature of teaching cannot be tightly specified, it is subject to political redefinitions by employers. The lack of clear boundaries in the labor process is often a major source of industrial conflict.

Academic studies of teachers, using time-and-motion techniques, tend to miss what teachers see as the core of their work, in particular its content, the process of learning, and the dilemma of relationships with students which rest on both care and authority (Steedman 1987). The curriculum is central to an analysis of the labor process. It defines the pupils' learning and at the same time it also defines the teachers' task. As an Australian teacher unionist put it, "curriculum is an industrial issue."

This relationship is clear in the debate on "deskilling." While teachers generally gained in skill and control over their work earlier in the twentieth century, it is argued that deskilling of teaching is a feature of the late twentieth century. This has been reflected in attempts to reassert control over curriculum. "Programmed learning" was an early version which displaced teachers from their key position in the processes and relationships of student learning and reoriented them toward administrative tasks. Examples of techniques used in the 1990s include curriculum packages produced by United States educational publishers, "computer-assisted learning" programs, and "basic skills" testing by means of standardized testing systems (Apple 1986).

Some curriculum "innovations" are said to be "teacher proof" because of the part they play in the control of curriculum and teachers. This link is often overlooked. Curriculum and administrative reforms (such as human relations management) are often justified educationally, in terms of their potential contribution to improved "educational outcomes," without making clear the implications for teachers' work. Indeed, teachers are often seen as a "constraint" to reform, and strategies are developed to minimize their effect in implementation.

Some research at the school level has indicated that significant deskilling does follow the introduction of packaged curricula, although some unexpected reskilling in bureaucratic techniques also occurs (Gitlin 1983). It is unclear how far this has taken place among teachers generally. These trends are opposed by both the industrial power of teacher unions, and the emotional complexity and practical judgements required in classroom work.

The programs that result in deskilling reflect a broader "managerial" perspective. This perspective views teaching as a technical activity, in which the results of academic research on learning or on organizational efficiency can be "applied." A succession of curriculum and administrative innovations have been introduced to this end, but found wanting. The longstanding failure to produce a "science" of education that works has fueled arguments that teaching must be seen as a craft rather than as a technical occupation.

There are two issues here. One emphasizes that teaching is based upon tacit rather than formal knowledge, and is mainly learned by example and by on-the-job experience rather than from codes or principles. The other emphasizes the way craft knowledge is specific to a particular group of workers and is protected by them, for instance against managerial attempts at redefinition or closer control. The "craft" conception captures important aspects of teachers' experience, and gives some insights into why the curriculum is a contested zone. However, this approach suggests an anachronistic picture of the isolated craft worker in a cottage, and plays down the extent to which teachers work collectively, especially outside the classroom.

3.3 The Industrial Dynamics of Schools

Like all other workplaces, schools have internal industrial politics. This point seems obvious, yet much research has missed it. For example, ethnographic or organizational studies of schools have commonly ignored their industrial relations, while work on industrial relations in education usually looks at the system, or union, but not at the school. Pioneering attempts to characterize the school as a workplace (e.g., Dreeben 1973) explored the character of authority, the school's technical features (such as the layout of classrooms and buildings), and the norms or culture of the school as an institution. This research found that top-down or bureaucratic patterns of authority conflicted with the demands of teacher professionalism. For this reason, among others, it was argued that there are chronic tensions around supervision in schools.

During most of the twentieth century there has been a general shift in schools from direct "line"

authority to more indirect forms of control. It has defined what constitutes an acceptable "professionalism," giving teachers some autonomy of action, but confining that autonomy within constraints, such as centrally controlled institutions, guidelines, and an ethos of schooling (Grace 1987). However, the scope for autonomy has been far from uniform between different countries or even between different systems within countries. There is some evidence, for instance, that teachers in private schools come under more insistent scrutiny about deportment and dress, religious observance, and private life ("morals") than teachers in state schools (Connell 1985).

Changes in the organization of schooling in the late twentieth century suggest that there have been moves toward more direct patterns of authority and control. The changing pattern of authority within schools, for example, is affected by the nature of the state, by the way it changes over time, and by its problems of legitimacy. The shift to indirect control and professionalism through much of the twentieth century has been part of a broader trend to develop the state and schooling as an interventionist and ameliorative agency within welfare capitalism. This social organization, based upon a regulatory state, has been challenged by social movements that seek to "roll back the state." They have favored social regulation predominantly through markets, with a small but strong state to ensure law and order. In schools, the trend has meant that authority operates through economic relations which are buttressed by direct control and hierarchical management in an emerging educational marketplace (Ball 1990).

The social organization of gender, especially the subordination of women, has particular implications for the school. Sexism in society at large has created difficulties for women as teachers, particularly in situations such as the maintenance of classroom control in a large mixed high school. Gender inequality has become obvious also in the serious under representation of women in educational administration—a live policy issue in many countries.

The large-scale structures of gender and class, race and generation, the organization of the state, and the international relations between states and economies, form a complex field of forces bearing on the school. Sometimes this field of social forces becomes evident as shifts in patterns of organization and regulation. In the 1990s such shifts are identified as transitions from bureaucratic to market organization of education, or as political struggles between forces of modernity or postmodernity (Hargreaves 1994). Within this field, and very much under its influence, the face-to-face participants in a school (the administrators, staff, students, and sometimes parents) negotiate an internal political order or "regime." This regime—the pattern of power, consent, alliance, and resistance that is temporarily established as the basis of a school's daily functioning—is central to the educational history of

707

a school. Likewise the regimes that predominate in a system's schools are central to its history as a system (Hunter 1994). There is therefore a social basis for the notorious conservatism of school systems, in school regimes that entrench the influence of groups who have most reason to resist change, notably middle-class, middle-aged, bureaucratically trained men.

Power generates resistance. Teachers, like other workers, are active in confronting, evading, or blunting control over their work. Where the overall policy of unions is strong (e.g., in Australian state schools) workplace unionism is a major form of defense. Teacher unionism, plus the state's historical shift to indirect control, has sometimes opened a space for industrial democracy. Where this is official policy, however symbolic, it can provide a venue for teachers to negotiate issues of control. In many schools, principals must win some kind of endorsement for their policies from the staff. Where unions are weak (as in much of the United States) resistance is more likely to be informal or individual. Yet it is notable that resistance occurs even in schools dominated by packaged curricula, with teachers asserting some control over how the packages work in the classroom (Gitlin 1983).

3.4 The Culture and Politics of Teachers' Work

The social patterning of teachers and their work has effects that are felt both in and beyond the classroom, school, or school system. Teachers contribute to an economics of schooling and to the production of meaning and significance in educational workplaces. They make and remake a culture and organization of work and so fuel political dynamics which cut across personal and institutional life and play a part in the broader social and historical movements of class and gender formation (Lawn and Grace 1987).

Life history research has revealed how teachers experience and adjust to contradictions in their experience; for example, how the experience of being a teacher of working-class origins in an English grammar school (Worpole 1985) or a Maori girl becoming a teacher in postwar New Zealand (Middleton 1987) shapes practice and, in some cases, politicizes it. Living these contradictions can turn a complex lived experience into a conscious understanding of the way one's space for action is shaped by social limits and possibilities which are made and can be remade through political action.

Resistance, conflict, debate, and struggle are central to political action. They also lead to the formation of distinctive cultural products: school organization, policy documents, and groups of people with distinctive ways of seeing and acting in the world. Pressures to redefine teachers' working conditions and employment relations are experienced differently by different teachers. The young and old see new reforming discourse, which advocates, for example, local management of schools, curriculum reform, and contract employment, as offering quite different patterns of constraint and opportunity. Teachers participate in the politics of reform as "Young Turks" or "Diehards," or by conservatively relinquishing public space in burnout, by withdrawing behind the classroom door, or by retiring early (Riseborough and Poppleton 1991). Deskilling and proletarianization are evident, but as heterogenous trends shaped by the division of labor. They affect men and women of different ages in different ways. They are not unidirectional in their "degradation of work," but appear as complex redefinitions of skill with implications for class and gender formation more generally (Ball 1988). These local, personal, and institutional politics form part of broader discursive politics through which different groups struggle to incorporate support for their experience and commitment. These politics are seen most clearly in policy debates over the course of educational reform (Ball 1990).

In all these cultural and political processes the shaping and making of teachers' work can become part of broader social and historical movements with long-term consequences. In South Africa, a colored woman teacher's commitment to educating her students brings her into conflict with the apartheid regime. It leads to conscious political involvement in the struggle against apartheid, and complex changing relations with her family, friends, students, and other teachers (Russell 1989). Economic crisis in the Philippines has been accommodated through a variety of personal austerity measures by Filipino teachers which have had implications on their immediate and longterm family life. It has also encouraged support for teacher action and organization (Del Fierro and Dalman 1987).

In the above cases, individuals' solutions to complex and contradictory circumstances have coalesced by sheer weight of numbers into a social force for remaking the social and educational order. Sometimes this has been consciously organized in collective action and political movements. In these movements the institutional setting is important. Research on nationalist independence movements in Africa has shown that before and after Independence there were quite different organizational and social arrangements which produced changing limits and constraints on teachers' action. Before Independence the space for teachers' work encouraged political mobilization. After Independence political mobilization was discouraged and teachers' energies were channeled into personal security and career advancement (Dove 1995).

4. Teachers' Work and Political Action

Teachers' work is a lens that opens up the study of teachers and their work. As the examples above have shown, however, there are significant ambiguities embedded in the concept of "teachers' work." Researchers can study teachers as workers, and their practice in employment and in professional and industrial politics. However, each of these frames is an abstraction and a methodological convenience which should not be seen as adequate in itself.

One set of ambiguities relates to "work." Teachers' work encompasses practices within employment and beyond: in families, communities, and other social movements. Teachers' work is simultaneously industrial and professional. Indeed the polar opposition commonly assumed between these two categories is empirically redundant and a good example of a politically significant cultural production. The social effects of teachers' work go beyond teaching and raise questions about the relationship between work and employment. It also challenges the familiar separation of education and work which suggests that students learn and workers work, and which establishes an association between learning, which is unpaid, and teaching, which is paid. This separation neglects that learning and work always go hand in hand because every workplace is also a learning place.

Another set of ambiguities centers on the "teacher." The teacher cannot be understood just as a teacher, as in individualist research, or just as a worker. The teacher should be seen as a social and historical actor involved in distinctive educative practices, as well as other practices, at the nexus of changing employment, family, and broader social relations and structures. Teachers are not the only agents of this educative practice, which raises questions about the social structures and processes that differentiate between the legitimated "teacher" as a social construction and the great range of other actors who educate, but beyond the classroom.

The Nicaraguan Literacy Crusade can be used to illustrate the complex interplay between economic and cultural production, and between teachers' work and political action (Arnove 1981). The Crusade was a mass movement which lifted Nicaraguan literacy levels. It was also a multilayered cultural product. Through its sheer existence, its materials, and its "teachers" (the *brigadistas*) the Crusade symbolized social justice and the popular democratic commitment of the Sandinista regime. One of its posters read:

Every home a classroom
Every table a desk
Every Nicaraguan a teacher!

For many Nicaraguans—and for those worldwide who press discourses of democracy, equality, and internationalism—this literacy campaign has been a significant resource which has been drawn on, and referred to, in ongoing cultural politics. For researchers of teachers' work it underlines the importance of treating categories with caution and can confirm that teachers' work is political action.

See also: Authority and Power in Educational Organizations; Effective Secondary Schools; Political Sociology of Teachers' Work; Sociology of Teaching

References

Acker S, David M E 1994 *Gendered Education: Sociological Reflections on Women Teaching and Feminism.* Open University, Buckingham

Apple M W 1986 *Teacher and Texts: A Political Economy of Class and Gender Relations in Education.* Routledge and Kegan Paul, London

Apple M W, Teitlebaum K 1986 Are teachers losing control of their skills and the curriculum? *J. Curric. St.* 18(2): 177–84

Arnove R S 1981 The Nicaraguan National Literacy Crusade of 1980. *Comp. Educ. Rev.* 25(2): 244–60

Ball S J 1988 Staff relations during the teachers' industrial action: Context, conflict, and proletarianisation. *Br. J. Sociol. Educ.* 9(3): 289–306

Ball S J 1990 *Politics and Policy Making in Education: Explorations in Policy Sociology.* Routledge and Kegan Paul, London

Braverman H 1974 *Labour and Monopoly Capital: The Degradation of Work in the Twentieth Century.* Monthly Review, New York

Connell R W 1985 *Teachers' Work.* Allen and Unwin, Sydney

Danylewycz M, Prentice A 1986 Revising the history of teachers: A Canadian perspective. *Interchange* 17(2): 135–46

del Fierro A C Jr, Dalman V M 1987 Coping mechanisms of elementary school teachers under economic crisis conditions in three southern Philippine regions. *Philippines Sociol. Rev.* 35: 11–25

de Lyon H, Widdowson F (eds.) 1988 *Women Teachers: Issues and Experiences.* Open University, Milton Keynes

Denscombe M 1980 The work context of teaching. *Br. J. Sociol. Educ.* 1: 279–92

Dove L A 1995 The work of schoolteachers as political actors in developing countries. In: Ginsburg M (ed.) 1995 *The Politics of Educators' Work and Lives.* Garland, New York

Dreeben R 1973 The school as a workplace. In: Travers R M W (ed.) 1973 *The Second Handbook of Research on Teaching.* Rand McNally, Chicago, Illinois

Gitlin A 1983 School structure and teachers' work. In: Apple M W, Wiess L (eds.) 1983 *Ideology and Practice in Schooling.* Temple University Press, Philadelphia, Pennsylvania

Goodson I, Ball S 1985 *Teachers' Lives and Careers.* Falmer Press, London

Grace G 1978 *Teachers, Ideology and Control: A Study in Urban Education.* Routledge and Kegan Paul, London

Grace G 1987 Teachers and the state in Britain: A changing relation. In: Lawn M, Grace G (eds.) 1987 *Teachers: The Culture and Politics of Work.* Falmer Press, London

Hargreaves A 1994 *Changing Teachers, Changing Time: Teachers' Work and Culture in the Postmodern Age.* Cassell, London

Harris K 1982 *Teachers and Classes: A Marxist Analysis.* Routledge and Kegan Paul, London

Hunter I 1994 *Rethinking the School: Subjectivity, Bureaucracy, Criticism.* Allen and Unwin, Sydney

Lawn M 1985 *The Politics of Teacher Unionism: International Perspectives.* Croom Helm, London

Lawn M 1996 *Modern Times?* Falmer, London

Lawn M, Ozga J 1981 The educational worker? A reassessment of teachers. In: Barton L, Walker S (eds.) 1981

Schools, Teachers and Teaching. Falmer Press, London

Lawn M, Grace G (eds.)1987 *Teachers: The Culture and Politics of Work.* Falmer Press, London

Middleton S 1987 Schooling and radicalisation: Life histories of New Zealand feminist teachers. *Br. J. Sociol. Educ.* 8(2): 169–89

Riseborough G F, Poppleton P 1991 Veterans versus beginners: A study of teachers at a time of fundamental change in comprehensive schooling. *Educ. Rev.* 43: 307–34

Russell D E H 1989 Life in a police state: A black South African woman who speaks out. *Women's Studies International Forum* 12(2): 157–66

Scarth J 1987 Teacher strategies: A review and critique. *Br. J. Sociol. Educ.* 8(3): 245–62

Steedman C 1987 Prisonhouses. In: Lawn M, Grace G (eds.) 1987

Theobald M R, Selleck R J W 1990 *Family, School and State in Australian History.* Allen and Unwin, Sydney

Waller W 1961 *The Sociology of Teaching.* Wiley, New York

Warren D 1989 *American Teachers: Histories of a Profession at Work.* Macmillan Inc., New York

Weiler K 1988 *Women Teaching for Change: Gender, Class and Power.* Bergin and Garvey, South Hadley, Massachusetts

Woods P 1979 *The Divided School.* Routledge and Kegan Paul, London

Worpole K 1985 Scholarship boy: The poetry of Tony Harrison. *New Left Review* No. 153: 63–74

Further Reading

Dove L A 1979 Teachers in politics in ex-colonial countries. *Journal of Comparative and Commonwealth Politics* 17: 176–91

Lipsky M 1980 *Street-level Bureauracracy: Dilemmas of the Individual in Public Service.* Sage, New York

Lortie D C 1975 *Schoolteacher: A Sociological Study.* University of Chicago Press, Chicago, Illinois

Thompson P 1989 *The Nature of Work: An Introduction to Debates on the Labour Process.* Macmillan, Basingstoke

Tropp A 1957 *The School Teachers: The Growth of the Teaching Profession in England and Wales from 1800 to Present Day.* Heinemann, London

Teaching, Realities of

A. Hargreaves

To speak of the realities of teaching is to address the nature and organization of teaching not in terms of ideals, fantasies, models, or rhetoric, but in terms of the complex actuality of the work, and the day-to-day shape it takes with real teachers, in real classrooms, in real schools. To speak of the realities of teaching, therefore, is to speak of teaching descriptively, not prescriptively: of how it is, more than how it should be. It is to see teaching holistically, as complex, interconnected sets of tasks, purposes, requirements, and constraints; rather than as fragmented domains of knowledge, skill, or motivation that can be addressed or improved in isolation. Understanding the realities of teaching and engaging with them effectively, therefore, entails understanding and engaging with what teachers actually do, rather than cajoling or exhorting them to do something better.

1. Change and Practicality

Educational reform and teacher reform, in particular, are often rather poor at recognizing the realities of teaching. Efforts to improve teaching quality have tended to focus on the characteristics of individuals —on knowledge, skill, and personal qualities—much more than on the patterns of work organization and leadership which limit or liberate teachers in their work. Poor teaching quality, it is commonly argued or assumed, tends to result from an absence of knowledge, skills, or qualities in individuals (for examples, see Department of Education and Science 1983). This implies a deficit model of teaching, where poor quality results from deficiencies in personality, gaps in learning, or weak matching of teachers' competencies to the tasks they are required to perform.

Teachers are not just technical learners, they are social learners too. As social learners, teachers actively interpret, make sense of, and adjust to the requirements their conditions of work place upon them. In this view, what some might judge to be "poor" teaching quality often results from reasoned and reasonable responses to occupational demands: from interpretive presences, not cognitive absences; from strategic strength, not personal weakness. "Poor" teaching quality, in this respect, often results from poor work environments. Similarly, enhanced work environments which are more collaborative and incorporate principles of recognition, reward, and risk-taking increase teachers' senses of efficacy (Ashton and Webb 1986) and the degree of positive influence they exert on student achievement (Rosenholtz 1989).

Recognizing that teachers are social learners draws attention not merely to their capacity for change, but also to their desires for change (and indeed for stability) (Louden 1991a). Political and administrative devices for bringing about educational change and improvement usually ignore, misunderstand, or override teachers' own desires. In this respect, the devices and desires of teacher development are often incongruent (Hargreaves 1993b). Change devices usually rely on principles of compulsion, constraint, or contrivance to get teachers to change. They presume that educational standards are low and young people are failing or dropping out because the practice of many teachers is deficient or misdirected. The remedy for these deficits and deficiencies, politicians and administrators believe, needs to be a drastic one, calling for decisive devices of intervention and control to make teachers more skilled, more knowledgeable, and more accountable.

At the heart of the realities of change for most teachers is the issue of whether it is practical. Judging changes by their practicality seems, on the surface, to amount to measuring abstract theories against the tough test of harsh reality, but there is more to it. In the ethic of practicality among teachers is a powerful sense of what works and what does not, not in the abstract, or even as a general rule, but for a particular teacher in a particular context. For teachers, the realities of teaching are the practicalities of teaching. To ask whether a new method is practical is therefore to ask much more than whether it works. It is also to ask whether it fits the context, whether it suits the person, whether it is tune with their purposes, and whether it helps or harms their interests.

2. Commitment and Purpose

Teaching is not just a technical business; it is also a moral one. There are two senses in which teaching is a moral enterprise. First, teachers are among the most important influences on the life and development of young children. They help create the generations of the future. Second, at the heart of teaching, as in many other kinds of professional action, is the making of discretionary judgments in situations of unavoidable uncertainty. Teaching is riddled with practical judgments that are also reflective ones, even if only in the most fleeting sense (Louden 1991b). For these decisions, there are few or no clear rules of thumb that can be applied in a systematic way from one situation to the next.

Because teaching is a moral craft, it has purpose for those who engage in it. There are things that teachers value, that they want to achieve through their teaching. There are also things they do not value, things they fear will not work or may actually do harm to the children in their charge. Teachers' purposes motivate what teachers do and explain why they often resist change which does not address those purposes. Stated somewhat differently, they are committed to these purposes. Nias (1989) describes three kinds of teacher commitment: vocational, professional, and career continuance. These forms of commitment do not describe three kinds of teacher; any one teacher may exhibit ele-

ments of each of the different forms. In many teachers, however, one of the forms is often dominant.

2.1 Vocational Commitment

This refers to the missionary character of teaching, to the care for and connectedness to young people which motivates many teachers in their work, especially at the primary or elementary level. What Gilligan (1982) calls the "ethic of care," where actions are motivated by concerns for care and nurturing of others and connectedness to others, is central among teachers of younger children. The primary teachers interviewed in Nias's (1989) study talked extensively about care, affection, and even love for their students. Book and Freeman (1986) note how purposes of care and nurturance are much more common as reasons for entering teaching among elementary than secondary school teachers. In Lortie's (1975) classic study of elementary teachers, the joys and satisfaction of caring for and working with young people were the prime psychic rewards of teaching.

Educational reform, however, is often propelled less by ethics of care than contrary (and arguably more stereotypically masculine) ones of responsibility, which stress professional obligations and improvements to planning and instruction. Ignoring the realities of teachers' purposes and vocational commitments is, in this regard, not only professionally disrespectful but also practically perverse. Neglect of teachers' purposes can lead to lowered teacher motivation and decreased effectiveness. Nias (1991) has described how the detailed demands of the National Curriculum in the United Kingdom have led to profound feelings of loss and bereavement among primary teachers, who no longer have time to care for and connect with their children's individual concerns in the ways they feel are important. Neufeld (1991) records similar responses among a group of Canadian elementary teachers pressed and stressed by the time demands of implementing a program of active learning to the exclusion of meeting their students' personal and emotional needs. Apple and Jungck (1992) in the United States describe how tendencies in teachers' work where teachers are becoming more subjected to the detailed, step-by-step requirements of prescribed programs, also erode their capacity to care for the young in the ways they would like.

Care is at the heart of the emotional and moral working life of many teachers. Reform efforts which do not recognize the centrality of care, fundamentally threaten or demean the emotional and moral character of teaching.

2.2 Professional Commitment

This describes the teacher's commitment to being knowledgeable, competent, and instructionally effective. Professional commitment is about doing a good job. As a source of satisfaction, professional commitment tends to strengthen once the earliest years of teaching have passed, and teachers begin to take pride in their own mastery, the breadth of their repertoires, and their capacity to improvise. Professional commitment as a prime commitment also tends to have more prominence among secondary school teachers than elementary school teachers. In secondary school teaching, professional commitment is mainly invested in subject mastery and subject expertise. Commitment to teaching a subject is the main reason why secondary teachers enter the profession (Book and Freeman 1986). Care for individuals is less important for them, a repeated difficulty that afflicts the capacity of many secondary schools to become more caring communities for their students (Hargreaves 1982).

In secondary school teachers' commitments to their academic subjects can be seen the intimate connection between the teacher's purpose and the teacher as a person. Subjects are not just intellectual communities. They are social and political communities as well. They bestow meaning and identity on those who teach in them. Secondary teachers are socialized into subject identities and commitments as school and university students. The subject department is often a more meaningful and visible community for them than that of the wider school. Subjects and their departments provide the major lines of career development and progression at the secondary school level.

Proposals for curriculum integration which challenge teachers' subjects are therefore construed as much more than rational attempts to reconstruct fields of knowledge and learning in tune with the needs and demands of contemporary times. They are also perceived and deeply experienced as threats to career, security, identity, and fundamental senses of competence. As Hargreaves (1980) points out, competence anxiety, the fear of appearing incompetent in front of one's colleagues, is perhaps the most basic anxiety of all in teaching. Proposals for curriculum integration therefore strike at fundamental and deep-seated realities of professional commitment, subject identities, and desires to retain competence among the teaching force.

2.3 Career-continuance Commitment

Career-continuance commitment is the commitment to remain in teaching for the security and extrinsic rewards it brings. Teachers can become committed *by* teaching, as well as *to* it. Teachers in later career who have put a lot of time and investment into their teaching, and have built up families, dependents, mortgages, and other life investments may feel obligated to stay in teaching even when innovation and change profoundly threaten their purposes and satisfactions.

Teachers who remain in teaching for these reasons are among those most prone to become disenchanted and resistant to change. However, the realities of teaching in mid-to-late career are more complex. Research undertaken by Huberman (1992), based on

interviews with 160 secondary school teachers in Switzerland, indicated that most teachers in mid-to-late career were unlikely to embrace innovation with enthusiasm. Two groups, whom Huberman describes as "defensive focuses" and "disenchanted" were deeply cynical about change. They had (accurately) predicted the demise of past innovations, steered well clear of them then and continued to do so now, or they had invested a lot in them only to be "sold out" as resources were withdrawn, the innovation collapsed, and the innovators moved on.

Other teachers, whom Huberman calls "positive focusers," were less dismissive but still tempered in their reactions and enthusiasms. They were pragmatic about school-wide innovations, having seen several come and go before. Feelings of mortality were also becoming stronger, leading to greater wishes to balance work with life and tendencies to become more serene, a discovery and development experienced rather later by men than by women (Krupp 1989). These positive focusers were prepared to change, but in ways which built on, instead of overturning, their past expertise and efforts: adding to their repertoires in their own classes, rather than transforming everything they did. The reality of mid-to-late career teaching is a reality in which modest, gradual, and respectful change may be embraced with willingness, but where radical transformative change will almost certainly not be (Fullan and Stiegelbauer 1991).

3. Career and Life Cycle Influences on Teachers

The issues of midcareer teaching in particular point to more general career and life cycle influences that have important impacts on how all teachers teach. Teachers in early career, especially when this coincides with youth, are typically preoccupied with classroom management and establishing competence. They will devote endless hours to their work and, once initial competence has been established, embrace innovation with all the time, energy, and commitment they can muster. Consequently, they are receptive to innovation, but also prone to burnout (Knowles 1988). At the early stages of career entry, young teachers may also still be in relatively early stages of personal ego development in ways that affect their capacity to work successfully and confidently with others, since teachers with poorly developed ego boundaries or sense of self, fear "invasion" when working with others. Young teachers entering the profession can be especially vulnerable here, since they are entering a profession with complex responsibilities and interpersonal relationships, often long before their own personal growth has matured (Nias 1989).

However, age and experience do not necessarily bring greater wisdom: they may also bring fixed views, outmoded understandings, dogmatism, and bigotry. Stoddart (1991), for instance, in case studies of teachers entering teaching through patterns of alternate certification designed to bring people of greater maturity and experience into the profession, found that:

> These individuals brought to teaching strong commitments and personal attributes which could have formed the basis for the development of outstanding professionals. Unfortunately, these attributes were not enhanced by systematic professional education. Faced with teaching dilemmas, they had limited resources with which to develop flexible responses . . . They developed a modal approach to practice which was shaped by the subject-specific curriculum and their own personal perspectives. They applied and misplaced these pedagogies with little opportunity to reflect on and critically analyze the consequences of their teaching actions. (p. 228)

Whatever the teacher's point in the life cycle, the need to reflect on and reconstruct experiences is demonstrable. This need is especially felt as teachers come to appreciate the profound and pervasive influences that their lives exert upon their work. Long-standing attachments to particular belief systems and ideologies can remain abiding influences on how teachers approach teaching and learning (Louden 1991b). Sometimes these commitments have important religious and spiritual dimensions which also influence their work, through, for instance, solicitous Catholicism (Woods 1981) or charismatic fundamentalism (Stoddart 1991). Ethnocultural attachments and identities can also affect teaching, most visibly where the teachers value more traditional, didactic approaches. Gender identity is also influential, though in varying and complex ways. Families and domestic obligations create an unwelcome triple or quadruple shift for many women (Acker 1990a), but for others they can be sources of strength, stability, support, and identity, personal anchors beyond the vocational vortex of work and career that help retain some sense of balance and perspective.

Intense and dramatic personal problems such as bereavement, divorce, family violence, or substance abuse are among the most obvious ways that teachers' lives intrude upon their work, sometimes impairing their performance. In schools where teachers are involved in collaborative working relationships of trust and support, the intermeshing of personal and professional lives is seen as normal and legitimate. In these schools, allowances are made for teachers who are sick, troubled, or stressed, and support is offered to them. Teachers here can show their vulnerabilities and share them with others.

If the research on teachers' lives has one flaw, it is its tendency to explain the relationship between teachers' lives and work in a one-sided way: with the life affecting the work but not vice versa. At its worst, this bias can lend (unintended) support to deficit-based explanations of teachers' problems which diagnose and treat them as personal and private problems when they may actually have their roots in the conditions and management of the workplace (Ashton and Webb

1986). It is important to remember also that problems in the workplace can have a profound impact on the quality of life outside it. This can happen positively as well as negatively. Indeed an important priority for future research on teachers' lives might well be to identify which patterns of schooling and teachers' work enrich rather than enervate the lives of teachers. In particular, there is a case for forging a bond between research on school improvement on the one hand and teachers' lives on the other; to see whether, in the long term, successful and innovative schools drain their teachers dry until nothing of their personal lives and selves is left, or whether they enrich and energize those lives through the ways they generate personal enjoyment and fulfillment.

4. Coping Strategies

Teaching is at least in part a matter of strategy. Teachers are products of their present and previous work environments. They are creatures of circumstance. The ways they teach evolve as strategies to pursue purposes that are important to them. These strategies develop as ways of adjusting to the particular pressures, contingencies, and expectations of their environment. Where these pressures are extreme, teachers' strategies can become desperate, a matter of sheer survival. Even in the most favorable circumstances, all teaching is in part a constructive trade-off (sometimes calculated, sometimes routine and taken for granted) between ideal purposes and practical realities. These constructive trade-offs, or coping strategies, are a key aspect of teaching.

Coping strategies connect the purpose and the person of teachers to the context in which they work. The connection of strategy to context is complex, for teachers' strategies are mediated by all kinds of other factors, such as the teacher's personal biography, career stage, educational purpose, and the ethos or institutional bias of the school. These complexities explain why attempts to "test" coping strategies theory by trying to establish a clean and clear one-to-one match between teaching strategies and the contexts in which they take place, have not been particularly successful. However, in connection with the other realities of teaching, the context of teachers' work remains extremely important in influencing teachers' actions and helping shape the coping strategies which characterize their work.

5. Context

Three forms of work context help frame the realities of teaching: continuing contexts, changing or contemporary contexts, and contexts of variability or diversity.

5.1 Continuing Contexts

The continuing contexts of teaching are to be seen in what Sarason (1990) calls the fundamental regularities

713

of teaching: the apparently fixed, pervasive, and intractable features of the work that define how it is done and that defy attempts to change it. These seemingly fixed regularities, however, have quite specific and deep historical roots (Cuban 1984). Modern school systems, as educational historians have noted, emerged as factory-like systems of mass education designed to meet the needs of manufacturing and heavy industry. They processed pupils in batches, segregated them into age-graded cohorts called "classes" or "standards," taught them in a standardized course or curriculum, and used teacher-centered methods of lecturing, recitation, question-and-answer, and seatwork. These systems of mass education for an increasingly massified society with large laboring classes were supplemented by more selective systems of state and private secondary education for commercial and social elites, rooted in academic and aristocratic traditions of contemplative study, disengaged from utilitarian concerns, and grounded in defined domains known as subjects that conferred cultural capital on those who successfully acquired them. These social and historical conditions have set the parameters and assumptions within which much of teachers' work takes place and which have come to define "real school" for many people. Punctuated lesson periods, age-segregated classes, the subject-based academic curriculum, and paper-and-pencil testing are therefore highly specific sociohistorical products, yet they have come to define a paradigm of teaching and teachers' work that is hard to break or reconstruct, even as the emerging educational needs of the postindustrial age seems to call for new patterns of teaching and teachers' work organization to meet them (Hargreaves 1993b).

5.2 Contemporary Contexts

Notwithstanding the realities and regularities of the continuing context of teachers' work by the accumulation and expansion of new tasks and responsibilities, this work is also changing in quite fundamental respects as the world outside schools also changes. Based on interviews with elementary teachers, Fullan and Hargreaves (1991) recorded teachers' perceptions of how their work is changing in terms of more "social work" responsibilities; the challenge of dealing with an increased range of abilities and behaviors in their classes (particularly since the move toward integration of special-needs students into ordinary classes); greater cultural and ethnic diversity and the demands this places on more diverse and sensitive programming; increased accountability and form-filling; and escalating amounts of time required to work, communicate, and meet with parents, principals, and other colleagues to meet the increasingly complex and pressing demands with which schools are having to deal. Two of the main explanations for this changing contemporary context are those of professionalization and intensification.

Arguments organized around the principle of professionalization emphasize the struggle for, and

in some cases the realization of, greater teacher professionalism through extension of the teacher's role. Teachers, especially those in elementary schools, are portrayed as having more experience of whole-school curriculum development, involvement in collaborative cultures of mutual support and professional growth, experience of teacher leadership, commitment to continuous improvement, and engagement with processes of extensive school-wide change. In these accounts, teaching is becoming more complex and more skilled. What Hoyle (1975) calls "extended teacher professionalism" and Nias (1989) more cautiously terms "bounded professionality" is, in this perspective, both an emerging reality and a point of aspiration.

A second line of argument is broadly derived from Marxist theories of the labor process that look at teaching less as a profession or craft, and more as a kind of work with its own distinctive and changing labor process. This approach highlights major trends towards deprofessionalization in teachers' work. Teachers' work is portrayed as becoming more routinized and deskilled, more and more like the degraded work of manual workers, and less and less like that of autonomous professionals. Teachers are depicted as being increasingly controlled by prescribed programs, mandated curricula, and step-by-step methods of instruction.

In addition, drawing on Larson's (1980) broader analysis of the labor process among professionals or semiprofessionals, it is claimed that teacher's work is becoming increasingly intensified, with teachers expected to respond to greater pressures and comply with multiplying innovations under conditions that are at best stable and at worst deteriorating. Intensification, it is argued, leads to reduced time for relaxation and relief of stress, lack of time to upgrade one's skills, insufficient opportunities to collaborate with one's co-workers, chronic and persistent overload with resulting dependency on outside experts and materials, cutting of corners and reductions in quality, and spreading oneself too thinly. Under this view, extended professionalism is a rhetorical ruse, a strategy for getting teachers to collaborate willingly in their own exploitation as more and more effort is extracted from them in the name of shared leadership and the like.

Hargreaves' (1992) investigation of 28 Canadian elementary teachers and their interpretations of and responses to additional preparation time which had been won by their teacher federations raises some critical questions about the intensification thesis and suggests important modifications to it. First, some teachers resisted additional time because it took them away from their own classes and the care they could offer them (it undermined their purposes). Second, preparation time opportunities for teacher collaboration and enhanced professionalism often became administratively contrived and controlled in ways that undermined that professionalism. Third, shortages of specialist expertise among teachers required to cover classes during preparation time perversely led to program dependency, deskilling, and reduction of quality in some of these classes (reproducing the effects of intensification in a context meant to combat it). Acker's (1990b) study of English primary school teachers and their work raises similar questions about being too ready to interpret the changes in teachers' work as ones that amount to deskilling.

The contemporary changes in teachers' work can neither be encompassed by heroic proclamations of increased professionalism, nor by critical theories of intensification and deskilling derived from neo-Marxist theories of the labor process. Unintended consequences, bureaucratic complexities, and the expanded expectations for teaching that follow in an increasingly postmodern society which is pluralistic, culturally diverse, informationally dense, suffused with uncertainty, and intensely influenced by accelerated change and the compressed character of time and space, all help to shape the contemporary context of teachers' work (Hargreaves 1993a).

6. Contexts of Diversity

As well as the continuing and contemporary contexts of teaching that affect most teachers and frame the realities of their work, there are also contexts of difference and diversity that lead to variations in the realities of teaching according to the settings in which it is performed. In a major study of secondary school work contexts, McLaughlin (1993) has conceptually and empirically delineated a range of such contexts and their impact on teachers' work, including the contexts of the students, the subject department, the school, the community, and the system.

Metz (1990) points out that teachers are in many respects defined by their students: successful, high status students reflect and reinforce the perceptions of status that attach to their teachers; and teachers will sometimes, as a result, seek to avoid contact with students who threaten to undermine these perceptions. This reality of teaching is one reason why many teachers avoid assignments to low-track classes if they can; it also provides a justification for detracking or destreaming to counter such inequities (Oakes 1985).

As mentioned earlier, the secondary school subject department provides a more immediate and meaningful context for many secondary teachers than their overall school. Departments vary in the strength of their culture, leadership, and support in ways that impact on the quality of teaching and on willingness to innovate. They also vary in terms of their shared beliefs about and practices in the areas of pedagogy, subject matter, assessment, and student grouping. Common innovations like curriculum integration or destreaming have a very different reality depending on the departments in which they are experienced.

The same can be said for the differences between communities in which schools are located. McLaughlin's (1993) study, for instance, indicates that teacher collaboration can take on very different meanings depending on the socioeconomic status of the community in which the school is embedded. In middle-class schools, collaboration tends to focus on program and academics. In working-class schools it is more oriented to dealing with the needs and demands of students.

7. Culture

Teachers' commitments, identities, and strategies are not established alone. They are built up and defined through interaction with others who are significant for them. Among these significant others are their colleagues. Teachers' relations with their colleagues comprise what have come to be called "cultures of teaching."

Hargreaves (1993a) distinguishes between two aspects of the teacher cultures: content and form. The content of teacher cultures consists of the substantive attitudes, values, beliefs, habits, assumptions, and ways of doing things that are shared within a particular teaching group or among the wider teaching community. Many different kinds of teacher cultures can be and have been differentiated by their content (e.g., academic, elementary, and developmental cultures; subject cultures).

The form of teacher cultures consists of the patterns of relationship among members of these cultures. It is through the forms of the teacher culture that the contents of these cultures are realized, reproduced, and redefined. Changes in beliefs, values, and attitudes among the teaching force, may, in this respect, be contingent upon prior or parallel changes in teachers' relations with their colleagues. Hargreaves identifies four forms of the teacher culture: individualism, balkanization, collaborative culture, and contrived collegiality.

7.1 Individualism

Individualism (also known as isolation or privatism), is characterized by situations in which teachers teach mainly alone in their insulated classroom "boxes," giving and receiving little help, advice, support, or feedback, and engaging in little joint planning or reflective dialogue about practice (Fullan and Stiegelbauer 1991). Individualism continues to be the dominant cultural form for most teachers. Although individualism is sometimes celebrated and justified as professional autonomy, history has created it, architecture and school timetables have reinforced it, and teachers have themselves actively and strategically retained it as a way of fending off the overwhelming constraints of bureaucracy. In addition, some teachers also actively elect to work individualistically to maintain care and contact with their own students and to experience the comfort and creativity of personal solitude against the pressures and cultural restraints of groupthink (Hargreaves 1992). While solitude at certain times for certain individuals seems educationally beneficial, widespread cultures of individualism appear to lead to personal insecurity, lowered levels of risk, and reduced levels of teaching quality (Rosenholtz 1989).

7.2 Balkanization

Balkanization is characterized by the fragmentation of teachers into separate and competing subgroups (such as subject departments) pursuing different self-interests in an environment where common purposes, joint understandings, and multiple group memberships are rare. Hargreaves and Macmillan (1992) argue that balkanization makes it difficult for teachers to establish common school goals, leads to inconsistency and redundancy in program and pedagogy, reinforces invidious political and status differences between different kinds of subjects and different forms of knowledge, and reduces teachers' opportunities to learn from one another across territorial boundaries. In balkanized cultures, the organizational whole is less than the sum of its parts.

7.3 Collaborative Cultures

Collaborative cultures among teachers are those where collegial relationships express principles of help, support, advice, planning, reflection, and feedback as joint enterprises. Little (1990) has identified four kinds of collegial relations among teachers which form a continuum from scanning and storytelling, to help and assistance, sharing and joint work. Only the latter, she argues, expressed in activities like team teaching, peer coaching, and action research, constitutes a strong form of collaboration. With Rosenholtz (1989), Little recognizes that these stronger forms reduce uncertainty, increase risk-taking, foster commitment to continuous improvement, and thereby raise teachers' senses of efficacy and, with that, the successes they have with their students (Ashton and Webb 1986). While advocacy for collaborative school cultures is increasing, they remain a relatively rare cultural reality of teaching.

7.4 Contrived Collegiality

This describes forms of collaboration that are administratively forced more than facilitated (Grimmett and Crehan 1992). While it can help provide structured frameworks to get collaboration going, more often it captures, contains, and constrains it, subordinating teachers' purposes to those of administrators and engaging teachers in efforts that are superficial, wasteful, or divisive. Contrived collegiality is evidenced in such measures as mandatory peer coaching, compulsory collaborative planning, and scheduled meetings with special education teachers. It is a form of collaboration that does not so much create empowerment, as entrapment, enticement, or enslavement.

8. Conclusion

The rhetorics of teaching quality and teacher development are often dominated by discourses of knowledge, skill, and competence. The realities of teaching quality and teacher development are more ones of commitment, context, culture, and career. Reform efforts are at last beginning to address some of these realities but it would be unrealistic not to acknowledge that there still remains a long way to go.

See also: Professional Socialization of Teachers; Sociology of Teaching; Teacher Burnout; Teacher Recruitment and Induction

References

Acker S 1990a Creating careers; Women teachers at work. *Curric. Inq.* 22(2): 141–63
Acker S 1990b Teachers' culture in an English primary school: Continuity and change. *Br. J. Sociol. Educ.* 11(3): 257–73
Apple M, Jungck S 1992 You don't have to be a teacher to teach in this unit: Teaching, technology, and control in the classroom. In: Hargreaves A, Fullan M (eds.) 1992 *Understanding Teacher Development*. Cassell, London
Ashton P, Webb R 1986 *Making a Difference: Teacher's Sense of Efficacy and Student Achievement*. Longman, New York
Book C, Freeman D 1986 Differences in entry characteristics of elementary and secondary teacher candidates. *J. Teach. Educ.* 37(2): 47–51
Cuban L 1984 *How Teachers Taught: Constancy and Change in American Classrooms (1890–1980)*. Longman, New York
Department of Education and Science 1983 *Teaching Quality*, Cmnd 8836. HMSO, London
Fullan M, Hargreaves A 1991 *What's Worth Fighting for in Your School?* Open University, Milton Keynes
Fullan M, Stiegelbauer S 1991 *The New Meaning of Educational Change*, 2nd edn. Cassell, London
Gilligan C 1982 *In a Different Voice: Psychological Theory and Women's Development*. Harvard University Press, Cambridge, Massachusetts
Grimmett P, Crehan E 1992 The nature of collegiality in teacher development: The case of clinical supervision. In: Fullan M, Hargreaves A (eds.) 1992 *Teacher Development and Educational Change*. Falmer Press, London
Hargreaves D 1980 The occupational culture of teaching. In: Woods P (ed.) 1980 *Teacher Strategies*. Croom Helm, London
Hargreaves D 1982 *The Challenge for the Comprehensive School: Culture, Curriculum and Community*. Routledge and Kegan Paul, London
Hargreaves A 1992 Cultures of teaching: A focus on change. In: Hargreaves A, Fullan M (eds.) 1992 *Understanding Teacher Development*. Cassell, London
Hargreaves A 1993a *Changing Teachers; Changing Times: Teachers' Work and Culture in the Postmodern Age*. Cassell, London
Hargreaves A 1993b Individualism and individuality: Reinterpreting the teacher culture. *Int. J. Educ. Res.* 19(3): 227–45
Hargreaves A, Macmillan R 1992 Balkanized secondary

schools and the malaise of modernity. Paper presented at the annual meeting of the American Educational Research Association, San Francisco, California

Hoyle E 1975 The study of schools as organizations. In: Machugh R, Morgan C (eds.) 1975 *Management in Education*. Ward Lock, London

Huberman M 1992 *The Lives of Teachers*. Cassell, London

Knowles J 1988 The failure of a student teacher: Becoming educated about teachers, teaching and self. Paper presented at the annual meeting of the American Educational Research Association, New Orleans, Louisiana

Krupp J 1989 Staff development and the individual. In: Caldwell S (ed.) 1989 *Staff Development: A Handbook of Effective Practices*. National Staff Development Council, Oxford, Ohio

Larson S 1980 Proletarianization and educated labour. *Theor. Society* 9: 131–75

Little J 1990 The persistence of privacy: Autonomy and initiative in teachers' professional relations. *Teach. Coll. Rec.* 91(4): 509–36

Lortie D 1975 *Schoolteacher*. University of Chicago Press, Chicago, Illinois

Louden W 1991a Collegiality, curriculum and educational change. *Curric. J.* 2(3): 361–73

Louden W 1991b *Understanding Teaching*. Cassell, London

McLaughlin M 1993 What matters most in teachers' workplace context? In: Little J W, McLaughlin M (eds.) 1993 *Cultures and Contexts of Teaching*. Teachers College Press, New York

Metz M 1990 How social class differences shape teachers' work. In: McLaughlin M, Talbert J, Basia N (eds.) 1990 *The Contexts of Teaching in Secondary Schools: Teachers' Realities*. Teachers College Press, New York

Neufeld J 1991 Curriculum reform and the time of care. *Curric. J.* 2(3): 283–300

Nias J 1989 *Primary Teachers Talking*. Routledge and Kegan Paul, London

Nias J 1991 Changing times, changing identities: Grieving for a lost self. In Burgess R (ed.) 1991 *Educational Research and Evaluation: For Policy and Practice?* Falmer Press, London

Oakes J 1985 *Keeping Track: How Schools Structure Inequality*. Yale University Press, New Haven, Connecticut

Rosenholtz S 1989 *Teachers' Workplace: The Social Organization of Schools*. Longman, New York

Sarason S 1990 *The Predictable Failure of School Reform*. Jossey-Bass, San Francisco, California

Stoddart T 1991 Learning to teach English and mathematics in an alternative route to certification. *Curric. J.* 2(3): 259–81

Woods P 1981 Strategies, commitment and identity: Making and breaking the teacher role. In: Barton L, Walker S (eds.) 1981 *Schools, Teachers, and Teaching*. Falmer Press, London

Teaching, Social Status

E. Hoyle

Social status of teaching refers to the relative standing of teaching as an occupation in a hierarchy of all occupations. This entry begins with an exploration of the concepts of occupational status and prestige. Next, the place of teaching within the occupational hierarchies of different societies as indicated by studies of occupational prestige will be described. The final three sections will consider explanations which account for the relative prestige of teaching.

1. Concepts of Status and Prestige

The terms "status," "prestige," and "esteem" are used synonymously in everyday language and very often in the sociological literature. They are also given different connotations by individual sociologists. However, as there are inconsistencies in these various usages the connotations to be used in this entry can be briefly outlined.

The social status of an individual—the degree to which he or she is accorded deference—is determined by a number of factors including wealth, education, gender, ethnicity, and life-style. However, in most developed and developing societies the major determinant of status is held to be occupation. Although a number of personal factors may shape the esteem in which individuals are held in their community—including, for example, how well a teacher is regarded as doing his or her job in school and in making a wider contribution to the community—these factors are less significant than membership in an occupation.

Occupational status is the regard in which an occupation is held in comparison with other occupations. Thus, occupational status turns upon the image of an occupation held by other members of society. To establish the nature of an occupational image, and hence status, is difficult. One can analyse natural speech about an occupation, examine how it is represented in the media, or use a variety of other means. By far the most sophisticated study in methodological terms has been carried out by Coxon and Jones (1978, 1979).

The term "occupational prestige" is widely used to refer to the outcome of studies in which people are asked to rate sets of occupations according to some criterion of "higher" or "lower" and a rank order of occupations is produced. Well over a hundred such studies have been undertaken worldwide. The occu-

717

pational lists have varied in size and content. The samples undertaking the ranking also have varied as have the instructions given to them.

"Schoolteaching" has appeared on virtually all the studies undertaken within this mode. Sometimes it has appeared as a single occupation, but other studies have subdivided it. One of the earliest studies of occupational prestige, undertaken specifically to determine the prestige of teaching, differentiated between primary and secondary teachers (Counts 1925). Most modern studies include hundreds of occupational titles in rank order—usually extrapolated from smaller samples of personal rankings—and differentiate not only between categories of teacher but also categories of principal. However, this entry, except where indicated, will focus on the general category of teacher.

2. The Occupational Prestige of Teaching

A number of studies have undertaken international comparisons of occupational prestige (e.g., Hodge et al. 1966) and have consistently demonstrated a high degree of correlation between occupational hierarchies despite variations in geographical location, stage of economic development, and point in time at which the study was undertaken. The most detailed analysis of these studies was carried out by Treiman (1977) who reviewed 85 studies carried out in 53 countries. The median correlation across studies was 0.81. Although the correlation is high, some studies show considerable variation by country, by region, and by characteristics of respondents.

He converted these findings into a single scale: the Standard International Occupational Prestige Score (SIOPS). Table 1 locates several teaching categories on the SIOPS continuum.

Data on the occupational prestige of teaching using SIOPS and other scales permit the following generalizations:

(a) Teaching is high in the range of all occupations.

(b) Teaching is relatively high within the group of public and personal service professions (e.g., nursing, social work, and police).

(c) Teaching is higher than that of skilled manual and white-collar occupations.

(d) Teaching is lower than that of the major professions, (e.g., medicine, law, and architecture).

Within the teaching profession as a whole:

(a) Principals are ranked more highly than classroom teachers.

(b) The rank order of teachers from high to low

Table 1

Twenty selected occupations from the Standard International Occupational Prestige Scale

	Scale score	Rank order
Judge	78	1=
Physician	78	1=
University professor	78	1=
Architect	72	4
Dentist	70	5
Physiotherapist	67	6
Airline pilot	66	7=
Middle-rank civil servant	66	7=
Electrical engineer	65	9
High school teacher	64	10=
Pharmacist	64	10=
Minister of religion	60	12
Surveyor	58	13
Primary school teacher	57	14
Social worker	56	15
Nurse	54	16
Actor	52	17
Preprimary school teacher	49	18=
Real estate agent	49	18=
Police officer	40	20

Source: Treiman (1977)

is: college, secondary school, elementary school, infant, and preschool (Bernbaum et al. 1969).

Variations in occupational prestige ratings require explanations in terms of cultural differences, whereas more general explanations are required in order to account for the relative consistency of the occupational prestige ratings over time and location. Three explanations are offered below, although they are not necessarily independent of one another.

3. The Social Functions of Teaching

The general form of this explanation is that occupational prestige is a reflection of the importance of the contribution to the well-being of society. This explanation is often termed the "functionalist" position. Treiman (1977), who uses the term "structuralist" for the same perspective, wrote that "the relative prestige of the social roles known as occupations is essentially invariant in all complex societies and that this must be so as a consequence of the inherent features of the division of labor as it exists in all societies" (p. 2). The implication is that those who fulfill key functions have knowledge, skill, power, privilege, and prestige.

There are, however, a number of arguments against this position. One alternative view is that the high prestige enjoyed by the professions owes more to their success in creating a market for a scarce resource and using the power thereby achieved to limit entry

(Larson 1977). Of course, the high correlations in prestige over time and location behove critics of the structural functionalist position to explain the consistency in the historical emergence of professional power.

The position of teaching below the major professions in the prestige hierarchy requires a critical look at the functionalist argument. There can be little doubt that education is a crucial social function in developed and developing societies. Teaching provides the transmission of the knowledge and skills required to sustain and enhance the quality of life in such societies. On this view, the functionalist argument appears less cogent than the argument that teaching has been unable to generate the power enjoyed by the major professions. There are two related reasons why this lack of power exists: the social characteristics of teachers, and the inherent nature of teaching as a professional activity.

4. The Social Characteristics of Teaching

A major barrier to enhanced status stems from the fact that teaching is by far the largest profession. Because the profession is so large, the total salary bill is high and thus individual salaries are depressed below those obtained in other professions. Moreover, because large numbers of teachers have constantly to be recruited, the status-bestowing characteristics of those recruited tend to be lower than those recruited to the major professions. The most important of these characteristics are social class background, gender, and academic achievement.

4.1 Social Class Background

The social class background of teachers is, on average, lower than that of entrants to the major professions and it is argued that this lower class background has a deleterious influence on status. However, apart from this broad generalization, reliable statements about the social class backgrounds of teachers are difficult to make, particularly as they have changed over time. Relatively few studies exist and they have mostly been undertaken in advanced societies. Moreover, relatively few studies (see Betz and Garland 1974 for an exception) take account of changes in the occupational structure over time. In industrialized societies, for example, there has been a shift from skilled craft occupations to technical service and quasiprofessional occupations.

As a very broad generalization relating to developed countries, one could say that teachers are recruited from the full range of social classes but with an underrepresentation from the highest and lowest social groups and with the modal background of all teachers increasing over time. Furthermore, women teachers come from a slightly higher social class background than men, and teachers in secondary schools come from a slightly higher social class background than those in elementary schools. These last two generalizations would at first seem to be incompatible since elementary schools tend to contain the highest proportion of women. Where detailed data exist, however, they show that the anomaly can be explained by the fact that the higher proportion of women in primary schools is offset by the considerably higher social class origins of both men and women in secondary schools.

Available data would indicate that there has been an increase in the social class background of teachers since the 1940s (Havighurst and Levine 1979, Bassett 1958, 1971). In Britain before the Second World War, for example, there were differences in social class backgrounds of teachers in the elementary schools and those in the highly selective secondary schools. However, in the postwar period, with the creation of secondary education for all, there was a degree of convergence between the social class background of teachers in the increasingly integrated system (Floud and Scott 1961). This trend has continued with the comprehensivization of secondary education.

4.2 Gender

The factor of gender functions relatively independently of social class background in the determination of the occupational prestige of teaching. There is a view that the relatively high proportion of women in teaching is detrimental to its social status because of the patriarchal attitudes which persist in many societies. However, whether or not this view is correct is difficult to demonstrate. One can only note that professions with a relatively low proportion of women (e.g., medicine and law) enjoy a higher occupational prestige than those with a relatively high proportion (e.g., teaching, nursing, and social work).

Because women tend to predominate in teaching in all societies one cannot deploy comparative data to test the proposition. One can note, however, that medicine enjoys a higher social status in the West than in the former Soviet Union where women predominate in the medical profession. As noted above, the prestige of primary school teachers, who are predominantly women, is lower than that for secondary school teachers, who are predominantly men. However, the relationship between gender and prestige is quite complex, involving both cultural and economic factors.

4.3 Academic Achievement

The academic achievements of teachers at all school levels is considerably higher than population averages. Nevertheless, the academic achievements of those who enter teaching is generally lower than those who enter the major professions. In the United Kingdom, for example, those entering Bachelor of Education (BEd) courses in colleges of education and polytechnics have lower school attainments than those entering BA and BS courses in universities. Furthermore, those who enter the one-year teacher training course in universities following their BA and BS degrees tend to have lower achievements (and come from slightly lower social class backgrounds) than those who enter other occupations (see Committee on Higher Education 1963).

5. The Nature of Teaching as an Activity

Class, gender, and academic achievement have been selected to indicate the characteristics of teachers which may help to determine their social status. However, although the data indicate social differences between those who enter teaching and those who enter other professions, these differences are not great and are perhaps diminishing. Moreover, as presented, the data imply a deficit model based on market forces and opportunity. Other determinants of teacher status are perhaps to be found in the nature of teaching as an occupational activity and the contexts in which teaching takes place.

Three factors inherent in teaching as an activity are related to the status of teaching. These factors are reviewed from the perspective of the lower standing of teaching vis-à-vis that of the major professions.

5.1 Knowledge and Skill

The knowledge and skills needed by teachers are regarded as being of a lower order than those required in the major professions. In this regard it is important to recognize that higher status generally is associated with specialization. This factor may account for the higher status of secondary school teachers relative to elementary and early childhood teachers. Furthermore, the uncertain relationship between educational and pedagogic theory, pedagogic practice, and learning outcomes detracts from its capacity to enhance its status.

5.2 Work Situation

The sustained relationship between teachers and pupils in an organized setting differs from the relatively infrequent contact which most professionals have with their clients in organizational settings or consultancy contexts. Thus, the work situation in which teachers find themselves may militate against the improved status of teaching.

5.3 Clients

Perhaps the most fundamental factor influencing the lower status of teaching vis-à-vis other professions is that teachers' immediate clients are children. In addition, virtually the entire adult population has had a sustained and direct experience of teachers at work. Thus, virtually everyone, to some extent, "accomplishes" schooling and leaves it behind as they leave behind their teachers. As Hoyle (1969) has noted, teachers are thus placed in an intermediate sta-

tus on a number of dimensions: childhood–adulthood ("A man amongst boys and a boy amongst men"), school–work ("Those who can, do, those who can't, teach"), moral idealism–moral realism (The school as "a museum of virtue," Waller 1965), the dissemination of knowledge–the creation of knowledge (The teacher as one who "spreads other people's butter," Geer 1966).

The fact that all have had the experience of schooling robs teaching of any status-enhancing mystique. Moreover, all have seen teachers constantly seeking to maintain control, a problem which is exacerbated where older pupils are in compulsory and often reluctant attendance. This image is powerful and does not apply to other major professions or "semi-professions" where client control is rarely an issue.

6. Conclusion

The occupational prestige of teachers lies in the upper reaches of all scales. The social background of teachers tends to be clustered around the center, suggesting that teaching represents upward social mobility, to some degree, for many. Teachers' educational qualifications are in the upper reaches of the distribution, as is their remuneration. Insofar as teacher status is regarded as "low," this statement can be made only in comparison with the major professions. In this regard there would seem to be limits to the degree to which teachers might enhance their status. These limits stem ultimately from the size of the profession and images of teachers and their work. Despite the high correlations between teachers' prestige ratings across countries, however, there are intercountry variations to indicate that the status of teaching is not wholly immutable.

See also: Sociology of Teaching; Teacher Recruitment and Induction; Teachers' Knowledge; Teachers' Work and Political Action

References

Bassett G W, 1958 The occupational background of teachers. *Aust. J. Educ.* 2: 79–90
Bassett G W 1971 The occupational background of teachers: Some recent data. *Aust. J. Educ.* 15: 211–14
Bernbaum G, Noble G, Whiteside T 1969 Intra occupational prestige differentiation in teaching. *Paedag. Eur.* 5: 1–59
Betz M, Garland J 1974 Intergenerational mobility rates of urban school teachers. *Soc. Educ.* 47: 511–22
Committee on Higher Education 1963 *Administrative, Financial and Economic Aspects of Higher Education* (Robbins Report), Appendix 2B. HMSO, London
Counts F A 1925 The social status of occupations. *Sch. Rev.* 33: 20–21
Coxon A P M, Jones C L 1978 *The Images of Occupational Prestige.* Macmillan, London

Coxon A P M, Jones C L 1979 *Class and Hierarchy: The Social Meaning of Occupations.* Macmillan, London

Floud J, Scott W 1961 Recruitment to teaching in England and Wales. In: Halsey A H, Floud J, Anderson C A (eds.) 1961 *Education, Economy and Society: A Reader in the Sociology of Education.* Free Press, New York

Geer B 1966 Occupational commitment and the teaching profession. *Sch. Rev.* 77(1): 31–47

Havighurst R J, Levine D U 1979 *Society and Education*, 5th edn. Allyn and Bacon, Boston, Massachusetts

Hodge R W, Treiman D J, Rossi P 1966 A comparative study of occupational prestige. In: Bendix R, Lipset S M (eds.) 1966 *Class, Status and Power: Social Stratification in Comparative Perspective,* 2nd edn. Free Press, New York

Hoyle E 1969 *The Role of the Teacher.* Routledge, London

Larson M 1977 *The Rise of Professionalism.* University of California Press, Berkeley, California

Treiman D J 1977 *Occupational Prestige in Comparative Perspective.* Academic Press, New York

Waller W 1965 *The Sociology of Teaching.* Wiley, New York

Women and the Professionalization of Teaching

K. A. Weiler

Contemporary proposals for school reform frequently include the demand that teaching be made more of a profession. The call for "professionalization" includes a demand for greater respect for teachers, but it also follows a model taken from such male dominated professions as medicine and law. Implicit in these calls for the greater professionalization of teaching are conceptions of hierarchy, competition, and rationalization that have raised concerns among feminist educators.

1. Historical Development of Professionalism

The concept of the professional developed in the late nineteenth century with the founding of associations to oversee and set standards of competence for a variety of occupations, and with the passage of licensing laws by the state. Medicine, law, and dentistry, for example, all became regularized and organized by both the state and their own associations. This conception of professionalism as it developed in the late nineteenth and early twentieth century was of a rational, orderly body of knowledge mastered by the specialist, the professional, who could be trusted by clients and the society at large to make decisions and act in the best interests of clients. The professional was an expert and, as such, entitled to both interpret and control social relationships.

This early twentieth century view of professionalism as the rational employment of advanced knowledge for the common good continues to be accepted unproblematically in many discussions of professionalization. A more critical approach has emerged, however, that views professionalism as an ideology, and as a means to police and control populations and to justify power and privilege for professionals as a "new class" (Bledstein 1976, Larson 1977). Feminist analyses of professionalism have focused on the class, gender, and racial bias of the ideal of the professional. Liberal feminist studies of professionalism have focused on the attempts of women to enter the professions and on the discrimination women faced and continue to face, emphasizing the intersection of conceptions of gender and professional ideas of "merit" and "competence" (Epstein 1970). As Glazer and Slater (1987) put it:

> In men, the drive for success was lauded as healthy ambition; in women, it was disdained as unfeminine . . . Certain men were seen as natural leaders; in women, leadership was always unnatural, especially if it meant supervising men. These attitudes were not easily compartmentalized. They permeated all areas of professional life and had a direct bearing on advancement, which itself depended on continual assessment and evaluation during training and beyond. (p. 12)

The most developed feminist critique of the concept of professionalism has come from a number of sociologists and historians who have studied nursing. Melosh (1982 p. 5), in her study of the history of nursing, argues that the concept of professionalism obscures the realities of what she calls "occupational culture." She argues that it is this cultural knowledge, "constructed from workers' accumulated experiences and their understandings of the work place . . . that guides and interprets the tasks and social relations of work." A similar line of argument has been put forward in feminist analyses of teaching as women's work.

2. Teaching and Professionalization

While professionalization and the ideological nature of the concept of the professional have been explored by historians and sociologists, in educational studies and policy statements the ideal of professionalism has tended to be accepted uncritically. Both sociologists of education and educational policymakers have accepted a hierarchy of occupations, with professionals at the top, as "natural" in contemporary societies.

This perspective derives from functionalist sociology and from the "common sense" view that the social world we observe is both natural and inevitable. The debate in education has concerned the location of teachers within an existing hierarchy of occupations, focusing on whether teachers are in fact professionals and whether they should strive for professional status. The articles in Etzioni's influential collection, *The Semi-Professions and Their Organization* (1969), for example, locate teaching with nursing and social work as "semi-professions," with less autonomy, privilege, and status than the established professions such as law or medicine. Etzioni points out that most of these occupations are filled by women, and therefore women's subordinate place in society is transferred to their jobs. This results in their never attaining the status of the "true" professions. Etzioni insists that he does not mean to be "prejudiced against a most attractive minority" but is simply reporting the facts (1969 p. viii). A similar line of analysis is found in the influential work of Lortie (1975). Both Lortie and Etzioni accept existing definitions of what it means to be a professional, and dispassionately note the ways in which teaching fails to meet these standards of elite knowledge and autonomy, in large part because most teachers are women.

The same uncritical acceptance of the concept of professionalism underlies the many education reports of the 1980s that emerged in industrialized countries such as the United States, the United Kingdom, Australia, and New Zealand. In the United States, both the Carnegie Report (1986) and the report of the Holmes Group (1987) have proposed the creation of more stringent certification requirements, merit pay, and a greater differentiation among teachers who have demonstrated "excellence." The Carnegie Report, for example, proposes that schools should be organized as hierarchies, with "lead teachers" who would achieve this position by sitting for a national examination and through seniority, and who would have greater pay and responsibility. A similar proposal has been put forward in Australia for the introduction of "advanced skill teachers." These reform proposals take for granted the desirability of following a model of professionalism taken from existing professional groups such as medicine or law.

The acceptance of professionalization as the most desirable model for teaching has not escaped criticism. Practicing teachers, while desirous of greater public recognition of the value of their work and certainly sympathetic to higher pay, have been suspicious of the schemes to create "lead teachers," "master teachers," or merit pay. Critics have noted the lack of clarity in what actually defines a "master teacher" and the emphasis on hierarchy and competition inherent in such schemes. They have also noted that schemes for the differentiation of teaching staffs and the creation of career ladders will in fact leave most teachers with even less autonomy and collective involvement in decisions about curriculum, pedagogy, and the organization of their workplace than they have in existing schools. At the same time that professionalization is trumpeted as necessary for the reform of education, the movement toward the deskilling of teachers through the introduction of prepackaged "teacher-proof" curricula, the increased reliance on standardized tests, and the continued call for expert control over the work of classroom teachers has strengthened a view of teachers as employees who require supervision and direction (Apple 1988, Densmore 1987).

3. "Professionalization" of Teaching: Feminist Critiques

Feminist scholars have expanded the critique of professionalism as ideology to consider what is implied when teaching is termed "women's work." While some liberal feminist educators have essentially accepted the idea of professionalization of teaching as desirable, and have argued that women teachers should be included in the professionalization of education, a growing number of feminist scholars in education have challenged the idea of professionalism itself.

3.1 Historical Genesis of Teaching as Women's Work

Teaching, particularly elementary school teaching, has been defined as "women's work" in most industrialized countries since the formation of state supported compulsory schooling in the late nineteenth and early twentieth centuries. The economic common sense behind hiring educated women, for whom there was virtually no other paid work available, was evident. Women teachers were cheap. An ideological defense of women teachers emerged at the same time, put forward in the mid-nineteenth century in the United States by such figures as Horace Mann and Catherine Beecher, which redefined teaching, in Beecher's famous phrase, as "women's true profession," because it called upon the virtues of compassion and nurturance that were the essence of womanly and motherly natures (Hoffman 1981). This use of the term "profession," of course, should be read with some caution, since both Beecher and Mann envisioned teaching as a brief period of an educated woman's life between her position as a daughter in her father's household and as wife in her future husband's household. This was hardly the concept of "professional" as applied to the male-dominated spheres of medicine and law.

By the end of the nineteenth century, with the rise of the first wave of feminism, an increasing number of women began to remain in teaching for much longer periods. With gains in women's higher education, more of these committed teachers rose to become principals and, in rural areas, county and even state superintendents of education. The numerical dominance of women teachers, along with the growing numbers of women teachers and administrators who made teaching a lifelong career, led to the "woman peril" panic of the early twentieth century, in which male educators argued that teaching was becoming "feminized," and that there was a desperate need to bring more men into teaching to make it more scientific and "professional." This vision of the educational professional emphasized scientific measurement and control; the nurturant and expressive work of women classroom teachers was ignored or rejected as unscientific. In the post-Second World War period, women were pushed out of most administrative positions in education and a model of schools staffed by women teachers and led by male administrators emerged, and in most cases continues to the present day.

3.2 Feminist Theories of Women's Psychology and Epistemology

One influential body of work with implications for a feminist critique of professionalism has emerged from developmental psychology, in particular the work of Gilligan (1982) and the jointly authored work of Belenky et al. (1986). These feminist psychologists claim to have identified a particular "women's way of knowing." In her studies of the moral development of young women, Gilligan has argued that girls and women hold different attitudes toward moral questions than do young men: boys and men base their statements on an abstract morality of rights, while girls and women make judgments from a contextual morality of responsibility and caring. Belenky et al. (1986) came to similar conclusions in their study of cognitive development. This approach applied to the work of women teachers can be seen in the work of Grumet (1988) and Pagano (1990) who have argued that teaching for women is similar to the emotional work of mothering.

A similar line of analysis can be found in the work of feminist philosophers like Noddings (1984, 1992) and Martin (1985). Martin, in her study of philosophies of women's education, argues that a fully developed conception of teaching should include the whole person, not just the abstract intellect, and that the traditionally "feminine" qualities of nurturance and caring are central. Noddings, a moral philosopher, proposes a feminist ethic based on caring. Like Grumet, she argues that nurturance and caring are essential to human relationships and to human society; these ideals should be acknowledged and celebrated as essential to relationships both in the family and public world. Her vision of teaching is modeled on the caring relationship of mother and child, not on the mastery and transmission of abstract knowledge. In this analysis, she defines professionalization as implying an elite knowledge and special language that separates teachers and administrators in schools from families and members of the community. It is an orientation "characterized by hierarchy, specialty, separation, objectification, and the loss of relation" (Noddings 1984 p. 200). Noddings (1984 p. 192) thus sees professionalization as a masculine project, "designed to detach the child from the world of relation and project him, as object, into

a thoroughly objectified world." In place of the model of bureaucratic schools dominated by professionals, Noddings proposes an image of circles and chains, in which parents, teachers, and members of the community would share decision-making and create a caring world in which children could learn and grow.

These feminist critiques have presented powerful challenges to the ideology of professionalism. However, they have also raised criticisms from other feminist educators: first, that these approaches have tended to universalize women and thus have ignored differences among women such as race, ethnicity, language, class, sexuality, and so forth; second, that they tend toward essentialism, in that they seem to imply that women and men have different "natures." The danger here is in accepting the earlier male view that it is part of the essential and universal nature of men to be rational and of women to be emotional.

3.3 The Feminist Analysis of Teaching as Work

Another line of feminist critique of the concept of professionalism emerges from the materialist analysis of teaching as work. This approach, similar to Smith's (1987) sociological analysis of the invisible work that maintains "everyday" reality, examines the kinds of relationships and activities that actually shape the work of teachers in classrooms. These analyses note the dangers of a feminist essentialism that echoes nineteenth-century conceptions of women as natural nurturers. Laird (1988 p. 461), for example, in her analysis of the current education reform reports in the United States, argues for the intellectual validity and strengths of a feminist pedagogy that would build on the kind of caring work women have traditionally done in schools and elsewhere, while acknowledging the dangers of a "subordinate and domesticated maternalism." Thus Laird argues for the deconstruction of the ideology of "woman's true profession" while calling for a recognition of the significance of the kinds of affective and caring work teachers have always done.

A more specific analysis of the effects of the ideology of professionalism on women teachers can be found in Freedman (1990) and Biklen (1995). Freedman points to the historic exclusivity of the White male-dominated professions and in particular, the distance such professionals have sought to maintain between themselves and their clients. Echoing Noddings, Freedman asks what the effect of such a model of professionalism will mean for the relationship of parents (which, as she points out, means mothers) and teachers. Like Noddings, Grumet, Laird, and others, Freedman argues for the essential role of caring and nurturing in the work of teachers. But she makes explicit the historical and social construction of this emotional work as women's work. Freedman argues that in place of the current model of the professional, teachers should demand changes in the organization of schools that would make the best teaching possible for all teachers, not just an elite. Biklen (1995) has argued

723

that teaching should be restructured to provide more autonomy and better pay and working conditions, but rejects the conventional model of professionalism as the source for these changes. As she points out, the hierarchical nature of most proposals for the professionalization of teaching assume relationships of subordination and exclusion that will create a climate of competition and privilege antithetical to a society based on collectivity and caring.

4. Conclusion

Feminist critics have viewed professionalism as a historical and social construct shaped by male-defined conceptions of elite knowledge as quantifiable, objective, and abstract. They have highlighted the family ideology that underlies the ideology of professionalism; they point out that the "professional" is in fact an autonomous man, with no domestic or familial obligations, who can depend on the emotional, affective work of women at work as well as in his home. Such feminist critiques challenge, either directly or implicitly, the underlying assumptions about knowledge that underlie mainstream discussions of professionalism in education. They emphasize the significance of compassion and caring in teaching and point to the need for the consideration of questions of power and material privilege that underlie claims to the need for "expert" professional control of education. Feminist critics have argued for respect and support for a vision of teaching that acknowledges the nurturance and caring traditionally provided by women. Although they recognize the appeal of the idea of professionalism for women whose work has been defined as subordinate and "unscientific," they also emphasize the dangers of simply adopting a male model of professionalism. They have argued instead for a "feminist professionalism," which would incorporate familial and child-caring responsibilities into the structure of work; democratize the school as a workplace, emphasizing community rather than autonomy as the ideal for teachers; and insist on the value of children for the whole society and thus raise the status and pay for those who teach.

See also: Feminist Approaches to the Curriculum; Gender and Education; Professional Socialization of Teachers

References

Apple M 1988 *Teachers and Texts: A Political Economy of Class and Gender Relations in Education.* Routledge, New York

Belenky M, Clinchy B, Goldberger N, Tarule J 1986 *Women's Ways of Knowing: The Development of Self, Voice and Mind.* Basic Books, New York

Biklen S K 1995 *School Work.* Teachers College Press, New York

Bledstein B 1976 *The Culture of Professionalism: The Middle Class and the Development of Higher Education in America.* W W Norton, New York

Carnegie Task Force on Teaching as a Profession 1986 *A Nation Prepared: Teachers for the 21st Century.* The Carnegie Foundation, New York

Densmore K 1987 Professionalism, proletarianization and teacher work. In: Popkewitz T (ed.) 1987 *Critical Studies in Teacher Education: Its Folklore, Theory and Practice.* Falmer Press, London

Epstein C 1970 *Woman's Place: Options and Limits in Professional Careers.* University of California Press, Berkeley, California

Etzioni A 1969 *The Semi-Professions and their Organization: Teachers, Nurses, Social Workers.* Free Press, New York

Freedman S 1990 Weeding women out of 'woman's true profession': The effects of the reforms on teaching and teachers. In: Biklen S, Antler J (eds.) *Changing Education. Women and Radicals and Conservators.* State University of New York Press, Albany, New York

Gilligan C 1982 *In a Different Voice.* Harvard University Press, Cambridge, Massachusetts

Glazer M, Slater M 1987 *Unequal Colleagues: The Entrance of Women into the Professions, 1890–1940.* Rutgers University Press, New Brunswick, New Jersey

Grumet M 1988 *Bitter Milk: Women and Teaching.* University of Massachusetts Press, Amherst, Massachusetts

Hoffman N 1981 *Woman's 'True' Profession: Voices from the History of Teaching.* Feminist Press, Old Westbury, New York

Holmes Group 1987 *Tomorrow's Teachers.* Holmes Group, East Lansing, Michigan

Laird S 1988 Reforming 'Woman's true profession': A case for "feminist pedagogy in teacher education?" *Harv. Educ. Rev.* 58(4): 449–63

Larson M 1977 *The Rise of Professionalism: A Sociological Analysis.* University of California Press, Berkeley, California

Lortie D 1975 *Schoolteacher.* University of Chicago Press, Chicago, Illinois

Martin J 1985 *Reclaiming a Conversation: The Ideal of the Educated Woman.* Yale University Press, New Haven, Connecticut

Melosh B 1982 *The Physician's Hand: Work Culture and Conflict in American Nursing.* Temple University Press, Philadelphia, Pennsylvania

Noddings N 1984 *Caring: A Feminine Approach to Ethics and Moral Education.* University of California Press, Berkeley, California

Noddings N 1992 *The Challenge to Care in Schools: An Alternative Approach to Education.* Teachers College Press, New York

Pagano J 1990 *Exiles and Communities: Teaching in the Patriarchal Wilderness.* State University of New York Press, Albany, New York

Smith D 1987 *The Everyday World as Problematic: A Feminist Sociology.* Northeastern University Press, Boston, Massachusetts

Further Reading

Acker S 1994 *Gendered Education.* Open University Press, London

Arnot M, Weiler K 1993 *Feminism and Social Justice in Education.* Falmer Press, London

Connell R W 1985 *Teacher's Work*. Allen and Unwin, Sydney

Freedman S, Jackson J, Boles K 1988 The other end of the corridor: The effect of teaching on teachers. In: Smythe J (ed.) 1988 *A "Critical Pedagogy" of Teacher Evaluation*. Deakin University Press, Deakin

Haskell T 1984 *The Authority of Experts*. Indiana University Press, Bloomington, Indiana

Kelly G 1989 *International Handbook of Women's Education*. Greenwood Press, New York

Lawn M, Grace G 1987 *Teachers: The Culture and Politics of Work*. Falmer Press, London

Middleton S 1993 *Educating Feminists*. Teachers College Press, New York

SECTION IX

Youth in Schools

Introduction: Youth and Schooling in Modern Society

L. J. Saha

The sociological study of youth is broader than that of secondary school students, even though the age categories overlap. The study of school students focuses primarily on the educational context, while the study of youth is much more broad, and includes life outside of school. As social categories, childhood, adolescence, and youth overlap somewhat. Childhood is generally regarded as that period which extends from infancy to the onset of puberty, that is about 12 or 13 years of age. Adolescence is generally defined as the period when a person's biological, psychological, and social characteristics are changing from childhood to adulthood.

While the notion of youth is somewhat problematic, the age group 15–19 years is generally thought to incorporate this social category, and therefore overlaps somewhat with the notion of adolescence. What is important is that all three of these social categories exist independently of education and schooling. Therefore, the study of youth incorporates life outside the school and includes topics related to leisure and pastime activities, peer groups in and outside of school, and youth employment, both full- and part-time. In spite of their independence from schooling, obviously much of what goes on outside of schools has an impact on, or is affected by, what goes on inside of schools.

The 11 articles in this section focus on aspects of childhood, adolescence, and the period of the life-cycle normally referred to as "youth." These articles focus particularly on the social and educationally-relevant activities in and out of schooling which are conventionally related to youth. Three articles relate to the characteristics of childhood and adolescence, four relate directly to youth and schooling, and the final four relate to aspects of youth not directly related to schooling.

In order to clearly conceptualize the period of adolescence and youth, Bjorklund and Cassel's article *Childhood* identifies the sometimes difficult boundary between childhood and adolescence. Many of the physical changes and social and emotional developments during childhood overlap with and extend into adolescence, and indeed affect the continuing developments in the later age period. The article by Lerner and Villarruel (*Adolescence*) describes the period of social and emotional development from childhood through adolescence. The authors identify a number of problems commonly associated with adolescence, ranging from problems with parents, sexuality, and the illicit use of drugs. Another characteristic of children and youth which impinges on school and out-of-school behavior is that of aggression. Perry (*Aggression, Development and Socialization*) reviews the literature on the biological bases and socialization influences on the development of aggression, and relates these to possible intervention strategies. These complexities of adolescence cannot be ignored in sociological studies of education, in particular those relating to teacher and student behavior. Violence in schools, in particular, is a subject of considerable importance and relates directly to the characteristics of adolescence.

The four articles relating youth to schooling are those by McCarthy and Peterson (*Student Roles in Classrooms*), Fraser (*Student Perceptions of Classrooms*), Bank (*Youth Friendships and Conflict in Schools*), and Altbach (*Student Political Activism and Student Movements*). McCarthy and Peterson, and Fraser focus on understandings about what goes on in classrooms. As McCarthy and Peterson point out, educational researchers previously concentrated on characteristics of teacher–student interaction in the classroom, but more recently have concentrated on understandings of what goes on in classrooms (the meanings which the participants attribute to classroom interaction) and the culture of the classroom. Fraser describes attempts to measure these understandings, and in particular how these understandings affect the learning environment.

Bank's article on *Youth Friendships and Conflict in Schools* focuses on the importance of friendship formation and its positive and negative consequences in schools. Of particular importance in this regard concerns the effects that friendships can have on learning. Finally, Bank demonstrates how conflict between youth both in and out of school may be a function of friendship maintenance. Altbach's article on *Student Political Activism and Student Movements* discusses those aspects of student culture which explain why some students become members of movements and many do not. While most student political activism takes place among university students, the possible link between secondary school experiences and future activism has yet to be thoroughly explored.

Obviously young people spend a large part of their social lives outside of schools. These activities largely take place within youth cultures and subcultures which set the behaviors of young people apart from that of the adult social world. Wilson (*Youth Cultures and Subcultures*) surveys the literature which documents the influence of youth cultures and subcultures in a range of settings, including the school and leisure activities. Of particular interest to social researchers has been the strength of deviant subcultures which often are resistant to the goals of schooling. Biddle (*Youth and Leisure*) provides further detail about the leisure activities of youth, including the residual nature of leisure activities (that is, activities not associated with school or work) and the commercialization of leisure activities. One important part of the leisure activity of youth is the media, both radio and television. The impact of the media on a wide range of youth behaviors is discussed in Comstock's article *Broadcasting and Technology: Effects on Children and Youth*.

Many of the concerns found in discussions of the nonschool behavior of youth are related to Lamoure's article *Youth Unemployment*, which explores the link between school and unemployment in modern societies. Lamoure discusses the social amd psychological consequences of youth unemployment and some policy measures which might help remedy its negative impact.

As the articles in this section make clear, youth represents a major component of all modern societies who live in a distinct biological, social, and psychological world. The sociological study of education cannot ignore the wider context of this world in the endeavor to understand the complexities of education itself. This complex world of youth has a major impact on what goes on in schools, both for individual students as well as for teachers, for classrooms, and for the climate of schools as well.

Adolescence

R. M. Lerner and F. A. Villarruel

In this article the characteristics of development in the adolescent period, that is, the second decade of life, are discussed. Adolescence may be defined as the period within the lifespan when most of a person's biological, psychological, and social characteristics are changing from what is considered childlike to what is considered adult. For the adolescent—the person experiencing this set of transitions—this period is a dramatic challenge, one requiring adjustment to changes in the self, in the family, and the peer group. In many societies, adolescents typically experience institutional changes as well, such as a change in school setting, or a transition from school to either the world of work or to college. For both adolescents and their parents, adolescence is a time of excitement and of anxiety, of happiness and of troubles, of discovery and of bewilderment, of breaks with the past and yet of continuations of childhood behavior.

Adolescence is a period about which much has been written, but until the 1970s, little was known. Until the 1970s when medical, biological, and social scientists began intensive studies of the adolescent period, there was relatively little sound scientific information available to verify or refute the romantic, literary characteristics of adolescence typical of the older literature. In the early 1990s, however, such information does exist, and it is not consistent with the idea that early adolescence is necessarily a stormy and stressful period.

Unfortunately, however, there is a major limitation in the status of the contemporary scientific literature about adolescent development. Most studies in the literature have involved the study of European or United States middle-class samples. There are only a few high-quality investigations that have studied adolescents from natural or cultural settings outside North America or Europe.

1. Key Generalizations about Adolescent Development

In the early 1990s, there is an increasingly more voluminous and sophisticated scientific literature about adolescence. The aforementioned limitations of this literature notwithstanding, it is possible to indicate several key generalizations that may be made about this period of life.

1.1 Multiple Levels of Context are Influential During Adolescence

Individual differences in adolescent development may be found throughout the world, involving different combinations of biological, psychological, and societal factors; no single influence (e.g., biology) acts alone or as the "prime mover" of change (Brooks-Gunn and Petersen 1983, Lerner 1987, Lerner and Foch 1987, Petersen 1988).

Accordingly, although adolescence is a period of extremely rapid transitions in such characteristics as height, weight, and body proportions (apart from infancy no other period of the life cycle involves such rapid changes) and although hormonal changes are part of the development of early adolescence, hormones are not primarily responsible for psychological or social developments taking place during this period (Petersen and Taylor 1980). The quality and timing of hormonal or other biological changes influence and are influenced by psychological, social, cultural, and historical factors (Elder 1980, Stattin and Magnusson 1990, Tanner 1991).

Global and pervasive effects of puberty do not seem to exist. When biological effects are found they interact with contextual and experiential factors (Stattin and Magnusson 1990). Accordingly, there is no evidence for general cognitive disruption over adolescence. Indeed, cognitive abilities increase over this period. Moreover pubertal timing is not predictive of gender differences on such tasks as spatial cognition. Girls' earlier maturation does not result in general sex differences in cognition (Graber and Petersen 1991).

1.2 Changing Relations Between Adolescents and Their Contexts Produce Development

The period of adolescence is one of continual change and transition between individuals and their contexts (Lerner 1987). These changing relations constitute the basic process of development in adolescence; they underlie both positive and negative outcomes during this period (Lerner 1984).

Accordingly, when the multiple biological, psychological, and sociocultural changes of adolescence occur simultaneously (e.g., when menarche occurs at the same time as a school transition), there is a greater risk of problems occuring in youth's development (Simmons and Blyth 1987). Indeed, in adolescence bad decisions (e.g., involving school, grades, sex, and drugs) have more negative consequences than in childhood, and the adolescent is more responsible for those consequences than in childhood (Petersen 1988). Nevertheless, most developmental trajectories across this period involve good adjustment on the part of the adolescent, and the continuation of positive parent–child relationships. Put simply, young adolescents are strongly tied to the family (e.g., Offer 1969).

Thus, adolescence is a good time for interventions involving the family. For instance, whereas minor parent–child conflicts (e.g., regarding chores and privileges) are normal in adolescence, major conflicts should be of concern to parents. However, the salience of the family in the adolescent period makes such conflicts an appropriate intervention target.

1.3 Individual Differences and Diversity

There are multiple pathways through adolescence. Inter-individual (between-person) and intra-individual (within-person) differences in development are the "rule" in this period of life.

Accordingly, there is diversity between and within each ethnic, racial, or cultural minority group. Therefore, general rules that confound class, race, and/or ethnicity do not apply (Lerner 1991). In regard to policies and programs, then, any intervention must be tailored to the specific target population, and in particular, to a group's developmental and environmental circumstances. However, because adolescents are so different from each other, no single policy or intervention can be expected to reach all of a given target population or to influence everyone in the same way.

Furthermore, normal adolescent development involves variability within the person as well as between people. Temperamental characteristics involving mood and activity level are good examples. There are differences among adolescents in such characteristics. In addition, individual adolescents may change over the course of their life in the quality of the temperament they manifest.

Thus, the breadth and depth of the high-quality scientific information available about development in adolescence underscores the diversity and dynamics of this period of life. The theoretically interesting and socially important changes of this period constitute one reason why the field of adolescence has attracted an increasing degree of scientific attention.

2. Biological Changes During Adolescence

The physical and physiological changes of adolescence typically span the second decade of life, involving early adolescence (around years 10–14 or 15), middle adolescence (years 15–17), and late adolescence (years 18–20). Within these stages of adolescence bodily and psychological changes do not proceed uniformly; however, a general sequence for these changes applies to most people (Katchadourian 1977, Tanner 1991).

It is useful to speak of phases of bodily changes in adolescence in order to draw important distinctions among various degrees and types of change. Bodily changes affect height, weight, fat and muscle distribution, glandular secretions, and sexual characteristics. When some of these exchanges have begun, but most are yet to occur, the person is said to be in the prepubescent phase (Schonfeld 1969). When most of those bodily changes that will eventually take place have been initiated, the person is in the pubescent phase. Finally, when most of those bodily changes have already occurred the person is in the postpubescent phase; this period ends when all bodily changes associated with adolescence are complete (Schonfeld 1969) (see *Childhood*).

2.1 Problems Associated with Pubertal Change

Although the sequence of the bodily changes of puberty is fairly uniform among individuals, there is considerable variation in the rate of change (Marshall and Tanner 1986). Some adolescents mature more rapidly or more slowly than their peers. Variations in the rate of bodily change in adolescence often affect psychological and social development.

For instance, delayed puberty and precocious puberty are related to insufficient production or the early production of hormones, respectively (Cutler 1991). Some physical problems may be known only to the adolescent initially. Painful menstruation, known as "dysmenorrhea," and the failure to menstruate, which is termed "amenorrhea," affect females and may have medical and/or emotional causes. Other physical disorders are externally noticeable: acne is an example of a problem which causes great concern to adolescents, since it is visible to others and is the most common disorder of medical significance during this period of life.

Moreover, because variations in height, weight, and muscle and fat distributions arise as a consequence of pubertal change, adolescents often become preoccupied with their own bodies (Lerner 1987). This focus is promoted by the character of thought processes during this period, and in some cases, adolescents' concerns with their own bodily changes can result in problems.

Moreover, the role of social context in shaping the behavioral effects of puberty helps explain why bodily changes among adolescents can also differ in relation to sociocultural and historical factors (e.g., Katchadourian 1977, Tanner 1991). The age of menarche, for example, varies among countries and even among different cultures within one country. Moreover, there has been a historical trend downward in the average age of menarche. Among European samples of youth there was a decrease of about four months per decade from about 1840 to about 1950 (Tanner 1991). This rate seems to have slowed down, but has not stopped (Marshall and Tanner 1986, Tanner 1991). Within United States samples, however, the decline in the age of menarche seems to have stopped about 1940; since that time 12.5 years has been the expected value for menarche among middle-class European–Americans. The most dramatic downward trend in the average age of menarche was evident in Japan. This trend in the average age of menarche is generally ascribed to the improved health and nutrition of children and adolescents, influences which are moderated by historical, cultural, and socioeconomic variables affecting a given society or group.

In sum, puberty both influences and is influenced by the adolescent's social world (the socioeconomic and nutritional characteristics of the nation, the family, the school, and peer group) and also by the other features of his or her development, such as cognitive changes (Elkind 1967, Keating 1991, Overton and Byrnes 1991).

3. Changes in the Social World of Adolescents

The adolescent's social world is broader and more complex than that of the infant and the child. The most notable social phenomenon of adolescence is the emergence of the marked importance of peer groups. The adolescent comes to rely heavily on the peer group for security and guidance; this is a time when such support is urgently needed, and perhaps only others undergoing the same transition can be relied upon to understand what is being experienced. Contrary to cultural stereotype, however, the family is also quite influential for adolescents (Steinberg 1991). It is useful to discuss, then, the relative influence of parents and peers in the development of adolescents.

3.1 The Influence of Parents and Peers

No social institution has a greater influence throughout development than the family. Most studies indicate that most adolescents have few, if any, serious disagreements with parents. Indeed, during adolescence very few families experience a major deterioration in the quality of the parent–child relationship (Steinberg 1991). Moreover, in choosing their peers, adolescents typically gravitate toward those who exhibit attitudes and values consistent with those maintained by the parents; these opinions are the beliefs ultimately adopted by the adolescents themselves (Guerney and Arthur 1983).

For instance, while peers affect adolescents in regard to such issues as educational aspirations and performance, in most cases there is convergence between family and peer influences. While it is the case that adolescents and parents have somewhat different attitudes about issues of contemporary social concern (e.g., politics, drug abuse, and sexuality), most of these differences reflect contrasts in the intensity of attitude rather than its direction. In other words, adolescents and parents are rarely diametrically opposed on a particular issue; rather, most generational differences simply involve different levels of support for the same position.

In sum, there is considerable diversity in the nature of parent–child relations in adolescence, and diversity related to the particular context within which youth and families develop. Whereas some of this diversity represents patterns of behavior that may be undesirable to both parents and their children (e.g., dropping out of school), for most youth there is a convergence between the attitudes and behaviors in which they engage and the views, desires, or expectations of their parents.

3.2 Pathways of Development Through Adolescence

Several studies have documented that, for most youth, adolescence is not a period of "storm and stress"; it is neither a period of wrenching oneself away from parents nor of frequent and inevitable problem behaviors.

For instance, Bandura (1964) observed that by adolescence most children had so thoroughly adopted parental values and standards that parental restrictions were actually reduced. In addition, Bandura noted that although the storm and stress idea of adolescence implies a struggle by youth to free themselves of dependence on parents, parents actually begin to train their children in childhood to be independent. Finally, Bandura found that the adolescent's choice of friends was not a major source of friction between adolescents and parents. Adolescents tended to form friendships with those who shared similar values. As such, the peers tended to support those standards of the parents that already had been adopted by the adolescents themselves.

Bandura points out, however that these observations do not mean that adolescence is an unstressful, problem-free period of life. Of course no period of life is devoid of crisis or adjustment problems, and any period of life may present particular adjustment problems for some people and not for others. Thus, caution must be exercised in attributing problems observed in one group of adolescents to all adolescents, or in generalizing from one culture to another.

From Bandura's (1964) study it may be concluded that: (a) even when storm and stress is seen in adolescence, it is not necessarily the result of events in adolescence, but instead may be associated with prior developments; and (b) storm and stress is not necessarily characteristic of the adolescent period: many possible types of adolescent development can occur.

The existence of such different paths through adolescence is supported by the results of other studies. Offer (1969) found three major routes through the adolescent period. He noted that there is a continuous-growth type of development that involves smooth changes in behavior. Young adolescents showing such development were not in any major conflict with their parents and did not feel either that parental rearing practices were inappropriate or that parental values were ones that they themselves did not share. Most adolescents fell into this category. A second type of pattern is surgent growth, where development involves abrupt change. Such rapid change does not necessarily involve the turmoil associated with storm and stress. Finally, however, Offer did identify a tumultuous-growth type of adolescent development, characterized by crisis, stress, and problems.

Thus, the belief that adolescence is a period of general disruption of parent–child ties, or the belief in the emergence of problematic social behaviors among virtually all youth, do not find support in the contemporary scientific literature. The facts of adolescent development allow the study of the social problems which do occur during this period to be put in an appropriate perspective. Problems such as drug and alcohol abuse and delinquency are quite significant; but these problems do not occur with a majority of contemporary youth, irrespective of racial, ethnic, or socioeconomic status. Nevertheless, it is important to highlight the nature of the social problems which do exist within this period of life. Although only a minority of youth exhibit these problems, on a population basis this frequency translates into millions of people.

3.3 Social Problems of Adolescence

Juvenile delinquency is defined in the United States as the violation of a law committed by a person prior to his or her 18th birthday, a violation which would have been a crime committed by an adult. In turn, a status offense is a violation of the law which involves a behavior which would not have been illegal if engaged in by an adult.

Some of the problems of adolescence which are classified as delinquent because, for instance, they involve a status offense, really signify more of an issue of poor social relationships than of criminality. For example, running away from home is technically considered a delinquent act, but it is really more than that. Between 750,000 and one million adolescents in the United States run away from home each year (Adams 1991). Home environments that involve rejection, neglect, disinterest, hostile control, parent–child conflict, inadequate supervision, and lack of family organization are associated with adolescents' running away (Adams 1991).

Thus, running away is a sign of a young person's inability to tolerate the social setting in which he or she resides. Leaving home may also be a way of telling parents that the home situation has become seriously intolerable, or it may be a way of indicating that help is needed.

Other problematic behaviors also skirt the borderlines between status offenses, social relationship issues, and actual illegality. Problems of teenage sexuality—unsafe sex, pregnancy, and childbearing—pertain both to status offenses and social relationships. In turn, issues of tobacco, alcohol, and drug abuse cross the borderlines between status offenses and illegality.

In regard to teenage sexuality, adolescents are not usually contraceptively protected when they begin sexual activity, and a large proportion are inadequately protected throughout adolescence. As an illustration of this point, about two-thirds of sexually active United States adolescent females either use no contraceptives at all or use only nonbarrier methods, such as withdrawal (Boyer and Hein 1991). As a result of such practices, there are hundreds of thousands of cases of sexually transmitted diseases and of pregnancies among adolescents each year in the United States. Between 30 and 40 percent of adolescent mothers have been impregnated by males who have not yet reached their 20th birthday (Elster 1991). About 15 percent of all Black males have, by the age of 19 years, fathered a child; corresponding rates among similarly aged Latino and European–American males are 11 percent and 6.5 percent respectively (Elster 1991).

Illicit use of drugs has been decreasing among youth in the United States. At the end of the 1970s, 60 percent of high school seniors reported having used marijuana; by the end of the 1980s the corresponding statistic was 44 percent. However, 51 percent of American high school seniors have tried at least one illicit drug (Kandel 1991). Moreover, almost all American high school seniors—92 percent—report some experience with alcohol. While 19 percent of the group report smoking cigarettes daily (Rauch and Huba 1991), and 66 percent have had at least some experience with cigarettes (Kandel 1991). Tobacco, alcohol, and drug use is initiated in early adolescence. Parents and teachers may model such behaviors to adolescents. If parents or teachers smoke, the probability of an adolescent doing so is increased significantly. Moreover, many "early users" of tobacco, alcohol, and drugs eventually develop habits of regular use.

Thus, there is a high proportion of adolescents for whom early use leads to continued adult use. Nevertheless, for many adolescents there is only a brief experimentation with such substances. Indeed, most adolescents recognize the dangers of drug, alcohol, and tobacco abuse, and it is still the case that for most youth problems of addiction do not arise.

Unfortunately, as noted above, given the proportion of adolescents who are involved in this and other risk behaviors, and the absolute number of youth that these proportions involve, there should be no complacency about this conclusion. Accordingly, at the very least there should be an examination of the individual and contextual factors that appear to put adolescents at risk of exhibiting the problem behaviors prominent during this period. In addition, it would be appropriate to study the individual and contextual factors that, when combined in intervention programs, appear to prevent the actualization of risk (see *Children and Youth at Risk*).

4. Risk And Prevention

Dryfoos (1990) has discussed the contrasting sets of individual and contextual factors that are associated with both the actualization and the prevention of risk behaviors in adolescence, that is, with substance use and abuse; with unsafe sex, adolescent pregnancy, and childbearing; with school failure and dropping out; and with crime and delinquency. Dryfoos found that there are six common characteristics involved in the occurrence during adolescence of one or more of these risk behaviors, and identified three individual and three contextual factors:

(a) *Age.* The earlier the initiation of any of the risk behaviors of adolescence, the more likely it is that the individual will engage in the behavior to a great extent and that he or she will suffer negative consequences.

(b) *Expectations for education and school grades.* All risk behaviors are associated with the adolescent's sense of self, especially insofar as self-perceived academic/scholastic competence is concerned (Harter 1983). Young people who do not expect to do well in school, and who do not in fact do well, are at risk for all the problem behaviors studied by Dryfoos (1990).

(c) *General behavior.* Inappropriate behaviors and inadequate conduct (e.g., acting out, truancy, and conduct disorders) are related to the appearance of risk behaviors.

(d) *Peer influences.* As noted by Stattin and Magnusson (1990), an individual's likelihood of engaging in problem behaviors is not simply due to individual factors (such as early pubertal maturation). In addition, contextual factors (e.g., the nature of the peer group within which the youth is embedded) are involved. Similarly, Dryfoos (1990) found that having peers who engage in risk behaviors, and having a low resistance to participating with peers, are factors associated with an adolescent's exhibiting such behaviors.

(e) *Parental influences.* Particular styles of parenting —that is, authoritarian or permissive styles, as compared to an authoritative one—place a youth "at-risk" for problem behaviors. Similarly, if parents do not monitor their children, or do not supervise, guide, or communicate with them effectively, there is a strong likelihood that an "at-risk" status will be actualized. In addition, if adolescents are not affectively tied to their parents by those positive ties which have been noted as being normal during this period (e.g., Douvan and Adelson 1966), risk behaviors are also likely to occur.

(f) *Neighborhood influences.* The community context also plays a role in the actualization of risk. A neighborhood characterized by poverty, or by urban, high-density living, is involved with risk actualization.

Dryfoos (1990) noted that a particular set of integrations among individual, familial, peer, and community "levels of organization" is involved in the actualization of risk behaviors among adolescents. In turn, however, there are other integrations, involving these several levels, that are involved in the design and delivery of successful prevention programs for "at-risk" youth.

In essence, then, there are multiple features of person and context that should be combined to design and deliver a successful program preventing the actualization of risk in adolescence. Building on the general developmental characteristics of the period, these programs, when attuned as well to the specific characteristics and needs of youths and their settings, will help adolescents avoid the development of risk behaviors.

In sum, Dryfoos (1990) indicated that there are grounds for optimism regarding the likely success of prevention efforts if these programs are designed and delivered sensitively. Above all, it must constantly be borne in mind that no one, single or isolated, effort is apt to succeed, given that risk behaviors are interrelated and influenced by a host of individual and contextual factors (see *Dropouts, School Leavers, and Truancy*).

5. Conclusion

Adolescence is a double-edged sword. It is a period potentially harboring myriad social problems. Yet the scientific evidence indicates that individual differences are prominent throughout adolescence, and that conditions exist or can be created to allow most young people to pass through this period with few, if any, major traumas. There is great resilience among youth (Werner and Smith 1982), and for most adolescents the period is one of quite favorable physical and mental health. Most adolescents can successfully meet the challenges of this transition period; they can assimilate in a coherent way the biological, cognitive, emotional, and social changes they are experiencing, and can form a useful (if sometimes provisional) self-definition. This sense of self, or identity, will allow youth to make decisions and commitments, first to educational paths, and then to careers and to other people. These decisions and commitments can eventuate in the adoption of roles (e.g., worker, spouse, and parent) beneficial to the advancement of society.

In sum, it may be concluded that, insofar as one limits one's generalizations to the samples studied within the contemporary scientific literature, young people have or can be given the personal, emotional, and social context resources necessary to meet successfully the biological, psychological, and social challenges of this period of life, leaving it with a developmentally new, but nevertheless useful, sense of self. Parents, educators, and other caregivers can be confident, then, that if a social context attuned to the developmental changes and individuality of youth is present, healthy and successful people will emerge from the period of adolescence.

See also: Aggression, Development and Socialization; Childhood; Children and Youth at Risk; Family and Schooling; Socialization

References

Adams G R 1991 Runaways, negative consequences for. In: Lerner R M, Petersen A C, Brooks-Gunn J (eds.) 1991, Vol. 1

Bandura A 1964 The stormy decade: Fact or fiction? *Psychol. Sch.* 1 (3): 224–31

Boyer C B, Hein K 1991 AIDS and HIV infection in adolescents: The role of education and antibody testing. In: Lerner R M, Petersen A C, Brooks-Gunn J (eds.) 1991, Vol. 1

Brooks-Gunn J, Petersen A C 1983 *Girls at Puberty: Biological and Psychosocial Perspectives.* Plenum Press, New York

Cutler G B Jr. 1991 Puberty, precocious, treatment of. In: Lerner R M, Petersen A C, Brooks-Gunn J (eds.) 1991, Vol. 2

Douvan E, Adelson J 1966 *The Adolescent Experience.* Wiley, New York

Dryfoos J G 1990 *Adolescent at Risk: Prevalence and Prevention.* Oxford University Press, New York

Elder G H Jr. 1980 Adolescence in historical perspective. In: Adelson J (ed.) 1980 *Handbook of Adolescent Psychology.* Wiley, New York

Elkind D 1967 Egocentrism in adolescence. *Child Dev.* 38: 1025–34

Elster A 1991 Fathers, teenage. In: Lerner R M, Petersen A C, Brooks-Gunn J (eds.) 1991, Vol. 1

Graber J A, Petersen A C 1991, Cognitive changes at adolescence: Biological perspectives. In: Gibson K R, Petersen A C (eds.) 1991 *Brain Maturation and Cognitive Development: Comparative and Cross-cultural Perspectives.* Aldine de Gruyter, New York

Guerney L, Arthur J 1983 Adolescent social relationships. In: Lerner R M, Galambos N L (eds.) 1983 *Experiencing Adolescence: A Sourcebook for Parents, Teachers, and Teens.* Teachers College Press, Columbia, New York

Harter S 1983 Developmental perspectives on the self-system. In: Mussen P H (ed.) 1983 *Handbook of Child Psychology. Vol. 4: Socialization, Personality, and Social Development,* 4th edn. Wiley, New York

Kandel D 1991 Drug use, epidemiology and developmental stages of involvement. In: Lerner R M, Petersen A C, Brooks-Gunn J (eds.) 1991, Vol. 2

Katchadourian H 1977 *The Biology of Adolescence.* Freeman, San Francisco, California

Keating D P 1991 Cognition, adolescent. In: Lerner R M, Petersen A C, Brooks-Gunn J (eds.) 1991, Vol. 1

Lerner R M 1984 *On the Nature of Human Plasticity.* Cambridge University Press, New York

Lerner R M 1987 A life-span perspective for early adolescence. In: Lerner R M, Foch T T (eds.) 1987

Lerner R M 1991 Changing organism-context relations as the basic process of development: A developmental contextual perspective. *Dev. Psychol.* 27: 27–32

Lerner R M, Foch T T (eds.) 1987 *Biological-psychosocial Interactions in Early Adolescence: A Life-span Perspective.* Erlbaum, Hillsdale, New Jersey

Marshall W A, Tanner J M 1986 Puberty. In: Falkner F, Tanner J M (eds.) 1986 *Human Growth. Vol. 2: Postnatal Growth, Neurobiology,* 2nd edn. Plenum Press, New York

Offer D 1969 *The Psychological World of the Teenager: A Study of Normal Adolescent Boys.* Basic Books, New York

Overton W F, Byrnes J P 1991 Cognitive development. In: Lerner R M, Petersen A C, Brooks-Gunn J (eds.) 1991, Vol. 1

Petersen A C 1988 Adolescent development. In: Rosenzweig M R (ed.) 1988 *Annual Review of Psychology,* Vol. 39. Annual Reviews, Inc., Palo Alto, California

Petersen A C, Taylor B 1980 The biological approach to adolescence: Biological change and psychological adaptation. In: Adelson J (ed.) 1980 *Handbook of Adolescent Psychology.* Wiley, New York

Rauch J M, Huba G J 1991 Drug use, adolescent. In: Lerner R M, Petersen A C, Brooks-Gunn J (eds.) 1991, Vol. 1

Schonfeld W A 1969 The body and the body image in adolescents. In: Caplan G, Lebovici S (eds.) 1969 *Adolescence: Psychosocial Perspectives.* Basic Books, New York

Simmons R G, Blyth D A 1987 *Moving into Adolescence: The Impact of Pubertal Change and School Context.* Aldine, Hawthorne, New Jersey

Stattin H, Magnusson D 1990 *Pubertal Maturation in Female Development.* Erlbaum, Hillsdale, New Jersey

Steinberg L 1991 Parent–adolescent relations. In: Lerner R M, Petersen A C, Brooks-Gunn J (eds.) 1991, Vol. 2

Tanner J 1991 Menarche, secular trend in age of. In: Lerner R M, Petersen A C, Brooks-Gunn J (eds.) 1991, Vol. 2

Werner E E, Smith R S 1982 *Vulnerable but Invincible.* McGraw-Hill, New York

Further Reading

Coleman J S, Husén T 1985 *Becoming Adult in a Changing Society.* OECD, Paris

Dornbusch S M et al. 1981 Sexual development, age, and dating: A comparison of biological and social influences upon one set of behaviors. *Child Dev.* 52(1): 179–85

Feldman S, Elliott G 1990 *At the Threshold: The Developing Adolescent.* Harvard University Press, Cambridge, Massachusetts

Hagen J W, Paul B, Gibb S, Wolters C 1990 Trends in research as reflected by publications in *Child Development*: 1930–1989. Paper presented at the Biennial Meeting of the Society for Research on Adolescence, Atlanta, Georgia

Kennedy R E 1991 Delinquency. In: Lerner R M, Petersen A C, Brooks-Gunn J (eds.) 1991, Vol. 1

Lerner R M, Petersen A C, Brooks-Gunn J (eds.) 1991 *Encyclopedia of Adolescence,* 2 Vols. Garland, New York

Petersen A C 1985 Pubertal development as a cause of disturbance: Myths, realities, and unanswered questions. *Genet. Psychol. Monogr.* 111: 207–31

Silbereisen R 1992 Adolescent behavior in context: Comparative analyses of beliefs, daily contexts, and substance use in West Berlin and Warsaw. In Featherman D L, Lerner R M, Perlmutter M (eds.) 1992 *Life-span Development and Behavior,* Vol. 11. Erlbaum, Hillsdale, New Jersey

Whiting B B, Whiting J W M 1991 Preindustrial world, adolescence in. In: Lerner R M, Petersen A C, Brooks-Gunn J (eds.) 1991, Vol. 2

Aggression, Development and Socialization

D. G. Perry

Aggression—that is, behavior aimed at harming another person—is a social problem of growing importance. This article discusses developmental patterns in aggression, theories of aggression, the roles of biology, socialization, and cognition in aggressive development, and intervention with aggressive children.

1. Developmental Patterns In Aggression

Three issues will be discussed in this section: developmental changes in the forms and elicitors of aggression, the stability of aggression, and sex differences in aggressive development.

1.1 Developmental Changes in the Forms and Elicitors of Aggression

Surprisingly little is known about how the forms and elicitors of aggression change with age. Over the preschool years, physical aggression decreases and verbal aggression increases (Parke and Slaby 1983). Much of the aggression of younger preschoolers is "instrumental" (aimed at retrieval of an object or privilege); "hostile" aggression (aimed at restoring self-esteem) develops later, presumably because it rests on the ability to infer the intentions and motives of an attacker (Hartup 1974). At any given age, there exists considerable trait-like cross-situational consistency in aggression: children who are the most (or least) aggressive in one context, such as the home, tend also to be the most (or least) aggressive in other contexts, such as the school (Perry and Bussey 1984).

1.2 Stability of Aggression

Aggression is highly stable over time, indeed about as stable as intelligence (Olweus 1979). The degree of stability varies inversely with both the length of the interval covered and the subjects' age at the time of first assessment. In one study, assessments of aggression among 10-year olds predicted their aggressiveness 22 years later (Eron et al. 1991). Aggressive children may remain aggressive because of biological factors, because they continue to live in environments conducive to aggression, because they retain cognitions conducive to aggression (e.g., the belief that aggression is successful), or because they elicit from the environment certain reactions (e.g., rejection from normal peers) that reinforce their aggression (Perry and Bussey 1984).

1.3 Sex Differences in Aggressive Development

At all ages males are more aggressive than females,

and this is true for verbal as well as physical aggression (Maccoby and Jacklin 1974). Aggression is about equally stable in boys and in girls, however (Olweus 1984). Reasons for the sex difference in aggression are unclear, but may involve biological factors (e.g., muscularity, temperament, hormones) as well as environmental ones (e.g., more physical punishment and encouragement of aggression for boys) Nature–nurture interplays may also be important. For example, boys' more active and resistant-to-control temperaments may elicit physical punishment from parents, which teaches the boys aggressive styles of interpersonal influence.

2. Theories of Aggressive Development

This section outlines three theories of aggression: ethological theory, psychoanalytic theory, and social cognitive theory.

2.1 Ethological Theory

Ethologists (e.g., Lorenz 1966) view aggression as instinctive behavior. In animals as well as humans, aggressive energy is thought to build up within the organism independently of external stimuli but to be periodically discharged or released by appropriate environmental elicitors, especially frustrations (goal blockages) and threats (e.g., territorial infringement). The theory emphasizes the importance of behavior patterns that have adaptive (survival) value for a species. Thus, the role of aggression in mate and resource selection and defense is emphasized. Moreover, within a species, groups often form dominance hierarchies, allowing group members to settle conflicts by exchanging signals of dominance and submission rather than by overt aggression. Thus, dominance hierarchies curb intragroup aggression.

Although the ethological perspective has yielded interesting data about the stimuli that regulate aggression in natural settings, the theory has been criticized for: (a) viewing aggression as a product of biologically programmed stimulus–response links that are minimally influenced by learning; (b) the absence of evidence to support the notion of an accumulating reservoir of aggressive energy; (c) the failure to acknowledge the role of higher cognition (e.g., values) in regulating aggression; and (d) the absence of data to support the "catharsis hypothesis," or the idea that observing and performing aggression depletes one of aggressive energy and reduces the inclination to further aggression.

2.2 Psychoanalytic Theory

Freud (1940) viewed people as biologically endowed with an aggressive drive that is aroused by frustrating and other ego-threatening events. When the drive is aroused, aggression may be expressed directly toward the provocateur (if no punishment is expected), or may be displaced, turned toward the self, suppressed, repressed, or otherwise defensively handled (especially if the aggressive impulses meet resistance from real-world or superego sources). If drive is aroused but not expressed, it accumulates. Moreover, if aggressive impulses are repressed rather than discharged, when the individual later encounters persons and events that are symbolically reminiscent of the originally frustrating circumstances, aggressive drive may be subconsciously aroused and motivate aggressive actions.

Although this theory recognizes the role of cognition (especially in the form of defensive transformations of aggressive drive), there exists little scientific evidence for the hypothesized defensive and subconscious processes. Also, like ethological theory, psychoanalytic theory has been criticized for its "hydraulic" properties, especially the idea that aggression springs from an invisible internal reservoir of energy that accumulates if unexpressed and is reduced through acts of vicarious and direct aggression (catharsis).

2.3 Social Cognitive Theory

According to social cognitive theory (Bandura 1986), children's social experiences influence how they mentally represent their social worlds and process social information; in turn, children's cognitions guide their social behavior. Much aggression is acquired through observing the aggression of others: by watching the behavior of playground bullies, television villains, and even their own parents acting as disciplinarians, children learn how to engage in a wide variety of harmful acts. Children are most likely to enact aggression, however, when they expect valued outcomes for it and believe they are capable of performing the requisite responses. Children learn about the likely consequences of aggression and about their ability to perform it partly through observation and partly through personal experiences. Children who see others rewarded for aggression, for example, may attempt aggression and, if successful, perceive themselves as capable aggressors.

In this theory, aggression comes under the control of internal self-regulatory processes. When children clearly see that society frowns on (or rewards) certain actions, they may internalize the standard, coming to experience guilt (or pride) for the behavior. For example, if children see that certain forms of aggression in certain situations or toward certain targets are inappropriate (e.g., physical aggression toward females, or aggression against someone whose frustrating behavior is unintentional), they may avoid acting aggressively under these circumstances for fear of self-censure. Not all children learn the same rules. Members of delinquent gangs, for example, may internalize the norm that violence and destruction are worthy of self-praise rather than self-blame.

Social cognitive theorists shun the concept of aggression as a reflexive reaction to frustration, but they do not deny the importance of frustrating and other aversive events in aggression. Indeed, they believe that aggression is often a response children learn to make when deprived, threatened, or hurt, especially if the children find aggression to be successful at improving their plight. Reactions to frustration and other arousing events are cognitively mediated, or depend on the individual's cognitive evaluation of the arousing event. For example, children who develop a style of blaming others for their mishaps and believe that aggression is an effective way to eradicate frustrations should be more likely to perform aggression than children who do not pin their misery on others or who can think of effective, nonaggressive solutions to conflicts. Considerable evidence supports the social cognitive perspective, as reviewed below.

3. Biological Bases of Aggression

Several biological factors affect aggressive development. First, body size, muscularity, and strength are correlated with aggression (Feshbach 1970). Second, physically unattractive children are more aggressive than attractive children (Langlois and Stephan 1981). Third, hormones influence aggression: injecting male hormones prenatally or early in development into animals of certain species enhances later aggressive reactions to certain stimuli (Parke and Slaby 1983, Reinisch 1981). Moreover, circulating levels of male hormones in adult men predict aggressive reactions to provocation and threat (Olweus et al. 1980). Fourth, children born with difficult, hot-headed, or oppositional temperaments are at risk of aggressive development (Bates et al. 1991, Olweus 1980, Thomas et al. 1978). Finally, identical twins are more similar than fraternal twins in aggressiveness (Plomin 1990).

The impacts of these biological factors upon aggression, however, are neither direct nor inevitable. Most biological factors interact with environmental ones to influence aggressive development. Muscular, strong children probably develop aggressive habits mainly when their forceful attempts to remove frustrations or to control others are allowed to succeed (Perry and Bussey 1984). Physically unattractive children may develop aggression mainly because adults and peers expect and elicit negative behavior from unattractive children (Langlois and Stephan 1981). Children with problem temperaments may elicit inept parental behaviors (e.g., erratic and harsh discipline, poor monitoring of the child) that promote child aggression.

736

Even hormonal influences hinge on social conditions (Cairns 1979).

4. Socialization Influences on Aggression

This section discusses influences of the family, the peer group, and the media on aggressive development.

4.1 Family Influences on Aggression

When children do not enjoy positive and emotionally satisfying relationships with their parents, or when the parents are inept at family management practices, the risk of aggressive development increases. These influences are discussed here.

Parental hostility and rejection are associated with child aggression (McCord 1979, Olweus 1980). It has also been suggested that the security of the child's attachments to caregivers figures in aggressive development (Ainsworth 1979, Sroufe 1983). Insecurely attached children are ones who have experienced an insensitive and emotionally unavailable caregiver and have come to display one of two styles of defensive coping to deal with the caregiver's unpredictability: excessive emotional dependence on the caregiver or excessive avoidance of the caregiver. Compared to securely attached children (who have experienced emphatic caregiving and can count on the caregiver's sensitive response at times of stress), insecurely attached children are expected to distrust others, to start fights, and to oppose others. Indeed, insecurely attached children are less compliant and more oppositional, with both parents and peers, than securely attached children. However, there is little evidence that insecurely attached children are actually more aggressive than securely attached children (Perry et al. 1992).

Inept family management practices can promote aggressive development. Among the parental practices that cause aggression are: (a) failure by the parents to monitor the child's whereabouts (Patterson and Stouthamer-Loeber 1984); (b) displays of violent behavior by at least one parent toward the child, toward siblings, or toward others outside the home (McCord 1979); (c) permissiveness in child-rearing (Baumrind 1973); (d) interparent or intraparent inconsistency in discipline (Martin 1975); and (e) ineffectual management of parent–child conflicts. The final item listed above requires elaboration. Patterson (1982) has shown that parents of aggressive children tend to be irritable and conflict-prone, in that they: (a) instigate numerous everyday family conflicts (e.g., by teasing, humiliating, or bossing their children); (b) have a low threshold for responding aversively to the moves of other family members; (c) allow family conflicts to escalate; and (d) respond unpredictably to escalated conflicts, by occasionally allowing their children to have their way, while at other times angrily assaulting them.

These findings support the hypothesis of social cognitive theory that environmental factors promote cognitions that encourage aggression. Parents who are aggressive, erratic, rejecting, and blaming not only teach their children to expect hostility and unpredictability in others but also communicate the message that aggression is an acceptable way of influencing others. Moreover, parents who intermittently allow their child to prevail during escalated conflicts teach the child that high-intensity coercion may succeed when lower-intensity efforts fail.

4.2 Peer Influences on Aggression

Children who acquire aggressive habits at home tend to take their aggression to the playground and school, where they often face rejection by normal peers, acceptance by deviant peers, and academic failure (Cairns and Cairns 1991, Patterson et al. 1991). Moreover, previously nonaggressive children may acquire aggressive habits from their peers, especially if they are frequently victimized by more aggressive children, try to defend themselves with counterattacks, and find these counterattacks to be successful (Patterson et al. 1967).

The fact that aggressive children are rejected by normal peers is important. Such rejection reduces the child's opportunities for normal socialization. Moreover, because normal peers treat aggressive children with open distrust and dislike, aggressive children's expectations that others are treating them with hostility are strengthened. This leads them to perceive hostility even when it is not there (e.g., when they are accidentally provoked) and therefore to behave aggressively when circumstances do not warrant it (Dodge 1986).

4.3 Media Influences on Aggression

Contrary to the catharsis hypothesis of ethological and psychoanalytic theories, but consistent with social cognitive theory, media violence increases rather than decreases children's aggressive tendencies (Bandura 1986, Perry et al. 1991). Evidence of this has been provided by both laboratory experiments and field studies. Field studies show that the relation between television violence and children's aggression is not readily explained by other variables (e.g., social class or a child's temperament).

Television violence has several effects, including: (a) teaching new styles of aggression; (b) teaching that aggression is effective; (c) desensitizing the viewer to violence and suffering, thereby decreasing the chance the viewer will aid others in distress; and (d) teaching the idea that aggression is commonplace, thereby making the viewer feel that aggression is acceptable and strengthening the viewer's tendency to perceive hostile intentions in others. Harmful effects of television violence are greater for, but not limited to, children who already possess favorable attitudes toward aggression, who have aggressive fantasies, or who are emotionally aroused when exposed to the violence (Perry et al. 1991).

5. Social Cognition and Aggression

As suggested by social cognitive theory, aggression is influenced by cognition. When responding to certain stimuli (e.g., provocation), aggressive children reveal deficits and biases in social information processing that lead them to respond aggressively (Dodge 1986, Perry et al. 1991). For example, compared to nonaggressive children, aggressive children tend to interpret ambiguously motivated provocations by others as acts of deliberate hostility, they have trouble thinking of nonaggressive solutions to conflicts, and they expect positive outcomes (control over a victim, increased self-esteem) for performing aggression. As reviewed above, inept family management, poor peer relations, and media violence are all implicated in the learning of cognitions that promote aggression. Discovering how cognitive factors interact with emotional factors to affect aggressive behavior is one important area for future study.

6. Intervention with Aggressive Children

According to the catharsis principle of ethological and psychoanalytic theories, intervention should involve activities that drain children of aggressive urges. This approach is not recommended, however, because encouraging children to enact (even in play) or to observe aggression increases rather than diminishes their aggressive tendencies (Parke and Slaby 1983).

As suggested by social cognitive theory, altering the environmental conditions that support aggression is a more promising approach to intervention. Intervention programs have been developed for both family and school settings. One successful family intervention idea involves teaching parents to reduce their aversive treatment of the child, to monitor the child, to resist the escalation of conflicts, to punish aggression consistently with time out (isolation), and to reward the child for acceptable social behavior (Patterson 1982). A successful school intervention idea involves increasing teachers', peers', and parents' awareness of bully/victim problems, developing clear rules against aggressive behavior, and providing support and protection for victimized children (Olweus 1978).

Coaching aggressive children in cognitive strategies designed to reduce aggression (teaching them to avoid assuming that others are acting with hostile intent, to be aware of the harmful consequences of aggression, to think of nonaggressive solutions to conflict, etc.) may also be helpful, but such cognitive retraining may not generalize to the natural environment unless real changes are also made in the environment to support the newly trained cognitions (Pepler and Rubin 1991). For example, aggressive children may continue to believe that peers are hostile unless peers can be induced to change their rejecting behavior, and aggressive children may not change their perceptions of the consequences of their actions unless consistent sanctions (e.g., time out) are actually applied to their behavior. Finally, training aggressive children in social skills (e.g., how to make friends, how to join a group of children at play) and tutoring them in academic skills may provide them with positive means of obtaining desired rewards, thereby reducing the need for antisocial behavior (Patterson 1982).

See also: Adolescence; Childhood; Children and Youth at Risk; Social Psychological Theories in Education; Socialization

References

Ainsworth M D S 1979 Infant–mother attachment. *Am. Psychol.* 34(10): 932–37

Bandura A 1986 *Social Foundations of Thought and Action: A Social Cognitive Theory*. Prentice-Hall, Englewood Cliffs, New Jersey

Bates J E, Bayles K, Bennett D S, Ridge B, Brown M M 1991 Origins of externalizing behavior problems at eight years of age. In: Pepler D J, Rubin K H (eds.) 1991

Baumrind D 1973 The development of instrumental competence through socialization. In: Pick A D (ed.) 1973 *Minnesota Symposium on Child Psychology*, Vol. 7. University of Minnesota Press, Minneapolis, Minnesota

Cairns R B 1979 *Social Development: The Origins and Plasticity of Interchanges*. Freeman, San Francisco, California

Cairns R B, Cairns B D 1991 Social cognition and social networks: A developmental perspective. In: Pepler D J, Rubin K H (eds.) 1991

Dodge K A 1986 A social information processing model of social competence in children. In: Perlmutter M (ed.) 1986 *Minnesota Symposium on Child Psychology*, Vol. 18. Erlbaum, Hillsdale, New Jersey

Eron L D, Huesmann L R, Zelli A 1991 The role of parental variables in the learning of aggression. In: Pepler D J, Rubin K H (eds.) 1991

Feshbach S 1970 Aggression. In: Mussen P H (ed.) 1970 *Carmichael's Manual of Child Psychology*, Vol. 2, 3rd edn. Wiley, New York

Freud S 1940 *The Ego and the Mechanisms of Defense*. Hogarth, London

Hartup W W 1974 Aggression in childhood: Developmental perspectives. *Am. Psychol.* 29(5): 336–41

Langlois J H, Stephan C 1981 Beauty and the beast: The role of physical attractiveness in the development of peer relations and social behavior. In: Brehm S S, Kassin S M, Gibbons F X (eds.) 1981 *Developmental Social Psychology: Theory and Research*. Oxford University Press, New York

Lorenz K 1966 *On Aggression*. Methuen, London

Maccoby E E, Jacklin C N 1974 *The Psychology of Sex Differences*, 2 Vols. Stanford University Press, Stanford, California

Martin B 1975 Parent–child relations. In: Horowitz F D (ed.) 1975 *Review of Child Development Research*, Vol. 4. University of Chicago Press, Chicago, Illinois

McCord J 1979 Some child-rearing antecedents of criminal behavior in adult men. *J. Pers. Soc. Psychol.* 37(9): 1477–86

Olweus D 1978 *Aggression in the Schools: Bullies and Whipping Boys*. Hemisphere, Washington, DC

Olweus D 1979 Stability of aggressive reaction patterns in males: A review. *Psychol. Bull.* 86(4): 852–75

Olweus D 1980 Familial and temperamental determinants of aggressive behavior in adolescent boys: A causal analysis. *Dev. Psychol.* 16(6): 644–66

Olweus D 1984 Development of stable aggression reaction patterns in males. In: Blanchard R, Blanchard C (eds.) 1984 *Advances in the Study of Aggression*, Vol. 1. Academic Press, New York

Olweus D, Mattson A, Schalling D, Low H 1980 Testosterone, aggression, physical and personality dimensions on normal adolescent males. *Psychos. Med.* 42(2): 253–69

Parke R D, Slaby R G 1983 The development of aggression. In: Hetherington E M (ed.) 1983 *Handbook of Child Psychology. Vol. 4: Socialization, Personality, and Social Development*. Wiley, New York

Patterson G R 1982 *Coercive Family Processes*. Castilia Press, Eugene, Oregon

Patterson G R, Capaldi D, Bank L 1991 An early starter model for predicting delinquency. In: Pepler D J, Rubin K H (eds.) 1991

Patterson G R, Littman R A, Bricker W 1967 Assertive behavior in children: A step toward a theory of aggression. *Monogr. Soc. Res. Child Dev.* 32(5) Serial No. 113: Whole issue

Patterson G R, Stouthamer-Loeber M 1984 The correlation of family management practices and delinquency. *Child Dev.* 55(4): 1299–307

Pepler D J, Rubin K H 1991 *The Development and Treatment of Childhood Aggression*. Erlbaum, Hillsdale, New Jersey

Perry D G, Bussey K 1984 *Social Development*. Prentice-Hall, Englewood Cliffs, New Jersey

Perry D G, Perry L C, Boldizar J P 1990 Learning of aggression. In: Lewis M, Miller S (eds.) 1990 *Handbook of Developmental Psychopathology*. Plenum, New York

Perry D G, Perry L C, Kennedy E 1992 Conflict and the development of antisocial behavior. In: Shantz C U, Hartup W W (eds.) 1992 *Conflict in Child and Adolescent Development*. Cambridge University Press, Cambridge

Plomin R 1990 *Nature and Nurture: An Introduction to Behavioral Genetics*. Brooks/Cole, Pacific Grove, California

Reinisch J M 1981 Prenatal exposure to synthetic progestins increases potential for aggression in humans. *Science* 211(4487): 1171–73

Sroufe L A 1983 Infant–caregiver attachment and patterns of adaptation in preschool: The roots of maladaptation and competence. In: Perlmutter M (ed.) 1983 *Minnesota Symposium in Child Psychology*, Vol. 16. Erlbaum, Hillsdale, New Jersey

Thomas A, Chess S, Birch H 1968 *Temperament and Behavior Disorders in Children*. New York University Press, New York

Broadcasting and Technology: Effects on Children and Youth

G. Comstock

Television is central in the effects of broadcasting and technology on children and youth, although it is important to place it in the context of other media and technological innovation. In the more developed countries, young people spend as much time on television as on school or sleep, and more than on any other leisure activity. The phenomena associated with television and other electronic media will occur elsewhere as they become more widely available. Five topics are discussed in this article: audience response, individual experience, cognitive outcomes, scholastic achievement, and behavioral influence.

1. Audience Response

The young audience for television and other mass media is huge. Large-scale studies in four countries—the United States (Schramm et al. 1961), the United Kingdom (Himmelweit et al. 1958), Canada (Williams 1985), and Sweden (Rosengren and Windahl 1989)—provide essentially corroborative information. By far the most time is devoted to television, although popular music becomes competitive in the preteens and adolescence. Issues concern audience size, the rank of viewing among other activities, the day and life cycle of exposure, preferences and time allocations among alternatives, and the place of the medium in family life.

1.1 Audience Size

Estimates of amount of viewing vary considerably. Audience measurement firms estimate that in the United States those aged 2–11 average about 30 hours a week, with the figure for those aged 12–17 about 20 percent lower. Academic analysts in both the United States (Kubey and Csikszentmihalyi 1990, Robinson 1990) and Western Europe (Rosengren and Windahl 1989) suggest between 2 and 2.5 hours a day, or 14–17.5 hours per week, as a more accurate figure for children, although all data concur that teenagers view less than younger children. Disparities among estimates are largely attributable to differences in measurement procedures; the more meticulous the procedure, typically the lower the estimate. Those estimates made by commercial firms may be inflated because: (a) households agreeing to provide data are more likely to have members who are more avid viewers or who will be overzealous in reporting; (b) the firms are more tolerant than academic researchers of inattention, engaging in other activities, and absence from the room.

In the United States, during the early prime-time period of 8–9 p.m., more than half of those aged 2–11 and about 40 percent of those aged 12–17 are viewers at any given moment, although individuals will enter and leave. Even the most conservative estimates conclude that young people spend a substantial amount of time on television.

1.2 Rank of Viewing

Children and youth in the more developed countries spend half or more of their leisure watching television. By the age of 9, twice as much time is being spent on television as in play. At very early ages, play is slightly ascendant. If there were no television, these young people would certainly spend more time with other media; however, equally certainly, some of the time would be allocated to other activities.

Nevertheless, the data in aggregate indicate that television does not typically interfere seriously with engaging in other pursuits (Comstock 1991). This is because people of all ages watch television when there are no other activities in which they prefer or are obligated to engage. Viewing does not so much detract from as reflect the absence of other opportunities and demands.

The principal exception is reading and the related activity of studying. Like watching television, both are sedentary. The three thus occupy a similar place in the ecology of daily life, and viewing may be preferred by many because it is less demanding. When television is combined with reading or studying, the latter two may suffer in quality—through the material chosen or degree of attention given to it.

1.3 Day and Life Cycle

Children and teenagers are similar in their daily cycle of viewing. The curve begins to rise in mid-afternoon, reaches an early peak around 5 p.m. and a later, higher peak between 8 and 9 p.m., and then declines. The principal differences are that children view more than teenagers, so their curve is slightly higher; teenagers go to bed later than children, so the decline in their curve occurs somewhat later; and about one fifth of children too young for school are viewing in the early morning compared to about 5 percent of teenagers.

Children begin viewing television regularly between the ages of 2 and 3. The amount viewed

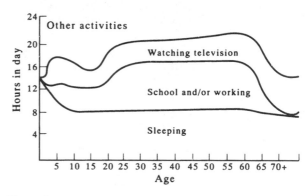

Figure 1
Viewing across the life cycle

typically increases over the elementary school years, declines during adolescence, experiences an increase with adulthood, and increases again in the late 50s and early 60s. Condry (1989) has charted viewing across the life cycle (Fig. 1), demonstrating that it is one of the major modes of time use in modern societies.

These cycles reflect the principal determinant of television use at all ages—time available, or opportunity (Comstock 1991). The shifts in viewing during the day and over the lifespan are the consequence of other obligations and preferred alternatives.

1.4 Preferences

Preferences among programs develop early, with almost all children by age 5 able to name one or more favorites. Two principal factors are age and gender. Very young children of both genders like animation. Males later shift toward action-adventure and females toward situation comedy and family drama. By the teenage years, viewing essentially parallels that of adults. Children enjoy seeing characters like themselves, but this is modulated by a preference for those of equal or higher status; thus, similar characters will be particularly enjoyed, while those who are different but have elevated status—typically, males, those older, and those of a particular ethnicity—will also be found pleasurable.

Television is the most widely used of the mass media throughout childhood and adolescence. By far the most frequent source is broadcast channels, although they may be received by cable; these are distantly followed, when available, by channels exclusive to cable and videocassette recorder (VCR) use. In the preteens and later, music listening increases and for some will become competitive in time consumption with television. Music videos typically make up a minority of music listening.

Moviegoing offers testimony on behalf of the general principle that media use is subordinate to social needs. The VCR greatly increases the viewing of movies by young people, and especially teenagers, including titles graded officially or unofficially as unsuitable for them. Much of this viewing is done alone. Thus, it is unlikely that the VCR will greatly affect moviegoing by teenagers because of the important needs that the activity serves—dating and interaction with peers outside the confines of the household. This is analogous to the introduction of television itself, which greatly depressed moviegoing generally but least so among teenagers (Comstock 1991, Himmelweit et al. 1958).

Video games, even where widely available, account for only a small fraction of the total time spent on the mass media. Nevertheless, they exemplify a component of an "electronic culture" among the young that is growing increasingly rich, with Greenberg and Lin (1989) finding in the United States that each of seven electronic devices (such as a personal computer, video camera, or compact disc player) was possessed by a majority of a sample of more than 400 teenagers.

Media use shifts with age. As they enter their teens, young people turn more toward print. This is especially pronounced among those of greater intellectual ability and among those from households of higher socioeconomic status. Among those ranking lower in these attributes, a shift in the same direction also occurs, but it is less sizable, and they are much more likely to remain heavy television viewers. Paradoxically, book reading declines in the teenage years; as with the decline in television viewing, this is partly explained by other activities and obligations taking precedence, and partly by the fact that the books that might be read at this age are much more substantial compared to those of earlier childhood. Enduring media habits are established between childhood and adolescence; from this period onward, certain people devote consistently greater attention to material that is related to coping with life, while others prefer escapist material. Schramm et al. (1961) contrasted these two preferences as "reality" and "fantasy" content.

1.5 Family Life

The family is an important arbiter of, as well as the social setting for, much of young persons' viewing. Household centrality of the medium is a major factor (Comstock 1991); in households where sets are on much of the time, where parents are heavy viewers, and where norms regulating exposure are minimal, children and teenagers themselves typically watch more television. The increase in multiset households (more than two-thirds of households in the United States) means that young persons and adults more frequently watch television alone. This precludes the possibility of parents offering judgments on the veracity, virtue, or artistry of what is portrayed, and hence conceivably influencing such judgments by young viewers. At the same time, television viewing accounts in television households for much of the time that teenagers spend with their parents. Kubey and Csikszentmihalyi (1990) found that family members rate themselves as less active, alert, and challenged

than when otherwise engaged with each other, and that heavy viewers rate themselves lower in such responses when engaged in other activities, suggesting to them that the medium "may be altering the general quality of family interaction toward greater passivity even when television is not being viewed" (p. 172). In contrast, Comstock (1991) concluded that there is "no justification . . . for thinking that television has debased family life" (p. 46); while undemanding, joint viewing is pleasurable or it would not be engaged in, and it is hardly devoid of interaction.

Parents typically do not impose stringent rules on viewing. In the United States only about half of parents say they do so regularly, and the forbidding of certain programs is more frequent than regulating the amount of time spent viewing. Effects attributable to time allocation rather than content thus particularly escape mitigation, and because rule-making is positively associated with socioeconomic status, especially in households that rate lower in levels of education and income.

2. Individual Experience

Three concepts aptly describe the typical experience of television. Although occasionally a particular program that is scrupulously sought out will be watched intently, the typical experience is exemplified by content indifference, low involvement, and monitoring.

2.1 Indifference to Content

The time available for viewing, rather than program content, is the principal factor in assembling the total audience for television. This applies at least as strongly to children and teenagers as to adults (Comstock 1991). Typically, the primary decision is whether to view; the secondary decision is which program to choose. It is at this second stage that viewers discriminate carefully among programs. This leads to a set of anomalies (Comstock 1991): despite the enormous variation in programming, television sets worldwide on the average are turned on for about the same number of hours per day; even with popular programs that are thought of as regularly viewed, few people see every offering; moreover, preferences in the sense of declared favorites are poor predictors of what those at any age will view, since they may not be scheduled when there is time available.

2.2 Low Involvement

The act of viewing has been defined as "a discontinuous, often interrupted, and frequently nonexclusive activity for which a measure in hours and minutes serves only as the outer boundary of possible attention" (Comstock et al. 1978 pp. 146–47). Typically, viewers are not deeply involved in what they are watching, and pay only partial attention. The major exception among young viewers is the devoted attention that young children give to animated cartoons.

2.3 Monitoring

Denotatively as well as connotatively, the term "monitoring" is more descriptive of the act of watching television than the term "viewing." The younger viewer pays sufficient attention to follow what is unfolding, using such cues as background music, gender of speaker, changes in voice level, shifts in camera angle, scene changes, the behavior portrayed, and the behavior of others in the room to guide attention to the screen. The amount of attention is based partly on comprehension and partly on the need to pay attention in order to comprehend. Thus the relationship between attention to the screen and age among young viewers is curvilinear, increasing as what is portrayed becomes increasingly comprehensible and then declining as less attention is required to follow what is unfolding (Comstock 1991). Attention is least for episodic and redundant elements, such as news, sports, and commercials, and most for unfamiliar narratives, such as movies.

3. Cognitive Outcomes

The influence of television on what young people think has been the focus of extensive inquiry. Three prominent areas of concern have been: general knowledge, advertising, and social relations.

3.1 General Knowledge

Programs designed to teach can be quite effective. Young viewers will acquire facts and alter their opinions in accordance with well-prepared didactic programming. However, there are a number of limitations on the use of television for educational purposes.

Television is primarily an entertainment medium, and young viewers approach it from that perspective. Salomon (1983) has introduced the concept of the "amount of invested mental effort" (AIME) in connection with this phenomenon. He found that television typically elicits little effort at learning; it is thought to be easy, and thus not to require much. As a result, even bright children may fail to learn from television.

Viewing may not be enough. In an evaluation involving several thousand young people in the United States of a public television series entitled *Freestyle*, which was designed to change the occupational stereotypes of preteens, Johnston and Ettema (1982) found that only when viewing was accompanied by reinforcing classroom discussions were outlooks changed.

Effects may be more constrained than intended. Johnston and Ettema found that *Freestyle* changed what young people thought it was alright for others to do but not what they thought was alright for themselves.

Since television began to be introduced on a widespread basis in the late 1940s, there have been numerous efforts to use it for formal instruction. Nowhere has in-school television been adopted as the centerpiece or even a major component of instruction,

although obviously it is widely used on a sporadic basis as a complement to teaching. Studies comparing live and televised instruction give neither mode a clear advantage in effectiveness; thus the failure of in-school television is a function of culture and norms, and not of pedagogical inadequacy.

With regard to public affairs, television has made the news part of growing up. For example, in the United States about half of children and teenagers are in the regular news audience (Comstock 1991). These young viewers are not necessarily close followers of news. On the contrary, it is only as they enter the teenage years that some will become motivated consumers of the news, and then these young people—who on the average will be of greater mental ability and from households higher in socioeconomic status—will be turning more toward print media. Nevertheless, the medium makes it almost impossible for parents to shield young people from the carnage and conflict that comprise so much news.

The "cultivation analysis" exemplified by Signorielli and Morgan (1990) initially maintained that television presents a somewhat monolithic, coherent picture of the world, so that the principal factor on which influence would be contingent was amount of viewing. The most discussed theme of this research has been the degree to which television may cultivate beliefs that the world is a hostile and dangerous place, through the high violence content of both entertainment and news. There has been much debate, but reformulations in the early 1990s (Comstock 1991) suggest that: (a) the type of programming predominantly viewed makes a major difference, and (b) while estimates about the hostility of the world in general indeed may be cultivated, expectations about personal vulnerability are not.

3.2 Advertising

Many of the world's media systems at least partially finance television programming and dissemination through the sale of time to advertisers. Two major issues concern the ethics of directing advertising at children and the desirability of nutritional choices encouraged by such advertising.

A great deal of research has been devoted to children's comprehension of commercials (Comstock 1991). It is clear that before the age of 8 most children do not understand the persuasive intent of advertising, and that the younger the children, the greater the proportion not comprehending. This should not be surprising, since this age also forms the threshold of Piaget's (1969) "stage of concrete operationalism" when children become better able to apply broad principles and to take the perspective of another, such as a vendor. The identification of commercials as different from programs, the association of such portrayals with the offering of goods that can be purchased, and the linking of products with the figures in commercials occurs earlier. Nevertheless, children below the age of

8 cannot judge commercials as adults would, and by that criterion they are exploited when advertising is directed at them.

Commercials are effective in shaping children's food choices (Comstock 1991). However, it is far clearer that they shift brand choices within genres, or choice of genre among nutritionally similar options, than that they influence basic diet. In the more developed countries, the effects of commercials cannot be isolated from those of the pervasive marketing to the young of brand-name food and drink—fast, precooked, packaged, soft, sugared—of which it is part, and as with most television-related phenomena, this circumstance will increasingly become the norm. Universally, however, culture, economics, family custom, and parental preference severely constrain any immediate influence of commercials on meaningful choices.

3.3 Social Relations

One principle widely applicable to the mass media is that they are influential when direct experience or other, more credible sources are absent (Comstock 1991). Two concrete instances involve ethnicity and gender.

The media influence what young people believe about those differing in ethnicity (Comstock 1991). The Payne Fund studies of the 1930s in the United States found that movies with powerful depictions of those in other lands could lastingly affect the beliefs about those people held by young viewers. Television typically is less powerful because of its emphasis on light entertainment and the fragmentary presentation of its portrayals in brief episodes. Nevertheless, television in early life and mass media in general later on are named by children and teenagers as major sources of such information.

Certainly, relations between the genders is an area where teenagers may lack direct experience and more credible sources. The large body of research on the effects of filmed erotica described by Donnerstein et al. (1987) supports the view that young males may become more callous toward females and more accepting of violence inflicted on them by males as a consequence of exposure to portrayals of women as the victims of assault, and particularly sexual assault. Such portrayals may constitute a rationale for victimization both by example and by the dehumanized status assigned to females. This is essentially the conclusion reached by a parliamentary group in the United Kingdom (Barlow and Hill 1986) with regard to "video nasties," or films featuring the brutalization of women.

4. Scholastic Achievement

There is no doubt that in the more developed countries the amount of television viewed is inversely associated with scholastic achievement. It is far less clear that television is a cause rather than the symptom. Four topics require attention: the nature and shape of the association, the effects of television on traits and abilities, direct evidence on causation, and the process most likely responsible for the observed correlations.

4.1 Association

The most convincing evidence comes from the United States, although data from Sweden are corroborative (Rosengren and Windahl 1989). The United States data encompass several million children and teenagers in eight statewide assessments (Neuman 1991) and a variety of independent surveys (Comstock 1991). These data present a picture that is highly consistent.

First, there is a negative relationship between amount of television viewed and achievement on standardized tests for the three basic skills: reading, writing, and mathematics. Second, the relationship holds for all ages, all social strata, and subjects other than the basic skills. Third, the relationship is most pronounced in the higher grades and among those from households higher in socioeconomic level.

There is some evidence, strongest for the lower grades, that the relationship is initially curvilinear, rising briefly with increased viewing before beginning the descent. In the California statewide evaluation, this was decidedly the case for those with limited English fluency for whom amount of viewing could be said to be curvilinearly but not negatively associated with achievement (Comstock 1991).

4.2 Traits and Abilities

Television variously has been hypothesized as affecting traits and abilities related to scholastic achievement. The review by Comstock (1991) concluded that the evidence does not suggest any pronounced effects. If impulse control or the ability to attend to the demands of instruction is adversely affected, it is only among the very young. If perceptual and spatial skills are improved, this occurs only passingly when television is new to children because the protracted instructional sequences for which such effects have been demonstrated are not matched didactically by entertainment television. Other media, such as print or radio, may evoke more imaginative activity, but it is unlikely that television has any effect on imaginative capability. One major field experiment (Williams 1985) recorded a decrease in one measure of creativity associated with the introduction of the medium, but no such effect was recorded for another, and there was no clear case of an inverse association between amount of contemporary viewing and creativity (Comstock 1991). In sum, effects on traits and abilities do not explain the negative relationship between viewing and achievement.

4.3 Direct Evidence

There is a paucity of direct evidence on whether television contributes causally. The authors of the major field experiment (Williams 1985) concluded that their data support such a view, but another analyst (Comstock 1991) argued that much in their data conflicted with that interpretation. In the very large data sets, the negative association survives controls for subject matter, grade level, socioeconomic status, and ethnicity. In several other smaller data sets in which additional variables are controlled, the negative association survives in a majority and none lead to a compelling case that it is an artifact of another variable. Thus the direct evidence does not discredit, and by failing to uncover an alternative explanation gives some support to, a causal contribution.

4.4 Process

An analysis (Comstock 1991) of the many pertinent studies indicates that much of the association is attributable to those less skilled or able watching more television—that is, those of lower mental ability, those lacking educational resources in the home, and those experiencing conflicts with parents, peers, or teachers. The amount of television viewed, in this respect, is a symptom. Nevertheless, the same analysis concluded that television is causally implicated in three ways: (a) by displacing time during the early years when the foundations are being laid for the basic skills; (b) by taking time away from the maintenance of those skills; and (c) by lowering the quality of reading, homework, and other school-related activities engaged in while watching television. The analysis concurs with the international inquiry of Beentjes and van der Voort (1988) who concluded that those most at risk are heavy viewers, viewers principally of entertainment, the intellectually more able, and the socioeconomically advantaged.

In sum, the data support Neuman (1991) in her assertion that the notion of a monolithic television effect is a "myth." The data point to what transpires during the critical skills-acquisition period and the amount of time spent on television both then and later as two major factors. Another crucial factor is the extent to which the material conveyed by the medium to the young viewer is more or less educative than what it displaces. Thus the relationships are not only with amount of viewing but also with the consumption of entertainment instead of information, and attributes enabling them to use time more constructively; this is represented by mental ability and socioeconomic status.

5. Behavioral Influence

The emulation of television and film portrayals by young viewers has been the subject of extensive research. Two topics require discussion: the empirical evidence, and its generalizability.

5.1 Empirical Evidence

There are a large number of laboratory-type experiments, pioneered by the work of the American psychologists Albert Bandura and Leonard Berkowitz, which demonstrate that exposure to a violent portrayal increases the aggressiveness of young viewers immediately thereafter (Comstock 1991). Bandura focused on the acquisition and later performance of the portrayed acts by children of nursery school age. Berkowitz focused on the increase among those of college age of aggression different in kind from that portrayed. Surveys of children and teenagers in Australia, Finland, the United Kingdom, Israel, Poland, and the United States (Comstock 1991, Huesmann and Eron 1986) confirm that those who watch greater amounts of violent entertainment are also on average more aggressive, and while there is some evidence that those who are more aggressive seek out such entertainment, neither this nor anything else that has been examined accounts fully for the association between viewing and behavior; thus, the surveys offer evidence that ordinary viewing of violence increases aggressiveness.

5.2 Generalizability

The credibility in regard to everyday behavior of the experiments, which represent the outcomes of manipulations occurring within a limited time framework and generally artificial circumstances, is greatly enhanced by the surveys, which reflect everyday behavior. The former document causation within the confines of the design, and raise the possibility that it may occur without; the latter record the relationships that would be expected if television had an everyday causal role, thereby extending validity to the experimental outcomes.

Additional data further extend generalizability. The meta-analysis, or quantitative aggregation, of 1,043 study outcomes by Hearold (1986) indicated that portrayals of constructive, or "prosocial," and those of antisocial behavior function analogously. Exposure on average was associated positively with similar behavior and negatively with contrasting behavior. The implication is that the price of violent entertainment is not only heightened antisocial but also diminished prosocial behavior. Other data suggest that while the antisocial evidence is strongest for interpersonal aggression, because it is the type of behavior to which most of the findings pertain, the pattern of positive associations between the viewing of violent entertainment and antisocial behavior remains unchanged when more serious forms, such as crime and delinquency, are examined (Comstock 1991). For example, the meta-analysis developed by Paik in 1991 includes a small cluster of such studies and the outcomes, while far smaller in magnitude, display the same pattern of positive, statistically significant outcomes as those for the enormously greater number of studies representing milder forms of aggression.

The factors on which antisocial effects are contingent also generalize or apply to other types of behavior. They fall into four categories (Comstock 1991): the efficacy, normativeness, and pertinence ascribed to the behavior, and the susceptibility of the viewer. Portrayals that depict reward, self-enhancement, or success; social acceptance and especially approval; or particular relevance to someone like the viewer in characteristics or circumstances are particularly likely to be taken as guides for behavior. In the antisocial case, frustration or anger exemplifies susceptibility; prosocial equivalents would be a motive to avoid harm, master a skill, or contribute to group achievement.

6. Conclusion

When available in the home, television is the first mass medium to which the young turn. The regular viewing that begins between the ages of 2–3 typically will continue throughout the maturing years. Television is the predecessor of a range of electronic media that become important to young people. Print will become more important as children enter their teens, and especially so for those of greater intellectual ability and from households higher in socioeconomic status. Viewing is a somewhat distinctive activity in which pleasure often derives from the act rather than from what is viewed, involvement is typically low, and attention frequently limited to whatever is necessary for comprehension. Nevertheless, viewing has implications during growing up for time use, scholastic achievement, beliefs, and behavior.

See also: Adolescence; Aggression, Development and Socialization; Childhood; Youth and Leisure

References

Barlow G, Hill A (eds.) 1986 *Video Violence and Children.* St Martin's Press, New York

Beentjes J W J, van der Voort T H A 1988 Television's impact on children's reading skills: A review of research. *Read. Res. Q.* 23(4): 389–413

Comstock G 1991 *Television and the American Child.* Academic Press, San Diego, California

Comstock G, Chaffee S, Katzman N, McCombs M, Roberts D 1978 *Television and Human Behavior.* Columbia University Press, New York

Condry J 1989 *The Psychology of Television.* Erlbaum, Hillsdale, New Jersey

Donnerstein E, Linz D, Penrod S 1987 *The Question of Pornography: Research Findings and Policy Implications.* Free Press, New York

Greenberg B S, Lin C 1989 Adolescents and the VCR boom: Old, new, and nonusers. In: Levy M R (ed.) 1989 *The VCR Age.* Sage, Newbury Park, California

Hearold S 1986 A synthesis of 1,043 effects of television on social behavior. In: Comstock G (ed.) 1986 *Public Communication and Behavior*, Vol. 1. Academic Press, New York

Himmelweit H T, Oppenheim A N, Vince P 1958 *Television and the Child: An Empirical Study of the Effect of Television on the Young.* Oxford University Press, London

Huesmann L R, Eron L D (eds.) 1986 *Television and the Aggressive Child: A Cross-national Comparison.* Erlbaum, Hillsdale, New Jersey

Johnston J, Ettema J S 1982 *Positive Images: Breaking Stereotypes with Children's Television.* Sage, Beverly Hills, California

Kubey R W, Csikszentmihalyi M (eds.) 1990 *Television and the Quality of Life: How Viewing Shapes Everyday Experience.* Erlbaum, Hillsdale, New Jersey

Neuman S B 1991 *Literacy in the Television Age: The Myth of the TV Effect.* Ablex, Norwood, New Jersey

Piaget J 1969 *The Mechanism of Perception.* Routledge and Kegan Paul, London

Robinson J P 1990 Television's effects on families' use of time. In: Bryant J (ed.) 1990 *Television and the American Family.* Erlbaum, Hillsdale, New Jersey

Rosengren K E, Windahl S 1989 *Media Matter: TV Use in Childhood and Adolescence.* Ablex, Norwood, New Jersey

Salomon G 1983 Television watching and mental effort: A social psychological view. In: Bryant J, Anderson D R (eds.) 1983 *Children's Understanding of Television: Research on Attention and Comprehension.* Academic Press, New York

Schramm W, Lyle J, Parker E B 1961 *Television in the Lives of Our Children.* Stanford University Press. Stanford, California

Signorielli N, Morgan M (eds.) 1990 *Cultivation Analysis: New Directions in Media Effects Research.* Sage, Newbury Park, California

Williams T M (ed.) 1985 *The Impact of Television: A Natural Experiment in Three Communities.* Academic Press, San Diego, California

Further Reading

Bandura A 1986 *The Social Foundations of Thought and Action: A Social Cognitive Theory.* Prentice-Hall, Englewood Cliffs, New Jersey

Berkowitz L 1984 Some effects of thoughts on anti- and prosocial influences of media events: A cognitive—neoassociation analysis. *Psych. Bull.* 95(3): 410–27

Greenfield P 1984 *Mind and Media: The Effects of Television, Video Games and Computers.* Harvard University Press, Cambridge, Massachusetts

Levine M 1996 *Viewing Violence.* Doubleday, New York

Van Evra J 1990 *Television and Child Development.* Erlbaum, Hillsdale, New Jersey

Zillmann D, Bryant J, Huston A C (eds.) 1994 *Media, Children, and the Family.* Erlbuam, Hillsdale, New Jersey

Childhood

D. F. Bjorklund and W. S. Cassel

In this article, important changes that occur during childhood are examined. Included in the survey are changes in: (a) physical growth; (b) social and emotional development; (c) language; and (d) cognition.

Childhood begins when infancy ends, and this, for the purposes of this entry, is with the advent of children's first two-word sentences, usually between the ages of 16 and 20 months. The word "infancy" derives from the Latin and translates roughly as "without language," or more literally, "no speech." Childhood is followed by adolescence, and the onset of puberty is used here as the endpoint of childhood. Thus, the period of childhood to be reviewed here ranges from the beginning of true productive language, at approximately 18 months, to the beginning of puberty, at about 12 or 13 years.

1. Physical and Motor Development

Different organs and physical systems develop at different rates. The head and the central nervous system grow most rapidly during the neonatal and early childhood periods, with the head and brain reaching about 90 percent of their adult size by age 5. The reproductive system grows the slowest, with sexual maturity being achieved at puberty. Although adolescence begins with the enlargement of the reproductive organs, there is a one- to two-year period of low fertility in both boys and girls, thus extending the period humans spend as nonreproductives (Tanner 1978).

Generally, boys and girls grow taller at about the same rate until approximately 11–12 years of age. During this same time, girls have a growth spurt for approximately two years that gives them a temporary height and strength advantage over boys. Thereafter, boys grow more rapidly than girls until about age 14 or 15, at which time children are practically fully grown (Tanner 1978).

By early childhood, children are walking, although the toddling 2-year old lacks the gross-motor skills of older children and adolescents. Children's gross-motor skills are refined over the preschool years, with children walking and running in a way that is qualitatively similar to adults by age 6. Fine-motor skills develop gradually over the preschool years. For example, children are not able to copy accurately a visual design until about 5 years of age, with substantial improvements in drawing skills still developing over the school years (Goodenough 1926). Such fine-motor skills are important in technological societies for writing and for many activities in traditional societies, such as weaving.

2. Social and Emotional Development

2.1 Parents' Influence on Children's Behavior

Social development of children follows a general pattern from home/self-centered to external/other-centered behavior. As children grow more physically capable, they become increasingly independent of their parents and experience the broader world outside of their homes. Contemporary behavioral genetics theories hold that genetic factors (a child's genotype) become increasingly influential with age in determining what environments children will experience, thus affecting greatly their social and intellectual development. In other words, with increasing age, children actively choose which activities they engage in, with these choices being heavily influenced by genetically determined dispositions (Scarr 1992).

However, children's relationships with their parents continue to influence their behavior outside the home. For example, emotional relationships between children and their parents tend to be stable from late infancy through childhood, with securely attached infants becoming securely attached children (Main et al. 1985). Moreover, quality of attachment in infancy (secure, insecure, or disorganized) has been found to be related to later social and intellectual development, with children who were rated as securely attached as infants or toddlers developing a better self-image, being more effective problem solvers, and being better liked by peers than children who were insecurely attached (e.g., Cohn 1990).

Parenting style also affects children's behavior. The children of authoritarian parents, who establish firm rules and frequently enforce them by use of physical punishment, often tend to be withdrawn, discontented, aggressive, and distrustful of others. Children of permissive parents, who generally exert little control over their children, often lack self-reliance, self-control, and explorative tendencies. Children of authoritative parents, who set clear standards and enforce rules with warmth and explanations, often are independent, socially responsive, self-controlled, explorative, and self-reliant (Baumrind 1967).

2.2 Development of Peer Relations

During the preschool years (ages 2–5), children's social interaction with peers increases substantially. As their interaction increases, so also do conflicts. Preschoolers who are friends fight with one another just as much as preschoolers who are only acquaintances. Conflicts are less intense between friends than between nonfriends and are more likely to result in nearly equal outcomes for the involved children (Hartup et al. 1988).

Many preschoolers take part in parallel play, two or more children playing near each other, possibly involved in similar activities but not engaged in mutual, or cooperative play. This semisocial parallel play may be a precursor to more social forms of interaction and truly cooperative play, which increases over early childhood as children become more able to take the perspective of others.

Throughout childhood, children segregate themselves into same-sex groups for play and other social activities; this same-sex segregation is universal and increases during the early school years (Maccoby and Jacklin 1987). Boys and girls play differently, with boys engaging in more rough-and-tumble play and centering their interactions on movable toys, whereas girls tend to engage in dramatic play and table activities. During the preschool years, and through adolescence, girls are more apt to play in smaller groups than boys.

Dominance hierarchies, or "pecking orders," in children's groups are established as a result of children testing each other in games and activities that produce clear winners and losers. Dominance hierarchies serve to reduce antagonism within the group, distribute scarce resources, and focus division of labor. Younger children are more apt to establish dominance hierarchies based upon their physical abilities to control other children. As children grow older, and most especially at puberty, other factors such as sexual maturity tend to become important in the establishment of a dominant position in the peer group (see Shaffer 1988).

2.3 Prosocial Behavior

The development of prosocial behavior, behavior that is intended to benefit others, is based on the development of empathy. Beginning at about age 2, children begin to understand that others have needs and feelings that are different from their own. Their empathic abilities improve as they become less egocentric (that is, less self-centered in their perspective-taking abilities) and as their role-taking abilities improve. By about age 11, children have developed a capacity for empathy with another person's life experience rather than simply with a single event in the person's life.

Sharing is seen in toddlers, but is more common in older children. Older preschool children are more prone to try to "help," such as assisting a parent or other adult accomplish some task. These forms of prosocial behavior increase over the school years to about 9 years of age when "helping" activities seem to level off (see Shaffer 1988).

2.4 Aggression in Children

Aggression is not limited to one gender or one age group of children, although boys, on average, are physically more aggressive than girls. The frequency and nature of aggressive behavior change with age. Aggressive behavior is common among young preschoolers, but decreases in frequency from ages 2 through 5. Levels of aggression are fairly stable over childhood, with aggressive toddlers becoming aggressive school age children (Cummings et al. 1989) (see *Aggression, Development and Socialization*).

2.5 Development of the Self

The development of the concept of the self is very important for social development. About 75 percent of children show some form of self-recognition (such as recognizing themselves in the mirror) by the age of 18–24 months. Late in their second year, children begin using pronouns in their language (*I, me, my,* and *mine*) that indicate a differentiation between themselves and others (Lewis and Brooks-Gunn 1979).

Initially, children's verbal references distinguishing themselves from others are centered on physical characteristics ("I'm stronger," "I'm bigger"). Only when children approach adolescence do they begin making more psychological, or abstract, references distinguishing themselves from others ("I'm happy," "I'm smart") (Montemayor and Eisen 1977).

3. Language Development

Beginning with their first combination of words into simple sentences at about 18 months, children's utterances become longer and more complex. Over the preschool years, children of all cultures learn the grammatical rules of their language, often applying them when not appropriate. This is reflected by overregularization, in which children use rules in situations where they do not apply (e.g., in English, saying "goed," "runned," or "mouses"). Children's syntax (the grammatical structure of their sentences) increasingly comes to resemble that of adults in their culture, as reflected by their formation of language constructions such as negatives, questions, and the use of relational terms. At all ages, children's receptive language (i.e., what they can understand) is more advanced than their productive language (i.e., what they can produce). By age 5, children's language greatly resembles that of adults. Although the structure of children's language does increase in complexity over the school years (e.g., in English, use of passive tense, more consistent noun/verb agreement), the differences between the grammar used by 6- and 7-year olds and by adults are subtle and minor (de Villiers and de Villiers 1978).

The ability to learn a new language is greatest in early childhood and wanes until adolescence, when second-language learning often becomes especially difficult. Adolescents and adults who learn the syntax of a second language successfully rarely sound like native speakers but continue to have decided accents, unlike children, who can master both the syntax and phonology of a new language "like a native."

Semantics (the meaning of language terms) also develops markedly through childhood. The number of words children have in their productive vocabularies grows rapidly beginning at about two years of age, increasing to between 8,000 and 14,000 words by the first grade, with individual words becoming more elaboratively encoded and associations with other words in memory becoming stronger and more numerous (see Bjorklund 1995).

Over childhood, children learn to categorize word concepts into natural language categories, first acquiring concepts at a basic level (e.g., chairs, cars) before learning to categorize according to superordinate categories (e.g., furniture, vehicles).

Children's representations can be expressed in terms of scripts, which are a form of schematic organization, with real-world events arranged in terms of temporal and causal relations between components of the event (e.g., who did what to whom and when). Preschool children's attempts at remembering sequences of events are based on scripts. Moreover, parents help young children form narratives in remembering events by asking them questions that focus on the important things to remember about events, such as who was involved, what was done, where did it occur, and what was the sequence of acts (see Fivush and Hudson 1990).

4. Cognitive Development

4.1 Representation

Developing alongside language late in the second year of life are imagery, fantasy play, and the ability to delay, or defer imitation. Piaget (1962) proposed that the representations of young children were symbolic but intuitive and illogical (preoperational period), becoming logical at some stage between the ages of five and seven years, although still tied to concrete objects (the stage of concrete operations). Beginning in early adolescence, children's thinking was described by Piaget as abstract, with "hypothetico-deductive reasoning" characterizing thought (formal operations).

Experiments by Flavell and his colleagues have shown the limits of symbolic representation in young children by investigating their knowledge about the distinction between appearance and reality (e.g., Flavell et al. 1986). For example, in some experiments, children watched as white milk was poured into a filtered glass to appear red, or they were shown objects that had uncharacteristic sounds or smells (e.g., socks that smelled like peanut butter). Questions to the children then focused on two areas: what the objects looked like, "how they look to your eyes right now"; and the actual identity of the objects, "how

they really and truly are." Somewhat surprisingly, Flavell et al. (1986) reported that most 3-year olds could not solve these apparently simple problems, even with explicit training, causing the authors to conclude that 3-year olds did not have even a minimal understanding of the appearance–reality distinction. Flavell et al. (1986) speculated that 3-year olds are unable to represent an object in more than one form at a time (dual encoding) and so base their answers on either the appearance (the milk looks red, so it really and truly is red) or the actual identity (the rock-like sponge is a sponge, so it looks like a sponge) of an object. With age, children become more adept at dual encoding, although it is not until late childhood or early adolescence before truly abstract distinctions can be made between the appearance and the reality of things.

During childhood, children develop naive "theories" of how the world works, and these theories reflect, in part, their representational abilities. For example, they learn what is animate and what is not, and what characteristics are attributed to the living and the nonliving. Children aged three and four develop theories of number, learning the one-to-one correspondence between count words and objects counted, that the last word in a count series reflects the total number of objects in the set (cardinal principle), and that anything, tangible or intangible, can be counted (Gelman and Gallistel 1978). They also develop a "theory of mind," which is a causal–explanatory framework to explain why people behave as they do. More specifically, they come to understand that other people's behavior is governed by their wants, wishes, hopes, and goals (i.e., their desires), and by their ideas, opinions and knowledge (i.e., their beliefs) (Perner 1991, Wellman 1990).

4.2 Learning and Remembering

Although most learning and memory tasks are mastered more easily by older than by younger children, there are some exceptions, notably in implicit memory. Implicit memory refers to memory for information that the individual did not explicitly set out to learn but was acquired in the process of performing related cognitive activity. For example, implicit memory is reflected in tasks where subjects are asked to make decisions about the perceptual characteristics of words (e.g., CHERRY: "Does it have an H in it?" or "Is it written in lower-case letters?") and later, unexpectedly, asked to recall the words or to complete word fragments (che—y). Because subjects do not attend explicitly to the meaning of words, performance on these tasks, when compared to proper controls, reflects the amount of information people acquire implicitly. Unlike explicit, or intentional, memory tasks, there are no age differences in implicit memory over childhood, suggesting that the processes of implicit memory are fully functional in school-age children (Naito 1990).

Age differences are dramatic, however, for explicit learning and memory tasks, where children intentionally attempt to solve problems. One popular approach to studying children's problem-solving behavior has been to evaluate strategies, usually defined as goal-directed, effortful, cognitive operations that are potentially available to consciousness.

Children aged two and three will use simple strategies to solve problems, such as staring at the place where a toy was hidden before they are allowed to retrieve it. Young children fail to use more complex strategies spontaneously, such as rehearsing or grouping items by meaning in a memory test; however, they can often be trained to use such strategies with corresponding improvements in their performance, a phenomenon referred to as "production deficiency." Research has found that when children are just learning to use a strategy there is a phase when they spontaneously produce the strategy without enhancing their task performance. Miller (1990) has referred to this as a "utilization deficiency," and describes it as a transition phase between nonstrategy use and effective strategic behavior.

Young children usually require more explicit training before they benefit from a strategy than older children, although even preschoolers will use a strategy when provided with familiar materials and clear instructions. Young children behave strategically only under highly favorable task conditions; with age, children broaden the situations in which they will use effective strategies (see Bjorklund 1995).

Age differences in explicit learning and memory tasks have been attributed to many different factors. For example, with age, children process information more quickly and experience less interference from both external sources (e.g., task-irrelevant stimuli) and internal sources (e.g., task-irrelevant thoughts) (Harnishfeger and Bjorklund 1993). Also, older children typically have more world knowledge than younger children, with the knowledge advantage influencing how information is processed (see Bjorklund 1995).

A particularly effective demonstration of the effect of knowledge on children's cognitive performance comes from an experiment by Schneider et al. (1989). In their study, third-, fifth-, and seventh-grade children were classified as either experts or novices for the game of soccer, and further classified, within each expertise group, as high or low IQ. The children were then given a text comprehension test on a soccer-related story. Soccer experts, regardless of their level of IQ, performed better than soccer novices. In short, having detailed background knowledge for the story overrode the effect of IQ on text comprehension.

Young children's problem-solving is often done "out loud" or by using physical prompts, and only in later childhood becomes covert. For example, preschool children will initially solve simple addition problems by physically counting their fingers or other external markers. They later count or add out loud, and only at the age of seven or eight years begin to solve problems of arithmetic mentally. Berk (1986) reported that the amount of "private speech" (i.e., children talking to themselves) while solving arithmetic problems was positively related to intelligence at Grade 1 but not at Grade 3, demonstrating that brighter children internalize their problem-solving sooner than less bright children.

Another factor that develops gradually over childhood and influences children's problem-solving is metacognition, namely, the knowledge a person has of his or her cognitive skills and the ability to monitor task performance and make adjustments toward achieving a goal. Older children are more aware of both endogenous and exogenous factors that influence attention, communication, imitation, memory, and reading than younger children and are better at evaluating the effectiveness of their attempts at task performance (see Bjorklund 1995). Young children generally overestimate their performance on cognitive tasks, thinking that they will remember more items on a memory test or achieve more in school than they actually will (Stipek and MacIver 1989).

Children's poor metacognition is generally viewed as a detriment to effective cognition, and understandably so. However, because young children are out of touch with their actual cognitive and physical abilities, they are less apt to be discouraged by their low levels of performance and thus tend to persist at tasks and attempt new ones where a better informed child, with a more realistic assessment of his or her performance, may not. This, and other aspects of young children's immature cognitive abilities, may actually be adaptive and should not be viewed as simply ineffective thinking that must be overcome by instructions (Bjorklund and Green 1992).

4.3 Culture, Schooling, and Cognitive Development

Humans have evolved certain cognitive abilities to deal with problems encountered over thousands of years, and it can be assumed that children worldwide possess the same basic neurological hardware for developing these cognitive skills. However, which skills develop and how they are expressed will vary with cultural experience. Different cultures will value and foster different cognitive skills. Cognition always occurs within a cultural context and can never be evaluated out of that context.

Perhaps the most dramatic differences in cognitive development are observed between children from schooled and nonschooled cultures. Children who attend school learn to divorce their thinking from specific contexts. They more readily classify information on the basis of abstract criteria, reason about things for which they have no prior knowledge, and use strategies to learn and remember information (Rogoff 1990). However, when given the proper contextual supports, unschooled children perform comparably to schooled children. For example, nonschooled children are much less apt to use memory strategies and thus they perform poorly on tasks in which they are asked to remember unrelated pieces of information (such as words). Performance differences disappear, however, when children are asked to remember contextually relevant information (Rogoff 1990).

5. The Significance of Childhood

Childhood in humans is longer than that of any other mammal. This extended childhood has great significance for the species. Humans, more than any other animal, depend on learning for survival. Moreover, human development cannot be understood out of the cultural context in which it occurs. Children require time to learn the complicated procedures and the social web of relationships at the center of all cultures, and the extended childhood provides the time needed to learn what must be learned. Humans are not the only species with complex social organization, but the variety of human cultures is far greater than that of any other species. The diversity of cultures in which any particular child may find himself or herself necessitates that learning be flexible. Unlike the social insects, children are not genetically programmed for certain social roles. Slow growth and prolonged childhood equips a person not only with time to learn the ways of their specific culture but also with mental and social flexibility, so that a given child can become a weaver, hunter, navigator, or computer programmer, depending on the cultural apprenticeship provided.

See also: Broadcasting and Technology: Effects on Children and Youth; Family, School, and Social Capital; Socialization

References

Baumrind D 1967 Child care practices anteceding three patterns of preschool behavior. *Genet. Psychol. Monogr.* 75(1): 43–88

Berk L E 1986 Relationship of elementary school children's private speech to behavioral accompaniment to task, attention, and task performance. *Dev. Psychol.* 22(5): 671–80

Bjorklund D F 1995 *Children's Thinking: Developmental Function and Individual Differences,* 2nd edn. Brooks/Cole, Pacific Grove, California

Bjorklund D F, Green B L 1992 The adaptive nature of cognitive immaturity. *Am. Psychol.* 47(1): 46–54

Cohn D A 1990 Child–mother attachment of six-year-olds and social competence at school. *Child Dev.* 61(1): 152–62

Cummings E M, Iannotti R J, Zahn-Waxler C 1989 Aggression between peers in early childhood: Individual continuity and developmental change. *Child Dev.* 60(4): 887–95

de Villiers J G, de Villiers P A 1978 *Language Acquisition.* Harvard University Press, Cambridge, Massachusetts

Fivush R, Hudson J A (eds.) 1990 *Knowing and Remembering in Young Children.* Cambridge University Press, Cambridge

Flavell J H, Green F L, Flavell E R 1986 The development of children's knowledge about the appearance–reality distinction. *Monogr. Soc. Res. Child Dev.* 51(1): 1–68

Gelman R, Gallistel C 1978 *The Child's Understanding of Number.* Harvard University Press, Cambridge, Massachusetts

Goodenough F L 1926 *The Measurement of Intelligence through Drawing.* Holt Publishing, Yonkers, New York

Harnishfeger K K, Bjorklund D F 1993 The ontogeny of inhibition mechanisms: A renewed approach to cognitive development. In: Howe M L, Pasnak R (eds.) 1993 *Emerging Themes in Cognitive Development. Vol. 1: Foundations.* Springer-Verlag, New York

Hartup W W, Laursen B, Stewart M I, Eastenson A 1988 Conflict and the friendship relations of young children. *Child Dev.* 59(6): 1590–1600

Lewis M, Brooks-Gunn J 1979 *Social Cognition and the Acquisition of Self.* Plenum Press, New York

Maccoby E E, Jacklin C N 1987 Gender segregation in childhood. In: Reese H W (ed.) 1987 *Advances in Child Development and Behavior,* Vol. 20. Academic Press, San Diego, California

Main M, Kaplan N, Cassidy J 1985 Security in infancy, childhood, and adulthood: A move to the level of representation. In: Bretherton I, Waters E (eds.) 1985 *Growing Points of Attachment Theory and Research.* University of Chicago Press, Chicago, Illinois

Miller P H 1990 The development of strategies of selective attention. In: Bjorklund D F (ed.) 1990 *Children's Strategies: Contemporary Views of Cognitive Development.* Erlbaum, Hillsdale, New Jersey

Montemayor R, Eisen M 1977 The development of self-conceptions from childhood to adolescence. *Dev. Psychol.* 13(4): 314–19

Naito M 1990 Repetition priming in children and adults: Age-related dissociation between implicit and explicit memory. *J. Exp. Child Psychol.* 50(3): 462–84

Perner J 1991 *Understanding the Representational Mind.* MIT Press, Cambridge, Massachusetts

Piaget J 1962 *Play, Dreams, and Imitation in Childhood.* Norton, New York

Rogoff B 1990 *Apprenticeship in Thinking: Cognitive Development in Social Context.* Oxford University Press, New York

Scarr S 1992 Developmental theories for the 1990s: Development and individual differences. *Child Dev.* 63(1): 1–19

Schneider W, Körkel J, Weinert F E 1989 Domain-specific knowledge and memory performance: A comparison of high- and low-aptitude children. *J. Educ. Psychol.* 81(3): 306–12

Shaffer D R 1988 *Social and Personality Development*, 2nd edn. Brooks Cole, Pacific Grove, California

Stipek D, MacIver D 1989 Developmental change in children's assessment of intellectual competence. *Child Dev.* 60(3): 521–38

Tanner J M 1978 *Fetus into Man: Physical Growth from Conception to Maturity.* Harvard University Press, Cambridge, Massachusetts

Wellman H M 1990 *The Child's Theory of Mind.* MIT Press, Cambridge, Massachusetts

Student Perceptions of Classrooms

B. J. Fraser

In contrast to earlier behaviorist views of students as passive recipients of information, late twentieth century theories of teaching and learning view students as being actively involved in their own learning and recognize the importance and relevance of student perceptions. Although this interest in students' perceptions is evident in the third edition of the *Handbook of Research on Teaching* (Wittrock 1986), it was largely absent from the first and second editions. Considerable research has provided insights into factors related to student perceptions as well as the associations between student perceptions and student outcomes.

The importance of students' perceptions is well supported by two lines of research. First, because research in numerous countries has revealed consistent differences between students' and teachers' perceptions (Fraser 1994), a focus on students' rather than teachers' perceptions is likely to be more productive in attempts to improve and understand classroom learning. Second, student perceptions help to explain student outcomes beyond the effects of student abilities, instructional methods, and curricular materials (Fraser 1986, Schunk and Meece 1992). Because teacher behaviors can be considered relevant only when they are perceived as cues by students, student perceptions can be thought of as mediators between instruction and student outcomes.

Schunk and Meece (1992) edited a collection of studies of both students' self-perceptions (of their abilities, competence, interests, and goals) and their social perceptions (of teachers, peers, events, and situations). In addition to providing evidence supporting the validity of student perceptions, this collection of research studies shows that the student's perceptions not only affect his or her own behavior, but that perceptions themselves are influenced by student attributes and situational cues. For example, gender differences in student perceptions have been documented (Meece and Courtney 1992) and student perceptions of classroom climate have been related consistently to student outcomes when student aptitude differences were controlled (Fraser 1986, Haertel et al. 1981).

1. Measuring Student Perceptions of Classrooms

In the late 1960s, the Learning Environment Inventory was used as part of the research and evaluation activities of Harvard Project Physics (Welch and Walberg 1972). Around the same time, Moos began developing social climate scales for a wide variety of human environments, including the Classroom Environment Scale for use in school settings (Moos and Trickett 1987).

Other instruments for assessing students' perceptions of classroom environment include the Individualized Classroom Environment Questionnaire, My Class Inventory, College and University Classroom Environment Inventory, Science Laboratory Environment Inventory, and Questionnaire on Teacher Interaction. Research involving the use of these instruments has been reviewed by Fraser (1986, in press) and Fraser and Walberg (1991).

2. Factors Related to Student Perceptions

Fraser (1986) tabulated 39 studies in which students' perceptions of their classrooms were employed as dependent variables in (a) curriculum evaluation studies, (b) investigations of differences between student and teacher perceptions of actual and preferred environment, and (c) studies involving other independent variables. One promising but largely neglected use of students' perceptions is as process criteria in evaluating innovations and new curricula. A study involving an evaluation of the Australian Science Education Project (ASEP) revealed that, in comparison with a control group, students in ASEP classes perceived their classrooms as being more satisfying and individualized and having a better material environment (Fraser 1986). The significance of this evaluation, as well as Welch and Walberg's (1972) evaluation of Harvard Project Physics in the United States, is that student perceptions differentiated revealingly between curricula, even when various outcome measures showed negligible differences.

The fact that most instruments which assess perceptions have different forms for assessing actual and preferred conditions and forms for teachers and students permits investigation of differences between students' and teachers' perceptions, and differences between the actual situation and that preferred by students or teachers. Fisher and Fraser's (1983) research revealed that, first, students preferred a more positive classroom environment than they perceived as being actually present and, second, teachers perceived a more positive classroom environment than did their students in the same classrooms. These results replicate studies in school classrooms in the United States, Israel, and Australia (Fraser in press), as well as in other settings such as hospital wards and work milieus (e.g., Moos 1974).

In a study by Wubbels et al. (1992) in the Netherlands, the majority of teachers (70 percent) perceived the classroom environment more favorably than their students. However, the perceptions of another group

751

of teachers (30 percent) were more negative than those of their students. Overall, this study suggested that teacher perceptions are shaped partly by their ideals about the learning environment (i.e., teachers' ideals can distort their perceptions of the actual learning environment). The discrepancy between teachers' and students' perceptions on average was larger for teachers who exhibited fewer behaviors that promoted student cognitive and affective outcomes than for teachers who exhibited more of those behaviors.

The third group of studies reviewed by Fraser (1986) shows that researchers in various countries have used students' perceptions as criterion variables in studies aimed at identifying how perceptions vary with such factors as teacher personality, class size, grade level, student gender, subject matter, the nature of the school-level environment, and the type of school. Studies into the transition from elementary to high school in the United States have revealed a deterioration in the perceived classroom environment when students move from generally smaller elementary schools to larger, departmentally organized lower secondary schools (Midgley et al. 1991). This decline could be attributable to less positive student relations with teachers and reduced student opportunities for decision-making in the classroom.

3. Associations Between Student Perceptions and Student Outcomes

A strong tradition in past research (Haertel et al. 1981) has shown that student perceptions of classroom environment account for appreciable amounts of variance in cognitive and affective learning outcomes, often beyond that attributable to background student characteristics. The practical implication from this research is that student outcomes might be improved by creating classroom environments found empirically to be conducive to learning.

Fraser (1994) has tabulated a set of 40 studies in which the effects of student perceptions of their classrooms on student outcomes were investigated in numerous countries. These studies involved a variety of cognitive and affective outcome measures, student perception instruments, and samples of students from a variety of grade levels.

The findings from prior research are highlighted in the results of a meta-analysis involving 734 correlations from 12 studies including 823 classes in eight subject areas containing 17,805 students in four nations (Haertel et al. 1981). Learning posttest scores and gains were found consistently and strongly to be associated with student perceptions of their classrooms, although correlations generally were higher in samples of older students and in studies employing collectivities such as classes and schools (in contrast to individual students) as the units of statistical analysis. In particular, higher achievement on a variety of

measures was found in classes perceived by students as having greater cohesiveness, satisfaction, and goal direction, and less disorganization and friction. In a study of science laboratory classes in Nigeria, Israel, the United Kingdom, Canada, the United States, and Australia, students' perceptions were more positive in settings in which integration between theory and laboratory classes was perceived to be greater (Fraser et al. 1992).

Fraser and Fisher (1983) used a person–environment interaction framework in exploring whether or not student outcomes depend, not only on student perceptions of the actual classroom environment, but also on the match between students' preferences and the actual environment. Overall, the findings suggest that similarity between actual and preferred environment could be as important as the actual environment in predicting student achievement of important affective and cognitive aims.

4. Current Trends and Desirable Future Directions

While speculations on numerous trends and directions can be offered, three topics are treated briefly in this section. They are school psychology, constructivist learning environments, and personal forms of scales.

4.1 School Psychology

Given the school psychologist's changing role, the work on student perceptions of classrooms provides a good example of an area that furnishes a number of ideas, techniques, and research findings that could be valuable in school psychology. Traditionally, school psychologists have tended to concentrate heavily and sometimes exclusively on their roles in assessing and enhancing academic achievement and other valued learning outcomes. Understanding student perceptions of classrooms enables school psychologists to become sensitized to subtle but important aspects of classroom life. Burden and Fraser (1993) report some ways in which students' perceptions were used in the United Kingdom in helping teachers change their classroom interactive styles, and in using discrepancies between students' perceptions of actual and preferred environment as an effective basis to guide improvements in their classrooms.

4.2 Constructivist Learning Environments

Traditionally, teachers have conceived their roles to be concerned with revealing or transmitting the logical structures of their knowledge, and directing students through rational inquiry toward discovering the predetermined universal truths expressed in the form of laws, principles, rules, and algorithms. Developments in history, philosophy, and sociology have provided educators with a better understanding of the nature of knowledge development. At the level of the individual learner, there has been a realization that meaningful learning is a cognitive process of making sense, or purposeful problem-solving, of the experiential world of the individual in relation to the totality of the individual's already constructed knowledge. This sense-making process involves active negotiation and consensus building. Because a new learning environment instrument was needed to assist researchers to assess the degree to which a particular classroom's environment is perceived by students to be consistent with a constructivist epistemology, and in order to assist teachers to reflect on their epistemological assumptions and reshape their teaching practice, the Constructivist Learning Environment Survey (CLES) was developed. The CLES includes the five scales of personal relevance, uncertainty, critical voice, shared control, and student negotiation (Taylor et al. in press).

4.3 Personal Forms of Student Perception Scales

There is potentially a major problem with nearly all existing classroom environment instruments when used to identify differences between subgroups within a classroom (e.g., boys and girls) or in the construction of case studies of individual students. The problem is that items are worded in such a way that they elicit an individual student's perceptions of the class as a whole, as distinct from that student's perceptions of his or her own role within the classroom. For example, items in the traditional class form of classroom environment instruments might seek students' opinions about whether "the work of the class is difficult" or whether "the teacher is friendly toward the class." In contrast, a personal form of the same items would seek opinions about whether "I find the work of the class difficult" or whether "the teacher is friendly toward me."

A vivid example of the way in which certain subgroups of students within a class perceived different subenvironments because of the teacher's differential treatment of them is provided by a study of "target" students (i.e., pupils who monopolized the verbal interaction during whole-class activities) (see Fraser 1994). It was found that target students perceived significantly greater levels of involvement and rule clarity than did nontarget students. Furthermore, these perceptions were consistent with classroom observations that the teachers directed more questions at target students and allowed them (and not other students) to call out answers without being asked. Similarly, Tobin et al.'s (1990) case studies of individual students revealed that meaningful differences in perceptions existed between certain students, and that those differences were consistent with the teacher's expectations of and attitudes toward individuals. The findings of these two studies highlight the need for a new generation of student perception instruments which are more capable of detecting the differences in perceptions between individuals or subgroups within the class.

Fraser et al. (1995) developed and validated parallel class and personal forms of both an actual and preferred version of the Science Laboratory Environment Inventory (SLEI), and reported three uses of the new personal form. First, students' perceptions on the class form were found to be systematically more favorable than their scores on the personal form, perhaps suggesting that students have a more detached view of the classroom as it applies to the class as a whole. Second, as hypothesized, gender differences in perceptions were somewhat larger on the personal form than on the class form. Third, although a study of associations between students' outcomes and their perceptions of the science laboratory revealed that the magnitudes of associations were comparable for class and personal forms, commonality analyses showed that each form accounted for appreciable amounts of outcome variance which was independent of that explained by the other form. This finding serves to justify the decision to evolve separate class and personal forms.

5. Conclusion

Outcome measures alone cannot provide a complete picture of the educational process, so student perceptions of classrooms also should be used to provide information about subtle but important aspects of classroom life. However, because teachers and students have systematically different perceptions of the learning environments of the same classrooms (the "rose-colored glasses" phenomenon), student feedback about classrooms is important in teacher education, staff development, and school improvement efforts.

See also: Social Psychological Theories in Education; Social Psychological Theories of Teaching; Sociology of Learning in School; Student Influences on Teaching; Student Roles in Classrooms

References

Burden R, Fraser B J 1993 Use of classroom environment assessments in school psychology: A British perspective. *Psychol. Sch.* 1993 30: 232–240

Fisher D L, Fraser B J 1983 A comparison of actual and preferred classroom environment as perceived by science teachers and students. *J. Res. Sci. Teach.* 20(1): 55–61

Fraser B J 1986 *Classroom Environment*. Croom Helm, London

Fraser B J 1994 Classroom and school climate. In: Gabel D (ed.) 1994 *Handbook of Research on Science Teaching and Learning*. Macmillan, New York

Fraser B J in press Science learning environments: Assessment effects and determinants. In Fraser B J, Tobin K (eds.) in press *International Handbook of Science Education*. Kluwer, Dordrecht, The Netherlands

Fraser B J, Fisher D L 1983 Student achievement as a function of person–environment fit: A regression surface analysis. *Br. J. Educ. Psychol.* 53(1): 89–99

Fraser B J, Giddings G J, McRobbie C J 1995 Evolution

and validation of a personal form of an instrument for assessing science laboratory classroom environments *J. Res. Sci. Teach.* 32(4): 399–422

Fraser B J, Walberg H J (eds.) 1991 *Educational Environments: Evaluation, Antecedents and Consequences.* Pergamon Press, Oxford

Haertel G D, Walberg H J, Haertel E H 1981 Sociopsychological environments and learning: A quantitative synthesis. *Br. Educ. Res. J.* 7(1): 27–36

Meece J L, Courtney D P 1992 Gender differences in students' perceptions: Consequences for achievement-related choices. In: Schunk D H, Meece J L (eds.) 1992

Midgley C, Eccles J S, Feldlaufer H 1991 Classroom environment and the transition to junior high school. In: Fraser B J, Walberg H J (eds.) 1991

Moos R H 1974 *The Social Climate Scales: An Overview.* Consulting Psychologists Press, Palo Alto, California

Moos R H, Trickett E J 1987 *Classroom Environment Scale Manual*, 2nd. edn. Consulting Psychologists Press, Palo Alto, California

Schunk D H, Meece J L (eds.) 1992 *Student Perceptions in the Classroom.* Erlbaum, Hillsdale, New Jersey

Taylor P S, Fraser B J, Fisher D L in press Monitoring constructivist classroom learning environments. *Int. J. Educ. Res.*

Tobin K, Kahle J B, Fraser B J (eds.) 1990 *Windows into Science Classrooms: Problems Associated with Higher-level Cognitive Learning.* Falmer Press, London

Welch W W, Walberg H J 1972 A national experiment in curriculum evaluation. *Am. Educ. Res. J.* 9(3): 373–83

Wittrock M C 1986 Students' thought processes. In: Wittrock M C (ed.) 1986 *Handbook of Research on Teaching*, 3rd. edn. Macmillan, New York

Wubbels T, Brekelmans M, Hooymayers H P 1992 Do teacher ideals distort the self-reports of their interpersonal behavior? *Teaching and Teacher Education* 8(1): 47–58

Further Reading

Raudenbush S, Bryk A S 1986 A hierarchical model of studying school effects. *Sociol. Educ.* 59(1): 1–17

Student Political Activism and Student Movements

P. G. Altbach

Students have been important political actors in many countries and in many circumstances. Most student activism has taken place at the postsecondary level, and this article will deal mainly with student political activism in colleges and universities. However, students have occasionally been politically involved in secondary schools as well. Student activism and student political organizations have had an immense and often ignored impact, not only on students and student cultures but also on academic institutions and sometimes on society. The most visible student organizations are activist political movements, which have received considerable attention, particularly in the aftermath of the volatile 1960s. Activist movements have not only had a significant impact on universities, but have occasionally created social unrest and sometimes revolution. However, there are many kinds of less dramatic student organizations, ranging from cultural and social organizations (including fraternities and sororities) to student publications and newspapers and athletic groups. This entry is mainly concerned with those organizations that have an impact on politics, culture, and society. It does not deal with the purely social element of extracurricular life, although for many students this is the most important aspect, or with the changing attitudes and values of students, which may influence the scope and nature of organizational life. It focuses on the organizational aspects of extracurricular life in higher education and stresses those parts that have a wider impact on both the university and society (Horowitz 1987).

The university is a particularly favorable environment for the development of organizations and movements among students. There is an active environment that stresses independent thought and analysis and intellectual values, theories, and ideals, that may call into question established social and political norms. University faculty, through their teaching and research, may also provide an atmosphere that legitimates dissent. It is the case, for example, that professors are often to the left of the broader society in their attitudes about politics and culture (Basu 1981).

In many countries, university authorities encourage extracurricular activities and organizations, often providing funds and space for them. There is a recognition that such activities are an important part of the experience of higher education and that the academic culture goes beyond the classroom. Universities are in most instances "age-graded" cultures where the majority of students are of a similar age and at a stage in life when they seek a sense of community. The academic culture also allows a considerable amount of free time to engage in extracurricular activities (Ben-David and Zloczower 1962). It is easy to communicate when students are centered on a campus. It should be kept in mind that the total combined membership of student groups is in almost all instances a minority, albeit significant, of the student population. Even in times of considerable politicization and activism, student involvement generally remains a minority phenomenon.

Academic communities also have some special characteristics that affect the nature of organizations and movements. Student generations are short, generally lasting 3 or 4 years, and thus it is sometimes a challenge to keep movements, and to a lesser extent organizations, alive through student generations. Students tend to be impatient, wanting change quickly, due in part to the brevity of student generations and in part to a certain impatience normal in young people. Students, especially in political organizations, tend to seek total solutions and be impatient with compromise. As Shils and others have pointed out, students are often antinomian—opposed to established authority— regardless of the perspectives of those in power (Shils 1969 pp. 1–34).

It is difficult to estimate the scope of student organizational involvement in different academic environments. Participation varies according to institutional tradition, period of time, facilities, and other factors. Even within a country, organizational participation may vary considerably. In the United States, elite colleges and universities with largely full-time and residential student populations generally have a higher level of involvement than "commuter schools" that attract many part-time and employed students who have little time for extracurricular activities. In many countries, there are few facilities available for organizational activities and this limits participation. There are also variations according to historical circumstances. During periods of considerable political consciousness, students tend to be involved in activist campus movements, swelling the numbers participating in organizations.

The impact of students on both university and society is often overlooked. This impact goes far beyond student political activist movements that have threatened governments. Student organizations are a major influence on the campus culture and ethos. They help to determine the self-image of the student body and strongly influence the ideas that permeate the institution. Student groups shape the political and cultural ideas of the institution as much as the faculty and curriculum. Student organizations influence and sometimes control the rules and regulations that govern campus life. For example, student opposition to *in loco parentis* in the United States at the end of the 1950s and in the 1960s forced academic institutions to give up many of the rules and regulations that governed student conduct (Horowitz 1987). In Western Europe, student reaction against deteriorating conditions during the rapid expansion of the 1960s led to significant reforms of higher education at this time (Altbach 1974). In West Germany and a few other countries, student ideas about the nature of reform had an impact on the dramatic changes that took place in many German universities at the time (Nitsch et al. 1965). Student unrest in India has led to the

canceling of examinations and other major changes in academic routines. The existence of active political and social organizations, as well as organizations such as fraternities and sororities, on campus can affect the opinions of the entire student body.

1. Multifaceted Student Organizational Culture

While national and institutional student cultures vary significantly, it is worth pointing out the scope of student organizations that exist on many campuses throughout the world.

1.1 Student Newspapers and Publications

Student newspapers and other publications are highly significant organizations on most campuses. Student newspapers are sometimes completely independent of administrative control, in some cases even being published off-campus or by independent companies. They are generally the most important means of communication among students and an outlet for student opinion on a variety of topics. Newspapers may be daily or published less frequently. Some are highly professional, while others are not. In many countries, experience in campus journalism often leads to a career in journalism. There are wide variations in the nature and scope of student newspapers. Some are highly political, seeking to convince the student body of a specific political position or ideology. Some seek to provide information about campus issues while others focus on national and international matters as well as university-based issues. Student newspapers generally constitute an organizational culture for those serving on the staff. Student newspapers also exist in secondary schools, although they are naturally less professional and in most instances more directly controlled by school authorities. However, secondary school newspapers often constitute a distinct subculture, frequently with political or cultural overtones. Students involved in the campus press often work long hours and find that the newspaper is an all-consuming activity.

Other student publications are also an important part of campus life. In the United States, most colleges and universities and many secondary schools publish yearbooks, featuring stories and pictures concerning campus life. Such books are designed, written, and frequently published by student groups. Many journals and other ephemeral publications appear from time to time on campuses, usually established and edited by students. Such publications may be political, cultural, or devoted to other pursuits. Student literary journals have a long-standing tradition in many countries and sometimes serve as the source of original intellectual work. As with newspapers, the student groups involved in editing such journals are generally close-knit and active.

The student press cannot be overestimated as an

important part of the organizational culture of a campus. Not only do such publications constitute a key means of communicating but they are also among the largest and most active student organizations. Newspapers can influence the campus, and other publications provide an outlet for creative writing. Student publications are among the most visible element of student organizational culture. They tend to be active even when other organizations may be dormant and can, if inclined, maintain a sense of political or social awareness in a university without overt activism. While student newspapers and other publications in secondary schools are less visible than those in higher education, they are often important, especially as a means of creating a sense of community among highly motivated students.

1.2 Fraternities and Sororities

Although limited to a relatively small number of countries, fraternities and sororities are important elements of student life. These organizations have been especially important in the United States and Germany, although their tradition goes back to medieval times. The tradition of students banding together for both social and living purposes dates back to the medieval "nations," or student communities based on country of origin in the medieval universities (Cobban 1975). In Germany, the *burschenshaften* (fraternities) have traditionally been an important part of German academic life, providing a social core to a highly fragmented academic culture. The traditional *burschenshaften* were conservative in culture and politics and often played a role in campus political affairs. They were also highly nationalistic and were a significant influence in the rise of German nationalism in the nineteenth century.

The United States fraternities and sororities provide a place to live on campus as well as a social focus for their student members. They tend to be relatively homogenous in membership, often in an effort to provide a congenial and unthreatening home for students challenged by a complex academic environment. Fraternities and sororities have seldom been overtly political in orientation, although they reflect conservative values and orientations. The "Greek movement," as the fraternities and sororities call themselves (because they have given themselves names based on letters in the Greek alphabet), has a long history in United States higher education, dating from the early nineteenth century (Allmendinger 1975). They have tended to play a more central part in campus life during relatively conservative periods. For example, their popularity declined significantly during the radical 1960s. Nonetheless, "Greeks" have been an important element in the student culture of most residential colleges and unversities and they remain active, although less important in the 1990s than in the 1950s and earlier. Relatively few other countries have significant fraternity–sorority movements. In most countries, students either live privately away from the campus or in

dormitories. Fraternities and sororities are extremely rare in secondary schools.

1.3 Religious Organizations

In many countries, religious organizations constitue an important part of student life in higher education but seldom in secondary schools. In the United States, for example, religious organizations representing virtually every major and many minor denominations and religions can be found at most large universities and colleges. These groups not only provide a spiritual focus for students but often provide a social center as well. Some religious organizations also have a political orientation. In the United States, fundamentalist Christian groups have been politically active against the legalization of abortion. At earlier periods, liberal Protestant organizations were at the forefront of civil rights and other progressive causes. Religious groups are also active in other countries. In India, nationalist-oriented Hindu organizations have been active in the universities and have involved large numbers of students in both religious and political activities as well as programs to assist the poor. In the Islamic world, fundamentalist Muslim groups have been among the strongest political influences in the universities and in some instances in society as well. The Islamic student movement is especially influential at the end of the twentieth century, dominating student political life in many Islamic countries. Islamic student organizations are powerful not only in higher education but also in secondary schools in many countries. The Islamic student movement constitutes a religious, cultural, and political force.

1.4 Student Unions and Governments

In most countries, students are organized into governmental structures to represent their interests and provide services at both the higher and the secondary levels. In some countries, there are national student unions that have both political and service functions as well as local student unions in individual universities. Generally, national student unions are federations of university-based student governments, which are in turn generally elected by the students. At times, national student unions have played an important national political role in influencing higher education policy and defending student interests (Fields 1970). National student unions, especially in Europe, have traditionally provided services to students such as low-cost travel arrangements.

Student governments or unions at individual universities and in many secondary schools often control a significant budget and provide services such as food, entertainment, reduced price tickets, and transportation. Student governments also represent student interests to the university and often appoint student representatives to academic committees and governing boards. At times, student governments have played significant political roles as well (Levine 1980). In the

United States, institution-based student governments sometimes reflect broader political concerns and often are thrust into a political role by campus events. In some cases, candidates for office have specifically political platforms, although in general overt politics are not part of the culture of student governments in the United States.

In other countries, student governments are often more politically involved and elections often have a political aura. In India and other countries, established political parties run candidates in student government elections and sometimes spend considerable amounts of money on campus to ensure that their candidates are elected. While less frequent, student governments in secondary schools sometimes play an important political role, especially in countries with very small higher education sectors. In a number of African countries, for example, secondary school student governments have sometimes been active in politics.

1.5 Cultural Organizations

Culture and politics are sometimes mixed on campus. For example, nationalist student organizations have often had a cultural component and sometimes emerged from cultural groups. Groups focusing on "countercultural" activities—certain kinds of music or art and, for example, in Eastern European countries, underground literature—often have a significant political as well as cultural function. Even when not overtly political, cultural organizations are an important force in most universities. Groups dealing with literature, drama, dance, and other forms of cultural expression involve many students, often providing both training and socialization for later careers.

2. Student Political Activism

Student politics is an important element of student organizations and movements. Political activism on campus is central because it has the greatest potential for affecting both the university and society. Activist movements have caused governments to topple and on a few occasions have implemented significant university reform (Walter 1968). These organizations involve highly motivated students, some of who become important in national politics. Activist movements tend to be among the best organized groups that are able to obtain very strong commitments from the students who are involved in them (Lipset 1976). It must be kept in mind, however, that student activist organizations are minority phenomena, involving a very small number of students in sustained organizational activity. Even when there are mass demonstrations on campus, those involved in them are generally a minority of the student body. This fact does not make student activist movements unimportant, but their scope and nature must be kept in careful perspective (Altbach 1989).

Activist movements are almost all oppositional in nature, opposing established governmental authority, university administrators, or others in authority. While most contemporary student movements are on the left in terms of their ideologies and politics, events in Eastern Europe, where students played a central role against Communist authorities, and in the Islamic world, where religious fundamentalism is currently the most potent political force on campus, indicate that there is no one universal student political orientation. Student political movements are both complex and highly significant to both the university and society.

2.1 Historical Perspectives

Student movements have a long history, and in many countries this historical tradition is part of the living memory of contemporary organizations. The involvement of students in the nationalist upsurge in Europe in the nineteenth century was very significant. German nationalist ideas percolated in the universities before becoming a key political force in society. Both students and professors played a central role in the nationalist uprisings of 1848 (Altbach 1969 pp. 451–74). Students were similarly active in the Italian nationalist movement, and in both cases were important in social movements that resulted in significant change in Europe.

Nationalist ideas spread to student movements emerging in the colonial areas of Africa and Asia and students emerged as key forces for independence in much of what is now the Third World (Emmerson 1968). For example, students from the Dutch East Indies studying at universities in the Netherlands in the first several decades of the twentieth century were exposed to nationalist ideas and created the concept of an Indonesian nation. Former student leaders such as Sukarno and Hatta became the most important leaders of the nationalist movement that eventually drove the Dutch from Indonesia and created a new nation (Bachtiar 1968 pp. 180–214). The role of Indonesian students was crucial not only in developing the ideas of the nationalist movement but later in the struggle against the Dutch. Students were a central force in the Indian nationalist movement as well. Ideas of nationalism, Marxism, and secularism were part of the Indian student experience while in the United Kingdom. Western-oriented universities in India also imparted nationalist orientations. Student movements emerged during the 1920s and were active in the struggle for independence that culminated in the departure of the British in 1947. Significantly, Indian student organizations were always situated on the left of the nationalist movement, often in opposition to the tactics of Gandhi (Altbach 1968). The traditions of student activism, established during the independence struggle in both Indonesia and India, continued after Independence and remained active in the early 1990s.

Historically, secondary schools have played a significant political role, although their importance has been overshadowed by university-based activism. In many colonial countries, the higher education sector was extremely small or even absent, and in these cases high schools often were hotbeds of nationalist political ferment. During the colonial period in Africa, where there were few postsecondary institutions, high-school students were often involved in nationalist agitation. There are similar examples in many Asian countries.

Late twentieth-century student movements are, for the most part, leftist. This has not always been the case. In fact, the nationalist influences of European student movements turned some of them to the right during the period after the First World War. In Germany, the major student organizations supported the Nazis both before and after Hitler came to power (Steinberg 1977). There were, of course, many student groups that opposed the Nazis as well. Similarly, in Italy the largest student groups supported Mussolini's Fascist movement. In France there was strong support in the universities for rightist nationalist movements during this period.

Another important historical example of student political activism is the significant student movement that emerged in Latin America in the first decades of the twentieth century, and which succeeded in virtually transforming Latin American higher education by forcing the adoption of far-reaching reforms (Walter 1968). The movement started in Argentina at the University of Cordoba and spread quickly throughout the continent, affecting the major institutions from Mexico in the north, to Chile in the south. The *reforma* established student participation in virtually all elements of academic decision-making, from the election of the rector to important curricular decisions. It also enshrined the notion of the university as an autonomous institution that could claim not only the freedom to control academic decisions but whose campus could not be entered by civil authority without the formal permission of university officials. The *reforma* fundamentally changed Latin American higher education and its impact continued to the early 1990s, although since the early 1970s severe political and economic pressures, military regimes, and the growth of private universities have weakened the power of the *reforma* ideals (Levy 1986).

Student movements are usually sporadic, seldom lasting very long. Even countries with high levels of activism exhibit considerable variation in levels of involvement and in the strength of student movements. It is to some extent possible to chart international trends in student political activism. The volatile 1960s were clearly a time of worldwide activism, and there were some international influences involved, although it seems clear that national student movements are largely motivated by national concerns.

The historical development of the United States student movement indicates the sporadic nature of student politics (Altbach 1974). While there was some campus unrest before the 1930s (including antislavery and then antidraft agitation in the period of the Civil War), the first major student movement emerged during the Depression of the 1930s, stimulated as much by foreign policy concerns (such as the civil war in Spain and a desire to keep the United States out of the Second World War) as by the economic crisis of the period. There was very little activism between 1941 and 1960. During the 1960s, student activism was stimulated by both the civil rights movement (started by Black college students in the south) and growing opinion on campus against the arms race. Escalation of the war in Vietnam brought student activism to its highest level of activity, culminating in nationwide campus disruptions and mass demonstrations in Washington, DC at the end of the decade. Once the war in Vietnam ended, campus activism declined to a very low level during the 1970s, with a minor resurgence of political interest in the late 1980s (Altbach and Cohen 1990). Similar fluctuations can be seen in student movements in other industrialized nations, although the reasons and the timing of course vary according to national, or even local, political and academic circumstances.

Historical consciousness is also important because countries that have a strong tradition of activism tend to see campus movements as more legitimate political actors than countries that have relatively weak activist traditions. It is particularly clear that where students played an important role in the shaping of national history, as in the Third World, activist movements are accepted as legitimate participants in the national political scene. In most Western countries, students have not been involved in key political events and, partly for this reason, are not generally accepted as actors on a societal political stage.

2.2 Ideological Variations

While most of the student activist movements of the post-Second World War period have been to one degree or another on the left, student movements in the 1990s show a significant, and perhaps widening, ideological range. It has been pointed out that there is considerable historical variety in student ideologies. The nationalist impulse, important historically, is difficult to characterize ideologically. Without question, nationalism continues to be an important force. The same is true of religion, particularly when it is combined with nationalism. The growth of Islamic fundamentalism as a powerful political force in the universities of the Islamic world is one of the major developments in student politics worldwide since the start of the 1980s.

It is difficult to characterize ideologically the extraordinarily important political role played by student activists in the political upheaval in Eastern Europe and to some extent in China in the late 1980s. Students were the primary motivating force in the political movement that led up to the Tiananmen Square massacre in June 1989 (Liu 1989). Chinese students seem to have been motivated by a desire for better jobs, complaints against corruption, and a demand for more democracy and freedom of expression. The students did not seem to have a clear perspective concerning their place in the ideological spectrum.

The role of students in the successful upheavals in Eastern Europe at the end of 1989 is clear. In every country (except perhaps Romania), university students and professors were the first important groups to protest against the government, and students often articulated and to an extent shaped the discontent felt by large numbers of people in those countries. Students were in part motivated by nationalism—a desire to see their countries free of external (Soviet) influence. A desire for freedom of expression and representative government also played an important role. The students were protesting against regimes that were unsuccessful in meeting the economic needs of the people. These demands are certainly anti-regime, and as been noted above, student movements tend in virtually all cases to be against established authority, but it is not clear whether the movements are on the left or on the right. The movements seem to be "anti-statist" in terms of the control of the economy, but it is not at all clear that they are "pro-capitalist." The ideological pedigree of several of the most important student activist movements of the postwar period is unclear. It is perhaps significant that these student movements became much less prominent and active in the aftermath of the collapse of the Communist regimes in Central and Eastern Europe.

Islamic fundamentalism is without question the most powerful force among students in Islamic countries. In countries such as Iran, Egypt, Algeria, and Malaysia, student movements that were at one time highly secularist and often leftist in orientation have been transformed into Islamic movements. The underlying reasons for this dramatic change have yet to be analyzed, but the phenomenon is clear. The failure of secular-minded governments throughout the Islamic world to achieve their goals of modernization, the continuing challenge of the Arab–Israeli conflict, and the breakdown of traditional values and the absence of widely accepted new norms may have all contributed to the rise of Islamic fundamentalism. So far, only Iran has become a fundamentalist state, although governments in many other countries from Malaysia to Algeria have become more religious in their orientation. These governments are also worried about political stability and about the future of the educated elite in the context of the new trend in the universities. There is no doubt that the power of the Islamic idea will remain a key force in the Islamic world.

Students have often tended to adhere to an all-encompassing ideology and to seek massive social change in an effort to create a utopian society. The rise of the Islamic movement may reflect such goals. More commonly in the twentieth century, students have looked to ideologies of the left to provide the path to a more perfect social order. The impact of Marxism and other socialist ideas has been perhaps the most

important influence on student movements around the world (Levitt 1984). During the 1960s, virtually all the powerful student movements of the period identified with the left and very often with Marxism, but without adherence to the Soviet Union or any other communist movement. There has been significant change since the 1960s, and the appeal of leftist alternatives has diminished.

The ideological orientation of student movements is less clear at the end of the twentieth century than it has been since the 1940s. The "failure" of countries identified with socialism to build just and successful societies, the rebirth of nationalism in many countries, the continuing problems of modernization and development in the Third World, and new issues such as the environment have all contributed to a lack of clarity concerning the ideological underpinnings of student activist movements.

2.3 Sociological Generalizations

While the research literature on student political movements is limited, relatively little is known about the backgrounds and motivations of student activists in most countries, and it is only possible to speculate about the causes of student unrest, some sociological generalizations are possible (Klineberg et al. 1979). While there are some counter examples, the following generalizations reflect the realities of many countries in the 1990s. Although very little is known about secondary school activism, there is some evidence that the generalizations noted here, based on research on university students, are applicable to high-school students as well.

Student activists come largely from the social sciences and to some extent from the humanities. Fields such as sociology and political science produce a significant proportion of student leaders. The content of the curriculum in these fields may contribute to an interest in activism; the social sciences are concerned with the problems of society. There is probably a degree of self-selection involved as well, with students who have an interest in social issues gravitating to disciplines that focus on these questions. Further, professors in these fields tend to be among the most liberal or radical in the university, no doubt contributing to such attitudes and values among students (Ladd and Lipset 1975). The intellectual atmosphere in the social sciences is more congenial to activism in both thought and action. At the other end of the activist spectrum, highly vocational fields such as management and agriculture tend to be much more conservative in terms of the attitudes of both faculty and students; the curriculum is vocationally focused as well. The culture of such fields does not seem to promote either radical ideologies or a tendency to become involved in activist movements.

Activist students have some common characteristics. Not surprisingly, they are more politically conscious and concerned about ideological issues than the majority of students. They tend to come from families with a higher level of income and education than the average student population. Students in most countries come from significantly more affluent families than the general population. The educational background of the parents tends to be much higher than average, and very often the political attitudes of the families of activists are to the left of the general population. Thus, activist students are very often from highly elite groups in their societies—groups that have benefited from existing societal arrangements. Activists tend to come from urban and cosmopolitan families. This is a key variable in developing countries where the majority of the population is rural and relatively uneducated. During the 1960s, much was made of a perceived "generational conflict" between student activists and their families (Feuer 1969). However, the data show that there is relatively little conflict among activists and their families (Keniston 1971).

3. Conclusion

It is said that students learn as much outside the classroom as in it during their university years. Without question student organizational culture plays an extraordinarily important role in the collegiate experience of students. Student groups provide socialization, give students a sense of belonging in what can be a difficult and sometimes alienating environment, and set up networks of support that often last throughout life and provide valuable skills.

The organizational network in most colleges and universities is highly complex and dense. Few realize how many student groups exist on campus or how they affect students. In the 1990s, as university authorities have yielded control over extracurricular activities to students, there is probably less concern about the nature of extracurricular organizational life than in the past, at least in the United States. Student organizations range from overtly political groups to purely social associations. Religion, culture, athletics, self-improvement, and aspects of the academic curriculum are all represented by such groups. The growing numbers of foreign students have their own nationality-based associations. In some cases, these groups are not very active and have only small numbers of participants. Other student groups are large and have significant budgets.

Student organizational culture varies from country to country and among academic institutions within a country. Traditionally, European universities have not had as strong a network of extracurricular organizations as United States universities. European students are older than their United States compeers and, except in the United Kingdom, there are few traditions of organized extracurricular life. In developing countries, there is often a large number of student groups, ranging from radical political movements to many social and religious organizations. There are also frequently more controls by campus administrators. There are significant variations within countries. In the United States, for example, student organizational life varies significantly from being very active in residential institutions to being much less dense in commuter schools and community colleges. Some institutions place emphasis on political organizations while others have a more active religious life.

The nature of both student culture and student political activism in secondary schools is much less clear everywhere. Except in periods of significant social unrest, secondary school students are generally not involved directly in politics. There are some exceptions to this generalization. For example, high school students were involved in the cultural revolution in China (Lin 1991, Chan 1985) and students have been sporadically involved in politics in some African countries where there are few university students. The relationship between political education and socialization in secondary schools and political activism is unclear (Massialas 1972).

This entry has focused significantly on political organizations and movements because they tend to be the most visible and vocal and they have had the greatest direct impact on both the educational system and society. Yet in terms of numbers of students involved or perhaps even in long-term effect on those involved in student organizations, activist movements are not necessarily the most important. The entire nexus of organizations and their different constituencies and functions are among the most important elements of contemporary academic life.

See also: Acquisition of Empowerment Skills; Conscientization and Mobilization; Political Socialization and Education; Youth Cultures and Subcultures

References

Allmendinger D F 1975 *Paupers and Scholars: The Transformation of Student Life in Nineteenth Century New England*. St. Martins, New York
Altbach E 1969 Vanguard of revolt: Students and politics in Central Europe, 1815–1948. In: Lipset S M, Altbach P (eds.) 1969 *Students in Revolt*. Beacon, Boston, Massachusetts
Altbach P (ed.) 1968 *Turmoil and Transition: Higher Education and Student Politics in India*. Basic Books, New York
Altbach P 1974 *Student Politics in America: A Historical Analysis*. McGraw-Hill, New York
Altbach P 1989 Perspectives on student political activism. *Comp. Educ.* 25: 97–110
Altbach P, Cohen R 1990 American student activism: The post-sixties transformation. *J. Higher Educ.* 61: 32–49
Bachtiar H 1968 Indonesia. In: Emmerson D (ed.) 1968 *Students and Politics in Developing Nations*. Praeger, New York
Basu A 1981 *Culture, Politics and Critical Academics*. Archana, Meerut

Ben-David J, Zloczower A 1962 Universities and academic systems in modern societies. *Eur. J. Sociol.* 3(1): 45–84

Chan A 1985 *Children of Mao: Personality Development and Political Activism in the Red Guard Generation.* Macmillan, London

Cobban A B 1975 *The Medieval Universities: Their Development and Organization.* Methuen, London

Emmerson D (ed.) 1968 *Students and Politics in Developing Nations.* Praeger, New York

Feuer L 1969 *The Conflict of Generations: The Character and Significance of Student Movements.* Basic Books, New York

Fields A B 1970 *Student Politics in France: A study of the Union Nationale des Etudiants de France.* Heinemann Educational, London

Horowitz H L 1987 *Campus Life: Undergraduate Cultures from the End of the Eighteenth Century to the Present.* University of Chicago Press, Chicago, Illinois

Keniston K 1971 *Youth and Dissent: The Rise of a New Opposition.* Harcourt Brace Jovanovich, New York

Klineberg O, Zavaloni M, Louis-Guerin L, Benbrika J 1979 *Students, Values and Politics: A Cross-cultural Comparison.* Free Press, New York

Ladd E C, Lipset S M 1975 *The Divided Academy: Professor and Politics.* McGraw-Hill, New York

Levitt C 1984 *Children of Privilege: Student Revolt in the Sixties.* University of Toronto Press, Toronto

Levine A 1980 *When Dreams and Heroes Died: A Portrait of Today's College Student.* Jossey-Bass, San Francisco, California

Levy D 1986 *Higher Education and the State in Latin America: Private Challenges to Public Dominance.* University of Chicago Press, Chicago, Illinois

Lin J 1991 *The Red Guards' Path to Violence: Political, Educational and Psychological Factors.* Praeger, New York

Lipset S M 1976 *Rebellion in the University.* University of Chicago Press, Chicago, Illinois

Liu S C 1989 The 1989 Peking student pro-democracy movement in retrospect. *Issues and Studies* 25:31–46

Massialas B (ed.) 1972 *Political Youth, Traditional Schools: National and International Perspectives.* Prentice Hall, Englewood Cliffs, New Jersey

Nitsch W et al. 1965 *Hochschule in der Demokratie.* Luchterhand, Berlin

Shils E 1969 Dreams of plentitude, nightmares of scarcity. In: Lipset S M, Altbach P G (eds.) 1969 *Students in Revolt.* Beacon, Boston, Massachusetts

Steinberg M S 1977 *Sabers and Brown Shirts: The German Students' Path to National Socialism, 1918–1935.* University of Chicago Press, Chicago, Illinois

Walter R J 1968 *Student Politics in Argentina: The University Reform and Its Effects, 1918–1964.* Basic Books, New York

Further Reading

Altbach P (ed.) 1974 *University Reform: Comparative Perspectives for the Seventies.* Schenkman, Cambridge, Masschusetts

Altbach P (ed.) 1989 *Student Political Activism: An International Reference Handbook.* Greenwood, Westport, Connecticut

Astin A, Astin H, Bayer A, Bisconti A 1975 *The Power of Protest.* Jossey-Bass, San Francisco, California

Barkan J 1975 *An African Dilemma: University Students, Development and Politics in Ghana, Tanzania and Uganda.* Oxford University Press, Nairobi

Caute D 1988 *The Year of the Barricades: A Journey Through 1968.* Harper and Row, New York

Cerych L, Sabatier P 1986 *Great Expectations and Mixed Performance: The Implementation of Higher Education Reforms in Europe.* Trentham Books, Stoke-on-Trent

Chu D 1989 *The Character of American Higher Education and Intercollegiate Sport.* SUNY Press, Albany, New York

Fass P 1977 *The Damned and the Beautiful: American Youth in the 1920s.* Oxford University Press, Oxford

Fields A B 1989 France. In: Altbach P (ed.) 1989

Gitlin T 1987 *The Sixties: Years of Hope. Days of Rage.* Bantam, Toronto

Hazary S C 1987 *Student Politics in India.* Ashish, New Delhi

Hendrick I G, Jones R L 1972 *Student Dissent in the Schools.* Houghton Mifflin, Boston, Massachusetts

Jayaram N 1989 India. In: Altbach P (ed.) 1989

Krauss E S 1974 *Japanese Radical Revisited: Student Protest in Postwar Japan.* University of California, Berkeley, California

Laqueur W 1962 *Young Germany: A History of the German Youth Movement.* Routledge and Kegan Paul, London

Liebman A, Walker K, Glazer M 1972 *Latin American University Students: A Six Nation Study.* Harvard University Press, Cambridge, Massachusetts

Touraine A 1971 (trans. Mayhew LFX) *The May Movement: Revolt and Reform.* Irvington, New York

Student Roles in Classrooms

S. J. McCarthey and P. L. Peterson

In the first edition of the *International Encyclopedia of Education*, student roles were conceptualized as behaviors characteristic of persons in a context (Tisher 1985). Researchers in the 1970s and early 1980s found that students in the typical classroom assumed a passive role, spending most of their time listening to the teacher (Goodlad 1984). Students talked no more than 30 percent of the time and this followed the teacher initiation–student response–teacher evaluation pattern (IRE) identified by Mehan (1979). Tisher (1985) suggested that classroom context influenced teachers' and students' observed behavior. For example, teachers in open classrooms asked more higher level cognitive questions than teachers in traditional classrooms. Thus, students in open classrooms received more opportunities to engage

761

in higher level responding than those in traditional classrooms.

Since 1985, researchers have shifted away from a view of classroom roles and practices that focus only on teachers' and students' observed behavior, toward a view that also considers the understandings and perspectives of students and teachers within the social context of classrooms and schools. According to this view, roles are created by participants within a social situation such as a classroom. An understanding of student roles, then, involves understanding not only the observed roles of students in classrooms, but also teachers' and students' assumptions and beliefs about these roles.

1. A New Role for Students in Classrooms

During the late 1980s and continuing into the 1990s, curriculum development efforts in literacy and mathematics have focused on creating a more active role for students (Anderson et al. 1984, National Council of Teachers of Mathematics 1989). In order for students to assume such a role, however, changes in the traditional conceptions of knowledge, tasks, and discourse are needed.

Underlying the student's traditionally passive classroom role is a conception of knowledge that places the authority for knowing with the teacher. The teacher's role is to transmit knowledge to students who simply receive the knowledge transmitted. Underlying the new role for students is a conception of knowledge as an active construction of meaning by the learner, often in collaboration with peers.

Classroom tasks in traditional classrooms involve the use of basal texts in reading and mathematics and an endless array of worksheets that teach skills. Reformers recommend that teachers engage students in new kinds of tasks such as reading authentic children's literature, working on real problems, interpreting texts from a variety of perspectives, solving mathematics problems using a variety of strategies and tools, keeping journals that document learners' thinking, writing for real audiences about topics of students' own choice, and having students pose and solve mathematics problems for themselves.

Finally in traditional classrooms, teachers typically control the discourse. They ask convergent, factual questions for which they know the answers. Students respond by providing specific answers and generating few questions of their own (Mehan 1979). New discourse patterns in literacy instruction include teacher–student and peer conferences that provide students with their peers' perspectives and interpretations of their reading and writing (DiPardo and Freedman 1988). New discourse patterns in mathematics classrooms involve students in negotiating mathematical meaning, discussing and explaining their thinking and strategies for solving problems, justifying their answers, and creating and posing new mathematical problems for themselves (Lampert 1990).

1.1 Student Responses and Teacher Diagnosis

The active role of students has been conceived as involving more extended student responses than has been typical in traditional classrooms. Students have the opportunity to engage in authentic tasks involving reading, writing, solving mathematical problems, and using mathematical tools. While the teacher controls classroom discourse, students have opportunities to provide ideas. The role of the teacher is to construct knowledge, diagnose students' needs, and develop instruction accordingly, while attempting to make learning meaningful for students. The student's role is to acquire this knowledge in a meaningful way.

An example of such a program in literacy is Reading Recovery. Developed in New Zealand to help children having trouble learning to read, Reading Recovery is designed to serve the lowest achieving readers in first-grade classrooms (Clay 1982). Teachers provide daily 30-minute lessons to individual children during which they involve students in reading small books and in writing their own messages. The teachers respond to the students on a minute-to-minute basis according to the student's strengths, needs, and interests. The teacher introduces students to predictable books that they often reread to develop fluency. Additionally, the student has the opportunity to read a new book each day to become familiar with important ideas in stories. While the student is reading, the teacher watches and records substitutions, self-corrections, and omissions to aid in selecting materials for the next day. Students also compose a message each day with the aid of the teacher (Pinnell et al. 1990). Research conducted in New Zealand indicated that students at risk of failure made accelerated progress while enrolled in the Reading Recovery program (Clay 1985). Studies in Ohio showed that students who had participated in Reading Recovery scored significantly higher than comparison children and retained their gains at least two years after the intervention (Pinnell 1989).

Stevenson and Stigler (1992) have portrayed a similar approach to mathematics teaching in their vignettes of selected Japanese classrooms. They have argued that the success of mathematics teaching in Japanese classrooms is related to several important features of active student roles. Students work on real world problems and manipulate concrete objects to model problem solutions. Students discuss their solution strategies in a small or large group. Finally, the teacher diagnoses and remediates students' misconceptions during group discussion. The student's role is to manipulate objects and construct representations; the teacher's role is to assure that correct representations are produced. Class discussion emphasizes meaning, yet is teacher-controlled.

1.2 Learning Expert Strategies from Experts

Some educators have attempted to make students more autonomous, active learners using programs designed to teach strategies that researchers have identified as being employed successfully by experts. These programs are characterized by direct modeling of strategies by the teacher or a student with students gradually assuming more responsibility. Conceptions of knowledge often derive from social constructivist notions, suggesting the importance of teacher scaffolding instruction for the learner (Vygotsky 1978) or from cognitive scientists' ideas of identifying strategies of experts or those more knowledgeable than the student and then teaching these strategies to novices (Romberg 1982). Again, these tasks are structured to promote a gradual internalization of problem-solving processes, emphasizing the learner's assuming metacognitive control (Baker and Brown 1984). Classroom discourse is often initiated by the teacher, but students gradually take over aspects of the dialogue and teach peers. Students assume an active role while receiving continued assistance from a person with greater expertise such as the teacher.

Palincsar and Brown (1989) developed what they term "reciprocal teaching" to increase both reading comprehension and the use of metacognitive strategies. Their premise is that students will come to internalize dialogue about text that is modeled by the teacher. The dialogue is structured around four strategies used by expert readers: summarizing, self-questioning, predicting, and clarifying. The teacher models these strategies and provides support as students gradually acquire the strategies to use independently in their reading, and students gradually take on more active roles in controlling the discourse. Reciprocal teaching has increased the reading comprehension of elementary- and junior-high students significantly; students were able to use the strategies independent of the teacher and to provide help to other students.

The Kamehameha Early Education Program (KEEP) has focused on altering discourse patterns during the reading of text to become more culturally congruent with the participation structures of native Hawaiians outside the classroom. Teachers use the experience–text–relationship (ETR) method that involves activating children's background experiences relevant to the text, close literal reading of the text, and the integration of information read with prior knowledge and experience. Teacher–student interactions are characterized by the talk story pattern in which students answer the teacher's questions without being called upon, building upon one another's answers. Studies suggest that a careful match between patterns of interaction and instructional goals can facilitate learning. The social organization of lessons permits students to show initiative and supports the transfer of control over text comprehension from teacher to student (Au and Kawakami 1986).

Cognitively Guided Instruction (CGI) is based on research on the development of young children's strategies for solving mathematics word problems (Carpenter and Moser 1982). The developers of CGI begin by sharing two research-based knowledge frameworks with teachers: (a) the framework of strategies that young children use in developing increasingly sophisticated approaches for solving mathematics word problems, and (b) the framework of problem types that children are able to solve. The assumption is that children construct knowledge by proceeding through a sequence of strategy development, and that the teacher's role is to facilitate the children's development of increasingly sophisticated problem-solving strategies. In CGI classrooms, elementary mathematics teaching is characterized by a focus on solving word problems and other nonroutine problems; use of multiple strategies by students to solve problems, including counters and other mathematics tools; and listening to students explain and show their strategies and solutions for solving problems. Students in CGI classrooms tended to achieve higher on tests of mathematical problem-solving than students in traditional classrooms, and to recall their number facts with equal or greater facility (Peterson et al. 1989).

1.3 Collaborative Roles in Learning

In this conception of the active learner, students are seen as being actively involved in the negotiation of shared meaning with others in a learning community. Like Dewey (1916), these educators see communication as both the means of learning and the substance of what is learned. Communication is intertwined with the notion of community, developing what Dewey referred to as "participation in a common understanding." Teachers and students, then, are jointly responsible for learning.

In collaboration with others in their learning community, students choose the tasks and materials they use and communicate and collaborate with one another in order to develop new knowledge. Students' roles are dynamic and changing, depending on the text or problem in which they are engaged. As advocated by Freire (1986) in teaching Brazilian students, "the teacher is no longer merely the-one-who-teaches, but one who is himself taught in dialogue with the students" (p. 67).

Within this conception of the active learner, educators have developed student-led "book clubs" and "literature circles." Students use the book clubs for several purposes including sharing their written responses to a text, clarifying points of confusion, discussing main themes in a book, relating the text to other texts, identifying an author's purpose, critiquing an author's success, and relating the text to their personal experiences (Raphael et al. 1992). In literature circles, students have choices about which books to read before joining the circle. The types of discussion questions depend on readers' interests. These discussions take the form of reacting to the book, reading aloud favorite parts, and raising questions about parts they do not understand. Members of the circle often present the book to the rest of the class (Harste et al. 1984). Smagorinsky and Fly (1992) suggested that such student-led discussions can be very successful, especially when the teacher has made the interpretive process explicit at an earlier point in time.

Peer writing conferences or response groups consist of small groups of students who respond to each other's written texts. DiPardo and Freedman (1988) suggested a variety of purposes for these conferences depending on teachers' and students' goals, including responding to writing, thinking collaboratively, writing collaboratively, and editing written text. Groups provide a forum for discussing the writing process, generating ideas, understanding the functions of an audience, and providing support for engaging in writing. The assumption is that students benefit from talking together because the writer's knowledge becomes available in the discourse; the beginner's work is supported through questions, comments, and suggestions of others; beginning writers have opportunities to practice orally ways of using written language; and talking about text makes clear to writers the value of their work (Florio-Ruane 1988). Studies suggest that peer groups for writing collaboratively or responding to writing can positively influence students' writing (Dahl 1988). The nature of the discourse is an important element in determining the kinds of revisions that students make in their texts (Gere and Abbott 1985). Finally, the quality of the discourse influences the learning of individual students (Daiute 1985, Fitzgerald and Stamm 1990).

Lampert (1990) discussed approaches to mathematics teaching where learning mathematics involves the negotiation of shared meaning among students and the teacher within the mathematical community which exists in each classroom. Students assume authority for knowing mathematics and for explaining and justifying their mathematical thinking to others in their community. Students' ideas and knowledge become available for debate and discussion as part of the classroom discourse. New ways of thinking and mathematical ideas are developed and learned by all members of the community, and learning occurs on the part of the teacher as well as the students.

2. Making Sense of Classrooms

Three ways that educators have conceived of students as playing more active roles in the classroom have been described. These conceptions should result in rather different classroom scenarios; different from traditional classrooms and different from each other. But how will developers' conceptions impact on what actually happens in classrooms and how will the actors—teachers and students—actually construe their roles?

Although new curricula, tasks, and discourse structures that embody more active roles for learners have been designed, these new curricula, tasks, discourse structures, and roles will be transformed by the participants in their particular contexts (Bruce and Rubin

1993). The roles students actually play in each classroom will depend on how curricula, tasks, discourse, and role structures are created and recreated within classrooms. Influential factors include the beliefs of the participants and the culture of the classroom.

2.1 Teachers' and Students' Beliefs About Subject Matter

Nickerson (1992) reviewed studies that show how the pupil's role in United Kingdom classrooms can vary dramatically according to the view of mathematics projected by the teacher. She contrasted pupil's roles as "accepting" versus "questioning" and suggested that pupils' participation in these different roles is related to the ideas they develop about mathematical knowledge. Similarly, Schoenfeld (1992) has shown how students' roles are intertwined with teachers' and students' existing beliefs about mathematical knowledge. Schoenfeld's analysis produced the following set of students' beliefs about the nature of mathematical knowledge.

(a) Mathematics problems have one and only one right answer.

(b) There is only one correct way to solve any mathematics problem, usually the rule the teacher has most recently demonstrated in class.

(c) Ordinary students cannot be expected to understand mathematics, they expect simply to memorize it and apply what they have learned mechanically and without understanding.

(d) Formal proof is irrelevant to processes of discovery or invention.

(e) Mathematics is a solitary activity, done by individuals in isolation.

(f) Students who have understood the mathematics they have studied will be able to solve any assigned problem in five minutes or less.

(g) The mathematics learned in school has little or nothing to do with the real world.

These beliefs have definite implications for students' roles. Students are expected to find the correct answer; to work alone; to memorize and apply procedures that are demonstrated by the teacher; to work quickly and efficiently; and to view their role as a "student" in school rather than as a lifelong "learner" in school and out.

Similarly, in the area of literacy, children and adults have a set of beliefs about text: what is, who created it, and how to evaluate it (Garner and Alexander in press). Once again these beliefs imply certain roles for students in the classroom.

2.2 Teachers' and Students' Beliefs About Teaching and Learning

The role of the student and what it means to be an

active learner in the classroom also depend on the beliefs teachers and students have about learning and teaching. For example, among 20 teachers who were implementing Cognitively Guided Instruction (CGI) in their classrooms, Peterson et al. (1989) observed substantial differences among teachers related to their beliefs about the role of the student and the teacher. Teachers who continued to see their roles as presenting knowledge rather than listening to students or facilitating children's construction of knowledge, implemented CGI by engaging in direct instruction and presenting the correct answer and correct mathematical strategy to be learned. Teachers who saw their roles as actively facilitating children's construction of knowledge created CGI classrooms where everyone listened to students' strategies for solving problems, tried to understand children's thinking, and encouraged the development of mathematical understanding.

In implementing new approaches to literacy learning, such as process writing and reciprocal teaching, teachers have "proceduralized" the substantive intervention and recreated the innovation within their existing conceptions of the learner, the teacher, and knowledge (Bruce and Rubin 1993). Florio-Ruane and Lensmire (1990), for example, found that teachers adopted and taught the steps of process writing, but did not alter their understandings of what it meant to be a good writer or the knowledge of authority relationships among teacher, student, and text.

2.3 The Culture of the Classroom and the School

The role of the student is one that is created solely within the context of the school. The role of the learner as conceived in school, however, is very different from the role of the learner in the contexts of work, family, and play where children and youth also learn (Resnick 1987). Outside of schools, children and youth often learn in authentic situations, such as apprenticeships (Collins et al. 1989) in which participants' work has real economic value and significance. What would happen if the role of learner were conceptualized within a community that is unbounded by school walls, but that encompasses the experiences of home and other learning contexts?

3. Transforming the Roles of Children and Youth as Learners in Schools and Out

Heath (in press) describes how effective organizations for inner-city youth in the United States differ from formal learning contexts in the ways in which learning and knowledge are conceived and the roles that youths play. She argues that formal learning contexts, such as schools, should change to encompass the following features:

(a)   Effective youth organizations have open frank discussions and make learning possible primarily through demonstration, apprenticeship, extensive practice, and peer evaluation.

(b)   Youth organizations place the control of knowledge within the group as team members committed to a central goal. Knowledge and skills blend together. The facts of a myth for a Ballet Folklorico dance go along with the skill inherent in specific dance routines.

(c)   Learning is cumulative, multidirectional, and displayed through a variety of different kinds of symbols: verbal, kinesthetic, musical, and visual.

(d)   Learning and thinking of the self as a learner for a set of purposes and goals of joint identification become synomous with one's life, just as knowing oneself as a member of a family unconsciously merges with an individual sense of identity (Heath in press).

Heath argues for changing schools to become more like effective youth organizations in order to create a "seamless life of thinking, development and learning." If such changes do come about, then in the next edition of the *International Encyclopedia of Education* this article will be transformed and retitled to reflect the role of the student as merged within the multifaceted roles of young learners growing up in a global community.

See also: Social Psychological Theories in Education; Social Psychological Theories of Teaching; Sociology of Learning in School; Student Influences on Teaching; Student Perceptions of Classrooms; Teachers' Roles

References

Anderson R C, Hiebert E H, Scott J A, Wilkinson I A G 1984 *Becoming a Nation of Readers: The Report of the Commission on Reading.* The National Institute of Education, Washington, DC

Au K H, Kawakami A J 1986 The influence of the social organization of instruction on children's text comprehension ability: A Vygotskian perspective. In: Raphael T E (ed.) 1986 *The Contexts of School-based Literacy.* Random House, New York

Baker L, Brown A L 1984 Metacognitive skills and reading. In: Pearson (ed.) 1984 *Handbook of Reading Research,* Vol 1. Longman, New York

Bruce B B, Rubin A 1993 *Electronic Quills: A Situated Evaluation of Using Computers for Writing in Classrooms.* Erlbaum, Hillsdale, New Jersey

Carpenter T P, Moser J M 1982 The development of addition and subtraction problem-solving skills. In: Carpenter T P, Moser J M, Romberg T A (eds.) 1982 *Addition and Subtraction: A Cognitive Perspective.* Erlbaum, Hillsdale, New Jersey

Clay M M 1982 *Observing Young Readers.* Heinemann, Portsmouth, New Hampshire

Clay M M 1985 *The Early Detection of Reading Difficulties.* Heinemann, Portsmouth, New Hampshire

Collins A, Brown J S, Newman S E 1989 Cognitive apprenticeship: Teaching the crafts of reading, writing, and mathematics. In: Resnick L (ed.) 1989 *Knowing, Learning and Instruction: Essays in Honor of Robert Glaser.* Erlbaum, Hillsdale, New Jersey

Dahl K 1988 Peer conferences as social contexts for learning about revision. In: Readance J (ed.) 1988 *Dialogues in Literacy Research.* National Reading Conference, Chicago, Illinois

Daiute C 1985 Do writers talk to themselves? In: Freedman S W (ed.) 1985 *The Acquisition of Written Language: Response and Revision.* Ablex, Norwood, New Jersey

Dewey J 1916 *Democracy and Education.* Macmillan, New York

DiPardo A, Freedman S W 1988 Peer response groups in the writing classroom: Theoretic foundations and new directions. *Rev. Educ. Res.* 58: 119–49

Fitzgerald J, Stamm C 1990 Effects of group conferences on first-grader's revisions of writing. *Written Communication* 7: 96–135

Florio-Ruane S 1988 How ethnographers of communication study writing in school. In: Readance J (ed.) 1988 *Dialogues in Literacy Research.* National Reading Conference, Chicago, Illinois

Florio-Ruane S, Lensmire T J 1990 Transforming future teachers' ideas about writing instruction *J. Curric. St.* 22: 277–89

Freire P 1986 *Pedagogy of the Oppressed.* Continuum Publishing, New York

Garner R, Alexander P (eds.) in press *Beliefs about Text and about Instruction with Text.* Erlbaum, Hillsdale, New Jersey

Gere A R, Abbott R D 1985 Talking about writing: The language of writing groups. *Research in the Teaching of English* 19: 362–85

Goodlad J I 1984 *A Place Called School.* McGraw-Hill, New York

Harste J C, Woodward V A, Burke C L 1984 *Language Stories and Literacy Lessons.* Heinemann, Portsmouth, New Hampshire

Heath S B in press Play for identity: Where the mind is everyday for inner-city youth. In: Mangieri J, Block C C (ed.) in press *Mindfulness: Increasing Thinking Abilities.* Harcourt, Brace, Jovanovich, New York

Lampert M 1990 When the problem is not the question and the solution is not the answer: Mathematical knowing and teaching. *Am. Educ. Res. J.* 27: 29–64

Mehan H 1979 *Learning Lessons.* Harvard University Press, Cambridge, Massachusetts

National Council of Teachers of Mathematics 1989 *Curriculum and Evaluation Standards for School Mathematics.* National Council of Teachers of Mathematics, Reston, Virginia

Nickerson M 1992 The culture of the mathematics classroom: An unknown quantity? In: Grouws D A (ed.) 1992 *Handbook of Research on Mathematics Teaching and Learning.* Macmillan, New York

Palincsar A S, Brown A L 1989 Classroom dialogues to promote self-regulated comprehension. In: Brophy J (ed.) 1989 *Advances in Research on Teaching*, Vol 1. JAI Press, Greenwich, Connecticut

Peterson P L, Carpenter T, Fennema E 1989 Teachers' knowledge of students' knowledge in mathematics problem solving: Correlational and case analyses. *J. Educ. Psychol.* 81: 558–69

Pinnell G S 1989 Reading Recovery: Helping at-risk children learn to read. *Elem. Sch. J.* 90 (2): 161–82

Pinnell G S, Fried M D, Estice R M 1990 Reading Recovery: Learning how to make a difference. *Read. Teach.* 43: 282–95

Raphael T E et al. 1992 Research directions: Literature and discussion in the reading program. *Lang. Arts* 69 (1): 54–61

Resnick L B 1987 Learning in school and out. *Educ. Researcher* 16 (9): 13–20

Romberg T 1982 An emerging paradigm for research on addition and subtraction skills. In: Carpenter T P, Moser J P, Romberg T A (eds.) 1982 *Addition and Subtraction: A Cognitive Perspective* Erlbaum, Hillsdale, New Jersey

Schoenfeld A 1992 Learning to think mathematically: Problem solving, metacognition, and sense making in mathematics. In: Grouws D A (ed.) 1993 *Handbook of Research on Mathematics Teaching and Learning.* Macmillan, New York

Smagorinsky P, Fly P K 1992 Patterns of discourse in small group discussions of literature. Paper presented at the Annual Meeting of the American Educational Research Association, San Francisco, California

Stevenson H, Stigler J 1992 *The Learning Gap.* Summit Books, New York

Tisher R P 1985 Student roles in the classroom. In: Husén T, Postlethwaite T N (eds.) 1985 *The International Encyclopedia of Education*, 1st edn. Pergamon Press, Oxford

Vygotsky L S 1978 *Mind in Society: The Development of Higher Psychological Processes.* Harvard University Press, Cambridge, Massachusetts

Youth and Leisure

B. J. Biddle

Concern about youth and leisure has been expressed widely, and a large amount of research has appeared concerning the leisure attitudes and behaviors of young people. Much of this effort has been driven by practical concerns, however, and has involved limited samples and questionable methods. Little integrative theory seems to have evolved concerning youth and leisure.

1. Concepts of Leisure

1.1 The Residual Concept of Leisure

In part, work on youth and leisure has been impaired because of confusions associated with the concept of leisure (see Kelly 1972, Poole 1983). A common meaning assigned to this term is that of activities that a person takes up after work or other duties are accomplished. Such a concept of leisure seems clear enough, but its use creates problems for the social analyst. Since the concepts of work and duty differ from context to context, so does the residual concept of leisure, and identical activities may be seen as part of "work" or "leisure" depending on the context in which those activities appear. To illustrate, most people would view a game of golf as a leisure activity, but real estate agents or stockbrokers may view golf games as necessary parts of their jobs.

In addition, the residual concept of leisure creates uncertainty about some types of activities, such as those associated with self-maintenance; for example, with studying and practicing, with religious observance, and with voluntary associations. Furthermore, what constitutes leisure for the person who is unemployed or who has only a few duties? These questions are particularly troubling when one considers the leisure of young people who rarely work on a full-time basis but, instead, are likely to be in schools or underemployed.

Finally, the residual concept of leisure gives analytic centrality to work rather than to what work accomplishes. Enthusiasm for work is common in capitalist economies, and most developed countries adopt strategies designed to promote work identification and effort. Theories of "the good life," however, stress that work should be engaged in not for itself alone but also because, if effective, it thereafter enables individuals to engage in rewarding and creative activities (see Kelly 1983). According to this latter perspective, leisure should be a central analytic concern, and a key task for education is to provide youth with instruction and motivation enabling them to enjoy creative leisure pursuits in their adult years.

Regardless of these questions, the residual concept of leisure is not only popular but has also generated a good deal of research. Various studies (e.g., Bhatty 1987) have constructed lists of leisure activities by asking respondents, including young people, to volunteer the names of activities they engage in during their "spare time" or "when they are not working or in school." These responses are then grouped into similarity clusters for subsequent analyses.

1.2 Leisure as Consummatory Activity

A second common approach pairs leisure with activities that the person considers consummatory: activities that are entered willingly and are enjoyed for their own sakes (Neulinger 1974, Hendry 1983, Csikszentmihalyi and Larson 1984). This second leisure concept also seems to be clear, but again it raises problems for the analyst. How does one judge work-related activities that are enjoyed by the person? And how does one classify nonwork activities that the person engages in for nonremunerative but instrumental reasons? The latter question, in particular, is relevant to young people who often engage in activities that

they may not enjoy in order to gain status or approval from peers.

Regardless of such problems, the consummatory concept of leisure has also generated significant research. Neulinger (1974) promoted a definition for leisure which stressed activities that the person enters willingly, that are intrinsically motivating, and that generate feelings of pleasure. Thus, three conditions are thought to be crucial for discriminating leisure events: (a) perceived freedom to enter the activity (Deci and Ryan 1975, Iso-Ahola 1980), (b) intrinsic motivation (Csikszentmihalyi 1975, Mannell 1979), and (c) positive affect (Neulinger 1986). This conceptualization has spawned studies in the United States on the perception of leisure, including studies concerned with youth (Kleiber et al. 1986, Ellis and Rademacher 1987, Hultsman and Kaufman 1990), and evidence suggests that the three conditions it posits are closely related for many Americans (Hultsman and Black 1989).

1.3 Other Conceptions of Leisure

Although popular, the residual and consummatory concepts of leisure are by no means exhaustive. Havighurst (1957) asked middle-aged people in the United States for the principal meanings that they associated with leisure. Although many respondents did volunteer meanings that were associated with the residual and consummatory concepts of leisure, others associated leisure with the opportunity to have contact with friends, enjoy new experiences, fill vacant time, and be creative. These answers appear to break new ground.

More recently, several studies have attempted to ascertain the dimensions of leisure using factor-analytic techniques. Kanters and Anderson (1989) asked youth from Ontario to rate recreational activities using a series of bipolar trait scales, and found three factors that seemed to represent the ways in which respondents thought about those leisure events: (a) simple–difficult, (b) exciting–dull, and (c) enjoyment of the activity context versus enjoyment of the activity itself. Again, these dimensions appear to enter new conceptual realms.

2. Troublesome Issues

The problem of defining leisure is also associated with several troublesome issues that are relevant to youth. First, when thinking about or studying leisure some authors list only activities that are socially approved, and yet if left to their own devices many persons will engage in activities that are not approved by the society at large. In particular, many young people engage in activities associated with violence, sexual conduct, drug use and other life-styles that the society may consider illegal or immoral (Bachman et al. 1978;

Larson and Kubey 1983). Should researchers consider such activities as part of "youth leisure"?

Second, many authors have argued that leisure is a product of affluence and is more prevalent in developed than non-developed nations (Kando 1975, Cross 1990). Less often noted is the fact that leisure is unequally distributed among population sectors within nations. Prior to the industrial revolution, leisure was presumably more often enjoyed by rich persons, whereas in developed nations in the 1990s it is more often the province of those who are frozen out of the work force, such as retired and young people. Since work is very important in developed societies, for retired and young people the filling of leisure time may become a problem rather than a blessing.

Third, most forms of leisure require artifacts, thus leisure activities fuel economic growth, and many people are occupied in selling leisure forms to potential consumers (Panelas 1983, Burton 1985). The servicing of leisure activities is important to the economy, and in analyzing leisure events attention should be paid not only to consumers but also to the producers of leisure products. Such arguments are particularly relevant to youth. Since youth in developed countries tend to have time on their hands, it seems hardly surprising that industries have sprung up to provide them with rock concerts, records, video arcades, motor cars, illegal drugs, and other items with which they can fill their leisure hours. Such industries have vested interests in promoting specific types of youth leisure.

Finally, people who participate in leisure activities are presumably affected by those events, and authors concerned with youth have often written about the consequences of leisure choice and participation. Sometimes this literature has concerned the manifest functions of leisure; indeed many school and recreation programs are designed to provide youth with leisure opportunities which should have "appropriate" effects on their participants (Spady 1970). Sometimes, however, authors have concerned themselves with the latent functions of youth leisure, particularly those associated with the reproduction of class, race, and the culture of sexism (Roberts 1983). Both of these literatures suggest that youth leisure is by no means an "innocent" set of events, but rather that it has consequences with which others are, or should be, concerned.

Although these issues have been discussed by some authors, others have ignored them or have made inadvertent assumptions about them that affected research.

3. Changing Conceptions of Youth

Research on youth and leisure has been affected by changing conceptions of the youth population. Apparently medieval societies had no concept of youth; indeed in such societies young people were considered

adults as soon as they could perform adult roles. Musgrove (1964) suggests that the concept of youth was invented by Rousseau, but that public schools and laws preventing child labor only gradually evolved in the nineteenth century as youth became less needed in the labor force. By the turn of the twentieth century (when G S Hall popularized the term "adolescent"), large numbers of postpubertal youth in developed countries were to be found in schools, but until the Second World War most of them left schooling for employment when this was legally allowed, at age 15 or so.

Since 1945, secondary and postsecondary education have rapidly expanded in the developed world, ever-larger proportions of youth are encouraged to remain in schools, colleges, and universities, and entry into full-time employment is now sometimes delayed until people are in their mid-20s or later. These trends have greatly expanded the population of those that might be considered as "youth," and have created significant problems for those young people who would rather work (or indeed, do anything else) than remain in formal education.

Whether they remained in or dropped out of formal schooling, youth in developed countries now constituted a large, significant, and growing sector of the population. Moreover, most young people had considerable free time and at least some discretionary income, and were thus able to develop their own styles of leisure. Some of these styles imitated or complemented the leisure styles of adults, but others challenged or posed problems for the larger community. Thus, the postwar years have generated a host of "youth cultures" and "youth movements," largely focused on leisure, that the adult world has considered problematic. A review of these developments in the United Kingdom and the United States is provided by Cross (1990) who suggests that British youth leisure has often expressed social-class concerns whereas American youth activities have more often reflected race or ethnicity and have been driven by commercial interests.

In short, some authors who have written about or studied youth leisure have focused on quite different populations than other authors who lived elsewhere and at other times.

4. Methods for Studying Youth Leisure

Although exceptions may be found, most empirical research on youth leisure has concerned either the attitudes of youth or their participation in leisure activities. In most studies of youth attitudes, investigators have prepared a list of activity terms and have asked young persons to rate each term using one or more judgmental scales. The major difficulty with such methods is that they may introduce bias because of unexamined criteria that the investigator used when selecting items and scales. For example, Kanters and Anderson (1989) asked respondents to rate 20 preselected "leisure activities" using 12 judgmental scales. Their study included no activities involving interaction with close friends, or behaviors that might be questioned on moral or legal grounds, and they did not explain their choice of rating scales.

In contrast, several methods have been used in studies of youth participation in leisure activities. Perhaps the simplest of these methods asks young respondents to report the time or emphasis they give to activities selected by the investigator (see e.g., Willits and Willits 1986), and such studies suffer from problems similar to those of the typical study of youth leisure attitudes. A more sophisticated method asks young people to volunteer examples of activities they enjoy or engage in frequently (see e.g., Poole 1983). These studies certainly reflect the interests and vocabularies of respondents, but they may also generate biased data because respondents do not think about, or may not want to talk about, certain kinds of leisure activities.

Stronger methods ask young people to generate records about the actual activities in which they engage. Several ways of generating such records have appeared. In "experience sampling" respondents are given electronic pagers, similar to those used by doctors, are "beeped" randomly from a central signal source, and are asked to complete a short questionnaire whenever they are beeped (see Kleiber et al. 1986). In other studies young respondents are asked to keep activity diaries or to provide retrospective accounts of their activities for specific time periods (Biddle et al. 1981). These methods provide a good deal of detail and again make use of the respondents' own vocabularies for activities. They too may generate bias because respondents can only describe the activities in which they have participated from their own, personal viewpoints.

The strongest methods for studying activities involves observing them directly, in situ, and techniques have been available for some years that could be used to generate such records for youth leisure. Unfortunately, these methods are quite expensive, and it is difficult to find studies that have employed them for investigating youth leisure. To this extent, then, there is only limited information about the details of youth participation in leisure.

5. Demographic Influences

Various demographic factors have already been investigated as generators of variance in the attitudes and participation of youth in leisure. For example, Iso-Ahola and Buttimer (1981) produced United States findings suggesting that youth rate leisure activities more highly (and work activities less highly) as they grow older, and Smith (1987) reported that British

youth increase their rates of leisure interaction with both friends and cross-sex partners as they age; Poole (1983) discovered sex differences in rates of reported leisure participation by Australian youth (males more often engaged in sports, females more often reported studying, housework, and interacting with friends); and various authors (e.g., Hendry 1983) have summarized and discussed social class differences in youth leisure pursuits in the United Kingdom. Unfortunately, most studies of demographic influences have reported data from only one country, and it is difficult to know whether or not their findings would generalize elsewhere.

6. Leisure and Schooling

Given the importance of schooling in the lives of youth, it is hardly surprising to learn that studies have also investigated the impact of schooling on youth leisure. Several of these studies have concerned relations between the curricular and leisure (extracurricular) programs of schools and have generated various findings. Some studies suggest that leisure activities are often seen as peripheral to the schools' central mission (Leigh 1971, Connell et al. 1975), others have reported positive relations between student academic progress and extracurricular participation (Campbell 1970, Rehberg and Schafer 1973), and still others have examined the effects of extracurricular participation on young people's status and peer associations (Coleman 1961, Spady 1970).

Other studies have examined whether school leisure programs have positive effects on the subsequent leisure attitudes or activities of youth, and most of these studies suggest that such effects are weak (see Hendry 1983). Still other studies have compared the leisure activities of youth who are in and out of schools. Hendry et al. (1984), for example, compared the leisure activities of in-school and out-of-school Scottish youth and found that the former reported participation in extracurricular activities and youth clubs whereas the latter reported more shopping and "hanging about." Such findings may be affected by nationality, however, a possibility explored by Biddle et al. (1981) in a study that compared youth activities among in-school and out-of-school youth in Australia and the United States. They found that whereas Australian school leavers were likely to engage in sports and organized recreation, American school leavers were more likely to report visiting with friends, loafing, and problem behaviors, and that these differences were generated by opportunity structures rather than preferences. In addition, the leisure activities of out-of-school youth appear to differ depending on whether or not they are employed (Hendry et al. 1984). Roberts et al. (1987) report that employment has somewhat different implications for young, out-of-school, British men and women in that it reinforces traditional, masculine roles for the former but provides relief from traditional, feminine constraints for the latter.

7. Effects of Leisure

Other studies have examined the effects of youth leisure participation through panel research. For example, Brooks and Elliott (1971) report positive correlations between the rates of young persons' participation in and satisfaction with leisure activities and measures of their "psychological health" at age 30. Lindsay (1984) found that participation in school activities was associated with involvement in voluntary social activities seven years later, and Scott and Willits (1989) found that the types of leisure activities reported by young people predicted the types of activities they reported in their early 50s. These results are impressive, but do they reveal causal relations? Such questions are addressed in panel studies by controlling for the effects of other variables that might account for relations between earlier and later events. Thus, Scott and Willits included controls for gender, general health, education, and income in their research, and to this extent one is more likely to assign causality to their findings. Nevertheless, most of the important questions about the effects of youth leisure seem not to have been studied in research to date.

8. The Commercialization of Youth Leisure

Finally, a host of studies have appeared that are concerned with specific types of youth leisure that are pushed by commercial interests. Many studies have appeared that concern youth use or abuse of alcohol, tobacco, and illegal substances; Condry and Keith (1983), Panelas (1983), and Ng and June (1985) explored the use of video games by youths; and various authors have examined the use or effects of television and rock music on youth (e.g., Larson and Kubey 1983, Morgan and Rothschild 1983, Peterson and Peters 1983, Burton 1985). Unfortunately, most of these studies ignore broader work on youth leisure and vice versa.

9. Conclusion

The topic of youth leisure has great fascination and has generated a good deal of research, but findings from this research have not cumulated well. Knowledge about this important topic will improve when more agreement is reached about the concept of leisure, integrative and testable theories concerning youth leisure are posed, and researchers are encouraged to study youth leisure in research designs that compare various contexts (such as two or more similar nations).

See also: Broadcasting and Technology: Effects on Children and Youth; Youth Cultures and Subcultures

References

Bachman J G, O'Malley P M, Johnston J 1978 *Adolescence to Adulthood: Change and Stability in the Lives of Young Men.* Institute for Social Research, University of Michigan, Ann Arbor, Michigan

Bhatty R 1987 Leisure-time world of youth. *Society and Leisure* 10: 339–44

Biddle B J, Bank B J, Anderson D S, Keats J A, Keats D M 1981 The structure of idleness: In-school and dropout adolescent activities in the United States and Australia. *Sociol. Educ.* 54(2): 106–19

Brooks J B, Elliott D M 1971 Prediction of psychological adjustment at age thirty from leisure time activities and satisfactions in childhood. *Hum. Dev.* 14: 51–61

Burton T L 1985 Rock music and social change, 1953–1978. *Society and Leisure* 8: 665–83

Campbell W J 1970 Some effects of size and organization of secondary schools on the experiences of pupils in extra-curricular behaviour settings. In: Campbell W J (ed.) 1970 *Scholars in Context: The Effects of Environment on Learning.* Wiley, Sydney

Coleman J S 1961 *The Adolescent Society: The Social Life of the Teenager and its Impact on Education.* Free Press, New York

Condry J, Keith D 1983 Educational and recreational uses of computer technology: Computer instruction and video games. *Youth Soc.* 15(1): 87–112

Connell W F, Stroobant R E, Sinclair K E, Connell R W, Rogers K W 1975 *12 to 20: Studies of City Youth.* Hicks Smith & Sons, Sydney

Cross G 1990 *A Social History of Leisure Since 1600.* Venture Publishing, State College, Pennsylvania

Csikszentmihalyi M 1975 *Beyond Boredom and Anxiety. The Experience of Play in Work and Games.* Jossey-Bass, San Francisco, California

Csikszentmihalyi M, Larson R 1984 *Being Adolescent.* Basic Books, New York

Deci E L, Ryan R 1975 *Intrinsic Motivation and Self-determination in Human Behavior.* Plenum Press, New York

Ellis G D, Rademacher C 1987 Development of a typology of common adolescent free time activities: A validation and extension of Kleiber, Larson, and Csikszentmihalyi. *J. Leisure Res.* 19(4): 284–92

Havighurst R J 1957 The leisure activities of the middle aged. *Am. J. Sociol.* 63: 152–62

Hendry L B 1983 *Growing Up and Going Out: Adolescents and Leisure.* Aberdeen University Press, Aberdeen

Hendry L B, Raymond M, Stewart C 1984 Unemployment, school and leisure: An adolescent study. *Leisure Stud.* 3(2): 175–87

Hultsman J T, Black D R 1989 Primary meta-analysis in leisure research: Results for Neulinger's *What Am I Doing?* instrument. *J. Leisure Res.* 21(1): 18–31

Hultsman J T, Kaufman J E 1990 The experience of leisure by youth in a therapeutic milieu: Implications for theory and clinical practice. *Youth Soc.* 21(4): 496–510

Iso-Ahola S E 1980 *The Social Psychology of Leisure and Recreation.* Wm C Brown, Dubuque, Iowa

Iso-Ahola S E, Buttimer K J 1981 The emergence of work and leisure ethic from early adolescence to early adulthood. *Journal of Leisure Research* 13(4): 282–88

Kando T M 1975 *Leisure and popular Culture in Transition.* C V Mosby, St. Louis, Missouri

Kanters M A, Anderson S C 1989 Cognitive structures of adolescent leisure behavior. *Society and Leisure* 12: 431–47

Kelly J R 1972 Work and leisure: A simplified paradigm. *J. Leisure Res.* 4(1): 50–62

Kelly J R 1983 *Leisure Identities and Interactions.* George Allen and Unwin, London

Kleiber D, Larson R, Csikszentmihalyi M 1986 The experience of leisure in adolescence. *J. Leisure Res.* 18(3): 169–76

Larson R, Kubey R 1983 Television and music: Contrasting media in adolescent life. *Youth Soc.* 15(1): 13–31

Leigh J 1971 *Young People and Leisure.* Routledge and Kegan Paul, London

Lindsay P 1984 High school size, participation in activities, and young adult social participation: Some enduring effects of schooling. *Educ. Eval. Policy Anal.* 6(1): 73–83

Mannell R C 1979 A conceptual and experimental basis for research in the psychology of leisure. *Society and Leisure* 11: 179–96

Morgan M, Rothschild N 1983 Impact of the new television technology: Cable TV, peers, and sex-role cultivation in the electronic environment. *Youth Soc.* 15: 33–50

Musgrove F 1964 *Youth and the Social Order.* Routledge and Kegan Paul, London

Neulinger J 1974 *The Psychology of Leisure.* Charles C Thomas, Springfield, Illinois

Neulinger J 1986 *What Am I Doing? The WAID.* The Leisure Institute, Dodgeville, New York

Ng D, June L 1985 Electronic leisure and youth: Kitchener arcade video game players. *Society and Leisure* 8: 537–48

Panelas T 1983 Adolescents and video games: Consumption of leisure and the social construction of the peer group. *Youth Soc.* 15(1): 51–65

Peterson G W, Peters D F 1983 Adolescents' construction of social reality: The impact of television and peers. *Youth Soc.* 15(1): 67–85

Poole M E 1983 *Youth: Expectations and Transitions.* Routledge and Kegan Paul, London

Rehberg R, Schafer W E 1973 Participation in interscholastic athletics and college expectation. *Am. J. Sociol.* 5: 732–40

Roberts K 1983 *Youth and Leisure.* George Allen and Unwin, London

Roberts K, Brodie D, Dench S 1987 Youth unemployment, and out-of-home recreation. *Society and Leisure* 10: 281–94

Scott D, Willits F K 1989 Adolescent and adult leisure patterns: A 37-year follow-up study. *Leisure Sci.* 11(4): 323–35

Smith D M 1987 Some patterns of reported leisure behavior of young people: A longitudinal study. *Youth Soc.* 18(3): 255–81

Spady W G 1970 Lament for the letterman: Effects of peer status and extra curricular activities on goals and achievements. *Am. J. Sociol.* 75: 680–702

Willits W L, Willits F K 1986 Adolescent participation in leisure activities: "The less, the more" or "the more, the more"? *Leisure Sci.* 8(2): 189–206

Youth Cultures and Subcultures

B. Wilson

This article examines the use of the concepts of culture and subculture in relation to research on the distinctive beliefs, values, and practices of young people, including so-called delinquent subcultures, and the value of the concepts in explaining patterns of achievement in schooling. The entry covers four main topics: the early use of the concept, particularly in studies of delinquency in the United States; the particular importance of schooling in the debates about youth cultures and subcultures, especially in relation to explanations of inequality; research on the "resistance" of male, working-class youth cultures in the United Kingdom in the 1960s and 1970s; and similar research in Europe on young people and cultural expressions of alienation.

1. Major Issues

The concepts of culture and subculture refer to the complex systems of beliefs, values, and practices which provide meaning for human groups, and a basis for action in response to problems which they encounter. Derived from the work of anthropologists, culture has been defined in more than 160 ways. This reflects various attempts to describe the ways in which human groups become cohesive, yet acknowledges the adaptiveness of human behavior, and conflicts within groups. The use of the concept of subculture applies specifically to the beliefs, values, and practices of particular social groups or divisions, often class- or age based, within larger stratified societies. Schooling has been an important element, in Western societies at least, in the framing of youth cultures and subcultures.

The concepts of youth culture and subculture have been used by social researchers in their efforts to investigate and explain several key issues. These have included:

(a) the characteristics, causes, and consequences of the distinctive "life-styles," and lives of particular groups of young people;

771

(b)   the interaction of different dimensions of social division in shaping the beliefs, values, and practices of young people;

(c)   the significance of the relationship between schooling and youth cultures, with two mutually reinforcing emphases: the contribution of schools in the production of youth cultures, and the significance of youth cultures in shaping educational achievement;

(d)   the use of various forms of media by particular subcultures to express their perspectives on their relationships with other social groups and dominant cultural forms; and

(e)   the significance of the cultural dimension in gender relations among young people—a task for which much of the theorizing about youth subcultures has proved to be inadequate.

Furthermore, these concepts were closely associated in the United States with an interest in youth problems, specifically delinquency, in the 1920s and 1930s. Similar interest emerged in the United Kingdom, Europe, and Australia during the 1960s.

2. Youth Subcultures and Delinquency

Cultural and subcultural theory has been an important component in the efforts by a number of United States researchers to explain delinquency among young men. Two distinct examples are discussed below.

2.1 The Chicago Social Ecology School

The significant contribution of the urban ecologists at the University of Chicago in the 1920s and 1930s was to examine the link between youth subcultures and territorial divisions. Based on detailed empirical research and related documentation, the researchers developed a notion of "natural areas," and attempted to identify connections between geography and delinquent practices (Park et al. 1967, see also Brake 1980). Their research was motivated by an interest in the association between young people, poverty, broader social trends associated with postwar developments and the Depression, and the expression of social disorganization in particular neighborhoods. While providing some innovative and significant examples of research (e.g., Thrasher 1927, Whyte 1943), this tradition made only a limited contribution to theoretical development. Their explanation drew on a broader understanding of urban and social forms as ecological systems within which particular geographic areas tended to retain their kinds of social characteristics, even as their populations changed. In this context, delinquent subcultures were seen to be a product of social disorganization and competing values. This thesis was beset by a basic tautology in that delinquency rates provided evidence of social disorganization between neighborhoods, which in turn was the cause of delinquency. Nevertheless, some of the detailed research was instructive in drawing attention to the complex structures of subcultural groups, and highlighted the similarities between delinquent and more respectable traditions (see Brake 1980 p. 32, also Matza 1969).

2.2 Delinquent Subcultures as Social Adaptation

Cohen (1955) also attempted to explain delinquent behavior by gangs of working-class boys. His account was framed in response to Merton's theory of structural tension resulting from the failure of certain groups to succeed in achieving the generally accepted social goals of material gain and social prestige. Cohen's view was that tendencies toward delinquency resulted not from "structural strain," but from the specific obstacles faced by working-class boys in achieving upward mobility. Whereas Merton had discussed the risks to society from failure to achieve social goals in terms of individual pathological response (anomie), Cohen emphasized the way in which the delinquent subculture provided a collective solution to a problem commonly experienced by working-class boys. The experience of schooling was critical, in that it set a "middle-class measuring rod" against which working-class boys, with different values and practices, were often doomed to fail.

Cohen's theories aroused considerable criticism and debate, but his work generated themes which have continued to be prominent in research on youth cultures and subcultures. One important variant on Cohen's work was introduced by Cloward and Ohlin (1961). Whereas Cohen had interpreted the problems faced by working-class boys in terms of their striving for social status, Cloward and Ohlin drew attention to the issue of economic justice. In their terms, the goals of material success may have been shared irrespective of class background, but some young men were able to achieve these goals only through illegal (delinquent) means. This issue has also been important in later work on youth cultures and educational achievement.

An immediate difficulty with this work is that delinquent behavior is by no means confined to working-class boys only. Quite different kinds of evidence and explanation are required to account for the extent of delinquent behavior across class groups.

3. Contributions to Subcultural Research in the United Kingdom

There have been some reservations among United Kingdom researchers about the relevance of United States subcultural theories for United Kingdom experience, mostly because of apparent differences in the historical development of social structures in the two societies. However, there has been considerable interest in subcultural investigations in the United Kingdom since the mid-1960s. Brake identified four approaches:

> First, there is the early social ecology of the working class neighbourhood carried out in the late fifties and the early sixties. Second, there is the relation of the delinquent subculture to the sociology of education, a tradition which is still continuing. This examines the relationship of leisure and youth culture as an alternative to achievement in school. Third, there is the cultural emphasis of the Centre for Contemporary Cultural Studies at Birmingham University . . . . Lastly, there are the contemporary neighbourhood studies which look at local youth groups, not as early social ecologists did, but in the light of influence by contemporary deviancy theory and social reaction. (Brake 1980 p. 50)

Of these, two have been particularly important, with implications both for policy initiatives and for stimulating further research. These are discussed in greater detail below.

3.1 Subcultures as a "Solution" to Conflict in Schools

Prompted by the work of Cohen on delinquent boys, Downes (1966) undertook research which led him to draw attention to the meaninglessness of school for many working-class young people, as a central aspect of any attempt to explain delinquency. The key aspect of the explanation was the effect of the structure and content of schooling in prompting dissociation from participation in schooling. Hence, the formation of subcultures is a reaction against the situation in which

> the adolescent is enjoined either to "better himself" or "to accept his station in life". To insulate themselves against the harsh implications of this creed, the adolescent in a "dead end" job in a "dead end" neighbourhood extricates himself from the belief in work as of any importance beyond the simple provision of income, and deflects what aspirations he has into areas of what has been termed "non-work." (Downes 1966 p. 273)

Hargreaves (1967) described in more detail the way in which schools contribute to the production of subcultures, sometimes in quite specific ways. His study focused on the practice of streaming in a working-class secondary school in the United Kingdom. He found that students who were placed in the higher streams of achievement had values which were congruent with those of the teachers, whereas students in the lower streams were antagonistic to schooling and the teachers, leading to the emergence of two quite distinct subcultures. Students in the "antischool" subculture who attempted to pursue academic achievement were mocked and ostracized by their classmates, and some students deliberately limited their school performance in order to enhance their status with their classmates. Hargreaves argued further that it was not only the institutionalization of streaming which produced

the subcultures, but also the allocation of particular teachers (either inexperienced or provocative) to the "antischool" streams.

Corrigan (1979) took this analysis a step further by focusing particularly on exploring what happens when students actively reject the school curriculum. Apart from highlighting the active part which students (and subcultures) play in the conflicts between schools and young people, he drew attention to the significance of broader social forces. His argument was that student rebellion was not just a matter of discipline, but a reflection of wider power relations. This is a theme which has been pursued extensively by researchers at the Centre for Contemporary Cultural Studies.

3.2 Cultural Studies and Youth Culture

A number of theoretical traditions came together in the United Kingdom during the 1970s, prompting the emergence of a new strand of research and theory on youth culture. Based at the Centre for Contemporary Cultural Studies (CCCS) at Birmingham University, the "new wave" drew on: the Marxist understanding of class structure and conflict; the traditional interest in delinquency and neighborhood; the new insights of deviancy theorists into processes of labeling and societal reaction; interest in the implications of policies adopted by state institutions such as schools and welfare agencies; and research on mass communications and expressive cultural forms.

The essence of the CCCS approach was first articulated in the work of Cohen (1972). His analysis of subcultures was derived from research on working-class life in an East London community. It focused on the interlinking of three strands of working-class life: the extended kinship network; the neighborhood as a physical space; and the local economy, which linked the workplace with family and neighborhood. The impact of postwar development on these social relations was profound, and left significant social, cultural, and material problems for those who remained, especially young people, who were forced to resolve complex tensions. In this context, subcultures formed among the young (especially males) in order "to express and resolve albeit 'magically' " (p. 23) the contradictions which were faced by both the parents and the young. As Brake noted (1980 p. 66), Cohen's analysis introduced the notion that the problems which subcultures set out to resolve were always experienced and resolved in ideological terms. Hence, subcultures prevented young people from challenging the real power relations with which they are confronted; the contradictions can only be relocated "in an imaginary relation" (p. 67).

A group of CCCS researchers attempted to present a more coherent and extensive analysis of youth cultures and subcultures in Hall and Jefferson (1976). Their starting point was similar to that of the Chicago school in the 1920s: the emergence of "youth" as a prominent social category and metaphor for social change in the postwar period. Clarke et al. (1976) identified five aspects of change which helped to promote this view of "youth": the relative affluence of postwar families; the emergence of mass communications which promoted the notion of mass or popular culture; the arrival of distinctive adolescent styles (see Hebdige 1979); secondary education for all, which meant that many young spent an increasing amount of time in age-specific institutions; and the war itself, which served to mark out those who were born subsequently as special. Against this backdrop, they argue that youth subcultures should be seen not only as ideological constructs but as protagonists in the struggles of class and age relations. At the very least, they *"win space for the young"*; beyond this,

> they adopt and adapt material objects—goods and possessions—and reorganise them into distinctive "styles" which express the collectivity of their being-as-a-group. These concerns, activities, relationships, materials become embodied in rituals of relationship and occasion and movement. (Clarke et al. 1976 p. 47)

The CCCS project acknowledges the ideological dimension of subcultures. Even though they may have set out to address real problems, their highly ritualized and symbolic forms were doomed to fail. As was implied in the title of Hall and Jefferson's book, *Resistance Through Rituals*, youth subcultures simply could not redress in material terms the specific issues of unemployment, educational disadvantage, low pay, and the diminishment of working-class labor.

One of the more prominent examples of the application of the CCCS approach was Willis's return to a persistent theme: the relationship between schooling and the formation of youth subcultures. Willis (1977) studied a group of working-class boys who described themselves as "lads," in opposition to others who viewed school positively, whom the lads called "ear'oles." The lads represented an oppositional culture, characterized by aggressive masculinity, within the school, and they rejected the forms of knowledge which it had to offer and its values in favor of cultural perspectives formed within the milieu of the shop floor. Willis undertook a detailed analysis of the relations between the lads and their school environment, and concluded that they were active participants in a process which prepared them for lives of labor, in the tradition of their parents' culture.

4. Responses to the Cultural Studies Approach

The work of the CCCS researchers has been the subject of considerable debate. Two major criticisms should be noted. The first is their failure to address effectively the issues of gender relations; "youth cultures and subcultures" effectively meant male subcultures. This can be partly explained by their greater visibility, but the absence of serious attention to girls' perspectives and

practices and the kinds of "imaginary" solutions which they constructed, with the exception of the work of MacRobbie (see MacRobbie and Nava 1984), remains a serious weakness.

By way of contrast, research in Australia by Walker (1988) and Wilson and Wyn (1987) has been able to explore the interaction of male and female youth cultures, indicating that interaction between males and females will reflect quite different assumptions about masculinity and femininity, depending on the circumstances. Wilson and Wyn found that both girls and boys perceived the sexual division of labor to be crucial, yet its actual form varied according to the context. What remained central was the issue of power, and its exercise in gender relations.

The other major, and related, criticism was that the CCCS researchers presented an overly romanticized view of male working-class subcultures. They tended to idealize the violence, sexism, and racism of these subcultures, and justify them in the context of broader inequalities (see Brake 1980 p. 69). Associated with this criticism is the observation that youth subcultures appear, in their terms, to be necessarily working class. As with the mistaken assumption that delinquency is a working-class problem, the failure to undertake studies of youth subcultures framed by other class backgrounds has been a significant limitation on theoretical understanding of young people's lives.

These criticisms raise a number of issues about the methodological practices of the CCCS researchers, and whether they came to identify too closely with their subjects. It also serves to draw attention to aspects of the CCCS theorizing which require considerable development.

4.1 Australian Studies

Nevertheless, the work of the CCCS researchers has stimulated a number of studies on the cultural dimension of class relations and on youth cultures in other countries. Walker (1988) studied male youth cultures in an urban Australian school, focusing on the hierarchy which formed between different groups of boys. Walker viewed cultures as

> problem-solving programmes, whose success, failure, development, change, and articulation with each other are to be explained by their interaction with the practical contexts in which the people whose programmes they are encounter everyday problems. (Walker 1988 p. 35)

Walker's study provided a rich picture of the significance of ethnicity, as well as class and gender, in the development of male youth cultures. Sport, in the form of Australian football, was central to the development of some kind of school spirit and unity. However, this was achieved at the expense of flouting the antiracist and antisexist values which were school policy.

A different approach was adopted by Dwyer et

al. (1984), who grounded their consideration of the importance of class cultures for educational outcomes in an analysis of the broader patterns of cultural formation. They identified four specific aspects of cultural formation, around which differences between the dominant cultural forms and working-class cultural perspectives could be considered. Although a tentative analysis, the study identified a number of structural and cultural arrangements which helped to explain the patterns of educational achievement found in Australian schools.

Wilson and Wyn (1987) drew on data from a number of studies of young people and their perspectives on the transition between school and work to examine the relationship between social division and cultural formation. Their evidence indicated that there are fundamental differences in the social experiences and priorities of young people, which inevitably link the cultural with the material dimensions of people's experience.

> An interplay of force and compliance, of mutual agreement and resistance is continually to be found in the circumstances within which social division is contested and maintained. While one of the outcomes of social division is "inequality", the process is one of relations of dependence and conflict between groups leading to the subordination of the interests of one group to those of another. (Wilson and Wyn 1987 p. 62)

This analysis drew attention to questions of power, and the more complex manner in which power can be exercised in order to advance the interests of some young people, educationally or otherwise, at the expense of others. These are issues which affect all young people, not only those who participate in subcultural activity.

4.2 Swedish Studies

In the early 1980s, the State Youth Council of Sweden undertook a major project on the "commercial child and youth culture" and its consequences for young people. This study drew on a concept of youth culture which emphasized a view of young people as "market," and revealed a lack of faith among young people about the future of their society. While they had hopeful visions of what society *might* be like, they did not expect them to be fulfilled. Their values and practices as consumers were shaped by social changes which had altered the character of social relationships and effectively denied young people any meaningful participation in the productive spheres of their society. Given the relative affluence of Swedish families and their children, the emergence of a preoccupation with consumption was almost inevitable (Henricksson 1983).

By the late 1980s, considerable research was being undertaken on the recreation and expressive interests of Swedish youth. Some, at least, of this work was influenced by the Birmingham approach to cultural

studies, and by the German theorist, Thomas Ziehe. The Youth Culture Research Program at Stockholm University has provided considerable impetus to this area of research, both through its conferences and publications and through its national research project on modernity, gender, style, and spheres. Its research has focused on distinguishing the different cultural meanings of differing types of media for various groups of young people. Music has been shown to be much more significant than, for example, television in the present period. Fornas et al. (1989) suggested that the impact of recent cultural modernization has given rock music, especially, a very important place in the lives of many Swedish teenagers. It provides: creative pleasure; access to a new language (words, tones, and visual styles); self-expansion; collective autonomy; and an alternative path to a career.

5. Age as a Category in Cultural Studies

The study of youth cultures and subcultures has made an important contribution to understanding the social context of schooling, and especially in understanding the ways in which youth subcultures and schooling interact and mutually shape each other. The differences between particular theorists in this regard indicate that it continues to be an area which warrants more research and theoretical development. The more documentation there is about the structure, values, and practices of youth subcultures in different parts of the world, the more data will be available for the analysis of these issues. Ethnographic studies on youth subcultures continue to be prominent not only in the countries discussed in this entry, but also in other parts of Europe, North America, and New Zealand.

A significant issue which requires further debate is the usefulness of age as an analytic category. As Allen has commented,

> Whilst the relations between those of different ages are of significance in all societies, to elevate these relations to a position in which stability, change, continuity and discontinuity are seen to be articulated through them is questionable. It is not the relations between ages which explain change or stability in societies, but change in societies which explains relations between different ages. (Allen 1968 p. 321)

The risk of focusing on age as a primary category of analysis is that young people will tend to be regarded as a distinctive group, with less attention being paid to the links in beliefs, values, and practices which they might share with their parents, more than with other groups of young people. At the very least, Allen's caution ought to indicate that it is important that attention to studies of youth culture should continue to be grounded in the broader theoretical and research developments in the sociology of education and cultural studies.

See also: Broadcasting and Technology: Effects on Children and Youth; Discipline in Schools; Resistance Theory; Youth and Leisure; Youth Friendships and Conflict in Schools

References

Brake M 1980 *The Sociology of Youth Cultures and Subcultures*. Routledge and Kegan Paul, London

Clarke J, Hall S, Jefferson T, Roberts 1976 Subcultures, cultures and class: A theoretical overview. In: Hall S, Jefferson T (eds.) 1976

Cloward R A, Ohlin L E 1961 *Delinquency and Opportunity*. Routledge and Kegan Paul, London

Cohen A 1955 *Delinquent Boys—The Culture of the Gang*. Free Press, New York

Cohen P 1972 *Subcultural Conflict and Working Class Community*, Working Papers in Cultural Studies 2. University of Birmingham, Birmingham

Corrigan P 1979 *Schooling the Smash Street Kids*. Macmillan, London

Downes D 1966 *The Delinquent Solution*. Routledge and Kegan Paul, London

Dwyer P, Wilson B, Woock R 1984 *Confronting School and Work: Youth and Class Cultures in Australia*. Allen and Unwin, London

Fornas J, Lindberg U, Sernhede O 1989 Under the surface of rock: Youth culture and late modernity. In: Fornas J (ed.) 1989 *Working Paper 89/1*. Centre for Mass Communication Research, Stockholm

Hall S, Jefferson T 1976 *Resistance Through Rituals: Youth Subcultures in Post-war Britain*. Hutchinson University Library, London

Hargreaves D 1967 *Social Relations in a Secondary School*. Routledge and Kegan Paul, London

Hebdige D 1979 *Subculture: The Meaning of Style*. Methuen, London

Henricksson B 1983 *Not for Sale: Young People in Society*. Aberdeen University Press, Aberdeen

MacRobbie A, Nava M 1984 *Gender and Generation*. Macmillan, London

Matza D 1969 *Becoming Deviant*. Prentice-Hall, Englewood Cliffs, New Jersey

Park R E, Burgess E W, McKenzie R D 1967 *The City*. University of Chicago Press, Chicago, Illinois

Thrasher F M 1927 *The Gang*. University of Chicago Press, Chicago, Illinois

Walker J 1988 *Louts and Legends*. Allen and Unwin, Sydney

Whyte W F 1943 *Street Corner Society: The Social Organisation of an Italian Slum*. University of Chicago Press, Chicago, Illinois

Willis P E 1977 *Learning to Labour*. Saxon House, London

Wilson B, Wyn J 1987 *Shaping Futures: Youth Action for Livelihood*. Allen and Unwin, Sydney

Youth Friendships and Conflict in Schools

B. J. Bank

Although theories and research focused on the friendships of children and adolescents have a long history, studies of such friendships that take account of school settings are more recent, and few studies have yet appeared that are centrally concerned with conflicts among students in schools. The older tradition of research and theorizing concerned with students' friendships has produced a well-established set of findings about the relationships between student characteristics and friendship formation. The smaller body of literature focused on friendships in schools has added information about the ways in which school characteristics affect friendship formation. Investigators in both traditions have participated in a lively debate concerned with the positive versus negative influences of friends on students' behaviors in school, and they have also begun to raise questions about the nature of student conflicts.

1. Relationships Between Student Characteristics and Friendship Formation

Of all the student characteristics that might affect friendship formation, the two that have produced the most reliable findings are age and gender. Studies conducted over several decades have found that friendship formation among younger children tends to be based on shared activities, and friends tend to be described by young children as playmates and helpers. In preschools, schools, and other settings, children are expected to get along with one another and to engage in coordinated activities. To these ends, adults have often been found to intervene in the interactions of young children and in the processes of their friendship formation.

As children get older, they are more likely to choose their own friends and to construct their friendships in interaction with one another. By middle childhood, reliable gender differences in friendship patterns also begin to appear. Whereas the friendships of girls are intensively focused on one or a few friends, boys both report and are observed to have more extensive friendship networks. In middle childhood, friendships also become characterized by more expressive intimacy, especially the friendships of females, which have consistently been found to be more expressive than those of males from middle childhood through adolescence and on into adulthood and old age. Even for males, however, friendships based on shared thoughts and feelings become more common as boys move toward adolescence, and teenagers of both sexes are more likely than younger children to describe their friends as confidantes.

Only since the late 1980s has research concerned with effects of social class on friendships in schools appeared, and most of these studies have been limited to secondary schools. A review of this research by Corsaro and Eder (1990) suggests that students from middle-class backgrounds, and especially those who are members of elite groups within the high school, are more likely to base their friendships on interests and activities, often switching friends as their interests change. In contrast, students from working-class backgrounds exhibit more loyalty to their friends, often to the point of avoiding those activities in which their friends are uninvolved. As a result, their friendship networks tend to be more stable and less extensive. Members of secondary school cliques and crowds in which working-class adolescents predominate are likely to view their personal networks as the continuous element in their lives, and their resistance to the formal school culture is well documented in a variety of national contexts.

Few studies have appeared examining the effects on friendships of nationality and national context, but Shlapentokh (1984) has used research into the role of friendship in the former Soviet Union as the basis for a theory about these effects. He begins by asserting that friendships often serve as a refuge for the individual against external threats, including threats from the state. He goes on to hypothesize that, all other things being equal, the lower the sense of security among people and the weaker their confidence in the future, the more intense and vital are their interpersonal relationships. It is for these reasons, Shlapentokh (1984) argues, that people from the former Soviet Union attribute to friendship a more prominent place in their system of values than do people from the United States, and oppressed minorities have closer personal relations than those of the dominant majority.

Despite this latter suggestion, the literature concerned with race and ethnicity contains surprisingly little research that compares the characteristics of friendships across groups. Instead, the major research question about race and friendship concerns the extent to which students select as friends other students whose race or ethnicity is the same as their own. This research has yielded a large body of evidence documenting the existence of racial homophily in several national contexts. In the United States, this preference for same-race friends seems to increase during primary school, reaching its highest level in junior high school, and then remaining at about the same level throughout high school.

The principle of homophily in friendship formation has also been documented for age, gender, social class, and a wide variety of opinions and behaviors. Unlike racial homophily, both gender and age homophily seem to decrease throughout adolescence, after reaching their peak in middle childhood. Some

of this decrease during the teenage years may be due to the formation of romantic or sexual liaisons, however, rather than to an increase in cross-sex or cross-age friendships per se. Although young children pay relatively little attention to such characteristics of potential friends as goals, values, or personal predispositions, students in the middle grades have been found to assign such characteristics great importance and to exhibit a strong preference for friends whose characteristics are similar to their own. This preference seems to decline slightly during the adolescent years, but there is no age group for whom similarities of any kind have been found to be negatively correlated with friendship formation.

Three major reasons have been offered to explain this strong tendency toward homophily. One of these is social pressure, which has been found by several investigators to inhibit the development of friendships that cross racial, gender, or social class lines. Adults often intervene to make certain that children select "appropriate" friends, and peers frequently do likewise. Especially among preadolescents, there seems to be a strong aversion to those who are different from themselves. In his description of a United States junior high school, Everhart (1983) gives vivid, and sometimes chilling, examples of the ways in which friendship groups demand conformity and reject anyone who deviates from the group norms for actions, interests, talk, dress, attitudes toward school, or treatment of peers.

A more benign and psychological reason for homophily in friendship selection is the set of assumptions that people tend to make about those who are similar to them. In particular, social psychologists have found that most people make the assumption that similar others will like them more than dissimilar others. This assumption, coupled with the well-documented tendency of people to like those who like them, produces more reciprocal liking among those who are similar than among those who are not. Both assumed and actual reciprocity of liking, in turn, have been found to be strong predictors of friendship selection and stability.

The third and most structural reason for homophily in friendship selection is proximity. Although it is not uncommon for researchers to find a few students who mention fantasy figures or famous personalities when asked to nominate their friends, most friends are selected from among people with whom the students have actually been in contact. Contact seems to be particularly necessary for what are called close friendships or strong ties in which students choose for their friends the same persons who choose them. Such choices, and the contacts that make them possible, depend on the available opportunities for interaction. Social structures can either facilitate or impede interactions among certain kinds of people, and considerable evidence exists to suggest that many social organizations sort and separate people who are dissimilar from one another while promoting interaction among those who are alike. This tendency is particularly noticeable in schools.

2. Effects of School Characteristics on Friendship Formation

Both across schools and within them, there is considerable segregation of students by age, gender, race, ethnicity, and social class. Some of this segregation is deliberately designed to promote connections among students from the same social background and to prevent contacts and friendships with students who are different. Some of this segregation is unintentional, however, and it often occurs even in those school systems that are sincerely dedicated to social integration and egalitarianism. Some of this unintended segregation is undoubtedly student initiated, but much of it seems to be perpetuated, and possibly created, by the many ways in which schools differentiate and group their students.

Epstein (1989) has identified a broad range of school characteristics that affect proximities among students and, therefore, possibilities for friendship formation. These school characteristics include architectural features of the school building and grounds, equipment and supplies, demographic features, the organization of extracurricular activities, and such characteristics of instructional methods as authority structures, evaluation and reward systems, ways of grouping students, task structures, and the amount of time teachers spend fostering exchanges of ideas among students.

Sometimes these characteristics vary across schools, with the result that some schools are friendlier than others. High participatory schools, for example, are defined by Epstein (1983b) as those in which both the school's architecture and its educational program combine to create a relatively high level of student participation in classroom decision-making. Compared to students in low participatory schools, those in high participatory schools were found to select more students as friends, to participate in more reciprocated friendships, and to select more friends from outside their own classroom.

Sometimes characteristics of classrooms within the same school have significant effects on friendship selection. One of these characteristics is curricular tracking. Such tracking includes specialized programs for academic and vocational students, student placements in core subjects on the basis of ability, and elective courses for students with particular talents or interests. Although tracking is usually designed for educational purposes, it also alters opportunities for peer interactions within the school. This opportunity structure directly affects friendship formation, and several studies have appeared showing that students are more likely to select friends from their own curricular track than from other tracks. Because the educationally relevant criteria used for tracking students are so highly correlated with their social background characteristics, tracking usually serves as a means for perpetuating segregation by age, gender, social class, race, and ethnicity.

Even though reducing proximity among students of diverse backgrounds seems to be an effective way of preventing friendships among them, encouraging contacts among diverse students does not guarantee friendly relations. In the case of race relations, for example, some studies (e.g., Bank et al. 1977) suggest that increased contact across racial lines is more likely to increase than decrease both perceptions of racial dissimilarity and interracial antipathy. Thus, the challenge for educators who would like to promote friendly behaviors among students of diverse backgrounds is to restructure school activities in ways that will help such students to see their similarities, rather than their differences, and to form positive opinions of one another. According to a growing body of research, these outcomes can be achieved if students participate in instructional groupings that are deliberately and carefully structured to meet these goals. Two interrelated group characteristics that have been found particularly likely to promote friendship formation among group members, even across racial lines, are task and reward interdependence.

In groups characterized by task interdependence, cooperation between students is emphasized by the teacher. All students in a group are expected to work together toward some common goal. Equal participation by all group members is encouraged, and tasks are structured in ways designed to equalize status differences. In some cooperative group methods, individuals are tested after their group experience and are given grades for their individual performance as well as a team score, based on the group average. In other cooperative group methods, students are praised and rewarded as a group, but not as individuals. In both cases, however, the rewards that students receive are dependent upon the help and cooperation they have given to and received from other group members.

Studies of cooperative learning generally support the conclusion that task and reward interdependence stimulate positive relations among students of different races or ethnicities, but many of these studies are experiments of relatively brief duration. Thus, it is not certain whether the positive relations among cooperative group members will continue after the group is dissolved. Nor is it clear whether task and reward interdependence among students of diverse backgrounds increases the heterogeneity of previously existing friendship groups. Nevertheless, it seems likely that schools and classrooms stressing greater proximity and cooperation among students will foster more friendships and more diversity in friendship networks than will schools and classrooms that limit contact and stress competition among their students.

3. *Influences of Friends on Students' Behaviors*

Although researchers and educators have often been willing, and sometimes eager, to seek ways to promote interracial and interethnic friendships among students, these propensities probably reflect a desire for racial harmony more than a positive view of student friendships per se. As Farrell (1990 p. 50) notes, "Many (American) teachers, in fact, fear that friendships in classrooms might work against learning and classroom management. Friends can reinforce each other to avoid work or to engage in disruptive and attention-getting behavior." This hostility toward friendships is similar to that which Vogel (1965) attributed to the Chinese Communist Party in the years after the People's Republic was established and which Shlapentokh (1984) described as the "hidden animosity toward friendship" in the state ideology of the former Soviet Union.

In support of teachers' suspicions that students' friendships undermine official educational goals, Everhart (1983) reports that the students in his ethnographic study prized their friendships above grades and rarely discussed the academic side of school with their friends. Similar findings have been reported by other researchers, especially in the United States. Csikszentmihalyi and Larson (1984), for example, asked a group of United States teenagers to carry electronic pagers for one week and to fill out reports of their activities and feelings whenever they were paged. This sampling of students' time revealed that the majority of the time these adolescents spent with friends was spent in leisure activities or maintenance tasks (such as eating or doing errands). Only 3.5 percent of the sampled time with friends was spent studying or doing other school-related productive work. Reports of students' feelings indicated that they enjoyed studying with friends more than studying alone or in the presence of family members, but they admitted to having more difficulty concentrating on studies when friends were present than when they were not.

In contrast to studies suggesting that friends have negative effects on student learning, there is considerable literature extoling the positive benefits of students' friendships. Several writers draw on the interpersonal development theory of Sullivan (1953) to argue that friendships help youngsters develop mutual respect and support, reciprocal commitment, and genuine, altruistic concern for each other. Buhrmester and Furman (1986), for example, have developed a neo-Sullivanian model of child development based on the assumption that children are actively motivated to establish new types of social relations as they get older, including the kinds of intimate, same-sex, preadolescent friendships with which Sullivan (1953) was primarily concerned. Buhrmester and Furman (1986) suggest that these new relationships benefit their participants by helping to fulfill their social needs, contributing to the growth of their social competencies, and remediating their adjustment problems.

Other positive consequences of friendship that have been argued in the literature include high or improved self-esteem, mastery of symbolic expression, realistic assessments of one's own abilities and achievements, acquisition of role-taking and communication skills, development of self-identity and autonomy, self-validation, development of creative and critical thinking, and the learning of moral principles and social rules. Regarding the latter, Youniss and Smollar (1985) have characterized close friendships as principled relationships in which adolescents learn the tenets of mutual caring, mutual respect, mutual trust, and symmetrical reciprocity. The latter principle seems to be a variant of the rule of fairness which young children are said to learn from their friendships.

Some of the claims about the influences of friendship seem contradictory. Some writers claim, for example, that close friends provide one another with the kinds of unconditional support they cannot gain in other relationships. It is hard to reconcile either this claim or the common assertion that friendships enhance self-esteem with the contention that friendships promote realistic self-assessments. Such inconsistencies may result from a lack of consensus among researchers about the best ways to measure friendships which may, in turn, account for the fact that evidence to support some of these claims is weak or inconsistent.

Another problem that characterizes some of the research concerned with the influence of friends is the failure to separate influence from selection. If, for example, friends have similar preferences, should this finding be interpreted to mean that friends influence each other's likes and dislikes, or should it be concluded that "birds of a feather flock together"? Although most research on the influence of friends continues to be cross-sectional, and thus is incapable of answering this question, some good, longitudinal studies have also appeared. In one of these, Kandel (1978) assessed the extent to which members of friendship dyads were alike in their frequency of current marijuana use, level of educational aspirations, political orientation, and participation in minor delinquency. She was able to show that about half of the similarity exhibited by the friendship pairs on these four measures was due to the process of selection in which similarity led to friendship, and the other half of the similarity resulted from the process of influence in which association led to similarity.

Whereas Kandel (1978) used behavioral self-reports, Epstein (1983a) obtained standardized achievement test scores in mathematics and English for the United States students she studied. She also asked them to nominate their three best friends from among their classmates. One year later, the achievements of these students were retested, and changes in their scores were calculated. Epstein (1983a) found that students with both high and low initial scores on achievement and high-scoring friends had significantly higher scores one year later than did students with low-scoring friends. Similar findings were obtained for report card grades in mathematics and English and for self-reports of college plans.

These findings suggest that the influence of friends is not necessarily a force antagonistic to the school's goals of achievement and academic success. Nevertheless, suspicious teachers and state authorities are correct in assuming that the influence of friends is not always supportive of official policies. Those who wish to make it so might follow the optimistic advice of Damon and Phelps (1989) concerning the ways in which educators can translate what is known about positive peer influences into an effective pedagogy that utilizes peer learning. More skeptical practitioners might heed the cautions of Cohen (1983) who argues that the friends students select for themselves have much more influence on them than nonselected peers, even if these peers are among the school elites.

4. Student Conflicts in Schools

Studies of friendships have become increasingly sensitive to the ways in which conflict is embedded in personal relationships. Preschool children tend to quarrel over possession of play materials and entry into peer groups (Corsaro and Eder 1990), and their conflicts often take the form of hitting and name-calling (Shantz 1987). Among older children, conflicts often occur when friends violate important rules, such as not helping a friend in need or breaking a promise (Shantz 1987). Among adolescents, conflicts often result from the paradoxical requirements of close friendships such as the tensions between autonomy and connection or between expressivity and instrumentality. These various kinds of conflicts rarely destroy close friendships. Instead, they are means for testing friendships and for developing social identity (Corsaro and Eder 1990).

Conflicts within friendships have also been found to be less frequent and severe than conflicts in other relationships, such as those with parents (Csikszentmihalyi and Larson 1984) or those in which a friendship group conflicts with individuals or collectivities external to the group (Everhart 1983). Regarding the latter, Fine (1981 p. 46) notes that the cruelty of the preadolescent boys he observed in the United States was "almost always expressed in the presence of friends. Insults seem(ed) to be expressed as much for reasons of self-presentation to one's peers as to attack the target." Similar observations were made by Connell et al. (1982) of boys in Australian secondary schools who often had to fight with other boys to prove their masculinity to themselves and their mates. Such findings suggest that conflicts in school can best be understood by using theories and research designs that also take account of the processes of friendship formation and influence among students.

See also: Discipline in Schools; School and Classroom Dynamics; Youth and Leisure

References

Bank B J, Biddle B J, Keats D M, Keats J A 1977 Normative, preferential and belief modes in adolescent prejudice. *Sociol. Q.* 18(4):574–88

Buhrmester D, Furman W 1986 The changing functions of friends in childhood: A neo-Sullivanian perspective. In: Derlega V J, Winstead B A (eds.) 1986 *Friendship and Social Interaction.* Springer-Verlag, New York

Cohen J 1983 Commentary: The relationship between friendship selection and peer influence. In: Epstein J L, Karweit N (eds.) 1983 *Friends in School: Patterns of Selection and Influence in Secondary Schools.* Academic Press, New York

Connell R W, Ashenden D J, Kessler S, Dowsett G W 1982 *Making the Difference: Schools, Families and Social Division.* Allen and Unwin, Sydney

Corsaro W A, Eder D 1990 Children's peer cultures. *Ann. Rev. Sociol.* 16:197–220

Csikszentmihalyi M, Larson R 1984 *Being Adolescent: Conflict and Growth in the Teenage Years.* Basic Books, New York

Damon W, Phelps E 1989 Strategic uses of peer learning in children's education. In: Berndt T J, Ladd G W (eds.) 1989 *Peer Relationships in Child Development.* Wiley, New York

Epstein J L 1983a The influence of friends on achievement and affective outcomes. In: Epstein J L, Karweit N (eds.) 1983 *Friends in School: Patterns of Selection and Influence in Secondary Schools.* Academic Press, New York

Epstein J L 1983b Selection of friends in differently organized schools and classrooms. In: Epstein J L, Karweit N (eds.) 1983 *Friends in School: Patterns of Selection and Influence in Secondary Schools.* Academic Press, New York

Epstein J L 1989 The selection of friends: Changes across the grades and in different school environments. In: Berndt T J, Ladd G W (eds.) 1989 *Peer Relationships in Child Development.* Wiley, New York

Everhart R B 1983 *Reading, Writing and Resistance: Adolescence and Labor in a Junior High School.* Routledge and Kegan Paul, Boston, Massachusetts

Farrell E 1990 *Hanging In and Dropping Out: Voices of At-Risk High School Students.* Teacher's College Press, New York

Fine G A 1981 Friends, impression management, and preadolescent behavior. In: Asher S R, Gottman J M (eds.) 1981 *The Development of Children's Friendships.* Cambridge University Press, Cambridge

Kandel D 1978 Homophily, selection, and socialization in adolescent friendships. *Am. J. Sociol.* 84(2): 427–36

Shantz C U 1987 Conflicts between children. *Child Dev.* 58(2): 283–305

Shlapentokh V 1984 *Love, Marriage, and Friendship in the Soviet Union: Ideals and Practices.* Greenwood, New York

Sullivan H S 1953 *The Interpersonal Theory of Psychiatry.* Norton, New York

Vogel E F 1965 From friendship to comradeship: The changes in personal relations in communist China. *China Quarterly* 21: 46–60

Youniss J, Smollar J 1985 *Adolescent Relations with Mothers, Fathers, and Friends.* University of Chicago Press, Chicago, Illinois

Further Reading

Epstein J L, Karweit N (eds.) 1983 *Friends in School: Patterns of Selection and Influence in Secondary Schools.* Academic Press, London

Gottman J M, Parker J G (eds.) 1987 *Conversations of Friends: Speculations on Affective Development.* Cambridge University Press, Cambridge

Hallinan M T 1986 School organization and interracial friendships. In: Derlega V J, Winstead B A (eds.) 1986 *Friendship and Social Interaction.* Springer-Verlag, New York

Rawlins W K 1992 *Friendship Matters: Communication, Dialectics, and the Life Course.* Aldine De Gruyter, Hawthorne, New York

Rubin K H, Ross H S (eds.) 1982 *Peer Relationships and Social Skills in Childhood.* Springer-Verlag, New York

Rubin Z 1980 *Children's Friendships.* Harvard University Press, Cambridge, Massachusetts

Salzinger S, Antrobus J, Hammer M (eds.) 1988 *Social Networks of Children, Adolescents, and College Students.* Erlbaum, Hillsdale, New Jersey

Youth Unemployment

J. Lamoure

For people of all ages, unemployment can mean economic and social exclusion. These phenomena are particularly acute among young people, who are also the chief victims of recessions; barely do they finish their studies before they often find themselves out of work. After a summary of how education and unemployment have developed in quantitative terms, this article details some of the effects of unemployment on young people's professional and social lives. Finally, it describes the major trends in educational and institutional solutions brought in by industrialized countries, as well as the limits of their effectiveness.

Youth unemployment, studied here in the context of industrialized countries, should not mask the gravity of the situation in developing countries: unemployment in the developing countries is even more dramatic, but the low number of people in regular jobs and the size of the unofficial sector give it a completely different significance and make it much harder to gauge the extent of the problem. Like adults, young people in the Third World live in very precarious circumstances, when they are not simply abandoned to beg in the streets. The problem here is not unemployment; quite often it is just a matter of the struggle to survive (UNESCO 1991). Furthering education and training can help to make young people more employable but—and this is even more true than in industrialized countries—only economic growth can provide a lasting solution to their problems. The confusion prevalent in the former Eastern bloc countries since the early 1990s has led to both a huge rise in unemployment and a breakdown in the social welfare systems that used to protect the young from economic exclusion. Although reliable information on youth unemployment in these countries is not yet available, it will probably become increasingly difficult for young people to find work over the next few years, especially as competition for jobs grows between school leavers and adults who lose their jobs from former state enterprises.

1. Education and Unemployment: Recent Developments

Defining the term "youth" has always presented a problem, according to whether it refers to the psychological development of individuals or their formation into a particular sociological or cultural group—especially their emergence in the 1950s as a group of consumers in their own right. School demography and the main statistical sources on unemployment agree that the 15–24 age group should be set apart because these are the ages at which young people in industrialized countries leave school or university and start to look for work. However, this demographic definition is insufficient, especially considering the state of the job market. Job seekers aged 15–19 without qualifications have only had a minimum of education, at best staying slightly beyond the minimum school-leaving age; those who leave the education system at the ages of 20–24 usually have a degree or higher education diploma of some kind. Work and unemployment obviously do not have the same meaning for these two age groups. Social, ethnic, and sexual differences reinforce the initial division into age groups, enabling groups particularly at risk from unemployment to be distinguished. Identifying these high-risk groups is one of the constant factors in policies aimed at combating youth unemployment. There are also geographical differences in the way the unemployed are distributed: more young people are out of work in areas hardest hit by economic recession and in the "pockets of poverty" of the suburbs or run-down city neighborhoods.

1.1 Longer Schooling

In all industrialized countries, the decade prior to 1992 has been characterized by young people continuing their studies longer before leaving school or university. In many countries—the United States, Germany, Belgium, and Denmark, for example—more than three-quarters of the 15–19 age group are still in the education system, and a quarter of those aged 20–24 are still studying. There are several reasons for this increase. First, families hope that investing in longer schooling will give their children a better chance of finding work, and the recession can only reinforce this attitude. Second, technological change means that there is greater pressure for new skills or a higher level of education, although this demand is felt more strongly in some economic sectors than in others. Finally, the fact that unemployment is high in most countries leads employers to be more demanding when taking on new staff and to give preference to candidates who have followed longer courses of education, have more qualifications, or who have already had some work experience.

When young people start looking for work, the limited opportunities on the job market widen the gap between those with degrees or diplomas and those who leave school with no qualifications or vocational training. Every country has some unemployed graduates, but there are fewer of them and they are likely to be out of work for less time than young people who have only had the legal minimum of education.

1.2 High Unemployment

The level of youth unemployment has been very high during the 1980s and 1990s: in 1980 this age group made up nearly half the total of unemployed, and even in the early 1990s, with the proportion of young people arriving on the job market smaller than previously, the figure is still around 40 percent. In some countries, the proportion of unemployed in the 19–24 age group is even increasing (see Table 1). Youth unemployment

has become a social and political problem which governments have tried to counter with specific measures, aimed both at helping unqualified young adults to acquire skills and at preventing them from falling into the social exclusion trap caused by lack of work and financial resources. Some of the wide variety of measures that have been introduced have been more effective than others, but the overall assessment is negative; they have not helped to eradicate youth unemployment, and industrialized societies are still facing a problem on which training policies have failed to make any impact.

2. The Consequences of Youth Unemployment

Although the most obvious consequence of unemployment is shortage of money, it also has destructuring effects not only on the general social and emotional behavior patterns of young people, but also on their future working lives. These factors tend to accumulate and reinforce one another and are closely connected with individual characteristics; the consequences of unemployment are more serious and long-lasting for young people from underprivileged social groups and for those with no qualifications. These factors are not peculiar to the young—they are frequently found among unemployed people of all ages, particularly those who have been out of work for long periods— but young people do seem to make up an especially vulnerable group.

2.1 Effects on Working Life

The consequences of unemployment not only concern young people with no qualifications, but also concern

Table 1
Percentage of young people unemployed in the 16–24 age group of the working population

	1981	1982	1983	1984	1985	1986	1987	1988	1989	1990
United States	14.3	17.0	16.4	13.3	13.0	12.7	11.7	10.6	10.5	10.7
Canada	13.3	18.8	19.8	17.8	16.3	15.1	13.7	12.0	11.3	12.8
Japan	4.0	3.9	4.5	4.9	4.8	5.2	5.2	4.9	4.5	4.3
Australia	10.8	12.9	17.9	16.5	14.3	14.5	14.6	12.8	10.4	13.3
New Zealand	—	—	—	—	—	7.9	8.0	10.9	13.5	14.1
Germany	6.5	9.5	10.7	9.9	9.5	8.6	8.1[a]	—	—	—
France	17.0	19.0[a]	19.7	24.4	25.6	23.4	23.0	21.7	19.1	19.3
United Kingdom	17.9	23.1[a]	23.4	21.8	21.5	20.5	17.3	11.8	8.3	8.1
Ireland	14.7	—	20.1	22.6	24.1	25.5	26.3	24.8	22.2	—
Italy	25.8	28.0	30.5	32.9	33.9	34.5	35.5	34.5	33.6	31.4
Finland	9.2	9.8	10.5	9.8	9.1	9.5	9.0	7.8	6.1	6.4
Netherlands	13.4[a]	18.6	24.9	25.2	22.9	20.0	14.8[a]	13.6	12.2	11.1
Norway	5.7	7.6	8.9	7.6	6.5	5.0	5.3	7.9	11.5	11.8
Spain	31.1	34.8	37.6	41.8	43.8	42.8	40.2	37.1	32.0	32.3
Portugal	14.6	14.6	18.3	19.6	19.5	17.8	13.7	11.5	11.4	10.2
Sweden	6.3	7.6	8.0	6.0	5.8	5.6	4.2[a]	3.3	3.0	3.5

Source: OECD, Directorate for Social Affairs, Manpower and Education
a Break in series

graduates with professional training. Their ability to find work is affected and so in the long run is the possibility that they may ever be able to find and keep stable employment.

2.1.1 Lower employability. Whether adults or young people are involved, any period of unemployment tends to reduce people's professional skills, especially for jobs that demand specific knowledge. Besides the traditional trades based on manual dexterity, other skills also have to be practiced if they are to remain effective. Being out of work for a few months can make it harder to pass recruitment tests; a secretary may type more slowly and a machine-tool operator's work may be less precise. At times when technologies are changing rapidly, the long-term unemployed may even find that their original professional skills have become obsolete. Young people hit by unemployment as soon as they leave school are in an even more critical situation than adults because usually they have not even had the chance to put into practice any skills they may have learned in school. The situation varies with different education systems. When at least a proportion of training is carried out by companies, as in Germany's *dual* system, it is more likely that the skills acquired will survive a period of unemployment.

2.1.2 Difficulty in keeping a stable job. It is important that a person's first job after a period of unemployment fulfills certain conditions. The job must have some relevance to the candidate's training and it must be fairly stable.

For young skilled workers, a series of temporary, unskilled jobs can be just as damaging to their future careers as being out of work as soon as they leave school. When both factors occur, finding a stable job is an enormous problem because the exclusion factor becomes self-perpetuating (Grapin and Lamoure 1979). The consequences are even more serious in countries such as France and the southern European countries, where finding a job depends to a great extent on the qualifications obtained at an early stage in the candidate's education.

A number of research projects have emphasized the fact that young people with no qualifications often have no career plans or social aspirations: in other words, the employment problems they are likely to have are intimately tied up with their own self-perception. This lack of identity is obviously reinforced by being out of work and partly explains the repeated failures of these young people to find employment (Pissart et al. 1990).

2.2 The Consequences for Social Life

Professional exclusion plays a part in social exclusion and it can break up the personality and can lead to psychological instability. Although the unemployed of all ages bear the scars of loneliness and withdrawal, it is the young who are most at risk from identity problems and social exclusion. Studies that have been carried out on these groups show that the social inequalities generated by schools are intensified by unemployment, leading to an "accumulation of handicaps" (OECD-CERI 1983).

2.2.1 Social identity problems. For its youngest victims, unemployment comes at a time when they are still going through the identity crisis linked to adolescence, and this aggravates the difficulty of finding their place in society. More generally, young people without jobs do not fit into any predetermined social category: they are no longer pupils, they are not yet workers, and their families still have to support them. This economic dependence is made worse by the fact that their parents may be out of work too. They are incapable of achieving the status of consumer so sought after in the culture of industrialized societies, and this is often a source of frustration.

2.2.2 From social difficulties to exclusion. The only chance these young unemployed have of a place in society lies in joining groups of people the same age, which in the worst cases may be gangs of petty criminals. While this is far from being a new phenomenon, it does seem to have grown in scale, especially in the run-down neighborhoods of large cities where it is associated with ethnic exclusion and unemployment. These gangs are all the more damaging because they enable their members to obtain illegal income above what they would earn doing a regular job. The exclusion then becomes endemic, and the victims' chances of finding employment look increasingly remote (White and Mcrae 1989).

The long-term impact of these difficulties in finding a place in society has yet to be fully assessed, but the studies that have been done indicate that such problems might have repercussions on the way the transition to adult life takes place.

3. The Solutions Put into Practice

Two general trends are emerging in industrialized countries: extending technical and professional education, and setting up after-school programs to help people find work and a place in society. Which of these tendencies takes precedence in any one country depends to a large extent on its educational history as well as the nature of its relations with industry. The two solutions are complementary insofar as they are both attempts to deal with the root causes of unemploymen, namely, a shortage of skills among young people and the restricted labor market. They also attempt to reduce the impact of unemployment on society.

3.1 Extending Technical and Professional Education

In most European countries, the increase in the length

of schooling has been accompanied by the growth of technical and professional training, with a number of clear differences according to country. During the 1980s in the Netherlands, Italy, Sweden, Germany, and France, professional training colleges or programs took in a growing proportion of young people, sometimes following the introduction of new forms of training such as the professional *baccalauréat* in France and Italy. Apprenticeship is not growing at the same rate, but deliberate policies have been brought in by the Netherlands and France to breathe new life into this form of training, both within and outside sectors of the economy where it is traditional. In Japan and the United States, the sluggish growth and low status of basic professional education in secondary schools is the result of the major part played by industry in training young people (Jallade 1988).

3.2 Helping People Find Work

The programs to help people enter employment are intended to complement the basic training facilities with a view to providing school leavers with a minimum of skills and protecting them against social exclusion by helping them develop behavior patterns that will help them find work. In some cases they are even given assistance in creating their own employment (Martinos 1986). The importance given to one or the other of these approaches is a question of changing attitudes to the causes of youth unemployment. In the early 1980s, youth unemployment was generally thought to be a cyclical phenomenon due to the modernization of companies as a result of technological progress, and due to training not being geared to the jobs available. This viewpoint gave rise to measures aimed at providing training and social assistance. However, since the mid-1980s, the introduction of measures linking economic and social factors as part of an overall policy of integrating young people into society and, more recently, the emphasis placed on creating new jobs and self-help, spring from the view that youth unemployment, far from being cyclical, has become a permanent factor in the new economic circumstances of Western countries.

The number and variety of measures taken in different countries makes any attempt at typology difficult. Only a few characteristics common to all of them can be distinguished: they are usually paid for out of public funds, they form an integral part of government policies against unemployment, and they involve a wide range of partners—schools and colleges, companies, local authorities, and, in some countries, private associations. They are aimed at tightly targeted groups chosen according to age (such as 16–18-year olds in France and 16–17-year olds in the United Kingdom) or according to educational background. One of the most wide-ranging initiatives in this respect is the United Kingdom's Youth Training Scheme which since 1983 has been aiming to provide about half a million young people with minimum qualifications, based on

alternance training combining work for a company and education at a school or college. Similar experiments are taking place in several European countries, but, as Jallade points out (1988), "where [alternance training programs] are well organized, [after-school training programs] prove to be unnecessary."

Although some of the measures to provide employment seem intended to offset the institutional rigidity of certain basic training systems, others are devised more as a way of helping young people find a place in society by giving them the chance to build up the "relationship capital" that is a vital complement to their "educational capital" in improving their employability. This is the thinking behind programs designed to involve people in the local economic and social fabric (economic adaptation), that seem to dominate the policies of the early 1990s. According to a comparative study of 50 such programs in Europe and the United States, their success depends on the following factors:

(a) keeping the programs firmly rooted in community self-help networks;

(b) making the programs part of a national economic or local development plan;

(c) making the best use of human resources and local infrastructure;

(d) using a wide range of institutional and financial partners suited to the needs of the people involved (Cauquil 1991).

In every case, providing people with a cultural identity seems to be a powerful tool for social adaptation and economic development. This means that the battle against youth unemployment is no longer just a matter of compensating for educational and/or social handicaps, which dominated the thinking behind the first measures introduced. It requires a search for synergy and shared concern between the young unemployed and local communities that may themselves be underprivileged.

4. Conclusion

The continuing high rate of youth unemployment shows the restricted usefulness of the measures introduced so far. In the final analysis, the countries with the fewest young people out of work are those where economic growth is strongest. Only economic recovery seems capable of providing an answer to the problem, In the meantime, technological choices and the organization of labor in industry must be implemented in such a way as to create more employment opportunities, while allowing businesses to remain competitive (D'Iribarne 1989).

Beyond this general situation, youth unemployment has generated new ways of looking at the links between education and training, on the one hand, and employment, on the other, especially concerning what can be expected from educational solutions:

(a) The limits to which increasing the duration of formal education may prove useful have been demonstrated, and "hopes of social change through schooling have given way to disappointment among social experts" (Rontopoulou 1986). Merely making young people stay in the education system longer has not in itself provided a contribution to greater employability. In fact, it actually increases differences in "educational capital" and social inequalities insofar as it is always young people from the lowest social categories who finish their studies soonest.

(b) In addition to providing compulsory education, training systems must in future be prepared to integrate greater flexibility into their planning and programs to answer the need for new skills, and to give people from previously excluded social strata access to further education. In most countries, this means fostering new kinds of relationships between all the players involved, and especially between schools and industry.

(c) The measures introduced to help young people find work have shown that teaching them professional skills is not enough to prepare them for working life. They must also be helped to improve their social skills, especially as education, by keeping them outside productive employment, is playing an increasingly important role in introducing them to society.

The broad range of measures taken to combat youth unemployment has highlighted the need to share the workload between official educational establishments and local or community initiatives on the one hand, and the various government bodies such as ministries or departments of education, labor, health, and social affairs on the other, all of which contribute logistically or financially to these measures. The ease with which all these bodies or their representatives communicate with one another varies from country to country, but this dialogue has become an unavoidable part of the new educational scene. Managing this overall effort in the sphere of education and securing employment has thus become extremely complicated. If sufficient care is not taken, human and financial resources could be wasted on a large scale, rendering the measures introduced so far less effective and the work undertaken less credible.

See also: Adolescence; Benefits of Education; Postliteracy: Concepts and Policies; Technological Change and Deskilling

References

Cauquil G 1991 De l'insertion sociale au développement territorial intégré. *Actualité de la formation permanente* 110: 26–37

D'Iribarne A 1989 *La compétitivité: Défi social, enjeu éducatif.* Presses du CNRS, Paris

Grapin P, Lamoure J 1979 Les premiers emplois: formation et expérience professionnelle. In: Grapin P, Lamoure J 1980 *Insertion professionnelle des jeunes, apparitions de nouvelles fonctions sociales.* Association des Ages, Paris

Jallade J P 1988 *Formation professionnelle à l'étranger: quels enseignements pour la France?* Commissariat Général du Plan, La documentation Française, Paris

Martinos H 1986 *Employment Creation in Local Labour Markets.* ILE Notebooks, No. 5, OECD, Paris

OECD-CERI 1983 *Les études et le travail vus par les jeunes* (Work and Study as Seen by Young People). OECD, Paris

Pissart F, Poncelet M, Voisin M 1990 Vivre en chômage. L'installation des jeunes sans emploi dans la vie adulte. *Revue française de sociologie* 31(4): 573–90

Rontopoulou J L 1986 *Des filières de relégation aux formations alternées des dispositifs d'insertion.* Université Paris V, Paris

UNESCO 1991 Enfances en péril. *Le Courrier de l'UNESCO* 10(44): 13–43

White M, Mcrae S 1989 *Young Adults and Long-Term Unemployment.* Policy Studies Institute Publications, London

Further Reading

Hartmann J 1985 Nouvelles formes de participation et de travail des jeunes en Suède. *Revue internationale des Sciences Sociales* 37(4): 491–506

Jallade J P 1982 *Alternance Training for Young People: Guidelines for Action.* European Community, Information Service, Washington, DC

McCleland K 1990 Cumulative disadvantage among the highly ambitious. *Sociol. Educ.* 63(2): 102–21

OECD 1984 *The Nature of Youth Unemployment: An Analysis for Policy Makers.* OECD, Paris

OECD 1985 *New Policies for the Young.* OECD, Paris

Squires G 1987 *Education and Training After Basic Education: Organization and Contents of Studies at the Post-Compulsory Level; General Report.* OECD, Paris

Educational Policy and Change

Introduction: New Developments in Education as an Agent of Change

L. J. Saha

One of the contradictions surrounding the relationship between education and social change is that education is both an agent of change in society, and in turn is changed by society (Fagerlind and Saha 1989). The focus on education at this macro level is determined by the specific characteristics of society. Thus the specific political, economic, and cultural systems of society will determine to what extent education operates as a relatively autonomous institution within society, or whether it is influenced or determined by the state or other social institutions (see Section IV, *Education and the State*).

The 16 articles in this section focus on education and change in the context of three general perspectives: (a) Education, Social Change, and Development; (b) Education and New Technology; and (c) Educational Policy and Planning. Together these articles locate education in a macro perspective, one more general than those found in Sections IV and V of this *Encyclopedia*, which are concerned with the systemic and structural aspects of education.

1. Education, Social Change, and Development

The first section consists of seven articles which address the relationship between education and social change. Two of the articles focus upon change, but from different perspectives. Hanna's article, *Social Change and Education*, addresses the role of education as a change agent partly from a cultural perspective and acknowledges that education is a change agent and is changed in various forms of cultural conflict. In this respect, Hanna discusses colonialism and Westernization, industrialization, and the impact of large-scale immigration on education processes. Hanna concludes with the observation that more needs to be known about the role of education in the conflicting processes of social reproduction and social change.

The article by Saha and Fagerlind (*Education and Development*) focuses on a specific aspect of social change, namely national development. By the latter the authors mean social, economic, and political development, both in a "modern" as well as in a "developing" context. Like Hanna they take a dialectical view of the relationship between education and society. The distinctiveness of their view is that they concentrate on the three institutions which play a major role in the development process: the economic, the political, and the socio/cultural. They also identify areas where further attention needs to be directed by those interested in the relationship between education and development, namely, the importance of literacy and gender for development, and the relative importance of vocational and academic education in the national development process.

The other articles in this section focus on specific aspects of education and change. The article by Solmon and Fagnano (*Benefits of Education*) discusses how education benefits both individuals and societies. It does not take a cost-benefit analysis approach, although the article does raise cost-benefit questions in the discussion of the benefits of education. The article by Carr-Hill (*Basic Education: Comparative and International Studies*) examines the importance of "basic" (primary) education and its role in promoting the development of a country. He examines the importance of primary education in terms of access and gender equity, but most importantly as the "cornerstone" of national development. Although human capital theory postulates that education improves the productivity of the workforce generally, in many developing countries the improvement in agricultural productivity is a crucial development strategy. The positive impact of formal schooling on agricultural productivity, particularly in developing countries, is clearly demonstrated by Moock and Addou's review of the literature in *Agricultural Productivity and Education*. The findings are consistent and particularly strong in "modernizing" countries. Of importance in the literature is that the amount of formal schooling to produce "functional literacy" is the minimum requirement for the improvement of agricultural productivity, a finding consistent with the argument in Carr-Hill's article. Nonformal education, however, does not seem to produce the same effect.

Torres, in his article *Adult Education for Development*, provides an excellent overview of the importance of adult education (sometimes called "nonformal education") in the national development process, even if the manner of contribution is somewhat problematic. Although adult education does not appear as clearly linked with improved productivity in the formal labor market, Torres maintains that it does make a contribution to informal economic activities. In this respect, his article complements the previous overviews in that adult education constitutes another strategy in the education-development process. Perhaps a more important aspect of adult education in the development process is the impact that it has on the creation of an aware and active citizenry, and in this respect its relationship to political processes in a country. Evans (*Conscientization and Mobilization*) discusses the political impact of adult education, sometimes called "popular education," in the consciousness raising and mobilization processes. Drawing primarily on the writings of Paulo Friere, he discusses how this form of adult education is used to achieve political objectives particularly in giving greater voice to those portions of the population who are less powerful and in less control of their own lives.

2. Education and New Technology

The second subsection consists of five articles and addresses the increasing impact of technology in the educational process. In the educational context, most discussions about technology refer to the rapid development of various forms of educational technology, but the study of the social impact of technology extends into the workforce as well. Thus the concern of the impact of technology in schooling, for example, applies to the use of technology to improve teaching and learning, and also learning to be comfortable with new technologies on the part of students, and acquiring the skills to adapt to new skill requirements as adults.

Conboy and White (*Social Implications of Educational Technology*) argue that questions of who has access to, participates in, or controls educational processes are key issues related to educational technology. Each of these questions raises issues of the changing nature of teaching and learning, of the relationship between teacher and student, and of inequalities resulting from unequal access and participation in newer educational technologies. One specific issue has been the extent to which educational technology has introduced a form of inequality between males and females. The article by Janssen Reinen and Plomp (*Gender and New Technology*) describes the evidence and implications of the fact that girls appear to have less access to and participate less in computer-based education both at home and at school. They argue that this pattern can be reversed, and provide examples to substantiate their claim.

A key link in the integration of educational technology into teaching and learning activities is obviously the teacher. Hativa addresses this topic in *Technology and the Classroom Teacher* and identifies major issues which surround the teacher. For example, Hativa argues that with the introduction of computers into the classroom, teachers become more like coaches and facilitators rather than information transmitters. Furthermore, the literature suggests that a large proportion of teachers use the computer in an inefficient manner, and there are many obstacles to effective use. However, Hatvia illustrates how these can be overcome, including major social and organizational changes of the curriculum and the classroom.

The final two articles in this section focus on the implications of technological change for the wider society. Carnoy (*Technological Change and Education*) provides an overview of the issues relating to the impact of technology on the workforce, and the type of training needed to prepare for entry into the workforce. This eventually leads to the decision as to whether vocational education or a general education better prepares youth for a changing work environment. While Carnoy accepts that the answer may, to some extent, depend on the growth level and development of a country, the answer must lie in the extent to which vocational training complements general education, and whether a combination of both is the preferred solution.

Spenner (*Technological Change and Deskilling*) provides a more specific examination of whether technology upgrades or downgrades the skill requirements for the workforce. Although the research evidence fails to provide a clear answer, the implications of changing skill requirements in the workforce for education are considerable. The expectation that education systems should produce graduates with specific or changing skills for a more technological society is one that underlies much of the debate about education today.

3. Educational Policy and Planning

One of the fundamental tensions regarding research in most disciplines is that between pure and applied research. Research which is oriented toward the testing of theory, for example, is often not oriented toward use by policymakers, and conversely research which is driven by the demands of policy and practice often fails to address some of the more fundamental questions of the discipline. This tension applies especially to educational research, irrespective of the disciplinary framework within which it is carried out. As already pointed out in the preface to this *Encyclopedia*, this has historically been the case with the sociology of education, where the labels of "educational sociology" and "sociology of education" were taken to represent the difference between normative research, which is oriented toward the development of policies, programs, and actions, and empirical (scientific) research, which is oriented to the "establishment of verified knowledge, internally consistent, cogent and adequate to its subject" (Hansen 1967 p. 16).

The four articles in this subsection address issues related to educational research and policymaking. Many of the points made above are treated in greater detail in Husén's article *Educational Research and Policymaking*. After describing the different values and environments within which researchers and policymakers work, Husén concludes that research can have an impact on policy decisions, but not often in the short term. As he observes, the findings of social science research often "creep" and "percolate" into the policymaking process.

The article by McGinn, *Politics of Educational Planning*, makes clear the political environment within which policy and planning decisions are carried out. Within this context, even in a decentralized planning environment, the competition for resources and competing interest groups rarely result in "rational" planning. Guthrie advances this view even further in his article *Globalization of Educational Policy and Reform* in which he documents evolving economic and social environments at the international level which are leading to the globalization of educational policies and movements toward educational reform. Benton's article on *Postliteracy: Concepts and Policies* addresses an issue which is increasingly common in most countries where the basic levels of literacy are proving inadequate to meet the higher skill needs of modern hi-tech industries. His discussion of policy needs across a number of countries pulls together and illustrates many of the observations and conclusions of other articles in this section.

References

Fagerlind I, Saha L J 1989 *Education and National Development: A Comparative Perspective*, 2nd edn. Pergamon Press, Oxford

Hansen D A 1967 The uncomfortable relation of sociology and education. In: Hansen D A, Gerstle J E (eds.) 1967 *On Education: Sociological Perspectives*. John Wiley & Sons, New York

(a) Education, Social Change, and Development

Adult Education for Development

C. A. Torres

This article discusses adult education for development. While a range of relevant research studies are reviewed, no specific reference is made to integrated rural development implementation strategies, nor is a systematic assessment of community education offered. The first section introduces the reader to adult education concepts, purposes, and principles. The following two sections discuss adult education and theories of national development, economic growth, and modernization theories, as well as theories of adult education for development, mobilization, participation, and empowerment with a particular focus on popular education models. In the conclusion, the mainstream models of adult education labeled as "clinical models" are discussed and confronted with an alternative model of "adult education as cultural politics." In this section, the challenges of social movements to adult education for development are noted.

1. Concepts and Principles

"Adult education" and "nonformal education" are sometimes used as interchangeable terms. Nonformal education is defined as "any organized, systematic educational activity carried out outside the framework of the formal system to provide selected types of learning to particular subgroups of the population (La Belle 1986 p. 2). Concepts, purposes, and principles of adult education are related to adult education origins, function, and the interaction between specific fields of practices and theoretical discourses which constitute adult education as an educational interdisciplinary hybrid.

Competing discourses clash over the definition of adult education itself. In historical terms, modern adult education relates to the postwar consensus trying to create a more educated and enlightened citizenship, avoiding the pitfalls in the socialization of citizens and the nurturing of a political culture which led to fascism and totalitarism in Europe. As a result, adult education mainstream programs share basic principles with liberalism, and contribute to social welfare politics. However, particularly in Latin America and Africa, adult education's origins also relate to the evangelical zeal of missionaries trying to convert native Latin Americans and Africans to Christianity. In the nineteenth and twentieth centuries, there were also clear expressions of adult education for national development linked to community activism and resistance to capitalist social relations.

At the most abstract level, a number of functions of adult and continuing education can be identified. Critical perspectives argue that a principal function of adult and continuing education is the maintenance of the social system and reproduction of existing social relations. According to this perspective, the manifest and latent functions of adult education tend to increase the socialization of individuals to adapt to the world of work in a knowledge-based society with growing diversification and specialization. A second approach emphasizes that adult and continuing education have a conservative function, contributing to the transmission of knowledge and the reproduction of culture. However, the culture that is transmitted and reproduced is the dominant culture, the canon of cultural literacy rather than the competing expressions or literacies of a society segmented by race, class, gender, religion, and diverse cultural narratives. In adult and continuing education, can one justifiably define what knowledge is worthwhile without asking who determines what is valid, worthwhile, relevant, pertinent, and needed knowledge?

Technocratic perspectives consider adult education to be part of a social mechanism to guarantee individual advancement and selection. Adult education thus becomes a vehicle toward upward mobility of the labor force—through contest mobility rather than sponsored mobility—and plays an important role in the moral and technical socialization of people. One of the most prominent early advocates of nonformal education as a key for national development is Philips Coombs. In his widely read contribution, Coombs (1968) indicates a number of educational problems that plague education at the international level, including the increasing demand for education, rapidly rising educational costs, inefficient management and teaching methods, the unsuitability of the output, and the scarcity of resources available for educational expansion. As solutions, Coombs suggests the introduction of capital intensive technologies, improved teacher training, increased foreign aid, and the promotion of rapid expansion of education through nonformal education.

Coombs's contribution reflects the optimism of the time and the faith that education will decisively contribute to development. It also reflects a certain mode of analysis, according to which persons and educational systems are held accountable for school failure, rather than the broader social structures. Thus, problems such as social inequality and regressive patterns of income distribution are a consequence of individual psychological deficit rather than inequalities in power, wealth, and influence. Coombs should be credited, however, with being one of the most articulate scholars distinguishing schooling and nonformal education as two sharply distinct teaching and learning systems.

Considering the sweeping changes brought about in industrial societies by new technologies and the re-organization of the division of labor with a growing service sector, many argue that a fundamental role of adult and continuing education relates to the pursuit of leisure time activities and institutional expansion. With more advanced technologies, there is more free time for individuals, particularly the middle classes which take advantage of this increase in free time, enrolling in adult education programs in the pursuit of aesthetic or artistic knowledge (i.e., courses in painting and art appreciation, and floral arrangements) or practical activities (e.g., courses in specialized cuisine, wine appreciation, carpentry, etc.). Hence, a growing relationship between adult education programs and gerontology has resulted from the increasing number of senior citizens who are free from the demands of work and seek fulfillment in continuing education programs.

Criticisms of the overly psychologized mode of analyses are well reflected in the political economy of adult education (Bock and Papagiannis 1983, Carnoy and Samoff 1990, Torres 1990, 1991). These authors emphasized the centrality of power and knowledge as a social construct, and therefore the basic questions they asked are not how nonformal education could contribute to social change but rather: (a) Who benefits from investing in nonformal education? (b) What is the nature of the complex relationship between schooling and nonformal education? (c) How does each differentially serve those social functions that education has always served—socialization, mobility management, and transmission of cognitive and noncognitive skills? (d) How do adult education and schooling systems differ in their patterns of recruitment, in their internal structural characteristics, and in their relationship to the occupational structure and the world of work?

In studies exploring the relationships between adult education and social change, it is argued that adult education plays a fundamental role in compensatory legitimation. More often than not, adult education systems constitute a second chance to improve academic performance and credentials, particularly with many adult education courses oriented to women entering the labor force after establishing a family, with the purposes of upgrading their skills, knowledge, and abilities. Viewed as compensatory legitimation, the uses of adult education in the production of a hegemonic culture legitimates inequalities (Torres 1990 pp. 171–74).

Finally, many practitioners and scholars argue that adult and continuing education for development should be understood as liberating education (Youngman 1986, Torres 1990, Freire and Macedo 1987, La Belle 1986). For liberation pedagogues, learning is related to critical understanding, contributing to the maturity and self-realization of individuals and communities. Liberation appears as an individual as well as a social goal. Adult education therefore constitutes an essential part in the practice of social transformation, and is not reduced to critical reflection or critical teaching.

Antecedents of adult education as community resistance or revival or social movements can also be found in Europe, Canada, and the United States. In this mode adult education refers to the strengthening of workers' education, community education, and nonformal education which is not to be controlled, legislated, regulated, or financed by the state, but by individual citizens, community members, and students. North American examples are the Antigonish Movement in the Canadian Maritime Eastern Provinces, and the Highlander Institute in the Appalachians. Similar examples can be traced back to workers' education in Argentina, Brazil, and Mexico, or to anarcosyndicalism propaganda and journalism oriented to enlighten workers and serving as a tool for mobilization and organization (Welton 1987, Horton and Freire 1990).

In spite of the richness and diversity of these and many other experiences, the most articulate expression of theories of adult education for national development relates to theories of economic growth, modernization, and human capital.

2. Adult Education and Theories of National Development: Economic Growth and Modernization Theories

Human Capital Theory works in the framework of a theory of modernization. The modernization approach considers education as a variable intimately linked to the processes of socioeconomic development. Development, in its turn, is conceived as growth of the social product, following the model of advanced Western societies. The underdevelopment of the Third World is explained in terms of individual personality traits. Individuals in industrial advanced capitalism cultivate the attitude of achievement, an universalistic perspective, and a specialized and functional division of labor, while traditional individuals in underdeveloped societies struggle helplessly with an orientation toward ascribed statuses, a particularistic perspective on the world, and a nonspecialized division of labor.

The human capital approach thus points to the necessity of identifying the mechanisms through which the passage from economic backwardness to economic development can be realized in different contexts. Literacy and basic education count among the privileged mechanisms for increasing contacts with modern societies (and their products), disorganizing traditional cultures (often of oral origin) which are considered an element of backwardness, and facilitating the development of social heterogeneity in the adoption of innovations.

Mark Blaug and others have noted that literacy and the basic education of adults in general contribute to economic development in diverse forms by: (a) increasing the productivity of the newly literate; (b) increasing the productivity of those who work with the newly literate; (c) expanding the diffusion of the general knowledge of individuals (training in health and infant nutrition) and generally reducing the cost of transmitting practical information; (d) stimulating the demand for technical training and vocational education; (e) acting as an instrument for selection of the most valuable elements of the population and enhancing their occupational mobility; (f) strengthening economic incentives (i.e., the tendency of people to respond positively to an increment of compensation for their efforts) (Blaug 1966). In these terms, literacy is seen as one of the most important elements in the process of modernization and the development of nations undergoing industrialization.

Diverse investigations have indicated there is a significant correlation between the percentage of illiterates and income per capita (0.84), as well as between illiteracy and industrialization (0.87). Further, the coefficient of multiple correlation for 54 countries between literacy, urbanization, recognition of the value of information, and political participation was 0.91. Psacharopoulos (1988) argues that:

> ... economists have established the link between increases in the educational level of the labor force and economic growth. Similarly, they have documented a direct link between increases in the level of schooling in the population and distributional equity. Sociologists have established the relationship between education and upward social mobility. Historians have documented the link between early rises in literacy and the economic take-off of nations. And a variety of other disciplines have established the relationship between education and further developmental outcomes like health, sanitation and fertility. (p. 1)

Along these lines regarding basic education, Marin and Psacharopoulos (1976) argue that giving primary education in Mexico to 10 percent of those who lack it, would reduce a measure of income inequality by 10 percent. Regarding the contributions of adult education to political development, Huntington (1968) claims that one of the most relevant aspects in the process of political modernization is the change in attitudes, values, and expectations—changes that are a direct consequence of literacy, education, increases in communications, the exposure to mass media, and urbanization.

In summary, the range of aims and goals of adult education for development as seen by human capital theorists vary from developing positive attitudes toward cooperation, work, community and national development, and further learning to the teaching of functional literacy and numeracy; from providing a scientific outlook toward health, agriculture, and the like to incorporating functional knowledge and skills; from preparing individuals to enter into the labor market or strengthening their current occupational position to making available functional knowledge and skills necessary for civic participation. These assumptions are overtly present in the documents of the Inter-Agency Commission, particularly in the background document of the important conference on Education for All held in Thailand in 1990 (IDRC 1991).

There are many criticisms of Human Capital Theory and its application to adult education. The contribution of basic education to growth may well be smaller than the early human capital theorists and development economists anticipated. The correlation between earnings and education picks up many other influences on earnings that are also correlated with schooling and training, but should not be attributed to them. Available evidence suggests that the wage structure to an extent depends upon variables exogenous to individual productivity. These variables include gender, race, the nature of a firm's market of goods, maintenance of class structure in the face of meritocratic rules, degree of monopoly power in the market, and/or social class background (Carnoy et al. 1979). Thus, differential rates of return to education are not primarily the result of inequality in the distribution of schooling, but refer instead to the basic unequal structures of capitalist societies. In addition, the role of the state in education and income policy is a crucial variable in determining income distribution. In this sense, taxation, wage fixing, price control, inflation, and employment policies are the means by which the state exercises this power —policies that are out of reach of adult education programs (Torres 1990).

A decisive standpoint from which to study the relationships between adult education, income distribution, and capital accumulation is the theory of labor market segmentation. According to this theory, labor market conditions can be understood as outcomes of four segmentation processes: (a) segmentation into primary and secondary markets, (b) segmentation within the primary sector, (c) segmentation by race, and (d) segmentation by gender. The primary and secondary segments are differentiated as follows:

> Primary jobs require and develop stable working habits; skills are often acquired on the job; wages are relatively high; and job ladders exist. Secondary jobs do not require

and often discourage stable working habits; wages are low; turnover is high; and job ladders are few. Secondary jobs are mainly (though not exclusively) filled by minority workers, women and youth. (Reich et al. 1975 p. 1)

Although the theory of segmented labor markets has a particular relevance to advanced industrial societies, it does help to understand that (adult) basic education in developing societies simply prepares people for improving their chances to enter the secondary labor markets. The notion of labor market segmentation duly cautions against assuming that education and training lead automatically to higher income distribution through increasing per capita productivity which leads, in turn, to higher earnings. Adult education does not train manual labor for all labor markets, but instead is oriented, in reality, toward the secondary work market, where the job stability is less, income low and fragmented, social benefits scarce or nonexistent, and the supply of barely qualified labor abundant. In this context, adult education could simply be preparing manual labor that will continue to function within capitalist modes of production, or it simply prepares people to assume a level of economic life marginalized from the mainstream economic lifeworld.

A major drawback of adult education programs underscored by Human Capital and modernization theories is that, by placing a strong emphasis on formal markets, they have virtually neglected informal labor markets, thus ignoring the actual and potential contribution of adult education planned in such markets. Hence, a discussion of informal labor markets is very relevant to adult education for development.

3. Informal Labor Markets and Adult Education

Informal labor markets refer to the informal economic activities undertaken by poor workers which not only generate income, but also promote efficient economic growth. Some of the characteristics of this specific labor force and market are: its units function with low capital investments and operating capital per worker; the workforce does not require high training levels, nor formal educational inputs; and their technical demands are minimal because their technology is simple or artisanal and the tools they use are either self-made or second-hand and obsolete (Sáenz 1989).

The existence of informal (urban) sectors poses a variety of complications for governments. These economies and labor sectors are difficult to tax, regulate, assess, or measure statistically. Indeed, even in Western European societies, informal labor (considered to be "social labor") can be characterized by "freedom of entry and exit, by considerable autonomy in the programming of activity as well as by non-discriminatory and legally guaranteed rights to income" (Offe 1985 p. 79).

In synthesis, the theoretical rationale of the human

capital approach has been challenged by a political economy of adult education. From this perspective a number of questions emerge: Does adult education and literacy contribute to increase output or does it allocate people to jobs with higher training requirements, productivity, and earning potential? Does adult education legitimize an unequal social structure and thereby contribute to higher output and acceptance of unequal work roles? Or, instead, does adult education reduce output through legitimizing a profit-making pattern of capital accumulation that is less than optimal for a particular society? Critical approaches will consider the role of adult education for development using analytical approaches which depart from classical human capital and modernization perspectives.

With very few exceptions, the success of adult education as rural education or education to broaden productive capacities and the distribution of goods and services in rural communities have been quite limited. At a more general and empirical level, the perception of the economic benefits of literacy and adult basic education in developing countries does not seem to be widely documented by empirical studies, with very few exceptions—Tanzania could be one of them. There do not seem to be studies that reflect these economic advantages of the investment in adult education (Bhola 1984).

Another critical objection to Human Capital Theory is the perspective of the diploma disease (Oxenham 1984), that is, the inflation of educational credentials such that employers are constantly creating newer and greater criteria of selection where employability is defined by educational characteristics. But even if after finishing primary school individuals were given the possibility of reaching better functional positions in an organization where they were already employed, or permitted to satisfy admission requirements to some occupation, there is no guarantee that in the immediate future that credential would not lose value as the education threshold of occupations rose.

This is a substantive problem confronting all postsecondary education programs, aggravated in the case of adult education for two reasons. First, because adult education often deals with the lowest levels of educational and occupational strata, and their educational credentials have low market value. Second, because at times adult education does not function in agreement with the criteria of supplying individuals with basic education credentials, but instead postulates the acquisition of skills and specific knowledge where credentials are not relevant.

Training of the labor force is a complex process. On occasion, once finished with their training and having achieved higher levels of technical ability, the workers remain outside the market of goods and services for which they were supposedly prepared in the first place. This occurs when the cost of employing a highly trained workforce exceeds the level of demand in relation to value and cost within the system (La

Belle 1986). At times, the educational supply of highly trained manual labor greatly exceeds its demand in a market that does not create work positions with the same speed, intensity, and diversity as the supply of education.

In conclusion, the economic advantages of adult education are at the very least debatable. The disparities between the mechanisms of employment and the qualification levels that adult education provide would seem to be growing. The issue is not only whether Human Capital Theory works or not in the context of developing countries—though there is enough evidence that it does not work as efficiently and smoothly as some of its proponents may suggest (La Belle 1986). The question is why adopt a single rationale or theory when many other theories or rationales for policy planning may also prove successful for development, mobilization, participation, and empowerment of individuals, families, and communities through adult education.

4. Adult Education for Development: Mobilization, Participation, and Empowerment

Arnove and Graff (1987) report that there are clearly neglected populations regarding literacy training in industrialized societies. Looking at several campaigns in a historical and comparative perspective, they have concluded that rural populations, the working class, ethnic and racial minorities, and women have been the last to receive literacy instruction and to gain access to advanced levels of schooling. Among all these groups, women have been the most disadvantaged group. Thomas (1983) pointed to the existence of large numbers of undereducated Canadians whose low levels of literacy might place serious limitations on their participating fully in the rights, responsibilities, and privileges of citizenship. Indeed, illiteracy becomes a political as well as a cultural problem in multiethnic and multicultural societies such as Canada, where special consideration needs to be given to indigenous populations (Indians and Inuit) and immigrant populations for whom English or French are not first languages (Thomas 1983 p. 13). Consequently, the provision of ESL (English as a Second Language) literacy in large reception centers is a matter of concern for specialists (Thomas 1983 p. 101).

Stromquist (1991) explores the manner in which women are either neglected or manipulated for nondemocratic ends in many national programs of adult education and literacy training. Stromquist attributes this situation to technical problems in the design and implementation of literacy training campaigns and adult education programs, and to patriarchal structures, well-reflected in a patriarchal state which regulates, controls, and manipulates the life of women in the Third World and industrialized societies.

Adult education may serve as a springboard for social organization, organized resistance, and the development of social movements. Zachariah (1987) has demonstrated how, drawing from the contributions of Gandhi and Freire, adult education becomes an important component of the Sarvodaya and Conscientization movements, both in India and Latin America, and how adult education plays a prominent role in the Popular Science Movement in India, particularly in the province of Kerala, India, and in Sri Lanka (Zachariah 1987). Adult education as workers' education is prominent in the many attempts to construct adult education for socialism in experiences as diverse as those in northwest China, Portugal, and Kenya (Youngman 1986), and in the consolidation of the most intriguing and successful example of workers and cooperative education in the experiences of the Mondragon Cooperatives in the Basque region of Spain.

4.1 Cultural Imperialism and Dependency Theories
Canadian adult educator Welton (1987) suggests that:

> Adult learning is more central to societal reproduction, resistance and transformation than that of the children. Resistance to and transformation of societal structures emerges from the adult population, and is premised upon men and women's ability to learn new ways of seeing the world and acting within it (p. 7).

Thus, adult education may contribute to social reproduction, resistance, and transformation in many ways. Carnoy (1974) has used theories of dependency to study the role of education in development. Emphasizing the structural asymmetry of power between nations and social classes, Carnoy has challenged the perceptions about the inherent good of educational investment in the Third World, linking education with power and the construction of knowledge. Carnoy and Samoff (1990) offer concrete cases of using education for social transformation, particularly nonformal education, in China, Mozambique, Tanzania, Cuba, and Nicaragua.

Revolutionary societies or societies in the process of social transition trying to change the basic principles of social reproduction of national capitalist societies have used nonformal education, and particularly literacy training (Arnove and Graff 1987, Torres 1991) as a means of social mobilization, trying at the same time to unleash social creativity, mass participation, and critical consciousness. However, planning and implementation of adult education programs require resources which are usually unavailable to governments in many developing countries. Thus, external aid and the contribution of nongovernmental Organizations (NGOs) is paramount to adult education for development.

4.2 Development Aid in Adult Education
Donor and lending agencies have mobilized resources for adult and basic education for many years. In fact, some adult education policies and programs of adult education could not have been implemented without the substantial and steady flow of external assistance

795

from international, multinational, and bilateral agencies. The role of UNESCO in advocating and supporting literacy training worldwide is widely acknowledged.

However, official international assistance seems to be diminishing quite rapidly (Morales-Gómez and Torres 1992) because the focus is shifting toward the problems of poverty, homelessness, and unemployment that many of the industrial countries face. In addition, there are changing priorities for international assistance brought about by the end of the Cold War, the demise of communism, and the realignment of hegemonic countries in the world. Even private, nongovernment organizations may be retracting their budgets and programs overseas, as a reflection of the changing priorities of international philanthropy and foreign aid policies.

There are reasons to believe that external assistance to adult education policies and programs in the last decade of the twentieth century will be less relevant for the development of the programs. Its demise as an effective player in the context of growing poverty and reduced state intervention in the Third World may result in smaller budgets for adult education, and consequently in the disenfranchisement of particular clientele from programs and policies, especially the poorest of the poor in developing countries. This trend toward deinvestment on the part of the state as well as that of bilateral and multilateral donor and lending agencies in adult education may have serious consequences in the long run. For instance, official development assistance from OECD countries does not exceed 0.36 percent of their combined Gross National Product (GNP), and the United States (the largest donor country in the world) contributes only 0.2 percent of its GNP. Bilateral aid in education dropped from 16.5 percent in 1979 to 10.7 percent in 1989 (Morales-Gómez and Torres in 1992).

Although it is difficult to estimate how much of that aid goes to adult education for development, it is conceivable that the policy preference of many international agencies toward mainly funding primary schooling, capacity building, and system management may hurt the chances of literacy, adult education, and training programs to receive sufficient funding. The option for adult education for development may rest on a multiplicity of initiatives undertaken by NGOs and community organizations, drawing from diverse epistemological, political, and socioeconomic perspectives. Many such initiatives are usually labeled as "popular education."

5. Conscientization and Popular Education

For popular educators, adult education is a field crossed by many ideologies, theories, and discursive narratives, and it has been placed (or thought of) at the service of diverse political and pedagogical projects for national development. Popular education is an educational paradigm critical of mainstream nonformal education, seeking to empower the marginalized and poor people (La Belle 1986, Gadotti 1990, Torres 1990, 1991). This perspective sees knowledge as a social construct and a process, and not merely as a product. Freire and many practitioners of popular education propose a nonauthoritarian but directivist pedagogy for liberation. The teacher is at the same time a student; the student is at the same time a teacher. The nature of their knowledge may differ, however, but as long as education is the act of knowing and not merely transmitting facts, students and teachers share a similar status and are linked together through a pedagogical dialogue characterized by horizontal relationships. The educational agenda will not necessarily be carried out in a classroom but in a "culture circle." Emphasis is placed on sharing and reflecting critically upon learner's experience and knowledge, both as a source or rough material for analyzing the "existential themes" of critical pedagogy, and as an attempt to demystify existing forms of false consciousness.

A main characteristic of liberation pedagogues has been their resistance to be organically linked to the apparatus of the capitalist state until a political regime exists which is sympathetic to the interests and demands of the popular sectors. Important differences exist between radical pedagogues and bureaucrats, decision-makers, and teachers located within these rather large educational bureaucratic structures, pursuing knowledge-guiding interests circumscribed by instrumental rationality (Mezirow 1985).

More than 20 years of implementation show that popular education will seek to design nonformal- and NGO-sponsored educational ventures rather than working within schools and other state-sponsored institutions. It is only since the mid-1980s that the intervention in school settings, with the notion of "public popular schooling" has been advanced by Freirean pedagogues (Gadotti 1990) in the context of Brazilian debates of school autonomy. Not surprisingly, many of the representatives of this pedagogy have worked, politically and professionally, within political parties, universities, and research centers as well as with organizations which have originated in or are linked to churches.

Some of the common features of popular education projects are summarized as follows:

First, they arise from a political and social analysis of the living conditions of the poor and their outstanding problems (such as unemployment, malnourishment, poor health) and attempt to engage the poor in individual and collective awareness of those conditions. Second, they base their educational practice on collective and individual previous experiences (as previous knowledge), and they work in groups rather than on an individual basis. Third, the notion of education provided by these projects is related to the concrete skills or abilities that they try to instill in the poor . . . and these projects strive to arouse self-reliance among the participants. Finally, these projects can be originated by governments, as in Colombia and Dominician Republic or, as in Nicaragua, with the collectives of popular education, and they may be directed toward adults as well as children. (Torres 1990 pp. 9–10)

Popular education projects are not restricted to Latin America. Projects such as the 150 hours of paid educational leave designed by the Italian workers around 1971–73; the struggle of the feminist movement in Geneva (Switzerland) in the early 1970s; the experience of education practice of the PAIGC (African Party for the Independence of Guinea and Cape Verde) liberation movement in Guinea-Bissau between 1973 and 1976 (Freire et al. 1980); or the *Kerala Sastra Sahitya Parishat* (Kerala Science Literature Society) are all considered experiences of popular education (Zachariah 1987).

There are epistemological, philosophical, and methodological problems associated with the notion of popular education (La Belle 1986, Torres 1990). In spite of these problems, popular education has helped to define, in its sharpest terms, one of the main roles attributed to adult education for development: how adult education can evolve into a form of cultural politics in the constitution of the citizenship. In this aspect, popular education models are in sharp contrast with mainstream adult education models.

6. Conclusion: Challenges for Development

The key features of mainstream adult education models are their liberal–pluralist ideological foundations, their technocratic rationale, and their premises of operating programs that deal with individual deficits in the learners—a set of pathologies that should be treated by experts through a complex system of referrals and treatment. They are based on observation, and the analysis of institutional events, with a focus on the relationship between teachers and learners. The basic approach is behaviorism, and in the North American tradition, it could be related to the clinical approach to supervision developed in the 1960s. These models can be labeled "clinical models of adult education."

For clinical models, individuals are mainly organized according to the requirements of production. The whole model depends on a conceptual repertoire organized by experts (adult education teachers, managers, planners) exerting exclusive authority in naming, diagnosing, assessing a treatment, suggesting a therapy, and predicting who in this process will improve and who will not. The paradigm uses a process–product approach, based on empirical measures, a strong emphasis on the psychological functions of the educational system, and the personalized power of teachers over learners. Clinical models of adult education are challenged by notions of adult education as cultural politics, and particularly for the attempts to implement adult education as part of broader social movements.

Adult education as cultural politics opposes these clinical models. In the well-established tradition of adult education for social change, it is argued that learning new ways of seeing and acting implies the development of new forms of cultural politics. For instance, literacy training programs should not only provide reading, writing, and numeracy, but should also be considered " . . . a set of practices that functions to either empower or disempower people" (Freire and Macedo 1987 p. viii). Adult education as cultural politics challenges the paternalistic mode of adult education discourse that seems dominant in the adult education field, because emancipatory adult education " . . . becomes a vehicle by which the oppressed are equipped with the necessary tools to reappropriate their history, culture, and language practices" (Freire and Macedo 1987 p. 159). This approach is in sharp contrast to mainstream adult education models.

In this context, adult education for development should result in the constitution of a social movement. Different state agencies—many of them associated with rural or extension education—have postulated that their adult education programs try: (a) to put education and knowledge at the service of the most impoverished sectors of society; (b) to use this education as a means of liberation to people and as a mechanism of social participation; (c) to use this education as an integrating part and as the initial stimulus of a broader social movement that challenges some of the functional irregularities of capitalism, such as imbalances in income distribution, imbalances between labor market sectors and dissenting actors, problems of providing the required services, and so on; (d) to contribute to the development of a just social space, where the limitation of state authoritarianism would be a desirable consequence; and (e) to promote national development, strengthening not only the identity of social actors but also reinforcing nationalist perspectives. These objectives for adult education relate to theories of social resistance or oppositional pedagogies.

Clinical models and adult-education-as-cultural-politics models both face the challenge of established and emerging social movements. The feminist challenge should be considered, allowing women learners to express their voices openly in the constitution and operation of the programs, considering the issues of power and relevance of adult education in the life of women, and making explicit that as the personal is political, the challenge of feminism should imply a drastic revision of the epistemological foundations of adult education as well as its social and pedagogical principles. The ecological challenge will help to review the connections of adult education with the world of work, and the notion of productivity at the expense of the environment and a social organization of labor that is alienating, hierarchical, undemocratic, and wasteful of resources. The challenge of human rights movements will help to promote basic notions of equality and egalitarian goals in the context of a basic respect for life and a tolerance for diversity and even citizenship opposition. The challenge of neighborhood associations and (religious) base communities will help adult education rediscover its community roots, emphasizing cooperation and joining efforts to reintegrate and reinvigorate communities, many of them deeply affected by the dynamics of capital accumulation at global scale. Hence, adult education for development may be linked with models of moral philosophy and moral education, so easily overlooked or dismissed as irrelevant when decisions in education are only seen as simply a matter of investment, expenditures, or political control.

Only by taking up these challenges can adult education programs emerge as part of a democratic social movement, and make a meaningful and lasting contribution to the development of individuals, families, communities, and nations in the world system.

See also: Agricultural Productivity and Education; Basic Education: Comparative and International Studies; Benefits of Education; Conscientization and Mobilization; Education and Development; Postliteracy: Concepts and Policies

References

Arnove R F, Graff H J (eds.) 1987 *National Literacy Campaigns: Historical and Comparative Perspectives* Plenum, New York

Bhola H S (ed.) 1984 *Campaigning for Literacy*. UNESCO Paris

Blaug M 1966 Literacy and economic development. *The Sch. Rev.* 74(4): 393–415

Bock J, Papagiannis G (ed.) 1983 *Nonformal Education and National Development*. Praeger, New York

Carnoy M 1974 *Education as Cultural Imperialism*. McKay, New York

Carnoy M et al. 1979 *Can Educational Policy Equalize Income Distribution in Latin America*. Saxon House, London

Carnoy M, Samoff J (ed.) 1990 *Education and Social Transformation in the Third World*. Princeton University Press, Princeton, New Jersey

Coombs P 1968 *The World Educational Crisis: A System Analysis*. Oxford University Press, New York

Freire P, Macedo D 1987 *Literacy: Reading the Word and the World*. Routledge and Kegan Paul, London

Freire P et al. 1980 *Vivendo e aprendendo. Experiencias do Idacen educação popular*. Brasilense, São Paulo

Gadotti M 1990 *Uma só escola para todos. Caminhos da autonomia escolar*. Vozes, Petrópolis

Horton M, Freire P 1990 *We Make the Road by Walking: Conversations on Education and Social Change*. Temple University, Philadelphia, Pennsylvania

Huntington S 1968 *Political Order in Changing Societies*. Yale University Press, New Haven, Connecticut

International Development Research Centre (IDRC) 1991 *Perspectives on Education for All*. IDRC, Ottawa

La Belle T J 1986 *Nonformal Education in Latin American and the Caribbean: Stability, Reform or Revolution?* Praeger, New York

Marin A, Psacharopoulos G 1976 Schooling and income Distribution. *Rev. Econ. Stat.* (58): 332–38

Mezirow J 1985 Critical transformation theory and the self-directed learner. In: Brookfield S (ed.) 1985 *Self-Directed Learning: From Theory to Practice*. Jossey-Bass, San Francisco, California

Morales-Gómez D, Torres C A 1992 Introduction: Education and development in Latin America. In: Morales-Gómez D, Torres C A (eds.) 1992 *Education, Policy and Social Change. Experiences from Latin America*. Praeger, Westport, Connecticut

Offe C 1985 *Disorganized Capitalism*. Polity Press, Cambridge

Oxenham J (ed.) 1984 *Education Versus Qualifications? A Study of Relationships Between Education, Selection for Employment and the Productivity of Labor*. George Allen and Unwin, London

Psacharopoulos G 1988 Critical issues in education and development: A world agenda. *Int. J. Educ. Dev.* 8(1): 1–7

Reich M et al. 1975 A theory of labor market segmentation. In: Carnoy M (ed.) 1975 *Schooling in a Corporate Society*. McKay, New York

Sáenz A 1989 Informal labor markets and education. Department of Educational Foundations, University of Alberta, Edmonton (mimeo)

Stromquist N 1991 *Women and Education in Latin America: Knowledge, Power and Change*. Lynne Rienner, Boulder, Colorado

Thomas A 1983 Adult illiteracy in Canada—A challenge (Occasional paper No. 42.) Canadian Commission for UNESCO, Ottawa

Torres C A 1990 *The Politics of Nonformal Education in Latin America*. Praeger, New York

Torres C A 1991 The state, nonformal education, and socialism in Cuba, Nicaragua, and Grenada. *Comp. Educ. Rev.* 35(1): 110–30

Welton M (ed.) 1987 *Knowledge for the People: The Struggle for Adult Learning in English-Speaking Canada 1828–1973*. OISE Press, Toronto

Youngman F 1986 *Adult Education and Socialist Pedagogy*. Croom Helm, London

Zachariah M 1987 New indigenous models of mass education and action: Lessons from the Kerala Sastra Sahitya Parishat (KSSP) of India. Paper presented at the World Congress of Comparative Education Societies, Rio de Janeiro, July 6–10

Agricultural Productivity and Education

P. R. Moock and H. Addou

Since the 1960s, a large number of studies have analyzed the effects of formal education on agricultural productivity. Most have estimated a "marginal product" of education by means of production function analysis. Some have looked also at education's "allocative effect" on agricultural productivity, in terms, for example, of a farmer's willingness to adopt profitable new technologies. This entry reviews the empirical literature in this area since 1978, picking up where an earlier survey (Lockheed et al. 1980) left off.

1. Education's Worker and Allocative Effects

It is argued that education should enhance both technical and allocative efficiency in production. Welch called these the "worker" and "allocative" effects of education. The worker effect is education's marginal product, "the increased output per change in education, holding other factor quantities constant" (Welch 1970 p. 42). It is education's contribution to the quality of the individual as a worker. The notion here is that increased education permits a worker to produce more output using any given quantity of physical inputs.

The allocative effect of education, on the other hand, refers to the more educated farmer's "ability to acquire and to decode information about costs and productive characteristics of other inputs" (Welch 1970 p. 42). A central aspect of the allocative effect is "the capacity to evaluate and adopt profitable new technologies" (Cotlear 1989 p. 75), for example the diversification of production to include different crops for sale, or the use of high-yielding hybrid seeds in lieu of traditional, home-grown seeds. Increased formal education enhances the worker's ability to make optimal decisions about the selection of outputs produced and also about the inputs used to produce particular outputs. Some studies have argued that the allocative effect is probably more important than the worker effect in terms of overall value added. (Dhakal et al 1987, Jamison and Moock 1984, Pudasaini 1983).

Studies on education and agricultural production commonly include years of formal schooling completed as one of several independent variables used to explain production levels or technological choice. The largest number of studies specify an engineering (single crop) or gross revenue production function to estimate education's contribution. Most make use of a Cobb–Douglas (C-D) function, in which dependent and independent variables are expressed as logarithmic transformations. Most use ordinary least squares (OLS) regression analysis to estimate the function. This approach has been used because the statistical results

are efficient and easy to interpret. The regression coefficient on any input in a log-log production function can be taken to be the constant elasticity of this factor in the production process.

Several studies have compared education's effects on agricultural productivity under traditional and modernizing conditions. Education has been found to be more effective in a modernizing environment, as Schultz (1975) reasoned should be the case.

The remainder of this entry is organized as follows. Section 2 recounts the findings up to and including the late 1970s as summarized in the earlier survey by Lockheed et al. (1980). Section 3 reports criticism in subsequent literature of the early studies and the survey. Section 4 summarizes the results of 14 studies published since 1978 analyzing 29 data sets from 12 countries in Africa, Asia, and the Americas and looking at the effect of education on agricultural productivity. The studies to be discussed are described in Table 1.

2. Early Findings

In a review of the literature up to 1978, Lockheed et al. (1980) developed a useful meta-analytic framework for examining the role of education in farm production. The authors were able to conclude that education has a positive effect on farmers' efficiency. To reach this conclusion, they reanalyzed 37 data sets from 18 studies in 13 countries. The studies they surveyed all used production functions to test the hypothesis that farmers' education influences farm productivity; outputs were regressed against factor inputs and education indicators.

The survey found that education was positively associated with farm production at the 0.05 probability level in 15 of 37 tests of the worker effect hypothesis. The regression coefficient was positive but not statistically significant in 16 other cases; in six cases, the coefficient was small but negative. The overall conclusion derived from the studies surveyed by Lockheed et al. (1980) was that, holding physical inputs constant, output could be expected to be about 7 percent higher on farms where the farmer had completed 4 years of elementary schooling as compared with no education at all.

The survey also reported evidence to support Schultz's hypothesis that the returns to education in production are greater in a modernizing environment. When the partial relationship between education and farm production was measured against degrees of modernization, the authors were able to conclude

Table 1
Studies published since 1980 and included in this survey

Author	Date	Country studied, year in which data collected, and sample characteristics
Azhar	1988	Pakistan, 1976–1977; entire irrigated region of Pakistan; data taken from survey conducted jointly by Pakistan WAPDA and World Bank; number of observations for high-yielding variety crops (1,370 wheat and 665 rice) and traditional crops (727 cotton and 720 sugarcane)
Butt	1984	Pakistan, 1977; 1,787 farms across the Indus Basin; survey jointly conducted by Pakistan WAPDA and World Bank; wheat, sugarcane, cotton, and sugar
Cotlear	1989	Peru, 1982–1983; 555 rural households in three regions of Peruvian highlands with varying degrees of technology: a modern region (the valley of Yanamarca), a traditional region (the pampa of Sangarara), and an intermediate region (the plateau of Chinchero)
Dhakal, Grabowski, and Belbase	1987	Nepal, 1973–1974; 600 farm families from six villages of the Nuwakot district in Nepal; maize, millet grown in the upland and in the lowland, paddy and wheat; data from Calkins (1976)
Duraisamy	1990	India, 1981–1982; 461 farm households in 12 villages in two development districts of Tamil Nadu; detailed information of 323 cultivated farms; analysis of paddy production
Grabowski and Pasurka	1988	Northern United States, 1860; sample of 109 farms; data: secondary source
Jameson	1988	Paraguay, 1976; 1,053 farms in eastern Paraguay; administered by Ministry of Agriculture and Livestock and USAID; focus on farm production, employment, and income
		Dominican Republic, 1976; 1,802 farms across the country; administered by Secretariat of State for Agriculture with USAID; focus on farm production, employment, and income
		Guatemala, 1974; 1,548 farms across the country; survey conducted by Ministry of Agriculture and USAID; analyze effects of credit on income, output, and employment
		Bolivia, 1977; 750 farms from Chiquisaca, Tarija, and Potosi; collected by USAID and Ministry of Rural Affairs and Agriculture; concentrated on farm income
Jamison and Moock	1984	Nepal, 1977–1978; 683 households in six panchayats of Bara district and six panchayats of Rautahat; early paddy, late paddy, and wheat; part of World Bank Research Project
Kalirajan and Shand	1985	India, 1977; random sample of 91 farmers in the Tamil Nadu State; growing high-yielding paddy varieties
Khandker	1986	Bangladesh, 1985; 364 farm households in Rangpur, Bogra, Sherpur, Tangail, Comilla, and Dhaka districts
Moock	1981	Kenya, 1971; 152 maize farmers in Vihiga division of Kakamega district in Kenya's Western Province
Phillips and Marble	1986	Guatemala, 1974; 1,348 small farmers across the country, excluding Peten region; survey administered by the Ministry of Agriculture with USAID support; analyze effect of credit on income, output, and employment
Pudasaini	1983	Nepal, 1981; random sample of 205 farmers of the Bara district (modernizing Terai) and 149 farmers of Gorkha district (traditional hill regions)
Ram and Singh	1988	Burkina Faso, 1980; 51 households from seven villages of the Mossi plateau area; part of a regional development project; data collected by personal interviews and questionnaires

that "the percentage gain [in productivity] as a result of 4 years of education is 10% higher in a modernizing environment than in a traditional environment" (Lockheed et al. 1980 p. 57).

Finally, the survey looked at the relationship between the farmer's exposure to agricultural extension services and farm output in 16 data sets. The survey reported that the regression coefficient on extension contact was significantly positive in eight cases, in one the coefficient was negative, and in the other seven there was no apparent effect of extension services on productivity.

3. Critique of Early Empirical Research

Work carried out in the 1980s has questioned the interpretations of Lockheed et al. as well as the empirical studies on which their survey was based. The survey has been criticized for its use of inadequate ad hoc classifications to define modernizing agriculture and for its inattention to the question of whether the observed relationship between education and agricultural productivity might not be the result of other factors related to both education and production, such as family background or land quality. Although some of the early studies used locational indicators as approximate control variables, most failed to include direct measures of such factors. Their absence from the analysis may have led to erroneous or exaggerated conclusions (Jamison and Moock 1984, Cotlear 1989).

The survey's "optimistic" conclusion regarding the impact of education on agricultural productivity has been further questioned in light of the fact that, although over 50 percent of the data sets surveyed by Lockheed et al. showed a positive association, this statistical effect was significant at the 0.05 level in only about half of these cases (Phillips and Marble 1986). Efforts to replicate findings on other sets of data have been only moderately successful in providing a consistent and strong relation, according to some critics (e.g., Jameson 1988).

Work in the 1980s has indicated the limitations of using either an engineering or gross revenue production function. Much of the effect of education on farm profits may be missed by taking this approach, since it measures only the worker effect and neglects the allocative effects on: (a) outputs produced, and (b) inputs selected. Several 1980s studies have suggested that education's total effect can be measured by estimating a value-added function, and the three separate effects (worker and two allocative effects) then measured by also estimating gross sales and engineering functions (Dhakal et al. 1987, Phillips and Marble 1986, Pudasaini 1983). "By simple manipulation [of the various coefficients] the three effects can be separated out" (Phillips and Marble 1986 p. 259). This requires more information, however, than most data sets actually contain, a problem encountered by most advocates of the complete approach (e.g., Pudasaini 1983, Phillips and Marble 1986).

The specification of the relationship between agricultural inputs and output as a C-D production function has also been subject to criticism. The restrictive assumptions implied by this specification have been questioned, including constant production elasticities of factor inputs and unitary elasticity of substitution between all pairs of inputs. Other authors have criticized the use of OLS regression analysis, as this approach results in estimation of an "average" function, with "efficient and inefficient farms . . . mixed in together so that the concept of inefficiency has no meaning" (Grabowski and Pasurka 1988 p. 316). Such critics argue for the use of a nonparametric estimation technique such as linear programing.

4. Studies in the 1980s

Studies published since the late 1970s have attempted to address some or all of the criticisms directed at the earlier studies reviewed by Lockheed et al. The 12 studies reviewed in this entry confirm, for the most part, the story that education has a positive effect on farmer efficiency. Table 2 reports the coefficients of education on productivity, listing the non-education variables controlled for in the regression equation and indicating whether or not the estimate relating to education is statistically significant at the 0.05 probability level. The table includes 78 tests of hypotheses relating to education's effects, drawing upon 29 data sets in 14 countries.

4.1 Years of Formal Schooling

Many of the findings reported in Table 2 are for the variable years of school completed. All but one of the 26 regression coefficients on this variable are positive, and 15 (58 percent) are statistically significant at the 0.05 level.

4.2 Levels of Formal Schooling

Fourteen regressions in Table 2 show the differential effects of "a few years" of school versus "more years," the cutoff between the two levels coming after three, four, five, or six years completed, depending on the study. All of the studies in Table 2 treat different schooling levels as categorical (dummy) variables rather than as continuous (spline) variables. In most of the studies, the missing category is "no education," although for his three Peruvian samples, Cotlear (1989) compares four to five years and six or more years wit three years or less, which is the omitted category in his regression equations.

When the schooling variable is collapsed in some such fashion, the prevailing result is that "a few years" of education shows no significant relation to agricultural productivity (true in 13 of 14 tests of the hypothesis), whereas "more years" of schooling does show a relation (in 9 of 14 cases, or 64%). The implication of these findings is that some minimum level of educational attainment, often argued to be the level at which the recipient achieves functional literacy and numeracy sufficient to be sustained over time, is required before any payoff is seen in the individual's performance as a farmer later in life.

4.3 Whose Education Is Relevant?

Table 2 suggests that the statistical effect of education on production probably differs depending on whose education is considered—that of the farm head, the farm manager, or all family members. In 4 of 13 cases (31%), the education level of the "farm head" has a significantly positive regression coefficient in the equation to explain farm output. The "farm manager," whom studies define as the person responsible for the day-to-day technical decisions on the farm, may

Table 2
Estimates of education's effect in studies of small-farm production

Country location study: author and date	Output variable (logarithmic transformation)	Sample size	Other variables controlled for in equation	Education variable (logarithmic transformation of nonbinary variables)	Coefficient on educ. variable (*t*-statistic in parentheses)
Africa					
Burkina Faso: Mossi Plateau (Ram and Singh 1988)	Farm income	51	None	Years of school completed: HH head	0.096 (2.7)[a]
				Yrs of school completed: all HH members	0.086 (2.14)[a]
			Land, labor, input, use, age, sex, value of livestock, credit, soil type, crop rotation, marketing, capital assets, no. of children, no. of wives, migration	Years of school completed: HH head	0.030 (1.27)
				Years of school completed: all HH members	0.070 (3.27)[a]
Kenya: Kakamega District (Moock 1981)	Maize output per acre	101	Plant population, rate of phosphate and nitrogen, labor, soil, interplanted crop, crop damage, insecticide, hybrid seed, area planted, migration, age, loan recipient	1–3 years of school completed: farm manager	−0.118 (−1.82)
				4 or more years of school completed: farm manager	0.182 (1.61)[a]
				Index of extension contact	0.030 (2.50)[a]
				(4 years schl) × (extension contact)	−0.037 (−1.76)
Asia					
Bangladesh: Ranpur, Bogra, Sherpur, Tangail, Comilla and Dhaka (Khandker 1986)	Gross value of farm outputs less expenditure on purchased inputs	364	Land; predicted wages of head, spouse, and family members	Years of schooling: male head of HH	0.143 (1.69)[a]
				Years of schooling: heads' wife	0.003 (0.09)[a]
				Years of schooling: other HH members	0.019 (0.50)
India: The Coimbatore District in Tamil Nadu (Kalirajan and Shand 1985)	Paddy production	91	Labor, fertilizer, capital, HYV seed, insecticide, farm size	Years of school completed: farm manager	0.102 (2.54)[a]
India: East Coimbatore and North Salem of Tamil Nadu (Duraisamy 1990)	Paddy production	323	Land, wage, labor, fertilizer, animal input, value of capital services	>4 yrs of school completed: farm manager	0.198 (2.93)[a]
				Extension dummy	0.130 (1.83)[a]
Nepal: Bara District (Pudasaini 1983)	Value of rice production	205	Land, family and hired labor, capital, age, schooling, machinery, bullock, use, fertilizer, farm size	Years of school completed: manager	0.011 (1.10)
				Extension dummy	0.004 (0.13)
				(School) × (extension)	−0.000 (−0.000)

Table 2 (cont)

Country location study: author and date	Output variable (logarithmic transformation)	Sample size	Other variables controlled for in equation	Education variable (logarithmic transformation of nonbinary variables)	Coefficient on educ. variable (*t*-statistic in parentheses)
Asia					
Nepal: Bara District (Pudasaini 1983)	Gross sales	205	Land, family and hired labor, capital, age, schooling, machinery, bullock use, fertilizer, farm size	Years of school completed: manager	0.030 (2.73)[a]
				Extension dummy	−0.013 (−1.00)
				(School) × (extension)	−0.001 (−0.50)
	Value added			Years of school completed: manager	0.050 (3.13)[a]
				Extension dummy	−0.008 (−0.42)
				(School) × (extension)	−0.003 (−1.00)
Nepal: Gorkha District (Pudasaini 1983)	Value of maize production	149	Land, family and hired labor, capital, age, schooling, machinery, bullock use, fertilizer, farm size	Years of school completed: manager	0.022 (1.29)
				Extension dummy	0.212 (0.99)
				(School) × (extension)	−0.004 (−1.33)
Nepal: Gorkha District (Pudasaini 1983)	Value of maize production	149	Land, family and hired labor, capital, age, schooling, machinery, bullock use, fertilizer, farm size	Years of school completed: manager	0.051 (4.25)[a]
				Extension dummy	−0.009 (−0.18)
				(School) × (extension)	0.001 (0.17)
	Value added			Years of school completed: manager	0.057 (4.57)[a]
				Extension dummy	−0.007 (−0.13)
				(School) × (extension)	0.000 (0.00)
Nepal: Bara and Rautahat Districts (Jamison and Moock 1984)	Value of early paddy production	443	Area cultivated, labor, percent female labor, percent male labor, animal use, capital, fertilizers, age, experience, SES background, occupation, numeracy, district	1–6 years of school completed: farm head	0.050 (0.63)
				>7 years of school completed: farm head	0.152 (1.25)
				Recent contact with extension agent	0.007 (0.11)
				Percent of HHs in area with extension contact	0.202 (0.12)
	Value of late paddy production	284		1–6 years of school completed: farm head	−0.048 (−0.52)
				>7 years of school completed: farm head	0.131 (1.08)
				Recent contact with extension agent	0.084 (1.01)
				Percent of HHs in area with extension contact	0.122 (0.48)

Table 2 (cont)

Country location study: author and date	Output variable (logarithmic transformation)	Sample size	Other variables controlled for in equation	Education variable (logarithmic transformation of nonbinary variables)	Coefficient on educ. variable (*t*-statistic in parentheses)
Asia					
Nepal: Bara and Rautahat Districts (Jamison and Moock 1984)	Value of wheat production	345	Area cultivated, labor, percent female labor, percent male labor, animal use, capital, fertilizers, age, experience, SES background, occupation, numeracy, district	1–6 years of school completed: farm head	−0.108 (−1.32)
				>7 years of school completed: farm head	0.271 (2.30)[a]
				Recent contact with extension agent	0.083 (1.26)
				Percent of HHs in area with extension contact	0.472 (2.85)[a]
Nepal: Nuwakot District (Dhakal *et al.* 1987)	Maize output in kilograms	600	Land, labor, farming experience, bullocks, family size, fertilizer	Average years of schooling of family members	0.036 (0.67)
	Gross sales				0.094 (2.17)[a]
	Value added				0.096 (2.23)[a]
Pakistan (Butt 1984)	Gross value of production	1,787	Land, labor, fertilizers, machinery, animal use, irrigation, age, schooling, owner operated	1–4 yrs of school: farm manager	0.070 (1.07)
				5+yrs of school: farm manager	0.107 (2.43)[a]
	Wheat output per acre	1,156	Acreage, owner operated	1–4 yrs of school: farm manager	0.037 (0.54)
				5+yrs of school: farm manager	0.186 (4.13)[a]
	Sugarcane output per acre	394		1–4 yrs of school: farm manager	0.0001 (0.00)
				5+yrs of school: farm manager	0.002 (0.26)
	Cotton output per acre	704		1–4 yrs of school: farm manager	0.012 (1.05)
				5+yrs of school: farm manager	0.202 (2.59)[a]
	Rice output per acre	604		1–4 yrs of school: farm manager	0.132 (1.14)
				5+yrs of school: farm manager	0.212 (2.92)[a]
Pakistan (Azhar 1988)	Output of wheat	1,370	Land, labor, fertilizers, irrigation	Years of school completed: farm manager	0.018 (4.06)[a]
	Output of rice	665			0.015 (2.69)[a]
	Output of cotton	727			0.014 (1.61)
	Output of sugar	720			−0.004 (−0.05)

Table 2 (cont)

Country location study: author and date	Output variable (logarithmic transformation)	Sample size	Other variables controlled for in equation	Education variable (logarithmic transformation of nonbinary variables)	Coefficient on educ. variable (*t*-statistic in parentheses)
Latin America					
Bolivia (Jameson 1988)	Value of farm production	750	Land, labor, seed, fertilizer, animal use, and machinery	Years of school completed: farm manager	0.138 (2.36)[a]
Dominican Republic (Jameson 1988)	Value of farm production	1,802	Land, labor, seed, fertilizer, animal use, and machinery	Years of school completed: farm manager	0.006 (1.90)[a]
Guatemala (Phillips and Marble 1986)	Value of corn production	1,384	land, labor, seed, fertilizer, machinery, animal use	Years of school completed: farm manager	0.028 (1.31)
				1–3 years of school completed: farm manager	0.006 (0.17)
				4+years of school completed: farm manager	0.065 (1.42)
Guatemala (Jameson 1988)	Value of farm Production	1,548	Land, labor, seed, fertilizer, animal use, and machinery	Years of school completed: farm manager	0.001 (0.40)
Paraguay (Jameson 1988)	Value of farm production	1,053	Land, labor, seed, fertilizer, animal use, and machinery	Years of school completed: farm manager	−0.006 (−0.31)
Peru: Valley of Yanamarca (Cotlear 1989)	Production of potatoes	254	Land, labor, animal, tractor, extension service, migration, credit, use of HYV	4–5 years of school completed: HH head	0.14 (1.27)
				6+years of school completed: HH head	0.37 (3.52)[a]
				Recent extension dummy	0.09 (0.84)
Peru: Plateau of Chinchero (Cotlear 1989)	Production of potatoes	151	Land, labor, animal, tractor, extension service, migration, credit, use of HYV	4–5 years of school completed: HH head	0.13 (1.35)
				6+years of school completed: HH head	0.24 (2.48)[a]
				Recent extension dummy	0.29 (3.42)[a]
Peru: The Pampa Sangarara (Cotlear 1989)	Production of potatoes	150	Land, labor, animal, tractor, extension service, migration, credit, use of HYV	4–5 years of school completed: HH head	0.13 (1.15)
				6+years of school completed: HH head	0.05 (0.56)
				Recent extension dummy	0.11 (0.66)
North America					
United States: Northern Region (Grabowski and Pasurka 1988)	Farm revenue	109	Land, age of head, family size	Literate: household head	0.108 (1.82)[a]

a Significant at 0.05 level

or may not be the same person as the farm head but is probably the more relevant agent to be considered when analyzing the effect of education on agricultural output. The educational attainment of the manager is positively related to production in 21 of 55 tests (38%) of the hypothesis.

A few studies have measured education as the average educational attainment of all family members on the farm. This variable shows a significantly positive relation to farm output in four out of six tests of the hypothesis. The farm manager or farm head, whichever may be the more relevant decision-maker, does not need to rely solely on his or her own expertise but, rather, can draw upon the collective expertise of all members of the family. By this logic, perhaps the best measure of education in the context of farm decision-making is that of the most educated family member— whoever that person may be, and however junior in the family hierarchy. No studies in the sample, however, have looked at this alternative measure.

4.4 Separate Estimates of Worker and Allocative Effects

Much of the empirical research, including most of the studies surveyed here, focuses on the worker effect of education, estimating a single crop or gross revenue production function, in which factor inputs are "held constant." Little or no attention is given to the farmer's choice either of outputs produced or factor inputs utilized. Many education and agricultural economists would argue that an informed selection of outputs and inputs is the essence of efficient farm production and, *ipso facto*, that the allocative effect of education is likely to be even more important than the worker effect.

Some of the studies surveyed here, such as the one by Jamison and Moock, which looked at paddy (rice) and wheat farmers in the Nepal Terai (1984), have specified probability (binary choice) models to explain a farmer's adoption or nonadoption of modern practices such as application of chemical fertilizers or use of a high-yielding seed variety, the profitability of which is assumed in the analysis. A significantly positive coefficient on an education variable in the logit or probit regression equation used to estimate the choice model indicates the existence of an allocative effect as posited by Welch and others.

For farm samples in other parts of Nepal, Pudasaini (1983) and Dhakal et al. (1987) have described and demonstrated an approach for actual quantification of the allocative effect of education. By estimating several equations and manipulating the regression results, both studies are able to conclude that the input selection effect is paramount among education's contributions to the profit-making of farmers.

4.5 Traditional and Modernizing Environments

The Nobel Prize-winning economist T. W. Schultz has argued (Schultz 1975) that education is likely to be much more effective under modernizing (i.e., rapidly changing) conditions than under very traditional and stable conditions. The survey by Lockheed et al. (1980) bears this hypothesis out. Of the studies surveyed here and summarized in Table 2, only two explicitly compared different groups of farmers who were living in more and less modern settings (Cotlear 1989) or who were engaged in more and less modern farming activities (Jamison and Moock 1984).

In Cotlear's Peruvian study, the statistical effect of formal schooling was greatest in Yanamarca, designated as "modernizing," and it was nonexistent in Sangarara, designated as "traditional." In Chinchero, designated as "intermediate" on the traditional-to-modern spectrum, the magnitude of the effect was intermediate, that is, between those found in the first two areas. For farmers in Nepal, Jamison and Moock observed a significantly positive worker effect of formal schooling in the production of wheat, a recently introduced crop, but not in the production of paddy, a traditional crop grown by all farm families in Nepal for countless generations.

4.6 Exposure to Agricultural Extension Services: Farm

Fourteen findings reported in Table 2 are concerned with the farmer's contact with the (government-provided) agricultural extension services. Only three of these (21%) are significant at the 0.05 level. Extension contact is quite crudely measured in most studies —nearly always a binary variable (recent contact or not) and self-reported by the farmers in the sample. This measure reveals nothing about the nature or the quality of the extension contact—the extension agent may have met with the farmer about some other matter and given no agricultural advice, or may have given bad advice. Even if correctly measured, extension contact is quite probably endogenous—less efficient farmers are visited more often by conscientious extension agents trying to enhance agricultural performance in an area.

4.7 Exposure to Agricultural Extension Services: Community

If extension exposure is measured, not by whether the individual farmer has been in contact with the extension services, but by the percentage of all farms in the same geographical area who have been in contact, then there is little chance that the individual's own farm performance is influencing the extension services received, and the question of endogeneity becomes moot. Moreover, it is quite likely that the impact of extension services on productivity in an area is indirect, at least in part. Extension services may affect productivity by changing the behavior of the most innovative farmers first, who then provide a demonstration of good farming practices for other farmers in the area. Finally, these practices are adopted by the less innovative farmers, whether or not they themselves have been in direct contact with an extension agent (see Rogers and Shoemaker 1971). The impact of community extension (percentage of farms reporting recent contact) is considered in a farm sample from Nepal by Jamison and Moock (1984). In three tests of the hypothesis, Jamison and Moock find one result to be significantly positive (for the "modern" wheat crop) and two to be not significantly different from zero (for the more traditional paddy crop in both the early and late growing seasons).

4.8 Interaction Between Formal Schooling and Extension Contact

A small number of studies have investigated the interaction between formal schooling and extension contact. It is not clear *ex ante* what this interaction term is expected to look like. A positive interaction might be assumed, implying that schooling and extension contact are complements—more schooling enables a farmer to benefit additionally from any given amount of extension exposure. On the other hand, a negative interaction is also plausible, suggesting that schooling and extension contact are substitutes—all farmers may benefit from extension contact, but the farmer with more schooling already has access to the information on best farming practices and benefits less from exten-

sion exposure than a farmer with less schooling. A zero nonsignificant interaction is also possible indicating that educational attainment and extension contact are both useful separately, but having the two in combination is no more useful in enhancing agricultural output than having either one by itself. In the sample of studies surveyed here, seven two-tailed tests are conducted of the hypothesis that there is a nonzero interaction between formal schooling and extension contact. For five the sign is negative (of which only one is significantly different from zero at the 0.10 probability level), and for two the sign is positive (neither of which is statistically significant).

5. Conclusion

There has developed since the 1960s a rich body of research on the relationship between education and agricultural productivity. Most of the empirical research has focused on samples of farmers in developing areas, where agricultural production is certainly more constrained by low levels of education than in more developed areas. Asian samples dominate the literature, probably because the data from Asia are better than from Africa or Latin America.

Although the findings include inconsistencies—

Table 3
Summary of findings in studies of education's effects

	Number of tests of hypothesis	Number of results significant at 0.05 level
Education variable		
Formal education, measured as:		
Years of school	26	15 (58%)
Dummy variables		
Some education	14	1 (7%)
More education	14	9 (64%)
Extension services received by:		
Household itself	14	3 (21%)
Community (households in area)	3	1 (33%)
Education × extension interaction	7	
Regression coefficient negative	5 71%	1 (20%)
Regression coefficient positive	2 29%	0 (0%)
Recipient of education/training		
Farm head	13	4 (31%)
Wife of head	1	0 (0%)
Farm manager	55	21 (38%)
Family members	6	4 (67%)
Region		
Africa	8	6 (75%)
Asia	53	18 (34%)
Americas	17	6 (35%)

they are particularly inconclusive in regard to nonformal education (namely, agricultural extension contact) as distinct from formal schooling—nevertheless, a reasonably clear pattern does emerge from the empirical literature, one that was first sketched by Lockheed et al. in their survey of studies through 1978. Much the same pattern is demonstrated here, based on 14 studies published since then. Table 3 summarizes the more recent findings, abstracting from Table 2 above.

In general, there is a positive relation between formal schooling and agricultural productivity. This relation is strong for educational attainment beyond some culturally defined threshold level, whereas it is weak or nonexistent for attainment below this level. The clear suggestion is that an individual who completes only a few years of school does not retain enough learning to benefit from it later as a farmer. Finally, the Schultzian hypothesis (the more modern and less traditional the farm activity which the farmer performs or the farming area in which the farmer lives, the stronger will be the relation between education and agriculture productivity) is generally borne out by studies conducted in the 1980s.

See also: Adult Education for Development; Basic Education: Comparative and International Studies; Benefits of Education; Education and Development; Postliteracy: Concepts and Policies

References

Azhar R A 1988 Education and technical efficiency in Pakistan's agriculture. *The Pakistan Dev. Rev.* 27(4), Pt. 2: 687–95

Butt M S 1984 Education and farm productivity in Pakistan. *Pakistan J. Appl. Econ.* 3(1): 65–82

Cotlear D 1989 The effects of education on farm productivity. *J. Dev. Planning* (UN Department of International Economic and Social Affairs) 19: 73–99

Dhakal D, Grabowski R, Belbase K 1987 The effect of education in Nepal's traditional agriculture. *Econ. Educ. Rev.* 6(1): 27–34

Duraisamy P 1990 Technical and allocative efficiency of education in agricultural production: A profit function approach. *Ind. Econ. Rev.* 25(1): 17–32

Grabowski R, Pasurka C 1988 Farmer education and economic efficiency: Northern farms in 1860. *Econ. Lett.* 28(4): 315–20

Jameson K P 1988 Education's role in rural areas in Latin America. *Econ. Educ. Rev.* 7(3): 333–43

Jamison D T, Moock P R 1984 Farmer education and farm efficiency in Nepal: The role of schooling, extension services, and cognitive skills. *World Dev.* 12(1): 67–86

Kalirajan K P, Shand R T 1985 Types of education and agricultural productivity: A quantitative analysis of Tamil Nadu rice farming. *J. Dev. Stud.* 21(2): 232–43

Khandker S R 1986 *Farmer Education and Farm Efficiency: The Role of Education Revisited.* Discussion Paper No. 506, Economic Growth Center, Yale University, New Haven, Connecticut

Lockheed M E, Jamison D T, Lau L J 1980 Farmer education and farm efficiency: A survey. *Econ. Dev. Cultural Change* 29(1): 37–76

Moock P R 1981 Education and technical efficiency in small-farm production. *Econ. Dev. Cultural Change* 29(4): 723–38

Phillips J M, Marble R P 1986 Farmer education and efficiency: A frontier production function approach. *Econ. Educ. Rev.* 5(3): 257–64

Pudasaini S P 1983 The effects of education in agriculture: Evidence from Nepal. *Am. J. Agricultural Econ.* 65(3): 509–15

Ram R, Singh R D 1988 Farm households in rural Burkina Faso: Some evidence on allocative and direct return to schooling, and male–female labor productivity differentials. *World Dev.* 16(3): 419–24

Rogers E M, Shoemaker F 1971 *Communication of Innovations*, 2nd edn. Free Press, New York

Schultz T W 1975 The value of the ability to deal with disequilibria. *J. Econ. Lit.* 13(3): 827–46

Welch F 1970 Education in production. *J. Pol. Econ.* 78(1): 35–59

Further Reading

Bowman M J 1991 The formation of human resources for farming and household work as vocations: Lessons for less developed countries. *Econ. Educ. Rev.* 10(1): 1–5

Eisemon T O, Nyamete A 1988 Schooling and agricultural productivity in western Kenya. *J. Eastern African Res. Dev.* 18: 44–66

Griliches Z 1964 Research expenditures, education, and the aggregate agricultural production function. *Am. Econ. Rev.* 54(6): 961–74

Hayami Y, Ruttan V W 1970 Agricultural productivity differences among countries. *Am. Econ. Rev.* 60(5): 895–911

Jamison D T, Lau L J 1982 *Farmer Education and Farm Efficiency.* Johns Hopkins University Press for The World Bank, Baltimore, Maryland

Khandker S R 1988 Input management ability, occupational patterns and farm productivity in Bangladesh agriculture. *J. Dev. Stud.* 24(2): 214–31

Moock P R 1976 The efficiency of women as farm managers: Kenya. *Am. J. Agricultural Econ.* 58(5): 831–35

Pudasaini S P 1982 Education and agricultural efficiency in Nepal, Discussion Paper No. 82–3. The World Bank, Washington, DC

Schultz T W 1964 *Transforming Traditional Agriculture.* Yale University Press, New Haven, Connecticut

Stefanou S E, Saxena S 1988 Education, experience, and allocative efficiency: A dual approach. *Am. J. Agricultural Econ.* 70(2): 338–45

Welch F 1978 The role of investments in human capital in agriculture. In: Schultz T W (ed.) 1978 *Distortions of Agricultural Incentives.* Indiana University Press, Bloomington, Indiana

Wu C C 1977 Education in farm production: The case of Taiwan. *Am. J. Agricultural Econ.* 59(4): 699–709

Basic Education: Comparative and International Studies

R. Carr-Hill

The term "basic education" has had a checkered history. When used in the North, it tends to refer to all or part of the compulsory cycle of schooling, which was established throughout Europe and North America in the nineteenth century. The term itself was popular among colonial administrators and, with a modified meaning, it became the general educational philosophy of UNESCO after the Second World War.

Much of this entry is based on data compiled by UNESCO about enrollments, etc. The reader should be warned that these data are notoriously inaccurate for several reasons (see Carr-Hill 1987), but they are the best we have.

1. Background

1.1 Definition

In the postwar period "basic" or "fundamental education" was based on the view that a sound general education should be provided through the vocational activities of the community. Although, in retrospect, this had resonance in the suggestions of, for example, Dewey (1915) and in indigenous forms of education, there were no obvious models at the time. Therefore, UNESCO set up several pilot projects to test the feasibility of this type of education. From being a temporary experiment, fundamental education became a panacea to reduce illiteracy in low-income countries.

After independence from colonial rule, however, this form of educational provision was seen as second-rate education "for the natives" and, as such, the term became discredited during the 1960s and 1970s. In its place, most newly independent nations adopted the more European model, found in Article 26 of the United Nations Declaration of Human Rights, and declared the goal of universal primary education (see Sect. 1.2).

The term "basic education" was gradually reintroduced into international public discourse after the "basic needs" initiatives of the International Labour Organization (ILO) during the mid-1970s. Because of the attention to minimum requirements inherent in the basic needs approach, the term now more typically refers to whatever is necessary for the attainment of minimum knowledge, skills, and values. This apparently simple term has, therefore, become variously a designation for preschool activities (or early childhood education), the primary cycle, adult literacy activities, and other "basic" education activities. In practice, however, the majority of writers use basic education to refer to activities within the primary cycle of education. Thus, early childhood education

and preschool activities tend to be seen as those components of the educational system which are *prior* to the primary cycle; and adult literacy and "other" basic education activities are seen as providing parallel complementary provision to the primary cycle but for groups who, for one reason or another, have failed to complete the primary cycle.

1.2 The 30-year Crusade for Universal Primary Education

In the early 1960s UNESCO held a series of conferences in different regions: in Karachi, Pakistan (1960); Addis Ababa, Ethiopia (1961); Santiago, Chile (1962); and Tripoli, Libya (1966). At these conferences, country delegates declared their intention to achieve Universal Primary Education (UPE) as soon as possible. The Karachi Plan of 1960 called for the provision of universal and free primary education of at least seven years by 1980. The Addis Ababa Plan of 1961 advocated that primary education be "universal, compulsory and free by 1980" (UNESCO 1961 p. 20), as did the Conference of Arab States. The Latin America Conference asked participating countries to "ensure that before the end of the present decade, all children can attend a primary education . . . not shorter than six years" (UNESCO 1962 p. 4). These international conferences had a substantial impact on developments over the following 20 years, first in terms of the emphasis upon quantitative expansion at the primary level (see Table 1), and second, in sustaining the belief in the importance of education for economic development.

Aggregate figures for the resources allocated to education overall and to primary education in particular during the 1960s, 1970s, and early 1980s are given by world region in Table 2. Resources increased as a proportion of gross national product (GNP) from 1960 to 1980 and then declined in Africa, Asia, and Latin America; the reverse happened in the Arab states. Note that, even though much less appears to be spent in sub-Saharan Africa, in terms of GNP per capita these countries spend about 15 percent of GNP per capita on preprimary and first level education, compared to around 11 percent in Southern Asia and 7 percent in Eastern Asia and the Latin America and the Caribbean.

Most countries in Asia and Latin America now have a gross enrollment ratio; that is, the numbers of children registered as attending school divided by the numbers of children of official school age, equal or close to, and sometimes greater than 100. This, however, has not happened everywhere (see Table 3). Although the numbers of pupils enrolled have increased enormously, the school-age population has

Table 1
Estimated total enrollment at the primary level in developing countries by world region (millions)

	Sub-Saharan Africa	Asia and Oceania	Latin America and Caribbean	Arab States	Total
1960	14.1[a]	85.0[c]	26.0	7.1	133.0
1970	20.3[a]	239.5 (105.8)[d]	46.6	12.6	319.0
1980	45.7[a]	323.7 (146.3)[d]	64.8	20.6	454.8
1985	51.5[a]	336.6 (133.7)[d]	69.6	24.8	482.5
1990	64.6[b]	338.2 (125.8)[d]	75.5	30.4	508.7
1993	70.6[b]	343.9 (123.0)[d]	80.8	52.3	547.6

Source: UNESCO 1967, 1977, 1988, 1995
a Not including South Africa   b Including South Africa   c Not including China   d Figure for China only

often increased even faster, so that educational systems appear to be chasing a receding target. In the case of Africa, Coombs (1985) calculated that, in order to reach a gross enrollment ratio of 100, countries of the region would have to increase total enrollment by 116 million between 1980 and 2000, compared to the smaller 55 million added (with enormous effort and sacrifice) between 1960 and 1980.

It has always been recognized that closing these gaps would require an enormous commitment. At one extreme, Illich (1971) and Reimer (1970) argued for an approach that was to be radically different from the costly pattern of providing formal schooling, but Nyerere (1977) and many others proclaimed UPE as the major priority in order to attain their development objectives, although Bray (1987) has queried that connection and indeed the rationale for aiming for UPE at all. On the whole, the latter viewpoint has prevailed. However there is now a growing concern over the affordability of UPE (e.g., Lee 1988). During the 1990s many countries, including some of the least developed, are devoting over 20 percent of government budgets to education, without being able to close the nonschooling gap in primary schools.

The quantitative shortfalls are important, but they are not the only issue. As Coombs stated:

Since 1945, all countries have undergone fantastically swift environmental changes, brought about by a number of concurrent worldwide revolutions—in science and technology, in economic and political affairs, in demographic and social structures. Educational systems have also grown and changed more rapidly than ever before. But they have adapted all too slowly in relation to the faster pace of events on the move all around them. The consequent disparity—taking many forms—between education systems and their environments is the essence of the worldwide crisis in education. (Coombs 1985 p. 5)

During the 20 years after 1945, some of these disparities became major problems. The issue of the relevance of transplanted curricula to developing countries, and particularly of the "vocational school fallacy" of tailoring curricula to a presumed pattern of agricultural employment, were hotly debated (e.g., Foster 1965). In some countries, the growing imbalance between the large cohorts of young people with secondary qualifications and their limited employment

Table 2
Estimated public expenditure on education (US dollars, billions at current prices) and as a percentage of gross national product (GNP)

	Sub-Saharan Africa		Asia and Oceania		Latin America and Caribbean		Arab states	
1960	0.4	2.6	3.9	2.2[a]	1.5	2.1	0.8	4.6
1970	1.4	3.9	13.5	3.0[b]	5.3	3.3	1.9	4.9
1980	10.7	5.2	92.5	4.6[b]	31.4	3.9	18.1	4.5
1990	15.2	5.3	67.6	3.4[b]	47.1	4.1	24.7	5.2
1992	15.4	5.7	61.5	3.3[b]	66.6	4.6	28.0	5.8

Source: UNESCO 1967, 1977, 1980, 1988, 1995: the earlier figures (up to 1980) have been calculated on a different basis from those for 1990 and 1992
a Not including China   b Figure for China only

Table 3
Number of countries with different levels of gross enrollment ratios, 1992 or latest year of available data

	Sub-Saharan Africa	Asia and Oceania	Latin America and Caribbean	Arab states	Least developed countries
100 or more	9	12	17	8	10
90–99	4	3	6	3	2
70–89	9	2	1	4	8
Up to 69	15	2	1	5	20
Total	37	19	25	20	40

Source: UNESCO 1995

opportunities led to increased popular pressure for the provision of further education to higher qualifications. In many countries, evidence accumulated of substantial disparities within the educational system. Everywhere, there emerged a growing concern over the quality of the educational services provided. In reviewing "the crisis" in the mid 1980s, Coombs, therefore, argued that: "Not only has the crisis been intensified by growing maladjustments between education systems and the rapidly changing world all around them, but ... *there is now a crisis of confidence in education itself*" (Coombs 1985 p. 9).

1.3 The Importance of Basic Education

For some, basic education is the cornerstone of national development. As early as 1963, for example, a major cross-national study (Bowman and Anderson 1963) claimed that a 40 percent literacy rate was a necessary condition for achieving even the first stages of development and economic growth. Although data such as these ignore the nineteenth-century experience of much of the currently industrialized North, the claim may now be true given the nature of production technology in the second half of the twentieth century. Nevertheless, as Table 4 shows, the growth in adult literacy rates has been slow. Although the percentage of illiterates is decreasing, the absolute number of illiterate people is increasing in most regions.

Many have argued that a basic education is an essential prerequisite for reducing infant mortality and facilitating the acceptability of family planning. Drawing on the data from the World Fertility Survey carried out in 40 countries during the second half of the 1970s, Caldwell et al. (1982) made particularly strong claims about the importance of each year in education in reducing infant mortality and overall fertility. For example, educated parents tend to care for and feed their children better, thereby reducing infant and child mortality. They also tend to have aspirations to upward mobility; in particular, educated women want, and are able, to take jobs outside the home. In addition, where education brings benefits, parental aspirations shift away from having more children in order to provide labor toward having fewer, better educated children. Others have argued that the spread of formal primary education has an effect upon attitudes toward and the use of "modern" farming practices, upon attitudes toward and the use of technology, and upon the possibilities of "modernizing" the society in general. Studies have shown that farmers' productivity is increased for every extra year of primary education (Jamison and Lau 1982).

A totally different view is taken by those who see universal primary education as a fundamental requirement for democracy. For them, the education system plays a more diffuse but no less important role in social terms. The type of educational system in a society not only reflects but also influences the parent culture. Education plays a part in forming and strengthening a sense of national cultural identity. Many also see education as "empowerment," giving a sense of civic rights and participation (e.g., Coombs 1985, Lind 1989).

These and other claims were repeated many times after 1960, leading to the eventual proclamation of the goal of "Education for All" at the World Conference held in March 1990 in Jomtien, Thailand. Although it is not clear that this proclamation has brought UPE any nearer than those of the earlier conferences, it has certainly brought "basic education" to the forefront of the aid and development agenda and even back into the educational journals!

Table 4
Literacy rates in developing countries by gender

	Males			Females		
	1970	1985	1995	1970	1980	1995
Developing countries of which	57.8	71.1	78.9	32.6	49.9	61.7
Sub-Saharan Africa	32.5	52.6	66.6	13.2	29.5	47.3
Eastern Asia	67.3	82.0	90.6	38.7	60.7	76.3
Southern Asia	44.8	55.6	62.9	16.9	27.9	35.6
Latin America and Caribbean	77.5	84.3	87.7	70.1	80.3	85.5
Arab states	39.5	59.2	68.4	13.7	31.5	44.2
Least developed countries	31.9	46.3	59.5	13.0	23.4	38.1
Developed countries	95.0	96.6	98.9	92.7	94.3	98.4

Source: UNESCO 1995
a Estimated percentage of literate adults in the population aged 15 years and over (estimate is based on numbers and proportions who have completed four years of schooling)   b The 1995 estimate is based on population estimates from the United Nations Population Division   c There have been changes in countries included between 1985 and 1995

2. Major Themes

Four themes have dominated empirical research on basic education:

(a) the issue of differential access to basic education for boys and girls and the influence of user charges on access of the poor;

(b) the equivalence problem, or what should count as literacy and numeracy;

(c) the quality of education provided, including the issues of retention;

(d) the importance of basic education for individual social advancement and social mobility.

2.1 The Question of Access

The phenomenon of mass education as it is presently understood is a comparatively recent development. It arose in Europe and North America during the late nineteenth century as a corollary to the widespread industrialization engendered by capitalism and the destruction of the family-based agrarian economy and artisan production in favor of mass production and organized labor. At the same time, in what were then seen as the underdeveloped regions of the world, formal education was mainly introduced by colonial social forces. Although in nearly all countries elementary education has become compulsory mass education, in many African and some Asian and Latin American countries, a significant proportion of girls and boys receive absolutely no formal schooling, or even drop out of elementary school. One issue then is, what governs access?

School enrollment, wastage, and absenteeism have all been found to be related to class background, ethnicity, income, and gender. Moreover, all these factors are interrelated. For example, social class and income differentials have been found to be influential in primary and secondary school enrollments in

Malaysia, India, Mexico, Ghana, Pakistan, Kenya, and Uganda.

The most obvious bias, because it is easily quantified, is against the education of girls. This is due, of course, to the lower status of women which is manifested among girls through: the significant contribution of female child labor in production and domestic work, the concern to control girl's contact with males, and the perception that the payoffs in terms of eventual wage employment for girls who have qualfied are minimal or nonexistent. Very few women have attained waged employment and, particularly in patrilineal systems, the future husband and his relatives usually benefit from wages rather than the girl or the girl's own family.

In the climate of the 1990s all these differentials are mediated by the perceived costs or lack of benefits of education to the individual or parents. Of course, what constitutes the "price" of places depends on the perspective adopted. Individuals, groups, communities, and society all face different price schedules. The emphasis in this entry is on direct costs to the parents in relation to their ability to pay and the opportunity costs that they perceive.

During the 1980s and 1990s many countries were forced to introduce so-called "adjustment policies." One consequence of these was a fall in family money incomes. At the same time many countries introduced or raised school fees. Although the fees do not appear large, they might well be substantial when considered as a proportion of average income (see Table 5 for data from Africa). Given the relationship between family income and participation, user charges will directly discriminate against the poor. However, if the user charge is too low or nonexistent, education provision will either be rationed (e.g., via a quota system) or the quality of the service will deteriorate. Both typically tend to disadvantage the poor more than the rich (Thobani 1983 p. 402). In reference to Malawi, Thobani suggested that the government could meet all

Table 5
Parental costs at the primary level in three countries in French-speaking Africa and Zambia 1986

Type of expenditure	Benin (range)	Mali (range)	Togo (range)	Zambia (range)
Registration fee, parents' associations, etc.	50–100	70	24–50	30–100
Materials	40–80	40–100	40–80	20–50
School uniforms	30–70	—	36–70	0–50
Total	120–250	110–170	100–200	50–200
Share (%) relative to GNP per capita (%)	7.6–16.0	12.2–18.8	7.2–14.4	5–20

Sources: Touré 1987 (Benin); Mali, Ministère de l'Education Nationale 1990 (Mali); Dougna 1987 (Togo); Kaluba *et al.* 1987 (Zambia)

three of its objectives in primary education (i.e., move towards UPE, reduce the average class size to 50, and finance expenditures) by charging appropriate fees. The poor would then be reached by special measures or a targeted fee structure.

If cost requires households to choose who is to receive additional schooling, girls will suffer. Since girls are perceived to have fewer chances than boys of being upwardly mobile and, therefore, of being eventually beneficial to the family, there may be a higher opportunity cost to the family in girls attending school because they are more useful at home. On the whole, however, these disparities are smaller at the first level, becoming larger with each step up the educational ladder.

Anderson and Bowman (1965) discussed forgone opportunities under two subheadings:

(a) forgone current production opportunities, including nonfamilial employment, child contributions to family enterprises, other production services in the house;

(b) forgone learning, including production skills learned through participation in family enterprises, traditional cultural values and behavior.

Thus, children who might have attended school in better times are excluded or are withdrawn from school in dire situations, such as times of drought, either because they are needed at home or in the fields, or because the family is forced to migrate.

There is some detailed evidence of basic education enrollments for Benin, Kenya, Nigeria, and Togo. Some areas have shown decreases and others increases. In Benin, the areas where the most decreases occur are three of the most fertile agricultural regions (Zou, Borgou, and Oweme). In Kenya, decreased enrollments have been concentrated in the coastal regions where there is a flourishing cocoa trade. In Nigeria, the largest decreases since 1981–82 were in Kano, Rivers, and Bauchi. The latter two states, together with the six other states that showed a decrease, are located either on the coast or in the regions of the Niger. In Togo, once again it is the agriculturally fertile regions that show the largest decreases. The suggestion, therefore, is that where the children have higher earning potential, they are more likely to be kept out of school. Moreover, there may be a higher opportunity cost to the parents in richer families if the children can be usefully employed on the farm.

2.2 The Equivalence Problem

The definition of basic education, while relatively clear, raises some problems because the primary cycle varies in length and quality between countries. For example, another commonly held view is that "universal primary education of at least four to six years can be regarded as the minimum requirement to sustain any kind of economic growth" (Fägerlind and Saha 1989

Table 6
Duration of first level of education in different world regions by number of countries

	Africa	Asia and Oceania	Latin America and Caribbean	Arab states	Total
3/4	2	7	0	1	10
5	2	12	1	2	17
6	26	10	19	12	67
7	11	1	8	—	20
8/9	2	2	7	5	16
Total	43	32	35	20	130

p. 91); yet clearly, not all countries agree even on the length of the first level of education (see Table 6). Although variations in quality are more elusive to document, they are no less evident on visiting schools in different countries. Any suggestion that there is a rough equivalence between two children who have completed a six-year primary cycle in, for example, Sweden and Zaire obviously has to be treated with caution (Stephens 1992).

Moreover, where the length of the compulsory cycle is extended and still referred to as primary education, there is obviously considerable room for doubt as to when the purpose shifts from providing education as a human right to education for the needs of an industrializing society. Indeed, this has become a concern among developed countries, with international surveys of the extent of "functional adult literacy" showing substantial proportions unable to reach the standards "required" for postindustrial economies (OECD, 1995)

2.3 Quality of Education

The measurement of the quality of schooling is a very big industry in the North (e.g., Ross and Mählck 1990). However, partly because of ideological disputes at the primary level over child-centered schooling versus more traditional methods, these studies have tended to concentrate on postprimary schooling. The issues of quality in primary education are fought over more in the South. Although there are some disagreements over what counts as quality (e.g., Cheng 1995, Daun 1995, Stephens 1991), the focus of most research has been on drop-out from schools, pupil achievement, and materials and teaching competence.

2.3.1 Retentivity of school by world region. A major indicator used to assess the comparative quality of differing school systems in the developing world is simply the extent to which they retain pupils after the first year of schooling or until they reach fourth, fifth, or sixth grade. From the global data given in Table

Table 7
Retention in schools by number of countries with percentage of 1991 cohort reaching grades 2 and 6

	Africa	Asia and Oceania	Latin America and Caribbean	Arab States	Total
90% and over reaching grade 2	17	12	13	15	57
Under 90% reaching grade 2	19	6	7	1	33
90% and over reaching grade 5	11	11	11	14	47
Under 90% reaching grade 5	26	5	9	1	41

Source: UNESCO 1995 calculated from Table 5, p. 134

7 it can be seen that there is a substantial dropout in the first year in many countries in the African region and, to a lesser extent, in Latin America and the Caribbean. In more than half the countries for which data are available, typically the countries with the most developed educational systems, fewer than 80 percent reach Grade 5.

The lack of retentivity of schools especially in the least developed countries has been the subject of extensive research in the years since Jomtien (e.g., Carron and Chau 1996, Daun 1995, Palme 1995).

2.3.2 Measures. of outcome. Given the emphasis on accountability in the 1990s, the lack of any systematic data on education achievements is an important gap. Although many countries, including developing countries, report pass rates of examinations for entry to or departure from a particular cycle or transition rates from one level to another, such rates are internal to that particular system and cannot easily be taken as a judgment upon the quality of the education provided or received. Hence the interest in the results of studies by the International Association for the Evaluation of Educational Achievement (IEA). The IEA has designed, with the cooperation of curriculum experts from several countries, "standard" tests in several subject areas and has related the levels of attainment "to instructional, economic and social factors which account for differences between students, schools and national systems of education" (Holmes 1980).

Groups of such tests have been administered to appropriate samples of pupils across a range of schools in several countries. There have been several rounds of testing, starting with the first mathematics study in 1967. Although the tests have been criticized as positivist and inconclusive by several authors (e.g., Holmes 1980 p.13), the results have been influential. When the results are compared (e.g., Heyneman and White 1986), Third World educational systems

fare badly. For example, in sub-Saharan Africa, the World Bank has pointed to poor performance among students in Nigeria and Swaziland on the IEA tests and to poor results in ad hoc studies in Malawi and a francophone African country. They concluded: "the quality of education in sub-Saharan Africa is below world standards" (World Bank 1988 p. 33).

At the same time, more detailed analysis suggests that the influence of the school upon achievement, relative to the influence of home background and socioeconomic circumstances, is greater among Third World countries than in the North. For example, a study by Kathuri (1986) of factors influencing the performance of pupils in the Kenyan Certificate of Education (CPE) concluded that efficient use of teaching methods, good administration, staff morale (not necessarily qualifications), as well as whether or not the pupil had attended nursery school, influenced examination performance. Most of these factors, though by no means necessarily inexpensive to modify, can be influenced by educational authorities. The pupil's socioeconomic background did *not* seem to influence performance to the same extent as in the North.

The apparent importance of school quality relative to the "impoverished" environment may simply be a consequence of socially selective enrollment. Those children who go to school, or more likely the parents of those children, are probably the most motivated. In systems with near 100 percent enrollment, motivation affects achievement, and a good proxy for this motivational factor would be home background; but in systems with much less than 100 percent enrollment, this variation in motivation *within* schools will be diminished because the least motivatied simply do not attend. Because the influence of home background upon achievement is reduced in this way, school characteristics appear to be more important.

2.3.3 Quality of educational services. In 1988 a World Bank report comments on sub-Saharan Africa as follows:

> Much of the evidence is indirect: supplies of key inputs (especially books and other learning materials) are critically low, and the use of those inputs has declined in relation to the use of teachers' time and of physical facilities. Less is known about the output performance of students. (World Bank 1988 p. 1)

Fuller (1986) showed how resource inputs to primary schools dropped, especially in low income countries, between 1970 and 1980 (see also Lockheed and Verspoor 1990). Decline in unit costs usually affects nonsalary items first because of the difficulty of cutting teacher salaries. The availability of books and other learning aids will decrease in the 1990s and school "quality" will also decline (World Bank 1988).

Eventually, of course, teachers' salaries are cut (Andersson and Rosengart 1987). However, it is unclear how such reduction affects teachers' behavior or presence in the classroom. Although declines or stagnations in expenditures at such low levels are obviously damaging,

> the question of how best to improve the quality of primary schooling becomes very important. Should the priority be to increase the number of trained teachers or to improve the quality of their training? Should it be to abandon double shift teaching or to reduce average class size? Should it be to increase the quantity and the quality of school books and equipment? (Colclough 1982 p. 182)

In terms of assessing the impact upon demand, what matters are the tangible characteristics of the school as perceived by the parents. Can the children go to school as expected or is the school often closed? Are there exercise books and text books; that is, sufficient learning materials for the children? More crudely, do the children learn how to read and write? There is little systematic evidence on how parents react to shortfalls in basic materials, on teacher absences, or on under-achievement of their children (e.g., Hoppers 1995, Schaeffer 1991). It may, therefore, appear that the reason for decline or stagnation in enrollments is due to lack of demand from parents. More probably, difficulties of supply interact with a fall-off in demand such that as resources decline (or stagnate), leading to a reduction in school materials and teachers' salaries, so, too, does the quality of education provided in the schools. Parents then see little point in continuing or attempting to educate their children.

2.4 Returns on Human Capital

The very rapid expansion of the "modern" school after independence, for example in African countries, was probably due to a perception that it was the best means of social advancement. The expected future net benefits included not only the incremental earnings attributable to additional schooling but also the access to more prestigious occupations and future gains in efficiency.

The belief in primary education as a means of social advancement may, however, be weakening so that the motivation to attend school is weaker. Indeed, if it is accepted that the driving force for attending school is economic betterment, then parental assessments of the job market relative to work in the traditional sector and of the relative advantage of schooling are crucial.

In many countries, the number of jobs available in the modern sector for those with educational qualifications has dropped or is growing more slowly than the growth in enrollments. This, in turn, leads to a drop in parental expectations about the likely future benefits to be gained from attending or completing primary education. The principal motivation for attending school becomes much less powerful: attendances will drop.

This does not necessarily mean that, as a whole, there is less demand for education. The difficulties of securing employment faced by those who have completed secondary or tertiary education has led in some countries to a "brain drain" where graduates take jobs abroad. It has also led to "schooling revolving around certification [because it is] the need for and desire for certificates rather than the knowledge which explain the popular demand for [secondary and tertiary] schooling" (Dore 1976 p. 80). This "diploma disease" is then further aggravated by employers demanding higher qualifications from applicants for the same job. While this may increase education costs, the returns from employment either at home or abroad are sufficiently valuable to keep educational demand high. So further education does not necessarily lose its popularity.

3. Trends

Given the hopes of the 1960s, the apparent stagnation in enrollments in the 1980s was a worrying development (Table 1). However, these figures are full of pitfalls for the unwary. The first problem is that the gross enrollment ratio in many countries is over 100, because of underage and overage children. Second, the problem arises that there are all kinds of political pressures on local authorities to increase the reported enrollments. Even when these biases are taken into account, it is difficult to interpret shifts. The rate of increase of the gross enrollment ratios in a country will depend on the *actual* level it has already reached (see Table 8) and in countries approaching universal enrollment, underage and overage enrollments become rarer; and it is always more difficult to enroll the last 10–15 percent than the first 85–90 percent of the school-age population (Blaug 1968 p. 16). In fact, the increases in gross enrollment ratios (GER) are largest in Africa where the 1980 GER was lowest (around 59%), and smallest in Latin America, where the 1980 GER was highest (around 82%). The correlation between the gross enrollment ratio in a country and increases in the ratio is large and negative at –0.69.

Table 8
Relationship between level of gross enrollment ratio 1980 and relative change from 1980 by number of countries

	Africa		Asia and Oceania		Latin America and Caribbean		Arab states	
Ratio	<0	0+	<0	0+	<0	0+	<0	0+
100 and over	3	7	3	7	5	12	5	5
90–100	5	2	1	4	3	2	1	1
Under 90	8	13	1	2	1	2	4	4
Total	16	22	5	13	9	16	10	10

Source: UNESCO 1995 calculated from Table 5, p. 134

Because of this inverse relationship, particular attention should be paid to those countries where enrollment ratios are low and declining. In the early 1990s there were 11 such countries where the gross enrollment ratios were below 90 and where there had been a decline since 1980. Six of these were in Africa: Central African Republic, Ghana, Guinea, Guinea-Bissau, Mali, and Somalia; three, in Asia: Afghanistan, Bangladesh, and Nepal; one, El Salvador, in Latin America; and one, the Democratic Republic of Yemen, among the Arab states.

4. Policy Issues in the Face of Declining Demand

Throughout the 1960s and 1970s there was an assumption that educational attainment would automatically increase demand for education; in other words, the introduction of formal education would have a "contagious" effect. An African child of illiterate parents who learned to read and do sums in primary school would want to go on to secondary school and, from there, would want to progress to university. Yet even if the child got no further than primary school, he or she would insist that his or her own children should do better. The social demand for education would thus build up across generations, regardless of what might be happening to the economy or to the resources available to education (Coombs 1985 p. 34), and regardless of the "real" need for learning. But this process no longer works; it now looks as if the demand for education falls short of an objective assessment of the level of learning "needed" in order to sustain the development of human resources. Many observers have noted a reluctance to enroll children for school, especially in rural areas, even when a school is available (e.g., Callewaert 1988, Hoppers 1995). This reluctance needs to be understood in order for appropriate policies to be developed. A wide range of possible factors have been discussed that are potentially amenable to policy, such as:

(a) the costs of schooling to households relative to their ability to pay;

(b) the expected future net benefits of schooling in terms of the opportunities for social mobility;

(c) the appropriateness of the "modern" school to the members of the community;

(d) the quality of the educational services offered from the parents' point of view.

The former two raise issues of efficiency and equity (see Sect. 4.1); the latter two, the question of whose school is it anyway (see Sect. 4.2). In turn, both raise questions about the extent and nature of an international commitment to "Education for All" (see Sect. 4.3).

4.1 Efficiency and Equity

Three questions will be examined in this section:

(a) How much does access matter, or does universalization dilute quality?

(b) Should the curriculum of basic education be terminal or a stepping stone to the next level?

(c) Who should pay, parents or the state?

4.1.1 UPE or quality? Although earlier debates contrasting a community-based vocational primary education with a more academic primary schooling have subsided, there is still considerable doubt, 30 years after the optimistic declarations by ministers of education at the World Regional Conferences, of the viability of the UPE goal. Indeed, although lip service is still paid to the goal of 100 percent enrollment, policy and political emphasis have been shifting to a concern for the deteriorating quality of educational provision (Carron and Chau 1996). This is partly because of the supposed reactions of parents to poor quality, but mostly because of the inefficiency of schooling as measured by drop out and repetition. The appropriate balance between quality and universality is still a very live issue.

4.1.2 Content of the basic education curriculum. There has been considerable debate on the curriculum content of the latter stages of the compulsory cycle in the industrialized countries—essentially over the balance between academic and vocational subjects. There is a parallel issue in developing countries as to the proper role of manual labor and/or prevocational training in the schools whilst, recently, the international community has tended to downplay the importance of these (Lockheed and Verspoor 1990), governments still promote manual labor and prevocational training in the name of "relevance" (Hoppers 1995).

During the 1960s and 1970s, there was a similar issue in the earlier stage of "basic education" in developing countries over whether the primary cycle should be seen as the first stage of a school career or as complete in itself. At the time, that issue led to debates over the appropriate language of instruction in many countries. For, if instruction is seen primarily as preparation for the second cycle, then local "tribal" languages are seen as a hindrance. If the primary cycle is seen as complete in itself, then the use of national or international languages may alienate primary school leavers from the community. Whilst few now maintain that the primary cycle should be seen as complete in itself because those who are vocal—the "middle-class"—tend to have higher aspirations for their children, a consensus does appear to be emerging that mother tongue in the first years of schooling (L1 teaching) not only encourages parents to enrol their children in school but is also more effective (Daun 1995, Lockheed and Verspoor 1990)

4.1.3 Who should pay? Lourie (1987) gave three good reasons why the public sector should remain the main provider of educational services:

> (a) social and economic *needs* for education are greater than private demand; (b) external *effects* of education extend beyond the individual and her or his household; (c) poverty must not be a *bar* to access to education. (Lourie 1987 p. 11)

Lourie also stated: "The momentum of enrolment growth takes place at the expense of the take home pay of teachers. Although teachers' annual remuneration expressed in terms of GNP per capita is higher than in OECD countries, it has tended to drop alarmingly" (Lourie 1987 p. 8). But the arguments continue. In the North, as a consequence of the "rolling back" of the state (in reality, more often a restructuring of the state to concentrate on essential social-control functions), there has been a move toward local management of schools. In the poorer countries of the South, the economic consequences of structural adjustment programs imply that, even though the rhetoric is for local control, communities have to rely progressively more on central funds while several governments have found it impossible to maintain expenditures (see Table 2). Indeed, even though the introduction of user charges has exacerbated the picture of declining demand in several countries, some still argue for privatizing schooling.

4.2 Whose School is it Anyway?

The latter discussion of "who should pay" raises the issue of control. In most industrialized countries, schools were originally local initiatives or sponsored by churches with local backing. In some cases this has meant that a relatively strong community school movement has survived (e.g., Sweden, United States). In the main, however, the state's role has been predominant.

Nevertheless, even in several developing countries where the model has been imported (some would say imposed), the community has been involved at least in building and maintaining the school, if not the teacher, in order for the school to survive. There are obvious, well-known examples such as the Harambee movement in Kenya, but even in situations where such support seems unlikely to be forthcoming villagers have helped to build the school.

Yet it must be remembered that for many developing countries, especially in Africa, widespread attendance at school is a recent and "Western" innovation. Thus, in most industrialized countries the primary school has long been the main instrument of social integration for children, so that formal schooling is almost universally accepted as having a central, fundamental value. That is not the case in many developing countries: indeed, in some areas, the "modern" school has been viewed as antagonistic to religious and secular traditional values (Daun 1995, Palme 1995).

On one level, this is a question of what is taught in school and how. Detailed discussion of the content of the curriculum and of the pedagogy adopted in the schools is inappropriate here. However, there are some clear incongruities in many curricula designed for basic education; for example, the in-depth study of literature, only focusing on a foreign country; or the study of world geography and history, but not of their own locality. Similarly, there are many teachers drafted into rural areas who feel ill at ease in that milieu.

There is also the wider question of whether the school, and the way it is organized, "fits in" to the local community. Is the school primarily seen as something imposed on the community from outside, or do the parents feel that they might be able to play a role in how it is run and even in what is taught? If the parents do not feel involved at all in the school, they will not make any particular effort to ensure that their children attend unless schooling ensures high status or economic returns.

Indeed, instead of asking why there has been stagnation in enrollments in primary schools in developing countries, it might more generally be asked whether parents in the industrialized countries will continue to encourage their children to stay on at a school that holds little prospect for their social and economic advancement.

4.3 International Support for Basic Education

For most of the post-Independence period, assistance agencies have ignored primary education. The massive flow of expatriates from North to South was to staff secondary and tertiary institutions. Educational reform and innovation concentrated on, for example, the diversification of the secondary school, although there was some European interest in adult education. At the same time the international agencies became increasingly concerned that their own dicta about the value of a minimum number of years of primary school were insufficient: what mattered was what went on in school. Hence the call, at the Jomtien World Conference on Education for All, for the international community to ensure not only that this goal be met by the year 2000, but that there be "an acceptable level of learning" in the schools.

Various estimates have been made of the extra resources required even to provide sufficient places in primary schooling, let alone to ensure the quality of the education provided. It is clear, however, that the low-income countries simply cannot afford the amounts required and that there has to be long-term, massive support for basic education if the EFA goal is to be reached in the first quarter of the twenty-first century.

Interest has, therefore, grown in monitoring the flow of aid. But, as two surveys, carried out for the International Consulative Forum on Education for All (King and Carr-Hill 1991) and for the Development Assistance Committee of the OECD (Carr-Hill and King

1992), showed (reinforced by Buchert 1995), donor agencies have great difficulty in reporting on their flow of aid to education. This is partly due to the difference between commitments and expenditures, partly because field offices have considerable latitude in the actual apportionment of aid, and partly because of the difficulty of clarifying project-related training.

With all these caveats, what was the picture of aid to education and to basic education in the late 1980s and early 1990s? First, it should be remembered that, according to the United Nations Development Programme's *Human Development Report*, 1991, the overall pattern of support to the education sector during the period 1979–89 registered a decline from 16.5 percent to 10.7 percent. In part, this can be accounted for by the rapid rise in the overall volume of aid given by Japan, which traditionally allocated little to education and which became the largest bilateral donor in 1991. Second, it should also be remembered that East European countries provided comparatively large amounts of educational aid, at least to universities, most of which was withdrawn by the early 1990s.

The major conclusion is that there is a very wide divergence between countries in the proportions of their aid devoted to basic education and that, if the EFA target is to be reached, there will have to be real signs of a "peace dividend."

See also: Agricultural Productivity and Education; Benefits of Education; Education and Development; Educational Expansion: Sociological Perspectives; Postliteracy: Concepts and Policies; Social Equality and Educational Planning in Developing Nations

References

Anderson C A, Bowman M J (eds.) 1965 *Education and Economic Development*. Aldine, Chicago, Illinois

Anderson G, Rosengart G 1987 *Education in Tanzania: Government Expenditure 1983–1987*. SIDA, Stockholm

Blaug M 1968 Cost-benefit analysis of educational expenditures in developing countries. In: Blaug M (ed.) 1968 *The Economics of Education. Vol. 1: Selected Readings*. Penguin, Harmondsworth

Bowman M J, Anderson C A 1963 Concerning the role of education in development. In: Gerty C (ed.) 1963 *Old Societies, New State*. Free Press, New York

Bray M 1986 If UPE is the answer what is the question? *Int. J. Educ. Dev.* 6(3): 147–58

Caldwell J 1982 *The Theory of Fertility Decline*. Academic Press, London

Callewaert G 1988 La chute des effectifs a l'école primaire en Guinea-Bissau. Presentation to seminar organized by SIDA and the IEE, Stockholm, February 1988

Carr-Hill R 1987 *Social Conditions in Sub-Sahara Africa*. Macmillan, London

Carr-Hill R A, King K 1992 *Aid to Basic Education: Flows, Policies and Modalities*. OECD, Paris

Carron G, Chau T M 1996 *The Quality of Primary Schools in Different Development Contexts*. IIEP Paris

Cheng K-M 1994 Quality of education as perceived in Chinese culture. In: Takala T (ed.) 1994 *Quality of Education in the Context of Culture in Developing Countries*. University of Tampere Press, Tampere

Colclough C 1982 The impact of primary schooling on economic development: A review of the evidence. *World Dev.* 10(3): 167–85

Coombs P H 1985 *The World Crisis in Education: A View from the Eighties*. Oxford University Press, New York

Daun H 1994 Holistic education, quality and technocratic criteria of competence—cases from Guinea-Bissau and Senegal. In: Takala T (ed.) 1994 *Quality of Education in the Context of Culture in Developing Countries*. University of Tampere Press, Tampere

Dewey J 1915 *The School and Society*, 2nd edn. University of Chicago Press, Chicago, Illinois

Dore R J 1976 *The Diploma Disease: Education, Qualifications and Development*. Allen and Unwin, London

Dougna K D 1987 *Crise économique et crise de l'éducation en Afrique* (IIEP/ KD/87–06). IIEP, Paris

Fägerlind I, Saha L J 1989 *Education and National Development: A Comparative Perspective*, 2nd edn. Pergamon Press, Oxford

Foster P J 1965 The vocational school fallacy in development planning. In: Anderson C A, Bowman M J (eds.) 1965

Fuller B 1986 Is primary school quality eroding in the Third World? *Comp. Educ. Rev.* 30(4): 491–507

Heyneman S P, White D (eds.) 1986 *The Quality of Education and Economic Development*. World Bank, Washington, DC

Holmes B 1980 *Comparative Education: Some Consideration of Method*. Allen and Unwin, London

Hoppers W 1994 Questioning the school. What room for the local perspective. In: Takala T (ed.) 1994 *Quality of Education in the Context of Culture in Developing Countries*. University of Tampere Press, Tampere

Illich I 1971 *Deschooling Society*. Harper and Row, New York

Jamison D T, Lau L J 1982 *Farmer Education and Farm Efficiency*. Johns Hopkins University Press, Baltimore, Maryland

Kaluba H, Karlsson M, Nystrom K 1987 Educational support to Zambia: Keeping up coverage and standards. In: Johnston A et al. 1987 *Educational and Economic Crises: The Cases of Mozambique and Zambia*. SIDA (Educational Division Documents No. 38), Stockholm

Kathuri N J 1986 *Factors that Influence the Performance of Pupils in CPE*. Bureau of Education Research, Kengalta University, Nairobi

King K, Carr-Hill R 1991 *Changing Patterns of Development Assistance to Basic Education*. UNESCO, Paris

Lee K H 1988 Universal primary education: An African dilemma. *World Dev.* 16: 1481–91

Lind A 1989 Literacy—a tool for the empowerment of women? *Nordic Association for the Study of Education in Developing Countries*, Stockholm, June 8–10, 1989

Lockheed M, Verspoor A 1990 *Improving Primary Education in Developing Countries: A Review of Policy Options*. World Bank, Washington, DC

Lourie S 1987 Are consequences of adjustment policies on education measurable? Lecture to the National Institute of Educational Planning and Administration, New Delhi, India, 2nd September 1987. International Institute for Educational Planning (IIEP/Dir/87.205), Paris

Mali, Ministère de l'Education Nationale 1990 Le financement de l'éducation. IIEP, Paris (mimeo)

Nyerere J 1977 *The Arusha Declaration: Ten Years After.* Government Printing Office, Dar es Salaam

Organisation for Economic Cooperation and Development 1995 *Functional Literacy.* OECD, Paris

Palme M 1994 How do we understand school failure and drop-out? Some suggestions based on studies on Mozambican primary education. In: Takala T (ed.) 1994 *Quality of Education in the Context of Culture in Developing Countries.* University of Tampere Press, Tampere

Reimer E 1970 *School is Dead: An Essay on Alternatives in Education.* Penguin, Harmondsworth

Ross K, Mählck L 1990 *Planning the Quality of Education.* IIEP, Paris

Schaeffer S 1991 A framework for collaborating for educational change Paris, IIEP Research and Studies Program Monograph No 3

Stephens D 1991 The quality of primary education in developing countries: who defines and who decides? *Comp. Educ.* 27(2)

Thobani M 1983 *Charging User Fees for Social Services: The Case of Education in Malawi.* World Bank, Washington, DC

Touré A 1987 Le problematique de financement de l'enseignement de base en République Populaire de Benin. Unpublished paper, IIEP, Paris

UNESCO 1960 *Conference of Ministers of Education in Asia.* UNESCO, Paris

UNESCO 1961 *Conference of African States on the Development of Education in Africa.* Final Report, Addis Ababa. UNESCO, Paris

UNESCO 1962 *Conference on Education and Economic and Social Development.* UNESCO, Paris

UNESCO 1966 *Conference of Ministers of Education and Ministers responsible for Economic Planning in the Arab States.* UNESCO, Paris

UNESCO 1967 *Statistical Yearbook.* UNESCO, Paris

UNESCO 1977 *Statistical Yearbook.* UNESCO, Paris

UNESCO 1980 *Statistical Yearbook.* UNESCO, Paris

UNESCO 1988 *Statistical Yearbook.* UNESCO, Paris

UNESCO 1995 *World Education Report.* 1995 UNESCO, Paris

World Bank 1988 *Education in Sub-Saharan Africa: Policies for Adjustment, Revitalisation and Expansion.* World Bank, Washington, DC

Benefits of Education

L. C. Solmon and C. L. Fagnano

Any discussion of educational benefits must start with two basic observations. The first is that people with more education usually differ from those with less education, though it is a matter of debate as to how far this results simply from education. The second observation is that individuals change as they obtain more schooling. Yet to what extent are changes the result of schooling? To what extent are they the effects of maturing generally or of other experiences unrelated to education? Ideally, study of these issues should consider two groups of individuals similar in all respects except for the fact that one experienced a particular type of education and the other did not. If advantages were observed only for those with the educational experience, then it would be possible to attribute those advantages to the education, since no other factors could account for the differences.

In the real world, as opposed to the ideal world of educational and social science research, it is impossible to study two identical groups, one with and one without education. In the first place, in situations where certain individuals or groups of individuals reach a certain level of education and other individuals or groups do not, there are clearly significant differences other than educational attainment between the individuals or groups. This has resulted in many attempts to hold constant statistically factors which differ between attenders and nonattenders, but which cannot be held constant by selection of experimental and control groups directly. The problem with attempts at statistical control is that one can never be certain that all important differences have been taken into account, because many factors may be either unthought of or unmeasurable.

1. The Dimensions of Educational Benefits

For all levels of education, the discussion of educational benefits must begin by asking a number of questions. The first of these is: who will benefit? There are several potential beneficiaries of the educational process. The first and most obvious is the student. However, even here it is impossible to look at benefits to students as a homogeneous group. Individuals enter the educational process with a variety of complementary and/or hindering characteristics which will either help or impede them in achieving what they seek. Thus individual characteristics of students must be considered in conjunction with benefits. One of the fundamental policy questions in this area is: what happens if certain students are able to benefit more or less from a particular type of education? Should different resources be provided for those with different needs, or does equality of educational opportunity demand that equal resources be provided for unequal students?

In addition to the students themselves, other groups of beneficiaries must be considered, such as others in society (nonstudents) who may or may not invest in the education of a student either directly (as in the case of family and friends) or indirectly (as in the case of individuals who support education by paying taxes). Benefits to individual students are easy to conceptualize: the student who learns to read in school is better-off than were he or she unable to read. In economic jargon this is known as a "private benefit" of education. The economist distinguishes private benefits from social benefits. Social benefits are ones that accrue to people other than those being educated. If a student graduates from medical school he or she will obviously obtain the benefits of high income and the satisfaction of curing the sick. However, if that medical doctor were to pursue a research career and eventually develop a cure for a major disease, the beneficiaries of his or her education would be not only the doctor who received income and acclaim, but also those who were saved from the disease by his or her discovery. Society is clearly better-off because of the education of that individual, and the individual has not appropriated all of the benefits of his or her education for him- or herself: others derive (social) benefits above and beyond those (private benefits) received by the individual doctor.

Basic economic analysis leads to the inference that if decisions are made by individuals who base their actions on the personal costs and benefits of education, and if net social benefits are produced by education, from society's perspective insufficient education will be purchased unless there is subsidy to potential purchasers. It is important to know what benefits accrue not only to students but to society at large in order to devise policies that achieve the socially optimal amount of education.

Most of the literature merely distinguishes between private and social benefits as discussed above. However, there is a third important group of beneficiaries from education at each of its levels: namely, those in the institutions who teach, administrate, and provide other services. This is important, because in many cases decisions are made within a school not for the benefit of students or society but for the benefit of those employed there.

At the elementary-school level, salaries are generally paid on the basis of degree attainments and seniority, not on the basis of an individual teacher's ability to impart knowledge or other educational benefits to students. At the level of higher education many compulsory courses in the humanities are maintained primarily to ensure that humanities faculties are able to maintain minimum class sizes in fields in which enrollments are declining. Additionally, administrators often decide to erect new buildings and expand the size of institutions, even if alternative uses of funds in developing a new curriculum or improving the quality of a smaller institution might have greater educational benefits to students. However, the former choices might lead to greater acclaim and individual power for particular administrators. It is therefore vital when evaluating educational decisions to ask in whose interest decisions have been made. By doing so, it will soon be discovered that, at all levels of education, decisions made can have a very different impact on individual students, on society at large, and on people employed in the institutions. This helps to explain why certain

objectives (or what some people regard as objectives) are not achieved in various educational settings.

Once the potential recipients of educational benefits have been identified, the various types of benefits should be considered. Certain benefits are explicit goals of educational institutions, such as enabling a grammar-school student to have a certain facility in reading, or ensuring that the chemistry graduate understands the various ways in which elements can be combined to form chemical compounds. In addition to benefits that are explicit goals, there can be unsought results or side effects, which may also be beneficial. Few colleges would admit to the explicit function of being a dating service, but one side-effect benefit of going to college for many individuals is the opportunity of meeting a future spouse during the college years.

Certain general aptitudes and characteristics are thought to result from attending school. These include an understanding of the value of democracy as opposed to a dictatorial form of government and the ability to think critically and reason well. Although various educational institutions would admit to the hope that their students would acquire these characteristics, they do not usually offer courses entitled "Appreciating Democracy" or "Thinking Critically." These skills might be the indirect effects of courses in civics, social studies, history, philosophy, English literature, and other subjects. Depending upon the degree of explicitness with which a goal is held, it may be more difficult to determine whether the goal is achieved. For example, most students obtain reading scores, thanks to the explicit nature of the desire to teach students to read. On the other hand, the appreciation of democracy or the ability to think critically are less measurable.

Whether the result of explicit or indirect behavior of students and educational institutions, a variety of possible educational benefits have been considered in the literature. These have been categorized according to whether they are psychological or behavioral; cognitive or affective; vocational or nonvocational; monetary or nonmonetary. It must be kept in mind that benefits of any of these types might accrue to students, society at large, or to those employed within the educational institutions.

Consideration of these categories of benefits again makes it clear that some are easier to identify than others. In their constant desire to conduct cost–benefit analyses, economists tend to consider benefits that can be evaluated in monetary terms. One school of economics views education in part as an investment in human capital, whereby expenditures of money and time are made to acquire education which increases individual productivity, value in the labor market, and income (Schultz 1963). However, vocational or monetary outcomes are only one type of benefit, and perhaps not the most important type. Others must be considered. There are also numerous psychological, behavioral, cognitive, and affective impacts of schooling, but these are very difficult to identify and, once identified, even more difficult to evaluate.

The problem is how to identify, assess, measure, and evaluate the benefits of education. As has already been noted, differences in individuals with different educational attainments cannot all be attributed to different educational experiences. The observation that a college graduate earns more than one with only a high school education should not lead to the conclusion that going to college necessarily yields higher income. It is possible that the college graduate is more intelligent and motivated than the high school graduate and that the college graduate would have earned more even had he or she not attended college. The problem is that basic intelligence, and more so motivation, are factors that affect income but are very difficult to isolate and measure.

The central issue of educational benefits is the question of what changes are effected by the educational experience. Methodologically, this implies that pre- and post-test measures on individuals are required that will identify changes caused by education. This has come to be known as the "value-added approach." In essence, knowing an individual's initial attributes and aptitudes would lead to a predicted achievement in some test or other. At the end of an educational experience one could determine actual achievement. By comparing the actual to the predicted achievement, one could observe the impact of the educational experience in this dimension. Even when that is done, if such a change is observed, it may not be attributable to the educational experience itself. Certain changes in individuals may be the result of normal maturation, which would have occurred with or without attendance at school. Other changes may be a function of such diverse factors as changes in national economic conditions or a divorce in the student's family. Thus, there is a need to net out or account for other noneducational factors which might confound the link between the educational experience and the changes observed in the students.

Assuming that this approach revealed that attendance at a particular institution led to a gain in a certain type of knowledge for a student, the question then becomes: how can the worth of such an achievement be evaluated? This issue is addressed by Bowen (1977) in his classic treatise *Investment in Learning.* There he asks: "What is the worth of the changes in individuals wrought by higher education?" Bowen suggests five different ways of making such a calculation, and applies each methodology specifically to higher education. His first way of evaluating changes in individuals is to argue that whatever is being spent on higher education is a measure of its worth; "the total expenditure on higher education would not have been made unless the students and their families, the citizenry, and philanthropic donors collectively thought the returns justified the outlays. . . . Nevertheless, that

American people do devote $85 billion of resources each year to higher education is some evidence that they value it highly" (p. 438). Bowen was writing in 1977. It is worth noting that, a decade and a half after his observation, Americans increased their expenditure on higher education in real terms by over 20 percent. Since education's share of gross national product remained constant or rose slightly, Americans apparently continued to value higher education long after Bowen conducted his analysis.

Bowen's second approach was to investigate the reactions of clients to their own college education. He concluded that "this evidence is far from conclusive—especially because the clients did not pay the whole cost. Yet the overwhelming favorable reaction of clients can only mean that something of great value was received by a larger majority of students" (p. 439). Bowen's third approach is to consider the possible increases in the capital value of human beings resulting from higher education. However repugnant, individuals are valued in connection with claims for damages in cases of death and disability; they are valued by implication when decisions are made about expenditures intended to save lives, as in air or highway travel or workplaces; and people value their own lives when they make decisions to accept premium pay for risky work assignments. Bowen describes the literature on valuing human lives and points out that if it were possible to determine the extent to which, say, college graduates' lives are valued more highly than those with less education, one could aggregate across all college graduates to determine the extra value of human lives resulting from college education.

A fourth approach for estimating the value of college education is to look at the sources of growth in the United States over a particular period and determine the extent to which higher education was responsible for that growth. The well-known Denison (1962, 1964, 1974, 1984) approach of accounting for growth in national income has led to the conclusion that instructional activities have paid their way handsomely in the history of the United States. The fifth approach to estimating the value of college education is to look at the rate of return on investments in college education. The problem with this approach is that it only takes into account the earnings or the increased earnings potential enjoyed by students as the result of college attendance. (It must be remembered that there are numerous other potential educational benefits beside an individual's higher earnings.)

Each of these approaches—namely, expenditure levels, reaction of clients, the incremental value of human lives, the contribution to economic growth, and the rate of return—is applicable to elementary, secondary, college, and postgraduate education. The point is that although evaluation of benefits might be difficult, that should not preclude them from being considered; nor should it lead to the conclusion that benefits that are difficult to evaluate are not valuable.

After considering identification and measurement problems, there are still more questions to ask. An important one is: when do educational benefits occur? Some benefits occur during the educational experience itself. For example, the opportunity to enjoy an entertaining and stimulating class is an educational benefit. Certain types of educational benefits could be assessed by querying students during the time they are engaged in education. Similarly, the social benefits of having a local high school football game to attend occur during the educational experience. Other educational benefits can be identified upon completion of an educational program. For example, reading scores at graduation can be compared with those at entry, and the increment in reading scores of elementary-school children over, say, a year of schooling determined. The pretest–posttest methodology can be used not only to identify changes in knowledge but also to consider changes in attitudes and values.

Looking for educational benefits only during the years of schooling or upon completion precludes a realistic assessment of a wide variety of additional possible educational benefits. Numerous benefits accrue at times well past the completion of education. There are also serious questions of whether or not the effects of education are long-lasting. The point here is that by looking only at benefits that accrue during the schooling experience or at its conclusion may give quite inaccurate results.

The most vivid example of this would be the results obtained by comparing the salaries of a high school graduate who has been at work for 4 years with that of a college graduate entering his first job. It would be naive to expect that the earnings of the college graduate would necessarily exceed those of the high school graduate who has had four years more experience. Also, it is often observed that graduates from "higher quality" college programs often earn less at the beginning than graduates from "lower quality" programs. These apparent paradoxes can be explained by several factors. In particular, the individual with more education, or with better education, has usually demonstrated a comparative advantage in learning and so will take a job that enables him or her to continue learning while earning a living and beginning a career. Most employers are unwilling to incur the cost of educating employees, particularly when the employee is able to change employers at any moment. The way for more highly educated, or better educated, individuals to learn on the job is to take lower initial salaries to compensate the employer for the cost of providing additional education or training. The expectation is that, after several years, the individuals who have been investing by taking lower salaries while learning on the job will receive a payoff not only from formal schooling but also from the additional human capital acquired on the job. Thus, more educated individuals are observed to begin with lower salaries than less educated individuals, but over the years their salaries

surpass those of people with less education, with the gap between the two groups widening over time.

If the educational benefit of higher earnings were to be evaluated at the time an individual with more or better education entered the labor market, it might be suggested that no educational benefit of this type existed because those with less or inferior education were earning more. It is necessary to observe income differentials after a substantial number of years in the labor market before it can be determined that there is an educational benefit in terms of higher income for the more highly educated.

Other impacts of education also occur some time after leaving college. It has generally been observed that the college years lead individuals to become increasingly more liberal in their political philosophy. However, other studies have shown that some years after their college experience, college graduates again become more conservative—indeed, even more conservative than they were upon entering college (Solmon and Ochsner 1978). This raises the question of whether the effect of education on political attitudes endures. It might be argued that the change to liberalism is a college impact (irrespective of whether it is a benefit) that is not enduring. Alternatively, the benefit under consideration might be identified as adopting a political philosophy that is in the student's best interest. During the college years, when educational subsidies and other types of support are a necessity, it is in the student's interest to advocate liberal causes. Afterward, when those liberal causes have to be financed by the individual's own tax payments, the educated person may see his or her interest as being served by a conservative ideology. In this sense, the understanding of different political philosophies might be viewed as an enduring effect of college. Finally, a student who would never have identified a course in English grammar as an educational benefit while struggling with the course might many years later recognize the tremendous value of that course when using the knowledge obtained to write the memoranda or speeches required in his or her particular line of work. Clearly, an assessment of educational benefits which stops at the time of graduation is an incomplete one.

Another question that must be asked is: what is it about education that caused or impeded the benefits? Is it the time in school? Is it the quality of the faculty staff, their teaching abilities, the physical plant, or other facilities? Is it the support services such as counseling, guidance, and the like? Is it the aptitude of students who attend? Or is it all of these things as they interacted with each other? In essence, much of the discussion of the impact or benefits of education at various levels to date has viewed education as a black box. That is, education is viewed as something people enter and leave. While in the box they change; but why they change is unknown.

Most studies that have attempted to identify particular factors such as quality of teachers and facilities generally have been forced to use highly aggregated measures of these inputs, thereby clouding the understanding of the actual interrelationship of particular factors with particular students. The most recent literature, particularly that dealing with educational impacts at the elementary or secondary school level, tends to emphasize the importance of looking at situations within schools and even within classrooms in order to understand what factors affect different students in different ways. There is clearly no universal answer to the question of what benefits accrue to whom during the educational process, nor will there be until it is known how individuals are affected by the various components of an educational experience.

2. Uses of Knowledge of Educational Benefits

The questions asked so far are fundamental to an understanding of the possible benefits of education at various levels. They are important because unless the benefits yielded by education are understood, various assessments and policy decisions will be made in a vacuum. It is necessary to know what benefits accrue from education in order to allocate resources not only among schools of various types and levels, but also between educational and other social programs. Educational benefits must also be appreciated in order to decide how to finance education at different levels. If benefits accrue to society in large amounts, this provides a justification for public subsidy. Alternatively, if virtually all benefits accrue to those who are educated, there are reasons to advocate self-financing of the education process, even if in the form of loans.

Educational benefits must also be identified in order to interpret the motivation of educators. What may seem irrational on one level may be explainable if it is appreciated that benefits accrue to those making the decisions. If those decisions are unjustified in terms of private and social educational objectives, action can be taken with full understanding of the situation. Basically, knowledge is required about educational benefits so that educational processes can be evaluated in terms of cost–benefit analysis (and associated resource allocation decisions) and in terms of assessing management.

The most overriding need to understand educational benefits is the result of the commitment of most countries to the achievement of equality of educational opportunity. In the first place, equal educational opportunity must be defined. Is it necessary for every student to attend any institution he or she chooses, or is it enough if every student has access to some but not all schools or colleges? Does access to the same amount of resources ensure equal opportunity? If so, does that mean that less able students should be given the same as more able students, even though more able students could reach the same levels of achievement with fewer resources? That is, does equal opportunity mean equal treatment in a particular educational institution, or

does it mean that each student should have the right to equal educational benefits? If the latter is the case, those with less aptitude or less ability to obtain educational benefits might require a different treatment, particularly a treatment that might be more costly than that needed by other students to achieve the same end. But unless it can be understood what educational benefits have been obtained, it is impossible to assess the extent to which a country has moved toward equality of educational opportunity.

3. Research on Benefits of Education

A considerable amount of research has been conducted on the educational benefits, impacts, and effects of each level of education. Yet for all levels, the research has focused on a very limited range of educational outputs and has not considered, in an empirical sense, a large number of other possible benefits. This section will summarize the major findings of the empirical research on educational benefits at both the elementary and secondary levels and at the higher education levels in the United States, where the research has been discussed in great detail. Some of the other possible benefits that have been discussed informally will also be considered, though they have rarely been documented and even more infrequently measured.

3.1 Elementary and Secondary Education

The literature on educational effects typically asks whether or not schools with different resource levels (and hence different inputs) have correspondingly differential impacts on students, where impacts are measured by some type of standardized achievement test. From the Coleman Report of the early 1960s (Coleman and Moynihan 1966), the results of the surveys, individually and in combination, have most frequently been interpreted to demonstrate that school differences account for little of the variations in students' outcome measures (McPartland and Karweit 1979). However, these and other authors have concluded that the pessimism inherent in the statement that "schools bring little influence to bear upon a child's achievement that is independent of his background and general social context" (Coleman and Moynihan 1966, p. 325) is basically unwarranted (Madaus 1980). Readers are encouraged to study these two papers for an excellent perspective on the research on early school effects. It is sufficient to note here that most scholars now reject the findings that effects of school variables on student achievement are minimal, because the evidence provided in the studies is inadequate to reach such conclusions. As McPartland and Karweit (1979) emphasized:

> Each study is based on naturally occurring variations of environments found in existing public schools and uses student samples that are non-randomly distributed across

schools. Because these studies do not meet the scientific standards for controlled experiments, methodological questions on the proper analysis and interpretation of non-experimental data apply to each of them. (p. 372)

The variety of criticisms of the school effects research can only be briefly listed here. The studies usually do not ask about the schools' objectives and then proceed to investigate the extent to which schools achieve these objectives. Schools certainly have many objectives other than to improve verbal ability or to maximize scores on standardized achievement tests. The dependent variables used in the most frequently cited studies probably do not represent either school achievements, even in such basic areas as reading or mathematics, or the appropriate goals of the schools and the teachers. Also, standardized tests are not linked to any common prescribed curriculum in the United States and so they are clearly testing some set of achievements that no single school particularly seeks. The test scores, therefore, come to reflect not achievement but how closely a particular school's curriculum parallels the curriculum implied by the test design.

The studies have also overlooked important environmental variations within the same schools, or have failed to measure the duration of exposure of different students to particular school factors. The typical model has implied that all students enter a black box (the school) and come out being somewhat different. In fact, different resources are targeted to certain students within the school (Oakes 1985). The characteristics of individual students must be linked with the teachers who actually taught them, rather than looking only at the impact of the average teacher. Yet the studies imply that all students within a school or school district are treated the same. Moreover, the learning consequences of additional instructional time and other resources may not be the same for all students, for all curricular units, or for all modes of classroom instruction. In sum, the variation of resources within schools available to students must be considered. Such work is dependent upon advances in research methodology that occurred from the mid-1980s onward. These will be discussed below.

The factors identified with school environment in the educational production function studies undertaken in the United States in the 1960s, 1970s and early 1980s tended to be fairly uniform throughout the country. These studies provided no information on how achievement related to school factors other than those in the restricted natural range. All schools have teachers with about the same level of education, classrooms with from about 10 to 45 students, and so on. It is not known if class sizes of 2 have different impacts from class sizes of 100 because there are not many of either size and rarely are the situations compared where a factor does and does not exist (e.g., all classrooms have a teacher). The small range of variation in the school measures causes two problems: since there is little variance in the explanatory variable, little of the variance in the dependent variable is explained, and nothing is known about the effects of variables with magnitudes outside the natural range.

There have also been a number of more technical problems with the school effects studies. When the aggregation level of certain background traits is too high, these can become confounded with measures of school resources. For example, it is clear how socioeconomic status might affect the achievement of a youngster (e.g., low socioeconomic status (SES) may lead to low appreciation of education and hence low motivation to achieve and low actual achievement). But an aggregate measure of SES for the student body is probably highly related to the community's and school's resources. The SES measure is correlated with a school's funds, and if entered into a regression model before the resource measure will prevent the latter from demonstrating much effect.

The problem concerning ordering of variables deserves emphasis. In the absence of longitudinal data, information on students' home background has usually been used as a proxy for students' initial status (to control for the aptitudes the student brings to school). Home or background variables were entered first, and it was thus erroneously assumed that these influenced achievement only prior to and independent of school influences. In estimating the relative importance of nonschool and school variables, all of their shared variation was assigned to the nonschool factors, resulting in an underestimate of the school effects.

From the mid-1980s onward there were considerable methodological advancements in school effects research. Statisticians developed regression models for handling hierarchical data that produced more accurate estimates of school effects. Techniques pioneered by Aitkin et al. (1986), Raudenbush and Bryk (1986, 1988), and Wilms and Raudenbush (1989) to analyze cross-sectional and longitudinal hierarchical data (i.e., data collected on individual pupils grouped into schools) became employed more widely. Barr and Dreeben (1983) observed that schooling is conducted in layers or levels and that what happens at one level will affect what happens at subsequent levels. Burstein (1980) demonstrated that the individual child should be the primary unit of analysis and then variables measured at other levels (classroom, school, district) should be incorporated into the analytical model.

Later school effects studies looked at the types of curriculum delivered to students and compared general or comprehensive public schools with other types of schools. Typically, these studies looked at schools serving inner-city minority students who tended to be most at risk for school failure. What has been reported from these projects is that schools which accelerated the learning of at-risk students tended to have greater success than schools that concentrated on remediation of these same types of students (Levin and Hopfenberg 1991). Additionally, several studies demonstrated that the previously reported relationship between social background and school achievement is weaker in Catholic schools than in public schools (Coleman et al. 1981, 1982). Also, it was found that students attending Catholic and special-purpose schools tended to have significantly different educational outcomes than their public school peers. That is, the percentage of at-risk students in the Catholic and special purpose schools who graduated from high school, who took the Scholastic Aptitude Test (SAT) and who scored above the mean for their group was greater than for the same types of students in typical public schools (Hill et al. 1990).

Using hierarchical linear modeling (HLM) techniques, Lee and Bryk (1989) identified characteristics of high schools that encouraged academic achievement and promoted an equitable distribution of achievement across diverse social classes. Their results indicated that organizational differences among Catholic and public schools exerted substantial impacts on students' achievements. For example, an equitable distribution of high achievement is enhanced when all students are required to take more academic courses. Additionally, when schools are small and resources unavailable for differentiating the academic program, this tends to promote broader academic achievement across all student groups. These findings supported the contention of other researchers that the normative environment and academic organization found in Catholic and special-interest schools appears to promote academic achievement independent of background variables.

Unfortunately, the use of these multilevel models did not solve all the problems associated with school effects research. Measurement and specification errors and the problem of multicollinearity continued to persist. (Multicollinearity is a problem confronted by statisticians and researchers in which two or more factors, any of which may account for a phenomenon, systematically vary together. In these circumstances, it is not possible to determine the unique contribution of any of these factors to the phenomenon being studied.) However, these new techniques did produce more precise estimates of variance between schools and students, as well as estimates of the effects of background variables in reducing or explaining these variables.

If conviction about the effectiveness of schools in imparting basic skills and knowledge to students has not been strongly supported by data, the other alleged benefits are supported even less. Schools have been credited with certifying people as being eligible for the next level of education. This could be a valuable sorting function, but as high school graduation in the United States has become more dependent on time spent and less on demonstrated achievement, and as admission to college has become more open and less based upon prior achievement, this function has declined in value.

One basic rationale for the education of youngsters has always been the custodial function. Schools keep children off the streets, reduce crime, free parents for work or leisure, and teach children the norms of civil society. The reader may decide if schools still perform these functions, and if so, how valuable they are. Schools have similarly been credited with serving a socialization function: teaching children how to get along, to share, to take turns, to dress, and to fit in. Whether this occurs and, if it does, whether it is a benefit are unclear. If any of these services were provided, both the students and the broader society would be affected. This is also the case with another long-alleged benefit, namely the entertainment services that a school provides for the community around it. These include athletic events, cultural activities, and extended educational programs.

In considering the benefits of precollege education other than providing knowledge and academically related skills and attitudes, it has become clear that many of them have become irrelevant to the mobile, heterogenous, mass-media society of the United States. These benefits were probably much more important at earlier stages in the social and economic development of the country.

3.2 Higher Education

The study of the benefits of higher education provides the opportunity to compare individuals who have achieved different numbers of years of schooling. That is, in addition to comparing those who attended different colleges, one can compare those with high school only to those who attend college without graduating, and to those with Associate of Arts degrees, bachelors' degrees, and postbaccalaureate training.

Economists focus on the private monetary or job- and career-related benefits received from colleges by those who attend and graduate not because they are only concerned with money, but because they want to see whether changes effected by college attendance enhance productivity (i.e., produce human capital) and thereby increase earnings. The questions are whether or not college attendance is likely to result in better jobs and higher earnings, and if so why?

The problem is of interest because the education–work fit has been the main justification for public support of higher education. Yet for the most part, career outcomes represent a private gain which should be purchased with private funds. Social benefits are the economic argument for public support. When the education–work fit seems less favorable, fewer people should be enrolling if labor market returns are all that matter, but subsidy moderates this. Subsidy should not be based on job outcomes, but it has been. Therefore, when the labor market becomes relatively less favorable for college graduates, subsidy declines, even though social benefits may still result.

What are the job-related benefits of higher education? The human capital theory (Schultz 1961) hypothesizes that the duration (quantity) and quality of education an individual obtains contribute to his or her human capital, which leads to greater productive capacity. It is also assumed that production capacity is reflected in higher earnings over a career if not immediately after graduation. An individual's human capital necessarily depends upon factors in addition to education (such as health, motivation, innate ability, and socioeconomic status). Thus the value of education in terms of earnings has been tested empirically by looking at the partial correlation between earnings and the quantity and quality of schooling while holding constant as many other factors that might affect earnings as possible. From the early work of Becker (1983), which looked at highly aggregated census data from 1950, to the later studies of Taubman and Wales (1974), Solmon (1981), Rumberger, (1987), and Murphy and Welch (1989), each of which analyzed a different longitudinal database, the human capital model seems to have been validated: everything else being equal, those with more and better education seem to earn more.

Obviously the earnings–education correlation is always substantially less than perfect. This led Jencks (Jencks et al. 1972) to minimize the value of education for earnings. Jencks argued that "Economic success seems to depend on varieties of luck and on-the-job competence that are only moderately related to family background, schooling or scores on standardized tests . . . . Competence . . . seems in most cases to depend more on personality than on technical skills" (p. 8). Of course, this argument merely points out that other factors that produce human capital are also important.

Other reasons for the imperfect relationship between education and earnings can also be suggested. There may be differences among educational programs in the extent to which they build human capital for the labor force (e.g., engineering courses) and the extent to which they provide consumption benefits unrelated to earning power (perhaps courses in the humanities). Similarly, jobs themselves yield not only monetary benefits, but also nonmonetary advantages. It is possible that advanced education might lead some people to highly desirable jobs that are relatively low-paying, but which have the attraction of providing other benefits such as satisfaction, challenge, and status. As examples, prestigious jobs in government and academe could be cited, which are often held by people who could be earning much more in other settings. The correlation between education and earnings may also break down somewhat when graduates produce a product or service that is not highly valued in the market. When demand for a product or service falls the price it can command also falls. For example, during the 1970s fewer students wanted to study the humanities than in the past. The supply of humanities teachers at that time exceeded the demand for them; therefore the wage rate for people with doctorates in the humanities fell (at least in inflation-adjusted dollars). This occurred even though the physical productivity of doctors in the humanities was not lower than it had been in the past (i.e., they could still teach the same things to the same number of students).

Finally, it is generally agreed that discrimination plays a role in preventing productivity from being reflected in higher earnings. The preference of certain employers for one type of worker (perhaps White males) over other types (perhaps women or minorities) would imply that at equal salaries the White males would be hired rather than equally productive women or minorities. Thus, for the latter groups to be hired by employers who discriminate, they must produce more to earn the same salary or accept lower salaries for equal productivity (Becker 1971). However, readers are warned to be cautious when deciding whether earnings differences are better explained by discrimination or productivity differences.

Some critics of the human capital model argue that the correlation between earnings and education is due to the fact that education, rather than enhancing productivity, serves merely as a screening device (Collins 1979, Dore 1976). One version of this argument claims that the more educated earn more because they are more productive but their productivity is due to nonschool factors. They would have been more productive than those with less education even had they not had as much schooling as they did. All education does is indicate to employers who is more productive. Thus, education is seen as no more than an expensive device for sorting the more from the less productive.

Another version of the screening argument is that employers think that college graduates are more productive even when they are not. This might result in those with more or higher prestige education being given special advantages, such as being put on a "fast track." Then they become more productive and successful even though education did not make them so.

The data, as much as they can, seem to support the argument that education serves to enhance productivity and thereby increases earnings, even though screening is also taking place (Layard and Psacharopoulos 1974, Chiswick 1973). From the mid-1970s the value of educational attainment (years) as a screen declined in the United States. Such a large proportion of college-aged people began to attend college, a college graduate was no longer a special person. Screening possibly then developed on the basis of quality of institution attended, major field of study, and grades.

Following the decline in the income advantage college graduates had over high school graduates in the mid-1970s, Freeman (1976) argued that the United States became an overeducated nation; that is, that too many people were getting too much schooling given the needs of the labor market. Immediately, several criticisms arose of Freeman's approach and of the work of others such as Berg (1971). Witmer (1978), after redoing Freeman's calculations, claimed to have found major errors. There were also problems with the way Berg defined "college level" jobs. Additionally, much of the decline in the high school–college wage gap was due to increases in wages for noncollege attenders working in craft industries or at minimum wage, both of which were irrelevant for people thinking of attending college. The 1980s witnessed a rebound in the rates of return to a college education which seemed to indicate that the experience of the 1970s was a temporary aberration in a general pattern of increasing returns to college education (Murphy and Welch 1989).

The "overeducated American" argument ignored the fact that unemployment for college graduates was substantially lower than for those who had not gone to college. It considered earnings only in the first job after college graduation, thus failing to recognize that if postschool on-the-job training is being acquired by college graduates, initial salaries will be misleading. In this case, the gap between college and high school salaries will widen over the years. Finally, the overeducation argument ignored the substantial nonmonetary benefits of college, which will be discussed below.

The fact remains that the United States' system of higher education has been distinguished by the high proportion of the population that has experienced it. In the 1960s, 45 percent of individuals aged 16–24 who graduated from high school during the preceding 12 months were enrolled in college, with others attending vocational programs in proprietary schools. By the early 1970s, over 50 percent of that group had enrolled, and by 1995 that rose to about 62 percent. There was also the prospect that many of those unable to attend immediately after high school would study at some college during their adult lives. Thus the question of oversupply should not have been unexpected in the American case (Cartter 1976). However, the benefits from college relating to income advantage and social prestige are inherently related to the supply and demand of college-educated workers. Whenever there is greater supply than demand, the price will go down and when there is greater demand and less supply, the price will go up. There were nearly 60 percent more holders of a bachelor's degree (a proxy for supply of college graduates) per dollar of gross domestic product per capita (a proxy for demand) available for jobs in 1976 than in 1960. This pattern reversed itself somewhat by 1995 when there were 6 percent fewer holders of a bachelor's degree per dollar of gross domestic product than in 1976, due to the post-baby-boomers' smaller population cohort attending college.

In the 1980s there was a rapid growth in the rate of return to a college education, due to the slowdown in the growth of the number of college graduates after the baby-boom. Murphy and Welch (1989) reported that "from 1979 to 1986, the earnings differential expanded from 32 percent to about 70 percent, so that by 1986 college/high school earnings differentials were larger

than ever" (p. 17). Again this was the result of the interplay between supply and demand. Between 1979 and 1986 there was a slowdown in the growth of the college population and an increase in the demand for college-educated workers. The college/noncollege relative wage has continued to rise during the early 1990s, but at a slower rate than in the 1980s (Bound and Johnson 1995). This is consistent with the increase in growth of college graduates once again as children of the boomers finished college.

Solmon (1981) asserted that years of schooling still pay off even in times of increasing supply. In college the major subject is important, as are quality of institution attended and grades; that is, college has always mattered even in regard to income. In 1977, 56 percent of 1970 freshmen regarded their jobs as closely related to their major subject, 19 percent as somewhat related, and 25 percent as not at all related. Most who held nonrelated jobs did so voluntarily, but this was less the case in later years. Those voluntarily in unrelated jobs were as satisfied as those in related jobs. Over 55 percent of those who held jobs related to their majors felt that their skills were not fully utilized. This implies that problems of underemployment are independent of the failure of the colleges to provide training that is relevant to work. Very few respondents to the survey were dissatisfied with their jobs. In 1977, 14 percent of 1970 freshmen were dissatisfied —far less than the 80 percent some were predicting —but only those employed full-time were considered. However, there may be a problem of college graduates involuntarily holding part-time jobs. Whether a particular job is a good one depends not only upon its links with education but also upon whether it provides the opportunity to use all one's skills, challenge, status, income, and opportunities for advancement.

Conversely, Rumberger (1986) suggested that additional schooling was not always automatically rewarded with higher earnings. According to Rumberger, schooling that is rewarded tends to be job-specific. That is, when workers acquire training based on their own or an independent judgment of what is needed on the job, that training is rewarded with higher salaries, while other nonjob-specific training may not be so rewarded. According to Rumberger, "This suggests that additional schooling is not completely unproductive, but simply that jobs constrain the ability of workers to fully utilize the skills and capabilities they acquire in school" (p. 46).

In other countries the proportion of the eligible population that has attended college is usually much lower than in the United States. Thus, if everything else were equal, the college graduate in other countries might be less likely to find himself or herself unappreciated in the job market, or forced to take a less prestigious job than those held by previous graduates. However, the problems of overeducation can surely occur despite lower postsecondary participation rates if the requirements of the economic system are for fewer college graduates than are available. This might be the case in many less developed countries (for example, where the agricultural sector dominates or where industry does not require high technology). Additionally, in some less developed countries, large numbers of college graduates study disciplines where demand is low (e.g., arts, letters, humanities) rather than those where demand is high (e.g., science, engineering, and business).

In the United States, it is difficult to argue that any level of saturation at the undergraduate level could result in overeducation in a general sense, because vocational outcomes are such a small part of the total benefits of education at that level. With regard to the job market, what is necessary for the individual might be wasteful for the overall economy (e.g., a bachelor's degree may be required in order to teach fourth-grade history, but there may not be a need for another history teacher). However, other benefits do not have this zero-sum game characteristic: additional enjoyment of classes, respect for democracy, better health habits, or appreciation of culture obtained by one student does not deprive others of receiving the same benefits.

In other countries a college first degree is more likely to serve as the final professional credential. For example, in Brazil even law and medicine are practiced by college graduates without any postbaccalaureate training. To the extent that vocational aims overpower other personal and societal goals for undergraduate education, then mismatches between demand and supply for graduates for various professional fields and disciplines become more of a reason to question the growth in undergraduate education.

Certainly the nonmonetary benefits of college (and education in general) are at least as important as the job-related monetary benefits of college. Perhaps the best summary of the research into educational benefits as changes in individuals and changes in society is provided by Bowen (1977). In his summary "Is Higher Education Worth the Cost?" Bowen begins by pointing out that, "The primary purpose of higher education is to change people in desirable ways. These changes may, in turn, have profound effects on the economy and the society and even on the course of history. But in the first instance the objective is to modify the traits and behavior patterns of individual human beings" (p. 432). These effects may occur in a variety of areas, including creativity, family planning, childcare, quality of schools, appreciation of arts, culture and learning, health service, political participation, understanding of social issues, acceptance of social change, and a sense of common culture and social solidarity.

A second type of social impact "is achieved through the manifold activities that we have called research and public service" (Bowen 1977 p. 445). Universities also serve to preserve the cultural heritage and advance the civilization. In addition, they provide direct community services such as health care, libraries,

museums, dramatic and musical performances, recreational facilities, and a consulting service. Higher education may also contribute to the quest for human equality.

These last benefits are vague, difficult to document, and even more difficult to evaluate. Related impacts of universities on society may be considered negative (e.g., if they produce research which culminates in the development of destructive weapons, if intolerance is the result of certain studies and so on).

Despite some minor shortcomings, Bowen's work has remained an authoritative voice regarding college effects. Indeed, a comparison of Pascarella and Terenzini's (1991) excellent and comprehensive review of the research with Bowen's 1977 work showed remarkably consistent findings. For example, Pascarella and Terenzini reported on college students' development of verbal, quantitative, and subject-matter competence by stating "our own estimates of the average gains in verbal and mathematical skills during college generally concur with those of Bowen" (p. 64). Regarding the personal adjustment and psychological well-being of college graduates they report, "Taken together, these estimates of average change are strikingly similar to the estimated overall change in psychological well-being reported by Bowen" (1977 p. 226). The same consistency is found regarding the attitude and value changes in graduates: "seniors as compared with freshman, place greater emphasis on the intrinsic value of liberal education and less on the instrumental value of education" (Bowen 1977 p. 273); and "estimates of magnitude of decline in traditional religious values are generally consistent with those reported by Bowen" (1977 p. 370).

4. Conclusion

Individuals are different and so all cannot expect to obtain all of the benefits that have been suggested. Some of the benefits become less potent as a level of education becomes less exclusive. There must also be negative impacts of schooling. Cost–benefit analysis must be undertaken by individuals in deciding whether the potential benefits they could receive from attending a particular educational institution are worth the costs. Similarly, society must ask whether the benefits it will receive from allocating public funds for education are worth as much as benefits that would be derived from alternative uses of these funds. The conclusion here is that for most individuals and for society as a whole, schooling is a good investment. However, like most economic goods, the incremental benefits from education probably get increasingly smaller after some point. Because substantial benefits derive from education it must be taken seriously, yet no one would be so rash as to claim that education can solve all of a nation's problems. Education is worth supporting, but too much cannot be expected of it.

See also: Agricultural Productivity and Education; Basic Education: Comparative and International Studies; Education and Development; Education, Occupation, and Earnings; Educational Expansion: Sociological Perspectives; Technological Change and Deskilling

References

Aitkin M A et al. 1986 Statistical modelling issues in school effectiveness studies. *J. Roy. Stat. Soc.* A 149 CD 1–43

Barr R, Dreeben R 1983 *How Schools Work.* University of Chicago Press, Chicago, Illinois

Becker G S 1971 *Economics of Discrimination*, rev. edn. University of Chicago Press, Chicago, Illinois

Becker G S 1983 *Human Capital: A Theoretical and Empirical Analysis, with Special Reference to Education*, 2nd edn. University of Chicago Press, Chicago, Illinois

Berg I 1971 *Education and Jobs: The Great Training Robbery.* Beacon, Boston, Massachusetts

Bound J, Johnson G 1995 What are the causes of rising wage inequality in the United States? *Econ. Policy Rev.* 1(1): 9–17

Bowen H R 1977 *Investment in Learning: The Individual and Social Value of American Higher Education.* Jossey-Bass, San Francisco, California

Burstein L 1980 The analysis of multilevel data in educational research and evaluation. In: Berliner D C (ed.) 1980 *Review of Research in Education.* American Educational Research Association, Washington, DC

Cartter A M 1976 *PhDs and the Academic Labor Market.* McGraw-Hill, New York

Chiswick B R 1973 Schooling, screening and income. In: Solmon L C, Taubman P J (eds.) 1973 *Does College Matter?* Academic Press, New York

Coleman J S, Hoffer T, Kilgore B S 1981 *Public and Private Schools. An Analysis of High School and Beyond: A National Longitudinal Study for the 1980s.* National Center for Educational Statistics, US Department of Education, Washington, DC

Coleman J S, Hoffer T, Kilgore B S 1982 *High School Achievement: Public, Catholic and Private Schools Compared.* Basic Books, New York

Coleman J S, Moynihan D P (eds.) 1966 *On Equality of Educational Opportunity.* National Center for Educational Statistics, Washington, DC

Collins R 1979 *The Credential Society: An Historical Sociology of Education and Stratification.* Academic Press, New York

Denison E F 1962 *The Source of Economic Growth in the United States and the Alternatives Before Us.* Committee for Economic Development, New York

Denison E F 1964 Measuring the contribution of education, and the residual, to economic growth. In: ECD Study Group in the Economics of Education 1964 *The Residual Factor and Economic Growth.* OECD, Paris

Denison E F 1974 *Accounting for United States Economic Growth 1929–1969.* The Brookings Institute, Washington, DC

Denison E F 1984 Accounting for slower growth: An update. In: Kendrick J (ed.) 1984 *International Comparisons of Productivity and Courses of Slowdowns.* Ballinger, Cambridge, Massachusetts

Dore R 1976 *The Diploma Disease: Education, Qualification*

and Development. University of California Press, Berkeley, California

Freeman R B (ed.) 1976 *The Overeducated American.* Academic Press, New York

Hill P T, Foster G E, Gendler T 1990 *High Schools with Character* (R-3944-RC). The Rand Corporation, Santa Monica, California

Jencks C S et al. 1972 *Inequality: A Reassessment of the Effect of Family and Schooling in America.* Basic Books, New York

Layard R, Psacharopoulos G 1974 The screening hypothesis and the returns to education. *J. Pol. Econ.* 82(5): 985–98

Lee V E, Bryk A S 1989 A multilevel model of the social distribution of high school achievement. *Sociol. Educ.* 62(3): 172–92

Levin H M, Hopfenberg W S 1991 Don't remediate accelerate! *Principal* 70(3): 11–13

Madaus G F 1980 *Schooling Effectiveness: A Reassessment of the Evidence.* McGraw-Hill, New York

McPartland J M, Karweit N 1979 Research on educational effects. In: Walberg H J (ed.) 1979 *Educational Environments and Effects: Evaluation Policy, and Productivity.* McCutchan, Berkeley, California

Murphy K, Welch F 1989 Wage premiums for college graduates: Recent growth and possible explanations. *Educ. Researcher* 18(4): 17–26

Oakes J 1985 *Keeping Track: How Schools Structure Inequality.* Yale University Press, New Haven, Connecticut

Pascarella E T, Terenzini P T 1991 *How College Affects Students: Findings and Insights from Twenty Years of Research.* Jossey-Bass, San Francisco, California

Raudenbush S W, Bryk A S 1986 A hierarchical model for studying school effects. *Sociol. Educ.* 59(1): 1–17

Raudenbush S W, Bryk A S 1988 Methodological advances in analyzing the effects of schools and classrooms on student learning. In: American Educational Research Association 1988 *Review of Research in Education.* American Educational Research Association, Washington, DC

Rumberger R W 1987 The impact of surplus schooling on productivity and earnings. *J. Hum. Resources*, 22(1): 24–50

Schultz T W 1961 Investment in human capital. *Am. Econ. Rev.* 51: 1–17

Schultz T W 1963 *The Economic Value of Education.* Columbia University Press, New York

Solmon L C 1981 New findings on the links between college education and work. *High. Educ.* 10(6): 615–48

Solmon L C, Ochsner N L 1978 New findings on the effects of college. In: American Association for Higher Education 1978 *Current Issues in Higher Education.* American Association for Higher Education, Washington, DC

Taubman P, Wales T 1974 *Higher Education and Earnings: College as an Investment and a Screening Device.* Report prepared for the Carnegie Commission on Higher Education and the National Bureau of Economic Research, General Series 101. McGraw-Hill, New York

US Department of Education 1996 *Digest of Education Statistics.* NCES 96–133

Wilms J D, Raudenbush S W 1989 A longitudinal hierarchical linear model for estimating school effects and their stability. *J. Educ. Meas.* 26(3): 209–32

Witmer D 1978 Shall we continue to pursue universal higher education? In: Solmon L C (ed.) 1978 *Reassessing the Link between Work and Education.* Jossey-Bass, San Francisco, California

Conscientization and Mobilization

D. R. Evans

The experience of educators, concerned clergy, and community workers in Latin America produced the realization that traditional approaches to education for adults were largely irrelevant for those who lived in poverty and misery, and, even worse, served to further entrench the structures and power relationships that were the causes of the problems. An alternative form of education was needed, one which allowed the learner to see the situation differently, understand the larger causes, and take personal responsibility to create changes. While many have been involved in the evolution of these ideas, they were crystallized by the thought and writing of Paulo Freire, a Brazilian educator, in his seminal work *Pedagogy of the Oppressed*, which introduced the concept of "conscientization." This and later writings proved enormously influential in the following decades, spreading slowly from Latin America to North America, and then echoed by the work of others in Asia and Africa.

Application of the insights of Freire and others to adult education took many forms, encapsulated by terms such as "conscientization," "nonformal education," "popular education," and "education for social mobilization." The use of these terms is varied and frequently overlapping, although distinctions are often argued fiercely on the basis of the ideological beliefs of proponents.

1. Conscientization

Although the concept of "conscientization" was known and used by other radical Catholics in Brazil before Paulo Freire, the term has come to be synonymous with him and his explication of it as an idea and a process. Mackie (1981) describes Freire's philosophy as an eclectic mixture which was not built up systematically, but which emerged and continues to be shaped through praxis—the continuing cycle of action and reflection. Freire drew upon a variety of European philosophers and from the many radical Catholics writing in the context of Latin America, yet his philosophy originated in his experiences with poor adults in the Third World and was addressed explicitly to the oppressed of the Third World. His pedagogy for adults is grounded in the social reality of the poor and the need to address their reality as the first priority in any approach to adult education.

1.1 Adult Literacy—Learning to Read the World and the Word

Initially, Freire's approach to adult education arose from his experiences with poor adults in Recife,

Brazil in his role as municipal coordinator for adult literacy. There he developed "culture circles" as alternative learning environments for adults where active, critical dialogue could take place. Work with the culture circles evolved into a more fully developed literacy method which can be briefly summarized in a few lines. Working with community members, Freire and his colleagues chose generative themes which reflected the social and political realities of the learners' lives—themes which engaged workers in problematizing their situation. These themes were then captured in a series of generative words which had the emotional impact needed to stimulate discussion and which contained the core phonemes of Portuguese. Typically they chose words with two or three syllables, beginning with words containing simple syllables common to the language such as "*tijolo*" (brick) or "*favela*" (slum). Each of the syllables could then be used to explore the family of syllables so that the "*ti*" in *tijolo* expands into the syllables "*ta te ti to tu*." From these syllables new words can be formed. A total of about 16 or 17 words was sufficient to cover the basic sounds for syllabic languages like Portuguese or Spanish (for a sample list of words, see Freire 1973 pp. 82–84). In Latin America, this approach is known as the "psychosocial method."

The first step, though, was to use a picture or drawing of the concept contained in the word to discuss its meaning in the local context. The picture of a brick provokes discussion of building with bricks, housing as a community problem, and the obstacles to better housing. The word itself was presented only after this discussion took place. He explicitly rejected primers which use an external message rather than the words and thoughts of the learners because he believed that they lead to domesticating rather than liberating education by encouraging uncritical acceptance.

Freire's approach to literacy has stimulated the development of literally hundreds of adaptations to a wide variety of literacy and adult education situations throughout the world. Srinivasan (1977) reports another approach, the Apperception–Interaction Method (AIM), that was used in functional literacy programs in the United States, Thailand, the Philippines, and Turkey. This method uses problem themes from the daily lives of learners, starting with a provocative photograph or drawing complemented by a short drama or narrative to stimulate discussion. A word or phrase is then introduced based on the theme. The Nicaraguan Literacy Crusade of the early 1980s also provides a good example. Miller (1985) describes the evolution of the methodology which used pictures, dialogue, and a series of 23 keywords beginning with the word "*la revolución*."

In many cases, there is tension between the desire to create primers which contain content viewed as essential, particularly in immediate postrevolutionary situations like Nicaragua, and Freire's pedagogy which argues that the themes and the conclusions must come from the learner if they are to be truly liberational. Srinivasan (1977 p. 91) feels similarly that materials must be truly open to local concerns rather than constraining the learners to react to content chosen by the curriculum designers. Most programs confront this tension when they move beyond pilot activities to larger scale implementation.

1.2 Conscientization—Overcoming the Psychology of Oppression

To interpret Freire's theory of conscientization as solely, or even primarily, a method for achieving adult literacy would seriously underestimate his importance. Following in the footsteps of Fromm, Fanon, and Memmi, Freire's theory is a description of the psychology of the oppressed, an analysis of how the oppressed and the oppressor behave, and a pedagogy for freeing both from the structures of oppression.

Conscientization is the humanization of people, transforming them from objects to subjects, from dehumanized individuals trapped in oppressive structures to more fully human beings (see Freire 1970 pp. 27–56). Since both oppressed and oppressor are trapped in the same structure, both are dehumanized and both need to be liberated. Liberation comes about through a painful process of rebirth in dialogue between humans, and between humans and the world. Critical and liberating dialogue must be part of a dialectical process between action and reflection, which Freire calls "praxis." Neither reflection nor action alone is sufficient.

The central point of Freire's philosophy is mirrored in the title of his book—*Pedagogy of the Oppressed* (1970). Oppression cannot be overcome by well-intentioned actions on the part of individual oppressors. Only the oppressed can initiate the process of praxis which has the power to free both themselves and their oppressors. The oppressed must move from seeing themselves as objects to people engaged in the vocation of becoming more fully human. In the process, they will come to understand that the oppressors are also trapped in the same dehumanizing structure. Only the oppressed can free themselves through a process of reflection and action to transform the dehumanizing situation. Conscientization is the process by which the oppressed liberate themselves and their oppressors.

Freire articulates three levels of consciousness which characterize individuals in the struggle to overcome oppression: magical, naive, and critical. In each stage, individuals name (problematize), reflect, and act in characteristic ways which reflect their stage of consciousness (see discussion in Smith 1976). These levels are characterized as follows:

(a) The magical state—conforming—is characterized by problem denial or avoidance, simplistic causality which focuses on things like lack of money or poor health, and inaction justified by fatalism or passively playing "host to the oppressor."

(b) The naive state—reforming—names the problem as individual oppressors who are bad, accepts the oppressor's ideology and explanations for what is essentially a good system, and actively plays "host to the oppressor" by defending them and blaming the oppressed for acting inappropriately.

(c) The critical state—transforming—names the problem as the whole dehumanizing structure, affirms the goodness of the oppressed and their values, and understands the contradictions that trap both the oppressors and the oppressed. The critical individual is self-actualizing, seeking to transform the system through acting as a subject, having faith in one's peers, and working to change the structure.

Conscientization is the process of growth through these stages, although the process is uneven, with individuals often regressing or being in different states simultaneously in different contexts.

Freire's lifetime of writing, speaking, and doing, the veritable library of references and writings which it has inspired, and the legion of followers who have been energized by his insights have all combined to have a significant effect on adult education efforts around the world. Anywhere there is a group which feels oppressed, one is almost certain to find an educational effort informed in part by Freire's analysis of oppression and his vision of a pedagogy which can liberate. These efforts are as much present in the First World—gays and lesbians, racial or ethnic groups, women's groups, native peoples—as they are in the Latin American setting in which Freire first worked.

2. Popular Education

La Belle (1986) documents a conceptual split between consciousness raising, as exemplified by Freire and others, and popular education for structural change. Torres (1990 p. 18) traces popular education back to at least the socialist education process in Mexico during the 1930s. Popular education, then and now, is characterized as being oriented toward political development, is highly participative and mobilizing with an emphasis on social change, and is sensitive to the structure of power in society. Freirean approaches became so well-known in the 1970s that they tended to be co-opted into official, government adult education programs which kept the rhetoric without being liberatory in nature. Partly in response to the perceived failure of consciousness raising and the nonformal education programs which sometimes incorporated it, popular education has gained new prominence, emphasizing social class, participatory organizations, and strategies for the transformation of society.

Current popular education is heavily influenced by the Marxist perspective of Antonio Gramsci, particularly his vision of cross-class coalitions to support change movements rooted in the lower classes and his concept of organic intellectuals—peasants and workers who serve as linkages between concrete knowledge and general knowledge, local and national issues, and social formation and the mode of production (Fals-Borda 1981). Gramsci argued for the organization of workers to counteract the hegemony of the state and its support for the interests of the dominant classes. The focus of popular education is therefore on preparing the lower classes to take advantage of opportunities to exercise power in an organized manner that will alter the balance of power in capitalist societies. This emphasis is in contrast to the more individualistic psychological and intellectual awareness produced by consciousness raising efforts. Popular education recognizes that consciousness raising is an important component of social change, but that it is inadequate on its own. Current popular education activities often begin with some form of participatory investigation by the community (referred to also as "action research," "participatory action research," or "participatory education"). Using a dependency perspective, Fals-Borda, for example, says that knowledge is produced by and reflects the class interests of the dominant groups. He promotes four techniques: collective research by the group to gather information, a critical recovery of local history from the perspective of the people, valuing and using popular culture to support social mobilization of the people, and production and diffusion of new knowledge generated by these methods. The organizations and the awareness created by participatory research constitutes the foundation for ongoing education and action for social change.

A typical example of a popular education activity is provided by the Learning Workshops Program in Chile which has been in operation since 1977 and has served over 10,000 children (Vaccarro 1990). The Learning Workshops are alternative learning centers for poor children who have dropped out of school. The workshops are run by community adults who serve as monitors and coordinators. They are trained with a participatory process which leads them to problematize the reality which has created the poverty and the children who are unable to learn in school. The workshop becomes an activity which is "appropriated" by the community as one way in which they can begin to transform their reality. The process of appropriation begins immediately, when the initial proposal offered

by an external agent is subject to discussion and modification by the participants and grows throughout the process until they become independent.

La Belle (1986 pp. 210–14) uses three goals to assess the outcomes of popular education: development of local participatory organizations, forging of linkages across and within social classes to generate power for the poor, and designing strategies to shift concentrations of power to the poor. He concludes that the evidence to date of success with popular education is limited: not being noticeably more successful than earlier community development approaches in building nondependent, participatory organizations, making some gains in forging within class alliances, and having little impact on power concentrations. However, the support for popular education approaches remains strong, partly because it provides a means for the oppressed to participate effectively in local development.

3. Conclusion

Conscientization and popular education are unique as development approaches because they originated in the Third World and speak from the realities of that setting, not from those of the First World. The rich ferment generated by peasants, workers, local leaders, intellectuals, and scholars, initially in Latin America but now increasingly throughout the world, has forced the development industry to recognize the social and human costs of dominant approaches to development. Yet within conscientization and popular education tensions continue to emerge between local generation of knowledge and the use of these techniques as a means for mobilizing a society in support of new national ideologies. The role of conscientization and social mobilization will continue striving to build effective linkages between micro-level and macro-level development, trying to balance national economic power with the rights and needs of people. For many knowledgeable and concerned educators, these approaches offer the only hopeful alternatives.

See also: Acquisition of Empowerment Skills; Adult Education for Development; Marxism and Educational Thought

References

Fals-Borda O 1981 The challenge of action research. *Development* 23(1): 55–61
Freire P 1970 *Pedagogy of the Oppressed*. Herder and Herder, New York
Freire P 1973 *Education for Critical Consciousness*. Seabury Press, New York
La Belle T J 1986 *Nonformal Education in Latin America and the Caribbean: Stability, Reform or Revolution?* Praeger, New York

Mackie R 1981 Contributions to the thought of Paulo Freire. In: Mackie R (ed.) 1981 *Literacy and Revolution: The Pedagogy of Paulo Freire*. Continuum, New York

Miller V 1985 *Between Struggle and Hope: The Nicaraguan Literacy Crusade*. Westview Press, Boulder, Colorado

Smith W A 1976 *The Meaning of Conscientizacao: The Goal of Paulo Freire's Pedagogy*. The Center for International Education, University of Massachusetts, Amherst, Massachusetts

Srinivasan L 1977 *Perspectives on Nonformal Adult Learning: Functional Education for Individual, Community, and National Development*. World Education, New York

Torres C A 1990 *The Politics of Nonformal Education in Latin America*. Praeger, New York

Vaccaro L 1990 Transference and appropriation in popular education interventions: A framework for analysis. *Harv. Educ. Rev.* 60(1): 62–78

Further Reading

Arnold A et al. 1991 *Educating for a Change. A Handbook for Community Educators*. Between the Lines/Doris Marshall Institute for Education and Action, Toronto

Barndt D 1989 *Naming the Moment: Political Analysis for Action: A Manual for Community Groups*. The Jesuit Centre, Toronto

de Kadt E 1970 *Catholic Radicals in Brazil*. Oxford University Press, Oxford

Fals-Borda O, Rahman M A (eds.) 1991 *Action and Knowledge: Breaking the Monopoly with Participatory Action-Research*. Apex Press, New York and Intermediate Technology Publications, London

Freire P 1972 *Cultural Action for Freedom*. Penguin, Harmondsworth

Freire P 1978 *Pedagogy in Process: The Letters to Guinea-Bissau*. Seabury Press, New York and Writers and Readers Publishing Cooperative, London

La Belle T J 1987 From consciousness raising to popular education in Latin America and the Caribbean. *Comp. Educ. Rev.* 31(2): 201–17

Magendzo S 1990 Popular education in nongovernmental organizations: Education for social mobilization. *Harv. Educ. Rev.* 60(1): 49–61

Zachariah M 1986 *Revolution through Reform: A Comparison of Sarvodaya and Conscientization*. Praeger Greenwood, New York

Education and Development

L. J. Saha and I. Fägerlind

The relationship between education and development has been the center of much discussion and controversy since the 1950s. Since that time, the conviction that education, in its formal form, makes a positive, and indeed an essential, contribution to the development of countries has shifted from unbridled optimism during the 1950s and 1960s to guarded hope and even despair in the 1990s (Fägerlind and Saha 1989). What was once thought to be a simple cause-and-effect relationship is now seen to be a highly complex one, and contingent upon many factors, not the least being the very understanding of education and of development (Saha 1995).

This entry will define education and development and discuss the changing nature of opinion about these two concepts. This will be followed by an examination of the various dimensions of national development and how education is related to each. Finally, some of the main issues in the understanding of the link between education and development will be addressed.

1. Education as an Agent of Change and Development

In the debates about whether and how education contributes to the development of a society there is often a neglect of what specifically the two concepts mean. With regard to development, the word is most often understood as economic development. For example, economists such as Psacharopoulos and Woodhall (1985) and Todaro (1989) define development as the improvement of a country's productive capacity. Although they acknowledge the importance of political and social factors in addition to the economic, these are seen as important primarily insofar as they help or hinder economic development.

Todaro (1989) added that development, particularly in the 1950s and 1960s, has "traditionally meant the capacity of a national economy, whose initial economic condition has been more or less static for a long time, to *generate and sustain* an annual increase in its gross national product at rates of perhaps 5 to 7% or more"(p. 86). Other writers, however, have argued that development is multifaceted, and includes changes in social structures and institutions, changes in social attitudes, values, and behaviors, and finally changes toward social and political equality and the eradication of poverty.

1.1 Definition of Development

Notions of how societies change and develop are not new or novel to current debates. From Classical Antiquity, through the Enlightenment, right up to modern times, there have always been ideas and theories about how societies change and develop. At the least, notions of development have included the realization of potential, irrespective of what that potential might be.

In the following discussion, development is defined in terms of three dimensions: (a) economic, (b) social/cultural, (c) political. As used here, economic development means the increase in the efficiency of the production system of a society. Social/cultural development includes changes in attitudes, values, and behaviors. Finally, political development is understood to mean the equal distribution of power and the absence of domination of any one group over another. Political development thus includes political participation, access to political positions, and the development of national integration, cohesion, and identity (Fägerlind and Saha 1989, Saha 1995).

1.2 Definition of Education

In this broader definition of development it is important to emphasize first the distinction between formal, informal, and nonformal education. Each of these is related differently to the process of development, and each type of education requires different types of policies in terms of education and development goals and strategies. Second, it is also important to distinguish between basic literacy, primary, secondary, and tertiary education. The strength of the relationship between these different levels of education and the development of a society requires specification. Finally, an enduring debate in formulating education policies for development is whether academic or vocational education programs are more appropriate for development strategies. The following sections most often refer to primary and secondary education with respect to development outcomes, but do not intend to preclude other forms of education from being considered in the development context. Some of these other forms of education and their relevance for development are addressed later in this entry.

2. Education and Economic Development

2.1 The Neoclassical View

The most common understanding of education and development is in terms of economic development. Models of economic growth have been dominant since the emergence of the eighteenth-century theories of progress of Adam Smith, John Stuart Mill, and others. Theories of economic progress agree that one, but not the main, component of progress is the human dimension, for example, the quality of the workforce and the skills that it possesses.

The underlying assumptions in the link between education and economic development are those of human capital theory, whereby any improvement in the health, skills, or motivation of the workforce are seen to improve the productivity of workers. Insofar as education brings about improvements in the quality of the human population, it is seen as a contribution to the economic growth of a country.

The economists who hold this view cite considerable evidence which they regard as supportive. For example, a review of 31 studies of rural areas showed that farmers with an educational attainment of four years increased their productivity by 8.7 percent (Lockheed et al. 1980). Although it is difficult to locate studies of the impact of education on the productivity of factory workers in single countries, the evidence available reported by Haddad et al. (1990) also points out that one consequence of higher levels of education is the opportunity to change to jobs with higher skill demands and incomes.

At an aggregate level Psacharopoulos (1985, 1994) has provided perhaps the most comprehensive evidence that investment in education does result in forms of economic growth. If one assumes that economic development can be defined in terms of rates of return, then his studies since the early 1970s merit attention. Beginning with a study of 32 countries in 1973, Psacharopoulos, by the mid-1990s, was able to demonstrate rates-of-return to investment in education for 78 countries. His findings show that in developing countries the social rates of return to primary schooling were between 17.9 and 24.3 percent (depending on region), compared to 12.8–18.2 percent and 11.2–12.3 percent for secondary and higher education, respectively. These figures were higher than the 14.4, 10.2, and 8.7 percent returns, respectively, for OECD countries, which clearly indicate declining returns with increasing levels of development (Psacharopoulos 1994).

However, in assessing the contribution of education to economic development it is necessary to take into account the difference between individual rates of return and social rates of return. Education may benefit the careers of individuals more than the careers of countries. In this respect Psacharopoulos's findings are even more interesting, for the rates of return to individuals are on the whole greater than those to society, and the discrepancies are greater for the higher education level than for the primary school level. Therefore, while it is appropriate to focus attention on the social rates of return to investment in education, it is also important to keep in mind the individual rates of return, as the latter may occur partly at the expense of the former.

Following his most recent analysis, Psacharopoulos summarized the implications of his findings as follows:

> The results of the update are fully consistent with and reinforce earlier patterns. Namely primary education continues to be the number one investment priority in developing countries, educating females is marginally more profitable than educating males, the academic secondary school curriculum is a better investment than the technical/vocational track, and the returns to education obey the

same rules as investment in conventional capital, i.e. they decline as investment is expanded. (Psacharopoulos 1994 p.1335)

Furthermore, Psacharopoulos repeated his conclusion from earlier studies that private rates of return to higher education represent a private advantage to university graduates because of the public subsidy of this level of education.

The use of rates of return as a guide to educational policy and investment has been controversial, in particular since the World Bank's 1995 policy review *Priorities and Strategies for Education* (World Bank 1995), where it was seen to have been endorsed. Bennell (1996), for example, has argued that the data and methods of the approach are flawed, the findings are too inconsistent, and that forward-looking education and development policies based exclusively on outcomes is inappropriate. (For a discussion of rates-of-return and policy see the special issue of *International Journal of Educational Development*, July 1996.)

2.2 Alternative Views

There are some economists who suggest that the relationship between education and development is not as straightforward as is implied by the neoclassicists. In the late 1960s Coombs (1968) argued that the expansion of educational facilities would not necessarily lead to economic growth, but rather to an economic crisis brought about by the costs of sustaining larger but inappropriate educational structures. More than a decade later Coombs's (1985) argument was more complex but not appreciably different.

In the late 1970s, Weiler (1978) called into question the priorities that the classical and neoclassical models of education and economic growth assumed. He questioned the notion that educational expansion would automatically lead to economic growth. He suggested that issues of equity, the relationship between education and work, and educational reform were among the three most important issues related to choice in educational policy-making, and that it is misleading to assume that investment in education will necessarily lead to economic growth.

The criticisms continued into the late 1980s and early 1990s. Blaug (1985) argued that the "golden years" of the economics of education ended in the early 1970s; since then there has been a realization that other factors besides the market affect changes in society. Blaug suggested that economists should direct their attention to the "screening hypothesis," the "incomplete employment contract," and labor market segmentation for explanations as to why educational expansion had not resulted in the level, or type, of economic growth desired. In essence, he argued that explanations about the link between education and development should include institutional and sociological factors in addition to economic factors.

Klees (1989) and Easton and Klees (1990) have argued that there are at least two alternatives to the human capital perspective in conceptualizing the relationship between education and economic development. The first is the institutionalist approach, whereby attention is directed to the patterns of social behavior that shape supply and demand for education (rather than the reverse), and the use to which it is put. In this context labor market segmentation and internal labor markets have been seen as important explanatory variables for the failure of investment in education to bring about the desired results (Easton and Klees 1990). The second is the radical economic perspective, or neo-Marxist political economy, which focuses on the ways that education leads to the reproduction of social inequalities, and the detrimental effects that these processes have on economic growth. Authors such as Bowles and Gintis (1976) and Carnoy and Levin (1985) have suggested that investment in education can and does have negative effects on economic growth. The failure of economists to take these factors into account leads to educational policies that result in more problems than are solved. In other words, educational expansion does not necessarily lead to economic growth.

2.3 Conclusions on Education and Economic Development

The belief that educational expansion will necessarily lead to economic growth is problematic. Although the notion of investment in education as human capital has dominated policy and planning since the 1960s, there is an emerging consensus that education may also have negative effects on economic growth. The problem is one of perspective and the resulting policies and plans, not of whether education has effects on the economy. Clearly the issues are related to questions of what kind of education, what kind of economic growth, and economic growth for whom? In spite of much research and debate, the links between education and the economy are not fully understood, and it would be erroneous to assume that consensus on this issue exists among academics and policymakers.

3. Education and Social Development

A preoccupation with the economic dimensions of development overlooks other ways in which education contributes to the development of a country. Social aspects of development may, in many respects, equal the economic in importance. Social dimensions of development include factors such as quality of life, modernity in attitudes, values, and beliefs, and the satisfaction of basic human needs. When these are not met, the effects of economic development on a country may be attenuated or blocked altogether. It is essential to take into account the ways in which education may or may not influence these factors to obtain a broader perspective on the overall relationship between education and development.

3.1 Education and Modernization

Although there is disagreement about the meaning and usefulness of the concept of modernization, largely because it is thought to be imprecise, multidimensional, and oriented toward the West, it has nevertheless been the object of much research. Furthermore, much of the policy and planning in the area of education and development, at least implicitly, assumes a modernization perspective.

Much of the research on modernization has been based on the definitions and measures of Inkeles, who first attempted to operationalize the notion of the "modern man" (Inkeles and Smith 1974). Following Inkeles and Smith, a modern person is characterized by the following: (a) openness to new experience; (b) readiness for social change; (c) awareness of diversity in attitudes and opinions, but the disposition to hold one's own views; (d) being fact-oriented in forming opinions; (e) focusing on the present and the future rather than the past; (f) possessing a sense of personal efficacy; (g) orientation to long-term planning; (h) trust in social institutions and in individuals; (i) placing a premium on technical skill; (j) showing high regard for education; (k) respect for the dignity of others; (l) understanding the logic underlying production and industry.

The basic thesis of Inkeles and others is that the path to modern development cannot occur without modern citizens. Furthermore, modernization theorists hold that people do not become modern except by participating in modern institutions, the chief of which are education (schools) and industry (factories).

There is evidence to support the notion that schools are important and effective modernizing institutions. People who attain higher levels of education (or who achieve at higher levels), also have higher levels of educational and occupational aspirations, less adherence to traditional customs and beliefs, an openness to new experiences, a willingness to migrate, and a reduction of family ties.

One of the early studies of modernization in which education played a part is found in Lerner (1964), who argued that that adults in the Middle East who had attained at least a secondary school education had higher levels of psychic empathy, that is, the ability to adjust efficiently to continually changing environments. Similar relationships between education and modernization were found in Mexico and Brazil. If one includes the notion of political interest and awareness as an indicator of modernization, Almond and Verba (1965) found that higher levels of education resulted in higher levels of political interest among respondents in the United States, United Kingdom, Germany, Italy, and Mexico. Inkeles and Smith (1974) found strong correlations between educational attainment and individual modernity in their study of adults in

Argentina, Chile, East Pakistan (Bangladesh), India, Israel, and Nigeria. The correlations were consistently higher than those between modernity and both exposure to mass media and occupational experience. In other words, education was the strongest modernizing agent of the three factors. Subsequent studies have reinforced these earlier findings.

Finally, in a study of the comparative effects of education and the mass media (in particular the Western cinema) on modernization, Delacroix and Ragin (1978) argued that the school is a domestically based modernizing institution while the mass media may or may not be. In their study of 49 less-developed countries, they concluded that the school had the potential to modernize without Westernizing, and that countries with strong state-sponsored programs (mobilizing regimes) used education as a modernizing agent more effectively than states with weaker programs.

3.2 Education and Modernization: A Critique

One of the important critiques of modernization as related to education is whether schooling inevitably leads to modernity. Armer and Youtz (1971) were among the first to suggest that under certain circumstances, schooling could have a traditionalizing rather than modernizing effect, and that it is the school curriculum rather than the school organization that accounts for this effect. Studies of Koranic schools have supported this notion; Wagner and Lofti (1980) found that Koranic schools actually inhibit the acquisition of modern values. Schools seem most successful as traditionalizing mechanisms in countries that have most strongly resisted foreign domination, such as Morocco, Nigeria, and Indonesia (Wagner 1985).

A further criticism of the modernization hypothesis is that many studies of modernity are based on attitude and value questionnaire items which are themselves similar to those espoused by Western-style schools. Thus studies of educational attainment and modernization are in fact studies of school learning generally. Second, because the school is a selective institution, it may be that the acquisition of modern values is due to factors other than the school itself. Persons already predisposed to the acquisition of modern values are the same as those predisposed to acquire more schooling.

Finally, the schooling and modernity thesis rests on the assumption that modernization inevitably leads to development. However, modernization can be detrimental to development. The "brain drain" of educated and skilled persons from developing countries, the disruption of social relationships as a result of the modernizing process, the destruction of useful traditional social institutions, and the creation of a modernized elite who are out of touch with the general population are but a few of the negative consequences of modernization on social development. When education produces a negative form of modernization in a society, then education can also have a negative impact on the social development of a country.

3.3 Education, Quality of Life, and Basic Human Needs

Another aspect of social development is quality of life and the meeting of basic human needs. When there are major disparities in the distribution of material goods —the lack of adequate food, shelter, and clothing— large proportions of populations are unable to contribute to the development process. Although education may not have a direct effect on the redistribution of resources, it can inhibit this process. For example, a study of the 32 states of Mexico concluded that literacy level was related to the provision of basic needs such as the eradication of infant mortality, nutrition, clean water, and healthcare. Furthermore it was argued that Mexico would lag behind other less developed countries in per capita income until these basic needs were met (Wood 1988).

The relationship between education and quality of life, and the meeting of basic human needs, parallels that of modernization in that both focus on changing people. However, they differ in that modernization involves social–psychological changes whereas a focus on quality of life and the meeting of basic human needs involves change in the physical and social conditions of the population. The impact of education on physical and social conditions is less direct than its impact on attitudes and values. It is not clear how an increase in educational level will necessarily result in more equitable distribution of physical and social conditions, particularly if higher levels of educational attainment are concentrated in a small selective elite group in society. In this respect, the improvement in quality of life and the meeting of basic human needs may depend on the level of political development in a country.

4. Education and Political Development

Political development can be defined in terms of high levels of political integration (i.e., high solidarity and low levels of conflict) and political participation (i.e., high levels of mobilization, such as voting and other forms of decision-making). These processes include political socialization, the preparation for political leadership, and political integration and the development of national political consciousness. Political development, in the form of political participation and the sharing of political power, may provide the "sufficient cause" for the link between education and economic and social development to occur.

4.1 Education, Political Socialization, and Citizenship

The importance of education for the inculcation of political attitudes, values, and behavior has been extensively researched (e.g., Renshon 1977). However, there are other important agents of political socialization which also merit attention, such as the media and the family. Research on the relative effects of these three agents of political socialization is not clear. Also unclear is the extent to which learning about politics and citizenship may occur differently in developed and less developed countries, or in different cultural settings.

While it is generally assumed that political socialization is functional for system maintenance (i.e., maintaining the status quo), it may be more correct to assume system persistence, that is, system maintenance plus change (Nathan and Remy 1977). Torney-Purta and Schwille (1986) have argued that no industrialized country has had complete success in imparting coherent and consistent civic values, partly because many desired values are in fact incompatible, such as democratic values (tolerance and equality) and support for the national government (national patriotism and trust in government). Furthermore, in some industrialized countries (the United States and United Kingdom) there is emphasis on individual success while in others (Japan, Greece, and Germany) security is seen as important. Ichilov (1991) reported that in Israel the effects of the school on knowledge about politics and democratic citizenship orientations are not uniform. Students who participate in class discussions, who are in academic rather than vocational programs, who are males of eastern ethnic origin, and who are members of disadvantaged groups are more affected by school experiences in the acquisition of these characteristics.

Ultimately, the effect of education on political socialization explains how societies change as well as how they persist. Because political learning occurs differently in countries with different structural characteristics, schools in some less developed countries socialize students toward political change rather than political stability, in spite of the official curriculum of the school or national ideology. This was the case in Kenya and Tanzania, where students rated developmental and modernizing problems as more important than the preservation of customs and tradition. Likewise in a comparative study of Colombia and the United States, it was found that American students held favorable political dispositions toward their government, while the opposite was true for Colombian students (Nathan and Remy 1977). Finally, it can happen that the political values taught in school may openly conflict with those of the political leadership, as Harber (1984) found in his study of the Hausa in Nigeria.

Thus education plays an important role in the political socialization of young people. However, the outcomes of that socialization process may support tradition or it may favor change and development.

4.2 Education and Political Leadership

One aspect of political socialization concerns the selection and preparation of political leaders. Sometimes political leaders are conservative and act to maintain the economic, social, and political system; at other times, they are major agents of change.

Although education systems are the normal avenue to political leadership, there are other avenues, such as the military, religion, or tradition. In many countries certain schools are known as the training grounds for elites, as in the United Kingdom and the United States.

In less developed countries the recruitment and training of political leadership are more problematic. Latukefu (1988) argued that in Papua New Guinea the traditional elite existed before the formal education system was established, and selection was based on knowledge about deities, mythology, and folklore. The modern elite, on the other hand, are products of the education system and follow a lifestyle very different from that of most of the population. But elite schools, by transmitting modern knowledge, ensure a claim to future elite status (Smith and Bray 1988).

However, if the gap between the elite and the general population is too great, there is a greater possibility of political instability. Thus the role of education in the preparation of political leadership includes both recruitment and selection for elite status; at the same time it ensures that elites maintain contact with the general population and helps to determine whether the elite is conservative or change-oriented. These aspects of the relationship between education and the development of political leadership are less well-known.

4.3 Education and Nation-building

The third aspect of political development to which education contributes concerns nation-building. Nation-building, in particular, refers in part to the development of a national identity and national consciousness. This process is closely linked to the legitimation of center-formation and the creation of a national culture. This requires the establishment of a national consensus regarding the political system itself. In addition to political socialization, education promotes citizenship and loyalty through the use of national symbols such as the flag, a national song or anthem, or a constitution, a monarch or other highly visible political leader (real or symbolic). The formation of the nation-state requires the breaking down of regional loyalties and identities, and their replacement with national loyalties and identities.

To the extent that less developed societies often experience weak levels of political consensus, high levels of regional or tribal loyalties, and high levels of tension and conflict, the importance of political development may enjoy equal priority to that of economic and social development. In such societies the expansion of education often serves to incorporate members into the state through the bestowal of citizenship. To this extent, the emergence of, and participation in a mass education system has been called a baptism "in a national history, a written language, national culture, and the mysteries of technical culture" (Meyer and Rubinson 1975 p. 146). By incorporating the individual into the nation-state, education strengthens the state and its institutions.

However, while education can serve as an agent for nation-building, it can also bring about divisions and conflict in society. Some writers have focused attention on education as a commodity that has often been unequally distributed in society, and thus has served as a source of advantage, of exclusion from social goods, and of social division rather than social integration and national consensus. Examples of this disintegrative effect of education have been documented in Nigeria, Kenya, and other developing countries.

Likewise, if education operates as an agent of political consensus and nation-building, then the most educated members of society should also be the most loyal and the most well-integrated. However, the pervasiveness of student activism in many societies, and the oppositional nature of many student movements, suggests that the integrative effect of education may be more problematic than is sometimes acknowledged. Nevertheless, as members of the educated elite, students are often nationalistic in their opposition to governments, particularly where those governments are totalitarian or controlled by outside interests, such as many former colonial regimes were. Thus, even student movements, either of the left or the right, can be seen as agents in the process of political development (Altbach 1991).

Like other aspects of education and political development, education may be a necessary but not sufficient condition for development to occur. One factor not often taken into account in the relationship between education and political development is the extent to which political systems actually control and structure the nature of the educational system.

4.4 Education as a Political Product

Political systems can shape the curriculum, the forms of assessment, discipline, and also the extent to which young people participate or leave the school system. In all societies decisions about education are made on the basis of what is expected from the schools. Whether vocational or academic programs are emphasized often depends on the skills desired or required by government decree in response to needs of the economic system.

The development status of a country is an important determinant of the shape of an educational system. The amount of funding available, the strength of traditional values, the extent to which the economy is based on agriculture or industry, are important inputs into what is expected of schools. Another important determinant is whether the economy is capitalist or socialist. Although the rapid collapse of many socialist economies in the early 1990s might suggest that socialism is not a viable economic form, it nevertheless made unique demands on educational systems, as does capitalism. Socialist education has been identified as more collectivity-oriented, more vocational, and more ideological than its capitalist counterpart.

While education can contribute to the development of a country in the ways described above, it can also be controlled by many aspects of the system. The interrelationship between education and its political, economic, and social system remains an important area for further research attention.

5. Issues in Education and Development

There are a number of issues that are likely to dominate education and development policies and strategies well into the twenty-first century. These will be briefly described in the final section of this entry.

5.1 Literacy

Literacy has always been associated with levels of development. Bowman and Anderson (1973) argued that a literacy rate of 40 percent is necessary but not sufficient for economic growth. Furthermore, high levels of industrialization are thought to require literacy levels of 70 to 80 percent. Although literacy rates remain low in many less developed countries, literacy campaigns and programs received high priority during the 1970s and 1980s in many newly independent countries such as Mozambique and Angola, and postrevolutionary countries such as Cuba and Nicaragua. These campaigns have served both developmental and ideological purposes, for the process of learning to read and write has often also involved learning about the social and economic goals of the new governments.

The problems related to literacy programs are those of sustaining effort until literacy goals are achieved for all members of society and literacy reaches a level where the gains will not be lost. A second problem concerns the maintenance of a literate environment, which includes the availability of newspapers and other reading materials. Finally, the priorities in literacy programs are such that often females and rural dwellers are the last to be targeted, the result being that in many less developed countries they remain the least literate and the most disadvantaged.

5.2 Gender Inequality

Women and girls have lagged behind men in literacy and educational attainments in virtually all developing countries. Furthermore, the disparity between women and men is increasing. According to Stromquist (1990), of the 154 million new illiterates in the world between 1960 and 1985, 133 million, or 86.4 percent were women. Women constitute one-third of the world's official paid labor force, they grow almost half the world's food, they perform most of the world's domestic work, and they provide more healthcare than all health services combined. Yet, in many countries, women cannot own land, they often work a double day,

and in many countries they do not enjoy equal political participation (Fägerlind and Saha 1989).

In spite of unequal educational participation and attainments, Psacharopoulos (1985) argued that "expanding the provision of school places to cover women is not only equitable but socially efficient as well" (p. 592). There are in many societies, however, cultural and institutional obstacles to the attainment of gender equality, against females as participants in the process of development and as recipients of the gains from development. With respect to barriers to education, The World Bank Policy Paper *Enhancing Women's Participation in Economic Development* (1994) identified the following: (1) low investments in women's education and health, (2) poor access for women to services and assets, (3) legal and regulatory barriers, and (4) the continuation of women's dual roles at home and at the marketplace.

The barriers are even more evident at the higher education level. In spite of considerable gains at the primary and secondary education levels, the gender gap at the higher education level remains pervasive. Subbarao et al. (1994), for example, have noted the following as contributing to low female participation rates in higher education: (1) low secondary school enrollments, (2) high dropout rates among females before the end of secondary school, and (3) the low levels of service and manufacturing oportunities which may discourage parents to send daughters to university because no job opportunities are seen at the end.

The equal education of women in all countries represents an important development objective, but one that has often been neglected. Although important gains continue to be made, the inequalities are sometimes subtle. Both as a development resource, and also in terms of justice, gender equity remains a major issue in educational issues that purport to promote development.

5.3 Vocational and Academic Education

The controversy about the advantages of vocational or academic secondary school curricula for development is largely related to attempts to match schooling with the needs of developing economies. The topic had its origins in Foster's (1966) contention that vocational schooling would never contribute to development goals as long as the academic curriculum was preferred for its employment prospects. Thus an enduring difficulty in many countries is the establishment of a curriculum that will provide needed labor force skills, and one that is also consistent with popular social demand.

The major difficulty with the coexistence of vocational and academic curricula is that they relate to two occupational sectors. They therefore tend to institutionalize and maintain inequalities in a society. While it is generally agreed that technical skills at all levels are needed in both agricultural and industrial economies, as long as the modern industrial sector is disproportionally rewarded, attempts to establish and promote vocational education will encounter difficulty.

Between 1950 and 1975, Benavot (1983) found that vocational education had declined on a global scale, a trend he associated with increasing emphasis on egalitarian ideologies. However, Psacharopoulos (1994) found that the social rate of return for technical/vocational education is lower (10.6 percent) than the rate of return for academic/general education (15.5 percent). In a survey of 21 studies, a World Bank report concluded that vocational education is not only more expensive than general education, but may not be the most cost-effective way of imparting desired technological skills (Haddad et al. 1990). For the latter, short-term training programs in institutes and firms may be the better alternative.

Vocational education remains an attractive, if not controversial, solution to the production of skills needed by many developing economies. Furthermore, it appears suitable for students not equipped for academic educational programs. However, in terms of social inequalities and adaptability to rapid change, it remains unclear which type of education contributes most to economic, social, and political development.

5.4 Equity and Efficiency

An issue facing all countries concerns decisions regarding equity and efficiency. Should emphasis be placed on keeping as many young people in school as long as possible, or should attention be directed mainly to those with proven ability to succeed to higher levels of schooling? The two processes are interrelated. At a global level, about 15 percent of all primary and secondary school students are repeaters, and as much as 20 percent of education budgets is spent on repeaters and future dropouts (Haddad et al. 1990).

The efficiency of schooling can be raised by improving inputs. Studies have shown that factors such as teacher quality, textbooks, homework, and time spent in school can improve student achievement (Saha 1983, Fuller 1987). However, it is not clear as to which inputs are most cost-effective, and because the teaching-learning process is complex, no one input alone will make a large impact on improvement on student performance. Nevertheless, the variation between schools in less developed countries is great enough to justify raising the quality of any of the inputs in order to raise performance substantially (Haddad et al. 1990).

6. Conclusion

There are other areas which are important in understanding the link between education and development, for example, adult education and higher education (Saha 1995, 1996) (see *Adult Education for Develop-*

ment and *Sociology of Higher Education*) These areas are beginning to receive the attention they deserve in studies of the relationship between education and development. In addition, new interpretations of development are emerging which include feminist, postcolonial and postmodernist theoretical perspectives, and these will have implications for understanding the role of education in a development context (Crush 1995, Marchand and Parpart 1995)

Overall, the evidence for the impact of education on economic, social, and political development is sufficient to dispel the skepticism that occurred in the late 1970s. However, the relationship is too complex to assume that any investment in education will produce the desired results. It is possible to overinvest in education, or to invest in the wrong kind of education. Because of expanding technologies and knowledge, it is virtually impossible for a country to pursue development policies without providing for an educated population. Education is a major agent for development, but only if it is adapted and used in a manner appropriate to the development needs of a particular country.

See also: Basic Education: Comparative and International Studies; Benefits of Education; Educational Expansion: Sociological Perspectives; Gender and Education; Institutional Approach to the Study of Education; Postliteracy: Concepts and Policies; Social Equality and Educational Planning in Developing Nations; Technological Change and Education

References

Almond G A, Verba S 1965 *The Civic Culture: Political Attitudes and Democracy in Five Nations: An Analytic Study*. Little, Brown & Co., Boston, Massachusetts

Altbach P G 1991 Student political activism. In: Altbach P G (ed.) 1991 *International Higher Education: An Encyclopedia*, Vol. 1. Garland, New York

Armer M, Youtz R 1971 Formal education and individual modernity in an African society. *Am. J. Sociol.* 76 (4): 604–26

Benavot A 1983 The rise and decline of vocational education. *Sociol. Educ.* 56 (2): 63–76

Bennell P 1996 Using and abusing rates of return: a critique of the World Bank's 1995 Education Sector Review. *Int. J. Educ. Dev.* 16(3): 235–48

Blaug M 1985 Where are we now in the economics of education? *Econ. Educ. Rev.* 4 (1): 17–28

Bowles S, Gintis H 1976 *Schooling in Capitalist America: Educational Reform and the Contradictions of Economic Life*. Basic Books, New York

Bowman M J, Anderson C A 1973 Human capital and economic modernization in historical perspective. In: Lane F C (ed.) 1973 *Fourth International Conference of Economic History*. Mouton de Gruyter, Paris

Carnoy M, Levin H 1985 *Schooling and Work in the Democratic State*. Stanford University Press, Stanford, California

Coombs P H 1968 *The World Educational Crisis: A Systems Analysis*. Oxford University Press, New York

Coombs P H 1985 *The World Crisis in Education: The View From the Eighties*. Oxford University Press, New York

Crush J (ed.) 1995 *Power of Development*. Routledge and Kegan Paul, London

Delacroix J, Ragin C 1978 Modernizing institutions, mobilization, and Third World development: A cross-national study. *Am. J. Sociol.* 84 (1): 123–50

Easton P, Klees S 1990 Education and the economy: Considering alternative perspectives. *Prospects* 20 (4): 413–28

Fägerlind I, Saha L J 1989 *Education and National Development: A Comparative Perspective*, 2nd edn. Pergamon Press, Oxford

Foster P 1966 The vocational school fallacy in development planning. In: Anderson C A, Bowman M J (eds.) 1965 *Education and Economic Development*. Frank Cass, London

Fuller B 1987 What school factors raise achievement in the Third World? *Rev. Educ. Res.* 57: 255–92

Haddad W D, Carnoy M, Rinaldi R, Regel O 1990 *Education and Development: Evidence For New Priorities*. World Bank Discussion Paper No. 95, World Bank, Washington, DC

Harber C R 1984 Development and political attitudes: The role of schooling in northern Nigeria. *Comp. Educ.* 20 (3): 387–403

Ichilov O 1991 Political socialization and schooling effects among Israeli adolescents. *Comp. Educ. Rev.* 35(3): 430–46

Inkeles A, Smith D H 1974 *Becoming Modern: Individual Change in Six Developing Countries*. Heinemann Educational, London

International Journal of Educational Development 1996 Special Issue: World Bank's Education Sector Review: Priorities and Strategies for Education. 16(3)

Klees S J 1989 The economics of education: A more than slightly jaundiced view of where we are now. In: Caillods F (ed.) 1989 *The Prospects For Educational Planning*. UNESCO, Paris

Latukefu S 1988 The modern elite in Papua New Guinea. In: Bray M, Smith P (eds.) 1988 *Education and Social Stratification in Papua New Guinea*. Longman Cheshire, Melbourne

Lerner D 1964 *The Passing of Traditional Society: Modernizing the Middle East*. Free Press, New York

Lockheed M E, Jamison D T, Lau L J 1980 Farmer education and farm efficiency: A survey. In: King T 1980 *Education and Income*. World Bank Staff Working Paper No. 402, World Bank, Washington, DC

Marchand M H, Parpart J L (eds.) 1995 *Feminism/Postmodernism/Development*. Routledge, London

Meyer J, Rubinson R 1975 Education and political development. In: Kerlinger F (ed.) 1975 *Review of Research in Education*. Peacock, Ithaca, Illinois

Nathan J A, Remy R C 1977 Comparative political socialization: A theoretical perspective. In: Renshon S A 1977 *Handbook of Political Socialization: Theory and Research*. Free Press, New York

Psacharopoulos G 1985 Returns to education: A further international update and implications. *J. Hum. Resources* 20: 583–604

Psacharopoulos G 1994 Returns to investment in education: a global update. *World Dev.* 22(9): 1325–43

Psacharopoulos G, Woodhall M 1985 *Education for Development: An Analysis of Investment Choices*. Oxford University Press, New York

Renshon S A (ed.) 1977 *Handbook of Political Socialization*. Free Press, New York

Saha L J 1983 Social structure and teacher effects on academic achievement: A comparative analysis. *Comp. Educ. Rev.* 27(1): 69–88

Saha L J 1995 Two decades of education and development: some reflections. In: Daun H, O'Dowd M, Zhao S (eds.) 1995 *The Role of Education in Development. From Personal to International Arenas*. Institute of International Education, Stockholm University

Saha L J 1996 Universities and national development: issues and problems in developing countries.. In: Morsy Z, Altbach P G (eds.) 1996 *Higher Education in an International Perspective: Critical Issues*. Garland Publishing, New York

Smith P, Bray M 1988 Educating an elite: Papua New Guinea enrolment in international schools. In: Bray M, Smith P (eds.) 1988 *Education and Social Stratification in Papua New Guinea*. Longman Cheshire, Melbourne

Stromquist N P 1990 Women and illiteracy: The interplay of gender subordination and poverty. *Comp. Educ. Rev.* 34(1): 95–111

Subbarao K, Raney L Dundar H, Howorth J 1994 *Women in Higher Education: Progress, Constraints, and Promising Initiatives*. World Bank Discussion Paper 244. The World Bank, Washington, DC

Todaro M P 1989 *Economic Development in the Third World*, 4th edn. Longman, London

Torney-Purta J, Schwille J 1986 Civic values learned in school: Policy and practice in industrialized nations. *Comp. Educ. Rev.* 30(1): 30–49

Wagner D A 1985 Islamic education: Traditional pedagogy and contemporary aspects. In: Husén T, Postlethwaite T N (eds.) 1985 *International Encyclopedia of Education*, 1st edn. Pergamon Press, Oxford

Wagner D A, Lofti A 1980 Traditional Islamic education in Morocco: Socio-historical and psychological perspectives. *Comp. Educ. Rev.* 24(2 Pt. 1): 238–51

Weiler H N 1978 Education and development from the age of innocence to the age of scepticism. *Comp. Educ.* 14(3): 179–98

Wood R H 1988 Literacy and basic needs satisfaction in Mexico. *World Dev.* 16(3): 405–17

World Bank 1994 *Enhancing Women's Participation in Economic Development*. A World Bank Policy Paper. The World Bank, Washington, DC

World Bank 1995 *Priorities and Strategies for Education: A World Bank Sector Review*. The World Bank, Washington, DC

Social Change and Education

J. L. Hanna

Education introduced through colonial and postcolonial modernism has had a key role in transforming indigenous peoples' lifestyles, but a lesser impact in changing their social status. The effect of education in transforming nonmainstream peoples (the poor, religious, immigrant, and ethnic and racial minorities) in complex urban industrial, suburban, and rural societies varies. In most societies, formal education has contributed to empowering women (Morgen 1989). Education has positively contributed to many immigrants' adaptation to the host society (Portes and Rumbaut 1996).

A calculated intervention and a means of social control, education is a process of learning and transmitting culture (explicit and hidden). Formal education includes structured social institutions (usually some kind of school), initiation, and apprenticeships. Informal education includes peer groups, family, and community and street life. Teachers, mass media, live performance (storytellers, drama, song, and dance), and visual arts are educational agents (Peacock 1968). Social change, intended or unintended, refers to variations in the relatively stable relationships that comprise a pattern of social organization within a culture and the associated values, beliefs, and behaviors. Policy-makers often expect Western education to promote social change as well as political, economic, and social development. Anthropological research reveals variable patterns.

1. Patterns of Change

How does education affect social institutions, norms, values, and the associated cultural symbols? Education may be an agent of change, a condition of change in a changing society, and an effect of change in other institutions. Technology, economic relations, ideology, and politics may cause social change. The success of education for social change depends largely upon the attitude of a child or adult targeted for education within the context of often competing cultures, economics, and politics.

There are, however, impediments to social change. Education may reinforce and maintain the existing social status quo. For example, a traditional elite obtains access to education, has better instruction and curriculum, and receives greater rewards for education, as in Morocco (Eickelman 1985). A form of education may be associated with domination by one group or generation over another. Lack of economic development (Foster 1965, Foner 1973) or discrimination (Torruellas et al. 1991) may prevent

social change through education. Unanticipated consequences of well-intentioned public policy may impede intended social change. For example, desegregation in the United States caused some school districts to lose middle-class role models and community activists associated with educational attainment and socioeconomic mobility (Wax 1980, Hanna 1988). Pre-existing incompatible sets of knowledge and language (bilingual or nonverbal) may act as impediments to education and social change.

2. Colonialism and Westernization

A dramatic uneven transformation began in the nineteenth century through Western colonialization of Africa, Asia, Latin America, and the Caribbean and the growth of a global communication and economic web. Groups in many parts of the Third World were illiterate until the colonial powers introduced modernization, including Western education, to advance their economic interests and to spread Christianity. This process catapulted small-scale subsistence societies into economies based on exchange. Their world views, life-styles, and material wants changed as a result (Wood 1985).

Not all peoples willingly acquiesced to become Western-educated or "tools" of the capitalist system. Some Nigerians, neither subordinate nor minority cultures, resisted the early alien establishment of an educational system external to the indigenous system with its own demands and rewards (Nwa-Chil 1976).

Formal Western education fostered nascent conceptions of social status that diverged from traditional models. Moreover, in such cases as India's untouchable caste, Western education permitted some new vertical social mobility, participation in mainstream society, and attainment of prestigious occupational positions (Lynch 1969). Learned Western notions of independence and self-reliance encouraged some men and women to consider new possibilities and to challenge the dominant powers. For example, the protests of university students helped colonized nations achieve political independence. A reservoir of unemployed school-leavers is sometimes mobilized for political action (Hanna 1975).

3. Complex Urban Industrial Societies

Nineteenth-century processes of industrialization ushered in mass schooling (Levine and White 1986). This catalyzed a radical shift in the parent–child relationship in both small-scale and complex societies and established that childhood was a time of preparation for an uncertain future. Children going to school no longer engaged in full-time productive work that contributed to the family. They required a larger share of family resources for clothes, study space, and satisfaction of new consumer tastes acquired outside the home.

Schools supply labor for dominant enterprises and, consequently, tend to reinforce the societal racial, ethnic, sexual, and class segmentation and inequality. Changes in patterns of production often led to school reform movements.

Since 1960 there has been an attempt in the United States to use education to bring "everyone" into middle-class society. Schools present an ideal picture of society and encourage expression of allegiance through colorful rituals, oaths, songs, and dances. However, educational credentials may not bring similar rewards to different social, ethnic, racial, or gender groups because of discrimination or exclusion from powerful social networks (Walsh 1996, Jipson 1995).

Resistance to formal education occurs through informal education in peer groups, gangs, and networks in the informal economy, including drug traffic and crime. This activity has caused people with economic resources and education to flee and leave some neighborhoods insulated and dangerous (Hanna 1992).

School-teachers often prepare students for jobs by encouraging them to work hard without guaranteeing that they will benefit from it. Consequently, students develop a system of resistance in order to retain some power in their present lives and to state how irrelevant they judge schoolwork to be. Youngsters' efforts to maintain control over their lives include creating a culture by means of defying the school, misbehaving badly, playing truant, name-calling, and aggression (Willis 1977, Everhart 1983, Bullivant 1987, Hanna 1988).

4. Societal Restructuring

Reflecting social change, education, nonetheless, tends to be conservative in terms of transforming social institutions (Bowles and Gintis 1976). Yet education may promote and secure social restructuring through the deliberate introduction of a form of education significantly different from that offered to the older generation. Noteworthy cases are Turkey under Kemal Atatürk in 1923, the Soviet Union in the 1920s, China with its Red Guards and ballet between 1966 and 1976, and Black slaves in the United States, Caribbean, and Latin America. Some caste-like groups may have lost the motivation to take advantage of opportunities in their own countries (Ogbu 1974, 1980).

5. Immigrants

Escapees from humble family and home, many of them self-selected or persecuted immigrants, have strong motivation to seek opportunities. They tend to fit into the existing system or to seek new economic niches.

A hallmark of the history of the United States is the country's openness to the improvement in the lot of many minorities. For example, in the early twentieth century Eastern European Jews formed a large proportion of the foreign stock in the country's public schools (Brumberg 1986). This encounter led to their successful assimilation into American society. Attendance was compulsory; a curriculum emphasized the English language, civics, and American moral and aesthetic values. Leaders of the established Jewish community in New York, largely of German background, were actively involved in the public school system. Immigrants themselves were eager to succeed and saw education as the avenue for upward mobility. Jews came with a socioeconomic and intellectual background congruent with demands of workforce and social life.

Punjabi Sikh immigrants have often outperformed both majority and long-established minority students despite significant cultural conflict between home and school life, little direct parental involvement, prejudice, language proficiency problems, and a depressed socioeconomic status (Gibson 1988). Believing good education offers social mobility to the middle class, and considering acculturation as additive not subtractive, parents have encouraged children to subordinate special cultural practices and to tolerate prejudice and hostilities. Rather than discard tradition, many immigrants have tried to give it new life and look.

In summary, the forces of reproducing social organization and the forces of change are in conflict. More needs to be known about the constellation of variables that determine the results.

See also: Education and Development; Reproduction Theory; Social Mobility, Social Stratification, and Education; Sociology of Education: An Overview

References

Bowles S, Gintis H 1976 *Schooling in Capitalist America: Educational Reform and the Contradictions of Economic Life.* Routledge and Kegan Paul, London
Brumberg S F 1986 *Going to America, Going to School: The Jewish Immigrant Public School Encounter in Turn-of-the-Century New York City.* Praeger, New York
Bullivant B M 1987 *The Ethnic Encounter in the Secondary School: Ethnocultural Reproduction and Resistance; Theory and Case Studies.* Falmer Press, London
Eickelman D 1985 *Knowledge and Power in Morocco: The Education of a Twentieth Century Notable.* Princeton University Press, Princeton, New Jersey
Everhart R B 1983 *Reading, Writing, and Resistance: Adolescence and Labor in a Junior High School.* Routledge and Kegan Paul, Boston, Massachusetts
Foner N 1973 *Status and Power in Rural Jamaica: A Study of Educational and Political Change.* Teachers College Press, New York
Foster P 1965 *Education and Social Change in Ghana.* Routledge and Kegan Paul, London
Gibson M A 1988 *Accommodation without Assimilation: Sikh Immigrants in an American High School.* Cornell University Press, Ithaca, New York

Hanna J L 1988 *Disruptive School Behavior: Class, Race, and Culture*. Holmes and Meier, New York

Hanna J L (ed.) 1992 Tough cases: School outreach for at-risk youth. Unpublished manuscript, US Department of Education, Office of Educational Research and Improvement, Washington, DC. Revised and expanded version in progress

Hanna W J (ed.) 1975 *University Students and African Politics*. Africana Publishing Corporation, New York

Jipson J, et al. 1995 *Repositioning Feminism and Education: Perspectives on Educating for Social Change*. Bergin and Garvey, Westport, Connecticut

Levine R A, White M I 1986 *Human Conditions: The Cultural Basis of Educational Development*. Routledge and Kegan Paul, New York

Lynch O M 1969 *The Politics of Untouchability: Social Mobility and Social Change in a City of India*. Columbia University Press, New York

Morgen S (ed.) 1989 *Gender and Anthropology: Critical Reviews for Research and Teaching*. American Anthropological Association, Washington, DC

Nwa-Chil C C 1976 Resistance to early Western education in Eastern Nigeria. In: Calhoun C J, Ianni F A J (eds.) 1976 *The Anthropological Study of Education*. Mouton, The Hague

Ogbu J U 1974 *The Next Generation: An Ethnography of Education in an Urban Neighborhood*. Academic Press, New York

Ogbu J U 1980 *Minority Education and Caste: The American System in Cross-Cultural Perspective*. Academic Press, New York

Peacock J L 1968 *Rites of Modernization: Symbolic and Social Aspects of Indonesian Proletarian Drama*. University of Chicago Press, Chicago, Illinois

Portes A, Rumbaut, R I (eds.) 1996 *Immigrant America: A Portrait*, 2nd edn. University of California Press, Berkeley, California

Torruellas R M, Benmayer R, Goris A, Juarbe A 1991 Affirming cultural citizenship in the Puerto Rican community: Critical literacy and the El Barrio popular education program. In: Walsh C E (ed.) 1991 *Literacy as Praxis: Culture, Language and Pedagogy*. Ablex, Norwood, New Jersey

Walsh C E 1996 *Education Reform and Social Change: Multicultural Voices, Struggles, and Visions*. Lawrence Erlbaum Associates, Mahwah, New Jersey

Wax M L (ed.) 1980 *When Schools are Desegregated: Problems and Possibilities for Students, Educators, Parents, and the Community*. Transaction Books, New Brunswick, New Jersey

Willis P E 1977 *Learning to Labour: How Working-class Kids Get Working-class Jobs*. Saxon House, Farnborough

Wood A E 1985 *Knowledge Before Printing and After: The Indian Tradition in Changing Kerala*. Oxford University Press, New Delhi

Further Reading

Gomez M 1993 *Legal Education for Social Change*. Law and Society Trust, Colombo, Sri Lanka

Kaestle C F 1980 *Education and Social Change in 19th Century Massachusetts*. Cambridge University Press, New York

Lee W O 1991 *Social Change and Educational Problems in Japan, Singapore and Hong Kong*. St. Martin's Press, New York

Medlin W K, Carpenter F, Cave W M 1965 *Education and Social Change: A Study of the Role of the School in a Technically Developing Society in Central Asia*. School of Education, University of Michigan, Ann Arbor, Michigan

Morales-Gomez D A, Torres C A 1992 *Education Policy and Social Change — Latin America*. Praeger, Westport, Connecticut

Rendon L I, Hope R O, and Associates 1996 *Educating a New Majority: Transforming America's Educational System for Diversity*. Jossey-Bass, San Fransisco, California

Weiler H 1996 *Educational Change and Social Transformation: Teachers, Schools, and Universities in Eastern Germany*. Falmer Press, London

Williamson F 1987 *Education and Social Change in Egypt and Turkey*. Macmillan, Houndmills

(b) Education and New Technology

Gender and New Technology

I. Janssen Reinen and T. Plomp

It is generally accepted that girls and boys should get equal opportunities to work with computers and that in education a situation should be avoided in which girls perceive this new technology as "something for boys" or, as computers are often being associated with mathematics and science, "for those who are good in maths or science." This kind of association may have serious implications for females because of the long history of reported gender differences in attitudes and achievement in mathematics and related disciplines. Daily practice concerning the use of computers in education by female and male students does not reflect the principle of equality (Durndell et al. 1987, Damarin 1989). In this article, the literature on "gender and computers" is summarized, suggestions for gender inclusive teaching and class organization are presented, and some development projects directed at closing the "gender gap" are summarized.

1. New Technologies: Factors Influencing the Performance and Participation of Girls

New technologies refer to all inventions and developments that lead to new ways of collecting, exchanging, or providing data. Examples of new technologies are videodisc, cable television, videotex and teletext, microcomputers, fiber optics, lasers, communication satellites, and data transmission networks. In the early 1990s, computer technology is the most dominant form of new technology in education. Within this setting, "gender and new technology" can therefore be considered synonymous with "gender and computers."

For the summary of research on equity and computers in the 1980s, Sutton's (1991) framework will be used, implying that equality in schools can be assessed in terms of input, processes, and outputs.

2. Input Variables: Access and Socialization

Differences in access to computers (at school as well as at home) and different socialization experiences are important contributors to the fact that computers are less used by women and girls (Siann et al. 1990). This

tendency holds at all age levels and across different educational settings.

2.1 Differences in Access

It is useful to distinguish access to computers at school from access at home (at least outside school). Sutton (1991) found that several studies came to contradictory conclusions concerning access to computers at school, but none of the studies reported greater access for girls. Computer use in free hours and after-school time is dominated by boys (Moore 1986).

Several authors found that females are significantly less likely to have access to home computers (Moore 1986, Durndell et al. 1987, Sutton 1991, Janssen Reinen and Plomp 1993). Furthermore, boys are significantly more likely to describe themselves as frequent users of computers outside school (Siann et al. 1990), and are also more likely to enroll in computer courses outside school and attend summer computer camps (Moore 1986). Thus, when both girls and boys have access to computers at home, girls work significantly less frequently with them (Doornekamp 1993, Janssen Reinen and Brummelhuis 1994)

> . . . home access to computers is likely to influence students' levels of comfort with computers . . . The negative consequences of inequity in access to computers at home are often evident in the schools where disparities in learning may result due to the limited availability female students have to home computers. (Campbell 1989 p. 217)

In summary, boys have more access to computers than girls, both at school and outside school. This gives them many advantages over girls in acquiring knowledge of and experience with computers.

2.2 Socialization Experiences

Differences in attitudes toward computers can be explained by the differential socialization of males and females which results in stereotypical sex-specific roles (Martin 1991, Shashaani 1994).

Generally, boys and girls are often socialized differently, which means that girls learn to adapt better to different roles and attitudes than boys (described as "sex specific socialization" by Klopper and Schleyper 1990); this could lead to different role models of male and female teachers in the school when computer use is involved. This socialization can, among others, take place through behavior stimulation of parents or through imitation of "significant others." One of the important "significant others" is the teacher (see Sect. 2). A major social barrier for females is the attitudes of parents and teachers who believe that computers are learning tools predominantly for males (Yeloushan 1989, Janssen Reinen and Plomp 1993).

Women respond more positively than men when asked to assess the ability and potential of "women in general" as computer users and scientists, but women view themselves individually as less comfortable, confident, and competent with computers than men do (Temple and Lips 1989, Janssen Reinen and Plomp 1993, Makrakis 1993). This phenomenon is referred to as the "we can but I can't paradox."

3. Process Variables: Equity Issues in School

At school level, several variables can influence gender inequality, such as teacher role models, organization issues, type of computer use, and teacher attitudes toward equity.

3.1 Female Role Models

A social barrier females face in computer usage is the lack of positive role models in the classroom (Yeloushan 1989, Pelgrum and Plomp 1991). The importance of female role models for the career perspective and interest of female students is indicated in several studies (Klopper and Schleyper 1990). It is expected that bringing girls into contact with females who work with computers professionally (e.g., as a teacher using computers) or introducing them to females with a career in computers (in, for instance, computer education courses) can be an important way in which to influence choices and performances of girls positively. An international comparative study in 1992 in both elementary and secondary education shows that in most countries, a majority of the staff positions (principals, computer coordinators, and teachers) is occupied by males and, as such, education does not seem to provide clear female role models to girls (Janssen Reinen and Plomp 1993).

3.2 Organization Issues

Engagement in social activities developed in the home and reinforced in school greatly affect how females interact with the computer (Yeloushan 1989). Involvement in cooperative and competitive social activities begins early in a child's life and is nurtured throughout the years. The performances of females is enhanced in cooperative learning situations whereas that of males is enhanced in competitive learning situations. The existence of cooperative activities in the school therefore seems to be positive for girls.

Gardner et al. (1986) and Moore (1986) conclude that girls in coeducational schools are more likely to be influenced by gender stereotypes in their attitudes to computers than their counterparts in single-sex schools, thus showing the importance of the social context of the school. Promoting "positive discrimination," that is, creating situations in which girls are the only ones working with computers (e.g., in special classes or during reserved time after school), seems to be important.

Further, a greater percentage of girls than boys indicated that a reason for not taking computer studies as a subject was timetabling difficulty (Gardner et al. 1986). This result is indicative for those schools where traditionally "feminine" subjects are timetabled against, for example, mathematics, physics, and in this case, computer studies. Another important issue refers to the fact that there seems to be a strong association in schools between computing and science subjects. Teachers of computer literacy courses are often mathematics or science teachers (Kar Tin 1995). When computers are being used as a tool in the current curriculum, this most often appears in the traditionally "masculine" subjects.

Janssen Reinen and Plomp (1993) conclude from an international comparative survey that in none of the countries do a majority of schools indicate that they have a special policy focusing on equal opportunities. In schools with such a policy, the most significant type of policy across countries is the training of female teachers and the selection of female supervisors; hardly any other policy is applied.

3.3 Type of Computer Use

Moore (1986) reports that gender differences do not exist uniformly across all types of computer use, but are found primarily in programming courses and voluntary activities. Sacks et al. (1994) report little or no gender difference in computer use for word processing. Both females and males are acquiring some experience with computers, but intellectual skills such as problem definition, organization of data, and specification of procedures are mostly taught in programming courses. The demands of programming are thought to be incompatible with socialized female values (Moore 1986) and females do not seem to find these courses relevant to their needs. Although there is no gender difference with respect to the question of whether students work with the computer at school, boys indicate that they work with the computer more frequently (Janssen Reinen and Brummelhuis 1994).

3.4 Teacher Attitudes

The attitude of teachers toward computer use is an important variable as well. If teachers feel that a subject is more important for one group of students than another, they are more likely to give them additional time and encouragement (Moore 1986). Male teachers have significantly greater self-confidence regarding computers (Janssen Reinen and Plomp 1993, Kar Tin 1995).

4. Output: Student Attitudes and Ability

4.1 Attitudes

In general, women are less positive about computers than men (Martin 1991, Siann et al. 1990, Temple and Lips 1989, Janssen Reinen and Plomp 1993, Shashaani 1994). Many factors may be involved in explaining these differences, including the fact that men or boys often have more experience with computers. Klopper and Schleyper (1990) mention three important factors contributing to the motivation of girls: (a) computer practice (how often they work with computers); (b) the availability of a computer at home; and (c) the attitudes of friends (if peers enjoy computers, the motivation of girls is higher).

As computer use is often associated with mathematics (Moore 1986, Pelgrum and Plomp 1991), females are more likely to combine negative attitudes toward mathematics with negative attitudes toward computers (Temple and Lips 1989, Damarin 1989). Todman and Dick (1993) found that gender differences in attitudes among primary school children were present but they were not widening throught the primary school years.

4.2 Ability

Temple and Lips (1989) found that women avoid studying computers not only because they dislike them, but because they are uncertain about their own abilities: uncertainty that is apparently reinforced by, among other things, the attitudes of their male peers.

Durndell et al. (1987) found that males knew significantly more about computers than females. One of the most important reasons for this is the difference in access and opportunities to practice with computers. Janssen Reinen and Plomp 1993 reported the results of a test on functional information technology administered among students in elementary and secondary education in a number of countries around the world. It was found that in most countries under study there was a significant difference between female and male students in knowledge about computers. The United States was one of the minority group of countries in which no such difference was found.

5. Suggestions for Improvement of Education Practice in Terms of Gender and Computers

The key to closing the gender gap in the use of computers is in recognizing its existence. Several authors (Fish et al. 1986, Moore 1986, Temple and Lips 1989, Damarin 1989, Siann et al. 1990) developed suggestions or strategies for improving educational practice and reducing inequities. These can be divided into several categories. There should be:

(a) more female teachers as role models for girls;

(b) teachers from other than science subjects who teach the subject of computer literacy or informatics;

(c) an increase in teachers' consciousness that gender differences are indeed a problem, and that different behavior patterns exist in the classroom;

(d) recognition of the fact that building comfort and confidence, rather than interest, in computer use may be more beneficial to female students.

Students should:

(a) pay explicit attention to career possibilities in the field of computers and informatics;

(b) be made aware of sex-role stereotyping.

In terms of curriculum development, it is important to:

(a) demonstrate many different computer applications, especially in computer education courses (Pelgrum and Plomp found in their international survey that this occurs only to a very limited extent);

(b) avoid a situation in which working with computers will be identified with mathematics and science activities (use the computer in all aspects of the curriculum);

(c) avoid gender bias in curriculum materials and assess software packages for sex stereotypes;

(d) select a language appealing to girls when teaching computer programming (there is some evidence that LOGO is more attractive to girls than, for example, BASIC—Pelgrum and Plomp found that in 1989 in elementary education LOGO is the most used language, and in secondary education, BASIC);

(e) ensure that instruction is attentive to the attitudes, feelings, and preferences students bring to the instructional situation.

With regard to grouping and teaching methods, it is necessary to:

(a) create peer role models of both sexes;

(b) make sure that girls and boys spend equal time at the keyboard (if students work in mixed groups on the computer);

(c) actively improve male students' attitudes toward female involvement with computers;

(d) emphasize the control students have over the system (when teaching about the computer);

(e) promote cooperative modes of instruction instead of competition, because women prefer the former.

In school organization:

(a) remove the image of the computer room as "male turf";

(b) ensure that rules for accessing computers guarantee sufficient opportunities for girls—this is particularly important in the free hours and after school;

(c) schedule computer education courses such that there are no obstacles in the way of girls attending.

6. Some Projects

Many development projects apply suggestions and strategies to influence the performance and participation of girls using computers in education positively. Some of them are discussed in this section; references to other projects are included in the Further Reading section.

6.1 SWITCH

Switch has been a campaign in Scotland, mounted by the Scottish Office, the University of Strathclyde, and the Equal Opportunities Commission aimed at encouraging Scottish Women Into The Computing Habit (SWITCH). Together with the Dundee College of Technology a short course in computing (called "Insight into Computing") has been offered for 14–15-year old girls, with the aim of influencing them positively about computers before they reach the stage at which they decide about their career. Some concrete goals for the course were (Farrow 1988):

(a) to provide an enjoyable encounter with computer activities;

(b) to encourage girls to believe that they can be successful in computing;

(c) to demonstrate a variety of computer applications;

(d) to encourage consideration of computing as a career.

A maximum of practical experience for girls was considered as one of the most important starting points. In addition, women were invited to speak about their successful career in computing. There were places for 60 students from schools in the region to attend the course.

The results show (Farrow 1988) that, where initially only 3 girls were positive about a career in computing, after the course 75 percent of girls showed a positive attitude. Girls responded most positively to those sessions that did not require too much theory in order to get a result.

6.2. Technika 10

Technika 10 is a Dutch organization which sets up technical and computer clubs regionally with female supervision for girls between 10 and 12 years. The aim is to make young girls aware of technique in an informal way in order to decrease their deficiency in this field and to increase their possibilities in society, ultimately leading to more girls and women participating in technical occupations. The age level chosen is important, because at the age of 12 children in the Netherlands have to choose the type of secondary school they wish to attend.

There is a great interest in the computer clubs. At least six meetings are needed before girls get a more positive attitude toward computers (Klopper and Schleyper 1990). These attitudes are manifest mainly in their self-assessment and decreasing computer fear.

6.3 The Computer Equity Expert Project

This national project in the United States, which aims to promote the participation of girls in computer, mathematics, and science courses and assist educators to close existing computer gaps in their schools, is part of the Women's Action Alliance Sex Equity in Education Program. From 1990 until 1993, a train-the-trainer approach was applied as follows:

(a) Two hundred educational trainers—teachers, building-level administrators, and district-level administrators who are specialists in computer education, gender equity, mathematics, and/or science—were selected from high schools in all states.

(b) During the summer of 1991, six day-long seminars were held for the trainers on the topics of gender equity in education; girls and women in mathematics and science; a feminist analysis of mathematics and science; and educational technology and training skills. Trainers learned to conduct in-service workshops on computer equity and to give technical assistance to faculty groups.

(c) In the autumn of 1991 trainers delivered workshops to the mathematics and science faculty members in their schools and coordinated the activities of teams of faculty, parents, and students to implement computer equity strategies through December 1992.

(d) In January 1992 a two-day follow-up session was organized for trainers to consolidate their skills.

(e) After the project, trainers were expected to continue their activities in other schools in their districts and states, thus building up a national network of computer equity experts.

Communication within the project took place via an electronic network (for brainstorming of ideas and exchange of information) and a bimonthly newsletter.

Fish et al. (1986) found that in the experimental schools girls showed even greater usage of computers than boys, whereas in the control schools boys appeared to use the computer more (although this difference was not statistically significant). It seems that strategies directed specifically at girls, such as girls-only computer time, and those emphasizing social context among same-sex peers are most effective.

See also: Sex Differences and School Outcomes; Social Implications of Educational Technology; Students in Classrooms, Gender and Racial Differences Among; Technology and the Classroom Teacher

References

Campbell N J 1989 Computer anxiety of rural middle and secondary school students. *J. Educ. Comp. Res.* 5(2): 213–20

Damarin S K 1989 Rethinking equity: An imperative for educational computing. *The Comp. Teacher* 16(7): 16–18

Doornekamp B G 1993 Students valuation of the use of computers in education. *Comput. Educ.* 21(1/2): 103–13

Durndell A, Macload H, Siann G 1987 A survey of attitudes to, knowledge about and experience of computers. *Comp. in Educ.* 11(3): 167–75

Farrow S 1988 Insight into computing for girls. *Comp. Educ.* 58(5): 5

Fish M C, Gross A L, Sanders J S 1986 The effect of equity strategies on girls' computer usage in school. *Comp. Human Behaviour* 2(2): 127–34

Gardner J R, McEwen A, Curry C A 1986 A sample survey of attitudes to computer studies. *Comp. Educ.* 10(2): 293–98

Janssen Reinen I A M, Brummelhuis A C A 1994 *Information technology and gender differences: Is there an unequality in computer use?* Internal Research report. University of Twente, Enschede, The Netherlands

Janssen Reinen I A M, Plomp 1993 Gender and computers: Another area of inequity in education? In: Pelgrum W J, Janssen Reinen I A M, Plomp T (eds.) 1993 *Schools, Teachers, Students and Computers: A Cross-national Perspective.* IEA, The Hague

Kar Tin L 1995 *Pathways to Computing in Schools: A Study of Teachers' Experiences in Integrating New Technology into their Teaching.* University of Melbourne Department of Education Policy and Management, Melbourne

Klopper D L, Schleyper Y G M 1990 *Zij wel, ik ook: an empirisch onderzoek naar de computerattitude van meisjes van 10–12 jaar.* Technika 10, Utrecht

Makrakis V 1993 Gender and computing in schools in Japan: The "we can, I can't" paradox. *Comput. Educ.* 20(2): 1991–98

Martin R 1991 School children's attitudes towards computers as a function of gender, course subjects and availability of home computers. *J. Comp. Assisted Learning* 7(3): 187–94

Moore B G 1986 Equity in education: Gender issues in the use of computers. A review and bibliography. ERIC Document Reproduction Service, No. ED 281 511. Washington, DC

Pelgrum W J, Plomp Tj 1991 *The Use of Computers in Education Worldwide.* Pergamon Press, Oxford

Sacks C H, Bellisimo Y, Mergendoller J 1994 Attitudes toward computers and computer use: The issue of gender. *J. Res. Comput. Educ.* 26(2): 256–69

Shashaani L 1994 Socio economic status, parents' sex-role stereotypes, and the gender gap in computing. *J. Res. Comput. Educ.* 26(3): 433–51

Siann G, Macload H, Glissov P, Durndell A 1990 The effect of computer use on gender differences in attitudes to computers. *Comp. Educ.* 14(2): 183–91

Sutton R E 1991 Equity and computers in the schools: A decade of research. *Rev. Educ. Res.* 61(4): 475–503

Temple L, Lips H M 1989 Gender differences and similarities in attitudes towards computers. *Comp. Human Behaviour* 5(4): 215–26

Todman J, Dick G 1993 Primary children and teachers' attitudes to computers. *Comput. Educ.* 20(2): 199–203

Yeloushan 1989 Social barriers hindering successful entry of females into technology-oriented fields. *Educ. Technol.* 29(11): 44–46

Further Reading

Culley L 1986 *Gender Differences and Computing in Secondary Schools.* Loughborough University of Technology, Loughborough

Hoyles C 1988 *Girls and Computers: General Issues and Case Studies of LOGO in the Mathematics Classroom.* University of London, London

Kay R H 1992 Understanding gender differences in computer attitudes, aptitude, and use: An invitation to build theory. *J. Res. Comput. Educ.* 25(2): 159–71

Sanders J S, Stone A 1986 *The Neuter Computer: Computers for Girls and Boys.* Neal-Shuman Publishers, New York

Social Implications of Educational Technology

I. Conboy and P. B. White

Educational technologies are usually based on information and communication technologies which allow for the storage, transmission, processing, and retrieving of information. When these are combined with advanced methods of instructional design, evaluation, and administration, these technologies can provide powerful educational tools. Educational technologies are not, however, merely neutral receptacles for "repackaging" old curricula or educational practices. The very process of adopting educational technology-based programs can have profound effects for who has access to, control of, and who participates in educational processes.

As a consequence, the social implications of educational technology revolve around issues of access to, participation in, and control of educational processes. These are essentially issues of social equity and are often the motivation for initiating educational programs based on educational technologies. But a more fundamental problem is the issue of control (Beniger 1986). For example, how do educational technology-based programs change the locus of control over the conception, administration, and delivery of educational programs? This set of questions deals with issues such as theories of knowledge, notions of appropriate pedagogy, and ultimately questions of social power and authority (Tehranian 1990).

Debate about the social and educational consequences of new communication technologies can be seen in ancient times, because new communications technology have always had implications for the distribution of power and authority in any society. Concern about the social and educational consequences of alphabetic writing, one of the earliest communication technologies, can be seen in Plato's *Phaedrus*. An examination of this text reveals a profound concern about the social and educational implications of a communications technology that would allow ready access to a hitherto restricted range of knowledge. The introduction of alphabetic writing meant that the traditional educational gatekeepers, the story-tellers or teachers, no longer had absolute control over the learning experiences of children. Access to information would be available to whoever could read. Issues of social control are persistent themes in the debate about the social implications of educational technologies. They are also persistent issues in general debates about the social effects of information and communication technology.

The implications of information and communications technologies for traditional forms of social control have been debated whenever a new information or communications technology became available.

In a parallel with the debate over alphabetic writing in Plato's time, motion pictures, radio, television, and computers have been the focus of sometimes anxious debate about their social consequences. In the latter part of the 1990s this debate has taken on a new urgency with the rapid development of the Internet and its ability to provide access to a wide range of information and entertainment, some of which is deemed to be unsuitable to children. But while the social consequences of these technologies have been debated, educators have experimented with harnessing these new media for educational purposes.

1. Current Knowledge

The short- and long-term effects of educational technology have been discussed by Dede (1981). Short-term effects have included greater access to education, high initial financial investments, increased centralization of resource production, changes to pre- and postservice teacher training, a bias toward certain clients, and a potential impact on the processes of human interaction in educational settings. According to Dede, long-term effects can include the differentiation of education from training, a creation of new definitions of intelligence, a higher overall rate of societal change, and the emergence of a different model of teaching and learning.

Dede called for thorough studies of the consequences of adopting educational technologies and a balance in emphasis between financial goals and the goals of ensuring that all groups have equal access to education. He proposed that educational technologies and curricula had to be designed to meet the diverse needs and backgrounds of students; that schools and teachers should be involved in important educational decisions; and that there should be an awareness of potential social change and cultural homogenization caused by educational technology.

In the time since Dede wrote this article, three issues stand out as significant challenges for educational technologists. The first, and most significant issue is the role of educational technology in the control of education and training. The second is the role of educational technology in the push for greater access to education and training. The third and final issue arises from concern about the role of educational technology in the growth in educational participation rates, particularly in developing nations.

1.1 Who Controls Education and Training?

A latent but potentially divisive issue for educational technologists is gathering momentum. In an effort to make their economies more competitive internationally, many national governments are becoming more interventionist by promoting various forms of educational technology. In response to these new forces, some educational technologists have expressed reservations about aspects of educational technology and its reliance on empirical analytical theories at the expense of more normative theories. Koetting and Januszewski (1991) have argued that if educational technologists persist with their limited views of educational theory and theory building they will cut themselves off from the cultural sciences and the variety of ways in which the world can be interpreted.

As Taylor and Swartz (1988) indicated, educational technology will be the site of a battle between those who see the basic premise of instructional technology to be that all instructional contingencies can be managed in any setting at any time and by groups such as women and ethnic communities who expect that their young people should engage collectively in the creation of knowledge, or people who think that "knowledge, like bread, is best made at the local level" (Taylor and Swartz 1988 p. 29).

Government concern about, and intervention into, education is increasing. Governments have called for "educational productivity" to become a key issue, with a shift in the focus of schools from educational processes to results and student performance (Dunham 1992). For example, one of the major justifications for the US National Information Infrastructure initiative was to improve the competitiveness of the national economy and the quality of education. As a consequence the linking of public libraries, schools and universities to the Internet has been a major goal of this program (National Telecommunications and Information Administration 1993 and United States Advisory Council on the National Information Infrastructure 1996). With mounting pressure on governments to use educational technology to serve what Watkins (1990 p. 72) referred to as "the new vocationalism and the resurgence of human capital theory," educational technologists will increasingly be caught in the cross fire. These issues of government versus individual and educator control over learning processes and outcomes are likely to become more prominent. Educators react to these pressures by expressing concern over predictive theories of learning which they see as controlling future action, with control becoming a part of the semantic content of knowledge (Striebel 1991).

On the other hand, governments seek justifiable and quantifiable outcomes, particularly for training. They set aggregate targets for education and training, and specify groups for special consideration. The question arises as to whose interests educational technology should serve.

In order to encourage the most efficient use of resources, there is a trend toward greater government coordination through the use of technology in education and training (Ramsey 1991). But Apple (1987) warned that in some cultures this approach could lead to the total prespecification of teaching processes and school curricula. There is a shift toward a greater reliance on prepackaged materials and software. This is a significant contrast with the old ways, which saw teachers having the time and skill to do their own curriculum planning and deliberation. Now they become isolated executors of someone else's plans, procedures, and evaluative mechanisms (Apple 1987).

Not only is there concern over the degree of government and central control. The high establishment costs of educational technology, such as satellite, beamed microwave and multimedia systems, usually require a partnership between education and private industry usually telephone and computer companies and publishing enterprises. Concern has been expressed about computer companies influencing the use of computers in schools (Yeomans 1991).

While in some educational cultures, such as that of the United States, where there is greater tolerance of the master–teacher concept, television broadcast programs such as TI-IN can openly promote the advantages of access to skilled university instructors. In other cultures this approach is not as acceptable. The involvement of owners of transmission capacity can lead to the downgrading of curriculum content, teacher professional development, and problems relating to administration. This is often exacerbated by a form of educational imperialism in the shape of interstate, intersector, and interinstitutional politics (Foks 1990). On the other hand, educational technology offers considerable scope for collaboration and sharing.

When educational technology and modern communication technology are used to deliver educational programs to isolated and culturally distinct areas, it will almost inevitably change the culture of that area. Native American and Australian Aboriginal groups are examples of this effect. Any centralist intervention in rural cultures runs the risk of eroding the concrete character of rural life (D'Cruz 1990).

In the past, print, and radio and television broadcasting provided a cost-effective way of disseminating information to a large number of people at a distance. But for the first time telecommunications-based systems such as the Internet can now provide a cost-effective method for establishing interactive communication links between providers of educational services and learners located in schools or in their homes. With open technical standards and rapidly reducing costs of communications bandwidth the Internet is set to become a widely available communications system which allows for two-way communications using a variety of textual, audio, and visual media. Because the Internet makes it possible for almost any organization or individual to be both a consumer and a publisher of information on the Internet, many of the barriers limiting publication using the old media have dissolved. To this extent the Internet democratizes control over educational resources and removes the barrier of distance. Publication on the Internet is inexpensive and immediately available worldwide.

1.2 The Challenge of Open Learning

Wider availability of educational technology has started to shift the focus of technology in education from distance education to the relatively new notion of open learning. Multimedia systems using interactive compact disk (CD-I) have raised the possibility of learners themselves exerting much more control over how and what they learn, when they learn, the speed at which they proceed through learning, and the form of assessment they undertake. There are now clear indications of more training occurring in the workplace rather than in separate education institutions. The possibility of using new media as a way of developing open learning communities has been recognized in UNESCO's *Learning Without Frontiers* program. This initiative sees open learning communities in terms of processes which are consistent with and responsive to the needs, interests and aspirations of individual learners in specific local contexts. The new media helps to enable processes which encourage a reexamination of the traditional roles of teachers and learners (Visser and Jain 1996).

Forms of education and training vary as to the degree of student or teacher control over content, time, setting, pace of learning, entry and exit points, credentialing, entry standards, levels of personal interaction with both teachers and peers, and recognition of prior learning. Generally, educators seek to provide learners with as much control over the learning process as possible, in the belief that learning will be increased if the learners themselves make some commitment to gaining the knowledge they believe will provide them with personal benefit. With this approach, the competencies that are taken as evidence of success are more general, and assessment is more open-ended and less structured.

In less structured or open learning modes, credit may be given for prior knowledge and experience, and there is a growing trend toward the increased use of modules of skills to free up student entry and exit points. While this approach provides the learner with some choice over the learning settings and content, often the form and content of individual modules will be predetermined, and there may be limitations on the extent to which a learner can follow up issues in personal face-to-face interaction with a teacher or tutor. The issue of personal interaction is controversial, as proponents of some educational technologies such as computer-mediated learning, question the degree to which students can actually follow up their individual concerns in standard classrooms (Bork 1990). Instead, they seek to provide opportunities for students to interact with learning programs of various types in order to offset the lack of personal face-to-face interaction.

Accompanying this trend is a greater emphasis on competency-based training where the focus is almost entirely on student outcomes rather than learning processes, and there is a move to segment elements of training into modules. As the economic push to use open learning techniques gathers momentum, there will be a shift in importance from real-time instruction delivered in specific purpose-designed training settings, to the design and delivery of multimedia training programs for use in a range of settings in delayed time. As a consequence, large-scale educational uses of technology will develop outside traditional educational settings (Mecklenburger 1990). This greater flexibility of learning and study venues is a direct consequence of developments in educational technology.

The comprehensive approach to using technology for distance education in Canadian and some United States projects, which includes accessing information using communications technology, taking part in electronic tutorials as well as delivering instruction, is pre-empting the notion of the "virtual group" (Romiszowski 1992). According to this approach, a major part of study beyond elementary years occurs outside the classroom using electronic data transmission between computers. Most activities normally associated with face-to-face instruction can occur within a fully developed "electronic community" However, new communications developments are unlikely to have significant effects in elementary schooling since children will still be required to interact together in groups for socializing purposes and to enable parents to work (Romiszowski 1992). Notwithstanding this, computer networking offers a strategy for joining teachers and students in "learning circles" where everyone is simultaneously teacher and learner (Riel 1990). Widespread access to the Internet creates the possibility of creating electronic links between teachers and students throughout the world. Ultimately this kind of development redefines the notion of the classroom.

1.3 Increasing Access to Education and Training

Governments and, increasingly, educational agencies perceive educational technology as a key contributor to delivering wider access to education and training particularly for disadvantaged groups, and for improving equity within their societies (Kahin and Keller 1995). "The notion that technology can be used to expand access to education implies, first of all, that teaching and learning can be taken out of the confines of existing schools and colleges, the more so in developing countries where the existing institutions cannot hope to cope with growing demands" (Reddi 1987 p.128).

In many developed Western countries convincing government, educational administrators, and the general public of the worth of educational technology is no small undertaking. Even so, some so-called Third World countries have embraced educational technology as a means of modernizing their educational systems. A joint cooperative arrangement between the Ministry of Education and Culture (MoEC), the State Television Network (TVRI) and Citra Televisi Pendidikan Indonesia, a private company, was launched in 1991 to produce educational television programs for secondary students (Sadiman 1992). Programs are broadcast for two hours each day and their purpose is to improve the quality of the teaching–learning process. In Nepal the Radio Education Teacher Training Project (RETT I) has used broadcast radio in its 10 years of operation to provide a 10-month training course to over 6,000 primary teachers (Upadhayay 1992). The broadcasts, along with accompanying printed materials, focused initially on teaching methodologies. However, teachers lacked expertise in primary school curriculum, and consequently the second phase of the program included instruction for teachers in primary school subjects.

Often in Western developed countries, government involvement in educational technology has been piecemeal and uncoordinated. However, there are tangible signs that governments may now be more receptive to using educational technology to improve education and training outcomes. In Australia there have been a number of government reports focusing at least in part on the role of educational technology in achieving educational outcomes. These include *An Apple for the Teacher?* (Australia, House of Representatives 1989), *Open Learning: Policy and Practice* (Johnson 1990), and *Towards a National Educational and Training Strategy for Rural Australians*. In the United States the Office of Technology has sponsored two influential reports: *Power On! New Tools for Teaching and Learning* (United States Congress 1988), and *Linking for Learning: A New Course for Education* (United States Congress 1989). These reports generate policy initiatives which establish agendas for educational change.

While governments can reasonably expect to generate savings in education budgets by reorganizing urban education, smaller student numbers dispersed over large areas mean that governments are faced with high costs per student in rural areas. There are pressing economic reasons for governments to look to alternative delivery forms in order to contain these costs. Computers and telecommunications are seen as tools that can make it easier for governments to meet their social obligations.

Access to additional education, resources, and expertise is one of the significant social effects of educational technology. Students who are beyond easy reach of schools and training centers have been catered for by distance education. Projects such as the Western Australian Art Access program (Moorhouse and Ellicott 1990), and Rural Outreach Education (Norris and Pyke 1990) are examples of initiatives that underscore technology for distance delivery.

Not only is instruction delivered in real and delayed time and provided over long distances, but there is also student access to information stored on databases and to electronic messaging systems. But there are concerns about using educational databases in education. These can divorce data from human contexts and inflate the importance given to impersonal data at the expense of the more anecdotal "lived experience" (Chandler 1990). The ease with which computers can deliver data can conceal the importance of the setting in which they are to be used. There is a danger that planners will feel that the solution to an educational and training problem simply lies in providing more information to the user in the form of computer data. Setting up a clearinghouse of information has come to be seen as an essential precursor to a successful project. Scant attention is paid to how the information is to be used, who will benefit from access to that information, and who will be adversely affected by the information.

One area where the use of technology is likely to have significant benefits is through increasing access to education for handicapped people. Technology is bringing undreamt-of benefits to groups of people who are at a disadvantage—the disabled, the infirm, and the elderly (Commonwealth Schools Commission 1988, Walker 1987).

1.4 Increasing Student Participation

Rural districts in Australia and other parts of the world tend to lag behind their urban counterparts in key educational outcomes, such as student participation rates in primary and secondary education and academic achievement. Further, it is not uncommon for rural populations to have less opportunity for participating in tertiary studies (Country Education Project 1988).

In Australia the federal government's specific objectives for rural education and training include increasing the nonmetropolitan school retention rates for Year 12 to 65 per cent; increasing the transfer rates of students from school to postschool education to levels comparable to those in metropolitan areas; and increasing overall participation in education and training so that the proportion of the nonmetropolitan workforce with qualifications after high school approaches the national average (Australia, Minister for Employment, Education and Training and Minister for Primary Industry and Energy 1989). Also, many rural authorities and associations are drawing urgent attention to education and other social needs at a time when there is a perception of rural decline (McGregor and Latchem 1991).

Distance educators sought to create the conversational mode characteristic of on-campus face-to-face instruction by addressing print materials to individual students and through personal written exchanges. Even so, the sometimes abstract, impersonal, and monotonous character of correspondence instruction had been criticized, and an attempt to remedy this has been made by using mass media and the telephone (Lefranc 1983). So called "conversational modes" of delivery returned to distance education with audioteleconferencing and gained further momentum from interactive approaches, which included using audiographics and video conferencing. These approaches are likely to develop further as telephone tariffs are reduced as a consequence of technological change and competitive pressures within the telecommunications industry and as the Internet becomes a low-cost, multipurpose, and multimodal communication system.

2. Emerging Trends and Issues for Further Research

The social and educational tensions that arose as a consequence of early communications technology in Classical Greece were a forerunner of the debates and concerns that have arisen as communications and educational technologies have been adopted by educators. For example, what are the cultural implications of using educational programs developed in one culture in another cultural setting? To what extent is the centralization of control inherent in large-scale curriculum and material development counteracted by the individual control afforded by other small-scale technologies? To what extent does the growing reliance of educational technologies on sophisticated information and storage and retrieval technologies make it difficult for poorer and less developed countries, or even poorer school systems in developed countries, to use those materials? To what extent does the interlinking of publishing and technology manufacturers mean that the production of educational materials will be vertically integrated? To what extent does individual access to media resources threaten a reduction in classroom activities and a reduced emphasis on human social interaction?

Modern educational technology has been driven from two, somewhat different directions. On the one hand, educational policymakers and educators have become increasingly aware of the shortcomings of existing traditional educational systems. On the other hand, developers and vendors of media and communication technologies have seen education as a market for their goods and services. It is this tension between educational needs and commercial objectives that permeates much of educational technology practice. The temptation to experiment with newer and ever more sophisticated media and communication systems sometimes overshadows the need to meet educational goals.

At other times the goals and assumptions implicit in educational technology-based programs can be changed. This happens when the control of education processes is moved from classroom teachers and publishers to a new range of professionals and organizational interests. Also, the scale of investment required for many educational technology programs

moves decision-making about content and process across regional boundaries to national and international production consortia. At the other end of the spectrum, curriculum design, small-scale publishing, and materials development can become the province of the classroom teacher.

These issues are likely to arise as new kinds of educational service providers emerge to tap the potential of the Internet. Publishers, software companies, and telecommunications carriers could create these new entities. Despite the diversity of language and culture, it is possible to foresee the development of international markets for educational services with Internet-based providers offering to diagnose the learning needs of students and to teach and evaluate students online. The economies of scale and the potential for commercial support which could be gained from these large-scale enterprises might be attractive to educational administrators with scarce financial resources.

Another major issue to be faced by educators is the growing commoditization of information (Mosco 1989). Information that was once freely available is now only available for a fee. This privatization of information and improved abilities to supply and bill for information use on demand will make it possible for educational activities to be seen as another revenue-generating enterprise by both public and private educational providers. The reduction of government involvement in educational activities and the privatization of education and training will be aided by educational technology and the information and communication systems that can deliver those programs across regional and national boundaries. When coupled with new modes of accreditation, educational technologies become an engine of significant educational change.

The privatization of education, or the reliance on user-pays principles, raises broad questions of social equity. What will governments provide for those who cannot pay? Will there be any guarantee of minimal educational standards for those who are unable to participate in the market for educational services? To some extent the questions raised by educational technology are merely a subset of questions that are raised by the decline of government-supported broadcasting and information activities and a growing societal-wide reliance on commercially oriented information and communication technologies.

See also: Gender and New Technology; Technological Change and Deskilling; Technological Change and Education; Technology and the Classroom Teacher

References

Apple M 1987 *Is the New Technology Part Of the Solution or Part Of the Problem*? Curriculum Development Centre, Canberra
Australia, House of Representatives 1989 *An Apple for*

the Teacher? Choice and Technology in Learning: Report of the House of Representatives Standing Committee on Employment, Education and Training, AGPS, Canberra

Australia, Minister for Employment, Education and Training and Minister for Primary Industry and Energy 1989 *A Fair Go: The Federal Government's Strategy for Rural Education and Training*. AGPS, Canberra

Beniger J R 1986 *The Control Revolution: Technological and Economic Origins of the Information Society*. Harvard University Press, Cambridge, Massachusetts

Bork A 1990 Schools for tomorrow. (mimeo)

Chandler D 1990 The educational ideology of the computer. *Br. J. Educ. Technol.* 21(3): 165–74

Commonwealth Schools Commission 1988 *Computers and the Realm of Ideas: An Interim Report on the Involvement of Disadvantaged Children with Computers*. Commonwealth Schools Commission, Canberra

Country Education Project 1988 *Three Times Less Likely: A Report on the Access of Country Students to Tertiary Institutions*. Country Education Project and Participation and Equity program, Melbourne

D'Cruz J V 1990 *Technology in Education: A Study of Policy and Practice in Rural Schools*, 2nd edn. Ministry of Education, Victoria

Dede C 1981 Educational, social and ethical implications of technological innovation. *Program. Learn. Educ. T.* 18(4): 204–13

Dunham E A 1992 *Educational Reform: The Critical Role of Information Technology*. Institute for Educational Leadership, Washington, DC

Foks J 1990 The politics of open learning. In: Atkinson R, McBeath C (eds.) 1990 *Open Learning and New Technology: Conference Proceedings*. Curtin University of Technology, Perth

Johnson R 1990 *Open Learning: Policy and Practice—A Discussion Paper Commissioned by the Department of Employment, Education and Training, Canberra*. AGPS, Canberra

Kahin B, Keller J 1995 *Public Access to the Internet*. MIT Press, Cambridge, Massachussetts

Koetting J R, Januszewski A 1991 Theory building and educational technology: Foundations for reconceptualization. Paper presented to ACET Convention, Orlando, Florida

Lefranc R 1983 The evolution of distance teaching in higher education: From correspondence to the new technologies, *Educational Media International* 20(1): 8–16

McGregor A L, Latchem C R 1991 *Networks for Learning: A Review of Access and Equity in Post-compulsory Education in Rural and Remote Areas of the State of Western Australia*. Western Australian Office of Higher Education, Perth

Mecklenburger J A 1990 Educational technology is not enough. *Phi Del. Kap.* 72(2): 105–08

Moorhouse J, Ellicott R 1990 Arts access: A history of open learning for country Western Australia. In: Atkinson R, McBeath C (eds.) 1990 *Open Learning and New Technology: Conference Proceedings*. Curtin University of Technology, Perth

Mosco V 1989 *The Pay-Per Society: Computers and Communication in the Information Age*. Ablex, Norwood, New Jersey

National Telecommunications and Information Administration 1993 *The National Information Infrastructure: Agenda for Action*. Department of Commerce, Washington, DC

Norris D, Pyke L 1990 Open learning in entrepreneurship. In: Atkinson R, McBeath C (eds.) 1990 *Open Learning and New Technology: Conference Proceedings*. Curtin University of Technology, Perth

Ramsey G 1991 The need for national policies in education. *Unicorn* 17(1): 34–41

Reddi U V 1987 Television in higher education: The Indian experience. *Media in Education and Development* 20(4): 128–33

Riel M 1990 A model for integrating computer networking with classroom learning. In: McDougall A, Dowling C (eds.) 1990 *Computers in Education*. North-Holland, Amsterdam

Romiszowski A J 1992 Developing interactive multi-media courseware and networks. *Proceedings of the International Interactive Multimedia Symposium*, Perth

Sadiman A S 1992 *Inservice Training for Teachers and Personnel in New Information Technologies in Indonesia: Country Report Presented to the Asia and the Pacific Seminar on Educational Technology, 1992*. Centre for Information Technology for Education and Culture, Ministry of Education and Culture, Jakarta

Striebel M 1991 Instructional design and human practice: What can we learn from Habermas' theory of technical and practical human interests? Paper presented at the ACET Convention, Orlando, Florida

Taylor W D, Swartz J B 1988 Instructional technology and proliferating world views. *Proceedings of Selected Research Papers Presented at the Annual Meeting of the Association for Educational Communications and Technology*. New Orleans, Louisiana

Tehranian M 1990 *Technologies of Power: Information, Machines and Democratic Prospects*. Ablex, Norwood, New Jersey

United States Advisory Council on the National Information Infrastructure 1996 *A Nation of Opportunity: Realizing the Promise of the Information Superhighway*. US Government Printing Office, Washington, DC

United States Congress 1988 *Power On! New Tools for Teaching and Learning*. Office of Technology Assessment, Congress of the United States, Washington, DC

United States Congress 1989 *Linking for Learning: A New Course for Education*. Office of Technology Assessment, Congress of the United States, Washington, DC

Upadhayay M P 1992 New information technologies in Nepal in formal and non-formal education: Current trends and future prospects. Paper presented to the Asia and Pacific Seminar on Educational Technology "New Information Technologies in Formal and Non-formal Education—Current Trends and Future Prospects," Tokyo

Visser J, Jain M 1996 *Towards Building Open Learning Communities: Re-contextualizing Teachers and Learners*. Learning Without Frontiers Coordination Unit, UNESCO, Paris

Walker D W 1987 Concerned technology. *Educational Media Int.* 24(2): 87–95

Watkins P 1990 Flexible manufacturing, flexible technology and flexible education: Visions of the post-Fordist economic situation. In: Dupe M (ed.) 1990 *Making the Links: Technology and Science, Industry and Education*. Ministry of Health, Education and the Arts, Canberra

Yeomans A R J 1991 Sociological aspects of computers in education. Paper presented to the ACET Convention, Orlando, Florida

Further Reading

Australia, Department of Employment 1991 *Open Access for Teachers, Professional Development: Towards a Cooperative National Framework for the Application of Distance Learning to the Professional Development of Teachers*. Department of Employment, Education, and Training, Canberra

Kirk J 1990 *Rural and Remote Learning Centres: The Point of Convergence for the Provision of Further Education by Alternative Delivery Systems*. Converging Technologies, Selected papers from EdTech90 (Conference of the Australian Society for Educational Technology). University of Sydney

Lundin R 1987 Some North American developments in communication technology and distance education. Paper delivered to the Australian and South Pacific External Studies Association (ASPESA) Forum, University of New England, Armidale

Romiszowski A 1990 Shifting paradigms in education and training. *Educ. Tech. Training Int.* 27(3): 233–37

Technological Change and Deskilling

K. I. Spenner

How does technological change alter the quantity and quality of jobs in parts or the whole of national economies? The answer to the question is of central importance to research and policy on education. Technological change directly and indirectly defines the demand for given mixtures of skills. A rapidly changing world of work implies different educational policies from one of little or slow change. In principle, technology and technological change shape the quality of the match between the skills and capabilities that workers bring to the labor force, and what jobs permit, demand, and allow. Technological change may constrain or enable new, more productive uses of human talent. Moreover, from the 1980s onward, technology and technological change have been directly implicated in the day-to-day conduct of education, for example, in issues surrounding computer literacy and the electronic classroom.

This article defines technology broadly to include product and process distinctions, the "hard" materials, things, and machines of producing goods and services, as well as the "soft" but changing ways of organizing production, people, and ideas (Cyert and Mowery 1987). The first section reviews the major theoretical positions, the second section considers methodological issues in research on technological change and deskilling, the third section summarizes the aggregate and case study evidence and suggests a synthesis, and the final section discusses several research frontiers.

1. Theoretical Positions

1.1 Upgrading Arguments

The upgrading position stems from the industrialization thesis and neoclassical economics (Kerr et al. 1964, Standing 1984). According to this argument, the division of labor evolves along the lines of greater differentiation and efficiency in industrial societies.

Technological changes increase productivity, requiring a broader variety of skills and higher average skills from the workforce. Automation and other forms of mechanization eliminate routine work. Jobs increasingly involve higher levels of complexity and discretion, both key dimensions of the skill demands of jobs, particularly white-collar, technical, and professional jobs, and in high-technology fields. Proponents of the industrialization thesis would cite the aggregate increase in levels of education and composition shifts in the occupational structure as evidence (Jaffe and Froomkin 1968, Bell 1973).

A related type of upgrading argument and line of evidence points to growing demand for managerial and professional workers in the 1980s and the rising wage-premium associated with a college degree. In the eyes of the human capital theorist, the rising wage-premiums are *prima facie* evidence of skill upgrading of the labor force, with technological change one of the generative factors.

Other versions of the upgrading thesis suggest that new technologies demand new forms of skill compared with the past, for example, with respect to computerization and flexible manufacturing systems, increased responsibilities for the whole of the production process, for teamwork and job interchangability, or higher abstraction skills and computer literacy (Adler 1983).

1.2 Downgrading Arguments

Downgrading arguments posit a decline in the quality and quantity of work because of changes in the nature of the labor process during the twentieth century (the web of social and technical aspects surrounding the activity of work). Technological change and automation are strategic instruments of managers, who use devices such as scientific management, numerical control, programmable automation, and the redesign of jobs to separate the execution of work from the conception of work (Braverman 1974, Wood 1982, Noble 1984). According to this argument, the job changes of the twentieth century include the dilution of traditional craft skills, and a growing mass of unskilled and semiskilled labor, particularly in clerical and selected white-collar fields. Other versions of the downgrading thesis point to a polarization in the changing labor force: differential growth of high-skill versus low-skill occupations and industries (Levin and Rumberger 1987), or deindustrialization, in which job loss and/or deskilling are secondary consequences of plant shutdowns, and national or international industry relocations.

Upgrading and downgrading studies consider a range of industrial market economies but concentrate on Canada, the United Kingdom, France, Germany, Japan, Sweden, and the United States (for reviews, see Cyert and Mowery 1987, Flynn 1988, Littler 1982, Spenner 1985, 1988, Wood 1989).

1.3 Mixed Change, Conditional, and Contingency Arguments

Mixed change arguments are more of a characterization of the empirical literature than a theoretical position: some sectors and jobs in the economy experience upgrading as a function of technological change, others experience downgrading, and the net result is little change in the skill requirements of work or offsetting trends in the composition of the occupational structure and the content of work (Horowitz and Herrnstadt 1966, Spenner 1979).

Conditional and contingency theories go beyond empirical description and specify a logic of one or more factors that condition the effects of technological change on jobs. For example, Flynn's (1988) model of the skill-training life cycle posits upgrading effects on jobs early in the life cycle of a technology. With the passage of time, the effects shift to mixed–neutral and then downgrading, as the technology is learned and segmented, as production processes are routinized, and as training shifts outside of firms to vocational and educational instutions. Form et al. (1988) postulate a multicomponent web of contingency factors that condition the effect of technological change on the quantity and quality of jobs. Depending upon measurement, the theory might generate 10s of conditioning factors, which comprise more a list of possibilities than a tight theory that answers the question "why?" Finally, the present author's synthesis of the empirical evidence postulates the uncertainty–contingency hypothesis discussed below (Spenner 1988). In brief, it states that technological change has no simple, single, or unitary effects on the quantity or quality of jobs. Rather, the effects of technological change on jobs are conditioned by market forces, by managerial strategies and actions, and by selected organizational factors.

2. Methodological Issues

Studies of technological change and upgrading–deskilling fall into two general types. Aggregate studies investigate the changes in skill levels of the economy over time, capturing a broad range of jobs. The upgrading tradition draws more upon aggregate studies. Case studies intensively investigate shifts in skill as a function of technological change in a narrower sampling of space, for example, for an occupation or in a single firm. Case studies have been more the domain of the downgrading tradition. The different designs have characteristic strengths and weakness, trading off population coverage for the ability to see the dynamics and detail of change.

A further distinction is helpful: the overall skill level of the economy or a subset thereof (i.e., jobs, firms) can change along two tracks, content and composition. Content changes refer to actual changes in the nature of jobs, apart from the numbers of workers in different types of jobs. Compositional changes refer to changes in the overall skill level that emanate from shifting distributions of workers to jobs, conceptually distinct from changes in the actual content of jobs. There is no logical reason why technological change need operate on skill levels in the same way or on the same schedule as for compositional and content changes. For example, the long-term effects of a technological change may be indirect and involve upgrading through job creation in certain industries (compositional shift). On the other hand, the short-term effects may involve content shifts in deskilling the jobs directly involved in the technological change.

Further, studies of technological change vary in their sampling of time and space. The case-study literature has concentrated heavily on manufacturing jobs, but has given relatively less attention to service industry jobs. Aggregate studies cover more jobs but only a few aggregate studies consider the era before the Second World War. The collected social science literature on technological change offers nothing approaching a full sampling of time and space for the twentieth century, particularly if one requires direct measures of skill at multiple points in time.

Finally, as economists have long known, "technology" is extraordinarily difficult to isolate and measure (Cyert and Mowery 1988). Technological change tends to occur in conjunction with a number of other changes, including changing factor conditions, supply–demand shifts, and larger demographic and social changes. Research designs often capture the gross effects of all changes but have difficulty isolating the net effects of technological change.

2.1 Meanings and Measures of Skill

The various meanings and measures of skill have been reviewed elsewhere (Spenner 1990). In general, substantial variability, but nonetheless progress, can be identified in the empirical research of the 1970s and 1980s. It is important to distinguish skill as a human attribute (internalized capabilities, forms of knowledge and so on) from the skill demands of jobs. A long tradition of research in education shows the match between the two is quite problematic, and is associated with issues of underemployment and overeducation (Berg and Gorelick 1970, Clogg and Shockey 1984, Smith 1986).

The research literature on technological change and skill changes offers a variety of conceptualizations of skill that vary on several issues (Spenner 1990 p. 400):

(a) social valuation; or what specific skills will be rewarded?

(b) social definition and construction; or what will custom, language, the construction of tasks, and the power of interested parties define as a skilled performance or job?

(c) supply, demand, and governance structures that determine transactions involving skills in people and jobs; or what logic—for example, efficiency or control—and what system (market, internal hierarchy) matches people to jobs, and translates technologies into mixtures of jobs with given skill demands and various forms of work organization?

The theoretical stance on these questions defines the conceptions of skill in the literature. For example, case studies in the downgrading tradition often assume strong forms of social construction of skill, key roles for managers in deciding valuation (versus the "market" or production functions), and control logics in addition to a logic of efficiency. Some of the variability in the findings of such studies may issue as much from variations in concepts and measures as it does from variation in the underlying phenomenon.

Measurement of jobs skills in the literature shows similar variability. Some studies continue to assume that the meaning of skill is so obvious that it need not be specified or measured but can be equated with education levels or labels for groups of occupations such as "white-collar," or "blue-collar." Other studies indirectly infer skill levels of jobs through wage levels. Studies of skill shifts and technological change in neoclassical economics provide illustration.

Since the early 1970s, research has relied increasingly on direct measures of skill, as provided by expert raters or systems (e.g., US Department of Labor 1977, Cain and Treiman 1981), or as provided through the self-reports of people about their jobs. Validity studies show a fairly reasonable degree of correlation between the two types of measure (for review see Spenner 1990). Nonetheless, each type of measure has strengths and weaknesses; progress in cumulative empirical research will require both.

A final measurement issue involves the specific dimensions of skill. Spenner (1990) shows studies that range from a single, often unspecified global dimension of skill, to one line of research that measures about 200 specific job features as dimensions of skill.

Here too, the research of the 1980s shows some convergence on multidimensional concepts and measures (versus unidimensional), and on two to five or so different dimensions.

Theoretical and empirical research suggest at least two broader organizing dimensions of skill: substantive complexity and autonomy control. Substantive complexity refers to the level, scope, and integration of mental (cognitive), manipulative, and interpersonal tasks in a job, following the classic distinction by job analysts of functional foci of data, people, and things in human–task interfaces. Aggregate studies and studies in the upgrading tradition frequently investigate skill conceived and measured as substantive complexity. Autonomy control refers to the discretion or leeway in a job to control the content, manner, and speed with which a task is done. Downgrading and case studies often consider this dimension of skill. The two dimensions are correlated for jobs in the United States economy, and studies have suggested a figure in the range of $r = 0.5$–0.7 (Spenner 1990).

3. Summary of Aggregate and Case-study Evidence

In brief, the empirical literature fails to provide a single or simple answer to the question of how technolgical change alters the quantity and quality of jobs. For example, Flynn (1988) reviews nearly 200 case studies in economics and finds substantial variability in outcomes, which she organizes with the skill-training life cycle model suggested earlier. The aggregate studies that cover all or a large portion of the United States economy and that use direct measures of skill at multiple time-points now number about 15. The case-study literature includes literally hundreds of studies. The summary here reflects this set of major aggregate studies, and a nonrandom sample of an equal number of major (frequently cited) case studies (see Spenner 1988).

The aggregate study evidence suggests several conclusions. First, the rate of change of the skill levels of jobs in the United States economy is evolutionary rather than revolutionary. The Canadian evidence is similar (Myles 1988). Second, there is no clear evidence of widespread or massive downgrading, particularly in studies of skill as substantive complexity. To the contrary, there is more consistent evidence of slow aggregate upgrading, particularly since the Second World War, and perhaps since the beginning of the twentieth century. No aggregate study evidence precedes this time frame. Third, studies of compositional shifts show slower net aggregate change; studies of content shifts show more dramatic change, but again in both upgrading and downgrading directions, with the net change fairly small. Fourth, aggregate studies of autonomy control are in short supply and are mixed, providing some hint or suggestion of an aggregate compositional downgrading in the autonomy control of jobs, but more a function of the massive movement out of self-employed farming (higher autonomy control) and into bureaucratized work settings (less autonomy control) over the course of the twentieth century. The larger changes involve a complicated web of specific technological changes. Fifth, both studies based on self-report measures of skill and studies based on expert-system measures of skill support these general conclusions.

The case-study evidence affords a related set of conclusions (Spenner 1988). First, case studies show more volatility in skill transformations and find more instances of downgrading, perhaps because of the concentration on autonomy control, or additionally, because of sample selection in overstudying changing occupations, industries, and firms, and understudying stable ones. Second, case studies concentrate on content shifts in work, again reporting more change of both upgrading and downgrading varities, but devoting less coverage to skill change through compositional shifts. Third, case studies suggest regional, industrial, and other variations in skill transformations. Fourth, and perhaps most importantly, case studies suggest that the effects of technological change on the skill levels of work are not necessarily simple, direct, or constant across settings and firms, and cannot be considered in isolation, that is, in the absence of contingency factors.

In summary, the aggregate and case-study evidence fails to provide consistent corroboration of simple versions of upgrading or deskilling arguments. If anything, there is slightly more support for upgrading arguments in the area of compositional shifts and skill as substantive complexity, but this support deteriorates if consideration is expanded to content shifts and skill as autonomy control. Interestingly, when the conclusions about skill dimensions are juxtaposed, it is possible that the world of work at the end of the twentieth century compared with a century before is more complicated in terms of its substantive complexity, but with less autonomy control to meet more complicated task demands. This hypothesis awaits comprehensive test.

One way to summarize the collected empirical literature is the uncertainty–contingency hypothesis (Spenner 1988). This hypothesis disavows simple, single, or unitary effects of technological change on skills. Rather, it posits intrinsic uncertainty and contingency in the relationship between technology and jobs. The uncertainty and contingency are not only in the state of knowledge about the relationship, but are built into the very character of how technology creates, destroys, and alters jobs. Technological change defines a new range of options and possibilities; other social and economic forces determine the specific of direction. The contingency factors fall into three general categories: market forces, managerial prerogatives, and organizational cultures. Selected evidence, as outlined below, suggests that any one of the contingency factors

or a combination of them are sufficiently powerful to alter or reverse (from net upgrading to downgrading, or vice versa) the effects of a technological change on the quality and quantity of jobs.

Market forces refer to classic economic dynamics of supply and demand, and the associated factor conditions in firms, industries, and sectors of the economy. For example, a resource-rich environment as defined in factor conditions and supply and demand levels may afford a more forgiving and expansive environment for content and compositional upgrading, whereas resource-lean environments might favor downgrading of job numbers and quality. Along these lines, Osterman (1986) found computerization in various industries led first to a stronger contraction in managerial and clerical labor, but after a number of years to lesser contraction, perhaps associated with bureaucratic reorganization and firms re-expanding into new products and markets over the longer term as a function of technological change.

Managerial prerogatives refer to the discretion of management to control the timing and nature of technological change. This includes decisions on whether to implement a technological change, what to implement, how to implement it, and who participates in the implementation (e.g., engineers, workers). A number of studies clearly suggest the central role played by managers. Kelley (1986, 1990) found differing managerial strategies produced all three outcomes —upgrading, downgrading, and mixed change—for the same technology change (computerized numerical control machinery) in a similar range of industrial settings in the United States, the United Kingdom, Germany, and Japan. Jaikumar (1986) found similar variability in outcomes as a function of managerial strategy and practice in the implementation of flexible manufacturing systems in Japanese and United States firms.

Organizational culture refers to the social and cultural system of the work environment in which technological change occurs. It includes classic demographic factors such as size, differention, hierarchy, and spans of control, but also belief systems and the norms and sources of power of different groups. Here too, there is suggestive evidence implicating a number of these factors.

Support for the uncertainty–contingency hypothesis comes more from a comparative overview of studies in the various disciplines than from a clear or comprehensive test in any single study. Further, the specific receipe of market forces, managerial strategies, and organizational cultures that produce upgrading or downgrading or more mixed results is not yet known. One of the main frontiers of research in this area will be to decipher this recipe for change, particularly if a parsimonious version exists. The major competing explanation to the uncertainty–contingency hypothesis for patterns in the empirical literature is Flynn's (1988) skill-training life cycle model. It explains the mixtures of upgrading and downgrading by stage in the life cycle of the technology: earlier stages produce upgrading and later stages produce downgrading. Studies that fail to control for life-cycle stage of technology produce a jumbled mixture of effects. The challenge to this explanation occurs in studies such as Kelley's (1986) and Jaikumar's (1986), in which the same technology at about the same life-cycle stage and in similar industrial settings still produces a range of effects, thus implicating other contingency factors such as managerial strategies.

4. Research Frontiers

The research literature on technological change and deskilling continues as an active, exciting, and fertile arena of ideas, with contributors from a number of disciplines including anthropology, economics, education, human systems engineering, managerial sciences, industrial psychology, and sociology. A number of frontiers shape future research.

First, while the 1980s research made considerable progress in moving toward replicable multidimesnsional concepts and measures of skill, considerable progress remains to be made. This includes national level-measurement and validation studies that regularly measure technological and job changes for sample universes, similar to other social indicator and assessment projects.

Second, better forums need to be developed to bring together ideas and contributors for publication and presentation. Research on technological change and skill change is truly interdisciplinary, yet often progress is slowed by lack of communication among contributors in different fields.

A third research frontier comprises arguments about a different future and new skills. The different future argument regards microelectronics and computerization as qualitatively different (Hirschhorn 1984). Earlier technological changes altered the physical dimensions of work; computerization has the potential to alter the intellectual requirements as well. The new skills argument is related, suggesting that new forms of work organization and high technology demand new forms of skill which are not adequately captured by earlier concepts and measures. Examples include teamwork or the requirements of a job to conceptualize an interrelated but remote system. Neither argument is resolved and both are in early stages of empirical investigation. The new skills argument depends centrally on the definition of skill. If a multidimensional conceptualization is at a sufficiently basic level (i.e., level, scope, and integration of mental, manipulative, and interpersonal tasks for substantive complexity), then it is not clear whether so-called "new" skills are qualitatively new, or whether they are quantitatively different levels of basic dimensions.

Finally, as technology has integrated the global economy and shortened horizons of time and space, the investigation of skill and technological change increasingly involves a comparative dimension, with cross-national and transnational dynamics and mechanisms. These range from differences between countries at the simplest level, to technology transfer, labor mobility, and skill shifts across national boundaries as a function of technological change. Beyond these, future research will also likely yield insight into whether the recipe that governs how technology changes job skills, researched in industrial market economies, has some broader applicability—namely, to Third World settings, to centralized state socialist economies, or to societies undergoing transformation.

See also: Benefits of Education; Education, Occupation, and Earnings; Technological Change and Education

References

Adler P 1983 Rethinking the skill requirements of new technologies. Working Paper HBS 84–27, Graduate School of Business Administration, Harvard University, Cambridge, Massachusetts

Bell D 1973 *The Coming of Post-industrial Society: A Venture in Social Forecasting.* Basic Books, New York

Berg I, Gorelick S 1970 *Education and Jobs: The Great Training Robbery.* Praeger, New York

Braverman H 1974 *Labor and Monopoly Capital: The Degradation of Work in the Twentieth Century.* Monthly Review Press, New York

Cain P, Treiman D J 1981 The Dictionary of Occupational Titles as a source of occupational data. *Am. Sociol. Rev.* 46(3): 253–78

Clogg C C, Shockey J W 1984 Mismatch between occupation and schooling: A prevalence measure, recent trends and demographic analysis. *Demography* 21(2): 235–57

Cyert R M, Mowery D C 1987 *Technology and Employment: Innovation and Growth in the U.S. Economy.* National Academy Press, Washington, DC

Cyert R M, Mowery D C (eds.) 1988 *The Impact of Technological Change on Employment and Economic Growth.* Harper Business, New York

Flynn P M 1988 *Facilitating Technological Change: The Human Resource Challenge.* Ballinger, Cambridge, Massachusetts

Form W, Kaufman R, Parcel T, Wallace M 1988 The impact of technology on work organization and work outcomes: A conceptual framework and research agenda. In: Farkas G, England P (eds.) 1988 *Industries, Firms, and Jobs: Sociological and Economic Approaches.* Plenum, New York

Hirschhorn L 1984 *Beyond Mechanization: Work and Technology in a Postindustrial Age.* MIT Press, Cambridge, Massachusetts

Horowitz M, Herrnstadt I 1966 Changes in skill requirements of occupations in selected industries. In: National Commission on Technology, Automation, and Economic Progress 1966 *Technology and the American Economy, Vol. 2 Appendix: The Employment Impact of Technological Change.* US Government Printing Office, Washington, DC

Jaffe A J, Froomkin J 1968 *Technology and Jobs, Automation in Perspective*. Praeger, New York

Jaikumar R 1986 Postindustrial manufacturing. *Harv. Bus. Rev.* 64(6): 69–76

Kelley M R 1986 Programmable automation and the skill question: A reinterpretation of the cross-national evidence. *Hum. Syst. Man.* 6: 223–41

Kelley M R 1990 New process technology, job design and work organization: A contingency model. *Am. Sociol. Rev.* 55(2): 191–208

Kerr C, Dunlop J T, Harbison C, Myers C A 1964 *Industrialism and Industrial Man: The Problems of Labor and Management in Economic Growth*. Oxford University Press, New York

Levin H, Rumberger R 1987 Educational requirements for new technologies: Visions, possibilities and current realities. *Educ. Policy* 1(3): 333–54

Littler C R 1982 *The Development of the Labour Process in Capitalist Societies: A Comparative Study of the Transformation of Work Organization in Britain, Japan and the USA*. Heinemann, London

Myles J 1988 The expanding middle: Some Canadian evidence on the deskilling debate. *Can. Rev. Sociol. Anthropol.* 25(3): 335–64

Noble D 1984 *Forces of Production: A Social History of Industrial Automation*. Knopf, New York

Osterman P 1986 The impact of computers on the employment of clerks and managers. *Ind. Lab. Rel. Rev.* 39(2): 175–86

Smith H L 1986 Overeducation and underemployment: An agnostic review. *Sociol. Educ.* 59(2): 85–99

Spenner K I 1979 Temporal changes in work content. *Am. Sociol. Rev.* 44(6): 968–75

Spenner K I 1985 The upgrading and downgrading of occupations: Issues, evidence, and implications for education. *Rev. Educ. Res.* 55(2): 125–54

Spenner K I 1988 Technological change, skill requirements and education: the case for uncertainty. In: Cyert R, Mowery D (eds.) 1988

Spenner K I 1990 Skill: Meanings, methods and measures. *Work Occup.* 17: 399–421

Standing G 1984 The notion of technological unemployment. *Int. Lab. Rev.* 123(2): 127–47

United States Department of Labor 1977 *Dictionary of Occupational Titles*, 4th edn. US Government Printing Office, Washington, DC

Wood S 1982 *The Degradation of Work? Skill, Deskilling and the Labour Process*. Hutchinson, London

Wood S 1989 *The Transformation of Work? Skill, Flexibility and the Labor Process*. Unwin Hyman, London

Technological Change and Education

M. Carnoy

Technological change has profound implications for production processes, the division of labor, and labor skills. This article assesses the extent of available knowledge about the spread of technology, its impact on skills, its consequences for educational policy at different stages of technological diffusion, and conversely, the effect of education on both the use and development of new technology. For the sake of presentation, the discussion focuses on the new information technology, since it is this that represents the most modern wave of worldwide change in production processes.

1. Technological Diffusion

The new microelectronic technologies are diffused in three major forms: (a) through their consumption (electronic consumer goods, such as radios, calculators, television sets, videocassette recorders, and video games, and through telephone availability); (b) through the use of information and telecommunications technologies in the production of traditional goods and services; and (c) through the development and production of high-technology products and processes themselves.

1.1 Consumer Electronics

Although the consumption of electronic goods is not usually regarded as technology diffusion, it does have an important impact on diffusion in three ways. First, there is a logical progression from the use of electronic and telecommunication products—even when imported—to their repair locally, and then to their local production. Second, there is a logical progression from the manufacture of simple electronic consumer goods to the manufacture of more complex computer and telecommunications systems, particularly when produced for export; both require similar quality control and production processes. Finally, and most important, certain electronic goods such as telephones also serve as the underlying infrastructure for a larger information–communication network.

The greater availability of telephones and improved worldwide communications have significant implications for the way developing economies can hook into the world economy. It is difficult to say precisely what "threshold" level of telecommunications access is needed for "high technification," but it appears to be approximately four to five telephone lines per 100 inhabitants.

1.2 Applications in Production of Traditional Goods and Services

The diffusion of computers and telecommunications as investment goods employed in the production of goods and services represents a different level of technological use from consumer electronics and consumer telephone use. New technology brought into the production process enhances productivity and quality control and creates the possibility of producing new goods and services associated with the collection, treatment, and dissemination of information: new goods and services which in turn can increase productivity in existing industry.

The process of the technology diffusion through such applications is undoubtedly complex (Rosenberg 1976, Rogers 1983, Dosi 1988). Enterprises in different countries adopt new technologies at different rates depending on a number of factors, including the sector in which they are situated (Pavitt 1984). Economic and social variation at the national level (e.g., the position of labor unions, state macroeconomic policies, the role of exports in the economy) also play a significant role in technology diffusion, in addition to conditions in firms themselves (Edquist 1985, Edquist and Jacobsson 1988).

But for true technology transfer to occur, "learning by using" (Rosenberg 1982) has to result in the adaptation and production of applications domestically as a result of importing technology. This may begin with the development and production of software applications or adapting quality control processes, but may eventually spread to the import-substitution of hardware. It is the first of these activities (software applications using imported hardware) which turns out to be far more important in terms of productivity, and far more indicative of technology diffusion than hardware production (Bhalla and James 1984). Research in the People's Republic of China (Bianchi et al. 1988) and Mexico (Miller 1986) suggests that the importation of new technology, both in the form of hardware and software without accompanying training in the use of the technology and the management of associated production processes (including quality control), creates minimal technology transfer and minimal higher productivity linkages to other firms.

1.3 The Production of High-tech Products

The last link in the technological diffusion process is the domestic production of high-tech goods and services. Such production sometimes refers to both consumer microelectronics and microelectronics for business applications. However, the two types of production require very different levels of quality control and research and development spending (hence management and labor skills), and should therefore be separated.

The development of both consumer electronic production and, even more so, microelectronics production for business purposes, depends on the presence of one or more of several key factors: (a) the availability of the management and labor skills associated with the production of high-tech goods and services; (b) supply conditions which attract transnational corporations to locate part of their production in that country for export to the world market; (c) the existence of a domestic market for such goods and services, which may be in large part the result of previous technology use; alternatively, development may depend initially on consumption by the state as part of modernizing the state sector (where the state is itself a producer of goods and services), or on the need of traditional industries to compete internationally in the sale of their products by improving their production technology; and (d) a structure of economic incentives that make it worthwhile for producers of final products to source high-tech inputs domestically, and worthwhile for local suppliers to invest in the production of such inputs.

There are several different national models in the Third World which have attempted to capture the rents associated with domestic production of business microelectronics. The Brazilian and Indian models attempt to develop autarkic production in order to satisfy domestic demand and to export to other, less developed countries (Evans 1986, Agarwal 1985). Although their high-tech products are not competitive with the products of developed countries in terms of quality, they assure the development of a domestic industry and assure that these countries can move up the "learning curve" most rapidly by actually producing the new technology.

In the South Korean model, which applies to Hong Kong, Singapore, and Taiwan (and, to a lesser extent, Malaysia), the first phase of development was represented by foreign companies assembling goods in the country for export to their domestic markets (see Kim 1986, Amsden 1989, Henderson 1988, Henderson and Castells 1987, Salih and Young 1989). Then, due to considerable investment by the South Korean government in education and research and development, Korea first began to produce consumer electronics and other consumer goods of its own using high-technology production processes, and then moved into the production of computers, all for export. This was simultaneously accompanied by domestic consumption of these products.

A third model is found in Mexico (and, on the periphery of Europe, Spain). Mexico is in a special situation, since it borders on the world's largest economic market and also as it is historically a major recipient of United States foreign investment. In this model, foreign firms assemble high-tech products in Mexico for the Mexican market and for export to the United States and other Latin American countries. These firms are committed to hiring Mexican engineers and technicians ("learning by doing"), who, it is hoped, will eventually develop their own firms producing high-tech goods and services (Miller 1986, Montoya 1988, Warman and Miller 1988).

A fourth and final model is that of the People's Republic of China. Here, a huge potential domestic market for electronic and communications equipment is used to attract foreign firms into joint ventures to transfer technology, much as in the Mexican model.

862

The difference between Mexico and China seems to be, however, that China is not attractive as an export platform for these foreign firms, although the Chinese would like it to be. And, unlike the Indians and Brazilians, China imports most of its new information technology for industrial applications in order to modernize manufacturing as rapidly as possible (Bianchi et al. 1988).

The data suggest that although diffusion has been limited, many developing countries in Asia and some in Latin America are already involved in the production and export of electronic goods and components. Many countries are importing new technologies. It is highly likely that production of new technologies in the developing world will increase, even though the research and development base for evolving and designing such products will remain concentrated in the Organisation for Economic Co-operation and Development (OECD) countries. This division of labor may change with the increasing importance of the software industry, which requires a much higher percentage of highly skilled labor.

2. Skill Effects

There is a long history of discussion among economists about the deskilling or reskilling effects of technology on labor. This discussion revolves around the issue of whether new technology decreases or increases the skills required in the workplace, hence lowering or raising the training and education needed by workers to do their jobs effectively. Without describing this literature in detail (see *Technological Change and Deskilling*) it is worthwhile summarizing its conclusions before going on to assess the wider relation between education and technology.

Spenner's review (1985) of results in the United States and Europe concludes that:

> There is no evidence that jobs, taken as a group, are experiencing dramatic upgrading and downgrading in terms of their skill requirements. This does not mean an absence of upgrading and downgrading changes but rather an approximate balancing in the direction and quantity of changes of an approximate conservation of total skill . . . It is intriguing that there are more hints of downgrading in studies of skill as autonomy-control and more hints of upgrading in studies of skill as substantive complexity, suggesting the possibility of divergent aggregate trends in the two dimensions of skill. (Spenner 1985 p. 141)

Spenner argues that, "the impacts of technology on skill levels are not simple, not necessarily direct, not constant across settings, and cannot be considered in isolation" (p. 146). The same innovation in different firms can alter skill requirements in different ways.

No research on developing countries is as detailed as Spenner's. However, a set of case studies in Asian countries (International Labour Organisation 1988) of automation in the banking, engineering, electrical appliance, and printing industries confirm Spenner's conclusions that it is difficult to identify deskilling or reskilling with automation. It seems that the new jobs being created do not require higher skills, only different skills. It also appears that the most likely workers to be made redundant when automation is introduced are unskilled workers, although this varies according to country and labor legislation. In some cases, such as in South Korea, new unskilled jobs for women were created by automation.

Intuitively, it would seem likely that, as manufacturing and services adopt more complex forms of production, more complex skills would be required. Yet Spenner's review suggests that this may not be the case. Even as new jobs are created that do require higher level skills, just as many jobs (in absolute terms) may be created that require lower level or unchanged skills (Rumberger and Levin 1984).

The changes are made even more complicated by shifts in the gender of those employed in the new manufacturing industries and services. Labor in high-tech industries—where they have an important research and development or software component—tends to be more highly educated but also more gender-stratified than either that in traditional manufacturing or the labor force as a whole. This has important implications for technological job displacement in traditional industries combined with expansion of production of new technologies. Although the production jobs involved may require similar levels of skill, microelectronics production employs a female production labor force. Males are hired into technical jobs—relatively highly educated managers, engineers, sales personnel, and technicians—demanding a different set of skills to those displaced from traditional manufacturing. Therefore, in countries where new technologies applied in traditional industries and services "release" workers, and the production of new technologies employs workers, there is very little absorption of the first by the second.

3. Implications for Education and Training Policies

3.1 The Complementarity of Schooling, Training, and New Technology

Education and training policies are key elements in the process of change occurring in the world economy, but these policies should be different at different levels of development. What is the basis for formulating such policies?

The traditional tools for analyzing public educational investment have been labor force planning and rates of return. Labor force planning attempts to use input–output analysis to predict educational "needs," given projected industry growth, fixed education–skill ratios, skill–job ratios, and job–industry ratios. The method was flawed from the start because none of these ratios was in reality fixed. Spenner's (1985) discussion makes clear that education and skill demand are not necessarily the same. Rumberger's (1981) study argues that education in the United States is increasing much more rapidly than skill requirements. Yet there have been few if any measures of changing skill requirements in other economies; hence most analysts use average education as a proxy for the "capacity to produce," or skill "availability" in the labor force.

Rate-of-return analysis also has its problems, especially when social rates of return are used to predict which levels and what kind of education and training should be subsidized by the state in order to maximize economic growth. Rapid technological change may make social rates of return in the 1990s obsolete in terms of where countries want to be or will be one or two decades hence. The future direction of an economy may well depend on the kind of educational investments made before the payoffs to that education are realized. As economies shift from agricultural to manufacturing and services and the educational system expands, the social rate of return to higher levels of education is seen to rise relative to lower levels (Carnoy 1972, Carnoy and Marenbach 1975, Ryoo et al. 1991, Knight and Sabot 1990).

The association of education with "capacity to produce" is inherently correct, particularly in terms of five variables: literacy, numeracy, socialization to "competence," (Inkeles and Smith 1974), the self-confidence to learn new skills, and the ability to adjust to change (Schultz 1989). In addition, high-level science, medical, mathematical, and management skills needed for certain kinds of production of goods and services can be associated with university education. Societies whose population has these capabilities seem to be more able and willing to learn a wide range of skills related to working with "new" technologies (i.e., new to them). A better "educated" population is more trainable into new jobs. And it is more likely to adopt new technologies and increase their own productivity by using them (Welch 1970). Schultz calls this the "adjustment to disequilibrium" (Schultz 1989).

This complementarity between new methods of production and the capacity to produce that is implied in what schools are supposed to teach is the most powerful argument for more education. As Cohen and Tyson (1989) contend, a better educated labor force will create the conditions for investing in new kinds of production and new organizations of production. This argument probably holds even in relatively low-income countries undergoing severe adjustments to the changing world economy.

Complementarity between education and new technology would contribute both to the diffusion of new growth-promoting technologies and to the employment-creation effect of technological change. A more literate, numerate, and socialized labor force would raise the rate of return to investing in new technology because it would be cheaper to train it to apply the new processes and to work in new kinds of work organizations. Moreover, in the case where labor is involved in making decisions on the use of new technology, it is more likely to use new technology and reap its benefits. An educated labor force would also represent one of the institutional conditions (in addition to a well-developed credit system, for example) required for the effects of technological change in particular firms and industries (lower prices or more employment and income) to spread to other firms and industries.

3.2 The Special Role of the University

Higher education plays a crucial role in technology transfer at two levels. First, it has the capability to develop the management skills required to utilize and organize the new technology; therefore, in terms of the analysis presented here, higher education is the key to the technology transfer process in those industries that use and produce information technology. Second, with the spread of science-based industries, the university is the site that can combine the basic research needed for the advance of such industries with the training of researchers and appliers of research for industry.

The rising rates of return in the larger, and higher educated, nonindustrialized countries (NICs) in part reflect this increasingly important economic role that the university plays in the labor force formation process. This role will increase in the future, especially in the NICs and the industrializing economies, and the more rapid the rate of growth and information-technology-orientation of the economy, the more important the university's role.

However, most universities in developing countries are not organized to combine research and training of undergraduates and graduates in the way required by the new technology and new organization of production. In Brazil, for example, the federal universities are expensive and inefficient, and produce relatively few research–training connections. Much of the teaching is not oriented toward problem-solving. In addition, space is not sufficiently utilized, keeping many qualified students out of the university system. Universities in Argentina and Mexico are much cheaper and much more crowded, but are similar in their lack of research and research–training connections. China's universities are almost purely training institutions, with research delegated to research centers that offer little training. Most developing countries' universities will have to undergo serious reforms if they are to enter into the information age.

Most countries also need to expand greatly their research program in both the universities and industry. Brazil, Argentina, and to some extent Mexico, have engaged in basic scientific research in universities and particularly research institutes. However, this effort has been small compared to the industrialized countries (Castells 1991).

The most telling variable is the degree of cross-activity between training and research on the one hand, and practical industrial applications, on the other hand, in the three institutions that conduct research and training in most societies: (a) universities, (b) research institutes, and (c) private and public businesses. The greater the presence of both research and training, and application activities in each of these institutions, and the greater the interaction between institutions, the greater the return to research and higher education.

3.3 The New Technology and Training

Training is also a complementary investment to new technology. Yet it must be viewed as complementary both to capital (and the technology associated with capital) and education (and the "technology" associated with education). Training can be divided into: (a) in-school training, or vocational education; (b) on-the-job training, both general and specific, designed for a particular type of production process; and (c) learning by doing, a form of on-the-job training directly connected to the production process itself.

In-school training/vocational education is most distant from the production process. It is designed to provide general skills directly applicable to the production of goods and services, and therefore falls somewhere between schooling and training. From the educators' point of view it has the distinct advantage of "taking care of" students who need preparation for the world of work but who do not perform especially well in abstract academic education. The emphasis centers more on deciding which kind of schooling and training best produces complementarity with new kinds of technology and production processes. Is vocational education more complementary to new methods of production than academic? And is vocational education more complementary than on-the-job training or learning by doing?

Grubb (1987) argues that the new information technologies' impact on skill demand should push the educational system away from vocational concerns into more general preparation of the population to think critically. In theory, this would make workers able to deal with a variety of higher quality jobs that require thought and decision-making rather than the repetitive work that characterizes Fordist technology. This approach would argue for investing in higher quality academic education rather than specific vocational, even if the two could be produced at same cost. In general, long-course vocational education is as expensive (or more so) than even relatively high-cost academic schooling.

A recent World Bank monograph (Middleton et al. 1990) makes the case that in-school vocational education, both because of its cost and its use of obsolete equipment, is not as complementary to changing technologies as in-firm training. This suggests that a more effective way to provide training is through direct sub-sidies to firms rather than through indirect subsidies via vocational education.

Nevertheless, there is still a case for vocational education in certain situations: (a) in countries characterized by high economic growth, especially where private enterprises are willing to bear part of its cost, or in vocations for high-growth industries (Chung 1990); (b) in situations where enterprises send workers who are already employed to be trained partially at the company's expense (examples are SENA in Colombia and SENAI in Brazil, but it should be remembered that the analyses of these programs were done in relatively high economic growth periods); (c) in countries characterized by low growth and increasing or high unemployment, short-course, self-employment-oriented training designed for new occupations in agriculture or the informal labor market may yield high returns provided that they focus on broader, "business" skills such as marketing and sales in addition to traditional production or service skills.

What is the complementarity of in-plant training to new technologies? It is commonly agreed that training programs are an important feature of successful firms producing high-technology products and those that use high-technology intensive capital (see, e.g., Shaiken and Herzenberg 1987). Less clear is the relationship of training programs to employee education and to work organization. Recent research in Mexico found that plants providing in-plant training generally geared it to certain "target" levels of education, and those targets were used in labor force hiring (Carnoy 1989). This held for production workers, as well as for management trainees and industrial engineers. There appears to be a significant relationship between the technology embodied in capital and work organization, the "optimum" level of education required of different kinds of employees who work with that capital or in that organization, and the in-plant training programs provided, although that optimum level may vary historically as the formal educational system expands. This suggests that "trainability" is as much a function of what is actually learned in various levels of schooling (the mathematics, science, and language arts curricula) as of graduates' sense of self-worth and capability. The first is an absolute consideration; employers producing particular products and using particular technology have a clear image of the minimum literacy and numeracy skills required for in-plant training in certain jobs. The availability of those school skills might be a condition of initial investment in such production. The second is relative: that is, how graduates are measured and how they measure themselves compared to others who are the same age and who are also seeking work at that point in time. A graduate with nine years of schooling in Mexico may well have a greater sense of capability than a high-school graduate in the United States. This relative notion of education is generally called its "screening" feature. The simpler the technology and the more hierarchical the organization, the less the complementarity between in-school education, in-plant training, and physical capital.

Learning by doing, unlike in-plant training, can be complemented by capital and especially by work organization. Once again, many questions arise: what is the complementarity of in-school education to learning by doing? Do more highly schooled workers learn more by doing with given capital (and therefore become more productive) than less schooled workers? Is in-plant formal training complementary to learning by doing, or are they relatively independent learning processes? Are certain types of work organization more complementary to learning by doing, given the schooling of workers and managers, than others (see Levin 1987)? Are there minimum levels of previous learning by doing which are required with certain kinds of technology or in certain industries and not in others?

The last wave of new technologies, new organizations of production, changing employment conditions, and the development of new sectors of production suggest that the complementarity of general, formal schooling, in-plant training, and learning by doing to capital investment are increasing over time and that general schooling plus on-the-job training is more complementary to new technologies than vocational schooling. The former combination is more likely to equip workers with the flexibility they require in such changing conditions. The analysis across types of sectors outlined above also suggests that different levels and conditions of development necessitate different decisions regarding schooling and training, and that many countries face the threat of being excluded from the new information revolution unless they restructure their economies and expand education and training programs with a focus on general and high-quality skill formation. The larger NICs could also fall far behind unless they, too, focus on university reform and greatly increased research and research-oriented training in higher education.

See also: Benefits of Education; Education, Occupation, and Earnings; Technological Change and Deskilling

References

Agarwal S M 1985 Electronics in India: Past strategies and future possibilities. *World Dev.* 13(3): 273–92

Amsden A 1989 *Asia's Next Giant: South Korea and Late Industrialization.* Oxford University Press, New York

Bhalla A S, James J 1984 New technology revolution: Myth or reality for developing countries? *Greek Econ. Rev.* 6 (3): 387–423

Bianchi P, Carnoy M, Castells M 1988 *Economic Modernization and Technology Transfer in the People's Republic of China.* Report No. 88–26. Center for Educational Research at Stanford, Stanford University, Stanford, California

Carnoy M 1972 The political economy of education. In: La

Belle T (ed.) 1972 *Education and Development in Latin America and the Caribbean.* Latin American Center, UCLA, Los Angeles, California

Carnoy M 1989 *Opening the Door: Education and Productivity.* Film produced by the International Labour Organisation, Geneva (VHS videotape, distributed by ILO, Geneva), 17 min

Carnoy M, Marenbach D 1975 The return to schooling in the United States, 1939–1969. *J. Hum. Resources* 10(3): 312–31

Castells M 1991 The university system: Engine of development in the new world economy. Paper prepared for the World Bank Seminar on Higher Education and Development, Kuala Lumpur (mimeo)

Chung Y-P 1990 The economic returns to vocational and technical education in a fast growing economy: A case study of Hong Kong. Unpublished doctoral dissertation, Stanford University, Stanford, California

Cohen S, Tyson L 1989 Technological change, competitiveness and the challenges confronting the American educational system. Berkeley Roundtable for International Economics, University of California, Berkeley, California (mimeo)

Dosi G 1988 Sources, procedures, and microeconomic effects of innovation. *J. Econ. Lit.* 26(3): 1120–71

Edquist C 1985 *Capitalism, Socialism and Technology: A Comparative Study of Cuba and Jamaica.* Zed Books, London

Edquist C, Jacobsson S 1988 *Flexible Automation: The Global Diffusion of New Technology in the Engineering Industry.* Basil Blackwell, Oxford

Evans P 1986 State, capital, and the transformation of dependence: The Brazilian computer case. *World Dev.* 14 (7): 791–808

Grubb N 1987 Responding to the constancy of change: New technologies and future demands on US education. In: Burke G, Rumberger R (eds.) 1987

Henderson J 1988 High technology production in Hong Kong and the making of a regional 'core'. Paper presented at the International Symposium of Technology Policy in the Americas, Stanford University, California

Henderson J, Castells M 1987 *Global Restructuring and Territorial Development.* Sage, Beverly Hills, California

Inkeles A, Smith D 1974 *Becoming Modern: Individual Change in Six Developing Countries.* Harvard University Press, Cambridge, Massachusetts

International Labour Organisation 1988 *Technological Change, Work Organization and Pay: Lessons from Asia.* Labor-Management Relations Series, No. 68. ILO, Geneva

Kim L 1986 New technologies and their economic effects: A feasibility study in Korea. Paper prepared for the United Nations University, New Technologies Centre Feasibility Study, Maastricht

Knight J B, Sabot R 1990 *Education, Productivity, and Inequality: The East African Natural Experiment.* World Bank/Oxford University Press, New York

Levin H 1987 Improving productivity through education and technology. In: Burke G, Rumberger R (eds.) 1987

Middleton J, Ziderman A, Van Adams A 1990 *Vocational Education and Training in Developing Countries.* World Bank, Washington, DC

Miller M 1986 High technology transfer: A case study of the Mexican computer electronics industry. Unpublished undergraduate honors thesis, Stanford University, California

Montoya A 1988 Telematics, knowledge and power in Mexican society: The policies of the Mexican State, 1970–1983. Unpublished Ph.D. dissertation, Stanford University, California (mimeo)

Pavitt K 1984 Patterns of technical change: Towards a taxonomy and a theory. *Res. Policy* 13(6): 343–73

Rogers E 1983 *Diffusion of Innovations*, 3rd edn. Free Press, New York

Rosenberg N 1976 *Perspectives on Technology*. Cambridge University Press, Cambridge

Rosenberg N 1982 *Inside the Black Box: Technology and Economics*. Cambridge University Press, Cambridge

Rumberger R 1981 *Overeducation in the US Labor Market*. Praeger, New York

Rumberger R, Levin H 1984 Forecasting the impact of new technologies on the future job market. *Technological Forecasting and Social Change* 27: 399–417

Ryoo J, Nam Y S, Carnoy M 1993 Rates of return to education in the Korea. *Econ. Educ. Rev.*

Salih K, Young M L 1989 Changing conditions of labour in the semiconductor industry in Malaysia. *Lab. Soc.* 14: 59–80 (special issue devoted to High Tech and Labor in Asia)

Schultz T 1989 Human capital in restoring equilibrium. Paper presented at the Conference on Human Capital and Economic Growth, Institute for the Study of Free Enterprise Systems, SUNY, Buffalo, New York

Shaiken H, Herzenberg S 1987 *Automation and Global Production. Automobile Engine Production in Mexico, the United States, and Canada*. University of California, Center for US–Mexican Studies, San Diego, California

Spenner K 1985 The upgrading and downgrading of occupations: Issues, evidence, and implications for education. *Rev. Educ. Res.* 55(2): 125–54

Warman J, Miller M 1989 *Competividad de la Industria Electrónica Mexicana: Estudios de caso*. Friedrich Ebert Foundation, Mexico City

Welch F 1970 Education in production. *J. Pol. Econ.* 78(1): 35–59

Further Reading

Burke G, Rumberger R (eds.) 1987 *The Future Impact of Technology on Work and Education*. Falmer Press, London

Castells M 1985 New technologies, world development, and structural transformation: The trends and the debate. Department of City and Regional Planning, University of California, Berkeley, California (mimeo)

Rumberger R, Levin H M 1989 Schooling for the modern workplace. Background paper No. 2 prepared for the Commission on Workforce Quality and Labor Market Efficiency, US Department of Labor, Washington, DC

Technology and the Classroom Teacher

N. Hativa

The teacher has a key role in the introduction of technology into the classroom and in its successful adoption and application. This article describes this role, the extent and patterns of the use of technology in the classroom, and factors that either promote or impede the successful integration of technology into the curriculum.

1. Teachers as Decision Makers in the Adoption and Use of Technology in the Classroom

During the twentieth century, there have been many attempts to penetrate schools with various technological innovations. Examples included the overhead projector, teaching machines, radio, 8 millimeter film, television, video-cassette recorders (VCRs), and computers. The majority of these technologies did not achieve widespread use in schools and did not survive the initial years of enthusiasm. The computer, on the other hand, has won widespread adoption and use, more than any of the other technologies.

Teachers are the most critical decision makers regarding the adoption and use of technology in schools. Concentrating on computers, teachers' decisions affect the type, frequency, and even the mere existence of computer experiences for students. Teachers also decide how to organize students' computer work socially: working individually, in pairs or in small groups, cooperatively or competitively. This social organization bears an important role in students' learning. Teachers' decisions regarding computer use in school are affected by their instructional style, flexibility in adapting to new teaching situations, attitudes toward computers, length of experience using computers in their own lessons, and their self-perception as computer users (Collis 1988).

2. Patterns of Teacher Use of Technology in the Classroom

A survey of teachers in 19 countries (China, India, Israel, Japan, New Zealand, and several countries in Europe) examined the use of computers in education. As a result of this study, Pelgrum and Plomp (1991) identified two major applications of computers in schools worldwide. First, there is an emphasis on learning about computers, primarily on the acquisition of operational skills in handling computers or learning programming languages. Second, there is an emphasis on using computers as an aid in teaching and learning traditional school subjects. This latter application is often referred to as the "integration of computers into the curriculum or into classroom teaching" (Sheingold et al. 1987). In this regard, the integration of computers in a school is regarded as successful when the computers are used in a variety of subjects by a large proportion of students and teachers (Meister 1984).

2.1 Integrating Computers into Classroom Instruction

The successful integration of computers throughout the curriculum—either for the purpose of learning traditional subjects or for tool use—is a major school goal (Sheingold et al. 1987). Teachers implement this integration in many different ways depending on their personal characteristics, teaching styles and methods, subject matter, and class level (Hadley and Sheingold 1993, OTA 1988). Teachers use computers in quite a wide range of pedagogical approaches: to individualize instruction, encourage individual and group problem solving, provide drill and practice for promoting basic skills, provide peer work with social-science simulations, simulate laboratory experiments, and perform real laboratory experiments using computer-attached sensors. They also use the computer as a tool for improving the students' productivity in accomplishing academic tasks (e.g., using word processors for writing or incorporating database management for analyzing data for students' projects).

In schools in the United States teachers are increasingly seeing the computer as a tool for improving students' productivity but they continue to use it also as a method of improving students' basic skills in mathematics or language arts. The higher the school level, the more the computer is used as an academic tool (Becker 1990). In elementary schools, the most frequent computer applications are self-exploratory activities for students, simulations, tutorials, drill-and-practice, and computer-based testing. A growing proportion of computer time is spent on instruction in keyboard techniques and in using word-processing programs. In lower secondary or middle schools computers are used most frequently for drill-and-practice and less frequently for self-exploratory activities. In upper secondary schools computers are used frequently as productivity tools or for teacher demonstration and exploration for the whole class (Becker 1990, Pelgrum and Plomp 1991).

A small proportion of teachers, identified as expert users of computers in schools (Sheingold and Hadley 1990), have been found to use a large software repertoire in multipurpose applications. They use tool-based computer environments to adapt and individualize tasks to students' needs and also operate small-group activity-based learning. They take multiple approaches to the use of computers in their classrooms for purposes as varied as demonstrating an idea in front of the class and individual student

remediation. Most commonly, students make their own products with the computer.

2.2 Location and Number of Computers and their Use by Teachers

Whether computers are located in a computer laboratory or distributed among classrooms strongly affects teacher and student attitudes toward computer use, the type of computer use, students' access to computers, and the extent to which teachers integrate computers into ongoing subject matter learning experiences.

Whole-class concurrent individualized activities can take place only if the number of computers is at least the same as the number of students. Similarly, pair work with computers for the whole class is possible only if the number of computers is at least one half the number of students. For these two types of whole-class computer activities, the computers are usually located in a special laboratory, networked to a central source of software that manages students' learning, assigns them learning activities, tests them frequently, and records their advancement. In situations where there are not enough computers for the whole class to work on concurrently, classes are split up and one group of students perform other activities while the others are working at the computer.

Computers located in the classrooms are usually stand-alone stations (not networked) that require separate loading and printing facilities. The most common arrangement in this case is to have two students share one computer and work cooperatively on drill-and-practice, problem solving, or similar tasks. A single computer in a classroom can also be used by the teacher in a variety of ways at various occasions. It can be used as a learning station for individual students, or can be attached to a large cathode ray tube (CRT) screen or to a projector on a large screen for presenting interactive demonstrations, experimentations, problem solving, and new concepts to the whole class.

In lower secondary and middle schools computers are most frequently located in a laboratory while in upper secondary schools they are in the classrooms; in elementary schools both arrangements are found (Pelgrum and Plomp 1991). Locating computers in laboratory at the high school level causes several problems. Many teachers choose not to interrupt their preferred teaching routines in order to relocate student activity to a laboratory. In addition, many teachers feel uncomfortable about working in a laboratory because it is perceived as the "territory" of a subgroup of staff, typically the teachers of computer science, mathematics, or physical sciences. Consequently, the laboratory is underutilized by the majority of teachers and overutilized by that subgroup of staff (Collis 1988).

2.3 Computerized Learning Environments and Teacher Role and Behavior

The integration of computers into the curriculum requires teachers to identify software that is relevant to the curriculum and specific lessons and to provide feedback and suggestions to their students as they use computers. For each type of computer-based activity, teachers need to provide either explicit teaching or individualized support. Consider the following two examples of basic computer-based activities.

Software that manages individualized student work in a computer laboratory often prints out a computerized class report on request. This report has proved an extremely helpful tool for the teacher in adapting instruction to the individual learner in and outside the computer laboratory. Teachers use it for tailoring individualized seatwork, for forming homogeneous groups of students to work together on problems in-class, and for providing explanations to the whole class on topics identified by the report as problematic to many students (Hativa et al. 1990).

In computer-based environments where students learn in groups, the interactivity of the computer software and its management of the content presented to students frees the teacher to observe the groups in action and to concentrate on leading the students in their analysis and discussions (OTA 1988). The role of the teacher shifts from that of provider of content-specific information to facilitator of students' own information organization skills. Instruction techniques shift away from the direct delivery of information toward greater emphasis on shaping students' mastery of the information and promoting thinking skills such as finding relevant information, solving problems, asking questions, thinking critically, and communicating ideas (Sheingold et al. 1987).

Does the introduction of computers into classrooms affect the teacher's role, behavior and methods? The study by Hativa et al. (1990) reveals that increased experience with students' individualized computer-based practice led to substantial changes in teacher behavior and in teaching methods. The most substantial change observed was a switch from frontal teaching, found in a high proportion of teachers new to computerized work, to individualized or achievement-based grouping of students, found in a high proportion of teachers experienced in this work. Similarly, for most of the exemplary computer-using teachers identified by Sheingold and Hadley (1990), computers did make a real difference in their teaching and in their expectations of student performance. The teachers began to expect more of their students, present more complex material, conduct better individualization in learning, encourage students' independent work, and promote student-centered classes. These teachers acted more as coaches and facilitators than as information transmitters. In summary, these teachers made their classrooms less teacher centered and more student centered and believed that the computer use changed their instruction and increased its effectiveness (Hadley and Sheingold 1993).

3. The Extent of Teachers' Use of Computers in Their Classes

In the United States the process of integrating computers into the curriculum has been relatively rapid. In a four-year period (1985–1989), the number of computer-using teachers doubled. In the early 1990s, 39 percent of all school teachers in the United States used computers in their classes. In other countries, the implementation of computers seems to be going much slower and to be at a much earlier stage. Outside the United States, computer applications in schools are still very limited. Learning about computers plays an important role, whereas the application of computers in existing subject areas frequently deals with drill and practice. Problem solving and simulation approaches, which are indicative of a more innovative approach to computer use in the classroom, are still rather scarce (Pelgrum and Plomp 1991).

However, teachers are still largely underutilizing computers. Marcinkiewicz's (1994) survey of elementary-school teachers reveals that 50 percent of them do not use computers at all for teaching even though computers are available in their schools. In addition, the mere number of computer-using teachers can be misleading. The important issue is the effectiveness of computer use in achieving the goals of instruction. Research that has examined this issue shows a striking discrepancy between teacher-reported use and actual use of computers for instruction. Computers are being used only minimally and without apparent focus or educational rationales. Many teachers still lack clear vision of how to teach effectively with computer technology. Moreover, many teachers resist using computers for instruction and find subtle ways to circumvent pressure to integrate computers into their teaching that comes from school principals, superintendents, and computer coordinators. These teachers either use the microcomputers as an extension of what they have already been doing in the classroom, make token gestures regarding computer use, or avoid using computers altogether (Hativa 1991).

In contrast to teachers who avoid using computers effectively, there are teachers who are expert and enthusiastic users of computers and who do provide intellectually exciting educational experiences at all grade levels. Teachers of this type, referred to as "expert computer-using teachers," were identified by Sheingold and Hadley (1990) and by Becker (1994) as constituting a broad cross-section of teachers from different regions and from different demographic and socioeconomic climates in the United States. They have their students use a wide variety of computer software in ways that are directly related to the teachers' major curricular goals.

In order to assess the actual impact of computers on school learning, the extent of effective computer use in schools and the proportion of expert computer-using teachers must be studied. Sheingold and Hadley's

(1990) survey cannot provide this information because it has identified expert teachers only on the basis of their reputation. Becker (1994), using a probability sample of schools in the United States, found that expert computer-using teachers constitute only 5 percent of all computer-using teachers and only 3 percent of all teachers of academic subjects. In other words, 95 percent of computer-using teachers use the computer ineffectively to a certain degree. This surprisingly high proportion suggests that computer applications in schools are not yet very effective.

4. Obstacles to the Adoption and Use of Technology by Teachers

The evidence presented in the above section points to a lack of proper integration of computers into classroom teaching. However, this phenomenon has been observed with most attempts to penetrate schools with new technologies during the twentieth century. Bosco (1988) summarizes:

> Television, 8mm film, radio, teaching machines, and even the telephone, were all touted as technologies which would improve instruction in the schools. There was considerable effort to turn television into an educational tool, but this effort has had little effect. Teachers cited the inconvenience of broadcast schedules and lack of appropriate programming as the most common barriers to use of TV. One might think the solution to these problems would have been the VCR. Most schools have TVs and VCRs, both of which are less expensive than computers, and there is much excellent video software available. Yet, the resolution of the perceived barriers has not resulted in significantly expanded use of video technology. (1988 p. 1)

What then are the impediments to the adoption of computer technology by teachers? Several sources (Hativa 1991, OTA 1988, Pelgrum and Plomp 1991, Wiske et al. 1988) indicate the following obstacles:

(a) *Lack of teacher knowledge and inadequate training.* Teachers are not trained properly to operate hardware, choose appropriate software, or integrate software into classroom instruction.

(b) *Logistics obstacles.* Teachers do not know what software is available, find that available software is inappropriate for their classes, and struggle with a single disk when they really need multiple disks. For many teachers, having to schedule the computer laboratory in advance and make arrangements to relocate the class constitute a logistical burden.

(c) *Extra burden on teacher time and effort in lesson preparation and planning.* The teacher needs to choose the appropriate software, learn to work with it and with the computer, and plan a fallback lesson in case the computer malfunctions. In addition, it takes substantial planning to match

software to the curriculum, and design separate activities for the students not using computers when there are not enough computers for a whole-class activity. Much computer software covers only one or a few instructional concepts; thus, the teacher needs to find the best way to incorporate sundry pieces of software into the overall curriculum.

(d) *Undesired changes in teacher role.* School reforms that attempted to foster student-centered classrooms have not taken root because the teacher-centered classroom has traditionally been accepted as the way to maintain order and to teach considerable instructional content to students. Since many computer applications produce changes in the traditional teacher role, they often fail to achieve widespread adoption. In addition, reducing the direct interaction between teacher and students as implied by many types of computer work reduces the likelihood of the psychological rewards that teachers experience with their teacher-centered instruction.

(e) *Difficulties in maintaining the traditional curriculum.* Teachers are reluctant to attempt innovative approaches when stringent curriculum requirements are reinforced by standardized tests. They feel accountable to uphold their professional responsibilities and to prepare their students to pass tests that constitute crucial gateways in their academic progress.

(f) *Fear.* The microcomputer produces strong anxiety among teachers. Teachers are afraid of the complex, technical nature of the microcomputer. Specifically, they fear that they are not able to use the hardware or software and that their students know more than they do about computers.

To conclude, the basic problem with the use of computer technology in schools is the attempt to incorporate it into the curriculum by adapting it to an existing infrastructure. Significant and innovative use of computers does not articulate well with the basic features of many classrooms. The effective use of computers requires social and organizational changes which take into consideration the fact that the classroom is an organizational entity with a well-established set of traditions and practices. This problem cannot be resolved by good hardware, software, and teacher training. Rather, only by direct confrontation with the elements in the classroom environment which create the logistical impediments to computer use can effective use of computers be increased.

5. Promoting the Successful Adoption of Technology in Schools

Despite the pessimism of the above section, several factors are related to the successful integration of computers into the curriculum and the classroom. Positive attitudes facilitate the adoption and use of technology by teachers. A crucial factor for teacher adoption of any innovation is having high satisfaction working with this innovation (Cuban 1984).

Positive attitudes toward integrating computers into teaching are formed as the result of the actual use of computers (Pelgrum and Plomp 1991). Sheingold and Hadley (1990) found that over time and with substantial experience—at least five to six years of teaching with computers—the exemplary computer-using teachers became increasingly comfortable and confident about using computers. Similarly, teacher satisfaction with computer-managed practice was found to be extraordinarily high for teachers who had used computers with their students for more than one year in comparison to teachers new to computer use (Hativa et al. 1990).

In addition to having substantial experience in teaching with computers, Hadley and Sheingold (1993) identified four additional conditions that must be met if teachers are to become exemplary school computer users. They are: (a) having high motivation for teaching; (b) receiving considerable support from their school and district in efforts for personal development as teachers; (c) being motivated by their students' using software tools for effective learning; and (d) having access in school to sufficient quantities of computers and to sophisticated technology (e.g., hard disk drives, laser printers, videodisc players). Similarly, Becker (1994) found that the likelihood of the development of exemplary teachers is enhanced in schools in which (a) social networks exist for fostering expert computer use; (b) there is sustained and widespread use of computers at the school for writing and publishing activities; (c) there is organized support for computer-using teachers in the form of staff development activities and a full-time computer coordinator role; and (d) acknowledgment of the resource requirements for effectively using computers, for example, smaller class sizes and funds for software acquisition.

6. Conclusion and Needs for Future Research

The successful integration of computers into classroom teaching has been accomplished by only a very small proportion of computer-using teachers worldwide. The use of the computer for learning in school constitutes a logistical burden for many teachers. To increase the integration of technology into the classroom, the existing school infrastructure must be changed dramatically. Future research should examine the behavior of teachers using computers in different innovative school and learning environments.

See also: Gender and New Technology; Social Implications of Educational Technology; Sociology of Teaching; Teachers' Knowledge; Teachers' Roles

References

Becker H J 1990 Computer use in United States schools: 1989. An initial report of US participation in the IEA Paper presented at the annual meeting of the American Educational Research Association, Boston, Massachusetts

Becker H J 1994 How exemplary computer-using teachers differ from other teachers: Implications for realizing the potential of computers in schools. *J. Res. Computing Educ.* 26(3): 291–321

Bosco J J 1988 *Structural Impediments to Computer Integration in Schools in the US 5th International Conference on Technology and Education*, Vol. I. CEP Consultants Ltd., Edinburgh

Collis B 1988 Manipulating critical variables: A framework for improving the impact of computers in the school environment. Paper presented at the annual meeting of EURIT, Lausanne

Cuban L 1984 *How Teachers Taught. Constancy and Change in American Classrooms 1890–1980*. Longman, New York

Hadley M, Sheingold K 1993 Commonalities and distinctive patterns in teachers' integration of computers. *Am. J. Educ.* 101(3): 261–315

Hativa N 1991 Teacher behavior and computer-based education. In: Husén T, Postlethwaite T N (eds.) 1991 *The International Encyclopedia of Education: Research and Studies*, Supplementary Vol. 2. Pergamon Press, Oxford

Hativa N, Shapira R, Navon D 1990 Computer-manager practice —effects on instructional methods and on teacher adoption. *Teach. Teach. Educ.* 6(1): 55–68

Marcinkiewicz H R 1994 Computers and teachers: Factors influencing computer use in the classroom. *J. Res. Computing Educ.* 26(2): 220–37

Meister G R 1984 *Successful Integration of Microcomputers in an Elementary School*. Program Report No. 84–A13, Institute for Research on Educational Finance and Goverance, Stanford University, Stanford, California

Office of Technology Assessment (OTA) Staff 1988 *Power On! New Tools for Teaching and Learning*. Technonic Publishing Co., Lancaster, Pennsylvania

Pelgrum W J, Plomp T 1991 *The Use of Computers in Education Worldwide*. Pergamon Press, Oxford

Sheingold K, Hadley M 1990 *Accomplished Teachers: Integrating Computers into Classroom Practice*. Center for Technology and Education, Bank Street College of Education, New York

Sheingold K, Martin M W, Endreweit M E 1987 Preparing urban teachers for the technological future. In: Pea R D, Sheingold K (eds.) 1987 *Mirrors of the Minds*. Ablex, Norwood, New Jersey

Wiske M S et al. 1988 *How Technology Affects Teaching*. Educational Technology Center, Education Development Center, Cambridge, Massachusetts

Further Reading

Dupagne M, Krendl K A (1992) Teachers' attitudes toward computers: A review of the literature. *J. Res. Computing Educ.* 24(3): 420–29

Wild M 1996 Technology refusal: Rationalising the failure of student and beginning teachers to use computers. *Br. J. Educ. Technol.* 27(2): 134–43

(c) Educational Policy and Planning

Educational Research and Policymaking

T. Husén

Educational research has two constituencies of practitioners: (a) teachers and school administrators; and (b) policymakers in education. Classroom practitioners expect educational research to help them improve the planning and execution of teaching. At the turn of the century the emerging psychology with its empirical and experimental methods was expected to provide guidelines for educational practice by identifying the facts and laws of learning, and by providing an understanding of individual development and individual differences. In his *Talks to Teachers on Psychology* (1899), William James underlined that education being an art and not a science could not deduce schemes and methods of teaching for direct classroom application out of psychology. "An intermediary inventive mind must make the application by using its originality" (p. 8). In order to bridge the gap between theory and practice, James tried over and over again to make his presentation of psychology less technical. In the preface to his book which appeared several years after the lectures were given for the first time he says: "I have found by experience that what my hearers seem least to relish is analytical technicality, and what they most care for is concrete practical application. So I have gradually weeded out the former, and left the latter reduced: and now that I have at least written out the lectures, they contain a minimum of what is deemed 'scientific' psychology and are practical and popular in the extreme" (p. III).

In general, there is a similar relationship between research and practice in policymaking. For a long time this relationship was, by both partners involved, conceived of in a rather simplistic way. Policymakers wanted research that primarily addressed their pressing problems within the framework of their perceptions of the world of education. They wanted findings that could be more or less directly applied to issues and problems under their consideration. Researches conceived of their role as expert problem solvers who advised policymakers what to do.

The problem of how research in education is related to policy-making was hardly studied before the 1960s. However, after this date, resources given to educational research grew markedly. Governments and private foundations within a period of a decade increased massively the funds for research in education, most of which was conducted by behavioral scientists. Hopes grew correspondingly high about what research might achieve in broadening the knowledge base for educational practice. Research was expected to provide recipes for the successful solution to classroom problems. Policymakers expected educational research to help them in the planning and execution of reforms that would improve the quality of a nation's schools. Typically, the enormous increase of funds for educational research under the provisions of the Elementary and Secondary Education Act passed by the United States Congress in 1965 was part of a big package of legislation on compensatory education being in its turn part of the Great Society program (Husén 1979).

In the 1960s the research and development (R & D) model which had been developed in science and technology was extended to the fields of education and social welfare. The model assumes a linear relationship between fundamental research, applied research, development of a prototype, its mass production, and dissemination in the field. The high hopes easily led to frustrations. Researchers began to be accused of coming up with "findings" which were "useless" to practitioners, be they school teachers or administrators, in schools or governments. There was a growing demand for "relevance."

The simplistic model of "linear" or "direct" application of research does not work in education for two main reasons. In the first place, education is, like other areas in the social realm, imbued with values. Educational research deals with a reality which is perceived differently depending upon ideological convictions and values held by both practitioner and researcher. The way a problem is conceptualized, how it is empirically studied and analyzed, and how the findings from studies are interpreted often depends very much on tacit or overt value assumptions. One typical example is research on bilingual education, the extent to which a minority child in a country with a main language should have an opportunity to be instructed in their mother tongue. Second, and often overlooked, are the widely different conditions under which researchers and policymakers operate. Studies of these conditions began in the 1970s.

The value problem in educational research has begun to be analyzed by educational philosophers. It is highlighted by the controversy between logical positivism or neopositivism which has dominated the social science scene since the 1940s and critical philosophies of various brands. The former takes the social reality educational research deals with as a fact and takes for granted that research can advance "objectively" valid statements about that reality. The role of the researcher vis-à-vis the policymaker is that of a technician: he or she provides the instrument or the expertise that policymakers and practitioners "use" in framing and implementing their plans and policies. The latter type of philosophy sees critical studies as a means of changing society and thereby more or less explicitly allows value premises to enter into the research process (see *Research Paradigms in Education*).

In the following discussion, the different conditions under which policymakers and researchers operate will be analyzed and the differences in ethos which guide endeavors in the respective categories will be described. After that, various research utilization models will be dealt with.

1. The Setting for Policymaking

Tensions between researchers and policymakers depend on certain constraints under which policy is shaped and implemented. Some of these have been discussed by Levin (1978) and by Husén and Kogan (1984).

Policymakers are primarily or even exclusively only interested in research that addresses problems which are on their agenda. This means that what researchers conceive as fundamental research which bears no or only a very remote relationship to the issues of the day is of little or no interest, if change in political regime or administration can mean a rearrangement of issues. For instance, the issues of private schools, educational vouchers, and busing took on quite a different importance under the Reagan as opposed to the Carter administration in the United States. In Europe after the Second World War the central issue in many countries was to what extent the structure of the mandatory school should be comprehensive with regard to intake of students and programs. In countries like Sweden, England and Wales, and the former Federal Republic of Germany many studies pertaining to the pedagogical and social aspects of comprehensiveness have been conducted and have been referred to extensively in the policy debate. In England, the 1944 Education Act with its provisions for tripartite, secondary education in grammar, technical, and modern schools, and the selection for grammar school (the so-called "11+ examination") became an issue of the first order and gave rise to a large body of research on methods of selection and their effects. The issue of equality of educational opportunity has been a major one in Europe and the United States since the 1950s and recently in many developing countries as well. It has consequently inspired a large volume of research (Husén 1975).

Politicians have party allegiances which influence not only what they regard as relevant, innocuous, or even dangerous research, but also their willingness to take research findings into account. Research, even if it addresses itself to a major issue on the political agenda, can be discarded or even rejected by one side in a political controversy if it does not support its views. Politicians, in the same way as court advocates, tend to select the evidence which they interpret as supporting their views.

Policymakers have their particular time horizon which in a parliamentary democracy tends to be rather narrow and determined not only by regular general elections, but also by the flow of policy decisions. Research which takes years to complete cannot be considered if the policymaker's timetable requires the outcomes of a research project or program to be available "here and now." Research findings have to be made available in time for the decisions that by necessity have to be taken, irrespective of the nature of the "knowledge base" on which the decision maker stands. He or she needs immediate access to findings. This is a dilemma which planners and policymakers in a government agency continuously have to face. On the one hand, strategic planning with a relatively broad time perspective goes on. On the other hand, operational decision-making is a continuous process which cannot wait for specially commissioned research to produce "relevant facts" of a rather simple, straightforward nature. This had led many administrators involved in policy-making to demand that research should be strictly decision- or policy-oriented and address problems "in the field" only.

Policymakers are concerned only with policies in a particular area of their own experience as politicians or administrators. They therefore tend to disregard the connections with other areas. Educational policies have been advanced in order to solve what basically are problems in the larger social context. For example, in the United States in the mid-1960s compensatory education programs with enormous federal funds were made available to local schools. The intention was to "break the poverty cycle" by providing better education and thereby enhancing the employability of the economically disadvantaged (Husén 1979).

Policymakers are in most cases not familiar with educational research or social science research in general. In particular, they are not familiar with the language researchers use in communicating with each other, a language that ideally serves precision in presenting theories and methods, but by laypersons is often perceived as empty jargon. The problem then is to disseminate research findings in such a way that they can be understood by "ordinary people."

2. The Setting for Research

Researchers operate under conditions that in several respects differ from those under which people of practical affairs in politics and administration operate. There are differences of background, social values, and institutional settings.

Researchers in education have traditionally been performing their tasks at teacher-training institutions, most frequently at universities. As a result of growing government involvement, research units have been established by public agencies as instruments of planning and evaluation. Researchers conduct their work according to paradigms to which they have become socialized during their graduate studies (see *Research Paradigms in Education*). They are in the first place anxious to preserve their autonomy as researchers from interferences by politicians or administrators. Second, their allegiance is more to fundamental or conclusion-oriented research than to applied or decision-oriented research. Third, and as a consequence of this orientation, they pay much more attention to how their research is received by their peers in the national or international community of scholars in their field of specialization than by their customers in public agencies. This means, among other things, that once a technical report has been submitted, the researcher tends to lose interest in what happens to their findings.

Researchers are much less constrained than policymakers with regard to what problems they can tackle, what kind of critical language they can employ, and, not least, how much time they can use in completing a study. An investigation by the Dutch Foundation for Educational Research (Kallen et al. 1982) found that the great majority of projects financed by the Foundation lagged behind the timetable agreed upon for their completion. In order to conduct an empirical field study properly several years are required. The relevant literature on the "state of the art" has to be reviewed, methods have to be developed, data have to be collected in the field, data have to be processed and analyzed, sufficient time has to be allowed for writing the report, and finally, it takes some time for critical reviews in scholarly journals to appear. This is a process which typically takes about four to six years. Thus, the researcher has a different time horizon to that of the policymaker, both in terms of how much time he or she can allow for a study and in terms of how his or her study fits into the ongoing research in the field. He or she perceives the study as an often humble contribution to an increasingly growing body of knowledge in a particular problem area.

Status in the research system depends upon the reputation that crystallizes from the continously ongoing review of a researcher's work by colleagues inside or outside his or her own institution. Whereas in an administrative agency status depends on seniority and position in the organizational hierarchy, it is in the long run the quality of a person's research and the recognition of this that determines the reputation in the scholarly community to which the researcher relates himself or herself.

3. Disjunctions between Researchers and Policymakers

The differences in settings and in value orientation between policymakers and educational researchers constitute what could be referred to as different kinds of ethos. It is even possible to speak of "two cultures." The research customers, the politicians, and/or the administrators/planners in a public agency are by necessity pragmatists. They regard research almost entirely as an instrument for achieving a certain policy or for use in planning or implementing certain administrative goals. They want research to be focused on priority areas of current politics.

University-based researchers are brought up in the tradition of "imperial, authoritative, and independent" Research with a capital R. In order to discharge properly what they regard as their task, academics tend to take an independent and critical attitude, not least toward government. They tend to guard anxiously their academic autonomy.

These differences in value orientation and outlook tend to influence the relationship between the policymaker and the researcher all the way from the initiation of a research project to the interpretation of its findings. The "researchworthiness" of a proposed study is assessed differently. The policymaker looks at its relevance for the issues on the agenda, whereas the researcher in the first place tends to assess it on the basis of "research-immanent" criteria, to what extent the proposed research can contribute to fundamental knowledge. The researcher wants to initiate studies without any particular considerations to the applicability of the findings and with the purpose of extending the frontiers of fundamental knowledge.

The fact that education by necessity deals with values anchored in various ideologies easily brings educational research into the turmoil of political controversy. Most regimes and administrations in power tend to perceive social science research with suspicion because of its critical nature. Those who want to preserve the status quo often tend to regard research as subversive radicalism. It is, however, in the nature of research to be in a literal sense "radical," that is to say, to go to the root (Latin "*radix*").

The close relationship between education and certain political and social philosophies has made it tempting for social scientists to become ideological evangelists. This has had an adverse effect on their credibility. The common denominator of what is understood by "academic ethos" is critical inquiry that does not spare partisan doctrines, not even the ones of the party to which the researcher belongs.

In the 1960s, social science and behavioral research on an unprecedented scale began to be supported by the government in countries such as the United States, Sweden, the United Kingdom, and the former Federal Republic of Germany. Social scientists began to have a strong appeal and provided the arguments liberal politicians needed in favor of programs in education and social welfare. The liberals had a strong confidence in what social science could achieve. This meant that economists, sociologists, and psychologists were commissioned to conduct research that was part of the implementation of various programs in education (Aaron 1978). At the same time, there was a quest for evaluation of these programs and increasingly a component of evaluation was included in planning them.

Soon discrepancies between expectations and actual research performances began to be aired and led to demands for accountability. There have been indications of a decreasing credibility on the part of policymakers vis-à-vis researchers since the early 1970s. Expert testimonies on major policy issues have been seen as inconclusive and inconsistent. Coleman's (1966) survey of equality of educational opportunity was interpreted to support desegregation in the public schools of the United States (Coleman 1966). His subsequent studies of busing were interpreted as providing counterevidence. Policymakers want, as President Truman once expressed it in talking about his economic advisors, "one-handed" advice and are not happy with "on the one hand—on the other hand." Furthermore, the credibility gap has been widened by allegations of ideologically imbued professional advice. In some countries, social scientists working in education have been accused of "Leftist leanings" and subversive intentions. Political preferences among social scientists have even led to the establishment of research institutions with different political orientations, such as Brookings Institution and the American Enterprise Institute in the United States.

There are some inherent difficulties for educational research to prove its usefulness. The committee which at the end of the 1970s evaluated the National Institute of Education pointed out that improvements in the learning and the behavior of students as a result of research endeavors are difficult to demonstrate. The committee gave three main reasons for this: (a) a low level of sophistication in the social sciences in comparison with the physical sciences does not allow "the luxury of predictable results;" (b) problems of bringing about and measuring changes in human learning and behavior are "vastly more complex" than those in the field of technological change; and (c) the need for improvement in education is so great that expectations on educational R & D have been set much higher than is possible to achieve.

The crucial problem behind many of the frustrations felt by customers of educational research is that research cannot provide answers to the value questions with which social issues, including those in education, are imbued. This means that research even of the highest quality and "relevance" can only provide partial information that has to be integrated with experience and human judgment. The Australian Minister of Education (Shellard 1979) quoted Glass as saying that there is more knowledge stored in the nervous systems of ten excellent teachers about how to manage classroom learning than what an average teacher could distill from all existing educational research journals.

Implied in what has been said so far are three major reasons for a "disjunction" between policymaking and research.

Research does not "fit" a particular situation. It might not at a given point in time be related to any political issue. Women's equal rights were for a long time a dead issue. But when they became an issue, they rapidly began to spur an enormous amount of research. But research addressing itself to issues on the agenda might come up with evidence that is out of phase with the policymaking process. As pointed out above, policymakers, like advocates, want to use research in order to support or legitimize a "prefabricated position." Often the situation occurs whereby research findings are in contradiction with or at least do not support the policy that a decision-making body or an agency wants to take or has already taken.

Research findings are, from the policymaker's point of view, not particularly conclusive. Furthermore, it is in the nature of the research process that in order to make a public issue "researchable" the overall problem has to be broken down into parts that more readily lend themselves to focused investigations.

A third major reason for the disjunctions between researchers and policymakers is ineffective dissemination. Research findings do not by themselves reach decision-makers and practitioners. Researchers seek recognition in the first place among their peers. They place high premium on reports that can enhance their academic reputation and tend to look with skepticism upon popularization. It has been suggested that this problem can be dealt with by middlepersons who can serve in the role of "research brokers" or policy analysts and can communicate to practitioners what appears to be relevant to them. A particular type of research broker is the one who conducts meta analyses of research, that is to say, reviews critically the existing research in a particular field in order to come up with relatively valid conclusions from the entire body of research.

4. Reviews of the "Utility" of Educational Research

The breakthrough in many countries for educational research with regard to institutionalization and, not least, funding came after the Second World War. Research was expected to serve educational policymakers and practitioners in planning and implementing educational reforms. Countries which provide examples are the United States, the United Kingdom, Sweden, and the former Federal Republic of Germany. However, the expectations bolstered by generous promises often led to disappointments.

Since the late 1970s, achievements of educational

research have been reviewed in a spirit of self-criticism and a quest for realism in their promises. It has been pointed out that, until the 1960s, educational research had come up with findings of significance which have had and still have an impact on educational policy and practice. Edward L Thorndike's studies of formal discipline and his establishment of the law of effect made their way into school teaching, as has also Arthur Gate's principle of active learning. The research that Kurt Lewin and his associates made on styles of classroom leadership have had their impact on the training of teachers and administrators. Binet and his successors have strongly influenced the practice in grouping and special education. Recent research which has had an impact is represented by Bloom's on mastery learning, studies of criterion-referenced testing, and the psychology of the reading process.

The National Academy of Education in the United States published in 1991 a report on "Research and the Renewal of Education." It was part of a project on funding priorities for educational research and therefore also reviewed what educational research could achieve. It was underscored that "learning exists outside of schools and that research must embrace education in its broadest contexts—including learning that takes place within families, communities, and in other settings." Research policy should be integrated with the research goals of social, economic, and health services. In proposing a research agenda, the Academy particularly singled out research on active learning over the lifespan, assessment and instructional relevance of testing, historically underserved minority groups, studies of schools as institutions, and the connection between teachers and teaching.

Social science research has been accused of giving divergent and confusing messages, with one researcher refuting the other. Policymakers and practitioners want "one authoritative voice." Coleman (1984) has proposed the setting up of "science courts" as a means of establishing pluralistic policy research. A study could begin by identifying the parties interested in a particular issue, and by describing the vested interests and their legitimacy. The research should be designed so as to address policy-relevant questions and, in doing so, introduce a dialectical element in the research process. The findings could then be subjected to competitive alternative analyses which in their turn could be reviewed by the "science court" which could see to it that the research is presented in an independent report. It should give room for alternative analyses and interpretations.

5. Models of Research Utilization

The way research, in particular social science research, is "utilized" in educational policymaking in general has been studied in the first place by political scientists. Important contributions to the conceptualization

have been made by Weiss (1979, 1980), and to the empirical study of the problem by both her and Caplan (1976).

In the first place, Weiss points out that "decisions" on policies or policy actions are not taken in the orderly and rational way that many think, namely that individuals authorized to decide sit down and ponder various options, consider relevant facts, and choose one of the options. Policies are decided upon in a much more diffuse way. What occurs is a complicated dynamic interaction between various interest groups, where, by means of arguments advanced by them, administrative considerations, and, not least, the inertia in the system, guidelines for action begin to emerge. The best way to characterize this process is to talk about "decision accretion."

Not least, researchers have been caught in rational and "knowledge-driven" models of how research findings relate to policymaking. Research findings rather "percolate" through public opinion to policymakers. Instead of the latter taking into consideration particular studies, they tend to be influenced by the total body of research in a particular field. Findings usually do not reach those in positions of influence via scientific and technical reports but to a large extent via the popular press and other mass media. A body of notions that forms a *commune bonum* of "what research has to say" is built up via diverse channels of popularization. Theoretical conceptions and specific findings are "trickling" or "percolating" down and begin to influence enlightened public opinion and, in the last run, public policy.

Weiss (1979) distinguishes between seven different "models" or concepts of research utilization in the social sciences. The first model is the R & D model which has dominated the picture of how research in the physical sciences is utilized. It is a "linear" process from basic research via applied research and development to application of new technology. There was a time in the 1960s and early 1970s when the R & D model was expected to apply in education by the development of programmed instruction and material for individualized teaching. Weiss points out that its applicability in the social sciences is heavily limited, since knowledge in this field does not readily lend itself to "conversion into replicable technologies, either material or social" (p. 427).

The second model is the problem-solving one, where results from a particular research project are expected to be used directly in a pending decision-making situation. The process can schematically be described as follows: identification of missing knowledge → acquisition of research information either by conducting a specific study or by reviewing the existing body of research → interpretation of research findings in the context given policy options → decision about policy to pursue.

This is the classical "philosopher-king" conception. Researchers are supposed to provide the knowledge and wisdom from which policymakers can derive guidelines for action. Researchers, not least in Continental Europe, for a long time liked to think of themselves as the ones who communicated to policymakers what "research has to say" about various issues. The problem-solving model often tacitly assumes consensus about goals, but social scientists often do not agree among themselves about the goals of certain actions, nor are they in agreement with the policymakers.

The third model is the interactive model which assumes "a disorderly set of interconnections and back-and-forthness" and an ongoing dialogue between researchers and policymakers.

The fourth model is the political one. Research findings are used as ammunition to defend a standpoint. An issue, after having been debated for quite some time in a controversial climate, leads to entrenched positions that will not be changed by new evidence. A frequent case is that policymakers in power have already made their decision before they commission research that will legitimize the policy for which they have opted.

The fifth model is the tactical one, whereby a controversial problem is "buried" in research as a defense against taking a decision at the present moment.

The sixth model is the "enlightenment" one, which according to Weiss (1979 p. 428) is the one through which "social science research most frequently enters the policy arena." Research tends to influence policy in a much more subtle way than is suggested by the word "utilization," which implies more or less direct use according to the first model. In the enlightenment model, research "permeates" the policy process, not by specific projects but by its "generalizations and orientations percolating through informed publics and coming to shape the way in which people think about social issues." Furthermore, without reference to any specific piece of evidence, research can sensitize policymakers to new issues, help to redefine old ones, and turn "nonproblems into policy problems." Empirical evidence appears to support this model. In a study where she was interviewing 155 policymakers in Washington, DC, Weiss found that 57 percent of them felt that they "used" research but only 7 percent could point to a specific project or study that had had an influence.

The seventh model in Weiss's taxonomy, finally, is referred to as "research-as-part-of-the-intellectual-enterprise-of-society" (research-oriented) model. Social science research together with other intellectual inputs, such as philosophy, history, journalism, and so on, contribute to widening the horizon for the debate on certain issues and to reformulating the problems.

In a presidential address to the American Educational Research Association, Shavelson (1988 pp. 4–5) takes as his point of departure the "uncertainty and the frustrations about the contributions of social science research." He seeks to reframe the issue of "utility" by suggesting "that the contributions lie not so much in immediate and specific applications but

rather in constructing, challenging, or changing the way policymakers and practitioners think about problems" (pp. 4–5). He points out that this grows out of a confusion of the two models, science versus social science (see *Research Paradigms in Education*). One cannot expect education research to lead to practices that make society happy, wise, and well-educated in the same way as the natural sciences lead to a technology that makes society wealthy. Educational research can influence policy and practice by alerting "policymakers and practitioners to problems, increase their commitments to working on a problem area, support a position held, legitimate decisions already made, or be used to persuade others about a position held" (pp. 4–5). The assumption that "educational research should have direct and immediate application to policy or practice rests on many unrealistic conditions" (pp. 4–5). Among these are relevance to a particular issue, provision of clear and unambiguous results, research being known and understood by policymakers, and findings implying other choices than those contemplated by policymakers.

6. Overcoming Disjunctions

The conclusion from analyses and studies of the relationships between research and educational policymaking is that the former has an influence in the long run but not usually in the short term following specific projects at specific points in time. The impact of research is exercised by the total body of information and the conceptualization of issues that research produces. It does not yield "products" in the same way as research in the physical sciences. In spite of misgivings about research as "useless" to practitioners and allegations that it contributes little or nothing to policies and practice, research in the social sciences tends to "creep" into policy deliberations. The "linear" R & D model of research utilization derived from science and technology does not apply in the field of social sciences relevant to educational issues. Nor does the problem-solving model which presupposes either value-free issues or consensus about the values implied.

Research "percolates" into the policymaking process and the notion that research can contribute is integrated into the overall perspective that policymakers apply on a particular issue. Thus the United States Department of Education in 1986 published a brochure under the title *What Works: Research About Teaching and Learning*. Its purpose was to "provide accurate and reliable information about *what works* in the education of our children" (p.V) and it was meant to be useful to all who deal with the education of children, from parents to legislators. It presents, in one or two pages for each problem, "a distillation of a large body of scholarly research" (p.V) by stating findings and spelling out their practical implications. Although most of the research presented relates to classroom practice there is also a considerable body relevant to policy issues. Such research findings contribute to the enlightenment of those who prepare decisions which usually are not "taken" at a given point in time, but are rather accretions (Husén and Kogan 1984).

See also: Globalization of Educational Policy and Reform; Policy-oriented Research; Politics of Educational Planning; Research Paradigms in Education

References

Aaron J H 1978 *Politics and the Professors: The Great Society in Perspective*. Brookings Institution, Washington, DC

Caplan N 1976 Social research and national policy: What gets used by whom, for what purposes, and with what effects? *Int. Soc. Sci. J.* 28: 187–94

Coleman J S 1984 Issues in the Institutionalisation of Social Policy. In: Husén T, Kogan M (eds.) 1984

Coleman J S et al. 1966 *Equality of Educational Opportunity*. United States Department of Health, Education and Welfare, Washington, DC

Husén T 1975 *Social Influences on Educational Attainment: Research Perspectives on Educational Equality*. OECD, Paris

Husén T 1979 Evaluating compensatory education. *Proceedings of the National Academy of Education*, Vol. 6. National Academy of Education, Washington, DC

Husén T, Kogan M (eds.) 1984 *Educational Research and Policy: How Do They Relate?* Pergamon Press, Oxford

James W 1899 *Talks to Teachers on Psychology: And to Students on Some of the Life's Ideals*. Longmans Green, London

Kallen D, Kosse G B, Wagenar H C (eds.) 1982 *Social Science Research and Public Policy Making: A Reappraisal*. National Foundation for Educational Research/Nelson, London

Levin H M 1978 Why isn't educational research more useful? *Prospects* 8(2): 157–68

Shavelson R J 1988 Contributions of educational research to policy and practice: Constructing, challenging, changing cognition. *Educ. Res.* 17 (7): 4–11, 22

Shellard J S (ed.) 1979 *Educational Research for Policy Making in Australia*. Australian Council for Educational Research, Hawthorn

United States Department of Education 1986 *What Works: Research About Teaching and Learning*. US Department of Education, Washington, DC

Weiss C H 1979 The many meanings of research utilization. *Public Admin. Rev.* 39: 426–31

Weiss C H 1980 Knowledge creep and decision accretion. *Knowledge: Creation, Diffusion, Utilization* 1: 381–404

Further Reading

Cronbach L J, Suppes P (eds.) 1969 *Research for Tomorrow's Schools: Disciplined Inquiry for Education: Report*. Macmillan, New York

Dutch Foundation for Educational Research 1978 *Programming Educational Research: A Framework for the Programming of Research Within the Context of the Objectives of the Foundation for Educational Research in the Netherlands*. Stichting voor Onderzoek van het Onderwijs (SVO), Dutch Foundation for Educational Research, Staatsuitgeverij, 's-Gravenhage

Her Majesty's Stationery Office (HMSO) 1971 *The Organisation and Management of Government R and D<ox> (The Rothschild Report)*. HMSO, London

Husén T 1968 Educational research and the state. In: Wall W D, Husén T (eds.) 1968 *Educational Research and Policy-making*. National Foundation for Educational Research, Slough

Husén T, Boalt G 1968 *Educational Research and Educational Change: The Case of Sweden*. Almqvist and Wiksell, Stockholm

Kogan M (ed.) 1974 *The Politics of Education: Edward Boyle and Anthony Crosland in Conversation with Maurice Kogan*. Penguin, Harmondsworth

Kogan M, Korman N, Henkel M 1980 *Government's Commissioning of Research: A Case Study*. Department of Government, Brunel University, Uxbridge

Lindblom C E, Cohen D K 1979 *Usable Knowledge: Social Science and Social Problem Solving*. Yale University Press, New Haven, Connecticut

Rein M 1980 Methodology for the study of the interplay between social science and social policy. *Int. Soc. Sci. J.* 32: 361–68

Rule J B 1978 *Insight and Social Betterment: A Preface to Applied School Science*. Oxford University Press, London

Suppes P (ed.) 1978 *Impact of Research on Education: Some Case Studies: Summaries*. National Academy of Education, Washington, DC

United States Office of Education 1969 *Educational Research and Development in the United States*. United States Government Printing Office, Washington, DC

Globalization of Educational Policy and Reform

J. W. Guthrie

Throughout the industrialized world, governments are seeking effective policies for enhancing economic productivity through education, employing economic incentives to promote the productivity and efficient administration of schooling, and searching for additional resources to meet increasing demands for education.

The purposes of this article are: (a) to describe the economic and social dynamics propelling the globalization of education policy and management reform internationally; (b) to suggest the probable nature of future education system administrative commonalities; and (c) to speculate as to the consequences of these changes for educational administration.

1. Purposes of Educational Reform

Nations increasingly view schooling as a strategic instrument for promoting national economic development. The primary policy objective in these instances is to enhance a nation's supply of human capital. Generally, the nations involved are ones that already have a large supply of material resources and are hoping to utilize their education systems to acquire even more. At the same time, the labor-intensive nature of instruction has resulted in dramatic increases in schooling costs in Western nations since the Second World War (Bottari et al. 1992). Thus there is frequently a policy tension as public officials attempt to use schooling to enhance national economic productivity while simultaneously keeping an eye open for ways to render schooling more efficient, shift school spending to the private sector, or reduce the growth of education costs. The policies that often result reflect this ambivalent, and sometimes antithetical, combination of purposes.

It should be added that international economic conditions are by no means the only forces shaping modern educational systems. The picture is made more complicated by the existence of national education reform efforts that stem from purely political purposes, are perhaps motivated by a nation's internal ideological dynamics, and are probably shaped by deep-seated historical conditions, religious beliefs, ethnic conflicts, and idiosyncratic practices.

Thus, given the multiplicity of national motives, and the complexity of national conditions, the observer cannot help but be struck by the remarkable similarity of internationally emerging educational policies. This convergence is particularly apparent in Western nations, which are the main subject of this article. However, it seems highly probable that, in time, global economic conditions will propel former East European and nonaligned nations in similar directions.

2. The Evolving Economic and Social Environment of Education

The explosion in electronic methods of conveying information, the creation of worldwide consumer markets, the existence of a growing international network of education reform ideas and informed educational policy experts, and vast reductions in the time and costs of international travel are stimulating a globalization of schooling. However, these forces only transmit ideas. The more likely explanation for their widespread adoption is a growing set of international economic and social imperatives (Morris 1989).

National economies are now global in their competitive outlook, internationally interdependent, insatiable in their quest for technological innovation, and crucially dependent upon the availability of human talent. Reliance upon a narrow intellectual elite appears increasingly outmoded. Modern manufacturing and service industry techniques demand a labor force capable of adjusting to new technologies and making informed production decisions. Educated and highly skilled human intelligence is increasingly viewed as a nation's primary economic resource, and it is needed in large amounts. The "new" strategic raw material, upon which economic productivity is ever more dependent, is "human capital" (Schultz 1971).

Modern economics, however, are not simply boosting or gently encouraging an already existing notion that education systems should enhance a nation's human capital resources. Rather, international economic forces are already beginning to reshape the forms of schooling across national boundaries. This "human capital imperative" is only likely to intensify over time. This globalization of education will occur primarily because nations can no longer easily protect their domestic producers from international economic forces. Failure to respond quickly to technological and organizational inventions can rapidly jeopardize a people's standard of living and a government's political future. Consequently, traditional educational values and institutions are being scrutinized by government officials who, in response to developing economic and social imperatives, believe that new educational policies and practices are necessary for their nation to become or remain successful.

Expansion of the populations served by schools and colleges, centralized curricula expectations, national educational objectives, expanded uses of standardized tests, growing dependence upon government agencies to collect and analyze school performance data, intensified efforts to link colleges and industry, and altered expectations for educational evaluation are among the predictable practical outcomes of this globalization movement.

Specific educational reform tactics and administrative procedures may differ from nation to nation, depending upon historic development patterns, contemporary politics, current resource levels, and operating structures. Regardless of the variety of national tactics, the long-term goal will be to utilize educated intellect as a strategic means for a nation to gain or retain an economically competitive position in the global marketplace. As a consequence, education systems increasingly will adopt similar characteristics.

3. What Will be the Converging Components of Global Reform?

Education reform—of preschool through secondary levels—is increasingly characterized by the following common components: (a) extension of publicly funded schooling to lower age groups, so-called "preschool"; (b) central government influence on the curriculum; (c) intensified instructional emphasis upon scientific and technological subject areas; (d) expanded use of standardized examinations and centralized evaluation procedures to measure student achievement and school performance; (e) wider dependence upon central government agencies to collect, synthesize, and report upon educational systems' performance; and (f) the devolution of greater operating authority to schools, bypassing conventional units of local educational governance.

3.1 Downward Expansion of Institutionalization

Involvement of ever-larger proportions of mothers in the workplace has created enormous political pressures in industrialized nations to provide publicly financed, or at least publicly subsidized or coordinated, childcare. Because schooling is an existing institution, and generally a publicly supported institution that eventually touches the life of almost every child, a policy connection is frequently made between childcare provision and schooling. Downward extension of schooling occasionally is boosted further by national desires to enhance the educational achievement of lower socioeconomic status, "at risk" youth. Thus, childcare and preschool services are provided, or at least are part of the policy debate, for children as young as three years of age (Bottari et al. 1992).

There is less agreement on the degree to which subject-matter content and specific schooling skills should be imposed upon children in preschool programs. The age at which children are capable of learning formally presented material is debatable. There is little controversy, however, regarding the usefulness of school "readiness" training. Increasingly, early childhood programs are expected not only to prepare young children for school in a social sense—to train them to follow adult directions, cooperate in a group setting, adhere to schedules, stand in lines, and so forth—but also to assist them in acquiring skills and habits useful in learning to read and count. Thus, even when specifically defined formal instruction is not extended to lower ages, institutionalization of children is occurring.

3.2 Centrally Defined Curriculum

Central governments increasingly specify the majority of subjects to be covered in primary and, particularly, secondary schools (Guthrie et al. 1991). Directives may include subject-matter guidelines, content frameworks, lesson plans, teaching modules, reading lists, bibliographies, lecture outlines, illustrative class activities, suggested experiments and field trips, sample examinations, and textbook preferences. This policy objective can also be accomplished more subtly by specifying subject-matter areas as either secondary school graduation or college admission requirements. In either event, the intent is to ensure that a minimal common core of subject material is conveyed to students.

Centrally imposed curriculum specifications seldom are intended to occupy the entire spectrum of what a school covers at a particular grade level. Almost always there is room left to supplement the curriculum at the discretion of local officials, governing boards, or educational professionals. Nevertheless, a predictable outcome is to limit discretion for students, or their families, to select from among only a relatively narrow list of elective courses. In nations that historically have not had a centrally determined curriculum, requirements will become more intense, and individual freedom to choose—by local officials, educators, and households—has been or will be reduced.

3.3 Emphasis on Mathematics, Science, and Technology

A corollary of the movement toward centrally determined curricula is an intensified concern for the subject areas of mathematics, science, and related technology. This emphasis applies to elementary, secondary, and tertiary schooling levels (Bottari et al. 1992). The justification is easy to understand. Modern economies are constructed on scientific discoveries and technological innovations—hence, the desire to use schooling to enhance national capacity for scientific research and technological development.

The hallmarks of this international movement are added expectations for mathematics and science instruction and expanded textbook treatments of science in the elementary grades, additional mathematics and science graduation requirements and college entrance criteria for secondary students, expanded undergraduate emphasis upon science in colleges, and vastly increased facilities and research funding at the graduate level.

3.4 Increased Reliance upon Pupil Performance Measures and Centralized Evaluation Procedures

The evolving mode for determining compliance with centrally issued curriculum mandates, and the increase in mathematics and science instruction, is governmentally developed or authorized tests of student achievement (Guthrie et al. 1991). Through psychometric procedures, test questions can be tied to curriculum objectives. These tests can be designed to provide data regarding each student's individual performance. They also can assess the overall performance of a school or other management unit, a school district, province, state, or an entire nation. Cost savings can be achieved for what otherwise is an unusually expensive undertaking by relying upon a variety of sampling techniques. The results can be generalized to the intended operating unit, without having to examine every student on every test item.

3.5 Expanded Central Reporting and Monitoring

A fifth point of international convergence is the development among nations of expanded government agencies and procedures for reporting and monitoring educational system performance (Guthrie 1991a). There are new, or substantially enlarged, government and quasi-government bureaus responsible for collecting, compiling, synthesizing, analyzing, and reporting education-related data. Moreover, the requirements placed upon operating subunits—states, provinces, and local education authorities—to supply information to the center are being increased.

A major component of this added emphasis upon data collection and analyses is the attention given to international comparison. Schooling contains few internally driven standards. This condition, when coupled with increasing global economic competition, renders international comparative information regarding student performance and school achievement ever more compelling to policymakers and the public.

3.6 Increased Operating Authority for Individual Schools

Education systems are tending to devolve greater operating discretion to individual school sites (Guthrie 1991b). This trend involves partially bypassing intermediate agencies—counties, shires, prefectures, parishes, boroughs, local education authorities, and local school districts. The stated intent of the reform is to empower local school officials, administrators, and in some instances teachers, with the ability to tailor instruction to the preferences and needs of their "clients"—pupils and their parents.

This reform appears to be impelled more by the desire to enhance educational productivity rather than efforts to increase economic productivity. Making decisions on the rim of the wheel, rather than at the hub, is how the movement is characterized in England and Wales. This strategy is consistent with modern private sector and organizational development dogma regarding the usefulness of maximized discretion at operating sites. By devolving management decisions to schools, it is easier to account for the use of resources and to pinpoint pupil performance. Thus, in addition to the prospect that it might enhance schooling productivity, school-site management may well also have a strong accountability and cost-cutting element.

This sixth point of global convergence—increased decision-making at the school site—appears at first glance to be paradoxical. In the face of growing centralization of school decision-making, why would greater operating authority be ceded to school sites? The frequent justification is that, whereas it is necessary for central authorities to specify the *what* of schooling, it is not appropriate, or even sensible, for them to specify the *how* (Davies and Ellison 1989).

4. Evolving Prospective Components

In addition to the common dimensions described above, modern reform movements in Western nations frequently include efforts: (a) to infuse schooling with features of the marketplace—competition and consumer choice; (b) to enhance teacher profession-

alization; (c) to identify policies that will enhance the education of under-participating or unmotivated youth. These three evolving components are further out on the policy horizon and their future likelihood is not yet as evident. Nevertheless, they are being discussed with sufficient frequency to justify mention (Guthrie and Pierce 1990).

4.1 Privatization and Choice

Proponents of this approach search for means by which schooling can be rendered more competitive, and clients—households and pupils—can be provided with an expanded range of choices about their education. The rationale for these proposals is mixed. The frequent fundamental assertion is that any organization with a guaranteed clientele, or a guaranteed source of financial support, will tend to become self-serving and less sensitive to the preferences and needs of clients. Hence, both in order to serve clients better and to render the institutions more efficient, steps must be taken to inject elements of the marketplace into schooling. Monopolies must be disbanded and competition encouraged.

A wide spectrum of choice proposals exists, some radical, some less so. Advocates of moderate choice would restrict household education selection solely to schools in the public sector. Other moderated choice plans restrict selection to schools within the public sector and only for a particular set of grades, or only if the movement of students enhances racial desegregation, or only if the household meets specified criteria, such as being below a minimum income level.

The more radical plans envision conversion of education—higher and lower—into a free market where all school services are provided privately. Government might subsidize, or even to some degree regulate, such services, but would not itself be a direct provider.

This evolving component has another related facet: "privatization." This involves putting various components of system operation out to tender by private providers. Privatized services can range from peripheral services such as trash removal and food catering all the way to integral features such as remedial reading or foreign language or vocational instruction. The policy objective is almost always to render an education system operation less costly. The closer to the core of instruction the proposals are, the more controversial they become, and the greater the resistance by education professionals.

4.2 Professionalization

Professionalization is also an incomplete or latent component of prospective Western education reform movements (Carnegie Forum on Education and the Economy 1986). Where it is found in the early 1990s, it has at least two dimensions, not all components of which are consistent. One is an effort to upgrade the quality of teachers by elevating entry standards. There is substantial policy debate about the most effective manner in which to achieve this objective. One avenue requires teaching-job candidates to have higher levels of academic preparation and (or sometimes "or") pass minimum competency tests. Elevating competency can also include requirements for an additional year of college preparation, possibly at the graduate level. The other policy avenue is to expand the pool of able candidates by liberating applicants from teacher training or pedagogical training requirements.

The second professionalization trend is an expansion of the degree of decision-making accorded to teachers. Such expanded decision arenas for teachers include participation in the recruitment and hiring of new teachers, the evaluation (including tenure decision) for probationary teachers, and the evaluation of tenured teachers. In addition, teachers in these expanded-discretion settings may take added responsibility for selecting curriculum materials, inservice training opportunities, and selection of administrators.

4.3 Underserved and Unmotivated Youth

Increasing discussion revolves around policies for enhancing the achievement and motivation of the large numbers of youth of lower socioeconomic status (SES) who may not be fully participating in or benefiting from schooling (Heyneman 1989). Whereas the relationship between education and national economic development is increasingly obvious to policymakers, the same relationship for individuals within a nation is not always as evident. International migrations of political and economic refugees, "guest" workers, alterations in family patterns, centuries of racial and class discrimination, widespread traffic in addictive drugs, and an assortment of other symptoms of social distress have created a sizable "underclass" in many industrialized nations.

In addition to their own unhappy personal conditions, individuals caught in debilitating circumstances threaten to increase public welfare costs substantially. Also, undereducated individuals represent lost labor. In many Western nations, youth population cohorts are shrinking. Faced with the prospect of a worker shortage, governments are beginning to assess means for enhancing the education of larger proportions of youth in order to increase the sophistication of their labor pool. However, no consensus has emerged regarding even the nature of the problem, let alone solutions to it. However, the expanding constellation of distressing conditions is provoking policy-level discussion about the problem and its relationship to schooling.

4.4 Absent Reform Components: Research and Technology

A striking feature of the situation outlined above is the absence of any significant central government reliance upon intensified educational research or development of technology to enhance schooling productivity and promote human capital formation. What would appear to be a natural response to spiraling costs of instruction, demands for spreading schooling to ever wider populations, and desires to link schooling to the growing realities of high-tech automation is virtually neglected by policymakers. This neglect occurs despite the fact that electronic and optical technology appear capable of revolutionizing instruction, making it far more individualized and eventually less expensive.

5. Professional Consequences

New economic imperatives are creating a different environment for educational professionals, even if only by way of the intensity with which these differences present themselves. The overarching change is in the degree to which education policy and practice are being politicized. This new environment includes the following:

(a) an increasing expectation that educational practitioners will be accountable to, and schooling results made understandable for, generalists and laypersons, not simply educational professionals and government specialists;

(b) educator involvement with a wider and more politically influential range of special interest groups and stakeholders directly interested in educational outcomes;

(c) an expansion of high-level general government agencies interested in, and perhaps responsible for, the management of education and schooling, and greater linkages between education agencies, government planning efforts, and the policy-making process;

(d) skepticism regarding evaluations undertaken by educators and consequently a greater reliance upon evaluation generalists; higher likelihood of competing and adversarial evaluations; intensified risk of advocacy imitating analysis; policymakers requiring systemic evaluation strategies; a greater reliance upon eclectic analytical tactics and expanded measurements;

(e) greater dependence upon internationally oriented performance comparisons.

6. A Concluding Concern

Despite a deep historical connection to industrial development and regardless of their immediate connection with the economy, schools traditionally have been expected to fulfill a substantial range of additional functions, both for society and for the individuals and households involved. Among the other-than-economic functions variously expected of schools are: acculturating new citizens; promoting religious, linguistic, and political indoctrination; inculcating government principles; ensuring social cohesion and civic order; preparing a citizenry for military participation; facilitating social mobility; developing artistic and aesthetic tastes; assisting in personal adjustment to society; and contributing to individual fulfillment.

Many of these other purposes are now being subordinated forcefully to national economic development in the last quarter of the twentieth century. Nevertheless, regardless of how exciting existing and prospective economically motivated reforms may appear, it is important to be mindful that other functions, even if currently diluted, still exist and undoubtedly will persist. Professional educators should thus be mindful of the many masters worthy of being served besides national economic development.

See also: Postliteracy: Concepts and Policies; Youth Unemployment

References

Bottari N, Duchene C, Tuijnman A (eds.) 1992 *Education at a Glance: OECD indicators.* OECD, Paris
Carnegie Forum on Education and the Economy 1986 *A Nation Prepared: Teachers for the 21st Century.* Carnegie Forum on Education and the Economy, Washington, DC
Davies B, Ellison L 1989 Changing financial provision leads to a radical reform of the English educational system. Paper presented at the annual meeting of the British Education Management and Administration Society, University of Leicester, 15–17 September 1989
Guthrie J W 1991a The world's evolving political economy and the emerging globalization of education: A set of extrapolations, interpolations, and predictions regarding the likely future internationalization of education policy. *Educ. Res. J.* 6: 1–15
Guthrie J W 1991b The world's new political economy is politicizing educational evaluation. *Educ. Eval. Policy Anal.* 13(3): 309–21
Guthrie J W, Binkley M, Wyatt T 1991 A survey of national assessment and examination practices in OECD countries. In: OECD International Indicators Project, Network A: Student Achievement Outcomes. INES Project General Assembly, Lugano, Switzerland, September 1991
Guthrie J W, Pierce L C 1990 The international economy and national education reform: A comparison of education reforms in the United States and Great Britain. *Oxford Rev. Educ.* 16(2): 179–205
Heyneman S P 1989 Paper presented at conference on Development Through Education, University College, Oxford, 26 September 1989
Morris C R 1989 The coming global boom. *Atlantic* 264(4): 53–54
Schultz T W 1971 *Investment in Human Capital.* Free Press, New York

Politics of Educational Planning

N. F. McGinn

Planning of education, once understood as a technical exercise best carried out by certified experts representing a single authority, increasingly is understood as a process by which disparate groups can join together to achieve consensus about goals and effective means to achieve them. The formal rationality of technical plans often ignores or masks the political objectives of planners, their employers, or other actors. The poor record of implementation of formal plans is attributed in large measure to this exclusion of political analysis. Planning that includes political decision-making has a better chance of effecting change.

1. Conceptions of Politics in Planning

Although the planning of education can be done by isolated individuals, the intended results are always social or collective: planners use their knowledge to devise strategies to affect the actions of others. This separation of knowledge and action is problematic. How can the planner gain an objective knowledge of the subjectivity that conditions the actor? In other words, if I as planner want to affect your behavior, how can I know why you do what you do?

One way to minimize this problem is to reduce the size of the unit for which planning is carried out, and to increase participation in the planning process. The form of decentralization called school-based management/shared decision-making (Hanson 1990) is one example; teachers participate in planning the activities of the school in which they work, they are both planners and actors.

This type of planning has been called transactive (Friedmann 1973, Warwick 1980) or interactive (Adams 1988), to suggest that planning is based on the dialectics between plan and reality (or action and consequence) and between the persons attempting to shape their collective future.

A second, more common type of educational planning locates the planner (as individual or group) outside the reality which is the object of planning, and applies the methods of objective science in an effort to overcome problems of subjectivity. The term "rational" has been pre-empted to apply to this kind of planning, an unfortunate choice that has caused much confusion because all planning requires the use of reason and information to choose among alternative methods to achieve goals.

The major difference between the two types of planning (and their many variants) is not their degree of rationality (or systematic use of information in the choice among alternatives for future action), but their assumptions about the extent to which the necessary information exists prior to the planning process. If objectives are fixed, alternative policies are already identified, and the environment is stable, then planning relies principally on technical (or policy) analysis to discover the alternative with most likelihood of achieving the objective. *Technical* problems are questions of the direction in which a set of actions will point. Can teachers be as effective with 14 years of education as compared to 16 years? What is the relative unit cost of providing teachers with 14 as opposed to 16 years of education? How many teachers are needed? Given the same set of facts, the answers to these questions will be the same for each analyst.

But if objectives are changed in the process as actors interact to construct alternatives, then prediction is more difficult, if not impossible, and the emphasis in planning shifts to political analysis and strategy. *Strategic* problems are questions of the viability of the actions taken. They deal with questions of power, of relationships between groups of persons with different and often opposing objectives. What groups are likely to favor extension of teacher education from 14 to 16 years? What groups are likely to oppose it? Are planners willing to pay the political cost of imposing this action even though most groups are against?

Although "politics" enters into both types of planning, their proponents differ about its meaning and acceptability. Perhaps both camps would accept a definition of politics as the contest between groups over what will be done (Thomas 1983), usually observed as " . . . the attempts (conscious and organized to some degree) to influence the inputs, processes, and outputs of education, whether by legislation, pressure group or union action, experimentation, private investment, local transactions, internal innovation or propaganda" (Archer 1981 p. 29). With this definition, to talk about the politics of educational planning is to talk about how planning is used to influence education. If one thinks that the purpose of planning is to influence education, planning is inherently political.

2. Politics in "Rational" Planning

When some planners distinguish between political and technical bases for educational planning their emphasis is not on *influence* but on the *validity* of the information used to identify means to ends. In this case "political" is often used as a pejorative, an ancient tradition dating at least from Plato who put politics and politicians on a lower level, further from the truth than the philosophers (today's scientists) who claim to rely more faithfully on reason and evidence in reaching their conclusions.

Champions of this approach argue that to the extent that one sticks to the facts one can avoid the introduction of any "ism" which distorts understanding and leads one away from effective planning. Reasonable people will agree on what the critical issues are, and careful research will indicate the correct responses (Psacharopolous 1990). Planning is the derivative of analysis; its function is to identify those policies that will result in the most efficient allocation of resources. Planning as policy analysis uses technical (i.e., supposedly nonpolitical) analysis and focuses on means, to achieve ends defined outside the planning process by politicians or "policy actors" (Psacharopolous 1986).

The ostensible objective of planning from this approach is plan-making, that is, the presentation of a set of policies specifying objectives to be achieved and means to achieve them. The plan is said to fail when the results do not match the promises of the plan. Plans fail for two major reasons: lack of political commitment, and the substantive content of the plan.

The extent of government and extra-government commitment for policies and plans is often overestimated by those who rely principally on the "rational" or technical approach to planning. After 10 years of implementation of a carefully constructed plan to increase enrollment of lower income students in secondary school in Jamaica, enrollment patterns had changed only slightly. Cogan (1983) describes how " . . . the upper and traditional middle classes, when threatened with changes in the educational system which could result in the loss of privilege, continue to assert effectively their influence in order to ensure control of the system" (p. 179). Some analysts choose to ignore politics in their plan-making. Rondinelli et al. (1990) define political analysis as distinct from economic or financial analysis, and cite research to the effect that World Bank project officers do more of the latter because there is so much to do. Political analysis is also avoided because it is difficult, and reduces the chances of project approval by Bank managers.

The second reason for plan failure, wrong content, is sometimes defined tautologically, to wit: "What I mean by a planning mistake, or disaster, is that a policy solution was adopted that was diametrically opposed to the one that should have been adopted for the educational system to have served the very purpose intended by the planner in the first place" (Psacharopolous 1986 p. 560). Here reasoning is circular because the proof that the policy solution should not have been adopted is that it did not work. Critiques of this kind often offer another solution, usually not yet tested and therefore not yet failed. Psacharopolous claims that the missing element in failed plans is "elementary economics," by which he apparently means the variables he would have included had he been asked. As the failed plans he criticizes were drawn up by other economists—some of great renown—the discussion is really about theories of economics rather than about careless application of techniques. Benveniste (1989) explains how "expert consensus" can gain credibility even without evidence to support it.

There is a third reason for plan failure, often ignored by "rational" planners: the process of making and carrying out the plan. From this perspective, plans fail because insufficient attention is given to those who will be responsible for their implementation. For example, Warwick et al. (1992) describe failures in implementation of five innovative projects in primary education in Pakistan. Failure of planners to take into account aspects of the culture in which these innovations were inserted is a major reason for their rejection and failure.

The implication in the first two explanations of plan failure is that with proper analysis and design, plans can be written that will be successful. In other words, the success of planning depends on the planner. If planners use the right theory and the right methods, then it will be possible to achieve the purposes they intend. "Politics" is sometimes included as an element in implementation but generally as an exogenous variable, or error term. Policy analysis often does not include political analysis.

3. Politics of Making Sure Plans are Implemented

Many "rational" planners do act politically. First, to have any chance of influencing policies and plans requires that:

> . . . the social researcher whose work is to enter the policy sphere should reach consensus with some important segment of policy actors on the basic value orientation of his work. For maximum research utility, the research should accept the fundamental goals, priorities, and political constraints of the key decision-making group. He should be sensitive to feasibilities and stay within the narrow range of low-cost, low-change policy alternatives. (Weiss in Friedmann 1987 p. 173)

Or, in other words, the policy analyst/planner can avoid (explicit) introduction of ideology into his or her analyses (only) by choosing to work within a particular one.

For some, it is self-evident that planners work for those in power (the Prince, to use Machiavelli's terminology), and that they are effective to the extent that they can help their Prince, or powerful clients, achieve their objectives. Planning is inherently political "because it makes a difference . . . something is changed that would not have been changed otherwise. This implies that social power has been utilized" (Benveniste 1989 p. 2).

Planners who are truly *technical* need not share the values of their Prince; they are sought for their technical expertise. But to ensure that their plans will make a difference, effective planners do more than just speak truth to power, they work to acquire power of their own. The power of information (both given and withheld) is well understood, but planners also seek to gain power through the construction of consensus, about: (a) what goals are or should be, (b) the extent to which goals are being realized, (c) causes of failure to reach goals, (d) the policy alternatives most likely to be effective, and (e) how best to carry out the designated policy.

Plans are implemented when they are credible, that is, believed, not just by persons expert in the technical aspects of the plan, but principally by those who will implement the plan and the "stakeholders" who will be affected by it (Rondinelli et al. 1990). Sophisticated statistics may impress some groups but for others images and metaphors that speak to common concerns may be more powerful. These may be more important in building coalitions and networks that actively support the plan (Benveniste 1989). Without attention to the interests and power of possible opponents and supporters of the plan, planners cannot serve their Prince well. The truth the Prince seeks includes politics: to be rational is to be political (Forester 1988). Strategic planners are chosen by their Princes because of their loyalty as well as their expertise.

At the same time, part of the power that planners can generate comes from their ability to appear as though their analyses are untainted by "mere political" considerations and as if their pronouncements are based on a dispassionate reading of the facts. Forester (1988) lists four ways in which planner analysts can manipulate information:

(a) deliberately using technical jargon and sophisticated analyses to obfuscate issues;

(b) appealing to openness and dependence on experts to create false assurance;

(c) arguing that a political issue is actually a technical issue;

(d) holding back information about other alternatives, misrepresenting the validity of analyses, and claiming success for untested options.

Planner analysts can also present information in order to increase comprehension, to develop merited trust, to generate legitimate consent, and to expand valid knowledge. Which choices are made depends on the ethical stance of the planner.

A further explanation for the low implementation rate of plans and policies is that they were never intended to be implemented as such. Plans and the policy analysis on which they are based can be part of the political strategy of a Prince seeking to legitimize a regime, to justify actions already taken, to distract attention from other policies more likely to mobilize opposition. Jalil and McGinn (1992) explain the repeated assertion of patently nonimplementable goals for universalization of primary education in Pakistan, by both conservative and progressive governments, as evidence of the use of planning in political strategy.

Even for the "rationalists" therefore, educational

planning is political, despite denials by technical analysts of any political consciousness. Examples of the
political actions of planners are found in case studies
of their practice (Benoit 1974, McGinn and Warwick
1979, McGinn and Schiefelbein 1979, Rideout and
Wilson 1975).

3.1 Who Are the Princes? What Are Their Objectives?

For the most part educational planners work for governments, as education is almost everywhere a responsibility of the state. In less centralized societies, each
level of government may have its own planning capability, but autonomous institutions often do planning
for state education. The list includes teacher unions,
political parties, business groups, churches, who from
time to time take positions on state policies and issue
recommendations of their own. These groups are more
important in the more industrialized countries. In the
Third World, planning for education is also done by
planners (generally called policy analysts) from international banks and bilateral assistance agencies. The
possibilities for conflict are obvious.

Strong central authorities and powerful national
and international groups see conflict between different groups with interests in education as a source
of confusion of their efforts to gain power through
"rational" analysis. Their planners can try to avoid
conflict through manipulation of information. Local
authorities and other relatively weak actors are more
likely to see confusion as a healthy expression of diversity through democracy, as an opportunity for their
participation in shaping outcomes. Their planners are
likely to use information to emphasize divergence in
interests and requirements, a strategy that is effective
only if combined with mobilization of all groups to
defend the interests of any that are attacked.

These processes are illustrated in the breakdown
of consensus about educational policy between the
central government, local government, and teachers
in the United Kingdom (Ranson 1985). Faced with
declining resources, the national state sought to extend
its control over education (and other sectors); concern
about content was less important than form of control.
Claiming to be seeking to reduce inefficiency the national government sought to reduce the power of local
education authorities, which had formed an alliance
with school heads and teachers. Planners within the
national Department of Education and Science (DES)
pursued two strategies to increase their control over
the policy-making (planning) process. First the DES set
up national committees ostensibly independent from
the DES, and using "objective" social science. Terms
of reference and to a large extent research data were
provided by the DES planners. The conclusions of the
advisory commissions were then used to legitimize
some actions, but ignored when they stood in the way
of DES objectives (Salter and Tapper 1981).

Resistance by teachers and local education authorities was ineffective because the two groups could

not form an effective alliance and failed to mobilize
citizen support. Jones (1985) argues that because the
official ideology of the teachers' union limits its alliances with groups outside education it cannot win in a
struggle with the national government about education
policies and plans.

Farrell (1986) describes the reaction of various
groups in Chilean society to the proposal by the
national government to equalize educational opportunity through the establishment of a "unified national school" (ENU). The government was a loosely
coupled coalition of left-wing parties ranging from
anticlericalists to Communists. Educational planning
was the responsibility of Socialists who for years had
championed the concept of a school to produce common citizens; there was little consultation between the
planners and other groups in the government about the
policy. The timing was not propitious. National and
foreign groups hostile to the government had succeeded in weakening the economy but popular opposition
had not yet crystallized. The ENU became the red
flag against which groups in opposition charged. An
important element of the attack was the presentation
of alternative proposals for education reform, prepared
by planners in opposition parties, the Catholic Church,
and the military. The ENU was defeated, and the
democratic government doomed to a military takeover.

The impact of transnational actors on national education planning is illustrated by research carried out
by Reimers (1990) who examined government expenditures on education in Latin America over time as
a function of the relative size of foreign debt. Until
the 1980s the relationship between size of debt and
proportion of spending on education was generally
positive; development plans based on easy credit reduced the need to choose between different sectors of
expenditure. In the 1980s, however, the International
Monetary Fund, concerned for what it considered the
high debt burden of countries relative to their export
earnings, imposed as a condition for further loans
reduction of government spending. Now governments
had to choose between sectors in order to stay in
power; in most countries spending on education was
reduced while spending on other sectors remained the
same or increased. These cuts came even though there
was an abundance of research demonstrating higher
rates of return from education than from other sectors.

3.2 Production and Application of Information

Information is the raw material of planning, and
much of the politics of planning deals with its production and application. Shaeffer and Nkinyangi (1983)
have produced a collection of cases on production of
research with specific attention to the environment in
which information for planning is produced. A common theme in the cases is how the source of funding
affects the topics that are chosen to be researched,
the definition of the research problem, and the audiences to whom results are presented. Governments

886

typically fund research to answer questions deriving from policies already under consideration. International agencies are an important source of funding for research in some developing countries, and " . . . they tend to share a concept of development that views the provision of information as the key to the solution of problems . . . The combined effect is to produce a powerful demand for a particular type of research . . ." (Court in Shaeffer and Nkinyangi 1983 p. 182), which emphasizes what is easy to change, rather than more fundamental problems such as inequality of income distribution or government corruption.

From one point of view, not too much should be made about the political determination of research for planning. Research shows that few policy decisions or plans are based directly on research (Fägerlind and Sjöstedt 1989) and statistical information is often of doubtful validity. Policymakers rely on trusted confidants and their own intuition more than on research reports. Even within such technocratic organizations as the World Bank the connection between research and actual field operations has been weak (Ayres 1983), explaining in part a weak correlation between World Bank policy statements and actual lending.

But research does contribute to general understanding of what are important issues, and what are possible solutions to them. Over time the statements of researchers becomes conventional wisdom, reported in the mass media and taken as given. From this emerges the intuitions of the decision-maker and the wisdom of the confidant. Over the long term, therefore, changing the content of research can contribute to changes in public and Princely support for positions now regarded with suspicion or disinterest.

3.3 Politics in the Planning of Decentralization of Education

Perhaps one of the most politicized topics of policy analysis and planning during the 1980s was decentralization. Proposing to shift the locus of governance or power necessarily raises political questions. Planning for decentralization has provided rich material for analysis of how politics enters into planning: "Decentralization is not an end in itself. Rather, it is a strategy for restructuring a school system to accomplish its goals more effectively and efficiently" (Rondinelli et al. 1990 p. 129). Whose goals, and efficiency from whose perspective, are the nub of the political question.

A major argument in decentralization plans is that central governments can no longer provide necessary funds. Technically clothed, this is a political position that takes as fixed how central governments have allocated the resources they have across sectors, and their political will to generate more resources. By defining certain factors as constraints or parameters planners rule out consideration of them as objectives.

Decentralization has been used by governments in order to redistribute power in society, weaken-

ing groups that threaten the regime's position. This is clearly illustrated in Mexico where the national Secretariat of Education has moved since the late 1970s to shift control of primary schools to state governments (controlled by the same party that has controlled the national government for 65 years). The process began when the Secretariat was taken over by technocrats drawing support from educated elites and business rather than from peasants and workers. They saw radical reform of education as necessary to economic growth, but anticipated opposition from the national teachers' union. Deconcentration of administration of primary education would require the union to negotiate with state governments, and reduce their influence in the national political arena. At the same time, the Secretariat sought to eliminate opposition in higher education by creation of an elaborate network of planning committees and budget offices staffed by persons linked to the technocrats. The government also relaxed its regulation of private universities (McGinn and Street 1986).

4. Politics in Interactive Planning

An alternative to plan-making is to understand the process of planning as the construction of possibilities for the future. Not all possibilities can be seen in advance because some will depend on the actions of others who also engage in planning. From this perspective successful planning requires the generation of consensus about both goals or objectives and means.

This approach to planning is overtly political. It includes the distribution of power as a central variable to be modified by the process of planning. In one variant, called "policy dialogue" by the international assistance agencies, conventional definitions of sovereignty or domain of authority are set aside as foreign lenders and donors insist that certain conditions be met by the government seeking funding. One justification for this kind of intervention is found in Bell (1974) who argues that planners (meaning here those working for the international assistance agencies) can be most effective in situations in which:

> the government is perceived neither by itself nor by others as a custodian of that difficult and ambiguous concept, the national interest. Rather it is an "operational" alliance between various interest groups which aim to grasp and preserve power, which also needs to be continuously cemented and possibly extended. (p. 70)

There has been no systematic treatment of the practice of policy dialogue, or its effects on the content and effectiveness of educational plans. It will be important to distinguish between instances of genuine dialogue, in which outcomes cannot be predicted from either set of planners' objectives, to instances of political manipulation in which the powerful impose their plans based on "rational" planning.

887

Policy dialogue as a form of planning is similar to the strategic planning carried out by private sector organizations in a competitive environment. "Rational" planning assumes a stable environment with few disagreements about the nature of the problem or situation. This may be a reasonable assumption only in highly centralized or authoritarian societies. Strategic planning, on the other hand, works best in a turbulent environment in which there are many organizations each with their own Prince and planners, constantly changing each other through interaction. What happens is intelligible, but not predictable. An effective planning approach in this situation is fundamentally inductive rather than "rationally deductive." The model is one of political decision-making. Strategy is required to guide actions beyond the foreseeable future (Bryson 1988).

The concept of strategic planning has also been adopted for public education in the United States, but with an important change (McCune 1986). Now emphasis is on development of community-wide consensus about what the goals of the education system should be. The task is not to plan to beat out competitors in the market but rather to satisfy multiple client populations often with competing goals. Once again politics are explicit; each group's goals and ideologies have to be made clear for them to be able to communicate effectively with other groups and to negotiate shared goals.

Strategic planning begins with definition of the mission (long-term objective) of the organization. The planner acts to collate and synthesize the expressions of the various groups within the organization; the Prince is now an aggregate. At each stage, from definition of performance standards to specification of budgets, the planner both suggests alternatives and attempts to synthesize suggestions made by the participants. In the process the mission and short-run objectives may be rewritten, as constituent groups become dissatisfied with what they are likely to achieve. The dominant method in these processes is communication rather than analysis: " . . . language, because it is based on 'consensual, intersubjective expectations,' carries the implicit building blocks for consensus of values as people attempt to identify and solve their own problems" (Adams 1988 p. 413).

The "rational" approach to planning has been described as a "search through a solution space of alternatives," while the interactive approach is one that treats "designing as making sense together" (Forester 1988 p. 121). The important alternatives do not yet exist when planning starts, therefore they cannot be discovered; instead they are brought into existence, they are constructed. Who participates in the construction process is critical to the success of the planning exercise; political criteria are primary and overt.

Strategic planning has been used in several American states and large cities such as Milwaukee and San Diego, and is also being used in New York City.

The experience is something like this described by a New York City Public Schools representative for one district (with 29,000 students) within New York City. A first problem was who should be included in the planning process.

> The experts recommend no more than 20 people. We wanted to include the custodians, police, fire, central office teachers, all the parts of the community, the different ethnic groups and so on. We ended up with 52 members. We selected them on the basis of whether in the past they had been outspoken for their group.

The various members participated in a three-day retreat that provided an opportunity for all groups to air their complaints and state their dreams for the education system, in a context of collective decision making for improvement. While some members worked in groups writing statements of the fundamental purpose or mission of the education system, others did an analysis of the strengths and weaknesses of the current organization. Collectively the participants identified areas for change, and strategies to bring that about. The draft plan was then distributed extensively throughout the community. The next step was evaluation of specific strategies.

> The central planning group had defined 13 strategies. We created focus teams made up of volunteers from the community. The consultants met with each leader of the 13 teams, and taught them how to write an action plan, and to develop a cost analysis. We did this over a 2–3-month period.

Community reactions helped the planning group to decide on a limited number of action plans to carry out during the first year. Budgets were drawn up, and an implementation plan developed. Central to this process was development of consensus about what should be done: "In the whole process, we decided consensually. No votes were taken. No decision could go forward until everyone agreed. If it wasn't possible to agree on a point, we dropped it. We finally accepted 6 of the 13 action plans, and put those into the plan" (interview by author with Colman Genn, New York City Public Schools, December 5, 1990).

5. Political Future of Educational Planning

Although educational planning as a centrally controlled activity carried out by a handful of highly trained experts may never regain the importance it was given in the 1950s and 1960s, planning is likely to proliferate in the future. The major impetus to the spread of planning has been, ironically, democracy, once considered threatened by the power of centralized and "rational" planning that excluded the voice of the people. The democracy that is emerging involves not just replacing self-appointed Princes with elected representatives, but also moving control over representatives closer to the citizenry. Decentralization, understood as moving the locus of control of education from larger toward smaller civic units, requires more rather than less planning. Decentralization requires planning in and by local units, and a new role for central planning in the promotion of equity and system-wide efficiency.

With more units doing planning, competing for resources, "rational" planning makes less sense; it would appear that some variety of interactive planning will be required. There is too little experience with strategic planning in education to know if it can in fact achieve the benefits claimed for it. Its use in some large education systems is, however, evidence that it is likely to continue to be tested in the crucible of reality.

See also: Policy-oriented Research

References

Adams D 1988 Extending the educational planning discourse: Conceptual and paradigmatic explorations. *Comp. Educ. Rev.* 32(4): 400–15

Archer M S 1981 Educational politics: A model for their analysis. In: Broadfoot P, Brock C, Tulasiewicz W (eds.) 1981 *Politics and Educational Change.* Croom Helm, London

Ayres R L 1983 *Banking on the Poor: The World Bank and World Poverty.* MIT Press, Cambridge, Massachusetts

Bell C L G 1974 The political framework. In: Chenery H et al. (eds.) 1974 *Redistribution with Growth.* Oxford University Press, New York

Benoit A 1974 *Changing the Educational System: A Colombian Case Study.* Weltforum Verlag, Munich

Benveniste G 1989 *Mastering the Politics of Planning.* Jossey-Bass, San Francisco, California

Bryson J M 1988 *Strategic Planning for Public and Nonprofit Organizations.* Jossey-Bass, San Francisco, California

Cogan J 1983 Jamaica: Education and the maintenance of the social class system. In: Thomas R M (ed.) 1983

Fägerlind I, Sjöstedt B 1989 *Review and Prospects of Educational Planning and Management in Europe.* Background Document for UNESCO International Congress on Planning and Management of Educational Development, Mexico. UNESCO, Paris

Farrell J P 1986 *The National Unified School in Allende's Chile: The Role of Education in the Destruction of a Revolution.* University of British Columbia Press, Vancouver

Forester J 1988 *Planning in the Face of Power.* University of California Press, Berkeley, California

Friedmann J 1973 *Retracking America: A Theory of Transactive Planning.* Anchor, Garden City, New York

Friedmann J (ed.) 1987 *Planning in the Public Domain: From Knowledge to Action.* Princeton University Press, Princeton, New Jersey

Hanson E M 1990 School-based management and educational reform in the United States and Spain. *Comp. Educ. Rev.* 34(4): 523–37

Jalil N, McGinn N 1992 Pakistan. In: Thomas R C (ed.)

1992 *Education's Role in National Development Plans.* Praeger, New York

Jones K 1985 The national union of teachers (England and Wales). In: Lawn M A (ed.) 1985 *The Politics of Teacher Unionism: International Perspectives.* Croom Helm, Beckenham

McCune S D 1986 *Guide to Strategic Planning for Educators.* Association for Supervision and Curriculum Development, Alexandria, Virginia

McGinn N, Schiefelbein E 1979 *Educational Planning in Chile.* Harvard Institute for International Development, Harvard University, Cambridge, Massachusetts

McGinn N, Street S 1986 Educational decentralization: Weak state or strong state? *Comp. Educ. Rev.* 30(4): 471–90

McGinn N, Warwick D P 1979, *The Evolution of Educational Planning in El Salvador: A Case Study.* Harvard Institute for International Development, Harvard University, Cambridge, Massachusetts

Psacharopolous G 1986 The planning of education: Where do we stand? *Comp. Educ. Rev.* 30(4): 560–73

Psacharopolous G 1990 Comparative education: From theory to practice, or are you A:\neo.* or B:*.ist? *Comp. Educ. Rev.* 34(3): 369–80

Ranson S 1985 Changing relations between centre and locality in education. In: McNay I, Ozga J (eds.) 1985 *Policy-making in Education: The Breakdown of Consensus.* Pergamon Press, Oxford

Reimers F 1990 *A New Scenario for Educational Planning and Management in Latin America: The Impact of the External Debt.* UNESCO/IIEP, Paris

Rideout W M Jr, Wilson D N 1975 The politics of national planning: The case of Zaire. *Educational Planning* 1(3): 35–63

Rondinelli D A, Middleton J, Verspoor A M 1990 *Planning Education Reform in Developing Countries: The Contingency Approach.* Duke University Press, Durham, North Carolina

Salter B, Tapper T 1981 *Education, Politics and the State: The Theory and Practice of Educational Change.* Grant McIntyre, London

Shaeffer S, Nkinyangi J A (eds.) 1983 *Educational Research Environments in the Developing World.* International Development Research Centre, Ottawa

Thomas R M (ed.) 1983 *Politics and Education: Cases from Eleven Nations.* Pergamon Press, Oxford

Warwick D P 1980 Planning as transaction In: Davis R G (ed.) 1980 *Issues and Problems in the Planning of Education in Developing Countries.* Harvard University, Center for Studies in Education and Development, Cambridge, Massachusetts

Warwick D P, Reimers F, McGinn N F 1992 The implementation of educational innovations: Lessons from Pakistan. *Int. J. Educ. Dev.* 12(4): 297–307

Further Reading

Archer M S 1979 *The Social Origins of Educational Systems.* Sage, London

Arnove R (ed.) 1982 *Philanthropy and Cultural Imperialism: The Foundations at Home and Abroad.* Indiana University Press, Bloomington, Indiana

Benveniste G 1970 *Bureaucracy and National Planning—A Sociological Case Study in Mexico.* Praeger, New York

Hardy C 1990 *Managing Strategy in Academic Institutions: Learning from Brazil.* De Gruyter, Hawthorne, New York

Kogan M 1978 *The Politics of Educational Change.* Fontana, London

Morales-Gomez D, Torres C A 1990 *The State, Corporatist Politics, and Educational Policy-Making in Mexico.* Praeger, New York

Schoppa L J 1991 *Education Reform in Japan: A Case of Immobilist Politics.* Routledge and Kegan Paul, London

Wirt F M, Kirst M W 1982 *Schools in Conflict: The Politics of Education.* McCutchan Publishing, Berkeley, California

Postliteracy: Concepts and Policies

L. Benton

Illiteracy is a problem not just in developing nations, but also in economically advanced countries. A significant proportion of working adults lack adequate skills in reading, writing, and numeracy, as various national assessment studies show. The problem has grave economic implications, particularly because economic restructuring since the mid-1970s has also altered jobs and increased skill requirements for some workers. Reforms aimed at addressing the problem in new ways include more participation by both labor unions and learners in program design, greater integration of literacy and work training, and efforts to build learning into job structures. Constraints on policy effectiveness are evident in the fragmented structure of various national literacy campaigns. "Postliteracy," if taken to mean achievement of universal basic literacy levels, still lies in the future.

In this article, the concept of postliteracy is discussed in relation to changes affecting the skill requirements of the labor force. Methodologies and issues in the measurement of functional illiteracy are presented, and postliteracy programs in different industrialized countries are described. Attention is also given to emerging trends and opportunities for the formation of a broad coalition to support the expansion of literacy training.

1. The Meaning of Postliteracy

The term "postliteracy" can be problematic if it is taken to imply the universal attainment of basic levels of literacy. Serious illiteracy problems persist even in the most advanced countries, and these problems affect not just populations that are perceived as "marginal" (e.g., immigrants, the unemployed, or school dropouts) but also significant, and perhaps growing, numbers of adult workers. One can therefore understand "literacy" to mean not a limited set of skills but a learned ability to interpret complex messages and codes of all kinds. "Postliteracy" is better defined, then, as the condition of countries where very basic abilities in reading and writing are indeed widely held, but where many cannot perform the literacy-related tasks needed to function fully at home, at work, and in civic life. This condition is shared by most economically advanced countries and by some developing countries. Particularly in the former, overcoming the problem of adult illiteracy is increasingly tied to the goal of enhancing international economic competitiveness.

This shift in the understanding of literacy is forcing policymakers to confront a series of new issues. One problem is how to assess the phenomenon of illiteracy in a meaningful way. Earlier measures of literacy, as discussed below, are at best crude indicators of the ability to complete various literacy-related tasks. New, more sophisticated methods of measurement have been developed, but they have not yet been widely used.

The new approaches to measuring illiteracy inevitably call attention to other problems that have been poorly perceived in the past. Levels of literacy that are actually required for individuals to function effectively in different contexts have rarely been systematically studied. Of particular importance is understanding the literacy requirements of jobs, including entirely new categories of jobs. This problem ties literacy research to broader investigations into the nature of economic change since the mid-1970s, when the advanced economies began the shift to a "post-Fordist" economy characterized by unstable markets, large-scale sectoral restructuring, and firm shake-ups. This process has involved the reorganization of many jobs and important shifts in the skill requirements for workers.

Related to both these issues is the question of how to alter government policies and programs. Surveying the efforts of national and local governments in some of the industrialized countries reveals a broad movement toward merging literacy concerns with economic goals. Although it is possible to point toward some particularly compelling experiments, no single strategy has gained a solid reputation for effectiveness. Even where government efforts share some similar features and are guided by similar concerns, differences in local and national politics tend to lead literacy policies across nations toward different outcomes.

2. *Measuring Functional Illiteracy*

The current situation contrasts with that of the early 1980s, when literacy was typically defined in terms of grade attainment. One advantage of this method was that data on grade completion were widely available, and it was thus possible to compare literacy rates defined by grade attainment internationally and also over time within individual countries. The drawback, of course, is that there was little evidence that grade attainment was an accurate indicator of literacy skills.

Rather than seeking to identify levels of basic literacy (the ability to write and/or decipher simple messages), most researchers now recognize the need to measure a more complex social construction, "functional literacy," or the ability to perform a complex range of tasks . The dimensions of the problem of functional illiteracy are just becoming known. Several national efforts to arrive at a more precise measure of the problem deserve mention.

A methodological approach developed in the 1975 Adult Performance Level (APL) survey in the United States was influential because it used performance tasks as indicators of literacy competency. A more complex method based on this approach was pioneered in the 1985 United States Department of Education survey of young adults (aged 21 to 25)—the National Assessment of Educational Progress (NAEP) (Kirsch and Jungeblut 1986). This survey assessed respondents' performance in three categories—prose literacy, document literacy, and quantitative literacy—and reported results by placing respondents' abilities along three scales corresponding to the differnt types of competencies. The authors of the study intended to shift the emphasis away from reporting flat rates of "illiteracy" or "functional illiteracy" and toward a more nuanced understanding of the problem.

The NAEP study showed that patterns of economic inequality paralleled the distribution of literacy skills. Poor minority groups performed at levels significantly lower than those of young White adults. The study also confirmed that classically defined illiteracy—the inability to read—was indeed a relatively small problem (affecting only about 2% of the sample), while a significant proportion of young adults were unable to complete many of the literacy-related tasks and only 10–40 percent could reliably complete the most complex, multistep tasks (Kirsch and Jungeblut 1986). The results of the NAEP survey encouraged the Department of Education to conduct a national adult literacy assessment for individuals aged 16 to 64 in 1992. In 1989, the Department of Labor also commissioned literacy assessments of three special populations of adults who were unemployed or in training.

Other attempts to assess the literacy problem nationally have been influenced by these efforts. A very comprehensive project is a 1989 study in Canada called the Survey of Literacy Skills Used in Daily Activities (LSUDA). This study surveyed 9,455 individuals between the ages of 16 and 69 with the goal of producing a separate test score for each respondent in reading, writing, and numeracy. The results confirmed that functional illiteracy is a significant problem, even though the majority of Canadian adults can read and would be classified as literate by standard proxy measures (Neice et al. 1992).

The study permitted a division of respondents into various categories of skill attainment and found that while relatively small proportions of respondents had no appreciable skills in reading, writing, and numeracy, significant proportions had skill levels that limited their abilities to complete daily functions. For example, 62 percent of Canadians were classified as reading at "level 4" (i.e., with skills that enabled them to complete most tasks and also gain further knowledge from printed materials); 22 percent of adult Canadians were classified as being able "to carry out simple reading tasks within familiar contexts with materials that are clearly laid out (level 3)"; and 16 percent of adults were found to have skills so limited that they could not understand most written material they would be likely to encounter in everyday life (Statistics Canada 1991). The study also found that reading, writing, and numeracy skills were closely linked to levels of schooling, to age, to region, and, for immigrants, to year of arrival in Canada.

Other countries have moved toward producing similar national assessments of literacy. France also revised the definition of functional illiteracy to include "individuals with difficulties in mastering basic skills" (*personnes en difficulté de maîtrise des savoirs de base*). A large-scale assessment of key skills was conducted in 1990 and was administered to a sample of 1,500 long-term unemployed individuals in five major cities: Paris, Marseilles, Lyon, Lille, and Toulouse. The skill areas analyzed were more extensive and were differently defined than in the studies in the United States and Canada. This survey, and other studies underway in France, promise to provide a much clearer profile of the functionally illiterate population in France than has been available to policymakers in the past.

An important finding shared across these studies is that although disadvantaged populations—migrants, young adults, minorities—may suffer disproportionately from literacy problems, they are likely to be outnumbered among the ranks of functional illiterates by apparently "mainstream" individuals, especially older, adult workers. This fact in turn suggests necessary revisions in the assessment of the effects of functional illiteracy on the economy and in the response to the problem through educational programs.

3. *Literacy and Work*

It has become commonplace to observe that workforce education problems in the advanced economies are related to the fact that such groups as women, young people, migrants, and minorities are growing quickly as a proportion of the workforce; because these groups have had a difficult time gaining equal access to education, the argument goes, they are less well-prepared for jobs. In fact, the sources of problems related to workforce preparedness are far more complex. Firm restructuring in response to widespread market instability has resulted in the reorganization of many jobs to entail a larger number and wider variety of tasks; it has also prompted the need to restructure the relationship of those tasks to others more frequently.

These shifts have been documented most clearly in manufacturing. So-called "Fordist" strategies of production for mass markets entailed the breakdown of jobs into easily performed tasks to which unskilled workers could be—at least in theory—indiscriminately assigned. Since the massive restructuring of those markets after the global crisis of the mid-1970s, firms have had to switch to strategies that emphasize production of short series, quick response to market shifts, and variability within product lines. One result has been a restructuring of jobs to allow for greater flexibility. Many unskilled jobs are disappearing, while skilled jobs tend to entail the performance of more varied tasks and a conceptual rather than a routine mastery of those tasks (Piore and Sabel 1984, Bailey 1989, Benton et al. 1991).

A similar transformation has also taken place in the services, where job creation in the advanced economies is the fastest. Although a rapid increase in the demand for low-level service workers is a feature shared by many of the advanced economies, this trend is part of a more complex story. Similar pressures as in manufacturing—to diversify product lines, to respond more quickly to market shifts, and to pursue specialized market niches—have led to a flattening of organizational structures. A larger percentage of the service workforce must have the communications skills necessary to participate directly in sales and customer/client service. As service firms work to distinguish themselves in the marketplace by developing proprietary technology and firm-specific procedures, workers must also learn to apply broad guidelines of action to specific cases and, moreover, to prepare to learn new guidelines as market positioning shifts again (Noyelle 1990, Benton et al. 1991).

These and other, related changes have meant that workers are being called on not only to arrive at work with a higher level of skills but also to be prepared to *learn at work*. Jobs for workers with very low literacy skills are disappearing. There is a noticeable trend within business toward providing in-house training to larger proportions of workers. This trend, in turn, feeds into a wider, growing movement in support of context-related instruction. Business interests, educators, and policy makers seem to be converging in support of a type of literacy training that promotes mastery of broad sets of skills by teaching their application to spe-

cific work-related tasks. This strategy contrasts with the more traditional approach of teaching basic skills as a step preparatory to, or at least separate from, job training.

4. Program Reforms

Several trends in program development appear to be shared across a range of more advanced countries. They are union participation in instruction, curriculum reform, the restructuring of work as a training strategy, and learner-centered instruction (see Benton and Noyelle 1992). Taken together, these trends share an emphasis on context-specific (especially work-centered) instruction for adults already in the workforce.

Although many firms and business leaders remain opposed to union participation in designing training, numerous ongoing experiments suggest that unions may be uniquely positioned to interpret training needs and encourage worker participation. In at least one country, Sweden, union participation in literacy training has been sweeping. The unions already had a strong tradition of participation in adult education, and they run high schools and other programs that target working adults. Union pressure prompted a 1985 policy requiring firms to set aside a portion of profits for a renewal fund partially dedicated to training. Although many firms have resisted using the funds to improve the skills of poorly educated workers, unions have pushed for such use. They have thus been important actors in creating and promoting programs that link basic skills and job skills training (Tuijnman 1989).

In the United States, union participation has been less consistently important, although a few cases suggest the promise of joint union–management training efforts. In the automobile industry, the United Auto Workers (UAW) has reached agreements with the three big automobile makers to co-manage training centers, accessible to workers at all education levels, that are richly funded through a "tax" on employee earnings. An example of even more direct union involvement is an innovative program in Ontario, Canada, run by the Ontario Federation of Labor. The Basic Education for Skills Training Program (BEST) is run entirely by unions and structured to emphasize the linkage between learning and workplace experience. The program is worker-run and worker-designed, and its success depends on the ability of the union to recruit and retain learners.

Curriculum trends in work-based, union-run programs are also apparent in other types of training. In many countries, traditional remedial adult training consists of standard high school equivalency training or basic skills instruction that varies little depending on the backgrounds or occupations of learners. But a trend toward developing *customized* curricula is clearly in place. In both North America and Western

Europe, various programs can be identified that use materials borrowed directly from work or community settings. Some publishers have also begun developing printed curricula customized for particular sectors or populations.

Such organizational and curricular changes are being complemented in a number of cases by strategies to restructure jobs themselves in ways that will encourage on-the-job learning. This trend is itself often simply an outcome of a more general strategy of firm competitiveness through increased flexibility and quick response to market shifts. In some places, though, the enhanced promise of learning on the job has become an explicit goal as well as an unintended outcome. Classic examples of such concerted efforts to increase worker participation as a means of enhancing competitiveness are manufacturing firms in the so-called "Third Italy," where employers encourage flexible production through flexible job assignments (Capecchi 1989).

Related to this trend toward structured learning on the job is a tendency to develop literacy programs that are "learner-centered." Community activists have been particularly outspoken in arguing that learners must play an active role in designing curricula and in devising methods of instruction. The BEST program described above, for example, works entirely with instructional materials provided by learners. In a community-based program run in Washington, DC, to take another example, learners identify practical, attainable goals (such as obtaining a driver's license) and gear learning specifically toward those goals. Such learner involvement is clearly tied to the other three trends of union participation, contextually structured curricula, and opportunities for learning at work.

5. Policy Responses

Whether or not these and other efforts will be effective appears to depend much on the larger institutional framework in which they operate. The national commitment to literacy training has varied over time and across countries. Patterns of government authority can also constrain literacy efforts in important ways. Consider the very different problems posed by the political contexts in the following cases.

In the United States, responsibility for literacy programs rests mainly at the state level. Although the federal government has recently publicized the problem of functional illiteracy, its support for actual programs remains limited. At the same time, the pressure on states to improve literacy training is increasing. With the decline of traditional manufacturing in many states, local and state governments seek to draw services and high-tech industry with the claim that they can provide highly trained workforces. Yet state policy makers have discovered that efforts to increase and improve literacy and basic skills training

are complicated by a highly fragmented funding and administrative structure that distributes responsibility for adult literacy training among a handful of programs (the two most important of these are the Job and Training Partnership Act, or JTPA, and Adult Basic Education, or ABE). Funding is also inadequate, with a total of US $1–$2 billion being spent each year by the federal government in all states (Chisman 1989).

In Canada, which has no Department of Education at the federal level, there is little federal involvement in literacy programs (Thomas 1983). This has been both a strength and a weakness for the country's literacy movement. One problem has been the unevenness of resources for literacy instruction. A few provinces have provided services to low-literate learners for decades and have backed scores of community groups involved in training, while others have left the task to traditional providers and have committed few resources. Yet lack of federal oversight has also given ambitious communities more room for experimenting with diverse providers and curricula. Thus providers in British Columbia can target loggers in need of retraining, while in Quebec funds can be used to help level educational opportunities for French and English speakers. In Canada, as in the United States, there remains a clear need for systems of evaluation of programs, as well as for administrative structures that can serve to replicate successful local programs reliably over a wider area.

In most European countries—with the possible exception of France and the United Kingdom—the perception until the late 1980s was that a major literacy problem did not exist. Yet recent evidence from the Netherlands and Sweden suggests that the need for some literacy and basic skills training extends beyond the immigrant population (Fransson and Larsson 1989). Perhaps better than any other national system among the developed countries, the Swedish system of adult education should be able to respond to this challenge using institutional arrangements already in place. The country has a well-established, multifaceted adult education system, with both national and local support (Abrahamsson 1988). Still, the system has tended in the past to benefit mostly those workers who already have average or above-average preparation, together with specially targeted populations such as immigrants or learning disabled students.

In France, the problem of illiteracy also used to be most closely associated with immigrants, but recent studies have signaled a much wider problem. Because illiteracy was thought of as a problem limited to special populations, programs have been separated from the rest of the education system. The result has been that literacy training programs of various kinds have remained fragmented. Some recent efforts promise to help. A national system of "individualized training credits" (*crédit-formation individualisé*) will allow school dropouts and others with low levels of schooling to qualify easily for remedial training.

These examples draw attention to some underlying constraints for expanding and improving literacy training. One constraint is the relationship of literacy initiatives to schooling in general. Where literacy training is considered an integral part of a system that serves citizens throughout their lives, as in Sweden, the necessary adjustments may be far easier to make. A second constraint is the relationship between national and local or regional politics. Local programs may be very innovative, but national support seems crucial to replicate successful strategies.

6. Conclusion

A valuable opportunity has emerged for the formation of a broad coalition to support the expansion of literacy training. Employers now recognize illiteracy as a problem they have to address directly, and many educators who once resisted emphasizing economic interests in the quest for universal literacy recognize that the best instructional methods often focus on skills needed by adults in the workplace. Local policy leaders also perceive that promoting literacy in the local workforce may be crucial to economic viability, given the new requirements of many firms. And learners, too, are becoming more active participants in planning the contents and goals of literacy and postliteracy programs. Whether or not effective action will result from this peculiar convergence of interests depends upon local and national political conditions and constraints. The opportunity, at least, clearly exists for building truly literate societies.

See also: Benefits of Education; Globalization of Educational Policy and Reform; Technological Change and Deskilling; Youth Unemployment

References

Abrahamsson K 1988 *Adult Literacy, Technology and Culture—Policies, Programs and Problems in Sweden.* Swedish National Board of Education, Stockholm

Bailey T 1989 *Changes in the Nature and Structure of Work. Implications for Employer-Sponsored Training.* Columbia University, New York

Benton L, Bailey T, Noyelle T, Stanback T 1991 *Employee Training and US Competitiveness: Lessons for the 1990s.* Westview Press, Boulder, Colorado

Benton L, Noyelle T (eds.) 1992 *Adult Illiteracy and Economic Performance.* OECD, Paris

Capecchi V 1989 The informal economy and the development of flexible specialization in Emilia Romagna. In: Portes et al. 1989 *The Informal Economy: Studies in Advanced and Less Developed Countries.* Johns Hopkins University Press, Baltimore, Maryland

Chisman F 1989 *Jump Start: The Federal Role in Adult Literacy.* Final Report of the Project on Adult Literacy. Southport Institute for Policy Analysis, Washington, DC

Fransson A, Larsson S 1989 *Who Takes a Second Chance? Implementing Education Equality in Adult Basic Education in a Swedish Context.* Report No. 1989–02. Department of Education and Educational Research, Gothenburg University, Gothenburg

Kirsch I, Jungeblut A 1986 *Literacy: Profiles of America's Young Adults.* Final Report. National Assessment of Educational Progress. Educational Testing Services, Princeton, New Jersey

Neice D, Adsett M, Rodney W 1992 Direct versus proxy measures of adult functional illiteracy: A preliminary re-examination. In: Benton L, Noyelle T (eds.) 1992

Noyelle T 1990 *Skills, Wages, and Productivity in the Service Sector.* Westview Press, Boulder, Colorado

Piore M, Sabel C 1984 *The Second Industrial Divide: Possibilities for Prosperity.* Basic Books, New York

Statistics Canada 1991 *Adult Literacy in Canada: Results of a National Study.* Minister of Industry, Science, and Technology, Ontario

Thomas A 1983 *Adult Illiteracy in Canada: A Challenge.* Occasional paper No. 42, Canadian Commission for UNESCO, Ottawa

Tuijnman A C 1989 *Further Education and Training in Swedish Working Life: A Discussion of Trends and Issues.* OECD, Paris

Further Reading

Fuchs-Brüninghoff E, Kreft W, Kropp U 1986 *Functional Illiteracy and Literacy Provision in Developed Countries: The Case of the Federal Republic of Germany.* UNESCO Institute for Education, Hamburg

Levine K 1986 *The Social Context of Literacy.* Routledge and Kegan Paul, London

Limage L 1987 Adult literacy policy in industrialized countries. In: Arnove R, Graff H (eds.) 1987 *National Literacy Campaigns.* Plenum, New York

Skagen A 1986 *Workplace Literacy.* American Management Association, New York

List of Contributors

Contributors are listed in alphabetical order together with their affiliations. Titles of articles which they have authored follow in alphabetical order, along with the respective page numbers. Where articles are co-authored, this has been indicated by an asterisk preceding the article title.

ACKER, S. (University of Toronto, Toronto, Canada)
Feminist Critiques of Educational Practices and Research 215–17

ADDOU, H. (Columbia University Teachers College, New York, USA)
*Agricultural Productivity and Education 799–808

ALTBACH, P. G. (Boston College, Massachusetts, USA)
Student Political Activism and Student Movements 754–61

ANDERSON, D. S. (Australian National University, Canberra, ACT, Australia)
Public and Private Schools: Sociological Perspectives 456–63

ANDERSON, J. (The Flinders University of South Australia, Adelaide, South Australia, Australia)
Content and Text Analysis 288–93

BANK, B. J. (University of Missouri, Columbia, Missouri, USA)
*Social Psychological Theories in Education 32–42; *Youth Friendships and Conflict in Schools* 776–81

BEHRMAN, J. R. (University of Pennsylvania, Philadelphia, Pennsylvania, USA)
*Family Status and Economic Status 625–30; **Kinship Studies* 635–41

BENAVOT, A. (Hebrew University of Jerusalem, Mount Scopus, Jerusalem, Israel)
Institutional Approach to the Study of Education 340–45

BENTON, L. (New Jersey Institute of Technology, Newark, New Jersey, USA)
Postliteracy: Concepts and Policies 890–94

BIDDLE, B. J. (University of Missouri, Columbia, Missouri, USA)
*Social Psychological Theories in Education 32–42; *Teachers' Roles* 697–702; *Youth and Leisure* 766–71

BJORKLUND, D. F. (Florida Atlantic University, Boca Raton, Florida, USA)
*Childhood 746–50

BOLAM, R. (National Development Centre, University of Bristol, Bristol, UK)
Teacher Recruitment and Induction 682–86

BRAUNGART, M. M. (State University of New York, Syracuse, New York, USA)
*Political Socialization and Education 521–27

BRAUNGART, R. G. (Syracuse University, Syracuse, New York, USA)
*Political Socialization and Education 521–27

BRAY, M. (University of Hong Kong, Hong Kong)
School Size and Small Schools 361–64

BROADFOOT, P. (School of Education, University of Bristol, Bristol, UK)
Sociology of Learning in School 187–93

BURBULES, N. C. (College of Education, University of Illinois, Champaign, Illinois, USA)
Marxism and Educational Thought 75–80

CARNOY, M. (School of Education, Stanford University, Stanford, California, USA)
Technological Change and Education 861–67

CARR-HILL, R. (University of York, York, UK)
Basic Education: Comparative and International Studies 809–19

CASSEL, W. S. (Florida Atlantic University, Boca Raton, Florida, USA)
*Childhood 746–50

CLIFTON, R. A. (University of Manitoba, Winnipeg, Manitoba, Canada)
Race and Ethnicity in Education 550–55

† COLEMAN, J. S. (University of Chicago, Chicago, Illinois, USA)
Family, School, and Social Capital 623–25

895

COLLINS, J. (State University of New York, Albany, New York, USA)
Family, School, and Cultural Capital 618–23

COLLOPY, R. M. B. (University of Michigan, Ann Arbor, Michigan, USA)
Student Influences on Teaching 667–70

COMSTOCK, G. (Syracuse University, Syracuse, New York, USA)
Broadcasting and Technology: Effects on Children and Youth 739–45

CONBOY, I. (Victoria Ministry of Education, Melbourne, Victoria, Australia)
Social Implications of Educational Technology 850–56

DAVIES, B. (University of New England, Armidale, New South Wales, Australia)
Gender Theories in Education 62–67

DAVIS, W. E. (University of Maine, Orono, Maine, USA)
Children and Youth at Risk 571–76

DENZIN, N. K. (University of Illinois, Urbana, Illinois, USA)
Biographical Research Methods 282–88

DIORIO, J. A. (University of Otago, Otago, New Zealand)
Sex Education 157–62

DONN, G. (University of Edinburgh, Edinburgh, UK)
Feminist Approaches to the Curriculum 130–35

DRONKERS, J. (Kohn Stamm Institute, University of Amsterdam, The Netherlands)
Educational Expansion: Sociological Perspectives 430–37; *Social Mobility, Social Stratification, and Education* 369–75

DWECK, C. S. (Columbia University, New York, USA)
Development of Achievement Motivation 517–20

DWORKIN, A. G. (University of Houston, Houston, Texas, USA)
Teacher Burnout 670–76

EKSTRAND, L. H. (Lund University, Malmö, Sweden)
Multicultural Education 345–55

ERICKSON, F. (University of Pennsylvania, Philadelphia, Pennsylvania, USA)
Schools as Sociocultural Systems 356–61

EVANS, D. R. (University of Massachusetts, Amherst, Massachusetts, USA)
Conscientization and Mobilization 830–33

EVERS, C. W. (Monash University, Clayton, Victoria, Australia)
Research in Education: Epistemological Issues 224–33

FÄGERLIND, I. (University of Stockholm, Stockholm, Sweden)
Education and Development 833–41

FAGNANO, C. L. (Milken Institute for Job and Capital Formation, Santa Monica, California, USA)
Benefits of Education 819–29

FARRELL, J. P. (Ontario Institute for Studies in Education, Toronto, Ontario, Canada)
Social Equality and Educational Planning in Developing Nations 473–79

FOSTER, W. (University of San Diego, San Diego, California, USA)
Administration of Education: Critical Approaches 43–50

FRASER, B. J. (Curtin University of Technology, Perth, Western Australia, Australia)
Student Perceptions of Classrooms 751–54

FULIGNI, A. J. (University of Michigan, Ann Arbor, Michigan, USA)
Home Environment and School Learning 630–35

GILBERT, R. (James Cook University, Townsville, Queensland, Australia)
Acquisition of Empowerment Skills 507–11

GINSBURG, M. B. (University of Pittsburgh, Pittsburgh, Pennsylvania, USA)
Political Sociology of Teachers' Work 657–62

GOOD, T. L. (University of Missouri, Columbia, Missouri, USA)
Teachers' Expectations 686–92

GORDON, D. (Bengurion University, Beer-Sheva, Israel)
Hidden Curriculum 484–87; *Neo-Marxist Approaches to Curriculum* 135–38

GROSSMAN, P. L. (University of Washington, Seattle, Washington, USA)
Teachers' Knowledge 692–97

GUTHRIE, J. W. (University of California, Berkeley, California, USA)
Globalization of Educational Policy and Reform 878–83

HAIG, B. D. (University of Canterbury, Christchurch, Canterbury, New Zealand)
Feminist Research Methodology 308–13

HALL, B. L. (Ontario Institute for Studies in Education, Toronto, Ontario, Canada)
Participatory Research 317–24

HALLINAN, M. T. (University of Notre Dame, Notre Dame, Indiana, USA)
School and Classroom Dynamics 491–97; *Social Foundations of School Choice* 365–69

HANNA, J. L. (University of Maryland, College Park, Maryland, USA)
Social Change and Education 842–44

HANUSHEK, E. A. (University of Rochester, Rochester, New York, USA)
Education Production Functions 297–303

HARGREAVES, A. (Ontario Institute for Studies in Education, Toronto, Ontario, Canada)
Teaching, Realities of 710–17

HATIVA, N. (Tel Aviv University, Tel Aviv, Israel)
Technology and the Classroom Teacher 867–71

HATTON, N. G. (University of Sydney, Sydney, Australia)
*Teacher Placement and School Staffing 677–82

HECKMAN, P. E. (University of Arizona, Tucson, Arizona, USA)
*Age Grouping of Students 401–04

HEYMAN, G. D. (University of Illinois, Champaign, Illinois, USA)
*Development of Achievement Motivation 517–20

HOYLE, E. (University of Bristol, Bristol, UK)
Teaching, Social Status 717–21

HUSÉN, T. (University of Stockholm, Stockholm, Sweden)
Educational Research and Policymaking 872–78; *Research Paradigms in Education* 241–46

JANSSEN REINEN, I. (University of Twente, Enschede, The Netherlands)
*Gender and New Technology 845–49

JARVIS, P. (University of Surrey, Guildford, UK)
Sociology of Adult Education 168–73

JOHNSON, D. W. (University of Minnesota, Minneapolis, Minnesota, USA)
*Social Psychological Theories of Teaching 163–67

JOHNSON, R. T. (University of Minnesota, Minneapolis, Minnesota, USA)
*Social Psychological Theories of Teaching 163–67

JUAN, S. (University of Sydney, Sydney, New South Wales, Australia)
Education of Indigenous Peoples 534–39

KAMAT, S. G. (University of Pittsburgh, Pittsburgh, Pennsylvania, USA)
*Political Sociology of Teachers' Work 657–62

KAPLAN, A. (University of Haifa, Haifa, Israel)
Research Methodology: Scientific Methods 234–41

KEEVES, J. P. (The Flinders University of South Australia, Adelaide, South Australia, Australia)
*Measurement of Social Background 218–24; **Sex Differences and School Outcomes* 555–64; *Trends in Quantitative Research Methods* 263–75

KELLAGHAN, T. (St Patrick's College, Dublin, Republic of Ireland)
Family and Schooling 606–13

KELLY, D. M. (University of British Columbia, Vancouver, British Columbia, Canada)
School Dropouts 582–86

KEMMIS, S. (Deakin University, Geelong, Victoria, Australia)
Action Research 276–82

KERDEMAN, D. (University of Washington, Seattle, Washington, USA)
*Hermeneutics 67–75

KIRK, D. (University of Queensland, Brisbane, Queensland, Australia)
Sociology of Physical and Health Education 193–201

KOTTE, D. (University of Hamburg, Hamburg, Germany)
*Sex Differences and School Outcomes 555–64

KUEBART, F. (Universität Bochum, Bochum, Germany)
Socialist Education Systems 381–87

ÖDMAN, P.-J. (University of Stockholm, Stockholm, Sweden)
Hermeneutics 67–75

OSER, F. K. (University of Fribourg, Fribourg, Switzerland)
Acquiring Attitudes and Values 504–07

OXENHAM, J. (University of Sussex, Falmer, UK)
Equality, Policies for Educational 443–52

PAYNE, M. A. (University of Waikato, Hamilton, New Zealand)
School–Parent Relationships 650–54

PERRY, D. G. (Florida Atlantic University, Boca Raton, Florida, USA)
Aggression, Development and Socialization 735–39

PESCHAR, J. L. (Groningen University, Groningen, The Netherlands)
Stratification in Educational Systems 387–92

PETERS, M. (University of Auckland, Auckland, New Zealand)
Postmodernism and Education 88–92

PETERSON, P. L. (Michigan State University, East Lansing, Michigan, USA)
Student Roles in Classrooms 761–66

PHILLIPS, D. C. (Stanford University, Stanford, California, USA)
Positivism, Antipositivism, and Empiricism 84–88

PLOMP, T. (University of Twente, Enschede, The Netherlands)
Gender and New Technology 845–49

POWELL, D. R. (Purdue University, West Lafayette, Indiana, USA)
Parent Involvement in Preschool Programs 642–47

RAUDENBUSH, S. W. (Michigan State University, East Lansing, Michigan, USA)
Effective Schools Research: Methodological Issues 304–08

SADKER, D. (The American University, Washington, DC, USA)
Sex Equity: Assumptions and Strategies 411–15

SADKER, M. (The American University, Washington, DC, USA)
Sex Equity: Assumptions and Strategies 411–15

SAHA, L. J. (Australian National University, Canberra, ACT, Australia)
Aspirations and Expectations of Students 512–17; *Classical Sociological Theories of Education* 11–21; *Education and Development* 833–41; *Introduction (Section III): Methodological Developments in the Sociology of Education* 213–14; *Introduction (Section X): New Developments in Education as an Agent of Change* 787–90; *Introduction (Section VI): Sociological Processes Within Schools* 481–83; *Introduction (Section VII): The Centrality of the Family in Educational Processes* 587–88; *Introduction (Section VIII): The Changing Social Role of the Teacher* 655–56 *Introduction (Section II): The Diversification of the Sociology of Education* 103–05; *Introduction (Section V): The Organizational Structure of Educational Systems* 393–94; *Introduction (Section IV): The Systemic Approach to the Study of Education* 301–02, *Introduction (Section I): Theoretical Developments in the Sociology of Education* 9–10; *Introduction (Section IX): Youth and Schooling in Modern Society* 727–28; *Measurement of Social Background* 218–24; *Sociology of Education: An Overview* 106–17

SCHNEEWIND, K. A. (University of Munich, Munich, Germany)
Family Influence on Human Development 614–17

SEDDON, T. (Monash University, Clayton, Victoria, Australia)
Teachers' Work and Political Action 702–10

SHIMONI, R. (Hebrew University, Jerusalem, Israel)
Parent Education 647–50

SKILBECK, M. (Organisation for Economic Co-operation and Development, Paris, France)
Social, Cultural, and Economic Factors Affecting Curriculum 498–503

SMALL, R. (Monash University, Clayton, Victoria, Australia)
Phenomenology and Existentialism 80–84

SOLMON, L. C. (Milken Institute for Job and Capital Formation, Santa Monica, California, USA)
Benefits of Education 819–29

SPENCER, D. A. (Arizona State University, Tempe, Arizona, USA)
Sociology of Teaching 206–12

SPENNER, K. I. (Duke University, Durham, North Carolina, USA)
Technological Change and Deskilling 856–61

STEVENSON, H. W. (University of Michigan, Ann Arbor, Michigan, USA)
Home Environment and School Learning 630–35

STROBER, M. H. (Stanford University, Stanford, California, USA)
Economics of Child Care 595–600; *Gender and Occupational Segregation* 545–49

STROMQUIST, N. P. (University of Southern California, Los Angeles, California, USA)
Gender and Education 539–44

STURMAN, A. (University of Southern Queensland, Toowoomba, Australia)
Loose Coupling and Educational Systems 452–56; *Socialization* 528–33

SUAREZ, T. M. (University of North Carolina, Chapel Hill, North Carolina, USA)
Needs Assessment 314–17

TACHIBANAKI, T. (Kyoto University, Kyoto, Japan)
Education, Occupation, and Earnings 293–97

† TAUBMAN, P. (University of Pennsylvania, Philadelphia, Pennsylvania, USA)
Family Status and Economic Status 625–30; *Kinship Studies* 635–41

TEESE, R. (University of Melbourne, Parkville, Victoria, Australia)
Reproduction Theory 92–97

THOMAS, R. M. (University of California, Santa Barbara, California, USA)
Religious Education 144–57

THOMPSON, F. (Temple University, Philadelphia, Pennsylvania, USA)
Family, School, and Cultural Capital 618–23

TORRES, C. A. (University of California, Los Angeles, California, USA)
Adult Education for Development 791–98

TREIMAN, J. E. (University of California, Riverside, California, USA)
Authority and Power in Educational Organizations 416–21

TROW, M. (University of California, Berkeley, California, USA)
Policy Analysis 138–44

TURNER, J. H. (University of California, Riverside, California, USA)
Contemporary Sociological Theories of Education 21–31

VAN DER PLOEG, S. W. (Kohn Stamm Institute, University of Amsterdam, The Netherlands)
Educational Expansion: Sociological Perspectives 430–37

VILLARRUEL, F. A. (Michigan State University, East Lansing, Michigan, USA)
Adolescence 729–34

WALKER, J. C. (University of Canberra, Canberra, ACT, Australia)
Research in Education: Epistemological Issues 224–33; *Resistance Theory* 97–102

WATSON, A. J. (University of New South Wales, Sydney, Australia)
Teacher Placement and School Staffing 677–82

WEILER, K. A. (Tufts University, Medford, Massachusetts, USA)
Women and the Professionalization of Teaching 721–25

WEINER, G. (South Bank University, London, UK)
Students in Classrooms, Gender and Racial Differences Among 565–70

WHITE, P. B. (LaTrobe University, Bundoora, Victoria, Australia)
Social Implications of Educational Technology 850–56

WILLMS, J. D. (University of British Columbia, Vancouver, British Columbia, Canada)
Effective Schools Research: Methodological Issues 304–08

WILLOWER, D. J. (Pennsylvania State University, University Park, Pennsylvania, USA)
Administration of Education as a Field of Study 118–25

WILSON, B. (University of Melbourne, Melbourne, Victoria, Australia)
Youth Cultures and Subcultures 771–76

WONG, K. K. (University of Chicago, Chicago, Illinois, USA)
Bureaucracy and School Effectiveness 421–27

YOGEV, A. (Tel Aviv University, Tel Aviv, Israel)
Second Chance Education and Alternative Routes 469–72

ZHAO, S. (University of Stockholm, Stockholm, Sweden)
Socialist and Capitalist Schooling: Comparative Perspectives 375–81

ZUBRZYCKI, J. (Australian National University, Canberra, ACT, Australia)
Classical Sociological Theories of Education 11–21

Name Index

The Name Index has been compiled so that the reader can proceed directly to the page where an author's work is cited, or to the reference itself in the bibliography. For each name, the page numbers for the bibliographic section are given first, followed by the page number(s) in parentheses where that reference is cited in text. Where a name is referred to only in text, and not in the bibliography, the page number appears only in parentheses.

The accuracy of the spelling of authors' names has been affected by the use of different initials by some authors, or a different spelling of their name in different papers or review articles (sometimes this may arise from a transliteration process), and by those journals which give only one initial to each author.

Subject Index

The Subject Index has been compiled as a guide to the reader who is interested in locating all the references to a particular subject area within the Encyclopedia. Entries may have up to three levels of heading. Where the page numbers appear in bold italic type, this indicates a substantive discussion of the topic. Every effort has been made to index as comprehensively as possible and to standardize the terms used in the index. However, given the diverse nature of the field and the varied use of terms throughout the international community, synonyms and foreign language terms have been included with appropriate cross-references. As a further aid to the reader, cross-references have also been given to terms of related interest.